Foundations of
Multidimensional and
Metric Data Structures

The Morgan Kaufmann Series in Computer Graphics and Geometric Modeling

The Morgan Kaufmann Series in Data Management Systems

Series Editor: Jim Gray, Microsoft Research

Foundations of Multidimensional and Metric Data Structures

Hanan Samet
University of Maryland, College Park

AMSTERDAM • BOSTON • HEIDELBERG • LONDON
NEW YORK • OXFORD • PARIS • SAN DIEGO
SAN FRANCISCO • SINGAPORE • SYDNEY • TOKYO

Morgan Kaufmann Publishers is an imprint of Elsevier

Publisher Diane D. Cerra
Publishing Services Manager George Morrison
Assistant Editor Asma Palmeiro
Editorial Intern Marisa Crawford
Cover Design © Picturequest Images
Cover Image Dick Hannus
Project Management Multiscience Press
Composition Multiscience Press & Windfall Software, using ZzTEX
Technical Illustration Dartmouth Publishing, Inc.
Copyeditor Ken DellaPenta
Proofreader Multiscience Press
Indexer Hanan Samet
Interior printer Maple-Vail Book Manufacturing Group
Cover printer Phoenix Color

Morgan Kaufmann Publishers is an imprint of Elsevier.
500 Sansome Street, Suite 400, San Francisco, CA 94111

This book is printed on acid-free paper.

Library of Congress Cataloging-in-Publication Data

Application submitted

ISBN 13: 978-0-12-369446-1
ISBN 10: 0-12-369-446-9

For information on all Morgan Kaufmann publications, visit our Web site at *www.mkp.com* or *www.books.elsevier.com*

Transferred to Digital Printing in 2011

In memory of

Gísli R. Hjaltason

Azriel Rosenfeld

Markku Tamminen

Contents

Foreword

Jim Gray, Microsoft Research

This book organizes the bewildering array of spatial and multi-dimensional indexing methods into a coherent field. Hanan Samet is the dean of "spatial data indexing." His two previous books have been the essential reference works for over a decade. This book unifies those previous books, and places the field in the broader context of indexing and searching for information in any metric space.

The book is encyclopedic. Nonetheless, it reads very well as a textbook that systematically develops the ideas. The four major chapters (points, objects, multidimensional intervals including rectangles, and high-dimensional data), are concise, copiously illustrated, and have exercises at the end of each section with detailed answers at the end of the book. The book includes tutorials on B-trees, linear hashing, and spiral hashing, has a huge bibliography (over 2,000 references), a detailed index compiled by the author, and a website (*http://www.cs.umd.edu/~hjs/quadtree/*) with demonstration programs and datasets.

There is no question that mastering this book will take time—but this book will be invaluable for those of us who struggle with spatial data, or with scientific datasets, or with graphics and vision problems involving volumetric queries, or with higher-dimensional datasets common in data mining.

Preface

The representation of multidimensional data is an important issue in diverse fields including database management systems (e.g., spatial databases, multimedia databases), computer graphics, game programming, computer vision, geographic information systems (GIS), pattern recognition, similarity searching (also known as similarity retrieval), solid modeling, computer-aided design (CAD), robotics, image processing, computational geometry, finite-element analysis, and numerous others. The key idea in choosing an appropriate representation is to facilitate operations such as search. This means that the representation involves sorting the data in some manner to make it more accessible. In fact, the term *access structure* or *index* is often used as an alternative to the term *data structure* in order to emphasize the importance of the connection to sorting.

The most common definition of "multidimensional data" is a collection of points in a higher dimensional space (i.e., greater than 1). These points can represent locations and objects in space as well as more general records where each attribute (i.e., field) corresponds to a dimension and only some, or even none, of the attributes are locational. As an example of nonlocational point data, consider an employee record that has attributes corresponding to the employee's name, address, sex, age, height, weight, and social security number. Such records arise in database management systems and can be treated as points in, for this example, a seven-dimensional space (i.e., there is one dimension for each attribute), although the different dimensions have different type units (i.e., name and address are strings of characters; sex is binary; while age, height, weight, and social security number are numbers). Note that the address attribute could also be interpreted in a locational sense using positioning coordinates such as latitude and longitude readings although the stringlike symbolic representation is far more common.

When multidimensional data corresponds to locational data, we have the additional property that all of the attributes usually have the same unit (possibly with the aid of scaling transformations), which is distance in space. In this case, we can combine the distance-denominated attributes and pose queries that involve proximity. For example, we may wish to find the closest city to Chicago within the two-dimensional space from which the locations of the cities are drawn. Another query seeks to find all cities within 50 miles of Chicago. In contrast, such queries are not very meaningful when the attributes do not have the same type. Nevertheless, other queries such as range queries that seek, for example, all individuals born between 1940 and 1960 whose weight ranges between 150 and 200 pounds are quite common and can be posed regardless of the nature of the attributes.

When multidimensional data spans a continuous physical space (i.e., an infinite collection of locations), the issues become more interesting. In particular, we are no longer just interested in the locations of objects, but, in addition, we are also interested in the space that they occupy (i.e., their extent). Some example objects with extent include lines (e.g., roads, rivers), intervals (which can correspond to time as well as space), regions of varying shape and dimensionality (e.g., lakes, counties, buildings, crop maps, polygons, polyhedra), and surfaces. The objects (when they are not points) may be disjoint or could even overlap.

Spatial multidimensional data is generally of relatively low dimension. However, there are many application domains where the data is of considerably higher dimensionality and is not necessarily spatial. This is especially true in databases for application domains such as multimedia and bioinformatics data, to name just two, where the data is a set of objects, and the high dimensionality is a direct result of attempts to describe the objects via a collection of features that characterize them (also known as a *feature vector*). For example, in the case of image data, some commonly used features include color, color moments, textures, shape descriptions, and so on, expressed using scalar values. Although such data falls into the class of point data, it often requires using very different representations than those that are traditionally used for point data. The problem is often attributed to the *curse of dimensionality* [159], which simply means that the indexing methods do not do as good a job of facilitating the retrieval of the objects that satisfy the query as is the case when the data has lower dimensionality.

The above discussion of nonspatial data of high dimensionality has been based on the premise that we know the features that describe the objects (and hence the dimensionality of the underlying feature space). In fact, it is usually quite difficult to identify the features, and thus we frequently turn to experts in the application domain from which the objects are drawn for assistance in this process. Nevertheless, often the features cannot be easily identified even by the domain experts. In particular, sometimes the only information available is a distance function that indicates the degree of similarity (or dissimilarity) between all pairs of objects in the database as well as how to compute the similarity between objects in the domain. Usually the distance function d is required to obey the triangle inequality, be nonnegative, and be symmetric, in which case it is known as a *metric* (also referred to as a *distance metric*). In this case, we resort to what are termed metric or distance-based representations, which differ from the more conventional representations in that the objects are now sorted with respect to their distance from a few key objects, known as *pivots*, rather than with respect to some commonly known reference point (e.g., the origin in the spatial domain), which may not necessarily be associated with any of the objects.

This book is about the representation of data such as that described above. It is organized into four chapters. Each chapter is like a part, sometimes as big as a book. Chapter 1 deals with the representation of point data, usually of low dimensionality. One of the keys to the presentation in this chapter is making a distinction between whether the representation organizes the data (e.g., a binary search tree) or the embedding space from which the data is drawn (e.g., a trie). Considerable attention is also devoted to issues that arise when the volume of the data is so high that it cannot fit in memory, and hence the data is disk resident. Such methods are characterized as bucket methods and have been the subject of extensive research in the database community.

Chapter 2 deals with the representation of objects. It focuses on object-based and image-based representations. These distinctions are analogous to those made in computer graphics where algorithms and decompositions of objects are characterized as being object-based or image-based corresponding to whether the representations result from the decomposition of the objects or the environment in which the objects are embedded, respectively. The central theme in this chapter is how the representations deal with the key queries of where and what—that is, given an object, we want to know its location, and, given a location, we want to know the identity of the object (or objects) of which it is a member. Efficiently responding to these queries, preferably with one representation, has motivated many researchers in computer graphics and related fields such as computer vision, solid modeling, and spatial databases, to name a few. This leads, in part, to a distinction between representations on the basis of being either object hierarchies, of which the R-tree [791] and its variants (commonly used in database applications) are examples, or space hierarchies, of which the pyramid and its variants (commonly used in computer vision applications) are examples. The representations that have been developed can also be differentiated on the basis of whether the objects are represented by their interiors or by their boundaries.

Chapter 3 deals with the representation of intervals and small rectangles. These representations are applicable in a number of important areas. For example, they are used in very large-scale integration (VLSI) design applications (also known as CAD), where the objects are modeled as rectangles for the sake of simplicity. The number of objects in these applications is quite large, and the size of the objects is several orders of magnitude smaller than that of the space from which they are drawn. This is in contrast to cartographic applications, where the sizes of the objects are larger. These representations are also used in game programming applications (e.g., [475, 476, 1025, 1456, 1890]), where their deployment is motivated by the fact that the objects are in spatial registration, thereby enabling efficient calculation of set-theoretic operations while not being as sensitive to changes in position as is the case for some other hierarchical representations that are based on a regular decomposition of the underlying space (e.g., the region quadtree). The representation of intervals is also of interest for applications that involve temporal data where intervals play a role (e.g., [951]). They can also be used for the representation of moving objects, which finds use in spatiotemporal databases (e.g., [21, 950, 1057, 1092, 1305, 2013] and the text of Güting and Schneider [790]).

Chapter 4 deals with the representation of high-dimensional data where the data is not spatial and the actual dimensionality of the data is also an issue. The key is that the data usually consists of features where the number and identity of the features that should be represented is not always clear. In particular, this data arises in applications such as multimedia, where the use of a large number of features to describe the objects is based on the premise that by increasing the number of features we are increasing our ability to differentiate between the objects for retrieval. An alternative is to make use of a distance function that measures the similarity (or dissimilarity) between the objects. A discussion of a number of distance-based indexes is included here.

Chapter 4 is motivated by the important problem of *similarity searching*—the process of finding and retrieving objects that are similar to a given object or set of objects. This process invariably reduces to finding the nearest or k nearest neighbors, and hence a considerable amount of attention is paid to this query by showing how to perform it efficiently for both distance-based and multidimensional indexing methods. The observation that, for high-dimensional data, the use of multidimensional indexing methods often fails to yield any improvement in performance over a simple sequential scan of the data is also addressed. This is in part due to the cost of computing distance in high dimensions, the nature of the data distribution, and the relatively low volume of available data vis-à-vis its dimensionality (i.e., the curse of dimensionality). One response is to take note of the observation that the "inherent dimensionality" of a dataset is often much lower than that of the underlying space. In particular, this has led to the development of techniques to reduce the dimensionality of the data using methods such as Singular Value Decomposition (SVD). An alternative solution that is discussed is how to make use of contractive embedding methods that embed the data in a lower-dimensional space, and then make use of a filter-and-refine algorithm in conjunction with multidimensional indexing methods to prune irrelevant candidates from consideration.

Many of the data structures that are presented in the four chapters are hierarchical. They are based either on the principle of recursive decomposition (similar to *divide-and-conquer* methods [27]) or on the aggregation of objects into hierarchies. Hierarchical data structures are useful because of their ability to focus on the interesting subsets of the data. This focusing results in an efficient representation and in improved execution times.

Hierarchical representations of spatial data were the subject of one of my earlier books [1637]. It dealt with the four basic spatial data types: points, rectangles, lines, and volumes. Many of these representations were based on variants of the quadtree and octree data structure that have been applied to many problems in a variety of domains. In this case, the term *quadtree* was used in a general sense to describe a class of representations whose common property was that they were based on the principle of recursive decomposition of space. They were differentiated on the following bases:

1. The type of data they are used to represent

2. The principle guiding the decomposition process

3. The resolution (variable or not)

This book is a considerable expansion of [1637] with approximately 10% overlap. Nevertheless there still remains a considerable amount of material from [1637] that has not been included in this book (e.g., from Chapters 4 and 5). One of the features of [1637] was the inclusion of detailed code for building and updating a number of data structures (at least one for each of the spatial data types point, lines, and rectangles). This code is also present in this book but is now part of the exercises and their solutions. In addition, the VASCO (Visualization and Animation of Spatial Constructs and Operations) [243, 244, 245, 246]) set of JAVA applets is available for use to illustrate many operations for a large number of the data structures presented in the current book (see *http://www.cs.umd .edu/~hjs/quadtree/index.html*). Readers interested in seeing how these methods are used in the context of an application should try the SAND Internet Browser [1644] at the same URL, which provides an entry point to explore their use in a geographic information system (GIS). The SAND Internet Browser is part of a considerably more complex system rooted in the QUILT quadtree GIS [1732], the SAND spatial database engine [71, 73], and the SANDTcl scripting tool for building spatial database applications [568, 570].

One substantial difference in the current book from [1637] is the inclusion of a part on high-dimensional data, representing approximately one third of the text (Chapter 4). In addition, almost all of the material on object-based and image-based representations in Chapter 2 is new. It is interesting to note that this material and the observation that most object representations are motivated by the desire to respond to the *what* and *where* queries served as the motivation for this book. Similarly, much of the material on point-based representations in Chapter 1 is also new with a particular emphasis on bucketing methods. In the case of linear hashing and spiral hashing, the explanations of the methods have been moved to Appendix B and C, respectively, while Chapter 1 focuses on how to adapt them to multidimensional data. Since the B-tree is really a fundamental foundation of the various bucket methods in Chapter 1 and of hierarchical object-based interior representations such as the R-tree in Chapter 2, an overview of B-trees has been included as Appendix A. This was motivated by our past experience with [1637], which revealed that often the extent to which readers were familiar with the B-tree did not match our expectations. Only Chapter 3, which deals with intervals and collections of rectangles, can be considered as both an update and an expansion of material in [1637] as it also contains a substantial number of new representations.

The main focus of this book is on representations and indexing methods rather than the execution of operations using them, which is the primary focus of another one of my books [1636]. Nevertheless, a few operations are discussed in greater detail. In particular, substantial coverage is given to the k-nearest neighbor finding operation in Sections 4.1 and 4.2 in Chapter 4. Its use in similarity searching is the main reason for the development of most of the representations discussed in this chapter. The related point location problem is also discussed in great detail in Sections 2.1.3.2 and 2.1.3.3 of Chapter 2. Another operation that is discussed in some detail (in Section 2.2.3.4 of Chapter 2) is simplification of surface data for applications in computer graphics and visualization. We assume that the representations and operations that we discuss are implemented in a serial environment although there has been a considerable interest in implementations in a parallel environment (e.g., [210, 213, 373, 470, 524, 532, 862, 898, 916, 997, 1182, 1719, 2006] and related references cited therein), as well as in making use of graphics processing units (GPU) (e.g., [739, 1146, 1815]).

Nevertheless there remain many topics for which justice requires a considerably more thorough treatment. However, due to space limitations, detailed discussion of them has been omitted, and, instead, the interested reader is referred to the appropriate literature. For example, surface representations are discussed in the context of boundary-based representations in Section 2.2 of Chapter 2. These are known as topological data structures. However, the area is much richer than what is covered here as can be seen by referring to the collection of papers edited by Rana [1536]. The presentation in Chapter 2 mentions simplification methods and data structures (Section 2.2.3.4) and hierarchical surface-based boundary representations (Sections 2.2.2–2.2.4). Simplification methods are also known as *Level of Detail (LOD) methods* and are reviewed comprehensively in the text by Luebke, Reddy, Cohen, Varshney, Watson, and Huebner [1212]. Additional work from the perspective of geometric modeling can be found in the texts by Bartels, Beatty, and Barsky [131], Mortenson [1316], Goldman [716], Farin [596], and Warren and Weimer [1962]. Many of the topics discussed here can also be classified under the category of *visual computing* (e.g., see Nielsen [1372]). Another related area in which our coverage is intentionally limited is real-time collision detection where speed is of the essence, especially in applications such as game programming. For a thorough treatment of this topic, see the recent texts by van den Bergen [198] and Ericson [564]. Similarly, representations for spatiotemporal data and moving objects are not discussed in great detail, and interested readers are referred to some of the references mentioned earlier.

Solid modeling is another rich area where the presentation has been limited to the boundary model (BRep), found in Section 2.2.1 of Chapter 2, which also includes a detailed discussion of variants of the winged-edge representation. For more detailed expositions on this and related topics, see the books by Mäntylä [1232], Hoffmann [870], and Paoluzzi [1457]. See also some early influential survey articles by Requicha [1555], Srihari [1798], and Chen and Huang [345]. Of course, there is also a much greater connection to computer graphics than that which is made in the text. This connection is explored further in another of my books [1636] and is also discussed in some early surveys by Overmars [1442] and Samet and Webber [1666, 1667].

Results from computational geometry, although related to many of the topics covered in this book, are only presented in the context of representations for intervals and collections of small rectangles (Sections 3.1 and 3.2 of Chapter 3) and the point location problem (Sections 2.1.3.2 and 2.1.3.3 of Chapter 2). For more details on early work involving some of these and related topics, the interested reader is encouraged to consult the texts by Preparata and Shamos [1511], Edelsbrunner [540], Boissonnat and Yvince [230], and de Berg, van Kreveld, Overmars, and Schwarzkopf [196], as well as the early collections of papers edited by Preparata [1509] and Toussaint [1884]. See also the surveys and problem collections by Edelsbrunner [539]. O'Rourke [1423], and Toussaint [1885]. This work is closely related to earlier research on searching as surveyed by Bentley and Friedman [173], the text of Overmars [1440], and Mehlhorn's [1282] text, which contains a unified treatment of multidimensional searching. For a detailed examination of similar and related topics in the context of external memory and massive amounts of data, see the survey of Vitter [1933].

Many of the data structures described in this book find use in spatial databases, geographic information systems (GIS), and multimedia databases. The close relationship between spatial databases and geographic information systems is evidenced by recent texts that combine results from the areas, such as those of Laurini and Thompson [1113], Worboys [2023], Günther [773], Rigaux, Scholl, and Voisard [1562], and Shekhar and Chawla [1746], as well as the surveys of Güting [784], Voisard and David [1938], and Shekhar, Chawla, Ravada, Fetterer, Liu, and Lu [1747].

For a slightly different perspective, see the text of Subrahmanian [1807], which deals with multimedia databases. Another related area where these data structures have been used is constraint databases, which are discussed in great detail in the recent text by Revesz [1559]. Note that, with the exception of the nearest neighbor finding operation, which is common to many of the fields spanned by this book, we do not discuss the numerous spatial database operations whose execution is facilitated by the data structures presented in this text, such as, for example, spatial join (e.g., [89, 262, 261, 772, 1072, 894, 934, 1195, 1207, 1223, 1415, 1474, 2076] as well as in a recent survey [935]), which are covered in some of the previously cited references.

In a similar vein, a number of survey articles have been written that deal with the representations that are described in this book from a database perspective, such as the one by Gaede and Günther [670]. The survey article by Samet [1642], however, combines a computer graphics/computer vision perspective with a database perspective. See also the earlier surveys by Nagy and Wagle [1335], Samet and Rosenfeld [1647], Peuquet [1490], and Samet [1628, 1632]. Others, such as Chávez, Navarro, Baeza-Yates, and Marroquín [334], Böhm, Berchtold, and Keim [224], Hjaltason and Samet [854, 855], and Clarkson [401], are oriented towards similarity searching applications.

The material in this book also has a strong connection to work in image processing and computer vision. In particular, the notion of a pyramid (discussed in Section 2.1.5.1 of Chapter 2) has a rich history, as can be seen in the collection of articles edited by Tanimoto and Klinger [1844] and Rosenfeld [1573]. The connection to pattern recognition is also important and can be seen in the survey by Toussaint [1882]. The pioneering text by Rosenfeld and Kak [1574] is a good early treatment of image processing and should be consulted in conjunction with the more recent text by Klette and Rosenfeld [1034], which makes the connection to digital geometry.

Nevertheless, given the broad and rapidly expanding nature of the field, I am bound to have omitted significant concepts and references. In addition, at times I devote a disproportionate amount of attention to some concepts at the expense of others. This is principally for expository purposes; in particular, I feel that it is better for the reader to understand some structures well rather than to receive a quick runthrough of buzzwords. For these indiscretions, I beg your pardon and still hope that you bear with me.

Usually my approach is an algorithmic one. Whenever possible, I have tried to motivate critical steps in the algorithms by a liberal use of examples. This is based on my strong conviction that it is of paramount importance for the reader to see the ease with which the representations can be implemented and used. At times, some algorithms are presented using pseudo-code so that readers can see how the ideas can be applied. I have deliberately not made use of any specific programming language in order to avoid dating the material while also acknowledging the diverse range in opinion at any given instance of time as to which language is appropriate. The main purpose of the pseudo-code is to present the algorithm clearly. The pseudo-code is algorithmic and is a variant of the ALGOL [1346] programming language, which has a data structuring facility incorporating pointers and record structures. I do not make use of object orientation although my use of record structures is similar in spirit to rudimentary classes in SIMULA [437] and FLEX [1008], which are the precursors of modern object-oriented methods. I make heavy use of recursion. This language has similarities to C [1017], C++ [1805], Java (e.g., [93]), PASCAL [952], SAIL [1553], and ALGOL W [137]. Its basic features are described in Appendix D. However, the actual code is not crucial to understanding the techniques, and it may be skipped on a first reading. The index indicates the page numbers where the code for each algorithm is found.

In many cases I also give an analysis of the space and time requirements of different data structures and algorithms. The analysis is usually of an asymptotic nature and is in terms of *big O* and Ω notation [1043]. The *big O* notation denotes an upper bound. For example, if an algorithm takes $O(\log_2 N)$ time, then its worst-case behavior is never any worse than $\log_2 N$. The Ω notation denotes a lower bound. As an example of its use, consider the problem of sorting N numbers. When we say that sorting is $\Omega(N \cdot \log_2 N)$ we mean that given any algorithm for sorting, there is some set of N input values for which the algorithm will require at least this much time.

At times, I also describe implementations of some of the data structures for the purpose of comparison. In such cases, counts such as the number of fields in a record are often given. However, these numbers are only meant to clarify the discussion. They are not to be taken literally, as improvements are always possible once a specific application is analyzed more carefully.

Each section contains a substantial number of exercises. Many of the exercises develop the material in the text further as a means of testing the reader's understanding, as well as suggesting future directions. When the exercise or its solution is not my own, I have credited its originator by preceding it with their name. The exercises have not been graded by difficulty. Usually, their solution does not require any mathematical skills beyond the undergraduate level. However, while some of the exercises are quite straightforward, the solutions to others require some ingenuity. Solutions, or references to papers that contain the solutions, are provided for a substantial number of the exercises that do not require programming. Of course, the reader is counseled to try to solve the exercises before turning to the solutions. The solutions are presented here as it is my belief that much can be learned by self-study (both for the student and, even more so, for the author!). The motivation for pursuing this approach was my wonderful experience on my first encounter with the rich work on data structures by Knuth [1044, 1045, 1046].

An extensive bibliography is provided. It contains entries for both this book and its companion predecessors [1636, 1637]. Each reference is annotated with one or more keywords and a list of the numbers of the book sections in which it is cited in the current text (denoted by F) or either of the other two texts (denoted by D for [1637] and A for [1636]) as well as in the exercises and solutions. Not all of the references that appear in the bibliography are cited in the text. They are included for the purpose of providing readers the ability to access as completely as possible the body of literature relevant to the topics discussed in the books. In order to increase the usefulness of these uncited references (as well as all of the references), a separate keyword index is provided that indicates some of the references in the bibliography that discuss them. Of course, this list is not exhaustive. For the more general categories (e.g., "points"), a second level index entry is often provided to narrow the search in locating relevant references. In addition, a name and credit index is provided that indicates the page numbers in this book on which each author's work is cited or a credit (i.e., acknowledgement) is made (e.g., in the main text, preface, appendices, exercises, or solutions).

My target audience is a varied one. The book is designed to be of use to professionals who are interested in the representation of spatial and multidimensional data and have a need for an understanding of the various issues that are involved so that they can make a proper choice in their application. The presentation is an algorithmic one rather than a mathematical one although the execution time and storage requirements are discussed. Nevertheless, the reader need not be a programmer nor a mathematician to appreciate the concepts described here. The material is useful not just to computer scientists. It is useful for applications in a diverse range of fields including geography, high-energy physics, engineering, mathematics, games, multimedia, bioinformatics, and other disciplines where location or the concept of a metric are important. The book can also be used in courses on a number of topics including databases, geographic information systems (GIS), computer graphics, computational geometry, pattern recognition, and so on, where the discussion of the data structures that it describes supplements existing material or serves as the central topic of the course. The book can also be used in a second course on data structures where the focus is on multidimensional and metric data structures. The organization of the material to be covered in these courses is discussed in greater detail below.

A Guide to the Instructor

This book can be used in a course on representations for multidimensional and metric data in multimedia databases, most likely at the graduate level. Such a course would include topics from the various parts as is appropriate to match the interests of the students. It would most likely be taught within a database framework, in which case the focus would be on the representation of points as in Chapter 1 and high-dimensional data in Chapter 4. In particular, the emphasis would be on bucket methods (Sections 1.1, 1.7, and 1.8 of Chapter 1), multidimensional indexing methods for high-dimensional data (Section 4.4 of Chapter 4), and distance-based indexing methods (Section 4.5 of Chapter 4). In addition, quite a bit of attention should be focused on representations based on object hierarchies such as the R-tree (Section 2.1.5.2 of Chapter 2).

The book can also be used in a computer graphics/computer vision/solid modeling framework, as well as part of a game programming course, in which case the emphasis would be on Chapters 2 and 3. In addition, it should include the discussion of some of the more basic representations of point data from Sections 1.1 and 1.4–1.6 of Chapter 1. Such a course could serve as a prerequisite to courses in computer graphics and solid modeling, computational geometry, database management systems (DBMS), multidimensional searching, image processing, and VLSI design applications. More specifically, such a course would include the discussions of interior-based representations of image data in Sections 2.1.1–2.1.3 of Chapter 2 and representations of image data by their boundaries in Sections 2.2.2 and 2.2.3 of Chapter 2. The representation of two-dimensional regions such as chain codes in Section 2.3.2 of Chapter 2 and polygonal representations in Section 2.2.2 of Chapter 2 and the use of point methods for focusing the Hough Transform in Section 1.5.1.4 of Chapter 1 should also be included as they are relevant to image processing.

The discussions of plane-sweep methods and their associated data structures such as the segment tree, interval tree, and priority search tree in Sections 3.1 and 3.2 of Chapter 3, and of point location and associated data structures such as the K-structure and the layered dag in Sections 2.1.3.2 and 2.1.3.3, respectively, of Chapter 2, are all relevant to computational geometry. Other relevant topics in this context are the Voronoi Diagram and the Delaunay triangulation and tetrahedralization in Sections 2.2.1.4– 2.2.1.7 of Chapter 2 as well as the approximate Voronoi diagram (AVD) in Section 4.4.5 of Chapter 4. The discussion of boundary-based representations such as the winged-edge data structure in Sections 2.2.1.1–2.2.1.3 of Chapter 2 is also relevant to computational geometry as well as to solid modeling. In addition, observe that the discussions of rectangle-representation methods and plane-sweep methods in Chapter 3 are of use for VLSI design applications.

Moreover, it is worth repeating the earlier comment that the discussion of bucket methods such as linear hashing, spiral hashing, grid file, and EXCELL, discussed in Sections 1.7 and 1.8 of Chapter 1, as well as the various variants of object hierarchies as typified by the R-tree in Section 2.1.5.2 of Chapter 2, are important in the study of database management systems. The discussion of topics such as k-d trees in Section 1.5 of Chapter 1, range trees in Section 1.2 of Chapter 1, priority search trees priority search tree in Section 1.3 of Chapter 1, and point-based rectangle representations in Section 3.3 of Chapter 3 are all relevant to multidimensional searching.

Another potential venue for using the book is a course on representations for spatial data either in a geography department where it would be part of a curriculum on geographic information systems (GIS) or within the context of course on spatial databases in a computer science department. Again, the material that would be covered would be a combination of that which is covered in a multimedia database course and the computer graphics/computer vision/solid modeling or game programming course. In this case, much of the material on the representation of high-dimensional data in Chapter 4 would be omitted although the material on nearest neighbor finding and approximate nearest neighbor finding (Sections 4.1–4.3 of Chapter 4) would be included. In addition, a greater emphasis would be placed on the representation of objects by their interiors (Section 2.1 of Chapter 2) and by their boundaries (Section 2.2 of Chapter 2).

This book could also be used in a second data structures course. The emphasis would be on the representation of spatial data. In particular, the focus would be on the use of the principle of "divide-and-conquer." Hierarchical data structures provide a good demonstration of this principle. In this case, the choice of topics is left to the instructor although one possible organization of topics would choose some of the simpler representations from the various chapters as follows.

From Chapter 1, some interesting topics include the fixed-grid method and some of its variants (Section 1.1); numerous variants of quadtrees such as the point quadtree (Section 1.4.1), PR quadtree (Section 1.4.2.2), k-d tree (Section 1.5), and variants thereof (Sections 1.5.1.4, 1.5.2.1, and 1.5.2.3); bucket methods such as the grid file (Section 1.7.2.1), EXCELL (Section 1.7.2.2), linear hashing (Section 1.7.2.3.1 and Appendix B); range trees (Section 1.2); priority search trees for points (Section 1.3); and the comparison of some of the structures (Section 1.9).

From Chapter 2, some interesting topics include the opening matter (preambles of both the chapter and of Section 2.1); unit-size cells (Section 2.1.1 with the exception of the discussion of cell shapes and tilings in Section 2.1.1.1); blocks (Sections 2.1.2.1–2.1.2.9); BSP tree (Section 2.1.3.1); winged-edge data structure (Sections 2.2.1.1 and 2.2.1.2); image-based boundary representations such as the MX quadtree and MX octree (Section 2.2.2.2), PM quadtree (Section 2.2.2.6), and PM octree (Section 2.2.2.7); and hierarchical object-based interior representations such as the R-tree (Section 2.1.5.2.1).

From Chapter 3, some interesting topics include the discussion of plane-sweep methods and data structures such as the segment tree (Section 3.1.1), interval tree (Section 3.1.2), and the priority search tree for rectangles and intervals (Section 3.1.3) and the MX-CIF quadtree (Section 3.4.1).

From Chapter 4, the most interesting topic is the incremental nearest neighbor algorithm (Sections 4.1.1–4.1.3). A brief introduction to distance-based indexing methods is also appropriate. In this case the most appropriate representations for inclusion are the vp-tree (Sections 4.5.2.1.1 and 4.5.2.1.1), the gh-tree (Section 4.5.3.1), and the mb-tree (Section 4.5.3.3).

Throughout the book, both worst-case optimal methods and methods that work well in practice are emphasized. This is in accordance with my view that the well-rounded computer scientist should be conversant with both types of algorithms. It is clear that the material in this book is more than can be covered in one semester. Thus the instructor will invariably need to reduce it as necessary. For example, in many cases, the detailed examples can be skipped or used as a basis of a term project or programming assignments.

Note that regardless of the course in which this book is used, as pointed out earlier, the VASCO [243, 244, 245, 246]) set of JAVA applets can be used to illustrate many operations for a large number of the data structures presented in the current book (see *http://www.cs.umd.edu/~hjs/quadtree/index.html*). In particular, for point data, it includes the point quadtree, k-d tree (also known as a point k-d tree), MX quadtree, PR quadtree, bucket PR quadtree, PR k-d tree, bucket PR k-d tree, PMR quadtree, PMR k-d tree, 2-d range tree (also known as a two-dimensional range tree), priority search tree, R-tree, and the PK-tree. For line data, it includes the PM_1 quadtree, PM_2 quadtree, PM_3 quadtree, PMR quadtree, bucket PM quadtree, and the R-tree. For collections of rectangles, it includes the MX-CIF quadtree, rectangle quadtree, bucket rectangle quadtree (also known as a bucket rectangle PM quadtree), PMR rectangle quadtree (also known as a PMR rectangle quadtree), PMR rectangle k-d tree, and R-tree. For all of these data structures, students can see how they are built step by step, and also how queries such as deletion, finding nearest neighbors, and overlap queries (which include the more general range query and corridor or buffer queries) are supported. In each case, the operation proceeds incrementally. Finally, an applet is also provided for the region quadtree that shows how it can be constructed from other region representations such as rasters and chain codes as well as how to obtain them from the region quadtree.

Instructors who adopt this book in a course are also welcome to use a comprehensive set of lecture notes in the form of Powerpoint/PDF presentations that help clarify many of the concepts presented in the book.

Acknowledgments

Over the years I have received help from many people, and for this I am extremely grateful to them. In particular, I would like to acknowledge the assistance and friendship of Gísli R. Hjaltason, whose sharp insight and critical thinking helped me clarify many of the concepts presented in this book over a very long time period during which we had daily discussions and interactions. He also set up all of the LaTeX typesetting macros that made it easy to assemble this book as well as drawing many of the figures and the original slides that accompany much of the text. I am deeply indebted to him. I would also like to acknowledge the many useful and critical discussions that I have had with Houman Alborzi as well as unstinting help in getting the final manuscript together. In addition, I have also been helped immensely by Jagan Sankaranarayanan, as well as Frantisek Brabec, Frank Morgan, and William Cheng in the preparation of the figures and the associated technical issues, and Brian Norberg in the preparation of the Powerpoint versions of many of the slides that accompany much of the text. I am deeply appreciative to Janice Perrone for providing logistical support in various daily tasks in which she was cheerfully assisted by David Madoo. I am grateful to Richard R. Muntz for generously providing office space, computer access, parking, mailing facilities, and most importantly being a sounding board at UCLA during many visits there. The system to compile the exhaustive bibliography was set up by Ron Sivan, and in the actual compilation process I was ably assisted by Nazanin Poorfarhani, Sze-Kit Hsu, Rene McDonald, and Astrid Hellmuth. Phil Bernstein, Per-Åke Larson, and Carlo Zaniolo graciously provided last-minute access to their personal library of conference proceedings to enable me to double-check some of my bibliography; of course, any errors are my responsibility.

At the same time, I would also like to thank again Robert E. Webber, Markku Tamminen, and Michael B. Dillencourt, who gave me much help in my first two books [1636, 1637], thereby making it much easier to write this book. I have also been extremely fortunate to work with Azriel Rosenfeld over the past thirty years. His dedication and scholarship have been a true inspiration to me. I deeply cherish our association. Finally, I want to also thank Gary D. Knott who introduced me to the field of multidimensional data structures by asking "how to delete in point quadtrees," and Charles R. Dyer who provided much interaction in the initial phase of my research when my focus was on computer vision applications of such data structures.

During the time that this book was written, my research was supported, in part, by the National Science Foundation, the Department of Energy, the Office of Policy Development and Research of the Department of Housing and Urban Development, and Microsoft Research. In particular, I would like to thank Tom Barclay, Larry Brandt, Dan Fay, Robert Grafton, Jim Gray, Dan Hitchcock, Howard Moraff, Rita Rodriguez, Mukesh Singhal, Jonathan Sperling, Bhavani Thuraisingham, Kentaro Toyama, and Maria Zemankova. I would also like to thank the support in previous years of the National Science Foundation, Defense Mapping Agency, US Army Engineering Topographic Laboratory, and the Harry Diamond Laboratory. In particular, I would like to thank Richard T. Antony, Su-Shing Chen, Y. T. Chien, Hank Cook, Phil J. Emmerman, Fred Esch, Joe Rastatter, Alan Saalfeld, and Larry Tokarcik. I am very appreciative of the support of all of them.

Aside, from the individuals named above, I have also benefited from discussions with many people over the past years. They have commented on various parts of the book and include Chuan-Heng Ang, Walid G. Aref, Lars Arge, John Arras, Renato Barrera, S. K. Bhaskar, Pedja Bogdanovich, Kaushink Chakrabarti, William Cheng, Larry S. Davis, Wiebren de Jonge, Daniel DeMenthon, Leila De Floriani, Michael B. Dillencourt, Sydney D'Silva, Claudio Esperança, Hakan Ferhatosmanoglu, Andre Folkers, Guilherme Fonseca, Mike W. Freeston, B. Brent Gordon, Eric Haines, Andreas Henrich, Michael E. Houle, Glenn S. Iwerks, Edwin Jacox, Ibrahim Kamel, Laveen N. Kanal, Simon Kasif, Benjamin B. Kimia, Hans-Peter Kriegel, Sam Lamphier, Nati

Linial, Paola Magillo, Maurizio Martelli, Songrit Maneewongvatana, Sharad Mehrotra, Daniel P. Miranker, David M. Mount, Richard R. Muntz, Michael Murphy, Brad G. Nickerson, Helmut Noltemeier, Aris M. Ouksel, Valerio Pascucci, Franco P. Preparata, Ari Rappoport, Manjit Ray, Azriel Rosenfeld, Peter Scheuermann, Günther F. Schrack, George Scott, Bernhard Seeger, Ben Shneiderman, Aya Soffer, Matti Tikkanen, Thatcher Ulrich, Amitabh Varshney, Robert E. Webber, Isaac Weiss, Peter Widmayer, Changjiang Yang, and Kaizhong Zhang.

The final preparation of the book was greatly aided by the helpful reviews of Charles R. Dyer, Jim Gray, Dinesh Manocha, Peter Revesz, Peter Scheuermann, Claudio T. Silva, and Bretton Wade. Their help and interest is very much appreciated. Similarly, I have been very fortunate to work with Diane Cerra of Morgan Kaufmann Publishers, who has been very patient with me during the many years that we have talked about the book, and I appreciate her confidence that it would happen. Most importantly, I am very grateful for her enthusiasm and for enabling me to reach my intended audience by ensuring the production of a book that is affordable while also being of the highest technical and production quality. During the years that I have been working on this book I have also benefited from discussions with representatives of other publishers and I am appreciative of the time they took to discuss the book with me. In particular, I would like to thank Peter Gordon, Alfred Hofmann, Ingeborg Mayer, David Pallai, Alice Peters, Simone Taylor, and Hans Wossner.

I was very fortunate to have the assistance of Ken DellaPenta in copy editing the book. Ken was amazing in terms of the number of technical errors that he caught, besides teaching me the Chicago Style and having the patience to answer my numerous questions. The actual composition and final layout of the book was ably handled by Paul C. Anagnostopoulos of Windfall Software, who capably incorporated the LaTeX macros and scripts that we developed into a viable system that could turn out the final version of the book using the ZzTeX system. I also appreciated his valuable technical advice. Darice Moore exhibited great patience in managing the interactions between the art house, the author, and compositor on getting the figures into shape. The production end was ably coordinated by Alan Rose, who kept us all on schedule and tactfully refereed the numerous production issues that invariably arise in such a big effort.

I would also like to acknowledge discussions with the following additional people on my other two books, which also had an effect on the contents of this book: James Arvo, Harvey H. Atkinson, Thor Bestul, Sharat Chandran, Chiun-Hong Chien, Jiang-Hsing Chu, Roger D. Eastman, Herbert Edelsbrunner, Christos Faloutsos, George (Gyuri) Fekete, Kikuo Fujimura, John Gannon, John Goldak, Erik G. Hoel, Liuqing Huang, Frederik W. Jansen, Ajay Kela, David Kirk, Per-Åke Larson, Dani Lischinski, Don Meagher, Randal C. Nelson, Glenn Pearson, Ron Sacks-Davis, Timos Sellis, Clifford A. Shaffer, Deepak Sherlekar, Li Tong, Brian Von Herzen, and David S. Wise.

Last, but not least, I would like to express my thanks and appreciation to my wife, Leila, for her love, encouragement, support, confidence, and patience during the too many years that this book took to complete. I would also like to thank my parents, Julius Samet and Lotte Samet, and in-laws, Ario De Floriani and Dalma Paravagna, for their support and belief in me, as well as my Uncle Seev Berlinger for his inspiration and imbuing me with the notion that your work should also be fun, as if it was your hobby. To all of them, I owe a lot and am forever indebted.

Multidimensional Point Data

The representation of multidimensional point data is a central issue in database design, as well as applications in many other fields, including computer graphics, computer vision, computational geometry, image processing, geographic information systems (GIS), pattern recognition, very large scale integration (VLSI) design, and others. These points can represent locations and objects in space, as well as more general records. As an example of a general record, consider an employee record that has attributes corresponding to the employee's name, address, sex, age, height, weight, and Social Security number. Such records arise in database management systems and can be treated as points in, for this example, a seven-dimensional space (i.e., there is one dimension for each attribute or key[1]), albeit the different dimensions have different type units (i.e., name and address are strings of characters; sex is binary; and age, height, weight, and Social Security number are numbers).

Formally speaking, a database is a collection of records, termed a *file*. There is one record per data point, and each record contains several attributes or keys. In order to facilitate retrieval of a record based on some of the values of attributes,[2] we assume the existence of an ordering for the range of values of each of these attributes. In the case of locational or numeric attributes, such an ordering is quite obvious because the values of these attributes are numbers. In the case of alphanumeric attributes, the ordering is usually based on the alphabetic sequence of the characters making up the attribute value. Other data such as color could be ordered by the characters making up the name of the color or, possibly, the color's wavelength. It should be clear that finding an ordering for the range of values of an attribute is generally not an issue; the only issue is what ordering to use!

The representation that is ultimately chosen for this collection depends, in part, on answers to the following questions:

1. What is the type of the data (e.g., is it discrete, is it continuous, is its domain finite)?

2. What operations are to be performed on the data?

3. Should we organize the data or the embedding space from which the data is drawn?

---

[1] We use the terms *key* and *attribute* (as well as *field*, *dimension*, *coordinate*, and *axis*) interchangeably in this chapter. We choose among them based on the context of the discussion, while attempting to be consistent with their use in the literature.

[2] This is also known as *secondary key retrieval* (e.g., [1046]) to distinguish it from *primary key retrieval*. In secondary key retrieval, the search is based on the value of more than just one attribute, as is the case in traditional searching applications where we are dealing with one-dimensional data.

4. Is the database static or dynamic (i.e., can the number of data points grow and shrink at will)?

5. Can we assume that the volume of data is sufficiently small so that it can all fit in main memory, or should we make provisions for accessing disk-resident data?

The type of the data is an important question. Of course, we must distinguish between data consisting of one and several attributes. Classical attribute values include bits, integers, real numbers, complex numbers, characters, strings, and so on. There is also the issue of whether the domain from which the data is drawn is finite (i.e., bounded) or not. This distinction is used, in part, to determine which of the data organizations in question 3 can be used. An alternative differentiation is on the basis of whether the data is discrete or continuous. In the case of data that is used in conventional scientific computations, discrete data corresponds to integers, while continuous data corresponds to real and complex numbers. In the case of spatial data, we have discrete data (by which we mean distinct samples or instances) such as points (which is the subject of this chapter and, to a lesser extent, Chapter 4), while continuous data consists of objects that take up space such as line segments, areas, surfaces, volumes, and so on (which are the subject of Chapter 2 and, to a lesser extent, Chapter 3). Similarly, temporal data can also be differentiated on the basis of whether it is discrete or continuous. In particular, concepts such as event time and transaction time are indicative of a discrete approach, while concepts such as rates are more indicative of a continuous approach in that they recognize that the data is constantly changing over time. In this book, we do not deal with temporal data (e.g., [951]) or the closely related concept of spatiotemporal data (e.g., [21, 950, 1305]).

The distinction in question 3 is formulated in terms of the notion of an *embedding space*. The embedding space is determined by the span of values of the data. For example, suppose that we have a set of employee records with a state-valued attribute called STATE whose embedding space is the set of names of the 50 U.S. states. In this case, our distinction is between organizing the employee records on the basis of the value of the STATE attribute (e.g., all employee records whose STATE attribute value starts with letters A–M in one group and all employee records whose STATE attribute value starts with letters N–Z in another group) or organizing the employee records on the basis of the value of this attribute for the record of a particular employee (e.g., if employee records are grouped into two groups based on whether the first letter of the value of their STATE attribute is less than or equal to the first letter of the value of the STATE attribute for the record corresponding to an employee named "John Smith").

As another example, in the case of a computer architecture where the representation of each data item is implemented by one word of 32 bits, then, for simple integer data, the embedding space spans the values 0 to $2^{32} - 1$, while it is considerably larger for real data, where it depends on the way in which the representation of simple real data is implemented (i.e., in the case of floating-point representation, the number of bits allocated to the mantissa and to the exponent). In both cases of the example above, the embedding space is said to be finite.

The distinction made in question 3 is often used to differentiate between one-dimensional searching methods (e.g., [1046]) that are tree-based from those that are trie-based. In particular, a *trie* [251, 635] is a branching structure in which the value of each data item or key is treated as a sequence of j characters, where each character has M possible values. A node at depth $k - 1$ ($k \geq 1$) in the trie represents an M-way branch depending on the value of the kth character (i.e., it has M possible values). Some (and at times all) of the data is stored in the leaf nodes, and the shape of the trie is independent of the order in which the data is processed.

For example, address computation methods such as radix searching [1046] (also known as *digital searching* and yielding structures known as *digital trees*) are instances of trie-based methods, since the boundaries of the partition regions of similarly valued data that result from the partitioning (i.e., branching) process are drawn from among locations that are fixed regardless of the content of the file. Therefore, these trie-based methods are said to organize the data on the basis of the embedding space from which they are drawn. Because the positions of the boundaries of the regions are fixed, the range of the embedding space from which the data is drawn must be known (said to be *bounded*). On the other hand, in one dimension, the binary search tree [1046] is an example of a tree-based method since the boundaries of different regions in the search space are determined by the data being stored. Such methods are said to *organize the data* rather than the embedding space from which the data is drawn. Note that although trie-based methods are primarily designed to organize integer-valued data since the partition values (i.e., the boundaries of the partition regions) are also integer valued, nevertheless they can also be used to organize real-valued data, in which case the real-valued data are compared to predetermined partition values (e.g., 0.5, 0.25, 0.75, in the case of real numbers between 0 and 1), which, again, are the boundaries of the partition regions. Of course, the data must still be bounded (i.e., its values must be drawn from within a given range).

The extension of a trie to multidimensional data is relatively straightforward and proceeds as follows. Assume d-dimensional data where each data item consists of d character sequences corresponding to the d attributes. Each character of the ith sequence has M_i possible values. A node at depth $k-1$ ($k \geq 1$) in the multidimensional trie represents an $\prod_{i=1}^{d} M_i$-way branch, depending on the value of the kth character of each of the d attribute values.[3] For attributes whose value is of numeric type, which is treated as a sequence of binary digits, this process is usually a halving process in one dimension, a quartering process in two dimensions, and so on, and is known as *regular decomposition*. We use this characterization frequently in our discussion of multidimensional data when all of the attributes are locational.

Disk-resident data implies grouping the data (either the underlying space based on the volume—that is, the amount—of the data it contains or the points, hopefully, by the proximity of their values) into sets (termed *buckets*), corresponding to physical storage units (i.e., pages). This leads to questions about their size and how they are to be accessed, including the following:

1. Do we require a constant time to retrieve a record from a file, or is a logarithmic function of the number of records in the file adequate? This is equivalent to asking if the access is via a directory in the form of an array (i.e., direct access) or in the form of a tree (i.e., a branching structure).

2. How large can the directories be allowed to grow before it is better to rebuild them?

3. How should the buckets be laid out on the disk?

In this chapter, we examine several representations that address these questions. Our primary focus is on dynamic data, and we concentrate on the following queries:

1. Point queries that determine if a given point p is in the dataset. If yes, then the result is the address corresponding to the record in which p is stored. This query is more accurately characterized as an *exact match query* in order to distinguish it from the related point query in the context of objects that finds all the objects that contain a given point (see, e.g., Section 3.3.1 of Chapter 3).

2. Range queries (e.g., region search) that yield a set of data points whose specified keys have specific values or values within given ranges. These queries include the partially specified query, also known as the *partial match query* and the *partial range query*, in which case unspecified keys take on the range of the key as their domain.

3. Boolean combinations of 1 and 2 using the Boolean operations **and**, **or**, and **not**.

---

[3] When the ith character sequence has less than k characters, there is no corresponding branching at depth $k-1$ for this attribute.

When multidimensional data corresponds to locational data, we have the additional property that all of the attributes have the same unit, which is distance in space.[4] In this case, we can combine the attributes and pose queries that involve proximity. Assuming a Euclidean distance metric, for example, we may wish to find all cities within 50 miles of Chicago. This query is a special case of the range query, which would seek all cities within 50 miles of the latitude position of Chicago and within 50 miles of the longitude position of Chicago.[5] A related query seeks to find the closest city to Chicago within the two-dimensional space from which the locations of the cities are drawn—that is, a nearest neighbor query, also sometimes referred to as the *post office problem* (e.g., [1046, p. 563]). This problem arises in many different fields, including computer graphics, where it is known as a *pick query* (e.g., [622]); in coding, where it is known as the *vector quantization problem* (e.g., [747]); and in pattern recognition, as well as machine learning, where it is known as the *fast nearest-neighbor classifier* (e.g., [514]). We do not deal with such queries in this chapter (but see [846, 848, 854] and Sections 4.1 and 4.2 of Chapter 4).

In contrast, proximity queries are not very meaningful when the attributes do not have the same type or units. For example, it is not customary to seek all people with age-weight combination less than 50 year-pounds (year-kilograms) of that of John Jones, or the person with age-weight combination closest to John Jones because we do not have a commonly accepted unit of year-pounds (year-kilograms) or a definition thereof.[6] It should be clear that we are not speaking of queries involving Boolean combinations of the different attributes (e.g., range queries), which are quite common.

The representations that we describe are applicable to data with an arbitrary number of attributes d. The attributes need not be locational or numeric, although all of our examples and explanations assume that all of the attributes are locational or numeric. In order to be able to visualize the representations, we let $d = 2$. All of our examples make use of the simple database of records corresponding to eight cities given in Figure 1.1.[7] Each record has three attributes, NAME, X, and Y, corresponding to their name and location. We assume that our queries retrieve only on the basis of the values of the X and Y attributes. Thus, $d = 2$, and no ordering is assumed on the NAME field. In particular, the NAME field is just used to aid us in referring to the actual locations and is not really part of the record when we describe the various representations in this chapter. Some of these representations can also be adapted to handle records where the attributes are nonlocational, as long as an ordering exists for their range of values. Moreover, Section 4.5 of Chapter 4 contains a discussion of how some of these representations can be adapted to handle records where the only information available is the relative distance between pairs of records.

NAME	X	Y
Chicago	35	42
Mobile	52	10
Toronto	62	77
Buffalo	82	65
Denver	5	45
Omaha	27	35
Atlanta	85	15
Miami	90	5

Figure 1.1
Sample list of cities with their *x* and *y* coordinate values.

---

[4] The requirement that the attribute value be a unit of distance in space is stronger than one that merely requires the unit to be a number. For example, if one attribute is the length of a pair of pants and the other is the width of the waist, then, although the two attribute values are numbers, the two attributes are not locational.

[5] The difference between these two formulations of the query is that the former admits a circular search region, while the latter admits a rectangular search region. In particular, the latter query is applicable to both locational and nonlocational data, while the former is applicable only to locational data.

[6] This query is further complicated by the need to define the distance metric. We have assumed a Euclidean distance metric. However, other distance metrics such as the City Block (also known as Manhattan) and the Chessboard (also known as maximum value) could also be used.

[7] Note that the correspondence between coordinate values and city names is not geographically accurate. We took this liberty so that the same example could be used throughout the chapter to illustrate a variety of concepts.

1.1 Introduction

There are many possible representations for a file of multidimensional point data. The feasibility of these representations depends, in part, on the number of attributes and their domains. At one extreme is a pure bitmap representation of the attribute space, with one bit reserved for each possible record (i.e., combination of attribute values) in the multidimensional point space to indicate whether it is present in the file. This representation is useful when the number of attributes d is small (i.e., $d \leq 2$) and the domains of the attributes are discrete and small (e.g., binary). Unfortunately, most applications have continuous domains, and the number of attributes exceeds two. Thus, we must look for other solutions.

The simplest way to store point data is in a sequential list. In this case, no ordering is assumed for any of the attributes. As an example, consider the set of records consisting of eight cities and their locations specified by their x and y coordinate values as shown in Figure 1.1. Given N records and d attributes to search on, an exact match query in such a data structure takes $O(N \cdot d)$ time since, in the worst case, the values of all of the attributes of each record must be examined (see Exercise 4).

Another very common technique is the *inverted file* [1046]. In this case, the roles of the records and the attributes are inverted: instead of keeping track of the values of the attributes of each record, we keep track of all records that have a particular value for a given attribute. In order to facilitate retrieval, all the records are sorted for the attribute on the basis of its value. The result is known as an *inverted list*. Often there are as many inverted lists as there are attributes.

There are many ways of implementing the inverted file. The simplest way is to maintain separate sorted lists for each attribute. For example, Figure 1.2 is such a representation for the data of Figure 1.1. There are two sorted lists: one for the x coordinate value and one for the y coordinate value. Note that the data stored in the lists are pointers into the set of records in Figure 1.1. Figure 1.2 makes use of sequential allocation for the inverted lists. We can also make use of linked allocation. In this case, we associate with each record as many linked lists as we have attributes, with the lists being linked in increasing or decreasing order of the values of the corresponding attributes. The result is known as a *multilist* (e.g., [1046]).

The most common use of the inverted list is to prune the search with respect to one key. In essence, the endpoints of the desired range for one key can be located very efficiently by using its corresponding sorted list. For example, this could be done by using a binary search with the aid of data structures such as the range tree [167, 176] (one-dimensional and the more general multidimensional range trees), as discussed in Section 1.2. When trying to execute a range query with respect to several keys, this resulting list is searched by brute force to obtain the records that satisfy the full range query (i.e., for the remaining keys). The average search has been shown in [649] to take $O(N^{1-1/d})$ time, under certain assumptions. This approach of making use of a sorted list for each coordinate has also been employed by Friedman, Baskett, and Shustek [649] (see also Section 4.6.1 in Chapter 4) as well as Nene and Nayar [1364], in conjunction with an algorithm to find neighbors in high-dimensional spaces (for other representations of such data, see Section 4.4 in Chapter 4).

It should be clear that the inverted list is not particularly useful for range queries involving several attributes because it can speed up the search for only one of the attributes (termed the *primary* attribute). Of course, we could execute the range query by performing a separate range query for each attribute and then intersect the result, but this is quite wasteful. The number of intersections can be reduced by sorting the records by applying a lexicographic ordering on the attributes, thereby forming a *combined index* [1214]. In essence, we have combined the attributes into a superattribute.

X	Y
Denver	Miami
Omaha	Mobile
Chicago	Atlanta
Mobile	Omaha
Toronto	Chicago
Buffalo	Denver
Atlanta	Buffalo
Miami	Toronto

Figure 1.2
Representation of the inverted file corresponding to the data of Figure 1.1 using separate sorted lists for each attribute.

Attribute			Page
A1	A2	A3	
A	1	b	1
A	1	c	2
A	2	a	3
A	2	d	4
A	3	a	5
B	2	a	6
B	3	b	7
B	3	c	8
C	3	d	9

Figure 1.3
Sample data with three attributes,
A1, A2, and A3.

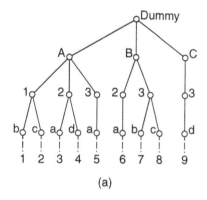

(a)

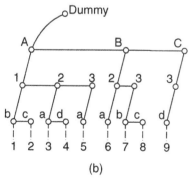

(b)

Figure 1.4
(a) The multiattribute tree (MAT)
and (b) the doubly chained tree
(DCT) corresponding to the file with
three different attributes given in
Figure 1.3.

The combined index is of limited value because it is useful only for a restricted subset of range queries where the values of the nonprimary attributes are left unspecified. In particular, given a record with d different attributes, the combined index enables the consecutive retrieval of records that satisfy range queries where a range is given for the primary attribute, exact matches are required for the values of the next i nonprimary attributes in lexicographic order, and the values of the remaining $d - 1 - i$ nonprimary attributes in lexicographic order are left unspecified. Thus, we have a variant of a partial match query (with respect to some of the nonprimary attributes in lexicographic order) and a partial range query (with respect to the remaining nonprimary attributes in lexicographic order). Nevertheless, using the combined index does result in replacing the need to intersect the results of range queries on the inverted lists of the individual attributes by the need to take the union of shorter lists that are disjoint.

Greater flexibility can be obtained by increasing the number of combined indexes by permuting the order in which the attributes are combined in the lexicographic order. The result is that a greater variety of partial range (i.e., partial match) queries can be handled. For example, with three attributes A, B, and C, all possible partial range (i.e., partial match) queries could be handled by making use of the following three lexicographically ordered combined indexes: ABC, BCA, and CAB. In general, given d attributes, it can be shown [1214] that we need $\binom{d}{\lfloor (d+1)/2 \rfloor}$ combined indexes to handle all possible partial range (i.e., partial match) queries (see Exercise 2). Shneiderman [1757] describes the *reduced combined index*, which structures the combined indexes in a treelike manner and thereby reduces their size, although their number is unchanged.

As we saw above, in order to achieve greater flexibility, the number of necessary combined indexes grows at a much faster rate than the number of attributes. Several alternative solutions have been proposed. These solutions can be decomposed into two classes. One class of solutions imposes an access structure on the values of the primary attribute, and then imposes another access structure on the remaining attributes in succession (often a recursive imposition of the same access structure) for each of the values of the first attribute. In essence, the combined index is being augmented with some form of random access so that the data can be accessed without being constrained totally by the inherent lexicographical order. Some examples of this approach include the doubly chained tree (DCT), which is closely related to the multiattribute tree and its variants, the quintary tree, the multidimensional B-tree (MDBT), and the kB-tree, as well as the multidimensional range tree and the priority search tree. The second class of solutions modifies the bitmap representation to form d-dimensional cells of ranges of attribute values so that all points whose attribute values fall within the range associated with cell c are associated with c. This is analogous to a compressed bitmap representation. A key difference between the two classes is that, in the first class, there exists an explicit ordering on the attributes, while no such ordering exists in the second class.

We first discuss briefly the first class of solutions. All of the members of this class of solutions are based on the same principle of constructing a skeleton m-ary tree that has one level per attribute. The first level consists of one child for each of the m different values of the first attribute (i.e., the primary attribute). Each child of the root, say child i with value a for the first attribute, serves as the root of a subtree with one child for each of the possible values of the second attribute given the value a for the first attribute. This process is repeated for the remaining children of the root and the remaining attributes for a total of d levels, assuming d attributes and that the root is at level 0. The result is characterized as a *multiattribute tree*[8] (e.g., [996]), although the representation predates the usage of the term. For example, given the file with three different attributes in Figure 1.3, Figure 1.4(a) is the corresponding multiattribute tree. Note that the multiattribute tree is similar to a trie, which forms the basis of digital searching (recall the discussion in the opening of this chapter). The difference is that

---

[8] Also sometimes denoted *MAT* but not here in order to avoid confusion with the medial axis transformation discussed in Section 2.1.2.2 of Chapter 2.

each node in the multiattribute tree only has as many children as there are different values for the attribute in the current set of records, instead of one child for each possible value of the attribute, as in the trie.

There are many implementations of the multiattribute tree. A simple implementation known as the *doubly chained tree* (DCT) [1817] links the children of each node (i.e., the *filial set* [1686]) instead of having a pointer from the root of each subtree to all of its children (see also [928, 961, 1365]). The result is that the m-ary tree is represented as a binary tree and is known as the *natural correspondence between a forest and a binary tree* [1044, p. 334], where the multiattribute tree serves as the forest. For example, Figure 1.4(b) is the doubly chained tree corresponding to the file with three different attributes given in Figure 1.3. Many variations on the implementation of the doubly chained tree have been proposed to enhance its performance in a database system (e.g., [305]). For example, often there is an additional pointer associated with each node that points back to the level containing the node's predecessor (i.e., an ancestor or parent link). Kashyap, Subas, and Yao [996] order the attributes in the doubly chained tree according to their probability of occurrence in a query, with the most likely ones being placed closer to the root. In addition, they propose to store records in pages in lexicographic order—that is, if record i is lexicographically lower than record j, then the page containing i is at a lower address than the page containing j. Further improvements are obtained by focusing on the pointer structure of the multiattribute tree such as removing redundant pointers [728].

Despite the various enhancements of the doubly chained tree described above, the worst-case execution time of an exact match query (i.e., point query) is still $O(N)$ due to the need to apply sequential search at each level (see Exercises 3 and 4). This worst-case execution time has been reduced to $O(d \cdot \log_2 N)$ time by Lien, Taylor, and Driscoll [1167], who replaced the linked list at each level of the doubly chained tree by a height-balanced binary search tree such as an AVL tree [15][9] (see Exercise 5). The drawback of the height-balanced binary search tree solution is that the balancing is only applied at the individual levels of the structure corresponding to the attributes instead of over the entire tree.

This drawback is addressed by the *quintary tree* [1133], which applies balancing over all the attributes (i.e., a form of "weight balancing"). In particular, assuming d attributes and a file of N records, the root node corresponds to the value of the first attribute, say $x_d = h$, forming a hyperplane. This hyperplane partitions the file into two subfiles, L and R, of at most $N/2$ records, instead of partitioning the different values of the first attribute into two sets of equal size as is done in the height-balanced binary search tree solution. In addition to the two subfiles L and R, assuming a d-dimensional space, we also project L and R onto the hyperplane, thereby forming two additional subfiles, LH and RH, in the $(d-1)$-dimensional hyperplane. These four subfiles (i.e., L, R, LH, and RH), as well as the subfile H of the records that lie on the hyperplane, form the subtrees of each node in the structure for a total of five subtrees, hence the term *quintary*. Note that when L and R correspond to one-dimensional data, then LH and RH are just sets of pointers to the records corresponding to the elements of L and R, respectively. The idea of projection is rooted in the empirical cumulative distribution function tree (ECDF tree) of Bentley and Shamos [180], which is used to determine the number of d-dimensional points dominated by a given query point (see Exercises 12 and 13).

Observe that the manner in which the quintary tree is constructed (i.e., the use of "weight balancing") ensures that at each node comparison approximately one-half of the records represented by the node's corresponding subfile will be pruned from consideration. This enables it to attain an $O(d + \log_2 N)$ execution time for an exact match query (see Exercise 8). Partial range queries for which the values of s out of d attributes are specified can take as much as $O(3^{d-s} \cdot (s + \log_2 N) + F)$ time, where F is

---

[9] The AV stands for Adelson-Velsky and the L stands for Landis, the originators of the structure.

the number of records found. This worst case arises when the s specified attributes are found at the deepest levels of the tree (see Exercise 9). Range queries take $O((\log_2 N)^d + F)$ time, where F is the number of records found (see Exercise 10).

The quintary tree has several drawbacks. First, it requires $O(N \cdot (\log_2 N)^d)$ space (see Exercise 6) and the same order of time to build (see Exercise 7). Second, it is primarily a static structure since insertions and deletions are quite costly as the amount of space that is needed implies that each record is represented $O((\log_2 N)^d)$ times. Clearly, despite having a good execution time behavior for the queries, a representation such as the quintary tree is not practical.

The desire to have both a dynamic behavior and to reduce the time needed to perform an exact match query to be $O(\log_2 N)$ has led to the use of B-trees [414] (see Appendix A) at each level of the doubly chained tree instead of height-balanced binary search trees. This is the basis of the multidimensional B-tree (MDBT) [1686] and kB-tree [786, 787] methods. Note that use of a multiway tree such as a B-tree also overcomes one of the drawbacks of binary trees: at each step of a search there are only two possible outcomes as there are only two children. In particular, the binary decision process can slow execution when each transition to a child corresponds to a disk access. Thus use of B-trees results in a significant reduction in the depth of the tree.

The *multidimensional B-tree* (MDBT) [1434, 1686] is a hierarchy of B-trees where the root of the hierarchy is a B-tree for the primary attribute. As in the doubly chained tree, for each distinct value v of the primary attribute p, there is a link to a distinct B-tree (corresponding to its filial set) for the values of the next attribute of all records for which $p = v$. This process is applied recursively to the remaining attributes. Therefore, for d-dimensional data, we have a hierarchy of B-trees that is d levels deep. The MDBT links the roots of all B-trees at each level, as well as providing an entry point at each level to the start of each such list. This facilitates partial range (i.e., partial match) queries that require sequential processing at each level. Formally, all filial sets (i.e., the roots of B-trees) at the same level i are linked in increasing order of their corresponding attribute values in their ancestor filial set at level $i - 1$. This ordering is recursive in the sense that the result is a lexicographic ordering of all of the B-trees at level i on the basis of the attribute values at levels 1 through $i - 1$.

For a B-tree of order M with N records, Scheuermann and Ouksel [1686] show that the height of the MDBT is $\log_M N$ under the assumption that the values of an attribute are uniformly distributed within its corresponding range and are independent of the other attribute values. However, when all of the records have different values for all of the attributes, the MDBT consists of a B-tree of height $\log_M N$ for the primary attribute, and each value of the primary attribute in this B-tree is connected to only one value at the next level, which in turn is connected to only one value, and so on. In other words, all the B-trees at the remaining levels for the remaining attributes are of height 1. Thus, the total height of the MDBT for this case is $(\log_M N) + d$ [1686]. Moreover, in the worst case, the height of the MDBT can be as high as $O(d \cdot \log_M N)$ (see Exercise 17).

The difference in these height values for the MDBT is overcome by the *kB-tree* of Güting and Kriegel [786, 787], which was developed independently of the MDBT. The kB-tree, like the MDBT, is also a hierarchy of B-trees where, whenever the B-trees at a particular level are of a different height, then these trees are repositioned (using techniques analogous to balancing in binary search trees) in such a way that the total height of the tree is never greater than $(\log_M N) + d$. This means that B-trees at the various levels, with the exception of those at the deepest level, do not have the property that all leaf nodes are at the same distance from the root. Such B-trees are known as *biased B-trees* [163]. Thus, the kB-tree is able to adapt better to the distribution of the records than the MDBT, while incurring a higher update cost than the MDBT. Performance studies encompassing updates, storage utilization, point queries (exact match), and range queries, including partial range (i.e., partial match), showed the relative performance of the kB-tree and MDBT to be comparable with a small edge (a few percentage points) for the kB-tree [1077, 1078].

The key difference between the kB-tree and the MDBT is that the kB-tree is balanced over all attributes, in contrast to the MDBT, which is only balanced within an attribute. Thus, we see that the kB-tree has been developed in the same spirit as the quintary tree in the sense that it makes use of a special case of weight balancing that is often applied to binary trees. However, unlike the quintary tree, where insertions and deletions destroy the balance, the kB-tree is able to maintain the balance in a dynamic environment.

Recall that in order to facilitate sequential processing, the roots of the B-trees at the levels of the MDBT are linked. This can also be done for the kB-tree. Further improvements in the speed can be obtained by defining a variant of the B^+-tree, termed a kB^+-tree [1076], which stores appropriate prefixes at the different levels of the resulting tree.

The multidimensional range tree [167, 176] imposes a one-dimensional range tree on the primary attribute, and then stores multidimensional range trees for the remaining attributes in the internal nodes of the one-dimensional range tree of the primary attribute. It is similar in spirit to the MDBT with the following difference: in the multidimensional range tree, there is a link in each node to a distinct multidimensional range tree for the remaining attributes, while in the MDBT, this link is to an MDBT, for the remaining attributes, with the same value of the first attribute. The multidimensional range tree is discussed in Section 1.2. The priority search tree [1266] forms the basis of another solution known as the *range priority tree* [535], which is also related to the range tree. The priority search tree makes use of a binary search tree whose leaf nodes form a one-dimensional range tree for one attribute, while its internal nodes form a heap for the remaining attribute. Such methods are discussed in Section 1.3.

The second class of solutions, and the one we focus on in the remaining sections of this chapter, modifies the bitmap representation to form d-dimensional cells of ranges of attribute values so that all points whose attribute values fall within the range associated with cell c are associated with c. This is analogous to a compressed bitmap representation.

The compressed bitmap representation has its roots in the multiattribute tree. As we saw above, one of the drawbacks of the multiattribute tree and its variants is that responding to queries requires some searching at each level of the tree. The use of a treelike structure with pointers speeds up the search process by limiting where the search takes place in contrast to the need to intersect the result of range queries on the inverted lists corresponding to the individual attributes when using the inverted file method. Nevertheless, the pointers do take up space. Pointers are not needed if we know that the number of children of each node at any given level is a constant. In particular, now the tree can be represented as a sequence of the nodes obtained via a depth-first traversal of the multiattribute tree (analogous to a lexicographical ordering of the relevant attribute values), and the appropriate children of each node are accessed by knowledge of the number of children that are present at each level.

Unfortunately, the requirement that the number of children of each node at any given level be a constant is somewhat difficult to satisfy in general as we cannot guarantee that the number of different values for each attribute is constant with respect to the value of its ancestor attribute in the multiattribute tree. However, if each child node in the tree corresponds to a range of values, then we can guarantee that the number of children at each level of each node is a constant. The result is that the leaf nodes correspond to d-dimensional cells that contain all the records (i.e., points) whose attribute values fall within the ranges that make up the boundaries of the cells. The resulting structure is known as the *multidimensional directory* (MDD) [1183]. Figure 1.5(a) is an example of a possible partition of a two-dimensional space that is induced by an MDD. The MDD has also been applied to high-dimensional data by McNames [1271] in the development of the principal axis tree (PAT), in which case the partition lines are no longer orthogonal. Instead, they are determined by recursively finding the directions of greatest variation in

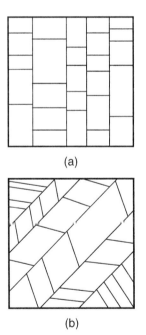

(a)

(b)

Figure 1.5
Example of a possible partition of a two-dimensional space that is induced by an MDD (a) when the partition lines are parallel to the coordinate axes and (b) when the partition lines have an orientation determined by the directions of greatest variation in the data within each region.

the data (termed the *principal axes*). Figure 1.5(b) is an example of such a partition in two dimensions. For more details about the principal axis tree, see Section 1.5.1.4.

When the number of different values of a particular attribute a is high in contrast to the number of ranges of values of a, then a is usually sufficient by itself to differentiate between the points. In this case, Liou and Yao [1183] suggest that a should not be included in the MDD, and instead the values of a are accessed via an inverted list. The resulting combination of the MDD and the inverted list is characterized as being a hybrid variant of the MDD [1183]. Formally, assuming a total of N records, G grid cells, and b_a ranges of values for a, and letting $|a|$ denote the number of different values for a in the dataset, then the hybrid variant of the MDD is used when $N/|a| \ll G/b_a$. For a discussion of how to choose the number of ranges for the attribute values, see [1183].

Although each attribute in the MDD is partitioned into the same number of ranges of values, the actual ranges differ for each range of values for the ancestor attribute in the multiattribute tree. This is a direct result of the fact that the order in which the attributes in the multiattribute tree are examined is important. The fixed-grid method (e.g., [173, 1046, 1584], also termed *multipaging* [1287, 1288]), avoids this difference by ensuring that each attribute is partitioned into the same ranges of values regardless of the ranges of values for the other attribute values. In other words, the fixed-grid method partitions the space from which the data is drawn into rectangular cells by overlaying it with a grid. Thus, the order in which the attributes in the multiattribute tree are examined is no longer relevant. Each grid cell c contains a pointer to another structure (e.g., a list) that contains the set of points that lie in c. Associated with the grid is an access structure to enable the determination of the grid cell associated with a particular point p. This access structure acts like a directory and is usually in the form of a d-dimensional array with one entry per grid cell or a tree with one leaf node per grid cell.

There are two ways of building a fixed grid. We can either subdivide the space into equal-sized grid cells or place the subdivision lines at arbitrary positions that are dependent on the underlying data. In essence, the distinction is between organizing the data to be stored and organizing the embedding space from which the data is drawn [1376]. In particular, when the grid cells are equal sized (termed a *uniform grid*), use of an array access structure is quite simple and has the desirable property that the grid cell associated with point p can be determined in constant time.

Figure 1.6 is an example of a uniform-grid representation corresponding to the data of Figure 1.1 with each grid cell having size 20×20. Assuming a 100×100 coordinate space, we have 25 squares of equal size. Assuming further that the origin is at the lower-left corner of the coordinate space, we adopt the convention that each square is open with respect to its upper and right boundaries and closed with respect to its lower and left boundaries (e.g., the point (60,75) is contained in the square centered at (70,70)). Also, all data points located at grid intersection points are said to be contained in the cell for which they serve as the SW corner (e.g., the point (20,20) is contained in the square centered at (30,30)).

When the width of each grid cell is twice the search radius for a rectangular range query,[10] then the average search time is $O(F \cdot 2^d)$, where F is the number of points that have been found [182]. The factor 2^d is the maximum number of cells that must be accessed when the search rectangle is permitted to overlap more than one cell. For example, to locate all cities within a 20×20 square centered at (32,37), we must examine the cells centered at (30,30), (50,30), (30,50), and (50,50). Thus, four cells are examined and, for our example database, the query returns Chicago and Omaha.

Multipaging [1287, 1288] is one of several examples of the fixed-grid method when the grid cells are not equal sized. In this case, in order to be able to use an array access

---

[10] This method can also be described as yielding an *adaptive uniform grid*, where the qualifier "adaptive" serves to emphasize that the cell size is a function of some property of the points (e.g., [632, 634]).

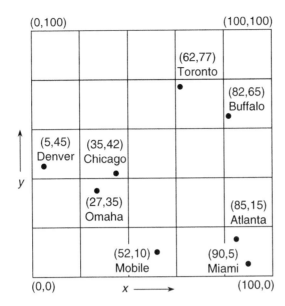

Figure 1.6
Uniform-grid representation corresponding to the data of Figure 1.1 with a search radius of 20.

structure, we must have a way of keeping track of their size so that we can determine the entry of the array access structure corresponding to the grid cell associated with point p. One way to do this is to make use of what are termed *linear scales* [1376] (also known as *axial directories* and *axial arrays* [1288]), which indicate the positions of the grid lines (or partitioning hyperplanes in $d > 2$ dimensions). Given a point p, we determine the grid cell in which p lies by finding the "coordinates" of the appropriate grid cell. The linear scales are usually implemented as one-dimensional trees containing ranges of values.

The use of an array access structure is fine as long as the data is static. When the data is dynamic, it is likely that some of the grid cells become too full while other grid cells are empty. This means that we need to rebuild the grid (i.e., further partition the grid or reposition the grid partition lines or planes) so that the various grid cells are not too full. However, this creates many more empty grid cells as a result of repartitioning the grid (i.e., empty grid cells are split into more empty grid cells). In this case, we have two alternatives.

The first alternative is to merge spatially adjacent empty grid cells into larger empty grid cells while splitting grid cells that are too full, thereby making the grid adaptive. The result is that we no longer make use of an array access structure to retrieve the grid cell that contains query point p. Instead, we make use of a tree access structure in the form of a k-ary tree, where k is usually 2^d. Thus, we have married a k-ary tree with the fixed-grid method. This is the basis of the point quadtree [614], as well as trie-based representations such as the MX quadtree [1628] and the PR quadtree [1413, 1637], which are all multidimensional generalizations of binary trees. They are discussed in Section 1.4.

As the dimensionality of the space increases, each level of decomposition of the quadtree results in many new cells since the fanout value of the tree is high (i.e., 2^d). This is alleviated by making use of a k-d tree [164, 168]. This is a binary tree, where at each level of the tree, we subdivide along just one of the attributes. This is discussed in Section 1.5.

The second alternative is to assign an ordering to all the grid cells and to impose a tree access structure on the elements of the ordering that correspond to nonempty grid cells. The effect of this alternative is analogous to using a mapping from d dimensions to one dimension, and then applying one of the one-dimensional access structures, such as a B-tree or a balanced binary tree, to the result of the mapping.[11] This is the subject of Section 1.6. Note that this alternative is applicable regardless of whether the grid cells are equal sized. Of course, if the grid cells are not equal sized (not discussed here), then we must also record their size in the element of the access structure.

At times, in the dynamic situation, the data volume becomes so large that a conventional tree access structure (i.e., with the limited fanout values described above) is inefficient. In particular, the grid cells can become so numerous that they cannot all fit into memory, thereby causing them to be grouped into sets (which we termed *buckets*) corresponding to physical storage units (i.e., pages) in secondary storage. This is the subject of Sections 1.7 and 1.8. In the case of a tree access structure, each bucket usually corresponds to a contiguous set of grid cells that forms a hyperrectangle in the underlying space. The problem is that, depending on the implementation of the tree access structure, each time we must follow a pointer, we may need to make a disk access.

This problem can be resolved in two ways. The first way is to retain the use of the tree access structure, say T, and also to aggregate the internal (i.e., nonleaf) nodes of T into buckets, thereby forming a multiway tree in the spirit of a B-tree (see Appendix A). The buckets whose contents are internal nodes of T correspond to subtrees of T, and their fanout value corresponds to the sum of the number of possible branches at the deepest level of each of the subtrees. The resulting structure is now a tree of buckets with a large fanout value, frequently referred to as a *tree directory*. Examples of such structures are the R-tree and the R^+-tree, which are discussed in great detail in Sections 2.1.5.2 and 2.1.5.3 of Chapter 2, respectively, as well as the k-d-B-tree, LSD tree, hB-tree, k-d-B-trie, and BV-tree, which are discussed in Section 1.7.1. In these structures, the buckets are formed by a grouping process that is applied in a top-down manner so that each bucket has a maximum number of elements. In contrast, in PK-tree methods, discussed in Section 1.8, the buckets are formed by a grouping process that is applied in a bottom-up manner so that each bucket has a minimum number of elements.

The second way is to return to the use of an array access structure. One difference from the array used with the static fixed-grid method described earlier is that now the array access structure (termed a *grid directory*) may be so large (e.g., when d gets large) that it resides on disk as well (although this is not the case for all of the representations that we present). Another difference is that the structure of the grid directory can be changed as the data volume grows or contracts. Each grid cell (i.e., an element of the grid directory) contains the address of a bucket (i.e., page) where the points associated with the grid cell are stored. Notice that a bucket can correspond to more than one grid cell. Thus, any page can be accessed by two disk operations: one to access the grid cell and one more to access the actual bucket. The mechanics of the management of the growth of the access structure is the interesting issue here and is the subject of Section 1.7.2.

Section 1.9 contains a comparison of the various representations that we present. It also discusses briefly how to adapt the representations to handle nonlocational attributes. In general, the representations that we have presented are good for range searching (e.g., finding all cities within 80 miles of Atlanta) as they act as pruning devices on the amount of search that will be performed. In particular, many points will not be examined since the grid cells that contain them lie outside the query range. Most of these representations are generally very easy to implement and have good expected execution times, although the execution times of algorithms that use some of them are often quite difficult to analyze from a mathematical standpoint. However, their worst cases, despite being rare, can be quite bad. This is especially true for the second class of solutions that were based on

---

[11] These mappings have been investigated primarily for purely locational or numeric multidimensional point data, in which case they can also be applied directly to the key values. They cannot be applied directly to the key values for nonlocational point data; instead, they can be applied only to the grid cell locations.

modifying the bitmap representation. These worst cases can be avoided by making use of members of the first class of solutions that were variants of range trees and priority search trees.

Exercises

1. Given a file containing N records with d attributes, implemented as an inverted list, prove that the average search for a particular record is $O(N^{1-1/d})$.

2. Given d attributes, show that $\binom{d}{\lfloor (d+1)/2 \rfloor}$ combined indexes are needed to handle all possible partial range (i.e., partial match) queries.

3. Given N records and d attributes, show that the worst-case execution time of an exact match query in a doubly chained tree is $O(N)$.

4. In the text, we mentioned that given N records and d attributes, the worst-case execution time of an exact match query in a sequential list takes $O(N \cdot d)$ time. An argument could be made that since d is a constant value, the query takes $O(N)$ time and thus is of the same order of magnitude as when it is executed on a doubly chained tree. Explain why such an argument fails.

5. Given N records and d attributes, show that the worst-case execution time of an exact match query, when the linked list at each level of the doubly chained tree has been replaced by a height-balanced binary search tree, is $O(d\log_2 N)$.

6. Prove that the quintary tree for N records and d attributes requires $O(N \cdot (\log_2 N)^d)$ space.

7. Prove that building a quintary tree for N records and d attributes takes $O(N \cdot (\log_2 N)^d)$ time.

8. Prove that an exact match query in a quintary tree with N records and d attributes takes $O(d + \log_2 N)$ time.

9. Prove that a partial range query in a quintary tree with N records and d attributes, where the values of s out of d attributes are specified, takes $O(3^{d-s} \cdot (s + \log_2 N) + F)$ time, where F is the number of records found.

10. Performing a range query in a quintary tree takes advantage of the auxiliary trees that are attached to each node. The algorithm is recursive [1133]. Assume that the ranges of the individual attribute values are given by $[l_i, r_i](1 \le i \le d)$. Let x denote the partitioning value at the root, and assume that the root partitions along attribute d. If x is not in the range $[l_d, r_d]$, then we descend to the L or R trees as is appropriate. Otherwise, we subdivide the interval into the two subintervals $[l_d, x)$ and $(x, r_d]$ and descend to the L and R trees, respectively, as well as descend the H tree. However, the next partition of these subintervals only results in descending the H, L, and RH trees or the H, R, and LH trees. For example, the next partition of the subinterval $[l_d, x)$ into $[l_d, w)$ and (w, x) only needs to descend the trees H, L, and RH (instead of R) because the interval (w, x) lies completely within $[l_d, r_d]$. Thus, we can ignore the value of attribute d by just considering the projections of the subfile on the R tree (i.e., the RH tree). This process is applied recursively at all levels. Prove that this algorithm takes $O((\log_2 N)^d + F)$ time, where F is the number of records found.

11. Modify the range query algorithm given in Exercise 10 in a quintary tree to work for a partial range query, where s out of d ranges of attribute values are specified. Show that it takes $O(3^{d-s} \cdot (\log_2 N)^s + F)$ time, where F is the number of records found.

12. The quintary tree is based on the ECDF tree of Bentley and Shamos [180]. The ECDF tree is used to indicate how many points are dominated by a query point q, where the point $x = (x_1, x_2, \ldots, x_d)$ is said to be *dominated* by $q = (q_1, q_2, \ldots, q_d)$ if and only if $x_i \le q_i$ for $i = 1, 2, \ldots, d$. This number is called the *ranking* of q and is also referred to as the *empirical cumulative distribution function*, hence the name of the data structure. The ECDF tree is constructed as follows. Find a hyperplane along one of the attributes a_i with the equation $a_i = r$ that divides the set of data into two subsets, A and B, where all elements of A have a_i values less than r, and all elements of B have a_i values greater than or equal to r. In addition, a set C is created of one lower dimension by projecting all elements of A onto the partitioning hyperplane. This process is applied recursively until we have either one point left or a subset with dimension one (i.e., just one attribute). Thus, the ECDF tree is a ternary tree. Associated

with each node is a number equal to one plus the number of records that lie in the left subtree (i.e., A using the above notation). Show how, using this information, the ranking (i.e., ECDF) of q can be computed in $O((\log_2 N)^d)$ time for N records in a d-dimensional space.

13. Given N records in a d-dimensional space, show that the amount of space needed to store an ECDF tree is $O(N \cdot (\log_2 N)^{d-1})$.

14. How would you use the ECDF tree to determine the number of d-dimensional points in a hyperrectangular query region with corners at $p = (p_1, p_2, \ldots, p_d)$ and $q = (q_1, q_2, \ldots, q_d)$ (i.e., a range query)?

15. How would you perform a range query in an MDBT?

16. How would you perform a partial range (i.e., partial match) query in an MDBT?

17. Given a file containing N records with d keys apiece, implemented as an MDBT with B-trees of order M, prove that the height can be as high as $O(d \cdot \log_M N)$.

18. Given a file containing records with d keys apiece, implemented using the uniform grid method such that each cell has a width equal to twice the search radius of a rectangular range query, prove that the average time for the range query is $O(F \cdot 2^d)$, where F is the number of records found and 2^d is the number of cells that must be accessed.

19. Assume a file containing records with d keys apiece and implemented using the fixed-grid method such that each cell has width equal to the search radius of a rectangular range query. Prove that the average time for the range query is $O(F \cdot 3^d/2^d)$, where F is the number of records found and 3^d is the number of cells that must be accessed.

1.2 Range Trees

The multidimensional range tree of Bentley and Maurer [167, 176] is an asymptotically faster search structure than the point quadtree and the k-d tree; however, it has significantly higher space requirements. It stores points and is designed to detect all points that lie in a given range.

The range tree is best understood by first examining the one-dimensional range searching problem. A one-dimensional range tree is a balanced binary search tree where the data points are stored in the leaf nodes and the leaf nodes are linked in sorted order by use of a doubly linked list. The nonleaf nodes contain midrange values that enable discriminating between the left and right subtrees. For example, Figure 1.7 is the one-dimensional range tree for the data of Figure 1.1 when it is sorted according to values of

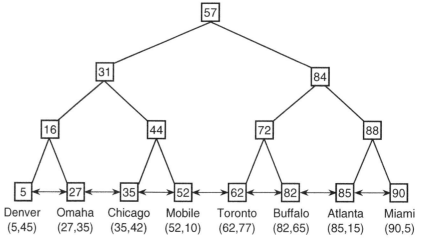

Figure 1.7
One-dimensional range tree for the *x* coordinate values of the data of Figure 1.1.

the x coordinate. A range search for $[B:E]$ is performed by procedure RANGESEARCH. It searches the tree and finds the node with either the largest value $\leq B$ or the smallest value $\geq B$, and then follows the links until reaching a leaf node with a value greater than E. For N points, this process takes $O(\log_2 N + F)$ time and uses $O(N)$ space. F is the number of points found.

Procedure RANGESEARCH assumes that each node has six fields, LEFT, RIGHT, VALUE, PREV, NEXT, and MIDRANGE. LEFT(P) and RIGHT(P) denote the left and right children, respectively, of nonleaf node P (they are null in the case of a leaf node). VALUE is an integer indicating the value stored in the leaf node. PREV(P) and NEXT(P) are meaningful only for leaf nodes, in which case they are used for the doubly linked list of leaf nodes sorted in nondecreasing order. In particular, PREV(P) points to a node with value less than or equal to VALUE(P), while NEXT(P) points to a node with value greater than or equal to VALUE(P). MIDRANGE(P) is a variant of a discriminator between the left and right subtrees—that is, it is greater than or equal to the values stored in the left subtree, and less than or equal to the values stored in the right subtree (see Exercise 2). The MIDRANGE field is meaningful only for nonleaf nodes. Note that by making use of a NODETYPE field to distinguish between leaf and nonleaf nodes, we can use the LEFT, RIGHT, and MIDRANGE fields to indicate the information currently represented by the PREV, NEXT, and VALUE fields, respectively, thereby making them unnecessary.

```
1   procedure RANGESEARCH(B, E, T)
2   /* Perform a range search for the one-dimensional interval [B:E] in the one-
        dimensional range tree rooted at T. */
3   value integer B, E
4   value pointer node T
5   if ISNULL(T) then return
6   endif
7   while not ISLEAF(T) do
8       T ← if B ≤ MIDRANGE(T) then LEFT(T)
9              else RIGHT(T)
10             endif
11  enddo
12  if not ISNULL(T) and VALUE(T) < B then T ← NEXT(T)
13  endif
14  while not ISNULL(T) and VALUE(T) ≤ E do
15      output VALUE(T)
16      T ← NEXT(T)
17  enddo
```

For example, suppose we want to perform a range search for [28:62] on the one-dimensional range tree in Figure 1.7. In this example, we assume that the VALUE field of the leaf nodes contains only the x coordinate values. We first descend the tree to locate, in this case, the node with the largest value ≤ 28 (i.e., (27,35)). Next, following the NEXT links, we report the points (35,42), (52,10), and (62,77). We stop when encountering (82,65).

A two-dimensional range tree is a binary tree of binary trees. It is formed in the following manner. First, sort all of the points along one of the attributes, say x, and store them in the leaf nodes of a balanced binary search tree (i.e., a range tree), say T. With each node of T, say I, associate a one-dimensional range tree, say T_I, of the points in the subtree rooted at I, where now these points are sorted along the other attribute, say y.[12] For example, Figure 1.8 is the two-dimensional range tree for the data of Figure 1.1,

---

[12] Actually, there is no need for the one-dimensional range tree at the root or its two children (see Exercise 6). Also, there is no need for the one-element, one-dimensional range trees at the leaf nodes, as the algorithms can make a special check for this case and use the data that is already stored in the leaf nodes (but see Exercise 5).

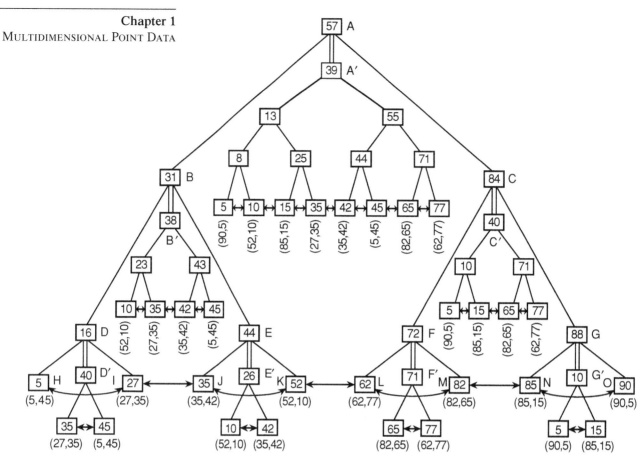

Figure 1.8
Two-dimensional range tree for the data of Figure 1.1.

where the x coordinate serves as the primary sort attribute. Notice the use of double vertical lines to indicate a link to the one-dimensional range tree associated with each nonleaf node, thereby distinguishing them from the single vertical lines used to indicate links to left and right children in the two trees. For N points, the two-dimensional range tree uses $O(N \cdot \log_2 N)$ space (see Exercise 7) and requires $O(N \cdot \log_2 N)$ time to build (see Exercise 8).

A range search for ($[B_x : E_x], [B_y : E_y]$) is performed by procedure 2DSEARCH, given below. It makes use of procedure 1DSEARCH, a variant of procedure RANGESEARCH not given here.[13] Procedure 2DSEARCH starts by descending the tree in search of the closest nonleaf node Q (in terms of the number of links that are descended) to the root whose midrange value lies between B_x and E_x. Let L_x and R_x be the leaf nodes in the two-dimensional range tree that are reported by a search for B_x and E_x, respectively, regardless of whether B_x and E_x are actually stored there. L_x and R_x are termed *boundary nodes*. For example, using Figure 1.8, if B_x is 24 and E_x is 74, then L_x and R_x are the leaf nodes containing (27,35) and (82,65), respectively. Q is known as the *nearest common ancestor* of L_x and R_x in T (hence the farthest from the root in terms of node links). Let $\{L_i\}$ and $\{R_i\}$ denote the sequences of nodes (excluding Q) that form the paths in T from Q to L_x and from Q to R_x, respectively.

Procedure 2DSEARCH assumes that each node has five fields: LEFT, RIGHT, MID-RANGE, RANGETREE, and POINT. LEFT, RIGHT, and MIDRANGE have the same meaning as in the one-dimensional range tree with the exception that MIDRANGE discriminates on the basis of the values of the x coordinate of the points represented by

---

[13] The difference is that in 1DSEARCH, the leaf nodes are points in two-dimensional space, while in RANGESEARCH, the leaf nodes are points in one-dimensional space.

the tree. RANGETREE(P) is the one-dimensional range tree for y that is stored at node

P. POINT is a pointer to a record of type *point* that stores the point that is associated with a leaf node. A *point* record has two fields, XCOORD and YCOORD, that contain the values of the x and y coordinates, respectively, of the point. The POINT field is not used for nonleaf nodes in the tree. Note that by making 2DSEARCH a bit more complicated, we can get by with just one of the POINT and RANGETREE fields (see Exercise 5).

For each node P that is an element of $\{L_i\}$, such that LEFT(P) is also in $\{L_i\}$, 2DSEARCH performs a one-dimensional range search for $[B_y:E_y]$ in the one-dimensional range tree for y associated with node RIGHT(P). For each P that is an element of $\{R_i\}$, such that RIGHT(P) is also in $\{R_i\}$, 2DSEARCH performs a one-dimensional range search for $[B_y:E_y]$ in the one-dimensional range tree for y associated with node LEFT(P). A final step checks (using procedure INRANGE not given here) if the points associated with the boundary nodes (i.e., leaves) L_x and R_x are in the two-dimensional range.

```
1  procedure 2DSEARCH(Bx, Ex, By, Ey, T)
2  /* Perform a range search for the two-dimensional interval ([Bx : Ex],
       [By : Ey]) in the two-dimensional range tree rooted at T. */
3  value integer Bx, Ex, By, Ey
4  value pointer node T
5  pointer node Q
6  if ISNULL(T) then return
7  endif
8  while not ISLEAF(T) do /* Find nearest common ancestor */
9     if Ex < MIDRANGE(T) then T ← LEFT(T)
10    elseif MIDRANGE(T) < Bx then T ← RIGHT(T)
11    else exit_while_loop /* Found nearest common ancestor */
12    endif
13 enddo
14 if ISLEAF(T) then
15    if INRANGE(POINT(T), Bx, Ex, By, Ey) then
16       output VALUE(T)
17    endif
18 else /* T is a nonleaf node and must process its subtrees */
19    Q ← T /* Save value to process other subtree */
20    T ← LEFT(T)
21    while not ISLEAF(T) do /* Process the left subtree */
22       if Bx ≤ MIDRANGE(T) then
23          1DSEARCH(By, Ey, RANGETREE(RIGHT(T)))
24          T ← LEFT(T)
25       else T ← RIGHT(T)
26       endif
27    enddo
28    if INRANGE(POINT(T), Bx, Ex, By, Ey) then
29       output VALUE(T)
30    endif
31    T ← RIGHT(Q)
32    while not ISLEAF(T) do /* Process the right subtree */
33       if MIDRANGE(T) ≤ Ex then
34          1DSEARCH(By, Ey, RANGETREE(LEFT(T)))
35          T ← RIGHT(T)
36       else T ← LEFT(T)
37       endif
38    enddo
39    if INRANGE(POINT(T), Bx, Ex, By, Ey) then
40       output VALUE(T)
41    endif
42 endif
```

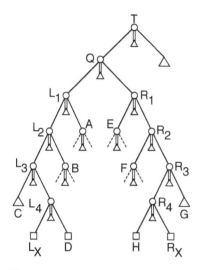

Figure 1.9
Example two-dimensional range tree
to illustrate two-dimensional range
searching.

For example, the desired closest common ancestor of L_X and R_X in Figure 1.9 is Q. One-dimensional range searches would be performed in the one-dimensional range trees rooted at nodes A, B, D, E, F, and H since 5 $\{L_i\} = \{L_1, L_2, L_3, L_4, L_X\}$ and $\{R_i\} = \{R_1, R_2, R_3, R_4, R_X\}$. For N points, procedure 2DSEARCH takes $O(\log_2^2 N + F)$ time, where F is the number of points found (see Exercise 9).

As a more concrete example, suppose we want to perform a range search for ([25:85],[8:16]) on the two-dimensional range tree in Figure 1.8. We first find the nearest common ancestor of 25 and 85, which is node A. The paths $\{L_i\}$ and $\{R_i\}$ are given by {B,D,I} and {C,G,N}, respectively. Since B and B's left child (i.e., D) are in the path to 25, we search the range tree of B's right child (i.e., E) and report (52,10) as in the range. Similarly, since C and C's right child (i.e., G) are in the path to 85, we search the one-dimensional range tree of C's left child (i.e., F), but do not report any results as neither (62,77) nor (82,65) is in the range. Finally, we check if the boundary nodes (27,35) and (85,15) are in the range, and report (85,15) as in the range.

The range tree also can be adapted easily to handle k-dimensional data. In such a case, for N points, a k-dimensional range search takes $O(\log_2^k N + F)$ time, where F is the number of points found. The k-dimensional range tree uses $O(N \cdot \log_2^{k-1} N)$ space (see Exercise 10) and requires $O(N \cdot \log_2^{k-1} N)$ time to build (see Exercise 11).

Exercises

1. Is there a difference between a balanced binary search tree, where all the data is stored in the leaf nodes, and a one-dimensional range tree?

2. The MIDRANGE field in the one-dimensional range tree was defined as a variant of a discriminator between the left and right subtrees in the sense that it is greater than or equal to the values stored in the left subtree, and less than or equal to the values stored in the right subtree. Why not use a simpler definition, such as one that stipulates that the MIDRANGE value is greater than all values in the left subtree and less than or equal to all values in the right subtree?

3. Why does procedure 2DSEARCH provide the desired result?

4. Prove that no point is reported more than once by the algorithm for executing a range query in a two-dimensional range tree.

5. Procedure 2DSEARCH makes use of a representation of the two-dimensional range tree where each node has a POINT and RANGETREE field. In fact, the POINT field is defined only for leaf nodes, while the RANGETREE field points to a one-dimensional range tree of just one node for leaf nodes. Rewrite 2DSEARCH, 1DSEARCH, and INRANGE so that they do not use a POINT field, and hence interpret the RANGETREE field appropriately.

6. Show that the one-dimensional range trees at the first two levels (i.e., at the root and the two children of the root) of a two-dimensional range tree are never used in procedure 2DSEARCH.

7. Show that $O(N \cdot \log_2 N)$ space suffices for a two-dimensional range tree for N points.

8. Show that a two-dimensional range tree can be built in $O(N \cdot \log_2 N)$ time for N points.

9. Given a two-dimensional range tree containing N points, prove that a two-dimensional range query takes $O(\log_2^2 N + F)$ time, where F is the number of points found.

10. Given a k-dimensional range tree containing N points, prove that a k-dimensional range query takes $O(\log_2^k N + F)$ time, where F is the number of points found. Also, show that $O(N \cdot \log_2^{k-1} N)$ space is sufficient.

11. Show that a k-dimensional range tree can be built in $O(N \cdot \log_2^{k-1} N)$ time for N points.

12. Write a procedure to construct a two-dimensional range tree.

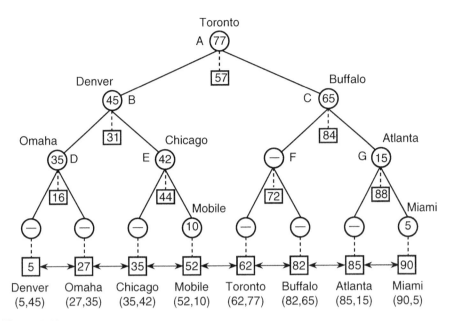

Figure 1.10
Priority search tree for the data of Figure 1.1. Each leaf node contains the value of its
x coordinate in a square box. Each nonleaf node contains the appropriate x coordinate
midrange value in a square box using a link drawn with a broken line. Circular boxes
indicate the value of the y coordinate of the point in the corresponding subtree with the
maximum value for its y coordinate that has not already been associated with a node at
a shallower depth in the tree.

1.3 Priority Search Trees

The *priority search tree* is a data structure that is designed for solving queries involving
semi-infinite ranges in two-dimensional space. A typical semi-infinite range query has
a range of the form $([B_x : E_x], [B_y : \infty])$. It is built in the following manner. Sort all
the points along the x coordinate and store them in the leaf nodes of a balanced binary
search tree, say T. We use a one-dimensional range tree in our formulation,[14] although in
some applications (e.g., the rectangle intersection problem as discussed in Section 3.1.3
of Chapter 3), the requirement of being able to insert and delete points in $O(\log_2 N)$
time, while still requiring the $O(N \cdot \log_2 N + F)$ search behavior, causes the balanced
binary search tree to be implemented using more complicated structures, such as a "red-
black" balanced binary tree [766] (see Appendix A), although in actuality, any variant of
a balanced binary tree could be used. Store midrange x coordinate values in the nonleaf
nodes. Next, proceed from the root node toward the leaf nodes. Associate with each node
I of T the point in the subtree rooted at I with the maximum value for its y coordinate
that is not already been associated with a node at a shallower depth in the tree. If no
such point exists, then leave the node empty. For N points, this structure uses $O(N)$
space (see Exercise 1) and requires $O(N \cdot \log_2 N)$ time to build (see Exercise 7).

For example, Figure 1.10 is the priority search tree for the data of Figure 1.1. In the
figure, square boxes contain the relevant x coordinate values (e.g., the midrange values
in the nonleaf nodes), while circular boxes contain the relevant y coordinate values (e.g.,
the maximums). Notice that the leaf nodes contain the points and are shown as linked
together in ascending order of the x coordinate value. The links for the x coordinate
values are used only if we conduct a search for all points within a given range of x
coordinate values. They are not used in the execution of the semi-infinite range query,
and thus they are frequently omitted from the implementation of the priority search tree.

---

[14] A Cartesian tree [1944] is an alternative. See Exercises 21 and 22.

It is not easy to perform a two-dimensional range query of the form $([B_x : E_x], [B_y : E_y])$ with a priority search tree. The problem is that only the values of the x coordinate are sorted. In other words, given a leaf node C that stores point (x_C, y_C), we know that the values of the x coordinate of all nodes to the left of C are smaller than or equal to x_C and the values of all those to the right of C are greater than or equal to x_C. On the other hand, with respect to the values of the y coordinate, we know only that all nodes below nonleaf node D with value y_D have values less than or equal to y_D; the y coordinate values associated with the remaining nodes in the tree that are not ancestors of D may be larger or smaller than y_D.

This is not surprising because a priority search tree is really a variant of a one-dimensional range tree in x (see Exercise 1 in Section 1.2) and a heap (i.e., priority queue) [1046] in y. A heap[15] enables finding the maximum (minimum) value in $O(1)$ time. More generally the largest (smallest) F out of N values can be determined in $O(F)$ time, but the F values are not sorted. Whether the heap is used to find the largest or smallest values depends on how it is constructed. The way in which we specify the priority search tree here enables finding the largest values.

Nevertheless, despite the difficulty in using priority search trees to perform a two-dimensional range query, priority search trees make it very easy to perform a semi-infinite range query of the form $([B_x : E_x], [B_y : \infty])$. The control structure is quite similar to that of procedure 2DSEARCH. Descend the tree looking for the nearest common ancestor of B_x and E_x, say Q. Apply the following tests during this descent, letting P be the point associated with the examined node, say T. If no such P exists, then we are finished with the entire subtree rooted at T as all points in T's subtrees have already been examined and reported as is appropriate. Examine the y coordinate value of P, say P_y. If $P_y < B_y$, then we are finished with the entire subtree rooted at T since P is the point with the maximum y coordinate value in T. Otherwise (i.e., $P_y \geq B_y$), check if the x coordinate value of P (i.e., P_x) is in the range $[B_x : E_x]$, and if yes, then P satisfies the query and is reported. At this point, determine if T is the nearest common ancestor by checking if B_x and E_x lie in T's left and right subtrees, respectively. If T is not the nearest common ancestor, then continue the descent in the left (right) subtree of T if E_x (B_x) is in the left (right) subtree of T.

Once Q has been found, process the left and right subtrees of Q using the appropriate step below, where T denotes the node currently being examined. In both cases, we apply the same sequence of tests described above to determine if an exit can be made due to having processed all points in the subtrees or if all remaining points are not in the y range.

1. Left subtree of Q: Check if B_x lies in the left subtree of T. If it does, then all of the points in the right subtree of T are in the x range, and we just check if they are in

---

[15] Briefly, a *binary heap* (usually referred to as simply a *heap*) is a variant of a binary search tree that has the property that the value of a node is greater than or equal to that of its two children. It can be implemented in a number of ways, including, when the tree is complete, as a mapping into an array so that all nodes at a given level are stored consecutively and immediately after the nodes at the preceding level. The advantage is that no pointers are needed. We can also define a d-heap, where a binary heap is the special case that $d = 2$. There are also binomial heaps [1943] and Fibonacci heaps [636]. They differ in the execution times of the operations that are performed on them. In particular, the principal differences between the binary heap and the binomial heap are that the union operation is $\Theta(n)$ for the former and $O(\log n)$ for the latter, while finding the maximum (minimum if the heap is defined so that the value of a node is less than or equal to that of its two children) is $\Theta(1)$ for the former and $O(\log n)$ for the latter. Fibonacci heaps have the property that the execution times of all operations are amortized and are $\Theta(1)$ for any operation that does not involve deletion (including union), while those that do involve deletion are $O(\log n)$. A particularly important property of the Fibonacci heap vis-à-vis the binary heap and the binomial heap is that the decrease-key operation is $\Theta(1)$ for the Fibonacci heap, while it is $\Theta(\log n)$ for both the binary and binomial heaps. This operation finds use when we want to decrease the value of the key attribute and to minimize the work needed to restructure the heap.

the y range, while recursively applying this step to the left subtree of T. Otherwise, recursively apply this step to the right subtree of T.

2. Right subtree of Q: Check if E_x lies in the right subtree of T. If it does, then all of the points in the left subtree of T are in the x range, and we just check if they are in the y range, while recursively applying this step to the right subtree of T. Otherwise, recursively apply this step to the left subtree of T.

The actual search process is given by procedure PRIORITYSEARCH. It assumes that each node has five fields: POINT, MIDRANGE, LEFT, RIGHT, and HEAPMAX. POINT, MIDRANGE, LEFT, and RIGHT have the same meaning as in the two-dimensional range tree. HEAPMAX is defined for all nodes. In particular, for any node I, HEAPMAX(I) points at the node C in the subtree S rooted at I such that YCOORD(POINT(C)) is greater than or equal to YCOORD(POINT(D)) for any other node D in S, such that neither C nor D is associated with a node at a depth in the tree that is shallower than the depth of I. As in the two-dimensional range tree, the POINT field is not used for nonleaf nodes in the tree, and, in fact, by making PRIORITYSEARCH a bit more complicated, we can get by with just one of the POINT and HEAPMAX fields (see Exercise 4).

PRIORITYSEARCH makes use of two auxiliary procedures, OUTOFRANGEY and YSEARCH. OUTOFRANGEY determines if all points in a subtree have already been output or if they are all outside the y range. YSEARCH performs a one-dimensional range search for the semi-infinite interval with respect to the y range.

```
1   procedure PRIORITYSEARCH(B_x, E_x, B_y, T)
2   /* Perform a semi-infinite range search for the two-dimensional interval
        ([B_x : E_x], [B_y : ∞]) in the priority search tree rooted at T. */
3   value integer B_x, E_x, B_y
4   value pointer node T
5   pointer node Q
6   if ISNULL(T) then return
7   while true do /* Find nearest common ancestor */
8       if OUTOFRANGEY(HEAPMAX(T), B_y) then return
9       elseif B_x ≤ XCOORD(POINT(HEAPMAX(T))) and
                XCOORD(POINT(HEAPMAX(T))) ≤ E_x then
10          output POINT(HEAPMAX(T))
11      endif
12      if ISLEAF(T) then return
13      elseif E_x < MIDRANGE(T) then T ← LEFT(T)
14      elseif MIDRANGE(T) < B_x then T ← RIGHT(T)
15      else exit_while_loop /* Found nearest common ancestor */
16      endif
17  enddo
18  /* T is a nonleaf node and must process its subtrees */
19  Q ← T /* Save value to process other subtree */
20  T ← LEFT(T)
21  while true do /* Process the left subtree */
22      if OUTOFRANGEY(HEAPMAX(T), B_y) then exit_while_loop
23      elseif B_x ≤ XCOORD(POINT(HEAPMAX(T))) then
24          output POINT(HEAPMAX(T))
25      endif
26      if ISLEAF(T) then exit_while_loop
27      elseif B_x ≤ MIDRANGE(T) then
28          YSEARCH(RIGHT(T), B_y)
29          T ← LEFT(T)
30      else T ← RIGHT(T)
31      endif
32  enddo
```

```
33    T ← RIGHT(Q)
34    while true do /* Process the right subtree */
35       if OUTOFRANGEY(HEAPMAX(T), B_y) then return
36       elseif XCOORD(POINT(HEAPMAX(T))) ≤ E_x then
37          output POINT(HEAPMAX(T))
38       endif
39       if ISLEAF(T) then return
40       elseif MIDRANGE(T) ≤ E_x then
41          YSEARCH(LEFT(T), B_y)
42          T ← RIGHT(T)
43       else T ← LEFT(T)
44       endif
45    enddo
```

```
1    Boolean procedure OUTOFRANGEY(P, B_y)
2    /* Check if all relevant points have already been output or if the y coordinate
        values of all points in the subtrees are too small. */
3    value pointer node P
4    value integer B_y
5    return(if ISNULL(P) then TRUE
6           else YCOORD(POINT(P)) < B_y
7           endif)
```

```
1    recursive procedure YSEARCH(T, B_y)
2    /* Perform a one-dimensional range search for the semi-infinite interval
        [B_y : ∞] in the priority search tree rooted at T. */
3    value pointer node T
4    value integer B_y
5    if ISNULL(T) then return
6    elseif OUTOFRANGEY(HEAPMAX(T), B_y) then return
7    else
8       output POINT(HEAPMAX(T))
9       YSEARCH(LEFT(T), B_y)
10      YSEARCH(RIGHT(T), B_y)
11   endif
```

For N points, performing a semi-infinite range query in this way takes $O(\log_2 N + F)$ time. F is the number of points found (see Exercise 2). To answer the two-dimensional range query ($[B_x : E_x], [B_y : E_y]$), perform the semi-infinite range query ($[B_x : E_x], [B_y : \infty]$) and discard all points (x, y) such that $y > E_y$.

As an example of the execution of a semi-infinite range query, suppose that we want to search for ([35:83],[50:∞]) in the priority search tree in Figure 1.10. We use Figure 1.11(a) to illustrate the space decomposition induced by the priority search tree of Figure 1.10. In the figure, horizontal lines correspond to the partitions caused by the HEAPMAX field values in the tree. The vertical lines correspond to the partitions caused by the MIDRANGE field values associated with the nonleaf nodes that have at least one child whose HEAPMAX field is not NIL.

The search proceeds as follows. We descend the tree starting at the root (i.e., A). The point associated with A is Toronto with a y coordinate value of 77, which is in the y range. The x coordinate value of Toronto is 62, which is in the range. Next, we find that A is indeed the nearest common ancestor since the midrange value is 57, which is between the x range values of 35 and 83. Thus, we prepare to descend both of A's left and right children.

We immediately cease processing the left subtree of A (i.e., B) since the maximum of the y coordinate values in B's subtrees is 45, which is less than the lower bound of the semi-infinite range of y (i.e., 50). Next, we process the root of the right subtree of A (i.e., C). The point associated with C is Buffalo, with a y coordinate value of 65, which is in the y range. The x coordinate value of Buffalo is 82, which is in the x range, and thus we output Buffalo as in the two-dimensional range. Next, we examine the midrange value of C, which is 84. This means that we need to descend only the left subtree of C (i.e., rooted at F) since the right subtree of C (i.e., rooted at G) is out of the x range. However, since there is no point associated with F, processing ceases because all nodes in F's subtrees have already been examined. Thus, the result is that points (62,77) and (82,65) are in the range ([35:83],[50:∞]).

Edelsbrunner [535] introduces a variation on the priority search tree, which we term a *range priority tree*, to obtain an $O(\log_2 N + F)$ algorithm for range searching in a two-dimensional space. Define an *inverse priority search tree* to be a priority search tree S such that with each node of S, say I, we associate the point in the subtree rooted at I with the minimum (instead of the maximum!) value for its y coordinate that has not already been stored at a shallower depth in the tree. For example, Figure 1.12 is the inverse priority search tree corresponding to Figure 1.10, and Figure 1.11(b) is the space decomposition induced by it. The range priority tree is a balanced binary search tree (i.e., a one-dimensional range tree), say T, where all the data points are stored in the leaf nodes and are sorted by their y coordinate values. With each nonleaf node of T, say I, that is a left child of its father, we store a priority search tree of the points in the subtree rooted at I. With each nonleaf node of T, say I, that is a right child of its father, we store an inverse priority search tree of the points in the subtree rooted at I. For N points, the range priority tree uses $O(N \cdot \log_2 N)$ space (see Exercise 13) and requires $O(N \cdot \log_2 N)$ time to build (see Exercises 14 and 15). However, unlike the priority search tree, dynamic updates (i.e., insertion and deletion) take $O(\log_2^2 N)$ time [535].

For example, Figure 1.13 is the range priority tree for the data of Figure 1.1, where the y coordinate serves as the primary sort attribute. Notice the use of double lines to indicate a link to the priority and inverse priority search trees associated with each nonleaf node, thereby distinguishing them from the single lines used to indicate links to left and right children in the two trees. In the figure, square boxes contain the relevant one-dimensional

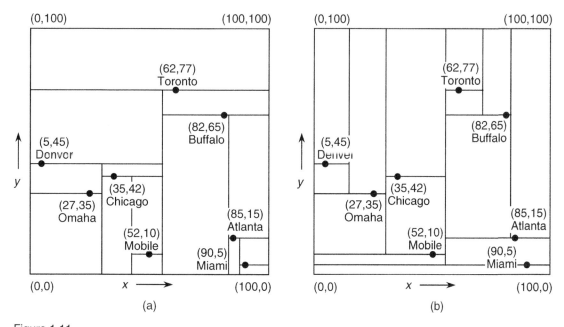

Figure 1.11
Space decomposition induced by (a) the priority search tree of Figure 1.10 and (b) the inverse priority search tree of Figure 1.12. Horizontal lines correspond to the partitions caused by the HEAPMAX field values in the tree. Vertical lines correspond to the partitions caused by the MIDRANGE field values associated with the nonleaf nodes that have at least one child whose HEAPMAX field is not NIL.

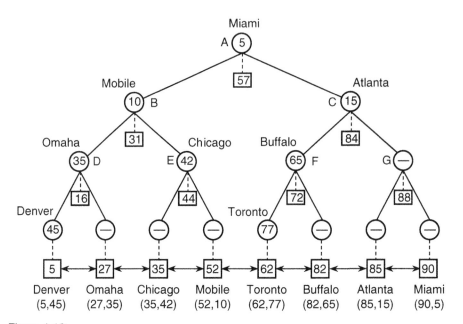

Figure 1.12
Inverse priority search tree for the data of Figure 1.1. Each leaf node contains the value of its *x* coordinate in a square box. Each nonleaf node contains the appropriate *x* coordinate midrange value in a box using a link drawn with a broken line. Circular boxes indicate the value of the *y* coordinate of the point in the corresponding subtree with the minimum value for its *y* coordinate that has not already been associated with a node at a shallower depth in the tree.

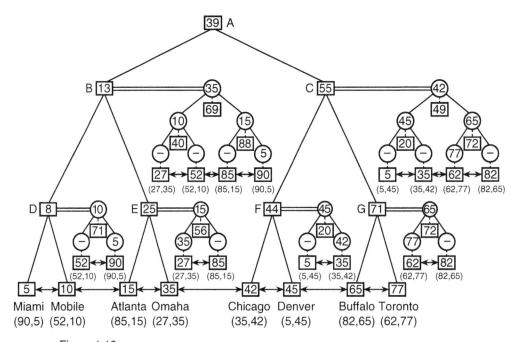

Figure 1.13
Range priority tree for the data of Figure 1.1. Square boxes contain the relevant one-dimensional range tree values (midrange values in the nonleaf nodes), and circular boxes contain the relevant heap values. The square boxes containing the midrange values in the priority and inverse priority search trees are linked to the appropriate nonleaf node by a broken line. Double horizontal lines indicate a link to the priority and inverse priority search trees associated with each nonleaf node, thereby distinguishing them from the single lines used to indicate links to left and right children in the two trees.

range tree values (e.g., the midrange values in the nonleaf nodes); circular boxes contain the relevant heap values (i.e., maximums for the priority search tree and minimums for the inverse priority search tree). Notice that, as in the priority search tree, the leaf nodes contain the points and are shown as linked together in ascending order of the x coordinate value. Again, as in the priority search tree, the links for the x coordinate values are used only if we conduct a search for all points within a given range of x coordinate values. They are not used in the execution of the two-dimensional range query, and thus they are frequently omitted from the implementation of the range priority tree.

Performing a range query for $([B_x : E_x], [B_y : E_y])$ using a range priority tree is done in the following manner (see also Exercise 12). We descend the tree looking for the nearest common ancestor of B_y and E_y, say Q. The values of the y coordinate of all points in the left child of Q are less than or equal to E_y. We want to retrieve just the ones that are greater than or equal to B_y. We can obtain them with the semi-infinite range query $([B_x : E_x], [B_y : \infty])$. This can be done by using the priority search tree associated with the left child of Q. The priority search tree is good for retrieving all points with a specific lower bound since it stores an upper bound and hence irrelevant values can be easily pruned.

Similarly, the values of the y coordinate of all points in the right child of Q are greater than or equal to B_y. We want to retrieve just the ones that are less than or equal to E_y. We can obtain them with the semi-infinite range query $([B_x : E_x], [-\infty : E_y])$. This can be done by using the inverse priority search tree associated with the right child of Q. The inverse priority search tree is good for retrieving all points with a specific upper bound since it stores a lower bound and hence irrelevant values can be easily pruned. Thus, for N points, the range query takes $O(\log_2 N + F)$ time, where F is the number of points found (see Exercise 17).

As an example, suppose we want to perform a range search for ([25:60],[15:45]) on the range priority tree in Figure 1.13. We first find the nearest common ancestor of 15 and 45, which is node A. Second, we search for ([25:60],[15:∞]) in the priority search tree attached to the left child of A (i.e., B), say p. The point (27,35) is associated with the root of p, and it is in the range. Hence, it is output. The left subtree of p is rejected because the y coordinate value associated with its root (i.e., 10) is less than the lower limit of the search range in y (i.e., 15). The elements of the right subtree of p are rejected because their x coordinate values are outside of the search range. Third, we search for ([25:60],[$-\infty$:45]) in the inverse priority search tree attached to the right child of A (i.e., C), say q. The point (35,42) is associated with the root of q, and it is in the range. Hence, it is output. The elements of the left subtree of q that have not been reported already (i.e., (5,45)) are rejected because their x coordinate values are outside of the search range. The right subtree of q is rejected because the y coordinate value associated with its root (i.e., 65) is greater than the upper limit of the search range in y (i.e., 45).

Exercises

1. Prove that a priority search tree for N points uses $O(N)$ space.

2. Prove that for a priority search tree with N points, a semi-infinite range query can be performed in $O(\log_2 N + F)$ time, where F is the number of points found.

3. Procedure PRIORITYSEARCH can be made considerably shorter by changing its structure slightly, as given below by procedure PRIORITYSEARCH2. The difference is that procedure PRIORITYSEARCH2 does not make explicit use of the result of finding the nearest common ancestor. This forces the repeated comparison of B_x and E_x with the MIDRANGE field value of the node even after the nearest common ancestor has been determined. However, it does enable procedure PRIORITYSEARCH2 to make use of recursion as there is no longer a need to distinguish between processing the right and left children of the nearest common ancestor, as well as testing if the node and its left child are on the path from the nearest common ancestor to B_x, or testing if the node and its right child are on the path from the nearest common

ancestor to E_x. Prove that for N points, procedure PRIORITYSEARCH2 executes the semi-infinite range query in $O(\log_2 N + F)$ time, where F is the number of points found. Which of PRIORITYSEARCH and PRIORITYSEARCH2 performs fewer comparison operations?

```
1   recursive procedure PRIORITYSEARCH2(B_x, E_x, B_y, T)
2   /* Perform a semi-infinite range search for the two-dimensional interval
        ([B_x : E_x], [B_y : ∞]) in the priority search tree rooted at T. */
3   value integer B_x, E_x, B_y
4   value pointer node T
5   if ISNULL(T) then return
6   elseif ISNULL(HEAPMAX(T)) then return
7       /* All relevant points have already been output */
8   elseif YCOORD(POINT(HEAPMAX(T))) < B_y then return
9       /* y coordinate values of all points in the subtrees are too small */
10  elseif B_x ≤ XCOORD(POINT(HEAPMAX(T))) and
           XCOORD(POINT(HEAPMAX(T))) ≤ E_x then
11      output POINT(HEAPMAX(T))
12  endif
13  if B_x ≤ MIDRANGE(T) then
14      if MIDRANGE(T) ≤ E_x then
15          PRIORITYSEARCH2(B_x, E_x, B_y, LEFT(T))
16          PRIORITYSEARCH2(B_x, E_x, B_y, RIGHT(T))
17      else PRIORITYSEARCH2(B_x, E_x, B_y, LEFT(T))
18      endif
19  else PRIORITYSEARCH2(B_x, E_x, B_y, RIGHT(T))
20  endif
```

4. Procedure PRIORITYSEARCH makes use of a representation of the two-dimensional range tree, where each node has a POINT and HEAPMAX field. In fact, the POINT field is defined only for leaf nodes, while the HEAPMAX field is defined for both leaf and nonleaf nodes. In particular, for leaf nodes, the HEAPMAX field either points to NIL or to itself; for nonleaf nodes, it points to either NIL or to a leaf node for which it is immediately dereferenced to obtain the corresponding POINT field value. Rewrite PRIORITYSEARCH, YSEARCH, and OUTOFRANGEY so that they do not use a POINT field, and hence interpret the HEAPMAX field appropriately.

5. In the original presentation of the priority search tree, two variants are defined [1266]. The first variant, which is the one described in the text, makes use of a one-dimensional range tree on the x coordinate value and stores midrange x coordinate values in the nonleaf nodes. The second variant does not store the midrange values. Instead, it is based on a trie search where the domain of the x coordinate value is repeatedly halved. Thus, the x coordinate values of all points in the left subtree are less than the partition value, while those of all points in the right subtree are greater than or equal to the partition value. This means that the midrange values are implicit to the tree. Prove that, in this case, no two data points in the priority search tree can have the same x coordinate value.

6. Suppose that you are using the second variant of the priority search tree as described in Exercise 5. Therefore, by the time we reach the final partition, there is just one value left. How can you get around the restriction that no two data points in a priority search tree have the same x coordinate value?

7. Prove that the construction of a priority search tree takes $O(N \cdot \log_2 N)$ time for N points.

8. Write a procedure to construct a priority search tree.

9. Write a procedure to construct an inverse priority search tree.

10. Modify procedure PRIORITYSEARCH to deal with an inverse priority search tree.

11. Can you extend the priority search tree to handle k-dimensional data? If yes, show how you would do it.

12. Consider the search for $([B_x : E_x], [B_y : E_y])$ in a range priority tree. The algorithm that we outlined first finds the nearest common ancestor Q of B_y and E_y, and the second step searches

for $([B_x : E_x], [B_y : \infty])$ in the priority search tree, say p, attached to the left child L of Q. Note that p is a superset of the objects that can satisfy the query. Making use of this observation, why can we not simplify the algorithm by descending as many right links of the left child L of Q as possible, until we encounter a nonleaf node S for which B_y is in the left subtree? Similarly, for the third step of the algorithm, the subsequent search is for $([B_x : E_x], [-\infty : E_y])$ in the priority search tree, say p, attached to the right child R of Q. Again, we note that p is a superset of the objects that can satisfy the query. Making use of this observation, why can we not simplify the search by descending as many left links of the right child R of Q as possible, until we encounter a nonleaf node S for which E_y is in the right subtree?

13. Prove that a range priority tree for N points uses $O(N \cdot \log_2 N)$ space.

14. Prove that the construction of a range priority tree takes $O(N \cdot \log_2 N)$ time for N points.

15. There are several ways of constructing a range priority tree with different execution times. As we pointed out in the text, for N points, the range priority tree can be constructed in $O(N \cdot \log_2 N)$ time (see Exercise 14). However, we could also build it in $O(N \cdot \log_2^2 N)$ time by constructing 2^i priority search trees at levels i $(1 \leq i \leq \log_2 N - 1)$. Describe this method in greater detail, and show that it takes $O(N \cdot \log_2^2 N)$ time.

16. Prove that insertion and deletion in a range priority tree with N points can be done in $O(\log_2^2 N)$ time.

17. Prove that for a range priority tree with N points, a two-dimensional range query can be performed in $O(\log_2 N + F)$ time, where F is the number of points found.

18. Can you extend the range priority tree to handle k-dimensional range queries? What is the order of the execution time of the query? How much space does it use?

19. Write a procedure to construct a range priority tree.

20. Write a procedure to search a range priority tree for a rectangular search region.

21. In the text, we characterized a priority search tree as a variant of a one-dimensional range tree in x and a heap (i.e., priority queue) in y. The priority search tree is somewhat wasteful of space as the nonleaf nodes duplicate some of the information stored in the leaf nodes. Vuillemin [1944] defines a *Cartesian tree*, which is a binary search tree in x and a heap in y. In this case, each point (a, b) is stored at just one node—that is, both nonleaf and leaf nodes contain data.[16] Construct a Cartesian tree for the data of Figure 1.1. Note that every conventional one-dimensional binary search tree that is constructed dynamically as the data is encountered (i.e., the first data item that is encountered serves as the root, the second data item is inserted as the right or left child of the root as is appropriate, etc.) is in fact a Cartesian tree, where there is a binary search tree on the one-dimensional data (represented as the x coordinate value) and a heap on the relative time (represented by the y coordinate value) at which the various elements were inserted in the binary search tree, with a higher priority being given to the elements that were inserted first.

22. Is the Cartesian tree defined in Exercise 21 unique? In other words, can you apply rotation operations to it to make it balanced?

---

[16] The *treap* [69, 1712] has the same structure as the Cartesian tree and is used by Aragon and Seidel to define what they term a *weighted randomized search tree*—a search structure for one-dimensional data with expected $O(\log N)$ behavior for search and update operations. The expected costs are independent of the data. In particular, a weighted, randomized search tree is defined as a treap where the key (i.e., analogous to the x coordinate value) is defined by the data, and the priority (represented by the y coordinate value) is a distinct, random value fixed when the corresponding element was inserted in the binary search tree. This formulation has the same execution time behavior for performing search and update operations as the skip list [1520], which has also been applied to a k-d tree [1204] for half-space range search, as well as to a PR quadtree [561] for a number of operations, including point location, approximate range searching, and approximate nearest neighbor finding.

1.4 Quadtrees

Recall from Section 1.1 that the quadtree is the result of imposing a tree access structure on a grid so that spatially adjacent empty grid cells are merged into larger empty grid cells. In essence, it is equivalent to marrying a k-ary tree, where $k = 2^d$, with the fixed grid. There are two types of quadtrees. The first is a point quadtree [614] where the subdivision lines are based on the values of the data points. The second is trie-based and forms a decomposition of the embedding space from which the data points are drawn.

In the rest of this section, we elaborate further on the differences between the point quadtree and the trie-based quadtree by showing how they are updated (i.e., node insertion and deletion) and how they are used for region searching. In particular, Section 1.4.1 presents the point quadtree. Section 1.4.2 discusses trie-based quadtrees, such as the PR and MX quadtrees. Section 1.4.3 contains a brief comparison of the point, PR, and MX quadtrees.

1.4.1 Point Quadtrees

In two dimensions, the point quadtree, invented by Finkel and Bentley [614], is just a two-dimensional binary search tree. The first point that is inserted serves as the root, and the second point is inserted into the relevant quadrant of the tree rooted at the first point. Clearly, the shape of the tree depends on the order in which the points were inserted. For example, Figure 1.14 is the point quadtree corresponding to the data of Figure 1.6.

The rest of this section is organized as follows. Section 1.4.1.1 shows how to insert a point into a point quadtree. Section 1.4.1.2 discusses how to delete a point from a point quadtree. Section 1.4.1.3 explains how to do region searching in a point quadtree.

1.4.1.1 Insertion

Inserting record r with key values (a, b) into a point quadtree is very simple. The process is analogous to that for a binary search tree. First, if the tree is empty, then allocate a new node containing r, and return a tree with it as its only node. Otherwise, search the tree for a node h with a record having key values (a, b). If h exists, then r replaces the record associated with h. Otherwise, we are at a NIL node, which is a child of type s (i.e.,

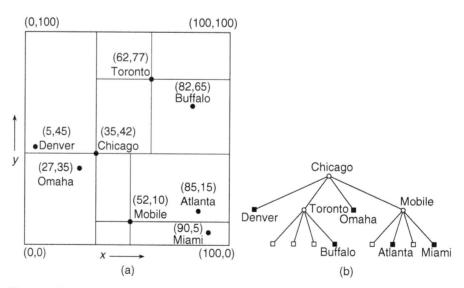

Figure 1.14
A point quadtree and the records it represents corresponding to the data of Figure 1.1:
(a) the resulting partition of space and (b) the tree representation.

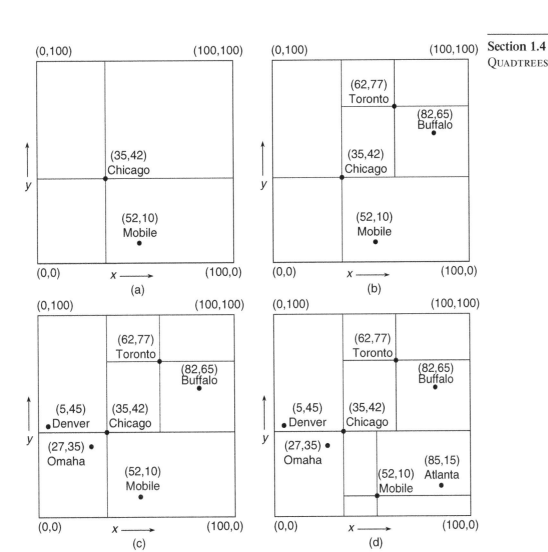

Figure 1.15
Sequence of partial block decompositions showing how a point quadtree is built when adding (a) Chicago and Mobile, (b) Toronto and Buffalo, (c) Denver and Omaha, and (d) Atlanta, corresponding to the data of Figure 1.1.

NW, NE, SW, or SE, as appropriate) of node c. This is where we make the insertion by allocating a new node t containing r and make t an s child of node c. The only difference from the binary search tree is the need to perform four-way comparisons at each node of the tree. In particular, at each node q with key values (e, f), we must determine the quadrant of the subtree rooted at q in which r lies. This is done by determining the position of point (a, b) with respect to (e, f). For example, the tree in Figure 1.14 was built for the sequence Chicago, Mobile, Toronto, Buffalo, Denver, Omaha, Atlanta, and Miami. Figure 1.15 shows how the tree was constructed in an incremental fashion for these cities by giving the appropriate block decompositions. In particular, Figure 1.15(a) corresponds to the tree after insertion of Chicago and Mobile, Figure 1.15(b) to the tree after insertion of Toronto and Buffalo, Figure 1.15(c) to the tree after insertion of Denver and Omaha, and Figure 1.15(d) to the tree after insertion of Atlanta.

To cope with data points that lie directly on one of the quadrant lines emanating from a data point, say P, we adopt the same conventions that were used for the grid method: the lower and left boundaries of each block are closed, while the upper and right boundaries of each block are open. For example, in Figure 1.14, insertion of Memphis with coordinate values (35,20) would lead to its placement somewhere in quadrant SE of the tree rooted at Chicago (i.e., at (35,42)).

The amount of work expended in building a point quadtree is equal to the total path length (TPL) [1044] of the tree as it reflects the cost of searching for all of the elements. Finkel and Bentley [614] have shown empirically that for N points, the TPL of a point quadtree under random insertion is roughly proportional to $N \cdot \log_4 N$, which yields an average cost $O(\log_4 N)$ of inserting, as well as searching for (i.e., a point query), a point. Devroye [484, 485] shows that the expected height of a point quadtree is logarithmic and asymptotic to $2c/d \ln N$, where $c = 4.31107$. Devroye and Laforest [486], as well as Flajolet, Gonnet, Puech, and Robson [618] have shown independently that the asymptotic expected cost of inserting the ith node in a random d-dimensional point quadtree is $(2/d)\ln i + O(1)$. Flajolet and Lafforgue [620] have made these results more precise by showing that random search has a logarithmic mean, and variance and is asymptotically distributed as a normal variable for all dimensions. Moreover, Flajolet, Labelle, Laforest and Salvy [619] have shown that these expected costs have explicit expressions and thus can be quantified precisely. Of course, the extreme case is much worse (see Exercise 9) and is a function of the shape of the resulting point quadtree. This is dependent on the order in which nodes are inserted into it. The worst case arises when each successive node is the child of the currently deepest node in the tree. Consequently, there has been some interest in reducing the TPL. Two techniques for achieving this reduction are described below.

Finkel and Bentley [614] propose one approach that assumes that all the nodes are known a priori. They define an *optimized point quadtree* so that given a node A, no subtree of A accounts for more than one-half of the nodes in the tree rooted at A. Building an optimized point quadtree from a file requires that the records in the file be sorted primarily by one key and secondarily by the other key. The root of the tree is set to the median value of the sorted file, and the remaining records are regrouped into four subcollections that will form the four subtrees of A. The process is applied recursively to the four subtrees.

This technique works because all records preceding A in the sorted list will lie in the NW and SW quadrants (assuming that the x coordinate value serves as the primary key), and all records following A will lie in the NE and SE quadrants. Thus, the requirement that no subtree can contain more than one-half of the total number of nodes is fulfilled. Of course, this construction method still does not guarantee that the resulting tree will be complete[17] (see Exercise 3).

The optimized point quadtree requires that all of the data points are known a priori. Overmars and van Leeuwen [1444] discuss an alternative approach that is a dynamic formulation of the above method—that is, the optimized point quadtree is built as the data points are inserted into it. The algorithm is similar to the one used to construct the conventional point quadtree, except that every time the tree fails to meet a predefined balance criterion, the tree is partially rebalanced using techniques similar to those developed by Finkel and Bentley to build the optimized point quadtree (for more details, see Exercise 6).

Exercises

Assume that each point in a point quadtree is implemented as a record of type *node* containing six fields. The first four fields contain pointers to the node's four children, corresponding to the directions (i.e., quadrants) NW, NE, SW, and SE. If P is a pointer to a node, and I is a quadrant, then these fields are referenced as CHILD(P, I). We can determine the specific quadrant in

---

[17] A t-ary tree containing N nodes is *complete* if we can map it onto a one-dimensional array so that the first element consists of the root, the next t elements are the roots of its t subtrees ordered from left to right, the next t^2 elements are the roots of all of the subtrees of the previous t elements again ordered from left to right, etc. This process stops once N is exhausted. Thus, each level of the tree, with the exception of the deepest level, contains a maximum number of nodes. The deepest level is partially full but has no empty positions when using this array mapping. For more details, see Knuth [1044, pp. 400–401].

which a node, say P, lies relative to its father by use of the function CHILDTYPE(P), which has a value of I if CHILD(FATHER(P), I) = P. XCOORD and YCOORD contain the values of the x and y coordinates, respectively, of the point. The empty point quadtree is represented by NIL.

1. Give an algorithm PTCOMPARE to determine the quadrant of a quadtree rooted at r in which point p lies.

2. Give an algorithm PTINSERT to insert a point p in a point quadtree rooted at node r. Make use of procedure PTCOMPARE from Exercise 1. There is no need to make use of the CHILDTYPE function.

3. Suppose that you could construct the optimized point quadtree (i.e., minimal depth) for N nodes. What is the worst-case depth of an optimized point quadtree?

4. What is the maximum TPL in an optimized point quadtree?

5. Analyze the running time of the algorithm for constructing an optimized point quadtree.

6. In the text, we intimated that the optimized point quadtree can also be constructed dynamically. Given δ ($0 < \delta < 1$), we stipulate that every nonleaf node with a total of m nodes in its subtrees has at most $\lceil m/(2-\delta) \rceil$ nodes in each subtree. Give an algorithm to construct such a point quadtree.

7. Prove that the depth of the optimized point quadtree constructed in Exercise 6 is always at most $\log_{2-\delta} n + O(1)$ and that the average insertion time in an initially empty data structure is $O(\frac{1}{\delta \log_2^2 N})$. n denotes the number of nodes currently in the tree, and N is the total number of nodes that have been inserted.

8. The TPL can also be reduced by applying balancing operators analogous to those used to balance binary search trees. Give the point quadtree analogs of the single and double rotation operators [1046, p. 461].

9. What is the worst-case cost of building a point quadtree of N nodes?

Figure 1.16
Idealized point quadtree deletion situation.

1.4.1.2 Deletion

There are several ways of deleting nodes in two-dimensional point quadtrees. The first, suggested by Finkel and Bentley [614], is quite simple in that we reinsert all nodes of the tree rooted at the deleted node. This is usually a very expensive process, unless the deleted node is a leaf node or its children are leaf nodes. In the rest of this section we describe a more complex, and more efficient, process developed by Samet [1618]. It may be skipped on an initial reading.

Ideally, we want to replace the deleted node (say A at (x_A, y_A)) with a node (say B at (x_B, y_B)), such that the region between the lines $x = x_A$ and $x = x_B$ and the region between the lines $y = y_A$ and $y = y_B$ are empty. The shaded area in Figure 1.16 illustrates this concept for nodes A and B in that A is deleted and replaced by B. We use the term *hatched* to describe the region that we would like to be empty. Unfortunately, finding a node that will lead to an empty hatched region involves a considerable amount of searching. In fact, it is not uncommon that such a node fails to exist (e.g., when deleting node A in Figure 1.17).

The algorithm we describe proceeds in a manner analogous to the method for binary search trees. For example, for the binary search tree of Figure 1.18, when node A is to be deleted, it can be replaced by one of nodes D or G—the two "closest" nodes in value. In the case of a point quadtree (e.g., Figure 1.17), it is not clear which of the remaining nodes should replace A. This is because no node is simultaneously the closest in both the x and y directions. We notice that no matter which of the nodes is chosen, some of the nodes will assume different positions in the new tree. For example, in Figure 1.17, if L replaced A, then J would no longer occupy the NW quadrant with respect to the root (which is now L instead of A) and thus J would need to be reinserted, along with some of its subtrees, in the quadrant rooted at F. Similarly, E and I would have to be reinserted, along with some of their subtrees, in the quadrant rooted at N.

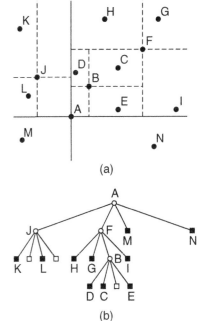

Figure 1.17
A point quadtree and the records it represents: (a) the resulting partition of space and (b) the tree representation.

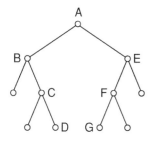

Figure 1.18
Example binary search tree.

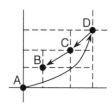

Figure 1.19
Example of the application of the candidate determination procedure to the NE quadrant of node A.

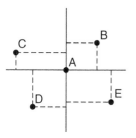

Figure 1.20
Example of a point quadtree with no "closest" terminal node.

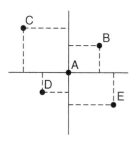

Figure 1.21
Example of a point quadtree with two nodes being "closest" to their bordering axes.

Our algorithm determines four candidate nodes for the replacement node, one for each quadrant, as follows. Let the primitive OPQUAD(i) denote the quadrant that is 180 degrees apart from quadrant i (e.g., OPQUAD('NW') = 'SE'). The candidate in quadrant i of the root r is obtained by starting at the node CHILD(r, i) and repeatedly following the branch corresponding to OPQUAD(i) until encountering a node having no subtree along this branch. Figure 1.19 shows how node B is selected as the candidate node from the NE quadrant of node A in an example where the NE child of A is D, the SW child of D is C, and the SW child of C is B. Note that this example is unrelated to the one in Figure 1.17. As a more complex example, in Figure 1.17, the candidates are B, J, M, and N.

Once the set of candidate nodes is found, an attempt is made to find the "best" candidate, which becomes the replacement node. There are two criteria for choosing the best candidate. Criterion 1 stipulates the choice of the candidate that is closer to each of its bordering axes than any other candidate and that is on the same side of these axes, if such a candidate exists. For example, in Figure 1.17, node B is the best candidate according to this criterion. Note that the situation may arise that no candidate satisfies criterion 1 (e.g., Figure 1.20) or that several candidates satisfy it (e.g., B and D in Figure 1.21). In such a case, criterion 2 chooses the candidate with the minimum L_1 metric value. Criterion 2 is also known as the *City Block metric* (or the *Manhattan metric*).

The L_1 metric is the sum of the displacements from the bordering x and y axes. To justify its use, we assume that the nodes are uniformly distributed in the two-dimensional space. Our goal is to minimize the area, that which is obtained by removing from the hatched region the rectangle whose opposite vertices are the root and candidate nodes (e.g., nodes A and B, respectively, in Figure 1.16).

Assume that the two-dimensional space is bounded, having sides of length L_X and L_Y parallel to the x and y axes, respectively. Let this space be centered at the node to be deleted. Assume further that the candidate node is at a distance of d_X and d_Y from the x and y axes, respectively. Under these assumptions, the remaining area is $L_X \cdot d_Y + L_Y \cdot d_X - 2 \cdot d_X \cdot d_Y$ (see Figure 1.22). We can ignore the area of the rectangle with sides d_X and d_Y because the candidate selection process guarantees that it is empty. As L_X and L_Y increase, as occurs in the general problem domain, the contribution of the $2 \cdot d_X \cdot d_Y$ term becomes negligible, and the area is proportional to the sum of d_X and d_Y.[18]

Criterion 2 is not sufficient by itself to insure that the selected candidate partitions the space so that the hatched region contains no other candidate. For example, see Figure 1.23, in which O has been deleted, and A satisfies criterion 2, but only C satisfies criterion 1. A pair of axes through C leaves all other candidates outside the hatched region, while a pair of axes through A results in B's being in the hatched region.

If no candidate is found to satisfy criterion 1, then criterion 2 guarantees that at least one of the candidates, say X, has the property that no more than one of the remaining candidates occupies the hatched region between the original axes and the axes passing through X. To see this, we examine Figure 1.20 and note that whichever candidate is selected to be the new root (say C in the NW quadrant), then the candidate in the opposite quadrant (i.e., SE) lies outside of the hatched region. In addition, the candidate in a quadrant on the same side of an axis as C, and to which axis C is closer (i.e., B), lies outside of the hatched region.

We are now ready to present the deletion algorithm. It makes use of the properties of the space obtained by the new partition to reduce the number of nodes requiring reinsertion. The algorithm consists of two procedures, ADJQUAD and NEWROOT. Let A be the node to be deleted, and let I be the quadrant of the tree containing B, the replacement node for A. Note that no nodes in quadrant OPQUAD(I) need to be

---

[18] Actually, this statement holds only for $L_X = L_Y$. However, this approximation is adequate for the purpose of this discussion.

reinserted. Now, separately process the two quadrants adjacent laterally to quadrant I using procedure AdjQuad, followed by application of procedure NewRoot to quadrant I.

Procedure AdjQuad proceeds as follows. Examine the root of the quadrant, say R. If R lies outside of the hatched region, then two subquadrants can automatically remain in the quadrant and need no further processing while the remaining subquadrants are separately processed by a recursive invocation of AdjQuad. Otherwise, the entire quadrant must be reinserted into the quadtree that was formerly rooted at A.

As an example of the effect of applying AdjQuad to the two quadrants laterally adjacent to the quadrant containing the replacement node, consider Figure 1.17, where node A is deleted and replaced by node B in the NE quadrant. J and the subquadrant rooted at K remain in the NW quadrant, while the subquadrant rooted at L is recursively processed. Eventually, L must be reinserted into the tree rooted at M. The SE quadrant of A (rooted at N) does not require reinsertion. The result of these manipulations is given in Figure 1.24, which shows the outcome of the entire deletion. Below, we explain how the contents of the quadrant containing the replacement node have been processed (i.e., I or NE in the example of Figure 1.17).

Once the nodes in the quadrants adjacent to quadrant I have been processed by AdjQuad, we apply procedure NewRoot to the nodes in I. Clearly, all of the nodes in subquadrant I of I will retain their position. Thus, NewRoot must be applied only to the remaining subquadrants of I. NewRoot starts by invoking AdjQuad to process the subquadrants adjacent laterally to subquadrant I. This is followed by an iterative reinvocation of NewRoot to subquadrant OpQuad(I). This iterative reinvocation process continues until an empty link in direction OpQuad(I) is encountered (i.e., at this point, we are at B, the node replacing the deleted node). Now, insert the nodes in the subquadrants adjacent to subquadrant I of the tree rooted at B in the quadrants adjacent to quadrant I of the tree rooted at A. Recall that by virtue of the candidate selection process, subquadrant OpQuad(I) of the tree rooted at B is empty. Also, subquadrant I of the tree rooted at B replaces subquadrant OpQuad(I) of the previous father node of B.

Figure 1.25 illustrates the subquadrants that NewRoot calls AdjQuad (labeled ADJ) to process when node O is deleted and the resulting tree is rooted at node 4. For the example of Figure 1.17, where node A is deleted and whose result is shown in Figure 1.24, application of NewRoot results in the tree rooted at G being left alone. Trees rooted at H and I are processed by AdjQuad. Trees rooted at D and E are reinserted in quadrants NW and SE, respectively. The tree rooted at C replaces B as the child of F in subquadrant SW.

The open and closed conventions that we adopted in Section 1.4.1.1 may at times result in the inability to apply procedure NewRoot. This is the case when at least one of the coordinate values of the point associated with the replacement node B and the root F of the quadrant I of the deleted node A that contains B are identical. In this case, the entire subtree rooted at F must be reinserted into the quadtree rooted at B. We must check for this situation at all stages where procedure NewRoot could possibly be applied. For example, it must be checked at nodes 1, 2, and 3 in Figure 1.25. Using our open and closed conventions that the lower and left boundaries of each block are closed, while the upper and right boundaries of each block are open, means that this situation can never arise when the replacement node is in the NE quadrant of the deleted node. However, it can easily arise in the remaining cases. For example, suppose that we are deleting node A at (0,0) and let B at (−5,3) in the NW quadrant of A be the replacement node. Moreover, let F at (−5,5) be the NW child of A. Before replacing A by B, F was in the NW quadrant of A. Once we replace A by B, F is in the NE quadrant of B due to the open and closed conventions, and thus we have to reinsert the entire subtree rather than take advantage of the pruning that is afforded by use of NewRoot. For more examples, see Exercise 3.

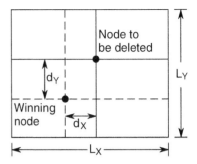

Figure 1.22
Example of a two-dimensional space.

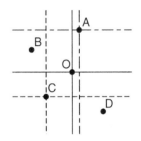

Figure 1.23
Example of the insufficiency of criterion 2 for an empty hatched region.

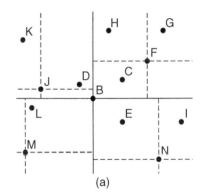

(a)

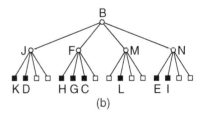

(b)

Figure 1.24
Result of deleting node A from the point quadtree of Figure 1.17 and replacing it with node B: (a) the resulting partition of space and (b) the tree representation.

33

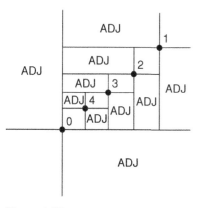

Figure 1.25
Subquadrants processed by procedure ADJQUAD (labeled ADJ) when node 0 is deleted and replaced by node 4.

Theoretical and empirical results for the above deletion method are described by Samet [1618]. It is shown theoretically that for data that is uniformly distributed, the average number of nodes requiring reinsertion is reduced by a factor of 5/6 (i.e., 83%) when the replacement node satisfies criteria 1 and 2. The relaxation of the requirement that the replacement node must satisfy criteria 1 and 2, and its substitution by a random selection of one of the candidates as the replacement node, caused the factor by which the average number of nodes required reinsertion to decrease to 2/3 (i.e., 67%). Of course, the candidate selection process becomes considerably simpler in this case.

The empirical tests led to the following interesting observations. First, the number of comparison operations is proportional to $\log_4 N$ versus a considerably larger factor when using the deletion method of Finkel and Bentley [614]. Second, the total path length (TPL) of the tree after deletion using Samet's method [1618] decreases slightly, whereas when Finkel and Bentley's method [614] is used, the TPL increases significantly. This data is important because it correlates with the effective search time (see also [182, 1132]). In other words, the smaller the TPL, the more quickly a node can be accessed.

It is interesting to observe that one of the main reasons for the complexity of deletion in point quadtrees is the fact that the data points also serve to partition the space from which they are drawn. The *pseudo quadtree* of Overmars and van Leeuwen [1444] simplifies deletion by using arbitrary points that are not in the set of data points being represented for the partitioning process. The pseudo quadtree is constructed by repeatedly partitioning the space into quadrants, subquadrants, and so on, until each subquadrant contains at most one data point of the original set. This means that the data points occur as leaf nodes of the pseudo quadtree. The partition points are chosen in a manner that splits the remaining set in the most balanced way.

Overmars and van Leeuwen show that for any N data points in a d-dimensional space, there exists a partitioning point such that every quadrant contains at most $\lceil N/(d+1) \rceil$ data points. They also demonstrate that the resulting pseudo quadtree has a depth of at most $\lceil \log_{d+1} N \rceil$ and can be built in $O(N \cdot \log_{d+1} N)$ time. For example, Figure 1.26 is the pseudo quadtree corresponding to the data of Figure 1.1. Efficient deletion and insertion in a pseudo quadtree require that the bound on the depth be weakened slightly (see Exercise 16).

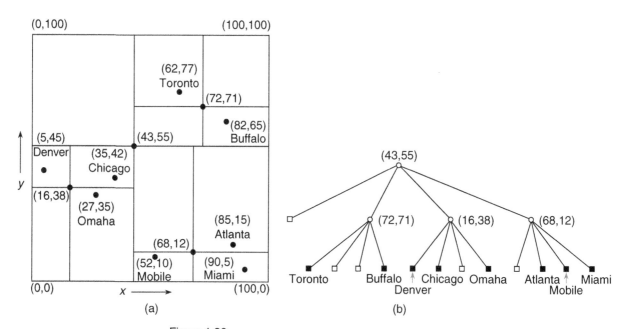

Figure 1.26
A pseudo quadtree and the records it represents corresponding to the data of Figure 1.1:
(a) the resulting partition of space and (b) the tree representation.

1. Assuming the same quadtree node implementation as in the exercises in Section 1.4.1.1, and that p points to the child in quadrant q of the node to be deleted, give an algorithm FINDCANDIDATE to determine the candidate in quadrant q.

2. Assuming the same quadtree node implementation as in the exercises in Section 1.4.1.1, give an algorithm PTDELETE for deleting a point stored in a node p from a point quadtree rooted at node r. The node does not have a FATHER field, although you may make use of the CHILDTYPE function. Make use of procedure PTCOMPARE from Exercise 1 in Section 1.4.1.1. Procedure PTDELETE implements procedures ADJQUAD and NEWROOT as described in the text. You can simplify the task by making use of primitives CQUAD(q) and CCQUAD(q), which yield the adjacent quadrants in the clockwise and counterclockwise directions, respectively, to quadrant q. Also, assume the existence of procedure INSERTQUADRANT(t, p), which inserts the nodes of the subtree rooted at node t in the subtree rooted at node p.

3. In the text, we pointed out that the open and closed conventions for the quadrants that we adopted in Section 1.4.1.1 may at times result in the inability to apply procedure NEWROOT. Using our conventions that the lower and left boundaries of each block are closed, while the upper and right boundaries of each block are open, we pointed out that this situation could not arise if the replacement node is in the NE quadrant of the deleted node. We gave an example of the occurrence of this situation when the replacement node B was in the NW quadrant of the deleted node A. Give examples of when this situation could arise when B is in the SE and SW quadrants of A, which is assumed to be at (0,0).

4. Suppose that a point quadtree node is implemented as a record with a FATHER field containing a pointer to its father. Modify procedure PTDELETE in the solution to Exercise 2 to take advantage of this additional field.

5. Let T be a tree containing N nodes with TPL(T) denoting its total path length. Prove that the sum of the sizes of its subtrees is TPL(T) + N. Show that this result holds for binary search trees and point quadtrees as well.

6. Define a *nontrivial* subtree to be a subtree with two or more nonempty subtrees. Let $Q(N)$ be the expected nontrivial subtree size in a complete point quadtree of N nodes. Prove that as N gets large, $Q(N)$ is $4 \cdot \log_4\left(\frac{3}{4} \cdot N\right) - 4/3$. Do not take the root of the subtree into account. Note that $Q(N)$ is the cost of deletion when the method of Finkel and Bentley [614] is used. A complete point quadtree is used because such a configuration minimizes the average cost of deletion in this case since, recalling Exercise 5, the sum of the subtree sizes for a given tree T containing N nodes is TPL(T) + N. This quantity is at a minimum when T is a complete tree.

7. Assuming a complete point quadtree of N nodes, let $r(N)$ denote the proportion of nodes that do not require reinsertion when using the deletion method of Samet [1618]. Let A and B be the deleted and replacement node, respectively, where B is a node returned by the candidate determination procedure (see procedure FINDCANDIDATE in Exercise 1). Assume further that the nodes are partitioned uniformly throughout the partition of the two-dimensional space rooted at A. Use a value of 1/2 for the probability that a node needs to be reinserted. Show that when B satisfies criteria 1 and 2, then $r(N)$ is 5/6 or 3/4, depending on whether none of the adjacent quadrants has its candidate replacement node in the hatched region. Similarly, show that $r(N)$ is 2/3 when the replacement node is chosen at random from the set of nodes returned by procedure FINDCANDIDATE.

8. Can you prove that the point quadtree deletion algorithm given by procedures ADJQUAD and NEWROOT is $O(\log_4 N)$?

9. Why do the resulting trees get bushier when the point quadtree deletion algorithm given by procedures ADJQUAD and NEWROOT is used?

10. Extend the deletion method of Samet [1618] to handle d-dimensional point quadtrees and compute $r(N)$.

11. Write an algorithm, BUILDPSEUDOQUADTREE, to construct a pseudo quadtree for two-dimensional data.

12. Given a set of N points in d-dimensional space, prove that there exists a partitioning point such that every quadrant contains $\lceil N/(d+1) \rceil$ points.

13. Given a set of N points in d-dimensional space, prove that there exists a pseudo quadtree for it with a depth of at most $\lceil \log_{d+1} N \rceil$.

14. Show that the upper bound obtained in Exercise 13 is a strict upper bound in that there exists a configuration of N points such that there is no corresponding pseudo quadtree with a depth less than $\lceil \log_{d+1} N \rceil$.

15. Prove that the pseudo quadtree of Exercise 13 can be built in $O(N \cdot \log_{d+1} N)$ time.

16. Prove that for any fixed δ $(0 < \delta < 1)$ there is an algorithm to perform N insertions and deletions in an initially empty d-dimensional pseudo quadtree such that its depth is always at most $\log_{d+1-\delta} n + O(1)$ and that the average transaction time is bounded by $O(\frac{1}{\delta \log_2^2 N})$. n denotes the number of nodes currently in the tree.

1.4.1.3 Search

The point quadtree, as well as the trie-based quadtree, is suited for applications that involve proximity search. A typical query seeks all nodes within a specified distance of a given data point—such as all cities within 50 miles of Washington, D.C. Since the mechanics of the search are the same for both point and trie-based quadtrees, in the rest of this discussion we use the term *quadtree* unless a distinction between the different quadtrees is necessary, in which case we restore the appropriate qualifier. The efficiency of the quadtree data structure lies in its role as a pruning device on the amount of search that is required. Thus, many records will not need to be examined.

For example, suppose that in the hypothetical database of Figure 1.1, we wish to find all cities within eight units of a data point with coordinate values (83,10). In such a case, there is no need to search the NW, NE, and SW quadrants of the root (i.e., **Chicago** located at (35,42)). Thus, we can restrict our search to the SE quadrant of the tree rooted at **Chicago**. Similarly, there is no need to search the NW and SW quadrants of the tree rooted at **Mobile** (i.e., located at (52,10)).

As a further illustration of the amount of pruning of the search space that is achievable with the quadtree, we make use of Figure 1.27. In particular, given the problem of finding all nodes within radius r of point A, the figure indicates which quadrants need not be examined when the root of the search space, say R, is in one of the numbered regions. For example, if R is in region 9, then all but its NW quadrants must be searched. If R is in region 7, then the search can be restricted to the NW and NE quadrants of R.

Similar techniques can be used to search for data points in any connected figure. For example, Finkel and Bentley [614] give algorithms for searching within a rectangular window of arbitrary size (also known as a *window query*). These algorithms are more general than the query that we examined here because they are applicable to both locational and nonlocational data. For example, such a query would seek to find all cities within 50 miles of the latitude position of Washington, D.C., and within 50 miles of the longitude position of Washington, D.C. The difference between these two formulations of the query is that the former admits a circular search region, while the latter admits a rectangular search region. In particular, the latter query is applicable to both locational and nonlocational data, while the former is applicable only to locational data. As a concrete example, suppose that we wish to find all people of a height between 5 and 6 feet (152.4 and 182.88 cm) and of a weight between 150 and 180 pounds (68 and 82 kg).

To handle more complex search regions, such as those formed by arbitrary hyperplanes (rather than ones that are parallel to one of the attribute axes, as in our examples), as well as convex polygons, Willard [2000] defines a *polygon tree*, where the x-y plane

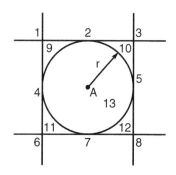

Problem: Find all nodes within radius r of point A

Solution: If the root is in region *I* (*I* =1...13), then continue to search in the quadrant specified by *I*

1. SE
2. SE,SW
3. SW
4. SE,NE
5. SW,NW
6. NE
7. NE, NW
8. NW
9. All but NW
10. All but NE
11. All but SW
12. All but SE
13. All

Figure 1.27
Relationship between a circular search space and the regions in which a root of a quadtree may reside.

is subdivided by J lines that need not be orthogonal, although there are other restrictions on these lines (see Exercise 6). When $J = 2$, the result is a point quadtree with nonorthogonal axes.

Thus, we see that quadtrees can be used to handle all three types of queries specified by Knuth [1046]. Range and Boolean queries are described immediately above, while simple queries (e.g., what city is located at a given pair of coordinate values) are a byproduct of the point quadtree insertion process described earlier. Nearest neighbor queries, as well as k-nearest neighbor queries, are also feasible [846, 848].

The cost of search in a point quadtree has been studied by Bentley, Stanat, and Williams [182] (see Exercise 2) and Lee and Wong [1132]. In particular, Lee and Wong show that in the worst case, range searching in a complete two-dimensional point quadtree takes $O(2 \cdot N^{1/2})$ time. This result can be extended to d dimensions to take $O(d \cdot N^{1-1/d})$ time and is derived in a manner analogous to that for a k-d tree, as discussed in Section 1.5. Note that complete point quadtrees are not always achievable, as seen in Exercise 3 in Section 1.4.1.1. Partial range queries can be handled in the same way as range searching. Lee and Wong [1132] show that when ranges for s out of d keys are specified, then the algorithm has a worst-case running time of $O(s \cdot N^{1-1/d})$.

Exercises

1. Write a procedure PTREGIONSEARCH that performs a region search for a circular region in a point quadtree. Repeat for a rectangular region.

2. Bentley and Stanat [181] define a *perfect point quadtree* of height m as a point quadtree with (1) 4^i nodes at level $m - i$, where the root is at level m, $0 \le i \le m - 1$, and (2) every node at the centroid of the finite space spanned by its subtrees. Assume a search space of $[0, 1]^2$ and a rectangular search region of sides of length x and y, where x and y are in $[0, 1]$. Find the expected number of nodes that are visited in a perfect point quadtree of height m when a region search procedure is applied to the above search region.

3. Bentley and Stanat [181] also define the concept of *overwork* of a search algorithm as the difference between the number of records visited and the number of records in the search region. Assume a search space of $[0, 1]^2$ with N records and a square search region of side length x, where x is in $[0, 1]$. Compare the amount of overwork for an inverted list (i.e., inverted file) and a perfect point quadtree.

4. Prove that the worst-case running time for a partial range query, such that ranges for s out of d keys are specified, is $O(s \cdot N^{1-1/d})$.

5. Perform an average case analysis for a region query in a point quadtree.

6. What are the restrictions on the choice of subdivision lines in Willard's polygon tree [2000]?

1.4.2 Trie-Based Quadtrees

From Section 1.4.1 we saw that for the point quadtree, the points of decomposition are the data points themselves (e.g., in Figure 1.14, Chicago at location (35,42) subdivides the two-dimensional space into four rectangular regions). Requiring that the regions resulting from the subdivision process be of equal size (congruent, to be precise) leads to a trie-based quadtree.

Trie-based quadtrees are closely related to the region quadtree representation of region data (see Section 2.1.2.4 in Chapter 2). Region quadtrees are built on the basis of recursively decomposing a region into four congruent blocks and stopping the decomposition whenever the block is homogeneous. In the case of region data, the homogeneity condition usually means that the area spanned by the block belongs to just one region (assuming that the underlying regions do not overlap). For example, Figure 1.28 shows a region and its corresponding region quadtree. There are many possible adaptations of the homogeneity condition for point data. For example, if we treat the points as elements

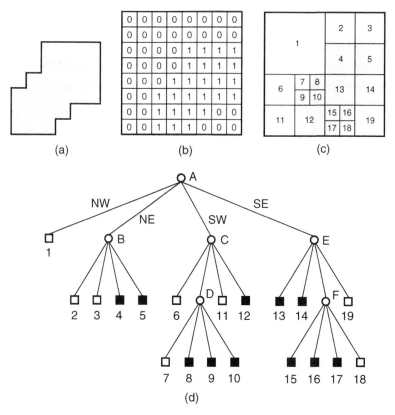

Figure 1.28
(a) Sample region, (b) its binary array representation, (c) its maximal blocks with the blocks in the region being shaded, and (d) the corresponding quadtree.

in a square matrix, then the homogeneity condition could be that the block contains no more than b nonzero elements (when $b = 1$, we have a PR quadtree). Alternatively, we could stipulate that all elements in the block must be zero or that the block contains just one element, which must be nonzero (an MX quadtree).

Although, conceivably, there are many other ways of adapting the region quadtree to represent point data, our presentation focuses on the MX and PR quadtrees. In particular, we discuss the MX quadtree in Section 1.4.2.1 and the PR quadtree in Section 1.4.2.2. We outline how they are created and updated as well as give a brief review of some of their applications. We omit a discussion of search operations because they are performed in the same manner as for a point quadtree (see Section 1.4.1.3).

1.4.2.1   MX Quadtree

There are several ways of adapting the region quadtree to represent point data. If the domain of the data points is discrete, and all attribute values are discrete and have the same type and range, then we can treat the data points as if they were black pixels in a region quadtree corresponding to a square image. An alternative characterization is to treat the data points as nonzero elements in a square matrix. We shall use this characterization in the subsequent discussion. In fact, we use the term *MX quadtree* to describe the structure on account of the analogy to the matrix (where *MX* denotes matrix), although the term *MX quadtrie* would probably be more appropriate.

The MX quadtree is organized in a similar way to the region quadtree. The difference is that leaf nodes are black, corresponding to regions of size 1×1, or empty (i.e., white and represented by NIL), in which case there is no restriction on their size. The leaf nodes correspond to the presence or absence, respectively, of a data point in the

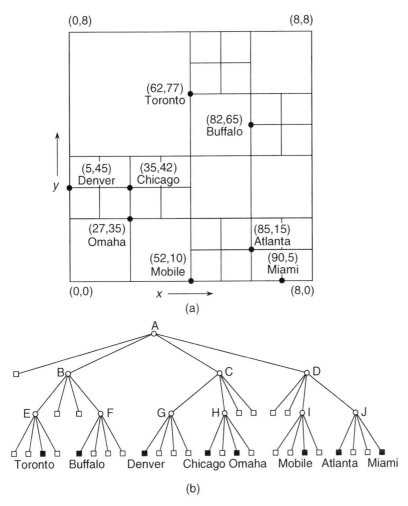

Figure 1.29
An MX quadtree and the records it represents corresponding to the data of Figure 1.1:
(a) the resulting partition of space and (b) the tree representation.

appropriate position in the matrix. For example, Figure 1.29 is the $2^3 \times 2^3$ MX quadtree corresponding to the data of Figure 1.1. It is obtained by applying the mapping f, such that $f(x) = x \div 12.5$ and $f(y) = y \div 12.5$, to the x and y coordinate values, respectively. The result of the mapping is reflected in the coordinate values in the figure.

Each data point in an MX quadtree corresponds to a 1×1 square. For ease of notation and operation using modulo and integer division operations, the data point is associated with the lower-left corner of the square. This adheres to the general convention followed throughout the text that the lower and left boundaries of each block are closed while the upper and right boundaries of each block are open. We also assume that the lower-left corner of the matrix is located at (0,0). Note that, unlike the region quadtree, when a nonleaf node has four black children, they are not merged. This is natural since a merger of such nodes would lead to a loss of the identifying information about the data points, as each data point is different. On the other hand, the empty leaf nodes have the absence of information as their common property, so four white children of a nonleaf node can be safely merged.

Data points are inserted into an MX quadtree by searching for them. This search is based on the location of the data point in the matrix (e.g., the discretized values of its x and y coordinates in our city database example). It is achieved by recursively descending the tree while comparing the location of the point with the implied coordinate values[19] of the root of the subtree being descended. The result of this comparison indicates which of the four subtrees is to be descended next. The search terminates when we have encountered a leaf node. If this leaf node is occupied by another record s, then s is replaced by a record corresponding to the data point being inserted (although the location is the same, some of the nonlocational attribute information may have changed). If the leaf node is NIL, then we may have to subdivide the space spanned by it repeatedly until it is a 1×1 square. This will result in the creation of nonleaf nodes. This operation is termed *splitting*. For a $2^n \times 2^n$ MX quadtree, splitting will have to be performed at most n times.

The shape of the resulting MX quadtree is independent of the order in which data points are inserted into it. However, the shapes of the intermediate trees do depend on the order. For example, Figure 1.30(a–d) shows how the tree was constructed in incremental fashion for Chicago, Mobile, Toronto, and Buffalo by giving the appropriate block decompositions.

Deletion of nodes from MX quadtrees is considerably simpler than for point quadtrees since all records are stored in the leaf nodes. This means that we do not have to be concerned with rearranging the tree as is necessary when a record stored in a nonleaf node is being deleted from a point quadtree. For example, to delete Omaha from the MX quadtree of Figure 1.29, we simply set the SW child of its father node, H, to NIL. Deleting Toronto is slightly more complicated. Setting the SW child of its father node, E, to NIL is not enough. We must also perform merging because all four children of E are NIL after deletion of Toronto. This leads to replacing the NW child of E's father, B, by NIL and returning nonleaf node E to the free storage list. This process is termed *collapsing* and is the counterpart of the splitting operation that was necessary when inserting a record into an MX quadtree.

Collapsing may take place over several levels. In essence, we apply the collapsing process repeatedly until we encounter a nearest common ancestor with an additional non-NIL child. As collapsing takes place, the affected nonleaf nodes are returned to the free storage list. For example, suppose that after deleting Toronto from Figure 1.29, we also delete Buffalo. The subsequent deletion of Buffalo means that nodes F and B are subjected to the collapsing process, with the result that the NE child of node A is set to NIL, and nonleaf nodes B and F are returned to the free storage list. The execution time of the deletion process is bounded by two times the depth of the quadtree. This upper bound is attained when the nearest common ancestor for the collapsing process is the root node.

Performing a range search in an MX quadtree is done in the same way as in the point quadtree. The worst-case cost of searching for all points that lie in a rectangle whose sides are parallel to the quadrant lines is $O(F + 2^n)$, where F is the number of points found and n is the maximum depth (see Exercise 5).

The MX quadtree is used in several applications. It can serve as the basis of a quadtree matrix manipulation system (see Exercises 6–10). The goal is to take advantage of the sparseness of matrices to achieve space and execution time efficiencies (e.g., [1, 647, 2007, 2010, 2011]. Algorithms for matrix transposition and matrix multiplication that take advantage of the recursive decomposition are easy to develop. Letellier [1150] makes use of the MX quadtree to represent silhouettes of hand motions to aid in the telephonic transmission of sign language for the hearing impaired. The region quadtree formulation of Hunter and Steiglitz [901, 905] (see Section 2.2.2.2 of Chapter 2) utilizes a three-color variant of the MX quadtree to represent digitized simple polygons. De Coulon and Johnsen [451] describe the use of the MX quadtree in the coding of black-and-white facsimiles for efficient transmission of images.

---

[19] The coordinate values are implied because they are not stored explicitly as they can be derived from knowledge of the width of the space spanned by the MX quadtree and the path from the root that has been descended. This is one of the properties of a trie.

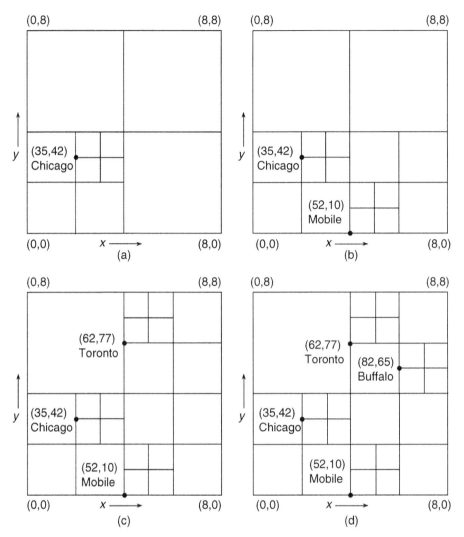

Figure 1.30
Sequence of partial block decompositions showing how an MX quadtree is built when adding (a) Chicago, (b) Mobile, (c) Toronto, and (d) Buffalo, corresponding to the data of Figure 1.1.

Exercises

In the following exercises assume that each point in an MX quadtree is implemented as a record of type *node* containing five fields. The first four fields contain pointers to the node's four children, corresponding to the directions (i.e., quadrants) NW, NE, SW, and SE. If *P* is a pointer to a node, and *I* is a quadrant, then these fields are referenced as CHILD(P, I). The fifth field, NODETYPE, indicates whether the node contains a data point (BLACK), is empty (WHITE), or is a nonleaf node (GRAY). There is no need to store information about the coordinate values of the data point since this is derivable from the path to the node from the root of the MX quadtree. The empty MX quadtree is represented by NIL.

1. Give an algorithm MXCOMPARE to determine the quadrant of a block of width $2 \times w$ centered at (w, w) in which a point (x, y) lies.

2. Give an algorithm MXINSERT for inserting a point p into an MX quadtree rooted at node r that spans a space of width w. Make use of procedure MXCOMPARE from Exercise 1.

3. Give an algorithm MXDELETE for deleting data point (x, y) from an MX quadtree rooted at node r that spans a space of width w. Make use of procedure MXCOMPARE from Exercise 1.

4. Write an algorithm to perform a range search for a rectangular region in an MX quadtree.

5. Show that the worst-case cost of performing a range search in an MX quadtree is $O(F + 2^n)$, where F is the number of points found, and n is the maximum depth. Assume a rectangular query region.

6. Letting a_{ij} and b_{ij} denote the elements of row i and column j of matrices A and B, respectively, the transpose of matrix A is matrix B with $b_{ij} = a_{ji}$. Give an algorithm to transpose a matrix represented by an MX quadtree.

7. How many interchange operations are needed to transpose an MX quadtree representation of a $2^n \times 2^n$ matrix so that it is not sparse (i.e., all blocks are of size 1)?

8. Compare the savings in space and time when a matrix is represented as an MX quadtree and as an array. Use the time required to perform a transpose operation as the basis of the comparison. You should assume the worst case, which occurs when there is no sparseness (i.e., all blocks are of size 1).

9. Give an algorithm for multiplying two matrices stored as MX quadtrees.

10. Unless there is a large number of square blocks of zeros, the MX quadtree is not a particularly attractive representation for matrix multiplication. The problem is that this is inherently a row and column operation. One possible alternative is to make use of a runlength representation (see Section 2.1.2.1 of Chapter 2, where it is termed a *runlength encoding* and is also known as a *runlength code*). This is a one-dimensional aggregation of consecutive, identically valued elements into blocks. The problem is that we would ideally like to have both the rows and columns encoded using this technique. Can you see a problem with using such a dual representation?

1.4.2.2 PR Quadtrees

The MX quadtree is feasible as long as the domain of the data points is discrete and finite. If this is not the case, then the data points cannot be represented using the MX quadtree because the minimum separation between the data points is unknown. This observation leads to an alternative adaptation of the region quadtree to point data, which associates data points (which need not be discrete) with quadrants. We call it a *PR quadtree* (*P* for point and *R* for region), although the term *PR quadtrie* would probably be more appropriate.

The PR quadtree is organized in the same way as the region quadtree. The difference is that leaf nodes are either empty (i.e., white) or contain a data point (i.e., black) and its coordinate values. A leaf node's corresponding block contains at most one data point. For example, Figure 1.31 is the PR quadtree corresponding to the data of Figure 1.1. To cope

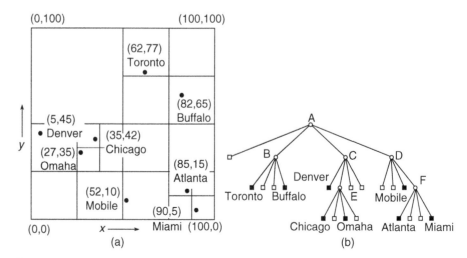

Figure 1.31
A PR quadtree and the records it represents corresponding to the data of Figure 1.1: (a) the resulting partition of space and (b) the tree representation.

with data points that lie directly on one of the quadrant lines emanating from a subdivision point, we adopt the convention that the lower and left boundaries of each block are closed, while the upper and right boundaries of each block are open. For example, in Figure 1.31, a point located at (50,30) would lie in quadrant SE of the tree rooted at (50,50).

A record r corresponding to data point (a,b) is inserted into a PR quadtree by searching for it. This is achieved by recursively descending the tree by comparing the location of the point with the location of the root of the subtree being descended. Note that the locations of the roots of the subtrees are not stored explicitly in the tree because they can be derived from knowledge of the space spanned by the PR quadtree and the path from the root that has been descended so far (this is one of the properties of a trie). If such a node t exists (i.e., containing (a,b)), then r replaces the record associated with t.

Actually, we don't really search for r. Instead, we search for the block h in which r belongs (i.e., a leaf node). If h is already occupied by another record s with different x and y coordinate values, say (c,d), then we must subdivide the block repeatedly (termed *splitting*) until records r and s no longer occupy the same block. This may cause a large number of subdivision operations, especially if the two points (a,b) and (c,d) are both contained in a very small quadtree block. A necessary, but insufficient, condition for this situation to arise is that the Euclidean distance between (a,b) and (c,d) is very small. As a result, we observe that every nonleaf node in a PR quadtree of a dataset consisting of more than one data point has at least two descendant leaf nodes that contain data points.

It should be clear that the shape of the resulting PR quadtree is independent of the order in which data points are inserted into it. However, the shapes of the intermediate trees do depend on the order. For example, the tree in Figure 1.31 was built for the sequence Chicago, Mobile, Toronto, Buffalo, Denver, Omaha, Atlanta, and Miami. Figure 1.32(a–d) shows how the tree was constructed in an incremental fashion for Chicago, Mobile, Toronto, and Buffalo by giving the appropriate block decompositions.

Deletion of nodes in PR quadtrees is considerably simpler than for point quadtrees since all records are stored in the leaf nodes. This means that there is no need to be concerned with rearranging the tree as is necessary when records stored in nonleaf nodes are being deleted from point quadtrees. For example, to delete Mobile from the PR quadtree in Figure 1.31, we simply set the SW child of its father node, D, to NIL.

Continuing this example, deleting Toronto is slightly more complicated. Setting the NW child of its father node, B, to NIL is not enough since now we violate the property of the PR quadtree that each nonleaf node in a PR quadtree of more than one record has at least two descendant leaf nodes that contain data points. Thus, we must also reset the NE child of A to point to Buffalo and return nonleaf node B to the free storage list. This process is termed *collapsing* and is the counterpart of the splitting operation that was necessary when inserting a record in a PR quadtree.

At this point, it is appropriate to elaborate further on the collapsing process. Collapsing can take place only when the deleted node has exactly one brother that is a non-NIL leaf node and has no brothers that are nonleaf nodes. When this condition is satisfied, we can perform the collapsing process repeatedly until we encounter the nearest common ancestor that has more than one child. As collapsing occurs, the affected nonleaf nodes are returned to the free storage list.

As an example of collapsing, suppose that we delete Mobile and Atlanta in sequence from Figure 1.31. The subsequent deletion of Atlanta results in Miami's meeting the conditions for collapsing to take place. Miami's nearest ancestor with more than one child is A. The result of the collapsing of Miami is that Miami becomes the SE child of A. Moreover, nonleaf nodes D and F become superfluous and are returned to the free storage list. The execution time of the deletion process is bounded by two times the depth of the quadtree. This upper bound is achieved when the nearest ancestor for the collapsing process is the root node.

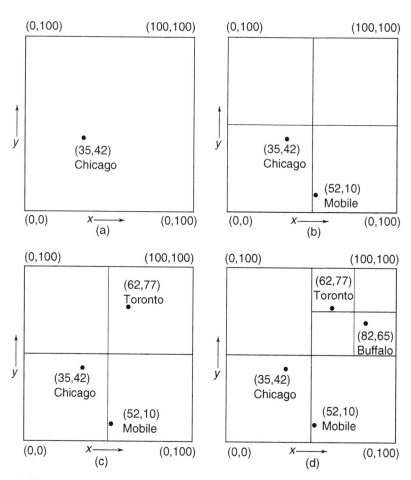

Figure 1.32
Sequence of partial block decompositions showing how a PR quadtree is built when adding (a) Chicago, (b) Mobile, (c) Toronto, and (d) Buffalo, corresponding to the data of Figure 1.1.

Analyzing the cost of insertion and deletion of nodes in a PR quadtree depends on the data points already in the tree. In particular, this cost is proportional to the maximum depth of the tree. For example, given a square region of side length s, such that the minimum Euclidean distance separating two points is d, the maximum depth of the quadtree can be as high as $\lceil \log_2((s/d) \cdot \sqrt{2}) \rceil$. Assuming that the data points are drawn from a grid of size $2^n \times 2^n$, for N data points the space requirements can be as high as $O(N \cdot n)$. This analysis is somewhat misleading because N and n do not necessarily grow in an independent manner. Often, the case is that the space requirements are proportional to N (see Exercises 5 and 6).

Performing a range search in a PR quadtree is done in basically the same way as in the MX and point quadtrees. The worst-case cost of searching for all points that lie in a rectangle whose sides are parallel to the quadrant lines is $O(F + 2^n)$, where F is the number of points found, and n is the maximum depth (see Exercise 8).

The PR quadtree is used in several applications. Anderson [49] makes use of a PR quadtree (termed a *uniform quadtree*) to store endpoints of line segments to be drawn by a plotter. The goal is to reduce pen plotting time by choosing the line segment to be output next whose endpoint is closest to the current pen position.

Rosenfeld, Samet, Shaffer, and Webber [1577] make use of the PR quadtree in a geographic information system as a means of representing point data in a consistent manner with region data that is represented using region quadtrees. In this way, queries can be made on different datasets that are partitioned at the same locations, assuming that

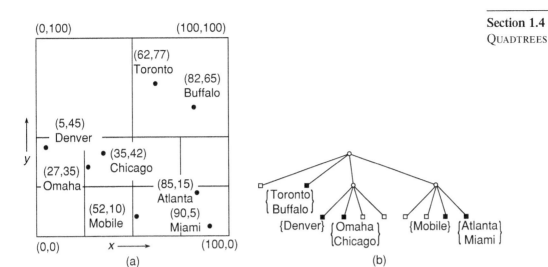

Figure 1.33
A bucket PR quadtree and the records it represents corresponding to the data of Figure 1.1 for bucket size 2: (a) the resulting partition of space and (b) the tree representation.

the space spanned by the datasets is of the same size and relative to the same origin. This enables answering queries such as finding all cities in wheat-growing regions by simply overlaying the crop map (represented by a region quadtree) and the city map (represented by a PR quadtree, assuming that the cities are treated as points). The overlay operation is implemented by traversing the two trees in tandem and making descents only if two nonleaf nodes in the same position in the tree are encountered (for more details, see [1636, Chapter 6]).

When the data is not uniformly distributed (e.g., when it is clustered), then the PR quadtree may contain many empty nodes, which in this case will cause it to become unbalanced. The imbalance may be overcome by aggregating the blocks corresponding to the nodes into larger blocks termed *buckets*. This is achieved by varying the decomposition rule so that a block is split only if it contains more than b points, where b is termed the *bucket capacity* [1258]. We use the term *bucket PR quadtree* to describe this representation. It should be clear that increasing the number of points permitted in a block reduces the dependence of the maximum depth of the PR quadtree on the minimum Euclidean distance separation of two distinct points to that of two sets of b points. For example, Figure 1.33 is the bucket PR quadtree corresponding to the data of Figure 1.1 when the bucket capacity is 2.

Nelson and Samet [1361, 1362] analyze the distribution of nodes in a bucket PR quadtree in terms of their occupancies for various values of the bucket capacity.[20] They model a quadtree as a collection of populations in which each population represents the set of nodes in the quadtree that have a particular occupancy. Thus, the set of all empty nodes constitutes one population, the set of all nodes containing a single point constitutes another population, and so on. Note that the individual populations contain nodes of different sizes.

As points are added to the bucket PR quadtree, each population grows in a manner that depends on the other populations. For example, when the bucket capacity is c, the probability of producing a new node with occupancy i depends both on the fraction of nodes with occupancy $i-1$ and on the population of full nodes (occupancy c), since nodes of any occupancy can be produced when a full node splits.

---

[20] The rest of the discussion in this section is somewhat technical and may be skipped.

The result of the analysis is the determination of a steady state where the proportions of the various populations are constant under addition of new points according to some data model (e.g., uniform distribution, Gaussian distribution). This steady state is taken as a representative distribution of populations from which expected values for structure parameters such as average node occupancies, are calculated.

The population model is an alternative to the use of a statistical analysis to define a "typical" structure. The statistical analyses are based on the computation, relative to some model of data distribution, of statistical sums over the space of possible data structure configurations. Statistical analyses for uniformly distributed data have been applied by Fagin, Nievergelt, Pippenger, and Strong to extendible hashing [579], Flajolet and Puech [621] to tries, Regnier to the grid file (see Section 1.7.2.1) [1550], and Tamminen to EXCELL (see Section 1.7.2.2) [1827].

The advantage of the population model is that dependencies between various populations and the steady state can be determined with relative ease. Moreover, the method is sufficiently flexible that it can be applied to other data structures in which the decomposition is determined adaptively by the local concentration of the data.

Nelson and Samet [1361, 1362] computed the average bucket occupancies for several different bucket capacities when points were generated under a uniform distribution. They found that the theoretical occupancy predictions were consistently slightly higher than the experimental values and that the size of the discrepancy had a cyclical structure. They use the terms *aging* and *phasing*, respectively, to describe these phenomena. They are explained briefly below.

The population model of bucket splitting assumes that the probability of a point falling into a node of type n_i (i.e., occupancy i) is proportional to the fraction of the total type n_i nodes. This means that the average size of a node is independent of its occupancy. In actuality, we have the situation that nodes with a larger area are formed before the nodes with a smaller area—hence, the origin of the term *aging*. These larger nodes will tend to have a slightly higher average occupancy than the smaller nodes. Therefore, to maintain a steady-state situation, the fraction of high occupancy nodes must be less than predicted by the model, with the result that we have more lower-occupancy nodes, thereby yielding a smaller average bucket occupancy.

When nodes are drawn from a uniform distribution, the nodes in the quadtree will tend to split and fill in phase with a logarithmic period repeating every time the number of points increases by a factor of four. In particular, all nodes of the same size tend to fill up and split at the same time. This situation is termed *phasing*. It explains why the average bucket occupancy for a fixed bucket size oscillates with the number of data points. In contrast, when the distribution of points is nonuniform (e.g., Gaussian), then, initially, there is oscillatory behavior; however, it damps out as node populations in regions of different densities get out of phase.

Ang and Samet [53, 55] propose an analysis technique that they term *approximate splitting* to calculate the approximate values of the average node distribution, which enables them to obtain an approximation of the population frequency distribution. This method was demonstrated to account for the aging and phasing phenomena and resulted in a closer match between the predicted and actual average node occupancies.

Exercises

In the following exercises assume that each point in a PR quadtree is implemented as a record of type *node* containing seven fields. The first four fields contain pointers to the node's four children corresponding to the four quadrants. If P is a pointer to a node, and I is a quadrant, then these fields are referenced as CHILD(P, I). The fifth field, NODETYPE, indicates whether the node contains a data point (BLACK), is empty (WHITE), or is a nonleaf node (GRAY). XCOORD and YCOORD contain the x and y coordinate values, respectively, of the data point. The empty PR quadtree is represented by NIL.

1. Give an algorithm PRCOMPARE to determine the quadrant of a block centered at (x, y) in which a point p lies.

2. Give an algorithm PRINSERT for inserting a point p in a PR quadtree rooted at node r, where r corresponds to an $lx \times ly$ rectangle centered at (x, y). Make use of procedure PRCOMPARE from Exercise 1.

3. Give an algorithm PRDELETE for deleting data point p from a PR quadtree rooted at node r, where r corresponds to an $lx \times ly$ rectangle centered at (x, y). Make use of procedure PRCOMPARE from Exercise 1.

4. Assume that the minimum Euclidean distance separating two points is d. Given a square region of side length s, show that $\lceil \log_2((s/d) \cdot \sqrt{2}) \rceil$ is the maximum depth of the PR quadtree.

5. Suppose that you are given N data points drawn from a grid of size $2^n \times 2^n$. Construct an example PR quadtree that uses $O(N \cdot n)$ space.

6. Under what situation does the PR quadtree use space proportional to N?

7. Write an algorithm to perform a range search for a rectangular region in a PR quadtree.

8. Show that the worst-case cost of performing a range search in a PR quadtree is $O(F + 2^n)$, where F is the number of points found and n is the maximum depth. Assume a rectangular query region.

    Exercises 9–16 are based on an analysis of PR quadtrees performed by Hunter [902].

9. Assume that you are given point data that is uniformly distributed in the unit square. What is the probability of a node at depth k containing a particular point?

10. Continuing the previous exercise, for a collection of v points, what is the probability that none of them lies in a given cell at depth k?

11. What is the probability that exactly one of the v points lies in a given cell at depth k?

12. What is the probability that a given cell at depth k contains two or more points (i.e., it corresponds to a parent node)?

13. Each node that contains two or more points must be a nonleaf node and hence will have four children. From the probability of the existence of a nonleaf node at depth k, derive the expected total number of nodes (i.e., leaf plus nonleaf nodes) at depth $k + 1$.

14. From the expected number of nodes at depth $k + 1$, derive the expected number of nodes in the entire PR quadtree, say E. Can you find a closed-form solution to it?

15. Calculate the ratio of E/v, the expected number of nodes per point. Does it converge?

16. Extend these results to data that is uniformly distributed in the m-dimensional unit hypercube.

1.4.3 Comparison of Point and Trie-Based Quadtrees

A comparison of point and trie-based quadtrees reduces, in part, to a comparison of their decomposition methods. In this discussion, we refer to the MX and PR quadtrees as trie-based quadtrees unless they differ in the context of the discussion. The trie-based quadtrees rely on regular decomposition (i.e., subdivision into four congruent rectangular regions). Data points are associated only with leaf nodes in trie-based quadtrees, whereas for point quadtrees, data points can also be stored at nonleaf nodes. This leads to a considerably simpler node deletion procedure for trie-based quadtrees. In particular, there is no need to be concerned about rearranging the tree, as is the case when nonleaf nodes are being deleted from a point quadtree.

A major difference between the two quadtree types is in the size of the rectangular regions associated with each data point. For the trie-based quadtrees, the space spanned by the quadtree is constrained to a maximum width and height. For the point quadtree, the space is rectangular and may, at times, be of infinite width and height. For the MX quadtree, this region must be a square with a particular size associated with it. This size is fixed at the time the MX quadtree is defined and is the minimum permissible separation between two data points in the domain of the MX quadtree (equivalently, it is the maximum number of elements permitted in each row and column of the corresponding matrix). For the PR quadtree, this region is also rectangular, but its size depends on what other data points are currently represented by nodes in the quadtree.

In the case of the MX quadtree, there is a fixed discrete coordinate system associated with the space spanned by the quadtree, whereas no such limitation exists for the PR quadtree. The advantage of such a fixed coordinate system is that there is no need to store coordinate information with a data point's leaf node. The disadvantage is that the discreteness of the domain of the data points limits the granularity of the possible differentiation between data points.

The size and shape of a quadtree are important from the standpoint of the efficiency of both space requirements and search operations. The size and shape of the point quadtree is extremely sensitive to the order in which data points are inserted into it during the process of building it. Assuming that the root of the tree has a depth of 0, this means that for a point quadtree of N records, its maximum depth is $N - 1$ (i.e., one record is stored at each level in the tree), and its minimum depth is $\lceil \log_4((3 \cdot N + 1)/4) \rceil$ (i.e., each level in the tree is completely full).

In contrast, the shape and size of the trie-based quadtrees is independent of the insertion order. For the MX quadtree, all nodes corresponding to data points appear at the same depth in the quadtree. The depth of the MX quadtree depends on the size of the space spanned by the quadtree and the maximum number of elements permitted in each row and column of the corresponding matrix. For example, for a $2^n \times 2^n$ matrix, all data points will appear as leaf nodes at a depth of n.

The size and shape of the PR quadtree depend on the data points currently in the quadtree. The minimum depth of a PR quadtree for $N > 1$ data points is $\lceil \log_4 N \rceil$ (i.e., all the data points are at the same depth), while there is no upper bound on the depth in terms of the number of data points. Recall from Section 1.4.2.2 that for a square region of side length s, such that the minimum Euclidean distance separating two points is d, the maximum depth of the PR quadtree can be as high as $\lceil \log_2((s/d) \cdot \sqrt{2}) \rceil$.

The volume of data also plays an important part in the comparison between the point and trie-based quadtrees. When the volume is very high, the MX quadtree loses some of its advantage since an array representation may be more economical in terms of space, as there is no need for links. Although the size of the PR quadtree was seen to be affected by the clustering of data points, especially when the number of data points is relatively small, this is not a factor in the size of a point quadtree. However, when the volume of data is large and uniformly distributed, the effect of clustering is lessened, and there should not be much difference in the space requirements between the point and PR quadtrees.

Exercises

1. Use the uniform distribution over [0,1] to construct two-dimensional point quadtrees, MX quadtrees, and PR quadtrees, and compare them using the criteria set forth in this section. For example, compare their total path length, maximum depth, and so on.

2. Perform an average case analysis of the cost of a partial range query (a subset of the range query) for a point quadtree and a PR quadtree when the attributes are independent and uniformly distributed.

1.5   K-d Trees

As the dimensionality (i.e., number of attributes) d of the underlying space increases, each level of decomposition of the quadtree results in many new cells since the fanout value of the tree is high (i.e., 2^d). This is alleviated by making use of variants of a *k-d tree* [164], a term in which k originally denoted the dimensionality of the space being represented. However, in many applications, the convention is to let the value of d denote the dimension, and this is the practice we have chosen to follow here. In principle, the k-d tree is a binary tree where the underlying space is partitioned on the basis of the value of just one attribute at each level of the tree instead of on the basis of the values of all d attributes, thereby making d tests at each level, as is the case for the quadtree. In other words, the distinction from the quadtree is that, in the k-d tree, only one attribute (or key) value is tested when determining the direction in which a branch is to be made.

Restricting the number of attributes that are tested at each level of the tree has several advantages over the quadtree. First, we make just one test at each level instead of d tests. Second, each leaf node in the quadtree is rather costly in terms of the amount of space required due to a multitude of NIL links. In particular, the node size gets rather large for a d-dimensional tree since at least $d + 2^d$ words (assuming that each pointer is stored in one word) are required for each node. Third, algorithms can be simplified because, at each recursive step, we have only two options since each node partitions the underlying space into only two parts. Finally, the same data structure (pointerwise) can be used to represent a node for all values of d, notwithstanding the partitioning axis values, which may need to be stored for some variants of the k-d tree.

The disadvantage of replacing a test of d values by a sequence of d tests is that, in the case of a k-d tree, decomposition in d-dimensional space has now become a sequential process as the order in which the various axes (i.e., attributes) are partitioned is important. In contrast, this ordering is of no consequence in the case of a quadtree because all d axes are partitioned simultaneously (i.e., in parallel). This lack of ordering has an advantage in a parallel environment: the key comparison operation can be performed in parallel for the d key values. Therefore, we can characterize the k-d tree as a superior serial data structure and the quadtree as a superior parallel data structure. For a discussion of the use of quadtrees for representing points in a multiprocessor environment, see Linn [1182]; Bestul [210] discusses their use in a data-parallel environment (e.g., [217]); Wise (e.g., [2006, 2008, 2009]) discusses their use for representing matrices in a parallel processing environment. There has also been a considerable amount of work on the processing of quadtree representations of region data in a parallel environment (e.g., [213, 373, 470, 524, 532, 898, 916, 997, 1719]).

The idea of replacing a test of d attribute values by a sequence of d tests is applicable to both point quadtrees and trie-based quadtrees, although it is applied more often to point quadtrees. The use of the term *k-d tree* to refer to the data structure is somewhat confusing as this term is used uniformly to refer to the point quadtree adaptation, whereas a consistent use of our terminology would result in terming it a *point k-d tree*. In fact, we will use this term whenever we need to differentiate it from the trie-based adaptation. There is no consistent terminology for the trie-based variant, although *k-d trie* would probably be the most appropriate. The region quadtree counterpart of the k-d tree is termed a *bintree* [1828].

In the rest of this section, we discuss several different variations of the k-d tree with a particular emphasis on the point k-d tree (i.e., the one that organizes the data to be stored rather than the embedding space from which the data is drawn). Section 1.5.1 discusses the point k-d tree, and Section 1.5.2 presents several variants of the trie-based k-d tree. There has also been an attempt to develop a hybrid splitting strategy [824] that combines the point k-d tree and the trie-based k-d tree to deal with situations where one approach is preferable to another in terms of worst-case tree depth, and so on. We do not discuss this approach further here. On another front, although it is beyond the scope of our discussion, we mention that lately there has been some interest in issues arising from the implementation of k-d trees in a peer-to-peer (P2P) setting (e.g., [676]).

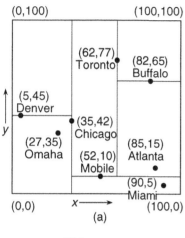

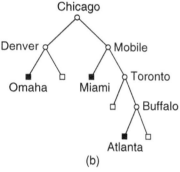

Figure 1.34
A k-d tree $(d = 2)$ and the records it represents corresponding to the data of Figure 1.1: (a) the resulting partition of space and (b) the tree representation.

1.5.1 Point K-d Trees

There are many variations of the point k-d tree. Their exact structure depends on the manner in which they deal with the following issues:

1. Is the underlying space partitioned at a position that overlaps a data point, or may the position of the partition be chosen at random? Recall that trie-based methods restrict the positions of the partitions points, thereby rendering moot the question of whether the partition actually takes place at a data point.

2. Is there a choice as to the identity of the partition axis (i.e., the attribute or key being tested)? If we adopt a strict analogy to the quadtree, then we have little flexibility in the choice of the partition axis in the sense that we must cycle through the d different dimensions every d levels in the tree, although the relative order in which the different axes are partitioned may differ from level to level and among subtrees.

The most common variant of the k-d tree (and the one we focus on in this section) partitions the underlying space at the data points and cycles through the different axes in a predefined and constant order. When we can apply the partitions to the underlying space in an arbitrary order rather than having to cycle through the axes, then we preface the name of the data structure with the qualifier *generalized*. For example, a generalized k-d tree also partitions the underlying space at the data points; however, it need not cycle through the axes. In fact, it need not even partition all of the axes (e.g., only partition along the axes that are used in queries [172]). In our discussion, we assume two-dimensional data, and we test x coordinate values at the root and at even depths (given that the root is at depth 0) and y coordinate values at odd depths.

We adopt the convention that when node P is an x-discriminator, then all nodes having an x coordinate value less than that of P are in the left child of P and all those with x coordinate values greater than or equal to that of P are in the right child of P. A similar convention holds for a node that is a y-discriminator. Figure 1.34 illustrates the k-d tree corresponding to the same eight nodes as in Figure 1.1.

In the definition of a discriminator, the problem of equality of particular key values is resolved by stipulating that records that have the same value for a particular key are in the right subtree. As an alternative, Bentley [164] defines a node in terms of a *superkey*. Given a node P, let $K_0(P)$, $K_1(P)$, and so on, refer to its d keys. Assuming that P is a j-discriminator, then for any node Q in the left child of P, $K_j(Q) < K_j(P)$; and likewise, for any node R in the right child of P, $K_j(R) > K_j(P)$. In the case of equality, a superkey, $S_j(P)$, is defined by forming a cyclical concatenation of all keys starting with $K_j(P)$. In other words, $S_j(P) = K_j(P) K_{j+1}(P) \ldots K_{d-1}(P) K_0(P) \ldots K_{j-1}(P)$. Now, when comparing two nodes, P and Q, we turn to the left when $S_j(Q) < S_j(P)$ and to the right when $S_j(Q) > S_j(P)$. If $S_j(Q) = S_j(P)$, then all d keys are equal, and a special value is returned to so indicate. The algorithms that we present below do not make use of a superkey.

The rest of this section is organized as follows. Section 1.5.1.1 shows how to insert a point into a k-d tree. Section 1.5.1.2 discusses how to delete a point from a k-d tree. Section 1.5.1.3 explains how to do region searching in a k-d tree. Section 1.5.1.4 discusses some variants of the k-d tree that provide more flexibility as to the positioning and choice of the partitioning axes.

1.5.1.1 Insertion

Inserting record r with key values (a, b) into a k-d tree is very simple. The process is essentially the same as that for a binary search tree. First, if the tree is empty, then allocate a new node containing r, and return a tree with r as its only node. Otherwise, search the tree for a node h with a record having key values (a, b). If h exists, then r replaces the record associated with h. Otherwise, we are at a NIL node that is a child of type s (i.e., 'LEFT' or 'RIGHT', as appropriate) of node c. This is where we make the insertion by

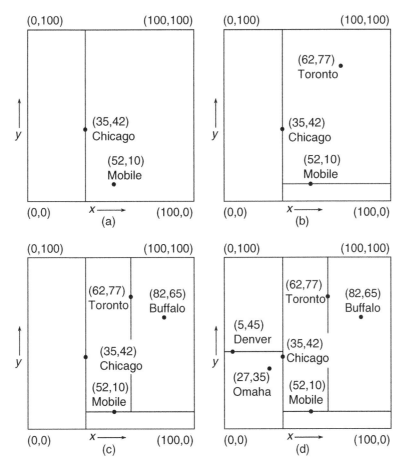

Figure 1.35
Sequence of partial k-d tree space partitions demonstrating the addition of (a) Chicago and Mobile, (b) Toronto, (c) Buffalo, and (d) Denver and Omaha, corresponding to the data of Figure 1.1.

allocating a new node t containing r and make t an s child of node c. The only difference from the binary search tree is that we compare x coordinate values at the root and at even depths of the tree and y coordinate values at odd depths of the tree. Bentley [164] shows that given N points, the average cost of inserting, as well as searching for (i.e., an exact match query), a node is $O(\log_2 N)$.

As in the case of point quadtrees, the shape of the resulting k-d tree depends on the order in which the nodes are inserted into it. Figure 1.34 is the k-d tree for the sequence Chicago, Mobile, Toronto, Buffalo, Denver, Omaha, Atlanta, and Miami. Figure 1.35(a–d) shows how the tree was constructed in an incremental fashion for these cities by giving the appropriate space partitions. In particular, Figure 1.35(a) corresponds to the space partition after insertion of Chicago and Mobile, Figure 1.35(b) to the space partition after insertion of Toronto, Figure 1.35(c) to the space partition after insertion of Buffalo, and Figure 1.35(d) to the space partition after insertion of Denver and Omaha.

It should be clear that in the insertion process described here, each node partitions the portion of the plane in which it resides into two parts. Thus, in Figure 1.34, Chicago divides the plane into all nodes whose x coordinate value is less than 35 and all nodes whose x coordinate value is greater than or equal to 35. In the same figure, Denver divides the set of all nodes whose x coordinate value is less than 35 into those whose y coordinate value is less than 45 and those whose y coordinate value is greater than or equal to 45.

As in the case of the point quadtree, the amount of work expended in building a k-d tree is equal to the total path length (TPL) of the tree as it reflects the cost of searching for all of the elements. Bentley [164] shows that the TPL of a k-d tree built by inserting N points in random order into an initially empty tree is $O(N \cdot \log_2 N)$ and thus the average cost of inserting a node is $O(\log_2 N)$. The extreme cases are worse since the shape of the k-d tree depends on the order in which the nodes are inserted into it, thereby affecting the TPL.

Exercises

Assume that each point in the k-d tree is implemented as a record of type *node* containing three plus d fields. The first two fields, Left and Right contain pointers to the node's two children, corresponding to the directions 'Left' and 'Right', respectively. If P is a pointer to a node, and I is a direction, then these fields are referenced as Child(P, I). At times, these two fields are also referred to as LoChild(P) and HiChild(P), corresponding to the left and right children, respectively. We can determine the side of the tree in which a node, say P, lies relative to its father by use of the function ChildType(P), which has a value of I if Child(Father$(P), I) = P$. Coord is a one-dimensional array containing the values of the d coordinates of the data point. If P is a pointer to a node, and I is a coordinate name, then these fields are referenced as Coord(P, I). The Disc field indicates the name of the coordinate on whose value the node discriminates (i.e., tests). The Disc field is not always necessary as, for example, when the relative order in which the different axes (i.e., coordinates) are partitioned is constant. In this case, it is easy to keep track of the discriminator type of the node being visited as the tree is descended. The empty k-d tree is represented by Nil.

1. Give an algorithm KdCompare to determine the child of a k-d tree rooted at r in which point p lies.

2. Give an algorithm KdInsert to insert a point p in a k-d tree rooted at node r. Make use of procedure KdCompare from Exercise 1. There is no need to make use of the ChildType function.

3. Modify procedures KdCompare and KdInsert to handle a k-d tree node implementation that makes use of a superkey in its discriminator field.

4. Prove that the TPL of a k-d tree of N nodes built by inserting the N points in a random order is $O(N \cdot \log_2 N)$.

5. Give the k-d tree analogs of the single and double rotation operators for use in balancing a binary search tree [1046, p. 461]. Make sure that you handle equal key values correctly.

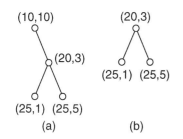

Figure 1.36
(a) Example of a two-dimensional k-d tree whose (b) right child is not a k-d tree.

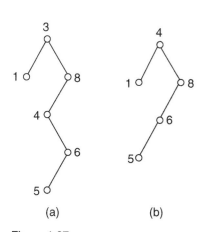

Figure 1.37
(a) Example of a binary search tree and (b) the result of deleting its root.

1.5.1.2 Deletion

Deletion of nodes from k-d trees is considerably more complex than it is for binary search trees. Observe that, unlike the binary search tree, not every subtree of a k-d tree is itself a k-d tree. For example, although Figure 1.36(a) is a k-d tree, its right subtree (see Figure 1.36(b)) is not a k-d tree. This is because the root node in a two-dimensional k-d tree discriminates on the value of the x coordinate, while both children of the root node in Figure 1.36(b) have x coordinate values that are larger than that of the root node. Thus, we see that special care must be taken when deleting a node from a k-d tree.

In contrast, when deleting a node from a binary search tree, we simply move a node and a subtree. For example, deleting node 3 from Figure 1.37(a) results in replacing node 3 with node 4 and replacing the left subtree of 8 by the right subtree of 4 (see Figure 1.37(b)). However, this cannot be done, in general, in a k-d tree as the nodes with values 5 and 6 might not have the same relative relationship at their new depths.

Deletion in a k-d tree can be achieved by the following recursive process. We use the k-d tree in Figure 1.38 to illustrate our discussion, and thus all references to nodes can be visualized by referring to the figure. Let us assume that we wish to delete the node (a,b) from the k-d tree. If both subtrees of (a,b) are empty, then replace (a,b) with the empty tree. Otherwise, find a suitable replacement node in one of the subtrees of (a,b), say (c,d), and recursively delete (c,d) from the k-d tree. Once (c,d) has been deleted, replace (a,b) with (c,d).

At this point, it is appropriate to comment on what constitutes a "suitable" replacement node. Recall that an x-discriminator is a node that appears at an even depth, and hence partitions its space based on the value of its x coordinate. A y-discriminator is defined analogously for nodes at odd depths. Assume that (a,b) is an x-discriminator. We know that every node in (a,b)'s right subtree has an x coordinate with a value greater than or equal to a. The node that will replace (a,b) must bear the same relationship to the subtrees of (a,b). Using the analogy with binary search trees, it would seem that we would have a choice with respect to the replacement node. It must either be the node in the left subtree of (a,b) with the largest x coordinate value or the node in the right subtree of (a,b) with the smallest x coordinate value.

Actually, we do not really have a choice as the following comments will make clear. If we use the node in the left subtree of (a,b) with the maximum x coordinate value, say (c,d), and if there exists another node in the same subtree with the same x coordinate value, say (c,h), then when (c,d) replaces node (a,b), there will be a node in the left subtree of (c,d) that does not belong there by virtue of having an x coordinate value of c. Thus, we see that, given our definition of a k-d tree, the replacement node must be chosen from the right subtree. Otherwise, a duplicate x coordinate value will disrupt the proper interaction between each node and its subtrees. Note that the replacement node need not be a leaf node.

The only remaining question is how to handle the case when the right subtree of (a,b) is empty. We use the k-d tree in Figure 1.39 to illustrate our discussion, and thus all references to nodes can be visualized by referring to the figure. This is resolved by the following recursive process. Find the node in the left subtree of (a,b) that has the smallest value for its x coordinate, say (c,d). Exchange the left and right subtrees of (a,b), replace the coordinate values of (a,b) with (c,d), and recursively apply the deletion procedure to node (c,d) from its prior position in the tree (i.e., in the previous left subtree of (a,b)).

With the aid of Figures 1.38 and 1.39, we have shown that the problem of deleting a node (a,b) from a k-d tree is reduced to that of finding the node with the smallest x coordinate value in a subtree of (a,b). Unfortunately, locating the node with the minimum x coordinate value is considerably more complex than the analogous problem for a binary search tree. In particular, although the node with the minimum x coordinate value must be in the left subtree of an x-discriminator, it could be in either subtree of a y-discriminator. Thus, search is involved, and care must be taken in coordinating this search so that when the deleted node is an x-discriminator at depth 0, only one of the two subtrees rooted at each odd depth is searched. This is done using procedure FINDDMINIMUM (see Exercise 1).

As can be seen from the discussion, deleting a node from a k-d tree can be costly. We can obtain an upper bound on the cost in the following manner. Clearly, the cost of deleting the root of a subtree is bounded from above by the number of nodes in the subtree. Letting TPL(T) denote the total path length of tree T, it can be shown that the sum of the subtree sizes of a tree is TPL(T) + N (see Exercise 5 in Section 1.4.1.2).

Bentley [164] proves that the TPL of a k-d tree built by inserting N points in a random order is $O(N \cdot \log_2 N)$, which means that the average cost of deleting a randomly selected node from a randomly built k-d tree has an upper bound of $O(\log_2 N)$. This relatively low value for the upper bound reflects the fact that most of the nodes in the k-d tree are leaf nodes. The cost of deleting root nodes is considerably higher. Clearly, it is bounded by N. Its cost is dominated by the cost of the process of finding a minimum element in a subtree, which is $O(N^{1-1/d})$ (see Exercise 6), since on every dth level (starting at the root), only one of the two subtrees needs to be searched.

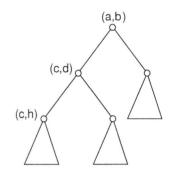

Figure 1.38
Example of a k-d tree illustrating why the replacement node should be chosen from the right subtree of the tree containing the deleted node.

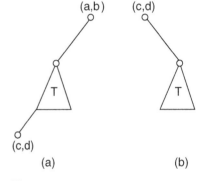

Figure 1.39
(a) Example k-d tree and (b) the result of deleting (a,b) from it.

As an example of the deletion process, consider the k-d tree in Figure 1.40(a, b). We wish to delete the root node A at (20,20). Assume that A is an x-discriminator. The node in the right subtree of A with a minimum value for its x coordinate is C at (25,50). Thus, C replaces A (see Figure 1.40(c)), and we recursively apply the deletion procedure to C's position in the tree. Since C's position was a y-discriminator, we seek the node with a minimum y coordinate value in the right subtree of C. However, C's right subtree was empty, which means that we must replace C with the node in its left subtree that has the minimum y coordinate value.

D at (35,25) is the node in the left subtree that satisfies this minimum value condition. It is moved up in the tree (see Figure 1.40(d)). Since D was an x-discriminator, we replace it by the node in its right subtree having a minimum x coordinate value. H at (45,35) satisfies this condition, and it is moved up in the tree (see Figure 1.40(e)). Again, H is an x-discriminator, and we replace it by I, the node in its right subtree with a minimum x coordinate value. Since I is a leaf node, our procedure terminates. Figure 1.40(f, g) shows the result of the deletion process.

In the above discussion, we had to make a special provision to account for our definition of a k-d tree node as a partition of space into two parts, one less than the key value tested by the node and one greater than or equal to the key value tested by the node. Defining a node in terms of a superkey alleviates this problem since we no longer always have to choose the replacing node from the right subtree. Instead, we now

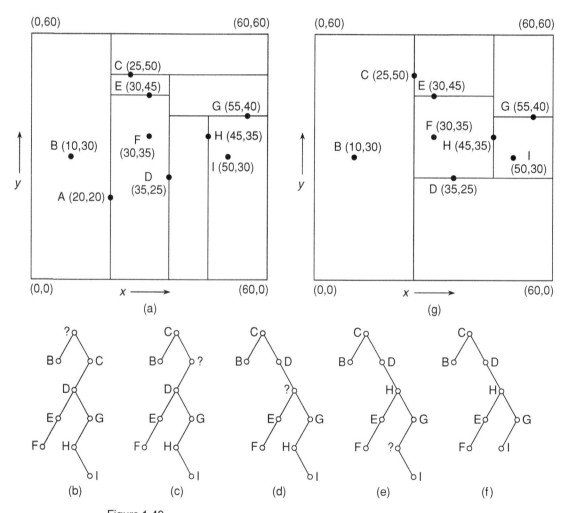

Figure 1.40
Example illustrating deletion in k-d trees where "?" indicates the node being deleted: (a) the original k-d tree, (b–f) successive steps in deleting node A, (g) the final k-d tree.

have a choice. The best algorithm is one that flip-flops between the left and right children, perhaps through the use of a random-number generator (see Exercise 5). Of course, node insertion and search are slightly more complex since it is possible that more than one key will have to be compared at each level in the tree (see Exercise 3 in Section 1.5.1.1 and Exercise 3 in Section 1.5.1.3).

Exercises

1. Given a node P in a k-d tree that discriminates on key D, write an algorithm, FINDDMINIMUM, to compute the D-minimum node in its left subtree. Repeat for the right subtree of P. Generalize your algorithm to work for either of the two subtrees.

2. Assuming the same k-d tree node implementation as in the exercises in Section 1.5.1.1, give an algorithm KDDELETE for deleting a point p from a k-d tree rooted at node r. The node does not have a FATHER field, although you may make use of the CHILDTYPE function. Make use of procedures KDCOMPARE and FINDDMINIMUM from Exercise 1 in Section 1.5.1.1 and Exercise 1 above, respectively.

3. Modify procedure KDDELETE in the solution to Exercise 2 to make use of a variant of FINDDMINIMUM that, in addition to returning the D-minimum node t, also returns t's CHILDTYPE values relative to its father f, as well as f.

4. Suppose that a k-d tree node is implemented as a record with a FATHER field containing a pointer to its father. Modify procedure KDDELETE in the solution to Exercise 2 to take advantage of this additional field.

5. Modify procedure KDDELETE in the solution to Exercise 2 to handle a k-d tree node implementation that makes use of a superkey in its discriminator field.

6. Prove that the cost of finding a D-minimum element in a k-d tree is $O(N^{1-1/d})$.

1.5.1.3 Search

Like quadtrees, k-d trees are useful in applications involving search. Again, we consider a typical query that seeks all nodes within a specified distance of a given point. The k-d tree data structure serves as a pruning device on the amount of search that is required; that is, many nodes need not be examined. To see how the pruning is achieved, suppose we are performing a region search of distance r around a node with coordinate values (a, b). In essence, we want to determine all nodes (x, y) whose Euclidean distance from (a, b) is less than or equal to r—that is, $r^2 \geq (a-x)^2 + (b-y)^2$.

Clearly, this is a circular region. The minimum x and y coordinate values of a node in this circle cannot be less than $a - r$ and $b - r$, respectively. Similarly, the maximum x and y coordinate values of a node in this circle cannot be greater than $a + r$ and $b + r$, respectively. Thus, if the search reaches a node with coordinate values (e, f), and KDCOMPARE$((a-r, b-r), (e, f)) = $ 'RIGHT', then there is no need to examine any nodes in the left subtree of (e, f). Similarly, the right subtree of (e, f) need not be searched when KDCOMPARE$((a+r, b+r), (e, f)) = $ 'LEFT'.

For example, suppose that we want to use the k-d tree in Figure 1.34 of the hypothetical database of Figure 1.1 to find all cities within three units of a point with coordinate values (88,6). In such a case, there is no need to search the left subtree of the root (i.e., Chicago with coordinate values (35,42)). Thus, we need examine only the right subtree of the tree rooted at Chicago. Similarly, there is no need to search the right subtree of the tree rooted at Mobile (i.e., coordinate values (52,10)). Continuing our search, we find that only Miami, at coordinate values (90,5), satisfies our request. Thus, we need examine only three nodes during our search.

Similar techniques are applied when the search region is rectangular, making the query meaningful for both locational and nonlocational data. In general, the search cost depends on the type of query. Given N points, Lee and Wong [1132] have shown that, in the worst case, the cost of a range search of a complete k-d tree is $O(d \cdot N^{1-1/d} + F)$,

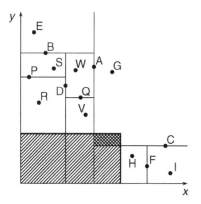

Figure 1.41
Example space partition for a k-d tree that illustrates the worst-case behavior for the k-d tree search procedure.

where F is the number of points found in the range. To see how this bound is obtained, we assume that $d = 2$ and, without loss of generality, consider a rectangular search region (see Exercise 1), marked as hatched in Figure 1.41. Although not explicitly shown in the figure, nodes G, H, R, and V are roots of subtrees that may also be in the shaded region. Similarly, nodes E, I, S, and W are also roots of subtrees that may also contain just one node, in which case they are leaf nodes. We use the number of nodes visited while searching the tree as a measure of the amount of work that needs to be expended.

Since we are interested in the worst case, we assume that B and C (see Figure 1.41) partition the tree rooted at A in such a way that the search region is overlapped by the regions rooted at B and C. If B is within the search region, then the subtree rooted at D need not be searched further. If B is outside of the search region (as is the case here), then E and its subtrees (if any) need not be searched further. Similarly, if F is within the search region, then H and its subtrees (if any) need not be searched further. Finally, when F is outside of the search region (as is the case here), then I and its subtrees (if any) need not be searched further. G is chosen in such a way that both of its subtrees will have to be searched. Further partitioning of G is analogous to a recursive invocation of this analysis two levels deeper in the tree than the starting level (see the cross-hatched region in Figure 1.41).

The analysis of the remaining subtrees of B and F (i.e., rooted at D and H) are equivalent to each other and enable the elimination of two subtrees from further consideration at every other level. For example, the children of the subtrees rooted at D are P and Q, with children rooted at R and S, and V and W, respectively. The subtrees (if any) rooted at S and W need no further processing.

We are now ready to analyze the worst case of the number of nodes that will be visited in performing a range search in a two-dimensional k-d tree. Let t_i denote the number of nodes visited when dealing with a k-d tree rooted at level i (where the deepest node in the tree is at level 0). Let u_j denote that number of nodes that are visited when dealing with a subtree of the form illustrated by the subtrees rooted at nodes D and H in Figure 1.41. This leads to the following recurrence relations:

$$t_i = 1 + 1 + 1 + t_{i-2} + u_{i-2} + 1 + u_{i-3}$$

$$u_j = 1 + 1 + 1 + 2 \cdot u_{j-2}$$

with initial conditions $t_0 = u_0 = 0$ and $t_1 = u_1 = 1$.

t_i and u_j can best be understood by referring to Figure 1.42, which is a treelike representation of the k-d tree of Figure 1.41. The terms in t_i correspond to nodes or subtrees rooted at A, B, C, G, D, F, and H, in order, while the terms in u_j correspond to nodes or subtrees rooted at D, P, Q, R, and V, in order. The square nodes in Figure 1.42 (e.g., E, I, S, and W) correspond to leaf nodes or roots of subtrees that have been pruned; they do not have to be searched.

When these relations are solved, we find that, under the assumption of a complete binary tree (i.e., $N = 2^n - 1$), t_n is $O(2 \cdot N^{1/2})$. Note that, unlike the point quadtree, a complete binary k-d tree can always be constructed (see the optimized k-d tree of Bentley [164] discussed in Section 1.5.1.1). In general, for arbitrary d, t_n is $O(d \cdot N^{1-1/d})$, and thus the worst-case cost of a range search for arbitrary d is $O(d \cdot N^{1-1/d} + F)$, where F is the number of points found in the range. The expected case is much better though and has been shown to be $O(\log_2 N + F)$ using a balanced variant of a k-d tree [181, 1767].

Partial range queries can be handled in the same way as range searching. Lee and Wong [1132] show that when ranges for s out of d keys are specified, the algorithm has a worst-case running time of $O(s \cdot N^{1-1/d} + F)$, where F is the number of points found in the partial range. For an alternative result, see Exercise 6.

As is the case for the point quadtree, the k-d tree can be used to handle all three types of queries specified by Knuth [1046]. The range query is described above, while

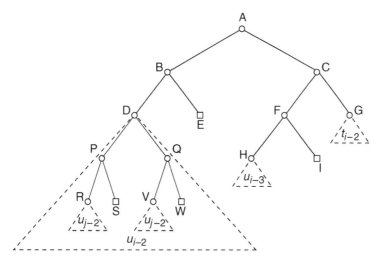

Figure 1.42
Tree representation of the space partition in Figure 1.41.

simple queries are a byproduct of the k-d tree insertion process. Boolean queries are straightforward. Range queries can be facilitated by use of a bounds array B[i] of $2 \cdot d$ elements stored at each node. It contains the range of values for all of the coordinates of the points stored in the k-d tree rooted at the node.

Exercises

1. Why was the search region in Figure 1.41 chosen to lie in the lower-left corner of the space instead of somewhere in the middle?

2. Write a procedure KDREGIONSEARCH to determine all the nodes in a given k-d tree that intersect a given rectangular region in d-dimensional space. Use a bounds array to facilitate your task. KDREGIONSEARCH should make use of a pair of auxiliary functions: one to determine if a subtree can be pruned, and the other to determine if a node is indeed in the search region.

3. Modify procedure KDREGIONSEARCH of Exercise 2 to handle a k-d tree node implementation that makes use of a superkey in its discriminator field.

4. Solve the recurrence relations for t_i and u_j used to analyze range searching in a k-d tree.

5. A partial range query is closely related to the range query. In this case, values are specified for s ($s < d$) of the keys, and a search is made for all records having such values for the specified keys. Show how you would use procedure KDREGIONSEARCH of Exercise 2 to respond to a partial range query.

6. Given a complete k-d tree of N nodes, where $N = 2^{d \cdot h} - 1$, and all leaf nodes appear at depth $d \cdot h - 1$, prove Bentley's [164] result that, in the worst case, $O(N^{(d-s)/d})$ nodes are visited in performing a partial range query with s out of d keys specified.

7. In Exercise 2 in Section 1.4.1.3, a *perfect point quadtree* was defined and used to analyze the expected number of nodes visited in performing a region query for a two-dimensional point quadtree. Define a *perfect k-d tree* in an analogous manner, and repeat this analysis.

8. Perform an average case analysis for region queries and partial range queries in a k-d tree.

1.5.1.4 Point K-d Tree Variants

Our formulation of the k-d tree and its ancestral predecessors (i.e., the fixed-grid and the point quadtree) has the property that all partition lines at a given level of subdivision are parallel to the coordinate axes. When more than one axis is partitioned at a given level in the tree, then all partition lines at a given level of subdivision are orthogonal.

If there is just one partition at a given level of subdivision (e.g., a k-d tree), then all partition lines at all nodes at this subdivision level are along the same axis and are orthogonal to all partition lines at the immediately preceding and subsequent level of subdivision. Moreover, we have assumed that the partitions cycle through the various axes in a predefined and constant order and that the partition lines must pass through the data points (with the exception of the trie-based methods).

Building k-d trees to satisfy these properties can lead to trees that are unbalanced and hence not very good for search operations. In particular, the total path length (TPL) may be quite high. There are several techniques for relaxing these rules with the effect that the resulting trees will be more balanced. Sproull [1797] contains a brief discussion of several such techniques, some of which are elaborated in greater detail in this section. Use of such techniques will reduce the TPL and, thereby, make subsequent searching operations faster. There are two approaches to reduce the TPL, one static and the other dynamic. They are discussed below.

The static approach assumes that all the data points are known a priori. Bentley [164] proposes an optimized k-d tree that is constructed in the same manner as the optimized point quadtree of Section 1.4.1.1. In this case, the partition lines must pass through the data points and still cycle through the various axes in a fixed and constant order.

Alternative static data structures incorporating an "adaptive partitioning" are the *adaptive k-d tree* of Friedman, Bentley, and Finkel [650], the *fair-split tree* of Callahan and Kosaraju [297], the *VAMSplit k-d tree* of White and Jain [1989] (see Section 1.7.1.7 for more details), and the *minimum-ambiguity k-d tree* [1226, 1228]. Unlike the standard k-d tree, and in the spirit of the pseudo quadtree of Overmars and van Leeuwen [1444] (see Section 1.4.1.2), data is stored only in the leaf nodes. In other words, the partition lines need not pass through the data points.[21] Moreover, the partition lines need not cycle through the various axes.

These methods are differentiated by the way in which the discriminator key and value are chosen. In the case of the adaptive k-d tree, the fair-split tree, and the VAMSplit k-d tree, at each level of subdivision, the discriminator is chosen to be the key for which the spread of the values of the key is a maximum. This spread can be measured by any convenient statistic, such as the variance (e.g., the VAMSplit k-d tree [1989]), or by the distance from the minimum to the maximum value (e.g., the adaptive k-d tree [650] and the fair-split tree [297]) usually normalized with respect to the median value, and so on.

Once the discriminator key has been chosen, we must select the discriminator value. A common choice is to use the median so that approximately one-half of the records will be in each subtree and hence the structure will be balanced (e.g., the adaptive k-d tree [650]). An alternative is to use the value that splits the range spanned by the key in half (e.g., the fair-split tree [297]). All records with key values less than the discriminator value are added to the left subtree, and all records with key values greater than or equal to the discriminator value are added to the right subtree. This process is continued recursively until there are only a few nodes left in a set, at which point they are stored as a linked list. Note that since we no longer require a cyclical discriminator sequence, the same key may serve as the discriminator for a node and its father, as well as its child. Thus, the resulting structure could also be characterized as an instance of a *generalized pseudo k-d tree*. We use this term in the rest of our discussion whenever the partition lines need not pass through the data points while leaving open the method for choosing the discriminator at each level of subdivision, in contrast with a conventional pseudo k-d tree where the discriminators cycle through the attributes in a given order as in the k-d tree. We also make use of this term in Section 1.7.1.

---

[21] Bentley [168] uses the qualifier *homogeneous* when describing a k-d tree where data is stored in both nonleaf and leaf nodes and the qualifier *nonhomogeneous* when describing a k-d tree where data is stored only in the leaf nodes.

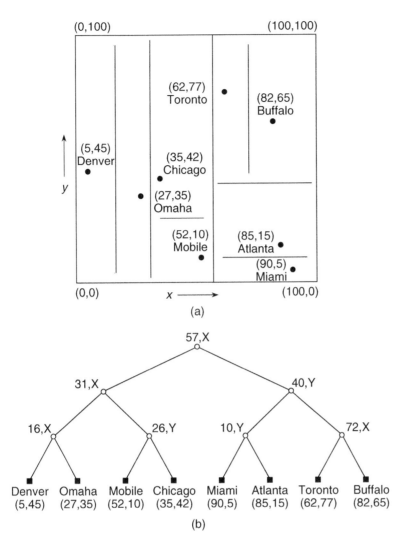

Figure 1.43
An adaptive k-d tree ($d = 2$) corresponding to the data of Figure 1.1: (a) the resulting partition of space and (b) the tree representation.

Figure 1.43 shows the adaptive k-d tree corresponding to the data of Figure 1.1. Note that although Figure 1.43(b) leads to the impression that the adaptive k-d tree is balanced, this is not necessarily the case. For example, when several nodes have the same value for one of their keys, then a middle value is impossible to obtain. The concept of a superkey is of no use in such a case.

Figure 1.44 shows the fair-split tree corresponding to the data of Figure 1.1. Note that the fair-split tree will not usually be balanced. The actual implementation of the fair-split tree also stores the ranges of the discriminator values in the tree (i.e., minimum bounding hyperrectangles of the underlying data). It is used for k-nearest neighbor queries and solving the N-body problem (e.g., [126]), in contrast to a previous solution by Greengard and Rokhlin [754].

In contrast to the adaptive k-d tree, fair-split tree, and the VAMSplit k-d tree, the minimum-ambiguity k-d tree [1226, 1228] chooses the discriminator key and value on the basis of the query distribution rather than the data distribution. The minimum-ambiguity k-d tree is motivated by the fact that, in high dimensions, partitioning methods such as the k-d tree (as well as others) do not help much in differentiating between the data. In particular, queries such as finding the k nearest neighbors result in examining most of the data anyway, especially when the data is uniformly distributed. Thus, a linear scan

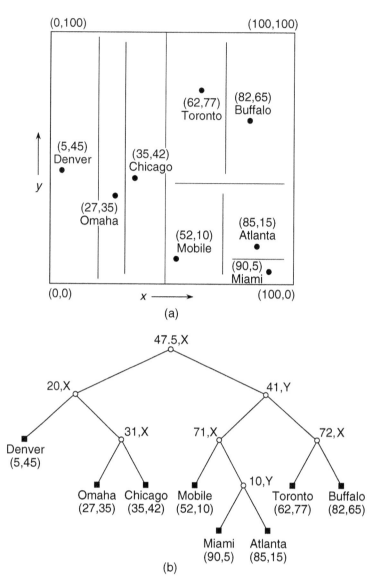

Figure 1.44
A fair-split tree ($d = 2$) corresponding to the data of Figure 1.1: (a) the resulting partition of space and (b) the tree representation.

of the data is often just as efficient as using an index, and there is no need to incur the cost of building the index (see Section 4.4.8 in Chapter 4). The minimum-ambiguity k-d tree is designed to deal with the case that high-dimensional data is clustered (and hence of an inherently lower dimensionality) by adapting the decomposition to the distribution of the query points so that nearest neighbor finding can be performed efficiently. This is done by finding a partitioning method that minimizes the expected number of times that both subtrees of a node must be visited when finding the nearest neighbor to a query point.

Finding such a partitioning is difficult from a theoretical standpoint as the extent of the clustering may not be so well defined. On the other hand, from a practical standpoint, examining the distance to every possible query point is also not feasible. So, instead, a subset of the query points, termed a *training set*, is used, and the quantity that is minimized is the maximum number of candidate nearest neighbors to the query points in the training set. Formally, this is the sum over the two subtrees, each denoted by i, of the product of the number of data points in i and the number of query points for whom the region spanned by the distance from query point p to the nearest data point

q has a nonempty intersection with i. This quantity is computed for every possible pair of subtrees along each of the keys, and the split is made along the key and value that minimize it. This process is repeated recursively until a block contains fewer than c points, where c is analogous to a bucket capacity.

The main drawback of the minimum-ambiguity k-d tree is the high number of training points that are needed for good performance (e.g., nine times the number of data points [1226, 1228]). This has a direct effect on the time needed to build it as the distance to the nearest neighbors must be computed for each of the elements of the training set. Moreover, the process of computing the discriminator key and value takes some time (see Exercise 7). The entire process of building the k-d tree with the training set is made faster by using the approximate nearest neighbor instead of the exact nearest neighbor [1226, 1228] (see Exercise 8). Experiments in terms of the number of nodes that are visited when finding approximate nearest neighbors with different approximation error tolerances for data of dimension 20 showed that the minimum-ambiguity k-d tree significantly outperformed the adaptive k-d tree for clustered data and query points from both a uniform distribution, as well as the same distribution as the data points [1226, 1228]. Nevertheless, due to the high cost of building it, the minimum-ambiguity k-d tree should only be used if the dataset is static, and the number of times it will be queried is far in excess of the number of training points needed for its construction.

It is interesting to observe that the manner in which the discriminator key and value are chosen in the minimum-ambiguity k-d tree is analogous to the way in which they are sometimes chosen for an R-tree when an R-tree node overflows (see Sections 2.1.5.2.1, 2.1.5.2.3, 2.1.5.2.4 of Chapter 2 and the related exercises). In particular, for the R-tree, we wish to partition the region in space containing bounding boxes (not necessarily disjoint) corresponding to the overflowing node into two parts so as to minimize the amount of overlap between the two parts. In this way, when subsequent search operations are performed (e.g., a variant of the point location query that finds the object that contains a given point when the R-tree is used to represent objects with extent, such as two-dimensional objects, or even the nearest neighbor query when the R-tree consists of bounding boxes of collections of points), the likelihood of visiting more than one subtree is reduced. The motivation in the minimum-ambiguity k-d tree is similar but with the difference that, in the minimum-ambiguity k-d tree representation of point data, the overlap is implicit since we do not actually store the search regions. Thus, the overlap is a property of the query instead of the data, which is the case in the R-tree, where it is also explicitly stored.

When the data volume becomes large, we may not want as fine a partition of the underlying space as is provided by the adaptive k-d tree and the other variants of the generalized pseudo k-d tree. In particular, it may be desirable for points to be grouped by proximity so that they can be processed together. The generalized pseudo k-d tree can be adapted to facilitate this, as well as to identify clusters of points, by grouping points by spatial proximity into buckets and using the generalized pseudo k-d tree decomposition rule (e.g., the one used for the adaptive k-d tree) to partition a bucket whenever it overflows its capacity. We term the result a *bucket generalized pseudo k-d tree*. We have already seen the use of bucketing in our definition of the bucket PR quadtree (see Section 1.4.2.2). However, in contrast to the bucket PR quadtree, in the bucket generalized pseudo k-d tree, the choice of both the key across which to split, as well as the positions of the partition lines, depends on the data. For example, consider Figure 1.45, the bucket generalized pseudo k-d tree corresponding to the data of Figure 1.1 when the bucket capacity is 2. The splitting rule uses as a discriminator the key whose values have the maximum range (i.e., the one used for the adaptive k-d tree, and hence the result can be described as an instance of the *bucket adaptive k-d tree*).

Henrich [825] discusses the general issue of bucket overflow in variants of k-d trees that make use of buckets. The examples and experiments are primarily in terms of bucket methods that employ a tree directory such as the LSD tree (see Section 1.7.1.3) where the nonleaf nodes are also bucketed. Nevertheless, the approach is much more general.

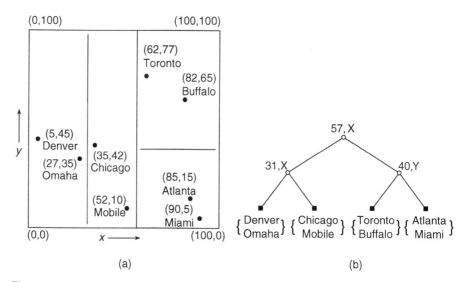

Figure 1.45
A bucket generalized pseudo k-d tree and the records it represents corresponding to the data of Figure 1.1 for bucket size 2: (a) the resulting partition of space and (b) the tree representation.

In particular, Henrich proposes to make use of rotation operations similar to those used in B-trees so that data is redistributed from the overflowing bucket to a sibling bucket that is not too full. In the case of a k-d tree, once the data is redistributed, we may also have to adjust the partition line. The problem is that the sibling may also be too full, in which case the redistribution process must be applied recursively to the sibling. Experiments [825] revealed that general application of recursive redistribution resulted in worse performance due to the fact that the trees became deeper. Thus, Henrich [825] suggests that redistribution should be applied only in the following two instances:

1. Between sibling buckets.

2. Recursively if the overflowing bucket and corresponding ancestor subtree are heavier (i.e., deeper) than the subtree that is receiving the overflowing data. Moreover, the recursion should be attempted for a limited number of levels of the tree (usually one, as, otherwise, the price of the increase in execution time for the redistribution process dwarfs the relative increase in storage utilization and decrease in tree depth).

Matsuyama, Hao, and Nagao [1258] use the bucket generalized pseudo k-d tree in a geographic information system. In this case, even though the spatial objects have extent (i.e., they correspond to entries such as regions and lines in two dimensions), they are treated as points by storing a corresponding representative point such as the object's centroid. A variant of the bucket generalized pseudo k-d tree is also used by Ooi, McDonell, and Sacks-Davis [1404, 1407]. In particular, they store the centroids of the objects and also associate with each node's partitioning line the maximum extent to the right (left), in terms of the coordinate j whose value is being tested, of all objects in the left (right) subtree. The result is termed a *spatial k-d tree* and is discussed further in Sections 1.7.1.2 and 3.3.2.5 of Chapter 3).

O'Rourke [1421, 1425] uses the bucket adaptive k-d tree, calling it a *Dynamically Quantized Space* (DQS), for cluster detection as well as for multidimensional histogramming to aid in focusing the Hough Transform (e.g., [514, 1122]). The *Dynamically Quantized Pyramid* (DQP) [1425, 1777] is closely related to the DQS in the sense that it is also used in the same application. Both the DQP and the DQS are instances of the bucket pseudo quadtree and the bucket generalized pseudo k-d tree, respectively, with the difference that in the DQP, the buckets are obtained by partitioning across all of the keys at each step while still varying the positions of the partition lines (the result is also called an irregular cell-tree pyramid and is discussed in Section 2.1.5.1 of Chapter 2). Below, we briefly describe the Hough Transform in order to show an application of these bucket methods. This discussion is very specialized and thus may be skipped.

Techniques such as the Hough Transform facilitate the detection of arbitrary sparse patterns, such as curves, by mapping them into a space where they give rise to clusters. A DQS (i.e., a bucket generalized pseudo k-d tree) has k attributes or dimensions corresponding to a set of parameters that can be mapped by an appropriate function to yield image patterns. The buckets correspond to the parameter regions. Associated with each bucket is a count indicating the number of times that an element in its region appears in the data. The goal is to find evidence for the presence of clusters in parameter space.

The DQS is particularly useful in parameter spaces of high dimension (i.e., $\gg 2$). However, for the sake of this discussion, we just look at two-dimensional data. In particular, consider a large collection of short edges and try to determine if many of them are collinear. We do this by examining the values of their slopes and y-intercepts (recall that the equation of a line is $y = m \cdot x + b$). It turns out that a high density of points (i.e., counts per unit volume) in the (m, b) plane is evidence that many collinear edges exist. We want to avoid wasting the space while finding the cluster (most of the space will be empty). To do this, we vary the sizes of the buckets (i.e., their parameter regions) in an attempt to keep the counts equal.

In two dimensions, the Hough Transform for detecting lines is quite messy unless each detected point has an associated slope. The same would be true in three dimensions, where we would want not only a position reading (x, y, z) but also the direction cosines of a surface normal (α, β, γ). We can then map each detection into the parameters of a plane, for example, (ρ, α, β), where ρ is the perpendicular distance from the plane to the origin. If there are many coplanar detectors, this should yield a cluster in the vicinity of some particular (ρ, α, β).

As the buckets overflow, new buckets (and corresponding parameter regions) are created by a splitting process. This splitting process is guided by the two independent goals of an equal count in each bucket and the maintenance of a uniform distribution in each bucket. This is aided by keeping a count and an imbalance vector with each bucket. When the need arises, buckets are split across the dimension of greatest imbalance. There is also a merging rule, which is applied when counts of adjacent neighbors (possibly more than two) are not too large, and the merges will not produce any highly unbalanced regions. This is especially useful if the data is dynamic.

The DQP addresses the same problem as the DQS with the aid of a complete bucket pseudo quadtree, which is known as a pyramid [1845] (see Section 2.1.5.1 of Chapter 2 for more details). Thus, for k attributes or dimensions, it is a full balanced tree where each nonleaf node has 2^k children. In this case, the number of buckets (i.e., parameter regions), and the relationship between fathers and children are fixed. The DQP differs from the conventional pyramid in that the partition points (termed *cross-hairs*) at the various levels are variable rather than fixed.

The partition points of a DQP are initialized to the midpoints of the different attributes. They are adjusted as data is entered. This adjustment process occurs at all levels and is termed a *warping process*. One possible technique when inserting a new data point, say P, in a space rooted at Q, is to take a weighted average of the position of P, say α, and of Q, say $(1 - \alpha)$. This changes the boundaries of all nodes in the subtree rooted at Q. P is recursively added to the appropriate bucket (associated with a leaf node), which causes other boundaries to change.

Figure 1.46 is an example of a two-dimensional DQP for three levels. It should be clear that regions grow smaller near inserted points and that the shape of the DQP depends on the insertion history, thereby providing an automatic focusing mechanism. The warping process is analogous to the splitting operation used in conjunction with a

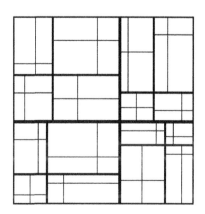

Figure 1.46
Example two-dimensional DQP for three levels.

DQS. The advantage of a DQP over the DQS is that it is easier to implement, and merging is considerably simpler. On the other hand, the DQP allocates equal resources for each dimension of the parameter space, whereas the DQS can ignore irrelevant dimensions, thereby yielding more precision in its focusing. Also, the DQS takes up less space than the DQP.

The drawback of methods such as the bucket generalized pseudo k-d tree (as exemplified by the DQS) and the DQP is that the result may not be aesthetically pleasing as the price of the balance is a bad aspect ratio. Intuitively, in two dimensions, this means that the lengths of the sides of a region differ greatly (such regions are characterized as *skinny* [516, 517], in contrast to others where the differences are not so great, which are characterized as *fat*). This makes them undesirable for applications such as drawing very large graphs using subgraphs (e.g., [516]). One way to define the *aspect ratio* in d dimensions is as the ratio of the smallest circumscribed hypersphere in R^d to the largest inscribed hypersphere in R^d, using any of the standard Minkowski distance metrics L_p (where, given the points (x_1, y_1) and (x_2, y_2), the distance is defined as $d_{L_p}((x_1, y_1), (x_2, y_2)) = ((x_1 - x_2)^p + (y_1 - y_2)^p)^{1/p}$ for integers $p \geq 1$).

Duncan, Goodrich, and Kobourov [516, 517] address the issue of finding a representation where the shapes of all of the resulting regions have an aspect ratio, as defined above, less than a particular value α (such regions are termed α-*balanced*), while also ensuring that the resulting regions are not too unbalanced in terms of the number of points that they contain. The resulting representation is termed a *balanced aspect ratio tree* (BAR tree) and has the property that for a set of N points, the depth is $O(\log N)$. However, unlike the variants of the bucket generalized pseudo k-d tree, not all of the leaf nodes of the BAR tree need to be at the same depth; nor is the maximum difference in their depths bounded by one.

Note that the requirement that the regions be α-balanced yields a structure that is very similar to the restricted quadtree [1453, 1771, 1772, 1940] and restricted bintree [513, 576, 651, 810, 1176, 1259, 1522, 1564, 1565] (see Section 2.2.4 of Chapter 2), where the widths of all adjacent blocks differ by at most a factor of 2. Other representations, such as the balanced box-decomposition tree (BBD-tree) of Arya, Mount, Netanyahu, Silverman, and Wu [100], which has $O(\log N)$ depth for N points, may result in α-balanced regions. However, the regions are not necessarily convex as some of the regions may have holes, making them unattractive for display purposes in applications such as graph drawing [516].

The basic structure of the BAR tree differs from that of the k-d tree by allowing an additional set of 2^d possible partitions (aside from the d axis-parallel ones) that correspond to all of the possible combinations where the magnitude of the relative changes in each of the d directions is the same (e.g., 45-degree-angled partitions in two dimensions, of which there are four).[22] Such partitions are termed *canonical cuts*, and the resulting regions are termed *canonical regions*. These additional partitions, coupled with the above definition of the aspect ratio, enable dealing with the situation that all of the points lie in a corner of the region. In this case, without the 45-degree-angled partitions, we would have arbitrarily skinny regions.

It is also desirable, once all of the canonical cuts have been applied, that the number of points in the resulting regions not be too unbalanced. This condition does not necessarily hold when all of the resulting regions are α-balanced. Thus, instead of requiring that the number of points in a region be cut roughly in half at every level, the BAR tree guarantees that the number of points is cut roughly in half every k levels ($k = 2$ for $d = 2$ and $k = d + 2$ in general), which is not always possible with an arbitrary k-d tree or a

---

[22] This is more general than the g-degrees rotated x-range [1923], which is used as an object approximation (see Section 2.1.1 in Chapter 2) and allows two parallel extra partitions for two-dimensional data, although the angle is arbitrary rather than being restricted to 45 degrees as in the BAR tree.

d-dimensional variant of the region quadtree (e.g., a region octree in three dimensions), while also guaranteeing that all of the resulting regions are α-balanced.

In particular, given a value β $(0.5 \leq \beta < 1)$, termed a *reduction factor*, we say that when an α-balanced region R (letting $|R|$ denote the number of points in R) is subdivided into two regions, R_1 and R_2, the following properties hold:

1. R_1 and R_2 are α-balanced.

2. $|R_1| \leq \beta|R|$, and $|R_2| \leq \beta|R|$.

The above is called a *one-cut*. A definition is also given for a *k-cut*, which divides an α-balanced region R into two regions, R_1 and R_2, such that

1. R_1 and R_2 are α-balanced.

2. $|R_2| \leq \beta|R|$.

3. Either $|R_1| \leq \beta|R|$, or R_1 is $(k-1)$-cuttable with a reduction factor β.

The main motivation for this subdivision process is that the application of the sequence of k canonical cuts $s_k, s_{k-1}, \ldots, s_2, s_1$ to region R will result in $k+1$ α-balanced regions, each containing no more than $\beta|R|$ points. In this case, we say that R is *k-cuttable*.

Duncan, et al. [517] prove that given a set of canonical cuts, if every possible α-balanced canonical region is k-cuttable with a reduction factor β, then a BAR tree with maximum aspect ratio α can be constructed with depth $O(k \log_{1/\beta} N)$ for any set S of N points (see Exercise 11). More importantly, they also prove that for $\alpha \geq 3d$ and $\beta \geq d/(d+1)$, any α-balanced canonical region R is $(d+2)$-cuttable. Using these results and the fact that the maximum depth of the BAR tree is $O(d^2 \log N)$ (see Exercise 12), they prove that a BAR tree with an appropriate maximum aspect ratio α can be constructed in $O(d^2 \cdot 2^d \log N)$ time, which for fixed dimensions is $O(N \log N)$. Thus, the BAR tree is balanced in two ways: clusters at the same level have approximately the same number of points, and each cluster region has a bounded aspect ratio.

Now, let us return to our more general discussion. Both the optimized and generalized pseudo k-d trees are static data structures, which means that we must know all of the data points a priori before we can build the tree. Thus, deletion of nodes is considerably more complex than for conventional k-d trees (see Section 1.5.1.2) since we must obtain new partitions for the remaining data. Searching in optimized and generalized pseudo k-d trees proceeds in an analogous manner to that in conventional k-d trees.

The dynamic approach to reducing the TPL in a k-d tree constructs the tree as the data points are inserted into it. The algorithm is similar to that used to build the conventional k-d tree, except that every time the tree fails to meet a predefined balance criterion, the tree is partially rebalanced. One radical approach, known as the *divided k-d tree* [1075], in the case of two-dimensional data, makes all subdivisions at the top of the tree along the first dimension value, and all subdivisions at the remaining levels on the dimension (of course, this idea can be generalized to higher dimensions). Thus, the result is somewhat similar to using a hierarchy of inverted lists (see Section 1.1). The actual implementation [1075] is based on a 2-3 tree [874] instead of a binary subdivision such as an AVL tree [15]. The key to this method is to make use of the ability to rebalance such a structure efficiently, thereby permitting it to have good dynamic behavior.

Overmars and van Leeuwen [1444] (see also Willard [1999]) rebalance the tree using techniques developed for constructing the optimized k-d tree. They present two variations: the first is analogous to the optimized point quadtree, and the second to the pseudo quadtree. One of the differences between these two approaches is that in the dynamic optimized k-d tree, the partition lines must pass through the data points, but this need not be the case for the dynamic pseudo k-d tree. This does not have an effect on searching. However, deletion will be considerably simpler in the dynamic pseudo k-d tree than in the dynamic optimized k-d tree.

Methods such as the dynamic optimized k-d tree and the dynamic pseudo k-d tree are characterized by Vaishnavi [1912] as yielding "severely" balanced trees in that they are generalizations of complete binary trees for one-dimensional data. As such, they can not be updated efficiently, and this has led Vaishnavi to propose a relaxation of the balancing criterion by generalizing the height-balancing constraint for a height-balanced binary search tree (also known as an AVL tree [15, 27]). This is done by storing data in a nested sequence of binary trees so that each nonleaf node P tests a particular key J. Each nonleaf node P has three children. The left and right children point to nodes with smaller and larger values, respectively, for the Jth key. The third child is the root of a $(k-1)$-dimensional tree containing all data nodes that have the same value for the Jth key as the data point corresponding to P.[23] The "rotation" and "double rotation" restructuring operations of height-balanced trees are adapted to the new structure. For N points, their use is shown to yield $O(\log_2 N + k)$ bounds on their search and update times (i.e., node insertion and deletion). Unfortunately, this data structure does not appear to be well suited for range queries.

The most drastic relaxation of the rule for the formation of the k-d tree is achieved by removing the requirements that the partition lines be orthogonal and parallel to the coordinate axes and that they pass through the data points. This means that the partition lines are arbitrary; thus, it is no longer meaningful to speak about the order in which the different coordinate axes are partitioned (e.g., [1797]). Also, the ancestral relationship (i.e., the common bond) between the k-d tree and the fixed-grid method is now meaningless as an array access structure to the results of the space partition is no longer possible.

Sproull [1797] suggests that the first partition line be obtained by computing the principal eigenvector of the covariance matrix of the data points. This axis, also known as the *principal axis*, points along the direction of the maximum variation in the data regardless of their orientation with respect to the coordinate axes.[24] This process is applied recursively to the resultant subsets. The same idea is used by McNames [1271] in his development of the principal axis tree (PAT). In this case, instead of a binary partition along the principal axis, the entire dataset is projected onto the principal axis, and the result is partitioned into $m \geq 1$ distinct regions such that each region has approximately the same number of points. This process is recursively reapplied to each of the point subsets until each subset contains fewer than m points. Note that the principal axis tree is analogous to the multidimensional directory (MDD) [1183] discussed in Section 1.1, with the difference that the partition lines are no longer orthogonal (see Figure 1.5(b)). The idea of performing more than one partition along an axis is also used in the X-Y tree [1334] and the equivalent treemap [1758] and puzzletree [479] (see Section 2.1.2.9 of Chapter 2) with the difference that the partitions are only made along the coordinate axes, and the number of partitions is permitted to vary at each node.

The *Binary Space Partitioning tree* (BSP tree) of Fuchs, Kedem, and Naylor [658] is an example of a k-d tree where the subdivision lines are not necessarily orthogonal or parallel to the coordinate axes and do not necessarily pass through the data points. Each subdivision line is really a hyperplane, which is a line in two dimensions and a plane in three dimensions. Thus, in two dimensions, each node's block is a convex polygon, while in three dimensions, it is a convex polyhedron.

The BSP tree is a binary tree where each child corresponds to a region. In order to be able to assign regions to the left and right subtrees, we need to associate a direction with each subdivision line. In particular, the subdivision lines are treated as separators

---

[23] The same principle is applied to the B-tree to yield the MDBT [1434, 1686] and the kB-tree [786, 787]. See Section 1.1 for more details.

[24] Singular Value Decomposition (SVD) (see Section 4.6.4.1 of Chapter 4) is also based on this principle.

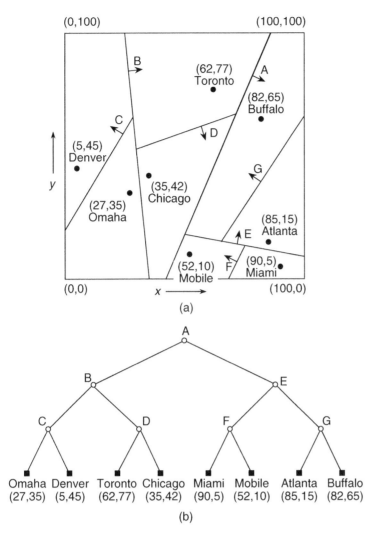

Figure 1.47
An adaptation of the BSP tree to points and the records it represents corresponding to the data of Figure 1.1: (a) the resulting partition of space and (b) the tree representation.

between two halfspaces.[25] Let the subdivision line have the equation $a \cdot x + b \cdot y + c = 0$. We say that the right subtree is the "positive" side and contains all subdivision lines formed by separators that satisfy $a \cdot x + b \cdot y + c \geq 0$. Similarly, we say that the left subtree is "negative" and contains all subdivision lines formed by separators that satisfy $a \cdot x + b \cdot y + c < 0$. As an example, consider Figure 1.47(a), which is one of many possible adaptations of the BSP tree to store the point data in Figure 1.1. Notice the use of arrows to indicate the direction of the positive halfspaces. Although in this example the tree is balanced, this need not be the case. Similarly, the subdivision lines may pass through the data points themselves.

Although we have presented the BSP tree as a point representation in this section, the real motivation for the development of the BSP tree was to expedite the process of visibility determination in scenes composed of polyhedral objects where the faces are coincident with the partitioning planes (assuming three-dimensional data). This is discussed is Section 2.1.3.1 of Chapter 2. Nevertheless, the BSP tree has also been used

---

[25] A (linear) *halfspace* in d-dimensional space is defined by the inequality $\sum_{i=0}^{d} a_i \cdot x_i \geq 0$ on the $d + 1$ homogeneous coordinates ($x_0 = 1$). The halfspace is represented by a column vector a. In vector notation, the inequality is written as $a \cdot x \geq 0$. In the case of equality, it defines a hyperplane with a as its normal. It is important to note that halfspaces are volume elements; they are not boundary elements.

by van Oosterom [1410, 1412] in the KD2-tree to represent objects as points in the same way that Ooi, McDonell, and Sacks-Davis used the bucket generalized pseudo k-d tree in their spatial k-d tree [1404, 1407]. In particular, the KD2-tree also stores the centroids of the objects and associates with each node P's subdivision line I two lines, L and R, both of which are parallel to I. L (R) is obtained by shifting I to the left (right), thereby expanding the space spanned by P's right (left) subtree so that it defines the smallest subspace that covers all of the objects whose centroids are stored in a's right (left) subtree. van Oosterom also defines a bucket variant of the KD2-tree, termed a *KD2B-tree* [1410, 1412], which is built using techniques similar to those employed in constructing an R-tree (see Section 2.1.5.2 of Chapter 2). In both the KD2-tree and the KD2B-tree, the leaf nodes also contain the minimum bounding spheres of the objects corresponding to the points stored therein as they provide a better approximation than the convex cells associated with the space that is spanned by the corresponding leaf nodes.

The BSP tree has also been used by Maneewongvatana and Mount [1229, 1230], who have adapted it to facilitate finding nearest neighbors in high dimensions by associating with each node a a bounding box in the form of a convex polyhedron, termed a *cover*, that contains every point in the d-dimensional space whose nearest data point is in the space spanned by a. The result is termed an *overlapped-split tree (os-tree)* (see Section 4.4.4 of Chapter 4 for more details) and is quite similar to an R-tree (see Section 2.1.5.2 in Chapter 2), except that the bounding boxes are not axis parallel. The resulting tree is formed in the same way as the KD2-tree of van Oosterom with the only difference being that, in the KD2-tree, the cover of a node corresponds to the extent of the objects whose centroids are associated with the node.

The *D-tree* of Xu, Zheng, Lee, and Lee [2035, 2036] is a generalization of the BSP tree where the subdivision lines are *polylines* (sequences of connected line segments of arbitrary orientation) instead of being restricted to be straight lines. In this case, the motivation of Xu et al. is to be able to represent an arbitrary partition of the underlying space instead of one that is based on a recursive halving of the underlying space, which is the case when using a k-d tree or a BSP tree. As an example, consider Figure 1.48(a), which is one of the many possible partitions of the underlying space spanned by the data points (i.e., cities) given in Figure 1.1 into regions so that there is one point per region, and Figure 1.48(b), one of the many possible D-trees for these eight regions. The

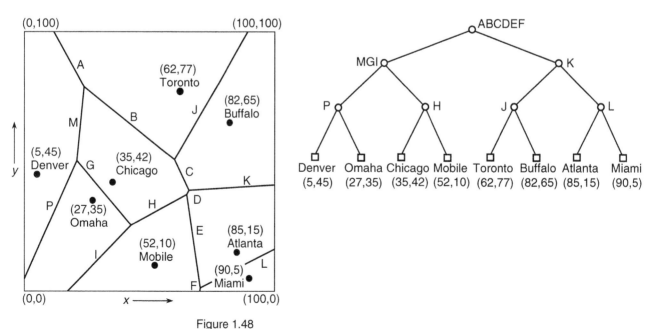

Figure 1.48
(a) An example partition of the underlying space containing the data in Figure 1.1 into regions and (b) one of a number of its possible D-tree representations.

nonleaf nodes in Figure 1.48(b) represent the polylines that correspond to the boundaries of the regions or groups of regions in Figure 1.48(a), and they have been labeled with the vertices that make them up (i.e., using the letters A–P). For example, the root is labeled with ABCDEF as it separates the regions containing Denver, Omaha, Chicago, and Mobile in the left subtree and Toronto, Buffalo, Atlanta, and Miami in the right subtree.

The particular partition of the underlying space consisting of the locations of the eight cities given by Figure 1.1 that is depicted in Figure 1.48(a) is known as the *Voronoi diagram* [1941] and is discussed in much greater detail in Sections 2.2.1.4 and 2.2.2.6 of Chapter 2 and Sections 4.4.4 and 4.4.5 of Chapter 4. Briefly, given a distinguished set of points s_i (termed *sites*), the Voronoi diagram is a partition of the underlying space into regions r_i, one per site s_i, so that each point p in the space spanned by a region r_i is closer to the site s_i of r_i than to the site s_j $(i \neq j)$ of any other region r_j. It should be clear that the partition of the underlying space given in Figure 1.48(a) has this property.

The main drawback of using subdivision lines that are polylines (i.e., as in the D-tree) instead of straight lines is that it significantly complicates the determination of which side of a line contains a query point, which is the cornerstone of the efficient execution of a point location query. This query is usually implemented by constructing an arbitrary infinite line l through the query point q and counting the number n of boundaries of the containing region r crossed by l (e.g., [622]). An odd (even) n means that q is inside (outside) r. The implementation is simplified considerably when we can ensure that, without loss of generality, no vertical line can intersect the boundary of r more than twice (a partition of space that has this property is called a *y-monotone subdivision* and is discussed in greater detail in Section 2.1.3.3.1 of Chapter 2). Unfortunately, the partition of the underlying space induced by the D-tree is not necessarily a y-monotone subdivision, and thus we cannot make use of a simple test such as "above-and-below" ("left-and-right" or any other orientation). Instead, we must resort to imposing an additional hierarchy on the D-tree's associated partition of the underlying space such as a hierarchy of triangulations as in the K-structure [1026] (see Section 2.1.3.2 of Chapter 2) or a hierarchy of "above-and-below" partitions consisting of groups of regions as in the separating chain method [1128] and the improved access structure for it known as the layered dag [541] (see Section 2.1.3.3 of Chapter 2). The problem is that these hierarchies invariably involve the addition of edges, thereby further partitioning the partition of the underlying space that is induced by the D-tree, and thus limiting its utility. In other words, the D-tree cannot be used effectively as an access structure on the original data without the imposition of an additional access structure on the D-tree itself.

Exercises

1. Write a procedure BUILDOPTIMIZEDKDTREE to construct an optimized k-d tree.

2. In the text, we indicated that the optimized k-d tree can also be constructed dynamically. Given δ $(0 < \delta < 1)$, show that there exists an algorithm to build such a tree so that its depth is always at most $\log_{2-\delta} n + O(1)$ and that the average insertion time in an initially empty data structure is $O(\frac{1}{\delta \log_2^2 N})$. In this case, n denotes the number of nodes currently in the tree, and N is the total number of nodes in the final tree.

3. Write a procedure BUILDADAPTIVEKDTREE to construct an adaptive k-d tree.

4. Analyze the running time of procedure BUILDADAPTIVEKDTREE.

5. Show that the average search time for a hypercube range query (i.e., all sides are of equal length) in an adaptive k-d tree of N nodes is $O(\log_2 N + F)$, where F is the number of answers and is relatively small in comparison to N.

6. Define a pseudo k-d tree in an analogous manner to that used to define the pseudo quadtree in Section 1.4.1.2. Repeat Exercise 16 in Section 1.4.1.2 for the pseudo k-d tree. In other words, prove that the same result holds for N insertions and deletions in a d-dimensional pseudo k-d tree.

when the data is clustered),[26] the tree contains many empty nodes and, thereby, becomes unbalanced. For example, inserting Amherst at location (83,64) in the PR k-d tree (PR quadtree) given in Figure 1.49 (Figure 1.31) will result in much decomposition to separate it from Buffalo, which is at (82,65). This effect is shown explicitly by the amount of decomposition necessary to separate Omaha and Chicago in the PR k-d tree given in Figure 1.49.

Exercises

1. Formulate a k-d tree variant of a matrix representation analogous to the MX quadtree (discussed in Section 1.4.2.1), and term it an *MX k-d tree* or an *MX bintree*. Give procedures MXKDINSERT and MXKDDELETE to insert and delete data points in an MX bintree.

2. Why would an MX k-d tree be a better matrix representation than the MX quadtree?

3. Each point in the MX k-d tree can be represented as a unique, one-dimensional number as a result of concatenating zeros and ones corresponding to left and right transitions in the tree while descending a path from the root to the point's leaf node. Such a representation is known as a *locational code*, which is discussed briefly in Section 1.8.5.1 and in much greater detail in Section 2.1.2.4 of Chapter 2. Assuming a $2^n \times 2^n$ image, a set of N points is represented by $N \cdot n$ bits. Devillers and Gandoin [483, 674] suggest that the space requirements can be reduced by using a method that encodes the set of N points using a string corresponding to a breadth-first traversal of the corresponding PR k-d tree, along with the cardinality of points in the subtrees. The first element of the output string is the number of points N encoded using $2 \cdot n$ bits. Next, output the number of points in the left subtree of the PR k-d tree using $\log_2(N + 1)$ bits. The number of points in the right subtree can be obtained by subtracting the number of points in the left subtree from the number of points in the father node. This process is repeated recursively for the nodes at the next level. The process ceases at each stage when a leaf node in the PR k-d tree is encountered. If the leaf node q corresponds to a point p, then the rest of the bits corresponding to the path from q to the corresponding node in the MX k-d tree are output. Assuming a uniform distribution data model so that when a nonleaf node (i.e., block) with c points is split, each of the children contains $c/2$ points, what is the expected number of bits needed to encode the N points?

4. Write a pair of procedures PRKDINSERT and PRKDDELETE to insert and delete, respectively, data points in a PR k-d tree.

5. Assuming that key values are uniformly distributed real numbers in [0,1) represented in binary, prove that the average depth of a PR k-d tree is $O(\log_2 N)$. Can you extend this result to PR quadtrees?

6. Perform an average case analysis of the cost of a partial range query (a subset of the range query) for a point k-d tree and a PR k-d tree when the attributes are independent and uniformly distributed.

1.5.2.2   Sliding-Midpoint K-d Tree

The lack-of-balance shortcoming of the PR k-d tree is evident when one side of the splitting hyperplane contains no data (termed a *trivial split*). An easy way to overcome this shortcoming is to make use of the *sliding-midpoint rule* [1226, 1228, 1319]. This is done by first splitting along the midpoint as in the PR k-d tree. If there are data points along both sides of the splitting hyperplane, then the split is retained. However, if a trivial split results, then the splitting hyperplane is moved (i.e., "slid") in the direction of the data until the first data point is encountered. The split is made so that one block contains this point while the other block contains the remaining points. This process is repeated recursively until each block contains just one point.[27] Thus, the sliding-midpoint k-d tree for N points has N leaf nodes, all of which are nonempty. For example, Figure 1.50

---

[26] See [1832] for an analysis of this situation.

[27] Actually, it is more common to halt the decomposition process whenever a block contains less than c points, where c is analogous to a bucket capacity. This is described below.

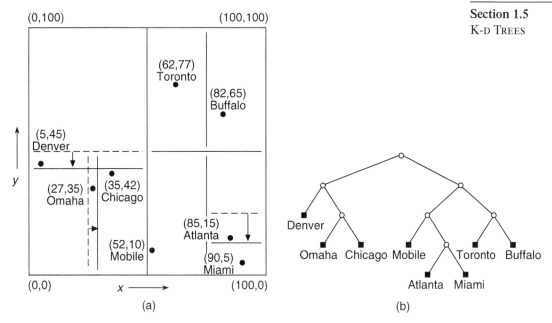

Figure 1.50
A sliding-midpoint k-d tree and the records it represents corresponding to the data of Figure 1.1: (a) the resulting partition of space and (b) the tree representation. Broken lines indicate the original position of the partition plane before it has been slid to its final position, which is indicated by a solid line.

shows the sliding-midpoint k-d tree corresponding to the data of Figure 1.1. Notice the use of broken lines to indicate the original position of the partition plane before it has been slid to its final position, which is indicated by a solid line. Observe also that unlike the PR k-d tree, the sliding-midpoint k-d tree is a static structure as we must know all of the points before making a decision to slide a partition plane.

Given N points (assuming different values for each attribute), the complexity of building a sliding-midpoint k-d tree of height h is $O(N \cdot h)$, which is the same as that of building an adaptive k-d tree of the same height. However, unlike the adaptive k-d tree, where h is $\log_2 N$, for the sliding-midpoint k-d tree, h can be as bad as n. Nevertheless, using a method due to Vaidya [1908], it is possible to build the sliding-midpoint k-d tree in $O(d \cdot N \cdot \log_2 N)$ time in dimension d (see Exercise 1).

The sliding-midpoint rule has a number of advantages over some other splitting rules. First of all, as mentioned above, it avoids the empty cells as is common in the PR k-d tree. It is interesting to observe that the real motivation for the sliding-midpoint rule is to slide the boundaries of the resulting cells toward the data clusters so that eventually, and ideally, the subsequent application of the recursive partitioning process will result in congruent cells with approximately the same number of data objects. In this respect, the sliding-midpoint rule can be said to be an adaptation of the adaptive k-d tree to an environment that makes use of regular decomposition.

The sliding-midpoint k-d tree helps overcome one of the drawbacks of the adaptive k-d tree. In particular, if the data points are highly clustered along some of the dimensions and vary greatly among the others, then the fact that the adaptive k-d tree repeatedly splits along the axis for which the points have the greatest spread means that the cells will be thin along some of the dimensions, thereby having a high aspect ratio. Therefore, in the adaptive k-d tree, a nearest neighbor query near the center of the data space may have to visit a large number of these thin cells. The sliding-midpoint k-d tree can also have cells with a high aspect ratio. However, in contrast to the adaptive k-d tree, a cell c in the sliding-midpoint k-d tree that has a high aspect ratio is adjacent to a cell c' that is fat along the same dimension i on which c is thin. This condition implies that in dimension

i, the number of cells of diameter s that can overlap a ball of radius r can be bounded as a function of d, s, and r (independent of the number of points in the data structure) [1226, 1227]. This property, called the *packing constraint*, is important for the efficiency of answering approximate nearest neighbor queries [100]. Thus, unlike the adaptive k-d tree, it is not possible to generate a long sequence of thin cells in the sliding-midpoint k-d tree, thereby lessening the effect of the high aspect ratio on nearest neighbor queries in the sliding-midpoint k-d tree.

Exercises

1. Given N d-dimensional points and assuming that a partitioning hyperplane for a k-d tree splitting rule in such a space can be obtained in $O(d)$ time, show that a k-d tree (e.g., using the sliding-midpoint rule) can be built in $O(d \cdot N \cdot \log_2 N)$ time.

2. The difference between the sliding-midpoint k-d tree and the PR k-d tree is that, whenever a split at a midpoint results in a trivial split, the splitting plane is moved (i.e., "slid") in the direction of the data until encountering the first data point a. The split is made so that one block contains this point while the other block contains the remaining points. In this case, we end up with one relatively large block containing a, while the remaining points are in the other blocks, which are smaller. Thus, if a is part of a cluster of points, then the blocks that contain the points are not necessarily of similar size. For some applications, such as finding nearest neighbors, it may be desirable for the blocks to be of equal size. One way to achieve this is to halt the movement of the splitting plane in the case of a trivial split at a position so that we have as large an empty node as possible. Let us use the term *open-sliding midpoint k-d tree* to describe the result. It should be clear that the open-sliding midpoint k-d tree will require more space than the sliding-midpoint k-d tree as now we also have empty nodes. Determine the worst-case space requirements of the open-sliding midpoint k-d tree as a function of the number of points n and the dimensionality d of the underlying space, and give an example that attains it.

1.5.2.3 Bucket PR K-d Tree and PMR K-d Tree

A very simple method for overcoming the lack of balance in the PR k-d tree is to treat each block in the PR k-d tree as a bucket of capacity b and to stipulate that the block is split whenever it contains more than b points. We present two instances of this method that are differentiated on the basis of how many tests they apply at each step when encountering a full bucket.[28] Having buckets of capacity b $(b > 1)$ reduces the dependence of the maximum depth of the PR k-d tree on the minimum Euclidean distance separation of two distinct points to that of two sets of at most b points apiece. This is a good solution as long as the cluster contains b or fewer points as, otherwise, we still need to make many partitions. The result is termed a *bucket PR k-d tree* (also known as a *hybrid k-d trie* [1413]) and is shown in Figure 1.51 for the data of Figure 1.1 when the bucket capacity is 2. The bucket PR k-d tree assumes a cyclic partitioning. If we permit the order in which we partition the various axes to vary rather than cycling through them in a particular order, then the result is termed a *bucket generalized k-d trie*. It is referred to extensively in Section 1.7.1.

The PMR k-d tree [1360, 1361, 1362] for points[29] is another example of a bucketing method. It addresses the clustering problem by making use of a concept related to bucket

---

[28] At times, an additional restriction on the bucketing criterion is placed so that after a bucket with more than b items is split, most of the data is not in just one of the regions corresponding to the newly formed buckets. For example, in their presentation of the BD-tree (see Section 1.5.2.6), Ohsawa and Sakauchi [1386, 1387] suggest that a bucket with Nb items can be split until none of the regions corresponding to the newly buckets contains more than $2N/3$ items. This splitting fraction is also used in the BBD-tree [100], where its use is justified from a theoretical standpoint (see Section 1.5.2.7 and Exercise 2 of that section).

[29] This structure was originally defined as a PMR quadtree, but its adaptation for k-d trees is straightforward: we vary the decomposition from 2^d blocks at each level to just 2 blocks at each level.

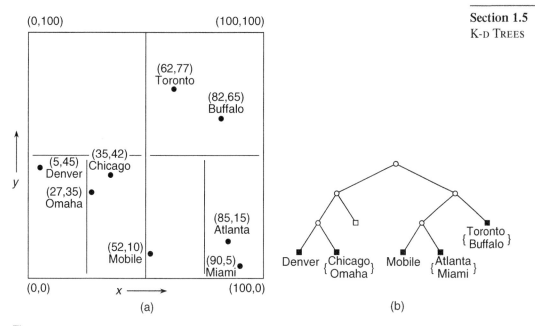

Figure 1.51
A bucket PR k-d tree and the records it represents corresponding to the data of Figure 1.1 for bucket size 2: (a) the resulting partition of space and (b) the tree representation.

capacity that we term a *splitting threshold*. Given a splitting threshold b, we say that if a block c contains more than b points, then it is split *once*, and only once. This is so even if one of the resulting blocks f still has more than b points. If, during the insertion of another point p, we find that p belongs in f, then f is split once, and only once. The idea is to avoid many splits when more than b points are clustered, and there are no other points in the neighborhood. The PMR k-d tree makes use of a cyclic partitioning.

On the other hand, a point is deleted from a PMR k-d tree by removing it from the node corresponding to the block that contains it. During this process, the occupancy of the node and its siblings is checked to see if the deletion causes the total number of points in them to be fewer than the predetermined splitting threshold. If the splitting threshold exceeds the occupancy of the node and its siblings, then they are merged, and the merging process is reapplied to the resulting node and its siblings. Notice the asymmetry between the splitting and merging rules. Also, observe that, unlike the bucket PR k-d tree, the shape of the PMR k-d tree does depend on the order in which the points were inserted.

Exercises

1. Let the size of a data item be bounded by h (i.e., the maximum total number of bits in the k keys), and let the bucket capacity be c. Suppose that a bucket in a bucket PR k-d tree overflows. Assuming that each bit has an equal probability of being 0 or 1, find the expected number of bits that must be tested to resolve the overflow.

2. Write a pair of procedures PMRKDINSERT and PMRKDDELETE to insert and delete, respectively, data points in a PMR k-d tree.

1.5.2.4 Path-Compressed PR K-d Tree

In this section, as well as the next section (i.e., Section 1.5.2.5), we use techniques similar to those used in classical trie-based searching to avoid testing bits of the key value that make no difference in the result (i.e., they do not differentiate between the data items that are present in the dataset).[30] Such a case arises when the key values have a common prefix. The Patricia trie [792, 1315], as used in digital searching [1046, p. 498], is one solution to this problem in the one-dimensional case. It makes use of the binary representation of the key values and replaces a sequence of two-way branches, where one result is always empty by a number that indicates which bit position should be tested next. In essence, we have compressed the sequence of tests. This technique is known as *path compression*. In some applications, knowing the results of the test enables us to reconstruct the values of the data items, which means that the leaf nodes of the tree need to store only the parts of the key values that have not been tested yet. In such a case, instead of storing the number of bits whose testing can be skipped, we often store their actual values. These values are represented by a binary bitstring (i.e., consisting of 1s and 0s) that indicates the values of the bits whose testing was skipped.

The application of path compression to a PR k-d tree involves taking parts of paths that consist of nonleaf nodes, all of whose siblings are empty (i.e., NIL), and compressing them so that all nonleaf nodes that have just one non-NIL child are eliminated. In particular, the nodes on these paths are replaced by one nonleaf node that indicates the results of the comparisons performed in accessing the first node in the path that has more than one non-NIL child. We term the result a *path-compressed PR k-d tree*. Path compression can also be applied to a PR quadtree and other related data structures. For example, Clarkson [396] suggests applying path compression to a multidimensional PR quadtree in one of a number of proposed solutions to the all nearest neighbors problem (i.e., given set A of multidimensional points, find the nearest neighbor in A of each point in A).

Figure 1.52 is the path-compressed PR k-d tree resulting from the application of path compression to the PR k-d tree given in Figure 1.49. Notice that some nonleaf nodes in Figure 1.52(b) are labeled with a variable-length bitstring consisting of 0s and 1s, where 0 and 1 correspond to the test results "<" and "≥," respectively. These bitstrings correspond to the tests that need not be performed (i.e., their corresponding path has been compressed). This information is necessary so that we know which bits to test at deeper levels of the tree.

For example, letting a correspond to the left child of the root of Figure 1.52(b), we have that a is equivalent to the left child of the root of Figure 1.49. Node a is labeled with 0, which indicates that the path from its equivalent in the original PR k-d tree in Figure 1.49 to its left child (i.e., 0) has been compressed by one level, as the right child of the left child of the root is empty in the original PR k-d tree in Figure 1.49. As another example, let b correspond to the right child of the left child of the root of Figure 1.52(b). b is equivalent to c, the right child of the left child of the left child of the root of Figure 1.49. From Figure 1.52(b), we find that b is labeled with 10, which indicates that the path from c (i.e., node b's equivalent in the original PR k-d tree in Figure 1.49) to the left child (i.e., 0) of c's right child (i.e., 1) has been compressed by two levels as both the left child of c and the right child of the right child of c are empty in the original PR k-d tree in Figure 1.49.

Path compression reduces the number of nodes in the tree by removing all empty leaf nodes and the tests that lead to them (represented by nonleaf nodes). This can be seen by examining Figure 1.52(a), which shows the blocks corresponding to the empty leaf nodes as shaded. Thus, given N records, the path-compressed PR k-d tree has N leaf nodes and $N - 1$ nonleaf nodes for a total of $2 \cdot N - 1$ nodes. However, the asymptotic expected average depth is not necessarily reduced. In this respect, the path-compressed PR k-d tree is analogous to the sliding-midpoint k-d tree—that is, they have the same number of nodes (but see Exercise 4). The difference is that, for the most part, the positions of

---

[30] If we are using bucketing, then the tests on the bits of the key values yield the address of a bucket that contains the data items present in the dataset. In the rest of the discussion in this and the remaining subsections, we speak of the actual data items rather than the bucket addresses.

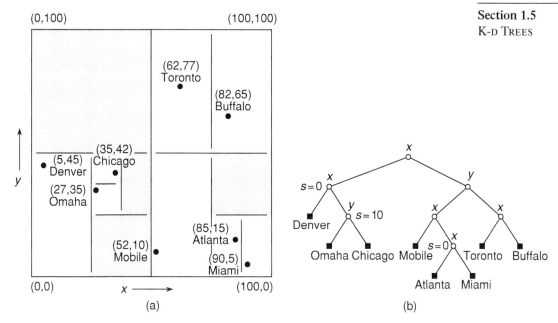

Figure 1.52
A path-compressed PR k-d tree and the records it represents corresponding to the data of Figure 1.1: (a) the resulting partition of space (nonexisting blocks corresponding to empty leaf nodes are shown shaded) and (b) the tree representation.

the partitions in the sliding-midpoint k-d tree are determined by the data rather than by the embedding space from which the data is drawn. Moreover, when a midpoint split is not appropriate in a sliding-midpoint k-d tree (i.e., a trivial split results), then one of the two resulting blocks always contains just one point while the remaining points are in the other block. In contrast, a node split in the path-compressed PR k-d tree can result in both nodes having more than one point. Thus, the path-compressed PR k-d tree is not necessarily as deep as the sliding-midpoint k-d tree (see Exercises 2 and 3).

Exercises

1. Write a pair of procedures PCPRKdInsert and PCPRKdDelete to insert and delete, respectively, data points in a path-compressed PR k-d tree.

2. Give an example where the path-compressed PR k-d tree is shallower than the corresponding sliding-midpoint k-d tree.

3. Is the maximum depth of the sliding-midpoint k-d tree always greater than or equal to that of the path-compressed PR k-d tree? Prove that this claim is true or give a counterexample.

4. Compare the space requirements of the path-compressed PR k-d tree and the sliding-midpoint k-d tree. Make sure to take into account the complexity of the nonleaf nodes.

5. Compare the open-sliding midpoint k-d tree described in Exercise 2 in Section 1.5.2.2 with the path-compressed PR k-d tree. Can you prove that the path-compressed PR k-d tree never has more nodes than the open-sliding midpoint k-d tree or never has a greater maximum depth? If not, give counterexamples for each case.

1.5.2.5 Path-Level Compressed PR K-d Tree

The depth of the path-compressed PR k-d tree can be reduced by applying level compression [51]. Operationally, we start at the root x of the path-compressed PR k-d tree and find the shortest path to a leaf node or a path-compressed node, say y at depth z relative to x, in the path-compressed PR k-d tree. An equivalent statement is that we are finding the largest complete subtree s rooted at x such that no element of s is a leaf or path-compressed node (with the possible exception of x) and compressing it. Now, all descendants of x at depth z are made children of x, which will now have 2^z nonempty children. This process is applied recursively (i.e., in a top-down manner) to the 2^z children of x at all levels. Of course, if $z = 1$, then no action takes place at x, and we reapply the process to the two children of x. The combination of level compression with path compression is termed *path-level compression*, and the result of the application of level compression to a path-compressed PR k-d tree is termed a *path-level compressed PR k-d tree*.

For example, Figure 1.53 is the path-level compressed PR k-d tree resulting from the application of level compression to the path-compressed PR k-d tree given in Figure 1.52. Notice that level compression was not applicable at the root of Figure 1.52(b) since the closest leaf or path-compressed nodes are children of the root. However, level compression was applicable at the right child of the root, say a, since the closest leaf or path-compressed nodes to a are at a depth of 2 relative to a.

Interestingly, path-level compression can be viewed as a single operation rather than treating path and level compression separately. In particular, if path compression can be applied over z levels, then path-level compression over z levels will result in two children. Furthermore, if perfect level compression can be applied over z levels (i.e., there are no leaf nodes, empty or not, at depth 1 through $z - 1$, and there are no empty leaf nodes at depth z), then path-level compression over z levels results in 2^z children. z is the maximum amount of level compression if all leaf nodes at depth z are nonempty, or there is at least one empty leaf node at depth $z + 1$. Our uniform treatment of path and level compression proceeds as follows. Starting at nonleaf node x, find the maximum depth w such that x has two sibling descendants at this and all shallower depths, where one of the descendants is a nonleaf node while the other sibling descendant is an empty leaf node. Let y be the nonleaf node descendant of x at depth w, and let z be the length of the shortest path from y to a nonempty leaf node descendant or 1 less than the length of the shortest path from y to an empty leaf node descendant, whichever is smaller. Path-level compression over $w + z$ levels results in node x having 2^z children corresponding to the 2^z descendants of y at depth z. x is also labeled with a sequence of 1s and 0s corresponding to the path from x to y. Note that if $w + z = 1$, then no path-level compression is performed.

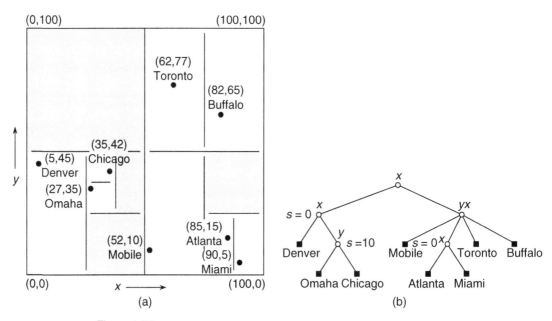

Figure 1.53

A path-level compressed PR k-d tree and the records it represents corresponding to the data of Figure 1.1: (a) the resulting partition of space (nonexisting blocks corresponding to empty leaf nodes are shown shaded) and (b) the tree representation.

Our definition of the path-level compressed PR k-d tree is static in the sense that the path and level compression is performed once we have all of the data. This is fine if the data does not change too often. Updates may involve a considerable restructuring of the tree. This poses a problem in real-time applications where reduction in the search length is one of the main reasons for the use of path-level compression. Thus, the data structure must also be capable of being updated dynamically. It is clear that the insertion and deletion of a point may cause both path and level compression and decompression to take place. Path compression and decompression by themselves are fairly simple as they are local in nature and do not involve changing too many nodes. On the other hand, path compression and decompression in conjunction with level compression may result in the need for level compression and decompression, which is more costly.

Nilsson and Tikkanen [1379] describe a dynamic way of building the path-level compressed PR k-d tree that takes into account level compression by relaxing the formal requirements of when level compression and decompression must take place, thereby defining a dynamic variant of the data structure. Recall that in the formal definition of the path-level compressed PR k-d tree, a node of size 2^z has exactly 2^z nonempty children. In the dynamic variant of the data structure, some of the children of a node are allowed to be empty in order to reduce the frequency of level reorganizations that need to be performed in order to maintain the property that the shortest path to a leaf or path-compressed node in the path-level compressed PR k-d tree is of length z. Otherwise, the alternating action of deletion and insertion of nodes at the same level can cause repeated reorganizations.

It should be clear that level decompression (i.e., contraction or halving of the size of a nonleaf node in the path-level compressed PR k-d tree) should take place as soon as one of the children of a nonleaf node in the path-level compressed PR k-d tree becomes empty. This is equivalent to saying that the decompression should occur as soon as the shortest path from a nonleaf node to a leaf or path-compressed node in a path-compressed PR k-d tree decreases (say from z to $z - 1$). Taking such an action in the path-level compressed PR k-d tree would result in much data movement, especially if nodes are deleted and inserted from the same level in alternating order. This situation is avoided by using a decompression threshold, say *low*, which sets a lower bound on the fraction of children that must be nonempty (equivalently, an upper bound on the fraction of children that can be empty). Thus, level decompression occurs only when the ratio of nonempty children to the total number of children of a node is less than *low*.

A similar principle is applied to level compression in the sense that it is performed in an anticipatory manner using a compression threshold, say *high*. Thus, given a nonleaf node x with 2^z children in a path-level compressed PR k-d tree, instead of waiting for the situation that both of the 2^z children of x are leaf or path-compressed nodes in the original path-compressed PR k-d tree, we perform level compression as soon as more than $high \cdot 2^{z+1}$ of the grandchildren of x correspond to leaf or path-compressed nodes in a path-compressed PR k-d tree. Nilsson and Tikkanen [1379] found that values of 0.25 for *low* and 0.5 for *high* give good performance.

Exercises

1. Write a pair of procedures PLCPRKDINSERT and PLCPRKDDELETE to insert and delete, respectively, data points in a path-level compressed PR k-d tree.

2. Implement the dynamic variant of the path-level compressed PR k-d tree.

1.5.2.6 BD-Trees

The path-compressed PR k-d tree and the path-level compressed PR k-d tree (with perfect level compression) are unique. The price of this uniqueness is that these trees are not always balanced. In this section, we describe the BD-tree (denoting Binary Division) devised by Ohsawa and Sakauchi [1386, 1387]. It makes use of what we term *test-concatenation techniques* to test simultaneously bits from several keys, as well as several bits from the same key, in a way that gives us freedom in choosing which data items appear in the left and right subtrees of the tree, thereby enabling the creation of a more balanced, as well as a more general, structure, but one that is not unique. The price of this freedom is that we must associate information with each nonleaf node that indicates which bit positions were tested and the value that each must have for the test to succeed, in which case the link to the left child is descended. Moreover, since the result of the test is binary (i.e., all bits must have the specified values for the test to hold), the test does not induce a partition of the underlying space into two congruent regions of space. In particular, only one of the two regions induced by the result of the test is guaranteed to be a hyperrectangle.

Although Ohsawa and Sakauchi describe the BD-tree as a bucket method for leaf nodes, in our initial discussion and example, we assume a bucket capacity of 1, which, in effect, leads to a structure that is similar to a path-compressed PR k-d tree. Nevertheless, the BD-tree in its full generality can represent a large range of block configurations and shapes, which, in fact, is far greater than that which can be obtained via the application of a PR k-d tree decomposition rule. Use of the PR k-d tree decomposition rule and the assumption of a bucket capacity of 1 means that the BD-tree can be formed in the same way as the path-compressed PR k-d tree—that is, paths in the PR k-d tree (also applicable to the PR quadtree) that consist of nonleaf nodes are compressed so that all nonleaf nodes with just one non-NIL child are eliminated. The compressed nonleaf nodes are replaced by one nonleaf node that indicates the results of the comparisons performed in accessing the first node in the path with more than one non-NIL child.

Even under these assumptions, there are still several important differences between the BD-tree and the path-compressed PR k-d tree. First of all, they differ in the format of the nonleaf nodes in the sense that, unlike the path-compressed PR k-d tree, the nonleaf nodes of the BD-tree contain more information than just the results of the comparisons that were eliminated by path compression. In particular, each nonleaf node a in the BD-tree contains a variable-length bitstring—termed a *discriminator zone expression* (DZE) by Ohsawa and Sakauchi—say s, consisting of 0s and 1s, that indicates the results of a sequence of tests involved in the formation of a PR k-d tree, starting at the root node, that lead to the formation of a region l deemed to be the left child of a.[31] The right child of a is accessed when the test result does not match the DZE of a. In other words, it corresponds to the part of the underlying space that remains if we do not descend to the left child of a. Thus, the right child actually corresponds to a region r that is not necessarily a hyperrectangle. This is the second important difference from the path-compressed PR k-d tree. In particular, like l, r corresponds to a bucket or set of buckets, and, in fact, in the BD-tree, the points may lie anywhere in r. In contrast, when the BD-tree is formed in the same way as a path-compressed PR k-d tree, r is also a hyperrectangle corresponding to the minimum enclosing block for the remaining points in a (i.e., not spanned by l) that can be generated by application of a PR k-d tree decomposition rule. Moreover, in this case, the right child of a is accessed by complementing the last binary digit of s. We say that 0 and 1 correspond to "<" and "≥," respectively.

Figure 1.54 shows how a BD-tree is constructed in an incremental fashion for the data of Figure 1.1—that is, Chicago, Mobile, Toronto, Buffalo, Denver, Omaha, Atlanta, and Miami are inserted in this order using a process that mimics the path-compressed PR k-d tree. All nonleaf nodes are labeled with their DZEs, assuming a sequence of alternating $x, y, x, y, \ldots$ tests, starting at the left end of the DZE. For example, in Figure 1.54(b), the root has a DZE of 0, which means that the left child corresponds to $x < 50$ (i.e., the left half of the space spanned by the quadtree). As a more complicated example, the left child of the root in Figure 1.54(e) has a DZE of 000, which means that the left child of the left child of the root corresponds to $x < 25$ and $y < 50$.

---

[31] We will see below in our more general definition of the BD-tree that the left child of a is sometimes a subset of l. More precisely, the left child of a is the intersection of the regions formed by a and l.

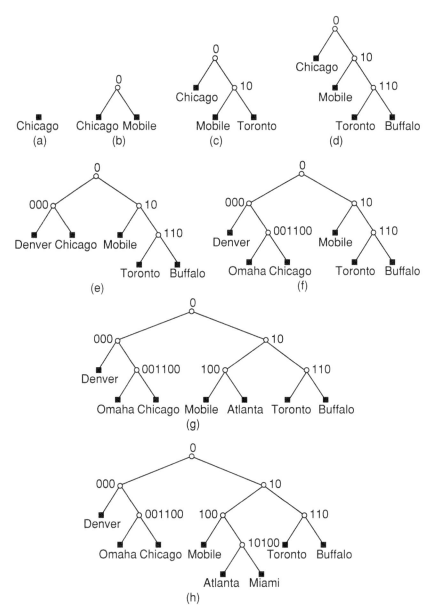

Figure 1.54
Sequence of partial BD-trees demonstrating the addition of (a) Chicago, (b) Mobile, (c) Toronto, (d) Buffalo, (e) Denver, (f) Omaha, (g) Atlanta, and (h) Miami, corresponding to the data of Figure 1.1.

Dandamudi and Sorenson [441] give a more precise and general definition of the BD-tree. They stipulate that if a node a represents a subset x of the space and is labeled with DZE s, then the left child of a corresponds to the region formed by the intersection of x and the space represented by s, while the right child of a corresponds to the region formed by the intersection of x and the complement of the space represented by s. Thus, unlike the case where the BD-tree and the path-compressed PR k-d tree were identical, we immediately see that the left child of a is not necessarily the same as the DZE s associated with a (e.g., block a in Figure 1.55(a) is a subset of the DZE 01). It is clear that using this more general definition means that there are many ways of forming a BD-tree since each region can be specified as the result of the intersection of more than one pair of regions. Thus, the BD-tree is not unique. In fact, rotation operations can be applied to reformulate the tests in the nonleaf nodes so that a greater degree of balancing is achieved. Such transformations are easy to express in terms of the DZEs [1387] and are

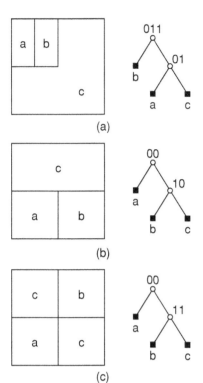

Figure 1.55
(a) Example of a BD-tree with shorter DZEs at deeper levels in the tree. (b, c) Examples of a BD-tree and the corresponding decomposition of the underlying space that cannot be generated by a PR k-d tree splitting rule that cycles through the x and y coordinates in this order. In this example node c corresponds to a merge of (b) two nonsibling adjacent blocks and (c) two noncontiguous blocks.

often the same as the rotation operations used to preserve balance in conventional binary search trees (e.g., AVL trees [15]). Moreover, there are no restrictions on the DZEs that are used to label nodes, and, in fact, the same DZE s can be used to label more than one node since the region corresponding to the left child of a is the intersection of the space spanned by a and s, and different values of a will lead to different results unless the result is empty, in which case we have a meaningless test at a.

It should be clear that this labeling scheme includes the one that we used earlier in the analogy with the path-compressed PR k-d tree, as well as permits the generation of blocks that need not be hyperrectangles (e.g., block c in Figure 1.55(a)). It has a number of interesting features. First of all, the intersection operation enables the use of shorter DZEs at deeper levels in the tree (e.g., DZE 01 leading to block a in Figure 1.55(a)). Second, it permits the specification of block configurations that correspond to a decomposition of the underlying space that could not be generated by a PR k-d tree decomposition rule, even though all blocks are hyperrectangles (e.g., block c in Figure 1.55(b), which is the result of merging nonsibling adjacent blocks, assuming a decomposition based on alternating $x, y, x, y, \ldots$ tests starting at the left). Moreover, it permits the specification of block configurations where a node corresponds to two noncontiguous blocks (e.g., the node corresponding to block c in Figure 1.55(c)).

It is important to point out again that, unlike the variants of the PR k-d tree that we discussed (i.e., bucket, bucket PMR, path-compressed, and path-level compressed), the BD-tree does not result in the partitioning of the underlying space into a collection of hyperrectangles. In particular, the BD-tree always results in the decomposition of a region into two regions, only one of which is guaranteed to be a hyperrectangle. In this respect, the decomposition of the underlying space induced by the BD-tree is closely related to the BBD-tree [100] (see Section 1.5.2.7 for more details), the BANG file [640], and, to a lesser extent, the hB-tree [1201, 1613] and the BV-tree [643] as they do not require the use of regular decomposition (see Section 1.7.1 for more detail about these two structures). One of the differences between the BD-tree and BBD-tree is that, in the BBD-tree, the region that is not a hyperrectangle is the set difference of two hyperrectangles, while this is not necessarily the case for the BD-tree (see Section 1.5.2.7 for more on the differences between the BD-tree and the BBD-tree). Thus, the set of possible block configurations is greater for the BD-tree than the BBD-tree. We also observe that the DZE associated with node a indicates only which bit combinations of the key values should be tested in order to separate the data in the subtree rooted at a. However, it should be clear that they are not the only bits that are tested when deciding which child of a to descend as we are using the results of the tests to specify a region that is then intersected with the region corresponding to a, which may involve testing more bits. Interestingly, although the DZE has a similar format to the bitstring used in the path-compressed and path-level compressed PR k-d trees, there is really no compression taking place in the BD-tree as the DZE is only used to identify the block via the identity and values of the combinations of bits of keys when the tests are conducted starting at the root node.

It should be clear that the BD-tree can be used for data of arbitrary dimensionality. Dandamudi and Sorenson [441, 443] provide more details on how to implement basic operations on BD-trees such as insertion and deletion, as well as answer exact match, partial range, and range queries. For an empirical performance comparison of the BD-tree with some variations of the k-d tree, see Dandamudi and Sorenson [440, 442].

The or Generalized BD-tree (GBD-tree) [1388] extends the BD-tree by bucketing the nonleaf nodes as well as the leaf nodes. In particular, the number of DZEs in each nonleaf node is one less than the number of children. To accomplish traversal of the structure, the DZEs are sorted in ascending order within a node, with longer strings coming first. Search is performed by traversing the sorted list of DZEs and following the link associated with the first matching DZE (i.e., whose corresponding block contains the query point or object). In addition, each nonleaf node p contains the minimum bounding rectangles that span all of the minimum bounding rectangles associated with the children of p.

1. Write a procedure to insert a point into a two-dimensional BD-tree.

2. Write a procedure to delete a point from a two-dimensional BD-tree.

3. Write a procedure to perform a point search in a two-dimensional BD-tree.

4. Write a procedure to perform a range search for a rectangular region in a two-dimensional BD-tree.

5. Implement a BD-tree with a bucket capacity of c. In particular, write procedures to insert and delete nodes from it. The key issue is how to handle bucket overflow and underflow. Try to use techniques analogous to those used for B-trees, such as rotation of elements between adjacent buckets that are not completely full.

1.5.2.7 Balanced Box-Decomposition Tree (BBD-Tree)

The *balanced box-decomposition tree* (BBD-tree) [100] is closely related to the BD-tree. It differs, in part, from the BD-tree by the shapes of the underlying regions and also by always having a logarithmic depth that comes at the cost of a more complex index construction procedure. Thus, for N records, its height is always $O(\log N)$. The BBD-tree need not be used with bucketing, although satisfaction of the balance criterion assures that, starting with a region containing m points, after descent by a constant number of levels in the tree (at most 4, as can be seen in Exercise 1), the number of points contained within each of the subregions will be no greater than $2m/3$ (see Exercise 2).[32] If this condition is not satisfied, then the offending region is split again. Unlike the BD-tree, each of the regions corresponding to a node has the shape of either a hyperrectangle or the set-theoretic difference of two hyperrectangles, one enclosed within the other. This shape condition also ensures that each of the regions is "fat"—in other words, each of the regions has an aspect ratio[33] less than some fixed constant. Clearly, using the Chessboard distance metric L_∞, this ratio is at most 2 for any k-d trie, such as a PR k-d tree.

The BBD-tree is constructed as follows for a set of N points. First, a bounding hypercube that contains all these points is computed. This hypercube is the region associated with the root of the tree. The construction proceeds by recursively subdividing each region into smaller subregions and distributing the points among these regions. The points are distributed through two operations termed *split* and *shrink*. They correspond to two different ways of subdividing a region, and thus they are represented by two different types of nodes in the tree. A split partitions a region by a hyperplane that is parallel to the hyperplanes formed by one of the coordinate axes. A shrink partitions a region by a box (termed a *partitioning box*) that lies within the original region. It partitions a region into two children, one lying inside the partitioning box (termed the *inner box*) and one lying outside of it (termed the *outer box*). Figure 1.56(a) is an example of a split operation, and Figure 1.56(b) is an example of a shrink operation. If a split is performed on a region that contains an inner box, then the splitting hyperplane cannot intersect the interior of this box. If a shrink is performed on a region that has an inner box, then this inner box will lie entirely inside the partitioning box.

The BBD-tree construction algorithm is given a region and a subset of the points associated with this region. Each stage of the algorithm determines how to subdivide the current region, through the use of either a split or a shrink operation, and then distributes the points among the child nodes. We will see that the split and shrink operations each achieve a different and desirable goal. A split operation is guaranteed to decrease the geometric size of the child regions by virtue of the way in which the inner and outer

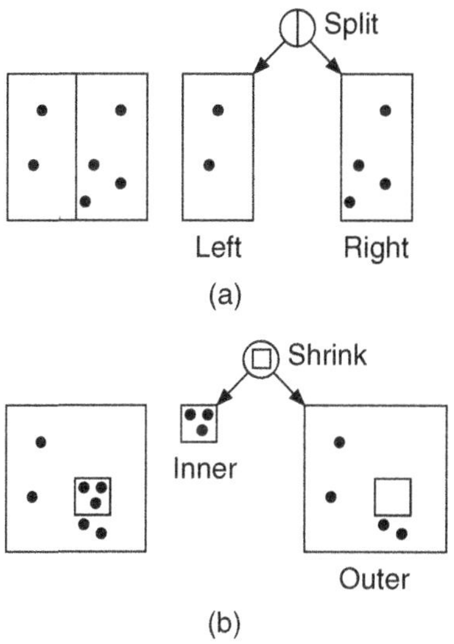

Figure 1.56
Example of (a) split and (b) shrink operations.

---

[32] Recall footnote 28 in this chapter.

[33] Recall from Section 1.5.1.4 that, using an appropriate distance metric, the aspect ratio of a cell is the radius of the smallest sphere that encloses the region to the radius of the largest sphere that is enclosed within the region.

Chapter 1
MULTIDIMENSIONAL POINT DATA

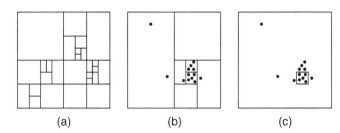

(a)   (b)   (c)

Figure 1.57
Examples of (a) midpoint split, (b) trial midpoint split, and (c) centroid shrink operations.

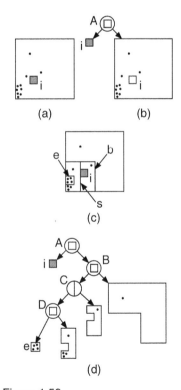

Figure 1.58
Centroid shrink with an inner box where the inner box i is separated from the region containing more than $2m/3$ of the remaining points: (a) initial situation, (b) the corresponding BBD-tree, (c) the first midpoint split s that separates i from the region containing more than $2m/3$ of the remaining points, and (d) the final BBD-tree.

boxes are chosen (but after a shrink operation, only the inner child is smaller). A shrink operation is guaranteed to decrease, by a constant factor, the number of points in each of the child regions (although this may not necessarily occur as a result of a split operation unless the points are uniformly distributed), and this implies that the tree has logarithmic depth. However, a shrink operation is much more complex than a split operation. The simplest strategy is to apply split and shrink operations at alternate levels of the tree. A more practical approach is always to split (since it is a simpler operation) and to resort to shrinking only when needed to maintain logarithmic depth. This process is repeated until a region is obtained with at most one point (or at most as many points as the bucket capacity in case of the use of bucketing), after which a leaf node is generated.

A split operation is performed by a hyperplane that passes through the center of the cell and is orthogonal to its longest side (with ties broken arbitrarily). The operation is termed a *midpoint split*. If only midpoint split operations are performed, then the resulting structure is a PR k-d tree (see Figure 1.57(a)) and the regions are termed *midpoint boxes*. It is easy to see that each of the midpoint boxes will have bounded aspect ratios as the ratio of the longest to shortest side is at most 2.

A shrink is performed as part of a global operation, termed a *centroid shrink*, which will generally produce up to three new nodes in the tree (two shrink nodes and one split node). Let m denote the number of data points associated with the current region. Note that if the region being shrunk is an outer box of a shrink node, then m does not include the points lying within the corresponding inner box. The goal of a centroid shrink is to decompose this region into a constant number of fat subregions, each containing at most $2m/3$ points.

The centroid shrink operation has two cases, depending on whether the current region has an inner box. We first consider the case in which the current region does not contain an inner box. A series of *trial midpoint split* operations is applied to the region (without altering the tree's structure). In each case, the recursion is applied only to the child having the greater number of points (see Figure 1.57(b)). This is repeated until the number of points in the current region is no more than $2m/3$. The inner box associated with this region serves as the partitioning box for the shrink operation, and thus the intermediate trial midpoint split operations are ignored. Observe that, just prior to the last split, there were at least $2m/3$ data points, and since the recursion is applied to the subregion with the larger number of data points, the partitioning box contains at least $m/3$ points. Thus, there are at most $2m/3$ points either inside or outside the partitioning box (see Figure 1.57(c)).

We now consider the case in which the current region contains an inner box (see Figure 1.58(a) and the corresponding tree in Figure 1.58(b), where A corresponds to the shrink node and i is the inner box). In this case, the repeated application of the above procedure might create a region with two inner boxes, which is prohibited by our definition of a region. This situation is remedied by use of a decomposition process that has at most three stages corresponding to a shrink, a split, and a shrink operation, in that order. Recall that i is the current inner box. Perform the trial-splitting process as in the case described above, where the current region did not contain an inner box, until one of the following two situations arises:

84

1. The first split **s** of the current region occurs that separates i from the region that contains more than $2m/3$ of the remaining points (i.e., splits the region containing i from the region containing more than $2m/3$ of the remaining points). Let **b** denote the region that was just split (see Figure 1.58(c)). Now, create a shrink node **B** whose partitioning box is b, and make node **B** the child corresponding to the outer box of **A**. Next, create a split node **C** corresponding to the split **s** that separates the majority of the points from i, and make **C** the child corresponding to the inner box of **B**. Now that the inner box i has been eliminated, we simply continue with the procedure described above for the case in which the current region does not contain an inner box, where a new shrink node **D** has been created with a partitioning box e (see Figure 1.58(d)).

2. The current region contains i and has no more than $2m/3$ of the points (where m does not include the points in i). Therefore, i is nested within the partitioning box, which is fine. Let **b** denote the current region (see Figure 1.59(c)). Now, create a shrink node **B** whose partitioning box is b, and make node **B** the child corresponding to the outer box of **A**.

As a more complex example, consider Figure 1.60, which has 21 points. We start with a set of trial midpoint splits, always recursing on the side having more points (see Figure 1.60(a)). The first centroid shrink is obtained when we encounter a cell that contains 14 points, which is $2m/3$ (see Figure 1.60(b) and the corresponding tree in

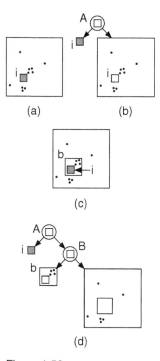

(a)   (b)

(c)

(d)

Figure 1.59
Centroid shrink with an inner box where the inner box i is not separated from the region containing more than $2m/3$ of the points. (a) Initial situation, (b) the corresponding BBD-tree, (c) the first midpoint split where neither of the regions contains more than $2m/3$ of the points and one of the resulting regions *b* contains i, and (d) the final BBD-tree.

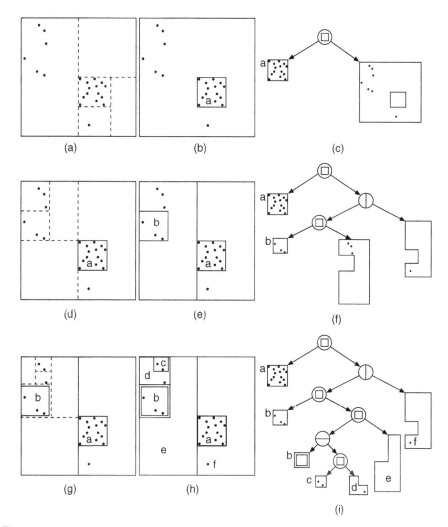

(a)   (b)   (c)

(d)   (e)   (f)

(g)   (h)

(i)

Figure 1.60
Complex example of the construction of a BBD-tree for a set of 21 points: (a), (d), and (g) denote trial midpoint splits with (b), (e), and (h) denoting their corresponding centroid shrinks, with corresponding trees in (c), (f), and (i).

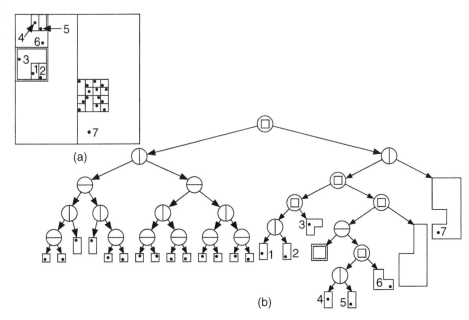

Figure 1.61
(a) Final decomposition and (b) its corresponding BBD-tree for the complex example in Figure 1.60.

Figure 1.60(c)). This cell, labeled a in Figure 1.60(b), corresponds to the inner box that will be subsequently decomposed further, but this is easy because we will need only midpoint splits (see Figure 1.61) when using the more practical approach to the construction of a BBD-tree discussed earlier.

Next, we decompose the outer box, which contains the remaining seven points. Again, we perform trial midpoint splits until producing a cell that contains three points (see Figure 1.60(d)). We could use either the cell in the upper left or the one immediately below as the inner box to complete the centroid shrink operation. We use the one immediately below (i.e., the one labeled b in Figure 1.60(e)). We cannot apply a shrink operation immediately at this point since this would produce a cell having two inner boxes. Therefore, we introduce the center vertical split to separate these two inner boxes. On the left side of this split, we apply a shrink operation (see Figure 1.60(e), whose corresponding tree is given in Figure 1.60(f)). Note that, in this case, we applied only a midpoint split and shrink operation as there was no need for an initial shrink operation to yield a centroid shrink.

At this point, we want to decompose the region that lies to the left of the vertical split and outside the inner box labeled b in Figure 1.60(g). There are a total of three points. We perform trial midpoint splits until we succeed in separating two points from the third (see the upper left of Figure 1.60(g)). This is the inner box labeled c in Figure 1.60(h). However, again, we cannot apply a shrink at this point as we need to separate inner box b from inner box c in Figure 1.60(h). To do this, we perform a shrink to surround these two boxes, then separate them with a horizontal line via a midpoint split and conclude by applying a shrink to the desired box c (see Figure 1.60(h), whose corresponding tree is given in Figure 1.60(i)). Notice that the tree in Figure 1.60(i) has two nodes labeled b. The one at the shallower level corresponds to an inner box, and the one at the deeper level corresponds to an outer box that is empty as the inner box completely fills the cell.

Finally, we need to decompose the regions a, b, and c, although we do not explain it here (see Figure 1.61(a) and the corresponding tree in Figure 1.61(b)). Notice that in the decomposition of region a, shrinking was not necessary, and thus we used repeated split operations as in the more practical approach for the construction of the BBD-tree discussed earlier.

The fact that centroid shrink operations are performed at every other level of the BBD-tree implies that the total number of nodes in the tree is $O(N)$ and that the BBD-tree has $O(\log N)$ height. It is easy to verify that every region has a bounded aspect ratio (because the inner boxes are a result of repeated midpoint split operations, which produce regions with an aspect ratio of at most 2) and that each leaf of the BBD-tree contains only a constant number of points. The use of midpoint splits guarantees that the partitioning hyperplanes do not intersect the interior of inner boxes.

Since the height of the BBD-tree is $O(\log N)$, and as at each level we must examine the N points for distribution into the appropriate children, the BBD-tree can be constructed in $O(dN \log N)$ time [100]. A direct implementation of the BBD-tree construction procedure given above is not efficient, however, because if the points in a cell are densely clustered in a very small region, then the number of midpoint splits needed to find the partitioning box cannot generally be bounded by a function of m. In particular, the number of necessary midpoint split operations depends on the minimum separation between the points. One way to remedy this problem is to compute the smallest midpoint box t that contains the data points prior to each split [396]. This remedy works because once t has been computed, the very next midpoint split operations will achieve a nontrivial partition of the points. Another implementation issue is how to partition the points after each split efficiently (see, e.g., [1908]).

As we pointed out before, it should be clear that the BBD-tree is somewhat similar to the BD-tree. Nevertheless, there are some differences. In particular, recall that one of the main differences is that the decomposition of space induced by a node in the BBD-tree is guaranteed to be either two hyperrectangles, or a hyperrectangle and the set difference of two hyperrectangles, while in the BD-tree the second region can be of arbitrary complexity. This increase in the complexity of the regions in the BD-tree makes it difficult to compute distances to the region, thereby complicating processes (such as nearest neighbor finding) that attempt to prune some regions from consideration.

Another difference between the BD-tree and the BBD-tree is that one usually knows all of the data points before building the BBD-tree (i.e., it is static using our characterizations), and the resulting height is always logarithmic, while the BD-tree is built one point at a time as the data points are encountered, and the attainability of the height bound is dependent on the number of rotations that are applied. However, see [207] for a variant of the BBD-tree that supports dynamic insertion and deletion.

Finally, the motivation for the BBD-tree is to support finding nearest neighbors efficiently by sometimes resorting to returning the approximate nearest neighbor (thereby looking at a predictable fraction of the data points rather than possibly having to look at all of the points in the worst case), which enables the attainment of an execution time bound that is inversely proportional to the approximation error tolerance ε [100] (see Section 4.3 of Chapter 4). The BBD-tree is used to support this purpose in the ANN library for approximate nearest neighbor searching [1319]. In contrast, the motivation for the BD-tree is to support good dynamic behavior as well as efficient exact match and partial range queries.

Exercises

1. Suppose that split and shrink operations are applied at alternate levels of the BBD-tree. Show that, starting with a region containing m points, the number of points contained within each of the subregions will be no greater than $2m/3$ after descent by at most four levels in the tree.

2. Consider a BBD-tree cell that has no inner box and contains b points. It was argued earlier that there exists a shrink operation that partitions this cell into an inner and outer box, each having no more than $2b/3$ points. Assuming that shrinks are based on midpoint splits, is it possible to prove that for any x, where $1/2 < x < 1$, there exists a shrink operation so that neither box has more than $b \cdot x$ points?

1.5.3 Conjugation Tree

The conjugation tree of Edelsbrunner and Welzl [546] (also termed the *Ham-Sandwich tree* [540]) is an interesting combination of a pseudo quadtree [1444] (Section 1.4.1.2), a pseudo k-d tree (Section 1.5.1.4), and a BSP tree [658] (Section 1.5.1.4) for points in the two-dimensional plane, while not being an instance of either of the structures. The motivation of the conjugation tree is to obtain a balanced structure where each quadrant contains approximately the same number of points.

The conjugation tree is formed as follows. Find a line L that bisects S into three subsets $S_{left}(L)$, $S_{right}(L)$, and $S_{on}(L)$, which correspond to the points that are to the left of, to the right of, and on L, respectively. Moreover, the size of each of the subsets $S_{left}(L)$ and $S_{right}(L)$ is bounded by $N/2$. If N is odd, then $S_{on}(L)$ cannot be empty, and in this case the bisecting line is unique if its direction is given. Next, find another line L', termed the *conjugate* of L, which simultaneously splits each of the point sets evenly (i.e., bisects them). Willard [2000] has shown that such a line is guaranteed to exist (also known as the *Ham-Sandwich Theorem*).[34] Once L' has been found, the same process is applied to find a conjugate for L', and so on. Each node in the conjugation tree contains the partitioning line segment L, pointers to the two subtrees, the number of points in the two subtrees, and the identity of the points that lie on L. The process halts when no points are left—that is, all points lie on some line, and thus $S_{left}(i)$ and $S_{right}(i)$ are empty for all lines i.

For example, Figure 1.62(a) is an example of the partition of the underlying space induced by a conjugation tree for the set of points given in Figure 1.1, augmented by eight additional points, P1–P8; Figure 1.62(b) shows the resulting tree, with the interior nodes labeled with the name of the partitioning line that caused its creation. It should be clear that the conjugation tree is a variant of a balanced pseudo quadtree and k-d tree, as well as a BSP tree. We use the characterization "pseudo" since the data is usually stored in the leaf nodes unless the partitioning lines coincide with some points. The structure is more like a BSP tree since the partitioning lines need not be axis-parallel; nor must they be orthogonal. The structure is neither a point quadtree nor a k-d tree since the partitions of the point sets that are induced by the conjugate lines are not carried out independently. In contrast, recall that in a point quadtree (k-d tree) each quadrant (half) is partitioned in a manner that is independent of its siblings, whereas this is not the case in the conjugation tree.

The conjugation tree is used by Edelsbrunner and Welzl to solve the halfplanar range search problem, which simply counts the number of points in a halfspace in $O(N^{0.695})$ time and $O(N)$ space (see Exercise 1). It is interesting to observe that the halfplanar range search problem is related to the point dominance problem that can be used to find the number of points in a hyperrectangular search region using an ECDF tree [180] (see Exercise 14 in Section 1.1). The conjugation tree can also be used to solve the line search problem that returns the number of points that lie on a given line segment. In this case, there is no need to keep track of the number of points in each subtree.

Exercises

1. Edelsbrunner and Welzl [543] use the following algorithm to perform a halfplanar range search (i.e., determine the number of points c) in a halfspace h in two-dimensional space. Let g denote the line that bounds h. Let $range(v)$ be the range of the space spanned by a node v, and let $int(v)$ be the intersection of g and $range(v)$. Initialize c, the count of the number of points in h,

---

[34] This theorem is really a discrete version of the Borsuk-Ulam Theorem [235, 540]. It is termed the *Ham-Sandwich Theorem* because of the analogy to the result of slicing a sandwich of ham so that there are two parts of equal amounts of bread and ham [540].

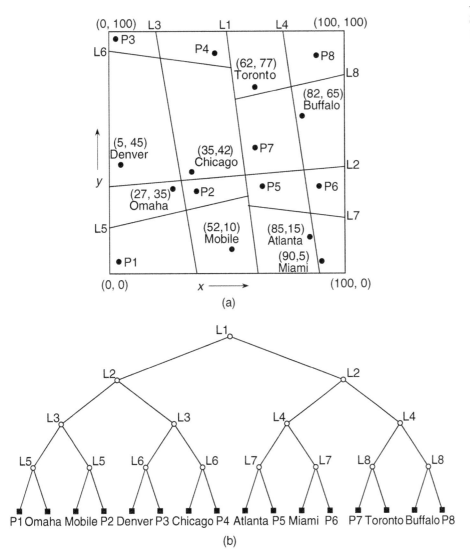

Figure 1.62
A conjugation tree and the records it represents corresponding to the data of Figure 1.1 augmented by eight additional points, P1–P8: (a) the resulting partition of space and (b) the tree representation with the interior nodes labeled with the name of the partitioning line that caused its creation.

to 0. Perform a search starting at the root, and at each node v, check the value of $int(v)$. There are two cases. If $int(v)$ is empty, then $range(v)$ is either contained in h, or its intersection with h is empty. In the former case, all points in the subtrees of v are in h, and c is incremented accordingly. In the latter case, no action is taken. If $int(v)$ is nonempty, then c is increased by the number of points in $S_{on}(v)$ that belong to h, and the two children are visited recursively, if they exist. Prove that this algorithm can be executed in $O(N^{0.695})$ time.

2. The conjugation tree is used to obtain a balanced structure in two dimensions, where each quadrant contains approximately the same number of points. This is achieved by appealing to the Ham-Sandwich Theorem, which guarantees the existence of a line in two dimensions that splits two point sets evenly. In d dimensions, the same theorem means that there exists a D-dimensional hyperplane h that simultaneously bisects d point sets $P_1, P_2, \ldots, P_d$. h is called a *Ham-Sandwich cut*. How can you obtain similar results in three dimensions and higher? In particular, can you construct an analog of the conjugation tree that would be balanced in a similar manner?

1.6 One-Dimensional Orderings

When point data is not uniformly distributed over the space from which it is drawn, then using the fixed-grid representation means that some of the grid cells have too much data associated with them. The result is that the grid must be refined by further partitions. Unfortunately, this leads to the creation of many empty grid cells, thereby wasting space. In Sections 1.4 and 1.5 we described how to eliminate some of the empty cells by aggregating spatially adjacent empty grid cells to form larger empty grid cells. However, not all spatially adjacent empty grid cells can be aggregated in this manner as the identities of the ones that can be aggregated are a function of the specific tree-based space decomposition process that was applied to generate them. In particular, recall that both the quadtree and the k-d tree are the result of a recursive decomposition process, and thus only empty grid cells that have the same parent can be aggregated.

In this section, we describe how to eliminate all empty grid cells by ordering all the grid cells (regardless of whether they are empty) and then imposing a tree access structure such as a balanced binary search tree, B-tree, and so forth, on the elements of the ordering that correspond to nonempty grid cells. The ordering is really a mapping from the d-dimensional space from which the data is drawn to one dimension. The mapping that is chosen should be invertible. This means that given the position of a grid cell in the ordering, it should be easy to determine its location. When the grid cells are not equal-sized but still result from a fixed grid, then we must also record the size of the nonempty grid cells.

There are many possible orderings with different properties (see Figure 2.5 and the accompanying discussion in Section 2.1 of Chapter 2). The result of drawing a curve through the various grid cells in the order in which they appear in the ordering is called a *space-filling curve* (e.g., [1603]). In this section, we elaborate further on two orderings: bit interleaving and bit concatenation. When all the attributes are either locational or numeric with identical ranges, then the orderings are applicable to the key values, as well as the locations of the grid cells. On the other hand, when some of the attributes are nonlocational, then the orderings are applicable only to the locations of the grid cells. In the latter case, we still need to make use of an additional mapping from the actual ranges of the nonlocational attribute values to the locations of the grid cells. We do not discuss this issue further here.

Bit interleaving consists of taking the bit representations of the values of the keys making up a record and forming a *code* consisting of alternating bits from each key value. For example, for $d = 2$, the code corresponding to data point $A = (X, Y) = (x_m x_{m-1} \ldots x_0, y_m y_{m-1} \ldots y_0)$ is $y_m x_m y_{m-1} x_{m-1} \ldots y_0 x_0$, where we arbitrarily deem key y to be the most significant. Figure 1.63 is an example of the bit interleaving mapping when $d = 2$. We have also labeled the codes corresponding to the cities of the example point set of Figure 1.1, which correspond to bit interleaving the result of applying the mapping f defined by $f(x) = x \div 12.5$ and $f(y) = y \div 12.5$ to the values of the x and y keys, respectively. Recall that the same mapping was used to obtain the MX quadtree of Figure 1.29. The drawback of using bit interleaving is the fact that it is not performed efficiently on general computers. Its complexity depends on the total number of bits in the keys. Thus, in d dimensions, when the maximum depth is n, the work required is proportional to $d \cdot n$.

Bit concatenation consists of concatenating the key values (e.g., for data point A, the concatenated code would be $y_m y_{m-1} \ldots y_0 x_m x_{m-1} \ldots x_0$). Bit concatenation is the same as row order or column order (depending on whether the y coordinate value or x coordinate value, respectively, is deemed the most significant). It is a classical ordering for storing images and is also known as *raster scan* or *scan order*.

Above, we have shown how to apply the orderings to the key values. Applying the orderings to the locations of the grid cells is easy. We simply identify one location in each grid cell c that serves as the representative of c. This location is in the same relative

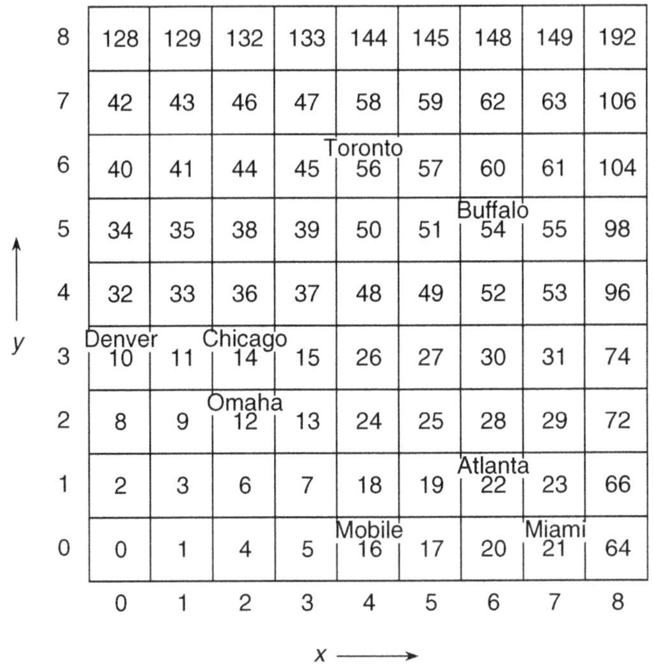

8	128	129	132	133	144	145	148	149	192
7	42	43	46	47	58	59	62	63	106
6	40	41	44	45	Toronto 56	57	60	61	104
5	34	35	38	39	50	51	Buffalo 54	55	98
4	32	33	36	37	48	49	52	53	96
3	Denver 10	11	Chicago 14	15	26	27	30	31	74
2	8	9	Omaha 12	13	24	25	28	29	72
1	2	3	6	7	18	19	Atlanta 22	23	66
0	0	1	4	5	Mobile 16	17	20	Miami 21	64
	0	1	2	3	4	5	6	7	8

y

$x \longrightarrow$

Figure 1.63
Example of the result of applying the bit interleaving mapping to two keys ranging in values from 0 to 8. The city names correspond to the data of Figure 1.1, scaled by a factor of 12.5 to fall in this range.

position in all of the grid cells (e.g., in two dimensions, this could be the location in the lower-left corner of each grid cell). Once the location has been identified, we simply apply the ordering to its corresponding key values. Again, if the grid cells can vary in size, then we must also record their size.

It should be clear that, in light of our interest in range searching, bit interleaving is superior to bit concatenation since the latter results in long, narrow search ranges, whereas the former results in squarer search ranges. This argument leads to the conclusion that bit concatenation is analogous to the inverted list method, while bit interleaving is analogous to the fixed-grid method. In fact, bit concatenation results in the records' being sorted according to a primary key, secondary key, and so on.

Range searching using a tree-based representation of the result of applying a one-dimensional ordering is fairly straightforward. Below, we show how it is performed for a binary search tree by an algorithm proposed by Tropf and Herzog [1891]. We use Figure 1.64, which is the binary search tree corresponding to the key values of Figure 1.1, encoded using bit interleaving as in Figure 1.63. The range is specified by the minimum and maximum codes in the search area. For example, to find all the cities within the rectangular area defined by (25,25), (50,25), (50,63), and (25,63), represented by codes 12, 24, 50, and 38 (see Figure 1.65), respectively, we must examine the codes between 12 and 50. The simplest algorithm is recursive and traverses the binary search tree starting at its root. If the root lies between the minimum and maximum codes in the range, then both subtrees must be examined (e.g., code 21 in Figure 1.64). Otherwise, one subtree needs to be searched (e.g., the left subtree of code 54 in Figure 1.64).

This algorithm is inefficient because many codes lie in the range between the minimum and maximum codes without being within the query rectangle, as illustrated by the two staircases in Figure 1.65. Codes above the upper staircase are greater than the maximum search range code; codes below the lower staircase are less than the minimum search range code. All remaining codes are potential candidates; yet, most are not in the query rectangle.

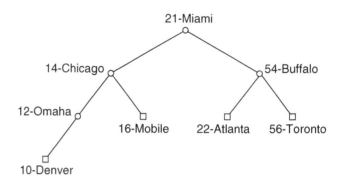

Figure 1.64
A binary search tree corresponding to the data of Figure 1.1, encoded using bit interleaving as in Figure 1.63.

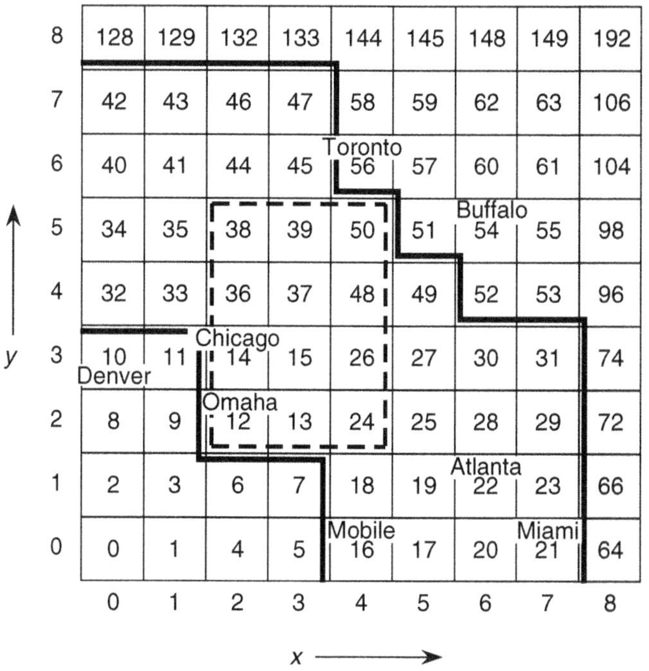

Figure 1.65
Illustration of the range search process when using bit interleaving.

To prune the search range when the root lies within the search range (e.g., code 21 in Figure 1.64), Tropf and Herzog define two codes, termed LITMAX and BIGMIN, which correspond to the maximum code in the left child and the minimum code in the right child, respectively, that are in the query rectangle. The subsequent search of the left child uses LITMAX as the maximum code in the range (e.g., 15 in the left subtree of Figure 1.64), and the search of the right child uses BIGMIN as the minimum code in the range (e.g., 24 in the right subtree of Figure 1.64), with the result that many codes are eliminated from consideration (e.g., codes between 16 and 23 in Figure 1.64) after examination of the root for the query rectangle between 12 and 50.

Experiments reported by Tropf and Herzog [1891] show that, given N records, for small hypercube ranges, the average number of records inspected is $O(d \cdot \log_2 N + F)$, where F is the number of records found. White [1992] shows how to perform the same task when using a B-tree as the underlying representation with the same order of execution time.

As pointed out earlier, the ordering methods that we have described can be applied to any of the representations that make use of a recursive decomposition process to generate a set of grid cells of unequal size. In this case, recall that since the mapping is no longer onto, we also need to record some information to enable us to determine the size of the grid cell. A simple, and different, way to obtain an ordering is to traverse the underlying tree access structure and assign successively higher numbers to the grid cells. The problem with such an approach is that there is no simple correlation between the number that is assigned to the grid cell and its actual location in space (i.e., the mapping is not invertible).

An alternative, and preferable, solution is to assign a unique number to each grid cell c in the resulting space decomposition, based on the path from the root of the access structure to c, and to record some information about the size of the partition that takes place at each level of the tree. In fact, this approach is equivalent to the solution that we proposed at the start of this section, which represents each nonempty block consistently by some easily identifiable location in the block (e.g., the one in the lower-left corner of the block) and then applies the mapping (e.g., bit interleaving) to it. The result of the mapping is stored in the one-dimensional access structure, along with the size information. In fact, this is the basis of a linear index into a two-dimensional spatial database developed by Morton [1317] (frequently referred to as a *Morton order*, where the result of applying the mapping to a block is referred to as its *Morton number*) and refined later by several other researchers, including Gargantini [684] and Abel and Smith [8].

As we can see, bit interleaving is quite a powerful idea. In the rest of this section, we give a brief historical background of its development and mention an interesting application. It is difficult to determine the origin of the notion of bit interleaving. The first mention of it was by Peano [1478]. Bentley [164] attributes bit interleaving to McCreight as a way to use B-trees to represent multidimensional data. The resulting B-tree is called an *N-tree* by White [1992], while Orenstein and Merrett [1420] term it a *zkd Btree*. Note that the result is different from the k-d-B-tree of Robinson [1567] (see Section 1.7.1.1). It was proposed by Tropf and Herzog [1891] to give a linear order to multidimensional data and to access it via a binary search tree or balanced variant thereof. Orenstein and Merrett [1420] use the term *Z order* to denote the resulting ordering, while reviewing its use in several data structures in the context of range searching. They use the Z order to build a variant of a binary search tree that they term a *zkd tree*, while cautioning that it differs from the conventional k-d tree since an inorder traversal of a k-d tree does not necessarily yield the nodes in Z order.

An interesting twist on bit interleaving that is claimed to improve the efficiency of partial range queries, and potentially also of range queries, is reported by Faloutsos [581]. The idea is to ensure that the codes of successive points in the result of bit interleaving differ by just one bit. The rationale for this idea is based on the belief of Faloutsos that diagonal transitions between successive points a and b in the ordering, as is the case for the Z order that characterizes the result of the conventional use of bit interleaving, are undesirable because they result from the fact that at least two values of corresponding bit positions in the binary representations of the key values of a and b are not the same. This is most visible when performing a partial range (i.e., partial match) query.

An encoding where the codes of successive points differ by just one bit is known as a *Gray code* [745] (see, e.g., [1264]).[35] It can be achieved by making sure that the transitions between successive points in the ordering are either in the horizontal direction

---

[35] The Gray code is motivated by a desire to reduce errors in transitions between successive gray-level values. Its one-bit difference guarantee is achieved by the following encoding. Consider the binary representation of the integers from 0 to $2^m - 1$. This representation can be obtained by constructing a binary tree, say T, of height m, where each left branch is labeled 0 while each right branch is labeled 1. Each leaf node, say P, is given the label formed by concatenating the labels of the branches taken by the path from the root to P. Enumerating the leaf nodes from left to right yields the binary integers 0

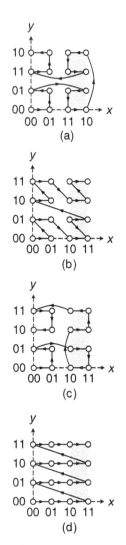

Figure 1.66
Orderings induced on points from
$\{0, 1, 2, 3\}$ and the result of the partial range query $x \geq 2$ shown shaded:
(a) Gray-coded key values and Gray-coded result of bit interleaving (double Gray order), (b) bit interleaving without Gray codes (Z order), (c) Gray-coded result of bit interleaving (Gray order), and (d) bit concatenation with y being more significant than x.

or in the vertical direction (assuming two-dimensional data) but not in both directions. This property is guaranteed to hold if only one bit in the binary representation of just one of the values of the keys changes with each transition. Faloutsos [581] achieves this by using a Gray code to encode each of the keys, and then making horizontal and vertical transitions between the encoded key values. For example, Figure 1.66(a) is the result of using a Gray code to encode the set of two-dimensional points from $\{0, 1, 2, 3\}$, and the arrows show the resulting ordering on the Gray-encoded values of the keys of the points, which has also been subjected to a Gray code. The shape of the ordering resulting from this encoding should be compared with Figure 1.66(b), which illustrates the situation when bit interleaving is applied without the prior application of the Gray code. The effect is to replace the diagonal transitions in Figure 1.66(b) with horizontal or vertical transitions in Figure 1.66(a).

In fact, the same effect of guaranteeing that the codes of successive points in the result of bit interleaving differ by one bit can be achieved by making sure that only one bit in the binary representation of the values of just one of the keys changes with each transition between successive elements of the result of bit interleaving the binary representations of the key values. This can be seen by the ordering given in Figure 1.66(c) (termed a *Gray order*). Thus, we see that there is no need to use a Gray code to encode the individual keys. In essence, Faloutsos applies the Gray code twice, once for each of the key values and once to the result of bit interleaving the Gray-coded key values. We use the term *double Gray order* to describe such an order. It is also interesting to observe that encoding the individual keys with the Gray code, as in the double Gray order suggested by Faloutsos [581], results in increasing the average distance in the original space between two successive points to 2.00, in contrast to 1.50, when only the result of the bit interleaving is encoded with a Gray code (Gray order), and 1.67, when no Gray coding is applied at all to the result of bit interleaving (Z order). An even lower average distance of 1.43 is obtained by using the U order proposed by Schrack and Liu [1698, 1192], which is analogous to the Z order, where the basic recursive pattern is a "U" instead of a "Z." For more detail on the derivation of this average distance, see Exercise 8 in Section 2.1.1.2 of Chapter 2.

In order to see the possible advantage using Gray code variants or the U order in a partial range query, suppose that $k = 2$, and the keys are x and y with ranges between 0 and 3. The query $x \geq 2$ means that we need to examine only one cluster of points (e.g., the shaded portion of Figure 1.66(a)) when bit interleaving is applied after coding the keys with their Gray codes (but see Exercise 6)—that is, using the double Gray order. In contrast, for the same query, using bit interleaving without a Gray code, termed a *Gray order*, means that we must examine two clusters of points (e.g., the shaded portion of Figure 1.66(b)). The same result holds when we just use the U order. Using bit concatenation such that key y is more significant than x, the same query requires that we examine four clusters of points (e.g., the shaded portion of Figure 1.66(c)).

Depending on how the data is structured, a multiplicity of clusters may have a significant impact on the cost of retrieving the answer. Variants of the Gray code and the U orders increase the size of the clusters for some instances of partial range queries. Faloutsos [582] has shown that for a partial range query, using the double Gray order never increases the number of clusters and can reduce the number of clusters by at most 50%. Faloutsos further conjectures that the use of the double Gray order has a similar

---

to $2^m - 1$. The Gray codes of the integers are obtained by constructing a new binary tree, say TP, such that the labels of some of the branches in TP are the reverse of what they were in T. The algorithm is as follows. Initially, TP is a copy of T. Next, traverse T in preorder (i.e., visit the root node, followed by the left and right subtrees). For each branch in T labeled 1, exchange the labels of the two descendant branches of its corresponding branch in TP. No action is taken for descendants of branches in T labeled 0. Enumerating the leaf nodes in TP from left to right yields the Gray codes of the integers 0 to 2^{m-1}. For example, for 8 gray levels (i.e., $m = 3$), we have 000, 001, 011, 010, 110, 111, 101, 100.

effect on range queries, although, at the present, this is an open problem. Note that these properties should also hold for the Gray and U orders. The overhead cost incurred by using Gray codes is that of the conversion process from a binary representation, which is linear in the size of the codeword [1551].

Exercises

1. Write an algorithm to perform bit interleaving of the x and y coordinate values of a point in an efficient manner.

2. Write a procedure BISEARCH to perform a range search for a rectangular region in a two-dimensional database implemented as a binary search tree with bit interleaving as the mapping function.

3. Assume a d-dimensional database implemented as a B-tree with bit interleaving as the mapping function. Write a procedure BTREESEARCH to perform a range search for a d-dimensional rectangular region.

4. Given a database of N records, prove that for a small, rectangular d-dimensional region, the range search in Exercise 3 takes $O(d \cdot \log_2 N + F)$ time, where F is the number of records found.

5. Give an algorithm for converting between a binary representation and a Gray code and vice versa.

6. Give an example partial range query involving keys x and y with ranges between 0 and 3 such that the use of Gray codes on the result of interleaving (i.e., double Gray order), as well as Gray order and U order, does not result in a decrease in the number of clusters from the number of clusters that result from normal bit interleaving.

7. Prove that for partial range queries, using Gray codes prior to bit interleaving (i.e., double Gray order) never increases the number of clusters and can reduce them by a maximum of 50%.

8. Derive a method of enumerating all the possible partial range queries for two keys. Also, evaluate the expected number of clusters when using bit concatenation, bit interleaving, and bit interleaving using Gray codes.

9. What is the effect on range queries of bit interleaving using Gray codes (e.g., using a double Gray order, Gray order, and even a U order)?

10. One of the problems with the Gray code encoding is the existence of long horizontal and vertical transitions between successive elements in the order. Find an ordering that avoids this problem (see Section 2.1.1.2 of Chapter 2).

1.7 Bucket Methods

When the data volume becomes very large, much of the data resides in secondary storage (e.g., disk) rather than in main memory. This means that tree access structures such as the quadtree and k-d tree variants discussed in Sections 1.4 and 1.5, which are based on making between 1 and d tests at each level of the tree, become impractical due to the limited fanout at each node. The problem is that each time we have to follow a pointer, we may have to make a disk access. This is far costlier than indirect addressing, which is the case when the tree resides entirely in main memory. This has led to the development of what are termed *bucket methods*.

There are many different bucket methods, as well as ways to distinguish between them. One way to do so is by noting whether they organize the data to be stored or the embedding space from which the data is drawn. An alternative, and the one we follow in this section, is to subdivide them into two principal classes. The first class consists of aggregating the data objects in the underlying space. The second class consists of decompositions of the underlying space with an appropriate access structure. It is important to note that not all of the methods can be classified so distinctly: some of them can be made to fit into both classes. We do not dwell on this issue further in this chapter.

The first class aggregates the actual data objects into sets (termed *buckets*), usually the size of a disk page in secondary memory so that the buckets are as full as possible. These methods still make use of a tree access structure, where each node in the tree is the size of a disk page, and all leaf nodes are at the same level. Thus, the fanout is much larger than in the quadtree (and, of course, the k-d tree). It should be clear that decomposing the underlying space is not a goal of these representations. Instead, they are more accurately classified as object hierarchies since they try to aggregate as many objects (points in our case) as possible into each node. When the nodes are too full, they are split, at which time some of the representations (e.g., the R-tree [791]) attempt to aggregate spatially proximate objects in the nodes resulting from the split. However, there is no guarantee that the space spanned by the collections of objects in the nodes (e.g., their convex hull, minimum bounding box, minimum bounding circle) is disjoint.

Nondisjointness is a problem for search algorithms because the path from the root of such structures (e.g., an R-tree) to a node that spans the space containing a given data point or object is not necessarily unique. In other words, the data point or object can be covered by several nodes of the R-tree; yet, it is found in only one of them. This results in more complex searches. No such problems exist when the decomposition of the space spanned by the collections of objects in the nodes is disjoint. Examples of such methods include the R^+-tree [593, 1718, 1803], which is really a k-d-B-tree [1567] with bounding boxes around the portions of space resulting from the decomposition. When the data objects have extent (e.g., nonpoint objects such as rectangles and lines), the disjointness requirement of these representations may result in decomposing the individual objects that make up the collection at the lowest level into several pieces. The disjointness requirement is usually expressed in the form of a stipulation that the minimum bounding boxes of the collection of objects at the lowest level of the tree (i.e., at the leaf nodes) be disjoint instead of that the minimum bounding boxes of the individual objects be disjoint.[36] The price that we pay for disjointness is that there is no longer a guarantee that each node will be as full as possible.

Neither the nondisjoint nor the disjoint object aggregation methods is discussed further in this chapter as each is covered in great detail in Sections 2.1.5.2 and 2.1.5.3, respectively, of Chapter 2, where their usage is discussed for nonpoint objects (e.g., region data). Of course, that discussion is also applicable for point data.

The above methods that are based on a disjoint decomposition of space can also be viewed as elements of the second class. The key property used to distinguish between the different elements of this class is whether the underlying space is decomposed into a grid of cells. When a grid is used, the access structure is usually an array (termed a *grid directory*). When a grid is not used, an access structure in the form of a tree is used (termed a *tree directory*). Such methods are the focus of the rest of this section. Tree directory methods are discussed in Section 1.7.1, and grid directory methods are discussed in Section 1.7.2. Section 1.7.3 concludes with a brief discussion of the analysis of the storage utilization of bucket methods.

1.7.1 Tree Directory Methods

The tree access structures that form the basis of bucket methods that make use of a tree directory differ from the quadtree and k-d tree access structures discussed in Sections 1.4

---

[36] Requiring the minimum bounding boxes of the individual objects to be disjoint may be impossible to satisfy, as is the case, for example, for a collection of line segments that all meet at a particular point.

and 1.5, respectively, in terms of the fanout of the nodes. As in the case of an R-tree, the data points are aggregated into sets (termed *point buckets* for the moment), where the sets correspond to subtrees S of the original access structure T (assuming variants of T with bucket size 1, where all data points are stored in the leaf nodes). They are made to look like the R-tree by also aggregating the internal (i.e., nonleaf) nodes of T into buckets (termed *region buckets* for the moment), thereby also forming a multiway tree (i.e., like a B-tree). This is in contrast to other bucket methods (e.g., the bucket PR quadtree, bucket PR k-d tree, bucket generalized k-d trie, and bucket PMR quadtree, discussed in Section 1.5.2), where only the contents of the leaf nodes are aggregated into buckets. The elements of the region buckets are regions. The tree access structures differ from the R-tree in the following respects:

1. The aggregation of the underlying space spanned by the nodes is often implicit to the structure.

2. All nodes at a given level are disjoint, and together they usually span the entire space.

In contrast, for the R-tree, the following must hold:

1. The spatial aggregation must be represented explicitly by storing the minimum bounding boxes that correspond to the space spanned by the underlying nodes making up the subtree.

2. The bounding boxes may overlap (i.e., they are not necessarily disjoint).

A region bucket R, whose contents are internal nodes of T, corresponds to a subtree of T, and its fanout value corresponds to the number of leaves in the subtree represented by R. Again, note that the leaves in the subtrees represented by the region bucket are internal nodes of the access structure T.

The use of a directory in the form of a tree to access the buckets was first proposed by Knott [1040]. The leaf nodes in a B^+-tree can also be used as buckets. Multidimensional point data can be stored in a B^+-tree by applying a linear ordering to it. In particular, such an ordering can be obtained by, for example, using bit interleaving, as mentioned in Section 1.6, and then storing the results in a B-tree (recall the zkd Btree). Unfortunately, in such a case, a B-tree node does not usually correspond to a k-dimensional rectangle. Thus, the representation is not particularly conducive to region searching.

Several different representations have been developed to overcome these deficiencies. They are the subject of the rest of this section, which is organized as follows. Section 1.7.1.1 describes the k-d-B-tree, which is the simplest tree directory method from a conceptual point of view. The drawback of the k-d-B-tree is the possible need to split many nodes when a node overflows. Section 1.7.1.2 outlines the hybrid tree, which is a variant of the k-d-B-tree that keeps track of some extra information so that the number of nodes that need to be split upon overflow is reduced at the expense of more costly search operations due to nondisjointness of the resulting regions. Section 1.7.1.3 presents the LSD tree, which is an alternative method of overcoming some of the drawbacks of the k-d-B-tree, although use of the LSD tree may lead to low storage utilization. Section 1.7.1.4 contains an overview of the hB-tree, which has better storage utilization than the LSD tree. This is achieved by removing the requirement that all blocks be hyperrectangles. Section 1.7.1.5 discusses methods where the underlying space from which the data is drawn is partitioned at fixed positions (i.e., based on a trie) rather than in a data-dependent manner as in the k-d-B-tree, LSD tree, and hB-tree. This includes the multilevel grid file, the buddy-tree, and the indextermBANG file. Section 1.7.1.6 explains the BV-tree, which is a novel method that has excellent performance guarantees for searching. All of the above techniques are dynamic. Section 1.7.1.7 describes a couple of static methods based on the generalized pseudo k-d tree.

1.7.1.1 K-d-B-Tree

A simple example of a method that makes use of a tree directory is the k-d-B-tree [1567]. It is best understood by pointing out that it is a bucket variant of a k-d tree similar in spirit to the bucket generalized pseudo k-d tree (see Section 1.5.1.4) in the following sense:

1. The partition lines need not pass through the data points.

2. There is no need to cycle through the keys.

3. All the data is in the leaf nodes.

The blocks corresponding to the leaf nodes of this variant are buckets of capacity b (termed *point pages*) where a bucket is split in two whenever it contains more than b points. What differentiates the k-d-B-tree from the bucket generalized pseudo k-d tree is that in order to form the k-d-B-tree, the nonleaf nodes making up subtrees of the bucket generalized pseudo k-d tree are also grouped into buckets of capacity c (termed *region pages*). In this case, c corresponds to the number of pointers in each subtree to point pages or other region pages. In other words, c is the number of leaf nodes in the extended binary tree[37] representation of the k-d tree corresponding to the space partition induced by the region page. Thus, c is the maximum number of regions that can make up a region page. Note that c does not have to be the same as b, and, in fact, it is usually smaller as the size of the individual entries in the region pages is usually larger since they represent the boundaries of regions.

As noted above, the nodes of the original bucket generalized pseudo k-d tree that make up each region page form a variant of a k-d tree T corresponding to the space partition induced by the region page. T stores region partitions in its nonleaf nodes and pointers to other region pages or point pages in its leaf nodes. Therefore, T is neither a generalized k-d tree since no actual data is stored in its nonleaf nodes; nor is T a generalized pseudo k-d tree as no actual data is stored in its leaf nodes. Thus, we term T a *generalized k^+-d tree* in recognition of its similarity in spirit to a B^+-tree since their nodes contain only partitions rather than actual data.

It is interesting to observe that obtaining a k-d-B-tree is equivalent to taking a bucket generalized pseudo k-d tree B and replacing it with a multiway tree B', which is a variant of a B^+-tree[38] where the nodes of B' are aggregates of subtrees of B containing a maximum of c elements. One of the reasons for stating that the resulting structure is a *variant* of the B^+-tree is that, unlike the B^+-tree, we cannot guarantee that each bucket in the k-d-B-tree will be 50% full. However, as in a B^+-tree, all point pages (i.e., leaf nodes) in a k-d-B-tree are at the same depth.

Of course, the resulting structure of the k-d-B-tree has many of the same properties as the B-tree, although updates (i.e., insertion and deletion) cannot always be achieved in analogous ways. In particular, when new data values are inserted into (deleted from) a B-tree, an overflowing (underflowing) bucket is either split (merged with an adjoining bucket) and a middle partition value promoted to (demoted from) the father bucket. Alternatively, we could try to make use of what is termed *deferred splitting* to rotate values from adjacent buckets. Unfortunately, the latter is not generally possible in the case of multidimensional point data (i.e., $d > 1$) as the buckets are not split on the basis of an ordering—that is, partitions are made on the basis of the relative positions (i.e., locations) of the points in the underlying space that is spanned by the bucket.[39] Moreover, recall that only the leaf nodes contain actual data.

---

[37] In an *extended binary tree*, each node is either a leaf node or has two children.

[38] We have an analogy with a B^+-tree rather than a B-tree because in the k-d-B-tree all the data points are in the leaf nodes, while the nonleaf nodes contain only the boundaries of the partitions.

[39] But see the MD-tree of Nakamura, Abe, Ohsawa, and Sakauchi [1337], which is a k-d-B-tree with a fanout of 3, where deferred splitting is actually handled by reconfiguring the splitting lines when necessary. The MD-tree is also used as the basis of the RMD-tree [1337], which represents two-

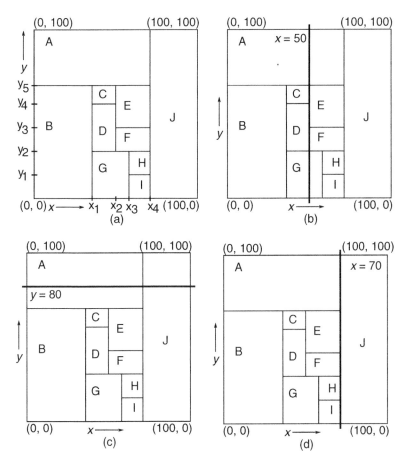

Figure 1.67
(a) A region page in a k-d-B-tree with capacity 9 that overflows. x_i $(1 \leq i \leq 4)$ and y_j $(1 \leq j \leq 5)$ denote the x-discriminator and y-discriminator values, respectively, of the corresponding k-d tree. The partitions are induced by splitting it into two region pages at (b) $x = 50$, (c) $y = 80$, and (d) $x = 70$.

If insertion of a point into the k-d-B-tree causes a point page p to overflow, then a partition line and axis are chosen and the corresponding bucket is split. This results in the creation of two new point pages s_1 and s_2, and the data in p is inserted into the appropriate new point page based on its position relative to the partition line. Finally, p is deleted from the region page f that contains it, while s_1 and s_2 are added to f.

Adding s_1 and s_2 to f may also cause f to overflow. If this is the case, then we pick a partition line l and axis in the region corresponding to f and split f into region pages f_1 and f_2. For example, consider the region page given in Figure 1.67(a) with x_i $(1 \leq i \leq 4)$ and y_j $(1 \leq j \leq 5)$ denoting the x-discriminator and y-discriminator values, respectively, of the corresponding k-d tree. Let the capacity of the region page be 9. As we can see, this page has ten regions and has overflowed. Suppose that we split it at $x = 50$ as shown in Figure 1.67(b). This means that we must check the relative positions of all of the regions corresponding to the elements of f with respect to the partition line l (e.g., $x = 50$ in Figure 1.67(b)). In particular, we must determine if they lie entirely to the left (e.g., regions B, C, and D in Figure 1.67(b)) or entirely to the right (e.g., regions E, F, H, I, and J in Figure 1.67(b)) of l and insert them into f_1 or f_2 as is appropriate. All elements e of f whose regions are intersected by l (e.g., regions A and G in Figure 1.67(b)) must be split and new regions created that are inserted into f_1 or f_2. This additional splitting process

dimensional objects as points in a four-dimensional space (see also Sections 3.3.2.2 and 3.3.2.3 of Chapter 3).

is applied recursively to the children of e and terminates upon reaching the appropriate point pages.

If a region page f has overflowed and f is not a root page of the k-d-B-tree, then f is deleted from its parent page g, the newly created region pages f_1 and f_2 are inserted into g, and the check for overflow is applied again (this time to g). If f has overflowed and f is a root page of the k-d-B-tree, then a new region page h is created containing region pages f_1 and f_2 as its elements and l as the partition line. Thus, we see that the k-d-B-tree grows at the root (i.e., its height increases by one), which is the same way that the B$^+$-tree grows.

Too many deletions may result in very low storage utilization. This can be overcome by either joining two or more adjacent point pages (i.e., catenating them), provided they are joinable (i.e., they have the same father region, their combined region forms a hyperrectangle, and the total number of points in the new page n does not cause n to overflow), or redistributing the contents of the adjacent point pages, which is the case when there is underflow in one of the point pages. If there is a reduction in the number of point pages, then this process is recursive in the sense that the parent region pages should be checked as well. For example, in Figure 1.67, region pages H and I are joinable. On the other hand, region page G is not joinable with region page H; nor is G joinable with region page I as neither of their combined regions forms a hyperrectangle. Note, however, that G is joinable with the combination H and I as their combined region does form a hyperrectangle. An alternative solution, which can also be applied in the case of overflow, is to reorganize the region pages by changing the positions (as well as the number) of partition lines. This will mean that descendant pages must be checked as well since this may cause the regions corresponding to the point pages to change, thereby necessitating the movement of points between pages, which may lead to overflow and creation of new partitions by going up the tree.

The drawback of the k-d-B-tree is that the insertion process is quite complex in the sense that we must be quite careful in our choice of a partition line l and partition axis when a region page f overflows. There are two problems. The first problem is that we must choose the new partition line so that the newly created region pages do not overflow. For example, suppose that we choose to partition region page f in Figure 1.67(a) at line l at $y = 80$ as shown in Figure 1.67(c). Recall that this page has capacity 9. Let f_1 and f_2 represent the newly created region page corresponding to the areas below and above $y = 80$, respectively. Therefore, all elements of f that are below l (e.g., regions B, C, D, E, F, G, H, and I in Figure 1.67(c)) are inserted into f_1, while all elements of f that are above l (e.g., none in Figure 1.67(c)) are inserted into f_2. In addition, the elements of f whose regions are intersected by l (e.g., A and J) must be split and new regions created that are inserted into f_1 and f_2. The result is that f_1 contains ten regions and has overflowed, which means that it must also be split, thereby causing the k-d-B-tree to grow by an additional level. With the appropriate choice of partition lines, this process can be applied repeatedly to create much larger k-d-B-trees. Clearly, this is undesirable, and we should choose another partition line and axis. In fact, it is not difficult to construct another example where both of the newly created region pages have overflowed (see Exercise 1).

The second problem is that even if neither of the newly created region pages f_1 and f_2 overflows, then we may still have to apply the splitting process recursively to f_1 and f_2, which may, in turn, cause a descent to the point pages. This recursive application of splitting can be avoided by choosing a partition line that is not intersected by any of the regions that make up the overflowing region page. For example, this is the case if we choose to partition the region page in Figure 1.67(a) at $x = 70$ as shown in Figure 1.67(d). By the very nature of the k-d tree, such a partition line can always be found (see Exercise 2). The shortcoming of such a partitioning is that it may lead to very poor storage utilization in the region pages.

1. Consider a k-d-B-tree. Give an example partition line and axis whose use to split an overflowing region page f with a capacity c (i.e., f has $c + 1$ regions) yields two newly created region pages, f_1 and f_2, that also overflow.

2. Why can we always find a partition line for a region page in a k-d-B-tree so that when a region page is split upon overflow, we do not have to apply the splitting process recursively to the child pages of the overflowing region page?

3. Write a procedure KDBINSERT to insert a point into a k-d-B-tree.

4. Write a procedure KDBDELETE to delete a point from a k-d-B-tree.

5. Write a procedure KDBPOINTQUERY to perform a point query in a k-d-B-tree.

6. Write a procedure KDBRANGEQUERY to perform a range query in a k-d-B-tree.

1.7.1.2 Hybrid Tree

It should be clear that in the k-d-B-tree the difficulty of choosing a partition line and axis that result in good space utilization without requiring further partitioning is a direct result of the requirement that the k-d-B-tree yield a disjoint decomposition of the underlying space. Chakrabarti and Mehrotra [317] suggest a modification of the k-d-B-tree, which they term a *hybrid tree* (see also Section 4.4.3 of Chapter 4), that avoids splitting the region and point pages that intersect the partition line l along partition axis a with value v by slightly relaxing the disjointness requirement. This is achieved by associating the intersecting pages with one of the two regions resulting from the partition, termed *low* and *high*, corresponding to the regions $a \le v$ and $a > v$, respectively. In addition, they replace the single partition line l by two partition lines l_{min} and l_{max}. l_{min} corresponds to the minimum value of coordinate a for all pages associated with region *high*, while l_{max} corresponds to the maximum value of coordinate a for all pages associated with region *low*. Of course, these changes may result in slower searches due to overlapping regions.

For example, if we partition the overflowing region page in the k-d-B-tree in Figure 1.67(a) at $x = 50$ as shown in Figure 1.67(b), then we must decide with which partition to associate the pages A and G that intersect the partition line. One solution is to associate A with the left partition and G with the right partition. In this case, instead of one partition line at $x = 50$, we now have two partition lines at $x = 70$ and $x = 40$, corresponding to the boundaries of regions *low* and *high*, respectively. Pages A, B, C, and D are associated with region *low*, while pages E, F, G, H, I, and J are associated with region *high*. An alternative is to retain the partition line at $x = 50$ for region *high* and just add the partition line at $x = 70$ for region *low*. In this case, the two regions have the same amount of data—that is, pages A, B, C, D, and G are associated with region *low*, while pages E, F, H, I, and J are associated with region *high*.

Recall from Section 1.5.1.4 that the same technique is used by Ooi, McDonell, and Sacks-Davis [1404, 1407] in their *spatial k-d tree* to represent a collection of objects with extent by storing their centroids in a k-d tree (see also Section 3.3.2.5 of Chapter 3). They keep track of the extent of the objects by associating with each nonleaf node, say P discriminating on coordinate a, information on the spatial extent of the objects stored in its two subtrees. In particular, they store the maximum value of coordinate a for the objects in the left child of P and the minimum value of coordinate a for the objects in the right child of P.

Associating two partition lines with each partitioned region is equivalent to associating a bounding box with each of the two regions *low* and *high*. The result is similar to an R-tree with the critical difference that the bounding box is not a minimum bounding box. In particular, if it were a minimum bounding box, then with each partition we would have to store the values of the partition line and axis, as well as $4 \cdot d$ values for the boundaries of the two minimum bounding boxes in d dimensions. Instead, with each partition, the hybrid tree stores just three values: the partition axis and two partition lines.

Thus, the space requirements, especially in high dimensions, are considerably lower. Of course, the drawback of not using a minimum bounding box is that we cannot eliminate as effectively the dead space in a region.

Chakrabarti and Mehrotra [317] propose to eliminate some of the dead space by using an approximation of a bounding box obtained by quantizing the space spanned by the minimum bounding box using a small number of bits to represent the coordinate values of the two corners of the bounding box. Assuming the use of b bits per dimension, this is equivalent to imposing a $2^b \times 2^b \times \ldots \times 2^b$ grid on the space spanned by the partition and recording the corners of the grid cells that are partially covered by the minimum bounding box. For example, using 4 bits (which is shown to yield good results), instead of 64 bits (which is needed to store the floating-point representation of each coordinate value in the unquantized representation), results in lowering the space requirements for the bounding box by a factor of 16. This idea was first proposed by Henrich [826] in adapting the LSD tree (see Section 1.7.1.3) to handle high-dimensional data.

Exercises

1. Write a procedure HYBRIDINSERT to insert a point into a hybrid tree.

2. Write a procedure HYBRIDDELETE to delete a point from a hybrid tree.

3. Write a procedure HYBRIDPOINTQUERY to perform a point query in a hybrid tree.

4. Write a procedure HYBRIDRANGEQUERY to perform a range query in a hybrid tree.

1.7.1.3   LSD Tree

The *Local Split Decision tree* (LSD tree) [829] chooses a partition line that is not intersected by any of the regions that make up the overflowing region page in the k-d-B-tree, thereby avoiding the need for a recursive invocation of the splitting process. This is achieved by partitioning each region page of the k-d-B-tree at the root of the generalized k^+-d tree corresponding to the space partition induced by the overflowing region page. As mentioned above, such a partitioning may lead to poor storage utilization by creating region pages that could be almost empty. An extreme example of this situation results from repeated partitions, assuming a bucket capacity c, that create two region pages whose underlying space is spanned by two generalized k^+-d trees, having 1 and c leaf nodes, respectively. Recall that these newly created pages contain pointers to region pages at the next, deeper level of the k-d-B-tree. Observe that a generalized k^+-d tree containing n leaf nodes can have a height as large as $n - 1$, where we assume that a tree with one leaf node has a height of 0. Thus, the generalized k^+-d tree corresponding to the space partition induced by a region page with c leaf nodes may have a height as large as $c - 1$.

Clearly, if the bucket capacity c (the number of pointers to region or point pages here) is large, then the maximum height of the generalized k^+-d tree corresponding to the space partition induced by a region page could also be large, thereby requiring many tests in performing basic operations on the data, such as an exact match query. The LSD tree alleviates this problem, in part, by choosing the maximum height h of the extended binary tree representation of the generalized k^+-d tree corresponding to the space partition induced by the region page to be $\lfloor \log_2 c \rfloor$. In other words, for a given value of c, h is chosen so that $2^h \leq c < 2^{h+1}$. Thus, the region page utilization is optimal when the generalized k^+-d tree corresponding to the space partition induced by the page is a complete binary tree (i.e., 2^h leaf nodes), while it is at its worst when the space partition is a linear binary tree (i.e., $h + 1$ leaf nodes). Notice also that when c is not a power of 2, then the region page utilization will never be 100%.

As in the k-d-B-tree, the LSD tree is best understood by assuming that we start with a variant of a bucket generalized pseudo k-d tree. Similarly, the key idea behind the LSD tree lies in distinguishing between the treatment of the nonleaf nodes of the tree (i.e., the bucket generalized pseudo k-d tree) from the treatment of leaf nodes that contain the actual data which are termed *data buckets* (i.e., point pages using the terminology of the k-d-B-tree). The nonleaf nodes are also grouped into pages of a finite capacity, termed *directory pages* (i.e., region pages using the terminology of the k-d-B-tree). The result is a variant of a B^+-tree where the root, termed an *internal directory page*, always resides in main memory and corresponds to the nonleaf nodes closest to the root of the bucket generalized pseudo k-d tree, while the nodes in the remaining levels, termed *external directory pages*, always reside in external storage. The root (i.e., the internal directory page) is a generalized k^+-d tree of finite size whose leaf nodes point to external directory pages or data buckets. Below, we first describe the external directory pages. This is followed by a description of the internal directory page. We use the LSD tree in Figure 1.68(a) to illustrate our explanation.

Each external directory page (as well as the internal directory page) is a generalized k^+-d tree implemented as an extended binary tree of a predefined maximum height h. The leaf nodes of each of the binary trees that make up an external directory page are either pointers to data buckets (i.e., point pages, using k-d-B-tree terminology) or other external directory pages (i.e., region pages using k-d-B-tree terminology). The internal nodes correspond to the partition values. The LSD tree definition stipulates that the lengths of the paths (in terms of the number of external directory pages that are traversed) from a particular leaf node in the internal directory to any data bucket are the same, while the lengths of the paths from different leaf nodes in the internal directory to any data bucket differ by at most one [829] (e.g., Figure 1.68(a)).

The pointer structure connecting the elements of the set of external directory pages and the data buckets yields a collection of trees (we are not speaking of the generalized k^+-d trees that make up each external directory page here). The internal nodes of these trees are external directory pages. Each internal node in each tree in this collection has a maximum fanout of 2^h. In addition, in each tree, the paths from the root to the leaf nodes (i.e., the data buckets) have the same length, in terms of the number of external directory pages, which is analogous to a stipulation that the trees are "balanced" (although the individual internal nodes may have a different degree). Moreover, the heights of any two trees can differ by at most one.

When insertion of a data item into the LSD tree causes a data bucket (i.e., a point page using k-d-B-tree terminology) to overflow, the data bucket is split according to several possible rules that include a rule that ensures that the number of data items in the resulting data buckets is approximately the same and a rule that ensures that the size of the space spanned by the two data buckets is the same. These rules are examples of what are termed *data-dependent* and *distribution-dependent* strategies, respectively.[40] The latter is similar to the trie-based decomposition strategies. They differ from the generalized pseudo k-d tree as they are based on a local, rather than a global, view (i.e., there is no need to know the entire dataset). The split will cause the addition of a data bucket (i.e., point page using k-d-B-tree terminology), which will cause an additional node to be inserted into the corresponding ancestor external directory page p. For a discussion of some ways to avoid splitting a data bucket by rotating data from the overflowing bucket to a sibling bucket that is not too full, see [824, 825] (see also Section 1.5.1.4).

External directory pages are split if the addition of the new data bucket causes their height to exceed the predefined maximum value h. If a split occurs, then the directory page is split at the root of its corresponding generalized k^+-d tree, and the split is propagated farther up the tree, which may, in turn, eventually cause a node to be added to the internal directory page.

---

[40] See Section 3.3.2.4 of Chapter 3 for a more detailed explanation in the context of the use of an LSD tree to store a collection of rectangles where each rectangle is represented by the representative point method.

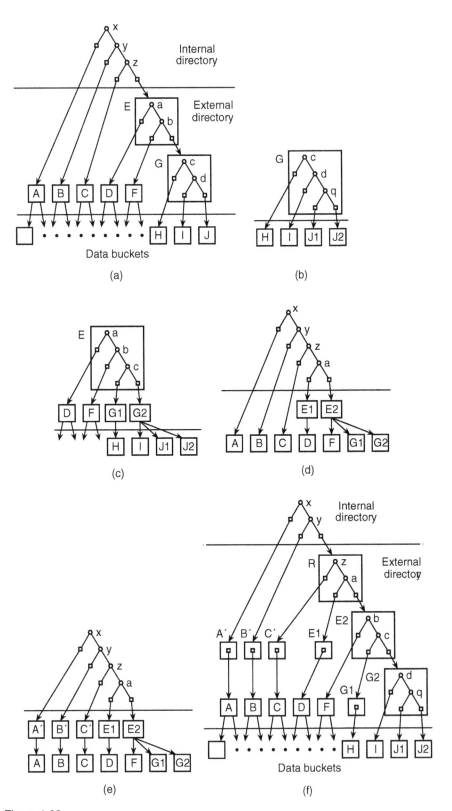

Figure 1.68

Example LSD tree showing the result of inserting a point in data bucket J, which causes it to overflow. (a) Original tree, (b) effect of splitting data bucket J on external directory page G, (c) effect of splitting external directory page G on external directory page E, (d) effect of splitting directory page E on the internal directory page, (e) effect of making new external directory pages upon detecting overflow of the internal directory page so that the lengths of all paths from the root of the internal directory page to any of the data buckets are the same, (f) final tree.

The internal directory page has a finite capacity i, which is the maximum number of leaf nodes that it can contain. Note that the leaf nodes correspond to the regions induced by the generalized k^+-d tree partition of the underlying space. i is usually much larger than the capacity of the external directory pages. The internal directory page is kept in main memory. Again, as in the case of the external directory pages, the internal directory page is an extended binary tree. When the internal directory page is too full, one of its subtrees s is made into an external directory page p, and s is removed from the internal directory page (we say that s has been *paged*). In this case, s is replaced by a leaf node that points to p. Subtree s is chosen to be as large as possible, subject to the predefined maximum height of an external directory page and the "path length to a bucket" constraint. The latter constraint implies that the path lengths, in terms of the number of external directory pages that are traversed, of all paths from the root of the subtree s to a data bucket must be the same and that the path length is the minimum of the permitted path lengths (recall that the path lengths may differ by one). Satisfaction of these constraints ensures that the external directory pages are as large as possible and also prevents the internal directory page from overflowing too often.

If the subtree s that was chosen has just one node, which must be a leaf node, then the size of the internal directory page has not been reduced. Recall that leaf nodes are pointers to external directory pages or data buckets. Thus, after paging subtree s consisting of just a single leaf node, a pointer to s must be included in the internal directory page in a newly created leaf node t, which means that the internal directory page is still overflowing. However, we have created a new external directory page consisting of one leaf node, and thus the path length l from t to all of the data buckets $\{B\}$ accessible from t has increased by one without violating our constraint that l be the same for all elements of $\{B\}$ and that l differ by at most one from those of the remaining trees that make up the collection of external directory pages. In this case, the paging algorithm must be reapplied, but now the algorithm has the opportunity to choose another subtree to make into an external directory page that hopefully consists of more than one leaf node.

For example, letting $i = 4$, $h = 2$, and $c = 4$, consider the situation when data bucket J overflows in the LSD tree whose directory map is given in Figure 1.68(a). Data bucket J is split into data buckets J1 and J2, with q serving as the new partitioning hyperplane that is promoted to the parent external directory page G (see Figure 1.68(b)). This causes G to have height 3, which is too large (as $h = 2$). Therefore, G is split into external directory pages G1 and G2, with partitioning hyperplane c serving as the new partition value that is promoted to the parent external directory page E (see Figure 1.68(c)). Again, this causes E to have height 3, which is too large. Therefore, E is split into external directory pages E1 and E2, with partitioning hyperplane a serving as the new partition value that is promoted to the parent, who is the internal directory page (see Figure 1.68(d)). This causes the internal directory page to overflow as it has pointers to five external directory pages while there is room for only four since $i = 4$.

At this point, the definition of the LSD tree requires that we locate the largest subtree s in the internal directory page such that the length of the path from its root, in terms of the number of external directory pages that are traversed, to a data bucket is a minimum and that we make s into an external directory page. Continuing our example, this means that we make, in order, external directory pages A$'$, B$'$, and C$'$ out of the leaf nodes that are the left children of the internal nodes x, y, and z, respectively, in Figure 1.68(d), yielding Figure 1.68(e). We now have the situation that the lengths of all paths from the internal directory page to any of the data buckets are the same. Of course, the internal directory page is still too full. Next, we convert the subtree rooted at internal node z in Figure 1.68(e), as it is the largest, into an external directory page as shown in Figure 1.68(f), and the insertion process is complete. Notice that the lengths of the paths to any data bucket are the same for any of the nodes in the resulting internal directory page, and they differ by just one for the different nodes in the resulting internal directory page.

It should be noted that the example we have described is a worst case in the sense that we had to make external directory pages that were essentially empty (i.e., did not correspond to a partition of the underlying space) when we created external directory pages A′, B′, and C′, as well as E1 and G1 in Figure 1.68(e). This worst case is unlikely to arise in practice because the capacity i for the internal directory page is usually chosen to be quite large, while the external directory pages and the data buckets are usually the size of a page in the underlying operating system. For example, in experiments reported in [829], the internal directory contained 1,000 nodes, while the external directory pages and data buckets were 512 bytes. Assuming an extended binary tree representation for the internal directory page leads to a value of 500 for i as the number of leaf nodes is one greater than the number of nonleaf nodes. Moreover, using eight bytes per node, the maximum number of nodes that can be stored in an external directory page is 64, which corresponds to an extended binary tree of height $h = 5$ as there are $2^5 = 32$ leaf nodes and $2^5 - 1 = 31$ nonleaf nodes. Thus, the page can hold as many as $c = 32$ pointers to other external directory pages and data buckets.

If a cyclic partition order is used, then there is no need to keep track of the partition axes. In this case, the generalized k^+-d tree in each external directory page is simplified considerably, and its extended binary tree representation can be stored using the complete binary tree array representation (which is also often used to represent heaps and is sometimes called a *sequential heap*).

It is interesting to observe (as in the k-d-B-tree) that the structure of the LSD tree is similar to that which would be obtained by taking a binary search tree B of height mh and replacing it with a multiway tree B' of height m, where the nodes of B' correspond to aggregates of subtrees of B of height h. Again, this is analogous to the motivating idea for a B-tree with the exception that the fanout at each node of B' is at most 2^h, whereas in a B-tree there is a predetermined minimum fanout, as well as a maximum fanout (usually related to the capacity of a page, which is also usually the case in the LSD tree [829]). The difference, of course, is that in the case of an LSD tree the binary search tree is a k-d tree, and each node in the resulting multiway tree represents a sequence of successive binary partitions of a hyperrectangular region.

Both the k-d-B-tree and the LSD tree result in the partitioning of the space corresponding to an overflowing region page into two region pages, each of which is a hyperrectangle. The k-d-B-tree permits quite a bit of latitude in the choice of the position of the partition line and identity of the partition axis at the expense of the possibility of further overflow on account of the need for further partitioning of the regions intersected by the partition line. In contrast, there is no further partitioning in the case of the LSD tree as each region page of the k-d-B-tree is partitioned at the root of the generalized k^+-d tree corresponding to the space partition induced by the overflowing region page. The drawback of this approach is that the storage utilization of the region pages resulting from the split may be quite poor.

Exercises

1. Write a procedure LSDINSERT to insert a point into an LSD tree.

2. Write a procedure LSDDELETE to delete a point from an LSD tree.

3. Write a procedure LSDPOINTQUERY to perform a point query in an LSD tree.

4. Write a procedure LSDRANGEQUERY to perform a range query in an LSD tree.

1.7.1.4 hB-Tree

The hB-tree [575, 1201] overcomes the low storage utilization drawback of the LSD tree by removing the requirement that the portions of the underlying space spanned by the region pages resulting from the split be hyperrectangles. Instead, the hB-tree splits each region page into two region pages so that each resulting region page is at least

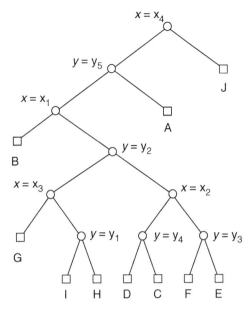

Figure 1.69
The generalized k+-d tree of the hB-tree node corresponding to the region page in Figure 1.67(a). The nonleaf nodes are labeled with the key that serves as the discriminator.

one-third full, thereby making the other region page no more than two-thirds full[41] (see Exercise 2). The portions of space spanned by the resulting region pages have the shapes of bricks with holes corresponding to region pages spanning a hyperrectangular space that has been extracted from the region page that has been split.[42] This analogy serves as the motivation for the name *holey brick tree* (hB-tree). Note that the one- to two-thirds balanced splitting property also holds for the point pages (see Exercise 3).

Each node corresponding to a region page in the hB-tree contains a generalized k+-d tree[43] describing a partition of a corresponding hyperrectangular area. However, the space spanned by the node may not cover the entire hyperrectangle. In this case, some of the generalized k+-d tree leaf nodes (corresponding to partitions of the hyperrectangle) are flagged as being external (denoted by ext) and thus spanned by other nodes of the hB-tree at the same level (such as its brothers). The best way to understand the hB-tree is to look at how it would deal with the overflowing region page, denoted by P, in Figure 1.67(a). It has 10 regions but its capacity is 9. Let Figure 1.69 be the generalized k+ d tree corresponding to the region page P in Figure 1.67 that has overflowed. In this case, the space spanned by P is a rectangle and thus none of the nodes in the corresponding k+-d tree are marked as being external. Notice that this example is quite simple as there are no external nodes in the generalized k+-d trees of any of the child nodes of P since they are all also rectangles. We shall look at more complex examples later.

First, we must determine how to split the overflowing region page, say P. This is done by traversing its corresponding generalized k+-d tree (i.e., Figure 1.69) in a top-down manner, descending at each step the subtree with the largest number of leaf nodes (i.e., regions). The descent ceases as soon as the number of regions in one of the subtrees, say

---

[41] This notion of minimum occupancy is also used in the BD-tree [1386, 1387] (see Section 1.5.2), the BANG file [640] (see Section 1.7.1.5), and the BV-tree (see Section 1.7.1.6).

[42] Note that subsequent splits may result in region pages that span areas that are not contiguous, but this is not a problem [1201].

[43] We characterize the structure using the qualifier *generalized* because the partitions need not be cyclic.

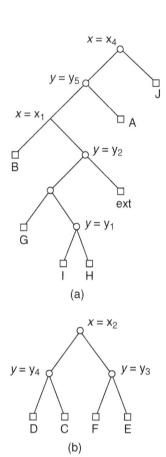

(a)

(b)

Figure 1.70
The generalized k$^+$-d trees associated with the results of splitting the hB-tree node corresponding to the region page in Figure 1.67(a) with the generalized k$^+$-d tree given in Figure 1.69 into nodes (a) Q and (b) S. Each nonleaf node is labeled with the key that serves as the discriminator.

S, lies between one-third and two-thirds of the total number of regions in the overflowing region page P. The space spanned by S corresponds to the brick that is being extracted from P.

In our example, the stopping condition is satisfied once we have made two left transitions, followed by two right transitions, in the generalized k$^+$-d tree of Figure 1.69. At this point, the brick that we will extract corresponds to the subtree of P's generalized k$^+$-d tree, consisting of the child nodes C, D, E, and F (i.e., these are hB-tree nodes at the next deeper level in the hB-tree). We let S refer to a new hB-tree node, consisting of the subtree of P's k$^+$-d tree, and let Q refer to the remaining portion of P[44] (i.e., the result of extracting S from P). The generalized k$^+$-d trees associated with Q and S are shown in Figure 1.70(a, b), respectively. Notice the use of the label ext in Figure 1.70(a) to mark the portions of the space covered by the generalized k$^+$-d tree (recall that this space is a hyperrectangle) that are spanned by another node in the hB-tree. This is needed because the underlying space spanned by its hB-tree node (i.e., S) is not a hyperrectangle. In contrast, no nodes are labeled ext in Figure 1.70(b) as the underlying space spanned by its hB-tree node (i.e., Q) is a hyperrectangle.

We must also propagate the result of the split to the father hB-tree node F of the node P corresponding to the overflowing region page (termed *posting* [1201]). In our example, after the split, we post a subtree that discriminates between Q and S to the father hB-tree node F. This results in merging the generalized k$^+$-d tree in Figure 1.71 into the generalized k$^+$-d tree for F. Of course, we must also check whether F has overflowed, which may cause further splitting and posting, eventually culminating in the growth of the hB-tree by one level.

From Figure 1.71, we see that the structure of the hB-tree is such that a particular region may appear more than once in the k-d tree that represents the node. Moreover, in the case of a node split as a result of node overflow, it is possible that some of the nodes in the hB-tree will have more than one parent (called the *multiple posting problem*). This means that the directory in the hB-tree is really a directed acyclic graph (i.e., there are no cycles, and the pointers are unidirectional), and thus is not actually a tree. As an example of this situation, consider the region page, say P, in Figure 1.72(a), whose generalized k$^+$-d tree is given in Figure 1.72(b). Suppose that P has overflowed. Of course, this example is too small to be realistic, but it is easy to obtain a more realistic example by introducing additional partition lines into the regions corresponding to A and B in the figure. In this case, we traverse P's k-d tree in a top-down manner, descending at each step the subtree with the largest number of leaf nodes (i.e., regions) and stopping as soon as the number of regions in one of the subtrees, say S, lies between one-third and two-thirds of the total number of regions in the overflowing region page P. In this example, this is quite easy as all we need to do is descend to the left subtree of the right subtree of the root. The result is the creation of two hB-tree nodes (Figure 1.72(c, d), where region A is now split so that it has two parent hB-tree nodes, and the partition line between these two parent hB-tree nodes is posted to the father hB-tree node of P.[45]

If subsequent operations result in further splits of region A, then we may have to post the result of these splits to all of the parent hB-tree nodes of A. For example, suppose that region A in Figure 1.72(a) is subsequently split into regions A and C as shown in Figure 1.73(a). In this case, the resulting hB-tree nodes are given by Figure 1.73(b, c)

---

[44] In an actual implementation, Q can occupy the same disk page as P did.

[45] The splitting procedure for the hB-tree would actually truncate the generalized k$^+$-d tree in Figure 1.72(c) to yield a single leaf node pointing to A. In general, this is done by traversing the generalized k$^+$-d tree from the root and discarding nonleaf nodes until neither of the children are external markers. However, in the hB$^\Pi$-tree [575], which is an adaptation of the hB-tree designed to provide better support for recovery and concurrency, such a truncation is not performed. This is because in the hB$^\Pi$-tree the external markers are replaced by *sibling pointers* whose value provides useful information. In particular, for a node P, a sibling pointer in its generalized k$^+$-d tree points to the node that was extracted (as a result of splitting) from P, whose underlying space spans the corresponding area.

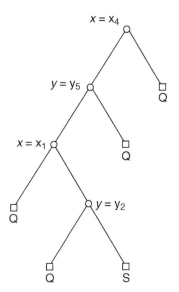

Figure 1.71
The generalized k⁺-d tree associated with the father of the hB-tree node corresponding to the region page in Figure 1.67(a) with the generalized k⁺-d tree given in Figure 1.69, which has been split into nodes Q and S, whose generalized k⁺-d trees are given by Figures 1.70(a) and (b), respectively. The nonleaf nodes are labeled with the key that serves as the discriminator.

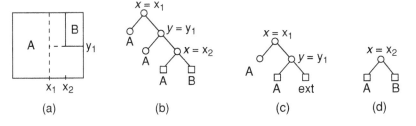

Figure 1.72
(a) Example region node where (b) is the generalized k⁺-d tree of its hB-tree node and whose overflow is resolved by partitioning it, thereby creating two hB-tree nodes having (c) and (d) as their generalized k⁺-d trees. The actual partition of the region page that is induced by the generalized k⁺-d trees is shown by the broken line in (a). Each nonleaf node of the generalized k⁺-d tree of the hB-tree nodes is labeled with the key that serves as the discriminator.

corresponding to Figure 1.72(c, d), respectively. Here we see that this could have possibly caused additional node splits to occur. The greater the number of such splits that take place, the more complicated the posting situation becomes. In fact, this complexity was later realized to cause a flaw in the original split and post algorithm for the hB-tree [574, 1614] and was subsequently corrected as part of the hB$^{\Pi}$-tree [575].

Exercises

1. Give an example point set with $4k$ points in two dimensions that cannot be partitioned by a vertical or a horizontal line into two sets, each of which has $2k$ points.

2. Prove that it is always possible to split a region page in an hB-tree into two region pages so that each resulting region page is at least one-third full, thereby making the other region page

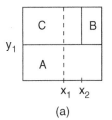

(a)

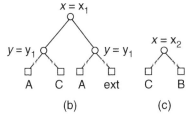

(b)   (c)

Figure 1.73
(a) Result of splitting region A in Figure 1.72(a) into regions A and C, and the resulting two hB-tree nodes having (b) and (c) as their generalized k⁺-d trees, which correspond to Figures 1.72(c) and (d), respectively. The actual partition of the region page that is induced by the generalized k⁺-d trees is shown by the broken line in (a). Each nonleaf node of the generalized k⁺-d tree of the hB-tree nodes is labeled with the key that serves as the discriminator.

no more than two-thirds full. Recall that the splitting of a region page is achieved by extracting a portion of the generalized k^+-d tree that describes the partitioning of the region page.

3. Prove that it is always possible to split a point page in an hB-tree into two point pages so that each resulting point page is at least one-third full, thereby making the other point page no more than two-thirds full.

4. Write a procedure HBINSERT to insert a point into an hB-tree.

5. Write a procedure HBDELETE to delete a point from an hB-tree.

6. Write a procedure HBPOINTQUERY to perform a point query in an hB-tree.

7. Write a procedure HBRANGEQUERY to perform a range query in an hB-tree.

1.7.1.5 K-d-B-Tries

Partitions in the k-d-B-tree (as well as the LSD tree and the hB-tree) are usually made in a data-dependent manner.[46] An alternative is to decompose recursively the underlying space from which the data is drawn into halves. The exact identity of the key being partitioned at each level of the decomposition process depends on the partitioning scheme that is used (e.g., whether we need to cycle through the keys). Such decompositions are characterized as being trie-based and have been used earlier in distinguishing between different forms of quadtrees (Sections 1.4.1 and 1.4.2) and k-d trees (Sections 1.5.1 and 1.5.2). Some examples of a trie-based decomposition are the PR k-d tree and the generalized k-d trie discussed in Section 1.5.2.

Trie-based decompositions have the obvious drawback of requiring many decomposition steps when the data is clustered, which results in empty subtrees. This is alleviated, in part, by making use of buckets, thereby leading to the bucket PR k-d tree and the bucket generalized k-d trie discussed in Section 1.5.2. The effects of clustering can be further mitigated by increasing the capacity of the buckets. Below, we discuss several extensions of the bucket generalized k-d trie (i.e., the multilevel grid file[47] [1087] and the buddy-tree [1710]) that have additional desirable characteristics. They differ from the bucket generalized k-d trie in that, as in the k-d-B-tree (and the LSD tree), they also aggregate the nonleaf nodes of the bucket generalized k-d trie. We use the term *k-d-B-trie* to refer to this general class of representations.

Our explanation of the k-d-B-trie is heavily influenced by the manner in which two of its variants, namely the multilevel grid file and the buddy-tree, are implemented. They yield a tighter decomposition of the underlying space in the sense that they eliminate some of the empty space that is inherent to the bucket generalized k-d trie. This is achieved by basing the overflow condition for an aggregated nonleaf node (i.e., a region page) on the number of nonempty regions or children that it comprises. Of course, other variants of the k-d-B-trie are also possible, and they often have different definitions. However, they all have in common the aggregation of the nonleaf nodes of a bucket generalized k-d trie and their organization using some variant of a k-d trie.

A k-d-B-trie has two types of pages: point pages (capacity b), containing the actual data, and region pages (capacity c) that contain pointers to point pages or to other region pages. Initially, we have one empty point page p and one region page r containing p that spans the entire underlying space U.[48] When p becomes full, p is split into two point pages, p_1 and p_2, using a variant of a recursive decomposition process described below. We may think of the splitting of p as the result of applying a sequence of halving

---

[46] But see the discussion of distribution-dependent decompositions in LSD trees [829].

[47] Although the qualifier *grid file* is used in the name of the data structure, it has little connection with the grid file as described in Section 1.7.2.1.

[48] Actually, most implementations dispense with the initial region page. However, in our explanation, we find it useful to assume its existence so that we can see how the underlying space is decomposed once the initial point page, which covered no space at the start, becomes full.

operations on the underlying space U. The sequence terminates once the last halving operation results in two nonempty halves, spanning u_1 and u_2. Since the k-d-B-trie is based on the bucket generalized k-d trie, the order in which the halving operations are applied to the domains of the different keys is permitted to vary. This leads to many possible different partitions of the underlying space and configurations of resulting point pages.

The result of the application of each halving operation to U is termed a *B-rectangle* [1710]. Thus, we see that u_1 and u_2 are B-rectangles. Depending on the configuration of the underlying space, we often find that p_i covers just a very small part of u_i. This will lead to inefficiencies in search, and thus we attempt to store a tighter approximation of the data in p_i. Let $M(p_i)$ be the minimum bounding rectangle of p_i.[49] Each minimum bounding rectangle $M(p_i)$ has a minimum bounding B-rectangle $B(M(p_i))$, termed the *B-region* of $M(p_i)$. The B-region of $M(p_i)$ is obtained by continuing the application of recursive halving operations to u_i. With each entry for a point page p_i in the father r, we associate the B-region of $M(p_i)$. Thus, we can now see that u_1 and u_2 may be obtained by the application of just one halving operation on the B-region of $M(p)$. In the following, when we speak of the B-region of a node o, we mean the B-region of the minimum bounding rectangle of the data in the subtree at o.

As an example of the tighter approximation that can be obtained, assuming a bucket capacity of 4, consider the insertion of point X into the point page in Figure 1.74(a). Figure 1.74(b) is one possible result of splitting the overflowing page into two nonoverflowing halves; Figure 1.74(c) shows the B-regions and minimum bounding rectangles that will be stored in the newly created region page. Thus, we see that the k-d-B-trie obtained in Figure 1.74(c) has smaller point pages than would have been the case had we not used the B-regions. At a cursory glance, we might think that the use of B-regions leads to the creation of more regions by virtue of the presence of the empty regions (e.g., the upper-right quarter of Figure 1.74(c), which is marked with diagonal lines). However, this is not a problem because the overflow condition for a region page depends only on the nonempty regions that it comprises.

Each region page r consists of the B-regions of its constituent pages, which form a *B-partition* of r. The B-partition has the property that its constituent B-regions are pairwise disjoint. Note that requiring that the B-regions are pairwise disjoint is stronger than just requiring that the minimum bounding rectangles of the child pages (which are point or region pages) are disjoint. For example, although the two minimum bounding rectangles A and B in Figure 1.75 are disjoint, their B-regions are not disjoint as they are, in fact, the same. Empty B-rectangles (corresponding to empty point or region pages) are not represented explicitly in the region page, and thus they are not counted when determining if the capacity of r has been exceeded.

Once the initial point page has been split, insertion continues into the existing point pages, with splits made as necessary until the number of B-regions (i.e., point pages) exceeds the capacity c of the region page r. At this point, we split r into two region pages, r_1 and r_2, by halving the B-region of r, and we propagate the split up the tree. If we are at the root of the tree, then we create a new region page, s, having r_1 and r_2 as its children. As this process of insertion is continued, s may eventually gain more children by virtue of splitting r_1 and r_2 until the number of region pages s comprises exceeds c, at which time another split operation is applied to s.

Of course, there are times when the newly inserted point q is not contained in any of the existing B-regions of the children of r. We have two options. The first is to extend the B-region of one of the children to cover q. The second is to create a new child with a B-region that covers q. Choosing the second option means that if we require the k-d-B-trie to be balanced (i.e., all point pages have to be at the same level), then we may have

---

[49] We assume that the sides of the minimum bounding rectangle are parallel to the axes corresponding to the keys.

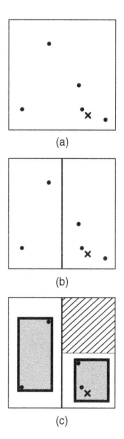

(a)

(b)

(c)

Figure 1.74
Example showing the insertion of point X into a point page of capacity 4 in k-d-B-trie: (a) original point page, (b) one possible result of splitting the overflowing point page into two halves, and (c) the B-regions and bounding rectangles (shown shaded) that will be stored in the newly created region page; empty regions that have no corresponding entry in the region page are marked with diagonal lines.

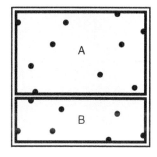

Figure 1.75
Example pair of disjoint minimum bounding rectangles (shown shaded) whose B-regions are not disjoint.

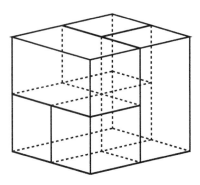

Figure 1.76
Example of a nonregular B-partition where each of the partitioning hyperplanes will pass through a B-region.

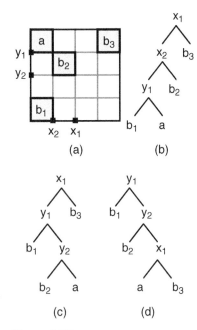

Figure 1.77
(a) A region page and the generalized k-d tries corresponding to three possible partitions upon overflow given in (b), (c), and (d). Each nonleaf node is labeled with the name of the key that serves as the discriminator.

to create a chain of new region pages, each of which contains just one element, until reaching the leaf level of the k-d-B-trie. Note that some implementations of the k-d-B-trie, such as the buddy-tree, allow it to be unbalanced. We usually try the first option because it leads to better storage utilization and use the second option only if the first option is not possible.

When a region page is split, we want to avoid the problem that arose in the k-d-B-tree where the partition of a region page could cause the partitioning of some of its constituent region pages. This problem is avoided by requiring that the B-partition corresponding to each region page form a generalized k-d trie[50] (such a B-partition is termed *regular* [1710]). For example, assuming a region page capacity of 4, the partition into five regions (three of which are $2 \times 1 \times 1$ hyperrectangles whose longest side is parallel to a different axis and two of which are $1 \times 1 \times 1$ cubes) given in Figure 1.76 [1710] is not regular. In particular, no hyperplane exists that can partition it into two disjoint sets. The above problem can arise in the k-d-B-trie only when two child pages of a region page are merged, which means that the merging process must ensure that the result of the merge does not violate the regularity requirement (see Exercise 1).

Observe that the generalized k-d trie need not be unique, which means that the B-partition need not be unique. For example, consider Figure 1.77(b–d), which shows three possible generalized k-d tries for the region page in Figure 1.77(a). Observe that in this figure, and for the purposes of facilitating the process of determining whether a B-partition is regular, each leaf node in the generalized k-d trie represents the largest possible bounding B-rectangle for the B-region corresponding to the node, thereby obviating the need for empty nodes.

It should be clear that each region page r in a k-d-B-trie is a collection of disjoint B-regions whose union (in terms of the portions of the underlying space that they span) is a subset of the underlying space spanned by r. This property is useful in making the k-d-B-trie a good structure for the execution of search queries (e.g., range queries) because we can avoid examining regions that cannot possibly contain data (e.g., notice the empty region in the upper-right corner of Figure 1.74(c)). Thus, the B-regions have similar properties to the minimum bounding boxes that form the basis of the R-tree. B-regions differ from minimum bounding boxes by virtue of the fact that their sizes and positions are restricted to being a result of the application of a recursive halving process to the underlying space.

Since each B-partition can be represented by a generalized k-d trie, we can represent the B-regions making up both the point and region pages of the k-d-B-trie compactly by just recording the minimum number of bits (i.e., the paths in the generalized k-d trie, one per key, to the B-region, with left and right transitions being represented by 0 and 1, respectively[51]) necessary to differentiate them from the remaining B-regions. Note that in this case we are representing the full generalized k-d trie in contrast to the one depicted in Figure 1.77, which employs just enough partitions to distinguish the different minimum bounding B-rectangles for the pages making up the B-partition. In contrast, in the k-d-B-tree, we need to store the whole partition value for each key.[52]

The k-d-B-trie has great flexibility in determining which nonfull point and region pages are to be merged when deletions take place, as well as when page splitting results in pages that are underfull. This permits the k-d-B-trie to have good dynamic behavior. In particular, assuming d-dimensional data, if we used a PR k-d tree instead of a generalized

---

[50] We could have also used the term *generalized k^+-d trie* to describe this k-d trie to reinforce the similarity of the representation of the nodes of the k-d-B-trie to those of the k-d-B-tree.

[51] A separate path for each key is needed instead of just one sequence of interleaved 0s and 1s because the attributes are not being tested in cyclic order and thus the correspondence between the identity of the tested attribute and the result of the test must be recorded.

[52] In fact, for some implementations of the k-d-B-tree, associated with each region entry in a region page is a rectangle, requiring two values for each key, representing the region.

k-d trie, then a page a could be merged with just one page (i.e., the brother of a). In contrast, in the k-d-B-trie, a can be merged with up to d pages corresponding to the d possible keys whose domain axes could have been split in half when a was created (i.e., as a result of a split). The pages with whom a can be merged are termed its *buddies*. In fact, the definition of a buddy could be made less restrictive by stipulating that two child pages, g and h, in region page p are buddies if the intersection of the B-region of their union with the B-regions of all remaining pages in p is empty. This means that the maximum number of pages with which a can be merged (i.e., buddies) is even greater than d (see [1706, 1710]). To see why this is true, recall that the B-regions of the child pages of a region page p can be represented by several different generalized k-d tries (whereas there is only one way to do so with a PR k-d tree). Therefore, a page b_i is a *buddy* of page a if a and b_i occur in sibling leaf nodes in some generalized k-d trie representing the partition of p. For example, in Figure 1.77, a can be merged with b_1, b_2, or b_3.

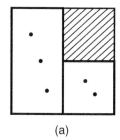

(a)

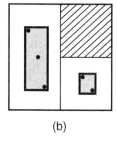

(b)

Figure 1.78
Example illustrating the difference between (a) a multilevel grid file and (b) a buddy-tree. Notice the use of minimum bounding rectangles (shown shaded) in (b).

There are several variants of the k-d-B-trie. The most notable are the multilevel grid file [1087] and the buddy-tree [1710]. The key difference between the multilevel grid file and the buddy-tree is the fact that in the buddy-tree a minimum bounding rectangle is stored for each of the child pages (instead of their B-regions, which may be computed from the minimum bounding rectangles as needed), while the multilevel grid file just stores the B-regions with the bitstring approach described above (see Figure 1.78). Another difference is that the buddy-tree exploits the less restrictive definition of a buddy, thereby permitting a page to be merged with a larger range of pages. In addition, the buddy-tree is not always balanced in order to prevent the existence of region pages with only one child page (see below for more details). Finally, the multilevel grid file employs a hashing function that is applied to the various keys prior to the application of the trielike decomposition process. This enables indexing on a wider variety of key types, such as strings of characters, and so on.

The fact that empty B-rectangles are not represented in a region page r leads to an interesting situation when a point q being inserted into r does not lie in the B-regions of any of the child pages of r. In other words, q is in an empty B-rectangle. Recall that the point insertion procedure is top-down in the sense that we start at the root of the k-d-B-trie and search for the point page containing q. The search ceases once we encounter such a point page or if we encounter an empty B-rectangle e in a region page r. In the latter case, we have two options. The first option is to attempt to enlarge one of the existing B-regions to accommodate the point. If this is not possible, then the second option is to create a new page for q. Let us look more closely at how we attempt to enlarge one of the existing B-regions. This is achieved by checking whether the B-region of q (i.e., the B-region of the minimum bounding rectangle of q) can be merged with the B-region of one of its buddies in r. If such a buddy a exists, and if a is not already filled to capacity, then we enlarge the B-region of a to accommodate q in the corresponding entry of region page r and continue by inserting q into a. If no nonfull buddy exists, then we resort to the second option and create a new point page v of one point.

The newly created point page should be at the deepest level of the k-d-B-trie. However, this would lead to a long sequence of region pages with just one nonempty entry. This is quite inefficient, and thus in some implementations of the k-d-B-trie (e.g., in the buddy-tree but not in the multilevel grid file), an unbalanced structure is used where the new point page v is added at the depth i of the empty B-rectangle t in which q fell. However, if this new point page v at depth i overflows at some later time, then v is pushed one level down in the k-d-B-trie to depth $i + 1$ and then split. This action is taken instead of splitting v at depth i and possibly having to split the region page w at depth $i - 1$ when w overflows as a result of the split at depth i.

Note that when the keys are clustered, methods such as the k-d-B-trie do not yield a very good partition of the underlying space. However, results of experiments with the buddy-tree [1710] show that the fact that empty B-rectangles are not represented explicitly ameliorates this drawback to such an extent that it is no longer significant.

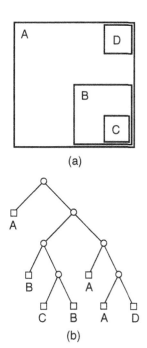

Figure 1.79
(a) Example illustrating a region
page in the BANG file and (b) its
corresponding PR k-d tree.

Nevertheless, the definition of the multilevel grid file does take this into consideration by virtue of the hashing functions that, we recall, are applied to the various keys prior to the application of the trielike decomposition process. However, it should be noted that, in general, it is quite difficult to devise an order-preserving hashing function that significantly reduces clustering. Moreover, the use of a non-order-preserving hashing function (which can be devised to spread the hash values virtually uniformly) is a drawback for range queries.

The BANG file [640, 641, 645, 646] is a variant of the k-d-B-trie that requires that the underlying space be decomposed by a sequence of partitions that cycle through the keys in a fixed order. Moreover, unlike other variants of the k-d-B-trie (such as the buddy tree and multilevel grid file), the BANG file removes the requirement that the portions of the underlying space that are spanned by the region pages be hyperrectangles. Instead, the BANG file requires only that the space spanned by the set of regions that make up each region page be describable by a PR k-d tree where the individual regions are unions of the blocks corresponding to collections of leaf nodes of the PR k-d tree. In this sense, the region pages are similar to those in the hB-tree except that the BANG file makes use of regular decomposition. In particular, as mentioned above, in the BANG file, the underlying space is decomposed by cycling through the various keys in a fixed and predetermined cyclic order (e.g., $xyxyx\ldots$). Thus, the BANG file is a variant of the k-d-B-trie in a similar way as the hB-tree is a variant of the k-d-B-tree.

As an example of the type of space decomposition permitted by the BANG file, consider the region page in Figure 1.79(a) and its corresponding PR k-d tree in Figure 1.79(b), which consists of the four regions, A, B, C, and D. Observe that, using the parlance of hB-trees, regions A and B play the role of holey bricks, regions B and D play the role of the bricks that are removed from A, and region C plays the role of the brick that is removed from B. In the BANG file, each of the various regions prior to the removal of the bricks is represented by a bitstring corresponding to the path from the root of the PR k-d tree of the region page to the nearest common ancestor of all leaf nodes belonging to the same region (i.e., the outer boundary of the original hyperrectangle before extraction of any bricks). For example, letting 0 correspond to branches to the left and below the partition line, while letting 1 correspond to branches to the right and above a partition line, we have that A is represented by the empty bitstring (as the nearest common ancestor is the root of the PR k-d tree), while B is represented by 10. The actual regions (i.e., their bit strings) are stored in a B-tree-like structure where, upon a split of a region page, each of the resulting region pages is at least one-third full, thereby making the other page no more than two-thirds full, as in the hB-tree (see Section 1.7.1.4). Another difference between the BANG file and the hB-tree (i.e., besides the BANG file's being based on a regular decomposition instead of allowing splits at arbitrary positions) is that this B-tree-like structure is a tree rather than a directed acyclic graph, as is the case for the hB-tree, since each region is only represented once in the BANG file.

The execution of operations, such as an exact match query, using the BANG file is facilitated by sorting the regions corresponding to each region page in the BANG file in order of increasing size of their blocks (i.e., prior to the removal of the bricks). The exact match query is performed by testing the regions for containment of the query point p in this order and stopping the search as soon as a region is found to contain p. This will guarantee that the smallest region enclosing p is selected. The process of searching for the block containing p can be implemented by sorting the bitstrings in lexical order (e.g., empty, 0, 011, 1, 101). Notice that this will order the bitstrings of larger blocks before the bitstrings of small blocks contained in them. The search itself is done by performing a prefix bit matching in the resulting list in reverse order (i.e., starting from the end) for the bitstring describing p. Unfortunately, this search process may take as much as $O(N)$ time when the N blocks are all nested within each other (i.e., the blocks are numbered b_i, $1 \le i \le N$, where b_i contains $N - i$ blocks). Thus, we see that, even though the original intent of the BANG file is to have a disjoint decomposition of the underlying space, the actual representation used here makes use of nondisjoint blocks and hence the more complex search time for the exact match query.

Freeston [645] overcomes the worst-case $O(N)$ execution time of the exact match query by modifying the BANG file so that the search paths are unique but at the loss of the minimal page occupancy guarantee. Ouksel and Mayer [1438] take an alternative approach to reducing the worst-case execution time of the exact match query. In particular, they reduce it to a function of the product of the logarithms of the number of nesting levels and the number of blocks by using a different implementation than Freeston [640] of the BANG file as the set of blocks prior to the removal of the bricks. They use a slightly modified form of the bitstring. In particular, all of the bitstrings have the same length, which is equal to the maximum possible level of decomposition, by padding them with zeros on the right and also by recording the length of the original unpadded bitstring. The resulting padded bitstrings are stored in a structure such as a B-tree and sorted in increasing order, with the length of the original unpadded bitstring serving as a secondary key to break ties. The padded bitstring is equivalent to a locational code, which is discussed briefly in Section 1.8.5.1 and in much greater detail in Section 2.1.2.4 of Chapter 2.

The key to Ouksel and Mayer's method is to partition the blocks into subsets where all members of a subset have the same nesting level (i.e., the number of containing ancestor blocks). Each of these subsets can be stored in a separate B-tree, and the result is called a *nested interpolation-based grid file* (NIBGF) [1438]. Note that the use of the term *grid file* is somewhat misleading as the NIBGF bears little resemblance to a grid file, being really a pointerless representation for the BANG file. In particular, the search is now a binary search through the various nesting levels. At each nesting level l that is tested, determine if the query point is covered by one of the blocks in the B-tree corresponding to the level. If it is, then the search proceeds at deeper nesting levels. If it is not, then the search proceeds at shallower nesting levels.

The worst-case execution time of this process is the product of the log of the number of nesting levels h and the cost of a B-tree lookup. A more precise analysis takes into account the fact that the B-trees at the different levels will differ in size, and thus the analysis is in terms of the number of B-tree nodes that must be examined. Letting h denote the number of nesting levels, Ouksel and Mayer show that the worst-case execution time is $O(\log_2 h \cdot \log_{\lfloor b/2 \rfloor} N)$ for a B-tree of order b (see Exercise 3). Special cases can yield tighter bounds. For example, if there are N nesting levels, then the cost is $O(\log_2 N)$ comparisons and corresponding B-tree node lookups. If there is just one nesting level, then only one B-tree node lookup is needed, and the cost is $O(\log_{\lfloor b/2 \rfloor} N)$ B-tree node lookup operations.

Ouksel and Mayer's solution is not just applicable to the BANG file. It is applicable to any representation that makes use of nondisjoint nested blocks, such as those resulting from the association of objects with their minimum enclosing quadtree or k-d tree blocks. Some examples include the MX-CIF quadtree [1009], R-file [909], and filter tree [1720] (see the discussion in Section 2.1.4.1 of Chapter 2 and Sections 3.4.1 and 3.4.2 of Chapter 3).

The use of bitstrings to represent the various regions in the BANG file is similar to that used in the BD-tree [1386, 1387][53] but quite different from the one used in the multilevel grid file [1087].[54] Nevertheless, a key difference between the BANG file and the BD-tree is the fact that the BD-tree does not aggregate the nonleaf nodes of the

---

[53] The difference is that in the BANG file the bitstrings corresponding to the regions are kept in a sorted list according to their size, while in the BD-tree they are kept in a binary tree. This results in a different search process, possibly visiting different regions, although, of course, the end result for both representations is the same!

[54] Recall that in the multilevel grid file, a set of bitstrings, one per key, is associated with each page since the keys are partitioned in arbitrary order rather than in a cyclic order as in the BANG file, thereby precluding the possibility of using just one bitstring, which is what is done in the BANG file. However, more importantly, in the multilevel grid file, the bitstrings represent rectangular regions, as in the BANG

structure into buckets. In particular, in the BD-tree, only the leaf nodes are aggregated into buckets. Therefore, the BANG file is related to the BD-tree in a way similar to how the k-d-B-tree is related to the bucket generalized pseudo k-d tree. An even more precise analogy is that the BANG file is related to the BD-tree in the same way as the k-d-B-trie (e.g., the buddy-tree or the multilevel grid file) is related to the bucket PR k-d tree as they all also make use of regular decomposition.

Exercises

1. Give an algorithm to test whether two pages in a k-d-B-trie can be merged. Recall that two pages can be merged only if the resulting page is not too full and if the result is a B-partition.

2. Do we need to test if the result of a page split in a k-d-B-trie is a B-partition?

3. Letting N denote the number of blocks, h the number of nesting levels, and b the bucket capacity of a B-tree node, show that the worst-case cost, in terms of B-tree node accesses, of an exact match query in a nested interpolation-based grid file (NIBGF) with N blocks is $O(\log_2 h \cdot \log_{\lfloor b/2 \rfloor} N)$.

4. Write a procedure BUDDYINSERT to insert a point into a buddy-tree.

5. Write a procedure BUDDYDELETE to delete a point from a buddy-tree.

6. Write a procedure BUDDYPOINTQUERY to perform a point query in a buddy-tree.

7. Write a procedure BUDDYRANGEQUERY to perform a range query in a buddy-tree.

8. What is the maximum number of possible buddies in a buddy-tree?

1.7.1.6 BV-Tree

The lifting of the requirement that the portions of the underlying space spanned by the region pages be hyperrectangles is a central principle behind the development of both the hB-tree and the BANG file. Recall that both the hB-tree and the BANG file are designed to overcome the cascading split problem that is common to the k-d-B-tree: the insertion of a split line may cause a recursive application of the splitting process all the way to the point pages. This means that we do not have a bound on the number of nodes in the directory structure as a function of the number of data points. Moreover, as we saw, the directory of the hB-tree is not a tree (recall that it is a directed acyclic graph) since it may be impossible to avoid the situation that some of the regions in the region page (i.e., directory node) that is being split will fall partially into both of the region pages resulting from the split.

The occurrence of this problem is addressed by Freeston [643] by use of a clever innovation. The innovation is to decouple [1640] the hierarchy inherent in the tree structure of the directory (where the node entries consist of point and region pages) from the containment hierarchy associated with the recursive partitioning process of the underlying space from which the data is drawn. Below, we use the term *BV-tree* to denote the tree structure of the directory obtained from applying the technique described in [643]. The goal is for the BV-tree to have properties similar to the desirable properties of the B-tree while avoiding the problems described above. In particular, a bounded range of depths (and hence a maximum) can be guaranteed for the BV-tree based on the maximum number of data points and capacity (i.e., fanout) of the point and region pages (they may differ). These bounds are based on the assumption that each point page is at least one-third full [643]. Moreover, in spite of the fact that the BV-tree is not quite balanced, search procedures always proceed level to level in the containment hierarchy. For exact match point search, this means that the number of steps to reach a point page is equal to the depth of the containment hierarchy. Note that in this section we use the

---

file, but all the regions in a given page are disjoint rather than being allowed to be nested, as is the case for the BANG file.

term *containment hierarchy* instead of *decomposition hierarchy* because it provides a more accurate description of the constraints on the decomposition process imposed by the BV-tree. We also use the term *directory node*, instead of the term *region page*, in order to reinforce the meaning that these pages are part of the directory and also to make the connection to the PK-tree [1952, 2043] (see Section 1.8), which is another representation that makes use of decoupling [1640] (now it is the grouping and partitioning processes that are decoupled). On the other hand, we continue to use the term *point page*, but in the PK-tree presentation, we use the term *point node* as the number of points in the node may be quite small.

This section is organized as follows. Section 1.7.1.6.1 defines the BV-tree. Section 1.7.1.6.2 describes how to build a BV-tree with the aid of a detailed example. Section 1.7.1.6.3 shows how to search a BV-tree for a region that contains a given point. Section 1.7.1.6.4 discusses the performance of the BV-tree in terms of its storage requirements. Section 1.7.1.6.5 concludes the presentation by reviewing some of the key properties of the BV-tree and compares it with some other representations, including the R-tree.

1.7.1.6.1 Definition

In order for the BV-tree technique to be applicable, the regions in the containment hierarchy are required to be disjoint within each level. Furthermore, the boundaries of regions at different levels of the containment hierarchy are also required to be nonintersecting. These requirements hold when the decomposition rules of both the BANG file and the hB-tree are used for the containment hierarchy. However, in the case of the BANG file, their satisfaction when splitting and merging nodes is almost automatic due to the use of regular decomposition; in the case of the hB-tree, we need to make use of an explicit k-d tree to represent the history of how the regions were split. In contrast, in the case of the BANG file, the splitting history is implicitly represented by the bitstring corresponding to each region.

As in the BANG file and in the hB-tree, there are two ways in which regions in the BV-tree are created that satisfy these properties. In particular, upon node overflow, the underlying space (e.g., Figure 1.80(a)) is recursively decomposed into disjoint regions either by splitting them into what we term *distinct regions* (e.g., Figure 1.80(b)) or *contained regions* (e.g., Figure 1.80(c)). Splitting into contained regions is achieved via the extraction of smaller-sized regions, thereby creating one region with holes. The disjointness of the regions at a particular level in the containment hierarchy ensures that the outer boundaries of the regions do not intersect (although they may touch or partially coincide). It can be shown that such partitions can be made so that each of the resulting partitions is at least one-third full (see Exercise 1). The BV-tree is built in a bottom-up manner so that data is inserted in point pages (of course, the search for the point page to insert into is done in a top-down manner). Overflow occurs when the point page is too full, at which time the point page is split, thereby leading to the addition of entries to the directory node that points to it, which may eventually need to be split when it points to more point pages than its capacity allows.

Before proceeding further, let us define some of the naming and numbering conventions that we use in our presentation. For a BV-tree of height h (i.e., with h levels of decomposition or containment), the levels in the containment hierarchy are numbered from 0 to h, where 0 is the deepest level (i.e., corresponding to point pages). Each level in the containment hierarchy has several regions associated with it that span the regions spanned by every point page or directory node in the immediately deeper level in the containment hierarchy. The levels in the directory hierarchy are numbered from 1 to h, with level 1 containing the leaf nodes whose entries are point pages. This convention enables a node at level v in the directory hierarchy to be (normally) associated with a region at level v in the containment hierarchy. For example, we can view the region representing the entire data space as being at level h in the decomposition hierarchy, and

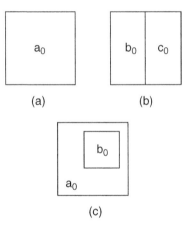

Figure 1.80
(a) Example region and the result of splitting it into (b) distinct regions or (c) contained regions.

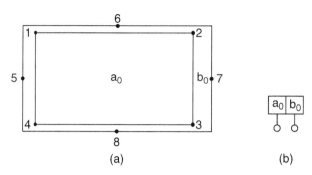

Figure 1.82
Initial step in creating a BV-tree: (a) containment hierarchy and (b) directory hierarchy.

1.7.1.6.2 Building a BV-Tree

The best way to see how the BV-tree works is to consider an example of how it is built. As mentioned above, each directory node a corresponds to a region in the underlying space. The entries in a contain regions and pointers to their corresponding point page or directory node (i.e., entries with regions at clevel 0 correspond to point pages, but regions at shallower clevels correspond to directory nodes). When a is at level i of the directory hierarchy, its entries may be at levels 0 to $i-1$ of the containment hierarchy. The entries whose corresponding regions are at clevels deeper than $i-1$ have been *promoted* to the node a, which is at a shallower dlevel in the directory, where they serve as *guards* of some of the entries in a. Each entry in a also contains information about the clevel of the region it contains, so we may distinguish between promoted and unpromoted entries.

Node a contains a maximum of m entries, where m is the fanout of a. Node a is split if it overflows—that is, if the total number of entries in a (not distinguishing between promoted and unpromoted entries) exceeds m. In our example, we assume a fanout value of 7 for the point pages and 4 for the directory nodes. When a directory node is split, the BV-tree definition [643] claims that it should be possible to distribute its entries in the newly created directory nodes a and b so that each of a and b is at least one-third full because this is one of the properties of the BV-tree that enables it to guarantee an upper bound on the maximum depth of the directory hierarchy. As we will see below, this may not always be possible for all fanout values, thereby requiring some adjustments in the definition of the fanout (see Section 1.7.1.6.4).

Let us start with a set of eight points, labeled 1–8. This means that the capacity (i.e., fanout) of the corresponding point page is exceeded, and thus it is split into two regions, thereby creating a_0 and b_0, containing points 1–4 and 5–8, respectively, and having a containment and directory hierarchy given in Figures 1.82(a, b), respectively.

Next, we add points 9–12, which cause a_0 to be split into a_0 and c_0, points 13–16, which cause a_0 to be split into a_0 and d_0, and points 17–20, which cause a_0 to be split into a_0 and e_0, as shown in Figure 1.83(a). However, this causes the single directory node to overflow, and it is split into two nodes whose corresponding regions are a_1 and b_1, as shown in Figure 1.83(b). Since region a_0 intersects both a_1 and b_1, while completely containing a_1, a_0 is promoted to the newly created directory node where it serves as a guard on region a_1. The resulting directory hierarchy is shown in Figure 1.83(c). Note that a_0 is the region that, if it were not promoted, we would have to split along the boundary of a_1. By avoiding this split, we also avoid the possibility of further splits at deeper levels of the directory hierarchy. Thus, the fact that a_0 appears at this shallower level in the directory hierarchy ensures that a_0 will be visited during any search of the BV-tree for a point on either side of the branch that would have been made if we would have split a_0, which we would have had to do if we did not promote it.

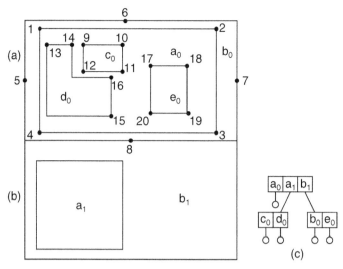

Figure 1.83
Second step in creating a BV-tree: (a) containment hierarchy at the deepest level (*clevel* = 0), (b) containment hierarchy at the shallowest level (*clevel* = 1), and (c) directory hierarchy.

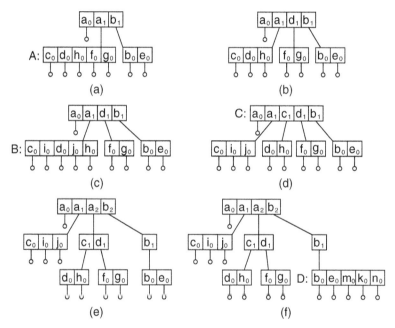

Figure 1.84
Sequence of intermediate directory hierarchies illustrating the node-splitting operations taking place when points are added to the BV-tree of Figure 1.82 until obtaining the BV-tree of Figure 1.85.

Now, suppose that more points are added so that the underlying space is split several times. We do not go into as much detail as before in our explanation, except to indicate one possible sequence of splits. We also no longer show the points in the point pages.

1. Split d_0 into d_0, f_0, and g_0, which is followed by splitting d_0 into d_0 and h_0. This results in the directory hierarchy given in Figure 1.84(a), where the directory node corresponding to a_1, labeled A, must be split as it overflows. Node A is split into two directory nodes whose corresponding regions are a_1 and d_1, resulting in the directory hierarchy given in Figure 1.84(b).

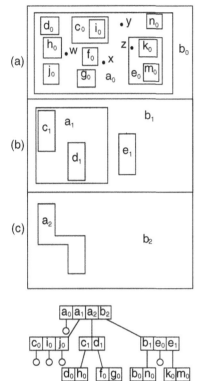

Figure 1.85
Final step in creating a BV-tree: (a) containment hierarchy at the deepest level (*clevel* = 0), (b) containment hierarchy at the intermediate level (*clevel* = 2), (c) containment hierarchy at the shallowest level (*clevel* = 3), and (d) BV-tree.

2. Split c_0 into c_0 and i_0, which is followed by splitting d_0 into d_0 and j_0. This results in the directory hierarchy given in Figure 1.84(c), where the directory node corresponding to a_1, labeled B, must be split as it overflows. Node B is split into two directory nodes whose corresponding regions are a_1 and c_1, resulting in the directory hierarchy given in Figure 1.84(d), where the directory node corresponding to the root, labeled C, must be split as it overflows.

3. Node C is split into two directory nodes whose corresponding regions are a_2 and b_2, resulting in the directory hierarchy given in Figure 1.84(e). Several items are worthy of note:

   (a) The directory node corresponding to the root also contains an entry corresponding to region a_1 because a_1 intersects both a_2 and b_2, while completely containing a_2. Thus, a_1 becomes a guard of a_2.

   (b) Since a_0 originally guarded a_1, a_0 continues to do so, and we find that a_0 is also promoted to the root of the directory hierarchy.

   (c) The directory node corresponding to region b_2 contains only the single region b_1. This means that our requirement that each directory node be at least one-third full is violated. This cannot be avoided in this example and is a direct result of the promotion of guards. This situation arises primarily at shallow dlevels when the fanout value is low compared to the height of the directory hierarchy. It is usually avoided by increasing the value of the fanout as described in Section 1.7.1.6.4.

4. Split e_0 into e_0, k_0, and m_0, which is followed by splitting a_0 into a_0 and n_0. This results in the directory hierarchy given in Figure 1.84(f), where the directory node corresponding to b_1, labeled D, must be split as it overflows. There are several ways to split D. One possibility, and the one we describe, is to split D into two directory nodes whose corresponding regions are b_1 and e_1, resulting in the directory hierarchy given in Figure 1.85(d). Since region e_0 intersects both e_1 and b_1, while completely containing e_1, e_0 is promoted to the directory node containing entries corresponding to b_1 and e_1, where e_0 serves as a guard on region e_1. The three levels that make up the final containment hierarchy are shown in Figure 1.85(a–c). Notice that we could have also split D so that the region e_1 contained regions e_0, k_0, and m_0. In this case, e_0 would not be needed as a guard in the directory node containing entries corresponding to regions b_1 and e_1.

Exercises

1. Suppose that a region r at level v in the containment hierarchy serves as a guard g for a region at level $v + 1$ in the containment hierarchy, and the directory node whose corresponding region is r overflows. How would you handle the situation? In particular, what are the ramifications of splitting r into two disjoint regions in contrast to one where one region contains the other?

2. How would you deal with deletion in a BV-tree?

1.7.1.6.3 Searching a BV-Tree

Having shown how to construct the BV-tree, we now examine the process of searching a BV-tree for the region that contains a point p (termed an *exact match search* here). The key idea behind the implementation of searching in the BV-tree is to perform the search on the containment hierarchy rather than on the directory hierarchy. At a first glance, this appears to be problematic because the BV-tree represents only the directory hierarchy explicitly, while the containment hierarchy is represented only implicitly. However, this is not a problem at all because the containment hierarchy can be, and is, reconstructed on the fly, as necessary, with the aid of the guards when performing the search. In particular, at each stage of the search, the relevant guards are determined, and they are carried down the directory hierarchy as the search proceeds. Note that, as we show below, all exact match searches are of the same length and always visit every level in the containment hierarchy (see Exercise 1).

We explain the search process in greater detail below. Initially, we differentiate between the searches depending on whether the directory node being searched is the root of the directory hierarchy, assumed to be at dlevel v. Recall that all unpromoted entries in the root correspond to regions at level $v - 1$ in the containment hierarchy. The search starts at the root of the directory hierarchy at dlevel v (assuming that the deepest directory node is at dlevel 1 and describes regions at level 0 in the containment hierarchy). It examines the regions corresponding to all of the entries (i.e., including the guards) and selects the smallest region r (corresponding to entry e_r) that contains the query point p. Entry e_r is termed the *best match*. The level $v - 1$ directory node at which the search is continued depends on whether e_r is a guard:

1. Entry e_r is not a guard: Continue the search at the directory node pointed at by e_r with a guard set formed by the current set of guards of e_r (as many as $v - 1$ guards, one for each of levels 0 through $v - 2$ in the containment hierarchy).

2. Entry e_r is a guard: Find the smallest region s containing r whose corresponding entry e_s is not a guard. It is easy to show that e_s must exist. The area spanned by s may also contain other regions, say the set O, corresponding to guards whose regions contain r. Continue the search at the directory node pointed at by e_s with a guard set consisting of e_r, the set of entries corresponding to the regions that make up O, and the guards that correspond to regions that contain s. The guards that correspond to regions that contain s are from levels in the containment hierarchy for which O does not contain guards. For each of these clevels, choose the guard that has the smallest region that contains p. In other words, the guard set can contain at most one guard for each of levels 0 through $v - 2$ in the containment hierarchy, for a maximum of $v - 1$ guards.

Searching at directory node a at dlevel u other than the root uses a similar procedure as at the root. Again, we wish to determine the level $u - 1$ directory node at which the search is to be continued. This is done by finding the smallest region r (termed the *best match*) containing p. The difference is that the best match is obtained by examining the guard g at clevel $u - 1$ (if it exists) of the u guards at clevels 0 through $u - 1$ that make up the guard set that was brought down from the previous search (i.e., from dlevel $u + 1$) and the entries in a that are not guards (note that it may be the case that none of the entries in a are guards, as can be seen by examining point w and the directory node whose corresponding region is a_2 in Figure 1.85(a)). There are two options:

1. If the best match is the region corresponding to g, then continue the search at the level $u - 1$ directory node pointed at by g. The guard set must also be updated as described below.

2. Otherwise, the best match is r, which corresponds to an entry in a (say e_r), and continue the search at dlevel $u - 1$ at the directory node pointed at by e_r. Use a guard set obtained by merging the matching guards found at dlevel u with those brought down from dlevel $u + 1$. Discard g, the clevel $u - 1$ guard brought down from dlevel $u + 1$ (if it exists), as g cannot be a part of a directory node at dlevel $u - 1$ since each entry at dlevel i of the directory hierarchy can contain at most $i - 1$ guards, and the search will next be on regions at clevel $u - 2$. Note that two guards at a given dlevel are merged by discarding the one that provides the poorer match.

Interestingly, there is really no need to differentiate the treatment of root nodes from that of nonroot nodes. In particular, in both cases, only the unpromoted nodes (i.e., entries whose corresponding regions are not guards) need to be examined. In the case of the root node, initially no guard set is brought down from the previous dlevel. Thus, it is initially empty. In this case, the new guard set is formed by finding the guard for each clevel that has the smallest region that contains p.

In order to understand the exact match search algorithm better, let us see how we find the regions in the BV-tree of Figure 1.85(a) that contain the points w, x, y, and z, which are a_0, a_0, a_0, and e_0, respectively. Notice that each region has been labeled with subscripts denoting its level in the containment hierarchy. This is also two less than the deepest level in the directory hierarchy at which it can serve as a guard, and one less than the deepest level in the directory hierarchy at which it will get carried down in the guard set.

1. The search for w first examines the root, at dlevel 3, and determines a_2 to be the best match. The search continues at the dlevel 2 directory node whose corresponding region is a_2 (i.e., containing c_1 and d_1) with a guard set consisting of a_0 and a_1. There is no match in the entries in a_2 (i.e., neither c_1 nor d_1 contains w), and thus we use the guard a_1 brought down from dlevel 3 as the best match. The search continues at the dlevel 1 directory node whose corresponding region is a_1 (i.e., containing c_0, i_0, and j_0) with a guard set consisting of a_0. Again, there is no best match in the entries in a_1 (i.e., neither c_0 nor i_0 nor j_0 contains w), but the guard a_0 contains w, and since the region corresponding to a_0 is at level 0 of the containment hierarchy, we are done. Therefore, w is in a_0.

2. The search for x first examines the root, at dlevel 3, and determines a_1 to be the best match. However, a_1 is a guard, and thus it finds the smallest nonguard region containing a_1, which is b_2. The search continues at the dlevel 2 directory node whose corresponding region is b_2 (i.e., containing b_1, e_0, and e_1) with a guard set consisting of a_0 and a_1. The best match in this node is b_1. However, the clevel 1 guard in the guard set is a_1, and its corresponding region is a better match. The search continues in the dlevel 1 directory node whose corresponding region is a_1 (i.e., containing c_0, i_0, and j_0) with a guard set consisting of a_0. There is no best match in this node, but the guard a_0 contains x, and since the region corresponding to a_0 is at level 0 of the containment hierarchy, we are done. Therefore, x is in a_0.

3. The search for y first examines the root, at dlevel 3, and determines a_0 to be the best match. However, a_0 is a guard, and thus it finds the smallest nonguard region containing a_0, which is b_2. The search continues at the dlevel 2 directory node whose corresponding region is b_2 (i.e., containing b_1, e_0, and e_1) with a guard set consisting of a_0. The best match in this node is b_1. There is no clevel 1 guard in the guard set, and the search continues at the dlevel 1 directory node whose corresponding region is b_1 (i.e., containing b_0 and n_0) with a guard set consisting of a_0 (we ignore e_0 as it does not contain y). There is no best match in b_1, but the guard a_0 contains y, and since the region corresponding to a_0 is at level 0 of the containment hierarchy, we are done. Therefore, y is in a_0.

4. The only difference in searching for z from searching for y is that the search is continued at the directory node whose corresponding region is b_1 (i.e., containing b_0 and n_0) with a guard set consisting of e_0, as it provides the better match (i.e., both e_0 and a_0 contain z, but a_0 contains e_0). Therefore, z is in e_0.

Exercises

1. Prove that all exact match searches in a BV-tree have the same length and always visit every level in the containment hierarchy.

2. Consider an exact match search for a point p in a BV-tree. This requires traversing the directory hierarchy of the tree while applying a process that finds the best match entry in a particular directory node a. When processing the root node, if the best match e_r corresponding to region r is a guard, then we need to find the smallest region s containing r whose corresponding entry e_s is not a guard. Prove that e_s exists.

3. Continuing Exercise 2, prove that any matching guards enclosed by region s also enclose r.

4. Let us try to generalize Exercise 2 to nodes other than the root. In particular, suppose that, during the search for a point p in a BV-tree, we have reached a nonroot node a at directory

level v. Note that this means that the nonguard entries in a correspond to regions at level $v - 1$ in the containment hierarchy. Let e_r, corresponding to region r, be the best match among the entries in a plus the clevel $v - 1$ entry in the guard set brought down from shallower levels. If e_r is a guard in a, then we need to find a region s containing r whose corresponding entry e_s is either a nonguard entry in a or is the clevel $v - 1$ member of the guard set (to see that e_s can be a nonguard, consider the search for z in Figure 1.85 where e_0 is the best match in the directory node whose corresponding region is b_2, although e_0 is enclosed by b_1 which is not a guard). Prove that e_s exists.

5. Suppose that you modify the exact match search procedure in a BV-tree so that when a search of a directory node a at level v finds that the best match is a guard g at clevel $v - 2$, then the search is continued in the level $v - 2$ directory node corresponding to g. This is instead of the regular search process, which leads to the following actions:

   (a) Finding the best match d in the entries in a that are not guards and applying the same process to the dlevel $v - 2$ entries in d, obtaining e as the best match.

   (b) Checking if e is a better match than the guard g at clevel $v - 2$ (if one exists) in the guard set that was brought down from the previous search (i.e., from dlevel v).

   In other words, if this modification is valid, then it would appear that there is no need to perform the search at the level $v - 1$ directory node once we have found that the best match at dlevel v is a guard. Prove or disprove the validity of this modification. If it is not valid, then construct a counterexample using the BV-tree of Figure 1.85.

1.7.1.6.4 Performance

Among the main reasons for the attractiveness of the BV-tree are its guaranteed performance for executing exact match queries, its space requirements in terms of the maximum number of point pages and directory nodes, and the maximum level of the directory structure necessary for a particular volume of data given the fanout of each directory node. The fanout is equal to the quotient of the number of bits in each node (i.e., page size) and the number of bits needed for each directory entry. The reason that these bounds exist for the BV-tree while they may not exist for the hB-tree is that in the BV-tree there is no need to worry about the multiple posting problem. Thus, each region is pointed at just once in the BV-tree.

The BV-tree performance guarantees are based in part on the assumption that each point page is at least one-third full [643]. This is justified by appealing to the proof given for the hB-tree's satisfaction of this property [1201] (and likewise for the BANG file). The presence of the guards complicates the use of the assumption that each directory node is at least one-third full (which holds for the hB-tree and the BANG file). For example, while illustrating the mechanics of the BV-tree insertion process, we saw an instance of a directory node split operation where the nodes resulting from the split were not at least one-third full (recall Figure 1.84(e)). This situation arose because of the presence of guards whose number was taken into account in the node occupancy when determining if a directory node had overflowed. However, the guards are not necessarily redistributed among the nodes resulting from the split. Instead, they are often promoted, thereby precipitating the overflow of directory nodes at shallower levels of the directory hierarchy.

At this point, let us reexamine the situation that arises when a directory node overflows. There are two cases, depending on whether the overflowing directory node is a guard node. We first deal with the case that the overflowing directory node is not a guard node. As mentioned earlier, a directory node at level v (assuming that the deepest directory node is at level 1) may have a maximum of $v - 1$ guards for each entry in it that is not a guard. An overflowing directory node a at level v has $F + 1$ entries. Let a be split into directory nodes b and c. Now suppose that, after the split, entry d in a serves as a guard for directory node c and that d has $v - 1$ guards in a. Therefore, d will be promoted as a guard to the directory node e at level $v + 1$ that serves as the father of a. In addition, we have to promote all of the $v - 1$ guards of d in a. This means that we have only $F + 1 - v$ entries to distribute into b and c, which must each be at least one-third full (i.e., contain at least $F/3$ entries each). Thus, we must be careful in our choice of F. In particular, if $F < 3v - 3$, then it is not possible to guarantee the one-third-full condition (e.g., when the promoted node has $v - 1$ guards so that a total of v nodes get promoted to dlevel $v + 1$).

Clearly, choosing F to be large is one way to increase the likelihood of avoiding such problems. An alternative method of avoiding this problem altogether is to permit the directory nodes to be of variable size and to take only the number of unpromoted entries into account when determining how to split an overflowing node. In this case, we can avoid most problems by increasing the capacity of a directory node at dlevel v to be $F \cdot v$, thereby guaranteeing enough space to store the maximum number of guards (i.e., $v - 1$) for each unpromoted entry in the directory node (see Exercises 5–7). Interestingly, this has little effect on the overall size of the directory since it can be shown that so few of the directory nodes are at the shallowest level [643]. An added benefit of permitting the directory nodes to vary in size and taking only the number of unpromoted entries into account is that now the execution time for the search query is the same as it would be for a balanced tree with the same number of point pages (assuming the same fullness-percentage guarantee).

We now deal with the case that the overflowing directory node is a guard node. This means that we must take into account the question of whether the two resulting nodes satisfy the same criteria for promotion as the original overflowing node [644]. If yes, then the situation is quite simple: the corresponding entry in the directory node at the next shallower level is replaced by entries for the two new guard nodes, and the overflow continues to be propagated if necessary. Otherwise, the situation is more complex as it may involve demotion, which may have an effect on the rest of the structure. Freeston [644] suggests that the demotion be postponed at the cost of requiring larger directory nodes. The exact details of this process are beyond the scope of our discussion.

The number of guards present also has a direct effect on the number of point pages and directory nodes in the BV-tree of dlevel v. It can be shown that regardless of the number of guards present, given the same fanout value F for both point pages and directory nodes, the ratio of directory nodes to point pages is $1/F$ [643] (see Exercise 4). Assuming that the deepest directory nodes are at level 1, the maximum number of point pages in a BV-tree of height v is F^v and arises when there are no guards (see Exercise 1 for a related result). This is the case when each directory node split results in two disjoint halves as no guards need to be promoted. The minimum number of point pages for a BV-tree of height v and fanout F is $F^v/v!$, where $F \gg v$, and arises when each directory node at level i contains $i - 1$ guards for each unpromoted entry in the node (see Exercises 2 and 3). From a practical standpoint, in order to accommodate the same number of point pages, for a fanout value of 24, a BV-tree of height 3 will have to grow to height 4. Similarly, BV-trees of heights 4 and 5 will have to grow to heights 6 and 10, respectively. For a fanout value of 120, the effect is even less pronounced. In particular, for this fanout value, BV-trees of heights 4 and 6 will have to grow to heights 5 and between 8 and 9, respectively. Thus, when the data pages are of size 1,024 bytes, a 200 GB file will contain about 200 M pages. These 200 M pages will fill up a BV-tree of height 4, and, in the worst case, will require the height of the BV-tree to grow by 1 to be of height 5.

Exercises

1. Prove that the maximum number of directory nodes in a BV-tree of height v and fanout F is approximately F^{v-1} for $F \gg 1$.

2. Prove that the minimum number of point pages in a BV-tree of height v and fanout F is approximately $F^v/v!$ for $F \gg v$.

3. Prove that the maximum number of directory nodes in the BV-tree of height v and fanout F for which the number of point pages is a minimum is approximately $F^{v-1}/v!$ for $F \gg v$.

4. Prove that the ratio of directory nodes to point pages in a BV-tree is $1/F$ regardless of whether a minimum or maximum number of guards is present.

5. Suppose that the directory nodes in the BV-tree are of varying size. In particular, assume that a directory node at level i of a BV-tree with fanout F is large enough to contain F unpromoted entries and $F \cdot (i - 1)$ guards (i.e., unpromoted entries). Show that the total number of point pages we can now have in the worst case of a BV-tree of height v and fanout F is $\approx F^v$ for $F \gg 1$.

6. Using the variable BV-tree node size assumption of Exercise 5, show that the total number of directory nodes we can now have in the worst case of a BV-tree of height v and fanout F is $\approx F^{v-1}$ for $F \gg 1$.

7. Using the variable BV-tree node size assumption of Exercises 5 and 6, prove that the ratio of directory nodes to point pages in a BV-tree is $1/F$ when the maximum number of guards is present.

8. Suppose that you use the variable BV-tree node size assumption of Exercises 5 and 6. This means that the directory nodes are not all the same size. Assuming that each directory node at level v originally required B bytes, the variable node size means that each node will be of size Bv bytes. Show that this modification leads to a very nominal growth in the number of bytes needed to represent the index nodes. In particular, given a BV-tree of height v and fanout F, prove that the space requirements for the index nodes is approximately BF^{v-1}—that is, B times the number of directory nodes as derived in Exercise 6. Thus, the increased size of the nodes close to the root has a negligible effect on the total size of the directory in that, when we use B bytes for each directory node, we also obtain an index size of BF^{v-1} in the best case.

1.7.1.6.5 Summary

The implementation of the searching process demonstrates the utility of the innovation in the design of the BV-tree. The directory is stored economically by reducing the number of nodes necessary due to the avoidance of needless splitting of regions. Recall that this was achieved by decoupling the directory hierarchy from the decomposition hierarchy.[55] Nevertheless, in order to perform searching efficiently (i.e., to avoid descending nodes needlessly, as is the case in the R-tree where the space containing the desired data can be covered by several nodes due to the nondisjoint decomposition of the underlying space), the regions must be split or at least examined in a way that simulates the result of the split, thereby posing apparently contradictory requirements on the data structure. In the BV-tree, this is avoided by the presence of the guards that are associated with the relevant nodes of the directory hierarchy. In fact, the guards are always associated with the directory node that corresponds to the nearest common ancestor of the directory nodes with whom they span some common portion of the underlying space. This is very similar to the notion of fractional cascading [339, 340], which is used in many computational geometry applications, such as the point location query (see Section 2.1.3.3.2 of Chapter 2).

Although up to now we have looked at the BV-tree as an attempt to overcome the problems associated with variants of the k-d-B-tree, the BV-tree can also be viewed as a special case of the R-tree that tries to overcome the shortcomings of the R-tree. In this case, the BV-tree is not used in its full generality since, in order for the analogy to the R-tree to hold, all regions must be hyperrectangles. Of course, although these analogies and comparisons are matters of interpretation, closer scrutiny does reveal some interesting insights.

---

[55] The decoupling idea is also used in the PK-tree (see Section 1.8), where the motivation is the decoupling of the tree structure of the partition process of the underlying space from that of the node hierarchy (i.e., the grouping process of the nodes resulting from the partition process) that makes up the tree directory. See also [462] for a related approach to triangular decompositions of surfaces, such as terrain data.

The main drawback of the k-d-B-tree and its variants is the fact that region splits may be propagated downwards. This is a direct result of the fact that regions must be split into disjoint subregions where one subregion cannot contain another subregion. The hB-tree attempts to overcome this problem, but it still suffers from the multiple posting problem. In this case, instead of splitting point pages into several pieces, directory nodes are referenced several times. In terms of efficiency of the search process, the multiple posting problem in the hB-tree is analogous to the multiple coverage problem of the R-tree. In particular, the multiple coverage problem of the R-tree is that the area containing a specific point may be spanned by several R-tree nodes since the decomposition of the underlying space is not disjoint. Thus, just because a point was not found in the search of one path in the tree does not mean that it would not be found in the search of another path in the tree. This makes search in an R-tree somewhat inefficient.

At a first glance, the BV-tree suffers from the same multiple coverage problem as the R-tree. This is true when we examine the directory hierarchy of the BV-tree. However, the fact that the search process in the BV-tree carries the guards with it as the tree is descended ensures that only one path is followed in any search, thereby compensating for the multiple coverage. Notice that what is really taking place is that the search proceeds by levels in the containment hierarchy, even though it may appear to be backtracking in the directory hierarchy. For example, when searching for point x in the BV-tree of Figure 1.85(a), we immediately make use of the guards a_0 and a_1 in our search of region b_2. We see that these three regions have quite a bit in common. However, as we descend the BV-tree, we find that some of the regions are eliminated from consideration, resulting in the pursuit of just one path. One way to speed the searches in the BV-tree is to organize each directory node into a collection of trees corresponding to the containment hierarchy represented by the node.

The use of the containment hierarchy in the BV-tree can be thought of as leading to a special case of an R-tree in the sense that the containment hierarchy serves as a constraint on the relationship between the regions that form the directory structure. For example, in the R-tree, the regions are usually hyperrectangles (termed *bounding hyperrectangles*), whereas in the BV-tree they can be of any shape. In particular, the constraint is that any pair of bounding hyperrectangles of two children a and b of an R-tree node r must be either disjoint, or one child must be completely contained within the other child (i.e., a is in b, or b is in a). In addition, if we were to build an R-tree using the BV-tree rules, then we would have to modify the rules as to the action to take when inserting a point (or, more generally, an object) that does not lie in the areas spanned by any of the existing bounding hyperrectangles. In particular, we must make sure that the expanded region does not violate the containment hierarchy requirements. Overflow must also be handled somewhat differently to ensure the promotion of guards so that we can avoid the multiple coverage problem. Of course, once this is done, the structure no longer satisfies the property that all leaf nodes be at the same level. Thus, the result is somewhat like the S-tree [22] (see Section 2.1.5.2 of Chapter 2), which is a variant of the R-tree designed to deal with skewed data.

It is interesting to note that when the underlying objects are not points, it may be impossible to guarantee satisfaction of the containment hierarchy requirements when the regions that form the elements of the directory structure are bounding hyperrectangles. In fact, an example of such an impossible case can be constructed when the minimum bounding objects of the underlying objects are hyperrectangles [36], as shown in Figure 1.86. In particular, the figure demonstrates a situation where it is not possible to split the boxes in the figure into two or more groups such that

1. each group is represented by a minimum bounding hyperrectangle, and

2. each group contains at least two of the rectangles in the figure, and

3. the minimum bounding hyperrectangles corresponding to the groups form a containment hierarchy (i.e., they are either pairwise disjoint, or one is contained within the other).

In this case, we may need to use more general and application-specific bounding structures and, most likely, also to require that the objects not overlap. The investigation of the exact relationship between the R-tree and the BV-tree is an issue for further study.

Exercises

1. Figure 1.86 shows a dataset with 12 rectangles that cannot be properly split into two sets that satisfy the containment hierarchy requirements. Can you find a generalized pattern for a set containing an arbitrarily large number of rectangles?

2. Investigate the relationship between the BV-tree and the R-tree. In particular, as outlined in the text, define an R-tree node-splitting rule that satisfies the containment hierarchy rules.

3. Suppose that the objects under consideration are not points and, instead, have extent (e.g., line segments and rectangles). What restrictions on the shape objects are necessary so that the BV-tree rules can be adapted for use with an R-tree or one of its variants?

1.7.1.7   Static Methods

The LSD tree, k-d-B-tree, hB-tree, k-d-B-trie, BANG file, and BV-tree are all dynamic structures where data is inserted at the leaf nodes, and splits are propagated upwards. Thus, they are often characterized as bottom-up data structures. A pair of related data structures are the VAMSplit (variance approximate median split) k-d tree [1989] and the VAMSplit R-tree [1989]. They differ from the LSD tree, k-d-B-tree, hB-tree, and BANG file in that they are static structures where the partitions (i.e., splits) are made in a top-down manner on the basis of knowledge of the entire dataset.

The *VAMSplit k-d tree* [1989] is really a bucket variant of the generalized pseudo k-d tree (e.g., the adaptive k-d tree) in the sense that each leaf node corresponds to a disk bucket or block of capacity b and thus we split a set of elements only if its cardinality exceeds b. Notice that the tree need not be complete. However, the depths of any two leaf nodes differ by at most one. The partitioning axis is chosen corresponding to the dimension with the maximum variance. The partitioning position is chosen with the goal that the leaf nodes (i.e., buckets) will be as full as possible. Thus, the partitioning position is not necessarily the median value along the partitioning axis (as in the adaptive k-d tree described in Section 1.5.1.4), although it is usually within a relatively close range of the median (hence the use of the qualifier *approximate median split*) [1989].

In particular, assuming a set of N nodes, if $N \leq 2b$, then we choose the median value as the partitioning position so that the left child has $\lfloor N/2 \rfloor$ elements, and the right child has $N - \lfloor N/2 \rfloor$ elements. Otherwise, $N > 2b$, and we choose a partitioning position so that the left child contains mb elements, where mb is the largest multiple of b that is less than $N/2$, and the right child contains the remaining elements. Such an action will minimize the number of leaf nodes in the final k-d tree by maximizing the number of completely full nodes so that at most two will not be full (see Exercise 3).

As an example, suppose that we have a set with 22 elements and bucket capacity of 5 for which we want to build a VAMSplit k-d tree. There are many ways to partition this set. Below, we consider only the way in which the partitioning positions are chosen, thereby assuming that the partitioning axes have already been determined. Figure 1.87(a) shows the size of the subtrees in the resulting k-d tree when the partitioning position is the median with six leaf nodes (i.e., buckets), and Figure 1.87(b) shows the resulting VAMSplit k-d tree when the partitioning position is chosen so as to minimize the total number of leaf nodes, which is five here. Note that although the difference in the number of leaf nodes is just one in this case, examples can be constructed with more elements where the difference in the number of leaf nodes is considerably higher.

Once the partitioning positions have been chosen, the internal nodes of the tree are aggregated into buckets of capacity c proceeding from the root downwards in a breadth-first traversal of the subtrees until enough nodes have been accumulated to

Figure 1.86
Example of a collection of hyperrectangle minimum bounding objects for which it is impossible to guarantee satisfaction of the containment hierarchy requirements—that is, the collection cannot be subdivided into two sets that both have at least two members and where the minimum bounding hyperrectangles of the sets are either disjoint or one is contained in the other.

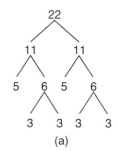

(a)

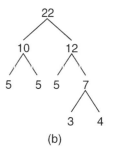

(b)

Figure 1.87
K-d trees with 22 elements and a bucket capacity of 5 that are built by using a partitioning position (a) at the median of the elements in the subtree and (b) at the position that minimizes the total number of leaf nodes (i.e., a VAMSplit k-d tree with no aggregation of the internal nodes). Each nonleaf node indicates the number of elements in the corresponding subtree.

fill the bucket (i.e., c). This process is applied recursively to the rest of the tree until the leaf nodes are encountered. The similarity to a top-down LSD tree and a top-down k-d-B-tree should be clear. The search performance of the VAMSplit k-d tree is enhanced by associating with each node i in the VAMSplit k-d tree a minimum bounding box of the part of the underlying space that is spanned by the internal nodes that have been merged into i. The result is termed a *VAMSplit R-tree* [1989]. However, unlike the real R-tree, minimization of overlap or coverage plays no role in deciding which internal nodes should be aggregated. This decision is based purely on the k-d tree splits. Thus, we see that the VAMSplit R-tree is related to the VAMSplit k-d tree in the same way that the R$^+$-tree [593, 1718, 1803] is related to the k-d-B-tree (see Section 2.1.5.3 of Chapter 2). In fact, a more appropriate name for the VAMSplit R-tree is a VAMSplit R$^+$-tree.

Exercises

1. Assuming a bucket size of 5, can you come up with a simpler example than that given in Figure 1.87 to illustrate the advantage of not using a partitioning position at the median of the set of elements in an adaptive k-d tree such as the VAMSplit k-d tree?

2. Give an algorithm to build a VAMSplit k-d tree.

3. Prove that the number of nonfull leaf nodes in a VAMSplit k-d tree is at most two.

4. Give an algorithm to build a VAMSplit R-tree.

1.7.2 Grid Directory Methods

There are several methods of decomposing the underlying space into a grid of cells, termed *grid cells*. The contents of the grid cells are stored in pages (termed *buckets*) in secondary memory. Some of the methods (e.g., grid file and EXCELL) permit a bucket to contain the contents of several grid cells but do not permit a grid cell to be associated with more than one bucket. Other methods (e.g., linear hashing and spiral hashing, also known as spiral storage) do not permit a bucket to contain the contents of more than one grid cell but do permit a grid cell to be associated with more than one bucket, in which case the additional buckets are known as *overflow buckets*. When more than one grid cell is associated with a bucket, then the union of these grid cells must form a d-dimensional hyperrectangle. The actual buckets associated with the grid cells are usually accessed with the aid of a directory in the form of an array (termed a *grid directory*) that can change as the data volume grows or contracts.

Below, we focus on what to do if the data volume grows to such an extent that either one of the grid cells or buckets is too full. There are several possible solutions. When a bucket is too full, we just split it. When a grid cell is too full, we usually need to make a new grid partition. In this case, the most extreme solution is to make a new grid by refining the entire grid of g d-dimensional grid cells by doubling it along all keys (i.e., halving the width of each side of a grid cell), thereby resulting in $2^d \cdot g$ grid cells. This is quite wasteful of space and is not discussed further here.

Whatever action we take, we must maintain the grid while also resolving the issue of the overflowing grid cell (usually by splitting it). This can be achieved by refining the partition along just one of the keys through the introduction of one additional partition. The drawback of such an action is that the grid cells are no longer equal sized. This means that, given a point, we cannot determine the grid cell in which it is contained without the aid of an additional data structure (termed a *linear scale* and discussed briefly in Section 1.1) to indicate the positions of the partitions. If there are originally $\prod_{i=1}^{d} g_i$ grid cells with $g_i - 1$ partition positions along key i, then, without loss of generality, refining key d results in $(g_d + 1) \cdot \prod_{i=1}^{d-1} g_i$ grid cells. This is the basis of multipaging [1287, 1288]) and the grid file [839, 840, 1376].

We can avoid the need for the linear scales by uniformly partitioning all grid cells in the same way, rather than just the cells in the $(d-1)$-dimensional hyperplane that passes through the overflowing grid cell. In essence, we halve the width of just one of the sides of each grid cell, thereby doubling the granularity of the decomposition along one of the axes. This results in doubling the total number of grid cells to yield $2 \cdot g$ grid cells. This is the basis of the EXCELL method [1822].

An alternative approach is to order the grid cells according to one of a subset of the one-dimensional orderings of the underlying space described in Section 1.6 and to use linear hashing to resolve an overflowing grid cell. In this case, we start with a grid of equal-sized grid cells (initially containing just one grid cell) that are split into two halves in succession in a consistent manner (i.e., along the same key), according to the particular one-dimensional ordering that is used, until all grid cells have been split, at which point the process is restarted with a split across the same or another key. The drawback of this method is that the grid cell that is split is not necessarily the one that has become too full. This is resolved by making use of what are termed *overflow buckets*.

It is important to observe that for linear hashing the grid directory is a one-dimensional array instead of a d-dimensional array as for the grid file and EXCELL. This is because the result of the hashing function is just an address in one dimension, although the underlying space is partitioned into sets of ranges of values that for most variants of linear hashing (with the notable exception of spiral hashing) correspond to grid cells in d dimensions. For most variants of linear hashing, the ranges have a limited set of possible sizes. In fact, if there is a one-to-one correlation between the numbering of the grid cells and the bucket labels, then there is no need for a grid directory in linear hashing.

The rest of this section is organized as follows. Section 1.7.2.1 describes the grid file. Section 1.7.2.2 presents EXCELL. Section 1.7.2.3 reviews linear hashing and explains how it can be adapted to handle multidimensional point data. Section 1.7.2.4 discusses some alternative implementations of linear hashing that address the drawback that the grid cell that has been split most recently is not necessarily the one that is full. This discussion also includes an explanation of how to adapt the related method of spiral hashing to multidimensional point data. Section 1.7.2.5 contains a brief comparison of the various bucket methods that make use of a grid directory.

1.7.2.1 Grid File

The *grid file* of Nievergelt, Hinterberger, and Sevcik [839, 840, 1376] is a variation of the fixed-grid method that relaxes the requirement that grid subdivision lines be equidistant. Its goals are to retrieve records with at most two disk accesses and to handle range queries efficiently. This is done by using a grid directory in the form of an array to the grid cells. All records in one grid cell are stored in the same bucket. However, several grid cells can share a bucket as long as the union of these grid cells forms a d-dimensional hyperrectangle in the space of the data. Although the regions of the buckets are piecewise disjoint, together they span the entire underlying space.

The purpose of the grid directory is to maintain a dynamic correspondence between the grid cells and the buckets. The grid directory consists of two parts. The first is a dynamic d-dimensional array, containing one entry for each grid cell. The values of the elements are pointers to the relevant buckets. Usually buckets will have a capacity of 10 to 1,000 points. Thus, the entry in the grid directory is small in comparison to a bucket. We are not concerned with how the points are organized within a bucket (e.g., linked list, tree). The grid directory is usually stored on disk as it may be quite large, especially when d is large.

The second part of the grid directory is a set of d one-dimensional arrays called *linear scales*. These scales define a partition of the domain of each key. They enable access to the appropriate grid cells by aiding the computation of their address based on the value

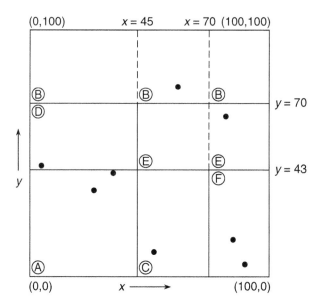

Figure 1.88
Grid file partition for the data corresponding to Figure 1.1.

of the relevant keys. The linear scales are kept in main memory. It should be noted that the linear scales are useful in guiding a range query, by indicating the grid cells that overlap the query range. The linear scales can also be implemented using binary trees (see Sections 1.7.2.3, 1.7.2.4.1, and 1.7.2.4.2, as well as Exercise 1).

Thus, we see that the two goals of the grid file are met. Any record is retrieved with two disk accesses: one disk access for the grid cell and one for the bucket. Of course, a variant of the grid file could also be formulated that guarantees that any record can be retrieved with i disk accesses by making use of a hierarchy of $i - 2$ grid files to organize the grid directory, each of which would be stored on disk. In fact, Hinrichs [840] describes such an approach, which he terms a *two-level grid file*, where the additional grid file is used to manage the grid directory. However, in order to obviate the need for a third disk access, Hinrichs proposes to store the first grid directory in main memory as well. Range queries are efficient, although, since the sizes of the grid cells (i.e., the ranges of their intervals) are not related to the query range, it is difficult to analyze the amount of time necessary to execute a range query.

As an example, consider Figure 1.88, which shows the grid file representation for the data of Figure 1.1. Once again, we adopt the convention that a grid cell is open with respect to its upper and right boundaries and closed with respect to its lower and left boundaries. The bucket capacity is two records. There are $d = 2$ different keys. The grid directory consists of nine grid cells and six buckets labeled A–F. We refer to grid cells as if they are array elements: grid cell (i, j) is the element in column i (starting at the left with column 1) and row j (starting at the bottom with row 1) of the grid directory.

Grid cells (1,3), (2,2), and (3,3) are empty; however, they do share buckets with other grid cells. In particular, grid cell (1,3) shares bucket B with grid cells (2,3) and (3,3), while grid cells (2,2) and (3,2) share bucket E. The sharing is indicated by the broken lines. Figure 1.89 contains the linear scales for the two keys (i.e., the x and y coordinates). For example, executing an exact match query with $x = 80$ and $y = 62$ causes the access of the bucket associated with the grid cell in row 2 and column 3 of the grid directory of Figure 1.88.

The grid file is attractive, in part, because of its graceful growth as more and more records are inserted. As the buckets overflow, we apply a splitting process, which results in the creation of new buckets and a movement of records. To explain the splitting process, let us examine more closely how the grid file copes with a sequence of insertion

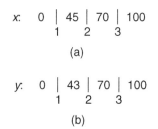

Figure 1.89
Linear scales for (a) x and (b) y corresponding to Figure 1.88.

operations. Again, we assume a bucket capacity of 2 and observe how a grid file is constructed for the records of Figure 1.1 in the order in which they appear there: Chicago, Mobile, Toronto, Buffalo, Denver, Omaha, Atlanta, and Miami.

The insertion of Chicago and Mobile results in bucket A being full. Insertion of Toronto leads to an overflow of bucket A, causing a split. We arbitrarily split along the y axis at $y = 70$ and modify the linear scale for key y accordingly. Toronto is inserted into B, the newly allocated bucket (see Figure 1.90(a)).

Next, we try to insert Buffalo and find that the bucket in which it belongs (i.e., A) is full. We split the x axis at $x = 45$ and modify the linear scale for key x. This results in the insertion of Buffalo in bucket C and the movement of Mobile from bucket A to bucket C (see Figure 1.90(b)). Note that, as a result of this split, both grid cells (1,2) and (2,2) share bucket B, although grid cell (1,2) is empty. Alternatively, we could have marked grid cell (1,2) as empty when the x axis was split. This has the disadvantage that, should

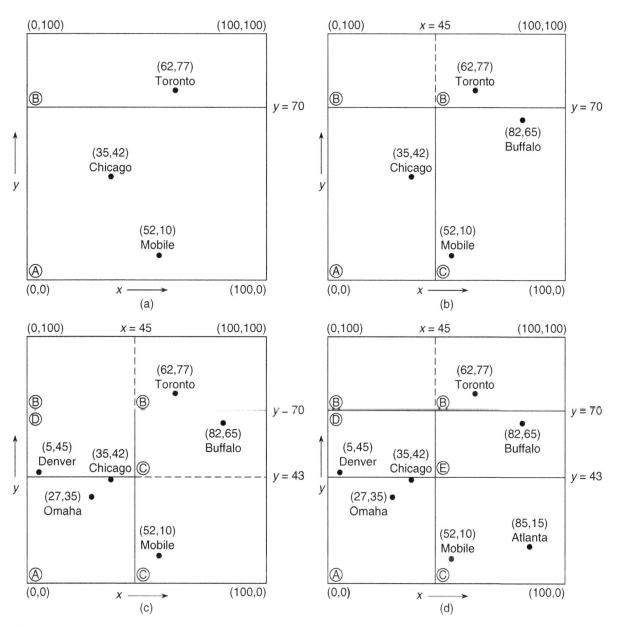

Figure 1.90
Sequence of partial grid partitions demonstrating the result of the insertion of (a) Chicago, Mobile, and Toronto, (b) Buffalo, (c) Denver and Omaha, and (d) Atlanta.

we later wish to insert a record into grid cell (1,2), we would either have to allocate a new bucket or search for a neighboring bucket that was not full and whose grid cells formed a convex region with grid cell (1,2).

The insertion of Denver proceeds smoothly. It is placed in bucket A. Omaha also belongs in bucket A, which means that it must be split again. We split the y axis at $y = 43$ and modify the linear scale for key y. In addition, we create a new bucket, D, to which Denver is moved, while Omaha and Chicago remain in bucket A (see Figure 1.90(c)). Note that as a result of this split, both grid cells (2,1) and (2,2) share bucket C, contributing Buffalo and Mobile, respectively.

Attempting to insert Atlanta finds it belonging in bucket C, which is full; yet, grid cell (2,1) is not full. This leads to splitting bucket C and the creation of bucket E. Bucket C now contains Mobile and Atlanta and corresponds to grid cell (2,1), while bucket E now contains Buffalo and corresponds to grid cell (2,2) (see Figure 1.90(d)). Note that we did not have to partition the grid in this case. Thus, no change needs to be made to the linear scales; however, the grid directory must be updated to reflect the association of grid cell (2,2) with bucket E instead of bucket C.

Finally, insertion of Miami finds it belonging to bucket C, which is full. We split the x axis at $x = 70$ and modify the linear scale for key x. A new bucket, F, is created to which Atlanta and Miami are moved (see Figure 1.88). Once again, we observe that as a result of this split, grid cells (2,3) and (3,3) share bucket B, although grid cell (3,3) is empty. Similarly, grid cells (2,2) and (3,2) share bucket E, although grid cell (2,2) is empty.

At this point, we are ready to elaborate further on the splitting process. From the above, we see that two types of bucket splits are possible. The first, and most common, arises when several grid cells share a bucket that has overflowed (e.g., the transition between Figure 1.90(c, d) upon the insertion of Atlanta).

In this case, we merely need to allocate a new bucket and adjust the mapping between grid cells and buckets.

The second type of a split arises when we must refine a grid partition. It is triggered by an overflowing bucket, all of whose records lie in a single grid cell (e.g., the overflow of bucket A upon insertion of Toronto in Figure 1.90(a)). In this case, we have a choice with respect to the dimension (i.e., axis) and location of the splitting point (i.e., we do not need to split at the midpoint of an interval). Without any external knowledge or motivation, a reasonable splitting policy is one that cycles through the various keys (e.g., first split on key x, then key y, key $x, \ldots$, as was done in Figure 1.90) and uses interval midpoints. This is the approach used in the grid file implementation [1376].

An alternative splitting policy is an adaptive one favoring one key over others. This is akin to a favored key in an inverted file. It results in an increase in the precision of answers to partially specified queries (i.e., partial range) where the favored key is specified. Such a policy is triggered by keeping track of the most frequently queried key (in the case of partial range queries) and by monitoring dynamic file content, thereby increasing the granularity of the key scales. Splitting at locations other than interval midpoints is also an adaptive policy.

The grid refinement operation is common at the initial stage of constructing a grid file. However, as the grid file grows, it becomes relatively rare in comparison with the overflowing bucket that is shared among several grid cells. Nevertheless, the frequency of grid refinement can be reduced by varying the grid directory as follows: Implement the grid directory as a d-dimensional array whose size in each dimension is determined by the shortest interval in each linear scale (i.e., if the linear scale for key x spans the range 0 through 64 and the shortest interval is 4, then the grid directory has 16 entries for dimension x).

This variation is a multidimensional counterpart of the directory used in extendible hashing [579] and is the basis of EXCELL [1822] (see Section 1.7.2.2). Its advantage is that a refinement of the grid partition will cause a change in the structure of the directory only if the shortest interval is split, in which case the grid directory will double in size. Such a representation anticipates small structural updates and replaces them by a large one. It is fine as long as the data is uniformly distributed. Otherwise, many empty grid cells will arise.

The counterpart of splitting is merging. There are two possible instances where merging is appropriate: bucket merging and directory merging. Bucket merging, the more common of the two, arises when a bucket is empty or nearly empty. Bucket-merging policy is influenced by three factors. First, we must decide which bucket pairs are candidates for merging. This decision can be based on a *buddy system* or a *neighbor system*.

In a *buddy system* [1042, 1044], each bucket, say X, can be merged with exactly one bucket, say B_j, in each of the d dimensions. Ideally, the chosen bucket, say B_j, should have the property that, at some earlier point, it was split to yield buckets X and B_j. We call this buddy the "true" buddy. For example, consider the grid directory of Figure 1.91, which contains buckets A–K and X. Assume that when a bucket is split, it is split into two buckets of equal size. Since $d = 2$, the only potential buddies of bucket X are I and J. We can keep track of the true buddies by representing the splitting process as a binary tree, thereby maintaining the buddy relationships.

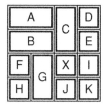

Figure 1.91
Example grid directory illustrating bucket merging when using the grid file.

In a *neighbor system*, each bucket can be merged with either of its two adjacent neighbors in each of the d dimensions (the resulting bucket region must be convex). For example, in the grid directory of Figure 1.91, bucket X can be merged with any one of its neighbors, buckets C, I, or J. Note that X cannot be merged with neighbor bucket G since the resulting bucket region would not be convex.

The second factor influencing bucket-merging policy deals with the ordering among possible choices should there be more than one candidate. In the case of the buddy system, we give priority to the true buddy. Otherwise, this factor is relevant only if it is desired to have varying granularity among keys. In particular, if the splitting policy favors some keys over others, the merging policy should not undo it.

The third factor is the merging threshold: when should a candidate pair of buckets actually be merged? It should be clear that the sum of the bucket occupancy percentages for the contents of the merged bucket should not be too large because, otherwise, it will soon have to be split. Nievergelt, Hinterberger, and Sevcik [1376] conducted simulation studies showing the average bucket occupancy to be 70% and suggest that this is an appropriate merging threshold for the occupancy of the resulting bucket.

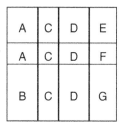

Figure 1.92
Example grid directory illustrating directory merging when using the grid file.

Directory merging arises when all the grid cells in two adjacent cross sections (i.e., slices along one axis) in the grid directory are associated with the same bucket. For example, consider the two-dimensional grid directory of Figure 1.92, where all grid cells in column 2 are in bucket C, and all grid cells in column 3 are in bucket D. In such a case, if the merging threshold is satisfied, then buckets C and D can be merged, and the linear scales modified to reflect this change.

Generally, directory merging is of little practical interest since, even if merging is allowed to occur, it is probable that splitting will soon have to take place. Nevertheless, there are occasions when directory merging is of use. First, directory merging is necessary in the case of a shrinking file. Second, it is appropriate when the granularity of certain keys is being changed to comply with the access frequency of the key. Third, it is a useful technique when attempting to get rid of inactive keys. In such a case, the key could be set to a "merge only" state. Eventually, the partition will be reduced to one interval, and the corresponding dimension in the grid directory can be removed or assigned to another key.

At times, it is desired to update an existing grid file with a large number of points at once. This is more efficient than updating the grid file one point at a time. This technique is known as *bulk insertion*. It can also be used to build the grid file from scratch, in which case it is also known as *bulk loading*. In the case of the grid file, the goal is to minimize the size of the grid file needed to ensure the absence of bucket overflow for a given dataset. This problem was first addressed by Li, Rotem, and Srivastava [1160], who were concerned with the bulk loading of grid files for two-dimensional data distributed across multiple sites in a "shared nothing" environment. They show how to partition the data among several processors and have each processor build its own grid file. Their method assumes an existing partition along one dimension and a fixed number of partitions along the remaining dimension. Given this assumption, they partition the remaining dimension optimally using a dynamic programming approach. Leutenegger and Nicol [1154] show that the dynamic programming approach is inefficient for large grid files and, instead, reformulate the problem as one of finding the smallest number of partitions in the remaining dimension for which the total overflow is zero. This enables them to use a fast heuristic algorithm instead of a slow and expensive dynamic programming algorithm.

As we pointed out, the grid file guarantees that any record can be retrieved with two disk accesses. This is fine for point queries (exact match); however, range queries require considerably more disk accesses. Kriegel [1078] reports on an empirical comparison of the grid file and a pair of versions of a multidimensional B-tree termed the *kB-tree* [786, 787] and the *MDBT* [1686] (see Section 1.1 for a brief description), as well as the inverted file. Kriegel's data [1078] show that when the keys are correlated and nonuniformly distributed, the grid file is superior with respect to insertions, deletions, and exact match queries, but the structures that are based on the B-tree variants are superior with respect to partial range queries. For range queries, the performance of the grid file is at best comparable to the B-tree variants and often worse. The performance of the inverted file is always worse than the alternatives. On the other hand, when the keys are independent and uniformly distributed, Kriegel [1078] points out that the grid file is expected to be superior on all counts. In all cases, the space requirements of the grid file are always lower than those of the B-tree variants. The relative performance of the kB-tree and the MDBT is comparable.

The grid file is similar to the multipaging method of Merrett and Otoo [1287, 1288]. Multipaging also uses a directory in the form of linear scales called *axial arrays*. However, instead of using a grid directory to access the data pages, multipaging accesses a data page and its potential overflow chain using an address that is computed directly from the linear scales. There are two variants of multipaging: static and dynamic. In static multipaging [1287], both the expected number of probes needed to access any record and the storage utilization are bounded. The result is similar to the fixed-grid method (recall Section 1.1) in that these values are used to determine the optimal partitioning of the grid. Thus, the method is designed to work when the data is known in advance. Dynamic multipaging [1288] is designed to work when the data is constantly changing and thus can deal with the case that the data pages grow and split at will. In this case, only the expected number of probes to access any record is bounded.

Comparing the grid file and multipaging, we find that the grid file uses multipaging as an index to the grid directory. Therefore, multipaging saves space by not requiring a grid directory, but this is at a cost of requiring bucket (i.e., data page) overflow areas. This means that multipaging can obtain good average-case performance, but it cannot guarantee record retrieval with two disk accesses. In addition, insertion and deletion in multipaging involves whole rows or columns (in the two-dimensional case) of data pages when splitting or merging data pages, while the grid file can split one data page at a time and localize more global operations in the grid directory. The absence of the grid directory in multipaging means that, in the case of dynamic multipaging, some attention must also be paid to how the resulting multipaging space is to be addressed. In this case, dynamic multipaging resembles some of the more sophisticated variants of linear hashing (see Section 1.7.2.4), and the issue is dealt with in a similar manner.

Exercises

1. The linear scales are implemented as one-dimensional arrays. They could also be implemented as binary trees. What would be the advantage of doing so?

2. Implement a database that uses the grid file to organize two-dimensional data.

3. The grid file is considered to be an instance of a bucket method with fanout 2 (i.e., the number of buckets into which an overflowing bucket is split, which also includes the B-tree, EXCELL, and EXHASH) and 0.69 average storage utilization [1376] (see the general discussion in Section 1.7.3). The *twin grid file* [907, 908] is a representation that makes use of two grid files and has been observed to result in improving the average storage utilization of the grid file to 90%. Give an intuitive explanation of why this is so.

4. How can you improve the performance of the twin grid file discussed in Exercise 3?

5. Calculate the expected size of the grid directory for uniformly distributed data.

1.7.2.2 EXCELL

The EXCELL method of Tamminen [1822] is similar in spirit to the grid file in that it also makes use of a grid directory and retrieves all records with at most two disk accesses. The principal difference between them is that grid refinement for the grid file splits only one interval in two and results in the insertion of a $(d-1)$-dimensional cross section. In contrast, a grid refinement for the EXCELL method splits all intervals in two (the partition points are fixed) for the particular dimension and results in doubling the size of the grid directory. This means that all grid cells are of the same size in EXCELL, but this is not the case for the grid file.

The result is that the grid directory grows more gradually when the grid file is used, whereas use of EXCELL reduces the need for grid refinement operations at the expense of larger directories, in general, due to a sensitivity to the distribution of the data. However, a large bucket size reduces the effect of nonuniformity unless the data consists entirely of a few clusters. The fact that all grid cells define equal-sized (and convex) regions has two important ramifications. First, it means that EXCELL does not require a set of linear scales to access the grid directory and retrieve a record with at most two disk accesses, as is needed for the grid file. Thus, grid directory access operations are considerably faster for EXCELL. Second, it means that the partition points are fixed and are not chosen on the basis of the data, as is the case for the grid file. Therefore, range queries are efficient with an execution time that is proportional to the number of buckets corresponding to the grid cells that make up the range being searched (i.e., to the size of the range). In contrast, the number of grid cells that make up a range in the grid file is not proportional to the size of the range.

An example of the EXCELL method is given in Figure 1.93, which shows the representation for the data in Figure 1.1. Here the x axis is split before the y axis. Again, the convention is adopted that a rectangle is open with respect to its upper and right boundaries and closed with respect to its lower and left boundaries. The capacity of the bucket is two records. There are $d = 2$ different keys. The grid directory is implemented as an array; in this case, it consists of eight grid cells (labeled in the same way as for the grid file) and six buckets labeled A–F. Note that grid cells (3,2) and (4,2) share bucket C, while grid cells (1,2) and (2,2), despite being empty, share bucket D. The sharing is indicated by the broken lines. Furthermore, when a bucket size of 1 is used, the partition of space induced by EXCELL is equivalent to that induced by a PR k-d tree [1413], although the two structures differ by virtue of the presence of a directory in the case of EXCELL.

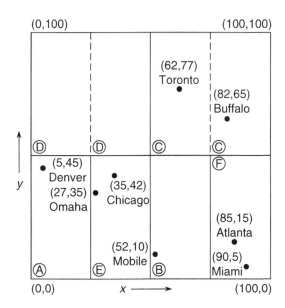

Figure 1.93
EXCELL representation for the data corresponding to Figure 1.1 when the *x* axis is split before the *y* axis.

As a database represented by the EXCELL method grows, buckets will overflow. This leads to the application of a splitting process, which results in the creation of new buckets and a movement of records. To explain the splitting process, we examine how EXCELL copes with a sequence of insertion operations corresponding to the data of Figure 1.1. Again, we assume a bucket capacity of 2 and that the records are inserted in the order in which they appear in Figure 1.1—that is, Chicago, Mobile, Toronto, Buffalo, Denver, Omaha, Atlanta, and Miami.

The insertion of Chicago and Mobile results in bucket A being full. Insertion of Toronto leads to an overflow of bucket A, which compels us to double the directory by splitting along key *x*. We split bucket A and move Mobile and Toronto to B, the newly allocated bucket (see Figure 1.94(a)). Next, we insert Buffalo and find that the bucket in which it belongs (i.e., B) is full. This causes us to double the directory by splitting along key *y*. We now split bucket B and move Toronto and Buffalo to C, the newly allocated bucket (see Figure 1.94(b)). Note that bucket A still contains Chicago and overlaps grid cells (1,1) and (1,2).

The insertion of Denver proceeds smoothly, and it is placed in bucket A. Omaha also belongs in bucket A, which has now overflowed. Since bucket A overlaps grid cells (1,1) and (1,2), we split it, thereby allocating a new bucket, D, such that buckets A and D correspond to grid cells (1,1) and (1,2), respectively (see Figure 1.94(c)). However, neither Denver, Chicago, nor Omaha can be moved to D, thereby necessitating a directory doubling along key *x*. We now split bucket A and move Chicago and Omaha to E, the newly allocated bucket (see Figure 1.94(d)). Note that buckets B, C, and D retain their contents, except that now each bucket overlaps two grid cells.

Next, Atlanta is inserted into bucket B. Insertion of Miami causes bucket B to overflow. Since B overlaps grid cells (3,1) and (4,1), we split it, thereby allocating a new cell, F, such that buckets B and F correspond to grid cells (3,1) and (4,1), respectively. Atlanta and Miami are moved to F (see Figure 1.93).

From the discussion, we see that two types of bucket splits are possible. The first, and most common, is when several grid cells share a bucket that has overflowed (e.g., the transition between Figures 1.94(d) and 1.93 caused by the overflow of bucket B as

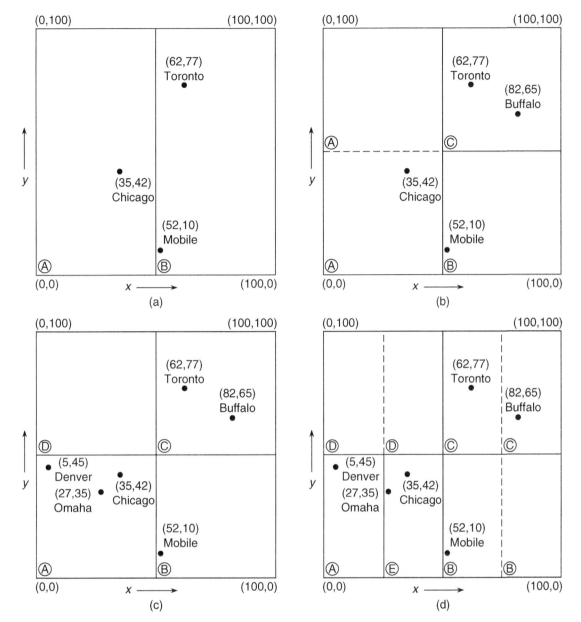

Figure 1.94
Sequence of partial EXCELL partitions demonstrating the result of the insertion of (a) Toronto, (b) Buffalo, and (c, d) Omaha.

Atlanta and Miami are inserted in sequence). In this case, we allocate a new bucket and adjust the mapping between grid cells and buckets.

The second type of a split causes a doubling of the directory and arises when we must refine a grid partition. It is triggered by an overflowing bucket that is not shared among several grid cells (e.g., the overflow of bucket A upon insertion of Toronto in Figure 1.94(a)). The split occurs along the different keys in a cyclic fashion (i.e., first split along key x, then y, then x, etc.).

For both types of bucket splits, the situation may arise that none of the elements in the overflowing bucket belongs to the newly created bucket, with the result that the directory will have to be doubled more than once. This is because the splitting points are fixed for EXCELL. For example, consider bucket A in Figure 1.95(a) with bucket capacity 2 and containing points X and Y. Insertion of point Z (see Figure 1.95(b)) leads

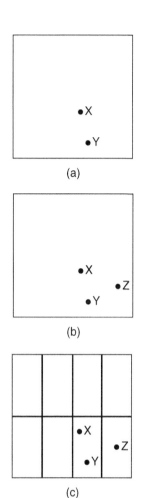

(a)

(b)

(c)

Figure 1.95
Example showing the need for three directory doubling operations using EXCELL when inserting point Z, assuming a bucket capacity of 2.

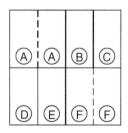

Figure 1.96
Example demonstrating the possibility of directory merging when using EXCELL.

to overflow of A and causes three directory doublings (see Figure 1.95(c)). In contrast, the fact that the splitting point is not fixed for the grid file means that it can be chosen so that only one grid refinement is necessary. Thus, we see that the size of the EXCELL grid directory is sensitive to the distribution of the data. However, a large bucket size reduces the effect of nonuniformity unless the data consists entirely of a few clusters.

The counterpart of splitting is merging. However, it is considerably more limited in scope for EXCELL than for the grid file. Also, it is less likely to arise because EXCELL has been designed primarily for use in geometrical applications where deletion of records is not so prevalent. There are two cases where merging is appropriate.

The first, and most common, is bucket merging, which arises when a pair of buckets is empty or nearly empty. The buckets that are candidates for merging, say X and Y, must be buddies in the sense that, at some earlier time, one of them was split, say X, to yield X and Y (e.g., A and E in Figure 1.93 but not A and C). Once such a bucket pair has been identified, we must see if its elements satisfy the merging threshold. In essence, the sum of the bucket occupancy percentages for the contents of the merged bucket should not be too large because, otherwise, it might soon have to be split.

The second instance where merging is possible is directory merging. It arises when either each bucket buddy pair in the grid directory meets the merging threshold (e.g., B and C, D, and E in Figure 1.96) or the bucket overlaps more than one grid cell (e.g., bucket A overlaps grid cells (1,2) and (2,2), and bucket F overlaps grid cells (3,1) and (4,1) in Figure 1.96). This is quite rare.

Exercise

1. Implement a database that uses EXCELL to organize two-dimensional data.

1.7.2.3   Linear Hashing

Linear hashing [1106, 1187] is a technique for avoiding drastic growth in the size of a hash table when it becomes too full (i.e., when a hash bucket overflows). In essence, use of linear hashing enables the hash table to grow by just one hash bucket, instead of doubling the number of hash buckets, as is the case with some hashing methods such as EXHASH [579], the extendible hashing function that forms the basis of EXCELL [1823].

This section is organized as follows. We first review the basic principles of linear hashing and show how to adapt it to handle multidimensional data (Section 1.7.2.3.1). This adaptation makes use of reversed bit interleaving as the hashing function. Next, we show how to implement linear hashing with multidimensional extendible hashing (MDEH) as the hashing function where the order in which overflowing buckets are split is more natural (Section 1.7.2.3.2). This is followed by an explanation of dynamic z hashing, which ensures that the newly created buckets are stored near each other (Section 1.7.2.3.3). We conclude with a brief discussion of linear hashing with partial expansions (LHPE), which addresses the issue that the load factors of the buckets that have just been split are much smaller than those of buckets that have not. In particular LHPE addresses this issue by splitting q buckets into $q + 1$ buckets, as done in some implementations of the B-tree (Section 1.7.2.3.4).

As the primary focus of this section is the adaptation of linear hashing to multidimensional data, the explanation of linear hashing is somewhat brief. Appendix B contains a more detailed explanation of linear hashing and how it is related to other methods, such as extendible hashing. Readers who are not familiar with linear hashing are encouraged to consult it first before continuing further in this section.

1.7.2.3.1 Adapting Linear Hashing to Multidimensional Data

Our adaptation is based on starting with a grid of equal-sized grid cells, ordering the grid cells using a mapping from d dimensions to one dimension (perhaps one of the orderings discussed in Section 1.6), and then, if necessary, splitting the grid cells one at a time in a manner consistent with the chosen order until all grid cells have been split. This results in creating a new grid of equal-sized grid cells, at which time the process is reapplied. Each bucket is associated with just one grid cell.

The key idea behind linear hashing is the decoupling of the decision as to which grid cell is to be split from the identity of the grid cell whose bucket has overflowed. This is a direct result of the predetermined order in which the grid cells are split. Since we must still deal with the fact that a bucket is too full, we have two types of buckets: primary and overflow. Each grid cell has a different primary bucket. When attempting to insert a data point p whose grid cell c's primary bucket b is full, then p is inserted into an overflow bucket associated with c. Generally, the overflow buckets are chained to the primary buckets. Assuming that there are m grid cells, we use a one-dimensional directory addressed from 0 to $m - 1$ to access the primary buckets associated with the grid cells. However, if there is a one-to-one correlation between the numbering of the grid cells and the primary bucket labels (as we will assume in our example), then there is no need for a grid directory.

Formally, we treat the underlying space as having a complete grid T imposed on it, said to be at *level n*, and a partial grid, T', said to be at level $n + 1$, where some of the grid cells in T have been split into two equal-sized parts.[56] n denotes the number of total grid partitions that have been applied, where a *total grid partition* means that the number of grid cells has doubled in size. Given a complete grid at level n, we have m ($2^n \le m \le 2^{n+1} - 1$) disjoint grid cells that span the entire underlying space: $2^{n+1} - m$ of the grid cells are d-dimensional hyperrectangles of size v (both in volume and orientation), while the remaining $2 \cdot (m - 2^n)$ grid cells are d-dimensional hyperrectangles of size $v/2$. The set of grid cells of size v are the ones that have not been split yet.

In order to make this method work, we need an ordering for the grid cells. In addition, we need a way to determine the grid cell associated with each data point. Moreover, if we do not assume a one-to-one correlation between the numbering of the grid cells and the primary bucket labels, then we also need a way to determine the directory element associated with each grid cell so that the relevant bucket can be accessed. Since we are using an ordering, we will need to make use of at least one mapping from d dimensions to one dimension.

In the following, we describe the approach that we use. Identify each grid cell c by the location of the point in the underlying space at the corner of c that is closest to the origin (e.g., the lower-leftmost corner for two-dimensional data with an origin at the lower-leftmost corner of the underlying space) and denote it as $l(c)$. Also, let $u(c)$ be the location of the point in the underlying space at the corner of c that is farthest from the origin (e.g., the upper-rightmost corner for two-dimensional data with an origin at the lower-leftmost corner of the underlying space).

We need two mappings. First, we need a mapping g from d dimensions to one dimension that assigns a unique number to each data point in d dimensions (i.e., an ordering). For this mapping, we use one of the orderings discussed in Section 1.6 that satisfies the properties given below. The ordering is implemented in such a way that the first element in the ordering corresponds to the point closest to the origin.

1. The position in the ordering of each data point p in grid cell c is greater than or equal to that of $l(c)$ (i.e., after)—that is, $g(p) \ge g(l(c))$.

2. The position in the ordering of each data point p in grid cell c is less than or equal to that of $u(c)$ (i.e., before)—that is, $g(p) \le g(u(c))$.

---

[56] Note that, in this case, the term *level* has the same meaning as *depth* for representations that make use of a tree or trie access structure. As we will see, in many other applications (e.g., the region quadtree, as well as the BV-tree in Section 1.7.1.6), the term *level* has a different meaning in the sense that it indicates the number of aggregation steps that have been performed.

3. The position in the ordering of any data point not in grid cell c is either before that of $l(c)$ or after that of $u(c)$.

All of these properties are satisfied for both bit interleaving and bit concatenation. Observe that these properties ensure that the ordering also applies to the grid cells. For both bit interleaving and bit concatenation, the ordering also indicates the order in which the grid cells are partitioned. In particular, the partition order is equal to the order from left to right in which the bits of the binary representation of the keys are combined to form the position of the point in the ordering.

Second, we need a mapping h from the one-dimensional representative k of each point p and grid cell c in a complete grid at level n (i.e., $k = g(p)$ and $k = g(l(c))$, respectively) to a number a in the range 0 to $m - 1$. The result of this mapping $a = h(k)$ serves as an index in the directory to access the buckets and is a one-dimensional array. The mapping h is such that the $2^{n+1} - m$ grid cells of size v are associated with directory addresses $m - 2^n$ through $2^n - 1$, and the remaining $2 \cdot (m - 2^n)$ grid cells of size $v/2$ are associated with directory addresses 0 through $m - 2^n - 1$ and 2^n through $m - 1$. Each directory element at address a contains the identity of the bucket corresponding to the grid cell associated with a.

Linear hashing implements the function h as two hash functions, h_n and h_{n+1}. The function $h_n(k) = k \bmod 2^n$ is used to access the buckets associated with the grid cells at directory addresses $m - 2^n$ through $2^n - 1$; $h_{n+1}(k) = k \bmod 2^{n+1}$ is used to access the buckets associated with the grid cells at directory addresses 0 through $m - 2^n - 1$ and those at directory addresses 2^n through $m - 1$. Such a file is said to be of level $n, n + 1$ so that the grid cells accessed by h_n are at level n and those accessed by h_{n+1} are at level $n + 1$. Note that when $m = 2^n$, no grid cells are accessed by h_{n+1}.

Our adaptation of linear hashing to multidimensional data requires a function g that has the property that all of the data points associated with a particular directory element (i.e., grid cell) are within a given range (recall properties 1–3). Unfortunately, this is not the case when we use the hash function $h_n(k) = k \bmod 2^n$, where $k = g(p)$. In particular, for any binding of k, $h_n(k)$ has the property that all of the points in a given directory element agree in the n least significant bits of k. Such a hash function is used to explain linear hashing in Appendix B. This is fine for random access; however, it does not support efficient sequential file access (in terms of spatial proximity) since different directory elements, and hence different buckets, must be accessed. On the other hand, if h_n would discriminate on the most significant bits of k, then all of the points mapped to a given directory element would be within a given range and hence in the same grid cell, thereby satisfying properties 1–3 of the mapping. Assuming k is of fixed length (i.e., the number of bits is fixed), this can be achieved by redefining the hashing function h_n to be $h_n(k) = reverse(k) \bmod 2^n$. An implementation of linear hashing that satisfies this property is termed *order preserving linear hashing* (OPLH).

In one dimension, OPLH is analogous to a trie. For multidimensional data (e.g., d dimensions), the same effect is obtained by combining the bits from the various keys (e.g., via interleaving, concatenation), reversing the result, and then performing a modulo operation. When the combination is based on bit interleaving, the result is analogous to a k-d trie, and its behavior for range searching is discussed in some detail in Section 1.6. In the rest of this section, we use the combination of bit interleaving as the function g whose result is reversed to form a hashing function that we term *reversed bit interleaving*, which we use in conjunction with linear hashing. We refer to this combination as *linear hashing with reversed bit interleaving* (LHRBI).

Reversed bit interleaving results in partitioning the underlying space in a cyclic manner. For example, assuming a bit interleaving order of $yxyxy\ldots$ (i.e., the y coordinate is the most significant), then the first partition splits every grid cell in two using the y coordinate, the second partition splits every grid cell in two using the x coordinate, the third partition splits every grid cell in two using the y coordinate, and so on. After each partition, the number of grid cells doubles. After each cycle of partitions (i.e., one partition per key), the number of grid cells grows by a factor of 2^d. Of course, a different partitioning order could be obtained by combining the keys in a different order. For example, we could have defined a similar function, termed *reversed bit concatenation*, that would complete all partitions along one key before starting a partition on another key. We refer to this combination as *linear hashing with reversed bit concatenation* (LHRBC). However, reversed bit concatenation has the drawback of favoring some of the keys over the others, and thus we do not discuss its use further here.

It is interesting to note that the use of reversed bit interleaving with linear hashing seems to have been proposed independently by Burkhard [282] (who terms it *shuffle order*), Orenstein [1414], and Ouksel and Scheuermann [1435] (see also [1829]). This combination is applied to range searching by Burkhard [282] and Orenstein and Merrett [1420], although they each used different search algorithms.

Now, let us briefly review the mechanics of linear hashing and then give an example of its use with multidimensional data. Recall that a file implemented using linear hashing has both primary and overflow buckets. One primary bucket is associated with each grid cell. The storage utilization factor, τ, is defined to be the ratio of the number of records (i.e., points) in the file to the number of positions available in the existing primary and overflow buckets.

When the storage utilization factor exceeds a predetermined value, say α, then one of the grid cells is split. When grid cell c associated with the directory element at address b is split, its records are rehashed using h_{n+1} and distributed into the buckets of the grid cells associated with directory elements at addresses b and $b + 2^n$. The identity of the directory element corresponding to the next grid cell to be split is maintained by the pointer s that cycles through the values 0 to $2^n - 1$. When s reaches 2^n, all of the grid cells at level n have been split, which causes n to be incremented and s to be reset to 0.

It is important to observe that a grid cell split does not necessarily occur when a point is inserted that lies in a grid cell whose primary bucket is full; nor does the primary bucket of the grid cell that is split have to be full. Nevertheless, the justification for using linear hashing is that eventually every bucket will be split, and, ideally, all of the overflow buckets will be emptied and reclaimed. This is similar to the rationale for analyzing algorithms using the amortization method [163].

As an example of the partitioning that results when g is bit interleaving, consider, again, the point set of Figure 1.1 after the application of the mapping $f(x) = x \div 12.5$ and $f(y) = y \div 12.5$ to the values of the x and y coordinates, respectively. The result of this mapping is given in columns 4 and 5 of Figure 1.97. Next, apply reversed bit interleaving to its keys to yield the mappings given in columns 6 and 7 of the figure, depending on whether we take the x coordinate as the most significant (column 6 and

NAME	X	Y	$f(X)$	$f(Y)$	CODEX	CODEY
Chicago	35	42	2	3	44	28
Mobile	52	10	4	0	1	2
Toronto	62	77	4	6	11	7
Buffalo	82	65	6	5	39	27
Denver	5	45	0	3	40	20
Omaha	27	35	2	2	12	12
Atlanta	85	15	6	1	37	26
Miami	90	5	7	0	21	42

Figure 1.97
Reversed bit interleaving applied to the result of applying $f(x) = x \div 12.5$ and $f(y) = y \div 12.5$ to the values of the x and y coordinates, respectively, of the point set in Figure 1.1.

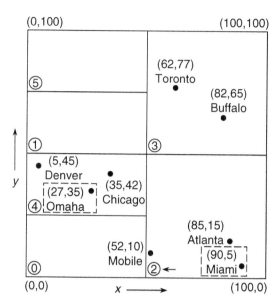

Figure 1.98
The representation resulting from applying linear hashing with reversed bit interleaving (LHRBI) corresponding to Figure 1.1. The y coordinate is assumed to be the most significant. Overflow bucket contents are enclosed by broken lines. A leftward-pointing arrow indicates the next bucket to be split.

labeled CODEX) or the y coordinate (column 7 and labeled CODEY). In our example, we treat the y coordinate as the most significant and thus make use of the values in column 7.

Assume that the primary and overflow buckets are both of size 2 and that a bucket will be split whenever τ, the storage utilization factor, is greater than or equal to 0.66 (i.e., $\alpha = 0.66$). We also assume that there is a one-to-one correlation between the numbering of the grid cells and the primary bucket labels and thus there is no need for a grid directory. Therefore, we use numbers to refer to both the grid cells and the primary buckets associated with them. Inserting the cities in the order Chicago, Mobile, Toronto, Buffalo, Denver, Omaha, Atlanta, and Miami yields the partition of the database shown in Figure 1.98, which has six primary buckets, labeled 0–5, and two overflow buckets. To explain the splitting process, we examine more closely how Figure 1.98 was obtained.

Initially, the file consists of just grid cell 0 and bucket 0, which is empty. The file is of level 0,1. The pointer to the next grid cell to be split, s, is initialized to 0. Chicago and Mobile, which lie in grid cell 0, are inserted in bucket 0, which yields $\tau = 1.00$. This causes grid cell 0 to be split and bucket 1 to be allocated. s retains its value of 0, and both Chicago and Mobile remain in bucket 0 (see Figure 1.99(a)).

Toronto lies in grid cell 1 and is inserted into bucket 1. However, now $\tau = 0.75$, thereby causing grid cell 0 to be split, s to be set to 1, bucket 2 to be allocated, and Mobile to be placed in it (see Figure 1.99(b)). Our file is now of level 1,2.

Next, we try to insert Buffalo, which lies in grid cell 1 and hence is inserted in bucket 1. However, now $\tau = 0.67$, thereby causing grid cell 1 to be split, s to be reset to 0, bucket 3 to be allocated, and Toronto and Buffalo to be placed in it (see Figure 1.99(c)).

Denver lies in grid cell 0 and is inserted into bucket 0. Omaha lies in grid cell 0, and hence it is inserted into bucket 0. However, now $\tau = 0.75$, thereby causing grid cell 0 to be split, s to be set to 1, bucket 4 to be allocated and and Denver and Chicago to be moved into it. Our file is now of level 2,3. Unfortunately, Omaha also lies in grid cell 4, but bucket 4 is full and thus an overflow bucket must be allocated and attached to grid cell 4, and Omaha is placed in it (see Figure 1.99(d)).

Atlanta lies in grid cell 2 and is placed in bucket 2. Miami also lies in grid cell 2 and is placed in bucket 2. However, now $\tau = 0.67$, thereby causing grid cell 1 to be split, s to be set to 2, and bucket 5 to be allocated. After the grid cell split, we still have too many items in bucket 2, and thus an overflow bucket must be allocated and attached to grid cell 2, and Miami is placed in it (see Figure 1.98).

Exercises

See also the exercises in Appendix B.

1. Does the Peano-Hilbert order (see Section 2.1.1.2 of Chapter 2) satisfy properties 1–3?

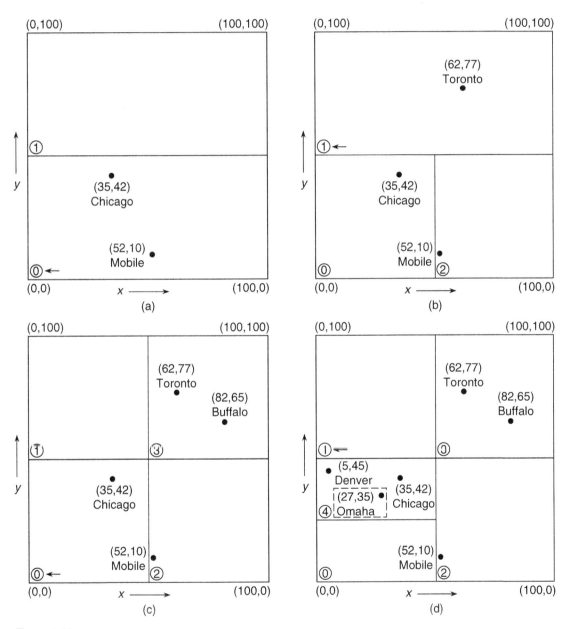

Figure 1.99
Snapshots of the representation resulting from applying linear hashing with reversed bit interleaving (LHRBI) after the insertion of (a) Chicago and Mobile, (b) Toronto, (c) Buffalo, and (d) Denver and Omaha. The y coordinate is assumed to be the most significant. Overflow bucket contents are enclosed by broken lines. A leftward-pointing arrow indicates the next bucket to be split.

2. Write a procedure LINRANGESEARCH to perform a range search for a rectangular region in a two-dimensional database implemented with linear hashing using reversed bit interleaving as the hashing function.

1.7.2.3.2 Multidimensional Extendible Hashing (MDEH)

The drawback of using linear hashing with reversed bit interleaving as the hashing function h is that the order in which the grid cells are split is not consistent with a splitting policy that introduces a $(d-1)$-dimensional partitioning hyperplane l (as in the grid file), and then splits the group of grid cells intersected by l (termed a *slice*), thereby creating an additional slice, before attempting to split other grid cells.[57] Such a splitting order is more in line with the manner in which the grid file grows and is frequently desired as it preserves some locality, at least across the key k that is being split. In particular, these grid cells are spatially contiguous within the range of k that has been split and hence are more likely to be full when the split is made (this is especially true when we use the PLOP hashing variant of linear hashing described in Section 1.7.2.4.2). Thus, we need another hashing function f. f must also stipulate the order in which the grid cells in the slice intersected by l are to be split and buckets allocated for them (as well as deallocated, if necessary, should there have been overflow buckets associated with some of the corresponding grid cells in l).

f results in partitioning the axes corresponding to the d keys in a cyclic manner, starting with one partition for each of the keys, thereby resulting in 2^d grid cells after completing the first cycle of partitions. Next, f cycles through the keys partitioning each key's axis twice, each key's axis four times on the next cycle, and so on.[58] As grid cells are partitioned, new ones are created and assigned numbers in increasing order, assuming that initially the entire set of data is in grid cell 0. The central property of f is that all the grid cells in slice a are split in two before any grid cells in any of the other slices are split, and the grid cells in a are split in the order in which they were created.[59] In contrast, the reversed bit interleaving hashing function h uses a different split policy in that it does not introduce a $(d-1)$-dimensional partitioning hyperplane. Instead, h results in splitting the grid cells in the order in which they were created, regardless of the identities of the slices in which they are contained.

In order to see this distinction between f and h, assume that the partitions are made on a cyclic basis $yxyxy\ldots$ (i.e., the y coordinate is more significant than the x coordinate). Figures 1.100 and 1.101 show the order in which the first 16 grid cells (starting with the initial grid cell 0) are partitioned for both h and f (also known as *MDEH*, as described below), respectively. The numbers associated with the cells correspond to the order in which they were created. Assume that the underlying space is a unit-sized square with an origin at the lower-left corner and that it is partitioned by a recursive halving process along the range of the corresponding key so that, after each cycle of partitions through all of the keys, the result is a grid of cells having a uniform width across all keys. The labels along the axes in Figure 1.101 indicate the relative time at which the partition was performed along the axis (subsequently referred to as the *partition number*).

Note that in the transition between Figure 1.100(b, c), grid cells 0 and 1 are split, thereby creating grid cells 4 and 5. However, these grid cells (i.e., 0 and 1) are not

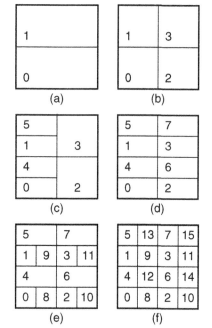

Figure 1.100
(a–f) The order in which the underlying space is partitioned during creation of the first 16 grid cells when applying linear hashing with reversed bit interleaving (LHRBI) (i.e., h), where the y coordinate is the most significant. The grid cells are numbered in the order in which they were created.

---

[57] This problem also holds for using linear hashing with reversed bit concatenation. We do not discuss it here as it favors some keys over others.

[58] We shall see later that the cyclic partitioning order is not a requirement of the definition of f. In other words, other partition orders are also possible as long as the number of partitions along the axis of each key doubles for each subsequent partitioning along that key. However, for the present, we assume a cyclic partition order.

[59] The grid cells in a that are being split were not necessarily created in immediate succession (i.e., they are not necessarily numbered in consecutive order). In other words, grid cell c_i in a is split before grid cell c_j in a if grid cell c_i was created earlier than grid cell c_j, although, of course, other grid cells in different slices than a could have been created in the time between the creation of c_i and c_j.

partitioned by the same one-dimensional hyperplane (which would be a line in two dimensions as is the case here). In contrast, the transition between Figure 1.101(b, c) does proceed by completely partitioning one slice before partitioning another slice. Thus, we find that the first two grid cells that are split (i.e., 0 and 2) are partitioned by the same hyperplane (i.e., the line $y = 0.25$), thereby creating grid cells 4 and 5.

Figure 1.102 shows the correspondence between the partition numbers in Figure 1.101 (i.e., the labels along the axes) and the numbers of the grid cells that are created by the first three partitions along each key (i.e., two cycles for each key) when $d = 2$. This correspondence can be calculated by using MDEH (*multidimensional extendible hashing*) [1428][60], which serves as the desired hashing function f, thereby obviating the need for the directory shown in Figure 1.102.

To convince ourselves that the MDEH function really does what it is supposed to do, let us determine the grid cell that contains the point ($x = 0.3$, $y = 0.6$). Once again, we assume that the underlying space of Figure 1.101 is a unit-sized square with an origin at the lower-left corner that is partitioned by a recursive halving process along the range of the corresponding key so that, after each cycle of partitions through all of the keys, the result is a grid of cells having a uniform width across all keys. The labels, S_x and S_y, along the axes in Figure 1.101 indicate the partition number that causes the creation of the ($d - 1$)-dimensional region of grid cells immediately to its right (for the x coordinate) or above (for the y coordinate). We also assume that the partitioning process has cycled through both keys twice, thereby resulting in Figure 1.101(f). This information is used to determine from Figure 1.101(f) that our query point is in the grid cell created by the second partition along the x axis and the first partition along the y axis. Looking up the entry in Figure 1.102 corresponding to $S_x = 2$ and $S_y = 1$ yields grid cell number 9, which is indeed the number associated with the grid cell containing the point in Figure 1.101(f).

Our explanation of how to determine the grid cell c that contains a point p at location r, with r_i ($1 \le i \le d$) as the values for key i, omitted one crucial step. In particular, we need to find a way to compute the partition numbers corresponding to the different partitioning hyperplanes for the keys so that they can be used as parameters to MDEH. In our explanation, the existence of d one-dimensional directories, such as those found along the axes of Figure 1.101(f), that correlate the locations of the partitioning hyperplanes with the partition numbers was implicitly assumed, when in fact such directories do not exist. When the partitions are obtained by a recursive halving process of the range of the keys that make up the underlying space (as is the case in this example), the equivalent effect of these one-dimensional directories can be achieved by applying the following five-step process to each key value r_k. Assume that key k has been partitioned q_k times such that $2^n \le q_k < 2^{n+1}$, where n is the number of times a full cycle of partitions has been made through k.

1. Determine the range t_k of values for key k.

2. Calculate the width w_k of a grid cell for key k (i.e., $w_k = t_k/2^{n+1}$).

3. Compute the position u_k ($0 \le u_k < 2^{n+1}$) of the grid cell containing r_k (i.e., $u_k = t_k \div w_k$).

4. Reverse the $n + 1$ least-significant bits of the binary representation of u_k to obtain v_k, which is the desired partition number.

5. If $v_k > q_k$, then recalculate v_k using steps 2–4 with 2^n instead of 2^{n+1} in steps 2 and 3.

An alternative to the five-step process described above is to use a set of d one-dimensional directories in the form of linear scales (as in the grid file), one per key,

---

60 Also referred to as the access function for a uniform extendible array of exponential varying order (UXAE). MDEH was first presented by Merrett and Otoo [1288] as the cornerstone of dynamic multipaging (see Section 1.7.2.1), which enables mapping the grid cells into a linear sequence in memory while permitting the dataset to grow dynamically.

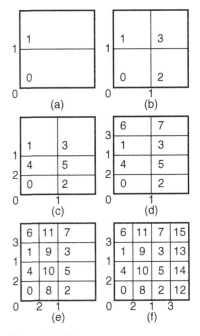

Figure 1.101
(a–f) The order in which the underlying space is partitioned during creation of the first 16 grid cells when using a hashing function that splits all grid cells within a slice before splitting other grid cells (i.e., f, which is also MDEH), where the y coordinate is the most significant. The grid cells are numbered in the order in which they were created. The labels along the axes indicate the relative time at which the partition was performed along the axis.

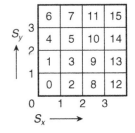

Figure 1.102
Correspondence between partition numbers (shown as horizontal and vertical axes of the table) and the number of the grid cells that are created by the first three partitions of the keys when all grid cells in one slice are split before splitting other slices. Assume that $d = 2$, where the y coordinate is the most significant. This table is the same as the function MDEH.

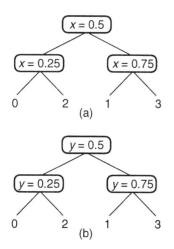

Figure 1.103
Linear scales showing the correspondence between coordinate values and partition numbers for the (a) x and (b) y axes, corresponding to the partition of the underlying space given in Figure 1.101(f). This can also be obtained by use of a five-step process outlined in the text.

implemented as binary trees (see Exercise 1). Each nonleaf node of the binary trees indicates the key value corresponding to the partition,[61] and the leaf nodes indicate the partition number. For example, Figure 1.103 shows the linear scales for the x and y axes corresponding to the partition of the underlying space given in Figure 1.101(f). Note that after each full cycle of partitions through the d keys, the linear scales are identical (as is the case in our example).

The method outlined above for determining the grid cell c that contains a point p given its location r demonstrates the second principal way in which f (i.e., MDEH) differs from the hashing functions used with linear hashing. In particular, c is not obtained by directly applying f to r (or to the result of reversing the bit interleaved or bit concatenated representation of the key values that make up r, as in linear hashing). Instead, c is determined by applying f to the partition numbers along the axes corresponding to the values of its keys that caused c to be created. The actual correspondence between partition numbers and key values is obtained by use of either the linear scales or the five-step process outlined above, given the number of times each key has been partitioned.

Upon some reflection, it should be apparent that f, in conjunction with the partition numbers, plays the same role as the table given in Figure 1.101(f) to indicate the two-dimensional correspondence between key values and grid cell numbers. Unfortunately, we do not have the luxury of having space to store this table, which is why we make use of f. It should be clear that the lack of this table is what sets linear hashing apart from the grid file (for which the table exists), which, after all, is the point of this discussion (i.e., how to avoid the table). Note that the use of the linear scales or the five-step process to calculate the partition numbers, which are then supplied as parameters to the hash function f to determine the grid cell containing the query point, obviates the need for the hashing function f to satisfy ordering properties 1–3 outlined in Section 1.7.2.3.1. In contrast, when using a hashing function that satisfies OPLH, we usually apply the hash function directly to the result of interleaving or concatenating the bits of the query point rather than computing the partition numbers corresponding to the coordinate values of the query point, as is the case when using MDEH.

Grid cells are split whenever the storage utilization factor τ exceeds a predetermined value, say α. We use a split index (termed an *expansion index* [1085]) in the form $E = (e_1, e_2, \ldots, e_d)$ to indicate which grid cell c is to be split next. The identity of c is determined by applying the MDEH hash function to the d values of e_i, where e_i is the partition number corresponding to key i. The actual split occurs by passing the $(d - 1)$-dimensional hyperplane corresponding to partition e_k through c. The split procedure is as follows. Assume that we are in the jth split cycle (meaning that we have cycled through the d keys $j - 1$ times) for key k. Thus, we must now apply 2^{j-1} partitions to k. We first determine the slice that is being partitioned (i.e., e_k, termed the *expansion slice*). Next, we check if we are splitting the first cell in slice e_k (i.e., $e_i = 0$ for all i, where $1 \leq i \leq d$ and $i \neq k$). In this case, we compute a partition point along key k that partitions the slice in two. Next, we split the cell.

Once a cell has been split, we check if all of the grid cells intersected by the current partition (i.e., in the expansion slice) have been split. If they have not, then we determine the next cell to be split, which is done in increasing lexicographic order of E, while holding e_k fixed. If they have, then, assuming that linear scales are used,[62] we update the linear scale of k to contain the partition value, as well as the new partition numbers, and reset the expansion index. We then proceed to the next partition on key k by incrementing e_k by 1, unless we are processing the final slice (i.e., the 2^{j-1}th slice in the current split

---

[61] There is no need to store the key value in the nonleaf nodes because they can always be determined from knowledge of their ranges and the path followed when descending from the root of the binary tree corresponding to the linear scale to the appropriate leaf node.

[62] In the rest of this discussion, we assume that linear scales are used as this will make the process general and enables it to be used with quantile hashing and PLOP hashing as described in Section 1.7.2.4.

cycle), in which case we proceed to the next key in cyclic order and possibly increase the cycle number j if $k = d$.

At this point, let us describe the process of determining the grid cell c associated with a query point $p = (p_1, p_2, \ldots, p_d)$ in more detail. As mentioned above, we look up the coordinate values of p in the linear scales (or use our five-step procedure) and obtain the partition numbers for the different keys, say s_i $(1 \leq i \leq d)$. We must now determine if c lies inside or outside the expansion slice as this indicates whether we can apply f directly to s_i to obtain the value of c. Assume that we are currently partitioning on key k. Therefore, from the expansion index E, we know that e_k denotes the partition number, thereby enabling the identification of the expansion slice for key k. We can determine whether c will be inside or outside the expansion slice by examining the values of s_i $(1 \leq i \leq d)$.

1. If $s_k = e_k$ and if the sequence s_i $(1 \leq i \leq d)$ is lexicographically less than E, then the grid cell containing p has already been expanded. This means that we have to recompute the partition number s_k, say q, for key k by including the expansion partition in the lookup process that uses the linear scales of key k (or use our five-step procedure). The function f is now applied to s_i $(1 \leq i \leq d)$ with q replacing s_k to yield the grid cell corresponding to c.

2. If c is outside the expansion slice, then we apply f to s_i $(1 \leq i \leq d)$ to yield the grid cell corresponding to c.

For example, consider the grid partition given in Figure 1.104(a) where the x coordinate is currently being partitioned (again assuming a cyclic order $yxyx\ldots$). In particular, we have cycled through the y axis twice and through the x axis once. We are currently in the second partition on the second cycle of the x axis with an expansion index value of $E = (2, 1)$ (denoting that the next grid cell to be split is the one formed by the second partition on y and the first partition on x). The corresponding linear scales are given to the left of the y axis and below the x axis. Let us first search for the point $(x = 0.3, y = 0.8)$. From the linear scales, we have that $S_y = 3$ and $S_x = 2$. Since $S_x \neq 1$, the grid cell containing $(x = 0.3, y = 0.8)$ is not in the expansion slice and thus the grid cell is obtained by applying MDEH (i.e., grid cell 11).

As another example, suppose that we search for the point $(x = 0.8, y = 0.6)$. From the linear scales, we have that $S_y = 1$ and $S_x = 1$. Since $S_x = 1$, the grid cell containing $(x = 0.8, y = 0.6)$ is in the expansion slice. Moreover, since $(S_y, S_x) = (1, 1) <^L (2, 1) = E$ (where $<^L$ denotes the lexicographic ordering), the grid cell containing $(x = 0.8, y = 0.6)$

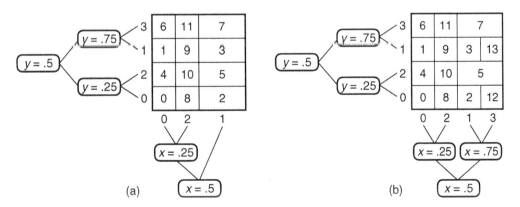

Figure 1.104
(a) Example grid partition illustrating the use of MDEH with the y coordinate being the most significant. Linear scales are given to the left of the y axis and below the x axis. The expansion index has a value $E = (2,1)$. (b) The modified linear scale for x to reflect the fact that the third partition on the x axis has not yet been completed but is used when the query point is in a grid cell in the expansion slice that has already been expanded.

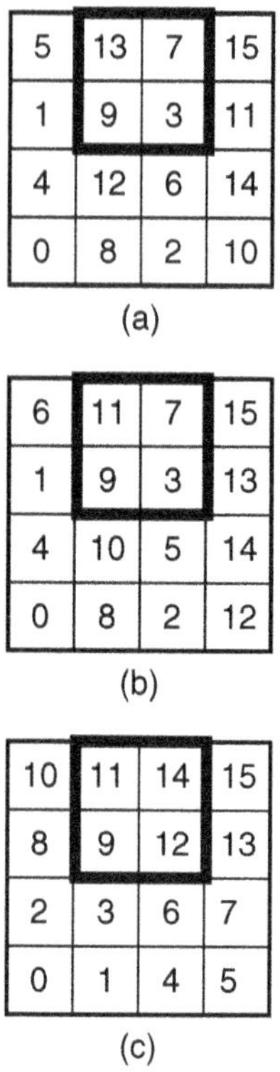

5	13	7	15
1	9	3	11
4	12	6	14
0	8	2	10

(a)

6	11	7	15
1	9	3	13
4	10	5	14
0	8	2	12

(b)

10	11	14	15
8	9	12	13
2	3	6	7
0	1	4	5

(c)

Figure 1.105
Correlation of grid cell addresses to the underlying space for (a) linear hashing with reversed bit interleaving (LHRBI), (b) MDEH, and (c) Morton order (i.e., conventional bit interleaving), where the y coordinate is the most significant after two complete cycles of splitting along the two keys. The heavy lines denote the boundaries of a 2×2 search window in the upper half of the underlying space.

has already been expanded. Therefore, we have to include this expansion in the linear scales (see Figure 1.104(b)) when looking up the value of S_x, which is now 3. Applying MDEH to $S_y = 1$ and $S_x = 3$ yields grid cell 13. Note that had we looked for the point $(x = 0.8, y = 0.8)$, we would have $S_y = 3$ and $S_x = 1$, which is also in the expansion slice. However, $(S_y, S_x) = (3, 1)$ is not lexicographically less than $E = (2, 1)$, and thus we can apply MDEH directly to obtain grid cell 5.

Exercises

1. What is the drawback of implementing the linear scales as one-dimensional arrays?

2. Give an algorithm for computing the value of MDEH for a set of partition numbers s_i ($1 \leq i \leq d$), where we have made j cycles through each key.

3. Write a procedure MDEHPOINTSEARCH to perform a point search (i.e., exact match query) in a two-dimensional database implemented with MDEH as the hashing function.

4. Write a procedure MDEHRANGESEARCH to perform a range search for a rectangular region in a two-dimensional database implemented with MDEH as the hashing function.

1.7.2.3.3 Dynamic Z Hashing

Hashing functions that satisfies OPLH (i.e., both LHRBI and LHRBC) and MDEH have the shortcoming that grid cells at consecutive addresses (i.e., buckets) are not usually in spatial proximity. Equivalently, grid cells that are in spatial proximity are not usually in consecutive addresses (i.e., buckets). If the numbers of the grid cells correspond to disk addresses (not an unreasonable assumption), then execution of queries such as multidimensional range queries (e.g., a hyperrectangular window query) usually results in a large number of seek operations. In order to see this, consider Figure 1.105, which shows the correlation of grid cells to the underlying space for linear hashing with reversed bit interleaving (Figure 1.105(a)), MDEH (Figure 1.105(b)), and the Morton order, which is the same as conventional bit interleaving (Figure 1.105(c)), where the y coordinate is the most significant after two complete cycles of splitting along the two keys. In particular, let us examine the grid cells that overlap the 2×2 search window in the upper half of each part of the figure (shown with a heavy line). Notice that only for conventional bit interleaving (i.e., the Morton order) are any of the covering grid cells at consecutive addresses. The goal is to make this number as large as possible.

The problem lies in the order in which the newly created grid cells are created. In particular, for a hashing function that satisfies OPLH (i.e., both LHRBI and LHRBC) and MDEH, when a grid cell is split, the grid cells resulting from the split are not stored in consecutive addresses. Thus, we need a method that preserves proximity by having the property that whenever a grid cell at address c is split, it must result in the creation of two grid cells at consecutive addresses, say at a and $a + 1$. Since the grid cell at address $c + 1$ is usually occupied, we cannot split c to create c and $c + 1$. Moreover, when the grid cell at address $c + 1$ is split, we would like its result to be near the result of splitting the grid cell at address c (i.e., a and $a + 1$). Interestingly, the Morton order does satisfy these requirements in that it has the property that a grid cell at address c is split into two grid cells at addresses $2c$ and $2c + 1$ (see Exercise 3). The Morton order is the basis of the z^+-order [906]. The difference from the Morton order is that the z^+-order enables the representation of the partition at times other than when a key is fully expanded (i.e., when we have doubled the number of grid cells as a result of splitting all of the grid cells for a particular key). When a key is fully expanded, the z^+-order is equivalent to the Morton order.

The central idea behind the z^+-order is to determine a sequence in which the grid cells are to be split so that the ordering is preserved. Assume that we have just completed L expansions, thereby having 2^L grid cells with addresses $0, 1, \ldots, 2^L - 1$, and we are now ready to start on the $L + 1$st expansion. Clearly, when we split the grid cell at address c to yield grid cells at addresses $2c$ and $2c + 1$, these grid cells must not be occupied.

This property does not hold if we try to split the grid cell at address 0. One way to ensure that this does not occur is to split the grid cells in decreasing order, starting with the grid cell at address $2^L - 1$, thereby creating grid cells at addresses $2^{L+1} - 2$ and $2^{L+1} - 1$. The problem with this approach is that it creates a large gap of unused grid cells, which contradicts the purpose of linear hashing—to extend the range of addresses in an incremental manner as needed. Moreover, it results in low storage utilization.

Ideally, if there are currently $4t$ grid cells in use (at addresses $0, 1, \ldots, 4t - 1$), then we want to place the newly created grid cells at addresses $4t$ and $4t + 1$. This means that we split the grid cell at address $2t$, thereby creating a gap (i.e., an unused grid cell) at $2t$. This is fine as long as we do not create too many gaps and if the gaps are small. Thus, any technique that we use must fill up the gaps as soon as possible, as well as minimize their number. The gaps are filled by splitting the predecessor grid cells. For example, suppose that after splitting the grid cell at address $2t$, we split the grid cell at address $2t + 1$, thereby creating grid cells at addresses $4t + 2$ and $4t + 3$. This means that we now have a gap at addresses $2t$ and $2t + 1$, which means that the next grid cell to be split is the one at address t. This process is continued recursively until all grid cells have been split, and we have 2^{L+1} grid cells at addresses $0, 1, \ldots, 2^{L+1} - 1$. This splitting method is termed *dynamic z hashing* [906].

As an example of dynamic z hashing, consider Figure 1.105(c), which corresponds to the mapping of grid cells and addresses when using the Morton order for the fourth expansion (i.e., $L = 4$). During the fifth expansion (i.e., $L = 5$), the grid cells are split in the following order, where we use the notation $(a{:}bc)$ to denote that the grid cell at address a has been split to create grid cells at addresses b and c: (8:16 17), (9:18 19), (4:8 9), (10:20 21), (11:22 23), (5:10 11), (2:4 5), (12:24 25), (13:26 27), (6:12 13), (14:28 29), (15:30 31), (7:14 15), (3:6 7), (1:2 3), (0:0 1).

As mentioned above, the cost of using the z^+-order is a lower storage utilization due to the existence of unused grid cells (i.e., gaps). The storage efficiency can be obtained by calculating the average number of gaps during a full expansion. Assuming that L full expansions have been carried out, it can be shown that the $L + 1$st expansion has an average of $L/2$ gaps (see Exercise 2) [906]. Experiments comparing the z^+-order with a variant of MDEH have shown that use of z^+-order for hyperrectangular range queries results in a significant reduction in the number of sequences of consecutive grid cells that need to be examined, thereby lowering the number of disk seek operations that will be needed and thus yielding faster execution times.

Exercises

1. Give an algorithm to implement dynamic z hashing.

2. Show that the average number of unused grid cells (i.e., the sizes of the gaps) during the $L + 1$st expansion when using the z^+-order is $L/2$.

3. One of the main properties that enables the Morton order to be used as the basis of dynamic z hashing is that a grid cell at address c is split into two grid cells at addresses $2c$ and $2c + 1$. Does this property also hold for the Peano-Hilbert order? If it does not hold, can you state and prove how often it does hold? Also, if it does not hold, can you find a similar property that does hold for the Peano-Hilbert order?

4. The z^+-order [906] was devised in order to ensure that when a grid cell is split in linear hashing, the newly created grid cells are in spatial proximity. The z^+-order makes use of a Morton order. Can you define a similar ordering, termed p^+-*order*, that makes use of a Peano-Hilbert order instead of a Morton order? If yes, give an algorithm for the splitting method that is analogous to dynamic z hashing (i.e., *dynamic p hashing*).

5. Compare the z^+-order and the p^+-order (i.e., the Morton and Peano-Hilbert orders as described in Exercise 4) in terms of their storage efficiency by examining the average number of gaps. The comparison should be analytic. If this is not possible, then use an experimental comparison.

6. Compare the z^+-order and the p^+-order (i.e., the Morton and Peano-Hilbert orders as described in Exercise 4) in terms of their efficiency in answering range queries by examining the average number of sequences of consecutive grid cells that are examined. The comparison should be analytic. If this is not possible, then use an experimental comparison. Do the results match the general comparison of the efficiency of the Morton and Peano-Hilbert orders described in [983]?

1.7.2.3.4 Linear Hashing with Partial Expansions (LHPE)

A general drawback of linear hashing is that, during each expansion cycle, the load factor of the buckets corresponding to the grid cells that have been split is only one-half of the load factors of the buckets corresponding to the grid cells that have not yet been split in the cycle. Thus, the records are not uniformly distributed over all of the buckets, thereby leading to worse query performance (e.g., search). The performance is worse because there are more overflow buckets to be searched. Larson [1105] proposes a variant of linear hashing termed *linear hashing with partial expansions* (LHPE) to overcome this problem. The key idea is that the number of grid cells is doubled in a more gradual manner through the application of a sequence of partial expansions.

For example, assuming that a file contains $2N$ buckets, the doubling can be achieved in a sequence of two partial expansions, where the first expansion increases the file size to 1.5 times the original size and the second expansion increases it to twice the original size. In particular, the original file is subdivided into N pairs of buckets, say 0 and N, 1 and $N + 1$, ..., $N - 1$ and $2N - 1$. Now, instead of splitting a bucket as in linear hashing, the first partial expansion creates a new bucket, $2N$, corresponding to the first pair 0 and N and rehashes their contents into buckets 0, N, and $2N$. This process is repeated until we have $3N$ buckets, at which time a similar second partial expansion is applied to N trios of buckets, where a new bucket is created for each trio of buckets until we have $4N$ buckets. The next time we need to allocate a new bucket, we start a new sequence of two partial expansions, resulting in the file growing to $6N$ and $8N$ buckets after each partial expansion.

It should be clear that we could use more than two partial expansions, say q, in which case each partial expansion would result in the number of buckets being increased by a factor of $1/q$ times the number of buckets at the beginning of each full expansion cycle. Interestingly, the choice of $q = 2$ seems to be the best from a performance standpoint since the more uniform load factor resulting from the larger number of partial expansions (thereby leading to a lower search cost due to the reduction in the number of overflow buckets) is not worth the higher bucket-splitting costs [1105].

Partial expansions can be easily used with a hashing function that satisfies OPLH (regardless of whether bit interleaving or bit concatenation is used). Using partial expansions with MDEH is a bit trickier because the expansion unit is a slice rather than a grid cell. This means that instead of expanding groups of individual grid cells, we must expand groups of slices. Kriegel and Seeger [1084] take this into consideration by proposing to split two adjacent slices into three on the first partial expansion for key k, followed by a split of three adjacent slices into four on the second partial expansion for k. They term the result *multidimensional order-preserving linear hashing with partial expansion* (MOLHPE) and give a function for its computation.

Exercise

1. Give an algorithm for computing the value of MDEH for a set of partition numbers s_i ($1 \le i \le d$) where we have made j cycles through each key and that uses two partial expansions (i.e., MOLHPE).

1.7.2.4 Alternative Implementations of Linear Hashing

Both linear hashing (regardless of whether the variant used is order preserving) and MDEH have the drawback that the grid cell that has been split most recently is not necessarily the one that is full. Three approaches, quantile hashing [1084, 1086], PLOP (denoting *piecewise linear order preserving*) hashing [1085], and spiral hashing [1106, 1247, 1324], discussed below, try to overcome this drawback by, in part, varying the range of values (i.e., in the underlying data domain) that can be associated with some of the grid cells (true for all three approaches) and by allowing some flexibility in choosing the next grid cells to be partitioned (true for PLOP hashing). Two of the approaches (i.e., quantile hashing and PLOP hashing) make use of MDEH as the underlying hashing function, while spiral hashing makes use of a hashing function that has similar properties to those used in OPLH as discussed in Section 1.7.2.3.1.

These approaches have the effect of permitting greater variability in the size of some of the grid cells, thereby differing from conventional linear hashing, as described in Section 1.7.2.3, where the number of possible sizes of the grid cells is quite limited.[63] Moreover, in both quantile and PLOP hashing, the space U spanned by the grid cell is still a hyperrectangle, although subsets of the individual grid cells no longer need to be similar. In contrast, in spiral hashing, U can have an arbitrary shape and, in fact, need not always be spatially contiguous.

A central difference between these three approaches is the action taken when the storage utilization factor is exceeded (i.e., the determination of which cell or group of cells is to be partitioned or, if there is no choice, where to place the partition).

1. Quantile hashing partitions a group of grid cells on the basis of a stochastic approximation of what the future distribution of the incoming data might look like for the associated quantile, which is always a power of 1/2.

2. PLOP hashing partitions a group of grid cells on the basis of which one contains the maximum number of data items.

3. Spiral hashing partitions the grid cell for which U is a maximum.

1.7.2.4.1 Quantile Hashing

Quantile hashing [1084, 1086] is just an implementation of the MDEH hashing function where, instead of partitioning each expansion slice of key k in half, we compute a partition point along key k that partitions the quantile associated with the slice so that approximately one-half of the incoming values that are in the range of the expansion slice will fall in each of the two resulting slices. For example, for the partition associated with the 1/2 quantile, its position is based on the estimate of the median along the key. Linear scales in the form of binary trees described in Section 1.7.2.3 are used to keep track of the actual partition points for each key, thereby enabling the correlation of the partitioning hyperplane with the partition numbers that are used as parameters to MDEH so that we can determine the grid cell associated with a particular point. The grid cell split procedure is the same as that used for the implementation of linear hashing with the MDEH hashing function (i.e., it makes use of the expansion index).

Figure 1.106 is an example of the type of partitioning of the underlying grid that is supported by quantile hashing. In essence, we have taken the partition of the underlying space given by Figure 1.101(f) and varied the positions of the partition lines from being the result of a recursive halving process. The actual partition points are recorded by the linear scales, which are given to the left of the y axis and below the x axis. Notice that, in the figure, we have also identified the quantiles in the nonleaf nodes by use of the

---

[63] In particular, when using linear hashing with a hashing function that satisfies order preserving linear hashing (OPLH) (as well as in EXCELL), there are two possible sizes for the grid cell, depending on whether the cell has been split in the current cycle of splits across the different keys. When MDEH is the hashing function, the range of grid cell sizes is larger as it depends on the number of times a particular slice has been split in the current cycle of splits across the different keys. However, the sizes of the grid cells differ only by factors that are powers of 2. Note that no matter which hashing function is used, for linear hashing, at any time after a complete cycle through all of the keys, all grid cells are of equal size.

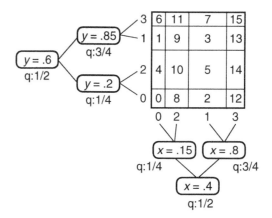

Figure 1.106
Example grid partition illustrating quantile hashing with the *y* coordinate being the most significant. Linear scales are given to the left of the *y* axis and below the *x* axis. The quantiles are also identified in the nonleaf nodes of the linear scales in the form of "q: quantile number."

notation "q: quantile value," although this is not necessary if we always use quantiles that are powers of 2. In particular, we can determine the quantile by noting the path followed when descending from the root of the linear scale to the appropriate leaf node.

The drawback of quantile hashing is that it assumes that the distribution of the incoming data does not change over time (i.e., it is stable). For example, if the data comes in a sorted order, say increasing without loss of generality, for a particular key (or lexicographically for all keys), then we have a problem as soon as we perform the first partition. In particular, the partition associated with the 1/2 quantile results in the first slice being repeatedly partitioned in future cycles, while no future data will ever be encountered that falls into its range. Another problem arises when the data tends to cluster around a few points in the underlying space (e.g., areas of dense population). If the cluster centers suddenly change, then quantile hashing will perform poorly (at least for a while) as it had adjusted the positions of its partitions according to the old and known cluster centers.

Exercises

1. Write a procedure QUANTILEPOINTSEARCH to perform a point search in a two-dimensional database implemented with quantile hashing.

2. Write a procedure QUANTILERANGESEARCH to perform a range search for a rectangular region in a two-dimensional database implemented with quantile hashing.

3. Give an algorithm for merging grid cells in a two-dimensional database of points implemented with quantile hashing.

1.7.2.4.2 Piecewise Linear Order Preserving (PLOP) Hashing

One way to overcome the drawbacks of quantile hashing that were pointed out in Section 1.7.2.4.1 is to apply repartitioning. Unfortunately, this is a costly process as it involves moving the positions of the partitions and, more importantly, moving the data in the corresponding grid cells. The alternative is to base the partitioning on the known data and to split the slices that contain the most data points. This is the basis of PLOP hashing [1085], which is a special case of dynamic multipaging [1288] (see Section 1.7.2.1). PLOP hashing is similar to quantile hashing in the sense that it cycles through the keys and doubles the number of partitions along each key's axis for each key on successive cycles.[64] However, the difference is that where in each cycle for a given key, quantile hashing splits each slice into two new slices, PLOP hashing may repeatedly split the same slice during the cycle if it turns out that it is the one that contains the most data points. Thus, PLOP hashing is much more suited to a dynamically changing distribution of data. Of course, both methods create the same number of new slices for key k during each cycle (i.e., they are doubled, thereby also doubling the number of grid cells). However, whereas in quantile hashing each grid cell is split during each cycle, in PLOP hashing some grid cells may never be split during a cycle, while other grid cells may be split many times by virtue of the fact that their containing slice is split many times during the cycle.

PLOP hashing is implemented by modifying the binary trees corresponding to the linear scales associated with the axes of the keys in quantile hashing, as well as the implementation of the MDEH hashing function. Once again, the nonleaf nodes record the positions of the partitions. However, the fact that the partitions may be applied to the same slice several times during a cycle means that the resulting binary tree is no longer "almost complete" in the sense that there is no longer a difference of at most one between the depths of all the leaf nodes, as is the case with quantile hashing. Each leaf node corresponds to a slice i and contains the number of the partition along the axis of key k that resulted in the creation of i. This number is used as the parameter to the MDEH function when attempting to determine the grid cell that contains a particular query point p at location l. In addition, each leaf node contains the number of data points in the corresponding slice. This number is used to determine which slice to partition next for key k when the storage utilization factor τ exceeds α and all grid cells in the slice that is currently being partitioned have already been expanded. Of course, whenever a slice is partitioned, a new nonleaf node t is created in the binary tree for the new partition, a new slice is allocated (with a partition number one higher than the current maximum for key k), and the count fields of the children of t are set. Note that the grid cell c associated with a particular point is determined in the same manner as with quantile hashing in the sense that the linear scales, in conjunction with the expansion index, are used to determine the appropriate partition numbers, which are then used as arguments to the MDEH function.

Figure 1.107(a) is an example of the type of partitioning of the underlying grid that is supported by PLOP hashing. The actual partition points are recorded by the linear scales, which are given to the left of the y axis and below the x axis. In essence, we have taken the partition of the underlying space given by Figure 1.101(f) and varied the positions of the partition lines from being the result of a recursive halving process. The linear scales in our figure are somewhat incomplete as their leaf nodes should also contain the number of data points in the corresponding slice. We have omitted this information here in the interest of reducing the complexity of the figure.

A number of interesting observations can be made by looking at this example (i.e., Figure 1.107(a)). First, note that some slices have been partitioned several times in a cycle, but others have not been partitioned at all during some cycles. Here we see that, on the first cycle, we partitioned the y axis at $y = 0.7$ and the x axis at $x = 0.3$. Second, notice that during the second cycle, slice 0 along the y axis was partitioned twice and likewise for slice 1 along the x axis. Third, we observe that when slice 0 along the x axis was split in the first cycle, the newly created slice 1 was associated with the right half of the underlying space. However, we could have also associated the newly created slice with the left half of the underlying space, as shown in Figure 1.107(b). Clearly, this is permissible as the linear scales provide the association of partition numbers with regions of the grid.

---

[64] As mentioned in the original definition of f (and MDEH), the requirement that we cycle through the axes is not necessary. Thus, both quantile hashing and PLOP hashing can be implemented without this requirement; this is pointed out at the end of this section.

Locating the grid cell containing a particular point with PLOP hashing is accomplished in the same way as for linear hashing with the MDEH hashing function. Once again, we find the leaf nodes in the binary trees of the linear scales that contain the region corresponding to the values of the keys, and then use the partition numbers recorded in the leaf nodes as arguments to MDEH. For example, let us first search for the point $(x = 0.4, y = 0.6)$. Using Figure 1.107(a), from the linear scales we have that $S_x = 1$ and $S_y = 2$. There is no expansion index here as we have completed two full cycles. Applying MDEH yields the grid cell **5**. Using Figure 1.107(b), from the linear scales we have that $S_x = 0$ and $S_y = 2$. There is no expansion index here as we have completed two full cycles. Applying MDEH yields the grid cell **4**.

Exercises

1. Why could you not implement the linear scales for PLOP hashing as one-dimensional arrays? In other words, why must they be implemented as binary trees?

2. Write a procedure PLOPPOINTSEARCH to perform a point search in a two-dimensional database implemented with quantile hashing.

3. Write a procedure PLOPRANGESEARCH to perform a range search for a rectangular region in a two-dimensional database implemented with PLOP hashing.

1.7.2.4.3 Spiral Hashing

Spiral hashing is the third approach that we discuss. Our presentation is quite brief and assumes that readers are familiar with it. Appendix C contains a more detailed explanation of spiral hashing. Readers who are not familiar with spiral hashing are encouraged to consult it first before continuing further in this section.

In this approach, we apply the same mapping g to a point p in d dimensions to yield a value k in one dimension, as in linear hashing. The difference is that the range of the mapping must be in $[0, 1)$. This is achieved by dividing the result $k = g(p)$ of the mapping by 2^s, where s is the total number of bits that make up the bit-interleaved or bit-concatenated value. Such an action has the same effect as the function $h_n(k) = reverse(k) \bmod 2^n$, where *reverse* corresponds to reversed bit interleaving or reversed bit concatenation. Recall that this definition of $h_n(k)$ ensures that all records in the same

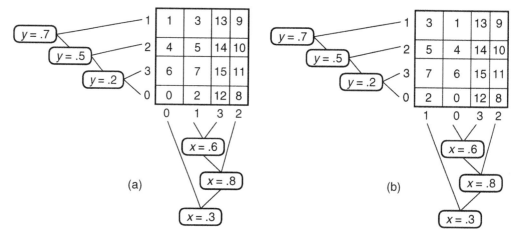

(a)   (b)

Figure 1.107
Example grid partition illustrating PLOP hashing with the y coordinate being the most significant. Linear scales are given to the left of the y axis and below the x axis. When slice 0 along the x axis is split in the first cycle, (a) the newly created slice 1 is associated with the right half of the underlying space, while in (b) it is associated with the left half of the underlying space. The leaf nodes of the linear scales should also contain the number of data points in the corresponding slice, although this is not shown here.

grid cell or bucket agree on the values of the n most-significant bits of k and hence they are within the same range.

Spiral hashing also decomposes the underlying values into disjoint ranges of k so that all points within a given range are stored in the same bucket (and possibly overflow buckets). Thus, the extent of the range is analogous to the concept of a grid cell in linear hashing. Moreover, as in linear hashing, a primary bucket of finite capacity is associated with each range, as are overflow buckets. The difference from linear hashing is that in spiral hashing, the ranges are not equal sized after a full cycle of splits for all keys. Again, as in linear hashing, buckets are split when the storage utilization factor τ exceeds a predetermined value α. Another difference from linear hashing is that the bucket b that is split is the one that corresponds to the largest-sized range. b's range is split into r ($r \geq 2$) unequal-sized ranges that are smaller than any of the existing ranges. As with linear hashing, establishing a one-to-one correlation between the values of the spiral hashing function $y(k) = \lfloor r^{x(k)} \rfloor$ and the primary bucket labels obviates the need for the one-dimensional array analog of the grid directory.

Using such a splitting policy, assuming a uniform distribution of data, the bucket corresponding to the range of values that is split is said to be more likely to have been full than the buckets that correspond to the smaller-sized ranges. Unfortunately, since the result of the one-dimensional mapping of the underlying space is no longer partitioned into equal-sized ranges (or a limited set of possible sizes at an instance that does not immediately follow a full cycle of splits for all keys) of values, there is less likelihood that the one-dimensional ranges correspond to a grid cell in d dimensions. This has the undesirable effect that the ranges of values in each partition are not always spatially contiguous, as is the case for linear hashing. This limits the utility of this technique.

For example, Figure 1.108 shows the result of applying spiral hashing to the points of Figure 1.1 under the same conditions that were used to construct Figure 1.98 for linear hashing. Once again, we assume a bit-interleaving ordering with the y coordinate being the most significant after application of the mapping f to the x and y coordinate values, where $f(x) = x \div 12.5$ and $f(y) = y \div 12.5$, respectively. However, as we divide the result of the interleaving by 2^s, where s is the number of bits (six in our example), there is no need for reversing the bits, as was done in the linear hashing example. The

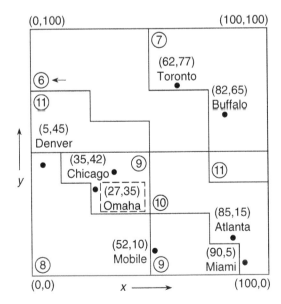

Figure 1.108
Spiral hashing representation using bit interleaving for the data of Figure 1.1. The y coordinate is assumed to be the most significant. Overflow bucket contents are enclosed by broken lines. A leftward-pointing arrow indicates the next bucket to be split.

primary and overflow bucket capacities are 2, and a bucket is split whenever τ, the storage utilization factor, is greater than or equal to 0.66 (i.e., $\alpha = 0.66$). The cities are inserted in the order Chicago, Mobile, Toronto, Buffalo, Denver, Omaha, Atlanta, and Miami.

Figure 1.109, in conjunction with Figure 1.108, shows the contents of the buckets and their corresponding spatial regions after the insertion of Chicago and Mobile (Figure 1.109(a)); Toronto (Figure 1.109(b)); Buffalo, Denver, and Omaha (Figure 1.109(c)); Atlanta (Figure 1.109(d)); and Miami (Figure 1.108). The steps in the insertion process are the same as those for the example in Appendix C shown in Figures C.6 and C.7. The only difference is that Figures 1.108 and 1.109 also show the spatial correspondence between the buckets and the corresponding regions of space. Notice that the spatial regions associated with bucket 11 are not spatially contiguous.

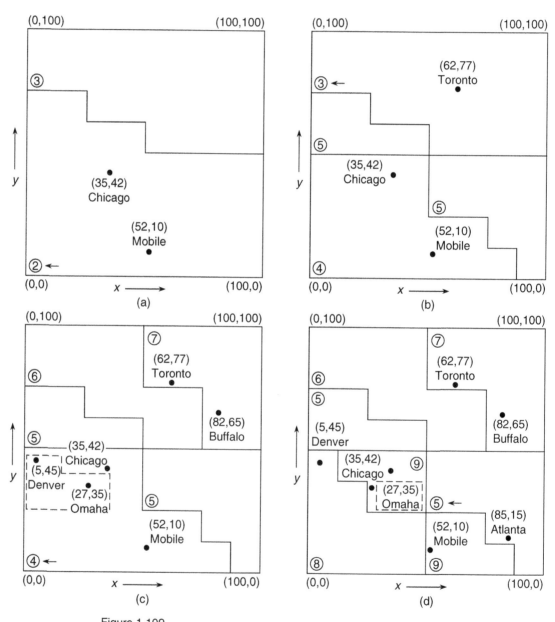

Figure 1.109
Sequence of spatial correspondences between the regions of space and the buckets created by spiral hashing using bit interleaving for the data of Figure 1.1, demonstrating the result of the insertion of (a) Chicago and Mobile, (b) Toronto, (c) Buffalo, Denver, and Omaha, and (d) Atlanta. Overflow bucket contents are enclosed by broken lines.

See also the exercises in Appendix C.

1. Suppose that spiral hashing is used to store two-dimensional point data, and each point is mapped to a value by use of bit interleaving. Prove that each bucket will span at most two spatially noncontiguous regions.

2. Suppose that spiral hashing is used to store point data of arbitrary dimension, and each point is mapped to a value by use of bit interleaving. What is the maximum number of spatially noncontiguous regions that can be spanned by a bucket?

3. Can you come up with a mapping for multidimensional point data to a value so that when it is used in conjunction with spiral hashing, each bucket will span just one spatially contiguous region?

4. Show the result of applying spiral hashing to the database of Figure 1.1 using reversed bit interleaving. Thus, instead of using the hashing function $h(k) = k/2^s$, where s is the total number of bits that make up the interleaved key value, use the function $h''(k) - reverse(k)/2^s$, in which *reverse* reverses the value of key k prior to the application of the hashing function. Again, assume that the cities are inserted in the order Chicago, Mobile, Toronto, Buffalo, Denver, Omaha, Atlanta, and Miami. Also, assume that the primary and overflow buckets are both of size 2, $r = 2$, and that a bucket will be split when τ, the storage utilization factor, is greater than or equal to 0.66. Is there a difference in this example between using the x coordinate as the most significant or the y coordinate?

5. Is there any advantage to using reversed bit interleaving with spiral hashing?

1.7.2.4.4 Summary

Our presentation of quantile hashing, PLOP hashing, and spiral hashing, assumed a cyclic partitioning order. This is not absolutely necessary. In other words, we can use a variant of MDEH that permits the partitions for the different keys to proceed in arbitrary order. For example, assuming three-dimensional data, one possible key partition order would be *zzxyzxxxxyy*.... Such an ordering is achieved by modifying the MDEH function [1288, 1428] to keep track of the order in which the keys were partitioned. This is not needed when using a cyclic order because, given the partition number and the cyclic order of the keys, we know the identity of the corresponding partitioning key. Of course, we still have the requirement that the number of partitions along each key's axis must double for each subsequent partitioning along that key. In fact, this partition-doubling requirement can also be dispensed with, as is the case in dynamic multipaging [1288], by also keeping track of the number of existing partitions at each application of a partition step for a key. Notice that the above variation of the partitioning order is also possible for spiral hashing, although, once again, we need to keep track of the order in which the keys are partitioned instead of via bit interleaving or bit concatenation, as is usually the case.

Exercises

1. Give an algorithm for computing the value of MDEH for an arbitrary partition order rather than a cyclic one. In other words, we do not have to cycle through the keys. For example, for three-dimensional data, a cyclic partitioning order is *zyxzyxzyx...zyx*, while *zzxyzxxxxyy...* is an example of an arbitrary order. Of course, we still have the requirement that the number of partitions along each key's axis must double for each subsequent partitioning along that key.

2. Give an algorithm for computing the value of MDEH for an arbitrary partition order rather than a cyclic one, as in Exercise 1, that permits partial expansions.

3. How would you completely generalize the implementation of PLOP hashing so that there is no need to complete a set of partitions along a key before starting to partition another key. In other words, the partitions on the keys can be sequenced arbitrarily without requiring that the number of grid cells be doubled for a key before a partition can be made on a different key. Moreover, there is no need to cycle through the keys.

4. One possible rationale for splitting all grid cells from one slice before splitting grid cells from another slice (as is the case when using the MDEH function) is that the grid cells in the slice are split in such an order that if grid cell c_i is split immediately before grid cell c_{i+1}, then c_i and c_{i+1} are spatially contiguous and hence more likely to be full. Does the spatial contiguity property always hold for successive splits of grid cells within a slice?

1.7.2.5 Comparison

Both the grid file and EXCELL guarantee that a record can be retrieved with two disk accesses: one for the d-dimensional grid directory element that spans the record (i.e., the grid cell in which its corresponding point lies) and one for the bucket in which it is stored. This is not necessarily the case for linear hashing methods (as well as their variants, including spiral hashing). The problem is that, although linear hashing methods often dispense with the need for a directory,[65] the possible presence of an unbounded number of overflow buckets means that each one must be accessed during an unsuccessful search for a record corresponding to a point that is spanned by a particular grid cell.

Although, for pedagogical purposes, the grid directories of Figures 1.88 and 1.93 were constructed in such a way that EXCELL required less grid cells than the grid file (8 versus 9), this is not generally the case. In fact, splitting points can always be chosen so that the number of grid cells and buckets required by the grid file is less than or equal to the number required by EXCELL. For example, if the space of Figure 1.88 were split at $x = 55$ and $y = 37$, then only four grid cells and buckets would be necessary.

Regnier [1550] has performed an analytical study of the directory size for the grid file under a uniform distribution. Comparison with similar studies for EXCELL [617, 1549] finds that the grid file appears to be asymptotically better than EXCELL, especially for nonuniform data distributions [1550]. However, for uniformly distributed data and large bucket sizes (e.g., larger than 50), EXCELL is preferred because it is easier to implement.

Interestingly, EXCELL can be characterized as a method that decomposes the underlying space into buckets of grid cells, where the space spanned by the buckets corresponds to blocks in a bintree decomposition of space (see Section 2.1.2.6 of Chapter 2), while the buckets corresponding to the individual grid cells are accessed by a directory in the form of an array. This decomposition of space is also identical to what is obtained by the bucket PR k-d tree. This close relationship between these methods causes EXCELL to be classified as a representation that employs regular decomposition. In particular, the buckets in EXCELL are created by a halving process.

The main difference between EXCELL and these representations is that the directory of EXCELL corresponds to the deepest level of a complete bintree or bucket PR k-d tree. Alternatively, we can say that EXCELL provides a directory to a space decomposition that is implemented as a bintree or bucket PR k-d tree. In particular, EXCELL results in faster access to the buckets since the k-d trie search step (i.e., following pointers in the tree) is avoided. However, if the longest search path in the tree has length s, then the EXCELL directory has 2^s entries.

From a superficial glance, EXCELL appears to be closely related to linear hashing with reversed bit interleaving as the hashing function. The reason for this observation is the fact that the space spanned by the buckets in the two methods resembles blocks in a bintree decomposition of space. For example, compare the decomposition induced by EXCELL when the x coordinate is split before the y coordinate (shown in Figure 1.93) with the result of applying linear hashing to the data of Figure 1.1 when the x coordinate is the most significant (shown in Figure 1.110).

---

[65] We use the qualifier *often* because, although linear hashing methods dispense with the need for a d-dimensional grid directory, a one-dimensional grid directory O may be needed to access the buckets associated with the grid cells unless there is a one-to-one correspondence between the numbering of the grid cells and the bucket labels, in which case there is no need for O.

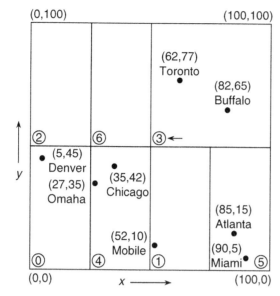

Figure 1.110
The representation resulting from applying linear hashing with reversed bit interleaving (LHRBI) corresponding to the data of Figure 1.1 when the *x* coordinate is taken as the most significant.

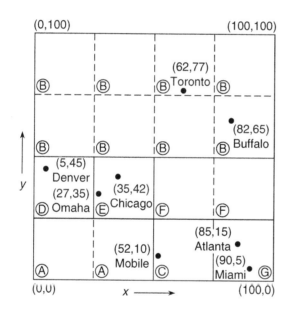

Figure 1.111
EXCELL representation corresponding to the data of Figure 1.1 when the *y* axis is split before the *x* axis.

Unfortunately, this similarity exists only when the buckets in EXCELL span no more than two grid cells. Recall that there is a one-to-one correspondence between primary buckets and grid cells in linear hashing, and for linear hashing with reversed bit interleaving (LHRBI) all grid cells are either of volume v or $v/2$. Greater variance in the volume of grid cells is not permitted for LHRBI (but see linear hashing with MDEH, as well as quantile hashing and PLOP hashing). For example, compare the decomposition induced by EXCELL when the *y* axis is split before the *x* axis (see Figure 1.111) with the result of applying LHRBI to the data of Figure 1.1 when the *y* coordinate is the most significant (see Figure 1.98). Letting v be the size of the next grid cell to be split in the linear hashing example (i.e., Figure 1.98), we see that, in the space decomposition induced by linear hashing, all buckets span regions (i.e., grid cells) of size v or $v/2$, while in the space decomposition induced by EXCELL (i.e., Figure 1.111), we have buckets that span regions of size $2v$ (e.g., bucket B), $v/2$ (e.g., A and F), and $v/4$ (e.g., C, D, E, and G). Thus, we see a bintree of four levels in the case of EXCELL but a bintree of just two levels in the case of LHRBI.

Other differences are that, in EXCELL, a bucket overflow may trigger a bucket split or a doubling of the directory, whereas, in linear hashing, at most two new buckets are allocated (one for a bucket split and one for an overflow bucket—recall the insertion of Omaha in the transition between Figure 1.99(c, d) in Section 1.7.2.3). In essence, using linear hashing, there is a more gradual growth in the size of the directory at the expense of the loss of the guarantee of record retrieval with two disk accesses. In addition, assuming equal bucket sizes and ignoring the situation of a directory split, linear hashing usually requires additional buckets since the bucket that is split is not necessarily the one that has overflowed.

Nevertheless, the relationship between EXCELL and LHRBI and MDEH is worthy of further comment. Disregarding our observations about the differing bucket sizes and just dealing with the grid cells that result from using EXCELL, a relationship does indeed exist. In particular, assuming an instance where linear hashing has applied all of the possible partitions for a specific key, and no key is partially partitioned, we find that both LHRBI and MDEH yield a decomposition of the underlying space U into grid cells, which is equivalent to EXCELL without requiring a d-dimensional grid directory.

At a first glance, a similar statement can be made about the relationship of PLOP hashing to the grid file. In particular, PLOP hashing appears to yield a partition of the underlying space U into grid cells, which is similar to that of the grid file without requiring a d-dimensional grid directory. Unfortunately, this statement is not quite true as PLOP hashing requires that the number of partitions along each key's axis double for each subsequent partitioning along that key and that, during the time at which we partition along a particular key, we cannot intersperse a partition along a different key. Thus, even though we do not have to cycle through the different keys, we must perform a complete partition along the key. In contrast, the grid file permits the partitions along the various keys to proceed in arbitrary order and allows an arbitrary number of partitions along each key's axis. In other words, key i may be partitioned once, followed by two partitions along key j, in turn followed by five partitions along key i, and so on.

A general problem that afflicts linear hashing (whether or not it is order preserving) is that the records may not be well distributed in the buckets when the data is not uniformly distributed. This means that overflow will be more common than with traditional hashing methods. It also has the effect of possibly creating a large number of sparsely filled buckets. Consequently, random access is slower since, in the case of overflow, several buckets may have to be examined. Similarly, sequential access will also take longer as several buckets will have to be retrieved without finding too many records. The problem is that all of the variants of linear hashing require that all buckets be stored at one or two levels. This has the advantage that at most two hash operations are required to determine the primary bucket to be accessed (see Exercise 1 in Appendix B).

Orenstein [1414] proposes a technique he terms *multi-level order preserving linear hashing* (MLOPLH) to be used with OPLH to deal with these problems. In particular, MLOPLH alleviates the sparseness problem by storing parts of the file in buckets at lower levels than n. Such buckets result from the combination of a sparse bucket with its brother(s). The major problem with MLOPLH is that now we may require $n + 1$ disk read operations (equal to the number of bucket accesses) to locate a bucket, whereas, previously, at most two hash operations were necessary.

The reason so many buckets may have to be accessed in MLOPLH is that linear hashing methods do not make use of a directory. Thus, encountering an empty bucket is the only way to detect that records of one bucket have been merged with those of another bucket at a lower level (see Exercise 3). Even more buckets will have to be accessed when deletion of a record causes a sparse bucket to be combined with its brother. In contrast, methods such as the grid file and EXCELL, which use a directory, do not suffer from such a problem to the same extent. The reason the sparseness issue can be avoided is that the directory indicates the buckets associated with each grid cell, and several grid cells can share a bucket.

Exercises

1. Why does linear hashing usually require at least as many buckets as EXCELL?

2. Given a large set of multidimensional point data, which of the bucket methods would you use? Take the volume of the data and its distribution into account. Can you support your choice using analytic methods?

3. Explain how MLOPLH [1414] looks up a value v.

4. Explain how MLOPLH splits a bucket.

5. Explain how MLOPLH merges two buckets.

1.7.3 Storage Utilization

In our discussion of the different bucketing methods, we often mentioned their storage utilization. In this case, we were referring to the extent that the buckets are full, given that they are split whenever they contain more elements than the bucket capacity. In particular, when a bucket of capacity b is full, it is split into n buckets, where n is the *fanout*. This is primarily of interest for methods that are based on a disjoint decomposition of the underlying space. These methods differ on the basis of whether they use a directory, the nature of the redistribution strategy, as well as the value of the fanout.

The storage utilization u of bucket method R that uses J buckets of capacity m to provide a total capacity of $a = Jm$ slots for storing v records has a value of v/a, where u ranges between 0 and 1. The fuller each bucket is (i.e., the closer the number of records that each bucket contains is to m), the smaller the value of J, and hence the larger the value of u. Thus, the greater the value of u, the more efficient R is in terms of storage utilization. Ang and Samet [53, 57] have shown that U, the average of u, under appropriate data distribution models, is $\frac{\ln n}{n-1}$ for a large number of bucketing methods subject to some constraints discussed below. Thus, it only depends on the fanout value n (i.e., how many buckets are needed when a full bucket is split), thereby enabling them to ignore the implementation details of the different bucket methods. This analysis assumes that the data is uniformly distributed. Of course, it should be clear that regardless of the nature of the bucket method used, it is often the case that U oscillates as the number of points increases since it is impossible for all buckets to be full always.

We note that the analysis of the average storage utilization has been carried out by a number of researchers for particular bucket methods. For example, EXHASH [579], B-trees [1151, 2046], and EXCELL [1827] are all instances of a bucket method of fanout 2, whose average storage utilization has been independently shown to be 0.69. Similarly, the PR quadtree (or, more appropriately, the PR quadtrie) is an instance of a bucket method of fanout 4, and its average storage utilization has been shown to be 0.46 [1827]. Most of these analyses assume that the data is drawn from a uniform distribution. However, these analyses were for the individual bucket methods rather than a general one. Ang and Samet's analysis is of interest because it is a unification of these results in a manner that is only dependent on the fanout and independent of the nature of the directory. In fact, Ang and Samet's analysis is a generalization from $n = 2$ to arbitrary values of n (thus applicable to any other trie-based bucketing method) of the analysis performed by Fagin, Nievergelt, Pippenger, and Strong [579] for EXHASH, which is based on an analysis by Knuth [1046, pp. 128–134]. The same generalization was also applied by

Ang and Samet to the analysis of Leung [1151] to obtain an approximate average storage utilization, which is equivalent to the mean of the average storage utilization.[66]

It is important to note that the analysis of Ang and Samet assumes that if a record is in a particular bucket, then it is equally likely to be in any of the children of the bucket in the case of a split. This assumption usually leads to a balanced structure and is thus useful for data structures based on digital searching (i.e., trie-based methods) or on the use of balancing (e.g., AVL trees [15] and balanced B-trees [2046]). In contrast, in the case of tree-based methods (e.g., binary search trees and point quadtrees), the order in which the data is encountered is important. Their analyses complement the above results. In particular, they are based on the use of generating functions (e.g., [880]) and, of course, yield different results (e.g., 0.33 for a point quadtree [880]).

1.8 PK-Trees

Wang, Yang, and Muntz [1952, 2043] use the term *PK-tree* to describe a family of data structures that are based on the application of a grouping technique whose effect, at a first glance, seems to be similar to bucketing; yet, is quite different in philosophy and result. In particular, the similarity lies in the fact that the basis of the decomposition process appears to be equivalent to a straightforward bucket method, such as the bucket PR quadtree and the bucket PR k-d tree. The key principle in the PK-tree is the use of a parameter k (known as a *k-instantiation value*) to stipulate the minimum number of objects or nodes that are grouped to form a node. In contrast, bucket methods use the parameter *bucket capacity* to stipulate a maximum number of objects or nodes that can be grouped together.

The PK-tree was originally developed as a means of representing high-dimensional point data in applications such as similarity searching, data mining, and bioinformatics databases. In particular, the originators of the PK-tree describe it as a spatial index and evaluate its performance with respect to conventional techniques, such as the X-tree [190] (see Section 4.4.1 in Chapter 4) and the SR-tree [999] (see Section 4.4.2 in Chapter 4). Unfortunately, as we will see in Sections 4.4.6 and 4.4.8 of Chapter 4, for most access methods that rely on the decomposition of the underlying space, performance for high-dimensional data is often unsatisfactory when compared with not using an index at all (e.g., [212]). Thus, the PK-tree is little known. However, it does have some very interesting properties whose utility extends beyond the domain of high-dimensional data, and it is in this context that we describe it here. In particular, it is useful for low-dimensional data like that found in applications such as spatial databases and geographic information systems (GIS).

This section is organized as follows. Section 1.8.1 motivates the development of the PK tree by reviewing the properties that it shares with bucket methods. Section 1.8.2 gives an overview of the PK-tree, and Section 1.8.3 presents a formal definition of the PK-tree. Section 1.8.4 compares the PK-tree with bucket methods. Section 1.8.5 describes how searching, insertion, and deletion are implemented in a PK-tree, as well as provides an outline of the underlying representation. Section 1.8.6 concludes the presentation by discussing some of the key properties of the PK-tree and continues the comparison with other methods.

---

[66] More precisely, the analysis of Fagin et al. was used by Ang and Samet to obtain the mean of the average storage utilization value. Note the distinction between "average," which corresponds to all trees with v points, and the "mean of the average," which deals with different values of v, the number of points. This is in contrast to the term *approximate average*, which is what Leung really derived in [1151].

1.8.1 Motivation

Recall that in the bucket method we recursively decompose the underlying space into disjoint blocks until the number of items in each block is less than or equal to the bucket capacity. The buckets are often the size of a disk page, and the bucket capacity is the maximum number of spatial objects that can be stored in the page. Once the underlying space has been decomposed into buckets, we usually make use of a directory to facilitate access (often referred to as an *access structure*). This directory is usually in the form of a tree and closely mimics the recursive decomposition (i.e., partitioning process). Without loss of generality, assuming two-dimensional data, in the case of a quadtree, each node in the tree has four children. Thus, we see that the leaf nodes correspond to buckets with a large capacity, while nonleaf nodes are generally small. A somewhat similar way to express this is that the fanout of the leaf nodes is high, while the fanout of the nonleaf nodes is generally small and, in the case of a quadtree, is a function of the dimensionality of the underlying space.

Ideally, we would also like to have a large fanout for the nonleaf nodes. This is the motivation for the development of the R-tree (see Section 2.1.5.2 in Chapter 2) and the bucket methods that make use of a tree directory (see Section 1.7.1). However, the R-tree results in a nondisjoint decomposition of the underlying space as it is based on the aggregation of the objects in the underlying space (actually the minimum bounding boxes or spheres of the objects). Instead, as we pointed out earlier, in this chapter we are interested in alternative methods based on a disjoint decomposition of the underlying space. Section 1.7.1 describes several such alternative methods that aggregate the nonleaf nodes to form larger nodes, thereby obtaining a larger fanout for the nonleaf nodes. In this section, we will see some of the ways in which the PK-tree differs from these methods.

One obvious way to increase the fanout in the nonleaf nodes is to aggregate the nonleaf nodes at several successive levels of decomposition into one nonleaf node. For example, in the case of a quadtree in two dimensions, instead of stipulating that each nonleaf node corresponds to a recursive aggregation of four children, we could stipulate that each nonleaf node corresponds to a recursive aggregation of 4^i children, where i is permitted to vary across nonleaf nodes at the same level, as well as at different levels. We use the term *quadgrid* to describe this technique; the "grid" suffix serves to remind us that the decomposition of the underlying two-dimensional space that is induced by the nonleaf node is analogous to that obtained by a grid of side length 2^i. The quadgrid is a form of level compression (recall the discussion of the path-level compressed PR k-d tree in Section 1.5.2). The problem with the quadgrid is the inflexibility of the adaptive nature. Notice that all children of a nonleaf node in the quadgrid are of the same size in the sense that their corresponding blocks span regions of the underlying space that have the same size. Ideally, we would like to have a bit more flexibility.

Using the above description of the quadgrid as a starting point, we point out that one of the key innovations of the PK-tree is the realization that all of the nodes at the same level of the hierarchy represented by the tree need not span identically sized regions in the underlying space. In other words, the principal idea behind the PK-tree is the decoupling of the tree structure of the partition process of the underlying space from that of the node hierarchy (i.e., the grouping process of the nodes resulting from the partition process) that makes up the tree directory. The PK-tree is a grouping technique and thus can be adapted to a number of different partitioning techniques. To understand what we mean by "decoupling," observe that the access structure for the blocks that correspond to the leaf nodes that result from the partitioning process may be different from the customary tree that caused the creation of the blocks. This decoupling idea also forms the basis of several bucket methods that make use of a tree directory described in Section 1.7.1. Note that the term *decoupling* could also be used to describe the differentiation of the construction of a spatial index with the aid of bulk loading (e.g., [87, 194, 1160]) from the

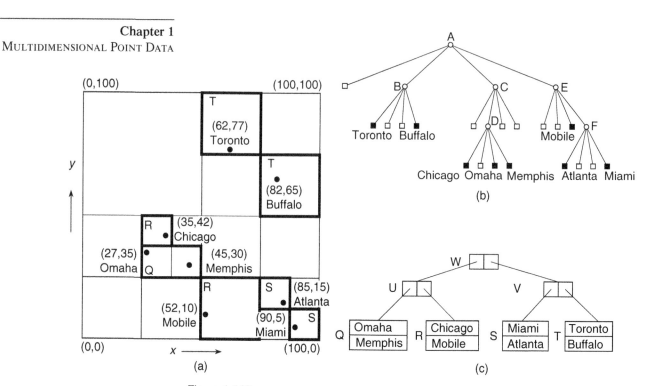

Figure 1.112
A PR quadtree and the records it represents: (a) the resulting partition of space, (b) the tree representation, and (c) one possible B$^+$-tree for the leaf blocks where each node has a minimum of two and a maximum of three entries. Each nonempty block in (a) has been labeled with the name of the B$^+$-tree leaf node in which it is a member.

process of building it incrementally (see Section 2.1.5.2.6 of Chapter 2). In other words, the term *decoupling* could be applied to many other processes used in the construction of spatial indexes besides the partitioning and grouping processes. Therefore, whenever we use the term, we make sure to qualify it appropriately unless there is no potential for confusion.

As an example of decoupling, we find that in many applications the blocks resulting from a region quadtree decomposition of the underlying space are represented by unique numbers (known as *locational codes* and discussed briefly below in Section 1.8.5.1), which are then aggregated into groups and stored in the leaf nodes of a B$^+$-tree (see the discussion in Section 2.1.2.4 in Chapter 2), which serves as the access structure (e.g., [2, 1577]). In the case of regular decompositions, such as the PR quadtree, we can reconstruct the PR quadtree just from knowledge of the locational codes of the nonempty leaf blocks, and thus the B$^+$-tree only needs to store the locatioal codes of these blocks—that is, we ignore the empty and nonleaf blocks. For example, Figure 1.112(c) is one possible B$^+$-tree corresponding to the leaf blocks of the PR quadtree whose block decomposition and corresponding tree representation are given in Figure 1.112(a, b), respectively. This PR quadtree is almost the same as the PR quadtree in Figure 1.31 except that Denver at (5,45) has been replaced by Memphis at (45,30). Each node of the B$^+$-tree in our example has a minimum of two and a maximum of three entries. We do not show the values of the locational codes of the contents of the leaf nodes of the B$^+$-tree. We also do not show the discriminator values that are stored in the nonleaf nodes of the B$^+$-tree. We have marked the leaf blocks of the PR quadtree in Figure 1.112(a) with the label of the leaf node of the B$^+$-tree of which it is a member (e.g., the block containing Chicago is in leaf node R of the B$^+$-tree).

It should be clear that the above combination of the PR quadtree and the B$^+$-tree has decoupled the tree structure of the partition process of the underlying space from the tree structure resulting from the grouping process. More precisely, the grouping process is based on proximity in the ordering of the locational codes and on the minimum and maximum capacity of the nodes of the B^+-tree. However, as we will see, in this, as well as in many of the bucket methods (including those described in Section 1.7.1), the region of space s spanned by node p of the B^+-tree does not necessarily have the same shape as the blocks that have been aggregated in p, whereas such a property holds for the PK-tree. In particular, in our example, in the case of a quadtreelike decomposition that makes use of regular decomposition, there is no guarantee that s is a square; this is the case, however, in the PK-tree when the PK-tree is based on a quadtreelike partitioning process that makes use of regular decomposition.

In fact, in our example, the resulting structure has the property that the space that is spanned by a leaf node of the B^+-tree (i.e., the blocks spanned by it) has a number of shapes, including a staircase (e.g., the leaf blocks in Figure 1.112(a), that make up leaf nodes S and T of the B^+-tree in Figure 1.112(c)), as well as noncontiguous regions (e.g., the leaf blocks in Figure 1.112(a) that make up leaf node R of the B^+-tree in Figure 1.112(c)). Of course, we could take the minimum bounding box of each node; however, now the problem is that the boxes will do a poor job of filtering due to a poor fit and also will not usually be disjoint. Similar problems arise for the minimum bounding boxes of the space aggregates corresponding to the nonleaf nodes of the B^+-tree. The problem is even more acute if we restrict the minimum bounding box to being one formed by the same rule as the partition process. In this case, the minimum bounding box can be as large as the underlying space (e.g., the minimum bounding quadtree block of leaf node R and nonleaf nodes U, V, and W of the B^+-tree in Figure 1.112(c)).

Interestingly, the same decoupling idea has also been used, albeit in a very different way, in the BV-tree [643] (see Section 1.7.1.6). However, the motivation for the decoupling in the BV-tree was different: to overcome a complication in disjoint space partitioning methods that lead to balanced trees (e.g., the BANG file [640, 641, 645, 646] and the hB-tree [1201, 1613] as discussed in Sections 1.7.1.5 and 1.7.1.4, respectively). In particular, the complication is that a node split may be such that one of the children of the split node becomes a child of both of the nodes resulting from the split.

1.8.2 Overview

The PK-tree can best be understood by examining an operational definition of its construction given the result of an existing partitioning process. If we view the partitioning process as forming a tree structure (termed a *partition tree*), then, in essence, each PK-tree node represents a subset of the nodes in the partition tree. The PK-tree is constructed by applying a bottom-up grouping process to the nodes of the corresponding partition tree where the partition tree nodes are merged into supernodes until a minimum occupancy, say k, has been attained.

The process starts by creating a PK-tree node for each node in the partition tree. We distinguish between the nodes that are formed for the points (i.e., the leaf blocks of the partition tree, some of which are empty) and the nodes formed for the blocks of the partition tree at higher levels (i.e., the nonleaf blocks), calling them *point nodes* and *directory nodes*, respectively. Next, we start grouping the nodes in bottom-up fashion, using the k-instantiation parameter k to decide how many and which nodes to group. At the deepest level, we eliminate all point nodes whose blocks do not contain a point (i.e., the empty ones) and remove them from their parents (i.e., the links to them). For a directory node a, we check the number of child nodes (which are nonempty), and if a has less than k child nodes, then we remove a and link its children to the parent of a.[67] This process is terminated at the root, which means that the root can have less than k

---

[67] Note that, as a result of this relinking process, the number of entries in a node is almost always greater than k. In Section 1.8.5.2, we show that there is indeed an upper bound on the number of entries in a node, which depends on k and the branching factor F of the underlying partitioning process.

children. The nodes of the partition tree that remain become nodes of the PK-tree and are said to be *k-instantiated*, and likewise for the blocks that correspond to them.

As an example, suppose that the partition tree is the PR quadtree given in Figure 1.112. We now show how to form the corresponding PK-tree, which we call a *PK PR quadtree*. Similar techniques could have been applied to other partition trees, such as a PR k-d tree, in which case we would have a *PK PR k-d tree*. We first find that node B in the PR quadtree has just two nonempty point node children, Toronto and Buffalo. Therefore, node B is removed and its children, Toronto and Buffalo, are linked to B's parent, A. Next, we find that directory node D in the PR quadtree has three nonempty point node children, Chicago, Omaha, and Memphis, which means that it is *k*-instantiated, and thus D is made a node of the PK-tree. However, D is the only nonempty child of its parent, directory node C of the PR quadtree. Therefore, C is removed, and its child, D, is linked to C's parent, A. Checking directory node F in the PR quadtree, we find that F has just two nonempty point node children, Atlanta and Miami. Therefore, node F is removed, and its children, Atlanta and Miami, are linked to F's parent, E. At this point, we have that directory node E in the PR quadtree has three point node children, Mobile, Atlanta, and Miami, which means that it is *k*-instantiated, and thus E is made a node of the PK-tree. Note that during this process we removed nodes B, C, and F of the partition tree, while only nodes A, E, and D of the partition tree are also in the PK-tree, besides the nodes corresponding to the data points. The result is that root node A of the PK-tree has four children corresponding to Toronto, Buffalo, and nodes D and E, which are the results of the *k*-instantiation of Chicago, Omaha, and Memphis, and of Mobile, Atlanta, and Miami, respectively. Figure 1.113(a) shows the decomposition of the underlying space, and Figure 1.113(b) is the corresponding tree structure. The boundaries of the blocks in Figure 1.113(a) that correspond to the nonleaf nodes in Figure 1.113(b) are drawn using heavy lines. The empty blocks in the first level of the decomposition of the underlying space induced by the PK PR quadtree in Figure 1.113(a) are shown shaded. Notice that all of the child blocks are similar but need not be congruent (i.e., they can be of different size, as is the case for blocks D and E); nor must the space spanned by their union equal

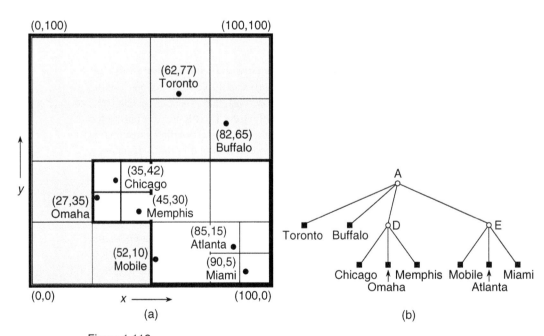

(a) (b)

Figure 1.113

A PK PR quadtree with $k = 3$ corresponding to the data in Figure 1.112: (a) the resulting partition of space and (b) the tree representation. The heavy lines indicate the boundaries of the blocks corresponding to the nonleaf nodes in the tree structure. Empty blocks in the first level of decomposition of the underlying space induced by the PK PR quadtree are shown shaded and are not represented in the tree structure.

the space spanned by their parent (as is the case for blocks D and E, whose union is not equal to that of their parent, A).

When $k = 2$, application of the above process to the PR quadtree yields the same result as applying path compression, which is discussed in Section 1.5.2 in the context of the path-compressed PR k-d tree, path-level compressed PR k-d tree, and the BD-tree. In particular, path compression occurs in the PK-tree because empty nodes in the original PR quadtree are not included in the PK-tree, and thus are not counted among the k or more children that make up each PK-tree nonleaf node. Of course, letting $k = 2$ when the partition tree is a PR k-d tree yields a PK PR k-d tree which is the same as a path-compressed PR k-d tree. However, notice that when $k > 4$ ($k > 2$), application of the above process to a partition tree that is a PR quadtree (PR k-d tree) yields a result similar to, but not the same as, applying level compression. The reason for the absence of equivalence here is that use of level compression aggregates all descendants of a node down to a fixed depth, whereas this is not a necessary condition in the case of a PK-tree. Thus, using a value of k that is greater than the branching factor of the underlying partitioning process yields a more flexible result than level compression.

The PK PR quadtree appears similar to a bucket PR quadtree, but unlike the bucket PR quadtree, each node in the PK PR quadtree has a minimum number of children instead of a maximum. This also applies to a PK-tree when the partition tree is not a PR quadtree.[68] Note that although all of the blocks that correspond to the children of a PK PR quadtree nonleaf node are squares, they are not all the same size, even though the space spanned by a nonleaf node in a PK PR quadtree is still a square. Observe also that when the partition tree is a variant of a quadtree, and k is larger than 4, then all nonleaf nodes, all of whose children are leaf nodes, in the partition tree are removed and do not appear in the PK-tree.

1.8.3 Definition

Given that the PK-tree really addresses the grouping process once a partitioning process yielding a partition tree has been chosen, it is not surprising that the actual, and formal, definition of the PK-tree is bottom up. In particular, given a value of k, where $k > 1$, the definition of the PK-tree is in terms of the concept of *k-instantiation*, where we say that a node or block in the partition tree is *k-instantiated* if it has a corresponding node or block in the PK-tree. We also say that a node or block a in the partition tree *directly contains* a k-instantiated node or block b if b is not contained by any k-instantiated node or block smaller than a. The PK-tree is the hierarchy that consists of just the k-instantiated nodes of the partition tree.

1. A nonempty leaf node (i.e., a point node) in the partition tree is k-instantiated.

2. A nonleaf node (i.e., a directory node) a in the partition tree is k-instantiated if a directly contains at least k k-instantiated nodes or blocks. In other words, if a's corresponding node b in the PK-tree has j ($j \geq k$) children c_i ($1 \leq i \leq j$), then each node in the partition tree that corresponds to one of c_i is both a descendant of a and is k-instantiated. Furthermore, there are no other k-instantiated nodes in the partition tree on the path from a to c_i.

3. The root node of the partition tree is k-instantiated (i.e., regardless of how many children its corresponding node in the PK-tree has).

---

[68] This statement is a bit loose in the sense that we will see that the nodes in both PK-tree and bucket methods have a minimum and maximum number of children. The real difference lies in the condition behind the node-formation process, which is a minimum in the case of the PK-tree and a maximum in the case of a bucket method.

In other words, unlike most tree definitions, which are often inductive, and where the base case is in terms of the root node of the partition tree (i.e., a tree with just one node) or an empty tree, in the PK-tree, the base case is in terms of the leaf nodes of the partition tree. Note that the above definition is rather cumbersome in light of the need to make a distinction between the nodes in the partition tree and the PK-tree. Nevertheless, it is necessary as there is a potential for confusion since we often use the term *node*. We will adopt the convention that whenever we speak of a node, we mean either a node of the PK-tree or a node of the partition tree. Usually, it will be clear from the context of the discussion which one is meant, but when it is not, we specify explicitly which type is meant.

The definition of the PK-tree is somewhat hard to understand as much of its significance lies in what is *not* k-instantiated. In particular, we have defined only whether a node in the original partition tree is k-instantiated. In addition, we must specify what is to become of nodes in the partition tree that are not k-instantiated. Notice also that our definition implies that empty children are not k-instantiated. A more explicit definition is that a nonleaf node a in the partition tree is *k-instantiated* (or equivalently *k-instantiable*) if a has at least k descendants c_i that are k-instantiated, and there are no other k-instantiated nodes between a and c_i. If a node q in the partition tree is not k-instantiated, then its children become children of the PK-tree node corresponding to the deepest ancestor a of q (i.e., a is the k-instantiated ancestor of q that is farthest from the root). Similarly, a k-instantiated node q, which is not a root node in the partition tree, is said to become *k-deinstantiated* when the number of nonempty children of its corresponding PK-tree node a, which is therefore also not a root node, falls below k. In this case, the fewer than k children of q's corresponding PK-tree node a are delinked from a and made children of g, the father of a, which must exist because q is not a root node, and a is returned to available storage to be reused again in the case of dynamic storage allocation. This definition of the PK-tree is a bit hard to visualize, which is why we also give the operational definition of the construction of the PK tree above.

What makes the PK-tree so attractive is that it is possible to make the internal nodes sufficiently large (i.e., by increasing their maximum capacity) so that each node can be stored efficiently in a disk page. The number of elements making up a PK-tree node differs on the basis of the underlying partition tree. For example, when the partition tree is a two-dimensional PR quadtree, then each node in the corresponding PK PR quadtree has a minimum of k children and a maximum of $4 \cdot (k - 1)$ children. Similarly, when the partition tree is a three-dimensional PR quadtree (i.e., a PR octree), then each node in the corresponding *PK PR octree* has a minimum of k children and a maximum of $8 \cdot (k - 1)$ children. Interestingly, when the partition tree is a PR k-d tree, then each node in the corresponding PK PR k-d tree has a minimum of k children and a maximum of $2 \cdot (k - 1)$ children, regardless of the dimensionality of the underlying space.

Of course, in order for the internal nodes of the PK-tree to have a large capacity, we must choose values of k larger than the branching factor of the corresponding partitioning process (i.e., 4 and 8, for the PR quadtree and PR octree, respectively). However, this is not really a problem as it simply means that we aggregate a larger number of nodes at each level of the tree. In fact, making k larger appears to increase the resemblance of the PK-tree to a quadgrid. However, the important difference is that, although in the case of a PK-tree with a quadtree partition tree, the k elements that are aggregated to form a node are squarelike, unlike the quadgrid, the blocks in the underlying space spanned by the individual aggregated elements need not necessarily be congruent (i.e., their corresponding sides do not have to have the same length).

1.8.4 Comparison with Bucket Methods

Earlier we mentioned that the PK PR quadtree (and, more generally, the PK-tree based on any partitioning process) resembles the bucket PR quadtree (or any variant of a bucket partitioning process, such as a bucket PR k-d tree). This was based on the apparent similarity of k-instantiation and bucketing. In fact, these two concepts are very different, although their effects are very similar. The most obvious difference, which was already pointed out, is that each node in the PK-tree is defined in terms of a minimum number of children, while in the bucket variants, each node is defined in terms of a maximum number of children. Another important difference is that bucketing is a top-down process, which means that for a bucket capacity k, the decomposition halts as soon as we encounter a block with k or fewer objects. Thus, we are seeking a maximum enclosing quadtree (or k-d tree) block for the k or fewer objects. In contrast, the k-instantiation in the PK-tree (as well as path compression) are bottom-up processes, and we are seeking the minimum enclosing quadtree (or k-d tree) block for the group of at least k objects.

This difference can be seen by observing that if a group of k objects exists in a block i of size $2^a \times 2^a$ that is embedded in a larger block j of size $2^b \times 2^b$ such that j contains no other objects, then a bucket method would use block j, while a PK-tree would use block i. Interestingly, the similarity between the two processes lies in the time at which they halt (i.e., as soon as possible!). In particular, the bottom-up process halts as soon as a block contains at least k objects, and the top-down process halts as soon as a block contains at most k objects.

K-instantiation, which is the principal idea behind the PK-tree, can be applied to other partitioning processes that are based on a disjoint decomposition of space (preferably a regular decomposition but not required) besides the PR quadtree (see Exercise 1 in Section 1.8.6). In particular, adapting the PK-tree to a two-dimensional PR k-d tree, yielding a PK PR k-d tree, we find that each node has a minimum of k children and a maximum of $2 \cdot (k-1)$ children. This resembles the classical B$^+$-tree definition (as well as an R-tree and other bucket variants discussed in Section 1.7.1) in terms of having nodes with a variable capacity; yet, each node is guaranteed to be at least half-full.

Of course, there are some important differences between the PK-tree and these bucket variants. In particular, the main difference is that, unlike the B$^+$-tree (and R-tree), the PK-tree is not necessarily balanced. The PK PR k-d tree is somewhat similar to the BD-tree (see Section 1.5.2.6), which is also a bucket method, but the PK-tree has the advantage that it is uniquely defined while the BD-tree is not. However, the nonuniqueness of the BD-tree does enable the BD-tree to be varied so that a more balanced structure can be achieved. The price of the balance is that the BD-tree does not decompose the underlying space into squares. Instead, the decomposition is into a collection of "holey bricks" (i.e., squares that possibly have smaller squares cut out) similar to that resulting from use of other bucket methods, such as the hB-tree (see Section 1.7.1.4) and the BANG file (see Section 1.7.1.5). This makes subsequent processing a bit difficult. Also, all but the leaf nodes in the BD-tree have a fanout of 2, whereas the fanout of all of the PK PR k-d tree nodes is much higher. The limited fanout of the nonleaf nodes in the BD-tree reduces the motivation for using it as a disk-resident data structure.

1.8.5 Operations

The PK-tree is a dynamic structure, which means that items can be inserted and deleted from an existing PK-tree without having to rebuild the structure for the entire dataset. Updating a PK-tree to add or remove a point p is a two-step process. The first step corresponds to a search for p. It starts at the root and proceeds in a top-down manner, guided by the decomposition rules for the specific partitioning process that has been chosen (e.g., PR quadtree, PR k-d tree). In essence, we are searching the blocks induced by the decomposition for the block b containing p. Once b has been found, the actual operation is performed, if possible (i.e., b is empty or does not contain p in the case of insertion, or b contains p in the case of deletion), and the grouping process is applied in a bottom-up manner, as necessary, to ensure that the result is a PK-tree. In the rest of this section, we discuss the representation of the PK-tree, as well as elaborate further on the searching process (Section 1.8.5.1) and the implementation of insertion (Section 1.8.5.2) and deletion (Section 1.8.5.3).

1.8.5.1 Representation and Searching

The mechanics of the search process are heavily dependent on the representation of the points and the nodes. The search for point p starts at the root and looks for the node whose corresponding block contains p. This is not so simple for the following reasons:

1. The blocks corresponding to the children of a node in the PK-tree are not necessarily the same size.

2. The union of the blocks corresponding to the elements of q is not necessarily equal to the block corresponding to q on account of the elimination of the empty children via a process analogous to path compression.

The child blocks (i.e., both point nodes and directory nodes) of each node a are represented by a unique number known as a locational code (see Section 2.1.2.4 of Chapter 2 for more detail). For example, such a number can be formed by applying bit interleaving to the binary representations of the coordinate values of an easily identifiable point in each block (e.g., its lower-left corner when the origin is in the lower-left corner of the underlying space as in Figure 1.112(a)) and concatenating this number with the base 2 logarithm of its block size—that is, i for a block of size 2^i. These locational codes are sorted in increasing order, thereby yielding an ordering (called a Morton order [1317] or Z order [1420]) equivalent to that which would be obtained by traversing the nonempty leaf nodes (i.e., blocks) of the tree representation of the decomposition of the embedding space from which the data is drawn in the order SW, SE, NW, and NE for a quadtree (or bottom, top, left, and right for a k-d tree). Of course, other orders, such as the Peano-Hilbert order [835], have also been used (e.g., [591, 937]).

Ordering the locational codes in increasing order facilitates searching for a particular point p as we can make use of a binary search for the block in a that contains p. This implementation poses a problem when a is a point node because the coordinate values of the points are usually specified with greater precision than is permitted by the resolution of the underlying space. Thus, it is usually stipulated that the underlying space has some finite resolution, and, therefore, the locational code of the point node is really the locational code of the 1×1 block that contains the point. In addition, besides the locational code, associated with each entry corresponding to child block b is a pointer to either the actual node in the PK-tree corresponding to b when b is a directory node in the partition tree, or a pointer to a record containing the rest of the information about the point (i.e., its coordinate values and any other relevant information). Of course, if two points fall into the same 1×1 cell, then they have the same locational code. However, they can still be distinguished because the combination of the locational code and pointer to the rest of the information about the point is unique. It is interesting to observe that the stipulation that the points are represented by 1×1 blocks means that the partition tree is actually an MX quadtree (e.g., [1637]), and the corresponding PK-tree is really a PK MX quadtree (see Figure 1.114). Now we see that every node in the PK MX quadtree is a minimum enclosing quadtree block of the points in the space spanned by its corresponding block (whereas this was not quite true for the blocks corresponding to the point nodes when the partition tree is a PR quadtree).

1.8.5.2 Insertion

Although our operational definition of the PK-tree has implied that we know all of the data items before building it (i.e., it is static), as we pointed out above, the PK-tree is a dynamic structure in the sense that data can be inserted and removed one at a time without our having to rebuild the structure from scratch. However, checks for k-instantiation

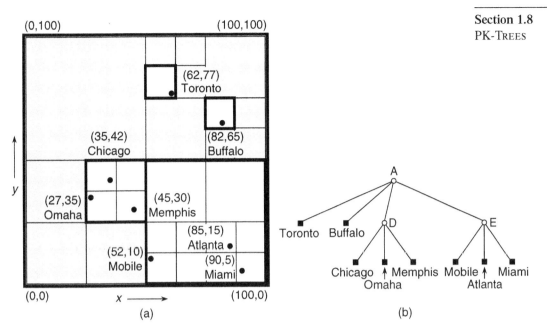

Figure 1.114
A PK MX quadtree with $k = 3$ corresponding to the data of Figure 1.112: (a) the resulting partition of space and (b) the tree representation. The heavy lines indicate the boundaries of the blocks corresponding to the nodes (leaf and nonleaf) in the first level of the tree structure. Empty blocks in the first level of decomposition of the underlying space induced by the PK MX quadtree are shown shaded and are not represented in the tree structure.

and k-deinstantiation may have to be applied at each level of the PK-tree during the grouping process. In particular, once the position where the point to be inserted or the point to be deleted has been found, we continuously check in a bottom-up manner for the applicability of k-instantiation or k-deinstantiation until it is no longer applicable, or we have reached the root of the structure. This is a direct consequence of the fact that the PK-tree is defined in a bottom-up manner (i.e., recall that the nodes of the PK-tree are always defined in terms of their descendants). The details of the insertion and deletion processes are given in the rest of this section and in Section 1.8.5.3, which follows immediately.

The insertion of a point p, which belongs in a block b of the partition tree, which is in turn contained in block c corresponding to nonleaf node q in the PK-tree, may result in the k-instantiation of an ancestor block b' of b in q. In this case, a new node t is created that corresponds to b', whose elements are p and $k - 1$ other elements of q. Observe that b' corresponds to the minimum enclosing block of p and the $k - 1$ elements of q that form t. Note also that t cannot contain more than k elements as, otherwise, t would have already existed since the block in the partition tree corresponding to t was not k-instantiated prior to the insertion of p. Node t is made an element of q, and t's $k - 1$ elements, excluding p, are removed from q. This action may cause the block in the partition tree corresponding to q (i.e., c) to cease being k-instantiated as fewer than k elements may be left in it (i.e., c is k-deinstantiated). This means that the elements of q must be made elements of the father f of q in the PK-tree. This process is applied recursively on f, with t taking on the role of p, as long as we end up with a node that contains fewer than k elements or encounter the root, at which time we halt. Recall that according to the definition of the PK-tree, the root's corresponding block in the partition tree is always k-instantiated, regardless of the number of nonempty children.

For example, consider the PK PR quadtree with $k = 5$ with points 1–4 and A–O and nonleaf nodes W–Z given in Figure 1.115(a). Figure 1.115(b) is the block decomposition of the underlying space of size $2^9 \times 2^9$ induced by the corresponding PR quadtree (i.e., the partition tree) where these points (and an additional point P that will be subsequently

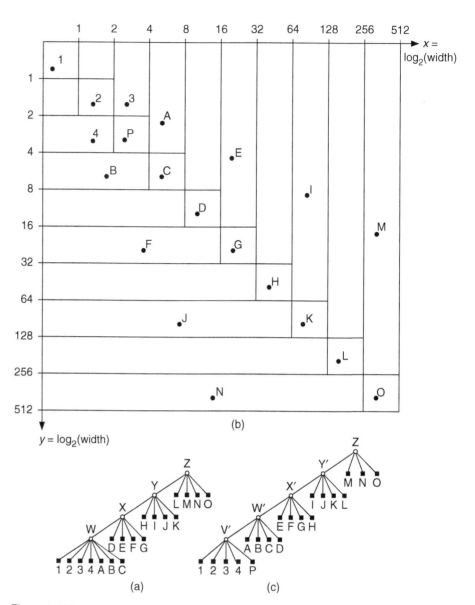

Figure 1.115
(a) Tree representation of an example PK PR quadtree for $k = 5$; (b) a block decomposition of the underlying space (at logarithmic scale but all blocks are square and of a width that is a power of 2), where the labeled points can lie so that the tree representation in (a) would be physically realizable; and (c) the result of inserting point P into the PK PR quadtree in (a).

inserted) lie. All blocks in Figure 1.115(b) are square, and the points can lie in any location in the square in which they are found. Note that the block decomposition in Figure 1.115(b) does not correspond to an MX quadtree since as soon as a block contains just one point, we halt the decomposition, whereas in the MX quadtree we would descend to the final level where each point is a 1×1 block. Of course, since the PK-tree effectively "path-compresses" all of the extra decomposition, there is no point in using the MX quadtree. Observe also that the example in Figure 1.115(b) is drawn using a logarithmic scale as the widths of the blocks at each successive level of decomposition are one half the widths of the blocks at the immediately preceding level. Figure 1.115(c) shows the result of inserting point P into the PK PR quadtree of Figure 1.115(a), given the physical interpretation of Figure 1.115(b). Nonleaf nodes V′–Y′ have been added during the insertion process, while nodes W–Y (see Figure 1.115(a)) have been removed.

Notice that the insertion of P has led to the k-instantiation of the partition tree node corresponding to the minimum enclosing block of it and points 1–4, thereby causing the creation of node V′ in Figure 1.115(c). In fact, this act of k-instantiation has caused the k-deinstantiation of the block in the partition tree corresponding to node W, as now it contains only four elements (i.e., A–C and V′), thereby causing the promotion of the partition tree blocks corresponding to points A–C and node V′ to node X. This causes the k-instantiation of the minimum enclosing partition tree block of points A–D and node V′ and the formation of a new node W′. This action results in the k-deinstantiation of the block in the partition tree corresponding to node X as now it contains only four elements (i.e., points E–G and node W′), thereby causing the promotion of the partition tree blocks corresponding to points E–G and node W′ to node Y. This causes the k-instantiation of the minimum enclosing partition tree block of points E–H and node W′ and the formation of a new node X′. Once again, this action results in the k-deinstantiation of the block in the partition corresponding to node Y, as now it contains only four elements (i.e., points I–K and node X′), thereby causing the promotion of the partition tree blocks corresponding to points I–K and node X′ to node Z. This causes the k-instantiation of the minimum enclosing partition tree block of points I–L and node X′ and the formation of a new node Y′. At this point, node Z remains with just four elements corresponding to points M–O and node Y′, but, as Z is the root of the tree, Z′'s corresponding block in the partition tree is k-instantiated by definition. Thus, we are done, and there is no need to be concerned about whether Z has fewer than k elements.

It is important to note that this example does not represent typical data because it corresponds to data that is extremely skewed. It was chosen because it represents the worst possible case for the insertion algorithm in the sense that it results in a k-instantiation and k-deinstantiation at each level of the PK-tree (for more details, see Section 1.8.6).

The actual insertion of a point p in a PK-tree rooted at node q with instantiation parameter k is given by procedure PKInsert. PKInsert is recursive and is invoked with the point to be inserted, pointers to the root of the subtree currently being processed (initially, the root of the entire PK-tree) and its father (initially Nil for the initial invocation), and the instantiation parameter k. We assume that nodes in the PK-tree are of type *node*. PKInsert accounts for the possibility that k-instantiation and k-deinstantiation could take place at all levels. This is achieved via the use of recursion. However, PKInsert is not efficient if k-instantiation and k-deinstantiation do not take place at all levels. In particular, we know that as soon as we have found a step at which k-instantiation cannot take place, we no longer have to check for it and can safely exit the procedure. Thus, a more efficient algorithm would not use recursion; however, we would still need to capture a history of the manner in which we descended to the current node from the root so that the equivalent of recursion unwinding could be executed. Alternatively, we could also benefit from a programming construct that enabled us to exit from a recursive instantiation of the procedure and from all remaining levels of recursion. Locations in the code where this feature would be useful are accompanied by a suitably phrased comment.

Procedure PKInsert makes use of the following auxiliary procedures: FindChild, MakeNodeAndAddAsChild, FormNodeForMinEnclosingBlockWithK-Items, RemoveChildsOfNewNodeFromFather, InsertNode, Count-Childs, and InsertChildsOfNode. These procedures are important as they correspond to the decomposition rules of the partition tree. Recall that the key idea in the PK-tree is the decoupling of the partition process from the grouping process. Thus, we should have one set of procedure implementations for a PR quadtree, another different set for an MX quadtree, and so on.

Procedure FindChild(P, Q) finds the child of node Q that contains point P. MakeNodeAndAddAsChild(P, Q) creates a new node t for point P, adds t as a child of node Q, and returns t as its value. FormNodeForMinEnclosingBlock-WithKItems(D, Q, K) finds the minimum enclosing block in the partition tree of element D in node Q with at least K elements and forms a new PK-tree node t corresponding to it that is returned as its value. In other words, it performs k-instantiation, if possible. Note that if Q is a root node with fewer than K elements and FORMNODEFOR-MINENCLOSINGBLOCKWITHKITEMS cannot find a block with K elements, then it returns Q as the value. Procedure REMOVECHILDSOFNEWNODEFROMFATHER(T, Q) removes the children of node T from node Q. INSERTNODE(T, Q) makes node T a child of node Q. COUNTCHILDS(Q) counts the number of elements (i.e., corresponding to nonempty children) in node Q. INSERTCHILDSOFNODE(Q, F) makes the children of node Q be children of node F, while REMOVENODEFROMFATHER(Q, F) removes the entry for node Q in node F, which is Q's father.

```
1   recursive node procedure PKINSERT(P, Q, F, K)
2   /* Attempt to insert point P in the PK-tree with parameter K rooted at node
         Q whose father is F. An empty PK-tree still has a nonempty root node
         with no entries in it. */
3   value pointer point P
4   value pointer node Q, F
5   value integer K
6   pointer node D, S, T
7   S ← FINDCHILD(P, Q)
8   D ←if ISNULL(S) then MAKENODEANDADDASCHILD(P, Q)
9       else PKINSERT(P, S, Q, K)
10      endif
11  T ← FORMNODEFORMINENCLOSINGBLOCKWITHKITEMS(D, Q, K)
12  if T = Q then
13      return Q /* Can exit completely as no k-instantiation has occurred */
14  else /* Propagate k-instantiation */
15      REMOVECHILDSOFNEWNODEFROMFATHER(T, Q)
16      INSERTNODE(T, Q)
17      if not ISNULL(F) and COUNTCHILDS(Q) < K then
18          /* propagate k-deinstantiation */
19          INSERTCHILDSOFNODE(Q, F)
20          REMOVENODEFROMFATHER(Q, F)
21          RETURNTOAVAIL(Q)
22          return T
23      else return Q /* Can exit completely as no further k-instantiation can */
24      endif           /* take place since no k-deinstantiation has occurred */
25  endif
```

It is interesting to observe that, at times, a node may temporarily contain more than the maximum possible number of elements, which is $F \cdot (k - 1)$ for a partition tree with a branching factor F. This is the case when k-deinstantiation takes place (i.e., right after k-instantiation, which, as we will see in Section 1.8.5.3, also occurs when a point is deleted rather than limited to occurring when a point is inserted) or when an insertion is made into a PK-tree node that is full. Suppose that node n contains $F \cdot (k - 1)$ elements. If we insert a new element into n, then n will momentarily contain $F \cdot (k - 1) + 1$ elements. Similarly, a k-deinstantiation involving n that replaces one of the elements in n by $k - 1$ elements from a child node results in n containing $F \cdot (k - 1) - 1 + (k - 1) = F \cdot (k - 1) + k - 2 = (F + 1) \cdot (k - 1) - 1$ elements. Of course, in both cases, the newly added elements of n will be immediately k-instantiated with other element(s) of n, and the node will once again contain a maximum of $F \cdot (k - 1)$ elements.[69]

---

[69] A more detailed explanation is as follows. Suppose that a block b' in node q becomes k-instantiated (via the insertion of a point, the promotion of $k - 1$ elements of the partition tree due to k-deinstantiation, or the invocation of procedure FORMNODEFORMINENCLOSINGBLOCKWITH-KITEMS). In this case, a new node t will be created corresponding to b' that has k elements. Node t is made an element of q, and t's k elements (or $k - 1$ elements if the k-instantiation has resulted from the

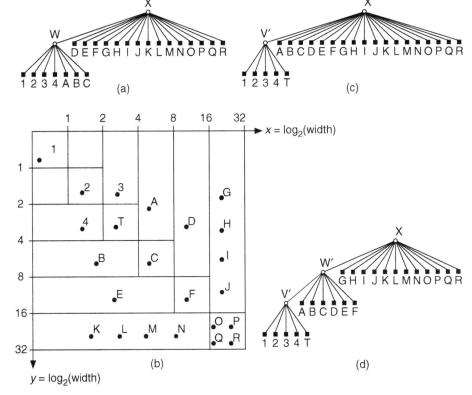

Figure 1.116
(a) Tree representation of an example PK PR quadtree for $k = 5$; (b) a block decomposition of the underlying space (at logarithmic scale but all blocks are square and of width that is a power of 2), where the labeled points can lie so that the tree representation in (a) would be physically realizable; (c) the tree representation after the combination of k-instantiation and k-deinstantiation resulting from inserting point T into the PK PR quadtree in (a); and (d) the final tree representation.

As an example of how this situation can arise, consider the PK PR quadtree with $k = 5$ with points 1–4 and A–R and nonleaf nodes W and X given in Figure 1.116(a). Figure 1.116(b) is a block decomposition of the underlying space of size $2^5 \times 2^5$, where these points (and an additional point T that will be subsequently inserted) lie. All blocks in Figure 1.116(b) are square, and the points can lie in any location in the square in which they are found. Observe also that Figure 1.116(b) is drawn using a logarithmic scale as the widths of the blocks at each successive level of decomposition are one-half the widths of the blocks at the immediately preceding level.

Inserting T into the PK PR quadtree of Figure 1.116(a), given the physical interpretation of Figure 1.116(b), has led to the k-instantiation of the partition tree node corresponding to the minimum enclosing block of it and points 1–4, causing the creation of node V′, as shown in Figure 1.116(c). In fact, this act of k-instantiation has caused the k-deinstantiation of the block in the partition tree corresponding to node W,

---

addition of a new point) are removed from q. This action may cause the block c in the partition tree corresponding to q to cease being k-instantiated, as fewer than k elements may be left in it (i.e., c is k-deinstantiated). The maximum number of elements remaining in q (including t) is $k - 1$. This means that the elements of q must be made elements of the father f of q. Thus, the number of elements in f grows by at most $k - 2$ as one of its elements (i.e., q), which has become k-deinstantiated, is replaced by $k - 1$ additional elements for a net gain of $k - 2$. Thus, if f already has the maximum number of elements (i.e., $F \cdot (k - 1)$), then the maximum number of elements in a node is really $(F + 1) \cdot (k - 1) - 1$. Of course, if this is the case, the newly added elements of f will be immediately k-instantiated with an element of f, and the maximum number of elements in the node will once again be $F \cdot (k - 1)$.

as now it contains only four elements (i.e., points A–C and node V'), thereby causing the promotion of the partition tree blocks corresponding to points A–C and node V' to node X, as shown in Figure 1.116(c). At this point, node X contains 19 elements, which is 3 more ($= k - 2$ when k is 5) than the possible maximum number of elements. However, this causes the k-instantiation of the minimum enclosing partition tree block of points A–F and node V', and a new node W' is formed, as shown in Figure 1.116(d). At this point, node X has 13 elements, and we are below the possible maximum number of elements.

Note that the physical size of a node (in bytes) is dictated by the chosen page size of the disk-resident tree file (often 4 kB). Thus, it is undesirable for the node to become larger than the physical size. There are essentially two ways to overcome this problem. The first is to allow the size of the nodes to exceed the physical size (i.e., the page size) when in memory (e.g., by allocating a larger memory block or by maintaining an overflow buffer of $k - 2$ elements, which is used only when a node overflows in the described manner). The second is to modify the code for the PK-tree update operations (i.e., both insertion and deletion algorithms) so that they avoid the overflow problem. In particular, before adding m elements to a node n (either through insertion or k-deinstantiation), we check whether we can k-instantiate these m new elements together with $k - m$ existing elements in n. If this is possible, then we perform the k-instantiation without adding the m elements to n; otherwise, it is safe to add the new elements without exceeding the maximum size.

Exercise

1. Write an iterative version of the PK-tree insertion algorithm, procedure PKINSERT, that does not perform unnecessary k-instantiation tests (i.e., the calls to procedure FORMNODE-FORMINENCLOSINGBLOCKWITHKITEMS) once we know that no more occurrences of k-instantiation are possible.

1.8.5.3 Deletion

Deletion of a point p that is an element of nonleaf node q in the PK-tree is handled in a similar manner to insertion. The difference from insertion is that deletion may result in the removal of nodes from the PK-tree whose corresponding blocks in the partition tree were formerly k-instantiated. If the block in the partition tree corresponding to q is still k-instantiated after the deletion, then no further action must be taken. Otherwise, q must be deallocated, and its remaining $k - 1$ elements are made elements of the father f of q in the PK-tree (i.e., the block in the partition tree corresponding to q is k-deinstantiated). The insertion of additional elements in f may mean that one of the subblocks, say b', of the partition tree block b corresponding to f that contains the newly inserted $k - 1$ elements, plus at least one other element, may become k-instantiated. In this case, a new node t will be created that corresponds to b'. Note that t can contain more than k elements. Node t is made an element of f, and t's elements are removed from f. This action may cause the block in the partition tree corresponding to f (i.e., b) to cease being k-instantiated, as fewer than k elements may be left in it (i.e., b is k-deinstantiated). This means that the elements of f must be made elements of the father g of f. This process is applied recursively on g, with t taking on the same role as p in the insertion process, as long as we end up with a node that contains fewer than k elements or encounter the root, at which time we halt. Recall that, according to the definition of the PK-tree, the root's corresponding block in the partition tree is always k-instantiated, regardless of the number of nonempty children.

For example, consider the PK PR quadtree with $k = 5$ with points 1–4, A–M, and P and nonleaf nodes V–Z in Figure 1.117(a). Figure 1.117(b) is the block decomposition of the underlying space of size $2^9 \times 2^9$ induced by the corresponding PR quadtree (i.e., the partition tree) where these points lie. All blocks in Figure 1.117(b) are square, and the points can lie in any location in the square in which they are found. Observe that the example in Figure 1.117(b) is drawn using a logarithmic scale as the widths of the

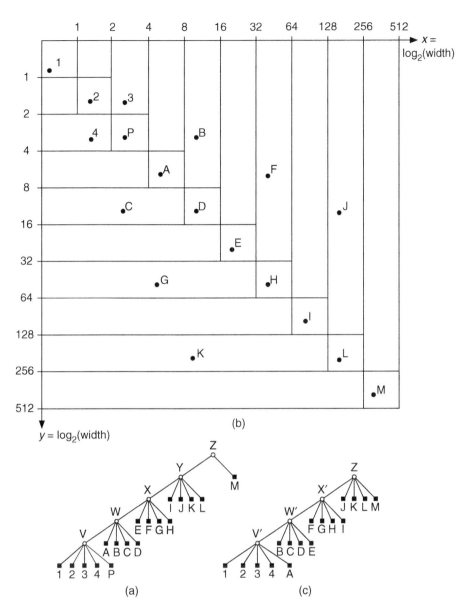

Figure 1.117
(a) Tree representation of an example PK PR quadtree for $k = 5$; (b) a block decomposition of the underlying space (at logarithmic scale but all blocks are square and of width that is a power of 2), where the labeled points can lie so that the tree representation in (a) would be physically realizable; and (c) the result of deleting point P from the PK PR quadtree in (a).

blocks at each successive level of decomposition are one-half the widths of the blocks at the immediately preceding level. Figure 1.117(c) shows the result of deleting point P from the PK PR quadtree of Figure 1.117(a), given the physical interpretation of Figure 1.117(b). Nonleaf nodes V–Z are the nonleaf nodes in the original PK-tree. Nodes V′–X′ have been added during the deletion process, while nodes V–Y have been removed.

Notice that the deletion of P has led to the k-deinstantiation of the partition tree node corresponding to V (as it has just four elements corresponding to points 1–4). This action results in the removal of node V in Figure 1.117(c) and the promotion of points 1–4 to node W. This causes the k-instantiation of the minimum enclosing partition tree block of the points 1–4 and the block corresponding to point A, and a new node V′ is formed that is made an element of node W. This action results in the k-deinstantiation of the block in the partition tree corresponding to node W, as now it contains only four elements (i.e., points B–D and node V′), thereby causing the promotion of the partition tree blocks corresponding to points B–D and node V′ to node X. This causes the k-instantiation of the minimum enclosing partition tree block of points B–E and node V′ and the formation of a new node W′ that is made an element of node X. This results in the k-deinstantiation of the block in the partition tree corresponding to node X, as now it contains only four elements (i.e., points F–H and node W′), thereby causing the promotion of partition tree blocks corresponding to points F–H and node W′ to node Y. This causes the k-instantiation of the minimum enclosing partition tree block of points F–I and node W′ and the formation of a new node X′ that is made an element of node Y. This results in the k-deinstantiation of the block in the partition tree corresponding to node Y, as now it contains only four elements (i.e., points J–L and node X′), thereby causing the promotion of the partition tree blocks corresponding to points J–L and node X′ to node Z, which is the root node with just one other element (i.e., M). At this point, node Z has five elements, but, as Z is the root of the tree, Z′'s corresponding block in the partition tree is k-instantiated by definition. Thus, we are done, and there is no need to be concerned about whether Z has fewer than k elements.

It is important to note that this example does not represent typical data but corresponds to data that is extremely skewed. It was chosen because it represents the worst possible case for the deletion algorithm in the sense that it results in a k-instantiation and k-deinstantiation at each level of the PK-tree (for more details, see Section 1.8.6).

The actual deletion of a point p in a PK-tree rooted at node q with instantiation parameter k is given by procedure PKDELETE. PKDELETE is recursive and is very similar to PKINSERT. PKDELETE is invoked with the point to be deleted, pointers to the root of the subtree currently being processed (initially the root of the entire PK-tree) and its father (initially NIL for the initial invocation), and the instantiation parameter k. PKDELETE accounts for the possibility that k-instantiation and k-deinstantiation could take place at all levels. This is achieved via the use of recursion. However, as we remark in our discussion of PKINSERT, PKDELETE is not efficient if k-instantiation and k-deinstantiation do not take place at all levels. In particular, we know that as soon as we have found a step at which k-instantiation can no longer take place, we no longer have to check for it and can safely exit the procedure. Thus, a more efficient algorithm would not use recursion; however, we would still need to capture a history of the manner in which we descended to the current node from the root so that the equivalent of recursion unwinding could be executed. Alternatively, we could also benefit from a programming construct that enabled us to exit from a recursive instantiation of the procedure and from all remaining levels of recursion. Locations in the code where this feature would be useful are accompanied by a suitably phrased comment.

Procedure PKDELETE makes use of the same auxiliary procedures as PKINSERT with the addition of ISPOINT and CHOOSECHILD. Recall from our discussion of PKINSERT that these procedures are important as they correspond to the decomposition rules of the partition tree, and there is one set of procedure implementations for the PR quadtree, another set for the MX quadtree, and so on. Procedure ISPOINT(S) determines if node S corresponds to a single point. CHOOSECHILD(Q) returns a pointer to one of the children of Q. This is useful in case any k-deinstantiation takes place at the level of the tree at which the deleted point was found.

```
1  recursive node procedure PKDELETE(P, Q, F, K)
2  /* Attempt to delete node P from the PK-tree with parameter K rooted at
        node Q whose father is F. An empty PK-tree still has a nonempty root
        node with no entries in it. */
3  value pointer point P
4  value pointer node Q, F
5  value integer K
6  pointer node D, S, T
7  S ← FINDCHILD(P, Q)
```

```
 8   if IsNull(S) then
 9       return Q /* P is not in the PK-tree and can exit completely */
10   elseif IsPoint(S) then
11       /* S must be point P as, otherwise, FindChild is Nil */
12       RemoveNodeFromFather(S, Q)
13       ReturnToAvail(S)
14       T ← ChooseChild(Q)
15   else
16       D ← PKDelete(P, S, Q)
17       T ← FormNodeForMinEnclosingBlockWithKItems(D, Q, K)
18       if T = Q then
19           return Q /* Can exit completely as no k-instantiation has occurred */
20       else /* Propagate k-instantiation */
21           RemoveChildsOfNewNodeFromFather(T, Q)
22           InsertNode(T, Q)
23       endif
24   endif
25   if not IsNull(F) and CountChilds(Q) < K then
26       /* propagate k-deinstantiation */
27       InsertChildsOfNode(Q, F)
28       RemoveNodeFromFather(Q, F)
29       ReturnToAvail(Q)
30       return T
31   else           /* Can exit completely as no further k-instantiation can */
32       return Q /* take place since no k-deinstantiation has occurred */
33   endif
```

Exercises

1. Write an iterative version of the PK-tree deletion algorithm, procedure PKDELETE, that does not perform unnecessary k-instantiation tests (i.e., the calls to procedure FORMNODE-FORMINENCLOSINGBLOCKWITHKITEMS) once we know that no more occurrences of k-instantiation are possible.

2. Suppose that after deletion we have the situation that a root node r has just one child s that is a nonleaf node. Should we make the children of s be children of r and delete s? An example of such a situation would arise after deleting point M from the PK PR quadtree in Figure 1.117(a).

1.8.6 Discussion

The examples in Figures 1.115 and 1.117 point out how and when the process of k-instantiation and k-deinstantiation can take place at all levels of the PK-tree. Notice that the particular configuration of data in our examples starts with (results in) each nonleaf node, save the root (which is always k-instantiated regardless of how many entries it has) at the end (start) of the insertion (deletion) process, being completely full (i.e., truly k-instantiated) with respect to the given value of k (i.e., $k = 5$ in our example). They represent the worst case of the PK-tree in the sense that insertion (deletion) of one point has caused the depth of the PK-tree to increase (decrease) by one level. However, it is the maximum possible increase (decrease) in depth due to the insertion (deletion) of a point. This is in contrast to the conventional PR quadtree, where the increase (decrease) in depth depends on the minimum separation between the newly added (deleted) point and the closest existing point to it in the tree. Similar examples of the worst case can be constructed for any value of k.

An additional important observation from these examples is that the maximum depth of a PK-tree with N nodes is $O(N)$, and thus the worst-case input/output time complexity to search (as well as update) is $O(N)$. Thus, we see that the PK-tree does not behave well (from the perspective of being a balanced structure) for skewed distributions of data as in our example, although Wang, Yang, and Muntz [1952] have shown that, under certain assumptions on the probability distribution of the data (including uniformly distributed data [2043]), the expected search cost is $O(\log N)$.

It is interesting to observe that, as in all methods based on the conventional application of regular decomposition, insertion and deletion of a point in a PK-tree may cause a substantial number of operations analogous to node splitting and merging, respectively, to take place. However, the process is not so clearly identifiable as one of pure merging (in the case of deletion, e.g., in a PR quadtree, a PR k-d tree, or an MX quadtree) and pure splitting (in the case of insertion, e.g., in a PR quadtree, a PR k-d tree, or an MX quadtree). The analogs of splitting and merging are the processes of k-instantiation and k-deinstantiation, respectively. However, both of these processes may take place in a PK-tree when inserting, as well as deleting, a point, whereas in the methods based on conventional application of regular decomposition, nodes are either split or merged but not both.

In fact, as we have seen, the amount of splitting and merging that is needed in a PK-tree may be as large as the maximum depth of the tree. This occurs because k-instantiation is defined in a bottom-up manner, resulting in the possible propagation of the effects of updates as high as the root. In contrast, in the methods that are based on pure path compression (i.e., path-compressed PR k-d tree, path-level compressed PR k-d tree, and the BD-tree), a node split or merge takes place just once rather than multiple times, as is the case for the structures from which they are derived (i.e., the PR and MX quadtrees and their corresponding k-d tree variants) as there are no empty nodes to merge. Notice that the PMR k-d tree and PMR quadtree (see Section 1.5.2) are somewhat anomolous in that the splits take place just once (assuming point objects), while the merges can happen across several levels.

The PK-tree still suffers from a sensitivity to skewness despite some claims to the contrary [1952, 2043]. This can be seen by the worst-case examples for $k = 5$ shown in Figures 1.115 and 1.117. The linear nature of the worst case of tree structures resulting from the use of a regular decomposition process that plagues all decomposition methods that are insensitive to the order of insertion can never be completely avoided. In contrast, the linear nature of the worst case of tree structures resulting from the use of methods that are not based on a regular decomposition process (e.g., the worst case of a binary search tree when the data is processed in sorted order and, likewise, for the worst case of the point quadtree) can be avoided by changing the order of insertion. Nevertheless, for the tree structures that result from the use of a regular decomposition process, we at least can avoid the tests that do not lead to differentiation between data. This is the effect of path compression in the path-compressed PR k-d tree, path-level compressed PR k-d tree, and the BD-tree. Moreover, the skewed data distributions are quite rare, and, in addition, the relatively large values of k ensure that the resulting trees are relatively shallow.

Interestingly, recalling Section 1.5.2, the PMR approach (both the PMR quadtree and the PMR k-d tree) is also motivated by a desire to avoid too many split operations. While the PMR approach does not employ path compression explicitly, it has the same effect when we recall that, with each newly added data item, we split the block containing it once, and only once. This can be viewed as a form of an inverse of path compression. In particular, in the bucket PR quadtree, the alternative to the PMR quadtree, we always split blocks whose occupancy is greater than the bucket capacity. The effect is that a block may be split and resplit repeatedly for the same insertion. In contrast, in the PMR quadtree, we protract the splitting process by performing it at most once for each insertion. We say that the effect is like the inverse of path compression because the fact that initially we perform only one split is analogous to performing path compression on all but one level. As more data items are added, we slowly undo the path compression by splitting the block each time it gains a member. Recall that this test elimination is what makes these representations similar in spirit to the Patricia trie [792, 1315].

In some sense, what we have achieved with structures such as the PK tree and those involving path and level compression that were discussed in Section 1.5.2, and, to a lesser degree, in the PMR k-d tree and PMR quadtree, is to make these structures more similar to the point quadtree and k-d tree in that each test leads to the differentiation between at least two data items. The result is that the space requirements are proportional to the number of data items instead of the inverse of the minimum separation between two data items. Thus, using the PK-tree and the related methods based on path and level compression has enabled us to achieve the best of both worlds in the sense that we have the benefits of regular decomposition while requiring $O(N)$ space, thereby avoiding the customary dependence on the resolution of the underlying space (i.e., the maximum number of decomposition steps).

An alternative characterization of what we have been able to achieve is that, in terms of the space requirements, we have the best of the image-space (i.e., regularity of the decomposition process, thereby enabling us to take advantage of the fact that the data is in registration, which facilitates set-theoretic operations) and object-space (i.e., $O(N)$ space requirements) representations. The latter is achieved primarily by virtue of the almost total elimination of empty children when a k-d tree variant is used (with the exception of the PMR k-d tree). This reduction in the space requirements has a direct impact on reducing the heights of the trees and hence the search time as tests are eliminated. However, it is important that we still do not have $O(\log N)$ guaranteed tree heights and searches, as is possible with object-space representations when data is moved in the structure after insertion to achieve balance. The possible downside of such an approach is that the resulting representation is not unique, whereas this is usually the case for most image-space methods.

Although we have stressed the differences between k-instantiation and bucketing, the concepts are related in that they both aggregate partition tree nodes into "supernodes" via the application of methods similar to level compression and, to a lesser extent, path compression. In particular, it should be clear that k-instantiation could also be defined in terms of the maximum enclosing quadtree (or k-d tree) block instead of the minimum enclosing quadtree block, but the insertion and deletion algorithms would be more complex (see Exercise 2). As we pointed out earlier, bucketing can be applied to most of the methods that involve path and level compression. The key advantage of the PK-tree is that bucketing (in the form of k-instantiation) is applied not just to the leaf nodes but also to the nonleaf nodes. The result, in the case of coupling the PK-tree with a PR k-d tree decomposition process, is a bucketing criterion that stipulates that each node has between k and $2 \cdot (k - 1)$ elements. Thus, instead of having just a maximum bucket occupancy, we also have a minimum bucket occupancy. This resembles the classical B-tree definition, which is the result of applying a variation of bucketing to a binary search tree. The advantage of using the PK-tree over the method described in Section 1.8.1, where the PR quadtree (as well as a PR k-d tree) was combined with a B^+-tree, is that in the PK PR k-d tree, the blocks corresponding to the area spanned by the data in the nodes (both leaf and nonleaf) are always similar in the sense that for d-dimensional data there are d possible hyperrectangular block shapes. Recall from the discussion of Figure 1.112 in Section 1.8.1 that this was not the case for the combination of the PR quadtree (or any other space decomposition method where the blocks are represented by locational codes) and a B^+-tree. Another advantage of the PK-tree is that, in the case of nonleaf nodes, the bucket elements can be points (i.e., objects) or pointers to child nodes, rather than having to be just one type. This was seen to yield greater flexibility.

The PK-tree appears to be similar to bucket methods based on regular decomposition, such as the k-d-B-trie discussed in Section 1.7.1. In particular, the bucketing condition is only in terms of the nonempty regions resulting from the application of regular decomposition of the underlying space. Similarly, k-instantiation is also only in terms of these nonempty regions. Nevertheless, there are some very important differences.

The most important difference is that in the PK-tree no distinction is made between data and directory nodes—that is, the PK-tree consists of the k-instantiated nodes of the corresponding partition tree (which may be data or directory nodes). Thus, points (or other objects) can appear in both leaf and nonleaf nodes of the PK-tree. This has the ramification that groups of points can stay grouped together in the same node for a much longer time than if bucketing was used. In particular, when using a bucket method, once two points are placed in the same bucket, they remain in the same bucket until it overflows, at which time they may be separated, whereas in the PK-tree these points are often moved between nodes as dictated by k-instantiation considerations. A drawback of having the points in both leaf and nonleaf nodes is that the fanout of the nonleaf nodes is potentially reduced, thereby leading to longer search paths since the height of the tree is longer. On the other hand, a drawback of storing only points in leaf nodes, as in the k-d-B-trie, is that the storage utilization of the leaf nodes may be low.

Another difference is that the PK-tree is defined in terms of a particular decomposition rule (i.e., the order in which the axes forming the underlying space are split is fixed). In contrast, the order is permitted to vary in the k-d-B-trie, thereby allowing a more compact representation of the regions that make up a nonleaf node and yielding a greater flexibility in splitting and merging of regions when updates take place. Of course, we could also use a variable splitting rule with the PK-tree, but this would complicate the process of detecting k-instantiation.

Exercises

1. How would you adapt the PK-tree to a partitioning process that is not based on a regular decomposition of the underlying space? In particular, can you adapt it to a conventional point quadtree or a k-d tree?

2. Rewrite procedures PKINSERT and PKDELETE for a PK-quadtree where the nonleaf nodes are defined in terms of a maximum enclosing quadtree block rather than a minimum enclosing quadtree block.

3. Write a procedure PKPOINTQUERY to perform a point query in a PK-tree.

4. Write a procedure PKRANGEQUERY to perform a range query in a PK-tree.

1.9 Conclusion

A principal motivation for our discussion of the representation of collections of multidimensional point data is the desire to be able to distinguish between the individual elements of the collections so that they can be retrieved efficiently on the basis of the values of their attributes. The key to the retrieval process is the fact that the values of the attributes can be ordered (i.e., a sort sequence exists for them). We are not concerned with retrieval on the basis of values that cannot be ordered. Much of our presentation (for both one-dimensional and multidimensional point data) has differentiated the representations on the basis of whether they organize the data to be stored according to its value (termed *tree-based* earlier) or whether they organize the values of the embedding space from which the data is drawn (termed *trie-based* earlier). In either case, the effect is to decompose the space (i.e., domain) from which the data is drawn into groups. The representations are further differentiated on the basis of how the ranges of the boundaries of the spatial units corresponding to the groups are determined, the nature of the grouping process, and how the groups are accessed.

In this section we present a taxonomy that includes many of the representations that were described in this chapter. Some of those that are not explicitly discussed here are

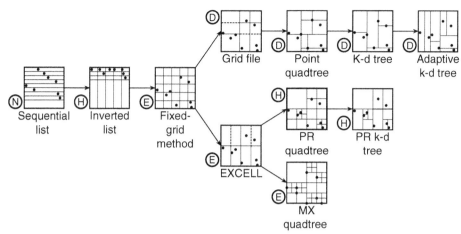

Figure 1.118
Tree representation of the interrelationship among the different data structures discussed in this chapter using the data in Figure 1.1.

a subject of Exercises 1–5. To understand their interrelationship better, we make use of Figure 1.118, a tree whose nodes are different representations. Each node in the tree is labeled with the name of the corresponding representation and contains a drawing that is an approximation of how it represents the two-dimensional data of Figure 1.1. The nodes of the tree are also labeled with a classification indicating whether they organize the data based on its values (denoted by D), organize the embedding space from which the data is drawn (denoted by E), or neither organize the data nor the embedding space from which it is drawn (denoted by N). We also makes use of an additional classification denoted by H indicating that the representation exhibits behavior that we associate with at least two of D, E, and N.

The depths of the nodes in the tree also convey important information on the relationship between the various data structures. We assume that the root of the tree is at depth 0. Our taxonomy reflects the fact that all of the representations are based on a decomposition of the underlying space into spatial elements termed *cells*. The tree reflects a progression from representations based on a fixed grid to ones based on an adaptive grid. The latter means that we have flexibility with respect to the size and shape of the cells. This progression also mirrors closely the transition from the use of access structures (i.e., directories) in the form of fixed grids (i.e., arrays) to trees in the sense that an adaptive grid usually requires some variant of a tree access structure. We make no special provision for the bucket methods that make use of a tree directory. Similarly, we make no special provisions for the methods that are used with the PK tree. In particular, we view them as natural methods of grouping more than one item in a cell. This is not the case for some of the bucket methods that make use of a grid directory that are shown in the tree, in which case we use a bucket capacity of 2. When the access methods are trees, there are many choices for the type of the tree. We do not assume a particular choice for the tree.

Note that our characterizations are not necessarily unique. Other characterizations are undoubtedly equally valid (see Exercise 8), and we may have omitted some characterizations or data structures (see Exercise 5). Nevertheless, we have tried to place each of the data structures discussed in the previous sections in an appropriate position relative to the other representations.

Depth 0 represents no identifiable organization of the data. The data is maintained in a sequential list that usually corresponds to the order in which it was inserted into the database. In the example in Figure 1.118, we have drawn the sequential list so that the elements are in the same order from top to bottom as they appear in Figure 1.1. The position of the point in each row corresponds to the value of its x coordinate.

Depth 1 corresponds to a partition of space that takes only one key into consideration. The inverted list appears at this depth and is characterized as hybrid. The key governing the partition exhibits behavior of type D. In contrast, the data values of the remaining keys have no influence on the way the space is organized and hence exhibit behavior of type N. In the example in Figure 1.118, we have assumed an inverted list for the key corresponding to the x coordinate. The position of the point in each entry corresponds to the value of its x coordinate. At this depth, we find the simplest types of cells.

At depth 2, all keys are taken into account, resulting in a partition that yields a decomposition into a fixed number of cells. Although we do not do so here, we could distinguish between cells of equal size and of varying size. The fixed-grid method, type E, is an example of the former. There are several ways of realizing cells of varying size, although they are not discussed in this chapter. For example, we could have a grid of cells of unequal size, which would require an additional data structure, such as linear scales, to locate the partition lines. Such a data structure would be of type D. Both this and the fixed-grid methods make use of a directory in the form of an array. An alternative is to use a recursive decomposition process to generate the partition into a fixed number of cells. An example of such a representation is the Dynamically Quantized Pyramid (DQP) [1777, 1425], which is a recursive decomposition into 2^d hyperrectangular cells that need not be of equal size. The DQP requires a directory in the form of a tree and would also be of type D.

Depth 3 is a generalization of depth 2. It permits the cells of the representations at depth 2 to vary in number. The amount of variation depends on the volume of the data. The goal is not to fill a cell beyond its capacity. Thus, the decomposition is adaptive. The fixed-grid method is refined to yield the grid file, type D, with cell boundaries that are allowed to vary, and EXCELL, type E, with cell boundaries at predetermined positions. Notice that the representations at this level (as well as most of the ones at depth 2) use directories in the form of arrays to access the data. However, in the case of the grid file, an additional access structure in the form of a tree is needed to determine the cell of the array that corresponds to a given point since the boundaries of the cells are free to vary. In addition, the representations at depth 3 enable the retrieval of a record in constant time.

The representations at depth 4 differ from those at depth 3 in that when a cell becomes too full (i.e., it overflows), only that particular cell is partitioned. In contrast, assuming d-dimensional data, at depth 3, a partition is made over a $(d-1)$-dimensional cross section. This means that we can no longer make use of a directory in the form of an array. Instead, we make use of directories in the form of a tree. The partition in the representations at depth 4 results in a cell's being decomposed into 2^d cells. At this depth, we find that the grid file is refined to yield the point quadtree of type D. EXCELL is refined to yield an MX quadtree of type E and a PR quadtree of type H. The PR quadtree is of type H because the partition points are fixed; however, the number of partition points depends on the relative position of the data points.

When a cell in one of the representations at depth 5 overflows, it is partitioned but decomposed into only two cells in contrast with 2^d for depth 4. The partitions that are made at the different levels in the relevant data structures cycle through the keys. At this depth, we find that the point quadtree is refined to yield a k-d tree of type D, and the PR quadtree is refined to yield a PR k-d tree of type H.

When a cell in one of the representations at depth 6 overflows, a partition is made using the key that has the greatest spread in values across the cell. Thus, we no longer need to cycle through the various keys as was done for the representations at depth 5. The adaptive k-d tree of type D (as well as the fair-split tree and the VAMSplit k-d tree) is an example of this class of data structure (also characterized as a generalized pseudo k-d tree in Section 1.5.1.4).

The representations at depth 4 to 6 are usually implemented using access structures in the form of a tree with fanout 2^d for depth 4 and fanout 2 for depths 5 and 6. However, they can also be implemented by representing each of the cells by a unique number n that corresponds to the location of some easily identifiable point in the block (i.e., its lower-right corner) and its size, also known as a locational code. n is stored in one of the one-dimensional access structures, such as a binary search tree or B-tree, along with the actual point that is associated with the cell. Such representations are discussed in greater detail in Sections 2.1.1.4 and 2.1.2.4 of Chapter 2. Observe that use of the tree access structure results in an implicit aggregation of the space spanned by the cells that are being aggregated. This is in contrast to representations that aggregate the objects (i.e., points) that are stored in the cells, in which case the space occupied by the points must be aggregated explicitly (e.g., by use of minimum bounding boxes as is done in the R-tree).

At this point, let us examine how some of the other representations that we discussed fit into our taxonomy. Representations such as the range tree and the priority search tree (as well as the range priority tree), although not shown explicitly in Figure 1.118, belong at depth 1 because they correspond to the result of the imposition of an access structure on the inverted list. Recall that the inverted list is nothing more than a decomposition of the underlying space into one-dimensional cells. The one-dimensional range tree provides an access structure on just one attribute, while the multidimensional range tree corresponds to the result of the recursive application of range trees of one fewer attribute to range trees. The drawback of the multidimensional range tree is the high space requirements since the data must be replicated. The priority search tree is like a range tree on one attribute (i.e., the one for which we have the inverted list) with the addition of a heap on the remaining attribute.

Notice that, with the exception of the grid file and EXCELL, we did not include the bucket methods that make use of a tree directory in our taxonomy. The reason is that the basic idea behind these bucket methods is the grouping of several items in a cell (e.g., the bucket PR quadtree), as well as the application of the grouping to the cells (e.g., the k-d-B-tree, k-d-B-trie, LSD tree, hB-tree, BV-tree, VAMSplit tree). However, the basic idea is still the same in the sense that the principle behind the underlying organization is one of the representations at depths 4–6. Of course, the difference is that the internal nodes of the tree have a higher fanout.

It is important to observe that our classification (i.e., Figure 1.118) has not included any of the data structures that are used to support the one-dimensional orderings. This is to be expected as once the data has been ordered in this way (regardless of whether the attributes are locational or nonlocational), we are representing the ordering rather than the actual data. The elements of the ordering are not multidimensional points in a true sense. Nevertheless, they can be viewed as multidimensional points of dimension 1. In this case, their representation fits into some of the categories that we have defined. For example, the binary search tree and B-tree would fit into the same classification as the point quadtree.

Notice also that our classification system did not contain any of the grid directory representations, such as linear hashing, quantile hashing, PLOP hashing, and spiral hashing, as they do not generally result in a new method of decomposing the underlying space. They are primarily implementations of the grid directory methods that provide an alternative in the form of a one-dimensional directory to the use of a d-dimensional directory, as in the grid file and EXCELL. In addition, they have the important property that, since the directory is one-dimensional, the directory can grow in a more gradual manner. In particular, the directory grows by one directory element (referred to as a *grid cell*) at a time instead of by doubling (as in EXCELL) or by the volume (in terms of the number of grid cells) of the $(d-1)$-dimensional cross section perpendicular to the key whose axis is being partitioned (as in the grid file).

Actually, the above statement that the one-dimensional grid directory methods do not result in a different decomposition of the underlying space is true only for linear hashing (with reversed bit interleaving as the hashing function), where the underlying space is decomposed as in EXCELL, and for quantile hashing and PLOP hashing, which decompose the underlying space as in the grid file. On the other hand, this statement is not true for spiral hashing, which is probably the most radically different of these one-dimensional directory methods as it is the only method whose use does not result in decomposing the underlying space into hyperrectangular d-dimensional cells. Moreover, not all of the regions resulting from the decomposition are spatially contiguous.

Thus, our failure to include linear hashing, quantile hashing, and PLOP hashing is justified, while spiral hashing does not seem to have any place in our classification, as our entire discussion has been predicated on the fact that the underlying space is decomposed into hyperrectangular d-dimensional cells. In retrospect, perhaps the right place to insert a family of methods that include spiral hashing is at a depth between 1 and 2, which would distinguish between methods on the basis of the shape of the underlying cell (see also Exercise 6), as well as on whether the cells need to be spatially contiguous. It should be clear that, at this point, we have really only scratched the surface in our attempt at a classification. Many other methods are possible and desirable.

A taxonomy similar to the one that we discussed is used by Aref and Ilyas [70] in their development of the *spatial partitioning generalized search tree* (SP-GiST), an extensible index structure that can be made to behave in the same way as many of the data structures described in this chapter, as well as those described in the remaining chapters. In particular, Aref and Ilyas present a class of primitives that support the class of space partitioning unbalanced trees. As in our taxonomy, the data structures that they support are differentiated on the basis of whether they organize the data based on its values or organize the embedding space from which it is drawn. Their structure depends on the following parameters:

1. The type of data (e.g., points, lines, rectangles, regions, surfaces, volumes, words, etc.),

2. The decomposition fanout (e.g., the number of partitions at each level),

3. A halting rule for the decomposition process, which could be a function of the size of the underlying space,

4. Whether or not single-arc nodes are allowed (i.e., a node can have just one child as is the case in the path-compressed PR k-d tree),

5. Bucket size.

The above parameters give a rough specification of the data structure. The actual implementation requires more detailed primitives. Aref and Ilyas decompose these additional primitives into two sets. The first set contains *interface parameters*, which enable a more precise definition of the structure. They are an expansion of the above parameters. For example, an interesting primitive is *PathShrink*, which describes the structure of the internal nodes of the tree. It has three possible values:

1. Never Shrink: The data is inserted in the node at the maximum possible level of decomposition (e.g., an MX quadtree for point data).

2. Leaf Shrink: The data is inserted into the first candidate leaf node encountered in the search process (e.g., a PR quadtree for point data).

3. Tree Shrink: Internal nodes are merged in order to eliminate all internal nodes with just one child (e.g., a path-compressed PR k-d tree, as well as the Patricia trie).

A related primitive is *NodeShrink*, which determines if empty partitions should be retained in the tree (e.g., empty nodes in trees such as the point, MX, PR quadtrees).

The second set of primitives contains *external methods*, which enable the user to specify the basic actions used in searching and building the tree:

1. Consistent: This enables navigating the tree during a search.

2. PickSplit: This defines how to split a node when building the structure and adding data.

3. Cluster: This defines how nodes are clustered into disk pages.

Note that if deletion is allowed, then an additional primitive is needed to deal with merging or removal of nodes.

The SP-GiST is similar in spirit to the *Generalized Search Tree* (GiST) [66 817], but with some very important differences. In particular, the goal of GiST is to provide a single implementation for indexes based on the B-tree, such as the R-tree in the spatial domain. GiST is designed to deal with indexes that are based on object hierarchies, which means that the key principle is one of object aggregation and the maintenance of a balanced structure. The fact that the objects occupy space is used in deciding the composition of the aggregates, but the underlying space is never decomposed, although the space occupied by the objects is aggregated. In contrast, SP-GiST is designed to deal with indexes that are based on space hierarchies that are a direct result of a recursive disjoint decomposition of the space in which the objects are embedded or drawn from (i.e., domain). This decomposition may be based on the space or on the values of the data in the space. Thus, there is no guarantee of balance. Note also that the domain need not be spatial (e.g., it can be text or any other type on which a linear ordering can be imposed). Therefore, the distinction between GiST and SP-GiST is that the former is designed to deal with object hierarchies while the latter is designed to deal with space hierarchies. This distinction is explored in much greater detail in Section 2.1 of Chapter 2.

At this point, let us briefly comment on the generality of the representations that we have described. Our presentation and examples have been in terms of records, all of whose attribute values were locational or numeric. As stated in the opening remarks of the chapter, most of these representations can be generalized so that they are also applicable to records that contain additional nonlocational attributes, as well as only nonlocational attributes. Below, we briefly discuss how to achieve this generalization.

The tree-based methods are easily extended to deal with nonlocational attributes. In this case, the partitions are made on the basis of the values of the attributes and make use of the ordering that is used for each attribute's value. Thus, representations such as the point quadtree, k-d tree, and adaptive k-d tree, as well as the range tree and the priority search tree, can be used. This ordering can also serve as the basis of an inverted list as well as a grid file.

Extension of the trie-based methods to deal with nonlocational attributes is a bit more complex. The main issue is that many of the representations that we have discussed are based on a binary subdivision of the underlying domain of the attributes, thereby resulting in trees with two-way branches. In the case of the locational attributes, which are always numbers, this is quite simple as we use the representation of the values of the numeric attributes as binary digits. When the nonlocational attribute values can be treated as sequences of characters with M possible values, then we have M-way branches instead of two-way branches. Thus, representations such as the PR quadtree and PR k-d tree are easily adapted to nonlocational attributes. Similarly, we can also adapt the fixed-grid method as well as EXCELL. In fact, the M possible values of each of the characters can also be viewed as being composed of $\lceil \log_2 M \rceil$ binary digits, and thus we can still use a two-way branch on the ordering of the individual characters making up the attribute's value.

Note that the MX quadtree cannot be adapted to the general situation where we have locational and nonlocational attributes. The problem is that the MX quadtree is appropriate only for the case that all of the attribute values have the same type and range. Moreover, the domain of the attribute values must be discrete. Of course, if these criteria are satisfied, then an appropriate variant of the MX quadtree can be used for nonlocational attributes.

Exercises

1. How does the pseudo quadtree fit into the taxonomy of Figure 1.118?

2. How does the optimized point quadtree fit into the taxonomy of Figure 1.118?

3. How does the BD-tree fit into the taxonomy of Figure 1.118?

4. How do the range tree, priority search tree, inverse priority search tree, and multidimensional range tree fit into the taxonomy of Figure 1.118?

5. The taxonomy shown in Figure 1.118 could be formulated differently. First, we qualify the E and D categories as being of type 1 or d, depending on whether they take one or d dimensions into account. Also, let depth 3 be characterized as a refinement of depth 2 with overflow handling. Add another data structure, termed a *pyramid*, that yields a 2^d growth in the directory upon a bucket overflow. Now, depth 4 can be recast as replacing a directory in the form of an array by a directory in the form of a tree. How would you rebuild depths 3–6 of Figure 1.118 using this new taxonomy?

6. How would you revise the taxonomy of Figure 1.118 to account for the fact that the shape of the cells into which the underlying space is decomposed need not be hyperrectangular (e.g., triangles)? In other words, include some decompositions that use these shapes. How does this generalize to dimensions higher than 2?

7. How would you revise the taxonomy of Figure 1.118 to account for the fact that the shape of the cells into which the underlying space is decomposed need not be hyperrectangular or spatially contiguous (e.g., spiral hashing)?

8. (Markku Tamminen) In the opening section of this chapter, several issues were raised with respect to choosing an appropriate representation for point data. Can you devise a taxonomy in the same spirit as Figure 1.118 using them? For example, let each depth of the tree correspond to a different property. At depth 0, distinguish between an organization of the data and an organization of the embedding space from which the data is drawn. At depth 1, distinguish between dynamic and static methods. At depth 2, distinguish between the number of keys on which the partition is being made. At depth 3, distinguish between the presence and absence of a directory. At depth 4, distinguish between the types of directories (e.g., arrays, trees). At depth 5, distinguish between bucket and nonbucket methods.

9. How would you adapt SP-GiST to deal with the PK-tree? Recall that the PK-tree decouples the partition process from the grouping process. Is it enough to modify the *PathShrink* and *NodeShrink* primitives?

10. The Euclidean matching problem consists of taking a set of $2 \cdot N$ points in the plane and decomposing it into the set of disjoint pairs of points so that the sum of the Euclidean distances between the components of each pair is a minimum. Would any of the representations discussed in this chapter facilitate the solution of this problem? Can you solve this problem by building a set of pairs, finding the closest pair of points, discarding it, and then applying the same procedure to the remaining set of points? Can you give an example that demonstrates that this solution is not optimal?

11. Exercise 10 proposes one solution to the Euclidean matching problem. An alternative solution proceeds in a manner analogous to that used in constructing the adaptive k-d tree in Section 1.5.1.4. In essence, we sort the points by increasing x and y coordinate values and then split them into two sets by splitting across the coordinate with the largest range. This process is applied recursively. Implement this method and run some experiments to show how close it comes to achieving optimality. Can you construct a simple example where the method of Exercise 10 is superior?

12. Suppose that you are given N points in a two-dimensional space and a rectangular window, say R, whose sides are parallel to the coordinate axes. Find a point in the plane at which the window can be centered so that it contains a maximum number of points in its interior. The window is not permitted to be rotated—it can be translated only to the point. Would any of the representations discussed in this chapter facilitate the solution of this problem?

2

Object-Based and Image-Based Image Representations

The representation of spatial objects and their environment is an important issue in applications of computer graphics, game programming, computer vision, image processing, robotics, pattern recognition, and computational geometry (e.g., [91, 1636, 1637, 1811]). The problem also arises in building databases to support them (e.g., [1638]). We assume that the objects are connected[1] although their environment need not be. The objects and their environment are usually decomposed into collections of more primitive elements (termed *cells*) each of which has a location in space, a size, and a shape. These elements can either be subobjects of varying shape (e.g., a table consists of a flat top in the form of a rectangle and four legs in the form of rods whose lengths dominate their cross-sectional areas), or they can have a uniform shape. The former yields an *object-based* decomposition; the latter yields an *image-based*, or *cell-based*, decomposition. Another way of characterizing these two decompositions is that the former decomposes the objects, while the latter decomposes the environment in which the objects lie. This distinction is used commonly in computer graphics to characterize algorithms as being either object-space or image-space, respectively [622].

Each of the decompositions has its advantages and disadvantages. They depend primarily on the nature of the queries that are posed to the database. The most general queries ask *where*, *what*, *who*, *why*, and *how*. The ones that are relevant to our application are *where* and *what* [1642]. They are stated more formally as follows:

1. Feature query: Given an object, determine its constituent cells (i.e., their locations in space).

2. Location query: Given a cell (i.e., a location in space), determine the identity of the object (or objects) of which it is a member, as well as the remaining constituent cells of the object (or objects).

Not surprisingly, the queries can be classified using the same terminology that we used in the characterization of the decomposition. In particular, we can either try to find the cells (i.e., their locations in space) occupied by an object or find the objects that overlap a cell (i.e., a location in space). If objects are associated with cells so that a cell contains the identity of the relevant object (or objects), then the feature query is analogous to retrieval by contents while the location query is analogous to retrieval by location. As we will see, it is important to note that there is a distinction between a location in space and the address where information about the location is stored, which, unfortunately, is often erroneously assumed to be the same.

---

[1] Intuitively, this means that a d-dimensional object cannot be decomposed into disjoint subobjects so that the subobjects are not adjacent in a $(d - 1)$-dimensional sense.

The feature and location queries are the basis of two more general classes of queries. In particular, the feature query is a member of a broader class of queries described collectively as being *feature-based* (also *object-based*), and the location query is a member of a broader class of queries described collectively as being *location-based* (also *image-based* or *cell-based*). In computational geometry, the location query is known as the *point location query* or *problem* (e.g., [1511, 196] and Sections 2.1.3.2 and 2.1.3.3). In other domains, it is also commonly referred to as a *point query*, in which case we must be careful to distinguish it from its narrower and broader definitions. In particular, in database applications, a point query has a narrower definition—it is really an exact match query as it seeks to determine if the data point corresponding to the location is in the database (e.g., [1046] and the introduction to Chapter 1), and thus whenever possible we use the term *exact match query* in this context. On the other hand, in computer graphics applications, the point query has a broader definition and is often synonymous with the related "pick" operation (e.g., [622]), which is used to find an object that contains a given location l, and if there is none, then to find the nearest object to l. In order to avoid overloading the term *point query* in this chapter we use the term *nearest object query* when a satisfactory response includes the nearest object should no object exist that contains l.[2] Therefore, in this chapter, the term *point query* has the same meaning as in Chapter 3, where the response is restricted to the objects that contain l. The class of location-based queries includes the numerous variants of the *window query*, which retrieves the objects that cover an arbitrary region (often rectangular). All of these queries are used in several applications including geographic information systems (e.g., [72, 1645]) and spatial data mining (e.g., [1953]).

The most common representation of the objects and their environment is as a collection of cells of uniform size and shape (termed *pixels* and *voxels* in two and three dimensions, respectively) all of whose boundaries (with dimensionality one less than that of the cells) are of unit size. Since the cells are uniform, there exists a way of referring to their locations in space relative to a fixed reference point (e.g., the origin of the coordinate system). An example of a location of a cell in space is a set of coordinate values that enables us to find it in the d-dimensional space of the environment in which it lies. Once again, we reiterate that it should be clear that the concept of the *location* of a cell in space is quite different from that of the *address* of a cell, which is the physical location (e.g., in memory, on disk), if any, where some of the information associated with the cell is stored. This distinction between the location in space of a cell and the address of a cell is important, and we shall make use of it often.

In most applications (including most of the ones that we consider here), the boundaries (i.e., edges and faces in two and three dimensions, respectively) of the cells are parallel to the coordinate axes. In our discussion, we assume that the cells making up a particular object are contiguous (i.e., adjacent) and that a different, unique value is associated with each distinct object, thereby enabling us to distinguish between the objects. Depending on the underlying representation, this value may be stored with the cells. For example, Figure 2.1 contains three two-dimensional objects, A, B, and C, and their corresponding cells. Note that, although it is not the case in this example, objects are allowed to overlap, which means that a cell may be associated with more than one object. Here we assume, without loss of generality, that the volume of the overlap must be an integer multiple of the volume of a cell (i.e., pixels, voxels, etc.).

The shape of an object o can be represented either by the interiors of the cells making up o, or by the subset of the boundaries of those cells making up o that are adjacent to the boundary of o. In particular, interior-based methods represent an object o by using the locations in space of the cells that make up o, while boundary-based methods represent o by using the locations in space of the cells that are adjacent to the boundary of o.

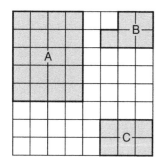

Figure 2.1
Example collection of three objects and the cells that they occupy.

---

[2] A more general term is *nearest neighbor query*, which is discussed in a more general context and in much greater detail in Sections 4.1–4.3 of Chapter 4.

In general, interior-based representations make it very easy to calculate properties of an object such as its mass and, depending on the nature of the aggregation process, to determine the value associated with any point (i.e., location) in the space covered by a cell in the object. On the other hand, boundary-based representations make it easy to obtain the boundary of an object.

Regardless of the representation that is used, the generation of responses to the feature and location queries is facilitated by building an index (i.e., the result of a sort) either on the objects or on their locations in space, and implementing it using an access structure that correlates the objects with the locations. Ideally, we want to be able to answer both types of queries with one representation. This is somewhat tricky, but, as we will show, it is doable.

The rest of this chapter is organized as follows. Section 2.1 discusses interior-based representations. These are the most prevalent, and thus this discussion forms the main part of the chapter. Section 2.2 discusses boundary-based representations. The discussion in these sections shows how some of the representations can be made more compact by aggregating similar elements. These elements are usually identically valued contiguous cells (possibly adjacent to identically oriented boundary elements) or even objects that, ideally, are in proximity. The representations can be made even more compact by recording only the differences between the elements. The use of difference-based compaction methods is the subject of Section 2.3. Many of the representations that we have described are based on the principle of recursive decomposition of the underlying space (as well as the aggregation of the results of the decomposition). Therefore, we conclude in Section 2.4 with a brief historical overview of this principle and some of its early uses.

As stated earlier, most of our discussion assumes that the objects can be decomposed into cells whose boundaries are parallel to the coordinate axes. Nevertheless, we discuss the representation of objects with boundaries that are hyperplanes (i.e., straight lines and planar faces for two- and three-dimensional objects, respectively), as well as objects with arbitrary boundaries (e.g., edges of arbitrary slope, nonplanar faces). In this case, the representation of the underlying environment is usually, but not always, based on a decomposition into cells whose boundaries are parallel to the coordinate axes.

2.1 Interior-Based Representations

In this section, we focus on interior-based representations. Section 2.1.1 examines representations based on collections of unit-size cells. An alternative class of interior-based representations of the objects and their environment removes the stipulation that the cells that make up the object collection be a unit size and permits their sizes to vary. The varying-sized cells are termed *blocks* and are the subject of Section 2.1.2. The representations described in Sections 2.1.1 and 2.1.2 assume that each unit-size cell or block is contained entirely in one or more objects. A cell or block cannot be partially contained in two objects. This means that either each cell in a block belongs to the same object or objects, or that all of the cells in the block do not belong to any of the objects. Section 2.1.3 permits both the blocks and the objects to be arbitrary polyhedra while not allowing them to intersect, although permitting them to have common boundaries. Section 2.1.4 permits a cell or block to be a part of more than one object and does not require the cell or block to be contained in its entirety in these objects. In other words, a cell or a block may overlap several objects without being completely contained in them. This also has the effect of permitting the representation of collections of objects whose boundaries do not coincide with the boundaries of the underlying blocks and also permitting them to intersect (i.e., overlap). Section 2.1.5 examines the use of hierarchies of space and objects that enable efficient responses to both the feature and location queries.

is really an ordering and hence its range is usually the integers (i.e., one-dimensional). When the data is multidimensional (i.e., cells in d-dimensional space where $d > 0$), it may not be convenient to use the location in space corresponding to the cell as an index since its range spans data in several dimensions. Instead, we employ techniques such as laying out the addresses corresponding to the locations in space of the cells in some particular order and then making use of an access structure in the form of a mapping function to enable the quick association of addresses with the locations in space corresponding to the cells. Retrieving the address is more complex in the sense that it can be a simple memory access, or it may involve an access to secondary or tertiary storage if virtual memory is being used. In most of our discussion, we assume that all data is in main memory, although, as we will see, several representations do not rely on this assumption.

Such an access structure enables us to obtain the contiguous cells (as we know their locations in space) without having to examine all of the cells. Therefore, we will know the identities of the cells that make up an object, thereby enabling us to complete the response to the location query with an implicit representation. In the rest of this section, we discuss several such access structures. However, before proceeding further, we wish to point out that the implicit representation could also be classified as *image-based* as it clearly lends itself to retrieval on the basis of knowledge only of the cells rather than of the objects. We shall make use of this characterization in Section 2.1.5.

The existence of an access structure also enables us to answer the feature query with the implicit representation, although this is quite inefficient. In particular, given an object o, we must exhaustively examine every cell (i.e., location l in space) and check if the address where the information about the object associated with l is stored contains o as its value. This will be time-consuming because it may require that we examine all the cells.

2.1.1.1 Cell Shapes and Tilings

There is a seemingly endless set of possible shapes for the unit-size cells. The shape that is ultimately chosen has a great effect on the operations and algorithms that can be executed on the data, especially in light of the fact that the unit-size cells will eventually be aggregated. The unit-size cells result from the application of a decomposition process to the underlying space (i.e., the environment containing the objects). In order to limit the verbosity of our explanation, we use the term *image* to refer to the environment comprising the unit-size cells that are in the objects and those that are not in any of the objects. In this section, unless otherwise stated, we restrict ourselves to the two-dimensional plane. In general, any planar decomposition that is used as a basis for an image representation should possess the following two properties:

1. The partition should be an infinitely repetitive pattern so that it can be used for images of any size.

2. The partition should be infinitely decomposable into increasingly finer patterns (i.e., higher resolution). This means that the size of the unit-size cells has no minimum.

Space decompositions can be classified into two categories, depending on the nature of the resulting shape. The shape can be either polygonal or nonpolygonal. Polygonal shapes are generally computationally simpler since their sides can be expressed in terms of linear relations (e.g., equations of lines). They are good for approximating the interior of a region. Also, they can be joined to form a tiling so that they span the entire space while being nonoverlapping.

On the other hand, the nonpolygonal shapes are more flexible since they provide good approximations, in terms of measures, of the boundaries (e.g., perimeter) of regions, as well as their interiors (e.g., area). Moreover, the normals to the boundaries of nonpolygonal shapes are not restricted to a fixed set of directions. For example, in the case of rectangular tiles, there is a 90 degree discontinuity between the normals to boundaries of adjacent tiles. This lack of continuity is a drawback in applications in fields like computer graphics where such tasks as shading make use of the directions of the surface. However, working with nonpolygonal shapes generally requires use of floating-point arithmetic; hence, it is usually more complex. Thus, we limit our discussion to polygonal shapes.

Bell, Diaz, Holroyd, and Jackson [157] discuss a number of polygonal tilings of the plane (i.e., tessellations) that satisfy property 1. Figure 2.2 illustrates some of these tessellations. They also present a taxonomy of criteria to distinguish between the various tilings. The tilings, consisting of polygonal tiles, are described by use of a notation that is based on the degree of each vertex as the edges (i.e., sides) of the "atomic" tile (i.e., unit-size cell) are visited in order, forming a cycle. For example, the tiling described by $[4.8^2]$ (see Figure 2.2(c)) has the shape of a triangle where the first vertex has degree four while the remaining two vertices have degree eight apiece.

A tiling is said to be *regular* if the atomic tiles are composed of regular polygons (i.e., all sides are of equal length, as are the interior angles). A *molecular tile* is an aggregation of atomic tiles to form a *hierarchy*, also more commonly referred to as a *block* in our discussion. The molecular tile (i.e., block) is not necessarily constrained to have the same shape as the atomic tile (i.e., unit-size cell). When a tile at level k (for all $k > 0$) has the same shape as a tile at level 0 (i.e., it is a scaled image of a tile at level 0), then the tiling is said to be *similar*.

Bell et al. focus on the *isohedral* tilings—a tiling is said to be isohedral if all the tiles are equivalent under the symmetry group of the tiling. A more intuitive way to conceptualize this definition is to assume the position of an observer who stands in the center of a tile having a given orientation and scans the surroundings. If the view is independent of the tile, then the tiling is isohedral. For example, consider the two tilings in Figure 2.3 consisting of triangles (Figure 2.3(a)) and trapezoids (Figure 2.3(b)). The triangles are isohedral, whereas the trapezoids are not, as can be seen by the view from tiles A and B.

In the case of the trapezoidal tiling, the viewer from A is surrounded by an infinite number of concentric hexagons, whereas this is not the case for B. In other words, the trapezoidal tiling is not periodic. Also, note that all of the tiles in Figure 2.3(a) are described by $[6^3]$, but those in Figure 2.3(b) are either $[3^2.4^2]$, $[3^2.6^2]$, or $[3.4.6^2]$ (i.e., the tiles labeled 1, 2, and 3, respectively, in Figure 2.3(b)). When the isohedral tilings are classified by the action of their symmetry group, there are 81 different types [761, 762]. When they are classified by their adjacency structure, as is done here, there are 11 types.

The most relevant criterion to our discussion is the distinction between limited and unlimited hierarchies of tilings (i.e., how the unit-size cells aggregate to form blocks). A *limited* tiling is not similar. A tiling that satisfies property 2 is said to be *unlimited*. Equivalently, in a limited tiling, no change of scale lower than the limit tiling can be made without great difficulty. An alternative characterization of an unlimited tiling is that each edge of a tile lies on an infinite straight line composed entirely of edges. Interestingly, the hexagonal tiling $[3^6]$ is limited. Bell et al. claim that only four tilings are unlimited. These are the tilings given in Figure 2.2(a–d). Of these, $[4^4]$, consisting of square atomic tiles (Figure 2.2(a)), and $[6^3]$, consisting of equilateral triangle atomic tiles (Figure 2.2(b)), are well-known regular tessellations [29]. For these two tilings, we consider only the molecular tiles given in Figure 2.4(a, b).

The tilings $[4^4]$ and $[6^3]$ can generate an infinite number of different molecular tiles where each molecular tile at the first level consists of n^2 atomic tiles ($n > 1$). The remaining nonregular unlimited triangular tilings, $[4.8^2]$ (Figure 2.2(c)) and $[4.6.12]$ (Figure 2.2(d)), are less understood. One way of generating $[4.8^2]$ and $[4.6.12]$ is to join the centroids of the tiles of $[4^4]$ and $[6^3]$, respectively, to both their vertices and the midpoints of their edges. Each of the tilings $[4.8^2]$ and $[4.6.12]$ has two types of hierarchy. $[4.8^2]$ has an ordinary hierarchy (Figure 2.4(c)) and a rotation hierarchy (Figure 2.4(e)),

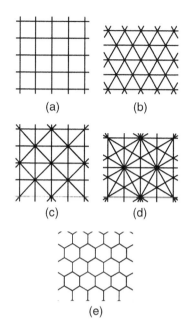

Figure 2.2
Sample tessellations: (a) $[4^4]$ square, (b) $[6^3]$ equilateral triangle, (c) $[4.8^2]$ isoceles triangle, (d) $[4.6.12]$ 30–60–90 right triangle, and (e) $[3^6]$ hexagon.

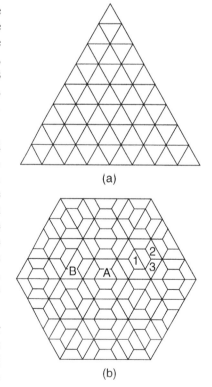

Figure 2.3
Examples of (a) isohedral and (b) nonisohedral tilings.

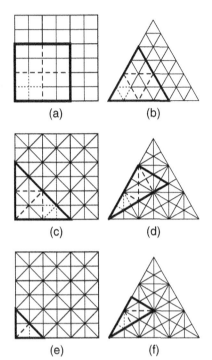

Figure 2.4
Examples illustrating unlimited
tilings: (a) $[4^4]$ hierarchy, (b) $[6^3]$
hierarchy, (c) ordinary $[4.8^2]$ hierarchy, (d) ordinary [4.6.12] hierarchy,
(e) rotation $[4.8^2]$ hierarchy, and (f)
rotation [4.6.12] hierarchy.

requiring a rotation of 135 degrees between levels. [4.6.12] has an ordinary hierarchy (Figure 2.4(d)) and a reflection hierarchy (Figure 2.4(f)), which requires a reflection of the basic tile between levels.

The distinction between the two types of hierarchies for $[4.8^2]$ and [4.6.12] is necessary as the tiling is not similar without a rotation or a reflection when the hierarchy is not ordinary. This can be seen by observing the use of dots in Figure 2.4 to delimit the atomic tiles in the molecular tile at the deepest level of the hierarchy (i.e., level 1) using our level-labeling conventions, which consider the atomic tiles to be at level 0). Similarly, broken lines are used to delimit the components of molecular tiles at the second level. For the ordinary $[4.8^2]$ and [4.6.12] hierarchies, each molecular tile at the first level consists of n^2 ($n > 1$) atomic tiles. In the reflection hierarchy of [4.6.12], each molecular tile at the first level consists of $3 \cdot n^2$ ($n > 1$) atomic tiles. On the other hand, for the rotation hierarchy of $[4.8^2]$, $2 \cdot n^2$ ($n > 1$) atomic tiles make up a molecular tile at the first level.

For example, in the case of the ordinary $[4.8^2]$ hierarchy, the level 1 molecular tiles that make up the level 2 molecular tile have the same orientation as the atomic tiles of the molecular tile at level 1. On the other hand, in the case of the rotation $[4.8^2]$ hierarchy, the level 1 molecular tiles that make up the level 2 molecular tile have the same orientation as the result of rotating the atomic tiles of the first molecular tile by 135 degrees in the counterclockwise direction. As another example, in the case of the ordinary [4.6.12] hierarchy, the atomic tiles of the first molecular tile have the same orientation as the level 1 molecular tiles that make up the level 2 molecular tile. On the other hand, in the case of the rotation [4.6.12] hierarchy, the level 1 molecular tiles that make up the level 2 molecular tile have the same orientation as the result of reflecting the atomic tiles of the first molecular tile about the shortest edge of the level 0 molecular tile, and repeating the reflection about the longest edge of the level 0 molecular tile.

To represent data in the Euclidean plane, any of the unlimited tilings could have been chosen. For a regular decomposition, the tilings $[4.8^2]$ and [4.6.12] are ruled out. Comparing "square" $[4^4]$ and "triangular" $[6^3]$ tilings, we find that they differ in terms of adjacency and orientation. Let us say that two tiles are *neighbors* if they are adjacent either along an edge or at a vertex. A tiling is *uniformly adjacent* if the distances between the centroid of one tile and the centroids of all its neighbors are the same. The adjacency number of a tiling is the number of different intercentroid distances between any one tile and its neighbors. In the case of $[4^4]$, there are only two adjacency distances, whereas for $[6^3]$, there are three adjacency distances.

A tiling is said to have *uniform orientation* if all tiles with the same orientation can be mapped into each other by translations of the plane that do not involve rotation or reflection. Tiling $[4^4]$ displays uniform orientation, while tiling $[6^3]$ does not. Under the assumption that uniform orientation and a minimal adjacency distance is preferable, we say that $[4^4]$ is more useful than $[6^3]$. $[4^4]$ is also very easy to implement. Nevertheless, $[6^3]$ has its uses. For example, $[6^3]$ is used when the space is the surface of a sphere (e.g., [1138]).

Of the *limited* tilings, many types of hierarchies may be generated [157]; however, in general, they cannot be decomposed beyond the atomic tiling without changing the basic tile shape. This is a serious drawback of the hexagonal tiling $[3^6]$ (Figure 2.2(e)) since the atomic hexagon can only be decomposed into triangles. Nevertheless, the hexagonal tiling is of considerable interest (e.g., [158, 234, 285, 706, 1149, 1293]). It is regular, has a uniform orientation, and, most importantly, displays a uniform adjacency (i.e., each neighbor of a tile is at the same distance from it). This property is one of the reasons for the appeal of the hexagonal tiling in strategic board games that involve control of space or reachability, and is often used as a means of modeling war games. We discuss this tiling further in Section 2.1.2.10.

1. Given a $[6^3]$ tiling such that each side of an atomic tile has a unit length, compute the three adjacency distances from the centroid of an atomic tile.

2. Repeat Exercise 1 for $[3^6]$ and $[4^4]$, again assuming that each side of an atomic tile has a unit length.

3. Suppose that you are given an image in the form of a binary array of pixels. The result is a square grid. How can you view this grid as a hexagonal grid?

2.1.1.2 Ordering Space

There are many ways of laying out the addresses corresponding to the locations in space of the cells, each having its own mapping function. Some of the most important ones for a two-dimensional space are illustrated in Figure 2.5 for an 8×8 portion of the space and are described briefly below. To repeat, in essence, what we are doing is providing a mapping from the d-dimensional space containing the locations of the cells to the one-dimensional space of the range of index values (i.e., integers) that are used to access a table whose entries contain the addresses where information about the contents of the cells is stored. The result is an ordering of the space, and the curves shown in Figure 2.5 are termed *space-filling curves* (e.g., [1603]).

Choosing among the space-filling curves illustrated in Figure 2.5 is not easy because each one has its advantages and disadvantages. Below, we review a few of their desirable properties, show how some of the two-dimensional orderings satisfy them, and provide some exercises to help you to explore them further:

■ The curve should pass through each location in space once and only once.

■ The mapping from the higher-dimensional space to the integers should be relatively simple and likewise for the inverse mapping. This is the case for all but the Peano-Hilbert order (Figure 2.5(d)). For the Morton order (Figure 2.5(c)), the mapping is obtained by interleaving the binary representations of the coordinate values of the location of the cell. The number associated with each cell is known as its *Morton number*. The Gray order (Figure 2.5(g)) is obtained by applying a Gray code (see footnote 35 in Section 1.6 of Chapter 1) to the result of bit interleaving, and the double Gray order (Figure 2.5(h)) is obtained by applying a Gray code to the result of bit interleaving the Gray code of the binary representation of the coordinate values. The U order (Figure 2.5(i)) is obtained in a similar manner to the Morton order, except for an intermediate application of $d - 1$ "exclusive or" ($\oplus$) operations on the binary representation of selected combinations of the coordinate values prior to the application of bit interleaving [1192, 1698] (see Exercise 7). Thus, the difference in cost between the Morton order and the U order in d dimensions is just the performance of additional $d - 1$ "exclusive or" operations. This is in contrast to the Peano-Hilbert order, where the mapping and inverse mapping processes are considerably more complex (see Exercises 5 and 6).

■ The ordering should be stable. This means that the relative ordering of the individual locations is preserved when the resolution is doubled (e.g., when the size of the two-dimensional space in which the cells are embedded grows from 8×8 to 16×16) or halved, assuming that the origin stays the same. The Morton, U, Gray, and double Gray orders are stable, while the row (Figure 2.5(a)), row-prime (Figure 2.5(b)), Cantor-diagonal (Figure 2.5(e)), and spiral (Figure 2.5(f)) orders are not stable (but see Exercises 1 and 2). The Peano-Hilbert order is also not stable, as can be seen by its definition (but see Exercise 3). In particular, in two dimensions, the Peano-Hilbert order of resolution $i + 1$ (i.e., a $2^i \times 2^i$ image) is constructed by taking the Peano-Hilbert curve of resolution i and rotating the NW, NE, SE, and SW quadrants by 90

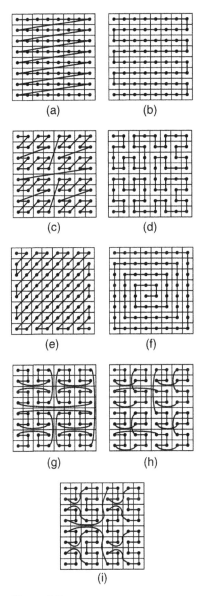

Figure 2.5
The result of applying several different space-ordering methods to an 8×8 collection of cells whose first element is in the upper-left corner: (a) row order, (b) row-prime order, (c) Morton order, (d) Peano-Hilbert order, (e) Cantor-diagonal order, (f) spiral order, (g) Gray order, (h) double Gray order, and (i) U order.

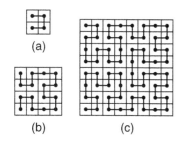

Figure 2.6
Peano-Hilbert curves of resolution
(a) 1, (b) 2, and (c) 3.

degrees clockwise, 0 degrees, 0 degrees, and 90 degrees counterclockwise, respectively. For example, Figure 2.6(a–c) gives the Peano-Hilbert curves of resolutions 1, 2, and 3, respectively.

- Two locations that are adjacent (i.e., in the sense of a $(d-1)$-dimensional adjacency, also known as 4-adjacent)[4] in space are neighbors along the curve and vice versa. In two dimensions, this means that the locations share an edge or a side. This is impossible to satisfy for all locations at all space sizes. However, for the row-prime, Peano-Hilbert, and spiral orders, every element is a 4-adjacent neighbor of the previous element in the sequence, while this is not the case for the other orders. This means that the row-prime, Peano-Hilbert, and spiral orders have a slightly higher degree of locality than the other orders.

- The process of retrieving the neighbors of a location in space should be simple.

- The order should be *admissible*—at each position in the ordering, at least one 4-adjacent neighbor in each of the lateral directions (i.e., horizontal and vertical) must have already been encountered. This is useful in several algorithms (e.g., connected component labeling [494]).[5] The row and Morton orders are admissible, while the Peano-Hilbert, U, Gray, and double Gray orders are not admissible. The row-prime, Cantor-diagonal, and spiral orders are admissible only if we permit the direction of the 4-adjacent neighbors to vary from position to position along the curve. For example, for the row-prime order, at positions on odd rows, the previously encountered 4-adjacent neighbors are the western and northern neighbors, while at positions on even rows, they are the eastern and northern neighbors.

The row order (Figure 2.5(a)) is of special interest to us because its mapping function is the one most frequently used by the multidimensional array (described in greater detail in Section 2.1.1.3), which is the most common access structure. Assuming that the first entry in the cell-address table indexed by the index has an index value of 0, location (a,b) in an 8×8 collection of cells is mapped to index value $8b + a$. An alternative ordering that is also used in the multidimensional array is known as *column order*; the difference from row order lies in the order in which the various dimensions are scanned. In the column order, the y coordinate value varies most rapidly; in the row order, the x coordinate value varies most rapidly. The one to choose is arbitrary, although the row order is preferred as it yields a lexicographic ordering when array references are of the form $T[i, j]$, corresponding to an element in row i and column j of array T (i.e., at location (j,i)).

The Morton order [1317] has a long history, having been first mentioned in 1890 by Peano [1478], and has been used by many researchers (e.g., [8, 684, 1420, 1992, 2017]). It is also known as a *Z order* [1420] and as an *N order* [1992]. The Peano-Hilbert order was first mentioned soon afterwards by Hilbert [835] and has also been used by a number of researchers (e.g., [591, 937]). The relationship of the Morton order to bit interleaving

---

[4] In two dimensions, the fact that two locations are *4-adjacent* means that the locations share an edge or a side. If the concept of adjacency also includes adjacency at a corner (i.e., diagonal adjacencies), then the locations are said to be *8-adjacent*.

[5] A *region*, or object, four-connected component is a maximal four-connected set of locations belonging to the same object, where a set S of locations is said to be *four-connected (eight-connected)* if for any locations p, q in S there exists a sequence of locations $p = p_0, p_1, \ldots, p_n = q$ in S, such that p_{i+1} is 4-adjacent (8-adjacent) to p_i, $0 \le i < n$. The process of assigning the same label to all 4-adjacent locations that belong to the same object is called *connected component labeling* (e.g., [1469, 1575]). A nonobject (often denoted as white) *region* or nonobject (white) eight-connected component is a maximal eight-connected set of locations that do not belong to any of the objects. The complement of all the regions that are contained in one of the objects consists of a union of eight-connected nonobject (white) regions. Exactly one of these nonobject (white) regions contains the infinite background of nonobject (white) locations. All the other nonobject (white) regions, if any, are called *holes* in the object regions. The set of object black regions, say R, is surrounded by the infinite nonobject (white) region, and R surrounds the other nonobject (white) regions, if any.

is discussed in greater detail in Section 1.6 of Chapter 1. Pascucci and Frank [1471, 1472] discuss the application of the Morton order to a multiresolution hierarchy where the full $2^n \times 2^n$ space of cells can be visualized as a hierarchy of n arrays a_i, each of size $2^i \times 2^i$ ($0 \leq i \leq n$), so that a_{i+1} is at twice the resolution of a_i, and one distinguished element of every 2×2 subset of of a_{i+1} is also an element of a_i. Their motivation is to support real-time progressive traversal and visualization of large grids of data that are too large to fit in memory and thus reside in external memory.

Although conceptually very simple, the U order introduced by Schrack and Liu [1192, 1698] is relatively recent. It is a variant of the Morton order but also resembles the Peano-Hilbert order. The primitive shape is a "U," which is the same as that of the Peano-Hilbert order. However, unlike the Peano-Hilbert order, and like the Morton order, the ordering is applied recursively with no rotation, thereby enabling it to be stable. The U order has a slight advantage over the Morton order in that more of the locations that are adjacent (i.e., in the sense of a $(d-1)$-dimensional adjacency) along the curve are also neighbors in space. This is directly reflected in the lower average distance between two successive positions in the order (see Exercise 8, where we see that this cost is also lower than that of the Gray and double Gray orders). However, the price of this is that, like the Peano-Hilbert order, the U order is also not admissible. Nevertheless, like the Morton order, the process of retrieving the neighbors of a location in space is simple when the space is ordered according to the U order.

Exercises

1. In the text, we said that the row order is not stable. This is true if the image grows by doubling or if its resolution is halved. Under what kinds of growth conditions is the row order stable?

2. In the text, we said that the spiral order is not stable. This is true if the image grows by doubling or if its resolution is halved. Under what kinds of growth conditions is the spiral order stable?

3. Examining the Peano-Hilbert order in Figure 2.5(d), it appears that, if we consider the 2×2 square in the upper-left corner and double the resolution to yield the 4×4 square in the upper-left corner, the relative positions of the cells in the 2×2 square in the upper-left corner are preserved. This seems to be contradictory to our claim that the Peano-Hilbert order is not stable. Explain why this is not the case.

4. Given a Morton ordering for a $2^n \times 2^n$ image, show how to determine the addresses associated with the locations that are adjacent to location c in the horizontal and vertical directions.

5. Give an algorithm to extract the x and y coordinates from a Peano-Hilbert order key.

6. Give an algorithm to construct the Peano-Hilbert key for a given point (x, y). Try to make it optimal.

7. Using "exclusive or" operations, show how to construct the U order key for a point.

8. Suppose that you are given a $2^n \times 2^n$ array of locations such that the horizontal and vertical distances between 4-adjacent locations are 1. What is the average distance between successive locations when the locations are ordered according to the orders illustrated in Figure 2.5? What about a random order?

9. Suppose that you are given a $2^n \times 2^n$ image. Assume that the image is stored on disk in pages of size $2^m \times 2^m$, where n is much larger than m. What is the average cost (in terms of disk page accesses) of retrieving a pixel and its 4-adjacent neighbors when the image is ordered according to the orders illustrated in Figure 2.5?

10. Given a Morton ordering for a $2^n \times 2^n$ image and the locations of a rectangle in the image, what is the location in the rectangle with the smallest Morton order value? Assume that the upper-left corner of the image is the first one in the Morton ordering.

11. Given a Peano-Hilbert ordering for a $2^n \times 2^n$ image and the locations of a rectangle in the image, what is the location in the rectangle with the smallest Peano-Hilbert order value? Assume that the upper-left corner of the image is the first one in the Peano-Hilbert ordering.

12. Given a U ordering for a $2^n \times 2^n$ image and the locations of a rectangle in the image, what is the location in the rectangle with the smallest U order value? What about the Gray and double Gray order values? Assume that the upper-left corner of the image is the first one in the U ordering.

13. The traveling salesman problem [1120] is one where a set of points is given, and it is desired to find the path of minimum distance such that each point is visited only once. This is an NP-complete problem [682]; and thus there is a considerable amount of work in formulating approximate solutions to it [170]. For example, consider the following approximate solution. Assume that the points are uniformly distributed in the unit square. Let d be the expected Euclidean distance between two independent points. Now, sort the points using the row order and the Morton order. Laurini [1111] simulated the average Euclidean distance between successive points in these orders and found it to be $d/2$ for the row order and $d/3$ for the Morton order. Can you derive these averages analytically? What are the average values for the other orders illustrated in Figure 2.5? What about a random order?

2.1.1.3 Array Access Structures

The multidimensional array (having a dimension equal to the dimensionality of the space in which the objects and the environment are embedded) is an access structure that, given a cell c at a location l in space, enables us to calculate the address a containing the identifier of the object associated with c. The array is only a conceptual multidimensional structure (it is not a multidimensional physical entity in memory) in the sense that it is a mapping of the locations in space of the cells into sequential addresses in memory. The actual addresses are obtained by the array access function (see, e.g., [1044], as well as the above discussion on space orderings), which is based on the extents of the various dimensions (i.e., coordinate axes). The array access function is usually the mapping function for the row order described above (although, at times, the column order is also used). Thus, the array enables us to implement the implicit representation with no additional storage except for what is needed for the array's descriptor. The descriptor contains the bounds and extents of each of the dimensions that are used to define the mapping function (i.e., they determine the values of its coefficients) so that the appropriate address can be calculated, given the cell's location in space.

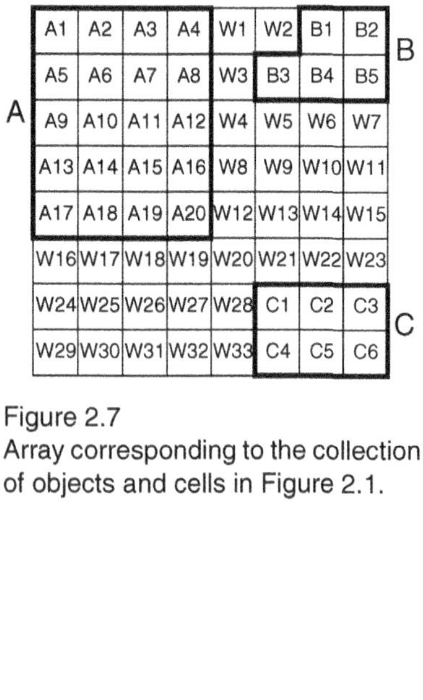

Figure 2.7
Array corresponding to the collection of objects and cells in Figure 2.1.

Figure 2.7 shows the contents of the array corresponding to the collection of two-dimensional objects and cells given in Figure 2.1. Each of the array elements $T[i, j]$ is labeled with an address that specifies where an identifier is stored that indicates the identity of the object (or objects) of which the corresponding cell at location (j, i) is a member. We have labeled array elements corresponding to cells of object O as Oi and the array elements corresponding to cells that are not in any of the objects as Wi, using the suffix i to distinguish between them in both cases. When there is no need to distinguish between the various objects, we use the labels *black* (also "1" and foreground) and *white* (also "0" and background) to characterize or differentiate between the cells that lie in any of the objects and those that are not in any of the objects, respectively.

The array is called a *random access structure* because the address associated with a location in space can be retrieved in constant time independently of the number of elements in the array and does not require any search. Note that we could store the object identifier o in the array element itself instead of allocating a separate address a for o, thereby saving some space.

The array is an implicit representation because we have not explicitly aggregated all the contiguous cells that make up a particular object. They can be obtained given a particular cell c at a location l in space belonging to object o by recursively accessing the array elements corresponding to the locations in space that are adjacent to l and checking if they are associated with object o. This process is known as depth-first connected component labeling (recall the definition of connected component labeling in footnote 5 in Section 2.1.1.2).

Interestingly, depth-first connected component labeling could also be used to answer the feature query efficiently with an implicit representation if we add a data structure such as an index on the objects (e.g., a table of object-location pairs, where *location* is one of the locations in space that make up *object*). Thus, given an object o we use the index to find a location in space that is part of o and then proceed with the depth-first connected component labeling as before. This index does not make use of the spatial coverage of the objects, and thus it can be implemented using conventional searching techniques such as hashing [1046]. In this case, we will need $O(N)$ additional space for the index, where N is the number of different objects. We do not discuss such indexes here.

Of course, we could also answer the location query with an explicit representation by adding an index that associates objects with locations in space (i.e., having the form location-objects). However, this would require $O(S)$ additional space for the index, where S is the number of cells. The $O(S)$ bound assumes that only one object is associated with each cell. If we take into account that a cell could be associated with more than one object, then the additional storage needed is $O(NS)$, if we assume n objects. Since the number of cells S is usually much greater than the number of objects N, the addition of an index to the explicit representation is not as practical as extending the implicit representation with an index of the form object-location as described above. Thus, it would appear that the implicit representation is more useful from the point of view of flexibility when taking storage requirements into account.

2.1.1.4 Tree Access Structures

The implicit representation can be implemented with access structures other than the array. This is an important consideration when many of the cells are not in any of the objects (i.e., they are empty). The problem is that using the array access structure is wasteful of storage, as the array requires an element for each cell, regardless of whether the cell is associated with any of the objects. In this case, we choose to keep track of only the nonempty cells.

We have two ways to proceed. The first is to use one of several multidimensional access structures, such as a point quadtree, k-d tree, or MX quadtree as described in Chapter 1. The second is to make use of one of the orderings of space shown in Figure 2.5 to obtain a mapping from the nonempty contiguous cells to the integers. The result of the mapping serves as the index in one of the familiar treelike access structures (e.g., binary search tree, range tree, B$^+$-tree) to store the address that indicates the physical location where the information about the object associated with the location in space corresponding to the nonempty cell is stored. In this discussion, we choose the second approach because often, when the dimensionality of the space (i.e., d) gets large, the implementation of the first approach resorts to use of the second approach anyway.

At this point, it is worthwhile to comment on what exactly is stored in the nodes of the treelike access structure that are associated with nonempty cells. First of all, as mentioned above, each node contains an address that indicates the physical location where the information about the object associated with the location in space corresponding to the nonempty cell is stored. As in the case of the array, we could store the object identifier o in the node of the tree itself rather than allocating a separate address a for o, thereby saving some space. In addition, each node of the tree must also store the index value (i.e., the result of the mapping) for the nonempty cell because, unlike the array, we do not have an entry for every cell, which would have enabled us to avoid having to store the index value. Note that if we did not store this index value, we would not be able to tell if the node in the tree corresponded to a particular location through the use of a comparison. The mapping that we use must have an inverse so that, given an index value, we can determine the corresponding location in space of the cell that is associated with it.

We demonstrate the use of a tree access structure with the mapping that yields a Morton order (i.e., Figure 2.5(c)) and use it as an index in the binary search tree. Figure 2.8 shows the result of applying a Morton ordering to an 8×8 collection of cells.

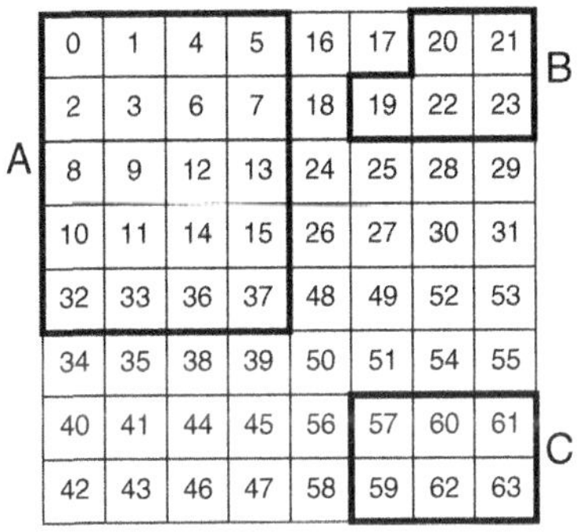

Figure 2.8
Result of applying a Morton ordering to an 8 × 8 collection of cells.

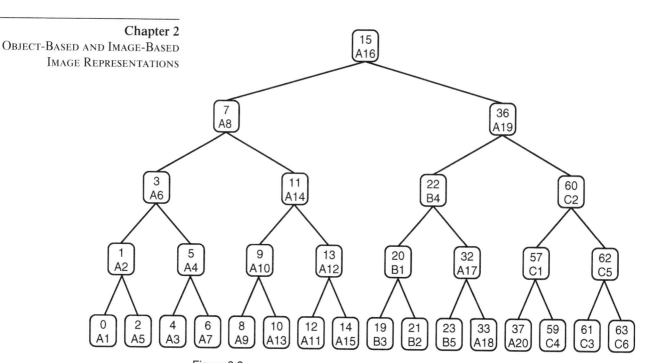

Figure 2.9
Result of applying a Morton order mapping to the collection of two-dimensional objects and cells in Figure 2.1 and storing the result in a binary search tree.

Figure 2.9 is the binary search tree for the collection of two-dimensional objects and cells given in Figure 2.1. Each node in the tree is labeled with the Morton order value of its corresponding cell c and an address a that specifies where an identifier is stored that indicates the identity of the object (or objects) of which c is a member. The address a in Figure 2.9 is the same as the one used in the corresponding cell in the array access structure in Figure 2.7. Notice that the empty cells (i.e., those labeled with Wi in the array access structure in Figure 2.7) are not present in Figure 2.9.

Regardless of which tree access structure is used, we can always determine the object o associated with a cell c at location l. We just apply the mapping (Morton ordering in our example) to l, yielding p (which is an address or an offset value from a base location), and then search for p in the tree (a binary search tree in our example). If p is not in the tree, then c is an empty cell; otherwise, we retrieve the object identifier o associated with it. Recall that retrieving the object identifier o associated with cell c only yields a partial response to the location query because we need to determine the remaining cells that make up o. This is achieved by accessing each of the cells adjacent to c and determining if they exist in the tree and if they do, then checking if they are associated with o. If the answer is yes to both of the above questions, then their adjacent cells are examined by a recursive application of this process. Note that for most of the orderings, we can determine the locations in space that are adjacent to c directly from the value of p without having to apply the mapping that yields the ordering or the inverse mapping (see Exercise 4 in Section 2.1.1.2). In fact, for some of the tree access structures (e.g., an MX quadtree [901, 905, 1637], which is a variant of the region quadtree, described in Section 2.1.2.4, that only merges empty cells), the adjacent cells can be determined by using just the structure of the tree (i.e., no arithmetic operations, such as those needed for address computation, are performed).

2.1.2 Blocks

An alternative class of representations of the objects and their environment removes the stipulation that the cells that make up the object collection be of unit size and permits their sizes to vary. The resulting cells are termed *blocks* and are usually rectangular with sides that are parallel to the coordinate axes (this is assumed in our discussion unless explicitly stated otherwise). The volume (e.g., area in two dimensions) of the blocks need not be an integer multiple of that of the unit-size cells, although this is frequently the case (and holds for all of the representations presented in this section). Observe that when the volumes of the blocks are integer multiples of that of the unit-size cells, we have two levels of aggregation in the sense that an object consists of an aggregation of blocks that are themselves aggregations of cells. Of course, it goes without saying that all the cells in a block belong to the same object or objects. In other words, the situation that some of the cells in the block belong to object o_1, while the others belong to object o_2 (and not to o_1), is not permitted.

The aggregation process that results in the blocks is usually guided by a set of rules, although this is not always the case in the sense that the process may also be arbitrary to a certain degree. It is usually easier to describe the aggregation process in a top-down manner by specifying an equivalent decomposition process of the underlying space that is occupied by the objects, and this is the way we will proceed in our discussion whenever possible. We start out by describing two aggregation methods that are not the result of a specific decomposition process. The first simply aggregates the unit-size cells into rectangular blocks of arbitrary size and position (see Section 2.1.2.1). The second finds a set of maximal blocks based on the distance of the unit-size cells from the boundary of the objects and is known as the medial axis transformation (MAT) (see Section 2.1.2.2).

When the decomposition is recursive, we have the situation that the decomposition occurs in stages and often, although not always, the results of the stages form a containment hierarchy. This means that a block b obtained in stage i is decomposed into a set of blocks b_j that span the same space. Blocks b_j are in turn decomposed in stage $i + 1$ using the same decomposition rule. Some decomposition rules restrict the possible sizes and shapes of the blocks, as well as their placement in space. Some examples include the following:

- All blocks at a particular stage are congruent.

- Blocks are similar at all stages (e.g., rectangles and isoceles triangles).

- All but one side of a block are unit-sized (e.g, runlength encoding).

- All sides of a block are of equal size (e.g., squares and equilateral triangles).

- All sides of each block are powers of 2.

These decomposition rules are described in Sections 2.1.2.3 to 2.1.2.9.

Other decomposition rules do not require that the blocks be axis parallel, while still others do not even require that the blocks be rectangular. For example, often, the blocks can be hexagonal (Section 2.1.2.10) or triangular (Section 2.1.2.11). As we pointed out in Section 2.1.1.1, hexagonal blocks find use in the implementation of strategic board games where the key is movement between adjacent spatial elements. Triangular blocks are often used in modeling the surface of a sphere using regular decomposition. In addition, the blocks may be disjoint or allowed to overlap. Clearly, the choice is large. These rules are described in greater detail in Sections 2.1.3 and 2.1.4.

2.1.2.1 Decomposition into Arbitrarily Sized Rectangular Blocks

The simplest decomposition rule is one that permits aggregation of identically valued cells in only one dimension. In essence, the decomposition assigns a priority ordering to the various dimensions; fixes the coordinate values of all but one of the dimensions, say i; and then varies the value of the ith coordinate and aggregates all adjacent cells belonging to the same object into a one-dimensional block. This technique is commonly used in image processing applications where the image is decomposed into rows that are scanned from top to bottom, and each row is scanned from left to right while aggregating all adjacent pixels (i.e., unit-size cells) with the same value into a block. The aggregation into one-dimensional blocks is the basis of *runlength encoding* [1595] (also see Section 2.3). The same techniques are applicable to higher-dimensional data as well.

The drawback of the decomposition into one-dimensional blocks described above is that all but one side of each block must be of unit width. The most general decomposition removes this restriction along all of the dimensions, thereby permitting aggregation along all dimensions. In other words, the decomposition is arbitrary. The blocks need not be uniform or similar—that is, the relative lengths of their sides need not satisfy any particular restriction such as being the same, which results in square blocks. The only requirement is that the blocks span the space of the environment. This general decomposition has the potential of requiring less space. However, its drawback is that the determination of optimal partition points may be a computationally expensive procedure (see Exercise 4 in Section 2.1.2.7). A closely related problem, decomposing a region into a minimum number of rectangles, is known to be NP-complete[6] if the region is permitted to contain holes [1179].

Sections 2.1.2.2 to 2.1.2.9 discuss the situation that the aggregation is subject to some rules as to which unit-size cells are to be aggregated. In this section, we assume that the blocks are disjoint, although, as we will later see, this need not be the case. We also assume that the blocks are rectangular with sides parallel to the coordinate axes, although, again, this is not absolutely necessary as there exist decompositions using other shapes as well (e.g., triangles, circles). For example, Figure 2.10 is an arbitrary block decomposition for the collection of objects and cells given in Figure 2.1. We have labeled the blocks corresponding to object O as Oi and the blocks that are not in any of the objects as Wi, using the suffix i to distinguish between them in both cases. When there is no need to distinguish between the various objects, we use the labels *black* (also "1" and foreground) and *white* (also "0" and background) to characterize or differentiate between the blocks whose cells all lie in any of the objects and those for which none of the constituent cells are in any of the objects, respectively. This characterization is used for all of the aggregations discussed in the rest of this section (i.e., Section 2.1.2).

It is easy to adapt the explicit representation to deal with blocks resulting from an arbitrary decomposition (which also includes the one that yields one-dimensional blocks). In particular, instead of associating a set with each object o that contains the location in space of each cell that makes up o, we need to associate with each object o the location in space and size of each block that makes up o. There are many methods for doing this, some of which are discussed in Section 3.3.1 of Chapter 3. One popular method is to specify the coordinate values of the upper-left corner of each block and the sizes of their various sides. This format is appropriate, and is the one we use, for the explicit representation of all of the block decompositions described in this section.

Using the explicit representation of blocks, both the feature and location queries are answered in essentially the same way as they were for unit-sized cells. The only

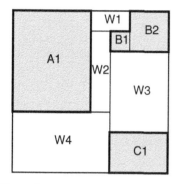

Figure 2.10
Arbitrary block decomposition for the collection of objects and cells in Figure 2.1.

---

[6] A problem is in NP if it can be solved nondeterministically in polynomial time. A nondeterministic solution process proceeds by "guessing" a solution and then verifying that the solution is correct. Assume that n is the size of the problem (e.g., for sorting, n is the number of records to be sorted). Intuitively, then, a problem is in NP if there is a polynomial $P(n)$ such that if one guesses a solution, it can be verified in $O(P(n))$ time, whether the guess is indeed a correct solution. Thus, it is the verification process that is the key to determining whether a problem is in NP, not the actual solution of the problem.

A problem is NP-complete if it is "at least as hard" as any other problem in NP. Somewhat more formally, a problem P_1 in NP is NP-complete if the following property holds: for all other problems P_i in NP, if P_i can be solved deterministically in $O(f(n))$ time, then P_i can be solved in $O(P(f(n)))$ time for some polynomial P. It has been conjectured that no NP-complete problem can be solved deterministically in polynomial time, but this is not known for sure. The theory of NP-completeness is discussed in detail in [682].

difference is that, for the location query, instead of checking if a particular location l in space is a member of one of the sets of cells associated with the various objects, we must check if l is covered by one of the blocks in the sets of blocks of the various objects. This is a fairly simple process as we know the location in space and size of each of the blocks.

An implementation of an arbitrary decomposition (which also includes the one that results in one-dimensional blocks) using an implicit representation is quite easy. We build an index based on an easily identifiable location in each block, such as its upper-left corner. We make use of the same techniques that were presented in the discussion of the implicit representation for unit-sized cells in Section 2.1.1.

In particular, we apply one of the orderings of space shown in Figure 2.5 to obtain a mapping from the coordinate values of the upper-left corner u of each block to the integers. The result of the mapping is used as the index in one of the familiar treelike access structures (e.g., binary search tree, range tree, B$^+$-tree) to store the address that indicates the physical location where the information about the object associated with the block with upper-left corner u is stored. Since we need to know the size of the block (i.e., the lengths of its sides), we also record this information, along with the address in the node of the tree corresponding to the block. An alternative approach is to forego the ordering and keep track of the upper-left corners of the blocks using one of several multidimensional access structures, such as a point quadtree, k-d tree, or MX quadtree (as described in Chapter 1). Again, each node in the tree contains the corresponding block's size and the address where more information can be found about the object associated with the corresponding block.

As in the case of unit-size cells, regardless of which access structure is used, we determine the object o associated with a cell at location l by finding the block b that covers l. If b is an empty block, then we exit. Otherwise, we return the object o associated with b. Notice that the search for the block that covers l may be quite complex in the sense that the access structures may not necessarily achieve as much pruning of the search space as in the case of unit-sized cells. In particular, this is the case whenever the space ordering and the block decomposition method to whose results the ordering is being applied do not have the property that all of the cells in each block appear in consecutive order. In other words, given the cells in the block e with minimum and maximum values in the ordering, say u and v, there exists at least one cell in block f distinct from e that is mapped to a value w, where $u < w < v$. Thus, supposing that the index is implemented using a treelike access structure, a search for the block b that covers l may require that we visit several subtrees of a particular node in the tree (see Exercise 1).

It is also important to recall that this yields only a partial response to the location query as we also want to determine the remaining blocks that make up object o. This is done by accessing the blocks adjacent to b and checking if they are associated with o. If they are, then their adjacent blocks are examined by a recursive application of this process.

The adjacent blocks are found by using the size information about block b and the location in space of b's upper-left corner to calculate points p_i that are adjacent to the faces (edges in two dimensions) of b and that must lie in the adjacent blocks. Next, we find the blocks b_i that contain p_i. Depending on the sizes of b_i, we may have to calculate additional neighboring points. This process can be quite tedious the less regularity exists in the decomposition process. For example, if all the blocks are of the same size, then there is just one adjacent block along each face. Otherwise, the number of adjacent blocks to b along face f can be as large as the surface area (length of an edge in two dimensions) of f. In the remaining subsections of this section, we discuss various decomposition rules that differ in the number of restrictions that they pose on the size and placement of the blocks, thereby simplifying the adjacency determination process.

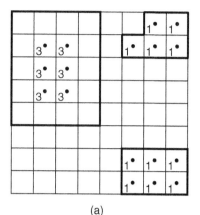

(a)

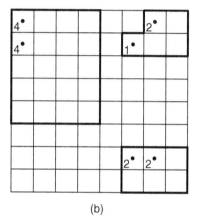

(b)

Figure 2.11
Medial axis transformation (MAT) for
the collection of objects and cells in
Figure 2.1 using a definition where
the maximal block is anchored at the
unit-size element at its (a) center and
(b) upper-left corner (i.e., CMAT).

Exercise

1. Given an arbitrary decomposition where each block is represented by the position of its upper-left corner in a Morton ordering, which is then used as an index in a binary search tree, show how to find the object o that is associated with a cell in location l.

2.1.2.2 Medial Axis Transformation (MAT)

In this section, we examine one of the earliest methods of aggregating unit-size cells with the same value (e.g., belonging to the same object). It proceeds as follows. For each unit-size cell c in object o, find the largest square s_c of width w_c (i.e., radius $w_c/2$) centered at c that is contained in o. s_c is called a *maximal block* if it is not contained in the largest square $s_{c'}$ of any other cell c' in o. Each object is completely specified by the maximal blocks, their widths, and the unit-size cells at their centers—that is, the set of triples (c, s_c, w_c)—since any point in o lies completely inside at least one maximal block. The set of these triples is called the *medial axis transformation* (MAT)[7] of o [221, 1575]. For example, Figure 2.11(a) is the MAT corresponding to the collection of two-dimensional objects in Figure 2.1 where we have specified only the maximal blocks of the objects. Each maximal block in the figure is specified by the unit-size cell at its center and its width. We usually do not construct the MAT of the regions containing the cells that are not in any of the objects (i.e., the background of the image).

The MAT is compact as long as the objects have simple shapes. However, the MAT is somewhat wasteful of space as some maximal blocks are contained in the unions of others. Furthermore, when the MAT is defined in the above manner, the widths of the blocks are restricted to being odd integers. This means that half the possible block widths are excluded. We can overcome this by redefining the maximal blocks to be anchored at the unit-size cell at one of their corners instead of at their centers. In particular, without loss of generality, suppose we use the unit-size cell in the upper-left corner of the maximal block as the anchor. Using this definition, we now construct the MAT as follows. For each unit-size cell c in object o, find the largest square s_c of width w_c (i.e., radius $w_c/2$) anchored at the upper-left corner of c that is contained in o. Again, s_c is called a *maximal block* if it is not contained in the largest square $s_{c'}$ of any other cell c' in o. We use the term *corner medial axis transformation* (CMAT) to distinguish this formulation of the MAT from the conventional MAT when necessary. For example, Figure 2.11(b) is the CMAT corresponding to the collection of two-dimensional objects in Figure 2.1 using this revised definition. Notice that the number of maximal blocks in the CMAT for this example case is significantly smaller than when the maximal blocks are anchored at the unit-size element in the center.

The block decomposition resulting from the MAT and CMAT is handled by the explicit and implicit representations in the same way as the arbitrary decomposition. Therefore, the feature and location queries are answered in the same way as described in Section 2.1.2.1. However, the fact that the decomposition is not disjoint does make the execution of the location query more complex for the implicit representation when we want to determine all of the blocks that make up the object associated with the given location as there are more of them since the decomposition is not disjoint.

The formulation of the MAT and CMAT that we have presented has been used as an object representation by several researchers. In particular, the TID of Scott and Iyengar [1702, 1703] is similar to the MAT (see also the squarecode of Oliver and Wiseman [1396] and the rectangular coding of Kim and Aggarwal [1022, 1023]).

At this point, we digress briefly and explain the rationale behind the original definition of the MAT in term of the unit-size cells in the centers of the maximal blocks instead of at some other positions (e.g., at the corners). Let S be the set of unit-size cells making up object o, and let $\overline{S}$ be the set of unit-size cells outside o. We say that for a

---

[7] MAT is sometimes used to denote the *multiattribute tree* discussed in Section 1.1 of Chapter 1.

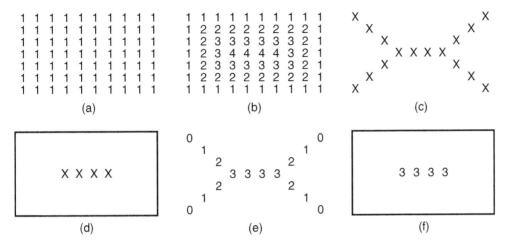

Figure 2.12

An array representation of a rectangle object, its distance values, its skeleton, and its MAT: (a) object, (b) its City Block and Chessboard distance metric values, (c) its skeleton using the City Block distance metric, (d) its skeleton using the Chessboard distance metric, (e) its MAT using the City Block distance metric, and (f) its MAT using the Chessboard distance metric.

point x and a set V, the distance $d(x, V)$ from x to the nearest point of V is defined as $d(x, V) = min\{d(x, y)|y \in V\}$, where d is a metric or distance function (also known as a distance metric). The set of elements in S having a distance from $\overline{S}$ that is greater than or equal to that of all of its "neighbors" in S constitutes a skeletal description of S and is called a *skeleton*. The definition of a skeleton also holds when p is a unit-size cell, in which case we measure the distance between the centers of the cells.

The nature of the skeleton depends on the distance metric that we choose (usually one of the Minkowski distance metrics L_p[8]). For example, consider the 7×10 rectangle object denoted by the array in Figure 2.12(a). The values of the City Block or Manhattan distance metric (i.e., L_1) and Chessboard or maximum value distance metric (i.e., L_∞) for this object are given by Figure 2.12(b), and the corresponding skeletons are given by Figure 2.12(c, d), respectively. The Euclidean distance metric (i.e., L_2) is more appropriate for the continuous case, although Figure 2.13 shows the skeleton corresponding to the rectangle object in Figure 2.12(a) when using it. In this case, the skeleton consists of line segments labeled a, b, c, d, and e. Use of the Euclidean distance metric has a physical analogy to what is left when the boundary of the object is set on fire. The skeleton is used as a compact representation of the objects in many applications in image processing (such as character recognition) where the essence of the object's shape is important.

The MAT is simply the set of elements in S making up the skeleton and their associated distance values to $\overline{S}$—that is, the maximal blocks of S that they span. Figure 2.12(e, f) shows the MATs of the rectangle of Figure 2.12(a) using its City Block and Chessboard distance metric values (given in Figure 2.12(b), which are identical for this example), respectively. Note that the MATs in Figure 2.12(e, f) have distance values that are one less than the values in Figure 2.12(b). This is due to a definition of the MAT as extending to the last unit-size element within the object rather than to the first unit-size element outside the image [1574]. Note that our initial formulation of the MAT in terms of the unit-size cells in the centers of the maximal blocks makes use of the Chessboard distance metric.

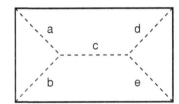

Figure 2.13

The skeleton corresponding to the rectangle object in Figure 2.12(a), using its Euclidean distance metric values.

---

[8] Recall that given the two-dimensional points (x_1, y_1) and (x_2, y_2), the Minkowski distance metric is defined as $d_{L_p}((x_1, y_1), (x_2, y_2)) = ((x_1 - x_2)^p + (y_1 - y_2)^p)^{1/p}$ for integers $p \geq 1$).

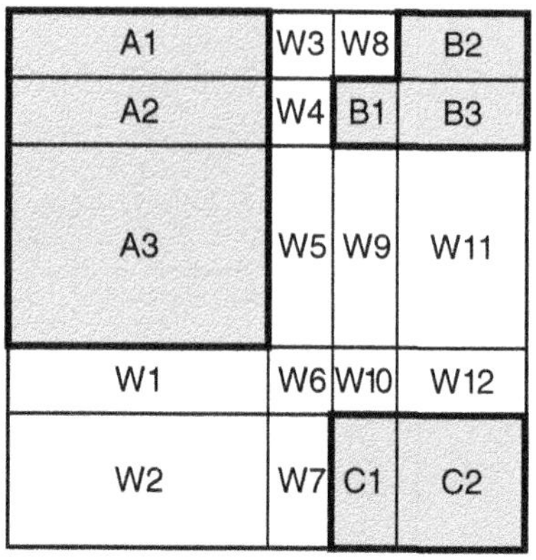

(a)

(b)

Array column	x range
1	[0,4)
2	[4,5)
3	[5,6)
4	[6,8)

(c)

Array row	y range
1	[0,1)
2	[1,2)
3	[2,5)
4	[5,6)
5	[6,8)

(d)

Figure 2.14
(a) Block decomposition resulting from the imposition of a grid with partition lines at arbitrary positions on the collection of objects and cells in Figure 2.1, yielding an irregular grid, (b) the array access structure, (c) the linear scale for the x coordinate values, and (d) the linear scale for the y coordinate values.

Exercises

1. Can you prove that a definition of the MAT where the maximal blocks are anchored at the unit-size elements in their upper-left corner (i.e., the CMAT) results in fewer blocks than one where the maximal blocks are anchored at the unit-size elements in their center?

2. Borgefors [233] discusses four different families of metrics for binary images. The most popular is the City Block/Chessboard metric family. Other families are the Chamfer metric, Octagonal metric, and D-Euclidean metric. The rationale is to enable a reasonable approximation of the Euclidean metric that is also easy and fast to implement. It should be clear that the City Block and Chessboard metrics are analogous to inner and outer approximations, respectively, to the Euclidean metric. The Chamfer, Octagonal, and D-Euclidean metrics are so-called "closer" approximations. Given a pair of points $p = (p_x, p_y)$ and $q = (q_x, q_y)$, arbitrary integers a and b, the (a,b) Chamfer metric, $d_{C(a,b)}(p,q)$, is defined as follows:

$$e = ||p_x - q_x| - |p_y - q_y||$$
$$f = \min\{|p_x - q_x|, |p_y - q_y|\}$$
$$d_{C(a,b)}(p,q) = a \cdot e + b \cdot f.$$

The pair of values (3,4) are used as a close approximation of the Euclidean metric. Compute $d_{C(3,4)}$ and the MAT for the rectangle of Figure 2.12(a).

3. Using the definition of the Chamfer metric in Exercise 2, what is the locus of points having $d_{C(a,b)}(p,q) \leq T$?

4. Using the definition of the Chamfer metric in Exercise 2, find the values of (a,b) that yield the Chessboard metric. Do the same for the City Block metric.

2.1.2.3 Irregular Grid

A very simple decomposition rule is one that partitions a d-dimensional space having coordinate axes x_i into d-dimensional blocks by use of h_i hyperplanes that are parallel to the hyperplane formed by $x_i = 0$ ($1 \leq i \leq d$). The result is a collection of $\prod_{i=1}^{d}(h_i + 1)$ blocks. These blocks form a grid of irregular-sized blocks rather than congruent blocks. There is no recursion involved in the decomposition process. For example, Figure 2.14(a) is an example block decomposition using hyperplanes parallel to the x and y axes for the collection of objects and cells given in Figure 2.1. We term the resulting decomposition an *irregular grid* as the partition lines are at arbitrary positions, in contrast to a *uniform grid* [632] where the partition lines are positioned so that all of the resulting grid cells are congruent.

The block decomposition resulting from the use of an irregular grid is handled by an explicit representation in the same way as the arbitrary decomposition. Finding a suitable implicit representation is a bit more complex as we must define an appropriate access structure. Although the blocks are not congruent, we can still impose an array access structure by adding d access structures, termed *linear scales*. The linear scales indicate the position of the partitioning hyperplanes that are parallel to the hyperplane formed by $x_i = 0$ ($1 \leq i \leq d$). Thus, given a location l in space, say (a,b) in two-dimensional space, the linear scales for the x and y coordinate values indicate the column and row, respectively, of the array access structure entry that corresponds to the block that contains l.

For example, Figure 2.14(b) is the array access structure corresponding to the block decomposition in Figure 2.14(a), and Figure 2.14(c, d) shows the linear scales for the x and y axes, respectively. In this example, the linear scales are shown as tables (i.e., array access structures). In fact, they can be implemented using treelike access structures such as a binary search tree, range tree, or segment tree. The representation described here is an adaptation for regions of the *grid file* [1376] data structure for points (see Section 1.7.2.1 of Chapter 1).

Our implementation of the access structures for the irregular grid yields a representation that is analogous to an *indirect uniform grid* in the sense that, given a cell at location *l*, we need to make $d + 1$ arraylike accesses (analogous to the two memory references involved with indirect addressing in computer instruction formats) to obtain the object *o* associated with it instead of just one array access when the grid is uniform (i.e., all the blocks are congruent and cell-sized). The first *d* accesses find the identity of the array element (i.e., block *b*) that contains *l*, and the last access determines the object *o* associated with *b*. Once we have found block *b*, we examine the adjacent blocks to obtain the rest of the cells making up object *o*, thereby completing the response to the location query by employing the same methods that we used for the array access structure for the uniform-sized cells. The only difference is that every time we find a block *b* in the array access structure associated with *o*, we must examine *b*'s corresponding entries in the linear scales to determine *b*'s size so that we can report the cells that make up *b* as parts of object *o*.

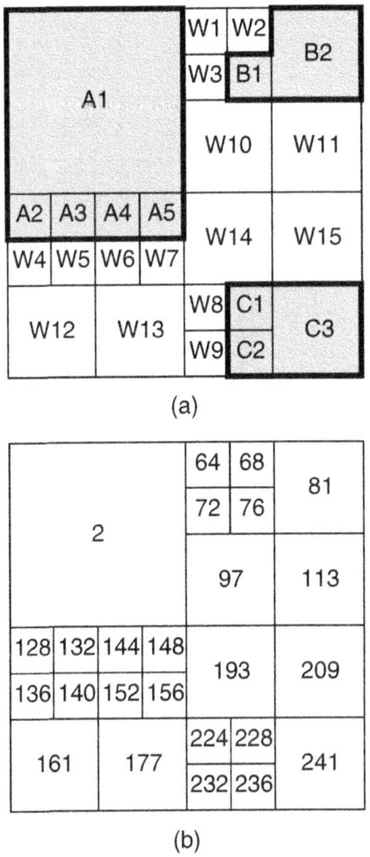

2.1.2.4 Region Quadtree and Region Octree

Perhaps the most widely known decompositions into blocks are those referred to by the general terms *quadtree* and *octree* [1636, 1637]. They are usually used to describe a class of representations for two- and three-dimensional data (and higher as well), respectively, that are the result of a recursive decomposition of the environment (i.e., space) containing the objects into blocks (not necessarily rectangular), until the data in each block satisfies some condition (e.g., with respect to its size, the nature of the objects it comprises, the number of objects in it). The positions and/or sizes of the blocks may be restricted or arbitrary. We shall see that quadtrees and octrees may be used with both interior-based and boundary-based representations. Moreover, both explicit and implicit aggregations of the blocks are possible.

There are many variants of quadtrees and octrees (see also Chapters 1 and 3), and they are used in numerous application areas, including high-energy physics, VLSI, finite-element analysis, and many others. Below we focus on *region quadtrees* [1035] and *region octrees* [901, 1276]. They are specific examples of interior-based representations for, respectively, two- and three-dimensional region data (variants for data of higher dimension also exist), that permit further aggregation of identically valued cells.

Region quadtrees and region octrees are instances of a restricted-decomposition rule, where the environment containing the objects is recursively decomposed into four or eight, respectively, rectangular congruent blocks until each block is either completely occupied by an object or is empty (see Exercise 2). Such a decomposition process is termed *regular*. For example, Figure 2.15(a) is the block decomposition for the region quadtree corresponding to Figure 2.1. We have labeled the blocks corresponding to object O as Oi and the blocks that are not in any of the objects as Wi, using the suffix i to distinguish between them in both cases. Such a quadtree is also known as a *multicolored quadtree* and is useful for applications such as a land use class map which associates colors with crops [1653]. When there is no need to distinguish between the various objects, we use the labels *black* (also "1" and foreground) and *white* (also "0" and background) to characterize or differentiate between the cells that lie in any of the objects and those that are not in any of the objects, respectively. Such a quadtree is also known as a *binary quadtree*.

Notice that in this case all the blocks are square, have sides whose size is a power of 2, and are located at specific positions. In particular, assuming an origin at the upper-left corner of the image corresponding to the environment containing the objects, the coordinate values of the upper-left corner of each block (e.g., (i, j) in two dimensions) of size $2^s \times 2^s$ satisfy the property that $a \bmod 2^s = 0$ and $b \bmod 2^s = 0$. For an example

(a)

(b)

Figure 2.15
(a) Block decomposition and (b) the corresponding locational codes for the region quadtree for the collection of objects and cells in Figure 2.1.

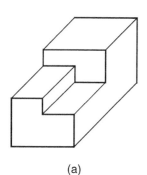

(a)

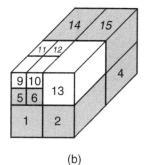

(b)

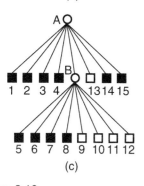

(c)

Figure 2.16
(a) Example three-dimensional object, (b) its region octree block decomposition, and (c) its tree representation.

of a region octree, see Figure 2.16(b), which is the block decomposition for the region octree corresponding to the three-dimensional staircaselike object in Figure 2.16(a).

It is interesting to note that Kawaguchi, Endo, and Matsunaga [1005] use a sequence of m binary-valued quadtrees to encode image data of 2^m gray levels, where the various gray levels are encoded by use of Gray codes (see footnote 35 in Section 1.6 of Chapter 1). This should lead to compaction (i.e., larger-sized blocks), since the Gray code guarantees that the binary representation of the codes of adjacent gray level values differ by only one binary digit. Note, though, that if the primary interest is in image compression, then there exist even better methods (see, e.g., [1508]); however, they are beyond the scope of this book (but see Chapter 8 of [1636]). In another context, Kawaguchi, Endo, and Yokota [1006] point out that a sequence of related images (e.g., in an animation application) can be stored compactly as a sequence of quadtrees such that the ith element is the result of performing an "exclusive or" operation on the first i images (see Exercise 5).

The region quadtree can be viewed as a special case of the medial axis transformation (MAT), which is discussed in Section 2.1.2.2. This can be seen by observing that in the case of the region quadtree, the widths of the maximal blocks of the MAT are restricted to be powers of 2, and the positions of their centers are constrained to being the centers of blocks obtained by a recursive decomposition of the underlying space into four congruent blocks. The notion of a MAT can be further adapted to the region quadtree by constraining only the positions of the centers of the blocks but not their sizes. The result is termed a *quadtree medial axis transform* (QMAT) [1626, 1630]. Thus, the blocks of the QMAT can span a larger area, as long as they are square-shaped. However, unlike the blocks of the region quadtree, the blocks of the QMAT are not disjoint.

The blocks of the QMAT are determined in the same way as the maximal blocks in the MAT. For each block b in the region quadtree for object o, find the largest square s_b of width w_b centered at b that is contained in o. s_b is called a *maximal block* if it is not contained in the largest square $s_{b'}$ of any other block b' in o. Each object is completely specified by the set of maximal blocks that it comprises. The set of blocks in the quadtree that correspond to these maximal blocks is called its *quadtree skeleton*. The QMAT is the quadtree whose object blocks are the elements of the quadtree skeleton, and whose nonobject blocks correspond to empty blocks in the original quadtree as well as the object blocks whose largest square centered in the block were found to be not maximal. Associated with each object block in the QMAT is the width of its corresponding maximal block. For example, Figure 2.17(b) is the block decomposition of the QMAT corresponding to the block decomposition of the region quadtree in Figure 2.17(a). Notice that, as we pointed out above, the maximal blocks corresponding to the blocks in the QMAT are not disjoint. Observe also that in order to enable larger maximal blocks, we assume that the area outside the array of unit-size cells corresponding to the space in which object o is embedded is also part of o (e.g., the area to the north, west, and northeast of block 1 in Figure 2.17(a)). It can be shown that the quadtree skeleton is unique (see Exercise 23) [1626, 1636].

A region quadtree can be implemented using an explicit representation by associating a set with each object o that contains its constituent blocks. Each block is specified by a pair of numbers corresponding to the coordinate values of its upper-left corner and the size of one of its sides. These numbers are stored in the set in the form $(i, j){:}k$, where (i, j) and k correspond to the coordinate values of the upper-left corner and size (in terms of a power of 2), respectively, of the block. For example, the explicit representation of the collection of blocks in Figure 2.1 is given by the sets A={(0,0):2,(0,4):0,(1,4):0,(2,4):0,(3,4):0}, B={(5,1):0,(6,0):1}, and C={(5,6):0,(5,7):0,(6,6):1}, which correspond to blocks {A1,A2,A3,A4,A5}, {B1,B2}, and {C1,C2,C3}, respectively.

An implementation of a region quadtree that makes use of an implicit representation is quite different. First of all, we allocate an address a in storage for each block b that

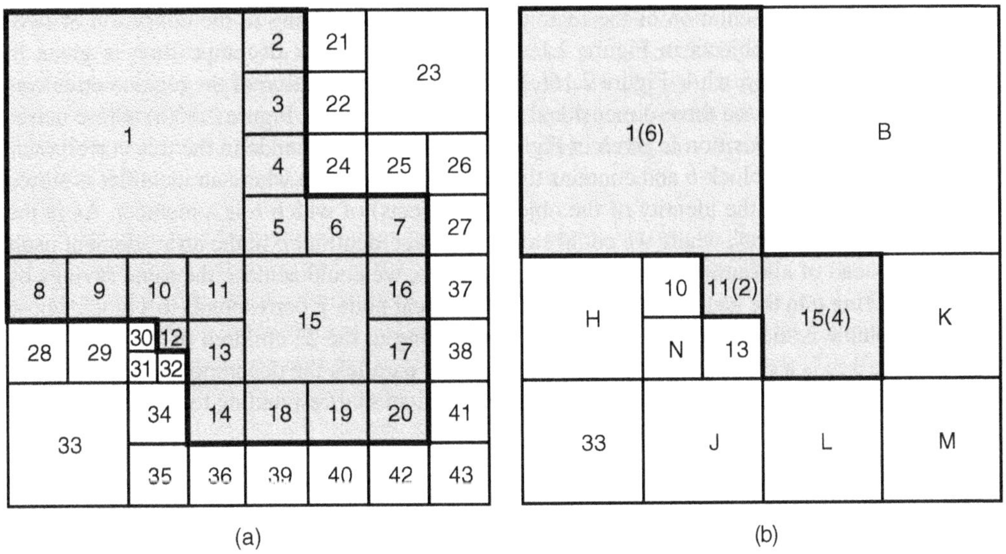

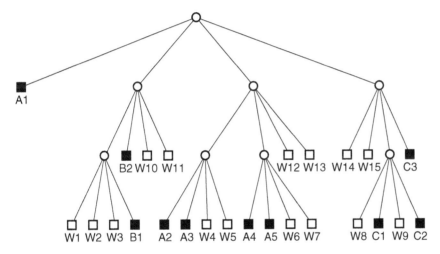

Figure 2.17
Block decomposition induced by (a) the region quadtree for an object and (b) its corresponding quadtree medial axis transform (QMAT). The radii (half the widths) of the corresponding maximal blocks are given in parentheses with each block label.

Figure 2.18
Tree representation for the region quadtree corresponding to the collection of objects and cells in Figure 2.1 whose quadtree block decomposition is given in Figure 2.16(a).

stores an identifier that indicates the identity of the object (or objects) of which b is a member. Second, it is necessary to impose an access structure on the collection of blocks in the same way as the array was imposed on the collection of unit-sized cells. Such an access structure enables us to determine easily the value associated with any point in the space covered by a cell without resorting to exhaustive search. Note that, depending on the nature of the access structure, it is not always necessary to store the location and size of each block with a.

There are many possible access structures. Interestingly, using an array as an access structure is not particularly useful as it defeats the rationale for the aggregation of cells into blocks unless, of course, all the blocks are of a uniform size, in which case we have the analog of a two-level grid.

The traditional, and most natural, access structure for a region quadtree corresponding to a d-dimensional image is a tree with a fanout of 2^d. For example, Figure 2.18 is

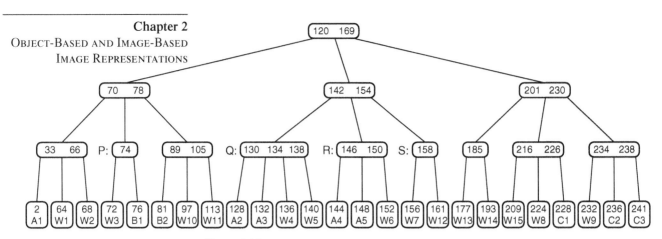

Figure 2.19
Result of applying a B$^+$-tree access structure to the locational codes of the collection of
objects whose quadtree block decomposition is given in Figure 2.15.

orders exhaust a quadtree block before exiting it. Note, however, that unlike the Peano-
Hilbert ordering, none of the Morton, U, Gray, and double Gray orderings traverses the
blocks in a spatially contiguous manner (i.e., for the Morton ordering the result has the
shape of the letter "N" or "Z" and is also known as *N order* [1992] and *Z order* [1420],
while for the U ordering the result has the shape of the letter "U"). The spatial contiguity
property has been shown to have a good effect on the efficiency of range queries [581],
thereby making a case for the use of the Peano-Hilbert order. In fact, Asano, Ranjan,
Roos, Welzl, and Widmayer [101] describe an order that has the same properties as the
Peano-Hilbert order except that for any square range query region, there are at most three
breaks in the spatial continuity of the curve, in contrast to four for the Peano-Hilbert order
(i.e., at most three out of four 4-adjacent subblocks of a square block are not neighbors
along the curve, in contrast to a possibility that all four 4-adjacent subblocks are not
neighbors in the Peano-Hilbert order). This property is useful for retrieval of squarelike
regions in the case of a range query when the data is stored on disk in this order as each
break in the continuity can result in a disk seek operation. Nevertheless, the Morton and
U orderings are useful due to the ease with which the mapping and the inverse mapping
can be constructed, as well as their other desirable properties described in Section 2.1.1.2.

An order 5 B$^+$-tree access structure for these locational codes is given in Figure 2.19.
It is important to note that although some of these treelike access structures also form a
containment hierarchy (e.g., the range tree and the B$^+$-tree), unlike the tree with fanout
2^d, the space spanned by the union of the blocks spanned by their nonleaf nodes does not
have to consist of similar blocks (e.g., nodes P and Q in Figure 2.19); nor does it have to
be a single block (e.g., node R in Figure 2.19); nor do the blocks that it comprises have
to be contiguous (e.g., node S in Figure 2.19). For a representation that does constrain
the blocks to be similar and the constituent blocks to be contiguous, see the discussion
of the PK-tree [1952, 2043] in Section 1.8 of Chapter 1.

Using an order M B$^+$-tree access structure for the locational codes of the blocks
corresponding to the leaf nodes reduces the execution time of the location query from
$O(n)$ (i.e., $O(\log 2^n)$) to $O(\log_M N)$, assuming that the sides of the environment are
of length 2^s and that there are N leaf nodes. Amir, Efrat, Indyk, and Samet [43] have
reduced this bound further to expected $O(\log n)$ time by using a hash table to store the
locational codes of both the leaf and nonleaf nodes of the tree access structure of the
quadtree (octree). Their result is based on the premise that given a query point q and a
depth k, we can use the hash table to determine in expected $O(1)$ time whether there exists
a block b at depth k (leaf or nonleaf) in the quadtree that contains q. It is well known that
this premise holds in general for a hash table (e.g., [422]). The expected $O(\log n)$ time is
obtained by repeated application of the above query in conjunction with a binary search
for q in the range of depths from 0 to n (see Exercise 18). In fact, given that q is in leaf

node v at depth h, the expected execution time is $O(\log h)$ when using an unbounded binary search on the range of depths in the order $1, 2, 4, 8, \ldots$ (see Exercise 19).

Regardless of the access structure that is used, we determine the object o associated with a cell at location l by finding the block b that covers l. Recall that this yields only a partial response to the location query as we also want to determine the remaining blocks that object o comprises. This is done by accessing the blocks adjacent[9] to b and checking if they are associated with o. If they are, then their adjacent blocks are examined by a recursive application of this process. This process is known as *neighbor finding* [1625, 1635]. The actual mechanics of this process depend on the nature of the access structure (for a detailed discussion, see Chapter 3 in [1636]).

Using an access structure in the form of a tree with fanout 2^d means that we can locate the adjacent blocks by just using the structure of the tree. For the sake of this discussion, assume that $d = 2$ and that each node p in the quadtree contains an additional pointer to its immediate ancestor. Here, we restrict ourselves to lateral neighbors (i.e., in the horizontal and vertical directions) that are of size greater than or equal to that of p. Now, to locate a lateral neighbor q of p, we follow ancestor links until finding the nearest common ancestor of p and q. Once the common ancestor is found, we descend along a path that retraces the ascending path with the modification that each step is a reflection of the corresponding prior step about an axis formed by the common boundary between the two nodes p and q.

For example, when attempting to locate the eastern neighbor of node A (i.e., node G) in the box in Figure 2.20, node D is their nearest common ancestor, while the eastern edge of the block corresponding to node A is the common boundary between node A and its neighbor G. The main idea behind this neighbor finding method can be understood by examining more closely how the nearest common ancestor of node p and its eastern neighboring node q of greater than or equal size are located. In other words, as we ascend links, how do we know that we have encountered the nearest common ancestor and that it is time to descend links? The answer is obtained by observing that the nearest common ancestor has p as one of the easternmost nodes of one of its western subtrees and q as one of the westernmost nodes of one of its eastern subtrees. Thus, as long as an ancestor r of p is in a subtree that is an eastern child (i.e., NE or SE), we must ascend the tree at least one more level before locating the nearest common ancestor. C code for this process, as well as the necessary tables, is given by procedure LATERALNEIGHBOR in Figure 2.20. This technique has been shown to require an average of four links to be followed for each neighbor of equal size that is being sought [1625]. If the neighbor is larger, then the algorithm is even faster because the descent step stops sooner [1625, 1636, 1652].

Neighbor finding can also be applied when using one of the alternative access structures that are based on finding a mapping from the domain of the blocks to a subset of the integers. In this case, neighbors are obtained by calculating their locational codes and then conducting a search for them in the relevant access structure. The calculation is made using binary arithmetic [1636, 1696]. The key idea (or trick) is to calculate the coordinate values of the upper-left corner of the neighboring block without having to decompose the locational code into its individual coordinate axes components and then composing them to form the new locational code.

Exercises

1. The region quadtree is an alternative to an image representation that is based on the use of an array or even a list. Each of these image representations may be biased in favor of the computation of a particular adjacency relation. Discuss these biases for the array, list, and quadtree representations.

---

[9] Adjacency between blocks from the same object is defined in an analogous manner to that for adjacent locations (i.e., pixels). In particular, two disjoint blocks, P and Q, are said to be *4-adjacent* if there exists a pixel p in P and a pixel q in Q such that p and q are 4-adjacent. The definition of 8-adjacency for blocks (as well as connected component labeling) is analogous.

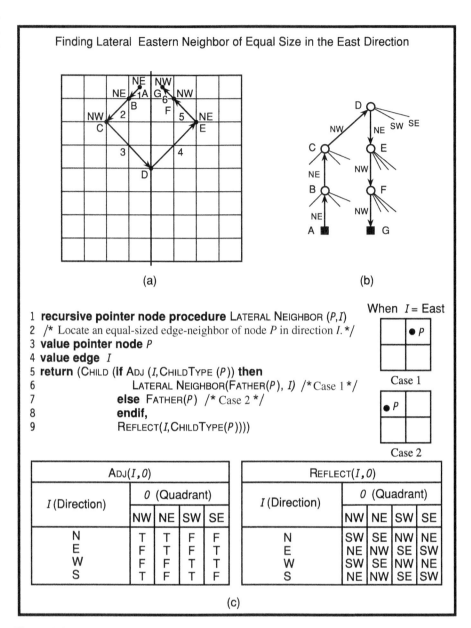

Finding Lateral Eastern Neighbor of Equal Size in the East Direction

(a)

(b)

```
1  recursive pointer node procedure LATERAL NEIGHBOR (P,I)
2  /* Locate an equal-sized edge-neighbor of node P in direction I. */
3  value pointer node P
4  value edge I
5  return (CHILD (if ADJ (I,CHILDTYPE (P)) then
6              LATERAL NEIGHBOR(FATHER(P), I) /* Case 1 */
7          else  FATHER(P)  /* Case 2 */
8          endif,
9          REFLECT(I,CHILDTYPE(P)))))
```

When I = East

Case 1

Case 2

ADJ($I,0$)				
I (Direction)	0 (Quadrant)			
	NW	NE	SW	SE
N	T	T	F	F
E	F	T	F	T
W	F	F	T	T
S	T	F	T	F

REFLECT($I,0$)				
I (Direction)	0 (Quadrant)			
	NW	NE	SW	SE
N	SW	SE	NW	NE
E	NE	NW	SE	SW
W	SW	SE	NW	NE
S	NE	NW	SE	SW

(c)

Figure 2.20
The process of locating the eastern neighbor of node A (i.e., G): (a) block decomposition, (b) the corresponding tree representation of the search process, and (c) C code of the algorithm and the necessary tables.

2. Given the array representation of a binary image, write an algorithm to construct the corresponding region quadtree.

3. Suppose that an octree is used to represent a collection of disjoint spheres. What would you use as a leaf criterion?

4. The quadtree can be generalized to represent data in arbitrary dimensions. As we saw, the octree is its three-dimensional analog. The renowned artist Escher [427] is noted for etchings of unusual interpretations of geometric objects such as staircases. How would you represent one of Escher's staircases?

5. Let $\oplus$ denote an "exclusive or" operation. Given a sequence of related images, $\langle P_n, P_{n-1}, \ldots, P_0 \rangle$, define another sequence $\langle Q_n, Q_{n-1}, \ldots, Q_0 \rangle$ such that $Q_0 = P_0$ and $Q_i = P_i \oplus Q_{i-1}$ for $i > 0$. Show that when the sequences P and Q are represented as quadtrees, replacing sequence P by sequence Q results in fewer nodes.

6. Prove that in Exercise 5 the sequence P can be reconstructed from the sequence Q. In particular, given Q_i and Q_{i-1}, determine P_i.

7. Suppose that you have an environment of width 32 and length 64. What are the permissible sizes of the blocks after the first region quadtree subdivision step?

8. Suppose that you have an environment of width 16 and length 24. Can the first region quadtree subdivision step result in two blocks of size 8×8 and two blocks of size 8×16? If not, explain why.

9. Given an image represented by a region quadtree with B black and W white nodes, how many additional nodes are necessary for the nonleaf nodes?

10. Given an image represented by a region octree with B black and W white nodes, how many additional nodes are necessary for the nonleaf nodes?

11. Consider the arbitrary placement of a square of size $2^m \times 2^m$ at any position in a $2^q \times 2^q$ image and then construct its corresponding region quadtree. Prove that in the best case $4 \cdot (q - m) + 1$ nodes are required while the worst case requires $4 \cdot p + 16 \cdot (q - m) - 27$ nodes. How many of these nodes are black and white, assuming that the square is black? Prove that, on the average, the number of nodes required is $O(p + q - m)$.

12. What are the worst-case storage requirements of storing an arbitrary rectangle in a quadtree corresponding to a $2^q \times 2^q$ image? Give an example of the worst case and the number of nodes it requires.

13. Assume that the probability of a particular pixel's being black is $\frac{1}{2}$ and likewise for its being white. Given a $2^q \times 2^q$ image represented by a quadtree, what is the expected number of nodes, say $E(q)$, in the quadtree? Also compute the expected number of black, white, and gray nodes.

14. Suppose that instead of knowing the probability that a particular pixel is black or white, we know the percentage of the total pixels in the image that are black. Given a $2^q \times 2^q$ image represented by a quadtree, what is the expected number of nodes in the quadtree?

15. Suppose that you are given a region quadtree, how would you obtain a uniform spatial sample of s black pixels from the black regions stored in the quadtree?

16. Prove that for a region such that w is the maximum of its horizontal and vertical extent (measured in pixel widths) and $2^{q-1} < w \le 2^q$, the optimal grid resolution when building its corresponding region quadtree is either q or $q + 1$. In other words, show that embedding the region in a larger area than $2^{q+1} \times 2^{q+1}$ and shifting it around will not result in fewer nodes.

17. Give an algorithm to find the optimal region quadtree, in terms of the minimum number of quadtree nodes, for an arbitrary binary image.

18. Assuming that an environment has sides of length 2^n, that the nodes of the region quadtree (octree) are represented by locational codes, and that the locational codes of both the leaf and nonleaf nodes are stored in a hash table, show that the leaf node v, and its depth h, containing query point q can be determined in expected $O(\log n)$ time. Assume further that given a depth k, we can use the hash table to determine in expected $O(1)$ time whether there exists a block b at depth k (corresponding to a leaf or a nonleaf node) in the quadtree that contains q.

19. Continuing Exercise 18, and, again, assuming an environment with sides of length 2^n, show that the block v at depth h containing q can be determined in expected $O(\log h)$ time instead of expected $O(\log n)$ time.

20. Suppose that you represent each block of a quadtree block decomposition by concatenating the result of applying bit interleaving to the coordinate values of one of the corners of each block (including the nonleaf blocks) and the size or depth of the block. Describe such an encoding so that when the locational codes of the leaf and nonleaf blocks of the quadtree appear in increasing order, the four sons of a node appear before their immediate ancestor when the children of the node corresponding to each nonleaf block are traversed in the order NW, NE, SW, SE. In other words, we have a bottom-up or postorder traversal of the tree.

21. Compare the use of the conventional locational code method with EPICT for representing three-dimensional data when the maximum number of bits in the locational code is 32 and 64. In other words, what is the maximum block size that can be represented using these two methods?

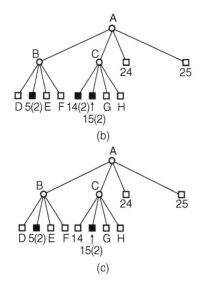

1(0)	2 (1/2)	5(2)		14(2)		15(2)	
3(0)	4 (1/2)						
6(0)	7 (1/2)	10 (1/2)	11 (1/2)	16 (1/2)	17 (1/2)	20 (1/2)	21 (1/2)
8(0)	9(0)	12(0)	13(0)	18(0)	19(0)	22(0)	23(0)
24(0)				25(0)			

(a)

(b)

(c)

Figure 2.21

(a) The region quadtree of an object and the tree representations of its corresponding QMATs using (b) property 3 and (c) property 3′. The radii (half the widths) of the maximal blocks are given in parentheses with each block label.

22. Give an algorithm for finding neighbors in the direction of a vertex (i.e., diagonal) for a region quadtree that is implemented using an access structure in the form of a tree with a fanout of 4.

23. A more precise definition of the quadtree skeleton of a collection of objects represented by a region quadtree is given as follows. Let B denote the set of quadtree blocks corresponding to the objects in the collection. For each block b in object o, let s_b of width w_b be the largest square centered at b that is contained in o. The quadtree skeleton consists of the set T of quadtree object blocks satisfying the following properties:

1. The set of pixels in $B = \cup_{t \in T} s_t$.

2. For any t in T, there does not exist b in B ($b \neq t$) such that $s_t \subseteq s_b$.

3. For each b in B, there exists t in T such that $s_b \subseteq s_t$.

Property 1 ensures that the entire collection of objects is spanned by the quadtree skeleton. Property 2 is termed the *subsumption property*—block j is *subsumed* by block k when $s_j \subseteq s_k$. Property 2 means that the elements of the quadtree skeleton are maximal blocks. Property 3 insures that no block in B requires more than one element of T for its subsumption; for example, the case that one-half of the block is subsumed by one element of T and the other half is subsumed by another element of T is not permitted. Prove that the quadtree skeleton of a collection of objects represented by a region quadtree is unique.

24. Property 2 in the definition of the quadtree skeleton in Exercise 23 means that the elements of the quadtree skeleton are the maximal blocks. Suppose that property 2 is modified as follows:

2′. For any t, in T, there does not exist u in T ($u \neq t$) such that $s_t \subseteq s_u$.

This results in ensuring that there are no extraneous elements in the quadtree skeleton. In other words, one element in the quadtree skeleton cannot be subsumed by another element in the quadtree skeleton. For example, for the region quadtree in Figure 2.17(a), this means that if the quadtree skeleton contains block 12, then it cannot contain block 11 as the maximal block of block 12 is subsumed by the maximal block of block 11. Is the resulting quadtree skeleton still unique?

25. Show that the modification of property 2 (i.e., property 2′) in the definition of the quadtree skeleton in Exercise 24 results in a QMAT with more blocks.

26. Property 3 of the definition of the quadtree skeleton in Exercise 23 does not yield a minimal set of blocks. For example, in the region quadtree of Figure 2.21(a), Property 3 requires that the quadtree skeleton contain blocks 5, 14, and 15, while, in actuality, blocks 5 and 15 are sufficient since together they subsume block 14. Thus, if we were interested in a minimal set of block,s we could modify property 3 as follows:

3′. There does not exist u in T such that $s_u \subseteq \cup_{t \in T \text{ and } t \neq u} s_t$.

Show that, although the number of blocks in the quadtree skeleton is reduced by this modification, the number of elements in the QMAT is not.

2.1.2.5 ATree

In some applications, we may require finer (i.e., more) partitions along a subset of the dimensions due to factors such as sampling frequency (e.g., when the blocks correspond to aggregates of point data), while needing coarser (i.e., fewer) partitions along the remaining subset of dimensions. This is achieved by loosening the stipulation that the region quadtree results in 2^d congruent blocks at each subdivision stage and replacing it with a stipulation that all blocks at the same subdivision stage (i.e., depth) i be partitioned into 2^{c_i} ($1 \leq c_i \leq d$) congruent blocks. We use the term *ATree* [222] to describe the resulting structure.

For example, Figure 2.22(a) is the block decomposition for the ATree for Figure 2.1, and Figure 2.22(b) is the corresponding tree access structure. We have labeled the blocks corresponding to object O as Oi and the blocks that are not in any of the objects as Wi, using the suffix i to distinguish between them in both cases. The nonleaf nodes are labeled with the partition axis or axes, which must be the same for all nodes at the same level. Note that all blocks at a particular level of subdivision e are partitioned in the same way (i.e., into the same number of congruent blocks along the same axes).

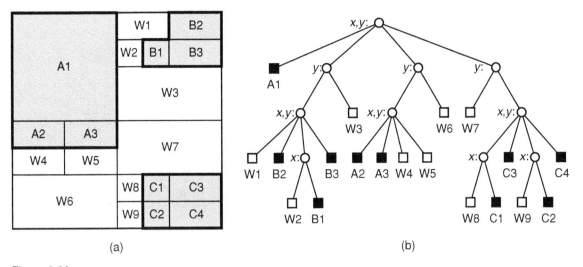

(a)

(b)

Figure 2.22
(a) Block decomposition for the ATree corresponding to the collection of objects and cells in Figure 2.1 and (b) the corresponding tree access structure. The nonleaf nodes are labeled with the partition axis or axes.

2.1.2.6 Bintree

As the dimensionality of the space (i.e., d) increases, each level of decomposition in the region quadtree results in many new blocks, as the fanout value 2^d is high. In particular, it is too large for practical implementation of the tree access structure. In this case, an access structure termed a *bintree* [1041, 1661, 1828] with a fanout value of 2 is used. The bintree is defined in a manner analogous to the region quadtree, except that at each subdivision stage, the space is decomposed into two equal-sized parts. In two dimensions, at odd stages we partition along the y axis, and at even stages we partition along the x axis. Of course, in d dimensions, the depth of the tree may increase by a factor of d. The bintree can also be viewed as a special case of the ATree where all blocks at subdivision stage i are partitioned into a predetermined subset of the dimensions of size 2^{c_i} blocks, where $c_i = 1$. Alternatively, the bintree is an adaptation of the PR k-d tree (see Section 1.5.2.1 of Chapter 1) to represent regions.

Figure 2.23(a) is the block decomposition for the bintree for Figure 2.1, and Figure 2.23(b) is the corresponding tree access structure. We assume that the first split is on the y coordinate value. We have labeled the blocks corresponding to object O as Oi and the blocks that are not in any of the objects as Wi, using the suffix i to distinguish between them in both cases. In general, in the case of d dimensions, we cycle through the different axes every d levels in the bintree.

The bintree can be generalized by relaxing the requirement that the decomposition steps cycle through the different axes while still requiring that at each subdivision stage the space be decomposed into two equal parts. We use the term *generalized bintree* to describe this structure. It is also known as the *Adaptive Hierarchical Coding* (AHC) structure [411]. For example, Figure 2.24(a) is the block decomposition for the generalized bintree for Figure 2.1, and Figure 2.24(b) is the corresponding tree access structure. Nonleaf nodes are labeled with the name of the axis of the partition. We have labeled the blocks corresponding to object O as Oi and the blocks that are not in any of the objects as Wi, using the suffix i to distinguish between them in both cases. The decision as to the coordinate on which to partition depends on the image. This technique may require some work to get the optimal partition from the point of view of a minimum number of nodes (see Exercise 5). Notice that the generalized bintree is not a special case of the ATree (see Exercise 1).

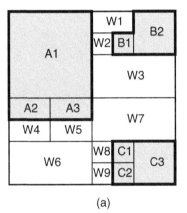

(a)

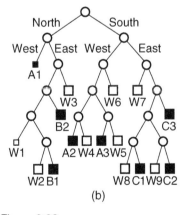

(b)

Figure 2.23
(a) Block decomposition for the bintree corresponding to the collection of objects and cells in Figure 2.1 and (b) the corresponding tree access structure. The splits alternate between the y and x coordinate values, with the first split being based on the y coordinate value.

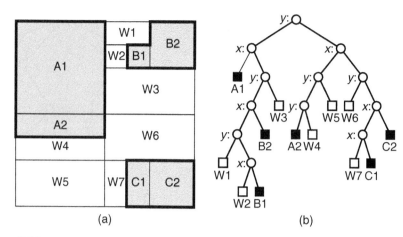

Figure 2.24
(a) Block decomposition for the generalized bintree corresponding to the collection of objects and cells in Figure 2.1 and (b) the corresponding tree access structure. The nonleaf nodes are labeled with the partition axes.

The block decomposition resulting from the use of a bintree (as well as an ATree and a generalized bintree) can be implemented using an explicit representation in the same way as the region quadtree. Although we presented the bintree in terms of an implicit representation that uses a tree access structure with a fanout value of 2, it can be implemented with other access structures (e.g., B^+-tree, etc.) that are applied once a mapping has been found from the domain of the blocks to that of the integers (e.g., locational codes). We do not discuss such techniques here, although it should be clear that they are quite easy to apply, as long as we know the order in which the decomposition process cycles through the axes in the case of the bintree or, in the case of the ATree, the identities of the partitions applied at each subdivision stage. For the generalized bintree, the situation is a bit more complex as we need to keep track of either the order in which the partitions were applied for each block or the size of each block.

Exercises

1. Why is the generalized bintree not a special case of the ATree?

2. What is the ratio of leaf nodes to nonleaf nodes in a bintree for a d-dimensional image?

3. What is a lower bound on the ratio of leaf nodes in a bintree to that in a region quadtree for a d-dimensional image? What is an upper bound? What is the average?

4. Is it true that the total number of nodes in a bintree is always less than that in the corresponding region quadtree?

5. Suppose that you use the AHC method. How many different rectangles and positions must be examined in building such a structure for a $2^n \times 2^n$ image?

2.1.2.7 Adaptation of the Point Quadtree for Regions

The region quadtree, as well as the bintree, is formed by a regular decomposition. This means that the blocks are congruent—that is, at each level of decomposition, all of the resulting blocks are of the same shape and size. We can also use decompositions where the sizes of the blocks are not restricted in the sense that the only restriction is that they be rectangular and be a result of a recursive decomposition process. In this case, the representations that we described must be modified so that the sizes of the individual blocks can be obtained. For example, the explicit representation (as described in the start of this section in conjunction with the example in Figure 2.10) needs to record both the coordinate values of the upper-left corner of each block and the lengths of its sides along the d coordinate axes, instead of just the length of one side as is the case for the region quadtree.

When using the implicit representation, we have several options. Since the decomposition process is recursive, we can use a tree access structure where, at each level of the tree, the positions of the partition lines are recorded. An example of such a structure is an adaptation of the point quadtree [614] to regions. Although the point quadtree was designed to represent points in a higher-dimensional space, the blocks resulting from its use to decompose space do correspond to regions. The difference from the region quadtree is that, in the point quadtree, the positions of the partitions are arbitrary, whereas they are a result of a partitioning process into 2^d congruent blocks (e.g., quartering in two dimensions) in the case of the region quadtree. For example, Figure 2.25(a) is the block decomposition for the point quadtree for Figure 2.1, and Figure 2.25(b) is the corresponding tree access structure. Nonleaf nodes are labeled with the location of the partition point. We have labeled the blocks corresponding to object O as Oi and the blocks that are not in any of the objects as Wi, using the suffix i to distinguish between them in both cases.

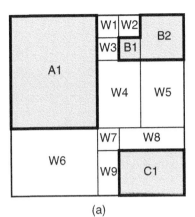

(a)

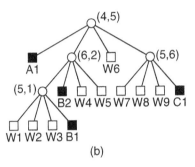

(b)

Figure 2.25
(a) Block decomposition for the point quadtree corresponding to the collection of objects and cells in Figure 2.1 and (b) the corresponding tree access structure. The (x, y) coordinate values of the locations of the partition points are indicated next to the relevant nonleaf nodes.

Exercises

1. (Ken-ichi Kanatani) The Fibonacci numbers consist of the sequence of numbers f_i that satisfy the relation $f_i = f_{i-1} + f_{i-2}$, with $f_0 = 1$ and $f_1 = 1$. There are a number of possible quadtree decomposition rules based on this sequence. One possible quadtree splitting rule is to restrict all shapes to squares with sides whose lengths are Fibonacci numbers. Is this rule feasible?

2. An alternative quadtree decomposition rule to the one proposed in Exercise 1 for a Fibonacci sequence is one that restricts the shapes to being rectangles whose sides have lengths that are either equal Fibonacci numbers or are successive Fibonacci numbers. This condition is termed the *2-d Fibonacci condition*. Give a formal specification of this condition for two dimensions in terms of a relation $g_{m,n}$ that must be satisfied. Can you generalize it to d dimensions?

3. Show that the 2-d Fibonacci condition given in Exercise 2 does not hold for all possible squares so that the smallest primitive unit is a 1×1 square?

4. Find a polynomial-time algorithm to decompose a region optimally so that its representation using the adaptation of a point quadtree requires a minimum amount of space (i.e., a minimum number of nodes). In other words, the decomposition lines need not split the space into four squares of equal size.

2.1.2.8 Adaptation of the K-d Tree for Regions

As in the case of the region quadtree, as the dimensionality d of the space increases, each level of decomposition in the point quadtree results in many new blocks since the fanout value 2^d is high. In particular, it is too large for a practical implementation of the tree access structure. Recall that in this case we resorted to the bintree, which is an access structure with a fanout value of 2. The same reasoning motivates the replacement of the point quadtree by a k-d tree [164] in an adaptation of a point quadtree to regions. As in the point quadtree, although the k-d tree was designed to represent points in a higher-dimensional space, the blocks resulting from its use to decompose space do correspond to regions. In fact, the k-d tree is the precursor of the bintree and, in its adaptation to regions, is defined in a similar manner in the sense that, for d-dimensional data, we cycle through the d axes every d levels in the k-d tree. The difference is that in the k-d tree the positions of the partitions are arbitrary, whereas they are a result of a halving process in the case of the bintree.

For example, Figure 2.26(a) is the block decomposition for the k-d tree for Figure 2.1, and Figure 2.26(b) is the corresponding tree access structure. Nonleaf nodes are labeled with the name of the axis of the partition and the location of the partition line. We have labeled the blocks corresponding to object O as Oi and the blocks that are not in any of the objects as Wi, using the suffix i to distinguish between them in both cases.

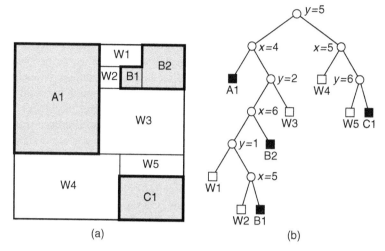

(a)   (b)

Figure 2.26

(a) Block decomposition for the k-d tree corresponding to the collection of objects and cells in Figure 2.1 and (b) the corresponding tree access structure. The splits alternate between the *y* and *x* coordinate values, with the first split being based on the *y* coordinate value. The locations of the splits are indicated next to the relevant nonleaf nodes.

The k-d tree can be further generalized so that the partitions take place on the various axes in an arbitrary order. In fact, the partitions need not be made on every coordinate axis. In this case, at each nonleaf node of the k-d tree, we must also record the identity of the axis that is being split. We use the term *generalized k-d tree* to describe this structure. For example, Figure 2.27(a) is the block decomposition for the generalized k-d tree for Figure 2.1, and Figure 2.27(b) is the corresponding tree access structure. Nonleaf nodes are labeled with the name of the axis of the partition and the location of the partition line. We have labeled the blocks corresponding to object O as Oi and the blocks that are not in any of the objects as Wi, using the suffix i to distinguish between them in both cases.

The generalized k-d tree is really an adaptation to regions of the adaptive k-d tree [650] and the dynamic pseudo k-d tree [1444], as well as the disk-based k-d-B-tree [1567] (see Section 2.1.5.3) and the LSD tree [829]. The similarity lies in the fact that they also permit the partitions to take place on the various axes in an arbitrary order and at arbitrary positions. Although all of these representations were originally developed for points, they can be also be easily adapted to handle regions.

The generalized k-d tree can also be regarded as a special case of the *Binary Space Partitioning tree* (BSP tree) [657, 658] discussed briefly as a point representation in Section 1.5.1.4 of Chapter 1. In particular, in the generalized k-d tree, the partitioning hyperplanes are restricted to being parallel to the axes, whereas, in the BSP tree, they have arbitrary orientations. The BSP tree is used in computer graphics to facilitate viewing. The BSP tree is discussed in greater detail in Section 2.1.3.1.

Similarly, the D-tree [2035, 2036] (discussed briefly in Section 1.5.1.4 of Chapter 1) is a further generalization of the BSP tree where polylines (sequences of connected line segments of arbitrary orientation) are used instead of partitioning hyperplanes of arbitrary orientation. Unfortunately, in order to efficiently execute a point location query, the D-tree requires the imposition of an additional data structure on its associated partition of the underlying space such as the K-structure [1026] (see Section 2.1.3.2) or the separating chain method [1128] and the improved access structure for it known as the layered dag [541] (see Section 2.1.3.3).

Exercises

1. Exercise 2 in Section 2.1.2.7 describes a quadtree decomposition rule for a Fibonacci sequence that restricts the shapes to being rectangles whose sides have lengths that are either equal

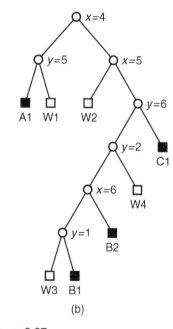

(a)

(b)

Figure 2.27

(a) Block decomposition for the generalized k-d tree corresponding to the collection of objects and cells in Figure 2.1 and (b) the corresponding tree access structure. The nonleaf nodes are labeled with the partition axes and the partition values.

Fibonacci numbers or are successive Fibonacci numbers. This condition was termed the *2-d Fibonacci condition*. Suppose that you use this rule in conjunction with a k-d tree instead of a quadtree. Show that this condition does not hold for all possible squares so that the smallest primitive unit is a 1×1 square.

2. From Exercises 1 and 3 in Section 2.1.2.7, we see that neither a quadtree nor a k-d tree can be used by itself as a basis for Fibonacci-based space decomposition. These solutions have assumed splitting rules that insure that vertical subdivision lines at the same level are colinear as are horizontal lines at the same level. For example, when using a quadtree splitting rule, the vertical lines that subdivide the NW and SW quadrants are colinear as are the horizontal lines that subdivide the NW and NE quadrants. One solution is to relax the colinearity restriction. However, the sides of the shapes must still satisfy the 2-d Fibonacci condition (see Exercise 2). An alternative is to combine the two rules so that either one can be used—that is, a stage can use either the k-d tree or quadtree-based rule. Explain this combined rule in greater detail.

2.1.2.9   X-Y Tree, Treemap, and Puzzletree

One of the shortcomings of the generalized k-d tree is that we can only decompose the underlying space into two parts along a particular dimension at each step. If we wish to partition a space into p parts along dimension i, then we must perform $p - 1$ successive partitions on dimension i. Once these $p - 1$ partitions are complete, we partition along another dimension. The *X-Y tree* of Nagy and Seth [1334] and the subsequently developed and equivalent *treemap* of Shneiderman [1758] (see also [153, 960, 1759]) and *puzzletree* of Dengel [478, 479, 480] are further generalizations of the k-d tree that decompose the underlying space into two or more parts along a particular dimension at each step so that no two successive partitions use the same dimension. In other words, the X-Y tree, treemap, and puzzletree compress all successive partitions on the same dimension in the generalized k-d tree. They are distinguished, in part, by their motivation. In particular, the original motivation for the treemap was a desire to visualize a containment hierarchy associated with one-dimensional data, while both the X-Y tree and the puzzletree were motivated by a desire to represent multidimensional region data. In any case, the underlying representation of the three methods is basically the same.

The treemap was developed as a means of visualizing data in the form of a one-dimensional containment hierarchy, such as a tree directory or an outline, by converting (i.e., "mapping") it into a planar space-filling map—that is, in effect, combining aspects of a Venn diagram with a pie chart [960, 1758]. The areas of the individual regions of space into which the nodes of the containment hierarchy are mapped is made proportional to a value of some attribute (i.e., the same attribute) of the data represented by the directory. For example, in the case of a tree directory for a computer file system, each nonleaf node in the hierarchy corresponds to a subdirectory, where its area in the visualization is proportional to the sum of the sizes of the constituent files (e.g., in megabytes), and, assuming that all levels of the directory hierarchy are visualized, each leaf node corresponds to an individual file, where its area in the visualization is proportional to the file's size. Of course, hierarchies involving other types of data are also possible.

The natural way of visualizing the treemap alternates the orientation of the boundaries of the regions corresponding to the different levels of the containment hierarchy region partitions between horizontal and vertical lines, thereby mimicking the compressed generalized k-d tree (termed *slice-and-dice* [1758]). Unfortunately, such a visualization leads to long, thin rectangles, which is not very pleasing from an aesthetic point of view. This has led to the development of techniques that make use of more "squarelike" aspect ratios for the individual regions (e.g.,[153, 1759]). The drawback of these techniques is that the implicit one-dimensional ordering of the leaf nodes of the containment hierarchy (e.g., a top-to-bottom or left-to-right ordering in an outline) is lost, and there is now a need to specify an ordering of the new layout (e.g., row-major or column-major in an array) if, indeed, the relative ordering is important, which is not always the case if grouping into categories is the key motivation for the containment hierarchy (e.g., a

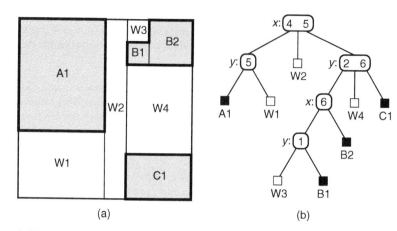

(a)

(b)

Figure 2.28
(a) Block decomposition for the puzzletree corresponding to the collection of objects and cells in Figure 2.1 and (b) the corresponding tree access structure. The nonleaf nodes are labeled with the partition axes and the partition values.

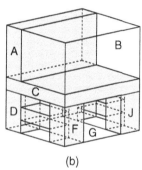

(a)

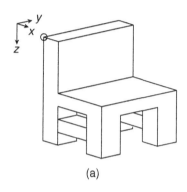

(b)

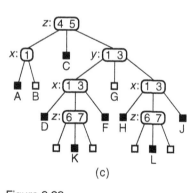

(c)

Figure 2.29
(a) A three-dimensional chair, (b) the block decomposition for its puzzletree, and (c) its corresponding tree access structure. The nonleaf nodes are labeled with the partition axes and the partition values, assuming an origin at the upper-left corner of the chair.

collection of photos). In some sense, these alternative region-representation techniques resemble the imposition of gridlike partitions at the various levels of the directory.

The X-Y tree was developed as a page representation for regions in optically scanned documents, and its presentation focused on issues related to its use in this application [1334]. However, Nagy and Seth do point out in passing that the X-Y tree could be extended to three and more dimensions, which could be useful for dealing with multipage documents as well as, possibly, with other applications. In contrast, the puzzletree was developed as an object representation with a detailed discussion of the ramifications of its use in the representation of both two- and three-dimensional objects. As our interest in this section is more in object representations, the discussion in the rest of this section follows the presentation of Dengel and hence is usually in terms of the puzzletree, especially in the context of objects, although almost all that we say is equally applicable to the X-Y tree and also to the original formulation of the treemap.

Figure 2.28(a) is the block decomposition for the puzzletree for Figure 2.1, and Figure 2.28(b) is the corresponding tree access structure. Notice that the puzzletree was created by compressing the successive initial partitions on $x = 4$ and $x = 5$ at depths 0 and 1, respectively, and likewise for the successive partitions on $y = 6$ and $y = 2$ at depths 2 and 3, respectively, in Figure 2.27. Nonleaf nodes are labeled with the name of the axis of the partition and the location of the partition line. We have labeled the blocks corresponding to object O as Oi and the blocks that are not in any of the objects as Wi, using the suffix i to distinguish between them in both cases.

The fact that the puzzletree compresses all successive partitions on the same dimension means that for $d = 2$ the partitions cycle through the different dimensions so that a different dimension is tested at each level of the decomposition. Note that for $d \geq 3$ a requirement that the partitions cycle through the various dimensions before being permitted to repeat may prevent us from being able to use certain more perceptually appealing block combinations. For example, consider the three-dimensional four-legged chair in Figure 2.29(a) whose corresponding puzzletree has the block decomposition given in Figure 2.29(b) and the tree access structure given in Figure 2.29(c). Here, we see the impossibility of cycling through all of the dimensions in an alternating manner.

The puzzletree is motivated by a desire to overcome the rigidity in the shape, size, and position of the blocks that result from the bintree (and to an equivalent extent, the region quadtree) partitioning process (because of its regular decomposition). In particular, in many cases, the decomposition rules ignore the homogeneity present in certain regions on account of the need to place the partition lines in particular positions as well as a possible limit on the number of permissible partitions along each dimension at each

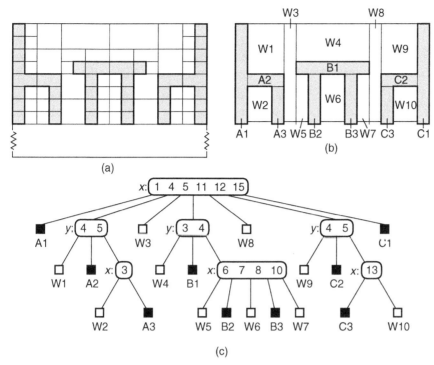

Figure 2.30
Block decomposition for the (a) bintree and (b) puzzletree corresponding to the front view of a scene containing a table and two chairs; (c) is the tree access structure for the puzzletree in (b).

decomposition step. Often, it is desirable for the block decomposition to follow the perceptual characteristics of the objects as well as to reflect their dominant structural features.

For example, consider a front view of a scene containing a table and two chairs. Figures 2.30(a, b) shows the block decompositions resulting from the use of a bintree and a puzzletree, respectively, for this scene, and Figure 2.30(c) is the tree access structure corresponding to the puzzletree in Figure 2.30(b). Notice the natural decomposition in the puzzletree of the chair into the legs, seat, and back and of the table into the top and legs. On the other hand, the blocks in the bintree (and, to a greater extent, in the region quadtree, although not shown here) do not have this perceptual coherence. Of course, we are aided here by the separability of the objects; however, this does not detract from the utility of the representation as it only means that the objects can be decomposed into fewer parts.

Constructing the puzzletree for a particular scene is a tricky matter. The problem is that, on the one hand, we want to decompose the scene into meaningful blocks. This requires some a priori high-level knowledge about the semantic meaning of the scene's constituent parts (e.g., a chair consists of four legs, a seat, and a back). On the other hand, we usually do not have this semantic information readily available when processing the scene. In other words, ideally, we would like the puzzletree construction to be omniscient. As this is impossible, we must resort to the use of heuristics about inferring meaningful two-dimensional blocks from easily derivable measures of one-dimensional block aggregations (see Exercise 1).

The puzzletree can be shown to require no more nodes than a region quadtree and often considerably fewer nodes. Of course, the construction process of the puzzletree is more complex than that of the region quadtree. In particular, the puzzletree is not unique and relies on heuristics to identify the dominant parts so that a perceptually meaningful decomposition is obtained when we start with a collection of cells. The drawback of the puzzletree (and other representations, such as the point quadtree, k-d tree, and generalized k-d, tree that do not use regular decomposition) is that, since the placement of the partition lines is arbitrary, a height-balanced decomposition (i.e., one that does not require too much space) will require that all the data be examined prior to building the structure. Otherwise, the structure can be skewed in a manner analogous to the worst-case behavior of a binary search tree, which is a linear list.

Of course, access structures aside from space partitions (e.g., multidimensional trees or trees that partition the space one dimension at a time) could be used as well. In this case, we again need to find a mapping from the domain of the blocks to a subset of the integers (i.e., to one dimension) and then to apply one of the familiar access structures (e.g., a binary search tree, range tree, B^+-tree). Since the sizes of the blocks are arbitrary, it does not make sense to use a mapping that concatenates the sizes to the result of interleaving the binary representations of the coordinate values of the upper-left corner of each block as was done for the regular decompositions. Instead, we employ the same techniques that we used for an arbitrary decomposition as described at the start of this section—that is, we apply one of the orderings shown in Figure 2.5 to obtain a mapping from the coordinate values of the upper-left corner u of each block to the integers.

Exercises

1. The key to building a puzzletree is identifying the blocks. Below, we describe a variation of a technique suggested in [478, 479, 480] to choose between performing a vertical or a horizontal partition at each stage. We illustrate our discussion with the collection of cells and objects in Figure 2.31(a). Decompose each row j, having length L, into maximal, one-dimensional, identically valued blocks (i.e., each block is associated with the same object), and calculate the value $H_j = \left(\sum_i x_i^2\right)/L^2$, where x_i denotes the width of the ith block in row j. Perform a similar calculation for the columns—that is, $V_j = \left(\sum_i y_i^2\right)/L^2$, where y_i denotes the length of the ith block in column j and L is the width of column j. Clearly, a value of $H_j = 1$ ($V_j = 1$) indicates that the row (column) consists of one solid block. Once these values have been computed, there are several ways to proceed, none of which is guaranteed always to yield the minimum number of leaf nodes. We choose the partitioning axis as the one that has the maximum H_j or V_j value (e.g., into columns for the objects in Figure 2.31(a)). Ties are broken in an arbitrary manner. Once we have chosen the partitioning axis, we partition so that adjacent columns (rows) with the maximum value V_j (H_j) and identical values in each cell form a block. This process is termed the *linear homogeneity heuristic*. Figure 2.31(a) is the block decomposition of the puzzletree resulting from its application to a collection of cells and objects whose corresponding tree access structure is given in Figure 2.31(b). Once the first level of partition has been chosen, the rest are chosen by adhering to the heuristic whenever possible. If successive application of this heuristic yields a partition on the same dimension, then the partitions are compressed. Is the puzzletree in Figure 2.28 constructed according to these rules?

2. Devise an algorithm to construct a puzzletree that makes use of the linear homogeneity heuristic described in Exercise 1.

3. Once a puzzletree has been generated, it is often possible to transform it into another puzzletree. For example, let a, b, and c be three node positions in a puzzletree, that are occupied by nonleaf nodes such that, without loss of generality, b and c test the x and y coordinate values, respectively, b has degree of 2, c is the only child of b that is a nonleaf node, all the children of c are leaf nodes, and b is a child of a. Therefore, by the definition of a puzzletree, the nonleaf node at position a tests the y coordinate value. One possible transformation interchanges the tests at positions b and c so that c becomes a test on the x coordinate value and b becomes a test on the y coordinate value. Once the interchange has occurred, we have two successive tests on the y coordinate value at positions a and b, and we can compress these two tests into one test. For example, referring to the tree access structure in Figure 2.28(b), this transformation is applicable to the partitions on $x = 6$ and $y = 1$ at depths 2 and 3, respectively, in the rightmost subtree of the root. What properties must node c satisfy (i.e., nature of the objects associated with it) so that this transformation does not result in an increase in the number of leaf nodes? Can it ever lead to a decrease in the number of leaf nodes?

4. At times, we can apply a technique, that we term *common partition elimination* (analogous to common subexpression elimination in compiler code optimization [28]) to yield more optimal partitions in terms of the number of blocks. This is the case when two sibling nonleaf nodes

have at least one common partition. For example, consider the block decomposition and tree access structure in Figure 2.32. The results of the partition at the root that yields the regions $5 \leq x < 6$ and $6 \leq x < 8$ are both subdivided further at $y = 2$ and $y = 6$. Hence, they share the common subsequent partitions $0 \leq y < 2$, $2 \leq y < 6$, and $6 \leq y < 8$. The regions corresponding to these subsequent partitions can be merged if they are identically valued (i.e., their blocks are associated with the same object or are not associated with any object). For example, the pair of blocks labeled W5 and W6 and the pair labeled C2 and C3 in Figure 2.32 can be merged into larger blocks labeled W4 and C1, respectively, as shown in Figure 2.28. Notice that the effect of the common partition elimination is the removal of the partition step at $x = 6$ from the root of the tree access structure, thereby reducing the size of the tree. The reason it is still present at depth 2 in Figure 2.28 is that the objects associated with blocks W3 and B1 are not the same as those associated with block B2. Give an algorithm COMPRESS to implement common partition elimination. In order to ease the expression of your solution, assume a recursive list representation [478, 479, 480] for the tree access structure where each node t in the tree is a list of three items having the format (A P S) where A is the split axis, P is a list containing the split locations, and S is a list containing the nodes or values corresponding to the children of t. We refer to these items by the field names A, P, and S. For example, the puzzletree corresponding to Figure 2.32 is (x (4 5 6) ((y (5) (A1 W1)) W2 (y (1 2 6) (W3 B1

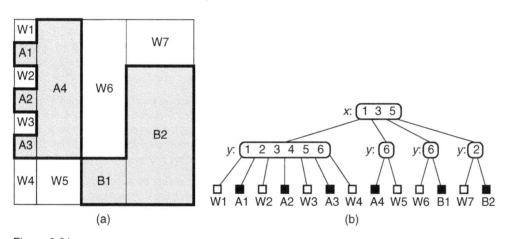

(a)   (b)

Figure 2.31
(a) Block decomposition of a puzzletree for a collection of cells and objects constructed according to the linear homogeneity heuristic and (b) the corresponding tree access structure.

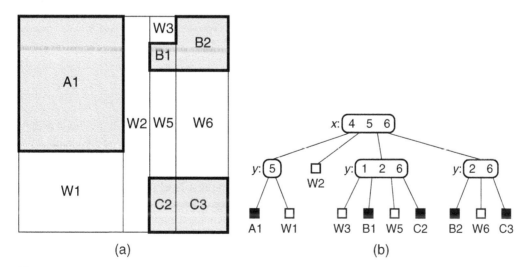

(a)   (b)

Figure 2.32
(a) An alternative block decomposition for a puzzletree corresponding to the collection of objects and cells in Figure 2.1 and (b) the corresponding tree access structure. The nonleaf nodes are labeled with the partition axes and the partition values.

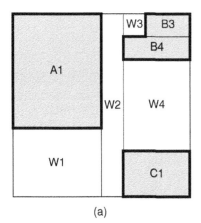

(a)

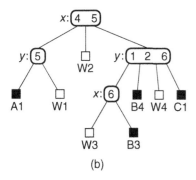

(b)

Figure 2.33
The puzzletree resulting from the application of a common partition elimination method to the puzzletree in Figure 2.32 that introduces new partitions whenever none are present: (a) resulting block decomposition and (b) the corresponding tree access structure. The nonleaf nodes are labeled with the partition axes and the partition values.

W5 C2)) (y (2 6) (B2 W6 C3)))). The inputs to procedure COMPRESS are the two sibling nodes being merged, the split axis separating them, and the split axis value.

5. Devise an algorithm COMPRESSTREE for the technique described in Exercise 4 to eliminate a partition for an implementation of a puzzletree that uses a tree access structure. The inputs to the algorithm are the axis u being partitioned, the partition value $p0$, and pointers to the two subtrees a and b corresponding to the two puzzletree nodes that are being merged. Assume that each nonleaf node has four fields: TEST, NUMCHILDS, CHILDS[1:NUMCHILDS], and V[1:NUMCHILDS], indicating the coordinate being tested, the number of children, pointers to the children, and the values of the coordinate being tested in increasing order, respectively. Note that in order to simplify the algorithms, V[NUMCHILDS] is always initialized to ∞. Each leaf node has a field called OBJECT that contains a pointer to the object associated with the block corresponding to the leaf node.

6. An alternative means of achieving common partition elimination to the one described in Exercise 4 is one that eliminates a partition step as well as introduces new partitions wherever the common partitions are not present [478, 479, 480]. For example, consider the block decomposition and tree access structure in Figure 2.32. In particular, focus on the partition at the root that yields the regions $5 \leq x < 6$ and $6 \leq x < 8$. They are both subdivided further at $y = 2$ and $y = 6$. Hence, they share the common partitions $0 \leq y < 2$, $2 \leq y < 6$, and $6 \leq y < 8$. In this case, we modify the technique discussed in Exercise 4 to create a new partition wherever a partition is not present so that we partition the region $0 \leq y < 2$ into $0 \leq y < 1$ and $1 \leq y < 2$. The result is shown in Figure 2.33. Give an algorithm called REPARTITION to implement this approach. Assume the same recursive list representation for the nodes that was used in Exercise 4. Again, the inputs to procedure COMPRESS are the two sibling nodes being merged, the split axis separating them, and the split axis value.

7. Give an example of a puzzletree, say t, for which common partition elimination using the method of Exercise 4 results in fewer leaf nodes, while common partition elimination using the method of Exercise 6 results in more nodes. The block decomposition in t is such that all the children of the two nodes in which the common partitions are found are leaf nodes. Also, t is constructed in accordance with the linear homogeneity heuristic.

8. Assume a puzzletree block decomposition where two sibling nodes a and b have common partitions, and the children of a and b are leaf nodes. Prove that the result of common partition elimination using the method of Exercise 4 never requires more leaf nodes than the method of Exercise 6. In this exercise, the puzzletree need not necessarily be constructed in accordance with the linear homogeneity heuristic.

9. Assume a puzzletree block decomposition constructed in accordance with the linear homogeneity heuristic and two sibling nodes a and b with common partitions. Can you prove that the result of common partition elimination using the method of Exercise 4 never requires more leaf nodes than the method of Exercise 6?

10. Assume that a puzzletree block decomposition is not necessarily constructed in accordance with the linear homogeneity heuristic and that two sibling nodes a and b have common partitions. Can you prove that the result of common partition elimination using the method of Exercise 4 never requires more leaf nodes than the method of Exercise 6?

2.1.2.10 Hexagonal Blocks

As we pointed out in Section 2.1.1.1, the drawback of a decomposition into hexagons is that they cannot be decomposed beyond that atomic tiling without changing the basic tile shape. Also, hexagonal unit-size cells cannot be aggregated into larger hexagonal cells. Nevertheless, there are a number of different hexagonal hierarchies of blocks that are distinguished by classifying the shape of the first-level molecular tile on the basis of the number of hexagons that it contains. Three of these tiling hierarchies are given in Figure 2.34 and are called *n-shapes*, where n denotes the number of atomic tiles in the first-level molecular tile. Of course, these n-shapes are not unique.

The 4-shape and the 9-shape have an unusual adjacency property in the sense that no matter how large the molecular tile becomes, contact with two of the tiles (i.e., the one above and the one below) is only along one edge of a hexagonal atomic tile, while contact with the remaining four molecular tiles is along nearly one-quarter of the perimeter of the corresponding molecular tile. The hexagonal pattern of the 4-shape and 9-shape molecular tiles has the shape of a rhombus. In contrast, a 7-shape molecular tile has a uniform contact with its six neighboring molecular tiles.

Given the various block shapes described above, the choice is usually made on the basis of the grid formed by the image sampling process. Square blocks are appropriate for square grids, and triangular blocks are appropriate for triangular grids. In the case of a hexagonal grid [285], the 7-shape hierarchy is frequently used since the shape of its molecular tile is more like a hexagon. It is usually described as *rosettelike* (i.e., a *septree*). Note that septrees have jagged edges as they are merged to form larger units (e.g., Figure 2.34(b)). The septree is used by Gibson and Lucas [706], who call it a *generalized balanced ternary* (GBT), in the development of algorithms analogous to those existing for region quadtrees.

Although the septree can be built up to yield large septrees, the smallest resolution in the septree must be decided upon in advance since its primitive components (i.e., hexagons) cannot later be decomposed into septrees. Therefore, the septree yields only a partial hierarchical decomposition in the sense that the components can always be merged into larger units, but they cannot always be broken down. For region data, a pixel is generally an indivisible unit and thus unlimited decomposition is not absolutely necessary. However, in the case of other data types such as points (see Chapter 1) and lines (see, e.g., Section 2.2.2.6), we find that the decomposition rules of some representations require that two entities be separated, which may lead to a level of decomposition not known in advance (e.g., a decomposition rule that restricts each square to contain at most one point). In this book, we restrict our discussion to hierarchies of rectangular blocks.

2.1.2.11 Triangular Blocks

Triangular blocks are used in triangular quadtrees that are based on a recursive decomposition of an equilateral triangle into four congruent blocks. Such a triangular decomposition results from using the $[6^3]$ tiling. Triangular blocks are also used in triangular bintrees that are based on a recursive decomposition of an isoceles triangle into two congruent blocks. Such a triangular decomposition results from using the $[4.8^2]$ tiling.

When the data lies on the surface of a sphere, a number of researchers have proposed the use of a representation based on an icosahedron (a 20-faced polyhedron whose faces are regular triangles) [520, 603]. The icosahedron is attractive because, in terms of the number of faces, it is the largest possible regular polyhedron. Each of the triangular faces can be further decomposed in a recursive manner into n^2 ($n > 1$) spherical triangles (the $[6^3]$ tiling).

Fekete and Davis [603] let $n = 2$, which means that, at each level of decomposition, three new vertices are generated by halving each side of the triangle; connecting them together yields four triangles. They use the term *property sphere* to describe their representation. The property sphere has been used in object recognition; however, it is also of potential use in mapping the Earth as it can enable accurate modeling of regions around the poles. For example, see Figure 2.35, which is a property sphere representation of some spherical data. In contrast, planar quadtrees are less attractive the farther we get from the equator due to distortions in planarity caused by the Earth's curvature. Of course, for true applicability for mapping, we need a closer approximation to a sphere than is provided by the 20 triangles of the icosahedron. Moreover, we want a way to distinguish between different elevations.

Dutton [520] lets $n = \sqrt{3}$, which means that, at each level of decomposition, one new vertex is created by connecting the centroid of the triangle to its vertices. The result is an alternating sequence of triangles so that each level is fully contained in the level that was created two steps earlier and has nine times as many triangles as that level. Dutton uses

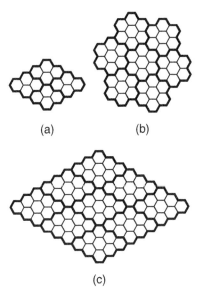

(a) (b)

(c)

Figure 2.34
Three different hexagonal tiling hierarchies: (a) 4-shape, (b) 7-shape, and (c) 9-shape.

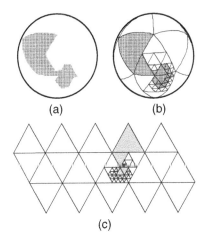

(a) (b)

(c)

Figure 2.35
Property sphere representation of some spherical data: (a) data, (b) decomposition on a sphere, and (c) decomposition on a plane.

the term *triacon* to describe the resulting hierarchy. As an example, consider Figure 2.36, which illustrates four levels of a triacon decomposition. The initial and odd-numbered decompositions are shown with heavy lines, and the even-numbered decompositions are shown with broken and thin lines.

The icosahedron is not the only regular polyhedron that can be used to model data that lies on a sphere. Others include the tetrahedron, hexahedron (more commonly known as a cube), octahedron, and dodecahedron, which have 4, 6, 8, and 12 faces, respectively. Collectively, these five polyhedra are known as the *Platonic solids* [1490]. The faces of the tetrahedron and octahedron are equilateral triangles, while the faces of the hexahedron and dodecahedron are squares and regular pentagons, respectively.

The dodecahedron is not an appropriate primitive because the pentagonal faces cannot be further decomposed into pentagons or other similar shapes. The tetrahedron and hexahedron (the basis of the octree) have internal angles that are too small to model a sphere properly, thereby leading to shape distortions.

Dutton [520] points out that the octahedron is attractive for modeling spherical data such as the globe because it can be aligned so that the poles are at opposite vertices, and the prime meridian and the equator intersect at another vertex. In addition, one subdivision line of each face is parallel to the equator. Of course, for all of the Platonic solids, only the vertices of the solids touch the sphere; the facets of the solids are interior to the sphere.

Other decompositions for data that lies on a sphere are also possible. Tobler and Chen [1877] point out the desirability of a close relationship to the commonly used system of latitude and longitude coordinates. In particular, any decomposition that is chosen should enable the use of meridians and parallels to refer to the data. An additional important goal is for the partition to be into units of equal area, which rules out the use of equally spaced lines of latitude (of course, the lines of longitude are equally spaced). In this case, the sphere is projected into a plane using Lambert's cylindrical projection [14], which is locally area preserving. Authalic coordinates [14], which partition the projection into rectangles of equal area, are then derived. For more details, see [1877].

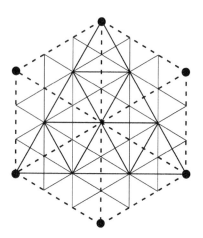

Figure 2.36
Example of a triacon hierarchy.

Exercises

1. Show how the property sphere data structure can be used to model the Earth. In particular, discuss how to represent landmass features, such as mountain ranges, crevices, and so on.

2. Suppose that you use an icosahedron to model spherical data. Initially, there are 20 faces. How many faces are there after the first level of decomposition when $n = 2$? When $n = \sqrt{3}$?

2.1.3 Nonorthogonal Blocks

In Section 2.1.1 we assumed that each unit-sized cell is contained entirely in one or more objects. In other words, no cell c is partially contained in one object o_1 and partially contained in another object o_2, or, even more generally, no cell c is partially contained in an object o_1 while the rest of c is contained in any other object. Similarly, in Section 2.1.2, we stipulate that the block decomposition rules all required that each cell in each block belong to the same object or objects or that the cells not belong to any objects. In other words, the situation in which some of the cells in a block belong to object o_1 while the others belong to object o_2 (and not to o_1) is not permitted. Of course, these restrictions are all subject to appropriate conventions with respect to blocks' being open and closed.

The above restrictions, coupled with the fact that both the blocks and the unit-sized cells are assumed to be axis parallel (i.e., with boundaries parallel to the coordinate axes), mean that we cannot represent objects whose boundaries do not coincide with the boundaries of the underlying blocks. A more general statement of this consequence is that we cannot represent polygonal objects whose sides are not parallel to the coordinate axes (i.e., non-axis-parallel objects).[10] In essence, the problem is that for such objects we cannot, in general, obtain a decomposition so that each cell or block is completely contained in a single object or is not in any object.

In this section, we loosen some of these restrictions so as to permit both the blocks and the objects to be arbitrary polyhedra (i.e., d-dimensional objects whose $(d-1)$-dimensional faces are hyperplanes). Nevertheless, unlike Sections 2.1.1 and 2.1.2, in this section, we do not permit the objects to intersect. However, we do permit the objects to be adjacent and, thereby, to have common boundaries. This means that we do include collections of polygons where the polygons form what is termed a *polygonal map*. Although most of our discussion is with respect to two-dimensional data (i.e., the sides of polygons and polygonal maps), it is often also relevant to higher-dimensional data.

It should be clear that, for both the implicit and explicit representations, we are now freed from the need to represent the individual objects as a collection of unit-sized cells or rectangular blocks. Thus, from now on, we speak only of blocks. In fact, collections of other shapes, such as triangles, trapezoids, and convex polygons (e.g., [261, 1081]), could be used. The rationale for using these shapes is that they can capture the geometry of the object more accurately than the rectangular blocks, as well as simplify the computation of point-in-object tests in comparison to performing the test on the entire object.

The rest of this section is organized as follows. First, we briefly present the BSP tree (Section 2.1.3.1), which is a generalization of the generalized k-d tree (see Section 2.1.2.8) that yields arbitrary-shaped blocks. We also mention the BSP tree in the context of point data in Section 1.5.1.4 of Chapter 1. Next, we describe the K-structure (Section 2.1.3.2) and the separating chain (Section 2.1.3.3), which are designed to respond to the location query (i.e., determining the object associated with a particular location in space) in optimal time and optimal space. This query is known as the *point location query* in the context of these representations, and this is how we will refer to it in Sections 2.1.3.2 and 2.1.3.3. The objects are decomposed into triangles in the case of the K-structure and into arbitrary-shaped blocks satisfying the property that they are intersected no more than twice by any vertical line in the case of the separating chain. Responses to the location query are facilitated by use of an access structure that is based on a hierarchy of blocks (BSP tree), triangulations (K-structure), and "above-and-below" partitions (separating chain). The discussion of the K-structure and the separating chain is quite detailed and thus may be skipped on a first reading.

2.1.3.1 BSP Tree

We have already mentioned the BSP tree [657, 658] in our discussions of the k-d tree in Section 1.5.1.4 of Chapter 1 and the generalized k-d tree in Section 2.1.2.8. In the discussion of the k-d tree, the BSP was presented as one of many methods of representing a collection of multidimensional points so that retrieval operations such as point and range queries can be efficiently represented. In this section, we view the BSP tree as an object and region representation. What differentiates the BSP tree from representations based on a regular decomposition (i.e., the region quadtree, ATree, and bintree) discussed in Section 2.1.2 is that the objects are being decomposed into blocks where at least one side (more generally one $(d-1)$-dimensional boundary for d-dimensional objects) of each block overlaps, even if only partially, the side (i.e., boundary) of one of the objects. Nevertheless, the BSP tree has been used by van Oosterom [1409, 1410] as an object representation in a manner analogous to the region quadtree. In particular, associated with each block b corresponding to a leaf node in the tree is a pointer to the object of which b is a member. The result is termed a *multiobject BSP tree*.

---

[10] To be more precise, we could not represent non-axis-parallel polygonal objects. Notice that, strictly speaking, our restrictions did not permit the representation of all hyperrectangular objects as such objects are required only to have boundaries that are orthogonal to each other, while not necessarily requiring the boundaries to be parallel to the coordinate axes.

As an example of the utility of the BSP tree, we show how it is used for retrieving the objects in an order that is consistent with their visibility from an arbitrary viewpoint (e.g., [941, 1357] and the references cited therein, as well as [196, Ch. 12]). In other words, the objects are retrieved (and displayed to the viewer) so that if object A occludes object B when viewed from viewpoint v, then B is retrieved (and displayed) before A (also known as *hidden-surface elimination*). The visibility problem is very similar to the point location query in the sense that a point is given (termed the *viewpoint*), and it is desired to determine all of the visible polygonal faces of the objects (i.e., the visible parts of the objects). We will focus on how the BSP tree is used to determine visibility in a three-dimensional scene. Of course, the BSP tree can be applied to objects of arbitrary dimensionality.

The utility of the BSP tree for visibility calculations can be understood best by examining its use for interobject visibility. Thus, for the moment, we assume that parts of an object are not occluded by other parts of the same object. This is true when the objects are convex. Suppose, further, that for the moment the objects are linearly separable. This is clearly the case if they are points and may be achievable for certain, but not all, collections of objects. Under these assumptions, partitioning the underlying space with a single hyperplane h results in giving visibility priority to all objects on the side of h that contains the viewpoint v over the objects on the other side of h. Determining the side of h in which v lies is achieved by taking the dot product of v and the normal to h.

It is important to note that a single hyperplane cannot order objects lying on the same side and thus cannot yield a total visibility ordering. One way of extending this idea to the remaining objects is to create a unique separating hyperplane for every pair of objects. However, for n objects, this would require $O(n^2)$ separating hyperplanes, which is too large. Instead, we can reduce the number of separating hyperplanes by recursively subdividing each of the regions resulting from the first hyperplane by introducing additional separating hyperplanes, assuming that the objects are linearly separable. This can be done with as few as n hyperplanes when none of the objects overlap the separating hyperplanes. In fact, we see that the resulting structure is indeed the BSP tree that we defined earlier. Visibility is now determined by traversing the tree so that at each node the child that is drawn first is the one that does not contain the viewpoint.

Of course, in general, we cannot assume that the objects are linearly separable and that parts of an object are not occluded by other parts of the same object. Thus, in the rest of this section, we examine the more general case, which must also account for intraobject visibility. We restrict ourselves to three-dimensional (i.e., polyhedra) objects, although, of course, the BSP tree can be applied to objects of arbitrary dimensionality. We assume that the partition of the underlying space is in terms of the object's faces, which are polygons (usually triangles as graphics hardware is optimized for displaying such polygons). Such partitions are called *autopartitions*. Although such autopartitions do not necessarily result in minimum-size BSP trees, they do produce reasonably sized ones.

Therefore, in our application domain, the underlying data consists of the polygonal faces $p_1, p_2, \ldots, p_n$ of a set of three-dimensional objects. The BSP tree is constructed by choosing an arbitrary polygonal face from this set, say p_k, and splitting the three-dimensional space along the plane in which p_k lies into two subsets, say $P_{k,L}$ and $P_{k,R}$. p_k is associated with the root of the tree.

$P_{k,L}$ and $P_{k,R}$ make up the two children of the root and correspond to the two halfspaces separated by this plane. We arbitrarily choose one of the sides of the polygonal face as the "front" side and say that $P_{k,L}$ corresponds to it, which means that $P_{k,R}$ corresponds to the "back" side. We associate $P_{k,L}$ and $P_{k,R}$ with the left and right subtrees, respectively, of the root. Thus, $P_{k,L}$ contains all polygonal faces that are in the left subtree, and $P_{k,R}$ contains all polygonal faces that are in the right subtree.

This decomposition process is applied recursively to $P_{k,L}$ and $P_{k,R}$ and terminates upon encountering empty sets.

Two items are worthy of further note. First, a polygonal face, say p_i, may be contained in both the left and right subtrees of a node in the BSP tree. Such a situation arises when p_i's plane intersects the plane of one of its ancestor nodes in the BSP tree. Second, the plane of a polygonal face is assumed to extend beyond the boundary of the polygon (i.e., it spans the entire underlying block). For example, the plane of the root's polygonal face partitions the entire scene. Moreover, for each subtree rooted at T, the polygonal face associated with T, say p_T, is extended so that p_T partitions the entire space of T.

One of the drawbacks of the BSP tree is that its shape is heavily dependent on the order in which the polygonal faces are processed and on the polygonal faces that are selected to serve as the partitioning planes. In the worst case, the BSP tree looks like a chain. Furthermore, the decomposition may be such that a polygonal face is contained in many subtrees. Such a situation arises in complex nonconvex scenes and will lead to large BSP trees. Nevertheless, it can be somewhat alleviated by choosing the root polygonal face more carefully at each stage of the BSP tree construction process.

For example, one heuristic is to choose the polygonal face, say M, in the set that splits the minimum number of the remaining polygonal faces in the set (see Exercise 5 for another approach). Fuchs, Abram, and Grant [657] have found that, in practice, there is no need to try out all possibilities to determine M. Instead, they follow a suggestion of Kedem [657] and just select a small subset of the polygonal faces at random, say S, to serve as candidates and then choose the polygonal face in S that splits the minimum number of the remaining polygonal faces in the set. In two dimensions, for n line segments, this method yields a BSP tree of expected size $O(n \log n)$ and can be constructed in $O(n^2)$ time [1475]. The execution time can be reduced to $O(n \log n)$ with the same size bound by using an approach that does not yield an autopartition [1475]. In three dimensions, for n polygonal faces that are triangles, the best-known method yields an autopartition BSP tree with expected size $O(n \log^2 n)$ and can be constructed in $O(n \log^3 n)$ time [18], although there exist sets of data for which the size is $\Omega(n^2)$ [1475]. Naylor observed that, in practice, three-dimensional BSP trees were usually of size $O(n \log n)$ [1353, 1354]. An analogous approach of avoiding a check of all possibilities was used by Samet [1618] in selecting a node to replace the deleted root of a point quadtree (see Section 1.4.1.2 of Chapter 1).

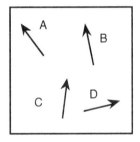

Figure 2.37
Example set of four line segments.

To illustrate the differences in the storage requirements of the BSP tree, we use a collection of line segments instead of polygonal faces because it is easier to visualize what is happening. Each line segment has a direction. We say that its "positive" side is the one to the right of the direction of the line segment. When the line segment is treated as a separator between two halfspaces, we say that the "positive" side is the one whose equation has the form $a \cdot x + b \cdot y + c \geq 0$, and the "negative" side is the one whose equation has the form $a \cdot x + b \cdot y + c < 0$.

For example, consider the four line segments labeled A, B, C, and D in Figure 2.37. Suppose that the BSP tree is constructed by letting B be the root. The positive subset consists of D, while the negative subset consists of A, C, and D. D appears in both subsets because D crosses B when it is extended and thereby serves as a separator between two halfspaces. Now, let us build the BSP tree for the negative subset. Letting C be the root, we find that A is in the negative subset, and D is in the positive subset. The resulting BSP tree is shown in Figure 2.38(a) and partitions the plane into six regions as shown in Figure 2.38(b).

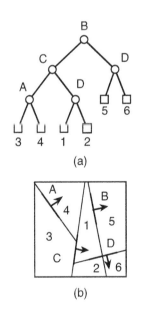

(a)

(b)

Figure 2.38
(a) The BSP tree corresponding to Figure 2.37 when B is the root and (b) the partition induced by it.

If, in the first step, we would have chosen C instead of B to be the root of the BSP tree, then the negative subset would consist of A, and the positive subset would consist of B and D. Now, let us build the BSP tree for the positive subset. Letting D be the root, we find that the positive subset is empty, and B is in the negative subset. The resulting BSP tree is

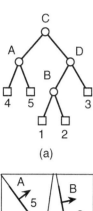

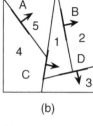

Figure 2.39
(a) The BSP tree corresponding to
Figure 2.37 when C is the root and
(b) the partition induced by it.

shown in Figure 2.39(a) and yields a partition of the plane into five regions as shown in Figure 2.39(b). Of course, there are many other BSP trees that can be constructed for this set of four line segments. For a discussion of what makes a good BSP tree, see [1353].

Using the BSP tree to determine visibility involves a traversal of the tree in an order that is determined by the position of the viewpoint, say V. Each node of the BSP tree partitions the relevant portion of the scene into two parts. They can be identified with respect to whether or not they contain V. In particular, for each node N in the BSP tree, let INCHILD(N, V) correspond to the child of N that contains V, and let OUTCHILD(N, V) correspond to the child that does not. There are two basic techniques.

The first technique assigns a visibility number to each polygon in the order in which it has been visited. This order depends on whether we are using a back-to-front or a front-to-back display algorithm. We shall assume a back-to-front algorithm. In such a case, the higher numbers correspond to a higher priority. They are assigned by traversing the BSP tree in such a way that, for a given node N, all the polygons in INCHILD(N, V) are given a lower number than N's polygon, and all the polygons in OUTCHILD(N, V) are given a higher number than N's polygon. It should be clear that this is nothing more than an inorder traversal with respect to the viewpoint. These priorities can be used by conventional hidden-surface elimination algorithms whenever a visibility determination must be made.

In fact, we do not even have to assign the visibility numbers. This observation forms the basis of the second technique which does not use the visibility numbers. Instead, the traversal is used to control a back-to-front (i.e., painter's) algorithm, which paints each polygon on the screen as it is encountered by the traversal. If one polygon overlaps another polygon, then the most recently painted polygon determines the color of the overlapped region. Given viewpoint V, BSP tree node N, and the previous definition of INCHILD and OUTCHILD, the polygons in OUTCHILD(N, V) are visited before the polygon in the root, which, in turn, is visited before the polygons in INCHILD(N, V). Correctness is assured since polygons that occlude other polygons are closer to the viewpoint and are visited later in the traversal.

Visibility orderings provide an alternative to the conventional use of the z-buffer algorithm for hidden-surface elimination. This algorithm is based on scan-converting the objects in the scene in an arbitrary order once the scene has been transformed so that the viewing direction is in the positive z direction. Scan-converting an object o determines which pixels in the projection are covered by o. These are the pixels where o is potentially visible. The z buffer algorithm makes use of a frame buffer and a z buffer to keep track of the objects that it has already processed. For each pixel, the frame buffer stores the intensity of the currently visible object among all of the objects that it has already processed, while the z buffer stores the corresponding z coordinate value. When a new object o is scan-converted, for each pixel p_o, the z value z_{p_o} of the corresponding point on the visible object is compared with the current z value z_p in the z buffer. If z_{p_o} is less than z_p, then o lies in front of the currently visible object in p, and the frame and z buffer values of pixel p are updated to reflect the fact that o is now the object visible at p.

The advantage of using a visibility ordering over the z buffer algorithm is that there is no need to compute or compare the z values. This is especially advantageous as this process can be subject to numerical errors. Moreover, it eliminates the need for space to store the z buffer, which can be substantial especially if used at subpixel resolution such as 4×4 in order to provide antialiasing.

BSP trees are used for a number of other applications besides visibility. For example, they have been used for set operations on polyhedra in solid modeling [1359, 1869], shadow generation [375], radiosity [302, 303], and beam tracing [436]. It has also been proposed to use the hierarchy of regions created by the partitioning process corresponding to the BSP tree as bounding volumes (e.g., [1357]) to speed up operations such as point location. The use of bounding volume hierarchies is described in much greater detail in Section 2.1.5.2.

Section 2.1
INTERIOR-BASED REPRESENTATIONS

Exercises

1. Write an algorithm to insert a line (polygonal face) into a BSP tree.

2. Write an algorithm to delete a line (polygonal face) from a BSP tree.

3. Suppose we define a predicate called CONFLICT(P_1,P_2) whose value is true if polygonal face P_1 intersects the halfspace of polygon P_2 and false otherwise. Is CONFLICT a symmetric relation? In other words, does CONFLICT$(P_1,P_2) =$ CONFLICT(P_2,P_1) always hold?

4. (David M. Mount) What is the physical interpretation when CONFLICT(P_1,P_2) and CONFLICT(P_2, P_1) are both true?

5. Fuchs, Kedem, and Naylor [658] suggest that the number of polygonal faces in a BSP tree for a given database of polyhedra can be reduced by choosing as the root node of each subtree that node which eliminates the maximum number of future splits. A future split exists between polygonal faces P_1 and P_2 if the value of CONFLICT(P_1,P_2) is true where CONFLICT is defined in Exercise 3. Write an algorithm to build a BSP tree that makes use of this method.

6. What is the minimum number of regions in the partition of a two- (three-) dimensional space that is induced by the BSP tree for n line segments (polygonal faces)?

7. Let us use the term *tessellation* to denote the partition of space induced by the construction of the BSP tree. Under what conditions is the tessellation independent of the order in which the BSP tree is built?

8. Suppose that the tessellation is independent of the order in which the BSP tree is built. What is the maximum number of polygons (polyhedra) that can be generated by n line segments (polygonal faces) in a two- (three-) dimensional space?

9. The BSP tree can be used to determine visibility by traversing the tree in an order that is determined by the position of the viewpoint, say V. Recall that each node of the BSP tree partitions the relevant portion of the scene into two parts. They can be identified with respect to whether they contain V. In particular, for each node N in the BSP tree, let INCHILD(N,V) correspond to the child of N that contains V, and let OUTCHILD(N,V) correspond to the child that does not. Give an algorithm that makes use of this idea to determine visibility from V when the scene is represented by a BSP tree.

2.1.3.2 K-Structure

The K-structure of Kirkpatrick [1026] is a hierarchical representation based on triangulation rather than a regular decomposition. It is not built directly from the list of line segments in a polygonal map, but, instead, it is built from a triangulation of the map. Briefly, a triangulation of a set of n points is a maximal subset of the $n \cdot (n-1)/2$ possible edges so that no edge crosses any other edge. Of course, there are many possible triangulations for a given set of points, and there are many methods of obtaining the triangulations (e.g., [1511]). It is important to note the distinction between a triangulation and the method of obtaining it. All of the triangulations contain the edges of the convex hull[11] of the points as the triangulations are maximal, and thus these edges could not have been eliminated by virtue of crossing any of the edges in the triangulation.

The notion of hierarchy in the K-structure is radically different from that of a quadtree: instead of replacing a group of triangles by a single triangle at the next higher level, a group of triangles is replaced by a smaller group of triangles. There is no proper

---

[11] A set is S *convex* if the presence of points x in S and y in S implies that the closed line segment xy is contained within S. The *convex hull* of a set S is the smallest convex set that contains S. An intuitive explanation is that the convex hull is equivalent to the set that is obtained by snapping a rubber band around a set of nails driven through the points of the set.

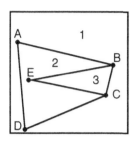

Figure 2.40
Sample polygonal map.

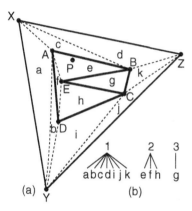

Figure 2.41
The first step in building the K-structure corresponding to Figure 2.40: (a) the result of the initial triangulation (newly introduced edges are shown by broken lines), and (b) the relationship between the triangles of (a) and the regions of Figure 2.40.

subset relationship between triangles at successive levels. In particular, a triangle at level i can be spanned by more than one triangle at level $i + 1$.

Triangles are grouped for replacement because they share a common vertex. The smaller group results from eliminating the common vertex and then retriangulating. This principle also forms the basis of one class of simplification methods for reducing the complexity of scenes for ease of display and other processes in computer graphics and visualization applications (see Section 2.2.3.4). At each level of the hierarchy, at least 1/24 of the vertices can be eliminated in this manner. Thus, the K-structure for a polygonal map of v vertices uses $O(v)$ space, and point location can be determined in $O(\log_2 v)$ time. Constructing a K-structure has a worst-case execution time of $O(v)$ for a triangular subdivision and $O(v \cdot \log_2 v)$ for a general one. The latter is dominated by the cost of triangulating the original polygonal map [834]. Below, we discuss the K-structure in greater detail, as well as illustrate how a K-structure is built for the polygonal map of Figure 2.40.

A K-structure is built by first enclosing the map with a bounding triangle anchored at points X, Y, and Z as shown in Figure 2.41(a). Next, we perform a plane-sweep triangulation by using the method of Hertel and Mehlhorn [834]. To do this, we assume that the vertices have been sorted in increasing order of their x coordinate values. Triangulation is achieved by sweeping (i.e., moving) a vertical line of infinite length from left to right along the x axis. Each time a vertex is encountered, edges are drawn from the vertex to all "visible" vertices to its left. Vertex V_2 is said to be *visible* from vertex V_1 if an edge can be drawn from V_1 to V_2 without intersecting an existing edge.

For the polygonal map of Figure 2.40, containing regions 1, 2, and 3, the vertices are processed in order X, Y, A, D, E, C, B, and Z. Processing vertex A results in creating edges AX and AY; D in DY; E in EA and ED; C in CY; B in BX; and Z in BZ and CZ. Figure 2.41(a) contains the outcome of the triangulation. The new edges are represented by broken lines. Region 1 consists of triangles a, b, C, d, i, j, and k; region 2 consists of triangles e, f, and h; and region 3 consists of triangle g. These inclusion relationships are shown in Figure 2.41(b).

Triangulating a polygonal map of v vertices has a worst-case execution time of $O(v \cdot \log_2 v)$. This is obtained in the following manner. Sorting the x coordinate values of the v vertices is $O(v \cdot \log_2 v)$. Sweeping the vertical line is $O(v)$. In addition, a $\log_2 v$ factor is contributed by the visibility computation at each vertex.

Before proceeding further, let us define some terms used in the construction of the K-structure, as well as in the analysis of its space and time requirements. A *K-vertex* is a vertex that has a degree of 11 or less. We can establish that at least half of the vertices are K-vertices in the following manner. According to a corollary of Euler's formula [801], any planar graph of v vertices (including a polygonal map) contains at most $3 \cdot v - 6$ edges. Since each edge contributes one edge to the degree of two vertices, the average degree of a vertex is ≤ 6. Therefore, at least half of the vertices have a degree of 11 or less and hence are K-vertices.

Two vertices are said to be *independent* if there is no edge connecting them. Each K-vertex is adjacent to, at most, 11 other K-vertices. Given a triangulated map with v_k K-vertices, at the minimum there is a partition into $v_k/12 \geq v/24$ sets of vertices, each of which has a representative K-vertex. These representative K-vertices are mutually independent.

The *neighborhood of a K-vertex* is defined as the polygon formed by the union of the triangles incident at the K-vertex. Since there are, at most, 11 such triangles for a given K-vertex, the polygon from the K-vertex's neighborhood has no more than 11 sides.

We are now ready to build the K-structure. Starting at a level corresponding to the result of the initial triangulation step, the next level of the K-structure is built in $O(v)$ time in the following manner. First, find a set S of mutually independent K-vertices. This can be done in $O(v)$ time from an edge-adjacency list of the map. Second, for each of the neighborhoods of an element of the set S, perform the following reduction: remove the K-vertex from the neighborhood, and retriangulate its polygon. Thus, the triangles of the neighborhood will be linked with a smaller collection of triangles that spans the same region. The remaining levels of the K-structure are formed from an iterative performance of the building procedure until a level is reached that contains a single triangle.

At each level, the cost of building the K-structure is proportional to the number of vertices at that level. Since each level of the K-structure contains at most 23/24 of the number of vertices that the previous level held, the total number of vertices processed in the construction is at most $24 \cdot v$. Furthermore, as each of the K-vertices is guaranteed to be of degree 11 or less, the cost of retriangulating any polygon is bounded. Thus, the K-structure can be built in $O(v)$ time. The number of levels in the K-structure is $O(\log_2 v)$.

Returning to our example, after the initial triangulation, we must identify the maximal subset of mutually independent K-vertices, remove them and their incident edges, and retriangulate. In Figure 2.41(a), we have several choices. We choose vertices B and D. Removing B and D and their incident edges leaves us with polygons XAYX, AECYA, XAECZX, and YCZY, which we label ε, δ, α, and β, respectively. Next, we retriangulate these polygons individually and obtain Figure 2.42(a). Polygons ε and β remain unchanged; polygon α consists of triangles α_1, α_2, and α_3; and polygon δ consists of triangles δ_1 and δ_2. These relationships are shown in Figure 2.42(b). The edges that were introduced during the retriangulation are represented by broken lines in Figure 2.42(a).

We now have seven triangles and must choose one of vertices A, E, and C as the independent K-vertex. We choose vertex A, and after removing it and its incident edges, we are left with polygons XYECX, XCZX, ECYE, and YCZY, which we label t, u, v, and w, respectively. After retriangulating the polygons individually, we obtain Figure 2.43(a), with broken lines corresponding to the added edges. Polygons u, v, and w remain unchanged, while polygon t consists of triangles t_1 and t_2. These relationships are shown in Figure 2.43(b).

Reapplying the algorithm to the five remaining triangles, we select vertex C as the independent K-vertex and remove it and its incident edges. The remaining polygons are XEYX and XEYZX, which we label q and r, respectively. Only polygon r needs to be retriangulated, resulting in triangles r_1 and r_2 as shown in Figure 2.44, with broken lines corresponding to the added edges. We now apply the algorithm for the final time to the three remaining triangles. Removing vertex E and its incident edges leaves us with a single triangle XYZX, which we label s as shown in Figure 2.45.

In general, the dynamic insertion of an edge into a K-structure takes $O(v)$ time in the worst case. This poor worst-case performance follows from the fact that the triangulation must be updated. The newly inserted edge could intersect $O(v)$ edges in the existing triangulation. For example, if the edge between vertices A and B is inserted into the triangulation of the polygon of Figure 2.46(a) (shown in Figure 2.46(b)), which has $2 \cdot v + 2$ vertices, then the new edge will intersect $2 \cdot v - 1$ edges in the triangulation. Updating the triangulation requires, at an absolute minimum, either the addition of a new vertex or the deletion of the old edge for each intersection of the new edge and an old edge. Hence $O(v)$ operations may be required.

On the other hand, the K-structure can always be updated in $O(v)$ time. To see this, observe that the triangulation can be updated by (1) removing all edges that intersect the new edge, (2) inserting the new edge, and (3) retriangulating the two polygonal regions on either side of the new edge. Step 1 takes $O(v)$ time, and step 2 takes $O(1)$ time. Step 3 can also be done in $O(v)$ time. This is because the two polygons that must be triangulated are *weakly edge visible* from the new edge (i.e., each point in the region is visible from some point on the edge), and polygons with this property can be triangulated in linear time. Once the triangulation is updated, the K-structure can be completely rebuilt in $O(v)$ time, as described earlier.

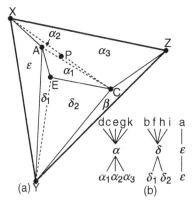

Figure 2.42
The second step in building the K-structure corresponding to Figure 2.40: (a) the result of retriangulating Figure 2.41 once vertices B and D and their incident edges have been removed (newly introduced edges are shown by broken lines), and (b) the relationship between the polygons resulting from (a) and the triangles of Figure 2.41.

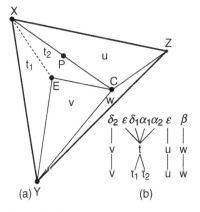

Figure 2.43
The third step in building the K-structure corresponding to Figure 2.40: (a) the result of retriangulating Figure 2.42 once vertex A and its incident edges have been removed (newly introduced edges are shown by broken lines), and (b) the relationship between the polygons resulting from (a) and the triangles of Figure 2.42.

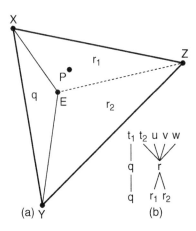

Figure 2.44
The fourth step in building the K-structure corresponding to Figure 2.40: (a) the result of retriangulating Figure 2.43 once vertex C and its incident edges have been removed (newly introduced edges are shown by broken lines), and (b) the relationship between the polygons resulting from (a) and the triangles of Figure 2.43.

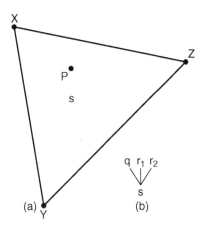

Figure 2.45
The final step in building the K-structure corresponding to Figure 2.40: (a) the result of retriangulating Figure 2.44 once vertex E and its incident edges have been removed, and (b) the relationship between the polygons resulting from (a) and the triangles of Figure 2.44.

Point location using the K-structure is relatively straightforward. In essence, at each level, the algorithm must determine the relevant triangle that contains the point. The key is that the comparison is made with at most 11 triangles. These 11 triangles form the neighborhood that contains the triangle in which the point was found at the previous level. Thus, since the number of levels is $O(\log_2 v)$, point location is solved in $O(\log_2 v)$ time.

As an example, suppose we wish to determine the region in the polygonal map of Figure 2.40 in which point P is located. Rather than give the values of the x and y coordinates of P, we have indicated its location by appropriately marking it in part (a) of Figures 2.41 to 2.45. Our explanation is facilitated by making use of part (b) of these figures.

Initially, we start with the triangle of Figure 2.45 and determine that P lies in triangle r_1. Moving down a level, we find r_1 in polygon r of Figure 2.44. Searching for P in r, we find that it lies in triangle t_2. Moving down a level, we find t_2 in polygon t of Figure 2.43. Searching for P in t we find that it lies in triangle α_2. Moving down a level, we find α_2 in polygon α of Figure 2.42. Searching for P in α, we find that it lies in triangle e. Moving down a level, we find e in region 2 of Figure 2.41, and we are done.

Exercises

1. Prove that a triangular subdivision on $v \geq 3$ vertices, such that each region (including the bounding region) is bounded by three line segments, has exactly $3 \cdot v - 6$ edges and $2 \cdot v - 4$ regions (including the bounding region).

2. Consider the more general case of an arbitrary triangulation with v vertices so that the convex hull of the triangulation has c vertices. Prove that the triangulation has $3 \cdot v - c - 3$ edges and $2 \cdot v - c - 2$ regions (i.e., triangles).

3. Prove that a convex polygon containing v vertices can be triangulated in $O(v)$ time.

4. Devise a data structure that enables the "visibility" computation of Hertel and Mehlhorn's triangulation method [834] to be performed in $O(\log_2 v)$ time.

5. There are many triangulation methods in use aside from the plane-sweep method of Hertel and Mehlhorn [834]. One such algorithm is known as the greedy method [1511]. Assume an arbitrary point set in the plane. The greedy method works by adding the edges in increasing order of length. It excludes an edge if a shorter edge intersects it. Prove that for v vertices and with appropriate data structures, the greedy method can be executed in $O(v^2 \log v)$ time.

6. The plane-sweep and greedy triangulations are defined by the algorithms used to obtain them. There also exist triangulations that are defined by specific optimization criteria on the resulting edges and triangles that they form. One example of such a ctierion is the "minimum-weight"triangulation (MWT) (e.g., [808]), which yields a triangulation with the smallest total edge length. For a point set in the plane, the problem of whether the minimum-weight triangulation can be computed in polynomial time is open, although it can be done in exponential time by brute-force methods. For a simple polygon (i.e., a polygon with nonintersecting edges and without holes), the minimum-weight triangulation can be obtained in polynomial time by using dynamic programming (e.g., [836]) as exemplified by the following algorithm. The key

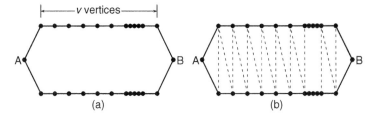

Figure 2.46
(a) A polygonal map and (b) its triangulation (broken lines correspond to the edges added by the triangulation).

idea is that given v vertices, for each edge e of the $O(v^2)$ possible edges, we assume that e is in the minimum-weight triangulation, and then determine the two vertices out of the $O(v)$ possible vertices that form the two triangles of the minimum-weight triangulation in which e participates. The algorithm is as follows:

- Let polygon Q have v vertices $p_1 p_2 \ldots p_v p_1$ appearing in successive order.

- Let $e_{i,j}$ denote an edge from p_i to p_j.

- Let $t_{i,j}$ be the MWT of the polygon with vertices $p_i p_{i+1} \ldots p_j p_i$, and let $w_{i,j}$ be its total edge length.

  (a) If edge $e_{i,j}$ is not a legal edge of the triangulation of Q (i.e., some part of it lies outside Q), then t_{ij} is undefined, and $w_{i,j} = \infty$.

  (b) If edge $e_{i,j}$ is a legal edge of the triangulation of Q, then there exists a vertex p_k in $t_{i,j}$ such that $p_i p_j p_k$ forms a triangle.

   i. p_k is found by solving $\min\{w_{i,k} + w_{k,j} \mid i < k < j\}$, and

   ii. $w_{i,j} = w_{i,k} + w_{k,j} + \text{length}(p_{i,j})$.

- Compute all $t_{i,j}$ and $w_{i,j}$ using dynamic programming. This is done with the aid of a pair of two-dimensional arrays t and w. Entry $t_{i,j}$ has value k, indicating the third vertex p_k of a triangle whose remaining vertices are p_i and p_j. Entry $w_{i,j}$ is the total edge length of the triangulation of the simple polygon with vertices in order $p_i p_{i+1} \ldots p_j p_i$.

- The MWT of Q is $t_{1,v}$, and this is the starting point for the application of steps 1 and 2, which are applied recursively.

The actual algorithm is executed by constructing array w (and simultaneously t) in order of increasing distances between the vertices corresponding to the indices of the array. In particular, we start with $w_{i,i+1} = \text{length}(p_{i,i+1})$ for all vertices i in increasing order. Next, we compute $w_{i,i+2} w_{i,i+3} \ldots w_{i,i+j} \ldots w_{i,i+v-1}$. For each value of j ($1 \leq j \leq v-1$), we vary i from 1 to $v - j$. Show that the MWT algorithm described above takes $O(v^3)$ time for a simple polygon.

7. Compare the approach described in Exercise 6 with one adapted from a suggestion of Posdamer [1504] that is based on sorting the vertices using a multidimensional point representation, such as a PR quadtree, and use a proximity criterion based on vertices being in the same block or in an adjacent block to determine which vertices should be connected to form an edge. This technique was originally developed for points in a three-dimensional space and, in fact, Posdamer [1504] suggests using a variant of a bucket PR octree where each block contains no more than three vertices.

8. An alternative triangulation, which is defined by specific optimization criteria on the resulting edges and triangles that they form, is the Delaunay triangulation (described in greater detail in Section 2.2.1.4). Briefly, the Delaunay triangulation has many useful properties. It is particularly attractive as the triangles are as close as possible to being equiangular, and thus it is good for interpolation of a surface (as discussed in Section 2.2.4). There are several algorithms to compute a Delaunay triangulation. They differ in part on the basis of the properties of the Delaunay triangulation that they exploit. We describe a pair of algorithms in Exercises 2 and 3 in Section 2.2.1.4 that make use of the property that none of the points in the point set being triangulated is in the circumcircles of any other triangle in the Delaunay triangulation (known as the *circle property*). Discuss how the Delaunay triangulation, as well as the greedy triangulation, method and the minimum-weight triangulation (MWT) described in Exercises 5 and 6, respectively, would be used in conjunction with the K-structure construction algorithm. Is any one of these triangulations superior to the others? How do they compare with the triangulation resulting from use of the plane-sweep method of Hertel and Mehlhorn? For a more thorough discussion of triangulations and triangulation methods, see [1597, 1965].

9. Give an $O(v)$ time algorithm and $O(v)$ space data structure to find a set S of mutually independent K-vertices given v vertices in the polygonal map.

10. Prove that for each independent K-vertex that has been removed in the construction of the K-structure, the number of triangles in the subsequent retriangulation has been reduced by two.

11. Write a procedure to do point location in a polygonal map that is represented by a K-structure.

12. The map overlay problem is related to the point location query, and its solution involves many of the issues discussed in this section and Section 2.1.3.3. In this case, you are given two

polygonal maps, and you are to overlay one of them on top of the other. This problem can be viewed as a generalization of the process of dynamic edge insertion: instead of inserting a single edge, you are now inserting a collection of edges (which happens already to be organized as a polygonal map). The goal is to achieve this in a manner that is more efficient than performing a sequence of dynamic line insertions. Write a set of procedures that will perform map overlay for the K-structure,

2.1.3.3 Separating Chain

The separating chain of Lee and Preparata [1128] is an alternative to the K-structure. Like the K-structure, the separating chain method also yields a hierarchical structure; however, this time, instead of using a hierarchy of triangulations, a hierarchy of "above-and-below" partitions consisting of groups of regions is used. In fact, the separating chain was developed before the K-structure. However, the execution time complexity of the access structure for the elements of each separating chain in the hierarchy used in the original formulation (i.e., a sorted list) was not as good as that of the K-structure. The layered dag of Edelsbrunner, Guibas, and Stolfi [541] provides an alternative access structure for the elements of each separating chain in the hierarchy so that the space requirements and time complexity of point location and structure building are the same as those for the K-structure. However, the constants of proportionality are smaller for the separating chain hierarchy when implemented with a layered dag than for the K-structure.

This section is organized as follows. We first outline the principles underlying the separating chain method, then show how it can be used to do point location when each separating chain in the hierarchy is implemented as a sorted list (Section 2.1.3.3.1). Next, we show how the separating chain solution to the point location query can be improved by using a layered dag access structure (Section 2.1.3.3.2) for the elements of each separating chain in the hierarchy. Unlike for the K-structure, our analyses of the orders of execution times and space requirements of solutions that make use of the separating chain are in terms of the number of edges, say m, in the polygonal map instead of the number of vertices, say v. However, by Euler's formula [801], for $v \geq 3$, we have that $m \leq 3 \cdot v - 6$, and thus the two quantities are of the same order of magnitude.

2.1.3.3.1 Overview

A polygonal map is said to be a *y-monotone subdivision* if no vertical line can intersect a region's boundary more than twice. Alternatively, the polygonal map is a *y*-monotone subdivision if every vertex of the map has at least one edge to its left and one edge to its right (see Exercise 1). For example, the polygonal map of Figure 2.47(a) is not a *y*-monotone subdivision because vertices J, L, and M have no edges to their right, and vertices A, B, and D have no edges to their left. This map has three regions labeled 1, 2, and 3. A vertical line through edges CE, DE, and DG crosses the boundary of region 1 three times. A *y*-monotone subdivision ensures that the "immediately above" relation is acyclic; that is, region 1 can either be below region 2 or above it, but it cannot be both below and above the same region.

A polygonal map is made into a *y*-monotone subdivision by a process termed *regularization*, which inserts additional edges, as well as two vertices at the extreme left and right of the polygonal map. For example, the broken lines in Figure 2.47(b) are the result of regularizing the polygonal map of Figure 2.47(a). It has eight regions, labeled 0–7; two additional vertices, α and δ, at the extreme left and right, respectively, of the map; and the new edges αA, αB, CD, JK, Lδ, and Mδ.

Of course, any triangulation can be used as the basis of a *y*-monotone subdivision, but, usually, regularization requires considerably fewer edges to be inserted than a triangulation (compare Figures 2.41 and 2.48, which are the results of triangulating and regularizing, respectively, the polygonal map of Figure 2.40). However, like triangulation, regularization of a polygonal map of m edges is performed by a plane-sweep

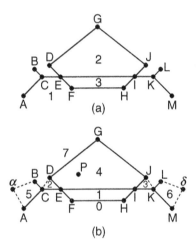

Figure 2.47
(a) Example polygonal map illustrating the use of separating chains and (b) the result of regularizing (a) with newly introduced edges represented by broken lines.

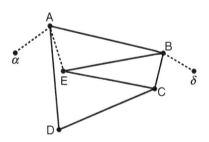

Figure 2.48
The result of regularizing the polygonal map of Figure 2.40. Newly introduced edges are shown by broken lines.

algorithm in $O(m \cdot \log_2 m)$ time. These definitions imply that the polygonal map has no vertical edges. However, this restriction is primarily a technical one and can be removed by the adoption of appropriate conventions (see Exercise 6).

As the polygonal map is regularized, the identity of each region immediately above and below each edge, say e, is stored with the edge using the fields ABOVE(e) and BELOW(e). In addition, a list is created of the vertices and edges of the regularized polygonal map in increasing order of x coordinate values. Once the polygonal map has been regularized, the regions are topologically sorted so that they are ordered according to an "above" relation.

Formally, given regions r_1 and r_2, r_1 is *above* r_2 (i.e., $r_1 \geq r_2$) if for every vertically aligned pair of points, (x, y_1) in r_1 and (x, y_2) in r_2, $y_1 \geq y_2$, and there is at least one pair where a strict inequality holds. It can be shown that the "above" relation is acyclic: it yields a partial ordering (see Exercise 8). For example, applying topological sort to the polygonal map of Figure 2.47(b) yields the regions in the order 0, 1, 2, 3, 4, 5, 6, and 7. The topological sort is performed by using the contents of the ABOVE field of each edge. Since there are m edges, this process takes $O(m)$ time [1044].

Assuming that there are n regions, let the result of the topological sort be a list of the regions in the order $R_0, R_1, \ldots, R_{n-1}$ such that $R_i \leq R_j$ implies that $i < j$. From this list we construct a complete binary tree for n regions, termed a *region tree*, such that the regions R_i appear as leaf nodes. The nonleaf nodes are labeled $S_1, S_2, \ldots, S_{n-1}$ so that an inorder traversal of the tree yields the nodes in the order $R_0, S_1, R_1, S_2, \ldots, S_{n-1}, R_{n-1}$. For example, Figure 2.49 shows such a tree for the eight regions of Figure 2.47(b).

A nonleaf node in the region tree is termed a *separator*. The separators correspond to polygonal lines of infinite length. These lines consist of edges of the y-monotone subdivision such that each polygonal line intersects every vertical line at exactly one point. In particular, each separator S_k serves as the boundary between regions R_i and R_j such that $i < k$ and $j \geq k$. In other words, a vertex or edge e belongs to S_k if and only if it is on the border of two regions, R_i and R_j, with $i < k \leq j$. It can be shown that the regions and separators satisfy the less than or equal ($\leq$) relation in such a way that $R_0 \leq S_1 \leq R_1 \leq S_2 \leq \ldots S_{n-1} \leq R_{n-1}$ (see Exercise 10). A consequence of this ordering is that if, for a given edge e, $R_i = $ BELOW(e) and $R_j = $ ABOVE(e), then edge e is contained in separators $S_{i+1}, S_{i+2}, \ldots, S_j$ and in no other separators (see Exercise 11). This result is referred to as the *edge-ordering property*.

The list of vertices making up a separator is termed a *separating chain*, and when no confusion is possible, the term *chain* is used to refer to it. For example, Figure 2.50 shows the result of labeling the nonleaf nodes of the region tree of Figure 2.49 with their chains. When the region tree is labeled in such a way, we shall call it a *chain tree*. The tree is rooted at the chain αACDEIJKMδ, which separates regions R_0–R_3 (i.e., 0, 1, 2, 3)

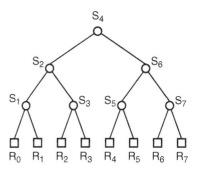

Figure 2.49
The region tree corresponding to the polygonal map of Figure 2.47. Region R_i corresponds to the region labeled with i.

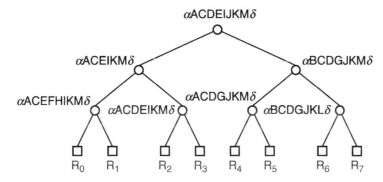

Figure 2.50
The chain tree resulting from labeling the internal nodes of the region tree of Figure 2.49 with their chains.

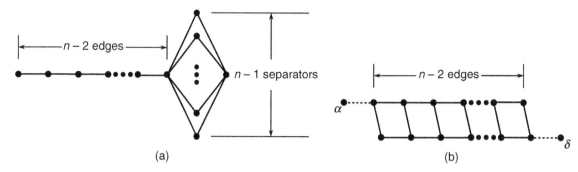

Figure 2.51
Example polygonal maps for which the length of each separator is n.

and regions R_4–R_7 (i.e., 4, 5, 6, and 7). The left child of the root is αACEIKMδ, which separates regions R_0 and R_1 (i.e., 0 and 1) from regions R_2–R_7 (i.e., 2, 3, 4, 5, 6, and 7).

Constructing the separators is a relatively straightforward process. To do this in an efficient manner, let us assume that the n regions are stored in a table, say R, indexed from 0 to $n-1$. Moreover, the ABOVE and BELOW information associated with each edge is the index of the region's entry in R. As an example, for the polygonal map of Figure 2.47(b), we have table R such that index 0 corresponds to region 0, 1 to region 1, ..., i to region i, and so forth. Therefore, for edge EI we find that ABOVE(EI) = 4 and BELOW(EI) = 1.

The construction process makes use of the property that the output of the regularization process is a list of the vertices and edges of the regularized polygonal map in order of increasing x coordinate values. This list is processed in order, and as each edge, say e, is visited, we obtain the values of the indices of the regions below it— that is, $i = \text{BELOW}(e)$ and $j = \text{ABOVE}(e)$, and then append e to each separator S_k such that $i < k \leq j$. The correctness of this process follows from the edge-ordering property. Therefore, we have shown that for a polygonal map with m edges, the separators can be constructed in $O(m)$ time.

The execution time of the separator construction process described above is somewhat misleading as it is heavily influenced by the manner in which the separators are represented. If each separator is represented as an array of all of the vertices and edges contained in it, then the storage requirements are quite high as some of the edges may appear in all but a small number of the separators. In particular, assuming n regions (i.e., $n-1$ separators), the average length of a separator can be as large as $O(n)$ for some classes of subdivisions (e.g., Figure 2.51). This would result in an $O(n^2)$ storage requirement, and the time to build the structure of separators would also be $O(n^2)$. The same example also shows that the storage requirements can be as high as $O(m^2)$.

The storage requirements can be reduced in applications such as point location by noting that when an edge is common to several separators, it is sufficient just to store it with the first separator, say S, that is encountered in a search down the chain tree (i.e., in a preorder traversal).[12] Assume the numbering convention for regions and separators discussed above and that edge e lies between regions R_a and R_b such that BELOW(e) = a and ABOVE(e) = b. In this case, S is the least (or nearest) common ancestor of a and b, and it is denoted by $lca(a,b)$. Using the edge-ordering property, it can be shown that any separator that contains e will be a descendant of the least common ancestor of a and b (see Exercise 12).

---

[12] The principle of associating key information with the nearest common ancestor has also been used by Edelsbrunner [534, 537, 538] as the basis of the interval tree to yield an efficient solution of the rectangle intersection problem (see Section 3.1.2 of Chapter 3).

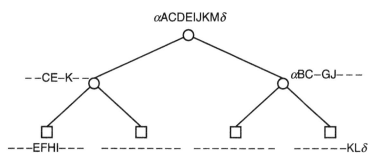

Figure 2.52
The gap tree corresponding to the chain tree of Figure 2.50.

The result of such a storage scheme for separators is that each edge needs to be stored only once in the chain tree, and thus a separator node need not contain all of the edges in its corresponding separating chain. This leads to the occurrence of breaks in the separating chain. These breaks are called *gaps*. We shall use the term *gap tree* to describe the variant of the chain tree that results from these economies.

Figure 2.52 shows the gap tree corresponding to Figure 2.50. Each nonleaf node is labeled with the edges that it contains by listing their vertices. A hyphen indicates the absence of an edge between a pair of vertices (i.e., a gap). Note that gaps may also arise at the extreme ends of a chain (e.g., there is a gap at the extreme left and right of the left child of the root in Figure 2.52).

The gap tree uses $O(m)$ space. Building a gap tree for the chain tree is done in the same way as before except that each edge needs to be inserted only once (i.e., in the separator of the least common ancestor). Insertion of an edge requires the ability to compute the index of the region corresponding to the least common ancestor of the regions adjacent to the edge. For a polygonal map of n regions, this process can take as much as $O(\log_2 n)$ time. However, it can be computed in $O(1)$ time by using bit manipulation techniques [541].

In such a case, a table of n values consisting of the values of the most significant bit in the binary representation of each of the indices from 0 to $n - 1$ is precomputed, and then the least common ancestor is computed by table lookup methods. This technique uses $O(n)$ space for the table (see Exercise 13). An alternative technique does not require additional storage but, instead, uses the reversal of the bit representation of the indices of the adjacent regions (see Exercise 14). This method takes $O(\log_2 n)$ time since the bits are reversed. Of course, the reverse function can also be precomputed and then accessed by use of table lookup techniques. This yields an $O(1)$ algorithm.

Now, let us consider the dynamic insertion of an edge into a polygonal map that is represented by a hierarchy of separating chains as in the gap tree. Let E denote the set of the edges introduced by the application of regularization to the original polygonal map. Addition of e may cause $O(v)$ new vertices to be added by virtue of the intersection of e with the set E. This means that the size of the gap tree (i.e., number of regions) will be dominated by the side effects of the regularization process. To avoid this situation, we must reapply the regularization step to the $O(v)$ vertices from which the intersected members of E emanated. In this special case, this process uses $O(v)$ space and time since the vertices are already sorted (see Exercise 16).

For example, consider the map of Figure 2.53(a), which consists of $4 \cdot v + 4$ vertices and resembles a collection of v toothlike objects. Figure 2.53(b) is the result of one way of regularizing this map where the added edges ($2 \cdot v$ of them) are shown with broken lines. In particular, we add edges to the left from vertices a_i to b_i ($1 \le i \le v$), edges to the right from a_i to b_{i+1} ($1 \le i < v$), and an edge from b_1 to A. Inserting an edge between vertices A and B into the original map intersects all of the edges that were added by the regularization. Thus, the nature of the $2 \cdot v$ vertices a_i and b_i requires that the map be regularized again since they must have edges to their right and left.

Point location in the gap tree is achieved by an algorithm that uses two levels of binary search. At each level of the tree, the entire relevant separating chain is searched for an edge or vertex whose projection on the x axis contains the x coordinate value of the query point. The individual separating chains are sorted by the x coordinate value of the leftmost vertices of their constituent edges. The gaps are not stored in the separating chains.

Initially, we search for an edge that partitions the set of regions bounded by R_0 at the bottom and R_{n-1} at the top. Let a and b designate the indices of the regions corresponding to the lower and upper boundaries, respectively, of the search space. The search starts at the separating chain stored at the root of the gap tree (i.e., $S_{lca(0,n-1)}$) with $a = 0$ and $b = n - 1$. Having found the appropriate edge, say e, we determine at which node of the gap tree to continue our search by examining the value of the y coordinate of the query point.

If the query point lies below e, then the search is resumed in the regions bounded by R_a and $R_{\text{BELOW}(e)}$. If it lies above e, then the search is resumed in the regions bounded by $R_{\text{ABOVE}(e)}$ and R_b. In either case, one of a and b is reset. If the query point lies on the edge, then the search ceases, and we say that the point lies in region $R_{\text{ABOVE}(e)}$. The actual node of the gap tree at which the search is resumed is equal to S_l, where l is the least common ancestor of a and b (i.e., $S_{lca(a,b)}$). We know that S_l is the separator that will contain the edge separating these regions by virtue of the way in which the gap tree was constructed (and by the edge-ordering property).

For example, to locate point P in the polygonal map of Figure 2.47(b), we search for it using Figure 2.52. We first examine the root that corresponds to the separator αACDEIJKMδ and find that it lies above edge EI. The search will continue in the separating chain stored in $S_{lca(\text{ABOVE}(EI),7)} = S_{lca(4,7)} = S_6$, which is αBC$--DGJ--$ (recall that the hyphens denote gaps). Repeating the search for P, we determine that it lies below edge DG. We are now through since $S_{lca(4,\text{BELOW}(DG))} = S_{lca(4,4)}$, which is region 4.

Although in this example we performed a test at successive levels of the gap tree, this need not be the case always. Many times, $S_{lca(a,b)}$ may be several levels down in the tree. To see this, let us try to locate point Q in the polygonal map of Figure 2.47(b). Again, we first examine the separator αACDEIJKMδ in the root of its gap tree in Figure 2.52. We find that Q lies below edge EI, and now $S_{lca(0,\text{BELOW}(EI))} = S_{lca(0,1)} = S_1$, which means that we have skipped a level.

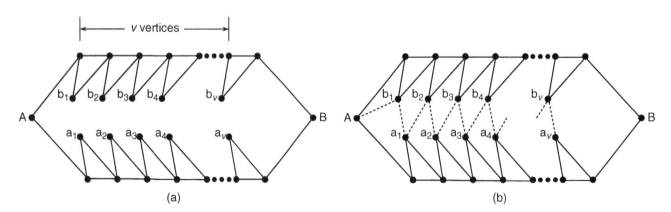

Figure 2.53
(a) A polygonal map and (b) its regularization (broken lines correspond to the edges added by the regularization).

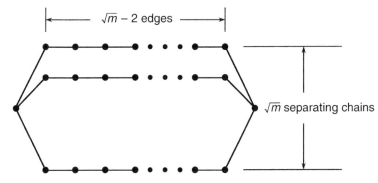

Figure 2.54
Example polygonal map for which point location using the gap tree requires $O(\log_2^2 m)$ time.

In the worst case, point location in the gap tree requires that we examine each separating chain on the path from the root of the tree to the desired region. Worse, we may also have to search each of these nodes in their entirety. For a regularized polygonal map with n regions and m edges, the binary search of each separating chain can be achieved in $O(\log_2 m)$ time. This assumes that the edges are sorted by the x coordinate value of their left vertex. Since the gap tree has $O(\log_2 n)$ levels, $O(\log_2 n)$ separating chains must be searched. Therefore, point location takes $O(\log_2 n \cdot \log_2 m) = O(\log_2^2 m)$ time. This bound is attainable as can be seen by constructing an example such as Figure 2.54, which has $\sqrt{m}$ separating chains (i.e., $\sqrt{m} + 1$ regions) where each chain contains $\sqrt{m}$ edges.

Exercises

1. Prove that defining a y-monotone subdivision in terms of not permitting a vertical line to cross a region's boundary more than twice is equivalent to requiring that each vertex have at least one edge to each of its right and left sides.

2. Does adding a new edge to a regularized polygonal map always preserve y-monotonicity?

3. Is the overlay of two y-monotone subdivisions always a y-monotone subdivision?

4. Prove that regularizing a polygonal map of m edges results in a y-monotone subdivision of $\leq 2 \cdot m$ edges.

5. Give an algorithm and data structure to regularize a polygonal map.

6. Discuss how the separating chain method can be modified to handle polygonal maps with vertical edges.

7. Can you devise an algorithm to perform regularization in time faster than $O(m \cdot \log_2 m)$?

8. Prove that the "above" relation is acyclic.

9. Is the following statement correct? If not, give a counterexample. For each separator in a chain tree, S_k, there exists at least one edge e in S_k such that for a vertical line passing through e at (x_e, y_e), all points (x_e, y) with $y \leq y_e$ are in the regions in the left subtree while those with $y > y_e$ are in the regions in the right subtree.

10. Assume a y-monotone subdivision such that $R_0 \leq R_1 \leq \cdots R_{n-1}$. Prove that $R_0 \leq S_1 \leq R_1 \leq S_2 \leq \cdots S_{n-1} \leq R_{n-1}$.

11. Assume a y-monotone subdivision such that $R_0 \leq R_1 \leq \cdots R_{n-1}$. Prove the edge-ordering property, which stipulates that if for a given edge e, $R_i = \text{BELOW}(e)$ and $R_j = \text{ABOVE}(e)$, then edge e is contained in separators $S_{i+1}, S_{i+2}, \ldots, S_j$ and in no other separators.

12. Suppose that edge e lies between regions R_a and R_b such that $\text{BELOW}(e) = a$ and $\text{ABOVE}(e) = b$. Prove that any separator in a chain tree that contains e will be a descendant of the least common ancestor of a and b.

13. Let $lca(i, j)$ denote the least common ancestor of i and j, where i and j are between 0 and $n-1$. Let $msb(i)$ denote the most significant bit of the binary representation of i, where i is between 0 and $n-1$. In other words, $msb(i) = lca(0, i)$. Compute $lca(i, j)$ in terms of msb. You should use a combination of Boolean operations such as "exclusive or" ($\oplus$), "complement" ($\neg$), "and" ($\wedge$), and so on.

14. Let $rev(k)$ denote a function that reverses the bits in the binary expansion of k. Using the definition of lca in Exercise 13, compute $lca(i, j)$ in terms of rev. You should use a combination of Boolean operations such as "exclusive or" ($\oplus$), "complement" ($\neg$), "and" ($\wedge$), and so forth.

15. In a gap tree, each separating chain is implemented as a list of the x coordinate values of the leftmost vertices of their gaps and edges. How would you cope with a query point that coincides with an endpoint of an edge?

16. Suppose that a new edge is inserted into a regularized polygonal map with $O(v)$ vertices that is represented by the separating chain method. Show that applying the regularization process again uses $O(v)$ space and time.

17. Let us reexamine the problem of inserting a new edge, say e, into a polygonal map that is represented by the separating chain method. Let E denote the set of the edges introduced by the application of regularization to the original polygonal map. Addition of e may cause new vertices to be added by virtue of the intersection of e with the set E. In the text and in Exercise 16, we mention that we remove all edges in E that intersect e and reapply the regularization process. Is this always a better method than simply adding new vertices whenever e intersects one of the elements of E?

18. Write a procedure GAPTREEPOINTLOCATION to perform point location in a gap tree.

2.1.3.3.2 Layered Dag

The main drawback of the algorithm for point location in a gap tree is that, for each level of the gap tree, the corresponding separating chain must be searched in its entirety (notwithstanding that the elements in the chain are sorted). It is preferable to restart the search in the vicinity of the edge or gap in the appropriate child. Thus, we want a pointer from each edge or gap on the separating chain, say e, to the edges on the separating chain of each child that overlaps e.

The problem is that an edge or gap of a parent may overlap many edges or gaps of the child. For example, in the polygonal map of Figure 2.47(b), edge EI in separating chain S_4 (or equivalently gap EI in separating chain S_2) overlaps edges EF, FH, and HI in separating chain S_1. Inserting these additional pointers has the potential to break up each separating chain at the x coordinate values of all of the vertices in the subdivision. Consequently, this could use quadratic space (i.e., $O(m^2)$).

To solve the problem described above, Edelsbrunner, Guibas, and Stolfi [541] propose a data structure that they call a *layered dag*. A layered dag is a separating chain that is augmented by a set of vertices. In particular, the layered dag, say L_u, corresponding to a separating chain, say S_u, is a set of *x-intervals* that covers the entire x axis. Each layered dag is implemented as a set of vertices and a set of edges and gaps. The x-intervals are specified in terms of these vertices, edges, and gaps. Each x-interval of L_u overlaps the x-projection of exactly one edge or gap of S_u and at most two x-intervals of the layered dags corresponding to the left and right children of S_u. As we shall see later, this condition enables us to keep the storage requirements of the resulting data structure linear.

Let L_u denote the layered dag of node u of a gap tree T whose separating chain is S_u. L_u is constructed by processing the separating chains in T in a bottom-up manner so that the layered dags corresponding to the children of u are built first. L_u consists of a set of vertices corresponding to union of the endpoints of the edges and gaps in S_u and every other vertex of those present in the layered dags of the left and right children of u. Duplicate vertices are removed. By convention, we assume that when u is a leaf node of T, then the children of L_u are empty. This process is applied recursively to every node of the gap tree. The result is that as the layered dags are constructed, at each level every

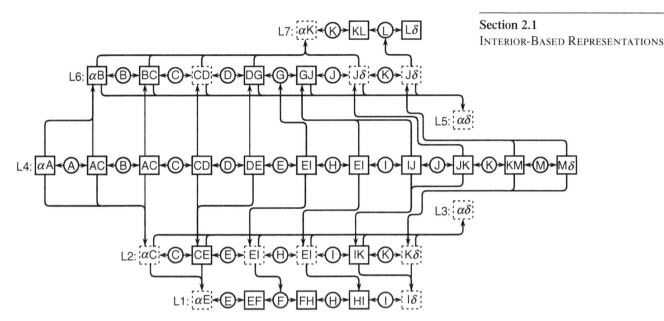

Figure 2.55
Layered dag representation of the gap tree of Figure 2.52.

other vertex is propagated towards the layered dag that corresponds to the root of the gap tree.

As an example, let us build the layered dags corresponding to the separating chains of the gap tree of Figure 2.52. Let L_i denote the result of applying the construction to S_i. Figure 2.55 shows the result of this construction. For the sake of the current discussion, we describe only how the elements making up each layered dag are determined. Thus, for the moment, we ignore the meaning of the interconnections between elements of the layered dag, as well as how they are formed. In the figure, vertices are depicted by circles, while x-intervals are shown by boxes between circles. In particular, x-intervals corresponding to edges are depicted by solid boxes, and those corresponding to gaps are depicted by broken boxes.

Before describing the correspondence between the layered dags of Figure 2.55 and the separating chains of the gap tree of Figure 2.52, we make the following two observations. First, the x-interval is labeled with the name of the edge or gap of which it is a subset; it is not necessarily labeled with the vertices to its immediate right and left. This situation arises when the x-interval is part of an edge or gap that extends beyond the endpoints of the x interval. For example, the x-interval corresponding to vertices A and B in L_4 in Figure 2.55 is labeled AC rather than AB since x-interval AC overlaps edge AB. Second, the layered dags do not include the dummy vertices at the extreme left and right (i.e., α and δ in Figure 2.47(b)) that are introduced by the regularization process. This means that we ignore them when building the layered dags corresponding to the separating chains. However, the x-intervals in which they participate are included in the layered dag.

In our example, the sets of x-intervals corresponding to L_1, L_3, L_5, and L_7 are identical to the edges and gaps making up S_1, S_3, S_5, and S_7, respectively. L_1 consists of vertices E, F, H, and I. L_3 and L_5 do not have any vertices. L_7 consists of vertices K and L.

L_2 is formed by combining vertices C, E, I, and K of S_2, and alternating vertices E and H of L_1. L_3 does not contribute any vertices. The result consists of vertices C, E, H, I, and K and the x-intervals between them: edges CE and IK, and gaps α C, EI, EI, and K δ.

L_6 is formed by combining vertices B, C, D, G, and J of S_6, and alternating vertex K of L_7. L_5 does not contribute any vertices. The result consists of vertices B, C, D, G, J, and K and the x-intervals between them: edges α B, BC, DG, and GJ, and gaps CD, J δ, and RJ δ.

L_4 is formed by combining vertices A, C, D, E, I, J, K, and M of S_4; alternating vertices C, H, and K of L_2; and alternating vertices B, D, and J of L_6. The result consists of vertices A, B, C, D, E, H, I, J, K, and M and the x-intervals between them: edges α A, AC, AC, CD, DE, EI, EI, IJ, JK, KM, and M δ; there are no gaps.

So far, we have described only the correspondence between the information stored in a layered dag and a chain node in the gap tree. We now show how the information in the layered dag is organized. This organization will be used subsequently in an algorithm to perform point location in $O(\log_2 m)$ time rather than $O(\log_2^2 m)$ time. We illustrate our presentation with Figure 2.55. We use the term *record* to refer to the box or circle in the figure that is associated with an x-interval. Our discussion makes heavy use of DOWN, UP, LEFT, and RIGHT links, which are all shown with the proper orientation in the figure.

As stated earlier, each x-interval, say I, of layered dag L_u corresponding to separating chain S_u of node u in the gap tree overlaps at most two x-intervals of the layered dags of the left and right children of u. We keep track of overlaps by using the two fields DOWN and UP in x-interval I's record. When x-interval I of L_u overlaps only one x-interval of the layered dags of the left (right) child of u, say $L_{\text{LEFT}(u)}$ ($L_{\text{RIGHT}(u)}$), then DOWN(I) (UP(I)) points to the overlapped x-interval's record. For example, x-interval HI in L_4 overlaps x-interval GJ in L_6, and thus its UP link is set to point to GJ's x-interval record. Notice that, in this example, x-interval HI is associated with edge EI since it is a subset of this edge.

When x-interval I overlaps two x-intervals of one or both children, then DOWN(I) (UP(I)) points to the record of the vertex that is common to the two overlapped x-intervals in $L_{\text{LEFT}(u)}$ ($L_{\text{RIGHT}(u)}$). This situation is facilitated by associating two fields LEFT and RIGHT with each vertex and letting them point to the x-intervals to the left and right of the vertex, respectively. For example, x-interval EH in L_4 overlaps both x-intervals DG and GJ in L_6, and thus its UP link is set to point to G's record in L_6.

Continuing the example above, we observe that x-interval EH is associated with edge EI since it is a subset of this edge. Note also that an x-interval can be overlapped by many x-intervals (e.g., CE in L_2 is overlapped by both CD and DE of L_4). Thus, it should be clear that the layered dag representation is not a tree. In fact, it resembles the K-structure. Not surprisingly, each vertex can be common only to one x-interval (see Exercise 2).

The cost of building the layered dag representation is easy to analyze. As we saw earlier, the process consists of processing the separating chains of the gap tree in a bottom-up manner. The DOWN (UP) links of L_u, corresponding to node u in the gap tree, are set by simultaneously traversing L_u and $L_{\text{LEFT}(u)}$ ($L_{\text{RIGHT}(u)}$) from left to right. Setting the LEFT and RIGHT links of the vertices is accomplished at the same time. The entire building process is linear in the number of edges in the gap tree (i.e., $O(m)$).

However, we must still show that the amount of space necessary to store the layered dags is $O(m)$. This can be seen by noting that the layered dags corresponding to the gap tree consist of sequences of vertices and then counting them. It can be shown that the total number of vertices in the layered dags is bounded by four times the number of edges in the regularized polygonal map (i.e., $4 \cdot m$).

An intuitive proof of this bound is obtained by observing that if the nodes of the gap tree that correspond to chains have a total of m edges, then there are $2 \cdot m$ vertices that serve as the endpoints of these edges. By the construction procedure, only one-half of these vertices are propagated to the parent chains, one-quarter to the grandparent chains, and so on, and the desired result follows by the properties of an infinite geometric series. For a more formal proof, see Exercise 3. Thus, the process of building the layered dag representation is $O(m)$ in space and time.

Point location in a layered dag representation is performed in a manner very similar to that in a gap tree. The only difference is that once the initial x-interval is located in the layered dag corresponding to the root of the gap tree, there is no need to search for it in the layered dags at the lower levels. The point is located by simply traversing the appropriate links in the layered dag representation. Let a and b designate the indices of the regions corresponding to the lower and upper boundaries, respectively, of the search space. They are initialized to 0 and $n - 1$, respectively.

Suppose we want to locate point P. We start at the layered dag, say L, corresponding to the root of the gap tree and search for the x-interval, say I, that contains the x coordinate value of P. Once we have found I, we must decide where to continue the search. Since I must correspond to an edge, say e, after the initial search, we now check the position of the y coordinate value of P relative to e. If P lies below (above) e, then we continue the search at the x-interval pointed at by $\text{DOWN}(I)$ ($\text{UP}(I)$) in the regions bounded by R_a and $R_{\text{BELOW}(e)}$ ($R_{\text{ABOVE}(e)}$ and R_b) and reset a and b as is appropriate. If P lies on e, then the search ceases, and we say that P lies in region $R_{\text{ABOVE}(e)}$.

x-interval I in L corresponds to an edge. However, in all subsequent steps of the algorithm, I can correspond to a gap or a vertex as well as an edge. When I corresponds to a gap, then there is no test to be performed on P. Nevertheless, we must descend to the appropriate x-interval in the layered dag of the next level. In this case, we have to reconstruct the result of a test at an x-interval at a previous level. This is done by comparing the value of b with the chain number[13] of the layered dag containing I, say c. If b is less than c, then we follow link $\text{DOWN}(I)$; otherwise, we follow link $\text{UP}(I)$. When I corresponds to a vertex, we check if P's x coordinate value is less than or equal to that of I, in which case we continue the search in x-interval $\text{LEFT}(I)$; otherwise, we continue in x-interval $\text{RIGHT}(I)$.

Note that the way we have described the organization of the vertices and x-intervals in the layered dag means that the only time that we have to perform a search is when we process L to locate the initial x-interval that contains P. This could be an $O(m)$ process in the worst case. All other searches are achieved by traversing the appropriate links— an $O(1)$ process per level for a total cost of $O(m + \log_2 n)$. The execution time can be reduced further by imposing an additional data structure in the form of a binary search tree on L.

This binary tree is built using the LEFT and RIGHT link fields of the nodes corresponding to the vertices in L. The leaf nodes of this tree consist of the x-intervals (i.e., edges), while the nonleaf nodes consist of the vertices. For example, Figure 2.56 is the modification of the layered dag representation of Figure 2.55 to include the binary search tree. This tree is rooted at vertex J, and thus all point location operations will start at node J. The result is that we have now reduced the cost of the point location operation to $O(\log_2 m)$ since m can be larger than n. Comparing point location in a layered dag with point location in a gap tree, we find that the two levels of binary searching have been replaced by a binary search in the root and an $O(1)$ search in the rest of the structure. This type of a transformation is an instance of a general technique known as *fractional cascading* [339, 340].

Procedure $\text{LAYEREDDAGPOINTLOCATION}$, given below, implements the point location algorithm using a layered dag. A layered dag is represented as a set of nodes of type *ldnode*, where each node has four fields. The TYPE field indicates whether the node corresponds to a vertex, edge, or gap. The remaining three fields depend on the type of data stored in the node.

A vertex node, say P, has three additional fields called LEFT, RIGHT, and XVAL. LEFT (RIGHT) points to the edge or gap nodes to the left (right) of P, and XVAL indicates the x coordinate value of P.

---

[13] Chains are assumed to be numbered from 1 to $n - 1$ as illustrated in Figure 2.49.

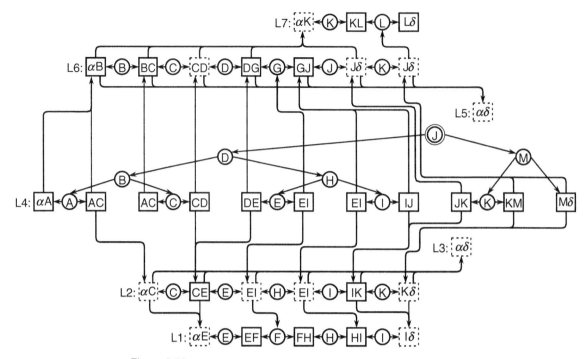

Figure 2.56
Layered dag representation of Figure 2.55 modified to include a binary search tree for the layered dag corresponding to the root of the gap tree.

An edge node, say E, has three additional fields called DOWN, UP, and EDGE. DOWN (UP) points to the edge, gap, or vertex nodes below (above) E, and EDGE points to a record of type *edge* describing edge E. A record of type *edge* has two fields called BELOW and ABOVE that indicate the regions immediately below and above it, respectively, as well as a field specifying the points it comprises, such as an equation of the line corresponding to it.

A gap node, say G, has three additional fields called DOWN, UP, and CHAINID. DOWN (UP) points to the edge, gap, or vertex nodes below (above) G, and CHAINID indicates the chain number of the node in the gap tree corresponding to the layered dag of which G is a member (i.e., u for L_u).

We also give a few more definitions. A point is implemented using a record of type *point* having two fields XCOORD and YCOORD corresponding to its x and y coordinate values, respectively. The relative position of the query point P with respect to an edge E (i.e., the side of E on which P lies) is determined with the aid of function FINDY, which takes the point P and the edge E as arguments and returns the value of the y coordinate of the point on E that has XCOORD(P) as the value of its x coordinate. Variables *Low* and *High* represent the lower and upper boundaries, respectively, of the search space.

1 **integer procedure** LAYEREDDAGPOINTLOCATION(P, T, N)
2 /* Search the layered dag representation of a polygonal map rooted at T for the region that contains point P and return its value. There are N regions in the polygonal map. The regions are numbered from 0 to $N - 1$. */
3 **value pointer point** P
4 **value pointer ldnode** T
5 **value integer** N
6 **integer** *Low, High*
7 **pointer edge** E
8 **real** Y
9 *Low* $\leftarrow 0$
10 *High* $\leftarrow N - 1$

```
11  while Low < High do
12    if TYPE(T) = 'EDGETEST' then
13      E ← EDGE(T)
14      /* Determine the y coordinate value of XCOORD(P) on the edge: */
15      Y ← FINDY(XCOORD(P), E)
16      if YCOORD(P) = Y then return ABOVE(E) /* P is on the edge */
17      elseif YCOORD(P) > Y then
18        /* P is above the edge */
19        T ← UP(T)
20        Low ← ABOVE(E)
21      else
22        /* P is below the edge */
23        T ← DOWN(T)
24        High ← BELOW(E)
25      endif
26    elseif TYPE(T) = 'XTEST' then
27      T ←if XCOORD(P) ≤ XVAL(T) then LEFT(T)
28         else RIGHT(T)
29         endif
30    else /* A gap test */
31      T ←if High < CHAINID(T) then DOWN(T)
32         else UP(T)
33         endif
34    endif
35  enddo
36  return Low
```

The layered dag and the K-structure are solutions for the point location query in a static environment. In other words, they assume that we know the positions of the vertices and edges of the subdivision of the underlying space (i.e., the polygonal map). There has also been a substantial amount of work on the dynamic point location problem. There are several solutions [103, 142, 357, 362, 365, 652, 653, 727, 1441, 1512, 1513, 1821] that differ in the amount of time it takes for a query to be answered or for edges and vertices to be inserted and deleted, as well as for some other operations such as vertex expansion and contraction (see [142, 357, 727] for overviews and summary tables). The key to the differences is the nature of the combination of the operations, the nature of the collection of the regions that can be handled, and whether the execution-time cost bounds are worst-case cost or amortized cost.

In particular, for n regions in a connected subdivision, Cheng and Janardan [357] execute the dynamic query in $O(\log_2^2 n)$ time with $O(n)$ space and $O(\log n)$ insertion and deletion (i.e, update) times. They use a combination of the interval tree [534, 537, 538] (see Section 3.1.2 of Chapter 3) and the priority search tree [1266] (see Section 1.3 of Chapter 1). Baumgarten, Jung, and Mehlhorn [142] also use $O(n)$ space and reduce the query execution time to $O(\log n \log \log n)$ in a general subdivision, while using amortized $O(\log n \log \log n)$ time for insertion and amortized $(\log^2 n)$ time for deletion. They use a combination of an interval tree, a segment tree [166] (see Section 3.1.1 of Chapter 3), fractional cascading [339, 340], and the combination of the interval tree and priority search tree used in [357]. Goodrich and Tamassia [727] obtain the same space and execution time bounds as Cheng and Janardan [357] for a monotone subdivision using a different data structure and also show how to perform vertex expansion and contraction in $O(\log n)$ time. They use an edge-ordered dynamic tree [562], which is an extension of the link-cut tree [1776].

Exercises

1. In the construction of the layered dag representation of the polygonal map of Figure 2.47(b), the alternating vertices were taken in the order first, third, fifth, and so on. Repeat this construction by taking them in the order second, fourth, sixth, and so forth.

2. In the layered dag representation of a polygonal map, explain why each vertex can be common only to one x-interval.

3. Prove that the total number of vertices in a layered dag representation of a regularized polygonal map of m edges is bounded by $4 \cdot m$. Use induction on the depth of the gap tree that serves as the basis of the construction of the layered dag representation. By letting a_u denote the number of edges in S_u, b_u the number of vertices in L_u, A_u the sum of a_v over all nodes v in the subtree rooted at u, and B_u the sum of b_v over all nodes v in the subtree rooted at u, the problem reduces to showing that $B_r \le 4 \cdot A_r = 4 \cdot m$ holds for the root node r of the gap tree.

4. Is the upper bound derived in Exercise 3 a least upper bound? Can you give an example where it is attained? If not, can you obtain a tighter bound?

5. The implementation of the layered dag described in the text is somewhat wasteful of space. Discuss how to reduce its space requirements.

6. The algorithm that we described for point location in a layered dag representation will usually visit $\log_2 n$ x-intervals, even if all but one of them correspond to gaps. In contrast, the algorithm that we described for point location in a gap tree made use of the gaps to skip some levels in the tree. Can you modify the structure of the layered dags and the point location algorithm to avoid the tests where the x-intervals correspond to gaps?

7. How would you adapt the layered dag to deal with the three-dimensional point location query? If this is not possible, explain why.

8. How would you compute map overlay (see Exercise 12 in Section 2.1.3.2) for two polygonal maps represented using a layered dag?

2.1.4 Arbitrary Objects

In this section, we loosen the restrictions on the cells, blocks, and objects in Sections 2.1.1 and 2.1.2 that prevented a cell or a block from being partially contained in several objects or that required a cell or a block to be contained in its entirety in a single object. In other words, a cell or a block may overlap several objects without being completely contained in these objects. Furthermore, we permit objects to be of arbitrary shapes rather than requiring their boundaries to be hyperplanes.

Loosening these restrictions enables the decoupling of the partition of the underlying space induced by the decomposition process from the partition induced by the objects. Again, as discussed in Section 2.1.3, the individual objects no longer need to be represented as collections of unit-sized cells or rectangular blocks. Instead, collections of other shapes, such as triangles, trapezoids, convex polygons, and so on, can be used. When there is no explicit relationship between the blocks and the objects that they contain (e.g., containment), then in addition to keeping track of the identities of all objects (or parts of objects) that can be covered by a block or part of a block, we must also keep track of the geometric descriptions of both the cells or blocks and the objects. This enables us to respond to the location query.

Note that without the geometric description, given a specific location l in space, finding the cell c or block b in which l is contained may not be enough to determine the identity of the object (or objects) of which l is a member, as well as the rest of the constituent cells of the object (or objects). Therefore, once we have located c or b, we must check the geometric description of the objects associated with c or b to see which ones contain l. By recording a pointer to the geometric description of the objects with each cell or block rather than the entire geometric description, we save much storage because the geometric description is recorded only once. Notice that once we have located the object (or objects) containing l, determining the remaining constituent cells of these objects is done in the same manner as described earlier (i.e., by use of appropriate variants of connected component labeling).

In Sections 2.1.2 and 2.1.3, we halted the decomposition process whenever a block was completely contained in an object or a set of objects. However, it is clear that this rule is impossible to satisfy in general, now that the boundaries of the objects need not coincide with the boundaries of the blocks that are induced by the decomposition process. Thus, we need to find an alternative way of halting the decomposition process. There are two natural methods for achieving this result, and they are the subject of this section:

1. Restrict the number of blocks that can cover an object (i.e., parts of it); this is termed *coverage-based splitting* [242] (Section 2.1.4.1).

2. Restrict the number of objects (or parts of objects) that can be covered by a block or part of a block; this is termed *density-based splitting* [242] (Section 2.1.4.2).

2.1.4.1 Coverage-Based Splitting

A common way of implementing coverage-based splitting is to set the number of blocks that can cover an object to 1. In particular, this block is usually the smallest possible block that contains the object. There are many ways of implementing this strategy. One of the earliest implementations is the MX-CIF quadtree [1009]. The MX-CIF quadtree [1009] is a quadtreelike regular decomposition rule that decomposes the underlying space into four congruent blocks at each stage (i.e., level) of the decomposition process so that each object is associated with its minimum enclosing quadtree block. Figure 2.57 is an MX-CIF quadtree, where we see that more than one object is associated with some of the nodes in the tree (e.g., the root and its NE child).

Since there is no limit on the number of objects that are associated with a particular block, an additional decomposition rule may be provided to distinguish between these objects. For example, in the case of the MX-CIF quadtree, a one-dimensional analog of the two-dimensional decomposition rule is used. In particular, all objects that are associated with a given block b are partitioned into two sets: those that overlap the vertical axis passing through the center of b and those that overlap the horizontal. Objects that overlap the center of b are associated with the horizontal axis. Associated with each axis is a one-dimensional MX-CIF quadtree (i.e., a binary tree), where each object o is associated with the node that corresponds to o's minimum enclosing interval. The MX-CIF quadtree is described in more detail in Section 3.4.1 in Chapter 3.

Note that the MX-CIF quadtree results in a decomposition of space into blocks that are not necessarily disjoint, although there is a containment relationship between them— that is, two blocks a and b are either disjoint, $a \subset b$, or $b \subset a$. Other researchers have also used the idea of associating each object with its minimum enclosing quadtree block. They differ in the manner in which they keep track of the minimum enclosing quadtree blocks. Abel and Smith [8] represent each block by its locational code (see Section 2.1.2.4) and store these locational codes in a B^+-tree [2]. Of course, each block must be stored as many times as there are objects for which it serves as the minimum enclosing quadtree block. The multiple instances of blocks with the same locational code can be distinguished by using a secondary key based on the actual object, such as its centroid.

The filter tree of Sevcik and Koudas [1720] keeps track of the minimum enclosing quadtree blocks by using a similar approach to that of Abel and Smith [2, 8] in that it makes use of a B-tree index. However, there are a couple of important differences. First, instead of having one B-tree for all of the blocks, the filter tree maintains one B-tree for each level in the quadtree. This means that all minimum enclosing quadtree blocks of a given size are associated with the same B-tree, and a $2^n \times 2^n$ image space may have as many as $n + 1$ B-trees. Second, the B-tree stores the Peano-Hilbert key corresponding to the centroid of the minimum bounding box of each object instead of the locational code of the minimum enclosing quadtree block of each object. Note that in the filter tree, as in the B^+-tree implementation of the MX-CIF quadtree, all of the objects with the same minimum enclosing quadtree block are stored contiguously.

The filter tree can be viewed as providing a variable number of grids, each one being at half the resolution of its immediate successor, where an object is associated with the grid whose cells provide the tightest fit. This concept is termed *multiresolution* and is

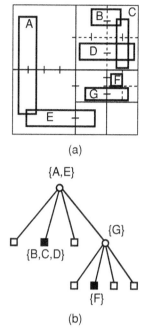

Figure 2.57
(a) Block decomposition induced by the MX-CIF quadtree for a collection of rectangle objects and (b) its tree representation.

expanded upon in Section 2.1.5.1. The filter tree is based on a regular decomposition of the underlying space. The multilayer grid file [1773] is similar to the filter tree. The difference is that each grid layer corresponds to separate grid file with its own partitions that are not necessarily related, as is the case in a regular grid, which forms the basis of the filter tree. As in the filter tree, each object o is inserted into the first grid file for which it fits in a grid block without having to partition o. The R-file [909] (see also Section 3.4.2 of Chapter 3) is a cross between the multilayer grid file and the MX-CIF quadtree in the sense that, instead of being associated with its minimum enclosing quadtree block, an object is associated with its minimum containing block among the existing quadtree (actually a regular decomposition k-d tree—that is, a bintree) blocks. One of the properties of the R-file is that just because the structure contains a block b, it need not necessarily contain its siblings (i.e., the blocks that result from the decomposition of b's parent block).

The R-file [909] is a modification of the multilayer grid file that is designed to overcome the observed low storage utilization by having just one directory instead of multiple directories. The R-file makes use of a regular decomposition in a spirit similar to the BANG file [640] (see Section 1.7.1.5 of Chapter 1) except that there is no use of holes (i.e., the bucket regions do not have the shapes of bricks with holes that correspond to regions that have been extracted as a result of the split process). In particular, one of its key features is that instead of splitting a bucket region into two halves (or four halves in the case of a quadtreelike approach), it retains the original bucket region and creates a new bucket for just one of the two halves of the original bucket region. The advantage of this method is that there is more flexibility in deciding which objects should be retained in the original bucket region and which ones should be moved to the newly created bucket region. Note that bucket regions do overlap in this case and that an object is not necessarily associated with the minimum containing block but, instead, is associated with its minimum containing block among the existing blocks. Like Abel and Smith's implementation of the MX-CIF quadtree [2] and other methods, the R-file stores a one-dimensional representative of the buckets (its locational code based on the Morton order) in a B-tree. In order to avoid searching unoccupied space, the R-file also associates with each bucket a minimum bounding box of the objects that it contains.

The drawback of restricting the number of blocks that can cover an object o to 1 (i.e., o's minimum enclosing quadtree block) is that the block tends to be rather large, on the average. In particular, in the worst case, a small object that straddles the top-level split partition will have the root as its minimum enclosing quadtree block (e.g., objects A and E are associated with the root in the MX-CIF quadtree in Figure 2.57).

An easy way to overcome this drawback is to decompose o's minimum enclosing quadtree block (or the result of another space decomposition method, such as a bintree) into smaller blocks, each of which minimally encloses some portion of o (or, alternatively, some portion of o's minimum bounding box). The expanded MX-CIF quadtree [9] is a simple example of such an approach where o's minimum enclosing quadtree block b is decomposed once into four subblocks s_i, which are then decomposed further until obtaining the minimum enclosing quadtree block for the portion of o, if any, that is covered by b_i (see Section 3.4.3 in Chapter 3 for more details).

Orenstein [1416] proposes the *error-bound* and *size-bound* methods for deciding how much decomposition to perform to yield the blocks covering object o. In the error-bound method, the minimum enclosing block is recursively split until level L is reached, where 0 is the level of the root and L is a user-specified level threshold. In the size-bound method, the minimum enclosing block is recursively split in a breadth-first manner (see Exercise 1), and the process is terminated once a threshold number S of blocks that collectively cover the space spanned by o has been obtained. For both methods, once enough splitting has been performed, the blocks that collectively cover o are shrunk so that each one minimally encloses the portion of o inside it, and sibling blocks that both cover o are coalesced. Thus, the possible number of resulting blocks ranges from 1 through 2^L for the error-bound method and from 1 through S for the size-bound method. Observe that both methods are equivalent for $S = 1/L = 0$ and for $S = 2^H/L = H$, where H is the height of the space decomposition hierarchy (i.e., the maximum number of levels), but other values lead to different results for the two methods.

Orenstein [1416] suggests that the error-bound method generally leads to better query performance than the size-bound method, and this has been confirmed by experiments [242]. Of course, regardless of the method used, there is an inherent conflict in their application because the greater the number of blocks used, the higher the quality of the approximation; yet, this has the undesirable result of increasing the processing cost for a number of queries as there are more blocks associated with each object (but see [668]). Thus, minimizing the number of objects is of interest (e.g., [669, 1417]). Regardless of which method is used, the results are stored in a zkd Btree [1420] (see Section 1.6 in Chapter 1).

Frank and Barrera [628, 630] and Ulrich [1901] take a different approach by retaining the restriction that each object can be covered by just one block. One solution is to expand the size of the space that is spanned by each quadtree block b of width w by a factor p ($p > 0$) so that the expanded block is of width $(1 + p) \cdot w$. In this case, an object would be associated with its minimum enclosing expanded quadtree block. It can be shown that the radius of the minimum bounding box for any object o that is associated with a block b of width w (on account of overlapping the horizontal or vertical axes that pass through the center of b while not lying within the expanded quadtree block of one of b's subblocks) must be larger than $p \cdot w/4$ (see Exercise 2). Otherwise (i.e., if the radius is smaller than $p \cdot w/4$), o is associated with a smaller block. The terms *cover fieldtree* [628, 630] and *loose quadtree* [1901] are used to describe the resulting structure. We use these terms interchangeably.

Ulrich [1901] advocates setting the block expansion factor p to 1. He argues that using block expansion factors much smaller than 1 increases the likelihood that the minimum enclosing expanded quadtree block is large and that letting the block expansion factor be much larger than 1 results in the areas spanned by the expanded quadtree blocks being too large, thereby having much overlap. For example, letting $p = 1$, Figure 3.26 in Chapter 3 is the loose quadtree corresponding to the collection of objects in Figure 2.57(a) and their MX-CIF quadtree in Figure 2.57(b). In this example, there are only two differences between the loose and MX-CIF quadtrees:

1. Rectangle object E is associated with the SW child of the root of the loose quadtree instead of with the root of the MX-CIF quadtree.

2. Rectangle object B is associated with the NW child of the NE child of the root of the loose quadtree instead of with the NE child of the root of the MX-CIF quadtree.

The loose quadtree and the cover fieldtree are similar to the quadtree medial axis transform (QMAT) [1626] (see Section 2.1.2.4), where the factor p is bounded by 2 (i.e., it is less than 2) [1624, 1626]. In this case, for a black block b of width w in a region quadtree, $p \cdot w/2$ represents the distance from the border of b to the nearest point that is on a boundary between a black and a white block in the structure. The QMAT is used as an alternative to the region quadtree representation of an image; it is an attempt to reduce the sensitivity of the storage requirements of the region quadtree to the position of the origin with respect to which it is built. The QMAT can also be used as a representation for a collection of objects, as is done with a loose quadtree and a cover fieldtree.

Frank and Barrera [628, 630] also propose shifting the positions of the centroids of blocks at successive levels of subdivision by half the width of the block that is being subdivided as yet another alternative approach to overcoming the problem of the minimum enclosing quadtree block of o being much larger than o (e.g., o's minimum bounding box). Figure 2.58 shows an example of such a subdivision. The result is termed a *partition fieldtree* by Frank and Barrera [628, 630] and is also similar to the overlapping pyramid of Burt, Hong, and Rosenfeld [286].

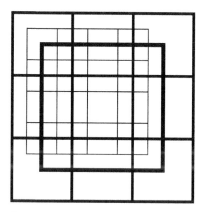

Figure 2.58
Example of the subdivision induced by a partition fieldtree.

We can make several observations about the partition fieldtree:

1. The boundaries of the blocks at different levels of decomposition will never coincide.

2. The grids formed by taking the set of blocks at the different levels of decomposition use a different origin for each level (i.e., the origin has been shifted).

3. The blocks at a given level of decomposition l do not form a refinement of the blocks at the previous level of decomposition $l-1$.

An important property of the partition fieldtree is that the relative size of the minimum enclosing quadtree block for object o is bounded with respect to the size of the minimum bounding box v of o. In particular, objects of the same size can be stored in nodes corresponding to larger blocks of at most three possible sizes, depending on their positions—that is, in the worst case, o will be stored in a block that is 2^3 (i.e., 8) times o's size (i.e., maximum width along the axes). In order to see how this worst-case situation can arise, consider a 32×32 universe with the origin at the lower-left corner and an object O slightly wider than unit size along the x axis and length ε ($0 < \varepsilon < 0.5$) along the y axis—that is, O's two opposite corners are at $(14-\delta, 16-\varepsilon)$ and $(15+\delta, 16+\varepsilon)$. We now show that the minimum enclosing quadtree block for O is of size $2^3 \times 2^3$. O does not fit in a block of size 1×1 due to its being of width $1+2\delta$. In particular, O is spanned by the 1×1 block A with corners at $(13.5, 15.5)$ and $(14.5, 16.5)$ and the 1×1 block B with corners at $(14.5, 15.5)$ and $(15.5, 16.5)$. These two blocks are spanned by the 2×2 block C with corners at $(13, 15)$ and $(15, 17)$ and the 2×2 block D with corners at $(15, 15)$ and $(17, 17)$. These two blocks are spanned by the 4×4 block E with corners at $(10, 14)$ and $(14, 18)$ and the 2×2 block F with corners at $(14, 14)$ and $(18, 18)$. These two blocks are spanned by the 8×8 block G with corners at $(12, 12)$ and $(20, 20)$, which is the minimum enclosing quadtree block. Figure 2.59 illustrates this situation.

Note that in the case of the cover fieldtree, we do not in general have a bound on the relative size of o's minimum enclosing quadtree block with respect to the size of o's minimum bounding box v. However, when $p = 1$, the block in which o is stored is at

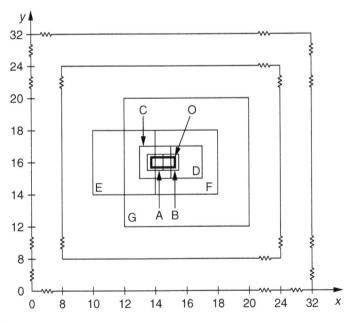

Figure 2.59
Example illustrating the largest possible minimum enclosing quadtree block in a partition fieldtree. In this case, the block is almost eight times larger than the object, in terms of the block width. The object is embedded in a 32×32 universe with the origin at the lower-left corner. The diagonally opposite corners of the object are at $(14-\delta, 32-\varepsilon)$ and $(15+\delta, 32+\varepsilon)$.

most twice o's size (i.e., maximum width). To see how this situation arises, recall that the radius of the minimum bounding box v for any object o that is associated with a block b of width w (on account of overlapping the horizontal or vertical axes that pass through the center of b while not lying within the expanded quadtree block of one of b's subblocks) must be larger than $p \cdot w/4$. The desired factor of 2 is obtained by setting the radius of v to be $w/4 + \delta$, where δ is close to 0. Note that as p approaches 0, the minimum size of the radius of v (i.e., $p \cdot w/4$) also decreases. In fact, for $p = 1/2$, the ratio of the size is at most 4; for $p = 1/4$, the ratio is at most 8. At $p = 1/8$, the ratio is at most 16, and we now find that the partition fieldtree yields a tighter fit than the cover fieldtree. Thus, $p = 1/4$ can be said to be the point at which the partition and cover variants of the fieldtree are approximately equivalent.

At this point, it is appropriate to review the distinction between the cover and partition fieldtrees. In both cases, the goal is to expand the area spanned by the subblocks of a block in order to reduce the size of the minimum enclosing quadtree block b when an object o overlaps the axes that pass through the center of b. In the case of the cover fieldtree, the area spanned by the four subblocks is expanded. In the case of the partition fieldtree, the number of covering subblocks is enlarged by offsetting their positions while retaining their sizes—that is, a set of 3×3 blocks of size $u/2^{i+1} \times u/2^{i+1}$ at level $i + 1$ spans a block of size $u/2^i$ at level i (assuming a universe of width u and a root at level i).

The result in both cases is that the subblocks span an area that overlaps the partition lines, which is something that would not be possible in a conventional quadtree (e.g., the region quadtree, MX-CIF quadtree, or any quadtree where the blocks are disjoint) since the edges of the blocks at successive levels of decomposition must coincide (i.e., they are collinear). Note that this distinction between the fieldtree (both the partition and the cover variants) and the conventional quadtree is always true for the partition fieldtree since it always shifts the positions of the centroids of the blocks at successive levels by one-half of the width of the field. However, this is not necessarily the case for the cover fieldtree when we use particular values of p such as 1. Nevertheless, there is also some coincidence for other values of p that are powers of 2 (both positive and negative).

Data structures employing coverage-based splitting have found use in many diverse applications. The MX-CIF quadtree [1009] was originally developed to represent design elements in applications in VLSI design (see Section 3.4.1 in Chapter 3). More recently it has been used to represent spatial objects in a peer-to-peer (P2P) setting [1846, 1847]. The fieldtree [628, 630] was developed to represent spatial objects in geographic information systems; the filter tree [1720] was developed for the same purpose in spatial databases, where it was also used for selectivity estimation [12]. Similarly, the loose quadtree and loose octree were also developed to represent spatial objects but in the context of game programming applications [1901].

Exercises

1. Why does the size-bound method split the minimum enclosing block in a breadth-first manner instead of a depth-first manner?

2. Show why the radius of the minimum bounding box for any object o that is associated with a block b of width w (on account of overlapping the horizontal or vertical axes that pass through the center of b while not lying within the expanded quadtree block of one of b's subblocks) in a loose quadtree must be larger than $p \cdot w/4$. Assume that p is the factor by which the width of the blocks has been expanded.

3. Ulrich [1901] proposes inserting an object o into a loose quadtree with $p = 1$ by determining the depth d of the tree at which o belongs (and thus the width of the containing block). d is obtained by observing that blocks at this depth can accommodate any object whose minimum bounding box has a radius r that is less than one-quarter of the width w of the edge of the expanded block at depth d, regardless of its position. An object whose minimum bounding box has a radius less than or equal to $w/8$ should be inserted at depth $d + 1$. The actual block into which o is to be inserted is identified by finding the block b at depth d that is closest to

the center of o's minimum bounding box. Once b has been determined, we observe that it is possible for a tighter fit on account of the positioning of o so that it can be contained in one of b's subblocks s in the sense that o is larger than s but fits into s's expanded block. This is done by checking to see if o fits in b's closest subblock. Can you derive an analogous procedure for arbitrary values of p?

2.1.4.2 Density-Based Splitting

Density-based splitting is formally specified as stipulating that a block is decomposed whenever it is covered by more than T $(T \geq 1)$ objects (or parts of them).[14] Such a rule is known as a *bucketlike* decomposition rule. The case $T = 1$ corresponds to halting the decomposition whenever each cell in the block b is an element of the same object o or is in no object. In other words, any cell c in b is either in o or in no object. Observe that even for the $T = 1$ case, the result is different from the block decomposition rule described in Section 2.1.2, which required that either all the cells in b be elements of the same object or all the cells in b be in none of the objects.

There are many variants of bucketlike block decomposition rules, depending in part on the nature of the objects being represented. Without loss of generality, in this section, we assume two-dimensional data.[15] In particular, we focus on how to deal with collections of arbitrary polygonal objects, thereby, of course, including rectangles, which are common in applications such as VLSI and CAD. In the case of polygons, the specific variant that is used also depends on whether the polygons themselves are the objects being decomposed, which is the case in this section, or if the decomposition rule is based on the primitive objects that make up the polygon (e.g., its vertices and/or edges), which is the case in the variants described in Section 2.2.2.8.

It is straightforward to formulate bucketlike variants of the different block decomposition rules described in Section 2.1.2. Without loss of generality, in the rest of this section, we assume a quadtreelike regular decomposition rule that decomposes the underlying space into four congruent blocks at each stage (i.e., level) of decomposition. As in Section 2.1.2, the results of successive stages form a containment hierarchy. Again, as in the previous section, once the decomposition process has terminated, the result is a set of disjoint blocks. Of course, other decomposition rules could be used such as those that, among others, do not require the blocks to be congruent at a particular stage and similar at successive stages (e.g., a point quadtree), do not subdivide into just two parts as do the k-d tree and bintree (e.g., an X-Y tree and puzzletree), or do not require that the blocks be axis parallel (e.g., a BSP tree) . We do not discuss such decomposition rules in this section (but see Section 2.1.3.1).

The bucketlike decomposition rule described above works well when the polygons are disjoint, and we use the term *bucket polygon quadtree* to describe the result. However, when the polygons are permitted to overlap or are adjacent, problems can arise: there exist polygon configurations for which the decomposition will never halt. In this case, our goal is to prevent as much unnecessary decomposition as possible but, at the same time, to minimize the amount of useful decomposition that is prevented from taking place. Overlapping polygons arise in several defense-analysis problems. For example, trafficability (also known as mobility) polygons are often overlapping [65]. In particular, it is frequently desired to find a path through a set of overlapping (thereby connected) polygons. Overlapping polygons also arise in VLSI and CAD applications, such as building plans. Adjacent polygons are discussed in greater detail a bit later in this section.

---

[14] Notice that the decomposition rule is not one that decomposes a block if it contains more than T objects. Such a rule may be difficult to satisfy in the sense that there would be very little decomposition after an initial level, as blocks usually contain portions of many objects rather than many objects in their entirety.

[15] Our discussion is also applicable to data of arbitrary dimensionality.

As an example of a block configuration for which the bucket polygon quadtree would require an infinite amount of decomposition, consider the situation when $Q > T$ polygons in block b are arranged so that polygon p_i is *completely contained* in polygon p_{i+1} for $1 \le i < Q$. Now, let us examine the instant when b contains T of the polygons. In this case, upon insertion of the $(T + 1)$st polygon, we are better off not even starting to decompose b, which now has $T + 1$ polygons, as we can never reach the situation that all the blocks resulting from the decomposition will be part of T or fewer polygons. For example, assuming $T = 2$, the block containing the three polygons in Figure 2.60(a) is not split upon insertion of the third polygon. In this case, the order of inserting the polygons is immaterial.

A decomposition rule that prevents more decomposition than one that halts the decomposition only upon complete containment is one that requires the mutual intersection of all of the polygons in block b, including the polygon p being inserted, to be nonempty in order to prevent decomposition (such a quadtree decomposition rule for a collection of rectangle objects is known as an RR_1 *quadtree* [1722]).[16] The mutual intersection rule is motivated by the desire to be able to deal with the situation in which many edges of the polygons have a common endpoint (e.g., in a polygonal subdivision of the plane where the polygons are adjacent but not overlapping). For example, assuming $T = 2$, the polygons in the block in Figure 2.60(b) are mutually intersecting, and thus the block is not split regardless of the order in which the polygons are inserted into it. In fact, the order in which the polygons are inserted is always immaterial when using the mutual intersection rule.

A decomposition rule that prevents even more decomposition than mutual intersection, and the one we suggest using, splits a block b that contains at least T polygons before inserting polygon p if p does not touch all of the polygons already contained in b. We say that two polygons p_1 and p_2 *touch* if p_1 and p_2 have at least one point in common (i.e., the polygons may overlap or just touch at their boundaries).[17] For example, assuming $T = 2$, inserting polygons 1, 2, and 3 in this order in Figure 2.60(c) avoids splitting the block. On the other hand, inserting the polygons in the order 1, 3, 2 in Figure 2.60(c) results in the block's being split. Thus, we see that the result of using the touching rule may be sensitive to the order in which the polygons are inserted. Notice that the touching rule would also not split the blocks in Figure 2.60(a, b), regardless of the order in which the polygons were inserted. This shows that the order in which the polygons are inserted is not always important for the touching rule.

It is interesting to observe that using a decomposition rule based on touching often prevents useful decompositions from taking place. For example, in Figure 2.60(c) it may be better to decompose the block. This is the case for the RR_2 *quadtree* [1722] for rectangles, whose adaptation to polygons results in a decomposition of a block b whenever b contains more than one distinct chain of connected or touching polygons. Nevertheless, although the mutual intersection rule is really a better decomposition rule than the touching rule in the sense that it allows more useful decomposition to take place, the use of the mutual intersection rule is not suggested because its computation for the general case of polygons of arbitrary shape is expensive.

Perhaps the most common type of collection of polygons is one where all the polygons are adjacent. This is called a *polygonal map* and results in the partition of the underlying image into connected regions. It arises in many cartographic applications, such as maps. For example, a map of the United States is a polygonal map where the polygons correspond to states, and the edges of the polygons correspond to state lines. Similarly, a map of the world is a polygonal map where the polygons correspond to countries, and the edges of the polygons correspond to the borders of countries. Polygonal

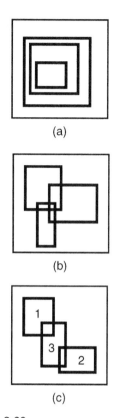

(a)

(b)

(c)

Figure 2.60
Examples of collections of three overlapping polygons and their effect on their containing block B that is not split when using (a) the completely contained decomposition rule or (b) the mutual intersection rule. (c) B is split when using the touching rule if the polygons are inserted in the order 1, 2, 3, but B is not split if the polygons are inserted in the order 1, 3, 2.

---

[16] The mutual intersection rule is *weaker* than the complete containment rule in the sense that complete containment implies mutual intersection.

[17] The touching rule is weaker than the mutual intersection rule in the sense that mutual intersection implies touching.

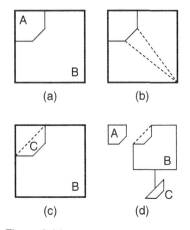

Figure 2.61
(a) Example block consisting of two
regions A and B. (b) The result of
decomposing B into three convex
regions. (c) The convex polygon
C that must be subtracted from
the convex hull of B to obtain B.
(d) The convex difference trees
corresponding to the polygons of
the entire block.

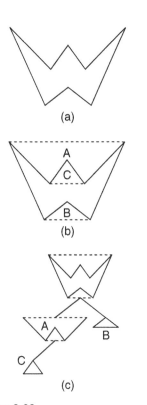

Figure 2.62
(a) Example W-like shape, (b) the
components that make up its CDT,
and (c) the actual tree.

maps arise in many applications. For example, they are used for crop coverages, soil types, land usage, and so on. In addition, they are used to represent the projections of elevation models. For example, given a set of elevations such as a Digital Terrain Model (DTM) or a Digital Elevation Model (DEM), we often fit an interpolating surface consisting of triangles on the set, which is called a triangulation. The projection of the triangulation onto the plane is also a polygonal map. Thus, the representation of a polygonal map is an important issue.

In the case of adjacent polygons, use of a bucketlike decomposition rule such as the bucket polygon quadtree can still result in an infinite amount of decomposition. However, the case of an infinite amount of decomposition due to more than T polygons being contained in each other is not possible as the polygons do not overlap. Nevertheless, infinite decomposition is still possible if the polygonal map has a vertex at which more than T polygons are incident. An interesting way to overcome this problem is to use a variant of a bucket polygon quadtree, developed originally for line segment objects [1360, 1362], known as the *PMR quadtree* (see also Section 2.2.2.8 for a discussion of its use for line segment objects). It decomposes the block just once if it is a part of more than T polygons. We term the result a *PMR polygon quadtree*. Such a rule means that the shape of the resulting tree depends on the order in which the polygons are inserted into it.

An alternative solution to that provided by the PMR polygon quadtree is to introduce an additional condition that halts the decomposition whenever the block b contains a single vertex v [1541]. The motivation for this rule is the fact that when a block b contains just one vertex v, it is often the case that all of the edges in b meet at v. Note that this rule does *not* preclude a block b from containing more than one vertex, provided that b does not contain more than T polygons. In fact, this is quite a common occurrence since each polygon consists of at least three vertices! We term the result a *vertex bucket polygon quadtree*.

Once the space has been partitioned into blocks, we need to consider the representations of the polygons that make up each block. There are several possible methods. The first is to leave them alone and just associate with each block a list of the polygons that overlap it. The elements of this list are usually pointers to a polygon table that contains the full geometric description of each polygon (e.g., a list of vertices or edges). Of course, we could also apply a spatial sorting technique to the polygons in each block (e.g., by the locations of their centroids). The second is to decompose them into a collection of convex regions [1541]. This is motivated by the fact that operations on convex polygons are more efficient than operations on general or simple polygons (e.g., point location). In particular, there are two choices for the decomposition into convex regions. The first is to represent each polygon in the block by a union of convex regions, and the second as a difference of convex regions.

Subdivision into a union of convex regions can be achieved easily by methods such as a triangulation. For example, polygon B in Figure 2.61(a) is decomposed into three convex regions (i.e., triangles) in Figure 2.61(b). In fact, optimal convex decompositions can also be achieved by introducing new points (known as *Steiner points*) [337], as well as without new points [751]. The disadvantage of a subdivision into a union of convex regions is that the number of resulting polygons can increase dramatically.

When the polygons are represented as a difference of convex regions, the number of resulting polygons is considerably smaller but still larger than just leaving them alone. This is achieved by using the convex difference tree (CDT) representation for simple polygons [1878]. In this case, a simple polygon is represented as a tree. The root of the tree contains the convex hull[18] of the polygon. There is one child for each connected component of the difference between the original polygon and the convex hull. The children are also convex difference trees, which means that they contain the convex hull

---

[18] See the definition in footnote 11 in Section 2.1.3.2

of their polygons. Thus, we see that the representation process is recursive, with the decomposition stopping once we get a connected component difference that is convex. As a simple example, the block in Figure 2.61(a) contains two polygons, A and B. Since B is not convex, its CDT is formed by subtracting convex polygon C, as shown in Figure 2.61(c), from the convex hull of B. The two CDTs corresponding to the polygons of the entire block are given in Figure 2.61(d). The broken lines in Figure 2.61(c, d) show the convex hull of B.

The W-like shape in Figure 2.62(a) is a more complicated example of a CDT. The broken lines in Figure 2.62(b) show the various components in the CDT for Figure 2.62(a), while Figure 2.62(c) is the actual tree. In particular, the root of Figure 2.62(c) corresponds to the convex hull of the W-like shape, while its left child corresponds to the convex hull of its upper connected region A, and its right child corresponds to the lower connected region B, which is a triangle and hence is not decomposed further. The left child of the root has one child corresponding to its lower connected component C.

When the polygons in a block are represented by their CDT, it has been suggested [1541] that the block be further subdivided on the basis of whether the total number of nodes in the CDT exceeds the splitting threshold T of the underlying polygon decomposition rule (i.e., the number of polygons or parts of them that can be covered by a block or a part of the block unless it possibly contains a vertex). Each time a block is decomposed, the CDTs of all polygons in the new subblocks are calculated, and all subblocks for which the total number of CDT nodes exceeds the splitting threshold are recursively subdivided.

Regardless of the value of T that is used, when all of the polygons meet at a single vertex, the blocks that contain such vertices may be a part of many polygons, thereby possibly complicating algorithms such as point location [1541]. One way to reduce this number and, more importantly, the number of polygons that can be a part of each block is to modify the polygonal map m by preprocessing it and applying a technique termed *vertex enlargement* to each vertex v at which more than T ($T \geq 3$) polygons are incident [1541]. Note that we discuss this technique not so much for its utility, which is unclear, but for the way in which it reduces the complexity of the map in a systematic manner.[19]

The basic operation in vertex enlargement is checking if each of the angles between the edges that meet at v in clockwise order is less than $180°$ (i.e., they form what is termed a *convex corner*). If this is the case, then v is replaced by a new small polygon at which all of these edges are incident (e.g., the polygonal map in Figure 2.63(a) is transformed to Figure 2.63(c) by the removal of vertex V). If this is not the case, then there is one angle that is greater than or equal to $180°$, and the new polygon contains v, but now the degree of v has been reduced to two (e.g., the polygonal map of Figure 2.63(d) is transformed to that of Figure 2.63(f) by the replacement of the four polygons incident at V with just two polygons). As long as the new vertices of the newly created polygons are sufficiently close to v, the new edges of the newly created polygons will not cross existing edges, and the result will be a legal polygonal map. This process is described more precisely and formally as follows, assuming that v has degree d:

1. For each polygon p in m with e edges such that successive adjacent edges e_1 and e_2 in clockwise order that are incident at v for which e_1 and e_2 form a convex corner, choose two points p_1 and p_2 on edges e_1 and e_2, respectively, so that the edge f between them does not cross any of the existing edges of the polygonal map. Replace p by a pair of polygons p' and p''. p' contains $e + 1$ edges and is formed by replacing the portions of the edges between p_1 and v and p_2 and v in p by a new edge f (e.g., polygon JKCD in Figure 2.63(b)). p'' is a triangle polygon formed by f and the edges between p_1 and v and p_2 and v (e.g., polygon VJK in Figure 2.63(b)).

---

[19] The rest of this discussion can be skipped on an initial reading.

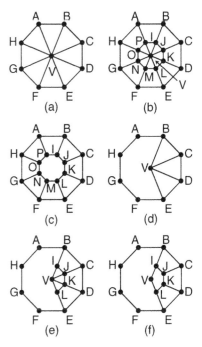

Figure 2.63
(a–c): Example of vertex enlargement where every pair of successive edges in clockwise order that are adjacent at vertex V form a convex corner: (a) initial polygonal map, (b) intermediate result after adding edges around V, and (c) final result after V has been removed. (d–f): Example of vertex enlargement where every pair of successive edges in clockwise order that are adjacent at vertex V form a convex corner with the exception of edges VE and VB: (d) initial polygonal map, (e) intermediate result after adding edges around V, and (f) final result after all but two of the edges incident at V have been removed.

2. For each polygon p with edges e_1 and e_2 incident at v such that there does not exist another polygon q with either edge e_1 or e_2 that does not have a convex corner at v; remove edges e_1 and e_2 (e.g., edges VI and VJ in polygon VJK in Figure 2.63(b), whose result is given in Figure 2.63(c), whereas this condition is not satisfied for the same edges and polygon in Figure 2.63(e)).

3. If v is isolated (i.e., it has degree 0), then mark the polygon q of d edges in which v is contained as having an enlarged vertex and remove v (e.g., vertex V in Figure 2.63(c)). Otherwise, v is a vertex of just two polygons, one of which, say q, has $d + 1$ edges where all pairs of adjacent edges form a convex angle, and both v and q are marked as corresponding to an enlarged vertex (e.g., vertex V and polygon VIJKL in Figure 2.63(f)).

Exercises

1. Why do we need to check for angles greater than 180° when checking for vertex enlargement?

2. Suppose that you apply vertex enlargement to a polygonal map. What is the minimum value of the maximum degree of any vertex in the resulting map, and how would you achieve this situation?

3. Consider a polygonal map. Suppose that you apply vertex enlargement in conjunction with a bucketing decomposition rule that decomposes a block whenever it is a part of more than T polygons. What is a reasonable value of T?

4. Suppose that you use a vertex bucket polygon quadtree (i.e., decomposition halts whenever a block is a part of no more than T polygons or contains just one vertex). Can you guarantee that using such a rule, the decomposition process for $T = 1$ will always halt? No vertex enlargement has been applied.

5. Suppose that you preprocess every polygonal map by applying vertex enlargement to all vertices that have degree greater than T ($T \geq 3$). Does this mean that we can now dispense with the stipulation that decomposition halts whenever a block contains just one vertex? In other words, does a decomposition rule that stipulates that decomposition halts whenever a block is a part of no more than T polygons yield the same decomposition as one that also halts the decomposition when the block contains just one vertex?

6. Suppose that a polygonal map has been decomposed to form a vertex bucket polygon quadtree. Next, recursively subdivide the block if its CDT contains more than T nodes. Prove that decomposition of the block based on the number of CDT nodes cannot lead to a reduction in the number of polygons in a node, thereby making it impossible for a situation to arise in which merging should be applied.

2.1.5 Hierarchical Interior-Based Representations

Assuming the presence of an access structure, the implicit interior-based representations described in Sections 2.1.1 and 2.1.2 are good for finding the objects associated with a particular location or cell (i.e., query 2), while requiring that all cells be examined when determining the locations associated with a particular object (i.e., the feature query). In contrast, the explicit interior-based representation that we described is good for the feature query, while requiring that all objects be examined when trying to respond to the location query. In this section, we focus on interior-based representations that enable both queries to be answered without possibly having to examine every cell.

This is achieved by imposing containment hierarchies on the representations. The hierarchies differ depending on whether the hierarchy is of space (i.e., the cells in the space in which the objects are found) or of objects. In the former case, we aggregate space into successively larger-sized chunks (i.e., blocks); in the latter, we aggregate objects into successively larger groups (in terms of the number of objects that they contain). The former is applicable to implicit (i.e., image-based) interior-based representations; the latter is applicable to explicit (i.e., object-based) interior-based representations. Thus, we see again that the distinction is the same as that used in computer graphics to distinguish between algorithms as being image space or object space [622], respectively.

The basic idea is that in image-based representations we propagate objects up the hierarchy, with the occupied space being implicit to the representation. Thus, we retain the property that associated with each cell is an identifier indicating the object of which it is a part. In fact, it is this information that is propagated up the hierarchy so that each element in the hierarchy contains the union of the objects that appear in the elements immediately below it.

On the other hand, in the object-based representations, we propagate the space occupied by the objects up the hierarchy, with the identities of the objects being implicit to the representation. Thus, we retain the property that associated with each object is a set of locations in space corresponding to the cells that make up the object. Actually, since this information may be rather voluminous, it is often the case that an approximation of the space occupied by the object is propagated up the hierarchy rather than the collection of individual cells that are spanned by the object. The approximation is usually the minimum bounding box for the object that is customarily stored with the explicit representation. Therefore, associated with each element in the hierarchy is a bounding box corresponding to the union of the bounding boxes associated with the elements immediately below it.

The use of the bounding box approximation has the drawback that the bounding boxes at a given level in the hierarchy are not necessarily disjoint. This can be overcome by decomposing the bounding boxes so that disjointness holds. The drawback of this solution is that an object may be associated with more than one bounding box, which may result in the object's being reported as satisfying a particular query more than once. For example, suppose that we want to retrieve all the objects that overlap a particular region (i.e., a window query) rather than a point, as is done in the location query.

It is very important to note that the presence of the hierarchy does not mean that the alternative query (i.e., the feature query in the case of a space hierarchy and the location query in the case of an object hierarchy) can be answered immediately. Instead, obtaining the answer usually requires that the hierarchy be descended. The effect is that the order of the execution time needed to obtain the answer is reduced from linear to logarithmic. Of course, this is not always the case. For example, the fact that we are using bounding boxes for the space spanned by the objects, rather than the exact space occupied by them, means that we do not always have a complete answer when reaching the bottom of the hierarchy. In particular, at this point, we may have to resort to a more expensive point-in-polygon test [622].

It is worth repeating that the only reason for imposing the hierarchy is to facilitate responding to the alternative query (i.e., the feature query in the case of a space hierarchy on the implicit representation and the location query in the case of an object hierarchy on the explicit representation). Thus, the base representation of the hierarchy is still usually used to answer the original query because, often, when using the hierarchy, the inherently logarithmic overhead incurred by the need to descend the hierarchy may be too expensive (e.g., when using the implicit representation with the array access structure to respond to the location query). Of course, other considerations, such as space requirements, may cause us to modify the base representation of the hierarchy, with the result that it will take longer to respond to the original query (e.g., the use of a treelike access structure with an implicit representation). Nevertheless, as a general rule, in the case of the space hierarchy, we use the implicit representation (which is the basis of this hierarchy) to answer the location query; in the case of the object hierarchy, we use the explicit representation (which is the basis of this hierarchy) to answer the feature query.

The rest of this section is organized as follows. We first show in Section 2.1.5.1 how to modify the implicit interior-based representations that are image based, and then, in Section 2.1.5.2, we address the explicit interior-based representations that are object-based. We conclude in Section 2.1.5.3 with a discussion of some disjoint object-based methods.

2.1.5.1 Image-Based Hierarchical Interior-Based Representations (Pyramids)

Our goal here is to be able to take an object o as input and return the cells that it occupies (the feature query) when using a representation that stores with each cell the identities of the objects of which it is a part. The most natural hierarchy that can be imposed on the cells to enable us to answer this query is one that aggregates every q cells, regardless of the values associated with them, into larger congruent blocks (unlike the aggregation of identically valued cells into multidimensional blocks, as in the region quadtree). This process is repeated recursively so that groups of q blocks are repeatedly aggregated into one block until there is just one block left. The value associated with the block b is the union of the names (i.e., object identifiers) of the objects associated with the cells or blocks that make up block b. The identities of the cells and blocks that are aggregated depends, in part, on how the collection of the cells is represented. For example, assuming a two-dimensional space, if the cells are represented as one long list consisting of the cells of the first row, followed by those of the second row, and so on, then one possible aggregation combines every successive q cells. In this case, the blocks are really one-dimensional entities.

The process that we have just outlined is described more formally below. We make the following assumptions:

- The blocks are rectangular with sides parallel to the coordinate axes.

- Each block contains q cells or q blocks so that, assuming d dimensions, $q = \prod_{j=1}^{d} r_j$, where the block has width r_j for dimension j ($1 \leq j \leq d$), measured in cells or blocks, depending on the level in the hierarchy at which the block is found.

- All blocks at a particular level in the hierarchy are congruent, with the different levels forming a containment hierarchy.

- There are S cells in the underlying space, and let n be the smallest power of q such that $q^n \geq S$.

- The underlying space can be enlarged by adding L empty cells so that $q^n = S + L$ and that each side of the underlying space along dimension j is of width $r_j{}^n$.

The hierarchy consists of the set of sets $\{C_i\}$ ($0 \leq i \leq n$), where C_n corresponds to the original collection of cells having $S + L$ elements, C_{n-1} contains $(S + L)/q$ elements corresponding to the result of the initial aggregation of q cells into $(S + L)/q$ congruent blocks, and C_0 is a set consisting of just one element corresponding to a block of size $S + L$. Each element e of C_i ($0 \leq i \leq n - 1$) is a congruent block whose value is the union of the values (i.e., sets of object identifiers) associated with the blocks of the q elements of C_{i+1}. The value of each element of C_n is the set of object identifiers corresponding to the objects of which its cell is a part.

The resulting hierarchy is known as a *cell pyramid* [1845][20] and is frequently characterized as a *multiresolution representation* since the original collection of objects is described at several levels of detail by using cells that have different sizes, although they are similar in shape. It is important to distinguish the cell pyramid from the region quadtree, which, as we recall, is an example of an aggregation into square blocks where the basis of the aggregation is that the cells have identical values (i.e., are associated with the same object, or objects if object overlap is permitted). The region quadtree is an instance of what is termed a *variable-resolution representation*, which, of course, is not limited to blocks that are square. In particular, it can be used with a limited number of nonrectangular shapes (most notably, triangles in two dimensions [157, 1637]).

---

[20] Actually, the qualifier *cell* is rarely used. However, we use it here to avoid confusion with other variants of the pyramid that are based on a hierarchy of objects rather than cells, as discussed in Section 2.1.5.2.

It is quite difficult to use the cell pyramid, in the form that we have described, to respond to the feature query and to the complete location query (i.e., to obtain all of the contiguous cells that make up the object associated with the query location) due to the absence of an access structure. This can be remedied by implementing a set of arrays A_i in a one-to-one correspondence to C_i ($0 \leq i \leq n$), where A_i is a d-dimensional array of side length $r_j^{\,i}$ for dimension j ($1 \leq j \leq d$). Each of the elements of A_i corresponds to a d-dimensional block of side length $r_j^{\,n-i}$ for dimension j ($1 \leq j \leq d$), assuming a total underlying space of side length $r_j^{\,n}$. The result is a stack of arrays A_i, termed an *array pyramid*, which serves as an access structure to collections C_i ($0 \leq i \leq n$). The array pyramid is an instance of an implicit interior-based representation consisting of array access structures. Of course, other representations are possible through the use of alternative access structures (e.g., different types of trees).

We illustrate the array pyramid for two dimensions with $r_1 = 2$ and $r_2 = 2$. Assume that the space in which the original collection of cells is found is of size $2^n \times 2^n$. Let C_n correspond to the original collection of cells. The hierarchy of arrays consists of the sequence A_i ($0 \leq i \leq n$) so that elements of A_i access the corresponding elements in C_i. We obtain C_{n-1} by forming an array of size $2^{n-1} \times 2^{n-1}$ with 2^{2n-2} elements so that each element e in C_{n-1} corresponds to a 2×2 square consisting of four elements (i.e., cells) in C_n and has a value consisting of the union of the names (i.e., labels) of the objects that are associated with these four cells. This process is applied recursively to form C_i ($0 \leq i \leq n-1$), where C_0 is a collection consisting of just one element whose value is the set of names of all the objects associated with at least one cell. The arrays are assumed to be stored in memory using sequential allocation with conventional orderings (e.g., lexicographically) and are accessed by use of the d-dimensional coordinate values of the cells. For example, Figure 2.64 is the array pyramid for the collection of objects in Figure 2.1.

Using the array pyramid, it is very easy to respond to the feature query: we just examine the relevant parts of the stack of arrays. For example, suppose that we want to determine the locations that make up object o, and we use the array pyramid consisting of arrays A_i ($0 \leq i \leq n$) in a two-dimensional space of size $2^n \times 2^n$ where the blocks are squares of side length 2^{n-i}. We start with A_0, which consists of just one element e, and determine if o is a member of the set of values associated with e. If it is not, then we exit, and the answer is negative. If it is, then we examine the four elements in A_1 that correspond to e and repeat the test. At this point, we know that o is a member of at least one of them as otherwise o could not have been a member of the set of values associated with element e of A_0. This process is applied recursively to elements of A_j that contained o (i.e., the appropriate elements of A_{j+1} are examined for $1 \leq j \leq n-1$) until we encounter A_n, at which time the process stops. The advantage of this method is that elements of A_{j+1} are not examined unless object o is guaranteed to be a member of the set of values associated with at least one of them.

The array pyramid uses a sequence of arrays as an access structure. An alternative implementation is one that imposes an access structure in the form of a tree T on the elements of the hierarchy $\{C_i\}$. One possible implementation is a tree of fanout q where the root T_0 corresponds to C_0, nodes $\{T_{ij}\}$ at depth i correspond to C_i ($1 \leq i \leq n-1$), and the leaf nodes $\{T_{nj}\}$ correspond to C_n. In particular, element t in the tree at depth j corresponds to element e of C_j ($0 \leq j \leq n-1$), and t contains q pointers to its q children in T_{j+1} corresponding to the elements of C_{j+1} that are contained in e. The result is termed a *cell-tree pyramid*. Figure 2.65 shows the cell-tree pyramid corresponding to the collection of objects and cells in the array in Figure 2.7. This example makes use of two-dimensional data with $r_1 = 2$ and $r_2 = 2$. In this case, notice the similarity between the cell-tree pyramid and the region quadtree implementation that uses an access structure that is a tree with a fanout of 4 (Figure 2.18).

Using the term *quadtree* in its most general sense (i.e., d-dimensional blocks whose sides need not be powers of 2 or of the same length), the cell-tree pyramid can be viewed as a complete quadtree (i.e., where no aggregation takes place at the deepest level or,

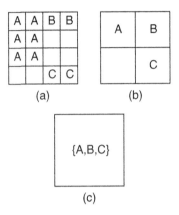

Figure 2.64
Array pyramid for the collection of objects and cells in Figure 2.1: (a) array A_2, (b) array A_1, and (c) array A_0. The block decomposition in Figure 2.1 corresponds to Array A_3.

equivalently, all leaf nodes are at the maximum depth of the tree). Nevertheless, there are some very important differences. The first difference, as we pointed out earlier, is that the quadtree is a variable-resolution representation, and the cell-tree pyramid is a multiresolution representation. The second, and most important, difference is that, in the case of the quadtree, the nonleaf nodes serve only as an access structure. They do not include any information about the objects present in the nodes and cells below them. This is why the quadtree, like the array, is not useful for answering the feature query. Of course, we could also devise a variant of the quadtree (termed a *truncated-tree pyramid* [1638]) that uses the nonleaf nodes to store information about the objects present in the cells and nodes below them (e.g., Figure 2.66). Note that both the cell-tree pyramid and the truncated-tree pyramid are instances of an implicit interior-based representation with a tree access structure.

Our definition of the pyramid was made in a bottom-up manner in the sense that we started with a block size and an underlying space size. Next, we expanded the size of the underlying space so that a containment hierarchy of congruent blocks at each level and similar blocks at different levels could be formed. We can also define a variant of the

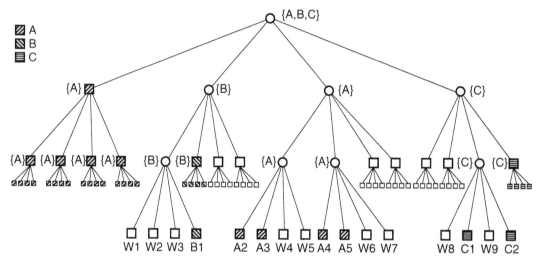

Figure 2.65
Cell-tree pyramid for the collection of objects and cells in Figure 2.1.

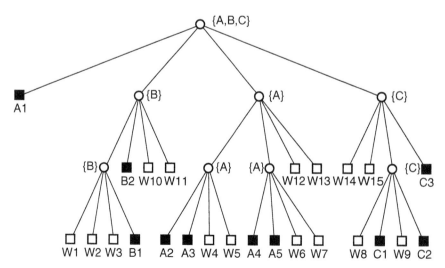

Figure 2.66
Truncated-tree pyramid for the collection of objects and cells in Figure 2.1.

pyramid where the requirements of block congruence at each level and block similarity at different levels are relaxed. This is a bit easier if we define the pyramid in a top-down manner as we can calculate the number of cells by which the underlying space needs to be expanded as the block sizes at the different levels are defined. It should be clear that the congruence requirement is more restrictive than the similarity requirement. If we relax the requirement that the blocks at different levels be similar, but retain the requirement that the blocks at each level be congruent, then we must store at each level i the size of the block q_i (i.e., the values of the individual components r_{ij} of $q_i = \prod_{j=1}^{d} r_{ij}$ for dimension j $(1 \le j \le d)$).

If we relax both the requirement that the blocks at the different levels be similar and the requirement that the blocks at each level be congruent, while still requiring that they form a containment hierarchy, then we are, in effect, permitting partitioning hyperplanes (i.e., lines in two dimensions) at arbitrary positions. In this case, we get a more general pyramid if we use a top-down definition as we can now have a different partition at each level. In this case, we have an irregular grid at each level, and thus we must store the positions of the partitioning hyperplanes (i.e., lines in two dimensions) at each level. We call the result an *irregular grid pyramid*. If the irregular grid is implemented with an array access structure, then the result is called an *irregular grid array pyramid*.

Other pyramid variants are also possible. For example, the *Dynamically Quantized Pyramid* (DQP) [1425, 1777] is a two-dimensional containment hierarchy where the blocks at the different levels are neither similar nor congruent. It differs from the irregular pyramid in that there is a possibly different 2×2 grid partition at each block at each level rather than one grid partition at each level. Figure 1.46 in Section 1.5.1.4 of Chapter 1 is an example of a DQP for $n = 3$. Notice the close similarity to a complete point quadtree [614]. The DQP finds use in cluster detection, as well as multidimensional histogramming. Of course, even more general variants are possible. In particular, we could use any one of the other recursive and nonrecursive decompositions described in Section 2.1.2 at each block with the appropriate access structure.

It is interesting to observe that the interior-based representations discussed in Section 2.1.3 that permit both the blocks and the objects to be arbitrary polyhedra (i.e., d-dimensional objects whose $(d-1)$-dimensional faces are hyperplanes), while still not permitting them to intersect and not permitting an object to overlap only a part of a block, can also be used as the basis of an image hierarchy. In particular, the BSP tree, K-structure, and layered dag are hierarchies of blocks, triangles, and "above-and-below" partitions, respectively. They are designed to facilitate responses to the location query (i.e., determining the object associated with a particular location in space). If with each nonleaf node we store the identities of the objects spanned by the underlying regions, then the feature query (i.e., determining the locations associated with a particular object) is very easy to answer. In fact, these structures are variants of the cell-tree pyramid, albeit with a very irregular decomposition of the underlying space.

Exercises

In Exercises 1–11, assume the use of an array pyramid over a $2^n \times 2^n$ space to store an object.

1. What is the maximum number of pyramid elements that must be examined in order to answer the feature query, assuming that only one object is stored in the pyramid?

2. Define the efficiency of the pyramid, E_p, to be the ratio of the maximum number of pyramid elements examined to the total number of cells in the space (i.e., the number of elements at the deepest level of the pyramid). E_p indicates the advantage of using the array pyramid hierarchy when answering the feature query with an implicit representation over the cost that would be incurred had we not used a hierarchy and, thereby, examined every cell. Define the overhead of the pyramid, O_p, to be the ratio of the maximum number of pyramid elements examined to the total number of cells in the space that satisfy the query (i.e., are associated with the object whose constituent cells the feature query is seeking). O_p indicates the overhead incurred in using the array pyramid hierarchy when answering the feature query with an

implicit representation instead of using an explicit representation. Compute E_p and O_p for an object that occupies just one cell.

3. Compute E_p and O_p for an object that occupies the entire space (i.e., $2^n \times 2^n$ cells).

4. Compute E_p and O_p for a linelike object that is one cell wide, is horizontal, and spans the entire space.

5. Compute E_p and O_p for a linelike object that is one cell wide and is diagonal so that one end is in the upper-left corner of the space while the other end is in the lower-right corner of the space.

6. Compute the worst-case E_p and O_p for an object that occupies a square of size 2×2 cells.

7. Compute average E_p and O_p values over all the possible positions of the 2×2 square.

8. Compute the worst-case E_p and O_p for an object that occupies a square of size $2^i \times 2^i$ cells ($1 \leq i \leq n - 1$).

9. Compute an average E_p and O_p for an object that occupies a square of size $2^i \times 2^i$ cells ($1 \leq i \leq n - 1$).

10. Compute the average worst-case E_p and O_p over all values of i ($1 \leq i \leq n - 1$) for an object that occupies a square of size $2^i \times 2^i$ cells.

11. Compute the average E_p and O_p over all values of i ($1 \leq i \leq n - 1$) for an object that occupies a square of size $2^i \times 2^i$ cells.

12. Compute the average worst-case E_p and O_p over all values of i ($1 \leq i \leq n - 1$) for an object that occupies a block of side length 2^i in a d-dimensional space.

13. Compute the average E_p and O_p over all values of i ($1 \leq i \leq n - 1$) for an object that occupies a block of side length 2^i in a d-dimensional space.

2.1.5.2 Object-Based Hierarchical Interior-Based Representations (R-trees, Bounding Box Hierarchies)

Our goal here is to be able to take a location a as input and return the objects in which a is a member (the location query) when using a representation that stores with each object the addresses of the cells it comprises (i.e., an explicit representation). The most natural hierarchy that can be imposed on the objects that would enable us to answer this query is one that aggregates every M objects (that are hopefully in close spatial proximity, although this is not a requirement) into larger objects. This process is repeated recursively until there is just one aggregated object left. Since the objects may have different sizes and shapes, it is not easy to compute and represent the aggregate object. Moreover, it is similarly difficult to test each one of them (and their aggregates) to determine if they contain a since each one may require a different test by virtue of the different shapes. Thus, it is useful to use a common aggregate shape and point inclusion test to prune the search.

The common aggregate shape and point inclusion test that we use assumes the existence of a minimum enclosing box (termed a *bounding box*) for each object. This bounding box is part of the data associated with each object and aggregate of objects. In this case, we reformulate our object hierarchy in terms of bounding boxes. In particular, we aggregate the bounding boxes of every M objects into a box (i.e., block) of minimum size that contains them. This process is repeated recursively until there is just one block left. The value associated with the bounding box b is its location (e.g., the coordinate values of its diagonally opposite corners for two-dimensional data). It should be clear that the bounding boxes serve as a filter to prune the search for an object that contains a.

In this section, we expand on hierarchies of objects that actually aggregate the bounding boxes of the objects. Section 2.1.5.2.1 gives an overview of object hierarchies and introduces the general concepts of an object pyramid and an object-tree pyramid, which provides a tree access structure for the object pyramid. Sections 2.1.5.2.2 to 2.1.5.2.4

present several aggregation methods. In particular, Section 2.1.5.2.2 discusses ordering-based aggregation methods. Section 2.1.5.2.3 discusses extent-based aggregation techniques, which result in the R-tree representation, and Section 2.1.5.2.4 describes the R*-tree, which is the best of the extent-based aggregation methods. Next, we discuss methods of updating or loading an object-tree pyramid with a large number of objects at once, termed *bulk insertion* (Section 2.1.5.2.5) and *bulk loading* (Section 2.1.5.2.6), respectively. Section 2.1.5.2.7 concludes the presentation by reviewing some of the shortcomings of the object-tree pyramid and discussing some of the solutions that have been proposed to overcome them. For a comparative look at these different aggregation methods, see the VASCO (Visualization and Animation of Spatial Constructs and Operations) [243, 244, 245, 246]) set of JAVA applets found at *http://www.cs.umd.edu/~hjs/quadtree /index.html*. The VASCO system also includes many other indexing techniques for points, lines, rectangles, and regions that are based on space decomposition (see also the SP-GiST system [70] described in Section 1.9 of Chapter 1), Other libraries that are based on object hierarchies include GiST [817] and XXL (Extensible and Flexible Library) [193].

Most of the research on the use of object hierarchies has been in the context of a sequential environment, and this is the focus of this section. Nevertheless, there has been some work in a parallel environment. In particular, Hoel and Samet [860, 865, 862, 861, 867, 869] discuss data-parallel algorithms for a number of spatial operations for R-trees. Note that this work involves the use of a large number of processors and should be contrasted with the work on "parallel R-trees" of Kamel and Faloutsos [982], where the parallelism involves issues in the distribution of R-tree data to multiple disks rather than multiple execution paths. There has also been some interest of late in issues arising from the implementation of R-trees in a peer-to-peer (P2P) setting (e.g., [1307]). These constructs are beyond the scope of this book and will not be discussed further.

2.1.5.2.1 Overview

The nature of the aggregation (i.e., using bounding boxes), the number of objects that are being aggregated at each step (as well as whether this number can be varied), and, most importantly, the decision as to which objects to aggregate are quite arbitrary although an appropriate choice can make the search process much more efficient. The decision as to which objects to aggregate assumes that we have a choice in the matter. It could be that the objects have to be aggregated in the order in which they are encountered. This could lead to poor search performance when the objects are not encountered in an order that correlates with spatial proximity. Of course, this is not an issue as long as we just have les than or equal to M objects.

It should be clear that the issue of choice only arises if we know the identities of all the objects before starting the aggregation process (unless we are permitted to rebuild the hierarchy each time we encounter a new object or delete an object) and if we are permitted to reorder them so that objects in aggregate i need not necessarily have been encountered prior to the objects in aggregate $i + 1$, and vice versa. This is not always the case (i.e., a dynamic versus a static database), although, for the moment, we do assume that we know the identities of all of the objects before starting the aggregation and that we may aggregate any object with any other object. Observe also that the bounding boxes in the hierarchy are not necessarily disjoint. In fact, the objects may be configured in space in such a way that no disjoint hierarchy is possible. By the same reasoning, the objects themselves need not be disjoint.

The process that we have just outlined can be described more formally as follows. Assume that there are N objects in the space, and let n be the smallest power of M such that $M^n \geq N$. Assume that all aggregates contain M elements with the exception of the last one at each level, which may contain less than M as M^n is not necessarily equal to N. The hierarchy of objects consists of the set D of sets $\{D_i\}$ ($0 \leq i \leq n$), where D_n corresponds to the set of bounding boxes of the individual objects; D_{n-1} corresponds to the result of the initial aggregation of the bounding boxes into N/M bounding boxes, each of which contains M bounding boxes of objects; and D_0 is a set containing just one element corresponding to the aggregations of all of the objects and is a bounding box that encloses all of the objects. We term the resulting hierarchy an *object pyramid*. Once again, we have a *multiresolution representation* as the original collection of objects is described at several levels of detail by virtue of the number of objects whose bounding boxes are grouped at each level. This is in contrast with the cell pyramid, where the different levels of detail are distinguished by the sizes of the cells that make up the elements at each level.

Searching an object pyramid consisting of sets D_i ($0 \leq i \leq n$) for the object containing a particular location a (i.e., the location query) proceeds as follows. We start with D_0, which consists of just one bounding box b and determine if a is inside b. If it is not, then we exit, and the answer is negative. If it is, then we examine the M elements in D_1 that are covered by b and repeat the test using their bounding boxes. Note that unlike the cell pyramid, at this point, a is not necessarily included in the M bounding boxes in D_1 as these M bounding boxes are not required to cover the entire space spanned by b. In particular, we exit if a is not covered by at least one of the bounding boxes at this level. This process is applied recursively to all elements of D_j for $0 \leq j \leq n$ until all elements of D_n have been processed, at which time the process stops. The advantage of this method is that elements of D_j ($1 \leq j \leq n$) are not examined unless a is guaranteed to be covered by at least one of the elements of D_{j-1}.

The bounding boxes serve to distinguish between occupied and unoccupied space, thereby indicating whether the search for the objects that contain a particular location (i.e., the location query) should proceed further. At a first glance, it would appear that the object pyramid is rather inefficient for responding to the location query because, in the worst case, all of the bounding boxes at all levels must be examined. However, the maximum number of bounding boxes in the object pyramid, and hence the maximum number that will have to be inspected, is $\sum_{j=0}^{n} M^j \leq 2N$.

Of course, we may also have to examine the actual sets of locations associated with each object when the bounding box does not result in any of the objects being pruned from further consideration since the objects are not necessarily rectangular in shape (i.e., boxes). Thus, using the hierarchy provided by the object pyramid results in at most an additional factor of 2 in terms of the number of bounding box tests while possibly saving many more tests. Therefore, the maximum amount of work to answer the location query with the hierarchy is of the same order of magnitude as that which would have been needed had the hierarchy not been introduced.

As we can see, the way in which we introduced the hierarchy to form the object pyramid did not necessarily enable us to make more efficient use of the explicit interior-based representation to respond to the location query. The problem was that once we determined that location a was covered by one of the bounding boxes, say b, in D_j ($0 \leq j \leq n-1$), we had no way to access the bounding boxes making up b without examining all of the bounding boxes in D_{j+1}. This is easy to rectify by imposing an access structure in the form of a tree T on the elements of the hierarchy D. One possible implementation is a tree of fanout M, where the root T_0 corresponds to the bounding box in D_0. T_0 has M links to its M children $\{T_{1k}\}$, which correspond to the M bounding boxes in D_1 that D_0 comprises. The set of nodes $\{T_{ik}\}$ at depth i correspond to the bounding boxes in D_i ($0 \leq i \leq n$), while the set of leaf nodes $\{T_{nk}\}$ correspond to D_n. In particular, node t in the tree at depth j corresponds to bounding box b in D_j ($0 \leq j \leq n-1$), and t contains M pointers to its M children in T_{j+1} corresponding to the bounding boxes in D_{j+1} that are contained in b. We use the term *object-tree pyramid* to describe this structure.

Figure 2.67 gives the specifications for the example object-tree pyramid shown in Figure 2.68(a) for a collection of nine rectangle objects with $M = 3$ (and thus $n = 2$). The rectangles are assumed to be embedded in a $2^6 \times 2^6$ grid with an origin in

Object	x_{left}	x_{right}	y_{bottom}	y_{top}	x_{centroid}	y_{centroid}	Peano-Hilbert code
A	3	8	6	36	5	21	904
B	25	34	34	38	29	36	2,017
C	33	37	21	36	35	28	3,423
D	21	38	23	27	29	25	658
E	6	26	3	8	16	5	275
F	31	35	15	19	33	17	3,496
G	23	38	11	14	30	12	420
1	23	26	25	36	24	30	700
2	27	35.5	14.5	20.5	31	17	598
3	16	22	3.5	7.5	19	5	284

Figure 2.67
Specifications for a collection of rectangles embedded in a $2^6 \times 2^6$ grid with an origin in the lower-left corner. The centroid values are truncated in order to be integers. The Peano-Hilbert order entry is based on coordinate values x_{centroid} and y_{centroid}.

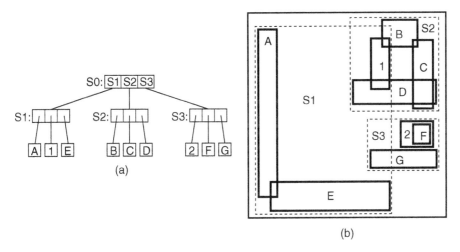

Figure 2.68
(a) Object-tree pyramid for a collection of rectangle objects whose specifications are given in Figure 2.67 with $M = 3$, and (b) the spatial extents of the objects and the bounding boxes of the nodes in (a). Notice that the leaf nodes in the index also store bounding boxes, although this is shown only for the nonleaf nodes.

the lower-left corner. Figure 2.68(b) shows the spatial extents of the objects and the bounding boxes of the nodes in Figure 2.68(a), with broken lines denoting the bounding boxes corresponding to the leaf nodes. Note that the object-tree pyramid is not unique. Its structure depends heavily on the order in which the individual objects and their corresponding bounding boxes are aggregated.

The object-tree pyramid that we have just described still has a worst case where we may have to examine all of the bounding boxes in D_j $(1 \le j \le n)$ when executing the location query or its variants (e.g., a window query). This is the case if query location a is contained in every bounding box in D_{j-1}. Such a situation, although rare, can arise in practice because a may be included in the bounding boxes of many objects (termed a *false hit*) as the bounding boxes are not disjoint, while a is contained in a much smaller number of objects. Equivalently, false hits are caused by the fact that a spatial object may be spatially contained in full or in part in several bounding boxes or nodes while being associated with just one node or bounding box.

However, unlike the object pyramid, the object-tree pyramid does guarantee that only the bounding boxes that contain a, and no others, will be examined. Thus, we have not improved on the worst case of the object pyramid although we have reduced its likelihood, because we may still have to examine $2N$ bounding boxes. It is interesting to observe that the object pyramid and the object-tree pyramid are instances of an explicit interior-based representation since it is still the case that associated with each object o is a set containing the addresses of the cells that it comprises. Note also that the access structure facilitates only the determination of the object associated with a particular cell and not which cells are contiguous. Thus, the object-tree pyramid is not an instance of an implicit interior-based representation.

The decision as to which objects to aggregate is an important factor in the efficiency of the object-tree pyramid in responding to the location query. The efficiency of the object-tree pyramid for search operations depends on its abilities to distinguish between occupied space and unoccupied space and to prevent a node from being examined needlessly due to a false overlap with other nodes.

The extent to which these efficiencies are realized is a direct result of how well our aggregation policy is able to satisfy the following two goals. The first goal is to minimize the number of aggregated nodes that must be visited by the search. This goal is accomplished by minimizing the area common to sibling aggregated nodes (termed *overlap*). The second goal is to reduce the likelihood that sibling aggregated nodes are visited by the search. This is accomplished by minimizing the total area spanned by the bounding boxes of the sibling aggregated nodes (termed *coverage*). A related goal to that of minimizing the coverage is minimizing the area in sibling aggregated nodes that is not spanned by the bounding boxes of any of the children of the sibling aggregated nodes (termed *dead area*). Note that this definition of dead area is slightly different from one that minimizes the part of the area that is spanned by the bounding box of any aggregated node that is not spanned by the bounding boxes of any of its children as it ignores the area that is spanned by the bounding boxes of children of siblings of the aggregated nodes. Dead area is usually decreased by minimizing coverage, and thus minimizing dead area is often not taken into account explicitly. Another way of interpreting these goals is that they are designed to ensure that objects that are spatially close to each other are stored in the same node. Of course, at times, these goals may be contradictory.

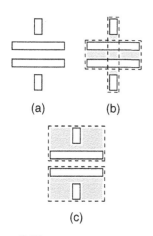

(a) **(b)**

(c)

Figure 2.69
(a) Four bounding boxes and the aggregations that would be induced (b) by minimizing the total area (i.e., coverage) of the covering bounding boxes of the two nodes and (c) by minimizing the area common (i.e., overlap) to the covering bounding boxes of the two nodes. The dead area for the two possible aggregations is shaded. Note that the dead area for one covering node may be part of the objects in another aggregated node, as in (b).

For example, consider the four bounding boxes in Figure 2.69(a). The first goal is satisfied by the aggregation in Figure 2.69(c); the second goal is satisfied by the aggregation in Figure 2.69(b). The dead area is shown shaded in Figure 2.69(b, c). Note that the dead area in Figure 2.69(b) is considerably smaller than the dead area in Figure 2.69(c) on account of the smaller amount of coverage in the children in Figure 2.69(b). Also observe that the dead area for the bounding box of one aggregated node may be part of the objects in another aggregated node, as seen in Figure 2.69(b).

These goals could be satisfied by using trial-and-error methods that examine all possible aggregations and choosing the one that yields the minimum amount of overlap or coverage among the constituent bounding boxes of the nodes, as well as among the nodes at a given level (e.g., Exercise 2 in Section 2.1.5.2.2). The cost is clearly prohibitive. These trial-and-error methods can be made more intelligent by use of iterative optimization [698] (see Exercise 3 in Section 2.1.5.2.2). However, the cost is still too high.

The aggregation techniques described above take the space (i.e., volume) occupied by (termed the *extent of*) the bounding boxes of the individual spatial objects into account. They are described in Sections 2.1.5.2.3 and 2.1.5.2.4. An alternative is to order the objects prior to performing the aggregation. However, in this case, the only choice that we may possibly have with respect to the identities of the objects that are aggregated is when the number of objects (or bounding boxes) being aggregated at each step is permitted to vary. The most obvious order, although it is not particularly interesting or useful, is one that preserves the order in which the objects were initially encountered (i.e., objects in aggregate i have been encountered before those in aggregate $i + 1$). The more common orders are based on proximity or on the values of a small set of parameters describing a common property that is hopefully related to the proximity (and, to a lesser degree, to the shape and extent) of the objects or their bounding boxes in one or all of the dimensions of the space in which they lie [983, 1303, 1588]. Ordering-based aggregation techniques are discussed in Section 2.1.5.2.2.

Exercise

1. Given a set of M rectangles, devise an algorithm to compute their minimum bounding box (i.e., rectangle). What is the execution time of the algorithm?

2.1.5.2.2 Ordering-Based Aggregation Techniques

The most frequently used ordering technique is based on mapping the bounding boxes of the objects to a representative point in a lower-, the same, or a higher-dimensional space and then applying one of the space-ordering methods described in Section 2.1.1.2 and shown in Figure 2.5 (see Exercise 23 in Section 2.1.5.2.4). We use the term *object number* to refer to the result of the application of space ordering.[21] For example, two-dimensional rectangle objects can be transformed into one of the following representative points (e.g., [1637]):

1. The centroid

2. The centroid and the horizontal and vertical extents (i.e., the horizontal and vertical distances from the centroid to the relevant sides)

3. The x and y coordinate values of the two diagonally opposite corners of the rectangle (e.g., the upper-left and lower-right corners)

4. The x and y coordinate values of the lower-right corner of the rectangle and its height and width.

For example, consider the collection of 22 rectangle objects given in Figure 2.70, where the numbers associated with the rectangles denote the relative times at which they were created. Figure 2.71 shows the result of applying a Morton order (Figure 2.71(a)) and Peano-Hilbert order (Figure 2.71(b)) to the collection of rectangle objects in Figure 2.70 using their centroids as the representative points.

Once the N objects have been ordered, the hierarchy D is built in the order D_n, $D_{n-1}, \ldots, D_1, D_0$, where n is the smallest power of M such that $M^n \geq N$. D_n consists of the set of original objects and their bounding boxes. There are two ways of grouping the items to form the hierarchy D: one-dimensional and multidimensional grouping.

In the one-dimensional grouping method, D_{n-1} is formed as follows. The first M objects and their corresponding bounding boxes form the first aggregate, the second M objects and their corresponding bounding boxes form the second aggregate, and so on. D_{n-2} is formed by applying this aggregation process again to the set D_{n-1} of N/M objects and their bounding boxes. This process is continued recursively until we obtain the set D_0 containing just one element corresponding to a bounding box that encloses all of the objects. Note, however, that when the process is continued recursively, the

---

[21] Interestingly, we will see that no matter which of the implementations of the object-tree pyramid is being deployed, the ordering is used primarily to build the object-tree pyramid, although it is used for splitting in some cases such as the Hilbert R-tree [984]. The actual positions of the objects in the ordering (i.e., the object numbers) are not usually recorded in the object-tree pyramid, which is somewhat surprising as this could be used to speed up operations such as point location.

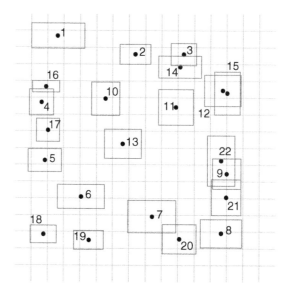

Figure 2.70
A collection of 22 rectangle objects, where the numbers associated with the rectangles denote the relative times at which they were created.

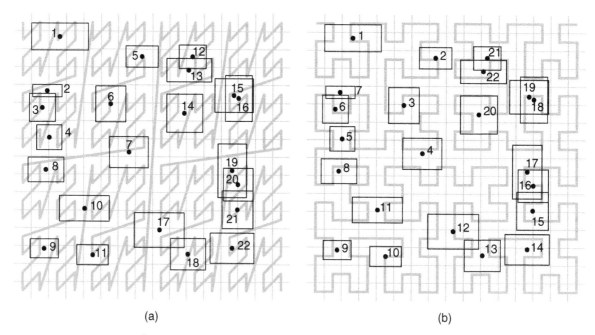

(a)　　　　　　　　　　　　　　　　　　(b)

Figure 2.71
The result of applying (a) a Morton order and (b) a Peano-Hilbert order to the collection of 22 rectangle objects in Figure 2.70 using their centroids as the representative points.

elements of the sets D_i $(0 \le i \le n - 1)$ are not necessarily ordered in the same manner as the elements of D_n.

There are several implementations of the object-tree pyramid using the one-dimensional grouping methods. For example, the *Hilbert packed R-tree* [983] is an object-tree pyramid that makes use of a Peano-Hilbert order. It is important to note that only the leaf nodes of the Hilbert packed R-tree are ordered using the Peano-Hilbert order. The nodes at the remaining levels are ordered according to the time at which they were created. For example, Figure 2.72(a) shows the bounding boxes corresponding to the first level of aggregation for the Hilbert packed R-tree for the collection of 22 rectangle objects in Figure 2.70 with $M = 6$. Similarly, Figure 2.72(b) shows the same result were we to build the same structure using a Morton order (i.e., a Morton packed R-tree), again with $M = 6$. Notice that there is quite a bit of overlap among the bounding boxes as the aggregation does not take the extent of the bounding boxes into account when forming the structure.

A slightly different approach is employed in the *packed R-tree* [1588], which is another instance of an object-tree pyramid. The packed R-tree is based on ordering the objects on the basis of some criterion, such as increasing value of the x coordinate or any of the space-ordering methods shown in Figure 2.5. Once this order has been obtained, the leaf nodes in the packed R-tree are filled by examining the objects in increasing order, where each leaf node is filled with the first unprocessed object and its $M - 1$ nearest neighbors that have not yet been inserted into other leaf nodes. Once an entire level of the packed R-tree has been obtained, the algorithm is reapplied to add nodes at the next level using the same nearest neighbor criterion, terminating when a level contains just one node. The only difference between the ordering that is applied at the levels containing the nonleaf nodes from that used at the level of the leaf nodes is that, in the former case we are ordering the bounding boxes while, in the latter case, we are ordering the actual objects.

Besides the difference in the way nonleaf nodes are formed, we point out that the packed R-tree construction process makes use of a proximity criterion in the domain of the actual data rather than the domain of the representative points, which is the case of the Hilbert packed R-tree. This distinction is quite important because it means that the Hilbert packed R-tree construction process makes no attempt to reduce or minimize coverage and overlap, which, as we shall soon see, are the real cornerstones of the R-tree data structure [791]. Therefore, as we point out below, this makes the Hilbert packed R-tree (and, to a lesser extent, the packed R-tree) much more like a B-tree that is constructed by filling each node to capacity. For example, Figure 2.72(c) shows the bounding boxes corresponding to the first level of aggregation for the packed R-tree for the collection of 22 rectangle objects in Figure 2.70. In this case, the objects were initially ordered using a Peano-Hilbert order.

The *sort-tile-recurse method* (STR method) of Leutenegger, López, and Edgington [1153] is an example of the multidimensional grouping method. Our explanation

(a) (b) (c)

Figure 2.72
The bounding boxes corresponding to the first level of aggregation for the (a) Hilbert packed R-tree, (b) Morton packed R-tree, and (c) packed R-tree (using a Peano-Hilbert order for the initial ordering) for the collection of 22 rectangle objects in Figure 2.70 with $M = 6$. The numbers associated with the rectangle objects in (a) and (b) denote the positions of their corresponding centroids in the order.

assumes, without loss of generality, that the underlying space is two-dimensional, although the extension of the method to higher dimensions is straightforward. Assuming a total of N rectangles and a node capacity of M rectangles per leaf node, D_{n-1} is formed by constructing a tiling of the underlying space consisting of s vertical slabs, where each slab contains s tiles. Each tile corresponds to an object-tree pyramid leaf node that is filled to capacity. Note that the result of this process is that the underlying space is being tiled with rectangular tiles, thereby resembling a grid, but, most importantly, unlike a grid, the horizontal edges of horizontally adjacent tiles (i.e., with a common vertical edge) do not form a straight line (i.e., are not connected). Using this process means that the underlying space is tiled with approximately $\sqrt{N/M} \times \sqrt{N/M}$ tiles and results in approximately N/M object-tree pyramid leaf nodes. The tiling process is applied recursively to these N/M tiles to form $D_{n-2}, D_{n-3}, \ldots$ until just one node is obtained.

The STR method builds the object-tree pyramid in a bottom-up manner. The actual mechanics of the STR method are as follows. Sort the rectangles on the basis of one coordinate value of some easily identified point that is associated with them, say the x coordinate value of their centroid. Aggregate the sorted rectangles into $\sqrt{N/M}$ groups of $\sqrt{NM}$ rectangles, each of which forms a vertical slab containing all rectangles whose centroid's x coordinate value lies in the slab. Next, for each vertical slab v, sort all rectangles in v on the basis of their centroid's y coordinate value. Aggregate the $\sqrt{NM}$ sorted rectangles in each slab v into $\sqrt{N/M}$ groups of M rectangles each. Recall that the elements of these groups form the leaf nodes of the object-tree pyramid. Notice that the minimum bounding boxes of the rectangles in each tile are usually larger than the tiles. The process of forming a gridlike tiling is now applied recursively to the N/M minimum bounding boxes of the tiles, with N taking on the value of N/M until the number of tiles is no larger than M, in which case all of the tiles fit in the root node, and we are done.

A couple of items are worthy of further note. First, the minimum bounding boxes of the rectangles in each tile are usually larger than the tiles. This means that the tiles at each level will overlap. Thus, we do not have a true grid in the sense that the elements at each level of the object-tree pyramid are usually not disjoint. Second, the ordering that is applied is quite similar to a row order (actually column order to be precise) as illustrated in Figure 2.5(a) where the x coordinate value serves as a primary key to form the vertical slabs while the y coordinate value serves as the secondary key to form the tiles from the vertical slabs. Nevertheless, the ordering serves only to determine the partitioning lines to form the tiles but is not used to organize the collection of tiles.

Leutenegger, et al. [1153] compare the results of the STR packing method with those of the Hilbert packed R-tree [983] and an incorrect version of the packed R-tree of Roussopoulos and Leifker [1588]. In particular, they erroneously assume that the packing occurs solely in the order of the x coordinate value of the centroid of each rectangle and do not use the nearest neighbor heuristic actually employed by Roussopoulos and Leifker [1588]. The comparison is in terms of the number of disk accesses made when performing point and region queries on point and region data. They find the STR method to be superior to the packed R-tree in all cases, whereas the result of the comparison of the STR method with the Hilbert packed R-tree is not so conclusive. For mildly skewed data, the STR method is usually better than the Hilbert packed R-tree, while for highly skewed data, neither method is always better than the other.

Notice that the STR method is a bottom-up technique. However, the same idea could also be applied in a top-down manner so that we originally start with M tiles that are then further partitioned. In other words, we start with $\sqrt{M}$ vertical slabs containing $\sqrt{M}$ tiles apiece. This is instead of the initial $\sqrt{N/M}$ vertical slabs containing $\sqrt{N/M}$ tiles in the bottom-up method. The disadvantage of the top-down method is that it requires that we make roughly $2\log_M N$ passes over all of the data, whereas the bottom-up method has the advantage of making just two passes over the data (one for the x coordinate value and one for the y coordinate value) since all recursive invocations of the algorithm deal with centroids of the tiles.

The top-down method can be viewed as an ordering technique in the sense that the objects are partitioned, thereby creating a partial ordering, according to their relative position with respect to some criterion such as a value of a statistical measure for the set of objects as a whole. For example, in the VAMSplit R-tree of White and Jain [1989], which is applied to point data, the split axis (i.e., x or y or z, etc.) is chosen on the basis of having the maximum variance from the mean in the distribution of the point data (for more detail, see Section 1.7.1.7 of Chapter 1). Once the axis is chosen, the objects are split into two equally sized sets constrained so that the resulting nodes are as full as possible. This process is applied recursively to the resulting sets.

Regardless of how the objects are aggregated, the object-tree pyramid is analogous to a height-balanced M-ary tree where only the leaf nodes contain data (objects in this case), and all of the leaf nodes are at the same level. Thus, the object-tree pyramid is good for static datasets. However, in a dynamic environment where objects are added and deleted at will, the object-tree pyramid needs to be rebuilt either entirely or partially to maintain the balance, order, and node-size constraints. In the case of binary trees, this issue is addressed by making use of a B-tree, or a B^+-tree if we wish to restrict the data (i.e., the objects) to the leaf nodes as is the case in our application. Below, we show how to use the B^+-tree to make the object-tree pyramid dynamic.

When the aggregation in the object-tree pyramid is based on ordering the objects, the objects and their bounding boxes can be stored directly in the leaf nodes of the B^+-tree. We term the result an *object B^+-tree*. The key difference between the object B^+-tree and the object-tree pyramid is that the B^+-tree (and likewise the object B^+-tree) permits the number of objects and nodes that are aggregated at each step to vary (i.e., the number of children per node). This is captured by the order of the B^+-tree: for an order (m,M) B^+-tree, the number of children per node usually ranges between $m \geq \lceil M/2 \rceil$ and M, with the root having at least two children unless it is a leaf node (see Appendix A). The only modification to the B^+-tree definition is in the format of the nodes of the object B^+-tree. In particular, the format of each nonleaf node p is changed so that if p has j children, then p contains the following three items of information for each child s:

1. A pointer to s

2. The maximum object number associated with any of the children of s (analogous to a key in the conventional B^+-tree)

3. The bounding box b for s (e.g., the coordinate values of a pair of diagonally opposite corners of b)

Notice that j bounding boxes are stored in each node corresponding to the j children instead of just one bounding box as called for in the definition of the object-tree pyramid. This is done to speed up the point inclusion tests necessary to decide which child to descend when executing the location query. In particular, it avoids a disk access when the nodes are stored on disk.

A leaf node p in the object B^+-tree has a similar format, with the difference that instead of having pointers to j children that are nodes in the tree, p has j pointers to records corresponding to the j objects that it represents. Therefore, p contains the following three items of information for each object s:

1. A pointer to the actual object corresponding to s

2. The object number associated with s

3. The bounding box b for s (e.g., the coordinate values of a pair of diagonally opposite corners of b)

Observe that unlike the object-tree pyramid, the object B^+-tree does store object numbers in both the leaf and nonleaf nodes in order to facilitate updates. The update algorithms (i.e., data structure creation, insertion, and deletion) for an object B^+-tree are identical to those for a B^+-tree with the added requirement of maintaining the bounding box information, while the search algorithms (e.g., the location query, window queries) are identical to those for an object-tree pyramid. The performance of the object B^+-tree for answering range queries is enhanced if the initial tree is built by inserting the objects in sorted order filling each node to capacity, subject to the minimum occupancy constraints, thereby resulting in a tree with minimum depth. Of course, such an initialization will cause subsequent insertions to be more costly because it will inevitably result in node split operations, although this would not necessarily be the case if the nodes were not filled to capacity initially. The *Hilbert R-tree* [984] is an instance of an object B^+-tree that applies a Peano-Hilbert space ordering (Figure 2.5(d)) to the centroid of the bounding boxes of the objects.[22]

Figure 2.73(a) shows the bounding boxes corresponding to the first level of aggregation for the Hilbert R-tree for the collection of 22 rectangle objects in Figure 2.70 with $m = 3$ and $M = 6$ when the objects are inserted in the order in which they were created (i.e., their corresponding number in Figure 2.70). Similarly, Figure 2.73(b) shows the corresponding result when using a Morton order instead of a Peano-Hilbert order. Notice that, for pedagogical reasons, the trees were not created by inserting the objects in sorted order as suggested above because, in this case, the resulting trees would be the same as the Hilbert packed R-tree and Morton packed R-tree in Figure 2.72(a, b), respectively.

As another example, consider Figure 2.74(a) which is the Hilbert R-tree for the collection of rectangle objects whose specifications are given in Figure 2.67 with $m = 2$ and $M = 3$. Figure 2.74(b) shows the spatial extent of the bounding boxes of the nodes in

---

[22] As we will see, the name *Hilbert B-tree* is more appropriate because the update algorithms (e.g., insertion) do not make use of the bounding box information to reduce the coverage and overlap, whereas this is the key to their operation in the R-tree [791]. Although experiments for the Hilbert R-tree and the very closely related Hilbert packed R-tree [983] (which is the result of the initial Hilbert R-tree construction process given N objects) exhibit good behavior, this is primarily on account of the use of pointlike data such as very small line segments. Experiments using objects with greater extent (e.g., longer line segments) may be different. The Hilbert R-tree is closely related to the *Hilbert tree* [1121], which applies the same ordering to a set of points and then stores the result in a height-balanced binary search tree (see also [1891], which makes use of a Morton order and a 1-2 brother tree [1430]).

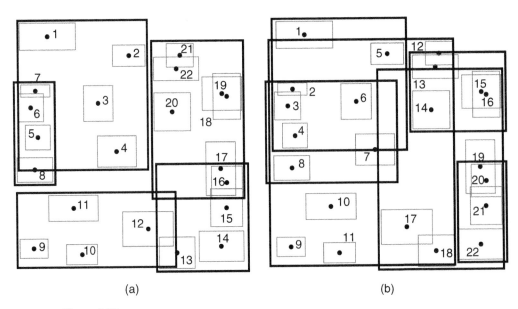

(a)   (b)

Figure 2.73
The bounding boxes corresponding to the first level of aggregation for the (a) Hilbert R-tree and (b) Morton R-tree for the collection of 22 rectangle objects in Figure 2.70 with $m = 3$ and $M = 6$.

Figure 2.74(a), with broken lines denoting the bounding boxes corresponding to the leaf nodes and gray lines denoting the bounding boxes corresponding to the subtrees rooted at the nonleaf nodes. Each node also indicates the Peano-Hilbert code of the centroid of the corresponding bounding box. We have filled each node to capacity, subject to the constraint that each node must have a minimal number of children. We have also tried to aggregate objects in each node based on the proximity of their positions in the Peano-Hilbert order.

Notice that there is much overlap between the bounding boxes of the nodes. Rearranging the objects that are aggregated in each node can alleviate this problem, but only to a very limited extent as the order of the leaf nodes must be maintained—that is, all elements of leaf node i must have a Peano-Hilbert order number less than all elements of leaf node $i + 1$. Thus, all we can do is change the number of elements that are aggregated in the node subject to the node capacity constraints. Of course, this means that the resulting trees are not unique. For example, in Figure 2.74, we could aggregate objects E and 3 into R3 and objects G, 2, and D into R4. However, the real problem is that objects 2 and F should be aggregated, but this is impossible as their corresponding positions in the Peano-Hilbert order are so far apart (i.e., 598 and 3496, respectively). The problem is caused, in part, by the presence of objects with nonzero extent and the fact that neither the extent of the objects nor their proximity is taken into account in the ordering-based aggregation techniques (i.e., they do not try to minimize coverage or overlap, which are the cornerstones of the R-tree). This deficiency was also noted earlier for the Hilbert packed R-tree. This is in contrast to experimental results [983] that encourage ordering the objects on the basis of the Peano-Hilbert order of their centroids. The problem is that these experiments were conducted with objects with little or no extent (i.e., pointlike objects or line segments with unit length).

Exercises

1. Give two possible representative points for circle objects.

2. What is the cost of an algorithm to build a packed R-tree that starts out by examining the N objects and finding the M objects with the smallest total bounding box, followed by the next M remaining objects with the smallest bounding box, until N/M bounding boxes have been obtained? This process is repeated recursively until there is just one box left [1588].

3. Write an algorithm to build a packed R-tree for a collection of two-dimensional objects that minimizes the total area covered by the bounding boxes at all of the levels.

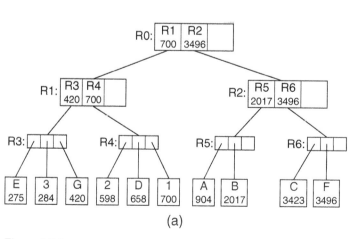

(a)

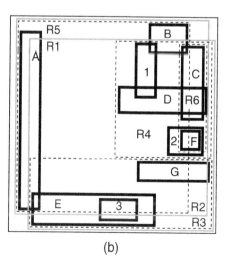

(b)

Figure 2.74
(a) Hilbert R-tree for a collection of rectangle objects whose specifications are given in Figure 2.67 with $m = 2$ and $M = 3$ and (b) the spatial extents of the bounding boxes.

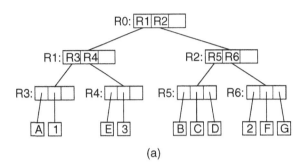

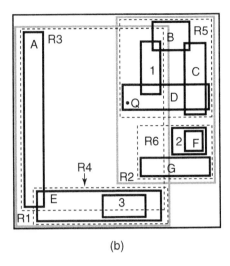

(a)

(b)

Figure 2.75

(a) R-tree for a collection of rectangle objects whose specifications are given in Figure 2.67 with $m = 2$ and $M = 3$ and (b) the spatial extents of the objects and the bounding boxes of the nodes in (a). Notice that the leaf nodes in the index also store bounding boxes, although this is shown only for the nonleaf nodes.

2.1.5.2.3 Extent-Based Aggregation Techniques

When the objects are to be aggregated on the basis of their extent (i.e., the space occupied by their bounding boxes), then good dynamic behavior is achieved by making use of an *R-tree* [791]. An R-tree is a generalization of the object-tree pyramid where, for an order (m,M) R-tree, the number of objects or bounding boxes that are aggregated in each node is permitted to range between $m \leq \lceil M/2 \rceil$ and M. On the other hand, it is always M for the object-tree pyramid. The root node in an R-tree has at least two entries unless it is a leaf node, in which case it has just one entry corresponding to the bounding box of an object. The R-tree is usually built as the objects are encountered rather than after all objects have been input. Of the different variations on the object-tree pyramid that we have discussed, the R-tree is the one used most frequently, especially in database applications.

Figure 2.75(a) is an example R-tree for a collection of rectangle objects whose specifications are given in Figure 2.67 with $m = 2$ and $M = 3$. Figure 2.75(b) shows the spatial extents of the objects and the bounding boxes of the nodes in Figure 2.75(a), with broken lines denoting the bounding boxes corresponding to the leaf nodes and gray lines denoting the bounding boxes corresponding to the subtrees rooted at the nonleaf nodes. Note that the R-tree is not unique. Its structure depends heavily on the order in which the individual objects were inserted into (and possibly deleted from) the tree.

Given that each R-tree node can contain a varying number of objects or bounding boxes, it is not surprising that the R-tree was inspired by the B-tree. This means that nodes are viewed as analogous to disk pages. Thus, the parameters defining the tree (i.e., m and M) are chosen so that a small number of nodes is visited during a spatial query (i.e., variants of the location query), which means that m and M are usually quite large.

The need to minimize the number of disk accesses also affects the format of each R-tree node. Recall that in the definition of the object-tree pyramid, each node p contains M pointers to p's children and one bounding box corresponding to the union of the bounding boxes of p's children. This means that in order to decide which of node p's children should be descended, we must access the nodes corresponding to these children to perform the point-inclusion test. Each such access requires a disk I/O operation. In order to avoid these disk I/O operations, the format of R-tree node p is modified so that p contains k ($m \leq k \leq M$) pointers to p's children and the k bounding boxes of p's children, instead of containing just one bounding box corresponding to the union of the bounding boxes of p's children as is the case for the object-tree pyramid.[23] Recall that this format is also used in the definition of a node in the object B$^+$-tree. Once again, we observe that the k point inclusion tests do not require any disk I/O operations at the cost of being able to aggregate a smaller number of objects in each node since m and M are now smaller, assuming that the page size is fixed.

As long as the number of objects in each R-tree leaf node is between m and M, no action needs to be taken on the R-tree structure other than adjusting the bounding boxes when inserting or deleting an object. If the number of objects in a leaf node decreases below m, then the node is said to *underflow*. In this case, the objects in the underflowing nodes must be reinserted, and bounding boxes in nonleaf nodes must be adjusted. If these nonleaf nodes also underflow, then the objects in their leaf nodes must also be reinserted. If the number of objects in a leaf node increases above M, then the node is said to *overflow*. In this case, it must be split, and the $M + 1$ objects that it contains must be distributed in the two resulting nodes. Splits are propagated up the tree.

Underflows in an R-tree are handled in an analogous manner to the way they are dealt with in a B-tree (see Exercise 7). In contrast, the overflow situation points out a significant difference between an R-tree and a B-tree. Recall that overflow is a result of attempting to insert an item t in node p and determining that node p is too full. In a B-tree, we usually do not have a choice (but see Exercise 2) as to the node p that is to contain t since the tree is ordered. Thus, once we determine that p is full, we must either split p or apply a rotation (also known as *deferred splitting*) process. On the other hand, in an R-tree, we can insert t into any node p, as long as p is not full. However, once t is inserted into p, we must expand the bounding box associated with p to include the space spanned by the bounding box b of t. Of course, we can also insert t in a full node p, in which case we must also split p.

The need to expand the bounding box of p has an effect on the future performance of the R-tree, and thus we must make a wise choice with respect to p. As in the case of the object-tree pyramid, the efficiency of the R-tree for search operations depends on its abilities to distinguish between occupied space and unoccupied space and to prevent a node from being examined needlessly due to a false overlap with other nodes. Again, as in the object-tree pyramid, the extent to which these efficiencies are realized is a direct result of how well we are able to satisfy our goals of minimizing coverage and overlap. These goals guide the initial R-tree creation process and are subject to the previously mentioned constraint that the R-tree is usually built as the objects are encountered rather than after all objects have been input.

In the original definition of the R-tree [791], the goal of minimizing coverage is the one that is followed. In particular, an object t is inserted by a recursive process that starts at the root of the tree and chooses the child whose corresponding bounding box needs to be expanded by the smallest amount to include t. As we will see, other researchers make use of other criteria such as minimizing overlap with adjacent nodes and even perimeter (e.g., in the R*-tree [152] as described in Section 2.1.5.2.4). Theodoridis and Sellis [1865] try to minimize the value of an objective function consisting of a linear combination of coverage, overlap, and dead area with equal weights. García, López, and Leutenegger [679] also make use of a similar objective function to build the entire R-tree in a top-down manner. The fact that nodes in the tree are constrained to be as full as possible means that there is no need to check all possible configurations of split positions and groupings of objects, which is otherwise exponential in N (i.e., $O(2^N)$).

---

[23] The A-tree [1607], different from the ATree discussed in Section 2.1.2.5, is somewhat of a compromise. The A-tree stores quantized approximations of the k bounding boxes of p's children, where the locations of the bounding boxes of p's children are specified relative to the location of the bounding box of p, thereby enabling them to be encoded with just a small number of bits. For more detail on other uses of such methods, see Section 4.4.3 of Chapter 4.

Not surprisingly, these same goals also guide the node-splitting process. In this situation, one goal is to distribute the objects among the nodes so that the likelihood that the two nodes will be visited in subsequent searches will be reduced. This is accomplished by minimizing the total area spanned by the bounding boxes of the resulting nodes (equivalent to what we have termed *coverage*). The second goal is to reduce the likelihood that both nodes are examined in subsequent searches. This goal is accomplished by minimizing the area common to both nodes (equivalent to what we have termed *overlap*). Again, we observe that, at times, these goals may be contradictory.

Several node-splitting policies have been proposed that take these goals into account. They are differentiated on the basis of their execution-time complexity and the number of these goals that they attempt to meet. An easy way to see the different complexities is to look at the following three algorithms [791], all of which are based on minimizing the coverage. The simplest is an exhaustive algorithm [791] that tries all possibilities. In such a case, the number of possible partitions is $2^M - 1$ (see Exercise 8). This is unreasonable for most values of M (e.g., $M = 50$ for a page size of 1,024 bytes).

The exhaustive approach can be applied to obtain an optimal node split according to an arbitrary cost function that can take into account coverage, overlap, and other factors. Interestingly, although we pointed out earlier that there are $O(2^M)$ possible cases to be taken into account, the exhaustive algorithm can be implemented in such a way that it need not require $O(2^M)$ time. In particular, Becker, Franciosa, Gschwind, Ohler, Thiemt, and Widmayer [146] present an implementation that takes only $O(M^3)$ time for two-dimensional data and $O(dM \log M + d^2 M^{2d-1})$ time for d-dimensional data.

García, López, and Leutenegger [680] present an implementation of the exhaustive approach that uses the same insight as the implementation of Becker et al. [146], which is that some of the boundaries of the two resulting minimum bounding boxes are shared with the minimum bounding box of the overflowing node. This insight constrains the number of possible groupings of the M objects in the node that is being split. The algorithm is flexible in that it can use different cost functions for evaluating the appropriateness of a particular node split. However, the cost function is restricted to being "extent monotone," which means that the cost function increases monotonically as the extent of one of the sides of the two bounding rectangles is increased (this property is also used by Becker et al. [146], although the property is stated somewhat differently).

Although the implementations of Becker et al. [146] and García, et al. [680] both find optimal node splits, the difference between them is that the former has the added benefit of guaranteeing that the node split satisfies some balancing criteria, which is a requirement in most R-tree implementations. The rationale, as we recall, is that in this way the nodes are not too full, which would cause them to overflow again. For example, in many R-tree implementations there is a requirement that the split be such that each node receive exactly half the rectangles or that each receive at least 40% of the rectangles. Satisfying the balancing criteria is more expensive, as could be expected, and, in two dimensions, the cost of the algorithm of Becker et al. [146] is $O(M^3)$, as opposed to $O(M^2)$ for the algorithm of García, et al. [680].

García, et al. [680] found that identifying optimal node splits yielded only modest improvements in query performance, which led them to introduce another improvement to the insertion process. This improvement is based on trying to fit one of the two groups resulting from a split of node a into one of a's siblings instead of creating a new node for every split. In particular, one of the groups is inserted into the sibling s for which the cost increase, using some predefined cost function, resulting from movement into s is minimized. Once a sibling s has been chosen, we move the appropriate group and reapply the node-splitting algorithm if the movement caused s to overflow. This process is applied repeatedly as long as there is overflow, while requiring that we choose among the siblings that have not been modified by this process. If we find that there is overflow in node i and there is no unmodified sibling left, then a new node is created containing one of the new groups resulting from the split of i. Even if each node overflows, this process is guaranteed to terminate because, at each step, there is one fewer sibling candidates for motion.

The process described above is somewhat similar to what is termed *forced reinsertion* in the R*-tree (see Section 2.1.5.2.4), with the difference that forced reinsertion results in reinsertion of the individual entries (i.e., objects in the case of leaf nodes and minimum bounding boxes in the case of nonleaf nodes) at the root, instead of as a group into one of the siblings. This reinsertion into siblings is also reminiscent of rotation (i.e., "deferred splitting") in the conventional B-tree with the difference being that there is no order in the R-tree, which is why motion into all unmodified siblings had to be considered. This strategy was found to increase the node utilization and, thereby, to improve query performance (by as much as 120% in experiments [680], compared with the Hilbert R-tree [984]).

The remaining two node-splitting algorithms have a common control structure that consists of two stages. The first stage "picks" a pair of bounding boxes j and k to serve as "seeds" for the two resulting nodes, while the second stage redistributes the remaining bounding boxes into the nodes corresponding to j and k. The redistribution process tries to minimize the "growth" of the area spanned by j and k. Thus, the first and second stages can be described as *seed picking* and *seed growing*, respectively.

The first of these seed-picking algorithms is a quadratic cost algorithm [791] (see Exercise 15) that initially finds the two bounding boxes that would waste the most area were they to be in the same node. This is determined by subtracting the sum of the areas of the two bounding boxes from the area of the covering bounding box. These two bounding boxes are placed in the separate nodes, say j and k. Next, the remaining bounding boxes are examined, and for each bounding box, say i, d_{ij} and d_{ik} are computed, which correspond to the increases in the area of the covering bounding boxes of nodes j and k, respectively, when i is added to them. Now, the bounding box r such that $|d_{rj} - d_{rk}|$ is a maximum is found, and r is added to the node with the smallest increase in area. This process is repeated for the remaining bounding boxes. The motivation for selecting the maximum difference $|d_{rj} - d_{rk}|$ is to find the bounding box having the greatest preference for a particular node j or k.

The second of these seed-picking algorithms is a linear cost algorithm [791] (see Exercise 11) that examines each dimension and finds the two bounding boxes with the greatest separation. Recalling that each bounding box has a low and a high edge along each axis, these two bounding boxes are the one whose high edge is the lowest along the given axis and the one whose low edge is the highest along the same axis. The separations are normalized by dividing the actual separation by the width of the bounding box of the overflowing node along the corresponding axis. The final "seeds" are the two bounding boxes having the greatest normalized separation among the d pairs that we found. The remaining bounding boxes are processed in arbitrary order and placed in the node whose bounding box (i.e., of the entries added so far) is increased the least in area as a result of their addition (see Exercise 19). Empirical tests [791] showed that there was not much difference between the three node-splitting algorithms in the performance of a window search query (i.e., in CPU time and in the number of disk pages accessed). Thus, the faster linear cost node-splitting algorithm was found to be preferable for this query, even though the quality of the splits was somewhat inferior.

An alternative node-splitting policy is based on minimizing the overlap. One technique that has a linear cost [60] applies d partitions (one for each of the d dimensions) to the bounding boxes in the node t being split, thereby resulting in $2d$ sets of bounding boxes. In particular, we have one set for each face of the bounding box b of t. The partition is based on associating each bounding box o in t with the set corresponding to the closest face along dimension i of b.[24] Once the $2d$ partitions have been constructed (i.e.,

---

[24] Formally, each bounding box o has two faces f_{oil} and f_{oih} that are parallel to the respective faces f_{bil} and f_{bih} of b, where l and h correspond to the low and high values of coordinate or dimension i.

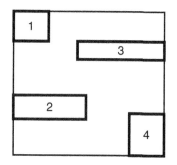

Figure 2.76
Example collection of rectangles
demonstrating a linear node-splitting
algorithm that minimizes overlap
rather than coverage.

each bounding box o has been associated with d sets), select the partition that ensures the most even distribution of bounding boxes. In case of a tie, choose the partition with the least overlap. In case of another tie, choose the partition with the least coverage. For example, consider the four bounding boxes in Figure 2.76. The partition along the x axis yields the sets $\{1,2\}$ and $\{3,4\}$, and the partition along the y axis yields the sets $\{1,3\}$ and $\{2,4\}$. Since both partitions yield sets that are evenly distributed, we choose the one that minimizes overlap (i.e., along the y axis).

The algorithm is linear as it examines each bounding box once along each dimension (actually, it is $O(dM)$ for M objects, but d is usually much smaller than M). Experiments with randomly generated rectangles [60] resulted in lower coverage and overlap than the linear and quadratic algorithms described above [791], which are based on minimizing the coverage. The window search query was also found to be about 16% faster with the linear algorithm based on minimizing overlap than with the quadratic algorithm based on minimizing coverage. The drawback of this linear algorithm (i.e., [60]) is that it does not guarantee that the two nodes resulting from the partition will contain an equal number of bounding boxes. This is because the partitions are based on proximity to the borders of the bounding box of the node being split. In particular, when the data is not uniformly distributed, although the resulting nodes are likely to have little overlap (as they are likely to partition the underlying space into two equal areas), they will most likely contain an uneven number of bounding boxes (see Exercise 21).

Extent-based aggregation techniques have also been applied to the representation of collections of moving rectangle objects, each of which is represented by a moving box. The result is an R-tree where the bounding boxes for a set of static rectangles are replaced by moving bounding boxes for a set of moving boxes (e.g., [296, 1610]). As in the case of R-trees, there are many ways of defining the moving bounding boxes. The *parametric R-tree* [296] and the *TPR-tree* [1610] (as well as the more recent improvement, the *TPR*-tree* [1855], which makes use of more sophisticated node-splitting and other basic algorithms for insertion and deletion) are two examples of such R-trees that are based on minimizing coverage, with the parametric R-tree providing tighter coverage vis-à-vis the TPR-tree. In particular, the parametric R-tree makes use of a minimum moving bounding box, termed a *time-parametric rectangle* [295], that takes the time intervals during which each of the individual rectangle objects are moving, which need not necessarily be the same, in calculating the moving bounding boxes of collections of moving bounding boxes. Thus, for example, in the time period $tp = [0, 10]$, some of the objects may only be moving during a subset of tp (e.g., object A is moving during $[0, 8]$ while object B is moving during $[4, 10]$). The minimum moving bounding boxes in the parametric R-tree are calculated on the basis of a principle similar to a convex hull. On the other hand, in the TPR-tree and the TPR*-tree the minimum moving bounding boxes assume that the objects are in motion during the entire time interval that is spanned by the minimum moving bounding box. The general discussion of moving objects is beyond the scope of this discussion.

Exercises

1. What is the difference between the definition of a node in an R-tree and a node in a B-tree?

2. In an R-tree, we always have a choice with respect to the node in which an object is to be inserted. This is not always the case in a B-tree. When do you have a choice as to the B-tree node in which an item with key k can be inserted?

For each dimension i, there are two sets S_{il} and S_{ih} corresponding to faces f_{bil} and f_{bih} of b, and the algorithm inserts o into S_{il} if $x_i(f_{oil}) - x_i(f_{bil}) < x_i(f_{bih}) - x_i(f_{oih})$ and into S_{ih} otherwise, where $x_i(f)$ is the ith coordinate value of face f. A similar idea of grouping bounding boxes by their proximity to the closest face along a particular dimension is also used in the priority R-tree [86], which is an R-tree designed for efficient bulk loading (see Section 2.1.5.2.6).

3. What is the maximum height of an R-tree of order (m,M) with N objects or bounding boxes (not nodes)?

4. What is the maximum number of nodes in an R-tree of order (m,M) with N objects or bounding boxes?

5. What is the total cost of inserting an object in an R-tree of order (m,M) when no node splitting is needed?

6. Write an algorithm to insert an object into an R-tree of order (m,M). You will have to choose one of the described techniques for splitting a full node with $M + 1$ records.

7. Write an algorithm to delete an object from an R-tree.

8. Prove that there are $2^M - 1$ possible partitions of a node in an R-tree of order (m,M) with $M + 1$ records into two nonempty subsets.

9. Theodoridis and Sellis [1865] suggest a seed-picking algorithm that sorts the bounding boxes of the objects in the node to be split according to some value such as the Peano-Hilbert code of their centroid and then uses the ones with the minimum and maximum value as the seeds. Compare the result of using this technique with the linear and quadratic node-splitting algorithms proposed by Guttman [791] based on reducing coverage, as well as the linear node-splitting algorithm based on reducing overlap proposed by Ang and Tan [60]. For the method of Theodoridis and Sellis [1865] use the same seed-growing algorithm as in the linear node-splitting algorithm based on reducing coverage.

10. Repeat the comparison in Exercise 9 by using the seed-picking algorithm of Theodoridis and Sellis [1865] in conjunction with a seed-growing algorithm that selects the node into which the objects are to be inserted by minimizing the value of an objective function consisting of a linear combination of coverage, overlap, and dead area with equal weights. Once the seeds have been chosen, the objects are processed using the ordering resulting from sorting the bounding boxes. In particular, if the last object was assigned to the group associated with the seed corresponding to the lowest (highest) value in the ordering, then the next object to be processed is the highest (lowest) valued one remaining in the ordering.

11. The seed-picking stage of the linear cost R-tree node-splitting algorithm proposed by Guttman [791] finds the two bounding boxes with the maximum normalized separation along all of the dimensions. This is based on a definition of separation in terms of the maximum distance between the farthest of the parallel sides of two bounding boxes. Suppose that the definition of farthest was changed to be the maximum separation between the closest of the parallel sides of the two bounding boxes [750]. Is the cost of the resulting algorithm still linear (i.e., $O(M)$) for an R-tree of order (m,M)?

12. Explain why the seeds picked by the quadratic cost R-tree node-splitting algorithm proposed by Guttman [791] tend to be small and far apart.

13. Suppose that the seeds picked by the quadratic cost R-tree node-splitting algorithm proposed by Guttman [791] are small. Suppose further that there exists a bounding box r far away from one of the seeds s where $d - 1$ of the coordinate values of r are almost in agreement with those of s. Show that r is highly likely to be the first to be distributed and will be distributed to the bounding box of s.

14. Let b_1 be the first bounding box to be redistributed by the quadratic cost R-tree node-splitting algorithm proposed by Guttman [791] and suppose that it is redistributed to seed s. Explain why the algorithm has a tendency to prefer seed s for the next bounding box b_2 to be redistributed. What happens to the remaining bounding boxes in this case (i.e., after b_1 and b_2 have been redistributed)?

15. Prove that the quadratic cost R-tree node-splitting algorithm proposed by Guttman [791] requires $O(M^2)$ time for an order (m,M) R-tree.

16. Both the linear and quadratic cost R-tree node-splitting algorithms proposed by Guttman [791] consist of a stage that picks seeds j and k, and a stage that redistributes the remaining bounding boxes into the nodes corresponding to j and k. The linear cost algorithm redistributes the remaining bounding boxes by inserting them into the node j or k whose bounding box is increased (i.e., that *grows*) the least by their addition. This is based on the principle of minimizing coverage. An alternative approach picks an axis in the first stage for which the normalized separation between the seeds is a maximum. In addition, instead of seed-growing,

an alternative redistribution algorithm is used that sorts the bounding boxes by their low value along the chosen split axis and then assigns the first $M/2$ bounding boxes to one node and the remaining bounding boxes to the other node [750]. In this case, there is no minimization of growth in the sense that, once the sort has taken place, the redistribution just depends on the value of M. Compare the performance of this alternative redistribution algorithm in conjunction with the following two approaches to picking the split axis:

(a) The axis with the greatest normalized separation for the two seeds j and k selected by the quadratic cost algorithm. The separations are normalized by dividing the actual separation by the length of the side of the bounding box of j and k along the appropriate axes.

(b) The variation on the technique used in the linear cost algorithm described in Exercise 11 that finds the two bounding boxes j and k with the maximum separation between the closest of the parallel sides of j and k.[25]

17. What is the cost of the variation of the node-splitting algorithm that makes use of the second technique in Exercise 16 for an R-tree of order (m,M)?

18. What is the drawback of using the alternative redistribution algorithm described in Exercise 16, which sorts the bounding boxes in an order (m,M) R-tree by their low value along the chosen split axis and then assigns the first $M/2$ bounding boxes to one node and the remaining bounding boxes to the other node [750]?

19. The seed-growing step of the linear cost node-splitting algorithm proposed by Guttman [791] redistributes the remaining bounding boxes in arbitrary order to the seed whose associated group's minimum bounding box is increased the least by the addition. Thus, if the bounding boxes happen to be redistributed in sorted order along one of the dimensions, then the algorithm is plagued by the same problem described in Exercise 14. In particular, once the first bounding box has been distributed to one of the seeds s, the redistribution step will tend to favor s for the next bounding box, and so on, and most of the bounding boxes will be distributed to s subject to the minimum storage utilization constraints. One way to avoid this problem completely is to redistribute the remaining bounding boxes one by one in arbitrary order to the seed whose original bounding box is increased the least by the addition. In this case, the order in which the bounding boxes are redistributed makes no difference in the final result. Perform a quantitative comparison of the two methods in terms of their coverage, overlap, and whether the resulting two nodes have approximately the same number of elements.

20. An alternative implementation of the seed-growing step of the linear cost node-splitting algorithm proposed by Guttman [791] is to remember the dimension i with the highest normalized separation and to redistribute the remaining bounding boxes to the seed whose associated group's minimum bounding box is increased the least along i by the addition. Perform a quantitative comparison of this method with the original method in terms of their coverage, overlap, and whether the resulting two nodes have approximately the same number of elements.

21. Ang and Tan [60] describe experiments that show that a linear R-tree node-splitting algorithm based on reducing overlap results in lower coverage and overlap than the linear and quadratic algorithms proposed by Guttman [791]. The experiments used randomly generated rectangles. In this case, the data is well-distributed throughout the underlying space, and thus the algorithm will naturally result in creating partitions that have approximately the same number of bounding boxes. In contrast, this may not be the case for nonrandom data. Perform a similar comparison using real data. The comparison should be qualitative and quantitative. The qualitative comparison should examine the resulting space decomposition, as in Figure 2.79 (discussed in Section 2.1.5.2.4). This can be achieved by choosing a sample dataset and drawing the output. The quantitative comparison should tabulate coverage and overlap, storage utilization, and the time for construction, as well as the times for intersection (i.e., determining all pairs of intersecting objects), window, and point queries.

22. Write an algorithm to perform a point query in an R-tree.

23. Consider an R-tree built for objects whose centroids and extents are uniformly distributed in the unit space and point queries that are also uniformly distributed over the same unit space.

---

[25] The first technique is erroneously attributed to [750] in [152], whereas the second technique is really the one described in [750].

Prove that the expected number of R-tree nodes visited by a point query is equal to the sum of the d-dimensional volumes of the bounding boxes of all of the nodes.

24. Write an algorithm to perform a window query in an R-tree.

25. Using the same environment as in Exercise 23, consider a rectangular window query to retrieve all objects whose bounding boxes have a nonempty intersection with window w having width w_i in dimension i. Prove that the expected number of R-tree nodes visited is $\sum_j \prod_{i=1}^{d} (b_{ji} + w_i)$, where b_j is the bounding box of R-tree node q_j, and b_{ji} is the width of b_j along dimension i.

26. Write an algorithm to find the nearest object to a point in an R-tree.

27. Write an algorithm to solve the rectangle intersection problem for an R-tree.

28. Prove that the worst-case execution time of the rectangle intersection problem for N rectangles using an R-tree is $O(N^2)$.

29. What is the expected cost of the rectangle intersection problem for N rectangles using an R-tree?

2.1.5.2.4 R*-Tree

Better decompositions in terms of less node overlap and lower storage requirements than those achieved by the linear and quadratic node-splitting algorithms have also been reported in [152], where three significant changes have been made to the R-tree construction algorithm, including a different node-splitting strategy. An R-tree that is built using these changes is termed an *R*-tree* [152].[26] These changes are described below. Interestingly, these changes also involve using a node-splitting policy that, at times, tries to minimize both coverage and overlap.

The first change is the use of an intelligent object insertion procedure that is based on minimizing overlap in the case of leaf nodes, while minimizing the increase in area (i.e., coverage) in the case of nonleaf nodes. The distinction between leaf and nonleaf nodes is necessary as the insertion algorithm starts at the root and must process nonleaf nodes before encountering the leaf node where the object will ultimately be inserted. Thus, we see that the bounding box b for an object o is inserted into the leaf node p for whom the resulting bounding box has the minimum increase in the amount of overlap with the bounding boxes of p's siblings (children of nonleaf node s). This is in contrast to the R-tree, where b is inserted into the leaf node p for whom the increase in area is a minimum (i.e., based on minimizing coverage). This part of the R*-tree object insertion algorithm is quadratic in the number of entries in each node (i.e., $O(M^2)$ for an order (m,M) R*-tree where the number of objects or bounding boxes that are aggregated in each node is permitted to range between $m \leq \lceil M/2 \rceil$) as the overlap must be checked for each leaf node child p of the selected nonleaf node s with all of p's $O(M)$ siblings (but see Exercise 4).

The second change is that when a node p is found to overflow in an R*-tree, instead of immediately splitting p as is done in the R-tree, first an attempt is made to see if some of the objects in p could possibly be more suited to being in another node. This is achieved by reinserting a fraction (30% has been found to yield good performance [152]) of these objects into the tree (termed *forced reinsertion*). Forced reinsertion is similar in spirit to rotation (also known as *deferred splitting*) in a conventional B-tree, which is also a technique developed to avoid splitting a node (see Exercise 1).

There are several ways of determining the objects to be reinserted. One suggestion is to sort the bounding boxes in p according to the distance of the centers of their bounding boxes from the center of the bounding box of p, and to reinsert the designated fraction

---

[26] The "*" is used to signify its "star"-like performance [1707] in comparison with R-trees built using the other node-splitting algorithms, as can be seen in examples such as Figures 2.77 and 2.79(b), discussed later in this section.

that is the farthest away. Once we have determined the objects to be reinserted, we need to choose an order in which to reinsert them. There are two obvious choices: from farthest to closest (termed *far-reinsert*) or from closest to farthest (termed *close-reinsert*). Beckmann, Kriegel, Schneider, and Seeger [152] make a case for using close-reinsert on the basis of the results of experiments. One possible explanation is that if the reinsertion procedure places the first object to be reinserted in p, then the size of the bounding box of p is likely to be increased more if far-reinsert is used rather than close-reinsert, thereby increasing the likelihood of the remaining objects' being reinserted into p as well. This has the effect of defeating the motivation for the introduction of the reinsertion process, which is to try to reorganize the nodes. However, it could also be argued that using far-reinsert is more likely to result in the farthest object being reinserted in a node other than p, on account of the smaller amount of overlap, which is one of the goals of the reinsertion process. Thus, the question of which method to use is not completely settled.

The sorting step in forced reinsertion takes $O(M \log M)$ time. However, this cost is greatly overshadowed by the fact that each invocation of forced reinsertion can result in the reinsertion of $O(M)$ objects, thereby increasing the cost of insertion by a factor of $O(M)$. One problem with forced reinsertion is that it can lead to overflow in the same node p again when all of the bounding boxes are reinserted in p or even to overflow in another node q at the same depth. This can lead to an infinite loop. In order to prevent the occurrence of such a situation, forced reinsertion is applied only once at each depth for a given object. Note also that forced reinsertion is applied in a bottom-up manner in the sense that resolving overflow in the leaf nodes may also lead to overflow of the nonleaf nodes, in which case we apply forced reinsertion to the nonleaf nodes as well. When applying forced reinsertion to a nonleaf node p at depth l, we reinsert only the elements in p and at depth l.

Forced reinsertion is quite important as, usually, an R-tree is built by inserting the objects one by one as they are encountered in the input. Thus, we do not usually have the luxury of processing the objects in sorted order. This can lead to some bad decompositions in the sense that the redistribution stage may prefer one of the seed nodes over the other in a consistent manner (see Exercise 14 in Section 2.1.5.2.3). Of course, this can be overcome by taking into account the bounding boxes of all of the objects before building the R-tree; but now the representation is no longer dynamic. Forced reinsertion is a compromise in the sense that it permits us to rebuild periodically part of the R-tree as a means of compensating for some bad node-placement decisions.

The third change involves the manner in which an overflowing node p is split. Again, as in the original R-tree node-splitting algorithm, a two-stage process is used. The difference is in the nature of the stages. The process follows closely an approach presented in an earlier study of the R-tree [750] (see Exercise 16 in Section 2.1.5.2.3), which did not result in the coining of a new name for the data structure! In particular, in contrast to the original R-tree node-splitting strategy [791], where the first stage picks two seeds for the two resulting nodes, which are subsequently grown by the second stage, in the R*-tree (as well as in the approach described in [750]), the first stage determines the axis (i.e., hyperplane) along which the split is to take place, and the second stage determines the position of the split. In two dimensions, for example, the split position calculated in the second stage serves as the boundary separating the left (or an equivalent alternative is the right) sides of the bounding boxes of the objects that will be in the left and right nodes resulting from the split.

Note that the result of the calculation of the split position in the second stage has the same effect as the redistribution step in the linear and quadratic cost R-tree node-splitting algorithms as it indicates which bounding boxes are associated with which node. In particular, as we will see below, the first stage makes use of the result of sorting the faces of the bounding boxes along the various dimensions. Moreover, it would appear that the first and last bounding boxes in the sort sequence play a somewhat similar role to that of the seeds in the original R-tree node-splitting algorithms. However, this comparison is false as there is no growing process in the second stage. In particular, these seeds do not grow in an independent manner in the sense that the bounding boxes b_i that will be assigned to their groups are determined by the relative positions of the corresponding faces of b_i (e.g., in two dimensions, the sorted order of their left, right, top, or bottom sides).

This two-stage process is implemented by performing $2d$ sorts (two per axis) of the bounding boxes of the objects in the overflowing node p. For each axis a, the bounding boxes are sorted according to their two opposite faces that are perpendicular to a. The positions of the faces of the bounding boxes in the sorted lists serve as the candidate split positions for the individual axes. There are several ways of using this information to determine the split axis and split position along the axis.

Beckmann et al. [152] choose the split axis as the axis a for which the average perimeter of the bounding boxes of the two resulting nodes for all of the possible splits along a is the smallest while still satisfying the constraint posed by m and M. An alternative approach (although not necessarily yielding the desired result as shown below and discussed further in Exercise 9) is one that chooses the split axis as the axis a for which the perimeter of the two resulting nodes is a minimum. Basing the choice on the value of the perimeter is related to the goal of minimizing coverage by favoring splits that result in nodes whose bounding boxes have a squarelike shape (see Exercise 7). Basing the choice of the split axis on the minimum average perimeter results in giving greater weight to the axis where the majority of the possible splits result in nodes whose bounding boxes have squarelike shapes (see also Exercise 9). This stage takes $O(dM\log M)$ time as the sort takes $O(M\log M)$ time for each axis while the average perimeter computation can be done in $O(M)$ time for each axis when scanning the faces of the bounding boxes in sorted order (see Exercise 8).

The position of the split along the axis a selected by the first stage is calculated by examining the two sorted lists of possible split positions (i.e., faces of the bounding boxes) for a and choosing the split position for which the amount of overlap between the bounding boxes of the two resulting nodes is the smallest (but see Exercises 10 and 21) while still satisfying the constraint posed by m and M. Ties are resolved by choosing the position that minimizes the total area of the resulting bounding boxes, thereby reducing the coverage. Minimizing the overlap reduces the likelihood that both nodes will be visited in subsequent searches. Thus, we see that the R*-tree's node-splitting policy tries to address the issues of minimizing both coverage and overlap. Determining the split position requires $O(M)$ overlap computations when scanning the bounding boxes in sorted order. Algorithms that employ this sort-and-scan paradigm are known as *plane-sweep techniques* [119, 1511, 1740].

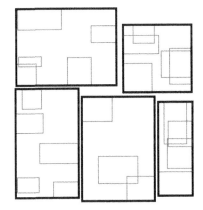

Figure 2.77 shows the bounding boxes corresponding to the first level of aggregation for an R*-tree in comparison to that resulting from the use of an R-tree that deploys the exhaustive (Figure 2.78(a)), linear cost (Figure 2.78(b)), quadratic cost (Figure 2.78(c)), and linear cost reducing overlap (Figure 2.78(d)) [60] node-splitting algorithms for the collection of 22 rectangles in Figure 2.71. It is quite clear from the figure, at least for this example dataset, that the combined criterion used by the R*-tree node-splitting algorithm that chooses the split that minimizes the sum of the perimeters of the bounding boxes of the two resulting nodes, as well as their overlap, seems to be working. Whether this is indeed the change in the definition that leads to this behavior is unknown (see Exercises 5 and 6).

Figure 2.77
The bounding boxes corresponding to the first level of aggregation for an R*-tree for the collection of 22 rectangles in Figure 2.71.

Figure 2.79 contains a more complex example consisting of a sample collection of 1,700 line-shaped objects (Figure 2.79(a)) for which R-trees have been constructed using different node-splitting rules using $m = 20$ and $M = 50$. In particular, it shows the space decomposition for this example dataset resulting from the use of the R*-tree (Figure 2.79(b)) in comparison to that resulting from the use of an R-tree that makes use of the linear cost (Figure 2.79(c)) and quadratic cost (Figure 2.79(d)) node-splitting algorithms. Notice the squarelike boxes corresponding to nodes at the bottom level of

(a)

(b)

(c)

(d)

Figure 2.78
The bounding boxes corresponding to the first level of aggregation for an R-tree built using different node-splitting policies: (a) exhaustive, (b) linear, (c) quadratic, and (d) the linear algorithm of [60] for the collection of 22 rectangles in Figure 2.71.

the R*-tree and the small amount of overlap between them. Again, as in the example in Figures 2.77 and 2.78, it is quite clear that the R*-tree behaves best.

Empirical studies have shown that use of the R*-tree node-splitting algorithm instead of the conventional linear and quadratic cost R-tree node-splitting algorithms leads to a reduction in the space requirements (i.e., improved storage utilization) ranging from 10% to 20% [152, 866], while requiring significantly more time to build the R*-tree [866]. The effect of the R*-tree node-splitting algorithms vis-à-vis the conventional linear and quadratic cost node-splitting algorithms on query execution time is not so clear due to the need to take factors such as paging activity, and node occupancy, into account [152, 866, 1303].

Although the definition of the R*-tree makes three changes to the original R-tree definition [791], it can be argued that the main distinction, from a conceptual point of view rather than based on its effect on performance, is in the way an overflowing node is split and in the way the bounding boxes are redistributed in the two resulting nodes.[27]

---

[27] On the other hand, it could also be argued that forced reinsertion is the most important distinction as it has the ability to undo the effect of some insertions that may have caused undesired increases in overlap and coverage.

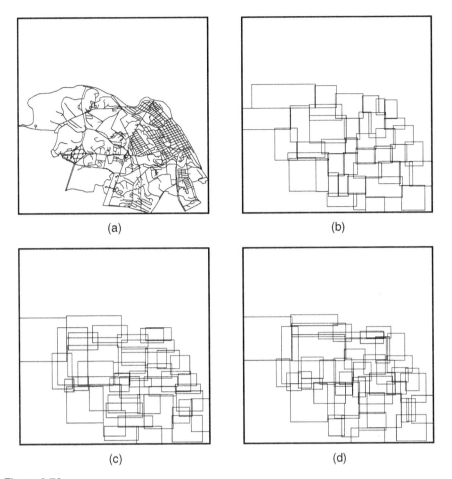

Figure 2.79
(a) A sample collection of 1,700 line-shaped objects and the space decomposition resulting from the use of (b) an R*-tree, as well as R-trees that make use of (c) linear cost and (d) quadratic cost node-splitting algorithms. All trees are order ($m = 20$, $M = 50$).

In particular, the original R-tree node-splitting algorithms [791] determine seeds, while the R*-tree algorithm determines a split axis and an axis split value. The bounding boxes of the objects are redistributed about these seeds and axis, respectively. At this point, it is important to reemphasize that the motivation for these redistribution strategies is to avoid the exhaustive search solution that looks at all possible partitions.

The R*-tree redistribution method first sorts the boundaries of the bounding boxes along each of the axes and then uses this information to find the split axis a (with respect to the minimum average perimeter of the bounding boxes of the resulting nodes) and split position (with respect to the minimal overlap once the split axis was chosen). This is a heuristic that attempts to approximate the solution to the d-dimensional problem (i.e., optimal partitioning with minimal coverage or overlap) with an approximation of the optimal one-dimensional solution along one of the axes (see Exercise 20). Intuitively, the validity of this approximation would appear to decrease as d (i.e., the dimensionality of the underlying space) increases since more and more splits are eliminated from consideration. However, the opposite conclusion might be true as it could be argued that although the number of eliminated splits grows exponentially with d, the majority of the eliminated splits are bad anyway. This is a problem for further study.

The remaining changes involving forced reinsertion and intelligent object insertion could have also been used in the R-tree construction algorithms. In particular, although the original R-tree definition [791] opts for minimizing coverage in determining the subtree into which an object is to be inserted, it does leave open whether minimizing coverage or overlap is best. Similarly, using forced reinsertion does not change the R-tree definition. It can be applied regardless of how a node is split and which policy is used to determine the node into which the object is to be inserted. The evaluation of the R*-tree conducted in [152] involves all three of these changes. An evaluation of R-trees constructed using these remaining changes is also of interest (see Exercises 5 and 6).

The node-splitting rules that form the basis of the R*-tree have also been used in conjunction with some of the methods for constructing instances of the object-tree pyramid such as the Hilbert packed R-tree. In particular, DeWitt, Kabra, Luo, Patel, and Yu [489] suggest that it is not a good idea to fill each leaf node of the Hilbert packed R-tree to capacity. Instead, they pack each leaf node i, say up to 75% of capacity, and then, for each additional object x to be placed in i, they check if the bounding rectangle of i needs to be enlarged by too much (e.g., more than 20% in area [489]) in order to contain x, in which case they start packing another node. In addition, whenever a node has been packed, the contents of a small number (e.g., 3 [489]) of the most recently created nodes are combined into a large node, which is then resplit using the R*-tree splitting methods. Although experiments show that these modifications lead to a slower construction time than that for the conventional Hilbert packed R-tree, the query performance is often improved (e.g., up to 20% in the experiments [489]).

Exercises

1. Explain why forced reinsertion is unlikely to be useful in a B-tree (i.e., why it would not necessarily enable us to avoid having to split a B-tree node)?

2. In the study of the linear R-tree node-splitting algorithm that is based on reducing overlap [60], all comparisons were made with a quadratic algorithm that was based on minimizing coverage (i.e., [791]). Conduct a similar study as in Exercise 21 for both random and real data using an R*-tree. This means that now the comparison uses a quadratic node-splitting algorithm that attempts to reduce both overlap and coverage as this is the motivation for the R*-tree.

3. What is the total cost of inserting an object into an R*-tree when no node splitting is needed?

4. When inserting an object into an R*-tree, we insert its bounding box b into the leaf node p for whom the resulting bounding box has the minimum increase in the amount of overlap with p's siblings that are children of nonleaf node s. This algorithm is quadratic in the number of entries in each node. We can improve on this bound by observing that insertion of b into the bounding boxes of sibling leaf nodes that are far from b is unlikely to result in minimizing the overlap. How would you take advantage of this to modify the insertion algorithm to avoid the quadratic cost and get an approximated minimum overlap solution?

5. Compare the performance of the R*-tree with R-trees that make use of the linear and quadratic cost node-splitting algorithms proposed by Guttman [791], both of which are implemented with forced reinsertion. The comparison should be qualitative and quantitative. The qualitative comparison should examine the resulting space decomposition as in Figure 2.79. This can be achieved by choosing a sample dataset and drawing the output. The quantitative comparison should tabulate coverage and overlap, storage utilization, and the time for construction, as well as the times for intersection (i.e., determining all pairs of intersecting objects), window, and point queries. You should use real data, if possible.

6. Compare the performance of the R*-tree with R-trees that make use of the linear and quadratic cost node-splitting algorithms proposed by Guttman [791], both of which are implemented with an intelligent object insertion procedure that is based on minimizing overlap in the case of leaf nodes, while minimizing the increase in area in the case of nonleaf nodes. Perform a similar comparison as in Exercise 5.

7. The R*-tree node-splitting rule tries to address both the issue of minimizing coverage and of minimizing overlap. Thus, it does not make use of a rule that minimizes just one of these factors. Instead, it makes use of a two-stage node-splitting process, where the first stage finds the axis along which the split takes place, and the second stage calculates the position of the split. Given that we want a rule that minimizes coverage while still leading to a reduction in overlap, explain why it may be better for the first stage that chooses the split axis to try to

minimize the average of the perimeters of the bounding boxes of the resulting nodes rather than to try to minimize the total area spanned (i.e., the coverage) by their bounding boxes?

8. Prove that once the faces of the bounding boxes have been sorted, when splitting an overflowing node in an R*-tree of order (m,M) in d dimensions, the split axis can be computed in $O(d \cdot M)$ time.

9. The first stage of the R*-tree node-splitting algorithm determines the axis a for which the average of the perimeters of the bounding boxes of the two nodes is the smallest, and the second stage calculates a split position s along axis a for which the amount of overlap between their bounding boxes is the smallest. Suppose that we modify the first stage of the R*-tree node-splitting algorithm to find the split axis a having the split position s' for which the perimeter of the bounding boxes resulting from the split is the smallest. What is the drawback of this approach with respect to the second stage of the node-splitting algorithm?

10. Suppose that you use the method described in Exercise 9 to determine the split axis when an R*-tree node overflows. In particular, it finds the split axis a having the split position s' for which the perimeter of the bounding boxes resulting from the split is the smallest. The second stage calculates a new (possibly different) split position s along axis a for which the amount of overlap between their bounding boxes is the smallest. Use the split position s' in the second stage, and dispense with the search for the split position that minimizes overlap. Explain why s' may not necessarily minimize overlap? Give an example of this phenomenon.

11. Despite the result of Exercise 10, compare the performance of using it with the variant described in Exercise 9 that computes the split position in the second stage and also with the conventional R*-tree definition that uses the split axis for which the average perimeter of the bounding boxes over all of the possible split positions for each axis is a minimum.

12. Repeat Exercise 5 with the variation of the R*-tree definition given in Exercise 9.

13. Repeat Exercise 6 with the variation of the R*-tree definition given in Exercise 9.

14. Repeat Exercise 5 with the variation of the R*-tree definition given in Exercise 10.

15. Repeat Exercise 6 with the variation of the R*-tree definition given in Exercise 10.

16. Suppose that the node-splitting algorithm in the R*-tree is modified to find the split axis a having the split position s for which the amount of overlap between the bounding boxes of the two resulting nodes is the smallest, and also use s as the position of the split. Compare the performance of using it with the variant described in Exercise 9 that finds the split axis a having the split position s' for which the perimeter of the bounding boxes resulting from the split is the smallest. Also compare it with the conventional R*-tree definition that uses the split axis for which the average perimeter of the bounding boxes over all of the possible split positions for each axis is a minimum.

17. Repeat Exercise 5 with the variation of the R*-tree definition given in Exercise 16.

18. Repeat Exercise 6 with the variation of the R*-tree definition given in Exercise 16.

19. Suppose that we modify the second stage of the R*-tree node-splitting algorithm so that, instead of choosing the split position for which the amount of overlap between the bounding boxes of the resulting nodes is the smallest, we choose the position for which the overlap along the split axis is minimized. This technique is useful if we choose to organize the elements of each R*-tree node using a k-d tree so that searching within the node is fast. In fact, this technique is used in the hybrid tree [317] (see Sections 1.7.1.2 of Chapter 1 and 4.4.3 of Chapter 4), which is a combination of an R-tree and k-d-B-tree for high-dimensional point data. First, project the bounding boxes on the split axis (i.e., the one-dimensional edges of the bounding boxes that are collinear with the split axis), thereby forming line segments. Second, sort the line segments into two sets on the basis of their left and right edges from left to right and right to left, respectively. Third, choose segments from the two sorted lists in alternating fashion, forming a left and a right partition until the minimum storage utilization constraints are satisfied. At this point, insert the remaining line segments in the partition that needs to be enlarged the least without worrying about the utilization. Once the minimum storage utilization constraints are satisfied, is the order in which the remaining line segments are inserted into the two partitions important?

20. Given a set of M bounding boxes of two-dimensional objects, suppose that you want to subdivide the set into two nonempty sets so that the sum of the perimeters of their bounding

boxes is minimized subject to the node-utilization constraints. This is a variant of the method used by Beckmann et al. [152] in the R*-tree that attempts to minimize the average perimeter of the bounding boxes of the two resulting nodes for all possible splits along the different axes. For two-dimensional data, this variant would be incorporated in the R*-tree node-splitting algorithm by decomposing this problem into four plane-sweep subproblems, one in each of the two dimensions and two sweep directions, as follows. Sort the left sides of all of the bounding boxes and then sweep a vertical line across this set stopping at every left boundary l, treating it as the separator between two sets L and R containing all of the bounding boxes whose left sides are less than or equal to l and those whose left sides are greater than l, respectively. Compute the sum of the perimeters of the bounding boxes of L and R retaining the position if it is smaller than the previous minimum. Repeat this sort-and-sweep process for the right sides of the bounding boxes and, likewise, for the top and bottom sides of the bounding boxes. Is this approach guaranteed to find the partitioning for which the sum of the perimeters of their bounding boxes is a minimum? In other words, is it possible that a better partition can be obtained where, without loss of generality, it is not the case that one of the nodes contains all of the bounding boxes whose left (right) sides are less than or equal to l and the other node contains all of the bounding boxes whose left (right) sides are greater than l? Note that the R*-tree algorithm only examines dM of the number of possible partitions, which is much smaller than the maximum number of possible partitions (see Exercise 8). Prove that this guarantee holds, or give a counterexample. If the guarantee does not hold, can you obtain an optimal solution by the use of an auxiliary data structure, such as a segment tree [166] or an interval tree [534, 537, 538], to keep track of the bounding boxes that are still active during the sweep process?

21. Repeat Exercise 20 for the problem of subdividing a set of M bounding boxes into two nonempty sets so that instead of minimizing the sum of their perimeters, we now try to minimize the area common to their bounding boxes.

22. As we saw, the R*-tree algorithms try to minimize the coverage, perimeter, and overlap in the node insertion process. Each of these factors is taken into account separately in different stages of the algorithm. An alternative approach is to define an objective function that takes these three factors, with appropriate weights, into account simultaneously and to try to minimize it. This objective function is applied when determining which node is to contain the new object, as well as during the node-splitting process. Investigate the use of this approach by defining some factors, and compare your results with the R*-tree node insertion algorithm that we described.

23. Measure the performance of point queries and window queries (in terms of the number of R-tree nodes visited) on packed R-trees for two-dimensional rectangle objects of your choice that have been transformed into the four representative point transformations described in the text and sorted using the row, Morton, and Peano-Hilbert orders. Generate the queries for uniformly distributed points and, likewise, for windows whose centroids and horizontal and vertical extents are drawn from a uniform distribution. Compare your results with those for an R-tree constructed using the R*-tree, linear cost, and quadratic cost node-splitting algorithms where the objects are inserted in the same order as in the packed R-tree for the corresponding space-ordering technique.

2.1.5.2.5 Bulk Insertion

Up to now, our discussion of building the object-tree pyramid has been differentiated on the basis of whether it is done in a static or a dynamic environment. The static methods, exemplified by the various packing methods, such as the packed R-tree, Hilbert packed R-tree, and the STR method, were primarily motivated by a desire to build the structure as quickly as possible. This is in addition to the secondary considerations of maximizing storage utilization and, possibly, faster query performance as a result of a shallower structure since each node is filled to capacity, thereby compensating for the fact that these methods may result in more coverage and overlap. The dynamic methods, exemplified by the R-tree and the R*-tree, were motivated equally by a desire to avoid rebuilding the structure as updates occur (primarily as objects are added and, to a lesser extent, deleted) and by a desire for faster query performance due to a reduction of coverage and overlap.

At times, it is desired to update an existing object-tree pyramid with a large number of objects at once. Performing these updates one object at a time using the implementations of the dynamic methods described above can be expensive. The CPU and I/O costs can be lowered by grouping the input objects prior to the insertion. This technique is known as *bulk insertion*. It can also be used to build the object-tree pyramid from scratch, in which case it is also known as *bulk loading*. In fact, we have seen several such techniques already in our presentation of the static methods that employ packing. The difference is that, although the bulk loading methods that we discuss in Section 2.1.5.2.6 are based on grouping the input objects prior to using one of the dynamic methods of constructing the object-tree pyramid, the grouping does not involve sorting the input objects, which is a cornerstone of the bulk loading methods that employ packing. We discuss the bulk insertion methods first.

A simple bulk insertion idea is to sort all of the m new objects to be inserted according to some order (e.g., Peano-Hilbert) and then insert them into an existing object-tree pyramid in this order [985]. The rationale for sorting the new objects is to have each new object be relatively close to the previously inserted object so that, most of the time, the nodes on the insertion path are likely to be the same, which is even more likely to be the case if some caching mechanism is employed. Thus, the total number of I/O operations is reduced. This technique works fine when the number of objects being inserted is small relative to the total number of objects. Also, it may be the best choice when the collection of new objects is spread over a relatively large portion of the underlying space, as, in such cases, the use of other methods (see below) may lead to excessive overlap (but see discussion of generalized bulk insertion (GBI) [381] below). It can be used with any of the methods of building an object-tree pyramid. A related approach, which also uses sorting, can be applied when the existing object-tree pyramid was built using one of the static methods, such as a packed R-tree. In this case, the new packed R-tree can be constructed by merging the sorted list of new objects with the sorted list of the existing objects, which is obtained from the leaf nodes of the existing packed R-tree. This approach is used in the cubetree [1587], a packed R-tree-like structure for data warehousing and online analytic processing (OLAP) [329]) applications, which is not discussed further here.

Another related bulk insertion method, due to Kamel, Khalil, and Kouramajian [985], first orders the new objects being inserted according to the Peano-Hilbert order and then aggregates them into leaf nodes, where each node is filled to a predetermined percentage of the capacity (e.g., 70%) as if we are building just the leaf nodes of a Hilbert packed R-tree for the new objects. These leaf nodes are inserted into an object-tree pyramid in the order in which they were built. Intuitively, the algorithm should yield a speedup of the order of the number of objects that can fit in a leaf node compared to inserting the objects one by one. Unfortunately, the algorithm is also likely to increase the degree of overlap in the existing object-tree pyramid and thus produce a worse index in terms of query performance. The reason for the increase in overlap is that the new leaf nodes may overlap existing leaf nodes in the object-tree pyramid. This is compounded by the fact that two new objects that are adjacent in Peano-Hilbert order (and thus inserted into the same node) may actually be far apart, leading to leaf nodes with large bounding rectangles. Empirical results reported support this observation [985]. In fact, the authors propose an alternative method of inserting the actual objects one at a time after sorting when the set of new objects is small or when it is spread over a large area as described above.

The *Small-Tree-Large-Tree* (STLT) method of Chen, Choubey, and Rundensteiner [347] can be viewed as a generalized variant of the method of Kamel, Khalil, and Kouramajian [985]: instead of inserting the leaf nodes of the object-tree pyramid T of the new data, it just inserts the root of T. First, an object-tree pyramid is built for the new data using any of the static or dynamic methods. Next, the root of the new object-tree pyramid T, of height h_T, is inserted into the existing object-tree pyramid E, of height h_E, using one of several dynamic R-tree insertion algorithms so that T ends up as an element in a node Q in E at depth $h_E - h_T - 1$. In other words, the leaf nodes of T are now at the same depth as the leaf nodes of E. Once the node Q has been determined, check if the insertion of T in Q will cause Q to overflow. If this is the case, then heuristics employing a combination of traditional dynamic R-tree and B-tree insertion techniques are used to make space for T. These heuristics attempt some local reorganization of the subtree rooted at Q in order to ensure that T can be inserted in one operation.

Although using the STLT method leads to significantly faster insertion compared with the dynamic insertion (i.e., when the objects are inserted one by one) when the new data covers the same area as the existing data, there is a considerable degradation in query performance due to the significant overlap between the nodes in T and E. In order to overcome this problem, Choubey, Chen, and Rundensteiner [381] introduce a new method (termed *Generalized Bulk Insertion* (GBI)) that uses cluster analysis to divide the new data into clusters. Small clusters (e.g., containing just one point) are inserted using a regular dynamic insertion method. On the other hand, for larger clusters, a tree is built and inserted using the STLT method. In other words, the STLT method is really a subcomponent of the GBI method. This reduces the amount of overlap, which can be very high for the STLT method. On the other hand, if there is little overlap between the nodes in T and E, then the query performance of the STLT method should be satisfactory.

It is interesting to observe the close relationship between the above three methods. In particular, all three methods reorganize the existing object-tree pyramid. They differ in the extent to which the new objects are interleaved with the objects in the existing object-tree pyramid. The cubetree method of Roussopoulos, Kotidis, and Roussopoulos [1587], as well as the one-object-at-a-time alternative method of Kamel, Khalil, and Kouramajian [985] that we described, merges the list of the individual new objects with the existing objects. On the other hand, the one-node-at-a-time method of Kamel, Khalil, and Kouramajian [985] and the GBI method of Chen, Choubey, and Rundensteiner [347] first build a partial or full object-tree pyramid for the new objects. The latter two methods differ in what parts of the new object-tree pyramid for the new objects are inserted into the existing tree. In particular, the method of Kamel, Khalil, and Kouramajian [985] inserts only the leaf nodes of the new object-tree pyramid. On the other hand, the GBI method of Chen, Choubey, and Rundensteiner [347] inserts only the root node of the new object-tree pyramid.

The result is that, in terms of construction time, the methods range in speed with the cubetree of Roussopoulos, Kotidis, and Roussopoulos [1587] and the one-object-at-a-time alternative method of Kamel, Khalil, and Kouramajian [985] as the slowest, followed by the one-node-at-a-time method of Kamel, Khalil, and Kouramajian [985] and the method of Chen, Choubey, and Rundensteiner [347] as the fastest. In contrast, query performance is best for the cubetree method of Roussopoulos, Kotidis, and Roussopoulos [1587] and the one-object-at-a-time alternative method of Kamel, Khalil, and Kouramajian [985] since the resulting tree is identical to that obtained had we constructed an object-tree pyramid for the new and old objects together using the same insertion order. The one-node-at-a-time method of Kamel, Khalil, and Kouramajian [985] is better than the GBI method of Chen, Choubey, and Rundensteiner [347] because more restructuring of the existing tree takes place. In fact, the method of Chen, Choubey, and Rundensteiner [347] will most likely result in very poor query performance after several successive applications because the amount of overlap will be quite high. Thus, we see that the costs of these methods reflect the trade-offs that must be made in choosing between fast construction and fast query performance.

Exercise

1. Perform an empirical comparison of the performance of the one-object-at-a-time and one-node-at-a-time methods of Kamel, Khalil, and Kouramajian [985] with the GBI method of Chen, Choubey, and Rundensteiner [347] for a window query of different window sizes.

2.1.5.2.6 Bulk Loading

The bulk loading methods that we describe [87, 194] are quite different from the bulk insertion methods described in Section 2.1.5.2.5 as the individual objects are inserted using the dynamic insertion rules. In particular, the objects are not preprocessed (e.g., via an explicit sorting step or aggregation into a distinct object-tree pyramid) prior to insertion as is the case for the bulk insertion methods. In particular, the sorting can be viewed as a variant of a lazy evaluation method, where the sorting is deferred as much as possible. Nevertheless, at the end of the bulk loading process, the data is ordered on the basis of the underlying tree structure and hence can be considered sorted. These methods are general in that they are applicable to most balanced tree data structures that resemble a B-tree, including a large class of multidimensional index structures, such as the R-tree. They are based on the general concept of the buffer tree of Arge [85], in which case each internal node of the buffer tree structure contains a buffer of records stored on disk. A main memory buffer is employed when transferring records from the buffer of a node to the buffers of its child nodes.

The basic idea behind the methods based on the buffer tree is that insertions into each nonleaf node of the buffer tree are batched. In particular, insertions into the buffer occur in association with the root node and slowly trickle down the tree as buffers are emptied when they are full. The buffers enable the effective use of available main memory, thereby resulting in large savings in I/O cost over the regular dynamic insertion method (although the CPU cost may be higher, in part, due to the large fanout when using one of the methods [194], as we shall see below). Nevertheless, the actual execution of a single insertion could be slower in comparison to a non–bulk loading method in the case that many overflowing buffers need to be trickled down.

When a buffer b_r associated with a nonleaf node r is full, the contents of b_r are distributed to the children of r (but see Exercise 1). During this process, only one block (i.e., the amount of data that can be transferred in one I/O operation from the disk to main memory) of records from the buffer of r needs to be in main memory, with one block of records from the buffers of each of its children. The distribution process depends on whether the children are nonleaf nodes or leaf nodes.

- If the children are nonleaf nodes, then the contents of b_r are inserted into the buffer b_{s_i} associated with one of the m children of r, say s_i ($1 \le i \le m$). Once the contents of all of the blocks in b_r have been emptied, a check is made to see if any of the buffers, say b_{s_i}, associated with the children of r are full. If they are, then the process is reapplied to the blocks in b_{s_i} and possibly to their children if they are full, and so on, until leaf nodes are encountered, at which time a node split is needed if the nodes contain more entries than the block size.

- If the children are leaf nodes, then the content of b_r is inserted into the leaf nodes (recall that only the nonleaf nodes have buffers). During the distribution process, some children of r (which are leaf nodes) may be split. If such a split causes r to have more than c children, then r is also split, and the remaining contents of b_r are distributed into the buffers of the two nodes resulting from the split.

It may be somewhat difficult to understand fully the actual process from the above recursive definition. In simpler terms, the process works as follows. We keep inserting into the buffer of the root node until its buffer is full. At this time, we distribute its content, as described above, and possibly reapply the process to the children if they are full, and so on, until encountering leaf nodes, at which time a node split is needed if the nodes contain more entries than the block size. Once all full buffers have been emptied, the root's buffer is filled with more data, and the insertion process is repeated.

Once all of the objects in the dataset have been processed, a pass is made over the buffer associated with the root node, and the remaining entries are inserted into the appropriate children of the tree rooted at the node. The same process is applied to the buffers associated with the children of the root and their descendants so that all nonempty buffers in the tree have been emptied. At this point, the leaf nodes of the object-tree pyramid have been constructed. Next, apply the same building process to the minimum bounding boxes of the leaf nodes, thereby constructing the level of the object-tree pyramid corresponding to the parents of the leaf nodes. This process is continued until the number of leaf nodes is less than the maximum capacity of an object-tree pyramid leaf node.

Buffer tree methods try to make maximum use of available memory by increasing the fanout c of each internal node of the tree structure. When distributing the contents of the buffer of an internal node s to the buffers of its children, we need one block of size B (i.e., the amount of space occupied by one disk block) for the internal node s and one block for each of its c children for reading s's buffer and writing the new buffer contents for the children. Thus, the internal memory requirements are $B \cdot (c + 1)$, in addition to the size of each internal node. Given an internal memory buffer of size M, we would choose c to be large enough so that the memory requirements are as close to M as possible. Note that c is much larger than B, which means that the intermediate object-tree pyramid is of a shallower maximum depth than the final object-tree pyramid. Thus, when buffer tree methods are applied to an object-tree pyramid, the intermediate tree has a larger fanout than the final object-tree pyramid.

Recall that the above method, proposed by van den Bercken, Seeger, and Widmayer [194], builds the object-tree pyramid recursively in stages in a bottom-up manner. There is one stage per level of the final object-tree pyramid, that has maximum depth d. At each stage i, an intermediate tree structure is built where the nodes at the deepest level correspond to the nodes at depth $d - i$ of the final object-tree pyramid. The drawbacks of this method are the need to build an intermediate structure and the multiple passes. These drawbacks are overcome by Arge, Hinrichs, Vahrenhold, and Vitter [87] by attaching buffers to nodes only at certain levels of a regular object-tree pyramid structure (i.e., the nodes have a normal amount of fanout to fill a disk page, whereas, in the method of van den Bercken et al. [194], the fanout depends on the amount of available main memory). In essence, assuming an intermediate tree fanout c and object-tree pyramid node fanout f, buffers are attached to object-tree pyramid nodes at depths where the total number of child nodes is approximately c^i. Such nodes are found at depths that are integer multiples of $\log_f c$. Therefore, all of the nodes of the object-tree pyramid exist as we distribute the objects, thereby avoiding the need to build the intermediate structure and thus enabling the object-tree pyramid to be built in one pass. In addition, as we will see below, this also makes the method of Arge et al. [87] suitable for bulk insertion.

The method of Arge et al. [87] has some other differences from the method of van den Bercken et al.[194], including the maximum size of the buffers and the specific details of how buffers are emptied. In particular, Arge et al. [87] propose to read the entire buffer contents to memory at the beginning of the distribution process rather than one block at a time. This reduces the overall seek time since it is paid only once rather than for each block. Furthermore, Arge et al. [87] also propose a method for increasing the storage utilization of the leaf nodes, which generally results in object-tree pyramids that have better query performance.

The construction of Arge et al. [87] yields the same object-tree pyramid as would have been obtained using conventional dynamic insertion methods without buffering (with the exception of the R*-tree, where the use of forced reinsertion is difficult to incorporate in the buffering approach). In contrast, this is not the case for the method of van den Bercken et al. [194], where as soon as the first stage has been completed, the next stage makes use of the minimum bounding boxes of the nodes at the immediately lower level of the tree. In addition, the method of [87] supports bulk insertions (as opposed to just initial bulk-loading) and bulk queries, and, in fact, intermixed insertions and queries. In contrast, bulk insertions are not so easy to support with the method of van den Bercken et al. [194] because only the intermediate structures have buffers associated with the internal nodes, whereas the final object-tree pyramid has no buffers.

Bulk loading is generally not nonblocking, although it may appear to be nonblocking to the user in the sense that, since the insertion must trickle down to the leaf nodes of the structure, the trickling down could be implemented in such a way that it is transparent to the user. In particular, it could be implemented using a thread (e.g., [1030]), in which case the next insertion should wait until the current operation is completed, although other operations could be executed simultaneously, thereby leading to the impression that the algorithm is nonblocking.

Exercise

1. When using the buffer tree method for the object-tree pyramid, if we always completely empty the buffer of node r when distributing its contents to its children, we may find that the buffers of some of the children of r will overflow before we have finished distributing the contents of r. How would you avoid this problem?

2.1.5.2.7 Shortcomings and Solutions

In this section, we point out some of the shortcomings of the object-tree pyramid, as well as some of the solutions. As we are dealing with the representations of objects, which are inherently of low dimension, we do not discuss the shortcomings and solutions for high-dimensional data, which are discussed in Section 4.4 of Chapter 4 (e.g., the X-tree [190]). One of the drawbacks of the object-tree pyramid (i.e., the R-tree, as well as its variants, such as the R*-tree) is that as the node size (i.e., page size—that is, M) gets large, the performance starts to degrade. This is somewhat surprising because, according to conventional wisdom, performance should increase with node size as the depth of the tree decreases, thereby requiring fewer disk accesses. The problem is that as the node size increases, operations on each node take more CPU time. This is especially true if the operation involves search (e.g., finding the nearest object to a point) as the bounding boxes in each node are not ordered [864].

This problem can be overcome by ordering the bounding boxes in each node using the same ordering-based aggregation techniques that were used to make the object-tree pyramid more efficient in responding to the location query. For example, we could order the bounding boxes by applying Morton or Peano-Hilbert space ordering to their centroids. We term the result an *ordered R-tree* (see Exercise 1). Interestingly, the ordered R-tree can be viewed as a hybrid between an object B^+-tree and an R-tree in the sense that nodes are ordered internally (i.e., by their constituent bounding box elements) using the ordering of the object B^+-tree, while they are ordered externally (i.e., vis-à-vis each other) using an R-tree.

Although the R-tree is height balanced, the branching factor of each node is not the same. Recall that each node contains between m and M objects or bounding boxes. This has several drawbacks. First, it means that the nodes are not fully occupied, thereby causing the tree structure to be deeper than it would be had the nodes been completely full. Therefore, the number of data objects in the leaf nodes of the descendants of sibling nonleaf nodes is not the same and, in fact, can vary quite greatly, thereby leading to imbalance in terms of the number of objects stored in different subtrees. This can have a detrimental effect on the efficiency of retrieval. Second, satisfying the branching factor condition often requires compromising the goal of minimizing total coverage, overlap, and perimeter. The packed R-tree and the Hilbert packed R-tree are two methods to overcome this problem as they initially have a branching factor of M at all but the last node at each level. However, they are not necessarily designed to meet our goals of minimizing total coverage, overlap, and perimeter.

The S-tree [22] is an approach to overcome the above drawbacks of the R-tree and its packed variants by trading off the height-balanced property in return for reduced coverage, overlap, and perimeter in the resulting minimum bounding boxes. The S-tree has the property that each node that is not a leaf node or a penultimate node (i.e., a node whose children are all leaf nodes) has M children. In addition, for any pair of sibling nodes (i.e., with the same parent) s_1 and s_2 with N_{s_1} and N_{s_2} objects in their descendants, respectively, we have that $p \leq N_{s_1}/N_{s_2} \leq 1/p$ $(0 < p \leq 0.5)$, where p, termed the *skew factor*, is a parameter that is related to the skewness of the data and governs the amount of trade-off, thereby providing a worst-case guarantee on the skewness of the descendants of the node. In particular, the number of objects in the descendants of each of a pair of sibling nodes is at least a fraction p of the total number of objects in the descendants of both nodes. This guarantee is fairly tight when p is close to 0.5, while it is quite loose when p is small. In other words, when $p = 0.5$, the difference in the number of objects that will be found in the subtrees of a pair of sibling nodes is within a factor of 2, whereas this ratio can get arbitrarily large in a conventional R-tree (see Exercise 6). In addition, the S-tree construction process makes use of an overlap factor parameter o (ranging between 0 and 1) defined to be the area covered by the intersection of the bounding boxes divided by the sum of the corresponding areas of the bounding boxes.

The *cost-based unbalanced R-tree* (CUR-tree) of Ross, Sitzmann, and Stuckey [1578] is another variant of an R-tree where the height-balanced requirement is relaxed in order to improve the performance of point and window queries in an environment where all the data is in main memory. In particular, the CUR-tree is constructed by considering the following two factors:

1. A cost model for the data structure (i.e., the R-tree) that accounts for the operations, such as reading the node and making the comparisons needed to continue the search

2. A query distribution model that includes uniformly distributed points and rectangular windows, as well as a skewed-point distribution

Unlike a conventional R-tree, operations on a CUR-tree are invoked not only upon overflow (and to a lesser extent underflow). Instead, upon every insertion and deletion, every node on the insertion path is examined to determine if its entries should be rearranged to lower the cost function. The result is that nodes can be split, and their entries can be promoted or demoted. Ross et al. [1578] compared the CUR-tree with the conventional R-tree and the R*-tree and found the performance of the CUR-tree for search queries to be better. Of course, the insertion time for the CUR-tree was found to be slower than both the conventional R-tree and the R*-tree. Note again that these comparisons and the cost model all assume that the data is in main memory, thereby somewhat limiting their applicability.

García, López, and Leutenegger [681] propose to improve the query performance of R-trees by restructuring the tree. Such restructuring can be performed after an R-tree has been built (termed *postoptimization*), say, for example, using one of the methods outlined in Section 2.1.5.2.6 (i.e., a static R-tree). Alternatively, a dynamically constructed R-tree can be restructured gradually as it is being updated (termed *incremental refinement*). Their approach consists of selecting a node e to be restructured and then applying the restructuring process to e and its ancestors. Several alternatives are proposed for choosing e; the simplest is to choose a point p at random and find a leaf node e that contains p. Once e has been determined, e is restructured by considering the siblings that overlap e (after recursively restructuring e's ancestors in the same manner). For each such sibling s, the entries in s are inserted into e, and s is deleted (i.e., s is merged with e). If e overflows, then split e (e.g., using an optimal node-splitting algorithm; see Section 2.1.5.2.3) and arbitrarily set e to one of the resulting nodes (while the other node is marked as having been processed already). Note that merging and resplitting overlapping sibling nodes e and s tends to reduce the amount of overlap among e and s (as resulting from the resplitting).

In the static case (i.e., postoptimization), García et al. [681] suggest performing n restructuring operations for a tree of n nodes. In the dynamic case (i.e., incremental refinement), García et al. [681] suggest performing a restructuring operation with some fixed probability for each insertion operation (e.g., so that 1 out of every 20 insertions leads to restructuring, on the average). Also, García et al. [681] point out that restructuring of an R-tree can be invoked during idle periods (e.g., at night). In an empirical study, for both the static and dynamic cases, such restructuring was found to reduce the query cost (in terms of the number of disk accesses) by 25–50%, while the cost of restructuring was relatively modest (i.e., 10% in the case of incremental refinement).

At a first glance, restructuring is similar to forced reinsertion in the case of an R*-tree (see Section 2.1.5.2.4). However, upon closer scrutiny, they are quite different. Forced reinsertion takes individual node entries and reinserts them at the root. In contrast, restructuring operates on groups of node entries by repeatedly merging and resplitting them, as necessary, in order to obtain better query performance through greater storage utilization and less overlap.

A shortcoming of all of the representations that are based on object hierarchies (i.e., including all of the R-tree variants) is that when the objects are not hyperrectangles, use of the bounding box approximation of the object eliminates only some objects from consideration when responding to queries. In other words, the actual execution of many queries requires knowledge of the exact representation of the object (e.g., the location query). In fact, the execution of the query may be quite complex using this exact representation. At times, these queries may be executed more efficiently by decomposing the object further into smaller pieces and then executing the query on the individual pieces, thereby overcoming the shortcoming associated with the approximation.

Some suggested implementations include a decomposition into shapes, such as triangles, trapezoids, convex polygons, and so on (e.g., [261, 1081]), as mentioned in Section 2.1.3 when discussing a representation of nonorthogonal objects (i.e., objects whose sides are not orthogonal) using a decomposition into nonorthogonal blocks. The TR*-tree [261, 1692] is an example of such a representation that decomposes each object in an R*-tree into a collection of trapezoids. The DR-tree [1142] is a related approach where the minimum bounding box is recursively decomposed into minimum bounding boxes until the volume of each box is less than a predefined fraction of the volume of the initial bounding box. The result of the decomposition process is represented as a binary tree, which is stored separately from the hierarchy that contains the minimum bounding boxes of the objects and can be processed in memory once it has been loaded. Of course, these techniques are also applicable to other R-tree variants.

Exercises

1. Implement an ordered R-tree using the different node-splitting algorithms (i.e., R*-tree, linear cost, and quadratic cost), and compare its performance with the corresponding nonordered versions. Implement the ordered R-tree by applying the Morton and Peano-Hilbert space orderings to their representative points. Use the following two types of representative points for the bounding boxes:

   (a) The centroid

   (b) The centroid and the horizontal and vertical extents (i.e., the horizontal and vertical distances from the centroid to the relevant sides)

   The comparison should include the time for construction, as well as the times for intersection (i.e., determining all pairs of intersecting objects), window, point, and nearest object queries. You should use real data, if possible (e.g., a collection of rectangle objects or lines).

2. Write an algorithm to perform a point query in an ordered R-tree.

3. Write an algorithm to perform a window query in an ordered R-tree.

4. Write an algorithm to find the nearest object to a point in an ordered R-tree.

5. Write an algorithm to solve the rectangle intersection problem for an ordered R-tree.

6. Consider an R-tree where each node contains between m and M objects or bounding boxes. The S-tree is designed to provide a guarantee of the relative difference in the number of objects found in the subtrees of two sibling nodes. In particular, for skewness factor p, given a pair of sibling nodes s_1 and s_2 with N_{s_1} and N_{s_2} objects in their descendants, respectively, we have that $p \leq N_{s_1}/N_{s_2} \leq 1/p$ ($0 < p \leq 0.5$). Show that the ratio N_{s_1}/N_{s_2} can get arbitrary large in an R-tree.

2.1.5.3 Disjoint Object-Based Hierarchical Interior-Based Representations (k-D-B-Tree, R^+-Tree, and Cell Tree)

In our descriptions of the object pyramid and the object-tree pyramid in Section 2.1.5.2, we observed that we may have to examine all of the bounding boxes at all levels when attempting to determine the identity of the object o that contains location a (i.e., the location query). This was caused by the fact that the bounding boxes corresponding to different nodes may overlap. Because each object is associated with only one node while being contained in possibly many bounding boxes (e.g., in Figure 2.75, rectangle 1 is contained in its entirety in R1, R2, R3, and R5), the location query may often require several nonleaf nodes to be visited before determining the object that contains a. This problem also arises in the R-tree, as seen in the following example.

Suppose that we wish to determine the identity of the rectangle object(s) in the collection of rectangles given in Figure 2.75 that contains point Q at coordinate values (22,24). We first determine that Q is in R0. Next, we find that Q can be in both or either R1 or R2, and thus we must search both of their subtrees. Searching R1 first, we find that Q can be contained only in R3. Searching R3 does not lead to the rectangle that contains Q, even though Q is in a portion of rectangle D that is in R3. Thus, we must search R2, and we find that Q can be contained only in R5. Searching R5 results in locating D, the desired rectangle. The drawback of the R-tree, as well as of other representations that make use of an object pyramid, is that, unlike those based on the cell pyramid, they do not result in a disjoint decomposition of space. Recall that the problem is that an object is associated with only one bounding box (e.g., rectangle D in Figure 2.75 is associated with bounding box R5; yet, it overlaps bounding boxes R1, R2, R3, and R5). In the worst case, this means that when we wish to respond to the location query (e.g., given a point, determining the containing rectangle in a rectangle database or an intersecting line in a line segment database, etc., in the two-dimensional space from which the objects are drawn), we may have to search the entire database. Thus, we need a hierarchy of disjoint bounding boxes.

An obvious way to overcome this drawback is to use one of the hierarchical image-based representations described in Section 2.1.5.1. Recall that these representations make use of a hierarchy of disjoint cells that completely spans the underlying space. The hierarchy consists of a set of sets $\{C_j\}$ $(0 \leq j \leq n)$, where C_n corresponds to the original collection of cells, and C_0 corresponds to one cell. The sets differ in the number and size of the constituent cells at the different depths, although each set is usually a containment hierarchy in the sense that a cell at depth i usually contains all of the cells below it at depth $i + 1$. The irregular grid pyramid is an example of such a hierarchy.

A simple way to adapt the irregular grid pyramid to our problem is to overlay the decomposition induced by C_{n-1} (i.e., the next to the deepest level) on the bounding boxes $\{b_i\}$ of the objects $\{o_i\}$, thereby decomposing the bounding boxes and associating each part of the bounding box with the corresponding covering cell of the irregular grid pyramid. Note that we use the set at the next deepest level (i.e., C_{n-1}) rather than the set at the deepest level (i.e., C_n) as the deepest level contains the original collection of unit-sized cells c_{nk} and thus does not correspond to any aggregation. The cells c_{jk} at the remaining levels j $(0 \leq j \leq n - 2)$ are formed in the same way as in the irregular grid pyramid—that is, they contain the union of the objects corresponding to the portions of the bounding boxes associated with the cells making up cell c_{jk}. Using our terminology, we term the result an *irregular grid bounding-box pyramid*. It should be clear that the depth of the irregular grid bounding-box pyramid is one less than that of the corresponding irregular grid pyramid.

The definition of the irregular grid pyramid, as well as of the other hierarchical image-based representations, stipulates that each unit-sized cell is contained in its entirety in one or more objects. Equivalently, a cell cannot be partially in object o_1 and partially in object o_2. The same restriction also holds for block decompositions, which are not hierarchical (see Section 2.1.2). In contrast, in the case of the irregular grid bounding-box pyramid, the fact that the bounding boxes are just approximations of the objects enables us to relax this restriction in the sense that we allow a cell (or a block in the case of the block decompositions of Section 2.1.2) to contain parts of the bounding boxes of several objects. In other words, cell (or block) b can be partially occupied by part of the bounding box b_1 of object o_1, by part of the bounding box b_2 of object o_2, and it may even be partially empty.

The irregular grid bounding-box pyramid is a hierarchy of grids, although the grid sizes are permitted to vary in an arbitrary manner between levels. This definition is still overly restrictive in the sense that we want to be able to aggregate a varying, but bounded, number of cells at each level (in contrast to a predefined number) that depends on the number of bounding boxes or objects that are associated with them so that we can have a height-balanced dynamic structure in the spirit of the B-tree. We also wish to use a hierarchy that makes use of a different block decomposition rule (e.g., a k-d tree, generalized k-d tree, point quadtree, bintree, region quadtree, thereby forming a bounding-box variant of the cell-tree pyramid that we describe as a *bounding-box cell-tree pyramid*) instead of a grid, as in the case of an irregular grid bounding-box pyramid.

Our solution is equivalent to a marriage of the bounding-box cell-tree pyramid hierarchy with one of the block decompositions described in Section 2.1.2. This is done by choosing a value M for the maximum number of cells (actually blocks) that can be aggregated and a block decomposition rule (e.g., a generalized k-d tree). As we are propagating the identities of the objects associated with the bounding boxes up the hierarchy rather than the space occupied by them, we use an object-based variant of the block decomposition rule. This means that a block is decomposed whenever it contains the bounding boxes of more than M objects rather than on the basis of the absence of homogeneity. Note that the occupied space is implicit to the block decomposition rule and thus need not be explicitly propagated up the hierarchy.

It should be clear that each object's bounding box can appear only once in each block as the objects are continuous. If more than M of the bounding boxes overlap each other in block b (i.e., they all have at least one point in common), then there is no point in attempting to decompose b further as we will never be able to find subblocks b_i of b so that each of b_i does not have at least one point in common with the overlapping bounding boxes. Observe also that although the block decompositions yield a partition of space into disjoint blocks, the bounding boxes at the lowest level of the hierarchy may not necessarily be disjoint. For example, consider a database of line segment objects and the situation of a vertex where five of the line segments meet. It is impossible for the bounding boxes of the line segments to be disjoint. The object-based variants of the block decomposition rules are quite different from their image-based counterparts discussed in Section 2.1.2, which base the decomposition on whether the space spanned by the block is completely covered by an object. It is important to reiterate that the blocks corresponding to the leaf nodes do not represent hyperrectangular aggregates of identically valued unit-sized cells, as in the conventional pyramid. Instead, they represent hyperrectangular aggregates of bounding boxes of objects or pieces thereof.

Without loss of generality, assuming a generalized k-d tree block decomposition rule, the hierarchy of sets $\{H_j\}$ $(1 \leq j \leq n)$ is defined as follows: H_0 consists of one block. H_1 consists of a subset of the nodes of a generalized k-d tree decomposition Z of the underlying space so that Z has a maximum of M elements whose corresponding blocks span the entire underlying space. H_2 is formed by removing from Z all nodes corresponding to members of H_1 and their ancestors and then applying the same rule that was used to form H_1 to each of the blocks in H_1 with respect to Z. In other words, H_2 consists of generalized k-d tree decompositions of the blocks h_{1k} $(1 \leq k \leq M)$ that make up H_1. Each element of H_2 contains no more than M blocks for a maximum of M^2 blocks. This process is repeated at each successive level down to the leaf level at depth $n - 1$. The nodes at the leaf level contain the bounding boxes of the objects or parts of the bounding boxes of the objects. The pyramid means that the hierarchy must be height balanced with all leaf nodes at the same level, and that the cells at depth j are disjoint and span the space covered by the cells at the immediately lower level at depth $j + 1$.

We term the resulting data structure a *generalized k-d tree bounding-box cell-tree pyramid* on account of the use of the generalized k-d tree as the building block of the pyramid and the use of a tree access structure, although it is more commonly known as a *k-d-B-tree* [1567] on account of the similarity of the node structure to that of a B-tree. If we had used the point quadtree or the bintree as the building block of the hierarchy, then we would have termed the result a *point quadtree bounding-box cell-tree pyramid* or a *bintree bounding-box cell-tree pyramid*, respectively. It is interesting to note that the k-d-B-tree was originally developed for storing pointlike objects (see the discussion in Section 1.7.1 of Chapter 1) although the extension to objects with extent is relatively straightforward, as shown here (but see Exercise 1).

Figure 2.80 is an example of one possible k-d-B-tree for the collection of rectangles whose specifications are given in Figure 2.67. Broken lines denote the leaf nodes, and thin lines denote the space spanned by the subtrees rooted at the nonleaf nodes. Of course, other variations are possible since the k-d-tree is not unique. This particular tree is of order (2,3) (i.e., having a minimum and maximum of two and three entries, respectively), although, in general, it is not possible always to guarantee that all nodes will have a minimum of two entries; nor is the minimum occupancy requirement a part of the definition of the k-d-B-tree. Notice that rectangle object D appears in three different nodes, while rectangle objects A, B, E, and G appear in two different nodes. Observe also that the example uses a partition scheme that cycles through the axes in the order x, y, x, y, and so on, although, as we shall see below, this cycling is not guaranteed to hold once objects are inserted and deleted.

Our definition of the structure was given in a top-down manner. In fact, the structure is often built in a bottom-up manner by inserting the objects one at a time. Initially, the hierarchy contains just one node corresponding to the bounding box of the single object. As each additional object o is processed, we insert o's bounding box b into all of the leaf nodes that overlap it. If any of these nodes become too full, then we split these nodes using an appropriate block decomposition rule and determine if the parent is not too full so that it can support the addition of a child. If it is not, then we recursively apply the same decomposition rule to the parent. The process stops at the root, in which case overflow will usually cause the hierarchy to grow by one level.

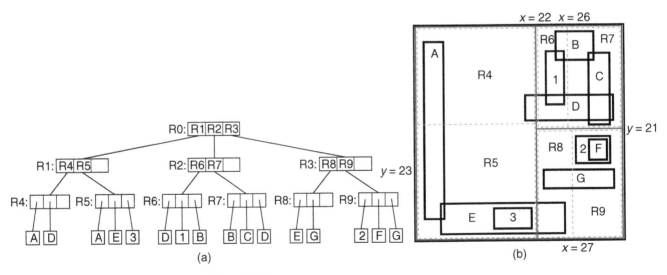

Figure 2.80
(a) k-d-B-tree for a collection of rectangle objects whose specifications are given in Figure 2.67 with $m = 2$ and $M = 3$ and (b) the spatial extents of the nodes. Notice that only in the leaf nodes are the bounding boxes minimal.

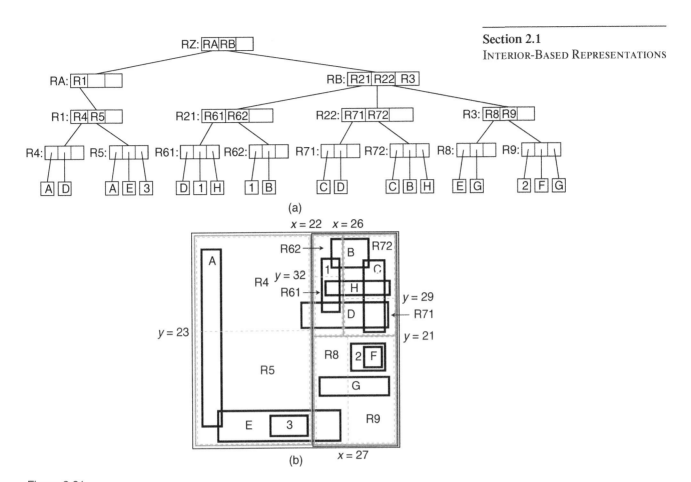

(a)

(b)

Figure 2.81
(a) k-d-B-tree resulting from the insertion of rectangle object H into the k-d-B-tree of Figure 2.80 when the root node is split at $x = 22$ and (b) the spatial extents of the nodes. Once the root node has been split, no further partitioning and reinsertion at deeper levels is needed. Notice that only in the leaf nodes are the bounding boxes minimal.

For example, consider the insertion of rectangle object H with a lower-left corner at (22,29) and an upper-right corner at (38,32) in the k-d-B-tree in Figure 2.80. H overlaps leaf nodes R6 and R7, and its insertion causes them to overflow. R6 is split into nodes R61 and R62 at $y = 32$, while R7 is split into nodes R71 and R72 at $y = 29$. These four nodes (i.e., R61, R62, R71, and R72) now become the children of node R2, which causes R2 to overflow. R2 is split at $x = 26$ into nodes R21 (containing nodes R61 and R62) and R22 (containing nodes R71 and R72).

These two nodes (i.e., R21 and R22) replace R2 as the children of the root node R0, along with R1 and R3, which now causes R0 to overflow. At this point, we split R0 along $x = 22$ into two nodes, RA and RB, where RA consists of node R1, and RB consists of nodes R21, R22, and R3. This causes the height of the tree to grow by one level, thereby resulting in the creation of a new root node RZ, as shown in the k-d-B-tree given in Figure 2.81. Notice that the resulting tree is no longer order (2,3).

The process that we have described is analogous to that used in a B-tree upon overflow. The difference is that there are several ways to deal with overflow, in the sense of where the node and the underlying space are to be partitioned. The most straightforward one is to split the node along the partition line that corresponds to the partition at the root of the k-d tree of the underlying space that is spanned by the node that has overflowed. In fact, this is the strategy pursued in the example illustrated in Figure 2.81. In particular, we split node R0 at $x = 22$ so that the newly created root node RZ has one child RA containing R1 and a second child RB containing R21, R22, and R3.

The advantage of splitting the node in this way is that once the node has been split, we do not need to worry about repartitioning nodes at lower levels in the tree. Interestingly, the same split strategy is also used in the LSD tree [829] (see Section 1.7.1.3 of Chapter 1, where its use for point data is discussed).

Unfortunately, an undesirable side effect of the split strategy described above is that the resulting tree may be unbalanced heightwise, which may cause it to be deeper than necessary. The LSD tree tries to address the issue of balance by having two types of nodes with varying capacities that do not contain objects (see Section 1.7.1.3 of Chapter 1 for more detail). In the k-d-B-tree, the issue of balance can be overcome by choosing another partition line, as well as an axis for partitioning the overflowing node. The drawback of such a solution is that this may force the repartitioning of nodes at deeper levels in the hierarchy and the reinsertion of the regions corresponding to the new partitions in the appropriate nodes.

In order to see the need for repartitioning, let us return to the example showing the result of inserting rectangle object H in the k-d-B-tree in Figure 2.80. Assume that all splits at levels deeper than the root have been made as in the earlier discussion and that we are now processing the root R0, which has overflowed (see Figure 2.81(b)). Now, instead of partitioning R0 at $x = 22$, we introduce a new partition at $x = 26$, yielding nodes RA and RB. Again, this causes the height of the tree to grow by one level, thereby resulting in the creation of a new root node RZ.

The difference from the partition that was performed at $x = 22$ is that we must now also repartition some of the nodes at deeper levels in the tree. In particular, we have to split node R3 into two parts: R31, which belongs in RA, and R32, which belongs in RB. Therefore, RA consists of R1, R21, and R31, while RB consists of R22 and R32. At the next level of the tree, we see that a further ramification of the split of R3 is that R8 has been split into two parts, R81 and R82. The effect of this split is that R81 is now a part of R31, and R82 is now a part of R32, which also contains R9. Figure 2.82 shows the result of pursuing this alternative.

When choosing the partition line and axis as in Figure 2.82(b), we must take care so that the newly created nodes do not overflow. For example, suppose that we choose to partition the overflowing node R0 in Figure 2.82(b) at line l at $y = 15$ (instead of at $x = 22$ or at $x = 26$ as in Figure 2.82(b)). Figure 2.83 shows the result of this partition at the level of node R0. Again, let RA and RB represent the newly created nodes corresponding to the area below and above $y = 15$, respectively. Therefore, all elements of R0 that are below l (e.g., none in Figure 2.81(b)) are inserted into RA, while all elements of R0 that are above l (e.g., regions R21 and R22 in Figure 2.81(b)) are inserted into RB. In addition, the elements of R0 whose regions are intersected by l (e.g., R1 and R3) must be split and new regions created, which are inserted into RA and RB.

The result is that RA contains two regions, while RB contains four regions. However, each node can contain a maximum of three entries. Therefore, RB has overflowed, which means that RB must also be split, thereby causing the k-d-B-tree to grow by yet an additional level. With the appropriate choice of partition lines, this process can be applied repeatedly to create much larger k-d-B-trees. Clearly, this is undesirable, and we should choose another partition line and axis. In fact, it is not difficult to construct another example where both of the newly created nodes have overflowed (see Exercise 1 in Section 1.7.1.1 of Chapter 1).

All of the example partitionings of the overflowing k-d-B-tree node that we have described result in the growth of the k-d-B-tree by one level. We propose to avoid this growth by making use of a technique analogous to rotation (also known as *deferred splitting*) in B-trees and R-trees (as discussed in Section 2.1.5.2). The idea is that instead of partitioning the overflowing node R into just two nodes, resulting in the growth of the height of the tree, we repartition the space S spanned by R several times (as long as R does not overflow), and then rebuild the k-d-B-tree in a top-down manner. Notice that in this case no new node is added when the process starts. Of course, we may have to

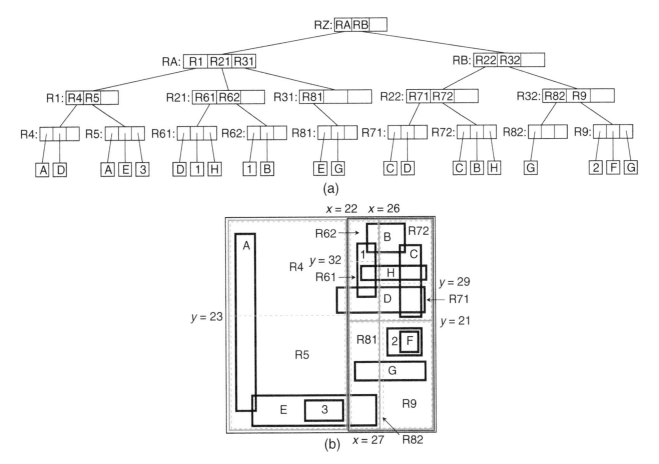

Figure 2.82

(a) k-d-B-tree resulting from the insertion of rectangle object H into the k-d-B-tree of Figure 2.80 when the root node is split at $x = 26$ and (b) the spatial extents of the nodes. Once the root node has been split, further partitioning is needed at deeper levels. Notice that only in the leaf nodes are the bounding boxes minimal.

perform many reinsertions, which may in turn result in the addition of nodes. We use the term *k-d-B-tree resplitting* to describe this overflow strategy.

As an illustration of the use of k-d-B-tree resplitting, let us return to the example showing the result of inserting rectangle object H in the k-d-B-tree in Figure 2.80. Assume that all splits at levels deeper than the root have been made as in the earlier discussion and that we are currently processing the root R0, which has overflowed (see Figure 2.81). We now repartition R0 at $x = 26$ into a left half, which is partitioned further at $y = 21$ into two halves, T1 and T2, and a right half, T3. In this case, the height of the tree stays the same. T1 is split into a left half, T4, at $x = 22$, which is similar to R4, and a right half, which is partitioned further at $y = 32$ into the two halves, R61 and R62. T2 is split at $x = 22$ into a left half, T5, which is similar to R5, and a right half, T8, which is similar to R8. T3 is split at $y = 21$ into a bottom half, T9, which is similar to R9, and a top half, which is partitioned further at $y = 29$ into the two halves, R71 and R72.

Figure 2.84 shows the result of using the k-d-B-tree resplitting overflow strategy. Notice that k-d-B-tree resplitting requires that we repartition a number of the original nodes. In particular, R5 is split into two parts: R51, which is inserted into T4, and R52, which is inserted into T5. Similarly, R8 is split into two parts: R81, which is inserted into T8, and R82, which is inserted into T9. In this case, the reinsertion is simple as these nodes are absorbed into the existing nodes as the subobjects that they comprise are identical. In other words, the merging does not cause the merged node to contain more objects, and hence it cannot overflow, thereby guaranteeing that there will be no more

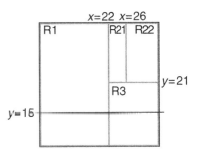

Figure 2.83

The result of partitioning the overflowing node R0 in Figure 2.81 at line $y = 15$.

reinsertion. For example, R82 consists of just a part of G and thus can be grafted onto the part of G that makes up T9 (the old R9). In general, using k-d-B-tree resplitting can become quite complex (as is also the case with rotation in a conventional B-tree), and thus its use is not recommended.

Variants of the bounding-box cell-tree pyramid, such as the k-d-B-tree, are good for answering both the feature and location queries. However, in the case of the location query, they act only as a partition of space. They do not distinguish between occupied and unoccupied space. Thus, in order to determine if a particular location a is occupied by one of the objects associated with cell c, we need to check each of the objects associated with c, which can be time-consuming, especially if M is large. We can speed this process by modifying the general definition of the bounding-box cell-tree pyramid so that a bounding box is stored in each node r in the hierarchy, regardless of r's depth, that covers the bounding boxes of the cells that make up r. Thus, associated with each node r is the union of the objects associated with the cells making up r, as well as a bounding box of the union of their bounding boxes. We term the result a *disjoint object pyramid*. Recall that the depth of any variant of the bounding-box pyramid is one less than that of the corresponding conventional pyramid, and the same is true for the disjoint object pyramid.

A key difference between the disjoint object pyramid and variants of the conventional pyramid, and to a lesser extent the bounding-box pyramid (including the bounding-box cell-tree pyramid), is that the elements of the hierarchy of the disjoint object pyramid are also parts of the bounding boxes of the objects rather than just the cells that make up the objects, which is the case for both variants of the bounding-box and conventional pyramids. The representation of the disjoint object pyramid, and of variants of the

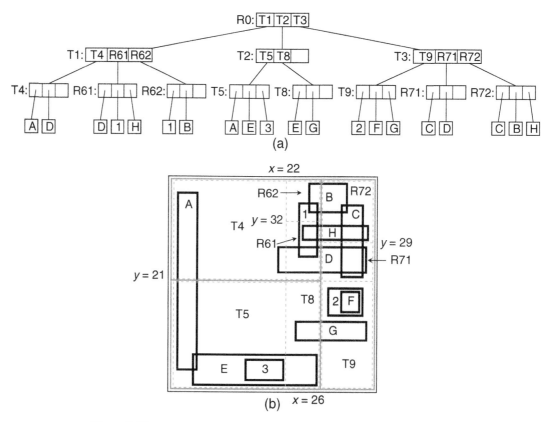

Figure 2.84
(a) k-d-B-tree resulting from the insertion of rectangle object H into the k-d-B-tree of Figure 2.80 when using the k-d-B-tree resplitting overflow strategy and (b) the spatial extents of the nodes. Notice that only in the leaf nodes are the bounding boxes minimal.

bounding-box pyramid such as the k-d-B-tree, is also much simpler as they both just decompose the objects until a criterion involving the number of objects present in the block, rather than one based on the homogeneity of the block, is satisfied. This results in avoiding some of the deeper levels of the hierarchy that are needed in variants of the conventional pyramid.

There are many variants of the disjoint object pyramid. They differ according to which of the block decomposition rules described in Section 2.1.2 is used. They are usually referred to by the general term R^+-tree [593, 1718, 1803] on account of their similarity to the R-tree since they both store a hierarchy of bounding boxes. However, the block decomposition rule is usually left unspecified, although a generalized k-d tree block decomposition rule is often suggested. An alternative is not to use any decomposition rule, in which case each node is just a collection of blocks, as in Figure 2.10.

R^+-trees are built in the same incremental manner as any of the bounding-box cell-tree pyramids that we have described (e.g., the k-d-B-tree). Again, as each additional object o is processed, we insert o's bounding box b into all of the leaf nodes that overlap it. If any of these nodes become too full, then we split them using the appropriate block decomposition rule and determine if the parent is not too full to support the addition of a child. If it is not, then we recursively apply the same decomposition rule to the parent. The process stops at the root, in which case the R^+-tree may grow by one level. The difference from the method used in the bounding-box cell-tree pyramids is that we also propagate the minimum bounding box information up the hierarchy. The entire process is analogous to that used in a B-tree upon overflow. The difference is that, at times, as is also the case for the k-d-B-tree, the decomposition at a nonleaf node may result in the introduction of a new partition that may force the repartitioning of nodes at deeper levels in the R^+-tree.

Figure 2.85 is an example of one possible R^+-tree for the collection of rectangles whose specifications are given in Figure 2.67. Broken lines denote the bounding boxes corresponding to the leaf nodes, and thin lines denote the bounding boxes corresponding to the subtrees rooted at the nonleaf nodes. In this case, we have simply taken the k-d-B-tree of Figure 2.80 and added bounding boxes to the nonleaf nodes. This particular tree is of order (2,3), although, in general, it is not possible always to guarantee that all nodes will have a minimum of two entries. Notice that rectangle D appears in three different

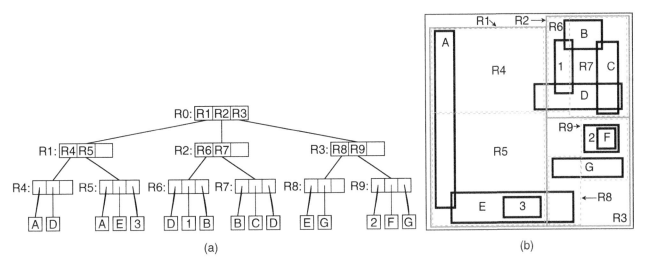

(a)   (b)

Figure 2.85
(a) R^+-tree for a collection of rectangle objects whose specifications are given in Figure 2.67 with $m = 2$ and $M = 3$ and (b) the spatial extents of the bounding boxes. Notice that the leaf nodes in the index also store bounding boxes, although this is shown only for the nonleaf nodes.

nodes, while rectangles A, B, E, and G appear in three different nodes. Of course, other variants are possible since the R$^+$-tree is not unique.

The *cell tree* of Günther [769, 774] is similar to the R$^+$-tree. The difference is that the nonleaf nodes of the cell tree are convex polyhedra instead of bounding rectangles. The children of each node, say P, form a binary space partition (BSP) [658] of P (see Section 2.1.3.1 and Section 1.5.1.4 of Chapter 1). The cell tree is designed to deal with polyhedral data of arbitrary dimension. As in the R$^+$-tree, the polyhedral data being represented may be stored in more than one node.

Exercises

1. We have discussed several methods of dealing with an overflowing node in a k-d-B-tree. One way to ensure greater balance in the tree is to partition the overflowing node at a position other than the one that corresponds to the partition at the root of the k-d tree of the underlying space spanned by the node (i.e., as in the LSD tree). The drawback of this solution is that we may have to repartition some of the nodes at deeper levels of the tree. We pointed out that these repartitions may lead to overflow, possibly resulting in an infinite loop. Why is this not a problem for point objects?

2. Compare the amount of information that must be stored in k-d-B-tree and R$^+$-tree nodes. Do they require the same amount of storage?

3. What are the minimum and maximum heights of an R$^+$-tree of order (m,M) with N objects (not nodes)?

4. Write an algorithm to insert an object into an R$^+$-tree, assuming a generalized k-d tree block decomposition rule.

5. Analyze the expected cost of inserting an object into an R$^+$-tree.

6. Write an algorithm to delete an object from an R$^+$-tree, assuming a generalized k-d tree block decomposition rule.

7. Write an algorithm to perform a point query in an R$^+$-tree.

8. Write an algorithm to perform a window query in an R$^+$-tree.

9. Prove that the worst-case execution time of the rectangle intersection problem for N rectangles using a R$^+$-tree is $O(N^2)$.

10. What is the expected cost of the rectangle intersection problem for N rectangles using a R$^+$-tree?

2.2 Boundary-Based Representations

Boundary-based representations are more amenable to the calculation of properties pertaining to shape (e.g., perimeter, extent). Not surprisingly, the nature of the boundaries plays an important role in the representation that is chosen. Often, the boundary elements of the objects are constrained to being hyperplanes (e.g., polygons in two dimensions and polyhedra in three dimensions), which may, in addition, be constrained to being axis-parallel. Much of the following presentation is in the context of such constraints unless explicitly stated otherwise, although we will also discuss the more general case.

Assuming that these two constraints hold, a simple representation is one that records the locations of the different boundary elements associated with each cell of each object and their natures (i.e., their orientations and the locations of the cells to which they are adjacent). For example, in two dimensions, the boundary elements are just the sides of the cells (i.e., unit vectors), while in three dimensions, the boundary elements are the faces of the cells (i.e., squares of unit area, with directions normal to the object). Boundary-based representations aggregate identically valued cells whose boundary elements have the same direction, rather than just identically valued cells as is done by interior-based representations. In two dimensions, the aggregation yields boundary elements that are vectors whose lengths can be greater than 1.

Whichever boundary-based representation is used and regardless of whether any aggregation takes place, the representation must also enable the determination of the connectivity between individual boundary elements. The connectivity may be implicit or explicit (e.g., by specifying which boundary elements are connected). Thus, we notice that this distinction (i.e., implicit versus explicit) between boundary-based representations is different from the one used with interior-based representations, which is based on the nature of the specification of the aggregation.

As an example of a boundary-based representation, let us consider two-dimensional objects for which the boundary elements are vectors. The location of a vector is given by its start and end vertices. An object o has one more boundary (i.e., a collection of connected boundary elements) than it has holes. Connectivity may be determined implicitly by ordering the boundary elements $e_{i,j}$ of boundary b_i of o so that the end vertex of vector v_j corresponding to $e_{i,j}$ is the start vertex of vector v_{j+1} corresponding to $e_{i,j+1}$. The result of applying such an ordering when identically valued cells whose boundary elements have the same direction are aggregated yields a representation known as the *polygon representation*. This term is also used to describe the representation of arbitrary objects whose boundaries need not be axis parallel.

In two dimensions, the most general example of a nonpolygonal object boundary is the curvilinear line segment. Straight line segments with arbitrary slopes are less general. A curvilinear line segment is often approximated by a set of line segments termed a *polyline*. In order to comply with our assumption that the objects are made up of unit-sized cells (i.e., pixels), we digitize the line and then mark the pixels through which it passes. An alternative is to classify the pixels on the basis of the slope of the part of the line that passes through them. One such representation is the *chain code* [638], in which case the slopes are restricted to the four or eight principal directions. The chain code is of particular interest when the slopes are restricted to the four principal directions as this is what is obtained when the boundaries of the objects are parallel to the coordinate axes. The chain code is discussed in more detail in Section 2.3.

In dimensions higher than 2, the relationship between the boundary elements associated with a particular object is more complex, as is its expression. Whereas in two dimensions we have only one type of boundary element (i.e., an edge or a vector consisting of two vertices), in $d > 2$ dimensions, given our axis-parallel constraint, we have $d - 1$ different boundary elements (e.g., faces and edges in three dimensions). As we saw, in two dimensions, the sequence of vectors given by a polygon representation is equivalent to an implicit specification of the boundary because each boundary element of an object can be adjacent to only two other boundary elements. Thus, consecutive boundary elements in the representation are implicitly connected. This is not possible in $d > 2$ dimensions; assuming axis-parallel objects comprising of unit-size, d-dimensional cells, there are 2^{d-1} different adjacencies per boundary element. Therefore, it is difficult to adapt the polygon representation to data of dimensionality greater than 2. Of course, it can be used to specify a spatial entity comprising of a sequence of edges in d-dimensional space that forms a cycle (i.e., the starting vertex is the same as the final vertex). However, the spatial entity need not be planar.

Nevertheless, in higher dimensions, we do have a choice between an explicit and an implicit boundary-based representation. The boundary model (also known as the *BRep* [141, 1637]) is an example of an explicit boundary-based representation. Observe that in three dimensions, the boundary of an object with planar faces is decomposed into a set of faces, edges, and vertices. The result is an explicit model based on a combined geometric and topological description of the object. The topology is captured by a set of relations that indicate explicitly how the faces, edges, and vertices are connected to

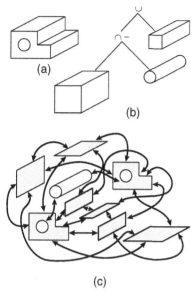

Figure 2.86
(a) A three-dimensional object, (b) its CSG tree, and (c) its boundary model.

each other. For example, the object in Figure 2.86(a) can be decomposed into the set of faces having the topology shown in Figure 2.86(c). The geometry of the faces can be specified by use of appropriate geometric entities (e.g., planes in the case of polyhedra). In d dimensions, the boundary of object o will be decomposed into d sets s_i ($0 \leq i < d$), where s_i contains all constituent i-dimensional elements of o. This forms the basis of the boundary model and is discussed in greater detail in Section 2.2.1. Although this representation is quite general, it is easy to constrain it to handle axis-parallel objects. We do not discuss this further here.

Constructive solid geometry (CSG) [1557] is another example of an implicit representation that is applicable to objects of arbitrary dimensionality. Although it is usually thought of as an interior-based representation, it also has a boundary-based interpretation. In the interior-based formulation, primitive instances of objects are combined to form more complex objects by use of geometric transformations and regularized Boolean set operations (e.g., union, intersection). The representation is usually in the form of a tree where the leaf nodes correspond to primitive instances and the nonleaf nodes correspond to the regularized Boolean set operations.[28] For example, the object in Figure 2.86(a) can be decomposed into three primitive solids with the CSG tree shown in Figure 2.86(b), where the operation A∩−B denotes set difference. The key is that this representation is procedural. Thus, it indicates how an item can be constructed—that is, what operations are necessary. Often these operations have physical analogs (e.g., drilling). A disadvantage of the CSG representation is that it is not unique. In particular, there are frequently several ways of constructing an object (e.g., from different primitive elements).

When the primitive instances in CSG are halfspaces, and the objects have planar faces, the result is an implicit boundary-based representation. In this case, the boundary of a d-dimensional object o consists of a collection of hyperplanes in d-dimensional space (i.e., the infinite boundaries of regions defined by the inequality $\sum_{i=0}^{d} a_i x_i \geq 0$, where $x_0 = 1$). We have one halfspace for each $(d-1)$-dimensional boundary element of o. Both of these representations (i.e., primitive instances of objects and halfspaces) are implicit because the object is determined by associating a set of regular Boolean set operations with the collection of primitive instances (which may be halfspaces), the result of which is the object. Again, although these representations are quite general, it is easy to constrain them to handle axis-parallel objects.

It is usually quite easy to determine the cells that make up an object (i.e., the feature query) when using boundary-based representations since the boundaries are usually associated with the individual objects. In contrast, one of the principal drawbacks of boundary-based representations is the difficulty of determining the value associated with an arbitrary point of the space given by a cell (i.e., the location query) without testing each boundary element using operations, such as point-in-polygon tests (e.g., [622]) or finding the nearest boundary element. The problem is that these representations are very local in the sense that, generally, they just indicate which boundary element is connected to which other boundary element rather than the relationships of the boundary elements to the space that they occupy. Thus, if we are at one position on the boundary (i.e., at a particular boundary element), we do not know anything about the rest of the boundary without traversing it element by element.

This situation can be remedied in two ways. The first is by aggregating the cells that make up the boundary elements of the objects and their environment into blocks, such as those obtained by using a region quadtree, a region octree, or a k-d tree variant, and then imposing an appropriate access structure on the blocks. Such methods are reviewed in Section 2.2.2. The second is by aggregating the boundary elements of the

---

[28] Regularized versions of the Boolean set operations [1555] are used in order to guarantee that the resulting objects correspond to our intuitive notion of solids. In such a case, the result of any Boolean set operation involving objects in d-space is always either null or has a nonzero d-dimensional measure. Regularized Boolean set operations form a Boolean algebra [1555] so that, for instance, De Morgan's laws hold for them.

objects themselves by using variants of bounding boxes to yield successively coarser approximations and then imposing appropriate access structures on the bounding boxes. These methods are presented in Section 2.2.3. Not surprisingly, the distinction between these representations is the same as that made earlier between image-based and object-based methods, respectively.

The boundary representations discussed above and in Sections 2.2.2 and 2.2.3 generally assume that the boundaries of the objects lie on hyperplanes or can be approximated by hyperplanes or some interpolation method. In these cases, the shape of the objects is the main focus of the applications that make use of these representations. In other applications, the main focus of the application is the boundary of the object, which is like a 2.5-dimensional image, such as a terrain, and is highly irregular. In this case, the object is treated as a surface boundary. This is the subject of Section 2.2.4.

2.2.1 The Boundary Model (BRep)

In this section, we assume that the objects are three-dimensional. We first give a general overview of the boundary model, or BRep (Section 2.2.1.1). The boundary model treats the objects as graphs whose basic elements are vertices, edge, and faces. There are a number of possible implementations of the boundary model. They are differentiated on the basis of being edge-based, such as the winged-edge data structure (Section 2.2.1.2), or vertex-based, such as the lath family of representations (Section 2.2.1.3). Face-based implementations are also possible and are shown to be duals of the vertex-based ones, although their utility is quite limited and thus they are only briefly mentioned (Section 2.2.1.3). The quad-edge data structure, results from a particular interpretation of the winged-edge data structure, whose use enables the simultaneous representation of the Voronoi diagram and the Delaunay triangulation of a given set of points (Section 2.2.1.4) and the constrained and conforming Delaunay triangulations (Section 2.2.1.5). Higher-dimension variants of the Delaunay triangulation, such as the Delaunay tetrahedralization, are also discussed briefly (Section 2.2.1.6). We conclude with a discussion of some applications of edge-based representation, such as the winged-edge data structure (Section 2.2.1.7).

2.2.1.1 Overview

The topology in the boundary model can be represented by a graph. Before proceeding further, let us review the definitions of a few terms. A graph is *planar* if it can be drawn on the plane in such a way that all the edges intersect only at vertices. Given a planar graph G, a *face* of G is an area of the plane bounded by edges of G that does not contain any edges or vertices of G in its interior. The *frontier* of a face is the set of all edges that "touch" it. The frontier of face f can also be specified in terms of the faces that share an edge or a vertex with f. Notice that a face is defined in terms of an area and not in terms of its boundary (i.e., the edges making it up). In particular, the frontier of a face need not be connected (e.g., the region with holes in Figure 2.87). Two faces are *adjacent* if they have at least one edge in common; however, their vertices need not necessarily be connected. We say that two faces f_i and f_j are *connected* if there is a sequence of distinct faces $(f_i, f_{i+1}, \ldots f_{j-1}, f_j)$ such that f_k is adjacent to f_{k+1} ($i \leq k < j$).

Our domain of three-dimensional objects is restricted to ones bounded by compact,[29] orientable, two-manifold surfaces [1326] (see Exercise 1 in Section 2.2.1.7).[30] In such a

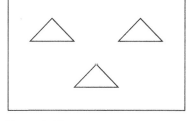

Figure 2.87
Example face with holes.

---

[29] The term *compact* means (1) topologically closed and (2) bounded. The closedness implies that for every edge e, e's endpoints are part of the surface and, for every face f, f's edges are part of the surface. The boundedness means that edges and faces that lead to infinity are not permitted.

[30] In the rest of this section, unless otherwise stated, when we use the term *two-manifold surface*, we mean *compact, orientable two-manifold surface*. Similarly, unless otherwise stated, when we use

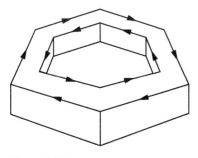

Figure 2.88
Example nut illustrating the concept
of a loop.

domain, only two faces may meet at an edge. Also, the faces are two-sided, thereby ruling out a Möbius strip and a Klein bottle. More general objects that do not satisfy the two-manifold surface condition fall into the class of nonmanifold objects and are beyond the scope of this book. Readers interested in representations for such objects should consult, for example, the radial-edge data structure of Weiler [1979], the extension of the half-edge data structure of Campagna, Kobbelt, and Seidel [301], and the partial-entity structure of Lee and Lee [1140], as well as additional representations described in the recent survey of De Floriani and Hui [457]. In three dimensions, it is convenient to view the nodes of the graph as the set of vertices, edges, and faces of the object. On the other hand, the arcs are the relations between pairs of these three entities. We elaborate on these relations later. We call the graph an *object graph*.

Vertices, edges, and faces form the three primitive topological entities of the object graph. The description of objects with multiply connected faces (e.g., holes) and internal cavities is facilitated by the addition of two higher-level, nonprimitive topological entities, termed the *shell* and the *loop*. A shell in an object O is defined as any maximally connected set of faces of O. For example, the object with an internal cavity formed by a cube within another cube has two shells, an internal shell and an external shell. A loop on a face f of O is defined as a closed chain of edges (i.e., a cycle) bounding f. For example, consider an object, such as a nut (e.g., Figure 2.88), in which case the top and bottom faces each have two loops, an internal loop and an external loop. Note that the set of nodes of the object graph has now been expanded to include the shell and the loop.

The boundary model is *unambiguous*—that is, each boundary model corresponds to a single object. It is also unique when the boundary is partitioned into maximally connected faces. This is especially relevant when the object has planar faces. In this case, we achieve such a partition when we merge all faces that are coplanar (provided that their union is connected).

The representation of the boundary model is conceptually hierarchical. Objects are decomposed into shells. Each shell is a collection of faces. Each face is represented by its surface equation and by a collection of its bounding loops. Each loop is a chain of edges. Often, a single curved edge is approximated by several linear segments. Each segment is represented by a pair of vertices that correspond to its endpoints.

The boundary model has both a geometric and topological component; neither is sufficient by itself to describe a three-dimensional object. The geometric component consists of the shape and location in space of each of the primitive topological entities. The topological component consists of a subset of the adjacency relationships between pairs of individual topological entities (e.g., edges and vertices). There are 25 different adjacency relationships—each one consists of a unique ordered pair from the five topological entities described above [1978]. Since the relationships are ordered, there is, for example, a difference between an edge-face relation and a face-edge relation. In particular, the edge-face relation associates with each edge the pair of faces that share it, while the face-edge relation associates with each face the edges that bound it.

It should be clear that the 25 different adjacency relationships are nothing more than a generalization of the vertex-based and edge-based representations of a graph to three dimensions. Note that the vertex-based representation associates with each vertex, say p, a list of all of the vertices, say V, that are connected to p by virtue of the existence of an edge between p and q, where $q \in V$. This is the same as a vertex-edge relationship.

the term *nonorientable two-manifold surface*, we mean *compact, nonorientable two-manifold surface*. Intuitively, a two-manifold surface is a surface in which the neighborhood of each point is topologically equivalent to an open disc or to an open half-disc if the surface has a boundary (e.g., the surface of a sphere does not have a boundary, while boundaries primarily arise when dealing with nonobjects such as terrains on a subset of the Earth).

The edge-based representation associates with each edge its constituent vertices. This is the same as an edge-vertex relationship.

Many of the data structures that have been proposed to represent the boundary model store the edge-vertex and edge-face relations. In this case, the representation of the object is accessed by knowing the identities of its edges. When the objects have multiple shells and multiply connected faces, then, for example, the edge-face and face-edge relations can be expressed as a combination of the edge-loop and loop-face and the face-loop and loop-edge relations, respectively [1978]. The advantage of introducing the combination involving the loop is that, from a hierarchical standpoint, the loop lies somewhere between a face and an edge.

At times, it is desirable to be able to access the information represented by the boundary model by using the identity of a particular face or vertex instead of just an edge. This is the motivation behind the symmetric structure [2016], which stores the face-edge and vertex-edge relations, as well as the edge-face and edge-vertex relations. A disadvantage of using relations such as the face-edge or vertex-edge is that the amount of information associated with the first element of the relation is not fixed.[31] For example, each instance of the face-edge relation contains the edges that bound the face, and each instance of the vertex-edge relation contains the edges that are incident at the vertex. On the other hand, for all relations in which the edge appears as the first element, the amount of information associated with an instance of the relation is fixed. This observation forms the basis of the *winged-edge data structure* of Baumgart [141]. It is an edge-based specification (i.e., it stores the edge-vertex and edge-face relations explicitly), and Section 2.2.1.2 describes an implementation of a special case of it that also stores the face-edge and vertex-edge relations implicitly.

Exercises

1. Give the boundary model representation for the parallelepiped of Figure 2.90 (discussed in Section 2.2.1.2) using a (a) face-vertex relation and (b) face-edge and edge-vertex relations.

2. What is the maximum number of loops with which an edge can be associated?

3. Can a face have more than two loops associated with it? If it can, then give an example.

4. Give two methods of implementing the loop-face relation. Which method is preferable?

5. Recalling that a loop l belongs to a face f if f contains all the edges forming l, what is the maximum number of faces with which a loop can be associated? Can you give an example?

2.2.1.2 Edge-Based Methods Using Winged Edges

In this section, we examine edge-based object representations. This means that we represent both the faces and the vertices of an object by the set of edges that they comprise and that are incident at them, respectively. Of course, many other representations are possible. In particular, each face could also be represented in terms of its constituent vertices, and, likewise, each edge could be represented in terms of the vertices that it comprises. The latter is the basis of what are termed *vertex-based object representations*. There are a number of ways of implementing these sets, ranging from a list to an adjacency matrix and differing by the amount of time needed to verify a particular adjacency, which is inversely related to the storage cost. In this and the next section, we discuss both edge-based and vertex-based object representations where the storage cost is proportional to the number of constituent edges and vertices, respectively, while the execution time cost of the queries that use them is proportional to the size of the query result set. In the rest of this section, we focus on the representation of the faces and vertices of the objects using the edges.

---

[31] In database terminology, this means that the relation violates the first normal form (i.e., 1nf) [554].

Assume that the faces of the objects do not have internal loops and are composed of a single shell.[32] Each face is represented as a sequence of the edges it comprises (i.e., a face-edge relation), while the edges are specified as ordered pairs of their constituent vertices (i.e., an edge-vertex relation). The sequence of edges must be oriented consistently. We adopt the convention that the edges are listed in a clockwise order as the face is viewed from the outside of the object. Since we are dealing with objects whose faces are compact, orientable two-manifolds, only two faces are adjacent at each edge. Therefore, each edge appears in only two faces, once in each of its orientations.

In other words, these consistency considerations (i.e., that the face is represented by a clockwise ordering of the edges that it comprises) mean that, given edge $e = (v_1, v_2)$, e appears in one face f as (v_1, v_2) and in the other face f' as (v_2, v_1). This information is captured by recording an orientation with each reference to e (i.e., positive or negative, corresponding to whether e is part of the face f for which e's direction makes e a part of a traversal of f in the clockwise or counterclockwise directions, respectively), although, as we shall see, the orientation is not always used. With this information, we can implement one part of the face data structure (i.e., the face-edge relation) as a table of fixed-length records by storing with each face only the identity of one of its constituent edges and a flag indicating the orientation of the edge. We use the term *face-edge table* to refer to this structure. Moreover, with each edge, say e, we keep track of the two edges that precede e and the two edges that follow e (one for each of the two faces in which e is a member). The result is that this part of the face data structure (i.e., the rest of the face-edge relation) is implemented as a linked list in which the pointers are stored as part of the edge records.

We represent the vertices of the objects as a sequence of the edges that are incident at them (i.e., a vertex-edge relation), while the edges are specified as ordered pairs of their constituent vertices (i.e., an edge-vertex relation). This sequence of edges must be oriented consistently. We adopt the convention that the edges are listed in a clockwise order as the vertex is viewed from the outside of the object. Since we are dealing with objects whose faces are compact, orientable two-manifolds, there is just one edge between any two vertices. Thus, each edge is incident at just two vertices, once at each of its two endpoints.

In other words, these consistency considerations (i.e., that the vertex is represented by a clockwise ordering of the edges incident at it) mean that, given edge $e = (v_1, v_2)$, e is incident at one vertex v_1 as (v_1, v_2) and at the other vertex v_2 as (v_2, v_1). This information is captured by recording an orientation with each reference to the edge (i.e., positive or negative, corresponding to whether the edge is directed into the vertex or away from the vertex, respectively), although, again, as we shall see, the orientation is not always used. With this information, we can implement one part of the vertex data structure (i.e., the vertex-edge relation) as a table of fixed-length records by storing with each vertex only the identity of one of its incident edges and a flag indicating the orientation of the edge. We use the term *vertex-edge table* to refer to this structure. Moreover, with each edge, say e, we keep track of the two edges that precede e and the two edges that follow e (one for each vertex that the edge comprises). The result is that this part of the vertex data structure (i.e., the rest of the vertex-edge relation) is implemented as a linked list in which the pointers are stored as part of the edge records.

The above combinations of vertex and face tables and edge records using records of uniform size form the basis of the *winged-edge representation* or *data structure* [141]. The rationale for the name is that the representation is based on visualizing each edge e as a line in space with a maximum of four wings, two at each of e's vertices, where the wings correspond to adjacent edges along e's two adjacent faces or, equivalently, to adjacent edges incident at e's two constituent vertices. Each edge is assigned an arbitrary

---

[32] Objects with multiple shells and faces with internal loops require further elaboration in the model (see [1977]).

direction (i.e., orientation) by designating one of its vertices as VSTART and the other as VEND so that the different wings and adjacent faces may be identified in a consistent manner. There are numerous variants of the winged-edge data structure. They differ in the interpretation of the wings (i.e., as adjacent edges along adjacent faces, adjacent edges incident at constituent vertices, or combinations thereof), in the amount of information that they store for each edge, and in whether they keep track of the orientations of the edges explicitly, or their orientation is checked each time the representation is navigated in the process of responding to a query.

Initially, we assume an interpretation of edge e's wings as adjacent edges along adjacent faces of e. Using this interpretation and the above orientation of e, let FCW(e) (FCCW(e)) denote the face f (f') adjacent to e such that e's direction makes e a part of a traversal of f (f') in the clockwise CW (counterclockwise CCW) direction. We use CF and CCF to refer to the next edges in a clockwise (C) and counterclockwise (CC), respectively, traversal of the edges that make up a face (F).[33] Alternatively, we can interpret edge e's wings as adjacent edges incident at the vertices that e comprises. In this case, we use CV and CCV to refer to the next edges in a clockwise (C) and counterclockwise (CC), respectively, traversal of the edges that are incident at a vertex (V).[34] These alternative naming conventions make it easier to see that the presence of the four wings enables us to obtain the edges that make up each face in both clockwise and counterclockwise orders and, likewise, to obtain the edges that are incident at each vertex in both of these orders. Figure 2.89(a) is an example of such an edge e, while Figure 2.89(b) illustrates an example of a physical interpretation of these concepts for an edge e of a parallelepiped where each face is viewed from the outside of the object, regardless of the direction of the edge that is actually stored.

We use the term *winged-edge-face* to describe the variant of the winged-edge data structure that results from the interpretation of edge e's wings as adjacent edges along adjacent faces of e. It can be summarized as capturing the following information for the relations involving vertices, edges, and faces, given edge e:

1. Edge-vertex relation: the two constituent vertices (VSTART(e) and VEND(e))

2. Edge-face relation: the two adjacent faces (FCW(e) and FCCW(e))

3. Edge-edge relation: the preceding edges (CCF(FCW(e)) and CCF(FCCW(e))) and the next edges (CF(FCW(e)) and CF(FCCW(e))) in the two faces, thereby incorporating the face-edge relation, as well as the vertex-edge relation when using an alternative interpretation of the wings of the edge.

Similarly, we use the term *winged-edge-vertex* to describe the variant of the winged-edge data structure that results from the interpretation of edge e's wings as adjacent edges incident at the vertices that make up e. It can be summarized as capturing the following information for the relations involving vertices, edges, and faces, given edge e:

1. Edge-vertex relation: the two constituent vertices (VSTART(e) and VEND(e))

2. Edge-face relation: the two adjacent faces (FCW(e) and FCCW(e))

---

[33] An equivalent naming convention for the wings that finds common use (e.g., [1232, 1637]) lets EPCW(e) (ENCW(e)) and EPCCW(e) (ENCCW(e)) denote the preceding P (next N) edges in a clockwise traversal of faces FCW(e) and FCCW(e), respectively. Note that the clockwise and counterclockwise directions are synonymous with next and preceding, respectively, given our assumption that the edge-edge relation stores a traversal of the edges in a clockwise order around a face in the winged-edge-face representation.

[34] Use of the equivalent naming convention for the wings described in footnote 33 (e.g., [1232, 1637]) results in ENCCW(e) (EPCW(e)) and ENCW(e) (EPCCW(e)) denoting the preceding P (next N) edges in a clockwise traversal of the edges incident at vertices VSTART(e) and VEND(e), respectively. Again, we note that the clockwise and counterclockwise directions are synonymous with next and preceding, respectively, given our assumption that the edge-edge relation stores a traversal of the edges incident at a vertex in a clockwise order in the winged-edge-vertex representation.

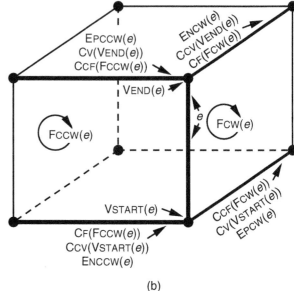

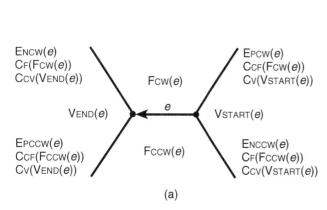

(a)

(b)

Figure 2.89
(a) Example of an edge e and its four wings and (b) the physical interpretation of e and its wings when e is an edge of a parallelepiped represented by the winged-edge data structure.

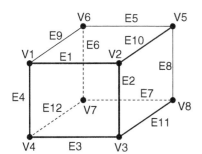

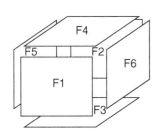

Figure 2.90
Sample parallelepiped with vertices (V1–V8), edges (E1–E2), and faces (F1–F6).

3. Edge-edge relation: the preceding edges ($\text{CCV}(\text{VSTART}(e))$ and $\text{CCV}(\text{VEND}(e))$) and the next edges ($\text{CV}(\text{VSTART}(e))$ and $\text{CV}(\text{VEND}(e))$) incident at the two vertices, thereby incorporating the vertex-edge relation, as well as the face-edge relation when using an alternative interpretation of the wings of the edge.

As an example of the winged-edge data structure, consider the parallelepiped in Figure 2.89(b), whose individual vertices, edges, and faces are labeled and oriented according to Figure 2.90. One possible implementation of a winged-edge representation for it is given by tables VERTEXEDGETABLE and FACEEDGETABLE in Figures 2.91 and 2.92, which correspond to the partial vertex-edge and face-edge relations, respectively, and the collection of edge records that make up the edge-edge relation given by Figure 2.93. Observe that VERTEXEDGETABLE and FACEEDGETABLE are really indexes (i.e., access structures) that enable an efficient response to queries on the basis of the value of a given vertex v or face f, such as finding all of the edges incident at v or the edges that f comprises, respectively, in both the clockwise and counterclockwise orders. This information is accessed by the field EDGE as the tables may contain additional information, such as the actual x, y, and z coordinate values of the vertex in the case of VERTEXEDGETABLE.

VERTEX v	X	Y	Z	EDGE
V1	X1	Y1	Z1	E1
V2	X2	Y2	Z2	E2
V3	X3	Y3	Z3	E3
V4	X4	Y4	Z4	E4
V5	X5	Y5	Z5	E5
V6	X6	Y6	Z6	E6
V7	X7	Y7	Z7	E7
V8	X8	Y8	Z8	E8

Figure 2.91
VERTEXEDGETABLE[v].

FACE f	EDGE
F1	E1
F2	E5
F3	E11
F4	E9
F5	E4
F6	E8

Figure 2.92
FACEEDGETABLE[f].

In particular, EDGE(VERTEXEDGETABLE[v]) = e contains a pointer to an edge record e that is incident at vertex v, while EDGE(FACEEDGETABLE[f]) = e contains a pointer to an edge record e that is part of face f.

It is also important to note that, given a pointer to an edge record e, the edge-edge relation makes use of fields CCFFCW(e), CVVSTART(e), CFFCW(e), CCVVEND(e), CCFFCCW(e), CVVEND(e), CFFCCW(e), and CCVVSTART(e), instead of CCF(FCW(e)), CV(VSTART(e)), CF(FCW(e)), CCV(VEND(e)), CCF(FCCW(e)), CV(VEND(e)), CF(FCCW(e)), and CCV(VSTART(e)), respectively. This is done in order to indicate that the pointer to the appropriate edge record in the corresponding field in the relation is obtained by storing it there explicitly instead of obtaining it by dynamically computing the relevant functions each time the field is accessed (e.g., the field CCFFCW(e) stores the value CCF(FCW(e)) directly rather than obtaining it by applying the function CCF to the result of applying FCW to e each time this field is accessed).

A crucial observation is that the orientations of the edges are not given either in VERTEXEDGETABLE or FACEEDGETABLE or in the edge-edge relation. The absence of the orientation is compensated for by the presence of the VSTART, VEND, FCW, and FCCW fields in the edge-edge relation. This means that, given a face f (vertex v), the edge e stored in the corresponding FACEEDGETABLE (VERTEXEDGETABLE) entry is not sufficient by itself to indicate the next or previous edges in f (incident at v) without checking whether f is the value of the clockwise FCW(e) or the counterclockwise FCCW(e) face field (v is the value of the start VSTART(e) or end VEND(e) vertex field) of record e in the edge-edge relation. Thus, the algorithms that use this orientationless representation must always check the contents of FCW(e) and FCCW(e) (VSTART(e) and VEND(e)) for the use of face f (vertex v). The same is also true upon making a transition from one edge to another edge when the edge has not been obtained from VERTEXEDGETABLE or FACEEDGETABLE.

As an example of the use of these tables, consider procedure EXTRACTEDGESOF-FACE given below, which extracts the edges of face f in either clockwise or counterclockwise order. Let e denote an edge in f, obtained from FACEEDGETABLE, and use the interpretation of e's wings as adjacent edges along adjacent faces of e (i.e., the winged-edge-face variant). For a clockwise ordering, if $f = $ FCW(e), then the next edge is CFFCW(e); otherwise, $f = $ FCCW(e), and the next edge is CFFCCW(e). For a counterclockwise ordering, if $f = $ FCW(e), then the next edge is CCFFCW(e); otherwise,

EDGE e	VSTART	VEND	FCW	FCCW	CCFFCW EPCW CVVSTART	CFFCW ENCW CCVVEND	CCFFCCW EPCCW CVVEND	CFFCCW ENCCW CCVVSTART
E1	V1	V2	F1	F4	E4	E2	E10	E9
E2	V2	V3	F1	F6	E1	E3	E11	E10
E3	V3	V4	F1	F3	E2	E4	E12	E11
E4	V4	V1	F1	F5	E3	E1	E9	E12
E5	V5	V6	F2	F4	E8	E6	E9	E10
E6	V6	V7	F2	F5	E5	E7	E12	E9
E7	V7	V8	F2	F3	E6	E8	E11	E12
E8	V8	V5	F2	F6	E7	E5	E10	E11
E9	V1	V6	F4	F5	E1	E5	E6	E4
E10	V5	V2	F4	F6	E5	E1	E2	E8
E11	V3	V8	F3	F6	E3	E7	E8	E2
E12	V7	V4	F3	F5	E7	E3	E4	E6

Figure 2.93
Edge-edge relation.

$f = \text{FCCW}(e)$, and the next edge is $\text{CCFFCCW}(e)$. This process terminates when we encounter the initial value of e again. For example, extracting the edges of face F1 in Figure 2.90 in clockwise order yields E1, E2, E3, and E4. The execution time of EXTRACTEDGESOFFACE is proportional to the number of edges in f as each edge is obtained in $O(1)$ time. This is a direct consequence of the use of FACEEDGETABLE, without which we would have had to find the first edge by a brute-force (i.e., a sequential) search of the edge-edge relation. Similarly, by making use of VERTEXEDGETABLE to obtain an edge incident at vertex v, we can extract the edges incident at v in time proportional to the total number of edges that are incident at v as each edge can be obtained in $O(1)$ time (see Exercise 2).

```
1   procedure EXTRACTEDGESOFFACE(f, CWFlag)
2   /* Extract the edges making up face f in clockwise (counterclockwise) order
        if flag CWFlag is true (false). */
3   value face f
4   value Boolean CWFlag
5   pointer edge e, FirstEdge
6   e ← FirstEdge ← EDGE(FACEEDGETABLE[f])
7   do
8       output e
9       if CWFlag then
10          e ←if FCW(e) = f then CFFCW(e)
11             else CFFCCW(e)
12             endif
13      else e ← if FCW(e) = f then CCFFCW(e)
14             else CCFFCCW(e)
15             endif
16      endif
17      until e = FirstEdge
18  enddo
```

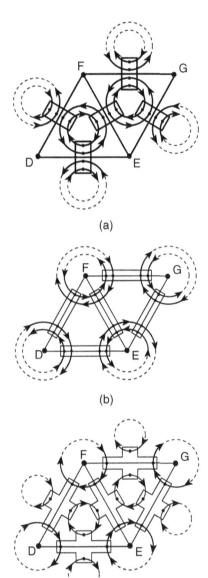

(a)

(b)

(c)

Figure 2.94
The physical interpretation of the (a) winged-edge-face, (b) winged-edge-vertex, and (c) quad-edge data structures for a pair of adjacent faces of a simple object. Assume an implementation that links the next and preceding edges in clockwise order for faces in (a), for vertices in (b), and next edges in clockwise order for both faces and vertices in (c).

The above interpretations are not the only ones that are possible. Another interpretation, among many others, which finds much use, interprets the four wings in terms of the next edges at each of the faces that are adjacent to e and the next edges incident at each of the two vertices that make up e. In this case, we have combined the interpretations of the wings $\text{CF}(\text{FCW}(e))$ and $\text{CF}(\text{FCCW}(e))$ as used in the winged-edge-face data structure with the interpretations of the wings $\text{CV}(\text{VSTART}(e))$ and $\text{CV}(\text{VEND}(e))$ as used in the winged-edge-vertex data structure. The result is known as the *quad-edge data structure* [767]. It keeps track of both the edges that make up the faces in the clockwise direction and the edges that are incident at the vertices in the clockwise direction.

The quad-edge data structure is of particular interest because it automatically encodes the dual graph, which is formed by assigning a vertex to each face in the original graph and an arc to each edge between two faces of the original graph. In other words, we just need to interpret the cycles through the edges around the vertices in the original graph as faces in the dual graph and the cycles through the edges that the faces comprise in the original graph as vertices in the dual graph. In addition, the exterior face, if one exists, in the original graph is also assigned a vertex in the dual graph, which is connected to every face in the original graph that has a boundary edge. This makes the quad-edge data structure particularly attractive in applications where finding and working with the dual mesh is necessary or useful. For example, this is the case when the mesh corresponds to a Voronoi diagram whose dual is the Delaunay triangulation (DT). We discuss this further in Section 2.2.1.4. Another advantage of the quad-edge data structure over the winged-edge-face and winged-edge-vertex data structures is that, in its most general formulation, the quad-edge data structure permits making a distinction between the two sides of a surface, thereby allowing the same vertex to serve as the two endpoints of an edge, as well as allowing dangling edges, and so on.

From the above, we see that the winged-edge-face, winged-edge-vertex, and quad-edge data structures are identical in terms of the information that they store for each edge (i.e., the edge-edge relation entries are the same). However, they do have different physical interpretations, as can be seen in Figure 2.94. In particular, this figure shows that both the winged-edge-face (Figure 2.94(a)) and winged-edge-vertex (Figure 2.94(b)) data structures associate two doubly linked circular lists with each edge e (one list for each of the two faces adjacent to e in the case of the winged-edge-face data structure and one list for each of the two vertices at which e is incident in the case of the winged-edge-vertex data structure), while the quad-edge data structure (Figure 2.94(c)) associates four singly linked circular lists with each edge e (one list for each of the two faces adjacent to e and one list for each of the two vertices that are incident at e). Thus, all three data structures make use of four circular lists, and, in fact, they are isomorphic in the sense that they all provide access to the same topological information with identical running times up to a constant factor.

It is interesting to point out that other combinations of four circular lists can be formed to yield additional physical interpretations of the winged-edge data structure. In particular, we could have also defined the quad-edge data structure in terms of the preceding edges in clockwise order for each of the two adjacent faces and incident vertices, which is the same as a counterclockwise order because "preceding" in clockwise order is equivalent to "next" in counterclockwise order. In fact, this implementation is used by the U.S. Bureau of the Census in the TIGER representation of road networks [280],[35] which are planar graphs and to whose representation our methods are applicable. As can be seen, many combinations are possible. However, not all combinations of next/preceding, clockwise/counterclockwise for the vertex/face pairs are allowed. In essence, the key to determining if a combination is permitted is to ascertain whether the combination permits obtaining all of the edges that make up a face and all of the edges that are incident at a vertex in constant time for both clockwise and counterclockwise traversal orders. For example, an invalid combination is one that keeps track of the next edges for the vertices that make up the edge in clockwise (counterclockwise) order while keeping track of the next edges that make up the adjacent faces in counterclockwise (clockwise) order. This combination will not let us obtain the edges that are incident at a vertex (that make up a face) in counterclockwise (clockwise) order in time proportional to the number of edges that are found (see Exercise 4 for the invalid combinations).

We can also try to make use of fewer circular lists (i.e., two), which essentially means that we are keeping track of a subset of the edge-edge relation. In particular, this is done in a data structure known as the *D-CEL* [1322], which, for a given edge e, stores either the preceding edges in the two faces (CCF(FCW(e)) and CCF(FCCW(e))) or the next edges in the two faces (CF(FCW(e)) and CF(FCCW(e))), but not both (see Figure 2.95(a), which corresponds to a clockwise traversal of the edges that make up the faces of the simple object in Figure 2.94, where there is one circle around each face that is adjacent to an edge). The D-CEL incorporates both the face-edge and vertex-edge relations with the limitation that, as a result, we can traverse either the faces (vertices) in clockwise (counterclockwise) order or the faces (vertices) in counterclockwise (clockwise) order, respectively, in time proportional to the number of edges, but not in both orders. The advantage of the D-CEL is that less information must be recorded for each edge, at the loss of some query-processing power. Of course, we still need the face-edge table and vertex-edge table to determine the edges associated with a face and a vertex, as well as the FCW, FCCW, VSTART, and VEND fields if we want to avoid keeping track of the orientation.

Note that we could also interpret the D-CEL data structure as storing either the preceding edges incident at each of the two vertices that make up the edges (CCV(VSTART(e)) and CCV(VEND(e))) or the next edges incident at each of the two vertices (CV(VSTART(e)) and CV(VEND(e))), but not both (see Figure 2.95(b), which corresponds to a counterclockwise traversal of the edges that are incident at the vertices of the simple object in Figure 2.94, where there is one circle around each vertex at which an edge is incident).

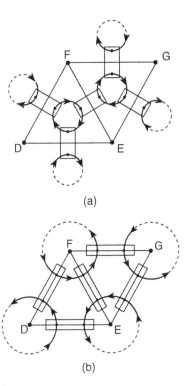

(a)

(b)

Figure 2.95
The physical interpretation of the (a) D-CEL-face and (b) D-CEL-vertex data structures for a pair of adjacent faces of the simple object in Figure 2.94. Assume an implementation that links the next edges in clockwise order for faces in (a) and in counterclockwise order for vertices in (b).

---

[35] Actually, the oriented variant (discussed later in this section) is the one used.

We distinguish between these two interpretations by using *D-CEL-face* to refer to the former and *D-CEL-vertex* to refer to the latter. From Figure 2.95, it is interesting to observe that, as in the case of the winged-edge-face, winged-edge-vertex, and quad-edge data structures, although the physical interpretations of the D-CEL-face and D-CEL-vertex data structures differ, for the traversal orders that we have used (i.e., clockwise around the faces and counterclockwise around the vertices), the two data structures are isomorphic (as are the winged-edge-face, winged-edge-vertex, and quad-edge data structures for all orders) in the sense that they all provide access to the same topological information with identical running times up to a constant factor. This isomorphism can be seen also when, given a traversal order o, say clockwise, without loss of generality, we interpret the D-CEL data structure so that, for each edge e, it stores the following information:

1. The preceding or next edge e' (i.e., in order o) in one of the faces f adjacent to e such that vertex v' is common to both e and e'

2. The next or preceding edge e'' around the vertex v'', in order opposite to o (i.e., counterclockwise, without loss of generality, in our example), where v'' is the other vertex of e

We can use *D-CEL-face-vertex* to refer to this variant of the D-CEL data structure. Note that the D-CEL-face-vertex data structure is not the same as a data structure that contains two singly linked lists so that there is one singly linked list around one of the two constituent vertices of each edge and one singly linked list around one of the two faces adjacent to each edge (see Exercise 7).

As we pointed out, our implementation of the winged-edge data structures ignores the orientation of the edges. This is possible because the identity of the faces that are adjacent to the edge, as well as the identity of the vertices at which the edge is incident, is stored explicitly in all of the variants of the data structure. Thus, knowing the identity of the face f (vertex v) that is being traversed enables the algorithms to determine the appropriate transition because, once an edge e is identified as either one of the edges in the face (incident at the vertex) via the face-edge (vertex-edge) table or as an intermediate edge in the face (incident at the vertex), then the orientation is determined by the face (vertex) field entry in the edge-edge relation whose value is f (v). Therefore, the algorithms must perform an extra lookup operation in the edge-edge relation before determining the next edge after e in the face f (incident at the vertex v), which is achieved by the tests $\text{FCW}(e) = f$ or $\text{FCCW}(e) = f$ ($\text{VSTART}(e) = v$ or $\text{VEND}(e) = v$).

By keeping track of the orientation, we can eliminate the extra lookup operation, thereby avoiding having to store the adjacent faces and incident vertices in the edge-edge relation—that is, removing the need for the FCW, FCCW, VSTART, and VEND fields. This allows us to have an implicit variant of the winged-edge data structure where the topology of the objects is decoupled from the information about the identities of the vertices, edges, and faces that the object comprises. Nevertheless, as we saw earlier, just knowing the identity of an edge is not sufficient to identify an object, as the edge can be a part of two faces; likewise, the edge can be incident at two vertices. Thus, in order to have an implicit winged-edge representation, our representation needs to be able to distinguish between the two faces (vertices) that are adjacent to (make up) the edge. In particular, the various next-edge fields of the edge-edge relation in the implicit variants of the winged-edge data structure must indicate more than just the next edge e—that is, they also need to indicate whether this next edge e is a part of a traversal of a clockwise or counterclockwise adjacent face (starting or ending vertex). Similarly, the face-edge (vertex-edge) table must indicate more than just an edge in the edge-edge relation corresponding to an edge e in the face (incident at the vertex)—that is, it also needs to indicate whether this edge e is a part of a traversal of a clockwise or counterclockwise adjacent face (starting or ending vertex). Therefore, in essence, the table entries (i.e., face-edge and vertex-edge) and next-edge fields of the edge-edge relation in an implicit winged-edge representation can be characterized as *oriented edges* in contrast to the unoriented edges in the explicit winged-edge representation (i.e., the nonoriented winged-edge data structure)

Vertex v	X	Y	Z	OrientedEdge
V1	X1	Y1	Z1	−E1
V2	X2	Y2	Z2	−E2
V3	X3	Y3	Z3	−E3
V4	X4	Y4	Z4	−E4
V5	X5	Y5	Z5	−E5
V6	X6	Y6	Z6	−E6
V7	X7	Y7	Z7	−E7
V8	X8	Y8	Z8	−E8

Figure 2.96
ORIENTEDVERTEXEDGETABLE[v].

Figures 2.96 to 2.98 illustrate an example of one possible implementation of the implicit winged-edge representation corresponding to the winged-edge representation given by the partial vertex-edge and face-edge relations in tables VERTEXEDGETABLE and FACEEDGETABLE of Figures 2.91 and 2.92, respectively, and the collection of edge records that make up the edge-edge relation given by Figure 2.93. In particular, tables ORIENTEDFACEEDGETABLE and ORIENTEDVERTEXEDGETABLE correspond to tables VERTEXEDGETABLE and FACEEDGETABLE, respectively. This implementation uses the orientation of the edges given by the VSTART and VEND fields in Figure 2.93. Notice that we have also included the VSTART, VEND, FCW, and FCCW fields in Figure 2.98, although they are not needed in the execution of most of the queries. We use the term *oriented winged-edge* representation to describe this structure.

The implementation in Figures 2.96 to 2.98 is such that a positive orientation value for a transition to edge e from one of the edges e' in the oriented edge-edge relation or in an ORIENTEDFACEEDGETABLE entry for face f indicates that e's direction makes e a part of a clockwise traversal of a clockwise adjacent face f (i.e., FCW$(e) = f$), while a negative orientation value indicates that e's direction makes e a part of a clockwise traversal of a counterclockwise adjacent face f (i.e., FCCW$(e) = f$). Similarly, in the context of the vertices, this assignment of orientations means that a positive orientation value for a transition to edge e from one of the edges e' in the oriented edge-edge relation or in an ORIENTEDVERTEXEDGETABLE entry for vertex v indicates that e's direction

Face f	OrientedEdge
F1	E1
F2	E5
F3	E11
F4	E9
F5	−E4
F6	−E8

Figure 2.97
ORIENTEDFACEEDGETABLE[f].

Edge e	Vstart	Vend	Fcw	Fccw	CcFFcw EpCw CvVstart	CFFcw EnCw CcvVend	CcFFccw EpCcw CvVend	CFFccw EnCcw CcvVstart
E1	V1	V2	F1	F4	E4	E2	E10	E9
E2	V2	V3	F1	F6	E1	E3	−E11	−E10
E3	V3	V4	F1	F3	E2	E4	E12	E11
E4	V4	V1	F1	F5	E3	E1	−E9	−E12
E5	V5	V6	F2	F4	E8	E6	E9	E10
E6	V6	V7	F2	F5	E5	E7	−E12	−E9
E7	V7	V8	F2	F3	E6	E8	E11	E12
E8	V8	V5	F2	F6	E7	E5	−E10	−E11
E9	V1	V6	F4	F5	−E1	−E5	−E6	−E4
E10	V5	V2	F4	F6	−E5	−E1	−E2	−E8
E11	V3	V8	F3	F6	−E3	−E7	−E8	−E2
E12	V7	V4	F3	F5	−E7	−E3	−E4	−E6

Figure 2.98
Oriented edge-edge relation.

makes e a part of a clockwise traversal of an ending vertex v of e (i.e., VEND$(e) = v$), and thus e is directed towards v. A negative orientation value indicates that e's direction makes e a part of a clockwise traversal of a starting vertex v of e (i.e., VSTART$(e) = v$), and thus e is directed away from v (see Exercise 5).

The entries in ORIENTEDFACEEDGETABLE, ORIENTEDVERTEXEDGETABLE, and the oriented edge-edge relation that correspond to pointers to oriented edges are implemented as pointers to records of type *edge_orientation_pair*, with two fields EDGE and ORIENT containing a pointer to the edge record in the oriented edge-edge relation corresponding to one of the edges e that are adjacent to the appropriate face f (incident at the appropriate vertex v) and e's orientation, as defined above, respectively. Observe the difference from the unoriented variant, where the corresponding entries were pointers to records of type *edge*. Again, as in the case of the edge-edge relation, we note that for a given edge e, the oriented edge-edge relation (Figure 2.98) makes use of fields CCFFCW(e), CVVSTART(e), CFFCW(e), CCVVEND(e), CCFFCCW(e), CVVEND(e), CFFCCW(e), and CCVVSTART(e), instead of CCF(FCW(e)), CV(VSTART(e)), CF(FCW(e)), CCV(VEND(e)), CCF(FCCW(e)), CV(VEND(e)), CF(FCCW(e)), and CCV(VSTART(e)), respectively. As we pointed out before, this is done in order to indicate that the appropriate edge value in the corresponding field in the table is obtained by storing it there explicitly instead of obtaining it by dynamically computing the relevant functions each time the field is accessed (e.g., the field CCFFCW(e) stores the value CCF(FCW(e)) directly rather than obtaining it by applying the function CCF to the result of applying FCW to e each time this field is accessed).

It should be clear that, as is the case with the explicit variants of the winged-edge data structures (i.e., the winged-edge-face, winged-edge-vertex, and quad-edge), the values for the various fields of the elements of the oriented edge-edge relation for all of the oriented variants are also still the same.

As an example of the use of these tables, consider procedure EXTRACTORIENTED-EDGESOFFACE, given below, which extracts the edges of face f in either clockwise or counterclockwise order. Let e denote an edge in f, obtained from the face-edge table ORIENTEDFACEEDGETABLE. For a clockwise ordering, if e's orientation is positive (i.e., $f = $ FCW(e)), then the next edge is CFFCW(e); otherwise, e's orientation is negative (i.e., $f = $ FCCW(e)), and the next edge is CFFCCW(e). For a counterclockwise ordering, if e's orientation is positive (i.e., $f = $ FCW(e)), then the next edge is CCFFCW(e); otherwise, e's orientation is negative (i.e., $f = $ FCCW(e)), and the next edge is CCFFCCW(e). This process terminates when we encounter the initial value of e again. For example, extracting the edges of face F1 in Figure 2.90 in clockwise order yields E1, E2, E3, and E4. Again, as in the nonoriented case, the execution time of EXTRACTORIENTEDEDGESOFFACE is proportional to the number of edges in f as each edge is obtained in $O(1)$ time. Note that, in contrast to the unoriented variant of the algorithm (i.e., procedure EXTRACTEDGESOFFACE), only one lookup operation in the oriented edge-edge relation is performed at each traversal step in the algorithm (although the oriented edge is accessed twice, once to determine the orientation and once to determine the next edge to which the transition is to be made). Similarly, by making use of the vertex-edge table ORIENTEDVERTEXEDGETABLE to obtain an edge incident at vertex v, we can extract the edges incident at v in time proportional to the total number of edges that are incident at v as each edge can be obtained in $O(1)$ time (see Exercise 6).

1 **procedure** EXTRACTORIENTEDEDGESOFFACE(f, *CWFlag*)
2 /* Extract the edges making up face f in clockwise (counterclockwise) order if flag *CWFlag* is true (false) in an oriented winged-edge-face data structure. For each edge e, a positive orientation value indicates that e's direction makes e a part of a traversal of a clockwise adjacent face f (i.e., FCW$(e) = f$), while a negative value indicates that e's direction makes e a part of a traversal of a counterclockwise adjacent face f (i.e., FCCW$(e) = f$). */

```
3   value face f
4   value Boolean CWFlag
5   pointer edge FirstEdge
6   pointer edge_orientation_pair p
7   p ← ORIENTEDEDGE(ORIENTEDFACEEDGETABLE[f])
8   FirstEdge ← EDGE(p)
9   do
10     output EDGE(p)
11     if CWFlag then
12         p ←if ORIENT(p) then CFFCW(EDGE(p))
13             else CFFCCW(EDGE(p))
14             endif
15     else p ←if ORIENT(p) then CCFFCW(EDGE(p))
16             else CCFFCCW(EDGE(p))
17             endif
18     endif
19     until EDGE(p) = FirstEdge
20  enddo
```

Notice that, theoretically speaking, the implicit representation does not contain any identifying information for the vertices and faces, which means that all query responses are in terms of edges. For example, a face would be identified by a list of its constituent edges, and a vertex would be identified by a list of the edges that are incident at it. As the latter method of identifying the vertices making up an edge is somewhat cumbersome, an edge is usually identified by its constituent vertices, which are obtained from an auxiliary table or are stored as part of the edge in the implicit representation, although they are not accessed during the process of determining the transitions to the next edges when traversing the edges incident at a vertex.

One of the drawbacks of the implicit representation is that responding to queries, such as finding the next or preceding edge to a particular edge e in face f (incident at vertex v) in order o, requires us to know if f (v) is a clockwise or counterclockwise adjacent face (starting or ending vertex). This is relatively easy in the case of queries that involve vertices (i.e., finding the preceding or next edge incident at vertex v relative to edge e), because, as we pointed out, the edge is usually identified by its constituent vertices, which are stored in an auxiliary table. Alternatively, we can augment the oriented winged-edge data structure by also storing this information along with the edge, although it is not accessed in determining transitions to the next edges when traversing the edges incident at a vertex. Without this information, we cannot tell if v is a starting or ending vertex of edge e unless we perform a search starting in the ORIENTEDVERTEXEDGETABLE entry corresponding to v and traverse all of the edges incident at v in order o in search of e. Similarly, in order to be able to respond to queries involving faces (i.e., finding the preceding or next edge in face f relative to edge e) as well, we should also augment the oriented winged-edge data structure with an auxiliary table that stores the adjacent faces for each edge. Otherwise, again, without this information, we cannot tell if f is a clockwise or counterclockwise adjacent face of edge e unless we perform a search starting in the ORIENTEDFACEEDGETABLE entry corresponding to f and traverse all of the edges making up f in order o in search of e. Therefore, incorporating these auxiliary tables into the oriented winged-edge data structure means that the augmented oriented winged-edge data structure is almost identical to the original winged-edge data structure with the difference that the execution of queries, such as finding all edges a face comprises (incident at a vertex), does not require more than one lookup operation in the oriented edge-edge relation per edge.

Note that knowing the orientation of the edge e whose next or preceding edge in f (or incident at v) is sought in the implicit representation only ensures that the next edge is along the same face or incident at the same vertex—that is, the same clockwise adjacent face (ending vertex) when the orientation is positive and the same counterclockwise

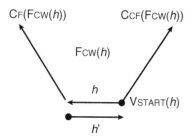

Figure 2.99
The physical interpretation of the fields of a half-edge-face data structure (i.e., the face variant of the half-edge data structure that is based on a traversal of the edges making up a face).

adjacent face (starting vertex) when the orientation is negative. However, knowing the orientation of the edge and $f(v)$ may lead to some confusion when e has a positive orientation and $f(v)$ is really the counterclockwise adjacent face (starting vertex) of e, and vice versa, when e has a negative orientation. In other words, a positive orientation means that $f = \text{FCW}(e)$ ($v = \text{VEND}(e)$), while a negative orientation means that $f = \text{FCCW}(e)$ ($v = \text{VSTART}(e)$).

The orientation issues described above are eliminated in the half-edge data structure [196], which decouples the clockwise and counterclockwise face (starting and ending vertex) information in the winged-edge data structure by storing each edge twice, once for each direction, where each instance is called a *half-edge* and each of the two half-edges corresponding to a single edge is referred to as the *companion half-edge* of the other half-edge. In particular, instead of n edges, we now have $2n$ directed half-edges. With each half-edge h, we record the following information (see Figure 2.99):

1. Starting vertex ($\text{VSTART}(h)$)

2. Companion half-edge (h')

3. Face ($\text{FCW}(h)$) along whose boundary h lies when moving in clockwise order

4. Preceding half-edge ($\text{CCF}(\text{FCW}(h))$) in clockwise order along the face on whose boundary h lies

5. Next half-edge ($\text{CF}(\text{FCW}(h))$) in clockwise order along the face on whose boundary h lies

Thus, the half-edge data structure is equivalent to a partition of the winged-edge data structure so that there is one element (i.e., half-edge) for each face in which the edge is a member. As in the winged-edge data structure, the half-edge data structure makes use of a face-edge table and vertex-edge table to determine the half-edges associated with a face and a vertex, respectively, although it identifies the relevant half-edges instead of the relevant edges, as in the corresponding winged-edge data structure. Similarly, as in the oriented winged-edge data structure, traversing the edges that make up a face is achieved with one lookup operation per edge in the half-edge data structure, in the sense that the information is encoded explicitly in the structure (again using $\text{CCFFCW}(h)$ and $\text{CFFCW}(h)$ instead of $\text{CCF}(\text{FCW}(h))$ and $\text{CF}(\text{FCW}(h))$, respectively). This is in contrast to the winged-edge data structure, where we saw that two lookup operations are needed for each traversal step. Note that traversing the edges that are incident at a vertex using the half-edge data structure is a bit more complex as we first need to find the incoming edge and then to use its companion half-edge, thereby obtaining the next edge incident at v in clockwise order. Observe that the variant of the half-edge data structure that we have presented above is defined in terms of a traversal of edges making up the faces. We can also construct a variant of the half-edge data structure that is defined in terms of a traversal of the edges that are incident at the vertices (see Exercise 11). When necessary, we differentiate between these two variants of the data structure by using the terms *half-edge-face* and and *half-edge-vertex* to refer to the former and the latter, respectively.

The only drawback of the half-edge data structure is the need to store the pointer to the companion half-edge, thereby requiring more storage than the winged-edge data structure (i.e., 10 items of information per edge instead of 8). However, we can save the space needed for the pointer to the companion half-edge by storing the two half-edges in consecutive locations. In this way, we need only determine which of the two half-edges we are currently processing and then access the companion half-edge. At this point, we can continue the traversal along the appropriate half-edge. This means that the storage requirements of the winged-edge and half-edge data structures are now the same.

Exercises

1. The face-edge, vertex-edge, and edge-edge relations that make up the winged-edge data structure can be viewed as a set of relations involving vertices, edges, and faces in a relational database management system. The format of the relations is often described as satisfying

several rules called *normal forms* (e.g., [554]). Do these relations satisfy the second normal form (2NF)? Do they satisfy the third normal form (3NF)? Do they satisfy the Boyce-Codd normal form (BCNF)?

2. Give an algorithm to extract the entire set of edges that is incident at each vertex when using the winged-edge-face data structure.

3. The winged-edge-face data structure is defined in such a way that the edge-edge relation encodes a traversal of the faces adjacent to an edge in clockwise order. In other words, we can obtain all of the edges adjacent to clockwise face f in clockwise (counterclockwise) order by following the CFFCW (CCFFCW) fields, while we can obtain all of the edges adjacent to counterclockwise face f' in clockwise (counterclockwise) order by following the CFFCCW (CCFFCCW) fields—that is, all edges e satisfy FCW$(e) = f$ in the former and FCCW$(e) = f'$ in the latter. Give a similar interpretation to the winged-edge-vertex data structure in terms of the traversal of edges incident at a vertex v in clockwise (counterclockwise) order around v where either all edges e satisfy VEND$(e) = v$ or VSTART$(e) = v$.

4. What are the invalid combinations of next/preceding, clockwise/counterclockwise for the vertex/face pairs that can be used to form a quad-edge data structure?

5. Can you give an explanation or rationalization for why the assignment of edge orientations used in the implementation of the implicit (i.e., oriented) winged-edge data structure when the transitions are interpreted in terms of being in the same face (i.e., a winged-edge-face data structure) so that positive (negative) orientations are associated with clockwise traversals of the clockwise (counterclockwise) adjacent faces correspond to clockwise traversals of the ending (starting) vertices when the transitions are interpreted in terms of being incident at the same vertex (i.e., a winged-edge vertex data structure)? In other words, why do we associate FCW and VEND (FCCW and VSTART) with the positive (negative) orientations instead of FCW and VSTART (FCCW and VEND)?

6. Write an algorithm ExtractOrientedEdgesIncidentAtVertex to extract the edges that are incident at vertex v in clockwise (counterclockwise) order in an oriented winged-edge-face data structure.

7. Can you define a variant of the D-CEL data structure that contains two singly linked lists so that there is one singly linked list around one of the two constituent vertices of each edge and one singly linked list around one of the two faces adjacent to each edge? Note that this variant is not the same as the D-CEL-face-vertex data structure.

8. How would you find the two vertices that make up an edge when using the half-edge-face data structure (i.e., the face variant of the half-edge data structure given in the text)?

9. Give an algorithm to extract the entire set of edges making up a face when using the half-edge-face data structure (i.e., the face variant of the half-edge data structure given in the text).

10. Give an algorithm to extract the entire set of edges that are incident at each vertex when using the half-edge-face data structure (i.e., the face variant of the half-edge data structure given in the text).

11. Define the half-edge-vertex data structure (i.e., the vertex variant of the half-edge data structure).

12. Repeat Exercise 8 for the half-edge-vertex data structure (i.e., the vertex variant of the half-edge data structure).

13. Repeat Exercise 9 for the half-edge-vertex data structure (i.e., the vertex variant of the half-edge data structure).

14. Repeat Exercise 10 for the half-edge-vertex data structure (i.e., the vertex variant of the half-edge data structure).

2.2.1.3 Vertex-Based and Face-Based Methods Using Laths

The winged-edge representation is an implementation of a BRep in terms of the edge-edge relation. It is an edge-based representation in that the boundary of the object is represented in terms of its edges, where there is one record for each edge. The advantage of this representation is that each record is of uniform size. Moreover, as we saw in Section 2.2.1.2, the winged-edge representation enables us to calculate the full set of adjacency relationships (termed *queries* below) involving the vertex, edge, and face primitive entities (i.e., all nine of them) in all orders (e.g., clockwise and counterclockwise around a vertex and a face, and opposite in the case of an edge) in time proportional to the size of the result set.

For example, using the winged-edge representation, we can extract the edges and vertices forming a face f or the edges and faces incident at a vertex v in both clockwise and counterclockwise orders in time proportional to the number of edges or vertices in f and the number of edges or faces incident at v, respectively. Of course, this assumes the presence of an index (i.e., access structure) that is really a pair of additional tables, known as FACEEDGETABLE and VERTEXEDGETABLE, that partially capture the vertex-edge and face-edge relations, thereby facilitating the search to locate an edge in face f or an edge incident at vertex v. The exact identity of the edge that is stored in the access structure is not important for most of the queries—that is, all that is required is the ability to locate one of the edges efficiently. In fact, other queries that can be performed using the same execution time include finding all edges incident at the two vertices of an edge, all faces sharing an edge or a vertex with a given face (i.e., a variant of the frontier of the face), and all vertices that share an edge with a given vertex. The remaining queries to determine all vertices incident at an edge and faces adjacent to an edge are performed by a simple lookup operation as this information is stored directly in the winged-edge and quad-edge data structures.

Uniform-sized representations that are vertex based are also possible. Their advantage is that the vertex is the simplest topological entity, whereas the edge and face are more complex and can be expressed in terms of the vertex objects they comprise. However, the drawback of the vertex-based methods is that we cannot have one record per vertex because the topological information associated with each vertex is more complex than that which is associated with each edge. In particular, whereas the full topological description of an object (i.e., in terms of the other primitive elements) can be obtained (i.e., derived) by knowing a subset of the edges that are associated with each edge as a direct result of the fact that each edge is associated with just two vertices and two faces (assuming a two-manifold), in contrast, there can be a variable number of edges and faces associated with each vertex. In other words, in order to obtain the full topological description of an object given each of its vertices, we need to know the full connectivity of each vertex, which precludes the use of a uniform-sized representation where there is one record per vertex. Similarly, if we want to use a face-based representation, we cannot have a uniform-sized representation where there is one record per face because there is a variable number of edges and vertices associated with each face.

Nevertheless, by examining the set of adjacency relations, we can have a uniform-sized representation where there is a variable number of records for each vertex. In particular, we observe that an object can be fully described by the set of all possible edge-face pairs (edge-face relation), the set of all possible edge-vertex pairs (edge-vertex relation), or the set of all possible face-vertex pairs (face-vertex relation) that it comprises whose cardinality is easily seen to be the same (i.e., twice the number of edges) in the absence of special treatment for boundaries (see Exercise 1). This idea is the principle behind the lath family of data structures of Joy, Legakis, and MacCracken [973], who use the term *lath* to denote a specific instance or element of these data structures. In particular, each object is described by the set of laths it comprises using the appropriate lath data structure. It should be clear that, being vertex based, in each of the different lath representations, a single vertex is associated with each lath, although in all cases, with the exception of a BRep that consists of an isolated vertex, more than one lath is associated with each vertex. Similarly, a single edge is associated with each lath; likewise, a single face is associated with each lath. Since an edge consists of two vertices, it is clear that two laths are associated with each edge. On the other hand, in the case of a face f, there are as many laths associated with f as there are vertices (equivalently, as many laths as there are edges) making up f. Moreover, for laths that do not involve a vertex explicitly such as the edge-face laths, the associated vertex is chosen in such a way that a unique vertex is associated with each of the laths that make up f.

In the rest of this section, we expand on the lath family of vertex-based data structures. It is organized as follows. Section 2.2.1.3.1 presents the different lath data structures for two-manifold objects. Section 2.2.1.3.2 shows how to use the lath data structures to handle unstructured meshes where the data has boundaries. Section 2.2.1.3.3 compares the different lath data structures while pointing out some of their desirable properties, as well as gives a brief description of face-based lath data structures. It also shows how most of the edge-based representations described in Section 2.2.1.2 can be formulated as combinations of vertex-based representations defined in terms of laths.

Exercise

1. Prove that, given a two-manifold object with no boundary edges, the number of possible edge-vertex pairs, the number of possible edge-face pairs, and the number of possible face-vertex pairs are all the same.

2.2.1.3.1 Lath Data Structures for Manifold Objects

Unlike the winged-edge data structure, the lath data structures do not encode the edge-edge relation. They also do not encode the edge-face, edge-vertex, or face-vertex relations (or, alternatively, the face-edge, vertex-edge, and vertex-face relations), although they are very similar. Instead, the basic entity of the lath data structure is one of the three combinations: edge-face, edge-vertex, or face-vertex.[36] In particular, let (a, b) denote the instance of the lath data structure that is being used, where a and b are bound to distinct elements of $\{vertex, edge, face\}$. Thus, the data structure encodes the $(a, b) - (a, b)$ relation (or, more generally, the lath-lath relation). In order to be able to execute the various queries, at the minimum, we must be able to navigate between instances (i.e., elements or laths) of the lath data structure that is being used. Therefore, given a specific lath (x, y) instance of lath data structure (a, b), we must be able to transition to the lath corresponding to the next object of type b for object x and to transition to the lath corresponding to the next object of type a for object y. We wish to execute the queries by storing the minimum amount of information with each instance of the data structure, which is three, corresponding to the associated vertex v and the two transitions, which are termed the *primitive transitions*. Thus, letting c denote *next*, each instance of the lath data structure (a, b) stores v and transitions ca and cb. Depending on the binding of a or b, we may have a choice between a transition to the next object or to a prior object. In particular, this is the case for vertices (v) and faces (f), in which case we speak of clockwise (c) and counterclockwise (cc) transitions instead of next and prior transitions, respectively. In the case of an edge (e), we only have a next (c) transition, which we characterize as transitioning to a *companion*.

Before presenting more precise definitions of the different lath data structures, we point out that all queries that involve laths are mappings from one lath to another lath or from one lath to a set of laths. Determining the corresponding edge, vertex, and face, or sets of laths often requires the execution of additional steps that usually involve a few lookup operations or at least a constant number of operations per element making up the result of the operation that is to be returned (e.g., if we want to return all vertices or edges that make up a face). We have seen similar considerations in terms of lookup costs in our discussion of the distinction between the half-edge data structure and the implicit (i.e., oriented) variants of the winged-edge data structure, on the one hand, versus the explicit variants of the winged-edge data structure, on the other hand, in determining the edges associated with a face or incident at a vertex (Section 2.2.1.2).

---

[36] We could have also used the terms *face-edge*, *vertex-edge*, and *vertex-face*, respectively.

It is also important to note that the lath data structures used in the vertex-based representations can be distinguished from the explicit winged-edge data structures that are based on the edge-edge relation by observing that the explicit winged-edge data structures include explicit information on both the topology of the faces containing the edges and the identity of the faces and vertices that are incident at them. In contrast, the lath data structures decouple these two pieces of information and only represent the topological information explicitly. In particular, only the vertices are represented explicitly in the lath data structures.

The identities of the faces that are adjacent to an edge, as well as the identity of one of the vertices that makes up an edge, are represented implicitly in the lath data structures instead of being stored explicitly, as is the case in the explicit winged-edge data structures. In addition, only a subset of the transitions from an edge to an adjacent edge along a face or incident at the same vertex is stored explicitly in the lath data structures, whereas a greater number of these transitions are stored explicitly in the winged-edge data structures. Therefore, for example, in order to identify the face or edge associated with a specific edge-face pair in an edge-face lath data structure, we need to retrieve all of the laths it comprises and look up the associated vertices, thereby enabling us to identify the face and edges in terms of their constituent vertices. This is not surprising given that the vertex is the primitive entity of the lath representations, and hence their characterization as being vertex based.

Of course, regardless of which lath data structure is used, we also need the analog of the face-edge and vertex-edge tables used in the winged-edge data structures to enable the execution of the queries. Recall that these tables serve as an index (i.e., access structure) that enables the search to locate an edge in face f or an edge incident at vertex v. In the case of the lath data structures, these tables record a lath (not necessarily unique) that is associated with the distinct instance of the relevant object type, which is an element of {*vertex,edge,face*}. Unlike the winged-edge data structures, where the principal element was an edge, the lath data structures are in terms of pairs of object types (i.e., edge-face, edge-vertex, and face-vertex), and thus we also need an edge-lath table instead of just a vertex-lath and a face-lath table. These three tables enable the efficient response to queries that seek, for example, all faces adjacent to and vertices making up a specific edge, all vertices and edges making up a specific face, and all edges and faces incident at a specific vertex—that is, the edge-face and edge-vertex relations, face-vertex and face-edge relations, and vertex-edge and vertex-face relations, respectively. We use the terms *face-lath table*, *vertex-lath table*, and *edge-lath table* to refer to these tables.

It should be clear that the execution of some of the queries may be faster (from a computational complexity standpoint) if additional information is stored or capable of being derived easily, for each instance of the lath data structure. In other words, although we only store information about two primitive transitions for each lath, some queries may be simpler to perform given information about the other nonprimitive transitions. For example, extracting the edges incident at a vertex v or the edges making up a face f in counterclockwise order is easier if the laths store explicit, or make it easy to derive, information about how to make counterclockwise transitions instead of just clockwise transitions.

In the following, we describe in greater detail three members of the lath family of data structures, one for each of the three combinations: edge-face, edge-vertex, and face-vertex. Letting (a,b) denote the instance of the lath data structure that is being described, where a and b are bound to two distinct elements of {*vertex,edge,face*}, and o is bound to the remaining element of the set, and assuming that the primitive transitions ca and cb are stored with each lath instance of (a,b), we also show how the other transitions cca, ccb, and co (as well as possibly ca and cb, if one of b or a, respectively, is bound to an element for which only transitions to the next laths are possible rather than transitions to both next and prior laths) can be made.

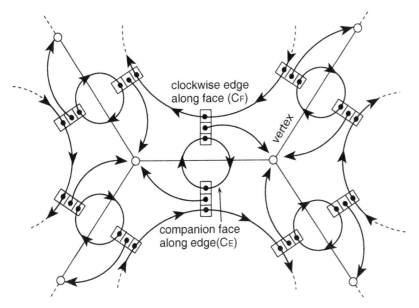

BOUNDARY-BASED
REPRESENTATIONS

Figure 2.100
Example set of split-face lath elements and some transitions.

We use the terms *split-face*, *split-vertex*, and *corner* to refer to the three lath data structures corresponding to the edge-face, edge-vertex, and face-vertex pairs, respectively. Our naming convention differs slightly from that of Joy, Legakis, and Mac-Cracken [973], who used the terms *split-edge*, *half-edge*, and *corner*, respectively. We have chosen this approach in order to avoid confusion with the well-known half-edge data structure [196] (see Section 2.2.1.2). Note that our naming conventions also capture the actions that lead to the creation of the pairs. In particular, a *split-face* denotes an edge-face pair, which results from splitting an edge record into two parts (one per adjacent face), while a *split-vertex* denotes an edge-vertex pair, which results from splitting an edge record into two parts (one per constituent vertex). A *corner* denotes a face-vertex pair, which corresponds to a corner of a face.

The lath-based split-face data structure represents the object by a lath record $L = (e, f)$ that contains the following information for the edge-face pair corresponding to edge e and face f, assuming the orientation in Figure 2.100:

1. A pointer to the vertex v associated with L

2. A pointer to the lath record corresponding to the other face f adjacent to e, as well as the vertex of edge e opposite to the one associated with L (i.e., the next edge-face pair along e)—that is, $\text{CE}(L)$

3. A pointer to the lath record corresponding to the next edge that follows L in a clockwise traversal of face f (i.e., the next edge-face pair along f)—that is, $\text{CF}(L)$

The nonprimitive transitions are defined as follows. $\text{CCV}(L)$ is obtained by $\text{CF}(\text{CE}(L))$, which is easy to compute as it makes use of the primitive transitions CE and CF. $\text{CV}(L)$ can be obtained by either successively traversing the laths representing face f using CF until obtaining a lath L' such that $\text{CF}(L') = L$ and then applying $\text{CE}(L')$ to obtain L'' so that $\text{CV}(L) = L''$, or by successively traversing the laths surrounding the vertex associated with L using CCV until obtaining a lath L' such that $\text{CCV}(L') = L$, which means that $\text{CV}(L) = L'$. $\text{CCF}(L)$ is obtained by $\text{CE}(\text{CV}(L))$. As we see, given lath $L = (e, f)$, whose associated vertex is v, the split-face lath representation is not conducive to finding the lath corresponding to the next edge incident at vertex v in the clockwise direction (CV) or the next edge in face f in the counterclockwise direction (CCF) efficiently. Figure 2.101 is an example of the split-face lath data structure for a pair of adjacent faces of the simple object in Figure 2.94.

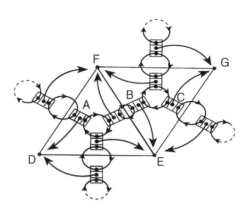

Figure 2.101
An example split-face lath data structure for a pair of adjacent faces of the simple object in Figure 2.94. Assume an implementation that links the laths corresponding to the next edges that make up a face in clockwise order. A pointer is shown from each lath to its associated vertex and to the lath corresponding to the face on the other side of the corresponding edge.

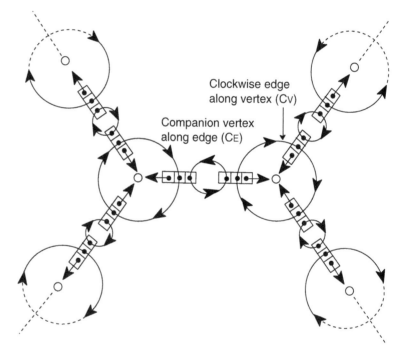

Figure 2.102
Example set of split-vertex lath elements and some transitions.

The lath-based split-vertex data structure represents the object by a lath record $L = (e, v)$ that contains the following information for the edge-vertex pair corresponding to edge e and vertex v, assuming the orientation in Figure 2.102:

1. A pointer to the vertex v associated with L

2. A pointer to the lath record that represents the same edge e as L but the opposite vertex of e (i.e., the next edge-vertex pair along e)—that is, $C_E(L)$

3. A pointer to the lath record corresponding to the next edge that follows L in a clockwise traversal of vertex v (i.e., the next edge-vertex pair along v)—that is, $C_V(L)$

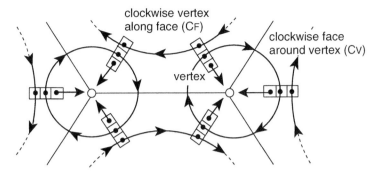

Figure 2.104
Example set of corner lath elements and some transitions.

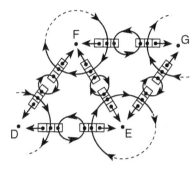

Figure 2.103
An example split-vertex lath data structure for a pair of adjacent faces of the simple object in Figure 2.94. Assume an implementation that links the laths corresponding to the next edges that are incident at a vertex in clockwise order. A pointer is shown from each lath to its associated vertex and to the lath corresponding to the vertex on the other side of the corresponding edge.

The nonprimitive transitions are defined as follows: $CCF(L)$ is obtained by $CE(CV(L))$, which is easy to compute as it makes use of the primitive transitions CE and CV. $CF(L)$ can be obtained in two ways. The first is by applying $CE(L)$ to obtain the lath L' of the same edge e but opposite vertex v' and then successively traversing the laths surrounding v' using CV until obtaining a lath L'' such that $CV(L'') = L'$, which means that $CF(L) = L''$. The second is by successively traversing the laths representing the face f in which L is a member using CCF until obtaining a lath L' such that $CCF(L') = L$, which means that $CF(L) = L'$. $CCV(L)$ is obtained by $CF(CE(L))$. As we see, given lath $L = (e, v)$, whose associated face is f, the split-vertex lath representation is not conducive to finding the lath corresponding to the next edge in face f in the clockwise direction (CF) or the next edge incident at vertex v in the counterclockwise direction (CCV) efficiently. Figure 2.103 is an example of the split-vertex lath data structure for a pair of adjacent faces of the simple object in Figure 2.94.

The lath-based corner data structure represents the object by a lath record $L = (f, v)$ that contains the following information for the face-vertex pair corresponding to face f and vertex v, assuming the orientation in Figure 2.104:

1. A pointer to the vertex v associated with L

2. A pointer to the lath record corresponding to the next vertex that follows L in a clockwise traversal of face f (i.e., the next face-vertex pair along f)—that is, $CF(L)$

3. A pointer to the lath record corresponding to the next face that follows L in a clockwise traversal of vertex v (i.e., the next face-vertex pair along v)—that is, $CV(L)$

The nonprimitive transitions are obtained as follows. $CE(L)$ is obtained by $CV(CF(L))$. $CCF(L)$ is obtained by $CE(CV(L))$. $CCV(L)$ is obtained by $CF(CE(L))$. All three nonprimitive transitions are easy to compute because they all make use of the primitive transitions CF and CV. It is interesting to note that, unlike the split-face and split-vertex lath representations, all of the transitions can be implemented in the corner lath representation in constant time, except along the boundary, as we point out in Section 2.2.1.3.2. Figure 2.105 is an example of the corner lath data structure for a pair of adjacent faces of the simple object in Figure 2.94.

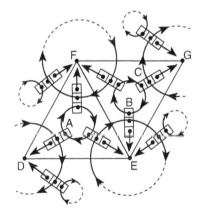

Figure 2.105
An example corner lath data structure for a pair of adjacent faces of the simple object in Figure 2.94. Assume an implementation that links the laths corresponding to the next edges that make up a face in clockwise order and likewise links the laths corresponding to the next edges that are incident at a vertex in clockwise order. A pointer is shown from each lath to its associated vertex.

Exercises

1. Why can we not define a lath data structure variant in which the primitive transitions are the pairs CF and CCF?

2. Repeat Exercise 1 for a lath data structure variant in which the primitive transitions are the pairs CV and CCV.

3. Given a lath L in a lath representation of a two-manifold object with no boundary edges, show that, regardless of which of the split-face, split-vertex, and corner lath representations is used, $\text{CE}(L)$ is uniquely determined.

4. Our definition of the split-face lath data structure assumes an orientation for each edge-face pair lath that is reflected by the vertex that is associated with each lath. Given that we are dealing with two-manifold objects, since an edge is made up of two vertices and is adjacent to two faces, there are two possible orientations for each lath. Referring to Figure 2.100, suppose that you reverse the orientation by associating the left, instead of the right, vertex with the lath. What effect does this change of orientation have on the definitions of the transitions for the split-face lath data structure in the case of objects?

5. Repeat Exercise 4 for the split-vertex lath data structure, referring to Figure 2.102.

6. Repeat Exercise 4 for the corner lath data structure, referring to Figure 2.104.

2.2.1.3.2 Lath Data Structures for Meshes with Boundaries

The data structures that we have described assume that the mesh corresponds to a manifold object (a two-manifold for three-dimensional objects with two-dimensional surfaces). They can also be used to describe unstructured two-dimensional meshes where the data has boundaries. This means that, unlike the three-dimensional object where all of the faces are part of the object, we also have a face that is not part of the object, termed the *boundary face*. Thus, some of the edges and vertices are members of the boundary of the mesh (i.e., of both the mesh and the boundary face). A key issue in the incorporation of a boundary is how to indicate its presence. There are a number of possible solutions.

The first is to add a flag to each lath record to indicate whether the associated vertex and edge combination is part of the boundary of a face in the mesh, in contrast to not being part of the boundary of any of the faces in the mesh, assuming that laths corresponding to vertex and edge combinations in the boundary face are not present. This is a simple solution whose cost is the storage that is required for the flag in the form of an additional bit in each lath record. An alternative solution, and the one that we adopt, is to overload one of the primitive operations (transitions to lath L') on the lath L to use the value NIL (i.e., L' is set to NIL) to indicate that L is part of the boundary (i.e., the vertex and edge combination associated with L corresponds to a boundary edge whose associated face f is not the boundary face and hence f is in the mesh) while the face f' associated with the next lath L' is the boundary face and hence f' is not in the mesh.

At this point, we discuss how to choose which of the primitive transitions in an instance $L = (x, y)$ of lath data structure (a, b) should use the value NIL when (x, y) is part of the boundary to indicate that the next instance $L' = (x', y')$ is part of the boundary face. We have at most two choices. We can either let the next (a, b) pair (i.e., lath) corresponding to an instance of object type b for instance x of object type a be NIL (i.e., $ca(L)$), or let the next (a, b) pair (i.e., lath) corresponding to an instance of object type a for instance y of object type b be NIL (i.e., $cb(L)$). The important criterion that dictates our choice is that the object instance and lath for which the transition is being performed must both be a boundary element and also be in the mesh for which it serves as a boundary element (otherwise, it might not be encountered during normal processing of the mesh), while the object instance and lath that is the result of the transition (i.e., that is pointed at and set to NIL) must be a part of the boundary (i.e., in the boundary face) and not be in the mesh for which it serves as a member of the boundary. In other words, in the latter case, we are not replacing an object instance that is on the boundary, while its corresponding lath is not, with NIL (this would be the case, for example, if, in the split-vertex lath data structure, we were to choose to set $\text{CV}(L)$ to NIL instead of choosing to set $\text{CE}(L)$ to NIL when L corresponds to a lath that is in the mesh).

Given the above considerations, the following transitions are the ones that are set to NIL to indicate that lath instance $L = (x, y)$ of the corresponding lath data structure is part of the boundary. For the split-face lath data structure, $\text{CE}(L)$ is set to NIL because it denotes the situation that L corresponds to a boundary edge object x, and its value is the next face object, which is the boundary face object. For the corner lath data structure, $\text{CV}(L)$ is set to NIL because it denotes the situation that L corresponds to a boundary vertex object y, and its value is the next face object, which is the boundary face object. For the split-vertex lath data structure, the situation is a bit more complex as neither of the objects x or y is the boundary face, while both x and y lie on the boundary. Thus, the decision must be made on the basis of which value is in the boundary face. In this case, we see that $\text{CE}(L)$ is set to NIL because it denotes the situation that L corresponds to a boundary edge object x and its value is the next vertex object y' whose associated lath $L' = (x, y')$ is part of the boundary face. In contrast, we do not set $\text{CV}(L)$ to NIL because it denotes the situation that L corresponds to a boundary vertex object y whose value is the next edge object x' whose associated lath $L'' = (x', y)$ is not on the boundary face.

Regardless of the lath data structure that is used, the manner in which we incorporate the boundary results in boundary edges that are distinguished from nonboundary edges by having only one lath associated with them instead of two—that is, the companion lath $\text{CE}(L)$ is not present when lath L is associated with boundary edge e, whether explicitly (as in the split-face and split-vertex lath data structures) or implicitly (as in the corner lath data structure), and thus $\text{CE}(L) = \text{NIL}$. It is easy to see that this is also true for the corner lath data structure that is not explicitly defined in terms of edge objects as $\text{CE}(L) = \text{CV}(\text{CF}(L))$, which is NIL for a face-vertex pair on the boundary. Therefore, disregarding the order, the set of laths corresponding to the boundary is uniquely determined once the order (clockwise or counterclockwise) and starting edge have been specified. Moreover, the same algorithm can be used to determine the set of boundary laths for all of the lath data structures (see Exercise 2). Nevertheless, some of the transitions for the different lath data structures must be modified to deal with the presence of NIL values and the absence of some of the companion laths of the boundary edges. This is discussed in greater detail below.

First of all, irrespective of which lath data structure is used, when lath L corresponds to a boundary edge e, no laths can follow L in the counterclockwise direction around vertex v associated with L, and thus $\text{CCV}(L)$ is always NIL. Since $\text{CCV}(L)$ is defined in terms of $\text{CE}(L)$ (i.e., $\text{CCV}(L) = \text{CF}(\text{CE}(L))$), the definition of CF is modified not to apply CF if $\text{CE}(L)$ is NIL and simply to return NIL as the result in this case. The absence of a companion lath means that nonprimitive transitions that involve transitions through the missing lath, as is the case when the transitions are in the form of a successive traversal of the laths surrounding v, cannot be used. Therefore, in the case of the split-face lath data structure, given lath L corresponding to edge-face pair (e, f), only use the definition of CV that successively traverses the laths representing face f using repeated invocations of CF until obtaining a lath L' such that $\text{CF}(L') = L$, followed by an application of $\text{CE}(L')$ to obtain L'' so that $\text{CV}(L) = L''$. Similarly, in the case of the corner lath data structure, given lath L corresponding to face-vertex pair (f, v), do not use the definition $\text{CCF}(L) = \text{CE}(\text{CV}(L))$. Instead, use a definition of CCF that successively traverses the laths representing the face f in which L is a member, using CF until obtaining a lath L' such that $\text{CF}(L') = L$ and thus $\text{CCF}(L) = L'$. For example, Figure 2.106(a) is the split-face lath data structure for the unstructured mesh corresponding to Figure 2.101 with laths on the boundary having NIL CE values, while Figure 2.106(c) is the corresponding corner lath data structure for Figure 2.105 with laths on the boundary having NIL CV values.

On the other hand, in the case of the split-vertex lath data structure, the absence of the companion lath $L' = (e, v')$ of the lath L corresponding to edge-vertex pair (e, v) when e is a boundary edge requires modifications to both primitive and nonprimitive transitions. First of all, L replaces L' as the next lath in clockwise order after lath $L'' = (e', v')$ around vertex v'—that is, $\text{CV}(L'') = L$ instead of $\text{CV}(L'') = L'$. In addition, since CCF is defined in terms of CV, $\text{CCF}(L'') = \text{CE}(\text{CV}(L''))$ must be redefined to yield L when $\text{CV}(L'') = L$ and $\text{CE}(\text{CV}(L'')) = \text{NIL}$. Second, as we pointed out above, the absence of a companion lath means that nonprimitive transitions that involve transitions through the missing lath, as is the case when the transitions are in the form of a successive traversal of the laths

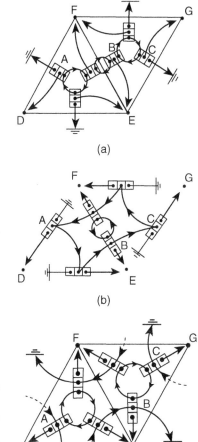

(a)

(b)

(c)

Figure 2.106
Examples of (a) split-face, (b) split-vertex, and (c) corner lath data structures for an unstructured mesh consisting of a pair of adjacent triangles analogous to the pair of adjacent faces in Figures 2.101, 2.103, and 2.105, respectively. Assume implementations that link the laths corresponding to the next edges that make up a face in (a) and (c) in clockwise order and that links the laths corresponding to the next edges that are incident at a vertex in (b) and (c) in clockwise order. A pointer is shown from each lath to its associated vertex. Laths on the boundary in (a) and (b) are shown with NIL CE values, while in (c) they are shown with NIL CV values.

surrounding v, cannot be used. Therefore, only use the definition of CF that successively traverses the laths representing the face f associated with L using repeated invocations of CCF until obtaining a lath L' so that $CCF(L') = L$, which means that $CF(L) = L'$. For example, Figure 2.106(b) is the split-vertex lath data structure for the unstructured mesh corresponding to Figure 2.103 with laths on the boundary having NIL CV values.

The main problem caused by the absence of a companion lath in our implementation for all three lath data structures is that a lath that corresponds to an edge of the boundary face (i.e., a companion lath of a boundary edge) cannot be returned as a valid value of a transition. In particular, this is the case when the companion lath is to be returned as the value of $CV(L)$, which is NIL, for a lath L associated with vertex v regardless of whether L corresponds to a boundary edge (e.g., laths A and B in the example split-face lath data structure in Figure 2.106(a), corresponding to boundary and nonboundary edges, respectively). This problem is encountered when we execute the query that seeks the laths corresponding to all of the edges incident at vertex v. The presence of the boundary means that, in general, obtaining a response to this query starting at the lath of an arbitrary edge requires making use of two successive traversals starting at v, one for each of the clockwise and counterclockwise directions around v.

Nevertheless, the response will not contain a lath corresponding to an edge of the boundary face. Assuming the orientations of the laths in Figures 2.100, 2.102, and 2.104, we can overcome this absence by using the lath L' corresponding to $CCF(L) = CE(CV(L))$ (e.g., C in Figure 2.106(a) for $CCF(B)$), which is obtained by successively traversing the laths representing the face f in which L is a member using CF until obtaining a lath L' such that $CF(L') = L$ and thus $CCF(L) = L'$. However, L' must be used with caution as the vertex v' associated with L' is not the same as the vertex v associated with L (e.g., vertex E is associated with lath B in Figure 2.106(a) while vertex G is associated with lath C $= CCF(B)$). Alternatively, we can choose to return NIL in this case. Note that, although we illustrated this problem with the aid of the split-face lath data structure, the problem also arises for the remaining lath data structures (i.e., split-vertex and corner, as can be seen in Figure 2.106(b, c) using the same laths and vertices).

A similar problem arises when the companion lath L' is to be returned as the value of $CE(L)$ for a lath L associated with boundary edge e such that L is in the mesh and not in the boundary face, while L' is in the boundary face and not in the mesh, and for which $CE(L) =$ NIL. This problem is encountered in all of the lath data structures when we execute the query that seeks the laths corresponding to all of the vertices that are incident at boundary edge e (see also Exercise 1). The presence of the boundary means that the response to this query starting at the lath L associated with edge e and vertex v involves the vertex v' associated with the companion lath L' whose associated edge is e where L' is in the boundary face. Thus, we cannot report L' because it is not present. However, assuming the orientations of the laths in Figures 2.100, 2.102, and 2.104, we can overcome this problem by using the lath L'' corresponding to $CF(L)$ (e.g., B in Figure 2.106 for $CF(C)$). This is a primitive transition for the split-face and corner lath data structures, but in the case of the split-vertex lath data structure, we make use of the definition of CF that successively traverses the laths representing the face f in which L is a member using CCF until obtaining a lath L'' such that $CCF(L'') = L$, which means that $CF(L) = L''$. However, regardless of which lath data structure is used, L'' must be used with caution as the edge e' associated with L'' is not the same as the edge e associated with L (e.g., edge EF is associated with lath B $= CF(C)$ in Figure 2.106, while edge EG is associated with lath C).

Joy et al. [973] incorporate the boundary in the split-vertex lath data structure in a different way, thereby avoiding some of the problems described above. Their implementation is based on an observation that given boundary edge-vertex lath instance $L = (x, y)$ and its companion lath instance $L' = (x, y')$, it is impossible for the instances of the next objects to be of object type *face*, which precludes the boundary face from serving as the object of the transition that is set to NIL as in the other lath data structures. Thus, they choose one of the instances of the object types in the two laths that is on the boundary and set the transition to the next instance of the other object type to NIL. In particular, they choose the lath and object type for which the transition is to an instance of the other object that is in the boundary face rather than on the boundary but not in the mesh. Therefore, $\text{CV}(L')$ is set to NIL because it denotes the situation that L' corresponds to a boundary vertex object y', and its value is the next edge object x' that is in the boundary, face and is not part of the boundary, as the role of x in L' is as an edge object which is on the boundary but not in the mesh. Note that this means that Joy et al. retain the definition of CE, where $\text{CE}(L') = L$ and $\text{CE}(L) = L'$.

The implementation of Joy et al. [973] described above has the property that, unlike the split-face and corner lath data structures, each boundary edge is represented by two laths instead of one. This means that incorporating the boundary in the split-vertex lath data structure using this implementation requires fewer modifications to the definitions of the transitions in the original variant described earlier that does not make provisions for the boundary. In particular, besides setting $\text{CV}(L')$ to NIL for all laths L' that are companions of laths L whose associated face is in the mesh while also having an associated edge that is on the boundary, we also need to guarantee that the remaining transitions are implemented in such a way that they avoid successive traversals of laths for which CV is NIL, unless this is the desired effect. This is achieved by ensuring that transitions that could be defined in terms of successive traversals of laths surrounding a vertex (using CV) are instead defined in terms of successive traversals of laths representing a face (using CCF). In particular, $\text{CF}(L)$ is implemented by successively traversing the laths representing the face f associated with L using CCF until obtaining the lath L'' such that $\text{CCF}(L'') = L$ and thus $\text{CF}(L) = L''$ (but see Exercise 5). For example, Figure 2.107 is the split-vertex lath data structure for the unstructured mesh corresponding to Figure 2.103 with laths on the boundary having NIL CV values.

In addition, the implementation of Joy et al. [973] means that tracing the boundary of the mesh represented by the modified split-vertex lath data structure uses a different algorithm (see Exercise 3) than the one used for the split-face and corner lath data structures (see Exercise 2). Actually, we can use the same algorithm (i.e., the one in Exercise 2) for all three lath data structures if we further modify the split-vertex lath data structure also to set $\text{CE}(L)$ to NIL for all laths L where $\text{CV}(L') = \text{NIL}$ for the companion lath L' of L—that is, the face associated with L is in the mesh while also having an associated edge that is on the boundary (see Exercise 16). In this case, $\text{CE}(L')$ is still pointing at L because, otherwise, there may be a loss in querying power for certain mesh configurations as some of the transitions may not be possible (see Exercise 15). Moreover, regardless of whether we make this modification (see Exercise 6) or not (see Exercise 4), we can also trace the boundary and provide the response in terms of the companion laths L' for which $\text{CV}(L') = \text{NIL}$.

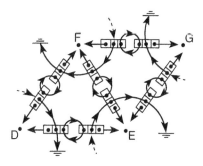

Figure 2.107
The implementation of Joy et al. [973] of the split-vertex lath data structure for an unstructured mesh consisting of a pair of adjacent triangles analogous to the pair of adjacent faces in Figure 2.103. Assume an implementation that links the laths corresponding to the next edges that are incident at a vertex in clockwise order. A pointer is shown from each lath to its associated vertex and to the lath corresponding to the vertex on the other side of the corresponding edge. Laths corresponding to boundary edges are shown with NIL CV values in the companion lath.

Exercises

1. In the text, we pointed out that our incorporation of the boundary resulted in boundary edges being distinguished from nonboundary edges by having only one lath associated with them instead of two—that is, the companion lath $\text{CE}(L)$ is not present when lath L is associated with boundary edge e, whether explicitly (as in the split-face and split-vertex lath data structures) or implicitly (as in the corner lath data structure), and thus $\text{CE}(L) = \text{NIL}$. This meant that the companion laths cannot be returned as valid values of a transition. We observed that this is a drawback because it means that some queries cannot be performed, such as determining the laths corresponding to all of the edges incident at a given vertex or the laths corresponding to all of the vertices that are incident at a given edge. The problem is that some of these laths are part of the boundary face. Are there any other queries that share this drawback?

2. Give a pair of algorithms to trace the laths corresponding to the edges that make up the boundary face of a lath data structure in both counterclockwise and clockwise orders where the response is in terms of the laths L for which $\text{CE}(L) = \text{NIL}$.

3. Repeat Exercise 2 for an implementation of the split-vertex lath data structure using the variant proposed by Joy et al. [973] where a boundary edge $e = (v_1, v_2)$ with vertices v_1 and v_2 is represented by the two edge-vertex pair laths $L = (e, v_1)$ and $L' = (e, v_2)$ such that L' is part of the boundary face where $\text{CE}(L) = L'$, $\text{CE}(L') = L$, and $\text{CV}(L') = \text{NIL}$.

4. Using the implementation of the split-vertex lath data structure of Joy et al. [973] that retains the companion laths L' of laths L for edges on the boundary of the mesh and for which $\text{CV}(L') = \text{NIL}$, give an algorithm to trace the boundary of the split-vertex lath data structure in both counterclockwise and clockwise orders by reporting the laths L' for which $\text{CV}(L') = \text{NIL}$, instead of the laths L for which $\text{CE}(L) = \text{NIL}$, as in Exercise 3. In other words, the response is in terms of the companion laths that correspond to edge-vertex pairs whose associated face is the boundary face. Note that this is only possible for this variant of the split-vertex lath data structure as it is the only one for which the companion laths of boundary edges are present (i.e., they are not present for the split-face and corner lath data structures).

5. Assume that the boundary has been incorporated in the split-vertex lath data structure using the method of Joy et al. [973] (i.e., by setting $\text{CV}(L')$ to NIL for the companion lath L' of the lath L that corresponds to a boundary edge). In the text we argued that, in this case, since $\text{CV}(L')$ is NIL, it is best not to define a nonprimitive transition in terms of successive traversals of laths surrounding a vertex (using CV). We followed this line of reasoning in the definition of the CF transition by basing it on the CCF transition rather than a successive traversal around the vertex associated with the companion of L using CV. However, closer scrutiny reveals that CCF is also defined in terms of CV–that is, $\text{CCF}(L) = \text{CE}(\text{CV}(L))$. How can you rationalize this apparent contradiction?

6. Repeat Exercise 4 for the modification of the split-vertex lath data structure discussed in the text where $\text{CE}(L)$ is also set to NIL for all laths L for edges on the boundary, when $\text{CV}(L') = \text{NIL}$ for the companion lath L' of L. Recall that $\text{CE}(L')$ is still set to L.

7. What is the cost of determining the laths that make up the boundary in counterclockwise order for the split-face lath data structure when the boundary is incorporated so that only one lath is associated with each edge?

8. What is the cost of determining the laths that make up the boundary in clockwise order for the split-face lath data structure when the boundary is incorporated so that only one lath is associated with each edge?

9. Repeat Exercise 7 for the corner lath data structure.

10. Repeat Exercise 8 for the corner lath data structure.

11. Repeat Exercise 7 for the split-vertex lath data structure.

12. Repeat Exercise 8 for the split-vertex lath data structure.

13. Repeat Exercise 7 for the implementation of Joy et al. [973] of the split-vertex lath data structure.

14. Repeat Exercise 8 for the implementation of Joy et al. [973] of the corner lath data structure.

15. Suppose that you incorporate a boundary edge in the split-vertex lath data structure so that the CE transitions of both laths that are associated with the boundary edge are NIL while retaining the same meaning for the remaining transitions—that is, boundary edge $e = (v_1, v_2)$ with vertices v_1 and v_2 is represented by the two edge-vertex pair laths $L = (e, v_1)$ and $L' = (e, v_2)$ such that L' is part of the boundary face, and $\text{CE}(L) = \text{CE}(L') = \text{CV}(L') = \text{NIL}$. Is there a loss in querying power in the sense that some of the queries that involve the boundary edges are no longer possible? If so, which queries and for what type of a mesh? Also, why do such problems not arise when only $\text{CV}(L')$ is set to NIL?

16. Is there a loss in querying power by making the modification of the split-vertex lath data structure discussed in the text where $\text{CE}(L)$ is also set to NIL (instead of L'), while still retaining the setting of $\text{CE}(L') = L$, for all laths L for edges on the boundary where $\text{CV}(L') = \text{NIL}$ for the companion lath L' of L?

17. Repeat Exercise 4 in Section 2.2.1.3.1 for unstructured meshes with boundaries.

18. Repeat Exercise 6 in Section 2.2.1.3.1 for unstructured meshes with boundaries.

2.2.1.3.3 Summary

In Section 2.2.1.2 we pointed out that by swapping the roles of the faces and vertices in the mesh and assigning an arc to each edge between two faces of the mesh, we obtain the dual of the mesh. This means that we interpret the cycles through the edges around the vertices of the original mesh as faces in the dual mesh and the cycles through the edges that make up the faces in the original mesh as vertices in the dual mesh. Doing this, we find that, if the mesh is represented by a split-face lath data structure, then each clockwise loop around a face is transformed into a clockwise loop around a vertex in the dual. Similarly, we find that if the mesh is represented by a split-vertex lath data structure, then each clockwise loop around a vertex is transformed into a clockwise loop around a face in the dual. Thus, the split-face lath data structure on the mesh induces a split-vertex lath data structure on the dual mesh, and vice versa—that is, the split-vertex lath data structure on the mesh induces a split-face lath data structure on the dual mesh (compare Figures 2.101 and 2.103).

Turning now to the corner lath data structure, we see that the dual mesh induced by the original mesh is also a corner lath data structure. In particular, a clockwise loop around a vertex in the original mesh is transformed into a clockwise loop around a face in the dual mesh, and a clockwise loop around a face in the original mesh is transformed into a clockwise loop around a vertex in the dual mesh. This duality is analogous to that exhibited by the interpretation of the four wings of each edge that led to the quad-edge data structure (recall Section 2.2.1.2), where we pointed out that one of the advantages of the quad-edge interpretation over the winged-edge-face and interpretations is that the dual graph is automatically encoded in the quad-edge data structure, as is also the case in the corner lath data structure.

The self-duality of the corner lath data structure and the fact that all transitions (i.e., CE, CF, CCF, CV, and CCV) can be implemented in constant time when we are not positioned at the boundary of the mesh make a strong case for preferring it. On the other hand, all three lath data structures have the same behavior when the mesh has a boundary in that not all of the transitions can be implemented in constant time. Moreover, incorporation of the boundary so that only one lath is associated with each boundary edge (i.e., the absence of the companion lath) means that some queries whose responses include objects whose corresponding laths are in the boundary face (e.g., finding all edges incident at a vertex or finding all vertices incident at an edge) fail to return these laths as part of the response, and thus the complete response to the query cannot be obtained. In the case of the split-vertex lath data structure, the implementation of Joy et al. [973] overcomes this problem by including the companion lath for boundary edges. Thus, assuming that a boundary edge e is represented by the laths L and L' such that $CF(L) = L'$ and $CV(L') = $NIL, we have that the laths that make up the boundary can be reported in two ways: using the laths L on the boundary of the mesh (see Exercise 3 in Section 2.2.1.3.2) and using the companion laths L' in the boundary face (see Exercise 4 in Section 2.2.1.3.2). It also requires less special handling for the transitions that involve boundary laths in the sense that only a CV primitive transition must be redefined, but this is at the expense of a different algorithm for tasks such as extracting the laths making up the boundary in both of the directions (compare Exercises 2 and 3 in Section 2.2.1.3.2). Note, though, that the method of incorporating the boundary that we have described does make it easy to obtain the laths making up the boundary in counterclockwise order for the corner and split-face lath data structures and in clockwise order for the split-vertex lath data structure, regardless of the implementation and whether the laths are in the mesh or in the boundary face. However, the process is complex for the reverse orders (see Exercises 7–14 in Section 2.2.1.3.2).

Contrary to claims by Joy et al, [973], the split-vertex lath data structure is the least suited to the incorporation of the boundary if we use just one lath (i.e., remove the companion lath) to represent elements on the boundary. The reason for their claim that the split-vertex lath data structure was the best suited for the incorporation of a boundary was that they retained the companion lath in their implementation. The implementation that we described was more consistent in the sense that all of the different lath data structures incorporated the boundary in the same way, and, in this case, we saw that the corner and split-face lath data structures are simpler in that the definitions of the transitions required the least amount of redefinition. In particular, in our implementation of the split-vertex lath data structure, almost all of the transitions needed to be redefined. However, in the case of the split-face and corner lath data structures we only needed to remove the companion lath that corresponded to the boundary face. Upon further reflection, this is not surprising as the face object is an explicit part of the split-face and corner lath data structures, and thus setting a transition to it to NIL is simple. In contrast, the face object is only implicitly represented in the split-vertex lath data structure, and hence the need for more complex methods for incorporating its presence.

It is worth mentioning that the three instances of the lath data structures (i.e., the split-face, split-vertex, and corner) that we described are not the only ones possible. In fact, given the presumed orientations of the laths in Figures 2.100, 2.102, and 2.104, we have a choice of eight possible structures as there are three possible combinations of two out of the three primitive entities, vertex, edge, and face. In particular, the remaining data structures are counterclockwise variants of the split-face (edge-face pair making use of CCF instead of CF), split-vertex (edge-vertex pair making use of CCV instead of CV), and corner (face-vertex making use of CCF with CCV instead of CF with CV) lath data structures, as well as two additional variants of the corner lath data structure that make use of a combination of a clockwise neighboring face (CF) with a counterclockwise neighboring vertex (CCV) and a combination of a counterclockwise neighboring face (CCF) with a clockwise neighboring vertex (CV).

The counterclockwise variants of the split-face (CE and CCF) and split-vertex (CE and CCV) lath data structures have the same duality properties (i.e., they are duals of each other) and execution time behavior as the clockwise variants except that their worst cases are obtained by interchanging clockwise and counterclockwise. The counterclockwise variant of the corner lath data structure (CCF and CCV) has the same desirable behavior as the clockwise variant of the corner lath data structure that we used. In particular, all transitions can be implemented in constant time when not positioned at the boundary of the mesh, and all queries can be executed in time proportional to the size of the result set. It is also a self-dual. The two additional variants of the corner lath data structure (CF with CCV and CCF with CV) are similar to the corner lath data structure in terms of behavior at the boundary of the mesh but do not have the constant time behavior for all transitions; nor are they strict duals of each other in the sense that the directions of the transitions are swapped in the dual. These two variants are termed the *corner* lath data structure* [973].

Note that, in the above, we assumed that the laths are oriented as in Figures 2.100, 2.102, and 2.104. If we also take into account the alternative orientations that are possible (i.e., two for each of the two possible lath data structures), then we have twice as many possible structures for a total of 16. Note that the difference between the additional eight data structures for the alternative orientation and the original ones lies in the implementation and semantics of the constituent transitions (see Exercises 4–6 in Section 2.2.1.3.1). Otherwise, they are identical to the original ones in terms of the transitions and directions that define them (e.g., the corner lath data structure is defined in terms of the CF and CV transitions for both orientations), as well as their execution time behavior and duality properties.

Besides self-duality and ignoring boundary considerations, the corner lath data structure consisting of face-vertex pairs and the quad-edge interpretation of the winged-edge data structure consisting of edges have other similarities. In particular, they have the same execution time behavior, enabling all of the transitions to be implemented in constant time and all queries to be executed in time proportional to the size of the query result set. Moreover, while the quad-edge data structure associates four singly linked circular lists (one for each of the faces adjacent to an edge and one for each of vertices incident at the same edge) in the same direction with each edge, the corner lath representation associates two singly linked circular lists (one for the vertex that makes up a face-vertex lath and one for the face that makes up the same face-vertex lath) in the same direction with each lath. However, since there are two face-vertex laths for each edge, the total number of elements in the two sets of circular lists associated with each element of the corner lath data structure is the same as the total number of elements in the four sets of circular lists associated with each element of the quad-edge data structure. In fact, given these observations, we could have also used the term *split-quad* to refer to the corner lath data structure to highlight the connection between it and the quad-edge data structure. In particular, in this way we see that the manner in which the corner lath representation is formed is equivalent to splitting an edge in the quad-edge interpretation of the winged-edge data structure into two in a manner analogous to the way in which an edge in the more general formulation of the winged-edge data structure was split into two parts, thereby creating the half-edge data structure [196]. In fact, perhaps a more appropriate name is *half-quad*.

Interestingly, the variants of the corner lath data structure, where the direction of the traversals of the transitions are not the same, do not lead to constant-time behavior for all transitions, which is analogous to the behavior of the variant of the quad-edge data structure where the direction of the two singly linked circular lists associated with the two vertices incident at the same edge and the direction of the two singly linked circular lists associated with the two faces adjacent to the same edge are not the same.

The execution time behavior of the split-face and split-vertex representations is similar to that of the D-CEL [1322] (see Section 2.2.1.2) where only two singly linked circular lists, one for each of the faces associated with the edge (D-CEL-face) or equivalently, under an alternative interpretation of the wings of the winged-edge data structure, one for each of the vertices at which the edge is incident (D-CEL-vertex) and in the same direction instead of four, are associated with each element of the winged-edge data structure. In fact, the D-CEL-face (D-CEL-vertex) data structure can be viewed as representing each edge e as a pair of edge-face (edge-vertex) laths that are companions of each other and that are elements of the split-face (split-vertex) lath data structure. The difference between the D-CEL and its lath counterparts is that the transitions in the D-CEL are in terms of edges rather than laths, which means that there is no need in the D-CEL for the transitions to the mutually companion laths. Given lath L, and letting $V(L)$, $F(L)$, $E(L)$, and $CE(L)$ denote its associated vertex, face, edge, and companion lath, respectively, Figure 2.108(a, b) shows the relationship between the two possible variants of the D-CEL and the corresponding split-face and split-vertex lath data structures, respectively, using the various interpretations of the wings of the winged-edge data structure in Figure 2.89.

Ignoring boundary considerations, the storage required for the lath data structures can be shown to be essentially the same as that for the winged-edge data structures. In particular, the winged-edge data structures have one record per edge, while the lath data structures have one record per lath (regardless of whether the lath corresponds to an edge-face, edge-vertex, or face-vertex pair), which is equal to twice the number of edges. However, each lath contains just three items of information, while each record of the winged-edge data structure contains between five and nine items of information, depending on whether we are dealing with an oriented variant of the winged-edge data structure. Recall that the oriented variants do not record any information about the vertices incident at the edge or about the faces adjacent to the edge. The three items of information in the lath account for half the pointers and half the vertices in the winged-edge data structure. Thus, it would seem that the oriented variants of the winged-edge data structure are slightly more efficient spacewise since the number of laths is twice the number of edges, which means that the amount of storage required by the lath data structure exceeds that required by the winged-edge data structure by a quantity equal to the number of edges.

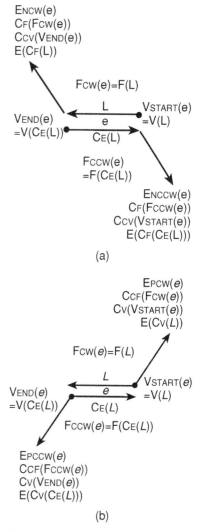

Figure 2.108
Examples of (a) D-CEL-face and (b) D-CEL-vertex data structures and the physical interpretations of their fields using the various interpretations of the wing of the winged-edge data structure in Figure 2.89, thereby yielding analogs of the (a) split-face and (b) split-vertex lath data structures.

Of course, since the oriented variant of the winged-edge data structure that we assumed does not store the identities of the vertices or faces explicitly, some queries are rather cumbersome. For example, in order to obtain a vertex that is represented implicitly in the oriented winged-edge data structure, we must retrieve all of the edges that are incident at it. On the other hand, the lath-based data structures do not store the identities of the edges or faces explicitly, and thus other queries are cumbersome. For example, in order to obtain a face that is represented implicitly in the lath-based data structure, we must retrieve the laths for all of its constituent vertices, while the identity of the associated faces is recorded explicitly in the nonoriented variant of the winged-edge data structures (two of them). Thus, the two data structures effectively use the same amount of storage, once we also store the associated face explicitly with the lath-based data structures, and we observe that the two vertices associated with each edge in the winged-edge data structure are distributed into the two companion laths in each of the lath-based data structures.

We have classified the lath representation as vertex-based. However, from duality considerations, we see that we can also define an equivalent face-based lath data structure where each lath contains a pointer to the face associated with the lath instead of the vertex. Once again, we will have three different representations identical to the split-face, split-vertex, and corner lath data structures. The only drawback of such face-based representations is that the identities of the edges and vertices that make up the faces will only be represented implicitly. Therefore, in order to identify the vertex or edge associated with a specific edge-vertex pair, we will need to retrieve all the laths that it comprises and look up the associated faces, which will enable us to identify the edge and vertex in terms of their adjacent and incident faces. This is not surprising given that the primitive entity of the redefined lath representations is the face, and hence their characterization as being face-based. Since we do not usually represent an object by its constituent faces, the face-based lath representations are not very useful.

At this point, we observe that the manner in which each edge is represented by two unique elements (i.e., a unique edge-face pair, a unique edge-vertex pair, and a unique face-vertex pair) in each of the variants of the lath data structures is reminiscent of the half-edge data structure described in Section 2.2.1.2. In particular, recall that the half-edge data structure was one of the methods proposed to resolve one of the drawbacks of the winged-edge representation—that is, the need to attribute a direction to an edge in order to be able to distinguish between the two faces that are adjacent to the edge, whereas in reality the edge has no direction. Another way of describing this drawback is to point out that, in the winged-edge representation, the single edge record serves a dual role of providing both directional information and information about the faces adjacent to the edge.

In fact, it is not too hard to see that the half-edge data structure that is based on a traversal of the edges that make up the faces is very closely related to the corner lath data structure. In particular, for each face-vertex lath L, the corner lath data structure records the transitions to both the next lath $\mathrm{C_F}(L)$ along the face F associated with L and to the next lath $\mathrm{C_V}(L)$ incident at the vertex V associated with L, and both in the same direction (i.e., clockwise in this example).

The key to the close relationship is the observation that the transition to the next lath $\mathrm{C_V}(L)$ incident at V is equivalent to the transition to the companion half-edge of the previous half-edge $\mathrm{C_E}(\mathrm{CC_F}(L))$ along F (see Figure 2.109). Recalling that, given half-edge L, the half-edge data structure is defined in terms of $\mathrm{C_E}(L)$, $\mathrm{C_F}(L)$, and $\mathrm{CC_F}(L)$ leads to the desired result as we have formulated $\mathrm{C_V}(L)$ in terms of two of the existing half-edge primitives (i.e., $\mathrm{C_E}(L)$ and $\mathrm{CC_F}(L)$). Alternatively, we can show that the transition to the companion half-edge $\mathrm{C_E}(L)$ of half-edge L is equivalent to the transition to the next lath $\mathrm{C_V}(\mathrm{C_F}(L))$ along the face associated with the next lath $\mathrm{C_F}(L)$ incident at V. Similarly, we know that we can obtain the transition to the half-edge $\mathrm{CC_F}(L)$ by simply following $\mathrm{C_E}(\mathrm{C_V}(L)) = \mathrm{C_V}(\mathrm{C_F}(\mathrm{C_V}(L)))$. Recalling that, given

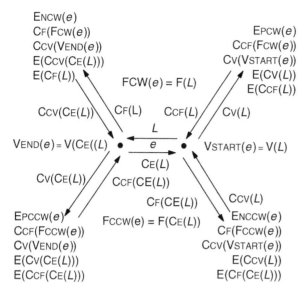

Figure 2.109
Example showing the relationship of the half-edge and corner lath data structures in terms of the physical interpretations of their fields using the various interpretations of the wing of the winged-edge data structure in Figure 2.89.

lath L, the clockwise variant of the corner lath data structure is defined in terms of $C_F(L)$ and $C_V(L)$ leads to the desired result as we have formulated both $C_E(L)$ and $C_{CF}(L)$ in terms of the two existing primitives of the clockwise variant of the corner lath data structure (i.e., $C_F(L)$ and $C_V(L)$).

A similar relationship can be obtained for the half-edge data structure that is based on a traversal of the edges that are incident at the vertices described in Exercise 11 of Section 2.2.1.2 (see Exercise 1 of this section). At this point, let us reemphasize that the key difference between the clockwise variant of the corner lath data structure and the half-edge data structure is that we can obtain L's companion lath by applying the pair of operations $C_V(C_F(L))$ in the corner lath data structure. This enables us to avoid the need to store the transition C_E to the companion explicitly, as is usually done in the half-edge data structure, although we have already pointed out that this can be avoided by storing the two half-edges in consecutive locations. Note also that, as in the corner lath data structure, there is no need to store the identity of the associated face explicitly in the half-edge data structure.

From the above discussion, it should be clear that the edge-based methods are simply combinations of the vertex-based methods where, usually, a pair of laths is associated with each edge. Moreover, as we pointed out before, just as there are a number of other possible lath data structures that can be obtained by varying the orientations of the laths and the pair of transitions that are recorded, there are also many other possible ways of combining pairs of laths to obtain variants of the winged-edge family of data structures. The variants that we have presented are the ones that find principal use. This is primarily due to their ability to respond to the basic queries, regardless of the order (i.e., clockwise and counterclockwise, or equivalently, next and preceding) in time proportional to the size of the query result set. Not all possible variants have this property. For example, as we point out in Section 2.2.1.2, a variant of the quad-edge data structure that keeps track of the transitions to the next edges along each of the two adjacent vertices for each edge, while keeping track of the transitions to the preceding edges along each of the two adjacent faces for each edge, does not have this execution time property for both directions. In particular, the execution time is proportional to the size of the result query set for just one of the orders.

Exercise

1. Show how the half-edge-vertex data structure (i.e., the vertex variant of the half-edge data structure) is closely related to the counterclockwise variant of the corner lath data structure In this case, recall from Exercise 11 of Section 2.2.1.2 that, given half-edge L, the vertex variant of the half-edge data structure is defined in terms of $Cv(L)$ and $Ccv(L)$.

2.2.1.4 Voronoi Diagrams, Delaunay Graphs, and Delaunay Triangulations

In Sections 2.2.1.2 and 2.2.1.3, we pointed out that an advantage of the quad-edge interpretation of the winged-edge data structure over the other interpretations (e.g., the winged-edge-face and winged-edge-vertex) is that the quad-edge data structure is a self-dual. As an example of where this duality is useful, consider the Voronoi diagram [1941] (also known as a Thiessen polygon [1870] and a Dirichlet domain [497]) and its dual, the Delaunay graph (e.g., [1424]), as shown in Figure 2.110. Briefly, given a set of points (termed *sites*), a Voronoi diagram is a partition of the plane into regions so that each point in a region is closer to its region's site than to any other site. These regions are termed *Voronoi regions* or *Voronoi cells*. For example, Figure 2.110(a) is the Voronoi diagram for the given set of points shown with solid circles, while the vertices of the diagram are shown with hollow circles.

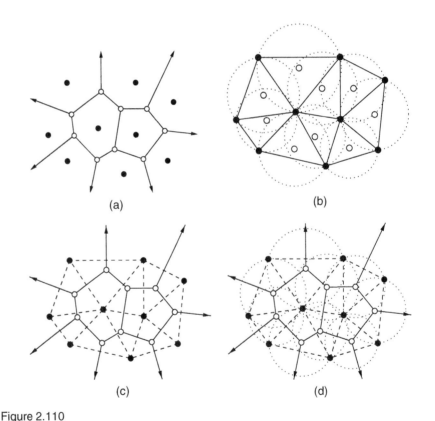

(a)   (b)

(c)   (d)

Figure 2.110
(a) Example Voronoi diagram, (b) its dual Delaunay triangulation and the corresponding circumcircles (shown with broken lines), (c) the result of superposing the Delaunay triangulation (shown with broken lines) on the Voronoi diagram, (d) the result of superposing the Delaunay triangulation (shown with broken lines) and the corresponding circumcircles (shown with broken lines) on the Voronoi diagram. The hollow circles denote the centers of the circumcircles and the vertices of the Voronoi diagram. The arrowheads on some of the edges of the Voronoi diagram correspond to "infinite" edges that meet at some infinite vertex.

A Voronoi diagram has many applications. For example, if we consider the sites as the locations of fire stations, then, using the Voronoi diagram, we can determine which fire station is the closest (using the Euclidean distance—that is, as the crow flies) to any point. Another example places distribution centers at the sites of the Voronoi diagram, and, as a result, we can tell what is the closest distribution center (as the crow flies) to a store located at any point. The process of determining the closest site to a query point is usually implemented by making use of an index on the regions or the boundaries that make up the Voronoi diagram (e.g., the K-structure and layered dag discussed in Section 2.1.3 or the representations discussed in Section 2.2.2) and executing a variant of a point location algorithm on the query point. These methods generally have a logarithmic behavior because they are based on sorting. Alternatively, we could also use a graph approach. In this case, we represent the Voronoi diagram as a graph where each site is a node, and there is an edge between any two sites whose Voronoi regions share an edge. Using this approach, finding the nearest site to a query point q is achieved by starting at an arbitrary site and making a transition along the edge that leads us to a site that is the closest to q. The algorithm terminates once we are at a site p such that no further transition can be made, and thus p is the nearest site. The drawback to this approach is that its worst-case execution time is $O(n)$, where n is the number of sites. Note that this approach to point location can be characterized as one that uses the A*-algorithm [1594], where the heuristic function that serves as the estimate of the cost from a given site s to the ultimate closest site corresponding to the Voronoi region v_q that contains q is the Euclidean distance from s to q.

The graph representation of the neighbor structure of the Voronoi diagram is called a *Delaunay graph*. As mentioned above, the Delaunay graph of a point set P is an embedding of the dual graph of the Voronoi diagram of P. It can be shown that the Delaunay graph of a planar point set is a plane graph (e.g., [196, Theorem 9.5]). Given a planar point set P, all the faces of the Delaunay graph of P are triangles if no four elements of P (i.e., sites of the Voronoi diagram of P) are cocircular. To see this, we observe that the vertices of the Voronoi diagram of P are equidistant from the sites of all of the Voronoi regions whose edges are incident at them. In particular, if a vertex v of the Voronoi diagram of P is a vertex for the Voronoi regions for the sites $p_1, p_2, \ldots, p_k$, then the corresponding face f in the Delaunay graph of P has $p_1, p_2, \ldots, p_k$ as its vertices, and they lie in a circle around v as they are all equidistant from v. In fact, f is convex and is a triangle if it consists of just three sites. When all the faces of the Delaunay graph are triangles, then we have a special case of the Delaunay graph known as the *Delaunay triangulation (DT)* [474]. Of course, a triangulation can be obtained for a Delaunay graph when there are four elements of P that are cocircular by adding edges as needed, although it is clear that the resulting triangulation will not be unique.

An equivalent way of defining the Delaunay triangulation of a set of points S is as a triangulation through the points in S so that none of the points in S are in the circumcircles of any other triangle (known as the *circle property*). The Delaunay triangulation is unique as long as no local configuration of four or more points in S is cocircular. Such a Delaunay triangulation is said to be *nondegenerate*, and likewise for a Voronoi diagram with sites S. For example, Figure 2.110(b) is the Delaunay triangulation for the set of points given in Figure 2.110(a), where the circumcircles of the triangles are shown using broken lines, while the centers of the circumcircles are shown with hollow circles. The Delaunay triangulation has several interesting properties that make it a desirable triangulation:

1. An edge between two points q and r in S is an edge of the Delaunay triangulation of S if and only if there exists at least one circle c through q and r such that no other point in S lies inside c (termed the *disc property*). This property is related to the circle property in the sense that satisfaction of the circle property implies satisfaction of the disc property.

2. It maximizes the minimum interior vertex angle, thereby avoiding small angles that cause distortion (termed the *minimum angle property*). This property can be stated more formally as follows: The Delaunay triangulation produces the lexicographically

largest possible nondecreasing sequence of angles in any triangulation of a given set of points. Thus if $a_1 \le a_2 \le \cdots \le a_i \le \cdots$ is the sequence of angles in a Delaunay triangulation and if $b_1 \le b_2 \le \cdots \le b_i \le \cdots$ is the sequence of angles in another triangulation of the same set of points, then there exists an i such that $a_i > b_i$.

3. Every interior edge of a Delaunay triangulation satisfies the *angle property*, which can be stated as follows: Let prq and qsp be two opposite interior angles of an arbitrary triangulation. The vertices $prqs$ (in that order) constitute the edge quadrilateral Q of the edge pq. Edge pq satisfies the angle property if it connects the opposite interior angles of Q having the largest sum—that is, if the angle rooted at r facing edge pq plus the angle rooted at s facing edge pq is smaller than or equal to the angle rooted at p plus the angle rooted at q (see also Exercise 4).

4. It is biased against large circumcircles.

5. It is biased against "thin" triangles.

6. The triangles are as close as possible to being equiangular.

7. It effectively chooses edges that connect natural neighbors. This means that the data points corresponding to the vertices of the Delaunay triangulation are closer to their mutual circumcenter than is any other data point. Thus, the Delaunay triangulation is a form of local optimization.

As pointed out above, the Delaunay triangulation is a special case of the Delaunay graph, which is the geometric dual of the Voronoi diagram. The actual physical interpretation of the duality is that the centers of the circumcircles of the triangles in the Delaunay triangulation (of which there is one for each face) serve as the vertices of the Voronoi diagram, while the sites of the Voronoi diagram (of which there is one per face) serve as the vertices of the Delaunay triangulation. Figure 2.110(c) shows the dual graph by superimposing the Delaunay triangulation (shown with broken lines) on top of the Voronoi diagram, while Figure 2.110(d) adds the circumcenters (shown with hollow circles) and circumcircles (shown with broken lines). In both cases, the centers of the circumcircles (which are also the vertices of the Voronoi diagram) are shown with hollow circles. Notice that the dual of the "infinite edges" of the Voronoi diagram (i.e., the edges that extend to infinity) are the edges of the convex hull[37] of the Delaunay triangulation (equivalently of its vertices), which are also elements of the Delaunay triangulation. We can imagine that these infinite edges of the Voronoi diagram all meet at some common point at infinity. This "infinite vertex" of the Voronoi diagram is the dual of the exterior face of the Delaunay triangulation. Although we cannot draw this infinite vertex, we show its implicit existence by attaching outgoing arrowheads to the infinite edges in Figure 2.110(a, c, d). It is interesting to observe that this additional "infinite vertex" of the Voronoi diagram is what makes the Voronoi diagram a compact two-manifold (and likewise for the exterior face of the Delaunay triangulation).

Exercises

1. Given a Delaunay triangulation, write an algorithm to construct its Voronoi diagram.

2. There are several ways of computing a Delaunay triangulation. They differ in part on the basis of the properties of the Delaunay triangulation that they exploit. For example, the following method [1268] makes use of the circle property of the Delaunay triangulation (i.e., that none of the points in the point set that is being triangulated is in the circumcircles of any other triangle in the triangulation). The method starts by computing the convex hull of the point set and then pushes into a queue each edge e whose orientation is such that the rest of the point set is to the left of e. While the queue is not empty, perform the following steps:

   (a) Pop an edge ab from the queue.

   (b) Find the point c to the left of ab so that the circle through a, b, and c is empty. Such an edge is guaranteed to exist by virtue of the circle property.

---

[37] See the definition in footnote 11 in Section 2.1.3.2.

(c) If ac is not in the Delaunay triangulation, then insert ac into the Delaunay triangulation, and push ac in the queue.

(d) If cb is not in the Delaunay triangulation, then insert cb into the Delaunay triangulation, and push cb in the queue.

Prove that, given a point set with v vertices, the algorithm takes $O(v^2)$ time. How can you reduce the execution time of the algorithm?

3. In Exercise 2, we showed how to compute the Delaunay triangulation in an inward manner by starting with the convex hull and adding edges while proceeding inwards. An alternative approach works in an outward manner [1964] as follows. Initially, start with one large triangle t that contains the entire point set. Select one point p at random and join p to the vertices of t. Now, apply the following algorithm to the remaining points in arbitrary order, starting with point q.

(a) Find all existing triangles whose circumcircles contain q. This can be done by finding the existing triangle abc (with vertices a, b, and c) that contains q and walking along its edges.

    i. If the circumcircle of triangle abd (i.e., adjacent to abc along edge ab) contains q, then recursively apply these steps to the triangles adjacent to abd along edges ad and bd.

    ii. Otherwise, apply this step to the edges adjacent to edge ab in triangle abc.

(b) Form a polygon from the union of the triangles found in step (a) and remove its interior edges.

(c) Form new triangles in the interior of the polygon obtained in step (b) by joining q to all of the polygon's vertices.

Some of the steps in the algorithm are justified as follows. The triangles found in step (a) are the only triangles that are affected by the insertion of q since the circumcircles of the remaining triangles are empty and thus belong to the new Delaunay triangulation as well. The new polygon formed in step (b) is star shaped since, for each edge ab and triangle abc that have been removed, q lies in the region bounded by ab and the circumcircle of abc, which means that q can "see" edges ac and bc. Watson [1964] claims that the circumcircles of the triangles formed in step (c) will not contain any of the remaining points as these points all lie on circumcircles that do not contain q and thus the resulting triangulation is a Delaunay triangulation. An alternative way of showing that step (c) yields a Delaunay triangulation is as follows. From step (a), we know that all of the edges that lie on the boundary of the star-shaped polygon are elements of the Delaunay triangulation. However, we must prove that the newly added edges from q to the vertices of the star-shaped polygon formed in step (c) are elements of the Delaunay triangulation. We want to show that the triangulation process in step (c) yields a Delaunay triangulation of the entire set of points. In particular, we want to show that the edges chosen in step (c) are Delaunay edges. We use contradiction. Consider convex quadrilateral $qdef$, where d, e, and f are adjacent vertices of the star-shaped polygon such that edge qe is not an edge of the Delaunay triangulation. We are not interested in nonconvex polygons as they have a unique triangulation. Let us swap qe with the opposite diagonal df of $qdef$. The circumcircle C of triangle def cannot be empty as, otherwise, it would have been a triangle of the Delaunay triangulation before the addition of q. C cannot contain q as, in this case, it would have been eliminated by step (a). Therefore, C must contain other points, which means that we cannot obtain a Delaunay triangulation of the star-shaped region by the swap operation. This contradicts the assumption that the original triangulation obtained in step (c) is not a Delaunay triangulation. Prove that given a point set with v vertices, the algorithm takes $O(v^2)$ time.

4. As we pointed out in the text, the angle property can be used to define the Delaunay triangulation in two dimensions in terms of the values of the sums of the interior angles that share each of the edge of a triangulation. The following definition of the Delaunay triangulation in two dimensions is based on similar reasoning. In particular, for points u and v, let us define α to be the largest angle seen by other points in the dataset S. That is, $\alpha = \max_{y \in S - \{u,v\}} \angle uyv$, and let $p \in S - \{u, v\}$ be the point such that $\alpha = \angle upv$. Note that the line passing through uv divides $S - \{u, v\}$ into two parts. Let S_p denote the points in $S - \{u, v\}$ that are on the same side of p with respect to line uv, and let O_p denote the set of points in $S - \{u, v\}$ that are on the other side of line uv. We have $O_p \cup S_p = S - \{u, v\}$. Prove that $\forall w \in O_p, \angle uwp \leq \pi - \alpha$ if and only if edge uv belongs to the Delaunay triangulation.

5. Suppose that you are given a two-dimensional polygonal map T (i.e., a set of edges and vertices) that is also a Voronoi diagram. How would you obtain the locations of its sites? What is the complexity of your algorithm? Assume that the vertices are in general position, which means that all Voronoi vertices have degree 3—that is, there are no sets of four or more sites that are cocircular, and some face of the Voronoi diagram has at least two vertices.

6. Repeat Exercise 5 for the more general case of the Voronoi diagram where the vertices are not required to be in general position (i.e., the vertices may have a degree higher than 3). What is the complexity of your algorithm?

2.2.1.5 Constrained and Conforming Delaunay Triangulations

Although the Delaunay triangulation is formally defined over a point set, in many applications (e.g., finite-element analysis, solutions to partial differential equations) the point set is usually defined by some shape. The fact that the Delaunay triangulation is defined over a point set means that the boundary triangles of the Delaunay triangulation are those with an edge on the convex hull of the point set. This has the effect of restricting the boundaries for the shapes for which we can compute a Delaunay triangulation to be convex. Therefore, if we simply compute the Delaunay triangulation of the vertices of a nonconvex polygon, we may find that not every edge of the polygon will be on the convex hull of the vertices and thus will not necessarily be a member of the Delaunay triangulation of the vertices. For example, Figure 2.111(b) is the Delaunay triangulation

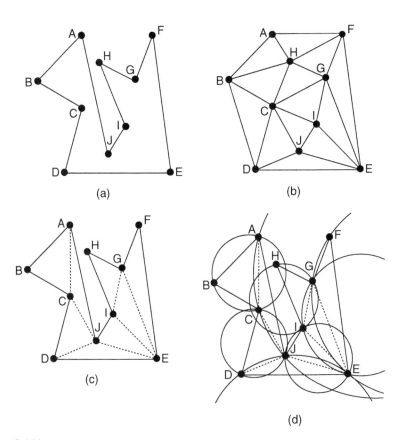

Figure 2.111
(a) Example nonconvex polygon, (b) the Delaunay triangulation of its vertices, (c) its constrained Delaunay triangulation (additional edges shown with broken lines), and (d) the result of superposing the circumcircles of the triangles of the constrained Delaunay triangulation.

of the vertices of the nonconvex polygon in Figure 2.111(a). Notice that edges AJ and HI of the original nonconvex polygon are not in the Delaunay triangulation of its vertices.

Often we wish to find the Delaunay triangulation of a nonconvex shape so that every edge of the polygon is a member of the Delaunay triangulation of the polygon. In fact, we want to handle the more general case where the point set defines a graph with edges that are straight lines in the plane and that need not necessarily be connected. Actually, the graph may even have isolated vertices as well as vertices with degree 1. The result is termed a *Planar Straight Line Graph* (PSLG) and is the subject of the rest of this discussion. Of course, the PSLG includes polygons (both convex and nonconvex) as well as polygonal maps (i.e., polygonal subdivisions). The requirement that every edge of the PSLG P be a member of the Delaunay triangulation of the point set of P is satisfied by the use of the constrained Delaunay triangulation [1131] or the conforming Delaunay triangulation [1600].

The constrained Delaunay triangulation [1131] of a PSLG P with vertex set Q is an adaptation of the Delaunay triangulation that modifies the circle property so that the interior of the circumcircle c of every triangle t contains no point of Q that is visible to all the three vertices of t. In other words, any vertices V that are in c cannot be seen by any of the vertices of t due to the existence of some additional edge that passes through t. This property is known as the *modified empty circle property*. For example, Figure 2.111(c) is the constrained Delaunay triangulation of the nonconvex polygon in Figure 2.111(a), while Figure 2.111(d) shows the circumcircles of the various triangles in the constrained Delaunay triangulation. Notice that the circumcircle of triangle ABC contains vertex H, which is not visible from A, B, and C because it is blocked by edge AJ, which passes through it. Similarly, the circumcircle of triangle GHI contains vertex C, which is not visible from G, H, and I because it is blocked by edge AJ, which passes through it.

The constrained Delaunay triangulation is unique [1127]. For an arbitrary PSLG with v vertices, Chew [361] gives an $O(v \log v)$ time algorithm to obtain its constrained Delaunay triangulation. This is optimal because, even when we ignore the constraints, if the vertices form a convex polygon, then a sorted order can be derived from any triangulation of the points and the constrained Delaunay triangulation is one instance of a triangulation. The lower bound follows from the well-known $O(v \log v)$ bound on sorting v points.

The conforming Delaunay triangulation [1600] inserts additional points, termed *Steiner points*, to ensure that all the edges of the PSLG P are members of the Delaunay triangulation of the point set of P. The Steiner points need only be placed on the existing edges of the PSLG P. This process is known as *edge refinement*. For example, Figure 2.112 is the conforming Delaunay triangulation of the nonconvex polygon in Figure 2.111(a). Three Steiner points K, L, and M have been added.

There are a number of algorithms for constructing a conforming Delaunay triangulation with different complexities in terms of execution time and the number of Steiner points that are inserted, which affects the quality of the resulting triangulation (e.g., [545, 1328, 1333, 1592, 1600]). Note that all of these methods make use of the disc property (i.e., an edge e of a PSLG P with vertex set V is an edge of the Delaunay triangulation of V if and only if there exists a circle around e that contains none of the points of V in its interior) to determine how to split an existing edge of the PSLG. For example, no particular algorithm was used to select the Steiner points in the conforming Delaunay triangulation in Figure 2.112, and, in fact, it may be possible to obtain a conforming Delaunay triangulation with just two Steiner points.

Exercises

1. Give an algorithm to obtain the constrained Delaunay triangulation of a nonconvex polygon.

2. Give an algorithm to obtain the conforming Delaunay triangulation of a nonconvex polygon.

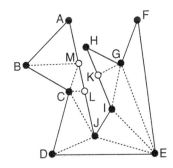

Figure 2.112
The conforming Delaunay triangulation of the nonconvex polygon in Figure 2.111(a) obtained by adding Steiner points K, L, and M. Only edges of the conforming Delaunay triangulation that lie within the polygon are shown. Edges of the conforming Delaunay triangulation that lie outside of the polygon have been removed.

2.2.1.6 Delaunay Tetrahedralizations

Neither the Voronoi diagram nor its geometric dual, the Delaunay graph and the special case of a Delaunay triangulation , is restricted to planar point sets. Both can be defined in arbitrary dimensions. For example, in three dimensions, the topological analog of the Delaunay triangulation is the Delaunay tetrahedralization, where the Delaunay graph is a tetrahedralization whenever no five sites are cospherical (i.e., lie on a sphere). Nevertheless, there are a number of properties of triangulations that do not generalize to three dimensions or higher. In the rest of this section, we examine some of the properties of triangulations that were discussed above that do not hold for tetrahedralizations and, therefore, also do not hold for the d-dimensional analog of the triangulation.

One of the biggest differences is that, unlike the planar case where the number of triangles in the triangulation of a particular point set is constant, the size of the tetrahedralization of a particular point set is not constant. For example, in two dimensions, a set of four points can be triangulated in two ways, depending on the choice of the diagonal of the quadrilateral formed by their convex hull. However, regardless of the diagonal that is chosen, there are only two triangles in the triangulation. In contrast, in three dimensions, for a given point set, the number of tetrahedra can vary dramatically. For example, consider a set of five points. It can have a number of different tetrahedralizations, some consisting of two tetrahedra and others consisting of three tetrahedra. In particular, Figure 2.113(a) shows a tetrahedralization of the point set {a,b,c,d,e} that yields the two tetrahedra (a,b,c,d) and (a,b,c,e) resulting from the sharing of triangle (a,b,c). On the other hand, Figure 2.113(b) shows a tetrahedralization of the same point set that yields the three tetrahedra (a,b,d,e), (a,c,d,e), and (b,c,d,e) resulting from the sharing of edge (d,e). Although in many real-world applications the number of tetrahedra for a given point set of size v is reasonable (e.g., $O(v)$ [1328, 1820]), examples can be constructed that have $O(v^2)$ tetrahedra [1328] and even a superlinear number of tetrahedra [563].

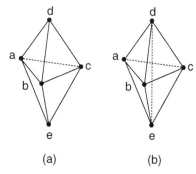

Figure 2.113
Example tetrahedralizations of a set of five points: (a) two tetrahedra resulting from the sharing of triangle abc and (b) three tetrahedra resulting from the sharing of edge de.

Another important difference is that there is no obvious generalization of the constrained Delaunay triangulation to three dimensions. It is clear that, given an arbitrary point set, we can always find a tetrahedralization. However, when the point set forms the three-dimensional analog of the PSLG (Planar Straight Line Graph), termed a *Piecewise Linear Complex* (PLC),[38] we cannot always find a tetrahedralization without having to add points (i.e., Steiner points) on the boundary or in the interior so that all edges of the tetrahedra are edges of the PLC (i.e., construct a conforming tetrahedralization regardless of whether it satisfies the Delaunay constraints). For example, Shewchuk [1752] points out that the PLC formed by the three nonintersecting line segments in Figure 2.114 cannot be tetrahedralized without some of the edges of the tetrahedra intersecting some of the edges of the PLC. In particular, any tetrahedron formed by choosing any four of the six vertices will be intersected by one of the three edges of the PLC. Therefore, the manner in which the remaining tetrahedra are formed is irrelevant, and thus this complex is not tetrahedralizable without the addition of Steiner points so that all edges of the tetrahedra are edges of the PLC. Deciding whether a set of line segments is tetrahedralizable without any Steiner points is an open problem [1328]. Murphy, Mount, and Gable [1328, 1329] present a point placement strategy for obtaining a conforming Delaunay tetrahedralization for a PLC P that, unlike other approaches (e.g., [1296, 1753]), makes no restrictions on the angles of P.

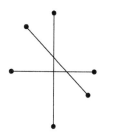

Figure 2.114
Example Piecewise Linear Complex consisting of three nonintersecting lines in three-dimensional space that cannot be tetrahedralized without some of the edges of the tetrahedra intersecting some of the edges of the PLC.

Even when the point set forms a polyhedron, an example can be given of a polyhedron that cannot be tetrahedralized without the addition of Steiner points so that all edges of

---

[38] The PLC is the most general adaptation of the PSLG to three dimensions. Unlike other definitions of three-dimensional "flat" objects that make various assumptions such as that every face of the object has simply connected boundaries or that the object's surface is a two-manifold, it makes no such assumptions. Thus, it is possible for three or more faces to be incident at an edge, for faces to have polygonal holes, to have isolated vertices and edges, and so forth. The only essential requirement is that the object be a topological complex, which means that, if faces intersect, then they must intersect along an edge; if edges intersect, then they must intersect at a vertex, and so forth.

the tetrahedra are edges of the polyhedron. Such a polyhedron is the Schönhardt Twisted Prism [1694], whose top view is shown in Figure 2.115. This polyhedron is formed by taking a prism whose top and bottom are triangles, followed by slightly twisting one of the triangle faces in its plane, and concluding by triangulating the three remaining faces that were quadrilaterals. These faces are triangulated by adding the reflex diagonals (i.e., the diagonals whose interior dihedral angle is greater than 180 degrees) so that the result is a nonconvex polyhedron. The twisted prism is constructed in such a way that the tetrahedra formed by taking any four of its vertices will have an edge that lies outside the polyhedron. In fact, since each vertex has degree 4 and there are only six vertices, only three tetrahedra can be formed as there is only one unconnected vertex for each vertex. However, these three tetrahedra do not cover the space spanned by the polyhedron, and thus the polyhedron is not tetrahedralizable unless Steiner points are inserted either on its boundary or in its interior. Deciding whether a polyhedron is tetrahedralizable with less than k Steiner points ($k > 1$) is NP-complete [1593] (recall footnote 6 in Section 2.1.2.1). For some algorithms for tetrahedralizing a nonconvex polyhedron by adding Steiner points, see [120, 335, 341, 959].

Figure 2.115
Example polyhedron consisting of a prism whose top and bottom are triangles, where the top triangle has been slightly twisted, and the three remaining faces that were quadrilaterals are diagonalized so that the resulting polyhedron is nonconvex.

Exercises

1. As we pointed out earlier, the Voronoi diagram is not restricted to planar point sets. It can be defined in arbitrary dimensions and likewise for its geometric dual, the Delaunay graph and the special case of a Delaunay triangulation. . The d-dimensional elements that are topologically equivalent to the triangle and a triangulation are known as *simplexes* and *simplicial complexes*, respectively (e.g., [870]). Describe the extension to d dimensions of the special cases of the Delaunay graph that yield constructs that are topological analogs of the Delaunay triangulation.

2. Suppose that you are given a point set S with $d + 2$ points in a d-dimensional space. The d-dimensional analog of the triangle is known as a d-dimensional simplex and is the convex hull of $d + 1$ points, while the d-dimensional topological equivalent of the triangulation is known as a d-dimensional simplicial complex (or *simplex* and *simplicial complex*, respectively, for short if there is no confusion about the dimensionality of the domain of the point set). How many different d-dimensional triangulations (simplicial complexes) of S are possible in terms of the number of d-dimensional simplexes in them?

2.2.1.7 Applications of the Winged-Edge Data Structure (Triangle Table, Corner Table)

The winged-edge data structure, as well as its variants (e.g., the quad-edge data structure), are not restricted to the representation of the surfaces of three-dimensional objects that are two-manifolds (e.g., [501], where they are applied to three-dimensional subdivisions). In particular, these representations can be applied to two-manifolds in any dimension. The key to their applicability is the cyclic nature of the neighborhood of any vertex or any face in a two-manifold (see Exercise 1), which can be represented with a simple linked list using the primitives "next" and "previous." In our examples with surfaces of three-dimensional objects, we have captured this cyclic nature by requiring that the two-manifolds be orientable and thus used the orientation concepts of clockwise and counterclockwise.[39] It is important to note that the winged-edge data structure and its variants can also be used to represent a nonorientable two-manifold surface (i.e.. a surface with no means of distinguishing between an inner and an outer face [870]), such as a Klein bottle or a Möbius strip. In this case, the orientation concepts of clockwise and counterclockwise are replaced by the simpler cyclic concepts of next and previous.

---

[39] Although these orientation concepts can be generalized to d dimensions, where the orientation of $d + 1$ points is defined to be the sign of the $(d + 1) \times (d + 1)$ determinant of homogeneous point coordinates [540], they no longer capture the cyclic nature (i.e., when $d \geq 3$). Thus, more complex representations would be required.

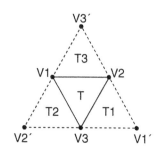

Figure 2.116
The physical representation of a sample triangle table entry.

As an application of the utility of the winged-edge data structure and its variants, recall that, in Section 2.2.1.4, we point out that the quad-edge data structure can be used to represent Voronoi diagrams and Delaunay triangulations in the plane, which are planar subdivisions. In the case of planar subdivisions where all the faces are triangles, we can use a simpler variation known as the *triangle table method* [714, 806] (see also Exercise 3). In this case, the basic unit is the triangle instead of the edge. In particular, we represent each triangle t by a six-tuple containing pointers to the three vertices that make up t and pointers to the entries in the triangle table to the three triangles that are adjacent to t along the edges of t. In addition, we have a vertex table that contains a pointer to the entry in the triangle table of one of the triangles that are incident at the vertex. Note that the triangle table stores the edges that make up each triangle implicitly as they can be derived from the vertices. The physical representation of a sample triangle table entry corresponding to triangle T, its three vertices V1, V2, and V3, and its three adjacent triangles T1, T2, and T3 is shown in Figure 2.116. The *corner table* method of Rossignac, Safanova, and Szymczak [1580] is equivalent to the triangle table method. The difference is that, instead of storing pointers to the adjacent triangles of t, the corner table stores pointers to the vertices of these triangles that are not in t (e.g., V1′, V2′, and V3′, instead of T1, T2, and T3, respectively, in Figure 2.116).

The analogy between the triangle table and the winged-edge data structure is that, with each triangle (the analog of a face in the winged-edge data structure), we have a fixed amount of information, in contrast with a face in the winged-edge data structure, which can have a varying number of edges. Thus, in the case of a triangular subdivision, we have two entities with which a fixed amount of information is associated (i.e., faces and edges, in contrast to just edges in the more general case). Storing the adjacent triangles to each triangle (the primitive entity) in the triangle table method is analogous to storing the two faces that are adjacent to each edge (the primitive entity) in the winged-edge data structure.

Higher-dimensional analogs of the triangle table method can be used to represent simplicial complexes (e.g., [870]) in higher dimensions.[40] For example, we can use a tetrahedron table for tetrahedralizations in three dimensions where we represent each tetrahedron t by an eight-tuple containing pointers to the four vertices that make up t and pointers to the entries in the tetrahedron table to the four tetrahedra that are adjacent to t along the faces of t. In addition, we have a vertex table that contains a pointer to the entry in the tetrahedron table of one of the tetrahedra that are incident at the vertex. Note that the tetrahedron table stores the edges and faces that make up each tetrahedron implicitly as they can be derived from the vertices since we are dealing with a simplicial complex of three dimensions.

Exercises

1. From the text, we see that for the polyhedral objects in which we are interested, each edge belongs to exactly two faces. This is one of three restrictions that lead to a two-manifold regardless of compactness or orientability. The other two restrictions are (1) that every vertex is surrounded by a single cycle of edges and faces, and (2) that faces may not intersect each other, except at common edges or vertices. An alternative definition is that a two-manifold is a connected surface where each point on the surface is topologically equivalent to an open disc [1978]. What are some examples of physically realizable objects that are not two-manifolds?

2. Using the definition of a two-manifold given in Exercise 1, are two-manifold objects closed under Boolean set operations?

---

[40] Recall from Exercise 2 in Section 2.2.1.6 that a *simplicial complex* is the topological equivalent of a triangulation in any dimension. It consists of simplexes, where a d-dimensional *simplex* is the convex hull of $d + 1$ points.

3. Peucker and Chrisman [1487] suggest an alternative method of representing a planar subdivision where all the faces are triangles that keeps track only of the vertices. It makes use of a vertex table that contains the coordinate values of each vertex. In addition, associated with each vertex v is a pointer to an entry in another table, termed a *connectivity table*, that contains a list of the vertices (actually pointers to the corresponding vertex table entries) that are connected to v in cyclic order. Given V vertices and T triangles, and ignoring the size of the vertex table, show that the connectivity table requires $3T + V$ storage units while the triangle table requires $6T$ storage units. In other words, the connectivity table requires about one-half the storage needed by the triangle table.

4. Given T triangles, prove that the storage requirements of the connectivity table method described in Exercise 3 are bounded by $5T + 4$. *Hint:* In your answer, you may want to make use of the following properties of a planar graph:

   (a) Given V vertices, E edges, and F faces (including the external face), according to Euler's formula, $V - E + F = 2$.

   (b) The sum of the face degrees is equal to twice the number of edges, and the same is true for the sum of the degrees of the vertices.

5. One of the shortcomings of a vertex-based method, such as the connectivity table method as described in Exercise 3, is that the triangles are only represented implicitly. This means that, given a vertex v, once we have identified a triangle $T = vv'v''$ by accessing vertices v and v'' through the connectivity table entry of v, we cannot identify in $O(1)$ time the triangle $t' = v'v''w$ such that t and t' have edge $v'v''$ in common. The *star-vertex data structure* of Kallmann and Thalmann [979] is designed to overcome this shortcoming of the connectivity table by storing an additional pointer with each vertex v' in the connectivity table of vertex v to the connectivity table entry of another vertex v'' that forms a triangle $t = vv'v''$. More precisely, for every triangle $t = vv'v''$, the entry corresponding to v' in the connectivity table of v contains a pointer to the entry corresponding to v'' in the connectivity table of v'. Similarly, the entry corresponding to v'' in the connectivity table of v contains a pointer to the entry corresponding to v' in the connectivity table of v''. This facilitates making a transition in $O(1)$ time from triangle t to the triangle t' that shares edge $v'v''$. Given V vertices and T triangles and ignoring the size of the vertex table, show that the connectivity table requires $6T + V$ storage units, thereby making it equivalent in functionality and storage requirements to the triangle table and corner table.

2.2.2 Image-Based Boundary Representations

In this section, we focus on image-based boundary representations of objects. This means that the environment in which the objects lie is recursively decomposed using some regular decomposition process. Below, we discuss several quadtreelike decompositions of the underlying space into four congruent blocks (or, in the case of three-dimensional data, octreelike decompositions into eight congruent blocks). Of course, other decompositions are possible (e.g., into noncongruent blocks, as well as a varying number of blocks), but, in the interest of space, we do not discuss them further here. In addition, we do not dwell on the nature of the access structures because the options are the same as those described in Section 2.1.2.

We start with the line quadtree (Section 2.2.2.1), where both the objects and their environment are composed of cells of uniform size and shape (i.e., pixels and voxels). This is overly restrictive, and hence we waive this requirement in the rest of the subsections. This means that, unlike Section 2.1, we no longer require that the boundaries of the objects (i.e., edges and faces in two and three dimensions, respectively) be axis parallel. This can be seen in the discussion of the MX quadtree and MX octree (Section 2.2.2.2), edge quadtree (Section 2.2.2.3), and face octree (Section 2.2.2.4), as well as of the adaptively sampled distance field, which is similar to a dual of the edge quadtree and face octree (Section 2.2.2.5). All of these representations can handle arbitrary boundaries. In fact, in Sections 2.2.2.9 and 2.2.2.10, we even waive the requirement that the objects and their environment be decomposed into polygonal cells by decomposing the underlying

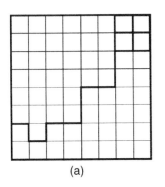

(a)

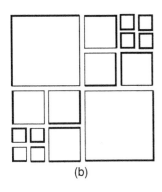

(b)

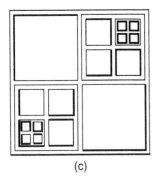

(c)

Figure 2.117
(a) Example partition of the plane into six objects (i.e., regions), (b) the block decomposition corresponding to its line quadtree, and (c) the tree access structure with blocks for the nonleaf nodes instead of the actual tree. All heavy lines indicate that an edge of the block is on the border of an object or the underlying space.

space into sectors of a circle and cones of a sphere for two- and three-dimensional data, respectively.

The remaining subsections deal with representations of objects whose boundaries are usually hyperplanes. In the case of two-dimensional data, besides two-dimensional objects whose boundaries are line segments, we also discuss the representation of data that is a collection of connected straight-line segments that partition the underlying space into a collection of polygons termed a *polygonal map* (or *map* for short). The PM quadtree family (Section 2.2.2.6) is an example of a representation that can deal with such data. In three dimensions, the data is a collection of objects with planar faces (i.e., polyhedra) and can be handled by the PM octree (Section 2.2.2.7), although we also show that the PM octree can be adapted to deal with more general data. As we will see, the vertices of the line segments and polyhedra play a crucial role in the decomposition that is induced by the PM quadtree and PM octree. The bucket PM quadtree and PMR quadtree (Section 2.2.2.8) relax this dependence on the vertices by basing the decomposition on the number of edges or faces that are present.

2.2.2.1 Line Quadtree

The simplest decomposition into blocks is obtained by using a region quadtree decomposition of the underlying space. Associated with each block b is the relevant information about the portion of the boundary e of the objects of which b is a part or the portion of the boundary e of the environment (i.e., the underlying space) in which the objects are embedded that is shared by b. This adaptation of the region quadtree serves as the basis of the line quadtree [1663, 1664].

The *line quadtree* partitions the underlying space via a recursive decomposition technique that successively subdivides the space until obtaining blocks (possibly single pixels) that have no boundary elements passing through their interior. With each block, a code is associated that indicates which of its four sides forms a boundary (not a partial boundary) of any single object (including the underlying space). Thus, instead of distinguishing blocks on the basis of whether they are part of the background and of the identity of the object in which they lie, we use the nature of the boundary information.

For example, Figure 2.117(b) is the block decomposition corresponding to the space partition given in Figure 2.117(a). Notice the use of heavy lines to denote the existence of a complete border on an edge e of a particular block b. The absence of a heavy line means that the edge e of b is not completely on the border of a block. In particular, e can be partially on the border. The extent of its presence on a border is determined by examining its neighbor c along the edge. In particular, if c along e is of equal size to that of a side of b, then e is not an edge of an object or of the underlying space.

Several access structures are possible. Using a tree access structure with fanout 4 is particularly attractive as we can store the boundary information in a hierarchical manner (i.e., in the nonleaf nodes). In essence, wherever a nonleaf node does not form a T-junction with any of the boundaries of its descendants along a particular edge e, then e is marked as being adjacent to a boundary by use of a heavy line. Figure 2.117(c) shows the blocks corresponding to all of the nodes (i.e., both leaf and nonleaf) in the tree access structure with fanout 4 for the line quadtree in Figure 2.117(a). Notice the use of heavy lines to denote the edges that are along the boundary, including that of the underlying space.

Exercises

1. Prove that the line quadtree of a polygonal map has the same number of nodes as does the region quadtree for the same map when each polygon is treated as a region of another color.

2. The definition of the line quadtree given here stores redundant information with many of the nonleaf nodes. This redundancy can be alleviated by recording the boundary information for

just two sides of each node instead of for all four sides. Let us refer to this structure as a *revised line quadtree*. This will affect the merging criteria since now we can merge four nodes only if their corresponding boundaries are identical. For example, suppose that for each node we record only the boundary information for its northern and eastern sides. Use the polygonal map of Figure 2.117(a) to show that the number of leaf nodes in the revised line quadtree is greater than the number of leaf nodes in the conventional line quadtree.

3. What is the maximum increase in the number of nodes in a revised line quadtree over the line quadtree?

2.2.2.2 MX Quadtree and MX Octree

Note that the line quadtree is also applicable to polygonal maps. In this case, the line segments are parallel to the coordinate axes. In fact, the line quadtree is really an approximation of an arbitrary polygonal map where the edges of the polygonal map are approximated by lines in the four principal directions. An alternative approximation is provided by the *MX quadtree* [901, 905]. In this case, the edges of the polygonal map are approximated by the pixels through which they pass.

For two-dimensional data such as a polygonal map, the MX quadtree is built by digitizing the line segments and labeling each unit-sized cell (i.e., pixel) through which it passes as of type BOUNDARY. The remaining pixels are labeled WHITE and are merged, if possible, into larger and larger quadtree blocks, as is done in the region quadtree. Figure 2.118(b) is the MX quadtree for the collection of line segment objects in Figure 2.118(a). A drawback of the MX quadtree is that it associates a thickness with a line. In addition, given an MX quadtree representation of a polygonal map, it is difficult to detect the presence of a vertex whenever five or more line segments meet. The problem is that, once the polygonal map has been digitized, thereby forming the basis of the MX quadtree, there is no one-to-one correspondence between them. At best, we can represent the intersection of four line segments (e.g., the vertex at which they meet) by four adjacent pixels. However, five or more lines will also likely be represented by four adjacent pixels.

A similar approximation for three-dimensional data, such as polyhedra or objects bounded by arbitrary surfaces, is provided by the *MX octree*, where the faces (as well as edges) of the object are approximated by the voxels through which they pass. The MX octree can be formed in a similar manner as the MX quadtree. In particular, we can make use of a scanning device, with the result that all voxels through which the surface passes are labeled as type *boundary*. The remaining voxels are labeled WHITE and are merged, if possible, into larger and larger octree blocks, as is done in the region octree. The MX octree has the same drawbacks as the MX quadtree. In particular, it is not invertible, and it is difficult to capture the incidence of many faces (and edges) at a vertex. We do not discuss the MX octree in great detail because its properties are similar to those of the MX quadtree.

The MX quadtree has the property that an upper bound can be derived on the number of nodes needed when using it to represent a simple polygon (i.e., with nonintersecting edges and without holes) [901]. It is obtained in the following manner. First of all, we observe that a curve of length $d + \varepsilon(\varepsilon > 0)$ can intersect at most six squares of side width d. Now consider a polygon, say G, having perimeter p, that is embedded in a grid of squares each of side width d. Mark the points at which G enters and exits each square. Choose one of these points, say P, as a starting point for a decomposition of G into a sequence of curves. Define the first curve in G to be the one extending from P until six squares have been intersected and a crossing is made into a different, seventh square. This is the starting point for another curve in G that intersects six new squares, not counting those intersected by any previous curve.

We now decompose G into a series of such curves. Since each curve adds at most six new squares and has length of at least d, we see that a polygon with perimeter p cannot intersect more than $6 \cdot \lceil p/d \rceil$ squares. Given a quadtree with a root at level q (i.e., the

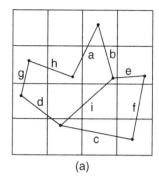

(a)

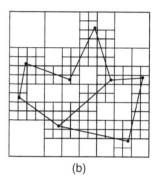

(b)

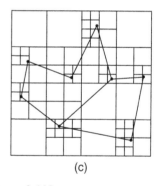

(c)

Figure 2.118
(a) Collection of line segments, (b) its MX quadtree, and (c) its edge quadtree.

grid of squares is of width 2^q), at level i each square is of width 2^i. Therefore, polygon G cannot intersect more than $B(i) = 6 \cdot \lceil p/2^i \rceil$ quadrants at level i. Recall that our goal is to derive an upper bound on the total number of nodes. This bound is attained when each boundary node at level i has three sibling nodes that are not intersected. Of course, only boundary nodes can have children, and thus no more than $B(i)$ nodes at level i have children. Since each node at level i is a child of a node at level $i + 1$, there are at most $4 \cdot B(i + 1)$ nodes at level i. Summing up over q levels (accounting for a root node at level n and four children), we find that the total number of nodes in the tree is bounded by

$$1 + 4 + \sum_{i=0}^{q-2} 4 \cdot B(i+1)$$

$$\leq 5 + 24 \cdot \sum_{i=0}^{q-2} \left\lceil \frac{p}{2^{i+1}} \right\rceil$$

$$\leq 5 + 24 \cdot \sum_{i=0}^{q-2} \left(1 + \frac{p}{2^{i+1}}\right)$$

$$\leq 5 + 24 \cdot (q - 1) + 24 \cdot p \cdot \sum_{i=0}^{q-2} \frac{1}{2^{i+1}}$$

$$\leq 24 \cdot q - 19 + 24 \cdot p.$$

Therefore, we have proved the following:

Theorem 2.1 *The quadtree corresponding to a polygon with perimeter p embedded in a $2^q \times 2^q$ image has a maximum of $24 \cdot q - 19 + 24 \cdot p$ (i.e., $O(p+q)$) nodes.*

Theorem 2.1 is also known as the *Quadtree Complexity Theorem*. In all but the most pathological cases (e.g., a small square of unit width centered in a large image), the q factor is negligible and thus the number of blocks is $O(p)$. The Quadtree Complexity Theorem also holds for three-dimensional data [1273] (i.e., represented by a MX octree), where perimeter is replaced by surface area, as well as for objects of higher dimensions d, for which it is proportional to the size of the $(d-1)$-dimensional interfaces between the objects [1948]. These results also hold for the region quadtree and region octree.

The most important consequence of the Quadtree Complexity Theorem is that it means that most algorithms that execute on a quadtree representation of an image (with an appropriate access structure), instead of simply imposing an array access structure on the original collection of cells, usually have an execution time proportional to the number of blocks in the image rather than the number of unit-sized cells.

In its most general case, the Quadtree Complexity Theorem indicates that the use of the quadtree representation, with an appropriate access structure, to solve a problem in d-dimensional space will lead to a solution whose execution time is proportional to the $(d-1)$-dimensional space of the surface of the original d-dimensional image. On the other hand, use of the array access structure on the original collection of cells results in a solution whose execution time is proportional to the number of cells that make up the image. Therefore, quadtrees and octrees act like dimension-reducing devices.

Exercises

1. The proof of Theorem 2.1 is based on a decomposition of the polygon into a sequence of curves, each of which intersects at most six squares. However, this bound can be tightened by examining patterns of squares to obtain minimum lengths and corresponding ratios of possible squares per unit length. For example, observe that once a curve intersects six squares, the next curve of length d in the sequence can intersect at most two new squares. In contrast, it is easy to construct a sequence of curves of length $d + \varepsilon (\varepsilon > 0)$ such that almost each curve intersects two squares of side length d. Prove that such a construction leads to an upper bound of the form $a \cdot q + b + 8 \cdot p$, where a and b are constants.

2. Decompose the polygon used in the proof of Theorem 2.1 into a sequence of curves in the following manner: Mark the points where G enters and exits each square of side width d. Choose one of these points, say P, and define the first curve in G as extending from P until four squares have been intersected and a crossing is made into a different fifth square. This is the starting point for another curve in G that intersects four new squares, not counting those intersected by any previous curve. Prove that all of the curves, except for the last one, must be of at least length d. Using this result, prove that the upper bound on the number of nodes in the MX quadtree is $16 \cdot n - 11 + 16 \cdot p$.

3. In this exercise and in Exercise 4, we show that the bounds given in Theorem 2.1 are attainable. We first look at the base 2 logarithm q of the image width. Consider a square of side width 2 that consists of the central four 1×1 squares in a $2^q \times 2^q$ image (see Figure 2.119). Prove that its MX quadtree has $16 \cdot q - 11$ nodes. This shows that the bound given in Theorem 2.1 is attainable

4. Continuing Exercise 3, we now show that the bound in terms of the perimeter given in Theorem 2.1 is attainable. Take a curve that follows a vertical line through the center of a $2^q \times 2^q$ image and lengthen it slightly by making it intersect all of the pixels on either side of the vertical line (see Figure 2.120). In particular, prove that as q increases, the total number of nodes in the corresponding MX quadtree approaches $8 \cdot p$, where $p = 2^q$.

5. Using a technique analogous to that used in Exercise 4, construct a polygon of perimeter p by approximating a square in the center of the image whose side is one-fourth the side of the image. Prove that its MX quadtree has approximately $8 \cdot p$ nodes.

6. Prove that $O(p + q)$ is a least upper bound on the number of nodes in a MX quadtree corresponding to a polygon. Assume that $p \leq 2^2 q$ (i.e., the number of pixels in the image). Equivalently, the polygon boundary can touch all of the pixels in the most trivial way but can be no longer. Decompose your proof into two parts, depending on whether p is greater than $4 \cdot q$.

7. Theorem 2.1 can be recast by measuring the perimeter p in terms of the length of a side of the image in which the polygon is embedded—that is, for a $2^q \times 2^q$ image, $p = p\prime \cdot 2^q$. Thus, the value of the perimeter no longer depends on the resolution of the image. Restating Theorem 2.1 in terms of $p\prime$ results in an MX quadtree having $O(p\prime \cdot 2^q + q)$ nodes. This means that the number of nodes in the MX quadtree doubles as the resolution is doubled, while the number of pixels in the array representation quadruples as the resolution is doubled. Can you prove a similar result for an arbitrary MX quadtree (rather than just one for a simple polygon)?

8. Prove the analog of Theorem 2.1 for a three-dimensional polyhedron represented as an octree (i.e., an MX octree). In this case, the perimeter corresponds to the surface area.

9. Prove the d-dimensional analog of Theorem 2.1 for the d-dimensional MX quadtree that corresponds to a d-dimensional polyhedron.

10. Assuming an image of resolution q that is not necessarily a polyhedron and measuring the perimeter, say p, in terms of the number of border pixels, prove that the total number of nodes in a d dimensional quadtree is less than or equal to $4 \cdot q \cdot p$.

11. Assuming an image of resolution q that is not necessarily a polyhedron and measuring the perimeter, say p, in terms of the number of border pixels, prove that the total number of black nodes in a d-dimensional quadtree is less than or equal to $(2^d - 1) \cdot q \cdot p/d$.

12. How tight are the bounds obtained in Exercises 10 and 11 for the number of nodes in a d-dimensional quadtree for an arbitrary region? Are they realizable?

2.2.2.3 Edge Quadtree

The MX quadtree results in a decomposition of the underlying space so that there is a unit-sized cell for each pixel through which an edge or curve passes, while all other cells are merged as much as possible using the quadtree aggregation rule (i.e., four sibling blocks of the same type are merged into a larger block of the same type). A slight reduction in the storage requirements can be achieved by halting the decomposition upon encountering a 2×2 cell through which an edge passes and then storing a templatelike representation of the edge [1401] (see also [1231]). This is quite similar to the MX quadtree, except that the data is now edges rather than points.

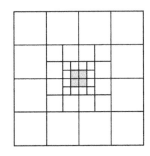

Figure 2.119
Example MX quadtree with $16 \cdot n - 11$ nodes.

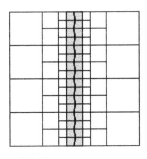

Figure 2.120
Example MX quadtree with approximately $8 \cdot p$ nodes.

The edge quadtree [1762, 1961] is a more general refinement of the MX quadtree based on the observation that the number of blocks in the decomposition can be reduced by terminating the subdivision whenever the block contains a single curve that can be approximated by a single straight line given an error tolerance value. Thus, the edge quadtree is defined for collections of line segments that are curves as well as straight lines. For example, Figure 2.118(c) is the edge quadtree for the collection of line segment objects in Figure 2.118(a) with a zero error tolerance.

It is interesting to observe that, in terms of the necessary storage requirements, Figure 2.118(b) represents the worst case of the edge quadtree in the sense that, since the underlying data is a polygonal map, and the error tolerance is zero, no approximation is taking place—that is, we are actually approximating straight lines with straight lines of zero error tolerance. This is why we have to decompose the underlying space to the maximum level of decomposition in the vicinity of corners or intersecting edges. Therefore, in the case of polygonal maps, using an edge quadtree with zero error tolerance results in quadtrees where long edges are represented by large blocks or a sequence of large blocks, while small blocks are needed in the vicinity of corners or intersecting edges. Of course, many blocks will contain no edge information at all. Nevertheless, it is important to note that when the curves are not straight lines, it is pointless to use the edge quadtree with a zero error tolerance because, in such a case, it yields the same result as the MX quadtree.

Another byproduct of using a zero error tolerance is that the maximum level of decomposition is determined by the resolution of the space in which the polygonal map is embedded since the cells at this depth are needed for the vertices and the locations where the edges or curves intersect. On the other hand, once a nonzero error tolerance is used, it determines the maximum level of decomposition, which need not be at the resolution of the underlying space (i.e. at the pixel level). Thus, the error tolerance value acts like a smoothing function. The error tolerance value can also be used to define a band around the original curve that serves to depict the extent of the approximation. Moreover, most importantly, use of a nonzero error tolerance means that the resulting approximation has induced a new polygonal map whose vertices are anchored on the quadtree subdivision lines. This is because we are approximating subcurves of the curve with a straight line whose vertices lie on the boundaries (i.e., edges) of the quadrant containing the approximating line—that is, we have created a piecewise linear approximation of the curve, which is the rationale for using the term *edge quadtree* to describe it. Thus, using a nonzero error tolerance enables the edge quadtree, to avoid having to decompose to the maximum resolution (i.e., the pixel level).

Actually, once we approximate a subcurve of the curve by a line and create the corresponding quadtree block, the approximating line of the next subcurve in the sequence is naturally anchored at the quadtree subdivision lines that now serve as the new vertices of the piecewise linear approximation of the curve. For example, the object in Figure 2.121(a) illustrates a more realistic application of the edge quadtree, where the object's boundary consists of curved lines. Figure 2.121(b) is the corresponding edge quadtree using a zero error tolerance, which is the same as the MX quadtree for the object boundaries that are neither straight lines nor points of intersection of straight lines. On the other hand, Figure 2.121(c) is an edge quadtree using an error tolerance of 0.4. As mentioned above, at times, the extent of the approximation is depicted by using a band, which is illustrated by Figure 2.121(d) for the edge quadtree in Figure 2.121(c). Notice that the bands of neighboring nodes overlap at the common quadrant boundary, but not completely. The union of all the bands of the curve defines a "thick curve" with a width that is twice the error tolerance that contains the true curvilinear boundary of the object. The result is analogous to what is obtained by using a strip tree [121] (see Section 2.2.3.1), with the distinction that the strip tree is an object-based representation while the edge quadtree is an image-based representation that uses regular decomposition.

Closely related to the edge quadtree is the *least square quadtree* [1248]. In that representation, leaf nodes correspond to regions that contain a single curve that can be

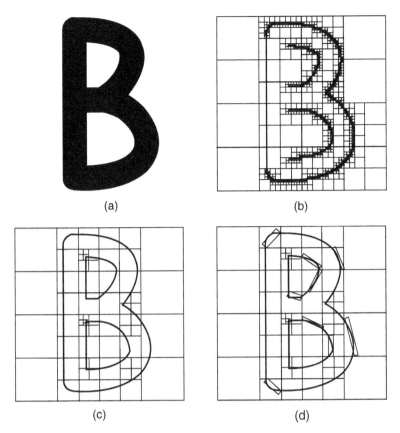

(a) (b)

(c) (d)

Figure 2.121
(a) Example object, (b) its edge quadtree with a zero error tolerance, (c) its edge quadtree with a 0.4 error tolerance, and (d) bands illustrating the extent of the approximation induced by (c).

approximated by K (fixed a priori) straight lines within a least square tolerance. This enables handling curved lines with greater precision and uses fewer nodes than the edge quadtree.

Exercise

1. Give an algorithm to construct an edge quadtree for a given polygonal map.

2.2.2.4 Face Octree

The region octree and the MX octree are difficult to work with when trying to represent objects whose faces are not restricted to being rectilinear. They both yield an approximation that is inadequate for many applications, such as solid modeling. Of course, if the faces are mutually orthogonal, then a suitable rotation operation can be applied to yield rectilinear faces. However, we are dealing with a more general case. One solution is to store surface normals in the visible surface nodes as discussed by Meagher [1279] (see Section 7.1.4 of [1636]). Chien and Aggarwal [369] show how to do this directly from boundaries of multiple silhouettes. We do not discuss this approach here.

An alternative solution, and the one we discuss in the remainder of this section, is to adapt the edge quadtree to three dimensions. Initially, we restrict our discussion to polyhedral objects. A simple adaptation is a variant of the MX octree that halts the decomposition whenever a block contains just one face. The result is termed a *face octree* [270, 1349]. An alternative adaptation, which is not used much, halts the decomposition whenever the block contains just one face or one edge, provided that all the faces in the block meet at this edge. The result is termed a *face-edge octree* [1349]. Observe that, in the former, decomposition occurs around an edge and a vertex, while, in the latter, decomposition occurs only around a vertex. In either case, the result is the three-dimensional analog of the edge quadtree where the objects are polyhedra instead of polygonal maps.

The storage requirements of the face octree—and, to a lesser extent, of the face-edge octree—can be reduced by modifying the halting condition for the decomposition process to be based on an error tolerance for a planar approximation of the surface. This halting condition forms the basis of a variant of the face octree proposed by Brunet [270] that, as in the case of polyhedral objects, only allows empty, full, and face nodes, where the face nodes contain the planar approximation, as well as a pointer to the complete geometrical description of the face (i.e., surface) that is being approximated. This variation of the face octree is very useful when the objects are not constrained to be polyhedra. In particular, it avoids the need to decompose around edges where the interior angle formed by the adjacent faces is small, as is the case for most objects. Thus, with this modification, the face-edge octree becomes less important, and we do not discuss it further here.

Although we have described the face octree in terms of objects with arbitrary surfaces, the face octree can also be used to represent polyhedra, in which case the representation is exact in the sense that it enables the reconstruction of the original polyhedron, provided that each face of the polyhedron is pointed at by at least one face node. The advantage of using a nonzero error tolerance in the case of polyhedra is that its use enables avoiding some of the decomposition that would otherwise be necessary around some of the edges and vertices. Numerous algorithms have been given for solid modeling operations involving face octrees (for polyhedra as well as objects with more general surfaces) as well as analyses of their storage requirements (e.g., [272, 274, 975, 1497, 1498, 1784]).

Every face node in a face octree can be interpreted as a three-dimensional hyperrectangle-shaped band of width equal to the error tolerance and oriented so that it is parallel to the planar approximation of the surface of the object. Thus, the surface can be viewed as a sequence of hyperrectangle-shaped bands. These bands change orientation at octant boundaries, and these positions play a role somewhat analogous to vertices when the object is a polyhedron. Using such an interpretation yields a result similar to the prism tree of Ponce and Faugeras [1501] and its predecessor, the polyhedral approximation [597] (see Section 2.2.3.2), which are three-dimensional generalizations of the strip tree [121] (see Section 2.2.3.1). The distinction is that the prism tree is an object-based representation while the face octree is an image-based representation that uses regular decomposition.

Exercise

1. Give an algorithm to construct a face octree for a given polyhedron.

2.2.2.5 Adaptively Sampled Distance Fields

The adaptively sampled distance field (ADF) of Frisken, Perry, Rockwood, and Jones [654, 655, 1482], applied to two- and three-dimensional data, yields a decomposition of the underlying space that is analogous to that obtained by the edge quadtree (Section 2.2.2.3) and face octree (Section 2.2.2.4), respectively. In fact, the adaptively sampled distance field can be viewed as the dual of the edge quadtree and face octree (see Exercise 3) in two and three dimensions, respectively. In this section, the discussion is primarily in terms of three-dimensional data because this is where the adaptively sampled distance field finds most use. Nevertheless, almost all of our comments are equally applicable to two-dimensional data, and, in fact, the example that we give makes use of a two-dimensional object as it is easier to visualize.

The basic idea is to represent an object by a *distance field*—a scalar field that specifies the distance to the nearest point on the surface of the object from every point in the space in which the object is embedded, where the distance is usually signed to distinguish between the inside and outside of the object [707]. The rationale for using the distance field is to overcome some of the drawbacks of methods based on volume graphics [1002].

Conventional representations (e.g., those that use collections of voxels or hierarchical aggregations of similarly valued voxels such as the region and MX octrees) are good for Boolean set operations and visualization of the interiors of the objects. The data usually originates as binary data. The discrete sampling process, by which the data is acquired and the associated representations are built, makes it difficult to use these representations to represent arbitrarily oriented surfaces very well. Estimation of surface normals for binary data is complicated by the fact that the discrete sampling process by which they have been acquired has led to the loss of prior information about the surface of the object. Moreover, the binary nature of the data inherently leads to abrupt changes in value at the surface of the object.

Being able to represent the surface accurately is important for a number of reasons [707]. For example, it is useful for dealing with interactions between different models, as in the case of the calculation of impact forces, which requires knowledge of the positions and surface normals of the contact points. Precise knowledge of the location and orientation of the surface is also needed for proper use of a lighting and shading model to obtain high-quality rendering. When the sample data is intensity based, the surfaces are not represented well enough because the intensity varies smoothly in the interiors of the objects while, as pointed out above, it varies rapidly (abruptly) at their surfaces. This makes shading in volume graphics difficult. During the rendering process, these abrupt changes are detected and used to determine the intensity and direction of the surface. In particular, these abrupt changes correspond to high spatial frequencies in the data, which means that high sampling rates are needed to reconstruct the image and its gradient near the surface.

Using a distance field has a number of important properties that overcome some of the above problems. First, the gradient of the distance field yields the direction of the surface normal. Second, unlike object representations that are based on intensity, the distance field varies smoothly across object surfaces, thereby avoiding high spatial frequencies at object boundaries. In other words, surfaces in sampled data, as is common in volume graphics, can be reconstructed accurately using low sampling rates. Thus, the distance fields are used to implicitly encode surfaces into the sampled volumetric data so that high-quality shading can be performed in volume rendering of such data. Although we mention an implicit encoding, the idea is similar to the manner in which we use a PM quadtree (Section 2.2.2.6) or a PM octree (see Section 2.2.2.7) to encode the line segment or face that passes through a block. In particular, instead of storing the full description of the intersecting curve or face with the block through which it passes, we only associate a pointer to the real data with the block.

The distance field permits a very precise description of the shape. However, its storage requirements are prohibitive as fine detail in the shape still requires dense sampling. The high storage costs associated with keeping the entire distance field are reduced by making use of an adaptively sampled distance field [655], which permits varying the sampling rates so that the density of the sampling is directly proportional to the variation of the field. Adaptively sampled distance fields are formed in an analogous manner to a region octree or an MX octree, with the difference being that, instead of decomposing the space until each block is either completely occupied by an object or empty (i.e., a region octree) or obtaining unit voxel-sized blocks through which the boundary of the shape passes (i.e., an MX octree), the space is decomposed whenever the distance field within the block is not well approximated by a trilinear interpolation of the block's corner values.

There are a number of ways of measuring the approximation error (e.g., relative, absolute, average), although no specific one is prescribed [655]. If the approximation error function is a relative one, then the sampling is more frequent around the object boundary, where the distance field is close to zero and hence the sampled distance field should follow the distance field more closely. On the other hand, if the approximation error function is an absolute one, then the approximation error threshold determines how far the sampled distance field can deviate from the actual distance field based on an absolute value. In this case, the sampling will be more uniform across the entire space.

If the application is only concerned with the distance field around the boundary of the object, then we can increase the approximation error threshold as the distance of the sampled points from the boundary of the object increases. The effect of such an approach is similar to a relative approximation error function. However, the problem is that such a solution tends to oversample at the boundary of the object. Hence, we can combine the two and use an absolute approximation error e_a if the sampled point p is sufficiently close to the boundary of the object, say within d of the boundary of the object, and use a relative approximation error e_r otherwise. Such an approximation error function e_p is given by

$$e_p = \min(e_a, e_r \times |d_p|)$$

which we characterize as an *adaptive approximation error*.

Being able to vary the approximation error at different locations is one of the main reasons for the attractiveness of the adaptively sampled distance field. This can be seen by observing that the distance field undergoes a change of sign at the boundary of the object as this is its zero-crossing. These changes are important and may require a relatively low approximation error threshold for their proper handling. On the other hand, the distance field undergoes rapid changes (i.e., points of discontinuity of the first derivative) at points on the skeleton (recall the definition in Section 2.1.2.2) of the object as the identity of the nearest object changes at these locations. In other words, the normal of the distance field surface is discontinuous at the object's skeleton, thereby requiring much decomposition in the skeleton's neighborhood when a low approximation error threshold is used, regardless of whether it is relative or absolute. On the other hand, there is little need for decomposition at the skeleton, and thus adaptively varying the approximation error threshold so that it is low around the boundary of the object and high at the neighborhood of the skeleton is very useful. In essence, an adaptive sampling of the distance field based on the values of the distance is being done, and hence the rationale for the name adaptively sampled distance field.

Regardless of how the approximation error threshold is measured, even highly curved edges and faces can be efficiently represented using adaptively sampled distance fields. In particular, since trilinear (bilinear) interpolation can represent curved surfaces (edges) well, cells with smoothly curved faces (edges) do not require many levels in the adaptively sampled distance field hierarchy, and thus much decomposition is only concentrated at corners, cusps, and sharp edges.

For example, Figure 2.122(a) is the adaptively sampled distance field for the two-dimensional object in Figure 2.121(a) using a relative approximation error threshold of 0.9. Notice the similarity in the decomposition to the edge quadtree in Figure 2.121(b, c). This is not surprising as it is a direct result of our observation of the duality of these representations.

It is interesting to observe that the distance field is somewhat of an indirect representation of the shape of an object as it describes the object by associating information with the parts of the space that are not occupied by it rather than the parts of the space that are occupied by it. In addition, note that, although the concept of distance is also used in the definition of a medial axis transformation (MAT) and a quadtree medial axis

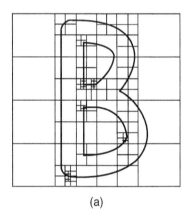

(a)

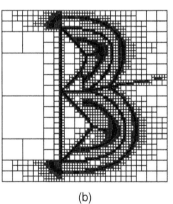

(b)

Figure 2.122
The adaptively sampled distance field for the two-dimensional object in Figure 2.121(a) using a relative approximation error threshold of (a) 0.9 and (b) 0.01.

transform (QMAT) (see Section 2.1.2.2),[41] thereby seeming similar to a distance field, they are different. In particular, the MAT and QMAT are methods of describing the interior of a shape by a collection of blocks of different radii (distance values), while the distance field describes the relationship of the boundary of the shape to the rest of the space (both inside and outside the object).

The decomposition induced by the adaptively sampled distance field is also closely related to the concept of a skeleton in the sense that some of the locations at which there is much decomposition in the adaptively sampled distance field coincide with the skeleton. This becomes more apparent when we examine Figure 2.122(b), which is the adaptively sampled distance field for the two-dimensional object in Figure 2.121(a) using a relative approximation error threshold of 0.01. In this case, the adaptively sampled distance field results in decomposing the underlying space around both the boundary of the shape and its skeleton. Here we see that the skeleton is computed for the region corresponding to the object (i.e., the solid part representing the letter "B") and its holes. Note that when the relative approximation error threshold is sufficiently high, as in the adaptively sampled distance field in Figure 2.122(a), there is no decomposition around the skeleton of the object.

Exercises

1. Give an algorithm to construct an adaptively sampled distance field for a given two-dimensional object.

2. Give an algorithm to construct an adaptively sampled distance field for a given three-dimensional object.

3. In the text, we pointed out that the adaptively sampled distance field can be viewed as the dual of the edge quadtree (face octree) in two (three) dimensions. Is there any correlation between the error tolerance used to define the edge quadtree (face octree) and the error used to create the bilinear (trilinear) interpolation approximation of the distance field within a block so that the resulting decompositions of the underlying space are the same? If there is not, then give a counterexample.

2.2.2.6 PM Quadtrees

The PM quadtree family [1360, 1665] (see also edge-EXCELL [1822]) represents an attempt to overcome some of the problems associated with the edge quadtree in the representation of a polygonal map. In particular, the edge quadtree is an approximation because vertices are represented by pixels. Also, when the lines are curves, the decomposition stops when they can be approximated by a single straight line for a predefined tolerance. There are several variants of the PM quadtree. These variants are either vertex based or edge based. They are all built by applying the principle of repeatedly breaking up the collection of vertices and edges (forming the polygonal map) until a subset is obtained that is sufficiently simple that it can be organized by some other data structure.

PM_1, PM_2, and PM_3 quadtrees [1665] are vertex based. The PM_1 quadtree is the simplest variant. Its decomposition rule stipulates that partitioning occurs as long as a block contains more than one line segment, unless the line segments are all incident at the same vertex, which is also in the same block. The fact that the structure is defined in a top-down manner means that each block is maximal. It should be clear that each block contains at most one vertex. For example, Figure 2.123(a) is the PM_1 quadtree corresponding to the collection of line segment objects in Figure 2.118(a).

The number of blocks in a PM_1 quadtree depends on the following three factors:

---

[41] Although the quadtree medial axis transform is defined for two-dimensional data, it is equally applicable for three-dimensional data.

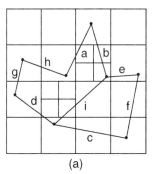
(a)

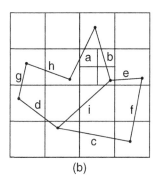
(b)

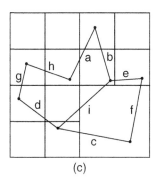
(c)

Figure 2.123
(a) PM_1 quadtree, (b) PM_2 quadtree, and (c) PM_3 quadtree for the collection of line segments of Figure 2.118(a).

1. The minimum separation between two vertices

2. The minimum separation between a vertex and a line segment

3. The minimum separation between two nonintersecting line segments in a block that contains no vertices

Given a polygonal map whose vertices are drawn from a grid (say $2^m \times 2^m$), and where line segments are not permitted to intersect at points other than the grid points (i.e., vertices), it can be shown that these factors imply that the maximum depth of any leaf node in a tree access structure for the PM_1 quadtree is bounded from above by $4m + 1$ [1656]. This is useful if we want to represent the collection of blocks using one of the alternative access structures to a tree discussed in Section 2.1.2. Recall that they are all based on finding a mapping from the domain of the blocks to a subset of the integers (i.e., to one dimension) and then applying one of the familiar treelike access structures (e.g., a binary search tree, range tree, B^+-tree). The depth bound enables a determination of the maximum amount of storage that will be necessary for the locational code of each block.

The amount of storage necessary to represent the PM_1 quadtree can be reduced by removing some of the factors on which its depth depends. For example, we can remove the dependence on the minimum separation between two nonintersecting line segments in a block that contains no vertices by modifying the definition of the PM_1 quadtree so that a block is not split if all of the line segments that it contains intersect at a vertex outside of the block. In other words, we modify the decomposition rule so that partitioning occurs as long as a block contains more than one line segment, unless the line segments are all incident at the same vertex, regardless of its location. The result is termed a *PM_2 quadtree* and is illustrated in Figure 2.123(b).

The amount of storage necessary to represent the PM_1 quadtree can be further reduced by removing the dependence on the minimum separation between a vertex and a line segment so that partitioning occurs only when a block contains more than one vertex. The result is termed a *PM_3 quadtree* and is illustrated in Figure 2.123(c). The PM_3 quadtree is the same as a PR quadtree (see Section 1.4.2.2 of Chapter 1), which is a representation for point data. As we see, the line segments play no role in the decomposition process. The sole dependence of the decomposition rule leading to the PM_3 quadtree on the existence of just one vertex per block shows why we say that the PM_3 quadtree is vertex based and, to a lesser extent, why we also say that the PM_1 and PM_2 quadtrees are vertex based. The PM_3 quadtree has been used by Ibbs [917] to store vector data in a commercial mapping program.

All variants of the PM quadtree (including the PMR quadtree discussed in Section 2.2.2.8 and the three-dimensional variants discussed in Section 2.2.2.7) are characterized as employing *spatial indexing* because, with each block, the only information that is stored is whether the block is occupied by the object or part of the object that is stored there. This information is usually in the form of a pointer to a descriptor of the object. For example, in the case of a collection of line segment objects in the PMR quadtree of Figure 2.128 (to be discussed in Section 2.2.2.8), the shaded blocks record only the fact that the line segments (i.e., a, b, and e) cross it or pass through it. The part of the line segment that passes through the block (or terminates within it) is termed a *q-edge* (*q-face* in three dimensions). It is determined by clipping [1568] an edge of the polygonal map against the border of the block through which it passes. Each q-edge in the block is represented by a pointer to a record containing the endpoints of the line segment of which the q-edge is a part [1360]. The pointer is really nothing more than a spatial index and hence the use of this term to characterize this approach. Thus, no information is associated with the shaded block as to what part of the line (i.e., q-edge) crosses it. Instead, this information is represented implicitly, and, as we point out above, it is obtained by clipping [622] the original line segment to the block. This is important because often the precision necessary to compute these intersection points is not available. This feature makes such representations particularly attractive for dealing with vector data (in contrast to raster data) and has led them to be called *vector quadtrees* (and *vector octrees* in three dimensions) [1666, 1667].

The PM_2 quadtree is particularly useful for storing polygonal maps that correspond to triangulations or, more generally, to polygonal maps where all vertices have degree 3 (e.g., nondegenerate Voronoi diagrams where no four sites are cocircular) as the space requirements are often considerably smaller than those of the PM_1 quadtree, while not being much larger than the PM_3 quadtree. This is especially true for the Delaunay triangulation, which satisfies the minimum angle property and thus maximizes the minimum interior angle, thereby implying that the constituent triangles are as close as possible to being equiangular (recall properties 2 and 6 of the Delaunay triangulation in Section 2.2.1.4). This can be seen in Figure 2.124(a–c), which shows the block decompositions induced by the PM_1, PM_2, and PM_3 quadtrees, respectively, for the Delaunay triangulation given in Figure 2.110(b) in Section 2.2.1.4, where the corresponding Voronoi diagram is shown using broken lines. Notice the difference in the maximum depth of the decomposition between the PM_1 and PM_2 quadtrees, while there is no difference in this example between the PM_2 and PM_3 quadtrees.

In fact, in such a case, instead of storing with each leaf block b the set of edges that pass through b, we use an alternative implementation where each leaf block b stores the vertex, if any, that is common to the edges that pass through b [453]. If only one edge passes through b, then one of its vertices is arbitrarily chosen to be stored. In any case, regardless of how many edges pass through b, the vertices are usually part of an auxiliary data structure (e.g., a triangle table or some other variant of the winged-edge data structure) that keeps track of the topological properties of the polygonal map. The auxiliary structure serves to facilitate a number of operations that involve visiting adjacent triangles that are necessary for updating the polygonal map in a consistent manner so that it remains a triangulation of a particular type or even operations such as point location. For another related application of the PM_2 quadtree, see the discussion of the approximate Voronoi diagram (AVD) [799] in Section 4.4.5 of Chapter 4. In particular, see the (3,0)-AVD [97, 98], which, for two-dimensional polygonal maps that correspond to Voronoi diagrams, yields an identical partition of the underlying space into blocks as does the PM_2 quadtree.

Exercises

Exercises 1–6 assume the following implementation for the PM quadtree. The basic entities are vertices and edges. Each vertex is represented as a record of type *point*, which has two fields called XCOORD and YCOORD that correspond to the x and y coordinate values, respectively, of the point. They can be real or integer numbers, depending on implementation considerations such as floating-point precision.

An edge is implemented as a record of type *line* with four fields, P1, P2, LEFT, and RIGHT. P1 and P2 contain pointers to the records containing the edge's vertices. LEFT and RIGHT are pointers to structures that identify the regions that are on the two sides of the edge. We shall use the convention that LEFT and RIGHT are with respect to a view of the edge that treats the vertex closest to the origin as the start of the edge.

Each node in a PM quadtree is a collection of q-edges, which is represented as a record of type *node* containing seven fields. The first four fields contain pointers to the node's four children corresponding to the directions (i.e., quadrants) NW, NE, SW, and SE. If P is a pointer to a node, and I is a quadrant, then these fields are referenced as CHILD(P, I). The fifth field, NODETYPE, indicates whether the node is a leaf node (LEAF) or a nonleaf node (GRAY). The sixth field, SQUARE, is a pointer to a record of type *square*, which indicates the size of the block corresponding to the node. It is defined for both leaf and nonleaf nodes. It has two fields CENTER and LEN. CENTER points to a record of type *point* that contains the x and y coordinate values of the center of the square. LEN contains the length of a side of the square that is the block corresponding to the node in the PM_1 quadtree.

DICTIONARY is the last field. It is a pointer to a data structure that represents the set of q-edges that are associated with the node. Initially, the universe is empty and consists of no

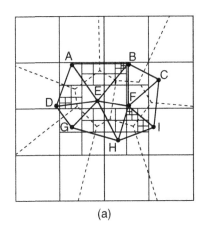

(a)

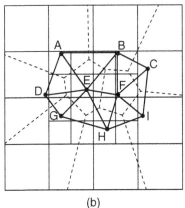

(b)

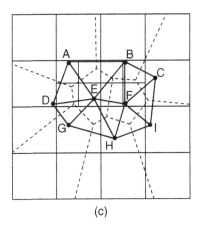

(c)

Figure 2.124
The block decompositions induced by the (a) PM_1, (b) PM_2, and (c) PM_3 quadtrees for the Delaunay triangulation given in Figure 2.110(b) of the set of sites {A, B, C, D, E, F, G, H, I} whose Voronoi diagram is given in Figure 2.110(a) and shown here using broken lines.

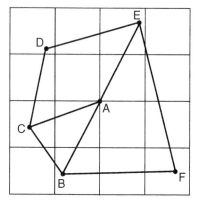

Figure 2.125
Example polygonal map where vertex A lies on the border of a quadtree node. The decomposition lines are those induced by a PM$_1$ quadtree definition in which a vertex is inserted in each of the nodes on whose border it lies.

edges or vertices. It is represented by a tree of one node of type LEAF whose DICTIONARY field points to the empty set.

In the implementation given here, the set of q-edges for each LEAF node is a linked list whose elements are records of type *edgelist* containing two fields, DATA and NEXT. DATA points to a record of type *line* corresponding to the edge of which the q-edge is a member. NEXT points to the record corresponding to the next q-edge in the list of q-edges. Although the set of q-edges is stored as a list here, it really should be implemented by a data structure that supports efficient updating and searching, as well as variants of set union and set difference operations.

1. Give an algorithm PMINSERT to insert a list of edges pointed at by p in the PM$_1$ quadtree rooted at r. Also write a procedure CLIPLINES to clip the edges to the blocks corresponding to the nodes. Assume the existence of predicates INTERSECTLINESQUARE and PTINSQUARE. INTERSECTLINESQUARE indicates if an edge has at least one point in common with a square (i.e., it intersects some of its boundaries or lies completely inside it) while PTINSQUARE indicates if a vertex lies in a square. They are responsible for enforcing the conventions with respect to vertices and edges that lie on the boundaries of blocks.

Assume that each vertex is a part of all nodes through which its incident q-edges pass, as shown in Figure 2.125. Note that this means that a vertex is a part of all nodes (and possibly more) through which its incident q-edges pass. This is why the NW, NE, and SE quadrants in the figure are split—that is, they contain vertices A and D, A and E, and A and F, respectively, which cannot be in the same node. Otherwise, if we follow the customary open and closed conventions described in Section 1.1 of Chapter 1 that the lower and left boundaries of each block are closed while the right and upper boundaries of each block are open (given an origin at the lower-left corner of the space spanned by the region that contains the line segments), then we will have a problem when at least three edges meet at a vertex on the border of a quadtree node such that two of the edges are in the open quadrant (i.e., the one not containing the vertex). These two edges may have to be decomposed to a very deep level in order to separate them (e.g., edges AB and AC in the SW quadrant of the figure).

Q-edges that lie on the border of a quadtree node or that pass through one of its corners are inserted into the quadrants for which the border is closed. Assuming the open and closed conventions described in Section 1.1 of Chapter 1, for a block b with center at p with four children, we have the following:

(a) Vertical edges coincident with the y axis through p are inserted into the NE and SE quadrants of b.

(b) Horizontal edges coincident with the x axis through p are inserted into the NW and NE quadrants of b.

(c) Diagonal edges from the NW quadrant of b to the SE quadrant of b are inserted into the NW, NE, and SE quadrants of b.

(d) Diagonal edges from the NE quadrant of b to the SW quadrant of b are inserted into the NE and SW quadrants of b.

Assume further that, whenever an edge e is inserted into the PM$_1$ quadtree, e does not intersect an existing edge. Otherwise, the block containing the intersection point will have to be decomposed forever as the intersection point is not treated as a vertex. In addition, it is assumed that e does not have an endpoint that is an existing isolated vertex (i.e., an edge with zero length). In the case of a PM$_1$ quadtree, e cannot already exist in the tree, unless each of e's q-edges are incident at the vertices of e. Otherwise, e's q-edges that are not incident at the vertices of e would occur more than once in a block b, which would cause the decomposition of b to go on forever. You need not check for the occurrence of duplicate instances of edges.

2. Give an algorithm PMDELETE to delete a list of edges pointed at by p from the PM$_1$ quadtree rooted at r. The process is analogous to that used in insertion. The difference is that, once the edge has been deleted, we process its ancestor nodes, and an attempt is made to merge their child nodes. The check for merging is analogous to the check for collapsing when deleting a point from a PR quadtree. The difference is that, for the PM$_1$ quadtree, a check for the possibility of merging is made at each level of the tree in which processing one of the children of a nonleaf node has resulted in the deletion of a q-edge. In particular, merging can occur if at least one of the children of a nonleaf node is a leaf node. There are two situations where merging must occur. The first situation arises when the deletion of an edge has resulted in four sibling leaf nodes having zero or one edge pass through them. The second situation is somewhat tricky. It arises when deletion causes all of the remaining edges in the descendants

of the nonleaf node, say N, to have a common vertex that lies in one of the children of N (not a descendant of N, who is not a child!). In this case, merging can occur, thereby making N a leaf node.

3. Modify procedure PMINSERT given in Exercise 1 to insert a list of edges pointed at by p in the PM_2 quadtree rooted at r. Again, assume that whenever an edge e is inserted into the PM_2 quadtree, e does not intersect an existing edge, and e does not have an endpoint that is an existing isolated vertex. Duplicate instances of an edge are allowed.

4. Modify procedure PMDELETE given in Exercise 2 to delete a list of edges pointed at by p in the PM_2 quadtree rooted at r.

5. Modify procedure PMINSERT given in Exercises 1 and 3 to insert a list of edges pointed at by p in the PM_3 quadtree rooted at r. Again, assume that whenever an edge e is inserted into the PM_3 quadtree, e does not intersect an existing edge, and e does not have an endpoint that is an existing isolated vertex. Duplicate instances of an edge are allowed.

6. Modify procedure PMDELETE given in Exercises 2 and 4 to delete a list of edges pointed at by p in the PM_3 quadtree rooted at r.

7. Prove that for a given polygonal map the average depth of a vertex node in a PM_3 quadtree is smaller than in a PM_2 (and PM_1) quadtree.

8. Using a random lines model and geometric probability as in the analysis of [1175], derive asymptotic bounds on the number of blocks that are necessary to store a triangulation using the different variants of the PM quadtree, the PMR quadtree (see Section 2.2.2.8), and the MX quadtree. Can you take advantage of the fact that you are using a PM_2 quadtree to represent the triangulation so that only the identity of the vertex, instead of the set of intersecting lines, is stored in each block, thereby making the amount of data stored in each block independent of the number of edges that intersect it?

9. How would you perform point location in a PM_1 quadtree? In this case, you wish to find the nearest q-edge to the query point q.

10. How would you compute map overlay (see Exercise 12 in Section 2.1.3.2) for two polygonal maps represented with the different variants of the PM quadtree?

11. Prove that two PM quadtrees can be overlaid in $O(v)$ time, where v is the number of vertices in the trees.

12. What are some issues in the use of PM quadtrees to represent collections of line segments in three-dimensional space? In other words, can you use, for example, a PM_1 quadtree to represent a collection of line segments in three-dimensional space where we recursively decompose the underlying space until each block contains at most one line segment or all of the line segments meet at a vertex within the block?

2.2.2.7 PM Octree

A more general adaptation of the MX octree to deal with three-dimensional objects that are polyhedra whose faces are not constrained to be rectilinear is obtained by modifying the decomposition rule of the face-edge octree so that it is also halted when all the faces and edges in the block meet at the same vertex, which is also in the block. This decomposition rule can be restated as stipulating that no block contains more than one face, edge, or vertex unless the faces all meet at the same vertex or are adjacent at the same edge inside the block. The result is analogous to what takes place in the neighborhood of a vertex node in the PM quadtree—that is, the decomposition around a node containing a vertex is halted as long as all of the edges that pass through the block are also incident at the vertex. Thus, we have defined the three-dimensional analog of the PM quadtree. Observe that, as in the PM quadtree family, the fact that the decomposition process is defined in a top-down manner means that each block is maximal. The result is usually called a *PM octree*, although the name *PM_1octree* is a more precise characterization for the adaptation that we have described. In our discussion, we use the term *PM octree* unless a more precise distinction is necessary.

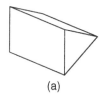

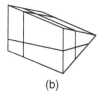

Figure 2.126
(a) Example three-dimensional object and (b) its corresponding PM_1 octree.

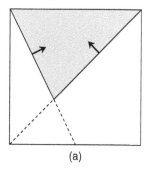

(a)

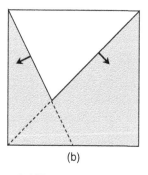

(b)

Figure 2.127
The two possible configurations for the cross section of an edge node in a PM octree: (a) a convex edge is the result of the intersection of the planes of the two faces that meet at the edge and (b) a concave edge is the result of the union of the plane of the two faces that meet at the edge. The arrows indicate the direction of the object relative to the faces. The broken lines correspond to the parts of the planes that do not form the boundary of the object. The shaded region corresponds to the object.

The space requirements of the PM octree are considerably harder to analyze than those of the region octree and the MX octree [1349] (see Exercise 6). Nevertheless, it should be clear that the PM octree for a given object is much more compact than the corresponding region octree. For example, Figure 2.126(b) is a PM octree decomposition of the object in Figure 2.126(a) (i.e., eight blocks with appropriate information about the primitives that lie in them).

At this point, let us briefly trace the history of the PM octree (see also [2020]). Quinlan and Woodwark [1526] describe a decomposition rule requiring that a leaf node contain at most one vertex. Otherwise, the node can either contain a number of faces or a number of edges and faces. The notion of a "number" is analogous to the manner in which Tamminen's edge-EXCELL method [1822, 1824] makes use of a bucket (see also Section 2.2.2.8) in the representation of a collection of line segments. The result is somewhat like a three-dimensional adaptation of a combination of EXCELL and a PM_3 quadtree. In fact, Tamminen [1822] does describe an adaptation of EXCELL for three-dimensional data in which faces take the place of line segments.

The PM octree formulation that we have described was reported almost simultaneously by three research groups who, of course, each gave it a different name [116, 308, 662]. Ayala, Brunet, Juan, and Navazo [116, 272] called it an *extended octree*. Carlbom, Chakravarty, and Vanderschel [308] called it a *polytree*. They say that it was initially investigated by Hunter [902], who termed it a *geometree*. They also state that the geometree is a simplification of a data structure described by Vanderschel [1915], who named it a *divided-leaf octal tree*. Fujimura and Kunii [662] termed it a *hierarchical space indexing method*. Regardless of its name(s), it is a useful method. The most extensive treatment of this data structure is to be found in the Ph.D. dissertation of Navazo [1349], who also points out the progressive transition from the MX octree to the face, face-edge, and PM_1 octrees. This work contains a detailed analysis of the storage requirements of the representation. It also includes algorithms for Boolean set operations involving it and for conversion between it and a boundary model.

An implementation of the PM octree consists of leaf nodes of type vertex, edge, and face, as well as empty and full, corresponding to the cell being completely outside or inside the object, respectively. Nevertheless, for the proper execution of many operations, the mere classification of the type of the node is not sufficient to characterize the object properly. At times, Carlbom, Chakravarty, and Vanderschel [308] store with each node the polygons determined by the boundary of the object that intersects the node. This is somewhat cumbersome and requires a considerable amount of extra information. Moreover, the vertices of the polygons cannot be specified exactly as most often they are not the vertices of the object. In particular, they are artifacts of the decomposition process. In fact, the edges of the polygons are analogous to the q-edges discussed in Section 2.2.2.6 in the context of the PM quadtree family. Thus, using that terminology, the polygons are more appropriately termed *q-faces*.

Navazo [1349] uses a more efficient representation. In the case of a face node, the equation of the plane of the face that is associated with the node is recorded with the node. In addition, the direction of the object relative to the face is noted. For nodes of type edge and vertex, the configuration of the faces (i.e., the planes) that make up the edge and vertex must also be recorded. This information is used to classify a point inside the node with respect to the object so that the PM octree can be built.

For example, in the case of an edge node, we must know if it is convex or concave. The two possibilities are shown in Figure 2.127. The intersection of the planes of the two faces that meet at the edge results in a convex edge (Figure 2.127(a)), and the union results in a concave edge (Figure 2.127(b)). Note the use of arrows to indicate the direction of the object relative to the planes of the faces. In the case of a vertex node, the situation is more complex because the number of possible configurations depends on the number of faces that are adjacent at the vertex.

In [1350], Navazo presents an elegant generalized treatment of vertices with n faces that permits the configurations to be classified on the basis of their constituent edge configurations and stores them by their type along with pointers to the plane equations of their faces. This generalized approach is then used as the basis of algorithms to compute Boolean set operations involving PM octrees (for another approach, see [307]).

One of the drawbacks of the PM octree as defined above (i.e., the PM_1 octree) is that it is possible to produce subtrees of arbitrary depth near the edges and vertices of the objects when two faces or edges are very close to each other because the decomposition only halts when all the faces meet at an edge in the block or all the faces meet at a vertex in the block. This results in what are termed *black holes* by Dürst and Kunii [519]. One way to overcome this problem is to resort to the face octree with a nonzero tolerance as described by Brunet [270] (see Section 2.2.2.4).

Wyvill and Kunii [2028] suggest overcoming this problem by halting the decomposition at some predetermined depth and classifying the corresponding nodes as *nasty* (e.g., [2028]). Such nodes are termed *terminal gray nodes* by Navazo [1349]. In this case, the nodes contain the same information as in the corresponding vertex node, thereby capturing the full geometry of the parts of the objects in the corresponding block.

Dürst and Kunii [519] suggest an alternative method of overcoming this problem by making use of what they call an *integrated polytree*. The integrated polytree is constructed using the same techniques employed by Samet and Webber [1665] that led to the formation of the PM_2 and PM_3 quadtrees, thereby yielding PM_2 and PM_3 octrees, respectively. The PM_3 octree is defined in the same manner as the PM_3 quadtree: we simply decompose the underlying space until each block contains at most one vertex.

The PM_2 octree is more complex. In particular, Dürst and Kunii suggest the use of three additional node types called *edge'*, *vertex'*, and *vertex''* so that there are now eight node types. The node types labeled with a prime and double prime symbol account for the possibility that the faces and edges that share a common vertex or edge may do so both inside and outside the block. The exact definition of the node types is now as follows (see Exercise 2):

1. *Empty:* completely inside the object

2. *Full:* completely outside the object

3. *Face:* contains one face

4. *Edge:* contains several faces and the edge at which they meet

5. *Vertex:* contains several faces, the edges at which they meet, and the vertex at which they meet; alternatively, contains one vertex and the edges and faces that meet at it

6. *Edge':* contains several faces, all of which meet at the same edge, which is outside the node

7. *Vertex':* contains several edges and the corresponding adjacent faces, all of which meet at the same vertex, which is outside the node

8. *Vertex'':* contains several faces, all of which meet at the same vertex, which is outside the node

It should be clear that not all of the above node types are needed in the sense that the definitions of the *edge* and *vertex* node types can be generalized so that the common edge or vertex can be both inside and outside the node. Thus, the revised definition of node type *edge* subsumes node type *edge'*, and the revised definition of the *vertex* node type subsumes both node types *vertex'* and *vertex''*. Therefore, the result would have the following form:

1. *Empty:* completely inside the object

2. *Full:* completely outside the object

3. *Face:* contains one face

4. *Edge:* contains several faces that meet at the same edge whether or not the edge is in the node

5. *Vertex:* contains several edges and faces that meet at the same vertex whether or not the vertex or the common edges are in the node

The advantage of the PM_2 octree is that the maximum depth of the tree is now bounded by the smallest distance between two elements (i.e., vertices, edges, or faces) that are topologically connected. Therefore, unlike the PM_1 octree, there are no black holes in the PM_2 octree. The same holds for the PM_3 octree. Nevertheless, Dürst and Kunii state that, whereas in the two-dimensional case the reduction in storage requirements when using a PM_2 quadtree over a PM_1 quadtree is not large, thereby leading to the formulation of the PM_3 quadtree, this is not the case in three dimensions, which is why, among other reasons, they omit the PM_3 octree from further consideration.

The definition of the PM octree that we have given makes an implicit assumption that objects are well-formed in the sense that at most two faces meet at a common edge. However, for our purposes, it is permissible to have more than two faces meet at a common edge. Of course, such a situation cannot arise when modeling solids that are bounded by compact, orientable two-manifold surfaces (i.e., only two faces may meet at an edge—see Exercise 1 in Section 2.2.1.7).[42] Nevertheless, the more general case is plausible when three-dimensional objects are represented by their surfaces.

Unfortunately, two-manifolds are not closed under Boolean operations. In other words, the result of applying such an operation between two two-manifold polyhedra can be a nonmanifold, which is not representable using an extended octree. This problem also arises with constructive solid geometry (CSG), in which case it is resolved by restricting the Boolean set operations to be regularized Boolean set operations (see the discussion in the prologue of Section 2.2). Instead, Brunet and Navazo [272] permit the representation of any nonmanifold object by adding a node type called a *Boolean node* to the *empty, full, face, edge, vertex,* and *terminal gray* node types. The Boolean node is a Boolean expression involving the individual face, edge, and vertex nodes that make up the solid in the cell. In order to reduce the storage requirements further, Brunet and Navazo [272] make use of another node type, called a *nearby node,* that halts the decomposition when a node contains two or more faces that meet at a vertex outside the node (i.e., a node of type *vertex″* using the terminology of Dürst and Kunii [519]).

Navazo, Fontdecaba, and Brunet [1352] discuss the conversion from a CSG representation to a PM octree. If the objects have planar faces, then the conversion process yields an exact representation. The algorithm proceeds in a top-down manner and employs pruning rules similar to those used by Samet and Tamminen [1658, 1662] in the conversion of a CSG tree to a bintree. The principal difference is that Navazo et al. also need to compute the vertex configuration that must be associated with each vertex node in the PM octree. The computational complexity of the algorithm is the same as that of Samet and Tamminen [1658, 1662] when the initial CSG tree is *well behaved*—that is, no faces are tangential to each other, which means that the boundaries of the objects do not coincide but are permitted to intersect along one-dimensional edges. The construction of a CSG tree from the PM octree is more complex (see Exercise 11).

With the above conversion algorithms at hand, the PM octree can serve as the basis of a hybrid solid modeling system. In such a case, a dual representation can be used, and operations will be performed in the model that most easily supports them. For example, Boolean set operations are more easily performed in the PM octree, as well as in other octrees such as the region quadtree, than in the boundary model. Similarly, recursive subdivision, as is present in the PM octree as well as in other octree variants, can facilitate the evaluation of CSG trees; e.g., the analysis [1143, 1144, 1947] and display [1525,

---

[42] By *oriented* we mean two-sided. Thus, it is not like a Möbius strip or a Klein bottle.

2019, 2021, 2022], as well as the computation of geometric properties, such as mass, of solid objects modeled by them. In other words, they can be performed more easily in the PM octree representation than in the CSG representation.

PM octree techniques have also been extended to handle curvilinear surfaces. Primitives, including cylinders and spheres, have been used in conjunction with a decomposition rule limiting the number of distinct primitives that can be associated with a leaf node [661, 2028]. In particular, the PM octree serves as the basis of the *PM-CSG tree* [2028]. In this case, the decomposition criteria are such that no block contains more than one CSG primitive. This representation does not handle a pure CSG representation as it does not permit a full complement of CSG operations. Instead, it uses a subset consisting of union and subtraction of sets (i.e., set difference). The set intersection operation is not allowed because, in this case, its constituent primitives cannot be separated so that each one is in only one block. Moreover, the set union operation is not general in that it requires that the two operand sets be disjoint. Thus, it is more like a set addition operation. This means that no two objects can occupy the same space. An alternative physical analogy is that the operations of set addition and subtraction correspond to gluing and cutting, respectively. For more details, see [1636, Section 5.5.2].

Another approach [1351] extends the concepts of face node, edge node, and vertex node to handle faces represented by biquadratic patches. The use of biquadratic patches enables a better fit with fewer primitives than can be obtained with planar faces, thereby reducing the size of the octree. The resulting decomposition and the contents of the blocks are quite similar to those obtained by use of the adaptively sampled distance field of Frisken et al. [654, 655, 1482] (see Section 2.2.2.5). The difficulty in organizing curved surface patches by using octrees lies in devising efficient methods of calculating the intersection between a patch and an octree node. Observe that, in this approach (i.e., [1351]), we are organizing a collection of patches in the image space. This is in contrast to decomposing a single patch in the parametric space by use of quadtree techniques, as discussed in [1636, Section 7.1.6].

Fujimura and Samet [663] treat time as an additional dimension (see also [708, 711, 933, 1658, 2050]) and use a PM octree to represent moving objects in the plane. Their goal is to perform path planning for a robot in an environment that contains moving obstacles. The environment is two-dimensional, and the obstacles are represented using PM_1 quadtrees. The addition of the time dimension yields a PM octree. A safe path is one in which the obstacles do not collide with each other or with the robot. The path is obtained by use of heuristic search.

Exercises

1. Give a precise definition of a PM_1 octree in terms of the number of vertices, edges, and faces that a block can contain.

2. At a first glance, it seems that the *vertex'* and *vertex''* node types in the definition of a PM_2 octree are identical. What is the difference between them?

3. Under what circumstances are the space requirements of the face octree less than those of the PM_1 octree?

4. Suppose that a vertex node is determined by three faces with plane equations h_1, h_2, and h_3. How many different configurations are possible when circular permutations are considered equivalent?

5. Suppose that a vertex node is determined by four faces with plane equations h_1, h_2, h_3, and h_4. How many different configurations are possible when circular permutations are considered equivalent?

6. In Section 2.2.2.2, we pointed out that the space requirements of the region octree of a polyhedral object are proportional to the object's surface area. Can you prove that the space requirements of the PM octree for a polyhedral object are proportional to the sum of the lengths of its edges?

7. Write an algorithm to compute the intersection of two objects represented by PM octrees.

8. Write an algorithm to compute the union of two objects represented by PM octrees.

9. Given a position of an observer, write an algorithm to display an object that is represented by a PM octree.

10. Write an algorithm to convert from a boundary model to a PM octree.

11. Write an algorithm to convert from a CSG representation to a PM octree.

12. Write an algorithm to convert from a PM octree to a boundary model.

13. Write an algorithm to convert from a PM octree to a CSG representation.

14. How would you solve the point location problem when a polyhedral subdivision is represented by a PM_1 octree?

2.2.2.8 Bucket PM Quadtree and PMR Quadtree

As mentioned above, the different variants of the PM quadtree that we have discussed are all vertex based. They differ in the degree to which the edges play in the decomposition process—that is, from some (PM_1), to little (PM_2), to none (PM_3). A drastic alternative is to remove completely the dependence of the decomposition on the vertices and just take into account the edges that make up the polygonal map. As we saw in the PM quadtrees, it is impossible for all of the blocks to contain just one line segment. Thus, one approach to defining an edge-based decomposition is to stipulate that each block is split until it contains no more that T line segments. In this case, T acts like a bucket capacity, and we term the result a *bucket PM quadtree*. The drawback of such a representation is that the decomposition does not stop in the neighborhood of a vertex v with degree greater than T (i.e., more than T edges are incident at v).

There are several options. The first option is analogous to ignoring the problem by setting an upper limit on the level of decomposition. The second option is to formulate bucketlike analogs of the vertex-based PM quadtrees where the bucketing condition involves the number of line segments that pass through the block. However, this is not as simple as it appears. The problem is that, if we add the proviso that a block is not split if it has T or fewer line segments, then we may violate the vertex condition. For example, a natural bucket analog of the PM_1 quadtree is one that decomposes the underlying space until each block b contains no more than T line segments or if all of the line segments in b meet at the same vertex v, which is in b. The bucket analog of the PM_2 quadtree will be defined similarly, with the added proviso that block b can contain more than T line segments if they all meet at the same vertex v, and v need not be in b. There is no logical bucket analog of the PM_3 quadtree as the number of line segments in the block plays no role in the decomposition process.

The shortcoming of these bucket decomposition rules is that, even though a block b may contain several vertices, no decomposition takes place when b has T or fewer line segments. Thus, the bucket analogs must be defined more directly in terms of the number of vertices that they permit. In other words, the primary condition is one that limits the number of vertices in each block, with the bucket capacity, in terms of the number of line segments, being a secondary condition.

Using such a condition priority, we define the bucketlike analogs of the PM_1 and PM_2 quadtrees as follows. A *bucket PM_1 quadtree* contains at most one vertex v per block and no line segments that do not meet at v. Each block that contains no vertices can contain at most T line segments. A *bucket PM_2 quadtree* is defined using a similar rule, with the added proviso that a block b that contains no vertices can contain more than T line segments if they all meet at the same vertex v where v is not in b. It is meaningless to define a bucketlike analog of the PM_3 quadtree because the number of line segments does not enter into the PM_3 quadtree decomposition rule, and thus we do not do so.

The third option is similar to the first option in the sense that it is motivated by the rationale that, since an infinite level of decomposition is possible, why not decompose the bucket PM quadtree just once each time an edge is inserted into a block that contains more than T line segments? Of course, the tree will still have a maximum level of decomposition; however, it will be attained only if there really is a lot of insertion activity in the blocks that are being repeatedly decomposed rather than just because we happened to insert a line segment having a vertex whose degree exceeded T. We say that the decomposition is based on a *probabilistic splitting rule*. We term the result a *PMR quadtree* [1360], an edge-based variant of the PM quadtree.

It should be clear that a PMR quadtree block is permitted to contain a variable number of line segments. The PMR quadtree is constructed by inserting the line segments one by one into an initially empty structure consisting of one block. Each line segment is inserted into all the blocks that it intersects or occupies in its entirety. During this process, the occupancy of each block that is intersected by the line segment is checked to see if the insertion causes it to exceed a predetermined *splitting threshold*. If the splitting threshold is exceeded, the block is split once, and only once, into four blocks of equal size.

Figure 2.128(e) is the PMR quadtree for the collection of line segment objects in Figure 2.118(a) with a splitting threshold value of 2. The nine line segments, labeled a–i, are inserted in alphabetical order. It should be clear that the shape of the PMR quadtree for a given polygonal map is not unique; instead, it depends on the order in which the line segments are inserted into it. In contrast, the shapes of the PM_1, PM_2, and PM_3 quadtrees, as well as their bucket analogs, are unique. Figure 2.128 shows some of the steps in the process of building the PMR quadtree of Figure 2.128(e). In each part of Figure 2.128, the line segment that caused the subdivision is denoted by a thick line, while the gray regions indicate the blocks where the most recent subdivisions have taken place.

The insertion of line segments c, e, g, h, and i cause the subdivisions in parts (a), (b), (c), (d), and (e), respectively, of Figure 2.128. The insertion of line segment i causes three blocks to be subdivided (i.e., the SE block in the SW quadrant, the SE quadrant, and the SW block in the NE quadrant). The final result is shown in Figure 2.128(e). Note the difference from the PM_1 quadtree in Figure 2.123—that is, the NE block of the SW quadrant is decomposed in the PM_1 quadtree, but the SE block of the SW quadrant is not decomposed in the PM_1 quadtree.

A line segment is deleted from a PMR quadtree by removing it from all the blocks that it intersects. During this process, the occupancy of the block and its siblings is checked to see if the deletion causes the total number of line segments in them to be fewer than the predetermined splitting threshold. If the splitting threshold exceeds the occupancy of the block and its siblings, then they are merged, and the merging process is reapplied to the resulting block and its siblings. Notice the asymmetry between the splitting and merging rules.

Notice that the splitting threshold is a different concept from the bucket capacity used in the definition of the bucket PM_1 and PM_2 quadtrees, although it plays the same role. Thus, it should be clear that the number of line segments in a PMR quadtree block can exceed the value of the splitting threshold. In fact, it can be shown [1637, Exercise 4.75, p. 268] that the maximum number of line segments in a PMR quadtree block is bounded by the sum of the splitting threshold and the depth of the block (i.e., the number of times the original space has been decomposed to yield this block). Interestingly, the number of line segments in a quadtree block can also exceed the bucket capacity T for the PM_3 quadtree and for both the PM_1 and PM_2 quadtrees, as well as their bucket analogs, since the presence of a vertex in a block b results in the possibility that b (as well as other blocks for the PM_2 quadtree) contains more than T line segments.

Once the decomposition into blocks has been obtained, we also need to decide how to organize the line segments that pass through the block. This is a relatively difficult issue to which not much attention has been paid in the past. However, the right choice has a dramatic effect on the performance of geometric operations as the blocks are often treated

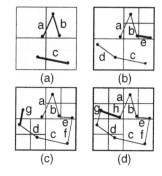

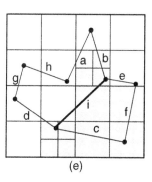

Figure 2.128
PMR quadtree for the collection of line segments of Figure 2.118(a): (a–e) snapshots of the construction process, with the final PMR quadtree given in (e). Gray regions indicate the blocks where the most recent subdivisions have taken place.

as buckets of nontrivial sizes (e.g., 32, 64, and even higher values). This is especially the case when the buckets take on the role of disk pages. Thus, the buckets provide an initial sort of the underlying space. However, once we access the appropriate bucket, we do not want to have to execute a sequential search to find the relevant data when the bucket can contain many elements. For example, some possibilities for line segments include the following:

1. Sort the lines on the basis of their nearness to one of the axes.

2. Sort the lines that meet at a vertex in clockwise or counterclockwise order.

3. Represent the portion of the line that passes through the block by its midpoint, and store it in a point representation such as a PR quadtree.

The PMR quadtree is very good for answering queries like finding the nearest line to a given point [863] (see [864] for an empirical comparison with hierarchical object representations, such as the R-tree and R^+-tree). It is preferred over the PM_1 quadtree (as well as the PM_2, PM_3, MX, and edge quadtrees) as it results in far fewer subdivisions. In particular, in the PMR quadtree, there is no need to subdivide in order to separate line segments that are very "close" or whose vertices are very "close," which is the case for the PM_1 quadtree. This is important since four blocks are created at each subdivision step. Thus, when many subdivision steps that occur in a PM_1 quadtree result in creating many empty blocks, the storage requirements of the PM_1 quadtree are considerably higher than those of the PMR quadtree. Generally, as the splitting threshold is increased, the storage requirements of the PMR quadtree decrease, while the time necessary to perform operations on it increases.

Using a random lines model and geometric probability (e.g., [1673]), it has been shown [1175] theoretically and empirically, using both random and real map data, that for sufficiently high values of the splitting threshold (i.e., ≥ 4), the number of blocks in a PMR quadtree is asymptotically proportional to the number of line segments and is independent of the maximum level of decomposition. In contrast, using the same model, the number of nodes in the PM_1 quadtree is a product of the number of lines and the maximal level of decomposition (i.e., n for a $2^n \times 2^n$ image). The same experiments and analysis for the MX quadtree confirmed the results predicted by the Quadtree Complexity Theorem, which is that the number of blocks is proportional to the total length of the line segments.

Exercises

Exercises 1–4 assume the use of the vertex bucket polygon quadtree defined in Section 2.1.4. In this case, decomposition halts whenever a block is a part of no more than T polygons or contains just one vertex.

1. Prove or disprove that the vertex bucket polygon quadtree decomposition rule yields the same decomposition as a bucket PM_1 quadtree decomposition rule for line segments.

2. Prove or disprove that the vertex bucket polygon quadtree decomposition rule yields the same decomposition as a bucket PM_2 quadtree decomposition rule for line segments.

3. Prove or disprove that the vertex bucket polygon quadtree decomposition rule yields the same decomposition as a PM_3 quadtree decomposition rule for line segments.

4. Consider a special case of the vertex bucket polygon quadtree where $T = 2$. Prove or disprove that the vertex bucket polygon quadtree decomposition is the same as one of the vertex-based PM quadtree decomposition rules for line segments.

5. Prove that the maximum number of line segments that can occur in a node in a PMR quadtree, say P, is the sum of the splitting threshold and the depth of the tree at which P is found.

6. Suppose that the set of line segments intersect but that their intersections are not considered as vertices (i.e., they are nonplanar). We saw that this does not pose a problem for the PMR quadtree. What about the PM_1, PM_2, and PM_3 quadtrees?

7. Prove that, on the average, if lines are drawn from a sample distributed uniformly in space and orientation, then the average number of quadrants intersected by a line passing through a quartered block is two. This can be done by showing that, for lines drawn from a set of parallel lines, say L, passing through the block at angle θ, the average number of blocks intersected by a line is two, independent of θ.

8. Assuming that the line segments that are stored in a node in the PMR quadtree are uncorrelated, use the result of Exercise 7 to compute the distribution of occupancies when a node is split into quadrants given a splitting threshold c. Normalize your result so that the expected total number of quadrants is four.

9. Prove that the average occupancy of the nodes produced when a PMR quadtree node is split is bounded and smaller than the size of the parent.

10. Continuing Exercise 9, prove that the average size of parent nodes in a PMR quadtree is also bounded by considering the case when the node occupancy i is greater than the splitting threshold c.

11. Give an algorithm to insert a line segment into a PMR quadtree.

12. Give an algorithm to delete a line segment from a PMR quadtree.

13. Do polygonal maps that correspond to Delaunay triangulations (see Section 2.2.1.4) behave better in the sense that their quadtree decompositions require fewer blocks than the quadtree decompositions of other triangulations of the same set of points? In other words, do they have some properties that avoid some of the bad, degenerate cases of many decompositions? For example, the Delaunay triangulation of a given set of points satisfies the minimum angle property, which means that it maximizes the minimum interior angle in the entire triangulation, thereby avoiding the presence of thin triangles that would cause much decomposition in the case of a PM_1 quadtree (and in a PM_2 quadtree to a lesser extent). Consider the various PM quadtree decompositions based on line segments, as well as the polygon decomposition rule that stipulates that decomposition halts whenever a block is a part of no more than T polygons or contains just one vertex (i.e., the vertex bucket polygon quadtree discussed in Section 2.1.4).

2.2.2.9 Sector Tree

In all of the previous sections, regardless of whether we have chosen to represent an object by its interior or by its boundary, the underlying space has been decomposed into polygonal blocks. This is the prevalent method in use today. However, for certain applications, the use of polygonal blocks can lead to problems. For example, suppose that we have a decomposition based on square blocks. In this case, as the resolution is increased, the area of the approximated region approaches the true value of the area. However, this is not true for a boundary measure such as the perimeter. To see this, consider a quadtree approximation of an isoceles right triangle where the ratio of the approximated perimeter to the true perimeter is $1/(2 + \sqrt{2})$ (see Exercise 1). Other problems include the discontinuity of the normals to the boundaries of adjacent tiles. Recall from Section 2.2.2.5 that overcoming this problem is one of the motivations behind adaptively sampled distance fields (ADFs).

There are a number of other ways of attempting to overcome these problems. The *hierarchical probe model* of Chen [352] is an approach based on treating space as a polar plane and recursively decomposing it into sectors. We say that each sector consists of an origin, two sides (labeled 1 and 2 corresponding to the order in which they are encountered when proceeding in a counterclockwise direction), and an arc. The points at which the sides of the sector intersect (or touch) the object are called *contact points*. (ρ, θ) denotes a point in the polar plane. Let (ρ_i, θ_i) be the contact point with the maximum value of ρ in direction θ_i. Each sector represents a region bounded by the points $(0,0)$, (ρ_1, θ_1), and (ρ_2, θ_2), where $\theta_1 = 2k\pi/2^n$ and $\theta_2 = \theta_1 + 2\pi/2^n$ such that k and n are nonnegative integers ($k < 2^n$). The arc between the two nonorigin contact points (ρ_1, θ_1) and (ρ_2, θ_2) of a sector is approximated by the linear parametric equations ($0 \le t \le 1$):

$$\rho(t) = \rho_1 + (\rho_2 - \rho_1) \cdot t \quad \theta(t) = \theta_1 + (\theta_2 - \theta_1) \cdot t.$$

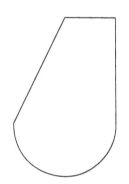

Figure 2.129
Example convex object.

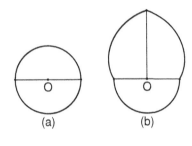

(a)   (b)

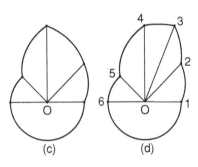

(c)   (d)

Figure 2.130
Successive sector tree approximations for the object of Figure 2.129:
(a) π intervals, (b) $\pi/2$ intervals, (c) $\pi/4$ intervals, and (d) $\pi/8$ intervals.

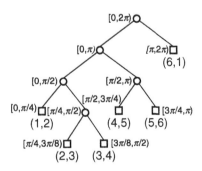

Figure 2.131
Binary tree representation of the sector tree of Figure 2.129.

Note that the interpolation curves are arcs of spirals due to the linear relation between ρ and θ. The use of the arcs of spirals to represent the boundary is what leads us to characterize the sector tree as a boundary representation.

The *sector tree* is a binary tree that represents the result of recursively subdividing sectors in the polar plane into two sectors of equal angular intervals. Thus, the recursive decomposition is only with respect to θ, not ρ. Initially, the universe is the interval $[0, 2\pi)$. The decomposition stops whenever the approximation of a part of an object by a sector is deemed adequate. The computation of the stopping condition is implementation dependent. For example, it can be the maximum deviation in the value of ρ between a point on the boundary and the corresponding point (i.e., at the same value of θ) on the approximating arc of a spiral. In fact, the use of the arcs of spirals to represent the boundary leads us to characterize the sector tree as a boundary representation.

In the presentation, we assume that the origin of the polar plane is contained within the object. See Exercise 7 for a discussion of how to represent an object that does not contain the origin of the polar plane. The simplest case arises when the object is convex. The result is a binary tree where each leaf node represents a sector and contains the contact points of its corresponding arc. For example, consider the object in Figure 2.129. The construction of its sector tree approximation is shown in Figure 2.130. The final binary tree is given in Figure 2.131, with interval endpoints labeled according to Figure 2.130(d).

The situation is more complex when the object is not convex. This means that each side of a sector may intersect the boundary of the object at an arbitrary, and possibly different, number of contact points. In the following, each sector will be seen to consist of a set of alternating regions that are within the object and outside the object. These regions are either three- or four-sided and have at least one side that is colinear with a side of the sector. We illustrate our discussion with the object of Figure 2.132(a), whose sector tree decomposition is given in Figure 2.132(b). The final binary tree is given in Figure 2.133. A better indication of the quality of the approximation can be seen by examining Figure 2.132(c), which contains an overlay of Figures 2.132(a) and 2.132(b).

When the boundary of the object intersects a sector at two successive contact points, say P and Q, that lie on the same side, say S, of the sector, then the region bounded by S and PQ must be approximated. Without loss of generality, assume that the region is inside the object. There are two choices. An inner approximation ignores the region by treating the segment of S between P and Q as part of the approximated boundary (e.g., the region between points 9 and 10 in sector $[9\pi/8, 5\pi/4)$ in Figure 2.132(b)).

An outer approximation inserts two identical contact points, say R and T, on the other side of the sector and then approximates the region by the three-sided region formed by the segment of S between P and Q and the spiral arc approximations of PR and QT. The value of R (and hence T) is equal to the average of the value of ρ at P and Q. For example, the region between points 4 and 5 in sector $[5\pi/4, 3\pi/2)$ in Figure 2.132(b) is approximated by the region formed with points C and D.

Of course, the same approximation process is applied to the part of the region that is outside the object. In Figure 2.132(b), we have an inner approximation for the region between points 7 and 8 in sector $[3\pi/2, 2\pi)$ and an outer approximation for the region between points 5 and 6 in sector $[9\pi/8, 5\pi/4)$, by virtue of the introduction of points A and B.

One of the drawbacks of the sector tree is that its use can lead to the creation of holes that do not exist in the original object. This situation arises when the decomposition is not carried out to a level of sufficient depth. For example, consider Figure 2.132(b), which has a hole bounded by the arcs formed by points A, B, 6, 7, C, D, and 5. This is a result of the inner approximation for the region between points 7 and 8 in sector $[3\pi/2, 2\pi)$ and an outer approximation for the region between points 4 and 5 in sector $[5\pi/4, 3\pi/2)$.

Of course, this situation can be resolved by further decomposition in either or both of sectors $[3\pi/2,2\pi)$ and $[5\pi/4,3\pi/2)$.

The result of the above approximation process is that each sector consists of a collection of three- and four-sided regions that approximate the part of the object contained in the sector. This collection is stored in the leaf node of the sector tree as a list of pairs of points in the polar plane. It is interesting to observe that the boundaries of the interpolated regions are not stored explicitly in the tree. Instead, each pair of points corresponds to the boundary of a region. Since the origin of the polar plane is within the object, an odd number of pairs of points is associated with each leaf node. For example, consider the leaf node in Figure 2.133 corresponding to the sector $[5\pi/4,3\pi/2)$. The first pair, together with the origin, define the first region (e.g., (6,7)). The next two pairs of points define the second region (e.g., (5,C) and (4,D)), with each successive two pairs of points defining the remaining regions.

The sector tree is a partial polar decomposition as the subdivision process is only based on the value of θ. A total polar decomposition would partition the polar plane on the basis of both ρ and θ. The result is analogous to a quadtree, and we shall term it a *polar quadtree*. There are a number of possible rules for the decomposition process (see Exercise 13). For example, consider a decomposition that recursively halves both ρ and θ at each level. In general, the polar quadtree is a variant of a maximal block representation. As in the sector tree, the blocks are disjoint. Unlike the sector tree, blocks in the polar quadtree do have standard sizes. In particular, all blocks in the polar quadtree are either three-sided (i.e., sectors) or four-sided (i.e., quadrilaterals, two of whose sides are arcs). Thus, the sides of polar quadtree blocks are not based on interpolation.

The sector tree can be used for performing many operations, some of which are easy to implement while others are more difficult. Boolean set operations, such as union and intersection, are straightforward. Scaling is trivial as the sector tree need not be modified. In particular, all values of ρ are interpreted as scaled by the appropriate scale factor. The

(a)

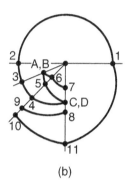

(b)

(c)

Figure 2.132
(a) Example object, (b) its sector tree description, and (c) a comparison of the sector tree approximation (thin lines) with the original object (thick lines). Note the creation of a hole corresponding to the region formed by points A, B, 6, 7, C, D, and 5.

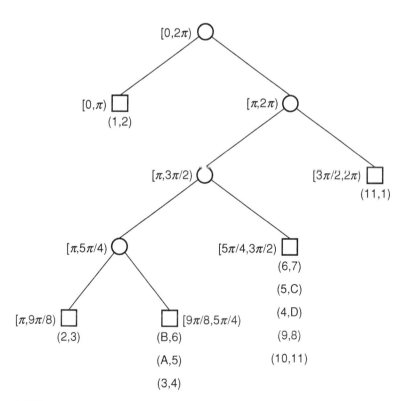

Figure 2.133
Binary tree representation of the sector tree of Figure 2.132.

number of nodes in a sector tree is dependent on its orientation—that is, on the points chosen as the origin and the contact point chosen to serve as $(\rho, 0)$. Rotation is not so simple: it cannot be implemented by simply rearranging pointers (but see Exercise 11). Translation is computationally expensive since the change in the relative position of the object with respect to the origin means that the entire sector tree must be reconstructed.

Exercises

1. Prove that, for an isoceles right triangle represented by a region quadtree, the ratio of the approximated perimeter to the true perimeter is $4/(2 + \sqrt{2})$.

2. Repeat Exercise 1 for a circle (i.e., find the ratio).

3. When the objects have linear sides, a decomposition of the underlying space into polygonal blocks is superior. How would you use the sector tree decomposition method with polygonal blocks?

4. In our discussion of the situation arising when the boundary of the object intersects a sector at two successive contact points, say P and Q, that lie on the same side, say S, of the sector, we assume that the region bounded by S and PQ is inside the object. Suppose that this region is outside the object. How does this affect the inner and outer approximations?

5. Can you traverse the boundary of an object represented by a sector tree by visiting each leaf node just once?

6. When using a sector tree, how would you handle the situation that the boundary of the object just touches the side of a sector without crossing it (i.e., a tangent if the boundary is differentiable)?

7. How would you use a sector tree to represent an object that does not contain the origin of the polar plane?

8. When you build a sector tree, the outer approximation always yields a three-sided region. Two of the sides are arcs of spirals with respect to a common origin. This implies a sharp discontinuity of the derivative at the point at which they meet. Can you devise a way to smoothen this discontinuity?

9. When you build a sector tree, does the inner approximation always underestimate the area? Similarly, does the outer approximation always overestimate the area?

10. Compare the inner and outer approximations used in building a sector tree. Is there ever a reason to prefer the outer approximation over the inner approximations (or vice versa)?

11. Define a complete sector tree in an analogous manner to a complete binary tree—that is, all leaf nodes are at the same level, say n. Prove that a complete sector tree is invariant under rotation in multiples of $2\pi/2^n$.

12. Write an algorithm to trace the boundary of an object that is represented by a sector tree.

13. Investigate different splitting rules for polar quadtrees. In particular, you do not need to alternate the splits—that is, you could split on ρ several times in a row, and so forth. This technique is used in the adaptive k-d tree [650] (see Section 1.5.1.4 of Chapter 1) by decomposing the quartering process into two splitting operations—one for the x coordinate and one for the y coordinate. What are the possible shapes for the quadrants of such trees (e.g., a torus, a doughnut, wheels with spokes)?

2.2.2.10 Cone Tree[43]

The *cone tree* is an extension of the sector tree of Chen [352] (see Section 2.2.2.9) to deal with three-dimensional data. In particular, it is a boundary representation of an object's surface where the space is treated as a polar sphere and is recursively decomposed into cones. The motivation for its development is the same as that for the sector tree. In particular, we want a representation that provides a good approximation, in terms of a measure, of both the boundary (e.g., surface area) of the object as well as its interior

---

[43] This section contains material of a specialized nature and can be skipped on an initial reading.

(e.g., volume). In addition, the normals to the surface should have a minimum amount of discontinuity between adjacent surface elements.

Let (ρ, θ, ϕ) denote a point in the polar sphere. θ and ϕ are called the *polar* and *azimuth* angles, respectively. θ ranges between 0 and π, and ϕ ranges between 0 and 2π. Each cone consists of an origin, four edges (alternatively, pairs of edges form sectors), and a spherical patch. The points at which the edges of the cones intersect (or touch) the object are called *contact points*.

Let $(\rho_{ij}, \theta_i, \phi_j)$ be the contact point with the maximum value of ρ in direction (θ_i, ϕ_j). Each cone (e.g., Figure 2.134) represents a region bounded by the points $(0,0,0)$, $(\rho_{11}, \theta_1, \phi_1)$, $(\rho_{12}, \theta_1, \phi_2)$, $(\rho_{21}, \theta_2, \phi_1)$, and $(\rho_{22}, \theta_2, \phi_2)$. $\theta_1 = k\pi/2^n$ and $\theta_2 = \theta_1 + \pi/2^n$, such that k and n are nonnegative integers ($k < 2^n$). $\phi_1 = 2m\pi/2^n$ and $\phi_2 = \phi_1 + 2\pi/2^n$, such that m and n are nonnegative integers ($m < 2^n$).

The spherical patch having the four nonorigin contact points as its corners is approximated by three parametric equations in s and t such that $0 \leq s \leq 1$ and $0 \leq t \leq 1$ (see Exercise 1). Note that the interpolation curves will be nonlinear functions of the parameters s and t. However, at the edges of the patch (e.g., $s = 0$, $s = 1$, $t = 0$, $t = 1$ in Figure 2.134), the approximation is a linear function.

The cone tree is analogous to a region quadtree that represents the result of recursively subdividing cones in the polar sphere into four cones of square spherical intervals (i.e., $\Delta\theta = \Delta\phi$). The spherical intervals form a two-dimensional space. Since the range of ϕ is twice as large as that of θ, the $\phi - \theta$ space is initially subdivided into two cones at $\phi = \pi$. All subsequent decompositions are into four cones of equal square spherical intervals. The decomposition stops whenever the approximation of a part of an object by the spherical patches represented by the cone is deemed adequate. The computation of the stopping condition is implementation dependent. In our presentation, we assume that the origin of the polar sphere is contained within the object.

Assume that the object is convex. Nonconvex objects are beyond the scope of our discussion. The result is a quadtree where each leaf node represents a spherical patch. It contains the contact points of its corresponding patch, which are the corners of the node's block. Unfortunately, there exist discontinuities in the approximated surfaces represented by the cone tree. The problem arises when adjacent blocks in the $\phi - \theta$ space are of different sizes. For example, consider the block decomposition in Figure 2.135. The approximated surface for block A is computed by using the contact points 1, 2, 3, and 5. The approximated surface for block B is computed by using the contact points 3, 4, 6, and 7. The approximated surface for block C is computed by using the contact points 4, 5, 7, and 8. We now see that the approximated surface of A does not match the approximated surface of B and C along the common side of their cone tree blocks (see Figure 2.136).

Chen suggests that this situation can be alleviated, in part, by replacing the contact points of the smaller block by points on the approximated surface of the larger adjacent block and subsequently subdividing the larger block if the error is too large. However, a better solution is to use an approach similar to the restricted quadtree [1453, 1771, 1772, 1940] (described in Section 2.2.4). In this case, nodes that have a neighbor whose level in the tree is more than one level deeper are subdivided further until the condition holds.

The cone tree can be used to facilitate the same kind of operations as the sector tree. For example, Boolean set operations, such as union and intersection, are straightforward. Scaling is trivial as the cone tree need not be modified. All values of ρ are interpreted as scaled by the appropriate scale factor. Rotating a cone tree is more complex than rotating a sector tree since two angles must be involved. Translation is expensive because the position of the object relative to the origin changes. Thus, the entire cone tree must be reconstructed.

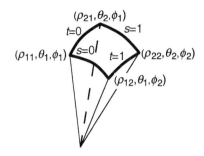

Figure 2.134
Example cone.

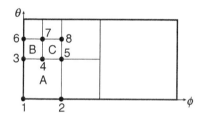

Figure 2.135
Example quadtree decomposition of a surface in $\phi - \theta$ space.

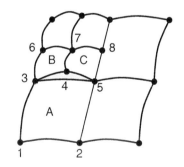

Figure 2.136
The cone tree representation of the left half of the surface in Figure 2.135. The shaded area represents a discontinuity in adjacent spherical patches.

Exercises

1. Give the three parametric equations in s and t for a spherical patch at points $(\rho_{11}, \theta_1, \phi_1)$, $(\rho_{12}, \theta_1, \phi_2)$, $(\rho_{21}, \theta_2, \phi_1)$, and $(\rho_{22}, \theta_2, \phi_2)$.

2. How would you use a cone tree to represent an object that is not convex?

3. How would you use a cone tree to represent an object that does not contain the origin of the polar sphere?

4. Write an algorithm to determine if a specific point is inside or outside an object represented by a cone tree.

5. How would you adapt the restricted quadtree [1453, 1771, 1772, 1940] (see Section 2.2.4) to avoid the discontinuities that are present in the approximated surfaces represented by a cone tree.

2.2.3 Object-Based Boundary Representations

In Sections 2.1.5.2 and 2.1.5.3, we examine two hierarchical representations (i.e., the R-tree and the R^+-tree) that propagate object approximations in the form of bounding boxes. In both of these cases, the location query is facilitated by imposing a tree access structure on the elements of the hierarchy. In this section, we review several related hierarchical representations of the boundaries of objects. Section 2.2.3.1 presents the strip tree and some variants for the representation of boundaries of two-dimensional objects. Section 2.2.3.2 discusses the prism tree, which is a generalization of the strip tree to the boundaries of three-dimensional objects. The bounding boxes used by these methods are variants of polyhedra as well as ellipses. Section 2.2.3.3 describes the HAL tree, which makes use of variants of spherical bounding boxes. Section 2.2.3.4 gives a brief overview of simplification methods that are commonly used in computer graphics to provide varying levels of detail for approximate display, as well as to speed up computations. They have been motivated by the need to process rapidly very large collections of polygons (usually triangles) on the surface of objects. They are closely related to the methods discussed in Sections 2.2.3.1 to 2.2.3.3 but differ in the motivation for their development and the extent of their use. All of these representations are also accompanied by a tree access structure so that the location query can be executed efficiently. Of course, other access structures could also be used, but they are not discussed here.

2.2.3.1 Strip Tree, Arc Tree, and BSPR

When using the R-tree or R^+-tree as an object approximation, the sides of the bounding boxes must be parallel to the coordinate axes of the space from which the objects are drawn. In contrast, the *strip tree* [121] is a hierarchical representation of a single curve that successively approximates segments of it with bounding boxes that do not require that the sides be parallel to the coordinate axes. The only requirement is that the curve be continuous; it need not be differentiable.

The strip tree data structure is supplemented by an access structure in the form of a binary tree whose root represents the bounding rectangle of the entire curve. For example, consider Figure 2.137, where the curve between points P and Q, at locations (x_P, y_P) and (x_Q, y_Q), respectively, is modeled by a strip tree. The rectangle associated with the root, A in this example, corresponds to a rectangular strip that encloses the curve, whose sides are parallel to the line joining the endpoints of the curve (i.e., P and Q). The curve is then partitioned in two at one of the locations where it touches the bounding rectangle (these are not tangent points as the curve only needs to be continuous; it need not be differentiable). Each subcurve is then surrounded by a bounding rectangle, and the partitioning process is applied recursively. This process stops when the width of each strip is less than a predetermined value. Figure 2.138 shows the binary tree corresponding to the decomposition into strips in Figure 2.137(a).

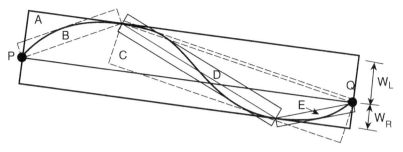

Figure 2.137
A curve and its decomposition into strips.

Figure 2.137 is a relatively simple example. In order to be able to cope with more complex curves such as those that arise in the case of objects rather than curves, the relationship between the bounding box and the underlying curve needs some further elaboration. In particular, closed curves and curves that extend past their endpoints require some special treatment. This issue can be resolved in several ways. One way is to change the nature of the bounding box. For example, we could make use of spherical bounding boxes as is done in the sphere tree (e.g., [895, 896, 1527]). However, there is really no need to do so as the strip tree can be modified so that such curves are enclosed by boxes that are split into two rectangular strips, and from now on the strip tree is used as before. For example, see Figure 2.139

For a related approach, see the *arc tree* [780]. The arc tree starts out by decomposing the curve into segments of equal length, thereby forming the deepest level in the hierarchy. Successive levels of the hierarchy are built by aggregating pairs, pairs of pairs, and so on. An access structure in the form of a complete binary tree (i.e., a one-dimensional pyramid) is imposed on the hierarchy. Thus, the result is analogous to imposing a one-dimensional uniform grid on the curve, where the width of each one-dimensional grid cell (i.e., interval) is based on the total length of the curve.

The arc tree makes use of ellipses as the bounding boxes for the subarcs. This, coupled with the fact that the aggregation is based on curve length, means that closed curves need no special treatment when represented by an arc tree. In particular, the foci of the ellipses are placed at the endpoints of each subarc, and the principal (i.e., major) axis is as long as the subarc. The result is that all subarcs lie completely within each ellipse, thereby obviating the need for special treatment for subarcs that extend past their endpoints (see Exercise 17). The drawback of the arc tree is that we need to be able to compute the length of an arc (see Exercise 16), which may be quite complex (e.g., if we have a closed form for the curve, then we need an elliptical integral).

The manner in which we have described the strip tree leads to it being characterized as top-down approach to curve approximation. The strip tree can also be built by a bottom-up process where the curve is assumed to be represented by a sequence of points. The construction process simply pairs up successive points and forms their strips, which are bounding boxes. It then pairs up the strips forming their strips, which are also bounding boxes. This process is applied repeatedly until one strip is obtained. It is interesting to note that the resulting approximations are not as good as those obtained by the top-down method.

The strip tree is rooted in the Douglas-Peucker line generalization algorithm [508] (also known as the *iterative endpoint fit* method in pattern recognition [514]). Generalization is a cartographic transformation from a large scale to a small scale (e.g.,[1269]), where large scale corresponds to less detail while small scale corresponds to more detail. The Douglas-Peucker algorithm is a top-down process whose input is a polyline L, which is a set of connected points $S = p_1 \ldots p_n$. The algorithm attempts to approximate L with another polyline L' whose vertices are a subset of S where each line segment in L' is an approximation of a subset of the line segments in L subject to a given error tolerance

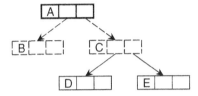

Figure 2.138
Strip tree corresponding to Figure 2.137.

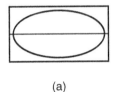

(a)

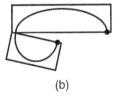

(b)

Figure 2.139
Strip tree representation of (a) a closed curve and (b) a curve that extends past its endpoints.

ε. Of course, other approximation-quality measures can be used, such as a minimum number of points or the preservation of the fractal dimension of the line (e.g., [1225]).

The Douglas-Peucker algorithm for arbitrary values of ε can be represented by a binary tree where the root corresponds to the line segment (p_1, p_n). The error for this approximation is determined by the point p_k in S, which has the greatest distance d from it. Now make p_k the root of the tree and store the error d, add two children to the tree corresponding to the line segments (p_1, p_k) and (p_k, p_n), and apply the process recursively to the two subtrees until all the points have been accounted for. The result is termed a *Binary Line Generalization Tree* (BLG-tree) [1410, 1411] (see also the PR-file 147).

Given an error tolerance ε, the Douglas-Peucker line generalization algorithm traverses the BLG-tree in a top-down manner and halts each time it encounters a node with an error tolerance less than ε. Interestingly, the distance values that are stored in the nodes of the BLG-tree do not necessarily become smaller as the tree is descended (see Exercise 24).

Note that the BLG-tree can be viewed as a generalization of the *Multi-scale Line Tree* [965, 966], which stores the result of the application of the Douglas-Peucker algorithm for several values of the error tolerance ε. In particular, the top level of the Multi-scale Line Tree corresponds to the points of the original line that are retained as a result of the application of the Douglas-Peucker algorithm at the coarsest error tolerance. Successive levels of the tree correspond to the result of the application of the Douglas-Peucker algorithm at finer error tolerances and contain the points that lie in between two points at the immediately preceding level. It should be clear that the BLG-tree is more general than the Multi-scale Line Tree as the BLG-tree does not require a commitment to a particular set of error tolerance values. Note also the similarity of the Multi-scale Line Tree to a multiresolution representation such as a pyramid.

Burton [293] defines a structure termed *Binary Searchable Polygonal Representation* (BSPR), which is closely related to the strip tree obtained by the bottom-up construction process in the sense that the BSPR is also a bottom-up approach to curve approximation. Once again, the primitive unit of approximation is a box; however, unlike the strip tree, in the case of the BSPR, all boxes are upright (i.e., they have a single orientation).

The curve to be approximated by the BSPR is decomposed into a set of *simple* sections, where each simple section corresponds to a segment of the curve that is monotonic in both the x and y coordinate values of the points it comprises. The tree is built by combining pairs of adjacent simple sections to yield *compound* sections. This process is repeatedly applied until the entire curve is approximated by one compound section. Thus, we see that leaf nodes correspond to simple sections, and nonleaf nodes correspond to compound sections. For a curve with 2^n simple sections, the corresponding BSPR has n levels. Thus, we see that, unlike the strip tree, which is constructed in a top-down manner, the BSPR does not allow for a variation in the approximation at the lowest level since the initial bounding boxes are determined by the simple sections (i.e., the monotonic curves).

As an example of a BSPR, consider the regular octagon in Figure 2.140(a) with vertices A–H. It can be decomposed into four simple sections: ABCD, DEF, FGH, and HA. Figure 2.140(b) shows a level 1 approximation to the four simple sections consisting of rectangles AIDN, DJFN, HMFK, and AMHL, respectively. Pairing up adjacent simple sections yields compound sections AIJF corresponding to AIDN and DJFN, and AFKL corresponding to HMFK and AMHL (see Figure 2.140(c)). More pairing yields the rectangle for compound section IJKL (see Figure 2.140(d)). The resulting BSPR tree is shown in Figure 2.140(e). Using the BSPR, Burton shows how to perform point-in-polygon determination and polygon intersection. These operations are implemented by tree searches and splitting operations.

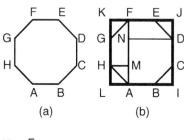

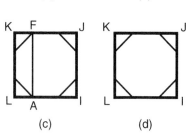

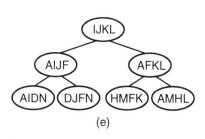

Figure 2.140
(a) A regular octagon, (b–d) the three successive approximations resulting from the use of BSPR, and (e) the resulting BSPR.

Strip trees and their variants are useful in applications that involve search (e.g., point inclusion) and set operations (e.g., intersection for interference detection). For example, suppose that we wish to determine if a road crosses a river. Using a strip tree representation for these features, answering this query requires that we perform an intersection of the corresponding strip trees. Three cases are possible, as is shown in Figure 2.141. Figure 2.141(a, b) corresponds to the answers NO and YES, respectively, while Figure 2.141(c) requires us to descend further down the strip tree. Notice the distinction between the task of detecting the possibility of an intersection and the task of computing the actual intersection, if one exists. The strip tree is well-suited to the former task. In particular, we often save much work when an intersection is impossible (e.g., [507, 1596]). The technique is similar to that used by Little and Peucker [1185] for bands (see Exercise 10). Other operations that can be performed efficiently by using the strip tree data structure include the computation of the length of a curve, areas of closed curves, intersection of curves with areas, point membership, and so on.

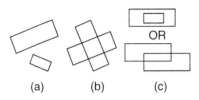

Figure 2.141
Three possible results of intersecting two strip trees: (a) null, (b) clear and (c) possible.

Exercises

1. The strip tree is designed primarily for the situation where a closed form representation of the curves is not known; otherwise, the strip tree is not so useful since many problems (e.g., curve intersection) can be solved directly. Thus, it is designed for the case that the curve is specified as an ordered sequence of points $t_0, t_1, \ldots, t_n$. Successive pairs of points define line segments, some of which may be collinear. The points are considered to be connected, although this restriction can be relaxed. The algorithm that we described for building a strip tree proceeds in a top-down manner. Given a sequence of n points, prove that this method takes $O(n \cdot \log_2 n)$ time.

2. Write a procedure TOPDOWNSTRIP to build a strip tree using the top-down method.

3. In the text, we also describe an alternative method of constructing a strip tree that proceeds in a bottom-up manner as follows. Take successive pairs of points, (t_0, t_1) (t_1, t_2) ... (t_{n-1}, t_n), and find their strips, say $S_0, S_1, \ldots, S_{n-1}$. Now, pair up these strips—that is, (S_0, S_1) (S_2, S_3) ..., and cover them with larger strips. Continue to apply this process until there is a single strip. Prove that this method takes $O(n)$ time.

4. Write a procedure BOTTOMUPSTRIP to build a strip tree using the bottom-up method.

5. Prove that the top-down method of constructing a strip tree always yields a tighter approximation of the curve than the bottom-up method.

6. Give an example curve where the rectangular strip has a larger area than the rectangle of minimum bounding area.

7. Why is it advantageous to use the rectangular strip in the top-down method instead of the rectangle of minimum bounding area?

8. Give an algorithm to construct the rectangle with minimum bounding area for an arbitrary curve.

9. Suppose that you are given two curves, C_1 and C_2, whose strip trees have depths d_1 and d_2, respectively. What is the worst-case order of the curve intersection algorithm?

10. Little and Peucker [1185] represent curves by bands that are strips of infinite length. They are analogous to the strip that is found at the root of the strip tree. Determining if two curves intersect reduces to determining if their bands intersect. The key idea is that, if they do, then the region formed by the intersection of their bands is used to clip the curves, bands are built for the clipped curves, and the algorithm is applied recursively. Implement this algorithm.

11. How would you use a strip tree to represent a closed curve whose corresponding region has a hole?

12. Write a procedure AREASTRIP to compute the area within a closed curve that is represented by a strip tree.

13. Write a procedure CURVEAREA to compute the intersection of a curve represented by a strip tree and an area represented by a strip tree. The result is the portion of the curve that overlaps the area.

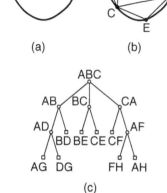

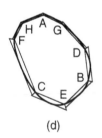

Figure 2.142
A two-dimensional prism tree: (a) object, (b) polyhedral approximation, (c) tree representation, and (d) prism tree.

14. Write a procedure AREAAREA to compute the intersection of two areas represented by strip trees. The result is an area.

15. Is the arc tree unique?

16. Suppose you are given a curve that is specified by $y = f(x)$. What is its length between points a and b?

17. Prove that every subarc in an arc tree is completely internal to its approximating ellipse.

18. How do you determine if a point is inside or outside an ellipse?

19. Write a procedure MEMBERAREAARC to determine whether a point is inside or outside an area represented by an arc tree.

20. What conditions must be satisfied by the ellipses of two subarcs of an arc tree if the subarcs intersect? Prove that your answer is true.

21. Write a procedure to compute the intersection points of two curves represented by arc trees.

22. Can you use the result of Exercise 21 to determine if two areas represented by arc trees overlap?

23. Write a procedure to compute the arc tree corresponding to the intersection of two areas represented by arc trees. How would you handle the situation arising when the two areas have some common edges?

24. Explain with an example why the distance values that are stored in the nodes of the BLG-tree do not necessarily become smaller as the tree is descended.

2.2.3.2 Prism Tree

The strip tree can also be generalized to represent boundaries of three-dimensional objects (i.e., their surface). These objects are usually polyhedra or the result of applying some process (such as range finding) to the original data that yields a polyhedron. The OBBTree of Gottschalk, Lin, and Manocha [735] is an example of such a generalization, where instead of a straight line joining the endpoints of the curve, principal component analysis (PCA) (e.g., [665]) is used to find the least-squares best-fit plane to the vertices of the objects (assuming polyhedral objects). Another example of such a generalization is the *prism tree* of Ponce and Faugeras [1501]. It is a hierarchical representation of an approximation that is used to model the surfaces of three-dimensional objects that are polyhedra of genus 0 (i.e., they have no holes). The prism tree is best understood by examining its predecessor, termed a *polyhedral approximation* [597].

To simplify the presentation, consider the construction of a polyhedral approximation of a two-dimensional object as in Figure 2.142(a). The object is initially modeled by a triangle with vertices that lie on the object's boundary. Assume for this example that the object is convex. Thus, no part of the triangle lies outside the object. For each side of the triangle, say E, find a point on the object's boundary, say M, whose distance from E is a local maximum. If the distance from M to E is greater than a predefined threshold, say ε, then repeat this step for the two new sides of the triangle formed by M and the endpoints of E. This process is repeated for all the new triangles until all of the approximations represented by their sides are within ε or the number of decomposition steps exceeds a predefined value. For example, Figure 2.142(b) is a possible polyhedral approximation for the object in Figure 2.142(a).

The polyhedral approximation provides a hierarchical representation of the boundary. The results of the process of successive subdivision of the boundary can be used by imposing a tree access structure on it where, with the exception of the root node, each node represents a straight line and the associated segment of the boundary. For example, Figure 2.142(c) is the tree structure corresponding to the polyhedral approximation of Figure 2.142(b). Notice that the root has three children, while all remaining nodes have two children. Often, the exact description of the segment of the boundary corresponding to the node is difficult to manipulate (e.g., detecting intersections between boundaries of adjacent objects). This is facilitated by storing a bounding box with each node. In this case, the bounding box is a quadrilateral approximation, in the form of a trapezoid, of the corresponding boundary segment. The resulting approximation is the two-dimensional version of the *prism tree*. For example, Figure 2.142(d) is the two-dimensional prism tree corresponding to the polyhedral approximation given in Figure 2.142(b). Notice that the shape of a trapezoid for a given boundary segment, say S, depends on the lines that approximate the segments that are adjacent to S.

To model three-dimensional objects (without holes), the polyhedral approximation uses tetrahedra and prisms (actually truncated pyramids) instead of triangles and quadrilaterals, respectively. The polyhedral approximation is built as follows. Start by forming a triangle, say T, that splits the surface of the object into two segments, S_1 and S_2. For each segment S_i, pick a point M_i on S_i such that the distance from S_i to T is a maximum. The result is a pair of tetrahedra with T as their common base and that form a triangular bipyramid (i.e., hexahedron), that serves as the initial polyhedral approximation. The rest of the approximation procedure consists of recursively attempting to replace each of the triangular faces of the tetrahedra with a new tetrahedron by finding the point M_i on triangular face F_i with the distance d_i to F_i that is a local maximum. If d_i exceeds a predefined error tolerance ε, then F_i is replaced by the tetrahedron formed by the three vertices of F_i and M_i; otherwise, F_i is retained as part of the approximation. The above decomposition process (termed a *split step*) is augmented with a couple of additional modifications to correct for

1. thin and elongated triangles,

2. edges between adjacent triangles for which the deviation from the actual surface is too large (termed an *adjustment step*).

Thin and elongated triangles are avoided by splitting each triangle T into three to six triangles instead of just three triangles. In particular, any edges that are common to two subdivided triangles are split at their points with the highest errors. It is important to observe that the triangles T_1 and T_2 that are split along edges appear at the same subdivision level and do not have the same immediate ancestor (i.e., they are not siblings when the decomposition process is represented as a tree). For example, Figure 2.143(b–e) shows the four ways the triangle in Figure 2.143(a) can be split.

When the deviation from the actual surface is too large for edges formed by vertices v_1 and v_2 between two adjacent triangles T_1 and T_2, the following adjustment step is applied. Add a new sample point M so that the space on the surface spanned by two adjacent noncoplanar triangles (e.g., Figure 2.144(a, b) is now spanned by four adjacent noncoplanar triangles (e.g., Figure 2.144(c, d), respectively). M satisfies the following three properties:

1. M is on the surface.

2. M is on the plane that bisects the two triangles that are being replaced.

3. Of all the points satisfying properties 1 and 2, M is the farthest from the edge that is being removed.

In particular, letting u_1 and u_2 be the two remaining vertices of T_1 and T_2, respectively, this adjustment tends to replace a pair of adjacent thin and elongated triangles T_1 and T_2 by four triangles u_1v_1M, u_2v_1M, u_1v_2M, and u_2v_2M, which are closer to being equiangular. There are two choices for the adjustment, depending on whether the elevation of M is lower than M's projection on the surface formed by the four vertices of the adjacent noncoplanar triangles (e.g., Figure 2.144(c)) or higher (e.g., Figure 2.144(d)).

The polyhedral approximation results in the modeling of a three-dimensional object by a collection of tetrahedra. The surface of the objects is represented by the visible triangular faces of the tetrahedra. As in the two-dimensional case, the result is a hierarchical representation of the boundary that can be used by imposing a tree structure where, with the exception of the root node, each node represents a triangular face and the associated portion of the surface. The root has two children, one for each of the tetrahedra that have

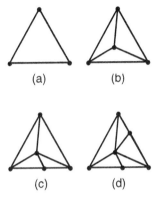

(a)   (b)

(c)   (d)

(e)

Figure 2.143
A triangle (a) and the four possible ways of splitting it: (b) split at an interior point and possible splits at (c) one edge, (d) two edges, and (e) three edges, depending on how many of the edges are common to two subdivided triangles at the same subdivision level.

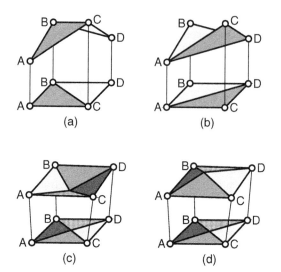

Figure 2.144
Illustration of the result of the adjustment step in the construction of a prism tree that replaces two adjacent triangles (a) and (b) whose common edge elevation deviates too much from the actual surface with four triangles, depending on whether the elevation of the new vertex is (c) lower or (d) higher than its projection on the surface formed by the four vertices of the adjacent noncoplanar triangles. This results in the deletion of the common edge.

a common triangular base. The remaining nodes have between three and six children if the decomposition step does not require an adjustment step; otherwise, there are just two children since a triangle has been replaced by two triangles instead of between three and six triangles.

Exercises

1. The prism tree is not a true generalization of the strip tree since the approximating shapes are rectangular parallelepipeds for the former while, for the latter, they are truncated pyramids. Is there an advantage to using trapezoids (truncated pyramids) over rectangles (rectangular parallelepipeds)?

2. Define a three-dimensional strip tree so that the approximating shapes are rectangular parallelepipeds.

3. What is the motivation for the adjustment step in the construction of the polyhedral approximation?

4. In the description of the prism tree approximation, it is stated that the surface of the object is represented by a collection of tetrahedra where, for each tetrahedron, at most three faces are visible. Why are there not three visible faces for each tetrahedron?

5. It would seem that using a collection of tetrahedra to approximate the surface of a polyhedron is not good for polyhedral-like objects because it may result in an approximating object with many points, where the solid angle formed by the three incident faces is less than 90°. How is this situation avoided in the algorithm for obtaining a polyhedral approximation?

6. In the adjustment step of the polyhedral approximation construction process, it is necessary to find adjacent triangles. How would you achieve this?

7. Write an algorithm to build a three-dimensional prism tree.

8. What is the space and time complexity of the process of building a three-dimensional prism tree for a polyhedron with n faces?

9. Consider a three-dimensional prism tree such that all faces of adjacent, approximating, truncated pyramids are coplanar. Must these coplanar faces also be identical?

10. Define a prism to be *regular* if the three nonparallel faces of the prism lie in the bisecting planes. Prove that, if the approximated surface is convex, then all prisms at all levels of the prism tree representation of the surface are regular.

11. Use the definition of a regular prism given in Exercise 10. Suppose that you are approximating an object with a concave surface. Is it possible for all the approximating prisms to be regular?

12. Adapt the definition of regularity given in Exercise 10 to a strip tree.

13. Give an algorithm to find the intersection of two three-dimensional objects represented by prism trees.

14. How would you extend the concepts of a polyhedral approximation and a prism tree to more general surfaces than genus 0?

2.2.3.3 HAL Tree

The development of hierarchical boundary-based object representations, such as the strip tree and the variants that we have discussed, has been motivated by the desire to speed up the processing of such objects by avoiding unnecessary operations. As we have seen, the speed up is accomplished by use of two mechanisms: approximation and localization [1927]. Approximating an object by using fewer elements enables faster display. The quality of the approximation depends on the extent to which it minimizes the loss of the sense of reality. Localization provides information about the volume and position of the boundary of the object in order to enable fast point location and testing for intersection (e.g., for applications such as interference detection and collision detection). Localization is achieved by making use of the hierarchies of bounding boxes.

Up to now, we have made use primarily of bounding boxes consisting of hyperrectangles (both aligned and not aligned with the coordinate axes), prisms, as well as spheres and ellipses. Spheres and ellipses have an advantage over some methods that make use of hyperrectangles (such as the strip tree) in that there is no need to make special provisions for closed curves or curves that extend past their endpoints. The principal advantage of spherical bounding boxes is that they are rotation invariant. Furthermore, testing for point inclusion (i.e., point-in-polygon) and intersection of bounding boxes is very simple for spherical bounding boxes. In particular, testing for point inclusion is just a matter of computing the distance from the point to the center of the sphere and comparing it with the radius of the sphere. Similarly, determining if two spheres intersect is just a matter of computing the distance between their corresponding centers and comparing it with the sum of their radii.

The drawback of spherical bounding boxes is that they are not very tight fitting, thereby resulting in the traversal of more levels in the hierarchy when performing some operations such as intersection testing. In fact, this is cited by Gottschalk et al. [735] as one of the reasons for the observed superior performance of hierarchies of non-axis-aligned bounding hyperrectangles, such as the OBBTree [735], over hierarchies of bounding spheres, such as the sphere tree (e.g., [895, 896, 1527]), in the context of interference detection (and also applicable to collision detection). Veltkamp's *hierarchical approximation and localization) tree* (HAL tree) [1927] is designed to overcome this drawback. In particular, in some cases, the HAL tree can provide an even tighter fit than a hierarchy of spherical bounding boxes by constraining the bounding boxes to being either the intersection of two discs or a disc and a halfspace when the objects are restricted, as before, to have planar faces and no holes. Below, we briefly describe how the HAL tree represents the boundary of a two-dimensional object.

The root of the HAL tree corresponds to the minimum bounding disc of the boundary of the object where at least two of the vertices of the object's boundary lie on the disc's boundary. The object's boundary is split into two parts by finding the two vertices, say v_1 and v_2, that are the farthest apart, thereby obtaining two polylines. These two polylines serve as the left and right children of the root. Notice that, in the case of the children of the root, the approximation of both polylines is the same line—that is, the straight line

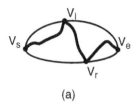

(a)

(b)

Figure 2.145
Example of a bounding box that is formed by the intersection of (a) two discs and (b) a disc and a halfspace. The boundary is shown with a thick line.

between v_1 and v_2. We now show how to form the minimum bounding box of a polyline $P = (v_s \ldots v_e)$ in the HAL tree. Let a denote the directed line from v_s to v_e. Let v_l (v_r) denote the vertex to the left (right) of a so that the disc formed by (v_s, v_e, v_l) $((v_s, v_e, v_r))$ contains all vertices to the left (right) of a. If there are no vertices to the left (right) of a, then the disc is replaced by the halfspace formed by the infinite extension of a. The minimum bounding box of the polyline is the intersection of the two discs (or a disc and a halfspace) corresponding to the sets of vertices on the two sides of a. Figure 2.145(a) is an example of a bounding box that is formed by the intersection of two discs, while Figure 2.145(b) is an example of a bounding box that is formed by the intersection of a disc and a halfspace.

Each polyline $P = (v_s \ldots v_e)$ is decomposed into two polylines, $P_1 = (v_s \ldots v)$ and $P_2 = (v \ldots v_e)$, by letting $v = v_l$ ($v = v_r$) if the curvature (radius) of the disc corresponding to v_l (v_r) is greater (smaller) than that of the curvature (radius) of the disc corresponding to v_r (v_l) (note that the radius of a halfspace is ∞). The rationale for the choice is the same as the one used in the Douglas-Peucker line generalization algorithm in the sense that v is the vertex that is furthest from the approximating line of the polyline. However, the difference is that, in the HAL tree, instead of v being the farthest vertex from the approximating line, we have that v lies on the disc segment that has largest maximal distance to that line. For example, $v = v_l$ in Figure 2.145(a, b). The process is applied recursively until the error of each edge is less than a given tolerance or an edge of the original polygon is encountered. It should be clear that testing for point inclusion and intersection of bounding boxes in the HAL tree is quite simple. In essence, we just apply the same tests as for spherical bounding boxes with the difference that the number of spheres involved in the test is doubled.

The HAL tree represents three-dimensional objects in a similar manner except that bounding spheres are used instead of bounding discs. Initially, a bounding sphere is constructed for the polyhedron object that touches at least three vertices of the polyhedron. These three vertices partition the surface of the polyhedron into two parts, termed *polysurfaces,* that are defined by determining the shortest paths of the edges of the polyhedron between these vertices. The initial approximation of these two polysurfaces is the triangle connecting the three vertices. These two polysurfaces form the left and right children of the root. Again, as in the two-dimensional case for the children of the root, the approximation of both polysurfaces is the same triangle. The minimum bounding box of each of the polysurfaces is obtained by determining the vertices, say v_l and v_r, of each polysurface on the two sides of the approximating triangle so that the bounding sphere formed by them and the vertices of the approximating triangle includes all vertices on the particular side. Having determined the bounding spheres of the two sides, the minimum bounding box of the polysurface is the intersection of the two spheres.

Each polysurface is decomposed into three polysurfaces using either v_l or v_r and the vertices of the corresponding approximating triangle (v_i, v_j, v_k). The choice of v_l or v_r depends on the curvature of the corresponding spheres. In any event, the resulting polysurfaces are approximated by triangles. Note that, in effect, the initial polyhedron is usually approximated by a pair of tetrahedra having a triangle as a shared common base.[44] Thus, each of the remaining nodes in the tree will have three children corresponding to the three exterior triangular faces of the tetrahedron that is being partitioned as a result of the approximation process.

Unfortunately, the process for decomposing the triangles that we have described will almost immediately result in the new triangles being very elongated because the angles at the vertices are subdivided at each decomposition stage. This leads to a very bad approximation. Thus, Veltkamp [1927] proposes heuristics that decompose the triangles

---

[44] If the object is a 2.5-dimensional image, such as the surface of a terrain, then, initially, we have just one tetrahedron where one side does not form part of the surface and hence is not decomposed further.

into more than three triangles. The drawback of these heuristics is that there is no longer a guarantee that the minimum bounding box is the intersection of two spheres, but, instead, may need to be their union. This arises because the two bounding spheres are constrained to pass through the vertices of the triangle. Of course, one can always find a single sphere that contains all of the vertices of the polyhedral surface, but this is contrary to our desire to find a tighter-fitting bounding box than a sphere or a hyperrectangle.

Observe that the approximation hierarchy that we have described is analogous to the prism tree [1501], which also makes use of one or two tetrahedra for the initial approximation of the polyhedron and then proceeds to approximate the triangular faces of the tetrahedra. However, the primary difference from the prism tree is the nature of the bounding boxes that, in the HAL tree, are intersections or unions of bounding spheres instead of prisms (i.e., truncated pyramids), which complicates its use. The fact that the minimum bounding box can be the union of the two bounding spheres makes the HAL tree unattractive in theory for such data unless further heuristics are devised to avoid this situation, although it rarely occurs in practice [1927]. Nevertheless, even if we are successful at one stage in obtaining a minimum bounding box that is the intersection of two bounding spheres, there is no guarantee that the bounding boxes at subsequent intermediate stages will indeed be the intersection of bounding spheres because they could, in fact, be unions of bounding spheres [1927].

Exercises

1. What is the complexity of constructing the HAL tree for a two-dimensional polygon with n vertices?

2. Show how a two-dimensional polygon with n vertices can be stored in a HAL tree with $O(n)$ space.

2.2.3.4 Simplification Methods and Data Structures

Hierarchical representations of the boundaries of objects play an important role in computer graphics and visualization applications. In particular, modern systems are required to process and display scenes of enormous complexity, which can be very time-consuming. One way to speed the process is to make use of special-purpose hardware. In this case, the scenes usually consist of very large collections of triangles (actually polygons that have been triangulated) as the triangle primitive is well-suited to the special-purpose graphics hardware for fast rendering. This has led to work in automatically simplifying the scenes by reducing the number of triangles that are necessary in order to take advantage of situations where full accuracy is not required or used. These methods are known as *simplification methods* (e.g., [392, 692, 812]) and are often supported by specialized data structures to enable viewing the scenes at varying levels of resolution (also known as *level of detail* [1212]). A data structure that exhibits such a behavior is frequently referred to as a *multiresolution model* (e.g., [692]). In this section, we give a brief overview of some simplification methods and the relevant data structures.

It should be clear that use of a simplification method results in an approximation of the surface of the objects (or objects in a scene). We assume three-dimensional data. The quality of the surface approximation is evaluated by several measures. A common measure is similarity of appearance where, for example, we can use the average sum of the squared differences in the intensities of corresponding pixels that are produced by the renderer (e.g., [1178]). The advantage of such a measure is that occluded regions play no role in the evaluation. The drawback is that we must be careful to sample adequately a wide range of viewpoints. An additional drawback is the fact that each sample usually requires an expensive rendering step.

This has led to the adoption of geometric measures of approximation error. In this case, the geometric similarity serves as a substitute for visual similarity while also yielding approximations that may be useful for applications other than rendering (e.g., collision detection). This duality has been termed *approximation and localization* in Section 2.2.3.3. The most commonly used geometric measures employ the Euclidean (i.e., L_2) and Chessboard (i.e., L_∞) distances. The advantage of the Euclidean distance is that it is better at indicating an overall fit, thereby discounting large but highly localized deviations. On the other hand, the Chessboard distance provides a global absolute bound on the distance between the original and the approximation, thereby providing quality guarantees.

One of the problems with measuring the distance between general surfaces (e.g., free-form surfaces) rather than terrainlike surfaces is that there is no single distinguished direction along which to measure the distance (in contrast to along the vertical direction corresponding to elevation in the case of terrain data). Thus, instead, the distance between closest pairs of points is used. This must be done for every point on both the original and approximating surface. In other words, for each point on the original surface, we find the closest point on the approximating surface, and for each point on the approximating surface, we find the closest point on the original surface—that is, we make use of a concept related to the Hausdorff distance (e.g., [911]).[45] Needless to say, in practice, such error measures are quite costly to compute exactly. Thus, they are usually computed by sampling the distances at a discrete set of points on the two surfaces (e.g., the Metro system [394]). Further computational savings are achieved by restricting the search for the closest point to a particular neighborhood for each sample point, thereby obtaining a localized distance (e.g., [692]).

The two most common surface simplification paradigms are refinement and decimation [692, 812]. A refinement algorithm starts with a coarse approximation and adds elements at each step, thereby resulting in more detail. In contrast, a decimation algorithm starts with the original surface and removes elements iteratively at each step. Another way of distinguishing between these two paradigms is to observe that refinement is a top-down process, while decimation is a bottom-up process.

An important distinction between different implementations of these paradigms is whether or not they perform topological simplification on the surface. Geometric simplifications reduce the number of primitives that describe the objects (e.g., the number of vertices, edges, and triangles when the primitive elements are triangles). Topological simplifications reduce the number of holes, tunnels, cavities, and so on. Some methods specifically prohibit topological simplification [408, 737]. This makes sense in applications such as medical imaging where, for example, preserving a hole in the image of an organ is much more important than preserving the exact shape of the surface. However, in most algorithms, the topology is simplified implicitly as a side effect of the geometric conditions that form the basis of the simplification. Nevertheless, there are algorithms that explicitly take the surface topology into account in conjunction with geometric simplification (e.g., [550, 804]).

---

[45] The Hausdorff distance between two sets A and B is the distance to the farthest nearest neighbor. It is computed by a two-step process. First, find the nearest neighbor in B of each element of a in A. Now, find the distance to the farthest nearest neighbor—that is, $h(A, B)$, where $h(A, B) = \max_{a \in A} \min_{b \in B} d(a, b)$. $h(A, B)$ is called the *directed Hausdorff distance*. It is not symmetric and thus is not a metric. Next, repeat the computation for the nearest neighbor in A of each element b in B. Now, again, find the distance to the farthest nearest neighbor—that is, $h(B, A)$, where $h(B, A) = \max_{b \in B} \min_{a \in A} d(b, a)$. The *Hausdorff distance* $H(A, B)$ is the maximum of $h(A, B)$ and $h(B, A)$—that is, $H(A, B) = \max(h(A, B), h(B, A))$.

The Hausdorff distance is used to measure the degree of mismatch between two sets. In essence, if the Hausdorff distance between A and B is δ, then every point of A must be within distance δ of at least one point of B and vice versa. The Hausdorff distance is a metric over all closed, bounded sets—that is, it is nonnegative and symmetric and obeys the triangle inequality.

The directed Hausdorff distance is useful in that, given $h(A, B) \leq \delta$, we know that, if we compute the expansion of B by δ (termed the Minkowski sum of B and δ) yielding B', then we are guaranteed that every point in A is in the expanded region B'—that is, $A \subset B'$.

For example, at times, we may want to perform both types of simplifications. In particular, it may be the case that further geometric simplification cannot be applied in the sense that certain geometric error tolerance criteria can no longer be satisfied without the application of some form of topological simplification. One simple way to obtain topological simplification that has been proposed is to roll a sphere over the boundary of the objects and fill up the regions that are not accessible to the sphere, thereby simplifying the topology in a gentle manner, after which further geometric simplification can be applied [550]. Observe that it is preferable to define the sphere using L_∞ instead of L_2 in order to ensure that the newly created regions can be described with planes rather than objects with spherical faces [550].

Note, however, that preserving topology may not necessarily be the most important consideration in the simplification. We may also need to be concerned about preserving the domain. In particular, if the objects in the image are two-manifolds, then the result of the simplification should also be a two-manifold. This is not the case, for example, when the result consists of two objects that are adjacent at a point or an edge. If the two objects are treated as one object, then that object is not a two-manifold. Notice the similarity to regularized Boolean set operations in constructive solid geometry (CSG), where, for example, we do not allow the intersection of two objects that have a common face (see the discussion in the opening of Section 2.2). In other words, while the intersection is allowed, the result is the empty set.

The refinement paradigm has a long history of usage in the simplification of curves and functions. The best-known example is the Douglas-Peucker line generalization algorithm for applications in cartography (see Section 2.2.3.1). It has also been widely used for terrain approximation where the typical implementation starts with the minimal approximation and iteratively inserts points where the approximating and original surfaces are the farthest apart. This is sometimes referred to as the *greedy insertion technique* [692].

The refinement paradigm has also been applied to the simplification of polygonal surfaces. Some examples include three-dimensional variants of the strip tree, such as the prism tree and the OBBTree (see Section 2.2.3.2). Nevertheless, the decimation method is the one that has been more commonly used for simplification. This stems, in part, from the difficulty of dealing with the topology of the original object. In particular, if we want to preserve the topology of the original object, then we must actually know it, and often this is not easy to discover. Thus, refinement is used more for surfaces that correspond to terrains, where the topology is relatively simple. Note that, as in the case of the refinement method, we will see that the simplification resulting from use of the decimation method is useful for other applications than display (e.g., collision detection).

There are three principal surface decimation methods: vertex clustering, vertex decimation, and face decimation. Vertex clustering works by spatially partitioning the vertices into a set of clusters and then merging all vertices in a cluster into one vertex. This is typically implemented by imposing a uniform grid on the data where each grid cell corresponds to a cluster and hence merging all vertices that lie in each grid cell (e.g., [1579]). For example, Figure 2.146(b) is the result of applying vertex clustering to the collection of polygons in Figure 2.146(a). It should be clear that vertex clustering can result in substantial modifications to the topology of the original object. In particular, some objects can be reduced to points (e.g., if all of the vertices lie in the same grid cell, as is the case for the object consisting of vertices A, B, and C in Figure 2.146(a), which becomes isolated vertex D in Figure 2.146(b)), while separate components can be joined together and thus the result is not required to be a two-manifold (e.g., objects E and F in Figure 2.146).

Observe that the results of vertex clustering are quite sensitive to the manner in which the grid is imposed on the data. Some of these problems can be overcome by use of an adaptive grid, such as an octree (e.g., [1211]). Another alternative to the uniform grid is the use of a set of cluster cells, such as cubes or spheres, about certain vertices [1205].

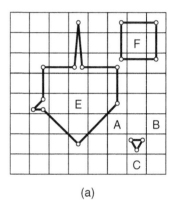

(a)

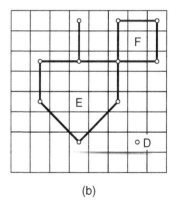

(b)

Figure 2.146
(a) A collection of polygons and (b) the result of applying vertex clustering to it.

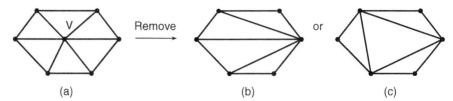

Figure 2.147
(a) An example triangulation, and (b, c) a couple of possible retriangulations of the result of removing vertex v.

Cells are centered around their vertex of highest weight, and when a vertex lies in the intersection of several cells, it is associated with the cell whose center is the closest.

There are many formulations of vertex decimation. The simplest formulation, termed *vertex removal* (e.g., [391, 1031, 1049, 1699, 1791]), initially ranks the vertices of the object according to their importance (e.g., the error that would result from their removal). At each step, a vertex is selected for removal, and all edges (faces) incident at it are removed from the object, thereby creating a hole. The hole is retriangulated (e.g., Figure 2.147). This process is repeated until the desired number of vertices is obtained or as long as the approximation error is within the desired tolerance. The retriangulation is often a constrained Delaunay triangulation (e.g., [1031, 1791]). Recall that vertex decimation also served as a central component of the K-structure construction process (see Section 2.1.3.2).

A more complex variant of vertex decimation is triangle decimation (e.g., [795]), where a triangle t is replaced by a new vertex v, thereby causing the removal of its constituent vertices $\{v_1, v_2, v_3\}$ and the replacement of the edges incident at them by new edges incident at v. This approach can be characterized as a *triangle collapse*. The triangle collapse differs from the vertex removal method. In particular, once the collapsed triangle has been chosen, the resulting surface is fully determined (i.e., there is no choice as to how it is to be retriangulated). In contrast, if we only perform triangle removal without the introduction of a new vertex, then the region forming the hole will be retriangulated, which might be time-consuming if the region has many vertices and is not convex.

The most common formulation of vertex decimation proceeds by the iterative contraction of vertex pairs. The vertex pair is replaced by a new vertex (termed *vertex simplification*) by virtue of a vertex or edge collapse operation. The result of the simplification process is often represented as a hierarchy of vertices, thereby serving as a basis for a multiresolution model.

The two main issues in vertex simplification are determining

1. the vertex pair (v_1, v_2) to be collapsed,

2. the position of the replacement vertex v.

Most of the algorithms use a simple greedy procedure to determine the sequence of vertex pairs to be contracted, where the cost metric is intended to reflect the extent of the geometric error that they introduce, which is to be minimized. Once the lowest-cost pair has been contracted, it is not reconsidered again. A simple approach for choosing the replacement vertex is to pick one of the two vertices v_1 or v_2 either at random or via some algorithm (e.g., [2031]). In this case, the solution is similar to the first formulation of vertex decimation that we described. However, a better approach is to position v so that some approximation error measure is minimized (termed *optimal placement* [692]). Nevertheless, the advantage of the first approach is that when it serves as the basis of a multiresolution model, less information needs to be stored as we have not introduced any new vertices.

The simplest cost metrics use local properties, such as minimizing the edge length (e.g., [2032]), making the dihedral angle as close as possible to 180 degrees (e.g., [837], or even minimizing the area affected by the collapse, and so on. Other more sophisticated cost metrics take the original surface into account (e.g., [408, 694, 763, 875, 1569]). For example, some methods (e.g., [875]) are based on the minimization of an energy function, one of whose primary components is a geometric term based on L_2. This method maintains a set of sample points on the original shape and uses the distance between these points and the corresponding closest points on the approximated shape to determine the geometric error. It is a simplified version of earlier work [878] that permitted edge swap and edge split operations, as well as made use of a more complex error metric that also included a term that penalized meshes with many vertices and a spring term that penalized long edges in the triangulation. Topological modifications are permitted as long as they reduce the global error. Note that the output vertices are not constrained to be a subset of the input vertices. This is a direct result of the positioning of v so that the error is minimized.

Other methods (e.g., [763]) compute a tolerance volume around the approximation so that the original surface is guaranteed to lie within that volume. This method is quite similar to the simplification envelope method [408, 1919], developed independently, which consists of approximations to offset surfaces (termed *envelopes*), where the only vertices that are removed are those that would create triangles that lay within the envelopes. On the other hand, some methods, such as [1177], only take the current approximation into account, thereby leading to a characterization as *memoryless*. In particular, this method is based on the preservation of local volume.

It is important to recall that a side effect of dealing with these issues using purely geometric considerations is that the original topology of the object may be implicitly simplified by the contraction. In fact, it has been proposed to loosen the requirement that an edge exist between the pair of vertices that are being contracted in order to enable the merging of topologically separate components during simplification (e.g., [694, 1502, 551]).

Vertex hierarchies are usually represented by binary trees where the leaf nodes are the vertices of the original object and the nonleaf nodes correspond to the vertex that is formed by the contraction. The resulting tree captures the sequence of collapse operations as well as the dependencies. It has been used for view-dependent reconstruction of surface approximations at runtime (e.g., [876, 1211, 2032]). It is interesting to note that vertex hierarchies can also be viewed as hierarchies of vertex neighborhoods, where the neighborhood of a vertex consists of its adjacent or incident faces (e.g., [692, 693, 1050, 1123]). In particular, when two vertices are contracted, their corresponding neighborhoods are merged to form a new neighborhood. Thus, each node in the hierarchy corresponds to a disjoint set of vertices on the original surface and, in fact, corresponds to the surface region formed by the union of the neighborhoods of all of the vertices in its set.

There are many ways of achieving face decimation. For example, the process of iterative contraction of vertex pairs can also be applied in such a way so as to merge the two faces adjacent to the collapsed edge. We use the term *face simplification* to describe this process. Its result is often represented as a hierarchy of faces, thereby serving as a basis for a multiresolution model. Face simplification is very reminiscent of the processes used to build a strip tree in a bottom-up manner. The difference is that, instead of starting with pixels or polylines, we start with a surface that has been triangulated and then, in a bottom-up manner, build a hierarchy of faces that are not necessarily triangles (and are rarely so). The *hierarchical face clustering* method of Garland, Willmott, and Heckbert [693, Ch. 8; 2004, Ch. 5; 695] is an example of such an approach. In this case, the initial triangular faces can be viewed as objects, and the hierarchical face clustering method chooses which faces to aggregate in the process of forming an object hierarchy.

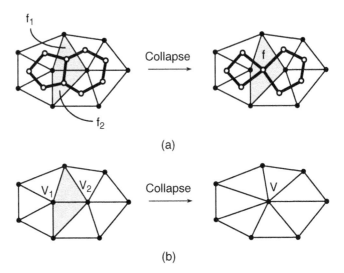

Figure 2.148
(a) Example of face collapsing in face simplification: the edge between the nodes corresponding to faces f_1 and f_2, denoted by hollow circles, on the left is collapsed leading to the merging of f_1 and f_2, yielding f, as shown on the right. (b) Example of vertex or edge collapsing in vertex simplification: the edge between vertices V_1 and V_2 on the left is collapsed, thereby merging V_1 and V_2 to yield the vertex V, as shown on the right.

Hierarchical face clustering is analogous to vertex simplification methods, where, now, the hierarchy is one of faces rather than one of vertices. They both have the same goal of yielding automatic simplification of highly detailed polygonal models into faithful approximations using fewer polygons. The key idea in hierarchical face clustering is the performance of face collapsing (e.g., Figure 2.148(a)) instead of vertex or edge collapsing (e.g., Figure 2.148(b)), as is done in vertex simplification, whose result can also be viewed as a hierarchy of sets of triangular faces. Face collapsing is achieved by operating on the dual of the original triangulated surface, where vertices in the dual correspond to faces in the original triangulated surface, and edges in the dual correspond to adjacent faces in the original triangulated surface.

An edge collapse in the dual is equivalent to merging faces in the original triangulated surface. The edge collapse in the dual is termed a *dual contraction* [695]. The result of applying many dual contractions is to obtain a face hierarchy. The surface is assumed to be a *manifold with boundary* (i.e., a surface all of whose points have a neighborhood that is topologically equivalent to a disc or half-disc) so that every surface edge has at most two adjacent faces.[46] This guarantees that the number of dual edges is no greater than the number of edges in the original surface mesh.

Face hierarchies cluster neighboring groups of faces instead of iteratively merging vertex neighborhoods, as in vertex hierarchies. In particular, each node in the vertex hierarchy corresponds to a disjoint set of vertices on the original surface. The node also corresponds to a surface region that is the union of the neighborhoods of all the vertices in its set. Because the face clusters are disjoint sets of faces, they also partition the surface in a well-defined way. In addition, face clusters are more likely to have a single normal that is a good match for the surface normals of the faces in the cluster, and thus are more likely to be nearly planar. In other words, the advantage of the face hierarchy over a vertex hierarchy is that local neighborhoods high in the vertex hierarchy are usually nonplanar (they are usually cone-shaped with the vertex at the apex). This is because any

---

[46] This assumption is motivated by the same rationale that led to polyhedral objects being assumed to be two-manifolds, in which each point has a neighborhood that is topologically equivalent to a disc; see Section 2.2.1.1. Note that a two-manifold is a manifold with boundary whose boundary is empty.

planar vertex neighborhood will be removed very early during the vertex simplification process. In addition, in the vertex hierarchy, the set of triangles on the original surface corresponding to a particular vertex may have a very irregular shape. In particular, most standard vertex simplification algorithms provide no mechanism to control this shape. Another drawback of hierarchies based on vertex simplification is that the bounding box of a node cannot be guaranteed to contain the surface of its children fully.

Briefly, in hierarchical face clustering, the face hierarchy is constructed iteratively by a greedy procedure that assigns a cost of contraction to each dual edge, and then the dual edge of minimal cost is contracted. Each iteration results in a partition of the original surface into disjoint sets of connected faces. This is in contrast to vertex simplification methods, where, after every iteration, the result is an approximate surface.

We now provide more detail on the process of constructing the face hierarchy. Start with an initial surface partition where each face of the original triangulated surface belongs to its own singleton cluster. The process of iterative dual contraction produces a sequence of partitions with successively fewer clusters. The process is greedy in the sense that it assigns a cost of contraction to each dual edge and inserts it into a priority queue that is sorted by the cost of its elements. It then extracts the dual edge $e = (v_1, v_2)$ of minimum cost from the priority queue and contracts it, forming a new dual vertex v_n. Next, it removes any dual edge $e = (v_i, v_j)$ from the priority queue, where v_j is equal to v_1 or v_2, and inserts a new dual edge $e_n = (v_i, v_n)$ with its associated cost into the priority queue. This process is continued until there is one face cluster for each connected component of the surface. It should be clear that while clusters are always connected sets of faces, they may have holes. The face hierarchy is represented as a binary tree where each nonleaf node corresponds to a dual contraction, and the leaf nodes are the faces of the original triangulated surface (e.g., Figure 2.149).

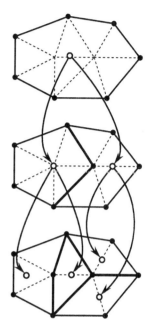

Figure 2.149
Example of a partial face hierarchy corresponding the triangulated surface in Figure 2.148.

One of the key issues with this construction method is deciding which faces to contract at each step. In other words, we would like to know what factors make for a good face cluster. This is the basis of the cost function. Garland, Willmott, and Heckbert [695] argue for the metric to be based primarily on planarity. In this case, using principal component analysis (PCA) (e.g., [665]), they find the least-squares best-fit plane to the vertices that make up the faces that make up the cluster. This will naturally tend to merge clusters that are collectively nearly planar. However, a surface may fold back on itself (termed a *foldover* [2032]). Thus, it will seem nearly planar, but the normal of the optimal plane will not be a good fit for all the surface normals of the constituent faces. In order to take this into account, an additional error term is used in the cost function that measures the average deviation of the plane normal from that of the individual surface normals.

It should be clear that, in some applications, planarity is not the only factor of importance. In particular, the shape of the face clusters should also be compact. This is achieved by using a measure termed *irregularity* (more commonly known as *circularity* [748]), which is defined as

$$\frac{P^2}{4\pi A'}$$

where P and A are the perimeter and area, respectively, of the face cluster. Irregularity indicates the extent to which the shape deviates from that of a circle (whose irregularity is 1). Irregularity is taken into account in the cost function by stipulating that the cost of merging two face clusters having irregularity γ_i to form a cluster with irregularity γ is

$$\text{cost} = \frac{\gamma - \max(\gamma_1, \gamma_2)}{\gamma}$$

If the irregularity of the resulting face cluster is greater than that of the face clusters that are merged, then the contraction of the edge incurs a penalty; otherwise, the cost is negative and is treated as a positive factor.

A drawback of the construction algorithm is the time needed to compute a fitting plane. Garland, Willmott, and Heckbert [695] suggest that the execution time can be reduced significantly by using PCA to compute the fitting planes only at the upper levels of the hierarchy and using a cheaper method to compute approximating planes at the lower levels of the hierarchy. In addition, the trees corresponding to the resulting hierarchies are not necessarily balanced. This can be resolved by either making use of parallel merging of a maximal independent set of dual edges (e.g., [2032]) or adding a balance bias to the error metric that is used to select the next edge to be collapsed.

The idea of iterative clustering is not new. It has been in use for many years, usually being applied to point sets (e.g., [48]), often in high dimensions, rather than to surface elements. Point sets are usually clustered on the basis of distance, whereas clustering surface elements requires taking into account factors such as adjacency and orientation. The simplification work of Kalvin and Taylor [980], resulting in "superfaces," is related to hierarchical face clustering. However, it differs in that it is based on growing the clusters around randomly chosen "seed" faces by adding faces one at a time until a planarity threshold is exceeded. This is in contrast to hierarchical face clustering, which works in a pairwise manner, producing a hierarchical structure of clusters rather than a single static partition that is heavily dependent on the choice of the seed faces. Some other related work includes an algorithm by DeRose, Kass, and Truong [481], which is only based on adjacency, and thus the elements of the clusters may possibly not be coplanar. The prism tree [1501], as mentioned earlier, is another example of a face clustering method.

The fact that the hierarchical face clustering method works in a bottom-up fashion and is useful for collision detection makes it conceptually similar to the BOXTREE of Barequet, Chazelle, Guibas, Mitchell, and Tal [125], which builds a bottom-up hierarchy of boxes by merging adjacent boxes. However, the BOXTREE is built in quite a different manner as Barequet et al. focus more on the properties of the bounding boxes rather than the surface regions that are being bounded. In particular, their definition of box adjacency is based on spatial overlap rather than on the connectivity of corresponding regions on the surface (e.g., planarity, normals, and compactness, as in the hierarchical face clustering method). They rank pairs of boxes for merging on the basis of properties of the resulting boxes, such as volume, rather than on the basis of any property of the local surface. Thus, the considerations are similar to those taken into account in other object-based hierarchies, such as the R-tree (see Section 2.1.5.2), where overlap and perimeter of the resulting bounding box are factors in deciding on how to group the boxes in an overflowing node. However, unlike the R-tree, the hierarchy is a binary tree and thus each node has an outdegree of 2. The BOXTREE is used in ray tracing applications.

The resulting face hierarchies can be used for many applications, including, but not limited to, surface simplification for ease of display. In the case of surface simplification for ease of display, the surface is partitioned into clusters whose boundaries are simplified, after which the clusters are retriangulated. Note that the result is similar to, but not the same as, that obtained by using the *superface* algorithm of Kalvin and Taylor [980]. The principal difference is that the superface algorithm seeks to minimize the maximum deviation of any point from its approximating plane, while the hierarchical face clustering method seeks to minimize the average deviation without guaranteeing any bound on the maximum.

One of the natural applications of the resulting face hierarchies is to serve as a basis for the construction of a hierarchy of bounding volumes (i.e., box). Each face cluster can be enclosed by a bounding volume on the basis of the best-fit plane for each cluster. The resulting hierarchy is similar to the OBBTree structure of Gottschalk, Lin, and Manocha [735] in that they also make use of Principal Component Analysis (PCA) to compute best-fit planes. However, their algorithm works in a top-down manner to partition the vertices of the original model. In contrast, the hierarchical face clustering method proceeds in a bottom-up manner to produce the bounding boxes. These bounding boxes are well approximated by a plane, which means that most nodes will correspond to surface regions with a reasonably well-defined orientation. This facilitates collision detection. Other applications of hierarchical face clustering include multiresolution radiosity [2004, 2005], computation of distance to the surface, and intersection queries useful in applications such as ray tracing. The key advantage over methods that are based on decompositions of the underlying space (such as variants of region octrees) is that the hierarchies are attached to the surface rather than to the entire space occupied by the surface.

The hierarchies that we have described are used to define a simplification method, and their results are often used to build a multiresolution model. Ideally, the multiresolution model should have approximately the same size as the most detailed approximation alone, although a small constant factor increase in size is usually acceptable. There are two types of multiresolution models: discrete and continuous. Discrete multiresolution models are usually based on having a set of increasingly simpler approximations (i.e., simplifications). These simplifications are usually performed offline in a preprocessing step at a fixed number of levels of resolution. The renderer selects a particular approximation to use and renders the approximation in the current frame. Discrete multiresolution models are adequate when a constant level of detail is needed.

Continuous multiresolution models enable the desired approximation to be extracted at runtime. They are useful for applications, such as terrain flyovers, dynamic walkthroughs, and so on, where the desired level of resolution is only known at runtime. In particular, they support view-dependent simplification (e.g., [459, 876, 1211, 2032]), where a particular scene may require several levels of resolution, depending on the position of the viewpoint, in the sense that parts of the scene at a greater distance can be displayed using a coarser resolution than nearby parts. A typical example is a terrain viewed at close range at an oblique angle, as might arise in a flight-simulator application. Thus, they permit a gradual transition to take place between different levels of resolution for different parts of an object or a scene, thereby providing a way of eliminating the visual "popping" effect. In addition, they support progressive transmission (e.g., [875, 1862]). Nevertheless, there are situations where a discrete model may be preferable to a continuous model. For example, the discrete model is simpler to program, has lower runtime requirements, and may be more amenable to the use of compression methods, such as triangle strips (e.g., [467, 549]), for faster display.

In the case of terrain data, a number of continuous representations have been developed. They are based on a regular adaptive subdivision of the terrain surface such as that provided by a region quadtree (e.g., [513, 576, 1176]). For more details, see Section 2.2.4. In the case of general triangulated surfaces, multitriangulations [460, 461] provide a general framework that encompasses most of the commonly used multiresolution models. This includes those methods that make use of vertex hierarchies (e.g., [764, 876, 877, 2032]), where the continuous multiresolution model is obtained as a byproduct of the decimation-based simplification algorithms used to construct them. The generality of the multitriangulation method lies in its independence of the simplification method used to construct the hierarchy and in its ability to capture the partial ordering, which enables the different triangulations to be extracted. In particular, one of the key features differentiating multitriangulation from other multiresolution models is its ability to represent the result of a simplification that makes use of an edge swap operation, in contrast to most multiresolution models that capture a sequence of vertex pair collapses (e.g., [875]).

Exercise

1. Give an algorithm to simplify a surface using the hierarchical face clustering method.

2.2.4 Surface-Based Boundary Representations

Section 2.2.3 has focused on object-based representations of the boundaries of two- and three-dimensional objects, such as polygons and polyhedra. However, in many applications, we are just interested in representing an arbitrary surface rather than the boundary of an entire object (i.e., a partial boundary). An especially important special case of this problem arises when we are really dealing with a 2.5-dimensional image—that is, for each pair (x, y) corresponding to the projection of the surface on the x-y plane, there corresponds a unique value of z (also known as an *elevation* value). In the rest of this section, we give a brief overview of hierarchical representations of 2.5-dimensional images in the context of processing topographic data (i.e., terrains). The data consists of elevation values sampled at various locations on the plane.

The goal is to reconstruct the surface. This reconstruction is facilitated by choosing a sampling process and representation that adapt to changes in the terrain. The most common method of sampling the data is to use a uniformly spaced rectangular or triangular grid known as a gridded Digital Terrain Model (DTM) or a Digital Elevation Model (DEM). In this case, we do not have to know where the special features are because the sampling process is given a resolution that ensures that any point on the surface is within a bounded distance of a sample point. An alternative method, which is more compact, is capable of capturing point and line features (e.g., peaks, pits, passes, ridges, and valleys) exactly by explicitly recording the elevations of the points corresponding to their location on the surface.

For both methods, the actual surface can be approximated by a network (termed a *mesh*) of planar nonoverlapping triangles. Interpolation is used to obtain the elevation at nonsample locations. In the former uniformly-spaced sampling method, all triangles are of equal size, and hence the interpolation uses the nearest samples. The drawback of this method is that some maxima and minima will be missed if they do not occur at sample points. In the latter more compact method, known as a *Triangular Irregular Network* (TIN) [1487], there is a high likelihood that the triangles are thin and elongated. This has the drawback that interpolation of the elevation of the nonsample point s, using the vertices of the triangle containing s, will not necessarily use the closest vertices to s. In other words, it is preferable that the triangles be as equiangular as possible. The Delaunay triangulation (DT) (see Section 2.2.1.4) is one approach to achieve such a goal. For a more thorough discussion of some of the earlier developed techniques, see the survey of De Floriani [452].

When the amount of data is large, the TIN approach becomes unwieldy in terms of storage requirements. In this case, there are two possible solutions. The first is a pyramidlike approach that represents the surface at different predefined levels of precision (i.e., multiple resolution). The second approach, and the one we focus on in this section, represents different parts of the surface at different levels of resolution. Representations based on such an approach are usually characterized as hierarchical. The hierarchical methods that are commonly used are based on either triangulations or rectangular decompositions.

Hierarchical triangular decomposition methods are differentiated on the basis of whether the decomposition is into three (termed *ternary*) or four (termed *quaternary*) [129, 722, 1790] subtriangles. Ternary hierarchical triangular decompositions are formed by taking an internal point p of one of the triangles, say T, and joining p to the vertices of T (e.g., Figure 2.150(a)). Quaternary hierarchical triangular decompositions are formed by joining three points, each on a different side of a given triangle (e.g., Figure 2.150(b)). The added points at which the subsequent decomposition takes place are usually the data points with the largest distance from the approximating triangle (edges) in the ternary (rectangular) triangular decomposition.[47] Hierarchical triangulations (i.e., triangular decompositions) are represented by trees, where the root corresponds to the initial enclosing rectangle; the out degree is 3 or 4, depending on the type of decomposition (i.e., whether it is ternary or quaternary, respectively). In the case of a ternary triangular decomposition, each triangle is adjacent to at most one triangle on each side.

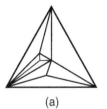

(a)

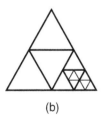

(b)

Figure 2.150
Example triangular decompositions:
(a) ternary and (b) quaternary.

---

[47] As we shall see, a more precise definition of the error involves projections of the points and the approximating triangle (edges).

In contrast, in the case of a quaternary triangular decomposition, each triangle may be adjacent to several triangles along a side.

Hierarchical triangulations result in the approximation of a surface, say S, by planar triangular patches whose vertices are a subset of the data points that define S. For each such patch, an approximation error is computed that is usually the maximum error of the data points with projections on the x-y plane overlapping the projection of the patch on the x-y plane. If the approximation error exceeds a predefined tolerance, then the patch is subdivided further. The resulting surface depends on the nature of the decomposition.

In the case of a ternary hierarchical triangular decomposition, the approximated surface described by the triangulation is usually continuous at every level. Formally, we say that the network, or mesh, is *conforming* as all polygons in the mesh have the same number of vertices and edges (i.e., three in the case of a ternary triangular decomposition). However, the triangles are often thin and elongated since the point at which the triangle is decomposed is internal to the triangle. Thus, equiangularity is generally not satisfied.

There are a number of ways of alleviating the elongation. We have already seen one way in our discussion of the prism tree in Section 2.2.3, where the triangular faces of the approximation of the object are decomposed using a ternary decomposition rule that splits each triangle into between three and six triangles instead of three. It should be clear that the prism tree can also be adapted to 2.5-dimensional data, in which case we simply have just one tetrahedron as the initial approximation instead of two.

Another way is to make use of the triacon hierarchy of Dutton [520], which creates an alternating containment hierarchy so that each level of decomposition is fully contained in the level that was created two steps previously. The partition fieldtree [628, 630] (see Section 2.1.4.1) treats a quadtree decomposition into squares on the plane in a similar manner.

Scarlatos and Pavlidis [1679] avoid the thin and elongated triangles by basing the approximation error that is the key to further decomposition of a triangular patch t on the maximum error along the edges of t, as well as the projection of the patch on the x-y plane. This results in five possible partitions of t as illustrated in Figure 2.151, termed an *adaptive hierarchical triangulation* (AHT). Let e be the maximum error allowed—that is, errors larger than e cause decomposition to take place. Let e_t denote the maximum error in t, and let e_i ($1 \le i \le 3$) denote the maximum error along edge i of t. Similarly, let the maximum errors occur at points p_t on t and p_i along e_i ($1 \le i \le 3$). Triangle t is decomposed depending on which of the following conditions hold:

1. Split at the interior (Figure 2.151(a)): If $e_t > e$ and $e_i < e$ for $1 \le i \le 3$, then split at p_t, and join p_t to the vertices of t.

2. Split at one edge (Figure 2.151(b)): If $e_i > e$, $e_t < e$, and $e_j < e$ for $j \ne i$, then split at p_i, and join p_i to the vertex opposite e_i.

3. Split at one edge and at the interior (Figure 2.151(c)): If $e_i > e$, $e_t > e$, and $e_j < e$ for $j \ne i$, then split at p_t and p_i, and join p_t to the vertices of t and to p_i.

4. Split at two edges (Figure 2.151(d)): If $e_i > e$, $e_j > e$ ($i \ne j$), and $e_k < e$ ($k \ne i$ and $k \ne j$), then split by joining p_i and p_j and also p_i (or p_j) to the vertex opposite to e_i (or e_j). The choice is arbitrary and can be made on the basis of the point with the largest error.

5. Split at three edges (Figure 2.151(e)): If $e_i > e$ for $1 \le i \le 3$, then split t by joining the three points on the edges—that is, p_1 to p_2, p_2 to p_3, and p_3 to p_1.

Notice that we do not distinguish between the case that the error on t is less than e and the case that it is greater than e when the error along just two (see Exercise 3) or three of the edges is greater than e (see Exercise 2).

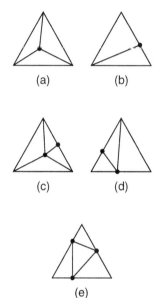

Figure 2.151
Possible partitions of a triangular patch when using the adaptive hierarchical triangulation method: (a) split at the interior, (b) split at one edge, (c) split at one edge and at the interior, (d) split at two edges, and (e) split at three edges.

This partitioning process is applied repeatedly until the maximum error on all triangle patches and their edges is less than the predefined maximum. Observe that a partition along the edge of one triangular patch t will also cause the adjacent triangular patch a to be partitioned. However, the condition for partitioning of a common edge of t and a depends only on the error value along the edge and not on the error in the adjacent triangles. It should be clear that partitions along an adjacent triangle a cascade to a's neighbors whenever more than one edge of a is split. Notice also the similarity of this approach to that used in the prism tree in Section 2.2.3, although one difference is the presence of condition 5 (Figure 2.151(e)), which is not accounted for in the prism tree.

Although the triangles resulting from the adaptive hierarchical triangulation are less likely to be thin and elongated in comparison to those obtained by the conventional ternary triangular decomposition, this problem does not disappear in its entirety. In order to increase the likelihood that the resulting triangles are as equiangular as possible, De Floriani and Puppo [463, 465] propose to use the Delaunay triangulation of each triangle whose maximum error exceeds the predefined tolerance. The result is termed a *hierarchical Delaunay triangulation* (HDT).

Notice that, in a realistic setting where the source data is a uniformly spaced rectangular or triangular grid, it is very unusual to find data points that lie on the edges of the triangles that are being decomposed. Thus, the solution is to consider any data point that lies within some small distance, say ε, of an edge of the triangular patch t that is being decomposed as lying on the edge. The area within ε of the edges of t is known as a *corridor* or a *buffer*. It is important to observe that the buffer also spans data in the triangular patches that are adjacent to t. The buffer is used with both the adaptive hierarchical triangulation and the hierarchical Delaunay triangulation.

The ternary hierarchical triangular decomposition is usually used when the surface is defined at points that are randomly located. De Floriani, Falcidieno, Nagy, and Pienovi [454, 455] discuss its use for surface interpolation, as well as its use as a data compression mechanism. We have also seen its use in the prism tree in Section 2.2.3.

In the case of a quaternary hierarchical triangular decomposition, each triangle can be adjacent to several triangles on each of its sides. The decomposition may be regular (e.g., [129, 603]) or based on the actual data (e.g., [722]). Thus, the approximated surface defined on it is generally not continuous (i.e., does not form a conforming mesh), thereby resulting in what are termed *cracks* (for more details, see, e.g., [1373], as well as the discussion below of hierarchical rectangular decompositions), unless all of the triangles are uniformly split—that is, the resulting tree is a complete quadtree. If the initial approximating triangle is equilateral, and the triangles are always subdivided by connecting their midpoints, then equiangularity holds, and the interpolation is ideal. The quaternary hierarchical triangular decomposition is especially attractive when the data points are drawn from a uniformly spaced grid.

Hierarchical rectangular decompositions are similar to hierarchical triangulations that are based on a quaternary decomposition. Of course, the difference is that a ternary hierarchical rectangular decomposition is meaningless. Thus, we often drop the qualifier "quaternary" when discussing them. Hierarchical rectangular decompositions are used when the data points are the vertices of a rectangular grid. In this case, a rectangle is split by choosing an internal point and joining it to its projections on the four sides of the rectangle. When the data is uniformly spaced, and the internal points are midpoints (e.g., [469, 1864]), the result is analogous to a region quadtree.

For example, Carlson [309] subdivides a surface into rectangular patches for use in algorithms that perform intersection of sculptured surfaces. Schmitt, Barsky, and Du [1690] use adaptive subdivision for surface fitting in conjunction with a parametric piecewise bicubic Bernstein-Bézier surface. They start with a rough approximating surface and recursively refine it where the data is poorly approximated. Chen and Tobler [355] evaluate the use of different approximations in each rectangular patch in terms of numerical accuracy, execution time, and storage.

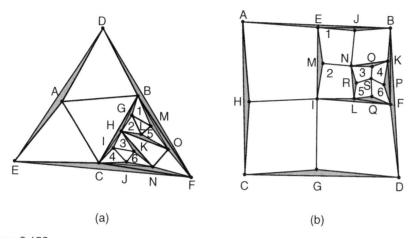

(a)   (b)

Figure 2.152
Example illustrating the alignment problem for a quaternary hierarchical decomposition
that makes use of (a) a triangular decomposition and (b) a rectangular decomposition.

A hierarchical rectangular decomposition has the same continuity problem as the quaternary hierarchical triangular decomposition (i.e., neither forms a conforming mesh). We discuss them together below using the term *quaternary hierarchical decomposition*. In particular, in a quaternary hierarchical decomposition, each triangle or rectangle can be adjacent to several triangles or rectangles on each of its sides since the triangles and rectangles are always subdivided by connecting the midpoints of their sides. The disadvantage of quaternary hierarchical decompositions is that, when we apply a planar triangulation to the three-dimensional points (i.e., the vertices with their elevation values) in the triangular decomposition or fit a patch (e.g., by using a ruled surface [622]) to them in the rectangular decomposition, the resulting surface is not continuous (termed the *alignment problem*) unless all of the triangles or rectangles in the underlying decomposition have been split uniformly—that is, the resulting quadtree (whether triangular or rectangular) is always complete. Figure 2.152(a, b) illustrates the alignment problem for a quaternary hierarchical decomposition on the plane that makes use of triangles and rectangles, respectively. Notice the cracks (shown shaded), which are the result of the discontinuity in the interpolated surfaces corresponding to the triangles and rectangles.

The alignment problem can be resolved for both of the quaternary hierarchical decompositions. In the case of a triangular decomposition, one solution is simply to use the interpolated point instead of the true point [128]. For example, in Figure 2.152(a), the elevation of point H used in triangles 2, 3, and HON would be replaced with the interpolated elevation at the midpoint of the edge between B and C. This is undesirable as we are giving up some of the original sample points. The same problem would arise in the case of a rectangular decomposition, where we would replace the elevation of point R in patches 3 and 5 in Figure 2.152(b) with the interpolated elevation at the midpoint of the edge between N and L.

Instead, it is better to decompose triangle ABC, as shown in Figure 2.153(a), into a hierarchy of triangles so that there are triangles in ABC adjacent to edge BC that are of the same size as triangles 1, 2, 3, and 4 in triangle BCF [602]. This is achieved by adding the points p, q, r, s, t, and u, as well as the edges between them (shown with light lines) and the vertices along edge BC (i.e., B, G, H, I, and C).

There are two types of newly added points. The first type are midpoints of known edges. The second type are midpoints of newly created edges lying between known vertices or midpoints of known edges. In the strictest sense, the first type do not represent new samples (since they lie on existing edges), while the second type do. In both cases, their elevation values are obtained by applying linear interpolation to the elevation values at the endpoints of these known or newly created edges. For example, q is obtained

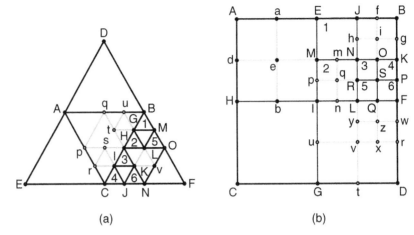

(a)　　　　　　　　　　　　　　(b)

Figure 2.153
Example illustrating how to resolve the alignment problem for a hierarchical quaternary decomposition corresponding to Figure 2.152 that makes use of (a) a triangular decomposition and (b) a rectangular decomposition. Newly added edges are shown with light lines.

by applying linear interpolation to the elevations at A and B. In contrast, both s and t are obtained by applying linear interpolation to the elevation at H and the interpolated elevation just computed at p and q, respectively.

Observe that a similar process must be applied to triangle HON in Figure 2.153(a) so that there are triangles in HON adjacent to edges HO and HN that are of the same size as triangles 2 and 5 in triangle BOH and triangles 3 and 6 in triangle HNC, respectively. This is achieved by adding the point v, as well as the edges between it and vertices L and K of triangles BOH and HNC, respectively.

Unfortunately, we are not yet through in the sense that we may also have to apply the same process to the other edge neighbors of triangle BCF (i.e., the ones adjacent along edges BF and CF). This is the case if their atomic triangles that share edges BM and CJ are larger than triangles 1 and 4, respectively.

A similar technique can be applied to a quaternary hierarchical rectangular decomposition, thereby obtaining a hierarchy of rectangles so that there are adjacent rectangles of equal size along the edges (see Figure 2.153(b)). For example, in Figure 2.153(b), there are rectangles in rectangle IFDG adjacent to edge IF that are the same size as rectangles 2, 5, and 6 in IFDG. As in the quaternary hierarchical triangular decomposition, several new points have been added. We decompose these points into two sets: those that lie on existing edges (e.g., n, r, t, u, and w) and those that do not (e.g., v, x, y, and z). The former, as in the case of the triangular decomposition, do not represent new samples since they are midpoints of known edges. However, their elevation values depend on the type of patch that is being fit through them.

The patch is defined by the four curves that make up its boundary. The simplest patch arises when the curves are linear, in which case the resulting patch is a ruled surface. Of course, more complex curves, such as quadratics, could be used, thereby leading to more complex surface patches. When the curves are linear, the elevation values of all newly added points that lie on existing edges are obtained by applying linear interpolation to the elevation values at the endpoints of the edges for which they serve as midpoints. For example, r is obtained by interpolating the elevations at D and F, while w is obtained by applying linear interpolation to the elevation at F and the interpolated elevation just computed at r.

The newly added points that do not lie on existing edges represent new samples. Thus, we must also obtain an elevation value for them. There are two choices for some of them since they fall at the midpoints of edges between the midpoints of both a horizontal and a vertical edge. We choose to take the average of the two interpolated values. For example, v is obtained by taking the average of the values obtained by applying linear interpolation to the elevation values at L and t and the elevation values at u and r. The same technique is applied to obtain the elevation value at z once we have obtained the elevation values at x, y, and w.

At this point, let us briefly compare the two different quaternary hierarchical decompositions. As we saw, both methods suffer from the alignment problem when we try to fit a surface through their vertices. However, as we have demonstrated, this problem can be overcome through the addition of the appropriate triangles and rectangles. For the triangular decomposition, we obtained a planar surface because we were able to use a planar triangulation. For the rectangular decomposition, we obtained a nonplanar surface because it is impossible to fit a plane through the four vertices of each rectangle.

It could be argued that a nonplanar surface is a better approximation of a nonplanar surface than a planar one, thereby making the rectangular decomposition more attractive than the triangular decomposition. Of course, we could also fit a nonplanar surface through the vertices of the triangles. However, it is well-known that the more sample points that are used in a surface patch, the better is the approximation of the underlying surface. Thus, such reasoning implies that the rectangular decomposition is preferable to the triangular decomposition.

An argument could also be made that the planar approximation of the surface provided by the triangle is preferable to the nonplanar approximation provided by the rectangle. This is especially true if ease of interpolation is an issue. In fact, we could also obtain a planar approximation using rectangles by splitting each rectangle into two triangles by adding a diagonal edge between two opposing vertices. There are two choices as shown in Figure 2.154. As long as the four vertices are not coplanar, one will result in a ridgelike planar surface (Figure 2.154(a)), while the other will result in a valleylike planar surface (Figure 2.154(b)). We usually choose the diagonal edge whose angle is the most obtuse.

Neither of the above solutions to the alignment problem that employ a quaternary hierarchical decomposition (whether they use a triangular or rectangular decomposition) yields a conforming mesh because not all of the polygons that make up the mesh have the same number of vertices and edges. Nevertheless, the quaternary hierarchical decomposition that makes use of a rectangular quadtree can form the basis of a conforming mesh and overcome the alignment problem. The idea is to apply a planar triangulation to the result of transforming the underlying rectangular quadtree to a restricted quadtree [1453, 1771, 1772, 1940]. The *restricted quadtree* has the property that all rectangles that are edge neighbors are either of equal size or of ratio 2:1. Such a quadtree is also termed a *1-irregular quadtree* [124], a *balanced quadtree* [204], and a *1-balanced quadtree* [1312]. A somewhat tighter restriction requires that all vertex neighbors either be of equal size or of ratio 2:1 (termed a *0-balanced quadtree* [1312]). It should be clear that a 0-balanced quadtree is also a 1-balanced quadtree but not vice versa (see Exercise 4).

Given an arbitrary quadtree decomposition, the restricted quadtree is formed by repeatedly subdividing the larger nodes until the 2:1 ratio holds. For example, Figure 2.155(a) is the restricted quadtree corresponding to the rectangular decomposition in Figure 2.152(b). Note that the SE quadrant of Figure 2.152(b) has to be decomposed once, in contrast to twice when building the hierarchy of rectangles in Figure 2.153(b). This method of subdivision is also used in finite-element analysis (e.g., [1147]) as part of a technique called *h-refinement* [1013] to refine adaptively a mesh that has already been analyzed, as well as to achieve element compatibility.

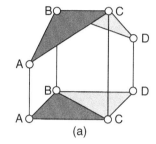

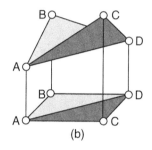

Figure 2.154
Example illustrating the ambiguity that results when each rectangle is split into two triangles by adding a diagonal edge between (a) vertices B and C and (b) vertices A and D.

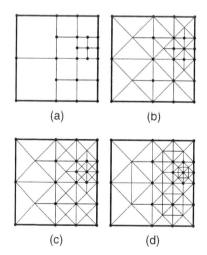

Figure 2.155
(a) Restricted quadtree corresponding to the rectangular decomposition in Figure 2.152(b) and the result of triangulating it using a (b) two-triangle rule, (c) four-triangle rule, and (d) eight-triangle rule.

A conforming triangular mesh is obtained by triangulating the rectangles in the restricted quadtree uniformly using one of the following three rules:

1. Decompose each atomic rectangle into two triangles in such a way that the partition line passes through the center of the rectangle's immediately containing node. If there is just one atomic rectangle, then the orientation of the partition line is arbitrary. For each triangle t whose adjacent triangle u is larger, if the bordering triangle u of any triangle t is larger, then recursively partition u in half until the resulting triangle shares an edge with t. Apply the decomposition to the newly created triangles as necessary (e.g., Figure 2.155(b)).

2. Decompose each atomic rectangle into four triangles, or one triangle per edge, unless the edge borders a smaller rectangle. In that case, two triangles are formed along the edge (e.g., Figure 2.155(c)).

3. Decompose each atomic rectangle into eight triangles, or two triangles per edge, unless the edge borders a larger rectangle. In that case, only one triangle is formed along the edge (e.g., Figure 2.155(d)).

Even though the decomposition into eight triangles requires more space than the decomposition into two and four triangles because it results in more triangles, it is nevertheless preferred [1940] as it avoids problems when displaying (i.e., shading [1568]) the resulting object (see also [1636, Section 7.1.6]).

If we are interested in reducing the number of triangles beyond the amount required by using the restricted quadtree with a decomposition into four triangles, then we can use a rule that decomposes each atomic rectangle into two triangles without first building a restricted quadtree where all rectangles that are edge neighbors are either of equal size or of ratio 2:1. We term the result a *restricted bintree*. It has been used by several researchers (e.g., [513, 576, 651, 702, 810, 1176, 1259, 1522, 1564, 1565]). Although we use the qualifier "restricted" to describe the structure, as we explain below, it is formed in a rather different way from the restricted quadtree.

The key idea behind the restricted bintree is that the square corresponding to the entire space spanned by the adaptively sampled rectangular grid is initially decomposed into two isoceles right triangles by using one of the two diagonals. These two isoceles right triangles are subsequently recursively decomposed into two isoceles right triangles by bisecting the right angle of each one as necessary. This process is continued until a conforming mesh is obtained (i.e., the resulting triangular mesh does not suffer from the alignment problem and thus there are no T-junctions, and all of the sample points are vertices of triangles). For example, Figure 2.156(b) is the restricted bintree corresponding to the rectangular decomposition in Figure 2.152(b). Notice that, as in the restricted quadtree, all adjacent triangles are either of equal size, or the length of the leg of one triangle t is half the length of the hypotenuse of its larger adjacent triangle u, or the length of t's hypotenuse is twice the length of the leg of its smaller adjacent triangle s.

The above definition of the restricted bintree is top down. We can also define the restricted bintree in a bottom-up manner. Such a definition resembles more closely the definition of the restricted quadtree with the four- or eight-triangle rule. In particular, the initial transformation of the rectangular decomposition in Figure 2.152(b) is such that each square block b corresponding to node a in the quadtree is split into two isoceles right triangles by the addition of a diagonal edge e that is oriented in such a way that e passes through the center of the parent of a (i.e., the immediately containing block). The only time we have a choice as to the orientation of the diagonal (i.e., from the NW corner to the SE corner or from the NE corner to the SW corner) is in the case of the block corresponding to the root, in which case either orientation is acceptable as there are only two triangles left anyway. Figure 2.156(a) shows the result of applying this triangulation process to the rectangular decomposition in Figure 2.152(b). Once we have obtained the initial triangulation, we decompose the remaining triangles until a conforming mesh is obtained (i.e., the resulting triangular mesh does not suffer from the alignment problem).

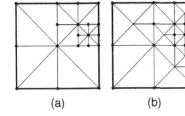

(a)   (b)

Figure 2.156
(a) Result of the initial step of forming the restricted bintree corresponding to the rectangular decomposition in Figure 2.152(b) using the bottom-up method and (b) the final restricted bintree so that the alignment problem is resolved.

At a first glance, the restricted bintree (Figure 2.156(b)) appears quite similar to the restricted quadtree with a decomposition into two triangles (Figure 2.155(b)). However, regardless of the how the restricted bintree is defined, we see that it does yield a different decomposition. In particular, the fact that, in order to obtain the restricted bintree, we did not initially have to build the restricted quadtree (i.e., decompose the underlying rectangles so that all adjacent rectangles are either of equal size or of ratio 2:1) meant that decomposition lines in rectangles that were created to ensure the 2:1 ratio could be eliminated if they were subdividing larger triangles. This may preclude the subsequent subdivision of larger adjacent triangles (e.g., the two triangles in the SW quadrant in Figure 2.156(b), which had to be subdivided in Figure 2.155(b)).

The principle of decomposing each element of the decomposition into two triangles can also be applied to a quaternary hierarchical decomposition that makes use of a triangular decomposition (e.g., Figure 2.152(a)) to obtain a conforming mesh. In this case, when two sides of a triangle have no sample points between their vertices, then we can repeatedly split the triangle into two triangles using the sample points on the other side as the vertices. For example, triangle ABC in Figure 2.152(a) would initially be split into triangles ACH and ABH. Since edges CH and BH contain sample points between their vertices, we split triangles ACH and ABH, resulting in triangles ACI, AIH, AHG, and ABG. In the case of triangle HON, the situation is more complicated as two of its sides contain sample points. For such a situation, it is best to decompose the triangle into four equilateral triangles after adding point v, which is the midpoint of edge NO (i.e., triangles HKL, KLv, KNv, and LOv). Once this is done, we split triangle FON into two triangles FNv and FOv. The result of the application of such a policy to the triangular decomposition in Figure 2.152(a) is shown in Figure 2.157(a).

The drawback of such a solution is that successive partitioning of a triangle and the resulting triangles into two triangles will lead to thin and elongated triangles. As mentioned earlier, equiangularity is preferred. In order to overcome this problem, it has been proposed to disallow a partition of triangle t into two triangles when the parent f of t has already been split into two triangles. Instead, the split of f into two triangles is undone, and f is now split into four equilateral triangles. These four triangles are split into two triangles as necessary to ensure that the alignment problem does not arise [124, 211]. For example, Figure 2.157(b) shows the result of the application of such a rule to triangle ABC in Figure 2.152(a). In particular, instead of splitting ABC into triangles ACH and ABH, followed by triangles ACI, AIH, AHG, and ABG, as in Figure 2.157(a), we now add points p and q at the midpoints of edges AC and AB, respectively, and split triangle ABC into the four equilateral triangles Apq, BHq, CHp, and Hpq. Of course, we must also split triangles AEC into triangles AEp and CEp, ABD into ADq and BDq, CHp into CIp and HIp, and BHq into BGq and GHq.

Exercises

1. Consider a hierarchical triangulation that is based on a ternary decomposition. Let t be the number of triangles and v the number of vertices. Prove that $t < 2 \cdot v$.

2. In the adaptive hierarchical triangulation method [1679], why is it not necessary to distinguish between the case that the error on t is less than e and the case that it is greater than e when the error along three of the edges is greater than e?

3. In the adaptive hierarchical triangulation method [1679], why is it not necessary to distinguish between the case that the error on t is less than e and the case that it is greater than e when the error along only two of the edges is greater than e?

4. Prove that a restricted quadtree where all vertex neighbors are either of equal size or of ratio 2:1 (i.e., a *0-balanced quadtree* [1312]) is also one where all edge neighbors are either of equal size or of ratio 2:1 (i.e., a *1-balanced quadtree* [1312]), but not vice versa.

5. Prove that the use of the restricted quadtree increases the number of nodes in the quadtree by at most a factor of 8.

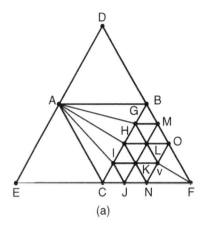

(a)

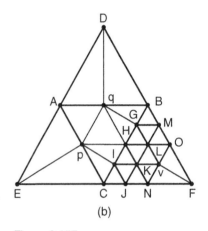

(b)

Figure 2.157
(a) Result of applying a two-triangle rule to resolve the alignment problem for the example quaternary decomposition that makes use of a triangular decomposition in Figure 2.152(a) and (b) result of replacing two successive partitions of a triangle and its two resulting triangles into two triangles by a partition into four triangles followed by appropriate partitions into two triangles.

6. Suppose that you define a restricted quadtree where each block is subdivided into a 3×3 set of congruent blocks instead of a 2×2 set of congruent blocks. Prove that the use of the restricted quadtree in this case increases the number of nodes in the quadtree by at most a factor of 6.

7. Suppose that you define a restricted triangular quadtree in the same manner as the restricted rectangle quadtree so that all edge neighbors are either of equal size or of ratio 2:1. Prove that the use of the restricted triangular quadtree in this case increases the number of nodes in the quadtree by at most a factor of 10.

8. Can you show that the use of a restricted d-dimensional quadtree where every $(d-1)$-dimensional neighbor is either of equal size or of ratio 2:1 increases the number of nodes in the quadtree by at most a factor of $3^d - 1$?

9. Consider a quaternary hierarchical decomposition that makes use of a rectangular decomposition implemented using a restricted bintree with a triangular mesh T. Suppose that a sample point is added at the midpoint of the hypotenuse h of triangle t in T. At this point, T must be adjusted to resolve the alignment problem. Prove that for each size z greater than or equal to that of t, no more than two triangles of size z will be split, and no triangles smaller than t will be split.

10. Evans, Kirkpatrick, and Townshend [576] point out that instead of using a restricted bintree that results in a hierarchy of isoceles right triangles, a similar subdivision of a 30-60 right triangle can be used. In this case, we start with one 30-60 right triangle, which is recursively decomposed as necessary into four 30-60 right congruent triangles of one-fourth the size. The 30, 60, and 90 degree vertices have degrees of 12, 6, and 4, respectively. Suppose that a sample point is added so that a triangle t needs to be split. Evans, Kirkpatrick, and Townshend [576] claim that, for each size z greater than or equal to that of t, at most 12 triangles of size z will be split, and no triangles smaller than t will be split. Prove that this is true.

2.3 Difference-Based Compaction Methods

Some interior-based and boundary-based representations (regardless of whether they are implicit or explicit) can be made more compact by making use of an ordering on the data whether it is the locations (i.e., the cells, blocks, boundary elements, etc.) or values that they record (if one exists). In particular, instead of just recording the actual values of the cells or the actual locations of the cells, such methods record the *change* (i.e., the difference) in the values of the cells or the locations of the cells where the value changes. The ordering is used to reconstruct the original association of locations with values (i.e., the feature query) or values with their locations (i.e., the location query) whenever we want to answer one of our basic queries for determining what locations are associated with a particular feature (i.e., the feature query) or what value is associated with a particular location (i.e., the location query). In other words, these compaction methods are not designed to facilitate responding to either the feature or location queries.

Naturally, this reconstruction process is costly because it requires traversing the entire representation (i.e., all the objects). However, this is not necessarily a problem when execution of the operations inherently requires that the entire representation be traversed (e.g., Boolean set operations, data structure conversion, erosion, dilation). On the other hand, operations that require the ability to access a cell at random in the representation (e.g., neighbor finding) are inefficient in this case unless an additional access structure is imposed on the compact representation. However, note that, if the representation records relative changes in the values rather than the actual values, then an access structure may not be of much use since we still need the reconstruction process to determine the value associated with a particular cell.

In this section, we discuss several difference-based compaction methods. We start with runlength encoding (Section 2.3.1), which is designed primarily for use with interior-based representations. Next, we review the chain code (Section 2.3.2), which is the classical method used to make boundary-based representations of two-dimensional data more compact. The chain code is inapplicable to data of dimensionality greater than

2. We conclude by presenting the vertex representation (Section 2.3.3). It uses the basic elements of the chain code (i.e., the vertices) to yield a variant of runlength encoding that is similar in spirit to constructive solid geometry (CSG) and that is applicable to the interiors of objects of arbitrary dimensionality. All of the sides (i.e., faces in dimensions higher than 2) of the objects in this section are restricted to being parallel to the coordinate axes (termed an *axis-parallel polygon*).[48]

2.3.1 Runlength Encoding

Runlength encoding [1595] is an example of a method that can be applied to make an interior-based representation, such as the array, more compact. The actual locations of the cells are not recorded. Instead, contiguous, identically valued cells are aggregated into one-dimensional rectangles for which only the value associated with the cells making up the rectangle and the length of the rectangle are recorded. The one-dimensional rectangles are ordered in raster-scan order, which means that row 1 is followed by row 2, and so on. The same technique is applicable to higher-dimensional data, in which case the one-dimensional rectangles are ordered in terms of the rows, planes, and so forth.

For example, consider the object in Figure 2.158(a), which is embedded in an 8×8 image array. The cells that make up the object are shown shaded. Assuming an origin at the upper-left corner and that the image is binary with B and W denoting foreground and background, respectively, we have a runlength encoding of (W,8), (W,8), (W,4), (B,4), (W,4), (B,4), (W,3), (B,5), (W,2), (B,6), (W,2), (B,4), (W,2), (W,2), (B,3), (W,3). Given the location of any cell c in one-dimensional rectangle r, the value associated with c can be computed by referring to the location of the starting position of the entire representation and accumulating the lengths of the one-dimensional rectangles encountered before the position of r in the ordering.

Runlength encoding can be made even more compact by just recording the change in the value associated with the cell rather than the value itself. We use the term *change-based runlength encoding* to describe this method, thereby distinguishing it from the previous variant, which we will refer to as *value-based runlength encoding* when the need arises.[49] Change-based runlength encoding is especially attractive in the case of a binary image, where we have just two possible values (i.e., 0 and 1 or B and W, respectively, in our examples). In this case, once we know the value associated with the first cell in each row, we do not need to keep track of the remaining values in the row. Thus, we just record the value of the first cell in each row, followed by a sequence of numbers corresponding to the lengths of the one-dimensional rectangles of alternating values. For example, given the image in Figure 2.158(a), we have the following change-based runlength encoding: (W,8), (W,8), (W,4,4), (W,4,4), (W,3,5), (W,2,6), (W,2,4,2), (W,2,3,3).

Runlength encoding can also be adapted to deal with rectangular aggregates (i.e., blocks) in higher dimensions. Once again, we assume that the locations of the blocks are not recorded. If the blocks are of a uniform size and orientation, then the adaptation is easy as it is analogous to a grid of cells of uniform size, and we apply the same methods as before. If the blocks are not of a uniform size, then the problem is more complex. Recall that since we do not record the locations of the blocks, we must make use of the ordering of the blocks. Such an ordering exists if there is a regularity to the manner in which the blocks of differing sizes are created. Of course, in such a case, we must specify the block sizes. A block decomposition that results from a regular decomposition of space, such as a region quadtree, region octree, bintree, has such an ordering.

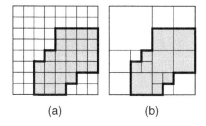

Figure 2.158
(a) Example object in an 8×8 image array and (b) its corresponding region quadtree block decomposition.

---

[48] Such an object was termed an *orthogonal polygon* in [566, 567, 569], although the term *axis-parallel polygon* is more appropriate, and we shall use it here.

[49] We use the general term *runlength encoding* whenever either of the two methods is applicable and no confusion is possible.

As an example, consider two-dimensional data represented by a region quadtree (i.e., a regular decomposition into four congruent rectangular blocks) where we ignore the imposed access structure (i.e., the tree). Its ordering is obtained in the same manner as the block decomposition—that is, we recursively decompose the embedding space into four congruent blocks (labeled NW, NE, SW, SE, in this order) until each block is either completely occupied by an object or is empty, at which time their size and value are placed in the list. For example, assuming a list of pairs (a, b), where a and b correspond to the value and size (i.e., power of 2), respectively, of each block, the region quadtree in Figure 2.158(b) corresponding to the object in Figure 2.158(a) is represented as (W,2), (W,1), (W,1), (B,1), (B,1), (W,1), (W,0), (B,0), (B,0), (B,0), (W,1), (B,1), (B,1), (B,1), (B,0), (B,0), (B,0), (W,0), (W,1).

This ordering can also be obtained by associating with each block b_i a unique base 4 number m_i formed by interleaving the bits in the binary representation of the x and y coordinate values of b_i's upper-left corner (termed a *Morton number* [1317, 1636]), assuming an origin at the upper-left corner of the image, and then sorting the m_i values in increasing order. The resulting order is the same as the *Morton order* (see Sections 2.1.1.2 and 2.1.2.4, as well as Figure 2.5(c)). We term this representation a Morton size ordering. It contains the same data.

Assuming a Morton size ordering representation, given the location of the upper-left corner of any cell c, and the size (must be a power of 2) of the space S in which the objects are embedded, then the value associated with c can be computed by an accumulation process that starts at the location of the upper-left corner of S. This is done by reconstructing the embedding space using the principle that, each time a block of width 2^m is encountered, it must be followed by three more blocks $\{b_1, b_2, b_3\}$, each of width 2^m or satisfying the constraint that the area spanned by the constituent blocks of b_i ($1 \le i \le 3$) have a total width of 2^m. As each block b of the Morton size ordering is added, we check if b contains c and report b's value as that of c when the containment test is satisfied.

From a theoretical standpoint, other orderings than the Morton order could be applied to the blocks (e.g., see Figure 2.5), thereby resulting in different block orders than that in the Morton size ordering. For example, we could try to use the Peano-Hilbert order given in Figure 2.5(d) to obtain a Peano-Hilbert size ordering. However, in this case, determining the value associated with a particular block or cell may be rather complex (see Exercise 8).

It is interesting to observe that an analogous representation to that of the Morton size ordering can be obtained by not completely ignoring the treelike nature of the block decomposition process, which is a tree having the property that each node has either four children or is one of the blocks. The ordering is obtained by traversing the resulting tree in the order NW, NE, SW, SE and forming a list of the values of the nodes or blocks encountered. Nonleaf nodes have a value that is different from those associated with the blocks (say I denoting a nonleaf node). In this case, there is no longer a need to record the size of the individual blocks, as in the Morton size ordering, since we can determine it by an accumulation process that keeps track of how many nonleaf nodes have been encountered in the traversal that starts at the root of the tree. This representation is also known as a *DF-expression* [1004] (denoting a depth-first traversal ordering). For example, the DF-expression of the region quadtree in Figure 2.158(b) is given by IWIWWBBIWIWBBBWBIBBIBBBWW. Some implementations of the DF-expression associate a value with each nonleaf node such as an average of the values of the descendants (e.g., [1395]) in which case an additional flag is needed to distinguish between the value types. Other implementations such as the *compressed quadtree* [2018] try to reduce the number of times that the same value of a leaf node appears by just keeping track of the nonleaf nodes by using a set of 52 patterns to describe the four possible value configurations of the children of each nonleaf node. For each pattern that has child leaf nodes, their values immediately follow the pattern in the list of values in the ordering.

The DF-expression stores the structure of the tree along with the values of the leaf nodes. Thus, in the case of a binary image, it may be a bit wasteful in its storage requirements because it requires two bits to encode each of the possible values, although there are really just three different values. An alternative is to separate the structure of the tree from that of the values of the leaf nodes by using two separate bitstrings [1830], termed a *linear tree* and a *color table*. The resulting structure is known as an *S-tree* [970]. The linear tree corresponds to the structure of the tree and uses 0 and 1 to represent nonleaf and leaf nodes, respectively. In the case of a binary image, the color table makes use of 0 and 1 to represent the values of the leaf nodes, while more than one bit is needed for each value when the image has a greater range of possible values. In order to simplify our examples, in the rest of this discussion, we assume, without loss of generality, that the image is binary. Both the linear trees and the color tables are formed by a preorder traversal of the underlying quadtree. For example, the S-tree corresponding to the region quadtree in Figure 2.158(b) has 010111101011111011011111 as its linear tree and 0001100111011111100 as its color table.

The space saving provided by the S-tree should be quite clear. For example, in the case of a binary image, the S-tree contains one bit (in the linear tree) for each nonleaf node in the original tree, while containing two bits (one in the linear tree and one in the color table) for each leaf node in the original tree. The trade-off is in the amount of time necessary to determine the value associated with a particular cell in the image as, now, the process takes twice as much time as in the DF-expression representation since two lists must be traversed in tandem (i.e., the linear tree and the color table). Again, we note that the S-tree could also be used for nonbinary images with even greater space-saving relative to the DF-expression.

The principal drawback of the S-tree, as well as the DF-expression, is the fact that determining the value associated with a particular cell may require that the entire representation be examined. This is quite time-consuming, especially for large images whose S-tree or DF-expression representation may span many pages. In this case, the S-tree is decomposed into several string segments that are stored on the different pages (e.g., we can distribute the bits of the string corresponding to the linear tree so that each group of consecutive m bits is on a separate page). This drawback can be overcome by identifying each string segment by the node N (leaf or nonleaf) in the original tree corresponding to the first element in the segment and then imposing an access structure on these node identifiers. This is the basis of the S^+-tree [970], which uses a B^+-tree as the access structure with the values of these node identifiers serving as the keys.[50] Below we describe the S^+-tree for binary images.

The simplest way of representing the first node N in each segment is to use the sequence of directional codes in the original tree corresponding to the path from the root of the tree to N. In this case, we can use the codes 0, 1, 2, and 3, corresponding to NW, NE, SW, and SE, respectively. Transitions are made in the B^+-tree on the basis of comparisons from left to right using these key values. Given two keys i and j, we say that $j > i$ whenever j is greater in value than i, once the two strings corresponding to i and j have been made the same length by padding the shorter one on the right with digits having the value D such that D is less than 0 in the sort sequence. Note that, if i is a substring of j, then $j > i$. Also, observe that the identifier consisting of the empty string corresponds to the root of the tree, which is not necessarily empty.

---

[50] The original formulation of the S-tree and S^+-tree makes use of a bintree [1041, 1661, 1828] (described in Section 2.1.2.6); however, this makes no difference here.

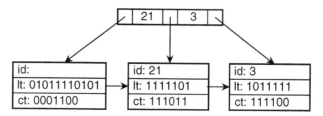

Figure 2.159
An S$^+$-tree corresponding to the region quadtree in Figure 2.158(b). "id," "lt," and "ct" denote the identifier, linear tree, and color table, respectively, for each leaf node in the tree. Note the presence of horizontal links in the leaf nodes of the tree in order to facilitate sequential access.

For example, the linear tree of the S-tree corresponding to the region quadtree in Figure 2.158(b) could be decomposed into three segments (of nearly equal size) on three consecutive pages as follows:

1. 010111101 with color table 000110 and no identifier (i.e., the root is the first node on the page).

2. 0111111 with color table 011101 and identifier 21. This is the portion of the tree starting with the NE child of the SW child of the root.

3. 011011111 with color table 1111100 and identifier 3. This is the portion of the tree starting with the SE child of the root.

The resulting S$^+$-tree is given in Figure 2.159. The identifier values are used as the index values in the nonleaf nodes of the B$^+$-tree. Note that the actual keys (i.e., the values of the identifiers) are also stored in the leaf nodes of the S$^+$-tree, which are linked, in order to facilitate operations on the actual data stored in the nodes, such as traversing the image in its entirety. In addition, observe that we have varied slightly the definition of the B$^+$-tree given in Appendix A in that, in our implementation, if a key value k is stored in a nonleaf node between pointers to subtrees p and q, then all key values in p are less than k, and all key values in q are greater than or equal to k.[51] For an extension of the S$^+$-tree to handle nonbinary images, see the S*-tree of Nardelli and Proietti [1345].

The Morton size ordering did not record the locations of the blocks. Instead, it just recorded their values and sizes in a particular order. As we saw, this information was sufficient to determine the value associated with any block or cell in the image, given its location. We can achieve a similar effect by just recording the locations of the blocks instead of their sizes, while still recording their values. In this case, we record the location of the block's upper-left corner and use the same ordering as in the Morton size ordering. In other words, its ordering is obtained in the same manner as the block decomposition—that is, by recursively decomposing the embedding space into four congruent blocks (labeled NW, NE, SW, and SE, in this order) until each block is either completely occupied by an object or is empty, at which time the location of the upper-left corner of the block and the block's value are placed in the list. We term the resulting representation a *Morton location ordering*. The presence of the ordering enables us to determine the size of the block.

For example, assuming a list of pairs (a, b), where a and b correspond to the value and location, respectively, of each block, the Morton location ordering representation of the region quadtree in Figure 2.158(b) corresponding to the object in Figure 2.158(a) is (W,(0,0)), (W,(4,0)), (W,(6,0)), (B,(4,2)), (B,(6,2)), (W,(0,4)), (W,(2,4)),

---

[51] This is in contrast to the other definition, which stipulates that, if a key value k is stored in a nonleaf node between pointers to subtrees p and q, then all key values in p are less than or equal to k, and all key values in q are greater than k.

(B,(3,4)), (B,(2,5)), (B,(3,5)), (W,(0,6)), (B,(2,6)), (B,(4,4)), (B,(6,4)), (B,(4,6)), (B,(5,6)), (B,(4,7)), (W,(5,7)), (W,(6,6)).

The size of each block in the Morton location ordering is determined by making use of its Morton number and that of the block that immediately follows it in the ordering. In particular, given the location of the upper-left corner of any block b in the set and the size M (must be a power of 2) of the space S in which the objects are embedded, the size of b is determined by taking the logarithm to the base 4 of the difference between the Morton numbers of the immediately following block in the ordering and b. The Morton number of the block following the last block in the ordering is M^2.

The key to understanding why the Morton location ordering works is to observe that the Morton order is a space-filling curve that accounts for all of the pixels in each block before moving to the next block in the block sequence. Thus, the Morton numbers of two successive blocks A and B in the sequence (where B follows A) differ by the size of A since the Morton number of a block corresponds to the first pixel in the block (i.e., the pixel in the upper-left corner of the block). For example, rewriting the Morton location ordering representation given above of the region quadtree in Figure 2.158(b) corresponding to the object in Figure 2.158(a) yields (W,0), (W,16), (W,20), (B,24), (B,28), (W,32), (W,36), (B,37), (B,38), (B,39), (W,40), (B,44), (B,48), (B,52), (B,56), (B,57), (B,58), (W,59), (W,60).

Given the location of the upper-left corner of any cell c, determining the value associated with c using a Morton location ordering is very easy. We simply construct the Morton number m_c corresponding to c and find the block b in the ordering with the largest Morton number that is less than or equal to m_c. This query can be executed even more efficiently if we impose an access structure on the Morton numbers such as a B^+-tree as now our search for the Morton number takes logarithmic time instead of being a sequential search. The ability to impose the access structure on the location field is an advantage of the Morton location ordering over the Morton size ordering, although, of course, the Morton location ordering does require more space than the Morton size ordering.

Both the Morton size and location orderings record the values and sizes or locations of each block in the image. This may be wasteful if the same value is associated with consecutive blocks in the image. One way to reduce the storage requirements is just to keep track of the blocks where the values change. This is not possible in the case of the Morton size ordering since only the sizes of the blocks are recorded and thus there is no easy way to identify the locations of the blocks where the values change. However, in the case of the Morton location ordering, such an approach does work since we can determine the size of the individual blocks in the ordering by making use of their Morton numbers and their relative position in the ordering. Thus, all we need to do is to keep track of the locations where the values change (i.e., the location of the first block in the ordering associated with each value), as well as the values. Such an adaptation of runlength encoding is termed *two-dimensional runlength encoding* [1115]. As in the case of the Morton location ordering, a sufficient location is the address of the upper-left corner of the block.

For example, assuming an origin at the upper-left corner of the space in which the objects are embedded, the two-dimensional runlength encoding of the region quadtree in Figure 2.158(b) is given by (W,(0,0)), (B,(4,2)), (W,(0,4)), (B,(3,4)), (W,(0,6)), (B,(2,6)), (W,(5,7)). Notice the similarity of this approach to the polygon representation of the boundary of an object that just records the locations of the vertices (i.e., the starting point of each vector).

Given the location of the upper-left corner of any cell c in the image, determining the value associated with c using a two-dimensional runlength encoding is done in the same manner as with the Morton location ordering. Once again, we simply construct the Morton number m_c corresponding to c and find the block b in the ordering with the largest Morton number that is less than or equal to m_c. As in the case of the Morton location ordering, this query can be executed even more efficiently if we impose an access structure on the Morton numbers of the blocks, such as a B^+-tree, as now our search for the Morton number takes logarithmic time instead of being a sequential search. We can also determine the locations and sizes of all of the blocks in the image using techniques similar to those used to compute the size of the blocks in the Morton location ordering (see Exercise 17).

As in the array representation, two-dimensional runlength encoding can be made more compact by just recording the change in the value associated with the block rather than the value itself. In fact, if the image is binary, then we need to record only the value of the first block in the ordering because all the rest of the blocks in the ordering will alternate in value (although we did not do so in our example). Another alternative to two-dimensional runlength encoding when the image is binary is just to record the locations and sizes of all blocks of a given color. The locations and sizes of the remaining blocks can be determined by a process similar to that used in determining the locations and sizes of the blocks of the same color in the two-dimensional runlength encoding (see Exercise 24).

Exercises

1. Give an algorithm to construct the value-based runlength encoding for an $M \times M$ image represented by an array.

2. Give an algorithm to determine the value associated with a cell c in an $M \times M$ image represented by a value-based runlength encoding.

3. Give an algorithm to construct the change-based runlength encoding for an $M \times M$ binary image represented by an array.

4. Give an algorithm to determine the value associated with a cell c in an $M \times M$ binary image represented by a change-based runlength encoding.

5. The runlength encoding that we have described traverses the cells in a row-by-row manner. An alternative is to traverse the cells in Morton order or Peano-Hilbert order. Repeat Exercises 1–4 for a runlength encoding based on a traversal of the cells in Morton and Peano-Hilbert order.

6. Give the Morton size ordering of the blocks of the region quadtree in Figure 2.15 in the form of a list of ordered pairs (a, b), where a and b correspond to the value and size (i.e., power of 2) of each block. Assume that the tree is traversed in the order NW, NE, SW, and SE.

7. Give an algorithm to determine the value associated with a cell c having an upper-left corner at location (x, y) in an $M \times M$ image (M is a power of 2) represented by a Morton size ordering.

8. Give an algorithm to determine the value associated with a cell c having an upper-left corner at location (x, y) in an $M \times M$ image (M is a power of 2) represented by a Peano-Hilbert size ordering.

9. Give the DF-expression for the region quadtree in Figure 2.15 assuming a traversal of the tree in the order NW, NE, SW, and SE.

10. Give an algorithm to determine the value associated with a cell c having an upper-left corner at location (x, y) in an $M \times M$ image (M is a power of 2) represented by a DF-expression.

11. Give an algorithm to determine the value associated with a cell c having an upper-left corner at location (x, y) in an $M \times M$ image (M is a power of 2) represented by an S-tree.

12. The original formulation of the S^+-tree [970] uses a slightly different representation for the identifier corresponding to the first node N in each segment S. If the node is the root of the tree (which is not necessarily empty), then the identifier is empty. If the tree consists of just one leaf node and no nonleaf nodes, then the identifier is 1. Otherwise, the identifier consists of a sequence of directional codes corresponding to the path from the root of the tree to N, where each code is represented by a variable-length sequence of the two binary digits 0 and 1 as follows:

(a) NW: 0,

(b) NE: 01,

(c) SW: 011,

(d) SE: 0111.

This string is equivalent to the linear tree encoding of a tree T containing N having the property that all leaf nodes at positions preceding N are of the same color R, where R is different from the color of N. This encoding of the identifier is termed the *linear prefix* of S. Of course, the first page has no linear prefix. Give an algorithm to build an S^+-tree using this representation of the identifier corresponding to the first node N in each segment S.

Assume the following implementation for the S^+-tree [970]. In order for each segment to be self-contained, corresponding parts of the linear tree and the color table are stored on the same page, as is the linear prefix. Each page is assumed to be of the same size. Since the goal is to utilize as much of the available storage on each page as possible, the linear prefix and the linear tree are represented as one consecutive bitstring, while the color table is represented as another bitstring. These two bitstrings are stored in the page as stacks that grow towards each other. Use of the stacks means that two top-of-stack pointers must be stored with each page to indicate the positions of their last elements as some of the positions in the page may be unoccupied. In order to distinguish between the linear prefix and the linear tree, the length of the linear prefix is also recorded with each page

13. In the original presentation of the S^+-tree [970], each page was required to terminate with a leaf node. Is this absolutely necessary?

14. In the original presentation of the S^+-tree, it is described as a variant of a prefix B^+-tree [144] (see Appendix A), whereas, as we have seen, it is really just a B^+-tree. Using the definition of an S^+-tree in terms of a linear prefix given in Exercise 12, explain how such a characterization could have been made. *Hint:* Think about the possible interpretations of the values that serve as the keys in the two data structures.

15. Why can we not compute the size of each block in the Morton location ordering directly from the locations of successive blocks in the list instead of having to use the difference between their Morton numbers? For example, why can we not use the maximum or minimum differences between the corresponding x and y coordinate values of their location entries?

16. Suppose that you use a Peano-Hilbert location ordering. How can you determine the size of each block b? Assume that, for each block b, we record the location of the pixel in b's upper-left corner.

17. Give an algorithm to determine the locations and sizes of all blocks of the same value in a two-dimensional runlength encoding, given the locations of the upper-left corners of two successive blocks b_1 and b_2 with Morton numbers C_1 and C_2, respectively. The result includes all blocks starting with b_1 up to, but not including, b_2.

18. Suppose that in the Morton location ordering, instead of recording the location of each block's upper left corner, the location of its lower-right corner (i.e., the location of the last pixel in the block is instead recorded). How would you compute the size of each block?

19. Suppose that the two-dimensional runlength encoding sequence is defined to consist of the last element of each subsequence of blocks of the same value rather than the first element. Give the resulting encoding of the region quadtree in Figure 2.158(b). Assume that the tree is traversed in the order NW, NE, SW, and SE.

20. Suppose that the two-dimensional runlength encoding sequence is defined to consist of the last element of each subsequence of blocks of the same value rather than the first element. Give a procedure similar to that given in Exercise 17 to reconstruct the Morton numbers of the blocks of the region quadtree given the Morton numbers of two successive blocks. If this is not possible, then how can you redefine the Morton number associated with each block so that it will work? Again, the inputs are the locations of the upper-left corners of two successive blocks b_1 and b_2 with Morton numbers C_1 and C_2, respectively.

21. Give the two-dimensional runlength encoding for the region quadtree in Figure 2.15. Assume that the tree is traversed in the order NW, NE, SW, and SE.

22. Give an algorithm to determine the value associated with a cell c having a upper-left corner at location (x, y) in an $M \times M$ image (M is a power of 2) represented by a two-dimensional runlength encoding.

23. Suppose that you base the two-dimensional runlength encoding on the Peano-Hilbert location ordering instead of the Morton location ordering. Give an algorithm to determine the value associated with a block b having an upper-left corner at location (x, y) in an $M \times M$ image (M is a power of 2) represented by this variant of the two-dimensional runlength encoding.

24. Consider a binary image for which only the locations and sizes of the black blocks are recorded. Give an algorithm to determine the locations and sizes of the white blocks.

25. Give an algorithm to determine the value associated with a cell c having an upper-left corner at location (x, y) in an $M \times M$ image (M is a power of 2) for which only the locations and sizes of the black blocks are recorded.

2.3.2 Chain Code

The same principles used in adapting runlength encoding to interior-based representations can also be used to a limited extent with some boundary-based representations. For example, in two dimensions, a common boundary-based representation is the chain code [638], which indicates the relative locations of the cells that make up the boundary of object o. In particular, it specifies the direction of each boundary element and the number of adjacent unit-sized cells that make up the boundary element. Given the location of the first cell in the sequence corresponding to the boundary of o, we can determine the boundary of o by just following the direction of the associated boundary element. Thus, there is no need to record the actual cells or their locations as now o is uniquely identified. Therefore, in the chain code, the locations of the boundary elements (i.e., the cells that are adjacent to them) are given implicitly while the nature of the boundary elements is given explicitly (i.e., the direction of the boundary element). Each object has a separate chain code. Of course, an object with holes (e.g., a doughnut) has several chain codes (i.e., 2 for a doughnut). In particular, it has one more chain code than holes. In the rest of this discussion, we assume, without loss of generality, that the objects do not have holes.

In order to see how the chain code is constructed, consider the object in Figure 2.158(a), which, as we recall, is embedded in an 8×8 image array. Assume boundary elements in the form of unit vectors in the four principal directions (corresponding to the boundaries of the cells) so that the interior of the object is always to the right of the unit vectors. Without loss of generality, represent the directions by integer numbers i ranging from 0 to 3 corresponding to a unit vector having direction $90 \cdot i$ degrees. In this case, starting from the lower-left corner of the object in Figure 2.158(a) and moving clockwise so that the interior of the object will be to the right of the unit vectors, the chain code for the boundary of the object is $1^3 0^1 1^1 0^1 1^2 0^4 3^4 2^2 3^1 2^1 3^1 2^3$, where the exponent is used as a shorthand notation to indicate the length (i.e., multiplicity) of the individual boundary elements in terms of the number of unit vectors they comprise. Notice the similarity of this approach to that used in obtaining the change-based runlength encoding from the value-based runlength encoding discussed earlier for the interior-based representations.

The chain code as described by us does not just record all of the possible changes that could be taking place in that it also records absolute values. In particular we recorded only the relative change of the locations of the cells adjacent to the boundary elements, while we recorded the absolute values of the directions of the boundary elements. Of course, we could also record the relative change in the directions of the boundary elements. We have just two possible changes in direction corresponding to a transition to the right (denoted as positive) or to the left (denoted as negative). A change in direction of 180 degrees would be meaningless as it would mean that the adjacent cell had zero area. Thus, we have achieved compression as, now, our directional component only requires one bit (corresponding to two possible choices) instead of two (corresponding to four possible choices), as is the case for the conventional chain code. Using such an implementation and assuming that the first element of the chain code must contain the direction, the chain code for the object in Figure 2.158(a) becomes $1^3 +^1 -^1 +^1 -^2 +^4 +^4 +^2 -^1 +^1 -^1 +^3$. Once again, the exponent is used as a shorthand notation to indicate the length (i.e., multiplicity) of the individual boundary elements in terms of the number of unit vectors they comprise.

Using any of the variants of the chain code that we have described, determining the value associated with a particular cell c is not easy. The problem is that the chain code does not provide a mechanism to find the closest part of the boundary to the location of c without reconstructing the boundary. In other words, there is no correlation between the boundary segments and their locations. We know only their absolute directions or directions relative to the immediately preceding boundary element. We do not know their starting and ending positions without reconstructing the entire boundary, which is possible as we do know the starting position of the boundary. This process is analogous in spirit to the accumulation process used to determine the value associated with a cell in the case of the runlength encoding, with the difference that now we are accumulating lengths of the boundary with the same direction rather than lengths of sequences of consecutive pixels with the same value. Once the boundary has been reconstructed, we can find the value by use of a point-in-polygon test (e.g., [622]), although it is a rather tedious task without the aid of an index (recall Section 2.2).

Exercises

1. Suppose that you use a chain code that records the relative change in the directions of the boundary elements. Prove that the number of positive transitions is always three more than the number of negative transitions. Assume that the object has no holes.

2. Suppose that you use a chain code that makes use of unit vectors in the four principal directions so that the interior of the object is always to the right of the unit vectors. Assume that the directions are represented by integer numbers i ranging from 0 to 3 corresponding to a unit vector having direction $90 \cdot i$ degrees. Prove that the sum of the lengths of the boundary elements encoded by 0 is equal to those encoded by 2. Similarly, prove that the sum of the lengths of the boundary elements encoded by 1 is equal to those encoded by 3.

2.3.3 Vertex Representation

Unfortunately, as we mentioned earlier, the chain code cannot be used for data in a higher dimension than 2 for the same reasons that the polygon representation cannot be used. The problem is that, regardless of the dimension of the underlying space, the boundary elements lie on hyperplanes whose dimension is one less than the space in which they are embedded, and, in these cases, no obvious natural order for traversing them exists.

Nevertheless, even though boundary elements cannot be easily ordered on the basis of connectivity, the fact that vertices serve as locations where change takes place can be used as the basis of a data structure, known as the *vertex representation* [1744], for the interiors of regions. The vertex representation is similar in spirit to runlength encoding. The regions are not restricted to polygons. In particular, they can also be collections of rasters.

The vertex representation was originally developed for storing and processing VLSI masks [1744]. It was recently extended to handle axis-parallel polygons of arbitrary dimension [566, 567]. It applies techniques similar to that of runlength encoding across several dimensions to axis-parallel polygons that are represented using blocks of arbitrary size located at arbitrary positions. Its use results in decomposing space into multidimensional blocks (not necessarily disjoint), which are aggregated using techniques, such as CSG (see Section 2.2), by attaching weights to the blocks. These weights enable the blocks to be manipulated in a manner analogous to the use of regularized set-union and set-difference operations in CSG. However, instead of using combining elements that are blocks of finite area or halfspaces as in CSG, the vertex representation makes use of *vertices* that serve as tips of infinite cones.

Each cone is equivalent to an unbounded object formed by the intersection of d halfspaces that are parallel to the d coordinate axes passing through a particular point, termed the *vertex*, which is the tip of the cone. As stated above, in some sense, the vertex representation resembles CSG where the primitive elements are halfspaces. In particular, the vertex plays the role of a CSG primitive, and the region that it represents is equivalent to the intersection of the halfspaces that pass through it. However, unlike CSG, the vertex representation of an object is unique (but see Exercise 3). The vertices have signs (termed *weights* and defined below) associated with them, indicating whether the space spanned by their cones is included in, or excluded from, the object being modeled. The space spanned by the union of the cones defines the object being modeled. It is interesting to observe that the cones corresponding to the vertices are like infinite blocks, thereby slightly resembling a region octree in the sense that the object being modeled is also defined by the union of the blocks. However, unlike the region octree, since the blocks need not be disjoint, the vertex representation of a particular object (i.e., the constituent blocks) is invariant under translation.

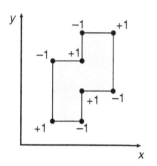

Figure 2.160
Example of a vertex representation for an axis-parallel polygon.

Ignoring for the moment the way in which the weights and vertices are determined (but see below), Figure 2.160 is an example of a vertex representation for an axis-parallel polygon. Notice that the vertices labeled with a weight of +1 correspond to infinite cones that are "included" while those labeled with a weight of -1 correspond to infinite cones that are "excluded."

Now, let us turn to a more formal definition of the vertex representation. The vertex representation is primarily designed to represent axis-parallel scalar fields (i.e., objects whose boundaries are parallel to the coordinate axes in our application). A scalar field is simply a function that maps points of the domain, which is a d-dimensional space, to scalar values. An axis-parallel scalar field is a scalar field where regions of the domain space that are mapped to the same value are delimited by faces parallel to the coordinate axes. Thus, each cone is a scalar field. The overall idea behind the use of the vertex representation for modeling axis-parallel polygons is to view the polygons as scalar fields where points inside the polygons are mapped to 1, and points outside the polygons are mapped to 0.

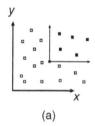

(a)

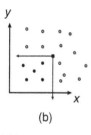

(b)

Figure 2.161
(a) A vertex (black dot) and some of the points influenced by it (black squares). (b) The point (black square) is influenced only by the vertices shown as black dots.

A vertex[52] v is defined as a pair (p, α), where p is the location of v (i.e., it is a point), and α is a nonzero integer value known as the *weight* of v. The weight α is used to determine the value of the scalar field anchored at location p. In particular, a vertex at a location $p = (p_1, p_2, \ldots p_d)$ with weight α has the effect of adding α to the mapping of all points $q = (q_1, q_2, \ldots q_d)$ such that $q_i \geq p_i$ for all $i = 1 \ldots d$ (see Figure 2.161(a)). As a consequence, we can tell if a point q is inside or outside the polygon by adding the weights of all vertices that contribute to its mapping—that is, a vertex at point p contributes to the mapping of q if and only if $p_i \leq q_i$ for all $i = 1 \ldots d$ (see Figure 2.161(b)). Therefore, given a particular cell c with a lower-left corner at location l, determining the value associated with c is a simple process, consisting of finding all vertices whose corresponding cones contain l and adding up their weights. An alternative way of characterizing this process is to say that we add the weights of all vertices whose location is dominated (e.g., [1511]) by l. The process of determining the relevant cones can be made efficient by using an index on the vertices, such as a variant of a point quadtree, point k-d tree, and so on (see Chapter 1).

The weights enable us to represent axis-parallel polygons as a collection of vertices by using negative weight values at some of the vertices. In particular, a set of vertices $V = \{v_1, v_2 \ldots v_n\}$ induces a scalar field $Q_V = \sum_{i=1}^{n} Q_{v_i}$. In other words, the scalar field induced by a set of vertices is the sum of the scalar field induced by each vertex separately.

---

[52] Note that we use the term *vertex* to refer to a mathematical entity that does not necessarily correspond to the common definition of "vertex" in geometry.

This means that the operation of addition is well defined for vertices. For example, recall Figure 2.160, which is the vertex representation for a simple polygon.

At this point, it is important to ask how we determine the locations that make up the vertices and their weights. Intuitively, the vertices are the locations where different boundary elements meet, and hence the boundary changes (i.e., it bends by 90 degrees). There are three methods of identifying the vertices. The first method is visual and is the natural and intuitive way. Once the location l of a vertex v has been identified, its weight may be determined by analyzing how the scalar field changes in the immediate neighborhood of l. For instance, in two dimensions, the scalar field must be evaluated immediately to the northeast, northwest, southeast, and southwest of l. Once this is done, it is possible to determine the weight of v by inspection (we discuss how to perform the actual computation below). Of course, more neighbors must be examined in three dimensions and higher. As we can see, this method is simple in two dimensions. However, it becomes increasingly more complex in three dimensions and higher because it requires that we be able to visualize the object, which is not an easy task, especially in four dimensions and higher.

The second method is very similar to the first method except that it is more formal. In particular, it consists of interpreting the vertex representation as a differential code for rasters and just retaining the locations with a nonzero weight. To explain why this works, we make two important observations. These observations are in the context of two-dimensional data, but the extensions to higher-dimensional data are not difficult. Our first observation is that, if a vertex p is placed at a certain point of the domain space, then its weight represents the difference between the sum of the fields induced by all other vertices that have p inside their cones and the actual value of the field inside the cone having its tip at p. For example, in Figure 2.162, p is inside the cones of vertices a, b, c, and d. Therefore, if we want to map the shaded region to the value S, then we must add to the representation a vertex placed at p with weight S−wgt(a)−wgt(b)−wgt(c)−wgt(d), where wgt(v) refers to the weight of vertex v.

Our second observation is based on a definition of the *weight of a cell c corresponding to a pixel* as being the weight of a vertex placed at the lower-left corner of c. Using this definition, we observe that the weight of a vertex that lies in the center of a 2×2 block of pixels is dependent only on the values of the pixels of the block. This observation is aided by considering the four adjacent cells (i.e., pixels) with values A, B, C, and D of a two-dimensional raster, as depicted in Figure 2.163. The cell with value A is influenced by vertices lying in regions R_1 and R_2, the cell with value B by vertices lying in region R_2, and the cell with value C by vertices lying in regions R_2 and R_3. Thus, if we want the upper-right cell to have a value of D, then a vertex should be placed at point p with weight equal to the difference between D and the weights of all vertices in regions R_1, R_2, and R_3. These weight sums can be rewritten in terms of A, B, C, and D by observing that

- A = sum(R_1)+sum(R_2),

- B = sum(R_2),

- C = sum(R_2)+sum(R_3).

From this we have that

- sum(R_1)=A−B,

- sum(R_2)=B,

- sum(R_3)=C−B.

Subtracting these values from D leads to the weight for the vertex at p being given by

$$\text{wgt(D)} = D - (A - B) - B - (C - B) = D + B - A - C.$$

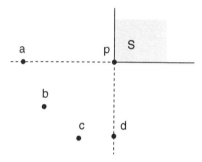

Figure 2.162
Vertices that influence the scalar field at a point p.

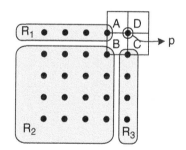

Figure 2.163
Example of how the interpretation of the vertex representation as a differential code for rasters is used to determine the weight of the vertex at p to be D + B − A − C.

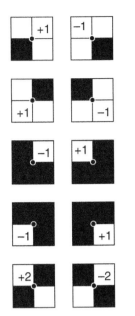

Figure 2.164
Pixel patterns that generate nonzero
vertex weights.

The importance of this second observation lies in the fact that it permits us to encode the images by computing the weight at a particular pixel (e.g., the one at the upper-right cell in a 2×2 block) without having to keep track of the weight sums over all possible regions. In particular, the weight at the upper-right corner depends only on the values of the pixels at the lower-left, lower-right, upper-right, and upper-left corners. Moreover, using this result, we see that, when we apply the differential coding scheme to a general raster, vertices (i.e., points with nonzero weights) will be generated only at certain positions. In order to see this, consider a two-dimensional raster representing a monochromatic image, where black pixels are mapped to 1 and white pixels to 0. We examine the 16 possible configurations of 2×2 pixels focusing on a pixel at position D using the labeling given in Figure 2.163. In particular, vertices will be generated in just 10 out of the 16 configurations, as depicted in Figure 2.164. By inspection, we notice that regions that are uniformly black or white, as well as regions containing strictly horizontal or vertical boundaries, do not generate vertices. In summary, not surprisingly, we find that only groups of pixels near corners of features generate nonzero codes (i.e., vertices).

The third method is procedural. It is best understood by examining the construction of the vertex representation of hyperrectangles in d dimensions. The idea is to sweep a hyperrectangle in $d - 1$ dimensions along the dth axis. The process starts out with the equivalent of a hyperrectangle in one dimension (x), which is an interval. In particular, it is the scalar field that maps the interval $[a_1, b_1]$ to 1 and all other points to 0. This field is represented with two vertices: one at $x = a_1$ with weight $+1$ and another at $x = b_1$ with weight -1.

Next, we transform this one-dimensional interval into a two-dimensional interval by adding to each vertex a second coordinate (y) equal to a_2. This results in a two-dimensional scalar field where the region of space being mapped to 1 is bounded by line $y = a_2$ but extends towards $+\infty$ along the y axis. Thus, we need to add two other vertices with coordinates (a_1, b_2) and (b_1, b_2) and weights -1 and $+1$, respectively, which will provide another boundary adjacent to line $y = b_2$.

This idea can be extended easily to higher dimensions. If we start with a set L of vertices representing a hyperrectangle in $(d - 1)$-dimensional space, then we may represent a hyperrectangle defined in d-dimensional space by a set L' obtained through the following process:

1. Copy L to L', adding a new coordinate to each vertex, say, a_d.

2. Append L to L', adding a new coordinate to each vertex, say, b_d, where $b_d > a_d$, and with weights changed from $+1$ to -1 and vice versa.

Figure 2.165 shows how this process can be repeated in order to build a vertex representation for a hyperrectangle in three dimensions—that is, a parallelepiped.

This method can also be applied to objects that need not be hyperrectangles. In particular, it can be applied to arbitrary rasters by using the sweep method to construct one-dimensional vertex representations for successive rows in the image, followed by sweeping the rows along the columns and subtracting the weights of vertices in corresponding positions. The same technique is applied to higher-dimensional data by applying the sweep-subtraction paradigm to the planes.

This procedure is best understood by examining the result of its application to the two-dimensional raster given in Figure 2.166(a). Figure 2.166(b) is the result of the application of the algorithm to the individual rows, and Figure 2.166(c) is the final vertex representation. Figure 2.166(a) is similar to the result obtained using traditional runlength encoding, which applies compression only in one dimension; the vertex representation, however, applies compression in the remaining dimensions as well, as seen in Figure 2.166(c). Since we are constructing a differential code, we must assume a reference value of 0 for the pixels that are outside the region spanned by the two-dimensional raster and on its boundary. Thus, when we process the first pixel of a row (as well as an entire row in the sweep of rows phase), we assume a (nonexistent) previous pixel (or entire row) with a value of 0.

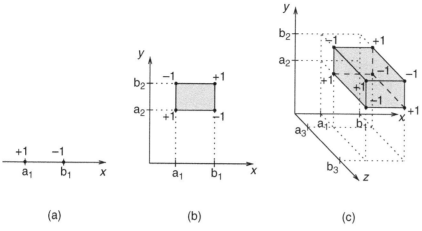

Figure 2.165
Construction of a hyperrectangle in three dimensions. The line segment from a_1 to b_1 shown in (a) is swept in the y-direction from a_2 to b_2 to form the two-dimensional rectangle given in (b), which in turn is swept along the z axis from a_3 to b_3, resulting in the 3-D parallelepiped given in (c).

It should be clear that the algorithm that we described for the hyperrectangles is a subset of the general algorithm given above in that the starting point of the one-dimensional interval corresponds to the cone that is included in the object, and the ending point of the one-dimensional interval corresponds to the cone that is excluded from the object. The general algorithm determines the weights of the locations that make up the vertices in a systematic manner by traversing the locations in each row, followed by the rows that make up each plane, and so on. This order is known as *inverse lexicographic order* and is illustrated in Figure 2.167 for the vertices a, b, c, and d, which would be visited in the order c, d, a, and b.

This traversal process is facilitated by storing the vertices in a list in the order in which they are visited (i.e., inverse lexicographic order). For example, in two dimensions, they are sorted first on the basis of their y coordinate value and then by their x coordinate value. This representation is termed a *vertex list*, and it has been used as the basis of several algorithms for operations on the vertex representation, including set operations [567, 565] and coarsening [569]. The utility of the vertex list representation is that it permits these algorithms to employ the plane-sweep paradigm (or line-sweep in two dimensions) [1511]. For example, in two dimensions, this is compatible with the sweeping of a line perpendicular to the y axis in the direction of increasing y coordinate values.

As an example of the utility of implementing the vertex representation using a vertex list, we examine the conversion of rasters to a vertex representation implemented as a vertex list. This is given below by the following recursive algorithm, called RASTERTOVLIST, with parameters d and R corresponding to the d-dimensional raster R being processed.

1. If $d = 1$, then for each pair of adjacent pixels $R(i)$, $R(i+1)$ at locations i and $i+1$, respectively, along the least significant coordinate value, compute $weight = R(i+1) - R(i)$. Output a vertex at location i if $weight$ is nonzero.

2. Otherwise (i.e., $d > 1$), for each pair of consecutive $(d-1)$-dimensional rasters $R(i)$ and $R(i+1)$ at i and $i+1$, respectively, along the dth coordinate value,

    (a) Compute vertex lists L_i and L_{i+1} for $(d-1)$-dimensional rasters $R(i)$ and $R(i+1)$, respectively, by recursive invocation of procedure RASTERTOVLIST (i.e., steps 1 and 2).

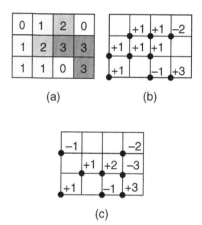

Figure 2.166
(a) A sample 2-D raster; in (b), each row was processed to yield 1-D vertex lists, and in (c), consecutive 1-D vertex lists are subtracted to yield a 2-D vertex list for the raster.

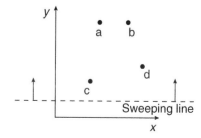

Figure 2.167
Vertices a, b, c, and d would be visited by the sweeping line in the order c, d, a, b.

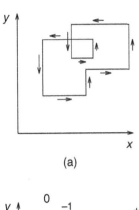

(a)

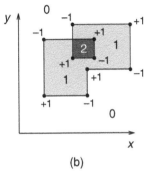

(b)

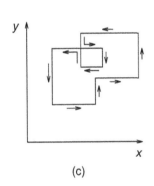

(c)

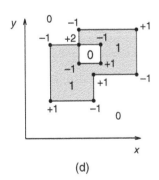

(d)

Figure 2.168
Example object whose vertex representations differ depending on how its boundary is interpreted. Interpreting the boundary as in (a) yields the vertex representation in (b), whereas interpreting it as in (c) results in the vertex representation given in (d).

(b) Compute $S = add(L_{i+1}, L_i, -1)$, which subtracts the two vertex lists.

(c) Make all vertices of S d-dimensional by appending i as the value of the dth coordinate value to their positions, and output them.

Given a particular cell c having a lower-left corner at location l, determining the value associated with c is achieved by finding all vertices whose corresponding cones contain l and adding up their weights. This process requires that we take into account the fact that we are dealing with a vertex list implementation of the vertex representation, which means that we need to process the list in a particular order. A simple approach would partially reconstruct the raster in an analogous manner to that used by chain-based runlength encoding (i.e., a process of accumulating changes in values) by scanning the vertex list element-by-element, adding up the weights of vertices that are "dominated" by l. A more elegant (and general, in terms of arbitrary dimensions) way of describing this process is to use a procedure that works in the inverse manner as the RASTERTOVLIST procedure given above (see Exercises 5 and 6).

The vertex list implementation of the vertex representation demonstrates why we say that the vertex representation is a variant of runlength encoding. In particular, observe that the only pixels for which values are recorded in the vertex list are those at which the pixel values change. The facts that the vertex list implementation of the vertex representation orders the pixels in raster-scan order (i.e., the pixel values in the image are ordered by rows) and that only changes in the values are recorded demonstrate why we say that the vertex representation is a variant of runlength encoding. The main difference from the process of runlength encoding for the multidimensional array described earlier that was applied only to the rows is that, in the case of the vertex representation, we are not restricted to blocks of a fixed size (e.g., squares or congruent blocks). Of course, this is not quite true because we restrict ourselves to congruent blocks of infinite size (anchored at the vertices). In essence, the vertex representation is a combination of an implicit interior-based representation and an implicit boundary-based representation in the sense that both the interiors and boundaries of regions are represented implicitly through the aid of a single vertex, which is the tip of a cone. Moreover, only the changes in the values are recorded. Therefore, we see that, using the vertex list implementation of the vertex representation, we have an ordering of the pixels, which is analogous to a raster-scan order (i.e., the pixel values in the image are ordered by rows).

The main difference from the process of runlength encoding for the multidimensional array described earlier that was applied only to the rows is that, in the case of the vertex representation, we are not restricted to blocks of a fixed size (e.g., squares or congruent blocks). Of course, this is not quite true as we restrict ourselves to congruent blocks of infinite size (anchored at the vertices). In essence, the vertex representation is a combination of an implicit interior-based representation and an implicit boundary-based representation in the sense that both the interiors and boundaries of regions are represented implicitly through the aid of a single vertex, which is the tip of a cone.

Exercises

1. Assume that axis-parallel polygons are scalar fields where points inside the polygons are mapped to 1, and points outside the polygons are mapped to 0. Given a vertex representation of a two-dimensional axis-parallel polygon, prove that any vertex p at a position given by (x_0, y_0) such that no other point (x, y) on the boundary of the polygon that satisfies $(x < x_0) \wedge (y < y_0)$ will have weight equal to $+1$.

2. How does the vertex representation deal with polygons containing holes?

3. In the text, we state that the vertex representation of an axis-parallel polygon is unique. How do you reconcile this statement with the fact that the object in Figure 2.168 can have two different vertex representations, depending on how its boundary is interpreted? In particular, interpreting the boundary as in (a) yields the vertex representation in (b), whereas interpreting it as in (c) results in the vertex representation given in (d).

4. It has been observed [567] that, in two dimensions, for a given simple axis-parallel polygon (i.e., non-self-intersecting), the weights of adjacent vertices along the border of the polygon always alternate between $+1$ and -1 as they are visited in clockwise or counterclockwise order. Prove that this is true.

5. Given a two-dimensional raster image represented by a vertex list, give an algorithm to determine the value associated with a location c. The algorithm should be an inverse of the procedure RASTERTOVLIST used to convert a raster to a vertex representation implemented as a vertex list.

6. Given an arbitrary d-dimensional raster image represented by a vertex list, give an algorithm to determine the value associated with a location c. The algorithm should be an inverse of the procedure RASTERTOVLIST used to convert a raster to a vertex representation implemented as a vertex list.

7. Assuming a vertex representation implemented as a vertex list, give an algorithm to perform set-theoretic operations such as union and intersection.

8. The vertex list implementation of the vertex representation orders the vertices in inverse lexicographic order. This is a variant of row order (recall the discussion in Section 2.1.1.2 and Figure 2.5(a)). Suppose that we order the vertices using another ordering, such as the Morton or the Peano–Hilbert order. How would this affect the implementation of some of the operations on vertex lists. For example, discuss the effect on the algorithm for set-theoretic operations in Exercise 7.

9. How would you extend the vertex list representation to deal with polygons whose faces are not axis parallel or not necessarily even orthogonal?

2.4 Historical Overview

In this section we give a brief, and very incomplete, historical overview of the method of recursive decomposition as used in the representation and processing of images and regions into blocks. There is a heavy emphasis on the quadtree and octree methods as these were the earliest and most prevalent examples of the use of this method. The origin of the principle of recursive decomposition is difficult to determine. Most likely its quadtree realization was first seen as a way of aggregating blocks of zeros in sparse matrices. Indeed, Hoare [858] attributes a one-level decomposition of a matrix into square blocks to Dijkstra. Morton [1317] used it as a means of indexing into a geographic database (i.e., it acts as a spatial index).

Warnock, in a pair of reports that serve as landmarks in the computer graphics literature [1959, 1961], described the implementation of hidden-line and hidden-surface elimination algorithms using a recursive decomposition of the picture area. The picture area is repeatedly subdivided into rectangles that are successively smaller while it is searched for areas that are sufficiently simple to be displayed.

Klinger [1035] and Klinger and Dyer [1036] applied these ideas to pattern recognition and image processing using the term *Q-tree* [1036]. Hunter [901] used them in an animation application and was the first to use the *quadtree* in such a context. In this text, we use the term *region quadtree* to describe the result, although, as we point out in Sections 1.4.2.1 and 1.4.2.2 of Chapter 1, a more precise term would be *quadtrie* as the resulting structure is really a trie [635] (recall the definition given in the opening discussion in Chapter 1).

Regardless of the terminology used, these applications were motivated by a desire to obtain a systematic way to represent homogeneous parts of an image. This resulted in what is currently known as the region quadtree. Thus, to transform the data into a region quadtree, a criterion must be chosen for deciding that an image is homogeneous (i.e., uniform). One such criterion is that the standard deviation of its gray levels is below a given threshold t. Using this criterion, the image array is successively subdivided into quadrants, subquadrants, and so on, until homogeneous blocks are obtained. This process

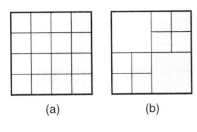

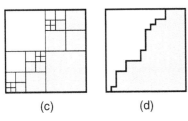

Figure 2.169
Example illustrating the split-and-
merge segmentation procedure: (a)
start, (b) merge, (c) split, and (d)
grouping.

1	2	3	4	5	6	7	8
9	10	11	12	13	14	15	16
17	18	19	20	21	22	23	24
25	26	27	28	29	30	31	32
33	34	35	36	37	38	39	40
41	42	43	44	45	46	47	48
49	50	51	52	53	54	55	56
57	58	59	60	61	62	63	64

Figure 2.170
Example pyramid A(3).

A	B	C	D
E	F	G	H
I	J	K	L
M	N	O	P

Figure 2.171
A(2) corresponding to Figure 2.170.

leads to a regular decomposition. If one associates with each leaf node the mean gray level of its block, then the resulting region quadtree will completely specify a piecewise approximation to the image where each homogeneous block is represented by its mean. The case where $t = 0$ (i.e., a block is not homogeneous unless its gray level is constant) is of particular interest since it permits an exact reconstruction of the image from its quadtree.

Note that the blocks of the region quadtree do not necessarily correspond to maximal homogeneous regions in the image. Often there exist unions of blocks that are still homogeneous. To obtain a segmentation of the image into maximal homogeneous regions, we must allow merging of adjacent blocks (or unions of blocks) as long as the resulting region remains homogeneous. This is achieved by a *split-and-merge segmentation algorithm* [879]. However, the resulting partition will no longer be represented by a region quadtree; instead, the final representation is in the form of an adjacency graph. Thus, the region quadtree is used as an initial step in the segmentation process.

For example, Figure 2.169(b–d) demonstrates the results of the application, in sequence, of merging, splitting, and grouping to the initial image decomposition of Figure 2.169(a). In this case, the image is initially decomposed into 16 equal-size square blocks. Next, the *merge step* attempts to form larger blocks by recursively merging groups of four homogeneous "siblings" (e.g., the four blocks in the NW and SE quadrants of Figure 2.169(b)). The *split step* recursively decomposes blocks that are not homogeneous (e.g., in the NE and SW quadrants of Figure 2.169(c)) until a particular homogeneity criterion is satisfied or a given level is encountered. Finally, the *grouping step* aggregates all homogeneous 4-adjacent black blocks into one region apiece; the 8-adjacent white blocks are likewise aggregated into white regions (see Figure 2.169(d)).

Quadtree methods have also been used in image understanding. Kelly [1015] introduced the concept of a *plan*, which is a small picture whose pixels represent gray-scale averages over 8×8 blocks of a larger picture. Needless effort in edge detection is avoided by first determining edges in the plan and then using these edges to search selectively for edges in the larger picture. Generalizations of this idea motivated the development of multiresolution image representations, for example, the recognition cone of Uhr [1898], the preprocessing cone of Riseman and Arbib [1563], and the pyramid of Tanimoto and Pavlidis [1845]. Of these representations, the pyramid is the closest relative of the region quadtree.

Given a $2^n \times 2^n$ image array, say $A(n)$, a *pyramid* is a sequence of arrays $\{A(i)\}$ such that $A(i-1)$ is a version of $A(i)$ at half the scale of $A(i)$, and so on, and $A(0)$ is a single pixel. The pyramid is discussed in Section 2.1.5.1, where we observe that the pyramid is a multiresolution representation, whereas the region quadtree is a variable resolution representation. Another analogy is that the pyramid is a complete quadtree [1044]. It should be clear that a pyramid can also be defined in a more general way by permitting finer scales of resolution than the power of 2 scale.

The above conventional definition of a pyramid is based on nonoverlapping 2×2 blocks of pixels. An alternative definition, termed an *overlapping pyramid*, uses overlapping blocks of pixels. One of the simplest schemes makes use of 4×4 blocks that overlap by 50% in both the horizontal and vertical directions [286]. For example, Figure 2.170 is a $2^3 \times 2^3$ array, say $A(3)$, whose pixels are labeled 1–64. Figure 2.171 is $A(2)$, corresponding to Figure 2.170, with elements labeled A–P. The 4×4 neighborhood corresponding to element F in Figure 2.171 consists of pixels 10–13, 18–21, 26–29, and 34–37. This method implies that each block at a given level participates in four blocks at the immediately higher level. Thus, the containment relations between blocks no longer form a tree. For example, pixel 28 participates in blocks F, G, J, and K in the next higher level (see Figure 2.172, where the four neighborhoods corresponding to F, G, J, and K are drawn as squares).

To avoid treating border cases differently, each level in the overlapping pyramid is assumed to be cyclically closed (i.e., the top row at each level is adjacent to the bottom row and likewise for the columns at the extreme left and right of each level). Once again, we say that the value of a node is the average of the values of the nodes in its block on the immediately lower level. The overlapping pyramid may be compared with the Quadtree Medial Axis Transform (QMAT) [1626, 1630] (see Section 2.1.2.4) in the sense that both may result in nondisjoint decompositions of space.

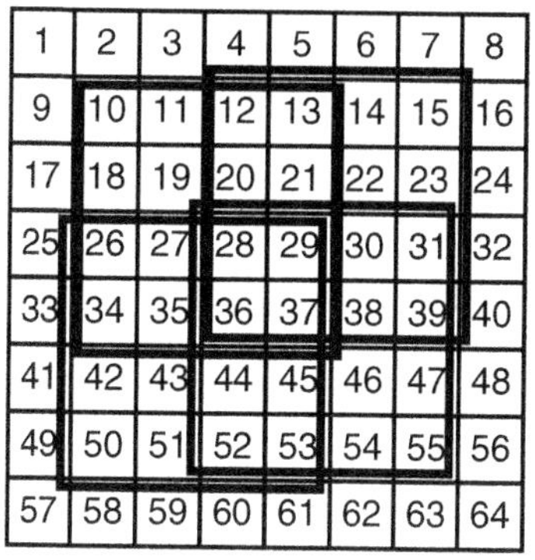

Pyramids have been applied to the problems of feature detection and extraction since they can be used to limit the scope of the search. Once a piece of information of interest is found at a coarse level, the finer-resolution levels can be searched. This approach was followed by Davis and Roussopoulos [447] in approximate pattern matching. Pyramids can also be used for encoding information about edges, lines, and curves in an image [1089, 1762]. One note of caution: the reduction of resolution has an effect on the visual appearance of edges and small objects [1842]. In particular, at a coarser level of resolution, edges tend to get smeared, and region separation may disappear. Pyramids have also been used as the starting point for a "split-and-merge" segmentation algorithm [1495].

Recursive decomposition methods have also been used to facilitate control in robotics and vision systems. The SRI robot project [1378] used a three-level decomposition of space to represent a map of the robot's world. Eastman [527] observed that recursive decomposition might be used for space planning in an architectural context and presents a simplified version of the SRI robot representation. Tucker [1894] uses quadtree refinement as a control strategy for an expert computer vision system.

The three-dimensional variant of the region quadtree—that is, the region octree—was developed independently by a number of researchers. Hunter [901] mentioned it as a natural extension of the region quadtree. Reddy and Rubin [1548] proposed the region octree as one of three representations for solid objects. The second is a three-dimensional generalization of the point quadtree of Finkel and Bentley [614]—that is, a decomposition into rectangular parallelepipeds (as opposed to cubes) with planes perpendicular to the x, y, and z axes. The third breaks the object into rectangular parallelepipeds that are not necessarily aligned with an axis. The parallelepipeds are of arbitrary sizes and orientations. Each parallelepiped is recursively subdivided into parallelepipeds in the coordinate space of the enclosing parallelepiped. Reddy and Rubin prefer the third approach for its ease of display.

Situated somewhere in between the second and third approaches of Reddy and Rubin is the method of Brooks and Lozano-Perez [268] (see also [1206]), who use a recursive decomposition of space into an arbitrary number of rectangular parallelepipeds, with planes perpendicular to the x, y, and z axes, to model space in solving the *findpath* or *piano movers* problem [1700] in robotics. This problem arises when, in planning the motion of a robot in an environment containing known obstacles, the desired solution is a collision-free path obtained by use of a search. Faverjon [599] discusses an approach to this problem that uses an octree, as do Samet and Tamminen [1658] and Fujimura and Samet [663]. Jackins and Tanimoto [932] adapted Hunter and Steiglitz's quadtree translation algorithm [901, 904] to objects represented by region octrees. Meagher [1276] developed numerous algorithms for performing solid modeling operations in an environment where the region octree is the underlying representation. Yau and Srihari [2050] extended the region octree to arbitrary dimensions in the process of developing algorithms to handle medical images.

Both quadtrees and octrees are frequently used in the construction of meshes for finite-element analysis. The use of recursive decomposition for meshes was initially suggested by Rheinboldt and Mesztenyi [1561]. Yerry and Shephard [2051] adapted the quadtree and octree to generate meshes automatically for three-dimensional solids represented by a superquadric surface-based modeler. This has been extended by Kela,

Figure 2.172
The overlapping block in which pixel 28 participates.

Voelcker, and Goldak [1014] (see also [1013]) to mesh boundary regions directly, rather than through discrete approximations, and to facilitate incremental adaptive analysis by exploiting the spatial index nature of the quadtree and octree.

Quadtree decompositions have also found much use in solving the *N-body problem* (also known as the *multibody problem*). In particular, the solutions involve reducing the computation time from $O(N^2)$ to $O(N \cdot \log N)$ and $O(N)$. Some examples include [50, 68, 126, 297, 571, 753, 755, 1001, 1608].

3

Intervals and Small Rectangles

The problem of how to represent the space spanned by collections of small rectangles arises in many applications. The space spanned by the rectangles can also be viewed as the d-dimensional Cartesian product of d one-dimensional intervals (i.e., spheres), and thus the problem is often cast as one of representing one-dimensional intervals. The most common application is one where rectangles are used to approximate other shapes for which they serve as the minimum enclosing objects (recall our discussion of the R-tree and other object-based hierarchical interior-based representations in Section 2.1.5.2 of Chapter 2). For example, rectangles can be used in cartographic applications to approximate objects such as lakes, forests, and hills [1258]. Of course, the exact boundaries of the object are also stored, but usually they are only accessed if a need for greater precision exists. Rectangles are also used for design rule checking in very large-scale integration (VLSI) design applications as a model of chip components for the analysis of their proper placement. Again, the rectangles serve as minimum enclosing objects. This process includes such tasks as determining whether components intersect and insuring the satisfaction of constraints involving factors such as minimum separation and width. These tasks have a practical significance in that they can be used to avoid design flaws.

The size of the collection depends on the application; it can vary tremendously. For example, in cartographic applications, the number of elements in the collection is usually small, and frequently the sizes of the rectangles are of the same order of magnitude as the space from which they are drawn. On the other hand, in VLSI design applications, the size of the collection is quite large (e.g., millions of components), and the sizes of the rectangles are several orders of magnitude smaller than the space from which they are drawn.

In this chapter, we focus primarily on how to represent a large collection of rectangles common in VLSI design applications. However, our techniques are equally applicable to other domains. We assume that all rectangles are positioned so that their sides are parallel to the x and y coordinate axes. Our presentation makes use of representations for one-dimensional intervals rooted in computational geometry as well as combines representations for multidimensional point data (see Chapter 1) and objects (see Chapter 2).

The principal tasks to be performed are similar to those described in Chapter 1. They range from basic operations, such as insertion and deletion, to more complex queries that include exact match, partial match, range, partial range, finding all objects (e.g., rectangles) in a given region, finding nearest neighbors with respect to a given metric for the data domain, and even join queries [1899]. The most common of these queries involves proximity relations and is classified into two classes by Hinrichs [839]. The first is an intersection query that seeks to determine if two sets intersect. The second is a subset relation and can be formulated in terms of enclosure (i.e., is A a subset of B?) or of containment (i.e., does A contain B?).

In describing queries involving these relations, we must be careful to distinguish between a point and an object. A *point* is an element in the d-dimensional space from which the objects are drawn. It is not an element of the space into which the objects may be mapped by a particular representation. For example, in the case of a collection of rectangles in two dimensions, a point is an element of the Euclidean plane and not a rectangle, even though we may choose to represent each rectangle by a point in some multidimensional space.

In this chapter, we focus on three types of proximity queries. The first, and most common, is the *point query*, which finds all the objects that contain a given point. It is important to distinguish this query from the point query discussed in Chapter 1 that seeks to determine if a given point p is actually in the dataset (more accurately described as an exact match query). The second type is a *point set query*, which, given a relation $\oplus$ and a set of points Q (typically a region), finds the set of objects S such that $S \oplus Q$ holds. An example is a query, more commonly known as a *window operation*, that finds all the rectangles that intersect a given region. In this example, the relation $\oplus$ is defined by $S \oplus Q$ if $S \cap Q \neq \emptyset$, and Q is the query window. The third type of query is a *geometric join query* (also known as a *spatial join query* [1415]), which, for a relation $\oplus$ and two classes of objects O_1 and O_2 with corresponding subsets S_1 and S_2, finds all pairs (P_1, P_2) with $P_1 \in S_1$, $P_2 \in S_2$, and $P_1 \oplus P_2$. An example is a query that determines all pairs of overlapping rectangles. In such a case, both O_1 and O_2 correspond to the set of rectangles, and $\oplus$ is the intersection relation. In our examples, S_1 and S_2 are usually the same subsets, although the more general problem can also be handled.

Initially, we present representations that are designed for use with the plane-sweep solution paradigm [119, 1511, 1740]. For many tasks, use of this paradigm yields worst-case optimal solutions in time and space. We examine its use in solving two problems:

1. Reporting all intersections between rectangles (the rectangle intersection problem—Section 3.1)

2. Computing the area of a collection of d-dimensional rectangles (the measure problem—Section 3.2)

We focus on the segment, interval, and priority search trees. They represent a rectangle by the intervals that form its boundaries. However, these representations are usually for formulations of the tasks in a static environment. This means that the identities of all the rectangles must be known if the worst-case time and space bounds are to hold. Furthermore, for some tasks, the addition of a single object to the database may force the reexecution of the algorithm on the entire database.

The remaining representations are for a dynamic environment. They are differentiated by the way in which each rectangle is represented. The first type of representation reduces each rectangle to a point in a usually higher-dimensional space and then treats the problem as if it involves a collection of points (Section 3.3). The second type is region-based in the sense that the subdivision of the space from which the rectangles are drawn depends on the physical extent of the rectangle—it does not just treat a rectangle as one point (Section 3.4). Many of these representations are variants of the quadtree. We show that these quadtree variants are very similar to the segment and interval trees that are used with the plane-sweep paradigm. Moreover, we observe that the quadtree serves as a multidimensional sort and that the process of traversing it is analogous to a plane sweep in multiple dimensions.

3.1 Plane-Sweep Methods and the Rectangle Intersection Problem

The term *plane sweep* is used to characterize a paradigm employed to solve geometric problems by sweeping a line (plane in three dimensions) across the plane (space in three dimensions) and halting at points where the line (plane) makes its first or last intersection with any of the objects being processed. At these points, the solution is partially computed so that at the end of the sweep a final solution is available. In this discussion, we are dealing with two-dimensional data. Assume, without loss of generality, that the line is swept in the horizontal direction and from left to right.

To use the plane-sweep technique, we need to organize two sets of data. The first set consists of the *halting points* of the line (i.e., the points of initial or final intersection). It is usually organized as a list of *x* coordinate values sorted in ascending order. The second set consists of a description of the status of the objects that are intersected by the current position of the sweep line. This status reflects the information relevant to the problem to be solved, and it must be updated at each halting point.

The data structure used to store the status must be able to handle updates, but it may take advantage of characteristics of the data discovered while the data was sorted. In other words, the data structure may use knowledge about the entire batch of updates. For this reason, these data structures are sometimes called *batched dynamic* [544]. The characteristics of this data structure will determine, to a large extent, the efficiency of the solution.

The application of plane-sweep methods to rectangle problems is much studied. The solutions to many of these problems require that the data be ordered in a manner that makes use of some variant of multidimensional sorting. In such cases, the execution times of optimal algorithms are often constrained by how fast we can sort, which, for N objects, usually means a lower bound of $O(N \cdot \log_2 N)$. At times, an increase in speed can be obtained by making use of more storage. The text of Preparata and Shamos [1511] contains an excellent discussion of a number of problems to which such techniques are applicable.

We assume that each rectangle is specified by four values, the x coordinate values of its two vertical sides and the y coordinate values of its two horizontal sides (equivalently, these are the x and y coordinate values of its lower-left and upper-right corners). We also assume that each rectangle is closed on its left and bottom sides and open on its top and right sides. Applying the same open-closed convention to the boundaries of a rectangle finds that its horizontal (vertical) boundaries are closed on their left (bottom) ends and open on their right (top) ends. Alternatively, the boundaries can be described as being *semiclosed*.

In this section, we focus on the efficient solution of the problem of reporting all intersections between rectangles and, to a lesser extent, on some related problems. Note that a naive way to report all intersections is to check each rectangle against every other rectangle. This takes $O(N^2)$ time for N rectangles. The plane-sweep solution of the problem consists of two passes. The first pass sorts the left and right boundaries (i.e., x coordinate values) of the rectangles in ascending order and forms a list. For example, consider the collection of rectangles given in Figure 3.1. Letting O_L and O_R denote the left and right boundaries of rectangle object O, the result of the first pass is a list consisting of 3, 6, 8, 21, 23, 25, 26, 31, 33, 34, 35, 37, 38, and 38, corresponding to A_L, E_L, A_R, D_L, G_L, B_L, E_R, F_L, C_L, B_R, F_R, C_R, D_R, and G_R, respectively.

The second pass sweeps a vertical scan line through the sorted list from left to right, halting at each one of these points. This pass requires solving a quasidynamic version of the one-dimensional intersection problem. At any instant, all rectangles whose horizontal boundaries intersect the scan line are termed *active rectangles*. (e.g., rectangles D, E, and G for a vertical scan line through $x = 24$ in Figure 3.1). We must report all intersections between a newly activated rectangle and currently active rectangles that lie on the scan line. The sweep process halts every time a rectangle becomes active (causing it to be inserted in the set of active rectangles) or ceases to be active (causing it to be deleted from the set of active rectangles). The key to a good solution is to organize the active rectangles so that intersection detection, insertion, and deletion are executed efficiently.

The first pass involves sorting, and thus it takes $O(N \cdot \log_2 N)$ time. Insofar as the second pass is concerned, each rectangle is nothing more than a vertical line segment (or equivalently, a one-dimensional interval). Several data structures can be used to

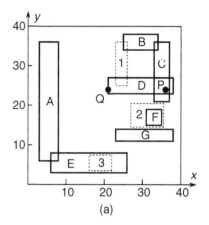

(a)

rectangle or point	x_L	x_R	y_B	y_T
A	3	8	6	36
B	25	34	34	38
C	33	37	21	36
D	21	38	23	27
E	6	26	3	8
F	31	35	15	19
G	23	38	11	14
1	23	26	25	36
2	27	35.5	14.5	20.5
3	16	22	3.5	7.5
P	36	—	24	—
Q	21	—	24	—

(b)

Figure 3.1
(a) A collection of rectangles. Members of the collection are designated by solid lines and labeled alphabetically (A–G). Query rectangles are designated by broken lines and labeled numerically (1–3). P and Q are query points. (b) The locations of the endpoints of the rectangles and the points in (a). For a rectangle, x_L and x_R correspond to its left and right boundaries, respectively, and y_B and y_T correspond to its bottom and top boundaries, respectively. For a point, x_L and y_B are its x and y coordinate values, respectively.

represent line segments. If we care only about reporting the intersections of boundaries (i.e., vertical boundaries with horizontal boundaries), then a balanced binary search tree is adequate to represent the bottom and top boundaries (i.e., y coordinate values) of the active rectangles [178] (see Exercise 6 in Section 3.1.4). Unfortunately, such a representation fails to account for intersections that result when one rectangle is totally contained within another rectangle.

In the rest of this section, we focus on solutions to the rectangle intersection problem that use the segment, interval, and priority search trees to represent the active line segments. We first explain the segment tree and then show how the order of the space requirements of the solution can be reduced by using either the interval or priority search trees, while still retaining the same order of execution time. Although the interval tree solution for the rectangle intersection problem requires less space than the segment tree solution, the segment tree is important due to its simplicity and finds use in a number of applications. We conclude by briefly explaining some alternative solutions and point out related problems that can be solved using the same techniques.

3.1.1 Segment Tree

The segment tree is a representation of a collection of line segments devised by Bentley [166]. It is useful for detecting all the intervals that contain a given point. It is best understood by first examining a simplified version that we call a *unit-segment tree*, which is used to represent a single line segment. For the moment, assume that the endpoints of the line segments of our collection are drawn from the set of integers $\{i \mid 0 \le i \le 2^h\}$. Let S be a line segment with endpoints l and r $(l < r)$. S consists of the set of consecutive unit intervals $[j:j+1)$ $(l \le j < r)$. The unit-segment tree is a complete binary tree of depth h such that the root is at level h, and nodes at level 0 (i.e., the bottom) represent the sequence of consecutive intervals $[j:j+1)$ $(0 \le j < 2^h)$. A node at level i in the unit-segment tree represents the interval $[p:p+2^i)$ (i.e., the sequence of 2^i consecutive unit intervals starting at p, where $p \bmod 2^i$ is 0).

Representing line segment S in a unit-segment tree is easy. We start at the root of the tree and check if its corresponding interval is totally contained in S. If yes, then we *mark* the node with S. In such a case, we say that S *covers* the node's interval. Otherwise, we repeat the process for the left and right children of S. This process visits at most four nodes at each level, while marking at most two of them. Thus, it is easy to see that inserting a line segment into a unit-segment tree in a top-down manner can be achieved in $O(h)$ time. An equivalent bottom-up description of this process is that a node is marked with S if all (i.e., both) the intervals corresponding to its children are totally contained in S, in which case, the children are no longer marked with S.

For an example of the unit-segment tree, consider a collection of line segments with integer endpoints that are in the range [0:16). In this case, there are 16 possible intervals, each of unit length. The unit-segment tree for a line segment named A of length 8 whose endpoints are at 3 and 11 is given in Figure 3.2. Note that the interval $[i:i+1)$ is represented by the node labeled i. From the figure, it is easy to observe the close analogy between the unit-segment tree and a one-dimensional region quadtree [1574] where the unit intervals are the one-dimensional analog of pixels. The analogy is completed by letting black (white) correspond to the labeled (unlabeled) nodes and merging brother nodes of the same color.

The unit-segment tree is inadequate for two reasons: it can represent only one line segment, and it is defined only for line segments with integer endpoints. The segment tree is an adaptation of the unit-segment tree that enables the use of one data structure to represent a collection of line segments with arbitrary endpoints by removing the restriction that the intervals be of uniform length and by replacing the mark at each node with a linked list of the names of the line segments that contain that node.

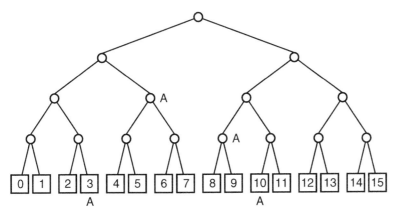

Figure 3.2
The unit-segment tree for the segment [3:11) labeled A in the range [0:16).

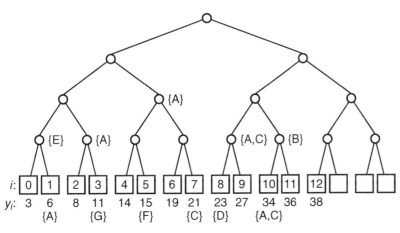

Figure 3.3
The segment tree for the set of line segments corresponding to the vertical boundaries of the rectangles in Figure 3.1. Terminal node i corresponds to the interval $[y_i:y_{i+1})$.

This adaptation is achieved in the following manner. Given a set of N line segments, we first sort their endpoints and remove duplicates to obtain $y_0, y_1, \ldots, y_m$ ($m < 2 \cdot N$). Next, we form the segment tree in the same way as the unit-segment tree with the exception that interval $[j:j+1)$ is replaced by the interval $[y_j:y_{j+1})$ ($0 \le j < 2^h$ and $2^{h-1} \le m < 2^h$). Each line segment S with endpoints y_l and y_r consists of the sequence of consecutive intervals $[y_j:y_{j+1})$ ($l \le j < r$).

A node at level i in the segment tree represents the interval $[y_p:y_{p+2^i})$ (i.e., the sequence of 2^i consecutive intervals starting at y_p, where $p \bmod 2^i$ is 0). Each node is marked with the names of all the line segments that cover the node's corresponding interval and that do not cover the corresponding interval of the parent node. As in the case of the unit-segment tree, a node and its brother cannot both be marked with the same line segment. The set of line segments associated with each node is represented as a doubly linked list. This will be seen to facilitate deletion of line segments.

For example, Figure 3.3 is the segment tree for the set of line segments that correspond to the vertical boundaries of the rectangles in Figure 3.1. Although there are 7 line segments, the segment tree contains 12 intervals as there are only 13 different endpoints. Since the segment tree is a complete binary tree, in this case it has 4 unused intervals. Each leaf node is labeled with its corresponding interval number and the leftmost endpoint of the interval—that is, node i corresponds to the interval $[y_i: y_{i+1})$. Nodes are also labeled with the sets of names of the line segments that cover their corresponding intervals. For example, the interval [23:34) is labeled with {A,C} because it is covered by these line segments.

Inserting a line segment into the segment tree is analogous to inserting it into the unit-segment tree. The only difference is that the line segment must also be inserted into the list of line segments associated with the node. It can be placed anywhere in the list, and thus we usually attach it to the front of the list. In a domain of N line segments, insertion (into the tree and list) takes $O(\log_2 N)$ time per line segment.

Deleting a line segment from a segment tree is somewhat more complex. We must remove the line segment from the doubly linked list associated with each node that contains it. This can be expensive since, in the worst case, it requires the traversal of $O(\log_2 N)$ linked lists, each containing $O(N)$ entries. This difficulty is avoided by maintaining an auxiliary table with one entry for each of the N line segments. Each table entry points to a list of pointers. Each pointer points to a list entry for the line segment in a node, say P, of the segment tree such that P's interval is covered by the line segment (see Exercise 3).

This table is built as the line segments are entered into the segment tree. It contains at most N entries and can be accessed or updated in $O(\log_2 N)$ time when implemented as a balanced binary search tree (or even in constant time, if implemented as an array, in which case each line segment must be represented by a unique integer in the range $1 \ldots N$). We can use an array instead of a dictionary because we know the identities of the rectangles in advance (i.e., it is a static environment).

A segment tree for N line segments has a maximum of $2 \cdot N$ leaf nodes. Each line segment covers the intervals of at most $2 \cdot \lceil \log_2 N \rceil$ nodes of the segment tree. At each of these nodes, deletion of the line segment can be performed in constant time since the segment lists that are associated with these nodes are implemented as doubly linked lists. Thus, the total cost of deleting a line segment is $O(\log_2 N)$. The segment tree has a total of $O(N)$ nodes and, since each line segment can appear in (i.e., cover) $O(\log_2 N)$ nodes, the total space required (including the auxiliary table) in the worst case is $O(N \cdot \log_2 N)$. Interestingly, Bucher and Edelsbrunner [277] have shown that the average space requirement for a segment tree is also $O(N \cdot \log_2 N)$.

Given F rectangle intersections, using a segment tree to determine the set of rectangles that intersect each other is somewhat complex [183] if we want to do it in $O(N \cdot \log_2 N + F)$ time. In particular, it involves considerably more work than just inserting a line segment and reporting the rectangles associated with the line segments that were encountered during the insertion process. We will indicate by means of an example why this is so, after we have described our algorithm.

Conceptually, the problem is quite straightforward. For each line segment S, with starting and ending points l and r, respectively, we want the set of line segments A such that $A_i \cap S$ is nonempty for each $A_i \in A$. Recalling that the segment tree is good for detecting all intervals that contain a given point, we formulate the problem as an infinite set of point queries: for each point p_i in line segment S, find all line segments that contain it. This process takes $O(\log_2 N)$ time for each point queried. To avoid looking at every point in S (an infinite number!), we can restrict our search to the endpoints of the line segments that are overlapped by S. An obvious, but unacceptable solution, is to store explicitly with each line segment the set of segments that intersect it at a total storage cost of $O(N^2)$.

A more reasonable solution, which makes use of the above restriction on the search, is given by Six and Wood [1774, 1775], who decompose the search into two disjoint problems. They make use of the obvious fact that any line segment with a starting point greater than r or with an ending point less than l does not intersect the line segment S. The first problem consists of determining all line segments with starting points less than l that have a nonempty intersection with S. The second problem consists of determining l that have a nonempty intersection with S. The second problem consists of determining all line segments with starting points that lie between l and r. Thus, there is really a need to be concerned only with an ordering that is based on the starting points.

One way to solve the first problem is to use a balanced binary search tree to store the starting points of the line segments. Now we search for all line segments with starting points that are less than l and check if the ending points are greater than l. Unfortunately, this could require us to examine every node in the tree (if l is large). An alternative solution is to perform a point query for point l on the segment tree representation of the line segments. To determine all the line segments that contain l, we simply locate the smallest interval containing it. Since a segment tree for N line segments has a maximum of $2 \cdot N$ leaf nodes, this search visits at most $\lceil \log_2 N \rceil + 1$ nodes, and for each node visited, we traverse its associated list of line segments and report them as containing l. This process takes $O(\log_2 N + F_l)$ time, where F_l is the number of line segments that contain l. Since a segment tree is used, the solution uses $O(N \cdot \log_2 N)$ space.

The second problem is solved by performing a range query for range $[l:r]$ on the set of starting points of the line segments. For this query, a one-dimensional range tree that stores the starting points of the line segments is ideal. Recall from Section 1.2 of Chapter 1 that a one-dimensional range tree is a balanced binary search tree where the data points are stored in sorted order in the leaf nodes that are linked in this order by use of a doubly linked list. Therefore, insertion and deletion are both $O(\log_2 N)$ processes.

A range query consists of locating the node corresponding to the start of the range, say L, and the closest node to the end of the range, say R, and then reporting the line segments corresponding to the nodes that lie between them by traversing the linked list of nodes. This process takes $O(\log_2 N + F_{lr})$ time, where F_{lr} is the number of line segments with starting points in $[l:r]$. Since a balanced binary search tree is used, it needs $O(N)$ space.

The combination of the point and range query solution uses $O(N \cdot \log_2 N)$ space and takes $O(N \cdot \log_2 N + F)$ time, where F is the number of rectangle intersections. At this point, let us see if we can improve on these bounds. Since the first pass also takes $O(N \cdot \log_2 N)$ time, the only room for improvement is in the space requirement, which is bounded from below by $O(N)$ as a result of using the range tree (i.e., a balanced binary search tree with double links between adjacent elements) for the range query.

Suppose that, instead of using a segment tree, we use an additional one-dimensional range tree for the ending points (as well as a one-dimensional range tree for the starting points). Now we perform a range query for range $[l:r]$ on the set of ending points of the line segments. Unfortunately, the results of the two range queries are not disjoint, so we will have to remove duplicates. The number of duplicate entries per range query can be as large as N, and we will have to sort them prior to removal. This means that the algorithm has a total worst-case execution time that can be as high as $O(N^2 \log_2 N)$.

Alternatively, we can try to determine the set of rectangles that intersect each other by just using a segment tree. The problem with this approach is that, upon insertion of a line segment, say S, in a segment tree, we cannot find all of the existing line segments in the tree that are totally contained in S, or partially overlap S, without examining every node in each subtree containing S. For example, consider the segment tree of Figure 3.3 without line segment A (i.e., for segments B, C, D, E, F, and G). Upon inserting line segment A into the node corresponding to interval $[14{:}23)$, the only way to determine the existence of line segment F (corresponding to the interval $[15{:}19)$) that is totally contained in A is to descend to the bottom of the subtree rooted at $[14{:}23)$.

The problem is not restricted to the situation of total containment as it also arises in the case of partial overlap. For example, consider the segment tree of Figure 3.3 without line segment B (i.e., for segments A, C, D, E, F, and G). Upon inserting line segment B into the node corresponding to interval $[34{:}38)$, the only way to detect the partial overlap of B with line segments A and C in the interval $[34{:}36)$ is to descend to the bottom of the subtree rooted at $[34{:}38)$. Checking for total containment or partial overlap in this way takes $O(N)$ time for each line segment, or $O(N^2)$ for all of the line segments. Thus, we must find a more satisfactory solution since we wish to perform this task in $O(N \cdot \log_2 N + F)$ time. This is achieved by using the interval tree and is the subject of the next section.

Exercises

1. Under what restriction is a segment tree equivalent to a unit-segment tree?

2. Is it true that, whenever two line segments overlap, at least one node in the segment tree will have more than one line segment associated with it?

3. The implementation of the segment tree described in the text makes use of an auxiliary table that contains an entry for each line segment. This entry points to a list of pointers, each of which points to a list entry for the line segment in a node of the segment tree whose intervals are covered by the line segment. Why is this a better solution than merely pointing to the node whose intervals are covered by the line segment?

4. Why can you not formulate the sweep pass of the rectangle intersection problem as locating all line segments that start within a given line segment and those that end within the line segment? In this case, there is no need for the segment tree; instead, use two one-dimensional range trees, one for the starting points and one for the ending points.

5. Given a point P on a line, devise an algorithm to find all intervals that contain P. This is known as a *stabbing query*. Assume that the intervals are represented using a segment tree. What is the order of the execution time of the algorithm when there are N intervals?

6. Suppose that we are interested only in the number of intervals that contain P. This is known as the *stabbing counting query*. Assume that the intervals are represented using a segment tree. Given N intervals, how quickly can you determine a solution to this query, and how much space does it require?

7. Give an algorithm to insert a line segment into a segment tree.

8. Give an algorithm to delete a line segment from a segment tree.

9. Give an algorithm to determine if a line segment intersects an existing line segment in a segment tree.

10. How would you use a segment tree to determine all of the one-dimensional intervals that are totally contained within a given one-dimensional interval? Given N intervals and F contained intervals, does your algorithm run in $O(\log_2 N + F)$ time? If not, explain why, and give an alternative solution.

11. How would you use a segment tree to determine all the one-dimensional intervals that contain a given one-dimensional interval? Given N intervals and F containing intervals, does your algorithm run in $O(\log_2 N + F)$ time? If not, explain why.

12. Give an algorithm to determine all pairs of intersecting rectangles using a segment tree.

3.1.2 Interval Tree

The problem discussed at the end of Section 3.1.1 with using the segment tree as the basis of the solution to the rectangle intersection problem can be overcome, in part, by making the following modifications. Link each marked node (i.e., a node whose corresponding interval overlaps at least one line segment), say P, to some of the nodes in P's subtrees that are marked. This can be implemented by an auxiliary binary tree with elements that are the marked nodes. Since each line segment can be associated with more than one node in the segment tree, the number of intersections that can be detected is bounded by $2 \cdot N^2 \cdot \log_2 N$ (see Exercise 1), and the number of different intersections is bounded by N^2. Removing duplicates will require sorting, and even use of the bin method [1976], which is linear, still leaves us with an $O(N^2 \cdot \log_2 N)$ process.

However, duplicate entries can be avoided by redefining the segment tree so that a line segment is associated only with one node: the nearest common ancestor[1] of all the intervals contained in the line segment (e.g., the node corresponding to the interval [3:38) for line segments A and C in Figure 3.3). The absence of duplicate entries also means that the space requirements can be reduced to $O(N)$.

The above modifications serve as the foundation for the development of the *interval tree* of Edelsbrunner [534, 537, 538] and the *tile tree* of McCreight [1265].[2] The difference between the interval tree and the tile tree is that the tile tree is based on a regular decomposition, while the interval tree is not. In the rest of this section, we discuss only the interval tree.

The interval tree is designed specifically to detect all intervals that intersect a given interval. It is motivated by the dual goals of reducing the space requirement to $O(N)$ while maintaining an execution time of $O(N \cdot \log_2 N + F)$. The interval tree solution also makes use of the decomposition of the search into two disjoint tasks:

1. Determining all line segments that overlap the starting point of the query line segment

2. Determining all line segments with starting points that lie within the query line segment

Once again, assume that we are given a set of N line segments such that line segment S_i corresponds to the interval $[l_i:r_i)$ where l_i and r_i are the left and right endpoints, respectively, of S_i. The endpoints of the N line segments are sorted (with duplicates removed) to obtain the sequence $y_0, y_1, \ldots, y_m$ ($m < 2 \cdot N$ and $2^{h-1} \leq m < 2^h$). The interval tree is a three-level structure in which the first (and principal) level is termed the *primary structure*, the second level is termed the *secondary structure*, and the third level is termed the *tertiary structure*. We shall illustrate our discussion with Figure 3.4, the interval tree for the set of line segments corresponding to the vertical boundaries of the rectangles in Figure 3.1.

The primary structure is a complete binary tree with $m + 1$ external (i.e., leaf) nodes such that, when the tree is flattened, and the nonleaf nodes are removed, then external node i corresponds to y_i. In Figure 3.4, the primary structure is denoted by solid lines. In our example, although there are 7 line segments, the primary structure contains only 13 external nodes as there are only 13 different endpoints. Each leaf node is labeled with its corresponding endpoint (i.e., y_i for leaf node i ($0 \leq i < 2 \cdot N$)). Each nonleaf node is assigned an arbitrary value, stored in the field VAL, that lies between the maximum value in its left subtree and the minimum value in its right subtree (usually their average). For example, the root node in Figure 3.4 is labeled 22.

Given a line segment corresponding to the interval $[l:r)$, we say that its *nearest common ancestor* in the interval tree is the nonleaf node containing l and r in its left and right subtrees, respectively. For example, in Figure 3.4, node 22 is the nearest common ancestor of line segment A, which corresponds to the interval [6,36).

Each nonleaf node in the primary structure, say v, serves as the key to a pair of secondary structures LS and RS that represent the sets of left and right endpoints, respectively, of the line segments for which v is the nearest common ancestor (i.e., they contain v's value). Elements of the sets LS and RS are linked in ascending and descending order, respectively. In Figure 3.4, the secondary structure is denoted by dotted lines

---

[1] The principle of associating key information with the nearest common ancestor is also used as the basis of an efficient solution of the point location query by Lee and Preparata [1128] (see Section 2.1.3.3.1 of Chapter 2) and later improved upon by use of fractional cascading [339, 340] by Edelsbrunner, Guibas, and Stolfi [541] (see Section 2.1.3.3.2 of Chapter 2).

[2] Preparata and Shamos [1511, pp. 323 and 373], as well as others (e.g., Cormen, Leiserson, Rivest, and Stein [422, p. 318], quoting Preparata and Shamos [1511]), mistakenly attribute the tile tree to the technical report preprint of [1266], which, in fact, describes the priority search tree.

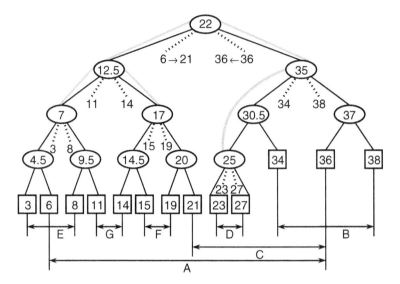

Figure 3.4
The interval tree for the set of line segments corresponding to the vertical boundaries of the rectangles in Figure 3.1. The primary structure is shown by solid lines. The secondary structure is shown by dotted lines. The tertiary structure is shown by gray lines with the active nodes circled with heavy lines. The interrelationships between the endpoints of the line segments are also shown.

emanating from each nonleaf node with a nonempty secondary structure. The sets LS and RS are distinguished by dotted lines emanating from the nonleaf node to its left and right sides, respectively.

When the sets LS and RS contain more than one entry, we show them as linked in increasing and decreasing order, respectively (e.g., LS of the root node shows 6 pointing to 21 since the corresponding intervals are [6:36) and [21:36)). Each starting (ending) point appears in LS (RS) as many times as there are line segments that have it as a starting (ending) point. For example, 36 appears twice in RS of the root node in Figure 3.4 as it is the ending point of line segments A and C. To support rapid insertion and deletion, the sets LS and RS are implemented as balanced binary search trees (as well as doubly linked lists).

Each nonleaf node in the primary structure has eight pointers: two to its left and right subtrees in the primary structure (LP and RP), two to the roots of LS and RS in the secondary structure, one to the minimum value in LS, one to the maximum value in RS, and two (LT and RT) to its left and right subtrees in the tertiary structure. The LT and RT pointers are discussed below.

A nonleaf node in the primary structure is marked *active* if its corresponding secondary structure is nonempty or both of its children have active descendants; otherwise, it is marked *inactive*. The active nodes of the primary structure form the tertiary structure, which is a binary tree. It is rooted at the root of the primary structure and is linked via the LT and RT fields of the nonleaf nodes of the primary structure. If node v of the primary structure is inactive, then LT(v) and RT(v) are Ω (i.e., pointers to NIL). If v is active, then LT(v) points to the closest active node in the left subtree of v (i.e., in LP(v)), and RT(v) points to the closest active node in the right subtree of v (i.e., in RP(v)). If there are no closest active nodes in the left and right subtrees of v, then LT(v) and RT(v), respectively, are Ω.

In Figure 3.4, the tertiary structure is denoted by gray lines linking all of the active nodes (e.g., nodes 22, 12.5, 7, 17, 35, and 25), also enclosed by thick ellipses. The tertiary structure is useful in collecting the line segments that intersect a given line segment. It enables us to avoid examining primary nodes with no line segments. Note that more than half of the elements of the tertiary structure (i.e., active nodes) have nonempty secondary structures (see Exercise 4).

Inserting the line segment $[l{:}r)$ in the interval tree is very simple. We start at the root and, using the primary structure, locate the first node v such that $l < \text{VAL}(v) < r$. In this case, we insert l into $\text{LS}(v)$ and r into $\text{RS}(v)$. Both of these processes can be achieved in $O(\log_2 N)$ time. Updating the tertiary structure requires us to traverse it in parallel with the primary structure and takes $O(\log_2 N)$ time. Deletion of a line segment is performed in a similar manner and with the same complexity.

Reporting the rectangle intersections in an interval tree is straightforward, although there are a number of cases to consider. Again, this task is performed while inserting a vertical line segment, say S corresponding to the interval $[l{:}r)$. During this process, we search for and report the line segments that overlap S (see Exercise 11). Assume that the interval tree is rooted at T_1. The search has the following three stages:

1. Start at T_1, and find the first node v such that $l < \text{VAL}(v) < r$.

2. Start at v, and locate l in the left subtree of v.

3. Start at v, and locate r in the right subtree of v.

This search involves the secondary structures of the nodes in the primary structure. The tertiary structure reduces the number of nodes in the primary structure with empty secondary structures that must be examined. Note that all of the overlapping line segments will be reported, and each will be reported only once as it is associated with the secondary structure of just one node in the primary structure.

In the following, we present the main ideas of the three stages. Figure 3.5 aids in the visualization of the symbols used in the explanation for $[l{:}r)$. All secondary and tertiary structures that are visited are marked with dotted and broken lines, respectively.

Let us start with stage 1. $\{T_i\}$ denotes the set of nodes encountered during the search for v. We use the insertion of line segment $[6{:}20)$ into the interval tree of Figure 3.4 as our example. The secondary structures associated with each T_i must be checked for a possible overlap with S. This is quite simple. Either $l < r < \text{VAL}(T_i)$ or $\text{VAL}(T_i) < l < r$.

If $r < \text{VAL}(T_i)$, then we need to report only the line segments in the secondary structure of T_i with starting points less than r (e.g., line segment A upon examining the nonleaf node with value 22). To achieve this, we visit $\text{LS}(T_i)$ in ascending order until we encounter a line segment with a starting point exceeding r. We then search the left subtree of T_i (i.e., $\text{LP}(T_i)$).

Similarly, if $\text{VAL}(T_i) < l$, then we need to report only the elements of the secondary structure of T_i with ending points greater than l. To do this, we visit $\text{RS}(T_i)$ in descending order until encountering a line segment with an ending point less than l. The search is then continued in the right subtree of T_i (i.e., $\text{RP}(T_i)$).

Both of these cases are executed in time proportional to the number of intersections reported. Once node v has been located, we report all elements of its secondary structure as intersecting S. In our example, we would report line segment G since v is the nonleaf node with value 12.5.

Now, let us understand stages 2 and 3. Since they are very similar, we just discuss stage 2. We use the insertion of line segment $[6{:}34)$ into the interval tree of Figure 3.4 as our example. In this case, v is the root of the tree (the nonleaf node with value 22). Let $\{L_i\}$ denote the set of nodes encountered during the search for l in this stage. Recall that $l < \text{VAL}(v)$. Either $l < \text{VAL}(L_i)$ or $\text{VAL}(L_i) < l$.

If $l < \text{VAL}(L_i)$, then S intersects every line segment in the secondary structure of L_i. S also intersects all the line segments in the secondary structures in the right subtree of L_i. The first set consists of just the line segments in $\text{RS}(L_i)$ (e.g., line segment G upon examining the nonleaf node with value 12.5). The second set is obtained by visiting

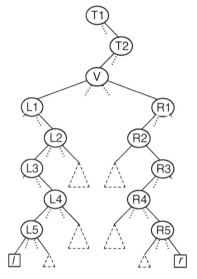

Figure 3.5
Example of an interval tree search for the interval $l{:}r$. All secondary structures that are visited are marked with dotted lines. All tertiary structures that are visited are marked with broken lines.

all of the active nodes in the right subtree of L_i, $RT(L_i)$ (e.g., line segment F during the processing of the nonleaf node with value 12.5 since F is associated with the active nonleaf node with value 17).

Notice the use of the pointers $LT(L_i)$ and $RT(L_i)$ in the tertiary structure to avoid visiting irrelevant nodes when forming the second set. Since more than half of the elements of the tertiary structure have nonempty secondary structures (see Exercise 4), the time necessary to execute this process is proportional to the number of intersections that are reported. The search is continued in the left subtree of L_i, $LT(L_i)$.

If $VAL(L_i) < l$, then we report the line segments in the secondary structure of L_i with ending points greater than l. To do this, we visit $RS(L_i)$ in descending order until encountering a line segment with an ending point less than l. This process is executed in time proportional to the number of intersections reported. The search is continued in the right subtree of L_i, $RT(L_i)$.

Solving the rectangle intersection problem using an interval tree uses $O(N)$ space and takes $O(N \cdot \log_2 N + F)$ time, where F is the number of rectangle intersections.[3] The space requirements are obtained by observing that, for N line segments, we need at most $2 \cdot N$ leaf nodes in the primary structure and likewise for the secondary structures. The tertiary structure is constructed from nodes in the primary structure, and thus it requires no additional space except for the pointer fields. Making use of the fact that the interval tree is a complete binary tree, the number of nonleaf nodes in the primary and secondary structures is bounded by $2 \cdot N - 1$.

The execution time requirements are obtained by noting that searching the primary structure for the starting and ending points of a line segment takes $O(\log_2 N)$ time. The number of nodes visited in the secondary structure is of the same order as the number of rectangle intersections that are found. Since at least one-half of the active nodes have nonempty secondary structures, the number of nodes visited in the tertiary structure is no more than twice the number of nodes visited in the secondary structure. Constructing the interval tree takes $O(N \cdot \log_2 N)$ time since the endpoints of the line segments forming the sides of the rectangles must be sorted.

Note that the interval tree that we have described is very different from what is termed an *interval tree* by Cormen, Leiserson, Rivest, and Stein [422, pp. 311–318], which simply stores the starting endpoint of each active vertical line segment in a balanced binary tree where each nonleaf node u also contains the maximum terminating endpoint of the vertical line segments stored in the subtree rooted at u. Thus, it is a balanced binary search tree in the starting endpoints of the active vertical line segments and a heap in the terminating endpoints of the active vertical line segments stored in each subtree. In fact, this structure is really a Cartesian tree [1944] (see Exercises 21 and 22 in Section 1.3 of Chapter 1). Unfortunately, the dual meaning of the term *interval tree* is not limited to Cormen et al. [422]. For example, this variant of the interval tree is characterized by some researchers (e.g., [89, 934]) as a *dynamic interval tree* since its use reduces the storage needed for the active list from $O(N)$ (actually more precisely $\Theta(N)$ due to the need to store the endpoints of all of the vertical line segments) to $O(A)$, where A is the maximum number of active vertical line segments at any particular moment. However, the cost of finding all intersecting pairs is now $O(N \cdot \log_2 N + F \cdot \log_2 N)$ because detecting all intervals that intersect a given interval in a dynamic interval tree with n nodes is $O(\min(n, k \cdot \log_2 n))$, where k is the number of intersections of the given interval [422]. The dynamic interval tree has found use in performing a spatial join query [89, 934] (see Exercises 14 and 15).

---

[3] For the tile tree, the execution time is $O(N \cdot \log_2(\max(N, K)) + F)$, where the horizontal boundaries of the rectangles are integers between 0 and $K - 1$. The execution time becomes $O(N \cdot \log_2 N + F)$ if the $2 \cdot N$ y coordinate values are first sorted and then mapped into the integers from 0 to $2 \cdot N - 1$.

1. Suppose that you modify the definition of the segment tree so that each marked node, say P, is linked (i.e., a node with a corresponding interval that overlaps at least one line segment) to the nodes in P's subtrees that are marked. Show that the number of intersections that can be detected is bounded by $2 \cdot N^2 \cdot \log_2 N$.

2. Can you implement the segment tree as a complete binary tree with $m + 1$ external nodes as was done for the interval tree—that is, merge the leaf nodes corresponding to the unused intervals? If so, the segment tree will have the same node configuration as the primary structure of the interval tree. If this is the case, show how the nodes will be marked.

3. The text describes stage 2 of the search involved in reporting all intersections with a vertical line segment S corresponding to the interval $[l:r)$. Complete the description of the search by showing what will be done in stage 3.

4. Why do more than half of the elements of the tertiary structure (i.e., active nodes) of the interval tree have nonempty secondary structures?

5. Assume that a set of intervals is stored using an interval tree. Given a point P on a line, devise an algorithm to find all intervals that contain P (i.e., a stabbing query). What is the order of the execution time of the algorithm when there are N intervals?

6. Can you use the interval tree to determine the number of intervals containing P (i.e., a stabbing counting query) without storing the identities of the intervals? In other words, just store the number of intervals with each nonleaf node.

7. Prove that solution of the rectangle intersection problem based on its decomposition into a point and region query does not report an intersection more than once.

8. Give an algorithm to insert a line segment into an interval tree. Remember, you must also update the secondary and tertiary structures.

9. Give an algorithm to delete a line segment from an interval tree. Remember, you must also update the secondary and tertiary structures.

10. How would you use an interval tree to determine all of the one-dimensional intervals that are completely contained within a given one-dimensional interval? Given N intervals and F contained intervals, does your algorithm run in $O(\log_2 N + F)$ time? If not, explain why.

11. Show that reporting the lines intersecting a line S corresponding to the interval $[l:r)$ in an interval tree can be done concurrently while inserting S instead by first inserting it and then checking for intersections with existing line segments.

12. How would you use an interval tree to determine all of the one-dimensional intervals that contain (i.e., enclose) a given one-dimensional interval? Given N intervals and F containing intervals, does your algorithm run in $O(\log_2 N + F)$ time? If not, explain why.

13. Give an algorithm to determine all pairs of intersecting rectangles using an interval tree. Remember that during this process you must also simultaneously traverse the tertiary structure.

14. Suppose that, instead of finding all pairs of intersecting rectangles from the same set, you want to find all pairs of intersecting rectangles from two different sets S_1 and S_2—that is, a true geometric join (or spatial join) query. How would you use an interval tree to solve this problem?

15. A drawback of using the interval tree for the spatial join query in Exercise 14 is that the size of each of the interval trees for the two sets S_1 and S_2 is $O(N)$ due to the need to keep track of the endpoints of all of the vertical line segments. Suppose that you have just a finite amount of memory available, say A such that $A << N$, for keeping track of the vertical line segments corresponding to the active rectangles. Devise an algorithm using the dynamic interval tree that does not fail when A is not large enough to store all of the active rectangles.

3.1.3 Priority Search Tree

Using an interval tree, as described in Section 3.1.2, yields an optimal worst-case space and time solution to the rectangle intersection problem. The interval tree solution requires that we know in advance the endpoints of all of the vertical intervals as they must be sorted and stored in a complete binary tree. Thus, given N rectangles, the storage requirement is always $O(N)$. The solution can be slightly improved by adapting the priority search tree of McCreight [1266] to keep track of the active vertical intervals.

In this case, the storage requirements for the sweep pass depend only on the maximum number of vertical intervals that can be active at any one time, say M. Moreover, there is no need to know their endpoints in advance, and thus there is no need to sort them. This also has an effect on the execution time of the algorithm since the data structure used to keep track of the endpoints of the vertical intervals is the determinative factor in the amount of time necessary to do a search. Therefore, when using the priority search tree, the sweep pass of the solution to the rectangle intersection problem can be performed in $O(N \cdot \log_2 M + F)$ time, rather than in $O(N \cdot \log_2 N + F)$ time. However, sorting the endpoints of the horizontal intervals, which is the first pass of the plane sweep, still takes $O(N \cdot \log_2 N)$ time.

The priority search tree has been described in Section 1.3 of Chapter 1. It keeps track of points in a two-dimensional space. Briefly, it is designed for solving queries involving semi-infinite ranges in such a space. A typical query has a range of the form $([L_x:R_x],[L_y:\infty])$. A priority search tree is built in the following manner. Sort all the points along the x coordinate, and store them in the leaf nodes of a balanced binary search tree, say S. We use a one-dimensional range tree in the following presentation so as to make the explanation easier to follow, although, as we will soon see, in order to be able to perform the sweep pass of the rectangle intersection problem in $O(N \cdot \log_2 M + F)$ time, we will need to implement the balanced binary search tree using a representation that enables us to insert and delete items in $O(\log_2 M)$ time (e.g., a red-black balanced binary tree [766], as described a bit more below and also in Appendix A). Continuing with the one-dimensional range tree implementation, store midrange x coordinate values in the nonleaf nodes. Next, proceed from the root node towards the leaf nodes. With each node of S, say I, associate the point in the subtree rooted at I with the maximum value for its y coordinate that has not already been stored at a shallower depth in the tree. If such a point does not exist, then the node is left empty.

Figure 3.6 is an example of the priority search tree. It is based on treating the vertical boundaries $[y_B,y_T]$ of the rectangles in Figure 3.1 as points (x, y). For N points, the priority search tree uses $O(N)$ storage (see Exercise 1 in Section 1.3 of Chapter 1). The priority search tree is good for performing a semi-infinite range query $([L_x:R_x],[L_y:\infty])$. For N points, this process takes $O(\log_2 N + F)$ time, where F is the number of points found (see Exercise 2 in Section 1.3 of Chapter 1). Notice that the leaf nodes of the priority search tree contain the points and are shown as linked together in ascending order of the y_B coordinate value. However, the links for the y_B coordinate values are used only if we conduct a search for all points within a given range of y_B coordinate values. They are not used in the execution of the semi-infinite range query, and thus they are frequently omitted from the implementation of the priority search tree.

It should be clear that the priority search tree in Figure 3.6 could never be realized for the example set of rectangles given in Figure 3.1. The reason is that it represents a situation in the sweep phase (i.e., a location with a particular x coordinate value) where all seven vertical intervals are simultaneously active, which is, of course, impossible given the positions of the horizontal intervals. Nevertheless, the figure does illustrate the data structure.

There are two keys to understanding the use of the priority search tree in solving the rectangle intersection problem. Assume, again, that all intervals are semiclosed (i.e., they are closed on their left ends and open on their right ends). First, each one-dimensional interval, say $[a:b)$, is represented by the point (a, b) in two-dimensional space. This two-dimensional space is represented by a priority search tree.

Second, we observe that the one-dimensional interval $[a:b)$ intersects the interval $[c:d)$ if and only if $a < d$ and $c < b$ (see Exercise 1). An equivalent observation is that

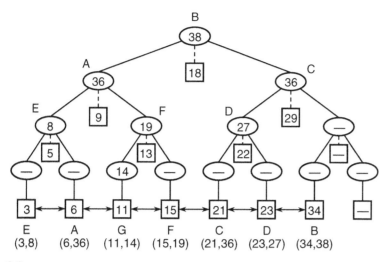

Figure 3.6
The priority search tree for the set of line segments corresponding to the vertical boundaries $[y_B,y_T)$ of the rectangles in Figure 3.1. Each vertical boundary $[y_B,y_T)$ is treated as a point (x,y) in a two-dimensional space. Each leaf node contains the appropriate y_B value in a square box. Each nonleaf node contains the appropriate y_B midrange value in a square box using a link drawn with a broken line. Circular boxes indicate the value of the y_T component of the line segment in the corresponding subtree with the maximum value for its y_T component that has not already been associated with a node at a shallower depth in the tree.

the point (c,d) lies in the range $([-\infty:b],(a:\infty])$. This equivalence means that to find all one-dimensional intervals that intersect the interval $[a:b]$, we need only perform the semi-infinite range query $([-\infty:b],(a:\infty])$ in the priority search tree. If the priority search tree contains M one-dimensional intervals, then this operation takes $O(\log_2 M + F)$ time, where F is the number of intersecting intervals found.

For the space and time bounds to be comparable or better than that of the interval tree, we must also show that a one-dimensional interval can be inserted and deleted from a priority search tree in $O(\log_2 M)$ time. Unfortunately, this cannot be guaranteed when the balanced binary search tree for the x (actually y_B) coordinate values is implemented using a one-dimensional range tree. In particular, the one-dimensional range tree is more of a static structure that requires the rearrangement of nodes and the resetting of links upon insertion and deletion, especially when $M = 2^i$ and $2^i + 1$, respectively, for arbitrary values of i. This problem is overcome by implementing the balanced binary search tree for the y_B coordinate values as a red-black balanced binary tree [766] (see Appendix A). The red-black balanced binary tree has the property that, for M items, insertions and deletions take $O(\log_2 M)$ time with $O(1)$ rotations [1858]. McCreight [1266] shows that the priority search tree adaptation of the red-black balanced binary tree can be maintained at a cost of $O(\log_2 M)$ per rotation (see Exercise 6). The use of a red-black balanced binary tree does not affect the $O(M)$ storage requirements of the priority search tree. Hence, the desired time and space bounds are achieved.

When the priority search tree is implemented as a red-black balanced binary tree, its node structure differs from the way it was defined in Section 1.3 of Chapter 1. In particular, the nonleaf nodes now also contain intervals corresponding to the endpoints of the vertical intervals $[y_B,y_T)$. The interval associated with a nonleaf node, say I, is the one whose left endpoint, say L, is the median value of the left endpoints of the intervals in I's subtrees. All intervals in I's left subtree have left endpoints that are less than or equal to L, and the intervals in I's right subtree have left endpoints that are greater than or equal to L.

Red-black trees enable the implementation of order 3 or order 4 B-trees (see Appendix A) (also known as 2-3 and 2-3-4 trees, respectively) as binary trees in a manner similar to the natural correspondence between a forest and a binary tree. Thus, all nodes are now uniform. In essence, in a red-black tree, the nodes of the order 3 and order 4 B-trees are represented as one-level binary trees consisting of zero or more red edges, while black edges are used to link up the nodes of the B-tree.

For example, Figure 3.7(a) shows a sample order 3 B-tree for the set of line segments corresponding to the vertical boundaries $[y_B, y_T)$ of the rectangles in Figure 3.1, where the sort key is the y_B coordinate value, while Figure 3.7(b) is the corresponding red-black tree. In both cases, we have included the corresponding y_T values. The edges of the red-black tree in Figure 3.7(b) are labeled with r and b to denote their color (red and black, respectively). The red-black tree also plays the role of a heap by associating with each node of P, say, I, the point in the subtree rooted at I with the maximum value for its y_T coordinate that has not already been stored at a shallower depth in the tree. If such a point does not exist, then the node is left empty. We show these values within a circle connected to the appropriate node with a broken line.

It should be clear that the red-black tree in Figure 3.7 could never be realized for the example set of rectangles given in Figure 3.1. The reason is that it represents a situation in the sweep phase (i.e., a location with a particular x coordinate value) where all seven vertical intervals are simultaneously active, which is, of course, impossible given the positions of the horizontal intervals. Nevertheless, the figure does illustrate the data structure.

Comparing the interval and priority search tree solutions to the rectangle intersection problem, we find that the priority search tree is considerably simpler from a conceptual standpoint than the interval tree. The execution time requirements of the priority search tree are lower when the sort pass is ignored. Also, the priority search tree enables a more dynamic solution than the interval tree because, for the priority search tree, only the endpoints of the horizontal intervals need to be known in advance. On the other hand, for the interval tree, the endpoints of both the horizontal and vertical intervals must be known in advance.

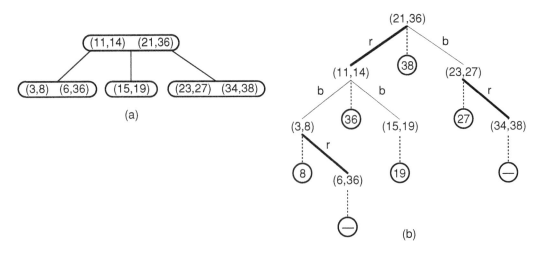

Figure 3.7
(a) The order 3 B-tree for the left endpoints (i.e., y_B) of the set of line segments corresponding to the vertical boundaries $[y_B, y_T)$ of the rectangles in Figure 3.1, and (b) its red-black tree which also shows the corresponding y_T value. Associated with each node I of the red-black tree is the value of the y_T component of the line segment in the subtree rooted at I with the maximum value for its y_T component that has not already been associated with a node at a shallower depth in the tree. This value is shown within a circle connected with a broken line.

Exercises

1. Prove that the one-dimensional interval [a:b) intersects the interval [c:d) if and only if a < d and c < b.

2. The adaptation of the priority search tree as a red-black balanced binary tree differs from the version of the priority search tree described in Section 1.3 of Chapter 1) in that the data items appear in both leaf and nonleaf nodes. Show that this does not cause any problems in executing the semi-infinite range query.

3. Give an algorithm to insert the interval [a:b) into a priority search tree.

4. Give an algorithm to delete the interval [a:b) from a priority search tree.

5. Prove that a point can be deleted from a red-black balanced binary tree of M items in $O(\log_2 M)$ time with $O(1)$ rotations.

6. Prove that the priority search tree adaptation of the red-black balanced binary tree can be maintained at a cost of $O(\log_2 M)$ per rotation.

7. Assume that a set of intervals is stored using a priority search tree. Given a point P on a line, devise an algorithm to find all intervals that contain P (i.e., a stabbing query). What is the order of the execution time of the algorithm when there are M intervals?

8. Give an algorithm that uses a priority search tree to find all one-dimensional intervals that partially overlap or are contained in a given one-dimensional interval.

9. Give an algorithm that uses a priority search tree to find all one-dimensional intervals [x:y] that completely contain (i.e., enclose) the one-dimensional interval [a:b].

10. In Section 1.3 of Chapter 1 an inverse priority search tree was defined to be a priority search tree in which, with each node of T, say I, we associate the point in the subtree rooted at I with the minimum (instead of the maximum!) value for its y coordinate that has not already been stored at a shallower depth in the tree. Give an algorithm that uses an inverse priority search tree to find all one-dimensional intervals [x:y] that are completely contained in the one-dimensional interval [a:b].

11. Repeat Exercise 10 by using a priority search tree instead of an inverse priority search tree.

12. Give an algorithm to determine all pairs of intersecting rectangles using a priority search tree.

3.1.4 Alternative Solutions and Related Problems[4]

The time requirements of the interval and priority search tree solutions of the rectangle intersection problem can be reduced further if we can make use of knowledge about the distribution of the data. Such an approach is reported by Bentley, Haken, and Hon [174]. They performed an empirical study on the distribution of components in VLSI design applications and determined that the rectangles are uniformly distributed. This distribution was used to organize the segments for the second pass so that the entire plane-sweep algorithm has a linear expected-time behavior.

Bentley et al. [174] obtained expected linear performance in the following manner. The sorting operation of the first pass takes expected linear time by use of the bin method [1976]. For the second pass, instead of using an interval tree to store the vertical segments that intersect the sweep line, bins of equal width are used. They are accessed by an array of pointers. Each bin contains a linked list of all the vertical segments that overlap it. The observed data was used to choose a bin width equal to the average width of a rectangle. This implies that each vertical segment is contained in two bins on average.

The linear expected time depends on an assumption that the expected number of rectangles per bin is a constant (i.e., independent of the number of rectangles N). This assumption means that the total number of bins is some multiple of $\sqrt{N}$, which is true

---

[4] The exercises in this section are quite difficult.

as long as the data is not highly clustered (e.g., under a uniform distribution).[5] Under these hypotheses, initialization of the bins is an $O(\sqrt{N})$ process. Inserting and deleting a vertical segment merely involves traversing a linked list of constant expected size. Checking a vertical segment, say S, for intersection with existing vertical segments is achieved by visiting the bins containing S and comparing S with the vertical segments stored within them. This is also achieved in constant time.

A related problem is finding the *containment set* (also known as the *inclusion* or *enclosure set*) of a collection of rectangles. The containment set is the set of all pairs of rectangles A and B such that A contains B. Variants of the segment tree are used by Vaishnavi and Wood [1910] to solve this problem in $O(N \cdot \log_2^2 N + F)$ time and $O(N \cdot \log_2^2 N)$ space (see Exercise 8). The space requirement is reduced to $O(N)$ by Lee and Preparata [1129], who map each rectangle to a point in four-dimensional space and solve a point dominance problem.

As described in the opening section of this chapter, the rectangle intersection problem is closely related to the following problems:

1. Determining all rectangles that are contained in a given rectangle (a containment query)

2. Determining all rectangles that enclose a given rectangle (an enclosure query)

3. Determining all rectangles that partially overlap or are contained in a given rectangle (a window query)

The plane-sweep approach is not appropriate for these problems since, regardless of the data structures employed (e.g., segment, interval, or priority search trees), sorting is a prerequisite, and thus any algorithm requires at least $O(N \cdot \log_2 N)$ time for N rectangles. In contrast, the naive solution of intersecting each rectangle with the query rectangle is an $O(N)$ process.

The problems described above can be solved by segment trees and interval trees without making use of a plane sweep (e.g., Exercises 15 and 24) [1442]. The key is to adapt these representations to store two-dimensional intervals (see Exercises 9 and 20) in a manner similar to that in which the two-dimensional range tree was developed from the one-dimensional range tree (see Section 1.2 of Chapter 1) [536, 542].

For example, for N rectangles, the execution time of the solution to the window query is $O(\log_2^2 N + F)$, where F is the number of rectangles that satisfy the query. The difference is in their storage requirements: the segment tree solution uses $O(N \cdot \log_2^2 N)$ space, while the interval tree solution uses $O(N \cdot \log_2 N)$ space. For both of these structures, judicious use of doubly linked lists insures that rectangles can be inserted and deleted in $O(\log_2^2 N)$ time (see Exercises 10 and 21). Of course, these structures must still be built, which takes $O(N \cdot \log_2^2 N)$ time in both cases (see Exercises 11 and 22). It is not clear how to adapt the priority search tree to store two-dimensional intervals.

The plane-sweep paradigm for solving the geometric problems discussed earlier in this section (e.g., the rectangle intersection problem) assumes that the set of rectangles is processed only once. It can be shown that for many of these problems, plane-sweep methods yield a theoretically optimal solution. A disadvantage is that such solutions assume a static environment.

In contrast, in a dynamic environment where update operations occur frequently (i.e., rectangles are added and deleted), the plane-sweep approach is less attractive. Plane-sweep methods require that the endpoints of all rectangles be known a priori and that the

---

[5] When the data is not uniformly distributed, the hierarchical methods described in Section 3.4 may prove more attractive since the bins are of different sizes. Such methods make use of a tree traversal in the order of a space-filling curve (see Section 2.1.1.2 of Chapter 2) instead of sweeping a line across one dimension.

endpoints be sorted prior to the sweep pass. This is not a major problem as it is easy to maintain a dynamically changing set of points in sorted order. A more serious problem is that in a dynamic environment, the sweep pass of a plane-sweep algorithm will usually have to be reexecuted since there is no data structure corresponding to it. Methods based on persistent search trees [509, 1675] may be useful in avoiding the reexecution of the sweep pass.

Dynamic environments can also arise when the rectangle objects are themselves in motion, and thus their motion is what leads to the occurrence of update operations (e.g., in moving objects databases). For example, a typical query seeks the number of moving objects that are within a query window at a particular instance or interval of time (e.g., [930]). One way to answer such queries is to use some of the representations that are based on object hierarchies, such as the parametric R-tree [296], TPR-tree [1610], and TPR*-tree [1855] mentioned in Section 2.1.5.2.3 of Chapter 2. Examples of related queries are aggregation queries such as the maximum number of moving objects that are within a query window at any time (e.g., [351, 1560]). They have received attention in constraint databases (e.g., [1559]) and spatiotemporal databases (e.g, [1203]) and are not discussed further here.

Exercises

1. The rectangle intersection problem is a special case of the problem of determining if any two of a set of N lines in the plane intersect. Give an $O(N \cdot \log_2 N)$ algorithm to solve the line intersection problem.

2. Suppose that you are given a set of N vertical line segments in the plane, say V, and a horizontal line segment, say H. Representing V as a segment tree, give an $O(\log_2^2 N + F)$ algorithm to find all elements of V that intersect H that uses $O(N \cdot \log_2 N)$ space. F is the number of intersecting elements.

3. Suppose that you are given a set of N arbitrary line segments in the plane, say L, and a rectilinear rectangle, say R. Using one-dimensional range trees and segment trees, give an $O(\log_2^2 N + F)$ algorithm to find all elements of L that intersect R that uses $O(N \cdot \log_2 N)$ space. F is the number of intersecting elements.

4. Suppose that, instead of reporting all intersecting rectangles, you want to report only if there is at least one pair of intersecting rectangles (including the case that a rectangle is totally enclosed in another rectangle). Once again, a plane-sweep method can be used with a scan from left to right. However, Bentley and Ottmann [177] suggest the use of a balanced binary search tree instead of a segment tree to organize the sorted list of bottom and top boundaries of the currently active rectangles during the sweep pass. Show how this technique can be used to yield a simpler $O(N \cdot \log_2 N)$ algorithm to detect the existence of an intersection. Assume that the boundaries are stored in both leaf and nonleaf nodes in the tree.

5. Why can you not use the balanced binary search tree method of Exercise 4 instead of the segment tree to report all intersections between rectangles? Give an example in which it fails to detect an intersection.

6. Given a collection of N rectangles with F intersections between their vertical and horizontal boundaries, how would you use the balanced binary search tree method of Exercise 4 to find all the intersections in $O(N \cdot \log_2 N + F)$ time and $O(N)$ space? In this problem, if rectangle A is totally contained in rectangle B, then A and B do not intersect.

7. Assume that the result of Exercise 6 is used to detect all rectangles that have intersections between their horizontal and vertical boundaries. Add another pass using a segment tree to report all pairs of rectangles in which one rectangle is totally enclosed by the other in $O(N \cdot \log_2 N + F)$ time. F is the number of pairs of rectangles that satisfy the query.

8. Using a segment tree, devise a plane-sweep algorithm to report all rectangles that are contained in other rectangles. In other words, for each rectangle in a collection of rectangles, report all the rectangles that are contained in it.

9. The segment tree can be adapted to represent rectilinear rectangles in a manner analogous to the way in which the one-dimensional range tree is extended to solve two-dimensional range

The unit-segment tree is analogous to a region quadtree in one dimension. This analogy is exploited by van Leeuwen and Wood [1145] in solving measure problems in higher-dimensional spaces (i.e, $d > 2$). A typical problem is the computation of the volume that is occupied by the union of a collection of three-dimensional rectangular parallelepipeds. In this case, they use a plane-sweep solution that sorts the boundaries of the parallelepipeds along one direction (say z) and then sweeps a plane (instead of a line) parallel to the x-y plane across it. At any instant, the plane consists of a collection of cross sections (i.e., two-dimensional rectangles). This collection is represented using a region quadtree, which is the two-dimensional analog of the segment tree.

The region quadtree, in this case, is a complete quadtree. It is built as follows. Note that there is a maximum of $2 \cdot N$ boundaries in all directions. First, sort the x and y boundaries of the parallelepipeds (removing duplicates), obtaining $x_0, x_1, \ldots, x_p$ ($p < 2 \cdot N$), $y_0, y_1, \ldots, y_q$ ($q < 2 \cdot N$), and $2^{h-1} \leq \max(p, q) < 2^h$. Assume, without loss of generality, that the boundaries are distinct. If they are not, then there are fewer subdivisions. Also, add enough subdivision lines so that there are 2^h subdivisions in each of x and y. This grid is irregular (i.e., the cells are of varying size). Next, form a fixed (termed *regular*) grid with an origin at the lower-left corner. Each cell in the regular grid with a lower-left corner at (i, j) corresponds to the cell in the irregular grid with (x_i, y_j) as its lower-left corner and is of size $(x_{i+1} - x_i) \times (y_{j+1} - y_j)$.

A node at level i in the region quadtree represents the two-dimensional interval corresponding to the Cartesian product of the intervals $[x_p : x_{p+2^i})$ and $[y_q : y_{q+2^i})$, where $p \bmod 2^i$ and $q \bmod 2^i$ are 0. The presence of a cross section of a particular parallelepiped (a rectangle) is represented by *marking* the nodes that overlap it (recall the definition of marking in the discussion of the computation of area). The rectangle (corresponding to the cross section) is inserted in the quadtree in a top-down manner that is analogous to the way a line segment is inserted in a segment tree. As in the computation of the area, we only need to record how many active parallelepipeds contain a particular node (i.e., how many times it is marked) and not their identities.

The volume is computed in the same way as the area. The difference is that now we keep track of the total area of the parts of the scan plane, say A_i at halting point Z_i, that overlap the cross sections of the parallelepipeds that are active just to the left of Z_i. This quantity is adjusted at each halting point by inserting or deleting the cross sections from the quadtree. The total volume is obtained by accumulating the product of this quantity with the difference between the current halting point and the next halting point—that is, $A_i \cdot (Z_i - Z_{i-1})$.

Insertion and deletion of a rectangle in a region quadtree is an $O(N)$ process, since a rectangle can appear in at most $O(N)$ nodes (see Exercise 12 in Section 2.1.2.4 of Chapter 2). Thus, we see that a plane-sweep algorithm employing the region quadtree will execute in time $O(N \cdot \log_2 N + N^2)$ or $O(N^2)$ as there are $O(N)$ halting points. The $O(N \cdot \log_2 N)$ term is contributed by the initial sort of the boundaries of the parallelepipeds.

This is an improvement over a solution of Bentley [166] that recursively performs a plane sweep across each of the planes (i.e., it reduces the area problem to N one-dimensional subproblems) for an execution time of $O(N^2 \cdot \log_2 N)$. Generalizing van Leeuwen and Wood's algorithm to d dimensions reduces the time requirement of Bentley's solution from $O(N^{d-1} \cdot \log_2 N)$ to $O(N^{d-1})$; however, this increases the space requirement from $O(N)$ to $O(N^2)$. The new bounds are achieved by recursively reducing the d-dimensional problem to N $(d-1)$-dimensional problems until we obtain the three-dimensional case and then solving each three-dimensional problem as discussed above.

The same technique is used by Lee [1126] to develop an algorithm to compute the maximum number of rectangles with a nonempty intersection (also termed a *maximum clique problem* [801]). Given N rectangles, the two-dimensional problem can be solved using a segment tree in $O(N \cdot \log_2 N)$ time and $O(N)$ space. In d dimensions, an adaptation of the region quadtree is used that solves the problem in $O(N^{d-1})$ time and $O(N^2)$ space. Note that these algorithms only yield the cardinality of the maximum clique; they do not report its members. The algorithm can be modified to report the members of the maximum clique with the same time bound but using $O(N \cdot \log_2 N)$ space when $d = 2$ and $O(N^3)$ space when $d > 2$. Lee points out that the solution to the maximum clique problem can be used to solve a rectangle placement problem (see Exercise 13).

Overmars and Yap [1445] have shown how to solve the d-dimensional measure problem in $O(N^{d/2} \cdot \log_2 N)$ time with $O(N)$ space. For $d \geq 3$, this is a significant improvement over the solutions of Bentley [166] and van Leeuwen and Wood [1145] described above. Below, we present Overmars and Yap's construction for three dimensions; the generalization to $d > 3$ is relatively straightforward. They also use a plane-sweep solution that sorts the boundaries of the parallelepipeds along one direction (say z) and then sweeps a plane parallel to the x-y plane across it.

At any instant, the plane consists of a collection of cross sections (i.e., two-dimensional rectangles). Elements of the collection are termed *active rectangles*. This collection is represented as a set of cells (very much like buckets). Each halting point of the sweep pass requires inserting or deleting an active rectangle. Overmars and Yap are able to perform each insertion into and deletion from the appropriate cells in $O(\sqrt{N} \cdot \log_2 N)$ time. This means that their algorithm runs in $O(N \cdot \sqrt{N} \cdot \log_2 N)$ time. The key to their algorithm is to partition the space into cells of a particular size so that their contents (i.e., rectangles) form a trellis (described below) and to use the properties of a trellis in an efficient way.

A *trellis* inside a rectangular cell is a collection of rectangles such that, for each rectangle, either its left and right (i.e., vertical) boundaries coincide with the cell boundary, or its top and bottom (i.e., horizontal) boundaries coincide with the cell boundary (see Figure 3.8). A *horizontal rectangle* is a rectangle whose left and right boundaries coincide with the cell boundary (e.g., rectangle H), and a *vertical rectangle* is a rectangle whose top and bottom boundaries coincide with the cell boundary (e.g., rectangle V).

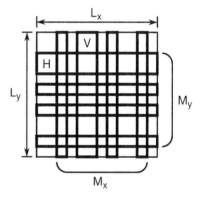

Figure 3.8
A trellis.

Trellises are useful because of the following property. Suppose that the cell is of width L_x and height L_y. Let M_x be the aggregate length of the projections of the union of the vertical rectangles on the x axis, and let M_y be the aggregate length of the projections of the union of the horizontal rectangles on the y axis. The area of the union of the rectangles forming the trellis is $M_x \cdot L_y + M_y \cdot L_x - M_x \cdot M_y$ (see Exercise 15).

To keep track of the total area of the union of rectangles in a trellis, it is necessary to keep track of only the lengths of the projections on the axes (i.e., the numbers M_x and M_y). This can be done by using two segment trees to store the two sets of projected intervals. It follows that if all the rectangles that are ever active within a cell form a trellis, and if there are k such rectangles, then the measure of the union of the rectangles can be updated at a cost of $O(\log_2 k)$ per insertion or deletion. Thus, the geometry of the trellis enables the exploitation of the fullness of the cell (i.e., bucket).

To exploit the properties of trellises, the plane containing the rectangles is partitioned as follows. First, the horizontal range is split into $\sqrt{N}$ intervals such that the interior of each interval contains at most $2 \cdot \sqrt{N}$ projections of vertical boundaries of rectangles. This partitions the region into $\sqrt{N}$ vertical *slabs*. Next, each slab is partitioned by horizontal segments into *cells*.

The partitioning within each slab makes use of the concept of a V-rectangle and an H-rectangle. If the interior of a slab contains at least one of the left and right (i.e., vertical) boundaries of a rectangle, then we call the rectangle a *V-rectangle* with respect to the slab. If the interior of the slab does not contain either of the left or right boundaries of a rectangle but does contain some portion of the rectangle's top or bottom (i.e., horizontal) boundaries, then we call the rectangle an *H-rectangle* with respect to the slab.

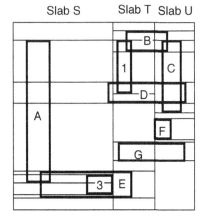

Figure 3.9
The partition of the collection of rectangles of Figure 3.1 into slabs and cells.

The partitioning of slabs into cells is performed as follows. Within each slab, a horizontal line is drawn through each top and bottom boundary of a V-rectangle and through every $\sqrt{N}$th top or bottom boundary of an H-rectangle. Since there are $\sqrt{N}$ slabs, it can be shown that the partitioning results in a total of $O(N)$ cells. Figure 3.9 is the result of applying this partition to the collection of rectangles in Figure 3.1, where query rectangles 1 and 3 are treated as members of the collection. The slabs are labeled S, T, and U. For example, in slab T, rectangles 1, B, D, and G are V-rectangles, while rectangle D is an H-rectangle.

To see that the partitioning does indeed yield $O(N)$ cells, we observe that there are at most $2 \cdot \sqrt{N}$ V-rectangles in each slab because of the way the x axis was partitioned. Therefore, there are at most $4 \cdot \sqrt{N}$ top and bottom boundaries of V-rectangles in each slab. Moreover, at most $2 \cdot \sqrt{N}$ top and bottom boundaries of H-rectangles are chosen to be cell boundaries within a slab. Hence, there are at most $6 \cdot \sqrt{N}$ cells in each slab. Our desired result of $O(N)$ cells follows since there are $\sqrt{N}$ slabs.

It is not hard to show (see Exercise 16) that the following properties hold for the partitioning:

1. The boundary of each rectangle intersects at most $O(\sqrt{N})$ cells.

2. Each cell intersects the boundary of at most $O(\sqrt{N})$ rectangles.

3. For each cell, the intersection of the rectangles with the cell forms a trellis.

To exploit the cell structure efficiently, a tree having these cells as its leaf nodes is built as follows. Within each slab, vertically adjacent cells are merged (creating a father node). This process continues until there is one node per slab. Then, neighboring slabs are merged. This tree, called an *orthogonal partition tree*, is a variant of the BSP tree (see Sections 1.5.1.4 of Chapter 1 and 2.1.3.1 of Chapter 2). The x coordinate value serves as the discriminator near the root of the tree, while the y coordinate value serves as the discriminator at the deeper nodes.

Since there are $O(\sqrt{N})$ slabs and $O(\sqrt{N})$ cells per slab, the orthogonal partition tree has a maximum depth of $O(\log_2 N)$. Figure 3.10 partially illustrates the orthogonal partition tree for Figure 3.9. In the figure, we only expand the portion corresponding to slab T (containing 11 cells). The cells in each slab are numbered in sequence starting from the top. Thus, the cell labeled T_i corresponds to the ith cell from the top of slab T.

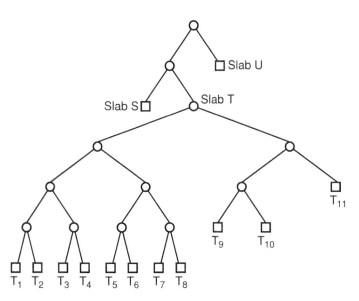

Figure 3.10
The orthogonal partition tree for Figure 3.9. Only slab T is fully expanded.

As the plane sweep progresses, data rectangles (i.e., two-dimensional cross sections of parallelepipeds) are added to the tree (i.e., become active) and deleted from it (i.e., become inactive). Each node P in the orthogonal partition tree has associated with it five fields, called LEFT, RIGHT, RECT, COUNT, and AREA. LEFT(P) and RIGHT(P) are the left and right children, respectively, of P. RECT(P) is the rectangle consisting of the union of the cells that are descended from P. This rectangle is called the *associated rectangle* of P. COUNT(P) is the number of active data rectangles that contain RECT(P). AREA(P) is the area of the intersection of the union of the active data rectangles with RECT(P). Associated with each leaf node are two segment trees for the trellis of rectangles in the corresponding cell. These segment trees store the projection of the vertical rectangles on the x axis and the projection of the horizontal rectangles on the y axis.

Initially, all segment trees associated with leaf nodes are empty, and all AREA and COUNT fields are zero. To insert rectangle R in the tree, we start at the root and proceed recursively as follows. Assume that we are processing node P. There are three cases. If rectangle R contains RECT(P), then we increment COUNT(P). Otherwise, there are two cases, depending on whether P is a leaf node. If P is a leaf node, then, by property 3, rectangle R is either a vertical or a horizontal rectangle of a trellis, and we insert it into the appropriate segment tree. If P is not a leaf node, then we insert rectangle R into the two children of P.

In all three cases, after the insertion, if COUNT(P) is nonzero, then we set AREA(P) to the area of RECT(P). Otherwise, if COUNT(P) is zero, then we set AREA(P) to the sum of AREA(LEFT(P)) and AREA(RIGHT(P)) (for a nonleaf node) or to the area of the trellis of rectangles in the corresponding cell (for a leaf node). Deleting a rectangle is done similarly (see Exercise 17).

Using the above structure, inserting rectangle R (i.e., making it active) requires at most $O(\sqrt{N} \cdot \log_2 N)$ time. To see that this is true, we observe that two classes of nodes are visited: leaf nodes and nonleaf nodes. By property 1, the boundary of any data rectangle intersects at most $O(\sqrt{N})$ leaf nodes. Updating the two segment trees of each leaf node intersected by R requires at most $O(\log_2 N)$ time. Therefore, $O(\sqrt{N} \cdot \log_2 N)$ time is sufficient to update the AREA fields of all leaf nodes that intersect R. For each leaf node that is visited, the path from the root visits at most $O(\log_2 N)$ nodes, for a total of $O(\sqrt{N} \cdot \log_2 N)$ nodes. For each leaf node that has been visited, the children of at most $O(\log_2 N)$ of the nodes that were encountered along the path starting from the root have their COUNT field updated. This accounts for all of the nodes that have their COUNT field updated.

The algorithm of Overmars and Yap uses $O(N \cdot \sqrt{N})$ space since there are $O(N)$ segment trees (one per cell), each using $O(\sqrt{N})$ storage (see Exercise 18). Overmars and Yap [1445] show that the total storage requirement can be reduced to $O(N)$ by using a technique called *streaming* due to Edelsbrunner and Overmars [544]. The basic idea behind streaming is to build only a portion of the tree at a time and to perform all updates to that portion of the tree together. In other words, the updates within the structure are grouped sequentially according to location within the structure, rather than according to the time at which they occur. For more details, see [544].

Exercises

1. Devise an $O(N \cdot \log_2 N)$ algorithm to compute the total length of a collection of N parallel line segments that can overlap. Overlapping parts should be counted only once.

2. Compute the total area spanned by the collection of rectangles in Figure 3.1. Letting $(x_{min}, y_{min}, x_{max}, y_{max})$ represent a rectangle, rectangles A, B, C, D, E, F, and G are at (3,6,8,36), (25,34,34,38), (33,21,37,36), (21,23,38,27), (6,3,26,8), (31,15,35,19), and (23,11,38,14), respectively. Overlapping parts should be counted only once.

3. Why is no node marked more than once in the computation of the total area spanned by the collection of rectangles in Figure 3.1? In particular, what about the nodes corresponding to intervals [23,34) and [34,36)?

4. Prove that an algorithm that uses a segment tree to compute the total area spanned by a collection of N rectangles uses $O(N)$ space.

5. Give a procedure SWEEPAREA to compute the area of a collection of possibly overlapping rectangles. Use the plane-sweep approach with a segment tree. You must code procedures to insert and delete the vertical boundaries of the rectangles into and from the segment tree.

6. Give a procedure SWEEPPERIMETER to compute the perimeter of a collection of possibly overlapping rectangles. Use the plane-sweep approach with a segment tree. You must code procedures to insert and delete the vertical boundaries of the rectangles from the segment tree.

7. Give a procedure MAX2DCLIQUE to compute the cardinality of the maximum clique of a collection of possibly overlapping rectangles. Use the plane-sweep approach with a segment tree.

8. Modify your solution to Exercise 7 so that the identities of the members of the maximum clique are also reported, not just the cardinality of the clique.

9. Give a procedure SWEEPVOLUME to compute the volume of a collection of possibly overlapping three-dimensional rectangles. Use the plane-sweep approach with a region quadtree. You must code procedures to insert and delete the x-y boundaries of the rectangles into and from the region quadtree.

10. Give a procedure SWEEPSURFACEAREA to compute the surface area of a collection of possibly overlapping three-dimensional rectangles. Use the plane-sweep approach with a region quadtree. You must code procedures to insert and delete the x-y boundaries of the rectangles into and from the region quadtree.

11. Give a procedure MAX3DCLIQUE to compute the cardinality of the maximum clique of a collection of possibly overlapping three-dimensional rectangles. Use the plane-sweep approach with a region quadtree.

12. Modify your solution to Exercise 11 so that the identities of the members of the maximum clique are also reported, not just the cardinality of the clique.

13. Consider the following rectangle placement problem. Given n points in a two-dimensional space and a rectangular window, say R, whose sides are parallel to the coordinate axes, find a point in the plane at which the window can be centered so that it contains a maximum number of points in its interior. The window is not permitted to be rotated; it can be translated only.

14. Consider a variation of the rectangle placement problem of Exercise 13 where the points are weighted. Find the location of R in which the sum of the weights of the points in it is maximized.

15. Consider a trellis inside a rectangular cell of width L_x and height L_y. Let M_x be the aggregate length of the projections of the union of the vertical rectangles on the horizontal axis, and let M_y be the aggregate length of the projections of the union of the horizontal rectangles on the vertical axis. Show that the area of the union of the rectangles forming the trellis is $M_x \cdot L_y + M_y \cdot L_x - M_x \cdot M_y$.

16. Show that properties 1, 2, and 3 used in the construction of Overmars and Yap's solution to the measure problem hold for $d = 3$.

17. Give an algorithm to delete a rectangle from an orthogonal partition tree when using Overmars and Yap's solution to the measure problem for $d = 3$.

18. Prove that each segment tree in Overmars and Yap's solution to the measure problem in three dimensions for N parallelepipeds uses $O(\sqrt{N})$ space.

19. Can you use Overmars and Yap's approach to compute the size of the maximum clique in time $O(N^{d/2} \cdot \log_2 N)$ with $O(N)$ space for N rectangles in a d-dimensional space?

20. Suppose that you apply Overmars and Yap's approach to report the members of the maximum clique for N rectangles in a d-dimensional space. What are the time and space requirements? In particular, how much space is needed to store the segment trees in each of the cells?

21. Why can you not use a $(d-1)$-dimensional region quadtree (e.g., an octree in three dimensions) to compute the measure of a d-dimensional space containing N rectangles in $O(N^2)$ time—that is, why can you not represent a $(d-1)$-dimensional cross section by a $(d-1)$-dimensional quadtree to get the execution time of the algorithm down to $O(N^2)$ and $O(N^{d-1})$ space?

22. Consider a collection of N right triangles so that two of the sides are always parallel to the x and y axes, and the third side has a negative slope. Devise an algorithm to compute the area of the collection. Can you get its execution time and space requirements to be $O(N \cdot \log_2 N)$ and $O(N)$, respectively?

23. Repeat Exercise 22 permitting the third side of the right triangle to have an arbitrary slope.

24. (Mark H. Overmars) Consider a collection of N arbitrary triangles. Devise an algorithm to compute the area of the collection. Can you get its execution time and space requirements to be $O(N \cdot \log_2 N)$ and $O(N)$, respectively?

3.3 Point-Based Methods

In this section, we first discuss the representation of rectangles as points (Section 3.3.1), and then examine the representation of the collection of points (Section 3.3.2) using some of the methods described in Chapter 1. We conclude with a summary of some of the properties of the representative point method (Section 3.3.3).

3.3.1 Representative Points

A common solution to the problem of representing a collection of objects is to approximate elements of the collection by simpler objects. One technique is to represent each object by using one of a number of primitive shapes that contain it. The discussion in Section 2.1.5.2 of Chapter 2 is primarily in the context of rectangle primitives; however, other shapes, such as triangles, circles, cubes, parallelepipeds, cylinders, spheres, and so on, can also be used.

This approach is motivated, in part, by the fact that it is easier to test the containing objects for intersection than it is to perform the test using the actual objects. For example, it is easier to compute the intersection of two rectangles than of two polygons for which the rectangles serve as approximations. More complex approximations can be created by composing Boolean operations and geometric transformations on instances of the primitive types. In fact, this is the basis of the constructive solid geometry (CSG) technique of representing three-dimensional objects [1555, 1935] as discussed in Section 2.2 of Chapter 2.

The advantage of using such approximations is that each primitive can be described by a small set of parameters and can, in turn, represent a large class of objects. In particular, if primitive P is described by d parameters, then each set of parameter values defines a point in a d-dimensional space assigned to the class of objects in which the members are all the possible instances of primitive P. Such a point is termed a *representative point*. Note that a representative point and the class to which it belongs completely define all of the topological and geometric properties of the corresponding object.

Most primitives can be described by more than one set of parameters. For example, using Cartesian coordinates, a circle is described by a representative point in three-dimensional space consisting of the x and y coordinate values of its center and the value of its radius. On the other hand, using polar coordinates, a circle can also be described by a representative point in three-dimensional space consisting of the ρ and θ coordinate values of its center and the value of its radius. For other primitives, the choices are even more varied. For example, the class of objects formed by a rectangle in two dimensions with sides parallel to the x and y coordinate axes is described by a representative point in four-dimensional space. Some choices for the parameters are as follows:

1. The x and y coordinate values of two diagonally opposite corners of the rectangle (e.g., the lower left and upper right), termed a *corner transformation* [1709]

2. The x and y coordinate values of a corner of the rectangle, together with its horizontal and vertical extents

3. The x and y coordinate values of the centroid of the rectangle, together with its horizontal and vertical extents (i.e., the horizontal and vertical distances from the centroid to the relevant sides)

The actual choice depends on the type of operations that we intend to perform on the objects formed by them.

Different parameters have different effects on the queries, and thus making the right choice is important. Hinrichs and Nievergelt [839, 841] lump the parameters into two classes: location and extension. Location parameters specify the coordinate values of a point, such as a corner or a centroid. On the other hand, extension parameters specify size, for example, the radius of a circle. This distinction is always possible for objects that can be described as Cartesian products of spheres of varying dimension.

Many common objects can be described in this way. For example, a rectangle is the Cartesian product of two one-dimensional spheres, and a cylinder is the Cartesian product of a one-dimensional sphere and a two-dimensional sphere. Whenever such a distinction between location and extension parameters can be drawn, the proximity queries described in the opening section of this chapter (i.e., intersection, containment, and enclosure) have cone-shaped search regions. The tip of the cone is usually in the subspace of the location parameters and has the shape of the query point or query object.

The importance of making the right choice can be seen by examining the class of one-dimensional intervals on a straight line. As an example, consider the collection of rectangles given in Figure 3.1. Each rectangle can be represented as the Cartesian product of two one-dimensional spheres corresponding to the sides that are given as horizontal and vertical intervals in Figure 3.11. These intervals can be represented using any of the three representations enumerated above.

Representation 1 yields an ordered pair (L, R) where L and R correspond to the left and right endpoints, respectively, of the interval. Figure 3.12 shows how the horizontal intervals are represented using this method. In most applications, the intervals are small.

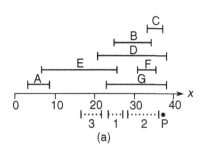

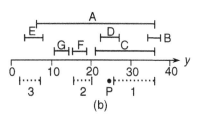

Figure 3.11
The (a) horizontal (i.e., x) and (b) vertical (i.e., y) intervals corresponding to the sides of the rectangles in Figure 3.1. Solid lines correspond to the rectangles in the collection, and dotted lines correspond to the query rectangles.

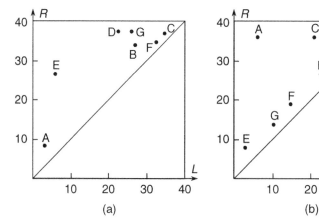

Figure 3.12
Representation of the (a) horizontal (i.e., x) and (b) vertical (i.e., y) intervals of Figure 3.1 as ordered pairs (L,R), where L and R are the left and right endpoints, respectively, of the interval (i.e., representation 1).

Therefore, for representation 1, *L* and *R* are very close in value. $L < R$ means that the representative points are clustered near and above the diagonal and that the lower half of the underlying space is empty.

The clustering means that the representative points are not well distributed. Therefore, any data structure for storing the collection of the representative points that is based on organizing the embedding space from which the data is drawn (e.g., address computation) into rectangular-shaped blocks, in contrast to one based on the actual representative points that are stored (e.g., comparative search), will have to pay a price for the large empty areas in the embedding space (e.g., at least one-half below the diagonal). Faloutsos and Rego [589] use representation 1 and overcome this price for the collection of the representative points by ignoring the empty half of the underlying space (i.e., embedding space in this discussion) and decompose the isoceles triangle corresponding to the nonempty half of the underlying space with a quadtreelike regular decomposition into four congruent isoceles triangles termed *triangular cells* (or *tri-cells* for short). This process is applied recursively whenever there are too many objects associated with a particular triangular cell. Note that if all the intervals are small (or have approximately the same width), the clustering about the diagonal (or a line parallel to the diagonal) results in decomposition of all of the triangular cells through which the diagonal passes.

On the other hand, Hinrichs and Nievergelt point out that separating the location parameters from the extension parameters results in a smaller underlying space (especially when the rectangles and corresponding intervals are small) that is filled more uniformly (but see Exercise 9). For example, representation 3 is used in Figure 3.13, where the horizontal intervals are represented as an ordered pair (C_x, D_x) such that C_x is the centroid of the interval and D_x is the distance from the centroid to the end of the interval. Note that no matter which representative point is used, some part of the underlying space will be empty. In the case of representation 1, the empty space consists of half the size of the underlying space and is a direct result of the stipulation that the starting endpoints of intervals are less than the terminating endpoints. In the case of representation 3, the empty space consists of two triangular regions at the upper-left and upper-right corners of the underlying space and is a direct result of a stipulation that both the starting and terminating endpoints of intervals lie in the underlying space. Of course, we could allow intervals that extend beyond the underlying space, but they are not likely to arise in a practical setting. The advantage of representation 3 over representation 1 is that these empty regions are generally very small since the intervals are small. Thus, the effect of the presence of the empty region is negligible (see Exercise 10). Representation 2 is similar to representation 3 (see Exercise 7).

Bearing the above considerations in mind, representation 3 seems to be the most appropriate. In such a case, a rectangle is represented by the four-tuple (C_x, D_x, C_y, D_y), interpreted as the Cartesian product of a horizontal and a vertical one-dimensional interval—that is, (C_x, D_x) and (C_y, D_y), respectively.[8] This representation is used by Hinrichs and Nievergelt [839, 841], and the following examples of its utility are due to them.

Proximity queries involving point and rectangular query objects are easy to implement. Their answers are conic-shaped regions in the four-dimensional space formed by the Cartesian product of the two interval query regions. This is equivalent to computing the intersection of the two query regions but is much more efficient. It also enables us to visualize our examples since the horizontal and vertical intervals correspond to the projections of the query responses on the C_x–D_x and C_y–D_y planes, respectively.

We illustrate our discussion with the collection of rectangles given in Figure 3.1, along with query point P and query rectangles 1, 2, and 3. Note that when the query objects are not individual points or rectangles, then the representation of a rectangle as

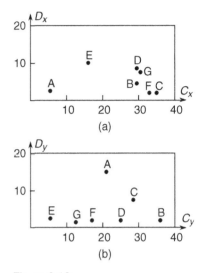

Figure 3.13
Representation of the (a) horizontal (i.e., *x*) and (b) vertical (i.e., *y*) intervals of Figure 3.1 as ordered pairs (C_x, D_x) and (C_y, D_y), where C_x and D_x are the centers and half-lengths, respectively, of the *x* interval, and C_y and D_y are the centers and halflengths, respectively, of the *y* interval (i.e, representation 3).

---

[8] The notation (C_x, D_x) corresponds to a point in a two-dimensional space. It is *not* the open one-dimensional interval whose left and right endpoints are at C_x and D_x, respectively.

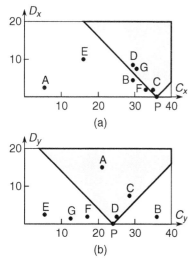

Figure 3.14
Search region for a point query on P for the (a) horizontal (i.e., *x*) and (b) vertical (i.e., *y*) intervals of Figure 3.1 when using representation 3. All intervals containing P are in the shaded regions. Intervals appearing in the shaded regions of both (a) and (b) correspond to rectangles that contain P.

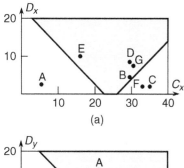

(a)

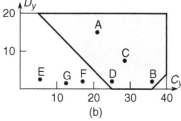

(b)

Figure 3.15
Search region for a window query on query rectangle 1 of Figure 3.1 for the (a) horizontal (i.e., *x*) and (b) vertical (i.e., *y*) intervals of that figure when using representation 3. All intervals that contain points of rectangle 1 are in the shaded regions. Intervals appearing in the shaded regions of both (a) and (b) correspond to rectangles that intersect rectangle 1.

the Cartesian product of two orthogonal intervals is not that useful (e.g., query regions in the form of an arbitrary line or circle as in Exercises 13 and 14, respectively).

For a point query, we wish to determine all intervals that contain a given point, say p. These intervals form a cone-shaped region with a tip that is an interval of length zero centered at p.[9] For example, the horizontal and vertical intervals containing P are shown shaded in Figure 3.14(a, b), respectively. To find all of the rectangles that contain a given point, we access a specific region in the four-dimensional space defined by the Cartesian product of the horizontal and vertical point-in-interval query regions. For example, P is in the set of rectangles with representative points in the intersection of the shaded portion of Figure 3.14(a, b)—that is, {C,D} is the intersection of {C,D,G} and {A,C,D}.

A window query is a bit more complex than a point query. In this case, the one-dimensional analog of this query is to find all intervals that overlap a given interval, say I. Again, the set of overlapping intervals consists of a cone-shaped region with a tip that is the interval I. For example, the horizontal and vertical intervals that overlap the horizontal and vertical sides of query rectangle 1 are shown shaded in Figure 3.15(a,b), respectively. To find all of the rectangles that overlap the query window, we access a specific region in the four-dimensional space defined by the Cartesian product of the horizontal and vertical interval-in-interval query regions. For example, query rectangle 1 overlaps the intersection of the shaded portion of Figure 3.15(a, b)—that is, {B,D} is the intersection of {B,D,E,G} and {A,B,C,D}.

For a containment query, the one-dimensional analog is to find all the intervals that are totally contained within a given interval, say I. The set of contained intervals consists of a cone-shaped region with a tip at I that opens in the direction of smaller extent values. This makes sense as all intervals within the cone are totally contained in the interval represented by the tip. For example, the horizontal and vertical intervals contained in the horizontal and vertical sides of query rectangle 2 are shown shaded in Figure 3.16(a, b), respectively. To find all of the rectangles that are contained in the query window, we access a specific region in the four-dimensional space defined by the Cartesian product of the horizontal and vertical contained-in-interval query regions. For example, query rectangle 2 contains the intersection of the shaded portion of Figure 3.16(a, b)—that is, {F}.

For an enclosure query, the one-dimensional analog is to find all the intervals that enclose the given interval, say I. The set of enclosing intervals consists of a cone-shaped region with a tip at I that opens in the direction of larger extent values. This is logical because the interval represented by the tip is contained (i.e., enclosed) by all intervals within the cone. To find all the rectangles that enclose the query window, we access a specific region in the four-dimensional space defined by the Cartesian product of the horizontal and vertical enclose-interval query regions. For example, the horizontal and vertical intervals that enclose the horizontal and vertical sides of query rectangle 3 are shown shaded in Figure 3.17 (a, b), respectively. For example, query rectangle 3 contains the intersection of the shaded portion of Figure 3.17(a, b)—that is, {E}.

In spite of the relative ease with which the above queries are implemented using the representative point method with representation 3, there are queries for which it is ill suited. For example, suppose that we wish to solve the rectangle intersection problem. In fact, no matter which of the three representations we use, to solve this problem we must intersect each rectangle with every other rectangle. The problem is that none of these representations is area oriented: they reduce a spatial object to a single representative point.

Although the extent of the object is reflected in the representative point, the final mapping of the representative point in the four-dimensional space does not result in the

---

[9] McCreight [1265] uses the same technique in conjunction with representation 1 to solve this problem (see Exercise 9). Note, though, that the search region is rectangle shaped in this case.

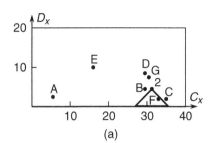

(a)   (b)

Figure 3.16
Search region for a containment query on query rectangle 2 of Figure 3.1 for the (a) horizontal (i.e., x) and (b) vertical (i.e., y) intervals of that figure when using representation 3. All intervals contained in one of the intervals forming rectangle 2 are in the shaded regions. Intervals appearing in the shaded regions of both (a) and (b) correspond to rectangles contained in rectangle 2.

preservation of nearness in the two-dimensional space from which the rectangles are drawn. In other words, two rectangles may be very close (and possibly overlap), yet the Euclidean distance between their representative points in four-dimensional space may be quite large, thereby masking the overlapping relationship between them. For example, even though rectangles B and D intersect query rectangle 1, we cannot easily tell if they intersect each other, except by checking their sizes.

So far, our discussion has emphasized representation 3. Nevertheless, of the three representations (i.e., 1, 2, and 3), representation 1 is a bit easier to work with in many applications. Recall that representations 2 and 3 have a component that indicates the extent of the rectangle (i.e., its width and height). In most applications, it is rare for this information (i.e., the extent) to be used on its own. On the other hand, it is very common (especially in geometric operations) to need to know the coordinate values of the corners of the rectangles or its sides (i.e., faces in higher dimensions).

Using representation 1, the two extreme corners specify the minimum and maximum coordinate values in the rectangle for any coordinate axis. The implementations of most geometric operations, such as point in rectangle, rectangle intersection, and distance from a point to a rectangle or between two rectangles, make use of this information. For instance, when testing whether a point is in a rectangle, we know that a point is not in the rectangle if, for any coordinate axis, the particular coordinate value of the point is outside the particular coordinate range of the rectangle (i.e., less than the minimum or greater than the maximum). This means that if we are using representations 2 and 3, then additional operations need to be performed to obtain the coordinate values of one (in the case of representation 2) or two (in the case of representation 3) corners of the rectangles. Besides making the source code implementing geometric operations less readable, this increases the number of arithmetic operations. However, in some cases, we can use clever coding tricks for representations 2 and 3 such that not many more, or even the same number of, arithmetic operations are used (see Exercise 18). In addition, we do want to point out that knowing the values of the extents is not without merit as it does make certain computations easier, such as computing areas.

Although most of our discussion has been in the context of representations 1, 2, and 3, other representative points are also commonly used. In particular, interestingly, even though a rectangle whose sides are parallel to the x and y axes requires the unique specification of four values, it is also frequently modeled by a representative point in a two-dimensional space. The representative point corresponds to the centroid of the rectangle or to one of its corners (e.g., lower left).

If rectangles are not permitted to overlap, then the above two-valued representation is sufficient to ensure that no two rectangles have the same representative point. Of course, since two values do not uniquely specify the rectangle, the remaining values are retained

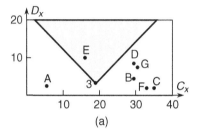

(a)

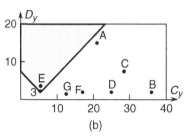

(b)

Figure 3.17
Search region for an enclosure query on query rectangle 3 of Figure 3.1 for the (a) horizontal (i.e., x) and (b) vertical (i.e., y) intervals of that figure when using representation 3. All intervals that enclose one of the intervals forming rectangle 3 are in the shaded regions. Intervals appearing in the shaded regions of both (a) and (b) correspond to rectangles that enclose rectangle 3.

in the record corresponding to the rectangle that is associated with the representative point. If rectangles are permitted to overlap, then such a representation means that there may be more than one record associated with a specific representative point.

Exercises

1. Suppose that the representative point corresponding to each rectangle is its centroid and that the collection of rectangles is represented using a PR quadtree. Moreover, rectangles are not permitted to overlap. What is the maximum horizontal or vertical separation of two rectangles with representative points that are contained in brother nodes in the PR quadtree (i.e., at level i in a $2^n \times 2^n$ image with a root at level n)?

2. Using the same representation and assumption about no overlapping rectangles as in Exercise 1, give an algorithm to determine the rectangle associated with a given point. If the representative point is stored in a block at level i, what is the maximum size of the neighborhood that may have to be searched to perform the operation?

3. How would you adapt representation 3 to represent a region quadtree for a binary image as a collection of representative points stored as a PR quadtree?

4. Prove that storing the region quadtree using a PR quadtree, such that the black nodes are representative points that correspond to the centers of black blocks, never requires more space (i.e., more nodes) than the region quadtree.

5. How would you represent a sphere in terms of location and extension parameters?

6. How many parameters are necessary to represent a rectangle in a general position in two-dimensional space?

7. Discuss the use of representation 2 for the representative points of the horizontal and vertical intervals making up the sides of a rectangle. Draw a graph such as Figures 3.11 and 3.12 for the horizontal intervals of Figure 3.1 using this representation. What are the advantages and disadvantages in comparison to representations 1 and 3?

8. Suppose that you are using representation 1 for the representative point of each interval in a collection of one-dimensional intervals. What is the shape of the search region for a query that seeks all the intervals that contain point p?

9. What is the relationship between representations 1 and 3?

10. The stipulation that the starting endpoints of intervals are less than their terminating endpoints means that one-half of the underlying space is empty in the case of representation 1. In the case of representation 3, the same stipulation means that the two triangular regions at the upper-left and upper-right corners of the underlying space are empty. Given that the intervals are drawn from the same space, the empty parts of the underlying space have the same area regardless of the representation. Therefore, assuming that the intervals are drawn from $[0, w]$, why do we say that representation 3 is superior to representation 1 when most of the intervals are very small (say of length s, where s is much smaller than w)?

11. How would you implement a point query for a collection of rectangles with a representative point that uses representation 1? Repeat for a point set query involving intersection (i.e., windowing), as well as the two subset relations (i.e., containment and enclosure).

12. How would you implement a point query for a collection of rectangles with a representative point that uses representation 2? Repeat for a point set query involving intersection (i.e., windowing), as well as the two subset relations (i.e., containment and enclosure).

13. Given a line from point (a, b) to point (c, d) and a collection of rectangles with a representative point that uses representation 3, describe the search regions for all of the rectangles intersected by the line and all the rectangles that enclose the line. Note that the line need not be horizontal or vertical.

14. Given a circle of radius r centered at point (a, b) and a collection of rectangles with a representative point that uses representation 3, describe the search regions for all of the rectangles intersected by the circle, the rectangles contained in their entirety in the circle, and the rectangles that enclose the circle.

15. Suppose that the representative point for a circle in the *x*-*y* plane uses representation 3. Describe the search regions for an object intersection query in which the object is (a) a point, (b) a line, (c) a circle, or (d) a rectangle.

16. Suppose that the representative point for a circle, say *C*, in the *x*-*y* plane uses representation 3. Describe the search regions for (a) all circles contained in *C* and, likewise, for (b) all circles enclosing *C*.

17. Consider a collection of two-dimensional objects and the implementation of a graphics editor that permits a graphical search-and-replace operation. Suppose that the objects are represented by their enclosing curves. Moreover, let each curve be approximated by a piecewise linear approximation. Give some possible representative points for the objects. Consider also the issue of translation, rotation, and scale invariance.

18. (Gísli R. Hjaltason) Compare the use of representations 1, 2, and 3 for the representative point of the horizontal and vertical intervals making up the sides of a rectangle when determining whether a point *p* is in rectangle *r*. Perform the comparison by giving the algorithms to compute the function and tabulate the number of different arithmetic and comparison operations. Note that on many CPU architectures, addition/subtraction and comparison operations are equally expensive. Note also that we ignore the cost of accessing the locations (i.e., via pointer manipulation) of the coordinate values of the point and the rectangle, which may itself involve some integer arithmetic operations, whereas the arithmetic operations on the coordinate values make use of floating-point arithmetic.

3.3.2 Collections of Representative Points

Once a specific representative point method is chosen for the rectangle, we can use the techniques discussed in Chapter 1 to organize the collection of representative points. Again, the choice of technique depends, to a large extent, on the type of operations that we will be performing. There are a number of techniques whose use has been proposed. In this section, we briefly describe the corner stitching method (Section 3.3.2.1) and the four-dimensional k-d tree (Section 3.3.2.2), as well as use of the grid file (Section 3.3.2.3), the LSD tree (Section 3.3.2.4), and two-dimensional representations, such as the PR quadtree and the k-d tree (Section 3.3.2.5).

3.3.2.1 Corner Stitching

Ousterhout [1439] represents the collection of representative points using a nonhierarchical approach where each rectangle, treated as if it were a point, is connected to its neighbors by means of links. This technique is termed *corner stitching*. In particular, for each rectangle, there are two links from the lower-left corner to the two neighbors to its left and bottom and two links from the top-right corner to the two neighbors to its top and right. This is analogous to using representation 1 for the representative point of the rectangle with no indexing to speak of for the individual rectangles.

The corner stitching representation imposes a partition of the plane that resembles a mosaic consisting of two types of tiles: space and solid. The solid tiles correspond to the rectangles. The space tiles correspond to the void space, if any, between the rectangles. The space tiles are maximal horizontal strips, which means that no space tile is adjacent to a space tile immediately to its left or right. The maximality restriction implies that the decomposition into space and solid tiles is unique.

Links exist between all types of tiles: solid tiles can be linked to both solid and space tiles, and likewise for space tiles. It can be shown that, for *N* rectangles, there are at most $3 \cdot N + 1$ space tiles (see Exercise 3). Figure 3.18 is an example of the space decomposition imposed by corner stitching for a nonoverlapping subset of the collection of rectangles given in Figure 3.1. The space tiles are delimited by solid and broken lines, while the rectangles are delimited by solid lines. The corner stitches (i.e., links) are also shown for some of the rectangles and space tiles. Although our discussion has been limited to the situation that the tiles are rectangles, corner stitching can also be used

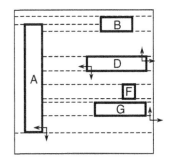

Figure 3.18
Example of the space decomposition imposed by corner stitching for a nonoverlapping subset of the collection of rectangles given in Figure 3.1. The rectangles are delimited by solid lines, while the space tiles are delimited by broken lines. Some of the corner stitches are shown.

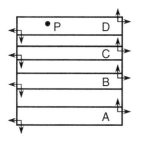

Figure 3.19
An example collection of rectangles A, B, C, and D illustrating the worst case of corner stitching when wishing to locate the rectangle associated with point P when the search starts at rectangle A and proceeds in an upward direction.

when the tiles are 45-degree trapezoids defined in such a way that their top and bottom sides are parallel to one of the axes while forming 45-, 90-, and 135-degree angles with the remaining sides [1245].

Corner stitching greatly facilitates operations that involve finding nearest neighbors. However, overlapping rectangles are not easily handled by it. Moreover, since the only way to move from one rectangle to another is through the links, in the worst case, accessing the rectangle associated with a given point requires that all rectangles be examined (see Exercise 5). This is a direct consequence of the fact that there is no index (i.e., none of the representations of collections of points described in Chapter 1 is used here). As an example of this worst case, consider the set of rectangles given in Figure 3.19. A is the first rectangle in the set. We wish to access the rectangle associated with point P, and we do so by traversing the up links shown in Figure 3.19. The worst case can be overcome by imposing an additional structure in the form of one of the hierarchical organizations described below while still retaining the links. However, in such a case, both the solid and space tiles must be represented in the structure. For a discussion of algorithms using corner stitching, see Shand [1741].

Exercises

1. Give an algorithm to insert a rectangle into a corner stitching representation.

2. Give an algorithm to delete a rectangle from a corner stitching representation.

3. Prove that, for N rectangles, the corner stitching representation implies a maximum of $3 \cdot N + 1$ space tiles.

4. Under what conditions is the number of space tiles fewer than $3 \cdot N + 1$?

5. Give an algorithm to find the rectangle that covers a particular point location when the rectangles are represented using corner stitching.

6. Give an algorithm to find all rectangles that intersect a given window when the rectangles are represented using corner stitching.

3.3.2.2 Balanced Four-Dimensional K-d Tree

Lauther [1114] and Rosenberg [1571] use representation 1 for the representative point and then use a balanced four-dimensional k-d tree (somewhat like the adaptive k-d tree discussed in Section 1.5.1.4 of Chapter 1 with the exception that the coordinates are tested in a cyclic order) to store the collection of representative points. Lauther discusses the solution of the rectangle intersection problem using the balanced four-dimensional k-d tree. The solution is an adaptation of the $O(N^2)$ algorithm. It first builds the tree (equivalent to a sorting process) and then traverses the tree in inorder and intersects each rectangle, say P, with the remaining unprocessed rectangles (i.e., the inorder successors of P).[10]

The balanced four-dimensional k-d tree can be used to solve the rectangle intersection problem by making use of the fact that two rectangles with sides parallel to the axes intersect if their projections on the x axis intersect and their projections on the y axis intersect. The one-dimensional analog of this condition has been used in the segment and interval tree solutions to the rectangle intersection problem (see Sections 3.1.1 and 3.1.2). More formally, we can restate this condition as stipulating that in order for rectangle Q to intersect rectangle P, all four of the following conditions must be satisfied:

1. $x_{\min}(Q) \le x_{\max}(P)$

2. $y_{\min}(Q) \le y_{\max}(P)$

---

[10] In this discussion, we use P to refer to both a rectangle and its corresponding node in the tree. The correct meaning should be clear from the context.

3. $x_{\min}(P) \leq x_{\max}(Q)$

4. $y_{\min}(P) \leq y_{\max}(Q)$

Armed with this formulation of the condition, we see that when the collection of representative points is represented as a balanced four-dimensional k-d tree (really, any variant of a four-dimensional k-d tree), we do not always have to visit all of the inorder successors of P since, whenever one of these conditions fails to hold at a node Q, then the appropriate subtree of Q need not be searched. These conditions can be restated in the following manner, which is more compatible with the way in which the balanced four-dimensional k-d tree is traversed:

5. $x_{\min}(Q) \leq x_{\max}(P)$

6. $y_{\min}(Q) \leq y_{\max}(P)$

7. $-x_{\max}(Q) \leq -x_{\min}(P)$

8. $-y_{\max}(Q) \leq -y_{\min}(P)$

Now, we build a balanced four-dimensional k-d tree with discriminators K_0, K_1, K_2, and K_3, corresponding to $x_{\min}$, $y_{\min}$, $-x_{\max}$, and $-y_{\max}$, respectively. Whenever we encounter node Q discriminating on K_d such that $K_d(Q) > K_{(d+2)\bmod 4}(P)$, then no nodes in the right subtree of Q need be examined further.

Solving the rectangle intersection problem as described above has an upper bound of $O(N^2)$ and a lower bound of $O(N \cdot \log_2 N)$. The lower bound is achieved when pruning is assumed to occur at every right subtree (see Exercise 6). When the rectangle intersection problem is posed in terms of conditions 5–8, the relation "$\leq$" between Q and P is said to be a *dominance relation* [1511]. In such a case, the intersection problem is called the *dominance merge* problem by Preparata and Shamos [1511]. Given F rectangle intersections, the algorithm of Preparata and Shamos solves the rectangle intersection problem in $O(N \cdot \log_2^2 N + F)$ time instead of the optimal $O(N \cdot \log_2 N + F)$ time.

A balanced four-dimensional k-d tree takes more time to build than an ordinary four-dimensional k-d tree since medians must be computed to assure balance. The balanced four-dimensional k-d tree makes point searches and region searches quite efficient. For such operations, the balanced four-dimensional k-d tree is preferable to corner stitching because of the implicit two-dimensional sorting of the rectangles. In addition, overlapping rectangles can be handled easily with the balanced four-dimensional k-d tree, whereas this is quite complicated with corner stitching. However, for operations involving finding nearest neighbors, corner stitching is superior to the balanced four-dimensional k-d tree.

Rosenberg compares the performance of the balanced four-dimensional k-d tree, a point method in his formulation, with linked lists[11] and the area-based quadtree approaches discussed in Section 3.4.1 and concludes that the point methods are superior. However, he only takes into account point and window queries. Comparisons using queries, such as finding all intersecting rectangles, may lead to a different conclusion.

Exercises

1. Can we say that whenever two rectangles intersect, then the corner of one rectangle is contained in the other rectangle?

2. By definition, each node in a balanced four-dimensional k-d tree that discriminates on key K_j serves as an upper bound for all the K_j values in the LoChild and as a lower bound for all the K_j values in the HiChild. To insure that point and region searches are efficient in the balanced four-dimensional k-d tree, it is useful to know more about the region below each node. Thus, a bounds array is stored with each node to indicate the information necessary to cut

---

[11] The rectangles are stored in a doubly linked list.

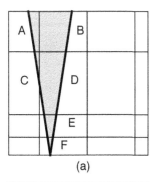

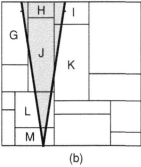

Figure 3.20
Blocks examined when searching
within a conic region for a collection
of rectangles represented by (a) a
grid file and (b) a k-d tree.

off unproductive search. For d-dimensional data, $2 \cdot d$ items are needed to specify completely the d-dimensional volume that is spanned by the node. Thus, for the four-dimensional trees used for the collection of rectangles, we need eight values at each node. Show that with each node, we really only need to store three values to specify the two regions (i.e., two-dimensional areas) that make up the LOCHILD and HICHILD of a node. Describe how they would be used to cut off the search. In addition, show that if the bounds array at a node only indicates the region spanned by the node, rather than the regions spanned by LOCHILD and HICHILD, then only two values are needed.

3. Give an algorithm to find all rectangles that intersect a given point (in two-dimensional space) when each rectangle is represented by a point in four-dimensional space and the collection of rectangles is organized by a balanced four-dimensional k-d tree.

4. Repeat Exercise 3 for all rectangles that intersect a rectangular window given by P.

5. Give an algorithm to determine all pairs of intersecting rectangles using a balanced four-dimensional k-d tree.

6. Prove that $O(N \cdot \log_2 N)$ is a lower bound on solving the rectangle intersection problem when using the balanced four-dimensional k-d tree.

3.3.2.3 Grid File

Hinrichs and Nievergelt [839, 840, 841] make use of the grid file (see Section 1.7.2.1 of Chapter 1) to organize the rectangles whose representative point uses representation 3. In particular, each rectangle is represented by the Cartesian product of a horizontal and a vertical one-dimensional interval, each of which is represented by a representative point using representation 3. The result is that proximity queries are answered by examining all grid blocks that intersect the cone-shaped search regions. Hinrichs and Nievergelt prefer this method to one based on a tree (e.g., the k-d tree) because the relevant grid blocks are in contiguous regions, whereas, in a tree, contiguous blocks may appear in different subtrees. Hinrichs and Nievergelt are quite concerned with reducing the number of disk access operations necessary to process such queries.

Figure 3.20(a) is an example of a conic-shaped search region for a grid file organization of rectangles. Figure 3.20(b) is an example of a conic-shaped search region for a k-d tree organization of rectangles. In the case of a grid file, blocks A, B, C, D, E, and F would be examined. On the other hand, for a k-d tree, blocks G, H, I, J, K, L, and M would be examined. Note that blocks I and K are in a different subtree of the k-d tree than blocks G, H, J, L, and M. In the worst case, solving the rectangle intersection problem when using a grid file takes $O(N^2)$ time. This is achieved by using the naive method of Section 3.1. However, the expected cost will be lower since it is assumed that the points corresponding to the rectangles are well distributed among the grid blocks.

Observe further that the conic shape of the search region resulting from the use of representation 3 for the representative points is transformed to a rectangle-shaped search region for a point query when representation 1 is used. Faloutsos and Rego [589] argue that this rectangle shape makes their method of using a quadtreelike decomposition of the underlying space into four congruent isoceles triangles (i.e., the tri-cell method discussed in Section 3.3.1) more appropriate for general queries of the nature that we have discussed. In particular, they claim that a subset of the collection of the triangular cells matches the query region better. Unfortunately, this is true only when the point query is the midpoint of the interval, in which case the search region corresponds to the middle two triangles at the top level of the decomposition. For other query points, as well as other queries (i.e., windowing and subsets), the situation is the same as for other representations for the underlying space of the collection of the representative points (e.g., the grid file).

Exercise

1. What is the expected cost of solving the rectangle intersection problem using the grid file?

3.3.2.4 LSD Tree

Henrich, Six, and Widmayer [829] makes use of the LSD tree (see Section 1.7.1.3 of Chapter 1) to organize the rectangles whose representative point uses representation 1. Of special interest is the manner in which they split an overflowing bucket. In particular, the splitting strategy takes into account the fact that representation 1 is used and that part of the underlying space is empty. As mentioned in Section 1.7.1.3 of Chapter 1, two splitting strategies are proposed: data dependent and distribution dependent.

The data-dependent split strategy is simple. Given a particular coordinate i in the original space along which the bucket is to be split, the split is made at the position that corresponds to the average value of the ith coordinate for all of the objects stored in the bucket.

The distribution-dependent strategy is more complex. It is a combination of two basic strategies, each of which is designed to deal with a special extreme case of the underlying data distribution. The first, denoted by SP_1, treats the intervals as if they have zero length (i.e., points), thereby assuming that the two endpoints of the interval are identical, and thus the idea is to divide the overflowing bucket into two cells that contain approximately the same number of objects. This means that the split position is the midpoint of the part of the diagonal that runs through the underlying space that overlaps the overflowing bucket (e.g., P_1 in Figure 3.21). This strategy is designed to deal with the case that the intervals are small relative to the underlying space. The second, denoted by SP_2, treats the intervals as if their representative points are uniformly distributed in the underlying space, and thus the idea is to divide the overflowing bucket into two cells that cover approximately the same area of the nonempty portion of the underlying space that ovelaps the bucket (e.g., P_2 in Figure 3.21).

The actual split position along coordinate i, denoted by SP, is a weighted sum of SP_1 and SP_2:

$$SP = \alpha \cdot SP_1 + (1 - \alpha) \cdot SP_2,$$

where $\alpha = \sqrt[10]{A_b / (u_i - l_i)^2}$, and A_b is the area of the part of the underlying space spanned by bucket b that is above the diagonal that runs through the space, while u_i and l_i are the minimum and maximum values, respectively, of the ith coordinate value of all points that are in the bucket that is being split. Assuming, without loss of generality, that the objects are rectangles, α has the property that, for large buckets (i.e., those that span a large part of the underlying space), SP approaches SP_1. On the other hand, for small buckets, SP approaches SP_2. This is appropriate: in the former case, the representative points tend to be clustered along the diagonal since their corresponding objects are much smaller than the underlying space; in the latter case, the representative points occupy a much larger portion of the underlying space as their corresponding objects are of approximately the same size as the underlying space. Not surprisingly, experiments [829] with collections of rectangles from both uniform and skewed distributions show a higher bucket utilization for the data-dependent splitting strategy than for the distribution-dependent splitting strategy, while the distribution-dependent strategy has a higher bucket utilization when the rectangles are inserted in sorted order (see Exercise 1).

Exercise

1. Explain why the bucket utilization for sorted data is expected to be higher for a distribution-dependent bucket-splitting strategy than for a data-dependent bucket-splitting strategy.

3.3.2.5 Two-Dimensional Representations

The techniques discussed in Sections 3.3.2.2 and 3.3.2.3 for organizing the collection of representative points assume that the representative point lies in four-dimensional space. Another possibility is to use a representative point in two-dimensional space and

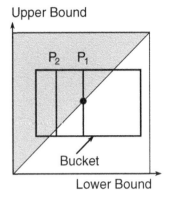

Figure 3.21
Possible split positions in an overflowing LSD tree bucket when using a distribution-dependent bucket-splitting strategy: (a) P_1 corresponds to a treatment of the intervals as having zero length and (b) P_2 corresponds to the assumption that the representative points of the intervals are uniformly distributed in the underlying space.

to represent the collection by one of the two-dimensional quadtree variants, such as the PR quadtree or the PR k-d tree. Recall that the PR quadtree is a regular decomposition quadtree that decomposes space until there is only one point per block (for more details, see Section 1.4.2.2 of Chapter 1).

As an example of the use of the PR quadtree, suppose that in our application we must perform a point query (i.e., determine the rectangles that contain a given point). In this case, when the representative point is the centroid, a PR quadtree requires that we search the entire data structure because the rectangle that is centered at a given point can lie in all of the quadrants. Of course, pruning can occur at deeper levels in the tree. In contrast, using the lower-left corner as the representative point may permit the pruning of up to three quadrants in the search. For instance, when the query point lies in the SW quadrant of a tree rooted at Q, then no rectangle with a representative point that lies in the NW, NE, or SE quadrants of Q can contain the query point.

One way to avoid having to search the entire data structure in the case of a point query when using a point representation, such as the PR quadtree or PR k-d tree, for the representative points that are centroids is to also associate with each block the corresponding minimum enclosing block. This approach, used by Freeston [646], stores the centroids of the objects in a BANG file, and with each block in the BANG file, he associates the minimum enclosing PR k-d tree block for the objects within it.

A similar approach serves as the basis of the *spatial k-d tree* of Ooi, McDonell, and Sacks-Davis [1404, 1407] to store the representative points that are the centroids of the objects (see also Sections 1.5.1.4 and 1.7.1.2 of Chapter 1 and Section 4.4.3 of Chapter 4).[12] Aside from storing the value and identity of the discriminating key, each nonleaf node, say P discriminating on key K_j, also contains information on the spatial extent of the objects stored in its two subtrees. In particular, it stores the maximum value of the j coordinate for the objects stored in LOCHILD(P) and the minimum value of the j coordinate for the objects stored in HICHILD(P). This information aids in reducing the number of nodes that need to be examined when executing a point query. However, in the worst case, the entire tree will still have to be searched.

Exercise

1. Suppose that you use the spatial k-d tree [1404, 1407]. Under what circumstances will a point query require that both children of a nonleaf node P be examined?

3.3.3 Summary

The representative point method finds much use. In particular, it is a very attractive solution when it is desired to integrate nonstandard data such as that found in spatial and image databases into a conventional database management system (e.g., relational), where the records are analogous to points in some high-dimensional space. In this case, the entire record can be indexed by one index (treating each record as a point in a high-dimensional space), or several indexes can be used for different attributes or subsets of the attributes. In fact, most of the indexes are usually one-dimensional, where there is one index for each of the attributes of a conventional type (e.g., textual attributes, numbers).

Another argument for the use of the representative point method as a basis for an index is its perceived utility as a clustering method. In particular, it preserves clustering in the index (e.g., [1787]) in the sense that objects of similar positions and size in the original space are placed together in a region of the transformed space. This is especially

---

[12] In addition see the KD2-tree of van Oosterom [1410, 1412] discussed in Section 1.5.1.4 of Chapter 1, where neither the objects nor the partition lines need be axis parallel (i.e., a BSP tree is used).

true when the objects overlap. It is interesting to note that proponents of building an index based on the representative point method argue against building an index based on the distance between objects in the original space because they do not believe that it is a good basis for clustering [1787]. In particular, they claim that a distance-based index breaks down when the objects overlap in that the distance between them is zero. This implies that the degree of similarity between pairs of objects in this case is the same, regardless of the sizes of the objects or the extent of the intersection. In addition, when the objects do not overlap, then they believe that the similarity between objects should not be the same just because their separation is the same. In other words, they believe that the extent of the objects should also be taken into account. However, this argument does not take into account the possibility of using a secondary similarity measure (e.g., [244]) that corresponds to the extent of the intersection in case of overlap and the sizes of the objects in the case of nonoverlap.

Nevertheless, it is important to note that the above clustering arguments break down when the objects are not of the same or similar size (e.g., one object is large and the other one is small, as is illustrated in Figure 3.22) but are close to each other in the original space (in terms of their distance). In this case, the objects are no longer clustered in the same region of the transformed space. This means that the search regions in the transformed space will be large. Proponents of the representative point method resolve this apparent contradiction by appealing to a definition of clustering where size is deemed to be more important than separation [1787].

In addition to its utility for clustering, proponents of the representative point method [1787, 1788] also maintain that the method yields good query performance compared to other spatial indexing methods. Usually, this is measured in terms of the number of page accesses to the underlying spatial index (e.g., for range queries in [1787] and for spatial join queries in [1788], both of which use a variant of the multilevel grid file [1087, 1987], which is also discussed in Section 1.7.1.5 of Chapter 1). Unfortunately, surprisingly, the experiments used to support this claim do not index on the representative point. In particular, in [1787, 1788], when the representative point method is applied to two-dimensional objects, only two of the four dimensions are split. However, this means that the spatial index on the representative points is effectively indexing only in a two-dimensional space, using two of the four dimensions. In other words, the result is equivalent to indexing only on two of the four elements of the representative point while also storing information about the other two elements in the spatial index. Although such an approach may be worthwhile and gives good results for certain queries (e.g., the simple QSF-tree [2057]), it cannot be used as evidence of the superiority of the representative point method over methods such as the R*-tree [152] as the index does not make use of any information about the extent of the objects. Of course, if the objects are all of approximately the same size, then the impact of this omission is lessened.

It has also been observed that the prime reason for the transformation of the query region from original space to the high-dimensional space of the representative point is to overcome the mismatch between the higher dimensionality of the data regions in the index and the lower dimensionality of the query region. This naturally leads to a mismatch in the shape of the transformed query regions and the data regions in the index (recall the discussion of the comparison of representations 1 and 3 in Section 3.3.2.3). The result is that many researchers (e.g., [822, 827, 1449]) resort to a transformation of the data regions in the index to a region in the lower-dimensional space of the query regions. As the regions in the lower-dimensional space of the query regions that correspond to the data regions in the index are generally much larger than the actual regions covered by the data, a minimum bounding box is often also associated with the data regions in the index [1449] in order to enable faster query processing. Further efficiencies can be gained in terms of the space needed to store the bounding box in the index nodes by formulating the box in terms of the original lower-dimensional space, and just using an approximation of it by virtue of quantizing the space spanned by the bounding box [822], as in the hybrid tree [317, 826] (see Sections 1.7.1.2 of Chapter 1 and 4.4.3 of Chapter 4). At this point,

Figure 3.22
Example of two objects that are close to each other in the original space but are not clustered in the same region of the transformed space when using a transformation such as the corner transformation.

having found it beneficial to make use of the inverse transformation, it is not unnatural to question the rationale for transforming the original data into the higher-dimensional space in the first place.

3.4 Area-Based Methods

The problem with using trees in conjunction with representative point methods, such as those discussed in Section 3.3, is that the placement of the node in the tree (i.e., its depth) does not reflect the size (i.e., the spatial extent) of the rectangle. It primarily depends on the location of the representative point. In this section, we focus on alternative representations provided by area-based methods that associate each rectangle with the blocks containing it or the blocks that it contains. The sizes and positions of these blocks may be predetermined, as is the case in an approach based on the region quadtree. However, this need not be the case; nor must the blocks be disjoint.

As an example of a representation based on the region quadtree, suppose that we represent each rectangle by its minimum enclosing quadtree block (i.e., a square). The rectangle is associated with the center of the quadtree block. Of course, more than one rectangle can be associated with a given enclosing square, and a technique must be used to differentiate among them. Observe that in this case we do not explicitly store a representative point. Instead, there is a predefined set of representative points with which rectangles can be stored. In some sense, this is analogous to hashing where the representative points correspond to buckets. These techniques, which we term *Caltech Intermediate Form* (CIF) *quadtrees*, have been developed independently by Kedem [1009] (called a *quad-CIF tree*) and by Abel and Smith [8]. In this section, we focus on a variant known as the *MX-CIF quadtree* [1009], which makes use of its one-dimensional variant to distinguish between the different rectangles that have the same minimum enclosing quadtree block. The MX-CIF quadtree has been discussed briefly in Section 2.1.4 of Chapter 2.

This section is organized as follows. Section 3.4.1 describes the MX-CIF quadtree in greater detail. Section 3.4.2 discusses alternative representations based on the MX-CIF quadtree that are designed to overcome some of its drawbacks, specifically as demonstrated by some inefficiencies in search queries. Section 3.4.3 outlines some quadtree-based alternatives that permit a rectangle to be associated with more than one quadtree block. Note that analyzing the space requirements of these representations, as well as the execution time of algorithms that use them, is quite difficult, as they depend heavily on the distribution of the data. In most cases, a limited part of the tree must be traversed, and thus the execution time depends, in part, on the depth and the shape of the tree.

3.4.1 MX-CIF Quadtree

This section is organized as follows. We first give a definition of the MX-CIF quadtree (Section 3.4.1.1). Next, we describe how operations such as insertion, deletion, and a number of variants of searching are executed for the MX-CIF quadtree (Section 3.4.1.2). We conclude with a comparison of the MX-CIF quadtree with a number of other representations (Section 3.4.1.3).

3.4.1.1 Definition

The *MX-CIF quadtree* associates each rectangle, say R, with the quadtree node corresponding to the smallest block that contains R in its entirety. Rectangles can be associated with both leaf and nonleaf nodes. Subdivision ceases whenever a node's block contains no rectangles. Alternatively, subdivision can also cease once a quadtree block is smaller

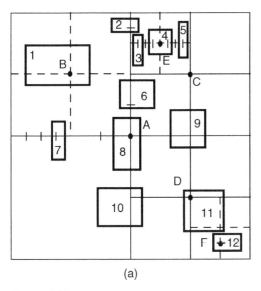

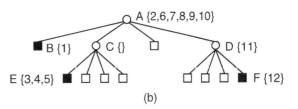

(a)   (b)

Figure 3.23
(a) A collection of rectangles and the block decomposition induced by its MX-CIF quadtree and (b) the tree representation of (a).

than a predetermined threshold size. This threshold is often chosen to be equal to the expected size of the rectangle [1009]. In this section, we will assume that rectangles do not overlap (but may touch), although our techniques can be modified to handle this situation. Figure 3.23 contains a set of rectangles and its corresponding MX-CIF quadtree. Once a rectangle is associated with a quadtree node, say P, it is not considered to be a member of any of the children of P. For example, in Figure 3.23, rectangle 11 overlaps the space spanned by both nodes D and F but is associated only with node D.

It should be clear that more than one rectangle can be associated with a given enclosing block (i.e., node). There are several ways of organizing these rectangles. Abel and Smith [8] do not apply any ordering. This is equivalent to maintaining a linked list of the rectangles. Another approach, devised by Kedem [1009], is described below.

Let P be a quadtree node, and let S be the set of rectangles that are associated with P. Members of S are organized into two sets according to their intersection (or the collinearity of their sides) with the lines passing through the centroid of P's block. We shall use the terms *axes* or *axis lines* to refer to these lines. For example, consider node P, whose block is of size $2 \cdot L_x \times 2 \cdot L_y$ and centered at (C_x, C_y). All members of S that intersect the line $x = C_x$ form one set, and all members of S that intersect the line $y = C_y$ form the other set. Equivalently, these sets correspond to the rectangles intersecting the y and x axes, respectively, passing through (C_x, C_y). If a rectangle intersects both axes (i.e., it contains the centroid of P's block), then we adopt the convention that it is stored with the set associated with the y axis.

These subsets are implemented as binary trees (really tries), which, in actuality, are one-dimensional analogs of the MX-CIF quadtree. For example, Figure 3.24 illustrates the binary tree associated with the x and y axes passing through A, the root of the MX-CIF quadtree of Figure 3.23. The subdivision points of the axis lines are shown by the tick marks in Figure 3.23.

Note that a rectangle is associated with the shallowest node in the binary tree that contains it. For example, consider Figure 3.25, which contains the binary trees associated with the x and y axes passing through E in the MX-CIF quadtree of Figure 3.23. In particular, we see that no rectangle is stored in the left (right) subtree of node XN (XM) in Figure 3.25(a) even though rectangle 4 contains it. In this example, rectangle 4 is associated with the y axis that passes through node E (i.e., node YE in Figure 3.25(b)).

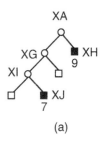

(a)

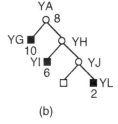

(b)

Figure 3.24
Binary trees for the (a) x axis and (b) (b) y axis passing through node A in Figure 3.23.

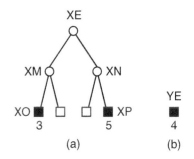

(a)   (b)

Figure 3.25
Binary trees for the (a) x axis and (b) y axis passing through node E in Figure 3.23.

3.4.1.2 Operations

We adopt the conventions that when rectangle R lies entirely within a block B, then R is associated with B if the left or bottom sides of R are collinear with axis lines of B. This is analogous to the open and closed conventions that we used for points in Chapter 1. Using these conventions, a rectangle is inserted into an MX-CIF quadtree by a top-down search for the position it is to occupy. As stated earlier, we assume that the input rectangle does not overlap (but may touch) any of the existing rectangles. This can be ascertained by preceding the insertion by a call to a procedure to determine if the rectangle intersects any of the existing rectangles (see procedure CIFSEARCH in Exercise 3).

The position to be occupied by a rectangle is determined by a two-step process. First, locate the first quadtree block such that at least one of its axis lines intersects the input rectangle. Second, having found such a block and an axis, say V, repeat the subdivision process for the V axis until locating the first subdivision point that is contained within the rectangle.

During the process of locating the destination position for the input rectangle, we may have to subdivide repeatedly the space spanned by the MX-CIF quadtree (termed *splitting*) and, in the process, create new nodes. As was the case for the MX quadtree, the shape of the resulting MX-CIF quadtree is independent of the order in which the rectangles are inserted into it, although the shapes of the intermediate trees are dependent on it.

Building an MX-CIF quadtree of maximum depth n for N rectangles has a worst-case execution time of $O(n \cdot N)$. This situation arises when each rectangle is placed at depth n[13] Therefore, the worst-case storage requirements are also $O(n \cdot N)$. Of course, the expected behavior should be better.

Deletion of nodes from MX-CIF quadtrees is analogous to the process used for MX quadtrees. The only difference is that collapsing needs to be performed for nodes in the binary trees (i.e., one-dimensional MX-CIF quadtrees) corresponding to the axes, as well as for the nodes in the MX-CIF quadtree. As an example, to delete rectangle 9 (i.e., the rectangle associated with node XH in the binary tree for the x axis through node A in Figure 3.24(a)) from the MX-CIF quadtree of Figure 3.23, we also delete the node XH as it has no left or right children. This requires us to set the right child of XH's father node, XA, to NIL.

Deleting rectangle 5 (i.e., node XP in the binary tree for the x axis through E in Figure 3.25(a)) is slightly more complex. Again, we delete the rectangle and the node XP since it has no left or right children. However, setting the right child of XP's father node, XN, to NIL is not enough. We must also perform merging since both children of XN are now NIL. This leads to replacing the right child of XN's father, XE, by NIL and returning XN and XP to the free storage list. This process is termed *collapsing* and is the counterpart of the splitting operation that was necessary when inserting a rectangle into an MX-CIF quadtree.

Collapsing can take place over several levels in both the binary tree and in the MX-CIF quadtree. In essence, collapsing is repeatedly applied in the binary tree until the nearest ancestor that has an additional non-NIL child is encountered. If the collapsing process brings us to the root of the binary tree (e.g., after deletion of rectangles 3, 4, and 5 from the MX-CIF quadtree of Figure 3.23), then further collapsing of MX-CIF quadtree nodes is possible only if both axes are empty. This process terminates when a nearest ancestor that has an additional non-NIL child or nonempty axes is encountered.

As the collapsing process takes place, the affected nodes are returned to the free storage list. For example, suppose that after deleting rectangle 5 from Figure 3.23, we

---

[13] n is the sum of the maximum depths of the MX-CIF quadtree and the binary tree.

also delete rectangles 3 and 4. This means that nodes XE, XM, and YE in Figure 3.25 are subjected to the collapsing process, with the result that the axes through E are empty. Since nodes E and E's ancestor, C, have empty axes and no other non-NIL children, collapsing is applicable, with the result that the NE child of A is set to NIL and nodes C, E, XE, XM, XO, and YE are returned to the free storage list.

The execution time of the deletion algorithm is bounded by two times the maximum depth of the MX-CIF quadtree (including the binary trees for the axes). This upper bound is attained when the nearest ancestor for the collapsing process is the root node.

The simplest search query in an MX-CIF quadtree is one that determines if a given rectangle overlaps (i.e., intersects) any of the existing rectangles. Range queries can also be performed. However, they are more usefully cast in terms of finding all the rectangles in a given area (i.e., a window query). Another popular query is one that seeks to determine if one collection of rectangles can be overlaid on top of another collection without any of the component rectangles intersecting one another.

These two operations can be implemented by using variants of algorithms developed for handling set operations (i.e., union and intersection) in region-based quadtrees [901, 905, 1760]. The range query is answered by intersecting the query rectangle with the MX-CIF quadtree. The overlay query is answered by a two-step process. First, intersect the two MX-CIF quadtrees. If the result is empty, then they can be safely overlaid, and we merely need to perform a union of the two MX-CIF quadtrees. It should be clear that Boolean queries can be easily handled.

When the rectangles are allowed to overlap, reporting the pairs of rectangles that intersect each other is achieved by traversing the MX-CIF quadtree and, for each node, examining all neighboring nodes that can contain rectangles intersecting it. In the worst case, for some rectangles, we may have to examine the entire MX-CIF quadtree. However, if this is the case, then the remaining rectangles will not require this much work. Nevertheless, the worst-case execution time of this task is $O(n \cdot N^2)$ for a tree of maximum depth n with N rectangles. The expected behavior should be better.

An alternative solution to the rectangle intersection problem can be formulated by adapting the plane-sweep method described in Section 3.1 to use the MX-CIF quadtree [1632]. This is quite straightforward and relies on the observation that a quadtree traversal is analogous to a two-dimensional plane sweep. The effect of the sort phase is obtained by the process of building the MX-CIF quadtree since a quadtree decomposition is equivalent to a multidimensional sort. The effect of the sweep phase is obtained by traversing the quadtree in some order (e.g., Morton order).

The border between the nodes that have been encountered in the traversal and those that have not is the analog of the scan line in the one-dimensional plane sweep. This border is known as the *active border* [1659, 1661] (see Sections 4.2.3 of [1636], 5.1.3 of [1636], and 6.3.3 of [1636]). The adaptation is completed by devising data structures to represent the active border with properties analogous to those of the segment and interval trees (i.e., space and time).

Note that in the plane-sweep solution described in Section 3.1, the sort was performed in one dimension, and the sweep was in the other direction. In contrast, in the MX-CIF quadtree solution, the sort and the sweep are both performed in the same direction.

The efficiency of operations such as search can be improved by associating with each node of the MX-CIF quadtree the two minimum bounding boxes of the rectangles that intersect each of the axis lines that emanate from the subdivision point. However, these additional fields will increase the complexity of the insertion and deletion procedures since these fields must always be updated.

Exercises

Exercises 1–5 assume the following implementation of the MX-CIF quadtree. The basic entities are the rectangles, nodes in the MX-CIF quadtree, and the nodes in the binary trees associated with each node in the MX-CIF quadtree. Let P denote a pointer to a record. A rectangle is represented by a record of type *rectangle* that has five fields that contain the coordinate values of its centroid, the distance from the centroid to the borders of the rectangle, and its name. $C(P, A)$ and $L(P, A)$ indicate, respectively, the coordinate values of the centroid, and the distance from the centroid to the border of the rectangle. A takes on the values 'X' and 'Y' corresponding to the names of the coordinate axes. The NAME field contains descriptive information about the rectangle stored at a node.

Nodes in the binary trees (i.e., one-dimensional MX-CIF quadtrees) of the set of rectangles that are associated with each node of the MX-CIF quadtree are represented by records of type *bnode* with three fields. There is one node of type *bnode* for each axis subdivision point that is contained in a rectangle or has descendants that contain rectangles. Two of the fields of a *bnode* record are called CHILD(P, I) and contain pointers to the left and right children of P, distinguished by I. The third field is called RECT and points to a record of type *rectangle* whose area contains the axis subdivision point, if such a rectangle exists and is not already included in the binary tree structure associated with an ancestor node in the quadtree structure.

Each node in the MX-CIF quadtree is represented by a record of type *cnode* that contains six fields. Four fields are termed CHILD(P, I), in which I corresponds to one of the four principal quadrant directions. The two remaining fields represent pointers to the binary trees for the rectangles that are associated with the node. These fields are called BIN(P, I), where I corresponds to one of the two axis names. Note that there is no need to store information about the coordinate values of nodes in the MX-CIF quadtree (in records of type *bnode* and *cnode*) since this information can be derived from the path to the node from the root of the MX-CIF quadtree. The algorithms assume that each rectangle is unique and does not overlap (but may touch) any other rectangle in the MX-CIF quadtree. In addition, an empty node is like an empty child and is represented by a NIL pointer in the direction of a quadrant that contains no rectangles.

1. Using the open and closed conventions described in this section, give an algorithm CIF-COMPARE to determine the quadrant in which the centroid of rectangle P lies relative to a grid subdivision point located at (C_x, C_y).

2. Using the open and closed conventions described in this section, give an algorithm BIN-COMPARE to determine the axis segment in which rectangle P lies relative to axis V subdivided at the coordinate value $V = C_V$. Make sure that your algorithm also works properly when the specification of the rectangles and of the underlying space is constrained to using integers.

3. Give an algorithm CIFSEARCH to determine if rectangle P overlaps (i.e., intersects) any of the existing rectangles in the MX-CIF quadtree rooted at R. Also, give an auxiliary procedure CROSSAXIS that is used by CIFSEARCH to determine if rectangle p overlaps any of the rectangles that are stored in the binary trees associated with the axes that pass through the centers of the blocks corresponding to the individual nodes of the MX-CIF quadtree. Assume the existence of Boolean-valued function RECTINTERSECT to indicate whether two rectangles overlap (i.e., the intersection must have a nonzero area—that is, two rectangles that share an edge do not intersect).

4. Give an algorithm CIFINSERT to insert rectangle P into the MX-CIF quadtree rooted at R. Also, give an auxiliary procedure INSERTAXIS to insert P into the binary tree rooted in the MX-CIF quadtree node in which P belongs.

5. Give an algorithm CIFDELETE to delete rectangle P from the MX-CIF quadtree rooted at R. Assume the existence of functions OPDIRECTION and OTHERAXIS to specify the spatial relationships among directions and axes. OPDIRECTION(D) yields the direction directly opposite to D. For example, OPDIRECTION('LEFT') = 'RIGHT', and OPDIRECTION('RIGHT') = 'LEFT', while OPDIRECTION('BOTH') is undefined. Given A as one of two coordinate axes, OTHERAXIS(A) returns the name of the second axis (i.e., OTHERAXIS('X') = 'Y' and OTHERAXIS('Y') = 'X').

6. Suppose that, in procedure BINCOMPARE in the solution to Exercise 2 you used the partial test "$C(P, V) - L(P, V) \leq C_V$" instead of "$C(P, V) - L(P, V) < C_V$" for rectangle P and coordinate axis V. What will happen when inserting two rectangles that share an edge that is

coincident with one of the coordinate axes? Assume that the specification of the rectangles and of the underlying space is constrained to using integers.

7. Suppose that, in procedure BINCOMPARE in the solution to Exercise 2 you used the partial tests "$C_V \leq C(P,V) + L(P,V)$" for rectangle P and coordinate axis V instead of "$C_V < C(P,V) + L(P,V)$", and "$C(P,V) - L(P,V) \leq C_V$" instead of "$C(P,V) - L(P,V) < C_V$", as described in Exercise 6. What will happen when inserting two rectangles that share an edge that is coincident with one of the coordinate axes? As in Exercise 6, assume that the specification of the rectangles and of the underlying space is constrained to using integers.

In Exercises 8–25 you are to implement functions that may be of use in an information-management system for handling a collection of small rectangles based on the MX-CIF quadtree. Assume that the rectangles do not overlap. An MX-CIF quadtree is built by a combination of procedures CREATERECTANGLE, which you are to write below, and a variant of CIFINSERT. A rectangle is created by specifying its centroid and distances to its borders and by assigning it a name for subsequent use. You will also want to keep the names in a directory so that rectangles can be retrieved by name without requiring an exhaustive search through the MX-CIF quadtree. This is useful when rectangles have not yet been inserted into the MX-CIF quadtree or after they have been removed.

8. Give a procedure CREATERECTANGLE to create a rectangle. It is invoked by a call of the form CREATERECTANGLE(N, C_x, C_y, L_x, L_y), where N is the name to be associated with the rectangle, C_x and C_y are the x and y coordinate values, respectively, of its centroid, and L_x and L_y are the horizontal and vertical distances, respectively, to its borders from the centroid.

9. What happens in procedure CIFINSERT when the rectangle being inserted is larger in width or height than the size of the root node?

10. Modify procedure CIFINSERT to take just one argument corresponding to the name of a rectangle and insert it into the MX-CIF quadtree, if it does not overlap any of the existing rectangles. To do this, you will need to invoke procedure CIFSEARCH. If two rectangles touch along a side or a corner, they are not said to overlap. You are to return TRUE if the query rectangle does not overlap any of the intersecting rectangles; otherwise, do not insert it, and return the name associated with one of the intersecting rectangles (i.e., if it intersects more than one rectangle).

11. Given the x and y coordinate values of a point, give a procedure DELETEPOINT to delete the rectangle in which the point is located. Make use of procedure CIFDELETE.

12. Given the x and y coordinate values of a point, give a procedure SEARCHPOINT to locate the rectangle, if any, that contains the point.

13. Given the x and y coordinate values of a point, say P, give a procedure NEARESTRECTANGLE to locate the rectangle, if any, whose side or corner is closest to P. Note that this rectangle could also be a rectangle that contains P, in which case the distance is 0.

14. Give a procedure DISPLAY to display the block decomposition corresponding to an MX-CIF quadtree on a screen. Assume that the space in which the rectangles are embedded is of size 128×128, with the origin at the lower-left corner having coordinate values (0,0). Note that the endpoints and widths of the rectangles need not be integers. Each rectangle is displayed by a rectangle with a border consisting of asterisks, while the name of the rectangle appears somewhere inside its boundary. The name is printed horizontally.

15. Give a function called LISTRECTANGLES to list all of the elements of a rectangle database in alphanumerical order. This means that, in the collating sequence, digits come before upper-case letters, which precede lower-case letters. Similarly, shorter identifiers precede longer ones. For example, a sorted list is 3DA, 5, A3D, A, AB. LISTRECTANGLES yields for each rectangle its name, the x and y coordinate values of its centroid, and the horizontal and vertical distances to its borders from the centroid. With this list, you are to include the coordinate values of each rectangle's lower-left corner and the lengths of its sides. This is of use in interpreting the display since sometimes it is not possible to distinguish the boundaries of the rectangles from the quadrant lines.

16. Give a procedure RECTINTERSECT to determine if the area of intersection of two rectangles is nonzero.

17. Give a procedure RECTTOUCH to determine if two rectangles touch (i.e., are adjacent along a side or a corner). Due to the limitations of a floating-point representation when checking for equality, which is needed in determining satisfaction of the touching condition, this operation is only meaningful when the specification of the rectangles and of the underlying space is constrained to using integers.

18. Give a procedure TOUCH to determine all of the rectangles in an MX-CIF quadtree that touch (i.e., are adjacent along a side or a corner) a given rectangle R. Note that R need not necessarily be in the MX-CIF quadtree. Due to the limitations of a floating-point representation when checking for equality, which is needed in determining satisfaction of the touching condition, this operation is only meaningful when the specification of the rectangles and of the underlying space is constrained to using integers.

19. Give a procedure WITHIN to determine all of the rectangles in the MX-CIF quadtree that lie within a given distance of a given rectangle, say R whose block is of size $2 \cdot L_x \times 2 \cdot L_y$ and centered at (C_x, C_y). This is the so-called *lambda problem* and is a variant of a range query. Given a distance d, WITHIN returns the names of all rectangles found to be $\leq d$ horizontal or vertical distance units from a side or corner of the query rectangle; otherwise it returns NIL. In essence, WITHIN constructs a query rectangle Q with the same centroid as R and distances $L_x + d$ and $L_y + d$ to the border. Now the query returns the identity of all rectangles whose intersection with the region formed by the difference of Q and R is not empty (i.e., any rectangle r that has at least one point in common with $Q - R$). In other words, we have a shell of width d around R, and we seek all the rectangles that have a point in common with this shell. Rectangle R need not necessarily be in the MX-CIF quadtree. Note that for this operation you must recursively traverse the tree to find the rectangles that overlap the query region.

20. Give a pair of procedures HORIZNEIGHBOR and VERTNEIGHBOR to find the nearest neighboring rectangle in the horizontal and vertical directions, respectively, to a given rectangle, say R. By "nearest" horizontal (vertical) neighboring rectangle, it is meant the rectangle whose vertical (horizontal) side, or extension, is closest to a vertical (horizontal) side of the query rectangle R. If the vertical (horizontal) extension of a side of rectangle r causes the extended side of r to intersect the query rectangle, then r is deemed to be at distance 0 and is thus not a candidate neighbor. In other words, the distance has to be greater than zero. HORIZNEIGHBOR and VERTNEIGHBOR return as their value the name of the neighboring rectangle if one exists; otherwise, NIL is returned. Rectangle R need not necessarily be in the MX-CIF quadtree. If more than one rectangle is at the same distance, then return the name of just one of them.

21. Give a procedure NEARESTNEIGHBOR to find the nearest rectangle, if any, to a given rectangle, say R. By "nearest," it is meant the rectangle C with a point on its side or at a corner, say P, such that the distance from P to a side or corner of R is a minimum. Rectangle R need not necessarily be in the MX-CIF quadtree. Note that rectangles that are inside R are not considered by this query. If no such rectangle exists (e.g., when the tree is empty or all of the rectangles in the tree are in R), then output an appropriate message. If more than one rectangle is at the same distance, then return the name of just one of them.

22. Give a pair of procedures DRAWHORIZNEIGHBOR and DRAWVERTNEIGHBOR to draw lines between the two neighbors found in Exercise 20. The difference between this procedure and DRAWHORIZNEIGHBOR and DRAWVERTNEIGHBOR is that in this case the query rectangle R must be in the MX-CIF quadtree.

23. Give a procedure LABEL that assigns the same label to all touching rectangles in the MX-CIF quadtree. By "touching" it is meant that the rectangles are adjacent along a side or a corner. Display the result of this operation by outputting the MX-CIF quadtree so that all touching rectangles are shown with the same label. Due to the limitations of a floating-point representation when checking for equality, which is needed in determining satisfaction of the touching condition, this operation is only meaningful when the specification of the rectangles and of the underlying space is constrained to using integers. This operation is known as *connected component labeling* (see footnote 5 in Section 2.1.1.2 of Chapter 2).

24. Give a procedure INTERSECTWINDOW to find all rectangles that intersect a rectangular window in an MX-CIF quadtree in which rectangles are not permitted to overlap.

25. Give a procedure CONTAINWINDOW to find all rectangles that are contained in a rectangular window in an MX-CIF quadtree in which rectangles are not permitted to overlap.

In Exercises 26–30, assume that the MX-CIF quadtree allows rectangles to intersect (i.e., overlap). Use an interval tree to organize the rectangles that cross the axes.

26. Give a procedure to insert a rectangle into an MX-CIF quadtree that permits overlap.

27. Give a procedure to delete a rectangle from an MX-CIF quadtree that permits overlap.

28. Give a procedure to find all rectangles that intersect a rectangular window in an MX-CIF quadtree that permits overlap.

29. Give a procedure to find all rectangles that are contained in a rectangular window in an MX-CIF quadtree that permits overlap.

30. Give a procedure to find all rectangles that enclose a rectangular window in an MX-CIF quadtree that permits overlap.

31. Analyze the expected cost of inserting a rectangle into an MX-CIF quadtree.

32. What is the expected cost of solving the rectangle intersection problem using the MX-CIF quadtree?

33. In the text, we mention that the rectangle intersection problem can be solved by using a plane-sweep technique that is based on a traversal of the MX-CIF quadtree. This requires a data structure with properties similar to the interval tree to represent the active border. Devise such a data structure. What are the space and time requirements of a solution to the rectangle intersection problem that uses it?

34. In Exercise 10 in Section 1.9 of Chapter 1, we discuss the Euclidean matching problem. Can you use a variant of the MX-CIF quadtree to try to attack this problem? You may wish to represent pairs of points as rectilinear rectangles having the two points as the extreme vertices. In particular, for each point, find the closest point and let them form a rectangle. It should be clear that a point may participate in more than one rectangle. The idea is to obtain a set of rectangles that cover all of the points, yet to have no common points (i.e., the rectangles do not touch). Give an example showing that it is not always possible to find such a set of nontouching rectangles.

35. Modify the method proposed in Exercise 34 so that it computes a solution without using the greedy-method heuristic (see Exercise 10 in Section 1.9 of Chapter 1).

3.4.1.3 Comparison with Other Representations

The MX-CIF quadtree is related to the region quadtree in the same way as the interval tree [534, 537, 538] is related to the segment tree [166]. The MX-CIF quadtree is the two-dimensional analog of the tile tree [1265] (see Section 3.1.2). The analogy is with the tile tree instead of the interval tree because the MX-CIF quadtree is based on a regular decomposition. In fact, the tile tree and the one-dimensional MX-CIF quadtree are identical when rectangles are not allowed to overlap.

At this point, it is also appropriate to comment on the relationship between the MX-CIF quadtree and the MX quadtree. The similarity is that the MX quadtree is defined for a domain of points with corresponding nodes that are the smallest blocks in which they are contained. Similarly, the domain of the MX-CIF quadtree consists of rectangles with corresponding nodes that are the smallest blocks in which they are contained. In both cases, there is a predetermined limit on the level of decomposition. One major difference is that in the MX-CIF quadtree, unlike the MX quadtree, all nodes are of the same type. Thus, data is associated with both leaf and nonleaf nodes of the MX-CIF quadtree. Empty nodes in the MX-CIF quadtree are analogous to white nodes in the MX quadtree.

Instead of using the one-dimensional analog of the MX quadtrees to organize the set of rectangles that are covered by a particular quadtree node, we could have adapted the one-dimensional analog of one of the other quadtree point representations discussed in Chapter 1. Not surprisingly, we find that the advantages and disadvantages are very similar to those outlined in Section 1.4.3 of Chapter 1. We briefly summarize them below. A more detailed comparison of the one-dimensional analogs of the point and

PR quadtrees is given in Section 3.4.2. Note that in this summary when we use the term *quadtree*, we are referring to the corresponding one-dimensional analog.

An advantage of the point quadtree (a binary search tree in one dimension!) is that the depth is reduced when the tree contains a small number of rectangles. This is also an advantage of the PR quadtree, although it is not necessarily true when the rectangles are very close. However, when we are using a point quadtree, deletion of a rectangle forces us to expend some work in locating a suitable replacement node. The shape of the point quadtree depends on the order in which the rectangles are inserted.

For the PR quadtree, the placement of the rectangle in the tree depends on what other rectangles are present. As rectangles are added to the PR quadtree, existing rectangles may have to be moved to positions farther away from the root (in a node distance sense). On the other hand, once a rectangle is inserted into the MX quadtree, it maintains that position forever since its position is independent of the order of insertion and of the other rectangles that are present. Another advantage of the MX and PR quadtrees over the point quadtree is that since they are based on a regular decomposition, there is no need to store the subdivision points.

Although our algorithms were generally defined under the assumption that the rectangles do not overlap (but may touch), this restriction can be removed quite easily. First, observe that when rectangles are permitted to intersect, there will often be more than one rectangle associated with a node of the one-dimensional MX-CIF quadtree that corresponds to a subdivision point. Thus, the issue becomes how to organize these rectangles. The simplest solution is to maintain a linked list of these rectangles. An even more natural solution is to use a tile tree to organize them.

Recall that the tile tree and the one-dimensional MX-CIF quadtree are identical when rectangles are not permitted to overlap. In such a case, the secondary structures of the tile tree consist of, at most, one rectangle. When the tile tree is used in this context, it is not a complete binary tree. Alternatively, the tile tree is not necessarily balanced since the subdivision points are fixed by virtue of regular decomposition rather than being determined by the endpoints of the domain of rectangles, as in the definition of the interval tree.

3.4.2 Alternatives to the MX-CIF Quadtree

One of the drawbacks of the MX-CIF quadtree is that region queries (e.g., a window query) are somewhat inefficient due to the possible need to examine the one-dimensional MX-CIF quadtrees stored at each node without necessarily finding any rectangles that satisfy the query. There are several problems:

1. The one-dimensional MX-CIF quadtrees that store the rectangles that overlap the partition lines may be quite deep due to the particular configuration of the rectangles that intersect the partition lines.

2. There are many empty one-dimensional MX-CIF quadtrees.

3. There is no easy way to prune the search when the query rectangle does not overlap any of the rectangles stored in the one-dimensional MX-CIF quadtrees.

One way of overcoming the first problem is to use the one-dimensional variants of the point quadtree and PR quadtree instead of the one-dimensional MX-CIF quadtree for the rectangles that overlap the partition lines. In Section 3.4.1.3, we point out that the one-dimensional variant of the point quadtree is not particularly useful as the partition points are not known in advance and deletion may be a bit more time-consuming. Moreover, partition points will depend on the order in which the data is processed, which may increase the complexity of operations between different data sets. The depth of the one-dimensional variant of the PR quadtree will in general be far less than that of the one-dimensional MX-CIF quadtree, although this is not necessarily the case when the rectangles are very close to one another. Moreover, in the case of the one-dimensional variant of the PR quadtree, the placement of the rectangle in the tree depends on what other rectangles are present. As rectangles are added to the one-dimensional variant of the PR quadtree, existing rectangles may have to be moved to positions farther away from the root (in a node distance sense). On the other hand, once a rectangle is inserted into the one-dimensional variant of the MX-CIF quadtree, it maintains that position forever since its position is independent of the order of insertion and of the other rectangles that are present. Another advantage of the one-dimensional variant of the PR quadtree (as well as of the one-dimensional variant of the MX-CIF quadtree) over the one-dimensional variant of the point quadtree is that since it is based on a regular decomposition, there is no need to store the subdivision points. Thus, the one-dimensional variant of the PR quadtree is more useful than the one-dimensional variant of the point quadtree.

Another way of overcoming the first problem addresses the fact that the size of rectangle r's minimum enclosing quadtree block b is not necessarily related to the size of r. In particular, b is often much larger than r, causing inefficiency in search operations due to a reduction in the ability to prune objects from further consideration. This situation arises when r overlaps the axes lines that pass through the center of b. Recalling Section 2.1.4.1 of Chapter 2, Frank and Barrera [628, 630], as well as Ulrich [1901], suggest expanding the size of the space that is spanned by each quadtree block b of width w by a factor p ($p > 0$) so that the expanded block will be of width $(1 + p) \cdot w$. In this case, r will be associated with its minimum enclosing expanded quadtree block. The terms *cover fieldtree* [628, 630] and *loose quadtree* [1901] are used to describe the resulting structure. For example, letting $p = 1$, Figure 3.26 is the loose quadtree corresponding to the collection of objects in Figure 2.57(a) and their MX-CIF quadtree in Figure 2.57(b) in Section 2.1.4.1 of Chapter 2. In this example, there are only two differences between the loose and MX-CIF quadtrees:

1. Rectangle object E is associated with the SW child of the root of the loose quadtree instead of with the root of the MX-CIF quadtree.

2. Rectangle object B is associated with the NW child of the NE child of the root of the loose quadtree instead of with the NE child of the root of the MX-CIF quadtree.

Frank and Barrera [628, 630] suggest an alternative solution as well, termed the *partition fieldtree*, which shifts the positions of the centroids of blocks at successive levels of subdivision by one-half of the width of the block that is being subdivided. This guarantees that the size of the minimum enclosing quadtree block for rectangle r is bounded by eight times the maximum extent of r [630]. The loose quadtree, as well as the two fieldtree variants, is discussed in greater detail in Section 2.1.4.1 of Chapter 2.

The second problem can be overcome by adapting the k-d tree so that partitions are made along just one axis at a time, and thus we have a variant of an MX-CIF k-d tree. The third problem can be overcome by storing minimum bounding rectangles with the nodes of the one-dimensional MX-CIF quadtrees.

These problems have led to the development of a number of variants of the MX-CIF quadtree that make use of the following modifications:

1. Upon insertion of a rectangle r, instead of halting the top-level decomposition (i.e., the two-dimensional quadtree) once the minimum enclosing quadtree block of r has been found or when the subdivision will yield a block smaller than the size of the smallest possible rectangle, modify the halting condition to take into account the number of rectangles associated with each block. In particular, also halt the decomposition once a block contains no more than T rectangles. Thus, the blocks act like buckets, where T is the *bucket capacity*. This means that rectangles are no longer necessarily associated with their minimum enclosing quadtree block. The result is termed an *adaptive quadtree* [1571].

2. Omit the one-dimensional MX-CIF quadtrees used to store the rectangles that overlap the partition lines.

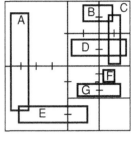

(a)

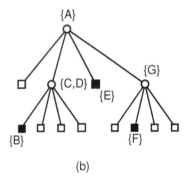

(b)

Figure 3.26
(a) Block decomposition induced by the loose quadtree for a collection of rectangle objects identical to those in Figure 2.57 in Section 2.1.4.1 of Chapter 2 and (b) its tree representation.

Some of these variants are discussed in the rest of this section and also in Section 3.4.3.

Pitaksanokul, Thanawastien, and Lursinsap [1496] make use of a bucketing solution where a block b is recursively decomposed into four equal-sized quadtree blocks when there are more than T rectangles in the space spanned by b. When a rectangle r overlaps one or both of the partition lines of a block, then r is associated with the quadrant of b that contains the lower-left corner of r. In order to support search queries, the minimum bounding rectangle of the rectangles stored in each block is also stored with the block. We will refer to this representation as a *bounded quadtree* (BQT) [1100]. Note that as in the MX-CIF quadtree, each rectangle r is associated with just one node a in the BQT, even though a may be smaller than r and, likewise, smaller than r's minimum enclosing quadtree block. Section 3.4.3 includes a discussion of more conventional adaptations of the bucketing method where the rectangles associated with the block b that is being decomposed may themselves have to be decomposed as they overlap the partition lines of b.

Lai, Fussell, and Wong [1100] overcome the above problems by employing variants of some of the proposed solutions. In particular, they use a bucket variant of an MX-CIF k-d tree with one-dimensional bucket variants of the PR k-d tree for the rectangles that intersect the partition lines in the case of a nonleaf node. In addition, they associate minimum bounding rectangles with each of the nonleaf nodes in the one-dimensional structures. They use the term *HV/VH tree* to describe their representation, although we use the term *bucket PR-CIF k-d tree* as it is more consistent with our terminology. Rectangles are allowed to overlap. There are two bucket capacities involved: one for the top-level two-dimensional bucket PR-CIF k-d tree corresponding to the maximum number of rectangles that can overlap a two-dimensional region before it must be split in two (termed a *region capacity*), and one for the one-dimensional bucket PR-CIF k-d tree corresponding to the maximum number of rectangles that can overlap a partition line (i.e., axis) before it must be split in two (termed an *axis capacity*). We use the terms *x-partition* (*y-partition*) to describe a line that partitions the underlying space at some value $x = C_x$ ($y = C_y$).

The two-dimensional bucket PR-CIF k-d tree is constructed by determining if the number of rectangles that overlap region r exceeds the region capacity. If it does not, then no further action is taken, and the rectangles are associated with the node corresponding to r. If it does, then r is split into two halves by cycling through the x and y coordinates in an alternating manner. Once r has been split (assume, without loss of generality, along the x axis at $x = C_x$), then all rectangles that have a nonempty intersection with $x = C_x$ are inserted into a one-dimensional bucket PR-CIF k-d tree that is associated with the node corresponding to r. The algorithm is applied recursively to the two sets of rectangles that do not intersect $x = C_x$, this time splitting the two sets along the y axis.

The one-dimensional bucket PR-CIF k-d tree is constructed by a similar process as the two-dimensional bucket PR-CIF k-d tree except that instead of determining if the number of rectangles that overlap a region exceeds the region capacity, we check if the number of rectangles that overlap the line l corresponding to the node exceeds the axis capacity. If it does not, then no further action is taken, and the rectangles are associated with the node corresponding to l. If it does, then l is split into two halves. Once l has been split into two halves, the rectangles that overlap the midpoint p of l are associated with the node corresponding to l, and the algorithm is applied recursively to the two sets of rectangles that do not overlap p.

In order to facilitate search operations, minimum bounding rectangles are associated with the nonleaf nodes of the one-dimensional bucket PR-CIF k-d trees. In particular, with each nonleaf node b of a one-dimensional bucket PR-CIF k-d tree for a y-partition (x partition), we record the minimum and maximum y (x) coordinate values of the rectangles stored in the tree rooted at b. In addition, we also record the minimum and maximum x (y) coordinate values of the rectangles stored in b. Moreover, in order to save execution time needed to recompute constantly the partition points by the recursive application of a halving process to the coordinate values of the boundary of the underlying space as the tree is traversed, the coordinate values of the partition axis and point are also stored with nonleaf nodes of both the two-dimensional and one-dimensional bucket PR-CIF k-d trees [1100].

Figure 3.27 is the bucket PR-CIF k-d tree for the set of rectangles given in Figure 3.23 using region and axis bucket capacities of 3. Figure 3.27(a) is the block decomposition, and Figure 3.27(b) is the corresponding tree representation. Notice that the pairing of the one-dimensional bucket PR-CIF k-d trees and the corresponding nonleaf nodes of the two-dimensional bucket PR-CIF k-d tree is shown with a horizontal line having a diagonal sawtooth pattern to the right of the node in the two-dimensional bucket PR-CIF k-d tree. We also use the same type of a line pattern to indicate that a set of rectangles associated with a node of the one-dimensional bucket PR-CIF k-d tree overlaps the midpoint of the partition axis (e.g., the node containing rectangle 8 in Figure 3.27(b)). In contrast, rectangle 9 is a leaf node of the one-dimensional bucket PR-CIF k-d tree associated with the right child of the root of the two-dimensional bucket PR-CIF k-d tree in Figure 3.27(b).

The execution of a region query is made quite efficient by avoiding some subsequent comparison operations when we determine that both children of a node of a one-dimensional or two-dimensional bucket PR-CIF k-d tree must be visited. For example, this situation arises in the case of a rectangular query window w that intersects the line l corresponding to partition axis a of two-dimensional bucket PR-CIF k-d tree node b and also intersects the midpoint p of l. This means that the set of rectangles S stored in the node c of the one-dimensional bucket PR-CIF k-d tree associated with b intersects w as the rectangles in the set have point p in common. Thus, no comparisons are needed for the elements of S. In fact, regardless of whether w intersects both l and p, we can always determine if each element of S intersects w with fewer than four comparison operations (see Exercise 3).

Similarly, we can also avoid some subsequent comparison operations when we determine that only one child of a one-dimensional bucket PR-CIF k-d tree must be visited. For example, this situation arises in the case of a rectangular query window w that intersects the line l corresponding to partition axis a of two-dimensional bucket PR-CIF k-d tree node b and does not intersect the midpoint p of l. Assume, without loss of generality, that x (y) is the partition axis, and let S denote the set of rectangles stored in the node c of the one-dimensional bucket PR-CIF k-d tree associated with b. When the right (top) edge of w is less than the x (y) coordinate value of p, then only the left child of c is processed. In this case, none of the elements of S intersects w if the right (top) edge of w is less than the minimum x (y) coordinate values of S. Similarly, when the left (bottom) edge of w is greater than the $x(y)$ coordinate value of p, then only the right child of c is processed. In this case, none of the elements of S intersects w if the left (bottom) edge of w is greater than the maximum $x(y)$ coordinate values of S.

The sets of rectangles that are associated with the leaf nodes of the two-dimensional bucket PR-CIF k-d trees and the nonleaf nodes of the one-dimensional bucket PR-CIF k-d trees are implemented as sequential lists. This is because the region and axis capacities are relatively small, and for such values, the overhead incurred by a complicated access structure is deemed not to be worthwhile [1100]. Note that it may be the case that the number of rectangles associated with a node in the one-dimensional bucket PR-CIF k-d tree may exceed the axis capacity. This situation arises when the number of rectangles that overlap the midpoint of the axis associated with the node exceeds the axis capacity. No further action is taken here.

Lai et al. [1100] conducted a number of experiments comparing the execution time for window queries and space requirements of the bucket PR-CIF k-d tree with the balanced four-dimensional k-d tree [1114, 1571], BQT [1496], and QLQT [1986] (a variant of a bucket rectangle PM quadtree, discussed in greater detail in Section 3.4.3, where the objects are rectangles instead of line segments, as in Section 2.2.2.8 of

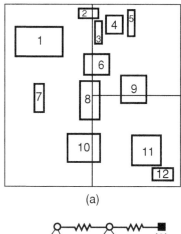

(a)

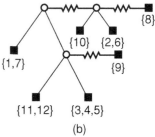

(b)

Figure 3.27
(a) The block decomposition induced by the bucket PR-CIF k-d tree for the collection of rectangles in Figure 3.23 using region and axis bucket capacities of 3 and (b) its tree representation. Horizontal lines with a diagonal sawtooth pattern denote a link from a nonleaf node of the two- and one-dimensional structure to the corresponding one-dimensional structure and list, respectively, that includes the rectangles that overlap the respective partition axis or point.

Chapter 2). Different bucket capacities were used to obtain the best performance for each representation (i.e., 8 for the one- and two-dimensional bucket PR-CIF k-d trees, and 32 for the BQT and QLQT methods). The bucket PR-CIF quadtree was over twice as fast as the balanced four-dimensional k-d tree and somewhat less than twice as fast as the BQT method. The QLQT method took approximately the same amount of time as the bucket PR-CIF k-d tree, sometimes taking less and sometimes taking more. The bucket PR-CIF k-d tree required 20% and 40% less space than the BQT method and balanced k-d tree, respectively. Moreover, the bucket PR-CIF k-d tree required between 60% and 100% less space than the QLQT method. This difference is primarily a result of the fact that the bucket PR-CIF k-d tree represents each rectangle in just one node of the tree, while the QLQT method usually uses considerably more nodes to represent each rectangle (four in these experiments). Thus, by using the bucket PR-CIF k-d tree, we achieve approximately the same execution time performance as the QLQT method with significantly lower space requirements. These results also serve to counter those of Rosenberg [1571] (mentioned in Section 3.3), who found the performance of the balanced four-dimensional k-d tree to be better than the MX-CIF quadtree. In other words, the use of the one-dimensional bucket PR-CIF k-d tree to represent the rectangles that span both sides of the line that partitions the underlying space appears to be useful.

The bucket PR-CIF k-d tree is very similar to the R-file of Hutflesz, Six, and Widmayer [909]. The R-file differs from the bucket PR-CIF k-d tree in that when a bucket overflow occurs, instead of splitting bucket region into two halves (or four quarters in the case of a quadtreelike approach), it retains the original bucket region and creates a new bucket for just one of the two halves of the original bucket region. It then distributes the rectangle objects into the smallest of the cells within which it lies in its entirety. The choice of the half to be retained is based on which one results in approximately the same number of objects in the region that has been split and the newly created region. In fact, the process may end up splitting the newly created region again if all of the objects will lie in the same region. Note that bucket regions do overlap in this case and that an object is not necessarily associated with its minimum containing quadtree or k-d tree block. Instead, it is associated with its minimum containing quadtree or k-d tree block among the existing blocks. Of course, if all of the objects overlap the partition line, then the region corresponding to the bucket cannot be split. In this case, an R-file of one less dimension is used, as is done for the MX-CIF quadtree and the bucket PR-CIF k-d tree.

For example, Figure 3.28 is the R-file for the set of rectangles given in Figure 3.23 using a bucket capacity of 3 for both the two- and one-dimensional R-files. We assume a PR k-d tree implementation and that the x coordinate is partitioned before the y coordinate. Figure 3.28(a–c) shows the block decomposition, and Figure 3.28(d) shows a tree representation of the resulting hierarchy that also includes the one-dimensional R-file associated with the block corresponding to the entire region (shown as the root of the tree). The two-dimensional R-file contains four blocks: one corresponding to the entire region (Figure 3.28(a)), two corresponding to its two descendants (Figure 3.28(b)), and one corresponding to the descendant of the top half of the right descendant (Figure 3.28(c)). The pairing of the one-dimensional R-file and the corresponding block of the two-dimensional R-file is shown with a horizontal line having a diagonal saw-tooth pattern to the right of the corresponding node in the tree representation of the two-dimensional R-file.

In this example, we find that the block corresponding to the entire region contains four rectangles (i.e., 2, 6, 8, and 10), which is more than the bucket capacity (Figure 3.28(a)). However, it cannot be decomposed further as these rectangles overlap the partition line of the block and thus we make use of a one-dimensional R-file that consists of one block corresponding to the length of the entire x partition (containing rectangles 8 and 10) and one block corresponding to the upper half of the partition (containing rectangles 2 and 6), as seen in Figure 3.28(d). Note that the empty white square nodes do not have a corresponding block in the R-file. They are only included to facilitate the visualization of which blocks are actually present in the R-file.

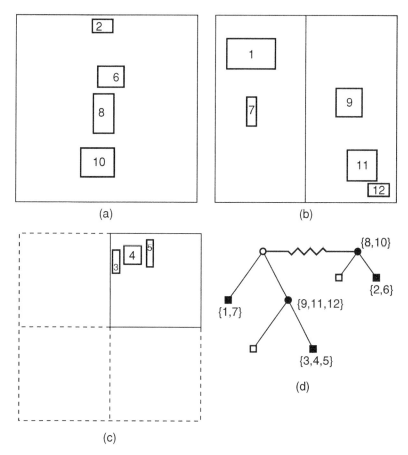

Figure 3.28
(a–c) The block decomposition induced by the R-file for the collection of rectangles in Figure 3.23 with a bucket capacity of 3 and (d) its tree representation. Horizontal lines with a diagonal sawtooth pattern denote the pairing of a one-dimensional R-file and the corresponding block of the two-dimensional R-file that has overflowed and whose rectangles overlap the partition axis. Empty white square nodes do not have a corresponding block in the R-file.

In order to avoid searching unoccupied space, the R-file also associates with each bucket a minimum bounding box of the objects that it contains. It is interesting to observe that the R-file is somewhat similar to the BANG file [640] (see Section 1.7.1.5 of Chapter 1) in the sense that some of the regions are nested in other regions. However, unlike the BANG file, region overlap is permitted in the R-file, and thus the nested regions are not removed from their containing regions (i.e., both the contained and containing regions are present in the R-file).

Like Abel and Smith's implementation of the MX-CIF quadtree [2] and other methods, the R-file is implemented by storing a one-dimensional representative of the buckets (the bucket's locational code based on the Morton number) in a B-tree. The organization and access of this B-tree that contains locational codes based on Morton numbers of overlapping blocks such as those present in the R-file, are addressed by Ouksel and Mayer [1438] in their development of the nested interpolation-based grid file (NIBGF), whose blocks overlap in much the same way as those in the R-file, although they are generated in a different manner. The motivation for the development of the NIBGF was to improve on the exhaustive search worst-case execution time of an exact match query in the BANG file. This worst-case execution time also arises for the more general, but analogous, point in the R-file.

Exercises

1. Draw the cover fieldtree for the collection of rectangles given in Figure 3.23 using $p = 1$.

2. Draw the partition fieldtree for the collection of rectangles given in Figure 3.23.

3. Show that, regardless of whether a rectangular query window w intersects the line l corresponding to partition axis a of two-dimensional bucket PR-CIF k-d tree node b or intersects the midpoint p of l, determining if each element of the set S of rectangles stored in the node c of the one-dimensional bucket PR-CIF k-d tree associated with b intersects w can be done with fewer than four comparison operations.

4. Give an algorithm to insert a rectangle into a bucket PR-CIF k-d tree.

5. Give an algorithm to delete a rectangle from a bucket PR-CIF k-d tree.

6. Give an algorithm to find the nearest rectangle to a given point in a bucket PR-CIF k-d tree.

7. Give an algorithm to retrieve all rectangles that overlap a rectangular query window in a bucket PR-CIF k-d tree.

8. Give an algorithm to insert a rectangle into an R-file.

9. Give an algorithm to delete a rectangle from an R-file.

10. Give an algorithm to find the nearest rectangle to a given point in an R-file.

11. Give an algorithm to retrieve all rectangles that overlap a rectangular query window in an R-file.

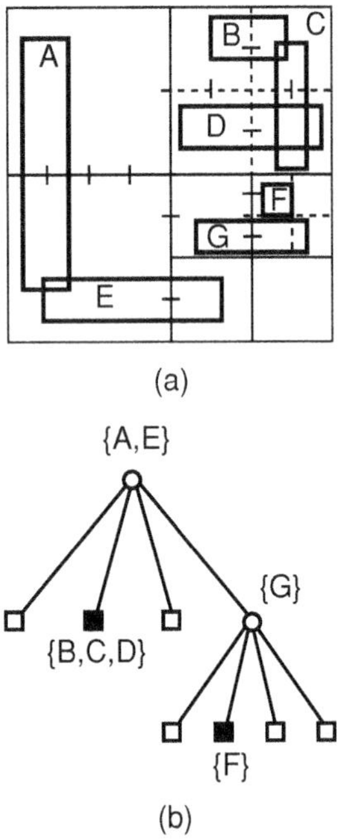

3.4.3 Multiple Quadtree Block Representations

Determining how many rectangles intersect a window (e.g., in the form of a rectangle) may be quite costly when using the MX-CIF quadtree and other representations that associate each rectangle with the smallest enclosing quadtree block. The problem is that the quadtree nodes that intersect the query rectangle may contain many rectangles that do not intersect the query rectangle; yet, each one of them must be individually compared with the query rectangle to determine the existence of a possible intersection.

For example, consider the MX-CIF quadtree in Figure 3.29, corresponding to the collection of rectangles given in Figure 3.1 (excluding the query rectangles). Unlike in the examples of the MX-CIF quadtree in the previous section, we permit the rectangles to overlap. Although query rectangle 1 (see Figure 3.1) is in the NE quadrant of the root of the MX-CIF quadtree, we still have to check some of the rectangles that are stored at the root of the entire quadtree since these rectangles could conceivably overlap rectangle 1.

This work could be avoided by using a more compact (in an area sense) representation of each rectangle. Such a representation would use more, and smaller, quadtree blocks to represent each rectangle, but the total area of the blocks would be considerably less than that of the smallest enclosing quadtree block. As a result, more rectangles would be eliminated from consideration by the pruning that occured during the search of the quadtree. A number of alternatives are available to achieve this effect. They are examined briefly below.

One possibility is to adapt the region quadtree to represent each rectangle. Such a representation leads to many nodes since its underlying decomposition rule requires that the block corresponding to each node be homogeneous (i.e., that it be totally contained within one of the rectangles or not be in any of the rectangles). Permitting rectangles to overlap forces a modification of the decomposition rule. In particular, it implies that decomposition ceases when a block is totally contained within one or more rectangles. However, if a block is contained in more than one rectangle, then it must be totally contained in all of them. We use the term *rectangle quadtree* to describe this representation.

(a)

(b)

Figure 3.29
(a) Block decomposition induced by the MX-CIF quadtree for the collection of rectangles in Figure 3.1 and (b) its tree representation.

Abel and Smith [9] present a less radical alternative. They propose that instead of using the minimum enclosing quadtree block, each rectangle be represented by a collection of enclosing quadtree blocks. They suggest that the collection contain a maximum of four blocks, although other amounts are also possible. The four blocks are obtained by determining the minimum enclosing quadtree block, say B, for each rectangle, say R, and then splitting B once to obtain quadtree blocks B_i ($i \in \{$NW, NE, SW, SE$\}$) such that R_i is the portion of R, if any, that is contained in B_i. Next, for each B_i, we find the minimum enclosing quadtree block, say D_i, that contains R_i. Now, each rectangle is represented by the set of blocks consisting of D_i. We term such a representation an *expanded MX-CIF quadtree*. As an example of the expanded MX-CIF quadtree, consider Figure 3.30, corresponding to the collection of rectangles of Figure 3.1. Several items are worthy of note. First, each node appears at least one level lower in the expanded MX-CIF quadtree than it did in the MX-CIF quadtree. Second, some of D_i may be empty (e.g., rectangle A in Figure 3.30 is covered by blocks 2 and 4; rectangle F in Figure 3.30 is covered by block 14). Third, the covering blocks are not necessarily of equal size (e.g., rectangle E in Figure 3.30 is covered by blocks 4 and 12). It should be clear that the area covered by the collection of blocks D_i is not greater than that of B.

The worst-case execution time for building the expanded MX-CIF quadtree and the space requirements are the same as for the MX-CIF quadtree: $O(n \cdot N)$ for a tree of maximum depth n with N rectangles. The worst-case execution time of the rectangle intersection problem is also the same as that for the MX-CIF quadtree: $O(n \cdot N^2)$. Abel and Smith suggest that the search process can be made more efficient by applying the splitting process again to the blocks D_i. Of course, the more times that we split, the closer we get to the region quadtree representation of the rectangles. Also, this increases the space requirement and the insertion and deletion costs.

A representation that is bit more general than the expanded MX-CIF quadtree and more closely related to the rectangle quadtree is to adapt the PM quadtree used for line segments in Section 2.2.2.6 of Chapter 2 to rectangles. We term the result a *bucket rectangle PM quadtree* (or *bucket rectangle quadtree*). This approach is used by Brown [269], who calls it a *multiple storage quadtree*. In this case, we recursively subdivide a block b into four equal-sized blocks until b contains no more than T rectangles, where T is the bucket capacity (see also [466], who subdivide b into a variable number c of blocks such that c is a power of 2 and varies from block to block, thereby reducing the ultimate depth of the tree and making accesses faster). Therefore, each rectangle can be associated with more than one node in the bucket rectangle PM quadtree. In order to avoid repeatedly storing rectangle r in all of the blocks intersected by r, the bucket rectangle PM quadtree just stores a pointer to r in these blocks. As with most PM quadtree implementations, each block contains a list of pointers to all of the rectangle objects that intersect it rather than the actual rectangles.

Numerous algorithms for operations in VLSI design applications have been developed that use the bucket rectangle PM quadtree (e.g., [887]). Weyten and De Pauw [1985] analyze the storage requirements of the bucket rectangle PM quadtree under uniform and Poisson data distribution models for the centers of the rectangles. The results of this analysis are used to predict the cost of a window query [1985].

The drawback of Brown's formulation of the bucket rectangle PM quadtree is that when executing a window query, some rectangle objects may be reported as intersecting the window several times. Brown overcomes this problem by marking each rectangle object the first time it is reported and then does not report any rectangle objects that have already been marked. Nevertheless, this solution has a shortcoming in the sense that, once the rectangle objects have been reported, the window must be processed again, and all marked rectangle objects must be unmarked.

Weyten and De Pauw [1986] avoid the need to unmark the rectangle objects that have been marked during the execution of the window query on the bucket rectangle PM

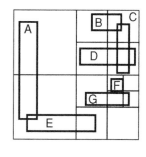

(a)

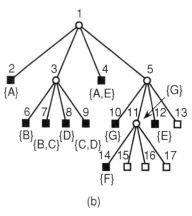

(b)

Figure 3.30
(a) Block decomposition induced by the expanded MX-CIF quadtree for the collection of rectangles in Figure 3.1 and (b) its tree representation.

481

quadtree by decomposing the list of rectangle objects that intersect each block into four lists, depending on which of the left or bottom sides of the block is intersected by the objects. There are four possible list types:

1. Neither the left nor bottom side of the block is intersected.

2. Only the left side of the block is intersected.

3. Only the bottom side of the block is intersected.

4. Both the left and bottom sides of the block are intersected.

The resulting representation is termed the *quad list quadtree* (QLQT) [1986]. The QLQT has the property that each rectangle object is a member of only one list of type 1, but it can be a member of several lists of types 2–4 (see Exercise 6). A window query on window w is executed without the need to mark by applying the following steps to each block b that it overlaps (see Exercise 7):

1. If b is completely contained in w, then examine all elements of lists of type 1 as their lower-left corner is in b.

2. If only the left (bottom) side of w intersects b, then examine all elements of lists of types 1 and 2 (1 and 3).

3. If both the left and bottom sides of w intersect b, then examine the elements of all four lists (i.e., types 1–4).

Recall from Section 3.4.2 that the QLQT method was compared with the BQT and bucket PR-CIF k-d tree and was found to require considerably more space than the bucket PR-CIF k-d tree, while the execution time of a general windowing algorithm was sometimes better and sometimes worse. The space requirements of the QLQT method could be reduced somewhat by making use of a larger bucket capacity than that used by the bucket PR-CIF k-d tree at the cost of increasing the time needed for some queries due to the higher number of items that must be searched in each node. In fact, this approach of increasing the bucket capacity is used by Lai, Fussell, and Wong [1101] in their development of the hinted quadtree, which is really just an improved implementation of the QLQT method.

The hinted quadtree is motivated by a desire to increase the efficiency of nearest neighbor searching, which is a primitive operation in VLSI geometry design rule checking. Lai et al. [1101] assume that, for a rectangle object of type t, the nearest neighbor will always be found within a given distance h_t (termed the *hinted distance*). Thus, their strategy is to expand the query rectangle by its corresponding hinted distance in the four principal directions, thereby creating a new rectangle w that serves as the query window. The nearest neighbor is found by executing a window query on w in the part of the space spanned by the minimum enclosing quadtree block of w, denoted by b_w, and returning the nearest object in the window. The determination of b_w is facilitated in the hinted quadtree by also storing with each rectangle r a pointer to its minimum enclosing quadtree block b_r, termed an *owner pointer*. If b_r does not fully contain b_w, then father pointers are traversed starting at b_r until the first block whose size is greater than or equal to that of b_w is reached. It should be clear that, in fact, the owner pointer is unnecessary as the minimum enclosing quadtree block of the query window can be obtained by simply descending the QLQT from the root. Thus, there is no real difference between the hinted quadtree and QLQT.

Lai et al. [1101] conducted some experiments comparing the hinted quadtree with BQT, the balanced four-dimensional k-d tree, QLQT, and the bucket PR-CIF k-d tree, where the bucket capacity of the hinted quadtree was 56, while the bucket capacity was 8 and 16 for the one- and two-dimensional bucket PR-CIF k-d trees, respectively. Neighbor searching was about 40% faster in the hinted quadtree than in the bucket PR-CIF k-d tree, but the build times and space requirements of the hinted quadtree were still worse than those of the bucket PR-CIF k-d tree, although they were better than those for QLQT.

The speedup in the neighbor searching is a direct result of the fact that in the hinted quadtree and QLQT the only nodes that need to be inspected are the leaf nodes that overlap the query window. On the other hand, the remaining methods must also inspect nonleaf nodes with descendant leaf nodes that overlap the query window. Of course, as mentioned earlier, the large bucket capacity used in the hinted quadtree limits its utility for queries that require the examination of the individual items in the bucket (e.g., mutual intersection) rather than simply reporting the ones that are present, as is the case for the window query. Moreover, the observed superiority of the hinted quadtree over the remaining representations [1101] for the nearest neighbor query implemented as a window query does not extend to other window queries as the size of the window was constrained in their experiments to be slightly larger than the rectangle objects stored in the structure. Thus, in general, the bucket PR-CIF k-d tree is still likely to be the most attractive of the alternatives that we have explored.

Exercises

1. Give a procedure called EXPANDEDINSERT to insert a rectangle R into an expanded MX-CIF quadtree. Rectangle R may overlap existing rectangles.

2. Analyze the expected cost of inserting a rectangle into an expanded MX-CIF quadtree.

3. Give a procedure called EXPANDEDWINDOW to find all rectangles that intersect a window in an expanded MX-CIF quadtree.

4. Analyze the cost of EXPANDEDWINDOW.

5. Prove that the worst-case execution time for building, the space requirements, and the worst-case execution time of the rectangle intersection problem for the expanded MX-CIF quadtree are the same as for the MX-CIF quadtree.

6. Show that the QLQT has the property that each rectangle object is a member of only one list of type 1, but it can be a member of several lists of types 2–4.

7. Show that the steps of the window query algorithm for the QLQT work properly in the sense that each rectangle object r that intersects window w is reported just once (i.e., there is no need for marking and unmarking, as in the bucket rectangle PM quadtree).

8. In order to implement the QLQT method, we need an efficient way to determine the nature of the intersection of a block and a rectangle object. How many different ways are there in which a rectangle object o intersects a block b? Give a method of classifying them.

4

High-Dimensional Data

Chapters 1 and 2 dealt with the representation of multidimensional points and objects, respectively, and the development of appropriate indexing methods that enable them to be retrieved efficiently. Most of these methods were designed for use in application domains where the data usually has a spatial component that has a relatively low dimension. Examples of such application domains include geographic information systems (GIS), spatial databases, solid modeling, computer vision, computational geometry, and robotics. However, there are many application domains where the data is of considerably higher dimensionality and is not necessarily spatial. This is especially true in pattern recognition and image databases where the data is made up of a set of objects, and the high dimensionality is a direct result of trying to describe the objects via a collection of features (also known as a *feature vector*). Examples of features include color, color moments, textures, shape descriptions, and so on, expressed using scalar values. The goal in these applications is often one of the following:

1. Finding objects having particular feature values (point queries).

2. Finding objects whose feature values fall within a given range or where the distance from some query object falls into a certain range (range queries).[1]

3. Finding objects whose features have values similar to those of a given query object or set of query objects (nearest neighbor queries). In order to reduce the complexity of the search process, the precision of the required similarity can be an approximation (approximate nearest neighbor queries).

4. Finding pairs of objects from the same set or different sets that are sufficiently similar to each other (all-closest-pairs queries). This is also a variant of a more general query commonly known as a *spatial join query*.

These queries are collectively referred to as *similarity searching* (also known as *similarity retrieval*), and supporting them is the subject of this chapter. The objective of the search can either be to find a few similar objects from a larger set or to match corresponding objects in two or more large sets of objects so that the result is a pairing of all of the objects from one set with objects in the other set. When the pairing is one-to-one (i.e., where for each distinct object in set A, we seek one nearest neighboring object in set B, which need not always be distinct), then the latter query is known as the *all nearest neighbors problem*. There is also the general problem (e.g., [226, 2030, 2066]), where B need not be the same as A, while in [297, 396, 1908], B is constrained to be

---

[1] When we are only interested in the number of objects that fall within the range, instead of the identity of the objects, then the query is known as a *range aggregation query* (e.g., [1853, 1203]).

the same as A),[2] and the distance semijoin for $k = 1$ [847]. An example of the utility of the latter is the *conflation problem*, which arises often in applications involving spatial data in GIS. In its simplest formulation, conflation is graph or network matching and is usually applied in a geographic setting to maps that are slightly out of alignment in a spatial sense (e.g., [155, 248, 344, 1598, 1599, 1601, 1958, 2033]). We do not deal with such searches in this book and, instead, focus on the former. Moreover, of the queries enumerated above, the nearest neighbor query also known as the *post office problem* (e.g., [1046, p, 563]), is particularly important and hence it is emphasized here. This problem arises in many different fields including computer graphics, where it is known as a *pick query* (e.g., [622]); in coding, where it is known as the *vector quantization problem* (e.g., [747]); and in pattern recognition, as well as machine learning, where it is known as the *fast nearest-neighbor classifier* (e.g., [514]). An apparently straightforward solution to finding the nearest neighbor is to compute a Voronoi diagram for the data points (i.e., a partition of the space into regions where all points in the region are closer to the region's associated data point than to any other data point) and then locate the Voronoi region corresponding to the query point. As we will see in Section 4.4.4, the problem with this solution is that the combinatorial complexity of the Voronoi diagram in high dimensions, expressed in terms of the number of objects, is prohibitive, thereby making it virtually impossible to store the structure, which renders its applicability moot. However, see the approximate Voronoi diagram (AVD) in Section 4.4.5, where the dimension of the underlying space is captured by expressing the complexity bounds in terms of the error threshold ε rather than the number of objects N in the underlying space.

The above is typical of the problems that we must face when dealing with high-dimensional data. Generally speaking, multidimensional problems such as these queries become increasingly more difficult to solve as the dimensionality increases. One reason is that most of us are not particularly adept at visualizing high-dimensional data (e.g., in three and higher dimensions, we no longer have the aid of paper and pencil). However, more importantly, we eventually run into the *curse of dimensionality*. This term was coined by Bellman [159] to indicate that the number of samples needed to estimate an arbitrary function with a given level of accuracy grows exponentially with the number of variables (i.e., dimensions) that it comprises. For similarity searching (i.e., finding nearest neighbors), this means that the number of objects (i.e., points) in the dataset that need to be examined in deriving the estimate grows exponentially with the underlying dimension.

The curse of dimensionality has a direct bearing on similarity searching in high dimensions in the sense that it raises the issue of whether or not nearest neighbor searching is even meaningful in such a domain. In particular, letting d denote a distance function that need not necessarily be a metric, Beyer, Goldstein, Ramakrishnan, and Shaft [212] point out that nearest neighbor searching is not meaningful when the ratio of the variance of the distance between two random points p and q, drawn from the data and query distributions, and the expected distance between them converges to zero as the dimension k goes to infinity—that is,

$$\lim_{k \to \infty} \frac{\text{Variance}[d(p,q)]}{\text{Expected}[d(p,q)]} = 0.$$

In other words, the distance to the nearest neighbor and the distance to the farthest neighbor tend to converge as the dimension increases. Formally, they prove that when the data and query distributions satisfy this ratio, then the probability that the farthest neighbor distance is smaller than $1 + \varepsilon$ of the nearest neighbor distance is 1 in the limit as the dimension goes to infinity and ε is a positive value. For example, they show that this ratio holds whenever the coordinate values of the data and the query point are independent

---

[2] Some of the solutions (e.g., [226, 1908, 2030]) try to take advantage of the fact that the nearest neighbor search needs to be performed on all points in the dataset and thus try to reuse the results of efforts expended in prior searches. They arise primarily in the context of database applications, where they are known as an *all nearest neighbor join* (ANN join).

and identically distributed, as is the case when they are both drawn from a uniform distribution. This is easy to see in the unit hypercube as the variance is smaller than the expected distance.

Assuming that d is a distance metric and hence that the triangle inequality holds, an alternative way of looking at the curse of dimensionality is to observe that, when dealing with high-dimensional data, the probability density function (analogous to a histogram) of the distances of the various elements is more concentrated and has a larger mean value. This means that similarity searching algorithms will have to perform more work. In the worst case, we have the situation where $d(x,x) = 0$ and $d(y,x) = 1$ for all $y \neq x$, which means that a similarity query must compare the query object with every object of the set. One way to see why more concentrated probability densities lead to more complex similarity searching is to observe that this means that the triangle inequality cannot be used so often to eliminate objects from consideration. In particular, the triangle inequality implies that every element x such that $|d(p,q) - d(p,x)| > \varepsilon$ cannot be at a distance of ε or less from q (i.e., from $d(p,q) \leq d(p,x) + d(q,x)$). Thus, if we examine the probability density function of $d(p,x)$ (i.e., on the horizontal axis), we find that when ε is small while the probability density function is large at $d(p,q)$, then the probability of eliminating an element from consideration via the use of the triangle inequality is the remaining area under the curve, which is quite small (see Figure 4.1(a) in contrast to Figure 4.1(b) where the density function of the distances is more uniform). This is not surprising because the sum of the area under the curve corresponding to the probability density function is 1. Note that use of the triangle inequality to eliminate objects from consideration is analogous to the application of the method of Friedman, Baskett, and Shustek [649] as well as Nene and Nayar [1364] for vector spaces, which eliminates a k-dimensional object $x = (x_0, x_1, \ldots, x_{k-1})$ from consideration as being within ε of $q = (q_0, q_1, \ldots, q_{k-1})$ if $|x_i - q_i| > \varepsilon$ for one of x_i where $0 \leq i \leq k-1$ (see Section 1.1 in Chapter 1).

These observations mean that nearest neighbor searching may be quite inefficient as it is very difficult to differentiate between the nearest neighbor and the other elements. Moreover, as we will see, seemingly appropriate indexing methods, analogous to those described in Chapters 1 and 2, which are designed to make it easier to avoid examining irrelevant elements, may not be of great help in this case. In fact, the experiments of Beyer et al. [212] show that the curse of dimensionality becomes noticeable for dimensions as low as 10–15 for the uniform distribution. The only saving grace is that real-world high-dimensional data (say of dimension k) is not likely to be uniformly distributed as its volume is much smaller than $O(c^k)$ for some small constant $c > 2$. Thus, we can go on with our discussion despite the apparent pall of the curse of dimensionality, which tends to cast a shadow on any arguments or analyses that are based on uniformly distributed data or queries.

Assuming that the curse of dimensionality does not come into play, query responses are facilitated by sorting the objects on the basis of some of their feature values and building appropriate indexes. The high-dimensional feature space is indexed using some multidimensional data structure (termed *multidimensional indexing*) such as those described in Chapters 1 and 2 or modifications thereof to fit the high-dimensional problem environment. Similarity search that finds objects similar to a target object can be done with a range search or a nearest neighbor search in the multidimensional data structure. However, unlike applications in spatial databases where the distance function between two objects is usually Euclidean, this is not necessarily the case in the high-dimensional feature space where the distance function may even vary from query to query on the same feature (e.g., [1591]). Unless stated otherwise, we usually assume that the distance is measured directly between points in the space (i.e., "as the crow flies" in a spatial context) rather than possibly being constrained to be along a network on which the points lie, as is useful in applications such as spatial databases. Nevertheless, we do cover the situation that distance is measured along a spatial network in Section 4.1.6. We also assume that the data and query objects are static rather than in motion (e.g., [162, 296, 889, 930,

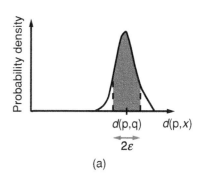

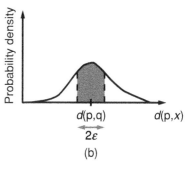

Figure 4.1
A probability density function (analogous to a histogram) of the distances $d(p,x)$ with the shaded area corresponding to $|d(p,q) - d(p,x)| \leq \varepsilon$: (a) a density function where the distance values have a small variation; (b) a more uniform distribution of distance values, thereby resulting in a more effective use of the triangle inequality to prune objects from consideration as satisfying the range search query.

931, 949, 1306, 1320, 1543, 1789, 1855, 1851, 2034, 2061], many of which make use of the TPR-tree [1610] and the TPR*-tree [1855], which are variants of an R-tree [791] and an R*-tree [152], respectively).

Searching in high-dimensional spaces is time-consuming. Performing point and range queries in high dimensions is considerably easier, from the standpoint of computational complexity, than performing similarity queries because point and range queries do not involve the computation of distance. In particular, searches through an indexed space usually involve relatively simple comparison tests. However, if we have to examine all of the index nodes, then the process is again time-consuming. In contrast, computing similarity makes use of distance, and the process of computing the distance can be computationally complex. For example, computing the Euclidean distance between two points in a high-dimensional space, say d, requires d multiplication operations and $d-1$ addition operations, as well as a square root operation (which can be omitted). Note also that computing similarity requires the definition of what it means for two objects to be similar, which is not always so obvious.

The previous discussion has been based on the premise that we know the features that describe the objects (and hence the dimensionality of the underlying feature space). In fact, it is often quite difficult to identify the features, and thus we frequently turn to experts in the application domain from which the objects are drawn for assistance in this process. Nevertheless, it is often the case that the features cannot be easily identified even by the domain experts. In this case, the only information that we have available is a distance function that indicates the degree of similarity (or dissimilarity) between all pairs of objects, given a set of N objects. Usually, it is required that the distance function d obey the triangle inequality, be nonnegative, and be symmetric, in which case it is known as a *metric* and also referred to as a *distance metric* (see Section 4.5.1). Sometimes, the degree of similarity is expressed by use of a similarity matrix that contains interobject distance values for all possible pairs of the N objects. Some examples of distance functions that are distance metrics include edit distances, such as the Levenshtein [1156] and Hamming [796] distances for strings[3] and the Hausdorff distance for images (e.g., [911] and footnote 45 in Section 2.2.3.4 of Chapter 2).

Given a distance function, we usually index the data (i.e., objects) with respect to their distance from a few selected objects. We use the term *distance-based indexing* to describe such methods. The advantage of distance-based indexing methods is that distance computations are used to build the index, but once the index has been built, similarity queries can often be performed with a significantly lower number of distance computations than a sequential scan of the entire dataset. Of course, in situations where we may want to apply several different distance metrics, then the drawback of the distance-based indexing techniques is that they require that the index be rebuilt for each different distance metric, which may be nontrivial. This is not the case for the multidimensional indexing methods that have the advantage of supporting arbitrary distance metrics (however, this comparison is not entirely fair since the assumption, when using distance-based indexing, is that often we do not have any feature values, as for example in DNA sequences).

There are many problems with indexing high-dimensional data. In fact, due to the complexity of handling high-dimensional data using a multidimensional index, we frequently find that the cost of performing queries using the index is higher than a sequential scan of the entire data (e.g., [212]). This is a result of the curse of dimensionality, which was discussed earlier. However, the "inherent dimensionality" of a dataset is often much lower than the dimensionality of the underlying space. For example, the values of some of the features may be correlated in some way. Alternatively, some of the features may

---

[3] The *Levenshtein edit distance* between two strings s and t is the number of deletions, insertions, or substitutions required to transform s into t. The *Hamming edit distance* between s and t, defined only when s and t are of the same length, is the number of positions in which s and t differ (i.e., have different characters).

not be as important as others in discriminating between objects and thus may be ignored
or given less weight (e.g., [838]). Therefore, there has been a considerable amount of
interest in techniques to reduce the dimensionality of the data. Another motivation for
the development of many dimension reduction techniques has been a desire to make use
of disk-based spatial indexes that are based on object hierarchies, such as members of
the R-tree family [791]. The performance of these methods decreases with an increase
in dimensionality due to the decrease in the fanout of a node of a given capacity since
usually the amount of storage needed for the bounding boxes is directly proportional to
the dimensionality of the data, thereby resulting in longer search paths.

In situations where no features but only a distance function are defined for the objects,
there exists an alternative to using distance-based indexes. In particular, methods have
been devised for deriving "features" purely based on the interobject distances [587, 886,
1181, 1950]. Thus, given N objects, the goal is to choose a value of k and find a set
of N corresponding points in a k-dimensional space so that the distance between the
N corresponding points is as close as possible to that given by the distance function
for the N objects. The attractiveness of such methods is that we can now index the
points using multidimensional data structures. These methods are known as *embedding
methods*[4] and can also be applied to objects represented by feature vectors as alternatives
to the traditional dimension reduction methods. In fact, one of these methods [587] is
inspired by dimension reduction methods based on linear transformations. Embedding
methods can also be applied when the features are known, in which case they can also
be characterized as dimension reduction techniques (e.g., [924]).

The rest of this chapter is organized as follows. Since our main motivation is similarity searching, we start with a description of the process of finding nearest neighbors
in Section 4.1. Here the focus is on finding the nearest neighbor rather than the k nearest
neighbors. Once the nearest neighbor has been found, the process that we describe can be
used to find the second nearest neighbor, the third, and so on. This process is incremental,
in contrast to an alternative method that, given an integer k, finds the k nearest neighbors
regardless of the order of their distance from the query object q. The advantage of this
approach over the incremental method is that the amount of storage is bounded by k, in
contrast to having possibly to keep track of all of the objects if their distance from q is
approximately the same. On the other hand, the advantage of the incremental approach
is that once the k nearest neighbors have been obtained, the $(k + 1)$-th neighbor can be
obtained without having to start the process anew to obtain $k + 1$ nearest neighbors.

Note that the problem of finding neighbors is somewhat similar to the point location
query, which was discussed in Section 2.1.3. In particular, in many algorithms, the first
step is to locate the query object q. The second step consists of the actual search. Most of
the classical methods employ a "depth-first" *branch and bound* strategy (e.g., [836]). An
alternative, and the one we describe in Section 4.1, employs a "best-first" search strategy.
The difference between the two strategies is that, in the best-first strategy, the elements
of the structure in which the objects are stored are explored in increasing order of their
distance from q. In contrast, in the depth-first strategy, the order in which the elements
of the structure in which the objects are stored are explored is a result of performing a
depth-first traversal of the structure using the distance to the currently nearest object to
prune the search. The depth-first approach is exemplified by the algorithm of Fukunaga
and Narendra [666] and is discussed in Section 4.2, where it is also compared with the
general incremental algorithm described in Section 4.1. During this comparison, we also
show how to use the best-first strategy when only the k nearest neighbors are desired.

The best-first process of finding nearest neighbors incrementally yields a ranking of
the objects with respect to their distance from the query object. This query has taken
on an importance of its own. For example, it forms the basis of the *distance join* [847,

---

[4] These methods are distinct and unrelated to embedding space organization methods discussed in
the opening text of Chapter 1 and throughout that chapter.

1756] query, where each element of A is paired up with elements in B, and the results are obtained in increasing order of distance. Another variant of this query is the *distance semijoin*, which arises when each element a in A can be paired up with just one element b in B, and we stipulate that b is the closest element in B to a, as well as report the results in increasing order of distance. This query is executed in a coroutine manner, obtaining as many results as necessary. When the query is executed by applying to A in its entirety, thereby letting the number of neighbors $k = |A|$, the result is equivalent to a discrete Voronoi diagram on B [847]. Moreover, by repeated application of the distance semijoin or distance join to the elements of one set A with respect to a second set B, and letting $k = 1$, the results of this query can be used as part of a process to find closest pairs (i.e., the all nearest neighbor join discussed earlier). The incremental algorithm finds use in many applications where the number of neighbors that are needed is not always known before starting the query (e.g., in forming query execution plans for query optimization in database applications).

In situations where complete accuracy is not critical, we can make use of the notion of approximate nearest neighbors. We explore two possible approaches to the problem. In the conventional approach, the approximation is the resulting quantitative error, which can be measured (Section 4.3). On the other hand, in the second, more unusual, approach, the approximation results from the assumption that "nearest neighbor" is an "equivalence" relation (Section 4.5.8), which, of course, is not generally true. For the first approach, we demonstrate how the performance of both the best-first and depth-first algorithms can be improved at the risk of having the objects reported somewhat out of order.

The presentation continues in Section 4.4, which presents some multidimensional indexing methods. Many of these methods are high-dimensional adaptations of techniques presented in Chapters 1 and 2. Section 4.5 outlines some distance-based indexing methods. Section 4.6 discusses a number of dimension reduction techniques and shows how some of them are used in conjunction with some of the indexing techniques presented in Chapters 1 and 2. Section 4.7 concludes by presenting a number of embedding methods. Note that many of the embedding methods (e.g., locality sensitive hashing [924]) could also have been discussed in the context of dimension reduction techniques. Our decision on the placement of the discussion depended on whether the emphasis was on the extent of the dimension reduction or on the satisfaction of other properties of the embedding.

4.1 Best-First Nearest Neighbor Finding

In this section, we present a general algorithm for finding nearest neighbors. Rather than finding the k nearest neighbors and possibly having to restart the search process should more neighbors be needed, our focus is on finding them in an incremental manner. The nature of such search is to report the objects in a dataset $S \subset \mathbb{U}$, one by one, in order of distance from a query object $q \in \mathbb{U}$ based on a distance function d, where $\mathbb{U}$ is the domain (usually infinite) from which the objects are drawn. The algorithm is a general version of the incremental nearest neighbor algorithm of [846, 848] that is applicable to virtually all hierarchical indexing methods for both spatial (point data and objects with extent) and metric data, in which case the index is based only on the distance between the objects (see Section 4.5). In order to make the discussion more concrete, we use the R-tree (recall Section 2.1.5.2 of Chapter 2) as an example data structure.

The rest of this section is organized as follows: In Section 4.1.1, we motivate the incremental nearest neighbor problem by examining some of the issues and proposed solutions. In Section 4.1.2, we introduce the basic framework for performing search in the form of a *search hierarchy*. In Section 4.1.3, we present a general incremental nearest neighbor algorithm, based on the abstract concept of a search hierarchy, as well as a discussion of its correctness. This algorithm can be adapted to virtually any data structure by a suitable definition of a search hierarchy, and we illustrate this in the case of the R-tree. Nevertheless, this algorithm can only handle indexes where each object is represented just once (e.g., an R-tree or an arbitrary index, provided that the data are points). However, in many applications the objects may be represented more than once in the index (i.e., there are duplicate instances since the object is decomposed into several pieces, as is the case for region data that is represented by a region quadtree). Section 4.1.4 contains an adaptation of the algorithm for such an environment. In Section 4.1.5, we show how the algorithm can be extended in a variety of ways, including setting limits on the distances of the result objects or on the number of result objects, reporting the objects in reverse order of distance (i.e., finding the *farthest* neighbor first), and computing skylines. Section 4.1.6 discusses how the algorithm can be used in a spatial network—that is, an environment where objects and the space in which their proximity is being measured are constrained to lie on a network, and the distance between them is measured along this network. Section 4.1.7 concludes the discussion by reviewing some related work, thereby placing the general incremental nearest neighbor algorithm in a proper perspective.

4.1.1 Motivation

Frequently, it is desired to obtain the neighbors in an incremental manner as they are needed since often we do not know in advance how many neighbors will need to be examined. For example, suppose that we want to find the nearest city to Chicago that has more than one million inhabitants. There are several ways to proceed. An intuitive solution is to guess some area range around Chicago and check the populations of the cities in the range. If we find a city with the requisite population, we must make sure that there are no other cities that are closer and that meet the population condition. This approach is rather inefficient because we have to guess the size of the area to be searched. The problem with guessing is that we may choose too small or too large a region. If the size is too small, the area may not contain any cities satisfying the population criterion, in which case we need to expand the region being searched. If the size is too large, we may be examining many cities needlessly.

A radical solution is to sort all the cities by their distances from Chicago. This is not very practical as we need to resort them each time we pose a similar query with respect to another query city. Moreover, sorting requires a considerable amount of extra work, especially when all that is usually needed to obtain the desired result is to inspect the first few nearest neighbors.

A less radical solution is to retrieve the closest k cities and determine if any of them satisfy the population criterion. The problem here lies in determining the value of k. As in the area range solution, we may choose too small or too large a value of k. If k is too small, failure to find a city satisfying the population criterion means that we have to restart the search with a value larger than k, say m. The drawback of this solution is that such a search forces us to expend work in finding the k nearest neighbors (which we already did once before) as part of the cost of finding the $m > k$ nearest neighbors. On the other hand, if k is too large, we waste work in calculating neighbors whose populations we will never check.

A logical way to overcome the drawbacks of the second and third solutions is to obtain the neighbors incrementally (i.e., one by one) as they are needed. In essence, we are browsing through the database on the basis of distance. The terms *distance browsing* [848] and *distance scan* [149]) are often used to describe this operation. The result is an incremental ranking of the cities by distance where we cease the search as soon as the secondary population condition is satisfied. The idea is that we want only a small, but unknown, number of neighbors. The incremental solution finds application in a much more general setting than our specialized query example. In particular, this includes queries that require the application of the "nearest" predicate to a subset s of the attributes of a relation (or object class) r. This class of queries is part of a more restricted, but very common, class that imposes an additional condition c usually involving attributes other than s. This means that the "nearest" condition serves as a primary condition, and condition c serves as a secondary condition. Using an incremental solution enables such a query to be processed in a pipelined fashion.

Of course, in the worst case, we will have to examine all (or most) of the neighbors even when using an incremental approach. This may occur if few objects satisfy the secondary condition (e.g., if none of the cities have the requisite population). In this case, it may actually be better to select first on the basis of the secondary condition (the population criterion in our example) before considering the "spatially nearest" condition, especially if an index exists that can be used to compute the secondary condition. Using a k-nearest neighbor algorithm may also be preferable, provided it is more efficient than the incremental algorithm for large values of k. It makes sense to choose this solution only if we know in advance how many neighbors are needed (i.e., the value of k), but this value can be estimated based on the selectivity of the secondary condition. These issues demonstrate the need for a query engine to make estimates using selectivity factors (e.g., [78, 1327, 1717]) involving the numbers of values that are expected to satisfy various parts of the query and the computational costs of the applicable algorithms.

4.1.2 Search Hierarchy

The incremental nearest neighbor algorithm is applicable whenever the search space can be represented in a hierarchical manner, provided that certain conditions hold. In this section, we define what we mean by "search hierarchy" and use the R-tree as a specific example. We assume an R-tree implementation in which each node contains an array of (*key*, *pointer*) entries, where *key* is a hyperrectangle that minimally bounds the data objects in the subtree pointed at by *pointer*. In an R-tree leaf node, the *pointer* is an object identifier (e.g., a tuple ID in a relational system), while in a nonleaf node, it is a pointer to a child node on the next lower level. If the geometric descriptions of the objects are simple (e.g., for points or line segments), then it is also possible to store the objects directly in the leaf nodes instead of their bounding rectangles. The maximum number of entries in each node is termed its *node capacity* or *fanout* and may be different for leaf and nonleaf nodes. The node capacity is usually chosen so that a node fills up one disk page (or a small number of them). Search operations on the R-tree are performed in a top-down manner with the bounding box serving as a filter to indicate if the tree should be descended further by following the corresponding pointer. The array of pairs associated with each node is usually not sorted and is thus searched using sequential search.

The algorithm operates on a finite set $S \subset \mathbb{U}$ of objects, a query object $q \in \mathbb{U}$, and a data structure T that organizes the set S or provides information about it. The search hierarchy is composed of elements e_t of several different types t, with $t = 0, \ldots, t_{max}$. Figure 4.2 depicts the search hierarchy for a set of 14 objects, A_0 through N_0, where there are three types of elements. As depicted in the figure, the search hierarchy forms a tree with the objects as leaves. Each element represents a subset of S, with an element e_0 of type 0 representing a single object in S. An element e_t of type t can give rise to one or more "child" elements of types 0 through t_{max}. Thus, the search problem for e_t is decomposed into several smaller subproblems. Often, all child elements are of the same type, but this is not a requirement. In this presentation, we assume that an element has only one "parent" in the search hierarchy and that each object is represented only once in the hierarchy. However, the algorithm can be adapted to handle multiple parents and duplicate object instances as well (see Section 4.1.4).

At this point, it may seem superfluous to use different types of elements, when they all merely represent subsets of S. However, for any particular search problem, the various element types represent different kinds of entities and therefore have different pieces of information attached to them. Furthermore, each specific search hierarchy will have

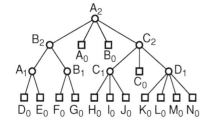

Figure 4.2
A sample search hierarchy for objects A_0 though N_0.

a different definition of what types of elements can be produced from each element type. In the example in Figure 4.2, for instance, elements of type 2 produce elements of types 2, 1, or 0, while elements of type 1 produce only elements of type 0. Elements of each type t, say e_t, have an associated distance function $d_t(q, e_t)$ for measuring the distance from a query object q to the elements of that type. $d_t(q, e_t)$ is computed when the parent element, say f, of e_t is processed, and thus its computation is based only on the specific information attached to f. Furthermore, for the algorithm to be practical, this computation must be substantially less expensive than the total cost of computing $d_0(q, e_0)$ for all the objects e_0 represented by e_t. In Section 4.1.3, it is shown that for the algorithm to be correct, it is sufficient that $d_t(q, e_t) \leq d_0(q, e_0)$ for any object e_0 in the subset represented by e_t. Some of the variants of the algorithm (e.g., farthest neighbors, as discussed in Section 4.1.5) make use of another set of distance functions, $\hat{d}_t(q, e_t)$, that bound from above the distances from q of the objects in a subtree (of course, $\hat{d}_0 = d_0$, so $\hat{d}_0$ is not really needed). In other words, $\hat{d}_t(q, e_t) \geq d_0(q, e_0)$ for any object e_0 in the subset represented by e_t.

In most cases, the search hierarchy arises naturally from the hierarchical structure of T. In the search hierarchy for the R-tree, for instance, we have three types of elements. Elements of type 0 are the spatial objects themselves, elements of type 1 are minimum bounding rectangles for single objects, and elements of type 2 represent R-tree nodes. The reason for distinguishing between the spatial objects and their bounding rectangles will become clear later. The distance functions are typically based on a distance metric $d_p(p_1, p_2)$ defined on points in the space, such as the Euclidean metric. Thus, for arbitrary spatial objects o_1 and o_2, we define $d(o_1, o_2) = \min_{p_1 \in o_1, p_2 \in o_2}\{d_p(p_1, p_2)\}$.[5] This definition serves as a basis for the distance functions for all three types of elements of the R-tree search hierarchy, the only difference being the types of the arguments. Given an object o and any rectangle r that bounds o (i.e., r can be the minimum bounding rectangle of o or the rectangle associated with any ancestor of the leaf node containing o), this definition guarantees that $d(q, r) \leq d(q, o)$, thus ensuring correctness (according to the sufficient condition for correctness given above). In fact, according to this definition, the distance functions obey an even stricter condition, namely, that $d_t(q, e_t) \leq d_{t'}(q, e_{t'})$ for any element $e_{t'}$ that is a descendant of e_t in the search hierarchy.

Exercise

1. Define a search hierarchy for an MX-CIF quadtree.

4.1.3 Algorithm

The key to the incremental nearest neighbor algorithm [846, 848] is that it traverses the search hierarchy in a "best-first" manner, like the classic A*-algorithm (e.g., see [1594]), instead of the more traditional depth-first or breadth-first traversals. In other words, at any step of the algorithm, the algorithm visits the element with the smallest distances from the query object among all unvisited elements in the search hierarchy (or, more accurately, all unvisited elements whose parents have been visited). This is done by maintaining a global list of elements, organized in increasing order of their distance from the query object, with the closest element to the query object being at the front of the list (i.e., it is the most easily accessible element in the list). A data structure that supports the necessary operations (i.e., inspect, insert, and delete a minimum element) is an instance of an abstract data type termed a *priority queue*. In order to break ties among elements having the same distance, priority is given to elements with lower type numbers, and

---

[5] In other words, if o_1 and o_2 have at least one point in common, then $d(o_1, o_2) = 0$. Otherwise, $d(o_1, o_2)$ equals the smallest distance between the boundaries of o_1 and o_2.

among elements of the same type, priority is given to elements deeper in the search hierarchy. This allows the algorithm to report neighbors as quickly as possible.

The general incremental nearest neighbor algorithm is given by procedure INC-NEAREST, where q is the query object, S is the set of objects, and T is a data structure that organizes S. Since no assumptions are made about the objects or the data structure, the algorithm is presented in terms of the search hierarchy induced by them. The algorithm starts off by initializing the priority queue with the root of the search space (lines 8–10). In the main loop, the element e_t closest to q is taken off the queue. If it is an object, we report it as the next nearest object (line 14). Otherwise, the child elements of e_t in the search hierarchy are inserted into the priority queue (line 17).

```
1   procedure INCNEAREST(q, S, T)
2   /* A best-first incremental algorithm that returns the nearest neighbors of q
        from the set of objects S organized using the search hierarchy T. */
3   value object q
4   value object_set S
5   value pointer search_hierarchy T
6   priority_queue Queue
7   pointer search_hierarchy e_t, e_t'
8   Queue ← NEWPRIORITYQUEUE()
9   e_t ← root of the search hierarchy induced by S and T
10  ENQUEUE(e_t, 0, Queue)
11  while not ISEMPTY(Queue) do
12      e_t ← DEQUEUE(Queue)
13      if t = 0 then /* e_t is an object */
14          Report e_t as the next nearest object
15      else
16          foreach child element e_t' of e_t do
17              ENQUEUE(e_t', d_t'(q, e_t'), Queue)
18          enddo
19      endif
20  enddo
```

Letting o_k be the kth object reported by the algorithm, observe that the nonobject elements on the priority queue (i.e., elements e_t with $t > 0$) at the time of reporting o_k essentially represent portions of the search hierarchy that did not have to be explored to establish o_k as the kth-nearest neighbor. Thus, if o_k is the last neighbor requested, those portions are said to be *pruned* by the algorithm, and all distance computations for objects descended from the nonobject elements on the priority queue are avoided. As we show at the end of this section using the notion of r-optimality, the algorithm achieves maximal possible pruning with respect to the given search hierarchy. Of course, if more neighbors are requested, some of those elements may be processed later. Nevertheless, the fact that their processing is deferred means that o_k is reported as quickly as possible.

Interestingly, in the spatial domain,[6] the algorithm can be viewed as having an initial phase that corresponds to an intersect query (or, if q is a point, a point location query). In particular, the algorithm first processes all elements e in the search hierarchy with $d(q,e) = 0$, namely, those elements that q intersects (fully or partially). Thus, at the conclusion of this initial phase, all leaf nodes in the spatial index intersecting q have been processed and their contents inserted into the priority queue, and all objects intersecting q have been reported. A similar observation also holds for many of the search hierarchies that correspond to the representations that we present in this book, especially the ones in Section 4.5.

---

[6] The algorithm is also applicable to multimedia data where we just have distance values indicating similarity or dissimilarity between objects, as discussed in Section 4.5.

To get a better idea of how the algorithm functions, let us examine how it behaves when applied to the R-tree for spatial data objects. Initially, the root of the R-tree (representing all the data objects) is placed in the priority queue. At subsequent steps, the element at the front of the queue (i.e., the closest element not yet examined) is retrieved, and this is repeated until the queue has been emptied. Thus, the algorithm processes the elements in the priority queue in increasing order of their distance from the query object. Informally, we can visualize the progress of the algorithm for a query object q as follows (see Figure 4.3, where q is the point q). We start by locating the leaf node(s) containing q. Next, imagine a circle centered at q being expanded from a starting radius of 0. We call this circle the *search region*. Note that for query objects other than points, the search region will have a more complex shape. Each time the circle hits the boundary of a node region, the contents of that node are put in the queue (and similarly for the bounding rectangle of an object), and each time the circle hits an object, we have found the object next nearest to q. We can characterize the contents of the priority queue based on their relationships with the search region. The elements still in the queue are outside the search region (but they all have parents that intersect the search region), while all elements that have been dequeued lie at least partially inside. Also, nodes whose bounding rectangles are fully contained in the search region will have had their entire subtrees already taken out of the priority queue. Therefore, all the queue elements are contained in nodes whose bounding rectangles intersect the boundary of the search region. Similarly, for all objects in the priority queue, their corresponding bounding rectangles intersect the boundary of the search region.

It should be clear now why a distinction was made between the spatial objects and their bounding rectangles in the R-tree implementation of the incremental nearest neighbor algorithm. This is on account of the fact that in most R-tree implementations the precise geometry of the objects is usually stored in a separate file on disk, whereas the bounding rectangles are stored directly in the leaf nodes of the R-tree. Thus, computing the distance from the query object to the bounding rectangle of an object is much less expensive than computing the distance to the object itself. When a leaf node in the R-tree is visited by the algorithm, the bounding rectangles for the objects in the leaf node are inserted into the priority queue. The actual distance from the query object to a data object is computed only when its bounding rectangle reaches the front of the priority queue.

In fact, at times, we can report an object as a nearest neighbor without ever having to compute its distance from the query object. Such a situation can arise when using an R-tree, where we recall that elements of type 1 represent minimum bounding rectangles of objects—that is, each element e_1 represents only one object. In particular, when processing such an element e_1, we can sometimes use the distance $\hat{d}_1(q, e_1)$ to report immediately the object o represented by e_1, without computing the actual distance $d(q, o)$. This can be done, provided that $\hat{d}_1(q, e_1) \leq D$, where D is the distance of the element at the front of the queue (i.e., after e_1 has been removed) since we then know that $d(q, o)$ is also no larger than D. This principle is generally applicable any time that one (or more) of the element types $t > 0$ represents single objects, and the upper-bound distance function $\hat{d}_t$ can be defined. The same insight can also be applied to farthest neighbor search, reversing the roles of d and $\hat{d}$ (see Section 4.1.5).

Deferring the computation of the actual distances usually leads to many fewer object distance computations, except when a large number of neighbors must be reported (i.e., k neighbors are required, where k is a significant fraction of N, the size of the dataset S). Hence, when the algorithm is terminated (i.e., enough neighbors have been obtained), any bounding rectangles present in the priority queue represent distance computations to objects that were avoided by their use. Of course, these benefits come at the cost of more priority queue operations. Similar considerations apply to other search structures.

The only drawback of the algorithm is that, in the worst case, the priority queue will be as large as the entire dataset. As an example, for an R-tree, the worst case of the

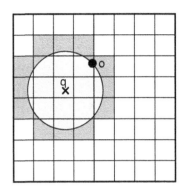

Figure 4.3
The circle around query object q depicts the search region after reporting o as next nearest object. For simplicity, the leaf nodes are represented by a grid; in most spatial indexes, the shapes of the leaf nodes are more irregular. Only the shaded leaf nodes are accessed by the incremental nearest neighbor algorithm. The region with darker shading is where we find the objects in the priority queue.

According to this definition, a nearest neighbor algorithm is r-optimal if it visits the same search hierarchy elements as would a range query with query radius $d(q, o_k)$ implemented with a top-down traversal of the search hierarchy. The incremental nearest neighbor algorithm is r-optimal (see Exercise 5). This is based on the fact that the algorithm reports the neighbors in order of nondecreasing distance if, for any object e_0 in the subtree represented by e_t, we have $d_t(q, e_t) \leq d_0(q, e_0)$ (see Exercise 4). This is known as the *correctness criterion* [851].

A basic premise underlying the satisfaction of r-optimality is that, for any object e_0 that has not been reported, there is a representative e_t in the priority queue (i.e., e_t is an ancestor of e_0 in the search hierarchy). This is clearly true initially since the root of the search hierarchy represents all the objects in S. The only actions of the algorithm are to remove objects from the priority queue and to replace search hierarchy elements with all their children. Thus, the algorithm never violates the premise.

Observe that the correctness criterion (i.e., $d_t(q, e_t) \leq d_0(q, e_0)$) does not actually guarantee that when a nonobject search hierarchy element e_t has been removed from the priority queue, no nonobject search hierarchy element $e_{t'}$ (in the subtree represented by e_t) with a smaller distance from the query object q can be inserted in the future and possibly removed in the future. In other words, it does not preclude the possibility that nonobject elements e_t and $e_{t'}$, where $d_t(q, e_t) > d_{t'}(q, e_{t'})$, could be processed in succession (by virtue of being removed from the priority queue in succession, although some other elements could have been inserted into the queue during this time).[7] The implication is that the algorithm has not necessarily visited all elements e_t with $d_t(q, e_t) \leq d(q, o_k)$ when the kth neighbor o_k of q is reported. However, this does not change the fact that object elements are obtained from the priority queue in order of distance. Often, however, the distance functions satisfy the stricter criterion that $d_t(q, e_t) \leq d_{t'}(q, e_{t'})$ for any element $e_{t'}$ that is a descendant of e_t in the search hierarchy. This was the case for the distance functions defined for the R-tree in Section 4.1.2. This stricter criterion guarantees that elements are obtained from the priority queue in order of increasing distance from the query object, regardless of their type.

It is also important to note that r-optimality does not imply that the incremental nearest neighbor algorithm for the given search hierarchy is necessarily optimal in some absolute sense (regardless of whether we consider the required number of distance computations or the overall work). First, actual search performance is highly dependent on the index structure that the search hierarchy is based on. Performance can suffer if the index structure poorly captures the inherent structure of the search space. Second, it is often possible to define more than one search hierarchy for a given index structure, each with different performance characteristics. In some cases, different choices of a search hierarchy even represent a trade-off between the amount of work required to maintain the priority queue operations and to compute the various distance functions (see [851, 854] for examples using indexing methods, such as those described in Section 4.5.7, that are just based on the distance between objects). Moreover, it is sometimes possible to tailor the incremental nearest neighbor algorithm more closely to the given index structure than is achieved with our general notion of search hierarchy. Finally, even for a specific search hierarchy, it is possible that a k-nearest neighbor algorithm is more efficient for any fixed value of k. Thus, some sacrifice in performance can be expected for the flexibility offered by the incremental aspect. However, when the number of desired neighbors is unknown prior to initiating the search, an incremental algorithm provides much better performance on the average than algorithms that require fixing the number of neighbors in advance (see [851] for the results of some experiments where this was observed).

---

[7] Such a situation could arise, for example, for a vp-tree [2052] (see Exercise 5 in Section 4.5.2.1.2), which is a distance-based indexing method for data arising in applications where the only available information is a distance function that indicates the degree of similarity (or dissimilarity) between all pairs of objects.

Exercises

1. Assuming that there are N uniformly distributed points in the two-dimensional interval $[0,1] \times [0,1]$, that the leaf nodes form a grid at the lowest level of the spatial index with average occupancy of c points per leaf node, and that the search region is completely contained in the data space, show that the expected size of the priority queue, when finding the k nearest neighbors with the general incremental algorithm, is $O(\sqrt{kc})$.

2. Continuing Exercise 1, show that the expected number of leaf nodes that are accessed to obtain the k nearest neighbors using the general incremental algorithm is $O(k + \sqrt{k})$.

3. Assume a typical priority queue implementation, such as a binary heap, for which the cost of each insertion and deletion operation is $O(\log m)$, where m is the size of the priority queue. Using the data model employed in Exercise 1 to analyze the expected size of the priority queue, what is the expected cost of the priority queue operations when finding the k nearest neighbors with the general incremental algorithm?

4. Let e_t be an arbitrary element in the search hierarchy. Prove that if for any object e_0 in the subtree represented by e_t, we have $d_t(q, e_t) \leq d_0(q, e_0)$ (i.e., the correctness criterion holds), then the INCNEAREST algorithm is guaranteed to report the neighbors in order of nondecreasing distance.

5. Prove that if the distance functions satisfy the correctness criterion, then the INCNEAREST algorithm is r-optimal.

4.1.4 Algorithm with Duplicate Instances of Objects

The algorithm given by procedure INCNEAREST can only handle indexes where each object is represented just once (e.g., an R-tree). This is fine when the multidimensional data consists of points. However, in many applications, such as computer graphics, geographic information systems (GIS), computer vision, and so on, the multidimensional data also has extent (e.g., lines, rectangles, regions, surfaces, volumes). In this case, it may not be desirable, or even possible, to represent the objects as points or by one entity such as a minimum bounding box (as is done in the R-tree). Instead, the domain of the data (i.e., the space occupied by the objects) is decomposed into blocks, and the index is used to facilitate the identification and access of the blocks that are occupied by the objects as well as to indicate the identity of the objects. Examples of such indexes include the region quadtree, members of the PM quadtree family, the R^+-tree, and so on.

Similar issues were raised in the discussion of hierarchical object-based representations of objects based on the interior of the space occupied by the objects in Chapter 2, where we made a distinction between nondisjoint (Section 2.1.5.2) and disjoint (Section 2.1.5.3) representations. Recall that such methods employ an object hierarchy coupled with bounding boxes for the objects in order to facilitate responses to queries such as finding the identity of the object that contains location a (i.e., query 2 of Chapter 2), while also enabling responses to queries such as finding all locations associated with a particular object (i.e., query 1 of Chapter 2). A hierarchy made up of disjoint bounding boxes enables avoiding the possibility of having to examine the bounding boxes of all of the objects, which could be the case with a hierarchy made up of nondisjoint bounding boxes since they might all span location a, even though location a could lie in just one of the objects. Disjointness can be achieved by decomposing the objects into several segments. The disadvantage of disjoint bounding boxes is the presence of duplicates in the sense that some objects may be reported several times for some queries such as finding all objects in a rectangular query region w since the object could have been decomposed into several segments, each of which overlaps a part of w. Nevertheless, there has been some work on developing algorithms for spatial queries that report objects just once, even though they may be duplicated in several blocks or nodes (e.g., [76, 80, 498]).

Extending the general incremental nearest neighbor algorithm to handle indexes that represent each object in all leaf nodes whose mutually nonintersecting regions intersect the object (e.g., the PMR quadtree, R$^+$-tree) means that we must be able to deal with the possible presence of duplicate instances of the objects in the search hierarchy. There are two issues here. The first is to make sure to detect all duplicate instances that are currently in the priority queue. The second is to avoid inserting duplicate instances of an object that has already been reported. Modifying the algorithm to resolve these issues involves the addition of just a few lines to procedure INCNEAREST, and the result is given by procedure INCNEARESTDUP. The resulting algorithm is also r-optimal (see Exercise 2).

```
1   procedure INCNEARESTDUP(q, S, T)
2   /* A best-first incremental algorithm that returns the nearest neighbors of q
        from the set of objects S organized using the search hierarchy T that per-
        mits duplicate instances of objects. */
3   value object q
4   value object_set S
5   value pointer search_hierarchy T
6   priority_queue Queue
7   pointer search_hierarchy e_t, e_t'
8   Queue ← NEWPRIORITYQUEUE()
9   e_t ←root of the search hierarchy induced by S and T
10  ENQUEUE(e_t, 0, Queue)
11  while not ISEMPTY(Queue) do
12      e_t ← DEQUEUE(Queue)
13      if t = 0 then /* e_t is an object */
14          while e_t = FRONTPRIORITYQUEUE(Queue) do
15              DEQUEUE(Queue) /* Remove duplicate object instances */
16          enddo
17          Report e_t as the next nearest object
18      else /* e_t is not an object */
19          foreach child element e_t' of e_t do
20              if t' > 0 or d_t'(q, e_t') ≥ d_t(q, e_t) then
21                  ENQUEUE(e_t', d_t'(q, e_t'), Queue)
22              endif
23          enddo
24      endif
25  enddo
```

It is easy to see that there are two differences from the original algorithm. The first difference is the test (i.e., the **if** statement) in line 20, which ensures that objects that have already been reported are not inserted into the queue again. Such a situation can only arise if we encounter an object o as a descendant of an ancestor element A where the distance of o from query object q is smaller than that of A from q. This situation, although valid in a disjoint index, is actually a violation of the correctness criterion, which stipulates that, for any object e_0 in the subtree represented by e_t, we have $d_t(q, e_t) \le d_0(q, e_0)$. Thus, we modify the correctness criterion to be "for all objects $o \in S$ (note that there could be multiple occurrences of particular objects), there exists at least one element e_0 in the search hierarchy that represents o and that satisfies $d_t(q, e_t) \le d_0(q, e_0)$ for all ancestors e_t of e_0." This modification ensures that each object o is detected early enough by the algorithm thereby allowing it to be reported at the appropriate time. However, duplicate instances of an object can still be inserted into the priority queue prior to the object being reported. The possibility of the occurrence of such an event is detected by the **if** statement in line 20; as a consequence, the insertion is not made. Note that the algorithm as presented assumes that elements of any type t can have objects as child elements, which is true for some structures (e.g., the PK-tree as discussed in Section 1.8 of Chapter 1). For structures in which only leaf nodes can contain objects, we can instead use two separate **for** loops, one for leaf nodes (with the **if** statement) and another for nonleaf nodes (without the **if** statement).[8]

The second difference deals with the possibility that there are multiple instances of an object o in the priority queue at the same time. This is checked explicitly in the loop in lines 14–16, by making use of the primitive FRONTPRIORITYQUEUE, which accesses the element at the front of the priority queue (which is also the closest one to the query object) without removing it, as would be the case if we were to use the DEQUEUE primitive. Thus, the duplicate instances of object o be ignored. For this to work properly (i.e., in order for all duplicate instances of an object in the queue to be retrieved in sequence), we make two stipulations. First, we stipulate that the objects will be ordered in the priority queue by their identity so that when the priority queue contains duplicate instances of two or more objects with the same distance, then all duplicate instances of one of the objects appear before all duplicate instances of the remaining objects. In other words, this ensures that duplicate instances of two different objects at the same distance are not obtained from the queue in an interleaved manner.

Second, we stipulate that nodes must be retrieved from the queue before spatial objects at the same distance. Otherwise, an object o may be retrieved from the queue and reported before a node A that contains o (i.e., A is an ancestor node, where we note that the presence of duplicate instances of objects means that an object may have more than one ancestor of a given type) that is at the same distance from the query object as o. The occurrence of such a situation means that o was contained in another node B that has already been dequeued by virtue of being an ancestor of o. Without such a stipulation, we would have the situation where when o was encountered again in node A, there would be no way of knowing that o had already been reported on account of being a descendant of B. Such situations are prevented from occurring by virtue of the fact that in order to break ties among elements having the same distance, priority is given to elements with higher type numbers (hence making objects have a lower priority than anything else). It is interesting to observe that this assignment of priorities represents a departure from the rule given in Section 4.1.3, where the emphasis was on reporting neighbors as soon as possible and thus ties among elements having the same distance were broken by giving priority to elements with lower type numbers.

Note that we explicitly check for duplicates in this manner (i.e., using the loop in lines 14–16) because, for many priority queue implementations (e.g., binary heap), it is not efficient to detect duplicates among the queue elements as these implementations only maintain a partial order among the elements. In other words, in such priority queue structures, the relative order among only some pairs of elements is represented at any given time (e.g., in a binary heap, we only know that the elements on a path from the root to a leaf are in increasing order, but two elements that are not on the same path may have any relative order). A possible alternative is to use a priority queue implementation that maintains a total order among all the queue elements (e.g., a balanced binary tree) and thus is able to detect duplicates efficiently.

Exercises

1. The modified correctness criterion presented above states that for all objects $o \in S$, there exists at least one element e_0 in the search hierarchy that represents o and that satisfies $d_t(q, e_t) \leq d_0(q, e_0)$ for all ancestors e_t of e_0. Prove that the INCNEARESTDUP algorithm is guaranteed to report the neighbors in order of nondecreasing distance if the correctness criteria holds.

2. Prove that if the distance functions satisfy the modified correctness criterion, then the INCNEARESTDUP algorithm is r-optimal.

---

[8] In a search hierarchy formulation, we could use e_1 to indicate leaf nodes (i.e., element type 1), and objects would only be children of this element type.

4.1.5 Algorithm Extensions (*K*-Nearest, *K*-Farthest, Skylines)

The incremental nearest neighbor algorithm is easily adapted to take advantage of imposed distance bounds (as in a range query), as well as maximum result size as in a k-nearest neighbor query, notwithstanding claims to the contrary [224]. In particular, given a maximum distance bound D_{max}, only elements having distances from q less than or equal to D_{max} need to be enqueued. A minimum distance bound D_{min} can be exploited in a similar way, but doing so requires the additional distance functions $\hat{d}_t(q, e_t)$ for each element type that provide an upper bound on the distances from q of the objects in the subtree represented by e_t. Taking advantage of such distance bounds reduces the size of the priority queue (since fewer items will be enqueued) and, consequently, the average cost of priority queue operations. However, the number of distance computations or the number of search hierarchy elements visited is not decreased when using D_{max}, and possibly not even when using D_{min}, depending on its value (in fact, utilizing D_{min} may even lead to worse performance as it requires computing the $\hat{d}$ distances). Recall that D_{min} was also mentioned in Section 4.1.3 in conjunction with a suggested method to reduce the size of the priority queue.

The simplest way of exploiting a maximum result size, say k, and performing a k-nearest neighbor query is simply to terminate the algorithm once k neighbors have been determined. Alternatively, the algorithm can be modified in such a way that the distance D_k from q of the kth candidate nearest neighbor o_k is used to reduce the number of priority queue operations. In this way, we avoid enqueueing elements with a distance greater than D_k from q, thereby pruning the search in the same way as we used D_{max} above. However, such a modification incurs the cost of additional complexity in the algorithm. In particular, knowing o_k means that we must keep track of the set L of k candidate nearest objects that have been encountered at any moment. Moreover, we must be able to identify and remove the element in L with the largest distance. This is done most easily by implementing L as a priority queue that is distinct from *Queue*, which now contains the remaining types of elements. Thus, we see that finding the k nearest neighbors makes use of two priority queues. Such an algorithm is given by procedure BFTRAV in Section 4.2.6.

A useful extension of the algorithm is to find the farthest neighbor of a query object q (i.e., the object in S that is farthest from q). This simply requires replacing $d_t(q, e_t)$ as a key for any element e_t in the priority queue with $-\hat{d}_t(q, e_t)$ (or, alternatively, ordering the elements in the priority queue in decreasing order of key values and using $\hat{d}_t(q, e_t)$ as a key value). Thus, once an object o has reached the front of the priority queue, we know that no unreported object has a greater distance from q.

Nevertheless, using a priority queue to support finding the farthest neighbors has the drawback that the performance of the algorithm that uses it is poor as usually many nodes must be examined before the first (i.e., farthest) object can be identified and reported, thereby making the priority queue quite large. The problem is that many objects tend to be at a similar distance from the query object as the farthest one. This drawback is actually more general in the sense that it is inherent to the task of finding the farthest neighbors as the initial search region is very large due to the large distance to the farthest neighbor. In contrast, when finding the nearest neighbors, the initial search region is small and thus the priority queue is also relatively small as the number of nodes in it is proportional to the size of the search region.

The incremental nearest neighbor algorithm can be applied in the skyline query [236] as well (e.g., [1462]). Below, we first give a brief review of the problem and then outline some of the alternative solutions that have been proposed. For an analysis of their computational costs, see Godfrey, Shipley, and Gryz [713], while for an estimation of the cardinality of the result sets, see [712]. Formally, given a dataset P of points

$p_1, p_2, \ldots, p_N$, the *skyline query*[9] (also known as the *Pareto operator* [379]) is defined to return a subset S of P (referred to as the *skyline points*) such that any point p_i of S is not dominated by any other point p_j in P, where we say that a point p_j *dominates* another point p_i if and only if none of the attribute values of p_j are greater than the corresponding attribute values of p_i (e.g., [1511]). The Pareto operator is well known, having been first formulated in 1906 by Pareto [1468] in a treatise on political economy.

As a common and simple example of a scenario in which a skyline query is useful, let us assume that we have a hotel database where the different attributes (i.e., features) include the average room rate per night and the distance from the hotel to the nearest beach. One possible query to this database would seek the hotel h whose average nightly rate and distance from the beach are both minimums—that is, h is both the cheapest hotel and the closest to a beach (not necessarily with respect to the same beach, in this example). For this scenario, we see that if such a hotel h exists, then h dominates all of the other hotels. Of course, a hotel that meets these requirements need not necessarily exist. Thus, the scope of the set of possible responses must be broadened, and it is precisely this set of responses that is returned by a skyline query. It is called a "skyline" query because its components serve as the extreme points of a wavefront very much like the tallest buildings in a city's skyline. The result is also similar to a convex hull, where we observe that a polygon is said to be convex if a line can be drawn between any of its constituent vertices without intersecting any of its constituent edges. Figure 4.5 is another example that shows the skyline with respect to the origin at the lower-left corner for the point data in Figure 1.1 of Chapter 1. The skyline consists of Denver, Omaha, Mobile, and Miami. We also see that Omaha dominates Chicago as well as Buffalo and Toronto. Similarly, Mobile dominates Toronto, Buffalo, and Atlanta. Denver only dominates Buffalo and Toronto, but no city is dominated by Miami.

There are many ways of computing the response to the skyline query. A simple way is to build the skyline set S as points are processed. Each time a new point p is encountered, first, remove any points in S that are dominated by p, and then insert p into S unless there exists some point t in S that dominates p, in which case p is ignored (i.e., pruned) [236]. The drawback of this solution, which is based on the well-known block-nested loop approach [733, 742], is its $O(N^2)$ complexity for N points. Its advantages are that no index needs to be built and that its complexity is independent of the dimension of the underlying space.

Chomicki, Godfrey, Gryz, and Liang [379] improve on the block-nested loop approach by first sorting the points according to some monotonic function of their attribute values that preserves dominance among the points (i.e., if point p_i dominates point p_j, then p_i precedes p_j) and then applying the block-nested loop algorithm. This method is known as the *sort-first strategy*. Ordering the processing of the points in this way ensures that once a point p is entered into the skyline set S, it is never dominated by any yet-to-be-processed point in the dataset, and thus p will never be removed from S. In other words, doing so improves the likelihood of pruning points and precludes the possibility of inserting them into the skyline set S only to have to remove them later. The drawback of this method is the need to sort the data before each invocation of the skyline query, which becomes readily apparent if the skyline query is invoked with respect to different reference query points. Godfrey, Shipley, and Gryz [713] further improve this approach by pruning points during the sorting phase. In essence, the sorting is now performed on a substantially smaller subset of the original data points. They show that for certain distributions of the data points, the algorithm is linear in the number of data points.

An alternative method to these two block-nested loop methods is based on a divide-and-conquer strategy of computing skylines for smaller sets and then merging

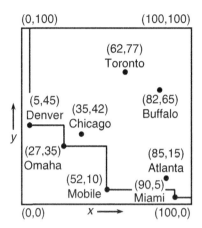

Figure 4.5
Denver, Omaha, Mobile, and Miami form the skyline for the point data in Figure 1.1 of Chapter 1 with respect to the origin at the lower-left corner.

---

[9] See also the *skyline cube* (also termed *skycube*) [1479, 2062], which is the set of skylines of all possible nonempty subsets of a given set of dimensions—that is, the skylines for the powerset of the dimensions.

them [236]. The advantage of this strategy is that it can handle large datasets as the entire dataset need not be in memory at the same time.

Other approaches make use of applications of the plane-sweep paradigm (see, e.g., [119, 1511, 1740], and the discussion in Section 3.1 of Chapter 3), which, in the case of the skyline query, differ by the distance metric used to determine the order in which the plane-sweep algorithm processes the candidate members of the skyline. Note that all of these methods are based on the implicit assumption that the underlying dimensional units of all of the attributes are the same or that the domains of their values (i.e., their ranges) have been normalized (i.e., by the application of suitable scale factors). Thus, for example, they cannot be applied directly (i.e., without normalization) to our hotel price and distance from the beach scenario. All of these methods are progressive in the sense that they can be halted once a sufficient number of skyline points has been obtained rather than having to wait until the entire set has been determined, as is the case for the block-nested loop method [236]. Moreover, two of the methods [1462, 1838] can be used to yield a "top-k" [306] variant of the skyline query, where the results are ordered by the value of the distance metric used to order the processing of the points in the plane-sweep algorithm, and the user has placed a limit k on the cardinality of the query result set.

Tan, Eng, and Ooi [1838] use a variant of the L_∞ distance metric defined in terms of "min" instead of "max." In particular, they process the points in increasing order of the minimum value of all of their attributes, while updating the attribute values of a fictitious point f that keeps track of the minimum value of all attributes that have been scanned so far (i.e., the halting points of the sweep process). During the sweep, for each point p that is encountered, a check is made if p is dominated by any of the existing skyline points, in which case p is discarded; otherwise, p is added to the skyline set. The process halts when all of the points have been processed or upon determining that f is dominated by one of the existing skyline points.

Kossmann, Ramsak, and Rost [1068] sweep the points in increasing order according to the L_2 distance metric from the origin, although any of the L_i ($i \geq 1$) Minkowski distance metrics could have been used. The first point p that is found, regardless of which of the Minkowski distance metrics is used, is guaranteed to be a skyline point. Next, the underlying space is partitioned into 2^d regions at p, at which time two of the regions can be pruned immediately from further processing as one of them, say a, is guaranteed to be empty by virtue of p's having been determined to be the closest point in a to the origin, while the other region, b, which is diametrically opposite to a, is also pruned as every point in b is dominated by p. At this point, the algorithm is applied recursively to the remaining regions. It is interesting to note that this process is equivalent to one used by Samet in a point quadtree deletion algorithm [1618] in determining which points residing in the quadrant that contains the replacement point p need to be reinserted into the newly formed quadtree rooted at p (recall the control structure of procedure NEWROOT described in Section 1.4.1.2 of Chapter 1). In fact, the points that must be reinserted are elements of the skyline. Note also that the initial process of determining p is the same as the first step in the selection process for the candidate points to replace the point to be deleted in the point quadtree.

Unfortunately, as Kossmann et al. [1068] point out, this approach does not work too well in dimensions greater than 2 as the process corresponds to a branching structure (i.e., tree) where, at each step, 2^d children are generated, of which only two are pruned from further processing, and hence the number of search subspaces grows to be as large as the number of objects N. Kossmann et al. propose to overcome this shortcoming by partitioning the underlying d-dimensional space at p into two pairwise disjoint regions along each of the d dimensions, thereby resulting in $2d$ overlapping regions. Of these d pairs of pairwise disjoint regions, retain the member of each pair that does not contain the region dominated by p (i.e., b in the above explanation, but see also Exercise 8). This results in d overlapping regions, at which point candidate skyline points are obtained as before for each region, and duplicate candidates are removed, although this does require search.

Papadias, Tao, Fu, and Seeger [1462] approach the problem by making use of a spatial index on the points (an R-tree) in their presentation, although in actuality any hierarchical spatial index could be used, and applying the incremental nearest neighbor algorithm described in this section to traverse the hierarchy in increasing order according to the L_1 distance metric from the origin. The advantage of using a spatial index instead of sorting the points with respect to the origin, or some other suitably chosen reference point, as in the sort-first block-nested loop strategy and the methods that employ plane-sweep, is that once the index has been built (which requires a variant of a sorting process), the same index can be used to respond to a skyline query with respect to any reference point. In other words, the index need not be rebuilt, whereas the sort-first block-nested loop strategy and the methods that employ plane sweep must sort the data each time the skyline query is executed with a different reference point. The algorithm makes use of a priority queue *Queue* to keep track of all objects and spatial index blocks that have been encountered so far whose L_1 distance from the origin is greater than the value of the object or block currently being processed by the algorithm.

At the outset of the algorithm, the priority queue *Queue* is initialized to the root of the search hierarchy, and the set of skyline points S is initialized to the empty set. The algorithm proceeds by removing the nearest entry i (which can be a point object or a nonobject block) to the origin in *Queue*, in terms of its L_1 distance, and checks if i is dominated by any of the existing skyline points in S. If it is, then i is discarded. Otherwise, there are two cases. If i is an object, then i is inserted into S. On the other hand, if i is a nonobject, then all of the children of i are inserted into *Queue* in a position consistent with their L_1 distance from the origin. Papadias et al. [1462] try to reduce the size of *Queue* by conditioning the insertion of a child j of i into *Queue* on the basis of j's not being dominated by any of the existing skyline points. However, we point out that when j is subsequently encountered at the front of *Queue*, we must still check if j is dominated by any of the skyline points in S as, in the intervening time period, additional points could have been added to S. Thus, the algorithm may be slowed down considerably if j does indeed get inserted into *Queue* after performing this check (see Exercise 9). Note that the traversal process of the search hierarchy is analogous to a plane-sweep method where the traversal order plays the same role as the sweep order.

Needless to say, the algorithm is progressive as this is one of the distinguishing characteristics of the incremental nearest neighbor algorithm that it deploys. Papadias et al. [1462] point out that at times it is desirable to report k elements of the skyline (i.e., a top-k skyline query) in a different order than that given by the distance metric L_1 used to control the traversal of the search hierarchy (i.e., the analog of the plane-sweep algorithm). In other words, the top-k skyline query expresses a preference [378, 1099] for an alternative weighting for the contributions of the attribute values to the equal weighting implicitly provided by the L_1 distance metric. In particular, they note that the dominance relation between two points yields a preference or nonpreference between them according to some scoring function (min in our examples). They propose to extend this notion of preference to a more general *preference function* that can also be used to order (i.e., rank) the skyline points. The ordering yielded by such a scoring function is consistent with that provided by the dominance relation, and both the orders in which the points are processed and the skyline points are produced as long as the function is monotonic in all of the attributes.

Note that this type of a scoring function is also used in the sort-first block-nested loop method of Chomicki et al. [379]. However, the key advantage of its use with the spatial index is that if the preference function changes, there is no need to modify the spatial index, whereas when the preference function changes, the sort-first block-nested loop strategy must be reinvoked to sort the points. The resorting step is necessary as the change in the preference function means that the order in which the elements of the skyline will be reported will change, which is important when executing a variant of a top-k skyline query. It is interesting to observe that this preference function plays the same role as the distance metric and can also be viewed as a composition of the distance metric and the normalization function that is needed when the domains of the attribute values differ.

A drawback of the implementation of the incremental nearest neighbor algorithm of Papadias et al. [1462] is that, in order to obtain the complete set of skyline points, the algorithm must traverse the entire search hierarchy, at which time the priority queue will be empty. This is in contrast with the algorithm of Tan et al. [1838], which has a condition to be checked for early termination that is not applicable when using the L_1 distance metric as done by Papadias et al. This raises the interesting point that the progressive variant of the skyline query could have also been implemented by using the incremental nearest neighbor algorithm in conjunction with any other distance metric in the Minkowski L_p family, such as L_2 or, even better, the variant of the L_∞ distance metric that makes use of a minimum instead of a maximum, as done by Tan et al. [1838] (see Exercise 10).

Skyline queries are only meaningful when an ordering exists on the value domains of the various attributes. The ordering is usually presumed to be total (e.g., [1068, 1462, 1838]), although the ordering can also be partial (e.g., [319]).[10] However, when the ordering is partial, caution must be exercised in the manner in which the partially ordered attributes are handled so that the skyline does not consist of all of the data points in the database, which will be the case if no ordering exists on the value domains of one or more of the attributes (i.e., neither a total or a partial ordering). As an example of a scenario where a partial ordering comes into play, suppose that our hotel database also includes an attribute corresponding to the amenities provided by each hotel. Suppose that we want to determine the hotels with the best amenities and the minimum prices and distances from the beach. In this case, the only ordering-related information that we have about the values of the amenities attribute is that some amenity values are deemed preferable to others. For example, valet covered parking can be viewed as a preferred amenity to covered self-parking, which in turn is preferable to street parking. Similar relationships can be constructed for other amenities. For example, a private beach can be viewed as preferable to a public beach; also, a private beach can be viewed as preferable to a swimming pool. Different classes of amenities could also be ordered, such as a stipulation that valet parking is preferable to a private beach. It is important to note that once we have different classes of amenities, there is also the possibility that an amenity that is preferred to all other amenities may not necessarily exist, although such a situation increases the likelihood that all objects will be in the result of the skyline query.

One possible method of coping with partially ordered attribute domains is to obtain a total ordering for them as a result of applying a process such as a topological sort

---

[10] Briefly, an ordering on a set S is said to be a *partial ordering* if there exists a relation among the elements of S, denoted by "$\leq$," satisfying transitivity (i.e., $a \leq b$ and $b \leq c$ implies $a \leq c$), reflexivity (i.e., $x \leq x$), and asymmetry (i.e., if $x \leq y$, then $y \leq x$ cannot hold unless $x = y$). Instances of the relation $a \leq b$ are often interpreted as indicating that a precedes or equals b. Therefore, if no such relation exists between some pair of objects u and v, then u and v can come in any order and thus u can precede v and also follow v. Partial orderings are used to describe many everyday sequences of actions and have been used to define processes such as construction and assembly where some tasks must be completed before others while other tasks can be carried out independently of each other (i.e., this is the case when no precedes relation holds between two objects). Partial orderings are to be contrasted with total orderings, where a *total ordering* is an ordering on S such that a relation R exists on S that yields a partial ordering on S, and for any two elements x and y, either $x \leq y$ or $y \leq x$ or $x = y$ holds. The total ordering differs from the partial ordering in that, in the total ordering, it is impossible for one of the above three relationships not to be satisfied for every possible pair of objects in S, whereas in the partial ordering, it is possible for objects to exist where none of the three relationships is satisfied. For example, letting u and v correspond to the prices of two hotels, in a total ordering, either $u \leq v$ or $v \leq u$ or $u = v$ holds. We also point out that no ordering is possible in the situation that the notion of a relation "$\leq$" between objects does not exist.

(e.g., [976, 1044]). In this case, though, we must be vigilant for false negatives that would incorrectly preclude certain objects from being in the skyline. For example, letting a be a partially ordered attribute such that, after generating a total ordering via the topological sort, we have that object x dominates object y, thereby possibly precluding y from being in the skyline, when, in fact, for the partially ordered attribute a, no ordering relationship exists between $a(x)$ and $a(y)$. Of course, x and y can still be prevented from being in the skyline if there exists another object z such that $a(z)$ has priority over both $a(x)$ and $a(y)$, provided that the other attribute values of x and y are also dominated by the corresponding attribute values of z. Note also that, although progressive skyline algorithms can be developed for partially ordered attribute domains, they cannot be characterized as top-k algorithms as the top-k objects are not unique due to the multitude of possible total orderings.

Exercises

1. Adapt procedure INCNEAREST to execute a maximum distance query (i.e., find all elements having distance from q less than D_{max}) in an incremental manner as described in the text.

2. Adapt procedure INCNEAREST to execute a minimum distance query (i.e., find all elements having distance from q greater than D_{min}) in an incremental manner as described in the text. You will need to make use of the additional distance functions $\hat{d}_t(q, e_t)$ for each element type that provide an upper bound on the distances from q of the objects in the subtree represented by e_t.

3. Adapt procedure INCNEAREST to execute a range query with a minimum and a maximum distance (i.e., find all elements having distance from q greater than D_{min} and less than D_{max}) in an incremental manner as described in the text.

4. Adapt procedure INCNEAREST to execute a maximum result query (i.e., the k nearest neighbors) in an incremental manner as described in the text.

5. Adapt procedure INCNEAREST to execute a maximum result query (i.e., the k nearest neighbors) by making use of the distance D_k from q of the kth candidate nearest neighbor o_k to reduce the number of priority queue operations as described in the text. In particular, use two priority queues, one for the objects and one for the remaining types of elements (i.e., nonobjects).

6. Adapt procedure INCNEAREST as described in the text to obtain a procedure INCFARTHEST that returns the farthest neighbors from object q in an incremental manner.

7. Adapt procedure INCNEARESTDUP as described in Section 4.1.4 to obtain a procedure INCFARTHESTDUP that returns the farthest neighbors from object q in an incremental manner while allowing duplicate object instances.

8. The modified skyline algorithm of Kossmann et al. [1068] partitions the underlying d-dimensional space at the closest point p to the origin into two pairwise disjoint regions along each of the d dimensions, thereby resulting in $2d$ overlapping regions. Of these d pairs of disjoint regions, the algorithm was described as retaining the member of each pair that does not contain the region dominated by p (i.e., b in the explanation of the basic two-dimensional algorithm). Can you also implement the algorithm by retaining the member of each pair that does not contain the region for which p is the closest point to the origin (i.e., a in the explanation of the basic two-dimensional algorithm)? If yes, which method is preferable?

9. In the text we point out that in their implementation of the incremental nearest neighbor algorithm for computing skyline queries, Papadias et al. [1462] try to reduce the size of the priority queue *Queue* by conditioning the insertion into *Queue* of a child j of a nonobject i that is not dominated by any of the elements in the set of skyline points S on the basis of j's not being dominated by any points in S. We point out that this may slow down the algorithm considerably due to the need to check for dominance twice, once upon insertion of j into *Queue* and once when j percolates to the front of *Queue*. Evaluate the utility of this conditioning step by comparing the size of *Queue* and the execution time (i.e., extra checks for dominance) when it is used to when it is not used.

10. Implement the skyline query using the incremental nearest neighbor algorithm with the distance metric employed by Tan et al. [1838]. In other words, the distance metric d_T is the

minimum of the attribute values so that for two-dimensional points (x_1, y_1) and (x_2, y_2), $d_T((x_1, y_1), (x_2, y_2)) = \min(|x_1 - x_2|, |y_1 - y_2|)$. Compare its performance with the implementation of Papadias et al. [1462], which makes use of the L_1 distance metric. In particular, what is the effect of the early termination condition on the size of the priority queue *Queue* and the execution times?

11. Develop a skyline algorithm that involves partially ordered attribute domains. Can you come up with a simpler solution than the one of Chan, Eng, and Tan [319]?

4.1.6 Nearest Neighbors in a Spatial Network

As mentioned in the opening section of this chapter, the nearest neighbor algorithms that we describe assume that the distance between two objects in the set of objects S is the shortest distance between them in the space in which they lie—that is, "as the crow flies." However, in many applications such a definition of distance is of limited value because both the set of objects S and the space in which their proximity is being measured are constrained to lie on a network such as a set of roads, air corridors, sea channels, and so on. In fact, even the choice of paths through the network may be constrained due to conditions such as road widths, weight limits, trafficability, aircraft separation rules, noise constraints, security zones, water depth variations, and so on. Such naturally occurring networks can be modeled as spatial networks. In particular, spatial networks are extensions of general graphs $G = (V, E)$, where now the vertices in the graph have fixed spatial positions. As an example, road networks are modeled as directed weighted graphs where the vertices (i.e., road intersections) have spatial positions specified using geographical coordinates—that is, pairs of latitude and longitude values. The edges are assigned suitable weights that model other imposed constraints, such as the distance between the constituent vertices. Note that other nonspatial attributes, often reflecting constraints, could also be associated with the edges, such as road widths, weight limits, speed limits, trafficability, and so on, for the particular road network. For all practical cases, the underlying graphs that form the basis of the spatial networks are assumed to be connected planar graphs. This is not an unreasonable assumption as road networks are connected (at least within a landmass such as a continent), although they do not have to be planar as can be seen by the presence of tunnels and bridges. In the case of water networks consisting of rivers, lakes, canals, and so on, the situation is somewhat different. We do not dwell on such situations here.

It is important to note that the objects that make up the set S from which the neighbors are drawn need not be the same as the set V of vertices of the spatial network, and the size of S is usually considerably smaller than that of V. The objects in S represent entities such as restaurants, hotels, gas stations, and so on. They may be coincident with the vertices of the spatial network, lie on the edges of the network, or even be off the network, in which case the algorithms assume that they are associated with the closest vertex in the network. For the purpose of this discussion, we assume that the set S of objects of interest is a subset of the set V of vertices.

A number of different algorithms (e.g., [1464, 1672]) have been proposed that make use of the incremental nearest neighbor algorithm in an environment where the distance is measured along a spatial network such as a set of roads (e.g., Figure 4.6(a), where the heavy dots are used to denote vertices with which the objects that are to be retrieved are associated). In other words, in order for an object o to be a neighbor of object q at distance d from q, there must be some path through the spatial network between q and o of length d. This is useful for obtaining more realistic nearest neighbors, especially in the context of applications where finding q's closest neighbor o is not an adequate answer by itself—that is, we must also actually be able to reach o on a path starting at q before reaching any other possible neighbors of q that might even be closer than o using a suitably chosen distance metric such as their Euclidean distance from q.

For example, Figure 4.6(b) is the result of the application of an incremental nearest neighbor algorithm to obtain the shortest paths between a query object associated with the vertex marked by X and its 17 nearest objects that are associated with a subset of the vertices of a spatial network in Figure 4.6(a). The objects associated with the vertices at the end of the paths in Figure 4.6(b) are labeled with a number corresponding to the relative rank of the lengths of the shortest paths to them from X, where lower numbers correspond to shorter paths. Observe that the object associated with vertex 3 is reported as a closer neighbor to X than the object associated with vertex 4, even though the spatial distance between X and 4 is less than the spatial (i.e., Euclidean) distance between X and 3.

One very simple way to use the incremental nearest neighbor algorithm to a spatial network is to note that the Euclidean distance between two objects q and u in the spatial network serves as a lower bound on the distance between them through the network (termed the *network distance*). This observation/restriction forms the basis of the *Incremental Euclidean Restriction* (IER) nearest neighbor algorithm of Papadias, Zhang, Mamoulis, and Tao [1464]. The IER algorithm uses a priority queue *Queue*, as well as an R-tree [791] to implement the search hierarchy T used to represent the set S of objects from which the neighbors are drawn (usually a subset of the vertices of the spatial network). IER starts by applying the incremental nearest neighbor algorithm to obtain a set L of k candidate nearest neighbors (recall Section 4.1.5) that are the k nearest neighbors of query object q in terms of their Euclidean distance from q. Once the k nearest Euclidean distance neighbors have been determined, IER computes the network distance from q to all of the elements of L (using a shortest-path algorithm such as Dijkstra's algorithm [491]), sorts them in increasing order of their network distance from q, and notes the farthest one o_k at network distance D_k from q. At this point, the incremental nearest neighbor algorithm is reinvoked to continue processing the remaining objects in increasing Euclidean distance from q until encountering an object o whose Euclidean distance from q is greater than D_k, at which time the algorithm terminates. Each time an object o is encountered whose Euclidean distance from q is less than D_k, then o's network distance d_o from q is computed, and if o is closer to q than one of the elements of L (i.e., $d_o < D_k$), then o is inserted into L, thereby removing o_k, and o_k and D_k are reset as is appropriate.

IER has several drawbacks. First of all, it is not really incremental in the sense that it does not obtain the nearest neighbors of q in increasing order of their network distance from q. Instead, it is only incremental in the sense that it operates in a filter-and-refine [1416] mode where it obtains its candidate objects for the filter test in increasing order of their Euclidean distance from q. However, the actual objects that it finds are not reported in increasing order of network distance. Thus, it is more of a k-nearest neighbor algorithm that performs filtering of candidates in increasing order of their Euclidean distance from the query object. This means that once IER has found the k nearest neighbors of q in terms of their network distance, it cannot be resumed to find the $(k + 1)$-th nearest neighbor. The second drawback is IER's constant need to evaluate the network distance along the shortest path from q to each object that it encounters. This can be quite expensive for large graphs and entails much repeated work as the shortest paths often have common subpaths.

Sankaranarayanan, Alborzi, and Samet [1672] describe an alternative algorithm, INCNEARESTSPATIALNETWORK (given further below), that overcomes both of these drawbacks. It is truly incremental in the sense that it reports the neighbors in increasing order of their network distance from q, and once it has reported the k nearest neighbors, it can be resumed to find the $(k + 1)$-th nearest neighbor. Their algorithm uses an all pair shortest-path algorithm (e.g., Dijkstra's algorithm [491]) to precompute the shortest paths between all pairs of vertices u and v in V in the graph $G = (V, E)$, although Sankaranarayanan et al. do not store the entire paths. Instead, they store partial information about the paths (i.e., the first edge along the shortest path from source

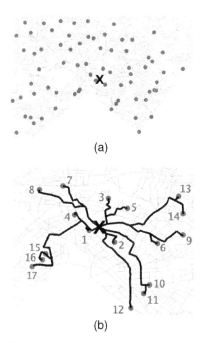

(a)

(b)

Figure 4.6
(a) A sample spatial network corresponding to Silver Spring, Maryland, with heavy dots denoting vertices with which the objects to be retrieved are associated and (b) the result of the application of an incremental nearest neighbor algorithm to obtain the shortest paths between a query object associated with the vertex marked by X and its 17 nearest objects that are associated with the subset of its vertices denoted by heavy dots. The objects associated with the vertices at the ends of the paths are labeled with their position number in an ordering based on increasing length of the shortest path from X to them along the spatial network.

(a)

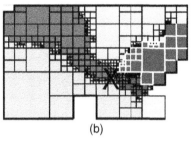

(b)

Figure 4.7
(a) Partition of the underlying space spanned by the spatial network in Figure 4.6(a) into regions r_i such that the shortest path from the vertex marked by X to a vertex in r_i passes through the same vertex among the six vertices that are adjacent to X (i.e., the shortest-path map of X) and (b) the blocks in the shortest-path quadtree corresponding to the regions in (a).

vertex u to destination vertex v), which enables the shortest path between u and v to be constructed in time proportional to the length of the path.

In particular, using the precomputed shortest-path information and the spatial position of the vertices, Sankaranarayanan et al. construct a map m_u, defined below, for each vertex (possible query object) u in the spatial network. Given vertex u_i, each map m_{u_i}, termed the *shortest-path map* of u_i, is a partition of the underlying space into M_{u_i} regions, where there is one region $r_{u_i j}$ for each vertex $w_{u_i j}$ ($1 \leq j \leq M_{u_i}$) such that there exists an edge $e_{u_i j}$ from u_i to $w_{u_i j}$. Region $r_{u_i j}$ spans the space occupied by all points v such that the shortest path from u_i to v contains edge $e_{u_i j}$ (i.e., the shortest path makes a transition through vertex $w_{u_i j}$). For example, Figure 4.7(a) is such a partition for the vertex marked by X in the road network of Figure 4.6(a). Sankaranarayanan et al. represent each m_{u_i} using a region quadtree (see also Exercise 5), termed a *shortest-path quadtree*, where there are M_{u_i} different disjoint regions $r_{u_i j}$. Each region $r_{u_i j}$ consists of the disjoint quadtree blocks that it comprises. Given our assumptions that the spatial network is planar and connected, the M_{u_i} regions $r_{u_i j}$ for vertex u_i are connected (see Exercise 2), ignoring possible floating-point precision errors in the underlying dataset. For example, Figure 4.7(b) is the block decomposition induced by the shortest-path quadtree on the shortest-path map of Figure 4.7(a).

Given source vertex u, destination vertex v, the shortest-path map m_u and shortest-path quadtree s_u associated with u, the next vertex t in the shortest path from u to v is the vertex w_j associated with the quadtree block of s_u in region r_j of m_u that contains v. The complete path from u to v is obtained by repeating the process, successively replacing u with t and replacing u's shortest-path quadtree with that of t, until u equals v.

There are a number of possible access structures that can be imposed on the set of blocks that make up the shortest-path quadtree. Sankaranarayanan et al. represent these blocks by their locational codes and impose a B$^+$-tree access structure on them. The blocks are known as Morton blocks (recall Section 2.1.2.4 of Chapter 2). This approach differs from that of Wagner and Willhalm [1945], who represent the individual regions $r_{u_i j}$ in map m_{u_i} for vertex u_i by their minimum bounding boxes, which must, in turn, be organized by an index for an object hierarchy such as an R-tree [791]. The drawback of the approach of Wagner and Willhalm is that the bounding boxes are not disjoint, which complicates future searches.

Sankaranarayanan et al. make use of the shortest-path quadtree representation of the shortest paths in a spatial network to facilitate finding neighbors in increasing order of their network distance along the spatial network from a query object in incremental order of network distance. Their algorithm is an adaptation of the general incremental nearest neighbor algorithm. It assumes the existence of a search hierarchy T (i.e., a spatial index) on a set of objects S (usually points in the case of spatial networks) that make up the set of objects from which the neighbors are drawn. For the sake of this discussion, we assume that S, as well as the set of query objects Q, is a subset of the vertices of the spatial network, although less restrictive definitions could also be permitted such as stipulating that elements of S and Q must lie on the network.

The algorithm of Sankaranarayanan et al. is facilitated by storing some additional information with each Morton block b to enable the computation of the range of network distances from the query object for shortest paths that pass through b. In particular, for a Morton block b in the shortest-path quadtree for the map m_q associated with a query vertex q, Sankaranarayanan et al. store a pair of values, λ^- (λ^+), that correspond to the minimum (maximum) ratio of the network distance (i.e., through the network) to the actual *spatial distance* (i.e., "as the crow flies") from q to all destination vertices in b.

At this point, let us elaborate on how the shortest-path quadtree is used to compute network distances. In particular, we first show how to compute the network distance between a query vertex q and a destination vertex v. We start by finding the block b in the shortest-path quadtree of q that contains v (i.e., a point location operation). By multiplying the λ^- and λ^+ values associated with b by the spatial distance between

q and v, we obtain an interval $[\delta^-, \delta^+]$, termed the *initial network distance interval*, which contains the range of the network distance between q and v. These two actions are achieved by procedure GETNETWORKDISTINTERVAL (not given here). Whenever it is determined that the initial network distance interval $[\delta^-, \delta^+]$ is not sufficiently tight, an operation, termed *refinement*, is applied that obtains the next vertex t in the shortest path between q and v using procedure NEXTVERTEXSHORTESTPATH (not given here). Having obtained t, we retrieve the shortest-path quadtree s_t for t and then calculate a new network distance interval $[\delta_t^-, \delta_t^+]$ by locating the Morton block b_t of s_t that contains v. The network distance interval of the shortest path between q and v is now obtained by summing the network distance from q to t (i.e., the weight of the edge from q to t) and $[\delta_t^-, \delta_t^+]$. Given a pair of vertices q and v and a length k for the shortest path between them, this process can be reinvoked at most another $k - 2$ times until reaching v.

We now show how to compute the network distance between a query vertex q and a block b of the search hierarchy T. First, we point out that in the case of a block, the concept of a network distance is complicated by the fact that there are usually many vertices within the block, and thus we need to specify somehow the vertex (vertices) for which we are computing the network distance. Instead, we compute a minimum network distance for the block using procedure MINNETWORKDISTBLOCK (not given here). The minimum possible network distance δ^- of q from b is computed by intersecting b with s_q, the shortest-path quadtree of q, to obtain a set of intersecting blocks B_q of s_q. For each element b_i of B_q, the associated λ_i^- value is multiplied by the corresponding MINDIST$(q, b_i \cap b)$ value to obtain the corresponding minimum shortest-path network distance μ_i^- from q to b_i. δ^- is set to the minimum value of μ_i^- for the set of individual regions specified by $b_i \cap b$. Note that the reason that block b can be intersected by a varying number of blocks b_i of B_q is that s_q and T need not be based on the same data structure (e.g., T can be an R-tree [791]), and even if they are both quadtree-based (e.g., T is a PR quadtree [1413, 1637]), s_q and T do not necessarily need to be in registration (i.e., they can have different origins, as can be seen in Figure 4.8).

The incremental nearest neighbor algorithm makes use of a priority queue *Queue* that is initialized to contain the root of the search hierarchy T and the root's network distance from the query object q. The principal difference between the spatial network adaptation of the incremental nearest neighbor algorithm and the conventional incremental nearest neighbor algorithm is that, in the case of a spatial network, objects are enqueued using their network distance interval (i.e., $[\delta^-, \delta^+]$) from the query object q, instead of just their minimum spatial distance from q. However, objects and blocks are still removed from *Queue* in increasing order of their minimum network distance from q (i.e., δ^-). When a nonleaf block b is removed from *Queue*, the minimum network distance is computed from q to all of the children of b, and they are inserted into *Queue* with their corresponding minimum network distances. When a leaf block b is removed from *Queue*, the objects (i.e., points) in b are enqueued with their corresponding initial network distance intervals, which are computed with the aid of the λ^- and λ^+ values associated with b.

On the other hand, when the incremental nearest neighbor algorithm processes an object p (i.e., when the most recently removed element from *Queue* corresponds to an object), it determines if the maximum network distance δ_p^+ of p is less than the minimum network distance δ_h^- of the element h that is currently at the top of the priority queue, in which case it exits because p is the desired neighbor. Otherwise, it attempts to tighten the network distance interval for p by applying one step of the refinement operation described earlier and then enqueues p with the updated network distance interval. Note that when the network distance intervals associated with an object p in *Queue* have been obtained via refinement, *Queue* must also keep track of the most recently determined intermediate vertex t on the shortest path from q to p and the network distance d from q to t along this path (see Exercise 4). Observe also that no such information need be recorded for blocks, and, in fact, each time we process a block, its associated intermediate vertex and minimum network distance are the query object q and 0, respectively.

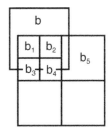

Figure 4.8
Example of the intersection of block b in a quadtree search hierarchy T with blocks b_1, b_2, b_3, b_4, and b_5 in the shortest-path quadtree.

1 **procedure** INCNEARESTSPATIALNETWORK(q, S, T)

2 /* A best-first incremental algorithm that returns the nearest neighbors of q from a set of objects S on a spatial network. S is organized using the search hierarchy T. It assumes that each element in the priority queue *Queue* has four data fields E, D, V, and I, corresponding to the entity x that *Queue* contains (which can be an object, leaf block, or nonleaf block), the network distance interval of x (just one value if x is not an object), the most recently determined vertex v via refinement when x is an object, and the network distance from q to v along the shortest path from q to x when x is an object. Note that ENQUEUE takes four arguments when the enqueued entity is an object instead of the usual two, and, in this case, the field names are specified in its invocation. */

3 **value object** q

4 **value object_set** S

5 **value pointer search_hierarchy** T

6 **priority_queue** *Queue*

7 **object** o

8 **vertex** v

9 **interval** i

10 **real** s

11 **pointer search_hierarchy** e, e_p

12 **priority_queue_entry** t

13 *Queue* ← NEWPRIORITYQUEUE()

14 e ← root of the search hierarchy induced by S and T

15 ENQUEUE($e, 0, Queue$)

16 **while not** ISEMPTY(*Queue*) **do**

17   t ← DEQUEUE(*Queue*)

18   e ← E(t)

19   **if** ISOBJECT(e) **then** /* e is an object */

20   **if** MAXNETWORKDISTINTERVAL(D(t))

21   < MINNETWORKDISTINTERVAL(

22   D(FRONTPRIORITYQUEUE(*Queue*))) **then**

23   Report e as the next nearest object

24   **else** /* Refinement operation */

25   v ← NEXTVERTEXSHORTESTPATH(

26   e, SHORTESTPATHQUADTREE(V(t)))

27   /* NEXTVERTEXSHORTESTPATH performs point location on e in the SHORTESTPATHQUADTREE of V(t) and returns the vertex v associated with the block or region containing V(t). */

28   s ← I(t) + EDGEWEIGHT(V(t), v)

29   /* EDGEWEIGHT(V(t), v) is the distance between V(t) and v */

30   i ← s + GETNETWORKDISTINTERVAL(

31   e, SHORTESTPATHQUADTREE(v))

32   ENQUEUE([E =]e, [D =]i, [V =]v, [I =]s, *Queue*)

33   **endif**

34   **elseif** ISLEAF(e) **then** /* e is a leaf block */

35   **foreach** object child element o of e **do**

36   /* Insert each object o in e in *Queue*, along with the network distance interval of o, which is obtained by performing a point location operation for the block containing o in the shortest-path quadtree of q. */

37   ENQUEUE([E =]o,

38   [D =]GETNETWORKDISTINTERVAL(

39   o, SHORTESTPATHQUADTREE(q)),

40   [V =]q, [I =]0, *Queue*)

41   **enddo**

```
42    else /* e is a nonleaf block */
43        foreach child element $e_p$ of e do
44            ENQUEUE($e_p$, MINNETWORKDISTBLOCK($q, e_p$), Queue)
45        enddo
46    endif
47 enddo
```

It is important to note that, as we have described earlier, although the approach of Sankaranarayanan et al. does precompute the shortest paths and the corresponding network distance value ratios between all possible vertices of the spatial network, it does not store the actual paths; nor does it store the network distances between the vertex pairs, which, for spatial networks with N vertices, can require as much as $O(N^3)$ and $O(N^2)$ space, respectively. Instead, it stores N shortest-path quadtrees s_{u_i}, one per vertex u_i ($1 \leq i \leq N$) corresponding to the various maps m_{u_i}. Assuming that each of the quadtrees s_{u_i} is embedded in a $2^n \times 2^n$ image, s_{u_i} requires $O(p_{u_i} + n)$ space, where p_{u_i} is the sum of the perimeters of the regions that make up m_{u_i} (recall the Quadtree Complexity Theorem in Section 2.2.2.2 of Chapter 2 [901]). This makes for a potentially considerably smaller contribution to the space requirements than the factor N associated with the methods that keep track of the network distance from each vertex to all remaining vertices as the number of different regions in the shortest-path quadtree of vertex v_i is equal to the outdegree of v_i. It is possible to obtain even lower space bounds by implementing the shortest-path map using one of the boundary-based quadtree representations such as the PM$_1$ quadtree [1665] and PMR quadtree [1360, 1362] discussed in Sections 2.2.2.6 and 2.2.2.8, respectively, of Chapter 2 (see Exercise 5).

Both the IER algorithm and the algorithm of Sankaranarayanan et al. make use of Dijkstra's algorithm to some extent, differing in whether the shortest paths are precomputed. Both algorithms make use of a priority queue to store candidate members of the set S from which the neighbors are drawn; however, only the algorithm of Sankaranarayanan et al. reports the neighbors in increasing order of network distance from the query object. An alternative is to use Dijkstra's algorithm directly. In this case, the priority queue Queue stores the vertices V of the spatial network, along with their network distances from q on the shortest path from q, and the elements are processed in increasing order of these network distances. This alternative forms the basis of the *Incremental Network Expansion* (INE) nearest neighbor algorithm of Papadias, Zhang, Mamoulis, and Tao [1464], which also permits the objects S to lie on the edges of the network.

The INE algorithm is implemented as follows. Queue is initialized to contain the vertices of the edge e on which q lies and their network distances from q. The set of the k candidate nearest neighbors is maintained in L and is initialized to the objects that lie on e and their network distances from q. At each step of INE, the vertex c at the front of Queue is removed, and each object o, if any, associated with an edge incident at c[11] is inserted into L with its network distance from q via c, say d_o, provided d_o is less than the network distance of the kth nearest neighboring object in L and that o is not already in L with a smaller associated network distance value. All vertices of the edges incident at c that have not yet been visited (i.e., removed from Queue) are inserted into Queue with their associated network distances from q. INE halts when the network distance between q and the kth nearest neighboring object in L is smaller than the network distance between c and q.

There are several differences between INE and Dijkstra's shortest-path algorithm. The first difference is that INE, as implemented above, is really a k-nearest neighbor algorithm, as is IER. INE does not obtain the k nearest neighbors of q in increasing network distance order from q, and thus it is not incremental. In contrast, the natural definition of Dijkstra's algorithm does obtain the neighbors incrementally. The second

---

[11] This step differs from the algorithm in [1464] which may miss some lower network distances to the objects via the closer vertex on the edge on which they lie.

Figure 4.9
A map of Silver Spring, Maryland, and the vertices, highlighted by circles, that are visited when applying Dijkstra's algorithm in determining the shortest path from the vertex marked by X to the vertex marked by V.

difference is that INE does not attempt to remove a vertex v that has not yet been visited from *Queue* (although it could, and should, do so) when INE encounters v as a result of being incident at c when dequeuing c. This variation potentially makes INE less efficient as the size of *Queue* is larger.

As we saw above, both INE and IER make heavy use of Dijkstra's algorithm, which is good for small spatial networks where it may not be worthwhile to precompute all of the shortest paths. Papadias et al. [1464] have shown the INE algorithm to outperform the IER algorithm, which is not surprising as the IER algorithm is constantly recomputing the shortest paths from q through the vertices on the shortest paths to its k nearest neighbors. However, for large spatial networks, applications of Dijkstra's algorithm to find the shortest path between two vertices such as INE can be expensive because it will visit a large proportion of the vertices in the spatial network, unless the distribution of the objects of S around q is dense as, in this case, fewer of the vertices or edges of G need to be visited. For example, Figure 4.9 shows the vertices that would be visited when finding the shortest path from the vertex marked by X to the vertex marked by V in the spatial network of Silver Spring, Maryland, of Figure 4.6. Here we see that 75.4% of the vertices are visited in the network (i.e., 3,191 out of a total of 4,233 vertices) in the process of obtaining a shortest path of length 75 edges.

Cho and Chung [377] try to improve on INE when the distribution of objects around q is sparse by preprocessing the spatial network to find vertices with a large outdegree (e.g., ≥ 3), termed *intersection vertices*, and computing the shortest paths from some small subset of them (elements of which are termed *condensing points*) to a predefined number m of their nearest neightboring objects. When the nearest neighbor algorithm encounters a condensing point c in the course of the search, the list L of k candidate nearest neighbors is updated with the m neighbors stored at c. Although the network distance to a neighbor v of c from q, denoted by $d(q, v)$, is unknown, Cho and Chung make use of the triangle inequality to approximate it with the network distance $d(q, c) + d(c, v)$. The result is that their algorithm encounters neighboring objects of q earlier than the INE algorithm, thereby enabling other vertices and objects to be pruned and consequently reducing the size of the priority queue. However, unfortunately, although the neighboring objects are encountered earlier, Cho and Chung do not provide a mechanism for the algorithm to terminate earlier as the network distance associated with an object o in L, such that o is a neighboring object of a condensing point, is an approximate network distance, and thus the algorithm only terminates when the search actually encounters these objects. Also, Cho and Chung's proposed improvement still does not make INE incremental. On the other hand, incremental algorithms such as the one of Sankaranarayanan et al. [1672] that we have described, which expend more time to precompute the shortest paths between all of the vertices of the spatial network, need not be concerned with these issues, and thus are more attractive, especially when many queries are posed to the spatial network.

Of course, there have been many other attempts at improving the performance of shortest-path algorithms such as Dijkstra's algorithm on large spatial networks, and the topic remains a subject of much research. Below, we describe some of the approaches. Filho and Samet [612] propose a method to speed up shortest-path computations on graphs that correspond to spatial networks by constructing a hierarchical auxiliary structure that aids path computations on G. This approach is an improvement on an earlier method of Jing, Huang, and Rundensteiner [958]. Goldberg and Harrelson [715] propose an alternative method to speed up path computations on spatial networks by embedding a set of pivots P at known positions (termed *landmarks*) in G. The network distances between all vertices and landmarks in G are precomputed and stored. Path computation between a source vertex u and a destination vertex v in G is sped up by making use of the network distance between u and v to a landmark $p_i \in P$. By applying constraints based on the triangle inequality, Goldberg and Harrelson are able to avoid visiting a substantial number of infeasible edges during the search process. Recall that the approach of Cho and Chung also makes use of the triangle inequality with the vertices that are condensing points playing the role of landmarks. Interestingly, the use of landmarks by both Goldberg and Harrelson and Cho and Chung can be viewed as a special case of the approach of Filho and Samet, where only one level of the hierarchical auxiliary structure is used.

Landmarks are also used by Kolahdouzan and Shahabi [1054] in a k-nearest neighbor finding algorithm where the objects from which the neighbors are drawn (a subset of the vertices of the spatial network) serve as sites of a Voronoi diagram. Shortest paths are precomputed between the Voronoi sites and vertices whose incident edges cross the boundaries of the Voronoi regions, termed *border vertices*. In this case, the $k > 1$ nearest neighbors of a query object q in Voronoi region r_q are obtained by making transitions to adjacent Voronoi regions of r_q with the aid of knowledge of the shortest-path network distances from the border vertices to the sites of the Voronoi regions in which they are contained. It should be clear that the border vertices play the role of landmarks. The algorithm is not incremental. Kolahdouzan and Shahabi [1053] have also adapted this method to the situation where the query object is in motion.

Linial, London, and Rabinovich [1181] describe an alternative method that constructs a Lipschitz embedding [1181] (see Section 4.7.2) consisting of a suitably chosen collection of subsets of the vertices of a general graph, where each subset serves as a coordinate. Shahabi, Kolahdouzan, and Sharifzdeh [1736] adapt this method for the special case that the general graph is a spatial network. Once the correspondence between coordinates and vertex subsets has been established, Shahabi et al. map each of the vertices in the spatial network into the high-dimensional vector space H formed by these coordinates. An approximate network distance between source vertex u and destination v is obtained by using the L_∞ Minkowski distance (i.e., the Chessboard metric) between their corresponding representations in H. Observe that Shahabi et al. do not compute the shortest path between u and v, although they claim that the approximate network distance that they obtain can be used as an estimate to guide the search for an approximate shortest path between them. However, it is important to point out that the distortion of the embedding (see Section 4.7.1) is $O(\log N)$, where N is the number of vertices in the spatial network. Gupta, Kopparty, and Ravishankar [781] describe a related approach that also makes use of embeddings in a high-dimensional space, which obtains exact network distances and shortest paths but requires that the edge weights be integers.

Exercises

1. Compare the performance of the incremental nearest neighbor algorithm in a spatial network when using a region quadtree [1672] and an R-tree [1945] for the regions of the shortest-path map of the query objects.

2. Recall that, for a given vertex u, its shortest-path map m_u is a partition of the underlying space into M_u regions where there is one region r_{uj} for each vertex w_j ($1 \leq j \leq M_u$) such that there exists an edge e_{uj} from u to w_j. Region r_{uj} contains the space occupied by all vertices v such that the shortest path from u to v contains edge e_{uj} (i.e., makes a transition through vertex w_j). Assuming that the spatial network is planar, prove that each of the M_u regions r_{uj} is connected.

3. How would you handle spatial networks that are both nonplanar and disconnected?

4. In the text, we mention that when the network distance intervals associated with a point p in *Queue* have been obtained via refinement, *Queue* must also keep track of the most recently determined intermediate vertex t on the shortest path from q to p and of the network distance from q to t along this path. Alternatively, instead of storing the network distance from q to t in *Queue*, suppose you stored the network distance interval from the intermediate vertex t to p. Is there any advantage to using this alternative?

5. Discuss the ramifications of representing the shortest-path map by imposing a variant of a PM quadtree such as the PM$_1$ quadtree [1665] or the PMR quadtree [1360, 1362] on the underlying subdivision of space instead of a region quadtree.

6. Given a spatial network, one way to store it is to build a spatial data structure such as one of the PM quadtree variants discussed in Sections 2.2.2.6 and 2.2.2.8, respectively, of Chapter 2. An alternative is to decompose the underlying space into regions so that the number of unconnected vertices in the region is kept low. Discuss how you would construct such a decomposition.

4.1.7 Related Work

Numerous algorithms exist for answering nearest neighbor and k-nearest neighbor queries. They are motivated by the importance of these queries in fields including geographical information systems (GIS), databases, pattern recognition, document retrieval, and learning theory. Almost all of these algorithms, many of them originating from the fields of pattern recognition and computational geometry, are for points in a d-dimensional vector space (e.g., [264, 530, 650, 666, 986, 1586, 1797]), but some allow for arbitrary spatial objects (e.g., [821, 863, 864]), although most of them restrict the query object to be a point.

Many of the above algorithms require specialized search structures (e.g., [100, 202, 666, 986]), but some employ commonly used spatial indexes such as those described in this book. For example, algorithms exist for the k-d tree (e.g., [264, 530, 650, 1331, 1797]), quadtree-related structures (e.g., [846, 848, 863]), the R-tree (e.g., [848, 1586, 1989]), the LSD tree [821], and others. In addition, many of the algorithms can be applied to other spatial indexes, some of which are discussed in Section 4.4. A number of approximate nearest neighbor algorithms have also been developed (e.g., [100, 202, 346, 387, 517, 608, 1226, 1229, 1230, 1286, 1971, 1989]). Some are discussed in Section 4.3 (i.e., [100, 346, 387, 517]), while others are discussed in Section 4.4.4 (i.e., [387, 1226, 1229, 1230]), Section 4.4.5 (i.e., [97, 98, 799]), and briefly in Section 4.4.8 (i.e., [387, 608, 1971]).

As we have pointed out in this section, frequently it is desired to obtain the neighbors in an incremental manner as they are needed since we often do not know in advance how many neighbors will have to be examined. Only a few of the above algorithms are incremental [821, 846, 848]. All of these incremental algorithms employ priority queues to organize the objects and to allow reporting the neighbors one by one. In addition, the algorithms of [821, 846, 848] also use a priority queue for the nodes of the index, enabling them to perform "best-first" traversal (i.e., at each step of the algorithms, the next node or object to visit is taken as the closest one to the query object that has yet to be visited).

The algorithm of [264] was developed for the k-d tree [164]. It is considerably different from the other algorithms [821, 846, 848] in that the algorithm of [264] stores only the data objects in the priority queue and uses a stack to keep track of the subtrees of the spatial data structure that have yet to be processed completely. This makes it necessary to use an elaborate mechanism to avoid processing the contents of a node more than once.

The algorithm of [821] was developed for the LSD tree [829]. It is very similar to the algorithm that we describe in Section 4.1.3 (presented in [846]) and was published at about the same time. The principal difference between [821] and the method that we have presented is that the LSD tree algorithm uses two priority queues, one for the data objects and another for the nodes of the spatial index, while our algorithm does not distinguish between the data objects and the nodes—that is, both nodes and data objects are stored in the same priority queue. This makes the algorithm of [821] a bit more complicated than the algorithm that we have presented, while the use of two priority queues does not offer any performance benefits according to experiments [848].

The incremental algorithm [846] that we have described in this section was initially developed for the PMR quadtree [1360], although its presentation was general and was easily adapted to an R-tree [848]. It was also recently adapted to be used with an MX-CIF quadtree in a peer-to-peer (P2P) setting [1848]. In addition, [848] has shown how an existing k-nearest neighbor algorithm [1586] can be transformed into a special case of the algorithm that we have presented. A byproduct of the transformation process is that the k-nearest neighbor algorithm has been simplified considerably.

Nearest neighbor algorithms have also been developed for general objects where the only restriction is that they reside in a metric space—that is, a distance metric is defined between any two objects. Methods for indexing such objects (e.g., [118, 241, 255, 283, 334, 389, 666, 851, 854, 1292, 1347, 1383, 1743, 1897, 1930, 1951, 2052]) are discussed in greater detail in Section 4.5. Most existing k-nearest neighbor algorithms for such distance-based indexes use a depth-first *branch and bound* strategy (e.g., [836]) as discussed in Section 4.2. A few algorithms employ best-first search, much like the general incremental nearest neighbor algorithm that we have described, but the full power of best-first search is not always exploited. Section 4.5 contains a detailed discussion of how to adapt the search hierarchies proposed in Section 4.1.2 and the general incremental nearest neighbor algorithm INCNEAREST to a number of the distance-based indexes.

4.2 The Depth-First K-Nearest Neighbor Algorithm

Perhaps the most common strategy for nearest neighbor finding employs the depth-first *branch and bound* method (e.g., [836]). Nearest neighbor finding algorithms that incorporate this strategy can be easily extended to find the k nearest neighbors, and this is how we describe them here. These algorithms are generally applicable to any index based on hierarchical clustering. The idea is that the data is partitioned into clusters that are aggregated to form other clusters, with the total aggregation being represented as a tree. The search hierarchies used by these algorithms are partly specific to vector data (e.g., [202, 530, 650, 666, 955, 986, 1103, 1199, 1331, 1374, 1586, 1797, 1989]), but they can be easily adapted to nonvector data (e.g., [118, 241, 255, 283, 334, 389, 851, 854, 1292, 1347, 1383, 1743, 1897, 1930, 1951, 2052], as discussed in Section 4.5), and this is how we present them here. This means that many of our derivations, unless stated otherwise, only make use of the triangle inequality rather than make an implicit assumption that the underlying space is a vector space with the Euclidean distance metric.

This section is organized as follows. The basic depth-first k-nearest neighbor algorithm is described in Section 4.2.1. Section 4.2.2 contains a detailed presentation of a number of pruning rules to avoid processing some of the clusters, as well as individual objects, when they can be shown to be farther from the query object q than any of the current k nearest neighbors of q. Section 4.2.3 discusses the effects of the manner in which the search hierarchy is formed on the pruning rules. Section 4.2.4 examines the effects of the order in which the clusters are processed on the performance of the algorithm. Section 4.2.5 incorporates some of the observations made in Sections 4.2.3 and 4.2.4 to yield a new and improved depth-first k-nearest neighbor algorithm. Besides using an estimate of the minimum distance at which a nearest neighbor can be found to eliminate some of the remaining clusters and objects from further consideration (referred to as MINDIST), the algorithm also makes use of an estimate of the maximum possible distance at which a nearest neighbor is guaranteed to be found in a cluster (referred to as MAXNEARESTDIST), which is new. Section 4.2.6 shows how to incorporate the MAX-NEARESTDIST estimate into a best-first algorithm. Section 4.2.7 gives an example where use of the MAXNEARESTDIST estimate does indeed improve the performance of both the depth-first and best-first k-nearest neighbor algorithms. Section 4.2.8 concludes with a comparison of the depth-first algorithm with the best-first algorithm with a particular emphasis on the use of the MAXNEARESTDIST estimate.

4.2.1 Basic Algorithm

A very general and basic depth-first k-nearest neighbor algorithm is given by procedures KNEAREST and DFTRAV, where q is the query object, k is the number of neighbors sought, S is the set of objects, and T is a data structure that organizes S. Since no assumptions are made about the objects or the data structure used to store them, the algorithm is presented in terms of the search hierarchy induced by them. The algorithm makes use of a set L that contains the k current candidate nearest neighbors along with their corresponding distance from q. L is implemented using a priority queue so that accessing the farthest of the k nearest neighbors, as well as updates (i.e., insertions and deletions of the k nearest neighbor), can be performed without needless exchange operations, as would be the case if L were implemented using an array. Each element e in L has two data fields E and D corresponding to the object o that e contains and o's distance from q (i.e., $d(q,o)$), respectively, and a number of fields corresponding to control information that is specific to the data structure used to implement the priority queue (e.g., a binary heap).

The algorithm is invoked by calling KNEAREST, which starts off by initializing L to be empty, thereby indicating that we have no candidate neighbors. D_k corresponds to an upper bound on the distance to the farthest of the k nearest neighbors (i.e., the kth-nearest neighbor) of q. D_k is initialized to ∞ because we have no candidate neighbors initially. D_k retains this initial value until either k actual neighbors have been found, or upper bounds on the distances to k distinct neighbors have been determined, in which case D_k is the maximum of these upper bounds. Thus, initially the algorithm is equivalent to a range query with the search range ε of ∞. The actual algorithm to find the k nearest neighbors of q is realized by the recursive procedure DFTRAV, which is invoked with e set to the root of the search hierarchy and the parameters L and D_k initialized as described above.

In DFTRAV, if the nonobject element e being visited is at the deepest level of the search hierarchy (usually referred to as a *leaf* or *leaf element*), then every object o in e that is nearer to q than the current kth-nearest neighbor of q (i.e., $d(q,o) < D_k$) is inserted into L using procedure INSERTL. If there are fewer than k candidate neighbors (determined with the aid of the function SIZE, which is not given here), then INSERTL invokes procedure ENQUEUE (not given here) to perform the actual insertion. Otherwise, if there are k candidate neighbors, then INSERTL dequeues the current farthest member (i.e., the kth-nearest member) from L using DEQUEUE (not given here)[12] and invokes ENQUEUE to perform the actual insertion. Next, if there are k

---

[12] Note the asymmetry between DEQUEUE, which removes the item at the front of the queue, and ENQUEUE, which inserts an item in its appropriate position in the queue. Procedure REMOVEPRIORITYQUEUE (not given here) is the complement of ENQUEUE in that it removes a specified element from the queue, which may involve a search.

candidate nearest neighbors after the insertion, then INSERTL resets D_k to the distance of the current farthest nearest neighbor, accessed by MAXPRIORITYQUEUE (not given here but equivalent to FRONTPRIORITYQUEUE when priority is given to elements at a maximum distance). Otherwise (i.e., e is not a leaf element), DFTRAV generates the immediate successors of e, places them in a list A known as the *active list* of child elements of e, and then proceeds to process them one by one by calling itself recursively.

1 **priority_queue procedure** KNEAREST(q,k,S,T)
2 /* A depth-first algorithm that returns a priority queue with the k nearest neighbors of q from the set of objects S organized using the search hierarchy T. */
3 **value object** q
4 **value integer** k
5 **value object_set** S
6 **value pointer search_hierarchy** T
7 **priority_queue** L
8 **pointer search_hierarchy** e
9 **integer** D_k
10 $L \leftarrow$ NEWPRIORITYQUEUE() /* L is the priority queue containing the k nearest objects */
11 $D_k \leftarrow \infty$ /* D_k denotes the distance of q's current kth candidate nearest object in L */
12 $e \leftarrow$ root of the search hierarchy induced by S and T
13 DFTRAV(q,k,e,L,D_k)
14 **return** L

1 **recursive procedure** DFTRAV(q,k,e,L,D_k)
2 /* Depth-first algorithm that recursively processes element e of a search hierarchy to determine the k nearest neighbors of q while using L to keep track of these neighbors with D_k as the distance of q's current kth candidate nearest object in L. */
3 **value object** q
4 **value integer** k
5 **value pointer search_hierarchy** e
6 **reference pointer priority_queue** L
7 **reference integer** D_k
8 **object** o
9 **pointer search_hierarchy** e_p
10 **pointer active_list** A
11 **if** ISLEAF(e) **then** /* e is a leaf with objects */
12   **foreach** object child element o of e **do**
13   Compute $d(q,o)$
14   **if** $d(q,o) < D_k$ **then**
15   INSERTL$(o,d(q,o),k,L,D_k)$
16   **endif**
17   **enddo**
18 **else**
19   Generate active list A containing the child elements of e
20   **foreach** element e_p of A **do**
21   DFTRAV(q,k,e_p,L,D_k)
22   **enddo**
23 **endif**

1 **procedure** INSERTL(e,s,k,L,D_k)
2 /* Insert object e at distance s from query object q into the priority queue L using ENQUEUE where D_k is the distance of q's current kth candidate nearest object in L. */
3 **value pointer search_hierarchy** e

4 **value integer** s, k
5 **reference pointer priority_queue** L
6 **reference integer** D_k
7 **if** SIZE$(L) = k$ **then**
8   DEQUEUE(L)
9 **endif**
10 ENQUEUE(e, s, L)
11 **if** SIZE$(L) = k$ **then**
12     $D_k \leftarrow$ D(MAXPRIORITYQUEUE(L))
13 **endif**

The general algorithm is a simple depth-first traversal of the treelike search structure. It visits every element of the search hierarchy. Clearly, better performance could be obtained by not visiting every element and its objects when it can be determined that it is impossible for an element to contain any of the k nearest neighbors of q. For example, this is true if we know that for every nonobject element e of the search hierarchy, $d(q, e) \leq d(q, e_0)$ for every object e_0 in e and that the relation $d(q, e) > D_k$ is satisfied.[13] In this case, line 21 of the **for** loop in DFTRAV is replaced by the following condition statement:

1 **if** $d(q, e_p) > D_k$ **then** skip processing e_p
2 **else** DFTRAV(q, k, e_p, L, D_k)
3 **endif**

Furthermore, given that $d(q, e) \leq d(q, e_0)$ for every object e_0 in e for all nonobject elements e, if we process the elements e_p of the active list A of e in order of increasing values of $d(q, e_p)$, then once we have found one element e_i in A such that $d(q, e_i) > D_k$, then $d(q, e_j) > D_k$ for all remaining elements e_j of A. This means that none of these remaining elements need to be processed, and we simply exit the loop and backtrack to the parent of e or terminate if e is the root of the search hierarchy. In this case, line 21 of the **for** loop in DFTRAV is replaced by the following condition statement:

1 **if** $d(q, e_p) > D_k$ **then** **exit_for_loop**
2 **else** DFTRAV(q, k, e_p, L, D_k)
3 **endif**

These modifications to DFTRAV and the rationale for making them should be familiar as they were used in our development of the general algorithm for finding the nearest neighbors of q in increasing order of their distance from q (i.e., INCNEAREST in Section 4.1.3). Recall that they enabled INCNEAREST to visit the various elements of the search hierarchy in increasing order of their distance from q, using a suitably defined distance metric. In particular, we saw that given a nonobject element e of the search hierarchy, using INCNEAREST we were able to avoid (actually only delay if we want all of the neighbors rather than just the k nearest neighbors) visiting all of the objects in e if $d(q, e) \leq d(q, e_0)$ for every object e_0 in e (termed the *correctness criterion* [851] in Section 4.1.3). Of course, INCNEAREST differs from the method discussed in this section in a significant manner by not being required to be depth first.

Exercises

1. Why is it worth sorting the elements e_p of the active list A of e in increasing order of $d(q, e_p)$ even though each one is only processed once?

2. Suppose that you want to find the k farthest neighbors instead of the k nearest neighbors. The basic idea is to keep track of the distance D_k to the current kth-farthest neighbor and, each

---

[13] This stopping condition ensures that all objects at the distance of the kth-nearest neighbor are examined. Of course, if the size of L is limited to k and if there are two or more objects at distance D_k, then some of them may not be reported in the set of q's k nearest neighbors.

time we encounter an object o, to check if $d(q,o) > D_k$, in which case o becomes one of the k farthest neighbors. In the case of a nonobject element e, if we know that the upper bound on the distance to q's farthest neighbor in e is less than D_k, then we can ignore e (i.e., e is pruned from further consideration), thereby enabling us to avoid visiting every nonobject element of the search hierarchy. Give a set of procedures KFARTHEST and DFTRAVFARTHEST corresponding to KNEAREST and DFTRAV, respectively, to achieve this. You may also have to modify procedure INSERTL.

3. Suppose that you use an alternative adaptation of the k-nearest neighbor algorithm that replaces all distances by their negation (recall the discussion in Section 4.1.5 of finding the k farthest neighbors using a best-first algorithm), while still making use of the definition of distance in terms of the upper bounds. Show how procedures and DFTRAV are affected by this change vis-à-vis the changes proposed in the solution to Exercise 2.

4. Suppose that you use a distance measure, as in Exercise 2, such that $d(q,e) \geq d(q,e_0)$ for every object e_0 in e for all nonobject elements e. How can you process the elements of the active list so that once we prune one element, all remaining elements need not be processed?

4.2.2 Pruning Rules

Fukunaga and Narendra [666] propose to use similar considerations to those outlined at the conclusion of Section 4.2.1, as well as others, to enhance the performance of the general depth-first k-nearest neighbor algorithm, although they do not require that the neighbors be reported in increasing order. These enhancements are based on observations similar to those that we use in Section 4.5.1 (as set forth in the various lemmas) to improve the efficiency of search algorithms in an environment that employs distance-based indexes, albeit in a somewhat different form.

Fukunaga and Narendra [666] achieve these enhancements by associating additional information with each element of the search hierarchy about its subelements. Their presentation assumes that the data is drawn from a vector space. In particular, with each element e_p, they associate its mean M_p and the distance $r_{p,max}$ from M_p to the farthest object within e_p. On the other hand, a dataset may consist of general objects where the only restriction is that the objects reside in a metric space—that is, a distance metric is defined between all pairs of objects, but no coordinate values are known. In this case, we propose to associate each element e_p with a representative object M_p that may or may not be in the dataset (although it usually is) and need not necessarily be in e_p. The distance $r_{p,max}$ from M_p to the farthest object in e_p is also stored. In the literature, M_p is known as a *pivot* [1897] or, less commonly, as a *routing object* [389]. While the work of Fukunaga and Narendra, as well as that of other researchers (e.g., Kamgar-Parsi and Kanal [986] and Larsen and Kanal [1103]), focuses on vector spaces, many of their conclusions are equally applicable to metric spaces. Thus, we present the following discussion in the more general context of metric spaces.[14]

Regardless of the interpretation placed on M_p, Fukunaga and Narendra [666] retain the results of the distance computations that were performed when obtaining the means (or pivots) and $r_{p,max}$ values of the clusters associated with the leaf elements of the search hierarchy. In other words, for each object o in leaf element e_p, $d(o, M_p)$ is stored with e_p. This is useful because knowledge of $d(o, M_p)$, in conjunction with the known distance of M_p from q and D_k (i.e., the distance from q to the current kth-nearest neighbor), will enable us to take advantage of the failure of satisfying the triangle inequality to show that o is too far from the query object q and thereby avoid computing $d(q,o)$.

Fukunaga and Narendra [666] define the distance $d(o, e_p)$ between an object o (as well as the query object q) and a nonobject element e_p with representative object

---

[14] In the rest of the discussion, although we refer to the distinguished element M_p as the *mean*, it should be clear that the discussion is equally applicable when the only restriction on the data is that it resides in a metric space, in which case the term *pivot* would be more appropriate.

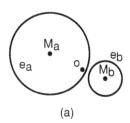

(a)

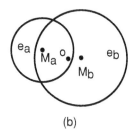

(b)

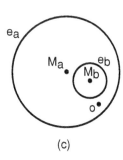

(c)

Figure 4.10
Examples illustrating that an object o is not necessarily associated with the element whose mean is closest to o. In particular, o is associated with element e_a, whose mean M_a is farther away from o than the mean M_b of element e_b.

M_p and maximum radius $r_{p,max}$ as $d(o, M_p)$. We use the term MEANORPIVOTDIST to describe this distance function—that is, MEANORPIVOTDIST$(o, e_p) = d(o, e_p) = d(o, M_p)$. Note that with this definition it is not generally true that $d(q, e_p) \leq d(q, e_0)$ for every object e_0 in e_p for all e_p that are not objects. However, on the other hand, with this definition, $d(o, e_p) = d(o, M_p)$ is not necessarily 0 when o or q, or both, are in e_p. Instead, $d(o, e_p) = d(o, M_p) = 0$ only holds if $o = M_p$.

We make the following observations:

1. The principal difference between the way vector data and metric data are handled is that, in the case of vector data, M_p usually does not correspond to one of the objects in the dataset, whereas for metric data, M_p usually corresponds to an object in the dataset, although, as we pointed out before, M_p need not be an element of e_p.

2. In the case of vector data, a representative other than the mean could be used (e.g., median).

3. Regardless of the nature of the underlying data, an object o is not necessarily associated with the element (e.g., cluster) whose representative object is the closest to o. In other words, o can be associated with element e_a with mean M_a while o's distance from the mean M_b of another element e_b is less—that is, $d(o, M_b) < d(o, M_a)$ (e.g., Figure 4.10). In the case of vector data, this means that the decomposition of the underlying space that is induced by the search hierarchy is not necessarily disjoint—that is, the blocks corresponding to the elements may overlap. Thus, when trying to insert a new object o, there could be several choices for the element in the search hierarchy that could contain o.

This information is used in five pruning rules that are described below. They are all presented here in a more general fashion than that used by Fukunaga and Narendra [666], Kamgar-Parsi and Kanal [986], and Larsen and Kanal [1103]. In particular, we consider the case of pruning a search for the k nearest neighbors; the others (i.e., [666, 986, 1103]) only consider the case of pruning a search for the nearest neighbor, although they do mention that the extension for the more general case can be made. In fact, as we see, often, although not always (i.e., for Pruning Rule 5), the modification is straightforward and usually only involves the replacement in the rules of the distance D_1 to the nearest neighbor with the distance D_k to the kth-nearest neighbor.

The pruning rules are motivated by a desire to prune some of the nonobject elements (and all of the objects that they contain) from further consideration when all of the objects that they contain are farther from the query object q than the distance D_k of the farthest of the current k candidate nearest neighbors. Similarly, in the case of an individual object o, o is pruned from further consideration by virtue of knowledge of o's distance from M_p (which was stored with the nonobject element e_p at the time of its formation), thereby rendering it farther from the query object than D_k. Pruning these elements and objects means that we can avoid needless distance computations between them and q given that we know that they cannot be members of the final set of the k nearest neighbors of q. Note that regardless of whether the pruned element is a nonobject element e_p or an object in e_p, the distance from q to M_p is computed (i.e., $d(q, M_p)$).

The pruning rules are embedded in procedure FNDFTRAV, given below, which is invoked by procedure KNEAREST instead of invoking DFTRAV. FNDFTRAV differs from DFTRAV in two main ways. First, naturally, it includes the various pruning rules proposed by Fukunaga and Narendra [666], as well as others proposed by Kamgar-Parsi and Kanal [986] and Larsen and Kanal [1103]. Second, following Fukunaga and Narendra [666], the algorithm processes elements in the active list in increasing order of MEANORPIVOTDIST(q, e_p)—that is, the distance of their representative objects from q. This is achieved by sorting the active list (line 26) prior to testing for the applicability of the pruning rules and processing the remaining elements (lines 35–40). Fukunaga and Narendra in their formulation of the algorithm repeatedly check if each element of the active list can be pruned prior to recursively invoking FNDFTRAV on a particular element (line 38) on the current member of the active list. This is not needed. Thus, we check if an element e_p can pruned just once, and this is done immediately before processing it (lines 36 and 37).

```
1   recursive procedure FNDFTRAV(q,k,e,L,D_k)
2   /* Depth-first algorithm that recursively processes element e of a search
        hierarchy to determine the k nearest neighbors of q while using L to
        keep track of these neighbors with D_k as the distance of q's current
        kth candidate nearest object in L. The algorithm makes use of Pruning
        Rules 1–4 for arbitrary values of k and Pruning Rule 5 for k = 1. */
3   value object q
4   value integer k
5   value pointer search_hierarchy e
6   reference pointer priority_queue L
7   reference integer D_k
8   object o
9   pointer search_hierarchy e_p
10  pointer active_list A
11  if ISLEAF(e) then /* e is a leaf with objects */
12      foreach object child element o of e do /* e has mean M and maximum
                                                  distance r_max */
13          if d(q,M) − d(o,M) > D_k then  /* Pruning Rule 2 */
14              Ignore object o
15          elseif d(o,M) − d(q,M) > D_k then  /* Pruning Rule 4 */
16              Ignore object o
17          else
18              Compute d(q,o)
19              if d(q,o) < D_k  then
20                  INSERTL(o,d(q,o),k,L,D_k)
21              endif
22          endif
23      enddo
24  else
25      Generate active list A containing the child elements e_p of e
26      /* The elements e_p of A are sorted in increasing order using
            MEANORPIVOTDIST(q,e_p) = d(q,M_p) and are always pro-
            cessed in this order */
27      if k = 1 then
28          foreach element e_p of A do  /*1 Pruning Rule 5 */
29              if d(q,M_p) > D_1 then   exit_for_loop
30              elseif d(q,M_p) + r_{p,min} < D_1   then
31                  D_1 ← d(q,M_p) + r_{p,min}
32              endif
33          enddo
34      endif
35      foreach element e_p of A do
36          if d(q,M_p) − r_{p,max} > D_k then ignore e_p  /* Pruning Rule 1 */
37          elseif r_{p,min} − d(q,M_p) > D_k then ignore e_p  /* Pruning Rule 3 */
38              FNDFTRAV(q,k,FIRST(A),L,D_k)
39          endif
40      enddo
41  endif
```

Fukunaga and Narendra [666] suggest that the search be sped up by applying the following pair of related pruning rules. The first rule prunes elements of the active list, and the second rule is used to prune individual objects.

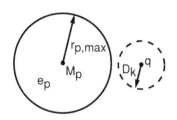

Figure 4.11
Example illustrating Pruning Rule 1, which eliminates element e_p and all its objects when $D_k + r_{p,max} < d(q, M_p)$.

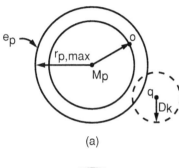

(a)

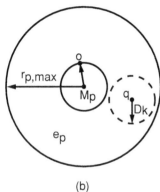

(b)

Figure 4.12
Examples illustrating Pruning Rule 2, which eliminates any object o in element e_p when $D_k + d(o, M_p) < d(q, M_p)$. Positioning of query object q so that (a) q is outside e_p, and (b) q is inside e_p.

- Rule 1: Element e_p in the active list with mean M_p and distance $r_{p,max}$ from M_p to the farthest object within e_p cannot contain the kth-nearest neighbor of query object q if $D_k + r_{p,max} < d(q, M_p)$ (see Exercise 1).

- Rule 2: Object o in element e_p at the deepest level of the search hierarchy with mean M_p and distance $r_{p,max}$ from M_p to the farthest object within e_p cannot be the kth-nearest neighbor of query object q if $D_k + d(o, M_p) < d(q, M_p)$ (see Exercise 2).

Rule 1 is illustrated by Figure 4.11 and is invoked in line 36. Rule 1 amounts to computing the minimum distance from the query object q to an object in e_p (referred to as MINDIST) and determining if it is greater than D_k, the distance from q to the farthest of the current k candidate nearest neighbors of q. In this case, there is no need to process any of the elements of e_p. Rule 1 is only meaningful when the distance of q from M_p renders it outside e_p—that is, $d(q, M_p) > r_{p,max}$.

Rule 2 is illustrated by Figure 4.12 and is invoked in lines 13–14. Rule 2 is related to Rule 1 in that it corresponds to the situation that, although some of the objects in e_p are sufficiently far from M_p to make them candidates for being the k nearest neighbors of q, object o is close enough to M_p to eliminate o from being one of the k nearest neighbors of q. Rule 2 is only meaningful when q is further from M_p than o—that is, when $d(q, M_p) > d(o, M_p)$ and also only when $d(q, M_p) > D_k$. However, given these constraints (i.e., $d(q, M_p) > d(o, M_p)$ and $d(q, M_p) > D_k$), for Rule 2 to be applicable, q can be both outside (Figure 4.12(a)) and inside e_p (Figure 4.12(b))—that is, $d(q, M_p)$ has an arbitrary value (i.e., it is independent of $r_{p,max}$).

Kamgar-Parsi and Kanal [986] improve the algorithm of Fukunaga and Narendra [666] by proposing an additional pair of related pruning rules, one of which is applied to elements of the active list (Pruning Rule 3), while the other is applied to the individual objects (Pruning Rule 4). They differ from Pruning Rules 1 and 2 by also associating with each element e_p the distance $r_{p,min}$ from the mean M_p to the closest object within e_p. This means that e_p has the shape of a multidimensional spherical shell, where $r_{p,min}$ and $r_{p,max}$ are the distances from M_p to e_p's internal and external spherical faces, respectively—that is, $r_{p,min}$ is the radius of e_p's inner spherical face, and $r_{p,max}$ is the radius of e_p's outer spherical face. Thus, whereas Pruning Rules 1 and 2 pertain to the outer spherical face of the spherical shell, Pruning Rules 3 and 4 pertain to the inner spherical face of the spherical shell.

- Rule 3: Element e_p in the active list with mean M_p and distance $r_{p,min}$ from M_p to the closest object within e_p cannot contain the kth-nearest neighbor of query object q if $D_k + d(q, M_p) < r_{p,min}$ (see Exercise 6).

- Rule 4: Object o in element e_p at the deepest level of the search hierarchy with mean M_p and distance $r_{p,max}$ from M_p to the farthest object within e_p cannot be the kth-nearest neighbor of query object q if $D_k + d(q, M_p) < d(o, M_p)$ (see Exercise 7).

Rule 3 is illustrated by Figure 4.13 and is invoked in line 37. Rule 3 amounts to computing the minimum distance from the query object q to an object in e_p and determining if it is greater than D_k, the distance from q to the farthest of the current candidate k nearest neighbors of q. In this case, there is no need to process any of the elements of e_p. The difference from Rule 1 is that, for Rule 3, e_p has the shape of a multidimensional spherical shell, and Rule 3 is only meaningful if q is inside the inner sphere of the spherical shell corresponding to e_p, whereas for Rule 1, regardless of whether e_p is a multidimensional spherical shell, q is outside the outer sphere of the spherical shell.

Rule 4 is illustrated by Figure 4.14 and is invoked in lines 15–16. Rule 4 is only meaningful when q is closer to M_p than o—that is, $d(q, M_p) < d(o, M_p)$. However, given this constraint (i.e., $d(q, M_p) < d(o, M_p)$), for Rule 4 to be applicable, q can be either inside e_p (Figures 4.14(b) and 4.14(d)) or inside the inner sphere of the spherical shell corresponding to e_p (Figures 4.14(a) and 4.14(c))—that is, $d(q, M_p)$ has an arbitrary value (i.e., it is independent of $r_{p,min}$).

Rule 4 is related to Rule 3 when q is inside the spherical shell or its inner sphere in a way analogous to that in which Rule 2 was determined to be related to Rule 1. In particular, Rule 4 corresponds to the situation that even though some of the objects in e_p are sufficiently close to M_p to make them candidates for being the k nearest neighbors of q, the distance of object o in e_p from M_p is far enough to eliminate o from being one of the candidates—that is, o cannot be one of the k nearest neighbors of q. Note that both Rules 3 and 4 are applicable regardless of whether $D_k < d(q, M_p)$ (See Figures 4.13(a) and 4.14(a, b)) or $D_k \geq d(q, M_p)$ (see Figures 4.13(b) and 4.14(c, d)). This is in contrast to Pruning Rules 1 and 2, where $D_k < d(q, M_p)$ must always hold.

When M_p is one of the objects in e_p, which means that $r_{p,min} = 0$, and q is in e_p, then Pruning Rule 4 is related to a well-known principle for nearest neighbor searching given by Feustel and Shapiro [610] (see also [1199]). This principle, which they call Lemma 2.1, states that, given the distance $d(q, p)$ from the query object q to some other object p, the distance from p to q's nearest neighbor o cannot be greater than $2d(q, p)$ (see Exercises 8–12). Feustel and Shapiro [610] use this principle as a heuristic to minimize the number of distance calculations in a metric space for a computer vision model matching application.

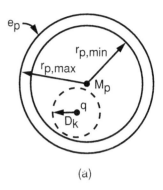

(a)

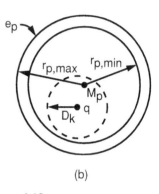

(b)

Figure 4.13
Examples illustrating Pruning Rule 3, which eliminates element e_p and all its objects when $D_k + d(q, M_p) < r_{p,min}$. Query object q is positioned so that (a) corresponds to $d(q, M_p) > D_k$, while (b) corresponds to $d(q, M_p) \leq D_k$.

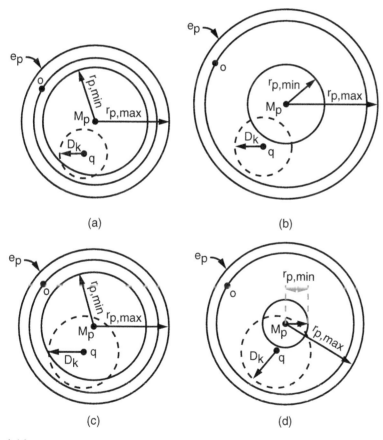

(a)   (b)

(c)   (d)

Figure 4.14
Examples illustrating Pruning Rule 4, which eliminates any object o in element e_p when $D_k + d(q, M_p) < d(o, M_p)$. Query object q is positioned so that (a) and (b) correspond to $d(q, M_p) > D_k$, while (c) and (d) correspond to $d(q, M_p) \leq D_k$. q is inside the inner sphere of the spherical shell corresponding to e_p in (a) and (c); q is in the spherical shell corresponding to e_p in (b) and (d).

Figure 4.15
Example illustrating a nearest neighbor searching principle that given objects p and q and the distance $d(q, p)$ between them, the distance from p of q's nearest neighbor o cannot be greater than $2d(q, p)$.

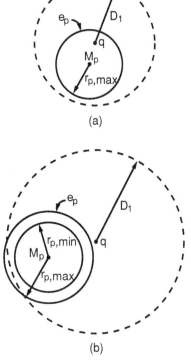

Figure 4.16
Examples illustrating the applicability of Pruning Rule 5, which resets the distance D_1 from q to its nearest neighbor during the insertion into the active list of element e_p, with M_p as the mean and $r_{p,max}$ and $r_{p,min}$ as the distances from M_p to the farthest and closest, respectively, objects within e_p: (a) if $d(q, M_p) + r_{p,max} < D_1$ and (b) if $d(q, M_p) + r_{p,min} < D_1$.

Obviously, the usefulness of this principle, as seen in Figure 4.15, depends heavily on the choice of p—that is, $d(q, p)$ must be small. If we choose p to be M_p, then we make the following four observations:

1. The pruning condition of Lemma 2.1 implies the pruning condition of Pruning Rule 4 (see Exercise 9).

2. In general, Lemma 2.1 is more widely applicable than pruning Rule 4 because it holds for any object p instead of just for M_p.

3. Whenever Pruning Rule 4 is applicable, then it has more pruning power than Lemma 2.1 (see Exercise 10).

4. For Lemma 2.1 to be applicable, q need not be inside e_p. However, in this case, Pruning Rules 1 and 2 provide tighter pruning.

Pruning Rules 1–4 make use of estimates of the minimum possible distance at which the nearest neighbor in nonobject element e can be found to avoid examining some nonobject elements of the search hierarchy. For $k = 1$, Fukunaga and Narendra [666] proposed one more pruning rule, which they characterize as a minor optimization, to be applied while constructing the active list A of child elements of e. In particular, assuming only the knowledge that $r_{p,max}$ is the distance from M_p to the farthest object in e_p, they point out that the distance from the query object q to its nearest neighbor cannot exceed $d(q, M_p) + r_{p,max}$. Thus, they suggest resetting D_1, the distance from q to its current nearest neighbor x, to the minimum of D_1 and $d(q, M_p) + r_{p,max}$ (see Exercise 13). In other words, the distance from q to the farthest possible object i of e_p is calculated (referred to as MAXDIST), and it is noted whether i can possibly serve as the nearest neighbor of q by virtue of being closer to q than x. Figure 4.16(a) illustrates a situation where this pruning rule, which we call Rule 5, is applicable. It is interesting to observe that at the time we find that Rule 5 is applicable to element e_p, the actual object in e_p that could serve as the nearest neighbor has not yet been identified. Instead, we are only setting an upper bound on the distance D_1 from q to it.

Larsen and Kanal [1103] improve upon Fukunaga and Narendra's [666] formulation of Pruning Rule 5 by taking advantage of the knowledge that $r_{p,min}$ is the distance from M_p to the closest object within e_p. In particular, they point out that the distance from the query object q to its nearest neighbor cannot exceed $d(q, M_p) + r_{p,min}$. Thus, they suggest resetting D_1, the distance from q to its current nearest neighbor x, to the minimum of D_1 and $d(q, M_p) + r_{p,min}$ (see Exercise 14).

In other words, the maximum possible distance from q to its nearest neighbor i in e_p is calculated (referred to as MAXNEARESTDIST), and it is checked whether i can possibly serve as the nearest neighbor of q by virtue of being closer to q than x— that is, we have determined the distance from q to its farthest possible nearest neighbor in e_p (i.e., MAXNEARESTDIST) instead of the distance to the farthest possible object in element e_p (i.e., MAXDIST) as in Fukunaga and Narendra's [666] formulation of this rule. Figure 4.16(b) illustrates a situation where this pruning rule, which from now on we refer to as Rule 5, is applicable. Again, as in the formulation of Fukunaga and Narendra [666], we observe that at the time we find that Rule 5 is applicable to element e_p, the actual object in e_p that could serve as the nearest neighbor has not yet been identified. Instead, we are only setting a minimum on the upper bound on the distance D_1 from q to it.

The extension of Pruning Rule 5 to find the k ($k > 1$) nearest neighbors is not immediate, although neither Fukunaga and Narendra [666] nor Larsen and Kanal [1103] give it any mention. In particular, note that we cannot simply reset D_k to $d(q, M_p) + r_{p,min}$ whenever $d(q, M_p) + r_{p,min} < D_k$. The problem is that the distance s from q to some of its k nearest neighbors may lie within the range $d(q, M_p) + r_{p,min} < s \leq D_k$, and thus resetting D_k to $d(q, M_p) + r_{p,min}$ may cause them to be missed, especially if child element e_p contains just one object. In other words, we must also examine the values of D_i ($1 \leq i < k$).

The problem is that, given the way in which Pruning Rule 5 is stated, its primary role is to set an upper bound on the distance from the query object to its nearest neighbor in a particular cluster. It is important to observe that this is not the same as saying that the upper bound computed by Pruning Rule 5 is the minimum of the maximum possible distances to the kth-nearest neighbor of the query object, which is not true. As we will see in Section 4.2.5, incorporating Pruning Rule 5 correctly for $k > 1$ requires a significant change in the algorithm. In particular, the way in which Pruning Rule 5 is used in k-nearest neighbor finding is to provide bounds for a number of different clusters. Once we have obtained k distinct such bounds, we have an estimate on the distance to the kth-nearest neighbor. Thus, we find that, as presented here using procedure FNDFTRAV, the depth-first k-nearest neighbor algorithm of Fukunaga and Narendra [666], even with the modification of Larsen and Kanal [1103], can make use of Pruning Rule 5 directly only for $k = 1$.

It should be clear that Pruning Rules 1–4 enable us to avoid the explicit computation of the distance from q to the individual subelements and objects of e_p. Moreover, these rules make use of existing distance computations that were performed when obtaining the means (or pivots) and $r_{p,max}$ values of the various elements (i.e., clusters). Thus, there is no need for additional distance computations. It is interesting to observe that Rules 1 and 2 prune objects from consideration on the basis of an upper bound on their distance from M_p, and Rules 3 and 4 prune objects from consideration on the basis of a lower bound on their distance from M_p. An alternative way of looking at this interpretation is to recall our characterization of nonobject element e_p as a multidimensional spherical shell, in which case Pruning Rules 1 and 2 are for a query object q that is not inside the inner sphere of the spherical shell corresponding to e_p, while Pruning Rules 3 and 4 are for a q that is either in the spherical shell or inside the inner sphere of the spherical shell corresponding to e_p. Pruning Rules 1 and 3 apply only when q is not in the spherical shell (i.e., Rule 1 for q outside the outer sphere of the spherical shell and Rule 3 for q inside the inner sphere of the spherical shell), while Pruning Rules 2 and 4 apply regardless of the position of q (i.e., Rule 2 for q in the spherical shell or outside the outer sphere of the spherical shell, and Rule 4 for q in the spherical shell or inside the inner sphere of the spherical shell). Note that Pruning Rule 5 also applies, regardless of the position of q. Finally, observe that Pruning Rule 5 can never be satisfied if either Pruning Rule 1 or 3 is applicable, and thus it need not be tested when either of them holds (see Exercise 16).

Rules 1 and 3 appear as part of Lemma 4.2, discussed in Section 4.5.1, where they serve as lower bounds on the distance from q to any object o such that $r_{p,lo} \leq r_{p,min} \leq d(o, M_p) \leq r_{p,max} \leq r_{p,hi}$, given $d(q, M_p)$. In addition, the formulation of Rule 5 given by Fukunaga and Narendra [666] (i.e., in terms of $d(q, M_p) + r_{p,max}$) also appears as part of this lemma, where the quantity $d(q, M_p) + r_{p,max}$ serves as an upper bound on the distance from q to an object o in the same range. In fact, Rules 1 and 3 and Fukunaga and Narendra's [666] formulation of Rule 5 could also be expressed in terms of the looser upper and lower bounds $r_{p,hi}$ and $r_{p,lo}$ instead of $r_{p,max}$ and $r_{p,min}$, respectively, as the proofs are identical. Similarly, Rules 2 and 4 also appear as part of Lemma 4.1, discussed in Section 4.5.1, where they serve as lower bounds on the distance from q to an arbitrary object o by knowing the distances $d(q, M_p)$ and $d(o, M_p)$. In fact, Rules 2 and 4 can be combined, as they are in Lemma 4.1, using the absolute value of the difference between $d(q, M_p)$ and $d(o, M_p)$—that is, o cannot be the kth nearest neighbor of q if $D_k < |d(q, M_p) - d(o, M_p)|$. These lemmas are used to facilitate range searching and nearest neighbor finding with different indexing methods in a metric space.

Exercises

1. Prove that element e_p in the active list with mean M_p and distance $r_{p,max}$ from M_p to the farthest object within e_p cannot contain the kth-nearest neighbor of query object q if $D_k + r_{p,max} < d(q, M_p)$, where D_k is the distance from q to the farthest of the current candidate k nearest neighbors—that is, prove that Pruning Rule 1 is correct.

2. Prove that object o in element e_p at the deepest level of the search hierarchy with mean M_p and distance $r_{p,max}$ from M_p to the farthest object within e_p cannot be the kth-nearest neighbor of query object q if $D_k + d(o, M_p) < d(q, M_p)$, where D_k is the distance from q to the farthest of the current candidate k nearest neighbors—that is, prove that Pruning Rule 2 is correct.

3. Feustel and Shapiro [610] make use of an alternative formulation of Pruning Rule 2 (which they call Lemma 2.2) that does not depend on the identification of a particular object to serve the role of M_p for the set of objects. In other words, the role of M_p is played by an arbitrary object rather than by the mean of a set or a pivot in the case of some metric data structures. Again, it makes use of the distance d_1 from query object q to some object n, and the distance d_2 from q to some other object p that plays the role of M_p in Rule 2, and that $d_1 < d_2$. The stipulation that $d_1 < d_2$ ensures that n plays the role of q's current nearest neighbor in the equivalence to Rule 2. Based on these distances, Lemma 2.2 stipulates that an arbitrary object o cannot be the nearest neighbor of q if o's distance from p is less than $d_2 - d_1$—that is, $d(o, p) < d_2 - d_1$. Prove this lemma.

4. Prove that Lemma 2.2 of Feustel and Shapiro [610], described in Exercise 3, is a special case of Pruning Rule 2 for $k = 1$. In other words, show that Rule 2 can be instantiated with the appropriate parameter bindings so that Lemma 2.2 holds.

5. Lemma 2.2 of Feustel and Shapiro [610], described in Exercise 3, is designed for use in pruning object o from further consideration as the nearest neighbor of query object q. In contrast, Pruning Rule 2 is designed for use in pruning object o from further consideration as the kth-nearest neighbor of query object q. How would you modify Lemma 2.2 so that it can also be used to prune object o from further consideration as the kth-nearest neighbor of query object q?

6. Prove that element e_p in the active list with mean M_p and distance $r_{p,max}$ from M_p to the farthest object within e_p cannot contain the kth-nearest neighbor of query object q if $D_k + d(q, M_p) < r_{p,min}$, where $r_{p,min}$ is the distance from M_p to the closest object within e_p, and D_k is the distance from q to the farthest of the current candidate k nearest neighbors—that is, prove that Pruning Rule 3 is correct.

7. Prove that object o in element e_p at the deepest level of the search hierarchy with mean M_p and distance $r_{p,max}$ from M_p to the farthest object within e_p cannot be the kth-nearest neighbor of query object q if $D_k + d(q, M_p) < d(o, M_p)$, where D_k is the distance from q to the farthest of the current candidate k nearest neighbors—that is, prove that Pruning Rule 4 is correct.

8. In the text, we point out that Pruning Rule 4 is related to Lemma 2.1 of Feustel and Shapiro [610] when M_p is one of the objects in e_p, which means that $r_{p,min} = 0$, and q is in e_p. In particular, Lemma 2.1 states that, given the distance $d(q, p)$ from the query object q to some other object p, if the distance from p to some other object o is greater than $2d(q, p)$, then o cannot be q's nearest neighbor. Prove this lemma.

9. Consider query object q in element e_p and M_p as an actual object in e_p, which means that $r_{p,min} = 0$. Prove that if Lemma 2.1 of Feustel and Shapiro [610], described in Exercise 8, holds, then so does Pruning Rule 4 of Kamgar-Parsi and Kanal [986]. In other words, Lemma 2.1 stipulates that o cannot be the nearest neighbor of q if $d(o, M_p) > 2d(q, M_p)$. You need to prove that, in this case, $d(o, M_p) > D_1 + d(q, M_p)$, which is the condition that must hold for Pruning Rule 4 to be applicable.

10. In the text, we stated that for $k = 1$, if M_p, o, and q are objects in e_p (which means that $r_{p,min} = 0$), and if p in Lemma 2.1 is chosen to be M_p, then Pruning Rule 4 has more pruning power than Lemma 2.1. Explain why this is true.

11. Lemma 2.1 of Feustel and Shapiro [610], described in Exercise 8, is designed for use in pruning object o from further consideration as the nearest neighbor of query object q. In contrast, Pruning Rule 4 is designed for use in pruning object o from further consideration as the kth-nearest neighbor of query object q. How would you modify Lemma 2.1 so that it can also be used to prune object o from further consideration as the kth-nearest neighbor of query object q?

12. A similar principle to Lemma 2.1 of Feustel and Shapiro [610], described in Exercise 8, is used to bound the maximum distance between any pair of objects a and b given the object p at a maximum distance from another object q—that is, $d(a, b) \le 2d(q, p)$ (see the discussion in Section 4.7.3.2). Prove it.

13. Justify the correctness of Fukunaga and Narendra's [666] formulation of Pruning Rule 5—that is, resetting the distance D_1 from q to its nearest neighbor to $d(q, M_p) + r_{p,max}$ whenever $D_1 > d(q, M_p) + r_{p,max}$ while constructing the active list A of child elements of e for finding the nearest neighbor to query object q. Assume that M_p is the mean of the elements of child element e_p, and $r_{p,max}$ is the distance from M_p to the farthest object within e_p.

14. Justify the correctness of Larsen and Kanal's [1103] formulation of pruning Rule 5—that is, resetting the distance D_1 from q to its nearest neighbor to $d(q, M_p) + r_{p,min}$ whenever $D_1 > d(q, M_p) + r_{p,min}$ while constructing the active list A of child elements of e for finding the nearest neighbor to query object q. Assume that M_p is the mean of the elements of child element e_p, and $r_{p,min}$ and $r_{p,max}$ are the distances from M_p to the closest and farthest, respectively, objects within e_p.

15. Assuming that KNEAREST using FNDFTRAV processes the elements e_p in the active list in increasing MEANORPIVOTDIST order, give an example that shows that Pruning Rule 5 can indeed be applied.

16. Consider nonobject element e_p with mean M_p and $r_{p,min}$ and $r_{p,max}$ as the distances from M_p to the closest and farthest, respectively, objects within e_p. Show that the condition for the applicability of Pruning Rule 5 (i.e., $d(q, M_p) + r_{p,min} < D_1$) can never be satisfied if either of Pruning Rules 1 or 3 are applicable, and thus Pruning Rule 5 need not be tested when they hold.

17. How would you adapt Pruning Rules 1–5 to facilitate finding the k farthest neighbors, as in Exercises 2 and 3 of Section 4.2.1?

18. Give the analog procedure FNDFTRAVFARTHEST of FNDFTRAV for finding the k farthest neighbors using the approach outlined in Exercise 2 in Section 4.2.1. Incorporate the modified Pruning Rules 1–5 given in Exercise 17.

19. Repeat Exercise 18 using the approach outlined in Exercise 3 of Section 4.2.1.

4.2.3 Effects of Clustering Methods on Pruning

Pruning Rules 1–5 have been presented in the context of a clustering method that clusters objects with respect to a cluster center M and the minimums and maximums on their distance values from M. In this section, we briefly examine some related clustering methods and their effect on the pruning rules.

First of all, we point out that Rules 3 and 4 are particularly useful when the partitions induced by the various cluster elements are such that an object o is not necessarily associated with the element whose cluster center (e.g., mean) is the closest to o. In other words, o can be associated with element e_a with mean M_a while o's distance from the mean M_b of another element e_b is less—that is, $d(o, M_b) < d(o, M_a)$ (e.g., recall Figure 4.10). Figure 4.17 is a more vivid illustration of such a scenario where M_b is an element of e_a and M_a is an element of e_b, and we see that e_b and all of its objects are eliminated by application of Rule 3 with respect to the given values of q and D_k, even though M_b is definitely one of the possible k nearest neighbors of q. Such a scenario can arise in the M-tree [389] (see Section 4.5.4.1), but it cannot arise in GNAT [255] (see Section 4.5.3.2). In the vector (and also spatial) domain, this scenario is analogous to a stipulation that the regions are not necessarily disjoint—that is, the region spanned by one cluster e_a can contain objects that are associated with another cluster e_b (e.g., the shaded area in Figure 4.17, assuming that each object is associated with just one cluster).

As we saw in Section 4.2.2, the cluster e_p is analogous to a bounding object, and the quantity $d(q, M_p) - r_{p,max}$ in Pruning Rule 1 can be interpreted as the minimum distance from the query object q to the bounding object, assuming that q is outside e_p. In the formulation of Rule 1, the bounding object is a ball centered at M_p of radius $r_{p,max}$. Similarly, recalling our analogy between e_p and a multidimensional spherical shell-like bounding object, the quantity $r_{p,min} - d(q, M_p)$ in Pruning Rule 3 can be interpreted as the minimum distance from q to the interior face of the bounding object, assuming that q is inside the inner sphere of the spherical shell corresponding to e_p. In both of these

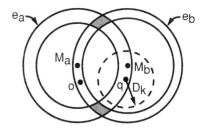

Figure 4.17
Example of the utility of Pruning Rules 3 and 4 when objects (including pivots) are not necessarily associated with the element, whose mean (pivot) is the closest. In particular, objects o and M_a are associated with element e_b, whose mean M_b is farther away from o than the mean M_a of element e_a. Similarly, M_b is associated with element e_a, whose mean M_a is farther away than M_b. Here, e_b and all of its objects are eliminated by application of Rule 3 with respect to the given values of q and D_k, even though M_b is definitely one of the possible k nearest neighbors of q. Area common to both elements e_a and e_b is shown shaded.

cases, we refer to the distance from q to e_p as MINDIST. These analogies hold for both a vector and a metric space.

It is important to note that the clusters above are not true minimum bounding objects due to the dependence on the cluster center M_p. For the cluster to be a true minimum bounding object, the cluster center M_p must be determined by the objects in the cluster and is not necessarily the sample mean. Moreover, the cluster must contain at least two distinct objects, as otherwise $r_{p,max}$ and $r_{p,min}$ are both zero, in which case the minimum bounding box is a point.

When the minimum bounding objects are hyperspheres (see Exercise 4 in Section 4.4.2) centered at an appropriately determined cluster center M_p, Pruning Rules 1–4 are applicable as stated. When the minimum bounding objects have other shapes such as hyperrectangles, then Pruning Rules 2 and 4 are applicable as stated with an appropriately determined cluster center, while Pruning Rules 1 and 3 must be reformulated in terms of the minimum distances from the query object to the minimum bounding hyperrectangles as $r_{p,min}$ and $r_{p,max}$ are not part of the definition of the minimum bounding object in this case (e.g., minimum bounding hyperrectangles).

On the other hand, in the same context (i.e., when the minimum bounding objects are hyperspheres), the issue of the applicability of Pruning Rule 5 is more complex. In particular, all of the statements that we make about the ramifications of Pruning Rule 5 are restricted to the case that $k = 1$—that is, to the situation that we are seeking the nearest neighbor as this is how the rule was presented in Section 4.2.2. However, as we will see in Section 4.2.5, the depth-first k-nearest neighbor algorithm of Fukunaga and Narendra [666] can be modified so that Pruning Rule 5 can be used for arbitrary values of k.

As we saw earlier, Pruning Rule 5 is considerably different from Pruning Rules 1–4 since its use does not result in pruning any elements in the active list. Instead, it is used to set an upper bound on the distance to the nearest neighbor, thereby enabling more elements and objects to be pruned by subsequent invocation of Pruning Rules 1–4. The upper bound computed by Pruning Rule 5 is the minimum of the maximum possible distances to the nearest neighbor of the query object. When the clusters are minimum bounding objects, sometimes it is possible to tighten Pruning Rule 5 even more than the form given by Larsen and Kanal [1103]—that is, to obtain a lower value for MAX-NEARESTDIST than $d(q, M_p) + r_{p,min}$. Note that our discussion of Pruning Rule 5 is in terms of finding the nearest neighbor rather than the k nearest neighbors as its primary role is to set a bound on the distance from the query object to its nearest neighbor in a particular cluster. Its use for finding the k nearest neighbors is independent of the nature of the clustering method, and hence is not discussed further here.

When the minimum bounding objects are hyperspheres, we first consider the situation that $r_{p,min}$ is unknown. In this case, let $r_{p,max}$ be the radius of the minimum bounding hypersphere of the objects in e_p whose center has been determined to be M_p. Assuming a Euclidean distance metric, it is easy to see that the maximum possible distance from the query object q to an object o in e_p that serves as the nearest neighbor of q arises when o lies in one of two positions a and b located diametrically opposite each other on the surface of the hypersphere so that the $(d-1)$-dimensional hyperplane passing through a, b, and M is perpendicular to the line joining M and q. Observe that a and b are equidistant from q and that the distance from q to either one of them is $\sqrt{d(q, M_p)^2 + r_{p,max}^2}$, the value of MAXNEARESTDIST (see Exercise 10). This quantity is clearly less than or equal to $d(q, M_p) + r_{p,max}$ (e.g., by the triangle inequality), which was the upper bound used by Fukunaga and Narendra [666] in their formulation of Pruning Rule 5 (i.e., MAXDIST). Figure 4.18 illustrates these concepts.

Now, suppose that $r_{p,min}$ is known, which corresponds to the situation that the minimum bounding object is a multidimensional spherical shell. We assume that the minimum bounding hypersphere with radius $r_{p,max}$ and centered at M_p coincident with

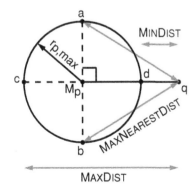

Figure 4.18
Example showing the calculation of MINDIST, MAXDIST, and MAXNEARESTDIST when the minimum bounding object is the minimum bounding hypersphere (e.g., an SS-tree) centered at M_p with radius $r_{p,max}$ and an unknown value of $r_{p,min}$, assuming a query point q and a Euclidean distance metric.

the outer sphere of the spherical shell is formed first. Next, given the above value of M_p, we determine the maximum bounding hypersphere with radius $r_{p,min}$ and centered at M_p coincident with the interior face of the spherical shell (i.e., the inner sphere) so that the interior is empty. From our earlier presentation of Pruning Rule 5, we know that the maximum possible distance from q to an object o of e_p that is on the interior face of e_p and that is to serve as the nearest neighbor of q is $d(q, M_p) + r_{p,min}$. In addition, from the immediately preceding derivation when $r_{p,min}$ was unknown, we also know that, assuming a Euclidean distance metric, the maximum possible distance from q to an object o of e_p that is on the exterior face of e_p and that is to serve as the nearest neighbor of q is $\sqrt{d(q, M_p)^2 + r_{p,max}^2}$. Thus, the maximum possible distance from q to an object o of e_p, which is a multidimensional spherical shell, that is to serve as the nearest neighbor of q is the minimum of $d(q, M_p) + r_{p,min}$ and $\sqrt{d(q, M_p)^2 + r_{p,max}^2}$, the value of MAXNEARESTDIST for the minimum bounding hypersphere, assuming a Euclidean distance metric. Note that the object that satisfies this minimum may in fact lie on the exterior face of the spherical shell (i.e., the outer sphere) when $r_{p,min}$ is not much different from $r_{p,max}$. On the other hand, the object that satisfies this minimum may lie on the interior face of the spherical shell (i.e., the inner sphere) when $r_{p,min}$ is much smaller than $r_{p,max}$.

It is interesting to observe that if the maximum bounding hypersphere with radius $r_{p,min}$ and centered at M_p coincident with the interior face of the spherical shell (i.e., the inner sphere) so that the interior is empty is formed first, then the maximum possible distance from q to its nearest neighbor on the interior face of the spherical shell is $\sqrt{d(q, M_p)^2 + r_{p,min}^2}$, assuming a Euclidean distance metric, which is always less than the maximum possible distance from q to its nearest neighbor on the exterior face (i.e., outer sphere) of the spherical shell. Thus, when forming the maximum bounding hypersphere corresponding to the interior face of the spherical shell first, there is no need to take the minimum bounding hypersphere corresponding to the outer face into account in determining the maximum possible distance to the nearest neighbor of q.

When the minimum bounding objects are hyperrectangles, and assuming that they are axis aligned, we take advantage of the fact that every face of the minimum bounding hyperrectangle b must contain at least one object. Thus, the farthest possible object from the query object q lies at the farthest corner f of b from q (i.e., MAXDIST). On the other hand, to obtain the minimum of the maximum possible distances from q to an object o in b that is to serve as the nearest neighbor we must determine the distances to the farthest points on each face of b from q and choose their minimum, the value of MAXNEAREST-DIST. An alternative definition of MAXNEARESTDIST(q, b) is as the distance from q to the closest corner of b that is "adjacent" to the corner f farthest from q.

When the objects have extent (rather than point objects), then the clusters are often formed in terms of their minimum bounding hyperrectangles. MINDIST, MAXDIST, and MAXNEARESTDIST are defined in the same manner as for the point objects. Once again, we take advantage of the fact that every surface of the minimum bounding hyperrectangle b must contain at least one point of the corresponding object's boundary. Figure 4.19 shows two examples of the calculation of MINDIST and MAXNEARESTDIST in two dimensions, which are depicted with a solid and a broken line, respectively. In both cases, f is the farthest corner from q and MAXDIST is the distance from q to it. However, notice that for the minimum bounding rectangle in Figure 4.19(a), the distance from q to a is less than the distance from q to b, thereby accounting for the value of MAX-NEARESTDIST being equal to the former rather than to the latter, while the opposite is true for Figure 4.19(b).

It is important to observe that the complexity of the computation of MINDIST, MAXDIST, and MAXNEARESTDIST is heavily dependent on the nature of the clustering process used to form the search hierarchy, as well as the domain of the data. For example, in d dimensions, the complexity of computing MAXNEARESTDIST is the same as that of MINDIST and MAXDIST when the cluster elements are minimum bounding

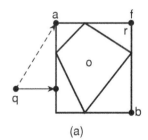

(a)

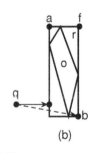

(b)

Figure 4.19
A pair of examples showing the relationship between MINDIST(solid line) and MAXNEARESTDIST(broken line) for a minimum bounding axis-aligned rectangle r. The distance of the object o from q is bounded from below by MINDIST(q,r) and from above by MAXNEARESTDIST(q,r). (a) Point a is closer to q than point b and in (b) point b is closer to q than point a. In both examples f is the farthest corner from q, and MAXDIST is the distance to it.

hyperspheres (i.e., $O(d)$), whereas when the cluster elements are minimum bounding hyperrectangles, the complexity of MAXNEARESTDIST is $O(d^2)$, while the complexity of MINDIST and MAXDIST in this case is just $O(d)$.

The above clustering methods can be viewed as making use of object hierarchies in the sense that when the data is drawn from a vector space, it is not necessarily the case that every point in the underlying space is guaranteed to be contained in one of the clusters; nor is it necessarily the case that each point in the underlying space is contained in just one cluster. In other words, they are not based on a disjoint decomposition of the underlying space, and possibly an aggregation of the regions resulting from the decomposition that satisfy these properties (i.e., disjointness and coverage). This is especially true in light of the nature of the aggregation method, which ensures that the aggregate clustering shapes are formed in the same way as the base clusters.

Other clustering methods can be devised that make use of a disjoint decomposition of the underlying space (e.g., a grid [955, 1374]). Again, all of the pruning rules are applicable with appropriate modifications similar to those made when using minimum bounding objects. Note that Pruning Rule 3 will not be applicable if the regions resulting from the decomposition do not have holes or voids (i.e., there are no regions whose shape is topologically equivalent to a spherical shell).

It is interesting to observe that, if for every nonobject element e_p the ball of radius $r_{p,min}$ centered at M_p is empty (i.e., besides not containing any objects of e_p by definition, this ball also does not contain any objects belonging to any other element e_o), then Pruning Rule 3 will never be invoked. This is a more general (and hence broader) specification than the one given by Larsen and Kanal [1103], who rely on the satisfaction of the following conditions in order to guarantee that Pruning Rule 3 cannot be applied:

1. The existence of a tessellation of the underlying space into regions (i.e., a partition into disjoint regions such that every point in the underlying space is in one of the regions), where

2. For each nonobject element e_p, its corresponding region contains the empty ball of radius $r_{p,min}$ centered at M_p, and

3. The members of the active list are visited in such an order so that all the elements that are visited on the first descent of the depth-first process (assuming that the clustering process results in a tree) contain the query object.

Although it seems that Pruning Rule 3 can never be invoked if the partition of the underlying space is disjoint, this is not the case because the ball of radius $r_{p,min}$ centered at M_p can contain an object that is not in e_p while still being empty with respect to e_p (i.e., locally empty by not containing any objects of e_p). In fact, as we stated before, all that is required for Pruning Rule 3 to be inapplicable is for the maximal empty balls (defined by $r_{p,min}$ for each e_p) to be globally empty.

Note also that in the case of data drawn from a metric space, the situation under which Pruning Rule 3 can be applied only arises when M_p does not correspond to an object in e_p, as otherwise $r_{p,min} = 0$. Moreover, if in such a case M_p is required to be an object in the dataspace, then our conclusions about the impossibility of invoking Pruning Rule 3 are inapplicable as the balls centered at M_p cannot be empty, whereas, in contrast, when the data is drawn from a vector space, M_p is not required to be an object in the dataspace.

Experiments by Kamgar-Parsi and Kanal [986] on finding the nearest neighbor for random two-dimensional data from both a Gaussian and uniform distribution showed that the number of distance computations that were eliminated by Rules 2 and 4 were about the same, and they were much greater than the number eliminated by Rules 1 and 3. In fact, use of each of Rules 2 and 4 resulted in eliminating approximately 40% of the distance computations, while use of each of Rules 1 and 3 resulted in eliminating between 1% and 3% of the distance computations. This is not surprising because Rules 2 and 4 involve elements at the deepest level of the search hierarchy (i.e., leaf elements and objects), and there are generally many more leaf elements than nonleaf elements and, likewise, more objects than nonobjects. Note that in these experiments, the random data was not sorted—that is, the first n samples that were generated were assigned to the first cluster, the second n samples to the second cluster, and so on. The rationale was to measure the performance of the four pruning rules in a manner independent of the clustering method. For example, Fukunaga and Narendra [666] used a hierarchical 3-means clustering method. In this way, Kamgar-Parsi and Kanal [986] demonstrated that their additional pruning rules (i.e., Rules 3 and 4) resulted in almost doubling the number of distance computations eliminated by Fukunaga and Narendra's algorithm, which only used Pruning Rules 1 and 2.

On the other hand, experiments by Larsen and Kanal [1103] with data that was clustered using clustering methods that satisfied the above conditions that ensure that Pruning Rule 3 will not be invoked also found that Pruning Rule 4 was invoked relatively rarely in comparison with Pruning Rule 2. Nevertheless, Pruning Rules 3 and 4 are important as they are general and formulated in a manner that is independent of the clustering method. In particular, recall the utility of these rules when the data is clustered, as in the example illustrated in Figure 4.17.

Exercises

1. Give an algorithm to compute the MINDIST function when the minimum bounding object is an axis-aligned hyperrectangle.

2. Give an algorithm to compute the MAXDIST function when the minimum bounding object is an axis-aligned hyperrectangle.

3. Give an algorithm to compute the MAXNEARESTDIST function when the minimum bounding object is an axis-aligned hyperrectangle.

4. How would you modify the MINDIST cost estimate function for an object hierarchy in the spatial domain where the minimum bounding object is the intersection of the minimum bounding hyperrectangle and the minimum bounding hypersphere of the objects (e.g., an SR-tree [999] as discussed in Section 4.4.2) instead of a hyperrectangle?

5. Repeat Exercise 4 for the MAXDIST cost-estimate function.

6. Repeat Exercise 4 for the MAXNEARESTDIST cost-estimate function.

7. How would you apply the depth-first k-nearest neighbor algorithm to an object hierarchy in an arbitrary metric space (e.g., an M-tree [389] as discussed in Section 4.5.4)?

8. Suppose you choose an arbitrary set of points in a vector space as cluster centers and then apply a clustering method that associates each point with its nearest cluster center. Show with an example that Pruning Rule 3 is applicable.

9. Can you prove that pruning Rule 3 is never invoked for data in a vector space that is clustered using a k-means algorithm (e.g., [1174, 1219])? Try this for one-dimensional data first. Can you prove this for arbitrary dimensions?

10. Consider the case that the minimum bounding object is a hypersphere. Formally, we say that B is the minimum enclosing hypersphere of P, a set of d-dimensional points, if and only if B is an enclosing hypersphere of P, and any hypersphere containing P has a radius greater than or equal to the radius of B. It can be shown easily that the minimum enclosing hypersphere B of a point set P is uniquely defined. Armed with this definition, given hypersphere B centered at c with radius r and query point q, and assuming a Euclidean distance metric, prove that MAXNEARESTDIST(q, B), the distance of the closest point $p \in P$ to q, cannot be greater than $\sqrt{d(q,c)^2 + r^2}$.

11. Suppose that the cluster centers M_i are chosen as the centroids of the clusters e_i and that r_i is the maximum distance from M_i to an object in e_i. Assuming a Euclidean distance metric, prove that MAXNEARESTDIST(q, e_i) is $\sqrt{d(q, M_i)^2 + r_i^2}$.

Exercises 12–16 consider the computation of the minimum distance from query object q to its farthest neighbor in minimum bounding object b (referred to as MINFARTHESTDIST) for different types of minimum bounding objects. Note that whereas the MAXNEARESTDIST function corresponds to the minimum of the maximum possible distances to the object o in b that is to serve as q's nearest neighbor, MINFARTHESTDIST is the maximum of the minimum possible distances from q to an object o in b that is to serve as q's farthest neighbor (see also Exercise 17 in Section 4.2.2 and its solution).

12. Give an algorithm to compute the MINFARTHESTDIST function when b is a minimum bounding object that is an axis-aligned hyperrectangle?

13. In the text, for the case that the minimum bounding object b is an axis-aligned hyperrectangle, we give an alternative definition of MAXNEARESTDIST(q, b) as the distance from q to the closest corner of b that is "adjacent" to the corner f farthest from q. It would seem that the analogous alternative definition of MINFARTHESTDIST(q, b) would be the distance from q to the farthest corner of b that is "adjacent" to the corner f nearest to q. Explain why this definition holds or fails to hold.

14. Assuming a Euclidean distance metric, what is MINFARTHESTDIST when the minimum bounding object b is the hypersphere e_p of radius $r_{p,max}$ whose center has been determined to be M_p, and $r_{p,min}$ is unknown?

15. Assuming a Euclidean distance metric, what is MINFARTHESTDIST when the minimum bounding object b is a multidimensional spherical shell e_p? Distinguish between the case that the minimum bounding hypersphere with radius $r_{p,max}$ and centered at M_p coincident with the exterior face of the spherical shell (i.e., outer sphere) is formed first and the case that the maximum bounding hypersphere with radius $r_{p,min}$ and centered at M_p coincident with the interior face of the spherical shell (i.e., inner sphere) so that the interior is empty is formed first.

16. Repeat Exercise 4 for the MINFARTHESTDIST cost-estimate function.

4.2.4 Ordering the Processing of the Elements of the Active List

As we pointed out before, generally speaking, regardless of the clustering method that is used, Fukunaga and Narendra's algorithm [666] processes the child elements e_p (which are not objects) in the active list in increasing MEANORPIVOTDIST order—that is, the distance from the query object to their means (i.e., M_p). The drawback of such an ordering is that the distance $r_{p,max}$ from M_p to the farthest object within e_p is not taken into account. In other words, a MEANORPIVOTDIST ordering results in giving priority to nearby elements whose $r_{p,max}$ values may be small over elements with larger $r_{p,max}$ values that are farther from the query object q—that is, for $d(q, M_a) > d(q, M_b)$, element e_a with mean M_a and farthest object at distance $r_{a,max}$ is deemed farther from query object q than element e_b with mean M_b and farthest object at distance $r_{b,max}$, even though e_a may contain an object o that is closer to q than any other object in e_b (e.g., see Figure 4.20). Alternatively, even though the elements e_p of the active list are processed in order of increasing values of $d(q, M_p)$, just because element e_b is processed before element e_a does not mean that e_a may not contain an object that is closer to q than any object in e_b. This means that the pruning of one element e_b of the active list cannot lead to the pruning of all remaining elements of the active list at the given level as they may contain objects that are in fact closer to q than any of the objects in the pruned element e_b. This is a direct consequence of the fact that when $d(q, e_p)$ is defined as MEANORPIVOTDIST, $d(q, e_p) \leq d(q, e_0)$ is not satisfied for every object e_0 in e_p.

Ideally, we would like to process the child elements in the active list in an order that is correlated with the likelihood of finding the k nearest neighbors. In particular, when the search hierarchy formed by the clustering method is a tree, which is the case in our discussion, we want to process the subtrees that are most likely to contain the k nearest neighbors (i.e., those closer to the query object) before those that are less likely to contain them and possibly to prune them from further consideration by virtue of being farther away from the query object than any of the members of the set L of the current candidate k nearest neighbors. This can be done with the aid of the pruning rules discussed in

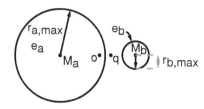

Figure 4.20
Example where element e_a contains an object o that is closer to q than any other object in element e_b. The ordering of Fukunaga and Narendra [666] deems e_b to be closer to q than e_a, while e_a is deemed closer using an ordering based on a distance d(q, e_p) between query object q and a nonobject element e_p of d(q, M_p) − r_p.

Section 4.2.2. This approach is analogous to a limited version of the A*-algorithm (e.g., see [1594]) used in heuristic search for a minimum-cost solution path from a start state to a goal state. In this case, an estimate is made of the cost of the solution (i.e., to the problem of finding the k nearest neighbors), and if the estimate is a lower bound on the total cost, then we are guaranteed to find the optimal solution.

Two other possible orderings for processing the child elements of an element of the active list that spring to mind are based on the cost-estimate functions MINDISTOBJECT and MAXDISTOBJECT. In particular, given cluster element n in the active list, estimate MINDISTOBJECT(q,n) is a lower bound on the distance between q and an object in the tree rooted at the search hierarchy element corresponding to n that is to serve as q's nearest neighbor. Similarly, estimate MAXDISTOBJECT(q,n) is an upper bound on the distance between q and an object in the tree rooted at the search hierarchy element corresponding to n that is to serve as q's nearest neighbor. Note that if n is not a leaf element, then we can define MAXDISTOBJECT(q,n) as the minimum value attained by MAXDISTOBJECT over all of the subtrees of n. MINDISTOBJECT(q,n) can also be defined recursively in the same manner. Unlike MEANORPIVOTDIST, MINDISTOBJECT and MAXDISTOBJECT are good estimates of where the nearest neighbor is to be found, but, unfortunately, the time needed to calculate them for n and its subtrees is proportional to the number of objects in n and its subtrees, which means that by the time we compute the ordering, we could have already found the closest neighbor. Thus, a better solution is needed.

The two additional orderings proposed above are easily improved upon by modifying the cost-estimate functions MINDISTOBJECT and MAXDISTOBJECT to yield MINDIST and MAXNEARESTDIST, respectively, so that given cluster element n in the active list, they are based only on the cluster associated with n instead of also being based on the objects in the subtrees of n. MINDIST and MAXNEARESTDIST are defined exactly in the same manner as they were in Section 4.2.3 in conjunction with Pruning Rule 5. In particular, for cluster c, MINDIST(q,c) is the least possible distance from the query object q to an object in c that can serve as q's nearest neighbor. Observe that MINDIST$(q,c) = 0$ when q is in c. Similarly, MAXNEARESTDIST(q,c) is the greatest possible distance between q and an object in c that can serve as q's nearest neighbor.

The orderings based on the MINDIST estimate have been used by a number of researchers (e.g., [955, 1374]) in conjunction with modifications of the clustering methods proposed by Fukunaga and Narendra [666] that replace the hierarchical treelike clustering by a multidimensional array so that the cluster elements are the array elements. Of course, using the array reduces the significance of the depth-first algorithm as the search hierarchy usually has either just one level or its depth is bounded by the dimensionality of the underlying dataspace. Roussopoulos, Kelley, and Vincent [1586] proposed using orderings based on the MINDIST and MAXNEARESTDIST estimates for an R-tree search hierarchy where the clusters are hyperrectangle minimum bounding objects, although, as we have seen, they are also applicable to other clustering methods.[15] The utility of these estimates lies in that often their calculation for an appropriate distance metric only requires knowledge of the size and shape of c rather than an examination of

---

[15] Roussopoulos et al. [1586] used the term MINMAXDIST instead of MAXNEARESTDIST as they were primarily concerned with objects that have extent and were trying to minimize the distance from the query object q to the farthest possible point on the $(d-1)$-dimensional faces of the d-dimensional minimum bounding hyperrectangles of the objects as each face must contain at least one point of the object—that is, they were trying to minimize the upper bound on the distance of the farthest possible point on the object, which accounts for the use of the term MINMAXDIST. On the other hand, a case could also be made for using the term MAXMINDIST to denote this quantity as we have an upper bound on the distance from q to the closest possible point of the object. However, in the more general context, when we disregard the nature of the data objects, Roussopoulos et al. [1586] were actually determining the maximum possible distance to the nearest neighbor, and this is why we use instead the term MAXNEARESTDIST in the rest of the discussion.

c's actual contents.[16] Note again that MAXNEARESTDIST is conceptually different from MAXDIST in that MAXDIST indicates the greatest possible distance from q to an object in c that need not necessarily be q's nearest neighbor. Nevertheless, MAXNEARESTDIST and MAXDIST sometimes have the same value in some domains, such as when the data is drawn from a metric space that is organized using a ball partitioning search hierarchy and the only information known about the balls is their radii (i.e., we do not know if the pivot objects are members of the balls).

In some sense, the MINDIST ordering represents the optimistic choice, MAX-NEARESTDIST represents the pessimistic choice, and MEANORPIVOTDIST behaves like a compromise. To see this, observe that if the active list is ordered in order of increasing value of MINDIST, and if cluster c_1 precedes cluster c_2 (i.e., MINDIST$(q,c_1) \leq$ MINDIST(q,c_2)), then, at best, c_1 contains an object o_1 at a distance close to its MINDIST value, such that DISTANCE$(q,o_1) \leq$ MINDIST(q,c_2). However, there is no guarantee that this will indeed be the case as c_2 may contain an object o_2 that is closer to q than o_1. On the other hand, if the active list is ordered in order of increasing value of MAX-NEARESTDIST so that MAXNEARESTDIST$(q,c_1) \leq$ MAXNEARESTDIST(q,c_2), then, in the worst case, the object in c_1 nearest to q is at distance MAXNEARESTDIST(q,c_1), which is no larger than MAXNEARESTDIST(q,c_2).

Regardless of which of the cost-estimate functions MINDIST and MAXNEAREST-DIST is used for ordering the processing of the elements of the active list, they sometimes have other uses in the depth-first k-nearest neighbor algorithm. In particular, since MINDIST represents the minimum distance at which an object could be found in a cluster c, MINDIST yields a means of pruning elements from the search, provided that a bound on the maximum distance to the kth-nearest neighbor is available. In particular, given the value of D_k, the distance from the query object q to the farthest of the k current candidate nearest neighbors, knowing that MINDIST is larger than D_k has the same effect as using Pruning Rule 1 of Fukunaga and Narendra [666], described in Section 4.2.2.

On the other hand, for any nonobject element e, MAXNEARESTDIST(q,e) is an upper bound on the distance of the object o in e nearest to q. In particular, MAX-NEARESTDIST can be used to tighten the search by resetting D_1 to the value of MAXNEARESTDIST(q,e) whenever MAXNEARESTDIST$(q,e) < D_1$. This has the same effect as using Pruning Rule 5. However, this technique, as well as Pruning Rule 5, can only be used in conjunction with a MINDIST ordering since the fact that MINDIST only provides a lower bound on D_1 makes it possible for elements of the active list that are subsequently processed to have MAXNEARESTDIST values that are lower than D_1. In contrast, when using the MAXNEARESTDIST ordering, we know that once we have processed element e and obtained D_1, then $D_1 \leq$ MAXNEARESTDIST(q,e), and thus Pruning Rule 5 is inapplicable as all remaining unprocessed elements of the active list have higher MAXNEARESTDIST values. Moreover, as we point out in Sections 4.2.2 and 4.2.3, it should be clear that MAXNEARESTDIST by itself does not help in pruning the search, as objects closer to q could be found in child elements of element e at positions in the ordering with higher MAXNEARESTDIST values. In this respect, MAXNEARESTDIST has the same drawback as MEANORPIVOTDIST.

Roussopoulos et al.'s [1586] implementation of the k-nearest neighbor algorithm uses MAXNEARESTDIST to prune any element e_1 in the active list such that MINDIST$(q,e_1) >$ MAXNEARESTDIST(q,e_2), where e_2 is some other element in the active list. However, this pruning method is only useful for $k = 1$. Moreover, it can be shown (e.g., [360, 848]) that regardless of how the active list is ordered, the facts that MINDIST$(q,e) \leq$ MAXNEARESTDIST(q,e) and that $D_1 \leq$ MAXNEARESTDIST(q,e) mean that this pruning method is of no use as these clusters will not be examined any-

---

[16] Of course, this statement is not completely true as the actual contents of c were examined at the time that c was originally formed.

way on account of the application of Pruning Rule 1, which will result in at least as much pruning (see Exercise 2).

At this point, let us summarize our observations about the utility of the MINDIST, MAXNEARESTDIST, and MEANORPIVOTDIST orderings. An advantage of ordering the elements e_p of the active list A of e according to increasing values of MINDIST(q, e_p) is that, by the definition of MINDIST, we have that MINDIST$(q, e_p) \leq d(q, e_0)$ for every object e_0 in e_p. Therefore, once we prune one element e_i in A of e on account of determining that MINDIST$(q, e_i) > D_k$, then we will know that MINDIST$(q, e_j) > D_k$ for all remaining elements e_j of the active list A of e. This means that none of these elements needs to be processed, and we simply exit the loop and backtrack to the parent of e or terminate if e is the root of the search hierarchy.

Therefore, from the above discussion, it does not appear that a MAXNEAREST-DIST (as well as MEANORPIVOTDIST) ordering is as useful as a MINDIST ordering. It is interesting to observe that if we are willing to forgo the use of Pruning Rule 5 (as is done in Roussopoulos et al.'s [1586] implementation of the depth-first k-nearest neighbor algorithm), then not using MAXNEARESTDIST for ordering the processing of the elements of the active list means that the CPU cost of the depth-first k-nearest neighbor algorithm is reduced since there is no need to compute the MAXNEAREST-DIST value of each cluster. This is especially important because MAXNEARESTDIST is usually more expensive to compute than MINDIST.

Notwithstanding the above, of course, examples can be constructed where using a MAXNEARESTDIST ordering leads to the examination of fewer minimum bounding objects than a MINDIST ordering (see Exercise 3), and vice versa (see Exercise 4), when finding the kth-nearest neighbor. This is true even if the depth-first k-nearest neighbor algorithm makes use of Pruning Rule 5 with the MINDIST ordering (i.e., for the case that $k = 1$), although the implementation of Roussopoulos et al. [1586] did not make use of Pruning Rule 5. The reason for the occasional superior performance of the MAXNEARESTDIST ordering is the better initial estimates of D_1 and its subsequent refinement, which can lead to some additional initial pruning.

Nevertheless, experiments reported by Roussopoulos et al. [1586], using a search hierarchy where the clusters are minimum bounding hyperrectangles organized in an R-tree, support the preference for the MINDIST ordering by finding that ordering the active list using MINDIST consistently performed better than using MAXNEARESTDIST. This was also confirmed in experiments reported by Hjaltason and Samet [848], who conclude that these results indicate that the optimism inherent in MINDIST usually provides a better estimate of the distance of the nearest object than the pessimism inherent in MAX-NEARESTDIST, so a MINDIST order will, in general, lead to finding the nearest object(s) earlier in the active list. Thus, the MINDIST order is the one that is usually used [848].

Exercises

1. Assume that KNEAREST using FNDFTRAV processes the elements e_p in the active list in increasing MINDIST order, and prove that Pruning Rule 5 can indeed be applied.

2. Roussopoulos et al. [1586] use the following three pruning strategies in their implementation of the depth-first k-nearest neighbor algorithm regardless of which of the cost-estimate functions MINDIST and MAXNEARESTDIST is used for ordering the processing of the elements of the active list. Roussopoulos et al. [1586] differentiate the strategies, in part, on the basis of whether they are applied before or after processing an element on the active list and term them *downward pruning* or *upward pruning*, respectively. Note that it can be shown [848] that it is not necessary to distinguish between downward and upward pruning in the sense that there is no need to remove items explicitly from the active list. Instead, we just test each element on the active list when its turn comes. Although these strategies were proposed for an R-tree search hierarchy that makes use of minimum bounding hyperrectangles, they are also applicable for arbitrary clusters, even though we do not present them here in this way.

(a) Strategy 1 is used in downward pruning. It allows pruning an element from the active list whose minimum bounding hyperrectangle r_1 is such that $\text{MINDIST}(q, r_1) > \text{MAXNEARESTDIST}(q, r_2)$, where r_2 is the minimum bounding hyperrectangle of some other element in the active list. This strategy, as formulated here, is only useful for $k = 1$.

(b) Strategy 2 prunes an object o when its distance from q is greater than $\text{MAXNEAREST-DIST}(q, r)$, where r is some minimum bounding hyperrectangle. Again, this strategy is only applicable when $k = 1$. Roussopoulos et al. [1586] claim that this strategy is of use in downward pruning, but Hjaltason and Samet [848] point out that its inclusion is somewhat puzzling since it does not help in pruning elements in the active list from the search. It is possible that the intent of Roussopoulos et al. [1586] is for Strategy 2 to be used to prune objects in leaf elements [848]. However, this does not appear to be particularly fruitful since it still requires that the objects be accessed and their distances from q be calculated [848]. Another possible explanation given by Hjaltason and Samet [848] for the inclusion of this strategy is that it can be used to discard the nearest object found in an element s in the active list after s has been processed. However, as Hjaltason and Samet [848] point out, the purpose of this is not clear since a better candidate will replace this object later on anyway.

(c) Strategy 3 prunes any element from the active list whose minimum bounding hyperrectangle r is such that $\text{MINDIST}(q, r) > D_k$. It is applicable for any value of k and in both downward and upward pruning.

As pointed out above, Strategy 2 is not a useful strategy. Show that even though Strategy 1 is only applicable when $k = 1$, applying Strategy 3 in upward pruning eliminates at least as many elements of the active list as applying Strategy 1 in downward pruning. In other words, show that there is no need to make use of Strategy 1.

3. Assume a search hierarchy where the clusters are minimum bounding hyperrectangles organized in a structure such as an R-tree. Letting $k = 1$, give an example of the depth-first algorithm where use of MAXNEARESTDIST to order the processing of elements of the active list for finding the k nearest neighbors of query point q examines the contents of fewer minimum bounding hyperrectangles than the use of MINDIST.

4. Assume a search hierarchy where the clusters are minimum bounding hyperrectangles organized in a structure such as an R-tree. Letting $k = 1$, give an example of the depth-first algorithm where use of MINDIST to order the processing of elements of the active list for finding the k nearest neighbors of query point q examines the contents of fewer minimum bounding hyperrectangles than the use of MAXNEARESTDIST.

5. How would you apply a depth-first k-nearest neighbor algorithm to a k-d tree representation of points?

6. Suppose that you want to find the k farthest neighbors instead of the k nearest neighbors. Discuss the relative merits of using MAXDIST and MINFARTHESTDIST to order the processing of the elements of the active list.

7. Assume a search hierarchy where the clusters are minimum bounding hyperrectangles organized in a structure such as an R-tree. Give an example of the depth-first algorithm where use of MINFARTHESTDIST to order the processing of elements of the active list for finding the kth-farthest neighbor of query point q examines the contents of fewer minimum bounding hyperrectangles than the use of MAXDIST.

8. Assume a search hierarchy where the clusters are minimum bounding hyperrectangles organized in a structure such as an R-tree. Give an example of the depth-first algorithm where use of MAXDIST to order the processing of elements of the active list for finding the kth-farthest neighbor of query point q examines the contents of fewer minimum bounding hyperrectangles than the use of MINFARTHESTDIST.

4.2.5 Improved Algorithm

In this section we make use of some of the observations made in Sections 4.2.3 and 4.2.4 to modify procedures FNDFTRAV and INSERTL, thereby yielding OPTDFTRAV and OPTINSERTL, respectively, which are given below. First, we incorporate a modified definition of MINDIST and use a MINDIST ordering to process the elements of the active list. We also indicate how to apply Pruning Rules 2 and 4 to nonobjects instead of just to objects. Next, we show how to modify the control structure of the original depth-first k-nearest neighbor algorithm of Fukunaga and Narendra [666] to enable the use of Pruning Rule 5 for arbitrary values of k. The result is a new algorithm that lies somewhere between the depth-first and best-first approaches, which we call the *maxnearest depth-first k-nearest neighbor algorithm*.

The discussion of MINDIST in Section 4.2.4 was for the most part silent about the shape of the nonobject cluster element e_p. Recall that in its most general form, e_p has the shape of a multidimensional spherical shell, where $r_{p,min}$ and $r_{p,max}$ are the distances from M_p to e_p's internal and external faces, respectively. Thus, we should have two bounding objects (hyperspheres) in this situation)—one for the interior face of the element and one for the exterior face. In this case, we redefine $d(q,e_p) = \text{MINDIST}(q,e_p)$ to be

$$\text{MINDIST}(q,e_p) = \begin{cases} r_{p,min} - d(q,M_p) & 0 \leq d(q,M_p) \leq r_{p,min} \\ 0 & r_{p,min} \leq d(q,M_p) \leq r_{p,max} \\ d(q,M_p) - r_{p,max} & r_{p,max} \leq d(q,M_p). \end{cases}$$

Making this modification enables us to combine Pruning Rules 1 and 3. Note that for this definition, the hyperspheres are not necessarily minimum bounding objects of the objects within them as we do not specify how M_p is chosen.

Despite the advantages cited above for using MINDIST to order the processing of elements of the active list, MEANORPIVOTDIST is still useful. In particular, when q is in a nonobject cluster element e_p of the search hierarchy, then we define $d(q,e_p) = \text{MINDIST}(q,e_p) = 0$, while this is not necessarily the case when we use the definition $d(q,e_p) = \text{MEANORPIVOTDIST}(q,e_p) = d(q,M_p)$. Thus, retaining MEANORPIVOTDIST enables us to distinguish between the different nonobject elements that contain q. In particular, we do this by using MEANORPIVOTDIST as a secondary order on all elements e_p in the active list such that $d(q,e_p) = \text{MINDIST}(q,e_p) = 0$. We also use MEANORPIVOTDIST as a secondary key when two elements have the same MINDIST values.

Recall that the tests for the applicability of Pruning Rules 2 and 4 are made when processing the objects in a leaf element e_p. In particular, for each object o in e_p, we examine the distance $d(o,M_p)$ from o to the mean or pivot M_p and try to apply the appropriate pruning rule to avoid computing the distance between o and q. The rationale for this is to make use of the distances from each o in e_p to M_p, which were computed when the cluster represented by e_p was formed.

In fact, there is no need to apply these tests for all of the objects. Instead, we propose to sort the objects in e_p in increasing order of their distance from M_p (i.e., using MEANORPIVOTDIST(o,M_p)) and to prune all objects o from consideration whose distance $d(o,M_p)$ from M_p is less than $d(q,M_p) - D_k$ (Pruning Rule 2) and greater than $d(q,M_p) + D_k$ (Pruning Rule 4), given that D_k is the distance from q to the farthest of its current k candidate nearest neighbors. In other words, any object o that is one of the k nearest neighbors of q must lie in the range $d(q,M_p) - D_k \leq d(o,M_p) \leq d(q,M_p) + D_k$. Notice that although D_k may change as more objects are examined, the fact that D_k is nonincreasing means that as more objects are processed, the new range is always a subrange of the original range (i.e., it decreases in size), and thus we are assured that we will not miss any objects. The objects are sorted in increasing MEANORPIVOTDIST order—that is, with respect to their distance from M_p. Note that there is no need to sort the objects in procedure OPTDFTRAV as the sort need only be performed once, and this is best done when the cluster represented by e_p is formed.

It is also interesting to observe that by ordering the objects o in e in terms of their distance from their mean or pivot object M (i.e., MEANORPIVOTDIST(o,M)), we are using an analogous principle to prune the processing of objects in a leaf element as we did to prune the processing of the child nonobject elements e_p in the active list A of nonleaf element e. Recall that this was done by ordering them using their distance from q (i.e., $\text{MINDIST}(q, e_p)$). The difference lies in the nature of the reference object for the sort—that is, with respect to M instead of q. Implementing this improvement requires that we find the first object o' such that $d(o', M) \geq d(q, M) - D_k$. This can be achieved by implementing the set of objects in leaf element e, say $O(e)$, as an array and executing a binary search on the set of object distances from M for the objects in e. Once the appropriate o' has been found, the distance between q and all other objects o in $O(e)$ is computed by stepping through $O(e)$ using $\text{NEXT}(O(e))$, and D_k is reset if necessary, until an object o'' is encountered such that $d(o'', M) > d(q, M) + D_k$, at which time we cease processing objects in e as none of the unprocessed objects can be one of the k nearest neighbors of q.

Note that when processing the child elements e_p of a nonleaf element e we did not need to find the first element of the active list whose distance from q was less than a given value as the distances (expressed in terms of MINDIST) are all lower bounds on D_k, and any nonleaf element whose distance from q is less than D_k can contain potential kth-nearest neighbor candidates. In particular, in the case of the active list of a nonleaf element, the pruning condition (i.e., the combination of Pruning Rules 1 and 3) only makes use of the ordering of the elements e_p of the active list (i.e., $\text{MINDIST}(q, e_p)$) with respect to their distances from q, whereas in the case of a leaf element e, the pruning condition (i.e., the combination of Pruning Rules 2 and 4) makes use of both the ordering of the objects (i.e., $\text{MEANORPIVOTDIST}(o, e) = d(o, M)$) with respect to their distances from the mean or pivot object M and the distance of the query object from M (i.e., $\text{MEANORPIVOTDIST}(q, e) = d(q, M)$).

Ciaccia, Patella, and Zezula [389] suggest that Pruning Rules 2 and 4 can also be applied to nonobject elements, instead of just to objects, in their adaptation of a best-first k-nearest neighbor algorithm for the M-tree. Below, we apply these rules to the depth-first algorithm as well. The idea is to prune some of the nonobject elements from the active list without having to compute their distances from q. In particular, for each nonobject element e with mean M whose elements e_p are also nonobjects with mean M_p and distance $r_{p,max}$ from M_p to the farthest object within e_p, this is achieved by storing the distance from M to the farthest and nearest object within e_p—that is, $\text{MAXDIST}(M, e_p) = d(M, M_p) + r_{p,max}$ and $\text{MINDIST}(M, e_p) = d(M, M_p) - r_{p,max}$, respectively. With this information at hand, while generating the active list A containing the nonobject child elements e_p of e, e_p is pruned if $d(q, M) - D_k > \text{MAXDIST}(M, e_p)$ when M is closer to the object at distance $\text{MAXDIST}(M, e_p)$ (and hence M_p as $d(M, M_p) < \text{MAXDIST}(M, e_p)$) than to q, and if $\text{MINDIST}(M, e_p) > D_k + d(q, M)$ when M is closer to q than to the object at distance $\text{MINDIST}(M, e_p)$ (and hence M_p as $d(M, M_p) > \text{MINDIST}(M, e_p)$). Notice that, in effect, the former corresponds to replacing Pruning Rule 2 for objects with o, M_p, $d(M_p, o)$, and M_p being closer to o than to q (Figure 4.12) with e_p, M, $\text{MAXDIST}(M, e_p)$, and M being closer to the object at distance $\text{MAXDIST}(M, e_p)$ than to q (Figure 4.21(a)), respectively. Similarly, the latter corresponds to replacing Pruning Rule 4 for objects with o, M_p, $d(M_p, o)$, and M_p being closer to q than to o (Figure 4.14) with e_p, M, $\text{MINDIST}(M, e_p)$, and M being closer to q than to e_p (i.e., the object at distance $\text{MINDIST}(M, e_p)$) (Figure 4.21(b)), respectively. Observe that the formulation of the rules in terms of MAXDIST and MINDIST leads to a more generalized formulation than the one of Ciaccia et al. [389] as it is applicable to a broader range of search hierarchies than the M-tree.

OPTDFTRAV has also been enhanced so that it need not apply the tests corresponding to Pruning Rules 2 and 4 to all nonobjects in a nonleaf node e with mean M when forming the active list. In this way, it can possibly avoid computing the distance from q to some of the individual nonobjects in e. In particular, the nonobjects in e are sorted in increasing MAXDIST order with respect to M (this is done when the search hierarchy is initially formed). This enables pruning all nonobjects e_p from consideration for which $\text{MAXDIST}(e_p)$ is less than $d(q, M) - D_k$ (Pruning Rule 2). The remaining nonobjects

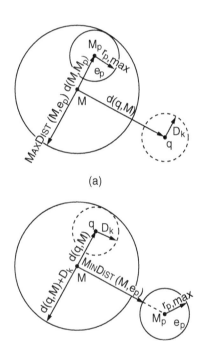

(a)

(b)

Figure 4.21
Examples illustrating Pruning Rules 2 and 4 for nonobject elements e_p in e with mean M: (a) Pruning Rule 2 eliminates any nonobject e_p in e when $D_k + \text{MAXDIST}(M, e_p) < d(q, M)$, for the case that M is closer to the object at distance $\text{MAXDIST}(M, e_p)$ than to q and (b) Pruning Rule 4 eliminates any nonobject e_p in e when $D_k + d(q, M) < \text{MINDIST}(M, e_p)$, for the case that M is closer to q than to e_p.

are only pruned if $\text{MINDIST}(M, e_p) > d(q, M) + D_k$ (i.e., Pruning Rule 4); otherwise, they are inserted into the active list.

As we pointed out in Section 4.2.2, it is not immediately clear how to adapt Pruning Rule 5 to deal with $k > 1$ neighbors. In order to visualize better the following discussion, we assume, without loss of generality, that the nonobject element e_p has the shape of a multidimensional spherical shell. Note that these hyperspheres are not necessarily minimum bounding objects of the objects within them as we do not specify how M_p is chosen. Therefore, in our examples, $\text{MAXNEARESTDIST}(q, e_p) = d(q, M_p) + r_{p,min}$, although the results also hold when using other values of MAXNEARESTDIST. One possible solution is that whenever we find that $d(q, M_p) + r_{p,min} < D_k$, we reset D_k to $d(q, M_p) + r_{p,min}$ if $D_{k-1} \leq d(q, M_p) + r_{p,min}$ (Figure 4.22(a)); otherwise, we reset D_k to D_{k-1} (Figure 4.22(b)). Nevertheless, this solution is problematic when $D_{k-1} > d(q, M_p) + r_{p,min}$ since, at this point, both D_k and D_{k-1} are the same (i.e., $D_k = D_{k-1}$), and from now on we will never be able to obtain a lower bound on D_k than D_{k-1}. The remedy is to add another explicit check to determine if $D_{k-2} \leq d(q, M_p) + r_{p,min}$, in which case we reset D_{k-1} to $d(q, M_p) + r_{p,min}$; otherwise, we reset D_{k-1} to D_{k-2}. Nevertheless, this remedy is only temporary as it will break down again if $D_{k-2} > d(q, M_p) + r_{p,min}$. However, we can just repeatedly apply the same method again until we find the smallest $i \geq 1$ such that $D_i > d(q, M_p) + r_{p,min}$. Once this value of i has been located, we set D_i to $d(q, M_p) + r_{p,min}$ after resetting D_j to D_{j-1} ($k \geq j > i$).

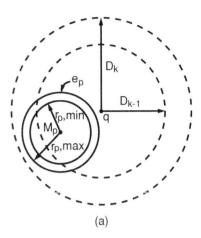

(a)

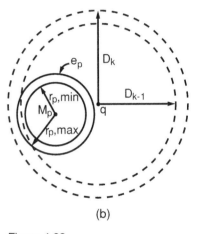

(b)

Figure 4.22
Examples illustrating the applicability of Larsen and Kanal's [1103] modification of Rule 5 used in the k-nearest neighbor algorithm of Fukunaga and Narendra [666] to reset the distance D_k from q to the farthest of its k neighbors upon inserting into the active list an element e_p of the active list with mean M_p. $r_{p,max}$ and $r_{p,min}$ are the distances from M_p to the farthest and closest objects, respectively, within e_p where $d(q, M_p) + r_{p,min} < D_k$ and D_k is reset to either (a) $d(q, M_p) + r_{p,min}$ if $D_{k-1} \leq d(q, M_p) + r_{p,min}$ or (b) D_{k-1} otherwise (i.e., if $D_{k-1} > d(q, M_p) + r_{p,min}$).

Unfortunately, the solution described above does not guarantee that the objects that are associated with the different $D_j (1 \leq j \leq k)$ values are unique. The problem is that the same object o may be responsible for the MAXNEARESTDIST value associated with both elements e_p and e_a of the search hierarchy that caused $d(q, M_p) + r_{p,min} < D_k$ and $d(q, M_a) + r_{a,min} < D_k$, respectively, at different times. Of course, this situation can only occur when e_p is an ancestor of e_a. However, it must be taken into account as, otherwise, the results of the algorithm are wrong.

In order to avoid this problem and to be able to make use of Pruning Rule 5, we expand the role played by the set L of the k nearest neighbors encountered so far so that it also contains nonobject elements corresponding to the elements of the active list along with their corresponding MAXNEARESTDIST values, as well as objects with their distance values from q [1639, 1643]. In particular, each time we process a nonobject element e of the search hierarchy, we insert in L all of e's child elements that make up e's active list, along with their corresponding MAXNEARESTDIST values (i.e., this replaces lines 28–33 in procedure FNDFTRAV). Moreover, in order to ensure that no ancestor-descendent relationship could possibly hold for any pair of items in L, before we process a nonobject element e of the search hierarchy (line 38 in procedure FNDFTRAV), we remove e's corresponding element from L using procedure REMOVEPRIORITYQUEUE (not given here). Therefore, the object o associated with the nonobject element u of L at a distance of MAXNEARESTDIST is guaranteed to be unique. In other words, o is not already in L; nor is o associated with any other nonobject element in L. It is also important to note that each of the entries u in L ensures that there is at least one object in the dataset whose maximum possible distance from q is the one associated with u.

1   **recursive procedure** OPTDFTRAV(q, k, e, L, D_k)
2   /* Depth-first algorithm that recursively processes element e of a search hierarchy to determine the k nearest neighbors of q while using L to keep track of these neighbors with D_k as the distance of q's current kth candidate nearest object in L. The algorithm makes use of the MAXNEAREST-DIST estimate and Pruning Rules 1–4 for both objects and nonobjects. */
3   **value object** q
4   **value integer** k
5   **value pointer search_hierarchy** e
6   **reference pointer priority_queue** L
7   **reference integer** D_k
8   **object** o

We implement Pruning Rule 5 by resetting D_k to $D(L_k)$ whenever, upon insertion of a nonobject element e_p into L with its corresponding MAXNEARESTDIST value, we find that L has at least k entries and that $D(L_k)$ is less than D_k as this corresponds to the situation that $d(q, M_p) + r_{p,min} < D_k$ (i.e., assuming that the nonobject element e_p contained in L_k has mean M_p and $r_{p,min}$ as the distance from M_p to the closest object within e_p). Recall that the same action of resetting D_k was also taken in procedures FNDFTRAV and INSERTL upon insertion of an object into L when L has k entries as can be seen by noting that MAXNEARESTDIST of an object o is just $d(q, o)$ as $r_{p,min} = 0$. Thus, we are able to use the unexplored nonobject elements of the active list for pruning in the sense that the distances from q of the farthest objects within them that can serve as the nearest neighbors enable us to calculate an upper bound D_k on the distance of the kth-nearest neighbor. Observe that it is important to distinguish between D_k, which is used in Pruning Rules 1–4 and $D(L_k)$, which serves as the basis of Pruning Rule 5. In particular, we see that defining D_k in terms of the minimum of D_k and $D(L_k)$ ensures that there are k distinct objects (even though they may not all have been identified) whose maximum distance from q is less than or equal to D_k. Of course, we do not reset D_k upon explicitly removing a nonobject element from L because D_k is already a minimum and thus cannot decrease further as a result of the removal of a nonobject element, although it may decrease upon the subsequent insertion of an object or nonobject.

Note that nonobjects can only be pruned after the successful application of Pruning Rules 1 or 3 (i.e., on the basis of their MINDIST values), in which case they should also be removed from L. Moreover, the fact that we are using the MINDIST ordering means that once we prune one of the child elements of nonobject element e in the active list A of e, we can prune all remaining elements in A since they all have larger MINDIST values as A is sorted in increasing MINDIST order. Therefore, all of these elements should be removed from L as well since each of their MAXNEARESTDIST values is greater than its corresponding MINDIST value and hence also greater than D_k. However, there is really no harm in not removing any of the pruned nonobjects from L as neither the pruned nonobjects nor their descendents will ever be examined again. Nevertheless, the pruned nonobjects take up space in L, which is why it may be desirable to remove them anyway.

The drawback of the solution that we have described is that the maximum size of L has grown considerably since it is no longer k. Instead, assuming that pruned nonobjects have been removed from L, the maximum possible size of L is k plus the maximum number of possible active list elements over all levels of the search hierarchy. For example, assuming N data items and that the clustering method makes use of a treelike search hierarchy with m as the branching factor, then the maximum size of L is $O(k + m \cdot \log N)$ and is attained when the depth-first search algorithm first encounters an object at the maximum depth, which is $O(\log N)$. Actually, it is interesting to note that the cost of increasing the size of L to include the maximum number of possible active list elements is not such a drawback as this amount of storage is needed by the recursion anyway due to the unexplored paths that remain at each level while descending to the deepest level of the search hierarchy.

Nevertheless, the facts that only nonobject elements with MINDIST values less than or equal to D_k are ever processed by the algorithm and that all of these nonobject elements have the same or larger corresponding MAXNEARESTDIST values mean that any nonobject element e whose MAXNEARESTDIST value is greater than the current value of D_k should not be inserted in L as D_k is nonincreasing, and thus were e to be inserted in L, it would never be examined subsequently, thereby implying that there will never be an explicit attempt to remove it. In fact, there is also no need to insert e in L when its MAXNEARESTDIST value is equal to the current value of D_k, regardless of how many elements are currently in L, as such an insertion will not enable us to lower the known value of D_k so that more pruning will be possible in the future (see Exercise 1). Otherwise, there is no reason to use L to keep track of the MAXNEARESTDIST values of the nonobjects.

Moreover, the fact that only the first k elements of L are ever examined by the algorithm (i.e., retrieved from L) when updating D_k in the case of an insertion into L means that there is no need for L ever to contain more than k elements. This simplifies the algorithm considerably. However, it does mean that when it comes to needing to remove a nonobject element e explicitly from L just before inserting into L all of e's child elements that make up e's active list along with their corresponding MAXNEARESTDIST values, it could be the case that e is no longer in L. This is because e may have been implicitly removed as a byproduct of the insertion of closer objects or nonobject elements whose corresponding MAXNEARESTDIST values are smaller than that of e and thereby resulted in the resetting of D_k.

The only tricky case is ensuring that a nonobject e is actually in L when we are about to attempt to remove e explicitly from L. In other words, we want to ensure that e has not already been removed implicitly. Of course, if e's MAXNEARESTDIST value is greater than D_k, then there is no need for any action because it is impossible for e to be in L, and thus we are guaranteed that e was implicitly removed from L. However, when e's MAXNEARESTDIST value is less than or equal to D_k, and there are several elements in L with distance D_k, we do not want to search needlessly for e, as may be the case if e had already been implicitly removed from L by virtue of the insertion of a closer object or a nonobject with a smaller MAXNEARESTDIST value. This needless search can be avoided by adopting some convention as to which element of L at distance D_k should be removed when there are several nonobjects in L having D_k as their MAXNEARESTDIST value, as well as objects at distance D_k.

We adopt the convention that objects have priority over nonobjects in the sense that, in terms of nearness, objects have precedence over nonobjects in L. This means that when nonobjects and objects have the same distance, the nonobjects appear closer to the maximum entry in the priority queue L, denoted by MAXPRIORITYQUEUE(L), which corresponds to the kth-nearest candidate neighbor. In particular, we stipulate that whenever insertion into a full priority queue results in dequeueing a nonobject element b, we check if the new MAXPRIORITYQUEUE(L) entry c corresponds to a nonobject with the same MAXNEARESTDIST value d, in which case c is also dequeued. This loop continues until the new MAXPRIORITYQUEUE(L) entry corresponds to an object at any distance including d or to a nonobject at any other distance d', or until L is empty. Note that D_k can only be reset if exactly one entry has been dequeued, and the distance of the new MAXPRIORITYQUEUE(L) entry is less than D_k. Otherwise, if we dequeue more than one entry, then, even though the distance of the new MAXPRIORITYQUEUE(L) entry may now be less than D_k, it cannot be used to reset D_k as L now contains fewer than k entries. In fact, it should be clear that D_k should not be reset because D_k has not been decreased since the only reason for the removal of the multiple nonobject entries is to avoid subsequent, possibly needless, searches when explicitly removing nonobject elements with MAXNEARESTDIST value D_k.

Following this convention, when a nonobject e is to be removed explicitly from L and e's MAXNEARESTDIST value is less than D_k, then e has to be in L because it is impossible for e to have been removed implicitly as D_k is nonincreasing. Therefore, we remove e and decrement the size of L. On the other hand, the situation is more complicated when e's MAXNEARESTDIST value is equal to D_k. First, if the maximum value in L (i.e., the one associated with MAXPRIORITYQUEUE(L)) is less than D_k, then e cannot be in L, and we do not attempt to remove e. Such a situation arises, for example, when we dequeue more than one nonobject because there are several nonobjects at distance D_k. Second, if the maximum value in L (i.e., the one associated with MAXPRIORITYQUEUE(L)) is equal to D_k, then there are two cases, depending on whether the entry c in MAXPRIORITYQUEUE(L) corresponds to an object or a nonobject. If c corresponds to an object, then nonobject e cannot be in L as we have given precedence to objects, and all nonobjects at the same distance are either in L or they are all not in L. If c corresponds to a nonobject, then nonobject e has to be in L as all of the nonobjects at the same distance have either been removed implicitly together or retained, and, in this case, by virtue of the presence of c in L, we know that they have been retained in L. Note that when we explicitly remove a nonobject at distance D_k from L, we do not remove all remaining nonobjects at the same distance from L as this needlessly complicates the algorithm with no additional benefit because they will all be removed implicitly together later if at least one of them must be implicitly removed due to a subsequent insertion into a full priority queue.

The advantage of expanding the role of L to contain nonobjects as well, instead of just containing objects, is that without this expanded role, when L contains h ($h < k$) objects, then the remaining $k - h$ entries in L are ∞. Therefore, as long as there are at least $k - h$ other entries in L that correspond to some nonobjects, we have a lower bound D_k than ∞. Moreover, the nonobjects in L often enable us to provide a lower bound D_k than if all entries in L were objects. In particular, this is the case when we have nonobjects with smaller MAXNEARESTDIST values than the k objects with the k smallest distance values encountered so far.

It is interesting to observe that the manner in which we incorporate Pruning Rule 5 in OPTDFTRAV enables the use of its result at a deeper level than the one at which it is calculated. In particular, the use of L to store the MAXNEARESTDIST values of some active nonobject elements means that a MAXNEARESTDIST value of an unexplored nonobject at depth i can be used to help in pruning objects and nonobjects at depth $j > i$. This is a significant improvement over the depth-first algorithm in FNDFTRAV, where the MAXNEARESTDIST value of a nonobject element at depth i could only be used to tighten the distance to the nearest neighbor (i.e., for $k = 1$) and prune nonobject elements at larger MINDIST values at the same depth i.

Unlike procedure FNDFTRAV, OPTDFTRAV incorporates Pruning Rule 5 in terms of MAXNEARESTDIST (lines 31–37) instead of $r_{p,min}$. This is preferable as we no longer need to be concerned about whether the data is drawn from a metric space rather than from a vector space, whether $r_{p,min}$ is known, or about the nature of the clustering method. Using MAXNEARESTDIST also enables us to distinguish between the use of $r_{p,min}$ in the definition of MINDIST where an unknown value of $r_{p,min}$ is equivalent to setting $r_{p,min}$ to 0, while when the value of $r_{p,min}$ is unknown in Pruning Rule 5, it is wrong to set $r_{p,min}$ to 0. In fact, when $r_{p,min}$ is unknown in Pruning Rule 5, then $r_{p,min}$ is set to $r_{p,max}$.

Notice that OPTDFTRAV is considerably different from Roussopoulos et al.'s [1586] implementation of the depth-first algorithm. Besides permitting a more general cluster element than a hyperrectangle minimum bounding object, OPTDFTRAV also incorporates Pruning Rules 2–5 instead of just Pruning Rule 1. In addition, OPTDFTRAV also tries to apply pruning to the objects in each of the leaf elements of the search structure and to the nonobjects in each of the nonleaf elements of the search structure, which is not done in the implementation of Roussopoulos et al. [1586].

Moreover, we observe that OPTDFTRAV is quite different from the original algorithm of Fukunaga and Narendra [666] in that OPTDFTRAV incorporates Pruning Rules 2–5 rather than just Pruning Rules 1, 2, and 5; it is also different from the enhanced version proposed by Kamgar-Parsi and Kanal [986], which incorporates Pruning Rules 1–4. OPTDFTRAV also differs from previous approaches including that of Larsen and Kanal [1103] by handling the k nearest neighbors instead of just the nearest neighbor (i.e., $k = 1$) in all of the pruning rules (especially Pruning Rule 5). Furthermore, use of the MINDIST ordering in conjunction with the MEANORPIVOTDIST ordering, as well as the application of the tighter pruning criteria, represents an improvement in terms of the number of objects that can eventually be pruned.

OPTDFTRAV processes each nonobject element e_p as a unit. This means that Pruning Rule 3 is inapplicable when the mean or pivot M_p is an element of e_p as then $r_{p,min} = 0$. This situation can be avoided, although we do not do so here, by modifying OPTDFTRAV to process the means or pivots M_p separately from the rest of the elements of nonobject element e_p (see Exercise 8 and Exercise 1 in Section 4.2.6). In particular, this will permit us to try to take advantage of the value of $r_{p,min}$, even when M_p is an element of e_p (i.e., permitting the use of Pruning Rule 3).

Exercises

1. How can a situation arise that there are two or more nonobjects in L with the same MAX-NEARESTDIST value?

2. Suppose that the search hierarchy is such that each cluster e_p, besides having a mean M_p, also has a maximum distance $r_{p,max}$, as is the case for the M-tree. Can you formulate the condition for the application of Pruning Rules 2 and 4 to be in terms of $r_{p,max}, d(q,M), d(M,M_p)$, and D_k, instead of in terms of MINDIST(M,e_p), MAXDIST(M,e_p), $d(q,M)$, $d(M,M_p)$, and D_k so that there is no need to make an explicit distinction between whether M is closer to M_p than to q?.

3. Prove that nonobject element e_p in the active list of nonobject element e with mean M and distance MAXDIST(M,e_p) from M to the farthest object within e_p, where M is closer to the object at distance MAXDIST(M,e_p) than to q, cannot contain the kth-nearest neighbor of query object q if $D_k + $ MAXDIST$(M,e_p) < d(q,M)$, where D_k is the distance from q to the farthest of the current candidate k nearest neighbors—that is, prove that Pruning Rule 2 for nonobjects is correct.

4. Prove that nonobject element e_p in the active list of nonobject element e with mean M and distance MAXDIST(M,e_p) from M to the farthest object within e_p and distance MINDIST(M,e_p) from M to the nearest object within e_p, where M is closer to q than to the object at distance MINDIST(M,e_p), cannot contain the kth-nearest neighbor of query object q if $D_k + d(q,M) < $ MINDIST(M,e_p), where D_k is the distance from q to the farthest of the current candidate k nearest neighbors—that is, prove that Pruning Rule 4 for nonobjects is correct.

5. Can you incorporate Pruning Rules 2 and 4 for nonobjects in OPTDFTRAV by sorting the nonobjects in nonleaf node e with mean M in MINDIST order with respect to M instead of MAXDIST order? If yes, then explain how this can be achieved; otherwise, explain why it cannot.

6. In the case of objects, Pruning Rules 2 and 4 are incorporated in OPTDFTRAV by first sorting the objects in e with mean M in increasing order of their distances from M, which are computed once and stored with e, and then only computing the distance $d(q,o)$ for the objects o whose distance from M lies between $d(q,M) - D_k$ and $d(q,M) + D_k$. In the case of nonobjects, they are incorporated by sorting the nonobjects in e with mean M in increasing MAXDIST order and only computing the distance $d(q,e_p)$ for the nonobjects e_p whose MAXDIST from M is greater than or equal to $d(q,M) - D_k$ and for which MINDIST from M is less than or equal to $d(q,M) + D_k$. Thus, there is no upper bound on the MAXDIST(M,e_p) values that must be checked, which is different from the incorporation of these rules for objects where there is both a lower and upper bound on the range. Explain why we cannot have both a lower and upper bound on the range in the case of nonobjects.

7. Suppose that we support the incorporation of Pruning Rules 2 and 4 for nonobjects in OPTDFTRAV by using two sorted lists in order to overcome the drawbacks of the current solution embodied by OPTDFTRAV as pointed out in Exercise 6. In particular, sort all nonobjects e_p in e in increasing and decreasing order with respect to M using MAXDIST and MINDIST, and store them in MX(e) and MN(e), respectively. The solution has two parts. First, find the first object e_p in MX(e) such that MAXDIST$(M,e_p) \geq d(q,M) - D_k$ and then insert each of the ensuing nonobjects e_i with mean M_i into the active list as long as $d(M_i,M) \leq d(q,M)$, which is equivalent to requiring that M be closer to e_i than to q. Next, find the first object e_p in MN(e) such that MINDIST$(M,e_p) \leq d(q,M) + D_k$ and then insert each of the ensuing nonobjects e_i with mean M_i into the active list as long as $d(M_i,M) > d(q,M)$, which is equivalent to requiring that M be closer to q than to e_i. Give a code fragment to implement this strategy by replacing lines 24–30 in OPTDFTRAV. Will this method work? In other words, is it guaranteed to insert all relevant nonobjects into the active list?

8. (Daniel DeMenthon) Modify procedure OPTDFTRAV to process the means or pivots M_p of nonobject element e_p separately from the rest of the elements of e_p so that you can take

advantage of $r_{p,min}$ even when M_p is an element of e_p (i.e., enabling the use of Pruning Rule 3).

9. Implement procedure KNEAREST with OPTDFTRAV and run it on some test data using an R-tree search hierarchy with minimum bounding hyperrectangles (e.g., an R*-tree [152]). Perform the comparison using different values of k. Is there a qualitative difference in performance comparable to that reported by Kamgar-Parsi and Kanal [986] with respect to the use of the various pruning rules? Also, compare its performance with that of an implementation that just makes use of Pruning Rule 1, as done by Roussopoulos et al. [1586].

10. Implement procedure KNEAREST with OPTDFTRAV as in Exercise 9, and compare its performance with that of the general incremental algorithm using an R-tree search hierarchy with minimum bounding hyperrectangles (e.g., an R*-tree [152]). Perform the comparison using different values of k. Is there a difference from the results reported in [848], which perform the comparison with the implementation of Roussopoulos et al. [1586], which only makes use of Pruning Rule 1?

11. How would you adapt Pruning Rules 2 and 4 so that each one can be applied to nonobject elements when finding the k farthest neighbors?

12. Give the analog procedure OPTDFTRAVFARTHEST of OPTDFTRAV for finding the k farthest neighbors using the approach outlined in Exercise 2 in Section 4.2.1. Incorporate the modified Pruning Rules 1–5 given in Exercise 17 of Section 4.2.2 as well as Pruning Rules 2 and 4 for nonobjects as in Exercise 11.

13. Repeat Exercise 12 using the approach outlined in Exercise 3 of Section 4.2.1.

4.2.6 Incorporating MAXNEARESTDIST in a Best-First Algorithm

Incorporating Pruning Rule 5 (i.e., MAXNEARESTDIST) in the depth-first k-nearest neighbor algorithm, resulting in what we call the maxnearest depth-first algorithm, can be viewed as providing a middle ground between a pure depth-first and a best-first k-nearest neighbor algorithm. In particular, assuming N data items, the priority queue L in the maxnearest depth-first algorithm behaves in a similar manner as the priority queue $Queue$ in the incremental implementation of the best-first k-nearest neighbor algorithm (i.e., so that it returns the k nearest neighbors while also enabling continuing the algorithm to obtain more neighbors, such as the $(k + 1)$-th, etc.), except that the upper bound on L's size is k, whereas the upper bound on the size of $Queue$ is $O(N)$. In contrast, in all of the versions of the depth-first algorithms that we have presented, the worst-case total storage requirements only depend on the nature of the search hierarchy (i.e., the maximum height of the search hierarchy, which is $O(\log N)$), instead of on the size of the dataset, as is the case for the best-first algorithm.

The difference in the maximum storage requirements of the depth-first and best-first algorithms is caused by several factors. First of all, in the incremental implementation of the best-first k-nearest neighbor algorithm, no objects or nonobjects can ever be deleted from the priority queue $Queue$ as they may eventually be needed. Second, even if the best-first algorithm is implemented to return only the k nearest neighbors, then $Queue$ may still be as large as the entire dataset. For example, recall from Figure 4.4 and the discussion in Section 4.1.3 that such a situation can arise when all of the leaf nonobject elements of the search hierarchy are within distance d from the query object q, while all of the data objects are farther away from q than d.

The best-first algorithm can be implemented to return only the k nearest neighbors by keeping track of the k nearest objects in a separate data structure, say C, and modifying the algorithm so that no objects are inserted into $Queue$ that are farther from q than the farthest of the current k candidate nearest neighbors.[17] As the k nearest objects must eventually be inserted into C when they reach the front of $Queue$, we might as well

---

[17] It should be clear that no nonobjects farther from q than the farthest of the current k candidate nearest neighbors should be inserted into $Queue$ since the fact that the nonobjects are processed in order

insert them into C immediately when they are first encountered and possibly remove them from C if closer objects are eventually encountered. This means that *Queue* now contains only nonobject elements, and, in fact, C is the same as L and thus we just make use of *Queue* and L. Such a solution was proposed by Hjaltason and Samet [851] and is described briefly in Section 4.1.5.

Procedure BFTRAV corresponds to this solution, with D_k again indicating the distance of the current kth-nearest neighbor of q (initialized to ∞). BFTRAV has a structure that combines features from both INCNEAREST in Section 4.1.3 and DFTRAV in Section 4.2.1. In this case, *Queue* is implemented in the same way as L, which means that each element e in *Queue* has two fields E and D, corresponding to the nonobject i that e contains and the value of MINDIST(q, i), respectively. *Queue* is initialized with the root of the search hierarchy and a MINDIST value of 0. Notice the use of INSERTL to insert objects in the priority queue L instead of ENQUEUE as in procedure INCNEAREST since L has a fixed size, which means that a check for L being full must be performed before the insertion is actually made.

```
1  priority_queue procedure BFTRAV(q, k, S, T)
2  /* A best-first nonincremental algorithm that returns a priority queue contain-
      ing the k nearest neighbors of q from the set of objects S organized using
      the search hierarchy T. */
3  value object q
4  value integer k
5  value object_set S
6  value pointer search_hierarchy T
7  integer D_k
8  priority_queue L, Queue
9  priority_queue_entry t
10 object o
11 pointer search_hierarchy e, e_p
12 L ← NEWPRIORITYQUEUE() /* L is the priority queue containing the k
                                nearest objects */
13 Queue ← NEWPRIORITYQUEUE()
14 e ←root of the search hierarchy induced by S and T
15 ENQUEUE(e, 0, Queue)
16 D_k ← ∞
17 while not ISEMPTY(Queue) do
18    t ← DEQUEUE(Queue)
19    e ← E(t)
20    if D(t) > D_k then
21       return L /* k nearest neighbors were found, and exit */
22    elseif ISLEAF(e) then /* e is a leaf with objects */
23       foreach object child element o of e do
24          Compute d(q, o)
25          if d(q, o) < D_k then
26             INSERTL(o, d(q, o), k, L, D_k)
27          endif
28       enddo
29    else
30       foreach child element e_p of e do
31          ENQUEUE(e_p, MINDIST(q, e_p), Queue)
32       enddo
33    endif
34 enddo
```

of increasing MINDIST values means that they will never be removed from *Queue* should they ever have been inserted.

35 **return** L

Thus, we see that the best-first algorithm given by BFTRAV uses the current k candidate nearest neighbors to prune objects from further consideration by not inserting them into *Queue* or L. On the other hand, the maxnearest depth-first algorithm (as implemented by OPTDFTRAV) also employs the estimate MAXNEARESTDIST to enable the use of the nonobject elements of the search hierarchy to speed up the convergence of D_k to its final value, thereby helping to prune the set of k candidate nearest neighbors instead of pruning only with the aid of the k nearest objects, as in the implementation of the best-first algorithm given by BFTRAV. It should be clear that the facts that a best-first algorithm examines the nonobject elements in increasing MINDIST order and that every nonobject element with MINDIST less than D_k must be examined together mean that no matter how fast the value of D_k converges to its final value, a best-first algorithm will never examine any extra nonobject elements. Therefore, use of an estimate such as MAXNEARESTDIST cannot have the same effect on a best-first algorithm as it can on a depth-first algorithm.

However, as we show below, the best-first algorithm given by BFTRAV can be adapted to use the estimate MAXNEARESTDIST to speed up the convergence of D_k to its final value and thereby reduce the size of *Queue* when finding the k nearest neighbors by checking if the MAXNEARESTDIST estimate for a given nonobject element e is less than D_k, in which case an entry corresponding to e is inserted in L. We characterize the result as a *maxnearest best-first k-nearest neighbor algorithm*. Such an algorithm is realized by procedure OPTBFTRAV as given below. It is a combination of BFTRAV and OPTDFTRAV and also incorporates Pruning Rules 1–4.

```
1   priority_queue procedure OPTBFTRAV(q,k,S,T)
2   /* A best-first nonincremental algorithm that returns a priority queue contain-
        ing the k nearest neighbors of q from the set of objects S organized using
        the search hierarchy T. The algorithm makes use of the MAXNEAREST-
        DIST estimate and Pruning Rules 1–4. */
3   value object q
4   value integer k
5   value object_set S
6   value pointer search_hierarchy T
7   integer D_k
8   priority_queue L, Queue
9   priority_queue_entry t
10  object o
11  pointer search_hierarchy e, e_p
12  L ← NEWPRIORITYQUEUE() /* L is the priority queue containing the k
                                       nearest objects */
13  ENQUEUE(e, MAXNEARESTDIST(q,e), L)
14  Queue ← NEWPRIORITYQUEUE()
15  e ← root of the search hierarchy induced by S and T
16  ENQUEUE(e, 0, Queue)
17  D_k ← ∞
18  while not ISEMPTY(Queue) do
19     t ← DEQUEUE(Queue)
20     e ← E(t)
21     if D(t) > D_k then
22        return L   /* k nearest neighbors were found, and exit */
23     elseif MAXNEARESTDIST(q,e) < D_k or
24            (MAXNEARESTDIST(q,e) = D_k
25              and D(MAXPRIORITYQUEUE(L)) = D_k
26              and not ISOBJECT(E(MAXPRIORITYQUEUE(L)))) then
27        REMOVEPRIORITYQUEUE(e, L)   /*1 Remove e from L */
28     endif
```

29 **if** ISLEAF(e) **then** /* e is a leaf with mean M and maximum distance r_{max} */

30 /* Assume all objects o in e are sorted in increasing order with respect to M */

31 Find first object o in O(e) such that $d(o, M) \geq d(q, M) - D_k$

32 **while** EXIST(o) **and** $d(o, M) \leq d(q, M) + D_k$ **do**

33 Compute $d(q, o)$ /* Pruning Rules 2 and 4 for objects */

34 **if** $d(q, o) < D_k$ **or** $(d(q, o) = D_k$ **and** SIZE(L) $< k)$ **then**

35 OPTINSERTL($o, d(q, o), k, L, D_k$)

36 **endif** /* Otherwise, o is too far or already have k objects o_i, $d(q, o_i) \leq D_k$ */

37 $o \leftarrow$ NEXT(O(e))

38 **enddo**

39 **else**

40 /* e is a nonleaf with mean M. Assume all nonobjects e_p in e are sorted in increasing MAXDIST order with respect to M and stored in C(e) */

41 Find first nonobject e_p in C(e) such that

42 MAXDIST(M, e_p) $\geq d(q, M) - D_k$

43 **while** EXIST(e_p) **do** /* Try to apply Pruning Rules 2 and 4 for nonobjects */

44 **if** MINDIST(M, e_p) $\leq d(q, M) + D_k$ **then**

45 /* Pruning Rules 2 and 4 for nonobjects do not hold */

46 **if** MINDIST(q, e_p) $\leq D_k$ **then**

47 /* Pruning Rules 1 and 3 do not hold */

48 **if** MAXNEARESTDIST(q, e_p) $< D_k$ **then**

49 OPTINSERTL(e_p, MAXNEARESTDIST(q, e_p), k, L, D_k)

50 **endif**

51 ENQUEUE(e_p, MINDIST(q, e_p), $Queue$)

52 **endif**

53 **endif**

54 $e_p \leftarrow$ NEXT(C(e))

55 **enddo**

56 **endif**

57 **enddo**

58 **return** L

OPTBFTRAV processes all nonobject elements in *Queue* in the order in which they appear in *Queue* (i.e., the element e at the front is processed first). We first remove e from *Queue* (lines 19–20) and also check if e should be explicitly removed from L using the same method as in OPTDFTRAV (lines 23–28). Recall that this step ensures that the objects that are associated with the different entries in L are unique. This removal step is missing in a variant of a best-first algorithm that uses MAXNEARESTDIST proposed by Ciaccia, Patella, and Zezula for the M-tree [389], thereby possibly leading to erroneous results. Next, we check if e is a leaf element, in which case we test for the applicability of Pruning Rules 2 and 4 using the same method as in OPTDFTRAV (lines 31–38). Otherwise, we examine each of e's child elements e_p that is not pruned by Pruning Rules 2 and 4 (lines 41–44) and insert e_p and its associated MINDIST(q, e_p) value into *Queue* (line 51) if MINDIST(q, e_p) is less than or equal to D_k, which is equivalent to determining that Pruning Rules 1 and 3 do not hold (line 46). Note that Pruning Rules 1–4 are used here to reduce the size of the priority queue *Queue* rather than for pruning nonobject elements from further processing, as in the depth-first algorithm OPTDFTRAV. When MINDIST(q, e_p) $\leq D_k$, we also check if e_p's associated MAXNEARESTDIST(q, e_p) value is less than D_k (line 48), in which case we use OPTINSERTL to insert e_p and MAXNEARESTDIST(q, e_p) into L and possibly reset D_k (line 49). As in OPTDFTRAV, this action may cause some elements (both objects and nonobjects) to be implicitly removed from L. Thus, the MAXNEARESTDIST estimate is used here to tighten the convergence of D_k to its final value.

As OPTBFTRAV proceeds, we find that the distances of the farthest object in L and the closest nonobject in *Queue* converge toward each other from ∞ and 0, respectively. OPTBFTRAV halts (line 21) once it encounters an element at the front of *Queue* whose associated distance value (i.e., MINDIST) is greater than D_k, the distance value associated with the object at the front of L (i.e., MAXDIST). This is another instance where Pruning Rules 1 and 3 are invoked, but this time it is done implicitly as their deployment is an inherent part of OPTBFTRAV by virtue of the use of MINDIST to order the processing of the nonobject elements. It is interesting to compare the use of Pruning Rules 1 and 3 in OPTBFTRAV with their use in the depth-first algorithm given by OPTDFTRAV, where they are used in conjunction with MINDIST to order the processing of the nonobject elements of the active list. However, the ordering in OPTDFTRAV is only local in the sense that it only involves the nonobject elements of the current active list, and thus once the pruning rules are found to be applicable, we only cease to process the nonobject elements of the current active list. In contrast, in OPTBFTRAV the ordering is global in the sense that it involves all of the nonobject elements, and thus once the pruning rules are found to be applicable, the algorithm terminates.

Notice that, in contrast to the depth-first algorithm OPTDFTRAV (recall Exercise 1 in Section 4.2.1), in the best-first algorithm OPTBFTRAV, the nonobject child elements e_p of nonobject element e (i.e., analogous to the elements of the active list of e in the case of the depth-first algorithm) need not be (and are not) sorted with respect to their distance (MINDIST or MAXNEARESTDIST) from q before we test for the possibility of insertion into L and enqueueing into *Queue* (lines 41–55). In particular, assuming that the active list contains T elements, there is no advantage to incurring the extra time needed to sort the child elements (i.e., an $O(T \log T)$ process) since all that the sort can accomplish is avoiding the tests (which is an $O(T)$ process). However, the nonobject child elements of e are sorted in increasing MAXDIST order with respect to the mean M of e in order to support the use of Pruning Rules 2 and 4 for nonobjects in both OPTDFTRAV and OPTBFTRAV.

Observe also that the facts that each time a nonobject element e is removed from the priority queue *Queue*, e is also removed from L if it is in L by virtue of its MAXNEAREST-DIST value's being less than D_k and that MINDIST$(q, e) \leq$ MAXNEARESTDIST(q, e) together ensure that there are no nonobject elements left in L when the best-first algorithm terminates (i.e., when the distance value associated with the first element in the priority queue *Queue* is greater than D_k), and thus the elements in L are the k nearest neighbors of q. This is of interest because, when the best-first algorithm terminates, it is quite likely that the priority queue *Queue* is not empty as we do not constantly check it for the presence of nonobject elements with associated distance values greater than D_k each time the value of D_k decreases.

In addition, we point out that in the maxnearest depth-first algorithm, the nonobject elements are inserted into L with their corresponding MAXNEARESTDIST values, whereas in any best-first algorithm (including the maxnearest best-first algorithm), the nonobject elements are inserted into the priority queue *Queue* with their corresponding MINDIST values. Moreover, note that for the best-first nearest neighbor algorithm to be correct, the MINDIST value of any nonobject element e must be less than or equal to the distance from the query object q to any object in e's descendants (recall Section 4.1.3), but in the maxnearest depth-first algorithm, neither is it the case that such a relationship holds between the MAXNEARESTDIST value of e and the objects in its descendants, nor is it required to hold for the correctness of the algorithm.

Exercises

1. (Daniel DeMenthon) Modify procedure OPTBFTRAV to process the means or pivots M_p of nonobject element e_p separately from the rest of the elements of e_p so that you can take

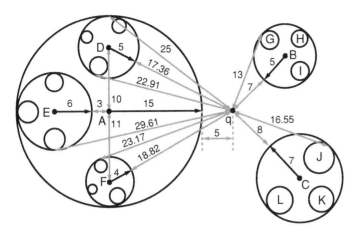

Figure 4.24
Example query object q and search hierarchy illustrating the ability of the MAXNEAREST-DISTestimate to lead to additional pruning in the depth-first algorithm and to a reduction in the size of the priority queue in the depth-first algorithm.

advantage of $r_{p,min}$ even when M_p is an element of e_p (i.e., enabling the use of Pruning Rule 3).

2. Give the analog procedure BFTRAVFARTHEST of BFTRAV for finding the k farthest neighbors in a best-first nonincremental manner using the approach outlined in Exercise 2 of Section 4.2.1.

3. Repeat Exercise 2 using the approach outlined in Exercise 3 of Section 4.2.1.

4. Give the analog procedure OPTBFTRAVFARTHEST of OPTBFTRAV for finding the k farthest neighbors in a best-first nonincremental manner using the approach outlined in Exercise 2 of Section 4.2.1. Incorporate the modified Pruning Rules 1–5 given in Exercise 17 of Section 4.2.2, as well as Pruning Rules 2 and 4 for nonobjects as in Exercise 11 of Section 4.2.5.

5. Repeat Exercise 4 using the approach outlined in Exercise 3 of Section 4.2.1.

4.2.7 Example

In this section we show with the aid of an example a situation where use of the MAX-NEARESTDIST estimate can lead to additional pruning in the depth-first algorithm and, likewise, to a reduction in the size of the priority queue in the best-first algorithm. In particular, we use query point q and the search hierarchy given in Figure 4.24 consisting of three clusters A, B, and C with MINDIST values 5, 7, and 8 and MAXNEARESTDIST values 25, 13, and 16.55, respectively. We determine the two nearest neighbors (i.e., $k = 2$). We assume that the data is embedded in a two-dimensional Euclidean space. The search hierarchy could be realized by an index such as the M-tree [389].

The depth-first algorithm as encoded by procedure OPTDFTRAV starts with D_2 and e initialized to ∞ and the nonobject element corresponding to the universe, respectively. It first generates the active list, consisting of A, B, and C, in this order due to the associated MINDIST values and the fact that none of A, B, and C have been pruned by Pruning Rules 2 and 4. Next, it examines the elements of the active list and constructs L, which contains $\{(B, 13), (A, 25)\}$ after processing the first two elements A and B. Once C has been processed, L contains $\{(B, 13), (C, 16.55)\}$ as the MAXNEARESTDIST value associated with A (i.e., 25) is greater than the MAXNEARESTDIST value associated with C (i.e., 16.55), and thus $D_2 = 16.55$. Next, the active list, which is unchanged, is processed in order of increasing MINDIST values. Therefore, cluster A, containing clusters D, E, and F, with MINDIST values 17.36, 23, and 18.82, and MAXNEARESTDIST values 22.91, 29.61, and 23.17, respectively, is processed first. Since A is not a leaf, we process its child elements in increasing MAXDIST order with respect to the mean of cluster A and generate the active list with all of them since none of them are pruned by Pruning Rule 2 (as they all have the same MAXDIST value of 15 and are all closer to the mean of cluster A than to q). The active list is sorted in increasing MINDIST order, which leads to D, F, and E. However, MINDIST(q, D) is 17.36, which is greater than $D_2 = 16.55$, and thus we do not process further any of the elements of A's active list, which means that D, E, and F have been pruned. Clearly, the two nearest neighbors of q cannot be in cluster A. However, if we had not used the MAXNEARESTDIST estimate to set the value of D_2, then we would have had to examine further elements or objects in D, E, and F. The algorithm continues by processing cluster B.

Applying the best-first algorithm as encoded by procedure OPTBFTRAV starts out with D_2 initialized to ∞ and the priority queue *Queue* initialized to the universe. At this point, it dequeues the universe from *Queue* and examines all of its constituent clusters in increasing MAXDIST order with respect to the mean of the universe (which is an arbitrary value, say 0, without loss of generality) as Pruning Rules 2 and 4 do not yield any pruning due to D_2's having an initial value of ∞. Assume, without loss of generality, that the initial order is A, B, and C. During this process, OPTBFTRAV constructs L, which contains $\{(B, 13), (A, 25)\}$ after processing the first two elements A and B, while entering them into *Queue* with their corresponding MINDIST values. Once C has been processed, L contains $\{(B, 13), (C, 16.55)\}$ as the MAXNEARESTDIST value associated with A (i.e., 25) is greater than the MAXNEARESTDIST value associated with C (i.e., 16.55), and thus $D_2 = 16.55$, while *Queue* contains A, B, and C in this order. Next, the closest element of *Queue* to q, which is A, is removed from *Queue*, but there is no need to adjust D_2 as the MAXNEARESTDIST value associated with A (i.e., 25) is greater than that of D_2, which is 16.55. Since A is not a leaf, we process its child elements in increasing MAXDIST order with respect to the mean of cluster A. As they all have the same MAXDIST value of 15, which means that none of them are pruned by Pruning Rule 2 (as they are all closer to the mean of cluster A than to q), we process them in arbitrary order, say D, E, and F, and check if their corresponding MINDIST values are greater than D_2. The fact that they are all greater than D_2 means that they could never contain the two nearest neighbors of q, and thus they are not enqueued in *Queue*. However, if we had not used the MAXNEARESTDIST estimate, then we would have had to enqueue D, E, and F as $D_2 = \infty$ initially, even though we would never dequeue them and hence never further examine elements or objects in them. Thus, the maximum possible size of the priority queue has been decreased by the use of the MAXNEARESTDIST estimate. The algorithm continues by processing cluster B, which is the closest element in *Queue* to q.

From this example, we see that use of the MAXNEARESTDIST estimate has enabled us to satisfy our goal of enhancing the performance of both the depth-first and best-first k-nearest neighbor algorithms. In particular, in the case of the depth-first algorithm, we have pruned elements from further processing, and in the case of the best-first algorithm, we have reduced the maximum possible size of the priority queue.

4.2.8 Comparison

In Sections 4.2.5 and 4.2.6, we have shown how to incorporate an estimate of the maximum possible distance at which a nearest neighbor is guaranteed to be found (termed MAXNEARESTDIST) to enhance the performance of both a depth-first branch and bound and a best-first k-nearest neighbor finding algorithm by virtue of yielding tighter initial estimates of D_k. Thus, we can start pruning elements of the search hierarchy (both objects and nonobjects) without having to wait until we have encountered the first k objects as this is the first time that D_k is reset from its initial value of ∞ in the traditional algorithms.

In the case of the depth-first algorithm, the enhancement lies in not having to process some of the nonobject elements of the search hierarchy, thereby making the algorithm faster with no increase in the storage requirements. On the other hand, in the case of the best-first algorithm, the enhancement lies in reducing the size of the priority queue *Queue* as the tighter initial estimates of D_k result in the insertion of fewer nonobject elements into *Queue*. The motivation for this is the observation that the nonobject elements that have not been inserted into *Queue* never would have been expanded anyway since their MINDIST values are greater than D_k, and thus there cannot be any reduction in execution time, which means that space in *Queue* should not be wasted to store them. An alternative rationale for this is to recall that, in the best-first algorithm, because the nonobject elements are examined in increasing order of D_k and because every nonobject element with MINDIST less than D_k must be examined no matter how fast the value of D_k is reduced, the algorithm will never examine any extra nonobject elements. Thus, use of an estimate such as MAXNEARESTDIST cannot have the same effect on a best-first algorithm as it can on a depth-first algorithm.

In general, it is well-known that depth-first k-nearest neighbor algorithms may achieve less pruning of the search space and therefore perform worse, as measured by the number of visited search hierarchy elements, than algorithms that apply best-first search on the same search hierarchy. The problem is that a depth-first algorithm must make local decisions about the next element to be visited, choosing among the children of a single element (the elements in the active list A of e that have not yet been visited) based on the current value of D_k. In contrast, a best-first algorithm makes global decisions about the next element to be visited. In particular, the global set of unvisited elements sorted by their distance from the query object that is maintained by the best-first algorithm essentially corresponds to the union of the unvisited portions of the active lists A in the depth-first algorithm for all elements e on the path from the root to the element that is currently being visited. Thus, while the best-first algorithm visits an element e only if $d(q,e) \leq d(q,o_k)$, where o_k is the kth-nearest neighbor 5 (since the elements are visited in order of distance), the depth-first algorithm may visit an element e_p with $d(q,e_p) > d(q,o_k)$, since D_k may be much larger than $d(q,o_k)$ for much of the duration of the search, especially early on.

Notice that these observations are also true for variants of the depth-first algorithms that attempt to improve performance by introducing aggressive pruning (effectively by reducing D_k), such as those described for the vp-tree by Chiueh [376].[18] Although such strategies can narrow the performance gap of a depth-first algorithm vis-à-vis a best-first algorithm, they cannot visit fewer elements in the search hierarchy than a best-first algorithm without taking the risk of missing some of the k nearest neighbors of q. In fact, when such an aggressive algorithm detects that too much pruning has taken place (which may well be a common occurrence), the search hierarchy must be traversed again, this time with less aggressive pruning. Hence, the average performance gain of aggressive pruning may be modest.

The manner in which we incorporated the MAXNEARESTDIST estimate in the maxnearest depth-first k-nearest neighbor algorithm (i.e., OPTDFTRAV) enables us to overcome the lower pruning power of the depth-first algorithm vis-à-vis the best-first algorithm as it enables the use of its result at a deeper level than the one at which it is calculated. In particular, the use of L to store the MAXNEARESTDIST values of some active nonobject elements means that a MAXNEARESTDIST value of an unexplored nonobject at depth i can be used to help in pruning objects and nonobjects at depth $j > i$. This is a significant improvement over the depth-first algorithm DFTRAV, where the MAXNEARESTDIST value of a nonobject element at depth i could only be used to tighten the distance to the nearest neighbor (i.e., for $k = 1$) and to prune nonobject elements at larger MINDIST values at the same depth i. Thus, we see that the manner

---

[18] Chiueh [376] suggested using an estimate of the upper bound on the distance to the nearest neighbor in each subtree to bound the search in that subtree, thus yielding an algorithm that performs a "bounded" nearest neighbor search of each subtree (in the reported experiments, a simpler strategy was employed that made use of an estimate of the maximum upper bound over all nodes of the vp-tree). Of course, if the upper bound estimate is too low, it may be necessary to apply the algorithm with a higher estimate.

in which MAXNEARESTDIST is used in OPTDFTRAV can be viewed as providing a middle ground between a pure depth-first and a best-first k-nearest neighbor algorithm by enabling more nonobject elements to be used in tightening the value of D_k.

On the other hand, the drawback of any best-first algorithm (including ours with the MAXNEARESTDIST estimate) is the need for the priority queue *Queue*, which, in the worst case, may be as large as the entire dataset. In contrast, as we pointed out, any implementation of the depth-first algorithm (including ours with the MAXNEAREST-DIST estimate) only requires storage for L (which is k) and the recursive calls of the algorithm corresponding to the depth of the search hierarchy, which is $O(\log N)$ for a dataset of size N. Note, however, that for k-nearest neighbor computation, when data is stored on disk, which is often the case in practical applications, the priority queue *Queue* is relatively small because it only contains pairs of disk page addresses and distances.

Of course, in the case of a ranking operation (i.e., when we must report the neighbors in an incremental manner without knowledge of the number of neighbors that will ultimately be required), this size drawback of best-first algorithms is irrelevant as no implementations of the depth-first algorithm (including one that makes use of OPTDFTRAV) can be used since they all prune some of the elements of the search hierarchy from further consideration. In other words, in order to be able to perform ranking, any implementation of the depth-first algorithm (including one that makes use of OPTDFTRAV) would need to retain these elements for possible further processing.

The manner in which we incorporate the MAXNEARESTDIST estimate in the max-nearest best-first k-nearest neighbor algorithm (i.e., OPTBFTRAV) enables us to reduce some of the storage requirements of the algorithm, thereby lessening the storage penalty incurred by using the best-first algorithm vis-à-vis the depth-first algorithm. Thus, we see that use of the MAXNEARESTDIST estimate enhances the performance of both the depth-first and best-first algorithms by addressing their shortcomings—that is, by reducing the execution time of the former and reducing the storage requirements of the latter, at no cost in extra execution time for the latter or extra storage requirements for the former.

It is important to note that the above comparison of the effects of the use of the MAX-NEARESTDIST estimate in the depth-first and best-first k-nearest neighbor algorithms does not address the relative performance of the two algorithms, which is a more general issue and beyond the scope of this discussion. Nevertheless, experiments conducted by Hjaltason and Samet [848] showed that for an R-tree spatial index, a best-first k-nearest neighbor algorithm implemented using procedure INCNEAREST performed better in terms of execution time than a depth-first algorithm implemented using the method of Roussopoulos et al. [1586]. In fact, Berchtold, Böhm, Keim, and Kriegel [186] have proved that the best-first algorithm is I/O optimal in terms of the number of disk page accesses when the query object and the data objects are points and $k = 1$. In particular, they show that the number of disk accesses is generally smaller than that needed by the depth-first algorithm (see Exercise 1). The I/O optimality of the general incremental algorithm is not surprising given our prior demonstration in Section 4.1.3 that it is r-optimal.

The depth-first k-nearest neighbor algorithm that we have presented, as embodied by procedure OPTDFTRAV, is very different from that of previous work. It differs considerably from Roussopoulos et al.'s [1586] implementation of the depth-first algorithm, which, like that of Larsen and Kanal [1103], only incorporates the MAXNEARESTDIST estimate for $k = 1$ instead of for arbitrary values of k. Moreover, besides being formulated in terms of a more general cluster element than a hyperrectangle minimum bounding object, OPTDFTRAV also applies pruning to the objects and nonobjects in each of the leaf and nonleaf elements, respectively, of the search structure (i.e., Pruning Rules 2 and 4), which is not done in the implementation of Roussopoulos et al. [1586]. Furthermore, we observe that OPTDFTRAV is very different from the original algorithm of Fukunaga and Narendra [666], as well as from the enhancements of Kamgar-Parsi and Kanal [986], neither of which make use of the MAXNEARESTDIST estimate.

The best-first k-nearest neighbor algorithm that we have presented as embodied by procedure OPTBFTRAV is different from a previous adaptation of INCNEAREST to the M-tree by Ciaccia et al. [389] (see Section 4.5.4.2) in the following respects. First, it incorporates the MAXNEARESTDIST estimate correctly for $k > 1$. Second, it is more general in that it is applicable to more search hierarchies, instead of being limited to the M-tree. Third, it contains a more efficient implementation of Pruning Rules 2 and 4 for both objects and nonobjects by sorting them with respect to the mean in each cluster. Finally, it takes advantage of the priority queue of nonobjects that remain to be visited by making the nonobject element with the smallest MINDIST value immediately accessible and by not having to remove explicitly previously enqueued nonobject elements with MINDIST values greater than D_k, as done by Ciaccia et al. [389].

Exercise

1. Give an example of a situation for point data where use of the general incremental algorithm to find the k nearest neighbors performs fewer page accesses than using an implementation of the depth-first algorithm that makes use of a MINDIST ordering (e.g., the one of Roussopoulos et al. [1586]). In order to simplify your task, use a minimum bounding hyperrectangle search hierarchy, and assume that each page is a minimum bounding hyperrectangle.

4.3 Approximate Nearest Neighbor Finding

In many applications, obtaining exact results is not critical. Therefore, users are willing to trade accuracy for improved performance. There are two principal methods of proceeding. The first method, and the one discussed in this section, is based on the use of an approximation error tolerance ε. In particular, the approximation criterion is that the distance between the query object q and the resulting candidate nearest neighbor o' is within a factor of $1 + \varepsilon$ of the distance to the actual nearest neighbor o—that is, $d(q, o') \leq (1 + \varepsilon) \cdot d(q, o)$ (see Exercise 1). This is the basis of the bulk of the work on approximate nearest neighbor search (e.g., [100]).

An alternative method is one where the approximation criterion is the result of treating the nearest neighbor relation as an "equivalence" relation, which is generally not true because the nearest neighbor relation is not necessarily symmetric or transitive and because of the absence of equivalence classes. This type of an approximation is the basis of the Spatial Approximation Sample Hierarchy (SASH) approximate search strategy [883, 884], which has been successfully deployed in applications involving very high dimensions, as well as those where only a similarity/dissimilarity measure is available that need not be a distance metric. This is discussed in more detail in Section 4.5.8.

Both the depth-first and best-first k-nearest neighbor algorithms can be adapted to return the approximate nearest neighbors using the first method, although it is more common to adapt the best-first algorithms, and this is the focus of this section (but see Exercises 3–5). The reason is that the motivation behind loosening the criterion as to what constitutes a nearest neighbor is to speed up the process, which is more in the spirit of the best-first algorithms that are inherently designed to cease processing as soon as the desired number of neighbors is found rather than possibly exploring the entire search hierarchy, as is the case for some of the depth-first algorithms. Regardless of whether the approximate k-nearest neighbor algorithm is an adaptation of the best-first or depth-first k-nearest neighbor algorithm, it is important to observe that, as a result, some of q's exact k nearest neighbors that are within a factor of $1 + \varepsilon$ of the distance D_k of q's approximate kth-nearest neighbor (including the exact kth-nearest neighbor o_k) may be missed (i.e., those neighbors o where $D_k/(1 + \varepsilon) \leq d(q, o) < D_k$).

A number of approximate k-nearest neighbor algorithms make use of a priority queue *Queue* to support a "best-first" traversal. Most of these algorithms (e.g., [100, 387, 1286])

From a practical point of view, in the incremental algorithm, enqueueing a nonobject element e_t with a larger distance value (i.e., by a factor of $1 + \varepsilon$ in this case) means that we delay its processing, thereby allowing objects to be reported "before their time." In particular, once e_t is finally processed, all of the objects o that we have reported satisfy $d(q, o) \leq (1 + \varepsilon) \cdot d_t(q, e_t)$ (which is greater than $d_t(q, e_t)$ if $\varepsilon > 0$). Therefore, it could be the case that there exists an object c in e_t with a distance $d(q, c) \leq d(q, o)$, yet o is reported before c. It should be clear that in this case the algorithm does not necessarily report the resulting objects in strictly increasing order of their distance from q. With this modification, for the object o'_k returned as the kth-nearest neighbor by the algorithm and the actual kth-nearest neighbor o_k, we have $d(q, o'_k) \leq (1 + \varepsilon) \cdot d(q, o_k)$.

The same technique of expanding all distances by a factor of $1 + \varepsilon$ can also be applied to the nonincremental best-first k-nearest neighbor algorithm given by procedure OPTBFTRAV to yield a best-first approximate k-nearest neighbor algorithm ANNOPTBFTRAV. In this case, we must also properly accommodate the MAX-NEARESTDIST estimate. The solution is to expand the distances (i.e., estimates and hence both MINDIST and MAXNEARESTDIST) of nonobject elements from q by $1 + \varepsilon$. These expanded distances are used in all comparisons with D_k, and the algorithm is simplified by also associating these expanded distances with the nonobjects in both L and $Queue$. In particular, the test for the applicability of Pruning Rules 1 and 3 becomes MINDIST$(q, e_p) \cdot (1 + \varepsilon) > D_k$ (line 46), the test for the applicability of Pruning Rules 2 and 4 for nonobjects becomes MAXDIST$(M, e_p) \geq d(q, M) - D_k/(1 + \varepsilon)$ (line 41) and MINDIST$(M, e_p) \leq d(q, M_p) + D_k/(1 + \varepsilon)$ (line 44), and the test for the insertion of nonobjects (i.e., Pruning Rule 5) in L by OPTINSERTL becomes MAXNEARESTDIST$(q, e_p) \cdot (1 + \varepsilon) < D_k$ (line 48). The distances associated with the nonobjects e_p that are inserted in $Queue$ and L become MINDIST$(q, e_p) \cdot (1 + \varepsilon)$ (line 51) and MAXNEARESTDIST$(q, e_p) \cdot (1 + \varepsilon)$ (line 49), respectively. The conditions involving MAXNEARESTDIST to determine whether it is necessary to remove a nonobject from L when processing its immediate descendants become MAXNEARESTDIST$(q, e) \cdot (1 + \varepsilon) < D_k$ (line 23) and MAXNEARESTDIST$(q, e) \cdot (1 + \varepsilon) = D_k$ (line 24). Observe that the depth-first k-nearest neighbor algorithm as given by procedures DFTRAV, FNDFTRAV, and OPTDFTRAV can be modified in the same way as OPTBFTRAV to yield depth-first approximate k-nearest neighbor algorithms ANNDFTRAV (see Exercise 3), ANNFNDFTRAV (see Exercise 4), and ANNOPTDFTRAV (see Exercise 5), respectively.

It is important to note that we must expand the values of both the MINDIST and MAXNEARESTDIST estimates rather than just that of the MINDIST estimate as otherwise we could have the situation that the ANNOPTBFTRAV algorithm terminates with some nonobjects in L where for some of these nonobjects, say b, MINDIST$(q, b) \leq$ MAXNEARESTDIST$(q, b) < D_k <$ MINDIST$(q, b) \cdot (1 + \varepsilon)$. In this case, the fact that MINDIST$(q, b) \cdot (1 + \varepsilon) > D_k$ results in b being pruned, and the fact that MAXNEAREST-DIST$(q, b) < D_k$ means that b is still in L. Thus, if the algorithm terminates at this point in the sense that MINDIST$(q, e) \cdot (1 + \varepsilon) > D_k$ for all remaining nonobjects e in $Queue$, then L may still contain some nonobjects. This means that the search hierarchy elements corresponding to each of these nonobjects, say b, will have to be searched to find the object o_b for which $d(q, o_b) \leq$ MAXNEARESTDIST$(q, b) < D_k$, which may be a time-consuming process, thereby defeating the purpose of finding the k approximate nearest neighbors instead of the exact k nearest neighbors. On the other hand, when the values of both the MINDIST and MAXNEARESTDIST estimates are expanded by $1 + \varepsilon$, then we know by virtue of MINDIST$(q, b) \leq$ MAXNEARESTDIST(q, b) that MINDIST$(q, b) \cdot (1 + \varepsilon) \leq$ MAXNEARESTDIST$(q, b) \cdot (1 + \varepsilon)$. Thus, the fact that MINDIST$(q, b) \cdot (1 + \varepsilon) > D_k$ means that MAXNEARESTDIST$(q, b) \cdot (1 + \varepsilon) > D_k$, and therefore b is not in L. In other words, L contains the k approximate nearest neighbors of q (which are objects).

As we pointed out, the key idea behind all of the methods that we have described is to delay the processing of nonobject elements (in the case of the incremental nearest neighbor algorithm and the best-first k-nearest neighbor algorithm) or avoid (in the case of the depth-first k-nearest neighbor algorithm) the processing of nonobject elements that are within a factor of $1 + \varepsilon$ of the distance of the actual kth-nearest neighbor of q. These methods can be viewed as enhancing Pruning Rules 1 and 3, as well as the nonobject variants of Pruning Rules 2 and 4, to deal with approximate nearest neighbors. The same principle could also be applied with similar results to objects that are within a factor of $1 + \varepsilon$ of the distance of the actual kth-nearest neighbor of q (see Exercises 3, 7, and 8). Moreover, we could also use this principle for pruning objects by incorporating it into the tests for the applicability of the object variants of Pruning Rules 2 and 4 (see Exercise 9).

Other methods for performing approximate nearest neighbor search can also be integrated into the general incremental nearest neighbor algorithm by similarly modifying the distances used in the priority queue. For example, the method of Chen, Bouman, and Dalton [346] is applicable to spatial and metric indexing methods that make use of spherical node regions (e.g., the SS-tree [1991] and the M-tree [389]). In particular, if b is a node in the structure having a reference object p and an associated radius of r, then for every object o stored in the subtree rooted at b, we have $d(p,o) \leq r$. Observe that if q is the query object, $d(p,q) - r$ is a lower bound on the distance $d(q,o)$ for o in the subtree rooted at b, and that this lower bound can be considered the distance between q and b when performing queries (see also the discussion of the vp-tree and Exercise 6 in Section 4.5.2.1.2).[19]

Like Arya et al. [100], Chen et al. [346] propose that the processing of b in best-first nearest neighbor algorithms (such as our incremental algorithm) be delayed by "inflating" the distance value $d(q,b)$, thus delaying or avoiding the processing of b. However, in the case of Chen et al., the distance is inflated by shrinking the radius of b by a factor of λ $(0 < \lambda \leq 1)$, resulting in the modified distance function $d'(q,b) = d(p,q) - \lambda \cdot r$. Notice that the extent to which the processing of b (and hence the objects in b) will be delayed depends on the radius of b, and thus nodes at the same distance will be processed in increasing order of their radii. In fact, it is not inconceivable that a small node b_s will be processed before a larger node b_l, even though b_l is closer to q than b_s. This is in contrast to the method of Arya et al. [100], where nodes are always processed in the order of their distance from q, even after their distances from q have been expanded. Observe that the approximation error is unbounded when using the method of Chen et al. (see Exercise 12).

From an intuitive standpoint, the two methods can be compared by noting that they differ in how they evaluate the likelihood that a particular bounding region will contain the nearest neighbor. In particular, the method of Chen et al. deems larger nodes as less likely to contain the nearest neighbor than smaller nodes at the same distance. On the other hand, the method of Arya et al. deems nodes that are farther away as less likely to contain the nearest neighbor than closer nodes, regardless of their size.

In some applications, even the willingness to settle for an approximate answer rather than an exact answer does not yield a solution procedure that is sufficiently fast. In particular, as we saw earlier, in high dimensions the effects of the curse of dimensionality come into play (i.e., for some data and query distributions, such as the uniform distribution, the difference between the distance to the nearest and the farthest neighbor approaches zero as the dimensionality increases), so that the approximate nearest neighbor algorithm (as does the exact nearest neighbor algorithm) spends most of the time deciding whether a particular candidate is good enough in comparison to the time it spends to locate it.

This consideration has led to a proposal to relax slightly the approximate nearest neighbor condition by stipulating a maximum probability δ for tolerating failure, thereby

---

[19] Note that $d(p,q) - r$ is a lower bound on $d(q,o)$ regardless of whether q is inside or outside b. Nevertheless, when q is inside b, then 0 is a tighter lower bound since $d(p,q) - r$ is then negative whereas distances are always nonnegative.

enabling the decision process to halt sooner at the risk δ of being wrong. This is the basis of the *probably approximately correct* (PAC) nearest neighbor method of Ciaccia and Patella [387]. Formally, an object o' is considered a PAC nearest neighbor of q if the probability that $d(q, o') \leq (1 + \varepsilon) \cdot d(q, o)$, where o is the actual nearest neighbor, is at least $1 - \delta$. In other words, given values of ε and δ, $1 - \delta$ is the minimum probability that o' is the $(1 + \varepsilon)$-approximate nearest neighbor of q. Equivalently, the probability that the effective error, defined as $d(q, o')/d(q, o) - 1$, is greater than ε is no more than δ. Ciaccia and Patella [387] show that, given some information about the distances between q and the data objects, we can derive an upper bound s on the distance between q and a PAC nearest neighbor o'. The distance bound s is then used during the actual nearest neighbor search as a preestablished halting condition—that is, the search can be halted once an object o' with $d(q, o') \leq s$ is located.

It is interesting to observe that using the PAC nearest neighbor method is analogous to executing a variant of a range query, where the range is defined by the distance bound s, which halts on the first object in the range. If no object is in the range, then the nature of the nearest neighbor algorithm that is used is important. In particular, if the objects are not indexed, then a sequential scan will end up examining all of the objects. In this case, it will either return no object or the closest one if it keeps track of the closest object found so far, which is the natural course of action. In contrast, if the objects are indexed, then a "best-first" nearest neighbor algorithm, regardless of whether it is incremental as ours is or nonincremental such as the one of Arya et al. [100] described above, will halt once it encounters the object at the minimum distance from the query object, subject to the approximation error tolerance ε. Thus, in this case, the range simply provides an additional stopping condition that is independent of the distance from the query point to the object that is currently the closest, which changes as the algorithm is executed.

The main difficulty in computing the PAC nearest neighbor lies in determining a relationship between δ and the distance bound s. Ciaccia and Patella assume that the relative distance distribution $F_q(x)$ of the query object q from an arbitrary object p is known—that is, $F_q(x) = Prob\{d(q, p) \leq x\}$. In other words, $F_q(x)$ is the probability that an object p is within distance x of q, which means that $1 - F_q(x)$ is the probability that p does not lie within distance x of q. Therefore, the probability that none of the N objects lies within distance x of q is $(1 - F_q(x))^N$, and thus the probability that at least one of the objects lies within distance x of q is $1 - (1 - F_q(x))^N$. This results in $G_q(x) = Prob\{d(q, NN(q)) \leq x\} = 1 - (1 - F_q(x))^N$ being the probability distribution for the distance to the nearest neighbor of q denoted by $NN(q)$. At this point, we define r as the distance bound so that $G_q(r) = \delta$. If G_q is invertible, then $r = G_q^{-1}(\delta)$ (see Exercises 14 and 15).

From the above, we have that the maximum probability that the nearest neighbor of q is closer than r is δ, and thus an algorithm that makes use of r as a halting condition can be said to be *probably correct* (PC), with r being a probably correct distance bound. However, we are interested in a probably approximately correct (PAC) distance bound. We now show that $s = (1 + \varepsilon) \cdot r$ is such a bound. Assume that $d(q, o') \leq s$ for some object o', and let o be the actual nearest neighbor of q. We now must show that $Prob\{d(q, o') \leq (1 + \varepsilon) \cdot d(q, o)\} \geq 1 - \delta$. In other words, we need to show that $1 - \delta$ is the minimum probability that o' is the $(1 + \varepsilon)$-approximate nearest neighbor of q. Rearranging terms, this goal can be rewritten as trying to show that $1 - Prob\{d(q, o') \leq (1 + \varepsilon) \cdot d(q, o)\} \leq \delta$. Appealing to the fact that $Prob\{X\} = 1 - Prob\{not(X)\}$, we have that $1 - Prob\{d(q, o') \leq (1 + \varepsilon) \cdot d(q, o)\} = Prob\{d(q, o') > (1 + \varepsilon) \cdot d(q, o)\}$. The right-hand side can be rewritten as $Prob\{d(q, o) < d(q, o')/(1 + \varepsilon)\}$, which equals $Prob\{d(q, o) \leq d(q, o')/(1 + \varepsilon)\}$ since the probability of real-valued variables being equal is zero (i.e., $Prob\{d(q, o) = d(q, o')/(1 + \varepsilon)\} = 0$). However, $Prob\{d(q, o) \leq d(q, o')/(1 + \varepsilon)\} = G_q(d(q, o')/(1 + \varepsilon))$, which is less than or equal to $G_q(r) = \delta$, and thus $s = (1 + \varepsilon) \cdot r$ can be used as the distance bound for the PAC nearest neighbor method. Note that $G_q(d(q, o')/(1 + \varepsilon)) \leq G_q(r)$ is a direct result of $d(q, o')/(1 + \varepsilon)) \leq r$ and the fact that G_q is a nondecreasing function.

As we saw above, $F_q(x)$ is the probability distribution of the distance from q to a random point, and $G_q(x)$ is the probability distribution of the distance from q to its closest point. Observe that as the number of points N goes to ∞, $G_q(x)$ approaches the constant function 1, while $F_q(x)$ is unchanged. On the other hand, as the dimension d goes to ∞, both $F_q(x)$ and $G_q(x)$ converge to the same value by virtue of the curse of dimensionality (i.e., the distance from the query point to a random point has the same distribution as the distance from the query point to the nearest point), assuming a uniform data and query distribution.

At this point, let us briefly review the PAC method. Earlier, we pointed out that use of the PAC method is similar to executing a range query on the basis of the distance bound that has been obtained. The effect of increasing ε is to increase the range. Thus, a probably correct nearest neighbor algorithm (i.e., with $\varepsilon = 0$) has the minimum range. Note that in the case of a probably correct nearest neighbor algorithm, δ is the maximum probability that the object o being reported as the nearest neighbor of query object q is wrong. In contrast, for a PAC nearest neighbor, δ is the maximum probability that the distance from q to o is more than a factor of $1 + \varepsilon$ of the distance to the real nearest neighbor. Note that neither ε nor δ indicates the effective error (i.e., the extent to which o is not the nearest neighbor), which has usually been found to be much smaller than ε. It is also important to observe that, in reality, it is difficult to make use of the PAC nearest neighbor algorithm as it is rare to have explicit knowledge of the distribution $F_q(x)$ and $G_q(x)$. This difficulty may be overcome by sampling the dataset [387]. For an alternative application of the PAC concept, see the discussion in Section 4.4.4 of the os-tree and the use of training sets to approximate a Voronoi diagram in high dimensions to find PAC nearest neighbors [1226, 1229].

There are a number of ways of adapting these methods for approximate farthest neighbor search. In this case, the approximation criterion is that the distance between the query object q and the resulting candidate farthest neighbor o' is within a factor of $1 + \varepsilon$ of the distance to the actual farthest neighbor o—that is, $d(q,o') \geq d(q,o)/(1+\varepsilon)$ (notice the slight difference from the definition of the approximate nearest neighbor). For example, the incremental farthest neighbor algorithm (see Exercise 6 in Section 4.1.5) can be modified so that a nonobject element $e_{t'}$ is always enqueued after shrinking its distance value by a factor of $(1+\varepsilon)$ (in contrast to expanding it by this value, as in the approximate variant of the incremental nearest neighbor algorithm). Again, as in the case of approximate nearest neighbor finding, this has the effect of delaying its processing, thereby allowing objects to be reported "before their time." In particular, for the approximate kth-farthest neighbor, we have that the distance between the query object q and the resulting candidate kth-farthest neighbor o'_k is within a factor of $1 + \varepsilon$ of the distance to the actual kth-farthest neighbor o_k—that is, $d(q,o'_k) \geq d(q,o_k)/(1+\varepsilon)$. Note that this method works even when we use the incremental nearest neighbor algorithm with distance $-\hat{d}_t(q,e_t)$ instead of $d_t(q,e_t)$ for any element e_t, as discussed in Section 4.1.5 (see Exercises 17–21).

The drawback of using a relative error bound, such as the one described above, for finding approximate farthest neighbors is that all of the points in S would tend to be the approximate farthest neighbor if all of the points in S were relatively close to each other, while the query object is far from them. Such a situation is common for high-dimensional point data. This has led Duncan, Goodrich, and Kobourov [517] to suggest an alternative criterion that stipulates that o' is an approximate farthest neighbor of q if $d(q,o') \geq d(q,o) - \varepsilon D$, where o is the actual farthest neighbor and D is the *diameter* of the point set S (i.e., the distance between the two farthest points in S). As we can see, this criterion is in terms of an *absolute error bound* based on D and, in the farthest neighbor case, can give a tighter bound than a *relative error bound* based on $d(q,o)$. This criterion can also be incorporated into the incremental nearest neighbor algorithm in a straightforward manner (see Exercise 23).

Exercises

1. An alternative definition of approximate nearest neighbor search is that the distance between the query object q and the resulting candidate nearest neighbor o' is within a factor of $1/(1-\varepsilon)$ of the distance to the actual nearest neighbor o—that is, $d(q,o') \le d(q,o)/(1-\varepsilon)$. What is the drawback of using such a definition?

2. In the text, we claim that procedures BFTRAV and ANNBFTRAV are equivalent when $\varepsilon = 0$. However, when we examine them more closely, we see that, whereas BFTRAV has line 31, ANNBFTRAV makes use of lines 31–32 to achieve this task. Explain the significance of this difference.

3. How would you adapt the basic depth-first k-nearest neighbor algorithm given by procedure DFTRAV in Section 4.2.1 to return the k approximate nearest neighbors, thereby yielding procedure ANNDFTRAV?

4. How would you modify procedure FNDFTRAV to return the k approximate nearest neighbors, thereby yielding procedure ANNFNDFTRAV?

5. How would you modify procedure OPTDFTRAV to return the k approximate nearest neighbors, thereby yielding procedure ANNOPTDFTRAV? Make sure to pay attention to the proper usage of MAXNEARESTDIST.

6. Suppose that Pruning Rule 5 is implemented in procedure OPTBFTRAV using the MAXDIST estimate instead of the MAXNEARESTDIST estimate. Suppose further that, in the approximate k nearest neighbor adaptation of OPTBFTRAV given by ANNOPTBFTRAV, only the value of the MINDIST estimate is expanded by $1 + \varepsilon$ (i.e., the value of the MAXDIST estimate is not expanded). How would you resolve the situation where ANNOPTBFTRAV terminates with some nonobjects in L?

7. The key idea behind the approximate nearest neighbor algorithms is to shrink the distances D_1 (D_k) from q to the closest (kth-nearest) object by a factor of $1 + \varepsilon$ and to ignore a nonobject element e_p and the objects it contains if the minimum distance from q to an object in e_p (i.e., MINDIST(q,e_p)) is greater than this shrunken distance. An alternative formulation of this idea is to expand the minimum distance MINDIST(q,e_p) from q to an object in e_p and to ignore e_p and its objects if the expanded distance is greater than D_1 (D_k). Can you also apply this idea at the object level in procedure ANNBFTRAV in the sense that an object o is ignored if the distance from q to o is greater than the shrunken distance D_1 (D_k) from q to the closest (kth-nearest) object (line 25)? Alternatively, can we ignore o in ANNBFTRAV if the expanded distance from q to o is greater than the distance D_1 (D_k) from q to the closest (kth-nearest) object (line 25)? Discuss the effect of adding these tests on the results of ANNBFTRAV.

8. Suppose that you apply the modification outlined in Exercise 7 to objects as well as nonobjects in variants of the approximate k-nearest neighbor algorithm that make use of the MAX-NEARESTDIST estimate, such as the adaptations of FNDFTRAV (line 19), OPTDFTRAV (line 17), and OPTBFTRAV (line 34) given by ANNFNDFTRAV (see Exercise 4), ANNOPTDFTRAV (see Exercise 5), and ANNOPTBFTRAV (see the text), respectively. From an initial glance, it would appear that this modification could cause the algorithm to terminate with some nonobjects in L—that is, not all of the elements in L are objects. For FNDFTRAV, k must be 1 for such a termination to arise. On the other hand, for OPTDFTRAV and OPTBFTRAV, it could arise when $k \ne 1$, and initially some of the k entries in L correspond to nonobjects. In particular, if we know that $d(q,o) > D_k/(1+\varepsilon)$ for all subsequently processed objects o, then the algorithms could terminate with L containing some nonobjects. This would mean that each of the individual nonobject elements b of L would have to be searched to find the object o_b for which $d(q,o_b) \le$ MAXNEARESTDIST$(q,b) < D_k$, which may be a time-consuming process, thereby defeating the purpose of finding the k approximate nearest neighbors instead of the exact k nearest neighbors. Prove or disprove that these modifications can cause these algorithms to terminate with some nonobjects in L—that is, not every element in L is an object.

9. How would you adapt Pruning Rules 2 and 4 (see Section 4.2.2) so that they can be used in the different approximate k-nearest neighbor algorithms to prune some objects from further consideration? Recall that the approximate k-nearest neighbor algorithms that we presented already incorporate Pruning Rules 1–4 to prune a nonobject and the objects it contains.

10. Suppose that you modify the incremental nearest neighbor algorithm INCNEAREST by expanding the key values of both the object and nonobject elements in the priority queue by a factor of $1 + \varepsilon$ instead of just expanding the key values of the nonobject elements as in ANNINCNEAREST. What is the resulting effect?

11. Suppose that you modify the incremental nearest neighbor algorithm INCNEAREST by expanding the key values of just the object elements in the priority queue by a factor of $1 + \varepsilon$ while leaving the key values for the nonobject elements unchanged. What is the resulting effect?

12. Show that the maximum approximation error ε when using the method of Chen et al. [346], so that the processing of a spherical minimum bounding box b centered at p is delayed by shrinking its radius r by λ ($0 < \lambda \leq 1$), is unbounded.

13. As discussed in the text, Chen et al. [346] propose that the processing of a block (i.e., nonobject element) b be delayed by shrinking b's radius by a factor of λ ($0 < \lambda \leq 1$) prior to evaluating its distance from q, which effectively increases the distance value for b (i.e., $d(q,b)$) used by the algorithm. We have given a number of possible rationales for this strategy. Can you give a theoretical justification for these rationales?

14. Consider a set of points uniformly distributed over the d-dimensional unit hypercube. Using the L_∞ distance metric, derive $F_q(x)$, $G_q(x)$, and $\delta = G_q^{-1}(x)$ to be used in the PAC nearest neighbor algorithm for a query point that coincides with the center of the hypercube and also for a query point that coincides with one of the 2^d corners.

15. Continuing Exercise 14 involving the PAC nearest neighbor algorithm, let $\delta = 0.01$, $N = 1,000,000$, and $d = 50$, and solve for x when the query point is in the center of the hypercube.

16. How would you extend the PAC nearest neighbor algorithm to finding the k nearest neighbors so that the exact search would retrieve the k best matches for the query object. This will require an estimate of the distance to the kth-nearest neighbor. Exercises 17–21 deal with adapting the specified procedures to obtain the k approximate farthest neighbors using the approach outlined in Exercise 3 of Section 4.2.1. All of the procedures use the relative error bound for finding the approximate kth-farthest neighbor. In other words, the distance between the query object q and the resulting candidate kth-farthest neighbor o_k' is within a factor of $1 + \varepsilon$ of the distance to the actual kth-farthest neighbor o_k—that is, $d(q,o_k') \geq d(q,o_k)/(1+\varepsilon)$. Note that in these exercises, this approximation criterion becomes $d(q,o_k') \leq d(q,o_k)/(1+\varepsilon)$ when all distances are replaced by their negation as in the approach in Exercise 3 of Section 4.2.1.

17. Adapt procedure ANNBFTRAV to obtain the k approximate farthest neighbors, thereby yielding procedure ANNBFTRAVFARTHEST.

18. Adapt procedure ANNINCNEAREST to obtain the approximate farthest neighbors in an incremental manner, thereby yielding procedure ANNINCFARTHEST.

19. Adapt procedure ANNOPTBFTRAV to obtain the k approximate farthest neighbors in a nonincremental best-first manner, thereby yielding procedure ANNOPTBFTRAVFARTHEST.

20. Adapt the depth-first procedure ANNFNDFTRAV in Exercise 4 to obtain the k approximate farthest neighbors in a depth-first manner, thereby yielding procedure ANNFNDFTRAVFARTHEST.

21. Adapt the depth-first procedure ANNOPTDFTRAV in Exercise 5 to obtain the k approximate farthest neighbors, thereby yielding procedure ANNOPTDFTRAVFARTHEST.

22. Adapt procedure INCNEAREST to obtain the approximate farthest neighbors in an incremental manner using the criterion proposed by Duncan et al. [517]. In particular, o' is an approximate farthest neighbor of q if $d(q,o') \geq d(q,o) - \varepsilon D$, where o is the actual farthest neighbor, and D is the diameter of the point set (i.e., the distance between the two farthest points).

23. Repeat Exercise 22 for obtaining the approximate nearest neighbors in an incremental manner. You will need to modify the criterion for the approximate farthest neighbor to the case of an approximate nearest neighbor. In other words, devise an absolute error bound.

4.4 Multidimensional Indexing Methods

In this section we discuss the issues that must be dealt with when trying to adapt the multidimensional indexing methods presented in Chapters 1 and 2 to high-dimensional data. Section 4.4.1 describes the X-tree, which attempts to address problems that arise if we cannot find a good partition (i.e., one that does not result in too much overlap) when using an indexing method that makes use of an object hierarchy (e.g., an R-tree). Section 4.4.2 presents indexing methods that make use of an object hierarchy where the bounding objects are spheres rather than rectangles. This is based on the premise that the bounding spheres are preferable for nearest neighbor queries that use the Euclidean distance metric. The efficiency of indexing methods that consist of a tree structure can be improved by reducing the number of levels in the tree. This can be achieved by increasing the fanout in each node and is the subject of Section 4.4.3. Sections 4.4.4 and 4.4.5 discuss indexing methods that try to take advantage of the partitioning of the underlying space provided by a Voronoi diagram to facilitate finding nearest neighbors in high dimensions.

Sections 4.4.6 and 4.4.7 present techniques to overcome the problem that most query regions overlap a high proportion of the leaf blocks that result from the index since it can be shown, at least for a uniform distribution, that most of the data lies at or near the surface. It is assumed that part of the data lies in external memory. Nevertheless, in this case, it is often preferable to scan the entire database sequentially instead of incurring the random access overhead costs associated with using the hierarchy of an index. In other words, in sequential access, we amortize the seek time over many disk blocks, but in random access, we must pay the price of a disk seek each time we access a disk block. In particular, using an index may be more costly than sequential access if as little as 15% of the data blocks are accessed [212]. Section 4.4.8 describes a number of indexing methods that are designed to work with a sequential scan of the database. They usually involve a reduction in the amount of data that is retrieved by reducing the size of the representative of each data object.

4.4.1 X-Tree

As we have observed in earlier chapters, there are two types of multidimensional objects: points having zero volume (Chapter 1) and objects with extent, such as spatial data (Chapter 2). The X-tree [190] is a variant of an object hierarchy such as an R-tree that is designed to handle high-dimensional point data as well as spatial data (i.e., with extent). In the X-tree, node splits are avoided if they will result in a high degree of overlap among the resulting nodes. In particular, if a node overflows and an appropriate split position cannot be found, then the node is enlarged such that it occupies two disk blocks. Such a node is termed a *supernode*. Supernodes can be further enlarged (i.e., if an appropriate split does not exist), so supernodes may consist of an arbitrary number of disk blocks. In fact, in an extreme case, the directory consists of a single supernode.

The X-tree applies two kinds of node-splitting policies, both of which result in splitting along a single dimension (in two approximately equal halves, if we assume uniformly distributed point data). The first policy is based on topological considerations—that is, attempts to minimize a combination of perimeter and overlap, such as the traditional R*-tree node-splitting policies. If the overlap among the nodes resulting from the split exceeds some threshold, a second node-splitting policy is applied instead. This policy splits the node along the dimension that was used when the first two children of the node were created. If this split is unbalanced (i.e., one child contains many more elements than the other), a supernode is created instead of performing the split. For point data, it can be shown that such a split is overlap free [190]. Furthermore, the likelihood of an overlap-free split existing for any other dimension decreases rapidly as the dimension of the underlying data increases [190]. A split history in the form of a binary tree is maintained for each nonleaf node to facilitate determining the overlap-free split dimension.

When two nodes resulting from a split have excessive overlap, it becomes highly likely that most queries end up accessing both nodes. Thus, the advantage of creating a supernode instead of splitting is that sequential access can be used to read all the blocks making up the supernode, instead of the random accesses that would be required to access the nodes resulting from a split. The result is a compromise between an index that makes use of a hierarchy and a sequential access. Such an approach enables the index to adapt gracefully between the R-tree, which is good for low-dimensional data, and a sequential access of the entire dataset when the dimensionality of the data is high. The X-tree was shown to outperform the R*-tree significantly for data of increasing dimensionality as high as 16 [190].

The notion of a supernode in the X-tree is similar to the concept of *oversized shelves* [771, 777, 778], which is used with representations that are based on a disjoint decomposition of the underlying space for representing data with extent to deal with the situation that the decomposition causes an object to be split too many times. In this case, the objects get stored in the oversized shelves that are associated with nonleaf nodes in the structure. This is in contrast with the X-tree, where all the data objects are stored in the leaf nodes, and only pointers to nodes at the next level and their corresponding minimum bounding boxes are stored in the nonleaf nodes.

4.4.2 Bounding Sphere Methods: Sphere Tree, SS-Tree, Balltree, and SR-Tree

In the above discussion (Section 4.4.1 and Chapter 2), we assume the use of bounding boxes in the form of minimum bounding hyperrectangles, although these can be extended to bounding boxes of arbitrary shapes. As we saw earlier, in applications that involve high-dimensional data, among the most common queries are those that find the nearest neighbors to a given object o or find all objects within a given distance from o. These queries usually use the Euclidean distance metric. In this case, the query region is a hypersphere rather than a hyperrectangle. This has led some researchers (e.g., [1991]) to argue that using bounding boxes in the shape of hyperspheres is preferable to ones shaped like hyperrectangles in spatial indexes that are object hierarchies (e.g., as the R-tree). This is based on the observation that the number of hyperrectangular data regions that are intersected by a hyperspherical query region tends to increase sharply as the dimensionality of the underlying space increases, regardless of the indexing method (i.e., the way in which the data regions are determined). For example, assuming that the data space is tiled by hypercubes of volume V, a hypersphere query region r with volume V will intersect at least 5 of the hypercube tiles for dimension 2 and 19 for dimension 3 (assuming that the hypersphere is fully inside the data space). In general, as the dimension d of the underlying space increases, the number of hypercube tiles with volume V of the underlying space intersected by r increases very rapidly in d (see Exercise 1).

The SS-tree of White and Jain [1991] is a representation that is similar in spirit to the R*-tree, which makes use of minimum bounding hyperspheres instead of minimum bounding hyperrectangles. The center of each minimum bounding hypersphere is the centroid of the points that have been aggregated to form it. The centroids are used in both the insertion and split algorithms. Each SS-tree node has a minimum of m and a maximum of M children. The SS-tree is equivalent to the sphere tree of van Oosterom and Claassen [1410, 1412], which was developed for representing objects with extent. They both use minimum bounding hyperspheres with the only difference between them being that the sphere tree is based on an R-tree while the SS-tree is based on an R*-tree. The SS-tree is also similar to the balltree of Omohundro [1399], which is based on a binary tree. The sphere tree of Hubbard [895, 896] also makes use of a hierarchy of spheres constructed in a somewhat different manner for collision detection among moving objects. One of the motivations for using the sphere as a minimum bounding box in this application is its rotation invariance [895].

The SS-tree insertion algorithm combines aspects of both the R-tree [791] and the R*-tree [152]. In particular, initially, an object o is inserted into the node whose centroid is the closest to the centroid of o. This step is similar to the first step of the R-tree insertion algorithm and is motivated by the desire to minimize the coverage of the existing nodes (but see Exercise 2).

Overflow in an existing SS-tree node is resolved in a similar manner to the way it is handled in an R*-tree in that forced reinsertion is used. In particular, if a node A is full, then a fraction of the elements in A are reinserted (e.g., 30% [1991]). The elements to reinsert are the ones farthest from the centroid. These elements are removed from A, the centroid and radius of A are adjusted, and the elements are inserted again into the SS-tree starting from the root. If A overflows again during the reinsertion, A is split rather than attempting reinsertion again. Note that this is different from the reinsertion convention of the R*-tree, where reinsertion is invoked on only one node at any given level (i.e., any node at the same level of A that overflows during the reinsertion process is split).

As in some implementations of the R-tree [750] and the R*-tree [152], a two-step process is used for splitting a node A. The first step is to find a split dimension. The dimension i that is split is the one with the highest variance for component i of the centroids of the elements in A. This process takes $O(M)$ time. The actual split position along dimension i is chosen by minimizing the variances for the $M + 2 - 2 \cdot m$ possible split positions with respect to the values of component i of the centroid of the resulting region. This process takes $O(M^2)$ time as computing the variance is an $O(M)$ process, and it must be done for each of the $O(M)$ possible split positions.[20] Of course, there are many other possible options for the way in which the split position or objects can be chosen. For example, we could take into account the variance of the centroid coordinate values along all of the dimensions as well as taking overlap and coverage into account (see Exercise 3).

Another advantage of using minimum bounding hyperspheres over minimum bounding hyperrectangles is that specifying a minimum bounding hypersphere requires slightly more than half the storage needed to describe a minimum bounding hyperrectangle. In fact, this was one of the motivations mentioned for the development of the sphere tree [1410, 1412]. In particular, in d dimensions, we need $d + 1$ values to specify a minimum bounding hypersphere (the d coordinate values of its centroid plus the radius) versus $2 \cdot d$ values to specify the minimum bounding hyperrectangle (the d coordinate values of two of its diagonally opposite corners). This means that the nodes in the SS-tree have a greater fanout, thereby reducing the height of the tree, which speeds up search. Nevertheless, the time needed to compute the minimum bounding hypersphere should be taken into account as it is considerably more complex than computing the minimum bounding hyperrectangles, especially as the dimension d increases (see Exercise 4) and when the faces of the hyperrectangles are parallel to the coordinate axes (see Exercise 1 in Section 2.1.5.2.1 of Chapter 2).

In experiments [999] on different datasets using a k-nearest neighbor algorithm [1586] for 16-dimensional data, the SS-tree performed better than the R*-tree in terms of CPU time and lower I/O operations (i.e., disk reads). Interestingly, in these experiments, the heights of the SS-tree and the R*-tree were usually the same, and thus the superiority of the SS-tree here was not a result of its lower fanout. Comparison with the VAMSplit R-tree [1989] (see Section 1.7.1.7 of Chapter 1) showed that the SS-tree performed slightly worse, but this was deemed a positive result given that the SS-tree is a dynamic method while the VAMSplit R-tree is a static method. However, in these comparisons, the height of the SS-tree was almost always one less than that of the VAMSplit R-tree, and thus the lower fanout of the SS-tree could have been the mitigating factor.

---

[20] White and Jain [1991] claim that this process takes $O(M)$ time instead of $O(M^2)$ time by virtue of restricting M to be equal to $2 \cdot m$. However, this need not be the case in general.

From the experiments [999], it was also observed that the average volume of the minimum bounding hyperrectangles in the R*-tree was much smaller than that of the minimum bounding hyperspheres in the SS-tree (approximately 2%), while the average diameter of the minimum bounding hyperspheres in the SS-tree was about 60% of that of the minimum bounding hyperrectangles in the R*-tree (i.e., the lengths of their diagonals). Although at a first glance it seems odd that regions with large diameters have small volumes, upon further reflection, this is not surprising. In particular, we note that in high dimensions, the length of the diagonal of a d-dimensional unit hypercube is $\sqrt{d}$, which is also the maximum diameter of the hypercube. For example, when $d = 16$, the maximum diameter of the unit hypercube is 4. Thus, given a set of points in the unit d-dimensional hypercube, the diameters of both the minimum bounding hypersphere and hyperrectangle range between 1 and $\sqrt{d}$. In contrast, the volume of the minimum bounding hyperrectangle ranges between 0 and 1, while the volume of the minimum bounding hypersphere ranges between 0 and

$$\left(\frac{\sqrt{d}}{2}\right)^d \frac{\pi^{d/2}}{\Gamma(d/2+1)}.$$

This is a considerably larger range of values. This means that there is less potential for overlap when using minimum bounding rectangles than minimum bounding spheres, and thus point location queries are faster when using minimum bounding hyperrectangles.

These observations mean that the SS-tree groups points into regions with short diameter, while the R*-tree groups points into regions with small volumes, which is to be expected given the node insertion and split policies that are being used. Katayama and Satoh [999] explain these results by appealing to their belief that the smallness of the diameter of the minimum bounding hyperspheres has a greater effect on the performance of nearest neighbor queries than their volume. This is especially true when using the Euclidean distance metric.

The drawback of using hyperspheres as bounding boxes is that it is impossible to completely cover the underlying space with a finite set of hyperspheres of arbitrary volume without overlap. This means that if hyperspheres are used as bounding boxes, it is highly likely there will be significant overlap among them no matter how hard we try to minimize it. This overlap will have negative effect on the efficiency of range queries and nearest neighbor queries.

The SR-tree [999] was motivated by the belief that the performance of the SS-tree for both search and nearest neighbor queries could be improved if the volume of the minimum bounding boxes (which are hyperspheres in the SS-tree) could be reduced because this would lead to less overlap between nodes. Results of experiments with a uniformly distributed set of 16 dimensional points [999] showed that the average volume of the minimum bounding hyperrectangles for the points in the minimum bounding hyperspheres was approximately 0.1% of the average volume of the minimum bounding hyperspheres themselves. Moreover, the average volume of the minimum bounding hyperrectangles for the points in the minimum bounding hyperspheres was approximately 5% of the average volume of the minimum bounding hyperrectangles obtained when using an R*-tree. The SR-tree takes advantage of these results by defining the bounding boxes to be the intersection of minimum bounding hypersphere and the minimum bounding hyperrectangle of the points, while it is constructed in basically the same way as the SS-tree with a few minor differences. The effect is to reduce significantly the volume of the bounding boxes. Thus, the SR-tree is a combination of an R*-tree (rather than the R-tree due to the use of forced reinsertion) and an SS-tree.

The main difference in the construction of the SR-tree from that of the SS-tree is in the way the minimum bounding boxes are updated upon insertion of a point. In particular, both the minimum bounding hypersphere and the minimum bounding hyperrectangle must be updated, and this information must be propagated upward toward the root. The minimum bounding hyperrectangles are updated in the same way as in the R-tree and R*-tree. The minimum bounding hypersphere of a parent node is updated by examining both the minimum bounding hyperspheres and hyperrectangles of the child nodes. The center of the minimum bounding hypersphere is computed in the same way as in the SS-tree—that is, each coordinate value is a weighted average of the corresponding coordinate value of the center of the child nodes. The weight is the number of elements in the child node. The radius of the minimum bounding hypersphere s of a parent node u is the minimum of the maximum distance from the center of s to a point on the minimum bounding hyperspheres of its children and the maximum distance from s to a point on the minimum bounding hyperrectangles of its children. In this way, the radii of the minimum bounding hyperspheres in the SR-tree are smaller than those in the SS-tree, thereby reducing the extent of the overlap of the minimum bounding hyperspheres.

The idea of letting the intersection of the minimum bounding hypersphere and hyperrectangle serve as the minimum bounding box is similar to the idea that forms the basis of the P-tree [939]. In this case, instead of using a minimum bounding hyperrectangle whose faces are parallel to the coordinate axes, the P-tree is based on the observation that the volume of a minimum bounding hyperrectangle can be reduced by dropping the restriction that it be axis aligned (i.e., that its faces be parallel to the coordinate axes). The cost of such a solution is the addition of $d - 1$ orientation parameters corresponding to the dimension of the data. Even further reductions in the volume can be achieved by making use of the intersection of several bounding hyperrectangles with different orientations. The result is a polygonal bounding box that serves as the basis of the P-tree. It is easy to see that the SR-tree corresponds to an adaptation of the P-tree without the restriction that the constituent bounding boxes be hyperrectangles (i.e., it uses the intersection of a hypersphere and a hyperrectangle). However, it is limited to two bounding boxes (of different type) rather than an arbitrary number as in the P-tree.

Notice that the SR-tree achieves a reduction in the volume of the bounding box in the SS-tree without having to increase the diameter, which is advantageous in the performance of nearest neighbor queries. However, there is a small price to pay in that the search for the nearest neighbors in the SR-tree must be modified so that the minimum distance from a query point p to a region q is no longer the minimum distance from p to the minimum bounding hypersphere of q. Instead, it is the longer of the minimum distance from p to the minimum bounding hypersphere of q and the distance from p to the minimum bounding hyperrectangle of q.

Searching for a point in an SR-tree is performed by using the minimum bounding hypersphere and minimum bounding hyperrectangle as filters. Notice that the object formed by the intersection is not used explicitly in the search, and thus there is no need to store it explicitly in the tree as it is too hard to compute and requires much storage. Thus, the minimum bounding boxes are stored implicitly in the SR-tree. In fact, the need to store both the minimum bounding hyperrectangle and the minimum bounding hypersphere for each node is one of the drawbacks of the SR-tree. In particular, the SR-tree requires almost 3 times the storage needed by the SS-tree and slightly more than 1.5 times the storage needed by the R-tree. This means that the fanout of intermediate nodes in the SR-tree is much smaller than that of the R-tree and the SS-tree, which leads to an increased height in the trees. This increase in height should lead to more I/O operations for the SR-tree in comparison with the SS-tree. Experiments [999] with 16-dimensional points showed that the number of nonleaf node I/O operations was indeed higher for the SR-tree than for the SS-tree. However, the number of leaf node I/O operations was much lower for the SR-tree than for the SS-tree, thereby resulting in an overall reduction in the total number of I/O operations for the SR-tree.

The same experiments also showed that the cost of creating an SR-tree was higher than that for an SS-tree while being lower than that for an R*-tree. The performance of the SR-tree for nearest neighbor queries resulted in the SR-tree's having a lower CPU time and number of I/O operations (i.e., disk reads) than the SS-tree for both uniformly distributed data and real data. For uniformly distributed data, the VAMSplit R-tree had better performance, but for real data, the SR-tree had slightly better performance. Again, as in the comparison of the SS-tree with the VAMSplit R-tree, the lack of degradation in the performance of the SR-tree vis-à-vis the VAMSplit R-tree is of importance as the SR-tree is a dynamic method while the VAMSplit R-tree is a static method. Nevertheless, in the case of uniformly distributed data of higher dimensionality (e.g., 32 and 64), the SR-tree (as well as the SS-tree) did not perform very well as they ended up accessing all of the leaf nodes in the tree. This is another case where sequential scan may be preferable to using an index.[21] The behavior of the SR-tree was better when the data was more clustered.

Exercises

1. Suppose that the underlying space is tiled with hypercubes of volume v. We have observed that a hypersphere query region r of the same volume (i.e., v) will intersect at least 5 of the hypercube tiles of the underlying space for dimension 2 and 19 for dimension 3. Can you generalize these observations in terms of d, the dimension of the underlying space? Assume that r is always inside the data space.

2. The initial step in the SS-tree insertion algorithm routes the object o to a leaf node of the tree, starting from the root. When choosing among the children of a nonleaf node n during the traversal, the algorithm selects the child node whose centroid is the closest to the centroid of o. This technique is motivated by a desire to reduce the coverage of the nodes. However, unfortunately, this is not always the result, and the use of this strategy may in fact increase the coverage and the overlap as compared to alternatives. In particular, suppose that the centroid of o is within the minimum bounding hypersphere of child node a of n while being closer to the centroid of child node b but not being within the minimum bounding hypersphere of b. In this case, the algorithm will descend to child node b, which will have to be expanded to contain o, and, as a result, overlap the minimum bounding hypersphere of a as well as increase the total coverage. In contrast, if we had chosen child node a, depending on the radii of the minimum bounding hyperspheres of o and a, then perhaps we would not have had to expand the minimum bounding hypersphere of a and thus not increase the overlap or coverage. In light of this observation, can you still give an explanation for the rationale of inserting o in the node whose centroid is closest to the centroid of o?

3. Devise alternative methods for partitioning an overflowing node A in the SS-tree, and compare their performance with the method of White and Jain [1991] that splits along the dimension i that has the highest variance and then chooses the split position with the minimum variance of component i of the centroids of the resulting region. In particular, devise methods that minimize overlap and coverage as in the conventional R-tree (see Section 2.1.5.2.3 of Chapter 2). This means trying to find two elements to serve as seeds and assigning the remaining elements to them so that the overlap or coverage, or both, of their minimum bounding spheres is minimized.

4. How would you compute the minimum bounding sphere for N points in a d-dimensional space?

5. Given a set of N uniformly distributed points in a unit d-dimensional hypercube, compute the expected diameter of the minimum bounding hypersphere for the points as a function of d and N.

6. Given a set of N uniformly distributed points in a unit d-dimensional hypercube, compute the expected volume of the minimum bounding hypersphere for the points as a function of d and N.

7. Given a set of N uniformly distributed points in a unit d-dimensional hypercube, can you prove that the minimum bounding hypersphere for the points has a smaller expected diameter than that of the minimum bounding hyperrectangle (defined as the length of the longest diagonal)? An intuitive explanation is that, as long as at least one point lies on each face of the unit hypercube, the minimum bounding hyperrectangle is identical to the unit hypercube. In

---

[21] However, it has been noted [212] that nearest neighbor search in uniformly distributed data may not make sense in high-dimensional spaces since there tends to be little difference in the distances to the various objects.

contrast, in order for the minimum bounding hypersphere to have a maximum diameter, there must be at least two points at a pair of diagonally opposite corners. In order for the claim to hold, you need to show that the latter event is less likely to occur than the event leading to the minimum bounding hyperrectangle being equivalent to the hypercube.

8. Given a set of N uniformly distributed points in a unit d-dimensional hypercube, can you prove that the minimum bounding hypersphere for the points has a larger expected volume than that of the minimum bounding hyperrectangle?

4.4.3 Increasing the Fanout: TV-Tree, Hybrid Tree, and A-Tree

As mentioned earlier, multidimensional indexing methods are attractive only if they result in better performance than using a sequential scan, which is fairly simple to execute as it only requires that we check the individual items one by one in sequence. Some of the bad performance of methods that are based on the use of an object hierarchy, such as the R-tree, SS-tree, SR-tree, and so on, for high-dimensional data can be attributed to the small fanout in each node of the structure. This is due to the increasing amount of information that must be stored in each node for the minimum bounding box as the dimensionality increases, which in turn causes the tree to get deeper, thereby resulting in more disk accesses.

One way to increase the fanout in each node is to limit the number of attributes that are tested at each level of the index hierarchy. The TV-tree (denoting *telescoping vector*) of Lin, Jagadish, and Faloutsos [1171] is an example of such an approach. In this case, the number of attributes that are tested at each level is fixed, although their identities can be varied from level to level, as well as from node to node at the same level. The same philosophy is used in the X-Y tree [1334] and the equivalent treemap [1758] and puzzletree [480] (see Section 2.1.2.9 of Chapter 2) with the difference that minimum bounding boxes are associated with each node in the TV-tree. The minimum bounding boxes are not restricted to hyperrectangles and, in fact, can be spheres constructed with any Minkowski distance metric L_p (where given the points (x_1, y_1) and (x_2, y_2), the distance is defined as $d_{L_p}((x_1, y_1), (x_2, y_2)) = ((x_1 - x_2)^p + (y_1 - y_2)^p)^{1/p})$. Note that when all the attributes are tested, then the TV-tree reduces to being equivalent to the SS-tree (which uses L_2 but could also use any other metric) in structure.

The attributes (i.e., features) that are tested in the TV-tree are termed *active* and are deemed to enable the best discrimination among the data. They are used for the initial discrimination phase. At some point, these features do not provide further discriminatory power, which occurs when all the feature vectors in a node share the same value in the first active attribute(s). In order to provide additional discriminatory power, other features are shifted into the active set while the currently active features are made inactive—hence the use of the term *telescoping*. Experiments have shown that the TV-tree leads to fewer disk accesses than the R*-tree for some datasets [1171].

The utility of the TV-tree is based on the assumption that features can be ordered according to "importance." It also depends on the assumption that sets of feature vectors will be likely to match exactly on some of the features, especially the "important" ones, as this is what will cause the shifting of features into and out of the active set. The first assumption is reasonable as an appropriate transform can be applied to some of the dimensions to obtain the most important ones (such as with principal component analysis or the discrete cosine transform [587] in the case of dynamic data; see Section 4.6). Unfortunately, the second assumption does not always hold in applications such as those in image databases where the feature values are real numbers and thus an exact match for these features is rare. This means that the TV-tree reduces to be an index on just the first few dimensions.

More significant reduction in the fanout in each node can be achieved by using the hybrid tree of Chakrabarti and Mehrotra [317] (see Section 1.7.1.2 of Chapter 1). The hybrid tree is a variant of the k-d-B-tree [1567] that shares some of the features of the R-tree [791]. In the hybrid tree, the partition regions in nonleaf nodes (i.e., the regions for the child nodes) are represented with a variant of the k-d tree [164] that allows overlap while minimum bounding boxes are associated with the child nodes. In particular, instead of representing the child node regions in a nonleaf node a with a list of minimum bounding boxes as is the case for an R-tree, the hybrid tree represents them as the leaf nodes of the k-d tree for a. Such a representation is much more compact than a list of bounding boxes, especially in high-dimensional spaces, as the same amount of fanout is obtained regardless of the dimensionality of the underlying space. In contrast, in the R-tree, the fanout is inversely proportional to the dimensionality of the underlying space.

However, the hybrid tree representation has the drawback that the child node regions are no longer minimal, in the sense that they may be larger than the minimum bounding box of the points in the subtree rooted at the child node. The extraneous area is termed *dead space* and can lead to reduced query performance. In particular, while during a query that has query region of r, a child node b may be accessed even though r only covers the dead space of b's region (as determined by the "k-d tree" in b's parent). The hybrid tree addresses this drawback by approximating the minimum bounding box of each child node region of a nonleaf node in a very compact form that is based on a quantization of the underlying space, thereby enabling it to be represented with fewer bits (this method was first proposed by Henrich [826]). Experiments with real data with dimension as high as 64 showed that the hybrid tree outperforms the SR-tree and sequential scan [317]. Nevertheless, as the dimension of the underlying space increases further, the advantage of the hybrid tree over sequential scan will vanish (at around dimension 100 [315]).

The A-tree of Sakurai, Yoshikawa, Uemura, and Kojima [1607] also uses a quantized approximation of the bounding boxes to reduce the space requirements in an R-tree for high-dimensional data. The idea is to modify the format of an internal node a so that instead of storing the bounding box of each of a's children, it stores an approximation of the bounding box of each child b where the approximation is a quantized bounding box relative to the location of the bounding box of a. The advantage is that at deeper nodes in the tree, the corresponding bounding boxes are smaller and thus their quantized approximation can be encoded with just a small number of bits. Such bounding boxes are characterized as being *virtual*: the complete bounding box of the set of objects in the space spanned by a is still stored with a, while the virtual bounding box of a is only associated with the node that points to a as one of its children.

4.4.4 Methods Based on the Voronoi Diagram: OS-Tree

One straightforward method of adapting the Voronoi diagram for nearest neighbor searching is to approximate each Voronoi region by its minimum bounding rectangle and then to construct an index in the form of an object hierarchy such as one of the variants of the R-tree as discussed in Section 2.1.5.2 of Chapter 2 [189] We do not discuss this approach here. Instead, we focus on the os-tree (denoting *overlapped-split tree*) [1226, 1229], which is an adaptation of the BSP tree to provide both a hierarchical approximation of the d-dimensional Voronoi diagram and an index to it in order to facilitate finding nearest neighbors in high dimensions. The idea is to associate with each node a a bounding box in the form of a convex polyhedron, termed a *cover*, that contains every point in the d-dimensional space whose nearest data point is in the space spanned by a. Therefore, the cover of a is really the d-dimensional polyhedron formed by the union of the Voronoi regions of the data points in a. This polyhedron is quite expensive to compute, and thus there are a number of alternatives that can be used. For example, one choice is the minimum convex bounding region—that is, the convex hull of the vertices of the union of the Voronoi regions. It should be clear that the covers of the children of a node will usually overlap (i.e., they are not disjoint), unless the node has only two data points (assuming a bucket size of 1) as the Voronoi bisector of two points is just a hyperplane. In other words, due to the requirement that the cover be convex, the cover of a can also contain points in the d-dimensional space whose nearest data point is not in a. In essence, the os-tree is an adaptation of an object hierarchy such as that used in the R-tree to the Voronoi diagram where the objects are the individual Voronoi regions (instead of the points) and the BSP tree is used like a skeleton to guide both the process of forming the bounding boxes, which are d-dimensional polyhedra, as well as the search.

Searching for the nearest neighbor to query point q in the os-tree is straightforward. Descend the tree and at each node visit the children whose covers contain q. Since the covers are not disjoint, both children may need to be visited. The efficiency of the solution depends on how tightly the covers surround the union of the Voronoi regions of the points in each node. Notice that the solution is simpler than one that uses the incremental nearest neighbor algorithm given in Section 4.1.3. In particular, it is analogous to the first component of that algorithm, which finds the block (i.e., leaf node) containing the query point. The difference is that the nondisjointness of the covers may result in more than one node's being visited at each level of the tree. An advantage is that actual distances between points are only computed when processing a leaf node. Of course, if more than one neighbor is sought, then the incremental nearest neighbor algorithm should be applied to the os-tree, which is possible.

The os-tree is constructed by recursively partitioning the cell corresponding to node a, containing point set S_a with cover c_a and bounded by the set of $(d-1)$-dimensional hyperplanes U_a, into two new cells using some partitioning hyperplane H_a. This results in the creation of two new nodes al and ar containing disjoint point sets S_{al} and S_{ar}, respectively, whose union is S_a and whose corresponding covers c_{al} and c_{ar} are computed as follows. At each partitioning step, compute the Voronoi bisector between S_{al} and S_{ar} (e.g., a sequence of connected line segments in two dimensions) and the corresponding Voronoi regions, v_{al} and v_{ar}, respectively, each of which is the union of the Voronoi regions of the individual points. Obtain covers c_{al} and c_{ar} by finding two parallel $(d-1)$-dimensional hyperplanes L and R having the property that $v_{al} \subset c_{al}$, where $c_{al} = U_a \cap L$, and $v_{ar} \subset c_{ar}$, where $c_{ar} = U_a \cap R$ (where the set operation $\cap$ is performed on the halfspaces induced by the hyperplanes).[22] The actual covers c_{al} and c_{ar} are the regions bounded by the subsets of $(d-1)$-dimensional hyperplanes $U_a \cup L$ and $U_a \cup R$, respectively. Note that L and R need not necessarily be parallel to the BSP partitioning hyperplane H_a; nor must they be parallel to each other. However, as we shall see below, making L and R parallel enables the detection of the children whose covers contain q with the same operation (i.e., the dot product of q and their normals, which are the same since they are parallel). Figure 4.25(a) shows the BSP tree node corresponding to a sample set of points and their Voronoi regions, as well as the node's cover, partitioning hyperplane, and Voronoi bisector. Figure 4.25(b) shows the result of partitioning the node, including the covers of the resulting nodes that are induced by the additional hyperplanes.

A critical shortcoming of the above solution is that it requires knowledge of the Voronoi diagram. This is a serious flaw as the combinatorial complexity of the d-dimensional Voronoi diagram grows exponentially with its dimension d—that is, for N points, the time to build and the space requirements can grow as rapidly as $\Theta(N^{d/2})$ as an example can be constructed that attains this bound [112]. In particular, the time to build is the storage cost plus the cost of sorting. In two dimensions, this cost is dominated

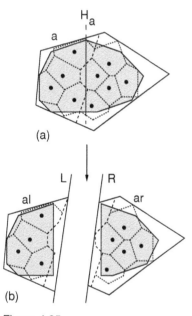

Figure 4.25
(a) The BSP tree node corresponding to a sample set of points and their Voronoi regions (shown with broken lines), as well as the node's cover, partitioning hyperplane H_a, and Voronoi bisector. (b) The result of partitioning the node in (a), including the covers of the resulting nodes that are induced by the additional hyperplanes L and R. The actual regions spanned by the nodes (in contrast to those spanned by the covers) are shaded.

---

[22] The addition of two arbitrary hyperplanes to bound the area spanned by the objects in the two subtrees is also used in the KD2-tree [1410, 1412] (see Section 1.5.1.4 of Chapter 1). In addition, it is used in the spatial k-d tree [1404, 1407] (see Sections 1.5.1.4 and 1.7.1.2 of Chapter 1 and Section 3.3.2.5 of Chapter 3) and the hybrid tree [317] (see Section 4.4.3 and Section 1.7.1.2 of Chapter 1) where the hyperplanes are restricted to being axis parallel.

by the time to sort, which is $O(N \log N)$. Therefore, the os-tree, as presented above, is impractical for high dimensions (even for moderate dimensions as low as $d = 10$) and not really usable. In order to overcome this shortcoming, Maneewongvatana and Mount [1230] modify the os-tree so that the covers correspond to unions of approximations of the Voronoi regions of the points rather than the unions of the actual Voronoi regions. This is achieved by the use of training points,[23] which are sample nearest neighbor queries whose results are used to delineate the boundaries of an approximate Voronoi diagram, where the approximate Voronoi diagram consists of approximate covers. For example, Figure 4.26 shows the result of forming an approximate cover for the set of sample points and node in Figure 4.25(a) using a set of training points. The broken line denotes the cover corresponding to the true Voronoi regions, the thick line denotes the cover corresponding to the approximate Voronoi regions, and the thin line denotes the boundary of the BSP tree node. Of course, the number of training points must be considerably larger than the number of data points as the training points are used to approximate boundaries that are already quite complex from a combinatorial standpoint. The result is termed a *probably correct os-tree*.

The drawback of this modification is that it can lead to errors: a query point q could be associated with the wrong nearest neighbor. This is the case when q is in the Voronoi region of a point p while not being in the approximate cover of the node containing p (e.g., whenever q is in any of the shaded regions in Figure 4.26). Let f, termed the *failure probability*, be the maximum probability of the occurrence of such an event. It can be shown that if the cover of each node in a probably correct os-tree contains the covers of its children, then f is the failure probability for search in the probably correct os-tree (see Exercise 1) [1226]. The result is an approximation of a Voronoi diagram, and an index is provided for it in the form of a BSP tree without ever actually having to construct the Voronoi diagram. This is an important point.

The probably correct os-tree is constructed in a similar manner to the conventional os-tree but with some key differences. Start at the root node, which corresponds to the entire set S of data points. For each node a corresponding to the point set S_a, determine if the number of data points in S_a is less than some threshold b (analogous to a bucket capacity), in which case the points are stored in a leaf node. Otherwise, split the cell corresponding to a into two new cells, thereby creating two new nodes al and ar containing disjoint data point sets S_{al} and S_{ar} whose union is S_a, where S_{al} and S_{ar} are of approximately equal size so that the resulting tree is balanced. Splitting the cell is actually a two-step process:

1. Choose the points that make up subsets S_{al} and S_{ar}.

2. Choose a partitioning plane I_a for the cell corresponding to a.

The first step introduces a partitioning plane H_a whose orientation is orthogonal to the direction of the greatest variation of the data points. This is achieved by using Principal Component Analysis (PCA) (e.g., [665]). In particular, the covariance matrix is computed for S_a, and the points are sorted according to their projection onto the eigenvector corresponding to the largest eigenvalue. S_{al} and S_{ar} are formed by the first and second halves, respectively, of the sequence. The eigenvalues are the variances along the directions of the corresponding eigenvector and indicate the relative strength of the correlation along that direction. Thus, without additional information about the distribution of the data points, separating the points on the basis of the first eigenvector is reasonable. For example, Figure 4.27 is an example of the result of applying PCA to a sample set of points. PCA is frequently used in dimension reduction (see Section 4.6.4.1) because the actual high-dimensional data does not usually span the entire space but, instead, is of some lower dimension. Use of this method for obtaining the partitioning

---

[23] The use of training points was inspired by Clarkson [400], who used them in a randomized (e.g., [1318, 1325]) nearest neighbor algorithm in a metric space, which, at times, with very low probability, may return the wrong answer.

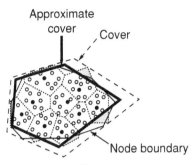

- Data points (S)
- Training points (T)

Figure 4.26
The approximate cover, drawn with a thick line, for the set of sample points and the node in Figure 4.25(a) obtained using the specified training points. The broken line corresponds to the cover for the true Voronoi regions, and the thin line is the boundary of the node. The shaded regions correspond to locations where the query points will be associated with the wrong nearest neighbor as they lie outside the approximate cover of the node.

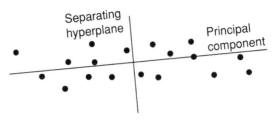

Figure 4.27
Example of the result of applying PCA to a sample set of points.

plane was first suggested by Sproull [1797] in a discussion of a k-d tree whose partitioning planes have an arbitrary orientation, a variant of a BSP tree for points (see Section 1.5.1.4 of Chapter 1).

It should be clear that once the points in S_a have been partitioned as described above, if the maximum of the projections of the elements in S_{al} is less than the minimum of the projections of the elements in S_{ar}, then there is an infinite number of possible choices for the separating hyperplane I_a. The second step tries to find a more appropriate orientation for I_a than the one used for the first step (i.e., H_a). The goal is to minimize the extent to which the Voronoi regions of the elements of S_{al} (S_{ar}) (measured by their d-dimensional volume) overlap the right (left) side of I_a. This will enable the covers to be tighter, thereby resulting in a more efficient search. The ideal solution is for I_a to coincide with the Voronoi bisector of the two sets S_{al} and S_{ar}, in which case there is zero overlap. This is generally impossible, so the next best solution is for I_a to be as close as possible in position and orientation to the Voronoi bisector of the two sets S_{al} and S_{ar}. However, as we do not know the Voronoi regions for the data points, we can try to find the position and orientation of I_a that minimizes the number of training points on the right side of I_a whose nearest neighbors are elements of S_{al} and the number of training points on the left side of I_a whose nearest neighbors are elements of S_{ar} (see Exercise 2).

This requires quite a bit of work as the number of training points is expected to be large. Thus, we need an alternative solution that is less complex. Maneewongvatana and Mount [1230] observe that most of the overlap can be accounted for by the data points that are closest to I_a. Therefore, they propose to position I_a so that it is coincident with the bisector of the edge that separates the two points p_{al} and p_{ar} in S_{al} and S_{ar}, respectively, which are the farthest apart subject to the additional constraints that all other points in S_{al} (S_{ar}) are to the left (right) of I_a and even farther from I_a than p_{al} (p_{ar}) (see also Exercise 3). Such a choice means that we are in essence ignoring the points that are far apart from I_a. They suggest that I_a be computed using the support vector machines (SVM) method [281, 1917] as it leads to a hyperplane that is farthest from the closest points on its two sides.

Formally, given the sets S_{al} and S_{ar}, the SVM method finds the hyperplane I_a with the highest margin, where the *margin* is defined as the sum of the distance from I_a to the nearest point p_{al} in S_{al} and the distance from I_a to the nearest point p_{ar} in S_{ar}, subject to the constraints that all points in S_{al} (S_{ar}) are to the left (right) of I_a. The SVM method formulates this as a nonlinear optimization problem and returns a set of points termed *support vectors*, as well as other coefficients that are used to determine I_a. The support vectors are the points that have a direct influence on the result. In particular, if a support vector is removed or modified, then the result may change, and thus other points in the original dataset may be removed with no change in the resulting hyperplane. For example, Figure 4.28 shows the resulting hyperplane and the support vectors for a small dataset. It is important to observe that one of the reasons for basing the choice of the separating hyperplane I_a on the SVM method rather than the PCA method is that the hyperplane resulting from the SVM method is more heavily influenced by the points that lie near it (i.e., it is local) while the one resulting from the PCA method is influenced by all of the points (i.e., it is global).

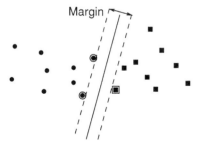

◉ ■ Support vector
● ■ Data point

Figure 4.28
Sample dataset and the resulting separating hyperplane and support vectors resulting from use of the SVM method.

The SVM method may take quite a bit of time to execute due to the need to satisfy the constraints on the relative positions of the points in S_{al} and S_{ar} with respect to I_a. This is generally much more complex than finding the distance between each point in one set and its nearest point in a second set (known as the *nearest foreign neighbor problem* [2047]).

One way to speed up the SVM method is to partition S_{al} and S_{ar} into smaller subsets, apply the SVM method to pairs of subsets, find the resulting support vectors, and then reapply the SVM method to sets making up the support vectors. The final application of the SVM method takes place once there are just two sets left [1226]. Of course, the result is an approximation of the hyperplane that would be obtained had the SVM method been applied to sets S_{al} and S_{ar} in their entirety rather their partitions.

Earlier we stated that our goal in the choice of I_a is to minimize the extent to which the Voronoi regions of the elements of S_{al} (S_{ar}) (measured by their d-dimensional volume) overlap the right (left) side of I_a. This assumes that the distribution of the query points is uniform in the regions where misclassification occurs. If this is not the case, then we may want to have an alternative way to measure the extent of the misclassification by enumerating the number of training points that are misclassified and minimizing it instead of the d-dimensional volume of the extent of the Voronoi regions that overlap the wrong side of I_a. This can be achieved by incorporating the minimization of the misclassification of training points into the constraints taken into account by the SVM method. Of course, this will result in a significant increase in the complexity of the SVM method due to the large number of training points, and hence this alternative is not used.

Once I_a has been determined, compute the nearest neighbor for each of the query points in the training set T_a, and partition T_a into two sets T_{al} and T_{ar}, depending on whether the nearest neighbor is in S_{al} or S_{ar}, respectively. Next, calculate the covers for the cells corresponding to nodes al and ar by computing two cover hyperplanes B_{al} and B_{ar} parallel to I_a that serve to bound the regions containing T_{al} and T_{ar}, respectively. These three hyperplanes (i.e., I_a, B_{al}, and B_{ar}) are stored with node a. Notice that the training points were not used in the determination of I_a, although they may provide some additional information, as discussed earlier. For example, Figure 4.29 shows the result of splitting a node in a probably correct os-tree corresponding to the set of data points and node in Figure 4.25. The shaded area in the root node corresponds to the overlap of the covers of the left and right children.

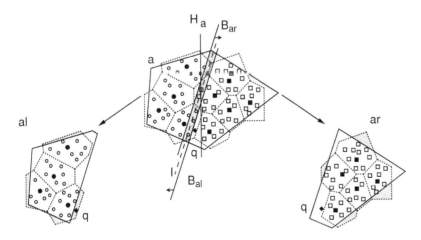

Figure 4.29
The result of splitting a node in a probably correct os-tree corresponding to the set of data points and the node in Figure 4.25. The shaded area in the root node corresponds to the overlap of the covers of the left and right children. The shaded areas in the left and right children correspond to locations where the query points will be associated with the wrong nearest neighbor as they lie outside the approximate cover of the node.

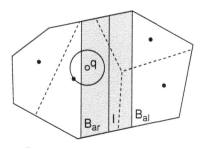

□ Overlap region

○ Query point

• Data point

-- Voronoi diagram

Figure 4.30
Sample query point q whose closest neighbor p is closer than the partitioning plane I_a, thereby precluding the need to visit the node that does not contain q.

Searching for the nearest neighbor to point q in the probably correct os-tree is done in a similar manner to that described earlier for the conventional os-tree. The search starts at the root node. At any internal node a (with hyperplanes I_a, B_{al}, and B_{ar}), find the location of the query point q with respect to the separating hyperplane I_a and the two cover hyperplanes B_{al} and B_{ar} (which define the covers of a's child nodes). This is done by taking the dot product of q and the normal to I_a, yielding v, and examining whether v is greater than or equal to the constant term of the equation corresponding to I_a, or if it is smaller. The fact that all three hyperplanes are parallel means that they all have the same normal, and thus only one dot product is needed for determining the location of q with respect to I_a, B_{al}, and B_{ar}, which can be done in $O(d)$ time. The only difference is in the comparand of the test. Armed with the result of the test, node al (ar) is visited first if q lies to the left (right) of I_a, while ar (al) is not visited unless q is in the cover region of ar (al), in which case it is visited next.

A minor optimization can avoid visiting ar (al) even if q is in the cover region of ar (al). This depends on the distance to q's current candidate nearest neighbor in the region corresponding to al (ar) being smaller than the distance from q to I_a. In this case, every point in S_{ar} (S_{al}) is on the other side of I_a and thus even farther from q. Therefore, no point in S_{ar} (S_{al}) can be a candidate nearest neighbor, which precludes visiting ar (al). Figure 4.30 illustrates such a situation.

The only way in which the above search can fail is if the query point q lies in the Voronoi region v_p of some point p, where p is in node b while the cover of b does not contain q. This is a direct result of the absence of training points in the neighborhood of q, thereby causing the covers to fail to capture properly the Voronoi regions of the data points. For example, the search will fail for any query point q that lies in the shaded regions in Figure 4.26 and in the left and right children in Figure 4.29. Maneewongvatana [1226] shows that if the set S of data points and the set T of training points are independent and identically distributed, then the probability of such a failure is approximately $|S|/|T|$ when $|T|$ is relatively large. Remarkably, this probability estimate is quite tight and was attained in a wide range of experiments [1230]. This is in contrast to most estimates in approximate nearest neighbor searching where the actual error was much less than the approximation error tolerance [387, 1226] (for more details, see below).

The $|S|/|T|$ failure probability means that the training set must be quite large in order to reduce it below some reasonable threshold when the volume of the data is of reasonable size with respect to the dimensionality of the underlying space, which somehow lessens the attractiveness of this method. Nevertheless, although the number of necessary training points seems large in comparison with the number of data points, it should be realized that the training points serve to approximate the Voronoi diagram, which is considerably more complex. Recall that the combinatorial complexity of the Voronoi diagram for N d-dimensional points can grow as rapidly as $\Theta(N^{d/2})$. For example, for $d = 30$ and $N = 4,000$, the combinatorial complexity is $4,000^{30}$, which is a huge number. In contrast, Maneewongvatana and Mount [1230] used training sets that were approximately 200 times the size of the datasets. Thus, the os-tree reduces the complexity from exponential to linear.

It is difficult to compare the os-tree with other representations as the concept of a failure probability is not present. However, finding the nearest neighbor with a failure probability is somewhat similar to approximate nearest neighbor finding. The idea is to find an approximation error tolerance ε that yields a failure error roughly equal to the failure probability. Note that the failure error is usually far less than the approximation error tolerance. Maneewongvatana and Mount [1229, 1230] conducted such a comparison of the os-tree with the sliding-midpoint k-d tree (see Section 1.5.2.2) for finding the nearest neighbor. The result when the failure error of approximate nearest neighbor finding for the sliding-midpoint k-d tree was roughly equal to that of the os-tree was comparable performance in terms of query time and number of nodes visited for 10 and 20 dimensions. On the other hand, the sliding-midpoint k-d tree usually performed better for 30 dimensions. Moreover, they found that the failure error was often as much as two orders of magnitude smaller than the approximation error tolerance (e.g., 0.0044 failure probability versus an epsilon value of 0.55 [1226]). Of course, the sliding-midpoint k-d tree was much faster to build.

These results show that the os-tree did reasonably well at approximating the Voronoi diagram in the lower dimensions (e.g., 10 and 20) but not so well in the higher dimensions (e.g., 30). The query time of the os-tree was hampered by the need to test the query point with respect to the partitioning hyperplane, which is an $O(d)$ operation, in contrast to a simple comparison of one coordinate value in the case of the sliding-midpoint k-d tree. This suggests that the idea of incorporating the approximation of the Voronoi diagram into the index is worthwhile, but perhaps better performance could be obtained if the index made use of partition planes that were parallel to the coordinate axes, as is usually done with a conventional k-d tree, while still retaining the notion of a cover that would also make use of axis-parallel boundaries (very similar to an R-tree). Of course, the trade-off is that the covers may not be as tight, thereby leading to larger overlap regions and more nodes being searched.

Maneewongvatana and Mount [1229] also examined the amount of overlap in the nodes, which they found to be surprisingly high. This is not really surprising when we realize that the amount of overlap is directly related to the number of training points. In particular, the greater the number of training points, the larger the cover associated with the node. However, the failure probability decreases with an increase in the number of training points. Thus, we have the seemingly contradictory result that the greater the overlap, the smaller is the failure probability. Actually, this is not surprising as the greater the amount of overlap, the smaller the chance of missing a nearest neighbor when descending the tree in the search process as the larger cover ensures that we descend both subtrees if necessary. Although the overlap ranged from 0.3 to 0.7, the maximum was attained at most of the levels of the tree, and it did not show a great variation with respect to the failure probability. This suggests that the work expended in the SVM method in choosing a good partitioning may not be worth the effort, thereby leading to faster construction of the os-tree. Moreover, it provides further confirmation of the hypothesis that a more computationally tractable bounding box (e.g., whose sides are axis parallel) may lead to performance improvements with possibly a small degradation in the accuracy as measured by the theoretical failure probability if a smaller number of training points is found to be needed. It should be clear that the utility of the os-tree needs to be investigated further.

Note that the idea of permitting the search to fail via the introduction of a failure probability is similar to that proposed by Ciaccia and Patella [387] for the computation of what are termed probably approximately correct (PAC) nearest neighbors (see Section 4.3). However, the difference is that Ciaccia and Patella assumed that the distribution of the distance between the query and data points is known. Moreover, they did not actually execute a nearest neighbor search. Instead, they used the knowledge of the distance distribution, approximation error tolerance, and a failure probability f to predict an expected distance d_f for which the probability that the nearest neighbor is closer than d_f is at most f, and then they proceeded to find a point within this distance of q that is deemed the nearest neighbor. Thus, they actually executed a variant of a range query where they stopped on the first object in the range.

Their approach has several drawbacks. First of all, the nearest neighbor distance is usually not independent of the position of the query point; nor is it independent of boundary effects. Second, notwithstanding the criticism of the above independence assumption, the distribution of the distance between the query and the data points is not generally known, thereby making the failure probability, which depends on it, difficult to compute. In contrast, in the method of Maneewongvatana and Mount [1229], the failure probability is shown to be a function of the ratio of the volume of the data and the number of training points, provided these two sets are independent and identically distributed.

Exercises

1. Given a probably correct os-tree where f holds for the leaf nodes, prove that if the cover of each node contains the covers of its children, then f is the failure probability for search in the tree.

2. When constructing the probably correct os-tree, once the points in S_a have been partitioned with the hyperplane H_a resulting from the use of the PCA method, it was proposed to find a more appropriate separating hyperplane I_a that minimizes the number of training points on the right side of I_a whose nearest neighbors are elements of S_{al} and the number of training points on the left side of I_a whose nearest neighbors are elements of S_{ar}. Would it not be more appropriate to choose the separating hyperplane I_a that minimizes the d-dimensional volume spanned by the training points on the right side of I_a whose nearest neighbors are elements of S_{al} and the volume spanned by the training points on the left side of I_a whose nearest neighbors are elements of S_{ar}? If yes, what are the drawbacks of such a choice?

3. When constructing the probably correct os-tree, what is the rationale for choosing the hyperplane that is farthest from the closest points on its two sides rather than one that is closer to the same two points?

(a)

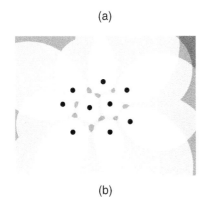

(b)

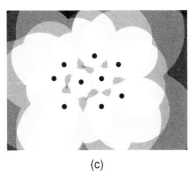

(c)

Figure 4.31
Partitions of the underlying space induced by the ε-nearest neighbor sets corresponding to the sites of the Voronoi diagram given in Figure 2.110(a) in Section 2.2.1.4 of Chapter 2 for (a) ε=0.10, (b) ε=0.30, and (c) ε=0.50. The darkness of the shading indicates the cardinality of the ε-nearest neighbor sets, with white corresponding to 1.

4.4.5 Approximate Voronoi Diagram (AVD)

Har-Peled [799] addresses the $\Theta(N^{d/2})$ space requirements of the d-dimensional Voronoi diagram of a point set S by approximating it with an implicit representation that he terms an *approximate Voronoi diagram* (AVD). The idea is to partition the underlying space using some arbitrary block decomposition rule so that, given a $\varepsilon \geq 0$, every block b is associated with some element r_b in S such that r_b is an ε-nearest neighbor for all of the points in b. The motivation for the AVD is to reduce the space requirements for a d-dimensional Voronoi diagram from $\Theta(N^{d/2})$ for N points to a quantity closer to linear, although not necessarily linear. In particular, Har-Peled [799] shows that, for a given value of ε, it is possible to construct an AVD in $O((N/\varepsilon^d)(\log N)(\log(N/\varepsilon)))$ time, taking up the same amount of space (i.e., the number of blocks is also $O((N/\varepsilon^d)(\log N)(\log(N/\varepsilon))))$ and to determine the ε-nearest neighbor of a query point q in $O(\log(N/\varepsilon))$ time.

Note that the Voronoi diagram is only implicitly represented in the AVD in the sense that the boundaries of the Voronoi regions are not explicitly stored in the blocks. This implicit representation is also a characteristic of using the mb-tree [1383] (see Section 4.5.3.3) to represent data drawn from either a vector or a metric space where the data are objects, termed *pivots*, with associated regions so that all objects that are associated with a pivot p are closer to p than to any other pivot. In this case, the boundaries of the regions are also represented implicitly (see Section 4.5.3.3 for more details).

There are many possible block decomposition rules. Regardless of the rule that is chosen for each block, the only requirement is that the intersection of the ε-nearest neighbor sets of all of the points in each block be nonempty. For example, Figure 4.31(a–c), corresponds to the partitions of the underlying space induced by the ε-nearest neighbor sets corresponding to the sites of the Voronoi diagram given in Figure 2.110(a) in Section 2.2.1.4 of Chapter 2 for $\varepsilon = 0.10, 0.30$, and 0.50, respectively. The darkness of the shading indicates the cardinality of the ε-nearest neighbor sets, with white corresponding to 1. The space requirements and the time complexity of nearest neighbor queries are reduced when the block decomposition rule yields blocks that are sufficiently "fat" (i.e., they have a good aspect ratio as discussed in Section 1.5.1.4 of Chapter 1). One possibility, for which the "fat" requirement holds, is to use a rule, such as the PR quadtree [1413, 1637] (see Section 1.4.2.2), that for multidimensional point data recursively decomposes the underlying space into congruent blocks (i.e., squares in two dimensions) until each block is either empty or contains at most one point.

In the case of the AVD, the decomposition rule is such that the underlying space is recursively decomposed into congruent blocks until the space spanned by each block b is associated with an element r_b in S (also known as the *sites* of the Voronoi diagram) such that r_b is an ε-nearest neighbor for every point in the space spanned by b. In this case, r_b is said to be associated with b. Of course, the same site r_b can be associated with several different blocks in the PR quadtree. Similarly, a particular block b can be associated with more than one site of the Voronoi diagram, say r_c in S, as well as r_b. This means that r_c is also an ε-nearest neighbor for every point in the space spanned by b. Naturally, the decomposition rule tries to avoid such multiple associations by stipulating that the blocks resulting from the decomposition be maximal. However, this stipulation can only reduce the likelihood of a multiple association; it cannot guarantee its absence.

For example, Figure 4.32(a) is the block decomposition induced by the AVD for a suitably chosen value of ε (e.g., 0.25) using a PR quadtreelike block decomposition rule for the Voronoi diagram given in Figure 2.110(a) in Section 2.2.1.4 of Chapter 2 and also shown using broken lines in the figure. Notice that due to space limitations, Figure 4.32(a) does not show the site that is associated with each block except for the block that contains the actual site, which is labeled with the site's name. One important difference from the PR quadtree is that there are no empty blocks in the block decomposition of the underlying space that is induced by the AVD. This is not surprising as each block must indicate the identity of its associated site.

Given a block decomposition rule, an access structure must be specified for the blocks. This is usually a tree of out degree 4 as in the tree representation of the PR quadtree in Figure 1.31(b) of Chapter 1. One shortcoming of such a tree representation is that its maximum depth may be high due to the need for a large number of empty blocks when much decomposition is required in order to separate the sites associated with a particular block or when the value of ε is very small so that much decomposition is needed to ensure that the entire space spanned by a block that straddles a boundary between adjacent regions of two sites can be associated with one of the relevant sites. In this case, Har-Peled [799] suggests using what he terms a "compressed quadtree" that avoids transitions through nonleaf nodes where the blocks corresponding to three of the child nodes are associated with the same site and no boundary of the Voronoi diagram passes through them. Many of these nodes and their corresponding blocks are eliminated from the data structure, and the blocks that remain are identified by recording the appropriate transitions to them from the root block via the use of suitably valued bit patterns. The exact number of nodes and blocks eliminated in this way depends on the value of ε and the minimum separation δ between the sites on the opposite sides of an edge of the Voronoi diagram. Thus, the blocks that remain are either squares or the differences between two squares, assuming, without loss of generality, two-dimensional data. This is analogous to the *path-compressed PR k-d tree* discussed in Section 1.5.2.4 of Chapter 1, except that here the tree has an out degree of 4 instead of 2. The same principle is used in other data structures discussed in Chapter 1, such as the BD-tree [1386, 1387] (Section 1.5.2.6), hB-tree [575, 1201] (Section 1.7.1.4), BANG file [640, 641, 645, 646] (Section 1.7.1.5), and balanced box-decomposition tree (BBD-tree) [100] (Section 1.5.2.7).

Arya, Malamatos, and Mount [97, 98] generalized the result of Har-Peled [799] to yield what they term a (t, ε)-*AVD* by allowing up to $t \geq 1$ elements $r_{ib}(1 \leq i \leq t)$ of S to be associated with each block b for a given ε, where each point in b has one of the r_{ib} as its ε-nearest neighbor. When the underlying space decomposition rule is based on a regular decomposition, the result is analogous to a bucket variant of the PR quadtree (i.e., the *bucket PR quadtree* discussed in Section 1.4.2.2 of Chapter 1) with bucket capacity t, where now, instead of halting the decomposition process whenever there are t or fewer points in a block b, we halt the decomposition process whenever the total number of different ε-nearest neighbors of the points in the space spanned by b is t or fewer. As long as the underlying space decomposition rule yields blocks that are sufficiently "fat," which is the case for the bucket PR quadtree, Arya et al. [98] are able to obtain AVDs that are more space efficient than the ones of Har-Peled [799], where

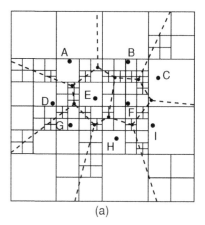

(a)

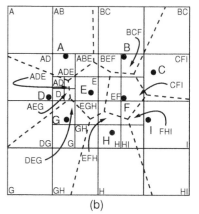

(b)

Figure 4.32
(a) The block decomposition induced by the AVD according to the definition of Har-Peled [799] for a suitably chosen value of ε (e.g., 0.25) using a PR quadtreelike–block decomposition rule for the point set {A,B,C,D,E,F,G,H,I} whose Voronoi diagram is given in Figure 2.110(a) in Section 2.2.1.4 of Chapter 2 and also shown here using broken lines and (b) the corresponding block decomposition induced by the (3,0)-AVD of Arya, Malamatos, and Mount [97, 98].

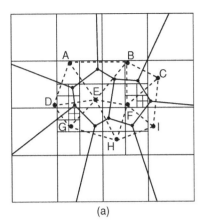

(a)

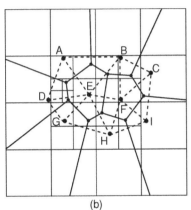

(b)

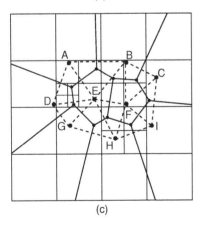

(c)

Figure 4.34
The block decompositions induced by the (a) PM$_1$, (b) PM$_2$, and (c) PM$_3$ quadtrees for the Voronoi diagram of the set of sites {A,B,C,D,E,F,G,H,I} whose Voronoi diagram is given in Figure 2.110(a) in Section 2.2.1.4 of Chapter 2 and shown here using broken lines.

tree (BBD-tree) [100]. All that remains is for each cell of the decomposition to select its representative. This can be done by running any existing algorithm for approximate nearest neighbor searching (e.g., the algorithm of Arya et al. [100]) applied to any point in the cell (e.g., its midpoint). The overall execution time is on the order of the product of the number of cells of the decomposition and the time needed to answer these approximate nearest neighbor queries using this auxiliary approximate nearest neighbor data structure (i.e., the BBD-tree). Har-Peled did not make use of well-separated pairs in his construction of the AVD [799] (i.e., for $t = 1$). Instead, he viewed the Voronoi diagram as a tournament, involving "spheres of influence" growing around each point. He used an approximation to the minimum spanning tree to determine the number of spheres and then used these spheres to guide the process of subdividing space.

For two-dimensional data, the block decomposition resulting from the bucket PR quadtree construction of Arya et al., using suitably chosen parameter values, is equivalent to an implicit variant of the PM quadtree [1665] family of hierarchical spatial data structures when the underlying data is a polygonal map (see Section 2.2.2.6 in Chapter 2). We use the qualifier *implicit* because the line segments are not explicitly present in the (t, ε)-AVD. For example, Figure 4.34(a–c) shows the block decompositions induced by the PM$_1$, PM$_2$, and PM$_3$ quadtrees,[24] respectively, for the Voronoi diagram given in Figure 2.110(a) in Section 2.2.1.4 of Chapter 2. From the figures, we see that the block decomposition induced by the (3,0)-AVD data structure (e.g., Figure 4.32(b)) is very similar to an implicit version of a PM$_2$ quadtree [1665]. A key difference is that the (t, ε)-AVD data structure is designed to represent only the special case of a polygonal map M that is a Voronoi diagram, whereas members of the PM quadtree family can be used to represent arbitrary polygonal maps, including the Delaunay triangulation, which is the dual of the Voronoi diagram. Moreover, the (t, ε)-AVD data structure only keeps track of the Voronoi sites (which are points) associated with each block. In contrast, members of the PM quadtree family keep track of the edges that make up the polygonal subdivision (i.e., the boundaries of the Voronoi regions), or, equivalently, the vertices of the polygonal map (i.e., the vertices of the Voronoi regions).

More specifically, recall that the PM$_2$ quadtree is a member of the PM quadtree family where the underlying space is recursively partitioned into four congruent blocks so that at most one edge of the polygonal map passes through each block b, unless all the edges that pass through b are incident at the same vertex v, regardless of whether v is in b. The PM$_2$ quadtree is usually implemented by keeping track of the set of edges that pass through each block. However, alternatively, as we pointed out in Section 2.2.2.6 of Chapter 2, the PM$_2$ quadtree can also be implemented in such a way that each leaf block b stores the vertex, if any, that is common to the edges that pass through b. If only one edge passes through b, then one of its vertices is arbitrarily chosen to be stored in b. In any case, regardless of how many edges pass through b, the vertices are usually part of an auxiliary data structure (e.g., a triangle table or some other variant of the winged-edge data structure) that keeps track of the topological properties of the polygonal map. When the polygonal map M is a Voronoi diagram where no four elements of S are cocircular, it is easy to see that the block decomposition of the underlying space induced by the (3,0)-AVD of M is equivalent to the block decomposition of the underlying space induced by the PM$_2$ quadtree for the edges of the Voronoi diagram (see Exercise 2). In other words, the set of blocks in the PM$_2$ quadtree and the (3,0)-AVD are identical, although they do contain different information. In particular, in the (3,0)-AVD, the blocks store the sites S of the Voronoi diagram, while in the PM$_2$ quadtree, the blocks store the vertices V of the Voronoi diagram (i.e., the circumcenters of the Delaunay triangulation of the underlying point set S, which is the dual of the Voronoi diagram). Thus, in this case, the

---

[24] There is no decomposition in the SW quadrant of the PM$_3$ quadtree in Figure 4.34(c) because in this example we assume that the Voronoi edges are semi-infinite lines. An alternative is to treat the Voronoi diagram as having pseudo vertices wherever the Voronoi edges intersect the boundary of the underlying space. In our example, this will cause the SW quadrant for the PM$_3$ quadtree to be decomposed once.

PM$_2$ quadtree of the Voronoi diagram of the point set S can be viewed as the dual of the (3,0)-AVD of S.

Notice that when the polygonal map M is a Voronoi diagram, the implementation in terms of the blocks of the PM$_2$ quadtree of M is more efficient spacewise than the implementation in terms of the blocks of the (3,0)-AVD of M as the (3,0)-AVD may need to store as many as three points of S in each block, whereas the PM$_2$ quadtree only needs to store at most one of the vertices of the Voronoi diagram in each block. Moreover, none of the blocks in the (3,0)-AVD of M are empty, but all blocks of the PM$_2$ quadtree through which no edges pass are empty. In many quadtree implementations (e.g., pointerless representations that make use of locational codes as described in Section 2.1.2.4 of Chapter 2), there is no need to keep track of the empty blocks as their identity can be derived from knowledge of the nonempty blocks (see Exercise 24 in Section 2.3.1 of Chapter 2, which shows how the locational codes of the empty blocks can be obtained from the locational codes of the nonempty blocks).

Of course, using such a pointerless implementation, given an arbitrary point q, determining the closest point of S, in the case of the PM$_2$ quadtree, will be more complex because this information is not explicitly present in the PM$_2$ quadtree data structure and thus can be most easily obtained by first constructing S by a process analogous to solving a linear system (see Exercises 5 and 6 in Section 2.2.1.4 of Chapter 2). An alternative, and more practical, solution is to augment the PM$_2$ quadtree data structure to store also the sites of the Voronoi diagram if they lie in a particular block. In this case, each block of the PM$_2$ quadtree will contain up to four points where at most three of the points correspond to sites, provided that we have a nondegenerate Voronoi diagram. Finding the site s associated with a particular point q requires locating the block b containing q and then searching b's adjacent blocks for a block c such that c contains a site s whose associated region also contains q. This search guarantees finding s as long as the search paths do not cross blocks that are associated with edges of the Voronoi diagram. This solution is not very efficient if there are many empty blocks. This drawback is overcome by reverting to a solution that associates a site with each block b of the PM$_2$ quadtree, which is essentially what is done in the (3,0)-AVD, except we now also keep track of the vertices of the Voronoi digram. Of course, still another alternative is to make use of the auxiliary structure that may be present that captures the topological properties of the polygonal map.

Exercises

1. Show how to construct a (t, ε)-AVD for a d-dimensional Voronoi diagram of N sites that uses $O(N)$ space and that can be used to answer an ε-nearest neighbor query in $O(\log N + (1/\varepsilon)^{(d-1)/2})$ time.

2. Prove that, in the case of a two-dimensional polygonal map M that is a Voronoi diagram where no four elements of S are cocircular, the (3,0)-AVD of M yields the same block decomposition of the underlying space as the PM$_2$ quadtree for the edges of M.

3. How would you adapt the analogy between the PM quadtree family and the (3,0)-AVD to three and more dimensions? In particular, devise an analog of the PM$_2$ quadtree in higher dimensions.

4.4.6 Avoiding Overlapping All of the Leaf Blocks

Most of the index structures that we have discussed are based on the principle that the data regions are recursively split into two when the data regions contain too many points—that is, each data region contains some maximum number of points. Such a splitting strategy can be implemented within many different structures (e.g., k-d tree, R-tree, hybrid tree, LSD tree). Berchtold, Böhm, and Kriegel [187] claim that one of the main reasons for the performance gaps of these index structures when dealing with high-dimensional data variability) along the different coordinates. Thus, for a given point v, the locational code $l(v)$ resulting from the transformation becomes

$$l(v) = \begin{cases} d_{min} \cdot c + v_{min} & \text{if } v_{min} + c \cdot \theta < c - v_{min} \\ d_{max} \cdot c + v_{max} & \text{otherwise} \end{cases}$$

What are the disadvantages of such an approach?

5. Can you define a variant of iMinMax that results in a partition of the d-dimensional underlying space into pyramids analogous to the extended pyramid technique rather than truncated pyramids. You will need to modify the definition of θ so that there is at least one variant for each coordinate.

6. In the text, we pointed out that the generalization of iMinMax to an arbitrary dataspace that need not be a vector space (but that has a distance function) resembles the top level of GNAT [255] (see Section 4.5.3.2). Does it also resemble the M-tree [389] (see Section 4.5.4)?

4.4.8 Methods Based on a Sequential Scan

As we pointed out in the previous subsections, as the dimensionality of the underlying space increases, the indexing methods that we have described become increasingly worse[25] and are often eventually outperformed by a simple sequential scan (also referred to as a *linear scan*) of the underlying data. The key advantage of sequential scan over hierarchical indexing methods is that the actual I/O cost for query algorithms (e.g., finding the nearest neighbor or the k nearest neighbors) is reduced because we can scan the data sequentially instead of at random. Accessing disk pages at random is likely to incur a disk seek overhead for each access, whereas sequential access only incurs one seek time overhead. Recall that the main reason for the poor performance of the hierarchical indexing methods is the fact that they do not discriminate well on high-dimensional data.

This has led a number of researchers to investigate methods that speed up the sequential scan method [185, 607, 1973]. Clearly, sequential scan must examine all of the data. Thus, the only way to reduce the work involved in the sequential scan is to reduce the proportion of the amount of each data object that is examined—that is, by not examining all of the features that characterize each object or each data point in its entirety. There are two principal methods of achieving this. The first way, which is quite simple, is to use a partial distance search (e.g., [356]). In this case, if the partial sum of the square differences (assuming Euclidean distance) of the features for a candidate exceeds the distance to the nearest neighbor found so far, then the candidate is rejected. In this case, we avoid examining some of the features completely.

The second way is a more general application of the idea. It takes all of the features into account at once, rather than sequentially, and then just examines a predefined part of each feature. This is the key to the efficiency of methods that scan the entire file, such as the VA-file [1973], the VA$^+$-file [607], and, in a more local manner, the IQ-tree [185]. These methods are the subject of the rest of this section. This idea has also been used in conventional indexing methods such as the hybrid tree [317] and the LSD^h tree [826] (see Section 4.4.3 and Section 1.7.1.2 in Chapter 1) to obtain a more compact, but less precise, representation of a minimum bounding box so that the fanout of a nonleaf node can be increased.

The *vector approximation file* (denoted *VA-file*) [1973] represents each object (i.e., a data point p in d-dimensional space) by a pair of values:

---

[25] More precisely, as the dimensionality of the underlying space increases, for some query and data distributions, such as the uniform distribution, the curse of dimensionality comes into play, and the performance of the indexing methods worsens.

1. An approximation of the d feature values using a bitstring of width b_i bits per feature i

2. A pointer to the tuple corresponding to p in the actual data file

Thus, the range of values of feature i is subdivided into 2^{b_i} slices. The boundaries of the slices are determined in such a way that all slices are approximately equally populated. Note that the boundaries of the slices are kept fixed as updates, such as insertions and deletions, are made to the data. However, periodic reorganizations can be performed when the distribution among slices becomes bad. The actual bitstrings for the individual feature are concatenated to form a larger bitstring of width $b = \sum_{i=1}^{d} b_i$ bits. The result is an approximation (actually a lossy compression) of the feature vector and hence the rationale for the use of the name *vector approximation* to describe the representation. Alternatively, we say that the vector is quantized.

The VA-file is a simple array or list of pairs with no particular order (i.e., the order of entries is simply the order in which the points were inserted). There is no spatial index imposed on it. Thus, the VA-file is nothing more than a representation of the original data that takes up less space. Nevertheless, it is important to observe that the VA-file is not a replacement for the original data, but, instead, it is an additional representation much like an index in the sense that it requires additional storage beyond that needed to store the original data.

In essence, the VA-file imposes a d-dimensional grid with 2^b hyperrectangular grid cells on the underlying dataspace, and each data point is represented by its grid cell. As we pointed out above, the actual representation of the grid cell is the concatenation of the bit values that it comprises, but, of course, it could also be represented by interleaving the corresponding bit values. The disadvantage of using bit interleaving is that this usually requires that each feature be approximated by the same number of bits, although it could be defined with a variable number of bits per feature, as done is in the BANG file [640]. Nevertheless, the fact that the VA-file is completely unordered means that the issue of using bit concatenation or some other encoding is most likely irrelevant.

Queries are processed using a two-stage procedure that, in essence, is a filter-and-refine algorithm [1416]. The first stage, corresponding to the filter step, applies a sequential scan to the VA-file instead of the original data file. During this process, candidate data points are generated that could satisfy the query. In particular, the grid cell c associated with each data point p is used to compute a lower bound on the distance from a query point q to p. This is the distance from q to the nearest boundary of c, or 0 if q is inside c. Similarly, an upper bound on the distance from q to p is the distance from q to the farthest point on the farthest boundary of c.

For example, for a range search (i.e., all points within radius r of query object q), a point p with grid cell c is a candidate if the lower bound on p's distance from q, based on c, falls within the range. Similarly, for a k-nearest neighbor query, a list is maintained of the k points that have been processed so far with the smallest upper bounds on their distance from q (again, based on their grid cells). Let D be the greatest of these k upper bounds. D is also an upper bound on the distance of the actual kth-nearest neighbor of q, and thus we ignore any grid cell c for which the lower bound on its distance from q is greater than D (i.e., the corresponding point p is not a candidate). This approach to finding nearest neighbors in a grid has been attributed to Elias by Rivest [1566] and is known as the *Elias algorithm* [403, 1566]. The Elias algorithm is typically only presented for the $k = 1$ case, but generalizing it to arbitrary k is not hard, as we saw above.

In the second stage, corresponding to the refine step, the elements in the candidate set obtained in the first stage are processed in increasing order of their lower-bound distances (i.e., using a priority queue mechanism such as a heap; see Exercise 1). For each element, the corresponding actual point representation p is accessed from disk, its distance from q is computed, and p is added to a (candidate) result set based on the query criteria. In the case of range searching, all of the points corresponding to the candidates must be examined, and those points satisfying the range criteria are added to the result set. However, for a k-nearest neighbor query, we can avoid examining all of the points corresponding to the candidates. In particular, the k-nearest neighbor query is implemented by again maintaining a candidate set, this time comprising the k points seen so far with the smallest actual distances from q. Let D be the greatest of these distances. The search is stopped as soon as a candidate element is encountered for which the lower bound on its distance from q is greater than D. Note that the nearest neighbor is obtained by letting $k = 1$. The same process is also used in many range and nearest neighbor query processing algorithms when we do not have easily identifiable features, and thus the indexing is based solely on the value of a distance function that indicates the similarity or dissimilarity between the pairs of objects (see Section 4.5).

Empirical studies [1973] show that the VA-file outperforms the X-tree, R*-tree, and the sequential scan methods for nearest neighbor searches on both random data as well as real datasets for dimensions ranging as high as 45. The performance of the VA-file was already better in all cases for dimensions greater than six.

The VA-file bears a close resemblance to the grid file [839, 840, 1376] (see Section 1.7.2.1 of Chapter 1). They both impose a grid on the underlying dataspace, and queries are processed by inspecting data that falls into relevant grid cells. Nevertheless, there are some important differences. First, in the VA-file, the relevant grid cells are obtained by a sequential scan of all of the grid cells, while in the grid file, the relevant grid cells are obtained by random access via the aid of the d linear scales (one per feature). Thus, the linear scales provide the index for the grid file. On the other hand, the VA-file has no index. Second, in contrast to the VA-file, in the grid file, the boundaries of the slices are modified as the underlying data changes (i.e., due to updates). Thus, the dynamic behavior of the VA-file may be bad, which means that, at times, the VA-file may have to be rebuilt. Actually, the VA-file need not necessarily be rebuilt as we may only need to move the points that are affected by the change in relevant slice boundaries. However, in order to determine these points, we will need to scan the VA-file in its entirety, which is somewhat time-consuming. Nevertheless, given the fact that the entire VA-file is always scanned for each query, the cost of this additional scan is less of an issue. In contrast, the same actions of moving points as a result of the change in the grid cell boundaries can be performed in the grid file via random access, and thus the grid file has good dynamic behavior.

The design of the VA-file makes the implicit assumption that the features are independent, or at least uncorrelated, as the number of bits used to represent each feature, as well as the boundaries of the slices corresponding to the grid cells, are obtained independently. Ferhatosmanoglu, Tuncel, Agrawal, and El Abbadi [607] address the situation where these assumptions do not hold—that is, when some of the features are less discriminatory than others or exhibit less variability, and so on. They propose to decorrelate the data by using the Karhunen-Loève Transform (KLT) [665]. Based on the KLT, they then examine the new features and allocate a varying number of bits to them, depending on their discriminating range. In addition, instead of dividing each range into equally populated or equally sized intervals, they use an optimal quantizer such as Lloyd's algorithm [1194], which is nothing more than a greedy heuristic for solving the k-means problem, thereby resulting in clustering (e.g., [1174, 1219]) that is adapted for one-dimensional data.

Ferhatosmanoglu et al. use the term *VA⁺-file* to describe the result of these modifications and show that the VA⁺-file is a significant improvement over the VA-file for a number of real datasets. This improvement is in terms of the I/O cost and is achieved due to having better approximations of the distances of the points to the queries. In other words, the lower and upper bounds are tighter, which means better filtering in the first stage of range and nearest neighbor algorithms (i.e., fewer candidates are obtained). Moreover, according to their experiments, the nearest neighbors are obtained by examining fewer candidates in the second stage of the algorithm, which must perform random disk I/O as the data objects are accessed in the order of their lower bound distances as determined from their grid cells.

The IQ-tree of Berchtold, Böhm, Jagadish, Kriegel, and Sander [185] also attempts to apply a more optimal quantization process, albeit based on a different philosophy. It is distinguished from the VA-file in several respects, with the most important being that the sequential scan is applied on a local basis, which has the consequence that a feature need not be quantized in the same way for the entire file. This enables a more optimal form of quantization to be used.

The IQ-tree is a three-level hierarchy. The first level contains an unordered list of minimum bounding rectangles (MBRs) of subsets of the dataset, obtained through a partitioning scheme described below. The second level consists of quantized data pages corresponding to the partitions at the first level. These quantized data pages are like mini VA-files for the data points in the MBR of each partition. These pages are of a fixed size, and the number of data points that they contain depends on the extent of the quantization (i.e., the number of bits allocated to each dimension). The third level consists of data pages that contain the full representation of the data points whose quantized representation is found on the second level. These data pages are of variable size. These pages are accessed only if the approximation at the second level is not enough to evaluate the query. Thus, we see that, in principle, when using the IQ-tree to respond to a query, the IQ-tree enables replacing the sequential scan of the VA-file corresponding to the entire dataset by a sequential scan of the file of MBRs of partitions of the underlying space and of the corresponding VA-file of the data points in the relevant MBRs. Therefore, the IQ-tree can be characterized as a hybrid of the VA-file and of hierarchical indexing methods such as the R-tree.

One of the main goals of Berchtold et al. [185] is to determine the optimal number of bits that should be assigned to the points in each partition. The partitions are formed by using a partitioning scheme such as that described by Berchtold, Böhm, and Kriegel [187] (see Section 4.4.6), originally proposed for fast bulk loading of high-dimensional indexes like the X-tree [190] (see Section 4.4.1). The initial step partitions the underlying data into s partitions using 1-bit quantization (i.e., each feature is quantized with 1 bit for a total of m bits for m features). Therefore, for d feature dimensions, each quantized data point occupies d bits. Thus, if a disk page can hold M such d bit-quantized values, then the initial partitioning is into $s = \lceil N/M \rceil$ partitions of approximately M points each, where N is the number of data points. Hence, we obtain a partitioning of the data points into the minimum number of nearly full data pages based on 1-bit quantization of each dimension (i.e., feature).

Next, each partition t is considered in turn, to see whether is worthwhile to split t into two parts, each with an equal number of points. Observe that after such a split, each part will only fill half a disk block if we still use 1-bit quantization. Therefore, we can double the number of bits for each dimension (i.e., feature), thus nearly filling two disk blocks to capacity. The decision as to whether or not to split the partition is made with the aid of a cost model. The idea is to find an appropriate trade-off between the increased accuracy obtained by splitting (since we have twice the number of bits per dimension) and the increased I/O cost of possibly accessing two disk blocks instead of one (i.e., depending on the likelihood of both parts being involved in a single query). The actual quantization is always performed with respect to the MBR of the partition that is being split, and all features are split the same number of times (i.e., the same number of bits is assigned to each feature). The splitting process is applied recursively with the number of bits of quantization per object doubled at each stage. The total number of splits is determined by the cost model, which also takes into account the costs of loading and processing the various levels of the directory [185].

The borders of the quantization cells in the IQ-tree are determined in the same way they are in the VA-file in that each range of a feature's quantized values has the same number of points. However, unlike in the VA-file, a feature need not be quantized using the same number of bits for the entire dataset; instead, in the IQ-tree, a different number of quantization bits can be used in each partition. However, all the features in a partition must be quantized using the same number of bits.

The query processing algorithms such as nearest neighbor finding are the same as for an R-tree or other spatial indexes (e.g., [846, 848]) with the exception that, instead of always resorting to the exact representation of a point, a quantized representation is used that plays the same role as the minimum bounding box of an object with extent, such as a line, surface, or volume. Furthermore, Berchtold et al. [185] adapt the algorithms to yield sequential access to disk blocks where possible. For nearest neighbor search, this involves estimating the access probabilities of disk pages. Note that, unlike the algorithms for the VA-file, instead of applying a sequential scan to the entire data file, for the IQ-tree, sequential scan is only applied to the file containing the MBRs of the partitions. Of course, a sequential scan is also used when examining the elements of a quantized data page. This is usually done for many spatial indexes, such as R-trees, where the elements of a leaf node have not been organized to permit fast access. Note that the quantized data page in the IQ-tree is similar to a VA-file with the difference that only the quantized representations of the points are stored, with no explicit pointer to the disk page at the third level that contains the full representation of the point.

Empirical studies [185] have shown the IQ-tree outperforming the VA-file, sequential scan, and the X-tree. These studies have demonstrated the benefit of indexing, which is something not really done in the VA-file. However, the dimensions of the data were generally low (up to 16) in contrast to those reported in studies of the VA-file [1973]. The effect of increasing the dimension of the data is an interesting subject for further study. Note that the performance of the IQ-tree could be improved upon by using the same methods employed by the VA$^+$-file [607] to improve on the VA-file. In particular, a different number of bits could be assigned to each feature in each partition, and an optimal quantizer could be used based on clustering instead of partitioning each range into equally populated regions.

The sequential scan can also be applied to the computation of approximate nearest neighbors. One of the simplest methods is to scan the actual objects sequentially and terminate once finding an object within some predefined distance s of the query object q. This is the basis of the sequential variant of the probably approximately correct (PAC) nearest neighbor method of Ciaccia and Patella [387] (see Section 4.3). Of course, deriving an appropriate value for s is challenging: with too small a value, the entire file must be scanned (i.e., no object is within distance s of q), and with too large a value, the object that is found is a poor candidate (e.g., if all objects are within distance s of q). Unfortunately, this method does not easily extend to finding the k nearest neighbors as we only have the estimate of the distance from the query object to the nearest neighbor and not to the k-nearest neighbor, thereby limiting its utility.

In the case of the VA-file, Weber and Böhm [1971] propose to obtain an approximate nearest neighbor by simply omitting the second step of the algorithm. However, this means that there is no need even to compute the upper-bound distances as they are only used to reduce the number of candidates for the second step. Thus, in order to determine the approximate k nearest neighbors, only the first pass needs to be performed, and the k elements with the k smallest lower bounds are retained.

A more drastic alternative to computing the approximate k nearest neighbors is limiting the number of pages that are scanned in sequence, retaining the k elements with the smallest distances from the query object, and deeming them the k nearest neighbors. Ferhatosmanoglu et al. [608] compare this approach with a number of other approaches that are based on limiting the amount of information (i.e., bits) that is available about each element (i.e., the number of bits per dimension), thereby also limiting the number of page accesses. These approaches include the VA-file, VA$^+$-file, and the result of decorrelating the data using the Karhunen-Loève Transform (KLT) [665]. In addition, the result is compared to a new method that makes use of clustering once the data has been decorrelated using the KLT. The method partitions the new features into groups of

d/s features according to the variance along each new feature axis (the variance, which is obtained as a byproduct of KLT, indicates the "spread" in data values along the axes) and applies a k-means clustering algorithm (e.g., [1174, 1219]) to all the data, but only in terms of the values of the group of the s most significant features. The closest cluster c to query point q is determined, and the k nearest elements in c to q are obtained. Next, the k elements in c are refined by including the values of the next s most significant features. These newly refined k elements are compared with the elements in the second closest cluster to q (using $2 \cdot s$ features this time), and, once again, the k nearest elements are determined. This process of increasing the number of clusters by one and the number of features by s is applied repeatedly until the quality of the result is deemed good enough.

One of the difficulties with applying any of the above approaches (except for PAC [387], which is only applicable for $k = 1$ and was not one of the approaches studied by Ferhatosmanoglu et al. [608]) to the determination of the approximate k nearest neighbors is that we have no a priori control over the quality of the resulting approximation. In particular, in contrast to conventional approximate k-nearest neighbor techniques, given an approximation error tolerance ε, we cannot stipulate that, as a result, all of the k elements are within a factor of $(1 + \varepsilon)$ of the distance to the real nearest neighbors. Thus, we need other measures of quality. One possible measure of quality is the number of elements in the set of k approximate nearest neighbors that should not have been returned (i.e., *false hits*) or the number of elements that should have been in the result but were not (i.e., *false dismissals*).

However, when computing the approximate k nearest neighbors, the number of false hits is always equal to the number of false dismissals. Thus, the quality of the result can be measured using either of these measures. For example, we could use the ratio of the number of false hits over k. Unfortunately, this ratio does not provide a good evaluation of the quality of the approximate k-nearest neighbor process. In particular, false hits that are far from the k nearest neighbors are less desirable than false hits that are close to the k nearest neighbors; yet, the ratio does not reflect this. Thus, a better measure is to compute a relative approximation error

$$D = \sum_{i=1}^{k} \|q - a_i\|^2 / \|q - r_i\|^2,$$

where q is the query point, and a_i and r_i ($1 \leq i \leq k$) are the corresponding approximate and exact result sets, respectively.

Using this quantity D, Ferhatosmanoglu et al. [608] show that, for a given number of pages that are accessed, the new method outperforms all three other methods, with the VA$^+$-file being second best, followed by the VA-file, and the method that applies no data reduction. In other words, to attain a given value of D, the new method requires that far fewer pages be accessed than the other methods. The same behavior also holds when the value of D is kept fixed while the volume of the dataset is allowed to grow. Nevertheless, D still depends on knowledge of the nearest neighbors, and thus it cannot be used to determine when enough pages have been accessed to obtain a good approximation. There is no obvious solution to this problem except possibly to use a distribution of D versus the number of pages that have been accessed for some prior queries to obtain an expected value of D and to use that value to choose the number of pages to be accessed.

Exercises

1. Queries on the VA-file, such as finding the k nearest neighbors, make use of a two-stage procedure such as a filter-and-refine algorithm. Why is it not necessary to sort the elements obtained in the first stage prior to starting to process them in the second stage?

2. Modify the IQ-tree by using some of the methods employed by the VA$^+$-file [607] to improve on the VA-file.

3. Adapt the IQ-tree to compute the k approximate nearest neighbors.

4.5 Distance-Based Indexing Methods

In many applications, we do not have easily identifiable features. In this case, the only available information is a distance function that indicates the degree of similarity (or dissimilarity) between all pairs of objects. Thus, searching is facilitated by indexing objects with respect to their distances from other objects. A number of such methods have been proposed over the past few decades, some of the earliest being due to Burkhard and Keller [283]. These methods generally assume that we are given a finite set S of N objects and a distance metric d indicating the distance values between them (collectively termed a *finite metric space*; for more details, see Section 4.5.1). Typical of distance-based indexing structures are *metric trees* [1896, 1897], binary trees that result in recursively partitioning a dataset into two subsets at each node. Uhlmann [1897] identified two basic partitioning schemes: *ball partitioning* and *generalized hyperplane partitioning*.

In ball partitioning, the dataset is partitioned based on distances from one distinguished object, sometimes called a *vantage point* [2052], into the subset that is inside and the subset that is outside a ball around the object (e.g., see Figure 4.39(a)). In generalized hyperplane partitioning, two distinguished objects p_1 and p_2 are chosen, and the dataset is partitioned based on which of the two distinguished objects is the closest—that is, all the objects in subset A are closer to p_1 than to p_2, while the objects in subset B are closer to p_2 (e.g., see objects p_1 and p_2 in Figure 4.39(b)). The asymmetry of ball partitioning (which is evident from Figure 4.39(a)) is a potential drawback of this method as the outer shell tends to be very narrow for metric spaces typically used in similarity searching (e.g., see [255]). In contrast, generalized hyperplane partitioning is more symmetric, in that both partitions form a "ball" around an object (see Figure 4.39(b)).

An alternative way of distinguishing between some of the different distance-based indexing methods is on the basis of whether they are pivot based or clustering based (e.g., [332]). Pivot-based methods choose a subset of the objects in the dataset to serve as distinguished objects, termed *pivot objects* (or more generally *pivots*), and classify the remaining objects in terms of their distances from the pivot objects. Pivot-based similarity searching algorithms make use of the known distances from the objects to different pivot objects to reduce the number of distance computations involving the query object that will be needed to respond to the query. The pivot objects, assuming without loss of generality that there are k of them, can often be viewed as coordinates in a k-dimensional space, and the result of the distance computation for object x is equivalent to a mapping of x to a point $(x_0, x_1, \ldots, x_{k-1})$, where coordinate value x_i is the distance $d(x, p_i)$ of x from pivot p_i. The result is very similar to embedding methods discussed in Section 4.7. Ball partitioning methods are examples of pivot-based methods. In addition, methods that make use of distance matrices that contain precomputed distances between some or all of the objects in the dataset [1292, 1930, 1951] are also examples of pivot-based methods. Note that the distance matrix methods differ from the ball partitioning methods in that they do not form a hierarchical partitioning of the dataset.

Clustering-based methods partition the underlying dataset into spatial-like zones called *clusters* that are based on proximity to a distinguished object known as the *cluster center*. In particular, once a set of cluster centers has been chosen, the objects that are associated with each cluster center c are those that are closer to c than to any other cluster center. Although the cluster centers play a similar role to the pivot objects, the principal difference is that an object o is associated with a particular pivot p on the basis of the distance from o to p, and not because p is the closest pivot to o, which would be the case if p were a cluster center. This distinction was already made in Figure 4.10 in conjunction with the discussion of the pruning methods used with the depth-first k-nearest neighbor algorithm in Section 4.2. Generalized hyperplane partitioning methods are examples of clustering-based methods. The *sa-tree* [1347], inspired by the Voronoi diagram, is another example of a clustering-based method. It records a portion of the Delaunay graph of the dataset, which is a graph whose vertices are the Voronoi cells,

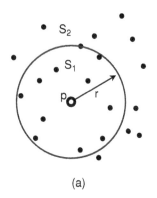

(a)

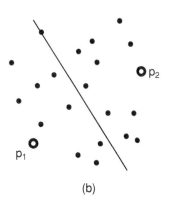

(b)

Figure 4.39
Possible top-level partitionings of a set of objects (depicted as two-dimensional points) in a metric tree using (a) ball partitioning and (b) generalized hyperplane partitioning.

with edges between adjacent cells. Although many of the clustering-based methods that we describe are hierarchical, this need not necessarily be the case.

It is interesting to observe that both pivot-based and clustering-based methods achieve a partitioning of the underlying dataset into spatial-like zones. However, the difference is that the boundaries of the zones are better defined in the case of pivot-based methods in the sense that they can be expressed explicitly using a small number of objects and a known distance value. In contrast, in the case of clustering-based methods, the boundaries of the zones are usually expressed implicitly in terms of the cluster centers, instead of explicitly, which may require quite a bit of computation to determine. In fact, very often, the boundaries cannot be expressed explicitly, as, for example, in the case of an arbitrary metric space (in contrast to a Euclidean space) where we do not have a direct representation of the "generalized hyperplane" that separates the two partitions.

Note that often the terms *cluster*, *cluster center*, and *pivot object* are used loosely without much attention to the nature of the indexing method with which they are being deployed (i.e., whether it is pivot based or clustering based). In particular, recall Section 4.2, where the cluster centers and cluster elements are actually pivots and collections of objects within a given distance of the pivots, respectively, in the context of the above discussion. Thus, in the rest of this section we usually use the term *pivot* in a collective sense to refer to any type of distinguished object that can be used during search to achieve pruning of other objects, following the convention of Chávez, Navarro, Baeza-Yates, and Marroquín [334]. In other words, a pivot $p \in S$ is an object for which we have some information about its distance from some or all objects in S. For example, for all objects $o \in S' \subseteq S$, we know one of the following:

1. The exact value of $d(p,o)$

2. That $d(p,o)$ lies within some range $[r_{lo}, r_{hi}]$ of values

3. That o is closer to p than to some other object $p' \in S$

In this section, we describe a number of distance-based indexing methods with an emphasis on how they can be used to find similar objects (i.e., range searching and nearest neighbors). The focus is on understanding the basic ideas behind the methods and on differentiating between them. Thus, we do not provide much detail about construction algorithms or devote much effort to comparing or contrasting the different methods. This section is organized as follows. In Section 4.5.1, we discuss properties of the distance metric useful for search pruning. This section is rather technical, and the reader may wish to skim over this section on first reading and refer back to it as needed. In Section 4.5.2, we describe the *vp-tree* [2052] and other variants of metric trees that employ ball partitioning. In Section 4.5.3, we present the *gh-tree* [1897] and other variants of metric trees that employ generalized hyperplane partitioning. In Section 4.5.3.3, we focus on the bisector tree [978] and the mb-tree [1383], which are representations based on generalized hyperplane partitioning that are analogous to classical space partitioning methods, such as the PR quadtree [1413, 1637] (see Section 1.4.2.2 in Chapter 1) with implicit rather than explicit boundaries of the regions formed by the partitions. In Section 4.5.4, we describe the *M-tree* [389], a dynamic and balanced metric tree variant suitable for disk-based implementation, which has features common to both pivot-based and clustering-based indexing methods. In Sections 4.5.5 and 4.5.6, we introduce the *Spatial Approximation tree (sa-tree)* [1347] and the *kNN graph* [1704], respectively, which are a pair of clustering-based methods. In Section 4.5.7, we describe *AESA* [1930] and *LAESA* [1292], methods that rely on distance matrices, which are variants of pivot-based methods. Finally, in Section 4.5.8, we present Spatial Approximation Sample Hierarchy (SASH), which enables distance-based indexing without requiring the triangle inequality. In this respect, it is similar to the kNN graph; however, it is much faster to construct, at the cost of having edges to objects that are likely to be nearest neighbors rather than to exact nearest neighbors, as in the kNN graph. In particular, indexing methods such as the kNN graph must compute the nearest neighbors as part of the process of forming the index, which will speed up the calculation of nearest neighbors in the future. In contrast, SASH constructs the index in an incremental manner by using the existing index for a set of objects to determine the approximate nearest neighbors of newly added objects.

4.5.1 Distance Metric and Search Pruning

As mentioned earlier, the indexed objects must reside in a finite metric space (S, d). This means that the distance function d must satisfy the following three properties, where $o_1, o_2, o_3 \in S$:

1. $d(o_1, o_2) = d(o_2, o_1)$ (symmetry)

2. $d(o_1, o_2) \geq 0, \ d(o_1, o_2) = 0$ iff $o_1 = o_2$ (nonnegativity)

3. $d(o_1, o_3) \leq d(o_1, o_2) + d(o_2, o_3)$ (triangle inequality)

When the distance function d satisfies these three properties, then d is said to be a *metric* as well as a *distance metric*. The indexing methods discussed in the remaining subsections are often applicable even when these three properties are relaxed. For example, it rarely matters if $d(o_1, o_2) = 0$ for some pairs of distinct objects o_1 and o_2 (in this case, d is often termed a *pseudometric*). Furthermore, adequate performance can often be attained even if the triangle inequality is occasionally violated,[26] but this leads to approximate results (i.e., we cannot guarantee that the nearest neighbors are obtained in strictly nondecreasing order of distance).

Of the distance metric properties, the triangle inequality is the key property for pruning the search space when processing queries. However, in order to make use of the triangle inequality, we often find ourselves applying the symmetry property. Furthermore, the nonnegativity property allows the discarding of negative values in formulas. Below, we enumerate a number of results that can be derived based on the metric properties. Our goal is to provide a foundation for use in later sections when we explain how to perform operations such as range searching and finding nearest neighbors. In particular, we provide lower and upper bounds on the distance $d(q, o)$ between a query object q and some object o, given some information about distances between q and o and some other object(s).

Recall that $S \in \mathbb{U}$, where $\mathbb{U}$ is some underlying set, usually infinite, and we assume that $(\mathbb{U}, d)$ is also a metric space (i.e., that d also satisfies the above properties on $\mathbb{U}$). For generality, we present our results in terms of $(\mathbb{U}, d)$ since a query object is generally not in S. In the first lemma, we explore the situation where we know the distances from an object p to both q and o (while the distance between q and o is unknown).

Lemma 4.1 *Given any three objects $q, p, o \in \mathbb{U}$, we have*

$$|d(q, p) - d(p, o)| \leq d(q, o) \leq d(q, p) + d(p, o) \tag{4.1}$$

Thus, knowing $d(q, p)$ and $d(p, o)$, we can bound the distance of $d(q, o)$ from both below and above.

Proof The upper bound is a direct consequence of the triangle inequality. For the lower bound, notice that $d(p, o) \leq d(p, q) + d(q, o)$ and $d(q, p) \leq d(q, o) + d(o, p)$, according to the triangle inequality. The first inequality implies $d(p, o) - d(p, q) \leq d(q, o)$, and the second implies $d(q, p) - d(o, p) \leq d(q, o)$. Therefore, combining these inequalities and making use of symmetry, we obtain $|d(q, p) - d(p, o)| \leq d(q, o)$, as desired. ∎

Figure 4.40(a) illustrates the situation where the lower bound $|d(\mathsf{q}, \mathsf{p}) - d(\mathsf{p}, \mathsf{o})|$ established in Lemma 4.1 is nearly attained. Clearly, in the figure, $d(\mathsf{q}, \mathsf{o})$ is nearly as small as $d(\mathsf{q}, \mathsf{o}) - d(\mathsf{p}, \mathsf{o})$. The opposite relationship (i.e., $d(\mathsf{q}, \mathsf{o})$ being nearly as small as $d(\mathsf{p}, \mathsf{o}) - d(\mathsf{q}, \mathsf{p})$) is obtained by exchanging q and o in the figure. Similarly,

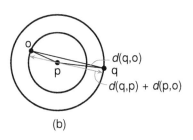

(a)

(b)

Figure 4.40
Illustration of distance bounds. Given $d(\mathsf{q}, \mathsf{p})$ and $d(\mathsf{p}, \mathsf{o})$, a lower bound (a) and an upper bound (b) can be established for $d(\mathsf{q}, \mathsf{o})$.

---

[26] Distance functions for DNA data that are based on edit distance are usually of this nature [1780].

Figure 4.40(b) illustrates the situation where the upper bound $d(\mathsf{q},\mathsf{p}) + d(\mathsf{p},\mathsf{o})$ is nearly attained.

The lower bound on $d(q,o)$ in Lemma 4.1 is also used in Pruning Rule 2 of Fukunaga and Narendra [666] and in Pruning Rule 4 of Kamgar-Parsi and Kanal [986], discussed in Section 4.2.2, to eliminate object o from consideration as q's kth-nearest neighbor in a depth-first k-nearest neighbor finding algorithm. We show this for $k = 1$, but the argument for arbitrary values of k is the same. To see this, we recall that both Rules 2 and 4 apply the triangle inequality to obtain a lower bound of $d(q, p) - d(p, o)$ and $d(p, o) - d(q, p)$, respectively, on the distance from q to o, with the difference depending on whether o is closer to p than q (Rule 2) or whether q is closer to p than o (Rule 4). This lower bound is used to eliminate o from being considered as the nearest neighbor of q when we know that a candidate nearest neighbor o' of q is at a distance of D_1 from q and that D_1 is less than $|d(q, p) - d(p, o)|$. In particular, in this case it is impossible for o to be a better candidate nearest neighbor of q than o' as o is farther from q than o'. Thus, we see that the lower bound on $d(q,o)$ given in Lemma 4.1 is also a lower bound on the distance to the nearest neighbor of q if o is to serve as q's nearest neighbor.

Use of the lower bound on $d(q,o)$ in Lemma 4.1 to eliminate objects from consideration is analogous to the application of the method of Friedman, Baskett, and Shustek [649], as well as that of Nene and Nayar [1364], for vector spaces who eliminate a k-dimensional object $x = (x_0, x_1, ..., x_{k-1})$ from consideration as being within ε of $q = (q_0, q_1, ..., q_{k-1})$ if $|x_i - q_i| > \varepsilon$ for one of x_i, where $0 \leq i \leq k - 1$ (see Section 1.1 in Chapter 1). A variant of this method is also advocated by Chávez, Marroquín, and Baeza-Yates [330]. It is interesting to note that all of these search strategies make an implicit assumption that the k-dimensional space is indexed with a set of inverted lists, one for the distance of the objects from each of the pivots. This is in contrast with a search strategy that assumes the existence of a more general multidimensional point access method such as those discussed in Chapter 1. Other instances where this technique is used include AESA [1930] (Section 4.5.7.1), LAESA [1292] (Section 4.5.7.2), the fixed-queries tree [118] (Section 4.5.2.4), and the fixed-queries array [331] (Section 4.5.2.4), which can all be viewed as variations of embedding methods (see Section 4.7) that map the distances between the objects into a k-dimensional space by finding k objects p_i known as *pivots*, and the result of the mapping of an object x is a point $(x_0, x_1, ..., x_{k-1})$ whose coordinate value x_i is the distance $d(x, p_i)$ of x from pivot p_i. An object x is pruned from further consideration as being within ε of query object q when $|d(q, p_i) - d(x, p_i)| > \varepsilon$ for some pivot p_i ($0 \leq i \leq k - 1$).

In the next lemma, we assume that we know the distance between q and p but that the distance between p and o is known only to be within some range. This is illustrated in Figure 4.41, where we show three different positions of the query object q. The lower bounds on the distances $d(\mathsf{q_1}, \mathsf{o})$ and $d(\mathsf{q_2}, \mathsf{o})$ are indicated with gray arrows, and the upper bound on $d(\mathsf{q_2}, \mathsf{o})$ is indicated with a gray broken arrow. It should be clear that the lower bound on $d(\mathsf{q_3}, \mathsf{o})$ is 0.

Lemma 4.2 *Let o and p be objects in $\mathbb{U}$ such that $r_{lo} \leq d(o, p) \leq r_{hi}$. The distance $d(q,o)$ from $q \in \mathbb{U}$ to o can be bounded as follows, given $d(q,p)$:*

$$\max\{d(q, p) - r_{hi}, r_{lo} - d(q, p), 0\} \leq d(q, o) \leq d(q, p) + r_{hi} \qquad (4.2)$$

Proof Again, we use the triangle inequality to prove these bounds. In particular, from the inequality $d(q, p) \leq d(q, o) + d(o, p)$ and the upper bound $d(o, p) \leq r_{hi}$, we obtain $d(q, p) - d(q, o) \leq d(o, p) \leq r_{hi}$, which implies that $d(q, p) - r_{hi} \leq d(q, o)$ (e.g., see $\mathsf{q_1}$ in Figure 4.41). Similarly, we can combine the triangle inequality and the lower bound on $d(o, p)$ to obtain $r_{lo} \leq d(o, p) \leq d(q, o) + d(q, p)$, which implies that $r_{lo} - d(q, p) \leq d(q, o)$ (e.g., see $\mathsf{q_2}$ in Figure 4.41). Either or both of these lower bounds can be negative (e.g., for $\mathsf{q_3}$ in Figure 4.41), whereas distance values are required to be nonnegative. Thus, the overall lower bound in Equation 4.2 is obtained by taking the maximum of zero and these two lower bounds. The upper bound in Equation 4.2 is obtained by a

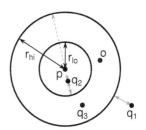

Figure 4.41
Illustration of distance bounds. Given that $r_{lo} \leq d(\mathsf{p}, \mathsf{o}) \leq r_{hi}$, we can establish lower and upper bounds on $d(\mathsf{q}, \mathsf{o})$. Three positions are shown for q, demonstrating three cases that can arise.

straightforward application of the triangle inequality and the upper bound on $d(o,p)$—that is, $d(q,o) \leq d(q,p) + d(o,p) \leq d(q,p) + r_{hi}$ (e.g., see the broken arrow from q_2 through p to the outer boundary in Figure 4.41). ∎

The lower bounds on $d(q,o)$ in Lemma 4.2 are also used in Pruning Rule 1 of Fukunaga and Narendra [666] and in Pruning Rule 3 of Kamgar-Parsi and Kanal [986], discussed in Section 4.2.2, to eliminate object o from consideration as q's kth-nearest neighbor in a depth-first k-nearest neighbor finding algorithm. We show this for $k = 1$, but the argument for arbitrary values of k is the same. To see this, we recall that Pruning Rule 1 makes use of the fact that, given any object o whose distance from object p is less than r_{hi}, the distance from o to another object q must be at least $d(q,p) - r_{hi}$, provided that the distance from q to p is larger than r_{hi}. This means that if we know that a candidate nearest neighbor of q is at a distance of D_1 from q and that D_1 is less than $d(q,p) - r_{hi}$, then it is impossible for o to be a better candidate nearest neighbor, and, in fact, no object o whose distance from p is less than r_{hi} can be the nearest neighbor of q.

Similarly, we recall that Pruning Rule 3 makes use of the fact that, given any object o whose distance from object p is greater than r_{lo}, the distance from o to another object q must be at least $r_{lo} - d(q,p)$, provided that the distance from q to p is smaller than r_{lo}. This means that if we know that a candidate nearest neighbor of q is at a distance of D_1 from q and that D_1 is less than $r_{lo} - d(q,p)$, then it is impossible for o to be a better candidate nearest neighbor, and in fact no object o whose distance from p is greater than r_{lo} can be the nearest neighbor of q. Thus, we see that the lower bounds on $d(q,o)$ given in Lemma 4.2 are also lower bounds on the distance to the nearest neighbor of q if o is to serve as q's nearest neighbor.

In addition, observe that the upper bound on $d(q,o)$ in Lemma 4.2 is also used in Fukunaga and Narendra's [666] formulation of Pruning Rule 5 discussed in Section 4.2.2 to bound the distance to the kth-nearest neighbor of q if o is to serve as q's kth-nearest neighbor in a depth-first k-nearest neighbor finding algorithm. To see this, we recall that Fukunaga and Narendra's [666] formulation of Pruning Rule 5 makes use of the fact that, given any object o whose distance from object p is less than r_{hi}, the distance from o to another object q must be no greater than $d(q,p) + r_{hi}$.

Note that Pruning Rules 1, 3, and 5 are formulated in terms of $r_{p,max}$ and $r_{p,min}$ instead of r_{hi} and r_{lo}, respectively. This means that objects o_{max} and o_{min} must exist at the maximum and minimum distances $r_{p,max}$ and $r_{p,min}$, respectively, from p. However, this is not a problem as the proof of Lemma 4.2 is identical as are the proofs of Pruning Rules 1, 3, and 5 with the alternative definitions.

In some situations, the distance $d(q,p)$ in Lemma 4.2 may not be known exactly. The next lemma establishes bounds on the distance from q to o in such circumstances.

Lemma 4.3 *Let o, p, and q be objects in $\mathbb{U}$ for which $d(o,p)$ is known to be in the range $[r_{lo}, r_{hi}]$ and $d(q,p)$ is known to be in the range $[s_{lo}, s_{hi}]$. The distance $d(q,o)$ can be bounded as follows:*

$$\max\{s_{lo} - r_{hi}, r_{lo} - s_{hi}, 0\} \leq d(q,o) \leq r_{hi} + s_{hi} \tag{4.3}$$

Proof Substituting s_{lo} for the first instance of $d(q,p)$ in Equation 4.2 can reduce only the lower bound. Thus, we find that $s_{lo} - r_{hi} \leq d(q,o)$. The same is true when substituting s_{hi} for the second instance of $d(q,p)$ in the equation as this instance is subtractive, which shows that $r_{lo} - s_{hi} \leq d(q,o)$. Similarly, substituting s_{hi} for the last instance of $d(q,p)$ in the equation increases the upper bound, so we obtain $d(q,o) \leq r_{hi} + s_{hi}$. ∎

Clearly, the roles of the two ranges in Lemma 4.3 are symmetric. For an intuitive understanding of the lower bound, imagine two shells around p, one with radius range $[r_{lo}, r_{hi}]$ (where o is allowed to reside) and the other with radius range $[s_{lo}, s_{hi}]$ (where q is allowed to reside). This is illustrated by the shaded arrow in Figure 4.42(a) where the minimum distance between q and o is equal to the space between the shells, if there is

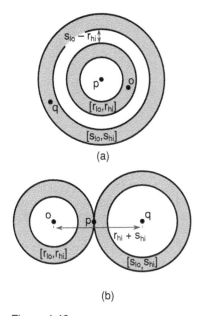

Figure 4.42
(a) The lower bound on $d(\mathsf{q},\mathsf{o})$ for the case when $d(\mathsf{p},\mathsf{o})$ is in the range $[r_{lo}, r_{hi}]$ and $d(\mathsf{p},\mathsf{q})$ is in the range $[s_{lo}, s_{hi}]$ and (b) illustration of how the upper bound on $d(\mathsf{q},\mathsf{o})$ can be attained when $d(\mathsf{p},\mathsf{o})$ and $d(\mathsf{p},\mathsf{q})$ are in these ranges.

any. Similarly, the upper bound can be understood by visualizing shells around q and o, with p at the outer edge of each shell, as illustrated in Figure 4.42(b).

In some distance-based indexes, such as those that use generalized hyperplane partitioning (see Section 4.5.3), objects are partitioned based on the relative closeness to two or more objects. Lemma 4.4 provides a result that we can use in such situations.

Lemma 4.4 *Let $o \in \mathbb{U}$ be an object that is closer to p_1 than to p_2 or equidistant from both (i.e., $d(p_1,o) \leq d(p_2,o)$). Given $d(q,p_1)$ and $d(q,p_2)$, we can establish a lower bound on $d(q,o)$:*

$$\max \left\{ \frac{d(q,p_1) - d(q,p_2)}{2}, 0 \right\} \leq d(q,o) \qquad (4.4)$$

Proof From the triangle inequality, we have $d(q,p_1) \leq d(q,o) + d(p_1,o)$, which yields $d(q,p_1) - d(q,o) \leq d(p_1,o)$. When combined with $d(p_2,o) \leq d(q,p_2) + d(q,o)$ (from the triangle inequality) and $d(p_1,o) \leq d(p_2,o)$, we obtain $d(q,p_1) - d(q,o) \leq d(q,p_2) + d(q,o)$. Rearranging yields $d(q,p_1) - d(q,p_2) \leq 2d(q,o)$, which yields the first component of the lower bound in Equation 4.4; the second component is furnished by nonnegativity. ∎

There are several ways of obtaining intuition about this result. One way is to observe that it is directly applicable to determining which Voronoi regions to examine when performing a range search in a Voronoi diagram (i.e., find all objects within ε of query object q). In essence, we compute the distance from q to each of the sites s_i of Voronoi region v_i and then choose the closest site s to q and eliminate every Voronoi region whose site s_i satisfies $(d(q,s_i) - d(q,s)) > 2 \cdot \varepsilon$ as the intersection of the Voronoi region v_i of s_i with the query range of radius ε centered at q is empty.

An alternative illustration of this result is obtained by considering the situation shown in Figure 4.43(a) where q lies on the line between p_1 and p_2 in a two-dimensional Euclidean space, closer to p_2. If o is closer to p_1, then o is to the left of the horizontal line midway between p_1 and p_2 that separates the regions in which objects are closer to p_1 or to p_2. Thus, $d(q,o)$ is lower bounded by the distance from q to the dividing line, which equals $(d(q,p_1) - d(q,p_2))/2$ for the particular position of q in the figure. If we move q up or down parallel to the dividing line (e.g., up in Figure 4.43(b) to position q'), then the distance from q' to the line is clearly unchanged (i.e., it is still $d(q,p_1) - d(q,p_2)$). However, the difference between $d(q',p_1)$ and $d(q',p_2)$ can be shown to decrease as both $d(q',p_1)$ and $d(q',p_2)$ increase, so the value of $(d(q',p_1) - d(q',p_2))/2$ will also decrease (see Exercise 3). In other words, we see that the distance from q to the dividing line in the figure is exactly $(d(q,p_1) - d(q,p_2))/2$, whereas $(d(q',p_1) - d(q',p_2))/2$ decreases as q' is moved while keeping the distance from q' to the dividing line constant. Therefore, the value $(d(q,p_1) - d(q,p_2))/2$ is indeed a lower bound on the distance from q to any point on the dividing line or from any point q' on the line parallel to the dividing line that passes through q, and thus it is also a lower bound on the distance between q and o. Note that this argument holds for all positions of q that are closer to p_2 than to p_1 as the initial position of q can be anywhere on the line between p_1 and p_2. Observe that without additional information, an upper bound on $d(q,o)$ cannot be established as o may be arbitrarily far away from p_1 or p_2.

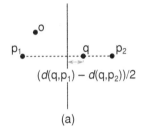

(a)

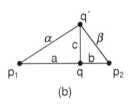

(b)

Figure 4.43
(a) Lower bound on $d(q,o)$ illustrated in a two-dimensional Euclidean space when q is on the line between p_1 and p_2, closer to p_2, while o is closer to p_1 and (b) the lower bound is shown to decrease when q is moved off the line (e.g., to q').

Exercises

1. Recall from footnote 3 of this chapter that the Hamming edit distance between two strings s and t, is defined only when s and t are of the same length, and is the number of positions in which s and t differ (i.e., have different characters). Show that the Hamming edit distance is a distance metric.

2. Recall from footnote 3 of this chapter that the Levenshtein edit distance between two strings s and t is the number of deletions, insertions, or substitutions required to transform s into t. Show that the Levenshtein edit distance is a distance metric.

3. Suppose that you are given points p_1, p_2, q, and o in a two-dimensional Euclidean space, where q is on the line between p_1 and p_2, closer to p_1, while o is closer to p_2, as shown in Figure 4.43(a). Move q in a direction parallel to the dividing line between p_1 and p_2 (e.g., up in Figure 4.43(a)) as shown by q′ in Figure 4.43(b). Show that the difference between $d(q,p_1)$ and $d(q,p_2)$ is decreasing as both $d(q,p_1)$ and $d(q,p_2)$ increase—that is, show that $(d(q′,p_1) - d(q′,p_2))/2 < (d(q,p_1) - d(q,p_2))/2$, while $d(q′,p_1) \geq d(q,p_1)$ and $d(q′,p_2) \geq d(q,p_2)$.

4.5.2 Ball Partitioning Methods

In this section, we discuss ball partitioning methods. Recall that in this case the dataset is partitioned based on distances from one distinguished object p into one subset that is inside and the subset that is outside a ball around the object (recall Figure 4.39(a)). The rest of this section is organized as follows. Section 4.5.2.1 describes the vp-tree. Section 4.5.2.2 presents the vp^{sb}-tree, which is a variant of the vp-tree that keeps track of additional distance information, as well as makes use of buckets in the leaf nodes. Section 4.5.2.3 introduces the mvp-tree, which increases the fanout of the nodes in the vp-tree by splitting the region corresponding to each node into more than two regions corresponding to more than two subsets. Section 4.5.2.4 contains a brief discussion of additional methods based on ball partitioning.

4.5.2.1 Vp-Tree

The *vantage point tree (vp-tree)* [2052] is the most commonly used ball partitioning method. In this section, we first describe the structure of the vp-tree and a number of ways of constructing it (Section 4.5.2.1.1). Next, we discuss how to perform range searching and how to find nearest neighbors incrementally (Section 4.5.2.1.2).

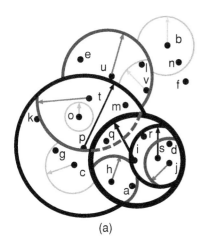

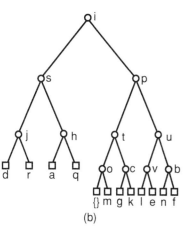

4.5.2.1.1 Structure

The vp-tree is an example of an indexing method that uses ball partitioning (and thus is a variant of the metric tree [1896, 1897]). In this method, we pick a pivot p from S (termed a *vantage point* in [2052]), compute the median r of the distances of the other objects to p, and then divide the remaining objects into roughly equal-sized subsets S_1 and S_2 as follows:

$$S_1 = \{o \in S \setminus \{p\} \mid d(p,o) < r\}$$
$$S_2 = \{o \in S \setminus \{p\} \mid d(p,o) \geq r\}$$

Thus, the objects in S_1 are *inside* the ball of radius r around p, while the objects in S_2 are *outside* this ball. Applying this rule recursively leads to a binary tree, where a pivot object is stored in each internal node, with the left and right subtrees corresponding to the subsets inside and outside the corresponding ball, respectively. In the leaf nodes of the tree, we would store one or more objects, depending on the desired capacity. An example of such a partition is shown in Figure 4.39(a). A more complex example is given by Figure 4.44(b), which is one possible vp-tree for a set of data objects that are points in a two-dimensional Euclidean space given in Figure 4.44(a). The circles in Figure 4.44(a) correspond to the balls, and the objects that serve as pivots are also surrounded by circles.

Note that the ball regions play a role somewhat similar to that of the bounding rectangles in the R-tree. In fact, we can define *bounding values* for each subset S_1 and S_2. In particular, for $o \in S_i$, we have $d(p,o) \in [r_{i,\mathrm{lo}}, r_{i,\mathrm{hi}}]$, for some bounding values $r_{i,\mathrm{lo}}$ and $r_{i,\mathrm{hi}}$. Given only the radius r, the known bounds are $[r_{1,\mathrm{lo}}, r_{1,\mathrm{hi}}] = [0,r]$ and $[r_{2,\mathrm{lo}}, r_{2,\mathrm{hi}}] = [r, \infty]$ (or, more accurately, $[0, r - \delta]$ and $[r, M]$, respectively, where $\delta \leq d(o,o_1) - d(o,o_2)$ and $M \geq d(o_1,o_2)$ for all o,o_1,o_2 in S). For the tightest bounds possible, all four bounding values can be stored in the node corresponding to p. This may yield improved search performance, but perhaps at the price of excessive storage

Figure 4.44
(a) Example set of objects that are points in the two-dimensional Euclidean space and (b) one possible vp-tree corresponding to them. The circles in (a) correspond to the balls, and the objects that serve as pivots are also surrounded by circles.

cost. Below, we use r_{lo} and r_{hi} to denote bounding values of S_1 or S_2 for statements or equations that apply to either subset.

The easiest method of picking pivots is simply to select at random. Yianilos [2052] argues that a more careful selection procedure can yield better search performance (but at the price of a higher construction cost). The method he proposes is to take a random sample from S and choose the object among the sample objects that has the best spread (defined in terms of the variance) of distances from a subset of S, also chosen at random. For a dataset drawn from a Euclidean space for which the data points are relatively uniformly spread over a hypercube c, this would tend to pick points near corners as pivots (the observation that such pivots are preferable was first made by Shapiro [1743]). Choosing such points as pivots can be shown to minimize the boundary of the ball that is inside c (e.g., the length of the boundary in Figure 4.45(a) is greater than that in Figure 4.45(b)), which Yianilos [2052] argues increases search efficiency. Some intuitive insight into the argument that the boundary is reduced as the pivot is moved farther from the center of c can be gained by considering that if we are allowed to pick points outside c as pivots, the resulting partitioning of the hypercube increasingly resembles a partitioning by a hyperplane (e.g., see Figure 4.45(c)). Notice that the areas of the two regions inside c formed by the partitioning tend to be about the same when the points are uniformly distributed, and the length of the partitioning arc inside c is inversely proportional to the distance between the pivot point and the center of c (see Figure 4.45). Observe also that the length l of the partitioning arc decreases even more as the pivot is moved farther away from c (e.g., see Figure 4.45(c)).

In the vp-tree, the ball radius is always chosen as the median r of the distances of the other objects to the pivot p so that the two subsets are roughly equal in size. Another possibility would be to split at the midpoint between the distances of the objects in $S \setminus \{p\}$ that are closest and farthest from p, as proposed by Chávez et al. [334] (and inspired by Burkhard and Keller [283]). This yields a partition into equal-width "shells" around p. Chávez et al. [334] argue that splitting at the midpoint yields better partitions for datasets whose "inherent dimensionality" is high as the objects outside the ball may reside in a thin "shell" when always splitting at the median [334]. However, the disadvantage of splitting at the midpoint is that the resulting tree is not balanced, as is the case when splitting at the median. Nevertheless, even when splitting at the median, the tree can become unbalanced if we support dynamic insertions, but this can be alleviated with periodic reorganization. For a discussion of how to handle dynamic datasets, see Fu, Chan, Cheung, and Moon, [656].

Exercises

1. Give an algorithm to insert an object in a vp-tree.

2. Give an algorithm to delete an object from a vp-tree.

3. Give an algorithm to construct a vp-tree. Use one of the pivot and radius value selection methods described in the text.

4. Compare a number of different methods of constructing a vp-tree by varying the radius r:

   (a) r is the median of the distances of all objects to the pivot object p.

   (b) r is the midpoint of the distances of the objects in $S \setminus \{p\}$ that are closest and farthest from p.

   (c) r is the average of the distances of the objects in $S \setminus \{p\}$ from p.

5. In ball partitioning, the surface of the sphere of radius r centered at p serves as a partitioning surface in the sense that the data has been partitioned into two sets, depending on whether it is inside the sphere or either on the surface of the sphere or outside it. Uhlmann [1896] suggests that the partition surface can be chosen according to the application at hand. How would you incorporate a generalized elliptical surface where the ellipse has pivots at p_1 and p_2 and a principal (i.e., major) axis r?

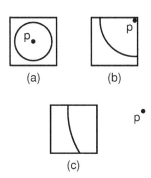

Figure 4.45
Depiction of partitions of a set of points in a two-dimensional Euclidean space, assumed to be uniformly distributed in a cube c, for pivot points (a) in the center of c, (b) in a corner of c, and (c) outside c.

6. Suppose that the partition surface in Exercise 5 is chosen so that it is the set of all objects whose distance from one of two pivots, say p_1, is r plus the distance from the other pivot, say p_2. What is the intuitive definition of this method?

4.5.2.1.2 Search

Clearly, search algorithms are fundamentally the same, regardless of how the pivot and ball radius are determined, since the basic structure is the same. For example, a range query for a query object q and query radius ε—that is, we wish to determine all objects o such that $d(q, o) \leq \varepsilon$—is most easily implemented with a depth-first traversal of the tree. In particular, when visiting a node n with pivot p and ball radius r, we must decide whether to visit the left or right child of n or both. Lemma 4.2 enables us to establish lower bounds on the distances from q to objects in the left and right subtrees. If the query radius is less than the lower bound for a subtree, there is no need to visit that subtree. For example, in Figure 4.46(a), the left subtree (for the objects inside the ball) need not be visited, but in Figure 4.46(b), the left subtree must be visited. Formally, from Equation 4.2 in Lemma 4.2, with $r_{lo} = 0$ and $r_{hi} = r$, we know that the distance from q to an object in the left subtree of n is at least $\max\{d(q, p) - r, 0\}$. Similarly, by applying the equation with $r_{lo} = r$ and $r_{hi} = \infty$, we know that the distance from q to an object in the right subtree of n is at least $\max\{r - d(q, p), 0\}$. Thus, we visit the left child if and only if $\max\{d(q, p) - r, 0\} \leq \varepsilon$ and the right child if and only if $\max\{r - d(q, p), 0\} \leq \varepsilon$. For a probabilistic analysis of the search process in a vp-tree, see Tasan and Özsoyoglu [1861].

We can also use a similar approach to design an incremental nearest neighbor algorithm for the vp-tree, by specifying the search hierarchy according to the framework presented in Section 4.1.2. Being that the vp-tree is hierarchical, the search hierarchy essentially falls out of the existing hierarchical structure. Thus, the elements of the search hierarchy correspond to the objects (type 0) and the nodes in the vp-tree (type 1). Again, we observe that the ball regions for the vp-tree nodes play the same role as bounding rectangles in the R-tree. The resulting search hierarchy for a small sample vp-tree is depicted in Figure 4.47. Note that elements of type 1 can produce elements of type 0 and 1.

We now define the distance functions d_t for the distance between the query object q and elements e_t of type t, $t = 0, 1$. Since elements e_0 of type 0 represent objects, d_0 is simply equal to d. As for d_1, recall that the value of $d_1(q, e_1)$ should be a lower bound on the distance $d(q, o)$ for any object o in the subhierarchy rooted at e_1. The information we have on hand to derive such a lower bound is the value of $d(q, p)$ and the fact that $d(p, o)$ is in the range $[r_{lo}, r_{hi}]$, where p is the pivot of the parent e_1, and $[r_{lo}, r_{hi}]$ defines the shell around p containing the objects in the subtree rooted at e_1 (i.e., $[0, r]$ if e_1 is a left child and $[r, \infty]$ if e_1 is a right child, where r is the ball radius). Thus, as we saw above for the range query, we can make use of Lemma 4.2, which gives lower and upper bounds on $d(q, o)$ based on exactly such information. In particular, the definition of d_1 as obtained from the lemma is

$$d_1(q, e_1) = \max\{d(q, p) - r_{hi}, r_{lo} - d(q, p), 0\}.$$

This definition of d_1 is general in that it accounts for e_1 being either a left child (in which case $r_{lo} = 0$ and $r_{hi} = r$) or a right child (in which case $r_{lo} = r$ and $r_{hi} = \infty$).[27] Furthermore, for either case, it also accounts for q being either inside or outside the region for e_1 (i.e., inside or outside the ball around p of radius r). Since the lemma guarantees that $d_1(q, e_1) \leq d(q, o)$ for any object o in the subtree rooted at e_1, we are

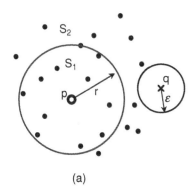

(a)

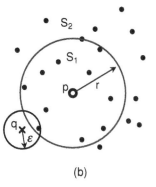

(b)

Figure 4.46
During a range query with query radius ε, the subtree corresponding to the inside of the ball need not be visited in (a) while it must be visited in (b).

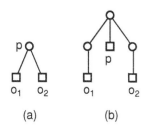

(a)   (b)

Figure 4.47
(a) An example vp-tree for three objects p, o_1, and o_2 and (b) the search hierarchy induced by the vp-tree.

---

[27] As we pointed out before, tight distance bounds for each subtree could be stored in each vp-tree node instead of just the median [2052], thereby causing d_1 and $\hat{d}_1$ to yield improved bounds. This can improve search performance but at the cost of an increase in the storage requirement (i.e., four distance values in each node instead of just one).

assured that the incremental nearest neighbor algorithm is correct when applied to the vp-tree search hierarchy that we have defined (see Section 4.1.3).

The upper-bound distance function $\hat{d}_1$ can also be derived from the result in Lemma 4.2 (i.e., by Equation 4.2):

$$\hat{d}_1(q, e_1) = d(q, p) + r_{hi}$$

where p and r_{hi} are defined as above. Recall that upper-bound distance functions are used when performing farthest-neighbor queries and when a minimum distance bound is imposed on the query results (see Section 4.1.5). The correctness of such algorithm variants is guaranteed by the lemma—that is, since $\hat{d}_1(q, e_1) \geq d(q, o)$ for any object o in the subtree rooted at e_1.

Given the search hierarchy defined above, incremental nearest neighbor search proceeds as described in Section 4.1.3. In particular, when the element obtained from the queue represents an object (i.e., is of type 0), we report it as the next nearest neighbor. Otherwise, the element is of type 1, representing a node n. If n is a nonleaf node with pivot p and ball radius r, we compute $d(q, p)$ and insert p into the priority queue as an element of type 0. Furthermore, the left and right children of n are inserted into the priority queue as elements of type 1 using the distance function defined above. If n is a leaf node, we perform the same action as for pivots of nonleaf nodes for the object(s) in the node.

Exercises

1. Implement the algorithm described in the text for a range query with query radius ε in a vp-tree.

2. Implement the algorithm described in the text to find the nearest neighbors in an incremental manner to a query object q in a vp-tree.

3. Implement the algorithm described in the text to find the farthest neighbors in an incremental manner to a query object q in a vp-tree.

4. Give an algorithm to find all objects within a range of distance values in an incremental manner from a query object q in a vp-tree (i.e., find all elements having distance from q greater than D_{min} and less than D_{max}).

5. In the discussion of the incremental nearest neighbor algorithm in Section 4.1.3, we pointed out that the correctness criterion (i.e., $d_t(q, e_t) \leq d_0(q, e_0)$ for any object e_o in the subtree represented by e_t) does not actually guarantee that when a nonobject search hierarchy element e_t has been removed from the priority queue, no nonobject search hierarchy element $e_{t'}$ (in the subtree represented by e_t) with a smaller distance from the query object q can be inserted in the future, and possibly be removed in the future. In other words, it does not preclude the occurrence of the situation that nonobject elements e_t and $e_{t'}$, where $d_t(q, e_t) > d_{t'}(q, e_{t'})$, could be processed in succession (by virtue of being removed from the priority queue in succession, although some other elements could have been inserted into the queue during this time). Give an example of how this situation can arise in a vp-tree.

6. In Section 4.3 we discuss the method of Chen et al. [346] for finding approximate nearest neighbors, which delays the processing of a node b by shrinking b's radius by a factor of λ ($0 < \lambda \leq 1$), thereby increasing the effective distance $d(b, q)$ between query object q and b as measured by the distance between q and the closest point in b (after its radius has been shrunk). How would you apply this idea to the vp-tree?

4.5.2.2 Vp^{sb}-Tree

When the vp-tree is constructed, we must compute the distances of an object o from each of the pivots on the path from the root to the leaf containing o. This information is useful as it can often be used during search either to prune o from the search or to include it in the search result without computing its distance. Based on this insight, Yianilos [2052] proposed a version of the vp-tree, termed the vp^s-tree, where we store, for each object (whether it functions as a pivot or is stored in a leaf node), its distance from all ancestral pivots (i.e., those higher in the tree on the path from the root). In the related vp^{sb}-*tree*, the leaf nodes can store more than one object, thus serving as "buckets."

Knowledge of the distances to the ancestral pivots is useful in performing a range query. In particular, consider an object o, one of its ancestral pivots p, and the query object q. Given $d(q,p)$ and $d(p,o)$, Lemma 4.1 allows us to bound the distance between q and o—that is, $|d(q,p) - d(p,o)| \le d(q,o) \le d(q,p) + d(p,o)$. Thus, when performing a range query with radius ε, we can safely discard o if $|d(q,p) - d(p,o)| > \varepsilon$ or directly include it in the result if $d(q,p) + d(p,o) \le \varepsilon$.

In order to take full advantage of all ancestral pivots, we define two functions $d_{\text{lo}}(q,o)$ and $d_{\text{hi}}(q,o)$ that provide upper and lower bounds on $d(q,o)$, respectively, for any object o:

$$d_{\text{lo}}(q,o) = \max_i\{|d(q,p_i) - d(p_i,o)|\} \text{ and}$$

$$d_{\text{hi}}(q,o) = \min_i\{d(q,p_i) + d(p_i,o)\}$$

where $p_1, p_2, \ldots$ are the ancestral pivots of o. Observe that when we evaluate these functions, no new distance computations are needed, as $d(q,p_i)$ will have been computed earlier in the query evaluation, and $d(p_i,o)$ is stored with o in its vp-tree node. Clearly, a straightforward application of Lemma 4.1 yields $d_{\text{lo}}(q,o) \le d(q,o) \le d_{\text{hi}}(q,o)$. Therefore, knowing that $d_{\text{lo}}(q,o) > \varepsilon$ means that we can discard object o from the result of a range query with radius ε, even if there exist several pivot objects v for which $|d(q,v) - d(v,o)| \le \varepsilon$. Similarly, knowing that $d_{\text{hi}}(q,o) \le \varepsilon$, we can include object o in the result, even if there exist several pivot objects v for which $d(q,v) + d(v,o) > \varepsilon$.

Incidentally, there is an interesting connection between d_{lo} and a class of mapping methods termed *Lipschitz embeddings* (see Section 4.7.2). In particular, the m ancestral pivots $p_1, \ldots, p_m$ of an object o can be regarded as m singleton sets, each of which corresponds to a coordinate axis, forming the mapping $h : S \to \mathbb{R}^m$, where $h(o)$ is the vector $(d(p_i,o))_i$. If we now map q and o according to h, the L_∞ distance $d_M(h(q), h(o))$ between $h(q)$ and $h(o)$ is equal to $d_{\text{lo}}(q,o)$.

Exercises

1. Give an algorithm to construct a vp^{sb}-tree with a bucket capacity b.

2. Give an algorithm to perform a range query for a query object q and query radius ε in a vp^{sb}-tree.

3. Give an algorithm to find the nearest neighbors in an incremental manner to a query object q in a vp^{sb}-tree.

4.5.2.3 Mvp-Tree

A potential criticism of vp-tree and related metric tree variants is that the fanout is low (i.e., just 2). As pointed out by Yianilos [2052], the vp-tree can gain higher fanout by splitting S into m subsets of roughly equal size instead of just two, based on $m + 1$ bounding values $r_0, \ldots, r_m$ (alternatively, we can let $r_0 = 0$ and $r_m = \infty$). In particular, S is partitioned into $S_1, S_2, \ldots, S_m$, where $S_i = \{o \in S \setminus \{p\} \mid r_{i-1} \le d(p,o) < r_i\}$. Observe that objects in the subsets lie on spherical "shells" around p. Applying this partitioning process recursively yields an m-ary tree. Range searching is performed in the same way as in the vp-tree using Equation 4.2 in Lemma 4.2, with r_{lo} and r_{hi} set to the proper values—that is, $r_{\text{lo}} = r_{i-1}$ and $r_{\text{hi}} = r_i$ for the child corresponding to S_i (unless tighter bounds are maintained).

Another variant of vp-trees that achieves a higher fanout, termed the *mvp-tree*, was suggested by Bozkaya and Özsoyoglu [241]. Each node in the mvp-tree is essentially equivalent to the result of collapsing the nodes at several levels of a vp-tree. There is one crucial difference between the mvp-tree and the result of such collapsing: only one pivot is used for each level inside an mvp-tree node (although the number of different ball radius values is unchanged). Thus, in an mvp-tree that corresponds to collapsing a vp-tree over every two levels, two pivots are used in each mvp-tree node with three ball radius values. An example of one possible top-level partitioning for such an mvp-tree is shown in Figure 4.48 which corresponds to the set of objects that are points in the two-dimensional space given in Figure 4.44(a). Figure 4.48(a) shows the partitioning of the underlying space, and Figure 4.48(b) shows the corresponding mvp-tree node. Range searching in an mvp-tree is performed in a manner analogous to that in the vp-tree with the difference that the search is decomposed into j stages, where there is one stage per pivot value.

The motivation for the mvp-tree is that fewer distance computations are needed for pivots during search since there are fewer pivots (e.g., for an mvp-tree node with two pivots, three pivots would be needed in the corresponding vp-tree). Observe that some subsets are partitioned using pivots that are not members of the sets, which does not occur in the vp-tree (e.g., p is used to partition the subset inside the ball around i in Figure 4.48(a)).

Bozkaya and Özsoyoglu [241] describe a number of modifications to the basic definition of the mvp-tree given above. First, they suggest using multiple partitions for each pivot, as discussed above. Hence, with k pivots per node and m partitions per pivot, the fanout of the nonleaf nodes is m^k. Furthermore, they propose storing, for each data object in a leaf node, the distances to some maximum number n of ancestral pivots (by setting a maximum n on the number of ancestral pivots, the physical size of all nodes can be fixed). This is analogous to the use of ancestral pivots in the vp^{sb}-tree, as described above, except that this distance information is maintained only in leaf nodes in the mvp-tree. Another minor departure from the vp-tree that enables additional pruning to take place is that each leaf node in the mvp-tree also contains k pivots (whereas pivots are not used in leaf nodes in the vp-tree). In addition, the distances between these pivots and the data objects are stored in the node (a version of the mvp-tree in which pivots are not used in leaves is also considered in [241]). Thus, the leaf node pivots essentially function like the ancestral pivots. The mvp-tree has found use in applications in bioinformatics databases (e.g., [1299]) when the data is on disk, and found to perform well when the pivots are chosen in a judicious manner (e.g., [1235]) in comparison to methods based on general hyperplane partitioning such as the gh-tree [1897] and more general methods such as the M-tree [389].

Exercises

1. Give an algorithm to construct an mvp-tree.

2. Give an algorithm to perform a range query for a query object q and query radius ε in an mvp-tree.

3. Give an algorithm to find the nearest neighbors in an incremental manner to a query object q in an mvp-tree.

4.5.2.4 Other Methods Related to Ball Partitioning

A number of additional proposals of search structures that employ some form of ball partitioning have been made. Below, we summarize some of these ball partitioning methods. Unless otherwise mentioned, finding similar objects (i.e., range searching and nearest neighbors) can be performed in these structures using similar techniques to those described in Sections 4.5.2.1 to 4.5.2.3.

The vp-tree, one of the most common instances of ball partitioning, is actually a special case of what Knuth terms a *post office tree*, whose proposal he attributes to Bruce McNutt in 1972 [1046, p. 563]. The difference is that each node in the post office tree is a vp-tree node (p, r) with the addition of a tolerance δ that is associated with the radius

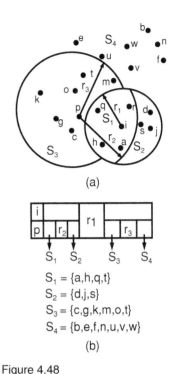

(a)

$S_1 = \{a,h,q,t\}$
$S_2 = \{d,j,s\}$
$S_3 = \{c,g,k,m,o,t\}$
$S_4 = \{b,e,f,n,u,v,w\}$

(b)

Figure 4.48
(a) Possible top-level partitioning for the set of objects that are points in the two-dimensional space given in Figure 4.44(a) in an mvp-tree where two pivots are used in each node and (b) a depiction of the corresponding mvp-tree node. The second pivot, p, partitions the inside of the ball for pivot i into subsets S_1 and S_2 and the outside of the ball into subsets S_3 and S_4.

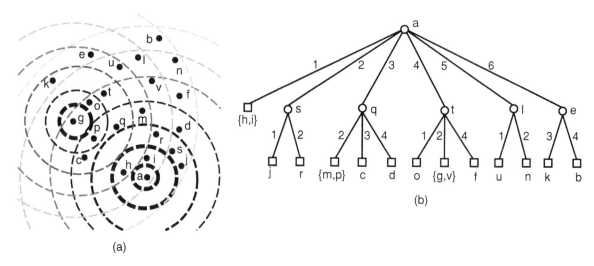

(a)

(b)

Figure 4.49
(a) Example set of objects that are points in the two-dimensional Euclidean space with broken circular lines denoting the boundaries of partitions around pivot objects a and g and (b) one possible bk-tree corresponding to them with bucket capacity 2.

r of the ball centered at p. In particular, given a value of δ, once pivot p and radius r have been chosen, the remaining objects are subdivided into two subsets S_1 and S_2 as follows:

$$S_1 = \{o \in S \setminus \{p\} \mid d(p,o) \leq r + \delta\}$$
$$S_2 = \{o \in S \setminus \{p\} \mid d(p,o) \geq r - \delta\}$$

Thus, the objects in S_1 are inside the ball of radius $r + \delta$, while the objects in S_2 are outside a ball of radius $r - \delta$. Of course, some objects lie both in S_1 and S_2—that is, all objects o where $|d(o,p) - r| \leq \delta$.[28]

Among the earliest published work on distance-based indexing is that of Burkhard and Keller [283]. One of the three structures they proposed employs ball partitioning and is frequently referenced as a *bk-tree*. However, the distance function was assumed to be discrete so that only a few different distance values are possible, say m. At the top level, some distinguished object $p \in S$ is chosen, and the remaining objects are partitioned into m subsets $S_1, S_2, \ldots, S_m$ based on their distance from p. Applying this process recursively yields an m-ary tree. The decomposition stops whenever the partition yields a set with b or fewer elements (b is a bucket capacity). For example, Figure 4.49(b) is one possible bk-tree for the set of data objects that are points in a two-dimensional Euclidean space given in Figure 4.44(a) with $b = 2$. The set of data objects is redrawn in Figure 4.49(a) with a pair of possible initial partitions around pivot objects a and g with broken circular lines, denoting the boundaries of the various subsets with respect to the pivot objects.

Clearly, in the bk-tree, p has the same role as a pivot in the vp-tree, and the result of the partitioning process is analogous to that of an m-ary vp-tree (see Section 4.5.2.3). In fact, as pointed out by Chávez et al. [334], a natural adaptation of the bk-tree to continuous distance functions is to choose the partition values $r_0, r_1, \ldots, r_m$ such that the objects are partitioned into m equiwidth shells around p. In other words, r_0 and r_m are chosen as the minimum and maximum distances, respectively, between p and objects in $S \setminus \{p\}$, and $r_i = \frac{i}{m}(r_m - r_0) + r_0$ for $i = 1, \ldots, m - 1$.

---

[28] The idea of a loose partition so that the children of a node are not disjoint is also used in the os-tree [1229, 1230] (see Section 4.4.4), the KD2-tree [1410, 1412] (see Section 1.5.1.4 of Chapter 1), the spatial k-d tree [1404, 1407] (see Sections 1.5.1.4 and 1.7.1.2 of Chapter 1 and Section 3.3.2.5 of Chapter 3), and the hybrid tree [317] (see Section 4.4.3 and Section 1.7.1.2 of Chapter 1).

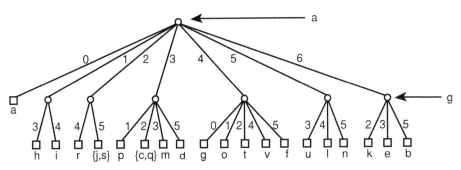

Figure 4.50
The fixed-queries tree corresponding to the set of objects that are points in the two-dimensional Euclidean space given in Figure 4.49(a). All branches at the root of the tree are with respect to pivot object a, and all branches at nodes that are sons of the root are with respect to pivot object g.

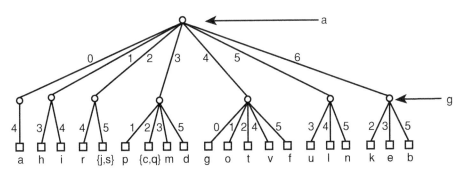

Figure 4.51
The fixed-height fixed-queries tree corresponding to the fixed-queries tree in Figure 4.50.

Baeza-Yates, Cunto, Manber, and Wu [118] proposed a variant of the bk-tree that they termed the *fixed-queries tree* (also known as an *fq-tree*). In this variant, all nodes at the same level in the tree use the same pivot, and the pivot objects also appear as data objects in leaf nodes of the tree (unlike the vp-tree or the bk-tree). For example, Figure 4.50 is the fixed-queries tree corresponding to the set of objects that are points in the two-dimensional Euclidean space given in Figure 4.49(a). All branches at the root of the tree are with respect to pivot object **a**, and all branches at nodes that are sons of the root are with respect to pivot object **g**. The rationale for using just one pivot per level is the same as in the mvp-tree [241] (see Section 4.5.2.3, although these two trees are quite different, as pointed out in Exercise 10)—that is, so that fewer distance computations are needed during search since only one distance computation is needed for visiting all nodes at a given level (as is the case when the search backtracks). The drawback is that the quality of the partitioning may suffer as a result of using fewer pivots.

Fixed-height variants of the fixed-queries tree were also proposed (termed the *fixed-height fixed-queries tree*) [118], where all leaf nodes are at the same level *h*. Thus, some internal nodes have only one child node (in cases where the node would otherwise have been a leaf node), and leaf nodes may contain arbitrary numbers of objects. For example, Figure 4.51 is the fixed-height fixed-queries tree corresponding to the fixed-queries tree in Figure 4.50.

Each object in the fixed-height fixed-queries tree has the same number of ancestral pivots, and thus requires the same number of distance computations when constructing the tree. This insight led to the proposal of the *fixed-queries array* (also known as an *fq-array*) [331], which is essentially a compact representation of the distances in a fixed-height fixed-queries tree in the form of an array of *h* numbers corresponding to the branches taken in the tree to reach the appropriate elements in the tree from the root.

The h numbers are the distances to the h pivots. For example, Figure 4.52 is the fixed-queries array corresponding to the fixed-height fixed-queries tree in Figure 4.51. The representation is made compact by encoding each of these numbers as a bitstring of b bits, which are concatenated to form a single number so that the most significant digits correspond to the pivots closer to the root. In the fixed-queries array, movements in the equivalent fixed-height fixed-queries tree are simulated with binary search.

It is interesting to repeat our observation (made in conjunction with the discussion of Lemma 4.1 that all three of the fixed-queries tree, fixed-height fixed-queries tree, and fixed-queries array methods can be viewed as variations of embedding methods (see Section 4.7) that map the distances between the objects into a k-dimensional space by using k pivots (i.e., the pivots at the different levels of these trees) as coordinates and the distances of the objects from the pivots as the coordinate values of the objects. In other words, the result of the mapping of an object x is a point $(x_0, x_1, \ldots, x_{k-1})$ whose coordinate value x_i is the distance $d(x, p_i)$ of x from pivot p_i. Lemma 4.1 enables pruning an object x from further consideration as being within ε of query object q when $|d(q, p_i) - d(x, p_i)| > \varepsilon$ for some coordinate corresponding to pivot p_i ($0 \leq i \leq k - 1$). Note that a similar observation was made in the discussion of the vp^{sb}-tree in Section 4.5.2.2, which is similar to these methods.

Yianilos [2053] proposed a variant of the vp-tree termed the *excluded middle vantage point forest* (see also [699]) that is intended for radius-limited nearest neighbor search—that is, where the nearest neighbor is restricted to being within some radius $r*$ of the query object. This method is based on the insight that most of the complexity of performing search in methods based on binary partitioning, such as the vp-tree, is due to query objects that lie close to the partition values, thereby causing both partitions to be processed. For example, in the vp-tree, these are objects q for which $d(q, p)$ is close to r, the partitioning value for a pivot p. The proposed solution is to exclude all data objects whose distances from a pivot are within $r*$ of the partition value (i.e., the ball radius). This process is applied to all pivots in the tree, and a new tree is built recursively for the set of all excluded objects. Thus, the final result is a forest of trees. Since the width of all exclusion regions is at least $2r*$, nearest neighbor search limited to a search region of radius $r*$ can be performed with no backtracking, but at the price of having to search all the trees in the forest. The fact that no backtracking is needed enables determining a worst-case bound on the search cost, based on the heights of the trees in the forest. Unfortunately, the method appears to provide good performance only for very small values of $r*$ [2053], which is of limited value in most similarity search applications.

Exercises

1. Give an algorithm to construct Burkhard and Keller's variant of the m-ary vp-tree (i.e., the bk-tree).

2. Give an algorithm to perform a range query for a query object q and query radius ε in the bk-tree.

3. Give an algorithm to find the nearest neighbors in an incremental manner to a query object q in the bk-tree.

4. Give an algorithm to construct a fixed-queries tree.

Object	a	h	i	r	j	s	p	c	q	m	d	g	o	t	v	f	u	l	n	k	e	b
Level 0	0	1	1	2	2	2	3	3	3	3	3	4	4	4	4	4	5	5	5	6	6	6
Level 1	4	3	4	4	5	5	1	2	2	3	5	0	1	2	4	5	3	4	5	2	3	5

Figure 4.52
The fixed-queries array corresponding to the fixed-height fixed-queries tree in Figure 4.51.

5. Give an algorithm to perform a range query for a query object q and query radius ε in a fixed-queries tree.

6. Give an algorithm to find the nearest neighbors in an incremental manner to a query object q in a fixed-queries tree.

7. Give an algorithm to construct a fixed-height fixed-queries tree.

8. Give an algorithm to perform a range query for a query object q and query radius ε in a fixed-height fixed-queries tree.

9. Give an algorithm to find the nearest neighbors in an incremental manner to a query object q in a fixed-height fixed-queries tree.

10. Compare the fixed-queries tree with the mvp-tree [241] (see Section 4.5.2.3).

11. Give an algorithm to construct a fixed-queries array.

12. Give an algorithm to perform a range query for a query object q and query radius ε in a fixed-queries array.

13. Give an algorithm to find the nearest neighbors in an incremental manner to a query object q in a fixed-queries array.

14. Chávez and Navarro [332] propose a linear variant of the vp-tree that only applies recursive decomposition to the subset outside the ball rather than to the subsets that are both inside and outside the ball as in the vp-tree. In particular, it initially picks a pivot p from S and a value r and divides the remaining objects into two subsets I and E corresponding to the objects inside and outside the ball, respectively, as follows:

$$I = \{o \in S \setminus \{p\} \mid d(p,o) < r\}$$
$$E = \{o \in S \setminus \{p\} \mid d(p,o) \geq r\}$$

This rule is applied recursively only to E. Thus, any search algorithm that is applied will process the objects in I exhaustively while being recursively invoked on the objects in E. The main rationale for this method is to take advantage of the fact that most of the objects will lie outside I for most reasonably chosen values of r, and thus there is no need to decompose I recursively. Give an algorithm to perform a range query on a set R for a query object q and query radius ε using this structure.

4.5.3 Generalized Hyperplane Partitioning Methods

In this section, we discuss generalized hyperplane partitioning methods. Recall that in this case two distinguished objects are chosen, and the dataset is partitioned based on which of the distinguished objects is the closest (recall Figure 4.39(b)). The rest of this section is organized as follows. Section 4.5.3.1 describes the gh-tree. Section 4.5.3.2 presents the Geometric Near-neighbor Access Tree (GNAT), which is a generalization of the gh-tree where more than two pivots may be chosen to partition the dataset in each node. Section 4.5.3.3 describes the bisector tree and the mb-tree, and Section 4.5.3.4 contains a brief discussion of additional methods based on generalized hyperplane partitioning.

4.5.3.1 Gh-Tree

Uhlmann [1897] defined a metric tree using generalized hyperplane partitioning, which has been termed a *generalized hyperplane tree (gh-tree)* by later authors [241, 255, 656]. Instead of picking just one object for partitioning, as in the vp-tree, this method picks two pivots p_1 and p_2 (e.g., the objects farthest from each other; see Exercise 3) and splits the set of remaining objects based on the closest pivot (see Figure 4.39(b)):

$$S_1 = \{o \in S \setminus \{p_1, p_2\} \mid d(p_1, o) \leq d(p_2, o)\} \text{ and}$$
$$S_2 = \{o \in S \setminus \{p_1, p_2\} \mid d(p_2, o) < d(p_1, o)\}$$

In other words, the objects in S_1 are closer to p_1 than to p_2 (or equidistant from both), and the objects in S_2 are closer to p_2 than to p_1. This rule is applied recursively, resulting in

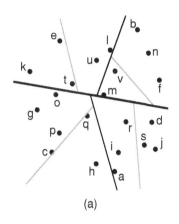

(a)

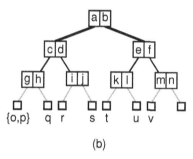

(b)

Figure 4.53
(a) A possible space partitioning produced by the gh-tree for a set of points in a two-dimensional Euclidean space and (b) its tree representation.

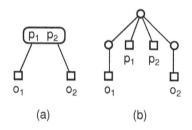

(a)   (b)

Figure 4.54
(a) An example gh-tree for four objects p_1, p_2, o_1, and o_2 and (b) the search hierarchy induced by the gh-tree.

a binary tree where the left child of a nonleaf node corresponds to S_1 and the right child corresponds to S_2. This rule can be restated as stipulating that S_1 contains all objects o such that $d(p_1, o) - d(p_2, o) \leq 0$. Clearly, the two subsets S_1 and S_2 can be very different in size. Uhlmann [1897] actually suggested partitioning based on a median value m, so that $d(p_1, o) - d(p_2, o) \leq m$ applies to roughly half the objects in S. For simplicity, we assume below that m is fixed at 0; the discussion is easily generalized to other values. Note also that the decomposition process is halted once the number of objects in each leaf node (corresponding to a cluster) is less than the desired capacity (which may be one). A sample gh-tree is shown in Figure 4.53 that makes use of the same data as in Figure 4.44(a). It is interesting to note, although it is beyond the scope of our discussion, that there have also been recent attempts to implement the gh-tree in a peer-to-peer (P2P) setting (e.g., [136]).

The term *generalized hyperplane partitioning* is derived from the fact that if the objects are points in an n-dimensional Euclidean space, then the resulting partitioning is equivalent to one based on an $(n-1)$-dimensional hyperplane like that used in a k-d tree (in a k-d tree, however, the partitioning planes are axis aligned). This hyperplane is the set of all points o that satisfy $d(p_1, o) = d(p_2, o)$. Consider how to compute a lower bound on the distance from a query object q to an object in one of the partitions, say, that for S_1. If q is in the partition (i.e., is closer to p_1), the lower bound is clearly zero. Otherwise, the lower bound is equal to the distance from q to the partitioning hyperplane, which is easy to compute in Euclidean spaces. For arbitrary metric spaces, however, we cannot form a direct representation of the "generalized hyperplane" that divides the two partitions since we assume that the interobject distances are the only available information.

Fortunately, even given the limited information available in the gh-tree, Lemma 4.4 shows that it is possible to derive a lower bound on the distance from q to some object in a partition[29] (though an upper bound cannot be determined since objects can be arbitrarily far from p_1 and p_2). In particular, for a range query with query radius ε, the left subtree (i.e., for S_1) must be visited if and only if

$$\frac{d(q, p_1) - d(q, p_2)}{2} \leq \varepsilon$$

and the right subtree (i.e., for S_2) must be visited if and only if

$$\frac{d(q, p_2) - d(q, p_1)}{2} \leq \varepsilon$$

We can also use a similar approach to design an incremental nearest neighbor algorithm for the gh-tree by specifying the search hierarchy according to the framework presented in Section 4.1.2. Our treatment is analogous to that used for the vp-tree in Section 4.5.2.1. Because the gh-tree is hierarchical, the search hierarchy essentially falls out of the existing hierarchical structure. Thus, the elements of the search hierarchy correspond to the objects (type 0) and the nodes in the gh-tree (type 1). Note that the ball regions for the gh-tree nodes play the same role as bounding rectangles in the R-tree. The resulting search hierarchy for a small sample gh-tree is depicted in Figure 4.54. Note that elements of type 1 can produce elements of type 0 and 1.

We now define the distance function d_1 for the distance between the query object q and elements e_1 of type 1. Recall that the value of $d_1(q, e_1)$ should be a lower bound on the distance $d(q, o)$ for any object o in the subhierarchy rooted at e_1. The information we have on hand to derive such a lower bound is the distance from q to the pivot value associated with e_1 and the distance from q to the pivot value associated with the brother of e_1. Thus, we can make use of Lemma 4.4, which gives a lower bound on $d(q, o)$ based on exactly such information. In particular, assuming that the parent of e_1 is pivoted at objects p_1 and p_2 so that the left child is associated with p_1 and the right child is associated with

---

[29] The bound in the lemma is clearly much weaker than that which would be obtained in a Euclidean space by using the hyperplane directly.

p_2, the definition of d_1 as obtained from the lemma is

$$d_1(q, e_1) = \begin{cases} \max\left\{\frac{d(q, p_1) - d(q, p_2)}{2}, 0\right\}, & \text{if } e_1 \text{ is a left child} \\ \max\left\{\frac{d(q, p_2) - d(q, p_1)}{2}, 0\right\}, & \text{if } e_1 \text{ is a right child} \end{cases}$$

This definition of d_1 is general in that, for either case, it also accounts for q's being either inside or outside the region for e_1. Since the lemma guarantees that $d_1(q, e_1) \le d(q, o)$ for any object o in the subtree rooted at e_1, we are assured that the incremental nearest neighbor algorithm is correct when applied to the gh-tree search hierarchy that we have defined (see Section 4.1.3).

Note that Lemma 4.4 does not provide an upper bound on the distance from q to any point o in a hyperplane-bounded region e_1 since objects can be arbitrarily far from p_1 and p_2 (recall Figure 4.43). However, by modifying the gh-tree data structure so that, in addition to the two pivots p_1 and p_2, each node also stores the radius of the balls around p_1 and p_2 that contain S_1 and S_2 [978] (i.e., $r_1 = \max_{o \in S_1}\{d(p_1, o)\}$ and $r_2 = \max_{o \in S_2}\{d(p_2, o)\}$), we can then use these radii in conjunction with Lemma 4.2 to define $\hat{d}_1$—that is,

$$\hat{d}_1(q, e_1) = \begin{cases} d(q, p_1) + r_1, & \text{if } e_1 \text{ is a left child} \\ d(q, p_2) + r_2, & \text{if } e_1 \text{ is a right child} \end{cases}$$

Observe that the addition of the radii of the balls around the pivots to the data structure means that we can also take them into account in the following definition of $d_1(q, e_1)$:

$$d_1(q, e_1) = \begin{cases} \max\{(d(q, p_1) - d(q, p_2))/2, d(q, p_1) - r_1, 0\}, & \text{if } e_1 \text{ is a left child} \\ \max\{(d(q, p_2) - d(q, p_1))/2, d(q, p_2) - r_2, 0\}, & \text{if } e_1 \text{ is a right child} \end{cases}$$

The rationale for the two choices for the lower bounds and taking their maximum is that the balls, which correspond to minimum bounding hyperspheres of the objects in the two partitions, are not necessarily disjoint. Thus, it could be the case that an object o lies in the hypervolume spanned by both balls, yet o is associated with just one of them. Observe that the query object q may itself lie in the ball corresponding to the objects in partition e_1, thereby accounting for the presence of 0 as one of the choices for d_{min}.

Given the search hierarchy defined above, incremental nearest neighbor search proceeds as described in Section 4.1.3. In particular, when the element obtained from the queue represents an object (i.e., is of type 0), we report it as the next nearest neighbor. Otherwise, the element is of type 1, representing a node n. If n is a nonleaf node with pivots p_1 and p_2, we compute $d(q, p_1)$ and $d(q, p_2)$ and insert both p_1 and p_2 into the priority queue. Furthermore, the left and right children of n are inserted into the priority queue as elements of type 1 using the distance function defined above. If n is a leaf node, we perform the same action as for pivots of nonleaf nodes for the object(s) in the node.

Note that Merkwirth, Parlitz, and Lauterborn [1286] make use of a similar, but nonincremental, approach to find the k nearest neighbors in a variant of a gh-tree that also stores the radii of the balls centered at the pivots that contain the objects associated with the pivots. The difference from our suggested approach is that Merkwirth et al. [1286] only store the nonleaf nodes in the priority queue sorted by a more precise, but equivalent (see Exercise 7), definition of $d_1(q, e_1)$ and sequentially scan the objects in the leaf nodes using Lemma 4.1 to try possibly to eliminate the need to compute their distance from q.

Exercises

1. Give an algorithm to insert an object in a gh-tree.

2. Give an algorithm to delete an object from a gh-tree.

3. Give an algorithm to construct a gh-tree. You need to come up with ways of choosing the pivots. Use the method described in the text that selects the objects farthest from each other.

(i.e., e_1) corresponding to S_1 (S_2) of the gh-tree is processed only if $\frac{d(q,p_1)-d(q,p_2)}{2} \leq \varepsilon$ ($\frac{d(q,p_2)-d(q,p_1)}{2} \leq \varepsilon$).

The advantage of the bisector tree over the gh-tree is that, at times, the lower bound $d(q,p_1) - r_1$ ($d(q,p_2) - r_2$) on $d(q,o)$ for all objects o in e_1 (i.e., $d(q,e_1)$, where we assume that e_1 is a nonobject element) is greater than the lower bound $\frac{d(q,p_1)-d(q,p_2)}{2}$ ($\frac{d(q,p_2)-d(q,p_1)}{2}$), which means that the bisector tree provides a tighter lower bound on the search in e_1 (i.e., $d(q,e_1)$). However, this is not always the case. In particular, when the covering balls associated with pivots p_1 and p_2 are not disjoint, the lower bound provided by the gh-tree is greater than the lower bound provided by the bisector tree. Both of these cases may result in some of the subtrees being descended needlessly. In fact, it is exactly for this reason that we use the following definition for $d_1(q,e_1)$ at the conclusion of the presentation of the gh-tree in Section 4.5.3.1:

$$d_1(q,e_1) = \begin{cases} \max\{(d(q,p_1) - d(q,p_2))/2, d(q,p_1) - r_1, 0\}, & \text{if } e_1 \text{ is a left child} \\ \max\{(d(q,p_2) - d(q,p_1))/2, d(q,p_2) - r_2, 0\}, & \text{if } e_1 \text{ is a right child} \end{cases}$$

The motivation for adding the covering balls to the gh-tree is to speed up the search by enabling the pruning of elements whose covering balls are farther from the query object than the current candidate nearest neighbor (the farthest of the k candidate nearest neighbors) or are outside the range for a range query. Naturally, the utility of the covering balls for pruning increases as their radii decrease. Thus, as the search hierarchy is descended, it is desirable for the covering balls to become smaller, thereby leading to more pruning. Unfortunately, the radii of the covering balls of the children are not necessarily smaller than the radii of the covering balls of their ancestors. For example, consider a two-dimensional space with a Euclidean distance metric as shown in Figure 4.56. Let p_a be at the origin, p_1 be at $(-2,3)$, p_2 be at $(-2,-3)$, o_1 be at $(4,3)$, and o_2 be at $(4,-3)$. Let o_1 and o_2 be the farthest objects from p_a. Moreover, let o_1 be the farthest object from p_1, and let o_2 be the farthest object from p_2. We now see that the radii of the covering balls around p_1 and p_2 are both 6 and are larger than the radius of the covering ball of p_a, which is 5.

Dehne and Noltemeier [473] characterize a child element in the bisector tree as *eccentric* when the radius of its covering ball is larger than the radius of the covering ball of its ancestor element. Eccentricity of children is disadvantageous for pruning because the radii of the covering balls increase as the search hierarchy is descended. The potential for having eccentric children is viewed by some (e.g., [473, 1383]) as a drawback of the bisector tree. Hence, it has been proposed to modify the definition of the bisector tree so that one of the two pivots in each nonleaf node n, except for the root, is inherited from its parent node—that is, of the two pivots in the parent of n, the one that is inherited is the one that is closer to each object in the subtree rooted at n. In other words, each pivot will also be a pivot in the child node corresponding to that pivot. Since this strategy leads to fewer pivot objects, its use can be expected to reduce the number of distance computations during search (provided the distances of pivot objects are propagated downward during search), at the possible cost of a worse partitioning and a deeper tree if the decomposition process is only halted when each mb-tree leaf node contains just one object. Of course, the radius of the covering ball around the pivots (i.e., the maximum distance to objects in the corresponding subtree) is also stored and used for pruning. The result is termed the *monotonous bisector tree* (abbreviated below as *mb-tree*) and was proposed by Noltemeier, Verbarg, and Zirkelbach [1383] (and used by Bugnion, Fei, Roos, Widmayer, and Widmer [278]). The mb-tree is a simpler form of the Voronoi tree [473], which is a ternary tree where each node contains between two and three pivot objects instead of just two objects, as in the mb-tree (see Exercises 6–8).

Mb-trees were originally intended for use with point data and Minkowski metrics. However, the mb-tree can be used with arbitrary metrics. An extension of the mb-tree, the *mb*-tree* [1383], accommodates complex objects, such as lines and polygons. The TLAESA method of Micó, Oncina, and Carrasco [1291] also uses an mb-tree-like search

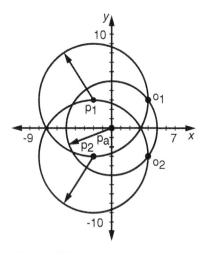

Figure 4.56
Example where the radii of the covering balls around pivots p_1 and p_2 in element e_a are greater than the radius of the covering ball around the pivot p_a in the ancestor element e of e_a.

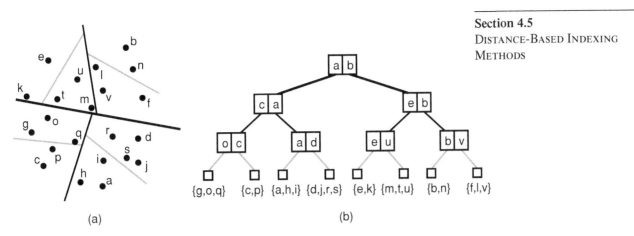

Figure 4.57
(a) A possible space partitioning produced by the mb-tree for the set of points in a two-dimensional Euclidean space of Figure 4.53 and (b) its tree representation.

structure in conjunction with a distance matrix to provide lower bounds on the distance from q to the pivot objects during search (see Section 4.5.7.3 for more details).

Figure 4.57(a) is an example of the space partitioning produced by an mb-tree corresponding to the set of points in the two-dimensional space stored in the gh-tree in Figure 4.53, and Figure 4.57(b) is its tree representation, where the same number of partitions were made at each level as in the corresponding gh-tree. Notice that two points are associated with each nonleaf node of the tree representation, thereby defining the partition of the underlying space, while each of the points is repeated in the next level of the tree. However, in the interest of saving storage, all of the points are actually stored in the leaf nodes of the mb-tree. Nonleaf nodes store pointers to their corresponding leaf node entries.

It should be clear that many different configurations are possible when constructing an mb-tree for a set of objects. This is because there are many options for which objects to choose as pivots at each step of the decomposition. In constructing our example mb-tree, we have followed a strategy that tries to associate approximately the same number of objects with each leaf node, while using the same initial partition as in the example gh-tree (i.e., using pivots a and b). Note also that if we decomposed the underlying space so that every leaf node contained just one point, then the resulting mb-tree would be considerably deeper than the corresponding gh-tree. In particular, for a set of $N(N > 1)$ objects, the fully decomposed mb-tree always requires $N - 1$ nonleaf nodes, but the corresponding gh-tree may need as few as $N/2$ nodes in total because each node can contain as many as two objects, and there is no need to distinguish between leaf and nonleaf nodes in a gh-tree as they are both used to store the points.

It is interesting to observe that the decomposition rule on which the mb-tree is based is analogous to a classical decomposition rule in applications involving vector space data, such as points, where a region is decomposed if it contains more than one point. This is the case for a PR quadtree [1413, 1637] (see Section 1.4.2.2 in Chapter 1) and the PR k-d tree [1413] (see Section 1.5.2 in Chapter 1). In particular, the analogy becomes more apparent when the comparison is made with the path-compressed PR k-d tree (see Section 1.5.2.4 in Chapter 1), as the mb-tree does not have any empty nodes, whereas both the PR k-d tree and its PR quadtree ancestor can have empty nodes that arise when all remaining nodes lie on the same side of the partitioning plane. For example, Figure 4.58(a, b) illustrates the block and tree representations of the mb-tree corresponding to the two-dimensional point data in Figure 1.1 of Chapter 1. Notice that the nonleaf nodes are labeled with the identity of the points whose partitioning line is captured by the node.

In the case of vector space data, the decomposition of the underlying space that is induced by the mb-tree is similar to that induced by variants of k-d trees [164], such as the adaptive k-d tree [650] and the BSP tree [658] (see Section 1.5.1.4 in Chapter 1). The BSP tree analogy is probably the easiest to compare as the partitioning planes in the BSP tree are not necessarily orthogonal. In particular, this similarity becomes very clear when we compare the BSP tree for the point data in Figure 1.1 of Chapter 1 given in Figure 1.47 (see Section 1.5.1.4 of Chapter 1) with the corresponding mb-tree in Figure 4.58. The analogy also holds for bucket variants of these structures where the decomposition is based on the region containing $k > 1$ points. In all of these examples, the pivot objects play the same role as the points. The principal difference is that the boundaries of the regions associated with the points are represented explicitly, while they are implicit in the mb-tree, and thus it is easy to use the mb-tree with data from an arbitrary metric space. In particular, in the latter, each partition is defined by two pivots and the set of objects that are closer to one of them than to the other. Thus, the pivot objects play a similar role to control points in Bézier methods in modeling curves and surfaces in computer-aided design applications (e.g., [622]) in the sense that just as the curve in the latter is implicitly defined by the control points, the partitioning hyperplanes in the former are also implicitly defined by the pivot points.

Sharing a pivot with an ancestor, as proposed for the mb-tree, has the effect of guaranteeing that children are not eccentric (i.e., that the radii of the covering balls around pivots p_1 or p_2 in element e_a, which form e_1, are not greater than the radius of the covering ball around the pivot p_a in the ancestor element e of e_a; see Exercise 1). This noneccentricity constraint on the radii of the covering balls is also satisfied when the more general stipulation that the distance from q to a nonobject element e_1 (i.e., $d(q, e_1)$) must be greater than or equal to the distance from q to an ancestor of e_1 (i.e., $d(q, e_a)$) holds—that is, they form a containment hierarchy and hence are monotonically nondecreasing.

It is important to note that, although it is impossible to have a containment hierarchy when the children are eccentric, a containment hierarchy may also fail to exist when the children are not eccentric and even when the hierarchy is formed by sharing a pivot with

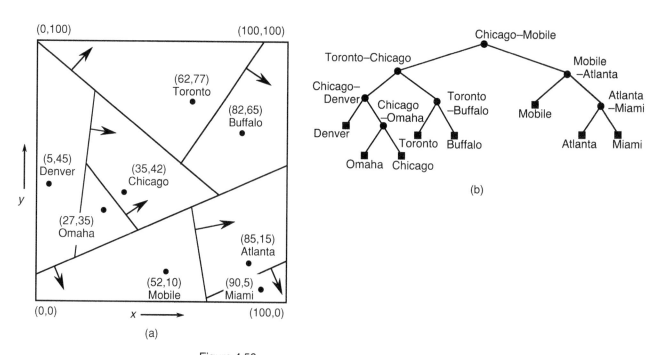

Figure 4.58
(a) A possible space partitioning produced by the mb-tree for the set of points corresponding to the data in Figure 1.1 of Chapter 1 and (b) its tree representation.

an ancestor, as in the mb-tree. For example, consider Figure 4.59, where the radius of the covering ball of child e_1 is smaller than the radius of the covering ball of its ancestor e_a, yet the covering ball of e_1 is not completely contained in the covering ball of e_a.

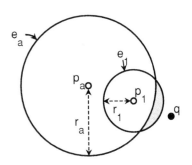

Merkwirth, Parlitz, and Lauterborn [1286] (see Exercise 7 in Section 4.5.3.1) ignore the issue of eccentricity and, instead, force a containment hierarchy to exist by basing the lower bound $d(q, e_1)$ on the maximum of the distance of q from the children and the distance of q from the parent (i.e., $d(q, e_a)$). They use a conventional bisector tree (also referred to as an augmented gh-tree in Section 4.5.3.1). Nevertheless, it can be shown (see Exercise 7 in Section 4.5.3.1) that for queries such as finding the nearest neighbors of q using the best-first method, the fact that the covering balls of the children do not contain any objects that are not in the covering balls of the ancestors means that taking the distance of the parent (i.e., $d(q, e_a)$) into account when computing $d(q, e_1)$ does not result in the pruning of more objects or nodes from the search process. Equivalently, failing to take the distance of the parent into account, and thus just using the distance from q of the children, does not cause additional objects or nodes to be visited during the search process. A similar statement can be made about range searching. The only requirement that must be met is that the distances of the nonobject elements be lower bounds for the distances of the object elements (as pointed out in Section 4.1.3). Thus, we can also safely ignore the issue of whether or not a containment hierarchy exists. In particular, whenever we process a nonobject element e_a and determine that the radius of the covering ball around the pivot in the ancestor (i.e., parent) element of e_a means that e_a's children must be visited, then whether or not the radii of the covering balls around the pivots of the children are larger than those of the covering balls around the pivot in the ancestor element of e_a has no effect on the extent of the pruning as the covering balls of the parent and the children contain the same objects (i.e., there are no additional objects in the hypervolume corresponding to the set difference of the covering balls of the child and its parent).

From the above we observe that the presence or absence of eccentric children is not really an issue in the bisector tree (and the suitably modified gh-tree). The real issue is similar to one that was raised earlier in our discussion of the incremental nearest neighbor algorithm in Section 4.1.3, where we pointed out that the correctness criterion (i.e., $d_t(q, e_t) \leq d_0(q, e_0)$ for any object e_o in the subtree represented by e_t) does not actually guarantee that when a nonobject search hierarchy element e_t has been removed from the priority queue, no nonobject search hierarchy element $e_{t'}$ (in the subtree represented by e_t) with a smaller distance from the query object q can be inserted, and possibly removed, in the future. In other words, it does not preclude the occurrence of the situation that nonobject elements e_t and $e_{t'}$, where $d_t(q, e_t) > d_{t'}(q, e_{t'})$, could be processed in succession (by virtue of their being removed from the priority queue in succession, although some other elements could have been inserted into the queue during this time). The latter situation arises in the bisector tree (and in a gh-tree that is augmented with covering balls) when eccentric children are present; it can also arise in a vp-tree (see Exercise 5 in Section 4.5.2.1.2). Note that, as we pointed out earlier, this situation is not limited to eccentric children in the bisector tree.

Exercises

1. Prove that none of the children in an mb-tree are eccentric.

2. Prove that, given $N > 1$ objects, the mb-tree requires $N - 1$ nodes.

3. Give an algorithm to construct an mb-tree.

4. Give an algorithm to perform a range query for a query object q and query radius ε in an mb-tree.

5. Give an algorithm to find the nearest neighbors in an incremental manner to a query object q in an mb-tree. Exercises 6–8 deal with the Voronoi tree [473], which is closely related to the mb-tree. Assuming a set of objects S, its Voronoi tree T is a ternary tree where each node

represents at least two, and at most three, objects of S, termed *pivots*. Of course, the root may represent just one object of S if S has just one object. The Voronoi tree is built in a manner analogous to that of the mb-tree. We first search for the node in which the new object o is to be inserted, starting at the root. If the current node U is not full, then insert o. If U is full and has no children, then create a new node V and insert o into V, as well as a redundant copy of the closest pivot p in U. Otherwise, determine the closest pivot p to o in U and descend to p's corresponding child.

6. Show that the Voronoi tree has no eccentric children.

7. Prove that the Voronoi tree is transitive in the sense that, given an object o stored in node U and letting $f(o,U)$ denote o's closest pivot in the immediate ancestor of U, $d(o, f(o,U)) = \min\{d(o, f(o,U'))\}$, where U' is in the set of ancestors of U.

8. Prove that a search for the nearest neighbor of an object stored in the root node of a Voronoi tree of height h can be done in $O(h)$ time.

4.5.3.4 Other Methods Related to Generalized Hyperplane Partitioning

The gh-tree and GNAT (as well as the M-tree, described in Section 4.5.4) can be considered special cases of a general class of hierarchical clustering methods, as described by Burkhard and Keller [283] and Fukunaga and Narendra [666] (recall Section 4.2.2). Using the description given by Burkhard and Keller [283], a set S of objects is clustered into m subsets $S_1, S_2, \ldots, S_m$ using some criterion usually based on proximity. Next, a pivot object p_i is chosen for each S_i, and the radius $r_i = \max_{o \in S_i}\{d(p_i, o)\}$ is computed.[30] This process is applied recursively to each S_i, possibly with a different number m of clusters each time. Observe that for performing search (e.g., range search), a lower bound on the distances from a query object q to all objects in S_i can be derived based on p_i and r_i according to Lemma 4.2, as was done for the vp-tree in Section 4.5.2.1.2 (i.e., letting $r_{\text{lo}} = 0$ and $r_{\text{hi}} = r_i$). Besides the above general formulation, Burkhard and Keller also described a specific method of clustering, where each cluster is a *clique*, which they define to be a set of objects R such that the greatest distance between any two objects in R is no more than some value D.[31] The clique property was found to reduce the number of distance computations and allow more pruning during search [283], at the price of high preprocessing cost (for determining the cliques).

The manner in which we described the hierarchies that make up the gh-tree, GNAT, monotonous bisector tree (mb-tree), and so on, implies that they are built in a top-down manner. For example, recall that the hierarchy in GNAT is built by initially choosing m of the objects to serve as pivots and then forming m sets, each of which contains the objects that are closest to the corresponding pivot. Each of these m sets are recursively processed to yield m or some other number of subsets. Alternatively, the hierarchy can also be built in a bottom-up manner. In this case, the algorithms generally assume that the objects are initially processed using some clustering method to obtain k clusters with k cluster centers. These clusters are subsequently processed by applying a hierarchical clustering method (e.g., [445, 666, 1311]). These methods are very similar to those used to obtain object hierarchies, such as the R-tree (Section 2.1.5.2 in Chapter 2), and, more specifically, object hierarchies that make use of minimum bounding hyperspheres, such as the SS-tree [1991], balltree [1399], and sphere tree [895, 896, 1410, 1412] (see Section 4.4.2).

There are many possible ways to perform the initial clustering at the bottom level of the hierarchy. For example, given a dataset S and an integer k, one way to proceed is to determine the k objects in S such that the maximum radius of the covering balls centered

---

[30] GNAT [255] maintains more comprehensive distance information in each node.

[31] If we consider the objects to be nodes in a graph with edges between objects whose distance is no more than D, a graph-theoretic clique in this graph corresponds to Burkhard and Keller's definition of a clique.

at these objects is minimized, assuming that each object is associated with its closest of these k objects. These k objects are known as k-*centers*. In other words, the process of finding the k-centers is equivalent to finding the k pivot objects so that the maximum distance from a k-center to an object in S is minimized.

Note that the pivots used by GNAT are not necessarily k-centers. The k-centers act like sites in a Voronoi diagram in the sense that all objects in each covering ball are closer to the corresponding k-center than to any other k-center. However, the converse is not generally true—that is, the sites in a Voronoi diagram are not necessarily k-centers. Observe also that the k-centers are not the same as the k-*means*, which are the k objects, not necessarily in S, that minimize the sum of the squares of the distances (usually using the Euclidean distance for objects in a vector space) of the individual objects from their closest k-mean. The k-median problem is similar to the k-center problem, with the difference that, in the former, it is the average radius of the covering balls that is minimized, and, in the latter, it is the maximum radius of the covering balls that is minimized.

Obtaining the k-centers is computationally complex (i.e., NP-hard [203]), and thus there is interest in obtaining what are termed *approximate k-centers*. In particular, assuming N objects, Gonzalez [723] describes an $O(N \cdot k)$ algorithm that yields the approximate k-centers such that the maximum radius is at most twice the optimum maximum radius resulting from the use of the actual k-centers (see Exercise 1). Hochbaum and Shmoys [859] proved that a better guarantee than twice the optimum maximum radius cannot be obtained in polynomial time (unless $P = NP$), while Feder and Greene [601] reduced the time bound for the algorithm of Gonzalez to $O(N \log k)$ in low dimensions by using a more efficient implementation. Dasgupta [445] and Moore [1311] address the issue of building the cluster hierarchy once the bottom level of the hierarchy has been built using methods similar to those of Gonzalez [723]. Moore uses the term *anchors hierarchy* to describe the resulting structure, which is similar to the balltree [1399] (see Section 4.4.2).

Micó, Oncina, and Vidal [1292] apply a variant of the Gonzalez [723] algorithm to find the k-medians (termed *base prototypes*) that are used in LAESA, where they behave like coordinates in a distance-based indexing method that makes use of a distance matrix that is similar in spirit to an embedding method (see Section 4.5.7.2). The difference is that, in this variant, it is the average distance from each object to the pivot set at each pivot selection step that is maximized; in the original formulation, it is the minimum distance from each object to the pivot set that is maximized. Charikar, Guha, Tardos, and Shmoys [325] also give an algorithm to obtain the approximate k-medians and prove that their average radius is at most eight times the optimum average radius from use of the actual k-medians (see Exercise 2).

Exercises

1. Assuming n objects, Gonzalez [723] proposed the following simple greedy algorithm called *farthest-point clustering* to determine the set C of approximate k-centers $c_1, \ldots, c_k$, which is initially empty, and to construct the corresponding sets $S_1, \ldots, S_k$.

    (a) Initially, pick an object v_0 in S at random to serve as the first approximate k-center and add it to C.

    (b) For $i = 1$ to $k - 1$ do the following:

        i. For every object $v \in S$, compute the distance from v to the current approximate k-center set $C = \{v_0, v_1, \ldots, v_{i-1}\}$—that is, $d_i(v, C) = \min_{c \in C} ||v - c||$.

        ii. From the set of objects $S - C$, find an object v_i that is farthest away from the current approximate k-center set C—that is, $d_i(v_i, C) = \max_{v \in S-C} \min_{c \in C} ||v - c||$.

        iii. Add v_i to C.

    (c) Return the set $C = \{v_0, v_1, \ldots, v_{k-1}\}$ as the set of k approximate k-centers.

Prove that the maximum radius obtained by this approximate algorithm is at most twice the optimum maximum radius resulting from the use of the actual k-centers. Your proof should make use of the following properties of the algorithm, letting $C_i = \{v_0, v_1, \ldots, v_{i-1}\}$ be the set of approximate k-centers after i iterations.

(a) The distance from each object to C does not increase as the approximate k-center algorithm progresses—that is, $d_j(v_j, C_j) \leq d_i(v_j, C_i)$ for $j \geq i$.

(b) For $j \geq i$, by definition, we have that $d_i(v_j, C_i) \leq d_i(v_i, C_i)$ as v_i at distance $d_i(v_i, C_i)$ is always the farthest object from an element of C_i after i iterations of the approximate k-center algorithm.

2. Show that the average radius obtained by the approximate k-medians algorithm of Charikar et al. [325] is at most eight times the optimum average radius from use of the actual k-medians.

3. Can you derive a bound on the quality of the bound obtained by the algorithm of Mico et al. [1292] for the k-medians similar to that obtained by Charikar et al. [325].

4.5.4 M-Tree

The distance-based indexing methods described in Sections 4.5.2 and 4.5.3 are either static, unbalanced, or both. Hence, they are unsuitable for dynamic situations involving large amounts of data, where a disk-based structure is needed. The M-tree [388, 389] is a distance-based indexing method designed to address this deficiency. Its design goal was to combine a dynamic, balanced index structure similar to the R-tree with the capabilities of static distance-based indexes. Below, we first describe the structure of the M-tree (Section 4.5.4.1) and then show how to perform search in it (Section 4.5.4.2)

4.5.4.1 Structure

In the M-tree, as in the R-tree, all the objects being indexed are referenced in the leaf nodes,[32] while an entry in a nonleaf node stores a pointer to a node at the next lower level, along with summary information about the objects in the subtree being pointed at. Recall that, in an R-tree, the summary information consists of minimum bounding rectangles for all the objects in the subtree. For arbitrary metric spaces, we cannot explicitly form the "regions" that enclose a set of objects in the same manner. Instead, in the M-tree, "balls" around pivot objects (termed *routing objects* in [389]) serve the same role as the minimum bounding rectangles in the R-tree. Clearly, the pivots in the M-tree have a function similar to that of the pivots in GNAT (see Section 4.5.3). However, unlike GNAT, all objects in S are stored in the leaf nodes of the M-tree, so an object may be referenced multiple times in the tree (once in a leaf node and as a pivot in one or more nonleaf nodes). For an object o in the subtree of a node n, the pivot p of that subtree is not always the one closest to o among all the pivots in n (i.e., we may have $d(p, o) > d(p', o)$ for some other pivot p' in n). In addition to this summary information, the entries in M-tree nodes also contain distance values that can aid in pruning during search, as is done in the vp^{sb}-tree (see Section 4.5.2.2).

More precisely, for a nonleaf node n, the entries are (p, r, D, T), where p is a pivot, r is the corresponding *covering radius*, D is a distance value (defined below), and T is a reference to a child node of n. For all objects o in the subtree rooted at T, we have $d(p, o) \leq r$. For each nonroot node, let *parent object* denote its associated pivot (i.e., the pivot in the entry pointing to it in its parent). The distance value stored in D is the distance $d(p, p')$ between p and the parent object p' of n. As we shall see, these parent distances allow more pruning during search than would otherwise be possible. Similarly, for a leaf node n, the entries consist of (o, D), where o is a data object, and D is the distance between o and the parent object of n. Clearly, the root has no parent, so $D = \infty$ for all the

---

[32] The objects can either be stored directly in the leaf nodes or externally to the M-tree, with object IDs stored in the leaf nodes.

entries in the root. Observe that the covering radius for a nonleaf entry is not necessarily the minimum radius for the objects in the corresponding subtree (except when the M-tree is bulk-loaded [386]).

Being a dynamic structure, the M-tree can be built gradually as new data arrives [389]. The insertion procedure first "routes" a new data object to a leaf node n, for each nonleaf node on the path, picking a child node that "best matches" the data object, based on heuristics. For example, a heuristic might first look for a pivot object whose "ball" includes the data object and pick the one closest to the data object if there is more than one such pivot. The insertion into n may cause overflow, causing n to be split and a new pivot to be selected. Thus, overflow may cascade up to the root, in which case the tree will actually grow in a bottom-up fashion. Ciaccia et al. [389] considered a number of heuristics for choosing the child node to route an object into and for splitting overflowing nodes. Bulk loading strategies [386, 1236] have also been developed for use when an M-tree must be built for an existing set of data objects. An example of root node partitioning in an M-tree for a set of objects is shown in Figure 4.60, where we have three pivot objects, p_1, p_2, and p_3. Notice that the regions of some of the three subtrees overlap. This may give rise to a situation where an object can be inserted into more than one subtree, such as the object marked o, which can be inserted into the subtree of either p_1 or p_3.

As pointed out above, the balls around the pivot objects in the M-tree play the same role as the minimum bounding rectangles in the R-tree. In fact, a more precise analogy is to the SS-tree [1991] and the sphere tree [1410, 1412] (see Section 4.4). There are a number of differences, though. In particular, the SS-tree and the sphere tree do not store parent distances as is done in the M-tree. In addition, the SS-tree and the sphere tree make use of geometric properties for some of the operations such as node splitting upon overflow, whereas this is not the case for the M-tree.

The M-tree has features common to both pivot-based and clustering-based indexing methods. The routing objects and the associated covering radii play the same role as the pivots in the pivot-based methods. On the other hand, the fact that an object is inserted into the ball of its closest pivot object when it is contained in the covering balls of more than one pivot object is a reminiscent of clustering-based methods. Nevertheless, when the object is not in the covering balls of any of the pivot objects, it is usually associated with the pivot whose covering is increased the least. This is reminiscent of techniques that minimize the coverage when inserting into an R-tree node. However, such a policy will not necessarily result in associating the new object with the closest pivot object. Therefore, it is not always a clustering-based strategy. Thus, we see that the M-tree is really a hybrid method combining features common to both pivot-based and clustering-based indexing methods.

Traina, Traina, Seeger, and Faloutsos [1888, 1889] introduced the *Slim-tree*, a variant of the M-tree with faster node-insertion and node-splitting algorithms. More importantly, the Slim-tree also features improved storage utilization, which is achieved, in part, by applying a postprocessing step, termed the *Slim-down* algorithm. This algorithm attempts to reduce the overlap among node regions by moving entries between sibling nodes in iterative fashion. In particular, in the case of slimming down leaf nodes, an object o stored in a leaf node n is a candidate for being moved if (1) o is the object in n that is farthest from n's parent object p, and (2) the region of a sibling n' of n also covers o. Having identified such a candidate o, o is moved from n to n', and the covering radius of n is reduced, if possible, depending on the distance between p and the next farthest object in n. An empirical study showed that these modifications led to a reduction in the number of disk accesses as compared to the original M-tree [1888].

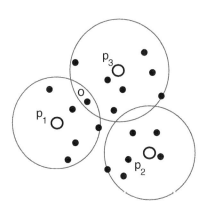

Figure 4.60
Possible top-level partitionings of a set of objects (depicted as two-dimensional points) in an M-tree. Objects that fall into more than one ball, like o, can be inserted into any of the corresponding subtrees.

Exercise

1. Give an algorithm to construct an M-tree.

4.5.4.2 Search

Range queries for query object q and query radius ε can be performed on the M-tree with a straightforward depth-first traversal, initiated at the root. Let n be a node that is being visited, and let p' be its parent pivot—that is, p' is the pivot for the entry in n's parent that points to n. In order to exploit the parent distance D stored in the entries of n (i.e., to avoid as much as possible the computation of the distances from q to the pivots p stored in the entries of n), the value of $d(q, p')$ must be propagated downward in the depth-first traversal as n is visited (since the root has no parent, we use $d(q, p') = \infty$ when processing the root and assume that $\infty - \infty$ evaluates to 0). Assume that n is a nonleaf node. We consider each entry (p, r, D, T) in turn. There are two cases:

1. If $|d(q, p') - D| - r > \varepsilon$, then the subtree pointed at by T need not be traversed, and thus the entry is pruned. In other words, we have found a lower bound on the distance from q to an object in the subtree pointed at by T and note that if this lower bound is greater than ε, then no object in this subtree can be in the range. This can be seen by making use of Lemmas 4.1 and 4.3. Lemma 4.1 yields a lower bound from q to any of the pivots (e.g., p) in node n. In this case, p and p' play the roles of o and p, respectively, in the lemma, which stipulates that $|d(q, p') - d(p', p)| = |d(q, p') - D| \leq d(q, p)$. The upper bound on the distance from q to any of the pivots (e.g., p) in node n is ∞. The distance from pivot p to any of the objects in the corresponding subtree T lies between 0 and r. We now apply Lemma 4.3 to obtain a lower bound on the distance from q to any object o in the subtree pointed at by T—that is, $r_{lo} = 0$, $r_{hi} = r$, $s_{lo} = |d(q, p') - D|$, and $s_{hi} = \infty$ yield $|d(q, p') - D| - r \leq d(q, o)$. Thus, as long as $\varepsilon < |d(q, p') - D| - r$, the subtree pointed at by T need not be traversed.

2. Otherwise, $|d(q, p') - D| - r \leq \varepsilon$. In this case, we can no longer avoid computing $d(q, p)$. However, having computed $d(q, p)$, we can still avoid visiting the node pointed at by T if the lower bound on the distance from q to any object o in T is greater than ε. This is the case if $d(q, p) - r > \varepsilon$ and is a direct result of applying Lemma 4.2, noting that the distance from p to o lies between 0 and r.

Leaf nodes are processed in a similar way: For each entry (o, D) in n with parent pivot p', we first check if $|d(q, p') - D| \leq \varepsilon$ (since we know from Lemma 4.1 that $|d(q, p') - d(p', o)| = |d(q, p') - D| \leq d(q, o)$, so if $\varepsilon < |d(q, p') - D| \leq d(q, o)$, we can immediately discard o without computing its distance), and only for such entries do we compute $d(q, o)$ and check whether $d(q, o) \leq \varepsilon$. Observe that, once again, we see that the parent distances sometimes allow us to prune node entries from the search based on the query radius ε, without computing the actual distances of the corresponding objects.

Finding nearest neighbors is more complicated. For k-nearest neighbor search, Ciaccia et al. [389] propose using the distance of the farthest candidate kth-nearest neighbor in place of ε in the pruning conditions.[33] This technique is discussed further below once we describe the more general incremental approach where the number of desired neighbors is not known in advance. In particular, for incremental nearest neighbor search, not knowing the number of desired neighbors in advance means that the search radius is unbounded, and thus the pruning condition used by Ciaccia et al. [389] is inapplicable. Hjaltason and Samet [851] overcome this drawback in their implementation of incremental nearest neighbor searching by introducing two new element types corresponding to approximate objects and approximate nodes to the search hierarchy. These new element types serve the same role as bounding rectangles in the case of an R-tree. Thus. they provide a simple way to order the subsequent processing of elements of both a leaf and nonleaf node without having to compute the actual distances of these elements from the

---

[33] This is a standard approach for solving this problem. For example, see Exercise 10 in Section 4.6.1.2, which deals with its use by Seidl and Kriegel [1716] to find nearest neighbors in an environment that employs dimensionality reduction.

query object. As we will see, this method can also be applied to obtain a more efficient solution to the k-nearest neighbor problem than the algorithm of Ciaccia et al. [389].

In particular, four types of elements are defined. Type 0 represents objects, type 1 represents approximate objects, type 2 represents nodes, and type 3 represents approximate nodes. Elements of type 1 and 3 are generated as a result of processing leaf nodes and nonleaf nodes, respectively. In particular, when processing a leaf (nonleaf) node n (i.e., when it reaches the front of the priority queue as an element of type 2), an element of type 1 (3) is generated from each of the entries in n. An element of type 0 is generated as a result of processing an element of type 1, and, similarly, each element of type 2 derives from an element of type 3. The distance functions for elements of type 1 through 3 are defined as follows:

$$d_1(q,e_1) = \max\{|d(q,p') - D|, 0\} \qquad (4.5)$$

$$d_2(q,e_2) = \max\{d(q,p) - r, 0\}$$

$$d_3(q,e_3) = \max\{|d(q,p') - D| - r, 0\}$$

where p' is the parent object, D is the corresponding distance for the node entry from which e_1 and e_3 were generated, and p and r are the pivot and covering radius for the node corresponding to e_2 and e_3. Using the same definitions, the upper-bound distance functions for types 1 through 3 are

$$\hat{d}_1(q,e_1) = d(q,p') + D$$

$$\hat{d}_2(q,e_2) = d(q,p) + r$$

$$\hat{d}_3(q,e_3) = d(q,p') + D + r$$

To support distance computations for descendants, we must associate certain information with each element. In particular, an element of type 1 must include the identity of the corresponding object; an element of type 2 must include a pointer to the corresponding node n and the distance $d(q,p')$, where p' is the parent object of n; and an element of type 3 must include p, r, and T, where (p,r,D,T) is the nonleaf node entry that gave rise to it. Note that a depth-first range search on this search hierarchy is equivalent to the range query algorithm described above.

The correctness of incremental nearest neighbor search with these definitions can be shown by applying the results in Section 4.5.1. In particular, for an element e_1 and the corresponding object o, $d_1(q,e_1) = |d(q,p') - D| = |d(q,p') - d(p',o)| \leq d(q,o) \leq d(q,p') + d(p',o) = |d(q,p') + D| = \hat{d}_1(q,e_1)$ follows from Lemma 4.1. For an element e_2 and an object o in its subtree, we have

$$d_2(q,e_2) = \max\{d(q,p) - r, 0\} \leq d(q,o) \leq d(q,p) + r = \hat{d}_2(q,e_2)$$

from Lemma 4.2. Finally, for an element e_3 and an object o in the subtree,

$$d_3(q,e_3) = \max\{|d(q,p') - D| - r, 0\}$$

$$= \max\{|d(q,p') - d(p',p)| - r, 0\} \leq d(q,o) \leq d(q,p') + d(p',p) + r$$

$$= |d(q,p') + D| + r$$

$$= \hat{d}_3(q,e_3)$$

follows from Lemmas 4.1, 4.2 and 4.3.

Observe that when $d_1(q,e_1)$ and $d_3(q,e_3)$ are computed for elements e_1 and e_3, respectively, the distance information that they are based on is already available, so no additional computation of actual distances is necessary. In particular, D is a distance value computed during the construction of the M-tree, and $d(q,p')$ was computed earlier in the processing of the query and stored in e_2, the node element from which e_1 or e_3 is generated (i.e., p' is the parent object of the node corresponding to e_2). Thus, assuming that incremental nearest neighbor search is terminated after object o_k has been reported, any element of type 1 that still remains on the priority queue represents an object that we were able to prune without computing its actual distance from q. A similar statement applies to elements of type 3.

The above general incremental algorithm can also be adapted to compute the k nearest neighbors, thereby obtaining an algorithm similar to one used by Ciaccia et al. [389] to solve the same problem. The k-nearest neighbor algorithm of Ciaccia et al. makes use of a priority queue containing the nodes of the M-tree (not the objects or the additional approximate elements introduced in the general incremental algorithm) and processes them in increasing order of their distance from the query object q. It uses the distance function $d_c(q,e) = \max\{d(q,p) - r, 0\}$, where p and r are the pivot and covering radius for node e, and d_c is the same as d_2 in Equation 4.5. As the algorithm obtains the actual neighbors (i.e., the objects) one by one, it computes the actual distance of each object using d and inserts the objects into a list L of the k candidate nearest neighbors. If the insertion causes L to contain more than k objects, then the object farthest from q is discarded.[34] Clearly, if all the objects in S were inserted into L in this way, L would eventually contain the actual k nearest neighbors. However, the algorithm can usually be terminated long before inserting all of the objects into L since an object is only inserted into L once the M-tree leaf node n that contains it is obtained from the priority queue—that is, when n is the unprocessed leaf node closest to q. In particular, the condition for terminating the search is $d_c(q,e) \geq D_k$,[35] where e represents the node that was most recently retrieved from the priority queue, and D_k is the distance of the current candidate kth-nearest neighbor in L (or ∞ if $|L| < k$). The reason that the search can be terminated at this point is that we know from Lemma 4.2 that $D_k \leq d_c(q,e) = \max\{d(q,p) - r, 0\} \leq d(q,o)$ for an M-tree node e and an object o in its corresponding subtree, and thus o cannot be one of the k nearest neighbors.

The way in which the algorithm of Ciaccia et al. makes use of a candidate list is analogous to placing the objects on the priority queue and terminating the search once the kth object has been retrieved from the priority queue. The primary difference is that, in the candidate list approach, at most k objects are remembered at any given time, whereas the priority queue can contain any number of objects in the general incremental algorithm. Note that the algorithm of Ciaccia et al. also uses D_k to prune entries locally as it processes nodes obtained from the priority queue. This local pruning takes the place of the approximate node and object elements used in the general incremental algorithm, which, as we recall, stores both the nodes and the objects in the priority queue. In particular, when processing a node n, using the distance functions in Equation 4.5, the algorithm of Ciaccia et al. prunes an entry in n if $d_1(q,e_1) \geq D_k$ or $d_3(q,e_3) \geq D_k$, depending on whether n is a leaf or a nonleaf node, respectively. Nevertheless, it should be clear that despite the use of such local pruning, the algorithm of Ciaccia et al. still results in more distance computations than in the general incremental algorithm, since D_k may converge slowly to its final value (i.e., $d(q,o_k)$, where o_k is the kth-nearest neighbor of q).

As an example of how use of the algorithm of Ciaccia et al. results in more distance computations than the general incremental algorithm, suppose that $D_k = 6$ for the current candidate kth-nearest neighbor. Moreover, suppose that we are currently processing a leaf node n with two objects a and b and that the "parent" object of n is p. Therefore, we know $d(q,p)$ (since it was computed when n was inserted into the priority queue), and we know $d(p,a)$ and $d(p,b)$ (since they are stored in the entries of M-tree node n). Furthermore, we know that $|d(q,p) - d(p,a)|$ and $|d(q,p) - d(p,b)|$ are lower bounds on $d(q,a)$ and $d(q,b)$, respectively. Let us assume that $|d(q,p) - d(p,a)| = 5$, $|d(q,p) - d(p,b)| = 3$,

---

[34] Of course, this distance is based on d rather than d_c as here we are dealing with an object rather than a node.

[35] This condition means that the algorithm will report exactly k neighbors regardless of how many objects are at the same distance from q as the kth-nearest neighbor. If it is desired to report all of the objects that are at the same distance from q as the kth-nearest neighbor, then the condition for terminating the search is modified to be $d_c(q,e) > D_k$.

$d(q,a) = 7$, and $d(q,b) = 4$. We first examine the execution of the general incremental algorithm. It inserts the "approximate" versions of a and b into the priority queue and uses the lower bound distance values 5 and 3, respectively. Assume that the next element that is removed from the priority queue is the "approximate" b, which would lead to computing $d(q,b)$ and inserting b on the priority queue. Next, the algorithm removes b from the queue, which is the next neighbor. If the search is now terminated, then the computation of $d(q,a)$ has been avoided.

To see why the general incremental algorithm is better in this example, we point out that, at the time the leaf node n was processed, the algorithm of Ciaccia et al. would compute both $d(q,a)$ and $d(q,b)$ since their lower bounds are both smaller than $D_k = 6$. In essence, Ciaccia et al.'s use of the lower-bound distances is local (as they are used to make an immediate decision about whether to compute the actual distance), whereas the general nearest neighbor algorithm makes a global use of them (by putting them on the priority queue, and only computing the actual distance once they are removed from the queue). In other words, the general incremental algorithm defers the computation of the distances via the use of the approximate objects and nodes. Nevertheless, both the general incremental algorithm and the algorithm of Ciaccia et al. explore the same number of M-tree nodes because, in both algorithms, these nodes are only explored once they reach the head of the priority queue, which happens in the same way in the two algorithms. However, use of the approximate node for n does result in deferring the computation of $d(q,p)$ and replacing it with a quantity that involves $|d(q,p') - D|$, which has already been computed before processing n. Thus, a distance computation has also been possibly avoided.

Exercises

1. Discuss the process of splitting an overflowing M-tree node and how to distribute the objects into the newly created nodes. Can you derive some techniques analogous to those used in the R*-tree [152] (see Section 2.1.5.2.4 in Chapter 2) to split an overflowing R-tree node?

2. Implement the algorithm described in the text to find the k nearest neighbors to a query object q in an M-tree.

3. Implement the algorithm described in the text to find the nearest neighbors in an incremental manner to a query object q in an M-tree.

4.5.5 Sa-Tree

The Voronoi diagram is a widely used method for nearest neighbor search in point data. For each "site" p, the Voronoi cell or region of p identifies the area closer to p than to any other site. Thus, given a query point q, nearest neighbor search simply involves identifying the Voronoi cell that contains q. In other words, we are given an underlying space $\mathbb{U}$ and a set of objects $S \subset \mathbb{U}$ (i.e., the "sites") such that, for each query object q into $\mathbb{U}$, we wish to find the nearest object in S to q (more generally the nearest k objects to or the objects within ε of q).

As we saw in Section 2.2.1.4 of Chapter 2, a somewhat indirect way of constructing a search structure for nearest neighbor search based on the Voronoi diagram is to build a graph termed a *Delaunay graph*, defined as the graph where each object is a node, and two nodes have an edge between them if their Voronoi cells have a common boundary.[36]

---

[36] In a conference version of [1347], Navarro used the term *Voronoi graph*, but the term *Delaunay graph* is a more appropriate term as it is closely related to the use of this concept in Section 2.2.1.4 of Chapter 2 (e.g., Delaunay triangulations), except that in the problem setting at hand, the edges in the Delaunay graph merely indicate that the Voronoi regions have a common boundary but do not have an associated geometric shape (e.g., they do not correspond to a particular curve or $(d-1)$-dimensional hyperplane, assuming that the objects are drawn from a d-dimensional space).

In other words, the Delaunay graph is simply an explicit representation of neighbor relations that are implicitly represented in the Voronoi diagram.

Searching a Delaunay graph for the nearest neighbor in S of a query point q in $\mathbb{U}$ starts with an arbitrary point in S and proceeds to a neighboring point in S that is closer to q as long as this is possible. Once we reach a point o in S where the points in its neighbor set $N(o)$ in S (i.e., the points connected to o by an edge) are all farther away from q than o, we know that o is the nearest neighbor of q. The reason this search process works on the Delaunay graph of a set of points is that the Delaunay graph has the property that if q is closer to a point p than to any of the neighbors of p in the Delaunay graph, then p is the point in S closest to q. The same search process can be used on any graph that satisfies this *Voronoi property*. In fact, for an arbitrary metric space $(\mathbb{U}, d)$, a Delaunay graph for a set $S \subset \mathbb{U}$ is a minimal graph that satisfies the Voronoi property (i.e., removing any edge would cause violation of the property). Thus, any graph that satisfies the Voronoi property must include a Delaunay graph as a subgraph. Note, however, that the Delaunay graph is not necessarily unique as there can be several such minimal graphs (possibly even with a different number of edges). In the rest this section, we define the sa-tree (Section 4.5.5.1), a data structure based on the Delaunay graph, and then show how to search it (Section 4.5.5.2).

4.5.5.1   Definition

The Voronoi diagram serves as the inspiration for the sa-tree [1347], a distance-based indexing method. Recall that in Section 4.5.3 we defined two other methods, the gh-tree and GNAT, that are also based on Voronoi cell-like partitioning. However, these structures make use of a hierarchical partitioning, where at each level the space is partitioned into two or more Voronoi cell-like regions. In contrast, the sa-tree attempts to approximate the structure of the Delaunay graph—hence its name, which is an abbreviation for *Spatial Approximation Tree*.

As we saw in Section 4.5.3.2, Voronoi cells (or, perhaps more accurately, Dirichlet domains [255]) for objects cannot be constructed explicitly (i.e., their boundaries specified) if only interobject distances are available. Moreover, it is possible to show [1347] that, without more information about the structure of the underlying metric space $(\mathbb{U}, d)$, just knowing the set of interobject distances for a finite metric space (S, d), $S \subset \mathbb{U}$, is not enough to enable the construction of a valid Delaunay graph for S based on d—that is, we also need information about the distances between the elements of S and the elements of $\mathbb{U}$. In other words, for the two sets $S \subset \mathbb{U}$ and $S' \subset \mathbb{U}'$ with identical interobject distances (i.e., (S, d) and (S', d') are isometric), possibly drawn from different underlying spaces $\mathbb{U}$ and $\mathbb{U}'$, (S, d) may have a Delaunay graph D that is not a Delaunay graph for (S', d'), or vice versa (see Exercise 1). Moreover, for any two objects a and b, a finite metric space (S, d) exists whose Delaunay graph contains the edge between a and b. Hence, given only the interobject distances for a set S, the only way to construct a graph G such that G satisfies the Voronoi property for all potential query objects in $\mathbb{U}$ (i.e., contains all the edges in the Delaunay graph) is for G to be the complete graph—that is, the graph containing an edge between all pairs of nodes (each of which represents an object in S). However, such a graph is useless for search as deciding on what edge to traverse from the initial object in S requires computing the distances from the query object to all the remaining objects in S (i.e., it is as expensive, $O(N)$, as brute-force search). The idea behind the sa-tree is to approximate the proper Delaunay graph with a tree structure that retains enough edges to be useful for guiding search, but not so many that an excessive number of distance computations is required to decide what node to visit next.

The sa-tree is defined as follows for a finite metric space (S, d) (see the example in Figure 4.61 to clarify some of the questions that may arise). An arbitrary object a is chosen as the root node of the tree (since each object is associated with exactly one node, we use the terms *object* and *node* interchangeably in this discussion). Next, a smallest possible set $N(a) \subset S \setminus \{a\}$ is identified, such that x is in $N(a)$ if and only if for all

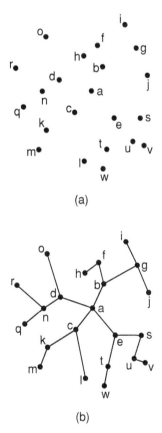

(a)

(b)

Figure 4.61
(a) A set of points in a two-dimensional Euclidean space and (b) its corresponding sa-tree constructed using the algorithm of [1347] when a is chosen as the root.

$y \in N(a) \setminus \{x\}$, $d(x,a) < d(x,y)$ (see Exercise 2). The set $N(a)$ is termed the *neighbor set* of a, by analogy with the Delaunay graph, and the objects in $N(a)$ are said to be the neighbors of a. Intuitively, for a legal neighbor set $N(a)$ (i.e., not necessarily the smallest such set), each object in $N(a)$ is closer to a than to the other objects in $N(a)$, and all the objects in $S \setminus N(a)$ are closer to one of the objects in $N(a)$ than to a. For example, the minimum neighbor set of a in Figure 4.62 is $N(\mathsf{a}) = \{\mathsf{d}\}$. The objects in $N(a)$ then become children of a. The remaining objects in S are associated with the closest child of a (i.e., the closest object in $N(a)$), and the subtrees are defined recursively in the same way for each child of a. As we shall see below, for the efficient implementation of search algorithms, it is useful to store in each node b the distance $d_{\max}(b)$ to the farthest object in the subtree rooted at b. More precisely, $d_{\max}(b) := \max_{o \in S_b} d(o,b)$, where S_b denotes the set of objects in the subtree rooted at b. Figure 4.61(b) shows a sample sa-tree for the set of two-dimensional points a–w given in Figure 4.61(a), with a chosen as the root. In this example, $N(\mathsf{a}) = \{\mathsf{b}, \mathsf{c}, \mathsf{d}, \mathsf{e}\}$. Note that h is not in $N(a)$ as h is closer to b than to a.

It should be clear that the definition of the sa-tree given above does not yield a unique solution. For example, such a situation arises when a is far from two of its neighbors b and c, which are close to each other, thereby resulting in the situation that both $N(a) = \{b\}$ and $N(a) = \{c\}$ satisfy the definition. Moreover, the fact that the neighbor set $N(a)$ is used in its definition (i.e., in a sense, the definition is self-referential) makes constructing a minimal set $N(a)$ expensive, and Navarro [1347] argues that its construction is an NP-complete problem. Thus, Navarro [1347] resorts to a heuristic for identifying the set of neighbors. This heuristic considers the objects in $S \setminus \{a\}$ in the order of their distance from a and adds an object o to $N(a)$ if o is closer to a than to the existing objects in $N(a)$ (see Exercise 3). In fact, for the points in Figure 4.61(a), the heuristic actually identifies the correct neighbor sets, and the sa-tree in Figure 4.61(b) was constructed using the heuristic with a chosen as the root. Nevertheless, the heuristic sometimes fails to find the minimal set of neighbors. An example of a situation where the heuristic would not find the minimal set of neighbors is shown in Figure 4.62, where approximate distances between four points a through d are labeled. The minimum neighbor set of a in this case is $N(\mathsf{a}) = \{\mathsf{d}\}$ (and $N(\mathsf{d}) = \{\mathsf{b}, \mathsf{c}\}$), whereas use of the heuristic would lead to $N(\mathsf{a}) = \{\mathsf{b}, \mathsf{c}\}$ (and $N(\mathsf{b}) = \{\mathsf{d}\}$).

Although the heuristic does not necessarily find the minimal neighbor set, it is deterministic in the sense that, for a given set of distance values, the same neighbor set is found (except for possible ties in distance values). Therefore, using the heuristic, the structure of the sa-tree is uniquely determined once the root has been chosen. In fact, Navarro [1347] formally redefines the sa-tree as the result of the application of this heuristic construction procedure. Thus, the initial minimality requirement in the sa-tree definition on the sizes of the individual neighbor sets seems to have been discarded.

Observe that different choices of the root lead to different tree structures. As an example, consider the distance matrix representing the interobject distances for the 18 objects a–r given in Figure 4.63. Figure 4.64(a) is the result of embedding these objects in the two-dimensional plane, assuming that the distance metric is the Euclidean distance, and assigning them a consistent set of coordinate values so that these distance values hold, while Figure 4.64(b) is the corresponding Delaunay graph, which for this particular embedding is a plane graph (e.g., [196, Theorem 9.5]) known as the Delaunay triangulation (DT) (i.e., the graph representation of the neighbor structure of the Voronoi diagram of the suitably embedded point set given by Figure 4.64(c)—see Section 2.2.1.4 of Chapter 2 for more details). Of course, it bears noting that for another embedding, not necessarily in the two-dimensional Euclidean plane, the Delaunay graph, in this case, is not necessarily a Delaunay triangulation. Figure 4.65(a–d) shows the sa-trees corresponding to the Delaunay graph realized by the planar embedding of Figure 4.64 when using objects r, a, d, b, respectively, as the roots. It is interesting to note that, from this example, we see that the sa-tree is not necessarily a subgraph of the Delaunay graph. In particular, when the sa-tree is rooted at a in Figure 4.65(b), we find the presence of edge hq, which is not present in the Delaunay graph in Figure 4.64(b).

Figure 4.62
An example of four points a, b, c, and d where the sa-tree construction algorithm does not find the minimal neighbor set N(a).

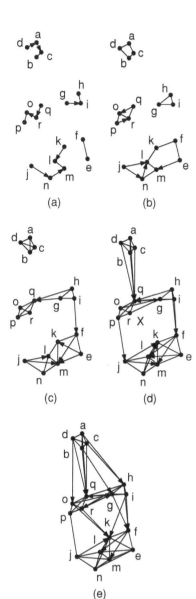

Figure 4.67
The kNN graphs for $k = 1...5$ corresponding to the data in Figure 4.63 using the planar embedding depicted in Figure 4.64(a): (a) $k = 1$, (b) $k = 2$, (c) $k = 3$, (d) $k = 4$, and (e) $k = 5$. Edges that are shown undirected correspond to bidirectional edges, which means that both vertices are in the k-nearest neighbor sets of each other.

vertex with corresponding object o has an edge to each of the vertices that correspond to the k nearest neighbors of o. As an example, consider the distance matrix representing the interobject distances for the 18 objects a–r in Figure 4.63 discussed in Section 4.5.5.1. Recall that Figure 4.64(a) is the result of embedding these objects in the two-dimensional plane, assuming that the distance is the Euclidean distance and assigning them a consistent set of coordinate values so that these distance values hold. In addition, Figure 4.64(b) is the corresponding Delaunay graph, which for this particular planar embedding is a plane graph known as the Delaunay triangulation. Figure 4.67(a–e) shows the kNN graphs for $k = 1...5$, respectively, corresponding to the data in Figure 4.63 using the planar embedding depicted in Figure 4.64. Edges in the graphs that are shown as undirected correspond to bidirectional edges, which means that both vertices are in the k nearest neighbor sets of each other.

Finding the nearest neighbor in S ($S \subset \mathbb{U}$) of query object q in $\mathbb{U}$ using the kNN graph can be achieved by using the same algorithm used in the Delaunay graph. In particular, start at an arbitrary object in S and proceed to a neighboring object in S that is closer to q as long as this is possible. Upon reaching an object o in S where the objects in its neighbor set $N(o)$ in S (i.e., the objects connected to o by an edge) are all farther away from q than o, we know that o is the nearest neighbor of q. Unfortunately, as can be seen from the different kNN graphs in Figure 4.67, there are situations where this algorithm will fail to yield the nearest neighbor. In particular, just because we found an object p whose k nearest neighbors are farther from the query object q than p does not necessarily mean that p is q's nearest neighbor, whereas this is the case in the Delaunay graph whenever we have found an object p, all of whose nearest neighbors (rather than just k) are farther from q.

There are several reasons for this failure. The first can be seen by examining Figure 4.67(a–c) where for low values of k (i.e., $k \le 3$), the kNN graphs are not connected, as is the case when the kNN graph consists of disconnected subgraphs corresponding to clusters. These clusters have the same effect on the search process as local minima or maxima in optimization problems. This shortcoming can be overcome by increasing k. However, this action does have the effect of increasing the storage requirements of the data structure by a factor of N for each unit increase in the value of k.

Nevertheless, even if we increase k so that the resulting kNN graph is connected, the algorithm may still fail to find the nearest neighbor. In particular, this is the case when the search halts at an object p, that is closer to q than any of p's k nearest neighbors but not necessarily closer to q than any of the objects that are in p's neighbor set but are farther from p than the k nearest neighbors of p. For example, consider the query object X in the kNN graph for $k = 4$ in Figure 4.67(d) positioned two-thirds of the way between k and r so that r is its nearest neighbor. Also consider a search that starts out at any one of objects e, f, j, k, l, m, n. In this case, assuming the planar embedding of Figure 4.64, the search will return k as the nearest neighbor instead of r. Again, this shortcoming can be overcome by further increasing the value of k. However, we do not have a guarantee that the true nearest neighbor will be found.

Sebastian and Kimia [1704] propose to overcome this drawback by extending the search neighborhood around the arbitrary object that is used as the starting point (termed a *seed*) of the search, as well as its closest neighbors obtained through use of the kNN graph, by a factor of $\tau \ge 1$. In particular, an object p_i is said to be τ-*closer* to q with respect to p if $d(p_i, q) \le \tau \cdot d(p, q)$. Armed with this definition, given an arbitrary object p, an element p_n belongs to the extended neighborhood $\text{EN}(p, q)$ of p with respect to query object q if there exists a path $p_0, p_1, ..., p_n$, where $p = p_0$ and p_i is τ-closer to q with respect to p for all $i = 1, ..., n - 1$. An object p is now reported as the nearest neighbor of q if it is closer to q than any other object in $\text{EN}(p, q)$. In essence, use of the extended neighborhood enables us to be able still to get to the nearest neighbor of q when the search is at an object p that is closer to q than any of p's k nearest neighbors but not necessarily closer to q than some of the objects that are reachable by transitioning via one of the k nearest neighbors of p. Note that the quality and performance of the search depends directly on the value of τ. In particular, if τ is sufficiently large, then the extended neighborhood will contain all of the objects, in which case there is no advantage to using the method over a search that involves all of the objects. Similarly, if τ is too small, then the extended neighborhood is small, and thus it may be the case that the true nearest neighbor will not be reported for some queries.

Unfortunately, use of the extended neighborhood will still not overcome the problem caused by the failure of the kNN graph to be connected. In particular, starting the search at a seed in a cluster, it is impossible to make a transition to the remaining clusters, even if the extended neighborhood factor τ is set to ∞. Thus, Sebastian and Kimia [1704] propose to use a multiple number of seeds chosen to be well separated and then to retain the closest neighbor of the objects that are returned as the nearest neighbor.

The notions of an extended neighborhood and multiple seeds are combined by Sebastian and Kimia [1704] to find the nearest neighbor by making use of a variant of the best-first search algorithm described in Section 4.1. In essence, they place the elements of the extended neighborhood in a priority queue *Queue*, sorted in increasing order of their distance from q, and at each step they pick the first element in *Queue* and attempt to move towards its neighbors that are τ-closer with respect to q than the current nearest neighbor of q. The search halts when the element at the front of *Queue* is not τ-closer to the current nearest neighbor of q. In order to minimize the effect of a possibly poor starting object, which is the case when the data is clustered so that the kNN graph is not connected, several starting objects are used as the seeds by initializing *Queue* with a few well-separated objects from the database, thereby increasing the likelihood that all of the components of the graph will be explored.

In experiments with synthetic and real data [1704], the true nearest neighbor was usually found by the algorithm, which was also relatively insensitive to the number of seeds for a given range of neighborhood extension parameter τ values, while also saving a good number of distance computations over a search that involved all objects. Note that, regardless of these experiments, this method may still yield an approximate nearest neighbor search (see Section 4.3) instead of an exact nearest neighbor search, as is the case in the sa-tree. Of course, exact nearest neighbor search in the sa-tree comes at the cost of some backtracking. However, there is also an element of backtracking involved in the kNN graph due to the use of a multiple number of seed objects.

Observe that the nearest neighbor search algorithm for the kNN graph does not make use of any of the properties of a metric space such as the triangle inequality (see Exercise 6). Thus, the algorithm would work correctly even if the distances between the objects were chosen arbitrarily. This is in contrast to the sa-tree, where the triangle inequality is an integral part of the search algorithm. Note also that using multiple seeds in the kNN graph nearest neighbor finding algorithm is somewhat similar to using different objects for the root in the sa tree. For example, recall Figure 4.65(a–d), which shows the sa-trees corresponding to the Delaunay graph realized by the planar embedding of Figure 4.64 when using objects r, a, d, and b, respectively, as the roots.

At this point, let us repeat that the motivation for the development of the kNN graph is to provide an approximation of the Delaunay graph. As we saw, one of the principal drawbacks of the kNN graph is that it is not necessarily connected, especially for low values of k. In the case of an embedding in the Euclidean plane, we can take advantage of some well-known properties of other approximations of the Delaunay graph, which are known to be connected by virtue of being supersets of the minimal spanning tree (MST) (e.g., [836]) of the vertices, while simultaneously being subsets of the Delaunay graph (i.e., the Delaunay triangulation in the Euclidean plane). For example, Figure 4.68(a) is the minimal spanning tree corresponding to the data in Figure 4.63 using the planar embedding depicted in Figure 4.64.

One such approximation is the relative neighborhood graph (RNG) [1883], where there is an edge between vertices u and v if, for all vertices p, u is closer to v than is p or v is closer to u than is p—that is, $d(u, v) \leq \max\{d(p, u), d(p, v)\}$ (see also Exercises 8–15).

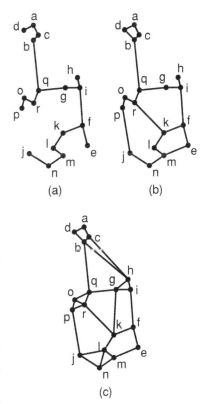

Figure 4.68
The (a) minimal spanning tree, (b) relative neighborhood graph, and (c) Gabriel graph corresponding to the data in Figure 4.63 using the planar embedding depicted in Figure 4.64(a).

data objects. The algorithm uses these lower bounds to guide the order in which objects are chosen to have their distances from the query object q computed and to eliminate objects from consideration (hopefully without computing their actual distances from q). In other words, AESA treats all N data objects as pivot objects when performing search. Although designed for finding nearest neighbors, AESA can also be used with almost no modification to perform range searching.

According to experiments presented in [1930], nearest neighbors can be obtained with AESA using remarkably few distance computations. In particular, AESA was observed to require at least an order of magnitude fewer distance computations than competing methods and was argued to have constant-time behavior with respect to the size of the dataset [1930]. These benefits are obtained at the expense of quadratic space complexity, quadratic time preprocessing cost, and linear time and storage overhead during search. Thus, although promising, the method is practical only for relatively small datasets of at most a few thousand objects. For example, for 10,000 data objects, the distance matrix occupies about 400 MB, assuming 4 bytes per distance value. Nevertheless, if distances are expensive to evaluate and if we can afford the large preprocessing cost, the search performance is hard to beat with other methods.

Of course, we could ask if it is really worthwhile to perform $N \cdot (N-1)/2$ distance computations between the objects, when by using brute force we can always find the nearest object to q using N distance computations. The payoff occurs when we can be sure that the set of objects is static, and that there will be many queries (more than N, assuming that preprocessing time and query time are of equal importance), and that most of these queries will be nearest neighbor queries for low numbers of neighbors or range queries with small query radii (otherwise, AESA will tend to require $O(N)$ distance computations, like the brute-force approach). The complexity arguments made in favor of AESA must also bear in mind that the constant-time claim refers to the number of distance computations, while the distance matrix has to be accessed many times for each query ($\Omega(N)$ for each nearest neighbor query[41]), although the distance computations are usually many orders of magnitude more complex than the operation of accessing the distance matrix.

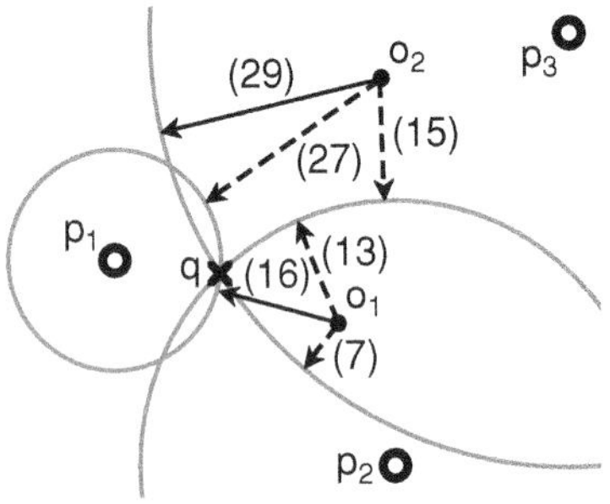

The key to the use of AESA [1930] in performing range searching and finding nearest neighbors is the property described in Lemma 4.1: for any objects o and p in the dataset S and any query object $q \in \mathbb{U}$, the following inequality holds:

$$|d(q,p) - d(p,o)| \leq d(q,o)$$

Thus, if $S_c \subset S$ is the set of objects whose distances from q have been computed, the greatest known lower bound $d_{\mathrm{lo}}(q,o)$ on $d(q,o)$ for any object $o \in S \setminus S_c$ is

$$d_{\mathrm{lo}}(q,o) = \max_{p \in S_c}\{|d(q,p) - d(p,o)|\} \tag{4.7}$$

An example of this computation is illustrated in Figure 4.73 for query object q and two objects o_1 and o_2 based on distances to three other objects, p_1, p_2, and p_3, in S_c, which serve as pivots. There are three directed lines emanating from each object o_1 and o_2 to the closest possible object position on the ball of radius $d(q,p)$ centered at each of the three different pivots p and passing through the query object q, where the solid line is the longest and its distance is used to compute the lower-bound distance $d_{\mathrm{lo}}(q,o)$, where o is one of o_1 and o_2 and q is the query object q. Observe that in this example, the lower bound on the distance from q for both objects o_1 and o_2 is quite close to the actual distance of the objects (16.5 and 31 for objects o_1 and o_2, respectively).

Figure 4.73
An example of the computation of the lower-bound distance d_{lo} for query object q and two objects o_1 and o_2 based on three pivots, p_1, p_2, and p_3. Three directed lines emanate from each object o_i to the closest possible object position on the ball of radius $d(q,p_j)$ centered at each of the three different pivots $p_j (j = 1...3)$ and passing through the query object q. The lines are labeled with these distance values (i.e., $|d(q,p_j) - d(p_j,o_i)|$) in parentheses. For each object o_i, the solid directed line is the longest, and its corresponding distance value is the one that is used in computing the lower-bound distance $d_{\mathrm{lo}}(q,o_i)$.

---

[41] To see why the number of accesses is at least proportional to N (i.e., $\Omega(N)$ instead of $O(N)$, which denotes at most), observe that even if the first object picked at random as the candidate nearest neighbor turns out to be the actual nearest neighbor, we still must access the distances between that object and all the other objects in order to establish that this is indeed the case.

AESA uses this lower bound in the algorithm for range searching with query radius ε to eliminate objects o in $S \setminus S_c$ whose lower-bound distances from q are greater than ε—that is, $d_{\text{lo}}(q,o) > \varepsilon$. For finding the nearest neighbor, the elimination criterion is objects o whose lower bound distances from q are greater than the distance from q of the nearest neighbor candidate o_n—that is, $d_{\text{lo}}(q,o) > d(q,o_n)$.[42] Hence, it maintains the set $S_u \subset S$ of objects whose distances from q have not been computed and that have not been eliminated based on their lower-bound distances.

Initially, the algorithm sets S_c to the empty set, S_u to S, and $d_{\text{lo}}(q,p)$ to 0 for all $p \in S$. At each step of the algorithm, the next object $p \in S_u$ whose distance is to be computed is chosen as the one whose lower-bound distance $d_{\text{lo}}(q,p)$ is smallest, with ties in lower-bound distances broken arbitrarily. Next, the algorithm computes $d(q,p)$ (which, we point out, may be very expensive), adds p to the result set if $d(q,p) \leq \varepsilon$ (in the case of finding the nearest neighbor, it instead updates the nearest neighbor candidate o_n if necessary), and then eliminates objects from S_u that cannot be within the range being searched (or that cannot be the nearest neighbor in the case of finding the nearest neighbor) as described above. The algorithm is terminated once S_u becomes empty—that is, once the greatest known lower-bound distance $d_{\text{lo}}(q,o)$ for each object $o \in S \setminus S_c$ is greater than ε (or $d(q,o_n)$ in the case of finding the nearest neighbor).

Observe that in the above algorithm, the lower-bound distance, $d_{\text{lo}}(q,o)$, for an object $o \in S_u$ need not be computed from scratch based on all $p \in S_c$ each time the algorithm makes use of it. Rather, the algorithm stores the current lower-bound distance for each object $o \in S_u$ and incrementally updates $d_{\text{lo}}(q,o)$ in each iteration as a new distance value is computed. Storing and maintaining this information accounts for the linear space and time overhead of the algorithm, besides the quadratic space and time cost for constructing and storing the distance matrix, respectively.

The rationale for picking the object p to process next based on the smallest lower bound $d_{\text{lo}}(q,p)$ is that, hopefully, such a choice ensures that p is relatively close to q. As pointed out by Vidal [1929], the closer p is to q, the greater the tendency is for $|d(p,o) - d(q,p)|$ to be large, which means that the lower bound $d_{\text{lo}}(q,o)$ is larger and hence the potential for pruning increases. Of course, other strategies for picking the next object are also possible.[43] Some possible strategies include picking the object at random, choosing the object with the greatest value of $d_{\text{lo}}(q,p)$, or even basing the choice on the upper bound $d_{\text{hi}}(q,p)$, where $d_{\text{hi}}(q,p) = \min_{o \in S_c}\{d(q,o) + d(p,o)\}$. Wang and Shasha [1951] explored several different strategies, which are described briefly in Section 4.5.7.3.

AESA is easily extended to a k-nearest neighbor algorithm by maintaining a list of the k candidate nearest neighbors seen so far and by using the largest distance among the k candidates for the elimination step. Unfortunately, this is not applicable for finding the nearest neighbors incrementally as the search radius is typically not bounded. Hjaltason and Samet [851] discuss a number of ways to define a search hierarchy based on the AESA framework so that the incremental nearest neighbor search algorithm in Section 4.1.3 can be applied. Of course, applying a range query algorithm to such a hierarchy should be equivalent to the algorithm presented above, in terms of the number of distance computations. Hjaltason and Samet [851] outline the definition of three search hierarchies, each of which has somewhat different characteristics. Conceptually, all three approaches involve the maintenance of two sets, S_c and S_u, of data objects, where

---

[42] If $d_{\text{lo}}(q,o) > \varepsilon$ is satisfied, we know that $d(q,o) > \varepsilon$; similarly, in the case of finding the nearest neighbor, $d_{\text{lo}}(q,o) > d(q,o_n)$ means that $d(q,o) > d(q,o_n)$ since $d_{\text{lo}}(q,o) \leq d(q,o)$.

[43] In the original formulation of AESA [1930], the selection criterion was actually based on picking the object $p \in S_u$ that minimizes the value of $\sum_{s \in S_c}\{|d(q,s) - d(s,p)|\}$ rather than that of $d_{\text{lo}}(q,p) = \max_{s \in S_c}\{|d(q,s) - d(s,p)|\}$, which Vidal [1929] later claimed was a better "approximation." One possible rationale for the claimed improvement is that the former minimizes the average lower bound, while the latter minimizes the maximum of the lower bounds, which yields a tighter lower bound.

$S = S_c \cup S_u$, whose distances from the query object have and have not been computed, respectively. Notice that in the case of incremental nearest neighbor search, S_u is larger than when it was used for range searching as no objects can be eliminated; instead, their reporting is deferred. In essence, they differ in the way in which S_u is represented, which has implications for the cost of maintaining the lower-bound distance, $d_{lo}(q, o)$, associated with each object $o \in S_u$.

Exercise

1. Give an algorithm to find the nearest neighbors in an incremental manner using AESA.

4.5.7.2 LAESA

Recall that AESA is impractical for all but the smallest datasets due to the large preprocessing and storage costs. LAESA (Linear AESA) [1292] alleviates this drawback by choosing a fixed number M of pivots (termed *base prototypes* by Micó, Oncina, and Vidal [1292]), whose distances from all other objects are computed. Thus, for N data objects, the distance matrix contains $N \cdot M$ entries rather than $O(N^2)$ for AESA (or more precisely $N(N-1)/2$ entries, assuming that only the lower triangular portion of the matrix is stored). An algorithm for choosing the M pivots is presented by Micó et al. [1292]. Essentially, this algorithm attempts to choose the pivots such that they are *maximally separated*—that is, as far away from each other as possible (a similar procedure was suggested by Brin [255] for GNAT, which is described in Section 4.5.3.2).

The LAESA search strategy is very similar to that of AESA, except that some complications arise from the fact that not all objects in S serve as pivot objects in LAESA (and the distance matrix does not contain the distances between nonpivot objects). In particular, as before, let $S_c \subset S$ be the set of objects whose distances from q have been computed, and let $S_u \subset S \setminus S_c$ be the set of objects whose distances from q have yet to be computed and that have not been eliminated.

The distances between the query object q and the pivot objects in S_c are used to compute a lower bound on the distances of objects in S_u from q, and these lower bounds allow eliminating objects from S_u whose lower-bound distances from q are greater than ε for range searching with query radius ε (for finding the nearest neighbor, the elimination criterion is objects whose lower-bound distances from q are greater than the distance from q of the current nearest neighbor candidate o_n). The difference here is that nonpivot objects in S_c do not help in tightening the lower-bound distances of the objects in S_u, as the distance matrix stores only the distances from the nonpivot objects to the pivot objects and not to the remaining objects. Thus, Micó et al. [1292] suggest treating the pivot objects in S_u differently from nonpivot objects when

1. selecting the next object in S_u to have its distance from q computed (since computing the distances of pivot objects early will help in tightening distance bounds) and

2. eliminating objects from S_u (since eliminating pivot objects that may later help in tightening the distance bounds is undesirable).

A number of possible policies can be established for this purpose. The policies explored by Micó et al. [1292] are simple and call for

1. selecting a pivot object in S_u over any nonpivot object and

2. eliminating pivot objects from S_u only after a certain fraction f of the pivot objects has been selected into S_c (f can range from 0% to 100%; note that if $f = 100\%$, pivots are never eliminated from S_u).

As with AESA, several possible strategies can be pursued for defining a search hierarchy within the framework of LAESA, as shown in [851]. However, since LAESA is practical for much larger datasets than AESA, some of the approaches that are feasible for AESA are too inefficient. Nevertheless, it is possible to define search hierarchies in which the use of the incremental nearest neighbor search algorithm in Section 4.1.3, without a priori knowledge of the result size, has the same cost as the LAESA nearest neighbor search strategy [851]. See Chávez et al. [330] for another search strategy that is in the spirit of the method of Nene and Nayar [1364].

It is interesting to repeat our observation (made in conjunction with the discussion of Lemma 4.1 in Section 4.5.1) that LAESA, and to a lesser extent AESA, can be viewed as variations of embedding methods (see Section 4.7) that map the distances between the objects into a k-dimensional space by using k pivots (i.e., the base prototypes in LAESA and all of the objects in AESA) as coordinates and the distances of the objects from the pivots as the coordinate values of the objects. In other words, the result of the mapping of an object x is a point $(x_0, x_1, \ldots, x_{k-1})$ whose coordinate value x_i is the distance $d(x, p_i)$ of x from pivot p_i. Lemma 4.1 enables pruning an object x from further consideration as being within ε of query object q when $|d(q, p_i) - d(x, p_i)| > \varepsilon$ for some coordinate corresponding to pivot p_i ($0 \le i \le k - 1$).

Exercise

1. Give an algorithm to find the nearest neighbors in an incremental manner using LAESA.

4.5.7.3 Other Distance Matrix Methods

Shapiro [1743] described a nearest neighbor algorithm, that is also applicable to range searching with query radius ε and is closely related to LAESA in that it also uses an $N \cdot M$ distance matrix based on M pivot objects. The order in which the data objects are processed in the search is based on their positions in a list $(o_1, o_2, \ldots)$ sorted by distance from the first pivot object p_1. Thus, the search is initiated at the object whose distance from p_1 is most similar to $d(q, p_1)$, where q is the query object—that is, the element at the position j (i.e., o_j) for which $|d(q, p_1) - d(p_1, o_j)|$ is minimized (this value is a lower bound on $d(q, o_j)$, as shown in Lemma 4.1). The goal is to eliminate object o_i from consideration as soon as possible, thereby hopefully avoiding the need to compute its distance from q. Therefore, assuming range searching, when object o_i is processed during the search, we check whether the pruning condition $|d(q, p_k) - d(p_k, o_i)| > \varepsilon$ (or $|d(q, p_k) - d(p_k, o_i)| > d(q, o_n)$ for finding the nearest neighbor, where o_n is the current candidate nearest neighbor) is satisfied for each pivot object $p_1, p_2, \ldots$ in turn until o_i can be eliminated; otherwise, we compute $d(q, o_i)$ and add o_i to the result set if $d(q, o_i) \le \varepsilon$ (in the case of finding the nearest neighbor, it instead updates the nearest neighbor candidate o_n if necessary). The search continues alternating in the two directions—that is, for $i = j + 1, j - 1, j + 2, j - 2, \ldots$, stopping in either direction when the pruning condition $|d(q, p_1) - d(p_1, o_i)| > \varepsilon$ (or $|d(q, p_1) - d(p_1, o_i)| > d(q, o_n)$ for finding the nearest neighbor) is satisfied.

Observe that Shapiro's algorithm is less sophisticated than LAESA in two ways:

1. The order used in the search is based on position in the sorted list ordered by distance from p_1.

2. Only the first pivot p_1 affects the order in which the data objects are processed.

In contrast, LAESA uses the lower-bound distances as determined by *all* pivot objects that have been applied so far to guide the search (i.e., to choose the pivot to use next and to decide when to compute the actual distances of data objects). In other words, rather than applying all pivots for each object in turn as done by Shapiro, LAESA applies each pivot in turn for all objects. Therefore, the difference can be characterized roughly in terms of processing the pivot-object distance matrix in row-major or column-major order.

Wang and Shasha [1951] have described a general search method based on distance matrices that is similar to AESA, which is applicable to a number of problems, including range searching and finding nearest neighbors. However, they allow for the case where only some of the distances have been precomputed, as in LAESA. In contrast to LAESA, Wang and Shasha make no assumptions about the pairs of objects for which the distance is precomputed (so that no distinction is made between pivot and nonpivot objects). In other words, we are given a set of interobject distances for arbitrary pairs of objects in S. Search is facilitated by the use of two matrices D_{lo} and D_{hi} (called *ADM* and *MIN* in [1951]), constructed on the basis of the precomputed distances, where $D_{lo}[i, j] \leq d(o_i, o_j) \leq D_{hi}[i, j]$, given some enumeration $o_1, o_2, ..., o_N$ of the objects in S.[44] In other words, all entries in D_{lo} and D_{hi} are initialized to 0 and ∞, respectively, except that the entries on their diagonals are set to 0, and if $d(o_i, o_j)$ has been precomputed, then $D_{lo}[i, j]$ and $D_{hi}[i, j]$ are both set to $d(o_i, o_j)$.

A dynamic programming algorithm is described by Wang and Shasha [1951] that utilizes a generalized version of the triangle inequality[45] to derive values for the entries of D_{lo} and D_{hi}, whose distance values are missing, in such a way that they provide as tight a bound as possible, based on the precomputed distances that are available. In particular, the generalized triangle inequality property was used by Wang and Shasha to derive rules for updating $D_{lo}[i, j]$ and $D_{hi}[i, j]$ based on the values of other entries in D_{lo} and D_{hi} (some of these rules use entries in D_{lo} to update entries in D_{hi}, and others do the opposite). At search time, the matrices D_{lo} and D_{hi} are augmented so that the query object q is treated as if it were object o_{N+1}. In particular, $D_{lo}[i, N+1]$ and $D_{hi}[i, N+1]$ are initialized to 0 and ∞, respectively. Observe that the values of $D_{lo}[i, N+1]$ and $D_{hi}[i, N+1]$ correspond to the definitions of $d_{lo}(q, o_i)$ and $d_{hi}(q, o_i)$, respectively, given in Section 4.5.7.1.

The range searching (as well as nearest neighbor) algorithm presented by Wang and Shasha [1951] follows the same general outline as AESA. Thus, any object o_i satisfying $D_{lo}[i, N+1] > \varepsilon$ (or $D_{lo}[i, N+1] > d(q, o_n)$ for finding the nearest neighbor, where o_n is the current candidate nearest neighbor) can be pruned from the search. The difference here is that when $d(q, o_k)$ is computed for some candidate object o_k, their method attempts to update $D_{lo}[i, j]$ and $D_{hi}[i, j]$ (by applying their generalized triangle inequality property) for all pairs of objects $o_i, o_j \in S$ whose actual distances are not available (i.e., they are either precomputed or computed during the search), thereby possibly yielding a tighter bound on $d(o_i, o_j)$. In contrast, in AESA, only the values of $d_{lo}(q, o_i)$ and $d_{hi}(q, o_i)$ are updated for all objects $o_i \in S$, corresponding to $D_{lo}[i, N+1]$ and $D_{hi}[i, N+1]$, respectively.

Since updating the entire matrices D_{lo} and D_{hi} can be expensive if done for all pairs at each stage of the algorithm, Wang and Shasha [1951] describe two alternatives, one of which is almost equivalent to the updating policy used in AESA. The difference is that in AESA, upper-bound distances are not maintained, whereas such upper bounds can be used to update the values of $d_{lo}(q, o)$ in the same way as is done for $D_{lo}[N+1, i]$ in the method of Wang and Shasha [1951]. Wang and Shasha [1951] identify four heuristics for picking the next candidate object during search. The next object o_i for which to compute $d(q, o_i)$ is chosen as the object in S_u (as defined in Section 4.5.7.1) having one of the following:

1. The least lower bound $D_{lo}[i, N+1]$

2. The greatest lower bound $D_{lo}[i, N+1]$

3. The least upper bound $D_{hi}[i, N+1]$

4. The greatest upper bound $D_{hi}[i, N+1]$

---

[44] Note that the matrices are symmetric and that their diagonals are 0. Thus, only the lower triangular part of each matrix is actually maintained.

[45] For example, based on $d(o_1, o_4) \geq d(o_1, o_3) - d(o_3, o_4)$ and $d(o_1, o_3) \geq d(o_1, o_2) - d(o_2, o_3)$, we can conclude that $d(o_1, o_4) \geq d(o_1, o_2) - d(o_2, o_3) - d(o_3, o_4)$.

According to their experiments, the best choice is the object with the least lower-bound distance estimate (i.e., heuristic 1), which is the same as is used in AESA. Incremental nearest neighbor search in this setting is implemented in the same manner as is done for AESA [851].

Micó et al. [1291] have proposed a hybrid distance-based indexing method termed *TLAESA* that makes use of both a distance matrix and hierarchical clustering, thereby combining aspects of LAESA [1292] (see Section 4.5.7.2) and the monotonous bisector tree (mb-tree) [1383] (see Section 4.5.3.3). The hierarchical search structure used by TLAESA applies the same variation on the gh-tree as is used in the monotonous bisector tree (mb-tree): two pivots are used in each node for splitting the subset associated with the node (based on which pivot is closer), where one of the pivots in each nonroot node is inherited from its parent. The search algorithm proposed by Micó et al. uses a partial distance matrix as in LAESA, thus introducing a second set of pivots (termed *base prototypes* by Micó et al. [1291]). Initially, the algorithm computes the distances between q and all distance matrix pivots. Next, when traversing the tree structure, TLAESA uses the distance matrix pivots to compute lower bounds on the distances of the tree pivots from q, rather than computing their actual distances from q. In other words, if $p_1, p_2, \ldots, p_M$ are the distance matrix pivots, and p is a tree pivot, a lower bound $d_{\mathrm{lo}}(q, p)$ on $d(q, p)$ is obtained by applying Lemma 4.1 to all the distance matrix pivots. Therefore, $d_{\mathrm{lo}}(q, p) \le d(q, p)$, where

$$ d_{\mathrm{lo}}(q, p) = \max_i \{|d(q, p_i) - d(p_i, p)|\} $$

Now, if r is the ball radius corresponding to the tree pivot p, $d_{\mathrm{lo}}(q, p) - r$ is the lower bound on the distances between q and all the objects in the subtree rooted at the child node corresponding to p (via Lemma 4.3, setting $r_{\mathrm{lo}} = 0$, $r_{\mathrm{hi}} = r$, $s_{\mathrm{lo}} = d_{\mathrm{lo}}(q, p)$, and $s_{\mathrm{hi}} = \infty$). The actual distances of data objects (other than distance matrix pivots) are then computed only when reaching leaf nodes of the tree.

Several other variants of AESA and LAESA have been developed (e.g., [1533, 1932]). For example, Ramasubramanian and Paliwal [1533] have presented a variant of AESA that is tailored to vector spaces, allowing them to reduce the preprocessing cost and space complexity to $O(nN)$, where n is the dimensionality of the vector space (thus, there are significant savings compared to $O(N^2)$ since $n \ll N$). This algorithm appears to be quite related to LAESA.

Although both AESA and LAESA usually lead to a low number of distance computations when searching, they do have an overhead of $O(N)$ in terms of computations other than distance. Vilar [1932] presents a technique termed *Reduced Overhead AESA* (or ROAESA for short), which is applicable to both AESA and LAESA, and reduces this overhead cost by using a heuristic to limit the set of objects whose lower-bound distances d_{lo} are updated at each step of the algorithm. In particular, rather than updating d_{lo} for all objects in S_u (to use the notation in Section 4.5.7.1), ROAESA partitions S_u into two subsets that are termed *alive* (S_a) and *not alive* (S_d), and only updates the d_{lo} values of the objects in S_a. ROAESA starts by picking an object o_1 whose distance from q is computed, and o_1 is entered into S_c. Next, it computes d_{lo} for all objects in $S_u = S \setminus S_c$ on the basis of o_1 and makes the object o_a in S_u with the lowest d_{lo} value alive—that is, initially, $S_a = \{o_a\}$ and $S_d = S \setminus \{o_a\}$.

In the main loop that constitutes the search, the object in S_a with the smallest d_{lo} value is picked as the next object whose distance is computed, and the d_{lo} values of the objects in S_a are updated. Then, in an inner loop, the objects in S_d are considered in order of their d_{lo} value (i.e., which was based on the initial object o_1) and made alive (i.e., moved from S_d to S_a) if their d_{lo} value is lower than the minimum of d_n and d_a, where d_n is the distance of the current candidate nearest neighbor and d_a is the minimum

d_{lo} of an object in S_a (note that d_a may change in each iteration of the inner loop).[46] Note that ROAESA has no effect for range searching as in this case d_n is replaced by ε, and now S_a is the set of all elements of S_u that have not been eliminated by virtue of their d_{lo} values being greater than ε.

Interestingly, some of the search hierarchies devised by Hjaltason and Samet [851] for finding nearest neighbors in an incremental manner using AESA and LAESA are related to Vilar's technique, as they also aim at reducing the amount of updating in a somewhat analogous, but more powerful, manner. In particular, in some of the search hierarchies that they proposed, S_u is partitioned into any number of subsets rather than just two (i.e., the alive and not alive objects in ROAESA), where a different number of objects in S_c are used to define d_{lo} for each subset.

Exercises

1. Give an algorithm to find the nearest neighbors in an incremental manner using Shapiro's algorithm.

2. Give an algorithm to find the nearest neighbors in an incremental manner using Wang and Shasha's algorithm.

3. Give an algorithm to find the nearest neighbors in an incremental manner using TLAESA.

4. Show that when all of the objects in S are sorted in the preprocessing step of AESA/LAESA on the basis of their distance from o_1, the first object that is entered into S_c, then all alive objects lie in consecutive locations in the sorted array. In other words, for all o_i that are alive, we have $x_{lo} \leq d(o_1, o_i) \leq x_{hi}$, for some values x_{lo} and x_{hi}.

4.5.8 SASH: Indexing without Using the Triangle Inequality

Neighborhood search strategies for the Delaunay graph and approximations such as the sa-tree [1347] (see Section 4.5.5) all make use of the triangle inequality to identify and prune search paths that are guaranteed not to lead to objects that belong to the query result set. However, as we demonstrated in Figure 4.1, when the dimensionality of the data increases, the curse of dimensionality causes the majority of interobject distances to be concentrated around their mean value, thereby drastically reducing the effectiveness of the triangle inequality in pruning search paths. The recently proposed *Spatial Approximation Sample Hierarchy* (SASH)[47] approximate search strategy [883, 884] attempts to circumvent this problem by appealing to the triangle inequality, regardless of whether or not it is satisfied for all objects, to establish links to objects that are likely to be neighbors of the query object, instead of using it, in the conventional manner, to eliminate objects that are guaranteed not to be neighbors.

This likelihood-based linking strategy can be understood best by considering the set S of objects, letting S' be a fixed random sample consisting of roughly half the objects of S, and assuming that we have some as-yet-unspecified search index that allows efficient approximate neighborhood queries to be performed over the points of S'. Consider the two points $x' \in S'$ and $x \in S \setminus S'$ in the vicinity of object q taken with respect to S (e.g., when seeking the nearest neighbors in S of q). The triangle inequality is but one of many possible embodiments of a "closeness" relationship that stipulates that if a is close to b, and if b is close to c, then a is close to c. In particular, the triangle inequality

---

[46] Vilar [1932] employs a performance-improvement technique in which all of the objects in S are sorted in the preprocessing step of AESA/LAESA on the basis of their distance from o_1. It can be shown (see Exercise 4) that this means that all alive objects lie in consecutive locations in the sorted array so that the next object to become alive will be one of the objects just beyond the region of alive objects.

[47] This notion of SASH is different from the SASH (Self Adaptive Set of Histograms) of Lim, Wand, and Vitter [1170].

$d(x',q) \leq d(x,q) + d(x',x)$), whether or not it is always satisfied, can be interpreted as indicating that when the distances from q to x and from x' to x are both very small, the distance from q to x' must also be small. In practice, this means that we can reasonably expect that if x is a highly ranked neighbor of both q and x' among the objects of $S \setminus S'$, then x' is also likely to be a highly ranked neighbor of q with respect to the set S' (e.g., when seeking the nearest neighbors in S' of q).

The key idea in the SASH method is to treat the approximate nearest neighbor relation as an equivalence relation, even though this is not generally true (see also [450, 2064] in the fuzzy logic area). In particular, the symmetry property does not hold in general—that is, x being an approximate nearest neighbor of x' does not mean that x' must be an approximate nearest neighbor of x. In addition, the transitivity property also does not hold in general—that is, x being an approximate nearest neighbor of q and x' being an approximate nearest neighbor of x do not mean that x' must be an approximate nearest neighbor of q. The process of constructing a SASH is analogous to a UNION operation, while the process of finding the approximate nearest neighbor is analogous to a FIND operation. Transitivity plays the same role as the triangle inequality, as discussed above, with the approximate nearest neighbor relation corresponding to the "$\leq$" relation on the distance values. Now, with the aid of this interpretation, we see better that instead of the conventional use of the triangle inequality to eliminate objects from consideration that are guaranteed not to be neighbors, the SASH method appeals to the triangle inequality, $d(x',q) \leq d(q,x) + d(x',x)$, regardless of whether or not it holds, to establish links to objects likely to be neighbors of query object q. Again, as mentioned above, this is based on the fact that when $d(q,x)$ and $d(x',x)$ are both very small, then $d(q,x')$ is also very small, a property that is analogous to "nearest." This leads us again to the implication that if $x \in S \setminus S'$ is a highly ranked neighbor of both q and $x' \in S'$ among objects in $S \setminus S'$, then x' is also likely to be a highly ranked neighbor of q among objects in S'. Now, given the assumption that the approximate nearest neighbor relation is an equivalence relation, by symmetry we have that x' is a highly ranked neighbor of x, combined with the premise that x is a highly ranked neighbor of q, leads us to conclude by transitivity that x' is a highly ranked neighbor of q.

The basic SASH approximate nearest neighbor search strategy exploits this closeness relationship, which generally, but not always, holds by using the neighbors of q in S' to generate candidate neighbors of q from among the objects of $S \setminus S'$. This action corresponds to the final step in a search strategy that is applied in a top-down manner to a hierarchy of successively larger subsets of the objects until encountering $S \setminus S'$. The hierarchy is built in two phases in a recursive manner starting with S. In the first phase, we initially partition S at random into two sets S' and another set $S \setminus S'$, each of which is approximately one-half the size of S. We then recursively apply the same partitioning process to S', thereby yielding S'' and $S' \setminus S''$, each of which is approximately one-half the size of S'. This halving process is applied to S'', and so on, to obtain successively smaller sets until obtaining a pair of sets, at least one of which contains just one object. Assuming that S contains N objects, we have $h = \lceil \log_2(N + 1) \rceil$ sets in the hierarchy. The complete hierarchy of h sets is called a *SASH*, and it is distinguished from subsets of the hierarchy by being identified as $SASH_h$. In general, $SASH_i$ ($1 \leq i \leq h$) corresponds to the first i subsets of the hierarchy starting at the root of the hierarchy. Using our example of subsets of S, we find that $SASH_{h-1}$ contains the objects in S' and, at times, we refer to it as the *subSASH*. Similarly, $SASH_{h-2}$ contains the objects in S'' and, again, at times, we refer to it as the *subsubSASH*. As an example, consider a set of 31 objects drawn from a one-dimensional space so that the distance between them is reflected by their horizontal separation. Figure 4.74 shows one example of how these 31 objects are distributed among the five sets that form a SASH hierarchy for this data.

Once the hierarchy of sets has been obtained in the first phase, we are ready to begin the second phase in the construction of a SASH. In this phase, a directed graph is constructed. The graph is defined so that for each object x in $SASH_i \setminus SASH_{i-1}$, there are at most p edges to x, one from each of p approximate nearest neighbors of x, which

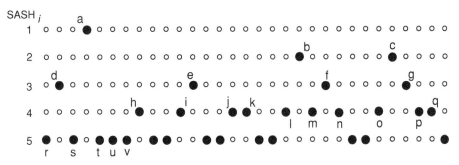

Figure 4.74
Example of how 31 objects drawn from a one-dimensional space so that the distance between them is reflected by their horizontal separation are distributed among the five sets that form a SASH hierarchy for this dataset. Labels are assigned to objects that are used in subsequent figures and are positioned (i.e., above or below the objects) in a manner that facilitates subsequent rendering of the SASH hierarchy.

are labeled x'_j $(1 \le j \le p)$ in $\text{SASH}_{i-1} \backslash \text{SASH}_{i-2}$, where p is a small, fixed, positive value. The graph corresponding to SASH_h is constructed recursively, making use of the graph corresponding to SASH_{h-1} and starting at the root said to be at level 1, which corresponds to SASH_1 and contains the root object. Again, we repeat that before starting the construction of the directed graph, the objects that form the various SASHes have been already determined by a random selection process as described above so that each level of a SASH contains approximately the same number of objects as the sum of the objects in the shallower levels.

The second phase starts at the root, which is said to be at level 1 corresponding to SASH_1, and constructs SASH_2. In general, assuming that we have constructed SASH_i for the objects at levels 1 through i, we construct SASH_{i+1} by using the edges in the directed graph that was already built for SASH_i to find the p approximate nearest neighbors in $\text{SASH}_i \backslash \text{SASH}_{i-1}$ of each object o in the set of objects at level $i + 1$ (i.e., $\text{SASH}_{i+1} \backslash \text{SASH}_i$). The p approximate nearest neighbors are obtained by a process described later. Once these p approximate nearest neighbors a_{oj} $(1 \le j \le p)$ are determined for each o, an edge is added from each of the a_{oj} to o. The rationale for this step is the assumption (recalling that it need not necessarily be true) that the approximate nearest neighbor relation is an equivalence relation and thus corresponds to making use of the symmetry property of the relation. If there are more than c edges emanating for a particular object b in $\text{SASH}_i \backslash \text{SASH}_{i-1}$, then only the edges to the closest c objects at level $i + 1$ are retained, while the remaining objects that had b as one of their p approximate nearest neighbors are said to be *rejected* by b. This process could result in objects that cannot be reached by a path starting from the root of a SASH (such objects are termed *orphan objects*). In order to avoid this situation, it is stipulated that there must be at least one edge to each object o at level $i + 1$ from an object t at level i, regardless of the distance from o to t, and hence an additional search is invoked to find some neighboring object that has excess capacity for a connection to it (see Exercise 10). This guarantees that o can be reached by subsequent searches that start at the root of the SASH hierarchy when executing an approximate k-nearest neighbor query. Once there is at least one edge to each object at level $i + 1$ from an object at level i, the construction of the directed graph corresponding to SASH_{i+1} is completed. The construction process is repeated at each successively deeper level of the SASH until the edges that complete the directed graph corresponding to SASH_h have been added.

At this point, it is important to reemphasize that all neighbors that were found during the process of constructing the directed graphs corresponding to the different SASHes are approximate, as for x at level i of the SASH (i.e., in $\text{SASH}_i \backslash \text{SASH}_{i-1}$), the set of candidate nearest neighbors is constrained to contain only objects at level $i - 1$ (i.e., in $\text{SASH}_{i-1} \backslash \text{SASH}_{i-2}$), rather than all of the objects in S, which is the usual case in nearest neighbor finding. Moreover, all of the neighboring objects at level i (i.e., that have incoming edges from objects at level $i - 1$) during the construction of $SASH_i$ were found by traversing the directed graph corresponding to the existing $SASH_{i-1}$.

One potential problem with this construction process is that an object may have many edges emanating from it to objects in the immediately deeper level. This is not surprising as it can easily arise, for example, when we have a cluster of objects C at level i around an object o at level $i - 1$ so that for each object b in C, b is closer to o than to any other object in $S \setminus C$ (e.g., as is the case for sites in a Voronoi diagram). This is why a firm limit c is placed on the number of connections each object of any $SASH_i \setminus SASH_{i-1}$ ($1 \le i < h$) can have to an object external to it (i.e., in $SASH_{i+1} \setminus SASH_i$). This limit on the out degree of SASH nodes permits better management of the execution time of the approximate k-nearest neighbor query. In practice, the limit is set at $c = 4p$.

The rationale for setting the limit c to $4p$ can be seen by examining the construction of the connections from the nonsubSASH objects to the nonsubsubSASH objects. In particular, we observe that if each of the $N/2$ nonsubSASH objects (i.e., in $SASH_h \setminus SASH_{h-1}$) is connected to at most its p nearest neighbors, then there is a total of approximately $p \cdot N/2$ connections (i.e., edges) distributed among the roughly $N/4$ objects of subSASH\subsubSASH (i.e., $SASH_{h-1} \setminus SASH_{h-2}$), for an average out degree of $2p$. As we pointed out above, the limit may cause some objects to be rejected. In order to minimize the number of rejections, c is chosen to be twice the average out degree. This is in the spirit of constructing a hash table in uniform hashing [1484] where the number of available locations is twice the minimum number of locations required to store all of the elements [884].

We now examine a simple example SASH as given by Figure 4.75. It is the SASH built by letting $p = 2$, and, in order to simplify the presentation, $c = 5$ for the set of 18 objects a–r whose distance matrix of interobject distances is given in Figure 4.63. Figure 4.64(a) is the result of embedding these objects in the two-dimensional plane, assuming that the distance metric is the Euclidean distance, and assigning the objects a consistent set of coordinate values so that these distance values hold. In this case, the full SASH has five levels, the subSASH contains the top four levels of the full SASH, the subsubSASH contains the top three levels of the full SASH, the subsubsubSASH contains the top two levels of the full SASH, and the subsubsubsubSASH contains just

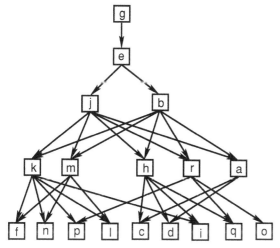

Figure 4.75
The SASH built by letting $p = 2$ and $c = 5$ for the set of 18 objects a–r whose distance matrix of interobject distances is given in Figure 4.63, while the result of embedding these objects in the two-dimensional plane, assuming that the similarity measure is the Euclidean distance, is given in Figure 4.64(a). The positions of the objects in the SASH figure depicted here do not reflect their true locations.

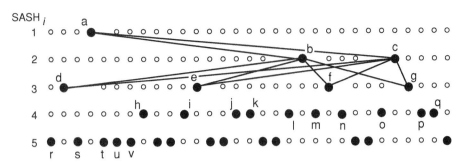

Figure 4.76
SASH$_1$, SASH$_2$, and SASH$_3$ corresponding to the SASH hierarchy given in Figure 4.74 with $p = 2$ and $c = 4$.

the top level of the full SASH (i.e., the root). Note that, although object k is one of the $p = 2$ nearest neighbors of objects {f,i,l,n,p,o}, since this set has more than $c = 5$ members, we must reject one of the objects, say o, as it is the farthest from object k. Observe, however, that all objects have at least one edge going into them.

In order to gain a better understanding of the SASH construction process, we turn to Figures 4.76–4.80, which illustrate how the directed graph corresponding to the full SASH is constructed level by level for the set of 31 objects drawn from a one-dimensional space whose distribution into five levels of a SASH hierarchy is given by Figure 4.74. In this example, we assume that $p = 2$ and $c = 4$. Figure 4.76 shows the result of the steps leading to SASH$_1$, SASH$_2$, and SASH$_3$. The construction of SASH$_1$, of course, is trivial as it consists of a single object serving as the root. For the next two levels, the small number of objects at the level means that at each stage of the SASH construction, every object at levels 2 and 3 has an edge directed towards each of the objects at levels 1 and 2, respectively, and, similarly, every object at levels 1 and 2 has an edge directed towards all objects at levels 2 and 3, respectively. Of course, once the edges of the directed graph from level i to level $i + 1$ have been determined, the edges from level $i + 1$ to level i are discarded, as is the case here, and thus the edges from level i to $i + 1$ are drawn without showing the direction explicitly.

Figure 4.77 shows the result of the step that leads to SASH$_4$. In this case, a bidirectional edge (illustrated by a solid line) between objects b and a at levels $i + 1$ and i ($i = 3$ here), respectively, denotes that b has determined a to be one of its p nearest neighbors in SASH$_i \setminus$ SASH$_{i-1}$ and that a has determined b to be one of its c nearest neighbors from the objects at level $i + 1$ (i.e., SASH$_{i+1} \setminus$ SASH$_i$) that have determined a to be one of their p nearest neighbors in SASH$_i \setminus$ SASH$_{i-1}$. On the other hand, a one-directional edge (illustrated by a broken line) from object b at level $i + 1$ to object a at level i denotes that b has determined a to be one of its p nearest neighbors in SASH$_i \setminus$ SASH$_{i-1}$ but that a has determined that b is not one of its c closest neighbors from the objects at level $i + 1$ (i.e., SASH$_{i+1} \setminus$ SASH$_i$) that have determined a to be one of their p nearest neighbors in SASH$_i \setminus$ SASH$_{i-1}$. In other words, a one-directional edge (illustrated by a broken line) from x to y reflects the fact that, in reality, the k-nearest neighbor relation is asymmetric. In this figure, we see one-dimensional edges (i.e., broken lines) from j and k to f, from l to e, from m to g, and from p and q to f. Of course, they are not present in the actual directed graph corresponding to SASH$_4$, which consists of just the solid edges.

Figure 4.78 shows the result of the step leading to SASH$_5$. The description of this step is analogous to that for the step that led to SASH$_4$. Once again, we use solid and broken lines to distinguish between bidirectional and one-directional edges. In this figure, we see one-dimensional edges (broken lines) from r, s, and t to h; and from s, t, u, and v to i. Of course, they are not present in the actual directed graph corresponding to SASH$_5$, which consists of just the solid edges.

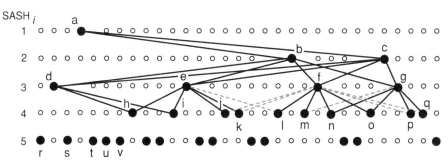

Figure 4.77
$SASH_4$ corresponding to the SASH hierarchy given in Figure 4.74 with $p = 2$ and $c = 4$. The solid lines correspond to the edges in the directed graph. The broken lines correspond to objects in $SASH_4 \backslash SASH_3$ whose nearest neighbors in $SASH_3 \backslash SASH_2$ do not find them to be among their $c = 4$ nearest neighbors in $SASH_4 \backslash SASH_3$.

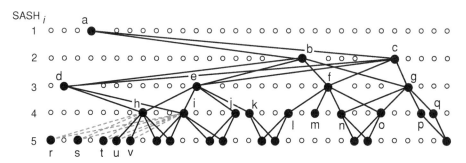

Figure 4.78
$SASH_5$ before the resolution of the presence of orphan objects corresponding to the SASH hierarchy given in Figure 4.74 with $p = 2$ and $c = 4$. The solid lines correspond to the edges in the directed graph. The broken lines correspond to objects in $SASH_5 \backslash SASH_4$ whose nearest neighbors in $SASH_4 \backslash SASH_3$ do not find them to be among their $c = 4$ nearest neighbors in $SASH_5 \backslash SASH_4$.

From Figure 4.78, we see that there are no edges from objects in $SASH_4 \backslash SASH_3$ to objects r, s, and t. In other words, r, s, and t are orphans. As each object must be reachable from the root, we double p, the number of nearest neighbors examined when attempting to establish links from r, s, and t to objects in $SASH_4 \backslash SASH_3$, and reapply the graph formation process. This enables r, s, and t to link to objects j and k, all of which, in turn, find s and t to be one of their $c = 4$ nearest neighbors from the objects in $SASH_5 \backslash SASH_4$ that find them as their nearest neighbors (ranging from p to $2p$ in this case) in $SASH_4 \backslash SASH_3$. This is shown in Figure 4.79, where we now see two additional one-dimensional edges (i.e., broken lines) from r to j and to k, as well as four additional solid edges (i.e., between j and s, j and t, k and s, and k and t).

From Figure 4.79, we see that object r remains an orphan as there are still no edges from objects in $SASH_4 \backslash SASH_3$ to it. Therefore, we now quadruple p, the number of nearest neighbors examined when attempting to establish links from r to objects in $SASH_4 \backslash SASH_3$ and reapply the graph formation process. This enables r to link to additional objects l, m, n, and o, all of which, in turn, find r to be one of their $c = 4$ nearest neighbors from the objects in $SASH_5 \backslash SASH_4$ that find them as their nearest neighbors (ranging from p to $4p$ in this case) in $SASH_4 \backslash SASH_3$. At this point, there are no orphans, and the resulting complete SASH is shown in Figure 4.80, where there are only solid lines as we no longer show the edges used to construct the SASH.

Now, let us turn to the problem of finding the approximate k nearest neighbors of q using the completed SASH. They are determined by the following procedure,

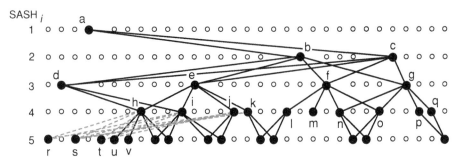

Figure 4.79
$SASH_5$ after doubling p, the number of nearest neighbors examined when attempting to establish links from orphan objects r, s, and t to objects in $SASH_4 \setminus SASH_3$, for the SASH hierarchy given in Figure 4.74 with $p = 2$ and $c = 4$. The solid lines correspond to the edges in the directed graph. The broken lines correspond to edges from objects in $SASH_5 \setminus SASH_4$ whose nearest neighbors in $SASH_4 \setminus SASH_3$ do not find them to be among their nearest neighbors (ranging from p to $2p$ in this case) in $SASH_5 \setminus SASH_4$.

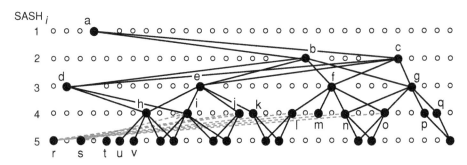

Figure 4.80
$SASH_5$ after quadrupling p, the number of nearest neighbors examined when attempting to establish links from orphan object r to objects in $SASH_4 \setminus SASH_3$, for the SASH hierarchy given in Figure 4.74 with $p = 2$ and $c = 4$.

which descends the SASH forming h sets U_i ($1 \le i \le h$), one at each level i, each of which consists of a set of as many as $f(k, i) = k_i$ approximate nearest neighbors of q. Once the h sets U_i have been formed, the k nearest neighbors of q taken from the union $U_1 \cup U_2 \cup \cdots \cup U_h$ are reported as the approximate k nearest neighbors of q. The actual sets U_i are formed as follows. U_1 is initialized to the root object r of the SASH (i.e., $SASH_1$). Next, those objects external to $SASH_1$ (i.e., $SASH_2 \setminus SASH_1$) that are connected by SASH edges to members of U_1 are tentatively placed in U_2. The set U_2 is then pruned by eliminating all but the k_2 closest objects to q. If U_2 contains fewer than k_2 objects, then no objects are pruned from it. This process is repeated for each level i in the SASH, forming U_{i+1} and retaining the k_{i+1} closest objects to q from the objects in $SASH_{i+1} \setminus SASH_i$ that are connected by SASH edges to members of $U_i \subseteq SASH_i \setminus SASH_{i-1}$. The process terminates with the construction of U_h from U_{h-1}. It is important to note that the rationale for following the links from objects in U_i to U_{i+1} in determining the sets of candidate approximate nearest neighbors for the k-nearest neighbor query is the assumption (recalling that it need not necessarily be true) that the approximate nearest neighbor relation is an equivalence relation and thus corresponds to making use of the transitivity property of the relation.

There are many ways of choosing $f(k, i)$. One possibility is to let $f(k, i) = k$ regardless of i. The drawback of this choice is that it leads to an $O(k \log_2 N)$ execution time for the query [884] (see Exercise 4). Instead, Houle and Sakuma [884] suggest that the quantity k_i depend on that of k_{i+1} ($1 \le i < h$), with k_h being initialized to k and the dependency being such that $k_1 = 1$. The rationale behind this choice follows from the definitions of S and S' and the fact that the objects of S' were chosen uniformly at random. In particular, roughly half the k nearest neighbors of q in S would be expected to belong to S' as well, regardless of the actual distribution of S and the choice of query object q. In order to be able to discover these neighbors from S', the ratio k_i/k_{i+1} should be at least $1/2$. The motivation for this choice is that by doing so, the number of candidate k-nearest neighbor objects generated at level $i+1$ (i.e., in $\mathrm{SASH}_{i+1}\backslash\mathrm{SASH}_i$) will exceed the number of expected k-nearest neighbor objects at level i (i.e., in $\mathrm{SASH}_i\backslash\mathrm{SASH}_{i-1}$). Ratios greater than $1/2$ would enable us to consider an even larger number of objects of $S\backslash S'$ as candidate neighbors of q, at the expense of execution time. Houle and Sakuma [884] use the quantity $k_i = k^{1-(h-i)/\log_2 N}$ in their implementation. For this quantity, the ratio k_i/k_{i+1} is guaranteed to lie between $1/2$ and 1 (see Exercise 9) and leads to an execution time of

$$
O\left(\frac{k^{1+\frac{1}{\log_2 N}}}{k^{\frac{1}{\log_2 N}} - 1} + \log_2 N\right)
$$

for the query (see Exercise 5). The execution time simplifies to $O(k)$ for practical choices of k and N (see Exercise 6). Note that for this definition of k_i, the number of candidate neighbors at each level is smoothly geometrically interpolated between 1 at the top (i.e., root) level of the SASH and k at the bottom level.

As an example of the process of determining the approximate k nearest neighbors, consider again the SASH in Figure 4.75, which has been constructed with the same values of $p=2$ and $c=5$. We want to find the three ($k=3$) neighbors of object c. Using $f(k, i) = k_i = k^{1-(h-i)/\log_2 N}$ to generate the sequence k_i and rounding the values of k_i to the nearest integer yields the sequence $k_i = (1, 1, 2, 2, 3)$. The sequence of sets U_i is formed as follows. U_1 is initialized to the root g of the SASH. U_2 is set to the objects reachable from U_1 is just object e, and, since $k_2 = 1$, we retain e in U_2. U_3 is set to the objects reachable from U_2, which are objects b and j, and, since $k_3 = 2$, we retain b and j in U_3. U_4 is set to the objects reachable from U_3, which are objects a, h, k, m, and r, and, since $k_4 = 2$, we retain a and h in U_4. U_5 is set to the objects reachable from U_4, which are objects c, d, i, and q, and, since $k_5 = 3$, we retain c, d, and q in U_5. The union of U_1, U_2, U_3, U_4, and U_5 is the set $\{$a,b,c,d,e,g,h,i,j,k,m,q,r$\}$, and the closest three neighbors to q are a, b, and c. If we exclude the query point c, then the closest three neighbors are a, b, and d.

One problem with using the sequence $f(k) = k_i = k^{1-(h-i)/\log_2 N}$ to determine how many neighbors to consider at level i in forming the sets U_i of approximate k nearest neighbors is that for small k, and large N, k_i is 1 for small values of i. This means that U_i consists of only one neighbor at shallower levels of the SASH, which will lead to a degradation in the performance of the search algorithm. In particular, at shallow levels i, as both k_i and the number of objects in $\mathrm{SASH}_i\backslash\mathrm{SASH}_{i-1}$ are relatively small, it could be the case that a greater proportion of the number of objects at level i (i.e., in $\mathrm{SASH}_i\backslash\mathrm{SASH}_{i-1}$) that are connected by an edge to elements of U_{i-1} are exact nearest neighbors than warranted by the small value of k_i, thereby possibly leading the subsequent search process to miss some neighbors as the low value of k_i means that they are not inserted in U_i. Houle and Sakuma [884] propose to overcome this problem by modifying the definition of k_i to ensure that a minimum number of objects is retained in U_i at each level of the search for the approximate k nearest neighbors of q.

pc is a good choice for this minimum and is justified as follows. As the SASH is constructed, for each object o at level $i+1$, we find its p approximate nearest neighbors at level i. Each of these p approximate nearest neighboring objects at level i, say b, can have as many as c edges to c different objects at level $i+1$ that deem b to be one of their p approximate nearest neighbors. Therefore, the p approximate nearest neighbors at level i of object o can be among the p approximate nearest neighbors of as many as pc objects at level $i+1$. So, by retaining at least pc objects in U_{i+1}, we are increasing the likelihood of o's presence in U_{i+1} should one of the p approximate nearest neighbors of

o have been in U_i (see also Exercise 8). Houle and Sakuma [884] found that, in practice, there was little difference in the accuracy of the results when a minimum value of $0.5pc$ was used instead of pc, and the execution time was lower with the smaller minimum value, thereby leading them to the redefinition of k_i as $k_i = \max\{k^{1-(h-i)/\log_2 N}, 0.5pc\}$.

At this point, it is interesting to observe the relationship between the kNN graph and SASH. In particular, in the kNN graph, there is an edge from every object to all of its exact k nearest neighbors drawn from the entire set S of objects. On the other hand, in SASH, there is an edge from every object o to as many as p of its approximate nearest neighbors drawn from samples of S of varying sizes depending on the level of the SASH at which o is found. We also note that both the kNN graph and SASH never actually evaluate the triangle inequality, either at construction time or at query time. Instead (at construction time), SASH trusts its subSASH to provide good approximate neighbors when needed, while the kNN graph makes use of the edges of the graph to find the required number of neighbors.

In addition, it is easy to see that the directed graph that makes up SASH is conceptually similar to the kNN graph. In both cases, the graphs have edges from their nodes, corresponding to objects, to other nodes corresponding to neighboring objects. There are several differences. The first is that SASH is more like a tree in the sense that there are no cycles, whereas the presence of cycles is always the case in the kNN graph when the k-nearest neighbor relation is symmetric. Of course, SASH is not a tree as there is usually more than one path from the root of the SASH to any object in the SASHes formed by the remaining levels. Actually, a more relevant characterization of SASH is that it is similar to a lattice.

A key difference is that each object a in the kNN graph has k edges to each of the k exact nearest neighbors of a. In contrast, each object a at level i of SASH has up to c edges to objects at level $i + 1$ for which a is one of the p nearest neighbors. In other words, instead of edges to the exact nearest neighboring objects, as in the kNN graph, in SASH, the edges are to objects that are likely to be nearest neighbors. In fact, SASH is similar to a reverse kNN graph where $k = p$, as the edges in SASH do indeed reflect the reverse of the links from objects at level $i + 1$ to their p nearest neighbors at level i (see Exercise 15). This analogy can be used to connect it to research results on the reverse nearest neighbor (RNN) problem (e.g., [162, 1060, 1674, 1800, 1801, 1854, 2041, 2042], as well as the distance semijoin (e.g., [847, 1756, 2030]), which addresses the problem in an implicit manner for $k = 1$, both of which are beyond the scope of this discussion.[48] In this context, the objects at level $i + 1$ connected to object o at level i are said to make up the *influence set* [1060] of o as they are the objects that have o as one of their p nearest neighbors at level i.

Both the kNN graph and SASH play the role of indexes. The difference lies in the way in which these indexes are constructed. In the case of the kNN graph, the index is built by finding the k nearest neighbors for each object. Without an existing index, which is the usual case, building the kNN graph is an $O(N^2)$ process (see also Exercise 14). In contrast, building a SASH is considerably more efficient as the fact that a SASH is built by adding levels one by one enables the construction process to make use of the index that it has already built for the existing levels. Thus, the process is incremental. Assuming N_i objects at level i of the SASH hierarchy and ignoring orphan objects, the fact that the p approximate nearest neighbors of each object at level $i + 1$ of the SASH can be obtained in $O(\log_2 N_i)$ time means that the directed graph for all of the levels can be constructed in $O(N \log_2 N)$ time as there is a total of N objects in SASH.

---

[48] Given a set of objects O and a set of locations S (termed *sites*) from the same spatial domain as O, the reverse nearest neighbors of site s are the objects $o \in O$ such that $\forall s_i \in S \ni s_i \neq s, d(o,s) \leq d(o,s_i)$, where d is a distance metric. The result is analogous to an implicit Voronoi diagram, where the Voronoi regions for a site s is defined by the space spanned by the objects that have s as their nearest neighbor.

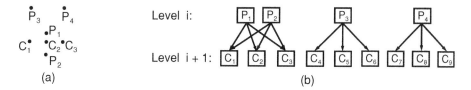

Figure 4.81

(a) Example illustrating an embedding of objects in two-dimensional space where (b) the directed graph of the resulting partial SASH shows that two of the objects P_3 and P_4 at level i are linked to the sets of three objects $\{C_4, C_5, C_6\}$ and $\{C_7, C_8, C_9\}$, respectively, at level i + 1, instead of to their nearest neighbors C_1, C_2, and C_3 at level i + 1.

The main drawback of SASH is that the links between an object a at level i and objects at level $i + 1$ are usually established on the basis of which objects o_j $(1 \leq j \leq p)$ at level $i + 1$ find a to be among the p approximate nearest objects to them[49] instead of on the basis of which of all of the objects at level $i + 1$ are found by a to be among the p approximate nearest objects. Thus, the key idea is to take advantage of a symmetry argument where an assumption is made that if a at level i is an approximate nearest neighbor of o at level $i + 1$, then o is also likely to be an approximate nearest neighbor of a, which we know is not generally true as the approximate nearest neighbor relation is not necessarily symmetric. The lack of symmetry is compensated for, in part, by the parameter c, which is used to determine the maximum number of objects at level $i + 1$ that can claim object a at level i as one of their p approximate nearest neighbors. By increasing c considerably above p and only retaining edges from a to the c closest objects at level $i + 1$ that find a as one of their p approximate nearest neighbors, SASH can avoid forming edges to objects that are not as near to a as other objects at level $i + 1$. However, regardless of the value of c, if an object at level $i + 1$ does not find object a as one of its p approximate nearest neighbors, then no edge can exist from a to o, even if o is in fact the nearest neighbor of a or one of the nearest neighbors of a at level $i + 1$.

In other words, the main drawback of SASH is that objects at level i will not necessarily be linked to their approximate nearest neighbors at level $i + 1$. Figure 4.81(a) is an example embedding of objects in a two-dimensional space whose partial SASH at levels i and i + 1 is given in Figure 4.81(b) with $p = 2$ and $c = 3$. In this case, each of objects C_1, C_2, and C_3 have P_1 and P_2 as their two approximate nearest neighbors, while each of C_4, C_5, C_6, C_7, C_8, and C_9 will have P_3 and P_4 as their two approximate nearest neighbors. Thus, the resulting SASH will have links directed from P_1 to C_1, C_2, and C_3; from P_2 to C_1, C_2, and C_3; from P_3 to C_4, C_5, and C_6; and from P_4 to C_7, C_8, and C_9. Notice that both P_3 and P_4 are not linked to their nearest neighboring objects at level i + 1. This means that if U_i at level i in the search for the k approximate nearest neighbors

---

[49] In fact, even this statement is not always true as can be seen in the presence of orphan objects. In particular, object o at level $i + 1$ of the SASH is an orphan object when none of the p objects at level i of the SASH, which o deems as its p approximate nearest objects, find o as one of their c nearest objects at the time of the formation of the SASH. In this case, Houle and Sakuma [884] suggest that the orphan o repeatedly increase the number of parent objects it attempts to link to (see Exercise 10) until it finds at least one parent a with open child slots that will accept the orphan o as a child (i.e., linked to fewer than c child approximate nearest neighbors). Thus, we see that it may be the case that an object a at level i of the SASH is linked to an object o at level $i + 1$ of the SASH that does not find a as one of its p approximate nearest objects at level i.

at level $i+1$ contains P_3 or P_4, or both, but does not contain P_1 or P_2, then the three nearest neighbors of P_3 and P_4 (i.e., C_1, C_2, and C_3) will not be in U_{i+1}, and there cannot be another P_j $(j > 4)$ in U_i with C_1, C_2, or C_3 as children since $c = 3$, and each of C_1, C_2, and C_3 at level $i+1$ can be a child of at most $p = 2$ parent objects at level i. Thus, the example illustrates the point that just because an object a at level i is one of the p approximate nearest neighboring objects of object b at level $i+1$ does not necessarily mean that b at level $i+1$ is one of the p approximate nearest neighbors of a at level i. Nevertheless, despite this example, it is important to bear in mind that the assignment of the objects to the various levels of the SASH hierarchy (i.e., which objects play the role of parents and children) is done at random. Therefore, even if we try to come up with a bad scenario of object placement, in fact, the sampling process tends to neutralize it.

The previous drawback of SASH was caused by the failure of the symmetry property to hold always. The failure of the transitivity property always to hold can also lead to some quirky pathological cases, occurring rarely at a very low probability, which will cause a query possibly to miss some of the nearest neighbors. In particular, the problem arises because, when we say that a relationship is transitive, then the relationship must be capable of being applied as many times as necessary. However, if we say that objects are within ε of each other, we cannot necessarily apply the within ε relation to a chain of objects $o_1, o_2, ..., o_i, ..., o_n$ and expect o_n to be within ε of o_1. Such an example is shown in the partial SASH given in Figure 4.82, where the objects are drawn from a one-dimensional space so that the distance between them is reflected by their horizontal separation. We say that Figure 4.82 is a partial SASH because not all of the elements in each level of the SASH are shown here. The basic idea illustrated by this example is that the data in the different levels of the SASH is distributed so that it is clustered in such a manner that we have two chains of nodes emanating from the root r: one leads very much to the left of r for a few levels and then veers to the right towards the query point q, while the second leads to the right, getting ever farther away from root r. Observe that Figure 4.82 does not show all of the objects; instead, we note that they are clustered around the two chains.

Now, without loss of generality, let us consider the task of finding the approximate $k = 2$ nearest neighbors of q. Applying the approximate k-nearest neighbor algorithm for the SASH will take us down the right chain from the root in the formation of the sets U_i of the k approximate nearest neighbors of q as we assume that there are enough nodes in the clusters for our purpose. Recall that U_{i+1} is formed by retaining the k_i nearest neighbors of q from the set of objects at level i that have edges leading into them from objects in U_i. Initially, we set $U_1 = \{r\}$ and form $U_2 = \{s, t\}$. At this point, it is clear from the figure that $d(s, q) >> d(t, q)$ and thus U_3 and subsequently generated sets U_i will be

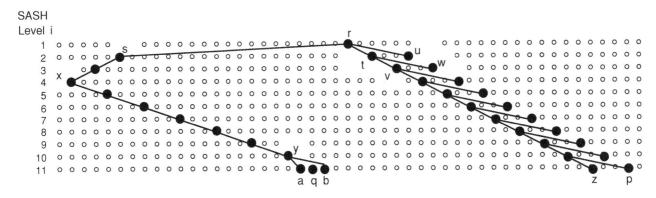

Figure 4.82
Example illustrating the partial SASH for an embedding of objects in a one-dimensional space where the assumption of transitivity will lead to r and t being reported as the approximate two nearest neighbors of q instead of a and b.

formed from the descendants of t. Thus, it is not hard to see that some of the nearest neighbors of q will be missed. In particular, we see that the path down the right chain from r through t will eventually lead us away from q. On the other hand, the path down the left chain from r through s is initially worse but eventually leads closer to q. However, our algorithm does not follow it and hence will miss reporting a and b as the two nearest neighbors of q and, instead, will report r and s as the two nearest neighbors of q.

Again, it is important to bear in mind our earlier observation made with respect to the drawback of the symmetry assumption that the assignment of the objects to the various levels of the SASH hierarchy at the time of its construction (i.e., choosing which objects play the role of parents and children) is done at random. Therefore, even if we try to come up with a bad scenario of object placement, as in this example, in fact, the sampling process used in the SASH construction tends to neutralize it. Moreover, we have additional redundancy in the SASH construction process when $p > 1$, and when performing a query, a wider search is conducted near the root of the SASH in order to preclude the descent from only following the bad branches. Another way of rationalizing the minimization of the likelihood of this bad case scenario is to observe that SASH transitivity fails in this way from a probabilistic standpoint in the same way that both quicksort [857] with random pivot (i.e., partition value) selection can lead to an $O(N^2)$ execution time for the sorting process, as well as by observing that a skip list [1520] with a randomly generated skip increment can lead to an $O(N)$ item retrieval time (i.e., search cost). Of course, both quicksort and the skip list generally perform quite well.

Although the design of SASH makes it inherently unsuitable for performing exact neighborhood queries, careful management of the parameters k_i and p, as well as additional restrictions on the maximum out degree c of the SASH structure, allow for very efficient approximate neighborhood queries at practical rates of accuracy, even for extremely high-dimensional datasets (in the hundreds of thousands or even millions of dimensions). Discussions of these and other implementation details, as well as experimental results for a variety of data types, can be found in [884]. The ability of SASH to cope with large, high-dimensional datasets makes it particularly well suited for applications such as k-nearest neighbor-based clustering [882], in which meaningful results can be obtained even when approximate neighborhood information is used.

Exercises

1. Give an algorithm to construct a SASH for a set of N objects and given values of p and c.

2. Show that a SASH takes $O(pN)$ storage for N objects.

3. Show that building a SASH takes $O(pcN \log_2 N)$ time for N objects, when we do not take into account the cost of dealing with orphan objects (see Exercise 10).

4. Show that the execution time of the algorithm for determining the approximate k nearest neighbors of q when $f(k,i) = k_i = k$ is $O(k \log_2 N)$ for N objects.

5. Show that the execution time of the algorithm for determining the approximate k nearest neighbors of q when $f(k,i) = k_i = \max\{k^{1-(h-i)/\log_2 N}, 0.5pc\}$ is

$$O\left(\frac{k^{1+\frac{1}{\log_2 N}}}{k^{\frac{1}{\log_2 N}} - 1} + \log_2 N\right)$$

6. Show that the execution time of the algorithm for determining the approximate k nearest neighbors of q, for N objects, when $f(k,i) = k_i = \max\{k^{1-(h-i)/\log_2 N}, 0.5pc\}$ in Exercise 5 simplifies to $O(k)$ when k is in $\Omega(N^\varepsilon)$ for any constant $\varepsilon > 0$.

7. Suppose that there are b candidate objects in the set of possible approximate k nearest neighbors at level $i + 1$. For given values of p and c, what is the range of the number of possible distinct candidate objects at level i through which these b candidates at level $i + 1$ could have been reached?

8. Suppose that there are a reachable candidate objects in the set of possible approximate k nearest neighbors at level i. For given values of p and c, what is the range of the number of possible distinct reachable candidate objects at level $i + 1$?

9. Show that the ratio k_i / k_{i+1} is guaranteed to lie between $1/2$ and 1 when $k_i = k^{1-(h-i)/\log_2 N}$.

10. While describing the construction of SASH, we point out that the existence of the limit c on the out degree of SASH nodes means that it may not be possible to connect some of the objects at level $i + 1$ to their p approximate nearest neighbors at level i. Such objects are said to be rejected (i.e., orphan objects), and attempts are made to connect them to some other nodes. Give a strategy to achieve this.

11. Consider the following alternative method of determining the k approximate nearest neighbors of query object q in the SASH that makes use of two sets U and V to accumulate the k approximate nearest neighbors. Initially, U is empty, and V is initialized to the root object r of the SASH hierarchy (i.e., SASH$_1$). Next, the objects in V are moved to U; also, all of the objects formerly in V are replaced by the objects in SASH$_2$\SASH$_1$ to which they are connected by edges in SASH. At this point, the k_2 closest objects to q from the objects in U and V are retained, which means that objects may be removed from both U and V. This process is repeated for each level i in SASH where at each level i, the objects in V that are moved to U are replaced by the objects in SASH$_{i+1}$\SASH$_i$ to which they are connected by edges in SASH. Once V has been reformed, the k_{i+1} closest objects to q from the objects in U and V are retained and the process is applied at level $i + 1$. The process terminates at level $h - 1$, at which time we extract the $k_h = k$ approximate nearest neighbors from U and V. Compare this method with the one of Houle and Sakuma [884] described in the text.

12. Give an algorithm to perform a range query for a query object q and query radius ε in a SASH.

13. Discuss the issues in devising an incremental approximate nearest neighbor algorithm for a SASH.

14. Consider EXSASH, a variant of SASH that is built on the basis of the kNN graph between subsets in the same way as SASH was built. It has the same recursive structure as SASH with $h = \lceil \log_2(N + 1) \rceil$ sets in the hierarchy. We start with a set of objects S. We first form a set S' about one-half the size of S. The set $S \setminus S'$ forms the deepest level of EXSASH$_h$. It is the same as the set EXSASH$_h$\EXSASH$_{h-1}$. The deepest level of EXSASH$_{h-1}$ is EXSASH$_{h-1}$\EXSASH$_{h-2}$. We connect each element in EXSASH$_{h-1}$\EXSASH$_{h-2}$ to its exact k_i nearest neighbors in EXSASH$_h$\EXSASH$_{h-1}$. Unlike SASH, no limit is placed on the number of incoming edges from objects at level i to a particular object at level $i + 1$. Thus, there is no need for parameters p and c in EXSASH, although orphan objects may exist at level i in EXSASH when there are no incoming edges into them from level $i - 1$. Notice the difference from a true kNN graph, where each object is linked to its exact k nearest neighbors. On the other hand, in EXSASH, an object at level i is linked to its exact k_i nearest neighbors at level $i + 1$. Compare EXSASH and SASH. What is the advantage and disadvantage of using EXSASH?

15. Suppose that you view SASH as a reverse kNN graph, as described in the text, so that the directions of the edges are reversed once the construction of the SASH has been completed. This means that the edges are directed from objects formerly at level $i + 1$ to as many as p of their approximate nearest neighbors at level i, and thus it behaves somewhat like EXSASH in Exercise 14. How would you use the reverse kNN graph to find nearest neighbors, and what are the pitfalls of such an approach, if any?

4.6 Dimension Reduction Methods

Database designers are often interested in reducing the dimension of their data. In particular, the motivation is to be able to perform search more efficiently using some indexing structure. For example, if the dimension of the data can be reduced to one, then the data can be ordered and an index built on it using conventional methods such as B-trees, thereby enabling it to be searched easily. However, for high-dimensional data, it is usually desirable to reduce to a dimension larger than one so as not to lose too much of the information inherent in the data, in which case a multidimensional indexing method can be employed.

Unfortunately, as we point out in Section 4.4.6, there are a number of difficulties associated with the use of multidimensional indexing methods for searching in high-dimensional spaces. In particular, most of the volume is rather close to the boundaries of the dataspace (which means that data objects tend to be close to the boundaries), and, in general, there is a relatively small amount of partitioning as most of the dimensions are split at most once. In addition, the distance between data objects tends to grow rather quickly (even in the unit hypercube) as the dimension increases. This means that even the search regions (i.e., the radii) for queries that only yield a few answers will have to be rather large. These effects cause multidimensional indexing methods to become inefficient as the dimensionality increases, typically at around 8–12 dimensions, and, in particular, they become less efficient than a simple sequential scan of the entire data (since the index uses relatively expensive random disk accesses) [212]. Briefly, the reason is that the search region tends to intersect most of the regions (corresponding to leaf and nonleaf nodes) of the index hierarchy [187].

Collectively, these and other effects arising as the dimensionality increases can be explained by appealing to the *curse of dimensionality* (e.g., [159] and described in the opening of this chapter). This problem is often overcome by reducing the dimensionality of the data, thereby making it feasible to use a multidimensional index in the search. Of course, this comes at the price of a reduction in the quality of the result of the query (as elaborated upon below) unless the original data is used to refine the query result.

Besides the effects of high-dimensional space that make it inherently difficult to perform searching, effects also arise that cause specific indexing methods to degenerate. For example, members of the R-tree [791] family (i.e., disk-based spatial indexes that make use of an object hierarchy) prune the search with the aid of bounding boxes (termed *filtering*) and make more exact comparisons using the original data (termed *refinement*). Recall that algorithms that follow such a query processing strategy are characterized as being filter-and-refine algorithms [1416].

One of the drawbacks of these spatial indexes (i.e., members of the R-tree family) is that the amount of information needed to keep track of the bounding boxes becomes quite large as the dimension of the underlying data increases. This means that the nodes, which usually correspond to disk pages, in the structures that represent the index have a small fanout. The small fanout causes the structures, which are variants of B-trees, to be deep, thereby increasing the I/O cost for search queries that must descend to the leaf nodes to perform the actual comparisons needed to satisfy the queries. Several techniques have been proposed for addressing this drawback, for example, reducing the storage cost of the bounding boxes (e.g., using k-d-tree-like techniques [317]), increasing the size of the nodes [190], or using bounding spheres [1991], as discussed in Section 4.4. Nevertheless, these techniques cannot escape the inherent effects that we have discussed above.

In this section, we focus on methods that reduce the dimension of a dataset, thereby enabling the use of efficient multidimensional indexing methods. The essential intuition behind dimension reduction is that, typically, the "inherent dimensionality" of a dataset is much lower than the dimensionality of the underlying space. In other words, the data objects often (roughly) lie on some lower-dimensional surface or manifold (e.g., a line or a sphere), and the implicit goal of dimension reduction methods is to reveal this structure. Of course, such methods differ in the extent to which they succeed in satisfying this goal. In addition, it is quite possible that the "inherent dimensionality" of the data is higher than the dimension to which the data is reduced. Thus, as we mentioned above, dimension reduction carries a price: the quality of query results when performing search operations in the dimension-reduced search space may suffer. In particular, queries may return objects that should not have been in the result (i.e., *false hits*), or objects that should have been in the query result may be missing (i.e., *false dismissals*).

Note that a number of the embedding methods discussed in Section 4.7 can also be described as dimension reduction methods (e.g., locality sensitive hashing (LSH) [924] in Section 4.7.4). However, they are discussed there because of the emphasis on properties of the embedding that enable them to be used for searching, whereas satisfaction of these properties for the methods discussed in this section is a straightforward matter.

4.6.1 Searching in the Dimension Reduced Space

A dimension reduction method can be thought of as providing a mapping f that transforms a vector v in the original space to a vector $f(v)$ in the transformed lower-dimension space. Letting d be the distance metric in the original space of dimensionality n, and letting d' be the distance metric in the *transformed* space of lower dimensionality k, we observe that most dimension reduction techniques attempt (implicitly or explicitly) to yield a mapping such that distances in the transformed space approximate the distances in the original space—that is, $d(v, u) \approx d'(f(v), f(u))$. In the rest of this section, we discuss properties of the mapping f that relate to search in the transformed space, first for range searching and then for nearest neighbor searching.

4.6.1.1 Range Queries

For a range query (often also termed an *epsilon query* [2026]), the query radius to be used in the transformed space is related to the query radius in the original space in a manner that depends on the dimension reduction method, as well as the distance metrics d and d'. Under the assumptions listed above, the most appropriate choice is usually to use the same query radius in the transformed space.

An interesting issue is the effect of increasing or decreasing the query radius for range search in the transformed space on the quality of the query results in the transformed space. If we reduce the query radius, then we obtain fewer incorrect candidates in the query result (i.e., fewer false hits), thereby increasing precision [1611]. On the other hand, this will most likely mean that we get fewer correct responses (i.e., more false dismissals), thereby decreasing recall [1611]. The opposite effect arises if the query radius is enlarged (i.e., precision is decreased but recall is increased). Formally, letting R_n and R_k denote the set of responses retrieved in the original and dimension reduced spaces, respectively, *precision* is $|R_n \cap R_k|/|R_k|$ and *recall* is $|R_n \cap R_k|/|R_n|$. Precision and recall are not the same for range queries (see Exercise 1). However, there are queries like finding the ith-nearest neighbor for which precision and recall are the same (see Exercise 1 in Section 4.6.1.2).

Ideally, we would like the query in the transformed space to include all the correct responses (i.e., 100% recall). This property can be achieved (while using the same query radius in the transformed space) if the dimension reduction method (i.e., transformation or mapping) has the property that the distance between the transformed objects in the dimension-reduced space is always less than the distance between the objects in the original space (i.e., the mapping is *contractive*). This property is known as the *pruning property*.

Pruning Property   Given a distance metric d in the original space, a distance metric d' in the transformed space, and a transformation f, then $d'(f(a), f(b)) \leq d(a, b)$ for any pair of objects a and b.

Of course, satisfaction of the pruning property does not prevent the precision from being arbitrarily bad since, in the worst case, the query result in the transformed space includes all the transformed objects (i.e., the precision is F/N, where F is the size of the correct query result, and N is the size of the dataset). The practical significance of the pruning property is that the distance in the transformed space between the transformed objects serves as a lower bound on the actual distance in the original space between the objects. In particular, the pruning property implies that if an object o in the original space is within a distance of r from a query object q, then $f(o)$ is also within a distance of r from $f(q)$. Thus, a range query in the transformed space with radius r for the query object $f(q)$ is guaranteed to yield no false dismissals.

Exercise

1. Show that precision and recall are not the same for a range query when using dimension reduction techniques.

4.6.1.2 Nearest Neighbor Queries

Unfortunately, in the case of nearest neighbor queries, the pruning property alone does not guarantee 100% recall. For such queries, a desirable property is for the relative ordering between objects to be preserved in the transformed space. This ensures that the result of performing a nearest neighbor query in the transformed space is identical to that obtained with a nearest neighbor query in the original space. This condition is stated as follows (termed the *proximity-preserving property*):

Proximity-Preserving Property Given a distance metric d in the original space, a distance metric d' in the transformed space, and a transformation f, then $d(a,b) \leq d(a,c)$ implies $d'(f(a), f(b)) \leq d'(f(a), f(c))$, for any objects a, b, and c.

The advantage of a transformation that is proximity preserving is that nearest neighbor queries can be performed directly in the transformed space. In contrast, when only the pruning property holds (which is usually the case in our examples), then 100% recall can be achieved for nearest neighbor queries by combining nearest neighbor search in the transformed space, thereby obtaining a set of candidates, with a refine step that uses the distance values in the original space to discard incorrect candidates. Note that if we rewrite the proximity-preserving property such that $d'(f(a), f(b)) > d'(f(a), f(c))$ implies $d(a,b) > d(a,c)$, then we can immediately see why there is no need to refine the candidate set when the proximity-preserving property holds.

An example of a proximity-preserving transformation is a scaling, a translation, or a combination thereof, in a vector space and when using any Minkowski distance metric L_p (where given the points (x_1, y_1) and (x_2, y_2), the distance is defined as $d_{L_p}((x_1, y_1), (x_2, y_2)) = ((x_1 - x_2)^p + (y_1 - y_2)^p)^{1/p}$). Rotation is proximity preserving when using the Euclidean distance metric in both the original and the transformed space and when there is no dimension reduction (but see Exercises 4 and 5 for other distance metrics that are not proximity preserving under rotation). However, there are many cases where the proximity-preserving property does not hold. For example, consider data in a two-dimensional space (x, y), a dimension reduction transformation that projects the data onto the x coordinate axis, and use the Euclidean distance in both the original and the transformed space. Observe that the point $p = (0,0)$ is closer to point $t = (2,2)$ than to point $u = (1, 10)$, but after the projection onto the x axis, p is closer to u than to t. In general, it is difficult to find combinations of transformations and distance metrics that satisfy the proximity-preserving property while also leading to a reduction in dimension, and thus we do not deal further with this property here.

Nevertheless, even without proximity preservation, we can still implement efficient nearest neighbor query algorithms that guarantee no false dismissals, given that f satisfies the pruning property.[50] Such algorithms use the filter-and-refine query processing

---

[50] Variants of the algorithms that allow a small error in the result (thereby yielding an approximate nearest neighbor) are also possible if we wish to trade off accuracy for a possible increase in efficiency.

strategy (e.g., [851, 1063, 1716]). In particular, in the filter step, the embedding space is used as a filter to produce a set of candidates. The satisfaction of the pruning property makes it possible to guarantee that the correct result is among the candidates. For example, if o is the actual nearest neighbor of the query object q, then the filter step must at the very least produce as candidates all objects o' such that $d'(f(q), f(o')) \leq d(q, o)$. In the refine step, the actual distance must be computed for all the candidates to determine the actual nearest neighbor.

To elaborate on how such a query is implemented, suppose that we want to find the nearest object to a query object q. We first determine the point $f(q)$ corresponding to q. Next, we examine the objects in the order of their distances from $f(q)$ in the embedding space. When using a multidimensional index, this can be achieved by using an incremental nearest neighbor algorithm [846, 848]. Suppose that point $f(a)$ corresponding to object a is the closest point to $f(q)$ at a distance of $d'(f(a), f(q))$. We compute the distance $d(a, q)$ between the corresponding objects. At this point, we know that any point farther from $f(q)$ than $d(a, q)$ cannot be the nearest neighbor of q since the pruning property guarantees that $d'(f(x), f(q)) > d(a, q)$, means that $d(x, q) > d(a, q)$ for any object x. Therefore, $d(a, q)$ now serves as an upper bound on the nearest neighbor search in the embedding space. We now find the next closest point $f(b)$ corresponding to object b subject to our distance constraint $d(a, q)$. If $d(b, q) < d(a, q)$, then b and $d(b, q)$ replace object a and $d(a, q)$ as the current closest object and upper-bound distance, respectively; otherwise, a and $d(a, q)$ are retained. This search continues until encountering a point $f(x)$ with distance $d'(f(x), f(q))$ greater than the distance to the current closest object, which is now guaranteed to be the actual closest object to q.

In fact, we may use the general version of the incremental nearest neighbor algorithm [851] described in Section 4.1.3 to find the nearest neighbor directly without needing to keep track explicitly of the upper-bound distance values above. This is achieved by extending the search hierarchy for T, the multidimensional index for $f(S)$, where S is the actual dataset whose dimension has been reduced by application of the transformation f, to include elements of S as well (i.e., in addition to those of $f(S)$). In the search hierarchy for T, the elements of type 0 are points in $f(S)$, while the other elements represent nodes in T (and/or possibly some other aspects of the data structure). When extending the search hierarchy for T to form the new search hierarchy, we increment the type numbers for all the element types of the search hierarchy of T and add the objects in S as the new elements of type 0. Thus, an element e_1 of type 1, representing a point $f(o)$, has as a child the element e_0 of type 0 that represents the corresponding object $o \in S$.

When T is an R-tree, the extension can be simplified further. In this case (recalling Section 4.1.3), the elements of type 1 were minimum bounding rectangles of the objects. However, each object $f(o)$ in $f(S)$ is actually a point, so its minimum bounding box is degenerate, and thus equivalent to $f(o)$. Therefore, the elements of type 1 in the (original) search hierarchy for the R-tree, representing minimum bounding rectangles, always have identical distances as do the corresponding elements of type 0 (i.e., in the original search hierarchy), which represent the points in $f(S)$ (recall from Section 4.1.2 that elements of type 2 represent R-tree nodes). Thus, the elements of type 1 can be thought of as representing the points in $f(S)$,[51] leaving us free to let the elements of type 0 represent the objects in S (replacing the original type 0) when extending the search hierarchy for R-trees.

The distance functions of the elements in the hierarchy are based on d and d', the distance functions for S and $f(S)$, respectively. In particular, for an element e_0 of type 0, $d_0(q, e_0) = d(q, o)$, where $o \in S$ is the object that corresponds to e_0. The distance function

---

[51] Since points occupy half as much space as rectangles, we could even replace the minimum bounding rectangles in the leaf nodes of the R-tree with the points themselves, thus doubling the capacity of the leaf nodes.

for elements of type 1, corresponding to points in $f(S)$, is defined as

$$d_1(q, e_1) = d'(f(q), f(o)) \tag{4.8}$$

where $f(o)$ is the point represented by e_1. An element of type $t \geq 2$ essentially represents a region in $\mathbb{R}^k$ (i.e., the dimension-reduced space) that contains all the points in the corresponding subtree. If T is an R-tree, for example, elements of type 2 represent nodes, which cover regions that are rectilinear hyperrectangles. Thus, for $t \geq 2$, we define the distance function

$$d_t(q, e_t) = \min_{p \in R}\{d'(f(q), p)\} \tag{4.9}$$

where R is the region covered by element e_t. Usually, Equation 4.9 can be evaluated with fairly simple geometric calculations (e.g., if d' is some Minkowski distance metric and T is an R-tree, the distance is equal to the distance between $f(q)$ and one of the faces of the hyperrectangle R, or zero if $f(q)$ is inside R).

Assuming that T is an R-tree, incremental nearest neighbor search using the above search hierarchy would proceed as follows (see procedure INCNEAREST). Initially, the root of the R-tree would be inserted on the priority queue as an element of type 2. If the element e_t taken off the queue is of type 2, representing a node u, we insert elements of type 1 (if u is a leaf node) or 2 (if u is a nonleaf node) into the priority queue based on the entries in u. If the element e_t that comes off the priority queue is of type 1, we insert the corresponding object as an element of type 0. Finally, if the element e_t is of type 0, we report the corresponding object as the next nearest neighbor. Figure 4.83 depicts how the algorithm would proceed on a small example consisting of three objects a, b, and c, and their transformed versions F(a), F(b), F(c), respectively, using transformation F. Both are shown here as two-dimensional points; we can also think of the figure as merely showing the relative distances of the objects from q and the mapped objects from F(q). Observe that the distance $d(\mathsf{q}, \mathsf{c})$ need not be computed by the algorithm since $\delta(\mathsf{F}(\mathsf{q}), \mathsf{F}(\mathsf{c})) > d(\mathsf{q}, \mathsf{b})$.

Exercises

1. Show that precision and recall [1611] are identical for finding the ith nearest neighbor when using dimension reduction techniques.

2. Consider data in a two-dimensional space (x, y) and a dimension reduction transformation f that projects the data onto the y coordinate axis. Use the Chessboard distance d_M in both the original and the transformed space, which, given the points (x_1, y_1) and (x_2, y_2), is defined as $d_M((x_1, y_1), (x_2, y_2)) = \max(|x_1 - x_2|, |y_1 - y_2|)$. Give an example to show that the proximity-preserving property does not hold in this case.

3. Repeat Exercise 2 for the City Block distance metric, which, given the points (x_1, y_1) and (x_2, y_2), is defined as $d_A((x_1, y_1), (x_2, y_2)) = |x_1 - x_2| + |y_1 - y_2|$.

4. Consider data in a two-dimensional space (x, y) and a rotation transformation. Use the Chessboard distance (see Exercise 2) in both the original and the transformed space. Show that the proximity-preserving property does not hold in this case.

5. Repeat Exercise 4 for the City Block distance metric.

6. Show that the proximity-preserving property can also be used to perform farthest neighbor queries directly in the transformed space.

7. Give an example where the proximity-preserving property holds while the pruning property does not hold.

8. Given a distance metric d in the original space, a distance metric d' in the transformed space, and a transformation f, Korn, Sidiropoulos, Faloutsos, Siegel and Protopapas [1063, 1064] use the following algorithm to find the k nearest neighbors to query object q. They first perform a standard k-nearest neighbor query on the multidimensional index that represents $f(S)$, using $f(q)$ as a query object and distance function d', resulting in a set R'' of k candidate nearest neighbors of q. Next, the algorithm computes the actual distances (based on d) of all the

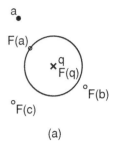

(a)

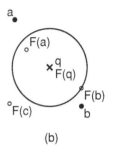

(b)

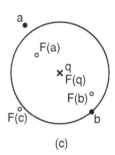

(c)

Figure 4.83
Progress of the incremental nearest neighbor algorithm on a small example involving three objects. Both the objects and their mapped versions are depicted as two-dimensional points. (a) The search region first reaches F(a), and $d(\mathsf{q}, \mathsf{a})$ is computed, (b) F(b) is reached next, causing $d(\mathsf{q}, \mathsf{b})$ to be computed, and (c) the object b is determined to be the nearest neighbor of q.

objects in R'' and determines the distance of the object farthest from q, $\varepsilon = \max_{o \in R''}\{d(q,o)\}$. A range query is then performed on $f(S)$ with a query radius of ε, resulting in a candidate set R'. Finally, the set R of the k nearest neighbors of q is determined by computing the distances of all objects in R' and retaining the k objects that are closest to q. Given that f is contractive, prove that this algorithm is correct by showing that R' contains the k nearest neighbors of q.

9. What are the drawbacks of the algorithm of Korn et al. [1063] described in Exercise 8 in terms of the quality of the estimate ε and the number of probes to the multidimensional index representing $f(S)$?

10. Seidl and Kriegl [1716] propose an improvement to the algorithm of Korn et al. [1063] described in Exercise 8 that is partially based on the incremental nearest neighbor search algorithm given in Section 4.1.3. In particular, the algorithm performs an incremental nearest neighbor query on the multidimensional index storing $f(S)$, using $f(q)$ as the query object and a distance measure d'. As the algorithm obtains the neighboring mapped objects one by one, it computes the actual distance of each object using d and inserts the objects into a list L of the candidate nearest neighbors of q (termed the *candidate list*). If this insertion causes L to contain more than k objects, then the object farthest from q (based on d) is discarded. Clearly, if all the objects in S were inserted into the candidate list L in this way, then L would eventually contain the actual k nearest neighbors. However, since the mapped objects are obtained from the incremental nearest neighbor query in order of the values of $d'(f(q), f(o))$, the algorithm can usually be terminated long before inserting all the objects into L. In particular, once $d'(f(q), f(o)) \geq D_k$ for the mapped object o just obtained from the incremental nearest neighbor query, where D_k is the distance of the current kth candidate nearest neighbor, the contractiveness of f guarantees that $d(q, o') \geq d'(f(q), f(o')) \geq D_k$ for all objects o' that have not yet been retrieved. Thus, when this condition arises, the candidate list L contains the actual k nearest neighbors of q, and the search can be halted. Note that in order to simplify our presentation of the algorithm, we assume that given any distance x, there is at most one object at this distance from q, although the algorithm as originally described by Seidl and Kriegel [1716] does report more than k neighbors when there is more than one object at the same distance from q as the kth-nearest neighbor.[52] Compare the algorithm of Seidl and Kriegel with an algorithm that uses the general version of the incremental nearest neighbor algorithm given in Section 4.1.3 that integrates L into the priority queue (i.e., stores both the objects and nodes of the multidimensional index on $f(S)$ in the priority queue) and terminates once k objects have been output (i.e., upon outputting the kth-nearest neighbor). In essence, whenever the algorithm encounters an object o (i.e., when $f(o)$ reaches the front of the priority queue), instead of inserting o into the candidate list L, it inserts o into the priority queue using $d(q, o)$ as the key. In particular, does one of the algorithms access more nodes of the multidimensional index than the other? Similarly, does one of the algorithms compute the distance between more pairs of objects than the other?

4.6.2 Using Only One Dimension

There are many techniques for reducing the dimension of the data when its dimension is known, as is the case when the data is represented as feature vectors in a high-dimensional space. The simplest technique is to ignore some of the features. It should be clear that in this case it is best to retain the most discriminating of the features (although this may take some work to determine).

The pruning property will always hold if the distance metric that is used for the single feature is suitably derived from the distance metric on all of the objects. For example, for any Minkowski distance metric L_p, the appropriate single-feature distance metric is always the same—that is, the absolute difference $|x_a - x_b|$, where x_a and x_b are the values of the retained feature for objects a and b, respectively. However, for this technique, the proximity-preserving property will hold typically only in the rare case that all the other features have the same value for all the objects.

---

[52] In this case, the algorithm is terminated once $d'(f(q), f(o)) > D_k$ instead of once $d'(f(q), f(o)) \geq D_k$ for the mapped object o just obtained from the incremental nearest neighbor query.

The most drastic, and easiest to implement, dimension reduction technique is to use just one of the given features (without applying any transformation). A drawback of this method, which we ignore below, is that many of the objects may be represented by the same point. This method forms the basis of the k-nearest neighbor algorithm of Friedman, Baskett, and Shustek [649]. Once the feature f has been chosen, all objects are sorted with respect to this feature (termed f-*distance*). The k nearest neighbors are found by processing the objects in increasing order of their f-distance from the query object q until encountering an object o such that its f-distance from q is greater than the actual distance from q to the kth-nearest neighbor found so far. Thus, they are making direct use of the pruning property as the f-distance between two objects is always less than the actual distance, and the search is halted once the f-distance is greater than the actual distance to the kth-nearest object.

The efficiency of the k-nearest neighbor algorithm of Friedman et al. [649] depends, in part, on which feature f is used. At its simplest, f is selected at random. However, it is clear that the feature with the smallest projected density will result in examining a smaller set of objects. This feature can be obtained globally or locally.

From a global perspective, f is the feature with the largest range (termed *spread*) of values. This requires that we examine all of the objects before starting the search. Once f has been identified, we sort the objects with respect to their f-distance.

From a local perspective, f is the feature with the largest expected range of values about the value of feature f for query object q (denoted by q_f). This is not so easy to determine. It requires that the objects be sorted with respect to all of the features. The local density around q depends on the expected number N' of objects that will be examined during the search. Friedman et al. [649] obtain N' from the radius of the expected search region, which is computed using a uniform distribution. The actual local density for each of the features i is determined by calculating the size of the range containing the $N'/2$ values less than or equal to q_i and the $N'/2$ values greater than or equal to q_i and choosing f as the one with the largest range.

Friedman et al. conducted a number of experiments comparing their algorithm with the brute-force method of examining all objects by varying k, the sample data sizes, and the dimension of the underlying space. They found that their method was considerably more efficient for different k and sample sizes and when the dimension of the underlying data was relatively small. However, once the dimension of the underlying space reached the value of 9, the effects of the curse of dimensionality become dominant, and the algorithm lost its advantage over the brute-force method. Of course, both the global and the local (to a lesser extent) methods are attractive only when the queries are performed many times as the preprocessing costs involved sorting the data.

Another technique of using just one dimension is one that is motivated by a desire to combine all of the different features into one representative feature by using some information from each of the features. For example, suppose that each object is represented by n different features, each of which has a 64-bit value. In this case, we can represent the object by a single number formed by concatenating the values of the most significant bit (or a small subset thereof) from each of the n different features.[53] This technique is similar to hashing and has the same drawback as the technique that retains only one of the features in that it is very likely that many of the objects will be represented by the same point. Satisfying the pruning property when using this technique is not simple, as is shown below for the space-ordering methods.

An alternative and related approach that is very well-known and frequently used in spatial databases transforms (i.e., maps) the feature vectors in high dimensions into one dimension by ordering the data using one of the various space-ordering methods such as

---

[53] We could also use the least-significant bit, although this is not particularly meaningful from the point of view of providing a summary (i.e., an approximation) of the values of the individual features.

features (more precisely, a linear combination of features) for a given set of feature vectors. Their use leads to a transformation of the original set of feature vectors S to obtain a new set of feature vectors S' where the individual features that make up S' are ranked by their importance, so that if we ignore the less important features by projecting onto the most important features, then we preserve much of the variation between the elements of the original set of feature vectors S.

The problem that we are addressing can be stated as follows. We are given a set of m n-dimensional feature vectors $\vec{f}_1, \vec{f}_2, \ldots \vec{f}_m$ that are to be transformed into a set of m k-dimensional feature vectors $\vec{t}_1, \vec{t}_2, \ldots \vec{t}_m$. The sets $\{\vec{f}_i \mid 1 \leq i \leq m\}$ and $\{\vec{t}_i \mid 1 \leq i \leq m\}$ of feature vectors can be written as an $m \times n$ matrix F and an $m \times k$ matrix T as follows:

$$F = \begin{pmatrix} f_{11} & f_{12} & \cdots & f_{1n} \\ f_{21} & f_{22} & \cdots & f_{2n} \\ \vdots & \vdots & \ddots & \vdots \\ f_{m1} & f_{m2} & \cdots & f_{mn} \end{pmatrix} \quad \text{and} \quad T = \begin{pmatrix} t_{11} & t_{12} & \cdots & t_{1k} \\ t_{21} & t_{22} & \cdots & t_{2k} \\ \vdots & \vdots & \ddots & \vdots \\ t_{m1} & t_{m2} & \cdots & t_{mk} \end{pmatrix}$$

From linear algebra, we know that any $m \times n$ matrix F, where the number of rows m is greater than the number of columns n, can be written as the product of three matrices U, Σ, and V as follows:

$$F = U \Sigma V^T \tag{4.10}$$

Equation 4.10 is known as the *singular value decomposition* of F (e.g., [721]). U is an $m \times n$ matrix consisting of a set of n orthonormal column vectors $\vec{u}_i$ (i.e., $\vec{u}_i \cdot \vec{u}_j = \delta_{ij}$ or, equivalently, $\sum_{h=1}^{m} U_{hi} U_{hj} = \delta_{ij}$, $1 \leq i \leq n$ and $1 \leq j \leq n$). This is the same as stating that $U^T U = I_n$. Similarly, $U U^T = I_m$. Σ is an $n \times n$ singular value matrix with nonnegative elements along its diagonal known as *singular values*:

$$\Sigma = \begin{pmatrix} \sigma_{11} & 0 & \cdots & 0 \\ 0 & \sigma_{22} & \cdots & 0 \\ \vdots & \vdots & \ddots & \vdots \\ 0 & 0 & \cdots & \sigma_{nn} \end{pmatrix}$$

V is an $n \times n$ orthonormal matrix where $V V^T = I_n$ and $V^T V = I_n$. The result of taking the singular value decomposition of a matrix F is the determination of a set of orthonormal column basis vectors $\vec{v}_1, \vec{v}_2, \ldots \vec{v}_n$. These basis vectors have the property that the original m feature vectors are spread out most widely along the $\vec{v}_1$ direction, then along the $\vec{v}_2$ direction, and so on. This is a direct result of the fact that the nonzero entries σ_{ii} in Σ correspond to the minimum variance of the data in F along the basis vectors in the $\vec{v}_i$ ($1 \leq i \leq n$) directions, assuming that the mean is at the origin. In order to take advantage of this property, we apply the transformation V to F, which in effect rotates the vectors that make up F in the direction that yields the best least squares fit (this is especially true once we start removing some of the dimensions, as discussed below). Therefore, the transformed feature vectors $\vec{t}_1, \vec{t}_2, \ldots \vec{t}_m$ are obtained by multiplying each vector $\vec{f}_i$ in the original matrix F with the basis matrix V. In other words, $FV = T = U\Sigma$, which can be verified by multiplying both sides of Equation 4.10 by V and taking note of the fact that $V^T V = I_n$.

V is known as the *SVD transform matrix*. It is the same matrix that transforms the coordinates in PCA. It is also the matrix corresponding to the KLT.[54] For details on how to compute the SVD transform matrix of a matrix (i.e., the matrix formed by the composition of the m n-dimensional feature vectors in our case), see [721, 1515]. The result of applying the rotation (i.e., via the SVD transform matrix) to the original data $\vec{f}_1, \vec{f}_2, \ldots \vec{f}_m$ (i.e., by computing FV) is a set of vectors $\vec{t}_1, \vec{t}_2, \ldots \vec{t}_m$ so that their

---

[54] The principal components correspond to the eigenvectors with the biggest eigenvalues. These are the leading elements in the matrix Σ. V is a rotation matrix, and it is equal to the T matrix (i.e., the result of the transformation) only if the elements of the F matrix are of the form $(1, 0, 0, \ldots 0)$, $(0, 1, 0, \ldots 0)$, $\ldots$, $(0, 0, 0, \ldots 1)$, and so forth.

lengths are preserved when measured using the Euclidean norm—that is, $\|\vec{f_i}\| = \|\vec{t_i}\|$ for $i = 1, \ldots, n$. This is a direct result of the fact that V is an orthogonal matrix (i.e., for any column or row vector $\vec{v_i}$ in V, we have that $\vec{v_i} \cdot \vec{v_j} = 0$ for $i \neq j$). It is also orthonormal (i.e., $\vec{v_i} \cdot \vec{v_j} = \delta_{ij}$), which means that V is an orthonormal transformation.[55] In particular, orthonormal transformations preserve the Euclidean norm of a vector. The practical significance of this property is that such transformations can rotate a point to a new location but cannot change its Euclidean distance from the origin.

We take advantage of this length-preserving property to reduce the dimension of the feature vectors in the transformed space to k by retaining only the k most significant values in Σ (i.e., the largest ones), thereby zeroing out the $n - k$ least significant values (i.e., the smallest ones). We also discard the corresponding entries in the T, U, and V matrices, yielding a new set of feature vectors $\vec{w_1}, \vec{w_2}, \ldots, \vec{w_m}$, where $\vec{w_i}$ ($1 \leq i \leq m$) corresponds to the first k features of $\vec{t_i}$. It is easy to see that for the Euclidean distance metric d_E, the distance between any two feature vectors $\vec{f_i}$ and $\vec{f_j}$ is greater than or equal to the distance between the corresponding transformed feature vectors $\vec{w_i}$ and $\vec{w_j}$, respectively, in the lower dimensional space. In other words, the pruning property holds as $d_E(\vec{w_i}, \vec{w_j}) \leq d_E(\vec{f_i}, \vec{f_j})$. Note that the pruning property does not hold for the result of the SVD transformation in the case of distance metrics other than d_E for both d and d' (e.g., the City Block and the Chessboard distance metrics) since their values are not preserved under rotation (see Exercises 1 and 2, respectively).

To summarize, the SVD method (as well as the KLT and PCA methods) is based on concepts from linear algebra and results in a linear transformation of the feature vectors into vectors whose coordinates are ordered based on "importance" (which is defined in terms of variance). This enables us to keep only the first few features of the transformed feature vectors while retaining as much information as possible. From a mathematical point of view, we computed the eigenvectors of the covariance matrix, sorted them in order of decreasing eigenvalue, chosen a value k ($k \leq n$), and then approximated each of the original n-dimensional feature vectors by its projection onto the first k eigenvectors.

The SVD method is data dependent, and thus is most appropriate in situations where the database is static (e.g., stored on CD-ROM) or changes little (at least in terms of data distribution). In particular, given m feature vectors in an n-dimensional feature space, computing the SVD transform matrix takes $O(m \cdot n^2)$ time and is thus quite expensive. Note that although the complexity is linear in terms of the number of feature vectors m, the value of the constants involved in the computation are quite high.

The time necessary to calculate the SVD transform matrix is the principal drawback of the SVD method. In particular, regardless of the amount of dimension reduction, we must always calculate the SVD transform matrix V using the entire data. Next, V is applied to each of the feature vectors in the input data to obtain the n-dimensional transformed feature vectors. During this step, we can reduce the dimension of the newly transformed feature vectors to k dimensions just by retaining the coordinates in the first k dimensions. Thus, only in this step is the execution time reduced by a factor proportional to the amount of dimension reduction. This data is then indexed using one of the multidimensional spatial indexes.

The SVD method, despite its slowness, is reasonable when the underlying datasets are static. However, the situation changes when the underlying datasets are dynamic. As data is inserted and deleted, we have two choices. We can simply reuse the existing SVD transform matrix to compute the dimension reduced transformed feature vector or recompute the SVD transform matrix. We can reuse the existing SVD transform matrix as long as the precision of the query responses does not degrade by too much (e.g., a 5% to 10% degradation is deemed tolerable [988]). Alternatively, the recomputation of the SVD transform matrix could also be triggered by a drop in the variance of the chosen

---

[55] Orthogonal transformations preserve relative angles while they do not necessarily preserve lengths, whereas orthonormal transformations preserve both relative angles and lengths.

dimensions (as a fraction of the total variance). The motivation for the recomputation is the fact that the features that make up the dimension-reduced transformed feature vector are supposed to be the ones with the greatest variance.

Recalculating the SVD transform matrix and rebuilding the index is quite an expensive proposition. Some incremental techniques have been proposed [321, 468] for recalculating the SVD transform matrix that reduce the complexity of the process from $O(m \cdot n^2)$ to $O(m \cdot r)$, where r is the rank of F, the matrix of the original m n-dimensional feature vectors. These techniques are of interest because r is usually much smaller than n, and thus the proportionality factor in the execution time complexity decreases from n^2 to r. Nevertheless, the process is still linear in the number of feature vectors m.

Kanth, Agrawal, El Abbadi, and Singh [988] propose to recompute the SVD transform matrix using a relatively small subset of the m feature vectors by making use of the aggregation information provided by the spatial index, thereby significantly reducing the complexity of the recomputation process. They also propose to reuse parts of the spatial index rather than always recomputing it. Their methods depend on the nature of the spatial index. They assume that the underlying spatial index is an object hierarchy such as an R-tree [791]. In particular, they make use of an SS-tree [1991] (see Section 4.4), which is an adaptation of an R*-tree [152] that makes use of bounding spheres instead of bounding rectangles. All of their experiments tested the behavior of finding the ith nearest neighbor with the Euclidean distance metric.

The subset of the m feature vectors used to recompute the SVD transform matrix is obtained by choosing a level in the R-tree for which Kanth et al. [988] feel that the distribution of the underlying data is well captured. Next, they calculate the centroid of the values in the subtrees at this level. The new SVD transform matrix (termed the *Approximate SVD transform matrix*) is computed with these centroid values. The larger the reduction in dimension (i.e., the lower the dimensionality of the reduced feature vectors), the smaller is the set of aggregated centroid values obtained at any given level as the fanout of the index nodes is higher (i.e., the number of nodes at the level below is smaller). Similarly, the size of the set of the aggregated values gets smaller as we get closer to the root. This is expected to make the Approximate SVD transform matrix less accurate, thereby leading to more approximation errors (i.e., a decrease in precision for queries to find the ith nearest neighbor).

Experiments [988] were conducted comparing the effects of using the Approximate SVD transform matrix and the regular SVD transform matrix. The SVD transform matrix was initially computed for approximately 12% of the data, dimension reduction was applied, the index was built, and the remaining data was inserted into the existing spatial index with the existing SVD transform matrix. At this point, the Approximate SVD transform matrix and the regular SVD transform matrix were computed for the entire dataset. The spatial index was not rebuilt. The effects of the use of these two matrices on precision were tabulated when the number of nearest neighbors was varied and also when the amount of dimension reduction was varied for a particular number (i.e., 21) of neighbors. Note that the spatial index was not used to calculate the nearest neighbors in this comparison because the goal was solely one of evaluating the quality of the approximation provided by the Approximate SVD transform matrix. If the spatial index were used, then the precision might also be affected by the different amounts of overlap and coverage for the R-trees corresponding to the two matrices.

Most of the experiments [988] used a level of aggregation immediately above that of the leaf nodes of the R-tree. Using this level of aggregation, while varying the amount of dimension reduction, led to two orders of magnitude of reduction in the execution time for the computation of the Approximate SVD transform matrix vis-à-vis the regular SVD transform matrix that took all of the data points into account. Use of the Approximate SVD transform matrix resulted in a very minor decrease in precision (ranging between 2% and 3%) in comparison to the regular SVD transform matrix for the different amounts of dimension reduction. Note that, although the use of dimension reduction resulted in different index node fanout values, its effect on the computation time of the Approximate SVD transform matrix was relatively minor aside from requiring fewer feature vectors for lower dimensions (as more feature vectors made up each aggregated value). This resulted in slightly lower overall precision than when the extent of the dimension reduction was higher, thus requiring a bit more time to calculate the query responses (i.e., to find the nearest neighbors). Nevertheless, since in all experiments' use of the Approximate SVD transform matrix had a relatively minor effect on precision, its use also had a relatively minor effect on query response time. Increasing the level of aggregation by one to a total of two levels above that of the leaf nodes of the R-tree led to a similar, further relative drop of precision. Observe also that all of these results with respect to the effect of using the Approximate SVD transform matrix on precision were not affected by varying the number of nearest neighbors.

Once the new SVD transform matrix has been constructed, its results must be incorporated into the spatial index. The first step is to transform all of the data points and store the results in the leaf nodes. Kanth et al. [988] propose three methods of incorporating the newly transformed points into the spatial index.

1. Build a new index from scratch.

2. Reuse the existing index while adjusting the extents of the bounding spheres of the SS-tree, which is the basis of the R*-tree used in the experiments. The extents of the bounding spheres are likely to increase as the SVD axes have been reoriented. This will degrade the query performance because the degree of filtering that can be achieved by the index is reduced.

3. Pick some level in the index and rebuild the index for each of the subtrees at the lower levels. The index is retained for all index nodes above this level, although the sizes of the bounding spheres for these nodes will have to be adjusted and most likely will have to be increased as the SVD axes have been reoriented. It should be clear that if we choose a level close to the root, then more memory is needed for the rebuilding process of the subtrees as a larger subtree needs to be manipulated. Each subtree is reconstructed using the VAMSplit method [1989] (see Section 1.7.1.7 of Chapter 1) where the partitioning process recursively splits the data items in the subtree until each partition fits in a single node (i.e., disk page). The partitioning axis is chosen corresponding to the dimension with the maximum variance, while the partitioning position is chosen so that the leaf nodes are as full as possible.

Kanth et al. [988] conducted experiments to evaluate the three methods when the new SVD transform matrix is the Approximate SVD transform matrix. Their experiments showed that method 3 worked almost as well as method 1 for query response time (within 10%), with a much lower cost of incorporating the new data into the index (almost 30 times faster), while being only twice as slow as method 2 for incorporating the new data into the index. The query response time for method 2 was almost twice that of methods 1 and 3 due to the much larger bounding spheres (sometimes their radius value tripled). These results held even as the extent of the reduction in dimension was varied. Method 3 was improved by selectively deleting some data items and reinserting them when it was determined that deleting them caused a considerable decrease in volume (e.g., a 50% decrease in the radius). Such a situation is a direct result of an item's not fitting into the subtree after application of the SVD transform matrix.

The SVD method and the accompanying dimension reduction may not always work for large databases when different subclusters are oriented along different axes as too much information can be lost, thereby leading to poor query performance. In this case, it is better first to identify the clusters, compute their individual SVD transform matrices, and then apply dimension reduction to the SVD transform matrices of the individual clusters [1873]. The methods of [988] are also applicable to the SVD transform matrices of the individual clusters.

Equation 4.11 is often referenced as Parseval's theorem [741, p. 1101]. Its validity can be seen by noting that the DFT is an example of a unitary transformation matrix M [701] (see Exercise 1). A matrix M is said to be *unitary* if the complex conjugate of the transpose of M (termed the *adjoint of M* and denoted by $M^\dagger$) is equal to the inverse of M. In other words $M^\dagger \cdot M = I$, where I is the identity matrix with 1s on the diagonal and 0s elsewhere. The adjoint (like the transpose for real-valued matrices) has the property that it interchanges the order of a product of two matrices A and B—that is,

$$(A \cdot B)^\dagger = B^\dagger \cdot A^\dagger$$

Using this property, while also recalling that matrix multiplication is distributive (i.e., $A \cdot (B+C) = A \cdot B + A \cdot C$) and associative (i.e., $A \cdot (B \cdot C) = (A \cdot B) \cdot C$), and rewriting the DFT as $\vec{X} = M \cdot \vec{x}$ enables us to verify equation 4.11:

$$
\begin{aligned}
\|\vec{X}\|^2 &= |(M \cdot \vec{x})^\dagger \cdot (M \cdot \vec{x})| \\
&= |(\vec{x}^\dagger \cdot M^\dagger) \cdot (M \cdot \vec{x})| \\
&= |\vec{x}^\dagger \cdot (M^\dagger \cdot M) \cdot \vec{x}| \\
&= |\vec{x}^\dagger \cdot \vec{x}| \\
&= \|\vec{x}\|^2
\end{aligned}
$$

Equivalently, taking the squares of the two sides of Equation 4.11, we have

$$\|\vec{x}\|^2 = \sum_{t=0}^{n-1} |x_t|^2 = \sum_{f=0}^{n-1} |X_f|^2 = \|\vec{X}\|^2 \tag{4.12}$$

It can be shown that the DFT is a linear transformation (see Exercise 4), and thus from Equation 4.11, we know that the DFT also preserves the Euclidean distance d_E between two sequences $\vec{x} = \{x_t | 0 \le t \le n-1\}$ and $\vec{y} = \{y_t | 0 \le t \le n-1\}$. In other words, the Euclidean distance between $\vec{x}$ and $\vec{y}$ is the same as the Euclidean distance between their corresponding DFTs $\vec{X}$ and $\vec{Y}$, respectively—that is,

$$d_E(\vec{x}, \vec{y}) = d_E(\vec{X}, \vec{Y})$$

Next, we apply dimension reduction by truncating the sequence forming the DFT $\vec{X}$ to k terms to form the new sequence $\vec{X}_k$, which is termed the *Compressed Discrete Fourier Transform* (CDFT) (or simply the *Compressed DFT*). Therefore, for $k \le n$, we have that

$$\|\vec{X}_k\|^2 = \sum_{f=0}^{k-1} |X_f|^2 \le \sum_{f=0}^{n-1} |X_f|^2 = \|\vec{X}\|^2 = \|\vec{x}\|^2 \tag{4.13}$$

This can be rewritten as

$$\|\vec{X}_k\| \le \|\vec{X}\| = \|\vec{x}\| \tag{4.14}$$

If we now keep the first k components (i.e., coefficients) of the DFTs $\vec{X}$ and $\vec{Y}$ of two sequences (i.e., feature vectors) $\vec{x}$ and $\vec{y}$ to yield $\vec{X}_k$ and $\vec{Y}_k$, respectively, then from Equations 4.13 and 4.14, we have that the Euclidean distance between $\vec{X}_k$ and $\vec{Y}_k$ is less than or equal to the Euclidean distance between $\vec{x}$ and $\vec{y}$. This can be formally stated as

$$\|\vec{X}_k - \vec{Y}_k\| \le \|\vec{x} - \vec{y}\| \tag{4.15}$$

Equation 4.15 is the same as the pruning property with the Euclidean distance:

$$d_E(\vec{X}_k, \vec{Y}_k) = d_E(\vec{x}, \vec{y})$$

Thus, we see that the pruning property holds for the CDFT when using the Euclidean distance. Note that the pruning property does not necessary hold for the CDFT when using other distance metrics (e.g., the City Block, Chessboard, or other distance metrics regardless of whether they are Minkowski distance metrics).

Although we have defined Equation 4.15 in terms of the first k coefficients of the DFT, it holds for any subset of k coefficients of the DFT. Thus, we broaden the definition of the CDFT to permit the subset to contain any of the coefficients of the DFT. Unfortunately, one of the main difficulties in using the DFT in a wide range of applications is deciding which of the coefficients should be retained as a result of dimension reduction when forming the CDFT.

This is in contrast to the SVD method, where the transformed coordinates are ordered by their discriminating power and thus we choose the k most discriminating transformed coordinates. Recall that, in the DFT, the coefficients of one feature vector are computed independently of the coefficients of the other feature vectors. The only intuition that we have about the coefficients is that the first one, X_0, corresponds to a mean value over all of the features that make up the feature vector, but we do not have such a simple intuitive interpretation for the remaining coefficients. Similarly, x_0 (the first feature in the feature vector) is equal to the mean value over all of the coefficients.

A number of researchers (e.g., [26, 588]) have argued for retention of the first k coefficients of the DFT. They use the DFT to represent one-dimensional sequences in time-series databases for applications such as stock market price movements, as well as exchange rate fluctuations over time. In order to reduce the volume of data, they retain only a few of the Fourier coefficients in the DFT (the k leading ones), which are stored as points in an R*-tree with dimension equal to the number of terms that make up the first few coefficients (usually the first two), thereby yielding four terms corresponding to the values of the real and imaginary components. The R*-tree is used to index the points. This method was applied to similarity queries [26] and finding subsequences [588] in time-series databases.[59]

Although not explicitly stated in [26], in the case of similarity queries, it is most likely that the second ($f = 1$) and third ($f = 2$) Fourier coefficients are used rather than the first two. The reason is that the time series is real valued, which means that the first ($f = 0$) Fourier coefficient has no imaginary part, and its real part is the mean of the time series. This has a number of ramifications. First, the true dimensionality of the feature vectors is three as one of the features is always zero. Second, if the corresponding elements of two sequences differ by a constant, then all of their coefficients will be the same except for the first one. In this case, if all of the coefficients are retained, then it is clear that the two series are very similar. However, if only two coefficients are retained, one of which is the first coefficient, then there will be a false impression that the two series are different when they are actually quite similar. Of course, if normalization is performed, as is often the case, then we have a time series with a zero mean and now the first coefficient is the same (i.e. both the real and imaginary parts are zero), for all of the time series, and once again it does not aid in discriminating between the different time series regardless of whether or not they differ by a constant. Thus, it is not advisable to use the first coefficient.

For finding subsequences, the situation is more complex, but the approach is similar. Faloutsos, Ranganathan, and Manolopoulos [588] assume that the smallest subsequence is of length w. Each time-series sequence of length l is decomposed into $l - w + 1$ subsequences starting at the first instance of time, and the DFT of each subsequence is computed. Next, the k leading coefficients of the DFT of each subsequence are represented as $2k$-dimensional points using the values of their real and imaginary components. The difference from the way similarity queries were handled is that the R*-tree does not index the points directly. Instead, the points (corresponding to subsequences) belonging to each different time-series sequence are connected to form a continuous curve, termed a *trail*, where there is one trail per sequence. Each trail is then decomposed into *subtrails* of appropriate length using heuristics (see Exercise 3), and minimum bounding boxes

---

[59] For a very different treatment of the two-dimensional problem for trajectories of moving objects, see [348].

are built for each subtrail (observe that the subtrails are not connected as they are formed by breaking up a sequence of points into subsequences). The R*-tree indexes the minimum bounding boxes of the subtrails that are aggregated. Note that the minimum boxes of the subtrails of a given trail may overlap. Furthermore, the subtrails that make up the minimum bounding boxes in the levels other than the leaf nodes do not have to belong to the same trail. Thus, the result is that the R*-tree is an index on all subsequences of length w.

Unlike the situation for similarity queries, as discussed above, it is not immediately obvious that the first ($f = 0$) Fourier coefficient should be omitted for finding subsequences. We point out that even if the time series of length l is normalized so that it has a zero mean, each subsequence of length w does not necessarily have a zero mean. In fact, how the mean is changing over successive subsequences can be important for finding a complete similar time series. In particular, a time series is mapped to a trail, and the shape of this trail is different depending on which Fourier coefficients are used for the feature vector. Thus, we may have better accuracy for the matches when the mean is included. To see this, suppose that we consider single-element feature vectors that just consist of the mean. In this case, the trail can be visualized as a time series of length $l - w + 1$ (i.e., we have $l - w + 1$ subsequences with one feature vector per subsequence). Considered as a time series, the trail would be equal to the low-pass-filtered original time series. The filter is a moving average of width w, and thus the trail would represent the essential shape of the time series. Therefore, it might be useful to include the mean. Whether its inclusion as one of the coefficients will improve the accuracy of the match is unknown as this is done using different choices of coefficients. On the other hand, if we search for a subsequence, then we will probably miss many matching subsequences if we include the mean. This can be seen by observing that, if the first coefficient is not omitted and if all the corresponding elements of two sequences differ by a constant, then the corresponding elements of their subsequences also differ by a constant, and all of their coefficients will be the same except for the first one. This will result in their having two different trails instead of having the same trail (since they will coincide). Given all of these considerations, it is probably better to ignore the first coefficient.

Matching subsequences subject to a given error tolerance ε are found by applying the same transformation to the query sequence q (i.e., compute the DFT of q, retain the same k coefficients as the data sequences, and represent the result as a $2k$-dimensional points using the amplitude values of their real and imaginary components). The search is conducted in the $2k$-dimensional space indexed by the R*-tree with a tolerance ε by finding overlapping bounding boxes. Once the bounding boxes are found, the corresponding subtrails are examined to determine which ones are within the desired tolerance, and the original subsequences are checked. Thus, we see that the bounding boxes serve to prune the search. Searches for larger subsequences are obtained by merging the results of the searches on the smaller subsequences.

The argument for retaining just the first few coefficients is made via an analogy to the problem of random walks. In particular, the first few coefficients represent the low-frequency components of the signal corresponding to the sequence, which are believed to be the dominant ones in this stock market price movements application [26, 588]. In fact, this was probably the case as the stock price movement data was relatively smooth and slow growing, thereby resulting in very few high-frequency components.

Experiments were conducted [26] using the R*-tree with a varying number of leading coefficients. The results showed that the search time increased as the number of leading coefficients increased, although the filtering was a bit better with more coefficients. Nevertheless, the overall search time still increased when taking into account the filtering time. The reason the search time increased with more leading coefficients was due to the increased complexity of the R*-tree search as the fanout of the nodes became smaller, and thus the tree was of greater height. However, no tests were conducted as to the effect of keeping the number of coefficients constant and varying which subset of the coefficients led to better performance. Of course, given the problem domain of one-dimensional sequences in time-series databases, as mentioned above, the lower coefficients correspond to lower-frequency components that reflect less abrupt changes, thereby enabling matching over a longer time period with a lesser emphasis on sudden local variations.

In contrast with the results reported above, Wu, Agrawal, El Abbadi, Singh, and Smith [2026] describe the results of experiments using texture images modeled with a DFT where the identities of the retained Fourier coefficients make a difference in the efficiency of the search time. In such application domains, the question of which coefficients of the DFT ought to be retained is open. We now examine more closely the nature of the Fourier coefficients following the presentation of Wu et al. [2026]. This is dependent on the assumption that the components of the original feature vectors are constrained to be real valued. There are n coefficients X_i ($0 \leq i \leq n - 1$). Given that the components of the original feature vector are real valued, we have that coefficient X_0 is a real number, and $X_{n/2}$ is also a real number if n is an even number, while the remaining coefficients are complex numbers. Again, noting that the components of the original feature vector are real valued, the remaining coefficients occur in complex conjugate pairs such that $X_{n-i} = X_i^*$, where we say that, if $A = a + bj$, then the complex conjugate A^* of A is $A^* = a - bj$. Thus, the sequence of coefficients $X_0, X_1, \ldots X_{n-1}$ can be rewritten as

$$X_0, X_1, \ldots, X_{n/2-1}, X_{n/2}, X_{n/2-1}^*, \ldots, X_2^*, X_1^*$$

where $X_{n/2}$ is nonexistent if n is odd. In this sequence, X_i is said to be the ith *harmonic* using signal-processing terminology.

As mentioned above, in contrast to the SVD,[60] the order in which the coefficients appear in the DFT, save for the first one, is not particularly meaningful for most applications, and thus the coefficients are often reordered when dimension reduction is performed. In particular, the close relationship between a coefficient X_i and its conjugate pair X_{n-i} (i.e., being the ith harmonic) leads to an ordering that retains conjugate pairs in the CDFT. This is done by reformulating what constitute the components of each DFT sequence using Equation 4.12 and the fact that $|X_i|^2 = |X_i^*|^2$ to obtain

$$\|\vec{X}\|^2 = |X_0|^2 + |X_1|^2 + |X_1^*|^2 + \cdots + |X_{n/2-1}|^2 + |X_{n/2-1}^*|^2 + |X_{n/2}|^2$$

$$= |X_0|^2 + 2|X_1|^2 + \cdots + 2|X_{n/2-1}|^2 + |X_{n/2}|^2$$

$$= |X_0|^2 + |\sqrt{2}X_1|^2 + \cdots + |\sqrt{2}X_{n/2-1}|^2 + |X_{n/2}|^2$$

Rewriting $\|\vec{X}\|^2$ in this manner enables us to obtain a new set of n coefficients for the purpose of approximating the Euclidean distance norm of the DFT $\vec{X}$ as follows:

$$X_0, \sqrt{2}Re(X_1), \sqrt{2}Im(X_1), \ldots, \sqrt{2}Re(X_{n/2-1}), \sqrt{2}Im(X_{n/2-1}), X_{n/2} \qquad (1.16)$$

We use the term *values* to describe the elements in Sequence 4.16 as they cannot be used as coefficients to recover the original feature vector from the DFT. Here, we have merged each pair of conjugates into a pair of single values corresponding to the real and imaginary parts of the corresponding coefficients by scaling them by a $\sqrt{2}$ factor. It should be clear that the pruning property holds regardless of the size or the identities of the elements in the subset of the values or coefficients that are used in the CDFT. Assuming that we are using the values in Sequence 4.16, using terminology from signal processing, the first value is what is usually referred to as the *DC* component of the signal and is equal to X_0, the second term corresponds to the average contribution of the real parts of X_1 and X_{n-1}, and the third term corresponds to the average contribution of the imaginary parts of X_1 and X_{n-1}. In other words, the second and third terms correspond to the real and imaginary components of the first harmonic, the fourth and fifth terms correspond to

---

[60] Recall that the algorithm that calculates the SVD transform matrix V produces the component basis vectors in the order of decreasing variability.

the real and imaginary parts of the second harmonic, and so on. If we restrict ourselves to dimension reduction using an odd number of dimensions (i.e., k components in the DFT), then we ensure that the harmonic contribution from each component is intact.

Despite the above reformulation of the components of the DFT, we still do not know for sure if the subset of the leading components (i.e., in increasing order of harmonics) is the right one. It could be that the leading components (if we truncate) are all zero, in which case we lose all information when we perform dimension reduction. Although this situation appears contrived, examples can be constructed that exhibit this behavior. In other words, regardless of how we reformulate the DFT, when we truncate the values or coefficients, we do not know if we have retained the most important ones. Again, we can be sure only that the first coefficient or value corresponds to an average over all the feature values (which could also be zero! and thus of not much help).

One way of overcoming this lack of knowledge is to look at all of the possible coefficients for all of the feature vectors and just pick the k dominant ones (i.e., the ones with the largest values). However, this cannot be done in a consistent manner because, for one feature vector, the last two coefficients could be dominant, while for another feature vector, the first two coefficients could be dominant. Thus, we must use some statistical measure, such as the largest mean (i.e., average) [2026] or the largest variance [988]. The result is termed a *Sorted DFT* (SDFT) [2026] when the Compressed DFT is formed with the k coefficients having the largest mean, and it is termed a *Variance DFT* (VDFT) [988] when the Compressed DFT is formed with the k coefficients having the largest variance. Keeping track of the coefficients with the largest mean or variance is quite simple and is achieved with a pair of constants M and V corresponding to the current value of the mean and variance, respectively, for each of the coefficients. Each time a new feature vector is added, we compute the coefficients of its DFT and update M and V. If there is a change in the set of k dominant coefficients, then we must recalculate the appropriate coefficients of the CDFT; otherwise, no additional work needs to be done.

Wu et al. [2026] compare the use of the CDFT and the SDFT with the SVD method. In order to make the comparison meaningful, comparisons are made using only an odd number of terms. In this way, whenever a CDFT or SDFT component is used, both its real and imaginary parts are taken into account. Thus, the harmonic contribution from each component is intact. Building the DFT for m feature vectors in n-dimensional space requires $O(m \cdot n^2)$ operations, which is the same number needed to calculate the SVD. However, the constant of proportionality involved in building the DFT is considerably lower. The number of operations involved in building the DFT can be further reduced to $O(mn \cdot \log n)$ when n is a power of 2 by calculating it using the Fast Fourier Transform (FFT) [421] (see Exercise 2). Computing the SDFT and the VDFT is a bit more complex as it requires keeping track of the mean and variance of the various coefficients.

Experiments have shown that the SVD method significantly outperforms the CDFT [2026]. Comparisons of the SVD method with the SDFT instead of the CDFT showed much better performance for the SDFT, which often rivaled the SVD method. In particular, this was the case for range queries with relatively small radius values and nearest neighbor queries with a small number of neighbors. These comparisons were more meaningful as they reflect a better the trade-off between the local nature of the SDFT (for a small radius and a small number of neighbors) and the global nature of the SVD method. Recall that the DFT method applies a fixed transformation (not dependent on the values of the feature vectors) to each feature vector (albeit some global information is used to determine the dominant coefficients in the case of the SDFT). In contrast, the SVD method applies a transformation (based on the values of all of the feature vectors) to each feature vector and finds optimal dimensions (i.e., in terms of the greatest amount of variation) by using a least squares fit to the feature vectors. Kanth et al. [988] compare the SVD method with the VDFT and show that the precision of nearest neighbor queries is higher for the SVD method. However, no data is given on the relative execution time for the two methods, which in certain cases could make the VDFT a viable alternative to the SVD method.

1. Prove that the DFT is a unitary transformation.

2. Show how the DFT can be computed in $O(n \log n)$ time for an n-dimensional feature vector.

3. In [588], curves (termed *trails*) formed by a sequence of points are decomposed into sub-curves (termed *subtrails*) formed by subsequences of points. Note that the subcurves are not connected. How would you decompose the curve into subcurves? What is a good criterion for the decomposition process? Recall that the subcurves are indexed by an R*-tree. Thus, are the conditions that make for a good R-tree decomposition (i.e., minimum overlap and minimum total area) also valid here? Alternatively, you may want to look at monotonicity of the subcurves.

4. Show that the DFT is a linear transformation.

5. Show that a shift in the time domain is equivalent to a rotation of the coefficients of the DFT.

4.6.5 Summary

Dimension reduction techniques have a number of drawbacks with respect to the ability to use them in conjunction with indexing methods so as to facilitate similarity searching:

1. As we have seen, search accuracy can suffer if the pruning property is not satisfied.

2. Most dimension reduction methods are tied to a specific distance metric (typically L_2, as in SVD/KLT/PCA discussed in Section 4.6.4.1 and DFT discussed in Section 4.6.4.2) and do not guarantee that the pruning property is satisfied for other distance metrics.

3. In order to be effective, they require that the data be strongly correlated, which means that, in the high-dimensional space, there are only a few independent dimensions, while the rest of the dimensions depend on them. This results in a loss of precision as many distinct points will be potentially mapped to the same representative point in the lower-dimension transformed space, which will result in degraded search performance.

4. Even if we reduce the number of dimensions, the resulting number may still be quite high with respect to the number of dimensions for which conventional indexing methods work well.

5. There are challenges in making them work in a dynamic environment, as the quality of the transformation may degrade (i.e., newly added data may not follow the same distribution as existing data), and thus it may be preferable to compute a new transformation based on the entire database. However, some work has been done to address this challenge (e.g., [988] for SVD).

4.7 Embedding Methods

Embedding methods are designed to facilitate similarity queries in an environment where we are given a finite set of N objects and a distance metric d indicating the distance values between them (collectively termed a *finite metric space*). As we discuss in Section 4.5, there are many applications where the cost of evaluating the distance between two objects is very high. Thus, the number of distance evaluations should be kept to a minimum, while (ideally) maintaining the quality of the result. At times, this distance function is represented by an $N \times N$ similarity matrix containing the distance d between every pair of objects. One way to approach this goal is to *embed* the data objects in a vector space so that the distances of the embedded objects as measured by a distance metric d' approximate the actual distances. Thus, queries can be performed (for the most part) on the embedded objects. In this section, we are especially interested in examining the issue of whether the embedding method returns the same query result as would be returned if the actual distances of the objects were used, thus ensuring that no relevant objects are left out (i.e., there are no false dismissals). In this context, particular attention is paid to SparseMap [886], a variant of Lipschitz embeddings [1181], and FastMap [587], which is inspired by the linear transformations discussed in Section 4.6.4.1 (e.g., KLT and the equivalent PCA and SVD). We also discuss locality sensitive hashing (LSH) [924] (Section 4.7.4), which is a method that combines an embedding into a Hamming space with a set of random projections into a subspace of the Hamming space. The key to its utility for similarity searching is its deployment in randomized approximate nearest neighbor algorithms. All three of these methods can be applied to arbitrary metric spaces.

This section is organized as follows. Section 4.7.1 contains an introduction to embedding methods, including a brief overview of multidimensional scaling. Section 4.7.2 describes Lipschitz embeddings, where the coordinate axes correspond to reference sets consisting of subsets of the objects. This includes a discussion of SparseMap. Section 4.7.3 presents the FastMap method. Section 4.7.4 discusses locality sensitive hashing in the context of randomized algorithms. As we point out earlier, embedding methods such as, locality sensitive hashing could have also been discussed in the context of dimension reduction techniques. We have placed them here as our emphasis is on how the distances in the embedding space approximate the actual distances.

Although it is not explicitly mentioned in the original presentations of some of the embedding methods (e.g., FastMap [587] and SparseMap [886]), we shall see below that it is desirable that the mapping F be such that distance functions d and d' obey the pruning property. Recall from Section 4.6.1 that the pruning property is satisfied if and only if $d'(F(a), F(b)) \leq d(a, b)$ for all pairs of objects a and b. Satisfaction of the pruning property is useful for responding to similarity queries (such as nearest neighbors) when using a spatial index that has been built on the result of the mapping. This is because the pruning property ensures 100% recall, which guarantees that no correct responses are missed. The bulk of the presentation in this section is drawn from the analysis of Hjaltason and Samet [850, 855] of the extent to which various embedding methods satisfy the pruning property.

Nevertheless, despite our focus on the extent to which F satisfies the pruning property (i.e., F is contractive), we also briefly discuss the alternative or additional notion of constructing an embedding that is proximity preserving. This turns out to be harder than merely requiring that the embedding be contractive. As we saw in Section 4.6.1.2, the proximity-preserving property is not commonly satisfied. Therefore, there has been some interest in devising embeddings that are approximately proximity preserving. One example of such a mapping is known as *BoostMap* and was developed by Athitsos, Alon, Sclaroff, and Kollios [106] (see also extensions [105, 107, 108]). BoostMap uses machine learning techniques to construct the mapping from a collection of one-dimensional embeddings that are classified as weakly proximity preserving. A mapping is said to be *weakly proximity preserving* if we know that, given triples of elements s, t, and u in the underlying data domain S, the following properties are both either true or false for more than half of all of the triples of elements:

1. $d(s, u) \leq d(t, u)$

2. $|f(s) - f(u)| \leq |f(t) - f(u)|$

In other words, whenever u is closer to s than to t, we want $f(u)$ to be closer to $f(s)$ than to $f(t)$ and vice versa (i.e., when $f(u)$ is closer to $f(s)$ than to $f(t)$, we want u to be closer to s than to t). The notion of being weakly proximity preserving is used to capture the fact that this property is necessarily satisfied for all triples in S.

Some possible weakly proximity preserving one-dimensional mappings include $f_r(s) = d(r, s)$, where r and s are both in S, and r serves as a parameter reference object, termed a *pivot*, which means that in effect we are computing the distance of the objects with respect to r. Another possibility, among many others, is to take the analog of a projection of an object s onto the line joining two parameter reference objects (i.e., two pivots) p and q—that is,

$$f_{p,q}(s) = \frac{d(p,s)^2 + d(p,q)^2 - d(q,s)^2}{2 \cdot d(p,q)}$$

The interpretation of this mapping as a projection only makes sense if the underlying domain S is a vector space; of course, the mapping is still valid regardless of the nature of S.

The AdaBoost machine learning technique (e.g., [648, 1682]) is used by BoostMap to construct an optimal linear combination of k of these weakly proximity preserving one-dimensional mappings, where "optimal" is with respect to the proximity-preserving property. In particular, the k one-dimensional mappings that make up the linear combination are used as the coordinates of an embedding into $\mathbb{R}^k$, and the coefficients a_j ($1 \le j \le k$) of the linear combination are used as the coefficients for a generalized L_1 distance, $D(X,Y) = \sum_{j=1}^{k} a_j \cdot |Y_j - X_j|$, where X and Y are in $\mathbb{R}^k$ (an image of S).

With this embedding and easily computable distance function, we can use an appropriate indexing technique, coupled with a filter-and-refine strategy, to perform nearest neighbor queries, although we may not achieve 100% recall as there is no guarantee that the embedding is completely proximity preserving. Note that the construction process of the embedding that we have described does not make any provisions for contractiveness or for a limited amount of distortion (i.e., the ratio of the distance in the embedding space to that in the original space). Of course, it is desirable for an embedding to be both contractive and proximity preserving, although neither is necessary for the other—that is, an embedding can be contractive while not being proximity preserving. Similarly, an embedding can be proximity preserving while not being contractive.

4.7.1 Introduction

The motivation behind the development of embedding methods is that, given a sufficiently high value of k, we can find a function F that maps the N objects into a vector space of dimensionality k, such that the distances between the points are approximately preserved when using a distance function d' in the k-dimensional space. In other words, for any pair of objects a and b, we have $d(a,b) \approx d'(F(a), F(b))$. Formally, the mapping F embeds a finite metric space (S,d) into a vector space $\mathbb{R}^k$ possessing a distance metric d', where $S \subset U$ is a dataset of N objects drawn from a universe U, and $d: U \to \mathbb{R}^+$ is the original distance function on U. The mapping $F: S \to \mathbb{R}^k$ is often said to be an *embedding*, and, if d' is the Euclidean distance metric, then F is a *Euclidean embedding*. Note that this problem setting also includes the situation where the N objects are described by an n-dimensional feature vector (this is an example of the case that the original distance function d is computed from the objects rather than existing in a distance matrix). In this case, the mapping F reduces the dimensionality of the problem setting from n to k.

In practice, our goal is to use a relatively low value for k in the mapping (i.e., $k \ll N$), while still achieving reasonable distance preservation. Observe that distance computation can be expensive (e.g., the Euclidean distance in very high-dimensional spaces), so the mapping F should ideally be fast to compute (i.e., take $O(N)$ time or $O(N \log N)$ time for the N objects rather than requiring the computation of the distances between all $O(N^2)$ pairs of objects), should preserve distance to a reasonable extent, and should provide a fast way of obtaining the k-dimensional point corresponding to the object.

At times, the distances between the objects are preserved exactly by the mapping F—that is, $d(a,b) = d'(F(a), F(b))$ for all objects $a, b \in S$. Of course, in this case, F is also proximity preserving. When this occurs, we say that (S,d) and $(\mathbb{R}^k, d')$ are *isometric* (strictly speaking, (S,d) is isometric to $(F(S), d')$, where $F(S) \subset \mathbb{R}^k$ is the image of S

under F). For example, this is possible when the data objects are originally drawn from a vector space, and d and d' are both Euclidean distance metrics. In this particular case, distance preservation among the N objects is ensured when $k = N - 1$ (but a much lower value suffices in most cases). However, usually, the distances cannot be preserved exactly for an arbitrary combination of d and d', regardless of the value of k (i.e., there is no guarantee that a distance-preserving mapping F exists).

As an example of a situation where distances cannot be preserved exactly, suppose that we are given four objects a, b, c, and e with a distance function d such that the distance between each pair in $\{a, b, c\}$ is 2, and the distance from e to each of a, b, and c is 1.1. This distance function d satisfies the triangle inequality. However, these four objects cannot be embedded into a three-dimensional Euclidean space (i.e., where d' is the Euclidean distance metric). In other words, we cannot position the objects in a three-dimensional space so that the Euclidean distance d' between the positions corresponds to the distance between the objects given by d. On the other hand, if the distance between e and the three remaining objects is at least $2/\sqrt{3}$, then such a positioning is possible by placing a, b, and c in a plane p and placing e on the line perpendicular to p that passes through the centroid of the triangle in p formed by a, b, and c.

Interestingly, the above embedding can be achieved if we use the City Block distance metric. In particular, we position objects a, b, and c at locations $(0,0,0)$, $(2,0,0)$, and $(1,1,0)$, respectively, and e at $(1,0,0.1)$. Thus, we see that we can often obtain better distance correspondence by being flexible in choosing the distance function d'. In fact, it is always possible to achieve exact distance preservation when d' is the Chessboard metric (L_∞). In one such embedding, there is one dimension for each object o_i, where $o_1, o_2, \ldots, o_N$ is an enumeration of the objects. Each object o is mapped by F into the vector $\{d(o, o_1), d(o, o_2), \ldots, d(o, o_N)\}$. For any pair of objects o_i and o_j, their distance in the embedding is $d'(F(o_i), F(o_j)) = d_M(F(o_i), F(o_j)) = \max\{|F(o_i) - F(o_j)|\} = \max_l\{|d(o_i, o_l) - d(o_j, o_l)|\}$. Observe that for any l, $|d(o_i, o_l) - d(o_j, o_l)| \le d(o_i, o_j)$ by the triangle inequality, while equality is achieved for $l = i$ and $l = j$, and thus distances are indeed preserved by F when using the Chessboard metric.

Notice that the number of dimensions in this distance-preserving embedding is rather high (i.e., $k = N$). Thus, we may want to define F in terms of a subset of the objects as done by Faragó, Linder, and Lugosi [595], although they do not indicate how to choose the k objects that form the subset. However, for lower values of k, it is possible that a better approximation of the original distances is obtained by a choice of d' other than L_∞. The same type of embedding is also used by Vleugels and Veltkamp [1934], who employ an application-dependent method to choose the k reference objects (e.g., in an application involving hue, the dominant colors of each of the objects differ), which are called *vantage objects*.

In most applications, it is not possible to achieve distance preservation given a particular choice for d' and k. In fact, we are often satisfied when the distance d' in the k-dimensional embedding space between the points that correspond to any pair of individual objects a and b is less than the true distance d between the objects in the original space—that is, $d'(F(a), F(b)) \le d(a, b)$. This property is known as the *pruning property* and is discussed in Section 4.6.1. As pointed out earlier, satisfaction of the pruning property is useful for responding to similarity queries (such as nearest neighbors) when using a spatial index that has been built on the result of the mapping. This is because the pruning property ensures 100% recall, which guarantees that no correct responses are missed.

The concept of *distortion* (e.g., [1181]) is frequently used for measuring the quality of an embedding procedure (i.e., a method that constructs a mapping F) or of a particular embedding F produced by such a procedure. Distortion measures how much larger or smaller the distances in the embedding space $d'(F(o_1), F(o_2))$ are than the corresponding distances $d(o_1, o_2)$ in the original space. In particular, the distortion is defined as $c_1 c_2$ when we are guaranteed that

$$\frac{1}{c_1} \cdot d(o_1, o_2) \leq d'(F(o_1), F(o_2)) \leq c_2 \cdot d(o_1, o_2) \qquad (4.17)$$

for all pairs of objects $o_1, o_2 \in S$, where $c_1, c_2 \geq 1$. In other words, the distance values $d'(F(o_1), F(o_2))$ in the embedding space may be as much as a factor of c_1 smaller and a factor of c_2 larger than the actual distances $d(o_1, o_2)$. Note that for a given embedding procedure, there may be no upper or lower bound on the distance ratio for the embeddings that it constructs, so c_1, c_2, or both may be infinite in this case. Of course, the distortion is always bounded for any given embedding F and finite metric space (S, d). A number of general results are known about embeddings—for example, that any finite metric space can be embedded in Euclidean space with $O(\log N)$ distortion [1181].

Another common measure of a particular embedding F with respect to a dataset S is *stress* [1090]. Stress measures the overall deviation in the distances (i.e., the extent to which they differ) and is typically defined in terms of variance:

$$\frac{\sum_{o_1, o_2} (d'(F(o_1), F(o_2)) - d(o_1, o_2))^2}{\sum_{o_1, o_2} d(o_1, o_2)^2}$$

Alternative definitions of stress may be more appropriate for certain applications. For example, the sum in the denominator may be on $d'(F(o_1), F(o_2))^2$, or the division by $d(o_1, o_2)^2$ may occur inside the sum (instead of in a separate sum). Multidimensional scaling (MDS) [1090, 1879, 2056] is a method of constructing F that is based on minimizing stress. It has been widely used for many decades, in both the social and physical sciences, for purposes such as visualizing and clustering the data resulting from experiments. MDS is defined in many ways, some of which even allow nonmetric distances (i.e., the triangle inequality is not required).

Minimizing stress is essentially a nonlinear optimization problem, where the variables are the $N \cdot k$ coordinate values corresponding to the embedding (i.e., k coordinate values for each of the N objects). Typically, solving such a problem involves starting with an arbitrary assignment of the variables and then trying to improve on it in an iterative manner using the method of steepest descent (e.g., [1090]). The result of the optimization is not always the embedding that achieves the absolute minimum stress, but instead it is one that achieves a local minimum (i.e., the minimization can be pictured as finding the deepest valley in a landscape by always walking in a direction that leads downhill; the process can thus get stuck in a deep valley that is not necessarily the deepest).

In principle, it is possible to make the result of MDS satisfy the pruning property by constraining the minimization of the stress with $O(N^2)$ pruning property conditions, one for each pair of objects—that is, to minimize

$$\sum_{a, b \subset S} (d'(F(a), F(b)) - d(a, b))^2 \bigg/ \sum_{a, b \subseteq S} d(a, b)^2$$

subject to the $O(N^2)$ conditions $d'(F(a), F(b)) - d(a, b) \leq 0$ (for all pairs $a, b \in S$). Note that simply minimizing the stress does not necessarily mean that the pruning property is satisfied. In particular, the stress could be minimized when the distance difference in the k-dimensional space (relative to the distance in the original space) increases by a large amount for one of the object pairs, whereas it decreases by just a small amount for all remaining pairs.

Unfortunately, MDS has limited applicability in similarity search, regardless of whether the resulting embedding satisfies the pruning property. This is partly due to the high cost of constructing the embedding, both in terms of the number of distance computations (i.e., $O(N^2)$, one for each pair of objects) and partly due to the inherent complexity of the optimization process. More seriously, when performing similarity queries, we must compute the embedding of the query object q, again, by minimizing stress subject only to varying the coordinate values of $F(q)$. Although the minimization process is itself expensive, the most serious drawback is that the distances of all objects in S from q must be computed in order to evaluate the stress—that is, $O(N)$ distance computations are required. This completely defeats the goal of performing similarity queries in terms of the embedding space, namely, to avoid as many distance computations as possible. In fact, after computing the distances of all objects in S from q, we can immediately tell what the result of the query should be, thereby making the embedding of q unnecessary.

The Karhunen-Loève Transform (KLT), as well as the equivalent Principal Component Analysis (PCA) and the Singular Value Decomposition (SVD) methods discussed in Section 4.6.4.1, are the optimal methods of linearly transforming n-dimensional points to k-dimensional points ($k \le n$). In particular, they minimize the *mean square error*—that is, the sum of the squares of the Euclidean distances between each n-dimensional point and its corresponding k-dimensional point (notice the similarity to minimizing the stress function in MDS described above). The goal of these methods is to find the most important features (more precisely, a linear combination of features) for a given set of feature vectors. The rationale behind them is that they can be interpreted as providing a new set of features ranked by their importance (i.e., their variation) so that if we ignore the less important (i.e., varying) ones by projecting onto the most important (i.e., varying) ones, then we preserve as much as possible of the variation between the original set of feature vectors as measured by the Euclidean distance between them.

These methods have several drawbacks. First, they cannot be applied when we are given only the distances between the objects (i.e., the distance function) and do not have the m-dimensional feature vectors. Second, they are very slow to compute, taking $O(N \cdot m^2)$ time, especially when there are many feature vectors (N), and the dimension m of the original space is very high.

Moreover, these methods are really meaningful only if d is the Euclidean distance metric and not one of the other Minkowski metrics. The reason is twofold. First, the other Minkowski metrics are not invariant under rotation. In other words, the distance between some pairs of points may increase or decrease, depending on the direction of the rotation. Second, variance is defined in terms of second powers, just like the Euclidean distance metric. Thus, the variance criteria that determine the rotation and, in turn, what axes to drop when reducing the dimensionality are inherently related to the Euclidean distance metric. In particular, the sum of the variances over all coordinate axes corresponds to the sum of the squared Euclidean distances from the origin to each point (recall that we are assuming that the mean along each dimension is at the origin). Therefore, dropping the axes having the least variance corresponds to reducing as little as possible the sum of the squared Euclidean distances from the origin to each point.

In contrast, as we will see, the embedding methods that we describe can be used with other distance metrics than the Euclidean distance metric. Moreover, they can be used with data from an arbitrary metric space (i.e., the only information about the data objects consists of the interobject distances). However, for some of the methods, such as FastMap, such usage is usually of limited interest as it does not necessarily satisfy the pruning property, and it may work only for very small values of k (even as small as just 1), instead of an arbitrary value of k when d is the Euclidean distance metric. However, the general class of Lipschitz embeddings does satisfy the pruning property, and, as we shall see, even the SparseMap method can be made to satisfy the pruning property.

Exercise

1. Devise an implementation of MDS where the variance in the difference of the distance values is minimized and the distance in the k-dimensional space satisfies the pruning property. If this is not possible, then give a counterexample.

4.7.2 Lipschitz Embeddings

A powerful class of embedding methods is known as *Lipschitz embeddings* [237, 962]. They are based on defining a coordinate space where each axis corresponds to a reference set that is a subset of the objects. This is the subject of this section, which is organized as follows. Section 4.7.2.1 defines a Lipschitz embedding. Section 4.7.2.2 describes how to select the reference sets. Section 4.7.2.3 presents an example of a Lipschitz embedding. Section 4.7.2.4 explains SparseMap, which is an instance of a Lipschitz embedding that attempts to reduce the computational cost of the embedding.

4.7.2.1 Definition

A Lipschitz embedding is defined in terms of a set R of subsets of S, $R = \{A_1, A_2, \ldots, A_k\}$.[61] The subsets A_i are termed the *reference sets* of the embedding. Let $d(o, A)$ be an extension of the distance function d to a subset $A \subset S$ such that $d(o, A) = \min_{x \in A}\{d(o, x)\}$. An embedding with respect to R is defined as a mapping F such that $F(o) = (d(o, A_1), d(o, A_2), \ldots, d(o, A_k))$. In other words, we are defining a coordinate space where each axis corresponds to a subset $A_i \subset S$ of the objects, and the coordinate values of object o are the distances from o to the closest element in each of A_i.

Notice that the distance-preserving L_∞ embedding that we describe in Section 4.7.1 is a special case of a Lipschitz embedding, where R consists of all singleton subsets of S (i.e., $R = \{\{o_1\}, \{o_2\}, \ldots, \{o_N\}\}$). Recall also the embedding of Faragó et al. [595], which made use of a subset of singleton subsets of S for a nearest neighbor search application (although they do not specify how to choose the objects that make up R). Another variation on a Lipschitz embedding is presented by Cowen and Priebe [426], where the number and sizes of the reference sets A_i are chosen based on an objective function that is meant to capture the quality of clustering that results. The distance-based indexing methods that make use of distance matrices described in Section 4.5.7 (e.g., see [130, 1292, 1743, 1930, 1951]) are also somewhat related to Lipschitz embeddings. These methods typically (e.g., see [1292]) make use of a matrix $D = (D_{ij})$ of distances, where $D_{ij} = d(o_i, p_j)$ and $T = \{p_1, p_2, \ldots, p_k\}$ is a set of k reference objects; for some methods (e.g., AESA [1930]), $T = S$ and $k = N$. The row vectors of D are equivalent to the result of a Lipschitz embedding using the singleton reference sets of objects in T. However, the search algorithms proposed for distance matrix methods do not explicitly treat the row vectors as if they represent points in geometric space (i.e., by using the Euclidean metric or some other Minkowski metric).

The intuition behind the Lipschitz embedding is that if x is an arbitrary object in the dataset S, some information about the distance between two arbitrary objects o_1 and o_2 is obtained by comparing $d(o_1, x)$ and $d(o_2, x)$ (i.e., the value $|d(o_1, x) - d(o_2, x)|$). This is especially true if one of the distances $d(o_1, x)$ or $d(o_2, x)$ is small. Observe that, due to the triangle inequality, we have $|d(o_1, x) - d(o_2, x)| \leq d(o_1, o_2)$, as illustrated in Figure 4.87. This argument can be extended to a subset A. In other words, the value $|d(o_1, A) - d(o_2, A)|$ is a lower bound on $d(o_1, o_2)$. This can be seen as follows. Let $x_1, x_2 \in A$ be such that $d(o_1, A) = d(o_1, x_1)$ and $d(o_2, A) = d(o_2, x_2)$. Since $d(o_1, x_1) \leq d(o_1, x_2)$ and $d(o_2, x_2) \leq d(o_2, x_1)$, we have $|d(o_1, A) - d(o_2, A)| = |d(o_1, x_1) - d(o_2, x_2)|$. Accounting for the fact that $d(o_1, x_1) - d(o_2, x_2)$ can be positive or negative, we have $|d(o_1, x_1) - d(o_2, x_2)| \leq \max\{|d(o_1, x_1) - d(o_2, x_1)|, |d(o_1, x_2) - d(o_2, x_2)|\}$. Finally, from the triangle inequality, we have $\max\{|d(o_1, x_2) - d(o_2, x_2)|, |d(o_1, x_1) - d(o_2, x_1)|\} \leq d(o_1, o_2)$. Thus, $|d(o_1, A) - d(o_2, A)|$ is a lower bound on $d(o_1, o_2)$. By using a set R of subsets, we increase the likelihood that the distance $d(o_1, o_2)$ between two objects o_1 and o_2 (as measured relative to other distances) is captured adequately by the distance in the embedding space between $F(o_1)$ and $F(o_2)$ (i.e., $d'(F(o_1), F(o_2))$).

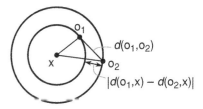

Figure 4.87
Demonstration of the distance bound $|d(o_1, x) - d(o_2, x)| \leq d(o_1, o_2)$. The objects o_1, o_2, and x are represented as points, and the distances between them by the lengths of the line segments between them.

---

[61] Note that the union of the set of elements comprising the subsets that make up R is not necessarily equivalent to S.

4.7.2.2 Selecting Reference Sets

With a suitable definition of R, the set of reference sets, we can establish bounds on the distance $d'(F(o_1), F(o_2))$ for all pairs of objects $o_1, o_2 \in S$, where d' is one of the L_p metrics. Such a definition was provided by Linial, London, and Rabinovich [1181], based in part on previous work by Bourgain [237]. In particular, in their definition [1181], R consists of $O(\log^2 N)$ randomly selected subsets of S, where each group of $O(\log N)$ subsets is of size 2^i, where $i = 1, \ldots, O(\log N)$. More concretely, the value $O(\log N)$ is typically approximately $\lfloor \log_2 N \rfloor$ (or perhaps $\lfloor \log_2(N-1) \rfloor$). Thus, $R = \{A_1, A_2, \ldots, A_k\}$, where $k = \lfloor \log_2 N \rfloor^2$, and A_i is of size 2^j with $j = \lfloor (i-1)/(\log_2 N) + 1 \rfloor$. The embedding proposed by Linial et al. [1181] is a variant of the basic Lipschitz embedding, where each coordinate value is divided by a factor that depends on k. In particular, if d' is the L_p metric, F is defined such that $F(o) = (d(o, A_1)/q, d(o, A_2)/q, \ldots, d(o, A_k)/q)$, where $q = k^{1/p}$. Given this definition, Linial et al. [1181] prove that F satisfies

$$\frac{c}{\lfloor \log_2 N \rfloor} \cdot d(o_1, o_2) \leq d'(F(o_1), F(o_2)) \leq d(o_1, o_2) \tag{4.18}$$

for any pair of objects $o_1, o_2 \in S$, where $c > 0$ is a constant.[62] Thus, the distortion in distance values (i.e., the relative amount of deviation of the distance values in the embedding space with respect to the original distance values) is guaranteed to be $O(\log N)$ (with high probability). The proof for the bound $c/\lfloor \log_2 N \rfloor d(o_1, o_2) \leq d'(F(o_1), F(o_2))$ is rather sophisticated [237, 1181] and is beyond the scope of this discussion. However, the bound $d'(F(o_1), F(o_2)) \leq d(o_1, o_2)$ is easy to show. In particular, for each $A_i \in R$, we have $|d(o_1, A_i) - d(o_2, A_i)| \leq d(o_1, o_2)$, as shown in Section 4.7.2.1. Thus, when d' is an arbitrary L_p distance metric,

$$d'(F(o_1), F(o_2)) = \left(\sum_{i=1}^{k} \left(\frac{d(o_1, A_i) - d(o_2, A_i)}{k^{1/p}} \right)^p \right)^{1/p} \tag{4.19}$$

$$\leq \left(k \cdot \frac{d(o_1, o_2)^p}{k} \right)^{1/p} = d(o_1, o_2) \tag{4.20}$$

A distortion of $O(\log N)$ may seem rather large and may render the embedding ineffective at preserving relative distances. For example, if the range of distance values is less than the distortion, then the relative order of the neighbors of a given object may be completely scrambled. However, note that $O(\log N)$ is a worst-case (probabilistic) bound. In many cases, the actual behavior is much better. For example, in a computational biology application [886, 1180], the embedding defined above was found to lead to good preservation of clusters, as defined by biological functions of proteins.

Notice that the mapping F as defined by Linial et al. [1181] satisfies the pruning property (i.e., it is contractive), which is advantageous in similarity search. In many other situations, only relative differences in distance are important in the embedding space, while the satisfaction of the pruning property is immaterial. In other words, the crucial information that we wish to retain is which objects are close to each other and which are far (i.e., a weak form of proximity preservation). An example of an application of this sort is cluster analysis [886, 1180]. In such situations, it may be more convenient to use the regular Lipschitz embedding definition of F with respect to the set of reference sets R defined in [1181] (i.e., without dividing by $k^{1/p}$). Recall that $k = \lfloor \log_2 N \rfloor^2$, thereby implying that $\sqrt{k} = \lfloor \log_2 N \rfloor$. Therefore, when the Euclidean distance metric is being used, this embedding guarantees distance bounds of

$$c \cdot d(o_1, o_2) \leq d_E(F(o_1), F(o_2)) \leq \lfloor \log_2 N \rfloor \cdot d(o_1, o_2)$$

for any pair of objects $o_1, o_2 \in S$, where $c > 0$ is a constant (with high probability).

---

[62] More accurately, since the sets A_i are chosen at random, the proof is probabilistic, and c is a constant with high probability.

Object	o_1	o_2	o_3	o_4	o_5	o_6	o_7	o_8	o_9	o_{10}
o_1	0	2	13	7	3	8	11	4	9	10
o_2	2	0	11	9	3	10	9	2	11	8
o_3	13	11	0	6	10	9	4	9	6	3
o_4	7	9	6	0	6	3	8	9	2	5
o_5	3	3	10	6	0	7	8	3	8	7
o_6	8	10	9	3	7	0	9	10	3	6
o_7	11	9	4	8	8	9	0	7	10	3
o_8	4	2	9	9	3	10	7	0	11	6
o_9	9	11	6	2	8	3	10	11	0	7
o_{10}	10	8	3	5	7	6	3	6	7	0

Figure 4.88
Distance matrix for 10 sample objects.

Reference Set	o_1	o_2	o_3	o_4	o_5	o_6	o_7	o_8	o_9	o_{10}
A_1	2	0	9	9	3	10	7	0	11	6
A_2	0	2	10	6	0	7	8	3	8	7
A_3	4	2	3	2	3	0	3	0	0	0
A_4	0	2	4	0	3	3	0	0	2	3

Figure 4.89
Four-dimensional coordinate values for the 10 objects based on the distances in Figure 4.88, as determined by a Lipschitz embedding with the four reference sets $A_1 = \{o_2, o_8\}$, $A_2 = \{o_1, o_5\}$, $A_3 = \{o_6, o_8, o_9, o_{10}\}$, and $A_4 = \{o_1, o_4, o_7, o_8\}$.

Unfortunately, the embedding of [1181] described above is rather impractical for similarity searching for two reasons. First, due to the number and sizes of the subsets in R, there is a high probability that all N objects appear in some set in R. Thus, when computing the embedding $F(q)$ for a query object q (which generally is not in S), we will need to compute the distances between q and practically all objects in S, which is exactly what we wish to avoid. Second, the number of subsets in R, and thus the number of coordinate values (i.e., dimensions) in the embedding, is relatively large—that is, $\lfloor \log_2 N \rfloor^2$. Even with as few as 100 objects, the number of dimensions is 36, which is much too high to index on efficiently with multidimensional indexing methods. These drawbacks are acknowledged in [1181], but addressing them is left for future work (the only suggestion made is to drop the sets A_i of largest sizes).

4.7.2.3 Example of a Lipschitz Embedding

We now give an example of Lipschitz embedding. Figure 4.88 shows the interobject distances between 10 objects (these distance values were constructed by positioning 10 two-dimensional points and measuring the L_1 distance between them). In this case, $\lfloor \log_2 N \rfloor = 3$, so we can have three reference sets of three different sizes (2, 4, and 8) for a total of nine dimensions. Since a set of size 8 contains nearly all of the objects, we instead choose to use only reference sets of sizes 2 and 4, and two sets of each size. Choosing objects at random, we arrive at the sets $A_1 = \{o_2, o_8\}$, $A_2 = \{o_1, o_5\}$, $A_3 = \{o_6, o_8, o_9, o_{10}\}$, and $A_4 = \{o_1, o_4, o_7, o_8\}$. The resulting four-dimensional coordinates are given in Figure 4.89. Here, we use the regular Lipschitz embedding, where coordinate value j for object o_i is $d(o_i, A_j)$, rather than $d(o_i, A_j)/k^{1/p}$ as specified by Linial et al. [1181]. For example, $d(o_4, A_2) = \min\{d(o_4, o_1), d(o_4, o_5)\} = \min\{7, 6\} = 6$.

We now give an example of how to compute the distance between two objects in the embedding space, when d' is the Euclidean distance metric. In particular, for objects o_3 and o_8, we have from Figure 4.89 that $F(o_3) = (9, 10, 3, 4)$ and $F(o_8) = (0, 0, 3, 0)$. Therefore,

$$d'(F(o_3), F(o_8)) = \sqrt{(9-0)^2 + (10-3)^2 + (3-0)^2 + (4-0)^2}$$
$$= \sqrt{81 + 49 + 9 + 16} = \sqrt{155} \approx 12.4$$

In comparison, their actual distance is $d(o_3, o_8) = 9$. Notice that in this case the distance in the embedding space is greater than the actual distance. In contrast, when we use the embedding of Linial et al. [1181], the distance in the embedding space will be about $12.4/\sqrt{4} = 6.2$. Also, if d' is the Chessboard distance metric (L_∞), the distance in the embedding space will be $\max\{9, 7, 3, 4\} = 9$, which happens to equal $d(o_3, o_8)$.

4.7.2.4 SparseMap

SparseMap [886] is an embedding method originally proposed for mapping a database of proteins into Euclidean space. It is built on the work of Linial et al. [1181] in that the same set of reference sets R is used. The SparseMap method [886] comprises two heuristics, each aimed at alleviating one of the drawbacks discussed in Section 4.7.2.2—that is, the potentially high cost of computing the embedding in terms of the number of distance computations that are needed and the large number of coordinate values. The first heuristic reduces the number of distance computations by calculating an upper bound $\hat{d}(o, A_i)$ instead of the exact value $d(o, A_i)$. The second heuristic reduces the number of dimensions by using a "high-quality" subset of R instead of the entire set, as defined in Section 4.7.2.2. Both heuristics have the potential to reduce the quality of the embedding in terms of the correspondence of distances in the original metric space and in the embedding space, but their goal [886] is to maintain the quality to the greatest extent possible. Note that the embedding used in SparseMap employs the regular Lipschitz embedding with respect to R, rather than the embedding proposed in [1181] (which divides the distances $d(o, A_i)$ by $k^{1/p}$), and uses the Euclidean distance metric.

In SparseMap, the coordinate values of the vectors are computed one by one. In other words, if $R = \{A_1, A_2, \ldots, A_k\}$ is the sequence of reference sets in order of size, we first compute $d(o, A_1)$ for all objects $o \in S$, next $d(o, A_2)$ for all objects o, and so on. Since evaluating $d(o, A_i)$ for any given object o can be very expensive in terms of distance computations, SparseMap adopts a heuristic that instead computes $\hat{d}(o, A_i)$, which is an upper bound on $d(o, A_i)$. This heuristic exploits the partial vector that has already been computed for each object, and only calculates a fixed number of distance values for each object (as opposed to $|A_i|$ distance values). In particular, for each object $x \in A_i$, it computes $d_E(F_{i-1}(o), F_{i-1}(x))$, where F_{i-1} is the embedding based on $A_1, \ldots, A_{i-1}$. On the basis of this approximate distance value, a fixed number l of objects in A_i having the smallest approximate distance value from o is picked, and the actual distance value $d(o, x)$ for each such object x is computed. The smallest distance value among those serves as the upper-bound distance value $\hat{d}(o, A_i)$, which becomes the ith coordinate value of the vector corresponding to o in the embedding.

The second heuristic involved in SparseMap reduces the dimensionality of the result and is termed *greedy resampling* in [886]. Greedy resampling is applied after the k coordinate axes have all been determined, and its goal is to reduce the number of coordinate axes to $k' < k$. Essentially, this means eliminating some of the reference sets A_i. A natural question is whether we cannot eliminate a poor reference set A_i before computing all the approximate distances $\hat{d}(o, A_i)$. However, the problem is that we cannot know whether a set A_i is good before evaluating $\hat{d}(o, A_i)$ (or $d(o, A_i)$) for each object o. The basic idea of greedy resampling is to start with a single "good" coordinate axis and then incrementally to add coordinate axes that maintain "goodness." In particular, initially, the coordinate axis whose sole use leads to the least stress [1090] is determined (this is somewhat analogous in spirit to basing the first coordinate axis on a pair of objects that are far apart in the FastMap method as described in Section 4.7.3). Unfortunately, calculating the stress requires computing distances for all pairs of objects, which is prohibitively expensive. Instead, the heuristic computes the stress based on some fixed number of object pairs (e.g., 4,000 in experiments in [886], which constituted 10% of the total number of pairs). Next, the coordinate axis that leads to the least stress when used in conjunction with the first axis is determined. This procedure is continued until the desired number of coordinate axes has been obtained.

A drawback of the embedding that forms the basis of SparseMap (i.e., the regular Lipschitz embedding on the reference sets, without taking the heuristics into account) is that it does not satisfy the pruning property (i.e., it is not contractive). In particular, the distance value in the embedding may be as much as a factor of $\log_2 N$ larger than the actual distance value. Two methods can be applied to obtain an embedding that satisfies the pruning property. First, the embedding proposed in [1181] (where the coordinate values are divided by $k^{1/p}$) can be employed, which does satisfy the pruning property. Second, the distance function d' can be modified to yield the same effect. In particular, if $d_p(F(o_1), F(o_2))$ is one of the Minkowski metrics, we can define $d'(F(o_1), F(o_1)) = d_p(F(o_1), F(o_2))/(k^{1/p})$. The advantage of modifying the distance function d' rather than the embedding itself is that it allows modifying the number of coordinate axes (for example, during the construction of the embedding and in the second SparseMap heuristic) without changing existing coordinate values. With either method, the embedding will satisfy Equation 4.18 for any distance metric L_p (i.e., subject to modification when using the second method).

Unfortunately, the heuristics applied in SparseMap do not allow deriving any practical bounds (in particular, bounds that rely on N, or k, or both) on the distortion resulting from the embedding. In particular, the first heuristic can lead to larger distances in the embedding space, thus possibly causing the pruning property to be violated (in contrast, the second heuristic can reduce only distances in the embedding space). This is because the value of $|\hat{d}(o_1, A_i) - \hat{d}(o_2, A_i)|$ may not necessarily be a lower bound on $d(o_1, o_2)$. To see why, note that the upper bound distances $\hat{d}(o_1, A_i)$ and $\hat{d}(o_2, A_i)$ can be larger than the actual distances $d(o_1, A_i)$ and $d(o_2, A_i)$ (which are the minimum distances from o_1 and o_2 to an object in A_i) by an arbitrary amount. In particular, we cannot rule out a situation where $\hat{d}(o_1, A_i) > \hat{d}(o_2, A_i) + d(o_1, o_2)$, in which case $|\hat{d}(o_1, A_i) - \hat{d}(o_2, A_i)| > d(o_1, o_2)$.

Thus, we see that in order to satisfy the pruning property, we must use the actual values $d(o, A_i)$ in the embedding, rather than an upper bound on these distances, as is done in SparseMap. Fortunately, there is a way to modify the first heuristic of SparseMap so that it computes the actual value $d(o, A_i)$ while still (at least potentially) reducing the number of distance computations [850, 855]. We illustrate this for the case when the Chessboard distance metric, d_M, is used as d' in the embedding space. Note that $d_M(F(o_1), F(o_2)) \leq d(o_1, o_2)$, as shown in Section 4.7.2.2 (the key observation is that $|d(o_1, A_i) - d(o_2, A_i)| \leq d(o_1, o_2)$ for all A_i). Furthermore, if F_i is the partial embedding for the first i coordinate values, we also have $d_M(F_i(o_1), F_i(o_2)) \leq d(o_1, o_2)$. In this modified heuristic for computing $d(o, A_i)$, instead of computing the actual distance value $d(o, x)$ for only a fixed number of objects $x \in A_i$, we must do so for a variable number of objects in A_i. In particular, we first compute the approximate distances $d_M(F_{i-1}(o), F_{i-1}(x))$ for all objects $x \in A_i$, which are lower bounds on the actual distance value $d(o, x)$. Observe that in SparseMap the approximate distances $d_E(F_{i-1}(o), F_{i-1}(x))$ are computed for each $x \in A_i$, which has the same cost complexity as evaluating $d_M(F_{i-1}(o), F_{i-1}(x))$, although the constants of proportionality are lower for d_M than for d_E. Next, we compute the actual distances of the objects $x \in A_i$ in increasing order of their lower-bound distances, $d_M(F_{i-1}(o), F_{i-1}(x))$. Let $y \in A_i$ be the object whose actual distance value $d(o, y)$ is the smallest distance value so far computed following this procedure. Once all lower-bound distances $d_M(F_{i-1}(o), F_{i-1}(x))$ of the remaining elements $x \in A_i$ are greater than $d(o, y)$, we are assured that $d(o, A_i) = d(o, y)$.

Even though we described our modified heuristic in terms of the Chessboard distance metric, by using a suitable definition of the distance function d', the heuristic can be applied to any Minkowski metric L_p. In particular, if k' is the current number of coordinate axes (at the completion of the process, $k' = k$), the distance function d' based on L_p is defined as

$$d'(F_{k'}(o_1), F_{k'}(o_2)) = \frac{\left(\sum_i |d(o_1, A_i) - d(o_2, A_i)|^p\right)^{1/p}}{(k')^{1/p}} \quad (4.21)$$

For any choice of p, this distance metric makes F satisfy the pruning property; note the similarity with Equation 4.20.

Moreover, observe that for fixed values of o_1, o_2, and $F_{k'}$, the function d' defined by Equation 4.21 increases with increasing values of p. For example, for $p = 1$, $d'(F_{k'}(o_1), F_{k'}(o_2))$ is the average among the coordinate value differences. On the other hand, for $p = \infty$, it is the maximum difference. Thus, the use of the Chessboard metric L_∞ would lead to the largest values of $d'(F_{k'}(o_1), F_{k'}(o_2))$ for any given choice of the sets A_i. For similarity queries, as well as for the modified heuristic described above, given a fixed set of reference sets A_i, this would therefore lead to the best possible pruning during search. To see why this is the case, suppose that we are performing a range query with query object q and query radius r, and we wish to report all objects o such that $d(q, o) \leq r$. Let o' be an object that is too far from q (i.e., $d(q, o') > r$). However, if $d'(F(q), F(o')) \leq r$, o' will be a part of the result set when performing a query in the embedding space. Thus, the situation can easily arise that $d'(F(q), F(o')) \leq r$ when basing d' on the City Block or Euclidean distance metrics (i.e., L_1 or L_2), but $d'(F(q), F(o')) > r$ when d' is based on the Chessboard distance metric L_∞. Such a hypothetical example is illustrated in Figure 4.90 with distance values r_1, r_2, and r_∞ corresponding to the use of L_1, L_2, and L_∞ distance metrics, respectively.

Although the modified heuristic presented above will likely lead to a higher number of distance computations than the SparseMap heuristic, the higher cost of the embedding (which mainly affects preprocessing) may be justified, as the resulting embedding satisfies the pruning property. This allows effective pruning in similarity queries, while obtaining accurate results, as we get 100% recall and thus do not miss any relevant answers.

One way to measure the quality of embeddings such as those produced by SparseMap is to use the concept of a cluster preservation ratio (CPR) [886]. It can be applied to a dataset when a known clustering exists for the objects. In particular, for each object o whose cluster is of size s, we find the s nearest neighbors in the embedding space and compute the fraction of cluster objects that are among these s neighbors. The CPR indicates the average ratio of cluster preservation over all objects in the dataset.

In order to study the validity of the SparseMap method, the results of various experiments are described in [886] in which the datasets consist of proteins (or more accurately, the amino acid sequences that make up each protein). This data is useful because these proteins have been studied extensively in terms of their biochemical functions, so proteins having similar functions can be grouped together. Therefore, we can test whether amino acid sequences representing these known proteins follow this grouping when an embedding is performed. The focus of the experiments is mainly on comparing the performance of SparseMap with that of FastMap [587], another embedding method proposed for similarity searching and described in greater detail in Section 4.7.3. Both methods are based on heuristics where some parameter controls the number of distance computations that are performed. In SparseMap, this is the number of actual distance computations performed in evaluating $\hat{d}(o, A_i)$, while in FastMap, it is the number of iterations performed in the pivot-finding process (see Section 4.7.3.2). Thus, the two methods can be made to perform approximately the same number of distance computations when obtaining a given number of coordinate axes. Using this technique, the embedding produced by SparseMap was of a higher quality than that produced by

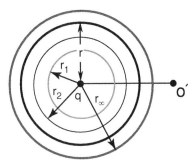

Figure 4.90
A hypothetical range query example where an object o′ is outside the distance range r from the query object q. The distance $d'(F(q), F(o'))$ from q to o′ in the embedding space will lie somewhere on the line between q and o′. Thus, this distance may lie inside the query range if d' is based on L_1 or L_2 but outside it if d' is based on L_∞.

FastMap in terms of stress and how well clusters are retained by the embedding using CPR [886], especially for a small number of coordinate axes. In addition, SparseMap was found to scale up better than FastMap, in terms of the time to perform the mapping, as the pattern in which the database is accessed leads to fewer disk I/Os.

4.7.3 FastMap

In this section, we explain how the FastMap method works in some detail. Recall from the introduction to Section 4.7, that FastMap was inspired by dimension reduction methods for Euclidean space that are based on linear transformations such as KLT (and the equivalent PCA and SVD) while also being applicable to arbitrary metric spaces. As we will see, FastMap is most useful for query processing when both d and d' are the Euclidean distance metric (i.e., the original objects are points in a multidimensional space) since these are the only cases in which satisfaction of the pruning property is guaranteed. This is primarily a result of the fact that many of the derivations used in the development of FastMap make an implicit assumption that d is the Euclidean distance metric in a vector space of varying dimensionality. Nevertheless, FastMap can be applied, with varying success, with other distance metrics as well as with data from an arbitrary metric space (i.e., the only information about the data objects consists of the interobject distances). However, in such cases, often some key aspects such as the pruning property will not necessarily hold; nor will we always be able to obtain as many as k coordinate axes. Similarly, due to the nature of the FastMap method, the best result is obtained when d', the distance function in the embedding space, is the Euclidean distance metric. Thus, unless otherwise stated, we assume d' to be the Euclidean distance metric.

This section is organized as follows. Section 4.7.3.1 gives an overview of the basic mechanics of the FastMap method. Section 4.7.3.2 describes how to obtain the pivot objects. Section 4.7.3.3 shows how to derive the first coordinate value. Section 4.7.3.4 indicates how to calculate the projected distance. Section 4.7.3.5 shows how to derive the remaining coordinate values. Section 4.7.3.6 discusses in great detail when the pruning property is satisfied. Section 4.7.3.7 points out the extent of the deviation of the distance in the embedding space from that in the original space (termed *expansion*). Section 4.7.3.8 discusses a heuristic that has been proposed to deal with the case that the projected distance is complex valued. Section 4.7.3.9 summarizes the properties of FastMap and the Lipschitz embeddings described in Section 4.7.2, while also briefly comparing FastMap with some other embeddings such as MetricMap [1950].

4.7.3.1 Mechanics of FastMap

The FastMap method works by imagining that the objects are points in a hypothetical high-dimensional Euclidean space of unknown dimension—that is, a vector space with the Euclidean distance metric. However, the various implications of this Euclidean space assumption are not explored by Faloutsos and Lin [587]. In the sequel, the terminology reflects the assumption that the objects are points (e.g., a line can be defined by two objects). The coordinate values corresponding to these points are obtained by projecting them onto k mutually orthogonal directions, thereby forming the coordinate axes of the space in which the points are embedded. The projections are computed using the given distance function d. The coordinate axes are constructed one by one, where at each iteration two objects (termed *pivot objects*) are chosen, a line is drawn between them that serves as the coordinate axis, and the coordinate value along this axis for each object o is determined by mapping (i.e., projecting) o onto this line.

Assume, without loss of generality, that the objects are actually points (this makes it easier to draw the examples that we use in our explanation) and that they lie in an m-dimensional space. We prepare for the next iteration by determining the $(m-1)$-dimensional hyperplane H perpendicular to the line that forms the previous coordinate axis and projecting all of the objects onto H. The projection is performed by defining

solving the following equation for x_a:

$$d(r,a)^2 - x_a^2 = d(s,a)^2 - (d(r,s) - x_a)^2 \tag{4.22}$$

Expanding terms in Equation 4.22 and rearranging yields

$$x_a = \frac{d(r,a)^2 + d(r,s)^2 - d(s,a)^2}{2d(r,s)} \tag{4.23}$$

Observe that Equation 4.22 is obtained by applying the Pythagorean theorem to each half of the triangle in Figure 4.92(a) (a similar interpretation applies to the case in Figure 4.92(b)). Since the Pythagorean theorem is specific to Euclidean space, here we have an instance where Faloutsos and Lin [587], in their development of the method, make the implicit assumption that d is the Euclidean distance metric. Thus, the equation is only a heuristic when used for general metric spaces. The implications of the use of this heuristic are explored in Section 4.7.3.6. In particular, we find that in this case the embedding produced by FastMap might not satisfy the pruning property, and this may cause the mapping process to terminate prematurely.

A number of observations can be made about x_a, based on Equation 4.23 and the selection of pivot objects. First, $x_r = 0$ and $x_s = d(r,s)$, as would be expected. Second, note that $|x_a| \leq d(r,s)$ (see Exercise 1). This implies that the maximum difference between two values x_a and x_b (i.e., the spread for the first coordinate axis as defined earlier) is $2d(r,s)$, which is equal to the maximum possible distance between any pair of objects, as shown in Section 4.7.3.2. In fact, it can be shown that the spread is never larger than the distance between the farthest pair of objects (see Exercise 2). Since the spread is at least $d(r,s)$ when r and s serve as the pivot objects (as $x_r = 0$ and $x_s = d(r,s)$), this implies that the spread obtained from pivots r and s is at least half of the maximum obtainable spread, which is $2d(r,s)$. Unfortunately, as we show in Section 4.7.3.6, it is possible that the distance functions used in subsequent iterations of FastMap do not satisfy the triangle inequality if d is not the Euclidean distance metric. Thus, the above bounds may not hold when determining the subsequent coordinate values. Note that Equation 4.23 is also used in BoostMap as one of two possible weakly proximity preserving mappings (see the preamble to Section 4.7).

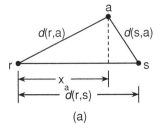

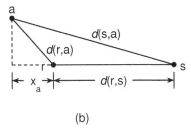

Figure 4.92
Examples of two possible positions for the projection of an object on the line joining the points corresponding to the pivot objects.

Exercises

1. Prove that $|x_a| \leq d(r,s)$ for any distance metric d, where x_a is the first coordinate value of a as defined in Equation 4.23 for pivot objects r and s (see Figure 4.92).

2. Let t and u be the two objects that are farthest apart of all the objects in S. Prove that for any distance metric d the spread (i.e., $\max_{a,b} |x_a - x_b|$ for any objects a and b) is never more than $d(t,u)$ for any choice of pivot objects.

4.7.3.4 Projected Distance

Before we can determine the second coordinate value for each object, we must derive d_H, the distance function for the distances between objects when projected onto the hyperplane H, as mentioned in Section 4.7.3.1. Figure 4.91(b) illustrates how the objects are projected onto the hyperplane H, and how the projected objects are used to determine the second coordinate axis. For expository purposes, assume that the underlying space is three-dimensional. In this case, points A and B are the projections of objects t and u, respectively, on the first coordinate axis (formed by the line joining the pivot objects r and s) with a separation of $|x_t - x_u|$. Points t' and u' are the projections of objects t and u, respectively, on the plane H that is perpendicular to the line between r and s that forms the first coordinate axis. Point C is the projection of u onto the line through t and t' parallel to the line through r and s. Thus, the distance between t' and u' equals the distance between C and u. The latter can be determined by applying the Pythagorean theorem since the angle at C in the triangle tuC is 90°. Therefore, we have

$$d(t,u)^2 = d(t,C)^2 + d(C,u)^2 = (x_t - x_u)^2 + d(t',u')^2 \qquad (4.24)$$

Thus, defining $d_H(t,u) = d(t',u')$ and changing the order of the terms, we obtain

$$d_H(t,u)^2 = d(t,u)^2 - (x_t - x_u)^2 \qquad (4.25)$$

Note that Equation 4.25 applies to any pair of objects t and u and not just to the ones that serve as pivots in the next iteration, as is the case in Figure 4.91(b). Also, note that Faloutsos and Lin [587] use the notation $d_H(t',u')$ rather than $d_H(t,u)$.

Observe that this is another occasion where Faloutsos and Lin [587], in their development of the method, make the implicit assumption that d is the Euclidean distance metric (or that (S,d) is isometric to a subset of some Euclidean space). This assumption has some undesirable side effects. For example, as we show in Section 4.7.3.6, if d is not a Euclidean distance metric, then it is possible for d_H to fail to satisfy the triangle inequality, which in turn may cause Equation 4.23 to produce coordinate values that violate the pruning property. Furthermore, violation of the pruning property in earlier iterations of FastMap may cause negative values of $d_H(a,b)^2$. This complicates the search for pivot objects as the square root of a negative value is a complex number, which in this case means that a and b (or, more precisely, their projections) cannot serve as pivot objects.

4.7.3.5 Subsequent Iterations

Each time we recursively invoke the FastMap coordinate determination method, we must determine the distance function d_H for the current set of projections in terms of the current distance function (i.e., the one that was created in the previous recursive invocation). Thus, the original distance function d is used only when obtaining the first coordinate axis. In subsequent iterations, d is the distance function d_H from the previous iteration. At this point, it is instructive to generalize Equations 4.23 and 4.25 to yield a recursive definition of the distance functions and the resulting coordinate values for each object. Before we do so, we must define a number of symbols, each representing the ith iteration of FastMap. In particular, x_o^i is the ith coordinate value obtained for object o, $F_i(o) = \{x_o^1, x_o^2, \ldots, x_o^i\}$ denotes the first i coordinate values of $F(o)$, d_i is the distance function used in the ith iteration, and p_1^i and p_2^i denote the two pivot objects chosen in iteration i (with the understanding that p_2^i is the farthest object from p_1^i). Now, the general form of Equation 4.23 for iteration i is

$$x_o^i = \frac{d_i(p_1^i,o)^2 + d_i(p_1^i,p_2^i)^2 - d_i(p_2^i,o)^2}{2d_i(p_1^i,p_2^i)} \qquad (4.26)$$

given the recursive distance function definition

$$d_1(a,b) = d(a,b) \qquad (4.27)$$
$$d_i(a,b)^2 = d_{i-1}(a,b)^2 - (x_a^{i-1} - x_b^{i-1})^2$$
$$= d(a,b)^2 - d_E(F_{i-1}(a), F_{i-1}(b))^2$$

As an example consider again Figure 4.88, which shows the interobject distances between 10 objects that were constructed by positioning 10 two-dimensional points and measuring the L_1 distance between them. We now show how FastMap obtains two-dimensional coordinate values for the objects. Seeing that the largest distance in the table is that between o_1 and o_3, we choose these objects as pivots. The result is shown as the first dimension in Figure 4.93 (i.e., in the first row), where the values are given to a precision of one fractional digit. In order to see how these values are determined, we derive the first coordinate value of o_5:

Coordinate	o_1	o_2	o_3	o_4	o_5	o_6	o_7	o_8	o_9	o_{10}
First	0.0	2.0	13.0	7.0	3.0	5.8	10.5	4.0	8.2	10.0
Second	4.4	1.0	4.4	8.5	3.7	9.7	0.7	0.0	10.2	2.8

Figure 4.93
Two-dimensional coordinate values for the 10 objects based on the distances in Figure 4.88, as determined by FastMap using o_1 and o_3 as pivot objects for the first coordinate axis and o_8 and o_9 for the second coordinate axis.

Object	o_1	o_2	o_3	o_4	o_5	o_6	o_7	o_8	o_9	o_{10}
o_1	0.0	0.0	0.0	0.0	0.0	29.8	9.9	0.0	13.3	0.0
o_2	0.0	0.0	0.0	56.0	8.0	85.2	8.1	0.0	82.2	0.0
o_3	0.0	0.0	0.0	0.0	0.0	29.8	9.9	0.0	13.3	0.0
o_4	0.0	56.0	0.0	0.0	20.0	7.7	51.5	72.0	2.5	16.0
o_5	0.0	8.0	0.0	20.0	0.0	40.9	7.2	8.0	36.6	0.0
o_6	29.8	85.2	29.8	7.7	40.9	0.0	59.0	96.6	3.3	18.7
o_7	9.9	8.1	9.9	51.5	7.2	59.0	0.0	6.2	94.7	8.7
o_8	0.0	0.0	0.0	72.0	8.0	96.6	6.2	0.0	103.1	0.0
o_9	13.3	82.2	13.3	2.5	36.6	3.3	94.7	103.1	0.0	45.9
o_{10}	0.0	0.0	0.0	16.0	0.0	18.7	8.7	0.0	45.9	0.0

Figure 4.94
Distances of the 10 sample objects as determined by the first projected distance function, d_H. The values in the table are actually the squared distances, $d_H(o_i, o_j)^2$.

$$\frac{d(o_1, o_5)^2 + d(o_1, o_3)^2 - d(o_3, o_5)^2}{2d o_1, o_3)} = \frac{3^2 + 13^2 - 10^2}{2 \cdot 13} = 78/26 = 3$$

Figure 4.94 shows the (squared) projected distances $d_H(o_i, o_j)^2$ for the 10 objects obtained by projecting them on the hyperplane H perpendicular to the line through the pivot objects o_1 and o_3. Again, the distance values are given to a precision of only one fractional digit. As an example of how these distance values are computed, we derive $d_H(o_5, o_6)^2$ with the help of Figure 4.93:

$$d_H(o_5, o_6)^2 = d(o_5, o_6)^2 - |x_5 - x_6|^2 \approx 7^2 - |3 - 5.8|^2 = 49 - 2.8^2 \approx 41.2$$

This value does not exactly match the value $d_H(o_5, o_6)^2 \approx 40.9$ found in Figure 4.94 due to roundoff error.

The largest distance value is $d_H(o_8, o_9)^2 \approx 103.1$, so the objects o_8 and o_9 (or, more precisely, their projected versions) get chosen as the second pair of pivot objects used to determine the values along the second dimension, as given in Figure 4.93. Again, let us show how the coordinate value for o_5 is determined, this time along the second coordinate axis:

$$\frac{d_H(o_8, o_5)^2 + d_H(o_8, o_9)^2 - d_H(o_9, o_5)^2}{2d_H(o_8, o_9)} \approx \frac{8 + 103.1 - 36.6}{2\sqrt{103.1}} \approx 74.5/20.3 \approx 3.7$$

The process of mapping the N objects to points in a k-dimensional space makes $O(k \cdot N)$ distance computations as there are $O(N)$ distance calculations at each of k iterations. It requires $O(k \cdot N)$ space to record the k coordinate values of each of the points corresponding to the N objects. It also requires a $2 \times k$ array to record the identities of the k pairs of pivot objects as this information is needed to process queries. Note that query objects are transformed to k-dimensional points by applying the same algorithm that was used to construct the points corresponding to the original objects, except that we use the existing pivot objects. In other words, given query object q, we obtain its k-dimensional coordinate values by projecting q onto the lines formed by the corresponding pivot objects using the appropriate distance function. This process is facilitated by recording the distance between the points corresponding to the pivot objects so that it need not be recomputed for each query, although this can be done if we do not want to store these distance values. The entire process of obtaining the k-dimensional point corresponding to the query object takes $O(k)$ distance computations (which is actually $O(1)$ if we assume that k is a constant), in contrast to the size of the database, which is $O(N)$.

Exercises

1. Show that the total number of distance computations performed by FastMap is $kP(N-1)$, assuming P iterations in the pivot-finding heuristic.

2. Prove that at least $k+1$ of the pivot objects in the process of constructing a point in k-dimensional space in the FastMap method are different, assuming that it is indeed possible to apply k iterations of FastMap.

3. Given N objects and a distance function that indicates the interobject distances, implement the FastMap algorithm to find the corresponding set of N points in a k-dimensional space.

4. Given N objects, a distance function that indicates the interobject distances query object q, and a set of N points in a k-dimensional space that have been obtained via the use of the FastMap algorithm, give an algorithm to find the point in the k-dimensional space corresponding to q.

4.7.3.6 Pruning Property

The embedding F produced by FastMap satisfies the pruning property when (S,d) is a subset of a Euclidean space (or isometric to such a subset). This is not surprising since key aspects of FastMap are based on a property unique to Euclidean spaces, namely, the Pythagorean theorem. In particular, both Equation 4.23, which computes a single coordinate value, and Equation 4.25, which computes the projected distance d_H used in the next iteration, are based on the Pythagorean theorem. Equivalently, FastMap can be seen to be based on the Euclidean distance metric's property of being invariant to rotation and translation. Below, we present an intuitive argument for the satisfaction of the pruning property by FastMap and show that total distance preservation can be achieved.

For (S,d_E), where $S \subset \mathbb{R}^m$ and d_E is the Euclidean distance metric, an iteration of FastMap essentially amounts to performing a rotation and a translation, followed by extracting the value of a coordinate axis. This is depicted in Figure 4.95 for pivot objects r and s. Notice that x_a for object $a \in S$ is simply the coordinate value along the new axis x′ since the Euclidean distance metric is invariant to rotation and translation. Furthermore, $d_H(a,b)$ as defined by Equation 4.25 can be shown to be equivalent to the Euclidean distance between the projections of a and b onto the hyperplane H. In general, we can show that $d_i(a,b) = d_E(a_i,b_i)$ for $a,b \in S$, where d_i is defined by Equation 4.27, and a_i and b_i are the projections of objects a and b, respectively, onto the intersection of the $i-1$ hyperplanes obtained in iterations 1 through $i-1$. Thus, we can obtain coordinate axis i by rotating and translating along the $(m-i+1)$-dimensional hyperplane formed by the intersection of these $i-1$ hyperplanes. After k iterations, Equation 4.27 yields $d_{k+1}(a,b)^2 = d_E(a_{k+1},b_{k+1})^2 = d_E(a,b)^2 - d'_E(F(a),F(b))^2$, where d'_E is the Euclidean distance metric for $\mathbb{R}^k$. Thus, since $d_E(a_{k+1},b_{k+1})^2 \geq 0$, we have $d_E(a,b)^2 - d'_E(F(a),F(b))^2 \geq 0$, which directly implies $d_E(a,b) \geq d'_E(F(a),F(b))$. In other words, F satisfies the pruning property.

We can also show that with enough iterations, F will preserve the distances between all objects. In particular, observe that projecting on an $(m-1)$-dimensional hyperplane in each iteration reduces the number of points by at least one since the two pivot points get projected to the same point. In other words, if S_i is the set of points obtained by projecting on the hyperplanes in iterations 1 through $i-1$, then $|S_i| \leq |S| - (i-1)$

(as each iteration reduces the number of points by one). Thus, since $|S_{k+1}| \geq 1$, this implies that $1 \leq N - k$ or $k \leq N - 1$, where $N = |S|$. Furthermore, when $k = m$, S_{k+1} is the result of projecting S onto a 0-dimensional hyperplane (i.e., a point), so $k \leq m$. In summary, after at most $\min\{m, N - 1\}$ iterations, all the points get projected to the same point. Therefore, $d_E(a_{k+1}, b_{k+1})$ is then zero for all objects $a, b \in S$, so $d_E(a, b) = d'_E(F(a), F(b))$, implying that total distance preservation is obtained.

Above, we saw that applying FastMap is essentially equivalent to applying a linear transformation involving translation and rotation and then retaining only some of the coordinate axes. Thus, FastMap works in a manner analogous to applying KLT (and the equivalent PCA and SVD) for dimension reduction as described in Section 4.6.4.1. However, we can expect that applying KLT (and the equivalent PCA and SVD) will yield a better approximation to the original distances as the coordinate axes with the greatest variance are the ones that are retained.

We also saw that the distances between all objects are preserved if $|S_{k+1}| = 1$ since all objects in S are then projected onto a single point in S_{k+1}. An interesting perspective is that even if F does not preserve all distances, F will still preserve the distances between some of the objects. In particular, the distances between any objects a and b that are projected onto the same point in S_{k+1} are preserved by the embedding since $d_{k+1}(a, b)$ is then zero. In fact, we can form equivalence classes for the objects based on the points in S_i such that objects mapped to the same point in S_i belong to the same equivalence class. Thus, the set of objects is partitioned into $|S_{k+1}| \leq N - k$ equivalence classes after k iterations of FastMap.

Figure 4.96 illustrates how FastMap maps objects a and b after having determined just one coordinate value, assuming that r and s are the pivot objects. Notice how it seems intuitively obvious that the distance between F(a) and F(b) is smaller than that between a and b. Unfortunately, intuition is misleading here as it is colored by the fact that we perceive the three-dimensional world around us as obeying Euclidean geometry. In particular, the relative lengths of the line segments between the points in Figure 4.96 can arise only if d is the Euclidean distance metric (or if (S, d) is isometric to a subset of a Euclidean vector space). Thus, we see that in the figure, $d(a, b)^2 = (x_a - x_b)^2 + D^2$ (according to the Pythagorean theorem), so we clearly have $d(a, b) \geq |x_a - x_b|$ (and thus the pruning property is satisfied). In general, we cannot assume that this relationship holds (i.e., D^2 may be negative!).

The pruning property is guaranteed to hold only when (S, d) is a subset of a Euclidean space, and d' is the Euclidean distance metric. There are two general scenarios where the pruning property is not guaranteed to hold. The first is when d is the Euclidean distance metric, and d' is a non-Euclidean distance metric. The second is when d is not the Euclidean distance metric (and (S, d) is not isometric to a subset of a Euclidean vector space), regardless of the nature of d', and is due to the implicit assumption in Equations 4.23 and 4.25 that d is the Euclidean distance metric.

An example of the first scenario occurs when the City Block (L_1) distance metric d_A is used for d'. To illustrate this, note that the City Block distance $d_A(F(1), F(2))$ between two points $F(1)$ and $F(2)$ may be greater than the Euclidean (L_2) distance $d_E(F(1), F(2))$ between the same points. For example, $d_A((0, 0), (3, 4)) = 7$ while $d_E((0, 0), (3, 4)) = 5$. Thus, we may have $d_A(F(a), F(b)) > d(a, b)$, even though $d_E(F(a), F(b)) \leq d(a, b)$, where $F(a)$ and $F(b)$ are the result of mapping a and b with FastMap. In fact, the pruning property is guaranteed to hold only if d' is the Euclidean distance metric (i.e., L_2) or some other Minkowski distance metric L_p, where $p \geq 2$ (see Exercise 1).

The second, and more serious, scenario where the pruning property does not hold occurs when d is not a Euclidean metric, regardless of the choice of d'. This is serious because the pruning property may be violated after determining any number of coordinate axes. In particular, this means that the value of $d_i(a, b)^2$ in Equation 4.27 can be negative (or zero) for any $i \geq 2$, which precludes using a and b as the pivot pair in iteration i of

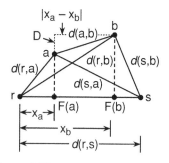

Figure 4.96
Example projection of two objects on the line joining the points corresponding to the pivot objects.

Object	a	b	c	e
a	0	10	4	5
b	10	0	8	7
c	4	8	0	1
e	5	7	1	0

Figure 4.97
Distance matrix for an example where Equation 4.23 causes the pruning property to be violated.

FastMap. Thus, the situation can arise that $d_i(a,b)^2 \leq 0$ for all pairs of objects a and b, in which case no more coordinate values can be determined (but see Section 4.7.3.8).

There are two possible causes for the violation of the pruning property. Equation 4.23 and Equation 4.25. Both are due to the implicit assumption made in deriving these equations that the Pythagorean theorem applies to the distance metric d. However, the Pythagorean theorem is unique to Euclidean spaces. As an example where Equation 4.23 causes the pruning property to be violated, consider objects a, b, c, and e, with the distance matrix given in Figure 4.97, for which satisfaction of the triangle inequality can be easily verified.

Since a and b are the objects that are the farthest apart, they are selected as the pivot objects in FastMap when determining the first coordinate axis. Following Equation 4.23, the values of the first coordinate of the points derived from objects c and e are as follows:

$$x_c = (4^2 + 10^2 - 8^2)/(2 \cdot 10) = 52/20 = 13/5$$

$$x_e = (5^2 + 10^2 - 7^2)/(2 \cdot 10) = 76/20 = 19/5$$

Thus, the distance between these one-dimensional points corresponding to objects c and e used in the first iteration of FastMap is $x_e - x_c = 6/5 = 1.2$, which is higher than the original distance between them, obtained from the distance matrix, which is 1. Thus the pruning property does not hold for c and e.

The pruning property is not directly, but indirectly, violated by Equation 4.25. In particular, if d is not a Euclidean distance metric, then Equation 4.25 may lead to a definition of d_H such that d_H does not satisfy the triangle inequality (thereby also failing to be a distance metric), and this, in turn, causes the pruning property to be violated in the next iteration of FastMap. We first show how the violation of the triangle inequality causes the pruning property to be violated.

Assuming that r and s are the pivot objects, the pruning property is violated if $d(r,a) < |x_r - x_a| = x_a$ (since $x_r = 0$). Now, let us explore what conditions are equivalent to $d(r,a) < x_a$, and thus give rise to a pruning property violation.

$$d(r,a) < x_a \Leftrightarrow d(r,a) < \frac{d(r,a)^2 + d(r,s)^2 - d(s,a)^2}{2d(r,s)}$$

$$\Leftrightarrow 2d(r,a)d(r,s) < d(r,a)^2 + d(r,s)^2 - d(s,a)^2$$

$$\Leftrightarrow d(s,a)^2 < d(r,a)^2 - 2d(r,a)d(r,s) + d(r,s)^2 = (d(r,a) - d(r,s))^2$$

$$\Leftrightarrow d(s,a) < |(d(r,a) - d(r,s))|$$

$$\Leftrightarrow d(s,a) + d(r,a) < d(r,s) \lor d(s,a) + d(r,s) < d(r,a)$$

Similarly, it can be shown that $d(s,a) < |x_s - x_a|$ if and only if $d(r,a) + d(s,a) < d(r,s) \lor d(r,s) + d(r,a) < d(s,a)$. Thus, we see that the pruning property is violated (for $d(r,a)$, $d(s,a)$, or both) if and only if the triangle inequality is violated for any of the distances between the two pivot objects r and s and an arbitrary object a.

Object	a	b	c	e
a	0	6	5	4
b	6	0	3	4
c	5	3	0	6
e	4	4	6	0

Figure 4.98
Distance matrix for an example where Equation 4.25 indirectly causes the pruning property to be violated.

Next, we give an example that actually results in d_H failing to satisfy the triangle inequality (thereby, also failing to be a distance metric). Consider objects a, b, c, and e, with the distance matrix given in Figure 4.98, for which satisfaction of the triangle inequality can be easily verified.

Following Equation 4.23, the values of the first coordinate of the points derived from c and e using a and b as the pivot objects are obtained as follows:

$$x_c = (5^2 + 6^2 - 3^2)/(2 \cdot 6) = 13/3$$

$$x_e = (4^2 + 6^2 - 4^2)/(2 \cdot 6) = 3$$

The distances between the projections of a, c, and e onto the hyperplane H that is orthogonal to the first coordinate axis follow from Equation 4.25:

$$d_H(a, c) = \sqrt{5^2 - (0 - 13/3)^2} \approx 2.494$$

$$d_H(a, e) = \sqrt{4^2 - (0 - 3)^2} \approx 2.647$$

$$d_H(c, e) = \sqrt{6^2 - (13/3 - 3)^2} \approx 5.850$$

Thus, we see that $d_H(a, c) + d_H(a, e) \approx 5.141$, which is less than $d_H(c, e)$, thereby violating the triangle inequality.

Thus far, we have examined the source of violation of the pruning property in FastMap and given examples where FastMap results in an embedding that does not satisfy the pruning property. This enables us to conclude that the embedding produced by FastMap may fail to satisfy the pruning property when d is not a Euclidean distance metric. It is possible to make an even stronger statement: if d is not a Euclidean distance metric, then FastMap will eventually result in an embedding that does not satisfy the pruning property if enough iterations are performed. Toward proving this, we first show that only a finite number of iterations can be applied in FastMap. At the start of this section, we used geometric arguments to show that when d is the Euclidean distance metric, the pivot objects used in an iteration of FastMap are effectively merged and are thereby indistinguishable in subsequent iterations. This is also true for arbitrary metric spaces. In particular, if r and s are pivot objects in iteration $i - 1$ of FastMap, it can be shown that $d_i(r, s) = 0$ and $d_i(r, t) = d_i(s, t)$ for an arbitrary object t, regardless of whether d_{i-1} satisfies the triangle inequality (see Exercise 2). Thus, r and s will have identical coordinate values for coordinate axes i through k. Furthermore, we can show that when the distances of any two objects r and s satisfy the distance property above (i.e., $d_i(r, s) = 0$ and $d_i(r, t) = d_i(s, t)$), then the distance between r and s is preserved by FastMap (see Exercise 3).

Based on this, we argue below that if (S, d) is a finite metric space that is not isometric to a subset of any Euclidean space, then repeated iterations of FastMap (i.e., k) will eventually result in a mapping F that violates the pruning property. We will show that $k < N - 1$. In particular, since (S, d) is not isometric to a subset of any Euclidean space, we know that no distance-preserving Euclidean embedding exists for (S, d). Thus, such an embedding cannot be produced by FastMap either. Also, note that $d_E(F_i(a), F_i(b))$ is nondecreasing in i for any objects $a, b \in S$. Therefore, the only way in which FastMap can be applied repeatedly without ever resulting in $d_E(F_i(a), F_i(b)) > d(a, b)$, for some objects a and b, is if an infinite series of iterations can be performed. Below, we show that at most $N - 2$ iterations can be performed by FastMap and that the final iteration necessarily will result in an embedding that does not satisfy the pruning property. In the process, we characterize the level of distance preservation among the objects obtained by the embedding.

The above observations can be used to define equivalence classes for data objects whose distances are preserved (in a similar way as we mentioned for Euclidean vector spaces). In particular, we say that two objects r and s (not necessarily pivot objects) belong to the same equivalence class in iteration i if $d_i(r, s) = 0$ and $d_i(r, t) = d_i(s, t)$ for all objects $t \in S$. Initially, each object belongs to a distinct equivalence class (except for objects having a distance of zero from each other). Furthermore, the fact that pivot objects become indistinguishable in the remaining iterations ensures that each iteration of FastMap causes the merger of at least two equivalence classes, namely, the ones containing the two pivot objects. Thus, the number of equivalence classes after i iterations is clearly at most $N - i$, as we initially have at most N equivalence classes and each iteration reduces the number of equivalence classes by at least one.

Since a distance-preserving embedding does not exist for (S, d), at least two equivalence classes must remain after the performance of the last iteration of FastMap (as the existence of just one equivalence class means that the embedding is distance preserving). Hence, the number of iterations k must satisfy $N - k \geq 2$, or $k \leq N - 2$. Furthermore, if no more iterations can be performed, then we must have $d_{k+1}(a, b)^2 < 0$ for any objects a and b from distinct equivalence classes since a and b could otherwise be chosen as the next pair of pivot objects, thereby allowing yet another iteration. However, Equation 4.27 then implies that $d(a, b)^2 - d_E(F_k(a), F_k(b))^2 < 0$, or, in other words, $d(a, b) < d_E(F(a), F(b))$, since $F = F_k$. Therefore, we have shown that F does not satisfy the pruning property (as $d' = d_E$). Moreover, since F was chosen in an arbitrary way (i.e., we made no assumption on the choices of pivot objects), we have shown that such a noncontractive embedding is always produced by FastMap, given enough iterations.

Exercises

1. Letting (S, d) be a subset of a Euclidean vector space and d' be some Minkowski distance metric L_p, prove that the embedding F produced by FastMap is guaranteed to satisfy the pruning property only if $p \geq 2$.

2. Letting r and s be the pivot objects in iteration $i - 1$ of FastMap, show that $d_i(r, s) = 0$ and $d_i(r, t) = d_i(s, t)$ for an arbitrary object t, regardless of whether d_{i-1} satisfies the triangle inequality.

3. Let r and s be data objects, not necessarily pivot objects. Show that if $d_i(r, s) = 0$ and $d_i(r, t) = d_i(s, t)$ for all objects t after $i - 1$ iterations of FastMap, then $d'(F(r), F(s)) = d(r, s)$ where F is the final embedding produced after k iterations of FastMap. In other words, show that the distance between r and s is preserved by F.

4.7.3.7 Expansion

Satisfaction of the pruning property means that $d'(F(o_1), F(o_2)) \leq d(o_1, o_2)$. We are also interested in how much larger the distances in the embedding space can be in comparison to the original distances. This is termed the *expansion* of F and is defined as

$$\max_{o_1, o_2} \left\{ \frac{d'(F(o_1), F(o_2))}{d(o_1, o_2)} \right\}$$

Note that if the expansion is not greater than 1, then F satisfies the pruning property. Furthermore, if we can derive an upper bound c on the expansion, then any embedding F

produced by FastMap can be made to satisfy the pruning property by defining $d'(o_1, o_2) = d_E(F(o_1), F(o_2))/c$ such that the expansion with respect to this d' is no more than 1. Unfortunately, the expansion of embeddings produced by FastMap when determining even just one coordinate is already relatively large (i.e., 3; see Exercise 1) [850], and for additional coordinates the expansion can be very large (see Exercise 2) [850].

Exercises

1. Prove that the expansion after determining one coordinate with FastMap is at most 3 and that this bound is tight.

2. As we saw in Section 4.7.3.6, the triangle inequality does not necessarily hold for the distance functions used in the second and subsequent iterations of FastMap. This means that the upper bound on the expansion derived in Exercise 1 holds only for the first coordinate value obtained by FastMap. The basic problem is that for iteration $i > 1$, the value of $d_i(r, s)^2$, as defined in Equation 4.27, may be less than or equal to zero for all objects s, even after several iterations of the pivot-finding heuristic (see Section 4.7.3.2). Moreover, even when $d_i(r, s)^2$ is found to be strictly positive, it can be arbitrarily close to zero, thereby yielding an arbitrarily large expansion. One solution is to set a strict lower bound on the distance between the pivot objects, based on the distance between the first pair of pivot objects. In other words, if r and s are the first two pivot objects, then any pivot objects t and u chosen in any subsequent iteration i must obey $d_i(t, u) \geq d(r, s)/\beta$, where $\beta > 1$ is some constant. Unfortunately, this requirement means that the pivot-finding heuristic may no longer succeed in finding a legal pair of pivots in a constant number of iterations, and the number of distance computations may become $O(N^2)$. An alternative solution is to terminate FastMap if a legal pivot pair is not found in $O(1)$ iterations of the pivot-finding process (see Section 4.7.3.2). This means that we may obtain fewer coordinate axes than desired. However, this is usually not a problem as a low number of coordinate axes is preferable in most applications. Nevertheless, it is still not clear that the original distances are adequately approximated in the embedding space in cases when legal pivots cannot be found in $O(N)$ distance computations. In any case, letting $d(r, s)/\beta$ ($\beta > 1$ is some constant) be the minimum distance value $d_2(t, u)$ for the pivot objects t and u used in the second iteration of FastMap (i.e., when finding the second coordinate value for each object), as well as for the distances between any two pairs of objects (using the original distance function), show that the expansion after determining two coordinates with FastMap is no more than $36\beta^2$.

4.7.3.8 Heuristic for Non-Euclidean Metrics

As we pointed out in Section 4.7.3.4, it is possible for the value $d_H(t, u)^2$ in Equation 4.25 to be negative when d is not a Euclidean distance metric. More generally, this implies that $d_i(a, b)^2$ may be negative for $i \geq 2$ in Equation 4.27. Such a situation is undesirable since it means that $d_i(a, b)$ becomes complex valued, which precludes the choice of a and b as the pair of pivot objects in iteration i of FastMap. Furthermore, since $d_i(a, b)^2$ can have a large negative value, such values can cause a large expansion in the distances between coordinate values determined by Equation 4.26, as discussed in Section 4.7.3.7.

Wang, Wang, Lin, Shasha, Shapiro, and Zhang [1950] introduce a heuristic to alleviate the situation that $d_i(a, b)^2$ may be negative for $i \geq 2$ in Equation 4.27. The heuristic defines $d_i(a, b)$ ($i \geq 2$) in such a way that it is always real valued but possibly negative:

$$d_i(a, b) = \begin{cases} \sqrt{d_{i-1}(a, b)^2 - (x_a^{i-1} - x_b^{i-1})^2} & \text{if } d_{i-1}(a, b)^2 \geq (x_a^{i-1} - x_b^{i-1})^2 \\ -\sqrt{(x_a^{i-1} - x_b^{i-1})^2 - d_{i-1}(a, b)^2} & \text{otherwise} \end{cases} \quad (4.28)$$

Equivalently, we can use the definition $d_i(a, b) = \text{sign}(d_i(a, b)^2) \cdot \sqrt{|d_i(a, b)^2|}$, where $d_i(a, b)^2$ is defined as in Equation 4.27. Although this heuristic apparently resolves the drawbacks of negative $d_i(a, b)^2$ values, it does not correct the fundamental problem with Equation 4.27, namely, that d_i may violate the triangle inequality if d is not the Euclidean distance metric (see the discussion in Section 4.7.3.6). Furthermore, notice that this formulation also means that if $d_i(a,b)$ is negative for some i, then $d_j(a,b)^2$ is not equal to $d(a,b)^2 - d_E(F_{j-1}(a), F_{j-1}(b))^2$ for all $j \geq i$.

Notice that when $d_i(a,b)$ is defined according to Equation 4.28, the value of $d_i(a,b)^2$ is always nonnegative, regardless of whether $d_i(a,b)$ is negative. Thus, in situations where Equation 4.27 leads to negative values, the coordinate value x_o^i for an object o as determined by Equation 4.26 can be different, depending on which definitions of d_i is used—that is, Equation 4.27 or 4.28. If we focus on the result of just one iteration of FastMap, neither definition of d_i is always better than the other in terms of how well distances are preserved. In particular, sometimes it is better to use Equation 4.27, and sometimes it is better to use Equation 4.28. However, the advantage of the definition in Equation 4.28 is that the value of $d_i(a,b)^2$ tends to decrease as i increases (i.e., as more iterations are performed). In particular, Equation 4.28 implies that $d_i(a,b)^2 = |d_{i-1}(a,b)^2 - (x_a^{i-1} - x_b^{i-1})^2|$, so $d_i(a,b)^2$ is only larger than $d_{i-1}(a,b)^2$ if $(x_a^{i-1} - x_b^{i-1})^2 > 2d_{i-1}(a,b)^2$. In contrast, according to Equation 4.27, the value of $d_i(a,b)^2$ is monotonically nonincreasing in i, so it can become a large negative value, which makes the mapping not very attractive in similarity searching applications as it results in a large expansion with concomitant adverse effects on search performance (see Section 4.7.3.7). Recall that any amount of expansion means that the distance in the embedding space becomes larger than the distance in the original space, thereby violating the pruning property (see Section 4.7.3.6).

The heuristic of Equation 4.28 enables the use of two objects a and b as a pivot pair even when $d_i(a,b)$ is negative. In contrast, such pairs cannot be utilized with Equation 4.27. However, it is not clear how appropriate such a choice of pivot objects is in terms of attempting to reduce the distance in the embedding space. In particular, the fact that $d_i(a,b)$ is negative implies that the distance between $F_{i-1}(a)$ and $F_{i-1}(b)$ is greater than $d(a,b)$, so using a and b as pivot objects further increases the amount by which the distance in the embedding space exceeds the distance in the original space (i.e., expansion).

In Section 4.7.3.6, we show that FastMap eventually results in an embedding that does not satisfy the pruning property if enough iterations are performed. This result still holds when the heuristic of Equation 4.28 is used. In particular, Equation 4.28, which defines the computation of the intermediate distance functions, is equivalent to Equation 4.27 unless the intermediate mapping F_{i-1} obtained in iteration $i-1$ already violates the pruning property. To see why they are otherwise equivalent, note that if i is the lowest value for which $d_{i-1}(a,b)^2 < (x_a^{i-1} - x_b^{i-1})^2$ for some objects a and b (thereby causing the invocation of the second case in Equation 4.28), then we can apply Equation 4.27 to show that $d(a,b)^2 < d_E(F_{i-1}(a), F_{i-1}(b))^2$ (i.e., F_{i-1} violates the pruning property). Furthermore, when F_{i-1} violates the pruning property, the final mapping F also violates the pruning property as $d_E(F_l(a), F_l(b))$ is monotonically nondecreasing in i (since, as we add coordinate axes, the distance can only get larger).

It is interesting to observe that the largest possible expansion when determining just one coordinate value is just as large with the heuristic as without (i.e., 3, as mentioned in Section 4.7.3.7). Nevertheless, for a larger number of coordinates, use of the heuristic may reduce the worst-case expansion somewhat, but it can still be large (e.g., 7 when determining two coordinate values) [850].

4.7.3.9 Summary and Comparison with Other Embeddings

In this section and in Section 4.7.2, we examine the embeddings of finite metric spaces and evaluate them in the context of their usage for similarity searching in multimedia databases with 100% recall. In similarity search, achieving 100% recall is important as it ensures that no relevant object is dropped from the query response. Particular attention has been paid to Lipschitz embeddings (as exemplified by SparseMap) and FastMap, which was inspired by dimension reduction methods for Euclidean space that are based on linear transformations such as KLT (and the equivalent PCA and SVD), while also being applicable to arbitrary metric spaces. When the resulting embedding satisfies the pruning property, 100% recall is achieved. Although Linial et al. [1181] have shown how to make the Lipschitz embeddings satisfy the pruning property, we prove that the speedup heuristics that make up the SparseMap adaptation result in an embedding that does not satisfy the pruning property. Moreover, we demonstrate how to modify the SparseMap heuristics so that the resulting embedding does indeed satisfy the pruning property.

In the case of FastMap, we first prove that it satisfies the pruning property when the data is drawn from a Euclidean vector space, and the distance metric in the embedding space is a Minkowski metric L_p ($p \geq 2$, which also includes the Euclidean distance metric). In their development of FastMap, Faloutsos and Lin [587] claim two advantages for FastMap over SVD:

1. SVD takes $O(N \cdot n^2)$ time while FastMap requires $O(N \cdot k)$ distance computations, each of which is $O(n)$, assuming that the data is drawn from an n-dimensional Euclidean vector space. Thus, a more accurate assessment of the execution time complexity of FastMap is $O(Nnk)$ in this setting.

2. FastMap can work for data drawn from an arbitrary metric space (i.e., the only information about the data objects consists of the interobject distances, which are required to satisfy the triangle inequality). SVD, on the other hand, only works for data drawn from a Euclidean vector space (i.e., a vector space with the Euclidean distance metric). Of course, d' for both SVD and FastMap can be any Minkowski distance metric L_p provided $p \geq 2$, although $p = 2$ is usually the most appropriate.

However, we show that the second advantage is somewhat mixed since, in the arbitrary metric space case, it is possible for FastMap not to satisfy the pruning property, which reduces the accuracy of similarity search queries (i.e., we can no longer guarantee 100% recall). We show that this is a direct result of the implicit assumption by Faloutsos and Lin [587] of the applicability of the Pythagorean theorem, which, in the case of a general metric space, can be used only as a heuristic in computing the projected distance values. In fact, this leads to definitions of distance functions at intermediate iterations that do not satisfy the triangle inequality and, thereby, fail to be distance metrics. Failure to satisfy the pruning property enables us to prove the following properties of FastMap for this situation:

1. Given a value k, application of FastMap may not always be possible in the sense that we are not guaranteed to be able to determine k coordinate axes.

2. The distance expansion (as well as the more general concept of distortion) of the embedding can be very large, as evidenced by the bounds that we gave, some of which were attainable, on how much larger the distances in the embedding space can be.

3. The fact that we may not be able to determine k coordinate axes limits the extent of achievable distance preservation. However, more importantly, failure to determine more coordinate axes does not necessarily imply that relative distances among the objects are effectively preserved.

4. The presence of many nonpositive, or very small positive, distance values (which can cause large expansion) in the intermediate distance functions (i.e., those used to determine the second and subsequent coordinate axes) may cause FastMap no longer to satisfy the claimed $O(N)$ bound on the number of distance computations in each iteration. In particular, finding a legal pivot pair may, in the worst case, require examining the distances between a significant fraction of all possible pairs of objects, or $\Omega(N^2)$ distance computations.

In Section 4.7.3.8, we describe a heuristic for non-Euclidean distance metrics in FastMap proposed by Wang et al. [1950]. This heuristic alleviates some of the drawbacks listed above. In particular, it should reduce the amount of distance expansion (as well as distortion) in the embedding, and the number of object pairs that do not qualify as pivots should be lower, thus reducing the likelihood of not satisfying the $O(N)$ bound on the number of distance computations in each iteration of FastMap. However, a detailed empirical study of the effect of the heuristic on actual datasets remains to be performed.

Wang et al. [1950, 1955, 2045] propose an interesting embedding, termed *MetricMap*, that has some similarity to SVD, FastMap, and a special class of Lipschitz embeddings. In essence, given a finite metric space (S, d), $2k$ of the objects (termed *reference objects*) are selected at random and used to form a coordinate space in $\mathbb{R}^{2k-1}$. In particular, one of the reference objects o_0 is mapped to the origin, while the remaining objects O_i ($1 \leq i \leq 2k - 1$) are mapped to unit vectors e_i in $\mathbb{R}^{2k-1}$. The interobject distances of the reference objects are used to form a matrix M that serves as the basis of a distance measure that preserves the distances between the reference objects. Through a process that resembles SVD, the k "most important" coordinate axes determined by M are established, from which a suitable linear transformation is computed. The k coordinate values for each object in S are then obtained by using the pairs (o_0, o_i) as pivots in a manner similar to FastMap and then applying the linear transformation. The result of MetricMap, like that of FastMap, may violate the pruning property if d is not the Euclidean distance metric. Furthermore, the way in which the original $2k$ reference objects are reduced down to $k + 1$ means that, even if d is Euclidean, the result may still violate the pruning property.

The distance function d' used on the coordinate values produced by MetricMap is *pseudo-Euclidean* in that it is defined in terms of the squares of the differences of the individual coordinate values just like the Euclidean distance metric. However, some of the coordinate axes may make a negative contribution to the overall distance between two points. Thus, in extreme cases, the squared distance between points can be negative. In order to produce the square root of such a negative value, MetricMap takes the square root of the absolute value and makes it negative (i.e., $-\sqrt{-D}$). This is similar to what was done in the FastMap heuristic to deal with non-Euclidean distance metrics. Thus, due to the possibility of negative distance values, the values produced by d' should really be termed "pseudo-distances" or "quasi-distances." In contrast, in a Euclidean space, all coordinate axes have a positive contribution to the overall distance so that the more coordinates that we have, the greater is the distance.

At a first glance, MetricMap appears to resemble the Lipschitz embedding of Faragó et al. [595] (mentioned in Sections 4.7.1 and 4.7.2.1) in that each of the reference objects except o_0 are, in some sense, used to construct a dimension in $\mathbb{R}^{2k-1}$. However, this resemblance is superficial as the values of each of the k coordinate axes in the final embedding are potentially influenced by all of the reference objects.

4.7.4 Locality Sensitive Hashing

Locality sensitive hashing (LSH) is a randomized algorithm for similarity searching developed by Indyk and Motwani [924]. A *randomized algorithm* is any algorithm that makes some random (or pseudorandom) choices (e.g., [398, 1318, 1325]. Randomized algorithms are usually characterized as being either Monte Carlo or Las Vegas. A *Monte Carlo randomized algorithm* [1318] is a randomized algorithm that may produce incorrect results, but with bounded error probability. In particular, a Monte Carlo algorithm gives more accurate results the more often it is invoked. On the other hand, a *Las Vegas randomized algorithm* (e.g., [397, 398, 1318]) is a randomized algorithm that always produces correct results, with the only variation from one run to another being its execution time.

One way to understand the difference between these two classes of randomized algorithms is to observe that a Monte Carlo algorithm yields a probabilistic result, while the Las Vegas algorithm yields a deterministic result. For example, the algorithm for finding the nearest neighbor in a kNN graph [1704] (see Section 4.5.6) is a Monte Carlo algorithm due to the use of pseudorandom seeds to identify the object at which the search starts. Thus, the more times we invoke the algorithm, using different seeds, the greater the likelihood of a correct answer. A bound on the error probability of this method should be derivable, hence justifying its characterization as a Monte Carlo algorithm (see Exercise 2). Therefore, the result of the search process is probabilistic, with some likelihood of an error. On the other hand, the nearest neighbor finding algorithm for a Delaunay graph [1424] (see Section 4.5.5) is a Las Vegas algorithm as the result is always correct, but the execution time varies depending on the starting object.

The approximate k-nearest neighbor algorithm for the SASH (Spatial Approximation Sample Hierarchy) method [883, 884] (see Section 4.5.8) is an example of an algorithm that is neither a Monte Carlo nor a Las Vegas algorithm. Recall that SASH uses a probabilistic algorithm to distribute the objects at the various levels. However, once the SASH has been constructed, all instantiations of an algorithm such as the one for finding the k nearest neighbors of a query object will have the same execution time and will return the same result, which may not be accurate; moreover, there is no known bound on the extent to which the answer deviates from the correct one. Thus, the SASH approximate k-nearest neighbor algorithm fails to be a Las Vegas algorithm on two counts. First, it does not necessarily yield the correct result, and, second, there is no variation in its execution time from one instantiation to another. The algorithm also fails to be a Monte Carlo algorithm in that repeated invocations with the same query object yield the same result—that is, neither does the accuracy of the answer change, nor is there a known bound on it.

The goal in LSH is to find a hashing function that is approximately distance preserving. LSH differs from other approaches by using a two-stage process that employs the embed-project-hash paradigm [510]. The key idea is for the hashing functions used in the two stages to be distance preserving, or at least to be approximate distance preserving within some tolerance.

Indyk and Motwani implement the first stage by embedding objects (usually point objects) drawn from $\mathbb{R}^d$ under a Minkowski L_p norm (i.e., distance metric) into the Hamming space $\{0, 1\}^i$ for some i, which is a vector space whose elements are strings of zeros and ones (i.e., bitstrings), and then use the L_1 distance metric (i.e., City Block). In essence, the value c_i of each feature f_i that makes up the multidimensional object at hand is mapped into a vector v_i in a Hamming space. In particular, letting feature value c_i be in range $[0, t]$ so that t is the integer greater than or equal to ($\geq$) the maximum among all feature values [709], v_i is represented by a string of c_i ones followed by $t - c_i$ zeros (e.g., the feature value 5 in the domain $[0, 7]$ is mapped into the bitstring 1111100, corresponding to five ones followed by two zeros). The vectors v_i are concatenated to form a single bitstring V (see also Exercise 3), which is an element of the Hamming space $\{0, 1\}^{td}$. It should be clear that this embedding, coupled with the L_1 distance metric, is distance preserving.

Indyk and Motwani implement the second stage by projecting the result V of the first stage onto an m-dimensional subspace of the Hamming space, which we term the *projection space*. This projection is achieved by drawing m bit positions at random with replacement. As we point out below, Indyk and Motwani show that coupling this embedding with the L_1 distance metric is approximately distance preserving within some tolerance.

Notice that this two-stage process involves two "hashing" functions. The first hashing function, h_1, corresponds to mapping the original data to the Hamming space. The second hashing function, h_2, corresponds to projecting from the Hamming space to the projection space. Queries are performed in the projection space. In order to make the approach practical, we need to be able to map a query object o in the original metric space to an object in the projection space, and this is achieved by making use of a third hashing function h_3 corresponding to the composition of h_2 and h_1 (i.e., $h_3 \equiv h_2 \circ h_1$). Note that the unary hashing function h_1 based on a Hamming space proposed by Indyk and Motwani [924] is just one of several possible hashing functions that could be used for the LSH function. In particular, Indyk [923] points out that similar hashing functions were used by Karp, Waarts, and Zweig [995] for the bit vector intersection problem and by Broder, Glassman, Manasse, and Zweig [265] in information-retrieval and pattern recognition applications.

As a more concrete example of LSH using the Hamming space, let us consider the set of records consisting of eight cities and their locations specified by their x and y coordinate values, as shown in Figure 1.1 in Chapter 1 and given in Figure 4.99. In order to make our example manageable, we have quantized the x and y coordinate values so that they lie in the range $[0, 7]$ by applying the mapping $f(x) = x \div 12.5$ and $f(y) = y \div 12.5$, respectively. The result of mapping the quantized coordinate values (i.e., $f(x)$ and $f(y)$) to the Hamming space is given by the function unary, and the result of the concatenation of the mappings is given by the function HS.

Figure 4.99 contains four examples of possible instances of projections involving three bit positions (i.e., $\{2,9,13\}$, $\{7,10,14\}$, $\{1,5,11\}$, and $\{8,12,14\}$). The physical interpretations of the mapping of the original data from the Hamming space to the projection space for these examples are given in Figure 4.100. In particular, the fact that $m = 3$ means that we are effectively mapping the objects into vertices of the unit cube. From this figure, we can quickly see that collisions exist whenever more than one object is mapped into the same vertex. Thus, by examining the locations in the original metric space of the objects associated with the same vertex of a cube (i.e., at a projected Hamming distance of 0), we find that some collisions, such as Chicago and Omaha for the $\{2,9,13\}$ projection instance (Figure 4.100(a)), can be characterized as "good" collisions as they are close to each other in both the original metric space and in the projected Hamming space. On the other hand, collisions such as Atlanta and Denver for the $\{8,12,14\}$ projection (Figure 4.100(d)) can be characterized as "bad' collisions as they are far from each other in the original metric space, while they are close to each other in the projected Hamming space.

It should be clear that the motivation for the formulation of h_3 is to reduce the probability of bad collisions to less than the probability of good collisions. Any hashing function that has this effect can be characterized as *locality preserving*, and such functions are termed *locality sensitive hashing functions* by Indyk and Motwani [924]. Indyk and Motwani [924] reduce the probability of bad collisions by increasing the number of different projections (i.e., increasing the number of hashing functions h_2) that are taken into account when computing the approximate nearest or k nearest neighbors to j. Notice that using this approach makes LSH a Monte Carlo randomized algorithm as the effect is to increase the accuracy of the query results by additional invocations. In this respect, the effect is reminiscent of (and analogous to) that which results from increasing the

NAME	ATTRIBUTE i		$f(i) = i \div 12.5$		HS = UNARY(X) & UNARY(Y)		PROJECTION INSTANCES			
	X	Y	$f(X)$	$f(Y)$	UNARY(X)	UNARY(Y)	$\{2,9,13\}$	$\{7,10,14\}$	$\{1,5,11\}$	$\{8,12,14\}$
Chicago	35	42	2	3	1100000	1110000	110	010	100	100
Mobile	52	10	4	0	1111000	0000000	100	000	100	000
Toronto	62	77	4	6	1111000	1111110	111	010	101	110
Buffalo	82	65	6	5	1111110	1111100	110	010	111	110
Denver	5	45	0	3	0000000	1110000	010	010	000	100
Omaha	27	35	2	2	1100000	1100000	110	000	100	100
Atlanta	85	15	6	1	1111110	1000000	100	000	110	100
Miami	90	5	7	0	1111111	0000000	100	100	110	000
q = Reno	5	55	0	4	0000000	1111000	010	010	001	100

Figure 4.99
Example of LSH using the data in Figure 1.1 in Chapter 1.

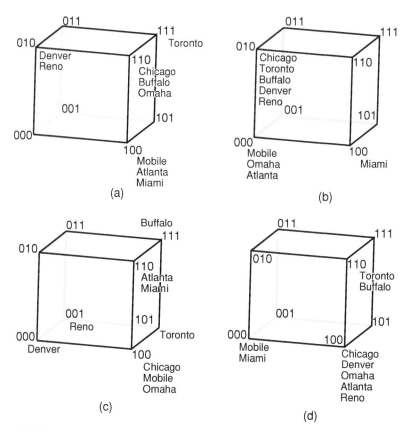

Figure 4.100
The physical interpretation of the mapping of the quantized representation of the original data in Figure 1.1 in Chapter 1 from the Hamming space to the projection space given by considering the three-bit position sequences (a) {2,9,13}, (b) {7,10,14}, (c) {1,5,11}, and (d) {8,12,14}.

number of seeds when finding the k nearest neighbors using the kNN graph. In addition, we can also attempt to increase the dimension m of the projected space to s as a means of reducing the number of additional projections a needed while maintaining the same number of bit positions drawn from the Hamming space (i.e., a total of $j \cdot m = a \cdot s$).

Executing a k-nearest neighbor query for q in LSH is accomplished by applying the hashing function h_3 to q, thereby obtaining q_p, and collecting all of the objects associated with q_p (i.e., these objects collide with q as they are associated with the same elements of the projection space and make up the *collision set* of q_p). This process is repeated j times, once for the j different projections, obtaining q_{pi} for each projection i ($1 \le i \le j$). At this point, we must decide what to report as the response to the query. One possible response to the k-nearest neighbor query is to report the k most frequently occurring objects in the j collision sets of q_{pi} for each projection i ($1 \le i \le j$). Of course, for some query objects, the situation could arise that the corresponding collision sets are empty. In this case, a reasonable solution is to examine the objects associated with elements of the projection space that are at an increasing distance from the elements q_{pi} for each projection i ($1 \le i \le j$).

As an example of the use of LSH, let us examine how it is used to determine the approximate nearest neighbor of $q =$ Reno at (5,55), whose corresponding embedding is shown in the last row and column of the table in Figure 4.99. We make use of the same four instances of projections involving three bit positions shown in Figure 4.99, whose physical interpretation of the mapping of the original data from the Hamming space to the projection space is given in Figure 4.100. Applying these four projections to $q =$ Reno, we find that q collides with Denver at object 010 for projection {2,9,13};

Object	Chicago	Mobile	Toronto	Buffalo	Denver	Omaha	Atlanta	Miami	q = Reno
Chicago		1	1	11	11	111	1		1
Mobile	3.6					1	11	111	1
Toronto	3.6	6.0		1					1
Buffalo	4.5	5.4	2.1						1
Denver	2.0	5.0	5.0	6.3					111
Omaha	1.0	2.8	4.5	5.0	2.2				1
Atlanta	4.5	2.2	5.4	4.0	6.3	4.1		1	1
Miami	5.8	3.0	6.7	5.1	7.6	5.4	1.4		
q = Reno	2.2	5.7	4.5	6.1	1.0	2.8	6.7	8.1	

Figure 4.101
The upper triangular half of the matrix, above the empty diagonal, indicates the unary representation of the number of times objects (a,b) are members of the collision list of the same element of the projection space for the projections given in Figure 4.99. The lower triangular half of the matrix, below the empty diagonal, indicates the interobject distances in the quantized original metric space.

with Chicago, Toronto, Buffalo, and Denver at object 010 for projection {7,10,14}; with an empty set at object 001 for projection {1,5,11}; and with Chicago, Omaha, Atlanta, and Denver at object 100 for projection {8,12,14}. Clearly, Reno collides most often with Denver, and hence Denver is returned as the approximate nearest neighbor of Reno. The upper triangular half of the matrix, above the empty diagonal, given in Figure 4.101 summarizes the various collision lists by indicating, using a unary representation, how many times each pair of objects, including Reno, collides, where, for example, the entry (Mobile, Miami) has a value of 111, denoting that Mobile and Miami occur three times as members of the collision lists of the same element of the projection space for the four instances of projections involving the three bit positions. The lower triangular half of the matrix, below the empty diagonal, gives the interobject distances in the quantized original metric space.

Assuming a d-dimensional metric space, N objects, and j projection instances, the approximate nearest neighbor query using LSH has an execution time of $O(d \cdot j)$ and requires $O(N \cdot (d + j))$ space. The fact that we repeat the process serves to reduce the likelihood that there are no collisions. If, in fact, we have no collisions for a particular query, then we could examine the objects associated with elements of the projection space that are at increasing distance from the elements q_{pi} for each projection i ($1 \leq i \leq j$), as mentioned earlier. Alternatively, we can increase the number of projections, but this is not very attractive as it is equivalent to rebuilding a hash table upon overflow, which is not always practical. Thus, such an occurrence serves as a reminder that LSH is an approximate nearest neighbor algorithm and has a probability of not returning the proper response.

Indyk and Motwani [924] prove that h_2 is approximately distance preserving within a tolerance, thereby justifying its use and thereby rendering h_3 also to be approximate distance preserving as h_3 is the result of composing h_2 with a distance-preserving hashing function h_1. This is done by appealing to the result of Frankl and Maehara [631] that improves upon the Johnson-Lindenstrauss Lemma [962], which states that given an ε and N points in a metric space, a mapping that projects onto some subspace defined by approximately $9\varepsilon^{-2} \ln N$ random lines is a distance-preserving mapping within an error of ε. Indyk [923] notes that this appeal to the improvement of the Johnson-Lindenstrauss Lemma by Frankl and Maehara is similar to that deployed by Kleinberg [1032] and Kushilevitz, Ostrovsky, and Rabani [1097] in their use of normal projections onto randomly chosen lines that pass through the origin in approximate nearest neighbor searching.

Note that, although we earlier characterized LSH as a Monte Carlo algorithm, Indyk [922] has also subsequently shown how the LSH method can be converted into a Las Vegas algorithm using a greedy set cover algorithm (e.g., [385]). The LSH method has been found to perform well in large databases where the data resides on disk [709]. It has found use in a number of applications in similarity searching of images in a number of computer vision applications (e.g., [700, 1523, 1737]).

Loosely speaking, LSH can be said to be similar in spirit to Lipschitz embeddings (see Section 4.7.2). Recall that in Lipschitz embeddings objects are embedded in a vector space where the coordinates consist of reference sets, each of which makes up a subset of the objects in the underlying domain S. The embedding is constructed by computing the distance of the embedded objects from the different reference sets, which is a form of a projection onto the reference sets. By using a sufficiently large number of randomly formed reference sets, the distortion of the values of distances in the embedding space is guaranteed to be bounded with a high probability. This is a form of approximate distance preservation. LSH replaces the "large" number of randomly formed reference sets by repeated application of the projection step using different elements of the embedding space that are somewhat analogous to reference sets in the Lipschitz embedding. The analogy can be made more concrete by appealing to the connection that we mentioned earlier between LSH and the solutions of Kleinberg [1032] and Kushilevitz, Ostrovsky, and Rabani [1097] in their use of random projections onto lines in approximate nearest neighbor searching. In particular, in this case, the random lines are analogous to the reference sets (see Exercise 4).

Exercises

1. Compare LSH and SASH for finding the approximate k nearest neighbors.

2. Derive a bound on the error probability of the algorithm for finding the nearest neighbor in a kNN graph, thereby demonstrating that it can be characterized as a Monte Carlo randomized algorithm.

3. At an initial glance, the mapping into a Hamming space that we described appears to resemble bit concatenation as described in Section 1.6 of Chapter 1 in the sense that the unary representations of the quantized values of the individual features that describe the multidimensional object are concatenated. Would using the analog of bit interleaving applied to the unary representation lead to improved performance?

4. (Sydney D'Silva) In the text, we argue that LSH is similar in spirit to Lipschitz embeddings (see Section 4.7.2). One way to rationalize this connection is to consider the related predecessor methods of Kleinberg [1032] and Kushilevitz, Ostrovsky, and Rabani [1097] that make use of random projections onto lines. In particular, we claim that the random choice of a subset of objects A_i and the mapping of each object o to $(d_1, d_2, .., d_k)$, where d_i is the distance from o to the nearest object in A_i, is akin to the random projections used in LSH. D'Silva [510] has observed that one of the difficulties with such an analogy is the absence of a common reference object with respect to which all of the distances that form the "coordinate" values are measured (e.g., an "origin" object) in the case of the Lipschitz embedding. In order to overcome this difficulty, D'Silva proposes to modify the Lipschitz embedding by imposing a point of origin O so that for each object o its mapping to tuple $(d_1, d_2, .., d_k)$ is such that d_i is the distance from the origin O to the closest object to o in A_i, instead of the distance from o to the closest object in A_i. The result is that this modified Lipschitz embedding is analogous to the method of Kleinberg [1032]. In order to complete the comparison, can you prove that the modified Lipschitz embedding is approximately distance preserving within a tolerance, thereby validating the relationship between Lipschitz embeddings and LSH?

Overview of B-Trees

Tree-based searching methods involve making branches based on the results of comparison operations. When the volume of data is very large, we find that often the tree is too large to fit in memory at once. Therefore, the tree is stored on many disk pages, and some of the pages might not be in memory at the time the comparison is made. In such an environment, the branches in the tree contain disk addresses, and it is not uncommon for a comparison operation to result in a page fault. This calls for search techniques known as *external searching*. The B-tree and its variants are the most commonly used external searching techniques and are the subject of this appendix.

When the tree is a binary tree, the number of page faults can be quite high. For example, for a binary tree of N records, the number of comparison operations is minimized if the binary tree is complete (a concept similar to global balance). In this case, we need to make approximately $\log_2 N$ comparisons before reaching a leaf node. If N is 2 million, then we will make 21 comparison operations, which potentially could cause 21 page faults. Thus, binary trees are not good for external searching.

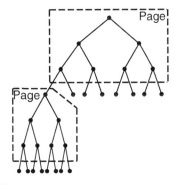

Figure A.1
8-ary tree.

Our goal is to minimize the number of page faults. There are several ways of achieving this goal. One way is to aggregate the results of the comparisons by delaying the branch operation to the missing page. For example, when N is 2 million, we can transform the complete binary tree of depth 21 to a complete tree of depth 7, where groups of seven key values are formed at every three levels of the tree. The result is that each node of the new tree has eight branches instead of two, and the effect is more like an 8-ary tree (see Figure A.1). Thus, we will have at most 7 page faults (instead of 21) when retrieving the data. It is important to note that we have separated the comparison operations from the branching process. This is clear in the figure, where we see the locality of the comparisons—that is, a branch is only attempted once the appropriate sequence of three comparisons has been executed.

The small page sizes (i.e., seven nodes), as in the example above, are widely used to improve cache locality of main memory data structures in modern processors where cache lines are typically 256 bytes at the present [746]. Nevertheless, when the above scheme is used, we usually aggregate more than seven key values. The aggregation is such that the result is stored on a page. It is not inconceivable to store as many as 500 key values on one of the pages. For example, if we store 511 key values on a page, then we have 512 branches and with at most three page faults, we can access over 128 million records. In fact, this is the basis of the *indexed-sequential file organization* (ISAM) [705] for storing data on disk. In this case, the first branch indicates a cylinder address, the second branch indicates a track along the cylinder, and the third address indicates the address of the record.

Another way to minimize the page faults is to use a multiway tree instead of a binary tree. A *multiway tree* is a generalization of a binary search tree where at each

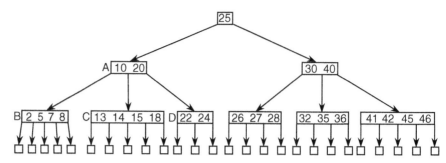

Figure A.2
Example of a B-tree of order 5.

nonleaf node, instead of testing just one key value and making a 2-way branch, we test m ($m \geq 1$) key values and make an ($m + 1$)-way branch. By being somewhat flexible about the capacity of each nonleaf node, we can guarantee that the resulting tree structure is balanced in the sense that all leaf nodes are at the same level. This is at the expense of leaving some of the space in each node unutilized. The result is known as a B-tree [143]. It has its roots in the 2-3 tree [874], which is a variant of a balanced binary search tree where all leaf nodes appear at the same level and every nonleaf node has two or three children. The B-tree is also related to the AVL tree [15, 27], which is a variant of a balanced binary search tree. The key difference between them is that the B-tree is globally balanced while the AVL tree is locally balanced (recall that the AVL tree only guarantees that the maximum depths of the two subtrees of any node differ by at most 1).

A B-tree of order m satisfies the following properties:

1. All leaf nodes appear at the same level and contain no key values (i.e., they are empty).

2. Unless the root is a leaf node, it has at least two children.

3. All nodes other than the root and the leaf nodes have at least $\lceil m/2 \rceil$ children.

4. A node has a maximum of m children.

5. A nonleaf node with j key values has $j + 1$ children.

For example, Figure A.2 is an example of a B-tree of order 5. Notice that each node has two, three, or four key values. The only exception is the root, which is permitted to have just one key value. In this example, we show the pointers to the empty leaf nodes (i.e., empty square boxes), although they are usually left out, as we will also do in the other examples. The leaf nodes are analogous to the external nodes in what is known as an *extended binary tree*.[1]

A nonleaf node containing j key values and $j + 1$ children has the following format:

$$p_0 k_1 p_1 k_2 p_2 k_3 \ldots k_{j-2} p_{j-2} k_{j-1} p_{j-1} k_j p_j$$

where $k_1 < k_2 < k_3 \ldots < k_j$, and p_i ($0 < i < j$) points to a node (i.e., subtree) containing key values ranging between k_i and k_{i+1}. p_0 points to a node containing key values less than or equal to k_1, while p_j points to a node containing key values greater than k_j. Our definition assumes that the key values are distinct (i.e., no duplicates). If this is not the case, then the definition of a node must be modified (see Exercise 1). There is a close relationship between nodes and pages in a B-tree. Often, we use the terms *node* and *page*

---

[1] In many applications, we find it useful for each node to be either a leaf node or to have k ($k > 1$) children. When $k = 2$, such a tree is called an *extended binary tree* because it can be constructed by taking a binary tree and replacing each null subtree by a special node.

interchangeably. It is easy to see that properties 1–5 guarantee that each page will be at least 50% full.

Searching for a record with key value k in a B-tree is very easy. Assume a nonleaf node format as given above. We start at the root node. The process is analogous to search in a binary search tree, with the exception that we must also perform a search within each nonleaf node. In particular, we must search for k among the k_i stored in the node. Either we find k and exit, or we find the largest i such that $k_i < k$ and retrieve the node pointed at by p_i. If we are at a leaf node, then the search is unsuccessful. When the nodes are large, it is preferable to use binary search within the node rather than sequential search.

Insertion in a B-tree is a bit more complex. We search for the record with key value k. An unsuccessful search leads us to the position where k should be inserted. This will be at the bottom of the tree in a leaf node t. We attempt to insert the record in the nonleaf node p containing the pointer to t. If node p is not already full (i.e., it contains less than $m - 1$ key values), then we make the insertion and exit. Otherwise, node p is full (i.e., it contains m key values after the insertion), a situation that is termed *overflow*. In this case, we split node p into two nodes, dividing the m key values as evenly as possible into two sets, and move the median key value to the ancestor node, say a. The same process is applied recursively to node a. The process terminates upon encountering a node that need not be split or if we are at the root node. If we are at the root node, and if it must be split, then we simply create a new node containing a single key value, and the process terminates.

As an example, consider the insertion of 16 into the B-tree in Figure A.2. We find that 16 belongs in node C and make the insertion. Node C is already full, and we have an overflow. Therefore, we split node C into two nodes, C1 and C2, and promote key value 15 to node A, which is not too full. The result is given in Figure A.3(a).

Alternatively, we can often perform the insertion without having to split any nodes by applying *rotation* (also known as *deferred splitting*). The basic idea is that whenever overflow occurs in node a, we examine the adjacent brother nodes to see if they are full. If one of the adjacent brother nodes, say b, is not full, then we perform a rotation from a to c, the father of a, and from c to b. For example, when inserting 16 into the B-tree in Figure A.2, we find that node C is full. However, adjacent brother node D is not full. So, we promote node 18 from C to A and demote 20 from A to D. The resulting B-tree, given in Figure A.3(b), satisfies properties 1–5 of the B-tree definition.

Formally, rotation is specified as follows. Assume that node a is full, and adjacent brother node b to the right of a is not full. Let c be the father node of a and b. Promote the maximum key value, d, in a to c, and demote to b the smallest key value, e, in c that is greater than d. A similar process is applied if the adjacent brother node that is not full is to the left of a instead of to the right (see Exercise 3). In general, although rotation avoids splitting a node (an operation analogous to allocating a new page), it is not a good idea to use it as its implementation becomes very complicated if the adjacent brother nodes are full.

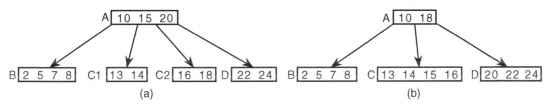

Figure A.3
The result of inserting 16 into the B-tree of Figure A.2 with (a) node splitting and (b) rotation. Only the subtree rooted at node A is shown.

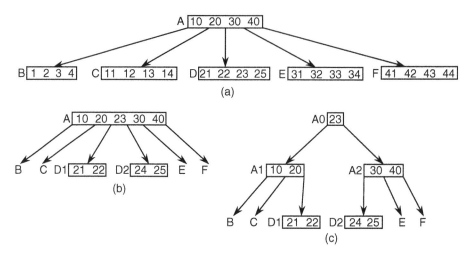

Figure A.4
(a) A B-tree awaiting insertion of 24, (b) an intermediate split of node D, and (c) the final result.

Notice that B-trees do not grow downwards. Instead, they grow from the top (i.e., at the root) since their depth can only increase when the root node splits (this happens relatively infrequently). For example, suppose we want to insert 24 into the B-tree in Figure A.4(a). We find that 24 belongs in node D and make the insertion. Unfortunately, node D is already full, and we have an overflow. Therefore, we split node D into two nodes, D1 and D2, and promote key value 23 to node A (see Figure A.4(b)). Again, we find that node A is already full, and we have an overflow. Thus, we split node A into two nodes, A1 and A2, and promote key value 23, thereby creating a new node, and the tree has grown by one level (see Figure A.4(c)).

Deletion in a B-tree is closely related to B-tree insertion. To delete a record with key value k, we start at the root and search for it. Once we find it, we continue searching for the maximum key value j that is less than k or for the minimum key value j greater than k. Key value j is found in node p, which is at the next to bottom level of the tree (i.e., the one containing the leaf nodes). j is moved to replace k. If node p contains at least $\lceil m/2 \rceil - 1$ key values after the move, then we are done. Otherwise, the node has too few key values, a situation that is termed *underflow*. In this case, we have two choices: rotation or merging.

Rotation is explained above in conjunction with B-tree insertion. Rotation can be applied if there is underflow in node a, while an adjacent brother node, say b, contains at least $\lceil m/2 \rceil$ key values. In this case, we rotate from b to c, the father of b, and from c to a. For example, when deleting 22 from the B-tree in Figure A.2, we find that there is underflow in node D. However, adjacent brother node C contains more than the minimum number of key values. So, we promote key value 18 from C to A and demote 20 from A to D. The resulting B-tree, given in Figure A.5(a), satisfies properties 1–5 of the B-tree definition.

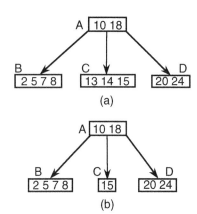

Figure A.5
The result of deleting 22 from the B-tree of Figure A.2 with node C containing (a) {13, 14, 15, 18} and (b) {15, 18}.

Rotation is not always possible. For example, if node C in Figure A.2 contained just two key values (e.g., 15 and 18) instead of four key values, then we would have underflow in adjacent brother nodes. In this case, rotation from C to A and from A to D would not solve our problem as now there would be underflow in node C instead of node D (see Figure A.5(b)). This calls for a more complex rotation algorithm. In particular, we would have to rotate key values over brothers that were not necessarily adjacent (e.g., promote 8 from B to A, demote 10 from A to C, promote 18 from C to A, and demote 20 from A to D), as well as over several levels. The implementation of such an algorithm is quite complicated. For this reason, in such cases, it is preferable to make use of merging.

When simple rotation among adjacent brothers is not possible, then we merge node p with one of its adjacent brother nodes (both of which contain $\lceil m/2 \rceil - 1$ key values)

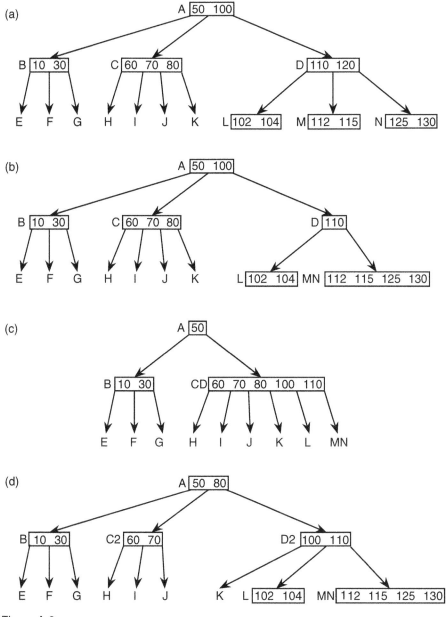

Figure A.6
(a) A B-tree awaiting deletion of 120, (b) the underflow created by its removal from node D,
(c) the overflow created by the merge of nodes C and D, and (d) the final result.

and demote the intermediate key value from the ancestor node, say *a*. This, in turn, can cause further underflow. In such a case, we continue applying the process recursively to node *a* and its ancestors. The process terminates upon encountering a node that need not be merged or if we are at the root node. If we are at the root node, and it used to contain a single key value but is now empty as a result of the demotion, then the root node is removed, and the process terminates. The result is that B-trees shrink from the top. Thus, the effect on tree growth of the deletion process is the reverse of the insertion process.

As an example of the deletion process using merging, suppose we want to delete 120 from the B-tree in Figure A.6(a). We first search for 120, and having found it in node D, we replace it by the maximum key value less than 120—that is, 115 in node M. This causes node M to underflow. Therefore, we merge nodes M and N and demote 115 from node D, thereby creating node MN (see Figure A.6(b)). Unfortunately, this causes node D to underflow. Thus, we merge node D with node C and demote 100 from node A, thereby creating node CD (see Figure A.6(c)). At this point, node CD is too full (i.e., overflow).

We split it into nodes C2 and D2 and promote 80 to node A2 (see Figure A.6(d)). At this point, we are done.

Note that deletion in Figure A.6 could have also been achieved by using rotation. In particular, we apply rotation to Figure A.6(b) by moving 100 from node A to node D, moving 80 from node C to node A, and linking node K to node D instead of to node C. However, if we modify Figure A.6(a) so that node C and key 100 are not present and stipulate that each of nodes E, F, and G contain just two keys, then rotation cannot be used. In this case, once again M and N will be merged to yield MN. This will cause an underflow in D, and it will be merged with B to yield BD, with 50 being demoted from A. We see that the depth of the B-tree has been reduced by one level.

B-trees are attractive because they are balanced, and storage utilization is at least 50% and is usually much better. Searching, insertion, and deletion can be performed in $O(d)$ time, where d is the depth of the B-tree. The number of disk retrievals and writes is at most $3d + 4$ for each operation (see Exercise 9).

Earlier, we mentioned that the B-tree is rooted in the 2-3 tree. In fact, it is a generalization of a 2-3 tree. In particular, each node in the corresponding B-tree has one or two key values, and the result is an order 3 B-tree. We can also define a 2-3-4 tree, which is the same as a B-tree of order 4, which means that each node contains between one and three key values. Both 2-3 and 2-3-4 trees require several different node types depending on the number of key values. Red-black balanced binary trees [766] enable the implementation of 2-3 and 2-3-4 trees as binary trees in a manner similar to the natural correspondence between a forest and a binary tree.[2] Thus, all nodes are now uniform.

In essence, in a red-black balanced binary tree, the nodes of the 2-3 and 2-3-4 trees are represented as one-level binary trees consisting of zero or more red edges, while black edges are used to link up the nodes of the 2-3 and 2-3-4 trees.[3] The implementation makes use of an additional one-bit field with each node that indicates if the incoming edge from its father is red or black. For example, Figure A.7(b) is the red-black balanced binary tree corresponding to the 2-3-4 tree in Figure A.7(a). Red edges are drawn with heavier lines and marked with r, while black edges are drawn with normal lines and marked with b.

We make the following observations. In the case of a 2-3 tree, the one-level binary tree has at most one edge, while it has at most two edges in the case of a 2-3-4 tree. The choice of whether a red edge is the left child or the right child of the root of the one-level binary tree corresponding to the 2-3 tree depends on which of the values in the node of the 2-3 tree is used as the root of the one-level binary tree. Also, it is easy to see that it is impossible to have two successive red edges in red-black balanced binary trees that correspond to 2-3 or 2-3-4 trees.

At this point, let us discuss the insertion of a record r with key value k in a red-black balanced binary tree corresponding to a 2-3 tree (see Exercise 15 for a discussion

---

[2] This correspondence arises from a concern that since a tree has a variable number of children, its implementation is somewhat cumbersome due to the need for extra storage to allow for a maximum number of children. An alternative solution is to represent the tree as a binary tree. In this case, the pointer structure of the tree rooted at t is modified so that each node in the corresponding binary tree rooted at u has two children, pointed at by LCHILD and RCHILD, say v and w, respectively. The LCHILD field of u is used to point to t's first child and results in the node v. The brothers of each node (i.e., the remaining children of t) are linked together in a list using the RCHILD field of v. Thus, the root u of the new binary tree has an empty RCHILD field w. This representation is also very useful for a forest, which is a set of zero or more disjoint trees. In this case, if the forest has at least two elements, then the RCHILD field v of the new binary tree rooted at u is no longer empty—that is, it points to the second member of the forest. The representation of a forest as a binary tree is known as the *natural correspondence* [1044] between a forest and a binary tree.

[3] Some descriptions of red-black balanced binary trees (e.g., [422]) assign colors to the nodes instead of the edges. In this case, a node is red if its parent is from the same node in the 2-3 or 2-3-4 tree; otherwise, it is black. In addition, if a node is red, then both of its children (if present) are black. Also, every path to a leaf node contains the same number of black nodes (see Exercise 13).

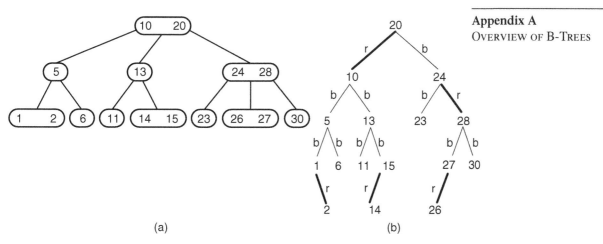

Figure A.7

(a) A 2-3-4 tree and (b) a corresponding red-black balanced binary tree. Red edges are drawn with heavier lines and marked with 'r' while black edges are drawn with normal lines and marked with 'b.'

of insertion into a red-black balanced binary tree corresponding to a 2-3-4 tree, which is a bit more complex as there are a few more cases to handle).[4] The algorithm is analogous to insertion in a B-tree in the sense that we first search for a record with key value k and find the leaf node y in which it belongs, make the insertion, determine if any splits are necessary, and propagate them up the tree. We make the insertion as a red edge d from some node x to y. Now, determine if a split is necessary. This is done by checking the color of the father edge f, which corresponds to an edge from a node w to x.

1. If f is black or empty (i.e., it does not exist), then test the brother edge b (if it exists) of d as x may have a child z.

   (a) If b is black or empty, then we are done.

   (b) If b is red, then we have a situation analogous to an overflow in a B-tree since nodes x, y, and z are like brothers. Thus, we change the colors of edges b and d to be black. Next, if f exists, then we change the color of f to be red and reapply steps 1 and 2 to f. Otherwise, if f does not exist, then we exit.

2. If f is red, then the configuration is an illegal 2-3 tree as we have two successive red edges. Therefore, we apply a single (Figure A.8(a)) or double (Figure A.8(b)) rotation as in the case of an AVL tree, which will make the two red edges brothers. This situation is not allowed in a 2-3 tree. Thus, we change the colors of these edges (i.e., d and f) to be black, make their father edge g red, and reapply steps 1 and 2 to edge g. Notice that, in this case, if edge g does not exist, then we are at the root, and we are done.

There are a number of ways of improving the performance of B-tree methods. Since they are primarily of interest for external (i.e., disk-based) searching, the focus is on reducing the number of disk accesses and on increasing the storage utilization. The number of disk accesses can be reduced by using a buffer pool of pages. In this case, a fixed number of pages are always kept in memory. We make use of a least recently used (LRU) page replacement policy to make room for a new page if all the pages in the buffer pool are full (i.e., we write to disk the page that was least accessed and replace it with the new page). Such a strategy is very efficient since the root page and some pages corresponding to the nodes at depth 1 will usually be in memory and will most likely

---

[4] This algorithm is complicated and may be skipped.

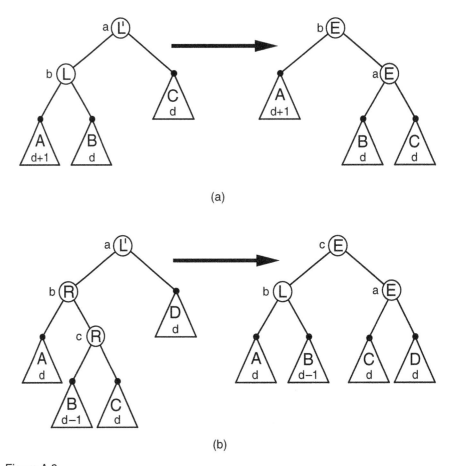

(a)

(b)

Figure A.8

Examples of right rotation operations in AVL trees. Each subtree is labeled with its depth. The labels L, R, and E associated with each node *n* are balance factors corresponding to the left subtree of *n* being one level deeper than, equal to, and one level shallower than, respectively, the right subtree of *n*. A right rotation is necessary when the depth of the left subtree of a node is more than one greater than the depth of the right subtree. L′ denotes this situation. (a) Example of an AVL tree (left) and the result of applying a single right rotation to it (right) when the balance factor of the left subtree is L. (b) Example of an AVL tree (left) and the result of applying a double right rotation to it (right) when the balance factor of the left subtree is R. The rotation is termed a double rotation because we first rotate the pair (b,c) to the left and then the pair (a,c) to the right.

have been accessed, thereby insuring that they will not be the ones chosen to be written out to make room for the new pages.[5]

When pages are modified (e.g., when an insertion and a split occur), we do not necessarily write the modified page to disk. Instead, we only write to disk when the modified page is the one chosen to be replaced by the buffer pool manager. We can try to delay writing the modified pages to disk by using a page replacement policy that replaces the least recently unmodified page instead of just the least recently accessed. However, if such a policy is followed, then we should be careful that the page that is written out is not the root page or one of the pages at depth 1.

There are a number of ways of increasing the storage utilization. One obvious improvement suggested by Knuth [1046] is to require that whenever a node split occurs, the *n* adjacent brother nodes be split to yield *n* + 1 adjacent nodes, each of which

---

[5] For a discussion of alternative strategies, including a most recently used (MRU) page replacement policy, see [380].

contains at least $\lfloor n \cdot (m-1)/(n+1) \rfloor$ key values so that storage utilization increases to $n/(n+1) \cdot 100\%$ instead of 50%, as in the conventional definition of a B-tree. When $n = 2$, the result is termed a B^*-tree [1046].

Other improvements suggested by Knuth [1046] include the use of different values of m at different levels of the tree. Assume that the nonleaf nodes are at levels 0 through d. This can be used to eliminate wasted space in the leaf nodes by making m be 1 at level $d + 1$. In fact, we observe that only nodes at level d contain pointers to Λ. Thus, we can dispense with level $d + 1$ and, instead, use a value of m at level d that is twice as large as that at all other levels than the root. In this way, we can store more key values in the nodes at the bottom level (i.e., d) of the B-tree.

A major improvement is made by limiting the amount of information stored in the nonleaf nodes. This has the effect of increasing the number of records that can be stored in each node, thereby reducing the maximum depth of the B-tree. There are several options. One option is just to store the key value plus a pointer to a page that contains the rest of the record's data.

In fact, using this option, we can also dispense with the empty leaf nodes. Knuth [1046] suggests that once the empty leaf nodes have been eliminated, only the nodes at the deepest level contain key values (henceforth referred to as *leaf nodes*, although they contain between $\lceil m/2 \rceil - 1$ and $m - 1$ key values). In this case, the nonleaf nodes only provide an index so that the appropriate leaf node that contains the desired record can be located. The nonleaf nodes can contain some of the same key values that are stored in the leaf nodes, but this need not be so. The only requirement is that if a key value k is stored in a nonleaf node between pointers to subtrees pointed at by p and q, then all key values in p are less than or equal to k, and all key values in q are greater than k.

These modifications to the B-tree definition result in what is called a B^+-tree [414]. B^+-trees still grow and shrink as do B-trees; however, key values are never passed up or down between levels of the tree. This also means that the leaf nodes in a B^+-tree are always at least half full instead of being empty as in the B-tree. Notice that since we no longer need the pointers to the empty leaf nodes (i.e., Λ), the space that they required can be used for the pointers to the pages that contains the rest of the data of the records associated with the key values stored in the node.

As an example of a B^+-tree, consider Figure A.9, which corresponds to the key values of the B-tree in Figure A.2. Notice that all the nodes at the deepest level contain key values, although their number is different from that shown in Figure A.2. We also observe that some of the key values have been duplicated in the nonleaf nodes (e.g., 25 and 40 in nonleaf nodes A and B, and C and D, respectively).

In fact, the nonleaf nodes in the B^+-tree need not contain the key values. In particular, if the key values are long strings of characters, we need only store enough characters to enable us to differentiate the key values in the subtrees. For example, to differentiate between jefferson and jones, we could use jefferson but actually jf is sufficient. Using

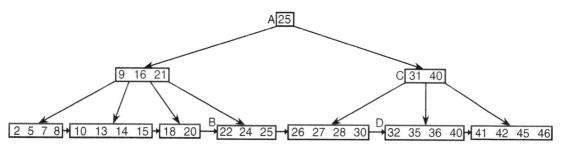

Figure A.9
The B^+-tree corresponding to the key values of the B-tree of Figure A.2.

the shortest possible key value enables us to store more key values in the nonleaf nodes, thereby resulting in shallower trees. This is known as a *prefix B^+-tree* [144].

A further improvement is to link all the leaf nodes in the B^+-tree by adding a pointer to each leaf node that points to the next leaf node in the sequence. This enables us to traverse the records in sequence without ever referencing the nonleaf nodes. The result is a representation that efficiently supports both random and sequential access.

Exercises

1. Modify the definition of a B-tree node to permit duplicate key values.

2. Prove that the number of leaf nodes in a B-tree is one greater than the number of key values.

3. Suppose that you are implementing insertion in a B-tree with rotation. How would you treat the case that the adjacent brother node b that is not full is to the left of the full node a?

4. Consider a B-tree of order m, and suppose that deletion has taken place and nodes a and b have been merged. Assume further that underflow has occurred in node a and that deletion of one more key value will cause node b to underflow as well. What is the total number of key values in the two adjacent brother nodes before the merge?

5. Given a B-tree of order m with N records, what is the maximum search length (i.e., in terms of levels)?

6. What is the maximum search length in a B-tree of order 512 with 128,000 records?

7. Given a B-tree of order m with p nodes at i levels (i.e., at depth 0 through $i-1$), prove that the total number of node splits that occur when building it is $p-i$.

8. Derive an upper bound on the average number of node splits per insertion in a B-tree of order m with N records.

9. What is the maximum number of disk accesses made when searching, inserting, and deleting in a B-tree with a root at depth 0 and leaf nodes at depth $d+1$?

10. Write an algorithm to insert a record into a B-tree.

11. Write an algorithm to delete a record from a B-tree.

12. What is the minimum number of key values that can be stored in a B-tree of order $m = 2a - 1$ ($a > 1$) with a root at depth 0 and leaf nodes at depth j?

13. A red-black balanced binary tree can also be defined in terms of node colors rather than edge colors. In particular, a node is red if its parent is from the same node in the 2-3 or 2-3-4 tree; otherwise, it is black. Moreover, if a node is red, then both of its children (if present) are black. Prove that every path to a leaf node in a red-black balanced binary tree contains the same number of black nodes.

14. Prove that the maximum depth of a red-black balanced binary tree is at most twice the maximum depth of the corresponding 2-3 or 2-3-4 trees.

15. What changes need to be made to the insertion algorithm given in the text for red-black trees corresponding to 2-3 trees so that it also works for 2-3-4 trees?

16. Write an algorithm for deletion in red-black balanced binary trees that correspond to 2-3 trees.

17. Write an algorithm for deletion in red-black balanced binary trees that correspond to 2-3-4 trees.

18. The insertion routine given in the text for B-trees is bottom up in the sense that we insert the key value at the deepest level followed by a node split if there is overflow, in which case the median key value is propagated up the tree where the same process is repeated. An analogous bottom-up algorithm for insertion into a red-black balanced binary tree that corresponds to a 2-3 tree is presented in the text. Devise a top-down insertion algorithm for a red-black balanced binary tree that corresponds to a 2-3-4 tree. In this case, you will split if necessary as you descend the tree when making the insertion. Assume that the key value is not yet in the tree.

19. Can you apply the same algorithm devised in Exercise 18 to insert into a 2-3 tree? If not, explain why.

20. Under what conditions can you apply the algorithm devised in Exercise 18 to insert into a B-tree of order m?

21. Suppose that you are implementing B-trees in a multiuser environment. In this case, once an insertion is taking place, all other users must be prevented from accessing all the nodes on the path from the root r to the leaf node i where the insertion is taking place. The rationale is that since the insertion process is bottom up, there is a possibility that a node split will be propagated all the way up to the root. How would the application of the top-down insertion process described in Exercise 18 to a B-tree (see Exercise 20) reduce the need to prevent the access of nodes on the path from r to i?

22. Implement a B-tree of order m as a binary tree. The idea is to use the analog of a red-black balanced binary tree where the red edges are used to link the contents of the order m nodes of the B-tree, and the black edges are used to link up the nodes of the B-tree.

23. What is the difference between searching for a record with a particular key value in a B^+-tree and for one in a B-tree?

24. What is the difference between deleting a record with a particular key value from a B^+-tree and one from a B-tree?

Linear Hashing

Linear hashing addresses the situation that arises when the hash table (usually consisting of buckets) is full or when the hash chains in a chaining method (attributed to Luhn by Knuth [1046, p. 547]) get too long. One solution is to expand the size of the hash table. Since the number of buckets (or chains in a chaining method) is usually fixed by the hash function, we must modify our hash function to generate more buckets. This modification should ideally require a minimal amount of rehashing—that is, only a few records should have to be moved to new buckets. Generally, most hashing methods do not allow the number of buckets to grow gracefully.

Knott [1040] suggests storing the buckets using a trie (see the definition in the opening section of Chapter 1) in the form of a binary tree (e.g., Figure B.1(a)). In this scheme, dealing with bucket overflow is rather trivial since the bucket is split into two parts (e.g., bucket B in Figure B.1(a) is split into buckets E and F in Figure B.1(b)). The problem with such a scheme is that accessing a bucket at depth l requires l operations. However, the tree is usually kept in memory, and thus these l operations are considerably faster than a disk access, and, in fact, only one disk access is required.

A more general formulation of Knott's approach is described by Larson [1104], who makes use of m binary trees, each of which contains just one leaf node initially. These leaf nodes correspond to buckets with a finite capacity c. Given a key k, applying a hash function h to k (i.e., $h(k)$) yields the binary tree that contains k. The collection of m one-node binary trees is analogous to a hash table with m buckets. As items are added to the hash table, the buckets corresponding to the leaf nodes become full, and thus they are expanded by splitting them, thereby creating two new buckets for each split. Subsequent insertions may cause these buckets also to fill up, thereby resulting in further splits. The splitting process is represented by a binary tree.

This method is analogous to the separate chaining method,[1] where, instead of placing the overflow buckets in a chain (i.e., linked list), we organize each bucket and its set of overflow buckets as a binary tree whose leaf nodes consist of these buckets. Thus, we have m binary trees. Note also that, unlike separate chaining, all buckets have the same capacity.

At this point, it is hard to see the advantage of using the binary tree organization of the overflow buckets over the separate chaining approach unless we can impose some access structure on the binary tree that enables us to avoid examining all of the buckets in the worst case of a search (whether or not it is successful). Larson [1104] proposes to

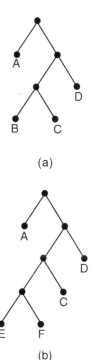

(a)

(b)

Figure B.1
Example illustrating the representation of a hash table as a binary tree and (b) the result of splitting bucket B into buckets E and F upon overflow.

---

[1] Briefly, in this case, we have a table of m hash values and pointers to m hash lists—that is, one for each hash value. The hash value is commonly referred to as a *bucket address* since, frequently, more than one key value is associated with it. The hash lists are used to store all of the records whose key values have the same hash value.

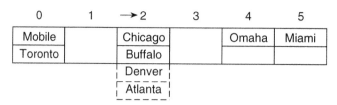

Figure B.4
Result of applying linear hashing to the data of Figure B.3. A rightward-pointing arrow indicates the next bucket to be split.

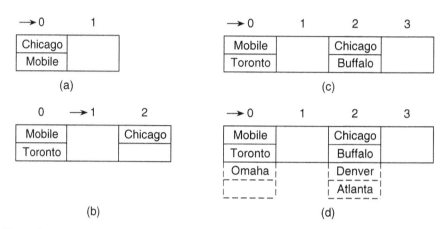

Figure B.5
Sequence of linear hashing bucket contents demonstrating the insertion of (a) Chicago and Mobile, (b) Toronto, (c) Buffalo, and (d) Denver, Omaha, and Atlanta. A rightward-pointing arrow indicates the next bucket to be split.

7 of Figure B.3, labeled CODEY). In our example, we treat the y coordinate as the most significant and thus make use of the values in column 7 of Figure B.3.[2] Assume that the primary and overflow buckets are both of size 2 and that a bucket will be split whenever τ, the storage utilization factor, is greater than or equal to 0.66 (i.e., $\alpha = 0.66$).

Figure B.4 shows the resulting bucket organization. In the figure, solid lines designate primary buckets, broken lines designate overflow buckets, and a rightward pointing arrow indicates the next bucket to be split. There are six primary buckets, labeled 0–5, and one overflow bucket. To understand the splitting process, let us examine more closely how linear hashing copes with a sequence of insertion operations. In particular, we observe how Figure B.4 is constructed for the records of Figure B.3 in the order in which they appear there: Chicago, Mobile, Toronto, Buffalo, Denver, Omaha, Atlanta, and Miami.

Initially, only bucket 0 exists, it is empty, and the file is of level 0,1. The pointer to the next bucket to be split, s, is initialized to 0. The insertion of Chicago and Mobile yields $\tau = 1.00$, causing bucket 0 to be split and bucket 1 to be allocated. s retains its value of 0, and both Chicago and Mobile remain in bucket 0 (see Figure B.5(a)). Toronto is inserted in bucket 0, but $\tau = 0.75$, which causes bucket 0 to be split, s to be set to 1, bucket 2 to be allocated, and Chicago to be placed in it (see Figure B.5(b)). Our file is now of level 1, 2. Next, we try to insert Buffalo. It belongs in bucket 2. However, now $\tau = 0.67$, causing bucket 1 to be split, s to be reset to 0, and bucket 3 to be allocated (see Figure B.5(c)).

---

[2] Note that, in an actual implementation, it is better to reverse the result of the interleaving as, in this case, points in the same bucket are in spatial proximity to each other. In fact, this is what is done in Section 1.7.2.3.1 of Chapter 1.

Attempting to insert Denver causes bucket 2 to overflow and leads to the allocation of an overflow bucket attached to bucket 2 once Denver has been placed in it. Similarly, inserting Omaha results in an overflow of bucket 0 and the allocation of an overflow bucket attached to 0 once Omaha has been placed in it. Atlanta belongs in bucket 2 and, since bucket 2 is full, it is placed into its overflow bucket (see Figure B.5(d)). Miami is inserted into bucket 1, resulting in $\tau = 0.67$. This causes bucket 0 to be split, s to be set to 1, bucket 4 to be allocated, and Omaha to be moved to bucket 4. Our file is now of level 2,3. Since bucket 0's overflow bucket is now empty, it is deallocated, yielding $\tau = 0.67$. Thus, bucket 1 is split, s is set to 2, bucket 5 is allocated, and Miami is moved to it (see Figure B.4).

Linear hashing as described above may require complex searches when many of the records hash to a subset of the buckets. Let S denote this subset. This means that several overflow buckets will be associated with each element of S. On the other hand, there will be few overflow buckets associated with the remaining primary buckets (i.e., not elements of S). Ramamohanarao and Sacks-Davis [1530] suggest that the linear hashing function used to distinguish between the primary buckets also be applied to distinguish between the contents of the overflow buckets for each of the primary buckets. This technique is called *recursive linear hashing*, and the result can be viewed as a separate file, termed an *overflow file*. This process is applied as many times as necessary (hence, the term *recursive*), each time creating an additional overflow file. However, in practice, it is rare for the hashing function to be applied more than three times [1530]. The only difference from the original application of the hashing function is that, for the second and subsequent applications of the hashing function, the overflow file is at a lower (i.e., smaller) level than that of the original file.

One problem with recursive linear hashing is that when primary bucket P is split, records in the overflow files that originally hashed to P may have to be moved either to a primary bucket or to another overflow file. A similar problem arises when two primary buckets are merged. Of course, these problems also arise with conventional linear hashing. Nevertheless, recursive linear hashing has the property that all records that originally hashed to P will be stored in a single bucket in each of the overflow files (see Exercise 18). Hence, the insertion costs for recursive linear hashing and for conventional linear hashing with optimal overflow bucket size [1105, 1529] are similar [1530]. (For more details on recursive linear hashing, see [1531].)

Exercises

1. Give an algorithm to look up a record with key value k in a file implemented with linear hashing of m buckets. The file is at level $n, n + 1$. In particular, do you use h_n first or h_{n+1}? If it makes a difference, explain why.

2. Discuss the issue of merging buckets for linear hashing—that is, when the storage utilization factor falls below a particular threshold, say β.

3. The insertion algorithm for linear hashing described in the text splits bucket s whenever insertion of a record causes the storage utilization factor, τ, to exceed a predetermined value. This is done even if bucket s does not overflow or if no records will move as a result of the bucket-splitting operation. Of course, allocating an overflow bucket is also a method of reducing the storage utilization factor. Modify the insertion algorithm so that when the storage utilization factor is too high and there is overflow, a split of bucket s only occurs if it will resolve the overflow; otherwise, allocate an overflow bucket. If there is no overflow, then split bucket s as before. Define a measure to compare these two methods, and do so analytically and empirically.

4. Show the result of applying linear hashing to the point set of Figure B.3 when the x coordinate is the most significant. Again, assume that the cities are inserted in the order Chicago, Mobile, Toronto, Buffalo, Denver, Omaha, Atlanta, and Miami. Draw the analogs of Figures B.4 and B.5.

5. Repeat the example shown in the text illustrating the mechanics of linear hashing by inserting the cities Chicago, Mobile, Toronto, Buffalo, Denver, Omaha, Atlanta, and Miami in this order when the x coordinate is the most significant. Draw the analogs of Figures B.4 and B.5.

Exercises 6–13 are based on an asymptotic analysis of linear hashing described by Larson [1106]. Assume that there are no deletions. The implementation is slightly different than the one described in the text. The capacity of the buckets is not restricted, and thus there is no need for overflow buckets. Each bucket is implemented as a linked list (i.e., a chain). In this case, the storage utilization factor τ is the total number of records in the table divided by the number of buckets.

6. Suppose that no bucket splits are ever allowed. Compute $s(\tau)$ and $u(\tau)$, the expected number of key value comparisons for a successful and unsuccessful search, respectively. In your answer, for the unsuccessful search case, assume that no key value comparison is necessary when the key value is hashed to an empty bucket.

7. For Exercises 7–13, assume that a bucket is split each time the storage utilization factor exceeds α. At any instant, let x ($0 \le x \le 1$) denote the fraction of the buckets that have been split and z the expected number of records in an unsplit bucket. The expected number of records in a split or new bucket is $z/2$. Show that $z = \alpha \cdot (1+x)$.

8. Let $S(\alpha, x)$ denote the expected number of key value comparisons for a successful search when a fraction x of the buckets have been split. Calculate $S(\alpha, x)$.

9. Calculate $U(\alpha, x)$, the expected length of an unsuccessful search.

10. When do the minimum expected search lengths occur?

11. When do the maximum expected search lengths occur?

12. Calculate the average search cost over a cycle (i.e., as x ranges from 0 to 1).

13. The cost of each insertion of a record can be decomposed into two parts. The first part is just the cost of placing the record at the end of the chain. The second part reflects the situation that a bucket is split, and the table is expanded. The cost of the first part is the same as that of an unsuccessful search and the cost of linking the record to the end of the chain. The second part arises with a probability of $1/\alpha$. Here, we must rehash each record on the chain and update some pointers. Calculate $A(\alpha, x)$, the expected number of rehashing operations per record that is inserted, and its average over a cycle.

14. Repeat the analyses of Exercises 6–13 when the primary buckets have a finite capacity, say c. This means that overflow buckets will be necessary. Assume an overflow bucket capacity of v.

15. Give an algorithm to insert a record with key value k into a file implemented with recursive linear hashing of m primary buckets that is at level $n, n+1$.

16. Give an algorithm to look up a record with key value k in a file implemented with recursive linear hashing of m primary buckets that is at level $n, n+1$.

17. Give an algorithm to delete a record with key value k from a file implemented with recursive linear hashing of m primary buckets that is at level $n, n+1$.

18. Prove that recursive linear hashing has the property that all records that originally hashed to primary bucket P will be stored in a single bucket in each of the overflow files.

Spiral Hashing

One of the drawbacks of linear hashing (see Appendix B) is that the order in which the buckets are split is unrelated to the probability of the occurrence of an overflow. In particular, all the buckets that are candidates for a split have the same probability of overflowing. Moreover, the expected cost of retrieving a record and updating the table of active buckets varies cyclically in the sense that it depends on the proportion of the buckets that have been split during a bucket expansion cycle (see Exercises 6–13 in Appendix B).

Proposed by Martin [1247], spiral hashing [324, 384, 1106, 1247, 1324] is a technique whose performance (i.e., the expected search length in a bucket) has been observed to be independent of the number (or fraction) of the buckets that have been split. Thus, it is said to have uniform performance (see Exercise 23). This is achieved by distributing the records in an uneven manner over the active buckets. Moreover, it always splits the bucket that has the highest probability of overflowing.

Spiral hashing is similar in spirit to linear hashing. To simplify our explanation, we identify the buckets by their addresses. The central idea behind spiral hashing is that there is an ever-changing (and growing) address space of active bucket addresses that is moving forward (e.g., Figure C.1). This is in contrast to linear hashing in which the active bucket addresses always range from 0 to $m - 1$. Recall that in linear hashing, when the bucket at address s is split, then a new bucket is created at location m, and the previous contents of bucket s are rehashed and inserted into buckets s and m, as is appropriate.

In the following discussion, we assume that a bucket can be split into r buckets rather than just two as was the case in our explanation of linear hashing. r is called the growth factor. We assume further that r is an integer; however, this restriction can be lifted. Let s and t denote the addresses of the first and last active buckets, respectively, so that each bucket with address i ($s \le i \le t$) is active. Define the storage utilization factor, τ, in the same way as for linear hashing—that is, the ratio of the number of records in the file to the number of positions available in the existing primary and overflow buckets. A bucket is split whenever τ exceeds a predetermined value, say α. When τ falls below a predetermined value, say β, buckets should be merged (i.e., the bucket-splitting process should be reversed). However, this has not been the subject of much research, and we ignore β here (see Exercise 5).

When the bucket at address s is split, say into r buckets, then r new buckets are allocated starting at bucket address $t + 1$, and the contents of bucket s are rehashed into these new buckets. Bucket address s is no longer used (but see Exercise 7), and the active bucket addresses now range from $s + 1$ to $t + r$. As we will see, the manner in which the hashing function is chosen guarantees that the expected load (i.e., the expected number of records per bucket) is always at a maximum at bucket s and is at a minimum at bucket

						7	8	9	10	11	12	13	14	15	16	17	18	19	20
					6	7	8	9	10	11	12	13	14	15	16	17			
				5	6	7	8	9	10	11	12	13	14						
			4	5	6	7	8	9	10	11									
		3	4	5	6	7	8												
	2	3	4	5															
1	2																		

Figure C.1

Example of a changing (and growing) address space of active bucket addresses with a growth factor $r = 3$. This means that when a bucket is split, three new buckets are created, and the bucket that has been split is no longer active.

t. Moreover, the expected load of bucket $i + 1$ is less than the expected load of bucket i ($s \leq i < t$).

The presentation is simplified considerably if we assume that initially there are $r - 1$ active buckets starting at address 1. For example, when $r = 2$, initially there is one active bucket starting at address 1; after the first split, there are two active buckets starting at address 2; after the second split, there are three active buckets starting at address 3; and so on. When $r = 3$, initially there are two active buckets starting at address 1; after the first split, there are four active buckets starting at address 2; after the second split, there are six active buckets starting at address 3; and so on. This splitting sequence (i.e., for $r = 3$) is illustrated in Figure C.1. In general, it can be shown that for arbitrary values of r, after the occurrence of s bucket-splitting operations, there are always $(s + 1) \cdot (r - 1)$ active bucket addresses (see Exercise 1).

The growth pattern described above can be modeled by observing the behavior of the function $y = r^x$. We know that $r^{x+1} - r^x = r^x \cdot (r - 1)$. Assume that bucket s has just been split. Letting $r^x = s + 1$, we find that $r^{x+1} - r^x = (s + 1) \cdot (r - 1)$, which is the number of active bucket addresses. Moreover, $r^x = s + 1$ is the address of the first active bucket, which means that the last active bucket is at $r^{x+1} - 1$. This relation serves as the basis of a combination of two hashing functions.

The first function, say $h(k)$, is used to map key value k uniformly into a value in $[0,1)$. Next, we map $h(k)$ into its bucket address, denoted by $y(h(k))$, such that $y(h(k))$ is in the range $[s + 1, s + 1 + (s + 1) \cdot (r - 1))$. This is achieved by the second function $y(h(k)) = \lfloor r^{x(h(k))} \rfloor$, where $x(h(k))$ is in the range $[\log_r(s + 1), \log_r(s + 1) + 1)$. The difficulty lies in defining $x(h(k))$. A simple solution is to let $x(h(k)) = \log_r(s + 1) + h(k)$. Unfortunately, in this solution, $x(h(k))$ changes whenever s changes. This is unacceptable as it means that whenever a bucket split occurs, all key values have to be rehashed.

What we want is a definition of $x(h(k))$ such that once bucket s has been split, all key values k whose previous $x(h(k))$ value was in the range $[\log_r(s), \log_r(s + 1))$ (i.e. key values in bucket s) are rehashed to one of the newly generated buckets by a new $x(h(k))$ in the range $[\log_r(s) + 1, \log_r(s + 1) + 1)$. In contrast, the new $x(h(k))$ value of all other key values whose previous $x(h(k))$ value was in the range $[\log_r(s + 1), \log_r(s) + 1)$ are unchanged. This is achieved by letting $x(h(k)) = \lceil \log_r(s + 1) - h(k) \rceil + h(k)$ (see Figure C.2 for $r = 2$). Therefore, $x(h(k))$ is a number in the range $[\log_r(s + 1), \log_r(s + 1) + 1)$ whose fractional part is $h(k)$. Thus, once key value k is hashed into a bucket with a particular bucket address, say b, key value k is guaranteed to continue to be hashed into b until b has been split.

Figure C.3 illustrates the use of the second hashing function $y(h(k))$ for $r = 2$. Given a bucket address, it shows the corresponding interval from $[0,1)$ that maps to the address and the proportion of the data that the bucket contains (labeled "relative load"). Notice that the relative load decreases as the bucket addresses increase (see also Figure C.4).

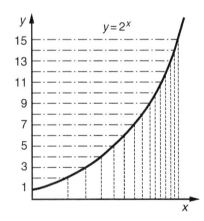

Figure C.2
The function $y = 2^x$.

Bucket Address	Hash Interval	Relative Load
1	[0.0000,1.0000)	1.0000
2	[0.0000,0.5849)	0.5849
3	[0.5849,1.0000)	0.4151
4	[0.0000,0.3219)	0.3219
5	[0.3219,0.5849)	0.2630
6	[0.5849,0.8073)	0.2224
7	[0.8073,1.0000)	0.1927
8	[0.0000,0.1699)	0.1699
9	[0.1699,0.3219)	0.1520
10	[0.3219,0.4594)	0.1375
11	[0.4594,0.5849)	0.1255
12	[0.5849,0.7004)	0.1155
13	[0.7004,0.8073)	0.1069
14	[0.8073,0.9068)	0.0995
15	[0.9068,1.0000)	0.0932

Figure C.3
Bucket address mapping for $r = 2$.

This verifies our claim that the bucket to be split is the one with the highest probability of overflowing.

Now, let us illustrate the use of spiral hashing by examining how the representation is built for the point set of Figure 1.1 of Chapter 1 when processing it one by one. First, apply the mapping f such that $f(x) = x \div 12.5$ and $f(y) = y \div 12.5$ to the values of the x and y coordinates, respectively. The result of this mapping is given in columns 4 and 5 of Figure C.5. Next, apply bit interleaving to its keys to yield the mappings given in columns 6 and 8 of Figure C.5. Two mappings are possible since we can either take the x coordinate value as the most significant (column 6 of Figure C.5, labeled CODEX) or the y coordinate value (column 8 of Figure C.5, labeled CODEY). Finally, reduce each interleaved value to a point in [0,1) by using $h(k) = k/64$ to yield columns 7 and 9 of Figure C.5. In our example, we treat the y coordinate as the most significant and thus make use of the values in columns 8 and 9 of Figure C.5. Assume that the primary and overflow buckets are both of size 2, $r = 2$, and that a bucket will be split whenever τ, the storage utilization factor, is greater than or equal to 0.66.

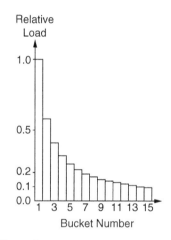

Figure C.4
Relative load of buckets 1–15 when $r = 2$.

NAME	X	Y	$f(X)$	$f(Y)$	CODEX	CODEX/64	CODEY	CODEY/64
Chicago	35	42	2	3	13	0.203125	14	0.218750
Mobile	52	10	4	0	32	0.500000	16	0.250000
Toronto	62	77	4	6	52	0.812500	56	0.875000
Buffalo	82	65	6	5	57	0.921875	54	0.843750
Denver	5	45	0	3	5	0.078125	10	0.156250
Omaha	27	35	2	2	12	0.187500	12	0.187500
Atlanta	85	15	6	1	41	0.640625	22	0.343750
Miami	90	5	7	0	42	0.656250	21	0.328125

Figure C.5
Bit interleaving (CODEX and CODEY) the result of applying $f(x) = x \div 12.5$ and $f(y) = y \div 12.5$ to the values of the x and y coordinates, respectively, of the point set in Figure 1.1 of Chapter 1, and dividing the result by 64.

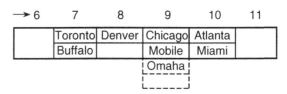

Figure C.6
Result of applying spiral hashing to the data of Figure C.5. A rightward-pointing arrow indicates the next bucket to be split.

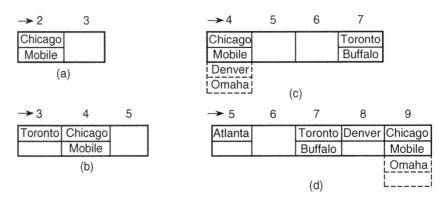

Figure C.7
Sequence of spiral hashing bucket contents demonstrating the insertion of (a) Chicago and Mobile, (b) Toronto, (c) Buffalo, Denver, and Omaha, and (d) Atlanta. A rightward-pointing arrow indicates the next bucket to be split.

Figure C.6 shows the resulting bucket organization. In the figure, solid lines designate primary buckets, broken lines designate overflow buckets, and a rightward-pointing arrow indicates the next bucket to be split. At the end of the construction process, there are six primary buckets, at addresses 6–11, and one overflow bucket. To understand the splitting process, let us examine more closely how spiral hashing copes with a sequence of insertion operations. In particular, we observe how Figure C.6 is constructed for the records of Figure C.5 in the order in which they appear there: Chicago, Mobile, Toronto, Buffalo, Denver, Omaha, Atlanta, and Miami.

Initially, only bucket 1 exists, and it is empty. The pointer to the last bucket to have been split, s, is initialized to 0. Applying the hashing function to Chicago and Mobile yields the values 0.21875 and 0.25, respectively. Since these values are in the range [0,1), they both belong to bucket 1, into which they are inserted. However, this results in $\tau = 1.00$, causing bucket 1 to be split, s to be set to 1, buckets 2 and 3 to be allocated, and both Chicago and Mobile to be moved to bucket 2 (see Figure C.7(a)) since their hash values are both in the range [0,0.5849). Bucket 1 is no longer active. Buckets 2 and 3 are now the active buckets.

Toronto hashes to 0.875. This value is in the range [0.5849,1), and Toronto is inserted into bucket 3. As a result of this action, $\tau = 0.75$, causing bucket 2 to be split, s to be set to 2, buckets 4 and 5 to be allocated, and both Chicago and Mobile to be moved into bucket 4 (see Figure C.7(b)) since their hash values fall in the range [0,0.3219). Bucket 2 is no longer active. The active buckets now range from 3 to 5.

Buffalo hashes to 0.84375. This value is in the range [0.5849,1), and Buffalo is inserted into bucket 3. However, now $\tau = 0.67$, causing bucket 3 to be split, s to be set to 3, buckets 6 and 7 to be allocated, and both Toronto and Buffalo to be moved into bucket 7 since their hash values fall in the range [0.8073,1). Bucket 3 is no longer active. The active buckets now range from 4 to 7.

Denver hashes to 0.15625. This value is in the range [0,0.3219), which belongs to bucket 4. However, attempting to insert Denver causes bucket 4 to overflow and leads to the allocation of an overflow bucket attached to bucket 4 once Denver has been placed into it. Omaha hashes to 0.1875. This value is in the range [0,0.3219), which belongs to bucket 4. Bucket 4 already has an overflow bucket associated with it, and thus Omaha is placed into it (see Figure C.7(c)).

Atlanta hashes to 0.34375. This value is in the range [0.3219,0.5849), which belongs to bucket 5. However, now $\tau = 0.70$, causing bucket 4 to be split, s to be set to 4, and buckets 8 and 9 to be allocated. In addition, Denver moves to bucket 8 since its value falls in the range [0,0.1699), while Chicago, Mobile, and Omaha belong in bucket 9 since they fall in the range [0.1699,0.3219). This means that an overflow bucket must be allocated and attached to bucket 9, and Omaha is placed into it (see Figure C.7(d)). Bucket 4 is no longer active. The active buckets now range from 5 to 9.

Miami hashes to 0.328125. This value is in the range [0.3219,0.5849), which belongs to bucket 5. But $\tau = 0.67$, causing bucket 5 to be split, s to be set to 5, buckets 10 and 11 to be allocated, and both Atlanta and Miami to be moved into bucket 10 (see Figure C.6) since they fall in the range [0.3219,0.4594). Bucket 5 is no longer active. The active buckets now range from 6 to 11.

The main advantage of spiral hashing over linear hashing is that the bucket that is split is the one that is most likely to overflow. There are two disadvantages to spiral hashing. The first is that the buckets that have been split are not reused (although they could be used also as overflow buckets). However, this problem can be overcome by using one of a number of alternative mappings between logical and physical addresses [1106, 1324] (see Exercises 7 and 10). The second is that it is computationally expensive to calculate a function such as $y = r^x$—that is, the bucket address. Of course, most programming languages have a runtime library where such functions are available. However, their computation is time-consuming since it usually requires a polynomial approximation.

Martin [1247] suggests replacing r^x by another function, $f(x)$, which is easier to compute. In particular, $f(x)$ is used to approximate r^x in [0,1] so that r^x is approximated in $[n, n+1]$ (n is an integer) by $r^n \cdot f(x-n)$. One such function, according to Martin, is

$$f(x) = \frac{a+b}{c-x} \quad (0 \le x \le 1).$$

The values of a, b, and c are obtained by calculating the value of f at three points. The most appropriate points are the endpoints—$x = 0$ and $x = 1$—and another point in [0,1], such as $x = 0.5$. We also need the inverse of $f(x)$, which is

$$x = \frac{c+b}{a-y}.$$

Larson [1106] reports on some experiments that compare spiral hashing with linear hashing, as well as unbalanced binary search trees, and an open addressing scheme that uses double chaining. In each case, the tables and trees are all stored in main memory. Using large files, averaging over many insertions, and different storage utilization factors, he found that linear hashing consistently outperformed spiral hashing in terms of average CPU time per key value in both loading the tables and searching them. The differences ranged from 1% to 20%. Larson attributes these differences primarily to the cost of address computation.

Further experiments with binary search trees showed that spiral hashing was faster at loading small key value sets than linear hashing; however, in all cases, searching was faster when hashing methods were used. A comparison of linear hashing with a traditional hash table implemented using double hashing, so that the costs of a periodic reorganization of the hash table are taken into account, resulted in a definite trend showing that the cost of linear hashing was usually lower (although at times slightly higher).

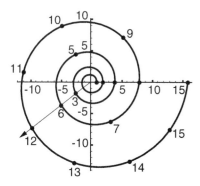

Figure C.8
Spiral corresponding to $\rho = e^{(\ln 2)\cdot\theta/2\pi} = 2^{\theta/2\pi}$.

When the tables and trees are not constrained to be stored in main memory, the results of the comparison may be different. Recall that the number of overflow records and their distribution over the buckets of the file (table) are different for linear and spiral hashing. In particular, at certain stages of a cycle, linear hashing has more overflow records clustered on a few pages. The expected search lengths per bucket depend on how these overflow records are handled. For example, some overflow-handling methods, such as linear probing [1046], are more sensitive to clustering of overflow records. In such a case, spiral hashing should have better performance than linear hashing. Moreover, since we are dealing with external files, the fact that spiral hashing has a higher address computation cost is not important.

At this point, it is interesting to explain the motivation for the qualifier "spiral" used to describe this variant of linear hashing. In the earlier discussion, we mapped each key value into a real number x, which was, in turn, mapped into an address y by the function $y = \lfloor r^x \rfloor$. This mapping can be rewritten in terms of polar coordinates, ρ and θ, as $\rho = \lfloor (e^j)^\theta \rfloor = \lfloor e^{j\theta} \rfloor$, with ρ, e^j, and θ taking on the roles of y, r, and x, respectively. This is the equation of a spiral. For example, Figure C.8 is the spiral corresponding to $\rho = e^{(\ln 2)\cdot\theta/2\pi}$ and is equivalent to $\rho = 2^{\theta/2\pi}$. Of course, any spiral (i.e., c^θ) can be used, not just the natural spiral.

Using polar coordinates in this way means that the active buckets are always within one complete arc of the spiral. For example, if the first active bucket is at $a = \lfloor e^{jb} \rfloor$ (i.e., at $\theta = b$), then the last active bucket is at $c = \lceil e^{j\cdot(b+2\pi)} \rceil - 1$. This is illustrated in Figure C.8 by the infinite line that emanates from the origin and passes through $\rho = 3, 6, 12, \ldots$. A bucket split has the effect that the active bucket at $\rho = a$ (i.e., at $\theta = b$) is split and its contents are distributed into buckets $c + 1$ through g, where $g = \lfloor e^{j\cdot(b+2\pi+\phi)} \rfloor$ and $\phi = (\ln(a+1))/j - b$. The value of ϕ is the solution of $a + 1 = e^{j\cdot(b+\phi)}$. Buckets $a + 1$ through g are now the active buckets.

Two items are worthy of further note. First, instead of using the hash function $h(k)$ to initially map key value k uniformly into $[0,1)$, we use a different hash function, say $h_\theta(k)$, to initially map key value k uniformly into a value in $[0, 2\pi)$. Second, the length of the arc of the spiral is also meaningful as it has a constant value between successive integer values of ρ (see Exercise 24); however, it has no relation to the capacity of the bucket.

Exercises

1. Prove that for arbitrary values of r, after the occurrence of s bucket-splitting operations, there are always $(s + 1) \cdot (r - 1)$ active bucket addresses.

2. Suppose that, regardless of the value of the growth factor r, there is initially just one active bucket. How does this affect the function that maps $h(k)$ to a bucket address?

3. Show the result of applying spiral hashing to the point set of Figure 1.1 of Chapter 1 subject to bit interleaving with the x coordinate being the most significant, as shown in columns 6 and 7 of Figure C.5. Again, assume that the cities are inserted in the order Chicago, Mobile, Toronto, Buffalo, Denver, Omaha, Atlanta, and Miami. Also, assume that the primary and overflow buckets are both of size 2, $r = 2$, and that a bucket will be split when τ, the storage utilization factor, is greater than or equal to 0.66. Draw the analogs of Figures C.6 and C.7.

4. Show the result of applying spiral hashing to the point set of Figure 1.1 in Chapter 1 subject to bit interleaving with the y coordinate being the most significant, as shown in columns 8 and 9 of Figure C.5 when the capacity of the buckets is not constrained to be finite. Instead, each bucket is implemented as a linked list (i.e., a chain). Thus, there is no need for overflow buckets. The storage utilization factor τ is the total number of points (i.e., cities) in the point set divided by the number of buckets. Again, assume that the cities are inserted in the order Chicago, Mobile, Toronto, Buffalo, Denver, Omaha, Atlanta, and Miami. Also, assume that $r = 2$ and that a bucket will be split when τ is greater than or equal to 0.66. Draw the analogs of Figures C.6 and C.7.

5. Discuss the issue of merging buckets—that is, when the storage utilization factor falls below a particular threshold, say β.

6. In the discussion of the use of polar coordinates, we calculated a value of ϕ to determine the buckets into which the contents of the split bucket were to be redistributed. It is given as the solution of $a + 1 = e^{j \cdot (b + \phi)}$. Why did we not use $a + 1 = \lfloor e^{j \cdot (b + \phi)} \rfloor$?

7. One of the deficiencies of the implementation of spiral hashing described in the text is that each time a bucket is split, its address is no longer used. This can be wasteful of storage. It would be nice if these locations could be reused. This is facilitated by making a distinction between a bucket's logical and physical addresses and finding a way to map a bucket's logical address to its physical address. This mapping is necessary for the implementation of all operations (e.g., insert, split, merge, access).

   Mullin [1324] suggests the following approach. Assume again that initially there are $r - 1$ buckets with logical addresses 1 through $r - 1$ occupying physical addresses 1 through $r - 1$. The first bucket that is split is at logical address 1. This split results in the creation of r new buckets at logical addresses r through $2 \cdot r - 1$. The buckets at logical addresses r through $2 \cdot r - 2$ are stored at physical addresses r through $2 \cdot r - 2$, while physical address 1 is reused to store the bucket at logical address $2 \cdot r - 1$. The second bucket that is split again results in the creation of r new buckets at logical addresses $2 \cdot r$ through $3 \cdot r - 1$. This time the buckets at logical addresses $2 \cdot r$ through $3 \cdot r - 2$ are stored at physical addresses $2 \cdot r - 1$ through $3 \cdot r - 3$, while physical address 2 is reused to store the bucket at logical address $3 \cdot r - 1$. It should be clear how the rest of the splits are handled. Give an algorithm that takes as its input the logical address of a bucket and returns its physical address.

8. The solution to Exercise 7 is specified using recursion. However, it is tail recursive and, thus, can be rewritten using iteration. Given a growth factor of r and a maximum logical bucket address t, what is the maximum number of iterations?

9. Assume that a bucket at physical address s is split. Let t be the maximum logical address that corresponds to physical address p. In such a case, the technique described in Exercise 7 creates r new buckets starting at logical addresses $t + 1$ through $t + r$. The buckets at logical addresses $t + 1$ through $t + r - 1$ are stored at physical addresses $p + 1$ through $p + r - 1$. The bucket at logical address $t + r$ is stored in physical address s. Suppose that, instead, we store the buckets at logical addresses $t + 2$ through $t + r$ in physical addresses $p + 1$ through $p + r - 1$ and store the bucket at logical address $t + 1$ at physical address s. Give an algorithm that takes as its input the logical address of a bucket and returns its physical address.

10. Mullin's [1324] technique of reusing the space occupied by the buckets that have been split requires the computation of an algorithm that maps a logical address to a physical address. As we saw in Exercise 8, its execution time may grow with the size of the logical address space. Can you avoid this growth by using a limited amount of extra space? In other words, devise a data structure that tries to reuse most of the buckets but is not guaranteed to reuse every bucket at each instance.

11. Suppose that the addresses corresponding to the buckets that have been split are reused as in Exercise 7. Repeat Exercise 5 in such an environment—that is, discuss the issue of merging buckets.

12. Suppose that the addresses corresponding to the buckets that have been split are reused as in Exercise 10. Repeat Exercise 5 in such an environment—that is, discuss the issue of merging buckets.

13. Suppose that the function $y = r^x$ is approximated by $r^n \cdot f(x - n)$, where $f(x - n) = a + b/(c - x + n)$ such that x is in $[n, n + 1]$. Calculate the values of a, b, and c for $r = 2$ by using $x = 0$, $x = 0.5$, and $x = 1$.

14. Suppose that the function $y = r^x$ is approximated by $r^n \cdot f(x - n)$, where $f(x - n) = a + b/(c - x + n)$ such that x is in $[n, n + 1]$. Does use of the approximation affect the bucket-splitting algorithm?

15. Suppose that $f(x)$ is approximated by a second-degree polynomial instead of by $a + b/(c - x)$. What is the disadvantage of such an approximation?

Exercises 16–21 are based on an asymptotic analysis of spiral hashing described by Larson [1106].

16. Assume that $r = 2$ and that there are no deletions. The implementation is slightly different from the one described in the text. The capacity of the buckets is not restricted, and thus there is no need for overflow buckets. Each bucket is implemented as a linked list (i.e., a chain). In this case, the storage utilization factor τ is the total number of records in the table divided by the number of buckets. Assume that the overall value of τ is kept constant at α ($\alpha > 0$). However, the expected value of τ for the different buckets can and does vary over the bucket address space. Assume a normalized address range $[1,2)$ as any address in the range $[2^x, 2^{x+1})$ can be normalized by multiplying it by 2^{-x}. Let $p(y)$ be the probability that a key value hashes to a normalized address in $[y, y + dy) \subseteq [1, 2)$. Show that $p(y)$ is $dy/(y \cdot \ln 2)$, and hence the probability density function is $1/(y \cdot \ln 2)$.

17. Assume that the expected value of the storage utilization factor of a bucket at address y, say $\tau(y)$, is proportional to the insertion probability at y. Use the result of Exercise 16 to show that $\tau(y) = \alpha/(y \cdot \ln 2)$.

18. Assume that each record is equally likely to be retrieved. Therefore, the probability that a successful search lands on a bucket at address y, say $q(y)$, is proportional to the storage utilization factor of the bucket. Show that $q(y) = 1/(y \cdot \ln 2)$.

19. Noting that each bucket is implemented as a linked list, calculate the expected cost of a successful search.

20. Noting that each bucket is implemented as a linked list, calculate the expected cost of an unsuccessful search.

21. When a record is inserted, its cost can be decomposed into two parts. The first part is just the cost of placing the record at the end of the chain. Its cost is the same as that of an unsuccessful search plus the cost of linking the record to the end of the chain. The second part reflects the situation that a bucket is split and the need to rehash its contents so that they can be properly distributed in the new buckets. This situation only arises for the first bucket. What is the expected number of extra hashing operations per record that is inserted?

22. What is the effect of using an arbitrary value of r in Exercises 16–21?

23. Prove that spiral hashing has uniform performance. In other words, prove that the expected search lengths in the buckets are independent of the table size, which in turn is a function of how many bucket-splitting operations have taken place.

24. Prove that the length of the arc of a spiral has a constant value between successive integer values of ρ (i.e., it is directly proportional to ρ).

Description of Pseudocode Language

The algorithms are given using pseudocode. This pseudocode is a variant of the AL-GOL [1346] programming language, which has a data structuring facility that incorporates pointers and record structures. We do not make use of object orientation, although our use of record structures is similar in spirit to rudimentary classes in SIMULA [437] and FLEX [1008], which are the precursors of modern object-oriented methods. We make heavy use of recursion. This language has similarities to C [1017], C++ [1805], Java (e.g., [93]), PASCAL [952], SAIL [1553], and ALGOL W [137]. Its basic features are described below. All reserved words are designated in bold face. This also includes the names (i.e., types) of predefined record structures.

A program is defined as a collection of functions and procedures. Functions are distinguished from procedures by the fact that they return values via the use of the **return** construct. Also, the function header declaration specifies the type of the data that it returns as its value. In the following the term *procedure* is used to refer to both procedures and functions.

All formal parameters to procedures must be declared, along with the manner in which they have been transmitted (**value** or **reference**). All local variables are declared. Global variables are declared and are specified by use of the reserved word **global** before the declaration. Variables and arrays may be initialized to prespecified values by prefacing the declaration with the reserved word **preload** and appending the reserved word **with** and the initialization values to the declaration.

"Short-circuit" evaluation techniques are used for Boolean operators that combine relational expressions. In other words, as soon as any parts of a Boolean **or** (**and**) are true (false), the remaining parts are not tested. This is similar to what is used in LISP [1263] but is different from PASCAL, where the order of the evaluation is deemed to be immaterial.

Record structures are available. An instance of a record structure of type **rec** is created by use of the command **create(rec)**. The result of this operation is a pointer to a record structure of the appropriate type. Pointers to record structures are declared by use of the reserved word **pointer**, which is followed by the name of the type of the record structure. Instances of record structures are referred by using functional notation where the field name is in the position of the function and the pointer is its argument. For example, if variable L points to an instance of a record structure of type **list**, then we use 'NEXT(L)' to refer to the NEXT field of this instance. Of course, L must be declared to be a pointer to a record structure of type **list** by using a declaration of the form '**pointer list** L'. Note the use of bold face for the specification of the type of the record structure since we assume that it has been predefined.

The fields of a record structure may be of any type including an array. For example, suppose that a record of type **rec** has a field called ARR, which is a one-dimensional array. Moreover, assume that L has been declared as a pointer to a record of type **rec**. We use $\text{ARR}(L)[I]$ to refer to the Ith element of the ARR field of the **rec** record pointed at by L.

The procedures are usually recursive and make heavy use of the **if-then-elseif-else-endif** mechanism to establish flow of control. The value of an **if-then-else-elseif** can be a statement or an expression. They are frequently used like a select statement in BLISS [2027] and are similar to a COND in LISP. They are often nested. Observance of the placement of **endif** insures a proper understanding of their semantics. In other words, they must nest properly. A procedure is a block of statements. Statements are either assignments, **if-then-else-elseif-endif** that are sets of statements, or sets of statements that are repeated (i.e., loops) within the **for-do-enddo**, **while-do-enddo**, and **do-until-enddo** constructs. The difference between **while-do-enddo** and **do-until-enddo** is the timing of the execution of the condition that must be satisfied for the loop to be repeated—that is, at the start and end, respectively.

There is a rich set of types. These types are defined as they are used. In particular, enumerated types in the sense of PASCAL are used heavily. For example, the type **quadrant** is an enumerated type whose values are NW, NE, SW, SE.

The array data type is treated as a special type of a record. However, there are some differences. Although an identifier that has been declared to be a record type is usually only used as a parameter to a function that allocates storage for an instance of the record type or to qualify the declaration of a pointer variable, when an identifier that has been declared to be an array appears by itself (i.e., without a suffix to indicate a particular array element, such as ARR instead of $\text{ARR}[I]$), then the identifier is treated as a pointer to an instance of the data type associated with the array declaration. This is useful when it is desired to pass an array as a parameter to a procedure or to return an entire array as the value of a procedure. Thus, in such cases, the array identifier is analogous to a pointer to a record having a type equal to that of the array declaration.

Storage for an array is allocated from a heap rather than from a stack. This means that there is a need for some form of garbage collection for array elements that are not pointed to by any of the currently accessible pointers (i.e., pointer variables). If an array is local to a procedure, then its storage is allocated upon entering the block in which the array is declared. If the array is transmitted as a formal 'value' parameter to a procedure, then its storage is allocated upon entry to the procedure, and its elements are set to the value they had in the corresponding array in the calling procedure. If the array is transmitted as a formal 'reference' parameter to a procedure, then the array occupies the same storage in both the calling and called procedures. It is the user's responsibility to make sure that the type declarations in the calling and called procedure match.

Two subtle points about memory management for arrays are worth noting. The first is that while storage for an array is usually deallocated when exiting from a procedure in which it has been declared or transmitted as a 'value' parameter, deallocation should not take place for an array that is returned as the value of a procedure. The second is that if an array name, say A, appears on the left-hand side of an assignment statement, and the right-hand side is an expression whose value is an array of the same type, then A is overwritten, and the original instance of the array that was bound to A is inaccessible once the assignment has taken place.

As an example of the first point above, let us examine the situation in which a procedure returns as its value an array that has been transmitted to it as a 'value' parameter. In such a case, once the called procedure has exited, there are two instances of the array, one of which is the value returned by the procedure, which is a (possibly modified) copy of the array that was transmitted as a parameter.

One shortcoming with the array data type is the absence of a true analogy with record structures. The problem is that the process of allocating storage for an array should be decoupled from its declaration (which is more like setting up a template). This is a shortcoming of many implementations, including the one described here. It could be overcome easily by replacing the reserved word **array** with the reserved word **array_pointer** whenever it is only desired to set up the template for the array, rather than also allocating the storage. For example, the declaration '**integer array_pointer** $\text{ARR}[0:N]$' would set up the template for array ARR without actually allocating the space for it, while '**integer array** $\text{ARR}[0:N]$' retains its original meaning of template declaration and storage allocation.

Note that the C language allows for either array declaration with allocation or without allocation (i.e., template declaration). However, in C, for the case of the array template, the actual size of the array cannot be specified. In other words, the template is really a pointer to an element of the type of the members of the array but cannot indicate how many elements are in the array.

Solutions to Exercises

Solutions to Exercises in Section 1.1

1. See [649].

2. There are $d!$ permutations of d attributes. It can be shown using symmetry arguments, as well as additional properties, that only $\binom{d}{\lfloor (d+1)/2 \rfloor}$ of the permutations are needed. For more details, see [1214], as well as [1046, pp. 577, 743–744].

3. The worst case is $N + d - 1$, where the first attribute value is different for all records, and now the remaining chains are one element long at each level.

4. In the case of a doubly chained tree, in the worst case, we only test one attribute value at a time for a total of $O(N)$ tests. On the other hand, in the case of a sequential list, in the worst case, we may have to test all attribute values of each record for a total of $O(N \cdot d)$ tests.

5. (Hans-Peter Kriegel) This worst case arises when the resulting tree has the depth $O(d \log_2 N)$. To see how this case arises, assume a configuration of N records in the following sequence. The first N/d records have N/d different values for the first attribute, and the remaining $d - 1$ attributes have arbitrary values. The first attribute value of the remaining $N \cdot (d-1)/d$ records is a constant, say c_1. The second set of N/d records in the sequence have N/d different values for the second attribute, and the remaining $d - 2$ attributes have arbitrary values. The second attribute value of the remaining $N \cdot (d-2)/d$ records is a constant, say c_2. This same process is applied for the remaining $d - 2$ sets of N/d records—that is, the ith set of N/d records in the sequence have N/d different values for the ith attribute and the remaining $d - i$ attributes have arbitrary values. The second attribute value of the remaining $N \cdot (d-i)/d$ records is a constant, say c_i. This results in a sequence of d height-balanced binary trees of height $\log_2 N/d$ apiece. Thus, the total height of the structure is $O(d \cdot \log_2 N/d) = O(d \cdot (\log_2 N - \log_2 d))$, which can be approximated by $O(d \log_2 N)$ since $d \ll N$.

6. Assume that all of the attribute values are distinct. This means that the subfile H of the records that lie on the partitioning hyperplane is empty as this maximizes the size of the left and right subtrees of each node. Let $S(N,d)$ denote the time needed to build the tree and solve the following recurrence relation [1133]:

$$S(N,d) = 2 \cdot S(N/2,d) + 2 \cdot S(N/2,d-1)$$

where $S(1,d) = O(d)$ and $S(N,1) = O(N \cdot \log_2 N)$. The recurrence relation indicates the space needed for the trees corresponding to the subfiles L and R, which contain $N/2$ records, and the subfiles LH and RH, which also contain $N/2$ records and are projections on the $(d-1)$-dimensional hyperplane. $S(N,1)$ is the space needed for the one-dimensional structure where at each level LH and RH are just sets of pointers to the records corresponding to the elements of L and H, respectively, and there are N records at each of the $\log_2 N$ levels. $S(1,d)$ is the space needed for a d-dimensional record that lies on the hyperplane corresponding to the record, and there are d levels in this structure with an empty right subtree and a nonempty left subtree as there are d attributes. The solution to this recurrence relation is $S(N,d) = O(N \cdot (\log_2 N)^d)$. For more details, see [1133].

7. The derivation is similar to that used for the cost of building a quinary tree in the solution of Exercise 6. Assume that all of the attribute values are distinct. This means that the subfile H of the records that lie on the partitioning hyperplane is empty as this maximizes the size of the left and right subtrees of each node. Let $P(N,d)$ denote the time needed to build the tree and solve the following recurrence relation [1133]:

$$P(N,d) = 2 \cdot P(N/2,d) + 2 \cdot P(N/2,d-1) + O(N),$$

where $P(1,d) = O(1)$ and $P(N,1) = O(N \cdot \log_2 N)$. The recurrence relation corresponds to the cost of constructing the trees for the subfiles L and R, which contain $N/2$ records, and the subfiles LH and RH, which also contain $N/2$ records and are projections on the $(d-1)$-dimensional hyperplane. The $O(N)$ factor corresponds to the cost of the actual partition process, including obtaining the median and the subfile H (which is empty by virtue of our distinctness assumption). $P(N,1)$ is the process of obtaining the binary search tree for the one-dimensional hyperplane. $P(1,d)$ is the cost of processing one d-dimensional record, which requires that a node with an empty left subtree (since there are no records with smaller attribute values) and a nonempty right subtree be created for each of the d attribute values. The solution to this recurrence relation is $P(N,d) = O(N \cdot (\log_2 N)^d)$. For more details, see [1133].

8. In the worst case, all of the attribute values are distinct, and thus the search may require that $\log_2 N$ levels be descended while testing the first attribute. In this case, we may need to test the values of all of the remaining attributes. For more details, see [1133].

9. The algorithm is similar to that used for the partial range query with the exception that we must search through all three trees at the next lower level whenever an attribute value is left unspecified. This work is maximized when the s specified attributes are at the s deepest levels of the tree. For more details, see [1133].

10. Each interval $[l_i, r_i](1 \le i \le d)$ can be subdivided into at most N subintervals at each level i. Therefore, the maximum number of nodes that are visited is bounded by $O(\log_2 N)^d)$ plus the number of records F that are found to satisfy the query—that is, $O((\log_2 N)^d + F)$.

11. The algorithm is the same as the range query algorithm except that we need to search through the attached three trees at the level whenever an attribute value is unspecified. This worst case occurs when the s specified attributes are at the s deepest levels of the tree. For more details, see [1133].

12. Using an ECDF tree, the ranking (i.e., ECDF) of q is determined as follows. If q falls in A, then no point in B can be dominated by q, and thus we only need to search A. Otherwise, q can dominate points in both A and B. However, in this case, since the value of the first attribute of any point in A is always smaller than the value of the first attribute of q, we only need to compare q with the projections of points in A—that is, the points in C. Letting $T(N,d)$ denote the time to compute the rank of q in a set of N records in d-dimensional space, we have the following recurrence relation: $T(N,d) = T(N/2,d) + T(N/2,d-1)$, where $T(N,1) = O(\log_2 N)$ and $T(1,d) = O(d)$, corresponding to a one-dimensional balanced binary search tree and a linear list, respectively. The solution to this recurrence relation is $T(N,d) = O((\log_2 N)^d)$.

13. Use the same solution process as in Exercise 12. Letting $S(N,d)$ denote the number of nodes in an ECDF tree for a set of N records in d-dimensional space, we have the following recurrence relation: $S(N,d) = 2 \cdot S(N/2,d) + S(N/2,d-1)$, where $S(N,1) = O(N)$ and $S(1,d) = O(d)$, corresponding to a one-dimensional balanced binary search tree and a linear list, respectively. The solution to this recurrence relation is $S(N,d) = O(N \cdot (\log_2 N)^{d-1})$.

14. Take the difference of the ranking of p and q.

15. Search the linked lists at the first level for values within the range of the first attribute and then recursively descend the links corresponding to the linked lists at the remaining levels that are within the range.

16. Start the search at the first level for which an attribute value or range is given. The rest of the process is analogous to that of a range query given in Exercise 15. The efficiency of the process is enhanced by the fact that all filial sets at the same level are linked.

17. (Hans-Peter Kriegel) The configuration is the same as the one used in Exercise 5 to show that the worst-case execution time for an exact match query when the linked list at each level of the doubly chained tree has been replaced by a height-balanced binary search tree is $O(d \log_2 N)$.

The only difference is that at each level we have a B-tree of depth $O(\log_M N)$ instead of a height-balanced binary search tree of depth $O(\log_2 N)$.

18. Assuming a uniform distribution of points in the cells, say c points per call, then the search must examine a maximum of 2^d cells for a total amount of work equal to $c \cdot 2^d$. Since the query region is a region having the width of a cell (i.e., the query region has width of twice the query radius), we would expect that $F = c$, Therefore, the amount of work is $F \cdot 2^d$.

19. Assuming a uniform distribution of points in the cells, say c points per call, then the search must examine a maximum of 3^d cells for a total amount of work equal to $c \cdot 3^d$. Since the query region is 2^d times the width of a cell, we would expect that $F = c \cdot 2^d$ or $c = F/2^d$. Therefore, the amount of work is $F \cdot 3^d/2^d$. Yuval [2063 describes an alternative approach that examines a smaller number of larger cells. In particular, given a fixed-grid with cells of edge length e, Yuval examines $d + 1$ cells of edge length $(d + 1) \cdot e$ so that using the same density of points per cell c, $c \cdot (d + 1)^{d+1}$ points would be examined although some points would be examined more than once, thereby reducing the total number of different points that are examined. Note that this number is always greater than $c \cdot 3^d$, the number of points examined in the solution to this exercise.

Solutions to Exercises in Section 1.2

1. Yes. In the one-dimensional range tree, the leaf nodes are linked in sorted order using a doubly linked list to facilitate retrieval of all elements within a given range in time proportional to the number of elements in the range.

2. The revised definition would cause problems for points with identical values. For example, suppose that there are eight points with identical values. In this case, it would be impossible to have a balanced tree with all values in left subtrees less than the MIDRANGE values.

3. The reason is that when B_x is less than MIDRANGE(P), then the x coordinate values of all points in the one-dimensional range trees that are searched in RIGHT(P) are greater than or equal to B_x and less than E_x. Similarly, the x coordinate values of all points in the one-dimensional range trees that are searched in LEFT(P) are less in value than E_x and greater than B_x.

4. The points that are found are unique; no point is reported twice since all one-dimensional range trees at a given level are disjoint. The one-dimensional range trees that are examined at the different levels are also disjoint.

5. When procedure 1DSEARCH is invoked, it must distinguish between a leaf node and a nonleaf node as the RANGETREE field points to a record of type *point* in the former and *node* in the latter. Moreover, care must be exercised in the search in the sense that only the specified node is tested and no transitions can be made via the NEXT field as it corresponds to another data structure—that is, the one-dimensional range tree for the x coordinate. Thus, the search should use procedure INRANGE in this case.

6. Procedure 2DSEARCH never makes use of the one-dimensional range trees of the nearest common ancestor and its two children. In the worst case, the nearest common ancestor is the root, and thus the one-dimensional range trees at the root and its two children are never used.

7. The balanced binary search tree, say T, for the main attribute uses $O(N)$ space. For each level of T, each data point occurs in exactly one of the one-dimensional range trees for the secondary attribute that are associated with the nonleaf nodes at that level. There are $O(\log_2 N)$ levels, and thus a total of $O(N \cdot \log_2 N)$ space suffices.

8. Building the range tree in x at the lowest level takes $O(N \cdot \log_2 N)$ for N points. The one-dimensional range trees for the y coordinate values are built based on the range trees for the x coordinate values. This is done by use of a merging process. In particular, the one-dimensional range tree in y at level i associated with node a is built by merging the two one-dimensional range trees in y associated with the two children of a at level $i + 1$. Since the y coordinate values of these two children are both sorted, we obtain the one-dimensional range tree at level i in time proportional to the number of points in the two merged one-dimensional range trees. The one-dimensional range trees at each level of the tree contain N points, and

since there are $\log_2 N$ levels, building the one-dimensional range trees for the y coordinate values takes $O(N \cdot \log_2 N)$ time. Thus, the total time to build the two-dimensional range tree is $O(N \cdot \log_2 N)$ (see also [169]).

9. To perform a range query, it takes $\log_2 N$ steps to locate the endpoints of the main attribute, plus $O(\log_2 N)$ time to locate the endpoints of the secondary attributes in each of the $O(\log_2 N)$ one-dimensional range trees of the secondary attribute, plus the time to sequence through the answers that are located.

10. Overmars [1442] (see also Bentley [169]) suggests using the solution of the following recurrence relation: Let $M(k, N)$ denote the space necessary for a k-dimensional range tree for N points. At each level of the k-dimensional range tree, at most $M(k - 1, N)$ space is used. Therefore, $M(k, N) \le \log_2 N \cdot M(k - 1, N)$, and the fact that $M(2, N) = O(N \cdot \log_2 N)$ leads to the desired result. The query time is analyzed in the same manner.

11. Use the same technique as in the solution to Exercise 10.

Solutions to Exercises in Section 1.3

1. The balanced binary search tree is equivalent to an extended binary tree. Such a tree with N leaf nodes has $N - 1$ nonleaf nodes.

2. Finding the nearest common ancestor requires at most $2 \cdot \log_2 N$ steps. Once the nearest common ancestor has been found, say Q, the search process may visit each point on the path from Q to B_x and E_x, even if it does not satisfy the query. All other nodes that are visited either cut off or satisfy the search. Of the nodes that cut off the search, at most $2 \cdot F$ are not on the path from Q to B_x and E_x. Empty nodes also cut off the search since their children have already been reported.

3. Procedure PRIORITYSEARCH2 performs more comparison operations than procedure PRIORITYSEARCH; however, they have the same execution time complexity. We prove this by showing that the number of comparison operations that they make differs by a constant factor. This can be seen once we are processing the left (right) subtree of the nearest common ancestor and have determined that the node and its left (right) child are on the path from the nearest common ancestor to B_x (E_x). In this case, there is no longer any need to test whether the remaining nodes in the right (left) child are in the x range. Procedure PRIORITYSEARCH does not perform these additional comparison operations while they are made by procedure PRIORITYSEARCH2. However, the number of additional comparison operations made in this manner is no more than $2 \cdot F$, which is the number of points found to satisfy the query. In all remaining cases, once the nearest common ancestor Q has been found, for nodes in the left (right) subtree of Q, procedure PRIORITYSEARCH compares only the MIDRANGE field of each node with respect to B_x (E_x), while procedure PRIORITYSEARCH2 compares both B_x and E_x. However, this doubles only the number of comparison operations and thus makes no difference in the order of complexity of the two procedures.

4. When procedure PRIORITYSEARCH is invoked, it must distinguish between an empty (i.e., NIL) value and a point for the HEAPMAX field, which it does already. Thus, we simply replace the use of POINT(HEAPMAX(i)) for any priority search tree node i with HEAPMAX(i). This causes no problems as its use is always prefaced by a test for being NIL by virtue of the prior invocation of OUTOFRANGEY.

5. Assuming N data points, after making $\log_2 N$ comparisons, exactly one point is found in the tree.

6. Use a derived pair $(f(x, y), y)$, where $f(x, y) = k \cdot x + y$. f is a mapping such that differences in x are more significant than differences in y. Of course, points must still be unique in the sense that every combination (x, y) must occur just once.

7. Build the one-dimensional range tree first on the x coordinate values of the points. This takes $O(N \cdot \log_2 N)$ time for N points. The next step is to build a heap on the basis of the y coordinate values of the points, which can be done in $O(N)$ time (e.g., [422]). This is easy to do. For the sake of this discussion, assume that the HEAPMAX field of each leaf node contains the actual value of the y coordinate of the point. Initialize the HEAPMAX field of all the nonleaf

nodes to $-\infty$ and apply an $O(N)$ heap creation algorithm (e.g., [422]). At the end of the heap creation process, nodes whose HEAPMAX field is $-\infty$ are the same as empty. Since the order of complexity of the heap creation process is less than that of the one-dimensional range tree construction process, the overall priority search tree construction process is still $O(N \cdot \log_2 N)$ time for N points.

12. The problem is that the priority search trees attached to the successive right children of L are all inverse priority search trees that do not support the semi-infinite range query $([B_x : E_x], [B_y : \infty])$. Similarly, the problem with the modification to the third step of the algorithm is that the inverse priority search trees attached to the successive left children of R are all priority search trees that do not support the semi-infinite range query $([B_x : E_x], [-\infty : E_y])$.

13. The balanced binary search tree is equivalent to an extended binary tree. Such a tree with N leaf nodes has $N - 1$ nonleaf nodes. Each node appears in one priority search tree or inverse priority search tree at each level. There are $\log_2 N$ levels.

14. The analysis is similar to that used in Exercise 8 in Section 1.2. Building the one-dimensional range tree in y takes $O(N \cdot \log_2 N)$ time. The total number of points in the priority and inverse priority search trees at each level is N. Each of these priority search trees consists of a one-dimensional range tree in x at the lowest level. Each of these one-dimensional range trees is built in time proportional to the number of points in it. To see this, we observe that the one-dimensional range trees in x at each level of the range priority tree are built using a merging process. In particular, the one-dimensional range tree in x at level i associated with node a is built by merging the two one-dimensional range trees in x associated with the two children of a at level $i + 1$. Since the x coordinate values of these two children are both sorted, we obtain the one-dimensional range tree at level i in time proportional to the number of points in the two merged one-dimensional range trees. The one-dimensional range trees in x at each level of the tree contain N points, and since there are $\log_2 N$ levels, building the one-dimensional range trees for the x coordinate values takes $O(N \cdot \log_2 N)$ time. The rest of each of the priority search trees is a heap in y, which can be built in time proportional to the number of points in it. Since there are N points at every level, and there are $\log_2 N$ levels, the heap creation part also takes $O(N \cdot \log_2 N)$ time.

15. At each level i ($1 \le i \le \log_2 N - 1$) of the range priority tree, we need to compute 2^i priority and inverse priority search trees (2^{i-1} of each) containing $N/2^i$ points apiece. Therefore, each level of the range priority tree takes $O(2^i \cdot N/2^i \cdot \log_2 N/2^i) = O(N \cdot \log_2 N/2^i)$ time to construct. Summing this quantity over i ($1 \le i \log_2 N/2$) yields approximately $N \cdot \log_2^2 N$, and the desired time bound is $O(N \cdot \log_2^2 N)$.

16. See [535].

17. Finding the nearest common ancestor requires at most $\log_2 N$ steps, and the remaining work is proportional to the number of points found.

21. See Figure S.1.

22. The Cartesian tree is unique as long as each x coordinate value and y coordinate value occurs at most once. This can be seen by observing that the root is the node with a maximum y coordinate value. Once the root has been chosen, the corresponding x coordinate value partitions the remaining points between the left and right subtrees. The recursive application of this process guarantees the uniqueness of the Cartesian tree. Thus, we cannot balance it by the use of rotation operations (unless some of the coordinate values occur more than once).

Solutions to Exercises in Section 1.4.1.1

1. 1 **quadrant procedure** PTCOMPARE(P, R)
    2 /* Return the quadrant of the point quadtree rooted at node R in which node P belongs. */
    3 **value pointer node** P, R
    4 **return(if** XCOORD(P) < XCOORD(R) **then**
    5   **if** YCOORD(P) < YCOORD(R) **then** 'SW'

```
6              else 'NW'
7           endif
8         elseif YCOORD(P) < YCOORD(R) then 'SE'
9         else 'NE'
10        endif)
```

2.
```
1   procedure PTINSERT(P, R)
2   /* Attempt to insert node P in the point quadtree rooted at node R. */
3   value pointer node P
4   reference pointer node R
5   pointer node F, T
6   quadrant Q
7   if ISNULL(R) then R ← P /* The tree at R is initially empty */
8   else
9     T ← R
10    while not ISNULL(T) and not EQUALCOORD(P, T) do
11      F ← T /* Remember the father */
12      Q ← PTCOMPARE(P, T)
13      T ← CHILD(T, Q)
14    enddo
15    if ISNULL(T) then CHILD(F, Q) ← P /* P is not already in the tree */
16    endif
17  endif
```

3. $\lfloor \log_2 N \rfloor$ when all points are collinear (i.e., they lie on a straight line).

4. The maximum path length in an optimized point quadtree of N nodes is $\lfloor \log_2 N \rfloor$. Therefore, the maximum TPL is $\sum_{i=1}^{\lfloor \log_2 N \rfloor} i \cdot 2^i$.

5. The ordering step on N elements is $O(N \cdot \log_2 N)$. Selecting the median at each level of recursion is $O(N)$. Regrouping the records is also $O(N)$. The depth of the recursion is the maximum path length bounded by $\lfloor \log_2 N \rfloor$. Therefore, the running time of the algorithm is $O(N \cdot \log_2 N)$.

6. Overmars and van Leeuwen [1444] use an algorithm similar to that used by Finkel and Bentley [614] to construct their version of an optimized point quadtree. Insert the nodes using the property that for every set of N points, a point quadtree can be built in $O(N \cdot \log_2 N)$ time such that for every nonleaf node with M nodes in its subtrees, every subtree contains at

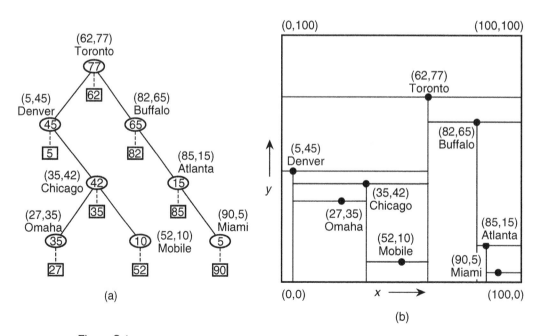

Figure S.1
A Cartesian tree.

most $\lceil M/2 \rceil$ nodes. Each subquadrant is repeatedly subdivided with respect to a point whose coordinate value is the median along a chosen axis. If the balance of the tree is destroyed upon the insertion of a point node, then rebuild the subtree rooted at the shallowest nonleaf node at which the tree is still balanced.

7. See [1444].

8. Finkel and Bentley [614, p. 4] suggest leaf balancing operations that they term *single balance* and *double balance*. Kersten and van Emde Boas [1018] report on an empirical study of different balancing operations.

9. $N \cdot (N-1)/2$, which arises when the tree is linear so that the insertion of the ith point requires $i-1$ comparison operations.

Solutions to Exercises in Section 1.4.1.2

1. 1 **pointer node procedure** FINDCANDIDATE(P,Q)
   2 /* P is a pointer to the child in quadrant Q of the node to be deleted. Starting at P, repeatedly follow the branch corresponding to OPQUAD(Q) until a node having no subtree along this branch is encountered. If P is initially NIL, then use INF to return a pointer to a fictitious point in the quadrant that is farthest from the deleted node (e.g., $(-\infty, -\infty)$ in the SW quadrant). */
   3 **value pointer node** P
   4 **value quadrant** Q
   5 **if** ISNULL(P) **then return** INF(Q)
   6 **endif**
   7 **while not** ISNULL(CHILD(P,OPQUAD(Q))) **do** $P \leftarrow$ CHILD(P,OPQUAD(Q))
   8 **enddo**
   9 **return** P

2. 1 **procedure** PTDELETE(P,R)
   2 /* Delete node P from the point quadtree rooted at node R. If the root of the tree was deleted, then reset R. */
   3 **begin**
   4 **value pointer node** P
   5 **reference pointer node** R
   6 **pointer node** J,T
   7 **quadrant** Q
   8 **if** HASNOCHILDS(P) **or** HASONLYONECHILD(P) **then**
   9   /* Set P's father to the child of P if one exists; otherwise, return NIL */
   10   $J \leftarrow$ FINDFATHER(P)
   11   **if** ISNULL(J) **then** $R \leftarrow$ NONEMPTYCHILD(P)
   12   **else** CHILD(J,CHILDTYPE(P)) $\leftarrow$ NONEMPTYCHILD(P)
   13   **endif**
   14   RETURNTOAVAIL(P)
   15   **return**
   16 **else** /* Find the "best" replacement node for P and rearrange the tree */
   17   $J \leftarrow$ "best" replacement node for P
   18   $Q \leftarrow$ quadrant of P containing J
   19   /* Copy the coordinate values of node J to node P */
   20   XCOORD(P) $\leftarrow$ XCOORD(J)
   21   YCOORD(P) $\leftarrow$ YCOORD(J)
   22   /* Rearrange the remaining quadrants */
   23   ADJQUAD(CQUAD(Q),OPQUAD(Q),CQUAD(Q),P,P)
   24   ADJQUAD(CCQUAD(Q),OPQUAD(Q),CCQUAD(Q),P,P)
   25   **if** PTCOMPARE(CHILD(P,Q),P) $\neq Q$ **then**
   26   /* Open-closed conventions force reinsertion */
   27     $T \leftarrow$ CHILD(P,Q)
   28   CHILD(P,Q) $\leftarrow$ NIL
   29   INSERTQUADRANT(T,P)

30 **else** NEWROOT(Q,CHILD(P,Q),P,P) /* Rearrange quadrant Q */
31 **endif**
32 RETURNTOAVAIL(J) /* Return node J to AVAIL since no longer need it */
33 **endif**

1 **recursive procedure** ADJQUAD(Q,D,S,F,R)
2 /* Rearrange subquadrant CHILD(F,S) of quadrant Q of the tree rooted at R.
  R is the node that has been deleted. D is the quadrant in which nodes in the
  subquadrant rooted at CHILD(F,S) may have to be reinserted. Otherwise, they
  remain in quadrant Q. */
3 **value quadrant** Q,D,S
4 **value pointer node** F,R
5 **pointer node** T
6 $T \leftarrow$ CHILD(F,S)
7 **if** ISNULL(T) **then return** /* An empty link */
8 **elseif** PTCOMPARE(T,R) $= Q$ **then**
9 /* Node T and subquadrants CHILD(T,Q) and CHILD(T,OPQUAD(D)) need
   no reinsertion */
10 ADJQUAD(Q,D,OPQUAD(Q),T,R) /* Rearrange subquadrant
            CHILD(T,OPQUAD(Q)) */
11 ADJQUAD(Q,D,D,T,R) /* Rearrange subquadrant CHILD(T,D) */
12 **else**
13 /* Unlink subquadrant S from F so that it will not be found upon reinsertion
   should it belong to the same quadrant */
14 CHILD(F,S) $\leftarrow$ NIL
15 INSERTQUADRANT(T,R)
16 **endif**

1 **recursive procedure** NEWROOT(Q,S,R,F)
2 /* Rearrange the quadrant containing the replacement node for the deleted node
  R—that is, quadrant Q of node R. S is the root of the subquadrant currently
  being processed and is a child of F. */
3 **value quadrant** Q
4 **value pointer node** S,R,F
5 **if** ISNULL(CHILD(S,OPQUAD(Q))) **then**
6 /* S is the replacement node. Insert its subquadrants and reset the father of the
   replacement node. */
7 INSERTQUADRANT(CHILD(S,CQUAD(Q)),R)
8 INSERTQUADRANT(CHILD(S,CCQUAD(Q)),R)
9 **if** $R \neq F$ **then** /* Reset the father of the replacement node */
10   CHILD(F,OPQUAD(Q)) $\leftarrow$ CHILD(S,Q)
11 **else** CHILD(F,Q) $\leftarrow$ CHILD(S,Q)
12 **endif**
13 **else**
14 /* Rearrange the quadrants adjacent to quadrant Q of the tree rooted at S and
   reapply NEWROOT to CHILD(S,OPQUAD(Q)) */
15 /* Rearrange subquadrant CHILD(S,CQUAD(Q)) */
16 ADJQUAD(Q,CQUAD(Q),CQUAD(Q),S,R)
17 /* Rearrange subquadrant CHILD(S,CCQUAD(Q)) */
18 ADJQUAD(Q,CCQUAD(Q),CCQUAD(Q),S,R)
19 /* Rearrange subquadrant CHILD(S,OPQUAD(Q)) */
20 **if** PTCOMPARE(CHILD(S,OPQUAD(Q)),R) $\neq Q$ **then**
21   /* Open-closed conventions force reinsertion */
22   $F \leftarrow$ CHILD(S,OPQUAD(Q))
23   CHILD(S,OPQUAD(Q)) $\leftarrow$ NIL
24   INSERTQUADRANT(F,R)
25 **else** NEWROOT(Q,CHILD(S,OPQUAD(Q)),R,S)
26 **endif**
27 **endif**

3. (a) Let us first examine the case that B at $(3,-5)$ is in the SE child of A. Let F at $(5,-5)$ be
   the SE child of A. Before we replaced A with B, F was in the SE quadrant of A. Once we
   replace A with B, F is now in the NE quadrant of B due to the open and closed conventions,

and thus we have to reinsert the entire subtree rather than take advantage of the pruning that is afforded by use of NEWROOT.

(b) Let us now examine the case that B is in the SW child of A. There are two subcases depending on the exact position of B. In both cases, let F at $(-5,-5)$ be the SW child of A.

    i. Let B be at $(-5,-3)$. Before we replaced A with B, F was in the SW quadrant of A. Once we replace A with B, F is now in the SE quadrant of B due to the open and closed conventions, and thus we have to reinsert the entire subtree rather than take advantage of the pruning that is afforded by use of NEWROOT.

    ii. Let B be at $(-3,-5)$. Before we replaced A with B, F was in the SW quadrant of A. Once we replace A with B, F is now in the NE quadrant of B due to the open and closed conventions, and thus we have to reinsert the entire subtree rather than take advantage of the pruning that is afforded by use of NEWROOT.

5. Use induction. Assume that the root is at depth 0. The result is clearly true for $N = 1$. Assume that it is true for $N = i$ and show that it is true for $N = i + 1$. Add the $(i + 1)$-th node at the bottom of the tree—say to a node at depth m—and let T' denote the new tree. TPL(T') increases by m. Also, each of the subtrees rooted at nodes at depths 0 through $m - 1$ in which the new node is a member have increased in size by 1 for a total increase of m. Furthermore, there is one additional subtree of size 1 corresponding to the $(i + 1)$-th node. The result follows, and holds for trees, as well as binary search trees and point quadtrees, since empty trees and orientation make no difference.

6. See [1618].

7. See [1618].

10. See [1617].

12. In the two-dimensional case, first divide the data points into two sets containing $\lceil N/3 \rceil$ and $\lfloor 2 \cdot N/3 \rfloor$ points. Next, divide the larger set into two parts containing $\lceil N/3 \rceil$ points each. This process is applied recursively. Overmars and van Leeuwen [1444] give more details.

13. See [1444].

14. Consider a collinear set of data points (i.e., a straight line). Alternatively, the set of points need have only monotonically increasing or monotonically decreasing coordinate values. If the line coincides with one of the axes lines, then the axes are rotated slightly.

15. See [1444].

16. See [1444] for a proof similar to that for Exercise 7 in Section 1.4.1.1.

Solutions to Exercises in Section 1.4.1.3

2. The subtrees at level $m - i$ form a regular checkerboard of 4^i squares. The expected number of squares intersected along the x and y directions is bounded by $x \cdot 2^i + 1$ and $y \cdot 2^i + 1$, respectively. Therefore, the number of squares at level i overlapped by the search rectangle is bounded by $(x \cdot 2^i + 1) \cdot (y \cdot 2^i + 1)$. Summing this quantity over all levels $0 \le i \le m - 1$, together with the fact that N, the number of nodes, is $(4^m - 1)/3$, yields $x \cdot y \cdot N + (x + y) \cdot \sqrt{3 \cdot N} + \log_4(3 \cdot N)$.

3. The expected number of records in a square search region is $N \cdot x^2$. The expected number of records visited in such a search in an inverted list is $N \cdot x$, and the expected overwork is $(1 - x) \cdot x \cdot N$. From Exercise 2 we have that for a square search region in a perfect point quadtree, the amount of overwork is approximately $2 \cdot x \cdot \sqrt{3 \cdot N}$. Thus, we see that the overwork for square search regions in perfect point quadtrees is asymptotically less than that for inverted lists.

4. See [1132].

6. See [2000].

Solutions to Exercises in Section 1.4.2.1

1. 1 **quadrant procedure** MXCOMPARE(X,Y,W)
    2 /* Return the quadrant of the MX quadtree of width $2 \cdot W$ centered at (W,W)
         in which data point (X,Y) belongs. */
    3 **value integer** X,Y,W
    4 **return**(**if** $X < W$ **then**
    5   **if** $Y < W$ **then** 'SW'
    6   **else** 'NW'
    7   **endif**
    8   **elseif** $Y < W$ **then** 'SE'
    9   **else** 'NE'
    10   **endif**)

2. 1 **procedure** MXINSERT(P,X,Y,R,W)
    2 /* Attempt to insert node P corresponding to data point (X,Y) in the MX
         quadtree rooted at node R of width W. If the tree is empty, then R is set
         to point to the new root. Nodes are created by use of CREATEPNODE.
         GRAY is used to specify nonleaf nodes. */
    3 **value pointer node** P
    4 **reference pointer node** R
    5 **value integer** X,Y,W
    6 **pointer node** T
    7 **quadrant** Q
    8 **if** $W = 1$ **then** /* The tree corresponds to a one-element dataset */
    9      $R \leftarrow P$
    10   **return**
    11 **elseif** ISNULL(R) **then**
    12     $R \leftarrow$ CREATEPNODE('GRAY') /* The tree at R is initially empty */
    13   **endif**
    14 $T \leftarrow R$
    15 $W \leftarrow W/2$
    16 $Q \leftarrow$ MXCOMPARE(X,Y,W)
    17 **while** $W > 1$ **do**
    18   **if** ISNULL(CHILD(T,Q)) **then**
    19   CHILD(T,Q)) $\leftarrow$ CREATEPNODE('GRAY')
    20   **endif**
    21     $T \leftarrow$ CHILD(T,Q)
    22     $X \leftarrow X$ **mod** W
    23     $Y \leftarrow Y$ **mod** W
    24     $W \leftarrow W/2$
    25     $Q \leftarrow$ MXCOMPARE(X,Y,W)
    26 **enddo**
    27 CHILD(T,Q) $\leftarrow P$

    1 **pointer node procedure** CREATEPNODE(C)
    2 /* Create a node with color C and return a pointer to it. */
    3 **value color** C
    4 **pointer node** P
    5 **quadrant** I
    6 $P \leftarrow$ CREATE(**node**)
    7 NODETYPE(P) $\leftarrow C$
    8 **for** I **in** {'NW','NE','SW','SE'} **do**
    9   CHILD(P,I) $\leftarrow$ NIL
    10 **enddo**
    11 **return** P

3. 1 **procedure** MXDELETE(X,Y,R,W)
    2 /* Delete the node corresponding to data point (X,Y) from the MX quadtree
         rooted at node R of width W. If (X,Y) is the only data point in the tree, then
         the root will be set to NIL. If all of (X,Y)'s brothers are NIL, then the nearest
         ancestor of (X,Y) that has more than one non-NIL child is set to point to NIL
         in the direction of (X,Y). The nonleaf nodes that are bypassed as a result of
         this collapsing process are returned to the free storage list. */

```
3    reference pointer node R
4    value integer X,Y,W
5    pointer node F,T,Temp
6    quadrant Q,Q_F
7    if IsNull(R) then return /* The tree is empty */
8    elseif W = 1 then /* The resulting tree is empty */
9        ReturnToAvail(R)
10       R ← Nil
11       return
12   endif
13   T ← R
14   F ← Nil
15   do /* Locate the quadrant in which (X,Y) belongs */
16       W ← W/2
17       Q ← MXCompare(X,Y,W)
18       if not(IsNull(Child(T,CQuad(Q))) and
19              IsNull(Child(T,OpQuad(Q))) and
20              IsNull(Child(T,CCQuad(Q)))) then
21           /* As the tree is descended, F and Q_F keep track of the nearest ancestor
                of (X,Y) with more than one child */
22           F ← T
23           Q_F ← Q
24       endif
25       T ← Child(T,Q)
26       X ← X mod W
27       Y ← Y mod W
28   until W = 1 or IsNull(T)
29   enddo
30   if IsNull(T) then return /* Data point (X,Y) is not in the tree */
31   else /* Collapse as much as possible */
32       T ← if IsNull(F) then R /* The entire tree will be collapsed */
33             else Child(F,Q_F)
34       Q ← 'NW'
35       while Gray(T) do /* Collapse one level at a time */
36          while IsNull(Child(T,Q)) do
37              Q ← CQuad(Q) /* Find non-Nil child */
38          enddo
39          Temp ← Child(T,Q)
40          Child(T,Q) ← Nil
41          ReturnToAvail(T)
42          T ← Temp
43       enddo
44       ReturnToAvail(T)
45       if IsNull(F) then R ← Nil  /* The tree contained just one node */
46       else Child(F,Q_F) ← Nil  /* Reset the link of the nearest ancestor */
47       endif
48   endif
```

5. The worst case arises when the boundaries of the rectangular query region intersect 2^n nodes (i.e., regions).

7. $\sum_{i=0}^{n-1} 4^i = (4^n - 1)/3$.

8. For a complete MX quadtree (i.e., where no sparseness occurs), the array representation requires one-third less space since the MX quadtree representation needs pointers. However, using the array, one-third more interchange operations must be performed while computing the transpose.

9. Wise [2006] observes that a quadtreelike decomposition admits a hybrid algorithm that uses *both* Strassen's recurrence [1804] and the conventional one (e.g., [578, Section 1.4]). The conventional recurrence requires eight quadrant multiplications, which is reduced when some of the quadrants correspond to nonleaf nodes that correspond to blocks of zeros. For example, only six quadrant multiplications are necessary when only one of the eight quadrants corresponds to a nonleaf node. The amount of reduction depends on how many such zero quadrants are present, but the improvement is profound with sparse matrices [1]. On larger

```
30              IsNull(Child(T,OpQuad(Q))) and
31              IsNull(Child(T,CcQuad(Q)))) then
32          /* As the tree is descended, F and Q_F keep track of the nearest ancestor
                of (X,Y) with more than one child */
33          F ← T
34          Q_F ← Q
35       endif
36       F_T ← T
37       T ← Child(T, Q)
38       X ← X+S_x[Q]*L_x
39       L_x ← L_x/2.0
40       Y ← Y + S_y[Q] * L_y
41       L_y ← L_y/2.0
42   until IsNull(T) or not Gray(T)
43   enddo
44   if IsNull(T) or
45      not(XCoord(P) = XCoord(T) and
46          YCoord(P) = YCoord(T)) then
47      return /* Node P is not in the tree */
48   else /* Determine if collapsing is possible */
49      ReturnToAvail(T)
50      Child(F_T, Q) ← Nil
51      S ← 0
52      for Q in {'NW','NE','SW','SE'} do
53          /* Determine the number of brother leaf nodes */
54          if not IsNull(Child(F_T, Q)) then
55              if Gray(Child(F_T, Q)) then return /* No collapsing is possible */
56              else S ← S + 1
57              endif
58          endif
59      enddo
60      if S > 1 then return /* No collapsing is possible */
61      else
62          T ←if IsNull(F) then R
63              else Child(F, Q_F)
64              endif
65          Q ← 'NW'
66          while Gray(T) do /* Collapse one level at a time */
67              while IsNull(Child(T, Q)) do
68                  Q ← CQuad(Q) /* Find the non-Nil child */
69              enddo
70              Temp ← Child(T, Q)
71              Child(T, Q) ← Nil
72              ReturnToAvail(T)
73              T ← Temp
74          enddo
75          if IsNull(F) then R ← T
76          else Child(F, Q_F) ← T
77          endif
78      endif
79   endif
```

4. The $\sqrt{2}$ term arises from the fact that the points may be at opposite corners of the smallest square of side width s/d.

5. Overmars [1442] suggests that the N points be chosen in such a way that they form $N/2$ clusters of two points each. These $N/2$ clusters are the leaf nodes of a complete PR quadtree of depth $\log_4(N/2)$ such that each leaf contains one cluster. At this point, each of the $N/2$ clusters must be further decomposed by use of the PR quadtree. The $N/2$ clusters of points are chosen in such a way that the elements of each cluster appear at the maximum depth in the PR quadtree (i.e., n). The result is that we need $O(N)$ space for the nodes at depth 0 through $\log_4(N/2)$ and $O((n - \log_4(N/2)) \cdot N)$ for the nodes at the remaining depths up to n. When 2^n is large in comparison to N, this is $O(N \cdot n)$.

6. This occurs when 2^n is $O(N)$ or smaller than N.

8. The worst case arises when the boundaries of the rectangular query region intersect 2^n nodes (i.e., regions).

9. $1/4^k$.

10. $\left(1 - \frac{1}{4^k}\right)^v$.

11. $\binom{v}{1} \cdot \frac{1}{4^k} \cdot \left(1 - \frac{1}{4^k}\right)^{v-1}$.

12. $1 - \left(1 - \frac{1}{4^k}\right)^v - \binom{v}{1} \cdot \frac{1}{4^k} \cdot \left(1 - \frac{1}{4^k}\right)^{v-1}$.

13. $4^{k+1} \cdot \left(1 - \left(1 - \frac{1}{4^k}\right)^v - \binom{v}{1} \cdot \frac{1}{4^k} \cdot \left(1 - \frac{1}{4^k}\right)^{v-1}\right)$.

14. $E = 1 + \sum_{k=0}^{\infty} 4^{k+1} \cdot \left(1 - \left(1 - \frac{1}{4^k}\right)^v - \binom{n}{1} \cdot \frac{1}{4^k} \cdot \left(1 - \frac{1}{4^k}\right)^{v-1}\right)$.

16. All instances of 2^2 or 4 are replaced by 2^m.

Solutions to Exercises in Section 1.4.3

2. See Exercise 6 in Section 1.5.2.1 and its solution for a related problem that has been addressed by Flajolet and Puech [621].

Solutions to Exercises in Section 1.5.1.1

1.
```
1   direction procedure KDCOMPARE(P, R)
2   /* Return the child of the k-d tree rooted at node R in which node P belongs. */
3   value pointer node P, R
4   return(if COORD(P, DISC(R)) < COORD(R, DISC(R)) then 'LEFT'
5           else 'RIGHT'
6           endif)
```

2.
```
1   procedure KDINSERT(P, R)
2   /* Attempt to insert node P in the k-d tree rooted at node R. */
3   value pointer node P
4   reference pointer node R
5   pointer node F, T
6   direction Q
7   if ISNULL(R) then /* The tree at R is initially empty */
8       R ← P
9       DISC(P) ← 'X' /* Assume without loss of generality that 'X' is the first
                            discriminator */
10  else
11      T ← R /* Initialize T since R is a reference variable */
12      while not ISNULL(T) and not EQUALCOORD(P, T) do
13          F ← T /* Remember the father */
14          Q ← KDCOMPARE(P, T)
15          T ← CHILD(T, Q)
16      enddo
17      if ISNULL(T) then /* P is not already in the tree */
18          CHILD(F, Q) ← P
19          DISC(P) ← NEXTDISC(F)
20      endif
21  endif
```

761

4. Bentley [164] shows that the probability of constructing a given k-d tree of N nodes by inserting N nodes in a random order into an initially empty k-d tree is the same as the probability of constructing the same tree by random insertion into a one-dimensional binary search tree. Once this is done, results that have been proved for one-dimensional binary search trees will be applicable to k-d trees. The proof relies on viewing the records as d-tuples of permutations of the integers $1, \ldots, N$. The nodes are considered random if all of the $(N!)^k$ d-tuples of permutations are permitted to occur. It is assumed that the key values in a given record are independent.

5. See [1912] for some hints.

Solutions to Exercises in Section 1.5.1.2

1.　1　**recursive pointer node procedure** FINDDMINIMUM(P, D)
　　2　/* Find the node with the smallest value for the D coordinate in the k-d tree
　　　　　rooted at P */
　　3　**value pointer node** P
　　4　**value direction** D
　　5　**pointer node** L, H
　　6　**if** ISNULL(P) **then return** NIL
　　7　**elseif** DISC(P) $= D$ **then** /* The 'MINIMUM' node is in the left subtree (i.e.,
　　　　　　　　　　　　　　　　　LOCHILD) */
　　8　　**if** ISNULL(LOCHILD(P)) **then return** P
　　9　　**else** $P \leftarrow$ LOCHILD(P)
　　10　　**endif**
　　11　**endif**
　　12　/* Now, DISC(P) $\neq D$. The 'MINIMUM' node is the node with the smallest D
　　　　　coordinate value of P, min(LOCHILD(P)), and min(HICHILD(P)) */
　　13　$L \leftarrow$ FINDDMINIMUM(LOCHILD(P), D)
　　14　$H \leftarrow$ FINDDMINIMUM(HICHILD(P), D)
　　15　**if not** ISNULL(H) **and** COORD(H, D) $\leq$ COORD(P, D) **then** $P \leftarrow H$
　　16　**endif**
　　17　**if not** ISNULL(L) **and** COORD(L, D) $\leq$ COORD(P, D) **then** $P \leftarrow L$
　　18　**endif**
　　19　**return** P

2.　1　**procedure** KDDELETE(P, R)
　　2　/* Delete node P from the k-d tree rooted at node R. If the root of the tree was
　　　　　deleted, then reset R. */
　　3　**value pointer node** P
　　4　**reference pointer node** R
　　5　**pointer node** F, N
　　6　$N \leftarrow$ KDDELETE1(P)
　　7　$F \leftarrow$ FINDFATHER(P, R, NIL)
　　8　**if** ISNULL(F) **then** $R \leftarrow N$ /* Reset the pointer to the root of the tree */
　　9　**else** CHILD(F, CHILDTYPE(P)) $\leftarrow N$
　　10　**endif**
　　11　RETURNTOAVAIL(P)

　　1　**recursive pointer node procedure** KDDELETE1(P)
　　2　/* Delete node P and return a pointer to the root of the resulting subtree. */
　　3　**value pointer node** P
　　4　**pointer node** F, R
　　5　**direction** D
　　6　**if** ISNULL(LOCHILD(P)) **and** ISNULL(HICHILD(P)) **then**
　　7　　**return** NIL /* P is a leaf */
　　8　**else** $D \leftarrow$ DISC(P)
　　9　**endif**
　　10　**if** ISNULL(HICHILD(P)) **then** /* Special handling when HICHILD is empty */

```
11      HiChild(P) ← LoChild(P)
12      LoChild(P) ← Nil
13   endif
14   R ← FindDMinimum(HiChild(P), D)
15   F ← FindFather(R, HiChild(P), P)
16   Child(F, ChildType(R)) ← KdDelete1(R) /* Reset the father of R */
17   LoChild(R) ← LoChild(P)
18   HiChild(R) ← HiChild(P)
19   Disc(R) ← Disc(P)
20   return R
```

```
1   recursive pointer node procedure FindFather(P, R, F)
2   /* Return the father of node P in the k-d tree rooted at R where F is the father
       of R. */
3   value pointer node P, R, F
4   return(if EqualCoord(P, R) then F
5           else FindFather(P, Child(KdCompare(P, R), R))
6           endif)
```

6. Assume the worst case: a complete k-d tree with the D discriminator found at depth $d - 1$. Therefore, all nodes at depth 0 through $d - 1$ will have to be visited (i.e., $2^d - 1$ nodes), while the right subtrees of nodes at depth $d - 1$ are pruned. This pruning occurs repeatedly at depths $h \cdot d - 1$, where $h > 0$. At all other depths, all nodes in nonpruned subtrees must be visited (e.g., all nodes at depth $h \cdot d$ through $h \cdot d - 1$ in the nonpruned subtrees). Summing up yields the desired result.

Solutions to Exercises in Section 1.5.1.3

1. If the search region would have been chosen in the middle of the space, then in the worst case, we would want the root of the k-d tree to partition the region somewhere in the middle. In this case, the subtrees contain identically shaped subregions of the original search region, and the analysis is applied recursively.

5. The search region is a $(d - s)$-dimensional hyperplane.

6. Assume the most pessimistic case: the first $d - s$ discriminators in the tree correspond to the $d - s$ unspecified keys of the partial range query. Therefore, all nodes at depth 0 through $d - s$ must be visited (i.e., $2^{d-s} - 1$ nodes), while pruning occurs at depth $d - s$ through $d - 1$, resulting in $t \cdot 2^{d-s-1}$ nodes being visited. This pruning occurs repeatedly at depth $h \cdot d - s$ through $h \cdot d - 1$. At all other depths, all nodes in nonpruned subtrees must be visited (e.g., all nodes at depth $h \cdot d$ through $h \cdot d - s$ in the nonpruned subtrees). Summing up yields the desired result.

Solutions to Exercises in Section 1.5.1.4

2. See [1444].

4. $N \cdot \log_2 N$ for N points.

5. See [650].

7. See [1226, 1228].

8. Compute the approximate nearest neighbors for each of the training points. For training point i, let d_{ei} be the distance to the exact nearest neighbor and d_{ai} be the distance to the approximate nearest neighbor. Therefore, $d_{ei} \leq d_{ai} \leq (1 + \varepsilon) \cdot d_{ei}$. When determining the discriminator key and value for partitioning the cell, use a distance d_{si} obtained by shrinking the distance d_{ai} to the approximate nearest neighbor of training point i by the factor $(1 + \varepsilon)$— that is, $d_{si} = d_{ai}/(1 + \varepsilon)$. The effect of the shrinking serves to decrease the likelihood that

the computation of the nearest neighbor of a training point needs to examine points in both halves of the cell that is being split as it enables a nearest point in the half of the cell that does not contain i to be ignored subject to the approximation error tolerance ε. Although it appears that the ε factor is accounted for twice—that is, once in the original determination of the approximate nearest neighbors and once in the determination of the discriminator key and value for the cell. This is not true, as can be seen by noting that $d_{ei}/(1+\varepsilon) \le d_{si} \le d_{ei}$. In other words, use of the distance to the actual approximate nearest neighbor means that we have not shrunken the nearest neighbor distance by the maximum amount for the given approximation error tolerance ε.

10. This is a result of the requirement that both R_1 and R_2 be α-balanced.

11. Start with an initial α-balanced canonical region. As this region is k-cuttable, use a sequence of k canonical cuts to subdivide the region into $k+1$ α-balanced canonical subregions so that each one contains fewer than βN of the points. Apply this process recursively to each of the resulting subregions until each subregion has fewer than some constant number of points (i.e., the bucket capacity). This process cannot be repeated more than $O(\log_{1/\beta}N)$ times down any path of subregions. Each time the process is applied, we obtain a binary tree of maximum depth k, and thus the maximum depth of the BAR tree is $O(k\log_{1/\beta}N)$ as desired [517].

12. $k = O(d)$ and $\beta = O(d/(d+1))$ implies $\log_{1/\beta}N = O(d\log N)$, and thus $O(k\log_{1/\beta}N) = O(d^2\log N)$ as desired.

14. No.

Solutions to Exercises in Section 1.5.2.1

2. It has a greater potential for saving space.

3. See [483], who obtain a result of $N \cdot (n - \log_2 N + 2.402)$.

5. See [1046, Section 6.3] for a proof for $d = 1$, which is generalized to hold for arbitrary values of d.

6. Flajolet and Puech [621] perform such an analysis for a k-d tree and a PR k-d tree and show that the PR k-d tree is asymptotically better than the k-d tree.

Solutions to Exercises in Section 1.5.2.2

1. See [297] for the basis of a solution.

2. (David M. Mount) In the worst case, $O(N \cdot d)$ leaf nodes are needed. To see how this situation can arise, consider the following point set consisting of N d-dimensional points $\{p_i|i=1\ldots N\}$ contained within the unit cube where the coordinate values for each point are identical. In particular, let $p_i = (1/2^i - \varepsilon, 1/2^i - \varepsilon, \ldots, 1/2^i - \varepsilon)$, where ε denotes an arbitrarily small quantity greater than 0, and the origin is the lower-left corner (minimum) corner. In (virtually) all instances (except where a point is separated and no slide occurs), the points will lie below the partitioning plane, and hence the slide will move the splitting plane to the left (lower coordinate value). For example, Figure S.2 illustrates this case for four points in two dimensions. The broken lines indicate the original position of the partition plane before it has been slid to its final position, which is indicated by a solid line.

The initial cell has corner points $(0,0,\ldots,0)$ and $(1,1,\ldots,1)$. Let x_1 be the first splitting axis. Since p_1's coordinate values are all $1/2 - \varepsilon$, the first partitioning plane is $x_1 = 1/2$, which is then slid to the left and is placed at $x_1 = 1/2 - \varepsilon$. The upper-right (maximum) corner of the resulting cell is $(1/2 - \varepsilon, 1, 1, \ldots, 1)$. The second splitting axis is x_2 as it is one of the axes along which the corresponding coordinate value has the maximum range (i.e., one of the longest sides of the cell). The partitioning plane is now $x_2 = 1/2$, which is then slid to the left and is

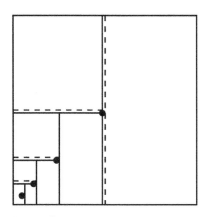

Figure S.2
Example of a set of four points in two dimensions illustrating how the worst case can arise that an open-sliding midpoint k-d tree can require $O(N \cdot d)$ leaf nodes.

placed at $x_2 = 1/2 - \varepsilon$. It yields a cell with an upper-right corner at $(1/2 - \varepsilon, 1/2 - \varepsilon, 1, 1, \ldots, 1)$. This partition-and-slide process is repeated d times, resulting in a cell whose upper-right corner is the point p_1.

Now, let us turn our attention to point p_2, all of whose coordinate values are $1/4 - \varepsilon$. The first split is at $x_1 = 1/2(1/2 - \varepsilon) = 1/4 - \varepsilon/2$. This split separates p_1 from p_2, and so is not slid. The lower-left corner of the cell containing p_2 is at the origin, while the upper-right corner is at $(1/4 - \varepsilon/2, 1/2 - \varepsilon, 1/2 - \varepsilon, \ldots, 1/2 - \varepsilon)$. The next splitting axis is x_2, which is bisected at $x_2 = 1/2(1/2 - \varepsilon) = 1/4 - \varepsilon/2$, which is then slid to the left and is placed at $x_2 = 1/4 - \varepsilon$. This partition-and-slide process is repeated once for each of the remaining coordinate values for a total of $d - 1$ times, and hence the final upper-right corner of this cell is located at $(1/4 - \varepsilon/2, 1/4 - \varepsilon, 1/4 - \varepsilon, \ldots, 1/4 - \varepsilon)$. Note that the value of the first coordinate is different from the rest because it was used to separate p_1 from p_2, and thus was not subject to sliding.

Next, we process p_3. Again, the first split will be on x_1. It is used to separate p_2 from p_3, and so is not slid. The process that we have just described is repeated for the remaining points, once per point, except for the last point. Therefore, we have made d partition-and-slide operations to separate p_1 from the rest of the points, while for each of the remaining points p_i ($1 < i < N$), we have made $d - 1$ partition-and-slide operations to separate p_i from p_{i-1}. Thus, for n points, we have a total of $d + (N - 2) \cdot d + 1 = (N - 1) \cdot d + 1$ partition operations of which $d + (N - 2) \cdot (d - 1) = (N - 1) \cdot (d - 1) + 1$ are partition-and-slide operations. Since each partition-and-slide operation results in the creation of one empty leaf node, we have $(N - 1) \cdot (d - 1) + 1 = O(N \cdot d)$ empty leaf nodes. Alternatively, since the total number of leaf nodes is one more than the number of partitions, and since there are N nonempty leaf nodes, the number of empty leaf nodes is N less than the number of partitions—that is, $1 + (N - 1) \cdot d + 1 - N = (N - 1) \cdot (d - 1) + 1$.

To see that the number of empty leaf cells is at most $N \cdot d$, we observe that each empty leaf node results from a partition-and-slide operation and hence is supported by a point. Each point can support at most d different empty leaf nodes, one for each coordinate or dimension. A point cannot support more than d different empty leaf nodes because this would imply that for some dimension it has been slid into from two different sides, which is impossible.

To see why this is impossible, consider an example in two dimensions, and suppose that point p has been slid into from a vertical split to the right of p. We now show how a slide could hit p from the other side. Assume that we make a subsequent vertical split to left of p. In order for such a split to be attempted, there must be some other point p' in the same cell as p (otherwise this would be a leaf). For a slide to take place, p' must be to the right of the midpoint split, as is p, since otherwise it is not a trivial split. Thus, the empty cell on the right side of p would be supported by p, and the empty cell on the left side of p would be supported by a different point p'. Therefore, we cannot slide into p from two different sides. Observe that if points are not in general position, and p and p' have the same x coordinate value, then p could be slid into from both sides. However, as this example shows, there must be at least two points p and p' sandwiched between the two lines, so the above argument still applies.

Solutions to Exercises in Section 1.5.2.3

1. The probability that i bit positions of c records are not sufficient to resolve the overflow (i.e., they have identical values) is $p_i = 2^{-ic}$, and the expected number of bits that must be compared is $E = \lim_{h \to \infty} \sum_{i=1}^{h} i \cdot p_{i-1} \cdot (1 - p_i)$. Orenstein [1413] shows that E is bounded by 28/9, and as c increases, it approaches 1.

Solutions to Exercises in Section 1.5.2.4

2. Make sure that at least one split results in more than one point in each node. For example, compare Figure S.3(a,b) and Figure S.3(c,d), which correspond to the block and tree representations of a path-compressed PR k-d tree and a sliding-midpoint k-d tree, respectively, for the same four-point dataset where the path-compressed PR k-d tree is shallower than the sliding-midpoint k-d tree.

Solutions to Exercises in Section 1.5.2.4

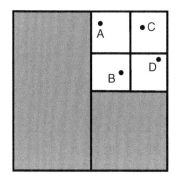

(a)

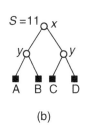

(b)

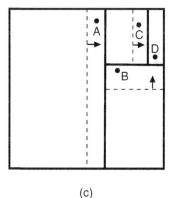

(c)

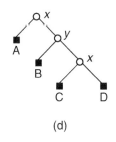

(d)

Figure S.3
The (a) block and (b) tree representations of a path-compressed PR k-d tree, for the same four-point dataset, that is shallower than its sliding-midpoint k-d tree with corresponding (c) block and (d) tree representations.

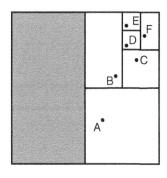

(a)

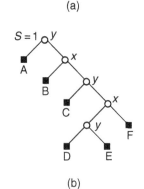

(b)

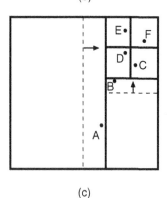

(c)

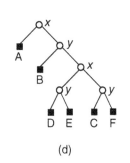

(d)

Figure S.4
The (a) block and (b) tree representations of a path-compressed PR k-d tree, for the same six-point dataset, that is deeper than its sliding-midpoint k-d tree with corresponding (c) block and (d) tree representations.

3. No, as can be seen by comparing Figure S.4(a,b) and Figure S.4(c,d), which correspond to the block and tree representations of a path-compressed PR k-d tree and a sliding-midpoint k-d tree, respectively, for the same six-point dataset where the path-compressed PR k-d tree is deeper than the sliding-midpoint k-d tree.

4. Both structures have the same number of leaf and nonleaf nodes. However, the nonleaf nodes of the path-compressed PR k-d tree are less complex than those of the sliding-midpoint k-d tree as they only need to store a bit pattern corresponding to the splits or coordinate values whose testing has been avoided, in contrast to the sliding-midpoint k-d tree where the full value of the split partition must also be recorded.

5. The path-compressed PR k-d tree avoids the worst case of the open-sliding midpoint k-d tree by not having any empty nodes, thereby enabling the retention of the property of having N leaf nodes for N points. Thus, the number of nodes in the path-compressed PR k-d tree is always less than or equal to the number of nodes in the open-sliding midpoint k-d tree. In particular, we see that the empty nodes that result in the worst case of the open-sliding midpoint k-d tree are avoided by the bitstring corresponding to the splits that have been avoided whose constituent bits indicate which coordinate values need not be tested as testing them will result in trivial splits. However, no such conclusion can be drawn about the relationship between the maximum depths of the path-compressed PR and open-sliding midpoint k-d trees. In particular, the maximum depth of the open-sliding midpoint k-d tree corresponding to the four-point dataset in Figure S.3 is deeper than that of the corresponding path-compressed PR k-d tree due to the presence of the two empty nodes at the left son of the root and the left son of the right son of the root. On the other hand, compare Figure S.5(a,b) and Figure S.5(c,d), which correspond to the block and tree representations of a path-compressed PR k-d tree and an open-sliding midpoint k-d tree, respectively, for the same eight-point dataset where the path-compressed PR k-d tree is deeper than the open-sliding midpoint k-d tree.

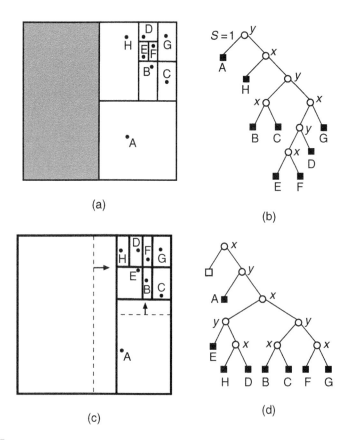

(a)

(b)

(c)

(d)

Figure S.5
The (a) block and (b) tree representations of a path-compressed PR k-d tree, for the same eight-point dataset, that is deeper than its open-sliding midpoint k-d tree with corresponding (c) block and (d) tree representations.

Solutions to Exercises in Section 1.5.2.5

2. See [1379].

Solutions to Exercises in Section 1.5.2.6

1. See [441].

2. See [441].

3. See [441].

5. See [441].

Solutions to Exercises in Section 1.5.2.7

1. When a centroid shrink operation is applied to a region with an inner box, we cannot create two inner boxes, and thus we must use a decomposition process that may require as many as one shrink, one split, and one shrink operation, each of which requires one additional level in the tree for a maximum of three additional levels. There is also one more level corresponding to the split of the alternating split and shrink sequence of operations. Of course, the split does not necessarily result in a reduction of the number of points in each of the child regions.

2. No. This is true only if $2/3 \leq x < 1$. If $x \geq 2/3$, then the BBD-tree shrink described earlier will trivially satisfy this requirement. However, if $x < 2/3$, consider an instance of a square cell c, where $b/3$ of the points are clustered near three of the four distinct corners of c. The first midpoint split will create two cells containing $b/3$ and $2b/3$ points each. The subsequent split applied to the cell containing $2b/3$ points will create two cells each containing $b/3$ points. An inner box based on midpoint splits either contains at least two clusters (and hence at least $2b/3$ points) or no more than one cluster (and hence the outer box has at least $2b/3$ points). Thus, the $2/3$ factor is tight. Notice that if we remove the restriction that splits occur along midpoint lines, then a more balanced decomposition may be possible, but the issue of maintaining cells of bounded aspect ratios must also be considered. See the BAR tree of Duncan et al. [516, 517], discussed in Section 1.5.1.4, for an alternative approach.

Solutions to Exercises in Section 1.5.3

1. Given a conjugation tree storing N points, the time required to perform a halfplanar search is given by the recurrence relation

$$Q(N) = Q(N/2) + Q(N/4) + O(\log_2 N)$$

This can be seen by observing that given an arbitrary node v of a conjugation tree T, the range of at least one of the grandchildren of v is either in h or has an empty intersection with h. This is because, given a pair of intersecting lines A and B in the plane, a third line C can only intersect three of the regions formed by the intersection of A and B. The $O(\log N)$ factor arises from the need to determine $int(v)$ (i.e., the intersection of g, the line which bounds h, with $range(v)$). This process can take as much as $O(\log_2 N)$ time as, at the maximum depth of the tree, $range(v)$ consists of $O(\log_2 N)$ line segments. In fact, this intersection test need not take as much as $O(\log_2 N)$ time even though the region corresponding to $range(v)$ gets more complicated in terms of the number of edges since, as the tree is descended, only one additional edge (i.e., line) needs to be tested at each new level. This recurrence relation is similar to the definition of a sequence of Fibonacci numbers and is solved in a similar manner to yield $Q(N) = O(N^{\log_2 1 + \sqrt{5} - 1}) = O(N^{0.695})$. Note that when solving the line search problem, the $O(\log_2 N)$ factor is needed as it corresponds to the complexity of searching the array of points that lie on the line stored at the node.

2. For three dimensions, we need to be able to find three planes that subdivide a set of N points into eight subsets, each of which is approximately of size $N/8$. This is possible [2048] but not via a sequence of Ham-Sandwich cuts as a Ham-Sandwich cut for four sets in three dimensions cannot be found [2048]. In general, it is known that in $d \geq 5$ dimensions, there are sets of N points such that no d hyperplanes can simultaneously equipartition them so that each d-dimensional "quadrant" can contain at most $N/2^d$ points [114]. The problem is open for $d = 4$ [540].

Solutions to Exercises in Section 1.6

3. See [1992].

4. See [1992].

6. The query $x < 2$.

7. See [582].

10. See the Peano-Hilbert order discussed in Section 2.1.1.2 of Chapter 2 and shown in Figure 2.5(d). It has the property that every element is a 4-adjacent neighbor of the previous element in the sequence. Goldschlager [718], Goodchild and Grandfield [725], and Witten and Wyvill [2012] give algorithms to extract the x and y coordinate values of a point given its Peano-Hilbert code. Fisher [616], Faloutsos and Roseman [591], Jagadish [937], and Liu and Schrack [1190, 1191] give algorithms to construct a Peano-Hilbert code for a point given its x and y coordinate values.

Solutions to Exercises in Section 1.7.1.1

1. Consider a region page f that spans the region with a lower-left corner at $(0,0)$ and upper-left corner at $(100, 10 \cdot (c+1))$. Let the region have $c+1$ horizontal regions of equal length that are parallel (i.e., partitions at $y_i = 10i$, $1 \leq i \leq c$). Now, introduce a partition at $x = 50$. The result is that f_1 and f_2 each contain $c+1$ regions, and thus both f_1 and f_2 overflow. Of course, this can be avoided by splitting along y such as at y_c (i.e., $y = y_c = 10c$).

2. We can choose the partition at the root of the k-d tree corresponding to the space partition induced by the overflowing region page.

Solutions to Exercises in Section 1.7.1.3

1. See [829].

2. See [829].

Solutions to Exercises in Section 1.7.1.4

1. Pick a point p inside a rectangle R, draw a horizontal and vertical line through p, and distribute the $4k$ points so that k points lie on each of the lines intersecting at p. It is impossible to partition R with a vertical or horizontal line so that each of the resulting partitions has $2k$ points [1201].

2. We use a constructive proof. Examine the root node of the generalized k$^+$-d tree. If one of the subtrees, say i, contains more than two-thirds of the nodes of the tree, then descend to i. This process is repeated until neither subtree of i contains more than two-thirds of the nodes in the

entire tree. In this case, at least one of the subtrees S contains at least one-third of the total number of nodes. Note that if neither subtree contained at least one-third of the total number of nodes, then the total number of nodes in both subtrees would be less than two-thirds, thereby contradicting the assumption that the subtree rooted at i has more than two-thirds of the total number of nodes in the tree. Thus, we can extract S from the whole tree and replace it with an external marker, resulting in two generalized k^+-d trees that both have at least one-third of the nodes in the original tree.

3. We only sketch a proof of the two-dimensional case here. For more details, including a proof for arbitrary dimensions, see [1201]. Let m_x and m_y be the median values along the x and y dimensions. If either of m_x or m_y splits the underlying space so that at least one-third of the points have x (y) coordinate values less than m_x (m_y) and at least one-third of the points have x (y) coordinate values greater than m_x (m_y), then we can use m_x (m_y) for splitting, and we are done. Otherwise, the problem is that at least one-third of the points have an x (y) coordinate value equal to m_x (m_y). In this case, we can show that at least one of the closed quadrants formed by the partition lines $x = m_x$ and $y = m_y$ contains between one-third and two-thirds of the points. To see this, we observe that less than one-third of the points are to the left of m_x (i.e., with a smaller x value) and less than one-third of the points are below m_y (i.e, with a smaller y value). Thus, at most two-thirds of the points are either on the left side or lower side. This means that at least one-third of the points have x and y values that are greater than or equal to m_x and m_y (i.e., lie in the closed top-right quadrant). We can make a similar argument to show that at least one-third of the points lie in the closed bottom-left quadrant. At this point, we see that at least one of these closed quadrants contains at most two-thirds of the points since, if both of the closed quadrants contain more than two-thirds of the points, then the sum of the number of points in the two quadrants (possibly subtracting one if they share a point) is larger than the total number of points. Therefore, we have established that at least one of the quadrants contains between one-third and two-thirds of the points. Similar techniques are used to establish this bound for higher dimensions.

4. See [1201].

Solutions to Exercises in Section 1.7.1.5

2. No, because the page being split is a leaf node in a k-d trie that is a B-partition before the split, and it remains so after the split.

3. Use the solution of Ouksel and Mayer [1438], which is essentially a two-stage binary search process. Assume for the moment that all blocks are in main memory, and thus each of the sets of blocks at a nesting level is represented by a balanced binary tree. Using binary search through the h nesting levels means that $\delta = \log_2(h + 1)$ nesting levels will be accessed. The maximum number of blocks contained in these nesting levels is $N - (h - \delta)$ as each of the nesting levels that has been bypassed by the search contains at least one block. Assuming that the δ examined nesting levels are numbered $s_1, s_2, \ldots s_\delta$, with $1 \le s_j \le h$ for $1 \le j \le \delta$, and letting $N_{s_1}, N_{s_2}, \ldots N_{s_\delta}$ denote their cardinality, then in the worst-case the binary search through the δ nesting levels will require accessing $\max\{\sum_{j=1}^{\delta} \log_2(N_{s_j} + 1) \mid \sum_{j=1}^{\delta} N_{s_j} \le N - (h - \delta)\}$ blocks. We know that $\sum_{j=1}^{\delta} \log_2(N_{s_j} + 1) = \log_2 \prod_{j=1}^{\delta}(N_{s_j} + 1)$, and since the logarithm is a monotonic function, the worst-case access quantity attains its maximum if and only if $\prod_{j=1}^{\delta}(N_{s_j} + 1)$ is maximal under the condition $\sum_{j=1}^{\delta} N_{s_j} \le N - (h - \delta)$. However, this maximum is attained if $N_{s_j} = (N - (h - \delta))/\delta$ for each $j, 1 \le j \le \delta$. Substituting this value in the worst-case access quantity yields

$$\delta \cdot [\log_2(\frac{N - (h - \delta)}{\delta} + 1)]$$
$$= \log_2(h + 1) \cdot [\log_2(N - h + 2 \cdot \log_2(h + 1)) - \log_2(\log_2(h + 1))].$$

This quantity is $O(\log_2 h \cdot \log_2 N)$. Now, suppose that each set of blocks at a nesting level is represented by a B-tree. In this case, we use a similar analysis to that used when the blocks are in a balanced binary search tree in main memory so that, in the worst case, the search through the h nesting levels will require accessing the following number of B-tree nodes:

$$\sum_{j=1}^{\delta} \log_{\lceil m/2 \rceil}(N_{s_j}+1)$$

$$= \log_2(h+1) \cdot [\log_{\lceil m/2 \rceil}(N-h+2 \cdot \log_2(h+1)) - \log_{\lceil m/2 \rceil}(\log_2(h+1))]$$

This quantity is $O(\log_2 h \cdot \log_{\lceil m/2 \rceil} N)$.

4. See [1710].

6. See [1710].

7. See [1710].

8. See Theorem 1 in [1710], whose proof can be found in [1706], which assumes that the smallest partition size on the domain of each key is the same.

Solutions to Exercises in Section 1.7.1.6.1

1. (Houman Alborzi)

   Proof   Let $n = |V|$. Mark all vertices v of $F(V)$ that have $n_V(v) \geq \lfloor \frac{1}{2}n \rfloor$. Observe that if any such vertex could be marked, then the marked vertices form a single path starting at a root of $F(V)$. Consider the two cases:

   (a) At least one vertex was marked. Now, consider u, the marked vertex with the minimum height. Observe that no children of u were marked as, otherwise, u does not have the minimum height. We either have

      i. $\lfloor \frac{1}{2}n \rfloor \leq n_V(u) \leq \lfloor \frac{2}{3}n \rfloor$. We let U be the set of regions in V contained by u.

      ii. $n_V(u) = \lfloor \frac{2}{3}n \rfloor + 1$. We let U be the set of regions in V properly contained by u.

      iii. $n_V(u) > \lfloor \frac{2}{3}n \rfloor + 1$. Notice that for all children w of u, we have $n_V(w) < \lfloor \frac{1}{2}n \rfloor$, and hence u has more than one child. Build X, a subset of children of u as follows. First, let X be the set of children of u. Next, arbitrarily remove elements of X until $\sum_{w \in X} n_V(w) \leq \lfloor \frac{2}{3}n \rfloor$. Now, in case $\sum_{w \in X} n_V(w) \geq \lceil \frac{1}{3}n \rceil$, let $U = X$. Otherwise, letting x denote the last element taken out from X, we have $\lfloor \frac{2}{3}n \rfloor < \sum_{w \in X} n_V(w) + n_V(x)$ and $\sum_{w \in X} n_V(w) < \lceil \frac{1}{3}n \rceil$. These two inequalities can be rewritten as $\lfloor \frac{2}{3}n \rfloor \leq \sum_{w \in X} n_V(w) + n_V(x) - 1$ and $\sum_{w \in X} n_V(w) \leq \lceil \frac{1}{3}n \rceil - 1$ as we know that for any integers i and j, $i < j$ implies that $i \leq j - 1$. Combining these relations and eliminating $\sum_{w \in X} n_V(w)$, we have that $\lfloor \frac{2}{3}n \rfloor - n_V(x) + 1 \leq \lceil \frac{1}{3}n \rceil - 1$, which can be rewritten as $\lfloor \frac{2}{3}n \rfloor - \lceil \frac{1}{3}n \rceil + 2 \leq n_V(x)$. This is simplified by noting that $\lfloor \frac{2}{3}n \rfloor + 1 \geq \lceil \frac{2}{3}n \rceil$ and $\lceil \frac{2}{3}n \rceil + 1 \geq \lceil \frac{1}{3}n \rceil + \lceil \frac{1}{3}n \rceil$ to yield the desired result $n_V(x) \geq \lceil \frac{1}{3}n \rceil$, and we let U be the set of regions in V contained by x.

   (b) No vertex was marked. Follow case (iii) above with X initially being the set of roots of V.

   In all cases above, we choose U to be a subset of V such that $\lceil \frac{1}{3}n \rceil \leq |U| \leq \lfloor \frac{2}{3}n \rfloor$. We let $S = V \setminus U$. Observe that in case (a), S encloses U, and in case (b), S and U are disjoint.   ∎

Solutions to Exercises in Section 1.7.1.6.2

1. Splitting the overflowing region r into two regions a and b that are disjoint may result in a situation where neither a nor b corresponds to guards (for this to happen, a or b must

have been shrunk so that their union is no longer the same as r), which means that a and b must be reinserted, thereby possibly causing other reinsertions while descending the directory hierarchy. For more details about the complexity of this process, see the brief discussion in Section 1.7.1.6.4 as well [644]. In contrast, if the resulting split is into contained regions, say a contains b, then there are two possibilities:

(a) The node corresponding to region a continues to guard the same regions as g while b does not. This means that a is retained as a guard at clevel v. b must be demoted to its proper position in the directory hierarchy using the search algorithm. In some cases, it could be that b also encloses other regions at a shallower clevel, and thus it must be properly inserted as their guard. This involves modifying the exact match search procedure to check if there exist other regions c that are contained in b and do not have a guard at clevel v that is contained in b, in which case b becomes their guard and any existing guard d of c at the same clevel is now the candidate for demotion. If c does have a guard at clevel v that is contained in b, then b is not a guard of c, and b is demoted to the next deeper dlevel (unless there is another region for which it can serve as a guard).

(b) b replaces g as a guard. This means that a is demoted using the same procedure as in (a).

Note that the eventual insertion of a demoted region may cause overflow of a directory node, in which case it is dealt with in the same way as discussed in the text. For more details, see [643].

2. The main issue with deletion in a BV-tree is how to redistribute the contents of the result of merging an underflowing directory node with another directory node (as well as how to choose it) while adhering to the minimum node occupancy conditions. The redistribution question is one of finding an appropriate splitting strategy for the merged directory nodes. See [642] for more details.

Solutions to Exercises in Section 1.7.1.6.3

1. Assume that the root of the directory hierarchy is at level v and that the deepest directory node is at level 1. The search starts at dlevel v. At each step, the search always descends to a node at the next deeper dlevel. This is done either through an unpromoted entry in the current node or an entry in the guard set representing a region at the next deeper clevel. The search terminates upon reaching a point page (corresponding to a region at clevel 0). Thus, all searches are of length v.

2. The unpromoted entries in the root of a BV-tree cover the entire dataspace spanned by the tree. Also, any region formed by the partitioning process is carved from this space. Thus, if no unpromoted entry e_s exists in the root that covers p, then this implies that no region in the whole tree covers p. In particular, there cannot be a guard e_r in the root that covers p.

3. Suppose that there is another matching guard e_t whose region t is contained by s. In this case, assume that t does not enclose r. Below we prove that this is impossible. Since both r and t are matching guards, r and t contain p, and thus they must intersect. However, according to the nonintersection boundary property, this can occur only if t contains r or vice versa. Since we assumed that t does not contain r, it must be that r contains t. However, this contradicts our original assumption that r was the best match guard as we have now found a better best match, namely e_t. Thus, any guards enclosed by region s also enclose r.

4. (Gísli R. Hjaltason) Since guards in a correspond to regions at a deeper level than $v - 1$ in the containment hierarchy, the fact that the best match e_r is a guard in a means that p is contained in a region at a deeper clevel than $v - 1$. A basic assumption of the BV-tree is that all regions that are not at the topmost level in the containment hierarchy must be covered by regions at a shallower clevel. Therefore, a region at level $v - 1$ in the containment hierarchy that contains p must exist. Let s be the smallest such region. Since the search led to a, the region b corresponding to a must contain p. Thus, s must either be contained in b, or b must be contained in s (this is a consequence of the nonintersection property of region boundaries). However, if s is contained in b, then e_s must be in a. Otherwise, if b is contained in s, then e_s

Solutions to Exercises in Section 1.7.2.3.2

1. Each time we had a partition, we would have to rearrange the contents of the arrays.

2. See [1428].

Solutions to Exercises in Section 1.7.2.3.3

1. See [906].

2. See [906].

3. The property does not hold in general, although it appears to hold one-half of the time. Can you prove that it holds exactly one-half of the time?

Solutions to Exercises in Section 1.7.2.3.4

1. See [1084].

Solutions to Exercises in Section 1.7.2.4.2

1. If they were implemented as arrays, then we could not capture the order in which the partitioning hyperplanes were applied. Varying this order is what distinguishes PLOP hashing from quantile hashing and conventional linear hashing with MDEH as the hashing function.

Solutions to Exercises in Section 1.7.2.4.3

3. See the Peano-Hilbert order discussed in Section 2.1 of Chapter 2 and shown in Figure 2.5(d) of Chapter 2. It has the property that every element is a 4-adjacent neighbor of the previous element in the sequence.

4. Reversed bit interleaving applied to the result of $f(x) = x \div 12.5$ and $f(y) = y \div 12.5$:

NAME	X	Y	$f(X)$	$f(Y)$	CODEX	CODEX/64	CODEY	CODEY/64
Chicago	35	42	2	3	44	0.687500	28	0.437500
Mobile	52	10	4	0	1	0.015625	2	0.031250
Toronto	62	77	4	6	11	0.171875	7	0.109375
Buffalo	82	65	6	5	39	0.609375	27	0.421875
Denver	5	45	0	3	40	0.625000	20	0.312500
Omaha	27	35	2	2	12	0.187500	12	0.187500
Atlanta	85	15	6	1	37	0.578125	26	0.406250
Miami	90	5	7	0	21	0.328125	42	0.656250

5. No. Since the hash function is of the form $h(k) = k/2^n$, reversed bit interleaving will have an effect analogous to that in which all records in a given bucket agree in the least significant digits. This is not quite true due to the nonuniformity of the relative load of the buckets.

Solutions to Exercises in Section 1.7.2.4.4

1. See [1288, 1428] for a discussion of how this might be achieved.

3. Although theoretically feasible, this would require a different hashing function than MDEH, whose specification and computation would be quite complex.

4. It is true for $d = 2$ when there are just 16 grid cells. For example, consider the splits that take place in the two methods once grid cells 0–7 have been created in Figures 1.100(d) and 1.101(d). Figures 1.100(e) and 1.101(e) show the resulting space decomposition after creating the same number of grid cells (i.e., 8–11) using the two methods. In particular, we find that using MDEH resulted in splitting 4 grid cells that are contiguous (i.e., 0, 4, 1, and 6), while this was not the case for the 4 grid cells that were split when using linear hashing with reversed bit interleaving (LHRBI) (i.e., 0–3). However, once more partitions are performed (e.g., 64 grid cells), this property no longer holds within a slice for grid cells that are split in succession.

Solutions to Exercises in Section 1.7.2.5

1. The reason is that buckets are not necessarily full when they are split by linear hashing. Also, linear hashing requires overflow buckets and makes use of a storage utilization factor in deciding when to split a bucket.

2. As long as the grid directory does not grow too large (i.e., there are not too many clusters of size larger than the bucket capacity), EXCELL seems to be the choice due to its simplicity and performance guarantees.

3. MLOPLH looks up a value as follows. Let $i = n + 1$. Start with $h_i(v)$, and assume that the result is bucket b. If $b \geq m$, then rehash using $h_i(v)$, where $i = n$, and again let the result be bucket b. In either case, if b is empty, then decrement i by 1 and rehash using h_i. This rehashing and decrementing process is repeated until either $i < 0$, or a nonempty bucket b is obtained, at which time we check to see if v is indeed in b.

Solutions to Exercises in Section 1.8.5.3

2. No. Doing this would violate the k-instantiation property because of the partition tree block corresponding to r is no longer the minimum enclosing quadtree block of its k elements. In particular, since the block corresponding to s is k-instantiated (based on the fact that s was a node in the PK-tree before the deletion), it should correspond to a node in the PK-tree after the deletion as its partition tree block is still k-instantiated.

Solutions to Exercises in Section 1.8.6

1. As long as the partitioning process stores the objects (i.e., points) in the leaf nodes, the PK-tree can be applied. The conventional point quadtree and the k-d tree store the objects (i.e., points) in both the leaf and nonleaf nodes. Thus, we cannot use them with the PK-tree. However, partitioning processes such as the pseudo quadtree and the pseudo k-d tree [1444] can be used.

Solutions to Exercises in Section 1.9

1. It is difficult to place the pseudo quadtree in the tree as, on the one hand, it is a refinement of the point quadtree of type D in a manner analogous to the way in which the adaptive k-d tree

is a refinement of the k-d tree. However, according to our taxonomy, this type of refinement belongs at depth 6, and we have nothing in the tree at depth 5 to lead into it. On the other hand, the pseudo quadtree can also be viewed as a refinement of the grid file of type D at the same level as the point quadtree. This is the choice that we make. Making such an adjustment means that depth 6 is no longer meaningful, and we move the adaptive k-d tree to depth 5 as a descendant of the pseudo quadtree.

2. We are confronted with the same choices as in Exercise 1, and we resolve the problem in the same manner. Thus the optimized point quadtree is added as a refinement of type D of the grid file at the same level as the point quadtree and the pseudo quadtree.

3. The BD-tree should be placed alongside the PR k-d tree because it is a PR k-d tree with a truncated path to each node. This path bypasses the tests when one child is empty.

4. The range tree should be placed as a descendant of the sequential list at the same level as the inverted list. It should be of type H as the key governing the partition exhibits behavior of type D, while the data values of the remaining keys have no influence on the way the space is organized and hence exhibit behavior of type N. The priority search tree, inverse priority search tree, and multidimensional range tree should all be placed as descendants of the range tree at the same level as the fixed-grid method and of type D. They are of type D as they organize the data to be stored.

5. At depth 3, EXCELL is now type D_1, the grid file is type D_1, and the pyramid is type E_d. At depth 4, the PR k-d tree is a type E_1 child of EXCELL, the PR quadtree is a type E_d child of the pyramid, the point quadtree is a type E_d child of the grid file, and the k-d tree is a type E_1 child of the grid file. At depth 5, the adaptive k-d tree is a type E_1 child of the k-d tree. How does the MX quadtree fit into the revised taxonomy?

6. Look at decompositions that make use of the Platonic solids in three dimensions.

10. A solution that proceeds by finding the closest pair of points in sequence need not be optimal as can be seen by considering the four points $(0,2)$, $(1,0)$, $(3,0)$, and $(4,2)$. The closest pair is $(1,0)$ and $(3,0)$. This means that the remaining pair is $(0,2)$ and $(4,2)$, which has a cost of 6. On the other hand, taking the pairs $(0,2)$ and $(1,0)$ followed by the pair $(3,0)$ and $(4,2)$ leads to a cost of $2 \cdot \sqrt{5}$, which, of course, is smaller. This is termed the greedy-method heuristic. The best known solution to the Euclidean matching problem using it is $O(N^{3/2} \cdot \log_2 N)$ [179]. Although the greedy-method heuristic is not optimal, Reingold and Tarjan [1552] have shown that the result of its use is never worse than $4/3 \cdot N^{\log_2 1.5}$. For other literature on this topic, see the survey of Avis [113] and Tarjan [1859]. For approximate solutions based on space-filling curves, see Section 2.1.1.2 of Chapter 2 as well as [133, 926].

Vaidya [1906] has developed an algorithm for finding the smallest Euclidean matching (i.e., for finding an exact solution) that runs in $O(N^{2.5} \cdot \log_2^4 N)$ time. Previously, the best upper bound for solving this problem was $O(N^3)$ [1119, 1859].

12. Lee [1126] suggests a transformation of the problem into an instance of the maximum clique problem (see Section 3.2 of Chapter 3 and the solution to Exercise 13 therein).

Solutions to Exercises in Section 2.1.1.1

1. $1/\sqrt{3}$, 1, $2/\sqrt{3}$.

2. $\sqrt{3}$ for $[3^6]$; 1 and $\sqrt{2}$ for $[4^4]$.

3. Treat every even-numbered row as if it has been shifted to the right (or left) by one-half of the interpixel distance.

Solutions to Exercises in Section 2.1.1.2

1. If the image grows by the addition of rows or shrinks by the removal of rows from the end.

2. If the image grows from the center outwards by the addition of shells on the outside or shrinks inwards by the removal of shells on the outside.

3. Recall the definition of the Peano-Hilbert order, which stipulates that orientation is a key part of the construction process. In fact, after doubling the resolution, the Peano-Hilbert order of the 4×4 square in the upper-left corner of Figure 2.5(d) should look like Figure 2.6(b). Note also that when we double the resolution to yield the 4×4 square in the upper-left corner, the spatial orientation of the final cell in the order with respect to that of the first cell in the order is not the same. In other words, the curve exits the 4×4 square in a different position—that is, assuming that the first cell is at the upper-left corner of a two-dimensional space, after an odd number of doublings, the Peano-Hilbert order exits at the upper-right corner of the space. On the other hand, after an even number of doublings, it exits at the lower-left corner. In contrast, all of the curves in Figure 2.6 exit the embedded space at the same position—that is, the lower-left corner of the space.

4. See Section 3.4.1 in [1636].

5. Assuming a $2^n \times 2^n$ image, an $O(n^2)$ algorithm is given in [725]. Algorithms are also given in [718, 2012]. An $O(n)$ algorithm can be achieved by inverting the algorithm given in [937].

6. See [591] for an $O(n^2)$ algorithm and [616, 937, 1190] for an $O(n)$ algorithm, assuming a $2^n \times 2^n$ image. The algorithm in [591] is the inverse of the algorithm given in [725] to obtain the x and y coordinate values of a number in the Peano-Hilbert order. For algorithms to construct and decode a Peano-Hilbert key in three dimensions, see [1191].

7. See [1192, 1698]. In two dimensions, let $x_{r-1}...x_1 x_0$ and $y_{r-1}...y_1 y_0$ represent the binary representation of the x and y coordinate values of a point (X, Y) in a $2^r \times 2^r$ space, and let $u_{2r-1}...u_1 u_0$ denote the corresponding location code when using a U order. In this case, assuming that the y coordinate value is the most significant, we have $u_{2i+1} = y_i$ and $u_{2i} = x_i \oplus y_i$ ($0 \le i \le r - 1$). Thus, to form the bit-interleaved value, we simply interleave the y coordinate values with the "exclusive or" of the x and y coordinate values. Of course, the order differs depending on which of the coordinate values is taken as the most significant. In three dimensions, the addition of the z coordinate, with $Z = z_{r-1}...z_1 x_0$, and letting z be the most significant coordinate yields $u_{3i+2} = z_i$, $u_{3i+1} = z_i \oplus y_i$, and $u_{3i} = z_i \oplus y_i \oplus x_i$ ($0 \le i \le r - 1$). The extension to d dimensions is straightforward.

8. For the row-prime, Peano-Hilbert, and spiral orders, it is 1. For the row order it is

$$\frac{(2^n - 1) \cdot (2^n + \sqrt{1 + (2^n - 1)^2})}{2^{2 \cdot n} - 1}$$

For the Cantor-diagonal order, it is

$$\frac{2^n \cdot (2^n + 3) - 4}{2^{2 \cdot n} - 1}$$

For the Morton order, it is

$$\frac{2^{2 \cdot n - 2}}{2^{2 \cdot n} - 1} \cdot \sum_{i=0}^{n-1} \frac{2 \cdot \sqrt{1 + (2^i - 1)^2} + \sqrt{1 + (2^{i+1} - 1)^2}}{2^{2 \cdot i}}$$

For the U order, it is

$$\frac{2^{2 \cdot n - 2}}{2^{2 \cdot n} - 1} \cdot \sum_{i=0}^{n-1} \frac{2 \cdot \sqrt{2^{2 \cdot i} + (2^i - 1)^2} + 1}{2^{2 \cdot i}}$$

For the Gray order, it is

$$\frac{2^{2 \cdot n - 2}}{2^{2 \cdot n} - 1} \cdot \sum_{i=0}^{n-1} \frac{3 \cdot 2^i}{2^{2 \cdot i}} = \frac{3}{2} \cdot \frac{2^{2 \cdot n} - 2^n}{2^{2 \cdot n} - 1}$$

For the double Gray order, it is

$$\frac{2^{2 \cdot n - 2}}{2^{2 \cdot n} - 1} \cdot \sum_{i=0}^{n-1} \frac{3 \cdot (2^{i+1} - 1)}{2^{2 \cdot i}} = \frac{2^{2 \cdot n + 1} - 3 \cdot 2^n + 1}{2^{2 \cdot n} - 1}$$

As n gets large (i.e., $n = 16$), these values converge to 2.0000, 1.6724, 1.5000, and 1.4387 for the double Gray, Morton, Gray, and U orders, respectively. Thus, the U order is the best of the approximations of the Peano-Hilbert order in terms of the average distance between successive positions, and the double Gray order is the worst. The latter confirms our observation in Section 1.6 of Chapter 1 that there is no need to Gray code the individual keys. Gotsman and Lindenbaum [734] discuss the inverse problem of correlating the distance between different locations along the space-filling curve to the Euclidean distance between their actual locations in space. This is done for a subset of space-filling curves where the distance in the original space between successive locations along the curve is 1 (e.g., the row-prime, Peano-Hilbert, and spiral orders) using a variant of a measure proposed by Pérez, Kamata, and Kawaguchi [1481].

9. For the Morton, Peano-Hilbert, U, Gray, and double Gray orders, it is $1 + 2^{2-m}$ as each page represents a $2^m \times 2^m$ block. The four corner pixels require that three pages be accessed; the remaining $4 \cdot (2^m - 2)$ pixels along the edges require that two pages be accessed; and as the neighbors of all other pixels are on the same page, only one page needs to be accessed. For the row order, it is $3 + 2^{1-2 \cdot m}$ as each page represents a portion of a row of size $2^{2 \cdot m}$. The first and last pixels require that four pages be accessed; the remaining pixels require that three pages be accessed.

10. The upper-left corner of the rectangle.

11. This is not as simple as for the Morton ordering. The orientation of the Peano-Hilbert ordering depends on whether the image width is an odd or even power of 2 (i.e., the value n in the image width 2^n). Once this is done, we recursively determine which of the quadrants of the image contain the rectangle, and then for each level of decomposition, we compute which part of the rectangle contains the point with the minimum Peano-Hilbert order value.

The interesting point is that this point need not necessarily be a corner of the rectangle. In fact, it is easy to see using contradiction that the only requirement is that this point lies on the boundary of the rectangle. In particular, suppose that the point p in rectangle r with the minimum Peano-Hilbert order value m does not lie on the boundary. Therefore, there must be some point q with a Peano-Hilbert order value $m - 1$ that is adjacent to p in the horizontal or vertical direction. If q does not lie on the boundary, then q must also be in the rectangle, which contradicts the fact that p was the point with the minimum Peano-Hilbert order value. Otherwise, q lies on the boundary, but this also contradicts the premise that p was the point with the minimum Peano-Hilbert order value and was not on the boundary. An alternative way of proving this is to recall that the Peano-Hilbert order value of a pixel corresponds to the number of the pixel's position along the Peano-Hilbert space-filling curve. The Peano-Hilbert space-filling curve, as drawn in Figure 2.5(d), starts at the top left of the space (the origin in this figure) and ends at the bottom left or top right depending on the whether the image width is an odd or even power of 2. Thus, for any rectangle, the Peano-Hilbert space-filling curve enters it at a pixel on the boundary (i.e., that pixel has the lowest Hilbert code for any in the rectangle). Otherwise, the Peano-Hilbert space-filling curve starts in the interior of the rectangle, which is clearly not the case since it starts at the origin (assuming the rectangle is fully inside the data space).

The actual process of determining the point in rectangle r with the minimum Peano-Hilbert order value is as follows. Initialize b with the root block. Test the child blocks of b in order of the Peano-Hilbert order value of their corner with the lowest Morton order value (that order depends on whether we are at an odd or even level of decomposition, which should not be too hard to calculate, although it is not trivial) to see if they intersect r. Set b to the first child block found to intersect and recursively reapply if b was not already a pixel. This process requires many intersection tests, and thus is fairly expensive (but not as expensive as computing the Peano-Hilbert codes of all locations along the boundary).

12. Unlike the Morton ordering, and as in the Peano-Hilbert ordering, the location in the rectangle with the smallest U order value is not the upper-left corner of the rectangle. Assuming that the upper-left corner of the image is the first one in the ordering, the problem arises when the upper-left corner of the rectangle is in the NW child of the root (and its NW child, etc.). This is resolved by applying the same recursive procedure as in the solution to Exercise 11. Similar issues arise for the Gray and double Gray orderings.

Solutions to Exercises in Section 2.1.2.1

1. Let p be the position of l in the Morton ordering. Check if p is in the block associated with the root of the binary search tree T. If it is, then exit. Else if p is less than the value associated with the root of T, then the block containing l must be in the left subtree, and we descend

the tree. Otherwise, p is greater than the value associated with the root of T, and we must examine both the left and right subtrees of T as there may be a block in the left subtree that contains l. As we can see, it is not possible to prune the search in all cases. The problem is that in the case of an arbitrary decomposition, the Morton ordering (as well as all other orderings in Figure 2.5) does not guarantee that all of the cells in each block will appear in consecutive order.

Solutions to Exercises in Section 2.1.2.2

3. It resembles a sawtooth approximation to a circle.

4. The Chessboard metric is represented by the pair $(1,1)$ since $d_M(p,q) = e + f$. The City Block metric is represented by the pair $(1,2)$ since $d_A(p,q) = e + 2 \cdot f$.

Solutions to Exercises in Section 2.1.2.4

1. The array, not surprisingly, has no such bias. The list is ordered by adjacency in one dimension. The region quadtree is ordered by adjacency in a hierarchical sense (i.e., by use of a parent relation).

2. There are several possible ways to proceed. The first mimics the top-down definition of the region quadtree and hence makes use of a top-down process. In practice, the construction process is bottom-up, and one usually uses one of two approaches. The first approach [1619] is applicable when the image array is not too large. In such a case, the elements of the array are often inspected in Morton order (Figure 2.5(c) and, more specifically, the order given by the labels in the array in Figure 2.8). By using such a method, a leaf node is never created until it is known to be maximal (this property is also shared by the Peano-Hilbert, Gray, double Gray, and U orders, given in Figures 2.5(d), 2.5(g), 2.5(h), and 2.5(i), respectively). An equivalent statement is that the situation does not arise in which four leaf nodes of the same color c necessitate the changing of the color of their parent from gray to c. For more details, see Section 4.1 of [1636].

   The second approach [1621] is applicable to large images. In this case, the elements of the image are processed one row at a time—for example, using row order (Figure 2.5(a)), which is also known as a *raster-scan order*. The corresponding region quadtree is built by adding pixel size nodes one by one in the order in which they appear in the file. For more details, see Section 4.2.1 of [1636]. This process can be time-consuming due to the many merging and node-insertion operations that need to take place.

   The above method has been improved by using a predictive method [1722, 1729], which only makes a single insertion for each node in the final quadtree and performs no merge operations. It is based on processing the image in row order (top to bottom, left to right), always inserting the largest node (i.e., block) for which the current pixel is the first (upper-leftmost) pixel. Such a policy avoids the necessity of merging since the upper-leftmost pixel of any block is inserted before any other pixel of that block. Therefore, it is impossible for four sibling nodes to be of the same color. This method makes use of an auxiliary array of size $O(2^n)$ for a $2^n \times 2^n$ image. For more details, see Section 4.2.3 of [1636].

3. No two spheres can occupy the same leaf node. In other words, each leaf node contains a part of just one sphere.

4. Since the staircases are usually infinite, a tree is inadequate, and a graph is necessary. Use an octgraph!

5. Compression is a result of the property of the exclusive or operation that $0 \oplus 0 = 0$ and $1 \oplus 1 = 0$.

6. $Q_i \oplus Q_{i-1} = (P_i \oplus Q_{i-1}) \oplus Q_{i-1} = P_i \oplus (Q_{i-1} \oplus Q_{i-1}) = P_i \oplus 0 = P_i$.

7. 16×32.

8. No. The four resulting blocks must be congruent. Thus, the only valid size is 8×12.

9. $(B + W - 1)/3$.

10. $(B + W - 1)/7$.

11. See [525].

12. $O(2^q)$. The worst case is a rectangle of width $2^q \times 2$ that straddles the x axis (i.e., one pixel on each side). It needs $5 + 16 \cdot 2^{q-2}$ nodes.

13. The probability that the entire image is black is $P_b(q) = (\frac{1}{2})$ Similarly, the probability that the entire image is white is $P_w(q) = (\frac{1}{2})^{2q}$. To find $E(q)$, solve the recurrence relation $E(q) = 4 \cdot E(q-1) + 1 - 4 \cdot (P_b(q) + P_w(q))$ with the initial condition $E(0) = 1$. The result is approximately $(29/24) \cdot 2^{2q}$. The expected number of black nodes, $B(q)$, is obtained by solving the recurrence relation $B(q) = 4 \cdot B(q-1) - 3 \cdot P_b(q)$ with the initial condition $B(0) = \frac{1}{2}$. The result is approximately $(29/64) \cdot 2^{2q}$. The expected number of white nodes is the same as $B(q)$, and the expected number of gray nodes is approximately $(29/96) \cdot 2^{2q} - 1/3$. For more details, see [383].

14. See [383].

15. See Olken and Rotem [1397], who discuss a number of sampling strategies for spatial databases involving both region quadtrees and R-trees [791].

16. See [757]. Intuitively, shifting the region may require fewer nodes as long as the region's maximum extent is such that the region occupies at least one block of size 1×1 in three horizontally (or vertically) adjacent blocks of size $2^m \times 2^m$. For the given value of w, the value of m is $q - 1$, and hence the $q + 1$ result follows.

17. Li, Grosky, and Jain [1161] developed the following algorithm. First, enlarge the image to be $2^{q+1} \times 2^{q+1}$, and place the region within it so that the region's northernmost and westernmost pixels are adjacent to the northern and western borders, respectively, of the image. Next, apply successive translations to the image of magnitude power of two in the vertical, horizontal, and corner directions, and keep count of the number of leaf nodes required. Initially, 2^{2q+2} leaf nodes are necessary. The following is a more precise statement of the algorithm:

    (a) Attempt to translate the image by (x, y), where x and y correspond to unit translations in the horizontal and vertical directions, respectively. Each of x and y takes on the values 0 or 1.

    (b) For the result of each translation in step (a), construct a new array at one-half the resolution. Each entry in the new array corresponds to a 2×2 block in the translated array. For each entry in the new array that corresponds to a single-color (not gray) 2×2 block in the translated array, decrement the leaf node count by 3.

    (c) Recursively apply steps (a) and (b) to each result of steps (a) and (b). This process stops when no single-color 2×2 block is found in step (b) (i.e., they are all gray), or if the new array is a 1×1 block. Record the total translation and the minimum leaf node count.

    Step (b) makes use of the property that for a translation of 2^k, there is a need to check only if single color blocks of size $2^k \times 2^k$ or more are formed. In fact, because of the recursion, at each step we check only for the formation of blocks of size $2^{k+1} \times 2^{k+1}$. Note that the algorithm tries every possible translation since any integer can be decomposed into a summation of powers of 2 (i.e., use its binary representation). In fact, this is why a translation of (0,0) is part of step (a). Although the algorithm computes the positioning of the quadtree with the minimum number of leaf nodes, it also yields the positioning of the quadtree with the minimum total number of nodes since the number of nonleaf nodes in a quadtree of T leaf nodes is $(T - 1)/3$.

18. See [43], where given a depth k, checking whether or not a block b at depth k exists that contains q is done by forming the locational code of q and then applying a mask with the trailing $d \cdot k$ bits set to 0, where d is the dimension of the underlying space (i.e., $d = 2$ and $d = 3$ for a region quadtree and octree, respectively). The actual check is a simple lookup in a hash table. The overall search process is a binary search on the depth k in the range $l \dots r$ where initially $l = 1$ and $r = s$. If b exists and if b corresponds to a leaf node, then the search halts with $v = b$ and $h = k$. If b exists and if b corresponds to a nonleaf node, then the search continues with another value k' in the range $k + 1 \dots r$, because if there is a block containing q, then its corresponding leaf node must be deeper in the tree structure (i.e., smaller). If b does not exist, then k is larger than h (i.e., b is at a deeper level than v), and the search must

be resumed at a shallower level with another value k' in the range $l \ldots k - 1$. Using a binary search ensures that the process terminates in $\log s$ steps as the query point must be contained in one of the blocks as they span the entire environment.

19. See [43], where an unbounded binary search on the range of depths in the order $1, 2, 4, 8, \ldots$ is used. The idea, an adaptation of the method of van Emde Boas [558], is that we repeatedly check for the presence of a block b at depth k that contains q while doubling the value of the depth k at each successive instantiation until we encounter a depth $k = k'$ for which the check fails. At this point, we apply a binary search in the range $k'/2 \ldots k'$ as in the solution to Exercise 18, but now we only need to perform at most $\log h$ checks for the presence of a block b at depth k that contains q. The total number of such checks is at most $2 \cdot \log h$.

20. Define a locational code where the right part contains the size of the block and the left part contains the result of applying bit interleaving to the coordinate values of the lower-right corner of the block.

21. When the maximum number of bits is 32, then the locational code can represent a three-dimensional image of side length 2^{10}, and EPICT can represent an image of side length 2^{11}. In contrast, when the maximum number of bits is 64, then the locational code can represent a three-dimensional image of side length 2^{19}, and EPICT can represent an image of side length 2^{21}. Thus, with a 64-bit locational code, EPICT enables the representation of a three-dimensional image with four times the resolution of that possible with a locational code.

22. See [1625, 1636, 1652]. Assume that we are trying to find the equal-sized neighbor of node P in direction I. Our initial aim is to locate the nearest common ancestor of P and its neighbor. We need to ascend the tree to do so. We must also account for the situation in which the ancestors of P and its neighbor are adjacent along an edge. Let N denote the node that is currently being examined in the ascent. There are three cases described below. They are implemented by procedure DIAGONALNEIGHBOR, which makes use of tables ADJ and REFLECT given in Figure 2.20, as well as COMMONEDGE given below. This procedure ignores the situation in which the neighbor may not exist (e.g., when the node is on the border of the image).

I (VERTEX)	COMMONEDGE(I,O)			
	Q (QUADRANT)			
	NW	NE	SW	SE
NW	Ω	N	W	Ω
NE	N	Ω	Ω	E
SW	W	Ω	Ω	S
SE	Ω	E	S	Ω

(a) As long as N is a child of type O such that ADJ(I, O) is true, we continue to ascend the tree. In other words, I's label is a subset of O's label.

(b) If the parent of N and the ancestor of the desired neighbor, say A, are adjacent along an edge, then calculate A using procedure LATERALNEIGHBOR given in Figure 2.20. This situation and the exact direction of A are determined by the table COMMONEDGE applied to I and the child type of N. Once A has been obtained, the desired neighbor is located by applying the retracing step outlined in step (c).

(c) Otherwise, N is a child of a type, say O, such that neither of the labels of the edges incident at vertex I is a subset of O's label. Its parent, say T, is the nearest common ancestor. The desired neighbor is obtained by simply retracing the path used to locate T, except that we now make diagonally opposite moves about the vertex shared by the neighboring nodes. This process is facilitated by use of the function REFLECT.

```
1  recursive pointer node procedure DIAGONALNEIGHBOR(P, I)
2  /* Locate an equal-sized vertex-neighbor of node P in direction I. */
3  value pointer node P
4  value vertex I
5  return(CHILD(if ADJ(I, CHILDTYPE(P)) then
6                    DIAGONALNEIGHBOR(FATHER(P), I)
7                  elseif COMMONEDGE(I, CHILDTYPE(P)) ≠ Ω  then
```

```
8                LATERALNEIGHBOR(FATHER(P),
9                              COMMONEDGE(I,CHILDTYPE(P)))
10         else FATHER(P)
11         endif,
12         REFLECT(I,CHILDTYPE(P))))
```

23. The proof follows [1626, 1636]. Assume that the quadtree skeleton is not unique. Let T_1 and T_2 both be quadtree skeletons of the same image—that is, $B = \cup_{t \in T_1} s_t$ and $B = \cup_{t \in T_2} s_t$. Assume, without loss of generality, that there exists $t1 \in T_1$ such that $t1 \notin T_2$. Therefore, by property 3, treating $t1$ as an element of B, there exists $t2 \in T_2 (t2 \neq t1)$ such that $s_{t1} \subseteq s_{t2}$. However, this contradicts property 2, which stipulates that, for any $t \in T_1$, there does not exist $b \in B$ ($b \neq t$) such that $s_t \subseteq s_b$. Hence, the quadtree skeleton of a collection of objects represented by a region quadtree is unique.

24. No. For example, for the region quadtree in Figure 2.17(a), both $\{1, 11, 15\}$ and $\{1, 12, 15\}$ would be legal quadtree skeletons.

25. Consider the region quadtree in Figure 2.17(a) where both $\{1, 11, 15\}$ and $\{1, 12, 15\}$ are legal quadtree skeletons. It is clear that the QMAT corresponding to $\{1, 12, 15\}$ results in more blocks than the QMAT corresponding to $\{1, 11, 15\}$ as block 12 is smaller than block 11 and thus the nonobject sibling blocks of block 12 must also be included in the QMAT.

26. The QMAT corresponding to the quadtree skeleton of Figure 2.21(a) using property 3 is given in Figure 2.21(b), and Figure 2.21(c) shows the QMAT corresponding to the quadtree skeleton using property $3'$. We see that the total number of blocks is the same. The only difference is that the additional blocks are represented by object blocks rather than empty blocks—for example, the node corresponding to block 14 in Figures 2.21(b) and 2.21(c). To see that this is always true, observe that for a block to be extraneous by virtue of property $3'$, it must be subsumed by its neighbors, which must themselves correspond to objects. Thus, the extraneous block, when represented by an empty block, cannot be merged with its neighbors to yield a larger block and must remain a part of the QMAT. In addition, the QMAT creation algorithm is considerably simpler when property 3 is used [1626, 1636].

Solutions to Exercises in Section 2.1.2.6

1. The ATree requires that all blocks at a particular level of subdivision e be partitioned in the same way (i.e., into the same number of congruent blocks along the same axes). This is not the case for the generalized bintree, as can be seen in Figure 2.24, where we see that some of the partitions at depth 3 are based on the value of the x coordinate, and others are based on the value of the y coordinate.

2. The same as for a binary tree: one more leaf node than nonleaf nodes. It is independent of d!

3. The lower bound is $1/2^{d-1}$, and the upper bound is 1.

4. No, since the number of nonleaf nodes in a bintree can be considerably larger than that in the corresponding region quadtree.

5. For a $2^n \times 2^n$ image, there are $(n + 1) \cdot (n + 1)$ different sizes of rectangles. For a given rectangle of size $2^i \times 2^j$, there are $(2^n/2^i) \cdot (2^n/2^j)$ positions where it can be placed when using the AHC method.

Solutions to Exercises in Section 2.1.2.7

1. No, as not all the shapes can be squares since we cannot aggregate these squares into larger squares that obey this rule.

2. In two dimensions, we have $g_{m,n} = g_{m-1,n-1} + g_{m-1,n-2} + g_{m-2,n-1} + g_{m-2,n-2}$, where $g_{m,n}$ corresponds to the area of the rectangle with sides of length f_m and f_n.

3. Consider a 3×3 square. It can only be split into two 1×2 rectangles, a 1×1 square, and a 2×2 square. The 1×2 rectangles cannot be further decomposed into 1×1 pixels using a quadtree splitting rule.

4. Dillencourt and Mount [492] propose the following solution. An optimal hierarchical decomposition of a binary image can be obtained by using a method based on dynamic programming [836]. Dynamic programming is a general technique in which a problem is solved by storing the solution to all subproblems and combining them appropriately. Assume an $M \times N$ image. The subproblems consist of the possible positions of the rectangles that correspond to the quadrants. There are at most $O(M^2 \cdot N^2)$ subproblems as there are $M \cdot N$ possible positions for the upper-leftmost corner of the rectangles, and for each of these rectangles, there are at most $M \cdot N$ positions for the lower-rightmost corner. Thus, the total storage is $O(M^2 \cdot N^2)$.

    The algorithm stores with each subproblem (i.e., rectangle) the best decomposition into quadrants, along with the number of rectangles in the decomposition. If the image is a single pixel (i.e., if $M = N = 1$), then there is only one way to subdivide the image—namely, not to subdivide it at all. Otherwise, the image may be subdivided into quadrants in $M \cdot N$ ways, as any grid point splits the image into four quadrants. For an $M \times N$ rectangle, this information is computed by examining all $(M - 1) \cdot (N - 1)$ possibilities, provided the information is known for all smaller rectangles.

    The heart of the algorithm is the computation of the solutions of the subproblems. The execution time of the algorithm is $O(M^3 \cdot N^3)$. This is obtained by noting that for each rectangle of size $i \times j$, there are $i \cdot j$ possible partitions, and they must all be examined. There are $(M - i + 1) \cdot (N - j + 1)$ rectangles of size $i \times j$. Since i and j vary from 1 to M and 1 to N, respectively, the result follows. Therefore, for an $N \times N$ image, the optimal quadtree can be computed in $O(N^6)$ time using $O(N^4)$ space.

Solutions to Exercises in Section 2.1.2.8

1. Consider a 3×3 square. It can only be split into 1×3 and 2×3 rectangles. The 1×3 square does not obey the 2-d Fibonacci condition; its sides are not of equal length, nor are they successive Fibonacci numbers.

2. When the lengths of the sides of a rectangle are equal, the rectangle is split into four rectangles such that the lengths of the sides satisfy the 2-d Fibonacci condition. When the lengths of the sides of a rectangle are not equal, the rectangle is split into two rectangles with the split along a line (an axis) that is parallel to the shorter (longer) of the two sides. Interestingly, the dimensions of the A-series of European paper are based on a Fibonacci sequence—that is, the elements of the series are of dimension $f_i \times f_{i-1}$ multiplied by an appropriate scale factor.

Solutions to Exercises in Section 2.1.2.9

1. The puzzletree in Figure 2.28 satisfies the linear homogeneity heuristic. Actually, use of the heuristic leads to two choices on the first level of partitioning. Assuming the rows and columns are numbered from 1 to 8, both row 5 and column 6 have the maximum linear homogeneity values of 1. In Figure 2.28 the initial partition was made on the two sides of column 6, resulting in partition lines $x = 4$ and $x = 5$.

3. The transformation will result in the same number of leaf nodes if at most one of the children of c corresponds to an empty region, and if the objects associated with the blocks of the remaining children are the same as the object associated with the block of child d of b, which is a leaf node. This is the best case as the transformation enables us to move a test only one level up in the tree. In this application of the transformation (e.g., see Figure 2.33), the number of tests stays the same, and so does the number of leaf nodes as it is always equal to one more than the number of tests (a direct result of properties of binary and multiway trees). In other cases (e.g., more than one child of c corresponds to an empty region), the interchange of the tests will cause the introduction of new tests and will create new leaf nodes. Another example of this increase would occur if blocks B1 and B2 in Figure 2.28 were associated with different

objects as this would force us to split the node corresponding to block B4 in Figure 2.33 at $x = 6$, thereby resulting in more leaf nodes.

4. In the following, we use $w[i]$ to refer to the ith element of list w.

```
1   node procedure COMPRESS(n1,n2,u,p0)
2   /* Merge the two nodes n1 and n2 that are partitioned along the u coordinate axis
        at value p0. */
3   value pointer node n1,n2
4   value axis u
5   value integer p0
6   list p1,p2,p3,c1,c2,c3
7   integer i,j,k,m,n,pi,pj
8   p1 ← P(n1)
9   p2 ← P(n2)
10  n ← LENGTH(p1)
11  m ← LENGTH(p2)
12  c1 ← S(n1)
13  c2 ← S(n2)
14  i ← j ← k ← pi ← pj ← 1
15  while not(i > n + 1 and j > m + 1) do
16     if (i > n and j > m) or p1 [i]=p2 [j] then
17        if pi = i and pj = j then
18           if c1 [i]=c2 [j] then c3 [k] ← c1 [i]
19           else c3 [k] ← MAKELIST(u p0 (c1 [i] c2 [j]))
20           endif
21        else
22           c3 [k] ← MAKELIST(u p0
23                              (A(n1) (p1 [pi ] ... p1 [i − 1])
24                                      (c1 [pi ] ... c1 [i]))
25                              (A(n2) (p2 [pj ] ... p2 [j − 1])
26                                      (c2 [pj ] ... c2 [j])))
27        endif
28        if p1 [i]=p2 [j] then p3 [k] ← p1 [i]
29        endif
30        i ← i + 1
31        j ← j + 1
32        k ← k + 1
33        pi ← i
34        pj ← j
35     elseif j > m and i ≤ n then i ← n + 1
36     elseif i > n and j ≤ m then j ← m + 1
37     elseif p1 [i] < p2 [j] then i ← i + 1
38     else j ← j + 1 /* p1 [i] > p2 [j] */
39     endif
40  enddo
41  return MAKELIST(A(n1) p3 c3)
```

5. The solution is a merge of two nodes.

```
1   pointer node procedure COMPRESSTREE(u,p0,a,b)
2   /* Merge the two two-dimensional puzzletree nodes pointed at by a and b that
        represent a partition on axis u at coordinate value p0 and return the result in
        c. The algorithm assumes that there is at least one common partition. */
3   value axis u
4   value integer p0
5   value pointer node a,b
6   integer i,j,k,m,n,pi,pj
7   pointer node c,d,e,f
8   c ← CREATE(node)
9   TEST(c) ← TEST(a)
10  k ← 0
11  i ← j ← 1
```

```
12   pi ← pj ← 0
13   while i ≤ NUMCHILDS(a) and j ≤ NUMCHILDS(b) do
14      if V(a)[i] < V(b)[j] then i ← i + 1
15      elseif V(b)[j] < V(a)[i] then j ← j + 1
16      else /* A common partition has been found */
17         k ← k + 1
18         if pi = i − 1 and pj = j − 1
19            and ISLEAF(CHILDS(a)[i]) and ISLEAF(CHILDS(b)[j])
20            and OBJECT(CHILDS(a)[i]) = OBJECT(CHILDS(b)[j]) then
21            /* A merge is possible */
22            V(c)[k] ← V(a)[i]
23            CHILDS(c)[k] ← CHILDS(a)[i]
24            pi ← i
25            i ← i + 1
26            pj ← j
27            j ← j + 1
28         else /* Create a new node one level deeper */
29            d ← CREATE(node)
30            CHILDS(c)[k] ← d
31            V(c)[k] ← V(a)[i]
32            TEST(d) ← u
33            NUMCHILDS(d) ← 2
34            V(d)[2] ← ∞
35            V(d)[1] ← p0
36            if pi = i − 1 then CHILDS(d)[1] ← CHILDS(a)[i]
37            else
38               /* Left child */
39               e ← CREATE(node)
40               CHILDS(d)[1] ← e
41               TEST(e) ← TEST(a)
42               NUMCHILDS(e) ← i − pi
43               n ← 1
44               for m ← pi + 1 step 1 until i − 1 do
45                  CHILDS(e)[n] ← CHILDS(a)[m]
46                  V(e)[n] ← V(a)[m]
47                  n ← n + 1
48               enddo
49               CHILDS(e)[n] ← CHILDS(a)[i]
50               V(e)[n] ← ∞
51            endif
52            if pj = j − 1 then CHILDS(d)[2] ← CHILDS(b)[j]
53            else
54               /* Right child */
55               F ← CREATE(node)
56               CHILDS(d)[2] ← f
57               TEST(f) ← TEST(b)
58               NUMCHILDS(f) ← j − pj
59               n ← 1
60               for m ← pj + 1 step 1 until j − 1 do
61                  CHILDS(f)[n] ← CHILDS(b)[m]
62                  V(f)[n] ← V(b)[m]
63                  n ← n + 1
64               enddo
65               CHILDS(f)[n] ← CHILDS(b)[j]
66               V(f)[n] ← ∞
67            endif
68         endif
69      endif
70   enddo
71   NUMCHILDS(c) ← k
72   return c
```

6.
```
1   node procedure REPARTITION(n1,n2,u,p0)
2   /* Merge the two nodes n1 and n2 that are partitioned along the u coordinate axis
       at value p0. */
3   value pointer node n1,n2
4   value axis u
5   value integer p0
6   list p1,p2,p3,c1,c2,c3
7   integer i,j,k,m,n
8   p1 ← P(n1)
9   p2 ← P(n2)
10  n ← LENGTH(p1)
11  m ← LENGTH(p2)
12  c1 ← S(n1)
13  c2 ← S(n2)
14  i ← j ← k ← 1
15  while not(i > n + 1 and j > m + 1) do
16     if c1 [i] = c2 [j] then c3 [k] ← c1 [i]
17     else c3 [k] ← MAKELIST(u p0 (c1 [i] c2 [j]))
18     endif
19     if not(i > n and j > m) then
20        if i > n then
21           p3 [k] ← p2 [j]
22           j ← j + 1
23        elseif j > m then
24           p3 [k] ← p1 [i]
25           i ← i + 1
26        elseif p1 [i] < p2 [j] then
27           p3 [k] ← p1 [i]
28           i ← i + 1
29        elseif p2 [j] < p1 [i] then
30           p3 [k] ← p2 [j]
31           j ← j + 1
32        else
33           p3 [k] ← p1 [i]
34           i ← i + 1
35           j ← j + 1
36        endif
37     else exit_while_loop ;
38     endif
39     k ← k + 1
40  enddo
41  return MAKELIST(A(n1) p3 c3)
```

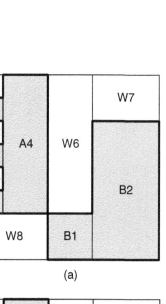

(a)

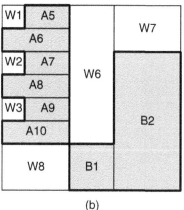

(b)

Figure S.7
Example puzzletree using the common partition elimination method of Exercises (a) 4 and (b) 6.

7. Consider the puzzletree given in Figure 2.31, which has 13 leaf nodes. The partitions at the root that yield the regions $0 \leq x < 1$ and $1 \leq x < 3$ are both subdivided further at $y = 6$, and they form the common partitions $0 \leq y < 6$ and $6 \leq y < 8$. The regions corresponding to the partition $6 \leq y < 8$ can be merged as neither is associated with any object. For the method in Exercise 4, the resulting block decomposition is given in Figure S.7(a) and has 12 leaf nodes (i.e., blocks). For the method in Exercise 6, the result is given in Figure S.7(b) and has 14 leaf nodes (i.e., blocks).

8. Each of the methods eliminates the same number of tests for each merge that takes place, which means one fewer leaf node for each eliminated test. The method described in Exercise 4 never creates new leaf nodes as it does not introduce new tests. When merging is not possible, it just rearranges the order in which tests are made on account of the factoring that has taken place as a result of the elimination of common tests. On the other hand, the method described in Exercise 6 creates new partitions accompanied by the introduction of additional tests wherever a merge is impossible, which increases the number of leaf nodes by one for each additional test.

Solutions to Exercises in Section 2.1.2.11

2. 80 and 60 faces, respectively.

Solutions to Exercises in Section 2.1.3.1

3. No. See the two-dimensional example in Figure 2.37, where line segment B does not intersect the halfspace of line segment D, whereas line segment D does intersect the halfspace of line segment B.

4. In two dimensions, P_1 and P_2 must intersect. In three dimensions, either P_1 and P_2 are coplanar, or else both P_1 and P_2 intersect the line along which their planes intersect (it does not imply that P_1 and P_2 intersect).

6. $n + 1$.

7. When all line segments (polygonal faces) span the entire two- (three-) dimensional space from which they are drawn. Alternatively, referring to Exercise 3, $\text{CONFLICT}(P_1, P_2) = \text{CONFLICT}(P_2, P_1)$ for every pair of line segments (polygonal faces).

8. $\sum_{i=0}^{d} \binom{n}{i}$ in a d-dimensional space.

9. There are two basic techniques [657]. The first technique assigns a visibility number to each polygon in the order in which it has been visited. This order depends on whether we are using a back-to-front or a front-to-back display algorithm. We shall assume a back-to-front algorithm. In such a case, the higher numbers correspond to a higher priority. They are assigned by traversing the BSP tree in such a way that for given node N, all the polygons in $\text{INCHILD}(N, V)$ are given a lower number than N's polygon, and all the polygons in $\text{OUTCHILD}(N, V)$ are given a higher number than N's polygon. It should be clear that this is nothing more than an inorder traversal with respect to the viewpoint. These priorities can be used by conventional hidden-surface elimination algorithms whenever a visibility determination must be made. In fact, we do not even have to assign the visibility numbers.

   The second technique does not use the visibility numbers. Instead, the traversal is used to control a back-to-front (i.e., painter's) algorithm that paints each polygon on the screen as it is encountered. If one polygon overlaps another polygon, then the most recently painted polygon determines the color of the overlapped region. Given viewpoint V, BSP tree node N, and the previous definition of INCHILD and OUTCHILD, the polygons in $\text{OUTCHILD}(N, V)$ are visited before the polygon in the root, which, in turn, is visited before the polygons in $\text{INCHILD}(N, V)$. Correctness is assured since polygons that occlude other polygons are closer to the viewpoint and are visited later in the traversal.

Solutions to Exercises in Section 2.1.3.2

1. Use induction on the number of vertices, and start with one triangle.

2. Use induction on the number of vertices, and start with one triangle.

3. Each vertex is visible from every other vertex. To obtain a triangulation, simply pick a vertex at random, and draw lines from it to the remaining vertices. This is an $O(v)$ process.

4. Sort the vertices seen so far by their y coordinate values. See [834], as well as [1282], for more details.

5. The greedy method cannot be performed in time faster than $O(v^2 \log(v^2)) = O(v^2 \log v)$ as we must first sort the edges in order of increasing length, and there are $O(v^2)$ possible edges. Checking if an edge intersects an existing edge in a partial triangulation takes at most $O(v)$ time as there are only $O(v)$ edges in a triangulation (see Exercise 2). The $O(v)$ time factor for checking the intersection of an edge with an existing edge can be reduced to $O(\log v)$ by use of a cleverer data structure [717] so that the entire greedy method can obtain a triangulation in $O(v^2 \log v)$ time and $O(v)$ space. Interestingly, Levcopoulos and Krznaric [1155] describe

a nongreedy algorithm to obtain the same triangulation in $O(v \log v)$ time. This algorithm can also be used to convert a Delaunay triangulation (see Exercise 8 and Section 2.2.1.4) into the same triangulation (i.e., the one obtained by the greedy method) in $O(v)$ time.

6. We look for p_k in step 2 by minimizing a quantity that takes $O(v)$ time and the process is performed for each of the $O(v^2)$ possible entries in w that correspond to the edges. Thus, the total time is $O(v^3)$.

9. Use an array of edge-adjacency lists such that there is one edge-adjacency list per vertex.

   (a) Identify all K-vertices.

   (b) Initially, the set of mutually independent K-vertices, say M, is empty.

   (c) Pick a K-vertex, say V, that has not been marked as not mutually independent with elements of M, and insert it into M. Now, mark all elements of V's edge-adjacency list as not mutually independent with M, and repeat until there are no vertices left. This process is $O(v)$ since we mark all edges, and by Euler's formula, given v vertices, the number of edges is $3 \cdot v - 6$. The data structure requires $O(v)$ array entries and $O(v)$ edge-adjacency list elements.

10. If the removed K-vertex had degree k, then its neighborhood (i.e., polygon) had k triangles and k sides. The triangulation of a k-sided polygon contains $k - 2$ triangles.

12. There is no obvious way to achieve map overlay using the K-structure. Nevertheless, since the triangulation forms a convex map, a plane-sweep algorithm can be used to do the overlay in $O(v \log_2 v + s)$ time and $O(v)$ space [1377], where s denotes the number of intersections of edges from the first map with edges from the second map, and v denotes the total number of vertices in the two maps. From this result, a new K-structure can be built in $O(v)$ time.

Solutions to Exercises in Section 2.1.3.3.1

1. Note that there are no regions to the left (right) of the extreme left (right) endpoints that are introduced by the regularization process.

2. Yes. Each vertex formed by the intersection of the new edge with an existing edge already has at least one edge to each of its right and left sides.

3. Yes. The intersection of any two y-monotone regions is always y-monotone.

4. A polygonal map of m edges has at most $m + 1$ vertices. Two of these vertices are at the extreme left and right of the map, and thus no edges are added to them. At most one edge can be added to each of the remaining $m - 1$ vertices since they must have at least either one edge to a vertex at their right or one edge to a vertex at their left.

5. Use a plane-sweep algorithm (see Section 3.1 of Chapter 3). First, sort the edges by their x coordinate values. Next, sweep a vertical line through the sorted list of edges. During the sweep, use a balanced binary search tree to represent the active intervals of the sweep line (i.e., crossed by edges), and order it by the y coordinate values.

6. For example, the vertex with the larger y coordinate value can be treated as the left vertex. The "immediately above" relation must be extended to mean "immediately right" in such a case. The general relation "above" becomes "right."

7. This is an open question.

8. Use contradiction.

9. No. Consider the case that regions R_i and R_j in the left and right subtrees, respectively, of S_k do not exist such that $R_i = \text{BELOW}(e)$ and $R_j = \text{ABOVE}(e)$.

10. See Theorem 8 in [541].

11. Edge e is contained in separator S_k if and only if S_k lies above region R_i and below region R_j for $i < k \leq j$.

12. Use the edge-ordering property and contradiction. In other words, assume that the least common ancestor does not contain e.

13. $lca(i, j) = j \wedge \neg(msb(i \oplus j) - 1)$ [541].

14. $lca(i, j) = rev(x \oplus (x - 1)) \wedge j$, where $x = rev(i \oplus j)$ [541].

15. Adopt the convention that each edge contains its left endpoint but not its right endpoint.

16. Use an array of edge-adjacency lists such that there is one edge-adjacency list per vertex. The reregularization process simply scans the array and, for each vertex whose edge-adjacency list does not contain vertices to the left (right), it adds the edge to the succeeding (preceding) vertex in the sorted list. By Euler's formula, this is an $O(v)$ space and time process.

Solutions to Exercises in Section 2.1.3.3.2

1. L_2 consists of vertices C, E, F, I, and K; the x-intervals making up edges CE and IK; and the gaps αC, EF, FI, and Kδ. L_6 consists of vertices B, C, D, G, J, and L; the x-intervals making up α B, BC, DG, and GJ; and the gaps CD, JL, and L δ. L_4 consists of vertices A, C, D, E, G, I, J, K, L, and M; the x-intervals making up edges α A, AC, CD, DE, EG, GI, IJ, JK, KL, LM, and M δ; there are no gaps.

2. If it were common to more than one x-interval, then the x-intervals would have to overlap, which is impossible.

3. See [541]. The inductive hypothesis is $B_v + b_v \leq 4 \cdot A_v$, which holds trivially for the leaf nodes of the gap tree. Letting $l(u)$ and $r(u)$ denote the left and right children of node u of the gap tree, $B_u = B_{l(u)} + B_{r(u)} + b_u$ and $A_u = A_{l(u)} + A_{r(u)} + a_u$. Moreover, $b_u \leq 2 \cdot a_u + (b_{l(u)} + b_{r(u)})/2$ since each edge in S_u contributes at most two vertices to L_u. Applying the inductive hypothesis to the subtrees using this inequality and the previous two equalities leads to the desired result.

5. For example, there is no need for links between vertices and adjacent x-intervals. Instead, the elements of the layered dag can be stored in consecutive memory locations by use of an array.

8. There is no obvious way to achieve map overlay using the layered dag. In particular, performing map overlay for the layered dag is more complex than for the K-structure since the map created by a y-monotone subdivision process is not convex. However, the algorithm still has the same execution time behavior and the same space requirement as the algorithm for the K-structure.

Solutions to Exercises in Section 2.1.4.1

1. A depth-first policy might reach the upper bound on the number of elements before some very large regions covering the object would have a chance to be split.

2. If the radius of the minimum bounding box for o is smaller than or equal to $p \cdot w/4$, then o will be associated with one of the subblocks of b of width $w/2$ whose expanded block is of width $(p + 1) \cdot w/2$. This situation arises when o overlaps the center point c of b, as well as at least one pair of two diametrically opposite points at a distance of $p \cdot w/4$ from c along at least one of the two axes that pass through c.

3. One issue here concerns how many subblocks will have to be checked for a tighter fit. Also, what is the guaranteed radius of o's minimum bounding box when it is stored at a given depth?

Solutions to Exercises in Section 2.1.4.2

1. If such an angle is present, then we cannot draw a line between the two edges that form this angle that will be part of a polygon that completely surrounds the vertex. Thus, we cannot eliminate the vertex.

2. After application of vertex enlargement to vertex v, the degree of v is either two or three. It is two if the angle between two of the adjacent edges originally incident at v was greater than $180°$; otherwise, it is three. Thus, we need to apply vertex enlargement to every vertex of degree greater than three, and we end up with a polygonal map where every vertex has a maximum degree of three.

3. Four, because polygonal maps often arise from road networks, in which case it is quite natural for four polygons to be incident at a vertex, and it does not make sense to replace it. In this case, a value of three for T does not make sense as often it will result in a T-like junction.

4. No. The problem arises when a block contains the edge of just one polygon. Unless the edge is along one of the sides of the block, the decomposition goes on forever.

5. No. Whenever a block b contains just one vertex v, there are two or three edges incident at v, thereby corresponding to two or three polygons. However, b can contain additional edges that are not incident at v. Each of these edges must pass through two sides of b as otherwise they would meet at a vertex in b, which would contradict our initial assumption that b contains only one vertex. If there are at least $T - 1$ such edges, then b could be a part of as many as $T - 1$ additional polygons, for a total of $T + 1$, thereby violating the decomposition rule.

6. Since each polygon has at least one CDT node, the number of CDT nodes is never smaller than the number of polygons. Therefore, it is impossible for the total number of CDT nodes in the four subblocks of a block that has been split according to the initial decomposition rule (i.e., based on the total number of polygons in a block) to be smaller than the bucket threshold. This means that we need not worry about merging.

Solutions to Exercises in Section 2.1.5.1

1. If the object occupies every element in the space, then $4^{n+1}/3 + 1$ elements of the pyramid will be examined.

2. $E_p = (4n + 1)/4^n$ and $O_p = 4n + 1$.

3. E_p and O_p are both $(4^{n+1} - 1)/(3 \cdot 4^n)$.

4. $E_p = (2^{n+2} - 3)/4^n$ and $O_p = (2^{n+2} - 3)/2^n$.

5. $E_p = (2^{n+2} - 3)/4^n$ and $O_p = (2^{n+2} - 3)/2^n$.

6. In the worst case, the square is positioned in the center of the image. $E_p = (5 + 16(n - 2))/4^n$ and $O_p = (5 + 16(n - 2))/4$.

Solutions to Exercises in Section 2.1.5.2.1

1. Determine the extreme left, right, top, and bottom sides by scanning all of the rectangles as they are not assumed to be sorted. This process takes $O(M)$ time.

Solutions to Exercises in Section 2.1.5.2.2

1. Use the circle center or the circle center plus the radius.

2. Assume, without loss of generality, that $N = M^n$. At the initial stage ($j = 1$), we must examine $\sum_{i=0}^{N/M-1} \binom{M+iM}{M}$ combinations. At stage j, we have N/M^{j-1} bounding boxes, and we

must examine $\sum_{i=0}^{N/M^j-1}\binom{M+iM}{M}$ combinations. Therefore, a total of $\sum_{j=1}^{n-1}\sum_{i=0}^{N/M^j-1}\binom{M+iM}{M}$ combinations are examined.

3. See [698] for an example algorithm that tries to minimize an objective function consisting of the sum of the areas of the bounding boxes.

Solutions to Exercises in Section 2.1.5.2.3

1. A node in a B-tree of order $2c + 1$ has c records and $c + 1$ children.

2. If the value k is such that there is no leaf node p containing two successive keys p_i and p_{i+1}, where $p_i \leq k \leq p_{i+1}$. In this case, there are two choices: either the leaf node containing the largest key q such that $q \leq k$, or the leaf node containing the smallest key s such that $k \leq s$.

3. $\lceil \log_m(N) \rceil$.

4. $\lceil N/m \rceil + \lceil N/m^2 \rceil + \cdots + 1$.

5. This requires a search starting at the root. At each level, we examine the M children of the node and descend the one for whom the corresponding block is increased the least by the addition. This takes $O(M \log_M(N))$ time.

7. Deletion of an object, say O, from an R-tree proceeds by locating the leaf node, say L, containing O and removing O from L. Next, adjust the bounding boxes on the path from L to the root of the tree while removing all nodes in which underflow occurs and adding them to the set U. Once the root node is reached, if it has just one child, then the child becomes the new root. The nodes in which underflow occurred (i.e., members of U) are reinserted at the root. Elements of U that correspond to leaf nodes result in the placement of their constituent bounding boxes in the leaf nodes, while other nodes are placed at a level so that their leaf nodes are at the same level as those of the whole tree.

8. For a set of $M + 1$ items, there are 2^{M+1} subsets. Of these subsets, we exclude the empty set and the set of $M + 1$ items, leaving $2^{M+1} - 2$ subsets. Removing duplicate partitions yields $2^M - 1$ partitions.

11. No. The new variant of the algorithm must compute the separation between every pair of bounding boxes (an $O(M^2)$ process) instead of the minimum separation between every bounding box and the upper and lower boundaries of the bounding box associated with the node that is being split (an $O(M)$ process).

12. In general, the farther apart the seeds are, the larger their combined bounding box is and the greater the amount of wasted space in their bounding box is. Also, the smaller their size is, the greater the area wasted when their area is subtracted from that of their combined bounding box. Thus, the combination of small seeds that are far part is ideal for maximizing the amount of wasted area [152].

13. Since s is so small and has almost the same coordinate values as r, r must also be very small, and the area increase relative to s will be very small as well, while the area increase from the other seed t may be large, thereby resulting in a large value of $|d_{rt} - d_{rs}|$ [152].

14. Since the bounding box of s was the first to be enlarged, it will be bigger than the bounding box of the other seed t. Thus, the enlarged bounding box of s needs less area enlargement to include bounding box b_2, which is the next one to be redistributed. Therefore, s will be enlarged again and again. Thus, the first $M - m$ bounding boxes may all be redistributed to the bounding box of s, which means that the remaining $m - 1$ bounding boxes are redistributed to the bounding box of t regardless of the minimum area enlargement computation [152]. This will result in a large overlap between the nodes s and t.

15. First, the algorithm must examine all possible pairs of bounding boxes to determine which combination wastes the most area. There are M^2 pairs of bounding boxes. Next, the algorithm computes, for each of the remaining bounding boxes, the preferred of new nodes i and j. This is also an $O(M^2)$ process as there are $2c$ area differences ($1 \leq c \leq M - 2$) computed at the remaining $M - 2$ stages.

16. See [152] for a comparison of the R*-tree (discussed in Section 2.1.5.2.4) and technique 1.

17. Seed-picking takes $O(M^2)$ time. The process of redistributing the remaining bounding boxes takes $O(M \log M)$ time as sorting is required. Thus, the algorithm takes $O(M^2)$ time.

18. The problem is that the algorithm blindly redistributes $M/2$ of the bounding boxes in one node and the remaining ones in the other node without taking any geometric factors into account, such as minimizing overlap or coverage. The result is that the split could be quite bad in the sense of having overlap, which could have been avoided by distributing more of the bounding boxes in one node than in another, as is done in the R*-tree (see Section 2.1.5.2.4) node redistribution algorithm. This algorithm is closely related in the sense that it also makes use of a sort of the bounding boxes according to one of their sides.

23. The probability that R-tree node q's bounding box b with volume v covers query point p is v. v is also the expected number of times that node q is visited in the search for p. Therefore, the expected number of nodes that are visited in the search for p is the sum of the volumes of the bounding boxes of all of the nodes in the R-tree [983]. This analysis assumes that the R-tree is implemented so that node p contains k ($m \leq k \leq M$) pointers to p's children and the k bounding boxes of p's children instead of containing just one bounding box corresponding to the union of the bounding boxes of p's children. Otherwise, we would have to make one more node access to determine whether the query point is covered by the bounding box of the root node.

25. Node q_j will be visited by the window query as long as the lower-right corner of the window has a nonempty intersection with the region of size $\prod_{i=1}^{d}(b_{ji} + w_i)$ that has the same upper-left corner as b_j. Thus, the probability that q_j is visited is $\prod_{i=1}^{d}(b_{ji} + w_i)$. This is also the expected number of times that node q_j is visited in the search for w. Therefore, the expected number of nodes that are visited in the search for w is the sum of the volumes of the expanded bounding boxes of all of the nodes in the R-tree, which is $\sum_j \prod_{i=1}^{d}(b_{ji} + w_i)$ [983].

26. See [1586] for an algorithm designed specifically for finding the nearest object in an R-tree. See also [846] for a general algorithm that works for arbitrary spatial data structures that ranks the objects according to their distance from the query point in an incremental manner.

28. Each rectangle may have to be tested against every other rectangle.

Solutions to Exercises in Section 2.1.5.2.4

1. The problem is that most of the keys that are reinserted would end up in the same node or a neighboring node, thereby achieving the same result as if we had rotated the overflowing items. The problem is that we usually do not have a choice of which record will contain a given key (see also the solution to Exercise 2 in Section 2.1.5.2.3).

3. This requires a search starting at the root. At each level other than the one containing the leaf nodes, we examine the M children of the node and descend the one for whom the corresponding block is increased the least by the addition. This takes $O(M \log_M(N))$ time. At the leaf level, given a parent node f, we need to check each of the children of f for overlap with all of its siblings, which takes $O(M^2)$ time for an order (m,M) R*-tree. Thus, the process takes $O(M^2)$ time.

4. For each child p of s, compute the increase in area resulting from the insertion of b in p. Sort the children of s in increasing order of area increase and select the first a entries forming a set I. Now insert b in the element of I for whom the resulting bounding box has the minimum increase in the amount of overlap with all remaining children of s. The answer is approximate as we did not check the overlap of each of the children of s [152].

7. Perimeter is often a better indication of spatial extent than area as we could have very long and thin slivers of minimal total area that span a large part of the node, thereby increasing the possibility of overlapping with the bounding box of the other node if the splitting axis is not perpendicular to the longest side of the bounding box. Thus, in the case of many parallel slivers, the choice of the split axis serves to insure that the slivers are separated with little overlap. Notice that the areas of the slivers can be made as small as possible, even approaching zero in the limit, while the perimeter does not go to zero and can be as big as twice the larger of the two sides of the bounding box of the node being split.

8. Instead of computing the averages along the axes and comparing them, it is simpler just to compare the sum of the perimeters along each axis. For a given sort order, perform a sweep of the bounding boxes in increasing order, starting with the first one, incrementally computing the union of the bounding boxes seen so far. For each legal group of bounding boxes (i.e., containing at least m entries and at most $M - m$ entries), compute the perimeter and add it to the perimeter sum for the corresponding axis. The same process is repeated in decreasing order starting with the last bounding box. Each of these processes computes the union of $M - m$ bounding boxes and performs $M - 2m$ perimeter computations, for a cost of $O(M)$. There are two sort orders for each axis, so the total cost of computing the perimeter sums is $O(dM)$. The final task of determining the minimum of the perimeter sums for the d axes can be done in $O(d)$ time.

9. The drawback of this approach is that it leads to a higher likelihood that the split position chosen in the second phase will result in a partition with a large perimeter. The reason is that the split position with the minimum perimeter is not necessarily the split position with the minimum coverage along the axis. In contrast, the approach that chooses the axis for which the average perimeter is the smallest results in a greater number of possible split positions with a low perimeter value.

10. The fact that s' may not necessarily minimize overlap can best be seen by considering an example consisting of a 10×10 grid with two bounding boxes b_1 and b_2 corresponding to sets of objects s_1 and s_2, respectively. b_1 is adjacent to the upper-left corner and has width 5 and height 4, and b_2 is adjacent to the lower-left corner and has width 8 and height 8. The sum of the perimeters of b_1 and b_2 is 50 with an overlapping area of 6. Suppose that we move a 1×1 object o in the lower-left corner of b_1 from s_1 to set s_2. This means that the new bounding box of the set $s_1 - o$ is now of height 3 and width 5 with perimeter 16, and the new bounding box of the set $s_2 + o$ is now of height 8 and width 10 with perimeter 36. The sum of the perimeters of the new bounding boxes is 52 with an overlapping area of 3. Thus, the split position that minimizes the sum of the perimeters of the constituent bounding boxes is not necessarily the one yielding a minimum overlap.

19. Yes. If we process them in increasing (decreasing) order from left to right (right to left), then the algorithm has a tendency to prefer the left (right) partition for the first insertion, and once the left (right) partition has been enlarged once, it is likely to be enlarged the least by the next element from left to right (right to left) in increasing (decreasing) order. Therefore, the left (right) partition will contain all of the remaining bounding boxes. This may result in a large overlap along the split axis. The same problem arose in the quadratic cost R-tree node-splitting algorithm proposed by Guttman [791] and is discussed in Exercise 14 in Section 2.1.5.2.3. A better solution is to continue to process the remaining line segments by choosing them in the same alternating fashion and increasing (decreasing) order from left to right (right to left) as before the determination that the storage utilization constraints have been satisfied.

20. An example can be constructed where the outlined approach does not find the partitioning for which the sum of the perimeters of the bounding boxes of the resulting nodes is a minimum. However, the evaluation of the quality of the partitioning obtained with the outlined approach in the use of R*-trees is an important one. Note that the problem of finding the partition into two sets of nodes for which the sum of the perimeters of their bounding boxes is a minimum can be solved using the method of Becker et al. [146] in $O(dM \log M + d^2 M^{2d-1})$ time for d-dimensional data subject to the minimum node occupancy constraints, whereas when these constraints are not required to hold, it can be solved in $O(M^d)$ time using the method of García et al. [680].

21. See the solution to Exercise 20. In particular, the optimal cost algorithms of Becker et al. [146] and García et al. [680] are applicable.

23. See [983] for the predictions of the results of such tests using the expected number of nodes calculated in Exercises 23 and 25 in Section 2.1.5.2.3. These calculations showed that a sort on the basis of the Peano-Hilbert order of the centroids of the objects results in the lowest expected number of retrieved R-tree nodes with respect to the other space orderings as well as the dynamic R-tree construction algorithms. Are your empirical results in agreement?

Solutions to Exercises in Section 2.1.5.2.6

1. Let $2 \cdot p \cdot B$ be the capacity of a buffer for a nonleaf node, where p is an integer, and B is the block size. If we distributed only the first $p \cdot B$ entries in a buffer each time the number of entries in the buffer exceeds $p \cdot B$, the size of the children's buffers will never be larger than $2 \cdot p \cdot B$.

Solutions to Exercises in Section 2.1.5.2.7

1. Compare your results to those reported in [983].

6. Let s_1 and s_2 be at depth i in the R-tree and let the leaf nodes be at depth j. Thus, the objects are at depth $j + 1$. Assume that s_1 has m children and s_2 has M children. Assume further that each of the descendants of s_1 has m children, and each of the descendants of s_2 has M children. Therefore, $N_{s_1} = m^{j-i+1}$ and $N_{s_2} = M^{j-i+1}$, and thus the ratio $N_{s_1}/N_{s_2} = (m/M)^{j-i+1}$ can get arbitrary large.

Solutions to Exercises in Section 2.1.5.3

1. Repartitioning may lead to overflow because the objects are being decomposed into subobjects. However, point objects cannot be further decomposed. Thus, repartitioning cannot create nodes that will overflow.

2. Each R^+-tree node must store the bounding box of its subtrees. This requires storing the coordinate values of the diagonally opposite corners of the bounding box (i.e., $2d$ values for d-dimensional data). On the other hand, each k-d-B-tree node p at depth h must just store the identity of the discriminating dimension and the coordinate value along this dimension (i.e., 2 items for each node and $2h$ values for the path from the root to p). The size of the block corresponding to p can be determined from the values of the discriminating dimensions and corresponding coordinate values of the ancestors of p.

3. This is complicated by the fact that, in general, it is not possible to guarantee that each node in an R^+-tree will contain a minimum of m items.

9. Each rectangle may have to be tested against every other rectangle.

Solutions to Exercises in Section 2.2.1.1

1. (a) Use two sets of lists. The first list contains the eight vertices and their coordinate values. The second list contains the faces. Each face is represented by a list of the identifiers corresponding to its constituent vertices.

   (b) Use three sets of lists. The first list contains the eight vertices and their coordinate values. The second list contains the faces, where each face is represented by a list of the identifiers corresponding to its constituent edges. The third list contains the twelve edges and the identifiers corresponding to their constituent vertices.

2. Two in the case of a two-manifold because an edge can touch at most two faces, each of which has a loop surrounding it.

3. Yes. For example, consider a hexagonal face with two holes. The holes are internal loops and still make up the boundary of the hexagon.

4. One way is to store with each loop all the faces that are incident at its edges. Another way is just to store the faces that contain all of the edges that make up the loop. The second alternative is superior since the importance of the loop-face relation is that, given a loop, we know which face(s) we are currently processing.

5. Two, in case each of the loop's edges touches the same two faces since an edge cannot touch more than two faces, and we have restricted all of the loop's edges to touch the same faces. For example, consider a cube. The surface of the cube consists of six squares. Assume that one of these squares, say s_o, contains a smaller square, say s_i. Now, one side of the cube contains the faces s_i and $s_o - s_i$. Let loop l be the external loop of the inner face s_i. l is also the internal loop of the outer face $s_o - s_i$.

Solutions to Exercises in Section 2.2.1.2

2. The ordering can be clockwise or counterclockwise. Let v denote the vertex and e the first edge incident at v obtained from the vertex-edge table VERTEXEDGETABLE. For a clockwise ordering, if $v = \text{VEND}(e)$, then the next edge is CVVEND(e); otherwise, $v = \text{VSTART}(e)$, and the next edge is CVVSTART(e). For a counterclockwise ordering, if $v = \text{VEND}(e)$, then the next edge is CCVVEND(e); otherwise, $v = \text{VSTART}(e)$, and the next edge is CCVVSTART(e).

```
1   procedure EXTRACTEDGESINCIDENTATVERTEX(v, CWFlag)
2   /* Extract the edges that are incident at vertex v in clockwise (counterclockwise)
        order if flag CWFlag is true (false) in a winged-edge-face data structure. */
3   value vertex v
4   value Boolean CWFlag
5   pointer edge e, FirstEdge
6   e ← FirstEdge ← EDGE(VERTEXEDGETABLE [v])
7   do
8      output e
9      if CWFlag then
10        e ←if VEND(e) = v then CVVEND(e)
11           else CVVSTART(e)
12           endif
13     else e ←if VEND(e) = v then CCVVEND(e)
14              else CCVVSTART(e)
15              endif
16     endif
17     until e = FirstEdge
18  enddo
```

3. We can obtain all of the edges incident at a starting vertex v in clockwise (counterclockwise) order by following the CVVSTART (CCVVSTART) fields, while we can obtain all of the edges incident at an ending vertex v in clockwise (counterclockwise) order by following the CVVEND (CCVVEND) fields—that is, all edges e satisfy $\text{VSTART}(e) = v$ in the former and $\text{VEND}(e) = v'$ in the latter.

4. Any combination that results in the faces being traversed in the opposite order to that of the vertices. This includes a combination of preceding/clockwise with next/clockwise and likewise for next/counterclockwise and preceding/counterclockwise. Other invalid combinations include preceding/clockwise and preceding/counterclockwise, next/clockwise and next/counterclockwise. Note that combinations such as next/clockwise and preceding/counterclockwise, and so on, are valid as they are the same.

5. In the case of edges in the same face, a positive orientation for the next edge e (i.e., a reference to it) means that e starts at the ending vertex of the current edge e' and is directed away from it. Similarly, in the case of edges incident at the same vertex, the next edge e must also terminate at the ending vertex of the current edge e' that corresponds to a positive orientation for e.

6. The algorithm is very similar to procedure EXTRACTORIENTEDEDGESOFFACE with the difference that the body in lines 11–16 is replaced by the analog of lines 9–14 in procedure EXTRACTEDGESINCIDENTATVERTEX, given in the solution to Exercise 2, and the use of ORIENTEDVERTEXEDGETABLE instead of ORIENTEDFACEEDGETABLE. One additional item of note is that the semantics of a positive (negative) orientation are reversed—that is, a negative orientation means that $\text{VSTART}(e) = v$, and a positive orientation means that $\text{VEND}(e) = v$.

```
1   procedure EXTRACTORIENTEDEDGESINCIDENTATVERTEX(v, CWFlag)
2   /* Extract the edges incident at vertex v in clockwise (counterclockwise) order
        if flag CWFlag is true (false) in an oriented winged-edge-face data structure.
        For each edge e, a negative orientation value indicates that e's direction makes
        e a part of a traversal of a starting vertex v of e (i.e., VSTART(e) = v), and
        thus e is directed away from v. On the other hand, a positive value indicates
        that e's direction makes e a part of a traversal of an ending vertex v of e (i.e.,
        VEND(e) = v), and thus e is directed towards v. */
3   value vertex v
4   value Boolean CWFlag
5   pointer edge FirstEdge
6   pointer edge_orientation_pair p
7   p ← ORIENTEDEDGE(ORIENTEDVERTEXEDGETABLE [v])
8   FirstEdge ← EDGE(p)
9   do
10      output EDGE(p)
11      if CWFlag  then
12          p ←if ORIENT(p) then CVVEND(EDGE(p))
13              else CVVSTART(EDGE(p))
14              endif
15      else p ←if ORIENT(p) then CCVVEND(EDGE(p))
16              else CCVVSTART(EDGE(p))
17              endif
18      endif
19      until EDGE(p) = FirstEdge
20  enddo
```

7. No. The problem is that many edges are incident at vertex v, and thus the exclusion of edge e from the singly linked list around vertex v means that we cannot have a valid singly linked list of edges around vertex v. Therefore, in effect, there is no singly linked list of edges around v, which means that this proposed data structure cannot be used to represent the necessary topological relationships. This can be seen by looking at the object consisting of a pair of adjacent triangular faces shown in Figure 2.95. In this case, forming a singly linked list around vertex E means that we cannot have any singly linked lists around vertices D F, and G. Thus, we cannot represent the object. A similar argument can be made about singly linked lists of edges around adjacent faces by considering a tetrahedron object where each of the four triangular faces is adjacent to all of the remaining three faces. Thus, we cannot represent this object either. Note that the D-CEL-face-vertex data structure does not qualify as an answer unless the various links (i.e., pointers to next or preceding edges) are shared between the vertex v at which they are incident and the face f along which they lie.

8. Obtain one vertex from each of the two companion half-edges.

11. The half-edge-vertex data structure is defined as follows. With each half-edge h, we record the following information (see Figure S.8):

   (a) Starting vertex (VSTART(h))

   (b) Companion half-edge (h')

   (c) Face (FCW(h)) along whose boundary h lies when moving in clockwise order

   (d) Preceding half-edge (CCV(VSTART(h))) in clockwise order around vertex VSTART(h)

   (e) Next half-edge (CV(VSTART(h))) in clockwise order around vertex VSTART(h)

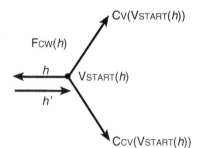

Figure S.8
The physical interpretation of the fields of a half-edge-vertex data structure (i.e., the vertex variant of the half-edge data structure that is based on a traversal of the edges that are incident at a vertex).

Solutions to Exercises in Section 2.2.1.3

1. Each edge has two vertices, and thus the number of edge-vertex pairs is two times the number of edges. Each edge is adjacent to two faces, and therefore the number of edge-face pairs is two times the number of edges. Each face-vertex pair corresponds to the presence of a vertex

in the face, and there are as many vertices in a face as there are edges. Therefore, for each face-vertex pair, there is one edge-face pair, and thus the number of face-vertex pairs is the same as the number of edge-face pairs, which is the same as the number of edge-vertex pairs.

Solutions to Exercises in Section 2.2.1.3.1

1. The problem is that, given lath L, knowing $\text{CF}(L)$ and $\text{CCF}(L)$ will only enable us to traverse the edges that make up the face f implicitly associated with L. The absence of a primitive transition involving laths associated with another face f' than f using either of CV, CCV, or CE precludes being able to make any transitions to laths corresponding to f'. Thus, we can only answer queries involving f, which is rather limiting.

2. The problem is that, given lath L, knowing $\text{CV}(L)$ and $\text{CCV}(L)$ will only enable us to traverse the edges incident at the vertex v explicitly associated with L. The absence of a primitive transition involving laths associated with another vertex v' other than v using either of CF, CCF, or CE precludes our being able to make any transitions to laths corresponding to v'. Thus, we can only answer queries involving v, which is rather limiting.

3. This is easy to see for the split-face and split-vertex representations as, by the nature of the objects' being two-manifolds, each edge is a member of two laths since it consists of two vertices and separates two faces. In the case of the corner representation, each lath corresponds to a face-vertex pair, which is an implicit representation of an edge's membership in a face. As we have a two-manifold object, the edge can be a member in just two faces, and thus we again have just two possible laths.

4. The main effect is that the order of applying the various transitions is reversed. $\text{CCV}(L)$ is obtained by $\text{CE}(\text{CF}(L))$. $\text{CV}(L)$ can be obtained either by first applying $\text{CE}(L)$ to obtain the lath L' of the same edge e but opposite face f', and then successively traversing the laths representing the face f' using CF until obtaining a lath L'' such that $\text{CF}(L'') = L'$, which means that $\text{CV}(L) = L''$, or by successively traversing the laths surrounding the vertex associated with L using CCV until obtaining a lath L' such that $\text{CCV}(L') = L$, which means that $\text{CV}(L) = L'$. $\text{CCF}(L)$ is obtained by $\text{CV}(\text{CE}(L))$. As we see, regardless of the orientation, the split-face lath data structure is not conducive to finding the lath corresponding to the next face in the counterclockwise direction (CCF) or the next vertex in the clockwise direction (CV) efficiently.

5. As can be seen from Figure 2.102, this alternative would result in no changes as all it means is that the right lath of the pair of split-vertex laths would be associated with the left vertex while the left lath of the pair of split-vertex laths would be associated with the right vertex. However, all transitions are the same.

6. The main effect is that the order of applying the various transitions is reversed. $\text{CE}(L)$ is obtained by $\text{CF}(\text{CV}(L))$. $\text{CCF}(L)$ is obtained by $\text{CV}(\text{CE}(L))$. $\text{CCV}(L)$ is obtained by $\text{CF}(\text{CF}(L))$

Solutions to Exercises in Section 2.2.1.3.2

2. For a counterclockwise order, first find a lath L for which $\text{CE}(L) = \text{NIL}$, report L, and set L' to $\text{CF}(L)$. Now, as long as $\text{CE}(L') \neq \text{NIL}$, set L' to $\text{CCV}(L')$; otherwise, report L' and set L' to $\text{CF}(L')$. Repeat this process until you encounter lath L again in an attempt to report it, at which time the traversal of the boundary face is complete. For a clockwise order, again, first find a lath L for which $\text{CE}(L) = \text{NIL}$, report L, and set L' to L. Now, as long as $\text{CE}(\text{CCF}(L')) \neq \text{NIL}$, set L' to $\text{CV}(L')$; otherwise, set L' to $\text{CCF}(L')$ and report L'. Repeat this process until you encounter lath L again in an attempt to report it, at which time the traversal of the boundary face is complete. Observe that the clockwise process is quite similar to the counterclockwise process in the sense that it can be obtained by simply replacing all clockwise transitions around a face (i.e., CF) by counterclockwise transitions (i.e., CCF) and all counterclockwise transitions around a vertex (i.e., CCV) by clockwise transitions (i.e., CV).

3. Replace all comparisons of $\text{CE}(L)$ with NIL in the solution to Exercise 2 by comparisons of $\text{CV}(\text{CE}(L))$ with NIL.

4. For a counterclockwise order, first find a lath L for which $\text{CV}(L) = \text{NIL}$, report L, and set L' to $\text{CCV}(L)$. Now, as long as $\text{CV}(\text{CE}(L')) \neq \text{NIL}$, set L' to $\text{CCV}(L')$; otherwise, report $\text{CE}(L')$ and set L' to $\text{CF}(L')$. Repeat this process until you encounter lath L again in an attempt to report it, at which time the traversal of the boundary face is complete. For a clockwise order, again, first find a lath L for which $\text{CV}(L) = \text{NIL}$, report L, and set L' to $\text{CE}(L)$. Now, as long as $\text{CV}(\text{CV}(L')) \neq \text{NIL}$, set L' to $\text{CV}(L')$; otherwise, report $\text{CV}(L')$ and set L' to $\text{CCF}(L')$. Repeat this process until you encounter lath L again in an attempt to report it, at which time the traversal of the boundary face is complete.

5. In the split-vertex lath data structure, each edge has two laths associated with it, regardless of whether it is a boundary edge. In the case of a boundary edge e whose associated lath is L and whose companion lath $L' = \text{CE}(L)$, we have $\text{CV}(L') = \text{NIL}$ and its associated face f' is actually the boundary face. It is meaningless to traverse the edges of f'. Therefore, in the case of a boundary edge e, the operation $\text{CCF}(L)$ is always applied to the lath L for which the associated face f is not the boundary face, and thus $\text{CV}(L)$ is not NIL, which means that $\text{CCF}(L) = \text{CE}(\text{CV}(L))$ can be used safely.

6. For a counterclockwise order, first find a lath L for which $\text{CE}(L) = \text{NIL}$, set L'' to $\text{CF}(L)$, and report $\text{CV}(L'')$. Now, as long as $\text{CE}(L'') \neq \text{NIL}$, set L'' to $\text{CCV}(L'')$; otherwise, set L'' to $\text{CF}(L'')$, and report $\text{CV}(L'')$. Repeat this process until you encounter lath L again in an attempt to obtain its companion, at which time the traversal of the boundary face is complete. For a clockwise order, again, first find a lath L for which $\text{CE}(L) = \text{NIL}$, and set L'' to L. Now, as long as $\text{CE}(\text{CCF}(L'')) \neq \text{NIL}$, set L'' to $\text{CV}(L'')$; otherwise, report $\text{CV}(L'')$, and set L'' to $\text{CCF}(L'')$. Repeat this process until you encounter lath L again after having reported its companion, at which time the traversal of the boundary face is complete.

7. Letting B denote the set of vertices that make up the boundary and $NEV(v)$ denote the number of edges incident at vertex $v \in B$, the cost is proportional to $\sum_{\{v \in B\}}(NEV(v) - 1)$.

8. Letting B denote the set of vertices that make up the boundary, $FV(v)$ denote the set of faces incident at vertex $v \in B$ excluding the boundary face, and $NEF(f)$ denote the number of edges that make up face f, the cost is proportional to $\sum_{\{v \in V\}}\sum_{\{f \in FV(v)\}}NEF(f)$.

9. Same as the solution to Exercise 7.

10. Same as the solution to Exercise 8.

11. Same as the solution to Exercise 8.

12. Same as the solution to Exercise 7.

13. Same as the solution to Exercise 8.

14. Same as the solution to Exercise 7.

15. Yes, there is a loss. In essence, it is now impossible to implement the CCF transition and thus to obtain the laths corresponding to the edges or vertices that make up a face that has at least two adjacent boundary edges (i.e., they have a vertex in common). No such problems arise when only $\text{CV}(L')$ is set to NIL because, in this case, we will be missing edges that lie in the boundary face. However, by virtue of the way we have defined the mesh, no such edges exist anyway.

16. When $\text{CV}(L') = \text{NIL}$, there are no possible transitions from L' except to L, and thus the absence of a transition from L to L' does not result in any loss of querying power.

17. The main difference caused by the change in orientation is that whereas with the previous definition, it was possible for some laths corresponding to some boundary edges to be incapable of being returned as a valid value for a CV transition, now the same possibility exists for a CCV transition. This can be overcome in part by returning a lath corresponding to the desired boundary edge but whose associated vertex is not the same as the one associated with L. In addition, once again, both the CV and CCF transitions must be implemented in terms of the definitions that make use of the successive traversals of the laths representing the face f in which the laths $\text{CE}(L)$ and L, respectively, are members.

18. The main difference caused by the change in orientation is that whereas with the previous definition, it was possible for some laths corresponding to some boundary edges to be

incapable of being returned as a valid value of a Cv transition, now the same possibility exists for a CCv transition. This can be overcome in part by returning a lath corresponding to the desired boundary edge but whose associated vertex is not the same as the one associated with L. In addition, once again, the CCF transition must be implemented in terms of the definition that makes use of the traversal of the laths representing the face f in which lath L is a member. Moreover, as $CE(L)$ is defined in terms of Cv (i.e., $CF(Cv(L))$), we must modify the definition of CF to not apply CF if $Cv(L)$ is NIL and simply to return NIL as the result in this case.

Solutions to Exercises in Section 2.2.1.3.3

1. For each face-vertex lath L, the counterclockwise variant of the corner lath data structure records the transitions to both the next lath $CCF(L)$ along the face F associated with L, to the next lath $CCV(L)$ incident at the vertex V associated with L and both in the same direction (i.e., counterclockwise in this example). The key to the close relationship is the observation that the transition to the next lath $CCF(L)$ along F is equivalent to the transition to the companion half-edge of the next half-edge $CE(Cv(L))$ incident at V. Recalling that, given half-edge L, the half-edge-vertex data structure is defined in terms of $CE(L)$, $Cv(L)$, and $CCv(L)$ leads to the desired result as we have formulated $CCF(L)$ in terms of two of the existing half-edge primitives (i.e., $CE(L)$ and $Cv(L)$). Alternatively, we can show that the transition to the companion half-edge $CE(L)$ of half-edge L is equivalent to the transition to the next lath $CCF(CCv(L))$ along the face associated with the next lath $CCv(L)$ incident at V. Similarly, we know that we can obtain the transition to the half-edge $Cv(L)$ by simply following $CE(CCF(L)) = CCF(CCv(CCF(L)))$. Recalling that, given lath L, the counterclockwise variant of the corner lath data structure is defined in terms of $CCF(L)$ and $CCv(L)$ leads to the desired result as we have formulated both $CE(L)$ and $Cv(L)$ in terms of the two existing primitives of the counterclockwise variant of the corner lath data structure (i.e., $CCF(L)$ and $CCv(L)$).

Solutions to Exercises in Section 2.2.1.4

1. Construct the perpendicular bisectors of the edges of the Delaunay triangulation. The bisectors meet in triplets at the circumcenters of the triangles, which are also the vertices of the Voronoi diagram.

2. Computing the convex hull takes $O(v \log v)$ time (e.g., [743, 1511]). The Delaunay triangulation has $O(v)$ edges. Step (b) takes $O(v)$ time, which can be reduced to $O(1)$ time if we use a grid [1260]. Steps (c) and (d) require $O(v)$ time, but they could be implemented in $O(\log v)$ time by assigning each edge a unique encoding and storing the edges in a balanced binary tree. Since steps (a) through (d) are iterated $O(v)$ times, the total cost is $O(v^2)$, and the result follows.

3. Step (a) takes $O(v)$ time as there are $O(v)$ triangles in a triangulation regardless of whether it is a Delaunay triangulation (see Exercise 2 in Section 2.1.3.2). Steps (b) and (c) take $O(v)$ time as there are at most $O(v)$ triangles found in step (a). Steps (a) through (c) are applied v times as there are v vertices, and the result follows. When the points are chosen in arbitrary order, the expected execution time is $O(v \log v)$ [765] due to the use of an amortized algorithm that enables the location of the points in an expected $O(\log v)$ time.

4. The proof consists of two parts, where the second part is more general than the first part:

   (a) When $\alpha < \pi/2$, showing that edge uv is in the Delaunay triangulation is straightforward. In particular, consider the minimum disc containing u and v, which is of diameter $d(u, v)$. Observe that for a point s, $\angle usv$ determines the location of s with respect to the disc. That is, $\angle usv < \pi/2$ if and only if s is outside the disc; $\angle usv > \pi/2$ if and only if s is inside the disc; and finally $\angle usv = \pi/2$ if and only if s is on the disc. It is now easy to see that when $\alpha < \pi/2$, the minimum disc containing u and v is empty. On the other hand, if the minimum disc contained vertex t, then $\angle utv \geq \pi/2$, and hence as $\alpha \geq \angle utv$, we would have $\alpha \geq \pi/2$, which is contrary to our initial assumption. Thus, from the disc property of the definition of the Delaunay triangulation, this means that edge uv is in the Delaunay triangulation.

(b) The general case, independent of the value of α, is a bit more complex. There are two cases due to the use of if and only if:

    i.   The assumption $\forall w \in O_p, \angle uwp \leq \pi - \alpha$ implies that edge uv is in the Delaunay triangulation.

Proof Let C denote the circle passing through u, v, and p. Let q denote a point on C that is not on the same side of uv as p. Chord uv divides C into two parts, C_p and C_q, such that $p \in C_p$ and $q \in C_q$. We know that $\angle upv + \angle uqv = \pi$ since the sum of these two inscribed angles is one-half of the sum of the arcs that they subtend, which is 2π. However, $\angle upv = \alpha$, and thus subtracting α from both sides of the equality yields $\angle uqv = \pi - \alpha$. Observe that if there is a point t inside C_p, then $\angle utv > \angle upv = \alpha$, and as we know that α is the largest such angle, we can conclude that there is no point inside C_p. We can also see that if there is a point t inside C_q, then $\angle utv > \pi - \alpha$. Now, since $\forall w \in O_p, \angle uwp \leq \pi - \alpha$, we can conclude that no point in O_p is inside C_q.

Note that by definition of S_p and C_q, no point of S_p could be inside C_q. Hence, we can see that no point of S is inside C. Therefore, by using the disc property, we have that edge uv is in the Delaunay triangulation. ∎

    ii. The assumption that edge uv is in the Delaunay triangulation implies that $\forall w \in O_p, \angle uwp \leq \pi - \alpha$.

Proof Consider point $w \in O_p$. We show that $\angle uwp <= \pi - \alpha$. As edge uv is in the Delaunay triangulation, from the disc property we know that there exists an empty disc D with center O passing through uv. Let C denote the boundary of D. As D is empty, neither p nor w is inside D. Consider points r and t, such that r is the intersection of C with line segment Op, and t is the intersection of C with line segment Ow. As r and t are points on C on opposite sides of chord uv, we have $\angle urv + \angle utv = \pi$ since the sum of these two inscribed angles is one-half of the sum of the arcs that make them up, which is 2π. As p is not inside C, we have $\angle upv \leq \angle urv$. Similarly, as w is not inside C, we have $\angle uwv \leq \angle utv$. Hence, $\angle upv + \angle uwv \leq \angle urv + \angle utv = \pi$, and thus $\angle upv + \angle uwv \leq \pi$. Noting that $\angle upv = \alpha$ and subtracting α from both sides yields the desired result that $\angle uwv \leq \pi - \alpha$. ∎

5. The fact that each vertex of the Voronoi diagram has degree 3 leads to the following elegant solution developed independently by Michael B. Dillencourt and Franco P. Preparata.

(a) Pick some face f of the Voronoi diagram, and let s_f be its site. Pick some vertex v_1 of f, and compute a line L_1 through v_1 such that s_f lies on L_1 (we discuss how to do this below).

(b) Pick some other vertex v_2 (not necessarily adjacent to v_1) of f, and, as in step (a), compute a line L_2 through v_2 such that s_f lies on L_2.

(c) s_f is the unique point of intersection of L_1 and L_2. Once we have determined s_f, we can find all the other sites by repeatedly reflecting s_f about the edges of the Voronoi diagram as each edge of the Voronoi diagram is the perpendicular bisector of the line joining the sites of its two adjacent Voronoi faces. Therefore, knowing s_f of face f, the reflection process about an edge e of f into the other face g adjacent to e determines the location s_g of the site of g.

Given a face f of a Voronoi diagram and a vertex v of f, the key to this algorithm is to find a line L_1 through v (actually a ray originating at v and passing through f) such that L is guaranteed to contain the generating site s_f of f. This is achieved as follows. Based on our initial assumption, each vertex of the Voronoi diagram has degree 3. Let v be a vertex of face f, and let va, vb, and vc be the edges, without loss of generality, in clockwise order that are incident at v with vertices a, b, and c, respectively. Assume that f is the face between va and

vb, g is the face between vb and vc, and h is the face between vc and va. Let s_f, s_g, and s_h be the generating sites of faces f, g, and h, respectively. Now, let us name the angles formed by v and its neighboring vertices and sites—that is, $r = \angle avb$, $s = \angle bvc$, $t = \angle cva$, $x = \angle avs_f$, $y = \angle bvs_g$, and $z = \angle cvs_h$. Note that we also have that $x = \angle s_h va$, $y = \angle s_f vb$, and $z = \angle s_g vc$ as the triangle pairs $s_h va$ and $s_f va$, $s_f vb$ and $s_g vb$, and $s_g vc$ and $s_h vc$ are congruent. From these relations, we have that $r = x + y$, $s = y + z$, and $t = x + z$. Subtracting $s = y + z$ from corresponding sides of $r = x + y$ yields $r - s = x - z$. Adding $r - s = x - z$ to corresponding sides of $t = x + z$ yields $r - s + t = 2x$, and solving for x yields $x = (r - s + t)/2$. At this point, we are done as we now know that the generating site s_f for face f is on the ray originating at v that makes an angle of $x = (r - s + t)/2$ with the ray va. This is L_1 from step (a) of the above algorithm. We now execute step (b) in the same manner to obtain L_2, and intersect the two rays to obtain s_f. Given a Voronoi diagram with N vertices, the running time of the algorithm after repeated application of step (c) is $O(N)$, assuming that the Voronoi diagram is represented using some reasonable planar graph structure. For example, use one of the variants of the winged-edge data structure discussed in Sections 2.2.1.2 and 2.2.1.3, or even a data structure that imposes a spatial index on the edges, such as one of the variants of the PM quadtree discussed in Sections 2.2.2.6 and 2.2.2.8. For more details on the use of the spatial index data structures in this context, see the discussion of the use of the PM$_2$ quadtree for the representation of a Voronoi diagram in Sections 2.2.2.6 of this chapter and 4.4.5 in Chapter 4. In particular, having chosen an appropriate data structure, determining the site for the first face takes $O(1)$ time. After that, traverse the faces of the Voronoi diagram in some depth-first order (which takes $O(N)$ time), and every time a new face is visited, its site is computed by reflecting the site of its parent across the edge that was just crossed to get from the parent face to the current face.

To elaborate further on the depth-first search process mentioned in the preceding paragraph, we note that, at times, we may be more interested in marking all of the edges of the faces of the polygonal map that is a Voronoi diagram with their associated sites instead of in just identifying all of the sites of the Voronoi diagram. In this case, once we have determined one site, say s_f of f, we trace all of the remaining edges in f and mark the relevant sides of the edges having s_f as its region's site. This is equivalent to a depth-first graph traversal where each edge is bidirectional. When the tracing process visits a side of an edge that has been visited already, we attempt to visit its other side and, if necessary, determine the site associated with its face. If both sides of an edge have been visited, then we backtrack. Thus, since a depth-first graph traversal can be performed in $O(N)$ time, we can also identify the sites associated with all of the edges of the Voronoi diagram in $O(N)$ time.

6. David M. Mount suggests turning to [807, 1616] for an alternative solution that addresses the more general variant of this problem by reducing it to a two-dimensional linear programming problem that can be solved in linear time, as well as the more general problem that, for a given integer k and an arbitrary polygonal map T, finds the set of k points, if one exists, whose Voronoi diagram contains every edge in T. Intuitively, this problem can be posed as a linear system as follows. Our solution assumes the two-dimensional plane but actually works in any dimension. Suppose that two Voronoi sites s_1 and s_2 are separated by an edge e of the Voronoi diagram. We do not know the coordinates of s_1 and s_2, but if we know the location (i.e., coordinate values) of s_1, then knowing that e is the perpendicular bisector of the edge formed by s_1 and s_2 enables us to fix the location of s_2. Thus, even though s_1 and s_2 have four degrees of freedom (two for each of the x coordinate values and two for each of the y coordinate values), the knowledge of the perpendicular bisector of the edge between them reduces this to two independent degrees of freedom. Therefore, as long as the number of Voronoi edges m exceeds the number of Voronoi sites n, the system will be fully constrained, and so, any linear solver (involving $2n$ variables and $2m$ equations) will provide the answer. Once the system has been solved and N sites have been obtained, it is possible in $O(N)$ time to verify that the topology of the planar subdivision is the same as the Voronoi diagram. This can be done by a simple traversal of the diagram. This verification step is necessary because the linear system of equations is typically overconstrained, and thus some of the constraints may have been omitted when solving the system. In particular, the problem with the linear programming solution is that it simply verifies that for each edge e in the Voronoi diagram there exists a pair of points whose bisector is collinear with e. However, the solution process does not verify the locations of the Voronoi vertices or that the edges are connected in the proper orientation to the Voronoi vertices. Note also that the solution may not be unique, as

is the case, for example, when we have the Voronoi diagram of just three sites. In particular, assume, without loss of generality, that all three sites lie on a unit circle centered at the origin. In this case, their Voronoi diagram consists of one Voronoi vertex at the origin and three semi-infinite edges. Now, observe that if we scale the coordinate values of the sites by any positive constant, they still lie on a scaled circle centered at the origin and their bisectors do not change, and we obtain exactly the same Voronoi diagram. The same result holds for a degenerate configuration where more than three sites lie on a circle (e.g., four sites that lie at the vertices of an origin-centered axis-aligned rectangle). Thus, again, we have a case where the Voronoi diagram does not determine its sites.

Solutions to Exercises in Section 2.2.1.6

1. In d dimensions, the topological analog of the Delaunay triangulation arises whenever no $d + 2$ vertices or points lie on the surface of a d-dimensional sphere.

2. $d - 1$, corresponding to the sharing of an edge, face, ..., and $(d - 1)$-dimensional face.

Solutions to Exercises in Section 2.2.1.7

1. Restriction (1) is violated by an hourglass object that consists of two pyramids. Restriction (2) is violated by a pyramid whose vertex or edge is adjacent to a flat surface.

2. No. For example, consider the hourglass object that consists of two pyramids. This object can be formed by the union of two pyramids, each of which is a two-manifold object, yet the result is not a two-manifold object.

3. The triangle table contains six items of information for each triangle (i.e., three pointers to the three constituent vertices and three pointers to the three adjacent triangles) for a total of $6T$. The storage requirements of the connectivity table are obtained as follows. Each triangle consists of three vertices, which means that each triangle participates in the connectivity list of three vertices. The planar subdivision formed by the triangulation also contains an exterior face that has H vertices ($H \leq V$). Thus, there is a total of $3T + H \leq 3T + V$ entries in the connectivity table, and the result follows, assuming that H is usually much smaller than V and T. Actually, the connectivity table also contains one end of a list marker for the list of each vertex, and thus the true storage requirement of the connectivity table is bounded by $3T + 2V$.

4. (David M. Mount) Assume a connected graph corresponding to a triangulation with V vertices, E edges, and T triangles. Let H denote the number of vertices on the exterior face. The number of faces F in the graph is $T + 1$ (counting the exterior face). All faces have degree 3 except the exterior face, which has degree H. Thus, the sum of face degrees is $3T + H$, which is equal to $2E$. Since H is not larger than V, we have $2E \leq 3T + V$. Combining this with Euler's formula we have

$$
\begin{aligned}
2 &= V - E + F \\
4 &= 2V - 2E + 2F \\
&\geq 2V - (3T + V) + 2 \cdot (T + 1) \\
&= 2V - 3T - V + 2T + 2 \\
&= V - T + 2
\end{aligned}
$$

Rearranging this inequality, we have that $V \leq T + 2$. From Exercise 3, we have that the connectivity table method requires $3T + 2V$ storage units. Replacing V with its upper bound $T + 2$ leads to the desired bound of $5T + 4$. Thus, we see that so long as $T \geq 4$, the connectivity table method using $3T + 2V$ storage units will be better from a space-efficiency standpoint than the triangle table method.

5. From Exercise 3, we have that the connectivity table of the connectivity table method requires $3T$ storage units, and since the connectivity table of the star vertex data structure contains twice as much information (i.e., one additional pointer per entry), we have that the star vertex data structure requires $6T + V$ storage units.

Solutions to Exercises in Section 2.2.2.1

1. The line quadtree is nothing but a region quadtree with additional information stored at the nonleaf nodes.

2. The SE quadrant of the line quadtree requires one node, whereas in the revised line quadtree, this quadrant requires four leaf nodes since the northern boundaries of the NW and NE subquadrants differ.

Solutions to Exercises in Section 2.2.2.2

1. Use $B(i) = 2 \cdot \lceil p/2^i \rceil$ instead of $B(i) = 6 \cdot \lceil p/2^i \rceil$ in the proof of Theorem 2.1.

2. Let the four squares defining each curve be called A, B, C, and D. If the curve is less than d in length, no two of A, B, C, and D can be d or more apart at their closest points and still permit the curve to enter a fifth different square. The rest of the proof is analogous to that of Theorem 2.1. In particular, use $B(i) = 2 \cdot \lceil p/2^i \rceil$ instead of $B(i) = 6 \cdot \lceil p/2^i \rceil$ in the proof of Theorem 2.1.

3. The MX quadtree contains 1 node at level q (i.e., the root node), 4 nodes at level $q - 1$, and 16 nodes at each of levels $q - 2$ through 0. Summing up yields the desired result.

4. The MX quadtree contains 1 node at level q (i.e., the root node), 4 nodes at level $q - 1$, and $4 \cdot 2^{q-i}$ nodes at level i, where i ranges between 0 and $q - 2$. Summing up yields $5 + 8 \cdot (2^q - 2)$, equal to $8 \cdot p - 11$.

6. When $p \le 4 \cdot q$, use the polygon of Figure 2.119 for the given value of q by extending the perimeter arbitrarily to achieve the desired value of p so that the extended polygon intersects all of the pixels that it intersected prior to the extension. This polygon requires at least $16 \cdot q - 11$ nodes, which is more than $p + q$ but is still less than $5 \cdot q$. When $p > 4 \cdot q$, construct a polygon in the form of a concatenated sequence of "U" patterns of minimal width. The components of the "U" are reduced in size or perturbed as necessary to yield a polygon of perimeter p. Since each pixel is a leaf, summing up the nodes at all levels yields at least $(4/3) \cdot p$ nodes or $(2/3) \cdot (p + q)$ as $p > q$.

8. See [1273] for a proof that the size of the MX octree is bounded by four times the surface area.

10. See [1948].

11. See [1948].

12. See [111] for some examples.

Solutions to Exercises in Section 2.2.2.5

3. When the boundaries of the object are straight lines (polygonal faces), then the resulting decompositions may be the same when using a zero error tolerance on the edge quadtree (face octree). Otherwise, the situation depends heavily on the shape of the object that is being represented.

Solutions to Exercises in Section 2.2.2.6

1. 1 **recursive procedure** PMINSERT(P, R)
    2 /* Insert the list of edges pointed at by P in the PM$_1$ quadtree rooted at R. The same procedure is used to insert in PM$_2$ and PM$_3$ quadtrees by replacing the calls to PM1CHECK by calls to PM2CHECK and PM3CHECK, respectively. */

```
3    value pointer edgelist P
4    value pointer node R
5    pointer edgelist L
6    quadrant I
7    L ← CLIPLINES(P, SQUARE(R))
8    if ISEMPTY(L) then return /* No new edges belong in the quadrant */
9    endif
10   if ISLEAF(R) then /* A leaf node */
11       L ← MERGELISTS(L, DICTIONARY(R))
12       /* MERGELISTS supports duplicate instances of an edge; otherwise, a conven-
             tional set union operation can be used */
13       if PM1CHECK(L, SQUARE(R)) then
14           DICTIONARY(R) ← L
15           return
16       else SPLITPMNODE(R)
17       endif
18   endif
19   for I in {'NW','NE','SW','SE'} do PMINSERT(L, CHILD(R, I))

1    recursive edgelist procedure CLIPLINES(L, R)
2    /* Collect all of the edges in the list of edges pointed at by L that have at least
         one point in common with the square pointed at by R (i.e., it intersects some
         of its boundaries or lies completely inside it). ADDTOLIST(X, S) adds element
         X to the list S and returns a pointer to the resulting list. */
3    value pointer edgelist L
4    value pointer square R
5    return(if ISEMPTY(L) then NIL
6            elseif INTERSECTLINESQUARE(DATA(L), R) then
7                ADDTOLIST(DATA(L), CLIPLINES(NEXT(L), R))
8            else CLIPLINES(NEXT(L), R)
9            endif)

1    Boolean procedure PM1CHECK(L, S)
2    /* Determine if the square pointed at by S and the list of edges pointed at by L
         form a legal PM₁ quadtree node. ONEELEMENT(L) is a predicate that indicates
         if L contains just one element. Assume that an isolated vertex (i.e., an edge
         with zero length) does not serve as an endpoint of another edge. */
3    value pointer edgelist L
4    value pointer square S
5    return(if ISEMPTY(L) then TRUE
6            elseif P1(DATA(L)) = P2(DATA(L)) then
7                ONEELEMENT(L) /* Isolated vertex */
8            elseif ONEELEMENT(L) then
9                /* Both vertices can lie outside the square */
10               not(PTINSQUARE(P1(DATA(L)), S) and
11                   PTINSQUARE(P2(DATA(L)), S))
12           elseif PTINSQUARE(P1(DATA(L)), S) and
13               PTINSQUARE(P2(DATA(L)), S)
14               /* Ensure that when a vertex is shared, other vertex is not in same
                     square */
15               then FALSE
16           elseif PTINSQUARE(P1(DATA(L)), S) then
17               SHAREPM12VERTEX(P1(DATA(L)), NEXT(L), S)
18           elseif PTINSQUARE(P2(DATA(L)), S) then
19               SHAREPM12VERTEX(P2(DATA(L)), NEXT(L), S)
20           else FALSE
21           endif)

1    recursive Boolean procedure SHAREPM12VERTEX(P, L, S)
2    /* The vertex pointed at by P is in the square pointed at by S. Determine if all
         the edges in the list of edges pointed at by L share P and do not have their
         other vertex within S. */
3    value pointer point P
```

```
 4   value pointer edgelist L
 5   value pointer square S
 6   return(if IsEMPTY(L) then TRUE
 7       elseif P = P1(DATA(L)) then
 8           not(PtInSquare(P2(DATA(L)),S)) and
 9           SharePM12Vertex(P,NEXT(L),S)
10       elseif P = P2(DATA(L)) then
11           not(PtInSquare(P1(DATA(L)),S)) and
12           SharePM12Vertex(P,NEXT(L),S)
13       else FALSE
14       endif)
```

```
 1   procedure SplitPMNode(P)
 2   /* Add four children to the node pointed at by P and change P to be of type
       GRAY. */
 3   value pointer node P
 4   quadrant I,J
 5   pointer node Q
 6   pointer square R
 7   /* Sₓ and S_y contain multiplicative factors to aid in the location of the centers of
       the quadrant children while descending the tree */
 8   preload real array Sₓ['NW','NE','SW','SE']
 9       with −0.25,0.25,−0.25,0.25
10   preload real array S_y['NW','NE','SW','SE']
11       with 0.25,0.25,−0.25,−0.25
12   for I in {'NW','NE','SW','SE'} do
13       Q ← Create(node)
14       Child(P,I) ← Q
15       for J in {'NW','NE','SW','SE'} do
16           Child(Q,J) ← NIL
17       enddo
18       NodeType(Q) ← 'Leaf'
19       R ← Create(square)
20       Center(R) ← Create(point)
21       XCoord(Center(R)) ← XCoord(Center(Square(P)))+
22                             Sₓ[I]∗Len(Square(P))
23       YCoord(Center(R)) ← YCoord(Center(Square(P)))+
24                             S_y[I]∗Len(Square(P))
25       Len(R) ← 0.5∗Len(Square(P))
26       Square(Q) ← S
27       Dictionary(Q) ← NIL ;
28   enddo
29   Dictionary(P) ← NIL
30   NodeType(P) ← 'Gray'
```

```
2.  1   recursive procedure PMDelete(P,R)
    2   /* Delete the list of edges pointed at by P from the PM₁ quadtree rooted at R.
          The same procedure is used to delete from PM₂ and PM₃ quadtrees by re-
          placing the calls to PossiblePM1Merge and TryToMergePM1 by calls to
          PossiblePM23Merge and TryToMergePM23. */
    3   value pointer edgelist P
    4   value pointer node R
    5   pointer edgelist L
    6   quadrant I
    7   L ← ClipLines(P,Square(R))
    8   if IsEMPTY(L) then return ; /* None of the edges is in the quadrant */
    9   endif
   10   if Gray(R) then
   11       for I in {'NW','NE','SW','SE'} do
   12           PMDelete(L,Child(R,I))
   13       enddo
   14       if PossiblePM1Merge(R) then
   15           L ← NIL
```

```
16        if TRYTOMERGEPM1(R, R, L) then
17            /* Merge the children of the gray node */
18            RETURNTREETOAVAIL(R)
19            DICTIONARY(R) ← L
20            NODETYPE(R) ← 'LEAF'
21        endif
22    endif
23    else DICTIONARY(R) ← REMOVEARG2FROMARG1(DICTIONARY(R), L)
24    /* REMOVEARG2FROMARG1 supports duplicate instances of an edge; other-
         wise, a conventional set difference operation can be used */
```

```
1   Boolean procedure POSSIBLEPM1MERGE(P)
2   /* Determine if the subtrees of the four children of the PM₁ quadtree node pointed
       at by P should be further examined to see if a merger is possible. Such a
       merger is feasible only if at least one of the four children of P is a LEAF. */
3   value pointer node P
4   return(ISLEAF(CHILD(P, 'NW')) or ISLEAF(CHILD(P, 'NE')) or
5          ISLEAF(CHILD(P, 'SW')) or ISLEAF(CHILD(P, 'SE')))
```

```
1   recursive Boolean procedure TRYTOMERGEPM1(P, R, L)
2   /* Determine if the four children of the PM₁ quadtree rooted at node P can be
       merged. Notice that the check for the satisfaction of the PM₁ decomposition
       conditions is with respect to the square associated with the original GRAY
       node, rooted at R, whose subtrees are being explored. Variable L is used to
       collect all of the edges that are present in the subtrees. */
3   value pointer node P, R
4   reference pointer edgelist L
5   if ISLEAF(P) then
6       L ← SETUNIONSAMEMULTIPLICITY(L, DICTIONARY(P))
7       /* SETUNIONSAMEMULTIPLICITY supports duplicate instances of an edge by
          making sure that edges that occur more than once in the sets maintain their
          multiplicity. If no duplicate instances are allowed, then can use a conven-
          tional set union operation. */
8       return TRUE
9   else return(TRYTOMERGEPM1(CHILD(P, 'NW'), R, L) and
10          TRYTOMERGEPM1(CHILD(P, 'NE'), R, L) and
11          TRYTOMERGEPM1(CHILD(P, 'SW'), R, L) and
12          TRYTOMERGEPM1(CHILD(P, 'SE'), R, L) and
13          PM1CHECK(L, SQUARE(R)))
14  endif
```

```
1   recursive procedure RETURNTREETOAVAIL(P)
2   /* Return the PM quadtree rooted at P to the free storage list. This process is
       recursive in the case of a PM₁ quadtree. */
3   value pointer node P
4   quadrant I
5   if ISLEAF(P) then return
6   else
7       for I in {'NW','NE','SW','SE'} do
8           RETURNTREETOAVAIL(CHILD(P, I))
9           RETURNTOAVAIL(CHILD(P, I))
10          CHILD(P, I) ← NIL
11      enddo
12  endif
```

3. Replace calls to procedure PM1CHECK in Exercise 1 by procedure PM2CHECK.

```
1   Boolean procedure PM2CHECK(L, S)
2   /* Determine if the square pointed at by S and the list of edges pointed at by
       L form a legal PM₂ quadtree node. SHAREPM12VERTEX is invoked with L
       instead of NEXT(L) because the edge might have one vertex in the square
       and share the other vertex with the list, which violates the PM₂ quadtree
       definition conditions. Assume that an isolated vertex (i.e., an edge with zero
       length) does not serve as an endpoint of another edge. */
```

3   **value pointer edgelist** L
4   **value pointer square** S
5   **return**(**if** IsEmpty(L) **then** True
6   **elseif** P1(Data(L)) = P2(Data(L)) **then**
7   OneElement(L) /* Isolated vertex */
8   **elseif** PtInSquare(P1(Data(L)), S) **and**
9   PtInSquare(P2(Data(L)), S)
10   /* Ensure that when a vertex is shared, the other vertex is not in
                same square */
11   **then** False
12   **elseif** SharePM12Vertex(P1(Data(L)), L, S) **or**
13   SharePM12Vertex(P2(Data(L)), L, S) **then** True
14   **else** False
15   **endif**)

4. Replace calls to procedures PossiblePM1Merge and TryToMergePM1 in PMDelete
   with calls to procedures PossiblePM23Merge and TryToMergePM23, respectively,
   to determine if an attempt should be made to merge the four children of a gray node after
   processing them—that is, the conditions of a PM_2 quadtree definition are satisfied. A merge
   is feasible only if all four children of a gray node are leaf nodes. This situation is checked
   by PossiblePM23Merge. If the merge is feasible, then TryToMergePM23 is applied
   to determine if the conditions of the definition of the PM_2 quadtree are satisfied by using
   PM2Check.

   1   **Boolean procedure** PossiblePM23Merge(P)
   2   /* Determine if an attempt should be made to merge the four children of the PM_2
          or PM_3 quadtree. Such a merger is feasible only if all four children of a gray
          node are leaf nodes. */
   3   **value pointer node** P
   4   **return**(IsLeaf(Child(P, 'NW')) **and** IsLeaf(Child(P, 'NE')) **and**
   5   IsLeaf(Child(P, 'SW')) **and** IsLeaf(Child(P, 'SE')))

   1   **Boolean procedure** TryToMergePM23(P, R, L)
   2   /* Determine if the four children of the PM_2 or PM_3 quadtree rooted at node P
          can be merged. Variable L is used to collect all of the edges that are present in
          the subtrees. Note that there is no need for parameter R, and the procedure is
          not recursive. The call to PM2Check is replaced by PM3Check when delet-
          ing from a PM_3 quadtree. */
   3   **value pointer node** P, R
   4   **reference pointer edgelist** L
   5   **quadrant** I
   6   **for** I **in** {'NW', 'NE', 'SW', 'SE'} **do**
   7       $L \leftarrow$ SetUnionSameMultiplicity(L, Dictionary(Child(P, I)))
   8   /* SetUnionSameMultiplicity supports duplicate instances of an edge by
              making sure that edges that occur more than once in the sets maintain their
              multiplicity. If no duplicate instances are allowed, then use a conventional
              set union operation. */
   9   **enddo**
   10 **return** PM2Check(L, Square(P))

5. Replace calls to procedures PM1Check and SharePM12Vertex in Exercise 1 with calls
   to procedures PM3Check and SharePM3Vertex, respectively. The PM_3 quadtree is
   somewhat different from the PM_1 and PM_2 quadtrees in that an isolated vertex is allowed
   to coexist in a leaf node along with the q-edges that do not intersect it. This is achieved by
   using Inf to represent a fictitious point at (∞, ∞) and to invoke SharePM3Vertex with it
   as the shared vertex.

   1   **recursive Boolean procedure** PM3Check(L, S)
   2   /* Determine if the square pointed at by S and the list of edges pointed at by L
          form a legal PM_3 quadtree node. Assume that an isolated vertex (i.e., an edge
          with zero length) does not serve as an endpoint of another edge. */
   3   **value pointer edgelist** L
   4   **value pointer square** S

5   **return**(**if** IsEMPTY(L) **then** TRUE
6   **elseif** P1(DATA(L)) = P2(DATA(L)) **then** /* Isolated vertex */
7   SHAREPM3VERTEX(INF, NEXT(L), S)
8   /* INF ensures that the remaining edges have no vertices in S */
9   **elseif** PTINSQUARE(P1(DATA(L)), S) **and**
10   PTINSQUARE(P2(DATA(L)), S)
11   /* Ensure that when a vertex is shared, the other vertex is not in
              same square */
12   **then** FALSE
13   **elseif** PTINSQUARE(P1(DATA(L)), S) **then**
14   SHAREPM3VERTEX(P1(DATA(L)), NEXT(L), S)
15   **elseif** PTINSQUARE(P2(DATA(L)), S) **then**
16   SHAREPM3VERTEX(P2(DATA(L)), NEXT(L), S)
17   **else** PM3CHECK(NEXT(L), S)
18   **endif**)

1   **recursive Boolean procedure** SHAREPM3VERTEX(P, L, S)
2   /* The vertex pointed at by P is the shared vertex in a PM_3 quadtree. It is in-
      side the square pointed at by S. Determine if all the edges in the list of edges
      pointed at by L either share P and do not have their other vertex within S, or
      do not have either of their vertices in S. When P is INF, then the rest of the
      edges have no vertex in S. */
3   **value pointer point** P
4   **value pointer edgelist** L
5   **value pointer square** S
6   **return**(**if** IsEMPTY(L) **then** TRUE
7   **elseif** P = P1(DATA(L)) **then**
8   **not**(PTINSQUARE(P2(DATA(L)), S)) **and**
9   SHAREPM3VERTEX(P, NEXT(L), S)
10   **elseif** P = P2(DATA(L)) **then**
11   **not**(PTINSQUARE(P1(DATA(L)), S)) **and**
12   SHAREPM3VERTEX(P, NEXT(L), S)
13   **else not**(PTINSQUARE(P1(DATA(L)), S)) **and**
14   **not**(PTINSQUARE(P2(DATA(L)), S)) **and**
15   SHAREPM3VERTEX(P, NEXT(L), S)
16   **endif**)

6. Replace the call to procedure PM2CHECK in TRYTOMERGEPM23 with a call to PM3CHECK to check if the conditions of a PM_3 quadtree definition are satisfied.

7. Since a vertex node in a PM_3 quadtree can contain edges that do not intersect the vertex, more vertex nodes appear at shallower levels. The result follows as the total number of vertex nodes is the same for all three variants of the PM quadtree, and thus fewer vertex nodes will appear in the deeper levels.

9. First, determine the quadtree block b of side length w containing q. The radius of the search region cannot be larger than $2w\sqrt{2}$, which is the case when b is empty as one of the siblings of b must contain a q-edge as otherwise the siblings would have been merged to yield a larger node. The actual search examines the blocks adjacent to b subject to the maximum search radius. Of course, the search radius is much smaller if b is not empty. For another approach, see the incremental nearest neighbor algorithm of Hjaltason and Samet [846, 848], as well as Section 4.1.3 of Chapter 4.

10. See [1665] for a solution for the PM_3 quadtree.

12. The difficulty is that unlike the two-dimensional plane, we cannot assume that two nonparallel lines will intersect.

Solutions to Exercises in Section 2.2.2.7

1. As we saw in the discussion of the PM quadtree, there are a number of possible PM_1 octree variants, largely depending on whether a vertex- or edge-based approach is pursued. In three

dimensions, the most logical approach is to adapt the PM_1 quadtree. In such a case, the resulting decomposition insures that each octree leaf node corresponds to a single vertex, a single edge, or a single face. The only exceptions are that a leaf node may contain more than one edge if all the edges are incident at the same vertex. Similarly, a leaf node may contain more than one face if all the faces are incident at the same vertex or edge. The result is termed a *PM octree*. The above subdivision criteria can be stated more formally as follows:

(a) At most, one vertex can lie in a region represented by an octree leaf node.

(b) If an octree leaf node's region contains a vertex, then it can contain no edge or face that is not incident at that vertex.

(c) If an octree leaf node's region contains no vertices, then it can contain at most one edge.

(d) If an octree leaf node's region contains no vertices and contains one edge, then it can contain no face that is not incident at that edge.

(e) If an octree leaf node's region contains no edges, then it can contain at most one face.

(f) Each region's octree leaf node is maximal.

2. In the case of the *vertex′* node type, the node also contains the edges at which the faces meet, but this is not the so for the *vertex″* node type.

3. For a polyhedron, the face octree requires more space than the PM_1 octree when the error tolerance is zero. However, as the error tolerance is increased, the use of the planar approximation could result in the elimination of edges and vertices by merging the faces and edges that are incident at them, thereby not eliminating the need to decompose around them and thus not requiring as much space as the PM_1 octree.

4. $h_1 \wedge h_2 \wedge h_3, h_1 \vee h_2 \vee h_3, (h_1 \wedge h_2) \vee h_3$, and $(h_1 \vee h_2) \wedge h_3$. The first two yield a vertex of a convex object, and the third and fourth yield the vertex of a concave object.

5. 12.

7. See [1352].

8. See [1352].

11. This is not possible when the CSG primitives are approximated in the PM octree. However, it is possible when the CSG tree is specified using halfspaces.

14. See the solution for the PM_1 quadtree in Exercise 9 in Section 2.2.2.6.

Solutions to Exercises in Section 2.2.2.8

1. They are not the same. The problem is that when block b in a vertex bucket polygon quadtree is a part of more than T polygons while containing just one vertex v, the edges of the polygons in b are not required to intersect at v. In this case, in the vertex bucket polygon quadtree b is not decomposed further, but b is decomposed further in the bucket PM_1 quadtree for line segments if the T line segments do not intersect at v.

2. They are not the same. The problem is that the only time that a block b in the vertex bucket polygon quadtree is permitted to be a part of more than T polygons is when b contains v. However, this is not necessarily the case in the bucket PM_2 quadtree for line segments as b can contain $L > T$ nonintersecting line segments and hence be a part of $L + 1$ polygons as long as all of the L line segments intersect at some vertex v, which could be outside b. This violates the decomposition rule for the vertex bucket polygon quadtree.

3. They are not the same. The problem is that a block b in the vertex bucket polygon quadtree can contain more than one vertex, but this is not possible for the PM_3 quadtree. Moreover, in the vertex bucket polygon quadtree, b can contain no vertices, in which case b is split if b is a part of more than T polygons, but b is not split in the case of a PM_3 quadtree.

4. The result is not equivalent to any of the PM quadtree decomposition rules for line segments.

(a) PM$_1$ quadtree for line segments: The problem is that in the vertex bucket polygon quadtree, the decomposition halts whenever a block contains just one vertex, but there is no stipulation that all the edges contained in the block must meet at the vertex as is required in the PM$_1$ decomposition rule for line segments.

(b) PM$_2$ quadtree for line segments: The problem is the same as for the PM$_1$ quadtree. In addition, the case where the line segments passing through the block intersect in the same vertex outside the block permits a block that does not contain a vertex to be a part of more than two polygons in the PM$_2$ quadtree for line segments, but this is not allowed in the vertex bucket polygon quadtree.

(c) PM$_3$ quadtree for line segments: The problem is that whenever a block b does not contain any vertices, the PM$_3$ quadtree for line segments does not restrict the number of line segments that can pass through b, while the vertex bucket polygon quadtree implicitly restricts it to just one line segment since the only way to have two polygons in a block is if the block contains just one line segment. Notice that, unlike the PM$_1$ quadtree for line segments, the two structures are identical when the block contains just one vertex as in both cases the line segments that pass through the block need not intersect at the vertex.

5. We use contradiction. Let X be the property that the number of line segments in a node is bounded from above by the splitting threshold plus the depth of the node. Assume the existence of a node, say P, at depth k in a tree built with splitting threshold m that contains n line segments, where $n > k + m$ (i.e., the existence of P contradicts property X). Also, assume that of the nodes that violate property X, node P is the closest one to the root. We have two cases: $k = 0$ (i.e., P is a root node) or $k > 0$. If $k = 0$, then we have a tree of just the one node P, which contains more items than the splitting threshold. Since line segments are inserted one at a time, P must have been created by inserting one line segment into a node, say Q, that previously contained $n - 1$ line segments. From $k = 0$ and $n > k + m$, we have $n - 1 \geq m$. However, since Q contains $n - 1$ line segments and must be at level 0 itself, it follows that upon inserting yet another line segment into a node Q that is already at or over threshold m, only leaf nodes at depth 1 will result. Therefore, k could not be zero, and hence P cannot be a root node.

Since P is not a root node, it has a parent node. Using analogous reasoning to that above yields the observation that P's parent, say PP, must be one level closer to the root and contains one fewer line segment prior to the creation of P. However, since $n > k + m$, it follows that $n - 1 > k - 1 + m$. Thus, PP will also violate property X and is one level closer to the root of the tree. This contradicts the assumption that P was the node closest to the root of the tree that could violate property X. Therefore, there can be no such node P that contradicts property X. Hence, property X is true—that is, for every node, the number of line segments in the node is bounded from above by the sum of the splitting threshold and the depth of the node.

6. This is not a problem for the PM$_3$ quadtree, but the PM$_1$ and PM$_2$ quadtrees will not be able to deal with it. The problem is that for the PM$_1$ and PM$_2$ quadtrees, it may be impossible to achieve a situation where each node contains just one line segment.

7. Every line in L passes through one, two, or three quadrants of the quartered block. Let A be a line perpendicular to the set L, and for any point P on A, let $q(P)$ be the number of quadrants intersected by the element of L that is perpendicular to A at P. A can be partitioned into sections depending on the value of $q(P)$. Because of the symmetry of the square block, the total length of the sections with $q(P) = 1$ is equal to the total length of the sections with $q(P) = 3$, independent of the value of θ. The value of $q(P)$ over the remainder of the intersection of A with L is 2. Therefore, the average number of quadrants intersected by the block is 2 [1361].

8. The expected number of quadrants of occupancy i produced by splitting a node of occupancy c is $\binom{n}{i} \cdot 2^{2-i}$.

9. From Exercise 7, we know that each quadrant has a 0.5 probability of intersecting each line segment in the parent node. Therefore, the average occupancy of the nodes produced is 0.5 times the occupancy of the parent node.

10. A node of occupancy $i > c$ must be produced by a split such that all i line segments intersect the same quadrant. Assuming a uniform distribution, the expected number of children for $i = c + 1$ is $4 \cdot 2^{c+1}$ per split; for $i = c + 2$, the expected number of children is $4 \cdot 2^{c+1} \cdot 4 \cdot 2^{c+2}$; and so on. Thus, the expected number of nodes with occupancy greater than c decreases exponentially with $i - c$.

12. Use procedure PMDELETE given in Exercise 2 in Section 2.2.2.6 with POSSIBLEPMR-MERGE and TRYTOMERGEPMR instead of POSSIBLEPM1MERGE and TRYTOMERGE-PM1, respectively.

Solutions to Exercises in Section 2.2.2.9

1. Let r be the length of the perpendicular sides of the triangle. The true perimeter is $2r + r\sqrt{2}$, and the approximated perimeter is $4r$.

2. $4/\pi$.

3. Use linear interpolation in x and y instead of ρ and θ for the arc of the sector. A combination of polygonal and nonpolygonal blocks could also be implemented by using an additional bit with each sector to indicate the block type.

4. The inner approximation means that the object is made larger since it is the part outside the object that is truncated. On the other hand, the outer approximation implies the addition of two newly created subregions to the collection represented by the sector.

5. No, because the boundary may repeatedly snake through a number of adjacent nodes.

6. Let P be the contact point in question, and let Q and R be the immediately preceding and following, respectively, contact points on the other side of the sector. Duplicate P in the sector's leaf node, and define a three-sided region bounded by the side of the sector between Q and R and the spiral arc approximations of PQ and PR.

7. The only difference is that when the origin of the polar plane is outside the object, each leaf node of a sector tree contains an even number of pairs of points instead of an odd number. Each successive two pairs of points define a region within the object.

8. Use different origins for the approximating arcs. In particular, the origins are on opposite sides of the arcs. For example, in Figure 2.132(b) the arc between points 5 and C would have an origin somewhere to the SW of the arc between points 4 and D.

9. No, for both approximations since this depends on the curvature of the boundary where the approximation takes place.

11. Rotation only requires rearranging pointers. All interpolations remain the same since each sector corresponds to an angular range of $2\pi/2^n$. Therefore, all the approximated arcs remain unchanged.

12. Traverse the tree in such a way that nodes corresponding to adjacent boundary segments are visited in sequence. Note that each leaf node may be visited more than once because the boundary may repeatedly snake through a number of adjacent nodes.

Solutions to Exercises in Section 2.2.2.10

1.
$$\rho(s,t) = \rho_{11} + (\rho_{12} - \rho_{11}) \cdot s + (\rho_{21} - \rho_{11}) \cdot t + (\rho_{22} - \rho_{21} - \rho_{12} + \rho_{11}) \cdot st$$
$$\theta(s,t) = \theta_1 + (\theta_2 - \theta_1) \cdot s \phi(s,t) = \phi_1 + (\phi_2 - \phi_1) \cdot t.$$

2. Each cone would be a collection of spherical patches similar to that used in the sector tree.

3. The only difference is that when the origin of the polar sphere is outside the object, then each leaf node of a cone tree contains an even number of spherical patches instead of an odd number. Each successive pair of patches defines a region within the object.

Solutions to Exercises in Section 2.2.3.1

1. At each level of the tree, we must examine n points to determine the points on the curve that are at a maximum distance from the line joining the curve's endpoints. The tree has $\log_2 n$ levels.

3. At each level of the tree, we must process one-half of as many rectangles as were processed on the previous level. Initially, we process $n + 1$ pairs of points to yield n rectangles. The result follows since we have a geometric series with a ratio of $1/2$.

5. In the top-down method, the enclosing rectangles are formed by using points on the curve, whereas in the bottom-up method, all rectangles at levels other than the deepest level are based on the strips. In other words, in the bottom-up method the width of the final rectangle is not necessarily the sum of the maximum distances to the curve from the line joining the endpoints of the curve.

7. Constructing the rectangular strip takes $O(N)$ time for N points since the perpendicular distance of each point from the line joining the curve's endpoints must be calculated. In contrast, constructing the rectangle of minimum bounding area for N points takes $O(N \cdot \log_2 N)$ time as the convex hull for the points must be obtained first.

8. See [639].

9. When all the strip segments in one tree intersect all the strip segments in the other tree, the algorithm will take $O(2^{d_1+d_2})$ time.

11. Represent it as two closed curves. Alternatively, draw an imaginary line across the area, and order the points so that the region is always to the right of the curve.

12. See [121].

13. The key is that if the intersection of any strip of the curve, say S_c corresponding to a node T_c, with the strip tree of the area, say T_a, is null, then (1) if any point on S_c is inside T_a, then every point in T_c is inside or on the boundary of T_a, and (2) if any point on S_c is outside T_a, then every point in T_c is outside T_a. See [121].

14. The key is to decompose the problem into two subproblems of intersecting curves with areas. Let T_1 and T_2 represent the strip trees corresponding to the two areas. First, intersect the curve corresponding to T_1 with the area corresponding to T_2 and then reverse the roles of the two strip trees. The final result is represented by the union of the previous two steps. See [121].

15. Not when the curve is closed.

16. $\int_a^b \sqrt{1 + f'^2(x)} \cdot dx$.

17. Use contradiction. The length of the major axis of the ellipse is equal to the length of the corresponding arc that is being approximated. An ellipse, say E, has the property that the sum of the distances from any point on E to the two foci is equal to the length of the major axis. Thus, the arc must be internal to the ellipse. The only way in which the arc can lie outside the ellipse is if its length exceeds the length of the major axis, which is a contradiction because the endpoints of the arc are the two foci of the ellipse.

18. Check if the sum of its distances from the foci of the ellipse is less than or greater than the length of the major axis of the ellipse.

19. Check if the approximation can be used instead of the actual curve. This requires the point to be outside the ellipses represented by the approximation. This can be tested using the result of Exercise 18. Traverse the arc tree in a breadth-first manner. Whenever the point is internal (external) to a node's ellipse, then the children of the node must (not) be tested. A conventional point inclusion test can be used once it has been determined that the approximation is sufficient.

20. The two ellipses must intersect, and the two foci of each ellipse must be external to the other ellipse.

21. See [769].

22. Yes, in principle, since an area is a closed curve. However, if the curves do not intersect, then their areas can still overlap as one area can be totally contained in the other. This can be determined by a point inclusion test.

23. See [769]. The common edges contribute to the output only if their orientation is identical when the curves of the areas are traversed in the same order (e.g., clockwise).

24. Consider a sawtoothlike polyline. The approximating line between the start and endpoints is a straight line that acts like an average, while the approximating line between alternating points has a larger error for the intermediate point.

Solutions to Exercises in Section 2.2.3.2

3. If only the split step is used, then even though the initial edges are very bad approximations of the surface, they are never removed.

4. The split and adjustment steps result in some faces being bases of new tetrahedra.

5. It is alleviated, in part, by the application of the adjustment step after each split step.

6. Use neighbor finding techniques similar to those discussed in Chapter 3 of [1636] (see [1501]).

9. No.

10. We prove that if the prism is not regular, then the surface is not convex. If the prism is not regular, then there is a line, lying outside the interior of the surface and in the bisecting plane, from a vertex on the surface to another point of intersection of the surface and the bisecting plane. This implies that the surface is not convex.

11. Yes.

14. Perform an initial step of subdivision into components of genus 0.

Solutions to Exercises in Section 2.2.3.3

1. The minimum bounding disc can be found in $O(n)$ time (see the solution to Exercise 4 in Section 4.4.2 of Chapter 4). Two vertices on the boundary of a disc that are the farthest apart can be found in $O(n\log_2 n)$ time [1511]. The new vertex to be included in the approximation polygon can be found in $O(n)$ time by testing the vertices sequentially. In the best case, the polygon is split into equally sized parts at each step, resulting in $\lceil \log_2 n \rceil$ iterations. The ith iteration processes 2^i polylines of size $n/2^i$, and thus in the best case, the HAL tree construction algorithm takes a total of $O(n) + O(\sum i = 0 \lceil \log_2 n \rceil 2^i \cdot (n/2^i)) = O(n\log_2 n)$ time. In the worst case, a polyline of j segments is split into one polyline of size 1 and one polyline of size $j - 1$ at each iteration. Thus, in the worst case, the algorithm takes a total of $O(n) + O(\sum i = 1nn) = O(n^2)$ time.

2. The root stores the smallest bounding disc and two of the vertices that lie on the disc. They define the initial two polylines. Each node in the remaining levels corresponds to a vertex that splits its corresponding polyline and the two discs that make up its minimum bounding box. There are as many nodes in the tree as there are vertices, and therefore the HAL tree takes $O(n)$ space.

Solutions to Exercises in Section 2.2.3.4

1. See [693, Ch. 8], [695], and [2004, Ch. 5].

Solutions to Exercises in Section 2.2.4

1. Each introduction of a new vertex causes the addition of two triangles.

2. The alternative would be to split at the interior if the error on t is greater than e (Figure 2.151(a)). However, such a split would not resolve the errors on the three original edges, and thus they would eventually have to be split.

3. There are four alternatives, none of which is useful:

   (a) Split at the interior (Figure 2.151(a)). However, as we saw in the solution to Exercise 2 such a split would not resolve the errors on the two original edges, and thus they would eventually have to be split.

   (b) Split at one edge (Figure 2.151(b)). However, this does not resolve the error on the other edge.

   (c) Split at one edge and at the interior (Figure 2.151(c)). However, this does not resolve the error on the other edge.

   (d) Split at three edges (Figure 2.151(e)). However, this results in a possibly needless split of one of the adjacent triangles.

4. If both vertex neighbors of a node along one of its edges e are of equal size, then it is impossible for the neighboring node along e to be of greater size. If one of the vertex neighbors along e is of greater size, then the neighbor along edge e can only be twice the size as, otherwise, the other vertex neighbor would be of greater than twice the size. It is easy to construct an example where all edge neighbors are of equal size or have a ratio of 2:1, while the vertex neighbors are larger than twice the size.

5. See the work of Moore [1312, 1313]. These bounds are better than the bound of 9 reported elsewhere [1300, 1981]. In fact, the bound of 9 reported by Weiser [1981] was really for the variant of the restricted quadtree where all vertex neighbors are either of equal size or of ratio 2:1 (termed a *0-balanced quadtree* [1312]).

6. See [1312].

7. See [1312], which is a better result than the factor of 13 originally reported in [1981].

8. See [1312].

9. This can be seen by construction. The newly added point will cause t to be split into two triangles, and likewise for the adjacent triangle u, if one exists, along h. If u is equal in size to t (i.e., h serves as a hypotenuse of u), then u is split just once. Otherwise, u must be split twice—once into two triangles of size equal to t and then one more split of one of these triangles. This second split is why we say that we may have to split two triangles of a given size. This process is applied repeatedly to the triangle v that is adjacent along the hypotenuse of u as long as the hypotenuse that is split is a leg of the adjacent triangle v. This process will stop once we are at the largest possible triangle (i.e., at the root of the restricted bintree).

Solutions to Exercises in Section 2.3.1

6. (A,2), (W,0), (W,0), (W,0), (B,0), (B,1), (W,1), (W,1), (A,0), (A,0), (W,0), (W,0), (A,0), (A,0), (W,0), (W,0), (W,1), (W,1), (W,1), (W,1), (W,0), (C,0), (W,0), (C,0), (C,1).

8. This is not as simple as for the Morton size ordering because the order of the subblocks of each block differs depending on the depth of the block and the size of the image.

9. IAIIWWWBBWWIIAAWWIAAWWWWIWWIWCWCC.

10. Reconstruct the space spanned by the quadtree while traversing the elements of the DF-expression until finding a leaf block that contains c.

11. Use a similar process as in the DF-expression. In essence, traverse the linear tree and the color table in tandem. Transitions are made in the color table only when a leaf node (i.e., 1) is encountered in the linear tree.

12. See [970].

14. There are two possible reasons for characterizing the resulting structure as a prefix B^+-tree. They both stem from the use of the term *linear prefix* to describe the keys.

(a) The S^+-tree makes use of a B-tree to store portions of the segments of the linear tree representation of the region quadtree. Each segment of the linear tree has a key that is its corresponding linear prefix. The B-tree is implemented as a B^+-tree where all data is in the leaf nodes and the keys are used as indexes stored in the nonleaf nodes. The keys are also stored in the leaf nodes along with their corresponding linear trees. The confusion stems from treating the key of the B-tree as the result of appending the linear tree to the linear prefix. In this case, the linear prefix plays the role of the prefix of the entire key. Thus, the issue of whether the S^+-tree is a B^+-tree or a prefix B^+-tree hinges solely on the nature of the key. However, since the original string corresponding to the linear tree has been decomposed into segments, each of which is stored in a separate page (leaf node) in the B-tree, it makes sense to treat each of these segments as the data that is stored in each node and the linear prefix as the key. Thus, the B^+-tree characterization seems more appropriate than the prefix B^+-tree characterization.

(b) In the original formulation of the S^+-tree, the segment stored on each page terminates with a leaf node. Now, instead of identifying each string segment S by F, which is the linear prefix of the node N in the original tree corresponding to the first element in S, use the linear prefix P of the last leaf node L in the immediately preceding segment of S. It is easy to show that F is the prefix of P. Thus, we see that if we identify each segment S by the last leaf node in the immediately preceding segment of S, then the S^+-tree is a prefix B^+-tree, while if we identify S by the first node in S, then the S^+-tree is a conventional B^+-tree.

15. None of the proposed solutions will work. The problem is the presence of "Z"-like transitions. In other words, given an $M \times M$ image, the difference in the x coordinate values of two successive 1×1 cells in the Morton order may be as large as $M - 1$, while the y coordinate values may differ by as much as $(M - 2)/2$.

16. Given that blocks a and b appear in consecutive positions in the ordering so that a precedes b, the size of a is equal to the logarithm to the base 4 of the maximum difference of the corresponding x and y coordinate values of their location entries. This works because successive elements in the Peano-Hilbert order are always edge neighbors (i.e., one of the coordinate values is the same for both of the successive elements).

17. Recall that given the Morton numbers of two successive blocks f_1 and f_2 in a Morton order, we can determine the size of block f_1 only from the Morton numbers of f_1 and f_2. Thus, in order to determine the size of f_1, we need to know the Morton number of the block that immediately follows f_1 in the Morton sequence.

First, determine the Morton number, say d_1, of the largest block in the Morton sequence that can follow the block having pixel C_1 at its upper-left corner. This is done by repeatedly incrementing C_1 by 4^L (L is initially 0) as long as the sum does not exceed C_2. Once d_1 has been found, its block is output in the list, C_1 is set to d_1, and the process is restarted. If C_2 is exceeded prior to finding a sibling block of the desired size—that is, $d_2 = C_1 + 4^{L-1}$ such that $d_2 \leq C_2$ and $C_2 < C_1 + 4^L$, then output the block corresponding to d_2, reset C_1 to d_2, and restart the process. The algorithm for decoding the two-dimensional runlength encoding is given by procedure DECODE2DRE below.

```
1   procedure DECODE2DRE(C₁, C₂)
2   /* Given two successive nodes with Morton numbers C₁ and C₂ in a two-
        dimensional runlength encoding of a quadtree, determine the Morton num-
        bers and sizes of all blocks whose Morton numbers are between C₁ and C₂,
        including C₁ but excluding C₂. */
3   value morton_number C₁, C₂
4   integer L
5   while C₁ < C₂ do
6       L ← 0
7       while C₁ + 4 ↑ L < C₂ and (C₁ mod 4 ↑ (L+1)) = 0 do
8           L ← L + 1
9       enddo
```

```
10    if C_1 + 4 ↑ L > C_2 then L ← L − 1
11    endif
12    output(C_1, L)
13    C_1 ← C_1 + 4 ↑ L
14  enddo
```

If the block with Morton number C_1 is not desired, then we need to make use of an additional variable T to store the initial value of C_1 and perform the output step only if C_1 is greater than its initial value T.

18. Given blocks a and b so that block a precedes block b in the ordering, then the size of b is determined by taking the logarithm to the base 4 of the difference between the Morton numbers of b and a. The Morton number of the block preceding the first block in the ordering is 0.

19. (W,(6,0)), (B,(6,2)), (W,(2,4)), (B,(3,5)), (W,(0,6)), (B,(4,7)), (W,(6,6)).

20. Such a definition leads to ambiguity in the sense that it is impossible to determine the sizes of the blocks. For example, consider the two-dimensional runlength encoding of the region quadtree in Figure 2.158(b) given by (W,(6,0)), (B,(6,2)), (W,(2,4)), (B,(3,5)), (W,(0,6)), (B,(4,7)), (W,(6,6)). In this case, we cannot tell if the block at (6,2) is of size 1×1 or 2×2. This problem can be resolved by encoding each leaf node using the Morton number of the pixel that occupies its lower-right corner (i.e., the last pixel). The resulting reconstruction is achieved by procedure DECODE2DRE2. Note that DECODE2DRE2 yields the blocks with Morton numbers ranging from C_1 to C_2, including C_2 but not C_1.

```
1   procedure DECODE2DRE2(C_1, C_2)
2   /* Given two successive nodes with Morton numbers C_1 and C_2 in a two-
        dimensional runlength encoding of a quadtree, determine the Morton num-
        bers and sizes of all blocks whose Morton numbers are between C_1 and C_2,
        including C_2 but excluding C_1. C_1 and C_2 are the Morton numbers of the
        pixels in the lower-right corners of the last elements of each subsequence of
        the same color. */
3   value morton_number C_1, C_2
4   integer L
5   while C_1 < C_2 do
6       L ← 0
7       while C_1 + 4 ↑ L < C_2 and ((C_1 + 1) mod 4 ↑ (L + 1)) = 0 do
8           L ← L + 1
9       enddo
10      if C_1 + 4 ↑ L > C_2 then
11          L ← L − 1
12      endif
13      C_1 ← C_1 + 4 ↑ L
14      output(C_1, L)
15  enddo
```

If the block with Morton number C_2 is not desired, then we perform the output step only if C_1 is less than C_2 in the algorithm.

21. (A,(0,0)), (W,(4,0)), (B,(5,1)), (W,(4,2)), (A,(0,4)), (W,(0,5)), (A,(2,4)), (W,(2,5)), (C,(5,6)), (W,(4,7)), (C,(5,7)).

23. The algorithm is the same as that for the two-dimensional runlength encoding based on the Morton location ordering.

24. See procedure WHITEBLOCKS in [1636, p. 38] for a similar algorithm.

Solutions to Exercises in Section 2.3.2

1. Positive transitions correspond to clockwise turns, and negative transitions correspond to counterclockwise turns. The chain code that we have defined is a *clockwise* chain code as

the image is always to the right of the boundary elements. For any object without holes, a clockwise chain code requires a minimum of four clockwise turns. This means that we record three positive transitions as the final positive transition that closes the curve is omitted from our code. Any counterclockwise turn requires an additional clockwise turn in excess of the minimum so that we can eventually proceed in a direction that will return us to the starting point. Thus, we have proven our desired result.

2. Since the object is closed, the chain code must terminate at its starting point. Thus, the number of unit vectors in these opposite directions must be the same.

Solutions to Exercises in Section 2.3.3

1. A vertex such as p is solely responsible for the mapping of the field in its immediate neighborhood. In particular, we want the mapping of (x_0, y_0) to be 1, and thus the vertex at that point must have a weight of $+1$ as there is no other point q on the boundary of the polygon that is dominated by the vertex at (x_0, y_0). The weights of points such as q could have led to the field in the neighborhood of (x_0, y_0) having a value of $+1$, but this is impossible as there are no such points.

2. The topology of the polygon is irrelevant when we think of the problem domain as one involving scalar fields as the topology of the polygon can be anything. It can have any number of holes or connected components. However, if we look at the problem as one of finding the weights of the vertices of the holes, then we could simply create the polygon without the holes, say A, and create the polygons of the holes, say B_i for the ith hole. We now compute the vertex representations of A and the individual holes B_i. Next, we calculate the vertex representation of $A - \sum_i B_i$ (i.e., by subtracting the vertex representations of the holes B_i from that of A).

3. The reason for the different vertex representation is the fact that the two cases correspond to a different definition of what is inside and outside the object. In (a) all elements of the object are termed to be inside as the object is interpreted as a polygon with a self-intersecting boundary, whereas in (c) it is interpreted as a concave polygon. The latter is also the case when we say that for two elements with a nonzero area that are considered as interior (i.e., inside of an object) to be in the same object, the elements must be adjacent along an edge (termed *4-adjacent*). On the other hand, the exterior elements of the object are adjacent along an edge or a vertex of the element (termed *8-adjacent*), and the exterior of the object is considered as one connected region. To summarize, what is ambiguous here is the representation of an object as a circular list of vertices and not its vertex representation.

4. Suppose that this is not true. Therefore, there must be at least one horizontal or vertical edge whose endpoints are marked by vertices with weights of equal sign. Without loss of generality, suppose that it is a horizontal edge delimited by two vertices a and b with weight $+1$, where a is to the left of b. The other cases (i.e., vertical edges as well as vertices with weight -1) are treated in an analogous manner. Let us analyze the scalar field along the edge. The fact that the weight of a is $+1$ and b is to the right of a means that the value of the field at a point infinitely close to the right of and above a must be 1, and that the value of the field at a point infinitely close to the right of and above a must be 0. In other words, the horizontal edge must mark the boundary between a region that is mapped to 0 (below the edge) and a region that is mapped to 1 (above the edge). Notice that the only other possibility (i.e., that the field below the edge is 1 and the field above the edge is 0) is impossible as it would lead to a value of the field above the edge as being 2 by virtue of the fact that the value of the field above a is 1 higher than the value of the field below a, thereby leading to a contradiction. As we walk along the edge in the direction of the rightmost vertex (b), the scalar field must also be mapped to 1. Suppose that this is not true at some point p along the way. In this case, p would have to be mapped to 0 since we allow only 0 and 1 as values of the scalar field. In order for p to be mapped to 0, there must exist some point q just below p that would have to be mapped to -1, which is not possible since we allow only 0 and 1 as values of the scalar field.

   Now, let us turn our attention to b. Using the same reasoning (i.e., that 0 and 1 are the only possible values of the scalar field), when we reach b we know that the scalar field at b can take on only values of 0 or 1. For this to be true, the fact that the weight at b is $+1$ means that there must exist some point p just below b where the scalar field is mapped to either -2 or -1, respectively, which as we will see is impossible. To see this, we make use of the relationship between the weight of a vertex at the upper-left corner of a 2×2 block of pixels and the values of the pixels as shown in Figure 2.163. In particular, we note that the scalar field at b is equal to the sum of the weight of b (which is $+1$), the scalar field just to the left of b (which is 1), the scalar field just below b at p, and the negation of the value of the scalar field below the edge (which is zero). If the scalar field at b is 0, then the scalar field at p must be -2. On the other hand, if the scalar field at b is 1, then the scalar field at p must be -1. Both of these cases are impossible as the only possible values for the scalar field are 0 and 1. Thus, we see that if a horizontal edge is delimited on the left by a vertex with weight $+1$, then it must be delimited on the right by a vertex with weight -1 and vice versa.

5. Use a procedure that works in the inverse manner to procedure RASTERTOVLIST. In two dimensions, instead of building successive one-dimensional lists and subtracting them pairwise, we extract consecutive one-dimensional prefixes of the two-dimensional list and add them together until the y coordinate value of the point is reached. The one-dimensional prefixes are lists consisting of all the vertices that have the same v coordinate value as the vertex at the head of the list. The inverse lexicographic ordering imposed on vertex lists guarantees that all such vertices are clustered at the beginning of the list, hence the term *prefix*. The weights of the vertices of the resulting one-dimensional list are then added together until reaching the x coordinate value of the point. The resulting sum of weights is the value of the desired location.

6. The algorithm is a generalization of the solution to Exercise 5. Assume that c has coordinate values $c_1 \ldots c_d$. The scalar field on a hyperplane given by $x_d = c_d$ can be represented by a $(d-1)$-dimensional vertex list which can be obtained as follows:

   (a) Take all vertices of the original vertex list such that their dth coordinate value is less than or equal to c_d.

   (b) Project these vertices onto a $d-1$-dimensional space by stripping their dth coordinate value. If two or more vertices assume the same position in the lower-dimensional space, then add their weights together and replace them with a single vertex with weight equal to their sum, provided that it is nonzero.

   Now, we repeat steps (a) and (b) using the resulting vertex list as input. Thus, we obtain vertex lists of increasingly lower dimension. After $d-1$ iterations, we obtain a one-dimensional vertex list corresponding to the scalar field along the line given by $x_d = c_d \wedge x_{d-1} = c_{d-1} \wedge \cdots \wedge x_2 = c_2$. At this point, all we need to do is evaluate the scalar field along this line at point $x_1 = c_1$, which is trivial. This process can be easily implemented by a recursive procedure. It should be clear that this procedure is equivalent to taking successive $(d-1)$-dimensional prefixes of the original vertex list, stripping the last coordinate value of each vertex, and then adding them together until reaching the hyperplane corresponding to $x_d = c_d$.

7. See [567].

8. Using the conventional row order vertex list ordering, it is simple to decompose a d-dimensional problem into a series of $(d-1)$-dimensional problems by examining prefixes, prefixes of prefixes, and so on. Recall from the solutions to Exercises 5 and 6 that a prefix of a d-dimensional vertex list is a sublist taken from the beginning of the list where all vertices have the same dth coordinate value. In fact, since all vertices of a prefix lie in the same hyperplane perpendicular to the dth coordinate axis, we do not need to keep the dth coordinate value of each vertex. Thus, we may make this list $(d-1)$-dimensional by removing (or simply disregarding) the last coordinate from the representation.

This approach was used, for example, in the solution to Exercise 6. Partial results obtained in the processing of the kth dimension are easily carried over to the processing of the $(k+1)$-th dimension by using a single k-dimensional vertex list.

On the other hand, suppose that we use a Morton order. In this case, a prefix of a list would correspond to the vertices that lie on a quadrant, octant, or the equivalent d-dimensional subregion. Therefore, depending on the dimensionality of the underlying space, the strategy for solving the problem would involve solving 4, 8, or 2^d subproblems (one for each subregion) and then combining their solutions to compute the solution for the whole region. Unfortunately, the vertices that lie in each subregion usually cannot be processed independently of those in the other subregions.

For instance, in two dimensions, if we use the standard x-y axis orientation with the origin at the lower-left corner, then the vertices of the SW quadrant can be processed independently of the others, but the vertices in the NW and SE quadrants need to take into consideration the vertices in the SW quadrant, and the vertices in the NE quadrant need to take into consideration the vertices in all of the quadrants.

Of course, we could employ the same techniques used in the processing of vertex lists ordered in row order lists to overcome this problem—that is, use vertex lists of lower dimension to transmit the result of the processing of earlier subregions to the processing of the remaining subregions. In the case of two dimensions, this would require that the processing of each quadrant produce (in addition to the transformed subregion) two one-dimensional lists that would hold the value of the regions along the northern and eastern borders, respectively.

As a concrete example, suppose that we want to evaluate the field inside the NE quadrant. In addition to the local changes that occur inside the quadrant itself, we must take into consideration the changes that are carried over from the processing of earlier quadrants. The changes that occurred in the SW quadrant can be summarized by a single vertex that dominates the entire NE quadrant. For convenience, let us position such a vertex at the lower-left corner of the NE quadrant. The weight of this vertex is the sum of the weights of all vertices in the SW quadrant. Now, let us consider the influence of all the vertices in the SE quadrant (with respect to the NE quadrant). Taken together, they define a series of semi-infinite regions whose southern boundary is the southern border of the NE quadrant and whose eastern and western boundaries are vertical lines. This series can be represented by a set of k vertices lying at the y coordinate value of the southern border of the NE quadrant having x coordinate values $x_1 \ldots x_k$, where the weight of the vertex lying at x_i is the sum of the weights of all vertices that lie on the vertical line $x = x_i$ inside the SE quadrant.

Similarly, the effect of the NW quadrant can be summarized by a set of n vertices placed over the western border of the NE quadrant and having y coordinate values equal to $y_1 \ldots y_n$, where the weight of the vertex at y_i is the sum of the weights of all vertices that lie on the horizontal line $y = y_n$ inside the NW quadrant.

In summary, the effect of one quadrant over the processing of another may be represented by vertex lists that describe how the field changes along their common boundary. In the cases that we have just described, we needed two one-dimensional lists (for quadrants that shared a common edge) plus a "zero"-dimensional list made up of a single vertex (for quadrants that are adjacent at a single point). In general, the processing of a d-dimensional subregion would require d $(d-1)$-dimensional lists, $d-1$ $(d-2)$-dimensional lists, $d-2$ $(d-3)$-dimensional lists, and so on.

Thus, the use of alternative orders does not reduce the complexity of the operations.

Solutions to Exercises in Section 3.1.1

1. The line segments are not permitted to overlap.

2. No. For example, consider the segment tree of Figure 3.3 without line segment C (i.e., for segments A, B, D, E, F, and G). Line segments A and E overlap, yet no node in the segment tree contains both of them.

3. The alternative solution requires that the list be traversed when attempting to remove the line segment. This could lead to an extra factor of N in the cost of deletion.

4. Multiple intersections are reported for line segments that are totally contained within other line segments. Removing duplicates requires sorting a set that may have more than N elements, and the algorithm may take more than $O(N \cdot \log_2 N)$ time.

5. Search for P starting at the root. Descend to the child whose interval contains P. Report all intervals associated with the nonleaf nodes on the path to the appropriate leaf node. This takes $O(\log_2 N + F)$ time, where F is the number of intervals that contain P. The $\log_2 N$ term results from the depth of the tree.

6. $O(N)$ space is used since only the number of intervals need be stored at each nonleaf node of the segment tree (instead of the identities of the intervals). Descending the tree takes $O(\log_2 N)$ time.

10. The segment tree is good for indicating all the one-dimensional intervals that contain a given point. It is not suitable for indicating which intervals lie within a given interval; a one-dimensional range tree is more appropriate. However, without additional structuring, many intervals that do not satisfy the query will be examined.

11. The segment tree is good for indicating all the one-dimensional intervals that contain a given point. One possible solution is to search for the endpoints of the given interval and take an intersection of the result. This takes more than $O(\log_2 N + F)$ time. Can you find a better solution?

Solutions to Exercises in Section 3.1.2

1. Each line segment can be marked in at most $2 \cdot \lceil \log_2 N \rceil$ nodes of the segment tree. There are N line segments that are tested for intersection with these nodes.

2. Yes. However, now the intervals represented by the nonleaf nodes are not of uniform size, but once we know the maximum number of intervals, there is no problem. The segment tree of Figure 3.3 would have its external nodes marked as in Figure 3.4 with the following differences. Node 10 would be marked with {B} instead of {A, C}, and node 11 would be marked with {B} instead of being unmarked. The only changes in the marking of the nonleaf nodes are that the left child of the right child of the root is marked with {A,C} instead of being unmarked, and the left child of the left child of the right child of the root is now unmarked instead of being marked with {A,C}.

3. The search is analogous to that used in stage 2. The difference is a replacement of l with r, L_i with R_i, $>$ with $<$, and all right children with left children and vice versa.

4. All leaf, and some nonleaf, nodes in the tertiary structure of the interval tree have nonempty secondary structures. The tertiary structure is a binary tree. A nonleaf node with an empty secondary structure must have two active children. The maximum number of such nonleaf nodes is one less than the total number of leaf nodes, all of which have a nonempty secondary structure. This result can also be obtained by viewing the tertiary structure as a variant of an extended binary tree.

5. The interval tree stabbing query is executed as follows. Search for P starting at the root. For each nonleaf node, say I, compare P with the value stored at I, say V_I. If P is less than V_I, then report all the intervals stored at I whose left endpoints are less than P. This takes time proportional to the number of intervals that contain P. Next, descend to the left child and repeat. If P is larger than V_I, then report all the intervals stored at I whose right endpoints are greater than P. Next, descend to the right child and repeat. This takes $O(\log_2 N + F)$ time, where F is the number of intervals that contain P. The $\log_2 N$ term results from the depth of the tree.

6. No. The problem is that the intervals that are stored with a nonleaf node of the interval tree do not span the entire interval associated with the node. Thus, we cannot execute the interval tree stabbing counting query.

7. Assume that the line segment $[l{:}r]$ is being processed. The point query returns all line segments $[a{:}b]$ such that $a < l \leq b$, and the range query returns all line segments $[c{:}d]$ such that $l \leq c < r$. Clearly, these two sets are disjoint.

10. If the task is to be achieved in $O(\log_2 N + F)$ time, then the interval tree needs modification, such as the addition of some auxiliary structures analogous to the secondary and tertiary structures. The problem is that presently the interval tree does not facilitate pruning. In particular, at each level of the tree a good part of the secondary structure may have to be searched without finding any intervals that satisfy the query.

11. Again, we start at the root and locate the first node v such that $l < \text{VAL}(v) < r$. At this point we update the secondary structure of v. We must also make v active if it was previously inactive. This means that we must keep track of its active predecessor in the tertiary structure while making the descent during the process of locating v. Once, this is done, the insertion is completed as no action is necessary in the subtrees of v.

12. See the solution to Exercise 10.

14. Construct two empty interval trees: one for S_1 and one for S_2. Without loss of generality, assume that the sweep line is a vertical line. Sort all of the rectangles in S_1 and S_2 by their left endpoints, thereby forming a set S_C. Process the elements in S_C in order. For each rectangle

r in S_1 (S_2), remove all inactive rectangles from the interval tree of S_2 (S_1); search for all rectangles in the interval tree of S_2 (S_1) that intersect r; and insert r in the interval tree of S_1 (S_2). Note that an intersection is reported only when the second rectangle of the intersecting pair in the sorted order is inserted into the appropriate interval tree, thereby avoiding reporting duplicate intersections. Assuming that there is a total of N rectangles in the two sets S_1 and S_2 and that there are F intersecting pairs, then the algorithm takes $O(N \cdot \log_2 N + F)$ time and $O(N)$ space.

15. When there is insufficient memory to store a current rectangle r in the appropriate dynamic interval tree, Jacox and Samet [934] propose recording r and continue the algorithm. Once the sweep pass is done, if some unprocessed rectangles remain, then an additional sweep pass is performed where only the rectangles that have not yet been processed (i.e., whose intersections have not yet been tested) are inserted into the appropriate dynamic interval tree, although all rectangles in S_1 (S_2) are checked for intersection with the rectangles in the dynamic interval tree of S_2 (S_1).

Solutions to Exercises in Section 3.1.3

1. Draw the intervals, and the result will be apparent.

5. See [1858].

6. See [1266].

7. Perform the semi-infinite range query $([-\infty:P],(P:\infty])$. It takes $O(\log_2 M + F)$ time, where F is the number of intersecting intervals found.

8. See [1266].

9. Perform the semi-infinite range query $([-\infty:a],(b:\infty])$ in search of the points (x, y).

10. Perform the semi-infinite range query $((a:\infty],[-\infty:b))$ in search of the points (x, y). This requires the use of an inverse priority search tree for the range of y. Since $x < b$, this can be simplified to $((a:b],[-\infty:b))$.

11. Perform the semi-infinite range query $([-\infty:b),(a:\infty])$ in search of the points (y, x). Since $a < y$, this can be simplified to $((a:b],(a:\infty])$.

Solutions to Exercises in Section 3.1.4

1. Use a plane-sweep method [1740]. Sort the endpoints of the line segments and then sweep a vertical line through the set. If some of the lines are vertical, then rotate the set slightly. The key is that if there are no intersections, then the relative ordering of the line segments will be the same through the entire sweep. Use a balanced binary search tree to record the segments that intersect the sweep line. A line segment is inserted into (deleted from) the tree each time a left (right) endpoint is encountered. An intersection has occurred if, upon deletion, the relative ordering between the line segment and its top and bottom neighbors has changed.

2. Use a one-dimensional range tree at each nonleaf node of the segment tree. The one-dimensional range tree is sorted by the x coordinate values of the vertical line segments associated with it. The one-dimensional range tree for m items uses $O(m)$ space. $O(\log_2 N + F)$ nodes may be examined at each level of the segment tree. There are $\log_2 N$ levels in the primary segment tree, and the result follows.

3. Overmars [1441] suggests decomposing this problem into two cases:

   (a) R contains an element of L. Build a two-dimensional range tree that contains the left endpoint of each element of L, and perform a range query with R.

   (b) An element of L intersects a boundary of R. Treat the horizontal and vertical boundaries of R separately. For the horizontal boundaries, project all the line segments on a vertical line, and build a segment tree for the projections. Let V denote the projections of the line segments. Find all elements of V that intersect either of the two horizontal boundaries using the result of Exercise 2. The vertical boundaries are handled in the same way with the exception that we use the projections of the line segments on a horizontal line.

The storage and execution time requirements follow from previous analyses of these problems. Reporting some intersections more than once is avoided by checking for the possibility of case 2 while performing case 1. A positive answer means that the reporting of the intersection is delayed until it is detected by case 2. This will increase F, the number of intersections, by at most a constant multiplicative factor, and thus the order of execution time is not affected.

4. Assume that the balanced binary search tree contains nodes corresponding to the top and bottom boundaries of all active rectangles (i.e., one node per boundary) and that bottom boundaries are smaller in magnitude than top boundaries. A type bit indicates whether the node serves as a bottom or top boundary. There is at least one pair of intersecting rectangles if, upon inserting a rectangle, say R, with bottom and top boundaries B and T, respectively, in the tree, one of the following conditions holds:

   (a) There exists a node L such that B and T are in different subtrees of L.

   (b) There exists a node L such that L corresponds to a bottom boundary, and one of either B or T is inserted as a right child of L.

   (c) There exists a node L such that L corresponds to a top boundary, and one of either B or T is inserted as a left child of L.

5. The algorithm proceeds as long as the boundaries in the tree are nonintersecting. Thus, it can be used to detect the occurrence of an intersection, but it can not be used to maintain a set of boundaries that are intersecting. For example, assuming that rectangles are specified by the pairs of coordinate values (x, y) of their lower-left and upper-right corners, consider the three rectangles (1,1) and (10,10); (3,7) and (9,9); and (5,3) and (7,5). Assuming a horizontal scan from left to right, the intersection of the rectangle specified by (5,3) and (7,5) with either of rectangles (1,1) and (10,10) or (3,7) and (9,9) is not detected.

6. Use a plane-sweep method [178]. Sort the left and right boundaries of the rectangles. Sweep a vertical scan line through them. Let T be the balanced binary search tree that represents the bottom and top boundaries of the active rectangles, and link them in ascending order. Each time a rectangle, with bottom and top boundaries b and t, respectively, becomes active (inactive), enter (remove) b and t in (from) T and output the line segments whose entries in T lie between b and t. The output step visits only the nodes in the range since T is linked in ascending order. The time and space requirements follow.

7. Sort the rectangles by their left and right endpoints as well as by the x coordinate value of their centroid. Sweep a vertical line through them. Each time a left (right) endpoint is encountered, the corresponding boundary is inserted into (deleted from) the segment tree. Each time a centroid point is encountered, say corresponding to rectangle R, the segment tree is searched for all segments that overlap R's y coordinate value. The rectangles corresponding to these segments either totally enclose R or intersect R [183].

8. See [1910].

9. The primary segment tree (containing the projections of the rectangles on the x axis) uses $O(N \cdot \log_2 N)$ storage as there are $O(N \cdot \log_2 N)$ possible segments. Each of these segments can appear in as many as $O(\log_2 N)$ positions in the secondary segment trees [536, 542].

10. Use doubly linked lists. Each rectangle can appear in $O(\log_2 N)$ nonleaf nodes in the primary segment tree. Each of these nonleaf nodes is the root of a secondary segment tree. Insertion in each of the relevant nodes in the secondary segment tree takes $O(\log_2 N)$ time.

11. The insertion of each rectangle takes $O(\log_2^2 N)$ time. There are N rectangles.

12. At each level of the primary segment tree, we perform a one-dimensional stabbing query on a segment tree. This takes $O(\log_2 N + F)$ time. There are $\log_2 N$ levels in the primary segment tree, and the result follows.

13. $O(N \cdot \log_2^d N)$ storage and $O(\log_2^d N + F)$ time for N points and F rectangles containing them.

14. Yes. Use the layered tree approach of Vaishnavi and Wood [1911] that makes use of additional pointers.

15. There are three possible cases:

    (a) R contains an element of V. Build a two-dimensional range tree that contains the lower-leftmost corner of each element of V, and perform a range query with R.

    (b) R is contained in some element of V. Build a two-dimensional segment tree for V, and perform a two-dimensional stabbing query for the lower-leftmost corner of R.

    (c) A side of R intersects a side of an element of V. Use the result of Exercise 2 to solve two problems. The first stores the line segments corresponding to the vertical sides of V in a segment tree and finds the elements of V that intersect either of the two horizontal sides of R. The second stores the line segments corresponding to the horizontal sides of V in a segment tree and finds the elements of V that intersect either of the two vertical sides of R.

    The storage and execution time requirements follow from previous analyses of these problems.

16. When performing cases (a) and (b), check for the possibility of case (c). A positive answer means that the reporting of the intersection is delayed until it is detected by case (c). This will increase F, the number of intersections, by at most a constant multiplicative factor, and thus the order of execution time is not affected.

20. Project the rectangles on the x axis, and store these intervals in a segment tree, say T. Let I be a nonleaf node in T, and let R_I denote the rectangles whose horizontal sides are associated with I. For each I, build an interval tree for the projections of R_I on the y axis. The primary segment tree uses $O(N \cdot \log_2 N)$ storage as there are $O(N \cdot \log_2 N)$ possible segments. Each of these segments appears in one node in the secondary interval tree [536, 542].

21. Use doubly linked lists. Each rectangle can appear in $O(\log_2 N)$ nonleaf nodes in the primary segment tree. Each of these nonleaf nodes is the root of a secondary interval tree. Insertion in each of the relevant nodes in the secondary interval tree takes $O(\log_2 N)$ time since this many nodes may have to be examined.

22. The insertion of each rectangle takes $O(\log_2^2 N)$ time. There are N rectangles.

23. At each level of the primary segment tree, we perform a one-dimensional stabbing query on an interval tree. This takes $O(\log_2 N + F)$ time. There are $\log_2 N$ levels in the primary segment tree, and the result follows.

24. See the solution to Exercise 15.

Solutions to Exercises in Section 3.2

1. Use a segment tree with a plane sweep once the endpoints of the lines have been sorted [166]. Fredman and Weide [637] have shown that it is $\Omega(N \cdot \log_2 N)$.

2. 453.

3. These intervals are contained in rectangles A and C, but the corresponding horizontal intervals do not overlap. Thus, these nodes are not marked for A and C at the same time.

4. We only need to record whether a node is covered by an interval (and how many times). The identity of the covering interval need not be recorded.

5. At each insertion and deletion, you must update the length of the overlap with the vertical scan line. This is done by recomputing the LEN fields of all nodes encountered during the insertion process with a COUNT field value of 0. It must also be recomputed for all nodes encountered during the deletion process with a COUNT field value that became 0 or that are ancestors of nodes with a COUNT field value that became 0. This is an $O(\log_2 N)$ process.

6. The procedure is very similar to that used for computing the area. The difference is that we must also take into account the contributions of the horizontal boundaries. In this case, we

must keep track of the number of disjoint segments in the segment tree. Each active disjoint segment $[y_b:y_t]$ at X_i contributes $2 \cdot (X_i - X_{i-1})$ to the perimeter unless there exists another segment $[y_a:y_b]$ or $[y_t:y_c]$. Besides keeping track of the lengths of the vertical segments that are in the interval corresponding to a node, the node also keeps track of twice the number of disjoint segments in its interval. In addition, each node contains two flags that indicate whether each of the endpoints of its corresponding interval is a bottom or top extreme of a segment in the segment tree. The space and time requirements are the same as for the computation of area. For more details, see [166, 1145].

7. See [1126].

9. At each insertion and deletion, you must update the area of the overlap with the scan plane. This is done by recomputing it for all nodes encountered during the insertion process that are currently unmarked. It must also be done for those nodes encountered during the deletion process that are no longer marked or are ancestors of nodes that are no longer marked. This is an $O(N)$ process.

11. See [1126].

13. Lee [1126] suggests that each point be treated as the center of a rectangle of size R. Now, compute the maximum clique (i.e., the identities of its members). Any point in the intersection of the maximum clique can be used as the center of R.

14. The solution is analogous to that of Exercise 13, except that, in the plane sweep, the total weights of the covering rectangles are recorded instead of their cardinality.

15. Use induction on the number of horizontal and vertical rectangles.

16. Property 1: Each top and bottom boundary goes through at most one cell in each slab. Each left and right boundary is totally contained in one slab.

    Property 2: Each cell can intersect at most $2 \cdot \sqrt{N}$ left and right boundaries of rectangles because of the way the slabs are defined. Each cell can intersect at most two top and bottom boundaries of V-rectangles and at most $\sqrt{N} + 1$ top and bottom boundaries of H-rectangles because of the way the cells are defined.

    Property 3: If the boundary of a rectangle intersects the cell, then the rectangle is either a V-rectangle or an H-rectangle with respect to the slab containing the cell. In the former case, the top and bottom boundaries of the rectangle are both cell boundaries, so the rectangle's intersection with the cell extends at least as far as the bottom and top boundaries of the cell (i.e., it is a vertical rectangle). In the latter case, the rectangle extends at least as far as the slab boundary in the left and right directions (i.e., it is a horizontal rectangle).

18. We only need to record whether a node is covered by an interval (and how many times). The identity of the covering interval need not be recorded.

21. Storing a $(d-1)$-dimensional rectangle in a $(d-1)$-dimensional quadtree of side length N uses $O(N^{d-2})$ space, and thus each insertion and deletion is an $O(N^{d-2})$ process.

24. An $O(N^2)$ time solution to this problem can be based on computing an arrangement of the lines forming boundaries of the triangles. An *arrangement* formed by a set of lines is the set of all bounded or unbounded polygonal regions (i.e., cells) determined by the lines. The arrangement formed by N lines in the plane can be computed in $O(N^2)$ time [543]. Once the arrangement has been obtained, we add up the area of all the cells in the arrangement that are contained in some triangle. It is not clear how to solve this problem in subquadratic time.

Solutions to Exercises in Section 3.3.1

1. 2^{i+1}.

2. A 4×4 area of blocks (i.e., 16 blocks) is the maximum since the rectangle corresponding to the representative point can have a side length that is bounded by four times the length of the block containing the representative point.

3. Each point of the PR quadtree corresponds to the center of each black block.

4. When a black block has three white brothers, then the block can be merged with its brothers to yield a node that is one level higher in the tree.

5. The center (C_x, C_y, C_z) is a location parameter, and the radius r is an extension parameter.

6. Five parameters are necessary: two for the centroid, two for the perpendicular extents, and one for the rotation from the horizontal line.

7. Representation 2 is similar to representation 3. It does not suffer from a large unpopulated underlying space as does representation 1.

8. Use Figure 3.12 as an illustration. It is a rectangular region whose upper-left corner coincides with the figure and whose lower-right corner is at (p, p) [1265].

9. Representation 3 is a clockwise rotation by 45 degrees of representation 1 subject to a scale factor of $\sqrt{2}$. Recall that representation 3 has two empty triangular regions at its upper-left and -right corners corresponding to the stipulation that both starting and terminating endpoints of intervals lie in the underlying space.

10. For representation 1, the representative points are clustered within a band of width $s/\sqrt{2}$ above the diagonal that runs through the underlying space. On the other hand, for representation 3, the representative points are clustered in a band of width s above the horizontal axis. In this case, we can shrink the underlying space when using representation 3 to be of size $w \times s$. On the other hand, when using representation 1, the underlying space does remain $w \times w$, unless some rotation is performed, in which case it is the same (i.e., $w\sqrt{2} \times s/\sqrt{2} = w \times s$), but the query processing will be more complex. Thus, the ratio of the useful space to the total underlying space is much larger when using representation 3 instead of representation 1.

11. The solution is identical to that for representation 3 subject to the clockwise rotation by 45 degrees of the search regions as described in the solution to Exercise 9.

13. A four-dimensional conelike region with the line at its tip and in the C_x-C_y plane.

14. A four-dimensional conelike region with the circle at its tip and in the C_x-C_y plane.

15. Three-dimensional conelike regions with the (a) point, (b) line, (c) circle, and (d) rectangle at its tip and in the C_x-C_y plane.

16. (a) A cone-shaped region whose tip is at C and that opens in the direction of smaller radius values.

    (b) A cone-shaped region whose tip is at C and that opens in the direction of larger radius values.

17. Kurlander and Bier [1096] suggest using the center of mass and the point farthest from the center of mass. If there is more than one such farthest point, then the representative point is not unique.

18. Let P denote a pointer to a record, and let A take on the names of the coordinate axes (i.e., 'X' and 'Y' in two dimensions). Let the query point be represented by a record of type *point* with a field $\mathrm{VAL}(P, A)$ indicating its coordinate values. Let the rectangle be represented by a record of type *rectangle* with fields $\mathrm{MIN}(P, A)$, $\mathrm{MAX}(P, A)$, $\mathrm{EXT}(P, A)$, $\mathrm{CENT}(P, A)$, and $\mathrm{HEXT}(P, A)$, corresponding to the minimum value along coordinate axis A, maximum value along coordinate axis A, extent along coordinate axis A, centroid along coordinate axis A, and half-extent along coordinate axis A, respectively. Each of the rectangle representations makes use of a subset of these fields.

    Using representation 1, we have the following code sequence, which requires at most two comparison operations for each coordinate axis.

```
1  value pointer point P
2  value pointer rectangle R
3  value axis I
4  if VAL(P, I) < MIN(R, I) or VAL(P, I) > MAX(R, I) then 'NOTINRECT'
5  endif
```

Using representation 2, we have the following code sequence, which requires one subtraction, one comparison, and one test for a negative result after a subtraction. In most machine architectures, a test for a negative result immediately after an arithmetic operation requires only a single conditional branch operation (an optimizing compiler should be able to exploit this property when compiling the code below).

```
1  value pointer point P
2  value pointer rectangle R
3  value axis I
4  integer X
5  X ← VAL(P, I) − MIN(R, I)
6  if X < 0 then 'NOTINRECT'
7  endif
8  if X > EXT(R, I) then 'NOTINRECT'
9  endif
```

Using representation 3, we have the following code sequence, which requires one subtraction, one comparison, one negation operation (which is typically an inexpensive operation), and one test for negative result from an arithmetic operation.

```
1  value pointer point P
2  value pointer rectangle R
3  value axis I
4  integer X
5  X ← VAL(P, I) − CENT(R, I)
6  if X < 0 then X ← −X
7  endif
8  if X > HEXT(R, I) then 'NOTINRECT'
9  endif
```

Solutions to Exercises in Section 3.3.2.1

3. Oustehout [1439] attributes the following proof to Carlo H. Séquin. Use induction. Insert the rectangles one at a time in order from right to left. When there is one rectangle, there are four space tiles. Each additional rectangle, say R, causes the creation of at most three new space tiles as follows. The top and bottom edges of R can each cause a space tile to be split, thereby creating one new space tile apiece. Only one new space tile will be created to the left of R since we are inserting them in right-to-left order and there can be no existing rectangle to the left of R at the time of its insertion. No additional space tile is created to the right of R. Note that the rectangles are inserted in a particular order to obtain the upper bound; however, the final configuration is independent of the order of insertion.

4. At least two of the rectangles have collinear edges.

5. Suppose that the search starts at one of the rightmost rectangles. First, move up or down until locating a tile whose vertical range covers the point. Next, move left or right until finding a horizontal range that contains the point. This may require several iterations due to vertical misalignment resulting from horizontal motion during the search [1439].

6. Locate a rectangle that intersects a corner of the window—say the lower-left corner. Now, use the links to traverse the set of rectangles with the window's boundaries serving to indicate the direction in which the traversal should proceed. Initially, up links are followed until a tile is encountered outside the window. Next, follow a right link and a down link.

Solutions to Exercises in Section 3.3.2.2

1. No. For example, consider rectangles C and D in Figure 3.1.

2. Let (K_0, K_1, K_2, K_3) represent a rectangle whose lower-left corner is at (K_0, K_1) and whose upper-right corner is at (K_2, K_3). Assume that node P is at level j of the four-dimensional k-d tree. Therefore, at P, we discriminate on key $K_{j \bmod 4}(P)$. With P are stored the lower and upper bounds of key $K_{j \bmod 4}$. The lower and upper bounds of the remaining keys are obtained

from the three ancestors of P in the four-dimensional k-d tree. Thus, only two bound values need to be stored at each node. However, these bound values may not be so useful. For example, when storing rectangles in a 4-d tree, the value of K_0 at the root is an upper bound for the left edges of rectangles in LoChild, which is of little use in cutting off searches.

Rosenberg [1571] suggests storing three values at each node, LoMinBound, HiMax-Bound, and OtherBound. LoMinBound corresponds to the minimum value of a left or bottom edge in LoChild, and HiMaxBound is the maximum value of a right or top edge in HiChild. For a node that discriminates on a left or bottom edge, OtherBound is the maximum value of a right or top edge in LoChild, while for a node that discriminates on a right or top edge, it is the minimum value of a left or bottom edge in HiChild. At the root we discriminate on the left edges of rectangles. LoMinBound is the minimum value of a left edge in LoChild. HiMaxBound is the maximum value of a right edge in HiChild. OtherBound is the maximum value of a right edge of a rectangle in LoChild. The minimum value of a left edge of a rectangle in HiChild is the value of the discriminator key (i.e., K_0).

Searches in LoChild are cut off if the left edge of the search region exceeds Other-Bound or if the right edge of the search region is less than LoMinBound. Searches in HiChild are cut off if the left edge of the search region exceeds HiMaxBound or the right edge of the search region is less than K_0. The cutoffs for searches at nodes in the remaining three levels are obtained in a similar manner. Of course, at odd depths of the tree (assuming that the root is at depth 0), the search cutoffs are in terms of the top and bottom edges of the search region.

6. Traversing the four-dimensional k-d tree is an $O(N)$ process. Every node must be intersected with the remaining nodes in the tree. Pruning at every right subtree means that the number of comparison operations that are made is $O(N \cdot \log_2 N)$ since this is the total path length, and for a node at depth L, at most L right subtrees will be examined.

Solutions to Exercises in Section 3.3.2.4

1. The rationale is the same as that in a binary search tree, where the worst-case depth arises when the points are inserted in sorted (i.e., increasing order). In other words, the fact that the data is constantly increasing means that as full buckets are split, some of the newly created buckets will never be inserted into again.

Solutions to Exercises in Section 3.3.2.5

1. If the maximum value in LoChild(P) is greater than the minimum value in HiChild(P), and the point lies between the maximum and minimum values.

Solutions to Exercises in Section 3.4.1.2

1.
```
1   quadrant procedure CifCompare(P, Cx, Cy)
2   /* Return the quadrant of the MX-CIF quadtree rooted at position (Cx, Cy) that
         contains the centroid of rectangle P. */
3   value pointer rectangle P
4   value real Cx, Cy
5   return(if C(P, 'X') < Cx then
6             if C(P, 'Y') < Cy then 'SW'
7             else 'NW'
8             endif
9           else if C(P, 'Y') < Cy then 'SE'
10          else 'NE'
11          endif)
```

2. 1 **direction procedure** BINCOMPARE(P, C_V, V)
    2 /* Determine whether rectangle P lies to the left of, right of, or contains the line
       $V = C_V$. */
    3 **value pointer rectangle** P
    4 **value real** C_V
    5 **value axis** V
    6 **return**(**if** $(C(P,V) - L(P,V)) < C_V$ **and** $C_V < (C(P,V) + L(P,V))$ **then**
    7   'BOTH'
    8   **else if** $C_V < C(P,V)$ **then** 'RIGHT'
    9   **else** 'LEFT'
    10   **endif**)

3. 1 **Boolean procedure** CIFSEARCH(P, R, C_x, C_y, L_x, L_y)
    2 /* Determine whether rectangle P intersects any of the rectangles in the MX-CIF
       quadtree rooted at node R. It corresponds to a region of size $2 \cdot L_x \times 2 \cdot L_y$
       centered at (C_x, C_y). */
    3 **value pointer rectangle** P
    4 **value pointer cnode** R
    5 **value real** C_x, C_y, L_x, L_y
    6 **quadrant** Q;
    7 /* S_x and S_y contain multiplicative scale factors to aid in the location of the cen-
       ters of the quadrant children while descending the tree */
    8 **preload real array** S_x['NW','NE','SW','SE'] **with** $-1.0, 1.0, -1.0, 1.0$
    9 **preload real array** S_y['NW','NE','SW','SE'] **with** $1.0, 1.0, -1.0, -1.0$
    10 **if** ISNULL(R) **then return** FALSE
    11 **else if not** RECTINTERSECT(P, C_x, C_y, L_x, L_y)) **then return** FALSE
    12 **else if** CROSSAXIS(P, BIN(R, 'Y'), C_y, L_y, 'Y') **or**
    13   CROSSAXIS(P, BIN(R, 'X'), C_x, L_x, 'X') **then**
    14   **return** TRUE
    15 **else**
    16   $L_x \leftarrow L_x/2.0$
    17   $L_y \leftarrow L_y/2.0$
    18   **for** Q **in** {'NW','NE','SW','SE'} **do**
    19   **if** CIFSEARCH(P, CHILD(R, Q), $C_x + S_x[Q] * L_x, C_y + S_y[Q] * L_y$,
    20   L_x, L_y)
    21   **then return** TRUE
    22   **endif**
    23   **return** FALSE
    24   **enddo**
    25 **endif**

    1 **Boolean procedure** CROSSAXIS(P, R, C_V, L_V, V)
    2 /* Determine whether rectangle P intersects any of the rectangles that are stored
       in the binary tree rooted at node R, which corresponds to a segment of the V
       axis of length $2 \cdot L_V$ centered at C_V. */
    3 **value pointer rectangle** P
    4 **value pointer bnode** R
    5 **value real** C_V, L_V
    6 **value axis** V
    7 **direction** D
    8 /* F_v contains multiplicative factors to aid in the location of the centers of the
       segments of the axis while descending the tree */
    9 **preload real array** F_v['LEFT','RIGHT'] **with** $-1.0, 1.0$
    10 **if** ISNULL(R) **then return** FALSE
    11 **elseif not** ISNULL(RECT(R)) **and**
    12   RECTINTERSECT(P, C(RECT(R), 'X'), C(RECT(R), 'Y'),
    13   L(RECT(R), 'X'), L(RECT(R), 'Y')) **then**
    14   **return** TRUE
    15 **else**
    16   $D \leftarrow$ BINCOMPARE(P, C_V, V)
    17   $L_V \leftarrow L_V/2.0$
    18   **return**(**if** $D =$ 'BOTH' **then**

```
19          CROSSAXIS(P,CHILD(R,'LEFT'),C_V − L_V,L_V,V) or
20          CROSSAXIS(P,CHILD(R,'RIGHT'),C_V + L_V,L_V,V)
21       else CROSSAXIS(P,CHILD(R,D),C_V + F_v[D] ∗ L_V,L_V,V)
22       endif)
23    endif
```

4.
```
 1    procedure CIFINSERT(P,R,C_x,C_y,L_x,L_y)
 2    /* Insert rectangle P into the MX-CIF quadtree rooted at node R. It corresponds
         to a region of size 2 · L_x × 2 · L_y centered at (C_x,C_y). If the tree is empty, then
         R is set to point to the new root. Procedure CREATE sets all pointer fields to
         NIL. */
 3    value pointer rectangle P
 4    reference pointer cnode R
 5    value real C_x,C_y,L_x,L_y
 6    pointer cnode T
 7    quadrant Q
 8    direction D_x,D_y
 9    /* S_x and S_y contain multiplicative scale factors to aid in the location of the cen-
         ters of the quadrant children while descending the tree */
10    preload real array S_x['NW','NE','SW','SE'] with −1.0,1.0,−1.0,1.0
11    preload real array S_y['NW','NE','SW','SE'] with 1.0,1.0,−1.0,−1.0
12    if ISNULL(R) then /* The tree at R is initially empty */
13       R ← CREATE(cnode)
14    endif
15    T ← R
16    D_x ← BINCOMPARE(P,C_x,'X')
17    D_y ← BINCOMPARE(P,C_y,'Y')
18    while D_x ≠ 'BOTH' and D_y ≠ 'BOTH' do
19       /* Locate the axis of the quadrant in which P belongs */
20       Q ← CIFCOMPARE(P,C_x,C_y)
21       if ISNULL(CHILD(T,Q)) then CHILD(T,Q) ← CREATE(cnode)
22       endif
23       T ← CHILD(T,Q)
24       L_x ← L_x/2.0
25       C_x ← C_x + S_x[Q] ∗ L_x
26       L_y ← L_y/2.0
27       C_y ← C_y + S_y[Q] ∗ L_y
28       D_x ← BINCOMPARE(P,C_x,'X')
29       D_y ← BINCOMPARE(P,C_y,'Y')
30    enddo
31    if D_x = 'BOTH' then /* P belongs on the y axis */
32       INSERTAXIS(P,T,C_y,L_y,'Y')
33    else INSERTAXIS(P,T,C_x,L_x,'X') /* P belongs on the x axis */
34    endif
```

```
 1    procedure INSERTAXIS(P,R,C_V,L_V,V)
 2    /* Insert rectangle P into the V binary tree rooted at MX-CIF node R. It corre-
         sponds to a segment of the V axis of length 2 · L_V centered at C_V. If the V
         axis is empty, then R is set to point to the new root. Procedure CREATE sets
         all pointer fields to NIL. */
 3    value pointer rectangle P
 4    reference pointer cnode R
 5    value real C_V,L_V
 6    value axis V
 7    pointer bnode T
 8    direction D
 9    /* F_v contains multiplicative factors to aid in the location of the centers of the
         segments of the axis while descending the tree */
10    preload real array F_v['LEFT','RIGHT'] with −1.0,1.0
11    T ← BIN(R,V)
12    if ISNULL(T) then /* The V axis at T is initially empty */
13       T ← BIN(R,V) ← CREATE(bnode)
```

14 **endif**

15 $D \leftarrow \text{BINCOMPARE}(P, C_V, V)$

16 **while** $D \neq$ 'BOTH' **do**

17   /* Locate the axis subdivision point that contains P */

18   **if** $\text{ISNULL}(\text{CHILD}(T, D))$ **then** $\text{CHILD}(T, D) \leftarrow \text{CREATE}(\textbf{bnode})$

19   **endif**

20    $T \leftarrow \text{CHILD}(T, D)$

21    $L_V \leftarrow L_V / 2.0$

22    $C_V \leftarrow C_V + F_v[D] * L_V$

23    $D \leftarrow \text{BINCOMPARE}(P, C_V, V)$

24 **enddo**

25 $\text{RECT}(T) \leftarrow P$

5.   1 **procedure** $\text{CIFDELETE}(P, R, C_x, C_y, L_x, L_y)$

2 /* Delete rectangle P from the MX-CIF quadtree rooted at node R. It corresponds to a region of size $2 \cdot L_x \times 2 \cdot L_y$ centered at (C_x, C_y). */

3 **value pointer rectangle** P

4 **reference pointer cnode** R

5 **value real** C_x, C_y, L_x, L_y

6 **pointer cnode** $T, F_T, R_B, TempC$

7 **pointer bnode** $B, F_B, TempB, T_B$

8 **quadrant** Q, Q_F

9 **direction** D, D_F

10 **axis** V

11 **real** C_V, L_V

12 /* S_x and S_y contain multiplicative scale factors to aid in the location of the centers of the quadrant children while descending the tree: */

13 **preload real array** $S_x[\text{'NW','NE','SW','SE'}]$ **with** $-1.0, 1.0, -1.0, 1.0$

14 **preload real array** $S_y[\text{'NW','NE','SW','SE'}]$ **with** $1.0, 1.0, -1.0, -1.0$

15 /* F_v contains multiplicative factors to aid in the location of the centers of the segments of the axis while descending the tree: */

16 **preload real array** $F_v[\text{'LEFT','RIGHT'}]$ **with** $-1.0, 1.0$

17 **if** $\text{ISNULL}(R)$ **then return** /* The tree is empty */

18 **endif**

19 $T \leftarrow R$

20 $F_T \leftarrow \text{NIL}$

21 **while** $\text{BINCOMPARE}(P, C_x, V \leftarrow \text{'X'}) \neq$ 'BOTH' **and**

22    $\text{BINCOMPARE}(P, C_y, V \leftarrow \text{'Y'}) \neq$ 'BOTH' **do**

23   /* Locate the quadrant in which P belongs */

24    $Q \leftarrow \text{CIFCOMPARE}(P, C_x, C_y)$

25   **if** $\text{ISNULL}(\text{CHILD}(T, Q))$ **then return** ; /* P is not in the tree */

26   **endif**

27   **if not** $\text{ISNULL}(\text{CHILD}(T, \text{CQUAD}(Q)))$ **or**

28   **not** $\text{ISNULL}(\text{CHILD}(T, \text{OPQUAD}(Q)))$ **or**

29   **not** $\text{ISNULL}(\text{CHILD}(T, \text{CCQUAD}(Q)))$ **or**

30   **not** $\text{ISNULL}(\text{BIN}(T, \text{'X'}))$ **or**

31   **not** $\text{ISNULL}(\text{BIN}(T, \text{'Y'}))$ **then**

32      $F_T \leftarrow T$ /* Reset F_T and Q_F, which keep track of the common ancestor MX-CIF node with more than one child or at least one nonempty axis. */

33      $Q_F \leftarrow Q$

34   **endif**

35    $T \leftarrow \text{CHILD}(T, Q)$

36    $L_x \leftarrow L_x / 2.0$

37    $C_x \leftarrow C_x + S_x[Q] * L_x$

38    $L_y \leftarrow L_y / 2.0$

39    $C_y \leftarrow C_y + S_y[Q] * L_y$

40 **enddo**

41 $V \leftarrow \text{OTHERAXIS}(V)$ /* Reset the axis since $V = C_V$ passes through P */

42 $R_B \leftarrow T$

43 $F_B \leftarrow \text{NIL}$

```
44   B ← BIN(T, V)
45   C_V ← if V = 'X' then C_x
46        else C_y
47        endif
48   L_V ← if V = 'X' then L_x
49        else L_y
50        endif
51   D ← BINCOMPARE(P, C_V, V)
52   while not ISNULL(B) and D ≠ 'BOTH' do
53      /* Locate the point along B's V axis containing P */
54      if not ISNULL(CHILD(B, OPDIRECTION(D))) or not ISNULL(RECT(B)) then
55         F_B ← B /* Reset the nearest ancestor binary tree node that has a rectangle
                      associated with it or more than one child. F_B and D_F keep track
                      of this information */
56         D_F ← D
57      endif
58      B ← CHILD(B, D)
59      L_V ← L_V / 2.0
60      C_V ← C_V + F_v[D] * L_V
61      D ← BINCOMPARE(P, C_V, V)
62   enddo
63   if ISNULL(B) or not SAMERECTANGLE(P, RECT(B)) then
64      return /* P is not in the tree */
65   elseif not ISNULL(CHILD(B, 'LEFT')) or
66          not ISNULL(CHILD(B, 'RIGHT')) then
67      RETURNTOAVAIL(RECT(B)) /* No collapsing is possible */
68      RECT(B) ← NIL
69   else /* Attempt to perform collapsing */
70      T_B ← if ISNULL(F_B) then BIN(R_B, V) /* Collapse the entire binary tree */
71           else CHILD(F_B, D_F)
72           endif
73      D ← 'LEFT'
74      while T_B ≠ B do /* Collapse the binary tree one level at a time */
75         if ISNULL(CHILD(T_B, D)) then D ← OPDIRECTION(D)
76         endif
77         TempB ← CHILD(T_B, D)
78         CHILD(T_B, D) ← NIL
79         RETURNTOAVAIL(T_B)
80         T_B ← TempB
81      enddo
82      RETURNTOAVAIL(RECT(B))
83      RETURNTOAVAIL(B)
84      if not ISNULL(F_B) then /* The V axis is not empty */
85         CHILD(F_B, D_F) ← NIL
86      else /* The V axis is empty, try to collapse MX-CIF nodes */
87         BIN(R_B, V) ← NIL
88         if not ISNULL(BIN(R_B, OTHERAXIS(V))) or
89            not ISNULL(CHILD(R_B, 'NW')) or
90            not ISNULL(CHILD(R_B, 'NE')) or
91            not ISNULL(CHILD(R_B, 'SW')) or
92            not ISNULL(CHILD(R_B, 'SE'))
93            then return /* No further collapsing is possible */
94         endif
95         T ← if ISNULL(F_T) then R /* Collapse the entire MX-CIF quadtree */
96             else CHILD(F_T, Q_F)
97             endif
98         while T ≠ R_B do /* Collapse one level at a time */
99            Q ← 'NW'
100           while ISNULL(CHILD(T, Q)) do Q ← CQUAD(Q)
101           enddo
102           TempC ← CHILD(T, Q)
```

831

```
103          CHILD(T, Q) ← NIL
104          RETURNTOAVAIL(T)
105          T ← TempC
106       enddo
107       RETURNTOAVAIL(R_B)
108       if ISNULL(F_T) then R ← NIL   /* The tree contained just one node */
109       else CHILD(F_T, Q_F) ← NIL   /* Reset the link of the nearest ancestor */
110       endif
111    endif
112 endif
```

6. For example, suppose that two rectangles i and j share an edge that is coincident with the y axis that passes through block b. Assume, without loss of generality, that rectangle i is adjacent to the y axis in the SE quadrant of b whose block we call c, while j is adjacent to the y axis in the SW quadrant of b whose block we call d. Now, we see that procedure CIFINSERT in the solution to Exercise 4 will insert i in block b while inserting j in block d. Thus we do not have a real problem except that i should really have been inserted into block c instead of b since c is smaller than b. However, the remaining operations such as CIFDELETE in this exercise still work correctly if this change is made.

7. Procedure INSERTAXIS in the solution to Exercise 4 will insert the first rectangle properly. However, insertion of the second rectangle will overwrite the RECT field of the node containing the result of the first insertion, thereby resulting in a loss of the first rectangle.

9. If the tree is empty, then the rectangle is inserted. This can be resolved by introducing a check for this case in procedure CIFINSERT.

16. Letting o and b denote the two rectangles, l and h denote the lower and high boundary, respectively, and x and y denote the two sides, we have

$$test = o_{lx} < b_{hx} \text{ and } b_{lx} < o_{hx} \text{ and } o_{ly} < b_{hy} \text{ and } b_{ly} < o_{hy}.$$

17. Letting o and b denote the two rectangles, l and h denote the lower and high boundary, respectively, and x and y denote the two sides, we have

$$test = ((o_{lx} = b_{hx} \text{ or } b_{lx} = o_{hx}) \text{ and } o_{ly} \leq b_{hy} \text{ and } b_{ly} \leq o_{hy}) \text{ or } ((o_{ly} = b_{hy} \text{ or } b_{ly} = o_{hy})$$
$$\text{and } o_{lx} \leq b_{hx} \text{ and } b_{lx} \leq o_{hx}).$$

34. Consider the four points $A = (5, 6)$, $B = (6, 5)$, $C = (0, 4)$, and $D = (4, 0)$. The closest point to A is B, the closest point to B is A, the closest point to C is A, and the closest point to D is B. The result is that the rectangles formed by A and C and by B and D intersect.

Solutions to Exercises in Section 3.4.2

3. There are several cases. Assume without loss of generality that l is an x partition. If w intersects l but does not intersect p, then we just need to compare the y coordinate values of the elements of S. If w does not intersect l, then we just need to compare one of the two x coordinate values of the elements of S while we still need to compare both of the y coordinate values of these elements.

Solutions to Exercises in Section 3.4.3

6. If subrectangle s of rectangle object r is an element of a list l of type 1, then the lower-left corner of r is also contained in l. However, r has just one lower-left corner, and there is just one subrectangle s that contains the lower-left corner. Thus, the subrectangle s containing the lower-left corner of r can be an element of only one list of type 1, and hence r can be pointed at by only one list of type 1.

7. When a block b is completely contained in window w, then for each subrectangle s of r that is an element of lists of type 2–4, there will be another subrectangle t of r that is in an adjacent block a to the left of, below, and to the southeast of b that is overlapped by w and can be reported when a is processed. When a block b is partially contained in w so that only the left (bottom) and not the bottom (left) side of b intersects w, then for each subrectangle s of r that is an element of lists of type 3 and 4 (2 and 4), there will be another subrectangle t of r that is in an adjacent block a below (to the left of) b that is overlapped by w and can be reported when a is processed. When a block b is partially contained in w so that both the left and bottom sides of b intersect w, then there are no adjacent blocks to the left of and below b that overlap w, and thus elements of all of the four lists associated with b must be examined for intersection with b and reported if they intersect w.

8. There are 16 cases corresponding to 4 instances of only one side of the block being intersected; 6 instances of two sides of the block being intersected, 4 of which correspond to the sides being adjacent and two of which correspond to the sides being opposite; 4 instances of three sides of the block being intersected; 1 instance of all sides being intersected; and 1 instance of none of the sides of the block being intersected. The type of intersection can be identified using a number ranging from 0 (all sides of the block being intersected) to 15 (none of the sides of the block being intersected). Letting o and b denote the object and block, respectively, l and h denote the lower and high boundary, respectively, and x and y denote the two sides, we have

$$test = (o_{lx} > b_{lx}) + 2 \cdot (o_{ly} > b_{ly}) + 4 \cdot (o_{hx} < b_{hx}) + 8 \cdot (o_{hy} < b_{hy})$$

Solutions to Exercises in Section 4.1.2

1. The elements of the search hierarchy for the MX-CIF quadtree correspond to the objects (type 0), while the remaining elements correspond to rectangular regions resulting from a quaternary or binary regular decomposition of the underlying space (types 1, 2, and 3), which play the same role as the bounding rectangles in the R-tree search hierarchy. In particular, we have elements corresponding to nodes in the two-dimensional MX-CIF quadtree (type 3), nodes in the one-dimensional MX-CIF quadtree corresponding to objects that overlap the horizontal (i.e., x) axis passing through the center of a block corresponding to a two-dimensional MX-CIF quadtree node (type 2), and nodes in the one-dimensional MX-CIF quadtree corresponding to objects that overlap the vertical (i.e., y) axis passing through the center of a block corresponding to a two-dimensional MX-CIF quadtree node (type 1). Elements of type 3 can produce elements of types 0, 1, 2, and 3;[1] elements of type 2 can produce elements of types 0 and 2; and elements of type 1 can produce elements of types 0 and 1. The use of quadtree blocks as elements in the MX-CIF quadtree search hierarchy is similar to the use of bounding rectangles in the R-tree search hierarchy, with the difference being that for the R-tree, we have minimum bounding rectangles, while for the MX-CIF quadtree, we have minimum enclosing square (i.e., quadtree) blocks and minimum enclosing rectangle blocks that are the result of the application of a recursive halving process along a single dimension of the corresponding two-dimensional MX-CIF quadtree block. The distance functions are defined in the same way as for the R-tree and hold for all of the combinations of argument types. As in the R-tree, the distance functions also obey the condition that $d_t(q, e_t) \leq d_{t'}(q, e_{t'})$ for any element $e_{t'}$ that is a descendant of e_t in the search hierarchy.

Solutions to Exercises in Section 4.1.3

1. See [821, 848]. Since we assume uniformly distributed points, the expected area of the search region is k/N, and the expected area of each of the leaf node regions is c/N. The area of

---

[1] Depending on the implementation, elements of type 3 could also produce elements of type 0 corresponding to objects that overlap the center of the corresponding quadtree block. For the sake of simplicity, we assume that the objects are associated only with nodes of the one-dimensional MX-CIF quadtree.

a circle of radius r is πr^2, so for the search region, we have $\pi r^2 = k/N$, which means that its radius is $r = \sqrt{\frac{k}{\pi N}}$. The leaf node regions are squares, so their side length is $s = \sqrt{c/N}$. It is easy to see [821] that the number of leaf node regions intersected by the boundary of the search region is the same as that intersected by the boundary of its circumscribed square. Each of the four sides of the circumscribed square intersects $\lfloor 2r/s \rfloor \leq 2r/s$ leaf node regions. Since each two adjacent sides intersect the same leaf node region at a corner of the square, the expected number of leaf node regions intersected by the search region is bounded by

$$4(2r/s - 1) = 4\left(\frac{2\sqrt{k/(\pi N)}}{\sqrt{c/N}} - 1\right) = 4\left(2\sqrt{\frac{k}{\pi c}} - 1\right).$$

It is reasonable to assume that, on the average, half of the c points in these leaf nodes are inside the search region, and the other half are outside. Thus, the expected number of points remaining in the priority queue (the points in the dark shaded region in Figure 4.3) is at most

$$\frac{c}{2}4\left(2\sqrt{\frac{k}{\pi c}} - 1\right) = 2c\left(2\sqrt{\frac{k}{\pi c}} - 1\right) = \frac{4}{\sqrt{\pi}}\sqrt{ck} - 2c \approx 2.26\sqrt{ck} - 2c,$$

which is $O(\sqrt{kc})$.

2. See [821, 848]. The number of points inside the search region (the light shaded region in Figure 4.3) is k. Thus, the expected number of points in leaf nodes intersected by the search region is at most $k + 2.26\sqrt{ck} - 2c$. Since each leaf node contains c points, the expected number of leaf nodes that were accessed to get these points is bounded by $k/c + 2.26\sqrt{k/c} - 2$, which is $O(k + \sqrt{k})$.

3. The number of objects inserted into the priority queue is $O(k + \sqrt{k})$, and the expected size of the queue is bounded by $O(\sqrt{k})$. Therefore, the total cost is $O(k + \sqrt{k}) \cdot O(\log \sqrt{k}) = O(k \log k)$. If we take the nonleaf nodes into account, then the cost becomes somewhat more complicated.

4. Follow the proof in [851]. Use contradiction. Assume that the condition holds for all elements of the search hierarchy and assume that e_0 and e_0' represent two objects, with $d_0(q, e_0) < d_0(q, e_0')$, that are reported out of order (i.e., e_0' first). This implies that, at some point, e_0' is the element in the queue with the smallest distance from q, while an element e_t that represents some subset that contains e_0 is also on the queue. In other words, $d_t(q, e_t) \geq d(q, e_0')$. However, since $d_t(q, e_t) \leq d_0(q, e_0) < d(q, e_0')$, we have $d_t(q, e_t) < d(q, e_0')$, contradicting the assumption that e_0' is reported before e_0. Thus, the desired result holds.

5. Follow the proof in [851]. Use contradiction. Let o_k be the kth-nearest neighbor to q, and assume that e_t is an element that was visited before o_k was reported, with $d_t(q, e_t) > d(q, o_k)$. This assumption means that when e_t was visited, some ancestor $e_{t'}$ of the element e_0 representing o_k in the search hierarchy existed in the priority queue, with $d_t(q, e_t) \leq d_{t'}(q, e_{t'})$. By the correctness criterion, we have $d_{t'}(q, e_{t'}) \leq d_0(q, e_0) = d(q, o_k)$, which implies that $d_t(q, e_t) > d_{t'}(q, e_{t'})$. This contradicts the initial assumption that e_t was visited before o_k was reported, so the desired result holds.

Solutions to Exercises in Section 4.1.4

1. The following is an informal proof. The modified correctness criterion guarantees that each object has at least one instance in the hierarchy for which the original correctness criteria holds. Thus, by the solution to Exercise 4 in Section 4.1.3, we are guaranteed that at least one instance of each object is reported at the proper time. Furthermore, the algorithm ensures (in the **if** statement in line 20) that object instances that do not satisfy $d_t(q, e_t) \leq d_0(q, e_0)$ (as $t' = 0$) for all ancestors e_t of e_0 are never inserted into the priority queue, and that all duplicate instances of the same object that do satisfy it are removed together (in lines 14–16).

2. Follow the proof in [851]. Use contradiction. Let o_k be the kth-nearest neighbor to q. By the modified correctness criterion, we know that at least one instance e_0 of o_k exists in the search hierarchy such that $d_t(q, e_t) \leq d_0(q, e_0)$ for all ancestors e_t of e_0. Now, by way of contradiction, assume that $e_{t'}$ is an element that was visited before o_k was reported, with $d_t(q, e_{t'}) > d(q, o_k)$.

This assumption means that when $e_{t'}$ was visited, some ancestor e_t of e_0 in the search hierarchy existed in the priority queue, with $d_{t'}(q, e_{t'}) \leq d_t(q, e_t)$. Since $d_t(q, e_t) \leq d_0(q, e_0)$, this implies that $d_{t'}(q, e_{t'}) \leq d_0(q, e_0) = d(q, o_k)$. However, this contradicts the assumption that $d_t(q, e_{t'}) > d(q, o_k)$, so the desired result holds.

Solutions to Exercises in Section 4.1.5

4. Keep a counter c that indicates how many neighbors have been reported, and halt the algorithm once $c = k$.

5. See procedure BFTRAV in Section 4.2.6.

6. As pointed out in the text, all that is needed to obtain INCFARTHEST is to replace $d_{t'}(q, e_{t'})$ in line 17 of INCNEAREST by $-\hat{d}_{t'}(q, e_{t'})$.

7. As pointed out in the text, there are two ways of modifying the incremental nearest neighbor algorithm to be an incremental farthest neighbor algorithm. The first is by replacing $d_t(q, e_t)$ as a key for any element e_t on the priority queue with $-\hat{d}_t(q, e_t)$ and thereby leaving the algorithm unchanged. The second orders the elements on the priority queue in decreasing order of key values, using $\hat{d}_t(q, e_t)$ as a key value. Note that there is no need to modify the use of FRONTPRIORITYQUEUE in line 14 as now the element at the front of the priority queue is the one with the maximum distance from q, and if it is an object, then it would be the next object to be reported. The only modification required is to change the sense of the test in line 20 to be "$t' > 0$ or $d_{t'}(q, e_{t'}) \leq d_t(q, e_t)$."

8. Since region a is empty, it can also be safely ignored. Ignoring b is preferable as it is nonempty, and thus we save the cost of checking if its points can be members of the skyline, which we already know to be impossible.

Solutions to Exercises in Section 4.1.6

2. This is proved easily by noting that from the point of view of a graph, ignoring the spatial embedding of its vertices, all of the vertices that make up each of the regions r_{uj} are connected. Therefore, the only way that the space spanned by one of these regions associated with vertex w_1 incident at u_1 can be disconnected, say consisting of two regions g_1 and g_2, is if the shortest path from u_1 to some vertex v_2 in g_2 would "jump" from vertex v_1 in g_1 over some region that is associated with a vertex w_2 incident at u_1, which is impossible since the spatial network is planar.

3. Nonplanar spatial networks may lead to disconnected regions. Disconnected spatial networks can be handled by using a special color to indicate that the vertices are unreachable from the source vertex.

4. No. Although the two methods are equivalent, the original method is preferable as it only stores two values, while the alternative stores three values since a range consists of two values.

5. The space complexity would decrease as can be seen by results reported by Lindenbaum, Samet, and Hjaltason [1175]. However, the actual regions would have to be vectorized to create a polygonal map that could be complex in terms of the number of edges.

6. See [1749].

Solutions to Exercises in Section 4.2.1

1. Because this may tighten the value of D_k so that there is no need to process the remaining elements of A of e.

2. Four changes are necessary in forming KFARTHEST and DFTRAVFARTHEST:

   (a) Replace the condition "$d(q,o) < D_k$" in line 14 of DFTRAV with the condition "$d(q,o) > D_k$."

   (b) Use an alternative definition of distance that incorporates the upper-bound information. This can be done if we know that for every nonobject element e of the search hierarchy, $d(q,e) \geq d(q,e_0)$ for every object e_0 in e and that the relation $d(q,e) < D_k$ is satisfied.[2] Assuming that this property holds, define $d(q,e)$ as the maximum (instead of the minimum) possible distance from q to any object e_0 in nonobject e. This distance function d is termed $\hat{d}$ by Hjaltason and Samet in [851], who use it in a best-first incremental farthest neighbor finding algorithm.

   (c) Change the priority queue implementation of L so that it is ordered in such a way that accessing the nearest (instead of the farthest) of the k farthest neighbors, as well as updating (i.e., inserting and deleting the kth-farthest neighbor), can be performed without needless exchange operations. In other words, modify INSERTL to use MINPRIORITYQUEUE, the distance from q to the current nearest of the k farthest neighbors, instead of MAXPRIORITYQUEUE in line 12. Note that MINPRIORITYQUEUE is equivalent to FRONTPRIORITYQUEUE when priority is given to elements at a minimum distance.

   (d) Initialize D_k to 0 before the first invocation of DFTRAV instead of to ∞.

3. There is no longer any need to replace the condition "$d(q,o) < D_k$" in line 14 of DFTRAV with the condition "$d(q,o) > D_k$" as it is equivalent to the condition "$-d(q,o) < -D_k$." Moreover, there is no need to modify the priority queue implementation of L as the first element will still correspond to the element with the maximum distance (which is now the nearest of the farthest elements due to the use of negative distances). The only modification needed is to initialize D_k to $-\infty$ before the initial invocation of DFTRAV instead of to ∞.

4. The property of the alternative distance measure that $d(q,e) \geq d(q,e_0)$ for every object e_0 in e for all nonobject elements e means that if we process the elements e_p of the active list A of e in order of decreasing values of $d(q,e_p)$, and once we have found one element e_i in A of e such that $d(q,e_i) < D_k$, then $d(q,e_j) < D_k$ for all remaining elements e_j of A of e. In particular, this guarantees that none of these remaining elements need to be processed, and we simply exit the loop and backtrack to the parent of e or terminate if e is the root of the search hierarchy.

Solutions to Exercises in Section 4.2.2

1. Let o be an object in e_p, which means that $d(M_p,o) \leq r_{p,max}$. From the triangle inequality, we have $d(q,o) + d(M_p,o) \geq d(q,M_p)$. Subtracting $d(M_p,o)$ from both sides and making use of the inequality $d(M_p,o) \leq r_{p,max}$ yields $d(q,o) \geq d(q,M_p) - d(M_p,o) \geq d(q,M_p) - r_{p,max}$. Therefore, if $d(q,M_p) - r_{p,max} > D_k$, which is the distance to the current kth-nearest neighbor of q, then o cannot be the kth-nearest neighbor of q, and, in fact, no object o of e_p can be the kth-nearest neighbor of q as they all satisfy $d(M_p,o) \leq r_{p,max}$. Rewriting $d(q,M_p) - r_{p,max} > D_k$ as $D_k + r_{p,max} < d(q,M_p)$ leads to the desired result.

2. From the triangle inequality, we have $d(q,M_p) \leq d(q,o) + d(M_p,o)$. Subtracting $d(M_p,o)$ from both sides yields $d(q,M_p) - d(M_p,o) \leq d(q,o)$. Therefore, if $d(q,M_p) - d(M_p,o) > D_k$, which is the distance to the current kth-nearest neighbor of q, then o cannot be the kth-nearest neighbor of q. Rewriting $d(q,M_p) - d(M_p,o) > D_k$ as $D_k + d(M_p,o) < d(q,M_p)$ leads to the desired result.

3. From the triangle inequality, we have $d(q,p) \leq d(q,o) + d(o,p)$. Subtracting $d(o,p)$ from both sides leads to $d(q,p) - d(o,p) \leq d(q,o)$. Replacing $d(q,p)$ with d_2 and making use of the inequality $d(o,p) < d_2 - d_1$ results in $d_2 - (d_2 - d_1) < d(q,o)$, which is simplified to yield

---

[2] This stopping condition ensures that all objects at the distance of the kth-farthest neighbor are examined. Note that if the size of L is limited to k, and if there are two or more objects at distance D_k, then some of them may not be reported in the set of q's k farthest neighbors.

$d_1 < d(q,o)$. This inequality means that n at a distance of d_1 is closer to q than o, and thus o cannot be q's nearest neighbor.

4. Rule 2 stipulates that object o in element e_p at the deepest level of the search hierarchy with mean M_p and distance $r_{p,max}$ from M_p to the farthest object within e_p cannot be the kth-nearest neighbor of query object q if $D_k + d(o, M_p) < d(q, M_p)$, where D_k is the distance from q to the farthest of the current candidate k nearest neighbors. This rule is applicable to arbitrary objects in the sense that M_p can also be one of the objects in e_p, and this is how we use it here. Letting $M_p = p$, $k = 1$, and $D_1 = d(q,n) = d_1$, we have $D_1 + d(o, p) < d(q, p)$, which is the same as $d_1 + d(o, p) < d_2$. This can be rewritten as $d(o, p) < d_2 - d_1$, which is Lemma 2.2, and the desired equivalence holds.

5. Set d_1 to be the distance of the current kth-nearest neighbor of q.

6. Let o be an object in e_p, which means that $d(M_p, o) \geq r_{p,min}$. From the triangle inequality we have $d(q, o) + d(q, M_p) \geq d(M_p, o)$. Subtracting $d(q, M_p)$ from both sides and making use of the inequality $d(M_p, o) \geq r_{p,min}$ yields $d(q, o) \geq d(M_p, o) - d(q, M_p) \geq r_{p,min} - d(q, M_p)$. Therefore, if $r_{p,min} - d(q, M_p) > D_k$, which is the distance to the current kth-nearest neighbor of q, then $d(q, o) > D_k$ and o cannot be the kth-nearest-neighbor of q, and in fact, no object o of e_p can be the kth-nearest neighbor of q as they all satisfy $d(M_p, o) \geq r_{p,min}$. Rewriting $r_{p,min} - d(q, M_p) > D_k$ as $D_k + d(q, M_p) < r_{p,min}$ leads to the desired result.

7. From the triangle inequality, we have $d(M_p, o) \leq d(q, M_p) + d(q, o)$. Subtracting $d(q, M_p)$ from both sides yields $d(M_p, o) - d(q, M_p) \leq d(q, o)$. Therefore, if $d(M_p, o) - d(q, M_p) > D_k$, which is the distance to the current kth-nearest neighbor of q, then $d(q, o) > D_k$ and o cannot be the kth-nearest neighbor of q. Rewriting $d(M_p, o) - d(q, M_p) > D_k$ as $D_k + d(q, M_p) < d(M_p, o)$ leads to the desired result.

8. (Feustel and Shapiro [610]) From the triangle inequality, we have $d(o, p) \leq d(q, o) + d(q, p)$. Making use of $d(o, p) > 2d(q, p)$, we have $2d(q, p) < d(o, p) \leq d(q, o) + d(q, p)$. Subtracting $d(q, p)$ from both sides of $d(o, p)$ leads to $d(q, p) < d(q, o)$, which is the desired result as it means that o is not the nearest neighbor of q as at least p is closer.

9. o cannot be the nearest neighbor of q if $d(o, M_p) > 2d(q, M_p)$. $d(o, M_p) > 2d(q, M_p)$ implies that $d(o, M_p) > d(q, M_p) + d(q, M_p)$. But, clearly $D_1 \leq d(q, M_p)$, which means that $d(o, M_p) > D_1 + d(q, M_p)$. This is Pruning Rule 4, and thus o cannot be the nearest neighbor of q.

10. Given the above constraints on k, $r_{p,min}$, M_p, o, and q, Pruning Rule 4 states that if $D_1 + d(q, M_p) < d(o, M_p)$, then o is not q's nearest neighbor. Similarly, Lemma 2.1 states that if $2d(q, M_p) < d(o, M_p)$, then o is not q's nearest neighbor. Now, since M_p is an object of e_p, and D_1 is the distance from q to its nearest known neighbor, we know that $D_1 \leq d(q, M_p)$. So, there are two cases:

    (a) If $D_1 = d(q, M_p)$, then Lemma 2.1 and Pruning Rule 4 are equivalent.

    (b) Otherwise, if $D_1 < d(q, M_p)$, which is the situation that we would normally expect to arise, then we see that $D_1 + d(q, M_p) < d(q, M_p) + d(q, M_p) = 2d(q, M_p)$. This last inequality implies that some object o may exist that cannot be pruned from the search by Lemma 2.1, while o can be pruned by Pruning Rule 4.

    This result, combined with the result of Exercise 9, means that, under the specified constraints, Pruning Rule 4 is tighter than Lemma 2.1.

11. Replace $d(q, p)$ with D_k, the distance to p, the current kth-nearest neighbor of q. In other words, restate Lemma 2.1 to stipulate that given a query object q and another object p that is the current kth-nearest neighbor of q, then any other object o such that $d(o, p) > 2d(q, p)$ cannot be the kth-nearest neighbor of q.

12. From the triangle inequality, $d(a, b) \leq d(a, q) + d(b, q)$ for any q. Choose q and let p be the object at a maximum distance from q, which means that $d(a, q) \leq d(q, p)$ and $d(b, q) \leq d(q, p)$. Therefore, $d(a, b) \leq d(a, q) + d(b, q) \leq d(q, p) + d(q, p) = 2d(q, p)$, which is the desired result.

13. From the triangle inequality, we have $d(q, M_p) + d(M_p, o) \geq d(q, o)$ for any object o in e_p. $d(M_p, o) \leq r_{p,max}$, and thus $d(q, M_p) + r_{p,max} \geq d(q, o)$. Therefore, if $D_1 \geq d(q, M_p) + r_{p,max}$, then $D_1 \geq d(q, o)$, and thus $d(q, M_p) + r_{p,max}$ is a better bound on the distance from q to its nearest neighbor.

14. Let o' be an object in e_p such that $d(M_p, o') = r_{p,min}$. There is at least one such object. From the triangle inequality, we have $d(q, o') \leq d(q, M_p) + d(M_p, o')$. By definition, $d(M_p, o') = r_{p,min}$, and thus $d(q, o') \leq d(q, M_p) + r_{p,min}$. Therefore, since there is an object o' within distance $d(q, M_p) + r_{p,min}$ of q, any object that is farther away may be removed from consideration. Therefore, the pruning distance D_1 may be safely reset to $\min(D_1, d(q, M_p) + r_{p,min})$.

15. Assume that $k = 1$. Consider element $e_a = (M_a, r_{a,max})$ with $d(q, M_a) = 1$ and $r_{a,max} = r_{a,min} = 20$, and element $e_b = (M_b, r_{b,max})$ with $d(q, M_b) = 2$ and $r_{b,max} = r_{b,min} = 4$. Since $r_{a,max} = r_{a,min} = 20$, we know that all of the objects in e_a are at a maximum distance $r_{a,max} = 20$ from M_a. Processing the active list in increasing MEANORPIVOTDIST order means that e_a is processed before e_b as $d(q, M_a)$ is less than $d(q, M_b)$. Thus, once e_a has been processed, we have that $19 \leq D_1 \leq 21$. Next, we process e_b, for which we know that $d(q, M_b) + r_{b,min} \leq 6$. When the active list A of e_b is generated, we can assume, without loss of generality, that its elements $e_i = (M_i, r_{i,max})$ can be formed in such a way that each of them satisfies $d(q, M_i) + r_{i,min} \leq 6 \leq 19$, and thus we can reset D_1 to 6.

16. If Pruning Rule 1 is satisfied, then $d(q, M_p) - r_{p,max} > D_1$, which means that $d(q, M_p) + r_{p,min} > D_1$, and thus Pruning Rule 5 cannot be applied. Similarly, if Pruning Rule 3 is satisfied, then $r_{p,min} - d(q, M_p) > D_1$, which means that $r_{p,min} + d(q, M_p) > D_1$, and thus Pruning Rule 5 cannot be applied. This should be obvious when we rewrite Pruning Rule 5 as MAXNEARESTDIST$(q, e_p) > D_1$ and Pruning Rules 1 and 3 as MINDIST$(q, e_p) > D_1$, and observe that MAXNEARESTDIST$(q, e_p) \geq$ MINDIST$(q, e_p) > D_1$.

17. The rationale for Pruning Rule 1 is that region E_k, containing all objects whose distance from q is greater than D_k, should be completely outside of element e_p, and thus it is possible to adapt it. The rationale for Pruning Rule 2 is that object o in e_p should be outside E_k while permitting the intersection of e_p and E_k to be nonempty, thereby making it possible to adapt it. However, Pruning Rules 3 and 4 are based on e_p having the shape of a multidimensional spherical shell and E_k being either completely inside the inner sphere of the spherical shell (i.e., Rule 3), or E_k being completely in the region formed by the union of the spherical shell e_p and the region spanned by the inner sphere of e_p, while o must be outside E_k and at the same time still be inside e_p (Rule 4). This means that Pruning Rules 3 and 4 rely on E_k being bounded, but E_k is unbounded, thereby making it impossible to adapt them. On the other hand, Pruning Rule 5 does not make use of the boundedness of E_k. The only important issue is whether e_p or its hole is totally contained within E_k, and thus Pruning Rule 5 is adaptable.

Alternatively, we could say that for finding the k farthest neighbors, Pruning Rules 3 and 4 are the same as Pruning Rules 1 and 2, respectively, in the sense that when q is completely inside the inner sphere of the spherical shell e_p (Rule 3), or when q is inside the union of e_p and the region spanned by the inner sphere of e_p, the only pruning that is possible is when the upper bound on the distance from q to any object in e_p (Rule 3) or to a specific object o (Rule 4) is less than D_k.

Pruning Rule 1 now stipulates that element e_p in the active list with mean M_p and distance $r_{p,max}$ from M_p to the farthest object within e_p cannot contain the kth-farthest neighbor of query object q if $D_k - r_{p,max} > d(q, M_p)$. In other words, Rule 1 amounts to computing the maximum distance from the query object q to an object in e_p (i.e., MAXDIST) and determining if it is less than D_k, the distance from q to the nearest of the current k candidate farthest neighbors of q. Rule 1 is illustrated by Figure S.9. Note that Rule 1 is applicable regardless of whether q is outside e_p (Figure S.9(a)) or in e_p (Figure S.9(b)). Moreover, it is also applicable even if e_p is a spherical shell.

Pruning Rule 2 now stipulates that object o in element e_p at the deepest level of the search hierarchy with mean M_p and distance $r_{p,max}$ from M_p to the farthest object within e_p cannot be the kth-farthest neighbor of query object q if $D_k - d(o, M_p) > d(q, M_p)$. Rule 2 is illustrated by Figure S.10. It is only meaningful when q is closer to M_p than D_k—that is, $d(q, M_p) < D_k$, and also only when $d(o, M_p) < D_k$. For this rule to be applicable, q can be both outside (Figure S.10(a)) and inside (Figure S.10(b)) e_p—that is, $d(q, M_p)$ has an arbitrary value (i.e., it is independent of $r_{p,max}$). In fact, D_k can also be such that all of the objects within D_k of q lie inside e_p (Figure S.10(c)).

Pruning Rules 1 and 2 make use of estimates of the maximum possible distance at which the farthest neighbor in nonobject element e can be found (i.e., MAXDIST) to prune the search process. The adaptation of Pruning Rule 5 makes use of estimates of the minimum possible distances at which the farthest neighbor can be found. The simplest way to do so is to use the minimum possible distance from q to an object in e (i.e., MINDIST) to tighten the estimate of

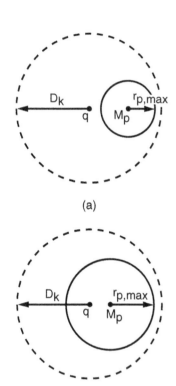

(a)

(b)

Figure S.9
Examples illustrating Pruning Rule 1 for computing the k farthest neighbors that eliminates element e_p and all its objects when $D_k - r_{p,max} > d(q, M_p)$: (a) query object q outside e_p, and (b) q inside e_p.

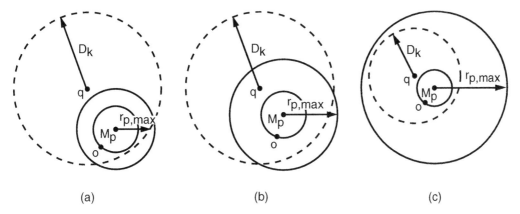

(a)   (b)   (c)

Figure S.10

Examples illustrating Pruning Rule 2 for computing the k farthest neighbors that eliminates any object o in element e_p when $D_k - d(o, M_p) > d(q, M_p)$: Query object q so that (a) query object q is outside e_p, (b) q is inside e_p, and (c) all of the objects within D_k of q lie inside e_p.

the distance to the farthest neighbor (i.e., D_1), which is an analog of the suggestion of Fukunaga and Narendra [666]. An even better estimate is to use the minimum possible distance from q to its farthest neighbor in e (referred to as MINFARTHESTDIST), which is an analog of the suggestion of Larsen and Kanal [1103].

The values of the MINDIST, MAXDIST, and MINFARTHESTDIST estimates are heavily dependent on the nature of the clustering process used to form the search hierarchy. For example, if all we know is that nonobject element e_p has mean M_p and distance $r_{p,max}$ from M to the farthest object within e, then the distance from q to its farthest neighbor cannot be smaller than $d(q, M_p) - r_{p,max}$ (i.e., MINDIST). In this case, Rule 5 results in setting D_1 to the maximum of D_1 and $d(q, M_p) - r_{p,max}$ (Figure S.11(a)), and we see that MINDIST and MINFARTHESTDIST are the same. On the other hand, if nonobject element e_p is a multidimensional spherical shell, then given that $r_{p,min}$ is the distance from M_p to the closest object within e_p, the distance from q to its farthest neighbor cannot be smaller than $d(q, M_p) - r_{p,min}$ (i.e., MINFARTHESTDIST). In this case, Rule 5 results in setting D_1 to the maximum of D_1 and $d(q, M_p) - r_{p,min}$ (Figure S.11(b)).

Note that, as in the case of the nearest neighbor, at the time we find that Rule 5 is applicable to element e_p, the actual object in e_p that could serve as the farthest neighbor has not yet been identified. Instead, all we are doing is setting a lower bound on the distance D_1 from q to it. The extension of Pruning Rule 5 to find the k ($k > 1$) farthest neighbors is not a simple matter, although it can be done, as discussed in Exercises 12 and 13 in Section 4.2.5.

18. FNDFTRAVFARTHEST is formed by modifying the priority queue as in the solution to Exercise 2 in Section 4.2.1 so that the first element in the priority queue L corresponds to the nearest of the k farthest neighbors instead of the farthest of the k nearest neighbors. The condition "$d(q, o) < D_k$" for the invocation of INSERTL in line 19 of FNDFTRAV is replaced with the condition "$d(q, o) > D_k$" in FNDFTRAVFARTHEST. D_k is initialized to 0 in KFARTHEST. Procedure FNDFTRAVFARTHEST does not use Pruning Rules 3 and 4, while Pruning Rules 1 and 2 are incorporated by replacing the conditions in lines 36 and 13 of FNDFTRAV with the conditions "$D_k > d(q, M_p) + r_{p,max}$" and "$D_k > d(q, M_p) + d(o, M_p)$," respectively. Pruning Rule 5 is incorporated by replacing the conditions in lines 29 and 30 of FNDFTRAV with "$d(q, M_p) < D_1$" and "$d(q, M_p) - r_{p,min} > D_1$," while D_1 in line 31 of FNDFTRAV is now reset to "$d(q, M_p) - r_{p,min}$." Finally, the elements of the active list in FNDFTRAVFARTHEST are sorted in decreasing order using MEANORPIVOTDIST$(q, e_p) = d(q, M_p)$ and are always processed in this order.

19. As in the solution to Exercise 3 in Section 4.2.1, replace all distances by their negation. Thus, $d(q, o)$ in lines 19 and 20 must be replaced with $-d(q, o)$. This means that the priority queue need not be modified in the sense that the first element still corresponds to the element with the maximum distance (which is now the nearest of the k farthest elements due to the use of negative distances). D_k is initialized to $-\infty$ in KFARTHEST. Pruning Rules 1 and 2 are incorporated by replacing the conditions in lines 36 and 13 of

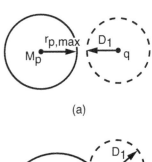

(a)

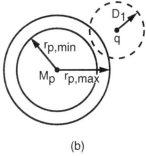

(b)

Figure S.11

Examples illustrating the applicability of Pruning Rule 5 for computing the farthest neighbor: (a) the MINDISTestimate that resets the distance D_1 from q to its farthest neighbor during the insertion into the active list of element e_p with M_p as the mean and distance $r_{p,max}$ from M_p to the farthest objects within e_p if $d(q, M_p) - r_{p,max} > D_1$, and (b) the MINFARTHESTDISTestimate that resets the distance D_1 from q to its farthest neighbor during the insertion into the active list of element e_p with mean M_p and r_{max} and r_{min} as the distances from M to the farthest and closest, respectively, objects within e_p if $d(q, M_p) - r_{p,min} > D_1$.

FNDFTRAV with the conditions "$D_k > d(q, M_p) + r_{p,max}$" and "$D_k > d(q, M) + d(o, M)$," respectively, which are rewritten as "$-d(q, M_p) - r_{p,max} > D_k$" and "$-d(q, M) - d(o, M) > D_k$," respectively, when we use negative distances (i.e., D_k is negative). Pruning Rule 5 is incorporated by replacing the conditions in lines 29 and 30 of FNDFTRAV with "$D_1 > d(q, M_p)$" and "$D_1 < d(q, M_p) - r_{p,min}$," respectively, which is rewritten as "$-d(q, M_p) > D_1$" and "$-d(q, M_p) + r_{p,min} < D_1$," respectively, when we use negative distances (i.e., D_1 is negative). In addition, D_1 in line 31 of FNDFTRAV is now reset to "$d(q, M_p) - r_{p,min}$," which is rewritten as "$-d(q, M_p) + r_{p,min}$" when we use negative distances. Finally, the elements of the active list in FNDFTRAVFARTHEST are sorted in increasing order using MEANORPIVOTDIST$(q, e_p) = -d(q, M_p)$ and are always processed in this order.

Solutions to Exercises in Section 4.2.3

1. Denote the query point by $q = (q_0, q_1, \ldots, q_{d-1})$ and the minimum bounding hyperrectangle by $H = [l_0, u_0] \times [l_1, u_1] \times \cdots \times [l_{d-1}, u_{d-1}]$. Moreover, let a_i be $l_i - q_i$ if $q_i < l_i$, $q_i - u_i$ if $u_i < q_i$, and 0 otherwise for $0 \leq i \leq d - 1$. Therefore, using the Euclidean distance metric, we have that MINDIST$(q, H) = \sqrt{\sum_{i=0}^{d-1} a_i^2}$.

2. Denote the query point by $q = (q_0, q_1, \ldots, q_{d-1})$ and the minimum bounding hyperrectangle by $H = [l_0, u_0] \times [l_1, u_1] \times \cdots \times [l_{d-1}, u_{d-1}]$. Moreover, let a_i be $|l_i - q_i|$ if $|l_i - q_i| > |q_i - u_i|$, and $|q_i - u_i|$ otherwise for $0 \leq i \leq d - 1$. Therefore, using the Euclidean distance metric, we have that MAXDIST$(q, H) = \sqrt{\sum_{i=0}^{d-1} a_i^2}$.

3. Denote the query point by $q = (q_0, q_1, \ldots, q_{d-1})$ and the minimum bounding hyperrectangle by $H = [l_0, u_0] \times [l_1, u_1] \times \cdots \times [l_{d-1}, u_{d-1}]$. Using the principle that every surface must contain a point, determine the farthest point on each surface and retain its minimum. For each dimension i, there are two surfaces. Clearly, the minimum of the maximums along dimension i will be attained at the surface that is closer to q. Therefore, let b_i be $|q_i - l_i|$ if $q_i \leq (l_i + u_i)/2$ and $|q_i - u_i|$ otherwise for $0 \leq i \leq d - 1$. Now, let a_j denote the distance to the farthest of the remaining possible corner points of the closest surface along dimension i, where a_j is $|q_j - l_j|$ if $q_j \geq (l_j + u_j)/2$ and $|q_j - u_j|$ otherwise for $0 \leq j \leq d - 1$ and $j \neq i$. Therefore, using the Euclidean distance metric, we have that MAXNEARESTDIST$(q, H) = \min_{0 \leq i \leq d-1} \sqrt{b_i^2 + \sum_{j=0, j \neq i}^{d-1} a_j^2}$.

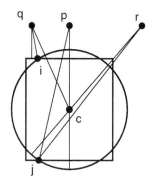

Figure S.12
Example showing the calculation of MINDIST and MAXDIST when the minimum bounding object is the intersection of the minimum bounding hyperrectangle and the minimum bounding hypersphere (e.g., an SR-tree).

4. The value of MINDIST depends on the relative position of the query object and the minimum bounding object. Katayama and Satoh [999] suggest using the maximum of the values of MINDIST for the minimum bounding hyperrectangle and for the minimum bounding hypersphere, which we denote by MINDISTSR. It is easy to see that MINDISTSR is a lower bound on the value of MINDIST by examining query point q in Figure S.12. From this figure it would appear that we should use the minimum of the distance from the query point to the points of intersection of the minimum bounding hypersphere with all of the surfaces of the minimum bounding hyperrectangle, which we call MINDISTINTER (i.e., i for query point q in Figure S.12). This solution is hinted at by Böhm, Berchtold, and Keim [224]. Unfortunately, MINDISTINTER may be too high as can be seen by examining query point p in Figure S.12. The real solution is to use a combination of these two methods. In particular, let p_r and p_s be the closest points to query point q on the minimum bounding hyperrectangle r and minimum bounding hypersphere s, respectively. If neither p_r nor p_s is on the minimum bounding object formed by the intersection of r and s, then the value of MINDISTSR is too low, and the correct value for MINDIST is MINDISTINTER. Otherwise, MINDISTSR is correct.

5. The value of MAXDIST also depends on the relative position of the query object and the minimum bounding object. We first form MAXDISTSR, which is the minimum of the values of MAXDIST for the minimum bounding hyperrectangle and for the minimum bounding hypersphere. It is easy to see that MAXDISTSR is an upper bound on the value of MAXDIST by examining query point p in Figure S.12. From this figure it would appear that we should use the maximum of the distance from p to the points of intersection of the minimum bounding hypersphere with all of the surfaces of the minimum bounding hyperrectangle, which we call MAXDISTINTER (i.e., j in Figure S.12). Unfortunately, MAXDISTINTER may be too low as can be seen by examining query point r in Figure S.12. The real solution is to use a combination of these two methods. In particular, let p_r and p_s be the farthest points from query

point q on the minimum bounding hyperrectangle r and minimum bounding hypersphere s, respectively. If neither p_r nor p_s is on the minimum bounding object formed by the intersection of r and s, then the value of MAXDISTSR is too high, and the correct value for MAXDIST is MAXDISTINTER. Otherwise, MAXDISTSR is correct.

6. Notwithstanding claims to the contrary [224], the value of MAXNEARESTDIST is obtained in an analogous manner to that when the minimum bounding object is a hyperrectangle. In particular, we find the farthest point on every surface that is a planar face (i.e., contributed by the minimum bounding hyperrectangle) and retain their minimum. Note that these points are the points of intersection of the minimum bounding hypersphere with all of the surfaces of the minimum bounding hyperrectangle.

7. One of the problems with forming an object hierarchy for an arbitrary metric space is that in a metric space, unlike in a vector space, where we can use a search hierarchy such as an R-tree that uses summary information in the form of clusters that are minimum bounding hyperrectangles for all of the objects in the subtree, we cannot explicitly form the "regions" that enclose a set of objects. The M-tree [389] makes use of "balls" around pivot objects, which play the same role as the minimum bounding hyperrectangles in the R-tree.

8. Consider a two-dimensional set of points with two clusters a and b centered at $M_a = (-5,0)$ and $M_b = (5,0)$, respectively, and a query point q at $(-1,0)$. Suppose that the nearest point p_b to q in b is at $(14,0)$ and that $r_{b,min}$ is 9. If we process cluster a first and the current nearest point to q is p at $(-3,0)$, then we can prune cluster b by applying Pruning Rule 3 as $D_1 + d(q, M_b) < r_{b,min}$—that is, $2 + 6 = 8 < 9$.

10. (Houman Alborzi) Assume that the contrary is true—that is, the distance of the closest point $p \in P$ to q is greater than $\sqrt{d(q,c)^2 + r^2}$. Thus,

$$\forall p \in P, d(p,q)^2 > d(q,c)^2 + r^2 \tag{S.1}$$

Below, we show that this assumption results in B not being a minimum enclosing hypersphere of P. There are two cases:

(a) $c = q$: In this case, Equation S.1 reduces to $\forall p \in P, d(p,c)^2 > r^2$, which means that the hypersphere B is not an enclosing hypersphere.

(b) $c \neq q$: Consider the line l passing through q and c. Project all points in P on this line, and consider a point p_t whose projection c_t on line l is the closest to q among all of the projected points (e.g., Figure S.13 for the two-dimensional case with points p_1, p_2, p_t in point set P, l passing through query point q and the center c of the minimum bounding hypersphere B of P, c_t being the projection of p_t on l, and q outside of B without loss of generality). Let $\vec{n}$ correspond to the unit vector oriented from q to c. Let $\alpha \vec{n} = \overrightarrow{c - q}, \alpha > 0$, where $\overrightarrow{c - q}$ denotes the vector pointing from q to c. Now, for point p_t we have

$$\forall p \in P, \overrightarrow{p - c} \cdot \vec{n} \geq \overrightarrow{p_t - c} \cdot \vec{n} \tag{S.2}$$

Letting $\varepsilon = \overrightarrow{p_t - c} \cdot \vec{n}$, we have $\forall p \in P, \overrightarrow{p - c} \cdot \vec{n} \geq \varepsilon$. For c_t, the projection of p_t on l, we have $c_t = c + \varepsilon \vec{n}$. Now, we show that $\varepsilon > 0$, which means that c_t is distinct from c and does not lie on the line segment between c and q.

$$\begin{aligned} d(p_t, q)^2 &= \overrightarrow{p_t - q} \cdot \overrightarrow{p_t - q} \\ &= (\overrightarrow{p_t - c} + \overrightarrow{c - q}) \cdot (\overrightarrow{p_t - c} + \overrightarrow{c - q}) \\ &= \overrightarrow{p_t - c} \cdot \overrightarrow{p_t - c} + \overrightarrow{c - q} \cdot \overrightarrow{c - q} + 2\overrightarrow{p_t - c} \cdot \overrightarrow{c - q} \\ &= d(p_t, c)^2 + d(c, q)^2 + 2\alpha \overrightarrow{p_t - c} \cdot \vec{n} \\ &= d(p_t, c)^2 + d(c, q)^2 + 2\alpha\varepsilon \end{aligned}$$

Therefore, solving for ε, we have

$$\varepsilon = \frac{d(p_t, q)^2 - d(p_t, c)^2 - d(c, q)^2}{2\alpha}$$

At this point, we show that $\varepsilon > 0$. Knowing that B contains p_t means that $d(p_t, c)^2 \leq r^2$ and thus replacing $d(p_t, c)^2$ by r^2 in the definition of ε yields $\varepsilon \geq \frac{d(p_t,q)^2 - r^2 - d(c,q)^2}{2\alpha}$.

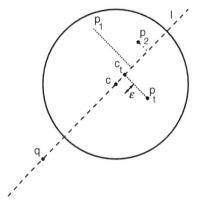

Figure S.13
Two-dimensional example illustrating the calculation of MAXNEAREST-DIST when the minimum bounding object is a hypersphere.

However, from Equation S.1, we have that $d(p_t, q)^2 > d(q, c)^2 + r^2$, which means that the numerator of the definition of ε is positive. This coupled with the fact that α is positive by definition means that $\varepsilon > 0$, and thus c_t is not between q and c.

Now, knowing that c_t is not between q and c, we show that the distance from c_t to all points of P is smaller than r, and thus B is not the minimum enclosing hypersphere of P. Formally, we show that, $\forall p \in P, d(p, c_t) < r$.

$$
\begin{aligned}
d(p, c_t)^2 &= \overrightarrow{p - c_t} \cdot \overrightarrow{p - c_t} \\
&= (\overrightarrow{p - c} - \varepsilon \vec{n}) \cdot (\overrightarrow{p - c} - \varepsilon \vec{n}) \\
&= \overrightarrow{p - c} \cdot \overrightarrow{p - c} + \varepsilon^2 \vec{n} \cdot \vec{n} - 2\varepsilon \overrightarrow{p - c} \cdot \vec{n} \\
&= d(p, c)^2 + \varepsilon^2 - 2\varepsilon \overrightarrow{p - c} \cdot \vec{n} \\
&\leq d(p, c)^2 + \varepsilon^2 - 2\varepsilon \overrightarrow{p_t - c} \cdot \vec{n} \qquad \text{from Equation S.2} \\
&\leq r^2 + \varepsilon^2 - 2\varepsilon^2 \\
&\leq r^2 - \varepsilon^2 \\
&< r^2 \qquad \text{as } \varepsilon > 0
\end{aligned}
$$

Therefore, B cannot be the minimum enclosing hypersphere as the distance from all points $p \in P$ to c_t is strictly less than r.

11. (Daniel DeMenthon) An intuitive explanation is that the centroid cannot lie outside the cloud of objects. Can you prove this more formally?

12. As in the computation of the MAXNEARESTDIST function, we take advantage of the fact that every face of the minimum bounding hyperrectangle b must contain at least one object. MINFARTHESTDIST is computed by determining the distances to the nearest points on each face of b from q and choosing their maximum. Denote the query point by $q = (q_0, q_1, \ldots, q_{d-1})$ and the minimum bounding hyperrectangle by $H = [l_0, u_0] \times [l_1, u_1] \times \cdots \times [l_{d-1}, u_{d-1}]$. Using the principle that every surface must contain a point, determine the nearest point on each surface and retain its maximum. For each dimension i, there are two surfaces. Clearly, the maximum of the minimums along dimension i will be attained at the surface that is farther from q. Therefore, let b_i be $u_i - q_i$ if $q_i \leq (l_i + u_i)/2$ and $q_i - l_i$ otherwise for $0 \leq i \leq d - 1$. Now, let a_j denote the distance to the nearest of the remaining possible corner points of the farthest surface along dimension i, where a_j is $l_j - q_j$ if $q_j < l_j$, $q_j - u_j$ if $u_j < q_j$, and 0 otherwise for $0 \leq j \leq d - 1$ and $j \neq i$. Therefore, using the Euclidean distance metric, we have that $\text{MINFARTHESTDIST}(q, H) = \max_{0 \leq i \leq d-1} \sqrt{b_i^2 + \sum_{j=0, j \neq i}^{d-1} a_j^2}$.

13. The MINFARTHESTDIST point is not always at a corner. For example, this is the case in Figure 4.19(a) where the MINFARTHESTDIST point is on the right edge of the minimum bounding rectangle with the same y coordinate value as the query object q. On the other hand, though, the MINFARTHESTDIST point for Figure 4.19(b) is at point b, which is a corner.

14. Same as MAXNEARESTDIST—that is, $\sqrt{d(q, M_p)^2 + r_{p,max}^2}$, as derived in the text for the same situation.

15. The two cases are handled as follows:

(a) The minimum bounding hypersphere with radius $r_{p,max}$ and centered at M_p coincident with the exterior face of the spherical shell is formed first. From the solution to Exercise 14 when $r_{p,min}$ is unknown, we know that the minimum possible distance from q to an object o of e_p that is on the exterior face of e_p and that is to serve as the farthest neighbor of q is $\sqrt{d(q, M_p)^2 + r_{p,max}^2}$. Next, given the above value of M_p, we determine the maximum bounding hypersphere with radius $r_{p,min}$ and centered at M_p coincident with the interior face of the spherical shell so that the interior is empty. From the discussion of Pruning Rule 5 in the solution to Exercise 17 in Section 4.2.2, we know that the minimum possible distance from q to an object o of e_p that is on the interior face of e_p and that is to serve as the farthest neighbor of q is $d(q, M_p) - r_{p,min}$. The value of MINFARTHESTDIST is the maximum of these lower bounds, which is $\sqrt{d(q, M_p)^2 + r_{p,max}^2}$. Thus, when forming the minimum bounding hypersphere corresponding to the exterior face of the spherical shell first, there is no need to take the maximum bounding hypersphere corresponding to the inner face into account in determining the minimum possible distance to the farthest neighbor of q.

(b) The maximum bounding hypersphere with radius $r_{p,min}$ and centered at M_p coincident with the interior face of the spherical shell so that the interior is empty is formed first. Using similar reasoning as in the solution to Exercise 14, we know that the minimum possible distance from q to an object o of e_p that is on the interior face of e_p and is to serve as the farthest neighbor of q is $\sqrt{d(q,M_p)^2 + r_{p,min}^2}$. From the discussion of Pruning Rule 5 in the solution to Exercise 17 in Section 4.2.2, we know that the minimum possible distance from q to an object o of e_p that is on the exterior face of e_p and which is to serve as the farthest neighbor of q is $d(q,M_p) - r_{p,max}$. The value of MINFARTHESTDIST is the maximum of these lower bounds, which is $\sqrt{d(q,M_p)^2 + r_{p,min}^2}$. Thus, when forming the maximum bounding hypersphere corresponding to the interior face of the spherical shell first, there is no need to take the minimum bounding hypersphere corresponding to the outer face into account in determining the minimum possible distance to the farthest neighbor of q.

16. MINFARTHESTDIST is obtained in an analogous manner to that in which we obtained MAXNEARESTDIST for the same minimum bounding object. In particular, we find the nearest (instead of the farthest) point on every surface that is a planar face (i.e., contributed by the minimum bounding hyperrectangle) and retain its maximum (instead of its minimum). Note that these points are the points of intersection of the minimum bounding hypersphere with all of the surfaces of the minimum bounding hyperrectangle.

Solutions to Exercises in Section 4.2.4

1. Assume that $k = 1$. Consider element $e_a = (M_a, r_{a,max})$ with $d(q, M_a) = 21$ and $r_{a,max} = r_{a,min} = 20$ so that MINDIST$(q, e_a) = 1$, and element $e_b = (M_b, r_{b,max})$ with $d(q, M_b) = 6$ and $r_{b,max} = r_{b,min} = 4$ so that MINDIST$(q, e_b) = 2$. Configure the objects in e_a so that they are all at a maximum distance from M_a so that the minimum distance D_1 from q is 11. Processing the active list in increasing MINDIST order means that e_a is processed before e_b as $d(q, M_a) - r_{a,max}$ is less than $d(q, M_b) - r_{b,max}$. Thus, once e_a has been processed, we have that $D_1 = 11$. Next, we process e_b for which we know that $d(q, M_b) + r_{b,min} \leq 10$. When the active list A of e_b is generated, we can assume, without loss of generality, that its elements $e_i = (M_i, r_{i,max})$ can be formed in such a way that each of them satisfies $d(q, M_i) + r_{i,min} \leq 10 \leq 11$, and thus we can reset D_1 to 10. The extension to arbitrary values of k is straightforward.

2. The proof follows the one given by Hjaltason and Samet [848] (see also Cheung and Fu [360] for a similar conclusion). Let r be the minimum bounding hyperrectangle of the element in the active list with the smallest MAXNEARESTDIST value. Using Strategy 1, we can prune any element in the active list with minimum bounding hyperrectangle r' such that MINDIST$(q, r') > $ MAXNEARESTDIST(q, r). However, Strategy 1 will not prune r or any element in the active list preceding it, regardless of the ordering used. If the active list is ordered based on MAXNEARESTDIST, this clearly holds since MINDIST$(q, r) \leq$ MAXNEARESTDIST(q, r). If the active list is ordered based on MINDIST, the elements preceding r have MINDIST values smaller than that of r, so their MINDIST values must also be smaller than MAXNEARESTDIST(q, r). Now, let us see what elements can be pruned from the active list by Strategy 3 after processing the element corresponding to r. In particular, at that point, from the definition of MAXNEARESTDIST, we have that the distance from q to o is less than or equal to MAXNEARESTDIST(q, r), where o is the candidate nearest object. Therefore, when Strategy 3 (based on MINDIST(q, o)) is now applied to the active list, it will prune at least as many elements as Strategy 1 (based on MAXNEARESTDIST(q, r)). Thus, we see that only Strategy 3 is needed for the implementation of Roussopoulos et al. [1586].

3. See Figure S.14, where the search for the nearest (i.e., $k = 1$) neighbor of q using the ordering MAXNEARESTDIST examines the contents of minimum bounding hyperrectangle B first, which is followed by examining the contents of minimum bounding hyperrectangle E. At this point, there is no need to examine the contents of E's sibling minimum bounding hyperrectangle F as it is farther from q than the farthest possible current candidate nearest neighbor

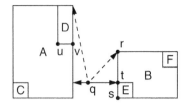

Figure S.14
Example where use of MaxNear-estDist(broken line) for ordering the processing of elements of the active list for finding the nearest neighbor of query point q results in examining the contents of fewer minimum bounding hyperrectangles than use of MinDist(solid line).

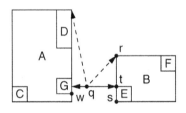

Figure S.15
Example where use of MinDist (solid line) for ordering the processing of elements of the active list for finding the nearest neighbor of query point q results in examining the contents of fewer minimum bounding hyperrectangles than the use of MaxNearestDist(broken line).

in E (represented by the point s). Next, we examine the contents of minimum bounding hyperrectangle A as its distance from q is less than the distance to s, and, in fact, is less than the distance from the closest possible current candidate nearest neighbor in E (represented by t). Regardless of the identity of the current candidate nearest neighbor (i.e., s or t), there is no need to examine the contents of minimum bounding hyperrectangles C and D as they are much farther from q than any possible current candidate nearest neighbor (i.e., s). On the other hand, ordering using MinDist examines the contents of minimum bounding hyperrectangle A first, which is followed by examining the contents of minimum bounding hyperrectangle D. Note that we must examine the contents of minimum bounding hyperrectangle D even if we apply Pruning Rule 5, which sets D_1 to MaxNearestDist(q, B) (i.e., the distance from q to r). In this case, D_1 is greater than MinDist(q, D) (i.e., the distance from q to v), which is why D must be examined. At this point, there is no need to examine the contents of D's sibling minimum bounding hyperrectangle C as it is farther from q than the farthest possible current candidate nearest neighbor in D (represented by the point u). Next, we examine the contents of minimum bounding hyperrectangle B as its distance from q is less than the distance to u and, in fact, is less than the distance from the closest possible current candidate nearest neighbor in D (represented by v). Regardless of the identity of the current candidate nearest neighbor (i.e., u or v), we examine the contents of minimum bounding hyperrectangle E as it is closer to q than any possible current candidate nearest neighbor (i.e., v). However, there is no need to visit E's sibling minimum bounding hyperrectangle F as it is farther from q than the farthest possible current candidate nearest neighbor in E (i.e., s), which is also closer than the closest possible current candidate neighbor resulting from visiting A and D (i.e., v). Thus, we find that in this example, using the MaxNearestDist ordering, we examine the contents of fewer minimum bounding hyperrectangles (i.e., B, E, A) than when using the MinDist ordering (i.e., A, D, B, and E).

4. See Figure S.15, where the search for the nearest (i.e., $k = 1$) neighbor of q using the ordering MaxNearestDist examines the contents of minimum bounding hyperrectangle B first, which is followed by examining the contents of minimum bounding hyperrectangle E. At this point, there is no need to examine the contents of E's sibling minimum bounding hyperrectangle F as it is farther from q than the farthest possible current candidate nearest neighbor in E (represented by the point s). Next, we examine the contents of minimum bounding hyperrectangle A as its distance from q is less than the distance to s and, in fact, is less than the distance from the closest possible current candidate nearest neighbor in E (represented by t). Regardless of the identity of the current candidate nearest neighbor (i.e., s or t), there is no need to examine the contents of minimum bounding hyperrectangles C and D as they are much farther from q than any possible current candidate nearest neighbor (i.e., s). However, the contents of minimum bounding hyperrectangle G must be examined as it is closer to q than any possible current candidate nearest neighbor (i.e., t). On the other hand, ordering using MinDist examines the contents of minimum bounding hyperrectangle A first, which is followed by examining the contents of minimum bounding hyperrectangle G. At this point, there is no need to examine the contents of either of G's sibling minimum bounding hyperrectangles C and D as they are farther from q than the farthest possible current candidate nearest neighbor in G (represented by the point w). For this example, we also do not need to examine the contents of minimum bounding hyperrectangle B as it is farther from q than any possible candidate nearest neighbor (i.e., w). Thus, we find that in this example, using the MinDist ordering, we examine the contents of fewer minimum bounding hyperrectangles (i.e., A and G) than when using the MaxNearestDist ordering (i.e., B, E, A, and G).

5. See Friedman, Bentley, and Finkel [650], who use the relationship between the value of the discriminator key at each nonleaf node of the k-d tree and the corresponding attribute value of the query point to decide which subtree (i.e., one of the two elements of the active list) to explore first. Pruning is achieved whenever the distance to the current nearest neighbor is less than the minimum distance to an unexplored subtree (i.e., Pruning Rule 1). The same technique is applied by Eastman and Zemankova [530] to find the nearest neighbor when only some of the attribute values of the query point are specified (termed a *partial match nearest neighbor query*).

6. The MaxDist ordering represents the optimistic choice. The MinFarthestDist ordering represents the pessimistic choice.

Solutions to Exercises in Section 4.2.5

1. One way is when L was initially set up when D_k was ∞. The second way is when we find ourselves at some point where a nonobject element has a MAXNEARESTDIST value x lower than D_k and there are other nonobject elements in L having x as their MAXNEARESTDIST value.

2. Ciaccia et al. [389] formulate Pruning Rules 2 and 4 for nonobjects for the M-tree by the condition $|d(q,M) - d(M,M_p)| > D_k + r_{p,max}$.

3. The proof is identical to the one for the correctness of Pruning Rule 1 in the solution to Exercise 1 in Section 4.2.2 with M instead of M_p and MAXDIST(M,e_p) instead of $r_{p,max}$.

4. The proof is identical to the one for the correctness of Pruning Rule 3 in the solution to Exercise 6 in Section 4.2.2 with M instead of M_p and MINDIST(M,e_p) instead of $r_{p,min}$.

5. Yes. Sorting the nonobjects in MINDIST order enables pruning all nonobjects e_p from consideration for which MINDIST(e_p) is greater than $d(q,M) + D_k$ (Pruning Rule 4). The remaining nonobjects are only pruned if MAXDIST$(M,e_p) < d(q,M) - D_k$ (i.e., Pruning Rule 2); otherwise, they are inserted into the active list. Note that in this case the nonobjects are sorted in decreasing, instead of increasing, order.

6. The reason is that in the case of an object o, regardless of whether M was closer to o than to q or M was closer to q than to o, in order for pruning to take place, we always tested the same quantity $d(o,M)$ for being outside of the range lying between $d(q,M) - D_k$ and $d(q,M) + D_k$. This was supported by storing the objects in e sorted by their distance from M. In contrast, in the case of a nonobject e_p with mean M_p, in order for pruning to take place, we test whether the quantity MAXDIST(M,e_p) is less than $d(q,M) - D_k$ when M is closer to e_p than to q or test whether the quantity MINDIST(M,e_p) is greater than $d(q,M) + D_k$ when M is closer to q than to e_p. Therefore, instead of testing just one quantity (i.e., $d(o,M)$) in the case of objects, we must test two different quantities in the case of nonobjects. Each sorting sequence (i.e., in increasing MAXDIST order as in OPTDFTRAV or in decreasing MINDIST order as in Exercise 5) supports one of the bounds. One possible approach to supporting both bounds is to maintain two sorted sequences with each nonleaf node e of the nonobjects in e: one in increasing MAXDIST order and one in decreasing MINDIST order (but see Exercise 7).

7. This algorithm is implemented with replacing lines 24–30 in OPTDFTRAV with the following code fragment:

```
1  /* Assume that all nonobjects e_p in e are sorted in both increasing and decreasing
       order with respect to M using MAXDIST and MINDIST, and stored in MX(e)
       and MN(e), respectively. Use INSERTACTIVELIST to generate the active list A
       containing the nonpruned elements of e sorted in increasing order with respect
       to q using MINDIST and MEANORPIVOTDIST as primary and secondary keys,
       respectively, and process A in this order. */
2  A ← Empty
3  Find first nonobject e_p in MX(e) such that
4      MAXDIST(M,e_p) ≥ d(q,M) − D_k
5  while EXIST(e_p) and d(M_p,M) ≤ d(q,M) do /* Pruning Rule 2 for nonobjects
                                                  */
6      INSERTACTIVELIST(e_p, A)
7      e_p ← NEXT(MX(e))
8  enddo
9  Find first nonobject e_p in MN(e) such that
10     MINDIST(M,e_p) ≤ d(q,M) + D_k
11 while EXIST(e_p) and d(M_p,M) > d(q,M) do /* Pruning Rule 4 for nonobjects
                                                  */
12     INSERTACTIVELIST(e_p, A)
13     e_p ← NEXT(MN(e))
14 enddo
```

This method will not work as it is not guaranteed to insert all relevant nonobjects into the active list. The problem is that the processing of the nonobjects in MX(e) in increasing order halts as soon as a nonobject e_a with mean M_a is found so that M is farther from M_a

than from q. This means that another nonobject e_b, with mean M_b where $\text{MAXDIST}(M,e_b) >$ $\text{MAXDIST}(M,e_a)$ while M is closer to M_b than to q, will not be inserted into the active list as a result of this part of the algorithm. Unfortunately, as M is closer to M_b than to M, e_b will also not be inserted into the active list by the second phase of the algorithm, which processes the nonobjects in $\text{MN}(e)$ in decreasing order and halts as soon as a nonobject e_c with mean M_c is found so that M is closer to M_c than to q. The same problem arises for another nonobject e_n, with mean M_n where $\text{MINDIST}(M,e_c) < \text{MINDIST}(M,e_n)$ while M is closer to q than to M_n, will not be inserted into the active list as a result of this part of the algorithm. Again, as M is closer to q than to M_n, e_n will not have been inserted into the active list by the first phase of the algorithm, which processes the nonobjects in $\text{MX}(e)$ and halts as soon as a nonobject e_a with mean M_a is found so that M_a is farther from M than from q. Thus, we cannot take advantage of sorting the nonobjects using MAXDIST and MINDIST as was done for objects.

11. As we pointed out in the solution to Exercise 17 in Section 4.2.2, it is not possible to adapt Pruning Rule 4 to the problem of finding the k farthest neighbors. On the other hand, Pruning Rule 2 can be easily adapted for nonobjects, in which case it stipulates that no object in nonobject e_p in nonobject element e, with mean M and $\text{MAXDIST}(M,e_p)$ as the distance from M to the farthest object within e_p, can be the kth-farthest neighbor of query object q if $D_k - \text{MAXDIST}(M,e_p) > d(q,M)$. Again, as in the case of objects, the rule is only meaningful when q is closer to M than D_k—that is, $d(q,M) < D_k$, and q can be anywhere (inside and outside e and likewise inside and outside e_p).

12. The code for OPTDFTRAVFARTHEST is almost the same, and the changes are similar to those described in the solution to Exercise 18 in Section 4.2.2. The main additional differences are the use of MAXDIST, MINFARTHESTDIST, and MINPRIORITYQUEUE instead of MINDIST, MAXNEARESTDIST, and MAXPRIORITYQUEUE, respectively. Moreover, all tests in terms of "$< D_k$" are changed to be in terms of "$> D_k$" (lines 19, 34, and 42 in OPTDFTRAV and line 20 in OPTINSERTL) and tests in terms of "$> D_k$" are changed to be in terms of "$< D_k$" (line 39 in OPTDFTRAV). Instead of being sorted and processed in increasing order, the elements of the active list in OPTDFTRAVFARTHEST are sorted in decreasing order with respect to q, using $\text{MAXDIST}(q,e_p)$ and $\text{MEANORPIVOTDIST}(q,e_p) = d(q,M_p)$ as the primary and secondary keys, respectively, and are processed in this order. Since there is no analog of Pruning Rule 4 when finding the k farthest neighbors, the code that handles Pruning Rule 2 is simplified considerably. In particular, Pruning Rule 2 for objects is implemented by storing the objects in leaf node e with mean M and maximum distance r_{max} sorted in decreasing order with respect to M, and they are processed in this order. The absence of the analog of Pruning Rule 4 means that there is no need in OPTDFTRAVFARTHEST for the analog of line 13 in OPTDFTRAV, and the condition "$d(o,M) \leq d(q,M) + D_k$" (line 15 in OPTDFTRAV) is replaced with the condition "$d(o,M) \geq D_k - d(q,M)$." Similarly, Pruning Rule 2 for nonobjects e_p in nonleaf e with mean M is implemented by again storing them in $C(e)$, but this time sorted in decreasing order with respect to M using MAXDIST instead of in increasing order. The actual implementation is simplified considerably by the inapplicability of Pruning Rule 4, which means that line 24 is omitted, as is the condition in line 27 for the insertion of e_p in A (i.e., the call of INSERTACTIVELIST). The actual condition for the pruning is incorporated by using "$\text{EXIST}(e_p)$ and $D_k - d(q,M) \leq \text{MAXDIST}(M,e_p)$" to condition the execution of the loop in lines 26–30.

13. Replace all distances by their negation. Thus, $d(q,o)$ in lines 17 and 18 must be replaced with $-d(q,o)$, and, similarly, D_k must be initialized to $-\infty$ in KFARTHEST instead of to ∞ as in KNEAREST. This means that the priority queue need not be modified in the sense that the first element still corresponds to the element with the maximum distance (which is now the nearest of the k farthest elements due to the use of negative distances). We also replace all uses of the distance functions MINDIST and MAXNEARESTDIST with MAXDIST and MINFARTHESTDIST, respectively, which, of course, are now negative. Again, the elements of the active list in OPTDFTRAVFARTHEST are sorted in increasing order (using a negative MAXDIST and $\text{MEANORPIVOTDIST}(q,e_p) = -d(q,M_p)$ as the primary and secondary keys, respectively) and are always processed in this order (which would really be a decreasing order if the distances were positive). Since there is no analog of Pruning Rule 4 when finding the k farthest neighbors, the code that handles Pruning Rule 2 is simplified considerably. In particular, in the case of objects, there is no need in OPTDFTRAVFARTHEST for the analog of line 13 in OPTDFTRAV, and the condition "$d(o,M) \leq d(q,M) + D_k$" (line 15 in OPTDFTRAV) is replaced with the condition "$d(o,M) \geq D_k - d(q,M)$," which is Pruning Rule 2 for finding the k farthest neighbors. Use of negative distances (i.e., D_k is negative)

causes this condition to be rewritten as "$-d(o,M) \leq D_k + d(q,M)$" and the objects in e to be processed in increasing order of their negative distance from M. Similarly, Pruning Rule 2 for nonobjects e_p in nonleaf e with mean M is implemented by again storing them in C(e), but this time sorted in increasing order with respect to M using negative MAXDIST distance values and processed in this order. The implementation is simplified considerably by the inapplicability of Pruning Rule 4, which means that line 24 is omitted, as is the condition in line 27 for the insertion of e_p in A (i.e., the call of INSERTACTIVELIST). The actual condition for the pruning is incorporated by using "EXIST(e_p) and $D_k - d(q,M) \leq$ MAXDIST(M,e_p)" to condition the execution of the loop in lines 26–30. Use of negative distances (i.e., D_k is negative) causes this condition to be rewritten as "$-$MAXDIST(M,e_p) $\leq D_k + d(q,M)$." No changes are needed in procedure OPTINSERTL.

Solutions to Exercises in Section 4.2.6

2. BFTRAVFARTHEST is almost the same as BFTRAV, and the changes are the same as those described in the solution to Exercise 2 of Section 4.2.1. Again, MINPRIORITYQUEUE and a definition of distance that incorporates upper bound information (i.e., MAXDIST) are used instead of MAXPRIORITYQUEUE and a definition of distance that incorporates lower-bound information (i.e., MINDIST), respectively. Similarly, all tests in terms of "$< D_k$" and "$> D_k$" are changed to be in terms of "$> D_k$" (line 25) and "$< D_k$" (line 20), respectively. No changes are needed in procedure INSERTL.

3. The result is similar to BFTRAV, and the modifications that are needed are virtually identical to those described in the solution of Exercise 3 of Section 4.2.1. Recall that in this case we replace all distances by their negation. Thus, $d(q,o)$ in lines 24–26 must be replaced with $-d(q,o)$, and, similarly, D_k must be initialized to $-\infty$ (line 16) instead of to ∞. This means that the priority queue need not be modified in the sense that the first element still corresponds to the element with the maximum distance (which is now the nearest of the farthest elements due to the use of negative distances). No changes are needed in procedure INSERTL.

4. OPTBFTRAVFARTHEST is almost the same as OPTBFTRAV, and the changes are similar to those described in the solution to Exercise 12 in Section 4.2.5. Again, MAXDIST, MINFARTHESTDIST, and MINPRIORITYQUEUE are used instead of MINDIST, MAXNEARESTDIST, and MAXPRIORITYQUEUE, respectively. Similarly, all tests in OPTBFTRAV in terms of "$< D_k$," "$> D_k$," and "$\leq D_k$" are changed to be in terms of "$> D_k$" (lines 23, 34, and 48), "$< D_k$" (line 21), and "$\geq D_k$" (line 46), respectively. Since there is no analog of Pruning Rule 4 when finding the k farthest neighbors, the code that handles Pruning Rule 2 is simplified considerably. In particular, Pruning Rule 2 for objects is implemented by storing the objects in leaf node e with mean M and maximum distance r_{max} sorted in decreasing order with respect to M, and they are processed in this order. The absence of the analog of Pruning Rule 4 means that there is no need in OPTBFTRAVFARTHEST for the analog of line 31 in OPTBFTRAV, and the condition "$d(o,M) \leq d(q,M) + D_k$" (line 32 in OPTBFTRAV) is replaced by the condition "$d(o,M) \geq D_k - d(q,M)$." Similarly, Pruning Rule 2 for nonobjects e_p in nonleaf e with mean M is implemented by again storing them in C(e), but this time sorted in decreasing order with respect to M using MAXDIST instead of in increasing order. The actual implementation is simplified considerably by the inapplicability of Pruning Rule 4, which means that line 41 is omitted, as is the condition in lines 44 and 53 for determining whether actual processing of e_p should continue. The actual condition for the pruning is incorporated by using "EXIST(e_p) and $D_k - d(q,M) \leq$ MAXDIST(M,e_p)" to condition the execution of the remaining instructions in lines 46–52. No changes are needed in procedure OPTINSERTL.

5. The modifications needed are virtually identical to those made in the transformation of OPTDFTRAV to OPTDFTRAVFARTHEST in Exercise 13 of Section 4.2.5. Recall that in this case, we replace all distances by their negation. Thus, $d(q,o)$ in lines 34 and 35 must be replaced with $-d(q,o)$, and, similarly, D_k must be initialized to $-\infty$ (line 17) instead of to ∞. This means that the priority queue need not be modified in the sense that the first element still corresponds to the element with the maximum distance (which is now the nearest of the farthest elements due to the use of negative distances). We also replace all uses of the distance functions MINDIST and MAXNEARESTDIST by MAXDIST and MINFARTHESTDIST, respectively, which, of course, are now negative. Interestingly, this has no effect on the manner in which

the priority queue is initialized in the sense that it is again initialized with the root of the search hierarchy but now with a MAXDIST value of 0 instead of with a MINDIST value of 0. As in OPTDFTRAVFARTHEST, the objects in leaf element e with mean M and maximum distance r_{max} are sorted in increasing order of their negative distance from M and are always processed in this order. Since there is no analog of Pruning Rule 4 when finding the k farthest neighbors, the code that handles Pruning Rule 2 is simplified considerably. In particular, in the case of objects, there is no need in OPTBFTRAVFARTHEST for the analog of line 31 in OPTBFTRAV. The failure to satisfy Pruning Rule 2 is incorporated by replacing the condition "$d(o,M) \leq d(q,M) + D_k$" (line 32 in OPTBFTRAV) with the condition "$D_k - d(q,M) \leq d(o,M)$," which is rewritten as "$-d(o,M) \leq D_k + d(q,M)$," when we use negative distances (i.e., D_k is negative). Similarly, Pruning Rule 2 for nonobjects e_p in nonleaf e with mean M is implemented by again storing them in C(e), but this time sorted in increasing order with respect to M using negative MAXDIST distance values and processed in this order. The implementation is simplified considerably by the inapplicability of Pruning Rule 4, which means that line 41 is omitted, as is the condition in lines 44 and 53 for determining whether actual processing of e_p should continue. The actual condition for the pruning is incorporated by using "EXIST(e_p) and $D_k - d(q,M) \leq$ MAXDIST(M,e_p)" to condition the execution of the remaining instructions in lines 46–52. Use of negative distances (i.e., D_k is negative) causes this condition to be rewritten as "$-$MAXDIST(M,e_p) $\leq D_k + d(q,M)$." No changes are needed in procedure OPTINSERTL.

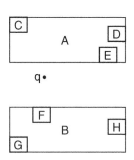

Figure S.16
Example of finding the nearest neighbor where using the general incremental algorithm performs fewer page accesses than using an implementation of the depth-first algorithm that makes use of a MINDISTordering such as the one of Roussopoulos et al. [1586].

Solutions to Exercises in Section 4.2.8

1. See Figure S.16, where A–F denote some of the pages that are to be accessed and we want to determine the nearest neighbor of query point q. The pages are specified in terms of their corresponding minimum bounding hyperrectangles and their relative spatial positions. We find that both algorithms process page A first. In particular, processing of the elements of the active list using the MINDIST ordering, an implementation of the depth-first algorithm, such as the one of Roussopoulos et al. [1586], places both A and B on the active list and processes A first. This means that at the next step, it processes the three children of A—that is, C, D, and E, with C being the first to be processed in the next stage. On the other hand, the general incremental algorithm inserts both A and B on the priority queue and removes A for processing first. This causes it to insert A's three children C, D, and E on the priority queue after B, which is closer to q. Next, the general incremental algorithm processes B and inserts its three children F, G, and H on the priority queue, where F is now at the front of the queue and is thus the first to be processed in the next stage. It is clear that F contains the nearest neighbor as the value of MINDIST(q,C) > MAXNEARESTDIST(q,F). Thus, we see that, at the very least, an implementation of the depth-first algorithm such as the one of Roussopoulos et al. [1586] will visit page C for naught.

Solutions to Exercises in Section 4.3

1. A problem arises when $\varepsilon \geq 1$, in which case the denominator is zero or negative, both of which are problematic: the former means that the approximate error is unbounded, while it is difficult to interpret the latter. Thus, we retain the original definition.

2. The difference is that ANNBFTRAV tries to avoid enqueueing nonobjects that are known to be too far away from q and thus will never be examined. Therefore, there is no need to enqueue them, possibly resulting in a smaller maximum size for the priority queue *Queue*.

3. The key idea behind approximate k-nearest neighbor finding is to ensure that for the object o'_k returned as the kth-nearest neighbor by the algorithm and the actual kth-nearest neighbor o_k, we have that $d(q,o'_k) \leq (1+\varepsilon) \cdot d(q,o_k)$. This is usually achieved by shrinking the distance D_k from q to the kth-nearest neighbor by $1 + \varepsilon$ or expanding the individual distances from q to the nonobjects by $1 + \varepsilon$. These shrunken or expanded distances are used in all comparisons that involve distances of nonobjects from q. However, since procedure DFTRAV does not make use of the distances of the nonobjects from q (i.e., it only makes use of distances

of the actual objects from q), we cannot report the approximate k nearest neighbors of q unless we modify the criteria for the applicability of the approximation to also involve the distances of the actual objects from q. In particular, we can only modify the test $d(q,o) < D_k$ (line 14) to be $d(q,o) < D_k/(1+\varepsilon)$ or $d(q,o) \cdot (1+\varepsilon) < D_k$ depending on whether distances are shrunk or expanded, respectively. For the effect of this modification on procedure ANNBF-TRAV, see Exercise 7. For its effect on procedures ANNFNDFTRAV, ANNOPTDFTRAV, and ANNOPTBFTRAV, see Exercise 8.

4. As in the modification of OPTBFTRAV to yield ANNOPTBFTRAV, the idea is to expand the distances of nonobject elements from q by $1+\varepsilon$. In this case, we do not employ the estimates MINDIST and MAXNEARESTDIST directly. Instead, each nonobject element e_p is assumed to have a representative element M_p with $r_{p,min}$ and $r_{p,max}$ as the distances from M_p to the closest and farthest object in e_p, respectively. The distances of the nonobject elements from q are expressed in terms of M_p, $r_{p,min}$, and $r_{p,max}$, and they are expanded in the comparisons with D_k. The tests for the applicability of Pruning Rules 1 and 3 become $(d(q,M_p) - r_{p,max}) \cdot (1+\varepsilon) > D_k$ (line 36) and $(r_{p,min} - d(q,M_p)) \cdot (1+\varepsilon) > D_k$ (line 37). The tests for the applicability of Pruning Rule 5 become $d(q,M_p) \cdot (1+\varepsilon) > D_1$ and $(d(q,M_p) + r_{p,min}) \cdot (1+\varepsilon) < D_1$ (lines 29 and 30, respectively). In the case that Pruning Rule 5 is found to be applicable, then we reset D_1 to the expanded distance $(d(q,M_p) + r_{p,min}) \cdot (1+\varepsilon)$ (line 31).

5. As in the modification of OPTBFTRAV to yield ANNOPTBFTRAV, the idea is to expand the distances (i.e., estimates and hence both MINDIST and MAXNEARESTDIST) of nonobject elements from q by $1+\varepsilon$. These expanded distances are used in all comparisons with D_k, and the algorithm is simplified by also associating these expanded distances with the nonobjects in L. The test for the applicability of Pruning Rules 1 and 3 becomes MINDIST$(q,e_p) \cdot (1+\varepsilon) > D_k$ (line 39), the test for the applicability of Pruning Rules 2 and 4 for nonobjects become MAXDIST$(M,e_p) \geq d(q,M) - D_k/(1+\varepsilon)$ (line 24) and MINDIST$(M,e_p) \leq d(q,M) + D_k/(1+\varepsilon)$ (line 27), and the test for the insertion of nonobjects (i.e., pruning Rule 5) in L by OPTINSERTL becomes MINDIST$(q,e_p) \cdot (1+\varepsilon) > D_k$ (line 32) and MAXNEARESTDIST$(q,e_p) \cdot (1+\varepsilon) < D_k$ (line 34). The distances associated with the nonobjects e_p that are inserted in L by OPTINSERTL become MAXNEARESTDIST$(q,e_p) \cdot (1+\varepsilon)$ (line 35). The conditions involving MAXNEARESTDIST to determine whether it is necessary to remove a nonobject from L when processing its immediate descendants become MAXNEARESTDIST$(q,e) \cdot (1+\varepsilon) < D_k$ and MAXNEARESTDIST$(q,e) \cdot (1+\varepsilon) = D_k$ (lines 42–47).

6. This means that each of the search hierarchy elements corresponding to each of these nonobjects, say b, is replaced with one of the objects in them. Note that there is no search involved here (in contrast to the situation when using the MAXNEARESTDIST estimate) as any object o_b in b satisfies the approximation criterion since MAXDIST$(q,b) < D_k$, even though MINDIST$(q,b) \cdot (1+\varepsilon) > D_k$.

7. If no use is made of the MAXNEARESTDIST estimate, as is the case in procedure ANNBF-TRAV, then this modification can be made easily. In fact, this is how the basic depth-first k-nearest neighbor algorithm given by procedure DFTRAV in Section 4.2.1 is adapted to return the k approximate nearest neighbors (see the solution of Exercise 3). Use of this modification reduces the number of update manipulations on L, at the cost of not lowering D_k. Moreover, its use may cause the expansion of some nonobjects that would have otherwise been pruned by virtue of the tighter values of D_k that could be obtained since objects within ε of D_k would not have been ignored. For example, suppose that $D_1 = 10$ with $\varepsilon = 0.2$. Using this modification, we ignore an object o with $d(q,o) = 8.5$ in the sense that D_1 is not reset to 8.5. Now, if we encounter a nonobject e with MINDIST$(q,e) = 7.6$, then we would have to process it as MINDIST$(q,e) = 7.6 < D_1/(1+\varepsilon) = 10/1.2 = 8.33$; whereas if we had not ignored o, then we could ignore e as MINDIST$(q,e) = 7.6 > D_1/(1+\varepsilon) = 8.5/1.2 = 7.08$. Notice that when the approximation error tolerance is applied at the object level, it is pointless not to apply it explicitly at the nonobject level as well, as otherwise more objects would be examined (i.e., the objects in the nonobjects that would have been pruned otherwise), while yielding the same resulting set of k approximate nearest neighbors.

8. It is impossible for the modified algorithms to terminate with nonobjects in L. We prove this by contradiction. Suppose that the algorithms terminate with a nonobject e_p in L. This means that MAXNEARESTDIST$(q,e_p) \cdot (1+\varepsilon) \leq D_k$. There are two ways in which this situation could arise. The first is if MINDIST$(q,e_p) \cdot (1+\varepsilon) > D_k$, which is always true for any unprocessed or pruned element e_p, but this is impossible in this case as MINDIST$(q,e_p) \leq$

MAXNEARESTDIST(q, e_p). The second is if for all objects o in e_p, $d(q, o) \cdot (1 + \varepsilon) > D_k$, which is also impossible as we know that for each nonobject e_p in L there exists at least one object o_p in e_p and its descendants with $d(q, o_p) \leq$ MAXNEARESTDIST(q, e_p) and thus $d(q, o_p) \cdot (1 + \varepsilon) \leq$ MAXNEARESTDIST$(q, e_p) \cdot (1 + \varepsilon) \leq D_k$. Therefore, when e_p and its descendants are processed by the algorithm, in the worst case, e_p will be replaced with o_p in L. Thus, it is impossible for the algorithms to terminate with nonobjects in L.

It is important to note that if the element e of L at distance D_k corresponds to a nonobject b such that $D_k =$ MAXNEARESTDIST$(q, b) \cdot (1 + \varepsilon)$, then the actual effect of making this modification is to defeat, in part, the motivation for using the approximate k nearest neighbors, which is to avoid the processing of the nonobject elements and to let some of the farther objects be elements of L as now all objects o that are encountered subsequently such that MAXNEARESTDIST$(q, b) < d(q, o) \leq D_k$ will be pruned from further consideration since the distance value of q from b that is associated with e has been expanded by a factor of $1 + \varepsilon$. Therefore, these objects o can no longer be reported "before their time." On the other hand, if e corresponds to an object, then use of this modification will result in pruning even more objects from consideration—that is, all objects o such that $d(q, o) < D_k \leq d(q, o) \cdot (1 + \varepsilon)$. In fact, in this case, the effect is the same as that observed in the solution to Exercise 7 in that some nonobjects may have to be processed that would have been otherwise pruned had a lower value of D_k been obtained by virtue of not having pruned some of the objects o where $d(q, o) \cdot (1 + \varepsilon) > D_k$ while $d(q, o) < D_k$.

9. Modify the conditions under which the rules are found to be applicable to be $D_k/(1 + \varepsilon) < d(q, M_p) - d(o, M_p)$ for Pruning Rule 2 and $D_k/(1 + \varepsilon) < d(o, M_p) - d(q, M_p)$ for Pruning Rule 4. For example, in the approximate k-nearest neighbor adaptation of OPTBFTRAV given by ANNOPTBFTRAV, the condition $d(o, M) \geq d(q, M) - D_k$ in line 31 of OPTBFTRAV becomes $d(o, M) \geq d(q, M) - D_k/(1 + \varepsilon)$. Similarly, the looping condition $d(o, M) \leq d(q, M) + D_k$ in line 32 becomes $d(o, M) \leq d(q, M) + D_k/(1 + \varepsilon)$. In addition, the tests $d(q, o) < D_k$ and $d(q, o) = D_k$ in line 34 become $d(q, o) < D_k/(1 + \varepsilon)$ and $d(q, o) = D_k/(1 + \varepsilon)$, respectively. Procedures FNDFTRAV and OPTDFTRAV are modified in the same way to yield ANNFNDFTRAV and ANNOPTDFTRAV, respectively.

10. The resulting algorithm is identical to the incremental nearest neighbor algorithm given by INCNEAREST as the objects are now reported in increasing order of their distance from the query object. Notice the difference from the result of Exercise 7.

11. The resulting algorithm still reports the neighbors in increasing order of their distance from the query object. However, the algorithm is less efficient than INCNEAREST as the result is to delay the time at which the nearest objects are reported as some nonobjects are processed before the objects that could have already been reported. Thus, more nonobject elements are processed, and the priority queue may possibly get needlessly larger.

12. (Houman Alborzi) Let the query object be q and $r \leq d(p, q)$. The effect of shrinking the radius of b centered at p by λ is that an object at a distance of $d(p, q) - r$ may be missed while an object at a distance of $d(p, q) - \lambda \cdot r$ is reported as a nearest neighbor. Therefore, the maximum approximation error is $(d(p, q) - \lambda \cdot r)/(d(p, q) - r) - 1 = (1 - \lambda) \cdot r/(d(p, q) - r)$. This value approaches infinity as r approaches $d(p, q)$, so the maximum approximation error is unbounded. A similar argument shows that the error is also unbounded if $r > d(p, q)$ as now the lower bound on the distance is 0 and dividing by 0 yields ∞.

14. When the query point coincides with the center of the hypercube, $F_q(x) = (2 \cdot x)^d$, and thus $G_q(x) = 1 - (1 - (2 \cdot x)^d)^N = \delta$. Solving for x in terms of δ, we have $x = (1 - (1 - (1 - \delta)^{1/N})^{1/d})/2$. On the other hand, when the query point coincides with one of the 2^d corners of the hypercube, $F_q(x) = x^d$, and thus $G_q(x) = 1 - (1 - x^d)^N = \delta$. Solving for x in terms of δ, we have $x = 1 - (1 - (1 - \delta)^{1/N})^{1/d}$.

15. From the solution of Exercise 14, we have that $x = (1 - (1 - (1 - \delta)^{1/N})^{1/d})/2$. Substituting for δ, N, and d, we have $x \approx 0.346$ [387], which means that the probability that the hypercube of width $2 \cdot 0.346$ centered at the center of the unit hypercube is empty is at least 0.99.

17. ANNBFTRAVFARTHEST is obtained as follows. Expand the distance D_k from q to the kth-farthest object o by a factor of $1 + \varepsilon$. Halt if the distance associated with the farthest nonobject e in *Queue* is greater than the expanded distance (line 20). Otherwise, if e is not a leaf, then only insert the nonobject child elements e_p of e into *Queue* for which the maximum distance from q to an object in e_p (i.e., MAXDIST(q, e_p)) is less than this expanded distance (line 31).

18. ANNINCFARTHEST is analogous to procedure INCFARTHEST in Exercise 6 in Section 4.1.5. Always shrink the distance value of a nonobject element $e_{t'}$ (i.e., the maximum distance from q to an object in $e_{t'}$ known as MAXDIST$(q, e_{t'})$) by a factor of $1 + \varepsilon$ before enqueueing it (line 19 of ANNINCNEAREST).

19. ANNOPTBFTRAVFARTHEST is analogous to procedure OPTBFTRAVFARTHEST in Exercise 5 in Section 4.2.6. Always shrink the distances (i.e., estimates and hence both MAXDIST and MINFARTHESTDIST, which are the analogs of MINDIST and MAXNEARESTDIST, respectively) of nonobject elements from q by $1 + \varepsilon$. These shrunken distances are used in all comparisons with D_k, and the algorithm is simplified by also associating these shrunken distances with the nonobjects in both L and *Queue*. In particular, the test for the applicability of Pruning Rule 1 becomes MAXDIST$(q, e_p)/(1 + \varepsilon) < D_k$ (line 46), and the test for the insertion of nonobjects (i.e., pruning Rule 5) in L by OPTINSERTL becomes MINFARTHESTDIST$(q, e_p)/(1 + \varepsilon) < D_k$ (line 48). The distances associated with the nonobjects e_p that are inserted in *Queue* and L become MAXDIST$(q, e_p)/(1 + \varepsilon)$ (line 51) and MINFARTHESTDIST$(q, e_p)/(1 + \varepsilon)$ (line 49), respectively. The conditions involving MINFARTHESTDIST to determine whether it is necessary to remove a nonobject from L when processing its immediate descendants become MINFARTHESTDIST$(q, e)/(1 + \varepsilon) < D_k$ and MINFARTHESTDIST$(q, e)/(1 + \varepsilon) = D_k$ (lines 23–28). Since there is no analog of Pruning Rule 4 when finding the k farthest neighbors, the code that handles Pruning Rule 2 is simplified considerably. As in OPTBFTRAVFARTHEST, we distinguish between the applicability of Rule 2 to objects and nonobjects. In the case of objects, the failure to satisfy Pruning Rule 2 for obtaining the k approximate farthest neighbors is incorporated by replacing the condition "$d(o, M) \leq d(q, M) + D_k$" (line 32 in OPTBFTRAV) by the condition "$D_k \cdot (1 + \varepsilon) - d(q, M) \leq d(o, M)$," which is rewritten as "$-d(o, M) \leq D_k \cdot (1 + \varepsilon) + d(q, M)$," when we use negative distances (i.e., D_k is negative). In the case of nonobjects, e_p in nonleaf e with mean M is implemented by again storing them in C(e), but this time sorted in increasing order with respect to M using negative MAXDIST distance values and processed in this order. The implementation is simplified considerably by the inapplicability of Pruning Rule 4, which means that line 41 is omitted, as is the condition in lines 44 and 53 for determining whether actual processing of e_p should continue. The actual condition for the pruning is incorporated by using "EXIST(e_p) and $D_k \cdot (1 + \varepsilon) - d(q, M) \leq$ MAXDIST(M, e_p)" to condition the execution of the remaining instructions in lines 46–52. Use of negative distances (i.e., D_k is negative) causes this condition to be rewritten as "$-$MAXDIST$(M, e_p) \leq D_k \cdot (1 + \varepsilon) + d(q, M)$." No changes are needed in procedure OPTINSERTL.

20. ANNFNDFTRAVFARTHEST is analogous to procedure FNDFTRAVFARTHEST in Exercise 19 in Section 4.2.2. Again, each nonobject element e_p is assumed to have a representative element M_p with $r_{p,min}$ and $r_{p,max}$ as the distances from M_p to the closest and farthest object in e_p, respectively. As in the solution to Exercise 19, always shrink the distances (i.e., estimates in terms of M_p, $r_{p,min}$, and $r_{p,max}$) of nonobject elements from q by $1 + \varepsilon$. These shrunken distances are used in all comparisons with D_k and D_1. In the case that Pruning Rule 5 is found to be applicable by virtue of comparisons that involve the shrunken distances, then we reset D_1 to the shrunken distance $(-d(q, M_p) + r_{p,min})/(1 + \varepsilon)$.

21. ANNOPTDFTRAVFARTHEST is analogous to procedure OPTDFTRAVFARTHEST in Exercise 13 in Section 4.2.5 and procedure ANNOPTDFTRAV in Exercise 5. As in the solution to Exercise 19, always shrink the distances (i.e., estimates and hence both MAXDIST and MINFARTHESTDIST, which are the analogs of MINDIST and MAXNEARESTDIST, respectively) of nonobject elements from q by $1 + \varepsilon$. These shrunken distances are used in all comparisons with D_k that correspond to Pruning Rules 1 and 5, and the algorithm is simplified by also associating these shrunken distances with the nonobjects in L. Pruning Rule 2 for objects and nonobjects is handled in the same way as in the solution to Exercise 19. In particular, in the case of objects, the inapplicability of pruning Rule 4 means that there is no need in ANNOPTDFTRAV for the analog of line 13 in OPTDFTRAV, and the failure to satisfy Pruning Rule 2 for obtaining the k approximate farthest neighbors is incorporated by replacing the condition "$d(o, M) \leq d(q, M) + D_k$" (line 15 in OPTDFTRAV) with the condition "$D_k \cdot (1 + \varepsilon) - d(q, M) \leq d(o, M)$," which is rewritten as "$-d(o, M) \leq D_k \cdot (1 + \varepsilon) + d(q, M)$," when we use negative distances (i.e., D_k is negative). In the case of nonobjects, e_p in nonleaf e with mean M is implemented by again storing them in C(e), but this time sorted in increasing order with respect to M using negative MAXDIST distance values and processed in this order. The implementation is simplified considerably by the inapplicability of Pruning Rule 4, which means that line 24 is omitted, as is the condition in line 27 for the

insertion of e_p in A (i.e., the call of INSERTACTIVELIST). The actual condition for the pruning is incorporated by using "EXIST(e_p) and $D_k \cdot (1+\varepsilon) - d(q,M) \leq$ MAXDIST(M,e_p)" to condition the execution of the loop in lines 26–30. Use of negative distances (i.e., D_k is negative) causes this condition to be rewritten as "$-$MAXDIST$(M,e_p) \leq D_k \cdot (1+\varepsilon) + d(q,M)$." No changes are needed in procedure OPTINSERTL.

23. We say that o' is an approximate nearest neighbor of q if $d(q,o') \leq d(q,o) + \varepsilon D$, where o is the actual nearest neighbor and D is the *diameter* of the point set (i.e., the distance between the two farthest points). Note that we do not want to define D in terms of the distance between the two nearest points as the rationale for using the relative error bound is for the data distribution to play a role in the quality of the approximation. Thus, a definition of D in terms of the two nearest points ignores the distance between the rest of the points.

Solutions to Exercises in Section 4.4.2

2. The rationale of the SS-tree insertion strategy is that, as a result of its use, the maximum radius for the minimum hypersphere among the child nodes of n tends to be smaller than for alternative strategies. However, coverage and overlap may be greater. For example, take the alternative strategy mentioned in the question—that is, that of inserting o into a child node a if a covers the centroid of o, even though the centroid of b is closer. The disadvantage of this strategy is that if this situation occurs repeatedly, a may get ever larger and, in particular, much larger than b, increasing the likelihood of overlap with other child nodes. Another alternative strategy is to insert o into the child node whose coverage is increased the least by the expansion. This strategy has the same drawback as the alternative above. In particular, let a and b be two child nodes of n that do not overlap each other, and imagine that a series of points is inserted into the tree, all falling on the line segment between the centroids of a and b, starting closest to the centroid of a and proceeding toward b. With a suitable spacing between the inserted points, a will always be chosen as its coverage is increased the least, even as the points start to be closer to the centroid of b, until a point is inserted close to b. Thus, the minimum bounding sphere for a keeps growing, possibly far beyond the center point between the centroids of a and b, while b stays the same. In contrast, with the SS-tree strategy, the sum of the volumes of a and b would be much less, and the radii of the minimum bounding hyperspheres of a and b would both be at most one-half of the distance between their centroids. From this discussion, we see that perhaps the real rationale for inserting o into the child node of n with the nearest centroid is that it tends to minimize the largest radius among the minimum bounding hyperspheres of the child nodes of n.

4. Preparata and Shamos [1511] discuss the $d = 2$ case. In particular, they point out that the minimum bounding circle is unique and is either the circumcircle of three of the points or is defined by two of them as a diameter. Algorithms can be devised that examine all pairs or triples of points and find the smallest circle that encloses the points. An obvious implementation of the algorithm takes $O(N^4)$ time and has been reduced to $O(N^2)$ by Elzinga and Hearn [556, 557]. This problem is known in operations research as the *minimax facilities location problem* [1511] and seeks the point $p_0 = (x_0, y_0)$ (i.e., the center of a circle) whose greatest distance to any point in a given set $S = \{x_i, y_i\}$ is a minimum—that is,

$$\min_{p_0} \max_i (x_i - x_0)^2 + (y_i - y_0)^2$$

Megiddo [1280, 1281] solves this by viewing it as an instance of a linear programming problem for which he obtains a deterministic $O(C_d \cdot N)$ algorithm, where $C_d = 2^{2^d}$. Thus, the minimum bounding sphere is computed in $O(N)$ time. Seidel [1711] devised a simpler randomized algorithm for linear programming with the same dependence on N. Welzl [1982] applied this randomized algorithm to the computation of the minimum bounding sphere in arbitrary dimensions and obtained an $O(C_d \cdot N)$ algorithm, where $C_d = d!$. Even tighter bounds can be obtained by making use of more recent randomized algorithms for linear programming, such as one by Matoušek, Sharir, and Welzl [1257], who obtain an $O(d^2 \cdot N + e^{\sqrt{d \cdot \ln d}})$ solution.

5. As we will see (Exercise 1 in Section 4.4.6), in high-dimensional spaces, most of the objects will tend to lie close to the boundary. Therefore, with a sufficient number of objects, we can expect that there is an object fairly close to each boundary hyperplane, so the minimum

bounding hypersphere can be expected to be almost as large as the circumscribing hypersphere for the unit hypercube.

6. Since the expected volume follows directly from the expected diameter, the result is obtained in the same manner as in Exercise 5.

8. The intuition for this result is that the maximum volume of the unit d-dimensional hypercube is 1, while the maximum volume of the minimum bounding hypersphere is quite large since the radius can be as large as $(\sqrt{d})/2$.

Solutions to Exercises in Section 4.4.4

1. By definition, $1 - f$ is the probability that when query point q is in the Voronoi region of a point p, q is also in the approximate cover of the node containing p. This is the probability that the search finds the correct answer when q is in a particular Voronoi region of a leaf node. If q is actually in the approximating cover of some leaf node a that contains p, then a must be visited since q is also in the covers of all of the nodes on the path from the root to a. Since the Voronoi regions of all of the leaf nodes constitute a partition of the entire space, every query point lies in some Voronoi region. Therefore, the probability that the search returns the correct answer is at least $1 - f$, and thus the probability that it fails to provide the right answer is at most f.

2. When the training points are uniformly distributed, then the choice based on the number of points is much easier to compute as there is no need to calculate d-dimensional volume, which is computationally complex. On the other hand, even if the training points are not uniformly distributed, a choice based on volume may not be attractive as the situation could arise that the volume spanned by the training points on the right side of I_a whose nearest neighbors are elements of S_{al} is large while containing just a few points, whereas the volume spanned by the training points on the left side of I_a whose nearest neighbors are elements of S_{ar} is small while containing many points. In this case, we would like to give greater weight to avoiding the misclassification in the region with the smaller volume as it contains more training points. Thus, minimizing the number of misclassified training points seems the best choice regardless of the distribution of the training points.

3. If the hyperplane is closer to the two points, then their Voronoi regions (as defined by the training points) are more likely to cross over to the other side of the hyperplane.

Solutions to Exercises in Section 4.4.5

1. See [98].

Solutions to Exercises in Section 4.4.6

1. Consider a unit hypercube in a 20-dimensional space. In this case, consider an outer shell consisting of the portion of the hypercube that lies within 10% of the outer boundary. This means that we have extracted a hypercube of volume $0.8^{20} = .01153$ of the volume of the hypercube. Assuming uniformly distributed data, this means that for 20-dimensional data, the outermost 10% of the hypercube contains 98.85% of the points. For even higher dimensions, such as 100, we find that the outermost 2% of the hypercube contains 98.31% of the data.

2. Böhm, Berchtold, and Keim [224] point out that it does not hold for all d. It is not hard to show that it holds for $d = 2$, and it is a bit more difficult for $d = 3$. However, it can be shown not to hold for $d = 9$. In particular, define a sphere around the point $a = (0.2, 0.2, ..., 0.2)$. The Euclidean distance from a to c is $\sqrt{9 \cdot 0.3^2} = 0.9$. Defining a sphere around a with a radius of 0.8 results in touching or intersecting all eight-dimensional surfaces of the space while not containing the center point c.

Solutions to Exercises in Section 4.4.7

1. See [188].

2. See [1408]. Letting $[x_{i1}, x_{i2}]$ $(1 \leq i \leq d)$ denote the range of coordinate i for the window w, the result is the points that satisfy the query, which is the union of the subqueries $w_i = [l_i, h_i]$ and is formed as follows:

$$
w_i = \begin{cases}
[i + \max_{1 \leq j \leq d} x_{j1}, i + x_{i2}] & \text{if } \min_{1 \leq j \leq d} x_{j1} + \theta \geq 1 - \max_{1 \leq j \leq d} x_{j1} \\
[i + x_{i1}, i + \min_{1 \leq j \leq d} x_{j2}] & \text{if } \min_{1 \leq j \leq d} x_{j2} + \theta < 1 - \max_{1 \leq j \leq d} x_{j2} \\
[i + x_{i1}, i + x_{i2}] & \text{otherwise}
\end{cases}
$$

The case $\min_{1 \leq j \leq d} x_{j1} + \theta \geq 1 - \max_{1 \leq j \leq d} x_{j1}$ means that all of the points that satisfy the query window w have been mapped to the 1 (maximum) face, and thus a point v that satisfies w is mapped to v_{max} and would have been mapped to the d_{max}th coordinate, and has a key of $d_{max} + v_{max}$. The subquery range for the d_{max}th coordinate is $[d_{max} + \max_{1 \leq j \leq d} x_{j1}, d_{max} + x_{d_{max}2}]$. Since v satisfies w, we have $v_i \in [x_{i1}, x_{i2}]$, $\forall i, 1 \leq i \leq d$. Moreover, we have $v_{max} \geq x_{i1}$, $\forall i, 1 \leq i \leq d$. This implies that $v_{max} \geq \max_{1 \leq i \leq d} x_{i1}$, $\forall i, 1 \leq i \leq d$. We also have $v_{max} \leq x_{d_{max}2}$. Therefore, we have $v_{max} \in [\max_{1 \leq i \leq d} x_{i1}, x_{d_{max}2}]$—that is, v can be retrieved using the d_{max}th subquery. Thus, the response to query w is a subset of the union of the responses to subqueries $w_i, 1 \leq i \leq d$.

Note that the range w_i is tight in the sense that if we let $w_i' = [l_i' + \varepsilon_l, h_i' - \varepsilon_h]$ for some $\varepsilon_l > 0$ and $\varepsilon_h > 0$. Consider a point $z = (z_1, z_2, \ldots, z_d)$ that satisfies w. Note that if $l_i < z_{max} < l_i + \varepsilon_l$, then we will miss z if w_i' has been used. Similarly, if $h_i - \varepsilon_h < z_{max} < \max_{1 \leq j \leq d} x_{j2}$, then we will miss z if w_i' has been used. Therefore, no w_i' provides the tightest bound that guarantees that no points will be missed.

Similarly, the case $\min_{1 \leq j \leq d} x_{j2} + \theta < 1 - \max_{1 \leq j \leq d} x_{j2}$ means that all of the points that satisfy the query window have been mapped to the 0 (minimum) face, and thus a point v that satisfies w is mapped to v_{min} and would have been mapped to the d_{min}th coordinate, and has a key of $d_{min} + v_{min}$.

The third case means that responses to the subqueries may be found in both the 1 (maximum) and 0 (minimum) faces, and thus there are two cases to consider. In the first case, v is mapped to the minimum face, its index key is $d_{min} + v_{min}$, and it is indexed on the d_{min}th coordinate. To retrieve v, we need to examine the d_{min}th subquery $[d_{min} + x_{d_{min}1}, d_{min} + x_{d_{min}2}]$. Now, we have $v_{min} \in [x_{d_{min}1}, x_{d_{min}2}]$ (since v is in the response) and thus the d_{min}th subquery will be able to retrieve v. The second case, which maps v onto the maximum face, is derived in a similar manner. It is easy to show that w_i is optimal and that narrowing its range may result in missing some points.

It is important to note that some of the subquery ranges may be empty as a result of the upper bound of the subquery range being smaller than the maximum of the lower bounds of the subquery ranges. In this case, there is no need to evaluate the subquery.

3. In two dimensions, the point common to all the regions is obtained by solving for x in $y = 1 - x - \theta$ and $y = x$, thereby getting $2 \cdot x = 1 - \theta$, which implies that $x = (1 - \theta)/2$. The generalization to higher dimensions is straightforward.

4. The ranges of values of the different coordinates may be quite different, and this is not taken into account by the value of c. In contrast, the use of the unit cube as the underlying space reflects the application of an appropriate scaling factor to each of the individual coordinate values.

6. No, as in the M-tree, the objects that are associated with a particular reference object (termed *pivot*) are not necessarily closer to the reference object than the other ones.

Solutions to Exercises in Section 4.4.8

1. As we want to quit as soon as possible (i.e., when encountering a candidate whose lower-bound distance is greater than the largest of the current k candidate nearest neighbors), sorting may be inefficient since, for N points, building a heap is an $O(N)$ process while sorting is an $O(N \cdot log_2 N)$ process.

Solutions to Exercises in Section 4.5.1

3. Refer to Figure 4.43(b), which depicts the relative distances for a query point q' that is above q. From $\alpha^2 = a^2 + c^2$, we obtain $\alpha^2 - a^2 = (\alpha - a)(\alpha + a) = c^2$ or $\alpha - a = \frac{c^2}{\alpha + a}$. In the same manner, we can show that $\beta - b = \frac{c^2}{\beta + b}$. Since q is closer to p_2, we have $a > b$ and $\alpha > \beta$, and therefore $\alpha + a > \beta + b$. Thus, $\alpha - a = \frac{c^2}{\alpha + a} < \frac{c^2}{\beta + b} = \beta - b$, implying that $\alpha - \beta < a - b$, and thus $(d(q',p_1) - d(q',p_2))/2 < (d(q,p_1) - d(q,p_2))/2$.

Solutions to Exercises in Section 4.5.2.1.1

5. The definition of the boundary of an ellipse in two dimensions is the set of all points p such that $d_E(p_1, p) + d_E(p_2, p) = r$. This can be generalized to any dimension and metric d by replacing d_E by d. The two subsets S_1 and S_2 are defined as follows:

$$S_1 = \{o \in S \setminus \{p_1, p_2\} \mid d(p_1, o) + d(p_2, o) < r\}$$
$$S_2 = \{o \in S \setminus \{p_1, p_2\} \mid d(p_1, o) + d(p_2, o) \geq r\}$$

6. In this case, we have what Uhlmann terms the *generalized hyperplane method* (see Section 4.5.3) [1897]. In essence, we have a hyperplane, which partitions the objects into two sets S_1 and S_2 depending on which of the pivots is closer (if $r = 0$) or which of the pivots is closer once the distance from p_1 has been decreased by r—that is, $d(p_1, o) - d(p_2, o) = r$. The two subsets S_1 and S_2 are defined as follows:

$$S_1 = \{o \in S \setminus \{p_1, p_2\} \mid d(p_1, o) - d(p_2, o) < r\}$$
$$S_2 = \{o \in S \setminus \{p_1, p_2\} \mid d(p_1, o) - d(p_2, o) \geq r\}$$

Solutions to Exercises in Section 4.5.2.1.2

5. (Gísli R. Hjaltason) Suppose that we have ball elements e_a and e_1 centered at pivots p_a and p_1 with ball radii r_a and r_1, respectively, so that e_1 is a son of e_a. Note that in this example we have that $d(p_1, p_a)$ is almost as large as r_a. In this case, it is possible for r_1 to be larger than $r_a - d(p_a, p_1)$, which means that the ball e_1 centered at pivot p_1 extends beyond the ball e_a centered at pivot p_a. Now, if q is chosen appropriately as in the figure, we may find that q is closer to e_1 than to e_a, as we wanted to show. Figure 4.59 in Section 4.5.3.3 illustrates this situation.

6. Each node A of the vp-tree partitions the domain S that it spans into two regions S_1 and S_2 based on a pivot p in S and a radius r so that S_1 contains all objects in S that lie within radius r of p and S_2 contains all objects in S whose distance from p is greater than r. We need to distinguish whether q lies in S_1 or in S_2 and the corresponding distance. If q lies in S_2, then the distance from q to S_1 is $d(q, p) - r$, and the result of shrinking S_1 is that its distance from q is $d(q, p) - \lambda \cdot r$. On the other hand, if q lies in S_1, then the situation is not so simple as now the distance from q to S_2 is $r - d(p, q)$ and shrinking S_2 requires that r be increased by a factor of $1 + 1 - \lambda$ instead of being reduced by a factor of λ. Therefore, the result of shrinking S_2 is that its distance from q is $(2 - \lambda) \cdot r - d(q, p)$.

Solutions to Exercises in Section 4.5.2.2

3. See [851].

Solutions to Exercises in Section 4.5.2.3

3. See [851].

Solutions to Exercises in Section 4.5.2.4

10. The only similarity is that they both use the same set of pivots at each node at a given level. They differ in several respects. The fixed-queries tree uses just one pivot at each level, while the mvp-tree uses a multiple number of pivots at a given level. The m-ary nature of the mvp-tree is derived from the multiple radius values used at each node at level i, which need not be the same for each node at level i. In contrast, the m-ary nature of the fixed-queries tree is derived from the partition values r_i ($i = 0, \ldots, m-1$) of the underlying data domain, which are centered about the different pivots but are the same for every node at level i.

14. Let L consist of the objects in the ball B with pivot c and radius r, and let E be the set of objects outside B. Compute $d(c,q)$. If R is empty, then exit. If $d(c,q) \leq \varepsilon$, then add c to the results of the query. If $d(c,q) \leq r + \varepsilon$, then search B in its entirety. If $d(c,q) \leq r - \varepsilon$, then apply all of these steps recursively to E.

Solutions to Exercises in Section 4.5.3.1

3. Faloutsos and Lin [587] suggest choosing an object a at random. Next, find the object r that is farthest from a. Finally, find the object s that is farthest from r. The last step can be iterated a number of times (e.g., 5 [587]) in order to obtain a better estimate of the pair that is farthest apart (see Section 4.7.3.2 for more details), although most implementations (e.g., [1270, 1272, 1286]) stop once they obtain the initial values for r and s.

4. For example, given that a and b are the objects that are the farthest apart, find two objects c and d separated by approximately $d(a,b)/2$ and at a distance of $d(a,b)/4$ from a and b, respectively.

7. This modification comes into play when q lies outside both e_1 and its parent e_a. Its rationale is that although the nesting property of the partitioning process means that d_{min} of the parent e_a of e_1 (based on the objects in the descendants of e_a) cannot be greater than the minimum distance from q to any object in e_1 and its descendants, the use of different pivots for the balls corresponding to partitions e_a and e_1 can result in d_{min} of e_a being greater than d_{min} for e_1. In particular, this happens because the union of the balls corresponding to e_1, and its parent e_a can be greater than the ball corresponding to e_a although the additional hypervolume does not contain any objects. Such a situation is depicted in Figure 4.59 in Section 4.5.3.3 and the solution to Exercise 5 in Section 4.5.2.1.2, where, without loss of generality, the partitions and the corresponding balls are identical. The fact that the additional hypervolume is empty means that there is no real harm in setting d_{min} to $d(q,p_1) - r_1$ in this case, which is less than $d(q,e_a)$, as no other node n with $d(q,n) < d(q,e_a)$ is presently on the priority queue by virtue of the fact that we take elements off the queue in increasing order of their distance from q.

Solutions to Exercises in Section 4.5.3.2

2. See [851].

Solutions to Exercises in Section 4.5.3.3

1. In essence, we need to prove that the covering radii of the balls around the pivots p_1 and p_2 corresponding to the children of element e_a are smaller than the radius of the covering ball

of pivot p_a in e_a. Assume without loss of generality that p_1 corresponds to the repeated pivot p_a. All objects that are closer to p_1 than to p_2 are in the ball around p_1, but the ball around p_a also includes the objects that are closer to p_2 than to p_1, and thus these objects cause the covering radius of the ball around p_a to be larger than the covering radius of the ball around p_1. Similarly, all objects that are closer to p_2 than to p_1 are in the ball around p_2, but the ball around p_a also includes the objects that are closer to p_2 than to p_1, and thus these objects cause the covering radius of the ball around p_a to be larger than the covering radius of the ball around p_2.

2. Use induction. When $N = 2$, only one node is needed. Each time we add an object, we add a node. The result follows.

6. The proof is analogous to the proof in Exercise 1 that none of the children in an mb-tree are eccentric. Again, we need to prove that the covering radii of the balls around the pivots p_1, p_2, and p_3 corresponding to the children of element e_a are smaller than radius of the covering ball of pivot p_a in e_a. Assume, without loss of generality, that p_1 corresponds to the repeated pivot p_a. All objects that are closer to p_1 than to p_2 or p_3 are in the ball around p_1, but the ball around p_a also includes the objects that are closer to p_2 or closer to p_3 than to p_1, and thus these objects cause the covering radius of the ball around p_a to be larger than the covering radius of the ball around p_1. Similarly, all objects that are closer to p_2 (p_3) than to p_1 are in the ball around p_2 (p_3), but the ball around p_a also includes the objects that are closer to p_2 (p_3) than to p_1 and thus these objects cause the covering radius of the ball around p_a to be larger than the covering radius of the ball around p_2 (p_3).

7. The process used to build the Voronoi tree ensures that at each stage we descend the path to the child corresponding to the closest of the pivots at the particular level. Note, however, that this process only ensures that the immediate ancestor is the closest of o's ancestor pivots. In particular, it does not ensure that there is no other closer object/pivot to o in the Voronoi tree.

8. The search for the nearest neighbor of an object o stored in the root node proceeds as follows. Descend the child corresponding to o. If we are at node U such that no such child exists, then o is one of the pivot objects contained in U. Next, descend in parallel down the one or two paths corresponding to the remaining pivots p_1 and p_2 in U to nodes V_1 and V_2, respectively. For each of the nodes V_1 and V_2 descend along the paths corresponding to the pivot in V_1 that is closest to o and the pivot in V_2 closest to o. When this process terminates, we have at most two candidate pivot objects, and the closest one to o is o's nearest neighbor. The correctness of this process (i.e., that the candidate pivot object that is closest to o is indeed o's nearest neighbor) is ensured by the fact that the Voronoi tree is transitive, as shown in Exercise 7.

Solutions to Exercises in Section 4.5.3.4

1. See [723]. Observe that once the approximate k-center algorithm has been applied k times (i.e., $i = k - 1$), we have the k approximate k-centers $\{v_0, v_1, \ldots, v_{k-1}\}$, which make up the set C_k. At this point, from property (b) we know that the object v_k, defined by $d_k(v_k, C_k) = \max_{v \in S - C_k} \min_{c \in C_k} ||v - c||$, is the farthest object in $S - C_k$ from its corresponding approximate k-center, where $d_k(v_k, C_k)$ is the distance of v_k from its corresponding approximate k-center. Now, let us examine the partition P of S resulting from the use of the actual k-centers (rather than the approximate ones). By the pigeonhole principle, in partition P, two of the $k + 1$ objects $\{v_0, v_1, \ldots, v_k\}$, say v_i and v_j, must be in the same cluster. Without loss of generality, we assume that this cluster has c as its k-center. From the triangle inequality, we have $||v_i - c|| + ||v_j - c|| \geq ||v_i - v_j||$. Letting $C_j = \{v_0, v_1, \ldots, v_{j-1}\}$, and assuming, without loss of generality, that $j > i$, we also know from property (b) that $||v_i - v_j|| \geq d_j(v_j, C_j)$ as v_j is the farthest object in $S - C_j$ from C_j at a distance of $d_j(v_j, C_j)$ and v_i is also in C_j resulting in its distance from v_j (i.e., $||v_i - v_j||$) being at least $d_j(v_j, C_j)$. In addition, we have that $d_j(v_j, C_j) \geq d_j(v_k, C_j)$ as, by definition, v_j at distance $d_j(v_j, C_j)$ is always the farthest object from an element of C_j after j iterations of the approximate k-center algorithm. Finally, given that $j \leq k$, from property (a) we have that $d_j(v_k, C_j) \geq d_k(v_k, C_k)$ as the distance from each object v (v_k in this case) to C ($C_a(j \leq a \leq k)$ in this case) does not increase as the approximate k-center algorithm progresses. At this point, knowing that $||v_i - c|| \leq \delta$

and $||v_j - c|| \le \delta$ means that $2\delta \ge d_k(v_k, C_k)$. Therefore, the maximum radius $d_k(v_k, C_k)$ obtained by the approximate k-center algorithm is at most twice the optimum maximum radius δ resulting from the use of the actual k-centers.

2. See [325]

Solutions to Exercises in Section 4.5.5.1

1. For example, suppose that $\mathbb{U} = \mathbb{U}' = \{a, b, c, x\}$, $d(a,b) = d(a,c) = d(b,c) = 2$ and $d'(a,b) = d'(a,c) = d'(b,c) = 2$. Furthermore, assume that $d(a,x) = 1$, $d(b,x) = 2$, and $d(c,x) = 3$, while $d'(a,x) = 3$, $d'(b,x) = 2$, and $d'(c,x) = 1$. If $S = S' = \{a, b, c\}$, the distance matrices for the two sets are the same. The graph with edges (a,b) and (a,c) (i.e., $N(a) = \{b,c\}$ and $N(b) = N(c) = \{a\}$) satisfies the Voronoi property for (S, d) since the nearest neighbor of any query object drawn from $\mathbb{U}$ can be arrived at starting at any object in S by only transitioning to neighbors that are closer to or at the same distance from the query object. Thus, this graph is a Delaunay graph for (S, d). However, it does not satisfy the Voronoi property for (S', d') since starting at b with $q = x$, b's only neighbor a is farther away from x than b is, so we cannot transition to the nearest neighbor c of x. Thus, it is not a Delaunay graph for (S', d'). It is interesting to note that the graph with edges (a,b) and (b,c) (i.e., $N(b) = \{a,c\}$ and $N(a) = N(c) = \{b\}$) satisfies the Voronoi property for both (S, d) and (S', d'), and thus it is a Delaunay graph for both (S, d) and (S', d'). Of course, this example does not invalidate our observation that knowledge of (S, d) is insufficient to determine the Delaunay graph.

2. (Houman Alborzi) One possible effect is that if all N objects are equidistant, then a definition in terms of $d(x, a) \le d(x, y)$ would yield a tree with one of the objects, say a, as the root, and all remaining $N - 1$ objects as a's immediate children, in contrast to a tree in the form of a linear list so that each node has a fanout of one.

3. Navarro [1347] makes use of the following "greedy" heuristic to identify the set of neighbors $N(a)$ of object a:

   (a) $N(a) \leftarrow \{\}$.

   (b) Process all objects x (besides a) in increasing order of distance from a.

   (c) If $d(x, a) < d(x, y)$ for all y in $N(a)$, then add x to $N(a)$.

   Although the algorithm does satisfy the criterion that any neighbor in $N(a)$ be closer to a than to any other neighbor in $N(a)$, it is a heuristic because the set $N(a)$ may not necessarily be the smallest possible set. An example of this is given in the text.

Solutions to Exercises in Section 4.5.5.2

1. *Proof* Following [851, 853], we divide the proof into two parts. First, we show that b' is closer to b than to any of the ancestors of b, and then we do the same for any of the children of the ancestors.

   Let c be an ancestor of b (or b itself), and let c' be the parent of c. We claim that b' is closer to c than to c', or, more accurately, $d(b', c) \le d(b', c')$. To show this, we will use contradiction. Assume that $d(b', c) > d(b', c')$. Since $c \in N(c')$, the definition of the neighbor set means b' should also be in $N(c')$, but this contradicts the original assumption that c is an ancestor of b (and, by extension, of b'). Thus, our claim holds, implying that the ancestors of b are progressively farther away from b' (or, more accurately, "farther away or equidistant"). Clearly, this implication subsumes the statement that we wished to prove, that b' is closer to b than to ancestors of b.

   Now, let a' be an ancestor of b (including, again, b itself), and let c be a member of $N(a')$ that is not an ancestor of b; the case of c being an ancestor was treated above. Suppose that b' is closer to c than to b—that is, $d(b', c) < d(b', b)$. Letting $c' \in N(a')$ be the ancestor of b among the siblings of c, we saw above that $d(b',b) \le d(b',c')$. This, coupled with our assumption about c, further implies that $d(b',c) < d(b',c')$. However, in this case, b' should have been associated with the subtree rooted at c instead of the one rooted at c', thereby contradicting the assumption that c is not an ancestor of b. Hence, b' cannot be closer to c than to b, and the proof is complete. ∎

2. Hjaltason and Samet [853] show that, unfortunately, the answer is no, as can be seen by examining the example in Figure S.17 from [853]. In the figure, the two-dimensional points b′ and c′ can be moved arbitrarily close to each other while maintaining the same sa-tree structure. Hence, an object b′ can easily be closer to some other object c′ than to its parent b if c′ is not among the "ancestor neighbors" of b. Therefore, objects that are not among the ancestor neighbors of b can be arbitrarily close to b′, thereby precluding their consideration as candidates for improving the pruning power.

3. Each of A's children e that is a leaf node is enqueued as an element of type 'node'. However, when each leaf node child e is subsequently dequeued, e's corresponding object a is enqueued as an element of type 'object' while no elements of type 'node' are enqueued as a has no children and thus $N(a)$ is empty. Therefore, SATREEINCNEAREST terminates in this case.

4. Simply include d_a inside the max{…} computation in line 22 of SATREEINCNEAREST.

5. *Proof* Following [853], we let $o_k \in S$ be the kth neighbor of q. When the nonmonotonic version of SATREEINCNEAREST reports o_k as the next neighbor of q, the priority queue, by the definition of DEQUEUE, contains no element with a key smaller than D_k. Clearly, the nonmonotonic version of SATREEINCNEAREST cannot visit any node not visited by the monotonic version, as the d_{lo} values computed in the former are never greater than those computed in the latter. Suppose $b \in S$ corresponds to an sa-tree node n that is visited by the nonmonotonic version of SATREEINCNEAREST, thus having a d_{lo} value smaller than $d(q,o_k)$. Since all the ancestors of n must be visited in order for n to be visited, the d_{lo} value for the ancestors must also be smaller than $d(q,o_k)$. The d_{lo} value computed for b by the monotonic version (i.e., by including d_a in the maximum computation of line 22) cannot be greater than that for the ancestors of n. Hence, these two facts imply that n is also visited by the monotonic version, so we have shown the two versions visit exactly the same set of nodes. ∎

6. When at node a that is not a root, we first determine the object $c \in \bigcup_{a' \in A(b)}(\{a'\} \cup N(a'))$, where b is in $N(a)$ such that $d(q,c)$ is minimized. When at node a that is a root, then c is set to a. In either case, the search now continues as before by visiting each child $b \in N(a)$, except those for which $(d(q,b) - d(q,c))/2 > \varepsilon$.

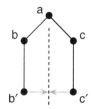

Figure S.17
A simple sa-tree for five two-dimensional points, with a as the root. The points b′ and c′ can move arbitrarily close to the broken line, as indicated by the gray arrows, without giving rise to a different tree structure.

Solutions to Exercises in Section 4.5.6

1. Yes. Just because there is an edge from p to a (i.e., a is one of the k nearest neighbors of p) does not necessarily mean that there is an edge from a to p (i.e., p is not necessarily one of the k nearest neighbors of a).

2. (Houman Alborzi) Use contradiction. Suppose that for vertex (i.e., object) u, its nearest neighbor v is not in the MST. In this case, by adding edge uv to the minimal spanning tree, we are forming a cycle in the tree that passes through u. This means that there exists another edge uw in the cycle where uw is longer than edge uv. Therefore, by removing edge uw, we have decreased the cost of the minimal spanning tree. This contradicts the assumption that we started with a minimal spanning tree and that the nearest neighbor v of u was not in the minimal spanning tree. Thus, the claim holds.

8. Show that each edge uv of the MST is in the RNG. In particular, for edge uv in the MST, we want to show that for all other vertices, w, $d(u,v) \le \max\{d(u,w),d(v,w)\}$. The inequality holds iff $d(u,v) \le d(u,w)$ or $(d(u,v) \le d(v,w))$. For any vertex w other than u or v, consider the possible edges uv, vw, and uw. uv is in the MST, and among the other two edges, at most one of them is in the MST as otherwise the three edges form a cycle, which is impossible as the MST cannot have any cycles. If uw is not in the MST, then $d(u,v) \le d(u,w)$ as otherwise the MST would have included uw instead of uv. Similarly, we can show that if vw is not

in the MST, then $d(u,v) \leq d(v,w)$. In other words, we have shown that $d(u,v) \leq d(u,w)$ or $(d(u,v) \leq d(v,w))$. Hence, by the definition of the RNG, uv is in the RNG. Therefore, every edge in the MST is in the RNG and thus the RNG is connected.

9. We can demonstrate an even stronger result than that the UNG is not connected. In particular, we show that it consists of isolated vertices or unconnected edges. Let us consider vertices u and v such that an edge uv exists in the UNG. If no such pair of vertices exists, then the graph is clearly unconnected. Now, consider any other vertex w. We show that neither edges uw nor vw are in the UNG, which means that the graph must be unconnected as there is no way to reach any vertex w from u or v. This can be seen by noting that since uv is in the UNG, we have from the definition of the UNG that $\min\{d(w,u),d(w,v)\} > d(u,v)$, which means that $d(w,u) > d(u,v)$, and $d(w,v) > d(u,v)$. From the definition of the UNG, this means that neither uw nor vw can be an edge in the UNG as v is closer to u than w is to u in the former, and u is closer to v than w is to v in the latter. Therefore, there are no edges incident at u and v, and thus we have an edge that is not connected to any other edges.

10. One possibility is to use it to detect two-element clusters and then use the pairs as cluster centers instead of single-element cluster centers.

11. It is easy to find nontrivial graphs where the DNG is connected. For example, this is the case when a third object is constrained to lie in the lune anchored at the two farthest objects.

12. (Houman Alborzi) Assume that the two vertices with the largest distances are u and v. Therefore, we know that $\max\{d(w,u),d(w,v)\} \leq d(u,v)$ holds for all vertices w. This is equivalent to stipulating that there does not exist a vertex w for which $\max\{d(w,u),d(w,v)\} > d(u,v)$, and by using the definition of the DNG , we see that edge uv must be in the DNG.

13. As in the case of the UNG, as discussed in the solution to Exercise 10, the DNG could be used to detect larger clusters in the sense that the initial two-element clusters could be larger.

14. It is easy to see that UNG $\subset$ RNG. For an edge to be included in the RNG, only the lune of the spheres must be empty, while for an edge to be included in the UNG , the union of the spheres must be empty, which also includes the lune.

15. In general, RNG $\cap$ DNG is not equal to the UNG as can be seen when there are just three objects in the dataset, and they are all equidistant. In this case, both the DNG and the RNG consist of three edges, while the UNG is empty. However, if all distances between pairs of vertices are different, then this relationship would hold. This relationship would also hold if we had slightly altered the definitions of the UNG and the DNG as follows:

- Edge uv is part of the UNG whenever the area defined by the objects p such that $\min\{d(p,u),d(p,v)\} < d(u,v)$ is empty.

- Edge uv is part of the DNG whenever the area defined by the objects p such that $\min\{d(p,u),d(p,v)\} < d(u,v) < \max\{d(p,u),d(p,v)\}$ is empty.

Given such definitions, RNG $\cap$ DNG = UNG as we observe that an edge can be included in the DNG regardless of whether the lune is empty, while the lune must be empty in the case of the RNG. However, these definitions were modified so that we could prove that the UNG is not connected.

16. In this case, $d_1(p,(u,v)) = d(p,u) + d(p,v)$, and the condition for the existence of an edge between u and v using bidistance metric $d_1(p,(u,v))$ is one that stipulates that the locus of all objects p at a distance $d_1(p,(u,v))$ from u and v that is less than $d(u,v)$ must be empty. In other words, for all objects p, we must have that $d(u,p) + d(v,p) \geq d(u,v)$. However, the condition $d(u,p) + d(v,p) \geq d(u,v)$ is the triangle inequality, which is always true for a distance metric d. The complete graph satisfies this condition, which means that in this graph, which we call the *Manhattan graph*, an edge exists between every pair of vertices.

17. From the definition of the RNG, we know that for an edge uv in RNG, $d(u,v) \leq \max\{d(p,u),d(p,v)\}$ for all other vertices p. Squaring both sides of the inequality leads to $d(u,v)^2 \leq \max\{d(p,u)^2,d(p,v)^2\}$, which implies that the inequality also holds for their sum and thus $d(u,v)^2 \leq d(p,u)^2 + d(p,v)^2)$. Therefore, edge uv is also in the GG.

18. It should be clear that whenever $\alpha \leq \pi/2$ in the original definition of the augmented Gabriel graph (AGG), the angles formed by the remaining vertices are also less than or equal to $\pi/2$.

This means that they are less than or equal to $\pi - \alpha$, which, of course, is greater than or equal to $\pi/2$. When $\alpha > \pi/2$, the condition for the existence of edge uv is still that for all other vertices w in the graph, $\angle u, w, v \leq \pi - \alpha$.

19. When $\alpha = \pi/2$, vertices p, u, and v form a right triangle, and thus the vertex p responsible for α has the property that $d(u, p)^2 + d(v, p)^2 = d(u, v)^2$. Using the fact that the vertices of the right triangle lie on a sphere of diameter $d(u, v)$, we have that for $\alpha < \pi/2$, p lies outside the sphere and hence $d(u, p)^2 + d(v, p)^2 \geq d(u, v)^2$, which means that the edge uv is in the Gabriel graph. On the other hand, for $\alpha > \pi/2$, p lies inside the sphere, and hence $d(u, p)^2 + d(v, p)^2 < d(u, v)^2$, and the edge uv is not in the Gabriel graph.

20. This definition is equivalent to stipulating that the disc whose boundary contains p, u, and v is empty, which is known as the disc property of the DT (see Section 2.2.1.4 of Chapter 2). It states that an edge uv exists in the DT if and only if there exists a disc with u and v on its boundary that does not contain any other vertex.

21. Consider the dataset with points $u = (0, 2, 0)$, $v = (0, -2, 0)$, $a = (1, 0, 0)$, $b = (-4, 0, 0)$, $c = (0.9, 0, 0.5)$, and $d = (0.9, 0, -0.5)$. Show that any sphere with u and v on its boundary contains at least one of a, b, c, or d. Hence, the DT does not contain edge uv. Also, show that the modification in Exercise 20 yields a graph with edge uv in it.

22. *Proof*   From Exercise 19, we have that $GG(E) \subset AGG(E)$ since every edge in the GG is in the AGG. However, the AGG may also contain other edges as well. Therefore, $MST(E) \subset RNG(E) \subset GG(E) \subset AGG(E)$. Showing that $AGG(E) \subset DT(E)$ is a bit trickier. The proof is similar to that used in the solution to Exercise 4 in Section 2.2.1.4 of Chapter 2. There are two cases to consider depending on whether $\alpha < \pi/2$ or $\alpha \geq \pi/2$.

(a) $\alpha < \pi/2$:. We show that if edge uv is in the AGG, then it is also in the DT. From the definition of α, we know that for all other vertices w, $\angle uwv \leq \alpha$. In addition, as $\alpha < \pi/2$, we have $\alpha < \pi/2 < \pi - \alpha$, and therefore $\angle uwv \leq \alpha < \pi/2 < \pi - \alpha$. We have just shown that $\angle uwv < \pi/2$, which means that all vertices w are outside the minimum disc (sphere in higher dimensions) enclosing u and v. Therefore, by the disc property, we know that uv is in the DT.

(b) $\alpha \geq \pi/2$: We show that if edge uv is in the AGG, then it is also in the DT. As uv is in the AGG, from the definition of the AGG we know that, for all other vertices w, $\angle uwv \leq \pi - \alpha$. Let D_{uvt} denote the disc passing through u, v, and an arbitrary point t. The line containing u and v divides the interior of disc D_{uvt} into two segments: segment S_t at the same side of t and segment O_t at the other side of point t. Now, consider the disc D_{uvp} passing through u, v, and p, remembering that $\alpha = \angle upv$. In this case, the line containing u and v divides the interior of D_{uvp} into two segments: segment S_p at the same side of p and segment O_p at the other side of point p.

We know that for all points t in S_p, the discs D_{uvt} formed by $t, u,$ and v will have larger radii than the disc D_{uvp} formed by $p, u,$ and v as the areas spanned by S_t are smaller than that spanned by S_p, which means that the angles $\angle utv$ are larger than the angle $\angle upv = \alpha$. Therefore, by the definition of the AGG, S_p cannot contain any vertices as any of the angles that they form with u and v would be larger than α, thereby contradicting the definition of the AGG.

Now, consider the case of points in O_p. Consider a point q on the disc D_{uvp} passing through u, v, and p such that q is not on the same side of uv as p. We know that $\angle upv + \angle uqv = \pi$ since the sum of these two inscribed angles is one-half of the sum of the arcs that they subtend, which is 2π. However, $\angle upv = \alpha$, and thus subtracting α from both sides of the equality yields $\angle uqv = \pi - \alpha$.

We now use the same reasoning as in the case of points in S_p. In particular, we know that for all points t in O_p, the discs D_{uvt} formed by $t, u,$ and v will have larger radii than the disc D_{uvq} formed by $q, u,$ and v (equivalently, D_{uvp} where q has been replaced by p) as the areas spanned by S_t are smaller than that spanned by O_p, which means that the angles $\angle utv$ are larger than the angle $\angle uqv = \pi - \alpha$. Therefore, by the definition of the

AGG, O_p cannot contain any vertices as any of the angles that they form with u and v would be larger than α, thereby contradicting the definition of the AGG. Thus, we have shown that the disc D_{uvp} does not contain any vertices, and hence by the disc property, we know that edge uv is in the DT.

Notice that the proof of case (b), as written, only applies to two dimensions. Nevertheless, it can be applied with a few more details in higher dimensions as well.

Therefore, since $GG(E) \subset AGG(E)$ and $AGG(E) \subset DT(E)$, we have now shown that $MST(E) \subset RNG(E) \subset GG(V) \subset AGG(E) \subset DT(E)$. ∎

From the proof we see that the AGG is more restricted than the DT as every edge in AGG is in the DT. We can also see this from the definition of the DT in terms of the statement of the definition of the AGG in Exercise 20. In particular, in the case of the AGG, the constraint on the angle formed by w, u, and v must be satisfied regardless of the side of the line or hyperplane on which w lies. On the other hand, in the case of the DT, the constraint must be satisfied only on the side of the line or hyperplane opposite to that containing p. Thus, an edge may fail to be in the AGG while still being in the DT.

23. It is easy to generalize this property to other L_p metrics or dimensions. In particular, notice that the minimum disc containing edge uv is centered at w such that $d(w,v) = d(w,u)$ and $d(w,v)$ is the smallest distance among all points of the space that are equidistant from u and v. So, for any space for which such a w can be found, the GG can be defined as having an edge uv iff for all other vertices t, $d(w,t) \geq d(w,u)$. Notice that this definition is equal to the one given in the text for any dimension when using the Euclidean distance.

25. (Houman Alborzi) Define $\angle u, p, v$ as

$$\arccos((dist(u,p)^2 + dist(p,v)^2 - dist(u,v)^2)/(2 \cdot dist(u,p) \cdot dist(p,v))).$$

Basing the definition only on distance values, rather than in terms of an angle that breaks down in non-Euclidean metrics, ensures that the definition can be applied to any other metric. Observe that as distances are drawn from a metric space, we can show that the argument of $\arccos()$ always lies between -1 and 1. Hence, the expression is always well defined. In particular, the expression results in the actual angle when the Euclidean metric is used. However, note that the definition does not guarantee that any of the properties of the AGG mentioned earlier will necessarily hold.

Solutions to Exercises in Section 4.5.7.1

1. See [851].

Solutions to Exercises in Section 4.5.7.2

1. See [851].

Solutions to Exercises in Section 4.5.7.3

4. Let $x = \min\{d_n, d_a\}$ denote the threshold value of d_{lo}, which is used to decide which objects to move from S_d to S_a. d_n is monotonically nonincreasing as it starts at ∞. d_a is monotonically nondecreasing as it starts with the smallest value in S_a (except for being ∞ when S_a is empty). Let o_i be an element of the alive set S_a. We want to show that $d(q,o_1) - x| \leq d(o_1,o_i) \leq x + d(q,o_1)$.

$$|d(q,o_1) - d(o_1,o_i)| \leq x \Rightarrow d(q,o_1) - d(o_1,o_i) \leq x \vee d(o_1,o_i) - d(q,o_1) \leq x$$

$$\Rightarrow d(o_1,o_i) \geq d(q,o_1) - x \vee d(o_1,o_i) \leq d(q,o_1) + x$$

$$\Rightarrow d(q,o_1) - x \leq d(o_1,o_i) \leq x + d(q,o_1).$$

Solutions to Exercises in Section 4.5.8

1. See [884].

2. At most p edges enter each object in the SASH, and there are N objects over the $h = \log_2 N$ levels of the SASH.

3. See [884].

4. There are $\log_2 N$ levels, and at each level i, we add k objects to set U_i, and the desired result follows. Note that the $0.5pc$ term in the computation of k_i that is used to ensure that at least $0.5pc$ objects are obtained at each level of the search is accounted for by the $\log_2 N$ term in the execution time.

5. The execution time is proportional to the work expended in forming the sets U_i ($1 \leq i \leq h$), which is proportional to the number of objects k_i found at level i as the SASH is descended:

$$\sum_{i=1}^{h} k^{1-(h-i)/\log_2 N}$$

$$= k^{1-h/\log_2 N} \sum_{i=1}^{h} (k^{1/\log_2 N})^i \leq k^{1-h/\log_2 N} \frac{k^{(h+1)/\log_2 N}}{k^{1/\log_2 N} - 1} \leq \frac{k^{1+1/\log_2 N}}{k^{1/\log_2 N} - 1}$$

The closed form, if any of this sum, varies depending on the relative magnitudes of k and N. Note that the $\log_2 N$ term arises from the $0.5pc$ term in the computation of k_i that is used to ensure that at least $0.5pc$ objects are obtained at each level of the search.

6. (Michael E. Houle) Substituting N^ε for all but one factor of k in the expression

$$\frac{k^{1+\frac{1}{\log_2 N}}}{k^{\frac{1}{\log_2 N}} - 1}$$

yields

$$k \frac{N^{\varepsilon \frac{1}{\log_2 N}}}{N^{\varepsilon \frac{1}{\log_2 N}} - 1}$$

which is equal to ck, where $c = \frac{2^\varepsilon}{2^\varepsilon - 1}$ is a constant, thereby leading to the desired result. We ignore that $\log_2 N$ term as N^ε dominates $\log_2 N$.

7. The minimum is b/c. It arises when as many as possible of the candidate objects at level $i + 1$ can be reached from the same object at level i, which is c for each such object at level i. The result follows as there are b reachable objects at level $i + 1$. The maximum is bp and is easy to see as each of the b objects at level $i + 1$ can have as many as p different approximate p nearest neighbors at level i.

8. The minimum is 0 as it could be that none of the reachable candidate objects at level i are among the p approximate nearest neighbors of the objects at level $i + 1$. The maximum is ac and arises when each of the a reachable candidate objects at level i is one of the p approximate nearest neighbors of as many different objects at level $i + 1$ as possible, assuming a maximum of c objects at level $i + 1$ for each of the a objects at level i. In other words, for each object in the reachable candidate objects at level $i + 1$, only one of its p approximate nearest neighbors at level i is in the set of reachable candidate objects at level i, and these approximate nearest neighbors are unique. Of course, there could be many more objects at level $i + 1$ than the reachable candidate objects at level $i + 1$.

9. $k_i/k_{i+1} = k^{1-(h-i)/\log_2 N}/k^{1-(h-(i+1))/\log_2 N} = k^{-1/\log_2 N} = 1/k^{1/\log_2 N}$, which is equal to 1 for $k = 1$, monotonically decreasing as k increases, and equal to $1/2$ when $k = N$.

10. Houle and Sakuma [884] suggest to apply a repeated doubling process in terms of the number of neighbors sought on subsequent iterations. Therefore, once the first p nearest objects are rejected, an attempt is made to connect to the $2p, 4p, \ldots, 2^i p$ nearest neighbors until a node with excess capacity is found.

11. The method proposed here immediately eliminates some candidates obtained early in the search process from further consideration when closer candidates have been found. In contrast,

once U_i has been computed for level i and we are processing level j ($j > i$), the method of Houle and Sakuma [884] does not examine U_i again until it is ready to report the k approximate nearest neighbors.

12. (Michael E. Houle) The algorithm is similar to that used for determining the approximate k nearest neighbors except that there are no fixed upper bounds k_i on the number of objects retained at each SASH level during the descent. Let W_i denote the set of objects that are retained at level i. W_1 is the root object. W_{i+1} is formed at level i by adding each object o at level $i + 1$ that is adjacent to at least one object in W_i. Next, any objects in W_{i+1} that do not lie in the search range are removed from W_{i+1} unless doing so will reduce the number of remaining objects so that it is less than $0.5pc$, in which case we retain the closest $0.5pc$ objects to q even if some of them lie outside the search range. The final range query result for q consists of the union of those objects retained over all SASH levels, minus those objects that lie outside the search range.

13. As the approximate k nearest neighbor algorithm for a SASH inherently finds a relatively large set of candidate neighbors before reducing it, one possible approach is to turn to this set for additional neighbors, although the fact that we only wanted k neighbors initially does influence the implementation of the approximate k nearest neighbor algorithm. Thus, there must be some way to reconsider some of the candidate nearest neighbors that were eliminated during the search for the approximate k nearest neighbors.

14. The advantage of SASH over EXSASH is that it takes $O(N_i^2)$ time to build EXSASH$_i$, assuming N_i objects in EXSASH$_i$\EXSASH$_{i-1}$, as, unlike in SASH, the existing edges in EXSASH$_{i-1}$ are of no use to us in determining the edges from the objects in EXSASH$_i$ \ EXSASH$_{i-1}$ to the objects in EXSASH$_{i+1}$\EXSASH$_i$. Of course, once the directed graph corresponding to EXSASH$_h$ has been built, EXSASH$_h$ is likely to yield more accurate results than SASH$_h$ as the edges reflect exact nearest neighbors rather than likely nearest neighbors.

15. Given a query object q, an immediate problem is finding an object or objects at level h that are close to q to start the search. The index represented by the reverse kNN graph does not provide any information to help find these objects. Thus, this step will require search, which could take as much as $O(N^2)$ time. Once these initial objects have been found, the search can proceed in the same way as in the kNN graph.

Solutions to Exercises in Section 4.6.1.1

1. This is easy to see when we realize that the number of responses for the query in the original and dimension reduced spaces are not necessarily the same assuming that we use the same query radius value.

Solutions to Exercises in Section 4.6.1.2

1. Letting R_n and R_k denote the set of responses retrieved in the original and dimension reduced spaces, respectively, remember that precision is equal to $|R_n \cap R_k|/|R_k|$ and recall is equal to $|R_n \cap R_k|/|R_n|$. However, $|R_k| = |R_n| = K$, and the result holds. Therefore, using recall and precision to measure the quality of a query to find the ith nearest neighbor is somewhat meaningless as they do not reflect the fact that the sets R_k and R_n may differ, even though their cardinality is the same.

2. Given points $a = (0,0)$, $b = (5,2)$, and $c = (7,1)$, we have that $d(a,b) = 5$ and $d(a,c) = 7$, while $d'(f(a), f(b)) = 2$ and $d'(f(a), f(c)) = 1$. $d(a, b) = 5 \leq d(a, c) = 7$, but $d'(f(a), f(b)) = 2 > d'(f(a), f(c)) = 1$ instead of the desired $d'(f(a), f(b)) \leq d'(f(a), f(c))$. Thus, the proximity-preserving property does not hold.

3. The proximity-preserving property does not hold as can be seen by using the same example as in the solution to Exercise 2.

4. The proximity-preserving property does not hold as can be seen by examining the points $a = (0,0)$, $b = (1,0)$, and $c = (.8, .8)$ and applying a rotation of 45 degrees counterclockwise.

In this case, using the Chessboard distance, before the rotation we have that $d(a,c) < d(a,b)$, but after the rotation f, we have that $d(f(a), f(c)) > d(f(a), f(b))$.

5. The proximity-preserving property does not hold as can be seen by using the same example as in the solution to Exercise 4.

6. Given a distance metric d in the original space, a distance metric d' in the transformed space, and a transformation f, then the proximity-preserving property stipulates that $d(a,b) \leq d(a,c)$ implies $d'(f(a), f(b)) \leq d'(f(a), f(c))$ for any objects a, b, and c. This property can be rewritten to be $d(a,c) \geq d(a,b)$ implies $d'(f(a), f(c)) \geq d'(f(a), f(b))$. Interchanging b and c yields the desired relationship: $d(a,b) \geq d(a,c)$ implies $d'(f(a), f(b)) \geq d'(f(a), f(c))$. Thus, when finding the farthest neighbors, whenever we have that $d'(f(a), f(b)) < d'(f(a), f(c))$ implies $d(a,b) < d(a,c)$, we do not have to refine the candidate list.

7. Consider a scaling transformation with the Euclidean distance metric. If the scaling factor is greater than 1, then the distance in the transformed space (which has been scaled upward) will be larger than the distance in the original space, and the pruning property is no longer meaningful as it is not satisfied. In particular, let c be the scaling factor, and let $a = (x_a, y_a)$ and $b = (x_b, y_b)$ be any two objects. Therefore, $d'(f(a), f(b)) = \sqrt{(cx_a - cx_b)^2 + (cy_a - y_b)^2} = \sqrt{c^2(x_a - x_b)^2 + c^2(y_a - y_b)^2} = c\sqrt{(x_a - x_b)^2 + (y_a - y_b)^2} = c \cdot d(a,b)$. So, for any c larger than 1, we have $d'(f(a), f(b)) > d(a,b)$.

8. By the contractiveness of f and the definition of ε, we know that $d'(f(q), f(o)) \leq d(q,o) \leq \varepsilon$ for all $o \subset R''$. Thus, since R' is the set of all o in S for which $d'(f(q), f(o)) \leq \varepsilon$, we have $R'' \subset R'$. Therefore, since R'' contains k objects, R' contains at least k objects, and thus the k nearest neighbors of q must be in R'.

9. The first is that ε may overestimate the distance of the kth nearest neighbor of q by a considerable margin [1716] so that R' may be significantly larger than necessary. Furthermore, the fact that two queries are issued to the multidimensional index that represents $f(S)$ (i.e., the k nearest neighbor query yielding R'' and the range query yielding R') means that some duplication of effort is inevitable.

10. The algorithm of Seidl and Kriegel [1716] is a k-nearest neighbor algorithm, requiring the number of desired neighbors to be known in advance, while the general version of the incremental nearest neighbor algorithm is an overall incremental process. The two algorithms have almost identical performance characteristics. The algorithm of Seidl and Kriegel halts upon encountering mapped object $f(o)$ such that $d'(f(q), f(o)) \geq D_k$, where D_k is the distance of the current candidate kth-nearest neighbor, as this implies that no other object exists with distance from q less than D_k. Thus, the algorithm performs the same number of object distance computations as the general version of the incremental nearest neighbor algorithm. However, the general version of the incremental nearest neighbor algorithm has a slight edge in that it sometimes accesses fewer multidimensional index nodes. To see this, suppose that Seidl and Kriegel's algorithm has just inserted an object into L that made it contain the actual k nearest neighbors—that is, D_k has reached its final value. If the next element obtained from the priority queue is a mapped object $f(o)$, then it will serve to establish the terminating condition, and Seidl and Kriegel's algorithm terminates without making any more node accesses than the general version of the incremental nearest neighbor algorithm. On the other hand, if the next element obtained from the priority queue is a multidimensional index node, then Seidl and Kriegel's algorithm will access that node, whereas the general version of the incremental nearest neighbor algorithm will not. However, since it's much more likely that the next element on the priority queue is a mapped object, Seidl and Kriegel's algorithm usually will not perform any more node accesses than the general version of the incremental nearest neighbor algorithm.

Solutions to Exercises in Section 4.6.2

2. Consider the points $(0,0)$ and $(1,1)$, whose Morton order difference is 3. The pruning property fails to hold for all of the Minkowski distance metrics L_p used for d since the Minkowski distance for thesepoints is at most 2 (when $p = 1$).

Solutions to Exercises in Section 4.6.4.1

1. (Isaac Weiss) Consider a point in two-dimensional space at location (a,b). Let $h = \sqrt{a^2 + b^2} = d_E((0,0),(a,b))$ be the Euclidean distance of (a,b) from the origin $(0,0)$. Letting $\theta = \text{atan}(a/b)$, the City Block distance $d_A((0,0),(a,b))$ of the point at location (a,b) from the origin can be written as a function of h and θ—that is, $d_A(h,\theta) = h(\sin(\theta) + \cos(\theta))$. It is easy to see that this function attains a maximum at $\theta = \pi/4$, and thus the City Block distance can increase and decrease as the points are rotated. In particular, for a given point (a,b) and the corresponding values of h and θ, the City Block distance value $d_A(a,b)$ is maximized when the coordinate axes are rotated by $\phi = \pi/4 - \theta$ degrees and minimized when the rotation is by $-\theta$ degrees.

2. Consider a point in two-dimensional space at location (a,b) and apply a rotation of $\theta = \text{atan}(a/b)$ degrees to the coordinate axes. In this case, the original value of the Chessboard distance metric d_M is $\max\{a,b\}$, but once the rotation has been applied, the value of d_M for the rotated point is $\sqrt{a^2 + b^2}$, which is larger than $\max\{a,b\}$.

Solutions to Exercises in Section 4.6.4.2

1. The proof follows the one in [701]. Let M be the DFT matrix. $M_{rs} = \exp(-j2\pi rs/n)/\sqrt{n}$. Therefore, the elements of the product of M and its adjoint $M^\dagger$ are given by

$$(M^\dagger \cdot M)_{rs} = \sum_{t=0}^{n-1} M_{rt}^\dagger M_{ts} = 1/n \sum_{t=0}^{n-1} \exp(-j2\pi t(r-s)/n)$$

The diagonal elements correspond to $r = s$.

$$(M^\dagger \cdot M)_{rr} = 1/n \sum_{t=0}^{n-1} \exp(0) = 1/n \sum_{t=0}^{n-1} 1 = 1$$

For the remaining terms, we note that we have a geometric sum with $x = \exp(-j2\pi(r-s)/n)$ for which we know that

$$\frac{1 - x^n}{1 - x} = 1 + x + x^2 + \cdots + x^{n-1}$$

Thus, we can rewrite $(M^\dagger \cdot M)_{rs}$ as

$$\frac{1}{n} \sum_{t=0}^{n-1} [\exp(-j2\pi(r-s)/n)]^j$$

$$= \frac{1}{n} \frac{1 - \exp(-j2\pi(r-s))}{1 - \exp(-j2\pi(r-s)/n)} = \frac{1}{n} \frac{1 - \cos(2\pi(r-s)) - j\sin(2\pi(r-s))}{1 - \exp(-j2\pi(r-s)/n)} = 0$$

Therefore, we have shown that $(M^\dagger \cdot M)_{rs} = \delta_{rs}$ as desired.

2. Decompose X_f as follows:

$$X_f = 1/\sqrt{n} \sum_{t=0}^{n-1} x_t \exp(-j2\pi ft/n)$$

$$= 1/\sqrt{n} \sum_{t=0}^{n/2-1} x_{2t} \exp(-j2\pi f(2t)/n) + 1/\sqrt{n} \sum_{t=0}^{n/2-1} x_{2t+1} \exp(-j2\pi f(2t+1)/n)$$

$$= 1/\sqrt{n} \sum_{t=0}^{n/2-1} x_{2t} \exp(-j2\pi f(2t)/n) + \exp(-j2\pi f/n)/\sqrt{n} \sum_{t=0}^{n/2-1} x_{2t+1} \exp(-j2\pi f(2t)/n)$$

$$= 1/\sqrt{n} \sum_{t=0}^{n/2-1} x_{2t} \exp(-j2\pi ft/(n/2)) + \exp(-j2\pi f/n)/\sqrt{n} \sum_{t=0}^{n/2-1} x_{2t+1} \exp(-j2\pi ft/(n/2))$$

$$= X_f^{even} + \exp(-j2\pi f/n) X_f^{odd}$$

Thus, instead of calculating one transform with n points, we now have two transforms, each having $n/2$ points: one transform for the even-numbered points and one for the odd-numbered points. This requires $O((n/2)^2) + O((n/2)^2) = O((n/2)^2)$ steps to calculate the transform, plus one final multiply and add operation to combine the results instead of the $O(n^2)$ steps that would have been required had we not performed this decomposition. Next, we repeatedly apply the same splitting procedure to the even and odd transforms until we have obtained single-point transforms. At this stage, we reassemble them via $\log_2 n$ multiplication and addition operations for a total of $O(n\log_2 n)$ steps. This results in quite a savings in the execution time when n is relatively large. This method is known as the Fast Fourier Transform (FFT) [421].

3. See [588].

4. We need to show that the DFT is preserved under addition (equivalent to translation and rotation in Euclidean space) and multiplication by a scalar.[3] Preservation under addition and multiplication by a scalar are straightforward to show as $\mathrm{DFT}(x + y) = \mathrm{DFT}(x) + \mathrm{DFT}(y)$ and likewise for $\mathrm{DFT}(\alpha \cdot x) = \alpha \cdot \mathrm{DFT}(x)$.

5. Rotation results in changing the phase of the coefficients of the DFT and not the amplitude. In particular, $\mathrm{DFT}(x_{t+\Delta t}) = \mathrm{DFT}(x_t) \cdot \exp(-j2\pi f \Delta t/n) = X_f \cdot \exp(-j2\pi f \Delta t/n)$.

Solutions to Exercises in Section 4.7.3.2

1. Assuming that we start with object o_1 and that at iteration j we find that object o_{j+1} is the farthest from object o_j and at a distance d_j, then no object can be repeated in the sequence as this would result in a contradiction. Note that the sequence d_j is increasing. Assume that o is an object that occurs twice in the sequence (i.e., $o = o_i = o_k$, where $i < k$). Since the sequence d_j is increasing, we have that $d_i < d_k$. However, this contradicts the fact o_{i+1} was the farthest object from o as now we find that o_{k+1} is even farther from o, which is impossible. Thus, an object can occur only once in the sequence.

3. Given objects a and b, from the triangle inequality we have that $d(a,b) \leq d(r,a) + d(r,b)$. Since s is the farthest object from r, $d(r,a) \leq d(r,s)$ and $d(r,b) \leq d(r,s)$. Therefore, $d(a,b) \leq d(r,a) + d(r,b) \leq d(r,s) + d(r,s) = 2d(r,s)$. As pointed out in the text, this bound is guaranteed to hold only for the first pair of pivot objects since it is possible that the distance functions used to determine the second and subsequent coordinate values may not satisfy the triangle inequality (see Section 4.7.3.6).

Solutions to Exercises in Section 4.7.3.3

1. First, we show that $x_a \leq d(r,s)$:

$$x_a = \frac{d(r,a)^2 + d(r,s)^2 - d(s,a)^2}{2d(r,s)}$$

$$\leq \frac{d(r,s)^2 + d(r,s)^2}{2d(r,s)} = d(r,s)$$

since $d(r,a) \leq d(r,s)$ and $d(s,a) \geq 0$. Second, we show that $-x_a \leq d(r,s)$:

---

[3] Note that the DFT is a general linear space, which is not necessarily a Euclidean space.

$$-x_a = \frac{d(s,a)^2 - d(r,a)^2 - d(r,s)^2}{2d(r,s)}$$

$$\leq \frac{(d(r,a) + d(r,s))^2 - d(r,a)^2 - d(r,s)^2}{2d(r,s)}$$

by the triangle inequality (i.e., $d(s,a) \leq d(r,a) + d(r,s)$)

$$= \frac{d(r,a)^2 + d(r,s)^2 + 2d(r,a)d(r,s) - d(r,a)^2 - d(r,s)^2}{2d(r,s)}$$

$$= \frac{2d(r,a)d(r,s)}{2d(r,s)} = d(r,a) \leq d(r,s)$$

2. Let r and s be pivot objects chosen according to the heuristic in Section 4.7.3.2, and let $d(t,u) = \alpha d(r,s)$. We know that $1 \leq \alpha \leq 2$ as $d(r,s) \leq d(t,u) \leq 2d(r,s)$. An upper bound on the value of x_a for any object a is easily derived given the upper bound of $d(r,s)$ for $d(r,a)$ and the lower bound of 0 on $d(s,a)$:

$$x_a = \frac{d(r,a)^2 + d(r,s)^2 - d(s,a)^2}{2d(r,s)}$$

$$\leq \frac{2d(r,s)^2}{2d(r,s)} = d(r,s)$$

To determine a lower bound on x_a, we appeal to the triangle inequality, which yields $|d(r,s) - d(s,a)| \leq d(r,a)$. Raising both sides to the second power yields

$$(d(r,s) - d(s,a))^2 = d(r,s)^2 + d(s,a)^2 - 2d(r,s)d(s,a) \leq d(r,a)^2$$

In other words, we have

$$d(r,a)^2 - d(s,a)^2 \geq d(r,s)^2 - 2d(r,s)d(s,a) \geq (1 - 2\alpha)d(r,s)^2$$

since $d(s,a) \leq d(t,u) = \alpha d(r,s)$. Substituting this lower bound into Equation 4.23 yields

$$x_a = \frac{d(r,a)^2 + d(r,s)^2 - d(s,a)^2}{2d(r,s)}$$

$$\geq \frac{(2 - 2\alpha)d(r,s)^2}{2d(r,s)} = (1 - \alpha)d(r,s).$$

Combining the upper and lower bounds on the value of x_a and the fact that $\alpha \leq 2$ yields the desired bound, $|x_a| \leq d(r,s)$. Furthermore, for any $\alpha \geq 1$ we can derive the maximum spread as

$$|x_a - x_b| \leq d(r,s) - (1 - \alpha)d(r,s) = \alpha d(r,s) = d(t,u)$$

Thus, the maximum spread is at most $d(t,u)$ for any choice of pivots, as desired.

Solutions to Exercises in Section 4.7.3.5

1. Each pivot-finding iteration requires $N - 1$ distance computations (as we do not need to compute the distance of the current object to itself). Thus, determining one pair of pivot objects requires $P(N - 1)$ distance computations. Since we assume k iterations of FastMap, the total number of distance computations is $kP(N - 1)$. Note that this derivation assumes that all the distances computed in the pivot-finding phase can be stored and used later in the coordinate computation phase. If there are too many objects to store all the distances in memory, then more distances may have to be computed.

2. The distance function used in the ith iteration is given in Equation 4.27. Once $d_i(r,s)^2$ for two objects r and s becomes nonpositive (i.e., zero or negative), the projections of r and s cannot be used as a pivot pair in any subsequent iterations. In particular, if r and s are used as a pivot pair in iteration $i - 1$, then $d_i(r,s) = 0$ and $d_i(r,t) = d_i(s,t)$ for an arbitrary object t. This can be shown by plugging the appropriate values into Equations 4.26 and 4.27 (see Exercise 2 in Section 4.7.3.7). Thus, r and s become indistinguishable in subsequent iterations of FastMap

and are in effect merged for the purpose of pivot pair selection. This can be interpreted as removing one of the pivot objects, say r, thereby reducing the number of objects by one. With this interpretation, we have $N - k$ objects left after k iterations. Since each of the k objects that were removed participated in a pivot pair and since at least one of the remaining objects has been used as a pivot, at least $k + 1$ distinct objects have been used as pivot objects. An alternative way of seeing this is to observe that it takes a minimum of $k + 1$ points to define a k-dimensional object. For example, two nonidentical points define a line, three noncollinear points define a plane, four noncoplanar points define a solid, and so on. The minimal object is termed a *simplicial complex* (e.g., [1326]). The simplicial complexes of dimension 1, 2, and 3 are lines, triangles, and tetrahedra, respectively.

3. See [587].

4. See [587].

Solutions to Exercises in Section 4.7.3.6

1. In the text, we show, that for a subset of a Euclidean vector space (S, d), FastMap satisfies the pruning property if d' is the Euclidean distance metric (i.e., L_2). Let $x = \{x_1, \ldots, x_m\}$ and $y = \{y_1, \ldots, y_m\}$ be arbitrary points in S. The L_p distance between x and y, $d_p(x, y) = \left(\sum_{i=1}^{m} |x_i - y_i|^p\right)^{1/p}$, can be shown to be nonincreasing as a function of p. Thus, if d_A is the L_1 metric, then $d_A(F(o_1), F(o_2)) \geq d_E(F(o_1), F(o_2))$, so we may have $d_A(F(o_1), F(o_2)) > d(o_1, o_2) \geq d_E(F(o_1), F(o_2))$. Therefore, F is not guaranteed to satisfy the pruning property if d' is L_1 (i.e., $p = 1$). This situation cannot arise if d' is some other Minkowski metric L_p, where $p \geq 2$, since $d'(F(o_1), F(o_2)) \leq d_E(F(o_1), F(o_2)) \leq d(o_1, o_2)$ for such a d'.

2. The following proof is from [850]. We first show that $d_i(r, s) = 0$. From Equation 4.26, we have

$$x_r^{i-1} = \frac{d_{i-1}(r, r)^2 + d_{i-1}(r, s)^2 - d_{i-1}(r, s)^2}{2d_{i-1}(r, s)} = 0$$

and

$$x_s^{i-1} = \frac{d_{i-1}(r, s)^2 + d_{i-1}(r, s)^2 - d_{i-1}(s, s)^2}{2d_{i-1}(r, s)} = d_{i-1}(r, s)$$

Substituting into Equation 4.27 we have

$$d_i(r, s)^2 = d_{i-1}(r, s)^2 - (x_r^{i-1} - x_s^{i-1})^2 = d_{i-1}(r, s)^2 - d_{i-1}(r, s)^2 = 0$$

Now, let t be an arbitrary object. Using Equations 4.26 and 4.27, we can compute the values of $d_i(r, t)^2$ and $d_i(s, t)^2$:

$$d_i(r, t)^2 = d_{i-1}(r, t)^2 - |x_r^{i-1} - x_t^{i-1}|^2 = d_{i-1}(r, t)^2 - (x_t^{i-1})^2$$

$$= d_{i-1}(r, t)^2 - \left(\frac{d_{i-1}(r, t)^2 + d_{i-1}(r, s)^2 - d_{i-1}(s, t)^2}{2d_{i-1}(r, s)}\right)^2$$

$$= \frac{4d_{i-1}(r, s)^2 d_{i-1}(r, t)^2 - (d_{i-1}(r, t)^2 + d_{i-1}(r, s)^2 - d_{i-1}(s, t)^2)^2}{4d_{i-1}(r, s)^2}$$

$$= \frac{1}{4d_{i-1}(r, s)^2} (4d_{i-1}(r, s)^2 d_{i-1}(r, t)^2 - d_{i-1}(r, s)^4$$

$$- d_{i-1}(r, s)^2 (d_{i-1}(r, t)^2 - d_{i-1}(s, t)^2) - (d_{i-1}(r, t)^2 - d_{i-1}(s, t)^2)^2)$$

$$= \frac{-d_{i-1}(r, s)^4 + 2d_{i-1}(r, s)^2 (d_{i-1}(r, t)^2 + d_{i-1}(s, t)^2) - (d_{i-1}(r, t)^2 - d_{i-1}(s, t))^2}{4d_{i-1}(r, s)^2}$$

and

$$d_i(s,t)^2 = d_{i-1}(s,t)^2 - |x_s^{i-1} - x_t^{i-1}|^2 = d_{i-1}(s,t)^2 - |d_{i-1}(r,s) - x_t^{i-1}|^2$$

$$= d_{i-1}(s,t)^2 - \left(\frac{d_{i-1}(s,t)^2 + d_{i-1}(r,s)^2 - d_{i-1}(r,t)^2}{2d_{i-1}(r,s)} \right)^2$$

$$= \frac{4d_{i-1}(r,s)^2 d_{i-1}(s,t)^2 - (d_{i-1}(s,t)^2 + d_{i-1}(r,s)^2 - d_{i-1}(r,t)^2)^2}{4d_{i-1}(r,s)^2}$$

$$= \frac{1}{4d_{i-1}(r,s)^2}(4d_{i-1}(r,s)^2 d_{i-1}(s,t)^2 - d_{i-1}(r,s)^4$$

$$- d_{i-1}(r,s)^2(d_{i-1}(s,t)^2 - d_{i-1}(r,t)^2) - (d_{i-1}(s,t)^2 - d_{i-1}(r,t)^2)^2)$$

$$= \frac{-d_{i-1}(r,s)^4 + 2d_{i-1}(r,s)^2(d_{i-1}(s,t)^2 + d_{i-1}(r,t)^2) - (d_{i-1}(s,t)^2 - d_{i-1}(r,t))^2}{4d_{i-1}(r,s)^2}$$

It should be clear that the final formulas for $d_i(r,t)^2$ and $d_i(s,t)^2$ are the same, even if the triangle inequality is not satisfied.

3. Since $d_i(r,s) = 0$, we have $d(r,s) = d_E(F_{i-1}(r), F_{i-1}(s))$, where the notation $F_{i-1}(v)$ denotes the $(i-1)$-dimensional partial vector for v determined in the first $i-1$ iterations. Furthermore, since $d_i(r,t) = d_i(s,t)$ for all objects t, coordinate values i through k will be the same for r and s. Thus, $d(r,s) = d_E(F(r), F(s))$, and since d' is the Euclidean distance metric d_E, we have $d(r,s) = d'(F(r), F(s))$ as desired.

Solutions to Exercises in Section 4.7.3.7

1. The following proof is from [850]. Using Equation 4.23 with pivot objects r and s, we can derive an upper bound on the expansion, with the help of the triangle inequality and the upper bound $d(r,s)$ on $d(r,a)$ and $d(r,b)$:

$$\frac{|x_a - x_b|}{d(a,b)} = \left| \frac{d(r,a)^2 - d(s,a)^2 - d(r,b)^2 + d(s,b)^2}{2d(r,s)d(a,b)} \right|$$

$$= \left| \frac{(d(r,a) - d(r,b))(d(r,a) + d(r,b)) + (d(s,b) - d(s,a))(d(s,b) + d(s,a))}{2d(r,s)d(a,b)} \right|$$

$$\leq \frac{|d(r,a) - d(r,b)|(d(r,a) + d(r,b)) + |d(s,b) - d(s,a)|(d(s,b) + d(s,a))}{2d(r,s)d(a,b)}$$

$$\leq \frac{d(a,b)(d(r,a) + d(r,b)) + d(a,b)(d(s,b) + d(s,a))}{2d(r,s)d(a,b)}$$

$$= \frac{d(r,a) + d(r,b) + d(s,b) + d(s,a)}{2d(r,s)}$$

$$\leq \frac{d(r,a) + d(r,b) + d(r,s) + d(r,b) + d(r,a) + d(r,s)}{2d(r,s)} \leq \frac{6d(r,s)}{2d(r,s)} = 3.$$

We now show that this bound is tight. Consider the following assignment of the distances among the objects a, b, r, and s, where $d(r,s)$ is left as a variable:

$$d(r,a) = d(r,s) \qquad d(s,a) = (2 - 2\alpha)d(r,s)$$
$$d(r,b) = (1 - \alpha)d(r,s) \qquad d(s,b) = (2 - \alpha)d(r,s)$$
$$d(a,b) = \alpha d(r,s)$$

The resulting distances clearly satisfy the triangle inequality for $0 < \alpha < 1$. Using these distance values leads to the following value of $|x_a - x_b|$:

$$|x_a - x_b| = \left| \frac{d(r,s)^2 - (2 - 2\alpha)^2 d(r,s)^2 - (1 - \alpha)^2 d(r,s)^2 + (2 - \alpha)d(r,s)^2}{2d(r,s)} \right|$$

$$= \left| \frac{1}{2}(1 - 4 - 4\alpha^2 + 8\alpha - 1 - \alpha^2 + 2\alpha + 4 + \alpha^2 - 4\alpha)d(r,s) \right|$$

$$= \left| \frac{1}{2}(-4\alpha^2 + 6\alpha)d(r,s) \right| = d(r,s)(3\alpha - 2\alpha^2)$$

Thus, dividing by $d(a,b) = \alpha d(r,s)$ gives the expansion on $d(a,b)$, namely, $3 - 2\alpha$. Clearly, as α approaches 0, the expansion approaches 3.

2. The following proof is from [850]. We derive an upper bound for

$$\frac{|x_a^2 - x_b^2|}{d(a,b)}$$

using the definitions from Section 4.7.3.5. Notice that the formula for $|x_a^2 - x_b^2|$ is symmetric in a and b, so we can use it without the absolute value operator. In the derivation, we make use of the lower bound $d(r,s)/\beta$ and the upper bound $2d(r,s)$ on any distance values. Furthermore, we use the bound obtained in Exercise 1. In particular, for any objects u and v, we obtain

$$d_2(u,v)^2 = d(u,v)^2 - |x_u - x_v|^2 \geq d(u,v)^2 - (3d(u,v))^2 = -8d(u,v)^2$$

Thus, applying Equation 4.26 with $i = 2$, the lower bound $-8d(u,v)^2$ on $d_2(u,v)^2$ derived above, the upper bound $d(u,v)^2$ on $d_2(u,v)^2$ derived above, and the bounds on the original distances, we obtain

$$\frac{x_a^2 - x_b^2}{d(a,b)} = \frac{d_2(p_1^2,a)^2 - d_2(p_2^2,a)^2 - d_2(p_1^2,b)^2 + d_2(p_2^2,b)^2}{2d_2(p_1^2,p_2^2)d(a,b)}$$

$$\leq \frac{d(p_1^2,a)^2 - (-8d(p_2^2,a)^2) - (-8d(p_1^2,b)^2) + d(p_2^2,b)^2}{2(d(r,s)/\beta)(d(r,s)/\beta)}$$

$$\leq \frac{4d(r,s)^2 + 8 \cdot 4d(r,s)^2 + 8 \cdot 4d(r,s)^2 + 4d(r,s)^2}{2d(r,s)^2/\beta^2}$$

$$= \frac{18 \cdot 4d(r,s)^2}{2d(r,s)^2/\beta^2} = \frac{72}{2/\beta^2} = 36\beta^2$$

This upper bound is not tight as the triangle inequality on the original distances and the pivot criteria for p_1^2 and p_2^2 prevent all the upper bounds used in the derivation from being realized simultaneously. It is difficult to derive a tighter bound that takes into account all of these criteria. Nevertheless, an attempt was made in [850] to construct an example exhibiting large expansion, through the use of a nonlinear optimization tool. The objective function describing the expansion involved 14 variables and the number of constraints (incorporating all the relevant criteria) was about 80. Due to this relatively large number, the optimizer frequently got stuck at local maxima rather than finding the true maximum. However, it was clear that the maximum expansion is at least proportional to β. For example, for $\beta = 5$ (which meant that the largest distance value was never more than 10 times larger than the smallest one), the optimizer was able to discover a legal assignment of distance values that yielded an expansion of about 30. For $\beta = 50$, it yielded an expansion of about 300, and for $\beta = 100$, it yielded an expansion of about 600.

Solutions to Exercises in Section 4.7.4

3. No. Remember that once we have mapped the objects into the Hamming space with hashing function h_1, the hashing function h_2 chooses m bitstring positions at random. Therefore, the ordering of the 1s and 0s that form the bitstring is irrelevant and thus using bit interleaving makes no difference, which is why the simpler method of bit concatenation is used in h_1.

4. You will probably need to appeal to the result of Frankl and Maehara [631] that improves upon the Johnson-Lindenstrauss Lemma [962] in much the same way as done by Indyk and Motwani [924], Kleinberg [1032], and Kushilevitz, Ostrovsky, and Rabani [1097].

Solutions to Exercises in Appendix A

2. Use the same proof technique used to show that there are $N + 1$ external nodes in an extended binary tree with N internal nodes. In particular, there is one leaf node for each key value in a node at the next to the bottom level (i.e., the one containing the leaf nodes), plus one for each predecessor node. Applying this reasoning recursively as we ascend the B-tree, we find that the root node has one fewer key value than its successors, where each successor corresponds to a leaf node. Thus, the total number of leaf nodes is one greater than the number of key values. In other words, given N key values, there are $N + 1$ leaf nodes.

3. Let c be the father node of a and b. Promote the minimum value, d, in a to c, and demote to b the key value, e, in c with the largest value that is less than d.

4. $m - 2$ if m is odd, and $m - 3$ if m is even.

5. From Exercise 2 we know that given N key values, there are $N + 1$ leaf nodes at depth i. The search length is maximized when each B-tree node has $\lceil m/2 \rceil$ key values. In this case, the number of nodes at depth 0, 1, 2, 3, ..., i is at least 1, 2, $2\lceil m/2 \rceil$, $2(\lceil m/2 \rceil)^2$, ..., $2(\lceil m/2 \rceil)^{i-1}$. The number of leaf nodes at depth i is $2(\lceil m/2 \rceil)^{i-1}$. Solving for i, we have $i \leq 1 + \log_{\lceil m/2 \rceil}((N + 1)/2)$.

6. 3.

7. Let r be the number of node splits. Let q be the number of nodes in the B-tree whose splitting creates one new node. This is the situation whenever the node that splits is not a root node. When the $i - 1$ root nodes split, we have $2(i - 1)$ new nodes. Therefore, we have $r = q + i - 1$ node splits, yielding $p = 1 + q + 2(i - 1)$ nodes, and thus $r = p - i$.

8. If there are p nodes in the B-tree, then there are at least $1 + (\lceil m/2 \rceil - 1) \cdot (p - 1)$ key values since the root has at least one key value, and all remaining nodes have at least $\lceil m/2 \rceil - 1$ key values. Therefore, $N \geq 1 + (\lceil m/2 \rceil - 1) \cdot (p - 1)$ or $p \leq 1 + (N - 1)/(\lceil m/2 \rceil - 1)$. From Exercise 7 we know that the number of node splits can be approximated by the number of nodes, and thus the average number of times that a node is split is less than $1/(\lceil m/2 \rceil) - 1$ per insertion of a record, assuming at least one node split.

9. Assume that each node is on a page. Nonleaf nodes are at levels 0 through d. Searching retrieves at most $d + 1$ pages (one per node) as we only know that the key value is not present when we reach a leaf node at depth $d + 1$ that is empty and does not involve a disk access. Insertion retrieves $d + 1$ disk pages (one per node) while searching for the key value and the node p in which it is to be inserted. Once p has been found, nodes may be split, and up to $d + 2$ new nodes can be created as a result of splitting. In this case, $2d + 3$ nodes will have to be written, which means $2d + 3$ disk accesses. Deletion retrieves $d + 1$ pages (one per node) while searching for the key value and the node p at depth d that contains its replacement key value. Once p has been found, nodes may be merged. Each merge involves the retrieval of an adjacent brother node, and the merged node must be written. A maximum of d merges can take place and d new nodes created, which means d disk accesses for the retrieval and d disk accesses for writing. If fewer than d merges occur, then a merge may be followed by a split.

12. The root node has at least two child nodes. There are at least two nodes at depth 1, and at the remaining depths 2 through j, there are at least $2a^{i-1}$ nodes at depth i. Summing up yields $1 + 2\sum_{i=1}^{j} a^{i-1}$, which is $1 + 2 \cdot (a^j - 1)/(a - 1)$ nodes. All but one of these nodes have $a - 1$ key values, and thus the total is $2a^j - 1$ key values.

13. This can be seen by observing that all leaf nodes in the red-black balanced binary tree correspond to nodes at the bottom level of the 2-3 or 2-3-4 tree. This means that the number of black edges from the root of the tree to the leaf nodes is the same for each leaf node. The red edges correspond to the case where the source node in the red-black tree is black, while the destination node is red. Thus, there is a one-to-one correspondence between the black edges and the black nodes on the path from the root to each leaf node, and our result follows.

14. The number of black edges on any path from the root of the tree to a leaf node is always the same. For every black edge there is at most one incoming red edge. Thus, the path from the root of the tree to any leaf node is at most twice the maximum depth of the original tree.

15. The case that the father edge f is black with two children that are red edges is now a valid node (i.e., it does not correspond to an overflow as in the 2-3 tree), and thus once we determine

that f is black, we can exit. Another change is when edge d is red, the father edge f of d is red, and the brother edge e of f is red. In this case, change the colors of both edges e and f to be black, change the color of the father g of f to be red, and reapply steps 1 and 2 to g. Notice that before this step, edge g had to be black as two consecutive red edges are not permitted. Finally, if edge d is red, the father edge f of d is red, and the brother edge e of f is black, then apply a single or double rotation to edges d and f, keeping the results red, and exit.

18. Descend the tree while doing the search. Whenever you encounter a node s with four children, no father, and key values a, b, and c, then split s as follows. Create a new node containing b, the median key value, and two children consisting of two new nodes s_1 and s_2 containing keys a and c, respectively, and attach the leftmost two children of s to s_1 and the rightmost two children of s to s_2. Whenever you encounter a node s with four children whose father f has exactly one more child x, then split s into nodes s_1 and s_2 with two children each, and transform f into a node with three children consisting of x, s_1, and s_2. Similarly, if the father node f has three children (i.e., x, y, and s), then apply the same transformation except that now f is transformed into a node with four children consisting of x, y, s_1, and s_2.

19. The algorithm cannot work because a node s with three children whose father f has two children cannot be split into a node containing one child and two children since a node with one child is not permitted in a 2-3 tree.

20. The top-down algorithm will work as long as m is even. The rule is that we descend the tree and whenever we encounter a node s with m children whose father f has i children, then we split s into nodes s_1 and s_2 with $m/2$ children each, transform f into a node with $i + 1$ children, and promote the median key value in s to f. Also, whenever the algorithm encounters a node s with m children and no father, then a new node is created with the median key value in s and two children each containing $m/2$ children. The algorithm will not work if m is odd as now $\lceil m/2 \rceil$ is also odd and is equal to $(m + 1)/2$. The problem is that when we split a node containing m children and promote a key value, we create one node with $\lceil m/2 \rceil$ children and one node with $\lfloor m/2 \rfloor$ children. The second node is not a valid node in a B-tree of order m when m is odd. Thus, the algorithm will not work in this case.

21. There is only a need to prevent access to the node being currently searched and its father. Once a split has taken place, subsequent searches and insertions can proceed as the resulting nodes can accommodate the additional child. Remember that if the parent f of the current node s could not have accommodated the extra child, then f would have been split before s.

22. Note that satisfying the properties of a B-tree will require extensive examination of the red-black balanced binary tree to determine the appropriate sequence of red and black edges corresponding to a node split or merge in a B-tree (i.e., satisfying the constraints on the minimum and maximum number of children in a B-tree node).

23. In a B^+-tree, the search is successful only if we find the key value in a leaf node. The presence of the desired key value in a nonleaf node of the B^+-tree does not mean that the corresponding record must be present, whereas this is true for a B-tree.

24. In a B^+-tree, the search for the key value to be deleted is only successful if it is found in a leaf node. If the search is successful, then the key value is deleted, and if the node meets the requirements of the B^+-tree definition, then nothing more needs to be done. Note that the deleted key value is not removed from the nonleaf nodes. In the B-tree, once the key value is found, we must replace it by the closest key value that appears in the next to the bottom level of the tree and then check if the resulting node meets the requirements of the B-tree definition.

Solutions to Exercises in Appendix B

1. Either one of h_n or h_{n+1} can be used first. The difference is in the mechanics of the lookup operation. Let $2^n \leq m \leq 2^{n+1} - 1$. Ignore the case where $m = 2^n$ because, in this case, only h_n is applicable. We apply h_{n+1} first. Let $h_{n+1}(k) = x$. If $x < m$, then we have found the location; otherwise, $x \geq m$, and we apply $h_n(k)$. Suppose that we apply h_n first. Let $h_n(k) = x$. If $x \geq m - 2^n$, then we have found the location; otherwise, $x < m - 2^n$, and we apply $h_{n+1}(k)$. Suppose that $x < m - 2^n$, and that $h_{n+1}(k) = 2^n + x$. If we had not applied h_{n+1} in this case,

and, instead, stored k in bucket x, then we would have had a problem in the future. To see this, we observe that since we are now at level $n, n+1$, the next time that bucket x is split, we will be at level $n+1, n+2$. This means that the records in bucket x will be rehashed using h_{n+2} and distributed into buckets x and $2^{n+1}+x$. However, at this time, if we want to look up the record with key value k with which we have been dealing, we will have to use hash function h_{n+1}, which will hash to bucket 2^n+x, and k will not be there.

2. There are two possibilities depending on whether s, the next bucket to be split, is nonzero. If s is nonzero, then bucket 2^n+s-1 is merged into bucket $s-1$, s is reset to $s-1$, and bucket 2^n+s-1 is no longer used. If s is zero, then bucket 2^n-1 is merged into bucket $2^{n-1}-1$, s is reset to $2^{n-1}-1$, bucket 2^n-1 is no longer used, and n is reset to $n-1$.

6. $s(\tau) = 1 + \tau/2$, and $u(\tau) = \tau$ (see [1046, p. 525]).

7. Calculate the expected number of records as a function of x and z and also as a function of x and α, and then solve for z. Therefore, $2 \cdot x \cdot (z/2) + (1-x) \cdot z = \alpha \cdot (2 \cdot x + 1 - x)$.

8. The probability of encountering a split group is x with an expected search length of $s(\alpha \cdot (1 + x)/2)$. On the other hand, for an unsplit group, it is $1-x$ with an expected search length of $s(\alpha \cdot (1+x))$. Therefore, $S(\alpha, x) = x \cdot s(\alpha \cdot (1+x)/2) + (1-x) \cdot s(\alpha \cdot (1+x))$, which reduces to $1 + \alpha \cdot (2 + x - x^2)/4$.

9. $U(\alpha, x) = x \cdot u(\alpha \cdot (1+x)/2) + (1-x) \cdot u(\alpha \cdot (1+x))$, which reduces to $\alpha \cdot (2 + x - x^2)/2$.

10. They arise when the expected number of records in all of the buckets is the same—that is, when $x = 0$ or $x = 1$. $S(\alpha, 0) = 1 + \alpha/2$ and $U(\alpha, 0) = \alpha$.

11. When $x = \frac{1}{2}$, $S(\alpha, \frac{1}{2}) = 1 + (\alpha/2) \cdot (\frac{9}{8})$, and $U(\alpha, \frac{1}{2}) = (\alpha/2) \cdot (\frac{9}{8})$.

12. $\bar{S}(\alpha) = \int_0^1 S(\alpha, x) dx = 1 + (\alpha/2) \cdot \frac{13}{12}$, and $\bar{U}(\alpha) = \int_0^1 U(\alpha, x) dx = (\alpha/2) \cdot \frac{13}{12}$.

13. $A(\alpha, x) = \alpha \cdot (1+x)/\alpha = 1 + x$, and $\bar{A}(\alpha, x) = \int_0^1 A(\alpha, x) dx = \frac{3}{2}$.

15. See [1530].

16. See [1530].

17. See [1530].

18. This should be apparent by noting that the overflow files are accessed with the same hashing function, albeit at a lower level. Thus, a bucket in the overflow file corresponds to "brother" primary buckets.

Solutions to Exercises in Appendix C

1. Use induction on s.

5. The last r buckets should be merged and their contents stored in bucket $s - 1$.

6. a is already an integer, and thus they are equivalent.

7. Mullin [1324] gives the following procedure:

```
1   recursive integer procedure PHYSICAL(L, R, Origin)
2   /* Given a spiral hashing implementation with a growth factor R and a
3       physical bucket addressing system starting at Origin, return the
4       physical bucket address corresponding to logical bucket address L. */
5   value integer L, R, Origin
6   integer Low, High
7   if L < R then return L
8   endif
9   High  ← (L + 1) ÷ R
10  Low   ← L ÷ R
11  return(if Low < High then PHYSICAL(Low, R, Origin)
12              /* This is a reused address */
13              else L - Low + Origin
14              endif)
```

8. $\log_r t$.

10. Larson [1106] suggests the use of a table of segments. Each segment contains a fixed number of buckets. As segments become full, new ones are allocated. Once all of the buckets in a particular segment have been split, then the segment can be reused. Of course, this requires a directory whose size is fixed.

13. $c = (2 - \sqrt{2})/(3 - 2\sqrt{2}) \approx 3.414$, $b = c \cdot (c - 1) \approx 8.243$, and $a = 2 - c \approx 1.414$.

14. Yes. A bucket split will now result in $r - 1$, r, or $r + 1$ new buckets, whereas previously r new buckets were always created.

15. A second-degree polynomial can be written as $(a \cdot x + b) \cdot x + c$, which requires four floating-point operations, whereas $a + b/(c - x)$ only requires three.

16. $p(y) = \log_2(y + dy) - \log_2 y = \log_2(1 + dy/y) \approx dy/(y \cdot \ln 2)$. This makes use of the fact that $\log_2 x = \ln x / \ln 2$ and $\ln(1 + x) \approx x$ for small x.

17. From the assumption about the expected value, there exists a constant c_1 such that $\tau(y) = c_1/(y \cdot \ln 2)$. The average storage utilization factor (i.e., overall value) is α, and solving the equation $\int_1^2 (c_1/(y \cdot \ln 2)) \cdot dy = \alpha$ yields $c_1 = \alpha$.

18. From the assumption that there exists a pair of constants c_2 and c_3 such that $q(y) = c_2 \cdot \tau(y) = c_2 \cdot \alpha/(y \cdot \ln 2) = c_3/y$. The value of c_3 is obtained by noting that the probability of landing on a bucket address in $[y, y + dy]$ is $q(y) \cdot dy$, and the probability of landing on some bucket in $[1,2]$ is 1. Solving the equation $\int_1^2 (c_3/y) \cdot dy = 1$ yields $c_3 = 1/\ln 2$.

19. From Exercise 6 in Appendix B, the expected number of key value comparisons for a successful search for a bucket at address y with a storage utilization factor of $\tau(y)$ is $1 + \tau(y)/2$. The expected cost of a successful search is then $\int_1^2 (1 + \tau(y)/2) \cdot q(y) \cdot dy = 1 + \alpha/(4 \cdot (\ln 2)^2) = 1 + (\alpha/2) \cdot 1.041$.

20. From Exercise 6 in Appendix B, the expected number of key value comparisons for an unsuccessful search for a bucket at address y with a storage utilization factor of $\tau(y)$ is $\tau(y)$. The expected cost of a successful search is then $\int_1^2 \tau(y) \cdot q(y) \cdot dy = \alpha/(2 \cdot (\ln 2)^2) = \alpha \cdot 1.041$.

21. This situation arises with a probability of $1/\alpha$—that is, for every $1/\alpha$ of the record insertions. The expected number of records in the first bucket is $\tau(1) = \alpha/\ln 2$, and thus the expected number of extra hashing operations is $\tau(1)/\alpha = 1/\ln 2 = 1.443$.

22. Instances of $\ln 2$ are replaced by $\ln r$.

23. See [384].

24. Using Cartesian coordinates, the arc length for the function $y = f(x)$ is $\int \sqrt{1 + (f'(x))^2} dx$. $f'(x)$ can be rewritten as dy/dx. Making the substitutions $x = \rho \cos\theta$, $y = \rho \sin\theta$, and $\rho = e^{j\theta}$ leads to the integral $\sqrt{1 + f^2} \cdot \int e^{j\theta} \cdot d\theta$. The value of this integral is $(\sqrt{1 + j^2}/j) \cdot e^{j\theta}$, which is $\rho \cdot \sqrt{1 + j^2} < /f$.

References

Each reference is followed by one or more keywords. It is also followed by a list of the sections in which it is referenced. The format is "F", "D", or "A", followed by the section number. "F" corresponds to this book, "D" corresponds to 1637, and "A" corresponds to 1636. "F.P", "D.P", and "A.P" denote the appropriate preface. "D.L" and "A.L" denote the corresponding appendices describing the pseudo-code language. The four appendices in this book are referenced by their corresponding one-letter label. "A" denotes the appendix describing the B-tree; "B" denotes the appendix describing linear hashing; "C" denotes the appendix describing spiral hashing; and "D" denotes the appendix describing the pseudo-code language. All references that are cited in the solutions to the exercises are associated with the section in which the exercise is found and are distinguished from the actual section that contains the exercise by the suffix "s". The indexes in this book are referenced by the following two-letter labels. "X.K" denotes the Reference Keyword Index. "X.A" denotes the Author and Credit Index. "X.S" denotes the Subject Index. In the case of this book, additional details are available by providing the page numbers within parentheses following the section number.

[1] S. K. Abdali and D. S. Wise. Experiments with quadtree representation of matrices. In *Proceedings of the International Symposium on Symbolic and Algebraic Computation (ISSAC'88)*, P. M. Gianni, ed., vol. 358 of Springer-Verlag Lecture Notes in Computer Science, pages 96–108, Rome, Italy, July 1988. [matrix methods] cited in D.2.6.1, D.2.6.1.s, F.1.4.2.1 (p. 40), F.1.4.2.1.s (p. 757)

[2] D. J. Abel. A B⁺-tree structure for large quadtrees. *Computer Vision, Graphics, and Image Processing*, 27(1):19–31, July 1984. [regions; B⁺-tree; MX-CIF quadtree] cited in A.2.1, A.2.1.1, A.4.2.3, F.1.8.1 (p. 166), F.2.1.2.4 (p. 214), F.2.1.4.1 (pp. 255–256), F.3.4.2 (p. 479)

[3] D. J. Abel. Comments on "detection of connectivity for regions represented by linear quadtrees". *Computers and Mathematics with Applications*, 10(2):167–170, 1984. [regions; connected component labeling; region quadtree] cited in A.5.1.3

[4] D. J. Abel. Some elemental operations on linear quadtrees for geographic information systems. *The Computer Journal*, 28(1):73–77, February 1985. [regions; region quadtree] cited in D.3.5.2

[5] D. J. Abel. SIRO-DBMS: a database tool-kit for geographical information systems. *International Journal of Geographical Information Systems*, 3(2):103–116, April–June 1989. [spatial database]

[6] D. J. Abel and D. M. Mark. A comparative analysis of some two-dimensional orderings. *International Journal of Geographical Information Systems*, 4(1):21–31, January 1990. [regions]

[7] D. J. Abel, B. C. Ooi, K.-L. Tan, R. Power, and J. X. Yu. Spatial join strategies in distributed spatial DBMS. In *Advances in Spatial Databases—4th International Symposium, SSD'95*, M. J. Egenhofer and J. R. Herring, eds., vol. 951 of Springer-Verlag Lecture Notes in Computer Science, pages 348–367, Portland, ME, August 1995. [rectangles; spatial join]

[8] D. J. Abel and J. L. Smith. A data structure and algorithm based on a linear key for a rectangle retrieval problem. *Computer Vision, Graphics, and Image Processing*, 24(1):1–13, October 1983. [rectangles; MX-CIF quadtree] cited in A.2.1.1, D.3.5, D.3.5.1, F.1.6 (p. 93), F.2.1.1.2 (p. 200), F.2.1.4.1 (p. 255), F.3.4 (p. 466), F.3.4.1.1 (p. 467)

[9] D. J. Abel and J. L. Smith. A data structure and query algorithm for a database of areal entities. *Australian Computer Journal*, 16(4):147–154, November 1984. [rectangles; expanded MX-CIF quadtree; geographic information systems (GIS)] cited in F.2.1.4.1 (p. 256), F.3.4.3 (p. 481)

[10] D. J. Abel and J. L. Smith. A simple approach to the nearest-neighbor problem. *Australian Computer Journal*, 16(4):140–146, November 1984. [points]

[11] A. Aboulnaga and W. G. Aref. Window query processing in linear quadtrees. *Distributed and Parallel Databases*, 10(2):111–126, September 2001. [regions; window query]

[12] A. Aboulnaga and J. F. Naughton. Accurate estimation of the cost of spatial selections. In *Proceedings of the 16th IEEE International Conference on Data Engineering*, pages 123–134, San Diego, CA, February 2000. [selectivity estimation] cited in F.2.1.4.1 (p. 259)

[13] S. Acharya, V. Poosala, and S. Ramaswamy. Selectivity estimation in spatial databases. In *Proceedings of the ACM SIGMOD Conference*, pages 13–24, Philadelphia, PA, June 1999. [spatial database; selectivity estimation]

[14] O. Adams. Latitude developments connected with geodesy and cartography. In *US Coast and Geodetic Survey Special Publication No. 67*. US Government Printing Office, Washington, DC, 1949. [map projections] cited in D.1.4.1, F.2.1.2.11 (p. 232)

[15] G. M. Adel'son-Vel'skiĭ and E. M. Landis. An algorithm for the organization of information. *Doklady Akademii Nauk SSSR*,

146:263–266, 1962. (English translation in *Soviet Math. Doklady* 3:1259–1263, 1962). [points; AVL tree] cited in D.2.4.1, D.2.7, F.1.1 (p. 7), F.1.5.1.4 (pp. 65–66), F.1.5.2.6 (p. 82), F.1.7.3 (p. 164), F.A (p. 718)

[16] P. K. Agarwal, L. Arge, and J. Erickson. Indexing moving points. In *Proceedings of the 19th ACM SIGACT-SIGMOD-SIGART Symposium on Principles of Database Systems (PODS)*, pages 175–186, Dallas, TX, May 2000. [moving objects]

[17] P. K. Agarwal, M. de Berg, J. Gudmundsson, M. Hammar, and H. J. Haverkort. Box-trees and R-trees with near-optimal query time. *Discrete and Computational Geometry*, 28(3):291–312, August 2002. [rectangles; R-tree]

[18] P. K. Agarwal, J. Erickson, and L. J. Guibas. Kinetic binary space partitions for intersecting segments and disjoint triangles. In *Proceedings of the 9th Annual ACM-SIAM Symposium on Discrete Algorithms*, pages 107–116, San Francisco, January 1998. [regions; volumes; BSP tree; moving objects] cited in F.2.1.3.1 (p. 235)

[19] P. K. Agarwal, E. F. Grove, T. M. Murali, and J. S. Vitter. Binary space partitions for fat rectangles. In *Proceedings of the 37th IEEE Annual Symposium on Foundations of Computer Science*, pages 482–491, Burlington, VT, October 1996. [rectangles; BSP tree]

[20] P. K. Agarwal, L. J. Guibas, H. Edelsbrunner, J. Erickson, M. Isard, S. Har-Peled, J. Hershberger, C. Jensen, L. Kavraki, P. Koehl, M. Lin, D. Manocha, D. Metaxas, B. Mirtich, and D. Mount. Algorithmic issues in modeling motion. *ACM Computing Surveys*, 34(4):550–572, December 2002. [spatiotemporal database; moving objects]

[21] P. K. Agarwal and C. M. Procopiuc. Advances in indexing for mobile objects. *IEEE Data Engineering Bulletin*, 25(2):25–34, June 2002. [spatiotemporal database; moving objects] cited in F.P (p. xvii), F.1 (p. 2)

[22] C. Aggarwal, J. Wolf, P. Yu, and M. Epelman. The *S*-tree: an efficient index for multidimensional objects. In *Advances in Spatial Databases—5th International Symposium, SSD'97*, M. Scholl and A. Voisard, eds., vol. 1262 of Springer-Verlag Lecture Notes in Computer Science, pages 350–373, Berlin, Germany, July 1997. [rectangles; object hierarchy; R-tree; S-tree] cited in F.1.7.1.6.5 (p. 128), F.2.1.5.2.7 (p. 301)

[23] C. C. Aggarwal. On the effects of dimensionality reduction on high dimensional similarity search. In *Proceedings of the 20th ACM SIGACT-SIGMOD-SIGART Symposium on Principles of Database Systems (PODS)*, pages 256–266, Santa Barbara, CA, May 2001. [high-dimensional data; dimension reduction; similarity searching]

[24] C. C. Aggarwal. An efficient subspace sampling framework for high-dimensional data reduction, selectivity estimation, and nearest-neighbor search. *IEEE Transactions on Knowledge and Data Engineering*, 16(10):1247–1262, October 2004. [high-dimensional data; dimension reduction; similarity searching]

[25] C. C. Aggarwal and D. Agrawal. On nearest neighbor indexing of nonlinear trajectories. In *Proceedings of the 22nd ACM SIGACT-SIGMOD-SIGART Symposium on Principles of Database Systems (PODS)*, pages 252–259, San Diego, CA, June 2003. [moving objects; nearest neighbor]

[26] R. Agrawal, C. Faloutsos, and A. N. Swami. Efficient similarity search in sequence databases. In *Proceedings of the 4th International Conference on Foundations of Data Organization and Algorithms (FODO)*, D. B. Lomet, ed., vol. 730 of Springer-Verlag Lecture Notes in Computer Science, pages 69–84, Chicago, October 1993. [points; time-series database; high-dimensional data; Discrete Fourier Transform (DFT)] cited in F.4.6.4.2 (pp. 677, 681–682)

[27] A. V. Aho, J. E. Hopcroft, and J. D. Ullman. *The Design and Analysis of Computer Algorithms*. Addison-Wesley, Reading, MA, 1974. [algorithms; general] cited in A.P, A.4.5, D.P, D.2.4.1, D.2.7, D.4.2.3, F.P (p. xvii), F.1.5.1.4 (p. 66), F.A (p. 718)

[28] A. V. Aho, R. Sethi, and J. D. Ullman. *Compilers: Principles, Techniques and Tools*. Addison-Wesley, Reading, MA, 1986. [compiler design; general] cited in F.2.1.2.9 (p. 228)

[29] N. Ahuja. On approaches to polygonal decomposition for hierarchical image representation. *Computer Vision, Graphics, and Image Processing*, 24(2):200–214, November 1983. [regions; tiling] cited in A.4.6, D.1.4.1, D.5.2, F.2.1.1.1 (p. 197)

[30] N. Ahuja. Efficient planar embedding of trees for VLSI layouts. In *Proceedings of the 7th International Conference on Pattern Recognition*, pages 460–464, Montréal, Canada, July 1984. [hardware]

[31] N. Ahuja and C. Nash. Octree representations of moving objects. *Computer Vision, Graphics, and Image Processing*, 26(2):207–216, May 1984. [volumes; region octree] cited in A.6.5.3

[32] N. Ahuja and J. Veenstra. Generating octrees from object silhouettes in orthographic views. *IEEE Transactions on Pattern Analysis and Machine Intelligence*, 11(2):137–149, February 1989. [volumes; region octree] cited in A.4.6, A.4.6.s, D.5.2, D.5.2.s

[33] K. Aizawa and A. Nakamura. Parsing of two-dimensional images represented by quadtree adjoining grammars. *Pattern Recognition*, 32(2):277–294, February 1999. [regions; picture grammars]

[34] J. Alander. Interval arithmetic methods in the processing of curves and sculptured surfaces. In *Proceedings of the 6th International Symposium on CAD/CAM*, pages 13–19, Zagreb, Yugoslavia, October 1984. [surfaces; interval arithmetic] cited in D.5.5.1

[35] J. Alander, K. Hyytia, J. Hamalainen, A. Jaatinen, O. Karonen, P. Rekola, and M. Tikkanen. Programmer's manual of interval package IP. Laboratory of Information Processing Report–HTKK–TKO–B59, Helsinki University of Technology, Espoo, Finland, 1984. [surfaces; interval arithmetic] cited in D.5.5.1

[36] H. Alborzi and H. Samet. BV-trees and R-trees for collections of extended objects represented by their minimum bounding hyper-rectangles. Computer Science Technical Report TR–4632, University of Maryland, College Park, MD, 2004. [rectangles; BV-tree; R-tree; R*-tree] cited in F.1.7.1.6.5 (p. 128)

[37] N. Alexandridis and A. Klinger. Picture decomposition, tree data-structures, and identifying directional symmetries as node combinations. *Computer Graphics and Image Processing*, 8(1):43–77, August 1978. [regions]

[38] V. V. Alexandrov and N. D. Gorsky. Recursive approach to associative storage and search of information in data bases. In *Proceedings of the Finnish-Soviet Symposium on Design and Application of Data Base Systems*, pages 271–284, Turku, Finland, 1980. [regions] cited in A.1.4, D.1.3

[39] V. V. Alexandrov, N. D. Gorsky, and A. O. Polakov. Recursive algorithms of data representation and processing. Leningrad Research Computer Center Technical Report 003, Academy of Sciences of the USSR, 1979. [regions; space-filling curve] cited in A.1.4, D.1.3

[40] M. Altenhofen and R. Diehl. Conversion of boundary representations to bintrees. In *Proceedings of the EUROGRAPHICS'88 Conference*, D. A. Duce and P. Jancene, eds., pages 117–127, Nice, France, September 1988. [volumes; boundary model (BRep)]

[41] S. Aluru. Greengard's N-body algorithm is not order N. *SIAM Journal on Scientific Computing*, 17(3):773–776, May 1996. [points; particle simulation; *N*-body problem]

[42] J. Amanatides. Ray tracing with cones. *Computer Graphics*, 18(3):129–135, July 1984. Also in *Proceedings of the SIGGRAPH'84 Conference*, Minneapolis, MN, July 1984. [volumes; ray tracing; antialiasing] cited in A.7.2.2, A.7.3, A.7.3.s

[43] A. Amir, A. Efrat, P. Indyk, and H. Samet. Efficient algorithms and regular data structures for dilation, location and proximity problems. *Algorithmica*, 30(2):164–187, 2001. Also see *Proceedings of the 40th IEEE Annual Symposium on Foundations of Computer Science*, pages 160–170, New York, October 1999 and University of Maryland Computer Science Technical Report TR–4201, November 2000. [regions; point location; image dilation] cited in F.2.1.2.4 (p. 216), F.2.1.2.4.s (pp. 780–781)

[44] N. An, S. Gurumurthi, A. Sivasubramaniam, N. Vijaykrishnan, M. T. Kandemir, and M. J. Irwin. Energy-performance trade-offs for spatial access methods on memory-resident data. *VLDB Journal*, 11(3):179–197, November 2002. [regions; energy-efficient data structures; packed R-tree; buddy-tree]

[45] N. An, J. Jin, and A. Sivasubramaniam. Toward an accurate analysis of range queries on spatial data. *IEEE Transactions on Knowledge and Data Engineering*, 15(2):305–323, March/April 2003. [range query]

[46] N. An, L. Qian, A. Sivasubramaniam, and T. Keefe. Evaluating parallel R-tree implementations on a network of workstations (extended abstract). In *Proceedings of the 6th ACM International Symposium on Advances in Geographic Information Systems*, R. Laurini, K. Makki, and N. Pissinou, eds., pages 159–160, Washington, DC, November 1998. [regions; R-tree; parallel processing]

[47] N. An, Z.-Y. Yang, and A. Sivasubramaniam. Selectivity estimation for spatial joins. In *Proceedings of the 17th IEEE International Conference on Data Engineering*, pages 368–375, Heidelberg, Germany, April 2001. [spatial join; selectivity estimation]

[48] M. R. Anderberg. *Cluster Analysis for Applications*. Academic Press, New York, 1973. [clustering; general] cited in F.2.2.3.4 (p. 398)

[49] D. P. Anderson. Techniques for reducing pen plotting time. *ACM Transactions on Graphics*, 2(3):197–212, July 1983. [points; PR quadtree] cited in A.6.2, D.2.6.2, F.1.4.2.2 (p. 44)

[50] R. J. Anderson. Tree data structures for N-body simulation. In *Proceedings of the 37th IEEE Annual Symposium on Foundations of Computer Science*, pages 224–233, Burlington, VT, October 1996. [points; particle simulation; *N*-body problem; k-d tree] cited in F.2.4 (p. 426)

[51] A. Andersson and S. Nilsson. Improved behaviour of tries by adaptive branching. *Information Processing Letters*, 46(6):295–300, July 1993. [points; trie; path compression; level compression; PR k-d tree] cited in F.1.5.2.5 (p. 77)

[52] F. P. Andresen, L. S. Davis, R. D. Eastman, and S. Kambhampati. Visual algorithms for autonomous navigation. In *Proceedings of the International Conference on Robotics*, pages 856–861, St. Louis, MO, March 1985. [regions] cited in A.9.2.s

[53] C.-H. Ang. *Analysis and applications of hierarchical data structures*. PhD thesis, Computer Science Department, University of Maryland, College Park, MD, June 1989. Also Computer Science Technical Report TR-2255. [regions; points; PR quadtree; image dilation] cited in F.1.4.2.2 (p. 46), F.1.7.3 (p. 163)

[54] C. H. Ang. An optimal quadtree translation algorithm. In *Advances in Spatial Databases—3rd International Symposium, SSD'93*, D. Abel and B. C. Ooi, eds., vol. 692 of Springer-Verlag Lecture Notes in Computer Science, pages 178–190, Singapore, June 1993. [regions]

[55] C.-H. Ang and H. Samet. Node distribution in a PR quadtree. In *Design and Implementation of Large Spatial Databases—1st Symposium, SSD'89*, A. Buchmann, O. Günther, T. R. Smith, and Y.-F. Wang, eds., vol. 409 of Springer-Verlag Lecture Notes in Computer Science, pages 233–252, Santa Barbara, CA, July 1989. [points; PR quadtree] cited in F.1.4.2.2 (p. 46)

[56] C.-H. Ang and H. Samet. Which is more efficient for window search bit interleaving or key-concatenation? Information Systems and Computer Science Technical Report TRD5/91, National University of Singapore, Singapore, May 1991. [points; window query]

[57] C. H. Ang and H. Samet. Approximate average storage utilization of bucket methods with arbitrary fanout. *Nordic Journal of Computing*, 3:280–291, 1996. Also University of Maryland Computer Science Technical Report TR-3618, March 1996. [points; B-tree; grid file; extendible hashing; EXCELL; ternary system] cited in F.1.7.3 (p. 163)

[58] C.-H. Ang, H. Samet, and C. A. Shaffer. A new region expansion for quadtrees. *IEEE Transactions on Pattern Analysis and Machine Intelligence*, 12(7):682–686, July 1990. Also see *Proceedings of the Third International Symposium on Spatial Data Handling*, pages 19–37, Sydney, Australia, August 1988. [regions; image dilation] cited in A.6.6, A.6.6.s

[59] C.-H. Ang and K.-P. Tan. The interval B-tree. *Information Processing Letters*, 53(2):85–89, January 1995. [intervals; temporal database; B-tree]

[60] C.-H. Ang and T. C. Tan. New linear node splitting algorithm for R-trees. In *Advances in Spatial Databases—5th International Symposium, SSD'97*, M. Scholl and A. Voisard, eds., vol. 1262 of Springer-Verlag Lecture Notes in Computer Science, pages 339–349, Berlin, Germany, July 1997. [regions; R-tree] cited in F.2.1.5.2.3 (pp. 285–288), F.2.1.5.2.4 (pp. 291–292, 294)

[61] M. Ankerst, B. Braunmüller, H.-P. Kriegel, and T. Seidl. Improving adaptable similarity query processing by using approximations. In *Proceedings of the 24th International Conference on Very Large Data Bases (VLDB)*, A. Gupta, O. Shmueli, and J. Widom, eds., pages 206–217, New York, August 1998. [points; similarity searching; nearest neighbor]

[62] M. Ankerst, H.-P. Kriegel, and T. Seidl. A multistep approach for shape similarity search in image databases. *IEEE Transactions on Knowledge and Data Engineering*, 10(6):996–1004, November/December 1998. [similarity searching]

[63] S. Ansaldi, L. De Floriani, and B. Falcidieno. Geometric modeling of solid objects by using a face adjacency graph representation. *Computer Graphics*, 19(3):131–139, July 1985. Also in *Proceedings of the SIGGRAPH'85 Conference*, San Francisco, July 1985. [volumes] cited in D.5.4

[64] R. Antony and P. J. Emmerman. Spatial reasoning and knowledge representation. In *Geographic Information Systems in Government*, B. K. Opitz, ed., vol. 2, pages 795–813. A. Deepak Publishing, Hampton, VA, 1986. [regions; spatial reasoning; data fusion]

[65] R. T. Antony. *Principles of Data Fusion Automation*. Artech House, Norwood, MA, 1995. [data fusion] cited in F.2.1.4.2 (p. 260)

[66] P. M. Aoki. Generalizing "search" in generalized search trees. In *Proceedings of the 14th IEEE International Conference on Data Engineering*, pages 380–389, Orlando, FL, February 1998. [object hierarchy; incremental nearest neighbor algorithm; GiST] cited in F.1.9 (p. 189), F.4.4.7 (p. 590)

[67] A. A. Appel. Some techniques for shading machine renderings of solids. In *Proceedings of the Spring Joint Computer Conference*, vol. 32, pages 37–45, Atlantic City, NJ, April 1968. [ray tracing] cited in A.7.2.1

[68] A. W. Appel. An efficient program for many-body simulation. *SIAM Journal on Scientific and Statistical Computing*, 6(1):85–103, January 1985. [points; particle simulation; *N*-body problem] cited in F.2.4 (p. 426)

[69] C. R. Aragon and R. G. Seidel. Randomized search trees. In *Proceedings of the 30th IEEE Annual Symposium on Foundations of Computer Science*, pages 540–545, Research Triangle Park, NC, October–November 1989. [balanced binary search tree; skip list; treap] cited in F.1.3 (p. 27)

[70] W. G. Aref and I. F. Ilyas. SP-GiST: an extensible database index for supporting space partitioning trees. *Journal of Intelligent Information Systems*, 17(2–3):215–240, December 2001. Also see *Proceedings of the 13th International Conference on Scientific and Statistical Database Management*, pages 49–58, Fairfax, VA, July 2001. [regions; GiST; SP-GiST] cited in F.1.9 (p. 188), F.2.1.5.2 (p. 271), F.4.4.7 (p. 590)

[71] W. G. Aref and H. Samet. An approach to information management in geographical applications. In *Proceedings of the 4th International Symposium on Spatial Data Handling*, vol. 2, pages 589–598, Zurich, Switzerland, July 1990. [SAND] cited in F.P (p. xviii)

[72] W. G. Aref and H. Samet. Efficient processing of window queries in the pyramid data structure. In *Proceedings of the 9th ACM SIGACT-SIGMOD-SIGART Symposium on Principles of Database Systems (PODS)*, pages 265–272, Nashville, TN, April 1990. Also in *Proceedings of the Fifth Brazilian Symposium on Databases*, pages 15–26, Rio de Janeiro, Brazil, April 1990. [spatial data mining; feature-based queries; location-based queries; pyramid] cited in F.2 (p. 192)

[73] W. G. Aref and H. Samet. Extending a DBMS with spatial operations. In *Advances in Spatial Databases—2nd Symposium, SSD'91*, O. Günther and H.-J. Schek, eds., vol. 525 of Springer-Verlag Lecture Notes in Computer Science, pages 299–318, Zurich, Switzerland, August 1991. [SAND] cited in F.P (p. xviii)

[74] W. G. Aref and H. Samet. Loading spatial features into the incomplete pyramid data structure. In *Proceedings of the Workshop on Geographic Database Management Systems*, G. Gambosi, M. Scholl, and H.-W. Six, eds., pages 138–160, Capri, Italy, May 1991. Springer-Verlag. [regions; spatial data mining]

[75] W. G. Aref and H. Samet. Optimization strategies for spatial query processing. In *Proceedings of the 17th International Conference on Very Large Databases (VLDB)*, G. M. Lohman, A. Sernadas, and

R. Camps, eds., pages 81–90, Barcelona, Spain, September 1991. [spatial query optimization]

[76] W. G. Aref and H. Samet. Uniquely reporting spatial objects: yet another operation for comparing spatial data structures. In *Proceedings of the 5th International Symposium on Spatial Data Handling*, pages 178–189, Charleston, SC, August 1992. [lines; duplicate removal] cited in F.4.1.4 (p. 499)

[77] W. G. Aref and H. Samet. Decomposing a window into maximal quadtree blocks. *Acta Informatica*, 30:425–439, 1993. Also University of Maryland Computer Science Technical Report TR–2771, October 1991. [regions; window query]

[78] W. G. Aref and H. Samet. Estimating selectivity factors of spatial operations. In *Optimization in Databases—5th International Workshop on Foundations of Models and Languages for Data and Objects*, A. Heuer and M. H. Scholl, eds., pages 31–40, Aigen, Austria, September 1993. Also in Technische Universität Clausthal Institut für Informatik Technical Report 93/9, Clausthal-Zellerfeld, Germany. [spatial query optimization; selectivity estimation] cited in F.4.1.1 (p. 492)

[79] W. G. Aref and H. Samet. A cost model for query optimization using R-trees. In *Proceedings of the 2nd ACM Workshop on Geographic Information Systems*, N. Pissinou and K. Makki, eds., pages 60–67, Gaithersburg, MD, December 1994. [regions; R-tree; spatial query optimization; selectivity estimation]

[80] W. G. Aref and H. Samet. Hashing by proximity to process duplicates in spatial databases. In *Proceedings of the 3rd International Conference on Information and Knowledge Management (CIKM)*, pages 347–354, Gaithersburg, MD, December 1994. [rectangles; duplicate removal] cited in F.4.1.4 (p. 499)

[81] W. G. Aref and H. Samet. The spatial filter revisited. In *Proceedings of the 6th International Symposium on Spatial Data Handling*, T. C. Waugh and R. G. Healey, eds., pages 190–208, Edinburgh, Scotland, September 1994. International Geographical Union Commission on Geographic Information Systems, Association for Geographical Information. [regions; spatial join]

[82] W. G. Aref and H. Samet. An algorithm for perspective viewing of objects represented by octrees. *Computer Graphics Forum*, 14(1):59–66, March 1995. Also University of Maryland Computer Science Technical Report TR–2757, September 1991. [volumes; region octree; perspective view]

[83] W. G. Aref and H. Samet. Cascaded spatial join algorithms with spatially sorted output. In *Proceedings of the 4th ACM Workshop on Geographic Information Systems*, S. Shekhar and P. Bergougnoux, eds., pages 17–24, Gaithersburg, MD, November 1996. [regions; spatial join]

[84] W. G. Aref and H. Samet. Efficient window block retrieval in quadtree-based spatial databases. *GeoInformatica*, 1(1):59–91, April 1997. Also see *Proceedings of the 3rd ACM Workshop on Geographic Information Systems*, pages 69–76, Baltimore, MD, December 1995. [regions; window query]

[85] L. Arge. *Efficient external-memory data structures and applications*. PhD thesis, Computer Science Department, University of Aarhus, Aarhus, Denmark, 1996. Also BRICS Dissertation Series Report DS–96–3. [rectangles; object hierarchy; R-tree; bulk loading; buffer tree] cited in F.2.1.5.2.6 (p. 299)

[86] L. Arge, M. de Berg, H. J. Haverkort, and K. Yi. The priority R-tree: a practically efficient and worst-case optimal R-tree. In *Proceedings of the ACM SIGMOD Conference*, pages 347–358, Paris, France, June 2004. [points; R-tree; object hierarchy; priority R-tree] cited in F.2.1.5.2.3 (p. 286)

[87] L. Arge, K. H. Hinrichs, J. Vahrenhold, and J. S. Vitter. Efficient bulk operations on dynamic R-trees. In *Proceedings of the 1st Workshop on Algorithm Engineering and Experimentation (ALENEX'99)*, M. T. Goodrich and C. C. McGeoch, eds., vol. 1619 of Springer-Verlag Lecture Notes in Computer Science, pages 328–348, Baltimore, MD, January 1999. [R-tree; bulk loading] cited in F.1.8.1 (p. 165), F.2.1.5.2.6 (pp. 299–300)

[88] L. Arge, O. Procopiuc, S. Ramaswamy, T. Suel, J. Vahrenhold, and J. S. Vitter. A unified approach for indexed and non-indexed spatial joins. In *Proceedings of the 7th International Conference on Extending Database Technology—EDBT 2000*, C. Zaniolo,

P. C. Lockemann, M. H. Scholl, and T. Grust, eds., vol. 1777 of Springer-Verlag Lecture Notes in Computer Science, pages 413–429, Konstanz, Germany, March 2000. [regions; spatial join]

[89] L. Arge, O. Procopiuc, S. Ramaswamy, T. Suel, and J. S. Vitter. Scalable sweeping-based spatial join. In *Proceedings of the 24th International Conference on Very Large Data Bases (VLDB)*, A. Gupta, O. Shmueli, and J. Widom, eds., pages 570–581, New York, August 1998. [spatial join] cited in F.P (p. xx), F.3.1.2 (p. 438)

[90] L. Arge, V. Samoladas, and J. S. Vitter. On two-dimensional indexability and optimal range search indexing. In *Proceedings of the 18th ACM SIGACT-SIGMOD-SIGART Symposium on Principles of Database Systems (PODS)*, pages 346–357, Philadelphia, PA, May–June 1999. [range query]

[91] R. Arman and J. K. Aggarwal. Model-based object recognition in dense range images—a review. *ACM Computing Surveys*, 25(1):5–43, March 1993. [volumes; object recognition; survey] cited in F.2 (p. 191)

[92] B. Arnaldi, T. Priol, and K. Bouatouch. A new space subdivision method for ray tracing CSG modeled scenes. *Visual Computer*, 3(2):98–108, August 1987. Also INRIA Rapport de Recherche No. 613, Rennes, France, February 1987. [volumes; image synthesis; ray tracing; constructive solid geometry (CSG)] cited in A.7.2.5

[93] K. Arnold and J. Gosling. *The JAVA™ Programming Language*. Addison-Wesley, Reading, MA, 1996. [JAVA; programming languages] cited in F.P (p. xx), F.D (p. 743)

[94] B. Aronov, H. Brönnimann, A. Y. Chang, and Y.-J. Chiang. Cost-driven octree construction schemes: an experimental study. In *Proceedings of the 19th Annual Symposium on Computational Geometry*, pages 227–236, San Diego, CA, June 2003. [volumes; region octree]

[95] E. Artzy, G. Frieder, and G. T. Herman. The theory, design, implementation, and evaluation of a three-dimensional surface detection algorithm. *Computer Graphics and Image Processing*, 15(1):1–24, January 1981. [volumes]

[96] J. Arvo and D. Kirk. Fast ray tracing by ray classification. *Computer Graphics*, 21(4):55–64, July 1987. Also in *Proceedings of the SIGGRAPH'87 Conference*, Anaheim, CA, July 1987. [volumes; ray tracing] cited in A.7.3, D.2.1

[97] S. Arya and T. Malamatos. Linear-size approximate Voronoi diagrams. In *Proceedings of the 13th Annual ACM-SIAM Symposium on Discrete Algorithms*, pages 147–155, Las Vegas, NV, January 2002. [regions; triangulations; Voronoi diagram; approximate Voronoi diagram (AVD); approximate nearest neighbor] cited in F.2.2.2.6 (p. 367), F.4.1.7 (p. 516), F.4.4.5 (p. 581)

[98] S. Arya, T. Malamatos, and D. M. Mount. Space-efficient approximate Voronoi diagrams. In *Proceedings of the 33rd Annual ACM Symposium on the Theory of Computing*, pages 721–730, Montréal, Canada, January 2002. [regions; triangulations; Voronoi diagram; approximate Voronoi diagram (AVD); approximate nearest neighbor] cited in F.2.2.2.6 (p. 367), F.4.1.7 (p. 516), F.4.4.5 (pp. 581–583), F.4.4.5.s (p. 853)

[99] S. Arya and D. M. Mount. Approximate nearest neighbor queries in fixed dimensions. In *Proceedings of the 4th Annual ACM-SIAM Symposium on Discrete Algorithms*, pages 271–280, Austin, TX, January 1993. [points; approximate nearest neighbor]

[100] S. Arya, D. M. Mount, N. S. Netanyahu, R. Silverman, and A. Y. Wu. An optimal algorithm for approximate nearest neighbor searching in fixed dimensions. *Journal of the ACM*, 45(6):891–923, November 1998. Also see *Proceedings of the 5th Annual ACM-SIAM Symposium on Discrete Algorithms*, pages 573–582, Arlington, VA, January 1994. [points; approximate nearest neighbor; BBD-tree; priority queue] cited in F.1.5.1.4 (p. 64), F.1.5.2.2 (p. 74), F.1.5.2.3 (p. 74), F.1.5.2.6 (p. 82), F.1.5.2.7 (pp. 83, 87), F.4.1.7 (p. 516), F.4.3 (pp. 557, 559, 561–562), F.4.4.5 (pp. 581, 584)

[101] T. Asano, D. Ranjan, T. Roos, E. Welzl, and P. Widmayer. Space-filling curves and their use in the design of geometric data structures. *Theoretical Computer Science*, 181(1):3–15, July 1997. [points; space-filling curve] cited in F.2.1.2.4 (p. 216)

[102] I. Ashdown. Octree color quantization. *C/C++ Users Journal*, 13(3):31–44, March 1995. [volumes; color quantization]

[103] M. J. Atallah, M. T. Goodrich, and K. Radimaer. Biased finger trees and three-dimensional layers of maxima. In *Proceedings of the 10th Annual Symposium on Computational Geometry*, pages 150–159, Stony Brook, NY, June 1994. [regions; dynamic point location] cited in F.2.1.3.3.2 (p. 253)

[104] P. R. Atherton. A scan-line hidden surface removal procedure for constructive solid geometry. *Computer Graphics*, 17(3):73–82, July 1983. Also in *Proceedings of the SIGGRAPH'83 Conference*, Boston, July 1983. [volumes; constructive solid geometry (CSG)] cited in D.5.5

[105] V. Athitsos, J. Alon, and S. Sclaroff. Efficient nearest neighbor classification using a cascade of approximate similarity measures. In *Proceedings of Computer Vision and Pattern Recognition'05*, pages 486–493, San Diego, CA, June 2005. [metric space embedding; BoostMap; AdaBoost; machine learning; FastMap] cited in F.4.7 (p. 686)

[106] V. Athitsos, J. Alon, S. Sclaroff, and G. Kollios. Boostmap: a method for efficient approximate similarity rankings. In *Proceedings of Computer Vision and Pattern Recognition'04*, pages 268–275, Washington, DC, June 2004. [metric space embedding; BoostMap; AdaBoost; machine learning; FastMap] cited in F.4.7 (p. 686)

[107] V. Athitsos, M. Hadjieleftheriou, G. Kollios, and S. Sclaroff. Query-sensitive embeddings. In *Proceedings of the ACM SIGMOD Conference*, pages 706–717, Baltimore, MD, June 2005. [metric space embedding; BoostMap; AdaBoost; machine learning; FastMap] cited in F.4.7 (p. 686)

[108] V. Athitsos and S. Sclaroff. Boosting nearest neighbor classifiers for multiclass recognition. In *Proceedings of the IEEE Workshop on Learning in Computer Vision and Pattern Recognition*, San Diego, CA, June 2005. [metric space embedding; BoostMap; AdaBoost; machine learning; FastMap] cited in F.4.7 (p. 686)

[109] H. H. Atkinson, I. Gargantini, and M. V. S. Ramanath. Determination of the 3d border by repeated elimination of internal surfaces. *Computing*, 32(4):279–295, October 1984. [volumes]

[110] H. H. Atkinson, I. Gargantini, and M. V. S. Ramanath. Improvements to a recent 3d border algorithm. *Pattern Recognition*, 18(3/4):215–226, 1985. [volumes]

[111] H. H. Atkinson, I. Gargantini, and T. R. S. Walsh. Counting regions, holes, and their nesting level in time proportional to their border. *Computer Vision, Graphics, and Image Processing*, 29(2):196–215, February 1985. [regions] cited in D.1.5.s, F.2.2.2.2.s (p. 803)

[112] F. Aurenhammer. Voronoi diagrams—a survey of a fundamental geometric data structure. *ACM Computing Surveys*, 23(3):345–405, September 1991. [Voronoi diagram; regions; points; survey] cited in F.4.4.4 (p. 574)

[113] D. Avis. A survey of heuristics for the weighted matching problem. *Networks*, 13(4):475–493, Winter 1983. [points; Euclidean matching problem; survey] cited in D.2.9.s, F.1.9.s (p. 776)

[114] D. Avis. On the partitionability of points sets in space. In *Proceedings of the Symposium on Computational Geometry*, pages 116–120, Baltimore, MD, June 1985. [points; lines; point quadtree] cited in F.1.5.3.s (p. 768)

[115] D. Ayala, F. Batlle, P. Brunet, and I. Navazo. Boolean operations between extended octrees. Llenguatges i Sistemes Informatics Department Technical Report LSI–91–31, Universitat Politecnica de Catalunya, Barcelona, Spain, 1991. [volumes; PM octree; extended octree]

[116] D. Ayala, P. Brunet, R. Juan, and I. Navazo. Object representation by means of nonminimal division quadtrees and octrees. *ACM Transactions on Graphics*, 4(1):41–59, January 1985. [volumes; PM octree; extended octree] cited in A.1.3, D.5.3, F.2.2.2.7 (p. 370)

[117] N. M. Aziz. A hierarchical model for spatial stacking. In *New Trends in Computer Graphics: Proceedings of the CG International'88*, N. Magnenat-Thalmann and D. Thalmann, eds., pages 267–274, Geneva, Switzerland, May 1988. Springer-Verlag. [volumes]

[118] R. A. Baeza-Yates, W. Cunto, U. Manber, and S. Wu. Proximity matching using fixed-queries trees. In *Proceedings of the 5th Annual Symposium on Combinatorial Pattern Matching*, vol. 807 of Springer-Verlag Lecture Notes in Computer Science, pages 198–212, Asilomar, CA, June 1994. [metric spaces; fixed-queries tree]

cited in F.4.1.7 (p. 517), F.4.2 (p. 517), F.4.5.1 (p. 601), F.4.5.2.4 (p. 611)

[119] H. S. Baird. Design of a family of algorithms for large scale integrated circuit mask artwork analysis. Technical Report PRRL–76–TR–062, RCA Laboratories, Princeton, NJ, May 1976. [rectangles; plane-sweep algorithms; hardware] cited in F.2.1.5.2.4 (p. 291), F.3 (p. 428), F.4.1.5 (p. 504)

[120] C. Bajaj and T. K. Dey. Convex decomposition of polyhedra and robustness. *SIAM Journal on Computing*, 21(2):339–364, April 1992. [volumes; conforming tetrahedralization] cited in F.2.2.1.6 (p. 353)

[121] D. H. Ballard. Strip trees: a hierarchical representation for curves. *Communications of the ACM*, 24(5):310–321, May 1981. Also see corrigendum, *Communications of the ACM*, 25(3):213, March 1982. [lines; strip tree] cited in D.4, D.4.1, D.4.1.s, D.5.7, F.2.2.2.3 (p. 360), F.2.2.2.4 (p. 362), F.2.2.3.1 (p. 382), F.2.2.3.1.s (p. 812)

[122] F. Banaei-Kashani and C. Shahabi. SWAM: a family of access methods for similarity-search in peer-to-peer data networks. In *Proceedings of the 13th International Conference on Information and Knowledge Management (CIKM)*, pages 304–313, Arlington, VA, November 2004. [points; similarity searching; peer-to-peer indexing]

[123] S. Bandyopadhyay and U. Maulik. Efficient prototype reordering in nearest neighbor classification. *Pattern Recognition*, 35(12):2791–2799, December 2002. [metric spaces; distance matrix]

[124] R. E. Bank, A. H. Sherman, and A. Weiser. Refinement algorithms and data structures for regular local mesh refinement. In *Scientific Computing, IMACS Transactions on Scientific Computation*, R. Stepleman, M. Carver, R. Peskin, W. F. Ames, and R. Vichnevetsky, eds., vol. 1, pages 3–17. North-Holland, Amsterdam, The Netherlands, 1983. [surfaces; triangulations; triangle meshes] cited in F.2.2.4 (pp. 405, 407)

[125] G. Barequet, B. Chazelle, L. J. Guibas, J. S. B. Mitchell, and A. Tal. BOXTREE: a hierarchical representation for surfaces in 3D. In *Proceedings of the EUROGRAPHICS'96 Conference*, J. Rossignac and F. X. Sillion, eds., pages 387–396, 484, Poitiers, France, August 1996. Also in *Computer Graphics Forum*, 15(3):387–396, 484, August 1996. [volumes; surfaces; minimum bounding box] cited in F.2.2.3.4 (p. 398)

[126] J. Barnes and P. Hut. A hierarchical $o(n \log n)$ force-calculation algorithm. *Nature*, 324(4):446–449, December 1986. [points; particle simulation; N-body problem] cited in F.1.5.1.4 (p. 59), F.2.4 (p. 426)

[127] R. Barrera, A. Frank, and K. Al-Taha. Temporal relations in geographic information systems: a workshop at the University of Maine. *SIGMOD RECORD*, 20(3):85–91, September 1991. [spatiotemporal database; geographic information systems (GIS)]

[128] R. Barrera and A. Hinojosa. Compression methods for terrain relief. Technical report, Engineering Projects Section, Department of Electrical Engineering, Polytechnic University of Mexico, Mexico City, Mexico, 1987. [surfaces; quaternary hierarchical triangular decomposition] cited in D.5.6, F.2.2.4 (p. 403)

[129] R. Barrera and A. M. Vazquez. A hierarchical method for representing terrain relief. In *Proceedings of the Pecora 9 Symposium: Spatial Information Technologies for Remote Sensing Today and Tomorrow*, pages 87–92, Sioux Falls, SD, October 1984. [surfaces; quaternary hierarchical triangular decomposition] cited in D.5.6, F.2.2.4 (pp. 400, 402)

[130] J. E. Barros, J. French, W. Martin, P. M. Kelly, and T. M. Cannon. Using the triangle inequality to reduce the number of comparisons required for similarity-based retrieval. In *Proceedings of the SPIE, Storage and Retrieval of Still Image and Video Databases IV*, I. K. Sethi and R. Jain, eds., vol. 2670, pages 392–403, San Jose, CA, January 1996. [metric spaces; nearest neighbor; distance matrix] cited in F.4.7.2.1 (p. 691)

[131] R. H. Bartels, J. C. Beatty, and B. A. Barsky. *An Introduction to Splines for use in Computer Graphics & Geometric Modeling*. Morgan-Kaufmann, Los Altos, CA, 1987. [splines; geometric modeling; general] cited in F.P (p. xix)

[132] J. J. Bartholdi III and P. Goldsman. Continuous indexing of hierarchical subdivisions of the globe. *International Journal of*

Geographical Information Science, 15(6):489–522, September 2001. [surfaces; space-filling curve]

[133] J. J. Bartholdi III and L. K. Platzman. A fast heuristic based on space-filling curves for minimum-weight matching in the plane. *Information Processing Letters*, 17(4):177–180, November 1983. [points; minimum-weight matching problem; space-filling curve] cited in D.2.9.s, F.1.9.s (p. 776)

[134] F. Bartling and K. Hinrichs. Probabilistic analysis of an algorithm for solving the k-dimensional all-nearest-neighbors problem by projection. *BIT*, 31(4):558–565, 1991. [points; all nearest neighbors query]

[135] I. Bartolini, P. Ciaccia, and F. Waas. FeedbackBypass: a new approach to interactive similarity query processing. In *Proceedings of the 27th International Conference on Very Large Data Bases (VLDB)*, P. M. G. Apers, P. Atzeni, S. Ceri, S. Paraboschi, K. Ramamohanarao, and R. T. Snodgrass, eds., pages 201–210, Rome, Italy, September 2001. [multimedia database; similarity searching]

[136] M. Batko, C. Gennaro, and P. Zezula. A scalable nearest neighbor search in P2P systems. In *Proceedings of the Second International Workshop on Databases, Information Systems, and Peer-to-Peer Computing*, W. S. Ng, B. C. Ooi, A. M. Ouksel, and C. Sartori, eds., vol. 3367 of Springer-Verlag Lecture Notes in Computer Science, pages 79–92, Toronto, Canada, August 2004. [metric spaces; nearest neighbor; peer-to-peer indexing] cited in F.4.5.3.1 (p. 614)

[137] H. Bauer, S. Becker, S. Graham, and E. Satterthwaite. ALGOL W (revised). Computer Science Technical Report STAN–CS–68–114, Stanford University, Stanford, CA, October 1968. [ALGOL W; programming languages] cited in A.P, A.L, D.P, F.P (p. xx), F.D (p. 743)

[138] M. A. Bauer. Set operations in linear quadtrees. *Computer Vision, Graphics, and Image Processing*, 29(2):248–258, February 1985. [regions; region quadtree]

[139] B. G. Baumgart. Winged–edge polyhedron representation. Computer Science Technical Report STAN–CS–320, Stanford University, Stanford, CA, 1972. [volumes; winged-edge representation; boundary model (BRep)] cited in A.7.1, D.5.4

[140] B. G. Baumgart. Geometric modeling for computer vision. Stanford Artificial Intelligence Laboratory Memo AIM–249 and Computer Science Technical Report STAN–CS–74–463, Stanford University, Stanford, CA, October 1974. [volumes; winged-edge representation; boundary model (BRep)] cited in D.5.4

[141] B. G. Baumgart. A polyhedron representation for computer vision. In *Proceedings of the 1975 National Computer Conference*, vol. 44, pages 589–596, Anaheim, CA, May 1975. [volumes; winged-edge representation; boundary model (BRep)] cited in D.5.4, F.2.2 (p. 313), F.2.2.1.1 (p. 317), F.2.2.1.2 (p. 318)

[142] H. Baumgarten, H. Jung, and K. Mehlhorn. Dynamic point location in general subdivisions. *Journal of Algorithms*, 17(1):342–380, July 1994. Also see *Proceedings of the 3rd Annual ACM-SIAM Symposium on Discrete Algorithms*, pages 250–258, Orlando, FL, January 1992. [regions; dynamic point location] cited in F.2.1.3.3.2 (p. 253)

[143] R. Bayer and E. M. McCreight. Organization and maintenance of large ordered indexes. *Acta Informatica*, 1(3):173–189, 1972. [points; B-tree] cited in F.A (p. 718)

[144] R. Bayer and K. Unternauer. Prefix B-trees. *ACM Transactions on Database Systems*, 2(1):11–26, March 1977. [points; B-tree; prefix B-tree] cited in F.2.3.1 (p. 415), F.A (p. 726)

[145] J. M. Beaulieu and M. Goldberg. Hierarchy in picture segmentation: a stepwise optimization approach. *IEEE Transactions on Pattern Analysis and Machine Intelligence*, 11(2):150–163, February 1989. [regions]

[146] B. Becker, P. G. Franciosa, S. Gschwind, T. Ohler, G. Thiemt, and P. Widmayer. Enclosing many boxes by an optimal pair of boxes. In *Proceedings of the 9th Annual Symposium on Theoretical Aspects of Computer Science (STACS)*, A. Finkel and M. Jantzen, eds., vol. 577 of Springer-Verlag Lecture Notes in Computer Science, pages 475–486, ENS Cachan, France, February 1992. [rectangles; R-tree] cited in F.2.1.5.2.3 (p. 284), F.2.1.5.2.4.s (p. 793)

[147] B. Becker, H.-W. Six, and P. Widmayer. Spatial priority search: an access technique for scaleless maps. In *Proceedings of the ACM SIGMOD Conference*, pages 128–137, Denver, CO, May 1991. [rectangles] cited in F.2.2.3.1 (p. 384)

[148] L. Becker, A. Giesen, K. Hinrichs, and J. Vahrenhold. Algorithms for performing polygonal map overlay and spatial join on massive data set. In *Advances in Spatial Databases—6th International Symposium, SSD'99*, R. H. Güting, D. Papadias, and F. H. Lochovsky, eds., vol. 1651 of Springer-Verlag Lecture Notes in Computer Science, pages 270–285, Hong Kong, China, July 1999. [regions; spatial join]

[149] L. Becker and R. H. Güting. Rule-based optimization and query processing in an extensible geometric database system. *ACM Transactions on Database Systems*, 17(2):247–303, June 1992. [spatial database; query optimization] cited in F.4.1.1 (p. 491)

[150] L. Becker, K. Hinrichs, and U. Finke. A new algorithm for computing joins with grid files. In *Proceedings of the 9th IEEE International Conference on Data Engineering*, pages 190–197, Vienna, Austria, April 1993. [points; spatial join; grid file]

[151] D. A. Beckley, M. W. Evens, and V. K. Raman. Multikey retrieval from K-d trees and quad-trees. In *Proceedings of the ACM SIGMOD Conference*, pages 291–301, Austin, TX, May 1985. [points; k-d tree; point quadtree]

[152] N. Beckmann, H.-P. Kriegel, R. Schneider, and B. Seeger. The R*-tree: an efficient and robust access method for points and rectangles. In *Proceedings of the ACM SIGMOD Conference*, pages 322–331, Atlantic City, NJ, June 1990. [points; rectangles; R-tree; R*-tree] cited in F.2.1.5.2.3 (pp. 283, 288), F.2.1.5.2.4 (pp. 289–292, 294, 296), F.3.3.3 (p. 465), F.4 (p. 488), F.4.2.5 (p. 548), F.4.4.2 (p. 568), F.4.5.4.2 (p. 629), F.4.6.4.1 (p. 674), F.2.1.5.2.3.s (p. 791), F.2.1.5.2.4.s (p. 792)

[153] B. B. Bederson, B. Shneiderman, and M. Wattenberg. Order and quantum treemaps: making effective use of 2d space to display hierarchies. *ACM Transactions on Graphics*, 21(4):833–854, October 2002. [regions; treemap; k-d tree; X-Y tree; puzzletree] cited in F.2.1.2.9 (p. 225)

[154] M. Beer. Interactive editing of cartographic raster images. *Photogrammetria*, 39(4–6):263–275, November 1984. [regions; region quadtree]

[155] C. Beeri, Y. Kanza, E. Safra, and Y. Sagiv. Object fusion in geographic information systems. In *Proceedings of the 30th International Conference on Very Large Data Bases (VLDB)*, M. A. Nascimento, M. T. Özsu, D. Kossmann, R. J. Miller, J. A. Blakely, and K. B. Schiefer, eds., pages 816–827, Toronto, Canada, September 2004. [map conflation] cited in F.4 (p. 486)

[156] S. B. M. Bell, A. Chadwick, A. P. R. Cooper, D. C. Mason, and P. A. V. Young. Handling four dimensional geo-coded data. In *Proceedings of the 4th International Symposium on Spatial Data Handling*, vol. 2, pages 918–927, Zurich, Switzerland, July 1990. [spatiotemporal database]

[157] S. B. M. Bell, B. M. Diaz, F. Holroyd, and M. J. Jackson. Spatially referenced methods of processing raster and vector data. *Image and Vision Computing*, 1(4):211–220, November 1983. [regions; tiling] cited in A.1.2, D.1.4.1, F.2.1.1.1 (pp. 197–198), F.2.1.5.1 (p. 266)

[158] S. B. M. Bell, F. C. Holroyd, and D. C. Mason. A digital geometry for hexagonal pixels. *Image and Vision Computing*, 7(3):194–204, August 1989. [regions; hexagonal tiling] cited in F.2.1.1.1 (p. 198)

[159] R. E. Bellman. *Adaptive Control Processes*. Princeton University Press, Princeton, NJ, 1961. [points; high-dimensional data; curse of dimensionality] cited in F.P (p. xvi), F.4 (p. 486), F.4.6 (p. 663)

[160] A. Belussi, E. Bertino, and A. Nucita. Grid based methods for estimating spatial join selectivity. In *Proceedings of the 12th ACM International Workshop on Advances in Geographic Information Systems*, I. F. Cruz and D. Pfoser, eds., pages 92–100, Washington, DC, November 2004. [spatial join; selectivity estimation]

[161] A. Belussi and C. Faloutsos. Estimating the selectivity of spatial queries using the 'correlation' fractal dimension. In *Proceedings of the 21st International Conference on Very Large Data Bases (VLDB)*, U. Dayal, P. M. D. Gray, and S. Nishio, eds., pages 299–310, Zurich, Switzerland, September 1995. [spatial database; selectivity estimation; fractal dimension]

[162] R. Benetis, C. S. Jensen, G. Karciauskas, and S. Saltenis. Nearest neighbor and reverse nearest neighbor queries for moving objects. In *Proceedings of the International Database Engineering and Applications Symposium*, M. A. Nascimento, M. T. Özsu, and O. R. Zaïane, eds., pages 44–53, Edmonton, Canada, July 2002. [points; moving objects; nearest neighbor; reverse nearest neighbor (RNN)] cited in F.4 (p. 487), F.4.5.8 (p. 658)

[163] S. W. Bent, D. D. Sleator, and R. E. Tarjan. Biased 2-3 trees. In *Proceedings of the 21st IEEE Annual Symposium on Foundations of Computer Science*, pages 248–254, Syracuse, NY, October 1980. [points; biased B-tree] cited in D.2.8.2, D.4.2.3, F.1.1 (p. 8), F.1.7.2.3.1 (p. 143), F.B (p. 731)

[164] J. L. Bentley. Multidimensional binary search trees used for associative searching. *Communications of the ACM*, 18(9):509–517, September 1975. [points; k-d tree] cited in A.1.3, D.1.4.1, D.2.3, D.2.4, D.2.4.1, D.2.4.1.s, D.2.4.2, D.2.4.3, D.2.7, F.1.1 (p. 11), F.1.5 (p. 49), F.1.5.1 (p. 50), F.1.5.1.1 (pp. 51–52), F.1.5.1.2 (p. 53), F.1.5.1.3 (pp. 56–57), F.1.5.1.4 (p. 58), F.1.6 (p. 93), F.2.1.2.8 (p. 223), F.4.1.7 (p. 516), F.4.4.3 (p. 573), F.4.5.3.3 (p. 620), F.1.5.1.1.s (p. 762)

[165] J. L. Bentley. A survey of techniques for fixed radius near neighbor searching. Stanford Linear Accelerator Center Technical Report SLAC–186 and Computer Science Technical Report STAN–CS–75–513, Stanford University, Stanford, CA, August 1975. [points; nearest neighbor; survey] cited in D.2.1

[166] J. L. Bentley. Algorithms for Klee's rectangle problems (unpublished). Computer Science Department, Carnegie-Mellon University, Pittsburgh, PA, 1977. [rectangles; segment tree; rectangle intersection problem] cited in D.3.2.1, D.3.3, D.3.3.s, F.2.1.3.3.2 (p. 253), F.2.1.5.2.4 (p. 296), F.3.1.1 (p. 430), F.3.2 (pp. 447–449), F.3.4.1.3 (p. 473), F.3.2.s (pp. 823–824)

[167] J. L. Bentley. Decomposable searching problems. *Information Processing Letters*, 8(5):244–251, June 1979. [points; range tree] cited in D.2.3, D.2.5, F.1.1 (pp. 5, 9), F.1.2 (p. 14)

[168] J. L. Bentley. Multidimensional binary search trees in database applications. *IEEE Transactions on Software Engineering*, 5(4):333–340, July 1979. [points; k-d tree; survey] cited in F.1.1 (p. 11), F.1.5.1.4 (p. 58)

[169] J. L. Bentley. Multidimensional divide-and-conquer. *Communications of the ACM*, 23(4):214–229, April 1980. [points] cited in F.1.2.s (p. 750)

[170] J. L. Bentley. *Writing Efficient Programs*. Prentice-Hall, Englewood Cliffs, NJ, 1982. [general; programming] cited in A.1.4, D.1.3, F.2.1.1.2 (p. 202)

[171] J. L. Bentley. K-d trees for semidynamic point sets. In *Proceedings of the 6th Annual Symposium on Computational Geometry*, pages 187–197, Berkeley, CA, June 1990. [points; k-d tree]

[172] J. L. Bentley and W. A. Burkhard. Heuristics for partial match retrieval data base design. *Information Processing Letters*, 4(5):132–135, February 1976. [points; partial match query; k-d tree] cited in F.1.5.1 (p. 50)

[173] J. L. Bentley and J. H. Friedman. Data structures for range searching. *ACM Computing Surveys*, 11(4):397–409, December 1979. [points; survey] cited in A.1.3, D.P, D.2.1, D.2.2, F.P (p. xix), F.1.1 (p. 10)

[174] J. L. Bentley, D. Haken, and R. W. Hon. Fast geometric algorithms for VLSI tasks. *Proceedings of the 20th IEEE COMPCON Conference*, pages 88–92, February 1980. Also Carnegie-Mellon University Computer Science Technical Report CMU–CS–80–111, April 1980. [rectangles; rectangle intersection problem] cited in D.3.2.4, F.3.1.4 (p. 443)

[175] J. L. Bentley and H. A. Maurer. A note on Euclidean near neighbor searching in the plane. *Information Processing Letters*, 8(3):133–136, March 1979. [points]

[176] J. L. Bentley and H. A. Maurer. Efficient worst-case data structures for range searching. *Acta Informatica*, 13:155–168, 1980. [rectangles; range tree] cited in D.2.3, D.2.5, F.1.1 (pp. 5, 9), F.1.2 (p. 14)

[177] J. L. Bentley and T. Ottmann. The complexity of manipulating hierarchically defined sets of rectangles. Computer Science Technical Report CMU–CS–81–109, Carnegie-Mellon University, Pittsburgh, PA, April 1981. [rectangles; rectangle intersection problem] cited in D.3.2.4, F.3.1.4 (p. 445)

[178] J. L. Bentley and T. A. Ottmann. Algorithms for reporting and counting geometric intersections. *IEEE Transactions on Computers*, 28(9):643–647, September 1979. [rectangles; rectangle intersection problem] cited in D.3.2, D.3.2.4.s, F.3.1 (p. 430), F.3.1.4.s (p. 822)

[179] J. L. Bentley and J. B. Saxe. Decomposable searching problems I: static-to-dynamic transformation. *Journal of Algorithms*, 1(4):301–358, December 1980. [points; Euclidean matching problem] cited in D.2.9.s, F.1.9.s (p. 776)

[180] J. L. Bentley and M. Shamos. A problem in multivariate statistics: algorithm, data structure, and applications. In *Proceedings of the 15th Allerton Conference on Communication, Control, and Computing*, pages 193–201, Monticello, IL, September 1977. [points; ranking query; quintary tree; ECDF tree] cited in F.1.1 (pp. 7, 13), F.1.5.3 (p. 88)

[181] J. L. Bentley and D. F. Stanat. Analysis of range searches in quad trees. *Information Processing Letters*, 3(6):170–173, July 1975. [points; range query; point quadtree; k-d tree] cited in D.2.3.3, F.1.4.1.3 (p. 37), F.1.5.1.3 (p. 56)

[182] J. L. Bentley, D. F. Stanat, and E. H. Williams Jr. The complexity of finding fixed-radius near neighbors. *Information Processing Letters*, 6(6):209–212, December 1977. [points; nearest neighbor] cited in D.2.2, D.2.2.s, D.2.3.2, D.2.3.3, F.1.1 (p. 10), F.1.4.1.2 (p. 34), F.1.4.1.3 (p. 37)

[183] J. L. Bentley and D. Wood. An optimal worst-case algorithm for reporting intersections of rectangles. *IEEE Transactions on Computers*, 29(7):571–577, July 1980. [rectangles; segment tree; rectangle intersection problem] cited in D.3.2.1, D.3.2.4.s, F.3.1.1 (p. 432), F.3.1.4.s (p. 822)

[184] S. Berchtold, C. Böhm, B. Braunmüller, D. A. Keim, and H.-P. Kriegel. Fast parallel similarity search in multimedia databases. In *Proceedings of the ACM SIGMOD Conference*, J. Peckham, ed., pages 1–12, Tucson, AZ, May 1997. [points; high-dimensional data; nearest neighbor; similarity searching]

[185] S. Berchtold, C. Böhm, H. V. Jagadish, H.-P. Kriegel, and J. Sander. Independent quantization: an index compression technique for high-dimensional data spaces. In *Proceedings of the 16th IEEE International Conference on Data Engineering*, pages 577–588, San Diego, CA, February 2000. [points; high-dimensional data; sequential scan; VA-file; IQ-tree] cited in F.4.4.8 (pp. 592, 595–596)

[186] S. Berchtold, C. Böhm, D. A. Keim, and H.-P. Kriegel. A cost model for nearest neighbor search in high-dimensional data space. In *Proceedings of the 16th ACM SIGACT-SIGMOD-SIGART Symposium on Principles of Database Systems (PODS)*, pages 78–86, Tucson, AZ, May 1997. [points; incremental nearest neighbor algorithm; cost model] cited in F.4.2.8 (p. 556)

[187] S. Berchtold, C. Böhm, and H.-P. Kriegel. Improving the query performance of high-dimensional index structures by bulk-load operations. In *Advances in Database Technology EDBT'98, Proceedings of the 1st International Conference on Extending Database Technology*, H.-J Schek, F. Saltor, I. Ramos, and G. Alonso, eds., vol. 1377 of Springer-Verlag Lecture Notes in Computer Science, pages 216–230, Valencia, Spain, March 1998. [points; high-dimensional data; bulk loading] cited in F.4.1.3 (p. 497), F.4.4.6 (pp. 585–586), F.4.4.8 (p. 595), F.4.6 (p. 663)

[188] S. Berchtold, C. Böhm, and H.-P. Kriegel. The pyramid-technique: towards breaking the curse of dimensionality. In *Proceedings of the ACM SIGMOD Conference*, L. Hass and A. Tiwary, eds., pages 142–153, Seattle, WA, June 1998. [high-dimensional data; pyramid technique; X-tree] cited in F.4.4.7 (pp. 587–590), F.4.4.7.s (p. 854)

[189] S. Berchtold, B. Ertl, D. A. Keim, H.-P. Kriegel, and T. Seidl. Fast nearest neighbor search in high-dimensional spaces. In *Proceedings of the 14th IEEE International Conference on Data Engineering*, pages 209–218, Orlando, FL, February 1998. [points; high-dimensional data; nearest neighbor; Voronoi diagram; minimum bounding box] cited in F.4.4.4 (p. 573)

[190] S. Berchtold, D. A. Keim, and H.-P. Kriegel. The X-tree: an index structure for high-dimensional data. In *Proceedings of the 22nd International Conference on Very Large Data Bases (VLDB)*, T. M.

Vijayaraman, A. P. Buchmann, C. Mohan, and N. L. Sarda, eds., pages 28–39, Mumbai (Bombay), India, September 1996. [points; high-dimensional data; X-tree; R-tree] cited in F.1.8 (p. 164), F.2.1.5.2.7 (p. 301), F.4.4.1 (pp. 566–567), F.4.4.6 (p. 587), F.4.4.8 (p. 595), F.4.6 (p. 663)

[191] S. Berchtold, D. A. Keim, and H.-P. Kriegel. Using extended feature objects for partial similarity retrieval. *VLDB Journal*, 6(4):333–348, November 1997. [regions; similarity searching]

[192] S. Berchtold, D. A. Keim, H.-P. Kriegel, and T. Seidl. Indexing the solution space: a new technique for nearest neighbor search in high-dimensional space. *IEEE Transactions on Knowledge and Data Engineering*, 12(1):45–57, January/February 2000. [points; high-dimensional data; nearest neighbor; Voronoi diagram]

[193] J. van den Bercken, B. Blohsfeld, J.-P. Dittrich, J. Krämer, T. Schäfer, M. Schneider, and B. Seeger. XXL—a library approach to supporting efficient implementations of advanced database queries. In *Proceedings of the 27th International Conference on Very Large Data Bases (VLDB)*, P. M. G. Apers, P. Atzeni, S. Ceri, S. Paraboschi, K. Ramamohanarao, and R. T. Snodgrass, eds., pages 39–48, Rome, Italy, September 2001. [R-tree; XXL] cited in F.2.1.5.2 (p. 271)

[194] J. van den Bercken, B. Seeger, and P. Widmayer. A generic approach to bulk loading multidimensional index structures. In *Proceedings of the 23rd International Conference on Very Large Data Bases (VLDB)*, M. Jarke, M. J. Carey, K. R. Dittrich, F. H. Lochovsky, P. Loucopoulos, and M. A. Jeusfeld, eds., pages 406–415, Athens, Greece, August 1997. [R-tree; bulk loading] cited in F.1.8.1 (p. 165), F.2.1.5.2.6 (pp. 299–300)

[195] J. van den Bercken, B. Seeger, and P. Widmayer. An evaluation of generic bulk loading techniques. In *Proceedings of the 27th International Conference on Very Large Data Bases (VLDB)*, P. M. G. Apers, P. Atzeni, S. Ceri, S. Paraboschi, K. Ramamohanarao, and R. T. Snodgrass, eds., pages 461–470, Rome, Italy, September 2001. [R-tree; bulk loading]

[196] M. de Berg, M. van Kreveld, M. Overmars, and O. Schwarzkopf. *Computational Geometry: Algorithms and Applications*. Springer-Verlag, Berlin, Germany, second revised edition, 2000. [computational geometry; general] cited in F.P (p. xix), F.2 (p. 192), F.2.1.3.1 (p. 234), F.2.2.1.2 (p. 328), F.2.2.1.3.1 (p. 333), F.2.2.1.3.3 (p. 343), F.2.2.1.4 (p. 347), F.4.5.5.1 (p. 631)

[197] M. de Berg, M. van Kreveld, and J. Snoeyink. Two- and three-dimensional point location in rectangular subdivisions. *Journal of Algorithms*, 18(2):256–277, March 1995. [rectangles; point location]

[198] G. van den Bergen. *Collision Detection in Interactive 3D Environments*. Morgan-Kaufmann, San Francisco, 2004. [game programming; collision detection; general] cited in F.P (p. xix), F.2.1.1 (p. 195)

[199] L. Berger, J.-P. Mariot, and C. Launay. A new formulation for fast image coding using quadtree representation. *Pattern Recognition Letters*, 13:425–432, June 1992. [regions; compression]

[200] P. Berkhin. Survey of clustering data mining techniques. Technical report, Accrue Software, San Jose, CA, 2002. [data mining; clustering; survey]

[201] M. Bern. Hidden surface removal for rectangles. In *Proceedings of the 4th Annual Symposium on Computational Geometry*, pages 183–192, Urbana-Champaign, IL, June 1988. [rectangles; hidden-surface removal]

[202] M. Bern. Approximate closest-point queries in high dimensions. *Information Processing Letters*, 45(2):95–99, February 1993. [points; approximate nearest neighbor] cited in F.4.1.7 (p. 516), F.4.2 (p. 517)

[203] M. Bern and D. Eppstein. Approximation algorithms for geometric problems. In *Approximation Algorithms for NP-hard Problems*, D. S. Hochbaum, ed., chapter 8, pages 296–345. PWS Publishing, Boston, 1997. [points; k-center problem] cited in F.4.5.3.4 (p. 623)

[204] M. Bern, D. Eppstein, and J. Gilbert. Provably good mesh generation. In *Proceedings of the 31st IEEE Annual Symposium on Foundations of Computer Science*, pages 231–241, St. Louis, MO, October 1990. [regions; finite element analysis; Delaunay triangulation (DT); mesh generation] cited in F.2.2.4 (p. 405)

[205] M. Bern, D. Eppstein, and S.-H. Teng. Parallel construction of quadtrees and quality triangulations. In *Algorithms and Data Structures—3rd Workshop, WADS'93*, F. K. H. A. Dehne, J. R. Sack, N. Santoro, and S. Whitesides, eds., vol. 709 of Springer-Verlag Lecture Notes in Computer Science, pages 188–199, Montréal, Canada, August 1993. [regions; triangulations; finite element analysis; mesh generation; restricted quadtree]

[206] S. N. Bespamyatnikh. An optimal algorithm for closest pair maintenance. In *Proceedings of the 11th Annual Symposium on Computational Geometry*, pages 152–161, Vancouver, Canada, June 1995. [points; closest pair problem]

[207] S. N. Bespamyatnikh. Dynamic algorithms for approximate neighbor searching. In *Proceedings of the 8th Canadian Conference on Computational Geometry*, pages 252–257, Ottawa, Canada, August 1996. [points; approximate nearest neighbor; BBD-tree] cited in F.1.5.2.7 (p. 87)

[208] P. W. Besslich. Quadtree construction of binary images by dyadic array transformations. In *Proceedings of the IEEE Conference on Pattern Recognition and Image Processing'82*, pages 550–554, Las Vegas, NV, June 1982. [regions; region quadtree]

[209] T. Bestul. A general technique for creating SIMD algorithms on parallel pointer-based quadtrees. In *Proceedings of the 10th International Symposium on Automated Cartography (AUTO-CARTO 10)*, pages 428–444, Baltimore, MD, March 1991. Also University of Maryland Computer Science Technical Report TR–2181, January 1989. [regions; points; lines; parallel processing]

[210] T. Bestul. *Parallel paradigms and practices for spatial data*. PhD thesis, Computer Science Department, University of Maryland, College Park, MD, April 1992. Also Computer Science Technical Report TR–2897. [regions; points; lines; data-parallel algorithms] cited in F.P (p. xviii), F.1.5 (p. 49)

[211] J. Bey. Tetrahedral grid refinement. *Computing*, 55:355–378, 1995. [surfaces; triangulations] cited in F.2.2.4 (p. 407)

[212] K. S. Beyer, J. Goldstein, R. Ramakrishnan, and U. Shaft. When is "nearest neighbor" meaningful? In *Proceedings of the 7th International Conference on Database Theory (ICDT'99)*, C. Beeri and P. Buneman, eds., vol. 1540 of Springer-Verlag Lecture Notes in Computer Science, pages 217–235, Berlin, Germany, January 1999. [points; high-dimensional data; nearest neighbor; curse of dimensionality] cited in F.1.8 (p. 164), F.4 (pp. 486–488), F.4.4 (p. 566), F.4.4.2 (p. 571), F.4.6 (p. 663)

[213] S. K. Bhaskar, A. Rosenfeld, and A. Y. Wu. Parallel processing of regions represented by linear quadtrees. *Computer Vision, Graphics and Image Processing*, 42(3):371–380, June 1988. [regions; parallel processing] cited in F.P (p. xviii), F.1.5 (p. 49)

[214] H. Bieri. Computing the Euler characteristic and related additive functionals of digital objects from their bintree representation. *Computer Vision, Graphics, and Image Processing*, 40(1):115–126, October 1987. [regions] cited in A.5.3

[215] H. Blanken, A. Ijbema, P. Meek, and B. van den Akker. The generalized grid file: description and performance aspects. In *Proceedings of the 6th IEEE International Conference on Data Engineering*, pages 380–388, Los Angeles, February 1990. [points; grid file]

[216] G. Blankenagel and R. H. Güting. External segment trees. *Algorithmica*, 12(6):498–532, December 1994. [rectangles; intervals; segment tree]

[217] G. E. Blelloch. Scan primitives and parallel vector models. Technical Report MIT/LCS/TR–463, Massachusetts Institute of Technology, Cambridge, MA, October 1989. [data-parallel algorithms] cited in F.1.5 (p. 49)

[218] R. Bliujute, C. S. Jensen, S. Saltenis, and G. Slivinskas. R-tree based indexing of now-relative bitemporal data. In *Proceedings of the 24th International Conference on Very Large Data Bases (VLDB)*, A. Gupta, O. Shmueli, and J. Widom, eds., pages 345–356, New York, August 1998. [bitemporal data; R-tree]

[219] B. Blohsfeld, D. Korus, and B. Seeger. A comparison of selectivity estimators for range queries on metric attributes. In *Proceedings of the ACM SIGMOD Conference*, pages 239–250, Philadelphia, PA, June 1999. [selectivity estimation]

[220] J. Bloomenthal. Polygonalization of implicit surfaces. Technical Report CSL–87–2, Xerox Palo Alto Research Center, Palo Alto, CA, May 1987. [surfaces]

[221] H. Blum. A transformation for extracting new descriptors of shape. In *Models for the Perception of Speech and Visual Form*, W. Wathen-Dunn, ed., pages 362–380. MIT Press, Cambridge, MA, 1967. [regions; medial axis transformation (MAT)] cited in A.1.3, A.9, D.1.2, F.2.1.2.2 (p. 208)

[222] P. Bogdanovich and H. Samet. The ATree: a data structure to support very large scientific databases. In *Integrated Spatial Databases: Digital Images and GIS*, P. Agouris and A. Stefanidis, eds., vol. 1737 of Springer-Verlag Lecture Notes in Computer Science, pages 235–248, Portland, ME, June 1999. Also University of Maryland Computer Science Technical Report TR–3435, March 1995. [volumes; ATree] cited in F.2.1.2.4 (p. 215), F.2.1.2.5 (p. 220)

[223] C. Böhm. A cost model for query processing in high dimensional spaces. *ACM Transactions on Database Systems*, 25(2):129–178, June 2000. [high-dimensional data; cost model; selectivity estimation]

[224] C. Böhm, S. Berchtold, and D. A. Keim. Searching in high-dimensional spaces: index structures for improving the performance of multimedia databases. *ACM Computing Surveys*, 33(3):322–373, September 2001. [points; high-dimensional data; nearest neighbor; survey] cited in F.P (p. xx), F.4.1.5 (p. 502), F.4.2.3.s (pp. 840–841), F.4.4.6.s (p. 853)

[225] C. Böhm, B. Braunmüller, F. Krebs, and H.-P. Kriegel. Epsilon grid order: an algorithm for the similarity join on massive high-dimensional data. In *Proceedings of the ACM SIGMOD Conference*, pages 379–390, Santa Barbara, CA, May 2001. [high-dimensional data; similarity join]

[226] C. Böhm and F. Krebs. Supporting KDD applications by the k-nearest neighbor join. In *Proceedings of 14th International Workshop on Database and Expert Systems Applications (DEXA'99)*, V. Marík, W. Retschitzegger, and O. Stepánková, eds., vol. 2352 of Springer-Verlag Lecture Notes in Computer Science, pages 504–516, Prague, Czech Republic, September 2003. [points; all nearest neighbors query] cited in F.4 (pp. 485–486)

[227] C. Böhm and H.-P. Kriegel. A cost model and index architecture for the similarity join. In *Proceedings of the 17th IEEE International Conference on Data Engineering*, pages 411–420, Heidelberg, Germany, April 2001. [similarity join; cost model]

[228] K. Böhm, M. Mlivoncic, H.-J. Schek, and R. Weber. Fast evaluation techniques for complex similarity queries. In *Proceedings of the 27th International Conference on Very Large Data Bases (VLDB)*, P. M. G. Apers, P. Atzeni, S. Ceri, S. Paraboschi, K. Ramamohanarao, and R. T. Snodgrass, eds., pages 211–220, Rome, Italy, September 2001. [similarity searching; VA-file]

[229] J.-D. Boissonnat and M. Teillaud. An hierarchical representation of objects: the Delaunay tree. In *Proceedings of the 2nd Annual Symposium on Computational Geometry*, pages 260–265, Yorktown Heights, NY, June 1986. [points; Delaunay triangulation (DT); Delaunay tree]

[230] J.-D. Boissonnat and M. Yvinec. *Algorithmic Geometry*. Cambridge University Press, Cambridge, United Kingdom, 1998. [computational geometry; general] cited in F.P (p. xix)

[231] A. Bolour. Optimality properties of multiple-key hashing functions. *Journal of the ACM*, 26(2):196–210, April 1979. [partial match query]

[232] F. Bonfatti and L. Cavazza. SECT: an effective coding technique for polygonal geographic data. *Computers & Graphics*, 12(3/4):503–513, 1988. [regions]

[233] G. Borgefors. Distance transformations in arbitrary dimensions. *Computer Vision, Graphics, and Image Processing*, 27(3):321–345, September 1984. [regions] cited in A.9.1, A.9.2, F.2.1.2.2 (p. 210)

[234] G. Borgefors. Distance transformations on hexagonal grids. *Pattern Recognition Letters*, 9(2):97–105, February 1989. [regions; hexagonal tiling; pseudo-Euclidean distance transformations] cited in F.2.1.1.1 (p. 198)

[235] K. Borsuk. Drei sätze über die *n*-dimensionale Euklidische sphäre. *Fundamenta Mathematicae*, 20:177–190, 1933. [points; lines] cited in F.1.5.3 (p. 88)

[236] S. Börzsönyi, D. Kossmann, and K. Stocker. The skyline operator. In *Proceedings of the 17th IEEE International Conference on Data Engineering*, pages 421–430, Heidelberg, Germany, April 2001. [points; skyline query; point dominance query; nearest neighbor] cited in F.4.1.5 (pp. 502–504)

[237] J. Bourgain. On Lipschitz embedding of finite metric spaces in Hilbert space. *Israel Journal of Mathematics*, 52(1–2):46–52, 1985. [metric space embedding; Lipschitz embedding] cited in F.4.7.2 (p. 691), F.4.7.2.2 (p. 692)

[238] A. Bowyer, P. J. Willis, and J. R. Woodwark. A multiprocessor architecture for solving spatial problems. *Computer Journal*, 24(4):353–357, November 1981. [hardware]

[239] A. Bowyer and J. Woodwark. *A Programmer's Geometry*. Butterworth's, Guilford, United Kingdom, 1983. Also second edition, 1988. [computer graphics; geometry; general]

[240] A. Bowyer and J. Woodwark. *Introduction to Computing with Geometry*. Information Geometers, Winchester, United Kingdom, 1993. [computer graphics; geometry; general]

[241] T. Bozkaya and M. Özsoyoglu. Indexing large metric spaces for similarity search queries. *ACM Transactions on Database Systems*, 24(3):361–404, September 1999. Also see *Proceedings of the ACM SIGMOD Conference*, J. Peckham, ed., pages 357–368, Tucson, AZ, May 1997. [metric spaces; mvp-tree] cited in F.4.1.7 (p. 517), F.4.2 (p. 517), F.4.5.2.3 (pp. 608–609), F.4.5.2.4 (pp. 611, 613), F.4.5.3.1 (p. 613), F.4.5.3.2 (p. 616)

[242] F. Brabec, G. R. Hjaltason, and H. Samet. Indexing spatial objects with the PK-tree (unpublished). Computer Science Department, University of Maryland, College Park, MD, 2001. [points; PK-tree] cited in F.2.1.4 (p. 255), F.2.1.4.1 (p. 257)

[243] F. Brabec and H. Samet. The VASCO R-tree JAVA™ applet. In *Visual Database Systems (VDB4). Proceedings of the IFIP TC2//WG2.6 Fourth Working Conference on Visual Database Systems*, Y. Ioannidis and W. Klas, eds., pages 147–153, L'Aquila, Italy, May 1998. Chapman and Hall. [VASCO; data structure visualization; R-tree; JAVA] cited in F.P (pp. xviii, xxiii), F.2.1.5.2 (p. 271)

[244] F. Brabec and H. Samet. Visualizing and animating R-trees and spatial operations in spatial databases on the worldwide web. In *Visual Database Systems (VDB4). Proceedings of the IFIP TC2//WG2.6 Fourth Working Conference on Visual Database Systems*, Y. Ioannidis and W. Klas, eds., pages 123–140, L'Aquila, Italy, May 1998. Chapman and Hall. [VASCO; data structure visualization; R-tree; PR quadtree; PM quadtree; JAVA] cited in F.P (pp. xviii, xxiii), F.2.1.5.2 (p. 271), F.3.3.3 (p. 465)

[245] F. Brabec and H. Samet. Visualizing and animating search operations on quadtrees on the worldwide web. In *Proceedings of the 16th European Workshop on Computational Geometry*, K. Kedem and M. Katz, eds., pages 70–76, Eilat, Israel, March 2000. [VASCO; data structure visualization; R-tree; PR quadtree; PM quadtree; JAVA] cited in F.P (pp. xviii, xxiii), F.2.1.5.2 (p. 271)

[246] F. Brabec, H. Samet, and C. Yilmaz. VASCO: visualizing and animating spatial constructs and operations. In *Proceedings of the 19th Annual Symposium on Computational Geometry*, pages 374–375, San Diego, CA, June 2003. [VASCO; data structure visualization; R-tree; PR quadtree; PM quadtree; JAVA] cited in F.P (pp. xviii, xxiii), F.2.1.5.2 (p. 271)

[247] I. C. Braid, R. C. Hillyard, and I. A. Stroud. Stepwise construction of polyhedra in geometrical modeling. In *Mathematical Models in Computer Graphics and Design*, K. W. Brodlie, ed., pages 123–141. Academic Press, New York, 1980. [volumes] cited in D.5.4

[248] S. Brakatsoulas, D. Pfoser, R. Salas, and C. Wenk. On map-matching vehicle tracking data. In *Proceedings of the 31st International Conference on Very Large Data Bases (VLDB)*, K. Böhm, C. S. Jensen, L. M. Haas, M. L. Kersten, P.-Å. Larson, and B. C. Ooi, eds., pages 853–864, Trondheim, Norway, September 2005. [map conflation] cited in F.4 (p. 486)

[249] B. Braunmüller, M. Ester, H.-P. Kriegel, and J. Sander. Efficiently supporting multiple similarity queries for mining in metric databases. In *Proceedings of the 16th IEEE International Conference on Data Engineering*, pages 256–267, San Diego, CA, February 2000. [metric spaces; similarity searching]

[250] J. E. Bresenham. Algorithm for computer control of a digital plotter. *IBM Systems Journal*, 4(1):25–30, 1965. [lines; cited in A.7.2.3.s, A.7.2.4

[251] R. de la Briandais. File searching using variable-length keys. In *Proceedings of the Western Joint Computer Conference*, pages 295–298, San Francisco, March 1959. [points; trie; digital searching] cited in F.1 (p. 2)

[252] E. Bribiesca. A new chain code. *Pattern Recognition*, 32(2):235–251, February 1999. [regions; chain code]

[253] E. Bribiesca. A chain code for representing 3D curves. *Pattern Recognition*, 33:755–765, 2000. [regions; chain code]

[254] S. Bright and S. Laflin. Shading of solid voxel models. *Computer Graphics Forum*, 5(2):131–137, June 1986. [volumes] cited in A.7.1.4

[255] S. Brin. Near neighbor search in large metric spaces. In *Proceedings of the 21st International Conference on Very Large Data Bases (VLDB)*, U. Dayal, P. M. D. Gray, and S. Nishio, eds., pages 574–584, Zurich, Switzerland, September 1995. [metric spaces; Voronoi diagram; GNAT] cited in F.4.1.7 (p. 517), F.4.2 (p. 517), F.4.2.3 (p. 529), F.4.4.7 (pp. 591–592), F.4.5 (p. 598), F.4.5.3.1 (p. 613), F.4.5.3.2 (pp. 616–617), F.4.5.3.4 (p. 622), F.4.5.5.1 (p. 630), F.4.5.7.2 (p. 646)

[256] T. Brinkhoff. *Der spatial join in gedatenbankensystemen*. PhD thesis, Ludwig-Maximilians Universität München, Munich, Germany, 1994. [regions; spatial join]

[257] T. Brinkhoff, H. Horn, H.-P. Kriegel, and R. Schneider. A storage and access architecture for efficient query processing in spatial database systems. In *Advances in Spatial Databases—3rd International Symposium, SSD'93*, D. Abel and B. C. Ooi, eds., vol. 692 of Springer-Verlag Lecture Notes in Computer Science, pages 357–376, Singapore, June 1993. [regions]

[258] T. Brinkhoff and H.-P. Kriegel. The impact of global clustering on spatial database systems. In *Proceedings of the 20th International Conference on Very Large Data Bases (VLDB)*, J. Bocca, M. Jarke, and C. Zaniolo, eds., pages 168–179, Santiago, Chile, September 1994. [spatial database]

[259] T. Brinkhoff, H.-P. Kriegel, and R. Schneider. Comparison of approximations of complex objects used for approximation-based query processing in spatial database systems. In *Proceedings of the 9th IEEE International Conference on Data Engineering*, pages 40–49, Vienna, Austria, April 1993. [regions; spatial join; query optimization]

[260] T. Brinkhoff, H.-P. Kriegel, R. Schneider, and B. Seeger. GENESYS: a system for efficient spatial query processing. In *Proceedings of the ACM SIGMOD Conference*, page 519, Minneapolis, MN, June 1994. [spatial database; R-tree]

[261] T. Brinkhoff, H.-P. Kriegel, R. Schneider, and B. Seeger. Multi-step processing of spatial joins. In *Proceedings of the ACM SIGMOD Conference*, pages 197–208, Minneapolis, MN, June 1994. [regions; R-tree; spatial join] cited in F.P (p. xx), F.2.1.1 (p. 195), F.2.1.3 (p. 233), F.2.1.5.2.7 (p. 303)

[262] T. Brinkhoff, H.-P. Kriegel, and B. Seeger. Efficient processing of spatial joins using R-trees. In *Proceedings of the ACM SIGMOD Conference*, pages 237–246, Washington, DC, May 1993. [lines; R-tree; spatial join] cited in F.P (p. xx)

[263] P. Brodatz. *Textures*. Dover, New York, 1966. [textures; general] cited in A.3.2.1

[264] A. J. Broder. Strategies for efficient incremental nearest neighbor search. *Pattern Recognition*, 23(1–2):171–178, January 1990. [points; incremental nearest neighbor algorithm; k-d tree] cited in F.4.1.7 (p. 516)

[265] A. Z. Broder, S. C. Glassman, M. S. Manasse, and G. Zweig. Syntactic clustering of the web. *Computer Networks*, 29(8–13):1157–1166, September 1997. Also see *Proceedings of the Sixth International World Wide Web Conference*, pages 391–404, Santa Clara, CA, April 1997. [points; high-dimensional data; approximate nearest neighbor] cited in F.4.7.4 (p. 713)

[266] A. Brodsky, C. Lassez, J. Lassez, and M. J. Maher. Separability of polyhedra for optimal filtering of spatial and constraint data. In *Proceedings of the 14th ACM SIGACT-SIGMOD-SIGART Symposium on Principles of Database Systems (PODS)*, pages 54–65, San Jose, CA, May 1995. [regions; minimum bounding box; constraint database] cited in F.2.1.1 (p. 195)

[267] J. Brooks, R. Muraka, D. Onuoha, F. Rahn, and H. A. Steinberg. An extension of the combinatorial geometry technique for modeling vegetation and terrain features. Technical Report NTIS AD–782–883, Mathematical Applications Group Inc., June 1974. [volumes] cited in A.7.2.2

[268] R. A. Brooks and T. Lozano-Perez. A subdivision algorithm in configuration space for findpath with rotation. In *Proceedings of the 8th International Joint Conference on Artificial Intelligence*, pages 799–806, Karlsruhe, West Germany, August 1983. [regions; configuration space; motion planning] cited in A.1.4, D.1.3, F.2.4 (p. 425)

[269] R. L. Brown. Multiple storage quad trees: a simpler faster alternative to bisector list quad trees. *IEEE Transactions on Computer-Aided Design*, 5(3):413–419, July 1986. [rectangles; PM quadtree; multiple storage quadtree] cited in F.3.4.3 (p. 481)

[270] P. Brunet. Face octrees: involved algorithms and applications. Department de Llenguatges i Sistemes Informatics Technical Report LSI–90–14, Universitat Politecnica de Catalunya, Barcelona, Spain, 1990. [volumes; face octree] cited in F.2.2.2.4 (pp. 361–362), F.2.2.2.7 (p. 371)

[271] P. Brunet and D. Ayala. Extended octtree representation of free form surfaces. *Computer-Aided Geometric Design*, 4(1–2):141–154, July 1987. [surfaces; PM octree; extended octree]

[272] P. Brunet and I. Navazo. Solid representation and operation using extended octrees. *ACM Transactions on Graphics*, 9(2):170–197, April 1990. [volumes; PM octree; extended octree] cited in F.2.2.2.4 (p. 362), F.2.2.2.7 (pp. 370, 372)

[273] P. Brunet, I. Navazo, and A. Vinacua. Octree detection of closed compartments. In *Proceedings of the 1st ACM Symposium on Solid Modeling Foundations and CAD/CAM Applications*, J. Rossignac and J. Turner, eds., pages 87–96, Austin, TX, June 1991. [volumes]

[274] P. Brunet, I. Navazo, and A. Vinacua. A modelling scheme for the approximate representation of closed surfaces. In *Geometric Modelling, Computing/Supplement 8*, G. E. Farin, H. Hagen, H. Noltemeier, and W. Knödel, eds., pages 75–90. Springer-Verlag, Vienna, Austria, 1993. [surfaces; face octree] cited in F.2.2.2.4 (p. 362)

[275] E. Bruzzone and L. De Floriani. Two data structures for building tetrahedralizations. *Visual Computer*, 6(5):266–283, November 1990. [volumes; tetrahedralizations]

[276] E. Bruzzone, L. De Floriani, and M. Pellegrinelli. A hierarchical spatial index for cell complexes. In *Advances in Spatial Databases—3rd International Symposium, SSD'93*, D. Abel and B. C. Ooi, eds., vol. 692 of Springer-Verlag Lecture Notes in Computer Science, pages 105–122, Singapore, June 1993. [volumes]

[277] W. Bucher and H. Edelsbrunner. On expected and worst-case segment trees. In *Advances in Computing Research: Computational Geometry*, F. P. Preparata, ed., vol. 1, pages 109–125. JAI Press, Greenwich, CT, 1983. [rectangles; segment tree] cited in D.3.2.1, F.3.1.1 (p. 432)

[278] E. Bugnion, S. Fei, T. Roos, P. Widmayer, and F. Widmer. A spatial index for approximate multiple string matching. In *Proceedings of the 1st South American Workshop on String Processing (WSP'93)*, R. Baeza-Yates and N. Ziviani, eds., pages 43–53, Belo Horizonte, Brazil, September 1993. [metric spaces; nearest neighbor; mb-tree] cited in F.4.5.3.3 (p. 618)

[279] Bureau of the Census. Technical description of the DIME system. In *Introductory Readings in Geographic Information Systems*, D. J. Peuquet and D. F. Marble, eds., chapter 7, pages 100–111. Taylor & Francis, London, United Kingdom, 1990. Originally published as The DIME Geocoding System, Report 4, Census Use Study, US Department of Commerce, Bureau of the Census, 1970. [lines] cited in D.4.4

[280] Bureau of the Census. *1990 Technical Documentation: Tiger/Line Census Files*. Washington, DC, 1991. [lines] cited in F.2.2.1.2 (p. 323)

[281] C. J. C. Burges. A tutorial on support vector machines for pattern recognition. *Data Mining and Knowledge Discovery*, 2(2):121–

167, June 1998. [support vector machines (SVM)] cited in F.4.4.4 (p. 576)

[282] W. A. Burkhard. Interpolation-based index maintenance. *BIT*, 23(3):274–294, 1983. [points; linear hashing] cited in D.2.7, D.2.8.2, F.1.7.2.3.1 (p. 143)

[283] W. A. Burkhard and R. Keller. Some approaches to best-match file searching. *Communications of the ACM*, 16(4):230–236, April 1973. [metric spaces; nearest neighbor; bk-tree] cited in F.4.1.7 (p. 517), F.4.2 (p. 517), F.4.5 (p. 598), F.4.5.2.1.1 (p. 605), F.4.5.2.4 (p. 610), F.4.5.3.4 (p. 622)

[284] P. A. Burrough. *Principles of Geographical Information Systems for Land Resources Assessment*. Clarendon Press, Oxford, United Kingdom, 1986. [geographic information systems (GIS); general] cited in A.P, D.P

[285] P. J. Burt. Tree and pyramid structures for coding hexagonally sampled binary images. *Computer Graphics and Image Processing*, 14(3):271–280, November 1980. [regions; pyramid; hexagonal tiling] cited in D.1.4.1, F.2.1.1.1 (p. 198), F.2.1.2.10 (p. 231)

[286] P. J. Burt, T. Hong, and A. Rosenfeld. Segmentation and estimation of image region properties through cooperative hierarchical computation. *IEEE Transactions on Systems, Man, and Cybernetics*, 11(12):802–809, December 1981. [regions; pyramid] cited in D.1.3, F.2.1.4.1 (p. 257), F.2.4 (p. 424)

[287] F. W. Burton and M. M. Huntbach. Lazy evaluation of geometric objects. *IEEE Computer Graphics and Applications*, 4(1):28–32, January 1984. [regions; lazy evaluation; region quadtree]

[288] F. W. Burton and J. G. Kollias. Comment on "the explicit quadtree as a structure for computer graphics". *The Computer Journal*, 26(2):188, May 1983. [regions; region quadtree] cited in A.2.1.1

[289] F. W. Burton, V. J. Kollias, and J. G. Kollias. Expected and worst-case requirements for quadtrees. *Pattern Recognition Letters*, 3(2):131–135, March 1985. [regions; lines; MX quadtree]

[290] F. W. Burton, V. J. Kollias, and J. G. Kollias. Real-time raster to quadtree and quadtree to raster conversion algorithms with modest storage requirements. *Angewandte Informatik*, 28(4):169–174, April 1986. [regions; region quadtree]

[291] F. W. Burton, V. J. Kollias, and J. G. Kollias. A general PASCAL program for map overlay of quadtrees and related problems. *Computer Journal*, 30(4):355–361, August 1987. [regions; map overlay; region quadtree]

[292] F. W. Burton, V. J. Kollias, and J. G. Kollias. Functional programming with quadtrees. *IEEE Software*, 6(1):90–97, January 1989. [regions; region quadtree; lazy evaluation]

[293] W. Burton. Representation of many-sided polygons and polygonal lines for rapid processing. *Communications of the ACM*, 20(3):166–171, March 1977. [lines; Binary Searchable Polygonal Representation (BSPR)] cited in D.4.1, D.4.1.s, F.2.2.3.1 (p. 384)

[294] A. R. Butz. Alternative algorithm for Hilbert's space-filling curve. *IEEE Transactions on Computers*, 20(4):424–426, April 1971. [regions; space-filling curve] cited in A.1.4, D.1.3

[295] M. Cai, D. Keshwani, and P. Z. Revesz. Parametric rectangles: a model for querying and animating spatiotemporal databases. In *Proceedings of the 7th International Conference on Extending Database Technology—EDBT 2000*, C. Zaniolo, P. C. Lockemann, M. H. Scholl, and T. Grust, eds., vol. 1777 of Springer-Verlag Lecture Notes in Computer Science, pages 430–444, Konstanz, Germany, March 2000. [rectangles; moving objects; time-parametric R-tree] cited in F.2.1.5.2.3 (p. 286)

[296] M. Cai and P. Revesz. Parametric R-tree: an index structure for moving objects. In *Proceedings of the 10th COMAD International Conference on Management of Data (COMAD)*, K. Ramamritham and T. M. Vijayaraman, eds., pages 57–64, Pune, India, December 2000. Tata McGraw-Hill. [rectangles; moving objects; time-parametric R-tree] cited in F.2.1.5.2.3 (p. 286), F.3.1.4 (p. 445), F.4 (p. 487)

[297] P. B. Callahan and S. R. Kosaraju. A decomposition of multidimensional point sets with applications to k-nearest-neighbors and n-body potential fields. *Journal of the ACM*, 42(1):67–90, January 1995. [points; k-d tree; *N*-body problem; well-separated pair decomposition; all nearest neighbors query; fair-split tree] cited

in F.1.5.1.4 (p. 58), F.2.4 (p. 426), F.4 (p. 485), F.4.4.5 (p. 582), F.1.5.2.2.s (p. 764)

[298] S. Cameron. Efficient intersection tests for objects defined constructively. *The International Journal of Robotics Research*, 8(1):3–25, February 1989. [volumes; collision detection; constructive solid geometry (CSG); interference detection]

[299] S. Cameron. Collision detection by four-dimensional intersection testing. *IEEE Transactions on Robotics and Automation*, 6(3):291–302, June 1990. [volumes; collision detection; constructive solid geometry (CSG); interference detection]

[300] S. A. Cameron. *Modelling solids in motion*. PhD thesis, University of Edinburgh, Edinburgh, Scotland, 1984. [volumes; moving objects] cited in D.5.5.1

[301] S. Campagna, L. Kobbelt, and H.-P. Seidel. Directed edges—a scalable representation for triangle meshes. *Journal of Graphics Tools*, 3(4):1–12, 1998. [surfaces; half-edge representation; triangle meshes; nonmanifold objects] cited in F.2.2.1.1 (p. 316)

[302] A. T. Campbell III. *Modeling global diffuse illumination for image synthesis*. PhD thesis, Department of Computer Sciences, University of Texas Austin, Austin, TX, December 1991. [volumes; BSP tree; radiosity] cited in F.2.1.3.1 (p. 236)

[303] A. T. Campbell III and D. S. Fussell. Adaptive mesh generation for global diffuse illumination. *Computer Graphics*, 24(4):155–164, August 1990. Also in *Proceedings of the SIGGRAPH'90 Conference*, Atlanta, GA, August 1990. [volumes; BSP tree; radiosity] cited in F.2.1.3.1 (p. 236)

[304] D. Cantone, A. Ferro, A. Pulvirenti, D. R. Recupero, and D. Shasha. Antipole tree indexing to support range search and k-nearest neighbor search in metric spaces. *IEEE Transactions on Knowledge and Data Engineering*, 17(4):535–550, April 2005. [metric spaces; nearest neighbor; vp-tree]

[305] A. F. Cardenas and J. P. Sagamang. Doubly-chained tree data base organization—analysis and design strategies. *The Computer Journal*, 20(1):15–26, February 1977. [points; doubly chained tree (DCT); multiattribute tree (MAT)] cited in F.1.1 (p. 7)

[306] M. J. Carey and D. Kossmann. On saying "enough already!" in SQL. In *Proceedings of the ACM SIGMOD Conference*, J. Peckham, ed., pages 219–230, Tucson, AZ, May 1997. [top-*k* query] cited in F.4.1.5 (p. 504)

[307] I. Carlbom. An algorithm for geometric set operations using cellular subdivision techniques. *IEEE Computer Graphics and Applications*, 7(5):44–55, May 1987. [volumes; polytree; PM octree] cited in D.5.3, F.2.2.2.7 (p. 371)

[308] I. Carlbom, I. Chakravarty, and D. Vanderschel. A hierarchical data structure for representing the spatial decomposition of 3D objects. *IEEE Computer Graphics and Applications*, 5(4):24–31, April 1985. [volumes; PM octree; polytree] cited in A.1.3, D.5.3, F.2.2.2.7 (p. 370)

[309] W. E. Carlson. An algorithm and data structure for 3-D object synthesis using surface patch intersection. *Computer Graphics*, 16(3):255–263, July 1982. Also in *Proceedings of the SIGGRAPH'82 Conference*, Boston, July 1982. [surfaces] cited in A.7.1.6, D.5.6, F.2.2.4 (p. 402)

[310] E. Caspary. *Sequential and parallel algorithms for ray tracing complex scenes*. PhD thesis, Electrical and Computer Engineering Department, University of California at Santa Barbara, Santa Barbara, CA, June 1988. [volumes; ray tracing]

[311] E. Catmull. Computer display of curved surfaces. In *Proceedings of the IEEE Conference on Computer Graphics, Pattern Recognition, and Data Structure*, pages 11–17, Los Angeles, May 1975. [surfaces] cited in A.7.1.6

[312] J. A. Cebrian, J. E. Mower, and D. M. Mark. Analysis and display of digital elevation models within a quadtree-based geographic information system. In *Proceedings of the 7th International Symposium on Automated Cartography (AUTO-CARTO 7)*, pages 55–64, Washington, DC, March 1985. [surfaces; digital elevation model (DEM)]

[313] R. L. T. Cederberg. Chain-link coding and segmentation for raster scan devices. *Computer Graphics and Image Processing*, pages 224–234, 1979. [lines; chain code]

[314] S.-H. Cha and S. N. Srihari. A fast nearest neighbor search algorithm by filtration. *Pattern Recognition*, 35(2):515–525, January 2002. [high-dimensional data; nearest neighbor]

[315] K. Chakrabarti. Personal communication. 2000. [high-dimensional data; hybrid tree; sequential scan] cited in F.4.4.3 (p. 573)

[316] K. Chakrabarti and S. Mehrotra. Dynamic granular locking approach to phantom protection in R-trees. In *Proceedings of the 14th IEEE International Conference on Data Engineering*, pages 446–454, Orlando, FL, February 1998. [points; R-tree; concurrency]

[317] K. Chakrabarti and S. Mehrotra. The hybrid tree: an index structure for high dimensional feature spaces. In *Proceedings of the 15th IEEE International Conference on Data Engineering*, pages 440–447, Sydney, Australia, March 1999. Also University of California at Irvine Information and Computer Science Technical Report TR–MARS–98–14, July 1998. [points; high-dimensional data; k-d-B-tree; hybrid tree] cited in F.1.7.1.2 (pp. 101–102), F.2.1.5.2.4 (p. 295), F.3.3.3 (p. 465), F.4.4.3 (p. 573), F.4.4.4 (p. 574), F.4.4.8 (p. 592), F.4.5.2.4 (p. 610), F.4.6 (p. 663)

[318] K. Chakrabarti and S. Mehrotra. Local dimensionality reduction: a new approach to indexing high-dimensional spaces. In *Proceedings of the 26th International Conference on Very Large Data Bases (VLDB)*, A. El Abbadi, M. L. Brodie, S. Chakravarthy, U. Dayal, N. Kamel, G. Schlageter, and K.-Y. Whang, eds., pages 89–100, Cairo, Egypt, September 2000. [points; high-dimensional data; nearest neighbor; dimension reduction]

[319] C.-Y. Chan, P.-K. Eng, and K.-L. Tan. Stratified computation of skylines with partially-ordered domains. In *Proceedings of the ACM SIGMOD Conference*, pages 203–214, Baltimore, MD, June 2005. Also see *Proceedings of the 21st IEEE International Conference on Data Engineering*, pages 190–191, Tokyo, Japan, April 2005. [points; skyline query; point dominance query; partial ordering; nearest neighbor] cited in F.4.1.5 (pp. 506, 508)

[320] K. C. Chan, I. A. Gargantini, and T. R. Walsh. Double connectivity filling 3d modeling. Computer Science Technical Report 155, University of Western Ontario, London, Ontario, Canada, December 1986. [volumes]

[321] S. Chandrasekharan, B. S. Manjunath, Y. F. Wang, J. Winkeler, and H. Zhang. An eigenspace update algorithm for image analysis. *CVGIP: Graphical Models and Image Processing*, 59(5):321–332, September 1997. [high-dimensional data; Singular Value Decomposition (SVD)] cited in F.4.6.4.1 (p. 674)

[322] J.-M. Chang and K. S. Fu. Extended k-d tree database organization: a dynamic multiattribute clustering method. *IEEE Transactions on Software Engineering*, 7(3):284–290, May 1981. [points; k-d tree; partial match query]

[323] S. K. Chang. *Principles of Pictorial Information System Design*. Prentice-Hall, Englewood Cliffs, NJ, 1989. [image database; general]

[324] Y.-I. Chang, C.-I. Lee, and W.-B. C. Liaw. Linear spiral hashing for expansible files. *IEEE Transactions on Knowledge and Data Engineering*, 11(6):969–984, November/December 1999. [points; spiral hashing] cited in F.C (p. 735)

[325] M. Charikar, S. Guha, E. Tardos, and D. B. Shmoys. A constant-factor approximation algorithm for the k-median problem (extended abstract). In *Proceedings of the 31st Annual ACM Symposium on the Theory of Computing*, pages 1–10, Atlanta, GA, May 1999. [points; k-median problem] cited in F.4.5.3.4 (pp. 623–624), F.4.5.3.4.s (p. 858)

[326] S. Chattopadhyay and A. Fujimoto. Bi-directional ray tracing. In *Computer Graphics 1987: Proceedings of the CG International'87*, T. L. Kunii, ed., pages 335–343, Karuizawa, Japan, May 1987. Springer-Verlag. [volumes; ray tracing]

[327] V. Chaudhary, K. Kumari, P. Arunachalam, and J. K. Aggarwal. Manipulations of octrees and quadtrees on multiprocessors. *International Journal of Pattern Recognition and Artificial Intelligence*, 8(2):439–455, April 1994. [regions; volumes; multiprocessing]

[328] B. B. Chaudhuri. Applications of quadtree, octree, and binary tree decomposition techniques to shape analysis and pattern recognition. *IEEE Transactions on Pattern Analysis and Machine Intelligence*, 7(6):652–661, November 1985. [regions; region quadtree; region octree]

[329] S. Chaudhuri and U. Dayal. Data warehousing and OLAP technology. *SIGMOD RECORD*, 26(1):65–74, March 1997. [data warehousing; online analytic processing (OLAP)] cited in F.2.1.5.2.5 (p. 297)

[330] E. Chávez, J. Marroquín, and R. Baeza-Yates. Spaghettis: an array-based algorithm for similarity queries in metric spaces. In *Proceedings String Processing and Information Retrieval and International Workshop on Groupware (SPIRE/CRIWG 1999)*, pages 38–46, Cancun, Mexico, September 1999. [metric spaces] cited in F.4.5.1 (p. 601), F.4.5.7.2 (p. 647)

[331] E. Chávez, J. Marroquín, and G. Navarro. Fixed queries array: a fast and economical data structure for proximity searching. *Multimedia Tools and Applications*, 14(2):113–135, June 2001. Also see *European Workshop on Content-Based Multimedia Indexing*, pages 57–64, Toulouse, France, October 1999. [metric spaces; curse of dimensionality; fixed-queries array] cited in F.4.5.1 (p. 601), F.4.5.2.4 (p. 611)

[332] E. Chávez and G. Navarro. An effective clustering algorithm to index high dimensional spaces. In *Proceedings String Processing and Information Retrieval (SPIRE 2000)*, pages 75–86, A Coruña, Spain, September 2000. [metric spaces; high-dimensional data; vp-tree] cited in F.4.5 (p. 598), F.4.5.2.4 (p. 613)

[333] E. Chávez and G. Navarro. Probabilistic proximity search: fighting the curse of dimensionality in metric spaces. *Information Processing Letters*, 85(1):39–46, January 2003. [high-dimensional data; similarity searching; curse of dimensionality]

[334] E. Chávez, G. Navarro, R. Baeza-Yates, and J. Marroquín. Searching in metric spaces. *ACM Computing Surveys*, 33(3):273–322, September 2001. Also University of Chile DCC Technical Report TR/DCC-99-3, June 1999. [metric spaces; survey] cited in F.P (p. xx), F.4.1.7 (p. 517), F.4.2 (p. 517), F.4.5 (p. 599), F.4.5.2.1.1 (p. 605), F.4.5.2.4 (p. 610)

[335] B. Chazelle. Convex partitions of polyhedra: a lower bound and worst-case optimal algorithm. *SIAM Journal on Computing*, 13(3):488–507, August 1984. [volumes; conforming tetrahedralization] cited in F.2.2.1.6 (p. 353)

[336] B. Chazelle. A functional approach to data structures and its use in multidimensional searching. *SIAM Journal on Computing*, 17(3):427–426, June 1988. [rectangles; functional programming; range query]

[337] B. Chazelle and D. Dobkin. Optimal convex decompositions. In *Computational Geometry*, G. T. Toussaint, ed., pages 63–133. North-Holland, Amsterdam, The Netherlands, 1985. [regions; convex region] cited in F.2.1.4.2 (p. 262)

[338] B. Chazelle and D. Dobkin. Intersection of convex objects in two and three dimensions. *Journal of the ACM*, 34(1):1–27, January 1987. [volumes; interference detection] cited in A.7.3.s

[339] B. Chazelle and L. J. Guibas. Fractional cascading: I. A data structuring technique. *Algorithmica*, 1(2):133–162, 1986. Also Digital Systems Research Center Technical Report 12, June 1986. [rectangles; lines; fractional cascading] cited in D.3.2.2, D.4.3.2, F.1.7.1.6.5 (p. 127), F.2.1.3.3.2 (pp. 251, 253), F.3.1.2 (p. 435)

[340] B. Chazelle and L. J. Guibas. Fractional cascading: II. Applications. *Algorithmica*, 1(2):163–191, 1986. Also Digital Systems Research Center Technical Report 12, June 1986. [rectangles; lines; fractional cascading] cited in D.3.2.2, D.4.3.2, F.1.7.1.6.5 (p. 127), F.2.1.3.3.2 (pp. 251, 253), F.3.1.2 (p. 435)

[341] B. Chazelle and L. Palios. Triangulating a non-convex polytope. *Discrete & Computational Geometry*, 5(5):505–526, 1990. [volumes; conforming tetrahedralization] cited in F.2.2.1.6 (p. 353)

[342] J. P. Cheiney and A. Touir. FI-Quadtree: a new data structure for content-oriented retrieval and fuzzy search. In *Advances in Spatial Databases—2nd Symposium, SSD'91*, O. Günther and H.-J. Schek, eds., vol. 525 of Springer-Verlag Lecture Notes in Computer Science, pages 23–32, Zurich, Switzerland, August 1991. [regions; similarity searching]

[343] C. Chen and H. Zou. Linear binary tree. In *Proceedings of the 9th International Conference on Pattern Recognition*, pages 576–578, Rome, Italy, November 1988. [regions]

[344] C.-C. Chen, C. A. Knoblock, C. Shahabi, Y.-Y. Chiang, and S. Thakkar. Automatically and accurately conflating orthoimagery and street maps. In *Proceedings of the 12th ACM International Workshop on Advances in Geographic Information Systems*, I. F. Cruz and D. Pfoser, eds., pages 47–56, Washington, DC, November 2004. [map conflation] cited in F.4 (p. 486)

[345] H. H. Chen and T. S. Huang. A survey of construction and manipulation of octrees. *Computer Vision, Graphics, and Image Processing*, 43(3):409–431, September 1988. [volumes; region octree; survey] cited in F.P (p. xix)

[346] J.-Y. Chen, C. A. Bouman, and J. C. Dalton. Hierarchical browsing and search of large image databases. *IEEE Transactions on Image Processing*, 9(3):442–455, March 2000. [metric spaces; approximate nearest neighbor] cited in F.4.1.7 (p. 516), F.4.3 (pp. 561, 565), F.4.5.2.1.2 (p. 607)

[347] L. Chen, R. Choubey, and E. A. Rundensteiner. Bulk-insertions into R-trees using the Small-Tree-Large-Tree approach. In *Proceedings of the 6th ACM International Symposium on Advances in Geographic Information Systems*, R. Laurini, K. Makki, and N. Pissinou, eds., pages 161–162, Washington, DC, November 1998. [points; bulk loading; bulk insertion; R-tree; STLT method] cited in F.2.1.5.2.5 (pp. 297–298)

[348] L. Chen, M. T. Özsu, and V. Oria. Robust and fast similarity search for moving object trajectories. In *Proceedings of the ACM SIGMOD Conference*, pages 491–502, Baltimore, MD, June 2005. [moving objects; similarity searching; time-series database] cited in F.4.6.4.2 (p. 681)

[349] L.-S. Chen, G. T. Herman, R. A. Reynolds, and J. K. Udupa. Surface shading in the cuberille environment. *IEEE Computer Graphics and Applications*, 5(12):33–43, December 1985. [volumes; shading] cited in A.7.1.4

[350] P.-M. Chen. A quadtree normalization scheme based on cyclic translations. *Pattern Recognition*, 30(12):2053–2064, December 1997. [regions]

[351] Y. Chen and P. Revesz. Max-count aggregation estimation for moving points. In *Proceedings of the 11th International Symposium on Temporal Representation and Reasoning (TIME 2004)*, pages 103–108, Tatihou Island, Normandie, France, July 2004. [rectangles; moving objects; aggregation query] cited in F.3.1.4 (p. 445)

[352] Y. C. Chen. An introduction to hierarchical probe model (unpublished). Department of Mathematical Sciences, Purdue University Calumet, Hammond, IN, 1985. [regions; sector tree; cone tree] cited in D.1.4.2, D.5.8, F.2.2.2.9 (p. 377), F.2.2.2.10 (p. 380)

[353] Z. T. Chen. Quadtree spatial spectrum: its generation and application. In *Proceedings of the International Symposium on Spatial Data Handling*, pages 218–237, Zurich, Switzerland, August 1984. [regions; quadtree spectrum]

[354] Z. T. Chen. A quadtree guides fast spatial searches in triangular irregular network (TIN). In *Proceedings of the 4th International Symposium on Spatial Data Handling*, vol. 1, pages 209–215, Zurich, Switzerland, July 1990. [surfaces; triangulations; triangulated irregular network (TIN)]

[355] Z. T. Chen and W. R. Tobler. Quadtree representations of digital terrain. In *Proceedings of Auto-Carto London*, vol. 1, pages 475–484, London, United Kingdom, September 1986. [surfaces; region quadtree] cited in D.5.6, F.2.2.4 (p. 402)

[356] D.-Y. Cheng, A. Gersho, B. Ramamurthi, and Y. Shoham. Fast search algorithms for vector quantization and pattern matching. In *Proceedings of the IEEE International Conference on Acoustics, Speech, and Signal Processing (ICASSP-84)*, vol. 1, pages 9.11.1–9.11.4, San Diego, CA, March 1984. [points; high-dimensional data; nearest neighbor; vector quantization] cited in F.4.4.8 (p. 592)

[357] S. W. Cheng and R. Janardan. New results on dynamic planar point location. *SIAM Journal on Computing*, 21(5):972–999, October 1992. [regions; dynamic point location; interval tree; priority search tree] cited in F.2.1.3.3.2 (p. 253)

[358] Y. Cheng. Mean shift, mode seeking, and clustering. *IEEE Transactions on Pattern Analysis and Machine Intelligence*, 17(8):790–799, August 1995. [points; mean shift analysis]

[359] R. Chestek, H. Muller, and D. Chelberg. Knowledge-based terrain analysis. In *Proceedings of the SPIE, Applications of Artificial Intelligence II*, vol. 548, pages 46–56, Mountain View, CA, 1985. [regions]

[360] K. L. Cheung and A. W.-C. Fu. Enhanced nearest neighbor search on the R-tree. *SIGMOD Record*, 27(3):16–21, September 1998. [points; R-tree; depth-first nearest neighbor algorithm] cited in F.4.2.4 (p. 536), F.4.2.4.s (p. 843)

[361] L. P. Chew. Constrained Delaunay triangulations. *Algorithmica*, 4(1):97–108, 1989. [surfaces; constrained Delaunay triangulation] cited in F.2.2.1.5 (p. 351)

[362] Y.-J. Chiang, F. P. Preparata, and R. Tamassia. A unified approach of dynamic point location, ray shooting, and shortest paths in planar maps. In *Proceedings of the 4th Annual ACM-SIAM Symposium on Discrete Algorithms*, pages 44–53, Austin, TX, January 1993. [regions; dynamic point location] cited in F.2.1.3.3.2 (p. 253)

[363] Y.-J. Chiang and C. T. Silva. I/O optimal isosurface extraction. In *Proceedings IEEE Visualization'97*, R. Yagel and H. Hagen, eds., pages 293–300, Phoenix, AZ, October 1997. [surfaces]

[364] Y.-J. Chiang and R. Tamassia. Dynamic algorithms in computational geometry. *Proceedings of the IEEE*, 80(9):1412–1434, September 1992. [intervals; survey]

[365] Y.-J. Chiang and R. Tamassia. Dynamization of the trapezoid method for planar point location. *International Journal of Computational Geometry Applications*, 2(3):311–333, 1992. [regions; dynamic point location] cited in F.2.1.3.3.2 (p. 253)

[366] C.-H. Chien and J. K. Aggarwal. A normalized quadtree representation. *Computer Vision, Graphics, and Image Processing*, 26(3):331–346, June 1984. [regions; region quadtree] cited in A.5.2

[367] C.-H. Chien and J. K. Aggarwal. A volume/surface octree representation. In *Proceedings of the 7th International Conference on Pattern Recognition*, pages 817–820, Montréal, Canada, July 1984. [volumes; region octree] cited in A.4.6, D.5.2

[368] C.-H. Chien and J. K. Aggarwal. Reconstruction and matching of 3-d objects using quadtrees/octrees. In *Proceedings of the 3rd Workshop on Computer Vision: Representation and Control*, pages 49–54, Bellaire, MI, October 1985. [volumes; region quadtree; region octree] cited in A.4.6, D.5.2

[369] C.-H. Chien and J. K. Aggarwal. Computation of volume/surface octrees from contours and silhouettes of multiple views. In *Proceedings of Computer Vision and Pattern Recognition'86*, pages 250–255, Miami Beach, FL, June 1986. [volumes; region octree] cited in A.7.1.4, D.5.3, F.2.2.2.4 (p. 361)

[370] C.-H. Chien and J. K. Aggarwal. Identification of 3-d objects from multiple silhouettes using quadtrees/octrees. *Computer Vision, Graphics, and Image Processing*, 36(2/3):256–273, November/December 1986. [volumes; region quadtree; region octree] cited in A.4.6, D.5.2

[371] C.-H. Chien and J. K. Aggarwal. Volume/surface octrees for the representation of three-dimensional objects. *Computer Vision, Graphics, and Image Processing*, 36(1):100–113, October 1986. [volumes; region quadtree; region octree] cited in A.4.6, A.4.6.s, D.5.2, D.5.2.s

[372] C.-H. Chien and J. K. Aggarwal. Shape recognition from single silhouettes. In *Proceedings of the 1st International Conference on Computer Vision*, pages 481–490, London, United Kingdom, June 1987. [volumes]

[373] C. H. Chien and T. Kanade. Distributed quadtree processing. In *Design and Implementation of Large Spatial Databases—1st Symposium, SSD'89*, A. Buchmann, O. Günther, T. R. Smith, and Y.-F. Wang, eds., vol. 409 of Springer-Verlag Lecture Notes in Computer Science, pages 213–232, Santa Barbara, CA, July 1989. [regions; region quadtree; parallel processing] cited in F.P (p. xviii), F.1.5 (p. 49)

[374] C.-H. Chien, Y. B. Sim, and J. K. Aggarwal. Generation of volume/surface octree from range data. In *Proceedings of Computer Vision and Pattern Recognition'88*, pages 254–260, Ann Arbor, MI, June 1988. [volumes; region octree] cited in A.4.6, A.4.6.s, D.5.2, D.5.2.s

[375] N. Chin and S. Feiner. Near real-time shadow generation using BSP-trees. *Computer Graphics*, 23(3):99–106, August 1989. Also

in *Proceedings of the SIGGRAPH'89 Conference*, Boston, July 1989. [volumes; BSP tree] cited in F.2.1.3.1 (p. 236)

[376] T. Chiueh. Content-based image indexing. In *Proceedings of the 20th International Conference on Very Large Data Bases (VLDB)*, J. Bocca, M. Jarke, and C. Zaniolo, eds., pages 582–593, Santiago, Chile, September 1994. [metric spaces; depth-first nearest neighbor algorithm; vp-tree] cited in F.4.2.8 (p. 555)

[377] H.-J. Cho and C.-W. Chung. An efficient and scalable approach to CNN queries in a road network. In *Proceedings of the 31st International Conference on Very Large Data Bases (VLDB)*, K. Böhm, C. S. Jensen, L. M. Haas, M. L. Kersten, P.-Å. Larson, and B. C. Ooi, eds., pages 865–876, Trondheim, Norway, September 2005. [lines; points; spatial networks; shortest path algorithm; nearest neighbor] cited in F.4.1.6 (p. 514)

[378] J. Chomicki. Querying with intrinsic preferences. In *Proceedings of the 8th International Conference on Extending Database Technology—EDBT 2002*, C. S. Jensen, K. G. Jeffery, J. Pokorný, S. Saltenis, E. Bertino, K. Böhm, and M. Jarke, eds., vol. 2287 of Springer-Verlag Lecture Notes in Computer Science, pages 34–51, Prague, Czech Republic, March 2002. [preference query] cited in F.4.1.5 (p. 505)

[379] J. Chomicki, P. Godfrey, J. Gryz, and D. Liang. Skyline with presorting. In *Proceedings of the 19th IEEE International Conference on Data Engineering*, pages 717–816, Bangalore, India, March 2003. [points; skyline query; point dominance query; nearest neighbor] cited in F.4.1.5 (pp. 503, 505)

[380] H. T. Chou and D. J. DeWitt. An evaluation of buffer management strategies for relational database systems. In *Proceedings of the 11th International Conference on Very Large Databases (VLDB)*, A. Pirotte and Y. Vassiliou, eds., pages 127–141, Stockholm, Sweden, August 1985. [buffer management] cited in F.A (p. 724)

[381] R. Choubey, L. Chen, and E A. Rundensteiner. GBI: a generalized R-tree bulk-insertion strategy. In *Advances in Spatial Databases— 6th International Symposium, SSD'99*, R. H. Güting, D. Papadias, and F. H. Lochovsky, eds., vol. 1651 of Springer-Verlag Lecture Notes in Computer Science, pages 91–108, Hong Kong, China, July 1999. [rectangles; R-tree; bulk insertion; Generalized Bulk Insertion (GBI)] cited in F.2.1.5.2.5 (pp. 297–298)

[382] Y. Chrysanthou and M. Slater. Computing dynamic changes to BSP trees. In *Proceedings of the EUROGRAPHICS'92 Conference*, A. Kilgour and L. Kjelldahl, eds., pages 321–332, Cambridge, United Kingdom, September 1992. Also in *Computer Graphics Forum*, 11(3):321–332, September 1992. [volumes; BSP tree]

[383] J.-H. Chu. Notes on expected numbers of nodes in a quadtree (unpublished). Computer Science Department, University of Maryland, College Park, MD, January 1988. [regions; region quadtree] cited in A.1.2.s, D.1.5.s, F.2.1.2.4.s (p. 780)

[384] J.-H. Chu and G. D. Knott. An analysis of spiral hashing. *The Computer Journal*, 37(8), 1994. Also University of Maryland Computer Science Technical Report TR–2107, September 1988. [points; spiral hashing] cited in D.2.8.2.2.s, F.C (p. 735), F.C.s (p. 875)

[385] V. Chvátal. A greedy heuristic for the set-covering problem. *Mathematics of Operations Research*, 4(3):233–235, August 1979. [points; set cover problem] cited in F.4.7.4 (p. 716)

[386] P. Ciaccia and M. Patella. Bulk loading the M-tree. In *Proceedings of the 9th Australasian Database Conference (ADC'98)*, pages 15–26, Perth, Australia, February 1998. [metric spaces; M-tree; bulk loading] cited in F.4.5.4.1 (p. 625)

[387] P. Ciaccia and M. Patella. PAC nearest neighbor queries: approximate and controlled search in high-dimensional and metric spaces. In *Proceedings of the 16th IEEE International Conference on Data Engineering*, pages 244–255, San Diego, CA, February 2000. [points; high-dimensional data; incremental nearest neighbor algorithm; approximate nearest neighbor] cited in F.4.1.7 (p. 516), F.4.3 (pp. 557, 559, 562–563), F.4.4.4 (pp. 578–579), F.4.4.8 (pp. 596–597), F.4.3.s (p. 850)

[388] P. Ciaccia and M. Patella. Searching in metric spaces with user-defined and approximate distances. *ACM Transactions on Database Systems*, 27(4):398–437, December 2002. [metric spaces; M-tree] cited in F.4.5.4 (p. 624)

[389] P. Ciaccia, M. Patella, and P. Zezula. M-tree: an efficient access method for similarity search in metric spaces. In *Proceedings of the 23rd International Conference on Very Large Data Bases (VLDB)*, M. Jarke, M. J. Carey, K. R. Dittrich, F. H. Lochovsky, P. Loucopoulos, and M. A. Jeusfeld, eds., pages 426–435, Athens, Greece, August 1997. [metric spaces; M-tree] cited in F.4.1.7 (p. 517), F.4.2 (p. 517), F.4.2.2 (p. 521), F.4.2.3 (pp. 529, 533), F.4.2.5 (p. 540), F.4.2.6 (p. 551), F.4.2.7 (p. 553), F.4.2.8 (p. 557), F.4.3 (p. 561), F.4.4.7 (p. 592), F.4.5 (p. 599), F.4.5.2.3 (p. 609), F.4.5.4 (p. 624), F.4.5.4.1 (pp. 624–625), F.4.5.4.2 (pp. 626–628), F.4.2.3.s (p. 841), F.4.2.5.s (p. 845)

[390] P. Ciaccia, M. Patella, and P. Zezula. A cost model for similarity queries in metric spaces. In *Proceedings of the 17th ACM SIGACT-SIGMOD-SIGART Symposium on Principles of Database Systems (PODS)*, pages 59–68, Seattle, WA, June 1998. [metric spaces; M-tree; cost model]

[391] A. Ciampalini, P. Cignoni, C. Montani, and R. Scopigno. Multiresolution decimation based on global error. *The Visual Computer*, 13(5):228–246, 1997. [surfaces; surface simplification; multiresolution modeling] cited in F.2.2.3.4 (p. 394)

[392] P. Cignoni, C. Montani, and R. Scopigno. A comparison of mesh simplification algorithms. *Computers & Graphics*, 22(1):37–54, February 1998. [simplification; multiresolution modeling] cited in F.2.2.3.4 (p. 391)

[393] P. Cignoni, E. Puppo, and R. Scopigno. Representation and visualization of terrain surfaces at variable resolution. *The Visual Computer*, 13(5):199–217, July 1998. [surfaces]

[394] P. Cignoni, C. Rocchini, and R. Scopigno. Metro: measuring error on simplified surfaces. *Computer Graphics Forum*, 17(2):167–174, June 1998. [surfaces; simplification; Hausdorff distance] cited in F.2.2.3.4 (p. 392)

[395] J. H. Clark. Hierarchical geometric models for visible surface algorithms. *Communication of the ACM*, 19(10):547–554, October 1976. [surfaces] cited in A.7.2.2

[396] K. L. Clarkson. Fast algorithm for the all nearest neighbors problem. In *Proceedings of the 24th IEEE Annual Symposium on Foundations of Computer Science*, pages 226–232, Tucson, AZ, November 1983. [points; all nearest neighbors query; path compression; PR quadtree] cited in F.1.5.2.4 (p. 76), F.1.5.2.7 (p. 87), F.4 (p. 485)

[397] K. L. Clarkson. Applications of random sampling in computational geometry, II. In *Proceedings of the 4th Annual Symposium on Computational Geometry*, pages 1–11, Urbana-Champaign, IL, June 1988. [points; Las Vegas randomized algorithm] cited in F.4.7.4 (p. 711)

[398] K. L. Clarkson. A randomized algorithm for closest-point queries. *SIAM Journal on Computing*, 17(4):830–847, August 1988. [points; nearest neighbor; Las Vegas randomized algorithm; post-office problem] cited in F.4.7.4 (p. 711)

[399] K. L. Clarkson. An algorithm for approximate closest-point queries. In *Proceedings of the 10th Annual Symposium on Computational Geometry*, pages 160–164, Stony Brook, NY, June 1994. [points; nearest neighbor]

[400] K. L. Clarkson. Nearest neighbor queries in metric spaces. In *Proceedings of the 29th Annual ACM Symposium on the Theory of Computing*, pages 609–617, El Paso, TX, May 1997. [points; approximate nearest neighbor] cited in F.4.4.4 (p. 575)

[401] K. L. Clarkson. Nearest-neighbor searching and metric space dimensions. In *Nearest-Neighbor Methods for Learning and Vision: Theory and Practice*, T. Darrell, P. Indyk, and G. Shakhnarovich, eds., pages 15–59. MIT Press, Cambridge, MA, 2005. [metric spaces; nearest neighbor; survey] cited in F.P (p. xx)

[402] R. D. Clay and H. P. Moreton. Efficient adaptive subdivision of Bézier surfaces. In *Proceedings of the EUROGRAPHICS'88 Conference*, D. A. Duce and P. Jancene, eds., pages 357–371, Nice, France, September 1988. [surfaces]

[403] J. G. Cleary. Analysis of an algorithm for finding nearest neighbors in Euclidean space. *ACM Transactions on Mathematical Software*, 5(2):183–202, June 1979. [points; nearest neighbor] cited in F.4.4.8 (p. 593)

[404] J. G. Cleary and G. Wyvill. Analysis of an algorithm for fast ray tracing using uniform space subdivision. *Visual Computer*, 4(2):65–83, July 1988. [volumes; ray tracing] cited in A.7.2.5

[405] M. Clemmesen. Interval arithmetic implementations using floating point arithmetic. Institute of Datalogy Technical Report 83/9, University of Copenhagen, Copenhagen, 1983. [interval arithmetic; general] cited in D.5.5.1

[406] E. Cohen, T. Lyche, and R. Riesenfeld. Discrete B-splines and subdivision techniques in computer-aided geometric design and computer graphics. *Computer Graphics and Image Processing*, 14(3):87–111, October 1980. [surfaces] cited in D.4, D.5.6

[407] J. Cohen and T. Hickey. Two algorithms for detecting volumes of convex polyhedra. *Journal of the ACM*, 26(3):401–414, July 1979. [volumes] cited in D.5.5

[408] J. Cohen, A. Varshney, D. Manocha, G. Turk, H. Weber, P. Agarwal, F. Brooks, and W. Wright. Simplification envelopes. In *Proceedings of the SIGGRAPH'96 Conference*, pages 119–128, New Orleans, LA, August 1996. [surfaces; polygon simplification] cited in F.2.2.3.4 (pp. 392, 395)

[409] M. F. Cohen and D. P. Greenberg. The hemi-cube: a radiosity solution for complex environments. *Computer Graphics*, 19(3):31–40, July 1985. Also in *Proceedings of the SIGGRAPH'85 Conference*, San Francisco, July 1985. [surfaces; radiosity] cited in A.7.4

[410] M. F. Cohen, D. P. Greenberg, D. S. Immel, and P. J. Brock. An efficient radiosity approach for realistic image synthesis. *IEEE Computer Graphics and Applications*, 6(3):26–35, March 1986. [surfaces; radiosity] cited in A.7.4

[411] Y. Cohen, M. S. Landy, and M. Pavel. Hierarchical coding of binary images. *IEEE Transactions on Pattern Analysis and Machine Intelligence*, 7(3):284–298, May 1985. [regions; bintree] cited in A.1.3, A.2.2, A.2.2.s, A.8, D.1.4.1, F.1.5.2.1 (p. 71), F.2.1.2.6 (p. 221)

[412] A. J. Cole. Compaction techniques for raster scan graphics using space-filling curves. *Computer Journal*, 30(1):87–96, February 1987. [regions; space-filling curve]

[413] A. J. Cole and R. Morrison. Triplex: a system for interval arithmetic. *Software—Practice and Experience*, 12(4):341–350, April 1982. [interval arithmetic] cited in D.5.5.1

[414] D. Comer. The ubiquitous B-tree. *ACM Computing Surveys*, 11(2):121–137, June 1979. [B-tree; B*-tree; B+-tree; survey] cited in A.2.1, A.2.1.1, A.2.1.4, A.4.2.3, D.2.7, D.3.2.3, D.3.5.3, D.4.2.3, F.1.1 (p. 8), F.A (p. 725)

[415] C. I. Connolly. Cumulative generation of octree models from range data. In *Proceedings of the International Conference on Robotics*, pages 25–32, Atlanta, GA, March 1984. [volumes; region octree] cited in A.4.6, D.5.2

[416] C. I. Connolly. The determination of next best views. In *Proceedings of the International Conference on Robotics*, pages 432–435, St. Louis, MO, March 1985. [volumes] cited in A.4.6, D.5.2

[417] P. Conti, N. Hitschfeld, and W. Fichtner. OMEGA—an octree-based mixed element grid allocator for the simulation of complex 3-d device structures. *IEEE Transactions on Computer-Aided Design*, 10(10):1231–1241, October 1991. [volumes; finite element analysis; mesh generation]

[418] B. G. Cook. The structural and algorithmic basis of geographic data base. In *Proceedings of the 1st International Advanced Study Symposium on Topological Data Structures for Geographic Information Systems*, G. Dutton, ed., Harvard Papers on Geographic Information Systems. Addison-Wesley, Reading, MA, 1978. [regions; database systems] cited in A.2.1.1

[419] R. L. Cook, T. Porter, and L. Carpenter. Distributed ray tracing. *Computer Graphics*, 18(3):137–145, July 1984. Also in *Proceedings of the SIGGRAPH'84 Conference*, Minneapolis, MN, July 1984. [volumes; ray tracing] cited in A.7.2.1, A.7.2.5

[420] R. L. Cook and K. E. Torrance. A reflectance model for computer graphics. *ACM Transactions on Graphics*, 1(1):7–24, January 1982. [surfaces; image synthesis; reflectance] cited in A.7.2.1

[421] J. W. Cooley and J. W. Tukey. An algorithm for the machine computation of complex Fourier series. *Mathematics of Computation*, 19(90):297–301, April 1965. [Fast Fourier Transform (FFT)] cited in F.4.6.4.2 (p. 684), F.4.6.4.2.s (p. 867)

[422] T. H. Cormen, C. E. Leiserson, R. L. Rivest, and C. Stein. *Introduction to Algorithms*. MIT Press/McGraw-Hill, Cambridge, MA, second edition, 2001. [algorithms; general] cited in F.2.1.2.4 (p. 216), F.3.1.2 (pp. 435, 438), F.A (p. 722), F.1.3.s (pp. 750–751)

[423] A. Corral, Y. Manolopoulos, Y. Theodoridis, and M. Vassilakopoulos. Closest pair queries in spatial databases. In *Proceedings of the ACM SIGMOD Conference*, W. Chen, J. Naughton, and P. A. Bernstein, eds., pages 189–200, Dallas, TX, May 2000. [points; distance join]

[424] A. Corral, M. Vassilakopoulos, and Y. Manolopoulos. Algorithms for joining R-trees and linear region quadtrees. In *Advances in Spatial Databases—6th International Symposium, SSD'99*, R. H. Güting, D. Papadias, and F. H. Lochovsky, eds., vol. 1651 of Springer-Verlag Lecture Notes in Computer Science, pages 251–269, Hong Kong, China, July 1999. [regions; spatial join; R-tree; region quadtree]

[425] M. S. Cottingham. A compressed data structure for surface representation. *Computer Graphics Forum*, 4(3):217–228, September 1985. [surfaces]

[426] L. J. Cowen and C. E. Priebe. Randomized non-linear projections uncover high-dimensional structure. *Advances in Applied Math*, 19:319–331, 1997. [metric space embedding; Lipschitz embedding] cited in F.4.7.2.1 (p. 691)

[427] H. S. M. Coxeter, M. Emmer, R. Penrose, and M. L. Teuber, eds. *M. C. Escher, Art and Science: Proceedings of the International Congress on M. C. Escher*. Elsevier North-Holland, New York, 1986. [Escher drawings] cited in A.1.2, D.1.2, F.2.1.2.4 (p. 218)

[428] E. Creutzburg. Complexities of quadtrees and the structure of pictures. Technical Report N/81/74, Friedrich-Schiller University, Jena, East Germany, 1981. [regions]

[429] F. C. Crow. Shadow algorithms for computer graphics. *Computer Graphics*, 11(2):242–248, Summer 1977. Also in *Proceedings of the SIGGRAPH'77 Conference* San Jose, CA, July 1977. [regions; volumes] cited in A.7.1.4

[430] F. Csillag and Å. Kummert. Spatial complexity and storage requirements of maps represented by region quadtrees. In *Proceedings of the 4th International Symposium on Spatial Data Handling*, vol. 2, pages 928–937, Zurich, Switzerland, July 1990. [regions; region quadtree; space requirements]

[431] B. Cui, B. C. Ooi, J. Su, and K.-L. Tan. Indexing high-dimensional data for efficient in-memory similarity search. *IEEE Transactions on Knowledge and Data Engineering*, 17(3):339–353, March 2005. Also see *Proceedings of the ACM SIGMOD Conference*, pages 479–490, San Diego, CA, June 2003. [high-dimensional data; dimension reduction; similarity searching]

[432] W. Cunto, G. Lau, and P. Flajolet. Analysis of *kdt*-trees: kd-trees improved by local reorganisations. In *Algorithms and Data Structures—Workshop WADS'89*, F. K. H. A. Dehne, J. R. Sack, and N. Santoro, eds., vol. 382 of Springer-Verlag Lecture Notes in Computer Science, pages 24–38, Ottawa, Canada, August 1989. [points; k-d tree]

[433] M. W. Cutlip. Verification of numerically controlled machine tool programs for 2.5-d parts using Z-tree solid modeling techniques. Master's thesis, George Washington University, Washington DC, 1986. [surfaces]

[434] M. Cyrus and J. Beck. Generalized two- and three-dimensional clipping. *Computers & Graphics*, 3(1):23–28, 1978. [line clipping] cited in A.7.2.3

[435] N. Dadoun, D. G. Kirkpatrick, and J. P. Walsh. Hierarchical approaches to hidden surface intersection testing. In *Proceedings of Graphics Interface'82*, pages 49–56, Toronto, Canada, May 1982. [volumes; ray tracing] cited in A.7.2.2, A.7.3, A.7.3.s

[436] N. Dadoun, D. G. Kirkpatrick, and J. P. Walsh. The geometry of beam tracing. In *Proceedings of the Symposium on Computational Geometry*, pages 55–61, Baltimore, MD, June 1985. [volumes; beam tracing; ray tracing] cited in A.7.2.2, A.7.3, F.2.1.3.1 (p. 236)

[437] O.-J. Dahl and K. Nygaard. SIMULA—an ALGOL-based simulation language. *Communications of the ACM*, 9(9):671–678, September 1966. [SIMULA; programming languages] cited in F.P (p. xx), F.D (p. 743)

[438] F. d'Amore and P. G. Franciosa. On the optimal binary plane partition for sets of isoteric rectangles. *Information Processing Letters*, 44(5):255–259, December 1992. [regions; rectangles; BSP tree]

[439] S. P. Dandamudi and P. G. Sorenson. Performance of a modified *k-d* tree. Department of Computational Science Technical Report 84–10, University of Saskatchewan, Saskatoon, Canada, 1984. [points; k-d tree]

[440] S. P. Dandamudi and P. G. Sorenson. An empirical performance comparison of some variations of the *k-d* tree and *BD* tree. *International Journal of Computer and Information Sciences*, 14(3):135–159, June 1985. [points; BD-tree; k-d tree] cited in D.2.6.2, F.1.5.2.6 (p. 82)

[441] S. P. Dandamudi and P. G. Sorenson. Algorithms for BD trees. *Software—Practice and Experience*, 16(12):1077–1096, December 1986. [points; BD-tree] cited in D.2.6.2, D.2.8.1.s, F.1.5.2.6 (pp. 81–82), F.1.5.2.6.s (p. 767)

[442] S. P. Dandamudi and P. G. Sorenson. Performance analysis of partial match search algorithms for BD trees. *Software—Practice and Experience*, 18(1):83–105, January 1988. [points; BD-tree] cited in F.1.5.2.6 (p. 82)

[443] S. P. Dandamudi and P. G. Sorenson. Improved partial match search algorithms for BD trees. *The Computer Journal*, 34(5):415–422, October 1991. [points; BD-tree] cited in F.1.5.2.6 (p. 82)

[444] A. Das, J. Gehrke, and M. Riedewald. Approximation techniques for spatial data. In *Proceedings of the ACM SIGMOD Conference*, pages 695–706, Paris, France, June 2004. [spatial join; range query; spatial query optimization; selectivity estimation]

[445] S. Dasgupta. Performance guarantees for hierarchical clustering. In *Proceedings of the 15th Annual Conference on Computational Learning Theory (COLT 2002)*, J. Kivinen and R. H. Sloan, eds., vol. 2375 of Springer-Verlag Lecture Notes in Computer Science, pages 351–363, Sydney, Australia, July 2002. [metric spaces; k-center problem] cited in F.4.5.3.4 (pp. 622–623)

[446] E. Davis. *Representing and acquiring geographic knowledge*. PhD thesis, Department of Computer Science, Yale University, New Haven, CT, 1984. [spatial reasoning]

[447] L. S. Davis and N. Roussopoulos. Approximate pattern matching in a pattern database system. *Information Systems*, 5(2):107–119, 1980. [regions] cited in A.1.4, D.1.3, F.2.4 (p. 425)

[448] W. A. Davis. Hybrid use of hashing techniques for spatial data. In *Proceedings of Auto-Carto London*, vol. 1, pages 127–135, London, United Kingdom, September 1986. [regions]

[449] W. A. Davis and X. Wang. A new approach to linear quadtrees. In *Proceedings of Graphics Interface'85*, pages 195–202, Montréal, Canada, May 1985. [regions; region quadtree]

[450] M. De Cock and E. E. Kerre. Approximate equality is no fuzzy equality. In *Proceedings of EUSFLAT 2001*, pages 369–371, Leicester, United Kingdom, September 2001. [fuzzy logic; equivalence relation; approximate nearest neighbor] cited in F.4.5.8 (p. 651)

[451] F. De Coulon and O. Johnsen. Adaptive block scheme for source coding of black-and-white facsimile. *Electronics Letters*, 12(3):61–62, February 1976. Also see erratum, *Electronics Letters* 12(6):152, March 18, 1976. [regions; MX quadtree] cited in A.2.2, D.2.6.1, F.1.4.2.1 (p. 40)

[452] L. De Floriani. Surface representations based on triangular grids. *Visual Computer*, 3(1):27–50, February 1987. [surfaces; survey] cited in D.5.6, F.2.2.4 (p. 400)

[453] L. De Floriani. Personal communication. 2004. [lines; triangulations; PM quadtree] cited in F.2.2.2.6 (p. 367)

[454] L. De Floriani, B. Falcidieno, G. Nagy, and C. Pienovi. A hierarchical structure for surface approximation. *Computers & Graphics*, 8(2):183–193, 1984. [surfaces; ternary hierarchical triangular decomposition] cited in D.5.6, F.2.2.4 (p. 402)

[455] L. De Floriani, B. Falcidieno, G. Nagy, and C. Pienovi. Efficient selection, storage and retrieval of irregularly distributed elevation data. *Computers & Geosciences*, 11(6):667–673, 1985. [surfaces; ternary hierarchical triangular decomposition] cited in D.5.6, F.2.2.4 (p. 402)

[456] L. De Floriani, B. Falcidieno, G. Nagy, and C. Pienovi. On sorting triangles in a Delaunay tessellation. *Algorithmica*, 6(4):522–532, 1991. [regions; triangulations]

[457] L. De Floriani and A. Hui. Data structures for simplicial complexes: an analysis and a comparison. In *Proceedings of the Third Eurographics Symposium on Geometry Processing*, M. Desbrun and H. Pottmann, eds., pages 119–128, Vienna, Austria, July 2005. [surfaces; winged-edge representation; triangle meshes; nonmanifold objects; boundary model (BRep); survey] cited in F.2.2.1.1 (p. 316)

[458] L. De Floriani and P. Magillo. Horizon computation on a hierarchical triangulated terrain model. *The Visual Computer, International Journal of Computer Graphics*, 11(3):134–149, 1995. [surfaces; triangulated irregular network (TIN)]

[459] L. De Floriani, P. Magillo, and E. Puppo. Building and traversing a surface at variable resolution. In *Proceedings IEEE Visualization'97*, R. Yagel and H. Hagen, eds., pages 103–110, Phoenix, AZ, October 1997. [surfaces; multiresolution modeling] cited in F.2.2.3.4 (p. 399)

[460] L. De Floriani, P. Magillo, and E. Puppo. Multiresolution representation and reconstruction of triangulated surfaces. In *Advances in Visual Form Analysis: Proceedings of the 3rd International Workshop on Visual Form (IWVF3)*, C. Arcelli, L. Cordella, and G. Sanniti di Baja, eds., pages 140–149. World Scientific, Capri, Italy, May 1997. [surfaces; triangulations; multitriangulation] cited in F.2.2.3.4 (p. 399)

[461] L. De Floriani, P. Magillo, and E. Puppo. VARIANT; a system for terrain modeling at variable resolution. *GeoInformatica*, 4(3):287–315, October 2000. [surfaces; multiresolution modeling] cited in F.2.2.3.4 (p. 399)

[462] L. De Floriani, P. Marzano, and E. Puppo. Multiresolution models for topographic surface description. *The Visual Computer*, 12(7):317–345, August 1996. [surfaces; multiresolution modeling] cited in F.1.7.1.6.5 (p. 127)

[463] L. De Floriani and E. Puppo. A hierarchical triangle-based model for terrain description. In *Proceedings of Theories and Methods of Spatio-Temporal Reasoning in Geographic Space, International Conference GIS—From Space to Territory: Theories and Methods of Spatio-Temporal Reasoning*, A. U. Frank, I. Campari, and U. Formentini, eds., vol. 639 of Springer-Verlag Lecture Notes in Computer Science, pages 236–251, Pisa, Italy, September 1992. [surfaces; triangulations] cited in F.2.2.4 (p. 402)

[464] L. De Floriani and E. Puppo. An on-line algorithm for constrained Delaunay triangulation. *CVGIP: Graphical Models and Image Processing*, 54(3):290–300, July 1992. [regions; constrained Delaunay triangulation]

[465] L. De Floriani and E. Puppo. Hierarchical triangulation for multiresolution surface description. *ACM Transactions on Graphics*, 14(4):363–411, October 1995. [surfaces; triangulations; multiresolution modeling] cited in F.2.2.4 (p. 402)

[466] W. De Pauw and L. Weyten. Multiple storage adaptive multi-trees. *IEEE Transactions on Computer-Aided Design*, 9(3):248–252, March 1990. [multiple storage quadtree] cited in F.3.4.3 (p. 481)

[467] M. F. Deering. Geometry compression. In *Proceedings of the SIGGRAPH'95 Conference*, pages 13–20, Los Angeles, August 1995. [surfaces; triangle strip] cited in F.2.2.3.4 (p. 399)

[468] R. D. Degroat and R. A. Roberts. Efficient numerically stabilized rank-one eigenstructure updating. *IEEE Transactions on Acoustic Signal Processing*, 38(2):301–316, February 1990. [high-dimensional data; Singular Value Decomposition (SVD)] cited in F.4.6.4.1 (p. 674)

[469] M. DeHaemer Jr. and M. J. Zyda. Simplification of objects rendered by polygonal approximations. *Computers & Graphics*, 15(2):175–184, 1991. [surfaces; simplification; region quadtree; multiresolution modeling] cited in F.2.2.4 (p. 402)

[470] F. Dehne and A. R. Chaplin. Hypercube algorithms for parallel processing of pointer-based quadtrees. *Computer Vision and*

Image Understanding, 62(1):1–10, July 1995. [regions; parallel processing] cited in F.P (p. xviii), F.1.5 (p. 49)

[471] F. Dehne, A. Fabri, M. Nassar, A. Rau-Chaplin, and R. Valiveti. Construction of d-dimensional hyperoctrees on a hypercube multiprocessor. *Journal of Parallel and Distributed Computing*, 23(2):256–261, November 1994. [hypervolumes; *d*-dimensional quadtree; parallel processing]

[472] F. Dehne, A. G. Ferreira, and A. Rau-Chaplin. Efficient parallel construction and manipulation of quadtrees. In *Proceedings of the 20th International Conference on Parallel Processing*, pages 255–262, Austin, TX, August 1991. [regions; region quadtree; parallel processing]

[473] F. Dehne and H. Noltemeier. Voronoi trees and clustering problems. *Information Systems*, 12(2):171–175, 1987. [metric spaces; Voronoi tree; gh-tree] cited in F.4.5.3.3 (pp. 618, 621)

[474] B. Delaunay. Sur la sphère vide. *Izvestia Akademia Nauk SSSR, VII Seria, Otdelenie Matematicheskii i Estestvennyka Nauk*, 7(6):793–800, October 1934. [surfaces; Voronoi diagram; Delaunay triangulation (DT)] cited in D.5.6, F.2.2.1.4 (p. 347)

[475] M. A. DeLoura, ed. *Game Programming Gems*. Charles River Media, Rockland, MA, 2000. [game programming; general] cited in F.P (p. xvii)

[476] M. A. DeLoura, ed. *Game Programming Gems 2*. Charles River Media, Hingham, MA, 2001. [game programming; general] cited in F.P (p. xvii)

[477] R. A. DeMillo, S. C. Eisenstat, and R. J. Lipton. Preserving average proximity in arrays. *Communications of the ACM*, 21(3):228–231, March 1978. [array representation] cited in A.3.2.1, A.3.2.1.2.s, A.4.2.2, F.2.1.2.4 (p. 214)

[478] A. Dengel. Object-oriented representation of image space by puzzletrees. *SPIE Visual Communications and Image Processing*, 1606:20–30, 1991. [regions; X-Y tree; k-d tree; puzzletree; treemap] cited in F.2.1.2.9 (pp. 225, 228–230)

[479] A. Dengel. Self-adapting structuring and representation of space. Technical Report RR–91–22, Deutsches Forschungszentrum für Künstliche Intelligenz, Kaiserslautern, Germany, September 1991. [regions; X-Y tree; k-d tree; puzzletree; treemap] cited in F.1.5.1.4 (p. 66), F.2.1.2.9 (pp. 225, 228–230)

[480] A. Dengel. Syntactic analysis and representation of spatial structures by puzzletrees. *International Journal of Pattern Recognition and Artificial Intelligence*, 9(3):517–533, June 1995. [regions; X-Y tree; k-d tree; puzzletree; treemap] cited in F.2.1.2.9 (pp. 225, 228–230), F.4.4.3 (p. 572)

[481] T. DeRose, M. Kass, and T. Truong. Subdivision surfaces in character animation. In *Proceedings of the SIGGRAPH'98 Conference*, pages 85–94, Orlando, FL, July 1998. [surfaces; mesh simplification; hierarchical face clustering] cited in F.2.2.3.4 (p. 398)

[482] O. Devillers. Tools to study the efficiency of space subdivision structures for ray tracing. In *Proceedings of the PIXIM'89 Conference*, pages 467–481, Paris, France, September 1989. [volumes; ray tracing]

[483] O. Devillers and P.-M. Gandoin. Geometric compression for interactive transmission. In *Proceedings IEEE Visualization 2000*, C. Hansen, C. Johnson, and S. Bryson, eds., pages 319–326, Salt Lake City, UT, October 2000. [points; k-d tree; progressive transmission] cited in F.1.5.2.1 (p. 72), F.1.5.2.1.s (p. 764)

[484] L. Devroye. A note on the height of binary search trees. *Journal of the ACM*, 33(3):489–498, July 1986. [points; point quadtree] cited in F.1.4.1.1 (p. 30)

[485] L. Devroye. Branching processes in the analysis of the heights of trees. *Acta Informatica*, 24(3):277–298, 1987. [points; point quadtree] cited in F.1.4.1.1 (p. 30)

[486] L. Devroye and L. Laforest. An analysis of random d-dimensional quad trees. *SIAM Journal of Computing*, 19(5):821–832, October 1990. [points; point quadtree] cited in F.1.4.1.1 (p. 30)

[487] P. M. Dew, J. Dodsworth, and D. T. Morris. Systolic array architectures for high performance CAD/CAM workstations. In *Fundamental Algorithms for Computer Graphics*, R. A. Earnshaw, ed., pages 659–694. Springer-Verlag, Berlin, West Germany, 1985. [hardware]

[488] A. K. Dewdney. Storing images: a cat in a quad tree. In *The Turing Omnibus: 61 Excursions in Computer Science*, chapter 44, pages 290–295. Computer Science Press, Rockville, MD, 1989. [regions; region quadtree]

[489] D. J. DeWitt, N. Kabra, J. Luo, J. M. Patel, and J. B. Yu. Client-server Paradise. In *Proceedings of the 20th International Conference on Very Large Data Bases (VLDB)*, J. Bocca, M. Jarke, and C. Zaniolo, eds., pages 558–569, Santiago, Chile, September 1994. [regions; rectangles; R-tree; geographic information systems (GIS)] cited in F.2.1.5.2.4 (p. 294)

[490] M. Dickerson, C. A. Duncan, and M. T. Goodrich. K-d trees are better when cut on the longest side. In *Proceedings of the 8th Annual European Symposium on Algorithms (ESA 2000)*, M. Paterson, ed., vol. 1879 of Springer-Verlag Lecture Notes in Computer Science, pages 179–190, Saarbrücken, West Germany, September 2000. [points; BAR tree; k-d tree]

[491] E. W. Dijkstra. A note on two problems in connexion with graphs. *Numerische Mathematik*, 1:269–271, 1959. [graphs; shortest path algorithm; spatial networks] cited in F.4.1.6 (p. 509)

[492] M. B. Dillencourt and D. M. Mount. Personal communication. 1987. [regions; dynamic programming] cited in A.1.3.s, D.1.2.s, F.2.1.2.7.s (p. 783)

[493] M. B. Dillencourt and H. Samet. Using topological sweep to extract the boundaries of regions in maps represented by region quadtrees. *Algorithmica*, 15(1):82–102, January 1996. Also see *Proceedings of the Third International Symposium on Spatial Data Handling*, pages 65–77, Sydney, Australia, August 1988 and University of California at Irvine Information and Computer Science Technical Report ICS TR 91-01. [regions; topological sweep; boundary following; region quadtree] cited in A.4.3.2, A.4.3.2.s

[494] M. B. Dillencourt, H. Samet, and M. Tamminen. A general approach to connected-component labeling for arbitrary image representations. *Journal of the ACM*, 39(2):253–280, April 1992. Also see Corrigendum, *Journal of the ACM*, 39(4):985, October 1992 and University of Maryland Computer Science Technical Report TR–2303, August 1989. [regions; connected component labeling] cited in A.5.1.1, A.5.1.1.s, A.5.1.3, F.2.1.1.2 (p. 200)

[495] I. Dinstein, D. W. L. Yen, and M. D. Flickner. Handling memory overflow in connected component labeling applications. *IEEE Transactions on Pattern Analysis and Machine Intelligence*, 7(1):116–121, January 1985. [regions; connected component labeling] cited in A.5.1.1

[496] M. Dippe and J. Swensen. An adaptive subdivision algorithm and parallel architecture for realistic image synthesis. *Computer Graphics*, 18(3):149–158, July 1984. Also in *Proceedings of the SIGGRAPH'84 Conference*, Minneapolis, MN, July 1984. [hardware; ray tracing] cited in A.7.2.5

[497] G. L. Dirichlet. Über die Reduction der positiven quadratischen Formen mit drie unbestimmten ganzen Zahlen. *Journal für die Reine und Angewandte Mathematik*, 40(3):209–227, 1850. [points; regions; nearest neighbor; Voronoi diagram] cited in F.2.2.1.4 (p. 346)

[498] J.-P. Dittrich and B. Seeger. Data redundancy and duplicate detection in spatial join processing. In *Proceedings of the 16th IEEE International Conference on Data Engineering*, pages 535–546, San Diego, CA, February 2000. [spatial join; duplicate removal] cited in F.4.1.4 (p. 499)

[499] D. P. Dobkin. Computational geometry and computer graphics. *Proceedings of the IEEE*, 80(9):1400–1411, September 1992. [computational geometry; computer graphics; survey]

[500] D. P. Dobkin and D. G. Kirkpatrick. Fast detection of polyhedral intersections. *Theoretical Computer Science*, 27(3):241–253, December 1983. [volumes] cited in A.7.3, A.7.3.s

[501] D. P. Dobkin and M. J. Laszlo. Primitives for the manipulation of three-dimensional subdivisions. *Algorithmica*, 4(1):3–32, 1989. [volumes] cited in F.2.2.1.7 (p. 353)

[502] D. P. Dobkin and R. J. Lipton. Multidimensional searching problems. *SIAM Journal on Computing*, 5(2):181–186, June 1976. Also see *Proceedings of the 6th Annual ACM Symposium on the Theory of Computing*, pages 310–316, Seattle, WA, April 1974. [points; point location]

[503] L. J. Doctor and J. G. Torborg. Display techniques for octree-encoded objects. *IEEE Computer Graphics and Applications*, 1(1):29–38, July 1981. [volumes; region octree] cited in A.2.1.2, A.7.1.4

[504] D. Dori and M. Ben-Bassat. Circumscribing a convex polygon by a polygon of fewer sides with minimal area addition. *Computer Vision, Graphics, and Image Processing*, 24(2):131–159, November 1983. [regions; minimum bounding box] cited in F.2.1.1 (p. 195)

[505] L. Dorst and R. P. W. Duin. Spirograph theory: a framework for calculations on digitized straight lines. *IEEE Transactions on Pattern Analysis and Machine Intelligence*, 6(5):632–639, September 1984. [lines]

[506] L. Dorst and A. W. M. Smeulders. Discrete representation of straight lines. *IEEE Transactions on Pattern Analysis and Machine Intelligence*, 6(4):450–463, July 1984. [lines; chain code]

[507] D. H. Douglas. It makes me so CROSS. In *Introductory Readings in Geographic Information Systems*, D. J. Peuquet and D. F. Marble, eds., chapter 21, pages 303–307. Taylor & Francis, London, United Kingdom, 1990. Originally published as Internal Memorandum, Harvard University Laboratory for Computer Graphics and Spatial Analysis, 1974. [lines; line intersection problem] cited in F.2.2.3.1 (p. 385)

[508] D. H. Douglas and T. K. Peucker. Algorithms for the reduction of the number of points required to represent a digitized line or its caricature. *The Canadian Cartographer*, 10(2):112–122, December 1973. [lines; generalization; Douglas-Peucker algorithm] cited in F.2.2.3.1 (p. 383)

[509] J. R. Driscoll, N. Sarnak, D. D. Sleator, and R. E. Tarjan. Making data structures persistent. *Journal of Computer and System Sciences*, 38(1):86–124, February 1989. [persistent search tree] cited in D.3.2.4, F.3.1.4 (p. 445)

[510] S. D'Silva. Personal communication. 2005. [metric space embedding; locality sensitive hashing (LSH)] cited in F.4.7.4 (pp. 712, 716)

[511] T. Dubitzki, A. Wu, and A. Rosenfeld. Parallel region property computation by active quadtree networks. *IEEE Transactions on Pattern Analysis and Machine Intelligence*, 3(6):626–633, November 1981. [regions; parallel processing]

[512] A. Duch and C. Martinez. On the average performance of orthogonal range search in multidimensional data structures. *Journal of Algorithms*, 44(1):226–245, July 2002. [points; k-d tree; range query]

[513] M. Duchaineau, M. Wolinsky, D. E. Sigeti, M. C. Miller, C. Aldrich, and M. B. Mineev-Weinstein. ROAMing terrain: real-time optimally adapting meshes. In *Proceedings IEEE Visualization'97*, R. Yagel and H. Hagen, eds., pages 81–88, Phoenix, AZ, October 1997. [surfaces; restricted bintree; triangle meshes] cited in F.1.5.1.4 (p. 64), F.2.2.3.4 (p. 399), F.2.2.4 (p. 406)

[514] R. O. Duda, P. E. Hart, and D. G. Stork. *Pattern Classification and Scene Analysis*. Wiley Interscience, New York, second edition, 2000. [pattern recognition; general] cited in F.1 (p. 4), F.1.5.1.4 (p. 62), F.2.2.3.1 (p. 383), F.4 (p. 486)

[515] T. Duff. Compositing 3-d rendered images. *Computer Graphics*, 19(3):41–44, July 1985. (also *Proceedings of the SIGGRAPH'85 Conference, San Francisco*, July 1985). [regions; z-buffer; image synthesis] cited in A.7.1.6

[516] C. A. Duncan, M. Goodrich, and S. Kobourov. Balanced aspect ratio trees and their use for drawing very large graphs. In *Graph Drawing—6th International Symposium, GD'98*, S. H. Whitesides, ed., vol. 1547 of Springer-Verlag Lecture Notes in Computer Science, pages 111–124, Montréal, Canada, August 1998. [points; BAR tree] cited in F.1.5.1.4 (p. 64), F.1.5.2.7.s (p. 767)

[517] C. A. Duncan, M. Goodrich, and S. Kobourov. Balanced aspect ratio trees: combining the advantages of *k*-d trees and octrees. *Journal of Algorithms*, 38(1):303–333, January 2001. Also see *Proceedings of the 10th Annual ACM-SIAM Symposium on Discrete Algorithms*, pages 300–309, Baltimore, MD, January 1999. [points; BAR tree; k-d tree; approximate nearest neighbor] cited in F.1.5.1.4 (pp. 64–65), F.4.1.7 (p. 516), F.4.3 (pp. 563, 565), F.1.5.1.4.s (p. 764), F.1.5.2.7.s (p. 767)

[518] M. J. Dürst and T. L. Kunii. Error-free image compression with gray scale quadtrees and its optimization. In *Proceedings of the International Workshop on Discrete Algorithms and Complexity*, pages 115–121, Fukuoka, Japan, November 1989. Also University of Tokyo Information Science Technical Report 88–024, December 1988. [regions; compression]

[519] M. J. Dürst and T. L. Kunii. Integrated polytrees: a generalized model for the integration of spatial decomposition and boundary representation. In *Theory and Practice of Geometric Modelling*, W. Strasser and H. P. Seidel, eds., pages 329–348. Springer-Verlag, Berlin, Germany, 1989. Also University of Tokyo Department of Information Science Technical Report 88–002, January 1988. [volumes; PM octree; polytree] cited in F.2.2.2.7 (pp. 371–372)

[520] G. Dutton. Geodesic modeling of planetary relief. *Cartographica*, 21(2&3):188–207, Summer & Autumn 1984. [surfaces; triacon hierarchy] cited in D.1.4.1, D.5.6, F.2.1.2.11 (pp. 231–232), F.2.2.4 (p. 401)

[521] G. Dutton. Locational properties of quaternary triangular meshes. In *Proceedings of the 4th International Symposium on Spatial Data Handling*, vol. 2, pages 901–910, Zurich, Switzerland, July 1990. [regions; triangular quadtree]

[522] N. Dwyer. Implementing and using BSP trees, fast 3-d sorting. *Dr. Dobb's Journal*, (232):46–49, 100–102, July 1995. [volumes; BSP tree]

[523] C. R. Dyer. Computing the Euler number of an image from its quadtree. *Computer Graphics and Image Processing*, 13(3):270–276, July 1980. Also University of Maryland Computer Science Technical Report TR–769, May 1979. [regions; Euler number; region quadtree] cited in A.5.3

[524] C. R. Dyer. A VLSI pyramid machine for hierarchical parallel image processing. In *Proceedings of the IEEE Conference on Pattern Recognition and Image Processing'81*, pages 381–386, Dallas, TX, August 1981. [hardware; parallel processing] cited in F.P (p. xviii), F.1.5 (p. 49)

[525] C. R. Dyer. The space efficiency of quadtrees. *Computer Graphics and Image Processing*, 19(4):335–348, August 1982. Also University of Illinois at Chicago Circle Information Engineering Technical Report KSL 46, March 1980. [regions; region quadtree; space requirements] cited in A.1.2, A.1.2.s, A.6.5.3.s, A.6.6, A.8.2.2, A.9.3.4, D.1.5, D.1.5.s, F.2.1.2.4.s (p. 780)

[526] C. R. Dyer, A. Rosenfeld, and H. Samet. Region representation: boundary codes from quadtrees. *Communications of the ACM*, 23(3):171–179, March 1980. Also University of Maryland Computer Science Technical Report TR–732, February 1979. [regions; chain code; region quadtree; boundary following] cited in A.4.3.2

[527] C. M. Eastman. Representations for space planning. *Communications of the ACM*, 13(4):242–250, April 1970. [regions; computer-aided design (CAD); robotics] cited in A.1.4, D.1.3, F.2.4 (p. 425)

[528] C. M. Eastman. Optimal bucket size for nearest neighbor searching in k-d trees. *Information Processing Letters*, 12(4):165–167, August 1981. [points; k-d tree; nearest neighbor]

[529] C. M. Eastman and K. Weiler. Geometric modeling using Euler operators. In *Proceedings of the 1st Conference on Computer Graphics in CAD/CAM Systems*, pages 248–259, Cambridge, MA, May 1979. [volumes] cited in D.5.4

[530] C. M. Eastman and M. Zemankova. Partially specified nearest neighbor searches using k-d-trees. *Information Processing Letters*, 15(2):53–56, September 1982. [points; k-d tree; depth-first nearest neighbor algorithm; partial match query] cited in F.4.1.7 (p. 516), F.4.2 (p. 517), F.4.2.4.s (p. 844)

[531] M. Edahiro, I. Kokubo, and T. Asano. A new point-location algorithm and its practical efficiency—comparison with existing algorithms. *ACM Transactions on Graphics*, 3(2):86–109, April 1984. [points]

[532] S. Edelman and E. Shapiro. Quadtrees in concurrent Prolog. In *Proceedings of the 14th IEEE International Conference on Parallel Processing*, pages 544–551, St. Charles, IL, August 1985. [regions; region quadtree; concurrent Prolog] cited in F.P (p. xviii), F.1.5 (p. 49)

[533] H. Edelsbrunner. Dynamic data structures for orthogonal intersection queries. Institute for Information Processing Technical Report 59, Technical University of Graz, Graz, Austria, October 1980. [rectangles]

[534] H. Edelsbrunner. Dynamic rectangle intersection searching. Institute for Information Processing Technical Report 47, Technical University of Graz, Graz, Austria, February 1980. [rectangles; interval tree; rectangle intersection problem] cited in D.3.2.2, D.4.3.2, F.2.1.3.3.1 (p. 244), F.2.1.3.3.2 (p. 253), F.2.1.5.2.4 (p. 296), F.3.1.2 (p. 435), F.3.4.1.3 (p. 473)

[535] H. Edelsbrunner. A note on dynamic range searching. *Bulletin of the EATCS*, (15):34–40, October 1981. [rectangles; range priority tree] cited in D.2.5, F.1.1 (p. 9), F.1.3 (p. 23), F.1.3.s (p. 751)

[536] H. Edelsbrunner. Intersection problems in computational geometry. Institute for Information Processing Technical Report 93, Technical University of Graz, Graz, Austria, June 1982. [rectangles; rectangle intersection problem] cited in D.3.2.4, D.3.2.4.s, F.3.1.4 (p. 444), F.3.1.4.s (pp. 822–823)

[537] H. Edelsbrunner. A new approach to rectangle intersections: part I. *International Journal of Computer Mathematics*, 13(3–4):209–219, 1983. [rectangles; rectangle intersection problem] cited in D.3.2.2, D.4.3.2, F.2.1.3.3.1 (p. 244), F.2.1.3.3.2 (p. 253), F.2.1.5.2.4 (p. 296), F.3.1.2 (p. 435), F.3.4.1.3 (p. 473)

[538] H. Edelsbrunner. A new approach to rectangle intersections: part II. *International Journal of Computer Mathematics*, 13(3–4):221–229, 1983. [rectangles; interval tree; rectangle intersection problem] cited in D.3.2.2, D.4.3.2, F.2.1.3.3.1 (p. 244), F.2.1.3.3.2 (p. 253), F.2.1.5.2.4 (p. 296), F.3.1.2 (p. 435), F.3.4.1.3 (p. 473)

[539] H. Edelsbrunner. Key-problems and key methods in computational geometry. In *Proceedings of the Symposium of Theoretical Aspects of Computer Science (STACS84)*, M. Fontet and K. Mehlhorn, eds., vol. 166 of Springer-Verlag Lecture Notes in Computer Science, pages 1–13, Paris, France, April 1984. [computational geometry; survey] cited in D.P, D.4, D.4.2.3, D.4.3, F.P (p. xix)

[540] H. Edelsbrunner. *Algorithms in Combinatorial Geometry*. Springer-Verlag, Berlin, West Germany, 1987. [computational geometry; survey] cited in D.P, D.4.3, F.P (p. xix), F.1.5.3 (p. 88), F.2.2.1.7 (p. 353), F.1.5.3.s (p. 768)

[541] H. Edelsbrunner, L. J. Guibas, and J. Stolfi. Optimal point location in a monotone subdivision. *SIAM Journal on Computing*, 15(2):317–340, May 1986. [regions; point location; layered dag] cited in D.P, D.3.2.2, D.4.3, D.4.3.2, D.4.3.2.s, F.1.5.1.4 (p. 69), F.2.1.2.8 (p. 224), F.2.1.3.3 (p. 242), F.2.1.3.3.1 (p. 245), F.2.1.3.3.2 (p. 248), F.3.1.2 (p. 435), F.2.1.3.3.1.s (pp. 788–789), F.2.1.3.3.2.s (p. 789)

[542] H. Edelsbrunner and H. A. Maurer. On the intersection of orthogonal objects. *Information Processing Letters*, 13(4,5):177–181, End 1981. [rectangles; rectangle intersection problem] cited in D.3.2.4, D.3.2.4.s, F.3.1.4 (p. 444), F.3.1.4.s (pp. 822–823)

[543] H. Edelsbrunner, J. O'Rourke, and R. Seidel. Constructing arrangements of lines and hyperplanes with applications. *SIAM Journal on Computing*, 15(2):341–363, May 1986. [rectangles; halfplanar range search; arrangements] cited in D.3.3.s, F.1.5.3 (p. 88), F.3.2.s (p. 824)

[544] H. Edelsbrunner and M. H. Overmars. Batched dynamic solutions to decomposable searching problems. *Journal of Algorithms*, 6(4):515–542, December 1985. [rectangles; rectangle intersection problem; streaming] cited in D.3.2, D.3.3, F.3.1 (p. 429), F.3.2 (p. 451)

[545] H. Edelsbrunner and T.-S. Tan. An upper bound for conforming Delaunay triangulations. *Discrete & Computational Geometry*, 104(2):197–213, 1993. [surfaces; conforming Delaunay triangulation] cited in F.2.2.1.5 (p. 351)

[546] H. Edelsbrunner and E. Welzl. Halfplanar range search in linear space and $o(n^{0.695})$ query time. *Information Processing Letters*, 23(6):289–293, December 1986. [points; halfplanar range search; conjugation tree] cited in F.1.5.3 (p. 88)

[547] M. J. Egenhofer and A. U. Frank. Towards a spatial query language: user interface considerations. In *Proceedings of the 14th International Conference on Very Large Databases (VLDB)*, F. Bachillon and D. J. DeWitt, eds., pages 124–133, Los Angeles, August 1988. [user interface]

[548] J. El-Sana and E. Bachmat. Optimized view-dependent rendering for large polygonal datasets. In *Proceedings IEEE Visualization 2002*, R. Moorehead, M. Gross, and K. I. Joy, eds., pages 77–84, Boston, October 2002. [surfaces; polygon simplification; k-d tree]

[549] J. El-Sana, F. Evans, A. Kalaiah, A. Varshney, S. Skiena, and E. Azanli. Efficiently computing and updating triangle strips for real-time rendering. *Computer-Aided Design*, 32(13):753–772, November 2000. [surfaces; triangle strip] cited in F.2.2.3.4 (p. 399)

[550] J. El-Sana and A. Varshney. Topology simplification for polygonal virtual environments. *IEEE Transactions on Visualization and Computer Graphics*, 4(2):133–144, June 1998. Also see *Proceedings IEEE Visualization'97*, R. Yagel and H. Hagen, eds., pages 403–410, Phoenix, AZ, October 1997. [surfaces; surface simplification; topology simplification] cited in F.2.2.3.4 (pp. 392–393)

[551] J. El-Sana and A. Varshney. Generalized view-dependent simplification. *Computer Graphics Forum*, 18(3):83–94, September 1999. [surfaces; surface simplification; view-dependent simplification] cited in F.2.2.3.4 (p. 395)

[552] G. Elber and M. Shpitalni. Octree creation via C. S. G. definition. *Visual Computer*, 4(2):53–64, July 1988. [volumes; constructive solid geometry (CSG); MX octree]

[553] E. W. Elcock, I. Gargantini, and T. R. Walsh. Triangular decomposition. *Image and Vision Computing*, 5(3):225–231, August 1987. [regions]

[554] R. Elmasri and S. B. Navathe. *Fundamentals of Database Systems*. Addison-Wesley, Upper Saddle River, NJ, fourth edition, 2004. [database systems; general] cited in F.2.2.1.1 (p. 317), F.2.2.1.2 (p. 329)

[555] G. A. Elmes. Data structures for quadtree-addressed entities on a spatial relational database. In *Proceedings of the International Geographic Information Systems (IGIS) Symposium: The Research Agenda*, vol. 2, pages 177–179, Arlington, VA, November 1987. [regions]

[556] D. J. Elzinga and D. W. Hearn. Geometrical solutions for some minimax location problems. *Transportation Science*, 6(4):379–394, November 1972. [minimum bounding hypersphere] cited in F.4.4.2.s (p. 852)

[557] D. J. Elzinga and D. W. Hearn. The minimum covering sphere problem. *Management Science*, 19(1):96–104, September 1972. [minimum bounding hypersphere] cited in F.4.4.2.s (p. 852)

[558] P. van Emde Boas. Preserving order in a forest in less than logarithmic time and linear space. *Information Processing Letters*, 6(3):80–82, June 1977. [point location] cited in F.2.1.2.4.s (p. 781)

[559] R. J. Enbody and H. C. Du. Dynamic hashing schemes. *ACM Computing Surveys*, 20(2):85–113, June 1988. [points; dynamic hashing; survey]

[560] J. Enderle, M. Hampel, and T. Seidl. Joining interval data in relational databases. In *Proceedings of the ACM SIGMOD Conference*, pages 683–694, Paris, France, June 2004. [intervals; spatial join]

[561] D. Eppstein, M. T. Goodrich, and J. Z. Sun. The skip quadtree: a simple dynamic data structure for multidimensional data. In *Proceedings of the 21st ACM Symposium on Computational Geometry*, pages 296–305, Pisa, Italy, June 2005. [points; skip quadtree; skip list; PR quadtree] cited in F.1.3 (p. 27)

[562] D. Eppstein, G. F. Italiano, R. Tamassia, R. E. Tarjan, J. Westbrook, and M. Yung. Maintenance of a minimum spanning forest in a dynamic planar graph. *Journal of Algorithms*, 13(1):33–54, March 1992. [regions; minimum spanning forest] cited in F.2.1.3.3.2 (p. 253)

[563] J. Erickson. Nice point sets can have nasty Delaunay triangulations. In *Proceedings of the 17th Annual Symposium on Computational Geometry*, pages 96–105, Medford, MA, June 2001. [volumes; Delaunay triangulation (DT)] cited in F.2.2.1.6 (p. 352)

[564] C. Ericson. *Real-Time Collision Detection*. Morgan-Kaufmann, San Francisco, 2005. [game programming; collision detection; general] cited in F.P (p. xix), F.2.1.1 (p. 195)

[565] C. Esperanca and H. Samet. Vertex representations and their applications in computer graphics. *The Visual Computer*, 14(5/6):240–256, 1998. [volumes; regions; vertex representation; orthogonal polygon] cited in F.2.1.1 (p. 195), F.2.3.3 (p. 421)

[566] C. Esperança. *Orthogonal objects and their application in spatial database*. PhD thesis, Computer Science Department, University of Maryland, College Park, MD, December 1995. Also Computer Science Technical Report TR–3566. [regions; vertex representation; spatial query optimization] cited in F.2.1.1 (p. 195), F.2.3 (p. 409), F.2.3.3 (p. 417)

[567] C. Esperança and H. Samet. Representing orthogonal multidimensional objects by vertex lists. In *Aspects of Visual Form Processing: Proceedings of the 2nd International Workshop on Visual Form (IWVF2)*, C. Arcelli, L. P. Cordella, and G. Sanniti di Baja, eds., pages 209–220, Capri, Italy, May 1994. World Scientific. [volumes; vertex representation] cited in F.2.1.1 (p. 195), F.2.3 (p. 409), F.2.3.3 (pp. 417, 421, 423), F.2.3.3.s (p. 818)

[568] C. Esperança and H. Samet. Spatial database programming using SAND. In *Proceedings of the 7th International Symposium on Spatial Data Handling*, M. J. Kraak and M. Molenaar, eds., vol. 2, pages A29–A42, Delft, The Netherlands, August 1996. International Geographical Union Commission on Geographic Information Systems, Association for Geographical Information. [SAND; scripting language; Tcl; programming languages] cited in F.P (p. xviii)

[569] C. Esperança and H. Samet. Orthogonal polygons as bounding structures in filter-refine query processing strategies. In *Advances in Spatial Databases—5th International Symposium, SSD'97*, M. Scholl and A. Voisard, eds., vol. 1262 of Springer-Verlag Lecture Notes in Computer Science, pages 197–220, Berlin, Germany, July 1997. [regions; vertex representation; orthogonal polygon; filter-and-refine] cited in F.2.1.1 (p. 195), F.2.3 (p. 409), F.2.3.3 (p. 421)

[570] C. Esperança and H. Samet. Experience with SAND/Tcl: a scripting tool for spatial databases. *Journal of Visual Languages and Computing*, 13(2):229–255, April 2002. [SAND; scripting language; Tcl; programming languages] cited in F.P (p. xviii)

[571] K. Esselink. The order of Appel's algorithm. *Information Processing Letters*, 41(3):141–147, March 1992. [points; particle simulation; N-body problem] cited in F.2.4 (p. 426)

[572] M. Ester, H.-P. Kriegel, and J. Sander. Spatial data mining: a database approach. In *Advances in Spatial Databases—5th International Symposium, SSD'97*, M. Scholl and A. Voisard, eds., vol. 1262 of Springer-Verlag Lecture Notes in Computer Science, pages 47–66, Berlin, Germany, July 1997. [points; spatial data mining]

[573] D. M. Esterling and J. Van Rosedale. An intersection algorithm for moving parts. In *Proceedings of the NASA Symposium on Computer-Aided Geometry Modeling*, pages 119–123, Hampton, VA, April 1983. [surfaces]

[574] G. Evangelidis, D. Lomet, and B. Salzberg. Node deletion in the hB$^\Pi$-tree. Computer Science Technical Report NU–CCS–94–04, Northeastern University, Boston, 1994. [points; hB-tree] cited in F.1.7.1.4 (p. 109)

[575] G. Evangelidis, D. Lomet, and B. Salzberg. The hB$^\Pi$-tree: a multi-attribute index supporting concurrency, recovery and node consolidation. *VLDB Journal*, 6(1):1–25, January 1997. Also see *Proceedings of the 21st International Conference on Very Large Data Bases (VLDB)*, U. Dayal, P. M. D. Gray, and S. Nishio, eds., pages 551–561, Zurich, Switzerland, September 1995. [points; hB-tree; concurrency] cited in F.1.7.1.4 (pp. 106, 108–109), F.4.4.5 (p. 581)

[576] W. Evans, D. Kirkpatrick, and G. Townsend. Right-triangulated irregular networks. *Algorithmica*, 30(2):264–286, 2001. Also University of Arizona Computer Science Technical Report 97–09, May 1997. [surfaces; restricted bintree; triangle meshes] cited in F.1.5.1.4 (p. 64), F.2.2.3.4 (p. 399), F.2.2.4 (pp. 406, 408)

[577] F. Fabbrini and C. Montani. Autumnal quadtrees. *Computer Journal*, 29(5):472–474, October 1986. [regions; region quadtree]

[578] V. N. Faddeeva. *Computational Methods of Linear Algebra*. Dover, New York, 1959. [linear algebra; general] cited in D.2.6.1.s, F.1.4.2.1.s (p. 757)

[579] R. Fagin, J. Nievergelt, N. Pippenger, and H. R. Strong. Extendible hashing—a fast access method for dynamic files. *ACM Transactions on Database Systems*, 4(3):315–344, September 1979. [points; extendible hashing] cited in D.2.7, D.2.8.1, D.2.8.2, F.1.4.2.2 (p. 46), F.1.7.2.1 (p. 135), F.1.7.2.3 (p. 140), F.1.7.3 (p. 163), F.B (p. 730)

[580] J. S. Falby, M. J. Zyda, D. R. Pratt, and R. L. Mackey. NPSNET: hierarchical data structures for real-time three-dimensional visual simulation. *Computers & Graphics*, 17(1):65–69, January/February 1993. [regions]

[581] C. Faloutsos. Multiattribute hashing using gray codes. In *Proceedings of the ACM SIGMOD Conference*, pages 227–238, Washington, DC, May 1986. [points; Gray code] cited in D.2.7, F.1.6 (pp. 93–94), F.2.1.2.4 (p. 216)

[582] C. Faloutsos. Gray codes for partial match and range queries. *IEEE Transactions on Software Engineering*, 14(10):1381–1393, October 1988. [points; double Gray order; partial match query] cited in D.2.7, D.2.7.s, F.1.6 (p. 94), F.1.6.s (p. 768)

[583] C. Faloutsos. Analytical results on the quadtree decomposition of arbitrary rectangles. *Pattern Recognition Letters*, 13(1):31–40, January 1992. [regions; region quadtree; space requirements]

[584] C. Faloutsos and V. Gaede. Analysis of n-dimensional quadtrees using the Hausdorff fractal dimension. In *Proceedings of the 22nd International Conference on Very Large Data Bases (VLDB)*, T. M. Vijayaraman, A. P. Buchmann, C. Mohan, and N. L. Sarda, eds., pages 40–50, Mumbai (Bombay), India, September 1996. [points; fractal dimension]

[585] C. Faloutsos, H. V. Jagadish, and Y. Manolopoulos. Analysis of the n-dimensional quadtree decomposition for arbitrary hyperrectangles. *IEEE Transactions on Knowledge and Data Engineering*, 9(3):373–383, May/June 1997. [hypervolumes; d-dimensional quadtree; space requirements]

[586] C. Faloutsos and I. Kamel. Beyond uniformity and independence: analysis of R-trees using the concept of fractal dimension. In *Proceedings of the 13th ACM SIGACT-SIGMOD-SIGART Symposium on Principles of Database Systems (PODS)*, pages 4–13, Minneapolis, MN, May 1994. [points; R-tree; fractal dimension]

[587] C. Faloutsos and K.-I. Lin. FastMap: a fast algorithm for indexing, data-mining and visualization of traditional and multimedia datasets. In *Proceedings of the ACM SIGMOD Conference*, pages 163–174, San Jose, CA, May 1995. [metric space embedding; FastMap] cited in F.4 (p. 489), F.4.4.3 (p. 572), F.4.7 (p. 686), F.4.7.2.4 (p. 696), F.4.7.3.1 (p. 697), F.4.7.3.2 (p. 699), F.4.7.3.3 (p. 700), F.4.7.3.4 (p. 701), F.4.7.3.9 (p. 710), F.4.5.3.1.s (p. 856), F.4.7.3.5.s (p. 869)

[588] C. Faloutsos, M. Ranganathan, and Y. Manolopoulos. Fast subsequence matching in time-series databases. In *Proceedings of the ACM SIGMOD Conference*, pages 419–429, Minneapolis, MN, June 1994. [points; intervals; R-tree; time-series database] cited in F.4.6.4.2 (pp. 677, 681–682, 685), F.4.6.4.2.s (p. 867)

[589] C. Faloutsos and W. Rego. Tri-cell—a data structure for spatial objects. *Information Systems*, 14(2):131–139, 1989. [rectangles; points; tri-cell; transformation technique] cited in F.3.3.1 (p. 455), F.3.3.2.3 (p. 462)

[590] C. Faloutsos and Y. Rong. DOT: a spatial access method using fractals. In *Proceedings of the 7th IEEE International Conference on Data Engineering*, pages 152–159, Kobe, Japan, April 1991. [points; space-filling curve]

[591] C. Faloutsos and S. Roseman. Fractals for secondary key retrieval. In *Proceedings of the 8th ACM SIGACT-SIGMOD-SIGART Symposium on Principles of Database Systems (PODS)*, pages 247–252, Philadelphia, PA, March 1989. [points; space-filling curve; Peano-Hilbert order] cited in F.1.8.5.1 (p. 172), F.2.1.1.2 (p. 200), F.1.6.s (p. 768), F.2.1.1.2.s (p. 777)

[592] C. Faloutsos, B. Seeger, A. J. M. Traina, and C. Traina Jr. Spatial join selectivity using power laws. In *Proceedings of the ACM SIGMOD Conference*, W. Chen, J. Naughton, and P. A. Bernstein, eds., pages 177–188, Dallas, TX, May 2000. [spatial join; selectivity estimation]

[593] C. Faloutsos, T. Sellis, and N. Roussopoulos. Analysis of object oriented spatial access methods. In *Proceedings of the ACM SIGMOD Conference*, pages 426–439, San Francisco, May 1987. [rectangles; R-tree; R$^+$-tree] cited in D.3.5.3, F.1.7 (p. 96), F.1.7.1.7 (p. 130), F.2.1.5.3 (p. 311), F.1.7.1.6.5.s (p. 773)

[594] N. P. Fan and C. C. Li. Computing quadtree medial axis transform by a multi-layered pyramid of LISP-processor arrays. In *Proceedings of*

896

Computer Vision and Pattern Recognition'88, pages 628–634, Ann Arbor, MI, June 1988. [hardware; quadtree medial axis transform (QMAT)]

[595] A. Faragó, T. Linder, and G. Lugosi. Fast nearest-neighbor search in dissimilarity spaces. *IEEE Transactions on Pattern Analysis and Machine Intelligence*, 15(9):957–962, September 1993. [metric space embedding; Lipschitz embedding] cited in F.4.7.1 (p. 688), F.4.7.2.1 (p. 691), F.4.7.3.9 (p. 711)

[596] G. Farin. *Curves and Surfaces for CAGD: A Practical Guide*. Morgan-Kaufmann, San Francisco, fifth edition, 2001. [geometric modeling; general] cited in F.P (p. xix)

[597] O. D. Faugeras, M. Hebert, P. Mussi, and J.-D. Boissonnat. Polyhedral approximation of 3-d objects without holes. *Computer Vision, Graphics, and Image Processing*, 25(2):169–183, February 1984. [surfaces; polyhedral approximation] cited in A.4.6, D.4.1, D.5.2, D.5.6, D.5.7, F.2.2.2.4 (p. 362), F.2.2.3.2 (p. 386)

[598] O. D. Faugeras and J. Ponce. Prism trees: a hierarchical representation for 3-d objects. In *Proceedings of the 8th International Joint Conference on Artificial Intelligence*, pages 982–988, Karlsruhe, West Germany, August 1983. [surfaces; prism tree] cited in D.4.1, D.5.6.s

[599] B. Faverjon. Obstacle avoidance using an octree in the configuration space of a manipulator. In *Proceedings of the International Conference on Robotics*, pages 504–512, Atlanta, GA, March 1984. [volumes; motion planning] cited in A.1.4, D.1.3, F.2.4 (p. 425)

[600] B. Faverjon. Object level programming of industrial robots. In *Proceedings of the IEEE International Conference on Robotics and Automation*, vol. 3, pages 1406–1412, San Francisco, April 1986. [volumes]

[601] T. Feder and D. H. Greene. Optimal algorithms for approximate clustering. In *Proceedings of the 20th Annual ACM Symposium on the Theory of Computing*, pages 434–444, Chicago, May 1988. [points; k-center problem] cited in F.4.5.3.4 (p. 623)

[602] G. Fekete. Rendering and managing spherical data with sphere quadtrees. In *Proceedings IEEE Visualization'90*, A. Kaufman, ed., pages 176–186, San Francisco, October 1990. [volumes; surfaces] cited in F.2.2.4 (p. 403)

[603] G. Fekete and L. S. Davis. Property spheres: a new representation for 3-d object recognition. In *Proceedings of the Workshop on Computer Vision: Representation and Control*, pages 192–201, Annapolis, MD, April 1984. Also University of Maryland Computer Science Technical Report TR–1355, December 1983. [surfaces; property sphere; quaternary hierarchical triangular decomposition] cited in D.1.4.1, D.5.6, F.2.1.2.11 (p. 231), F.2.2.4 (p. 402)

[604] G. Fekete and L. Treinish. Sphere quadtrees: a new data structure to support the visualization of spherically distributed data. In *Proceedings of the SPIE/SPSE, Symposium on Electronic Imaging Science and Technology*, E. J. Farrell, ed., vol. 1259, pages 242–253, Santa Clara, CA, February 1990. [volumes; surfaces; quaternary hierarchical triangular decomposition]

[605] J. Feng, N. Mukai, and T. Watanabe. Incremental maintenance of all-nearest neighbors based on road network. In *Proceedings 17th International Conference on Industrial and Engineering Applications of Artificial Intelligence and Expert Systems, IEA/AIE 2004*, R. Orchard, C. Yang, and M. Ali, eds., vol. 3029 of Springer-Verlag Lecture Notes in Computer Science, pages 164–169, Ottawa, Canada, May 2004. [lines; points; spatial networks; all nearest neighbors query; distance semijoin]

[606] H. Ferhatosmanoglu, I. Stanoi, D. Agrawal, and A. El Abbadi. Constrained nearest neighbor queries. In *Advances in Spatial and Temporal Databases—7th International Symposium, SSTD'01*, C. S. Jensen, M. Schneider, B. Seeger, and V. J. Tsotras, eds., vol. 2121 of Springer-Verlag Lecture Notes in Computer Science, pages 257–278, Redondo Beach, CA, July 2001. [points; constrained neighbor]

[607] H. Ferhatosmanoglu, E. Tuncel, D. Agrawal, and A. El Abbadi. Vector approximation based indexing for non-uniform high dimensional data sets. In *Proceedings of the 9th International Conference on Information and Knowledge Management (CIKM)*, pages 202–209, McLean, VA, November 2000. [points; high-

dimensional data; sequential scan; VA-file; VA$^+$-file] cited in F.4.4.8 (pp. 592, 594, 596–597)

[608] H. Ferhatosmanoglu, E. Tuncel, D. Agrawal, and A. El Abbadi. Approximate nearest neighbor searching in multimedia databases. In *Proceedings of the 17th IEEE International Conference on Data Engineering*, pages 503–511, Heidelberg, Germany, April 2001. [points; high-dimensional data; sequential scan; VA-file; VA$^+$-file; approximate nearest neighbor] cited in F.4.1.7 (p. 516), F.4.4.8 (pp. 596–597)

[609] V. Ferruci and G. Vaněček. A spatial index for convex simplicial complexes. In *Advances in Spatial Databases—2nd Symposium, SSD'91*, O. Günther and H.-J. Schek, eds., vol. 525 of Springer-Verlag Lecture Notes in Computer Science, pages 361–380, Zurich, Switzerland, August 1991. [volumes]

[610] C. D. Feustel and L. G. Shapiro. The nearest neighbor problem in an abstract metric space. *Pattern Recognition Letters*, 1(2):125–128, December 1982. [metric spaces; nearest neighbor] cited in F.4.2.2 (pp. 525, 528), F.4.2.2.s (p. 837)

[611] R. P. Feynman, R. B. Leighton, and M. Sands. *The Feynman Lectures on Physics*. Addison-Wesley, Reading, MA, 1963. [physics; general] cited in A.7.1.4

[612] G. G. Filho and H. Samet. A hybrid shortest path algorithm for intra-regional queries in hierarchical shortest path finding. Computer Science Technical Report TR–4417, University of Maryland, College Park, MD, November 2002. [points; lines; spatial networks; shortest path algorithm] cited in F.4.1.6 (p. 515)

[613] U. Finke and K. H. Hinrichs. The quad view data structure—a representation for planar subdivisions. In *Advances in Spatial Databases—4th International Symposium, SSD'95*, M. J. Egenhofer and J. R. Herring, eds., vol. 951 of Springer-Verlag Lecture Notes in Computer Science, pages 29–46, Portland, ME, August 1995. [regions; winged-edge representation]

[614] R. A. Finkel and J. L. Bentley. Quad trees: a data structure for retrieval on composite keys. *Acta Informatica*, 4(1):1–9, 1974. [points; point quadtree] cited in A.1.3, A.1.4, D.1.2, D.1.3, D.1.4.1, D.2.1, D.2.3, D.2.3.1, D.2.3.1.s, D.2.3.2, D.2.3.3, F.1.1 (p. 11), F.1.4 (p. 28), F.1.4.1 (p. 28), F.1.4.1.1 (p. 30), F.1.4.1.2 (pp. 31, 34–35), F.1.4.1.3 (p. 36), F.2.1.2.7 (p. 223), F.2.1.5.1 (p. 269), F.2.4 (p. 425), F.1.4.1.1.s (pp. 752–753)

[615] A. Fischer and M. Shpitalni. Accelerating the evaluation of volumetric modelers by manipulating CSG trees and DAGs. *Computer-Aided Design*, 23(6):420–434, July 1991. [volumes]

[616] A. J. Fisher. A new algorithm for generating Hilbert curves. *Software—Practice and Experience*, 16(1):5–12, January 1986. [regions; space-filling curve; Peano-Hilbert order] cited in F.1.6.s (p. 768), F.2.1.1.2.s (p. 777)

[617] P. Flajolet. On the performance evaluation of extendible hashing and trie searching. *Acta Informatica*, 20:345–369, 1983. [points; EXCELL; extendible hashing] cited in F.1.7.2.5 (p. 160)

[618] P. Flajolet, G. Gonnet, C. Puech, and J. M. Robson. Analytic variations on quadtrees. *Algorithmica*, 10(6):473–500, December 1993. Also see *Proceedings of the 2nd Annual ACM-SIAM Symposium on Discrete Algorithms*, pages 100–109, San Francisco, January 1991. [points; point quadtree] cited in F.1.4.1.1 (p. 30)

[619] P. Flajolet, G. Labelle, L. Laforest, and B. Salvy. Hypergeometrics and the cost structure of quadtrees. *Random Structures and Algorithms*, 7(2), 1995. [points; point quadtree] cited in F.1.4.1.1 (p. 30)

[620] P. Flajolet and T. Lafforgue. Search costs in quadtrees and singularity perturbation asymptotics. *Discrete & Computational Geometry*, 12(2):151–175, September 1994. [points; point quadtree] cited in F.1.4.1.1 (p. 30)

[621] P. Flajolet and C. Puech. Partial match retrieval of multidimensional data. *Journal of the ACM*, 33(2):371–407, April 1986. Also see *Proceedings of the 24th IEEE Annual Symposium on Foundations of Computer Science*, pages 282–288, Tucson, AZ, November 1983. [points; trie; partial match query] cited in D.2.6.3.s, D.2.8.1, F.1.4.2.2 (p. 46), F.1.4.3.s (p. 761), F.1.5.2.1.s (p. 764)

[622] J. D. Foley, A. van Dam, S. K. Feiner, and J. F. Hughes. *Computer Graphics: Principles and Practice*. Addison-Wesley, Reading, MA, second edition, 1990. [computer graphics; general] cited in

A.4.6, D.5.2, F.1 (p. 4), F.1.5.1.4 (p. 69), F.2 (pp. 191–192), F.2.1.5 (p. 265), F.2.2 (p. 314), F.2.2.2.6 (p. 366), F.2.2.4 (p. 403), F.2.3.2 (p. 417), F.4 (p. 486), F.4.5.3.3 (p. 620)

[623] A. C. Fong. A scheme for reusing label locations in real time component labeling of images. In *Proceedings of the 7th International Conference on Pattern Recognition*, pages 243–245, Montréal, Canada, July 1984. [regions; connected component labeling] cited in A.5.1.1

[624] L. Forlizzi, R. H. Güting, E. Nardelli, and M. Schneider. A data model and data structures for moving objects databases. In *Proceedings of the ACM SIGMOD Conference*, W. Chen, J. Naughton, and P. A. Bernstein, eds., pages 319–330, Dallas, TX, May 2000. [moving objects]

[625] A. R. Forrest. Computational geometry in practice. In *Fundamental Algorithms for Computer Graphics*, R. A. Earnshaw, ed., pages 707–724. Springer-Verlag, Berlin, West Germany, 1985. [computational geometry; survey]

[626] A. Fournier and P. Poulin. A ray tracing accelerator based on a hierarchy of 1D sorted lists. In *Proceedings of Graphics Interface'93*, pages 53–61, Toronto, Canada, May 1993. [volumes; ray tracing]

[627] A. Frank. Applications of DBMS to land information systems. In *Proceedings of the 7th International Conference on Very Large Databases (VLDB)*, C. Zaniolo and C. Delobel, eds., pages 448–453, Cannes, France, September 1981. [regions]

[628] A. Frank. Problems of realizing LIS: storage methods for space related data: the fieldtree. Technical Report 71, Institute for Geodesy and Photogrammetry, ETH, Zurich, Switzerland, June 1983. [regions; fieldtree] cited in F.2.1.4.1 (pp. 257, 259), F.2.2.4 (p. 401), F.3.4.2 (p. 475)

[629] A. U. Frank. Properties of geographic data: requirements for spatial access methods. In *Advances in Spatial Databases—2nd Symposium, SSD'91*, O. Günther and H.-J. Schek, eds., vol. 525 of Springer-Verlag Lecture Notes in Computer Science, pages 225–234, Zurich, Switzerland, August 1991. [survey]

[630] A. U. Frank and R. Barrera. The Fieldtree: a data structure for geographic information systems. In *Design and Implementation of Large Spatial Databases—1st Symposium, SSD'89*, A. Buchmann, O. Günther, T. R. Smith, and Y.-F. Wang, eds., vol. 409 of Springer-Verlag Lecture Notes in Computer Science, pages 29–44, Santa Barbara, CA, July 1989. [regions; fieldtree] cited in F.2.1.4.1 (pp. 257, 259), F.2.2.4 (p. 401), F.3.4.2 (p. 475)

[631] P. Frankl and H. Maehara. The Johnson-Lindenstrauss lemma and the sphericity of some graphs. *Journal of Combinatorial Theory Series A*, 44(3):355–362, 1987. [metric space embedding; Lipschitz embedding] cited in F.4.7.4 (p. 715), F.4.7.4.s (p. 871)

[632] W. R. Franklin. Adaptive grids for geometric operations. *Cartographica*, 21(2&3):160–167, Summer & Autumn 1984. [regions; uniform grid] cited in A.1.3, D.2.2, F.1.1 (p. 10), F.2.1.2.3 (p. 210)

[633] W. R. Franklin and V. Akman. Building an octree from a set of parallelepipeds. *IEEE Computer Graphics and Applications*, 5(10):58–64, October 1985. [volumes; region octree] cited in A.4.6, A.4.6.s, D.5.2, D.5.2.s

[634] W. R. Franklin, N. Chandrasekhar, M. Kankanhalli, M. Seshan, and V. Akman. Efficiency of uniform grids for intersection detection on serial and parallel machines. In *New Trends in Computer Graphics: Proceedings of the CG International'88*, N. Magnenat-Thalmann and D. Thalmann, eds., pages 288–297, Geneva, Switzerland, May 1988. Springer-Verlag. [regions; uniform grid] cited in A.1.3, D.2.2, F.1.1 (p. 10)

[635] E. Fredkin. Trie memory. *Communications of the ACM*, 3(9):490–499, September 1960. [points; trie; digital searching] cited in A.1.3, D.1.2, D.2.1, D.2.6, F.1 (p. 2), F.2.4 (p. 423)

[636] M. L. Fredman and R. E. Tarjan. Fibonacci heaps and their uses in improved network optimization algorithms. *Journal of the ACM*, 34(3):596–615, July 1987. [Fibonacci heap; priority queue] cited in F.1.3 (p. 20)

[637] M. L. Fredman and B. Weide. On the complexity of computing the measure of $\cup[a_i, b_i]$. *Communications of the ACM*, 21(7):540–544, July 1978. [intervals; measure problem] cited in D.3.3.s, F.3.2.s (p. 823)

[638] H. Freeman. Computer processing of line-drawing images. *ACM Computing Surveys*, 6(1):57–97, March 1974. [lines; chain code; survey] cited in A.4.3, D.P, D.4, D.4.4, F.2.2 (p. 313), F.2.3.2 (p. 416)

[639] H. Freeman and R. Shapira. Determining the minimum area encasing rectangles for an arbitrary closed curve. *Communications of the ACM*, 18(7):409–413, July 1975. [regions; minimum bounding box] cited in D.4.1.s, F.2.2.3.1.s (p. 812)

[640] M. Freeston. The BANG file: a new kind of grid file. In *Proceedings of the ACM SIGMOD Conference*, pages 260–269, San Francisco, May 1987. [points; BANG file] cited in D.2.6.2, F.1.5.2.6 (p. 82), F.1.7.1.4 (p. 107), F.1.7.1.5 (pp. 114–115), F.1.8.1 (p. 167), F.2.1.4.1 (p. 256), F.3.4.2 (p. 479), F.4.4.5 (p. 581), F.4.4.8 (p. 593)

[641] M. Freeston. The comparative performance of BANG indexing for spatial objects. In *Proceedings of the 5th International Symposium on Spatial Data Handling*, vol. 1, pages 190–199, Charleston, SC, August 1992. [points; BANG file] cited in F.1.7.1.5 (p. 114), F.1.8.1 (p. 167), F.4.4.5 (p. 581)

[642] M. Freeston. A general solution of the n-dimensional B-tree problem. Computer Science Technical Report ECRC–94–40, ECRC, Munich, Germany, 1994. [points; BV-tree; decoupling] cited in F.1.7.1.6.2.s (p. 771)

[643] M. Freeston. A general solution of the n-dimensional B-tree problem. In *Proceedings of the ACM SIGMOD Conference*, pages 80–91, San Jose, CA, May 1995. [points; k-d-B-tree; BV-tree; decoupling] cited in F.1.5.2.6 (p. 82), F.1.7.1.6 (p. 116), F.1.7.1.6.2 (p. 120), F.1.7.1.6.4 (pp. 125–126), F.1.8.1 (p. 167), F.1.7.1.6.2.s (p. 771), F.1.7.1.6.4.s (p. 772)

[644] M. Freeston. On the complexity of BV-tree updates. In *Constraint Databases and Their Applications—2nd International Workshop on Constraint Database Systems, CDB'97*, V. Gaede, A. Brodsky, O. Günther, D. Srivastava, V. Vianu, and M. Wallace, eds., vol. 1191 of Springer-Verlag Lecture Notes in Computer Science, pages 282–293, Delphi, Greece, January 1997. [points; BV-tree; decoupling] cited in F.1.7.1.6.4 (p. 126), F.1.7.1.6.2.s (p. 771)

[645] M. W. Freeston. Advances in the design of the BANG file. In *Proceedings of the 3rd International Conference on Foundations of Data Organization and Algorithms (FODO)*, W. Litwin and H.-J. Schek, eds., vol. 367 of Springer-Verlag Lecture Notes in Computer Science, pages 322–338, Paris, France, June 1989. [points; BANG file] cited in F.1.7.1.5 (pp. 114–115), F.1.8.1 (p. 167), F.4.4.5 (p. 581)

[646] M. W. Freeston. A well-behaved file structure for the storage of spatial objects. In *Design and Implementation of Large Spatial Databases—1st Symposium, SSD'89*, A. Buchmann, O. Günther, T. R. Smith, and Y.-F. Wang, eds., vol. 409 of Springer-Verlag Lecture Notes in Computer Science, pages 287–300, Santa Barbara, CA, July 1989. [regions; BANG file] cited in F.1.7.1.5 (p. 114), F.1.8.1 (p. 167), F.3.3.2.5 (p. 464), F.4.4.5 (p. 581)

[647] J. D. Frens and D. S. Wise. Auto-blocking matrix-multiplication, or tracking BLAS3 performance from source code. In *Proceedings of the 1997 ACM Symposium on Principles and Practice of Parallel Programming*, pages 206–216, Las Vegas, NV, June 1997. Also in *SIGPLAN Notices*, 32(7):206–216, July 1997. [matrix methods] cited in F.1.4.2.1 (p. 40)

[648] Y. Freund and R. E. Schapire. Experiments with a new boosting algorithm. In *Machine Learning, Proceedings of the Thirteenth International Conference (ICML'96)*, L. Saitta, ed., pages 148–156, Bari, Italy, July 1996. [machine learning; AdaBoost] cited in F.4.7 (p. 687)

[649] J. H. Friedman, F. Baskett, and L. J. Shustek. An algorithm for finding nearest neighbors. *IEEE Transactions on Computers*, 24(10):1000–1006, October 1975. [points; nearest neighbor] cited in D.2.2, D.2.2.s, F.1.1 (p. 5), F.4 (p. 487), F.4.4.7 (pp. 589, 591), F.4.5.1 (p. 601), F.4.6.2 (pp. 669–670), F.1.1.s (p. 747)

[650] J. H. Friedman, J. L. Bentley, and R. A. Finkel. An algorithm for finding best matches in logarithmic expected time. *ACM Transactions on Mathematical Software*, 3(3):209–226, September 1977. [points; adaptive k-d tree; depth-first nearest neighbor algorithm] cited in D.1.4.2, D.2.4.1, F.1.5.1.4 (p. 58), F.2.1.2.8 (p. 224), F.2.2.2.9 (p. 380), F.4.1.7 (p. 516), F.4.2 (p. 517), F.4.5.3.3 (p. 620), F.1.5.1.4.s (p. 763), F.4.2.4.s (p. 844)

[651] A. Friedrich, K. Polthier, and M. Schmies. Interpolation of triangle hierarchies. In *Proceedings IEEE Visualization'98*, D. Ebert, H. Hagen, and H. Rushmeier, eds., pages 391–396, Research Triangle Park, NC, October 1998. [surfaces; restricted bintree; triangle meshes] cited in F.1.5.1.4 (p. 64), F.2.2.4 (p. 406)

[652] O. Fries. *Suchen in dynamischen planaren Unteteilungen*. PhD thesis, Universität des Saarlandes, Saarbrücken, Germany, 1990. [regions; dynamic point location] cited in F.2.1.3.3.2 (p. 253)

[653] O. Fries, K. Mehlhorn, and S. Näher. Dynamization of geometric data structures. In *Proceedings of the Symposium on Computational Geometry*, pages 168–176, Baltimore, MD, June 1985. [regions; point location; dynamic point location; fractional cascading] cited in F.2.1.3.3.2 (p. 253)

[654] S. F. Frisken and R. N. Perry. Adaptively sampled distance fields. In *SIGGRAPH Tutorial on New Directions in Shape Representations*, Los Angeles, August 2001. [volumes; surfaces; edge quadtree; face octree; adaptively sampled distance fields (ADF)] cited in F.2.2.2.5 (p. 362), F.2.2.2.7 (p. 373)

[655] S. F. Frisken, R. N. Perry, A. P. Rockwood, and T. R. Jones. Adaptively sampled distance fields: a general representation of shape for computer graphics. In *Proceedings of the SIGGRAPH'00 Conference*, pages 249–254, New Orleans, LA, July 2000. [volumes; surfaces; edge quadtree; face octree; adaptively sampled distance fields (ADF)] cited in F.2.2.2.5 (pp. 362–364), F.2.2.2.7 (p. 373)

[656] A. W.-C. Fu, P. M.-S. Chan, Y.-L. Cheung, and Y. S. Moon. Dynamic vp-tree indexing for n-nearest neighbor search given pairwise distances. *VLDB Journal*, 9(2):154–173, July 2000. [metric spaces; vp-tree; nearest neighbor] cited in F.4.5.2.1.1 (p. 605), F.4.5.3.1 (p. 613)

[657] H. Fuchs, G. D. Abram, and E. D. Grant. Near real-time shaded display of rigid objects. *Computer Graphics*, 17(3):65–72, July 1983. Also in *Proceedings of the SIGGRAPH'83 Conference*, Boston, July 1983. [volumes; BSP tree] cited in A.1.3, A.7.1.5, D.1.4.1, F.2.1.2.8 (p. 224), F.2.1.3.1 (pp. 233, 235), F.2.1.3.1.s (p. 787)

[658] H. Fuchs, Z. M. Kedem, and B. F. Naylor. On visible surface generation by a priori tree structures. *Computer Graphics*, 14(3):124–133, July 1980. Also in *Proceedings of the SIGGRAPH'80 Conference*, Seattle, WA, July 1980. [volumes; BSP tree] cited in A.1.3, A.7.1, A.7.1.5, A.7.3, D.1.4.1, D.2.4, D.3.5.3, F.1.5.1.4 (p. 66), F.1.5.3 (p. 88), F.2.1.2.8 (p. 224), F.2.1.3.1 (pp. 233, 237), F.2.1.5.3 (p. 312), F.4.5.3.3 (p. 620)

[659] D. R. Fuhrmann. Quadtree traversal algorithms for pointer-based and depth-first representations. *IEEE Transactions on Pattern Analysis and Machine Intelligence*, 10(6):955–960, November 1988. [regions; connected component labeling; region quadtree]

[660] A. Fujimoto and K. Iwata. Accelerated ray tracing. In *Computer Graphics: Visual Technology and Art: Proceedings of Computer Graphics Tokyo'85*, T. L. Kunii, ed., pages 41–65, Tokyo, Japan, April 1985. Springer-Verlag. [volumes; ray tracing]

[661] A. Fujimoto, T. Tanaka, and K. Iwata. ARTS: accelerated ray-tracing system. *IEEE Computer Graphics and Applications*, 6(4):16–26, April 1986. [volumes; ray tracing; PM octree] cited in A.7.2.2, A.7.2.3, A.7.2.3.s, A.7.2.4, D.5.3, F.2.2.2.7 (p. 373)

[662] K. Fujimura and T. L. Kunii. A hierarchical space indexing method. In *Computer Graphics: Visual Technology and Art: Proceedings of Computer Graphics Tokyo'85*, T. L. Kunii, ed., pages 21–33, Tokyo, Japan, April 1985. Springer-Verlag. [volumes; PM octree] cited in A.1.3, D.5.3, F.2.2.2.7 (p. 370)

[663] K. Fujimura and H. Samet. A hierarchical strategy for path planning among moving obstacles. *IEEE Transactions on Robotics and Automation*, 5(1):61–69, February 1989. Also University of Maryland Computer Science Technical Report TR–1736, November 1986. [volumes; motion planning; PM octree; time dimension] cited in A.1.4, A.6.6.s, A.7.2.4, D.1.3, D.5.3, F.2.2.2.7 (p. 373), F.2.4 (p. 425)

[664] K. Fujimura, H. Toriya, K. Yamaguchi, and T. L. Kunii. Oct-tree algorithms for solid modeling. In *Computer Graphics: Theory and Applications*, T. L. Kunii, ed., pages 69–110. Springer-Verlag, Tokyo, Japan, 1983. [volumes] cited in A.6.5.3

[665] K. Fukunaga. *Introduction to Statistical Pattern Recognition*. Academic Press, Boston, second edition, 1990. [pattern recognition; general] cited in F.2.2.3.2 (p. 386), F.2.2.3.4 (p. 397), F.4.4.4 (p. 575), F.4.4.7 (p. 591), F.4.4.8 (pp. 594, 596), F.4.6.4.1 (p. 671)

[666] K. Fukunaga and P. M. Narendra. A branch and bound algorithm for computing k-nearest neighbors. *IEEE Transactions on Computers*, 24(7):750–753, July 1975. [points; metric spaces; depth-first nearest neighbor algorithm; branch-and-bound nearest neighbor algorithm] cited in F.4 (p. 489), F.4.1.7 (pp. 516–517), F.4.2 (p. 517), F.4.2.2 (pp. 521–524, 526–527, 529), F.4.2.3 (pp. 530, 533), F.4.2.4 (pp. 534–536), F.4.2.5 (pp. 539, 541, 546), F.4.2.8 (p. 556), F.4.5.1 (pp. 601–602), F.4.5.3.4 (p. 622), F.4.2.2.s (p. 839)

[667] K. R. Gabriel and R. R. Sokal. A new statistical approach to geographic variation. *Systematic Zoology*, 18:259–278, 1969. [points; Gabriel graph (GG); Delaunay triangulation (DT)] cited in F.4.5.6 (p. 640)

[668] V. Gaede. Geometric information makes spatial query processing more efficient. In *Proceedings of the 3rd ACM Workshop on Geographic Information Systems*, pages 45–52, Baltimore, MD, December 1995. [redundancy] cited in F.2.1.4.1 (p. 257)

[669] V. Gaede. Optimal redundancy in spatial database systems. In *Advances in Spatial Databases—4th International Symposium, SSD'95*, M. J. Egenhofer and J. R. Herring, eds., vol. 951 of Springer-Verlag Lecture Notes in Computer Science, pages 96–116, Portland, ME, August 1995. [redundancy] cited in F.2.1.4.1 (p. 257)

[670] V. Gaede and O. Günther. Multidimensional access methods. *ACM Computing Surveys*, 20(2):170–231, June 1998. Also International Computer Science Institute Report TR–96–043, October 1996. [points; survey] cited in F.P (p. xx)

[671] M. Gahegan and R. Iverach. A hybrid edge and region quadtree. In *Proceedings of the 8th International Symposium on Spatial Data Handling*, T. K. Poiker and N. Chrisman, eds., pages 701–712, GIS Lab, Department of Geography, Simon Fraser University, Burnaby, British Columbia, Canada, July 1998. International Geographical Union, Geographic Information Science Study Group. [regions; lines]

[672] M. N. Gahegan. An efficient use of quadtrees in a geographical information system. *International Journal of Geographical Information Systems*, 3(3):210–214, July 1989. [regions; geographic information systems (GIS)]

[673] I. Galperin and R. L. Rivest. Scapegoat trees. In *Proceedings of the 4th Annual ACM-SIAM Symposium on Discrete Algorithms*, pages 165–174, Austin, TX, January 1993. [points; k-d tree]

[674] P.-M. Gandoin and O. Devillers. Progressive lossless compression of arbitrary simplicial complexes. *ACM Transactions on Graphics*, 21(3):372–379, July 2002. Also in *Proceedings of the SIGGRAPH'02 Conference*, San Antonio, TX, July 2002. [points; progressive transmission; k-d tree] cited in F.1.5.2.1 (p. 72)

[675] P. Ganesan, M. Bawa, and H. Garcia-Molina. Online balancing of range-partitioned data with applications to peer-to-peer systems. In *Proceedings of the 30th International Conference on Very Large Data Bases (VLDB)*, M. A. Nascimento, M. T. Özsu, D. Kossmann, R. J. Miller, J. A. Blakely, and K. B. Schiefer, eds., pages 444–455, Toronto, Canada, September 2004. [points; range query; peer-to-peer indexing]

[676] P. Ganesan, B. Yang, and H. Garcia-Molina. One torus to rule them all: multidimensional queries in P2P systems. In *Proceedings of the Seventh International Workshop on the Web and Databases ('WebDB' 2004)*, S. Amer-Yahia and Gravano L, eds., pages 19–24, Maison de la Chimie, Paris, France, June 2004. [points; range query; peer-to-peer spatial indexing; k-d tree] cited in F.1.5 (p. 49)

[677] P. Gao and T. R. Smith. Space efficient hierarchical structures: relatively addressed compact quadtrees for GISs. *Image and Vision Computing*, 7(3):173–177, August 1989. Also see *Proceedings of the International Geographic Information Systems (IGIS) Symposium: The Research Agenda*, vol. 2, pages 405–414, Arlington, VA, November 1987. [regions; region quadtree]

[678] G. Garcia and J. F. Le Corre. Geometrical transformations on binary images represented by quadtrees. In *Proceedings of MARI'87 (Intelligent Networks and Machines)*, pages 203–210, Paris, France, May 1987. [regions; region quadtree]

[679] Y. J. García, M. A. López, and S. T. Leutenegger. A greedy algorithm for bulk loading R-trees. In *Proceedings of the 6th ACM International Symposium on Advances in Geographic Information Systems*, R. Laurini, K. Makki, and N. Pissinou, eds., pages 163–164, Washington, DC, November 1998. Also see the extended version in University of Denver Computer Science Technical Report 97–02, 1997. [regions; R-tree; bulk loading] cited in F.2.1.5.2.3 (p. 283)

[680] Y. J. García, M. A. López, and S. T. Leutenegger. On optimal node splitting for R-trees. In *Proceedings of the 24th International Conference on Very Large Data Bases (VLDB)*, A. Gupta, O. Shmueli, and J. Widom, eds., pages 334–344, New York, August 1998. [rectangles; R-tree] cited in F.2.1.5.2.3 (pp. 284–285), F.2.1.5.2.4.s (p. 793)

[681] Y. J. García, M. A. López, and S. T. Leutenegger. Post-optimization and incremental refinement of R-trees. In *Proceedings of the 7th ACM International Symposium on Advances in Geographic Information Systems*, Claudia Bauzer Medeiros, ed., pages 91–96, Kansas City, MO, November 1999. [rectangles; R-tree] cited in F.2.1.5.2.7 (p. 302)

[682] M. R. Garey and D. S. Johnson. *Computers and Intractability, A Guide to the Theory of NP-Completeness*. W. H. Freeman and Co., San Francisco, 1979. [general] cited in A.1.3, A.1.4, D.1.2, D.1.3, F.2.1.1.2 (p. 202), F.2.1.2.1 (p. 206)

[683] I. Gargantini. Detection of connectivity for regions represented by linear quadtrees. *Computers and Mathematics with Applications*, 8(4):319–327, 1982. [regions; connected component labeling; region quadtree] cited in A.2.1.1, A.5.1.3, D.1.5

[684] I. Gargantini. An effective way to represent quadtrees. *Communications of the ACM*, 25(12):905–910, December 1982. [regions; region quadtree; neighbor finding] cited in A.2.1.1, A.3.4.2, D.1.5, D.2.6.2, F.1.6 (p. 93), F.2.1.1.2 (p. 200), F.2.1.2.4 (p. 215)

[685] I. Gargantini. Linear octrees for fast processing of three dimensional objects. *Computer Graphics and Image Processing*, 20(4):365–374, December 1982. [volumes; region octree] cited in A.2.1.1, A.3.3

[686] I. Gargantini. Translation, rotation and superposition of linear quadtrees. *International Journal of Man-Machine Studies*, 18(3):253–263, March 1983. [regions; region quadtree] cited in A.2.1.1, A.6.3, A.6.5.3

[687] I. Gargantini. The use of linear quadtrees in a numerical problem. *SIAM Journal of Numerical Analysis*, 20(6):1161–1169, December 1983. [regions; region quadtree; numerical methods]

[688] I. Gargantini and H. H. Atkinson. Linear quadtrees: a blocking technique for contour filling. *Pattern Recognition*, 17(3):285–293, 1984. [regions; connected component labeling; region quadtree]

[689] I. Gargantini, M. V. S. Ramanath, and T. R. S. Walsh. Linear octtrees: from data acquisition or creation to display. In *Proceedings of Computer Graphics'86*, T. L. Kunii, ed., vol. 3, pages 615–621, Anaheim, CA, May 1986. National Computer Graphics Association (NCGA). [volumes; region octree]

[690] I. Gargantini and Z. Tabakman. Linear quad- and oct-trees: their use in generating simple algorithms for image processing. In *Proceedings of Graphics Interface'82*, pages 123–127, Toronto, Canada, May 1982. [regions; volumes; region octree; region quadtree]

[691] I. Gargantini, T. R. Walsh, and O. L. Wu. Viewing transformations of voxel-based objects via linear octrees. *IEEE Computer Graphics and Applications*, 6(10):12–21, October 1986. [volumes; region octree]

[692] M. Garland. Multiresolution modeling: survey and future opportunities. In *EUROGRAPHICS'99 State of the Art Report (STAR)*, Milan, Italy, September 1999. [surfaces; simplification; multiresolution modeling; survey] cited in F.2.2.3.4 (pp. 391–395)

[693] M. Garland. *Quadric-based polygonal surface simplification*. PhD thesis, School of Computer Science, Carnegie-Mellon University, Pittsburgh, PA, May 1999. Also Computer Science Technical Report CMU–CS–99–105. [surfaces; surface simplification; multiresolution modeling; hierarchical face clustering] cited in F.2.2.3.4 (p. 395), F.2.2.3.4.s (p. 813)

[694] M. Garland and P. S. Heckbert. Surface simplification using quadric error metrics. In *Proceedings of the SIGGRAPH'97 Conference*, pages 209–216, Los Angeles, August 1997. [surfaces; polygon simplification] cited in F.2.2.3.4 (p. 395)

[695] M. Garland, A. Willmott, and P. S. Heckbert. Hierarchical face clustering on polygonal surfaces. In *Proceedings of the ACM Symposium on Interactive 3D Graphics*, pages 49–58, 245, Research Triangle Park, NC, March 2001. [surfaces; hierarchical face clustering; surface simplification; multiresolution modeling] cited in F.2.2.3.4 (pp. 395–397), F.2.2.3.4.s (p. 813)

[696] P. C. Gaston and T. Lozano-Perez. Tactile recognition and localization using object models: the case of polyhedra on a plane. *IEEE Transactions on Pattern Analysis and Machine Intelligence*, 6(3):257–266, May 1984. [volumes; robotics] cited in D.4.1

[697] N. K. Gautier, S. S. Iyengar, N. B. Lakhani, and M. Manohar. Space and time efficiency of the forest-of-quadtrees representation. *Image and Vision Computing*, 3(2):63–70, May 1985. [regions; forests of quadtrees]

[698] D. M. Gavrila. R-tree index optimization. In *Proceedings of the 6th International Symposium on Spatial Data Handling*, T. C. Waugh and R. G. Healey, eds., pages 771–791, Edinburgh, Scotland, September 1994. International Geographical Union Commission on Geographic Information Systems, Association for Geographical Information. Also University of Maryland Computer Science Technical Report TR–3292, June 1994. [points; rectangles; packed R-tree] cited in F.2.1.5.2.1 (p. 274), F.2.1.5.2.2.s (p. 791)

[699] C. Gennaro, P. Savino, and P. Zezula. Similarity search in metric databases through hashing. In *Proceedings of the 3rd International Workshop on Multimedia Information Retrieval (MIR'01)*, pages 1–5, Ottawa, Canada, October 2001. [metric spaces] cited in F.4.5.2.4 (p. 612)

[700] B. Georgescu, I. Shimshoni, and P. Meer. Mean shift based clustering in high dimensions: a texture classification example. In *Proceedings of 9th International Conference on Computer Vision*, pages 456–463, Nice, France, October 2003. [metric space embedding; mean shift analysis; locality sensitive hashing (LSH); approximate nearest neighbor] cited in F.4.7.4 (p. 716)

[701] N. Gershenfeld. *The Nature of Mathematical Modeling*. Cambridge University Press, Cambridge, United Kingdom, 1999. [mathematical modeling; general] cited in F.4.6.4.1 (p. 671), F.4.6.4.2 (pp. 676, 680), F.4.6.4.2.s (p. 866)

[702] T. Gerstner. Multiresolution compression and visualization of global topographic data. *GeoInformatica*, 7(1):7–32, March 2003. [surfaces; triangulations; level of detail (LOD); restricted quadtree] cited in F.2.2.4 (p. 406)

[703] M. Gervautz. Three improvements of the ray tracing algorithm for CSG trees. *Computers and Graphics*, 10(4):333–339, 1986. [volumes; ray tracing; constructive solid geometry (CSG)]

[704] T. M. Ghanem, R. Shah, M. F. Mokbel, W. G. Aref, and J. S. Vitter. Bulk operations for space-partitioning trees. In *Proceedings of the 20th IEEE International Conference on Data Engineering*, pages 29–41, Boston, March 2004. [SP-GiST; bulk loading; GiST]

[705] S. P. Ghosh and M. E. Senko. File organization: on the selection of random access index points for sequential files. *Journal of the ACM*, 16(4):569–579, October 1969. [points; ISAM] cited in F.A (p. 717)

[706] L. Gibson and D. Lucas. Vectorization of raster images using hierarchical methods. *Computer Graphics and Image Processing*, 20(1):82–89, September 1982. [regions; hexagonal tiling] cited in D.1.4.1, F.2.1.1.1 (p. 198), F.2.1.2.10 (p. 231)

[707] S. F. F. Gibson. Using distance maps for accurate surface representation in sampled volumes. In *Proceedings of the 1998 Symposium on Volume Visualization*, pages 23–30, Research Triangle Park, NC, October 1998. [volumes; surfaces; edge quadtree; face octree; adaptively sampled distance fields (ADF)] cited in F.2.2.2.5 (p. 363)

[708] R. Gillespie and W. A. Davis. Tree data structures for graphics and image processing. In *Proceedings of the 7th Conference of the Canadian Man-Computer Communications Society*, pages 155–161, Waterloo, Ontario, Canada, June 1981. [regions; time dimension] cited in A.7.1.4, D.5.3, F.2.2.2.7 (p. 373)

[709] A. Gionis, P. Indyk, and R. Motwani. Similarity search in high dimensions via hashing. In *Proceedings of the 25th International*

Conference on Very Large Data Bases (VLDB), M. P. Atkinson, M. E. Orlowska, P. Valduriez, S. B. Zdonik, and M. L. Brodie, eds., pages 518–529, Edinburgh, Scotland, September 1999. [metric space embedding; similarity searching; approximate nearest neighbor; locality sensitive hashing (LSH)] cited in F.4.7.4 (pp. 712, 716)

[710] A. S. Glassner. Space subdivision for fast ray tracing. *IEEE Computer Graphics and Applications*, 4(10):15–22, October 1984. [volumes; ray tracing; neighbor finding] cited in A.7.2.2, A.7.2.3, A.7.2.5

[711] A. S. Glassner. Spacetime ray tracing for animation. *IEEE Computer Graphics and Applications*, 8(2):60–70, March 1988. [volumes; ray tracing; time dimension] cited in D.5.3, F.2.2.2.7 (p. 373)

[712] P. Godfrey. Skyline cardinality for relational processing. In *Proceedings of the 3rd International Symposium on Foundations of Information and Knowledge Systems (FoIKS)*, D. Seipel and J. M. Turull-Torres, eds., vol. 2942 of Springer-Verlag Lecture Notes in Computer Science, pages 78–97, Wilheminenburg Castle, Austria, February 2004. [points; skyline query; point dominance query; cost model] cited in F.4.1.5 (p. 502)

[713] P. Godfrey, R. Shipley, and J. Gryz. Maximal vector computation in large data sets. In *Proceedings of the 31st International Conference on Very Large Data Bases (VLDB)*, K. Böhm, C. S. Jensen, L. M. Haas, M. L. Kersten, P.-Å. Larson, and B. C. Ooi, eds., pages 229–240, Trondheim, Norway, September 2005. [points; skyline query; point dominance query; cost model] cited in F.4.1.5 (pp. 502–503)

[714] C. Gold, T. D. Charters, and J. Ramsden. Automated contour mapping using triangular element data structures and an interpolant over each irregular triangular domain. *Computer Graphics*, 11(2):170–175, Summer 1977. Also in *Proceedings of the SIGGRAPH'77 Conference*, San Jose, CA, July 1977. [regions; triangle table; triangulations] cited in F.2.2.1.7 (p. 354)

[715] A. V. Goldberg and C. Harrelson. Computing the shortest path: A* search meets graph theory. In *Proceedings of the 16th Annual ACM-SIAM Symposium on Discrete Algorithms*, pages 156–165, Vancouver, Canada, January 2005. [lines; points; spatial networks; shortest path algorithm] cited in F.4.1.6 (p. 515)

[716] R. Goldman. *Pyramid Algorithms: A Dynamic Programming Approach to Curves and Surfaces for Geometric Modeling*. Morgan-Kaufmann, San Francisco, 2003. [geometric modeling; general] cited in F.P (p. xix)

[717] S. Goldman. A space efficient greedy triangulation algorithm. *Information Processing Letters*, 31(4):191–196, May 1989. [regions; triangulations] cited in F.2.1.3.2.s (p. 787)

[718] L. M. Goldschlager. Short algorithms for space-filling curves. *Software—Practice and Experience*, 11(1):99–100, January 1981. [regions; space-filling curve] cited in A.1.4, D.1.3, D.2.7.s, F.1.6.s (p. 768), F.2.1.1.2.s (p. 777)

[719] J. Goldstein and R. Ramakrishnan. Contrast plots and P-Sphere trees: space vs. time in nearest neighbor searches. In *Proceedings of the 26th International Conference on Very Large Data Bases (VLDB)*, A. El Abbadi, M. L. Brodie, S. Chakravarthy, U. Dayal, N. Kamel, G. Schlageter, and K.-Y. Whang, eds., pages 429–440, Cairo, Egypt, September 2000. [points; high-dimensional data; curse of dimensionality; nearest neighbor]

[720] R. A. Goldstein and R. Nagel. 3-D visual simulation. *Simulation*, 16(1):25–31, January 1971. [volumes] cited in A.7.2.5.s

[721] G. H. Golub and C. F. van Loan. *Matrix Computations*. Johns Hopkins University Press, Baltimore, MD, third edition, 1996. [matrix methods; numerical methods; general] cited in F.4.4.7 (p. 591), F.4.6.4.1 (pp. 671–672)

[722] D. Gomez and A. Guzman. Digital model for three-dimensional surface representation. *Geo-Processing*, 1:53–70, 1979. [surfaces; quaternary hierarchical triangular decomposition] cited in D.5.6, F.2.2.4 (pp. 400, 402)

[723] T. F. Gonzalez. Clustering to minimize the maximum intercluster distance. *Theoretical Computer Science*, 38:293–306, October 1985. [points; k-center problem] cited in F.4.5.3.4 (p. 623), F.4.5.3.4.s (p. 857)

[724] M. F. Goodchild. Tiling large geographical databases. In *Design and Implementation of Large Spatial Databases—1st Symposium, SSD'89*, A. Buchmann, O. Günther, T. R. Smith, and Y.-F. Wang,

eds., vol. 409 of Springer-Verlag Lecture Notes in Computer Science, pages 137–146, Santa Barbara, CA, July 1989. [surfaces; tiling]

[725] M. F. Goodchild and A. W. Grandfield. Optimizing raster storage: an examination of four alternatives. In *Proceedings of the 6th International Symposium on Automated Cartography (AUTO-CARTO 6)*, vol. 1, pages 400–407, Ottawa, Canada, October 1983. [regions; space-filling curve] cited in A.1.4, A.1.4.s, D.1.3, D.1.3.s, D.2.7.s, F.1.6.s (p. 768), F.2.1.1.2.s (p. 777)

[726] M. F. Goodchild and Y. Shiren. A hierarchical spatial data structure for global geographic information systems. *CVGIP: Graphical Models and Image Understanding*, 54(1):31–44, January 1992. [surfaces; regions]

[727] M. T. Goodrich and R. Tamassia. Dynamic trees and dynamic point location. *SIAM Journal on Computing*, 28(2):612–636, April 1998. [regions; dynamic point location] cited in F.2.1.3.3.2 (p. 253)

[728] V. Gopalakrishna and C. E. Veni Madhavan. Performance evaluation of attribute-based tree organization. *ACM Transactions on Database Systems*, 5(1):69–87, March 1980. [points; multiattribute tree (MAT)] cited in F.1.1 (p. 7)

[729] C. M. Goral, K. E. Torrance, D. P. Greenberg, and B. Battaile. Modeling the interaction of light between diffuse surfaces. *Computer Graphics*, 18(3):213–222, July 1984. Also in *Proceedings of the SIGGRAPH'84 Conference*, Minneapolis, MN, July 1984. [surfaces; radiosity; shading] cited in A.7.2.1, A.7.4

[730] D. Gordon and S. Chen. Front-to-back display of BSP trees. *IEEE Computer Graphics and Applications*, 11(5):79–85, September 1991. [volumes; BSP tree]

[731] D. Gordon and R. A. Reynolds. Image space shading of three-dimensional objects. *Computer Vision, Graphics, and Image Processing*, 29(3):361–376, March 1985. [volumes; shading] cited in A.7.1.4

[732] N. D. Gorsky. On the complexity of the quadtree and 2d-tree representations for binary pictures. In *Proceedings of the COST-13 Workshop on From the Pixels to the Features*, Bonas, France, August 1988. [regions]

[733] L. R. Gotlieb. Computing joins of relations. In *Proceedings of the ACM SIGMOD Conference*, pages 55–63, San Jose, CA, May 1975. [relational join; block-nested loop join] cited in F.4.1.5 (p. 503)

[734] C. Gotsman and M. Lindenbaum. On the metric properties of discrete space-filling curves. *IEEE Transactions on Image Processing*, 5(5):794–797, May 1996. [points; space-filling curve; Peano-Hilbert order] cited in F.2.1.1.2.s (p. 778)

[735] S. Gottschalk, M. C. Lin, and D. Manocha. OBBTree: a hierarchical structure for rapid interference detection. In *Proceedings of the SIGGRAPH'96 Conference*, pages 171–180, New Orleans, LA, August 1996. [volumes; minimum bounding box; strip tree; interference detection; OBBTree] cited in F.2.1.1 (p. 195), F.2.2.3.2 (p. 386), F.2.2.3.3 (p. 389), F.2.2.3.4 (p. 398)

[736] H. Gouraud. Continuous shading of curved surfaces. *IEEE Transactions on Computers*, 20(6):623–629, June 1971. [surfaces; shading] cited in A.7.1.4

[737] A. Gourdon. Simplification of irregular surface meshes in 3d medical images. In *Computer Vision, Virtual Reality and Robotics in Medicine—1st International Conference, CVRMed'95*, N. Ayache, ed., vol. 905 of Springer-Verlag Lecture Notes in Computer Science, pages 413–419, Nice, France, April 1995. [surfaces; surface simplification] cited in F.2.2.3.4 (p. 392)

[738] L. Gouzènes. Strategies for solving collision-free trajectories problems for mobile and manipulator robots. *The International Journal of Robotics Research*, 3(4):51–65, Winter 1984. [volumes]

[739] N. K. Govindaraju, B. Lloyd, W. Wang, M. C. Lin, and D. Manocha. Fast computation of database operations using graphics processors. In *Proceedings of the ACM SIGMOD Conference*, pages 215–226, Paris, France, June 2004. [GPU] cited in F.P (p. xviii)

[740] I. G. Gowda, D. G. Kirkpatrick, D. T. Lee, and A. Naamad. Dynamic Voronoi diagrams. *IEEE Transactions on Information Theory*, 29(5):724–731, September 1983. [regions; Voronoi diagram]

[741] I. S. Gradshteyn and I. M. Ryzhik. *Tables of Integrals, Series, and Products*. Academic Press, San Diego, CA, fifth edition, 1979. [general] cited in F.4.6.4.2 (p. 680)

[742] G. Graefe. Query evaluation techniques for large databases. *ACM Computing Surveys*, 25(2):73–170, June 1993. [query evaluation; survey] cited in F.4.1.5 (p. 503)

[743] R. L. Graham. An efficient algorithm for determining the convex hull of a finite planar set. *Information Processing Letters*, 1:132–133, 1972. [points; convex hull] cited in F.2.2.1.4.s (p. 799)

[744] A. G. Gray and A. W. Moore. 'N-body' problems in statistical learning. In *Advances in Neural Information Processing Systems 13*, T. K. Leen, T. G. Dietterich, and V. Tresp, eds., pages 521–527, Denver, CO, November 2000. MIT Press. [points; particle simulation; N-body problem]

[745] F. Gray. Pulse code communication. United States Patent Number 2632058, March 17, 1953. [points; Gray code] cited in F.1.6 (p. 93)

[746] J. Gray. Personal communication. 2005. [B-tree] cited in F.A (p. 717)

[747] R. M. Gray. Vector quantization. *IEEE Acoustics, Speech and Signal Processing Magazine*, 1(2):4–29, April 1984. [regions; vector quantization; survey] cited in F.1 (p. 4), F.4 (p. 486)

[748] S. B. Gray. Local properties of binary images in two dimensions. *IEEE Transactions on Computers*, 20(5):551–561, May 1971. [regions] cited in F.2.2.3.4 (p. 397)

[749] S. A. Green and D. J. Paddon. Exploiting coherence for multiprocessor ray tracing. *IEEE Computer Graphics and Applications*, 9(6):12–26, November 1989. [volumes; ray tracing; multiprocessing]

[750] D. Greene. An implementation and performance analysis of spatial data access methods. In *Proceedings of the 5th IEEE International Conference on Data Engineering*, pages 606–615, Los Angeles, February 1989. [regions; points; R-tree] cited in F.2.1.5.2.3 (pp. 287–288), F.2.1.5.2.4 (p. 290), F.4.4.2 (p. 568)

[751] D. H. Greene. The decomposition of polygons into convex parts. In *Advances in Computing Research: Computational Geometry*, F. P. Preparata, ed., vol. 1, pages 235–259. JAI Press, Greenwich, CT, 1983. [regions; convex region] cited in F.2.1.4.2 (p. 262)

[752] N. Greene, M. Kass, and G. Miller. Hierarchical Z-Buffer visibility. In *Proceedings of the SIGGRAPH'93 Conference*, pages 231–238, Anaheim, CA, August 1993. [volumes; scan conversion; z-buffer; pyramid]

[753] L. Greengard. Fast algorithms for classical physics. *Science*, 265:909–914, August 1994. [points; particle simulation; N-body problem] cited in F.2.4 (p. 426)

[754] L. Greengard and V. Rokhlin. A fast algorithm for particle simulations. *Journal of Computational Physics*, 73(2):325–348, December 1987. [points; particle simulation; N-body problem] cited in F.1.5.1.4 (p. 59)

[755] L. F. Greengard. *The rapid evaluation of potential fields in particle systems*. PhD thesis, Department of Computer Science, Yale University, New Haven, CT, 1987. [points; particle simulation; N-body problem] cited in F.2.4 (p. 426)

[756] M. Greenspan, G. Godin, and J. Talbot. Acceleration of binning nearest neighbor methods. In *Proceedings of Vision Interface 2000*, pages 337–344, Montréal, Canada, May 2000. [points; metric spaces; nearest neighbor]

[757] W. I. Grosky and R. Jain. Optimal quadtrees for image segments. *IEEE Transactions on Pattern Analysis and Machine Intelligence*, 5(1):77–83, January 1983. [regions; optimal region quadtree; space requirements] cited in A.1.2, A.1.2.s, A.4.3.1.s, D.1.5, D.1.5.s, F.2.1.2.4.s (p. 780)

[758] W. I. Grosky, M. Li, and R. Jain. A bottom-up approach to constructing quadtrees from binary arrays. Computer Science Technical Report CSC–81–011, Wayne State University, Detroit, MI, 1981. [regions; region quadtree construction] cited in A.4.1

[759] W. I. Grosky, P. Neo, and R. Mehrotra. A pictorial index mechanism for model-based matching. In *Proceedings of the 5th IEEE International Conference on Data Engineering*, pages 180–187, Los Angeles, February 1989. [image database; general]

[760] M. G. Gross, O. G. Staadt, and R. Gatti. Efficient triangular surface approximations using wavelets and quadtree data structures. *IEEE Transactions on Visualization and Computer Graphics*, 2(2):130–143, June 1996. [surfaces; triangulations; wavelets]

[761] B. Grünbaum and G. C. Shephard. The eighty-one types of isohedral tilings in the plane. *Mathematical Proceedings of the Cambridge Philosophical Society*, 82(2):177–196, September 1977. [regions; tiling] cited in D.1.4.1, F.2.1.1.1 (p. 197)

[762] B. Grünbaum and G. C. Shephard. *Tilings and Patterns*. W. H. Freeman and Co., New York, 1987. [regions; tiling] cited in D.1.4.1, F.2.1.1.1 (p. 197)

[763] A. Guéziec. Surface simplification with variable tolerance. In *Proceedings of the 2nd International Symposium on Medical Robotics and Computer Assisted Surgery (MRCAS'95)*, pages 132–139, Baltimore, MD, November 1995. [surfaces; surface simplification] cited in F.2.2.3.4 (p. 395)

[764] A. Guéziec, F. Lazarus, G. Taubin, and W. Horn. Surface partitions for progressive transmission and display, and dynamic simplification of polygonal surfaces. In *Proceedings of the 3rd Symposium on the Virtual Reality Modeling Language (VRML'98)*, S. N. Spencer, ed., pages 25–32, Monterey, CA, February 1998. [surfaces; polygon simplification; progressive transmission] cited in F.2.2.3.4 (p. 399)

[765] L. J. Guibas, D. E. Knuth, and M. Sharir. Randomized incremental construction of the Delaunay and Voronoi diagrams. *Algorithmica*, 7(4):381–413, 1992. [regions; Delaunay triangulation (DT); Voronoi diagram] cited in F.2.2.1.4.s (p. 799)

[766] L. J. Guibas and R. Sedgewick. A dichromatic framework for balanced trees. In *Proceedings of the 19th IEEE Annual Symposium on Foundations of Computer Science*, pages 8–21, Ann Arbor, MI, October 1978. [points; balanced binary search tree; red-black tree] cited in D.2.5, D.3.2.3, F.1.3 (p. 19), F.3.1.3 (pp. 440–441), F.A (p. 722)

[767] L. J. Guibas and J. Stolfi. Primitives for the manipulation of general subdivisions and the computation of Voronoi diagrams. *ACM Transactions on Graphics*, 4(2):74–123, April 1985. Also see *Proceedings of the 15th Annual ACM Symposium on the Theory of Computing*, pages 221–234, Boston, April 1983. [point location; quad-edge representation; Voronoi diagram; Delaunay triangulation (DT); boundary model (BRep)] cited in F.2.2.1.2 (p. 322)

[768] D. Gunopulos, G. Kollios, V. J. Tsotras, and C. Domeniconi. Selectivity estimators for multidimensional range queries over real attributes. *VLDB Journal*, 14(2):137–154, April 2005. [points; selectivity estimation; range query; cost model]

[769] O. Günther. *Efficient structures for geometric data management*. PhD thesis, Computer Science Division, University of California at Berkeley, Berkeley, CA, 1987. Also vol. 37 of Lecture Notes in Computer Science, Springer-Verlag, Berlin, West Germany, 1988 and Electronics Research Laboratory Memorandum UCB/ERL M87/77. [regions; cell tree] cited in D.3.5.3, D.4.1, D.4.1.s, F.2.1.5.3 (p. 312), F.2.2.3.1.s (pp. 812–813)

[770] O. Günther. The design of the cell tree: an object-oriented index structure for geometric databases. In *Proceedings of the 5th IEEE International Conference on Data Engineering*, pages 598–605, Los Angeles, February 1989. [regions; R-tree; cell tree]

[771] O. Günther. Evaluation of spatial access methods with oversize shelves. In *Proceedings of the Workshop on Geographic Database Management Systems*, G. Gambosi, M. Scholl, and H.-W. Six, eds., pages 177–193, Capri, Italy, May 1991. Springer-Verlag. Also Forschungsintitut für anwendugsorientierte Wissensverarbeitung and the University of Ulm Technical Report FAW–TR–900017, December 1990. [points; regions; rectangles; R-tree; cell tree; oversized shelf] cited in F.4.4.1 (p. 567)

[772] O. Günther. Efficient computation of spatial joins. In *Proceedings of the 9th IEEE International Conference on Data Engineering*, pages 50–59, Vienna, Austria, April 1993. [regions; spatial join] cited in F.P (p. xx)

[773] O. Günther. *Environmental Information Systems*. Springer-Verlag, Berlin, Germany, 1998. [geographic information systems (GIS); general] cited in F.P (p. xix)

[774] O. Günther and J. Bilmes. Tree-based access methods for spatial databases: implementation and performance evaluation. *IEEE Transactions on Knowledge and Data Engineering*, 3(3):342–356, September 1991. Also University of California at Santa Barbara Computer Science Technical Report TRCS88–23, October 1988. [volumes; cell tree] cited in D.3.5.3, F.2.1.5.3 (p. 312)

[775] O. Günther and A. Buchmann. Research issues in spatial databases. *SIGMOD RECORD*, 19(4):61–68, December 1990. Also in *IEEE*

Data Engineering Bulletin, 13(4):35–42, December 1990. [spatial database; general]

[776] O. Günther and S. Dominguez. Hierarchical schemes for curve representation. *IEEE Computer Graphics and Applications*, 13(3):55–63, May 1993. [lines; arc tree; survey]

[777] O. Günther and V. Gaede. Oversize shelves: a storage management technique for large spatial data objects. *International Journal of Geographical Information Science*, 11(1):5–32, 1997. [points; regions; rectangles; R-tree; cell tree; oversized shelf] cited in F.4.4.1 (p. 567)

[778] O. Günther and H. Noltemeier. Spatial database indices for large extended objects. In *Proceedings of the 7th IEEE International Conference on Data Engineering*, pages 520–526, Kobe, Japan, April 1991. [points; regions; rectangles; R-tree; cell tree; oversized shelf] cited in F.4.4.1 (p. 567)

[779] O. Günther, V. Oria, P. Picouet, J.-M. Saglio, and M. Scholl. Benchmarking spatial joins à la carte. In *Proceedings of the 10th International Conference on Scientific and Statistical Database Management*, M. Rafanelli and M. Jarke, eds., pages 32–41, Capri, Italy, July 1998. [regions; spatial join]

[780] O. Günther and E. Wong. The arc tree: an approximation scheme to represent arbitrary curved shapes. *Computer Vision, Graphics, and Image Processing*, 51(3):313–337, September 1990. [lines; arc tree] cited in F.2.2.3.1 (p. 383)

[781] S. Gupta, S. Kopparty, and C. Ravishankar. Roads, codes, and spatiotemporal queries. In *Proceedings of the 23rd ACM SIGACT-SIGMOD-SIGART Symposium on Principles of Database Systems (PODS)*, pages 115–124, Paris, France, June 2004. [moving objects; spatial networks; shortest path algorithm] cited in F.4.1.6 (p. 515)

[782] R. H. Güting. An optimal contour algorithm for iso-oriented rectangles. *Journal of Algorithms*, 5(3):303–326, September 1984. [rectangles]

[783] R. H. Güting. Gral: an extensible relational system for geometric applications. In *Proceedings of the 15th International Conference on Very Large Databases (VLDB)*, P. M. G. Apers and G. Wiederhold, eds., pages 33–44, Amsterdam, The Netherlands, August 1989. [spatial database]

[784] R. H. Güting. An introduction to spatial database systems. *VLDB Journal*, 3(4):401–444, October 1994. [spatial database; survey] cited in F.P (p. xix)

[785] R. H. Güting, T. de Ridder, and M. Schneider. Implementation of the ROSE algebra: efficient algorithms for realm-based spatial data types. In *Advances in Spatial Databases—4th International Symposium, SSD'95*, M. J. Egenhofer and J. R. Herring, eds., vol. 951 of Springer-Verlag Lecture Notes in Computer Science, pages 216–239, Portland, ME, August 1995. [spatial database; realms]

[786] R. H. Güting and H.-P. Kriegel. Multidimensional B-tree: an efficient dynamic file structure for exact match queries. In *Proceedings of the 10th Annual Gesellschaft für Informatik Conference*, R. Wilhelm, ed., pages 375–388, Saarbrücken, West Germany, September 1980. [points; kB-tree] cited in D.2.8.2, F.1.1 (p. 8), F.1.5.1.4 (p. 66), F.1.7.2.1 (p. 136)

[787] R. H. Güting and H.-P. Kriegel. Dynamic k-dimensional multiway search under time-varying access frequencies. In *Proceedings of the 5th Gesellschaft für Informatik Conference on Theoretical Computer Science*, P. Deussen, ed., vol. 104 of Springer-Verlag Lecture Notes in Computer Science, pages 135–145, Karlsruhe, West Germany, March 1981. [points; kB-tree] cited in D.2.8.2, F.1.1 (p. 8), F.1.5.1.4 (p. 66), F.1.7.2.1 (p. 136)

[788] R. H. Güting and W. Schilling. A practical divide-and-conquer algorithm for the rectangle intersection problem. *Information Sciences*, 42(2):95–112, July 1987. [rectangles; rectangle intersection problem]

[789] R. H. Güting and M. Schneider. Realm-based spatial data types: the ROSE algebra. *VLDB Journal*, 4(2):243–286, April 1995. Also see *Advances in Spatial Databases—3rd International Symposium, SSD'93*, D. Abel and B. C. Ooi, eds., pages 14–35, Singapore, June 1993. [spatial database; realms]

[790] R. H. Güting and M. Schneider. *Moving Objects Databases*. Morgan-Kaufmann, San Francisco, 2005. [spatiotemporal database; moving objects; general] cited in F.P (p. xvii)

[791] A. Guttman. R-trees: a dynamic index structure for spatial searching. In *Proceedings of the ACM SIGMOD Conference*, pages 47–57, Boston, June 1984. [rectangles; R-tree] cited in D.2.8.1, D.3.5, D.3.5.3, F.P (p. xvi), F.1.7 (p. 96), F.2.1.5.2.2 (pp. 277, 280), F.2.1.5.2.3 (pp. 282–288), F.2.1.5.2.4 (pp. 290, 292–294), F.4 (pp. 488–489), F.4.1.6 (pp. 509–511), F.4.4.2 (p. 568), F.4.4.3 (p. 573), F.4.6 (p. 663), F.4.6.4.1 (p. 674), F.2.1.2.4.s (p. 780), F.2.1.5.2.4.s (p. 793)

[792] G. Gwehenberger. Use of a binary tree structure for processing files. *Elektronische Recheanlagen*, 10(5):223–226, October 1968. [points; Patricia trie] cited in F.1.5.2.4 (p. 76), F.1.8.6 (p. 183)

[793] N. I. Hachem and P. B. Berra. Key-sequential access methods for very large files derived from linear hashing. In *Proceedings of the 5th IEEE International Conference on Data Engineering*, pages 305–312, Los Angeles, February 1989. [points; linear hashing]

[794] M. Hadjieleftheriou, G. Kollios, P. Bakalov, and V. J. Tsotras. Complex spatio-temporal pattern queries. In *Proceedings of the 31st International Conference on Very Large Data Bases (VLDB)*, K. Böhm, C. S. Jensen, L. M. Haas, M. L. Kersten, P.-Å. Larson, and B. C. Ooi, eds., pages 877–888, Trondheim, Norway, September 2005. [spatiotemporal pattern retrieval]

[795] B. Hamann and J.-L Chen. Data point selection for piecewise trilinear approximation. *Computer-Aided Geometric Design*, 11(5):477–489, October 1994. [surfaces; simplification; triangle collapse] cited in F.2.2.3.4 (p. 394)

[796] R. W. Hamming. Error-detecting and error-correcting codes. *Bell System Technical Journal*, 29(2):147–160, April 1950. [edit distance] cited in F.4 (p. 488)

[797] J. Han and M. Kamber. *Data Mining: Concepts and Techniques*. Morgan Kaufmann, San Francisco, 2000. [data mining; general]

[798] P. Hanrahan. Using caching and breadth-first search to speed up ray-tracing. In *Proceedings of Graphics Interface'86*, pages 56–61, Vancouver, Canada, May 1986. [volumes; ray tracing]

[799] S. Har-Peled. A practical approach for computing the diameter of a point set. In *Proceedings of the 17th Annual Symposium on Computational Geometry*, pages 177–186, Medford, MA, June 2001. [points; approximate Voronoi diagram (AVD); farthest point pair; minimum bounding hypersphere; approximate nearest neighbor] cited in F.2.2.2.6 (p. 367), F.4.1.7 (p. 516), F.4.4.5 (pp. 580–582, 584), F.4.7.3.2 (p. 699)

[800] R. M. Haralick. Some neighborhood operations. In *Real Time/Parallel Computing Image Analysis*, M. Onoe, K. Preston, and A. Rosenfeld, eds. Plenum Press, New York, 1981. [regions; connected component labeling] cited in A.5.1.1

[801] F. Harary. *Graph Theory*. Addison-Wesley, Reading, MA, 1969. [graphs; general] cited in A.5.3, D.3.3, D.3.5.2, D.4.2.3, D.4.3, D.4.3.1, D.4.3.2, F.2.1.3.2 (p. 238), F.2.1.3.3 (p. 242), F.3.2 (p. 448)

[802] D. M. Hardas and S. N. Srihari. Progressive refinement of 3-d images using coded binary trees: algorithms and architecture. *IEEE Transactions on Pattern Analysis and Machine Intelligence*, 6(6):748–757, November 1984. [volumes; computed tomography; k-d tree; progressive transmission] cited in A.8.3, A.8.3.s

[803] V. Hayward. Fast collision detection scheme by recursive decomposition of a manipulator workspace. In *Proceedings of the IEEE International Conference on Robotics and Automation*, vol. 2, pages 1044–1049, San Francisco, April 1986. [volumes]

[804] T. He, L. Hong, A. Varshney, and S. Wang. Controlled topology simplification. *IEEE Transactions on Visualization and Computer Graphics*, 2(2):171–184, June 1996. [surfaces; polygon simplification] cited in F.2.2.3.4 (p. 392)

[805] B. W. Heal. Node partitioning in an octree display pipeline. *Computer Graphics Forum*, 9(3):205–211, September 1990. [volumes]

[806] B. R. Heap. Algorithms for the production of contour maps over an irregular triangular mesh. Computer Science Technical Report NAC 10, National Physical Laboratory, Teddington, United Kingdom, 1972. [regions; triangulations; triangle table] cited in F.2.2.1.7 (p. 354)

[807] D. G. Heath and S. Kasif. The complexity of finding minimal Voronoi covers with applications to machine learning. *Computational Geometry*, 3(5):289–305, November 1993. [points; Voronoi diagram] cited in F.2.2.1.4.s (p. 801)

[808] L. S. Heath and S. V. Pemmaraju. New results for the minimum weight triangulation problem. *Algorithmica*, 12(6):533–552, December 1994. [triangulations] cited in F.2.1.3.2 (p. 240)

[809] D. J. Hebert. Symbolic local refinement of tetrahedral grids. *Journal of Symbolic Computation*, 17(5):457–472, May 1994. [volumes; tetrahedralizations]

[810] D. J. Hebert. Cyclic interlaced quadtree algorithms for quincunx multiresolution. *Journal of Algorithms*, 27(1):97–128, April 1998. [surfaces; restricted bintree; triangle meshes] cited in F.1.5.1.4 (p. 64), F.2.2.4 (p. 406)

[811] M. S. Hecht. *Flow Analysis of Computer Programs*. Elsevier North-Holland, New York, 1977. [flow analysis; general] cited in A.4.3.2

[812] P. Heckbert and M. Garland. Survey of polygonal surface simplification algorithms. In *SIGGRAPH'97 Tutorial on Multiresolution Surface Modeling*, Los Angeles, August 1997. [surfaces; polygon simplification; multiresolution modeling; survey] cited in F.2.2.3.4 (pp. 391–392)

[813] P. S. Heckbert and P. Hanrahan. Beam tracing polygonal objects. *Computer Graphics*, 18(3):119–127, July 1984. Also in *Proceedings of the SIGGRAPH'84 Conference*, Minneapolis, MN, July 1984. [volumes; ray tracing] cited in A.7.2.2, A.7.3, A.7.3.s

[814] J. Hecquard and R. Acharya. Connected component labeling with linear octree. *Pattern Recognition*, 24(6):515–531, 1991. [volumes; connected component labeling; region octree]

[815] M. Heller. Triangulation algorithms for adaptive terrain modeling. In *Proceedings of the 4th International Symposium on Spatial Data Handling*, vol. 1, pages 163–174, Zurich, Switzerland, July 1990. [surfaces; triangulations]

[816] J. M. Hellerstein, E. Koutsoupias, and C. H. Papadimitriou. On the analysis of indexing schemes. In *Proceedings of the 16th ACM SIGACT-SIGMOD-SIGART Symposium on Principles of Database Systems (PODS)*, pages 249–256, Tucson, AZ, May 1997. [rectangles]

[817] J. M. Hellerstein, J. F. Naughton, and A. Pfeffer. Generalized search trees for database systems. In *Proceedings of the 21st International Conference on Very Large Data Bases (VLDB)*, U. Dayal, P. M. D. Gray, and S. Nishio, eds., pages 562–573, Zurich, Switzerland, September 1995. [R-tree; B-tree; GiST] cited in F.1.9 (p. 189), F.2.1.5.2 (p. 271), F.4.4.7 (p. 590)

[818] R. Helm, K. Marriott, and M. Odersky. Constraint-based query optimization for spatial databases. In *Proceedings of the 10th ACM SIGACT-SIGMOD-SIGART Symposium on Principles of Database Systems (PODS)*, pages 181–191, Denver, CO, May 1991. [constraint spatial database; query optimization]

[819] P. Henderson. *Functional Programming: Application and Implementation*. Prentice-Hall International, Englewood Cliffs, NJ, 1980. [functional programming; general] cited in A.7.3

[820] T. C. Henderson and E. Triendl. Storing feature description as 2-d trees. In *Proceedings of the IEEE Conference on Pattern Recognition and Image Processing'82*, pages 555–556, Las Vegas, NV, June 1982. [regions]

[821] A. Henrich. A distance-scan algorithm for spatial access structures. In *Proceedings of the 2nd ACM Workshop on Geographic Information Systems*, N. Pissinou and K. Makki, eds., pages 136–143, Gaithersburg, MD, December 1994. [points; incremental nearest neighbor algorithm; best-first nearest neighbor algorithm; ranking query; priority queue; LSD tree] cited in F.4.1.3 (p. 496), F.4.1.7 (pp. 516–517), F.4.1.3.s (pp. 833–834)

[822] A. Henrich. Adapting the transformation technique to maintain multi-dimensional non-point objects in k-d-tree based access structures. In *Proceedings of the 3rd ACM Workshop on Geographic Information Systems*, pages 37–44, Baltimore, MD, December 1995. [points; k-d tree; transformation technique] cited in F.3.3.3 (p. 465)

[823] A. Henrich. Adapting a spatial access structure for document representations in vector space. In *Proceedings of the 5th International Conference on Information and Knowledge Management (CIKM)*, K. Barker and M. T. Özsu, eds., pages 19–26, Rockville, MD, November 1996. [points; k-d tree; LSD tree]

[824] A. Henrich. A hybrid split strategy for k-d-tree based access structures. In *Proceedings of the 4th ACM Workshop on Geographic Information Systems*, S. Shekhar and P. Bergougnoux, eds., pages 1–8, Gaithersburg, MD, November 1996. [points; k-d tree; LSD tree] cited in F.1.5 (p. 49), F.1.7.1.3 (p. 103)

[825] A. Henrich. Improving the performance of multi-dimensional access structures based on k-d-trees. In *Proceedings of the 12th IEEE International Conference on Data Engineering*, S. Y. W. Su, ed., pages 68–75, New Orleans, LA, February 1996. [points; k-d tree; LSD tree] cited in F.1.5.1.4 (pp. 61–62), F.1.7.1.3 (p. 103)

[826] A. Henrich. The LSD^h-tree: an access structure for feature vectors. In *Proceedings of the 14th IEEE International Conference on Data Engineering*, pages 362–369, Orlando, FL, February 1998. [points; high-dimensional data; similarity searching; LSD tree] cited in F.1.7.1.2 (p. 102), F.3.3.3 (p. 465), F.4.4.3 (p. 573), F.4.4.8 (p. 592)

[827] A. Henrich and J. Möller. Extending a spatial access structure to support additional standard attributes. In *Advances in Spatial Databases—4th International Symposium, SSD'95*, M. J. Egenhofer and J. R. Herring, eds., vol. 951 of Springer-Verlag Lecture Notes in Computer Science, pages 132–151, Portland, ME, August 1995. [transformation technique] cited in F.3.3.3 (p. 465)

[828] A. Henrich and H.-W. Six. How to split buckets in spatial data structures. In *Proceedings of the Workshop on Geographic Database Management Systems*, G. Gambosi, M. Scholl, and H.-W. Six, eds., pages 212–244, Capri, Italy, May 1991. Springer-Verlag. [points]

[829] A. Henrich, H.-W. Six, and P. Widmayer. The LSD tree: spatial access to multidimensional point and non-point data. In *Proceedings of the 15th International Conference on Very Large Databases (VLDB)*, P. M. G. Apers and G. Wiederhold, eds., pages 45–53, Amsterdam, The Netherlands, August 1989. [points; rectangles; LSD tree] cited in F.1.7.1.3 (pp. 102–103, 106), F.1.7.1.5 (p. 110), F.2.1.2.8 (p. 224), F.2.1.5.3 (p. 308), F.3.3.2.4 (p. 463), F.4.1.7 (p. 517), F.1.7.1.3.s (p. 768)

[830] F. Herbert. Fractal landscape modeling using octrees. *IEEE Computer Graphics and Applications*, 4(11):4–5, November 1984. [surfaces; region octree; fractal landscape modeling]

[831] F. Herbert. Solid modeling for architectural design using octpaths. *Computers & Graphics*, 9(2):107–116, 1985. [volumes]

[832] M. Herman. Fast path planning in unstructured, dynamic, 3-d worlds. In *Proceedings of the SPIE, Applications of Artificial Intelligence 3*, pages 505–512, Orlando, FL, April 1986. [volumes]

[833] M. Herman. Fast, three-dimensional, collision-free motion planning. In *Proceedings of the IEEE International Conference on Robotics and Automation*, vol. 2, pages 1056–1063, San Francisco, April 1986. [volumes; motion planning]

[834] S. Hertel and K. Mehlhorn. Fast triangulation of the plane with respect to simple polygons. *Information and Control*, 64(1–3):52–76, January/February/March 1985. Also see *Proceedings of the 1983 International Conference on the Fundamentals of Computation Theory (FCT)*, M. Karpinski, ed., pages 207–218, Borgholm, Sweden, August 1983. [regions; triangulations] cited in D.4.3.1, D.4.3.1.s, F.2.1.3.2 (pp. 238, 240), F.2.1.3.2.s (p. 787)

[835] D. Hilbert. Ueber stetige abbildung einer linie auf flächenstück. *Mathematische Annalen*, 38:459–460, 1891. [regions; space-filling curve; Peano-Hilbert order] cited in A.1.4, A.4.1, D.1.3, F.1.8.5.1 (p. 172), F.2.1.1.2 (p. 200)

[836] F. S. Hillier and G. J. Lieberman. *Introduction to Operations Research*. Holden-Day, San Francisco, 1967. [operations research; general] cited in A.1.3.s, D.1.2.s, F.2.1.3.2 (p. 240), F.4 (p. 489), F.4.1.7 (p. 517), F.4.2 (p. 517), F.4.5.6 (pp. 639, 641), F.2.1.2.7.s (p. 783)

[837] P. Hinker and C. Hanson. Geometric optimization. In *Proceedings IEEE Visualization'93*, G. M. Nielson and R. D. Bergeron, eds., pages 189–195, San Jose, CA, October 1993. [surfaces; vertex simplification] cited in F.2.2.3.4 (p. 395)

[838] A. Hinneburg, C. C. Aggarwal, and D. A. Keim. What is the nearest neighbor in high dimensional spaces? In *Proceedings of the 26th International Conference on Very Large Data Bases (VLDB)*,

A. El Abbadi, M. L. Brodie, S. Chakravarthy, U. Dayal, N. Kamel, G. Schlageter, and K.-Y. Whang, eds., pages 506–515, Cairo, Egypt, September 2000. [points; high-dimensional data; nearest neighbor; curse of dimensionality] cited in F.4 (p. 489), F.4.6.4 (p. 671)

[839]   K. Hinrichs. *The grid file system: implementation and case studies of applications*. PhD thesis, Institut für Informatik, ETH, Zurich, Switzerland, 1985. [points; rectangles; grid file] cited in D.2.8.2, D.3.1, D.3.4, F.1.7.2 (p. 130), F.1.7.2.1 (p. 131), F.3 (p. 427), F.3.3.1 (pp. 454–455), F.3.3.2.3 (p. 462), F.4.4.8 (p. 594)

[840]   K. Hinrichs. Implementation of the grid file: design concepts and experience. *BIT*, 25(4):569–592, 1985. [rectangles; grid file] cited in D.2.8.2, D.3.4, F.1.7.2 (p. 130), F.1.7.2.1 (pp. 131–132), F.3.3.2.3 (p. 462), F.4.4.8 (p. 594)

[841]   K. Hinrichs and J. Nievergelt. The grid file: a data structure designed to support proximity queries on spatial objects. In *Proceedings of WG'83, International Workshop on Graphtheoretic Concepts in Computer Science*, M. Nagl and J. Perl, eds., pages 100–113, Haus Ohrbeck (near Osnabrück), West Germany, 1983. Trauner Verlag. [rectangles] cited in D.3.1, D.3.4, F.3.3.1 (pp. 454–455), F.3.3.2.3 (p. 462)

[842]   K. Hinrichs, J. Nievergelt, and P. Schorn. An all-round sweep algorithm for 2-dimensional nearest-neighbor problems. *Acta Informatica*, 29(4):383–394, July 1992. [points; nearest neighbor]

[843]   D. S. Hirschberg. On the complexity of searching a set of vectors. *SIAM Journal on Computing*, 9(1):126–129, February 1980. [points]

[844]   G. R. Hjaltason. *Incremental algorithms for proximity queries*. PhD thesis, University of Maryland, College Park, MD, September 2000. [points; high-dimensional data; spatial database; incremental nearest neighbor algorithm; similarity searching; contractiveness; metric space embedding] cited in F.4.1.3 (p. 497)

[845]   G. R. Hjaltason, M. Ray, H. Samet, and I. Weiss. Using spatial sorting and ranking in model-based object recognition. In *Proceedings of the 14th International Conference on Pattern Recognition*, A. K. Jain, S. Venkathesh, and B. C. Lovell, eds., vol. 1, pages 1347–1349, Brisbane, Australia, August 1998. [lines; image invariants; ranking query; spatial join; distance join]

[846]   G. R. Hjaltason and H. Samet. Ranking in spatial databases. In *Advances in Spatial Databases—4th International Symposium, SSD'95*, M. J. Egenhofer and J. R. Herring, eds., vol. 951 of Springer-Verlag Lecture Notes in Computer Science, pages 83–95, Portland, ME, August 1995. [incremental nearest neighbor algorithm; best-first nearest neighbor algorithm; ranking query; priority queue] cited in F.1 (p. 4), F.1.4.1.3 (p. 37), F.4.1 (p. 490), F.4.1.3 (p. 493), F.4.1.7 (pp. 516–517), F.4.4.8 (p. 596), F.4.6.1.2 (p. 666), F.2.1.5.2.3.s (p. 792), F.2.2.2.6.s (p. 808)

[847]   G. R. Hjaltason and H. Samet. Incremental distance join algorithms for spatial databases. In *Proceedings of the ACM SIGMOD Conference*, L. Hass and A. Tiwary, eds., pages 237–248, Seattle, WA, June 1998. [points; distance join; distance semijoin; incremental nearest neighbor algorithm] cited in F.4 (pp. 486, 489–490), F.4.5.8 (p. 658)

[848]   G. R. Hjaltason and H. Samet. Distance browsing in spatial databases. *ACM Transactions on Database Systems*, 24(2):265–318, June 1999. Also University of Maryland Computer Science Technical Report TR–3919, July 1998. [incremental nearest neighbor algorithm; best-first nearest neighbor algorithm; ranking query; R-tree; priority queue] cited in F.1 (p. 4), F.1.4.1.3 (p. 37), F.4.1 (p. 490), F.4.1.1 (p. 491), F.4.1.3 (pp. 493, 496–497), F.4.1.7 (pp. 516–517), F.4.2.4 (pp. 536–538), F.4.2.5 (p. 548), F.4.2.8 (p. 556), F.4.4.8 (p. 596), F.4.5.5.2 (p. 634), F.4.6.1.2 (p. 666), F.2.2.2.6.s (p. 808), F.4.1.3.s (pp. 833–834), F.4.2.4.s (p. 843)

[849]   G. R. Hjaltason and H. Samet. Improved bulk-loading algorithms for quadtrees. In *Proceedings of the 7th ACM International Symposium on Advances in Geographic Information Systems*, Claudia Bauzer Medeiros, ed., pages 110–115, Kansas City, MO, November 1999. [lines; bulk loading; PMR quadtree]

[850]   G. R. Hjaltason and H. Samet. Contractive embedding methods for similarity searching in metric spaces. Computer Science Technical Report TR–4102, University of Maryland, College Park, MD, February 2000. [points; high-dimensional data; metric space embedding; contractiveness; Lipschitz embedding; FastMap; SparseMap] cited in F.4.7 (p. 686), F.4.7.2.4 (p. 695), F.4.7.3.7 (p. 708), F.4.7.3.8 (p. 709), F.4.7.3.6.s (p. 869), F.4.7.3.7.s (pp. 870–871)

[851]   G. R. Hjaltason and H. Samet. Incremental similarity search in multimedia databases. Computer Science Technical Report TR–4199, University of Maryland, College Park, MD, November 2000. [points; high-dimensional data; similarity searching; incremental nearest neighbor algorithm] cited in F.4.1.3 (p. 498), F.4.1.7 (p. 517), F.4.2 (p. 517), F.4.2.1 (p. 520), F.4.2.6 (p. 549), F.4.3 (p. 559), F.4.5.4.2 (p. 626), F.4.5.5.2 (pp. 634, 637), F.4.5.7.1 (p. 645), F.4.5.7.2 (pp. 646–647), F.4.5.7.3 (pp. 649–650), F.4.6.1.2 (p. 666), F.4.1.3.s (p. 834), F.4.1.4.s (p. 834), F.4.2.1.s (p. 836), F.4.5.2.2.s (p. 855), F.4.5.2.3.s (p. 856), F.4.5.3.2.s (p. 856), F.4.5.5.2.s (p. 858), F.4.5.7.1.s (p. 862), F.4.5.7.2.s (p. 862)

[852]   G. R. Hjaltason and H. Samet. Speeding up construction of PMR quadtree-based spatial indexes. *VLDB Journal*, 11(2):109–137, October 2002. Also University of Maryand Computer Science Technical Report TR–4033, July 1999. [lines; bulk loading; PMR quadtree]

[853]   G. R. Hjaltason and H. Samet. Improved search heuristics for the sa-tree. *Pattern Recognition Letters*, 24(15):2785–2795, November 2003. [metric spaces; sa-tree; incremental nearest neighbor algorithm; best-first nearest neighbor algorithm] cited in F.4.5.5.2 (pp. 634, 637), F.4.5.5.2.s (pp. 858–859)

[854]   G. R. Hjaltason and H. Samet. Index-driven similarity search in metric spaces. *ACM Transactions on Database Systems*, 28(4):517–580, December 2003. [metric spaces; high-dimensional data; similarity searching; incremental nearest neighbor algorithm; best-first nearest neighbor algorithm; survey] cited in F.P (p. xx), F.1 (p. 4), F.4.1.3 (p. 498), F.4.1.7 (p. 517), F.4.2 (p. 517), F.4.5.5.2 (p. 634)

[855]   G. R. Hjaltason and H. Samet. Properties of embedding methods for similarity searching in metric spaces. *IEEE Transactions on Pattern Analysis and Machine Intelligence*, 25(5):530–549, May 2003. Also University of Maryland Computer Science Technical Report TR–4102, February 2000. [points; high-dimensional data; metric space embedding; contractiveness; Lipschitz embedding; FastMap; SparseMap] cited in F.P (p. xx), F.4.7 (p. 686), F.4.7.2.4 (p. 695)

[856]   G. R. Hjaltason, H. Samet, and Y. Sussmann. Speeding up bulk-loading of quadtrees. In *Proceedings of the 5th ACM International Workshop on Advances in GIS*, pages 50–53, Las Vegas, NV, November 1997. [lines; bulk loading; PMR quadtree]

[857]   C. A. R. Hoare. Quicksort. *Computer Journal*, 5(1):10–15, February 1962. [quicksort] cited in F.4.5.8 (p. 661)

[858]   C. A. R. Hoare. Notes on data structuring. In *Structured Programming*, O. J. Dahl, E. W. Dijkstra, and C. A. R. Hoare, eds., page 154. Academic Press, London, United Kingdom, 1972. [matrix methods] cited in A.1.4, D.1.3, F.2.4 (p. 423)

[859]   D. S. Hochbaum and D. B. Shmoys. A best possible heuristic for the k-center problem. *Mathematics of Operations Research*, 10(2):180–184, May 1985. [points; k-center problem] cited in F.4.5.3.4 (p. 623)

[860]   E. Hoel and H. Samet. Data-parallel spatial join algorithms. In *Proceedings of the 23rd International Conference on Parallel Processing*, vol. 3, pages 227–234, St. Charles, IL, August 1994. [lines; data-parallel algorithms; R-tree; spatial join] cited in F.2.1.5.2 (p. 271)

[861]   E. Hoel and H. Samet. Performance of data-parallel spatial operations. In *Proceedings of the 20th International Conference on Very Large Data Bases (VLDB)*, J. Bocca, M. Jarke, and C. Zaniolo, eds., pages 156–167, Santiago, Chile, September 1994. [lines; data-parallel algorithms; spatial join; R-tree; PMR quadtree; R$^+$-tree] cited in F.2.1.5.2 (p. 271)

[862]   E. G. Hoel. *Spatial data structures and query performance in the sequential and data-parallel domains*. PhD thesis, Computer Science Department, University of Maryland, College Park, MD, December 1995. Also Computer Science Technical Report TR–3584. [lines; data-parallel algorithms; R-tree; spatial join] cited in F.P (p. xviii), F.2.1.5.2 (p. 271)

[863] E. G. Hoel and H. Samet. Efficient processing of spatial queries in line segment databases. In *Advances in Spatial Databases—2nd Symposium, SSD'91*, O. Günther and H.-J. Schek, eds., vol. 525 of Springer-Verlag Lecture Notes in Computer Science, pages 237–256, Zurich, Switzerland, August 1991. [lines; PMR quadtree; R-tree; R$^+$-tree; nearest neighbor] cited in F.2.2.2.8 (p. 376), F.4.1.7 (p. 516)

[864] E. G. Hoel and H. Samet. A qualitative comparison study of data structures for large line segment databases. In *Proceedings of the ACM SIGMOD Conference*, M. Stonebraker, ed., pages 205–214, San Diego, CA, June 1992. [lines; PMR quadtree; R-tree; R$^+$-tree; nearest neighbor] cited in F.2.1.5.2.7 (p. 301), F.2.2.2.8 (p. 376), F.4.1.7 (p. 516)

[865] E. G. Hoel and H. Samet. Data-parallel R-tree algorithms. In *Proceedings of the 22nd International Conference on Parallel Processing*, vol. 3, pages 47–50, St. Charles, IL, August 1993. [lines; data-parallel algorithms; R-tree] cited in F.2.1.5.2 (p. 271)

[866] E. G. Hoel and H. Samet. Benchmarking spatial join operations with spatial output. In *Proceedings of the 21st International Conference on Very Large Data Bases (VLDB)*, U. Dayal, P. M. D. Gray, and S. Nishio, eds., pages 606–618, Zurich, Switzerland, September 1995. [lines; spatial join; R-tree; R*-tree] cited in F.2.1.5.2.4 (p. 292)

[867] E. G. Hoel and H. Samet. Data-parallel primitives for spatial operations. In *Proceedings of the 24th International Conference on Parallel Processing*, vol. 3, pages 184–191, Oconomowoc, WI, August 1995. [lines; data-parallel algorithms; R-tree; R$^+$-tree] cited in F.2.1.5.2 (p. 271)

[868] E. G. Hoel and H. Samet. Data-parallel primitives for spatial operations using PM quadtrees. In *Proceedings of Computer Architectures for Machine Perception*, V. Cantoni, L. Lombardi, M. Mosconi, M. Savini, and A. Setti, eds., pages 266–273, Como, Italy, September 1995. [lines; data-parallel algorithms]

[869] E. G. Hoel and H. Samet. Data-parallel polygonization. *Parallel Computing*, 29(10):1381–1401, October 2003. [data-parallel algorithms; polygonization; PM quadtree; R-tree] cited in F.2.1.5.2 (p. 271)

[870] C. M. Hoffmann. *Geometric & Solid Modeling*. Morgan-Kaufmann, San Mateo, CA, 1989. [solid modeling; general] cited in F.P (p. xix), F.2.2.1.6 (p. 353), F.2.2.1.7 (pp. 353–354)

[871] F. C. Holroyd and D. C. Mason. Efficient linear quadtree construction algorithm. *Image and Vision Computing*, 8(3):218–224, August 1990. [regions]

[872] T. H. Hong and M. Shneier. Describing a robot's workspace using a sequence of views from a moving camera. *IEEE Transactions on Pattern Analysis and Machine Intelligence*, 7(6):721–726, November 1985. [volumes] cited in A.4.6, D.5.2

[873] T. H. Hong and M. Shneier. Rotation and translation of objects represented by octrees. In *Proceedings of the 1987 IEEE International Conference on Robotics and Automation*, vol. 2, pages 947–950, Raleigh, NC, March–April 1987. [volumes; region octree]

[874] J. E. Hopcroft. 2-3 tree (unpublished), 1970. [points; balanced binary search tree; B-tree; 2-3 tree] cited in F.1.5.1.4 (p. 65), F.A (p. 718)

[875] H. Hoppe. Progressive meshes. In *Proceedings of the SIGGRAPH'96 Conference*, pages 99–108, New Orleans, LA, August 1996. [surfaces; simplification; vertex pair collapse] cited in F.2.2.3.4 (pp. 395, 399)

[876] H. Hoppe. View-dependent refinement of progressive meshes. In *Proceedings of the SIGGRAPH'97 Conference*, pages 189–198, Los Angeles, August 1997. [surfaces; surface simplification; view-dependent simplification] cited in F.2.2.3.4 (pp. 395, 399)

[877] H. Hoppe. Smooth view-dependent level-of-detail control and its application to terrain rendering. In *Proceedings IEEE Visualization'98*, D. Ebert, H. Hagen, and H. Rushmeier, eds., pages 35–42, 516, Research Triangle Park, NC, October 1998. [surfaces; polygon simplification] cited in F.2.2.3.4 (p. 399)

[878] H. Hoppe, T. DeRose, T. Duchamp, J. McDonald, and W. Stuetzle. Mesh optimization. In *Proceedings of the SIGGRAPH'93 Conference*, pages 19–26, Anaheim, CA, August 1993. [surfaces; surface simplification] cited in F.2.2.3.4 (p. 395)

[879] S. L. Horowitz and T. Pavlidis. Picture segmentation by a tree traversal algorithm. *Journal of the ACM*, 23(2):368–388, April 1976. [regions; split-and-merge segmentation] cited in A.1.3, D.1.2, F.2.4 (p. 424)

[880] M. Hoshi and P. Flajolet. Page usage in a quadtree index. *BIT*, 32(3):384–402, 1992. [points; k-d tree] cited in F.1.7.3 (p. 164)

[881] M. Hoshi and T. Yuba. A counter example to a monotonicity property of k-d trees. *Information Processing Letters*, 15(4):169–173, October 1982. [points; k-d tree]

[882] M. E. Houle. Navigating massive data sets via local clustering. In *Proceedings of the 9th ACM SIGKDD Conference on Knowledge Discovery and Data Mining*, pages 547–552, Washington DC, August 2003. [metric spaces; approximate nearest neighbor] cited in F.4.5.8 (p. 661)

[883] M. E. Houle. SASH: a spatial approximation hierarchy for similarity search. Technical Report RT0517, IBM Tokyo Research Lab, Tokyo, Japan, March 2003. [metric spaces; approximate nearest neighbor] cited in F.4.3 (p. 557), F.4.5.8 (p. 650), F.4.7.4 (p. 712)

[884] M. E. Houle and J. Sakuma. Fast approximate similarity search in extremely high-dimensional data sets. In *Proceedings of the 21st IEEE International Conference on Data Engineering*, pages 619–630, Tokyo, Japan, April 2005. [metric spaces; approximate nearest neighbor] cited in F.4.3 (p. 557), F.4.4.5 (p. 582), F.4.5.8 (pp. 650, 653, 656–659, 661–662), F.4.7.4 (p. 712), F.4.5.8.s (pp. 863–864)

[885] P. Houthuys. Box sort, a multidimensional method for rectangular boxes, used for quick range searching. *Visual Computer*, 3(4):236–249, December 1987. [rectangles]

[886] G. Hristescu and M. Farach-Colton. Cluster-preserving embedding of proteins. Technical report, Department of Computer Science, Rutgers University, Piscataway, NJ, 1999. [metric space embedding; Lipschitz embedding; SparseMap; FastMap] cited in F.4 (p. 489), F.4.7 (p. 686), F.4.7.2.2 (p. 692), F.4.7.2.4 (pp. 694–697)

[887] P. Y. Hsiao and W. S. Feng. Using a multiple storage quad tree on a hierarchical VLSI compaction scheme. *IEEE Transactions on Computer-Aided Design*, 9(5):522–536, May 1990. [rectangles; bucket rectangle PM quadtree] cited in F.3.4.3 (p. 481)

[888] P. K. Hsiung and R. Thibadeau. Accelerating ARTS. *Visual Computer*, 8(3):181–190, March 1992. [volumes; ray tracing]

[889] H. Hu, J. Xu, and D. L. Lee. A generic framework for monitoring continuous spatial queries over moving objects. In *Proceedings of the ACM SIGMOD Conference*, pages 479–490, Baltimore, MD, June 2005. [moving objects] cited in F.4 (p. 487)

[890] C.-Y. Huang and K.-L. Chung. Fast operations on binary images using interpolation-based bintrees. *Pattern Recognition*, 28(3):409–420, March 1995. [regions; bintree]

[891] C.-Y. Huang and K.-L. Chung. Faster neighbor finding on images represented by bincodes. *Pattern Recognition*, 29(9):1507–1518, September 1996. [regions; bintree; neighbor finding]

[892] Y.-W. Huang, N. Jing, and E. A. Rundensteiner. A cost model for estimating the performance of spatial joins using R-trees. In *Proceedings of the 9th International Conference on Scientific and Statistical Database Management*, Y. E. Ioannidis and D. M. Hansen, eds., pages 30–38, Olympia, WA, August 1997. [regions; R-tree; spatial join; cost model]

[893] Y.-W. Huang, N. Jing, and E. A. Rundensteiner. Integrated query processing strategies for spatial path queries. In *Proceedings of the 13th IEEE International Conference on Data Engineering*, A. Gray and P.-Å. Larson, eds., pages 477–486, Birmingham, United Kingdom, April 1997. [lines; shortest path algorithm; spatial join]

[894] Y.-W. Huang, N. Jing, and E. A. Rundensteiner. Spatial joins using R-trees: breadth-first traversal with global optimizations. In *Proceedings of the 23rd International Conference on Very Large Data Bases (VLDB)*, M. Jarke, M. J. Carey, K. R. Dittrich, F. H. Lochovsky, P. Loucopoulos, and M. A. Jeusfeld, eds., pages 396–405, Athens, Greece, August 1997. [spatial join; R-tree] cited in F.P (p. xx)

[895] P. M. Hubbard. Collision detection for interactive computer graphics applications. *IEEE Transactions on Visualization and Computer Graphics*, 1(3):218–230, September 1995. [volumes; collision

detection; sphere tree] cited in F.2.1.1 (p. 195), F.2.2.3.1 (p. 383), F.2.2.3.3 (p. 389), F.4.4.2 (p. 567), F.4.5.3.4 (p. 622)

[896] P. M. Hubbard. Approximating polyhedra with spheres for time-critical collision detection. *ACM Transactions on Graphics*, 15(3):179–210, July 1996. [volumes; collision detection; sphere tree] cited in F.2.1.1 (p. 195), F.2.2.3.1 (p. 383), F.2.2.3.3 (p. 389), F.4.4.2 (p. 567), F.4.5.3.4 (p. 622)

[897] D. A. Huffman. A method for the construction of minimum-redundancy codes. *Proceedings of the IRE*, 40(9):1098–1101, September 1952. [Huffman code] cited in A.8, A.8.3

[898] Y. Hung. *Parallel processing of geometric representations on SIMD computers*. PhD thesis, Computer Science Department, University of Maryland, College Park, MD, 1987. [regions; parallel processing] cited in F.P (p. xviii), F.1.5 (p. 49)

[899] Y. Hung and A. Rosenfeld. Parallel processing of linear quadtrees on a mesh-connected computer. *Journal of Parallel and Distributed Computing*, 7(1):1–27, August 1989. [regions; parallel processing]

[900] A. Hunter and P. J. Willis. A note on the optimal labeling of quadtree nodes. *The Computer Journal*, 33(5):398–401, October 1990. [regions; region quadtree]

[901] G. M. Hunter. *Efficient computation and data structures for graphics*. PhD thesis, Department of Electrical Engineering and Computer Science, Princeton University, Princeton, NJ, 1978. [regions; volumes; MX quadtree] cited in A.1.2, A.1.3, A.1.4, A.3.2.2, A.3.2.2.s, A.4.3.1, A.4.4, A.4.4.s, A.5.1.2, A.5.1.2.s, A.5.2, A.5.3, A.6.3, A.6.3.2, A.6.3.2.s, A.6.5.1, A.7.1.1, A.7.1.2, A.9.2, D.1.2, D.1.3, D.1.5, D.2.6.1, D.3.5.1, D.4.2.1, D.4.2.4.s, D.5.5.1, F.1.4.2.1 (p. 40), F.2.1.1.4 (p. 204), F.2.1.2.4 (p. 211), F.2.2.2.2 (p. 357), F.2.4 (pp. 423, 425), F.3.4.1.2 (p. 469), F.4.1.6 (p. 513)

[902] G. M. Hunter. Geometrees for interactive visualization of geology: an evaluation. Technical report, System Science Department, Schlumberger-Doll Research, Ridgefield, CT, 1981. [volumes; PM octree; geometree] cited in A.1.3, D.2.6.2, D.5.3, F.1.4.2.2 (p. 47), F.2.2.2.7 (p. 370)

[903] G. M. Hunter. Three-dimensional frame buffers for interactive analysis of three-dimensional data. *Optical Engineering*, 25(2):292–295, February 1986. [hardware]

[904] G. M. Hunter and K. Steiglitz. Linear transformation of pictures represented by quad trees. *Computer Graphics and Image Processing*, 10(3):289–296, July 1979. [regions; MX quadtree] cited in A.1.4, A.3.2.2, A.4.4, A.6.5.1, D.1.3, F.2.4 (p. 425)

[905] G. M. Hunter and K. Steiglitz. Operations on images using quad trees. *IEEE Transactions on Pattern Analysis and Machine Intelligence*, 1(2):145–153, April 1979. [regions; MX quadtree] cited in A.1.2, A.3.2.2, A.3.2.2.s, A.4.3.1, A.4.4, A.4.4.s, A.5.1.2, A.5.1.2.s, A.5.2, A.5.3, A.6.3, A.6.3.2, A.6.5.1, A.7.1.1, A.7.1.2, A.9.2, D.1.5, D.2.6.1, D.3.5.1, D.4.2.1, D.4.2.4.s, D.5.5.1, F.1.4.2.1 (p. 40), F.2.1.1.4 (p. 204), F.2.2.2.2 (p. 357), F.3.4.1.2 (p. 469)

[906] A. Hutflesz, H.-W. Six, and P. Widmayer. Globally order preserving multidimensional linear hashing. In *Proceedings of the 4th IEEE International Conference on Data Engineering*, pages 572–579, Los Angeles, February 1988. [points; linear hashing; dynamic z hashing] cited in F.1.7.2.3.3 (pp. 150–151), F.1.7.2.3.3.s (p. 774)

[907] A. Hutflesz, H.-W. Six, and P. Widmayer. The twin grid file: a nearly space optimal index structure. In *Advances in Database Technology—EDBT'88, Proceedings of the 1st International Conference on Extending Database Technology*, J. W. Schmidt, S. Ceri, and M. Missikoff, eds., pages 352–363, Venice, Italy, March 1988. [points; twin grid file] cited in F.1.7.2.1 (p. 137)

[908] A. Hutflesz, H.-W. Six, and P. Widmayer. Twin grid files: space optimizing access schemes. In *Proceedings of the ACM SIGMOD Conference*, pages 183–190, Chicago, June 1988. [points; twin grid file] cited in F.1.7.2.1 (p. 137)

[909] A. Hutflesz, H.-W. Six, and P. Widmayer. The R-file: an efficient access structure for proximity queries. In *Proceedings of the 6th IEEE International Conference on Data Engineering*, pages 372–379, Los Angeles, February 1990. [rectangles; points; R-file] cited in F.1.7.1.5 (p. 115), F.2.1.4.1 (p. 256), F.3.4.2 (p. 478)

[910] A. Hutflesz, P. Widmayer, and C. Zimmerman. Global order makes spatial access faster. In *Proceedings of the Workshop on Geographic*

[911] *Database Management Systems*, G. Gambosi, M. Scholl, and H.-W. Six, eds., pages 161–176, Capri, Italy, May 1991. Springer-Verlag. [points]

[911] D. P. Huttenlocher, D. A. Klanderman, and W. Rucklidge. Comparing images using the Hausdorff distance. *IEEE Transactions on Pattern Analysis and Machine Intelligence*, 15(9):850–863, September 1993. [Hausdorff distance] cited in F.2.2.3.4 (p. 392), F.4 (p. 488)

[912] D. Ibaroudene and R. Acharya. Coordinate relationships between vertices of linear octree nodes and corners of the universe. *Computers & Graphics*, 15(3):375–381, 1991. [volumes; region octree]

[913] D. Ibaroudene and R. Acharya. Linear hypertree for multi-dimensional image representation. *Information Sciences*, 68(1 and 2):123–154, February 1993. [hypervolumes; d-dimensional quadtree]

[914] D. Ibaroudene and R. Acharya. Parallel display of objects represented by linear octrees. *IEEE Transactions on Parallel and Distributed Systems*, 6(1):79–85, January 1995. [volumes]

[915] D. Ibaroudene, V. Demanjenko, and R. S. Acharya. Adjacency algorithms for linear octree nodes. *Image and Vision Computing*, 8(2):115–123, May 1990. [volumes; region octree]

[916] O. H. Ibarra and M. H. Kim. Quadtree building algorithms on an SIMD hypercube. *Journal of Parallel and Distributed Computing*, 18(1):71–76, May 1993. [regions; region quadtree; parallel processing] cited in F.P (p. xviii), F.1.5 (p. 49)

[917] T. J. Ibbs and A. Stevens. Quadtree storage of vector data. *International Journal of Geographical Information Systems*, 2(1):43–56, January–March 1988. [lines; PM quadtree] cited in F.2.2.2.6 (p. 366)

[918] H. A. H. Ibrahim. The connected component labeling algorithm on the NON-VON supercomputer. In *Proceedings of the Workshop on Computer Vision: Representation and Control*, pages 37–45, Annapolis, MD, April 1984. [regions; connected component labeling]

[919] T. Ichikawa. A pyramidal representation of images and its feature extraction facility. *IEEE Transactions on Pattern Analysis and Machine Intelligence*, 3(3):257–264, May 1981. [regions; pyramid]

[920] D. S. Immel, M. F. Cohen, and D. P. Greenberg. A radiosity method for non-diffuse environments. *Computer Graphics*, 20(4):133–142, August 1986. Also in *Proceedings of the SIGGRAPH'86 Conference*, Dallas, TX, August 1986. [surfaces; radiosity] cited in A.7.4

[921] P. Indyk. On approximate nearest neighbors in non-Euclidean spaces. In *Proceedings of the 39th IEEE Annual Symposium on Foundations of Computer Science*, pages 148–155, Palo Alto, CA, November 1998. [points; high-dimensional data; approximate nearest neighbor]

[922] P. Indyk. Dimensionality reduction techniques for proximity problems. In *Proceedings of the 11th Annual ACM-SIAM Symposium on Discrete Algorithms*, pages 371–378, San Francisco, January 2000. [metric space embedding; locality sensitive hashing (LSH); approximate nearest neighbor] cited in F.4.7.4 (p. 716)

[923] P. Indyk. Nearest-neighbor searching in high dimensions. In *Handbook of Discrete and Computational Geometry*, J. E. Goodman and J. O'Rourke, eds., chapter 39. CRC Press, Boca Raton, FL, second edition, 2004. [metric space embedding; locality sensitive hashing (LSH); approximate nearest neighbor; survey] cited in F.4.7.4 (pp. 713, 715)

[924] P. Indyk and R. Motwani. Approximate nearest neighbors: towards removing the curse of dimensionality. In *Proceedings of the 30th Annual ACM Symposium on the Theory of Computing*, pages 604–613, Dallas, TX, May 1998. [metric space embedding; locality sensitive hashing (LSH); approximate nearest neighbor; curse of dimensionality] cited in F.4 (pp. 489–490), F.4.6 (p. 664), F.4.7 (p. 686), F.4.7.4 (pp. 711, 713, 715), F.4.7.4.s (p. 871)

[925] A. Inselberg and B. Dimsdale. Parallel coordinates: a tool for visualizing multi-dimensional geometry. In *Proceedings IEEE Visualization'90*, A. Kaufman, ed., pages 361–378, San Francisco, October 1990. [parallel coordinates; visualization]

[926] M. Iri, K. Murota, and S. Matsui. Linear-time approximation algorithms for finding the minimum-weight perfect matching on a plane. *Information Processing Letters*, 12(4):206–209, August 1981. [points; Euclidean matching problem] cited in D.2.9.s, F.1.9.s (p. 776)

[927] M. G. B. Ismail and R. Steele. Adaptive pel location coding for bilevel facsimile signals. *Electronics Letters*, 16(10):361–363, May 1980. [regions] cited in A.8.2.3

[928] K. E. Iverson. *A Programming Language*. John Wiley & Sons, New York, 1962. [APL; programming languages] cited in F.1.1 (p. 7)

[929] G. S. Iwerks and H. Samet. The spatial spreadsheet. In *Proceedings of the 3rd International Conference on Visual Information Systems (VISUAL99)*, D. P. Huijsmans and A. W. M. Smeulders, eds., pages 317–324, Amsterdam, The Netherlands, June 1999. [spatial database]

[930] G. S. Iwerks, H. Samet, and K. Smith. Continuous k-nearest neighbor queries for continuously moving points with updates. In *Proceedings of the 29th International Conference on Very Large Data Bases (VLDB)*, J. C. Freytag, P. C. Lockemann, S. Abiteboul, M. J. Carey, P. G. Selinger, and A. Heuer, eds., pages 512–523, Berlin, Germany, September 2003. [moving objects; nearest neighbor] cited in F.3.1.4 (p. 445), F.4 (p. 487)

[931] G. S. Iwerks, H. Samet, and K. Smith. Maintenance of spatial semijoin queries on moving points. In *Proceedings of the 30th International Conference on Very Large Data Bases (VLDB)*, M. A. Nascimento, M. T. Özsu, D. Kossmann, R. J. Miller, J. A. Blakely, and K. B. Schiefer, eds., pages 828–839, Toronto, Canada, September 2004. [moving objects; distance semijoin] cited in F.4 (p. 488)

[932] C. L. Jackins and S. L. Tanimoto. Oct-trees and their use in representing three-dimensional objects. *Computer Graphics and Image Processing*, 14(3):249–270, November 1980. [volumes; region octree] cited in A.1.4, A.6.5.2, D.1.3, F.2.4 (p. 425)

[933] C. L. Jackins and S. L. Tanimoto. Quad-trees, oct-trees, and *k*-trees—a generalized approach to recursive decomposition of Euclidean space. *IEEE Transactions on Pattern Analysis and Machine Intelligence*, 5(5):533–539, September 1983. Also University of Washington Computer Science Technical Report 82–02–02. [hypervolumes; region octree; time dimension] cited in A.3.2.3, A.5.1.2, A.5.1.3, A.5.2, D.5.3, F.2.2.2.7 (p. 373)

[934] E. Jacox and H. Samet. Iterative spatial join. *ACM Transactions on Database Systems*, 28(3):268–294, September 2003. [rectangles; spatial join; interval tree] cited in F.P (p. xx), F.3.1.2 (p. 438), F.3.1.2.s (p. 821)

[935] E. Jacox and H. Samet. Spatial join techniques. Computer Science Technical Report TR–4730, University of Maryland, College Park, MD, June 2005. [spatial join; survey] cited in F.P (p. xx)

[936] K. J. Jacquemain. The complexity of constructing quadtrees in arbitrary dimensions. In *Proceedings of the Seventh International Workshop on Graphtheoretic Concepts in Computer Science (WG'81)*, J. R. Mühlbacher, ed., pages 293–301, Linz, Austria, June 1981. Hanser Verlag. [points; point quadtree]

[937] H. V. Jagadish. Linear clustering of objects with multiple attributes. In *Proceedings of the ACM SIGMOD Conference*, pages 332–342, Atlantic City, NJ, June 1990. [points; space-filling curve; transformation technique; Peano-Hilbert order] cited in F.1.8.5.1 (p. 172), F.2.1.1.2 (p. 200), F.1.6.s (p. 768), F.2.1.1.2.s (p. 777)

[938] H. V. Jagadish. On indexing line segments. In *Proceedings of the 16th International Conference on Very Large Data Bases (VLDB)*, D. McLeod, R. Sacks-Davis, and H.-J. Schek, eds., pages 614–625, Brisbane, Australia, August 1990. [lines; Hough transform]

[939] H. V. Jagadish. Spatial search with polyhedra. In *Proceedings of the 6th IEEE International Conference on Data Engineering*, pages 311–319, Los Angeles, February 1990. [rectangles; P-tree] cited in F.2.1.1 (p. 195), F.4.4.2 (p. 570)

[940] H. V. Jagadish, B. C. Ooi, K.-L. Tan, C. Yu, and R. Zhang. iDistance: an adaptive B$^+$-tree based indexing method for nearest neighbor search. *ACM Transactions on Database Systems*, 30(2):364–397, June 2005. [metric spaces; high-dimensional data; pyramid technique; iMinMax] cited in F.4.4.7 (p. 591)

[941] A. James. *Binary space partitioning for accelerated hidden surface removal and rendering of static environments*. PhD thesis, School of Information Systems, University of East Anglia, Norwich, United Kingdom, August 1999. [volumes; BSP tree; hidden-surface removal] cited in F.2.1.3.1 (p. 234)

[942] F. W. Jansen. Data structures for ray tracing. In *Data Structures for Raster Graphics*, F. J. Peters, L. R. A. Kessener, and M. L. P. van Lierop, eds., pages 57–73. Springer-Verlag, Berlin, West Germany, 1986. [volumes; ray tracing] cited in A.7.2.3

[943] F. W. Jansen. *Solid modelling with faceted primitives*. PhD thesis, Department of Industrial Design, Delft University of Technology, Delft, The Netherlands, September 1987. [volumes] cited in D.5.5

[944] F. W. Jansen and R. J. Sutherland. Display of solid models with a multi-processor system. In *Proceedings of the EUROGRAPHICS'87 Conference*, G. Marechal, ed., pages 377–387, Amsterdam, The Netherlands, August 1987. [multiprocessing] cited in D.5.5

[945] F. W. Jansen and J. J. van Wijk. Fast previewing techniques in raster graphics. In *Proceedings of the EUROGRAPHICS'83 Conference*, P. J. W. ten Hagen, ed., pages 195–202, Zagreb, Yugoslavia, September 1983. [volumes; ray tracing] cited in A.7.2.5

[946] G. E. M. Jared and T. Varady. Synthesis of volume modeling and sculptured surfaces in BUILD. In *Proceedings of the CAD'84 Conference*, pages 481–495, Brighton, United Kingdom, 1984. [surfaces]

[947] J. W. Jaromczyk and G. T. Toussaint. Relative neighborhood graphs and their relatives. *Proceedings of the IEEE*, 80(9):1502–1517, September 1992. [points; relative neighborhood graph (RNG); Delaunay graph; Gabriel graph (GG); Delaunay triangulation (DT); minimum spanning tree (MST)] cited in F.4.5.6 (pp. 640–641)

[948] J. F. Javis, C. N. Judice, and W. H. Ninke. A survey of techniques for the image display of continuous tone images on a bilevel display. *Computer Graphics and Image Processing*, 5(1):13–40, March 1976. [regions] cited in A.6.3.1

[949] C. S. Jensen, J. Kolář, T. B. Pedersen, and I. Timko. Nearest neighbor queries in road networks. In *Proceedings of the 11th ACM International Symposium on Advances in Geographic Information Systems*, E. Hoel and P. Rigaux, eds., pages 1–8, New Orleans, LA, November 2003. [spatial networks; nearest neighbor; moving objects] cited in F.4 (p. 488)

[950] C. S. Jensen and S. Saltenis. Towards increasingly update efficient moving-object indexing. *IEEE Data Engineering Bulletin*, 25(2):35–40, June 2002. [spatiotemporal database; moving objects] cited in F.P (p. xvii), F.1 (p. 2)

[951] C. S. Jensen and R. T. Snodgrass. Temporal data management. *IEEE Transactions on Knowledge and Data Engineering*, 11(1):36–44, January/February 1999. [temporal database] cited in F.P (p. xvii), F.1 (p. 2)

[952] K. Jensen and N. Wirth. *PASCAL User Manuel and Report*. Springer-Verlag, New York, second edition, 1974. [PASCAL; programming languages] cited in A.P, A.L, D.P, F.P (p. xx), F.D (p. 743)

[953] C. Jermaine, E. Omiecinski, and W. G. Yee. Maintaining a large spatial database with T2SM. In *Proceedings of the 9th ACM International Symposium on Advances in Geographic Information Systems*, pages 76–81, 2001. [regions; R-tree; linear file]

[954] D. Jevans and B. Wyvill. Adaptive voxel subdivision for ray tracing. In *Proceedings of Graphics Interface'89*, pages 164–172, London, Ontario, Canada, June 1989. [volumes; ray tracing]

[955] Q. Jiang and W. Zhang. An improved method for finding nearest neighbors. *Pattern Recognition Letters*, 14(7):531–535, July 1993. [points; depth-first nearest neighbor algorithm] cited in F.4.2 (p. 517), F.4.2.3 (p. 532), F.4.2.4 (p. 535)

[956] H. Jin, B. C. Ooi, H. T. Shen, C. Yu, and A. Zhou. An adaptive and efficient dimensionality reduction algorithm for high-dimensional indexing. In *Proceedings of the 19th IEEE International Conference on Data Engineering*, pages 87–98, Bangalore, India, March 2003. [high-dimensional data; dimension reduction]

[957] J. Jin, N. An, and A. Sivasubramaniam. Analyzing range queries on spatial data. In *Proceedings of the 16th IEEE International Conference on Data Engineering*, pages 525–534, San Diego, CA, February 2000. [range query]

[958] N. Jing, Y.-W. Huang, and E. A. Rundensteiner. Hierarchical encoded path views for path query processing: an optimal model and its performance evaluation. *IEEE Transactions on Knowledge and Data Engineering*, 10(3):409–432, May 1998. [lines; points; spatial networks; shortest path algorithm] cited in F.4.1.6 (p. 515)

[959] B. Joe. Geompack: a software package for the generation of meshes using geometric algorithms. *Advances in Engineering Software and Workstations*, 13(5–6):325–331, September 1991. [volumes; conforming tetrahedralization] cited in F.2.2.1.6 (p. 353)

[960] B. Johnson and B. Shneiderman. Tree-maps: a space filling approach to the visualization of hierarchical information structures. In *Proceedings IEEE Visualization'91*, G. M. Nielson and L. Rosenbloom, eds., pages 284–291, San Diego, CA, October 1991. Also University of Maryland Computer Science Technical Report TR–2657, April 1991. [regions; treemap; k-d tree; X-Y tree; puzzletree] cited in F.2.1.2.9 (p. 225)

[961] L. R. Johnson. On operand structure, representation, storage, and search. Technical Report RC–603, IBM Research, 1962. [doubly chained tree (DCT)] cited in F.1.1 (p. 7)

[962] W. Johnson and J. Lindenstrauss. Extensions of Lipschitz mappings into a Hilbert space. *Contemporary Mathematics*, 26:189–206, 1984. [metric space embedding; Lipschitz embedding] cited in F.4.7.2 (p. 691), F.4.7.4 (p. 715), F.4.7.4.s (p. 871)

[963] A. Jonas and N. Kiryati. Digital representation schemes for 3d curves. *Pattern Recognition*, 30(11):1803–1816, November 1997. [lines; survey]

[964] C. B. Jones. Data structures for three-dimensional spatial information systems in geology. *International Journal of Geographical Information Systems*, 3(1):15–31, January–March 1989. [volumes]

[965] C. B. Jones and I. M. Abraham. Design considerations for a scale independent cartographic database. In *Proceedings of the 2nd International Symposium on Spatial Data Handling*, pages 384–398, Seattle, WA, July 1986. [lines; strip tree; Douglas-Peucker algorithm] cited in F.2.2.3.1 (p. 384)

[966] C. B. Jones and I. M. Abraham. Line generalization in a global cartographic database. *Cartographica*, 24(3):32–45, Autumn 1987. [lines; strip tree; Douglas-Peucker algorithm] cited in F.2.2.3.1 (p. 384)

[967] C. B. Jones, D. B. Kinder, and J. M. Ware. The implicit triangulated irregular network and multiscale spatial databases. *The Computer Journal*, 37(1):43–57, 1993. [surfaces; triangulated irregular network (TIN)]

[968] C. B. Jones and J. M. Ware. Nearest neighbor search for linear and polygonal objects with constrained triangulations. In *Proceedings of the 8th International Symposium on Spatial Data Handling*, T. K. Poiker and N. Chrisman, eds., pages 13–21, GIS Lab, Department of Geography, Simon Fraser University, Burnaby, British Columbia, Canada, July 1998. International Geographical Union, Geographic Information Science Study Group. [regions; nearest neighbor; constrained triangulation]

[969] J. Jones and S. S. Iyengar. Space and time efficient virtual quadtrees. *IEEE Transactions on Pattern Analysis and Machine Intelligence*, 6(2):244–247, March 1984. [regions; forests of quadtrees] cited in A.2.1.4

[970] W. de Jonge, P. Scheuermann, and A. Schijf. S⁺-trees: an efficient structure for the representation of large pictures. *CVGIP: Image Understanding*, 59(3):265–280, May 1994. Also see *Advances in Spatial Databases—2nd Symposium, SSD'91*, O. Günther and H.-J. Schek, eds., pages 401–419, Zurich, Switzerland, August 1991. [regions; S-tree; S⁺-tree; DF-expression] cited in F.2.3.1 (pp. 411, 414–415), F.2.3.1.s (p. 815)

[971] R. C. Joshi, H. Darbari, S. Goel, and S. Sasikumaran. A hierarchical hex-tree representational technique for solid modelling. *Computer & Graphics*, 12(2):235–238, 1988. [volumes]

[972] K. I. Joy and M. N. Bhetanabhotla. Ray tracing parametric surface patches utilizing numerical techniques and ray coherence. *Computer Graphics*, 20(4):279–285, August 1986. Also in *Proceedings of the SIGGRAPH'86 Conference*, Dallas, TX, August 1986. [surfaces; ray tracing]

[973] K. I. Joy, J. Legakis, and R. MacCracken. Data structures for multiresolution representation of unstructured meshes. In *Hierarchical and Geometrical Methods in Scientific Visualization*, G. Farin, B. Hamann, and H. Hagen, eds., pages 143–170. Springer-Verlag, Berlin, Germany, 2003. [volumes; winged-edge representation; lath; quad-edge representation; boundary model (BRep)] cited in F.2.2.1.3 (p. 330), F.2.2.1.3.1 (p. 333), F.2.2.1.3.2 (pp. 338–340), F.2.2.1.3.3 (pp. 341–342)

[974] A. Juan, E. Vidal, and P. Aibar. Fast k-nearest-neighbors searching through extended versions of the approximating and eliminating search algorithm. In *Proceedings of the 14th International Conference on Pattern Recognition*, A. K. Jain, S. Venkathesh, and B. C. Lovell, eds., vol. 1, pages 828–830, Brisbane, Australia, August 1998. [metric spaces; points; nearest neighbor]

[975] R. Juan-Arinyo and J. Solé. Constructing face octrees from voxel-based volume representations. *Computer-Aided Design*, 27(10):783–791, 1995. [volumes; face octree] cited in F.2.2.2.4 (p. 362)

[976] A. B. Kahn. Topological sorting of large networks. *Communications of the ACM*, 5(11):558–562, November 1962. [points; topological sort] cited in F.4.1.5 (p. 507)

[977] J. T. Kajiya. The rendering equation. *Computer Graphics*, 20(4):143–150, August 1986. Also in *Proceedings of the SIGGRAPH'86 Conference*, Dallas, TX, August 1986. [volumes; ray tracing; radiosity] cited in A.7.2.1

[978] I. Kalantari and G. McDonald. A data structure and an algorithm for the nearest point problem. *IEEE Transactions on Software Engineering*, 9(5):631–634, September 1983. [points; metric spaces; nearest neighbor; Voronoi diagram; bisector tree] cited in F.4.5 (p. 599), F.4.5.3.1 (p. 615), F.4.5.3.2 (p. 616), F.4.5.3.3 (p. 617)

[979] M. Kallmann and D. Thalmann. Star-vertices: a compact representation for planar meshes with adjacency information. *Journal of Graphics Tools*, 6(1):7–18, 2001. [surfaces; winged-edge representation; triangle meshes; nonmanifold objects; star-vertex data structure] cited in F.2.2.1.7 (p. 355)

[980] A. D. Kalvin and R. H. Taylor. Superfaces: polygonal mesh simplification with bounded error. *IEEE Computer Graphics and Applications*, 16(3):64–77, May 1996. [surfaces; mesh simplification; hierarchical face clustering] cited in F.2.2.3.4 (p. 398)

[981] S. Kambhampati and L. S. Davis. Multiresolution path planning for mobile robots. *IEEE Journal of Robotics and Automation*, 2(3):135–145, September 1986. [regions; path planning]

[982] I. Kamel and C. Faloutsos. Parallel R-trees. In *Proceedings of the ACM SIGMOD Conference*, M. Stonebraker, ed., pages 195–204, San Diego, CA, June 1992. Also University of Maryland Computer Science Technical Report TR–2820, January 1992. [regions; R-tree] cited in F.2.1.5.2 (p. 271)

[983] I. Kamel and C. Faloutsos. On packing R-trees. In *Proceedings of the 2nd International Conference on Information and Knowledge Management (CIKM)*, pages 490–499, Washington, DC, November 1993. [points; Hilbert-packed R-tree] cited in F.1.7.2.3.3 (p. 152), F.2.1.5.2.1 (p. 275), F.2.1.5.2.2 (pp. 276, 278, 280, 281), F.4.4.6 (p. 587), F.2.1.5.2.3.s (p. 792), F.2.1.5.2.4.s (p. 793), F.2.1.5.2.7.s (p. 794)

[984] I. Kamel and C. Faloutsos. Hilbert R-tree: an improved R-tree using fractals. In *Proceedings of the 20th International Conference on Very Large Data Bases (VLDB)*, J. Bocca, M. Jarke, and C. Zaniolo, eds., pages 500–509, Santiago, Chile, September 1994. [points; space-filling curve; Hilbert R-tree] cited in F.2.1.5.2.2 (pp. 275, 280), F.2.1.5.2.3 (p. 285), F.4.4.7 (p. 589)

[985] I. Kamel, M. Khalil, and V. Kouramajian. Bulk insertion in dynamic R-trees. In *Proceedings of the 7th International Symposium on Spatial Data Handling*, M. J. Kraak and M. Molenaar, eds., pages 3B.31–3B.42, Delft, The Netherlands, August 1996. International Geographical Union Commission on Geographic Information Systems, Association for Geographical Information. [points; R-tree; bulk insertion] cited in F.2.1.5.2.5 (pp. 297–298)

[986] B. Kamgar-Parsi and L. N. Kanal. An improved branch and bound algorithm for computing k-nearest neighbors. *Pattern Recognition Letters*, 3(1):7–12, January 1985. [points; depth-first nearest neighbor algorithm; branch-and-bound nearest neighbor algorithm] cited in F.4.1.7 (p. 516), F.4.2 (p. 517), F.4.2.2 (pp. 521–522, 524,

528), F.4.2.3 (pp. 532–533), F.4.2.5 (pp. 546, 548), F.4.2.8 (p. 556), F.4.5.1 (pp. 601–602), F.4.5.3.2 (p. 616)

[987] K. Kanatani. Personal communication. 1985. [regions; Fibonacci numbers] cited in D.1.4.1

[988] K. V. R. Kanth, D. Agrawal, A. El Abbadi, and A. Singh. Dimensionality reduction for similarity searching in dynamic databases. *Computer Vision and Image Understanding*, 75(1/2):59–72, July/August 1999. Also see *Proceedings of the ACM SIGMOD Conference*, L. Hass and A. Tiwary, eds., pages 237–248, Seattle, WA, June 1998. [points; high-dimensional data; similarity searching; Singular Value Decomposition (SVD); dimension reduction] cited in F.4.6.4.1 (pp. 673–675), F.4.6.4.2 (p. 684), F.4.6.5 (p. 685)

[989] K. V. R. Kanth, S. Ravada, J. Sharma, and J. Banerjee. Indexing medium-dimensionality data in Oracle. In *Proceedings of the ACM SIGMOD Conference*, pages 521–522, Philadelphia, PA, June 1999. [regions; R-tree]

[990] C. T. Kao. Efficient/practical algorithms for geometric structures: convex hulls, Delaunay triangulations and Voronoi diagrams. Computer Science Technical Report TR–2958, University of Maryland, College Park, MD, September 1992. [regions; Delaunay triangulation (DT); Voronoi diagram]

[991] M. R. Kaplan. Space-tracing: a constant time ray-tracer. In *SIGGRAPH Tutorial on the Uses of Spatial Coherence in Ray-Tracing*, San Francisco, July 1985. [volumes; ray tracing] cited in A.7.2.2

[992] M. R. Kaplan. The use of spatial coherence in ray tracing. In *Techniques for Computer Graphics*, D. F. Rogers and R. A. Earnshaw, eds., pages 173–193. Springer-Verlag, New York, 1987. Also in *Proceedings of the International Summer Institute on the State of the Art in Computer Graphics*, Stirling, Scotland, United Kingdom, June 1986. [volumes; ray tracing] cited in A.7.2.2, A.7.2.3, A.7.2.4

[993] R. G. Karlsson. Greedy matching on a grid. *BIT*, 28(1):19–26, 1988. [points; Euclidean matching problem]

[994] O. Karonen, M. Tamminen, P. Kerola, M. Mitjonen, and E. Orivouri. A geometric mine modeling system. In *Proceedings of the 6th International Symposium on Automated Cartography (AUTO-CARTO 6)*, vol. 1, pages 374–383, Ottawa, Canada, October 1983. [volumes]

[995] R. M. Karp, O. Waarts, and G. Zweig. The bit vector intersection problem (preliminary version). In *Proceedings of the 36th IEEE Annual Symposium on Foundations of Computer Science*, pages 621–630, Milwaukee, WI, October 1995. [points; high-dimensional data; approximate nearest neighbor] cited in F.4.7.4 (p. 713)

[996] R. L. Kashyap, S. K. C. Subas, and S. B. Yao. Analysis of the multiple-attribute-tree data organization. *IEEE Transactions on Software Engineering*, 3(6):451–466, November 1977. [points; multiattribute tree (MAT); doubly chained tree (DCT)] cited in F.1.1 (pp. 6–7)

[997] S. Kasif. Optimal parallel algorithms for quadtree problems. *CVGIP: Image Understanding*, 59(3):281–285, May 1994. Also see *Proceedings of the 5th Israeli Symposium on Artificial Intelligence, Vision, and Pattern Recognition*, pages 353–363, Tel Aviv, Israel, December 1988. [regions; region quadtree; parallel processing] cited in F.P (p. xviii), F.1.5 (p. 49)

[998] J. Katajainen and M. Koppinen. Constructing Delaunay triangulations by merging buckets in quadtree order. *Fundamenta Informaticae*, 11(3):275–288, September 1988. [regions; Delaunay triangulation (DT)]

[999] N. Katayama and S. Satoh. The SR-tree: an index structure for high-dimensional nearest neighbor queries. In *Proceedings of the ACM SIGMOD Conference*, J. Peckham, ed., pages 369–380, Tucson, AZ, May 1997. [points; high-dimensional data; SR-tree; minimum bounding hypersphere; minimum bounding box] cited in F.1.8 (p. 164), F.2.1.1 (p. 195), F.4.2.3 (p. 533), F.4.4.2 (pp. 568–570), F.4.2.3.s (p. 840)

[1000] N. Katayama and S. Satoh. Distinctiveness-sensitive nearest neighbor search for efficient similarity retrieval of multimedia information. In *Proceedings of the 17th IEEE International Conference on Data Engineering*, pages 493–502, Heidelberg, Germany, April 2001. [high-dimensional data; nearest neighbor; similarity searching]

[1001] J. Katznelson. Computational structure of the *n*-body problem. *SIAM Journal on Scientific and Statistical Computing*, 10(4):787–815, July 1989. [points; particle simulation; *N*-body problem] cited in F.2.4 (p. 426)

[1002] A. Kaufman, ed. *Volume Visualization*, Los Alamitos, CA, 1991. IEEE Computer Society Press. [volumes; general] cited in F.2.2.2.5 (p. 363)

[1003] A. Kaufman, D. Forgash, and Y. Ginsburg. Hidden surface removal using a forest of quadtrees. In *Proceedings of the 1st IPA Conference on Image Processing, Computer Graphics, and Pattern Recognition*, A. Kaufman, ed., pages 85–89, Jerusalem, Israel, June 1983. Information Processing Association of Israel. [volumes; forests of quadtrees] cited in A.7.1.1

[1004] E. Kawaguchi and T. Endo. On a method of binary picture representation and its application to data compression. *IEEE Transactions on Pattern Analysis and Machine Intelligence*, 2(1):27–35, January 1980. [regions; DF-expression] cited in A.1.4, A.2.2, A.3.4.4, A.5.1.3, D.1.3, D.1.5, D.5.4, F.2.3.1 (p. 410)

[1005] E. Kawaguchi, T. Endo, and J. Matsunaga. Depth-first picture expression viewed from digital picture processing. *IEEE Transactions on Pattern Analysis and Machine Intelligence*, 5(4):373–384, July 1983. [regions; DF-expression] cited in A.1.3, A.2.2, A.6.3, A.8, D.1.2, F.2.1.2.4 (p. 212)

[1006] E. Kawaguchi, T. Endo, and M. Yokota. DF-expression of binary-valued picture and its relation to other pyramidal representations. In *Proceedings of the 5th International Conference on Pattern Recognition*, pages 822–827, Miami Beach, FL, December 1980. [regions; DF-expression] cited in A.1.3, A.1.4, D.1.2, D.1.3, F.2.1.2.4 (p. 212)

[1007] E. Kawaguchi and R. I. Taniguchi. Coded DF–expression for binary and multi-valued picture. In *Proceedings of the 9th International Conference on Pattern Recognition*, pages 1159–1163, Rome, Italy, November 1988. [regions; DF-expression]

[1008] A. C. Kay. FLEX; a flexible extensible language. Master's thesis, University of Utah, Salt Lake City, UT, 1968. [FLEX; programming languages] cited in F.P (p. xx), F.D (p. 743)

[1009] G. Kedem. The quad-CIF tree: a data structure for hierarchical on-line algorithms. In *Proceedings of the 19th Design Automation Conference*, pages 352–357, Las Vegas, NV, June 1982. Also University of Rochester Computer Science Technical Report TR–91, September 1981. [rectangles; MX-CIF quadtree] cited in D.3.5, D.3.5.1, F.1.7.1.5 (p. 115), F.2.1.4.1 (pp. 255, 259), F.3.4 (p. 466), F.3.4.1.1 (p. 467)

[1010] D. A. Keim. Efficient geometry-based similarity search of 3d spatial databases. In *Proceedings of the ACM SIGMOD Conference*, pages 419–430, Philadelphia, PA, June 1999. [volumes; similarity searching; R-tree]

[1011] A. Kela. Programmers guide to the PADL-2 octree processor output system. Production Automation Project Input/Output Group Memo 15, University of Rochester, Rochester, NY, January 1984. [rectangles; finite element analysis]

[1012] A. Kela. Hierarchical octree approximations for boundary representation-based geometric models. *Computer-Aided Design*, 21(6):355–362, July/August 1989. [volumes; boundary model (BRep)]

[1013] A. Kela, R. Perucchio, and H. Voelcker. Toward automatic finite element analysis. *Computers in Mechanical Engineering*, 5(1):57–71, July 1986. [finite element analysis] cited in A.P, A.1.4, A.7.1.6, D.1.3, D.5.6, F.2.2.4 (p. 405), F.2.4 (p. 426)

[1014] A. Kela, H. Voelcker, and J. Goldak. Automatic generation of hierarchical, spatially addressable finite-element meshes from CSG representations of solids. In *International Conference on Accuracy Estimates and Adaptive Refinements in Finite Element Computations*, pages 221–234, Lisbon, Portugal, June 1984. [finite element analysis; constructive solid geometry (CSG)] cited in A.1.4, D.1.3, F.2.4 (p. 426)

[1015] M. D. Kelly. Edge detection in pictures by computer using planning. In *Machine Intelligence*, B. Meltzer and D. Michie, eds., pages 397–

409. American Elsevier, New York, 1971. [regions] cited in A.1.4, D.1.3, F.2.4 (p. 424)

[1016] E. W. Kent, M. O. Shneier, and T. H. Hong. Building representations from fusions of multiple views. In *Proceedings of the IEEE International Conference on Robotics and Automation*, vol. 3, pages 1634–1639, San Francisco, April 1986. [volumes]

[1017] B. W. Kernighan and D. M. Ritchie. *The C Programming Language*. Prentice-Hall, Englewood Cliffs, NJ, 1978. [C; programming languages] cited in A.P, A.L, D.P, F.P (p. xx), F.D (p. 743)

[1018] M. L. Kersten and P. van Emde Boas. Local optimizations of QUAD trees. Informatica Rapport IR–51, Free University of Amsterdam, Amsterdam, The Netherlands, June 1979. [points; point quadtree] cited in D.2.3.1.s, F.1.4.1.1.s (p. 753)

[1019] K. Kim, S. K. Cha, and K. Kwon. Optimizing multidimensional index trees for main memory access. In *Proceedings of the ACM SIGMOD Conference*, pages 139–150, Santa Barbara, CA, May 2001. [regions; minimum bounding box]

[1020] S.-W. Kim, W.-S. Cho, M.-J. Lee, and K.-Y. Whang. A new algorithm for processing joins using the multilevel grid file. In *Proceedings of the 4th International Conference on Database Systems for Advanced Applications (DASFAA'95)*, T. W. Ling and Y. Masunaga, eds., vol. 5, pages 115–123, Singapore, April 1995. [points; multilevel grid file; spatial join]

[1021] S.-W. Kim and K.-Y. Whang. Asymptotic directory growth of the multilevel grid file. In *International Symposium on Next Generation Database Systems and Their Applications*, pages 257–264, September 1993. [points; multilevel grid file]

[1022] Y. C. Kim and J. K. Aggarwal. Rectangular coding for binary images. In *Proceedings of Computer Vision and Pattern Recognition'83*, pages 108–113, Washington, DC, June 1983. [regions] cited in A.1.3, A.9.3.4, D.1.2, F.2.1.2.2 (p. 208)

[1023] Y. C. Kim and J. K. Aggarwal. Rectangular parallelepiped coding: a volumetric representation of three-dimensional objects. *IEEE Journal of Robotics and Automation*, 2(3):127–134, September 1986. [regions; volumes] cited in A.1.3, A.9.3.4, D.1.2, F.2.1.2.2 (p. 208)

[1024] Y.-M. Kim and S.-B. Park. Complementary quadtree. *Image and Vision Computing*, 11(7):413–418, September 1993. [regions]

[1025] A. Kimse, ed. *Game Programming Gems 4*. Charles River Media, Hingham, MA, 2004. [game programming; general] cited in F.P (p. xvii)

[1026] D. Kirkpatrick. Optimal search in planar subdivisions. *SIAM Journal on Computing*, 12(1):28–35, February 1983. [regions; point location; K-structure] cited in D.P, D.4.3, F.1.5.1.4 (p. 69), F.2.1.2.8 (p. 224), F.2.1.3.2 (p. 237)

[1027] Y. Kitamura and F. Kishino. A parallel algorithm for octree generation from polyhedral shape representation. In *Proceedings of the 13th International Conference on Pattern Recognition*, vol. IV, pages 303–309, Vienna, Austria, August 1996. [volumes; region octree; parallel processing]

[1028] M. Kitsuregawa, L. Harada, and M. Takagi. Join strategies on KD-tree indexed relations. In *Proceedings of the 5th IEEE International Conference on Data Engineering*, pages 85–93, Los Angeles, February 1989. [points; k-d tree]

[1029] V. Klee. Can the measure of $\cup[a_i, b_i]$ be computed in less than $0(n\log n)$ steps? *American Mathematical Monthly*, 84(4):284–285, April 1977. [rectangles; measure problem] cited in D.3.3, F.3.2 (p. 447)

[1030] S. Kleiman, D. Shah, and B. Smaalders. *Programming with Threads*. SunSoft Press. Prentice-Hall, Englewood Cliffs, NJ, 1996. [threads; programming languages] cited in F.2.1.5.2.6 (p. 301)

[1031] R. Klein, G. Liebich, and W. Strasser. Mesh reduction with error control. In *Proceedings IEEE Visualization'96*, R. Yagel and G. M. Nielson, eds., pages 311–318, San Francisco, October 1996. [simplification; Hausdorff distance] cited in F.2.2.3.4 (p. 394)

[1032] J. M. Kleinberg. Two algorithms for nearest-neighbor search in high dimensions. In *Proceedings of the 29th Annual ACM Symposium on the Theory of Computing*, pages 599–608, El Paso, TX, May 1997. [metric space embedding; approximate nearest neighbor] cited in F.4.7.4 (pp. 715–716), F.4.7.4.s (p. 871)

[1033] A. Kleiner and K. E. Brassel. Hierarchical grid structures for static geographic data bases. In *Proceedings of Auto-Carto London*, vol. 1, pages 485–496, London, United Kingdom, September 1986. [regions]

[1034] R. Klette and A. Rosenfeld. *Digital Geometry: Geometric Methods for Digital Picture Analysis*. Morgan-Kaufmann, San Francisco, 2004. [digital geometry; general] cited in F.P (p. xx)

[1035] A. Klinger. Patterns and search statistics. In *Optimizing Methods in Statistics*, J. S. Rustagi, ed., pages 303–337. Academic Press, New York, 1971. [regions; region quadtree] cited in A.1.3, A.1.4, D.1.2, D.1.3, F.2.1.2.4 (p. 211), F.2.4 (p. 423)

[1036] A. Klinger and C. R. Dyer. Experiments in picture representation using regular decomposition. *Computer Graphics and Image Processing*, 5(1):68–105, March 1976. [regions; region quadtree] cited in A.1.3, A.1.4, A.2.1.1, D.1.2, D.1.3, F.2.4 (p. 423)

[1037] A. Klinger and M. L. Rhodes. Organization and access of image data by areas. *IEEE Transactions on Pattern Analysis and Machine Intelligence*, 1(1):50–60, January 1979. [regions] cited in A.2.1.1, A.3.2.2

[1038] J. T. Klosowski, M. Held, J. S. B. Mitchell, H. Sowizral, and K. Zikan. Efficient collision detection using bounding volume hierarchies of k-DOPs. *IEEE Transactions on Visualization and Computer Graphics*, 4(1):21–36, January 1998. [volumes; minimum bounding box; collision detection; k-DOP] cited in F.2.1.1 (p. 195)

[1039] J. Knipe and X. Li. A new quadtree decomposition reconstruction method. In *Proceedings of the 13th International Conference on Pattern Recognition*, vol. II, pages 364–369, Vienna, Austria, August 1996. [regions; region quadtree; compression]

[1040] G. D. Knott. Expandable open addressing hash table storage and retrieval. In *Proceedings of SIGFIDET Workshop on Data Description, Access and Control*, pages 187–206, San Diego, CA, November 1971. [points; linear hashing; extendible hashing] cited in D.2.8.1, D.2.8.2, F.1.7.1 (p. 97), F.B (p. 729)

[1041] K. Knowlton. Progressive transmission of grey-scale and binary pictures by simple efficient, and lossless encoding schemes. *Proceedings of the IEEE*, 68(7):885–896, July 1980. [regions; bintree] cited in A.1.3, A.8, A.8.1, A.8.3, D.1.4.1, F.2.1.2.6 (p. 221), F.2.3.1 (p. 411)

[1042] K. C. Knowlton. A fast storage allocator. *Communications of the ACM*, 8(10):623–625, October 1965. [dynamic storage allocation; buddy system] cited in F.1.7.2.1 (p. 135), F.B (p. 731)

[1043] D. E. Knuth. Big omicron and big omega and big theta. *SIGACT News*, 8(2):18–24, April-June 1976. [algorithms; general] cited in A.P, D.P, F.P (p. xx)

[1044] D. E. Knuth. *The Art of Computer Programming: Fundamental Algorithms*, vol. 1. Addison-Wesley, Reading, MA, third edition, 1997. [algorithms; general] cited in A.P, A.1.4, A.2.1.4, A.3.2.1, D.P, D.1.3, D.2.3.1, D.2.8.2, D.4.3.2, F.P (p. xxi), F.1.1 (p. 7), F.1.4.1.1 (p. 30), F.1.7.2.1 (p. 135), F.2.1.1.3 (p. 202), F.2.1.3.3.1 (p. 243), F.2.4 (p. 424), F.4.1.5 (p. 507), F.A (p. 722), F.B (p. 731)

[1045] D. E. Knuth. *The Art of Computer Programming: Seminumerical Algorithms*, vol. 2. Addison-Wesley, Reading, MA, third edition, 1998. [algorithms; general] cited in F.P (p. xxi)

[1046] D. E. Knuth. *The Art of Computer Programming: Sorting and Searching*, vol. 3. Addison-Wesley, Reading, MA, second edition, 1998. [algorithms; general] cited in A.P, A.1.3, D.P, D.1.2, D.2.1, D.2.2, D.2.3.1, D.2.3.3, D.2.4.1, D.2.4.3, D.2.5, D.2.6.2, D.2.6.2.s, D.2.8.2, D.2.8.2.1.s, F.P (p. xxi), F.1 (pp. 1–4), F.1.1 (pp. 5, 10), F.1.3 (p. 20), F.1.4.1.1 (p. 31), F.1.4.1.3 (p. 37), F.1.5.1.1 (p. 52), F.1.5.1.3 (p. 56), F.1.5.2.4 (p. 76), F.1.7.3 (p. 163), F.2 (p. 192), F.2.1.1.3 (p. 194), F.2.1.1.3 (p. 203), F.4 (p. 486), F.4.5.2.4 (p. 609), F.A (pp. 724–725), F.B (p. 729), F.C (p. 740), F.1.1.s (p. 747), F.1.5.2.1.s (p. 764), F.B.s (p. 874), F.X.K (p. 947)

[1047] H. Kobayashi, T. Nakamura, and Y. Shigei. Parallel processing of an object space for image synthesis using ray tracing. *Visual Computer*, 3(1):13–22, February 1987. [volumes; ray tracing; parallel processing] cited in A.3.3

[1048] H. Kobayashi, S. Nishimura, H. Kubota, T. Nakamura, and Y. Shigei. Load balancing strategies for a parallel ray-tracing system based on constant subdivision. *Visual Computer*, 4(4):197–209, October 1988. [volumes; ray tracing; parallel processing]

[1049] L. Kobbelt, S. Campagna, and H.-P. Seidel. A general framework for mesh decimation. In *Proceedings of Graphics Interface'98*, W. Davis, K. Booth, and A. Fournier, eds., pages 43–50, Banff, Alberta, Canada, May 1998. [surfaces; surface simplification; vertex decimation] cited in F.2.2.3.4 (p. 394)

[1050] L. Kobbelt, S. Campagna, J. Vorsatz, and H.-P. Seidel. Interactive multi-resolution modeling on arbitrary meshes. In *Proceedings of the SIGGRAPH'98 Conference*, pages 105–114, Orlando, FL, July 1998. [surfaces; surface simplification; vertex decimation] cited in F.2.2.3.4 (p. 395)

[1051] P. Koistinen. Interval methods for constructive solid geometry: display via block model conversion. Master's thesis, Helsinki University of Technology, Helsinki, Finland, May 1988. [volumes; interval arithmetic] cited in D.5.5.1

[1052] P. Koistinen, M. Tamminen, and H. Samet. Viewing solid models by bintree conversion. In *Proceedings of the EUROGRAPHICS'85 Conference*, C. E. Vandoni, ed., pages 147–157, Nice, France, September 1985. [volumes; bintree] cited in A.7.1.4

[1053] M. R. Kolahdouzan and C. Shahabi. Continuous k-nearest neighbor queries in spatial network databases. In *Proceedings of the 2nd International Workshop on Spatio-Temporal Database Management STDBM'04*, J. Sander and M. A. Nascimento, eds., pages 33–40, Toronto, Canada, August 2004. [lines; points; spatial networks; nearest neighbor; shortest path algorithm] cited in F.4.1.6 (p. 515)

[1054] M. R. Kolahdouzan and C. Shahabi. Voronoi-based k nearest neighbor search for spatial network databases. In *Proceedings of the 30th International Conference on Very Large Data Bases (VLDB)*, M. A. Nascimento, M. T. Özsu, D. Kossmann, R. J. Miller, J. A. Blakely, and K. B. Schiefer, eds., pages 840–851, Toronto, Canada, September 2004. [lines; points; spatial networks; nearest neighbor; Voronoi diagram] cited in F.4.1.6 (p. 515)

[1055] G. Kollios, D. Gunopulos, and V. J. Tsotras. On indexing mobile objects. In *Proceedings of the 18th ACM SIGACT-SIGMOD-SIGART Symposium on Principles of Database Systems (PODS)*, pages 261–272, Philadelphia, PA, May–June 1999. [moving objects]

[1056] G. Kollios, D. Papadopoulos, D. Gunopulos, and V. J. Tsotras. Indexing mobile objects using dual transformations. *VLDB Journal*, 14(2):238–256, April 2005. [points; moving objects]

[1057] G. Kollios, V. J. Tsotras, D. Gunopulos, A. Delis, and M. Hadjieleftheriou. Indexing animated objects using spatiotemporal access methods. *IEEE Transactions on Knowledge and Data Engineering*, 13(5):758–777, November/December 2001. [video database; moving objects] cited in F.P (p. xvii)

[1058] C. P. Kolovson and M. Stonebraker. Segment indexes: dynamic indexing techniques for multi-dimensional interval data. In *Proceedings of the ACM SIGMOD Conference*, pages 138–147, Denver, CO, May 1991. [rectangles]

[1059] J. Koplowitz and J. DeLeone. Hierarchical representation of chain-encoded binary image contours. *Computer Vision and Image Understanding*, 63(2):344–352, March 1996. [lines]

[1060] F. Korn and S. Muthukrishnan. Influence sets based on reverse nearest neighbor queries. In *Proceedings of the ACM SIGMOD Conference*, W. Chen, J. Naughton, and P. A. Bernstein, eds., pages 201–212, Dallas, TX, May 2000. [points; distance join; reverse nearest neighbor (RNN)] cited in F.4.5.8 (p. 658)

[1061] F. Korn, S. Muthukrishnan, and D. Srivastava. Reverse nearest neighbor aggregates over data streams. In *Proceedings of the 28th International Conference on Very Large Data Bases (VLDB)*, pages 814–825, Hong Kong, China, August 2002. [points; reverse nearest neighbor (RNN)]

[1062] F. Korn, B.-U. Pagel, and C. Faloutsos. On the "dimensionality curse" and the "self-similarity blessing". *IEEE Transactions on Knowledge and Data Engineering*, 13(1):96–111, January/February 2001. [points; high-dimensional data; nearest neighbor; curse of dimensionality; fractal dimension]

[1063] F. Korn, N. Sidiropoulos, C. Faloutsos, E. Siegel, and Z. Protopapas. Fast nearest neighbor search in medical image databases. In *Proceedings of the 22nd International Conference on Very Large Data Bases (VLDB)*, T. M. Vijayaraman, A. P. Buchmann, C. Mohan, and N. L. Sarda, eds., pages 215–226, Mumbai (Bombay), India, September 1996. [medical image database; nearest neighbor] cited in F.4.6.1.2 (pp. 666–668)

[1064] F. Korn, N. Sidiropoulos, C. Faloutsos, E. Siegel, and Z. Protopapas. Fast and effective retrieval of medical tumor shapes. *IEEE Transactions on Knowledge and Data Engineering*, 10(6):889–904, November/December 1998. [medical image database; nearest neighbor] cited in F.4.6.1.2 (p. 667)

[1065] M. R. Korn and C. R. Dyer. 3-d multiview object representations for model-based object recognition. *Pattern Recognition*, 20(1):91–103, 1987. Also University of Wisconsin Computer Science Technical Report TR 602, June 1985. [surfaces]

[1066] M. Kornacker, C. Mohan, and J. M. Hellerstein. Concurrency and recovery in generalized search trees. In *Proceedings of the ACM SIGMOD Conference*, J. Peckham, ed., pages 62–72, Tucson, AZ, May 1997. [GiST; concurrency]

[1067] H. Kosch and S. Atnafu. Processing a multimedia join through the method of nearest neighbor search. *Information Processing Letters*, 82(5):269–276, June 2002. [points; distance semijoin; nearest neighbor]

[1068] D. Kossmann, F. Ramsak, and S. Rost. Shooting stars in the sky: an online algorithm for skyline queries. In *Proceedings of the 28th International Conference on Very Large Data Bases (VLDB)*, pages 275–286, Hong Kong, China, August 2002. [points; skyline query; point dominance query; nearest neighbor] cited in F.4.1.5 (pp. 504, 506–507)

[1069] R. K. Kothuri and S. Ravada. Efficient processing of large spatial queries using interior approximations. In *Advances in Spatial and Temporal Databases—7th International Symposium, SSTD'01*, C. S. Jensen, M. Schneider, B. Seeger, and V. J. Tsotras, eds., vol. 2121 of Springer-Verlag Lecture Notes in Computer Science, pages 404–421, Redondo Beach, CA, July 2001. [regions]

[1070] R. K. V. Kothuri, S. Ravada, and D. Abugov. Quadtree and R-tree indexes in Oracle spatial: a comparison using GIS data. In *Proceedings of the ACM SIGMOD Conference*, pages 546–557, Madison, WI, June 2002. [R-tree; MX quadtree]

[1071] N. Koudas, B. C. Ooi, H. T. Shen, and A. K. H. Tung. LDC: enabling search by partial distance in a hyper-dimensional space. In *Proceedings of the 20th IEEE International Conference on Data Engineering*, pages 6–17, Boston, March 2004. [high-dimensional data; similarity searching]

[1072] N. Koudas and K. C. Sevcik. Size separation spatial join. In *Proceedings of the ACM SIGMOD Conference*, J. Peckham, ed., pages 324–335, Tucson, AZ, May 1997. [spatial join] cited in F.P (p. xx)

[1073] N. Koudas and K. C. Sevcik. High dimensional similarity joins: algorithms and performance evaluation. In *Proceedings of the 14th IEEE International Conference on Data Engineering*, pages 466–475, Orlando, FL, February 1998. [high-dimensional data; similarity join]

[1074] E. Koutsoupias and D. S. Taylor. Tight bounds for 2-dimensional indexing schemes. In *Proceedings of the 17th ACM SIGACT-SIGMOD-SIGART Symposium on Principles of Database Systems (PODS)*, pages 52–58, Seattle, WA, June 1998. [points; range query]

[1075] M. J. van Kreveld and M. H. Overmars. Divided *k-d* trees. *Algorithmica*, 6(6):840–858, 1991. [points; divided k-d tree] cited in F.1.5.1.4 (p. 65)

[1076] H.-P. Kriegel. Variants of multidimensional B-trees as dynamic index structures for retrieval in database systems. In *Proceedings of the Eighth International Workshop on Graphtheoretic Concepts in Computer Science (WG'82)*, H.-J. Schneider and H. Göttler, eds., pages 109–128, Neuenkirchen (near Erlangen), West Germany, 1982. Hanser Verlag. [points; kB$^+$-tree] cited in F.1.1 (p. 9)

[1077] H.-P. Kriegel. Performance of index structures for databases. In *Proceedings of WG'83, International Workshop on Graphtheoretic Concepts in Computer Science*, M. Nagl and J. Perl, eds., pages 151–166, Haus Ohrbeck (near Osnabrück), West Germany, 1983. Trauner Verlag. [points; kB-tree; grid file; multidimensional B-tree (MDBT)] cited in F.1.1 (p. 9)

[1078] H.-P. Kriegel. Performance comparison of index structures for multikey retrieval. In *Proceedings of the ACM SIGMOD Conference*, pages 186–285, Boston, June 1984. [points; kB-tree; grid file;

multidimensional B-tree (MDBT)] cited in D.2.8.2, F.1.1 (p. 9), F.1.7.2.1 (p. 136)

[1079] H.-P. Kriegel, T. Brinkhoff, and R. Schneider. The combination of spatial access methods and computational geometry in geographic database systems. In *Advances in Spatial Databases—2nd Symposium, SSD'91*, O. Günther and H.-J. Schek, eds., vol. 525 of Springer-Verlag Lecture Notes in Computer Science, pages 5–21, Zurich, Switzerland, August 1991. [regions]

[1080] H.-P. Kriegel, P. Heep, S. Heep, M. Schiwietz, and R. Schneider. An access method based query processor for spatial databases. In *Proceedings of the Workshop on Geographic Database Management Systems*, G. Gambosi, M. Scholl, and H.-W. Six, eds., pages 273–292, Capri, Italy, May 1991. Springer-Verlag. [spatial database; general]

[1081] H.-P. Kriegel, H. Horn, and M. Schiwietz. The performance of object decomposition techniques for spatial query processing. In *Advances in Spatial Databases—2nd Symposium, SSD'91*, O. Günther and H.-J. Schek, eds., vol. 525 of Springer-Verlag Lecture Notes in Computer Science, pages 257–276, Zurich, Switzerland, August 1991. [regions; minimum bounding box] cited in F.2.1.3 (p. 233), F.2.1.5.2.7 (p. 303)

[1082] H.-P. Kriegel and M. Schiwietz. Performance comparison of point and spatial access methods. In *Design and Implementation of Large Spatial Databases—1st Symposium, SSD'89*, A. Buchmann, O. Günther, T. R. Smith, and Y.-F. Wang, eds., vol. 409 of Springer-Verlag Lecture Notes in Computer Science, pages 89–114, Santa Barbara, CA, July 1989. [points; R-tree]

[1083] H.-P. Kriegel, T. Schmidt, and T. Seidl. 3d similarity search by shape approximation. In *Advances in Spatial Databases—5th International Symposium, SSD'97*, M. Scholl and A. Voisard, eds., vol. 1262 of Springer-Verlag Lecture Notes in Computer Science, pages 11–28, Berlin, Germany, July 1997. [regions; similarity searching]

[1084] H.-P. Kriegel and B. Seeger. Multidimensional order preserving linear hashing with partial expansions. In *Proceedings of the 1st International Conference on Database Theory (ICDT'86)*, G. Ausiello and P. Atzeni, eds., vol. 243 of Springer-Verlag Lecture Notes in Computer Science, pages 203–220, Rome, Italy, September 1986. [points; linear hashing] cited in F.1.7.2.3.4 (p. 152), F.1.7.2.4 (p. 153), F.1.7.2.4.1 (p. 153), F.1.7.2.3.4.s (p. 774)

[1085] H.-P. Kriegel and B. Seeger. PLOP–hashing: a grid file without directory. In *Proceedings of the 4th IEEE International Conference on Data Engineering*, pages 369–376, Los Angeles, February 1988. [points; PLOP hashing] cited in F.1.7.2.3.2 (p. 148), F.1.7.2.4 (p. 153), F.1.7.2.4.2 (p. 154)

[1086] H.-P. Kriegel and B. Seeger. Multidimensional quantile hashing is very efficient for nonuniform distributions. *Information Sciences*, 48(2):99–117, July 1989. Also see *Proceedings of the 3rd IEEE International Conference on Data Engineering*, pages 10–17, Los Angeles, February 1987. [points; quantile hashing] cited in F.1.7.2.4 (p. 153), F.1.7.2.4.1 (p. 153)

[1087] R. Krishnamurthy and K.-Y. Whang. Multilevel grid files. Technical report, IBM T. J. Watson Research Center, Yorktown Heights, NY, 1985. [points; multilevel grid file; buddy-tree] cited in F.1.7.1.5 (pp. 110, 113, 115), F.3.3.3 (p. 465)

[1088] K. Kronlof and M. Tamminen. A viewing pipeline for discrete solid modeling. *Visual Computer*, 1(1):24–36, July 1985. [volumes; bintree]

[1089] W. G. Kropatsch. Curve representations in multiple resolutions. In *Proceedings of the 8th International Conference on Pattern Recognition*, pages 1283–1285, Paris, France, October 1986. [lines; pyramid] cited in A.1.4, D.1.3, F.2.4 (p. 425)

[1090] J. B. Kruskal and M. Wish. Multidimensional scaling. Technical report, Sage University Series, Beverly Hills, CA, 1978. [metric space embedding; multidimensional scaling (MDS)] cited in F.4.7.1 (p. 689), F.4.7.2.4 (p. 694)

[1091] A. Kumar. G-tree: a new data structure for organizing multidimensional data. *IEEE Transactions on Knowledge and Data Engineering*, 6(2):341–347, April 1994. [points; B-tree; BD-tree; k-d-B-tree]

[1092] A. Kumar, V. J. Tsotras, and C. Faloutsos. Designing access methods for bitemporal databases. *IEEE Transactions on Knowledge and Data Engineering*, 10(1):1–20, January/February 1998. [temporal database] cited in F.P (p. xvii)

[1093] P. S. Kumar and M. Manohar. On probability of forest of quadtrees reducing to quadtrees. *Information Processing Letters*, 22(3):109–111, March 1986. [regions; forests of quadtrees]

[1094] T. L. Kunii, I. Fujishiro, and X. Mao. G-quadtree: a hierarchical representation of gray-scale digital images. *Visual Computer*, 2(4):219–226, August 1986. [regions; region quadtree]

[1095] T. L. Kunii, T. Satoh, and K. Yamaguchi. Generation of topological boundary representations from octree encoding. *IEEE Computer Graphics and Applications*, 5(3):29–38, March 1985. [volumes; region octree] cited in D.5.4

[1096] D. Kurlander and E. A. Bier. Graphical search and replace. *Computer Graphics*, 22(4):113–120, August 1988. Also in *Proceedings of the SIGGRAPH'88 Conference*, Atlanta, GA, August 1988. [regions; graphical search and replace; user interface] cited in D.3.4.s, F.3.3.1.s (p. 825)

[1097] E. Kushilevitz, R. Ostrovsky, and Y. Rabani. Efficient search for approximate nearest neighbor in high dimensional spaces. In *Proceedings of the 30th Annual ACM Symposium on the Theory of Computing*, pages 614–623, Dallas, TX, May 1998. [metric space embedding; approximate nearest neighbor] cited in F.4.7.4 (pp. 715–716), F.4.7.4.s (p. 871)

[1098] T. Kushner, A. Wu, and A. Rosenfeld. Image processing on ZMOB. *IEEE Transactions on Computers*, 31(10):943–951, October 1982. [regions; hardware; parallel processing]

[1099] M. Lacroix and P. Lavency. Preferences: putting more knowledge into queries. In *Proceedings of the 13th International Conference on Very Large Databases (VLDB)*, P. M. Stocker and W. Kent, eds., pages 217–225, Brighton, United Kingdom, September 1987. [preference query] cited in F.4.1.5 (p. 505)

[1100] G. G. Lai, D. Fussell, and D. F. Wong. HV/VH trees: a new spatial data structure for fast region queries. In *Proceedings of the 30th ACM/IEEE Design Automation Conference*, pages 43–47, Dallas, TX, June 1993. [rectangles; bounded quadtree (BQT); MX-CIF quadtree; HV/VH tree] cited in F.3.4.2 (pp. 476–477)

[1101] G. G. Lai, D. S. Fussell, and D. F. Wong. Hinted quad trees for VLSI geometry DRC based on efficient searching for neighbors. *IEEE Transactions on Computer-Aided Design of Integrated Circuits and Systems*, 15(3):317–324, March 1996. [rectangles; hinted quadtree] cited in F.3.4.3 (pp. 482–483)

[1102] J. M. Lane, L. C. Carpenter, T. Whitted, and J. F. Blinn. Scan line methods for displaying parametrically defined surfaces. *Communications of the ACM*, 23(1):23–34, January 1980. [surfaces] cited in A.7.1.6

[1103] S. Larsen and L. N. Kanal. Analysis of k-nearest neighbor branch and bound rules. *Pattern Recognition Letters*, 4(2):71–77, April 1986. [points; depth-first nearest neighbor algorithm; branch-and-bound nearest neighbor algorithm] cited in F.4.2 (p. 517), F.4.2.2 (pp. 521–522, 526–527, 529), F.4.2.3 (pp. 530, 532–533), F.4.2.5 (pp. 541, 546), F.4.2.8 (p. 556), F.4.5.3.2 (p. 616), F.4.2.2.s (p. 839)

[1104] P.-Å. Larson. Dynamic hashing. *BIT*, 18:184–201, 1978. [dynamic hashing] cited in F.B (pp. 729–730)

[1105] P.-Å. Larson. Linear hashing with partial expansions. In *Proceedings of the 6th International Conference on Very Large Databases (VLDB)*, F. H. Lochovsky and R. W. Taylor, eds., pages 224–232, Montréal, Canada, October 1980. [points; linear hashing] cited in D.2.8.2, F.1.7.2.3.4 (p. 152), F.B (p. 733)

[1106] P.-Å. Larson. Dynamic hash tables. *Communications of the ACM*, 31(4):446–457, April 1988. [points; linear hashing; spiral hashing] cited in D.2.8.2, D.2.8.2.2.s, F.1.7.2.3 (p. 140), F.1.7.2.4 (p. 153), F.B (pp. 730, 734), F.C (pp. 735, 739, 742), F.C.s (p. 875)

[1107] P.-Å. Larson. Linear hashing with separators—a dynamic hashing scheme achieving one-access. *ACM Transactions on Database Systems*, 13(3):366–388, September 1988. [points; linear hashing]

[1108] L. J. Latecki and R. Lakämper. Shape similarity measure based on correspondence of visual parts. *IEEE Transactions on Pattern Analysis and Machine Intelligence*, 22(10):1185–1190, October 2000. [regions; turning angle; similarity searching; image database]

[1109] L. J. Latecki and R. Lakämper. Application of planar shape comparison to object retrieval in image databases. *Pattern Recognition*, 35(1):15–29, January 2002. [regions; turning angle; similarity searching; image database]

[1110] M. Lattanzi and C. A. Shaffer. An optimal boundary to quadtree conversion algorithm. *CVGIP: Image Understanding*, 53(3):303–312, May 1991. [regions; chain code; region quadtree construction; boundary following]

[1111] R. Laurini. Graphical data bases built on Peano space-filling curves. In *Proceedings of the EUROGRAPHICS'85 Conference*, C. E. Vandoni, ed., pages 327–338, Nice, France, September 1985. [regions; space-filling curve] cited in A.1.4, D.1.3, F.2.1.1.2 (p. 202)

[1112] R. Laurini. Manipulation of spatial objects by a Peano tuple algebra. Computer Science Technical Report TR–1893, University of Maryland, College Park, MD, July 1987. [regions; space-filling curve]

[1113] R. Laurini and D. Thompson. *Fundamentals of Spatial Information Systems*. Academic Press, San Diego, CA, 1992. [geographic information systems (GIS); general] cited in F.P (p. xix)

[1114] U. Lauther. 4-dimensional binary search trees as a means to speed up associative searches in design rule verification of integrated circuits. *Journal of Design Automation and Fault-Tolerant Computing*, 2(3):241–147, July 1978. [rectangles; k-d tree] cited in D.3.4, F.3.3.2.2 (p. 460), F.3.4.2 (p. 477)

[1115] J. P. Lauzon, D. M. Mark, L. Kikuchi, and J. A. Guevara. Two-dimensional run-encoding for quadtree representation. *Computer Vision, Graphics, and Image Processing*, 30(1):56–69, April 1985. [regions; two-dimensional runlength encoding] cited in A.2.1.3, A.3.4.1, A.5.1.3, F.2.3.1 (p. 413)

[1116] Lavakusha, A. K. Pujari, and P. G. Reddy. Linear octrees by volume intersection. *Computer Vision, Graphics, and Image Processing*, 45(3):371–379, March 1989. [volumes; region octree]

[1117] Lavakusha, A. K. Pujari, and P. G. Reddy. Polygonal representation by edge k-d trees. *Pattern Recognition Letters*, 11(6):391–394, April 1990. [lines; regions]

[1118] J. Lavenberg. Fast view-dependent level-of-detail rendering using cached geometry. In *Proceedings IEEE Visualization 2002*, R. Moorehead, M. Gross, and K. I. Joy, eds., pages 259–265, Boston, October 2002. [surfaces; polygon simplification; restricted bintree]

[1119] E. Lawler. *Combinatorial Optimization: Networks and Matroids*. Holt, Rinehart and Winston, New York, 1976. [network optimization; general] cited in D.2.9.s, F.1.9.s (p. 776)

[1120] E. L. Lawler, J. K. Lenstra, A. H. G. Rinnooy-Kan, and D. B. Shmoys. *The Traveling Salesman Problem: A Guided Tour of Combinatorial Optimization*. John Wiley & Sons, New York, 1985. [traveling salesman problem] cited in A.1.4, D.1.3, F.2.1.1.2 (p. 202)

[1121] D. Lea. Digital and Hilbert *k-d* trees. *Information Processing Letters*, 27(1):35–41, February 1988. [points; Hilbert tree] cited in F.2.1.5.2.2 (p. 280)

[1122] V. F. Leavers. Survey: which Hough transform? *CVGIP: Image Understanding*, 58(2):250–264, September 1993. [Hough transform; survey] cited in F.1.5.1.4 (p. 62)

[1123] A. W. F. Lee, W. Swedens, P. Schröder, L. Cowsar, and D. Dobkin. MAPS: multiresolution adaptive parameterization of surfaces. In *Proceedings of the SIGGRAPH'98 Conference*, pages 95–104, Orlando, FL, July 1998. [surfaces; surface simplification] cited in F.2.2.3.4 (p. 395)

[1124] D.-H. Lee and H.-J. Kim. SPY-TEC: an efficient indexing method for similarity search in high-dimensional data spaces. *Data and Knowledge Engineering*, 34(1):77–97, July 2000. [points; high-dimensional data; pyramid technique; SPY-TEC] cited in F.4.4.7 (p. 587)

[1125] D.-H. Lee and H.-J. Kim. An efficient nearest neighbor search in high-dimensional data spaces. *Information Processing Letters*, 81(5):239–246, March 2002. [points; high-dimensional data; pyramid technique; SPY-TEC]; incremental nearest neighbor algorithm] cited in F.4.4.7 (p. 587)

[1126] D. T. Lee. Maximum clique problem of rectangle graphs. In *Advances in Computing Research: Computational Geometry*, F. P. Preparata, ed., vol. 1, pages 91–107. JAI Press, Greenwich, CT, 1983. [rectangles; maximum clique problem] cited in D.2.9.s, D.3.3, D.3.3.s, F.3.2 (p. 448), F.1.9.s (p. 776), F.3.2.s (p. 824)

[1127] D. T. Lee and A. K. Lin. Generalized Delaunay triangulation for planar graphs. *Discrete & Computational Geometry*, 1:201–217, 1986. [regions; constrained Delaunay triangulation] cited in F.2.2.1.5 (p. 351)

[1128] D. T. Lee and F. P. Preparata. Location of a point in a planar subdivision and its applications. *SIAM Journal on Computing*, 6(3):594–606, July 1977. [regions; point location; separating chain method] cited in D.3.2.2, D.4.3, D.4.3.2, F.1.5.1.4 (p. 69), F.2.1.2.8 (p. 224), F.2.1.3.3 (p. 242), F.3.1.2 (p. 435)

[1129] D. T. Lee and F. P. Preparata. An improved algorithm for the rectangle enclosure problem. *Journal of Algorithms*, 3(3):218–224, September 1982. [rectangles; point dominance query] cited in D.3.2.4, F.3.1.4 (p. 444)

[1130] D. T. Lee and F. P. Preparata. Computational geometry—a survey. *IEEE Transactions on Computers*, 33(12):1072–1101, December 1984. [computational geometry; survey]

[1131] D. T. Lee and B. J. Schachter. Two algorithms for constructing a Delaunay triangulation. *International Journal of Computer and Information Sciences*, 9(3):219–242, June 1980. [regions; constrained Delaunay triangulation] cited in F.2.2.1.5 (p. 351)

[1132] D. T. Lee and C. K. Wong. Worst-case analysis for region and partial region searches in multidimensional binary search trees and balanced quad trees. *Acta Informatica*, 9(1):23–29, 1977. [points; k-d tree; point quadtree; range query] cited in D.2.3, D.2.3.2, D.2.3.3, D.2.3.3.s, D.2.4.3, F.1.4.1.2 (p. 34), F.1.4.1.3 (p. 37), F.1.5.1.3 (pp. 55–56), F.1.4.1.3.s (p. 755)

[1133] D. T. Lee and C. K. Wong. Quintary trees: a file structure for multidimensional database systems. *ACM Transactions on Database Systems*, 5(4):339–353, September 1980. [points; quintary tree; multiattribute tree (MAT)] cited in F.1.1 (pp. 7, 13), F.1.1.s (pp. 747–748)

[1134] J.-H. Lee, Y.-K. Lee, and K.-Y. Whang. A region splitting strategy for physical database design of multidimensional file organizations. In *Proceedings of the 23rd International Conference on Very Large Data Bases (VLDB)*, M. Jarke, M. J. Carey, K. R. Dittrich, F. H. Lochovsky, P. Loucopoulos, and M. A. Jeusfeld, eds., pages 416–425, Athens, Greece, August 1997. [points]

[1135] J.-T. Lee and G. G. Belford. An efficient object-based algorithm for spatial searching, insertion and deletion. In *Proceedings of the 8th IEEE International Conference on Data Engineering*, F. Golshani, ed., pages 40–47, Tempe, AZ, February 1992. [regions; minimum bounding box]

[1136] M. Lee, L. De Floriani, and H. Samet. Constant-time neighbor finding in hierarchical tetrahedral meshes. In *Proceedings of the 2001 International Conference on Shape Modeling and Applications*, pages 286–295, Genova, Italy, May 2001. [volumes; tetrahedralizations; neighbor finding]

[1137] M. Lee, L. De Floriani, and H. Samet. Constant-time navigation in four-dimensional nested simplicial meshes. In *Proceedings of the 2004 International Conference on Shape Modeling and Applications*, pages 221–230, Genova, Italy, June 2004. [hypervolumes; neighbor finding]

[1138] M. Lee and H. Samet. Navigating through triangle meshes implemented as linear quadtrees. *ACM Transactions on Graphics*, 19(2):79–121, April 2000. Also see *Proceedings of the 8th International Symposium on Spatial Data Handling*, T. K. Poiker and N. Chrisman, eds., pages 22–33, GIS Lab, Department of Geography, Simon Fraser University, Burnaby, British Columbia, Canada, July 1998. International Geographical Union, Geographic Information Science Study Group; and University of Maryland Computer Science Technical Report TR–3900, April 1998. [surfaces; triangulations; spherical representation; neighbor finding] cited in F.2.1.1.1 (p. 198)

[1139] M.-L. Lee, W. Hsu, C. S. Jensen, B. Cui, and K. L. Teo. Supporting frequent updates in R-trees: a bottom-up approach. In *Proceedings of the 29th International Conference on Very Large Data Bases (VLDB)*, J. C. Freytag, P. C. Lockemann, S. Abiteboul, M. J. Carey, P. G. Selinger, and A. Heuer, eds., pages 608–619, Berlin, Germany, September 2003. [rectangles; R-tree]

[1140] S.-H. Lee and K. Lee. Partial entity structure: a compact non-manifold boundary representation based on partial topological entities. In *Proceedings of the 6th ACM Symposium on Solid Modeling and Applications*, pages 159–170, Ann Arbor, MI, June 2001. [surfaces; partial-entity structure; nonmanifold objects] cited in F.2.2.1.1 (p. 316)

[1141] S.-S. Lee, S.-J. Horng, H.-R. Tsai, and S.-S. Tsai. Building a quadtree and its application on a reconfigurable mesh. *Pattern Recognition*, 29(9):1571–1579, September 1996. [regions; region quadtree]

[1142] Y.-J. Lee and C.-W. Chung. The DR-tree: a main memory data structure for complex multi-dimensional objects. *Geoinformatica*, 5(2):181–207, June 2001. [regions; R-tree; R$^+$-tree; DR-tree] cited in F.2.1.5.2.7 (p. 303)

[1143] Y. T. Lee and A. A. G. Requicha. Algorithms for computing the volume and other integral properties of solids. I. Known methods and open issues. *Communications of the ACM*, 25(9):635–641, September 1982. [volumes; solid modeling; constructive solid geometry (CSG); survey] cited in D.5.5, F.2.2.2.7 (p. 372)

[1144] Y. T. Lee and A. A. G. Requicha. Algorithms for computing the volume and other integral properties of solids. II. A family of algorithms based on representation conversion and cellular approximation. *Communications of the ACM*, 25(9):642–650, September 1982. [volumes; solid modeling; constructive solid geometry (CSG)] cited in D.5.5, D.5.5.1, F.2.2.2.7 (p. 372)

[1145] J. van Leeuwen and D. Wood. The measure problem for rectangular ranges in *d*-space. *Journal of Algorithms*, 2(3):282–300, September 1981. [rectangles; measure problem] cited in D.3.3, D.3.3.s, F.3.2 (pp. 448–449), F.3.2.s (p. 824)

[1146] S. Lefebvre, S. Hornus, and F. Neyret. Octree textures on the GPU. In *GPU Gems 2*, M. Pharr, ed. Addison-Wesley, Upper Saddle River, NJ, 2005. [volumes; surfaces; textures; region octree; GPU] cited in F.P (p. xviii)

[1147] P. Leinen. Data structures and concepts for adaptive finite element methods. *Computing*, 55:325–354, 1995. [surfaces; finite element analysis; triangulations; survey] cited in F.2.2.4 (p. 405)

[1148] D. A. Lelewer and D. S. Hirschberg. Data compression. *ACM Computing Surveys*, 19(3):261–296, September 1987. [regions; compression; survey] cited in A.8

[1149] L. N. Lester and J. Sandor. Computer graphics on a hexagonal grid. *Computers & Graphics*, 8(4):401–409, 1984. [regions; hexagonal tiling; antialiasing] cited in F.2.1.1.1 (p. 198)

[1150] P. Letellier. *Transmission d'images à bas débit pour un système de communication téléphonique adatée aux sounds*. PhD thesis, Université de Paris-Sud, Paris, France, September 1983. [regions; MX quadtree] cited in D.2.6.1, F.1.4.2.1 (p. 40)

[1151] C. H. C. Leung. Approximate storage utilization of B-trees: a simple derivation and generalizations. *Information Processing Letters*, 19(12):199–201, November 1984. [B-tree] cited in F.1.7.3 (pp. 163–164)

[1152] S. T. Leutenegger and M. A. López. The effect of buffering on the performance of R-trees. *IEEE Transactions on Knowledge and Data Engineering*, 12(1):33–44, January/February 2000. Also see *Proceedings of the 15th IEEE International Conference on Data Engineering*, pages 164–171, Sydney, Australia, March 1999. [regions; R-tree]

[1153] S. T. Leutenegger, M. A. López, and J. Edgington. STR: a simple and efficient algorithm for R-tree packing. In *Proceedings of the 13th IEEE International Conference on Data Engineering*, A. Gray and P.-Å. Larson, eds., pages 497–506, Birmingham, United Kingdom, April 1997. [rectangles; R-tree; STR method] cited in F.2.1.5.2.2 (pp. 277–278)

[1154] S. T. Leutenegger and D. M. Nicol. Efficient bulk-loading of gridfiles. *IEEE Transactions on Knowledge and Data Engineering*, 9(3):410–420, May/June 1997. [points; bulk loading; grid file] cited in F.1.7.2.1 (p. 136)

[1155] C. Levcopoulos and D. Krznaric. The greedy triangulation can be computed from the Delaunay triangulation in linear time. *Computational Geometry: Theory and Applications*, 14(4):197–220, December 1999. [regions; triangulations] cited in F.2.1.3.2.s (p. 787)

[1156] V. A. Levenshtein. Binary codes capable of correcting deletions, insertion, and reversals. *Cybernetics and Control Theory*, 10(8):707–710, 1966. [edit distance] cited in F.4 (p. 488)

[1157] A. Li and G. Crebbin. Octree encoding of objects from range images. *Pattern Recognition*, 27(5):727–739, May 1994. [volumes]

[1158] C. Li, E. Y. Chang, H. Garcia-Molina, and G. Wiederhold. Clustering for approximate similarity search in high-dimensional spaces. *IEEE Transactions on Knowledge and Data Engineering*, 14(4):792–808, July/August 2002. [points; high-dimensional data; approximate nearest neighbor]

[1159] H. Li, M. A. Lavin, and R. J. LeMaster. Fast Hough transform: a hierarchical approach. *Computer Vision, Graphics, and Image Processing*, 36(2/3):139–161, November/December 1986. [regions; Hough transform]

[1160] J. Li, D. Rotem, and J. Srivastava. Algorithms for loading parallel grid files. In *Proceedings of the ACM SIGMOD Conference*, pages 347–356, Washington, DC, May 1993. [points; grid file; parallel processing; bulk loading] cited in F.1.7.2.1 (p. 136), F.1.8.1 (p. 165)

[1161] M. Li, W. I. Grosky, and R. Jain. Normalized quadtrees with respect to translation. *Computer Graphics and Image Processing*, 20(1):72–81, September 1982. [regions; optimal region quadtree; space requirements] cited in A.1.2, A.1.2.s, A.4.3.1.s, A.9.3.4, D.1.5, D.1.5.s, F.2.1.2.4.s (p. 780)

[1162] S.-X. Li and M. H. Loew. Adjacency detection using quadcodes. *Communications of the ACM*, 30(7):627–631, July 1987. [regions; region quadtree; neighbor finding]

[1163] S.-X. Li and M. H. Loew. The quadcode and its arithmetic. *Communications of the ACM*, 30(7):621–626, July 1987. [regions; region quadtree]

[1164] S. Liao, M. A. Lopez, and S. T. Leutenegger. High dimensional similarity search with space filling curves. In *Proceedings of the 17th IEEE International Conference on Data Engineering*, pages 615–622, Heidelberg, Germany, April 2001. [high-dimensional data; similarity searching; space-filling curve]

[1165] F. D. Libera and F. Gosen. Using B-trees to solve geographic range queries. *Computer Journal*, 29(2):176–181, April 1986. [regions; region quadtree; B-tree]

[1166] D. Libes. Modeling dynamic surfaces with octrees. *Computers & Graphics*, 15(3):383–387, 1991. [surfaces; region octree]

[1167] Y. E. Lien, C. E. Taylor, J. R. Driscoll, and M. L. Reynolds. Binary search tree complex—towards the implementation of relations. In *Proceedings of the International Conference on Very Large Databases (VLDB)*, D. S. Kerr, ed., pages 540–542, Framingham, MA, September 1975. [points; multiattribute tree (MAT)] cited in F.1.1 (p. 7)

[1168] M. L. P. van Lierop. Geometrical transformations on pictures represented by leafcodes. *Computer Vision, Graphics, and Image Processing*, 33(1):81–98, January 1986. [regions; region quadtree] cited in A.6.3.3, A.6.5.2

[1169] M. L. P. van Lierop. Intermediate data structures for display algorithms. In *Data Structures for Raster Graphics*, F. J. Peters, L. R. A. Kessener, and M. L. P. van Lierop, eds., pages 39–55. Springer-Verlag, Berlin, West Germany, 1986. [regions]

[1170] L. Lim, M. Wang, and J. S. Vitter. SASH: a self-adaptive histogram set for dynamically changing workloads. In *Proceedings of the 29th International Conference on Very Large Data Bases (VLDB)*, J. C. Freytag, P. C. Lockemann, S. Abiteboul, M. J. Carey, P. G. Selinger, and A. Heuer, eds., pages 369–380, Berlin, Germany, September 2003. [selectivity estimation] cited in F.4.5.8 (p. 650)

[1171] K.-I. Lin, H. V. Jagadish, and C. Faloutsos. The TV-tree—an index structure for high-dimensional data. *VLDB Journal*, 3(4):517–542, October 1994. Also University of Maryland Computer Science Technical Report TR–3296, July 1994. [points; high-dimensional data; dimension reduction; TV-tree] cited in F.4.4.3 (p. 572)

[1172] S. Lin, M. T. Özsu, V. Oria, and R. T. Ng. An extendible hash for multi-precision similarity querying of image databases. In *Proceedings of the 27th International Conference on Very Large Data Bases (VLDB)*, P. M. G. Apers, P. Atzeni, S. Ceri, S. Paraboschi, K. Ramamohanarao, and R. T. Snodgrass, eds., pages 221–230, Rome, Italy, September 2001. [similarity searching; image database]

[1173] X. Lin, X. Zhou, and C. Liu. Efficient computation of a proximity matching in spatial databases. *Data and Knowledge Engineering*, 33(1):204–241, April 2000. [points; distance semijoin; spatial data mining]

[1174] Y. Linde, A. Buzo, and R. M. Gray. An algorithm for vector quantizer design. *IEEE Transactions on Communication Theory*, 28(1):84–95, January 1980. [vector quantization; k-means problem] cited in F.4.2.3 (p. 533), F.4.4.8 (pp. 594, 597)

[1175] M. Lindenbaum, H. Samet, and G. R. Hjaltason. A probabilistic analysis of trie-based sorting of large collections of line segments in spatial databases. *SIAM Journal on Computing*, 35(1):22–58, September 2005. Also see *Proceedings of the 10th International Conference on Pattern Recognition*, vol. II, pages 91–96, Atlantic City, NJ, June 1990 and University of Maryland Computer Science TR–3455.1. [lines; space requirements; PMR quadtree; PM quadtree; MX quadtree] cited in F.2.2.2.6 (p. 369), F.2.2.2.8 (p. 376), F.4.1.6.s (p. 835)

[1176] P. Lindstrom, D. Koller, W. Ribarsky, L. F. Hodges, N. Faust, and G. A. Turner. Real-time continuous level of detail rendering of height fields. In *Proceedings of the SIGGRAPH'96 Conference*, pages 109–118, New Orleans, LA, August 1996. [surfaces; restricted bintree; triangle meshes] cited in F.1.5.1.4 (p. 64), F.2.2.3.4 (p. 399), F.2.2.4 (p. 406)

[1177] P. Lindstrom and G. Turk. Fast and memory efficient polygonal simplification. In *Proceedings IEEE Visualization'98*, D. Ebert, H. Hagen, and H. Rushmeier, eds., pages 279–286, Research Triangle Park, NC, October 1998. [surfaces; polygon simplification] cited in F.2.2.3.4 (p. 395)

[1178] P. Lindstrom and G. Turk. Image-driven simplification. *ACM Transactions on Graphics*, 19(3):204–241, July 2000. [surfaces; polygon simplification] cited in F.2.2.3.4 (p. 391)

[1179] A. Lingas. The power of non-rectilinear holes. In *Proceedings of the 9th International Colloquium on Automata, Languages, and Programming*, M. Nielsen and E. M. Schmidt, eds., vol. 140 of Springer-Verlag Lecture Notes in Computer Science, pages 369–383, Aarhus, Denmark, July 1982. [regions] cited in A.1.3, D.1.2, F.2.1.2.1 (p. 206)

[1180] M. Linial, N. Linial, N. Tishby, and G. Yona. Global self organization of all known protein sequences reveals inherent biological signatures. *Journal of Molecular Biology*, 268(2):539–556, May 1997. [similarity searching; bioinformatics database] cited in F.4.7.2.2 (p. 692)

[1181] N. Linial, E. London, and Y. Rabinovich. The geometry of graphs and some of its algorithmic applications. *Combinatorica*, 15:215–245, 1995. Also see *Proceedings of the 35th IEEE Annual Symposium on Foundations of Computer Science*, pages 577–591, Santa Fe, NM, November 1994. [metric space embedding; Lipschitz embedding; spatial networks] cited in F.4 (p. 489), F.4.1.6 (p. 515), F.4.7 (p. 686), F.4.7.1 (pp. 688–689), F.4.7.2.2 (pp. 692–693), F.4.7.2.3 (pp. 693–694), F.4.7.2.4 (pp. 694–695), F.4.7.3.9 (p. 710)

[1182] J. Linn. General methods for parallel searching. Digital Systems Laboratory Technical Report 81, Stanford University, Stanford, CA, May 1973. [points; multiprocessing] cited in D.2.4.4, F.P (p. xviii), F.1.5 (p. 49)

[1183] J. H. Liou and S. B. Yao. Multi-dimensional clustering for data base organizations. *Information Systems*, 2(4):187–198, 1977. [points; multidimensional directory (MDD)] cited in F.1.1 (pp. 9–10), F.1.5.1.4 (p. 66)

[1184] R. J. Lipton and R. E. Tarjan. Application of a planar separator theorem. In *Proceedings of the 18th IEEE Annual Symposium on Foundations of Computer Science*, pages 162–170, Providence, RI, October 1977. [regions] cited in D.4.3

[1185] J. J. Little and T. K. Peucker. A recursive procedure for finding the intersection of two digital curves. *Computer Graphics and Image Processing*, 10:159–171, 1979. [lines; line intersection problem] cited in D.4.1, F.2.2.3.1 (p. 385)

[1186] J. J. Little and P. Shi. Ordering points for incremental TIN construction from DEMs. *GeoInformatica*, 7(1):33–53, March 2003. [surfaces; triangulated irregular network (TIN)]

[1187] W. Litwin. Linear hashing: a new tool for file and table addressing. In *Proceedings of the 6th International Conference on Very Large Databases (VLDB)*, F. H. Lochovsky and R. W. Taylor, eds., pages 212–223, Montréal, Canada, October 1980. [points; linear hashing] cited in D.2.7, D.2.8.2, F.1.7.2.3 (p. 140), F.B (p. 730)

[1188] W. Litwin, M.-A. Neimat, and D. A. Schneider. LH*—linear hashing for distributed files. In *Proceedings of the ACM SIGMOD Conference*, pages 327–336, Washington, DC, May 1993. [points; distributed indexing; linear hashing]

[1189] W. Litwin and T. Risch. LH*G: a high-availability scalable distributed data structure by record grouping. *IEEE Transactions on Knowledge and Data Engineering*, 14(4):923–927, July/August 2002. [points; distributed indexing; peer-to-peer indexing]

[1190] X. Liu and G. F. Schrack. Encoding and decoding the Hilbert order. *Software—Practice and Experience*, 26(12):1335–1346, December 1996. [points; space-filling curve; Peano-Hilbert order] cited in F.1.6.s (p. 768), F.2.1.1.2.s (p. 777)

[1191] X. Liu and G. F. Schrack. An algorithm for encoding and decoding the 3-d Hilbert order. *IEEE Transactions on Image Processing*, 6(9):1333–1337, September 1997. [points; space-filling curve; Peano-Hilbert order] cited in F.1.6.s (p. 768), F.2.1.1.2.s (p. 777)

[1192] X. Liu and G. F. Schrack. A new ordering strategy applied to spatial data processing. *International Journal Geographical Information Science*, 12(1):3–22, January 1998. [points; U order; space-filling curve] cited in F.1.6 (p. 94), F.2.1.1.2 (pp. 199, 201), F.2.1.1.2.s (p. 777)

[1193] B. Lloyd and P. Egbert. Horizon occlusion culling for real-time rendering of hierarchical terrains. In *Proceedings IEEE Visualization 2002*, R. Moorehead, M. Gross, and K. I. Joy, eds., pages 403–409, Boston, October 2002. [surfaces; restricted quadtree]

[1194] S. P. Lloyd. Least squares quantization in PCM. *IEEE Transactions on Information Theory*, 28(2):127–135, March 1982. [vector quantization] cited in F.4.4.8 (p. 594)

[1195] M.-L. Lo and C. V. Ravishankar. Spatial joins using seeded trees. In *Proceedings of the ACM SIGMOD Conference*, pages 209–220, Minneapolis, MN, June 1994. [rectangles; R-tree; spatial join] cited in F.P (p. xx)

[1196] M.-L. Lo and C. V. Ravishankar. Generating seeded trees from data sets. In *Advances in Spatial Databases—4th International Symposium, SSD'95*, M. J. Egenhofer and J. R. Herring, eds., vol. 951 of Springer-Verlag Lecture Notes in Computer Science, pages 328–347, Portland, ME, August 1995. [rectangles; spatial join]

[1197] M.-L. Lo and C. V. Ravishankar. Spatial hash-joins. In *Proceedings of the ACM SIGMOD Conference*, pages 247–258, Montréal, Canada, June 1996. [rectangles; spatial join]

[1198] M.-L. Lo and C. V. Ravishankar. The design and implementation of seeded trees: an efficient method for spatial joins. *IEEE Transactions on Knowledge and Data Engineering*, 10(2):136–152, January/February 1998. [rectangles; spatial join]

[1199] P. Lockwood. A low cost DTW-based discrete utterance recognizer. In *Proceedings of the 8th International Conference on Pattern Recognition*, pages 467–469, Paris, France, October 1986. [points; depth-first nearest neighbor algorithm] cited in F.4.2 (p. 517), F.4.2.2 (p. 525)

[1200] D. Lomet. A review of recent work on multi-attribute access methods. *SIGMOD Record*, 21(3):56–63, September 1992. [points; survey]

[1201] D. Lomet and B. Salzberg. The hB-tree: a multi-attribute indexing method with good guaranteed performance. *ACM Transactions on Database Systems*, 15(4):625–658, December 1990. Also see *Proceedings of the 5th IEEE International Conference on Data Engineering*, pages 296–304, Los Angeles, February 1989 and Northeastern University Computer Science Technical Report NU–CCS–87–24, 1987. [points; hB-tree] cited in D.2.6.2, F.1.5.2.6 (p. 82), F.1.7.1.4 (pp. 106–108), F.1.7.1.6.4 (p. 125), F.1.8.1 (p. 167), F.4.4.5 (p. 581), F.1.7.1.4.s (pp. 768–769)

[1202] D. B. Lomet. Bounded index exponential hashing. *ACM Transactions on Database Systems*, 8(1):136–165, March 1983. [points; extendible hashing] cited in F.B (p. 730)

[1203] I. F. V. López, R. T. Snodgrass, and B. Moon. Spatiotemporal aggregate computation: a survey. *IEEE Transactions on Knowledge and Data Engineering*, 17(2):271–286, February 2005. [spatiotemporal database; aggregation query; survey] cited in F.3.1.4 (p. 445), F.4 (p. 485)

[1204] M. A. López and B. G. Nickerson. Analysis of half-space range search using the *k*-d search skip list. In *Proceedings of the 14th Canadian Conference on Computational Geometry*, S. Wismath, ed., pages 58–62, Lethbridge, Alberta, Canada, August 2002. [points; skip list; k-d tree] cited in F.1.3 (p. 27)

[1205] K.-L. Low and T.-S. Tan. Model simplification using vertex-clustering. In *Proceedings of the ACM Symposium on Interactive 3D Graphics*, pages 75–81, Providence, RI, April 1997. [surfaces; simplification; vertex clustering] cited in F.2.2.3.4 (p. 393)

[1206] T. Lozano-Perez. Automatic planning of manipulator transfer movements. *IEEE Transactions on Systems, Man, and Cybernetics*, 11(10):681–698, October 1981. [regions; collision detection; motion planning] cited in A.1.4, D.1.3, F.2.4 (p. 425)

[1207] H. Lu, R. Luo, and B. C. Ooi. Spatial joins by precomputation of approximations. In *Proceedings of the 6th Australasian Database Conference*, Australian Computer Science Communications, volume 17, number 2, pages 132–142, Glenelg, South Australia, Australia, January 1995. Also in *Australian Computer Science Communications*, 17(2):143–152, January 1995. [regions; spatial join] cited in F.P (p. xx)

[1208] H. Lu and B. C. Ooi. Spatial indexing: past and future. *IEEE Data Engineering Bulletin*, 16(3):16–21, September 1993. [points; survey]

[1209] H. Lu, B. C. Ooi, and K.-L. Tan. On spatially partitioned temporal join. In *Proceedings of the 20th International Conference on Very Large Data Bases (VLDB)*, J. Bocca, M. Jarke, and C. Zaniolo, eds., pages 546–557, Santiago, Chile, September 1994. [points; intervals; spatiotemporal database]

[1210] W. Lu and J. Han. Distance-associated join indices for spatial range search. In *Proceedings of the 8th IEEE International Conference on Data Engineering*, F. Golshani, ed., pages 284–292, Tempe, AZ, February 1992. [points; spatial join index]

[1211] D. Luebke and C. Erickson. View-dependent simplification of arbitrary polygonal environments. In *Proceedings of the SIGGRAPH'97 Conference*, pages 199–208, Los Angeles, August 1997. [surfaces; polygon simplification] cited in F.2.2.3.4 (pp. 393, 395, 399)

[1212] D. Luebke, M. Reddy, J. D. Cohen, A. Varshney, B. Watson, and R. Huebner. *Level of Detail for 3D Graphics*. Morgan-Kaufmann, San Francisco, 2003. [surfaces; level of detail (LOD); surface simplification; polygon simplification; general] cited in F.P (p. xix), F.2.2.3.4 (p. 391)

[1213] G. Lueker. A data structure for orthogonal range queries. In *Proceedings of the 19th IEEE Annual Symposium on Foundations of Computer Science*, pages 28–34, Ann Arbor, MI, October 1978. [points; range query] cited in D.2.3

[1214] V. Y. Lum. Multi-attribute retrieval with combined indexes. *Communications of the ACM*, 13(11):660–665, November 1970. [points; combined index] cited in F.1.1 (pp. 5–6), F.1.1.s (p. 747)

[1215] R. Lumia. A new three-dimensional connected components algorithm. *Computer Vision, Graphics, and Image Processing*, 23(2):207–217, August 1983. [volumes; connected component labeling] cited in A.5.1.1, A.5.1.2, A.5.1.3

[1216] R. Lumia. Rapid hidden feature elimination using an octree. In *Proceedings of the IEEE International Conference on Robotics and Automation*, vol. 1, pages 460–464, San Francisco, April 1986. [volumes; ray tracing]

[1217] R. Lumia, L. Shapiro, and O. Zuniga. A new connected components algorithm for virtual memory computers. *Computer Vision, Graphics, and Image Processing*, 22(2):287–300, May 1983. [regions; connected component labeling] cited in A.5.1, A.5.1.1, A.5.1.2, A.5.1.3, A.5.1.3.s

[1218] L. D. MacDonald and K. S. Booth. Heuristics for ray tracing using space subdivision. *Visual Computer*, 6(3):153–166, June 1990. Also see *Proceedings of Graphics Interface '89*, pages 152–163, London, Ontario, Canada, June 1989. [volumes; BSP tree; ray tracing]

[1219] J. MacQueen. Some methods for classification and analysis of multivariate observations. In *Proceedings of the 5th Berkeley Symposium on Mathematics, Statistics, and Probability*, vol. 1,

pages 281–297, Berkeley, CA, 1967. [vector quantization; k-means problem] cited in F.4.2.3 (p. 533), F.4.4.8 (pp. 594, 597)

[1220] H. G. Mairson and J. Stolfi. Reporting and counting intersections between two sets of line segments. In *Theoretical Foundations of Computer Graphics and CAD*, R. A. Earnshaw, ed., pages 307–325. Springer-Verlag, Berlin, West Germany, 1988. [lines]

[1221] J. Makino. Comparison of two different tree algorithms. *Journal of Computational Physics*, 88(2):393–408, June 1990. [points; particle simulation; *N*-body problem]

[1222] N. Mamoulis and D. Papadias. Integration of spatial join algorithms for processing multiple inputs. In *Proceedings of the ACM SIGMOD Conference*, pages 1–12, Philadelphia, PA, June 1999. [spatial join]

[1223] N. Mamoulis and D. Papadias. Multiway spatial joins. *ACM Transactions on Database Systems*, 26(4):424–475, December 2001. [spatial join] cited in F.P (p. xx)

[1224] N. Mamoulis and D. Papadias. Slot index spatial join. *IEEE Transactions on Knowledge and Data Engineering*, 15(1):211–231, 2003. [regions; R-tree; spatial join]

[1225] B. B. Mandelbrot and J. W. Van Ness. Fractional Brownian motions, fractional noises and applications. *SIAM Review*, 10(4):422–437, October 1968. [fractal dimension] cited in F.2.2.3.1 (p. 384)

[1226] S. Maneewongvatana. *Multi-dimensional nearest neighbor searching with low-dimensional data*. PhD thesis, Computer Science Department, University of Maryland, College Park, MD, 2001. [points; high-dimensional data; approximate nearest neighbor; Voronoi diagram; minimum-ambiguity k-d tree; os-tree; probably-approximately correct nearest neighbor; sliding-midpoint k-d tree] cited in F.1.5.1.4 (pp. 58–59, 61), F.1.5.2.2 (pp. 72, 74), F.4.1.7 (p. 516), F.4.3 (p. 563), F.4.4.4 (pp. 573, 575, 577–579), F.1.5.1.4.s (p. 763)

[1227] S. Maneewongvatana and D. M. Mount. It's okay to be skinny, if your friends are fat. In *Proceedings of the 4th Annual Center for Geometric Computing Workshop on Computational Geometry*, Baltimore, MD, October 1997. Electronic edition. [points; packing constraint; sliding-midpoint k-d tree] cited in F.1.5.2.2 (p. 74)

[1228] S. Maneewongvatana and D. M. Mount. Analysis of approximate nearest neighbor searching with clustered point sets. In *Proceedings of the 6th DIMACS Implementation Challenge Workshop*, Baltimore, MD, January 1999. No proceedings published. [points; sliding-midpoint k-d tree; minimum-ambiguity k-d tree] cited in F.1.5.1.4 (pp. 58–59, 61), F.1.5.2.2 (p. 72), F.1.5.1.4.s (p. 763)

[1229] S. Maneewongvatana and D. M. Mount. The analysis of a probabilistic approach to nearest neighbor searching. In *Algorithms and Data Structures—7th International Workshop, WADS 2001*, F. K. H. A. Dehne, J. R. Sack, and R. Tamassia, eds., vol. 2125 of Springer-Verlag Lecture Notes in Computer Science, pages 276–286, Providence, RI, August 2001. [points; high-dimensional data; approximate nearest neighbor; Voronoi diagram; BSP tree] cited in F.1.5.1.4 (p. 68), F.4.1.7 (p. 516), F.4.3 (p. 563), F.4.4.4 (pp. 573, 578–579), F.4.5.2.4 (p. 610)

[1230] S. Maneewongvatana and D. M. Mount. An empirical study of a new approach to nearest neighbor searching. In *Proceedings of the 3rd Workshop on Algorithm Engineering and Experimentation (ALENEX'01)*, vol. 2153 of Springer-Verlag Lecture Notes in Computer Science, pages 172–187, Washington, DC, January 2001. [points; high-dimensional data; approximate nearest neighbor; Voronoi diagram; BSP tree; os-tree] cited in F.1.5.1.4 (p. 68), F.4.1.7 (p. 516), F.4.4.4 (pp. 575–576, 578), F.4.5.2.4 (p. 610)

[1231] M. Manohar, P. S. Rao, and S. S. Iyengar. Template quadtrees for representing region and line data present in binary images. *Computer Vision, Graphics, and Image Processing*, 51(3):338–354, September 1990. [lines; regions; template quadtree] cited in D.4.2.1, F.2.2.2.3 (p. 359)

[1232] M. Mäntylä. *An Introduction to Solid Modeling*. Computer Science Press, Rockville, MD, 1987. [solid modeling; general] cited in D.P, D.5.1, D.5.4, F.P (p. xix), F.2.2.1.2 (p. 319)

[1233] M. Mäntylä and R. Sulonen. GWB: a solid modeler with Euler operators. *IEEE Computer Graphics and Applications*, 2(7):17–31, September 1982. [volumes; boundary model (BRep)] cited in D.5.4

[1234] M. Mäntylä and M. Tamminen. Localized set operations for solid modeling. *Computer Graphics*, 17(3):279–288, July 1983. Also in

917

Proceedings of the SIGGRAPH'83 Conference, Detroit, July 1983. [volumes]

[1235] R. Mao, W. Xu, S. Ramakrishnan, G. Nuckolls, and D. P. Miranker. On optimizing distance-based similarity search for biological databases. In *Proceedings of the 2005 IEEE Computational Systems Bioinformatics Conference (CSB'05)*, pages 351–361, 2005. [metric spaces; mvp-tree; bioinformatics database] cited in F.4.5.2.3 (p. 609)

[1236] R. Mao, W. Xu, N. Singh, and D. P. Miranker. An assessment of a metric space database index to support sequence homology. In *Proceedings of the 3rd IEEE International Symposium on BioInformatics and BioEngineering (BIBE2003)*, pages 375–382, Bethesda, MD, March 2003. [metric spaces; M-tree; bioinformatics database] cited in F.4.5.4.1 (p. 625)

[1237] X. Mao, T. L. Kunii, I. Fujishiro, and T. Noma. Hierarchical representations of 2d/3d gray-scale images and 2d/3d two-way conversion. *IEEE Computer Graphics and Applications*, 7(12):37–44, December 1987. [regions]

[1238] D. Marble, H. Calkins, and D. Peuquet, eds. *Readings in Geographic Information Systems*. SPAD Systems, Williamsville, NY, 1984. [spatial database; geographic information systems (GIS)]

[1239] A. Margalit and G. D. Knott. An algorithm for computing the union, intersection or difference of two polygons. *Computers & Graphics*, 13(2):167–183, 1989. Also University of Maryland Computer Science Technical Report TR–1995, March 1988. [regions; polygon set operations] cited in A.4.6.s, D.5.2.s

[1240] D. M. Mark. The use of quadtrees in geographic information systems and spatial data handling. In *Proceedings of Auto-Carto London*, vol. 1, pages 517–526, London, United Kingdom, September 1986. [regions; region quadtree; geographic information systems (GIS)]

[1241] D. M. Mark. Neighbor-based properties of some orderings of two-dimensional space. *Geographical Analysis*, 22(2):145–157, April 1990. [space-filling curve]

[1242] D. M. Mark and D. J. Abel. Linear quadtrees from vector representations of polygons. *IEEE Transactions on Pattern Analysis and Machine Intelligence*, 7(3):344–349, May 1985. [regions; region quadtree] cited in A.4.3.1

[1243] D. M. Mark and J. A. Cebrian. Octtrees: a useful data-structure for the processing of topographic and sub-surface area. In *Proceedings of the 1986 ACSM-ASPRS Annual Convention*, vol. 1: Cartography and Education, pages 104–113, Washington, DC, March 1986. [surfaces; digital elevation model (DEM); triangulated irregular network (TIN)]

[1244] D. M. Mark and J. P. Lauzon. The space efficiency of quadtrees: an empirical examination including the effects of 2-dimensional run-encoding. *Geo-Processing*, 2:367–383, 1985. [regions; region quadtree; space requirements] cited in A.2.1.3

[1245] D. Marple, M. Smulders, and H. Hegen. Tailor: a layout system based on trapezoidal corner stitching. *IEEE Transactions on Computer-Aided Design*, 9(1):66–90, January 1990. [rectangles; corner stitching] cited in F.3.3.2.1 (p. 460)

[1246] S. C. Marsh. Fine grain parallel architectures and creation of high-quality images. In *Theoretical Foundations of Computer Graphics and CAD*, R. A. Earnshaw, ed., pages 728–753. Springer-Verlag, Berlin, West Germany, 1988. [hardware]

[1247] G. N. N. Martin. Spiral storage: incrementally augmentable hash addressed storage. Theory of Computation Technical Report 27, Department of Computer Science, University of Warwick, Coventry, United Kingdom, March 1979. [points; spiral hashing] cited in D.2.8.2, F.1.7.2.4 (p. 153), F.C (pp. 735, 739)

[1248] J. J. Martin. Organization of geographical data with quad trees and least square approximation. In *Proceedings of the IEEE Conference on Pattern Recognition and Image Processing'82*, pages 458–463, Las Vegas, NV, June 1982. [lines; least square quadtree] cited in D.4.2.1, F.2.2.2.3 (p. 360)

[1249] M. Martin, D. M. Chiarulli, and S. S. Iyengar. Parallel processing of quadtrees on a horizontally reconfigurable architecture computing system. In *Proceedings of the 15th IEEE International Conference on Parallel Processing*, pages 895–902, St. Charles, IL, August 1986. [regions; region quadtree; parallel processing]

[1250] R. R. Martin and M. M. Anguh. Quadtrees, transforms, and image coding. *Computer Graphics Forum*, 10(2):91–96, June 1991. [regions; compression; region quadtree]

[1251] W. N. Martin and J. K. Aggarwal. Volumetric descriptions of objects from multiple views. *IEEE Transactions on Pattern Analysis and Machine Intelligence*, 5(2):150–158, March 1983. [volumes] cited in A.4.6, D.5.2

[1252] D. C. Mason. Dilation algorithm for a linear quadtree. *Image and Vision Computing*, 5(1):11–20, February 1987. [regions; image dilation] cited in A.6.6

[1253] D. C. Mason and M. J. Callen. Comparison of two dilation algorithms for linear quadtrees. *Image and Vision Computing*, 6(3):169–175, August 1988. [regions; image dilation]

[1254] C. Mathieu, C. Puech, and H. Yahia. Average efficiency of data structures for binary image processing. *Information Processing Letters*, 26(2):89–93, October 1987. [regions; space requirements]

[1255] J. Matoušek. Efficient partition trees. *Discrete & Computational Geometry*, 8(3):315–334, 1992. [points; BSP tree]

[1256] J. Matoušek. Geometric range searching. *ACM Computing Surveys*, 26(4):421–461, December 1994. [points; range query; survey]

[1257] J. Matoušek, M. Sharir, and E. Welzl. A subexponential bound for linear programming. *Algorithmica*, 16(4/5):498–516, October/November 1996. [linear programming; minimum bounding hypersphere] cited in F.4.4.2.s (p. 852)

[1258] T. Matsuyama, L. V. Hao, and M. Nagao. A file organization for geographic information systems based on spatial proximity. *Computer Vision, Graphics, and Image Processing*, 26(3):303–318, June 1984. [points; bucket PR quadtree; k-d tree] cited in D.2.8.1, D.3, F.1.4.2.2 (p. 45), F.1.5.1.4 (p. 62), F.3 (p. 427)

[1259] J. M. Maubach. Local bisection refinement for N-simplicial grids generated by reflection. *SIAM Journal on Scientific Computing*, 16(1):210–227, January 1995. [regions; surfaces; restricted bintree; triangle meshes] cited in F.1.5.1.4 (p. 64), F.2.2.4 (p. 406)

[1260] A. Maus. Delaunay triangulation and the convex hull of n points in expected linear time. *BIT*, 24:151–163, 1984. [regions; Delaunay triangulation (DT)] cited in F.2.2.1.4.s (p. 799)

[1261] P. Mazumder. Planar decomposition for quadtree data structure. *Computer Vision, Graphics, and Image Processing*, 38(3):258–274, June 1987. [regions; region quadtree]

[1262] P. Mazumder. A new strategy for octtree representation of three-dimensional objects. In *Proceedings of Computer Vision and Pattern Recognition'88*, pages 270–275, Ann Arbor, MI, June 1988. [volumes; region octree]

[1263] J. McCarthy. Recursive functions of symbolic expressions and their computation by machine, part I. *Communications of the ACM*, 3(4):184–195, April 1960. [LISP; programming languages] cited in A.L, F.D (p. 743)

[1264] E. J. McCluskey. *Introduction to the Theory of Switching Circuits*. McGraw-Hill, New York, 1965. [hardware; general] cited in A.1.3, D.1.2, F.1.6 (p. 93)

[1265] E. M. McCreight. Efficient algorithms for enumerating intersecting intervals and rectangles. Technical Report CSL–80–09, Xerox Palo Alto Research Center, Palo Alto, CA, June 1980. [rectangles; tile tree; rectangle intersection problem] cited in D.3.2.2, D.3.4, D.3.4.s, F.3.1.2 (p. 435), F.3.3.1 (p. 456), F.3.4.1.3 (p. 473), F.3.3.1.s (p. 825)

[1266] E. M. McCreight. Priority search trees. *SIAM Journal on Computing*, 14(2):257–276, May 1985. Also Xerox Palo Alto Research Center Technical Report CSL–81–5, January 1982. [rectangles; priority search tree] cited in D.2.5, D.3.2.3, D.3.2.3.s, F.1.1 (p. 9), F.1.3 (p. 26), F.2.1.3.3.2 (p. 253), F.3.1.2 (p. 435), F.3.1.3 (pp. 440–441), F.3.1.3.s (p. 821)

[1267] D. M. McKeown Jr. and J. L. Denlinger. Map-guided feature extraction from aerial imagery. In *Proceedings of the Workshop on Computer Vision: Representation and Control*, pages 205–213, Annapolis, MD, April 1984. [regions]

[1268] D. H. McLain. Two dimensional interpolation from random data. *Computer Journal*, 19(2):178–181, May 1976. Also see Corrigendum, *Computer Journal*, 19(4):384, November 1976. [regions; Delaunay triangulation (DT)] cited in F.2.2.1.4 (p. 348)

[1269] R. B. McMaster and K. S. Shea. *Generalization in Digital Cartography*. Association of American Geographers, Washington, DC, 1992. [generalization] cited in F.2.2.3.1 (p. 383)

[1270] J. McNames. A nearest trajectory strategy for time series prediction. In *Proceedings of the International Workshop on Advanced Black-Box Techniques for Nonlinear Modeling*, pages 112–128, Leuven, Belgium, July 1998. [points; depth-first nearest neighbor algorithm] cited in F.4.5.3.1.s (p. 856)

[1271] J. McNames. A fast nearest-neighbor algorithm based on a principal axis search tree. *IEEE Transactions on Pattern Analysis and Machine Intelligence*, 23(9):964–976, September 2001. [points; nearest neighbor; principal components analysis (PCA); multidimensional directory (MDD)] cited in F.1.1 (p. 9), F.1.5.1.4 (p. 66)

[1272] J. McNames, J. A. K. Suykens, and J. Vanderwalle. Winning entry of the K. U. Leuven time series prediction competition. *International Journal of Bifurcation and Chaos*, 9(8):1485–1500, August 1999. [points; depth-first nearest neighbor algorithm] cited in F.4.5.3.1.s (p. 856)

[1273] D. Meagher. Octree encoding: a new technique for the representation, manipulation, and display of arbitrary 3-D objects by computer. Electrical and Systems Engineering Technical Report IPL–TR–80–111, Rensselaer Polytechnic Institute, Troy, NY, October 1980. [volumes; region octree; MX octree] cited in A.1.2, A.1.2.s, D.1.5, D.1.5.s, D.5.5.1, F.2.2.2.2 (p. 358), F.2.2.2.2.s (p. 803)

[1274] D. Meagher. Computer software for robotic vision. In *Proceedings of SPIE, Robotics and Industrial Inspection*, vol. 360, pages 318–325, San Diego, CA, August 1982. [volumes; region octree]

[1275] D. Meagher. Efficient synthetic image generation of arbitrary 3-d objects. In *Proceedings of the IEEE Conference on Pattern Recognition and Image Processing'82*, pages 473–478, Las Vegas, NV, June 1982. [volumes; region octree]

[1276] D. Meagher. Geometric modeling using octree encoding. *Computer Graphics and Image Processing*, 19(2):129–147, June 1982. [volumes; region octree] cited in A.1.4, A.5.1.3, A.6.5.2, A.6.5.3.s, A.7.1.4, A.7.1.4.s, D.1.3, F.2.1.2.4 (p. 211), F.2.4 (p. 425)

[1277] D. Meagher. The octree encoding method for efficient solid modeling. Electrical and Systems Engineering Technical Report IPL–TR–032, Rensselaer Polytechnic Institute, Troy, NY, August 1982. [volumes; region octree] cited in A.2.1.2

[1278] D. Meagher. Octree generation, analysis and manipulation. Electrical and Systems Engineering Technical Report IPL–TR–027, Rensselaer Polytechnic Institute, Troy, NY, 1982. [volumes; region octree] cited in D.5.1, D.5.5.1

[1279] D. Meagher. The Solids Engine: a processor for interactive solid modeling. In *Proceedings of the NICOGRAPH'84 Conference*, pages A–2, 1–11, Tokyo, Japan, November 1984. [volumes; region octree] cited in A.7.1.4, D.5.3, D.5.5, F.2.2.2.4 (p. 361)

[1280] N. Megiddo. Linear time algorithms for linear programming in R^3 and related problems. *SIAM Journal on Computing*, 12(4):759–776, November 1983. [linear programming; minimum bounding hypersphere] cited in F.4.4.2.s (p. 852)

[1281] N. Megiddo. Linear programming in linear time when the dimension is fixed. *Journal of the ACM*, 31(1):114–127, January 1984. [linear programming; minimum bounding hypersphere] cited in F.4.4.2.s (p. 852)

[1282] K. Mehlhorn. *Multi-dimensional Searching and Computational Geometry*. Springer-Verlag, Berlin, West Germany, 1984. [computational geometry; general] cited in D.P, D.4.3.1.s, F.P (p. xix), F.2.1.3.2.s (p. 787)

[1283] G. G. Mei and W. Liu. Parallel processing for quadtree problems. In *Proceedings of the 15th IEEE International Conference on Parallel Processing*, pages 452–454, St. Charles, IL, August 1986. [regions; region quadtree; parallel processing]

[1284] S. Menon, P. Gao, and T. R. Smith. Multi-colored quadtrees for GIS: exploiting bit-parallelism for rapid Boolean overlay. In *Proceedings of the International Geographic Information Systems (IGIS) Symposium: The Research Agenda*, vol. 2, pages 371–383, Arlington, VA, November 1987. [regions; region quadtree]

[1285] S. Menon and T. R. Smith. Multi-component object search using spatial constraint propagation. In *Proceedings of the International Geographic Information Systems (IGIS) Symposium: The Research Agenda*, vol. 2, pages 281–293, Arlington, VA, November 1987. [regions]

[1286] C. Merkwirth, U. Parlitz, and W. Lauterborn. Fast exact and approximate nearest neighbor searching for nonlinear signal processing. *Physical Review E (Statistical Physics, Plasmas, Fluids, and Related Interdisciplinary Topics)*, 62(2):2089–2097, August 2000. [points; best-first nearest neighbor algorithm; approximate nearest neighbor] cited in F.4.1.7 (p. 516), F.4.3 (pp. 557, 559), F.4.5.3.1 (pp. 615–616), F.4.5.3.2 (p. 616), F.4.5.3.3 (p. 621), F.4.5.3.1.s (p. 856)

[1287] T. H. Merrett. Multidimensional paging for efficient database querying. In *Proceedings of the International Conference on Management of Data*, pages 277–289, Milan, Italy, June 1978. [points; multipaging] cited in D.2.8.2, F.1.1 (p. 10), F.1.7.2 (p. 130), F.1.7.2.1 (p. 136)

[1288] T. H. Merrett and E. J. Otoo. Dynamic multipaging: a storage structure for large shared data banks. In *Proceedings of the 2nd International Conference on Improving Database Usability and Responsiveness*, P. Scheuermann, ed., pages 237–254, Jerusalem, Israel, June 1982. Academic Press. Also McGill University Computer Science Technical Report SOCS–81–26. [points; multipaging; multidimensional extendible hashing (MDEH)] cited in D.2.8.2, F.1.1 (pp. 10–11), F.1.7.2 (p. 130), F.1.7.2.1 (p. 136), F.1.7.2.3.2 (p. 147), F.1.7.2.4.2 (p. 154), F.1.7.2.4.4 (p. 159), F.1.7.2.4.4.s (p. 775)

[1289] R. D. Merrill. Representations of contours and regions for efficient computer search. *Communications of the ACM*, 16(2):69–82, February 1973. [lines] cited in D.4.4

[1290] J. Michener. Personal communication. 1980. [regions; chain code] cited in A.4.3.1.s

[1291] L. Micó, J. Oncina, and R.C. Carrasco. A fast branch & bound nearest neighbor classifier in metric spaces. *Pattern Recognition Letters*, 17(7):731–739, June 1996. [metric spaces; nearest neighbor; distance matrix; TLAESA] cited in F.4.5.3.3 (p. 618), F.4.5.7.3 (p. 649)

[1292] L. Micó, J. Oncina, and E. Vidal. A new version of the nearest-neighbour approximating and eliminating search algorithm (AESA) with linear preprocessing-time and memory requirements. *Pattern Recognition Letters*, 15(1):9–17, January 1994. Also see *Proceedings of the 11th International Conference on Pattern Recognition*, vol. II, pages 557–560, The Hague, The Netherlands, August–September 1992. [metric spaces; nearest neighbor; distance matrix; LAESA] cited in F.4.1.7 (p. 517), F.4.2 (p. 517), F.4.5 (pp. 598–599), F.4.5.1 (p. 601), F.4.5.3.4 (pp. 623–624), F.4.5.7.2 (p. 646), F.4.5.7.3 (p. 649), F.4.7.2.1 (p. 691)

[1293] L. Middleton and J. Sivaswamy. Edge detection in a hexagonal-image processing framework. *Image and Vision Computing*, 19(14):1071–1081, December 2001. [hexagonal tiling] cited in F.2.1.1.1 (p. 198)

[1294] D. J. Milford and P. J. Willis. Quad encoded display. *IEE Proceedings E(GB)*, 131(3):70–75, May 1984. [hardware; region quadtree]

[1295] D. J. Milford, P. J. Willis, and J. R. Woodwark. Exploiting area coherence in raster scan displays. In *Proceedings of Electronic Displays'81*, pages 34–46, London, United Kingdom, 1981. [hardware]

[1296] G. L. Miller, D. Talmor, S.-H. Teng, N. Walkington, and H. Wang. Control volume meshes using sphere packing: generation, refinement, and coarsening. In *Proceedings of the 5th International Meshing Roundtable*, pages 47–61, Pittsburgh, PA, October 1996. [volumes; conforming Delaunay tetrahedralization; Steiner points] cited in F.2.2.1.6 (p. 352)

[1297] R. Miller and Q. F. Stout. Pyramid computer algorithms for determining geometric properties of images. In *Proceedings of the Symposium on Computational Geometry*, pages 263–269, Baltimore, MD, June 1985. [regions; pyramid]

[1298] M. Minsky and S. Papert. *Perceptrons: An Introduction to Computational Geometry*. MIT Press, Cambridge, MA, 1969. [perceptrons; general] cited in A.5.3

[1299] D. Miranker, W. Xu, and R. Mao. MoBIoS: a metric-space DBMS to support biological discovery. In *Proceedings of the 15th International Conference on Scientific and Statistical Database Management*, S. Nittel and D. Gunopulos, eds., pages 241–244, Cambridge, MA, July 2003. [bioinformatics database] cited in F.4.5.2.3 (p. 609)

[1300] J. S. B. Mitchell, D. M. Mount, and S. Suri. Query-sensitive ray shooting. *International Journal of Computational Geometry Applications*, 7(4):317–347, August 1997. Also see *Proceedings of the Tenth Annual ACM Symposium on Computational Geometry*, pages 359–368, Stony Brook, NY, June 1994. [volumes; ray tracing; restricted quadtree] cited in F.2.2.4.s (p. 814)

[1301] B. G. Mobasseri. Soft-linked quadtree: a cascaded ring structure using flexible linkage concept. In *Proceedings of Computer Vision and Pattern Recognition'88*, pages 622–627, Ann Arbor, MI, June 1988. [regions; region quadtree]

[1302] B. G. Mobasseri. A generalized solution to the quadtree expected complexity problem. *Pattern Recognition Letters*, 16(5):443–456, May 1995. [regions; region quadtree]

[1303] A. Moitra. Spatiotemporal data management using R-trees. In *Proceedings of the ACM Workshop on Advances in Geographic Information Systems*, N. Pissinou, ed., pages 28–33, Arlington, VA, November 1993. [rectangles; R-tree] cited in F.2.1.5.2.1 (p. 275), F.2.1.5.2.4 (p. 292)

[1304] M. F. Mokbel, W. G. Aref, and I. Kamel. Analysis of multidimensional space-filling curves. *GeoInformatica*, 7(3):179–210, September 2003. Also see *Proceedings of the 10th International Symposium on Advances in Geographic Information Systems*, A. Voisard and S.-C. Chen, eds., pages 149–154, McLean, VA, November 2002. [points; space-filling curve]

[1305] M. F. Mokbel, T. M. Ghanem, and W. G. Aref. Spatio-temporal access methods. *IEEE Data Engineering Bulletin*, 26(2):40–49, June 2003. [spatiotemporal database; moving objects] cited in F.P (p. xvii), F.1 (p. 2)

[1306] H. Mokhtar, J. Su, and O. H. Ibarra. On moving object queries. In *Proceedings of the 21st ACM SIGACT-SIGMOD-SIGART Symposium on Principles of Database Systems (PODS)*, pages 188–198, Madison, WI, June 2002. [points; moving objects; nearest neighbor] cited in F.4 (p. 488)

[1307] A. Mondal, Y. Lifu, and M. Kitsuregawa. P2PR-Tree: an R-tree-based spatial index for peer-to-peer environments. In *Current Trends in Database Technology—EDBT 2004 Workshops*, W. Lindner, M. Mesiti, C. Turker, Y. Tzitzikas, and A. Vakali, eds., vol. 3268 of Springer-Verlag Lecture Notes in Computer Science, pages 516–525, Heraklion, Crete, Greece, March 2004. [points; peer-to-peer R-tree; peer-to-peer spatial indexing] cited in F.2.1.5.2 (p. 271)

[1308] C. Montani and R. Scopigno. Quadtree/octree-to-boundary conversion. In *Graphics Gems II*, J. Arvo, ed., pages 202–218. Academic Press, Boston, 1991. [regions; region quadtree; region octree]

[1309] B. Moon, H. V. Jagadish, C. Faloutsos, and J. H. Saltz. Analysis of the clustering properties of the Hilbert space-filling curve. *IEEE Transactions on Knowledge and Data Engineering*, 13(1):124–141, January/February 2001. Also University of Maryland Computer Science Technical Report TR–3611, 1996. [points; range query; space-filling curve; fractal dimension]

[1310] B. Moon and J. H. Saltz. Scalability analysis of declustering methods for multidimensional range queries. *IEEE Transactions on Knowledge and Data Engineering*, 10(2):310–327, March/April 1998. [points; range query]

[1311] A. W. Moore. The anchors hierarchy: using the triangle inequality to survive high-dimensional data. In *Proceedings of the 16th Conference on Uncertainty in Artificial Intelligence*, pages 397–405, San Francisco, July 2000. [points; metric tree; M-tree; k-center problem] cited in F.4.5.3.4 (pp. 622–623)

[1312] D. Moore. The cost of balancing generalized quadtrees. In *Proceedings of the 3rd ACM Symposium on Solid Modeling and Applications*, C. Hoffman and J. Rossignac, eds., pages 305–311, Salt Lake City, UT, May 1995. [surfaces; restricted quadtree] cited in F.2.2.4 (pp. 405, 407), F.2.2.4.s (p. 814)

[1313] D. W. Moore. *Simplicial mesh generation with applications*. PhD thesis, Department of Computer Science, Cornell University, Ithaca, NY, December 1992. Also Computer Science Technical Report 92–1322. [surfaces; restricted quadtree] cited in F.2.2.4.s (p. 814)

[1314] R. E. Moore. *Methods and Applications of Interval Analysis*. SIAM, Philadelphia, PA, 1979. [interval arithmetic; general] cited in D.5.5.1

[1315] D. R. Morrison. PATRICIA—practical algorithm to retrieve information coded in alphanumeric. *Journal of the ACM*, 15(4):514–534, October 1968. [points; Patricia trie] cited in F.1.5.2.4 (p. 76), F.1.8.6 (p. 183)

[1316] M. E. Mortenson. *Geometric Modeling*. John Wiley & Sons, New York, 1985. [geometric modeling; general] cited in A.7.1.6, F.P (p. xix)

[1317] G. M. Morton. A computer oriented geodetic data base and a new technique in file sequencing. Technical report, IBM Ltd., Ottawa, Canada, 1966. [regions; space-filling curve; Morton order] cited in A.1.4, A.2.1.1, A.4.1, D.1.2, D.1.3, D.2.7, F.1.6 (p. 93), F.1.8.5.1 (p. 172), F.2.1.1.2 (p. 200), F.2.3.1 (p. 410), F.2.4 (p. 423)

[1318] R. Motwani and P. Raghavan. *Randomized Algorithms*. Cambridge University Press, New York, 1994. [randomized algorithms; Las Vegas randomized algorithm; Monte Carlo randomized algorithm; general] cited in F.4.4.4 (p. 575), F.4.7.4 (p. 711)

[1319] D. M. Mount and S. Arya. ANN: a library for approximate nearest neighbor searching. In *Proceedings of the 2nd Annual Center for Geometric Computing Workshop on Computational Geometry*. electronic edition, Durham, NC, October 1997. [points; approximate nearest neighbor; sliding-midpoint k-d tree; BBD-tree] cited in F.1.5.2.2 (p. 72), F.1.5.2.7 (p. 87)

[1320] K. Mouratidis, M. Hadjieleftheriou, and D. Papadias. Conceptual partitioning: an efficient method for continuous nearest neighbor monitoring. In *Proceedings of the ACM SIGMOD Conference*, pages 634–645, Baltimore, MD, June 2005. [moving objects; nearest neighbor] cited in F.4 (p. 488)

[1321] S. P. Mudur and P. A. Koparkar. Interval methods for processing geometric objects. *IEEE Computer Graphics and Applications*, 4(2):7–17, February 1984. [surfaces; interval arithmetic] cited in D.5.5.1, D.5.6

[1322] D. E. Muller and F. P. Preparata. Finding the intersection of two convex polyhedra. *Theoretical Computer Science*, 7(2):217–236, October 1978. [regions; winged-edge representation; Voronoi diagram; Delaunay triangulation (DT); boundary model (BRep)] cited in F.2.2.1.2 (p. 323), F.2.2.1.3.3 (p. 343)

[1323] J. K. Mullin. Unified dynamic hashing. In *Proceedings of the 10th International Conference on Very Large Databases (VLDB)*, U. Dayal, G. Schlageter, and L. H. Seng, eds., pages 473–480, Singapore, August 1984. [points; spiral hashing; linear hashing]

[1324] J. K. Mullin. Spiral storage: efficient dynamic hashing with constant performance. *Computer Journal*, 28(3):330–334, August 1985. [points; spiral hashing] cited in D.2.8.2, D.2.8.2.2.s, F.1.7.2.4 (p. 153), F.C (pp. 735, 739, 741), F.C.s (p. 874)

[1325] K. Mulmuley. *Computational Geometry: An Introduction Through Randomized Algorithms*. Prentice Hall, Englewood Cliffs, NJ, 1994. [computational geometry; randomized algorithms; general] cited in F.4.4.4 (p. 575), F.4.7.4 (p. 711)

[1326] J. R. Munkres. *Elements of Algebraic Topology*. Prentice Hall, Englewood Cliffs, NJ, second edition, 2000. [topology; general] cited in F.2.2.1.1 (p. 315), F.4.7.3.5.s (p. 869)

[1327] M. Muralikrishna and D. J. DeWitt. Equi-depth histograms for estimating selectivity factors for multi-dimensional queries. In *Proceedings of the ACM SIGMOD Conference*, pages 28–36, Chicago, June 1988. [points; selectivity estimation] cited in F.4.1.1 (p. 492)

[1328] M. Murphy. *Delaunay triangulations and control-volume mesh generation*. PhD thesis, Computer Science Department, University of Maryland, College Park, MD, May 2002. [volumes; conforming Delaunay triangulation; tetrahedralizations] cited in F.2.2.1.5 (p. 351), F.2.2.1.6 (p. 352)

[1329] M. Murphy, D. M. Mount, and C. W. Gable. A point-placement strategy for conforming Delaunay tetrahedralization. *International Journal of Computational Geometry and Applications*, 11(6):669–

683, December 2001. Also see *Proceedings of the Eleventh Annual ACM-SIAM Symposium on Discrete Algorithms*, pages 67–74, San Francisco, January 2000. [volumes; conforming Delaunay tetrahedralization; Steiner points] cited in F.2.2.1.6 (p. 352)

[1330] M. Murphy and S. S. Skiena. Ranger: a tool for nearest neighbor search in high dimensions. In *Proceedings of the 9th Annual Symposium on Computational Geometry*, pages 403–404, San Diego, CA, May 1993. [data structure visualization; nearest neighbor]

[1331] O. J. Murphy and S. M. Selkow. The efficiency of using k-d trees for finding nearest neighbors in discrete space. *Information Processing Letters*, 23(4):215–218, November 1986. [points; k-d tree; nearest neighbor] cited in F.4.1.7 (p. 516), F.4.2 (p. 517)

[1332] O. J. Murphy and S. M. Selkow. Finding nearest neighbors with Voronoi tessellations. *Information Processing Letters*, 34(1):37–41, February 1990. [points; nearest neighbor; Voronoi diagram]

[1333] L. R. Nackman and V. Srinivasan. Point placement for Delaunay triangulation of polygonal domains. In *Proceedings of the 3rd Canadian Conference on Computational Geometry*, pages 37–40, Vancouver, Canada, August 1991. [surfaces; conforming Delaunay triangulation; Steiner points] cited in F.2.2.1.5 (p. 351)

[1334] G. Nagy and S. Seth. Hierarchical representation of optically scanned documents. In *Proceedings of the 7th International Conference on Pattern Recognition*, pages 347–349, Montréal, Canada, July 1984. [regions; X-Y tree; k-d tree; puzzletree; treemap] cited in F.1.5.1.4 (p. 66), F.2.1.2.9 (pp. 225–226), F.4.4.3 (p. 572)

[1335] G. Nagy and S. Wagle. Geographic data processing. *ACM Computing Surveys*, 11(2):139–181, June 1979. [lines; geographic information systems (GIS); survey] cited in A.P, D.P, D.4, D.4.4, F.P (p. xx)

[1336] K. N. R. Nair and R. Sankar. An approach to geometric modeling of solids bounded by sculptured surfaces. *Computers and Graphics*, 11(2):113–120, 1987. [volumes]

[1337] Y. Nakamura, S. Abe, Y. Ohsawa, and M. Sakauchi. Efficient hierarchical structures for spatial objects: MD-tree and RMD-tree. In *Proceedings of the 2nd Far-East Workshop on Future Database Systems*, Q. Chen, Y. Kambayashi, and R. Sacks-Davis, eds., vol. 3, pages 116–124, Kyoto, Japan, April 1992. World Scientific. [points; MD-tree; RMD-tree] cited in F.1.7.1.1 (p. 98)

[1338] Y. Nakamura, S. Abe, Y. Ohsawa, and M. Sakauchi. A balanced hierarchical data structure for multidimensional data with highly efficient dynamic characteristics. *IEEE Transaction on Knowledge and Data Engineering*, 5(4):682–694, August 1993. Also see *Proceedings of the 9th International Conference on Pattern Recognition*, pages 1109–1112, Rome, Italy, November 1988. [points; MD-tree]

[1339] S. K. Nandy and L. M. Patnaik. Linear time geometrical design rule checker based on quadtree representation of VLSI mask layouts. *Computer-Aided Design*, 18(7):380–388, September 1986. [regions; region quadtree]

[1340] S. K. Nandy and L. M. Patnaik. Algorithm for incremental compaction of geometrical layouts. *Computer-Aided Design*, 19(5):257–265, June 1987. [regions; region quadtree; MX-CIF quadtree]

[1341] S. K. Nandy and I. V. Ramakrishnan. Dual quadtree representation for VLSI designs. In *Proceedings of the 23rd Design Automation Conference*, pages 663–666, Las Vegas, NV, June 1986. [regions; MX-CIF quadtree]

[1342] E. Nardelli and G. Proietti. Efficient secondary memory processing of window queries on spatial data. *Information Sciences*, 84(1–2):67–83, May 1995. [regions; window query]

[1343] E. Nardelli and G. Proietti. Time and space efficient secondary memory representation of quadtrees. *Information Systems*, 22(1):25–37, March 1997. [regions; region quadtree; space requirements]

[1344] E. Nardelli and G. Proietti. Probabilistic models for images and quadtrees: differences and equivalences. *Image and Vision Computing*, 17(9):659–665, July 1999. [regions; region quadtree; space requirements]

[1345] E. Nardelli and G. Proietti. An efficient spatial access method for spatial images containing multiple non-overlapping features.

Information Systems, 25(8):553–568, December 2000. [regions; S*-tree] cited in F.2.3.1 (p. 412)

[1346] P. Naur (ed.), J. W. Backus, F. L. Bauer, J. Green, C. Katz, J. McCarthy, A. J. Perlis, H. Rutishauser, K. Samuelson, B. Vauquois, J. H. Wegstein, A. van Wijngaarden, and M. Woodger. Report on the algorithmic language ALGOL 60. *Communications of the ACM*, 3(5):299–314, May 1960. [ALGOL; programming languages] cited in A.P, A.L, D.P, F.P (p. xx), F.D (p. 743)

[1347] G. Navarro. Searching in metric spaces by spatial approximation. *VLDB Journal*, 11(1):28–46, August 2002. Also see *Proceedings String Processing and Information Retrieval and International Workshop on Groupware (SPIRE/CRIWG 1999)*, pages 141–148, Cancun, Mexico, September 1999. [metric spaces; sa-tree; nearest neighbor] cited in F.4.1.7 (p. 517), F.4.2 (p. 517), F.4.5 (pp. 598–599), F.4.5.5 (p. 629), F.4.5.5.1 (pp. 630–632), F.4.5.5.2 (pp. 633–634, 636), F.4.5.6 (p. 637), F.4.5.8 (p. 650), F.4.5.5.1.s (p. 858)

[1348] G. Navarro and N. Reyes. Fully dynamic spatial approximation trees. In *String Processing and Information Retrieval—9th International Symposium (SPIRE 2002)*, A. H. F. Laender and A. L. Oliveira, eds., vol. 2476 of Springer-Verlag Lecture Notes in Computer Science, pages 254–270, Lisbon, Portugal, September 2002. [metric spaces; sa-tree] cited in F.4.5.5.1 (p. 632)

[1349] I. Navazo. *Contribució a les tècniques de modelat geomètric d'objectes polièdrics usant la codificació amb arbres octals*. PhD thesis, Department de Metodes Informatics, Universitat Politècnica de Catalunya, Barcelona, Spain, January 1986. [volumes; PM octree; extended octree; MX octree; boundary model (BRep)] cited in A.1.3, D.5.3, F.2.2.2.4 (pp. 361–362), F.2.2.2.7 (pp. 370–371)

[1350] I. Navazo. Extended octtree representation of general solids with plane faces: model structure and algorithms. *Computers & Graphics*, 13(1):5–16, 1989. [volumes; PM octree; extended octree] cited in D.5.3, F.2.2.2.7 (p. 371)

[1351] I. Navazo, D. Ayala, and P. Brunet. A geometric modeller based on the exact octtree representation of polyhedra. *Computer Graphics Forum*, 5(2):91–104, June 1986. [volumes; PM octree; extended octree; boundary model (BRep)] cited in A.7.1.6, A.7.2.2, A.7.4, D.5.3, F.2.2.2.7 (p. 373)

[1352] I. Navazo, J. Fontdecaba, and P. Brunet. Extended octtrees, between CSG trees and boundary representations. In *Proceedings of the EUROGRAPHICS'87 Conference*, G. Marechal, ed., pages 239–247, Amsterdam, The Netherlands, August 1987. [volumes; PM octree; extended octree; CSG tree] cited in D.5.3, D.5.3.s, F.2.2.2.7 (p. 372), F.2.2.2.7.s (p. 809)

[1353] B. Naylor. Constructing good partitioning trees. In *Proceedings of Graphics Interface'93*, pages 181–191, Toronto, Canada, May 1993. [volumes; BSP tree] cited in F.2.1.3.1 (pp. 235–236)

[1354] B. F. Naylor. *A priori based techniques for determining visibility*. PhD thesis, Department of Computer Science, University of Texas at Dallas, Dallas, TX, May 1981. [volumes; BSP tree; hidden-surface removal] cited in F.2.1.3.1 (p. 235)

[1355] B. F. Naylor. Binary space partitioning trees: an alternative representation of polytopes. *CAD*, 22(4):250–252, May 1990. [volumes; BSP tree]

[1356] B. F. Naylor. SCULPT: an interactive solid modeling tool. In *Proceedings of Graphics Interface'90*, pages 138–148, Halifax, Newfoundland, Canada, May 1990. [volumes; BSP tree]

[1357] B. F. Naylor. A tutorial on binary space partitioning trees. In *SIGGRAPH Tutorial on the Representations of Geometry for Computer Graphics*, New Orleans, LA, August 1996. [regions; volumes; BSP tree; survey] cited in F.2.1.3.1 (pp. 234, 236)

[1358] B. F. Naylor. Binary space partitioning trees. In *Handbook of Data Structures and Applications*, D. Mehta and S. Sahni, eds., chapter 20. CRC Press, Boca Raton, FL, 2005. [volumes; BSP tree; survey]

[1359] B. F. Naylor, J. Amanatides, and W. Thibault. Merging BSP trees yields polyhedral set operations. *Computer Graphics*, 24(4):115–124, August 1990. Also in *Proceedings of the SIGGRAPH'90 Conference*, Dallas, TX, August 1990. [volumes; BSP tree] cited in F.2.1.3.1 (p. 236)

[1360] R. C. Nelson and H. Samet. A consistent hierarchical representation for vector data. *Computer Graphics*, 20(4):197–206, August 1986. Also in *Proceedings of the SIGGRAPH'86 Conference*, Dallas, TX, August 1986. [lines; PMR quadtree] cited in A.1.3, D.4.2.3, D.5.5.2, F.1.5.2.3 (p. 74), F.2.1.4.2 (p. 262), F.2.2.2.6 (pp. 365–366), F.2.2.2.8 (p. 375), F.4.1.6 (pp. 513, 516), F.4.1.7 (p. 517)

[1361] R. C. Nelson and H. Samet. A population analysis of quadtrees with variable node size. Computer Science Technical Report TR–1740, University of Maryland, College Park, MD, December 1986. [points; PMR quadtree; bucket PR quadtree] cited in D.2.8.1, D.4.2.3, D.4.2.3.4.s, D.5.5.2, F.1.4.2.2 (pp. 45–46), F.1.5.2.3 (p. 74), F.2.2.2.8.s (p. 810)

[1362] R. C. Nelson and H. Samet. A population analysis for hierarchical data structures. In *Proceedings of the ACM SIGMOD Conference*, pages 270–277, San Francisco, May 1987. [points; PMR quadtree; bucket PR quadtree] cited in D.2.8.1, F.1.4.2.2 (pp. 45–46), F.1.5.2.3 (p. 74), F.2.1.4.2 (p. 262), F.4.1.6 (pp. 513, 516)

[1363] K. Nemoto and T. Omachi. An adaptive subdivision by sliding boundary surfaces for fast ray tracing. In *Proceedings of Graphics Interface'86*, pages 43–48, Vancouver, Canada, May 1986. [surfaces; ray tracing]

[1364] S. A. Nene and S. K. Nayar. A simple algorithm for nearest neighbor search in high dimensions. *IEEE Transactions on Pattern Analysis and Machine Intelligence*, 19(9):989–1003, September 1997. [points; high-dimensional data; nearest neighbor] cited in F.1.1 (p. 5), F.4 (p. 487), F.4.5.1 (p. 601), F.4.5.7.2 (p. 647)

[1365] A. Newell, ed. *Information Processing Language–V Manual*, Englewood Cliffs, NJ, 1961. Prentice-Hall. [IPL–V; programming languages] cited in F.1.1 (p. 7)

[1366] M. E. Newell. The utilization of procedure models in digital image synthesis. Computer Science Technical Report UTEC–CSc–76–218, University of Utah, Salt Lake City, UT, Summer 1975. [volumes] cited in A.7.2.2

[1367] R. T. Ng and J. Han. Efficient and effective clustering methods for spatial data mining. In *Proceedings of the 20th International Conference on Very Large Data Bases (VLDB)*, J. Bocca, M. Jarke, and C. Zaniolo, eds., pages 144–155, Santiago, Chile, September 1994. [points; spatial data mining]

[1368] R. T. Ng and J. Han. CLARANS: a method for clustering objects for spatial data mining. *IEEE Transactions on Knowledge and Data Engineering*, 14(5):1003–1016, September/October 2002. [points; spatial data mining]

[1369] V. Ng and T. Kameda. Concurrent accesses to R-trees. In *Advances in Spatial Databases—3rd International Symposium, SSD'93*, D. Abel and B. C. Ooi, eds., vol. 692 of Springer-Verlag Lecture Notes in Computer Science, pages 142–161, Singapore, June 1993. [rectangles; R-tree; concurrency]

[1370] X. Ni and M. S. Bloor. Performance evaluation of boundary data structures. *IEEE Computer Graphics and Applications*, pages 66–77, November 1994. [volumes]

[1371] B. G. Nickerson and S. Hartati. Constructing orientation adaptive quadtree. In *Proceedings of Graphics Interface'90*, pages 190–195, Halifax, Newfoundland, Canada, May 1990. [regions; region quadtree; space requirements]

[1372] F. Nielsen. *Visual Computing: Geometry, Graphics, and Vision*. Charles River Media, Hingham, MA, 2005. [visual computing; general] cited in F.P (p. xix)

[1373] G. M. Nielson, D. Holliday, and T. Roxborough. Cracking the cracking problem with Coons patches. In *Proceedings IEEE Visualization'99*, D. Ebert, M. Gross, and B. Hamman, eds., pages 285–290, San Francisco, October 1999. [surfaces; triangulations] cited in F.2.2.4 (p. 402)

[1374] H. Niemann and R. Goppert. An efficient branch-and-bound nearest neighbor classifier. *Pattern Recognition Letters*, 7(2):67–72, February 1988. [points; depth-first nearest neighbor algorithm; branch-and-bound nearest neighbor algorithm; uniform grid] cited in F.4.2 (p. 517), F.4.2.3 (p. 532), F.4.2.4 (p. 535)

[1375] J. Nievergelt. 7 ± 2 criteria for assessing and comparing spatial data structures. In *Design and Implementation of Large Spatial Databases—1st Symposium, SSD'89*, A. Buchmann, O. Günther, T. R. Smith, and Y.-F. Wang, eds., vol. 409 of Springer-Verlag

Lecture Notes in Computer Science, pages 3–27, Santa Barbara, CA, July 1989. [survey]

[1376] J. Nievergelt, H. Hinterberger, and K. C. Sevcik. The grid file: an adaptable, symmetric multikey file structure. *ACM Transactions on Database Systems*, 9(1):38–71, March 1984. [points; grid file] cited in D.2.1, D.2.8.2, F.1.1 (pp. 10–11), F.1.7.2 (p. 130), F.1.7.2.1 (pp. 131, 134–135, 137), F.2.1.2.3 (p. 210), F.4.4.8 (p. 594)

[1377] J. Nievergelt and F. P. Preparata. Plane-sweep algorithms for intersecting geometric figures. *Communications of the ACM*, 25(10):739–746, October 1982. [regions; plane-sweep algorithms] cited in D.4.3.3.s, F.2.1.3.2.s (p. 788)

[1378] N. J. Nilsson. A mobile automaton: an application of artificial intelligence techniques. In *Proceedings of the 1st International Joint Conference on Artificial Intelligence*, pages 509–520, Washington, DC, May 1969. [regions; robotics] cited in A.1.4, D.1.3, F.2.4 (p. 425)

[1379] S. Nilsson and M. Tikkanen. An experimental study of compression methods for dynamic tries. *Algorithmica*, 33(1):19–33, 2002. [points; path compression; level compression; PR k-d tree] cited in F.1.5.2.5 (p. 79), F.1.5.2.5.s (p. 767)

[1380] T. Nishita and E. Nakamae. Continuous tone representation of three-dimensional objects taking account of shadows and interreflection. *Computer Graphics*, 19(3):23–30, July 1985. Also in *Proceedings of the SIGGRAPH'85 Conference*, San Francisco, July 1985. [volumes; shading] cited in A.7.2.1

[1381] V. B. Nitya, N. Sridevi, and A. K. Pujari. Linear octree by volume intersection using perspective silhouettes. *Pattern Recognition Letters*, 13(11):781–788, November 1992. [volumes; region octree; perspective view]

[1382] H. Noborio, S. Fukuda, and S. Arimoto. Construction of the octree approximating three-dimensional objects by using multiple views. *IEEE Transactions on Pattern Analysis and Machine Intelligence*, 10(6):769–782, November 1988. [volumes; region octree] cited in A.4.6, D.5.2

[1383] H. Noltemeier, K. Verbarg, and C. Zirkelbach. A data structure for representing and efficient querying large scenes of geometric objects: mb*-trees. In *Geometric Modelling, Computing/Supplement 8*, G. E. Farin, H. Hagen, H. Noltemeier, and W. Knödel, eds., pages 211–226. Springer-Verlag, Vienna, Austria, 1993. Also see *Data Structures and Efficient Algorithms*, B. Monien and T. Ottmann, eds., vol. 594 of Springer-Verlag Lecture Notes in Computer Science, pages 186–211, Berlin, Germany, 1992. [points; metric spaces; nearest neighbor; mb-tree; mb*-tree] cited in F.4.1.7 (p. 517), F.4.2 (p. 517), F.4.4.5 (p. 580), F.4.5 (p. 599), F.4.5.3.2 (p. 616), F.4.5.3.3 (p. 618), F.4.5.7.3 (p. 649)

[1384] V. T. Noronha. A survey of hierarchical partitioning methods for vector images. In *Proceedings of the 3rd International Symposium on Spatial Data Handling*, pages 185–200, Sydney, Australia, August 1988. [rectangles; survey]

[1385] T. Ohler. The multi class grid file: an access structure for multi class range queries. In *Proceedings of the 5th International Symposium on Spatial Data Handling*, vol. 1, pages 260–271, Charleston, SC, August 1992. [points; grid file]

[1386] Y. Ohsawa and M. Sakauchi. The BD-tree—a new n-dimensional data structure with highly efficient dynamic characteristics. In *Proceedings of Information Processing'83*, R. E. A. Mason, ed., pages 539–544, Paris, France, September 1983. North-Holland. [points; BD-tree] cited in D.2.6.2, F.1.5.2.3 (p. 74), F.1.5.2.6 (p. 79), F.1.7.1.4 (p. 107), F.1.7.1.5 (p. 115), F.4.4.5 (p. 581)

[1387] Y. Ohsawa and M. Sakauchi. Multidimensional data management structure with efficient dynamic characteristics. *Systems, Computers, Controls*, 14(5):77–87, 1983. Translated from *Denshi Tsushin Gakkai Ronbunshi*, 66–D(10):1193–1200, October 1983. [points; BD-tree] cited in D.2.6.2, F.1.5.2.3 (p. 74), F.1.5.2.6 (pp. 79, 81), F.1.7.1.4 (p. 107), F.1.7.1.5 (p. 115), F.4.4.5 (p. 581)

[1388] Y. Ohsawa and M. Sakauchi. A new tree type data structure with homogeneous nodes suitable for a very large spatial database. In *Proceedings of the 6th IEEE International Conference on Data Engineering*, pages 296–303, Los Angeles, February 1990. [points; rectangles; GBD-tree; BD-tree] cited in F.1.5.2.6 (p. 82)

[1389] T. Ohya, M. Iri, and K. Murota. Improvements of the incremental method for the Voronoi diagram with computational comparison of various algorithms. *Journal of the Operations Research Society of Japan*, 27(4):306–337, December 1984. [regions; Voronoi diagram]

[1390] F. Okawara, K. Shimizu, and Y. Nishitani. Data compression of the region quadtree and algorithms for set operations. Department of Computer Science Report CS–88–6, Gumma University, Gumma, Japan, July 1988. Translated from *Proceedings of the 36th All-Japan Conference on Information Processing*, pages 73–74, Tokyo, Japan, March 1988. [regions] cited in A.2.1.2

[1391] N. Okino, Y. Kakazu, and H. Kubo. TIPS–1: technical information processing system for computer-aided design, drawing and manufacturing. In *Computer Languages for Numerical Control: Proceedings of the Second IFIP/IFAC International Conference on Programming Languages for Machine Tools (PROLAMAT'73)*, J. Hatvany, ed., pages 141–150, Budapest, Hungary, January 1973. North Holland. [volumes] cited in D.5.5

[1392] M. A. Oliver. Two display algorithms for octrees. In *Proceedings of the EUROGRAPHICS'84 Conference*, K. Bo and H. A. Tucker, eds., pages 251–264, Copenhagen, Denmark, September 1984. [volumes; region octree]

[1393] M. A. Oliver. Display algorithms for quadtrees and octtrees and their hardware realization. In *Data Structures for Raster Graphics*, F. J. Peters, L. R. A. Kessener, and M. L. P. van Lierop, eds., pages 9–37. Springer-Verlag, Berlin, West Germany, 1986. [regions; region quadtree; region octree]

[1394] M. A. Oliver, T. R. King, and N. E. Wiseman. Quadtree scan conversion. In *Proceedings of the EUROGRAPHICS'84 Conference*, K. Bo and H. A. Tucker, eds., pages 265–276, Copenhagen, Denmark, September 1984. [regions; region quadtree] cited in A.4.2.2

[1395] M. A. Oliver and N. E. Wiseman. Operations on quadtree-encoded images. *Computer Journal*, 26(1):83–91, February 1983. [regions; region quadtree; DF-expression] cited in A.2.1.1, A.2.2, F.2.3.1 (p. 410)

[1396] M. A. Oliver and N. E. Wiseman. Operations on quadtree leaves and related image areas. *Computer Journal*, 26(4):375–380, November 1983. [regions; region quadtree] cited in A.6.4, A.9.3.4, F.2.1.2.2 (p. 208)

[1397] F. Olken and D. Rotem. Sampling from spatial databases. In *Proceedings of the 9th IEEE International Conference on Data Engineering*, pages 199–208, Vienna, Austria, April 1993. [regions; sampling strategies; region quadtree; R-tree] cited in F.2.1.2.4.s (p. 780)

[1398] D. R. Olsen Jr. and C. N. Cooper. Spatial trees: a fast access method for unstructured graphical data. In *Proceedings of Graphics Interface'85*, pages 69–74, Montréal, Canada, May 1985. [regions]

[1399] S. M. Omohundro. Five balltree construction algorithms. Technical Report TR–89–063, International Computer Science Institute, Berkeley, CA, December 1989. [regions; balltree; k-d tree; minimum bounding hypersphere] cited in F.2.1.1 (p. 195), F.4.4.2 (p. 567), F.4.5.3.4 (pp. 622–623)

[1400] S. M. Omohundro. Bumptrees for efficient function, constraint, and classification learning. In *Advances in Neural Information Processing Systems 3*, R. P. Lippmann, J. E. Moody, and D. S. Touretzky, eds., pages 693–699, Denver, CO, November 1990. Morgan-Kaufmann. [regions; points; balltree]

[1401] J. O. Omolayole and A. Klinger. A hierarchical data structure scheme for storing pictures. In *Pictorial Information Systems*, S. K. Chang and K. S. Fu, eds., vol. 80 of Lecture Notes in Computer Science, pages 1–38. Springer-Verlag, Berlin, West Germany, 1980. [regions; MX quadtree] cited in D.4.2.1, F.2.2.2.3 (p. 359)

[1402] B. C. Ooi, C. H. Goh, and K.-L. Tan. Fast high-dimensional data search in incomplete databases. In *Proceedings of the 24th International Conference on Very Large Data Bases (VLDB)*, A. Gupta, O. Shmueli, and J. Widom, eds., pages 357–367, New York, August 1998. [points; high-dimensional data]

[1403] B. C. Ooi, P. Kalnis, K.-L. Tan, and R. Zhang. Generalized multi-dimensional data mapping and query processing. *ACM Transactions on Database Systems*, 30(3), September 2005. [high-dimensional data; GiST; iMinMax; pyramid technique] cited in F.4.4.7 (p. 590)

[1404] B. C. Ooi, K. J. McDonell, and R. Sacks-Davis. Spatial kd-tree: an indexing mechanism for spatial database. In *Proceedings of the 11th International Computer Software and Applications Conference COMPSAC*, pages 433–438, Tokyo, Japan, October 1987. [rectangles; spatial k-d tree] cited in D.2.8.1, D.3.4, F.1.5.1.4 (pp. 62, 68), F.1.7.1.2 (p. 101), F.3.3.2.5 (p. 464), F.4.4.4 (p. 574), F.4.5.2.4 (p. 610)

[1405] B. C. Ooi and R. Sacks-Davis. Query optimization in an extended DBMS. In *Proceedings of the 3rd International Conference on Foundations of Data Organization and Algorithms (FODO)*, W. Litwin and H.-J. Schek, eds., vol. 367 of Springer-Verlag Lecture Notes in Computer Science, pages 48–63, Paris, France, June 1989. [spatial query optimization]

[1406] B. C. Ooi, R. Sacks-Davis, and K. J. McDonell. Extending a DBMS for geographic applications. In *Proceedings of the 5th IEEE International Conference on Data Engineering*, pages 590–597, Los Angeles, February 1989. [rectangles; points; spatial k-d tree]

[1407] B. C. Ooi, R. Sacks-Davis, and K. J. McDonell. Spatial indexing in binary decomposition and spatial bounding. *Information Systems*, 16(2):211–237, 1991. [rectangles; spatial k-d tree] cited in F.1.5.1.4 (pp. 62, 68), F.1.7.1.2 (p. 101), F.3.3.2.5 (p. 464), F.4.4.4 (p. 574), F.4.5.2.4 (p. 610)

[1408] B. C. Ooi, K.-L. Tan, C. Yu, and S. Bressan. Indexing the edges—a simple and yet efficient approach to high-dimensional indexing. In *Proceedings of the 19th ACM SIGACT-SIGMOD-SIGART Symposium on Principles of Database Systems (PODS)*, pages 166–174, Dallas, TX, May 2000. [pyramid technique; high-dimensional data; iMinMax] cited in F.4.4.7 (pp. 589–590), F.4.4.7.s (p. 854)

[1409] P. van Oosterom. A modified binary space partitioning tree for geographic information system. *International Journal of Geographical Information Systems*, 4(2):133–146, April–June 1990. [lines; BSP tree] cited in F.2.1.3.1 (p. 233)

[1410] P. van Oosterom. *Reactive data structures for geographic information systems*. PhD thesis, Department of Computer Science, Leiden University, Leiden, The Netherlands, December 1990. [geographic information systems (GIS); BSP tree; sphere tree; KD2-tree; KD2B-tree] cited in F.1.5.1.4 (p. 68), F.2.1.1 (p. 195), F.2.1.3.1 (p. 233), F.2.2.3.1 (p. 384), F.3.3.2.5 (p. 464), F.4.4.2 (pp. 567–568), F.4.4.4 (p. 574), F.4.5.2.4 (p. 610), F.4.5.3.4 (p. 622), F.4.5.4.1 (p. 625)

[1411] P. van Oosterom and J. van den Bos. An object-oriented approach to the design of geographic information systems. *Computers & Graphics*, 13(4):409–418, 1989. [regions; geographic information systems (GIS); BLG-tree] cited in F.2.2.3.1 (p. 384)

[1412] P. van Oosterom and E. Claassen. Orientation insensitive indexing methods for geometric objects. In *Proceedings of the 4th International Symposium on Spatial Data Handling*, vol. 2, pages 1016–1029, Zurich, Switzerland, July 1990. [rectangles; BSP tree; k-d-B-tree; sphere tree; KD2-tree; KD2B-tree] cited in F.1.5.1.4 (p. 68), F.2.1.1 (p. 195), F.3.3.2.5 (p. 464), F.4.4.2 (pp. 567–568), F.4.4.4 (p. 574), F.4.5.2.4 (p. 610), F.4.5.3.4 (p. 622), F.4.5.4.1 (p. 625)

[1413] J. A. Orenstein. Multidimensional tries used for associative searching. *Information Processing Letters*, 14(4):150–157, June 1982. [points; PR quadtree; PR k-d tree] cited in A.1.3, D.2.6.2, D.2.7, D.2.8.1, D.2.8.1.s, D.2.8.2, F.1.1 (p. 11), F.1.5.2.1 (p. 71), F.1.5.2.3 (p. 74), F.1.7.2.2 (p. 137), F.4.1.6 (p. 511), F.4.4.5 (p. 580), F.4.5 (p. 599), F.4.5.3.3 (p. 619), F.1.5.2.3.s (p. 765)

[1414] J. A. Orenstein. A dynamic hash file for random and sequential accessing. In *Proceedings of the 9th International Conference on Very Large Databases (VLDB)*, M. Schkolnick and C. Thanos, eds., pages 132–141, Florence, Italy, October 1983. [points; linear hashing] cited in D.2.7, D.2.8.2, F.1.7.2.3.1 (p. 143), F.1.7.2.5 (pp. 162–163)

[1415] J. A. Orenstein. Spatial query processing in an object-oriented database system. In *Proceedings of the ACM SIGMOD Conference*, pages 326–336, Washington, DC, May 1986. [points; spatial join] cited in F.P (p. xx), F.3 (p. 428)

[1416] J. A. Orenstein. Redundancy in spatial databases. In *Proceedings of the ACM SIGMOD Conference*, pages 294–305, Portland, OR, June 1989. [points; regions; redundancy; filter-and-refine] cited in

F.2.1.4.1 (pp. 256–257), F.4.1.6 (p. 509), F.4.4.7 (p. 590), F.4.4.8 (p. 593), F.4.6 (p. 663)

[1417] J. A. Orenstein. Strategies for optimizing the use of redundancy in spatial databases. In *Design and Implementation of Large Spatial Databases—1st Symposium, SSD'89*, A. Buchmann, O. Günther, T. R. Smith, and Y.-F. Wang, eds., vol. 409 of Springer-Verlag Lecture Notes in Computer Science, pages 115–134, Santa Barbara, CA, July 1989. [lines; redundancy; Z order; spatial join] cited in F.2.1.4.1 (p. 257)

[1418] J. A. Orenstein. A comparison of spatial query processing techniques for native and parameter spaces. In *Proceedings of the ACM SIGMOD Conference*, pages 343–352, Atlantic City, NJ, June 1990. [points; transformation technique]

[1419] J. A. Orenstein. An object-oriented approach to spatial data processing. In *Proceedings of the 4th International Symposium on Spatial Data Handling*, vol. 2, pages 669–678, Zurich, Switzerland, July 1990. [object-oriented spatial database]

[1420] J. A. Orenstein and T. H. Merrett. A class of data structures for associative searching. In *Proceedings of the 3rd ACM SIGACT-SIGMOD-SIGART Symposium on Principles of Database Systems (PODS)*, pages 181–190, Waterloo, Ontario, Canada, April 1984. [points; zkd Btree; linear hashing; Z order] cited in A.1.4, D.1.3, D.2.7, D.2.8.2, F.1.6 (p. 93), F.1.7.2.3.1 (p. 143), F.1.8.5.1 (p. 172), F.2.1.1.2 (p. 200), F.2.1.2.4 (p. 216), F.2.1.4.1 (p. 257)

[1421] J. O'Rourke. Dynamically quantized spaces for focusing the Hough transform. In *Proceedings of the 7th International Joint Conference on Artificial Intelligence*, pages 737–739, Vancouver, Canada, August 1981. [points; dynamically quantized space (DQS); Hough transform;] cited in D.2.8.1, F.1.5.1.4 (p. 62)

[1422] J. O'Rourke. Computing the relative neighborhood graph in the L_1 and L_∞ metrics. *Pattern Recognition*, 15(3):189–192, 1982. [points; relative neighborhood graph (RNG); Delaunay triangulation (DT)] cited in F.4.5.6 (p. 641)

[1423] J. O'Rourke. Computational geometry. *Annual Reviews in Computer Science*, 3:389–411, 1988. [computational geometry; general] cited in D.P, F.P (p. xix)

[1424] J. O'Rourke. *Computational Geometry in C*. Cambridge University Press, Cambridge, United Kingdom, second edition, 1998. [computational geometry; general] cited in F.2.2.1.4 (p. 346), F.4.7.4 (p. 712)

[1425] J. O'Rourke and K. R. Sloan Jr. Dynamic quantization: two adaptive data structures for multidimensional spaces. *IEEE Transactions on Pattern Analysis and Machine Intelligence*, 6(3):266–280, May 1984. [points; dynamically quantized pyramid (DQP); dynamically quantized space (DQS); Hough transform] cited in D.2.8.1, F.1.5.1.4 (p. 62), F.1.9 (p. 186), F.2.1.5.1 (p. 269)

[1426] D. N. Oskard, T. H. Hong, and C. A. Shaffer. Spatial mapping system for autonomous underwater vehicles. In *Proceedings of the SPIE, Sensor Fusion: Spatial Reasoning and Scene Interpretation*, vol. 1003, pages 439–450, Cambridge, MA, November 1988. [regions]

[1427] W. Osse and N. Ahuja. Efficient octree representation of moving objects. In *Proceedings of the 7th International Conference on Pattern Recognition*, pages 821–823, Montréal, Canada, July 1984. [volumes; region octree] cited in A.6.5.3

[1428] E. J. Otoo. A mapping function for the directory of multidimensional extendible hashing. In *Proceedings of the 10th International Conference on Very Large Databases (VLDB)*, U. Dayal, G. Schlageter, and L. H. Seng, eds., pages 493–506, Singapore, August 1984. [linear hashing; grid file; multidimensional extendible hashing (MDEH); PLOP hashing] cited in F.1.7.2.3.2 (p. 147), F.1.7.2.4.4 (p. 159), F.1.7.2.3.2.s (p. 774), F.1.7.2.4.4.s (p. 775)

[1429] E. J. Otoo and H. Zhu. Indexing on spherical surfaces using semi-quadcodes. In *Advances in Spatial Databases—3rd International Symposium, SSD'93*, D. Abel and B. C. Ooi, eds., vol. 692 of Springer-Verlag Lecture Notes in Computer Science, pages 510–529, Singapore, June 1993. [surfaces]

[1430] T. Ottmann and D. Wood. 1-2 brother trees or AVL trees revisited. *Computer Journal*, 23(3):248–255, August 1980. [points; 1-2 brother tree] cited in D.2.7, F.2.1.5.2.2 (p. 280)

[1431] A. A. Ouksel, M. Sayal, and P. Scheuermann. EPICT: an efficient pixel interleaving compression technique for binary images. Technical report, Electrical and Computer Engineering Department, Northwestern University, Evanston, IL, 1998. [regions; EPICT; DF-expression] cited in F.2.1.2.4 (p. 215)

[1432] M. Ouksel. The interpolation-based grid file. In *Proceedings of the 4th ACM SIGACT-SIGMOD-SIGART Symposium on Principles of Database Systems (PODS)*, pages 20–27, Portland, OR, March 1985. [points]

[1433] M. Ouksel and J. Abdul-Ghaffar. Concurrency in multidimensional linear hashing. In *Proceedings of the 3rd International Conference on Foundations of Data Organization and Algorithms (FODO)*, W. Litwin and H.-J. Schek, eds., vol. 367 of Springer-Verlag Lecture Notes in Computer Science, pages 233–240, Paris, France, June 1989. [points; concurrency; linear hashing]

[1434] M. Ouksel and P. Scheuermann. Multidimensional *B*-trees: analysis of dynamic behavior. *BIT*, 21(4):401–418, 1981. [points; multidimensional B-tree (MDBT)] cited in F.1.1 (p. 8), F.1.5.1.4 (p. 66)

[1435] M. Ouksel and P. Scheuermann. Storage mappings for multidimensional linear dynamic hashing. In *Proceedings of the 2nd ACM SIGACT-SIGMOD-SIGART Symposium on Principles of Database Systems (PODS)*, pages 90–105, Atlanta, GA, March 1983. [points; linear hashing] cited in D.2.7, D.2.8.2, F.1.7.2.3.1 (p. 143)

[1436] M. Ouksel and A. Yaagoub. The interpolation-based bintree and encoding of binary images. *CVGIP: Graphical Models and Image Understanding*, 54(1):75–81, January 1992. [regions; bintree]

[1437] M. A. Ouksel, V. Kumar, and C. Majumdar. Management of concurrency in interpolation based grid file organization and its performance. *Information Sciences*, 78(1–2):129–158, May 1994. [points; grid file; concurrency]

[1438] M. A. Ouksel and O. Mayer. A robust and efficient spatial data structure. *Acta Informatica*, 29(4):335–373, July 1992. [points; BANG file; nested interpolation-based grid file (NIBGF)] cited in F.1.7.1.5 (p. 115), F.3.4.2 (p. 479), F.1.7.1.5.s (p. 769)

[1439] J. K. Ousterhout. Corner stitching: a data structuring technique for VLSI layout tools. *IEEE Transactions on Computer-Aided Design*, 3(1):87–100, January 1984. [rectangles; corner stitching] cited in D.3.1, D.3.4, D.3.4.s, F.3.3.2.1 (p. 459), F.3.3.2.1.s (p. 826)

[1440] M. H. Overmars. *The Design of Dynamic Data Structures*. vol. 156 of Lecture Notes in Computer Science. Springer-Verlag, New York, 1983. [points; general] cited in D.P, D.2.1, F.P (p. xix)

[1441] M. H. Overmars. Range searching in a set of line segments. In *Proceedings of the Symposium on Computational Geometry*, pages 177–185, Baltimore, MD, June 1985. [rectangles; regions; segment tree; dynamic point location] cited in D.3.2.4.s, F.2.1.3.3.2 (p. 253), F.3.1.4.s (p. 821)

[1442] M. H. Overmars. Geometric data structures for computer graphics: an overview. In *Theoretical Foundations of Computer Graphics and CAD*, R. A. Earnshaw, ed., pages 21–49. Springer-Verlag, Berlin, West Germany, 1988. [rectangles; survey] cited in D.P, D.2.1, D.2.5.s, D.2.6.2.s, D.3.2.4, F.P (p. xix), F.3.1.4 (p. 444), F.1.2.s (p. 750), F.1.4.2.2.s (p. 760)

[1443] M. H. Overmars. Point location in fat subdivisions. *Information Processing Letters*, 44(5):261–265, December 1992. [regions; point location]

[1444] M. H. Overmars and J. van Leeuwen. Dynamic multi-dimensional data structures based on quad- and *k–d* trees. *Acta Informatica*, 17(3):267–285, 1982. [points; optimized point quadtree; pseudo quadtree; optimized k-d tree; pseudo k-d tree] cited in D.2.3.1, D.2.3.1.s, D.2.3.2, D.2.3.2.s, D.2.4.1, D.2.4.1.s, F.1.4.1.1 (p. 30), F.1.4.1.2 (p. 34), F.1.5.1.4 (pp. 58, 65), F.1.5.3 (p. 88), F.2.1.2.8 (p. 224), F.1.4.1.1.s (pp. 752–753), F.1.4.1.2.s (p. 755), F.1.5.1.4.s (p. 763), F.1.8.6.s (p. 775)

[1445] M. H. Overmars and C. K. Yap. New upper bounds in Klee's measure problem. In *Proceedings of the 29th IEEE Annual Symposium on Foundations of Computer Science*, pages 550–556, White Plains, NY, October 1988. [rectangles; measure problem] cited in D.3.3, F.3.2 (pp. 449, 451)

[1446] E. A. Ozkarahan and M. Ouksel. Dynamic and order preserving data partitioning for database machines. In *Proceedings of the*

11th International Conference on Very Large Databases (VLDB), A. Pirotte and Y. Vassiliou, eds., pages 358–368, Stockholm, Sweden, August 1985. [points]

[1447] B.-U. Pagel, F. Korn, and C. Faloutsos. Deflating the dimensionality curse using multiple fractal dimensions. In *Proceedings of the 16th IEEE International Conference on Data Engineering*, pages 589–598, San Diego, CA, February 2000. [high-dimensional data; curse of dimensionality; fractal dimension]

[1448] B.-U. Pagel and H.-W. Six. Are window queries representative for arbitrary range queries? In *Proceedings of the 15th ACM SIGACT-SIGMOD-SIGART Symposium on Principles of Database Systems (PODS)*, pages 150–160, Montréal, Canada, June 1996. [rectangles; window query]

[1449] B.-U. Pagel, H.-W. Six, and H. Toben. The transformation technique for spatial objects revisited. In *Advances in Spatial Databases—3rd International Symposium, SSD'93*, D. Abel and B. C. Ooi, eds., vol. 692 of Springer-Verlag Lecture Notes in Computer Science, pages 73–88, Singapore, June 1993. [points; transformation technique] cited in F.3.3.3 (p. 465)

[1450] B.-U. Pagel, H.-W. Six, and P. Widmayer. Towards an analysis of range query performance in spatial data structures. In *Proceedings of the 12th ACM SIGACT-SIGMOD-SIGART Symposium on Principles of Database Systems (PODS)*, pages 214–221, Washington, DC, May 1993. Also Informatik Berichte 137, Fern Universität, Hagen, Germany, November 1992. [points; range query]

[1451] B.-U. Pagel, H.-W. Six, and M. Winter. Window query-optimal clustering of spatial objects. In *Proceedings of the 14th ACM SIGACT-SIGMOD-SIGART Symposium on Principles of Database Systems (PODS)*, pages 86–94, San Jose, CA, May 1995. [points; window query]

[1452] A. G. Pai, H. Usha, and A. K. Pujari. Linear octree of a 3d object from 2d silhouettes using segment tree. *Pattern Recognition Letters*, 11(9):619–623, September 1990. [volumes; region octree; segment tree]

[1453] R. Pajarola. Large scale terrain visualization using the restricted quadtree triangulation. In *Proceedings IEEE Visualization'98*, D. Ebert, H. Hagen, and H. Rushmeier, eds., pages 19–26, Research Triangle Park, NC, October 1998. [surfaces; restricted quadtree; triangulations] cited in F.1.5.1.4 (p. 64), F.2.2.2.10 (pp. 381–382), F.2.2.4 (p. 405)

[1454] R. Pajarola, M. Antonijuan, and R. Lario. QuadTin: quadtree based triangulated irregular networks. In *Proceedings IEEE Visualization 2002*, R. Moorehead, M. Gross, and K. I. Joy, eds., pages 395–402, Boston, October 2002. [surfaces; restricted quadtree; triangulated irregular network (TIN)]

[1455] J. Palimaka, O. Halustchak, and W. Walker. Integration of a spatial and relational database within a geographic information system. In *Proceedings of the 1986 ACSM-ASPRS Annual Convention*, vol. 3: Geographic Information Systems, pages 131–140, Washington, DC, March 1986. [regions; geographic information systems (GIS)]

[1456] K. Pallister, ed. *Game Programming Gems 5*. Charles River Media, Hingham, MA, 2005. [game programming; general] cited in F.P (p. xvii)

[1457] A. Paoluzzi. *Geometric Programming for Computer-Aided Design*. Wiley, Chichester, United Kingdom, 2003. [solid modeling; general] cited in F.P (p. xix)

[1458] D. Papadias, N. Mamoulis, and V. Delis. Algorithms for querying by spatial structure. In *Proceedings of the 24th International Conference on Very Large Data Bases (VLDB)*, A. Gupta, O. Shmueli, and J. Widom, eds., pages 546–557, New York, August 1998. [spatial join; topological relations]

[1459] D. Papadias, N. Mamoulis, and Y. Theodoridis. Processing and optimization of multiway spatial joins using R-trees. In *Proceedings of the 18th ACM SIGACT-SIGMOD-SIGART Symposium on Principles of Database Systems (PODS)*, pages 44–55, Philadelphia, PA, May–June 1999. [spatial join; R-tree]

[1460] D. Papadias, T. Sellis, Y. Theodoridis, and M. J. Egenhofer. Topological relations in the world of minimum bounding rectangles: a study with R-trees. In *Proceedings of the ACM SIGMOD Conference*, pages 92–103, San Jose, CA, May 1995. [rectangles; R-tree; topological relations]

[1461] D. Papadias, Q. Shen, Y. Tao, and K. Mouratidis. Group nearest neighbor queries. In *Proceedings of the 20th IEEE International Conference on Data Engineering*, pages 301–312, Boston, March 2004. [points; nearest neighbor]

[1462] D. Papadias, Y. Tao, G. Fu, and B. Seeger. Progressive skyline computation in database systems. *ACM Transactions on Database Systems*, 30(1):41–82, March 2005. Also see *Proceedings of the ACM SIGMOD Conference*, pages 467–478, San Diego, CA, June 2003. [points; skyline query; point dominance query; nearest neighbor] cited in F.4.1.5 (pp. 502, 504–508)

[1463] D. Papadias, Y. Tao, K. Mouratidis, and C. K. Hui. Aggregate nearest neighbor queries in spatial databases. *ACM Transactions on Database Systems*, 30(2):529–576, June 2005. [points; aggregate nearest neighbor]

[1464] D. Papadias, J. Zhang, N. Mamoulis, and Y. Tao. Query processing in spatial network databases. In *Proceedings of the 29th International Conference on Very Large Data Bases (VLDB)*, J. C. Freytag, P. C. Lockemann, S. Abiteboul, M. J. Carey, P. G. Selinger, and A. Heuer, eds., pages 802–813, Berlin, Germany, September 2003. [lines; points; nearest neighbor; spatial networks; shortest path algorithm] cited in F.4.1.6 (pp. 508–509, 513–514)

[1465] A. Papadopoulos and Y. Manolopoulos. Nearest neighbor queries in shared-nothing environments. *GeoInformatica*, 1(4):369–392, December 1997. [points; nearest neighbor; R-tree; parallel processing]

[1466] A. Papadopoulos and Y. Manolopoulos. Performance of nearest neighbor queries in R-trees. In *Proceedings of the 6th International Conference on Database Theory (ICDT'97)*, F. N. Afrati and P. Kolaitis, eds., vol. 1186 of Springer-Verlag Lecture Notes in Computer Science, pages 394–408, Delphi, Greece, January 1997. [nearest neighbor; R-tree]

[1467] A. Papadopoulos, P. Rigaux, and M. Scholl. A performance evaluation of spatial join processing strategies. In *Advances in Spatial Databases—6th International Symposium, SSD'99*, R. H. Güting, D. Papadias, and F. H. Lochovsky, eds., vol. 1651 of Springer-Verlag Lecture Notes in Computer Science, pages 286–307, Hong Kong, China, July 1999. [regions; spatial join]

[1468] V. Pareto. *Manuale di Economia Politica, con una Introduzione alla Scie nza Sociale*. Società Editrice Libraria, Milan, Italy, 1906. English translation *Manual of Political Economy* by A. S. Schwier, Augustus M. Kelley, New York, 1971. [economics; skyline query; point dominance query] cited in F.4.1.5 (p. 503)

[1469] C. M. Park and A. Rosenfeld. Connectivity and genus in three dimensions. Computer Science Technical Report TR–156, University of Maryland, College Park, MD, May 1971. [volumes; connected component labeling] cited in A.5.1, A.5.1.1, D.1.1, F.2.1.1.2 (p. 200)

[1470] H.-H. Park, G.-H. Cha, and C.-W. Chung. Multi-way spatial joins using R-trees: methodology and performance evaluation. In *Advances in Spatial Databases—6th International Symposium, SSD'99*, R. H. Güting, D. Papadias, and F. H. Lochovsky, eds., vol. 1651 of Springer-Verlag Lecture Notes in Computer Science, pages 229–250, Hong Kong, China, July 1999. [regions; spatial join; R-tree]

[1471] V. Pascucci and R. J. Frank. Global static indexing for real-time exploration of very large regular grids. In *Proceedings of the 2001 ACM/IEEE Conference on Supercomputing*, page 2 (electronic edition), Denver, CO, November 2001. [regions; volumes; space-filling curve; Morton order] cited in F.2.1.1.2 (p. 201)

[1472] V. Pascucci and R. J. Frank. Hierarchical indexing for out-of-core access to multi-resolution data. In *Hierarchical and Geometrical Methods in Scientific Visualization*, G. Farin, B. Hamann, and H. Hagen, eds., pages 225–241. Springer-Verlag, Berlin, Germany, 2003. [regions; volumes; space-filling curve; Morton order] cited in F.2.1.1.2 (p. 201)

[1473] J. Patel, J. B. Yu, N. Kabra, K. Tufte, B. Nag, J. Burger, N. Hall, K. Ramasamy, R. Lueder, C. Ellmann, J. Kupsch, S. Guo, J. Larson, D. DeWitt, and J. Naughton. Building a scalable geo-spatial DBMS: technology, implementation, and evaluation. In *Proceedings of the*

ACM SIGMOD Conference, J. Peckham, ed., pages 336–347, Tucson, AZ, May 1997. [spatial database]

[1474] J. M. Patel and D. J. DeWitt. Partition based spatial-merge join. In *Proceedings of the ACM SIGMOD Conference*, pages 259–270, Montréal, Canada, June 1996. [rectangles; spatial join] cited in F.P (p. xx)

[1475] M. S. Paterson and F. F. Yao. Efficient binary space partitions for hidden-surface removal and solid modeling. *Discrete & Computational Geometry*, 5(5):485–503, 1990. Also see *Proceedings of the Fifth Symposium on Computational Geometry*, pages 23–32, Saarbrücken, Germany, June 1989. [volumes; BSP tree; hidden-surface removal] cited in F.2.1.3.1 (p. 235)

[1476] M. S. Paterson and F. F. Yao. Optimal binary space partitions for orthogonal objects. *Journal of Algorithms*, 13(1):99–113, March 1992. Also see *Proceedings of the 1st Annual ACM-SIAM Symposium on Discrete Algorithms*, pages 100–106, San Francisco, January 1990. [volumes; BSP tree]

[1477] E. A. Patrick, D. R. Anderson, and F. K. Bechtel. Mapping multidimensional space to one dimension for computer output display. *IEEE Transactions on Computers*, 17(10):949–953, October 1968. [points] cited in A.1.4, D.1.3

[1478] G. Peano. Sur une courbe qui remplit toute une aire plaine. *Mathematische Annalen*, 36:157–160, 1890. [regions; space-filling curve; Morton order] cited in A.1.4, D.1.3, D.2.7, F.1.6 (p. 93), F.2.1.1.2 (p. 200)

[1479] J. Pei, W. Jin, M. Ester, and Y. Tao. Catching the best views of skyline: a semantic approach based on decisive subspaces. In *Proceedings of the 31st International Conference on Very Large Data Bases (VLDB)*, K. Böhm, C. S. Jensen, L. M. Haas, M. L. Kersten, P.-Å. Larson, and B. C. Ooi, eds., pages 253–264, Trondheim, Norway, September 2005. [points; skyline query; point dominance query; skyline cube] cited in F.4.1.5 (p. 503)

[1480] S. V. Pemmaraju and C. A. Shaffer. Analysis of the worst case complexity of a PR quadtree. *Information Processing Letters 49*, pages 263–267, 1994. [points; PR quadtree]

[1481] A. Pérez, S. Kamata, and E. Kawaguchi. Peano scanning of arbitary size images. In *Proceedings of the 11th International Conference on Pattern Recognition*, vol. III, pages 565–568, The Hague, The Netherlands, August–September 1992. [points; space-filling curve; Peano-Hilbert order] cited in F.2.1.1.2.s (p. 778)

[1482] R. N. Perry and S. F. Frisken. Kizamu: a system for sculpting digital characters. In *Proceedings of the SIGGRAPH'01 Conference*, pages 47–56, Los Angeles, August 2001. [volumes; surfaces; edge quadtree; face octree; adaptively sampled distance fields (ADF)] cited in F.2.2.2.5 (p. 362), F.2.2.2.7 (p. 373)

[1483] F. Peters. An algorithm for transformations of pictures represented by quadtrees. *Computer Vision, Graphics, and Image Processing*, 32(3):397–403, December 1985. [regions; region quadtree] cited in A.6.5.1

[1484] W. W. Peterson. Addressing for random access storage. *IBM Journal of Research and Development*, 1(2):130–146, April 1957. [uniform hashing] cited in F.4.5.8 (p. 653)

[1485] E. G. M. Petrakis and C. Faloutsos. Similarity searching in medical image databases. *IEEE Transactions on Knowledge and Data Engineering*, 9(3):435–447, May/June 1997. [medical image database; similarity searching; regions; R-tree]

[1486] T. Peucker. A theory of the cartographic line. *International Yearbook of Cartography*, 16:134–143, 1976. [lines] cited in D.4.1

[1487] T. Peucker and N. Chrisman. Cartographic data structures. *American Cartographer*, 2(2):55–69, April 1975. [surfaces; survey; triangulated irregular network (TIN)] cited in D.4.4, D.5.6, F.2.2.1.7 (p. 355), F.2.2.4 (p. 400)

[1488] D. J. Peuquet. Raster processing: an alternative approach to automated cartographic data handling. *American Cartographer*, 6(2):129–139, April 1979. [regions] cited in D.4.4

[1489] D. J. Peuquet. A hybrid data structure for the storage and manipulation of very large spatial data sets. *Computer Vision, Graphics, and Image Processing*, 24(1):14–27, October 1983. [regions] cited in D.4.4

[1490] D. J. Peuquet. A conceptual framework and comparison of spatial data models. *Cartographica*, 21(4):66–113, 1984. Reprinted in D.

J. Peuquet and D. F. Marble, *Introductory Readings in Geographic Information Systems*, pages 250–285, Taylor & Francis, London, United Kingdom, 1990. [survey] cited in A.P, D.P, D.1.4.1, F.P (p. xx), F.2.1.2.11 (p. 232)

[1491] D. J. Peuquet. An algorithm for calculating minimum Euclidean distance between two geographic features. *Computers & Geosciences*, 18(8):989–1001, September 1992. [regions; range query]

[1492] J. L. Pfaltz and A. Rosenfeld. Computer representation of planar regions by their skeletons. *Communications of the ACM*, 10(2):119–122, February 1967. [regions]

[1493] D. Pfoser and C. S. Jensen. Indexing of network constrained moving objects. In *Proceedings of the 11th ACM International Symposium on Advances in Geographic Information Systems*, E. Hoel and P. Rigaux, eds., pages 25–32, New Orleans, LA, November 2003. [spatial networks; nearest neighbor; moving objects; R-tree]

[1494] B. T. Phong. Illumination for computer generated images. *Communications of the ACM*, 18(6):311–317, June 1975. [surfaces; shading; hidden-surface removal] cited in A.7.1.4, A.7.2.1

[1495] M. Pietikäinen, A. Rosenfeld, and I. Walter. Split-and-link algorithms for image segmentation. *Pattern Recognition*, 15(4):287–298, 1982. [regions; pyramid; split-and-merge segmentation] cited in A.1.4, D.1.3, F.2.4 (p. 425)

[1496] A. Pitaksanonkul, S. Thanawastien, and C. Lursinsap. Comparisons of quad trees and 4-D trees. *IEEE Transactions on Computer-Aided Design*, 8(11):1157–1164, November 1989. [rectangles; bounded quadtree (BQT); MX-CIF quadtree] cited in F.3.4.2 (pp. 476–477)

[1497] N. Pla-Garcia. Boolean operations and spatial complexity of face octrees. *Proceedings of the EUROGRAPHICS'93 Conference*, 12(3):153–164, September 1993. [volumes; face octree] cited in F.2.2.2.4 (p. 362)

[1498] N. Pla-Garcia. *Techniques for modeling solids with smooth boundary*. PhD thesis, Departament de Llenguatges i Sistemes Informàtics, Universitat Politècnica de Catalunya, Barcelona, Spain, June 1993. [volumes; face octree] cited in F.2.2.2.4 (p. 362)

[1499] J. Ponce. Prism trees: an efficient representation for manipulating and displaying polyhedra with many faces. Artificial Intelligence Memo 838, Massachusetts Institute of Technology, Cambridge, MA, April 1985. [surfaces; prism tree] cited in D.4.1

[1500] J. Ponce and D. Chelberg. Localized intersections computation for solid modelling with straight homogeneous generalized cylinders. In *Proceedings of the 1987 IEEE International Conference on Robotics and Automation*, vol. 3, pages 1481–1486, Raleigh, NC, March–April 1987. [volumes]

[1501] J. Ponce and O. Faugeras. An object centered hierarchical representation for 3d objects: the prism tree. *Computer Vision, Graphics, and Image Processing*, 38(1):1–28, April 1987. [surfaces; prism tree] cited in D.4.1, D.5.6, D.5.7, D.5.7.s, F.2.2.2.4 (p. 362), F.2.2.3.2 (p. 386), F.2.2.3.3 (p. 391), F.2.2.3.4 (p. 398), F.2.2.3.2.s (p. 813)

[1502] J. Popovich and H. Hoppe. Progressive simplicial complexes. In *Proceedings of the SIGGRAPH'97 Conference*, pages 217–224, Los Angeles, August 1997. [surfaces; polygon simplification] cited in F.2.2.3.4 (p. 395)

[1503] T. Porter and T. Duff. Compositing digital images. *Computer Graphics*, 18(3):253–259, July 1984. Also in *Proceedings of the SIGGRAPH'84 Conference*, Minneapolis, MN, July 1984. [surfaces; compositing] cited in A.7.1.1, A.7.1.1.s

[1504] J. L. Posdamer. Spatial sorting for sampled surface geometries. In *Proceedings of SPIE, Biostereometrics'82*, R. E. Herron, ed., pages 152–163, San Diego, CA, August 1982. [surfaces; region octree] cited in A.4.6, A.7.1.6, D.5.2, F.2.1.3.2 (p. 241)

[1505] M. Potmesil. Generating octree models of 3d objects from their silhouettes in a sequence of images. *Computer Vision, Graphics, and Image Processing*, 40(1):1–29, October 1987. [volumes; region octree] cited in A.4.6, D.5.2

[1506] G. V. S. Prabhakar Reddy, H. J. Montas, A. Shirmohammadi, and H. Samet. Quadtree-based triangular mesh generation for finite element analysis of heterogeneous spatial data. In *Proceedings of the International ASAE Annual Meeting*, Sacramento, CA, July–August 1988. [regions; finite element analysis; mesh generation]

[1507] S. Pramanik and J. Li. Fast approximate search algorithm for nearest neighbor queries in high dimensions. In *Proceedings of the 15th IEEE International Conference on Data Engineering*, page 251, Sydney, Australia, March 1999. [high-dimensional data; approximate nearest neighbor]

[1508] W. K. Pratt. *Digital Image Processing*. Wiley-Interscience, New York, 1978. [image processing; general] cited in A.1.3, D.1.2, F.2.1.2.4 (p. 212)

[1509] F. P. Preparata, ed. *Advances in Computing Research: Computational Geometry*, vol. 1. JAI Press, Greenwich, CT, 1983. [computational geometry; general] cited in D.P, F.P (p. xix)

[1510] F. P. Preparata and S. J. Hong. Convex hulls of finite sets of points in two and three dimensions. *Communications of the ACM*, 20(2):87–93, February 1977. [regions; convex hull] cited in A.7.3.s

[1511] F. P. Preparata and M. I. Shamos. *Computational Geometry: An Introduction*. Springer-Verlag, New York, 1985. [computational geometry; general] cited in D.P, D.3, D.3.2, D.3.4, D.4.3, D.5.6, F.P (p. xix), F.2 (p. 192), F.2.1.3.2 (pp. 237, 240), F.2.1.5.2.4 (p. 291), F.2.3.3 (pp. 418, 421), F.3 (p. 428), F.3.1 (p. 429), F.3.1.2 (p. 435), F.3.3.2.2 (p. 461), F.4.1.5 (pp. 503–504), F.2.2.1.4.s (p. 799), F.2.2.3.3.s (p. 813), F.4.4.2.s (p. 852)

[1512] F. P. Preparata and R. Tamassia. Fully dynamic point location in a monotone subdivision. *SIAM Journal on Computing*, 18(4):811–830, August 1989. [points; dynamic point location] cited in F.2.1.3.3.2 (p. 253)

[1513] F. P. Preparata and R. Tamassia. Dynamic planar point location with optimal query time. *Theoretical Computer Science*, 74(1):95–114, July 1990. [regions; dynamic point location] cited in F.2.1.3.3.2 (p. 253)

[1514] F. P. Preparata and R. Tamassia. Efficient point location in a convex spatial cell-complex. *SIAM Journal on Computing*, 21(2):267–280, April 1992. Also see *Proceedings of the 1989 Workshop on Algorithms and Data Structures (WADS'89)*, F. Dehne, J. R. Sack, and N. Santoro, eds., vol. 382 of Springer-Verlag Lecture Notes in Computer Science, pages 3–11, Ottawa, Canada, August 1989. [points; volumes; point location]

[1515] W. H. Press, S. A. Teukolsky, W. T. Vetterling, and B. P. Flannery. *Numerical Recipes in C: The Art of Scientific Computing*. Cambridge University Press, Cambridge, United Kingdom, second edition, 1992. [numerical methods; general] cited in F.4.6.4.1 (p. 672)

[1516] T. Priol and K. Bouatouch. Experimenting with a parallel ray-tracing algorithm on a hypercube machine. Rapport de Recherche 843, IRISA, Campus de Beaulieu, Rennes, France, 1988. [volumes; ray tracing]

[1517] G. Proietti and C. Faloutsos. Analysis of range queries and self-spatial join queries on real region datasets stored using an R-tree. *IEEE Transactions on Knowledge and Data Engineering*, 12(5):751–762, September/October 2000. [regions; R-tree; range query]

[1518] G. Proietti and C. Faloutsos. Accurate modeling of region data. *IEEE Transactions on Knowledge and Data Engineering*, 13(6):874–883 November/December 2001. [regions]

[1519] C. Puech and H. Yahia. Quadtrees, octrees, hyperoctrees: a unified analytical approach to tree data structures used in graphics, geometric modeling, and image processing. In *Proceedings of the Symposium on Computational Geometry*, pages 272–280, Baltimore, MD, June 1985. [hypervolumes; *d*-dimensional quadtree] cited in A.3.2.1

[1520] W. Pugh. Skip lists: a probabilistic alternative to balanced trees. *Communications of the ACM*, 33(6):668–676, June 1990. [points; skip list] cited in F.1.3 (p. 27), F.4.5.8 (p. 661)

[1521] R. Pulleyblank and J. Kapenga. The feasibility of a VLSI chip for ray tracing bicubic patches. *IEEE Computer Graphics and Applications*, 7(3):33–44, March 1987. [hardware; ray tracing] cited in A.7.2.5

[1522] E. Puppo. Variable resolution triangulations. *Computational Geometry Theory and Applications*, 11(3–4):219–238, 1998. [surfaces; restricted bintree; triangulations] cited in F.1.5.1.4 (p. 64), F.2.2.4 (p. 406)

[1523] A. Qamra, Y. Meng, and E. Y. Chang. Enhanced perceptual distance functions and indexing for image replica recognition. *IEEE Transactions on Pattern Analysis and Machine Intelligence*, 27(3):379–391, March 2005. [metric space embedding; locality sensitive hashing (LSH); approximate nearest neighbor] cited in F.4.7.4 (p. 716)

[1524] G. Qian, Q. Zhu, Q. Xue, and S. Pramanik. The ND-tree: a dynamic indexing technique for multidimensional non-ordered discrete data spaces. In *Proceedings of the 29th International Conference on Very Large Data Bases (VLDB)*, J. C. Freytag, P. C. Lockemann, S. Abiteboul, M. J. Carey, P. G. Selinger, and A. Heuer, eds., pages 620–631, Berlin, Germany, September 2003. [moving objects]

[1525] P. Quarendon. A general approach to surface modeling applied to molecular graphics. *Journal of Molecular Graphics*, 2(3):91–95, September 1984. [surfaces] cited in F.2.2.2.7 (p. 372)

[1526] K. M. Quinlan and J. R. Woodwark. A spatially-segmented solids database—justification and design. In *Proceedings of CAD'82 Conference*, A. Pipes, ed., pages 126–132, Brighton, United Kingdom, 1982. Butterworths. [volumes; PM octree] cited in A.1.3, D.5.3, F.2.2.2.7 (p. 370)

[1527] S. Quinlan. Efficient distance computation between non-convex objects. In *Proceedings of the IEEE International Conference on Robotics and Automation*, vol. 4, pages 3324–3329, San Diego, CA, May 1994. [volumes; sphere tree; minimum bounding box; interference detection] cited in F.2.2.3.1 (p. 383), F.2.2.3.3 (p. 389)

[1528] V. V. Raghavan and C. T. Yu. A note on a multidimensional searching problem. *Information Processing Letters*, 6(4):133–135, August 1977. [points; point location]

[1529] K. Ramamohanarao and J. W. Lloyd. Dynamic hashing schemes. *Computer Journal*, 25(4):478–485, November 1982. [points; recursive linear hashing] cited in D.2.8.2, F.B (p. 733)

[1530] K. Ramamohanarao and R. Sacks-Davis. Recursive linear hashing. *ACM Transactions on Database Systems*, 9(3):369–391, September 1984. [points; recursive linear hashing] cited in D.2.8.2, D.2.8.2.1.s, F.B (p. 733), F.B.s (p. 874)

[1531] K. Ramamohanarao and R. Sacks-Davis. Partial match retrieval using recursive linear hashing. *BIT*, 25(3):477–484, 1985. [points; partial match query; recursive linear hashing] cited in D.2.8.2, F.B (p. 733)

[1532] V. Raman and S. S. Iyengar. Properties and applications of forests of quadtrees for pictorial data representation. *BIT*, 23(4):472–486, 1983. [regions; forests of quadtrees] cited in A.2.1.4

[1533] V. Ramasubramanian and K. K. Paliwal. An efficient approximation-elimination algorithm for fast nearest neighbour search based on a spherical distance coordinate formulation. *Pattern Recognition Letters*, 13(7):471–480, July 1992. [metric spaces; nearest neighbor; distance matrix; LAESA] cited in F.4.5.7.3 (p. 649)

[1534] V. Ramasubramanian and K. K. Paliwal. Fast *k*-dimensional tree algorithms for nearest neighbor search with application to vector quantization encoding. *IEEE Transactions on Signal Processing*, 3(40):518–531, March 1992. [points; nearest neighbor; vector quantization]

[1535] V. Ramasubramanian and K. K. Paliwal. Fast nearest-neighbor search algorithms based on approximation-elimination search. *Pattern Recognition*, 33(9):1497–1510, September 2000. [metric spaces; distance matrix; AESA; survey] cited in F.4.7.3.2 (p. 699)

[1536] S. Rana, ed. *Topological Data Structures for Surfaces: An Introduction to Geographical Information Science*. John Wiley & Sons, Chichester, United Kingdom, 2004. [surfaces; general] cited in F.P (p. xix)

[1537] S. Ranade. Use of quadtrees for edge enhancement. *IEEE Transactions on Systems, Man, and Cybernetics*, 11(5):370–373, May 1981. [regions; edge enhancement]

[1538] S. Ranade, A. Rosenfeld, and J. M. S. Prewitt. Use of quadtrees for image segmentation. Computer Science Technical Report TR–878, University of Maryland, College Park, MD, February 1980. [regions; region quadtree]

[1539] S. Ranade, A. Rosenfeld, and H. Samet. Shape approximation using quadtrees. *Pattern Recognition*, 15(1):31–40, 1982. Also University of Maryland Computer Science Technical Report TR–847, December 1979. [regions; shape approximation] cited in A.8.1, A.8.1.s, A.8.2.1

[1540] S. Ranade and M. Shneier. Using quadtrees to smooth images. *IEEE Transactions on Systems, Man, and Cybernetics*, 11(5):373–376, May 1981. Also University of Maryland Computer Science Technical Report TR–894, April 1980. [regions; region quadtree; smoothing]

[1541] A. Rappoport. Using convex differences in hierarchical representations of polygonal maps. In *Proceedings of Graphics Interface'90*, pages 183–189, Halifax, Newfoundland, Canada, May 1990. [regions; convex difference tree (CDT)] cited in F.2.1.4.2 (pp. 262–263)

[1542] A. Rappoport. The extended convex differences tree (ECDT) representation for n-dimensional polyhedra. *International Journal of Computational Geometry Applications*, 1(3):227–241, 1991. [volumes; convex difference tree (CDT)]

[1543] K. Raptopoulou, A. N. Papadopoulos, and Y. Manolopoulos. Fast nearest-neighbor query processing in moving-object databases. *GeoInformatica*, 7(2):113–137, June 2003. [points; moving objects; nearest neighbor] cited in F.4 (p. 488)

[1544] S. Rasetic, J. Sander, J. Elding, and M. A. Nascimento. A trajectory splitting model for efficient spatio-temporal indexing. In *Proceedings of the 31st International Conference on Very Large Data Bases (VLDB)*, K. Böhm, C. S. Jensen, L. M. Haas, M. L. Kersten, P.-Å. Larson, and B. C. Ooi, eds., pages 934–945, Trondheim, Norway, September 2005. [spatiotemporal range query; moving objects; R-tree]

[1545] H. Ratschek and J. Rokne. *Computer Methods for the Range of Functions*. Ellis Horwood, Chichester, United Kingdom, 1984. [interval arithmetic; general] cited in D.5.5.1

[1546] S. Ravada and J. Sharma. Oracle8i spatial: experiences with extensible databases. In *Advances in Spatial Databases—6th International Symposium, SSD'99*, R. H. Güting, D. Papadias, and F. H. Lochovsky, eds., vol. 1651 of Springer-Verlag Lecture Notes in Computer Science, pages 355–359, Hong Kong, China, July 1999. [spatial database]

[1547] S. Ravindran and M. Manohar. Algorithm for converting a forest of quadtrees to a binary array. *Image and Vision Computing*, 5(4):297–300, November 1987. [regions; forests of quadtrees]

[1548] D. R. Reddy and S. Rubin. Representation of three-dimensional objects. Computer Science Technical Report CMU–CS–78–113, Carnegie-Mellon University, Pittsburgh, PA, April 1978. [volumes; minimum bounding box] cited in A.1.4, D.1.3, F.2.1.1 (p. 195), F.2.4 (p. 425)

[1549] M. Regnier. Evaluation des performances du hachage dynamique. Thèse de troisième cycle, Université d'Orsay, Paris, France, 1983. [points; grid file] cited in F.1.7.2.5 (p. 160)

[1550] M. Regnier. Analysis of grid file algorithms. *BIT*, 25(2):335–357, 1985. [points; grid file] cited in D.2.8.1, D.2.8.2.3.s, D.3.4, F.1.4.2.2 (p. 46), F.1.7.2.5 (p. 160), F.1.7.2.1.s (p. 773)

[1551] E. M. Reingold, J. Nievergelt, and N. Deo. *Combinatorial Algorithms: Theory and Practice*. Prentice-Hall, Englewood Cliffs, NJ, 1977. [combinatorial algorithms; general] cited in D.2.7, F.1.6 (p. 95)

[1552] E. M. Reingold and R. E. Tarjan. On the greedy heuristic for complete matching. *SIAM Journal on Computing*, 10(4):676–681, November 1981. [points; Euclidean matching problem] cited in D.2.9.s, F.1.9.s (p. 776)

[1553] J. F. Reiser. SAIL. Stanford Artificial Intelligence Laboratory Memo AIM–289, Stanford University, Stanford, CA, August 1976. [SAIL; programming languages] cited in A.P, A.L, D.P, F.P (p. xx), F.D (p. 743)

[1554] L. Relly and A. Wolf. A storage manager for the development of spatial data structures, a performance analysis. In *IGIS'94: Geographic Information Systems, International Workshop on Advanced Research in Geographic Information Systems*, J. Nievergelt, T. Roos, H.-J. Schek, and P. Widmayer, eds., pages 168–177, Monte Verità, Ascona, Switzerland, March 1994. [points; spatial database]

[1555] A. A. G. Requicha. Representations of rigid solids: theory, methods, and systems. *ACM Computing Surveys*, 12(4):437–464, December 1980. [volumes; solid modeling; constructive solid geometry (CSG); survey] cited in A.P, A.7.1.4, D.P, D.3.4, D.5.1.s, D.5.5, D.5.5.1, F.P (p. xix), F.2.2 (p. 314), F.3.3.1 (p. 453)

[1556] A. A. G. Requicha and J. R. Rossignac. Solid modeling and beyond. *IEEE Computer Graphics and Applications*, 12(5):31–44, September 1992. [volumes; solid modeling; survey]

[1557] A. A. G. Requicha and H. B. Voelcker. Solid modeling: a historical summary and contemporary assessment. *IEEE Computer Graphics and Applications*, 2(2):9–24, March 1982. [volumes; solid modeling; constructive solid geometry (CSG); survey] cited in D.5.5, F.2.2 (p. 314)

[1558] A. A. G. Requicha and H. B. Voelcker. Solid modeling: current status and research directions. *IEEE Computer Graphics and Applications*, 3(7):25–37, October 1983. [volumes; solid modeling; constructive solid geometry (CSG); survey] cited in D.5.5

[1559] P. Revesz. *Introduction to Constraint Databases*. Springer-Verlag, New York, 2002. [constraint database; general] cited in F.P (p. xix), F.3.1.4 (p. 445)

[1560] P. Revesz and Y. Chen. Efficient aggregation on moving objects. In *Proceedings of the 10th International Symposium on Temporal Representation and Reasoning / 4th International Conference on Temporal Logic (TIME 2003)*, pages 118–127, Cairns, Australia, July 2003. [rectangles; moving objects; aggregation query] cited in F.3.1.4 (p. 445)

[1561] W. C. Rheinboldt and C. K. Mesztenyi. On a data structure for adaptive finite element mesh refinements. *ACM Transactions on Mathematical Software*, 6(2):166–187, June 1980. [regions; finite element analysis] cited in A.1.4, D.1.3, F.2.4 (p. 425)

[1562] P. Rigaux, M. Scholl, and A. Voisard. *Spatial Databases with Application to GIS*. Morgan-Kaufmann, San Francisco, 2002. [spatial database; geographic information systems (GIS); general] cited in F.P (p. xix)

[1563] E. M. Riseman and M. A. Arbib. Computational techniques in the visual segmentation of static scenes. *Computer Graphics and Image Processing*, 6(3):221–276, June 1977. [regions; preprocessing cone; pyramid] cited in A.1.4, D.1.3, F.2.4 (p. 424)

[1564] M. C. Rivara. Algorithms for refining triangular grids suitable for adaptive and multigrid techniques. *International Journal Numerical Engineering*, 20(4):745–756, April 1984. [surfaces; restricted bintree; triangle meshes] cited in F.1.5.1.4 (p. 64), F.2.2.4 (p. 406)

[1565] M. C. Rivara. Fully adaptive multigrid finite element software. *ACM Transactions on Mathematical Software*, 10(3):242–264, September 1984. [surfaces; restricted bintree; triangle meshes] cited in F.1.5.1.4 (p. 64), F.2.2.4 (p. 406)

[1566] R. L. Rivest. On the optimality of Elias's algorithm for performing best-match searches. *Information Processing 74*, pages 678–681, 1974. [points; nearest neighbor; Elias algorithm] cited in F.4.4.8 (p. 593)

[1567] J. T. Robinson. The K-D-B-tree: a search structure for large multidimensional dynamic indexes. In *Proceedings of the ACM SIGMOD Conference*, pages 10–18, Ann Arbor, MI, April 1981. [points; k-d-B-tree] cited in D.2.7, D.2.8.1, D.3.5.3, F.1.6 (p. 93), F.1.7 (p. 96), F.1.7.1.1 (p. 98), F.2.1.2.8 (p. 224), F.2.1.5.3 (p. 306), F.4.4.3 (p. 573)

[1568] D. F. Rogers. *Procedural Elements for Computer Graphics*. McGraw-Hill, New York, 1985. [computer graphics; general] cited in A.1.3, A.4.5, A.4.6, A.4.6.s, A.5.1.1, A.6, A.6.4, A.7.1.2, A.7.1.4, A.7.2.3, A.7.2.4, D.4.2.3, D.5.2, D.5.2.s, D.5.6, F.2.2.2.6 (p. 366), F.2.2.4 (p. 406)

[1569] R. Ronfard and J. Rossignac. Full-range approximation of triangulated polyhedra. In *Proceedings of the EUROGRAPHICS'96 Conference*, J. Rossignac and F. X. Sillion, eds., pages 67–76, Poitiers, France, August 1996. [surfaces; surface simplification] cited in F.2.2.3.4 (p. 395)

[1570] C. Ronse. Codage en liste d'arbres quaternaires. *Technique et Science Informatiques*, 7(2):235–245, 1988. [regions; LISP]

[1571] J. B. Rosenberg. Geographical data structures compared: a study of data structures supporting region queries. *IEEE Transactions on Computer-Aided Design*, 4(1):53–67, January 1985. [rectangles; k-d tree] cited in D.3.4, D.3.4.s, F.3.3.2.2 (p. 460), F.3.4.2 (pp. 475, 477–478), F.3.3.2.2.s (p. 827)

[1572] A. Rosenfeld. Digital straight line segments. *IEEE Transactions on Computers*, 23(12):1264–1269, December 1974. [lines; digital geometry]

928

[1573] A. Rosenfeld, ed. *Multiresolution Image Processing and Analysis*. Springer-Verlag, Berlin, West Germany, 1984. [multiresolution image processing; pyramid; general] cited in A.P, A.4.2.3, D.P, F.P (p. xx)

[1574] A. Rosenfeld and A. C. Kak. *Digital Picture Processing*. Academic Press, New York, second edition, 1982. [image processing; general] cited in A.P, A.5.2, A.7.4.s, A.8.1, A.9.1, A.9.3.4, D.P, D.3.2.1, F.P (p. xx), F.2.1.2.2 (p. 209), F.3.1.1 (p. 430)

[1575] A. Rosenfeld and J. L. Pfaltz. Sequential operations in digital picture processing. *Journal of the ACM*, 13(4):471–494, October 1966. [regions; connected component labeling] cited in A.1.3, A.5.1, A.5.1.1, A.5.1.2, A.9, D.1.1, D.1.2, F.2.1.1.2 (p. 200), F.2.1.2.2 (p. 208)

[1576] A. Rosenfeld, H. Samet, C. Shaffer, and R. E. Webber. Application of hierarchical data structures to geographical information systems. Computer Science Technical Report TR–1197, University of Maryland, College Park, MD, June 1982. [QUILT; geographic information systems (GIS); region quadtree] cited in A.1.2, A.3.2.3, A.6.4, A.6.5.2, D.1.5

[1577] A. Rosenfeld, H. Samet, C. Shaffer, and R. E. Webber. Application of hierarchical data structures to geographical information systems: phase II. Computer Science Technical Report TR–1327, University of Maryland, College Park, MD, September 1983. [QUILT; geographic information systems (GIS); region quadtree] cited in A.2.1, A.2.1.1, D.2.6.2, F.1.4.2.2 (p. 44), F.1.8.1 (p. 166)

[1578] K. A. Ross, I. Sitzmann, and P. J. Stuckey. Cost-based unbalanced R-trees. In *Proceedings of the 13th International Conference on Scientific and Statistical Database Management*, pages 203–212, Fairfax, VA, July 2001. [regions; rectangles; R-tree; CUR-tree] cited in F.2.1.5.2.7 (p. 302)

[1579] J. Rossignac and H. Borrel. Multi-resolution 3D approximations for rendering complex scenes. In *Modeling in Computer Graphics: Methods and Applications*, B. Falcidieno and T. L. Kunii, eds., pages 455–465. Springer-Verlag, Berlin, Germany, 1993. [surfaces; polygon simplification; vertex clustering] cited in F.2.2.3.4 (p. 393)

[1580] J. Rossignac, A. Safanova, and A. Szymczak. 3D compression made simple: Edge-Breaker on a corner table. In *Proceedings of the 2001 International Conference on Shape Modeling and Applications*, pages 278–283, Genova, Italy, May 2001. [surfaces; winged-edge representation; triangulations; corner table; triangle table; boundary model (BRep)] cited in F.2.2.1.7 (p. 354)

[1581] J. R. Rossignac and A. A. G. Requicha. Depth-buffering display techniques for constructive solid geometry. *IEEE Computer Graphics and Applications*, 6(9):29–39, September 1986. [volumes; solid modeling; constructive solid geometry (CSG)] cited in D.5.5

[1582] D. Rotem. Spatial join indices. In *Proceedings of the 7th IEEE International Conference on Data Engineering*, pages 500–509, Kobe, Japan, April 1991. [points; grid file; spatial join index]

[1583] S. D. Roth. Ray casting for modeling solids. *Computer Graphics and Image Processing*, 18(2):109–144, February 1982. [volumes; ray tracing] cited in A.4.6, A.7.2.2, A.7.2.5.s, D.5.2, D.5.5

[1584] J. B. Rothnie Jr. and T. Lozano. Attribute based file organization in a paged memory environment. *Communications of the ACM*, 17(2):63–69, February 1974. [points; multiattribute tree (MAT)] cited in F.1.1 (p. 10)

[1585] N. Roussopoulos, C. Faloutsos, and T. Sellis. An efficient pictorial database system for PSQL. *IEEE Transactions on Software Engineering*, 14(5):639–650, May 1988. [regions; PSQL]

[1586] N. Roussopoulos, S. Kelley, and F. Vincent. Nearest neighbor queries. In *Proceedings of the ACM SIGMOD Conference*, pages 71–79, San Jose, CA, May 1995. [rectangles; R-tree; depth-first nearest neighbor algorithm; branch-and-bound nearest neighbor algorithm] cited in F.4.1.7 (pp. 516–517), F.4.2 (p. 517), F.4.2.4 (pp. 535–538), F.4.2.5 (pp. 546, 548), F.4.2.8 (pp. 556–557), F.4.4.2 (p. 568), F.2.1.5.2.3.s (p. 792), F.4.2.4.s (p. 843), F.4.2.8.s (p. 848)

[1587] N. Roussopoulos, Y. Kotidis, and M. Roussopoulos. Cubetree: organization of and bulk incremental updates on the data cube. In *Proceedings of the ACM SIGMOD Conference*, J. Peckham, ed., pages 89–111, Tucson, AZ, May 1997. [points; online analytic processing (OLAP); R-tree; cubetree; bulk insertion] cited in F.2.1.5.2.5 (pp. 297–298)

[1588] N. Roussopoulos and D. Leifker. Direct spatial search on pictorial databases using packed R-trees. In *Proceedings of the ACM SIGMOD Conference*, pages 17–31, Austin, TX, May 1985. [points; packed R-tree; PSQL] cited in D.2.8.1, D.2.8.1.s, D.3.5.3, F.2.1.5.2.1 (p. 275), F.2.1.5.2.2 (pp. 277–278, 281)

[1589] S. M. Rubin and T. Whitted. A 3-dimensional representation for fast rendering of complex scenes. *Computer Graphics*, 14(3):110–116, July 1980. Also in *Proceedings of the SIGGRAPH'80 Conference*, Seattle, WA, July 1980. [volumes; minimum bounding box] cited in A.7.2.2

[1590] R. Ruff and N. Ahuja. Path planning in a three-dimensional environment. In *Proceedings of the 7th International Conference on Pattern Recognition*, pages 188–191, Montréal, Canada, July 1984. [volumes; path planning]

[1591] Y. Rui, T. S. Huang, and S. Mehrotra. Content-based image retrieval with relevance feedback in MARS. In *Proceedings of the 1997 IEEE International Conference on Image Processing*, pages 815–818, Santa Barbara, CA, October 1997. [image database] cited in F.4 (p. 487)

[1592] J. Ruppert. A Delaunay refinement algorithm for quality 2-dimensional mesh generation. *Journal of Algorithms*, 18(3):548–585, May 1995. [surfaces; conforming Delaunay triangulation] cited in F.2.2.1.5 (p. 351)

[1593] J. Ruppert and R. Seidel. On the difficulty of triangulating three-dimensional non-convex polyhedra. *Discrete & Computational Geometry*, 7:227–253, 1992. [volumes; conforming tetrahedralization] cited in F.2.2.1.6 (p. 353)

[1594] S. Russel and P. Norvig. *Artificial Intelligence: A Modern Approach*. Prentice Hall, Englewood Cliffs, NJ, second edition, 2003. [artificial intelligence; general] cited in F.2.2.1.4 (p. 347), F.4.1.3 (p. 493), F.4.2.4 (p. 535)

[1595] D. Rutovitz. Data structures for operations on digital images. In *Pictorial Pattern Recognition*, G. C. Cheng, R. S. Ledley, D. K. Pollock, and A. Rosenfeld, eds., pages 105–133. Thompson Book Co., Washington, DC, 1968. [regions; runlength encoding] cited in A.1.3, A.2.1.3, A.4.2, A.9, D.1.2, F.2.1.2.1 (p. 206), F.2.3.1 (p. 409)

[1596] A. Saalfeld. It doesn't make me nearly as CROSS, some advantages of the point-vector representation of line segments in automated cartography. *International Journal of Geographical Information Systems*, 1(4):379–386, October–December 1987. [lines; line intersection problem] cited in F.2.2.3.1 (p. 385)

[1597] A. Saalfeld. Triangulated data structures for map merging and other applications geographic information systems. In *Proceedings of the International Geographic Information Systems (IGIS) Symposium: The Research Agenda*, vol. 3, pages 3–13, Arlington, VA, November 1987. [regions; triangulations] cited in A.4.6, D.4.3.1, D.5.2, F.2.1.3.2 (p. 241)

[1598] A. Saalfeld. Classifying and comparing spatial relations of computerized maps for feature matching applications. *Journal of Official Statistics*, 4(2):125–140, 1988. [map conflation] cited in F.4 (p. 486)

[1599] A. Saalfeld. Conflation: automated map compilation. *International Journal Geographical Information System*, 2(3):217–228, September 1988. [map conflation] cited in F.4 (p. 486)

[1600] A. Saalfeld. Delaunay edge refinements. In *Proceedings of the 3rd Canadian Conference on Computational Geometry*, pages 33–36, Vancouver, Canada, August 1991. [surfaces; conforming Delaunay triangulation; Steiner points] cited in F.2.2.1.5 (p. 351)

[1601] A. Saalfeld. *Conflation: automated map compilation*. PhD thesis, Computer Science Department, University of Maryland, College Park, MD, May 1993. Also Computer Science Technical Report TR–3066. [map conflation] cited in F.4 (p. 486)

[1602] A. Saalfeld. Sorting spatial data for sampling and other geographic applications. *GeoInformatica*, 2(1):37–57, March 1998. [points]

[1603] H. Sagan. *Space-Filling Curves*. Springer-Verlag, New York, 1994. [points; space-filling curve; survey] cited in F.1.6 (p. 90), F.2.1.1.2 (p. 199)

[1604] S. C. Sahinalp, M. Tasan, J. Macker, and Z. M. Özsoyoglu. Distance based indexing for string proximity search. In *Proceedings of the 19th IEEE International Conference on Data Engineering*, pages 125–136, Bangalore, India, March 2003. [metric spaces; approximate nearest neighbor]

[1605] M. Sakauchi and Y. Ohsawa. General framework for N-dimensional pattern data management. In *Proceedings of the International Symposium on Image Processing and Its Applications*, M. Onoe, ed., pages 306–316, Roppongi, Japan, January 1984. [points; BD-tree]

[1606] Y. Sakurai, M. Yoshikawa, R. Kataoka, and S. Uemura. Similarity search for adaptive ellipsoid queries using spatial transformation. In *Proceedings of the 27th International Conference on Very Large Data Bases (VLDB)*, P. M. G. Apers, P. Atzeni, S. Ceri, S. Paraboschi, K. Ramamohanarao, and R. T. Snodgrass, eds., pages 231–240, Rome, Italy, September 2001. [similarity searching; ellipsoid query]

[1607] Y. Sakurai, M. Yoshikawa, S. Uemura, and H. Kojima. Spatial indexing of high-dimensional data based on relative approximation. *VLDB Journal*, 11(2):93–108, October 2002. Also see *Proceedings of the 26th International Conference on Very Large Data Bases (VLDB)*, A. El Abbadi, M. L. Brodie, S. Chakravarthy, U. Dayal, N. Kamel, G. Schlageter, and K.-Y. Whang, eds., pages 516–526, Cairo, Egypt, September 2000. [regions; high-dimensional data; R-tree; A-tree] cited in F.2.1.5.2.3 (p. 283), F.4.4.3 (p. 573)

[1608] J. K. Salmon and M. S. Warren. Skeletons from the treecode closet. Caltech Concurrent Supercomputing Consortium Technical Report CCSF–28–92, California Institute of Technology, Pasadena, CA, October 1992. [points; particle simulation; *N*-body problem; treecode] cited in F.2.4 (p. 426)

[1609] S. Saltenis and C. S. Jensen. Indexing of moving objects for location-based services. In *Proceedings of the 18th IEEE International Conference on Data Engineering*, pages 463–472, San Jose, CA, February 2002. [moving objects]

[1610] S. Saltenis, C. S. Jensen, S. T. Leutenegger, and M. A. López. Indexing the positions of continuously moving objects. In *Proceedings of the ACM SIGMOD Conference*, W. Chen, J. Naughton, and P. A. Bernstein, eds., pages 331–342, Dallas, TX, May 2000. [moving objects; R-tree; TPR-tree] cited in F.2.1.5.2.3 (p. 286), F.3.1.4 (p. 445), F.4 (p. 488)

[1611] G. Salton. *Automatic Text Processing: The Transformation Analysis and Retrieval of Information by Computer*. Addison-Wesley, Reading, MA, 1989. [information retrieval; general] cited in F.4.6.1.1 (p. 664), F.4.6.1.2 (p. 667)

[1612] B. Salzberg. Grid file concurrency. *Information Systems*, 11(3):235–244, 1986. [points; grid file]

[1613] B. Salzberg. *File Structures: An Analytic Approach*. Prentice-Hall, Englewood Cliffs, NJ, 1988. [database systems; general] cited in D.2.6.2, F.1.5.2.6 (p. 82), F.1.8.1 (p. 167)

[1614] B. Salzberg. On indexing spatial and temporal data. *Information Systems*, 19(6):447–465, September 1994. [points; spatiotemporal database; hB-tree; survey] cited in F.1.7.1.4 (p. 109)

[1615] B. Salzberg and D. B. Lomet. Spatial database access methods. *SIGMOD RECORD*, 20(3):6–15, September 1991. [points; survey]

[1616] S. Salzberg, A. L. Delcher, D. G. Heath, and S. Kasif. Best-case results for nearest-neighbor learning. *IEEE Transactions on Pattern Analysis and Machine Intelligence*, 17(6):599–608, June 1995. [points; regions; Voronoi diagram] cited in F.2.2.1.4.s (p. 801)

[1617] H. Samet. Deletion in k-dimensional quadtrees (unpublished). Computer Science Department, University of Maryland, College Park, MD, 1977. [points; point quadtree] cited in D.2.3.2.s, F.1.4.1.2.s (p. 755)

[1618] H. Samet. Deletion in two-dimensional quad trees. *Communications of the ACM*, 23(12):703–710, December 1980. [points; point quadtree] cited in A.7.1.5, D.2.3.2, D.2.3.2.s, F.1.4.1.2 (pp. 31, 34–35), F.2.1.3.1 (p. 235), F.4.1.5 (p. 504), F.1.4.1.2.s (p. 755)

[1619] H. Samet. Region representation: quadtrees from binary arrays. *Computer Graphics and Image Processing*, 13(1):88–93, May 1980. Also University of Maryland Computer Science Technical Report TR–767, May 1979. [regions; region quadtree construction] cited in A.4.1, D.1.2, D.1.2.s, F.2.1.2.4.s (p. 779)

[1620] H. Samet. Region representation: quadtrees from boundary codes. *Communications of the ACM*, 23(3):163–170, March 1980. Also University of Maryland Computer Science Technical Report

TR–741, March 1979. [regions; chain code; region quadtree construction; boundary following] cited in A.4.3.1

[1621] H. Samet. An algorithm for converting rasters to quadtrees. *IEEE Transactions on Pattern Analysis and Machine Intelligence*, 3(1):93–95, January 1981. Also University of Maryland Computer Science Technical Report TR–766, May 1979. [regions; runlength encoding; region quadtree construction] cited in A.4.2.1, D.1.2, F.2.1.2.4.s (p. 779)

[1622] H. Samet. Computing perimeters of images represented by quadtrees. *IEEE Transactions on Pattern Analysis and Machine Intelligence*, 3(6):683–687, November 1981. Also University of Maryland Computer Science Technical Report TR–755, April 1979. [regions; region quadtree; perimeter computation] cited in A.5.2, A.9.2, A.9.3.3

[1623] H. Samet. Connected component labeling using quadtrees. *Journal of the ACM*, 28(3):487–501, July 1981. Also University of Maryland Computer Science Technical Report TR–756, April 1979. [regions; connected component labeling; region quadtree] cited in A.5.1.2, A.5.1.3, A.9.2

[1624] H. Samet. Distance transform for images represented by quadtrees. *IEEE Transactions on Pattern Analysis and Machine Intelligence*, 4(3):298–303, May 1982. Also University of Maryland Computer Science Technical Report TR–780, July 1979. [regions; region quadtree] cited in A.9.2, F.2.1.4.1 (p. 257)

[1625] H. Samet. Neighbor finding techniques for images represented by quadtrees. *Computer Graphics and Image Processing*, 18(1):37–57, January 1982. Also University of Maryland Computer Science Technical Report TR–857, January 1980. [regions; neighbor finding] cited in A.3.2.1, A.3.2.3, A.5.1.2, F.2.1.2.4 (p. 217), F.2.1.2.4.s (p. 781)

[1626] H. Samet. A quadtree medial axis transform. *Communications of the ACM*, 26(9):680–693, September 1983. Also see corrigendum, *Communications of the ACM*, 27(2):151, February 1984 and University of Maryland Computer Science Technical Report TR–803. [regions; quadtree medial axis transform (QMAT)] cited in A.8, A.9.3, F.2.1.2.4 (p. 212), F.2.1.4.1 (p. 257), F.2.4 (p. 425), F.2.1.2.4.s (p. 782)

[1627] H. Samet. Algorithms for the conversion of quadtrees to rasters. *Computer Vision, Graphics, and Image Processing*, 26(1):1–16, April 1984. Also University of Maryland Computer Science Technical Report TR–979, November 1980. [regions; region quadtree; runlength encoding] cited in A.4.2.2

[1628] H. Samet. The quadtree and related hierarchical data structures. *ACM Computing Surveys*, 16(2):187–260, June 1984. Also University of Maryland Computer Science Technical Report TR–1329, November 1983. [survey] cited in A.P, D.P, F.P (p. xx), F.1.1 (p. 11)

[1629] H. Samet. Data structures for quadtree approximation and compression. *Communications of the ACM*, 28(9):973–993, September 1985. Also University of Maryland Computer Science Technical Report TR–1209, August 1982. [regions; progressive transmission; lossless compression; forests of quadtrees] cited in A.8, A.8.2.2

[1630] H. Samet. Reconstruction of quadtrees from quadtree medial axis transforms. *Computer Vision, Graphics, and Image Processing*, 29(3):311–328, March 1985. Also University of Maryland Computer Science Technical Report TR–1224, October 1982. [regions; quadtree medial axis transform (QMAT)] cited in A.9.3.3, F.2.1.2.4 (p. 212), F.2.4 (p. 425)

[1631] H. Samet. A top-down quadtree traversal algorithm. *IEEE Transactions on Pattern Analysis and Machine Intelligence*, 7(1):94–98, January 1985. Also University of Maryland Computer Science Technical Report TR–1237, December 1982. [regions; region quadtree] cited in A.3.2.3, A.3.2.3.s, A.4.3.1, A.5.1.2, A.5.1.3, A.5.2, A.9.2

[1632] H. Samet. Hierarchical representations of collections of small rectangles. *ACM Computing Surveys*, 20(4):271–309, December 1988. Also University of Maryland Computer Science Technical Report TR–1967, January 1988. [rectangles; survey] cited in D.P, D.3.5.1, F.P (p. xx), F.3.4.1.2 (p. 469)

[1633] H. Samet. Hierarchical spatial data structures. In *Design and Implementation of Large Spatial Databases—1st Symposium,*

SSD'89, A. Buchmann, O. Günther, T. R. Smith, and Y.-F. Wang, eds., vol. 409 of Springer-Verlag Lecture Notes in Computer Science, pages 193–212, Santa Barbara, CA, July 1989. [survey]

[1634] H. Samet. Implementing ray tracing with octrees and neighbor finding. *Computers & Graphics*, 13(4):445–460, 1989. Also University of Maryland Computer Science Technical Report TR–2204, February 1989. [volumes; ray tracing; neighbor finding] cited in A.7.2

[1635] H. Samet. Neighbor finding in images represented by octrees. *Computer Vision, Graphics, and Image Processing*, 46(3):367–386, June 1989. Also University of Maryland Computer Science Technical Report TR–1968, January 1988. [volumes; neighbor finding] cited in A.3.3, A.3.4, F.2.1.2.4 (p. 217)

[1636] H. Samet. *Applications of Spatial Data Structures: Computer Graphics, Image Processing, and GIS*. Addison-Wesley, Reading, MA, 1990. [general] cited in D.P, D.1.2, D.1.2.s, D.1.3, D.1.4.1, D.1.5, D.2.1, D.2.4, D.2.6.2, D.2.7, D.2.8.2, D.3.1, D.3.5.1, D.3.5.2, D.4, D.4.2.2.s, D.4.2.3, D.5.2, D.5.3, D.5.4, D.5.4.s, D.5.5.2, D.5.6, D.5.7.s, F.P (pp. xviii–xix, xxi, xxiv), F.1.4.2.2 (p. 45), F.2 (p. 191), F.2.1.2.4 (pp. 211–212, 214, 217), F.2.2.2.4 (p. 361), F.2.2.2.7 (p. 373), F.2.2.4 (p. 406), F.2.3.1 (p. 410), F.3.4.1.2 (p. 469), F.2.1.1.2.s (p. 777), F.2.1.2.4.s (pp. 779, 781–782), F.2.2.3.2.s (p. 813), F.2.3.1.s (p. 816), F.R (p. 877)

[1637] H. Samet. *The Design and Analysis of Spatial Data Structures*. Addison-Wesley, Reading, MA, 1990. [general] cited in A.P, A.1, A.1.2, A.1.2.s, A.1.3, A.1.3.s, A.2.1.1, A.2.1.3, A.4.2.3, A.4.5, A.4.5.s, A.4.6, A.6.5.1.s, A.7.1, A.7.1.2, A.7.1.4, A.7.1.5, A.7.1.6, A.7.2.2, A.7.2.4, A.9.3.1, F.P (pp. xvii–xviii, xxi, xxiv), F.1.1 (p. 11), F.1.8.5.1 (p. 172), F.2 (p. 191), F.2.1.1.4 (p. 204), F.2.1.2.4 (p. 211), F.2.1.5.1 (p. 266), F.2.1.5.2.2 (p. 275), F.2.2 (p. 313), F.2.2.1.2 (p. 319), F.2.2.2.8 (p. 375), F.4.1.6 (p. 511), F.4.4.5 (p. 580), F.4.5 (p. 599), F.4.5.3.3 (p. 619), F.R (p. 877)

[1638] H. Samet. Spatial data structures. In *Modern Database Systems, The Object Model, Interoperability and Beyond*, W. Kim, ed., pages 361–385. ACM Press and Addison-Wesley, New York, 1995. [survey] cited in F.2 (p. 191), F.2.1.5.1 (p. 268)

[1639] H. Samet. Depth-first *k*-nearest neighbor finding using the MaxNearestDist estimator. In *Proceedings of the 12th International Conference on Image Analysis and Processing*, pages 486–491, Mantova, Italy, September 2003. [points; depth-first nearest neighbor algorithm] cited in F.4.2.5 (p. 541)

[1640] H. Samet. Decoupling partitioning and grouping: overcoming shortcomings of spatial indexing with bucketing. *ACM Transactions on Database Systems*, 29(4):789–830, December 2004. Also University of Maryland Computer Science Technical Report TR–4523, August 2003. [points; decoupling; object hierarchy; BV-tree; PK-tree; R-tree] cited in F.1.7.1.6 (pp. 116–117)

[1641] H. Samet. Indexing issues in supporting similarity searching. In *Advances in Multimedia Information Processing—5th Pacific Rim Conference on Multimedia, PCM'04*, K. Aizawa, Y. Nakamura, and S. Satoh, eds., vol. 3332 of Springer-Verlag Lecture Notes in Computer Science, pages 463–470 of vol. 2, Tokyo, Japan, November 2004. [metric spaces; high-dimensional data; similarity searching; survey]

[1642] H. Samet. Object-based and image-based object representations. *ACM Computing Surveys*, 36(2):159–217, June 2004. Also University of Maryland Computer Science Technical Report TR–4526, September 2003. [survey; R-tree] cited in F.P (p. xx), F.2 (p. 191)

[1643] H. Samet. K-nearest neighbor finding using the MaxNearestDist estimator. Computer Science Technical Report TR–4757, University of Maryland, College Park, MD, October 2005. [points; depth-first nearest neighbor algorithm; best-first nearest neighbor algorithm] cited in F.4.2.5 (p. 541)

[1644] H. Samet, H. Alborzi, F. Brabec, C. Esperança, G. R. Hjaltason, F. Morgan, and E. Tanin. Use of the SAND spatial browser for digital government applications. *Communications of the ACM*, 46(1):63–66, January 2003. [SAND; geographic information systems (GIS); user interface] cited in F.P (p. xviii)

[1645] H. Samet and W. G. Aref. Spatial data models and query processing. In *Modern Database Systems, The Object Model, Interoperability*

and Beyond, W. Kim, ed., pages 338–360. ACM Press and Addison-Wesley, New York, 1995. [spatial database; survey] cited in F.2 (p. 192)

[1646] H. Samet and A. Kochut. Octree approximation and compression methods. In *Proceedings of the 3D Data Processing Visualization and Transmission Conference*, pages 460–469, Padua, Italy, June 2002. [regions; progressive transmission; compression]

[1647] H. Samet and A. Rosenfeld. Quadtree representations of binary images. In *Proceedings of the 5th International Conference on Pattern Recognition*, pages 815–818, Miami Beach, FL, December 1980. [regions; region quadtree; survey] cited in A.P, D.P, F.P (p. xx)

[1648] H. Samet, A. Rosenfeld, C. A. Shaffer, R. C. Nelson, and Y. G. Huang. Application of hierarchical data structures to geographic information systems: phase III. Computer Science Technical Report TR–1457, University of Maryland, College Park, MD, November 1984. [QUILT; geographic information systems (GIS); region quadtree] cited in A.1.2, A.6.6, D.1.5, D.4.2.4

[1649] H. Samet, A. Rosenfeld, C. A. Shaffer, R. C. Nelson, Y. G. Huang, and K. Fujimura. Application of hierarchical data structures to geographic information systems: phase IV. Computer Science Technical Report TR–1578, University of Maryland, College Park, MD, December 1985. [QUILT; geographic information systems (GIS); region quadtree] cited in A.4.2.3, A.6.3.3, A.6.5.3

[1650] H. Samet, A. Rosenfeld, C. A. Shaffer, and R. E. Webber. Quadtree region representation in cartography: experimental results. *IEEE Transactions on Systems, Man, and Cybernetics*, 13(6):1148–1154, November/December 1983. [QUILT; geographic information systems (GIS); region quadtree]

[1651] H. Samet, A. Rosenfeld, C. A. Shaffer, and R. E. Webber. A geographic information system using quadtrees. *Pattern Recognition*, 17(6):647–656, November/December 1984. [QUILT; geographic information systems (GIS); region quadtree] cited in A.2.1.2, A.3.4.1, A.8.2.1, D.4.2.4

[1652] H. Samet and C. A. Shaffer. A model for the analysis of neighbor finding in pointer-based quadtrees. *IEEE Transactions on Pattern Analysis and Machine Intelligence*, 7(6):717–720, November 1985. Also University of Maryland Computer Science Technical Report TR–1432, August 1984. [regions; neighbor finding] cited in A.3.2.1, F.2.1.2.4 (p. 217), F.2.1.2.4.s (p. 781)

[1653] H. Samet, C. A. Shaffer, R. C. Nelson, Y. G. Huang, K. Fujimura, and A. Rosenfeld. Recent developments in linear quadtree-based geographic information systems. *Image and Vision Computing*, 5(3):187–197, August 1987. [QUILT; geographic information systems (GIS); region quadtree] cited in A.1.3, A.2.1.2, A.3.2.1, A.3.4.1, A.8.2.1, D.1.2, D.4.2.4, F.2.1.2.4 (p. 211)

[1654] H. Samet, C. A. Shaffer, and R. E. Webber. Digitizing the plane with cells of non-uniform size. Computer Science Technical Report TR–1619, University of Maryland, College Park, MD, January 1986. [lines; PM quadtree] cited in A.1.3.s, D.4.2.3, D.4.2.3.1.s

[1655] H. Samet, C. A. Shaffer, and R. E. Webber. The segment quadtree: a linear quadtree-based representation for linear features. In *Data Structures for Raster Graphics*, F. J. Peters, L. R. A. Kessener, and M. L. P. van Lierop, eds., pages 91–123. Springer-Verlag, Berlin, West Germany, 1986. Also see *Proceedings of Computer Vision and Pattern Recognition 85*, pages 385–389, San Francisco, June 1985 and University of Maryland Computer Science Technical Report TR–1550, August 1985. [lines]

[1656] H. Samet, C. A. Shaffer, and R. E. Webber. Digitizing the plane with cells of non-uniform size. *Information Processing Letters*, 24(6):369–375, April 1987. [lines; PM quadtree] cited in A.1.3.s, D.4.2.3, F.2.2.2.6 (p. 366)

[1657] H. Samet and M. Tamminen. Experiences with new image component algorithms. In *Proceedings of the EUROGRAPHICS'84 Conference*, K. Bo and H. A. Tucker, eds., pages 239–249, Copenhagen, Denmark, September 1984. [volumes; connected component labeling]

[1658] H. Samet and M. Tamminen. Bintrees, CSG trees, and time. *Computer Graphics*, 19(3):121–130, July 1985. Also in *Proceedings of the SIGGRAPH'85 Conference*, San Francisco, July 1985. [volumes; CSG tree; bintree; time dimension] cited in A.1.4,

A.7.2.4, D.1.3, D.5.3, D.5.5, D.5.5.1, F.2.2.2.7 (pp. 372–373), F.2.4 (p. 425)

[1659] H. Samet and M. Tamminen. Computing geometric properties of images represented by linear quadtrees. *IEEE Transactions on Pattern Analysis and Machine Intelligence*, 7(2):229–240, March 1985. Also University of Maryland Computer Science Technical Report TR–1359, December 1983. [regions; connected component labeling; region quadtree] cited in A.3.4.4, A.5.1.3, A.5.3, A.6.3.3, D.3.5.1, F.3.4.1.2 (p. 469)

[1660] H. Samet and M. Tamminen. A general approach to connected component labeling of images. Computer Science Technical Report TR–1649, University of Maryland, College Park, MD, August 1986. Also see *Proceedings of Computer Vision and Pattern Recognition 86*, pages 312–318, Miami Beach, FL, June 1986. [regions; connected component labeling] cited in A.5.1.1, A.5.1.1.s, A.5.1.3

[1661] H. Samet and M. Tamminen. Efficient component labeling of images of arbitrary dimension represented by linear bintrees. *IEEE Transactions on Pattern Analysis and Machine Intelligence*, 10(4):579–586, July 1988. [volumes; connected component labeling; bintree] cited in A.1.3, A.3.4.4, A.4.2.3, A.4.6, A.5.1.2.s, A.5.1.3, A.6.3.3, A.9.2, D.1.4.1, D.3.5.1, D.5.2, F.2.1.2.6 (p. 221), F.2.3.1 (p. 411), F.3.4.1.2 (p. 469)

[1662] H. Samet and M. Tamminen. Approximating CSG trees of moving objects. *Visual Computer*, 6(4):182–209, August 1990. Also University of Maryland Computer Science Technical Report TR–1472, January 1985. [volumes; CSG tree; bintree] cited in D.5.3, D.5.5, D.5.5.1, D.5.5.1.2.s, F.2.2.2.7 (p. 372)

[1663] H. Samet and R. E. Webber. On encoding boundaries with quadtrees. Computer Science Technical Report TR–1162, University of Maryland, College Park, MD, February 1982. [lines; line quadtree] cited in A.3.2.3, D.4.2.2, F.2.2.2.1 (p. 356)

[1664] H. Samet and R. E. Webber. On encoding boundaries with quadtrees. *IEEE Transactions on Pattern Analysis and Machine Intelligence*, 6(3):365–369, May 1984. [lines; line quadtree] cited in D.4.2.2, F.2.2.2.1 (p. 356)

[1665] H. Samet and R. E. Webber. Storing a collection of polygons using quadtrees. *ACM Transactions on Graphics*, 4(3):182–222, July 1985. Also see *Proceedings of Computer Vision and Pattern Recognition'83*, pages 127–132, Washington, DC, June 1983 and University of Maryland Computer Science Technical Report TR–1372, February 1984. [lines; PM quadtree] cited in A.1.3, A.7.2.2, D.4.2.3, D.4.3.3, D.4.3.3.s, F.2.2.2.6 (p. 365), F.2.2.2.7 (p. 371), F.4.1.6 (pp. 513, 516), F.4.4.5 (p. 584), F.2.2.2.6.s (p. 808)

[1666] H. Samet and R. E. Webber. Hierarchical data structures and algorithms for computer graphics. Part I. Fundamentals. *IEEE Computer Graphics and Applications*, 8(3):48–68, May 1988. Also University of Maryland Computer Science Technical Report TR–1752, January 1987. [computer graphics; survey] cited in A.P, A.6.3.3, D.P, F.P (p. xix), F.2.2.2.6 (p. 367)

[1667] H. Samet and R. E. Webber. Hierarchical data structures and algorithms for computer graphics. Part II. Applications. *IEEE Computer Graphics and Applications*, 8(4):59–75, July 1988. Also University of Maryland Computer Science Technical Report TR–1752, January 1987. [computer graphics; survey] cited in A.P, D.P, F.P (p. xix), F.2.2.2.6 (p. 367)

[1668] H. Samet and R. E. Webber. A comparison of the space requirements of multi-dimensional quadtree-based file structures. *Visual Computer*, 5(6):349–359, December 1989. Also University of Maryland Computer Science Technical Report TR–1711, September 1986. [regions; region quadtree; region octree; space requirements] cited in A.2.1.2

[1669] H. Samet and R. E. Webber. Data structures to support Bézier-based modeling. *Computer-Aided Design*, 23(3):162–176, April 1991. [Bézier curve]

[1670] V. Samoladas and D. P. Miranker. A lower bound theorem for indexing schemes and its application to multidimensional range queries. In *Proceedings of the 17th ACM SIGACT-SIGMOD-SIGART Symposium on Principles of Database Systems (PODS)*, pages 44–51, Seattle, WA, June 1998. [rectangles; range query]

[1671] J. Sandor. Octree data structures and perspective imagery. *Computers and Graphics*, 9(4):393–405, 1985. [volumes; region octree; perspective view]

[1672] J. Sankaranarayanan, H. Alborzi, and H. Samet. Efficient query processing on spatial networks. In *Proceedings of the 13th ACM International Symposium on Advances in Geographic Information Systems*, pages 200–209, Bremen, Germany, November 2005. [lines; points; spatial networks; shortest path algorithm; best-first nearest neighbor algorithm; incremental nearest neighbor algorithm] cited in F.4.1.6 (pp. 508–509, 514–515)

[1673] L. A. Santaló. *Integral Geometry and Geometric Probability*, vol. 1 of *Encyclopedia of Mathematics and Its Applications*. Addison-Wesley, Reading, MA, 1976. [geometric probability; general] cited in F.2.2.2.8 (p. 376)

[1674] R. F. Santos Filho, A. J. M. Traina, C. Traina Jr., and C. Faloutsos. Similarity search without tears: the OMNI family of all-purpose access methods. In *Proceedings of the 17th IEEE International Conference on Data Engineering*, pages 623–630, Heidelberg, Germany, April 2001. [points; reverse nearest neighbor (RNN); distance semijoin] cited in F.4.5.8 (p. 658)

[1675] N. Sarnak and R. E. Tarjan. Planar point location using persistent search trees. *Communications of the ACM*, 29(7):669–679, July 1986. [regions; post-office problem; point location; persistent search tree] cited in D.3.2.4, F.3.1.4 (p. 445)

[1676] J. B. Saxe. On the number of range queries in *k*-space. *Discrete Applied Math*, 1(3):217–225, November 1979. [points; range query]

[1677] L. Scarlatos and T. Pavlidis. Hierarchical triangulations using terrain features. In *Proceedings IEEE Visualization'90*, A. Kaufman, ed., pages 168–175, San Francisco, October 1990. [surfaces; triangulations; triangulated irregular network (TIN)]

[1678] L. Scarlatos and T. Pavlidis. Adaptive hierarchical triangulation. In *Proceedings of the 10th International Symposium on Automated Cartography (AUTO-CARTO 10)*, pages 234–246, Baltimore, MD, March 1991. [surfaces; triangulations]

[1679] L. Scarlatos and T. Pavlidis. Hierarchical triangulation using cartographic coherence. *CVGIP: Graphical Models and Image Processing*, 54(2):147–161, March 1992. [surfaces; triangulations; triangle meshes] cited in F.2.2.4 (pp. 401, 407)

[1680] L. L. Scarlatos. *Spatial data representations for rapid visualization and analysis*. PhD thesis, Computer Science Department, State University of New York at Stony Brook, Stony Brook, NY, August 1993. [surfaces; triangulations]

[1681] L. L. Scarlatos and T. Pavlidis. Optimizing triangulations by curvature equalization. In *Proceedings IEEE Visualization'92*, A. E. Kaufman and G. M. Nielson, eds., pages 333–339, Boston, October 1992. [surfaces; triangulations]

[1682] R. E. Schapire and Y. Singer. Improved boosting algorithms using confidence-rated predictions. *Machine Learning*, 37(3):297–336, December 1999. [machine learning; AdaBoost] cited in F.4.7 (p. 687)

[1683] H. Schek and W. Waterfeld. A database kernel system for geoscientific applications. In *Proceedings of the 2nd International Symposium on Spatial Data Handling*, pages 273–288, Seattle, WA, July 1986. [spatial database]

[1684] I. D. Scherson and E. Caspary. Data structures and the time complexity of ray tracing. *Visual Computer*, 3(4):201–213, December 1987. [volumes; ray tracing] cited in A.7.2.5

[1685] I. D. Scherson and E. Caspary. Multiprocessing for ray tracing: a hierarchical self-balancing approach. *Visual Computer*, 4(4):188–196, October 1988. [volumes; ray tracing; multiprocessing]

[1686] P. Scheuermann and M. Ouksel. Multidimensional *B*-trees for associative searching in database systems. *Information Systems*, 7(2):123–137, 1982. [points; multiattribute tree (MAT); multidimensional B-tree (MDBT)] cited in D.2.8.2, F.1.1 (pp. 7–8), F.1.5.1.4 (p. 66), F.1.7.2.1 (p. 136)

[1687] M. Schiwietz. *Organization and query processing of spatial objects*. PhD thesis, Ludwig-Maximilians Universität München, Munich, Germany, 1993. In German. [regions; minimum bounding box] cited in F.2.1.1 (p. 195)

[1688] M. Schiwietz and H.-P. Kriegel. Query processing of spatial objects: complexity versus redundancy. In *Advances in Spatial Databases—*

3rd International Symposium, SSD'93, D. Abel and B. C. Ooi, eds., vol. 692 of Springer-Verlag Lecture Notes in Computer Science, pages 377–396, Singapore, June 1993. [regions; minimum bounding box] cited in F.2.1.1 (p. 195)

[1689]   F. Schmitt and B. Gholzadeh. Adaptive polyhedral approximation of digitized surfaces. In *Proceedings of SPIE, Computer Vision for Robots*, vol. 595, pages 101–108, Cannes, France, December 1985. [surfaces; progressive polyhedral approximation]

[1690]   F. J. M. Schmitt, B. A. Barsky, and W. H. Du. An adaptive subdivision method for surface-fitting from sampled data. *Computer Graphics*, 20(4):179–188, August 1986. Also in *Proceedings of the SIGGRAPH'86 Conference*, Dallas, TX, August 1986. [surfaces] cited in D.5.6, F.2.2.4 (p. 402)

[1691]   B. Schneider. Geomorphologically sound reconstruction of digital terrain surfaces from contours. In *Proceedings of the 8th International Symposium on Spatial Data Handling*, T. K. Poiker and N. Chrisman, eds., pages 657–667, GIS Lab, Department of Geography, Simon Fraser University, Burnaby, British Columbia, Canada, July 1998. International Geographical Union, Geographic Information Science Study Group. [surfaces; digital terrain model (DTM)]

[1692]   R. Schneider and H.-P. Kriegel. The TR*-tree: a new representation of polygonal objects supporting spatial queries and operations. In *Computational Geometry – Methods, Algorithms and Applications*, H. Bieri and H. Noltemeier, eds., vol. 553 of Springer-Verlag Lecture Notes in Computer Science, pages 249–264, Bern, Switzerland, March 1991. [regions; minimum bounding box; TR*-tree] cited in F.2.1.5.2.7 (p. 303)

[1693]   R. Schneider and H.-P. Kriegel. Indexing the spatiotemporal monitoring of a polygonal object. In *Proceedings of the 5th International Symposium on Spatial Data Handling*, vol. 1, pages 200–209, Charleston, SC, August 1992. [regions; spatiotemporal database]

[1694]   E. Schönhardt. Über die zerlegung von dreieckspolyedern in tetraeder. *Mathematische Annalen*, 98:309–312, 1928. [volumes; tetrahedralizations; Schönhardt Twisted Prism] cited in F.2.2.1.6 (p. 353)

[1695]   P. Schorn and J. Nievergelt. Wie wachsen quad-bäume? *Informatik-Spektrum*, 12(2):97–101, April 1989. [regions; region quadtree; space requirements]

[1696]   G. Schrack. Finding neighbors of equal size in linear quadtrees and octrees in constant time. *CVGIP: Image Understanding*, 55(3):221–230, May 1992. [regions; volumes; neighbor finding] cited in F.2.1.2.4 (p. 217)

[1697]   G. Schrack and I. Gargantini. Mirroring and rotating images in linear quadtree form with few machine instructions. *Image and Vision Computing*, 11(2):112–118, March 1993. [regions]

[1698]   G. Schrack and X. Liu. The spatial U-order and some of its mathematical characteristics. In *Proceedings of the Pacific Rim Conference on Communications, Computers, and Signal Processing*, pages 416–419, Victoria, British Columbia, Canada, May 1995. [points; U order; space-filling curve] cited in F.1.6 (p. 94), F.2.1.1.2 (pp. 199, 201), F.2.1.1.2.s (p. 777)

[1699]   W. J. Schroeder, J. A. Zarge, and W. E. Lorenson. Decimation of triangle meshes. *Computer Graphics*, 26(2):65–70, July 1992. Also in *Proceedings of the SIGGRAPH'92 Conference*, Chicago, July 1992. [surfaces; polygon simplification] cited in F.2.2.3.4 (p. 394)

[1700]   J. T. Schwartz and M. Sharir. A survey of motion planning and related geometric algorithms. *Artificial Intelligence*, 37(1–3):157–169, December 1988. [regions; motion planning; survey] cited in A.1.4, D.1.3, F.2.4 (p. 425)

[1701]   J. T. Schwartz, M. Sharir, and A. Siegel. An efficient algorithm for finding connected components in a binary image. Computer Science Division Technical Report 38, Courant Institute of Mathematical Sciences, New York University, New York, February 1985 (Revised July 1985). [regions; connected component labeling] cited in A.5.1.1

[1702]   D. S. Scott and S. S. Iyengar. A new data structure for efficient storing of images. *Pattern Recognition Letters*, 3(3):211–214, May 1985. [regions; TID] cited in A.1.3, A.9.3.4, D.1.2, F.2.1.2.2 (p. 208)

[1703]   D. S. Scott and S. S. Iyengar. TID—a translation invariant data structure for storing images. *Communications of the ACM*, 29(5):418–429, May 1986. [regions; TID] cited in A.1.3, A.9.3.4, A.9.3.4.s, D.1.2, F.2.1.2.2 (p. 208)

[1704]   T. B. Sebastian and B. B. Kimia. Metric-based shape retrieval in large databases. In *Proceedings of the 16th International Conference on Pattern Recognition*, R. Kasturi, D. Laurendau, and C. Suen, eds., vol. 3, pages 291–296, Quebec City, Canada, August 2002. [metric spaces; kNN graph; sa-tree; shape retrieval] cited in F.4.4.5 (p. 582), F.4.5 (p. 599), F.4.5.6 (pp. 637–639, 641), F.4.7.4 (p. 711)

[1705]   R. Sedgewick. *Algorithms*. Addison-Wesley, Reading, MA, 1983. [algorithms; general] cited in A.5.1.1

[1706]   B. Seeger. *Design and implementation of multidimensional access methods*. PhD thesis, Computer Science Department, University of Bremen, Bremen, Germany, 1989. (In German). [points; buddy-tree] cited in F.1.7.1.5 (p. 113), F.1.7.1.5.s (p. 770)

[1707]   B. Seeger. Personal communication. 1990. [R-tree; R*-tree] cited in F.2.1.5.2.4 (p. 289)

[1708]   B. Seeger. Performance comparison of segment access methods implemented on top of the buddy-tree. In *Advances in Spatial Databases—2nd Symposium, SSD'91*, O. Günther and H.-J. Schek, eds., vol. 525 of Springer-Verlag Lecture Notes in Computer Science, pages 277–296, Zurich, Switzerland, August 1991. [rectangles; intervals; buddy-tree]

[1709]   B. Seeger and H.-P. Kriegel. Techniques for design and implementation of efficient spatial access methods. In *Proceedings of the 14th International Conference on Very Large Databases (VLDB)*, F. Bachillon and D. J. DeWitt, eds., pages 360–371, Los Angeles, August 1988. [points; survey] cited in F.3.3.1 (p. 454), F.4.6.3 (p. 670)

[1710]   B. Seeger and H.-P. Kriegel. The buddy-tree: an efficient and robust access method for spatial data base systems. In *Proceedings of the 16th International Conference on Very Large Databases (VLDB)*, D. McLeod, R. Sacks-Davis, and H.-J. Schek, eds., pages 590–601, Brisbane, Australia, August 1990. [points; buddy-tree; multilevel grid file] cited in F.1.7.1.5 (pp. 110–113), F.1.7.1.5.s (p. 770)

[1711]   R. Seidel. Small-dimensional linear programming and convex hulls made easy. *Discrete and Computational Geometry*, 6(5):423–434, 1991. [linear programming; randomized algorithms] cited in F.4.4.2.s (p. 852)

[1712]   R. Seidel and C. R. Aragon. Randomized search trees. *Algorithmica*, 16(4/5):464–497, October/November 1996. [skip list; treap] cited in F.1.3 (p. 27)

[1713]   T. Seidl. *Adaptable similarity search in 3-d spatial database systems*. PhD thesis, Ludwig-Maximilians University, Munich, Germany, 1998. [similarity searching; nearest neighbor]

[1714]   T. Seidl and H.-P. Kriegel. A 3d molecular surface representation supporting neighborhood queries. In *Advances in Spatial Databases—4th International Symposium, SSD'95*, M. J. Egenhofer and J. R. Herring, eds., vol. 951 of Springer-Verlag Lecture Notes in Computer Science, pages 240–258, Portland, ME, August 1995. [volumes; protein docking; nearest neighbor]

[1715]   T. Seidl and H.-P. Kriegel. Efficient user-adaptable similarity search in large multimedia databases. In *Proceedings of the 23rd International Conference on Very Large Data Bases (VLDB)*, M. Jarke, M. J. Carey, K. R. Dittrich, F. H. Lochovsky, P. Loucopoulos, and M. A. Jeusfeld, eds., pages 506–515, Athens, Greece, August 1997. [points; similarity searching]

[1716]   T. Seidl and H.-P. Kriegel. Optimal multi-step k-nearest neighbor search. In *Proceedings of the ACM SIGMOD Conference*, L. Hass and A. Tiwary, eds., pages 154–165, Seattle, WA, June 1998. [points; nearest neighbor; similarity searching] cited in F.4.5.4.2 (p. 626), F.4.6.1.2 (pp. 666, 668), F.4.6.1.2.s (p. 865)

[1717]   P. G. Selinger, M. M. Astrahan, D. D. Chamberlin, R. A. Lorie, and T. G. Price. Access path selection in a relational database management system. In *Proceedings of the ACM SIGMOD Conference*, pages 23–34, Boston, June 1979. [query optimization; selectivity estimation] cited in F.4.1.1 (p. 492)

[1718]   T. Sellis, N. Roussopoulos, and C. Faloutsos. The R^+-tree: a dynamic index for multi-dimensional objects. In *Proceedings of the 13th International Conference on Very Large Databases (VLDB)*, P. M. Stocker and W. Kent, eds., pages 71–79, Brighton, United Kingdom, September 1987. Also University of Maryland Computer

Science Technical Report TR–1795, 1987. [rectangles; R-tree; R$^+$-tree] cited in D.3.5.3, F.1.7 (p. 96), F.1.7.1.7 (p. 130), F.2.1.5.3 (p. 311), F.1.7.1.6.5.s (p. 773)

[1719] H. Senoussi and A. Saoudi. Quadtree algorithms for template matching on mesh connected computer. *International Journal of Pattern Recognition and Artificial Intelligence*, 9(2):387–410, April 1995. Also see *Proceedings of Computer Architectures for Machine Perception*, M. A. Bayouni, L. S. Davis, and K. P. Valavanis, eds., pages 27–33, New Orleans, LA, December 1993. [regions; region quadtree; parallel processing] cited in F.P (p. xviii), F.1.5 (p. 49)

[1720] K. Sevcik and N. Koudas. Filter trees for managing spatial data over a range of size granularities. In *Proceedings of the 22nd International Conference on Very Large Data Bases (VLDB)*, T. M. Vijayaraman, A. P. Buchmann, C. Mohan, and N. L. Sarda, eds., pages 16–27, Mumbai (Bombay), India, September 1996. [points; filter tree; MX-CIF quadtree] cited in F.1.7.1.5 (p. 115), F.2.1.4.1 (pp. 255, 259)

[1721] C. A. Shaffer. Personal communication. 1985. [regions; perimeter computation] cited in A.5.2

[1722] C. A. Shaffer. *Application of alternative quadtree representations*. PhD thesis, Computer Science Department, University of Maryland, College Park, MD, June 1986. Also Computer Science Technical Report TR–1672. [regions; region quadtree; RR$_1$ quadtree; RR$_2$ quadtree] cited in A.4.2.3, A.6.3.3.s, A.8.2.3, A.9.3.1.s, A.9.3.4, A.9.3.4.s, D.1.2, D.3.5.2, D.3.5.2.s, D.5.2, F.2.1.4.2 (p. 261), F.2.1.2.4.s (p. 779)

[1723] C. A. Shaffer. An empirical comparison of vectors, arrays, and quadtrees for representing geographic data. In *Proceedings of the International Colloquium on the Construction and Display of Geoscientific Maps Derived from Databases*, pages 99–115, Dinkelsbühl, West Germany, December 1986. Also in *Geologisches Jahrbuch*. vol. 104 of *A*, pages 99–115, 1988. [regions; lines]

[1724] C. A. Shaffer. A formula for computing the number of quadtree node fragments created by a shift. *Pattern Recognition Letters*, 7(1):45–49, January 1988. [regions; space requirements] cited in A.6.5.3.s

[1725] C. A. Shaffer. Bit interleaving for quad- or octrees. In *Graphics Gems*, A. S. Glassner, ed., pages 443–447 and 759–762. Academic Press, Boston, 1990. [regions]

[1726] C. A. Shaffer and P. R. Brown. A paging scheme for pointer-based quadtrees. In *Advances in Spatial Databases—3rd International Symposium, SSD'93*, D. Abel and B. C. Ooi, eds., vol. 692 of Springer-Verlag Lecture Notes in Computer Science, pages 89–104, Singapore, June 1993. [regions]

[1727] C. A. Shaffer, Ramana Juvvadi, and Lenwood S. Heath. Generalized comparison of quadtree and bintree storage requirements. *Image and Vision Computing*, 11(7):402–412, September 1993. Also Virginia Polytechnic Institute and State University Computer Science Technical Report TR 89–23, June 1989. [regions; space requirements]

[1728] C. A. Shaffer and H. Samet. An in–core hierarchical data structure organization for a geographic database. Computer Science Technical Report TR–1886, University of Maryland, College Park, MD, July 1987. [regions; pyramid] cited in A.2.2

[1729] C. A. Shaffer and H. Samet. Optimal quadtree construction algorithms. *Computer Vision, Graphics, and Image Processing*, 37(3):402–419, March 1987. [regions; region quadtree construction] cited in A.4.2.3, A.6.3.3.s, D.1.2, D.5.2, F.2.1.2.4.s (p. 779)

[1730] C. A. Shaffer and H. Samet. An algorithm to expand regions represented by linear quadtrees. *Image and Vision Computing*, 6(3):162–168, August 1988. [regions; image dilation] cited in A.6.6

[1731] C. A. Shaffer and H. Samet. Set operations for unaligned linear quadtrees. *Computer Vision, Graphics, and Image Processing*, 50(1):29–4, April 1990. Also Virginia Polytechnic Institute and State University Computer Science Technical Report TR 88–31, 1988. [regions; region quadtree] cited in A.6.3.3, A.6.3.3.s, A.6.5.3

[1732] C. A. Shaffer, H. Samet, and R. C. Nelson. QUILT: a geographic information system based on quadtrees. *International Journal of Geographical Information Systems*, 4(2):103–131, April–June 1990. Also University of Maryland Computer Science Technical Report TR–1885.1, July 1987. [QUILT; geographic information

systems (GIS); region quadtree] cited in A.2.1.2, A.3.4.1, A.6.6, A.8.2.1, D.4.2.4, F.P (p. xviii)

[1733] C. A. Shaffer and Q. F. Stout. Linear time distance transforms for quadtrees. *CVGIP: Image Understanding*, 54(2):215–223, September 1991. Also Virginia Polytechnic Institute and State University Computer Science Technical Report TR 89–7, 1989. [regions; region quadtree] cited in A.9.2

[1734] C. A. Shaffer and M. T. Ursekar. Large scale editing and vector to raster conversion via quadtree spatial indexing. In *Proceedings of the 5th International Symposium on Spatial Data Handling*, vol. 2, pages 505–513, Charleston, SC, August 1992. [lines]

[1735] E. Shaffer and M. Garland. Efficient adaptive simplification of massive meshes. In *Proceedings IEEE Visualization 2001*, T. Ertl, K. Joy, and A. Varshney, eds., pages 127–134, San Diego, CA, October 2001. [surfaces; BSP tree; polygon simplification]

[1736] C. Shahabi, M. R. Kolahdouzan, and M. Sharifzadeh. A road network embedding technique for k-nearest neighbor search in moving object databases. *GeoInformatica*, 7(3):255–273, September 2003. Also see *Proceedings of the 10th International Symposium on Advances in Geographic Information Systems*, A. Voisard and S.-C. Chen, eds., pages 94–100, McLean, VA, November 2002. [lines; points; spatial networks; shortest path algorithm; Lipschitz embedding] cited in F.4.1.6 (p. 515)

[1737] G. Shakhnarovich, P. A. Viola, and T. Darrell. Fast pose estimation with parameter-sensitive hashing. In *Proceedings of 9th International Conference on Computer Vision*, pages 750–759, Nice, France, October 2003. [metric space embedding; locality sensitive hashing (LSH); approximate nearest neighbor; pose estimation] cited in F.4.7.4 (p. 716)

[1738] M. I. Shamos. *Computational geometry*. PhD thesis, Department of Computer Science, Yale University, New Haven, CT, 1978. [computational geometry; general] cited in D.4.3

[1739] M. I. Shamos and D. Hoey. Closest-point problems. In *Proceedings of the 16th IEEE Annual Symposium on Foundations of Computer Science*, pages 151–162, Berkeley, CA, October 1975. [points] cited in A.6.3.2, D.4.3

[1740] M. I. Shamos and D. Hoey. Geometric intersection problems. In *Proceedings of the 17th IEEE Annual Symposium on Foundations of Computer Science*, pages 208–215, Houston, TX, October 1976. [points; plane-sweep algorithms] cited in D.3, D.3.2.4.s, F.2.1.5.2.4 (p. 291), F.3 (p. 428), F.4.1.5 (p. 504), F.3.1.4.s (p. 821)

[1741] M. A. Shand. Algorithms for corner stitched data-structures. *Algorithmica*, 2(1):61–80, 1987. [rectangles; corner stitching] cited in D.3.4, F.3.3.2.1 (p. 460)

[1742] M.-Z. Shao and N. I. Badler. Analysis and acceleration of progressive refinement radiosity method. In *Proceedings of the 4th Eurographics Workshop on Rendering*, M. Cohen, C. Puech, and F. Sillion, eds., pages 247–280, Paris, France, June 1993. [radiosity]

[1743] M. Shapiro. The choice of reference points in best-match file searching. *Communications of the ACM*, 20(5):339–343, May 1977. [metric spaces; nearest neighbor; distance matrix] cited in F.4.1.7 (p. 517), F.4.2 (p. 517), F.4.5.2.1.1 (p. 605), F.4.5.3.2 (p. 616), F.4.5.7.3 (p. 647), F.4.7.2.1 (p. 691)

[1744] J. Shechtman. Processamento geométrico de máscaras VLSI. Master's thesis, Universidade Federal do Rio de Janeiro, Rio de Janeiro, Brazil, April 1991. [volumes; vertex representation] cited in F.2.3.3 (p. 417)

[1745] R. Shekhar, E. Fayyad, R. Yagel, and J. F. Cornhill. Octree-based decimation of marching cubes surfaces. In *Proceedings IEEE Visualization'96*, R. Yagel and G. M. Nielson, eds., pages 335–342, San Francisco, October 1996. [surfaces; region octree; marching cube algorithm]

[1746] S. Shekhar and S. Chawla. *Spatial Databases: A Tour*. Prentice-Hall, Englewood-Cliffs, NJ, 2003. [spatial database; general] cited in F.P (p. xix)

[1747] S. Shekhar, S. Chawla, S. Ravada, A. Fetterer, X. Liu, and C.-T. Lu. Spatial databases—accomplishments and research needs. *IEEE Transactions on Knowledge and Data Engineering*, 11(1):36–44, January/February 1999. [spatial database; survey] cited in F.P (p. xix)

[1748] S. Shekhar, A. Kohli, and M. Coyle. Path computation algorithms for advanced traveller information system (atis). In *Proceedings of the 9th IEEE International Conference on Data Engineering*, pages 31–39, Vienna, Austria, April 1993. [lines; spatial networks; shortest path algorithm]

[1749] S. Shekhar and D.-R. Liu. CCAM: a connectivity-clustered access method for networks and network computations. *IEEE Transactions on Knowledge and Data Engineering*, 9(1):102–119, January/February 1997. [spatial networks] cited in F.4.1.6.s (p. 835)

[1750] S. Shekhar, C.-T. Lu, S. Chawla, and S. Ravada. Efficient join-index-based spatial-join processing: a clustering approach. *IEEE Transactions on Knowledge and Data Engineering*, 14(6):1400–1421, November/December 2002. [spatial join index]

[1751] M. S. Shephard, H. L. de Cougny, R. M. O'Bara, and M. W. Beall. Automatic grid generation using spatially based trees. In *Handbook of Grid Generation*, J. F. Thompson, B. K. Soni, and N. P. Weatherill, eds., chapter 15. CRC Press, Boca Raton, FL, 1999. [finite element analysis; MX quadtree; restricted quadtree]

[1752] J. R. Shewchuk. *Delaunay refinement mesh generation*. PhD thesis, School of Computer Science, Carnegie-Mellon University, Pittsburgh, PA, May 1997. Also Computer Science Technical Report CMU–CS–97–137. [volumes; tetrahedralizations] cited in F.2.2.1.6 (p. 352)

[1753] J. R. Shewchuk. Tetrahedral mesh generation by Delaunay refinement. In *Proceedings of the 14th Annual Symposium on Computational Geometry*, pages 86–95, Minneapolis, MN, June 1998. [volumes; conforming Delaunay tetrahedralization; Steiner points] cited in F.2.2.1.6 (p. 352)

[1754] F. Y. Shih and W.-T. Wong. An adaptive algorithm for conversion from quadtree to chain codes. *Pattern Recognition*, 34(3):631–639, March 2001. [regions; region quadtree; chain code]

[1755] K. Shim, R. Srikant, and R. Agrawal. High-dimensional similarity joins. *IEEE Transactions on Knowledge and Data Engineering*, 14(1):156–171, January/February 2002. [high-dimensional data; similarity join]

[1756] H. Shin, B. Moon, and S. Lee. Adaptive and incremental processing for distance join queries. *IEEE Transactions on Knowledge and Data Engineering*, 15(6):1561–1578, 2003. Also see *Proceedings of the ACM SIGMOD Conference*, W. Chen, J. Naughton, and P. A. Bernstein, eds., pages 343–354, Dallas, TX, May 2000. [points; distance join; distance semijoin] cited in F.4 (p. 490), F.4.5.8 (p. 658)

[1757] B. Shneiderman. Reduced combined indexes for efficient multiple attribute retrieval. *Information Systems*, 2(4):149–154, 1977. [points; reduced combined index] cited in F.1.1 (p. 6)

[1758] B. Shneiderman. Tree visualization with tree-maps: 2-d space-filling approach. *ACM Transactions on Graphics*, 11(1):92–99, January 1992. Also University of Maryland Computer Science Technical Report TR–2645, April 1991. [regions; treemap; k-d tree; X-Y tree; puzzletree] cited in F.1.5.1.4 (p. 66), F.2.1.2.9 (p. 225), F.4.4.3 (p. 572)

[1759] B. Shneiderman and M. Wattenberg. Ordered treemap layouts. In *Proceedings IEEE Symposium on Information Visualization'01*, pages 73–78, San Diego, CA, October 2001. [regions; visualization; treemap; k-d tree; X-Y tree; puzzletree] cited in F.2.1.2.9 (p. 225)

[1760] M. Shneier. Calculations of geometric properties using quadtrees. *Computer Graphics and Image Processing*, 16(3):296–302, July 1981. Also University of Maryland Computer Science Technical Report TR–770, May 1979. [regions] cited in A.5.2, A.6.3.2, D.3.5.1, F.3.4.1.2 (p. 469)

[1761] M. Shneier. Path-length distances for quadtrees. *Information Sciences*, 23(1):49–67, February 1981. Also University of Maryland Computer Science Technical Report TR–794, July 1979. [regions; region quadtree] cited in A.9.2

[1762] M. Shneier. Two hierarchical linear feature representations: edge pyramids and edge quadtrees. *Computer Graphics and Image Processing*, 17(3):211–224, November 1981. Also University of Maryland Computer Science Technical Report TR–961, October 1980. [lines; edge pyramid; edge quadtree] cited in A.1.4, A.7.1.2, D.1.3, D.4.2.1, F.2.2.2.3 (p. 360), F.2.4 (p. 425)

[1763] M. O. Shneier, R. Lumia, and M. Herman. Prediction-based vision for robot control. *Computer*, 20(8):46–55, August 1987. [volumes; region octree]

[1764] M. Shpitalni. Relations and transformations between quadtree encoding and switching function representation. *Computer-Aided Design*, 19(5):266–272, June 1987. [regions; region quadtree]

[1765] R. B. Shu and M. S. Kankanhalli. Efficient linear octree generation from voxels. *Image and Vision Computing*, 12(5):297–303, June 1994. [volumes; region octree]

[1766] C. E. Silva. Alternative definitions of faces in boundary representation of solid objects. Production Automation Project Technical Memorandum TM–36, University of Rochester, Rochester, NY, 1981. [volumes; surfaces; boundary model (BRep)] cited in D.5.4

[1767] Y. V. Silva Filho. Average case analysis of region search in balanced *k-d* trees. *Information Processing Letters*, 8(5):219–223, June 1979. [points; k-d tree] cited in F.1.5.1.3 (p. 56)

[1768] Y. V. Silva Filho. Optimal choice of discriminators in a balanced *k-d* binary search tree. *Information Processing Letters*, 13(2):67–70, November 1981. [points; k-d tree]

[1769] A. da Silva and H. Duarte-Ramos. A progressive trimming approach to space decomposition. In *Proceedings of the 4th International Symposium on Spatial Data Handling*, vol. 2, pages 951–960, Zurich, Switzerland, July 1990. [lines; finite element analysis]

[1770] A. P. Sistla, C. T. Yu, C. Liu, and K. Liu. Similarity based retrieval of pictures using indices on spatial relationships. In *Proceedings of the 21st International Conference on Very Large Data Bases (VLDB)*, U. Dayal, P. M. D. Gray, and S. Nishio, eds., pages 619–629, Zurich, Switzerland, September 1995. [regions; similarity searching]

[1771] R. Sivan. *Surface modeling using quadtrees*. PhD thesis, Computer Science Department, University of Maryland, College Park, MD, February 1996. Also Computer Science Technical Report TR–3609. [surfaces; restricted quadtree] cited in F.1.5.1.4 (p. 64), F.2.2.2.10 (pp. 381–382), F.2.2.4 (p. 405)

[1772] R. Sivan and H. Samet. Algorithms for constructing quadtree surface maps. In *Proceedings of the 5th International Symposium on Spatial Data Handling*, vol. 1, pages 361–370, Charleston, SC, August 1992. [surfaces; restricted quadtree] cited in F.1.5.1.4 (p. 64), F.2.2.2.10 (pp. 381–382), F.2.2.4 (p. 405)

[1773] H.-W. Six and P. Widmayer. Spatial searching in geometric databases. In *Proceedings of the 4th IEEE International Conference on Data Engineering*, pages 496–503, Los Angeles, February 1988. [rectangles; multilayer grid file] cited in F.2.1.4.1 (p. 256)

[1774] H.-W. Six and D. Wood. The rectangle intersection problem revisited. *BIT*, 20(4):426–433, 1980. [rectangles; segment tree; rectangle intersection problem] cited in D.3.2.1, F.3.1.1 (p. 432)

[1775] H. W. Six and D. Wood. Counting and reporting intersections of *d*-ranges. *IEEE Transactions on Computers*, 31(3):181–187, March 1982. [rectangles; segment tree; rectangle intersection problem] cited in D.3.2.1, F.3.1.1 (p. 432)

[1776] D. D. Sleator and R. E. Tarjan. A data structure for dynamic trees. *Journal of Computer System Sciences*, 26(3):362–391, June 1983. [regions; link-cut tree] cited in F.2.1.3.3.2 (p. 253)

[1777] K. R. Sloan Jr. Dynamically quantized pyramids. In *Proceedings of the 7th International Joint Conference on Artificial Intelligence*, pages 734–736, Vancouver, Canada, August 1981. [points; dynamically quantized pyramid (DQP); Hough transform] cited in D.2.8.1, F.1.5.1.4 (p. 62), F.1.9 (p. 186), F.2.1.5.1 (p. 269)

[1778] K. R. Sloan Jr. and S. L. Tanimoto. Progressive refinement of raster images. *IEEE Transactions on Computers*, 28(11):871–874, November 1979. [regions; progressive transmission] cited in A.8.3

[1779] T. Smith, D. Peuquet, S. Menon, and P. Agarwal. A knowledge-based geographical information system. *International Journal of Geographical Information Systems*, 1(2):149–172, April–June 1987. [regions]

[1780] T. F. Smith and M. S. Waterman. Identification of common molecular subsequences. *Journal of Molecular Biology*, 147(1):195–197, 1981. [edit distance] cited in F.4.5.1 (p. 600)

[1781] J. M. Snyder and A. H. Barr. Ray tracing complex models containing surface tessellations. *Computer Graphics*, 21(4):119–128, July 1987. Also in *Proceedings of the SIGGRAPH'87 Conference*, Anaheim, CA, July 1987. [volumes; surfaces; ray tracing]

[1782] J. P. Snyder. *Map Projections - A Working Manual*. United States Government Printing Office, Washington, DC, 1987. [surfaces; map projections]

[1783] C. Sobhanpanah and I. O. Angell. Polygonal mesh and quad-tree display algorithms for nonconvex crystal structures. *Computers & Graphics*, 10(4):341–349, 1986. [regions; region quadtree]

[1784] J. Solé Bosquet. *Parallel operations on octree representation schemes*. PhD thesis, Departament de Llenguatges i Sistemes Informàtics, Universitat Politècnica de Catalunya, Barcelona, Spain, October 1996. [volumes; face octree] cited in F.2.2.2.4 (p. 362)

[1785] N. Solntseff and D. Wood. Pyramids: A data type for matrix representation in PASCAL. *BIT*, 17(3):344–350, 1977. [matrix methods; pyramid; Strassen's algorithm]

[1786] D. M. Y. Sommerville. *An Introduction to the Geometry of N Dimensions*. Methuen, London, United Kingdom, 1929. [geometry; general]

[1787] J.-W. Song, K.-Y. Whang, Y.-K. Lee, and S.-W. Kim. The clustering property of corner transformation for spatial database applications. In *Proceedings of the IEEE COMPSAC'99 Conference*, pages 28–35, Phoenix, AZ, October 1999. [points; corner transformation; transformation technique] cited in F.3.3.3 (pp. 464–465)

[1788] J.-W. Song, K.-Y. Whang, Y.-K. Lee, M.-J. Lee, and S.-W. Kim. Spatial join processing using corner transformation. *IEEE Transactions on Knowledge and Data Engineering*, 11(4):688–695, July/August 1999. [points; corner transformation; transformation technique] cited in F.3.3.3 (p. 465)

[1789] Z. Song and N. Roussopoulos. *K*-nearest neighbor search for moving query point. In *Advances in Spatial and Temporal Databases—7th International Symposium, SSTD'01*, C. S. Jensen, M. Schneider, B. Seeger, and V. J. Tsotras, eds., vol. 2121 of Springer-Verlag Lecture Notes in Computer Science, pages 79–96, Redondo Beach, CA, July 2001. [points; moving objects] cited in F.4 (p. 488)

[1790] D. L. G. Sotomayor. Tessellation of triangles of variable precision as an economical representation for DTM's. In *Proceedings of the Digital Terrain Models DTM Symposium*, pages 506–515, St. Louis, MO, May 1978. [surfaces; quaternary hierarchical triangular decomposition] cited in D.5.6, F.2.2.4 (p. 400)

[1791] M. Soucy and D. Laurendeau. Multiresolution surface modeling based on hierarchical triangulation. *Computer Vision and Image Understanding*, 63(1):1–14, January 1996. [surfaces; triangulations; multiresolution modeling] cited in F.2.2.3.4 (p. 394)

[1792] J. Spackman and P. Willis. The smart navigation of a ray through an oct-tree. *Computers & Graphics*, 15(2):185–194, 1991. [volumes; region octree; neighbor finding; ray tracing]

[1793] J. N. Spackman. *Scene decompositions for accelerated ray tracing*. PhD thesis, School of Mathematical Sciences, University of Bath, Claverton Down, United Kingdom, February 1990. Also Computer Science Technical Report 90–33. [volumes; ray tracing]

[1794] L. R. Speer. A new subdivision method for high-speed, memory-efficient ray shooting. In *Proceedings of the 3rd Eurographics Workshop on Rendering*, A. Chalmers, D. Paddon, and F. Sillion, eds., pages 45–59, Bristol, England, May 1992. Consolidation Express. [volumes; ray tracing]

[1795] L. R. Speer, T. D. DeRose, and B. A. Barsky. A theoretical and empirical analysis of coherent ray tracing. In *Computer-Generated Images—The State of the Art*, N. Magnenat-Thalmann and D. Thalmann, eds., pages 11–25. Springer-Verlag, Tokyo, Japan, 1985. Also see *Proceedings of Graphics Interface'85*, pages 1–8, Montréal, Canada, May 1985. [volumes; ray tracing] cited in A.7.3

[1796] G. Sperling, M. Landy, Y. Cohen, and M. Pavel. Intelligible encoding of ASL image sequences at extremely low information rates. *Computer Vision, Graphics, and Image Processing*, 31(3):335–391, September 1985. [regions; American Sign Language (ASL) images]

[1797] R. F. Sproull. Refinements to nearest-neighbor searching in *k*-dimensional trees. *Algorithmica*, 6(4):579–589, 1991. [points; nearest neighbor; k-d tree] cited in F.1.5.1.4 (pp. 58, 66), F.4.1.7 (p. 516), F.4.2 (p. 517), F.4.4.4 (p. 576)

[1798] S. N. Srihari. Representation of three-dimensional digital images. *ACM Computing Surveys*, 13(1):399–424, December 1981. [volumes; survey] cited in A.P, D.P, F.P (p. xix)

[1799] S. K. Srivastava and N. Ahuja. Octree generation from object silhouettes in perspective views. *Computer Vision, Graphics, and Image Processing*, 49(1):68–84, January 1990. Also see *Proceedings of the IEEE Computer Society Workshop on Computer Vision*, pages 363–365, Miami Beach, FL, November 1987. [volumes; region octree; perspective view] cited in A.4.6, D.5.2

[1800] I. Stanoi, D. Agrawal, and A. El Abbadi. Reverse nearest neighbor queries for dynamic databases. In *Proceedings ACM SIGMOD Workshop on Research Issues in Data Mining and Knowledge Discovery*, D. Gunopulos and R. Rastogi, eds., pages 44–53, Dallas, TX, May 2000. [points; distance join; reverse nearest neighbor (RNN)] cited in F.4.5.8 (p. 658)

[1801] I. Stanoi, M. Riedewald, D. Agrawal, and A. El Abbadi. Discovery of influence sets in frequently updated databases. In *Proceedings of the 27th International Conference on Very Large Data Bases (VLDB)*, P. M. G. Apers, P. Atzeni, S. Ceri, S. Paraboschi, K. Ramamohanarao, and R. T. Snodgrass, eds., pages 99–108, Rome, Italy, September 2001. [points; distance join; reverse nearest neighbor (RNN)] cited in F.4.5.8 (p. 658)

[1802] J. R. Stenstrom and C. I. Connolly. Building wire frames from multiple range views. In *Proceedings of the IEEE International Conference on Robotics and Automation*, vol. 1, pages 615–620, San Francisco, April 1986. [volumes]

[1803] M. Stonebraker, T. Sellis, and E. Hanson. An analysis of rule indexing implementations in data base systems. In *Proceedings of the 1st International Conference on Expert Database Systems*, pages 353–364, Charleston, SC, April 1986. [rectangles; R-tree; R⁺-tree] cited in D.3.5.3, F.1.7 (p. 96), F.1.7.1.7 (p. 130), F.2.1.5.3 (p. 311), F.1.7.1.6.5.s (p. 773)

[1804] V. Strassen. Gaussian elimination is not optimal. *Numerische Mathematik*, 13(4):354–356, August 1969. [matrix methods] cited in D.2.6.1.s, F.1.4.2.1.s (p. 757)

[1805] B. Stroustrup. *The C++ Programming Language*. Addison-Wesley Longman, Reading, MA, third edition, 1997. [C++; programming languages] cited in F.P (p. xx), F.D (p. 743)

[1806] N. Stuart. Quadtree GIS—pragmatics for the present, prospects for the future. In *Proceedings of GIS/LIS'90*, pages 373–382, Anaheim, CA, November 1990. [regions; region quadtree; geographic information systems (GIS)]

[1807] V. S. Subrahmanian. *Principles of Multimedia Database Systems*. Morgan-Kaufmann, San Francisco, 1998. [multimedia database; general] cited in F.P (p. xix)

[1808] K. R. Subramanian and D. S. Fussell. Applying space subdivision techniques to volume rendering. In *Proceedings IEEE Visualization'90*, A. Kaufman, ed., pages 150–159, San Francisco, October 1990. [volumes; ray tracing; k-d tree]

[1809] K. R. Subramanian and B. Naylor. Representing medical images with partitioning trees. In *Proceedings IEEE Visualization'92*, A. E. Kaufman and G. M. Nielson, eds., pages 147–154, Boston, October 1992. [regions; BSP tree]

[1810] S. Subramanian and S. Ramaswamy. The P-range tree: a new data structure for range searching in secondary memory. In *Proceedings of the 6th Annual ACM-SIAM Symposium on Discrete Algorithms*, pages 378–387, San Francisco, 1995. [points; range query]

[1811] P. Suetens, P. Fua, and A. J. Hanson. Computational strategies for object recognition. *ACM Computing Surveys*, 24(1):5–61, March 1992. [volumes; object recognition; survey] cited in F.2 (p. 191)

[1812] K. G. Suffern. Recursive space subdivision techniques for rendering implicitly defined surfaces. In *Proceedings of the 7th Australian Conference on Computer Graphics AUSGRAPH'89*, pages 239–249, Sydney, Australia, July 1989. [surfaces]

[1813] K. G. Suffern. An octree algorithm for displaying implicitly defined mathematical functions. *Australian Computer Journal*, 22(1):2–10, February 1990. Also New South Wales Institute of Technology School of Computing Sciences Technical Report 87.9, December 1987. [surfaces; perspective view]

[1814] K. G. Suffern. Quadtree algorithms for contouring functions of two variables. *The Computer Journal*, 33(5):402–407, October 1990.

Also New South Wales Institute of Technology Computing Sciences Technical Report 87.1, February 1987. [surfaces]

[1815] C. Sun, D. Agrawal, and A. E. Abbadi. Hardware acceleration for spatial selections and joins. In *Proceedings of the ACM SIGMOD Conference*, pages 455–466, San Diego, CA, June 2003. [spatial join; GPU] cited in F.P (p. xviii)

[1816] K. Sung. A DDA octree traversal algorithm for ray tracing. In *Proceedings of the EUROGRAPHICS'91 Conference*, F. H. Post and W. Barth, eds., pages 73–85, Vienna, Austria, September 1991. [volumes; ray tracing; neighbor finding]

[1817] E. H. Sussenguth Jr. Use of tree structures for processing files. *Communications of the ACM*, 6(5):272–279, May 1963. [points; doubly chained tree (DCT)] cited in F.1.1 (p. 7)

[1818] I. E. Sutherland, R. F. Sproull, and R. A. Schumacker. A characterization of ten hidden–surface algorithms. *ACM Computing Surveys*, 6(1):1–55, March 1974. [surfaces; hidden-line removal; hidden-surface removal; survey] cited in A.1.2, A.7, A.7.1, D.1.2, D.2.1

[1819] R. Szeliski and H.-Y. Shum. Motion estimation with quadtree splines. *IEEE Transactions on Pattern Analysis and Machine Intelligence*, 18(12):1199–1210, December 1996. Also see *Proceedings of 5th International Conference on Computer Vision*, pages 757–763, Cambridge, MA, June 1995. [regions; pyramid; motion estimation]

[1820] D. Talmor. *Well-spaced points for numerical methods*. PhD thesis, School of Computer Science, Carnegie-Mellon University, Pittsburgh, PA, August 1997. Also Computer Science Technical Report CMU–CS–97–164. [volumes; tetrahedralizations] cited in F.2.2.1.6 (p. 352)

[1821] R. Tamassia. An incremental reconstruction method for dynamic planar point location. *Information Processing Letters*, 37(2):79–83, January 1991. [regions; dynamic point location; triangulations] cited in F.2.1.3.3.2 (p. 253)

[1822] M. Tamminen. The EXCELL method for efficient geometric access to data. *Acta Polytechnica Scandinavica*, 1981. Also Mathematics and Computer Science Series No. 34. [points; regions; EXCELL; edge-EXCELL] cited in A.1.3, D.2.8.2, D.4.2.3, D.5.3, F.1.7.2 (p. 131), F.1.7.2.1 (p. 135), F.1.7.2.2 (p. 137), F.2.2.2.6 (p. 365), F.2.2.2.7 (p. 370)

[1823] M. Tamminen. Order preserving extendible hashing and bucket tries. *BIT*, 21(4):419–435, 1981. [points; extendible hashing] cited in D.2.7, F.1.7.2.3 (p. 140)

[1824] M. Tamminen. Efficient spatial access to a data base. In *Proceedings of the ACM SIGMOD Conference*, pages 47–57, Orlando, FL, June 1982. [lines; EXCELL; edge-EXCELL] cited in D.5.3, F.2.2.2.7 (p. 370)

[1825] M. Tamminen. The extendible cell method for closest point problems. *BIT*, 22(1):27–41, 1982. [points; extendible hashing; nearest neighbor; EXCELL]

[1826] M. Tamminen. Hidden lines using the EXCELL method. *Computer Graphics Forum*, 1(3):96–105, September 1982. [lines; EXCELL]

[1827] M. Tamminen. Performance analysis of cell based geometric file organizations. *Computer Vision, Graphics, and Image Processing*, 24(2):168–181, November 1983. [points; regions; EXCELL] cited in D.2.8.1, F.1.4.2.2 (p. 46), F.1.7.3 (p. 163)

[1828] M. Tamminen. Comment on quad- and octtrees. *Communications of the ACM*, 27(3):248–249, March 1984. [regions; volumes; bintree] cited in A.1.3, A.2.1.2.s, D.1.4.1, F.1.5 (p. 49), F.2.1.2.6 (p. 221), F.2.3.1 (p. 411)

[1829] M. Tamminen. Efficient geometric access to a multirepresentation geo-database. *Geo-Processing*, 2:177–196, 1984. [lines; EXCELL] cited in D.2.8.2, F.1.7.2.3.1 (p. 143)

[1830] M. Tamminen. Encoding pixel trees. *Computer Vision, Graphics, and Image Processing*, 28(1):44–57, October 1984. [regions; bintree] cited in A.2.2, D.5.4, F.2.3.1 (p. 411)

[1831] M. Tamminen. Metric data structures—an overview. Laboratory of Information Processing Science Report–HTKK–TKO–A25, Helsinki University of Technology, Espoo, Finland, 1984. [points; survey]

[1832] M. Tamminen. On search by address computation. *BIT*, 25(1):135–147, 1985. [points; PR quadtree; PR k-d tree] cited in D.2.6.2, F.1.5.2.1 (p. 72)

[1833] M. Tamminen and F. W. Jansen. An integrity filter for recursive subdivision meshes. *Computers & Graphics*, 9(4):351–363, 1985. [surfaces] cited in A.7.1.6

[1834] M. Tamminen, O. Karonen, and M. Mäntylä. Ray-casting and block model conversion using a spatial index. *Computer-Aided Design*, 16(4):203–208, July 1984. [volumes; ray tracing; EXCELL] cited in A.7.2.2, A.7.2.3

[1835] M. Tamminen, P. Koistinen, J. Hamalainen, O. Karonen, P. Korhonen, R. Raunio, and P. Rekola. Bintree: a dimension independent image processing system. Laboratory of Information Processing Science Report–HTKK–TKO–C9, Helsinki University of Technology, Espoo, Finland, 1984. [volumes; bintree] cited in D.5.5.1, D.5.5.1.1.s

[1836] M. Tamminen and H. Samet. Efficient octree conversion by connectivity labeling. *Computer Graphics*, 18(3):43–51, July 1984. Also in *Proceedings of the SIGGRAPH'84 Conference*, Minneapolis, MN, July 1984. [volumes; region octree; bintree] cited in D.5.4, D.5.4.s

[1837] M. Tamminen and R. Sulonen. The EXCELL method for efficient geometric access to data. In *Proceedings of the 19th Design Automation Conference*, pages 345–351, Las Vegas, NV, June 1982. [points; regions; EXCELL]

[1838] K.-L. Tan, P.-K. Eng, and B. C. Ooi. Efficient progressive skyline computation. In *Proceedings of the 27th International Conference on Very Large Data Bases (VLDB)*, P. M. G. Apers, P. Atzeni, S. Ceri, S. Paraboschi, K. Ramamohanarao, and R. T. Snodgrass, eds., pages 301–310, Rome, Italy, September 2001. [points; skyline query; point dominance query; nearest neighbor] cited in F.4.1.5 (pp. 504, 506–507)

[1839] K.-L. Tan, B. C. Ooi, and D. J. Abel. Exploiting spatial indexes for semijoin-based join processing in distributed spatial databases. *IEEE Transactions on Knowledge and Data Engineering*, 12(6):920–937, November/December 2000. [regions; R-tree; spatial data mining]

[1840] H. T. Tanaka. Accuracy-based sampling and reconstruction with adaptive meshes for parallel hierarchical triangulation. *Computer Vision and Image Understanding*, 61(3):335–350, May 1995. [surfaces; triangulations; restricted quadtree]

[1841] Z. Tang and S. Lu. A new algorithm for converting boundary representation to octree. In *Proceedings of the EUROGRAPHICS'88 Conference*, D. A. Duce and P. Jancene, eds., pages 105–116, Nice, France, September 1988. [volumes; region octree]

[1842] S. L. Tanimoto. Pictorial feature distortion in a pyramid. *Computer Graphics and Image Processing*, 5(3):333–352, September 1976. [regions; pyramid] cited in A.1.4, D.1.3, F.2.4 (p. 425)

[1843] S. L. Tanimoto. Image transmission with gross information first. *Computer Graphics and Image Processing*, 9(1):72–76, January 1979. [regions; pyramid] cited in A.8.3

[1844] S. L. Tanimoto and A. Klinger, eds. *Structured Computer Vision*. Academic Press, New York, 1980. [pyramid; general] cited in A.P, D.P, F.P (p. xx)

[1845] S. L. Tanimoto and T. Pavlidis. A hierarchical data structure for picture processing. *Computer Graphics and Image Processing*, 4(2):104–119, June 1975. [regions; pyramid] cited in A.1.4, A.8.3, D.1.3, D.2.8.1, F.1.5.1.4 (p. 63), F.2.1.5.1 (p. 266), F.2.4 (p. 424)

[1846] E. Tanin, A. Harwood, and H. Samet. Indexing distributed complex data for complex queries. In *Proceedings of the 4th National Conference on Digital Government Research*, pages 81–90, Seattle, WA, May 2004. [regions; rectangles; peer-to-peer spatial indexing; distributed indexing; Chord method] cited in F.2.1.4.1 (p. 259)

[1847] E. Tanin, A. Harwood, H. Samet, S. Nutanong, and M. Truong. A serverless 3D world. In *Proceedings of the 12th ACM International Workshop on Advances in Geographic Information Systems*, I. F. Cruz and D. Pfoser, eds., pages 157–165, Washington, DC, November 2004. [regions; volumes; peer-to-peer spatial indexing; distributed indexing; Chord method] cited in F.2.1.4.1 (p. 259)

[1848] E. Tanin, D. Nayar, and H. Samet. An efficient nearest neighbor algorithm for P2P settings. In *Proceedings of the 5th National Conference on Digital Government Research*, pages 21–28, Atlanta,

GA, May 2005. [regions; rectangles; peer-to-peer spatial indexing; distributed indexing; nearest neighbor; Chord method] cited in F.4.1.7 (p. 517)

[1849] Y. Tao, R. Cheng, X. Xiao, W. K. Ngai, B. Kao, and S. Prabhakar. Indexing multi-dimensional uncertain data with arbitrary probability density functions. In *Proceedings of the 31st International Conference on Very Large Data Bases (VLDB)*, K. Böhm, C. S. Jensen, L. M. Haas, M. L. Kersten, P.-Å. Larson, and B. C. Ooi, eds., pages 922–933, Trondheim, Norway, September 2005. [probablistic range query; U-tree]

[1850] Y. Tao and D. Papadias. Adaptive index structures. In *Proceedings of the 28th International Conference on Very Large Data Bases (VLDB)*, pages 418–429, Hong Kong, China, August 2002. [rectangles; R-tree]

[1851] Y. Tao and D. Papadias. Spatial queries in dynamic environments. *ACM Transactions on Database Systems*, 28(2):101–139, June 2003. Also see *Proceedings of the ACM SIGMOD Conference*, pages 334–345, Madison, WI, June 2002. [moving objects; nearest neighbor; TPR*-tree; R-tree; TPR-tree] cited in F.4 (p. 488)

[1852] Y. Tao and D. Papadias. Performance analysis of R*-trees with arbitrary node extents. *IEEE Transactions on Knowledge and Data Engineering*, 16(6):653–668, June 2004. [regions; R*-tree]

[1853] Y. Tao and D. Papadias. Range aggregate processing in spatial databases. *IEEE Transactions on Knowledge and Data Engineering*, 16(12):1555–1570, December 2004. [points; aggregation query] cited in F.4 (p. 485)

[1854] Y. Tao, D. Papadias, and X. Lian. Reverse kNN search in arbitrary dimensionality. In *Proceedings of the 30th International Conference on Very Large Data Bases (VLDB)*, M. A. Nascimento, M. T. Özsu, D. Kossmann, R. J. Miller, J. A. Blakely, and K. B. Schiefer, eds., pages 744–755, Toronto, Canada, September 2004. [high-dimensional data; reverse nearest neighbor (RNN)] cited in F.4.5.8 (p. 658)

[1855] Y. Tao, D. Papadias, and J. Sun. The TPR*-tree: an optimized spatio-temporal access method for predictive queries. In *Proceedings of the 29th International Conference on Very Large Data Bases (VLDB)*, J. C. Freytag, P. C. Lockemann, S. Abiteboul, M. J. Carey, P. G. Selinger, and A. Heuer, eds., pages 790–801, Berlin, Germany, September 2003. [moving objects; TPR*-tree; R-tree] cited in F.2.1.5.2.3 (p. 286), F.3.1.4 (p. 445), F.4 (p. 488)

[1856] Y. Tao, J. Zhang, D. Papadias, and N. Mamoulis. An efficient cost model for optimization of nearest neighbor search in low and medium dimensional spaces. *IEEE Transactions on Knowledge and Data Engineering*, 16(10):1169–1184, October 2004. [points; cost model; nearest neighbor]

[1857] R. E. Tarjan. Efficiency of a good but not linear set union algorithm. *Journal of the ACM*, 22(2):215–225, April 1975. [set union algorithm] cited in A.5.1.1

[1858] R. E. Tarjan. Updating a balanced search tree in $O(1)$ rotations. *Information Processing Letters*, 16(5):253–257, June 1983. [balanced binary search tree] cited in D.3.2.3, D.3.2.3.s, F.3.1.3 (p. 441), F.3.1.3.s (p. 821)

[1859] R. E. Tarjan. *Data Structures and Network Algorithms*. SIAM, Philadelphia, PA, 1984. [network algorithms; general] cited in D.2.9.s, F.1.9.s (p. 776)

[1860] R. E. Tarjan and J. van Leeuwen. Worst-case analysis of set union algorithms. *Journal of the ACM*, 31(2):245–281, April 1984. [set union algorithm] cited in A.5.1.1

[1861] M. Tasan and Z. M. Özsoyoglu. Improvements in distance-based indexing. In *Proceedings of the 16th International Conference on Scientific and Statistical Database Management*, M. Hatzopoulos and Y. Manolopoulos, eds., pages 161–170, Santorini, Greece, June 2004. [metric spaces; nearest neighbor; vp-tree] cited in F.4.5.2.1.2 (p. 606)

[1862] G. Taubin, A. Guéziec, W. Horn, and F. Lazarus. Progressive forest split compression. In *Proceedings of the SIGGRAPH'98 Conference*, pages 123–132, Orlando, FL, July 1998. [surfaces; simplification; progressive compression] cited in F.2.2.3.4 (p. 399)

[1863] J. Tayeb, Ö. Ulusoy, and O. Wolfson. A quadtree-based dynamic attribute indexing method. *The Computer Journal*, 41(3):185–200, March 1998. [lines; moving objects]

[1864] D. C. Taylor and W. A. Barrett. An algorithm for continuous resolution polygonalizations of a discrete surface. In *Proceedings of Graphics Interface'94*, pages 33–42, Banff, Alberta, Canada, May 1994. [surfaces; simplification; level of detail (LOD); triangulated irregular network (TIN)]; region quadtree cited in F.2.2.4 (p. 402)

[1865] Y. Theodoridis and T. Sellis. Optimization issues in R-tree construction. In *IGIS'94: Geographic Information Systems, International Workshop on Advanced Research in Geographic Information Systems*, J. Nievergelt, T. Roos, H.-J. Schek, and P. Widmayer, eds., pages 270–273, Monte Verità, Ascona, Switzerland, March 1994. Also National Technical University of Athens Knowledge and Database Systems Laboratory Report KDBSLAB–TR–93–08, October 1993. [rectangles; R-tree] cited in F.2.1.5.2.3 (pp. 283, 287)

[1866] Y. Theodoridis and T. K. Sellis. A model for the prediction of R-tree performance. In *Proceedings of the 15th ACM SIGACT-SIGMOD-SIGART Symposium on Principles of Database Systems (PODS)*, pages 161–171, Montréal, Canada, June 1996. [rectangles; R-tree; cost model]

[1867] Y. Theodoridis, E. Stefanakis, and T. K. Sellis. Cost models for join queries in spatial databases. In *Proceedings of the 14th IEEE International Conference on Data Engineering*, pages 476–483, Orlando, FL, February 1998. [spatial join; cost model]

[1868] Y. Theodoridis, E. Stefanakis, and T. K. Sellis. Efficient cost models for spatial queries using R-trees. *IEEE Transactions on Knowledge and Data Engineering*, 12(1):19–32, January/February 2000. [R-tree; cost model]

[1869] W. C. Thibault and B. F. Naylor. Set operations on polyhedra using binary space partitioning trees. *Computer Graphics*, 21(4):153–162, July 1987. Also in *Proceedings of the SIGGRAPH'87 Conference*, Anaheim, CA, July 1987. [volumes; BSP tree] cited in F.2.1.3.1 (p. 236)

[1870] A. H. Thiessen. Precipitation averages for large areas. *Monthly Weather Review*, 39(7):1082–1084, July 1911. [points; regions; nearest neighbor; Voronoi diagram] cited in F.2.2.1.4 (p. 346)

[1871] J. P. Thirion. Tries: data structures based on a binary representation for ray tracing. In *Proceedings of the EUROGRAPHICS'90 Conference*, C. E. Vandoni and D. A. Duce, eds., pages 531–542, Montreux, Switzerland, September 1990. [volumes; ray tracing]

[1872] A. L. Thomas. Geometric modeling and display primitives towards specialized hardware. *Computer Graphics*, 17(3):299–310, July 1983. Also in *Proceedings of the SIGGRAPH'83 Conference*, Detroit, July 1983. [hardware] cited in D.5.5

[1873] A. Thomasian, V. Castelli, and C.-S. Li. Rcsvd: recursive clustering with singular value decomposition for dimension reduction in content-based retrieval of large image/video databases. Technical Report RC 20704, IBM T. J. Watson Research Center, Yorktown Heights, NY, January 1997. [points; high-dimensional data; similarity searching; Singular Value Decomposition (SVD)] cited in F.4.6.4.1 (p. 675)

[1874] M. Tikkanen, M. Mäntylä, and M. Tamminen. GWB/DMS: a geometric data manager. In *Proceedings of the EUROGRAPH-ICS'83 Conference*, P. J. W. ten Hagen, ed., pages 99–111, Zagreb, Yugoslavia, September 1983. [volumes]

[1875] R. B. Tilove. Exploiting spatial and structural locality in geometric modeling. Production Automation Project Technical Memorandum TM–38, University of Rochester, Rochester, NY, 1981. [volumes] cited in D.5.5.1

[1876] R. B. Tilove. A null-object detection algorithm for constructive solid geometry. *Communications of the ACM*, 27(7):684–694, July 1984. [volumes; constructive solid geometry (CSG)] cited in D.5.5.1, D.5.5.2

[1877] W. Tobler and Z. T. Chen. A quadtree for global information storage. *Geographical Analysis*, 18(4):360–371, October 1986. [surfaces] cited in D.1.4.1, F.2.1.2.11 (p. 232)

[1878] S. B. Tor and A. E. Middleditch. Convex decomposition for simple polygons. *ACM Transactions on Graphics*, 3(4):244–265, October 1984. [regions; convex difference tree (CDT)] cited in F.2.1.4.2 (p. 262)

[1879] W. S. Torgerson. Multidimensional scaling: theory and method. *Psychometrika*, 17(1):401–419, 1952. [metric space embedding; multidimensional scaling (MDS)] cited in F.4.7.1 (p. 689)

[1880] K. E. Torrance and E. M. Sparrow. Theory for off-specular reflection from roughened surfaces. *Journal of the Optical Society of America*, 57:1105–1114, September 1967. [surfaces; optics; reflectance] cited in A.7.2.1

[1881] D. Tost, A. Puig, and I. Navazo. Visualization of mixed scenes based on volumes and surfaces. In *Proceedings of the 4th Eurographics Workshop on Rendering*, M. Cohen, C. Puech, and F. Sillion, eds., pages 281–293, Paris, France, June 1993. [volumes; surfaces; face octree]

[1882] G. T. Toussaint. Pattern recognition and geometrical complexity. In *Proceedings of the 5th International Conference on Pattern Recognition*, pages 1324–1346, Miami Beach, FL, December 1980. [computational geometry; survey] cited in D.P, D.4, D.4.2.3, D.4.3, F.P (p. xx)

[1883] G. T. Toussaint. The relative neighborhood graph of a finite planar set. *Pattern Recognition*, 12(4):261–268, 1980. [points; relative neighborhood graph (RNG); Delaunay triangulation (DT)] cited in F.4.5.6 (pp. 639–640)

[1884] G. T. Toussaint, ed. *Computational Geometry*. North-Holland, Amsterdam, The Netherlands, 1985. [computational geometry; general] cited in F.P (p. xix)

[1885] G. T. Toussaint. What is computational geometry? *Proceedings of the IEEE*, 80(9):1347–1363, September 1992. [computational geometry; survey] cited in F.P (p. xix)

[1886] G. T. Toussaint and D. Avis. On a convex hull algorithm for polygons and its application to triangulation problems. *Pattern Recognition*, 15(1):23–29, 1982. [regions; triangulations]

[1887] C. Traina Jr., A. J. M. Traina, and C. Faloutsos. Distance exponent: a new concept for selectivity estimation in metric trees. In *Proceedings of the 16th IEEE International Conference on Data Engineering*, page 195, San Diego, CA, February 2000. [metric spaces; selectivity estimation]

[1888] C. Traina Jr., A. J. M. Traina, C. Faloutsos, and B. Seeger. Fast indexing and visualization of metric data sets using slim-trees. *IEEE Transactions on Knowledge and Data Engineering*, 14(2):244–260, March/April 2002. [metric spaces; M-tree; Slim-tree] cited in F.4.5.4.1 (p. 625)

[1889] C. Traina Jr., A. J. M. Traina, B. Seeger, and C. Faloutsos. Slim-trees: high performance metric trees minimizing overlap between nodes. In *Proceedings of the 7th International Conference on Extending Database Technology—EDBT 2000*, C. Zaniolo, P. C. Lockemann, M. H. Scholl, and T. Grust, eds., vol. 1777 of Springer-Verlag Lecture Notes in Computer Science, pages 51–65, Konstanz, Germany, March 2000. [metric spaces; M-tree; Slim-tree] cited in F.4.5.4.1 (p. 625)

[1890] D. Treglia, ed. *Game Programming Gems 3*. Charles River Media, Hingham, MA, 2002. [game programming; general] cited in F.P (p. xvii)

[1891] H. Tropf and H. Herzog. Multidimensional range search in dynamically balanced trees. *Angewandte Informatik*, 23(2):71–77, February 1981. [points; range query] cited in D.2.7, F.1.6 (pp. 91–93), F.2.1.5.2.2 (p. 280)

[1892] Y.-H. Tsai, K.-L. Chung, and W.-Y. Chen. A strip-splitting-based optimal algorithm for decomposing a query window into maximal quadtree blocks. *IEEE Transactions on Knowledge and Data Engineering*, 16(4):519–523, April 2004. [regions; region quadtree; window query]

[1893] L. W. Tucker. *Computer vision using quadtree refinement*. PhD thesis, Department of Electrical Engineering and Computer Science, Polytechnic Institute of New York, Brooklyn, NY, May 1984. [regions; neighbor finding; region quadtree] cited in A.3.2.3

[1894] L. W. Tucker. Control strategy for an expert vision system using quadtree refinement. In *Proceedings of the Workshop on Computer Vision: Representation and Control*, pages 214–218, Annapolis, MD, April 1984. [regions; quadtree refinement] cited in A.1.4, D.1.3, F.2.4 (p. 425)

[1895] T. Tzouramanis, M. Vassilakopoulos, and Y. Manolopoulos. Overlapping linear quadtrees: a spatio-temporal access method. In

Proceedings of the 6th ACM International Symposium on Advances in Geographic Information Systems, R. Laurini, K. Makki, and N. Pissinou, eds., pages 1–7, Washington, DC, November 1998. [regions; intervals; spatiotemporal database]

[1896] J. K. Uhlmann. Metric trees. *Applied Mathematics Letters*, 4(5):61–62, 1991. [metric spaces; nearest neighbor; metric tree] cited in F.4.5 (p. 598), F.4.5.2.1.1 (pp. 604–605), F.4.5.5.2 (p. 636)

[1897] J. K. Uhlmann. Satisfying general proximity/similarity queries with metric trees. *Information Processing Letters*, 40(4):175–179, November 1991. [metric spaces; nearest neighbor; metric tree; vp-tree; gh-tree] cited in F.4.1.7 (p. 517), F.4.2 (p. 517), F.4.2.2 (p. 521), F.4.5 (pp. 598–599), F.4.5.2.1.1 (p. 604), F.4.5.2.3 (p. 609), F.4.5.3.1 (pp. 613–614), F.4.5.5.2 (p. 636), F.4.5.2.1.1.s (p. 855)

[1898] L. Uhr. Layered "recognition cone" networks that preprocess, classify, and describe. *IEEE Transactions on Computers*, 21(7):758–768, July 1972. [regions; recognition cone; pyramid] cited in A.1.4, D.1.3, F.2.4 (p. 424)

[1899] J. D. Ullman. *Principles of Database Systems*. Computer Science Press, Rockville, MD, second edition, 1982. [database systems; general] cited in D.3.1, F.3 (p. 427)

[1900] T. Ulrich. Continuous LOD terrain meshing using adaptive quadtrees. In *gamasutra.com*. February 2000. *http://www.gamasutra.com/features/20000228/ulrich_01.htm*. [surfaces; level of detail (LOD); restricted quadtree]

[1901] T. Ulrich. Loose octrees. In *Game Programming Gems*, M. A. DeLoura, ed., pages 444–453. Charles River Media, Rockland, MA, 2000. [regions; loose octree; loose quadtree; MX-CIF quadtree; fieldtree] cited in F.2.1.4.1 (pp. 257, 259), F.3.4.2 (p. 475)

[1902] A. Unnikrishnan, P. Shankar, and Y. V. Venkatesh. Threaded linear hierarchical quadtrees for computation of geometric properties of binary images. *IEEE Transactions on Software Engineering*, 14(5):659–665, May 1988. [regions; connected component labeling; region quadtree]

[1903] A. Unnikrishnan and Y. V. Venkatesh. On the conversion of raster to linear quadtrees. Technical report, Department of Electrical Engineering, Indian Institute of Science, Bangalore, India, May 1984. [regions; region quadtree] cited in A.4.2.1.s

[1904] A. Unnikrishnan, Y. V. Venkatesh, and P. Shankar. Connected component labeling using quadtrees—a bottom-up approach. *Computer Journal*, 30(2):176–182, April 1987. [regions; connected component labeling; region quadtree]

[1905] A. Unnikrishnan, Y. V. Venkatesh, and P. Shankar. Distribution of black nodes at various levels in a linear quadtree. *Pattern Recognition Letters*, 6(5):341–342, December 1987. [regions]

[1906] P. M. Vaidya. Geometry helps in matching. In *Proceedings of the 20th Annual ACM Symposium on the Theory of Computing*, pages 422–425, Chicago, May 1988. [points; Euclidean matching problem] cited in D.2.9.s, F.1.9.s (p. 776)

[1907] P. M. Vaidya. Approximate minimum weight matching on points in k-dimensional space. *Algorithmica*, 4(4):569–583, 1989. [points; minimum-weight matching problem]

[1908] P. M. Vaidya. An $O(n\log n)$ algorithm for the all-nearest-neighbor problem. *Discrete & Computational Geometry*, 4(2):101–115, 1989. Also see *Proceedings of the 27th IEEE Annual Symposium on Foundations of Computer Science*, pages 117–122, Toronto, Canada, October 1986. [points; all nearest neighbors query] cited in F.1.5.2.2 (p. 73), F.1.5.2.7 (p. 87), F.4 (pp. 485–486)

[1909] P. M. Vaidya. Space-time trade-offs for orthogonal range queries. *SIAM Journal on Computing*, 18(4):748–758, August 1989. [points; range query]

[1910] V. Vaishnavi and D. Wood. Data structures for the rectangle containment and enclosure problems. *Computer Graphics and Image Processing*, 13(4):372–384, August 1980. [rectangles; segment tree] cited in D.3.2.4, D.3.2.4.s, F.3.1.4 (p. 444), F.3.1.4.s (p. 822)

[1911] V. Vaishnavi and D. Wood. Rectilinear line segment intersection, layered segment trees and dynamization. *Journal of Algorithms*, 3(2):160–176, June 1982. [rectangles; layered tree] cited in D.3.2.4.s, F.3.1.4.s (p. 823)

[1912] V. K. Vaishnavi. Multidimensional height-balanced trees. *IEEE Transactions on Computers*, 33(4):334–343, April 1984. [points;

balanced binary search tree] cited in D.2.4.1, D.2.4.1.s, F.1.5.1.4 (p. 66), F.1.5.1.1.s (p. 762)

[1913] V. K. Vaishnavi. Multidimensional balanced binary trees. *IEEE Transactions on Computers*, 38(7):968–985, July 1989. [points; balanced binary search tree]

[1914] K. E. Van Camp. A quadcode class for mapping. *The C Users Journal*, 10(8):17–32, August 1992. [regions; region quadtree]

[1915] D. J. Vanderschel. Divided leaf octal trees. Research Note, Schlumberger-Doll Research, Ridgefield, CT, March 1984. [volumes; PM octree; divided-leaf octal tree] cited in A.1.3, D.5.3, F.2.2.2.7 (p. 370)

[1916] G. Vaněček. Brep-index: a multidimensional space partitioning tree. *International Journal of Computational Geometry Applications*, 1(3):243–261, 1991. [volumes; BSP tree]

[1917] V. Vapnik. *Statistical Learning Theory*. John Wiley & Sons, New York, 1998. [support vector machines (SVM)] cited in F.4.4.4 (p. 576)

[1918] T. Varady and M. J. Pratt. Design techniques for the definition of solid objects with free-form geometry. *Computer Aided Geometric Design*, 1:207–225, 1984. [surfaces]

[1919] A. Varshney. *Hierarchical geometric approximations*. PhD thesis, Department of Computer Science, University of North Carolina, Chapel Hill, NC, 1994. Also Computer Science Technical Report TR94–050. [surfaces; simplification] cited in F.2.2.3.4 (p. 395)

[1920] M. Vassilakopoulos and Y. Manolopoulos. Analytical comparison of two spatial data structures. *Information Systems*, 19(7):569–582, October 1994. [regions; region quadtree; bintree; space requirements]

[1921] M. Vassilakopoulos and Y. Manolopoulos. Dynamic inverted quadtree: a structure for pictorial databases. *Information Systems*, 20(6):483–500, 1995. [regions; feature-based queries; location-based queries; pyramid]

[1922] M. Vassilakopoulos, Y. Manolopoulos, and K. Economou. Overlapping quadtrees for the representation of similar images. *Image and Vision Computing*, 11(5):257–262, June 1993. [regions; region quadtree]

[1923] H. M. Veenhof, P. M. G. Apers, and M. A. W. Houtsma. Optimisation of spatial joins using filters. In *Advances in Databases, Proceedings of 13th British National Conference on Databases (BNCOD13)*, C. A. Goble and J. A. Keane, eds., vol. 940 of Springer-Verlag Lecture Notes in Computer Science, pages 136–154, Manchester, United Kingdom, July 1995. [regions; spatial join; minimum bounding box] cited in F.1.5.1.4 (p. 64), F.2.1.1 (p. 195)

[1924] J. Veenstra and N. Ahuja. Octree generation from silhouette views of an object. In *Proceedings of the International Conference on Robotics*, pages 843–848, St. Louis, MO, March 1985. [volumes; region octree] cited in A.4.6, D.5.2

[1925] J. Veenstra and N. Ahuja. Efficient octree generation from silhouettes. In *Proceedings of Computer Vision and Pattern Recognition'86*, pages 537–542, Miami Beach, FL, June 1986. [volumes; region octree] cited in A.4.6, A.4.6.s, D.5.2, D.5.2.s

[1926] J. Veenstra and N. Ahuja. Line drawings of octree-represented objects. *ACM Transactions on Graphics*, 7(1):61–75, January 1988. [volumes; region octree] cited in D.5.4

[1927] R. C. Veltkamp. Hierarchical approximation and localization. *The Visual Computer*, 14(10):471–487, 1998. [lines; regions; strip tree; HAL tree] cited in F.2.2.3.3 (pp. 389–391)

[1928] S. Venkatesh and D. Kieronska. Distributed quadtree processing of vector data. In *Proceedings of the 1st International Workshop on Parallel Processing*, pages 388–393, Bangalore, India, December 1994. [lines; parallel processing]

[1929] E. Vidal. New formulation and improvements of the nearest-neighbour approximating and eliminating search algorithm (AESA). *Pattern Recognition Letters*, 15(1):1–7, January 1994. [metric spaces; nearest neighbor; distance matrix; AESA] cited in F.4.5.7.1 (pp. 643, 645)

[1930] E. Vidal Ruiz. An algorithm for finding nearest neighbors in (approximately) constant average time. *Pattern Recognition Letters*, 4(3):145–157, July 1986. [metric spaces; nearest neighbor; distance matrix; AESA] cited in F.4.1.7 (p. 517), F.4.2 (p. 517), F.4.5

(pp. 598–599), F.4.5.1 (p. 601), F.4.5.7.1 (pp. 643–645), F.4.7.2.1 (p. 691)

[1931] T. Vijlbrief and P. van Oosterom. The GEO++ system: an extensible GIS. In *Proceedings of the 5th International Symposium on Spatial Data Handling*, pages 40–50, Charleston, SC, August 1992. [spatial database]

[1932] J. M. Vilar. Reducing the overhead of the AESA metric-space nearest neighbour searching algorithm. *Information Processing Letters*, 56(5):265–271, December 1995. [metric spaces; nearest neighbor; distance matrix; ROAESA] cited in F.4.5.7.3 (pp. 649–650)

[1933] J. S. Vitter. External memory algorithms and data structures dealing with massive data. *ACM Computing Surveys*, 33(2):209–271, June 2001. [points; external memory representations; survey] cited in F.P (p. xix)

[1934] J. Vleugels and R. C. Veltkamp. Efficient image retrieval through vantage objects. *Pattern Recognition*, 35(1):69–80, January 2002. [metric spaces; vp-tree] cited in F.4.7.1 (p. 688)

[1935] H. B. Voelcker and A. A. G. Requicha. Geometric modeling of mechanical parts and processes. *IEEE Computer*, 10(12):48–57, December 1977. [volumes; solid modeling; constructive solid geometry (CSG); survey] cited in D.3.4, D.5.5, F.3.3.1 (p. 453)

[1936] A. Voigtmann, L. Becker, and K. Hinrichs. A hierarchical model for multiresolution surface reconstruction. *Graphical Models and Image Processing*, 59(5):333–348, September 1997. [surfaces; multiresolution modeling]

[1937] A. Voisard. *Bases de données géographiques: du modeéle de données a l'interface utilisateur*. PhD thesis, L'université de Paris-Sud—Orsay, Paris, France, October 1992. [spatial database; user interface]

[1938] A. Voisard and B. David. A database perspective on geospatial data modeling. *IEEE Transactions on Knowledge and Data Engineering*, 14(2):226–243, March/April 2002. [spatial database; survey] cited in F.P (p. xix)

[1939] B. Von Herzen. Applications of surface networks to sampling problems in computer graphics. Computer Science Technical Report Caltech-CS–TR–88–15, California Institute of Technology, Pasadena, CA, 1988. [surfaces; restricted quadtree] cited in A.7.1.6, D.5.6, D.5.8

[1940] B. Von Herzen and A. H. Barr. Accurate triangulations of deformed, intersecting surfaces. *Computer Graphics*, 21(4):103–110, July 1987. Also in *Proceedings of the SIGGRAPH'87 Conference*, Anaheim, CA, July 1987. [surfaces; restricted quadtree] cited in A.7.1.6, D.5.6, D.5.8, F.1.5.1.4 (p. 64), F.2.2.2.10 (pp. 381–382), F.2.2.4 (pp. 405–406)

[1941] G. Voronoi. Nouvelles applications des paramètres continus à la théorie des formes quadratiques. Deuxième mémoire: Recherches sur les parallèllòedres primitifs. Seconde partie. *Journal für die Reine und Angewandte Mathematik*, 136(2):67–181, 1909. [points; regions; nearest neighbor; Voronoi diagram] cited in F.1.5.1.4 (p. 69), F.2.2.1.4 (p. 346)

[1942] J. Vörös. A strategy for repetitive neighbor finding in images represented by quadtrees. *Pattern Recognition Letters*, 18(10):955–962, October 1997. [regions; neighbor finding]

[1943] J. Vuillemin. A data structure for manipulating priority queues. *Communications of the ACM*, 21(4):309–315, April 1978. [binomial heap; priority queue] cited in F.1.3 (p. 20)

[1944] J. Vuillemin. A unifying look at data structures. *Communications of the ACM*, 23(4):229–239, April 1980. [points; Cartesian tree] cited in F.1.3 (pp. 19, 27), F.3.1.2 (p. 438)

[1945] D. Wagner and T. Willhalm. Geometric speed-up techniques for finding shortest paths in large sparse graphs. In *Proceedings of the 11th Annual European Symposium on Algorithms (ESA 2003)*, G. Di Battista and U. Zwick, eds., vol. 2832 of Springer-Verlag Lecture Notes in Computer Science, pages 776–787, Budapest, Hungary, September 2003. [lines; points; spatial networks; shortest path algorithm; R-tree] cited in F.4.1.6 (pp. 510, 515)

[1946] M. Walker, R. S. Lo, and S. F. Cheng. Hidden line detection in polytree representations. *Computers and Graphics*, 12(1):65–69, 1988. [volumes; polytree]

[1947] A. F. Wallis and J. R. Woodwark. Creating large solid models for NC toolpath verification. In *Proceedings of the CAD'84 Conference*, pages 455–460, Brighton, United Kingdom, 1984. [volumes] cited in D.5.5, F.2.2.2.7 (p. 372)

[1948] T. R. Walsh. On the size of quadtrees generalized to *d*-dimensional binary pictures. *Computers and Mathematics with Applications*, 11(11):1089–1097, November 1985. [hypervolumes; *d*-dimensional quadtree; space requirements] cited in A.1.2, A.1.2.s, D.1.5, D.1.5.s, F.2.2.2.2 (p. 358), F.2.2.2.2.s (p. 803)

[1949] T. R. Walsh. Efficient axis-translation of binary digital pictures by blocks in linear quadtree representation. *Computer Vision, Graphics, and Image Processing*, 41(3):282–292, March 1988. [volumes; region octree] cited in A.6.5.3, A.6.5.3.s

[1950] J. T.-L. Wang, X. Wang, K.-I. Lin, D. Shasha, B. A. Shapiro, and K. Zhang. Evaluating a class of distance-mapping algorithms for data mining and clustering. In *Proceedings of the ACM SIGKDD International Conference on Knowledge Discovery and Data Mining*, pages 307–311, San Diego, CA, August 1999. [metric space embedding; MetricMap; FastMap] cited in F.4 (p. 489), F.4.7.3 (p. 697), F.4.7.3.8 (p. 708), F.4.7.3.9 (pp. 710–711)

[1951] T. L. Wang and D. Shasha. Query processing for distance metrics. In *Proceedings of the 16th International Conference on Very Large Databases (VLDB)*, D. McLeod, R. Sacks-Davis, and H.-J. Schek, eds., pages 602–613, Brisbane, Australia, August 1990. [metric spaces; distance matrix] cited in F.4.1.7 (p. 517), F.4.2 (p. 517), F.4.5 (p. 598), F.4.5.7.1 (p. 645), F.4.5.7.3 (pp. 647–648), F.4.7.2.1 (p. 691)

[1952] W. Wang, J. Yang, and R. Muntz. PK-tree: a spatial index structure for high dimensional point data. In *Proceedings of the 5th International Conference on Foundations of Data Organization and Algorithms (FODO)*, K. Tanaka and S. Ghandeharizadeh, eds., pages 27–36, Kobe, Japan, November 1998. Also University of California at Los Angeles Computer Science Technical Report 980032, September 1998. [points; PK-tree; decoupling] cited in F.1.7.1.6 (p. 117), F.1.8 (p. 164), F.1.8.6 (p. 182), F.2.1.2.4 (p. 216)

[1953] W. Wang, J. Yang, and R. R. Muntz. STING: a statistical information grid approach to spatial data mining. In *Proceedings of the 23rd International Conference on Very Large Data Bases (VLDB)*, M. Jarke, M. J. Carey, K. R. Dittrich, F. H. Lochovsky, P. Loucopoulos, and M. A. Jeusfeld, eds., pages 186–195, Athens, Greece, August 1997. [regions; pyramid; feature-based queries; spatial data mining] cited in F.2 (p. 192)

[1954] W. Wang, J. Yang, and R. R. Muntz. An approach to active spatial data mining based on statistical information. *IEEE Transactions on Knowledge and Data Engineering*, 12(5):715–728, September/October 2000. [points; spatial data mining]

[1955] X. Wang, J. T.-L. Wang, K.-I. Lin, D. Shasha, B. A. Shapiro, and K. Zhang. An index structure for data mining and clustering. *Knowledge and Information Systems*, 2(2):161–184, May 2000. [metric space embedding; MetricMap; FastMap] cited in F.4.7.3.9 (p. 711)

[1956] Y. Wang and W. A. Davis. Octant priority for radiosity image rendering. In *Proceedings of Graphics Interface'90*, pages 83–91, Halifax, Newfoundland, Canada, May 1990. [volumes; radiosity]

[1957] G. J. Ward, F. M. Rubinstein, and R. D. Clear. A ray tracing solution for diffuse interreflection. *Computer Graphics*, 22(4):85–92, August 1988. Also in *Proceedings of the SIGGRAPH'88 Conference*, Atlanta, GA, August 1988. [volumes; ray tracing]

[1958] J. M. Ware and C. B. Jones. Matching and aligning features in overlayed coverages. In *Proceedings of the 6th ACM International Symposium on Advances in Geographic Information Systems*, R. Laurini, K. Makki, and N. Pissinou, eds., pages 28–33, Washington, DC, November 1998. [map conflation] cited in F.4 (p. 486)

[1959] J. E. Warnock. A hidden line algorithm for halftone picture representation. Computer Science Technical Report TR 4–5, University of Utah, Salt Lake City, UT, May 1968. [regions; hidden-line removal] cited in A.1.4, A.7.1, A.7.1.2, D.1.3, F.2.4 (p. 423)

[1960] J. E. Warnock. The hidden line problem and the use of halftone displays. In *Pertinent Concepts in Computer Graphics—Proceedings of the 2nd University of Illinois Conference on Computer Graphics*, M. Faiman and J. Nievergelt, eds., pages 154–163, Urbana-Champaign, IL, March 1969. University of Illinois Press. [regions; hidden-line removal] cited in A.7.1

[1961] J. E. Warnock. A hidden surface algorithm for computer generated half tone pictures. Computer Science Technical Report TR 4–15, University of Utah, Salt Lake City, UT, June 1969. [regions; hidden-surface removal; edge quadtree] cited in A.1.4, A.7.1.2, D.1.3, D.4.2.1, F.2.2.2.3 (p. 360), F.2.4 (p. 423)

[1962] J. Warren and H. Weimer. *Subdivision Methods for Geometric Design: A Constructive Approach*. Morgan-Kaufmann, San Francisco, 2002. [geometric modeling; general] cited in F.P (p. xix)

[1963] W. Waterfeld, A. Wolf, and D. U. Horn. How to make spatial access methods extensible. In *Proceedings of the 3rd International Symposium on Spatial Data Handling*, pages 321–335, Sydney, Australia, August 1988. [spatial database]

[1964] D. F. Watson. Computing the *n*-dimensional Delaunay tessellation with application to Voronoi polytopes. *Computer Journal*, 24(2):167–172, May 1981. [regions; Delaunay triangulation (DT)] cited in F.2.2.1.4 (p. 349)

[1965] D. F. Watson and G. M. Philip. Systematic triangulations. *Computer Vision, Graphics, and Image Processing*, 26(2):217–223, May 1984. [regions; triangulations] cited in A.4.6, D.4.3.1, D.5.2, F.2.1.3.2 (p. 241)

[1966] T. C. Waugh and R. G. Healey. The GEOVIEW design: a relational data base approach to geographical data handling. In *Proceedings of the 2nd International Symposium on Spatial Data Handling*, pages 193–212, Seattle, WA, July 1986. [spatial database]

[1967] R. E. Webber. *Analysis of quadtree algorithms*. PhD thesis, Computer Science Department, University of Maryland, College Park, MD, March 1984. Also Computer Science Technical Report TR–1376. [regions; lines; PM quadtree] cited in A.3.3.4, A.4.3.1, A.4.3.1.s, A.4.3.2, A.5.1.2, A.5.1.2.s, D.4.2.3

[1968] R. E. Webber. Personal communication. 1985. [lines; PM quadtree] cited in A.3.2.1

[1969] R. E. Webber and M. B. Dillencourt. Compressing quadtrees via common subtree merging. *Pattern Recognition Letters*, 9(3):193–200, April 1989. Also University of Maryland Computer Science Technical Report TR–2137, October 1988. [region quadtree; common subcube elimination]

[1970] R. E. Webber and H. Samet. Linear-time border-tracing algorithms for quadtrees. *Algorithmica*, 8(1):39–54, 1992. Also University of Maryland Computer Science Technical Report TR–2309, August 1989. [regions; boundary following; region quadtree]

[1971] R. Weber and K. Böhm. Trading quality for time with nearest-neighbor search. In *Proceedings of the 7th International Conference on Extending Database Technology—EDBT 2000*, C. Zaniolo, P. C. Lockemann, M. H. Scholl, and T. Grust, eds., vol. 1777 of Springer-Verlag Lecture Notes in Computer Science, pages 21–35, Konstanz, Germany, March 2000. [points; high-dimensional data; sequential scan; incremental nearest neighbor algorithm; approximate nearest neighbor] cited in F.4.1.7 (p. 516), F.4.4.8 (p. 596)

[1972] R. Weber, K. Böhm, and H.-J. Schek. Interactive-time similarity search for large image collections using parallel VA-files. In *Proceedings of the 16th IEEE International Conference on Data Engineering*, page 197, San Diego, CA, February 2000. [points; high-dimensional data; sequential scan; VA-file; parallel processing]

[1973] R. Weber, H.-J. Schek, and S. Blott. A quantitative analysis and performance study for similarity-search methods in high-dimensional spaces. In *Proceedings of the 24th International Conference on Very Large Data Bases (VLDB)*, A. Gupta, O. Shmueli, and J. Widom, eds., pages 194–205, New York, August 1998. [points; high-dimensional data; sequential scan; VA-file] cited in F.4.4.8 (pp. 592, 594, 596)

[1974] W. Weber. Three types of map data structures, their ANDs and NOTs, and a possible OR. In *Proceedings of the 1st International Advanced Study Symposium on Topological Data Structures for Geographic Information Systems*, G. Dutton, ed., Harvard Papers on Geographic Information Systems. Addison-Wesley, Reading, MA, 1978. [database systems; general] cited in A.2.1.1

[1975] H. Weghorst, G. Hooper, and D. P. Greenberg. Improved computational methods for ray tracing. *ACM Transactions on Graphics*, 3(1):547–55, January 1984. [volumes; ray tracing] cited in A.7.2.1, A.7.2.2

[1976] B. W. Weide. Statistical methods in algorithm design and analysis. Computer Science Technical Report CMU–CS–78–142, Carnegie-Mellon University, Pittsburgh, PA, August 1978. [bin method] cited in D.3.2.2, D.3.2.4, F.3.1.2 (p. 434), F.3.1.4 (p. 443)

[1977] K. Weiler. Edge-based data structures for solid modeling in a curved-surface environment. *IEEE Computer Graphics and Applications*, 5(1):21–40, January 1985. [volumes; winged-edge representation; boundary model (BRep)] cited in D.5.4, F.2.2.1.2 (p. 318)

[1978] K. Weiler. *Topological structures for geometric modeling*. PhD thesis, Computer and Systems Engineering Department, Rensselaer Polytechnic Institute, Troy, NY, August 1986. [volumes; winged-edge representation; boundary model (BRep)] cited in D.5.4, F.2.2.1.1 (pp. 316–317), F.2.2.1.7 (p. 354)

[1979] K. Weiler. The radial-edge data structure: topological representation for non-manifold geometric boundary modeling. In *Geometric Modeling for CAD Applications*, M. J. Wozny, H. W. McLaughlin, and J. L. Encarnaçao, eds., pages 3–36. North-Holland, Amsterdam, The Netherlands, 1988. Also in *Proceedings of the IFIP WG 5.2 Working Conference*, Rensselaerville, NY, May 1986. [surfaces; half-edge representation; radial-edge representation; nonmanifold objects; boundary model (BRep)] cited in F.2.2.1.1 (p. 316)

[1980] K. Weiler and P. Atherton. Hidden surface removal using polygon area sorting. *Computer Graphics*, 11(2):214–222, Summer 1977. Also in *Proceedings of the SIGGRAPH'77 Conference*, San Jose, CA, July 1977. [volumes; hidden-line removal; hidden-surface removal] cited in A.7.1, A.7.1.3, A.7.3

[1981] A. Weiser. *Local-order adaptive finite-element methods with a posteriori error estimators for elliptic partial differential equations*. PhD thesis, Yale University, New Haven, CT, 1981. [surfaces; restricted quadtree; finite element analysis] cited in F.2.2.4.s (p. 814)

[1982] E. Welzl. Smallest enclosing disks (balls and ellipsoids). In *Proceedings of New Results and New Trends in Computer Science*, H. Maurer, ed., vol. 555 of Springer-Verlag Lecture Notes in Computer Science, pages 359–370, Graz, Austria, June 1991. [linear programming; minimum bounding hypersphere] cited in F.4.4.2.s (p. 852)

[1983] J. Weng and N. Ahuja. Octrees of objects in arbitrary motion: representation and efficiency. *Computer Vision, Graphics, and Image Processing*, 39(2):167–185, August 1987. [volumes; region octree] cited in A.6.5.1, D.5.5.1

[1984] K. H. Werner, S. Yie, F. M. Ottliczky, H. B. Prince, and H. Diebel. ME CAD geometry construction, dimensioning, hatching, and part structuring. *Hewlett-Packard Journal*, 38(5):16–29, May 1987. [points]

[1985] L. Weyten and W. De Pauw. Performance predictions for adaptive quad tree graphical data structures. *IEEE Transactions on Computer-Aided Design*, 8(11):1218–1222, November 1989. [rectangles; bucket rectangle PM quadtree; quad list quadtree (QLQT)] cited in F.3.4.3 (p. 481)

[1986] L. Weyten and W. De Pauw. Quad list quad data structures: a geometrical data structure with improved performance for large region queries. *IEEE Transactions on Computer-Aided Design*, 8(3):229–233, March 1989. [rectangles; bucket rectangle PM quadtree; quad list quadtree (QLQT)] cited in F.3.4.2 (p. 477), F.3.4.3 (pp. 481–482)

[1987] K.-Y. Whang. The multilevel grid file—a dynamic hierarchical multidimensional file structure. In *Proceedings of the 2nd International Conference on Database Systems for Advanced Applications (DASFAA'91)*, A. Makinouchi, ed., pages 449–459, Tokyo, Japan, April 1991. [points; multilevel grid file] cited in F.3.3.3 (p. 465)

[1988] K.-Y. Whang, J.-W. Song, J.-W. Chang, J.-Y. Kim, W.-S. Cho, C.-M. Park, and I.-Y. Song. Octree-R: an adaptive octree for efficient ray tracing. *IEEE Transactions on Visualization and Computer Graphics*, 1(4):343–349, December 1995. [volumes; region octree; ray tracing]

[1989] D. A. White and R. Jain. Algorithms and strategies for similarity retrieval. Technical Report VCL–96–101, Visual Computing Laboratory, University of California, San Diego, CA, 1996. [points; high-dimensional data; approximate nearest neighbor; similarity searching; VAMSplit R-tree; VAMSplit k-d tree] cited in F.1.5.1.4 (p. 58), F.1.7.1.7 (pp. 129–130), F.2.1.5.2.2 (p. 279), F.4.1.7 (p. 516), F.4.2 (p. 517), F.4.4.2 (p. 568), F.4.6.4.1 (p. 675), F.1.7.1.7.s (p. 773)

[1990] D. A. White and R. Jain. Similarity indexing: algorithms and performance. In *Proceedings of the SPIE, Storage and Retrieval of Still Image and Video Databases IV*, I. K. Sethi and R. Jain, eds., vol. 2670, pages 62–73, San Jose, CA, January 1996. [points; similarity searching]

[1991] D. A. White and R. Jain. Similarity indexing with the SS-tree. In *Proceedings of the 12th IEEE International Conference on Data Engineering*, S. Y. W. Su, ed., pages 516–523, New Orleans, LA, February 1996. [points; high-dimensional data; nearest neighbor; similarity searching; R-tree; minimum bounding hypersphere; VAMSplit k-d tree; SS-tree; sphere tree] cited in F.2.1.1 (p. 195), F.4.3 (p. 561), F.4.4.2 (pp. 567–568, 571), F.4.5.3.4 (p. 622), F.4.5.4.1 (p. 625), F.4.6 (p. 663), F.4.6.4.1 (p. 674)

[1992] M. White. N-trees: large ordered indexes for multi-dimensional space. Statistical Research Division, US Bureau of the Census, Washington, DC, 1982. [points; space-filling curve; N order] cited in A.1.4, D.1.3, D.2.7, D.2.7.s, F.1.6 (pp. 92–93), F.2.1.1.2 (p. 200), F.2.1.2.4 (p. 216), F.1.6.s (p. 768)

[1993] R. A. White and S. W. Stemwedel. The quadrilateralized spherical cube and quad-tree for all sky data. In *Astronomical Data Analysis Software and Systems I*, D. M. Worrall, C. Biemesderfer, and J. Barnes, eds., vol. 25 of *Astronomical Society of the Pacific Conference Series*, pages 379–381, San Francisco, 1992. [surfaces]

[1994] T. Whitted. An improved illumination model for shaded display. *Communications of the ACM*, 23(6):343–349, June 1980. [surfaces; shading] cited in A.7.2, A.7.2.1, A.7.2.2, A.7.2.5, A.7.3

[1995] J. Wilhelms and A. van Gelder. Octrees for faster isosurface generation. *ACM Transactions on Graphics*, 11(3):201–227, July 1992. Also see *Proceedings of the ACM Workshop on Volume Visualization*, pages 57–62, San Diego, CA, December 1990 and *Computer Graphics*, 24(5):57–62, November 1990. [surfaces; isosurface octree]

[1996] J. Wilhelms and A. van Gelder. Multi-dimensional trees for controlled volume rendering and compression. In *Proceedings of the 1994 Symposium on Volume Visualization*, pages 17–18, Washington, DC, October 1994. [volumes]

[1997] L. M. Wilke and G. F. Schrack. Filling boundaries by insertion and traversal in a linear quadtree domain. In *Proceedings of the Pacific Rim Conference on Communications, Computers, and Signal Processing*, pages 399–402, Victoria, British Columbia, Canada, May 1995. [regions; region quadtree]

[1998] L. M. Wilke and G. F. Schrack. Improved mirroring and rotation functions for linear quadtree leaves. *Image and Vision Computing*, 13(6):491–495, August 1995. [regions; region quadtree]

[1999] D. E. Willard. Balanced forests of *k-d* trees as a dynamic data structure. Aiken Computation Lab Technical Report TR–23-78, Harvard University, Cambridge, MA, 1978. [points; k-d tree] cited in D.2.4.1, F.1.5.1.4 (p. 65)

[2000] D. E. Willard. Polygon retrieval. *SIAM Journal on Computing*, 11(1):149–165, February 1982. [points; polygon tree] cited in D.2.3, D.2.3.3, D.2.3.3.s, F.1.4.1.3 (pp. 36–37), F.1.5.3 (p. 88), F.1.4.1.3.s (p. 755)

[2001] D. E. Willard. New data structures for orthogonal range queries. *SIAM Journal on Computing*, 14(1):232–253, February 1985. [points]

[2002] R. Williams. The goblin quadtree. *Computer Journal*, 31(4):358–363, August 1988. [regions; region quadtree]

[2003] P. Willis and D. Milford. Browsing high definition colour pictures. *Computer Graphics Forum*, 4(3):203–208, September 1985. [hardware]

[2004] A. Willmott, P. S. Heckbert, and M. Garland. Face cluster radiosity. In *Rendering Techniques: Proceedings of the 10th Eurographics Workshop on Rendering*, D. Lischinski and G. Ward Larson, eds., pages 293–304, Granada, Spain, June 1999. Springer-Verlag.

[surfaces; hierarchical face clustering; surface simplification; radiosity] cited in F.2.2.3.4 (pp. 395, 398), F.2.2.3.4.s (p. 813)

[2005] A. J. Willmott. *Hierarchical radiosity with multiresolution meshes*. PhD thesis, School of Computer Science, Carnegie-Mellon University, Pittsburgh, PA, December 2000. Also Carnegie-Mellon University Technical Report CMU–CS–00–166. [surfaces; hierarchical radiosity; surface simplification; multiresolution modeling; global illumination; hierarchical face clustering] cited in F.2.2.3.4 (p. 398)

[2006] D. S. Wise. Representing matrices as quadtrees for parallel processors. *Information Processing Letters*, 20(4):195–199, May 1985. Also see *ACM SIGSAM Bulletin*, 18(3):24–25, August 1984. [matrix methods] cited in D.2.6.1.s, F.P (p. xviii), F.1.5 (p. 49), F.1.4.2.1.s (p. 757)

[2007] D. S. Wise. Matrix algebra and applicative programming. In *Functional Programming Languages and Computer Architecture*, G. Kahn, ed., vol. 274 of Springer-Verlag Lecture Notes in Computer Science, pages 134–153, Portland, OR, September 1987. [matrix methods] cited in D.2.6.1, F.1.4.2.1 (p. 40)

[2008] D. S. Wise. Ahnentafel indexing into Morton-ordered arrays, or matrix locality for free. In *Proceedings of the 6th International Euro-Par Conference on Parallel Processing, PARPRO'00*, A. Bode, T. Ludwig, and R. Wismüller, eds., vol. 1900 of Springer-Verlag Lecture Notes in Computer Science, pages 774–783, Munich, Germany, January 2000. [parallel processing; matrix methods] cited in F.1.5 (p. 49)

[2009] D. S. Wise, C. L. Citro, J. J. Hursey, F. Liu, and M. A. Rainey. A paradigm for parallel matrix algorithms: scalable Cholesky. In *Proceedings of the 11th International Euro-Par Conference on Parallel Processing (Euro-Par 2005)*, J. C. Cunha and P. D. Medeiros, eds., vol. 3648 of Springer-Verlag Lecture Notes in Computer Science, pages 687–698, Lisbon, Portugal, August 2005. [matrix methods] cited in F.1.5 (p. 49)

[2010] D. S. Wise and J. Franco. Costs of quadtree representation of non-dense matrices. *Journal of Parallel and Distributed Computing*, 9(3):282–296, July 1990. Also Indiana University Computer Science Technical Report 229, October 1987. [matrix methods] cited in D.2.6.1, F.1.4.2.1 (p. 40)

[2011] D. S. Wise, J. D. Frens, Y. Gu, and G. A. Alexander. Language support for Morton-order matrices. In *Proceedings of the 2001 ACM Symposium on Principles and Practice of Parallel Programming*, pages 24–33, Snowbird, UT, June 2001. Also in *SIGPLAN Notices*, 36(7):24–33, July 2001. [matrix methods] cited in F.1.4.2.1 (p. 40)

[2012] I. H. Witten and B. Wyvill. On the generation and use of space-filling curves. *Software—Practice and Experience*, 13(6):519–525, June 1983. [regions; space-filling curve] cited in A.1.4, D.1.3, D.2.7.s, F.1.6.s (p. 768), F.2.1.1.2.s (p. 777)

[2013] O. Wolfson. Moving objects information management: the database challenge. In *Proceedings of 5th International Workshop on Next Generation Information Technologies and Systems NGITS 2002*, pages 75–89, Caesarea, Israel, June 2002. [moving objects; survey] cited in F.P (p. xvii)

[2014] O. Wolfson, P. Sistla, B. Xu, J. Zhou, and S. Chamberlain. DOMINO: databases for moving objects tracking. In *Proceedings of the ACM SIGMOD Conference*, pages 547–549, Philadelphia, PA, June 1999. [moving objects]

[2015] E. K. Wong and K. S. Fu. A hierarchical-orthogonal-space approach to collision-free path planning. *IEEE Journal of Robotics and Automation*, 2(1):42–53, March 1986. [volumes; motion planning]

[2016] T. C. Woo. A combinatorial analysis of boundary data structure schemata. *IEEE Computer Graphics and Applications*, 5(3):19–27, March 1985. [volumes; symmetric structure] cited in D.5.4, F.2.2.1.1 (p. 317)

[2017] J. R. Woodwark. The explicit quad tree as a structure for computer graphics. *Computer Journal*, 25(2):235–238, May 1982. [regions; region quadtree] cited in A.2.1.1, F.2.1.1.2 (p. 200), F.2.1.2.4 (p. 215)

[2018] J. R. Woodwark. Compressed quad trees. *Computer Journal*, 27(3):225–229, August 1984. [regions; region quadtree; DF-expression] cited in F.2.3.1 (p. 410)

[2019] J. R. Woodwark. Generating wireframes from set-theoretic solid models by spatial division. *Computer-Aided Design*, 18(6):307–315, July–August 1986. [volumes; constructive solid geometry (CSG)] cited in D.5.5, F.2.2.2.7 (p. 373)

[2020] J. R. Woodwark. Comments on "extended octtrees". *Computers & Graphics*, 13(4):529, 1989. Also see Letters to the Editor, *Computers & Graphics*, 14(1):137–138, 1990. [volumes; extended octree; PM octree] cited in F.2.2.2.7 (p. 370)

[2021] J. R. Woodwark and K. M. Quinlan. The derivation of graphics from volume models by recursive subdivision of the object space. In *Proceedings Computer Graphics 80 Conference (CG-80)*, R. J. Lansdown, ed., pages 335–343, Brighton, United Kingdom, August 1980. Online Publishers. [volumes; constructive solid geometry (CSG); PM octree] cited in D.5.5, D.5.5.1, F.2.2.2.7 (p. 373)

[2022] J. R. Woodwark and K. M. Quinlan. Reducing the effect of complexity on volume model evaluation. *Computer-Aided Design*, 14(2):89–95, March 1982. [volumes; constructive solid geometry (CSG); PM octree] cited in D.5.5, D.5.5.1, F.2.2.2.7 (p. 373)

[2023] M. Worboys. *GIS A Computing Perspective*. Taylor & Francis, London, United Kingdom, 1995. [spatial database; geographic information systems (GIS); general] cited in F.P (p. xix)

[2024] A. Y. Wu, T. H. Hong, and A. Rosenfeld. Threshold selection using quadtrees. *IEEE Transactions on Pattern Analysis and Machine Intelligence*, 4(1):90–94, January 1982. [regions; region quadtree; threshold selection]

[2025] C.-H. Wu, S.-J. Horng, and P.-Z. Lee. A new computation of shape moments via quadtree decomposition. *Pattern Recognition*, 34(7):1319–1330, July 2001. [regions; region quadtree; moments]

[2026] D. Wu, D. Agrawal, A. El Abbadi, A. Singh, and T. R. Smith. Efficient retrieval for browsing large image databases. In *Proceedings of the 5th International Conference on Information and Knowledge Management (CIKM)*, K. Barker and M. T. Özsu, eds., pages 11–18, Rockville, MD, November 1996. [points; high-dimensional data; Singular Value Decomposition (SVD); Discrete Fourier Transform (DFT)] cited in F.4.6.1.1 (p. 664), F.4.6.4.2 (pp. 677, 683–684)

[2027] W. A. Wulf, D. B. Russell, and A. N. Habermann. BLISS: a language for systems programming. *Communications of the ACM*, 14(12):780–790, December 1971. [BLISS; programming languages] cited in A.L, F.D (p. 744)

[2028] G. Wyvill and T. L. Kunii. A functional model for constructive solid geometry. *Visual Computer*, 1(1):3–14, July 1985. [volumes; ray tracing; constructive solid geometry (CSG); PM-CSG tree] cited in A.7.2.2, A.7.2.3, A.7.2.4, D.5.3, D.5.5, D.5.5.2, F.2.2.2.7 (pp. 371, 373)

[2029] G. Wyvill, T. L. Kunii, and Y. Shirai. Space division for ray tracing in CSG. *IEEE Computer Graphics and Applications*, 6(4):28–34, April 1986. [volumes; ray tracing; constructive solid geometry (CSG)] cited in A.7.2.2, D.5.5.2, D.5.5.2.s

[2030] C. Xia, J. Lu, B. C. Ooi, and J. Hu. Gorder: an efficient method for KNN join processing. In *Proceedings of the 30th International Conference on Very Large Data Bases (VLDB)*, M. A. Nascimento, M. T. Özsu, D. Kossmann, R. J. Miller, J. A. Blakely, and K. B. Schiefer, eds., pages 756–767, Toronto, Canada, September 2004. [points; all nearest neighbors query; distance semijoin] cited in F.4 (pp. 485–486), F.4.5.8 (p. 658)

[2031] J. C. Xia, J. El-Sana, and A. Varshney. Adaptive real-time level-of-detail-based rendering for polygonal models. *IEEE Transactions on Visualization and Computer Graphics*, 3(2):171–183, September 1997. [surfaces; surface simplification] cited in F.2.2.3.4 (p. 394)

[2032] J. C. Xia and A. Varshney. Dynamic view-dependent simplification for polygonal models. In *Proceedings IEEE Visualization '96*, R. Yagel and G. M. Nielson, eds., pages 327–334, San Francisco, October 1996. [surfaces; surface simplification] cited in F.2.2.3.4 (pp. 395, 397–399)

[2033] D. Xiong and J. Sperling. Semiautomated matching for network database integration. *ISPRS Journal of Photogrammetry and Remote Sensing*, 59(1–2):35–46, August 2004. [map conflation] cited in F.4 (p. 486)

943

[2034] X. Xiong, M. F. Mokbel, and W. G. Aref. SEA-CNN: scalable processing of continuous k-nearest neighbor queries in spatio-temporal databases. In *Proceedings of the 21st IEEE International Conference on Data Engineering*, pages 643–654, Tokyo, Japan, April 2005. [moving objects; nearest neighbor] cited in F.4 (p. 488)

[2035] J. Xu, B. Zheng, W.-C. Lee, and D. L. Lee. Energy efficient index for querying location-dependent data in mobile broadcast environments. In *Proceedings of the 19th IEEE International Conference on Data Engineering*, pages 239–250, Bangalore, India, March 2003. [points; nearest neighbor; D-tree] cited in F.1.5.1.4 (p. 68), F.2.1.2.8 (p. 224)

[2036] J. Xu, B. Zheng, W.-C. Lee, and D. L. Lee. The D-tree: an index structure for planar point queries in location-based wireless services. *IEEE Transactions on Knowledge and Data Engineering*, 16(12):1526–1542, December 2004. Also see *Proceedings of the 19th IEEE International Conference on Data Engineering*, pages 239–250, Bangalore, India, March 2003. [points; nearest neighbor; D-tree] cited in F.1.5.1.4 (p. 68), F.2.1.2.8 (p. 224)

[2037] X. Xu, J. Han, and W. Lu. RT-tree: an improved R-tree index structure for spatiotemporal databases. In *Proceedings of the 4th International Symposium on Spatial Data Handling*, vol. 2, pages 1040–1049, Zurich, Switzerland, July 1990. [rectangles; spatiotemporal database; R-tree]

[2038] H. Yahia. *Analyse des structures de donné arborescentes représentant des images*. PhD thesis, Université de Paris-Sud, Paris, France, December 1986. [regions]

[2039] K. Yamaguchi, T. L. Kunii, K. Fujimura, and H. Toriya. Octree-related data structures and algorithms. *IEEE Computer Graphics and Applications*, 4(1):53–59, January 1984. [volumes; region octree] cited in A.4.6, A.6.5.3, A.7.1.4, A.7.1.4.s, D.1.4.1, D.5.2

[2040] K. Yamaguchi, T. L. Kunii, D. F. Rogers, S. G. Satterfield, and F. A. Rodriguez. Computer-integrated manufacturing of surfaces using octree encoding. *IEEE Computer Graphics and Applications*, 4(1):60–65, January 1984. [volumes; region octree]

[2041] C. Yang and K.-I. Lin. An index structure for efficient reverse nearest neighbor queries. In *Proceedings of the 17th IEEE International Conference on Data Engineering*, pages 485–492, Heidelberg, Germany, April 2001. [points; reverse nearest neighbor (RNN); distance semijoin] cited in F.4.5.8 (p. 658)

[2042] C. Yang and K.-I. Lin. An index structure for improving nearest closest pairs and related join queries in spatial databases. In *Proceedings of the International Database Engineering and Applications Symposium*, M. A. Nascimento, M. T. Özsu, and O. R. Zaïane, eds., pages 140–149, Edmonton, Canada, July 2002. [points; reverse nearest neighbor (RNN); distance semijoin] cited in F.4.5.8 (p. 658)

[2043] J. Yang, W. Wang, and R. Muntz. Yet another spatial indexing structure. Computer Science Technical Report 97040, University of California at Los Angeles, Los Angeles, November 1997. [points; PK-tree; decoupling] cited in F.1.7.1.6 (p. 117), F.1.8 (p. 164), F.1.8.6 (p. 182), F.2.1.2.4 (p. 216)

[2044] S. N. Yang and T. W. Lin. An efficient connected component labeling algorithm for images represented by linear quadtrees. In *Proceedings of the 7th Scandinavian Conference on Image Analysis*, pages 1086–1093, Alborg, Denmark, August 1991. [regions; connected component labeling; region quadtree]

[2045] Y. Yang, K. Zhang, X. Wang, J. T.-L. Wang, and D. Shasha. An approximate oracle for distance in metric spaces. In *Proceedings of the 9th Annual Symposium on Combinatorial Pattern Matching*, M. Farach-Colton, ed., vol. 1448 of Springer-Verlag Lecture Notes in Computer Science, pages 104–117, Berlin, Germany, July 1998. [metric space embedding; FastMap; MetricMap] cited in F.4.7.3.9 (p. 711)

[2046] A. C. Yao. On random 2-3 trees. *Acta Informatica*, 9(2):159–168, 1978. [points; 2-3 tree] cited in F.1.7.3 (pp. 163–164)

[2047] A. C. C. Yao. On constructing minimum spanning trees in k-dimensional space and related problems. *SIAM Journal on Computing*, 11(4):721–736, November 1982. [points; nearest foreign neighbor problem] cited in F.4.4.4 (p. 577)

[2048] F. F. Yao, D. P. Dobkin, H. Edelsbrunner, and M. S. Paterson. Partitioning space for range queries. *SIAM Journal on Computing*, 18(2):371–384, April 1989. [points; halfplanar range search] cited in F.1.5.3.s (p. 768)

[2049] M.-M. Yau. Generating quadtrees of cross-sections from octrees. *Computer Vision, Graphics, and Image Processing*, 27(2):211–238, August 1984. [regions; volumes; region quadtree; region octree] cited in A.7.1.4, A.7.1.4.s

[2050] M.-M. Yau and S. N. Srihari. A hierarchical data structure for multidimensional digital images. *Communications of the ACM*, 26(7):504–515, July 1983. [hypervolumes; time dimension] cited in A.1.4, A.2.1.2, A.4.2.3, A.4.6, A.4.6.s, D.1.3, D.5.2, D.5.2.s, D.5.3, F.2.2.2.7 (p. 373), F.2.4 (p. 425)

[2051] M. A. Yerry and M. S. Shephard. A modified quadtree approach to finite element mesh generation. *IEEE Computer Graphics and Applications*, 3(1):39–46, January–February 1983. [regions; finite element analysis] cited in A.1.4, D.1.3, F.2.4 (p. 425)

[2052] P. N. Yianilos. Data structures and algorithms for nearest neighbor search in general metric spaces. In *Proceedings of the 4th Annual ACM-SIAM Symposium on Discrete Algorithms*, pages 311–321, Austin, TX, January 1993. [metric spaces; depth-first nearest neighbor algorithm; vp-tree] cited in F.4.1.3 (p. 498), F.4.1.7 (p. 517), F.4.2 (p. 517), F.4.5 (pp. 598–599), F.4.5.2.1 (p. 604), F.4.5.2.1.1 (pp. 604–605), F.4.5.2.1.2 (p. 606), F.4.5.2.2 (p. 607), F.4.5.2.3 (p. 608), F.4.5.3.2 (p. 616), F.4.5.5.2 (p. 636)

[2053] P. N. Yianilos. Excluded middle vantage point forests for nearest neighbor search. In *Proceedings of the 6th DIMACS Implementation Challenge Workshop*, Baltimore, MD, January 1999. No proceedings published. Also technical report, NEC Research Institute, Princeton, NJ, July 1998. [metric spaces; vp-tree] cited in F.4.5.2.4 (p. 612)

[2054] P. N. Yianilos. Locally lifting the curse of dimensionality for nearest neighbor search. In *Proceedings of the 11th Annual ACM-SIAM Symposium on Discrete Algorithms*, pages 361–370, San Francisco, January 2000. [metric spaces; nearest neighbor]

[2055] M. L. Yiu, N. Mamoulis, and D. Papadias. Aggregate nearest neighbor queries in road networks. *IEEE Transactions on Knowledge and Data Engineering*, 17(6):820–833, June 2005. [spatial networks; aggregation query]

[2056] F. W. Young and R. M. Hamer. *Multidimensional Scaling: History, Theory, and Applications*. Lawrence Erlbaum Associates, Hillsdale, NJ, 1987. [metric space embedding; multidimensional scaling (MDS)] cited in F.4.7.1 (p. 689)

[2057] B. Yu, R. Orlandic, and M. Evens. Simple QSF-trees: an efficient and scalable spatial access method. In *Proceedings of the 8th International Conference on Information and Knowledge Management (CIKM)*, pages 5–14, Kansas City, MO, November 1999. [intervals; corner transformation; transformation technique; simple QSF-tree] cited in F.3.3.3 (p. 465)

[2058] C. Yu, S. Bressan, B. C. Ooi, and K.-L. Tan. Querying high-dimensional data in single-dimensional space. *VLDB Journal*, 13(2):105–119, May 2004. [pyramid technique; high-dimensional data; iMinMax]

[2059] C. Yu, B. C. Ooi, K.-L. Tan, and H. V. Jagadish. Indexing the distance—an efficient method to KNN processing. In *Proceedings of the 27th International Conference on Very Large Data Bases (VLDB)*, P. M. G. Apers, P. Atzeni, S. Ceri, S. Paraboschi, K. Ramamohanarao, and R. T. Snodgrass, eds., pages 421–430, Rome, Italy, September 2001. [metric spaces; high-dimensional data; pyramid technique; iMinMax] cited in F.4.4.7 (p. 591)

[2060] S. Yu, M. van Kreveld, and J. Snoeyink. Drainage queries in TINs: From local to global and again. In *Proceedings of the 7th International Symposium on Spatial Data Handling*, M. J. Kraak and M. Molenaar, eds., pages 13A.1–13A.14, Delft, The Netherlands, August 1996. International Geographical Union Commission on Geographic Information Systems, Association for Geographical Information. [surfaces; triangulated irregular network (TIN)]

[2061] X. Yu, K. Q. Pu, and N. Koudas. Monitoring k-nearest neighbor queries over moving objects. In *Proceedings of the 21st IEEE International Conference on Data Engineering*, pages 631–642, Tokyo, Japan, April 2005. [moving objects; nearest neighbor] cited in F.4 (p. 488)

[2062] Y. Yuan, X. Lin, Q. Liu, W. Wang, J. X. Yu, and Q. Zhang. Efficient computation of the skyline cube. In *Proceedings of the 31st International Conference on Very Large Data Bases (VLDB)*, K. Böhm, C. S. Jensen, L. M. Haas, M. L. Kersten, P.-Å. Larson, and B. C. Ooi, eds., pages 241–252, Trondheim, Norway, September 2005. [points; skyline query; point dominance query; skyline cube] cited in F.4.1.5 (p. 503)

[2063] G. Yuval. Finding near neighbors in k-dimensional space. *Information Processing Letters*, 3(4):113–114, March 1975. [points; nearest neighbor] cited in F.1.1.s (p. 749)

[2064] L. Zadeh. Similarity relations and fuzzy orderings. *Information Sciences*, 3:177–200, 1971. [fuzzy logic; equivalence relation; approximate nearest neighbor] cited in F.4.5.8 (p. 651)

[2065] P. Zezula, P. Savino, G. Amato, and F. Rabitti. Approximate similarity retrieval with M-trees. *VLDB Journal*, 7(4):275–293, December 1998. [metric spaces; M-tree]

[2066] J. Zhang, N. Mamoulis, D. Papadias, and Y. Tao. All-nearest-neighbors queries in spatial databases. In *Proceedings of the 16th International Conference on Scientific and Statistical Database Management*, M. Hatzopoulos and Y. Manolopoulos, eds., pages 297–306, Santorini, Greece, June 2004. [points; all nearest neighbors query] cited in F.4 (p. 485)

[2067] J. Zhang, M. Zhu, D. Papadias, Y. Tao, and D. L. Lee. Location-based spatial queries. In *Proceedings of the ACM SIGMOD Conference*, pages 443–454, San Diego, CA, June 2003. [moving objects]

[2068] R. Zhang, B. C. Ooi, and K.-L. Tan. Making the pyramid technique robust to query types and workloads. In *Proceedings of the 20th IEEE International Conference on Data Engineering*, pages 313–324, Boston, March 2004. [high-dimensional data; pyramid technique]

[2069] J. Zhao and W. A. Davis. Fast display of octree representations of 3d objects. In *Proceedings of Graphics Interface'91*, pages 160–167, Calgary, Canada, June 1991. [volumes; region octree]

[2070] B. Zheng and D. L. Lee. Informtion dissemination via wireless broadcast. *Communications of the ACM*, 48(5):105–110, May 2005. [points; nearest neighbor; D-tree; grid-partition index] cited in F.4.4.5 (p. 582)

[2071] X. Zhou, D. J. Abel, and D. Truffet. Data partitioning for parallel spatial join processing. In *Advances in Spatial Databases—5th International Symposium, SSD'97*, M. Scholl and A. Voisard, eds., vol. 1262 of Springer-Verlag Lecture Notes in Computer Science, pages 178–196, Berlin, Germany, July 1997. [regions; spatial join; parallel processing]

[2072] X. Y. Zhou and W. A. Davis. Parallel processing of linear quadtrees for robotics. In *Proceedings of Graphics Interface'90*, pages 197–204, Halifax, Newfoundland, Canada, May 1990. [regions; region quadtree; parallel processing]

[2073] H. Zhu, J. Su, and O. H. Ibarra. An index structure for spatial joins in linear constraint databases. In *Proceedings of the 15th IEEE International Conference on Data Engineering*, pages 636–643, Sydney, Australia, March 1999. [spatial join; constraint database]

[2074] M. Zhu, D. Papadias, J. Zhang, and D. L. Lee. Top-k spatial joins. *IEEE Transactions on Knowledge and Data Engineering*, 17(4):567–579, April 2005. [spatial join; top-*k* query]

[2075] S. G. Ziavras and N. A. Alexandridis. Improved algorithms for translation of pictures represented by leaf codes. *Image and Vision Computing*, 6(1):13–20, February 1988. [regions; region quadtree]

[2076] G. Zimbrao and J. M. de Souza. A raster approximation for processing of spatial joins. In *Proceedings of the 24th International Conference on Very Large Data Bases (VLDB)*, A. Gupta, O. Shmueli, and J. Widom, eds., pages 558–569, New York, August 1998. [spatial join] cited in F.P (p. xx)

[2077] J. E. Zolnowsky. *Topics in computational geometry*. PhD thesis, Department of Computer Science, Stanford University, Stanford, CA, 1978. Also Computer Science Technical Report STAN–CS–78–659. [points; k-d tree; nearest neighbor]

Reference Keyword Index

Each keyword is followed by a set of numbers corresponding to the references in the bibliography with which it is associated. The result is an inverted file [1046] (see Section 1.1 in Chapter 1). The categories "general," "high-dimensional data," "lines," "points," "rectangles," "regions," "surfaces," and "volumes" have been omitted since they have too many entries to be useful.

multiprocessing [327, 749, 944, 1182, 1685]

multiresolution image processing [1573]

multiresolution modeling [391–392, 459, 461–462, 465, 469, 692–693, 695, 812, 1791, 1936, 2005]

multitriangulation [460]

mvp-tree [241, 1235]

MX octree [552, 1273, 1349]

MX quadtree [289, 451, 901, 904–905, 1070, 1150, 1175, 1401, 1751]

MX-CIF quadtree [2, 8, 1009, 1100, 1340–1341, 1496, 1720, 1901]

N order [1992]

N-body problem [41, 50, 68, 126, 297, 571, 744, 753–755, 1001, 1221, 1608]

nearest foreign neighbor problem [2047]

nearest neighbor [25, 61, 130, 136, 162, 165, 182, 184, 189, 192, 212, 224, 236, 278, 283, 304, 314, 318–319, 356, 377, 379, 398–399, 401, 403, 497, 528, 610, 649, 656, 719, 756, 838, 842, 863–864, 930, 949, 968, 974, 978, 1000, 1053–1054, 1062–1064, 1067–1068, 1271, 1291–1292, 1306, 1320, 1330–1332, 1347, 1364, 1383, 1461–1462, 1464–1466, 1493, 1533–1534, 1543, 1566, 1713–1714, 1716, 1743, 1797, 1825, 1838, 1848, 1851, 1856, 1861, 1870, 1896–1897, 1929–1930, 1932, 1941, 1991, 2034–2036, 2054, 2061, 2063, 2070, 2077]

neighbor finding [684, 710, 891, 1136–1138, 1162, 1625, 1634–1635, 1652, 1696, 1792, 1816, 1893, 1942]

nested interpolation-based grid file (NIBGF) [1438]

network algorithms [1859]

network optimization [1119]

nonmanifold objects [301, 457, 979, 1140, 1979]

numerical methods [687, 721, 1515]

OBBTree [735]

object hierarchy [22, 66, 85–86, 1640]

object recognition [91, 1811]

object-oriented spatial database [1419]

online analytic processing (OLAP) [329, 1587]

operations research [836]

optics [1880]

optimal region quadtree [757, 1161]

optimized k-d tree [1444]

optimized point quadtree [1444]

orthogonal polygon [565, 569]

os-tree [1226, 1230]

oversized shelf [771, 777–778]

P-tree [939]

packed R-tree [44, 698, 1588]

packing constraint [1227]

parallel coordinates [925]

parallel processing [46, 209, 213, 373, 470–472, 511, 524, 898–899, 916, 997, 1027, 1047–1048, 1098, 1160, 1249, 1283, 1465, 1719, 1928, 1972, 2008, 2071–2072]

partial match query [172, 231, 322, 530, 582, 621, 1531]

partial ordering [319]

partial-entity structure [1140]

particle simulation [41, 50, 68, 126, 571, 744, 753–755, 1001, 1221, 1608]

PASCAL [952]

path compression [51, 396, 1379]

path planning [981, 1590]

Patricia trie [792, 1315]

pattern recognition [514, 665]

Peano-Hilbert order [591, 616, 734, 835, 937, 1190–1191, 1481]

peer-to-peer indexing [122, 136, 675, 1189]

peer-to-peer R-tree [1307]

peer-to-peer spatial indexing [676, 1307, 1846–1848]

perceptrons [1298]

perimeter computation [1622, 1721]

persistent search tree [509, 1675]

perspective view [82, 1381, 1671, 1799, 1813]

physics [611]

picture grammars [33]

PK-tree [242, 1640, 1952, 2043]

plane-sweep algorithms [119, 1377, 1740]

PLOP hashing [1085, 1428]

PM octree [115–116, 271–272, 307–308, 519, 661–663, 902, 1349–1352, 1526, 1915, 2020–2022]

PM quadtree [244–246, 269, 453, 869, 917, 1175, 1654, 1656, 1665, 1967–1968]

PM-CSG tree [2028]

PMR quadtree [849, 852, 856, 861, 863–864, 1175, 1360–1362]

point dominance query [236, 319, 379, 712–713, 1068, 1129, 1462, 1468, 1479, 1838, 2062]

point location [43, 197, 502, 541, 558, 653, 767, 1026, 1128, 1443, 1514, 1528, 1675]

point quadtree [114, 151, 181, 484–486, 614, 618–620, 936, 1018, 1132, 1617–1618]

polygon set operations [1239]

polygon simplification [408, 548, 694, 764, 804, 812, 877, 1118, 1177–1178, 1211–1212, 1502, 1579, 1699, 1735]

polygon tree [2000]

polygonization [869]

polyhedral approximation [597]

polytree [307–308, 519, 1946]

pose estimation [1737]

post-office problem [398, 1675]

PR k-d tree [51, 1379, 1413, 1832]

PR quadtree [49, 53, 55, 244–246, 396, 561, 1413, 1480, 1832]

preference query [378, 1099]

prefix B-tree [144]

preprocessing cone [1563]

principal components analysis (PCA) [1271]

priority queue [100, 636, 821, 846, 848, 1943]

priority R-tree [86]

priority search tree [357, 1266]

prism tree [598, 1499, 1501]

probablistic range query [1849]

probably-approximately correct nearest neighbor [1226]

programming [170]

programming languages [93, 137, 437, 568, 570, 928, 952, 1008, 1017, 1030, 1263, 1346, 1365, 1553, 1805, 2027]

progressive compression [1862]

progressive polyhedral approximation [1689]

progressive transmission [483, 674, 764, 802, 1629, 1646, 1778]

property sphere [603]

protein docking [1714]

pseudo k-d tree [1444]

pseudo quadtree [1444]

pseudo-Euclidean distance transformations [234]

PSQL [1585, 1588]

puzzletree [153, 478–480, 960, 1334, 1758–1759]

pyramid [72, 285–286, 752, 919, 1089, 1297, 1495, 1563, 1573, 1728, 1785, 1819, 1842–1845, 1898, 1921, 1953]

pyramid technique [188, 940, 1124–1125, 1403, 1408, 2058–2059, 2068]

quad list quadtree (QLQT) [1985–1986]

quad-edge representation [767, 973]

quadtree medial axis transform (QMAT) [594, 1626, 1630]

quadtree refinement [1894]

quadtree spectrum [353]

quantile hashing [1086]

quaternary hierarchical triangular decomposition [128–129, 603–604, 722, 1790]

query evaluation [742]

query optimization [149, 259, 818, 1717]

quicksort [857]

QUILT [1576–1577, 1648–1651, 1653, 1732]

quintary tree [180, 1133]

R*-tree [36, 152, 866, 1707, 1852]

R+-tree [593, 861, 863–864, 867, 1142, 1718, 1803]

R-file [909]

R-tree [17, 22, 36, 46, 60, 79, 85–87, 146, 152, 190, 193–195, 218, 243–246, 260–262, 316, 347, 360, 381, 424, 489, 586, 588, 593, 679–681, 750, 770–771, 777–778, 791, 817, 848, 860–867, 869, 892,

Author and Credit Index

When the page number of an index entry refers to a credit (such as an acknowledgement of a solution or of aid in the preparation of the book), then the page number is in italics. Index entries corresponding to authors indicate the page numbers on which a work of the corresponding author is either cited or appears in the bibliography. A page range for an individual indicates that each page in the range cites a work of the corresponding author, or is part of the bibliography in which case it contains at least one work of the corresponding author.

Subject Index

When the page number of an index entry refers to a definition, then the page number is in italics. When the index entry appears in a footnote, then the letter "n" is appended to the page number. A page range for a topic indicates that either the topic is discussed in the given page range or that each page in the range mentions the topic.

Printed and bound by CPI Group (UK) Ltd, Croydon, CR0 4YY

03/10/2024

01040320-0020